FEDERAL CIVIL RULES HANDBOOK

2023

By

STEVEN BAICKER-McKEE

Joseph A. Katarincic Endowed Chair
in Legal Process and Civil Procedure
Associate Professor of Law
Duquesne University School of Law

WILLIAM M. JANSSEN

Professor of Law
Charleston School of Law

WITH CONTRIBUTING AUTHORS

K. MARK HALL
KATIE MCELVEEN
DANIELLE MRDJENOVICH

For Customer Assistance Call 1-800-328-4880

Mat #42820884

ISBN: 978-1-731-92433–9

PREFACE TO THE 2023 HANDBOOK

This is the 30th edition of the *Federal Civil Rules Handbook*! It has been a labor of love since we started writing it in the early 1990s, and we have been so grateful for our *Handbook*'s reception. It is used by hundreds of thousands of lawyers, judges, and legal scholars across and outside the country, and over the past 30 years, the *Handbook* has been cited hundreds of times by federal trial and appellate court judges and in thousands of scholarly articles. We regularly hear from you, our readers, about how you've come to depend on the *Handbook* and how it helps you in your practices, along with suggestions for features or information that would improve it; all those emails warm our hearts. Thank you.

Our goal in creating the *Handbook* nearly 30 years ago was to design a resource to address what seemed, then, a truly unmet need: to provide practitioners, judges, and scholars with easy-to-find, quickly understood, citation-supported, legally reliable answers to pressing questions in federal civil practice. The main options then for applying the federal rules were an unannotated copy of the Rules themselves, which lacked nuance or guidance, or a costly multi-volume treatise that included more scholarly and historical background than most practitioners needed in the moment. The *Handbook*, we hoped, would bridge the gap as a pragmatic but adequately thorough and comprehensive guide to applying the Rules.

The *Handbook* has found its place in that middle ground. It remains a single-volume, soft-bound, annually-updated resource containing the Rules' text accompanied by a dependable, up-to-date commentary on how the Rules operate in practice. In this period of remote working, the *Handbook* serves an enhanced purpose, allowing individual lawyers to take with them to their home or workplace, in a single volume, what amounts to an entire federal practice library.

The format of the *Handbook* remains familiar. It begins with an introduction to **general concepts in federal practice** (jurisdiction, removal and remand, venue and *forum non conveniens*, the *Erie* doctrine, and preclusion). Each Rule is then set out and discussed in turn, beginning with the **current text of each Rule**, a quick summary of each Rule's "**Purpose and Scope,**" an introduction to the "**Core Concept**" of each Rule's various subsections, and "**Applications**" which describe (with accompanying citations) how those various subsections function in practice. The *Handbook* also includes a bundle of practitioner-helpful added features: a complete set of all of the **Advisory Committee Notes** to the Rules, an orienting summary to **federal appellate practice**, the text of often-consulted sections of the **federal Judiciary Code** (Title 28), a description of **federal multidistrict litigation** (MDL), and the full text of both the federal **appellate rules** (with forms), as amended through December 1, 2022, and the federal **evidence rules**.

What's New in this 2023 Edition:

- **More than 1,600 New Citations:** This edition contains more than *1,600 new citations*, most to opinions from the Nation's federal courts decided between Fall 2021 and late Summer 2022.
- **December 1, 2022 Amendments to the Federal Civil and Appellate Rules:** This edition introduces and discusses the *amendment to Rule 7.1* of the Federal Rules of Civil Procedure, which adds an important disclosure requirement for cases appearing in federal courts under diversity jurisdiction. It also includes the addition of the Supplemental Rules for Social Security Review Actions Under 42 U.S.C.A. § 405(g) and the amendments to Rules 25 and 42 of the Federal Rules of Appellate Procedure.
- **Tracking COVID-19:** This edition tracks the court opinions addressing the logistical challenges presented by COVID-19, such as requests to take depositions remotely and requests for continuances.
- **New U.S. Supreme Court Opinions:** As always, we carefully track the Supreme Court's procedural rulings. This edition incorporates *Kemp v. United States*, where the Court determined that Rule 60(b)(1)'s authority to reopen a judgment for "mistake, inadvertence, surprise, or excusable neglect" includes legal errors made by a federal judge.
- **Enhanced Federal Practice Summaries:** This edition includes a comprehensively revised and reformatted treatment of removal and remand and issue and claim preclusion designed to offer practitioners added guidance in these two important areas of federal practice.

With each edition of the *Handbook*, we end our Preface with the same invitation. Please email us, write us, or phone us with any recommendations on how to improve the *Handbook*. (Contact information for each of us appears in *The Authors*, the section that follows this Preface.) We consider carefully every such recommendation we receive. Reader advice has often helped us to sharpen the *Handbook* and make it a more useful, valuable, and responsive tool for practitioners and jurists. Thank you, in advance, for your thoughts. We appreciate them all!

THE AUTHORS

NOVEMBER 2022

THE AUTHORS

STEVEN BAICKER-MCKEE is an Associate Professor of Law at the Duquesne University School of Law and is the Joseph A. Katarincic Endowed Chair in Legal Process and Civil Procedure. He teaches Civil Procedure, Environmental Law, and Pretrial Litigation Simulation, and was voted Professor of the Year by the students. He is co-author of *A Student's Guide to the Federal Rules of Civil Procedure*, used by law students across the country, *Learning Civil Procedure*, a law school text book, *Practicing Civil Discovery*, a law school text exploring the strategic and practical aspects of civil discovery, and *Mastering Multiple Choice—Federal Civil Procedure*, a study aid for the bar examination and for law students. He the author/editor of the *Federal Litigator*, a monthly publication summarizing developments in federal practice, and the author of numerous book chapters and articles.

Prior to joining Duquesne University, Mr. Baicker-McKee was a litigator at Babst Calland in Pittsburgh for more than 20 years, serving on the firm's Operating Committee and Board of Directors. He has been recognized as one of the Outstanding Lawyers of America and elected to the Academy of Trial Lawyers.

Mr. Baicker-McKee received his B.A. from Yale University, then spent the next several years building fine furniture and custom cabinets in Charlottesville, Virginia before attending law school. He received his J.D from Marshall-Wythe School of Law, College of William and Mary, where he was on the Board of Editors of the *William and Mary Law Review*.

Mr. Baicker-McKee resides in Pittsburgh, Pennsylvania with his wife, Carol. Mr. Baicker-McKee is grateful for her love and support, and that of his three children, Kyle, Eric, and Sara, and his parents, Joe and Macky Baicker.

WILLIAM M. JANSSEN is a Professor of Law at the Charleston School of Law in Charleston, South Carolina. Mr. Janssen teaches courses in civil procedure, products liability, mass torts, and first amendment law. He has been honored six times by the students of his law school as their "Professor of the Year." He is also the author or co-author of other books, book chapters, articles, and bar preparation materials on civil procedure, including *Federal Civil Procedure Logic Maps*, a collection of "mind-maps" graphically illustrating principles of federal civil practice; *A Student's Guide to the Federal Rules of Civil Procedure*, an annual resource for law students; *Mastering Multiple Choice—Federal Civil Procedure*, a workbook for bar exam prep and for law students; *Practicing Civil Discovery*, an experiential coursebook for learning discovery; and *Rice's Attorney-Client Privilege in the United States* (contributing author), a treatise examining the privilege. Before his appointment to the faculty in Charleston, Mr. Janssen was a litigation partner, the Chair of Life Sciences Practices, and a member of the Executive Committee at the Midatlantic law firm of Saul Ewing LLP, with whom he practiced for almost seventeen years. He focused his private practice in pharmaceutical and medical device risk management and litigation. Mr. Janssen is a member of the International Association of Defense Counsel and the Food and Drug Law Institute.

Mr. Janssen graduated from Saint Joseph's University in Philadelphia and The American University, Washington College of Law, in Washington, D.C. He served as Executive Editor of the *American University Law Review* and as a member of the Moot Court Board. After law school, Mr. Janssen clerked for the Honorable James McGirr Kelly, on the United States District Court for the Eastern District of Pennsylvania, and for the Honorable Joseph F. Weis, Jr., on the United States Court of Appeals for the Third Circuit.

Mr. Janssen thanks his family and friends for teaching him that you have not truly lived until you've answered, for the thousandth time: "No, we're still not done with that book yet." Mr. Janssen dedicates this effort to his parents, Bill and Catherine, and to TMcP.

The authors welcome any comments, suggestions, or critiques of this book. Their telephone numbers and email addresses are provided below.

Steven Baicker-McKee
(412) 396-2258
baickermckees@duq.edu (email)
William M. Janssen
(843) 377-2442
wjanssen@charlestonlaw.edu (email)

THOMSON REUTERS PROVIEW™

This title is one of many now available on your tablet as an eBook.

Take your research mobile. Powered by the Thomson Reuters ProView™ app, our eBooks deliver the same trusted content as your print resources, but in a compact, on-the-go format.

ProView eBooks are designed for the way you work. You can add your own notes and highlights to the text, and all of your annotations will transfer electronically to every new edition of your eBook.

You can also instantly verify primary authority with built-in links to WestlawNext® and KeyCite®, so you can be confident that you're accessing the most current and accurate information.

To find out more about ProView eBooks and available discounts, call 1-800-328-9352.

Summary of Contents

PART I THE RULES AND JUDICIAL RULEMAKING 1

PART II GENERAL CONCEPTS IN FEDERAL CIVIL PRACTICE:
PERSONAL JURISDICTION, SUBJECT-MATTER JURISDICTION, REMOVAL AND REMAND, VENUE AND FORUM NON CONVENIENS, THE ERIE DOCTRINE, AND PRECLUSION (RES JUDICATA AND COLLATERAL ESTOPPEL) 13

PART III-A AN ORIENTATION TO YEARS OF MAJOR RULE AMENDMENTS 181

PART III FEDERAL RULES OF CIVIL PROCEDURE WITH COMMENTARY AND PRACTICE POINTERS 185

PART IV APPENDIX OF FORMS 1511

PART V MULTIDISTRICT LITIGATION 1513

PART VI APPELLATE PROCEDURE 1523

PART VII TITLE 28, JUDICIARY AND JUDICIAL PROCEDURE—SELECTED PROVISIONS 1625

PART VIII ADVISORY COMMITTEE NOTES 1693

PART IX FEDERAL RULES OF EVIDENCE FOR UNITED STATES COURTS 2053

PART X USCOURTS.GOV 2087

Index

Table of Contents

PART I THE RULES AND JUDICIAL RULEMAKING

A AN INTRODUCTION TO THE FEDERAL RULES OF CIVIL PROCEDURE

§ 1.1 INTRODUCTION

§ 1.2 CREATING THE FEDERAL RULES OF CIVIL PROCEDURE

B THE PROCESS OF JUDICIAL RULEMAKING

§ 1.3 INTRODUCTION

§ 1.4 HOW THE RULES ARE AMENDED

§ 1.5 SUMMARY OF RULEMAKING PROCEDURES

§ 1.6 CIVIL RULE AMENDMENTS IN 2022

PART II GENERAL CONCEPTS IN FEDERAL CIVIL PRACTICE: *PERSONAL JURISDICTION, SUBJECT-MATTER JURISDICTION, REMOVAL AND REMAND, VENUE AND FORUM NON CONVENIENS, THE ERIE DOCTRINE, AND PRECLUSION (RES JUDICATA AND COLLATERAL ESTOPPEL)*

A OVERVIEW—FEDERAL JUDICIAL POWER

§ 2.1 A Primer on Invoking Federal Judicial Power

B PERSONAL JURISDICTION

§ 2.2 Introduction

§ 2.3 Step #1—Legislative Authority

§ 2.4 Step #2—Constitutional (Due Process) Authority

§ 2.5 Acquiring *In Personam* Jurisdiction

§ 2.5a *In Personam* Circumstance #1—Consent to Jurisdiction

§ 2.5b *In Personam* Circumstance #2—In-State Service (Transient or "Tag") Jurisdiction

§ 2.5c *In Personam* Circumstance #3—Contacts-Based Jurisdiction

§ 2.5c1 *In Personam* Circumstance #3—Contacts-Based Jurisdiction—Specific Jurisdiction

§ 2.5c2 *In Personam* Circumstance #3—Contacts-Based Jurisdiction—General Jurisdiction

§ 2.6 Acquiring *In Rem* Jurisdiction

§ 2.7 Acquiring *Quasi In Rem* Jurisdiction

§ 2.8 Notice and an Opportunity to Be Heard—Another Prerequisite for Exercising Personal Jurisdiction

C SUBJECT-MATTER JURISDICTION

§ 2.9 Introduction

§ 2.10 Federal Question Jurisdiction

§ 2.11 Diversity Jurisdiction

§ 2.11a The First Requirement: Complete Diversity of Citizenship

§ 2.11b The Second Requirement: Amount in Controversy

§ 2.11c Diversity Jurisdiction in Class Actions and Mass Torts

§ 2.12 Supplemental Jurisdiction

D REMOVAL AND REMAND

§ 2.13 Removal

§ 2.14 Removal Procedure

§ 2.15 Removal of Class Actions

§ 2.16 Post-Removal Procedures and Remand

E VENUE AND *FORUM NON CONVENIENS*

§ 2.17 Venue

§ 2.17a Venue Transfer and *Forum Non Conveniens*

F THE *ERIE* DOCTRINE

§ 2.18 Introduction

§ 2.18a The Namesake: *Erie R.R. Co. v. Tompkins* and its Propgeny

§ 2.18b *Erie* Today, and the Sources of Federal Procedure

§ 2.18c Identifying the Law to Apply

§ 2.18d A Residue of Federal Common Law

G PRECLUSION (RES JUDICATA AND COLLATERAL ESTOPPEL)

§ 2.19 Introduction

§ 2.20 Claim Preclusion (*Res Judicata*)

§ 2.21 Issue Preclusion (Collateral Estoppel)

PART III-A AN ORIENTATION TO YEARS OF MAJOR RULE AMENDMENTS

PART III FEDERAL RULES OF CIVIL PROCEDURE WITH COMMENTARY AND PRACTICE POINTERS

I SCOPE OF RULES; FORM OF ACTION

Rule 1 Scope and Purpose

Rule 2 One Form of Action

II COMMENCING AN ACTION; SERVICE OF PROCESS, PLEADINGS, MOTIONS, AND ORDERS

Rule 3 Commencing an Action
Rule 4 Summons
Rule 4.1 Serving Other Process
Rule 5 Serving and Filing Pleadings and Other Papers
Rule 5.1 Constitutional Challenge to a Statute—Notice, Certification, and Intervention
Rule 5.2 Privacy Protection For Filings Made with the Court
Rule 6 Computing and Extending Time; Time for Motion Papers

III PLEADINGS AND MOTIONS

Rule 7 Pleadings Allowed; Form of Motions and Other Papers
Rule 7.1 Disclosure Statement
Rule 8 General Rules of Pleading
Rule 9 Pleading Special Matters
Rule 10 Form of Pleadings
Rule 11 Signing Pleadings, Motions, and Other Papers; Representations to the Court; Sanctions
Rule 12 Defenses and Objections: When and How Presented; Motion for Judgment on the Pleadings; Consolidating Motions; Waiving Defenses; Pretrial Hearing
Rule 13 Counterclaim and Crossclaim
Rule 14 Third-Party Practice
Rule 15 Amended and Supplemental Pleadings
Rule 16 Pretrial Conferences; Scheduling; Management

IV PARTIES

Rule 17 Plaintiff and Defendant; Capacity; Public Officers
Rule 18 Joinder of Claims
Rule 19 Required Joinder of Parties
Rule 20 Permissive Joinder of Parties
Rule 21 Misjoinder and Nonjoinder of Parties
Rule 22 Interpleader
Rule 23 Class Actions
Rule 23.1 Derivative Actions
Rule 23.2 Actions Relating to Unincorporated Associations
Rule 24 Intervention
Rule 25 Substitution of Parties

V DISCLOSURES AND DISCOVERY

Rule 26 Duty to Disclose; General Provisions Governing Discovery
Rule 27 Depositions to Perpetuate Testimony
Rule 28 Persons Before Whom Depositions May Be Taken
Rule 29 Stipulations About Discovery Procedure
Rule 30 Depositions by Oral Examination
Rule 31 Depositions by Written Questions

Rule 32 Using Depositions in Court Proceedings
Rule 33 Interrogatories to Parties
Rule 34 Producing Documents, Electronically Stored Information, and Tangible Things, or Entering onto Land, for Inspection and Other Purposes
Rule 35 Physical and Mental Examinations
Rule 36 Requests for Admission
Rule 37 Failure to Make Disclosures or to Cooperate in Discovery; Sanctions

VI TRIALS

Rule 38 Right to a Jury Trial; Demand
Rule 39 Trial by Jury or by the Court
Rule 40 Scheduling Cases for Trial
Rule 41 Dismissal of Actions
Rule 42 Consolidation; Separate Trials
Rule 43 Taking Testimony
Rule 44 Proving an Official Record
Rule 44.1 Determining Foreign Law
Rule 45 Subpoena
Rule 46 Objecting to a Ruling or Order
Rule 47 Selecting Jurors
Rule 48 Number of Jurors; Verdict; Polling
Rule 49 Special Verdict; General Verdict and Questions
Rule 50 Judgment as a Matter of Law in a Jury Trial; Related Motion for a New Trial; Conditional Ruling
Rule 51 Instructions to the Jury; Objections; Preserving a Claim of Error
Rule 52 Findings and Conclusions by the Court; Judgment on Partial Findings
Rule 53 Masters

VII JUDGMENT

Rule 54 Judgment; Costs
Rule 55 Default; Default Judgment
Rule 56 Summary Judgment
Rule 57 Declaratory Judgment
Rule 58 Entering Judgment
Rule 59 New Trial; Altering or Amending a Judgment
Rule 60 Relief from a Judgment or Order
Rule 61 Harmless Error
Rule 62 Stay of Proceedings to Enforce a Judgment
Rule 62.1 Indicative Ruling on a Motion for Relief That is Barred by a Pending Appeal
Rule 63 Judge's Inability to Proceed

VIII PROVISIONAL AND FINAL REMEDIES

Rule 64 Seizing a Person or Property
Rule 65 Injunctions and Restraining Orders
Rule 65.1 Proceedings Against a Security Provider
Rule 66 Receivers
Rule 67 Deposit into Court
Rule 68 Offer of Judgment
Rule 69 Execution
Rule 70 Enforcing a Judgment for a Specific Act
Rule 71 Enforcing Relief For or Against a Nonparty

IX SPECIAL PROCEEDINGS

Rule 71.1 Condemning Real or Personal Property
Rule 72 Magistrate Judges: Pretrial Order
Rule 73 Magistrate Judges: Trial by Consent; Appeal
Rule 74 Method of Appeal from Magistrate to District Judge Under Title 28, U.S.C. § 636(c)(4) and Rule 73(d) [Abrogated]
Rule 75 Proceedings on Appeal from Magistrate to District Judge Under Rule 73(d) [Abrogated]
Rule 76 Judgment of the District Judge on the Appeal Under Rule 73(d) and Costs [Abrogated]

X DISTRICT COURTS AND CLERKS: CONDUCTING BUSINESS; ISSUING ORDERS

Rule 77 Conducting Business; Clerk's Authority; Notice of an Order or Judgment
Rule 78 Hearing Motions; Submission on Briefs
Rule 79 Records Kept by the Clerk
Rule 80 Stenographic Transcript as Evidence

XI GENERAL PROVISIONS

Rule 81 Applicability of the Rules in General; Removed Actions
Rule 82 Jurisdiction and Venue Unaffected
Rule 83 Rules by District Courts; Judge's Directives
Rule 84 Forms [Abrogated]
Rule 85 Title
Rule 86 Effective Dates

SUPPLEMENTAL RULES SET #1

Rule A Scope of Rules
Rule B In Personam Actions: Attachment and Garnishment
Rule C In Rem Actions: Special Provisions
Rule D Possessory, Petitory, and Partition Actions
Rule E Actions in Rem and Quasi in Rem: General Provisions
Rule F Limitation of Liability
Rule G Forfeiture Actions In Rem

SUPPLEMENTAL RULES SET #2

Rule 1 Review of Social Security Decisions Under 42 U.S.C. § 405(g)
Rule 2 Complaint
Rule 3 Service
Rule 4 Answer; Motions; Time
Rule 5 Presenting the Action for Decision
Rule 6 Plaintiff's Brief
Rule 7 Commissioner's Brief
Rule 8 Reply Brief

PART IV APPENDIX OF FORMS

PART V MULTIDISTRICT LITIGATION

§ 5.1 Introduction
§ 5.2 The Federal Multidistrict Litigation Statute, 28 U.S.C.A. § 1407

PART VI APPELLATE PROCEDURE

§ 6.1 Introduction
§ 6.2 Step One: Appealability
§ 6.3 Step Two: Time for Taking an Appeal
§ 6.4 Step Three: Procedure for Taking an Appeal
§ 6.5 Step Four: Stays Pending Appeal
§ 6.6 Step Five: The Appeal Process
§ 6.7 Step Six: Appeals to the United States Supreme Court
§ 6.8 *Federal Rules of Appellate Procedure* (Effective July 1, 1968; amendments effective December 1, 2022)

TITLE I APPLICABILITY OF RULES

Rule 1 Scope of Rules; Definition; Title
Rule 2 Suspension of Rules

TITLE II APPEAL FROM A JUDGMENT OR ORDER OF A DISTRICT COURT

Rule 3 Appeal As of Right—How Taken
Rule 3.1 Appeal From a Judgment of a Magistrate Judge in a Civil Case [Abrogated]
Rule 4 Appeal As of Right—When Taken
Rule 5 Appeal By Permission
Rule 5.1 Appeal By Leave under 28 U.S.C. § 636(c)(5) [Abrogated]
Rule 6 Appeal in a Bankruptcy Case
Rule 7 Bond for Costs on Appeal in a Civil Case
Rule 8 Stay or Injunction Pending Appeal
Rule 9 Release in a Criminal Case
Rule 10 The Record on Appeal
Rule 11 Forwarding the Record
Rule 12 Docketing the Appeal; Filing a Representation Statement; Filing the Record

Rule 12.1 Remand After an Indicative Ruling by the District Court on a Motion for Relief That Is Barred by a Pending Appeal

TITLE III APPEALS FROM THE UNITED STATES TAX COURT

Rule 13 Appeals from the Tax Court
Rule 14 Applicability of other Rules to Appeals from the Tax Court

TITLE IV REVIEW OR ENFORCEMENT OF AN ORDER OF AN ADMINISTRATIVE AGENCY, BOARD, COMMISSION, OR OFFICER

Rule 15 Review or Enforcement of an Agency Order—How Obtained; Intervention
Rule 15.1 Briefs and Oral Argument in a National Labor Relations Board Proceeding
Rule 16 The Record on Review or Enforcement
Rule 17 Filing the Record
Rule 18 Stay Pending Review
Rule 19 Settlement of a Judgment Enforcing an Agency Order in Part
Rule 20 Applicability of Rules to the Review or Enforcement of an Agency Order

TITLE V EXTRAORDINARY WRITS

Rule 21 Writs of Mandamus and Prohibition, and other Extraordinary Writs

TITLE VI HABEAS CORPUS; PROCEEDINGS IN FORMA PAUPERIS

Rule 22 Habeas Corpus and Section 2255 Proceedings
Rule 23 Custody or Release of a Prisoner in a Habeas Corpus Proceeding
Rule 24 Proceeding in Forma Pauperis

TITLE VII GENERAL PROVISIONS

Rule 25 Filing and Service
Rule 26 Computing and Extending Time
Rule 26.1 Disclosure Statement
Rule 27 Motions
Rule 28 Briefs
Rule 28.1 Cross-Appeals
Rule 29 Brief of an Amicus Curiae
Rule 30 Appendix to the Briefs
Rule 31 Serving and Filing Briefs
Rule 32 Form of Briefs, Appendices, and other Papers
Rule 32.1 Citing Judicial Dispositions
Rule 33 Appeal Conferences

Rule 34 Oral Argument
Rule 35 En Banc Determination
Rule 36 Entry of Judgment; Notice
Rule 37 Interest on Judgment
Rule 38 Frivolous Appeal—Damages and Costs
Rule 39 Costs
Rule 40 Petition for Panel Rehearing
Rule 41 Mandate: Contents; Issuance and Effective Date; Stay
Rule 42 Voluntary Dismissal
Rule 43 Substitution of Parties
Rule 44 Case Involving a Constitutional Question When the United States or the Relevant State Is Not a Party
Rule 45 Clerk's Duties
Rule 46 Attorneys
Rule 47 Local Rules By Courts of Appeals
Rule 48 Masters

§ 6.9 Appendix of Forms to the *Federal Rules of Appellate Procedure*

Form 1A Notice of Appeal to a Court of Appeals From a Judgment of a District Court
Form 1B Notice of Appeal to a Court of Appeals From an Appealable Order of a District Court.
Form 2 Notice of Appeal to a Court of Appeals From a Decision of the United States Tax Court
Form 3 Petition for Review of Order of an Agency, Board, Commission or Officer
Form 4 Affidavit Accompanying Motion for Permission to Appeal in Forma Pauperis
Form 5 Notice of Appeal to a Court of Appeals from a Judgment or Order of a District Court or a Bankruptcy Appellate Panel
Form 6 Certificate of Compliance with Type-Volume Limit
Form 7 Declaration of Inmate Filing
Appendix 1 Length Limits Stated in the Federal Rules of Appellate Procedure

PART VII TITLE 28, JUDICIARY AND JUDICIAL PROCEDURE—SELECTED PROVISIONS

§ 144 Bias or Prejudice of Judge
§ 451 Definitions
§ 452 Courts Always Open; Powers Unrestricted by Expiration of Sessions
§ 455 Disqualification of Justice, Judge, or Magistrate
§ 636 Jurisdiction, Powers, and Temporary Assignment
§ 1251 Original Jurisdiction
§ 1253 Direct Appeals from Decisions of Three-Judge Courts
§ 1254 Courts of Appeals; Certiorari; Certified Questions
§ 1257 State Courts; Certiorari
§ 1291 Final Decisions of District Courts
§ 1292 Interlocutory Decisions

§ 1331 Federal Question
§ 1332 Diversity of Citizenship; Amount in Controversy; Costs
§ 1333 Admiralty, Maritime and Prize Cases
§ 1334 Bankruptcy Cases and Proceedings
§ 1335 Interpleader
§ 1337 Commerce and Antitrust Regulations; Amount in Controversy, Costs
§ 1338 Patents, Plant Variety Protection, Copyrights, Mask Works, Designs, Trademarks, and Unfair Competition
§ 1339 Postal matters
§ 1340 Internal Revenue; Customs Duties
§ 1343 Civil Rights and Elective Franchise
§ 1345 United States As Plaintiff
§ 1346 United States As Defendant
§ 1349 Corporation Organized under Federal Law As Party
§ 1357 Injuries under Federal Laws
§ 1359 Parties Collusively Joined or Made
§ 1361 Action to Compel an Officer of the United States to Perform His Duty
§ 1367 Supplemental Jurisdiction
§ 1369 Multiparty, Multiforum Jurisdiction
§ 1390 Scope
§ 1391 Venue Generally
§ 1397 Interpleader
§ 1400 Patents and Copyrights, Mask Works, and Designs
§ 1401 Stockholder's Derivative Action
§ 1402 United States As Defendant
§ 1404 Change of Venue
§ 1406 Cure or Waiver of Defects
§ 1407 Multidistrict Litigation
§ 1412 Change of Venue
§ 1441 Removal of civil actions
§ 1442 Federal Officers or Agencies Sued or Prosecuted
§ 1442a Members of Armed Forces Sued or Prosecuted
§ 1443 Civil Rights Cases
§ 1445 Nonremovable Actions
§ 1446 Procedure for removal of civil actions
§ 1447 Procedure after Removal Generally
§ 1448 Process after Removal
§ 1449 State Court Record Supplied
§ 1451 Definitions
§ 1453 Removal of Class Actions
§ 1631 Transfer to Cure Want of Jurisdiction
§ 1651 Writs
§ 1652 State Laws As Rules of Decision
§ 1653 Amendment of Pleadings to Show Jurisdiction
§ 1654 Appearance Personally or by Counsel
§ 1655 Lien enforcement; absent defendants
§ 1657 Priority of Civil Actions

§ 1658 Time Limitations on the Commencement of Civil Actions Arising under Acts of Congress
§ 1691 Seal and Teste of Process
§ 1692 Process and Orders Affecting Property in Different Districts
§ 1695 Stockholder's Derivative Action
§ 1696 Service in Foreign and International Litigation
§ 1697 Service in Multiparty, Multiforum Actions
§ 1731 Handwriting
§ 1732 Record Made in Regular Course of Business; Photographic Copies
§ 1733 Government Records and Papers; Copies
§ 1734 Court Record Lost or Destroyed, Generally
§ 1735 Court Record Lost or Destroyed Where United States Interested
§ 1738 State and Territorial Statutes and Judicial Proceedings; Full Faith and Credit
§ 1739 State and Territorial Nonjudicial Records; Full Faith and Credit
§ 1746 Unsworn Declarations under Penalty of Perjury
§ 1781 Transmittal of Letter Rogatory or Request
§ 1782 Assistance to Foreign and International Tribunals and to Litigants before Such Tribunals
§ 1783 Subpoena of Person in Foreign Country
§ 1784 Contempt
§ 1785 Subpoenas in Multiparty, Multiforum Actions
§ 1821 Per Diem and Mileage Generally; Subsistence
§ 1826 Recalcitrant Witnesses
§ 1914 District Court; Filing and Miscellaneous Fees; Rules of Court
§ 1915 Proceedings in Forma Pauperis
§ 1917 District Courts; Fee on Filing Notice of or Petition for Appeal
§ 1920 Taxation of Costs
§ 1924 Verification of Bill of Costs
§ 1927 Counsel's Liability for Excessive Costs
§ 1961 Interest
§ 1963 Registration of Judgments for Enforcement in Other Districts
§ 1964 Constructive Notice of Pending Actions
§ 2071 Rule-Making Power Generally
§ 2072 Rules of Procedure and Evidence; Power to Prescribe
§ 2101 Supreme Court; Time for Appeal or Certiorari; Docketing; Stay
§ 2104 Reviews of State Court Decisions
§ 2106 Determination
§ 2107 Time for Appeal to Court of Appeals
§ 2111 Harmless Error
§ 2201 Creation of Remedy
§ 2202 Further Relief
§ 2283 Stay of State Court Proceedings
§ 2284 Three-Judge Court; When Required; Composition; Procedure
§ 2361 Process and Procedure

§ 2401 Time for Commencing Action Against United States
§ 2402 Jury Trial in Actions Against United States
§ 2403 Intervention by United States or a State; Constitutional Question
§ 2404 Death of Defendant in Damage Action
§ 2408 Security Not Required of United States
§ 2411 Interest
§ 2412 Costs and Fees
§ 2413 Executions in Favor of United States
§ 2414 Payment of Judgments and Compromise Settlements
§ 2415 Time for Commencing Actions Brought by the United States
§ 2416 Time for Commencing Actions Brought by the United States—Exclusions

PART VIII ADVISORY COMMITTEE NOTES

§ 8.1 Introduction to the Committee Notes—The Civil Rules' "Legislative History"
§ 8.2 Full Text of the Advisory Committee Notes

I SCOPE OF RULES—ONE FORM OF ACTION

Rule 1 Scope and Purpose of Rules
Rule 2 One Form of Action

II COMMENCEMENT OF ACTION; SERVICE OF PROCESS, PLEADINGS, MOTIONS AND ORDERS

Rule 3 Commencement of Action
Rule 4 Summons
Rule 4.1 Service of other Process
Rule 5 Service and Filing of Pleadings and other Papers
Rule 5.1 Constitutional Challenge to a Statute—Notice, Certification, and Intervention
Rule 5.2 Privacy Protection for Filings Made with the Court
Rule 6 Time

III PLEADINGS AND MOTIONS

Rule 7 Pleadings Allowed; Form of Motions
Rule 7.1 Disclosure Statement
Rule 8 General Rules of Pleading
Rule 9 Pleading Special Matters
Rule 10 Form of Pleadings
Rule 11 Signing of Pleadings, Motions, and other Papers; Representations to Court; Sanctions
Rule 12 Defenses and Objections—When and How Presented—By Pleading or Motion—Motion for Judgment on the Pleadings
Rule 13 Counterclaim and Cross-Claim
Rule 14 Third Party Practice
Rule 15 Amended and Supplemental Pleadings

Rule 16 Pretrial Conferences; Scheduling; Management

IV PARTIES

Rule 17 Parties Plaintiff and Defendant; Capacity
Rule 18 Joinder of Claims and Remedies
Rule 19 Joinder of Persons Needed for Just Adjudication
Rule 20 Permissive Joinder of Parties
Rule 21 Misjoinder and Non-Joinder of Parties
Rule 22 Interpleader
Rule 23 Class Actions
Rule 23.1 Derivative Actions by Shareholders
Rule 23.2 Actions Relating to Unincorporated Associations
Rule 24 Intervention
Rule 25 Substitution of Parties

V DEPOSITIONS AND DISCOVERY

Rule 26 General Provisions Governing Discovery; Duty of Disclosure
Rule 27 Depositions Before Action or Pending Appeal
Rule 28 Persons Before Whom Depositions May Be Taken
Rule 29 Stipulations Regarding Discovery Procedure
Rule 30 Depositions upon Oral Examination
Rule 31 Depositions upon Written Questions
Rule 32 Use of Depositions in Court Proceedings
Rule 33 Interrogatories to Parties
Rule 34 Production of Documents and Things and Entry upon Land for Inspection and Other Purposes
Rule 35 Physical and Mental Examinations of Persons
Rule 36 Requests for Admission
Rule 37 Failure to Make Disclosure or Cooperate in Discovery: Sanctions

VI TRIALS

Rule 38 Jury Trial of Right
Rule 39 Trial by Jury or by the Court
Rule 40 Assignment of Cases for Trial
Rule 41 Dismissal of Actions
Rule 42 Consolidation; Separate Trials
Rule 43 Taking of Testimony
Rule 44 Proof of Official Record
Rule 44.1 Determination of Foreign Law
Rule 45 Subpoena
Rule 46 Exceptions Unnecessary
Rule 47 Selection of Jurors
Rule 48 Number of Jurors—Participation in Verdict
Rule 49 Special Verdicts and Interrogatories
Rule 50 Judgment As a Matter of Law in Jury Trials; Alternative Motion for New Trial; Conditional Rulings
Rule 51 Instructions to Jury: Objection

Rule 52 Findings by the Court; Judgment on Partial Findings
Rule 53 Masters

VII JUDGMENT

Rule 54 Judgments; Costs
Rule 55 Default
Rule 56 Summary Judgment
Rule 57 Declaratory Judgments
Rule 58 Entry of Judgment
Rule 59 New Trials; Amendment of Judgments
Rule 60 Relief from Judgment or Order
Rule 61 Harmless Error
Rule 62 Stay of Proceedings to Enforce a Judgment
Rule 62.1 Indicative Ruling on a Motion for Relief That is Barred by a Pending Appeal
Rule 63 Inability of a Judge to Proceed

VIII PROVISIONAL AND FINAL REMEDIES

Rule 64 Seizure of Person or Property
Rule 65 Injunctions
Rule 65.1 Security: Proceedings against Sureties
Rule 66 Receivers Appointed by Federal Courts
Rule 67 Deposit in Court
Rule 68 Offer of Judgment
Rule 69 Execution
Rule 70 Judgment for Specific Acts; Vesting Title
Rule 71 Process in Behalf of and Against Persons Not Parties

IX SPECIAL PROCEEDINGS

Rule 71.1 Condemnation of Property
Rule 72 Magistrate Judges; Pretrial Orders
Rule 73 Magistrate Judges; Trial by Consent and Appeal
Rule 74 Method of Appeal From Magistrate Judge to District Judge Under Title 28, U.S.C. § 636(c)(4) and Rule 73(d)
Rule 75 Proceedings on Appeal from Magistrate Judge to District Judge under Rule 73(d)
Rule 76 Judgment of the District Judge on the Appeal under Rule 73(d) and Costs

X DISTRICT COURTS AND CLERKS

Rule 77 District Courts and Clerks
Rule 78 Motion Day
Rule 79 Books and Records Kept by the Clerk and Entries Therein
Rule 80 Stenographer; Stenographic Report or Transcript As Evidence

XI GENERAL PROVISIONS

Rule 81 Applicability in General
Rule 82 Jurisdiction and Venue Unaffected
Rule 83 Rules by District Courts; Judge's Directives
Rule 84 Forms
Rule 85 Title
Rule 86 Effective Date

SUPPLEMENTAL RULES FOR CERTAIN ADMIRALTY AND MARITIME CLAIMS

Rule A Scope of Rules
Rule B In Personam Actions: Attachment and Garnishment
Rule C In Rem Actions: Special Provisions
Rule D Possessory, Petitory, and Partition Actions
Rule E Actions in Rem and Quasi in Rem: General Provisions
Rule F Limitation of Liability
Rule G Forfeiture Actions In Rem

PART IX FEDERAL RULES OF EVIDENCE FOR UNITED STATES COURTS

ARTICLE I GENERAL PROVISIONS

Rule 101 Scope; Definitions
Rule 102 Purpose
Rule 103 Rulings on Evidence
Rule 104 Preliminary Questions
Rule 105 Limiting Evidence That Is Not Admissible Against Other Parties or for Other Purposes
Rule 106 Remainder of or Related Writings or Recorded Statements

ARTICLE II JUDICIAL NOTICE

Rule 201 Judicial Notice of Adjudicative Facts

ARTICLE III PRESUMPTIONS IN CIVIL CASES

Rule 301 Presumptions in Civil Cases Generally
Rule 302 Applying State Law to Presumptions in Civil Cases

ARTICLE IV RELEVANCE AND ITS LIMITS

Rule 401 Test for Relevant Evidence
Rule 402 General Admissibility of Relevant Evidence
Rule 403 Excluding Relevant Evidence for Prejudice, Confusion, Waste of Time, or Other Reasons
Rule 404 Character Evidence; Other Crimes, Wrongs or Acts
Rule 405 Methods of Proving Character
Rule 406 Habit; Routine Practice
Rule 407 Subsequent Remedial Measures
Rule 408 Compromise Offers and Negotiations

Rule 409 Offers to Pay Medical and Similar Expenses
Rule 410 Pleas, Plea Discussions, and Related Statements
Rule 411 Liability Insurance
Rule 412 Sex-Offense Cases: The Victim's Sexual Behavior or Predisposition
Rule 413 Similar Crimes in Sexual-Assault Cases
Rule 414 Similar Crimes in Child-Molestation Cases
Rule 415 Similar Acts in Civil Cases Involving Sexual Assault or Child Molestation

ARTICLE V PRIVILEGES

Rule 501 Privilege in General
Rule 502 Attorney-Client Privilege and Work Product; Limitations on Waiver

ARTICLE VI WITNESSES

Rule 601 Competency to Testify in General
Rule 602 Need for Personal Knowledge
Rule 603 Oath or Affirmation to Testify Truthfully
Rule 604 Interpreter
Rule 605 Judge's Competency as a Witness
Rule 606 Juror's Competency as a Witness
Rule 607 Who May Impeach a Witness
Rule 608 A Witness's Character for Truthfulness or Untruthfulness
Rule 609 Impeachment by Evidence of a Criminal Conviction
Rule 610 Religious Beliefs or Opinions
Rule 611 Mode and Order of Examining Witnesses and Presenting Evidence
Rule 612 Writing Used to Refresh a Witness's Memory
Rule 613 Witness's Prior Statement
Rule 614 Court's Calling or Examining a Witness
Rule 615 Excluding Witnesses

ARTICLE VII OPINIONS AND EXPERT TESTIMONY

Rule 701 Opinion Testimony by Lay Witnesses
Rule 702 Testimony by Expert Witnesses
Rule 703 Bases of an Expert's Opinion Testimony
Rule 704 Opinion on an Ultimate Issue
Rule 705 Disclosing the Facts or Data Underlying an Expert's Opinion
Rule 706 Court-Appointed Expert Witnesses

ARTICLE VIII HEARSAY

Rule 801 Definitions That Apply to This Article; Exclusions from Hearsay
Rule 802 The Rule Against Hearsay
Rule 803 Exceptions to the Rule Against Hearsay — Regardless of Whether the Declarant Is Available as a Witness

Rule 804 Exceptions to the Rule Against Hearsay — When the Declarant Is Unavailable as a Witness
Rule 805 Hearsay Within Hearsay
Rule 806 Attacking and Supporting the Declarant's Credibility
Rule 807 Residual Exception

ARTICLE IX AUTHENTICATION AND IDENTIFICATION

Rule 901 Authenticating or Identifying Evidence
Rule 902 Evidence That Is Self-Authenticating
Rule 903 Subscribing Witness's Testimony

ARTICLE X CONTENTS OF WRITINGS, RECORDINGS, AND PHOTOGRAPHS

Rule 1001 Definitions That Apply to This Article
Rule 1002 Requirement of the Original
Rule 1003 Admissibility of Duplicates
Rule 1004 Admissibility of Other Evidence of Content
Rule 1005 Copies of Public Records to Prove Content
Rule 1006 Summaries to Prove Content
Rule 1007 Testimony or Statement of a Party to Prove Content
Rule 1008 Functions of the Court and Jury

ARTICLE XI MISCELLANEOUS RULES

Rule 1101 Applicability of the Rules
Rule 1102 Amendments
Rule 1103 Title

PART X USCOURTS.GOV

Index

PART I
THE RULES AND JUDICIAL RULEMAKING

Table of Sections

A. AN INTRODUCTION TO THE FEDERAL RULES OF CIVIL PROCEDURE

Sec.

1.1 Introduction

1.2 Creating the Federal Rules of Civil Procedure

B. THE PROCESS OF JUDICIAL RULEMAKING

1.3 Introduction

1.4 How the Rules Are Amended

1.5 Summary of Procedure

1.6 Civil Rule Amendments in 2022

A. AN INTRODUCTION TO THE FEDERAL RULES OF CIVIL PROCEDURE

§ 1.1 Introduction

The Federal Rules of Civil Procedure ("Rules") took effect on Friday, September 16, 1938. They established the manner of practice for civil litigation in the federal trial courts. The Rules are national in scope. They apply in all federal districts, to all federal trial judges, and for all civil actions and proceedings (except where specifically exempted by the Rules themselves).[1] This result—a nationally uniform system of federal procedures—was one of the important objectives of adopting the Rules in the first place.

The constitutionality of the Rules flows from the authority granted Congress in Article III of the U.S. Constitution to establish a federal judiciary.[2] Where one of the Rules squarely addresses a matter of procedure, and that Rule is found to be both constitutional and in accordance with Congress's direct or delegated rulemaking authority, that Rule will govern—notwithstanding any contrary State law.[3] None of the Rules has

---

[1] *See* Rule 1; Rule 81.

[2] *See Hanna v. Plumer*, 380 U.S. 460, 472, 85 S. Ct. 1136, 14 L.Ed.2d 8 (1965) ("the constitutional provision for a federal court system (augmented by the Necessary and Proper Clause) carries with it congressional power to make rules governing the practice and pleading in those courts").

[3] *See Gasperini v. Ctr. for Humanities, Inc.*, 518 U.S. 415, 428 n.7, 116 S. Ct. 2211, 135 L. Ed. 2d 659 (1996).

ever been declared to be invalid.[4]

Today, the Rules are supplemented in nearly all federal districts with a set of "Local Rules," and many individual federal judges have supplemented them further by adopting "Chambers Policies" or "Standing Orders." None of those locally-adopted procedures are permitted to be inconsistent with the national Rules.[5] Moreover, many States have used the Rules as a template for crafting their own State procedures, and State courts occasionally refer to the Rules as a respected resource for interpreting their own State rules.[6]

§ 1.2 Creating the Federal Rules of Civil Procedure

Federal trial courts are located within the boundaries of the various States, territories, and the District of Columbia.[1] They were created during the first few months of the first session of the first U.S. Congress.[2] In that same law, known today as the Judiciary Act of 1789, Congress authorized federal courts to prepare rules for practice in their courtrooms, so long as those procedures were not "repugnant to the laws of the United States."[3] But that first Congress also instructed that, until further notice, each federal court was to conform its "writs and executions" in all "suits at common law" to match those "now used or allowed" in the State where that federal court was sitting.[4] The syntax of this law tied federal procedure not just to local State practice, but even more restrictedly to that State practice as it existed in September 1789 (making no adjustment for intervening State law changes and providing no guidance for federal courts formed in newly-admitted States).[5] In 1872, Congress reformed the "static" nature of this required federal conformity by directing that federal practice, pleadings, and other proceedings be generally conformed "as near as may be" to the practice, pleadings, and other proceedings governing practice "existing at the time" in

---

[4]*See Shady Grove Orthopedic Assocs., P.A. v. Allstate Ins. Co.*, 559 U.S. 393, 407, 130 S. Ct. 1431, 1442, 176 L. Ed. 2d 311 (2010) ("we have rejected every statutory challenge to a Federal Rule that has come before us").

[5]*See* Rule 83(a)(1).

[6]*See, e.g., Laffitte v. Bridgestone Corp.*, 674 S.E.2d 154, 162 n.10 (S.C. 2009) (federal decisions interpreting a federal Rule (which State rule mirrors) accepted as "persuasive authority" in correctly interpreting that State rule).

[1]Only two of the federal districts span outside the boundary of the States in which they sit—the District of Wyoming encompasses territory in Montana and Idaho (because the district includes all of Yellowstone National Park), *see* 28 U.S.C.A. § 131; and the District of Hawai'i encompasses other Pacific Island territories of the United States, *see* 28 U.S.C.A. § 91. Every other federal district court lies entirely within a single State or territory.

[2]*See* Judiciary Act of 1789, ch. 20, §§ 2-3, 1 Stat. 73, 73-74 (Sept. 24, 1789).

[3]*See* Judiciary Act of 1789, ch. 20, § 17, 1 Stat. 73, 83 (Sept. 24, 1789).

[4]*See* Process Act of 1789, ch. 21, § 1, 1 Stat. 93, 93 (Sept. 29, 1789).

[5]*See* CHARLES ALAN WRIGHT, LAW OF FEDERAL COURTS § 61 (5th ed. 1994).

the State courts of the particular State within which each federal court was located.[6] This conformity approach to federal practice had the effect of closely aligning each federal court's procedures to its host State's procedures, but in doing so, it allowed for federal procedures to differ—sometimes markedly—from one federal district to the next. Thus, how a lawyer practiced civil litigation in federal court in Boston might be quite different from the norms that prevailed in federal court in Richmond.

The story was different for suits in equity. For those types of disputes, Congress had directed the Supreme Court to prepare a special set of equity rules for use in the federal courts.[7] But even there, the obsolesce of the equity procedures soon proved troublesome.[8]

As the Nation grew in size, in population, and in legal complexity, these State-by-State variations in legal claims and antiquated procedures in equity suits became increasingly unsatisfactory. The Federal Rules of Civil Procedure were drafted to address these concerns. The goal was ambitious—to craft a single, nationally uniform set of procedures to govern civil litigation in every federal trial court across the Nation. After a lengthy, sometimes pitched battle in the federal legislature, Congress enacted the Rules Enabling Act of 1934, directing the Supreme Court to merge law cases and equity claims into a single, unified type of civil case that would be litigated in a single type of federal tribunal which would apply a newly-crafted, uniform set of federal procedures.[9] To assist in this imposing task, the Supreme Court commissioned a distinguished group of lawyers and law professors to prepare a draft of the Rules; their handiwork was then adopted by the Court about three years later in December 1937, reported to Congress in January 1938, and took effect in September 1938.[10]

As drafted, the Rules were destined to do far more than simply unify federal practice across the country. As one of the principal co-drafters of the Rules explained on the eve of the Rules taking effect: "The rules are really so simple that it is hard for those who are familiar with the technique of the modern litigation to

[6] *See* Conformity Act of 1872, ch. 255, § 5, 17 Stat. 196, 197 (June 1, 1872).

[7] *See* An Act for Regulating Processes in the Courts of the United States, ch. 36, § 2, 1 Stat. 275, 276 (May 8, 1792).

[8] *See* CHARLES ALAN WRIGHT, LAW OF FEDERAL COURTS § 61 (5th ed. 1994).

[9] *See* Rules Enabling Act of 1934, ch. 49, 48 Stat. 1064 (Mar. 8, 1934) (codified at 28 U.S.C.A. § 2072).

[10] For a contemporary summary of the drafting of the Rules, *see* generally Charles E. Clark, *The Proposed Federal Rules of Civil Procedure*, 22 A.B.A. J. 447 (1936); Charles E. Clark, *The New Federal Rules of Civil Procedure: The Last Phase—Underlying Philosophy Embodied in Some of the Basic Provisions of the New Procedure*, 23 A.B.A. J. 976 (1937).

appreciate how simple they are."[11] The Rules were prepared with a master, defining purpose: "to eliminate technical matters by removing the basis for technical objections, to make it as difficult as impossible, for cases to go off on procedural points, and to make litigation as inexpensive, as practicable and as convenient, as can be done."[12] In scope, effect, and influence on the practice of civil litigation in America, the Rules were little short of revolutionary.

In the many decades that have followed their promulgation, the Rules have been amended on numerous occasions to meet new challenges, address unforeseen developments and technological advances, and resolve shortcomings later discovered. The process for amending the Rules is not unlike the process by which they were originally drafted. Congress directed the formation of a "Judicial Conference of the United States," a body of federal judges from throughout the country to continuously study the operation and effect of the Rules in practice, and to recommend to the U.S. Supreme Court revisions to those Rules as may be "desirable to promote simplicity in procedure, fairness in administration, the just determination of litigation, and the elimination of unjustifiable expense and delay."[13] The work of the Conference is coordinated through committees on the various sets of federal rules, and those committees, in turn, make recommendations to the Conference. Before Rules are adopted, public consideration and comment is invited on prospective drafts. Only after the committees, the Conference, and the U.S. Supreme Court are all satisfied that an amendment is in order, will a revision to the Rules be delivered to Congress for legislative consideration. Congress, however, need not formally act on the proposed amendments. Under the terms of the Rules Enabling Act, Rule amendments take effect on December 1 of the year of submission unless Congress acts legislatively to modify or block them.[14]

The Rules amendment process is discussed in greater detail below.

---

[11]Edson R. Sunderland, *The New Federal Rules*, 45 W. Va. L. Q. 5, 30 (1938).

[12]Edson R. Sunderland, *The New Federal Rules*, 45 W. Va. L. Q. 5, 30 (1938).

[13]See 28 U.S.C.A. § 331.

[14]*See* 28 U.S.C.A. § 2074.

B. THE PROCESS OF JUDICIAL RULEMAKING

§ 1.3 Introduction

The federal rules govern procedure, practice, and evidence in the federal courts. They set forth the procedures for the conduct of court proceedings and serve as a pattern for the procedural rules adopted by many State court systems.

Authority

The Congress has authorized the federal judiciary to prescribe the rules of practice, procedure, and evidence for the federal courts, subject to the ultimate legislative right of the Congress to reject, modify, or defer any of the rules. The authority and procedures for promulgating rules are set forth in the Rules Enabling Act. 28 U.S.C.A. §§ 2071 to 2077.

The Judicial Conference of the United States is also required by statute to "carry on a continuous study of the operation and effect of the general rules of practice and procedure." 28 U.S.C.A. § 331. As part of this continuing obligation, the Conference is authorized to recommend amendments and additions to the rules to promote

- simplicity in procedure,
- fairness in administration,
- the just determination of litigation, and
- the elimination of unjustifiable expense and delay.

The Rules Committees

The Judicial Conference's responsibilities as to rules are coordinated by its Committee on Rules of Practice and Procedure, commonly referred to as the "Standing Committee." 28 U.S.C.A. § 2073(b). The Standing Committee has five advisory committees, dealing respectively with the appellate, bankruptcy, civil, criminal, and evidence rules. 28 U.S.C.A. § 2073(a)(2). The Standing Committee reviews and coordinates the recommendations of the five advisory committees, and it recommends to the Judicial Conference proposed rules changes "as may be necessary to maintain consistency and otherwise promote the interests of justice." 28 U.S.C.A. § 2073(b).

The Standing Committee and the advisory committees are composed of federal judges, practicing lawyers, law professors, State chief justices, and representatives of the Department of Justice. Each committee has a reporter, a prominent law professor, who is responsible for coordinating the committee's agenda and drafting appropriate amendments to the rules and explanatory committee notes.

The Assistant Director for Judges Programs of the Administrative Office of the United States Courts currently serves as secretary to the Standing Committee, coordinates the operational aspects of the rules process, and maintains the records of the committees. The Rules Committee Support Office of the Administrative Office provides the day to day administrative and legal support for the secretary and the committees.

Open Meetings and Records

Meetings of the rules committees are open to the public and are widely announced. All records of the committees, including minutes of committee meetings, suggestions and comments submitted by the public, statements of witnesses, transcripts of public hearings, and memoranda prepared by the reporters, are public and are maintained by the secretary. Copies of the rules and proposed amendments are available from the Rules Committee Support Office. The proposed amendments are also published on the Judiciary's website <http:\\www.uscourts.gov>.

§ 1.4 How the Rules Are Amended

The pervasive and substantial impact of the rules on the practice of law in the federal courts demands exacting and meticulous care in drafting rule changes. The rulemaking process is time-consuming and involves a minimum of seven stages of formal comment and review. From beginning to end, it usually takes two to three years for a suggestion to be enacted as a rule.

The process, however, may be expedited when there is an urgent need to enact an amendment to the rules.

All interested individuals and organizations are provided an opportunity to comment on proposed rules amendments and to recommend alternative proposals. The comments received from this extensive and thorough public examination are studied very carefully by the committees and generally improve the amendments. The committees actively encourage the submission of comments, both positive and negative, to ensure that proposed amendments have been considered by a broad segment of the bench and bar.

STEP 1 INITIAL CONSIDERATION BY THE ADVISORY COMMITTEE

Making suggestions for changes

Proposed changes in the rules are suggested by judges, clerks of court, lawyers, professors, government agencies, or other individuals and organizations. They are considered in the first instance by the appropriate advisory committees (appellate, bankruptcy, civil, criminal, or evidence). Suggestions for changes, additions, or deletions must be submitted in writing to the secretary, who acknowledges each letter and distributes it to the chair of the Standing Committee and the chair and reporter of the advisory committee.

The reporter normally analyzes the suggestions and makes appropriate recommendations to the advisory committee. The suggestions from the public and the recommendations of the reporter are placed on the advisory committee's agenda and are normally discussed at its next meeting. The advisory committees usually meet twice a year, and they also conduct business by telephone and correspondence.

Consideration of suggestions

In considering a suggestion for a change in the rules, the advisory committee may take several courses of action, including:

1. Accepting the suggestion, either completely or with modifications or limitations:
2. Deferring action on the suggestion or seeking additional information regarding its operation and impact;
3. Rejecting a suggestion because it does not have merit or would be inconsistent with other rules or a statute; or
4. Rejecting a suggestion because, although it may be meritorious, it simply is not necessary or important enough to warrant the significant step of an amendment to the federal rules.

The secretary is required, to the extent feasible, to advise the person making a suggestion of the action taken on it by the advisory committee.

Drafting Rules Changes

When an advisory committee decides initially that a particular change in the rules would be appropriate, it normally asks its reporter to prepare a draft amendment to the rules and an explanatory committee note. The draft amendment and committee note are discussed and voted upon at a committee meeting.

The Standing Committee has a style subcommittee that works with the respective advisory committees in reviewing proposed amendments to ensure that the rules are written in clear and consistent language. In addition, the reporter of the Standing Committee and the reporters of the five advisory committees are encouraged to work together to promote clarity and consistency among the various sets of federal rules.

STEP 2 PUBLICATION AND PUBLIC COMMENT

Once an advisory committee votes initially to recommend an amendment to the rules, it must obtain the approval of the Standing Committee, or its chair, to publish the proposed amendment for public comment. In seeking publication, the advisory committee must explain to the Standing Committee the reasons for its proposal, including any minority or separate views.

After publication is approved, the secretary arranges for printing and distribution of the proposed amendment to the bench and bar, to publishers, and to the general public. More than 10,000 persons and organizations are on the mailing list, including

- federal judges and other federal court officers,
- United States attorneys,
- other federal government agencies and officials,
- State chief justices,
- State attorneys general,
- legal publications,
- law schools,
- bar associations, and
- interested lawyers, individuals, and organizations requesting distribution.

In order to promote public comment, the proposed amendments are sent to points of contact that have been established with 53 State bar associations.

The public is normally given 6 months to comment in writing to the secretary regarding the proposed amendment. In an emergency, a shorter time period may be authorized by the Standing Committee.

During the 6-month comment period, the advisory committee schedules one or more public hearings on the proposed amendments. Persons who wish to appear and testify at the hearings are required to contact the secretary at least 30 days before the hearings.

STEP 3 CONSIDERATION OF THE PUBLIC COMMENTS AND FINAL APPROVAL BY THE ADVISORY COMMITTEE

At the conclusion of the public comment period, the reporter is required to prepare a summary of the written comments received from the public and the testimony presented at the hearings. The advisory committee then takes a fresh look at the proposed rule changes in light of the written comments and testimony.

If the advisory committee decides to make a substantial change in its proposal, it may provide a period for additional public notice and comment.

Once the advisory committee decides to proceed in final form, it submits the proposed amendment to the Standing Committee for approval. Each proposed amendment must be accompanied by a separate report summarizing the comments received from the public and explaining any changes made by the advisory committee following the original publication. The advisory committee's report must also include minority views of any members who wish to have their separate views recorded.

STEP 4 APPROVAL BY THE STANDING COMMITTEE

The Standing Committee considers the final recommendations of the advisory committee and may accept, reject, or modify them. If the Standing Committee approves a proposed rule change, it will transmit it to the Judicial Conference with a recommendation for approval, accompanied by the advisory committee's reports and the Standing Committee's own report explaining any modifications it made. If the Standing Committee makes a modification that constitutes a substantial change from the recommendation of the advisory committee, the proposal will normally be returned to the advisory committee with appropriate instructions.

STEP 5 JUDICIAL CONFERENCE APPROVAL

The Judicial Conference normally considers proposed amendments to the rules at its September session each year. If approved by the Conference, the amendments are transmitted promptly to the Supreme Court.

STEP 6 SUPREME COURT APPROVAL

The Supreme Court has the authority to prescribe the federal rules, subject to a statutory waiting period. 28 U.S.C.A. §§ 2072, 2075. The Court normally transmits proposed rules amendments to the Congress by May 1 of each year. 28 U.S.C.A. §§ 2074, 2075.

STEP 7 CONGRESSIONAL REVIEW

The Congress has a statutory period of at least 7 months to act on any rules prescribed by the Supreme Court. If the Congress does not enact legislation to reject, modify, or defer the rules, they take effect as a matter of law on December 1. 28 U.S.C.A. §§ 2074, 2075.

§ 1.5 Summary of Rulemaking Procedures

Action	Date
STEP 1	
• Suggestion for a change in the rules. (*Submitted in writing to the secretary.*)	At any time.
• Referred by the secretary to the appropriate advisory committee.	Promptly after receipt.
• Considered by the advisory committee.	Normally at the next committee meeting.
• If approved, the advisory committee seeks authority from the Standing Committee to circulate to bench and bar for comment.	Normally at the same meeting or the next committee meeting.
STEP 2	

Action	Date
• Public comment period.	6 months.
• Public hearings.	During the public comment period.
STEP 3	
• Advisory committee considers the amendment afresh in light of public comments and testimony at the hearings.	About one or two months after the close of the comment period.
• Advisory committee approves amendment in final form and transmits to the Standing Committee.	About one or two months after the close of the comment period.
STEP 4	
• Standing Committee approves amendment, with or without revisions, and recommends approval by the Judicial Conference.	Normally at its June meeting.
STEP 5	
• Judicial Conference approves amendment and transmits to the Supreme Court.	Normally at its September session.
STEP 6	
• The Supreme Court prescribes the amendment.	By May 1.
STEP 7	
• Congress has statutory time period in which to enact legislation to reject, modify, or defer the amendment.	By December 1.

Action	Date
• Absent Congressional action, the amendment becomes law.	December 1.

§ 1.6 Civil Rule Amendments in 2022

This year, the U.S. Supreme Court has promulgated one amendment to the Federal Rules of Civil Procedure, which takes effect on December 1, 2022:

- **Rule 7.1:** to extend this Rule's corporate disclosure obligation to intervenors (not just existing parties), and to impose a citizenship disclosure obligation for diversity cases.

This amendment is discussed in greater depth in Part III of this *Handbook*.

PART II
GENERAL CONCEPTS IN FEDERAL CIVIL PRACTICE: *PERSONAL JURISDICTION, SUBJECT-MATTER JURISDICTION, REMOVAL AND REMAND, VENUE AND FORUM NON CONVENIENS, THE ERIE DOCTRINE, AND PRECLUSION (RES JUDICATA AND COLLATERAL ESTOPPEL)*

Table of Sections

A. OVERVIEW—FEDERAL JUDICIAL POWER

Sec.

2.1 A Primer on Invoking Federal Judicial Power

B. PERSONAL JURISDICTION

2.2 Introduction
2.3 Step #1—Legislative Authority
2.4 Step #2—Constitutional (Due Process) Authority
2.5 Acquiring *In Personam* Jurisdiction
2.5a — Circumstance #1—Consent to Jurisdiction
2.5b — Circumstance #2—In-State Service (Transient or "Tag") Jurisdiction
2.5c — Circumstance #3—Contacts-Based Jurisdiction
2.5c1 — Specific Jurisdiction
2.5c2 — General Jurisdiction
2.6 Acquiring *In Rem* Jurisdiction
2.7 Acquiring *Quasi In Rem* Jurisdiction
2.8 Notice and an Opportunity to Be Heard—Another Prerequisite for Exercising Personal Jurisdiction

C. SUBJECT-MATTER JURISDICTION

2.9 Introduction
2.10 Federal Question Jurisdiction
2.11 Diversity Jurisdiction
2.11a —The First Requirement: Complete Diversity of Citizenship
2.11b —The Second Requirement: Amount in Controversy
2.11c —Diversity Jurisdiction in Class Actions and Mass Torts
2.12 Supplemental Jurisdiction

D. REMOVAL AND REMAND

2.13 Removal
2.14 Removal Procedure
2.15 Removal of Class Actions.
2.16 Post-Removal Procedures and Remand

E. VENUE AND *FORUM NON CONVENIENS*

2.17 Venue

2.17a Venue Transfer and *Forum Non Conveniens*

F. THE *ERIE* DOCTRINE

2.18 Introduction
2.18a —The Namesake: *Erie R.R. Co. v. Tompkins* and its Progeny
2.18b —*Erie* Today, and the Sources of Federal Procedure
2.18c —Identifying the Law to Apply
2.18d —A Residue of Federal Common Law

G. PRECLUSION (RES JUDICATA AND COLLATERAL ESTOPPEL)

2.19 Introduction
2.20 Claim Preclusion (Res Judicata—)
2.21 Issue Preclusion (*Collateral Estoppel*)

A. OVERVIEW—FEDERAL JUDICIAL POWER

§ 2.1 A Primer on Invoking Federal Judicial Power

The Federal Rules of Civil Procedure (referred to throughout this *Handbook* as the "Rules") establish requirements for practicing civil litigation in the Nation's federal trial courts.[1] But the Rules are not the only source of procedural law governing federal civil litigation. In addition to these national Rules, each federal district has promulgated local procedural rules that apply to cases pending in that district. Most federal judges also have developed a further set of procedures (typically called "Chambers Rules") that apply to cases pending in their courtrooms. All local procedures must be consistent with, and not duplicative of, the national Rules,[2] and they, like the national Rules, carry the force and effect of law.[3] Accordingly, practitioners must know and abide by the national Federal Rules of Civil Procedure as well as the rules set both by the federal district where their lawsuit is pending and by the federal district judge before whom they will be appearing.

Still other sources of law also set federal civil litigation procedure. The U.S. Constitution imposes limits on how and when federal courts may operate,[4] as do laws enacted by the U.S. Congress[5] and treaties to which the United States of America is a signatory.[6]

Thus, proficiency with the national Rules forms just a part of

---

[1]For a discussion of the drafting history of the Rules and the process for their amendment, see *supra* Part I.

[2]*See* Rule 83(a).

[3]*See Hollingsworth v. Perry*, 558 U.S. 183, 191 (2010); *Weil v. Neary*, 278 U.S. 160, 169 (1929).

[4]*See, e.g.*, U.S. CONST. amend. V ("No person shall be . . . deprived of . . . property, without due process of law . . .").

[5]*See, e.g.*, 28 U.S.C. § 1332 (establishing federal subject-matter jurisdiction on the basis of diversity of citizenship); 28 U.S.C. § 1446 (establishing procedures for removal of State lawsuit to federal court).

[6]*See, e.g.*, Hague Convention on the Service Abroad of Judicial and

the federal civil litigator's practice obligations. As their text makes clear, the Federal Rules of Civil Procedure do not "extend" or "limit" the authority of, or proper situs for, federal civil litigation.[7] Accordingly, determining that one of the Rules permits an act does not answer the preliminary, foundational question of whether the court has the judicial power to hear a lawsuit in which that act would occur. This Part II, *General Concepts in Federal Civil Practice*, offers a survey of these essential but non-Rule-based elements of civil litigation.

* * *

An irreducible, threshold requirement for federal civil litigation is a judge with the lawful authority to rule. That authority begins in the U.S. Constitution. Article III created the federal judicial power of the United States, installed a national Supreme Court, and set the permissible reach of this federal power.[8] Article I invested Congress with the right to create inferior federal courts and to enact laws "necessary and proper" for those courts' fair and efficient operation.[9] And the Fifth Amendment restricts a federal judge from exercising his or her power in a manner that would offend the Due Process Clause.[10] Due process, in turn, requires both that the defendant (or the defendant's property) be brought within the court's jurisdiction ("personal" jurisdiction) and that the tribunal be "competent" by "the law of its creation" to rule "upon the subject-matter of the suit" ("subject-matter" jurisdiction).[11]

The Supreme Court has chided itself for using the terms "jurisdiction" and "jurisdictional" a bit imprecisely in the past,[12] but today those words are understood as confined to constitutional and statutory constraints on a federal judge's authority to rule—

Extrajudicial Documents in Civil or Commercial Matters, Nov. 15, 1965, 20 U.S.T. 361, T.I.A.S. No. 6638, 658 U.N.T.S. 163 (entered into force Feb. 10, 1969).

[7]*See* Rule 82. *See also Owen Equip. & Erection Co. v. Kroger*, 437 U.S. 365, 370 (1978) ("it is axiomatic that the Federal Rules of Civil Procedure do not create or withdraw federal jurisdiction").

[8]*See* U.S. CONST. art. III.

[9]*See* U.S. CONST. art. I, § 8, cl. 9 & 18. II. *See also Jinks v. Richland Cty.*, 538 U.S. 456, 462, 123 S. Ct. 1667, 155 L. Ed. 2d 631 (2003) (Congress authorized to enact court procedures " 'conducive to the due administration of justice' in federal court" and " 'plainly adapted' to that end") (citations omitted).

[10]*See, e.g.*, U.S. CONST. amend. V. The Constitution's guarantee of due process extends to State courts as well, but through the Fourteenth Amendment. *See infra* § 2.4 (**"Two Different Due Process Clauses"**).

[11]*See Pennoyer v. Neff*, 95 U.S. 714, 733 (1877). *See also Ins. Corp. of Ireland v. Compagnie des Bauxites de Guinee*, 456 U.S. 694, 701 (1982).

[12]See *Kontrick v. Ryan*, 540 U.S. 443, 454 (2004) ("less than meticulous" in using term); *Steel Co. v. Citizens for a Better Env't*, 523 U.S. 83, 90 (1998) ("a word of many, too many, meanings") (citation omitted). *See generally Nutraceutical Corp. v. Lambert*, ___ U.S. ___, 139 S. Ct. 710, 714, 203 L. Ed. 2d 43 (2019) (time limits set by federal rule, rather than by congressional statute, are not jurisdictional).

namely, "personal" jurisdiction and "subject-matter" jurisdiction.[13] Over the years, the law has evolved on how these two predicates for judicial power operate. But the law has remained constant on at least one point. When the judge's jurisdiction is missing, she or he "cannot proceed at all" and is, instead, authorized to take only two actions: to declare that jurisdiction is absent and to dismiss the case.[14]

"Personal" jurisdiction is the authority of a federal judge to enter a ruling that will bind the particular litigants in the lawsuit.[15] It protects nonresident defendants from being unfairly "haled into a distant and possibly inconvenient forum."[16] It is conferred by behavior: either by voluntarily submitting to the judge's power to rule on the dispute[17] or by voluntarily choosing to engage with the forum in some manner deemed sufficient to permit a judge there to rule on the dispute.[18] Because it is anchored in a litigant's willing conduct, an objection to personal jurisdiction is considered a defense that can be waived or forfeited.[19] Personal jurisdiction is acquired through service of process.[20] Personal jurisdiction is discussed in Sections 2.2 through 2.8 of this Part II and in Authors' Commentary to Rule 12(b)(2) in Part III.

"Subject-matter" jurisdiction is the authority of a federal judge to enter a binding ruling in a particular type of lawsuit.[21] Unlike personal jurisdiction's function of protecting individuals against inconvenience, subject-matter jurisdiction is treated as an irreducible structural restraint on a federal judge's authority to adjudicate.[22] To rule without subject-matter jurisdiction is "to

---

[13]*See Ruhrgas AG v. Marathon Oil Co.*, 526 U.S. 574, 577 (1999) ("Jurisdiction to resolve cases on the merits requires both authority over the category of claim in suit (subject-matter jurisdiction) and authority over the parties (personal jurisdiction), so that the court's decision will bind them.").

[14]*See Ex Parte McCardle*, 74 U.S. 506, 514 (1868).

[15]*See Burger King Corp. v. Rudzewicz*, 471 U.S. 462, 471–72 (1985) (constitutional due process "protects an individual's liberty interest in not being subject to the binding judgments of a forum with which he has established no meaningful 'contacts, ties, or relations' ").

[16]*See Carlsbad Tech., Inc. v. HIF Bio, Inc.*, 556 U.S. 635, 639 (2009) (citation omitted).

[17]*See Pennoyer v. Neff*, 95 U.S. 714, 733 (1877) (voluntary appearance).

[18]*See World-Wide Volkswagen Corp. v. Woodson*, 444 U.S. 286, 297 (1980) ("allows potential defendants to structure their primary conduct with some minimum assurance as to where that conduct will and will not render them liable to suit").

[19]*See Ins. Corp. of Ireland v. Compagnie des Bauxites de Guinee*, 456 U.S. 694, 703 (1982). *See also* Rule 12(h)(1).

[20]*See BNSF Ry. Co. v. Tyrrell*, 581 U.S. __, 137 S. Ct. 1549, 1556 (2017); *Omni Cap. Int'l, Ltd. v. Rudolf Wolff & Co.*, 484 U.S. 97, 104 (1987).

[21]*See United States v. Morton*, 467 U.S. 822, 828 (1984).

[22]*See Steel Co. v. Citizens for a Better Env't*, 523 U.S. 83, 101 (1998) ("an essential ingredient of separation and equilibration of powers, restrain-

act ultra vires."[23] Consequently, subject-matter jurisdiction cannot be conferred by litigants' consent nor can a defect in subject-matter jurisdiction be waived or forfeited.[24] Instead, federal judges have an independent, affirmative duty to check their own subject-matter jurisdiction, defects in subject-matter jurisdiction can be raised at any time (even after final judgment), and if subject-matter jurisdiction is found to be lacking, dismissal is compelled.[25] Testing for a judge's subject-matter jurisdiction is essential, but it need not always precede a personal jurisdiction inquiry. There is "no unyielding . . . hierarchy" among types of jurisdiction and, while it may be customary to examine subject-matter jurisdiction first, it is not necessarily improper to begin a judicial power inquiry with personal jurisdiction.[26] Subject-matter jurisdiction, along with its companion concepts of removal and remand, are discussed in Sections 2.9 and 2.16 of this Part II and in Authors' Commentary to Rule 12(b)(1) in Part III.

Although not a jurisdictional principle, "**venue**" represents yet another restriction on a federal judge's power to rule. Venue proposes to select for the litigation a convenient geography; like personal jurisdiction, venue endeavors to safeguard defendants against an unfair or inconvenient place for trial.[27] Also like personal jurisdiction, venue is considered a defendant's personal privilege and, thus, may waived or forfeited.[28] Venue is discussed in Sections 2.17 and 2.17a of this Part II and in Authors' Commentary to Rule 12(b)(3) in Part III.

Following orientations to personal jurisdiction, subject-matter jurisdiction, and venue, this *General Concepts in Federal Civil Practice* portion of the *Handbook* concludes with two final doctrines to round out the federal practitioner's toolbox of core litigation principles:

- The ***Erie* doctrine** supplies the sometimes-byzantine process by which federal judges select the law to be applied in

---

ing the courts from acting at certain times"); *U.S. Catholic Conf. v. Abortion Rts. Mobilization, Inc.*, 487 U.S. 72, 77 (1988) ("the central principle of a free society that courts have finite bounds of authority, some of constitutional origin, which exist to protect citizens from . . . the excessive use of judicial power").

[23]*See Steel Co. v. Citizens for a Better Env't*, 523 U.S. 83, 101–02 (1998). *See also Mansfield, C. & L. M. R. Co. v. Swan*, 111 U.S. 379, 382 (1884) ("the rule, springing from the nature and limits of the judicial power of the United States, is inflexible and without exception").

[24]*See Ashcroft v. Iqbal*, 556 U.S. 662, 671 (2009) (no forfeiture or waiver); *Ins. Corp. of Ireland v. Compagnie des Bauxites de Guinee*, 456 U.S. 694, 702 (1982) (no consent).

[25]*See Henderson ex rel. Henderson v. Shinseki*, 562 U.S. 428, 434 (2011); *Arbaugh v. Y&H Corp.*, 546 U.S. 500, 506–07 (2006). *See also* Rule 12(h)(3) ("If the court determines at any time that it lacks subject-matter jurisdiction, the court must dismiss the action.").

[26]*See Ruhrgas AG v. Marathon Oil Co.*, 526 U.S. 574, 578 (1999).

[27]*See Leroy v. Great W. United Corp.*, 443 U.S. 173, 180 & 183–84 (1979).

[28]*See Leroy v. Great W. United Corp.*, 443 U.S. 173, 180 (1979).

federal civil litigation. It is discussed in Sections 2.18 through 2.18d of this Part II.

- The **preclusion doctrines**—"claim preclusion" (traditionally labeled "res judicata") and "issue preclusion" (traditionally labeled "collateral estoppel")—assess a litigant's right to re-try all or a portion of a claim that had been litigated earlier. They are discussed in Sections 2.19 through 2.21 of this Part II.

B. PERSONAL JURISDICTION

Table of Sections

2.2 Introduction
2.3 Step #1—Legislative Authority
2.4 Step #2—Constitutional (Due Process) Authority
2.5 Acquiring *In Personam* Jurisdiction
2.5a — Circumstance #1—Consent to Jurisdiction
2.5b — Circumstance #2—In-State Service (Transient or "Tag") Jurisdiction
2.5c — Circumstance #3—Contacts-Based Jurisdiction
2.5c1 — Specific Jurisdiction
2.5c2 — General Jurisdiction
2.6 Acquiring *In Rem* Jurisdiction
2.7 Acquiring *Quasi In Rem* Jurisdiction
2.8 Notice and an Opportunity to Be Heard—Another Prerequisite for Exercising Personal Jurisdiction

§ 2.2 Introduction

CORE CONCEPT

Personal jurisdiction concerns "the court's power to exercise control over the parties" to a lawsuit.[1] It is the *litigant*-focused type of jurisdiction. It examines whether it is lawful and fair for a judge to exercise coercive judicial power to issue a ruling that would bind *these* particular persons, *these* particular entities, or *these* particular things (or parcels of property). That power derives (ordinarily) from two sources—an authorizing statute and constitutional tolerance. Those sources operate in tandem. Governments set the territorial reach of their courts by statute; the ensuing use of that reach as exercised by those courts must then not offend constitutional due process. Consequently, personal jurisdiction is a two-step inquiry.[2] Unless both steps are met, the court will lack personal jurisdiction over that defendant and may not proceed to bind the defendant with a judicial ruling,

---

[1]*See Leroy v. Great W. United Corp.*, 443 U.S. 173, 180 (1979).

[2]*See Motus, LLC v. CarData Consultants, Inc.*, 23 F.4th 115, 121 (1st Cir. 2022) (must be statutorily authorized and consistent with constitutional due process); *Charles Schwab Corp. v. Bank of Am. Corp.*, 883 F.3d 68, 82 (2d Cir. 2018) (same). *See also Viasystems, Inc. v. EBM-Papst St. Georgen GmbH & Co., KG*, 646 F.3d 589, 594 (8th Cir. 2011) ("Even if personal jurisdiction over a defendant is authorized by the forum state's long-arm statute, jurisdiction can be asserted only if it comports with the strictures of the Due Process Clause.").

absent the defendant's consent or waiver.[3] Comportment with an authorizing statute is forum-specific and will vary depending on the court system. Satisfying federal due process is nationally uniform by court system, though interpretative nuances sometimes persist among federal circuits (in the absence of unifying precedent from the U.S. Supreme Court). If personal jurisdiction is statutorily authorized and constitutionally permissible, it may be acquired through proper service of process (or its waiver).[4]

The law has traditionally grouped personal jurisdiction into two broad categories: *in personam* jurisdiction (where the judge's power rests on authority over a defendant's person) and *in rem / quasi in rem* jurisdiction (where the judge's power rests on authority over a defendant's property located within the territory of the court).[5]

APPLICATIONS

Must Be Proper as to Each Party, Each Claim

Personal jurisdiction under one or the other of these categories must exist as to each party[6] and each claim[7] in a lawsuit.

- *Federal Question Lawsuits:* The majority view among the courts of appeals holds that the 5th Amendment does not excuse the requirement that a proper Rule 4(k) basis for personal jurisdiction must exist as to each party and each claim in a federal question lawsuit, absent an express congressional authorization otherwise.[8]
- *Pendent Personal Jurisdiction:* Some courts have ruled

[3] *Cf. United Techs. Corp. v. Mazer*, 556 F.3d 1260, 1275 n.15 (11th Cir. 2009) (because personal jurisdiction failed under the legislative step, court did not proceed on to consider the constitutional step).

[4] *See BNSF Ry. Co. v. Tyrrell*, 581 U.S. —, 137 S. Ct. 1549, 1556 (2017); *Omni Cap. Int'l, Ltd. v. Rudolf Wolff & Co.*, 484 U.S. 97, 104 (1987). *See also Schwab Short-Term Bond Mkt. Fund v. Lloyds Banking Grp. PLC*, 22 F.4th 103, 121 (2d Cir. 2021) (noting three requirements for personal jurisdiction: proper service, statutory basis, and constitutional comportment).

[5] *See Shaffer v. Heitner*, 433 U.S. 186, 199 (1977).

[6] *See Rush v. Savchuk*, 444 U.S. 320, 332 (1980). *Accord Bristol-Myers Squibb Co. v. Superior Ct.*, 582 U.S. —, 137 S. Ct. 1773, 1783 (2017).

[7] *See Charles Schwab Corp. v. Bank of Am. Corp.*, 883 F.3d 68, 83 (2d Cir. 2018); *Dental Dynamics, LLC v. Jolly Dental Grp., LLC*, 946 F.3d 1223, 1228 (10th Cir. 2020).

[8] *Compare Fischer v. Fed. Express Corp.*, 42 F.4th 366, 370–88 (3d Cir. 2022) (non-resident opt-in FLSA claimants could not assert personal jurisdiction over defendant when their claims did not arise from or relate to defendant's in-State activities, notwithstanding that lead plaintiffs' claims had proper personal jurisdiction), *and Vallone v. CJS Sols. Grp., LLC*, 9 F.4th 861, 865–66 (8th Cir. 2021) (same result, because personal jurisdiction must be assessed claim by claim), *with Canaday v. Anthem Cos.*, 9 F.4th 392, 398–404 (6th Cir. 2021) (same result, Congress could have, but did not, authorize nationwide service in FLSA actions, so host State's personal jurisdiction limits apply), *and Waters v. Day & Zimmermann NPS, Inc.*, 23 F.4th 84, 92–100 (1st Cir. 2022) (although non-resident opt-in FLSA

that if the trial judge possesses personal jurisdiction as to certain of a litigant's claims in the lawsuit, the judge might also exercise "pendent" personal jurisdiction over that litigant's remaining claims in the lawsuit so long as they arise out of the same "common nucleus of operative facts" as the claims for which personal jurisdiction exists.[9]

How to Challenge Personal Jurisdiction

A judge's exercise of personal jurisdiction can be challenged by filing a pre-answer motion to dismiss on that ground. If a party files no pre-answer motions, the objection can be raised in that party's responsive pleading and must be thereafter dutifully preserved. In certain circumstances, the objection may be asserted by collateral attack following a default. The process for pursuing each of these options is discussed in Part III of this text.[10]

Burden of Proving Personal Jurisdiction

Ordinarily, the party invoking the court's personal jurisdiction bears the burden of demonstrating that it exists.[11] Thus, that burden typically falls on the plaintiff, but usually is not triggered unless and until the defendant contests the court's right to exercise personal jurisdiction.[12] The nature of the burden and how it is carried depends on the manner of the defendant's challenge. Those logistics are discussed in depth in Part III of this text.[13]

Jurisdictional Discovery

On occasion, a party may contend that its adversary is, alone, in possession of the facts needed to show that sufficient forum-related contacts exist (or do not exist) to allow personal jurisdiction. In such circumstances the presiding judge may grant limited discovery so that the seeking party can endeavor to obtain that jurisdictional evidence. Before authorizing such discovery, judges normally require the seeking party to propose more than a hopeful fishing expedition. Instead, that party ordinarily must make a good faith showing that its targeted discovery might lead to facts confirming the existence of

---

claimants might lack 14th Amendment ability to initiate lawsuit against defendant, once named plaintiff acquired proper personal jurisdiction over defendant, 5th Amendment permitted non-resident opt-in claimants' joinder),

[9]*See Laurel Gardens, LLC v. Mckenna*, 948 F.3d 105, 123–24 (3d Cir. 2020); *Action Embroidery Corp. v. Atl. Embroidery, Inc.*, 368 F.3d 1174, 1180–81 (9th Cir. 2004). *But cf. Canaday v. Anthem Cos., Inc.*, 9 F.4th 392, 401–02 (6th Cir. 2021) (questioning whether such jurisdiction exists).

[10]*See infra* Rule 12(b)(2) and accompanying authors' commentary.

[11]*See Luv N' care, Ltd. v. Insta-Mix, Inc.*, 438 F.3d 465, 469 (5th Cir. 2006).

[12]*See UMG Recordings, Inc. v. Kurbanov*, 963 F.3d 344, 350 (4th Cir. 2020); *Curry v. Revolution Lab'ys, LLC*, 949 F.3d 385, 392 (7th Cir. 2020).

[13]*See infra* Rule 12(b)(2) and accompanying authors' commentary ("**Burden of Proof**", "**Types of Challenges**", "**Legal Test**").

personal jurisdiction over the adversary.[14] If jurisdictional discovery is allowed, it will take place within the Rules governing discovery discussed later in this text.[15]

§ 2.3 Step #1—Legislative Authority

CORE CONCEPT

The first step in establishing personal jurisdiction is satisfying the forum's legislative requirements for the exercise of judicial power over the particular defendant. Each legislature is entitled to determine how much personal jurisdiction authority to impart to its courts, and a judge's exercise of personal jurisdiction must be faithful to that limit.[1] Of course, a litigant's consent to personal jurisdiction may excuse an inability to satisfy the legislature's requirements.[2] Remember, though, that in addition to this first step (satisfying the forum's legislative requirements), every exercise of personal jurisdiction must also provide the defendant with due process (the second step), as explained in the next section.

APPLICATIONS

State-Granted Power: Resident Defendants

State legislatures often grant their courts very broad judicial authority over defendants who reside within their borders. (For personal jurisdiction purposes, "reside" often means more than temporary presence—it generally means citizenship.) South Carolina is a good example. Its legislature grants the South Carolina courts the authority to exercise personal jurisdiction over any cause of action against a defendant who is domiciled in the State, organized under the laws of the State, or maintains its principal place of business in the State.[3]

State-Granted Power: Non-Resident Defendants

When the defendant does not reside within the State's borders, the grant of personal jurisdiction by the State legislatures is (and must be) more tightly constrained. These grants, often called "long-arm statutes," can vary greatly by State. Florida is a good example of this type of authority. Its legislature permits the Florida courts to exercise personal jurisdiction over a non-resident defendant as to a cause of action

---

[14]*See* Authors' Commentary to Rule 12(b)(2) (**"Allowing Pre-Ruling Jurisdictional Discovery"**).

[15]*See infra* Rules 26–37 and accompanying authors' commentary.

[1]*See Chloe v. Queen Bee of Beverly Hills, LLC*, 616 F.3d 158, 169 (2d Cir. 2010) (must satisfy New York's long-arm statute, then due process); *Diamond Crystal Brands, Inc. v. Food Movers Int'l, Inc.*, 593 F.3d 1249, 1263 (11th Cir. 2010) (courts "must engage in a statutory examination that is independent of, and distinct from, the constitutional analysis to ensure that both, separate prongs of the jurisdictional inquiry are satisfied").

[2]*See Knowlton v. Allied Van Lines, Inc.*, 900 F.2d 1196, 1199 (8th Cir. 1990) (consent-based personal jurisdiction "exist[s] independently of long-arm statutes").

[3]*See* S.C. CODE § 36-2-802.

arising from nine different categories of Florida-related behavior, including: operating a business in Florida, committing a tort in Florida, breaching a contract in Florida, or insuring a person located in Florida.[4]

State-Granted Power: "Unenumerated" Authority

Other State legislatures grant their courts "unenumerated" judicial authority, permitting those courts to exercise personal jurisdiction to the greatest extent that the U.S. Constitution will tolerate. Wyoming is a good example of this type of "unenumerated" grant.[5] In such States, the two-step personal jurisdiction inquiry (*i.e.,* legislative authority first, then due process comportment) functionally conflates into a single constitutional inquiry.[6]

State-Granted Power: Hybrid Authority

Still other State legislatures follow a hybrid approach, granting specific categories of approved "long-arm" reach along with a later generalized grant of "unenumerated" judicial authority. Illinois is an example of the hybrid approach: it sets out fourteen specific categories of qualifying Illinois-related conduct that could confer jurisdiction, which it follows with a generalized grant of personal jurisdiction "on any other basis now or hereafter permitted by" the State and federal constitutions.[7]

Federally-Granted Power (Personal Jurisdiction in Federal Courts)

The allowable personal jurisdiction reach of the federal courts is set out in Rule 4(k) of the Federal Rules of Civil Procedure, which is discussed elsewhere in this text.[8] By way of overview, that Rule grants the federal courts the right to exercise personal jurisdiction in four circumstances:

- *Borrowed State Statute:* when the State courts in the State where the federal court is located would be able to exercise personal jurisdiction over the defendant; or
- *Congress Allows:* when Congress, by particular federal statute, sets some special reach for a federal court's exercise of personal jurisdiction in certain types of lawsuits; or
- *The 100-Mile Bulge Rule:* when the defendant is joined

[4]*See* FLA. STAT. § 48.193(1)(a).

[5]*See* WYO. STAT. § 5-1-107(a) ("A Wyoming court may exercise jurisdiction on any basis not inconsistent with the Wyoming or United States constitution.").

[6]*See Carmona v. Leo Ship Mgmt., Inc.*, 924 F.3d 190, 193 (5th Cir. 2019) ("the two inquiries merge"); *Xilinx, Inc. v. Papst Licensing GmbH & Co. KG*, 848 F.3d 1346, 1353 (Fed. Cir. 2017) ("the two inquiries collapse into a single inquiry"). *See also Helicopteros Nacionales de Colombia, S.A. v. Hall*, 466 U.S. 408, 413 (1984) (because long-arm statute reaches as far as due process allow, "the only question remaining for the court to decide was whether [the exercise of personal jurisdiction] was consistent with the Due Process Clause").

[7]*See* 735 ILL. COMP. STAT. § 5/2-209(a) & (c).

[8]*See infra* Rule 4(k) and accompanying authors' commentary.

into the lawsuit by Rule 14 (third-party practice/impleader) or Rule 19 (required party joinder) and served within a federal district that is not more than 100 miles from where the lawsuit is pending; or

- *National-Contacts Personal Jurisdiction:* when the defendant is being sued for a claim arising under federal law and is not subject to the personal jurisdiction of any individual U.S. State's courts, so long as exercising personal jurisdiction would be consistent with the federal Constitution and federal laws.

§ 2.4 Step #2—Constitutional (Due Process) Authority

CORE CONCEPT

The second step in establishing personal jurisdiction—the "constitutional" step—is satisfied if the judge's exercise of legislatively-granted personal jurisdiction authority will not offend the due process guarantee enshrined in the U.S. Constitution.[1] Thus, the Constitution acts as an outer limit of personal jurisdiction authority: judges may make full use of the personal jurisdiction authority granted them by their legislatures, but only so long as doing so would not offend constitutional due process.

APPLICATIONS

Two Different Due Process Clauses

The U.S. Constitution contains two Due Process Clauses. The first, in the Fifth Amendment, imposes the due process constraint when federal courts rule.[2] The second, in the Fourteenth Amendment, imposes the same constraint when State courts rule.[3] It had been assumed that the Fifth Amendment Due Process Clause and the Fourteenth Amendment Due Process Clause tested for personal jurisdiction in the same manner. The Supreme Court, though, has not yet confirmed this assumption,[4] and lower courts disagree on the Clauses' respective impacts on the allowable reach of personal jurisdiction.[5]

---

[1]*See Ins. Corp. of Ireland v. Compagnie des Bauxites de Guinee*, 456 U.S. 694, 703 (1982) (Due Process Clause "is the only source of the personal jurisdiction requirement" constitutionally.

[2]*See* U.S. CONST. amend. V ("No person shall . . . be deprived of . . . property, without due process of law").

[3]*See* U.S. CONST. amend. XIV, § 1 ("nor shall any State deprive any person of . . . property, without due process of law"). ("No person shall . . . be deprived of . . . property, without due process of law").

[4]*See, e.g., Bristol-Myers Squibb Co. v. Superior Court*, 582 U.S. —, 137 S. Ct. 1773, 1780, 1783–84 (2017); *Omni Capital Int'l, Ltd. v. Rudolf Wolff & Co.*, 484 U.S. 97, 102 n.5 (1987).

[5]*Compare Waters v. Day & Zimmermann NPS, Inc.*, 23 F.4th 84, 92–100 (1st Cir. 2022) (in federal FLSA collective action lawsuit, although non-resident opt-in claimants might lack 14th Amendment ability to

The Meaning of "Due Process"

The Due Process Clauses ordinarily bar a judge from reaching out to render a binding judgment against anyone with whom the forum has "no meaningful 'contacts, ties, or relations.' "[6] In this way, the Clauses are understood as protecting litigants from being burdened by the chore of having to travel to a distant or inconvenient forum in order to see that justice is done.[7] This protection rests in the liberty interests of the litigants.[8] Consequently, a litigant's behavior and reasonable expectations are central to the constitutional inquiry. By permitting the exercise of judicial power only over those who "should reasonably anticipate being haled into court" in that particular forum, due process "gives a degree of predictability to the legal system that allows potential defendants to structure their primary conduct with some minimum assurance as to where that conduct will and will not render them liable to suit."[9]

Although the "primary concern" is the "burden" that litigating in the forum will impose on a defendant, the due process inquiry "also encompasses the more abstract matter of submitting to the coercive power of a State that may have little legitimate interest in the claims in question."[10] Convenience, alone, does not answer that nuance.[11] Indeed, jurisdiction might be prohibited even when the defendant would actually be inconvenienced only slightly (or not at all) and even when the chosen forum has a strong interest in applying its law and can do so efficiently.[12] This is so because of the territorial limitations on each State's sovereignty: each State has the sovereign author-

---

initiate lawsuit against defendant, once named plaintiff acquired proper personal jurisdiction over defendant, 5th Amendment permitted nonresident opt-in claimants' joinder), *with Canaday v. Anthem Cos.*, 9 F.4th 392, 398–404 (6th Cir. 2021) (Congress could have, but did not, authorize nationwide service in FLSA actions, so host State's personal jurisdiction limits apply); *and Vallone v. CJS Sols. Grp., LLC*, 9 F.4th 861, 865–66 (8th Cir. 2021) (same result, because personal jurisdiction must be assessed claim by claim, so FLSA claims with no connection to Minnesota were properly excluded). *See also Fischer v. Fed. Express Corp.*, 42 F.4th 366, 370–88 (3d Cir. 2022) (joining Sixth and Eighth Circuits' view).

6. *See Burger King Corp. v. Rudzewicz*, 471 U.S. 462, 471–72 (1985) (quoting *Int'l Shoe Co. v. Washington*, 326 U.S. 310, 319 (1945)).

7. *See World-Wide Volkswagen Corp. v. Woodson*, 444 U.S. 286, 292 (1980).

8. *See Ins. Corp. of Ireland v. Compagnie des Bauxites de Guinee*, 456 U.S. 694, 702–03 (1982) ("protects an individual liberty interest;" "represents first of all an individual right").

9. *See World-Wide Volkswagen Corp. v. Woodson*, 444 U.S. 286, 297 (1980).

10. *See Bristol-Myers Squibb Co. v. Superior Ct.*, 582 U.S. __, 137 S. Ct. 1773, 1780–81 (2017) (citations omitted).

11. *See Bristol-Myers Squibb Co. v. Superior Ct.*, 582 U.S. __, 137 S. Ct. 1773, 1780–81 (2017) ("more than a guarantee of immunity from inconvenient or distant litigation[:] They are a consequence of territorial limitations on the power of the respective States.' ") (citation omitted).

12. *See Bristol-Myers Squibb Co. v. Superior Ct.*, 582 U.S. __, 137 S. Ct.

ity to try cases in its own courts and the companion power to limit the encroaching reach of sister States into its borders.[13] At base, then, the due process constraints on personal jurisdiction "reflect two sets of values—treating defendants fairly and protecting 'interstate federalism.' "[14]

Judges must have constitutionally adequate personal jurisdiction over every party or thing over which they will act. Consequently, due process must be satisfied as to everyone and every claim in the lawsuit.[15]

Consequences of Violating Due Process

If a judge were to violate the constitutional due process limit on personal jurisdiction and, without a consent or waiver, issue a ruling nonetheless, that decision would be void in the place where it was entered and not entitled to full faith and credit (including enforcement) anywhere else.[16]

Certain Parties Not Protected by Due Process

A few narrow classes of defendants fall outside the scope of the Constitution's due process protection. American States are not considered "persons" encompassed by the Due Process Clause,[17] nor are sovereign foreign nations.[18]

§ 2.5 Acquiring *In Personam* Jurisdiction

CORE CONCEPT

When a judge exercises personal jurisdiction over a defendant's person, he or she is invoking *in personam* personal jurisdiction. This type of personal jurisdiction can be exercised over natural persons (people) or entities (like corporations, partnerships, and other sorts of associations).[1] Whether *in personam* jurisdiction is conferred depends, initially, on the "legislative" step, discussed above. Exercises of *in personam* personal jurisdiction satisfy the next inquiry, the "constitutional" step, when the judge's use of coercive authority over each party is not fundamentally unfair or unreasonable. Due process allows *in personam* jurisdiction in

---

1773, 1780–81 (2017) (quoting *World-Wide Volkswagen Corp. v. Woodson*, 444 U.S. 286, 294 (1980)).

[13]*See Bristol-Myers Squibb Co. v. Superior Ct.*, 582 U.S. ___, 137 S. Ct. 1773, 1780 (2017).

[14]*See Ford Motor Co. v. Montana Eighth Jud. Dist. Ct.*, 592 U.S. ___, 141 S. Ct. 1017, 1025 (2021). *See also J. McIntyre Mach., Ltd. v. Nicastro*, 564 U.S. 873, 884 (2011) (plurality opinion: "[W]hether a judicial judgment is lawful depends on whether the sovereign has authority to render it.").

[15]*See Rush v. Savchuk*, 444 U.S. 320, 332 (1980).

[16]*See World-Wide Volkswagen Corp. v. Woodson*, 444 U.S. 286, 291 (1980).

[17]*See South Carolina v. Katzenbach*, 383 U.S. 301, 323 (1966).

[18]*See Price v. Socialist People's Libyan Arab Jamahiriya*, 294 F.3d 82, 96–100 (D.C. Cir. 2002). *But cf. Livnat v. Palestinian Auth.*, 851 F.3d 45, 49 (D.C. Cir. 2017) (exclusion applies only to sovereign foreign states, not necessarily to all foreign governmental entities).

[1]*See Shaffer v. Heitner*, 433 U.S. 186, 204 n.19 (1977) (*Int'l Shoe* standard "govern[s] actions against natural persons as well as corporations").

three circumstances: (1) when the party consents to the exercise of that jurisdiction; (2) when the party is served with original process while voluntarily present in the State where the judge is sitting; or (3) when the party has a sufficient connection (or "contacts") with that State to deem jurisdiction proper. Each is discussed, in turn, in Sections 2.5a, 2.5b, 2.5c, 2.5c1, and 2.5c2 below.

APPLICATIONS

Effect of an *In Personam* Judgment

When a court issues a lawful judgment *in personam*, that ruling is a binding one that may thereafter be enforced against the defendant wherever that defendant (or that defendant's property) may be found.[2]

§ 2.5a *In Personam* Circumstance #1—Consent to Jurisdiction

CORE CONCEPT

Because personal jurisdiction is intended to ensure that a party will not be obligated to litigate in an unfair or unreasonable forum, the parties are entitled to a voice in making that assessment. They are usually allowed to surrender this protection voluntarily if they find it in their interests to do so[1] (and, if they do, that surrender is ordinarily confined just to the setting in which it is given).[2] They may also lose this protection involuntarily if they fail to properly or timely assert it.[3]

APPLICATIONS

Consent By Plaintiffs Presumed

Personal jurisdiction battles are ordinarily initiated by defendants, not plaintiffs. In most cases, defendants are the parties who are being summoned to appear in a court not of their choosing. Plaintiffs, by contrast, have chosen the forum in which they filed, are therefore deemed to have consented to

---

[2] *See Shaffer v. Heitner*, 433 U.S. 186, 210 (1977) ("The Full Faith and Credit Clause . . . makes the valid in personam judgment of one State enforceable in all other States."); *Eurasia Int'l, Ltd. v. Holman Shipping, Inc.*, 411 F.3d 578, 584 n.1 (5th Cir. 2005) ("A judgment in personam imposes personal liability on a party and may therefore be satisfied out of any of the party's property within judicial reach.").

[1] *See Pennoyer v. Neff*, 95 U.S. 714, 733 (1877) (voluntary appearance). *See also J. McIntyre Mach., Ltd. v. Nicastro*, 564 U.S. 873, 880 (2011) ('a person may submit to a State's [personal jurisdiction] authority in a number of ways," including "explicit consent").

[2] *See Charles Schwab Corp. v. Bank of Am. Corp.*, 883 F.3d 68, 88 (2d Cir. 2018) (party's consent to jurisdiction in one case extends only to that case, and "in no way opens that party up to other lawsuits in the same jurisdiction in which consent was given") (citation omitted).

[3] *See Ins. Corp. of Ireland v. Compagnie des Bauxites de Guinee*, 456 U.S. 694, 704–05 (1982). *See also* Rule 12(h)(1) and Authors' Commentary to Rule 12(h)(1).

that court's power to rule, and ordinarily will not be heard to complain about that forum's exercise of personal jurisdiction over them.[4] This is not to say, however, that plaintiffs' consent is unrestricted—they may, by advance agreement, limit their forum choices (*e.g.*, in forum selection clauses).

Consent By Advance Agreement

By prior agreement or contract, parties can consent to a court's personal jurisdiction (though not, of course, to subject-matter jurisdiction).[5] This is true even where the forum the parties have selected would not otherwise have had personal jurisdiction over those parties.[6] These sorts of agreements—"forum selection clauses"—are routinely included in many business contracts; by including such clauses, the contracting parties negotiate, at the outset of their agreement, for the place where any future dispute under the contract will be heard and resolved.[7] As a due process matter, these clauses are generally upheld so long as they are contractually valid, absent some extraordinary circumstance.[8] A forum selection clause like this might, for example, be invalid when there was substantially unequal bargaining power or duress among the parties that gave one side an unconstitutionally unfair advantage in choosing the jurisdiction or if there was no fair link between the chosen forum and the parties or their cause of action (*e.g.*, in a contract made in Georgia and to be performed by Georgians entirely in Georgia, the clause selects the Pacific Island of Guam as the forum for any litigation as a way of disincentivizing the filing of lawsuits).[9]

Consent By Waiver

A party can also consent to the court's exercise of personal jurisdiction by failing to timely, properly object to the court's

---

[4] *See Adam v. Saenger*, 303 U.S. 59, 67–68 (1938). *See also United States v. Swiss Am. Bank, Ltd.*, 191 F.3d 30, 35 (1st Cir. 1999) ("a plaintiff ordinarily consents to a court's jurisdiction by filing suit").

[5] *See National Equip. Rental, Ltd. v. Szukhent*, 375 U.S. 311, 315–16 (1964).

[6] *See National Equip. Rental, Ltd. v. Szukhent*, 375 U.S. 311, 315–16 (1964) ("settled" law that "parties to a contract may agree in advance to submit to the jurisdiction of a given court").

[7] *See Burger King Corp. v. Rudzewicz*, 471 U.S. 462, 472 n.14 (1985).

[8] *See Atl. Marine Const. Co. v. U.S. Dist. Ct.*, 571 U.S. 49, 62 (2013).

[9] *See Kawasaki Kisen Kaisha Ltd. v. Regal-Beloit Corp.*, 561 U.S. 89, 109–10 (2010) ("imposes a venue 'so gravely difficult and inconvenient that [the plaintiff] will for all practical purposes be deprived of his day in court' ") (citation omitted); *Scherk v. Alberto-Culver Co.*, 417 U.S. 506, 519 n.14 (1974) (not enforceable if clause "was the product of fraud or coercion"). *Cf. Carnival Cruise Lines, Inc. v. Shute*, 499 U.S. 585, 594–95 (1991) (passengers failed to meet "heavy burden of proof" to set aside clause in standard passage contract, where place of litigation was not "remote alien forum," where no fraud, bad faith, or overreaching was present, and where "fundamental fairness" was not otherwise violated).

authority.[10] This sort of consent can be done intentionally (where the party is willing to have the court proceed when personal jurisdiction would otherwise be improper) or unintentionally (by neglectfully failing to raise an objection, failing to do so properly or timely, failing to seasonably press for a ruling on the objection once made, or otherwise behaving in a way that demonstrates a willingness to submit to the court's adjudicatory authority).[11]

Consent By Challenging Personal Jurisdiction

The act of arguing to a court that it lacks personal jurisdiction is a submission to that court's authority to issue a ruling; it could, theoretically risk a finding of consent-by-waiver. Historically, lawyers would evade that risk by announcing their intention to make a "special appearance" for the limited purpose of contesting jurisdiction and nothing else.[12] That maneuver is no longer needed in federal court: the Rules abolished the distinction between "special" and "general" appearances.[13] Today, not only are federal litigants permitted to raise personal jurisdiction objections without fear of impliedly consenting to the very jurisdiction they are contesting, but they are allowed (and, sometimes, even required) to combine with that jurisdictional challenge other preliminary defenses and objections they might then have.[14]

Consent for the Limited Purpose of Determining Jurisdiction

A party who objects to a court's personal jurisdiction is, however, always deemed to have consented to that court's jurisdiction for the limited purpose of having that court determine

---

[10]*See* Rules 12(b)(2), 12(g), and 12(h)(1). *See also infra* Authors' Commentary to Rule 12(b)(2) ("**Timing and Waiver**").

[11]*See Burger King Corp. v. Rudzewicz*, 471 U.S. 462, 472 n.14 (1985); *Ins. Corp. of Ireland v. Compagnie des Bauxites de Guinee*, 456 U.S. 694, 703 (1982). *See also* Rule 12(h)(1) and Authors' Commentary to Rule 12(h)(1).

[12]*See Harkness v. Hyde*, 98 U.S. 476, 479 (1878). *See also Baldwin v. Iowa State Traveling Men's Ass'n*, 283 U.S. 522, 524–25 (1931).

[13]*See Blessing v. Chandrasekhar*, 988 F.3d 889, 899 (6th Cir. 2021); *Orange Theatre Corp. v. Rayherstz Amusement Corp.*, 139 F.2d 871, 874 (3d Cir.1944). *See also Blessing*, 988 F.3d at 899 (defense attorney's entry of appearance is not waiver of personal jurisdiction defense); *Lewellen v. Morley*, 909 F.2d 1073, 1077 (7th Cir. 1990) (defendants' entry of appearance does not excuse need to serve process).

[14]*See* Rule 12(g) & 12(h). *See also Martinez v. Picker Int'l, Inc.*, 635 F. Supp. 658, 658–59 (D.P.R. 1986) (purpose of those Rules was "to dispense with the technicality of making special appearances to challenge jurisdiction or risk submission"). *See generally Orange Theatre Corp. v. Rayherstz Amusement Corp.*, 139 F.2d 871, 874 (3d Cir.1944) ("A defendant need no longer appear specially to attack the court's jurisdiction over him. He is no longer required at the door of the federal courthouse to intone that ancient abracadabra of the law, de bene esse, in order by its magic power to enable himself to remain outside even while he steps within. He may now enter openly in full confidence that he will not thereby be giving up any keys to the courthouse door which he possessed before he came in.").

whether personal jurisdiction exists.[15]

Consent By Counterclaiming

A plaintiff against whom a counterclaim is asserted is ordinarily deemed to have consented to personal jurisdiction on that counterclaim by the act of having filed the original complaint.[16] This seems true whether the counterclaim is compulsory or permissive.[17] It is unsettled whether filing an *in rem* action similarly constitutes consent to personal jurisdiction on a counterclaim.[18] From a defendant's perspective, the result is often different. Although the courts are not unanimous on the question, many hold that a defendant does not forfeit an otherwise properly asserted personal jurisdiction objection by filing a counterclaim (or crossclaim or third-party/impleader claim).[19]

§ 2.5b *In Personam* Circumstance #2—In-State Service (Transient or "Tag") Jurisdiction

CORE CONCEPT

A defendant who is served with original process while physically present within a State may be subject to the personal jurisdiction of the State and federal trial courts within that State.[1] This authority is often referred to as "tag" or "transient presence" personal jurisdiction. For this type of personal jurisdiction, it is irrelevant, for due process purposes, whether the defendant, when served, was living in the State or just passing through, whether the duration of the presence was lengthy or brief, and whether the lawsuit was related or unrelated to the defendant's in-State

---

[15] *See Ins. Corp. of Ireland v. Compagnie des Bauxites de Guinee*, 456 U.S. 694, 706 (1982). *See also Transaero, Inc. v. La Fuerza Aerea Boliviana*, 162 F.3d 724, 729 (2d Cir. 1998) ("[W]hen a defendant appears and challenges jurisdiction, it agrees to be bound by the court's determination on the jurisdictional issue.").

[16] *See Adam v. Saenger*, 303 U.S. 59, 67–68 (1938); *Leman v. Krentler-Arnold Hinge Last Co.*, 284 U.S. 448, 451 (1932).

[17] *See Trade Well Int'l v. United Cent. Bank*, 825 F.3d 854, 859 (7th Cir. 2016).

[18] *Compare U.S. v. One Lear Jet Aircraft*, 836 F.2d 1571, 1576–77 (11th Cir. 1988) (en banc) (filing *in rem* action does not usually equal consent to personal jurisdiction), *with U.S. v. 51 Pieces of Real Property Roswell, N.M.*, 17 F.3d 1306, 1313 (10th Cir. 1994) (rejecting *One Lear Jet Aircraft*; concluding that government submits to personal jurisdiction upon filing forfeiture action).

[19] *See United States v. Ligas*, 549 F.3d 497, 502 (7th Cir. 2008) ("general rule" that defendants do not waive jurisdictional defenses by including counterclaim, a cross-claim, or a third-party claim in answer); *Rates Tech. Inc. v. Nortel Networks Corp.*, 399 F.3d 1302, 1308 (Fed. Cir. 2005) (same). *But cf. Halliburton Energy Servs., Inc. v. Ironshore Specialty Ins. Co.*, 921 F.3d 522, 540 n.15 (5th Cir. 2019) (noting exception where defendant asserts new claims against new parties that do not arise out of same transaction or occurrence as original action).

[1] *See Pennoyer v. Neff*, 95 U.S. 714, 733 (1877).

activities.[2]

Personal jurisdiction premised on in-State service upon the defendant has a longstanding lineage.[3] It traces its roots back to an era when personal jurisdiction was viewed in territorial terms only. Because a sovereign was understood to possess the exclusive right to act within its territory, anyone found within those borders was thereby amenable to that sovereign's judicial authority—provided the sovereign asserted that power against the defendant personally (through service of process) and did so while the defendant was still present within the territory.[4] Although the rigidity of this territorial view of personal jurisdiction was relaxed as cross-border activities increased during the 20th Century, in-State service has persisted as a constitutionally sound basis for asserting judicial authority.[5] Nothing in the recent personal jurisdiction case law seems to have undercut the settled nature of "tag".[6] Today, because of this long history, defendants are considered to be on "fair notice" that their decision to voluntarily enter a State exposes them to personal jurisdiction if they are served while present there.[7]

For in-State service to confer personal jurisdiction, however,

---

[2] *See Burnham v. Superior Ct.*, 495 U.S. 604, 619 (1990) (plurality opinion).

[3] *See Burnham v. Superior Ct.*, 495 U.S. 604, 610 (1990) (plurality opinion) ("Among the most firmly established principles of personal jurisdiction in American tradition is that the courts of a State have jurisdiction over nonresidents who are physically present in the State."); *id.* at 615 ("We do not know of a single state or federal statute, or a single judicial decision resting upon state law, that has abandoned in-state service as a basis of jurisdiction. Many recent cases reaffirm it."); *id.* at 636–37 (Brennan, J., concurring) ("that American courts have announced the rule for perhaps a century . . . provides a defendant voluntarily present in a particular State *today* 'clear notice that [he] is subject to suit' in the forum").

[4] *See Burnham v. Superior Ct.*, 495 U.S. 604, 610–20 (1990) (plurality opinion); *Pennoyer v. Neff*, 95 U.S. 714, 721–23 (1877).

[5] *See Burnham v. Superior Ct.*, 495 U.S. 604, 619–21 (1990) (plurality opinion). *See also J. McIntyre Mach., Ltd. v. Nicastro*, 564 U.S. 873, 880 (2011) (persons submit to forum's personal jurisdiction by "[p]resence within a State at the time suit commences through service of process"); *Luv N' care, Ltd. v. Insta-Mix, Inc.*, 438 F.3d 465, 469 n.2 (5th Cir. 2006) ("Federal courts may also always assume jurisdiction over a defendant in any action in which there is personal, in-state service of process.").

[6] *See, e.g., Loughlin v. Goord*, 558 F. Supp. 3d 126, 139–42 (S.D.N.Y. 2021) (rejecting argument that recent case law undermined "tag" jurisdiction); *JLB LLC v. Egger*, 462 F. Supp. 3d 68, 78 (D. Mass. 2020) (accepting "tag" as settled law); *Mohamad v. Rajoub*, 2018 WL 1737219, at *7 (S.D.N.Y. Mar. 12, 2018), aff'd, 767 Fed. Appx. 91 (2d Cir. 2019) (rejecting contention that recent cases altered "well-settled principles" of "tag"); *Senju Pharm. Co. v. Metrics, Inc.*, 96 F. Supp. 3d 428, 437 (D.N.J. 2015) ("did not disturb the consent-by-in-state service rule described in *Burnham*"). *But cf. Jaramillo v. Naranjo*, 2014 WL 4898210, at *4–*5 (S.D. Fla. Sept. 30, 2014) (surmising, without deciding, that recent precedent "severely undercut" foreign citizens' amenability to "tag").

[7] *See Burnham v. Superior Ct.*, 495 U.S. 604, 624–25 (1990) (plurality opinion); *id.* at 636–37 (Brennan, J., concurring). *See also Shaffer v. Heitner*, 433 U.S. 186, 218 (1977) (Stevens, J.,

the served defendant must have been in the State voluntarily and not lured there by fraud.[8] Thus, abducting a person and driving him into the State or frightening a person into entering the State with a concocted tale of a dire family illness will likely disqualify the "tag" from conferring personal jurisdiction.

APPLICATIONS

Reasonableness / Fairness Inquiry

The Supreme Court's most detailed discussion of "tag" jurisdiction appeared in a 1990 opinion. Although all nine Justices agreed that "tag" jurisdiction was constitutionally proper in that case, one nuance divided them. Four Justices believed that the longstanding "pedigree" of "tag" jurisdiction supplies automatic constitutional validation, without any further inquiry into reasonableness or fairness.[9] Four other Justices resisted that view, and would perform an "independent inquiry" into the reasonableness and fairness of exercising "tag"-based personal jurisdiction in each individual case, albeit with three narrowing caveats—"tag" is considered to be "consistent" with a defendant's "reasonable expectations," is "entitled to a strong presumption" of constitutionality, and, "as a rule," ought to be understood as satisfying due process.[10] Because neither view received support from a majority of the Court, the necessity for a separate case-specific inquiry into reasonableness / fairness remains uncertain nationally.[11]

"Tagging" a Corporation

Although it is discussed only sporadically in the case law, some courts have ruled that personal jurisdiction cannot be acquired over a corporation by "tagging" one of its officers who might be visiting the forum State. Those courts often reason that because corporations are recognized as a legal entity, separate and apart from their owners and employees, "tagging" a

---

concurring) ("If I visit another State . . ., I knowingly assume some risk that the State will exercise its power over . . . my person while there. My contact with the State, though minimal, gives rise to predictable risks.").

[8]*See Commercial Mut. Acc. Co. v. Davis*, 213 U.S. 245, 256 (1909) ("if a person is induced by artifice or fraud to come within the jurisdiction of the court for the purpose of procuring service of process, such fraudulent abuse of the writ will be set aside upon proper showing"); *Manitowoc W. Co. v. Montonen*, 639 N.W.2d 726, 729 (Wis. 2002) (same). *See generally infra* Authors' Commentary to Rule 4 ("**Immunity from Service**").

[9]*See Burnham v. Superior Ct.*, 495 U.S. 604, 621 (1990) (plurality opinion) (conducting no independent inquiry, "leaving that judgment to the legislatures" who may amend their "tag" rule; "for our purposes, its validation is its pedigree, as the phrase "*traditional notions* of fair play and substantial justice" makes clear.").

[10]*See Burnham v. Superior Ct.*, 495 U.S. 604, 629, 637, & 639 (1990) (Brennan, J., concurring).

[11]*See, e.g., El-Maksoud v. El-Maksoud*, 568 A.2d 140, 142–44 (Ch. Div. 1989) (adopting plurality view, approving "tag" jurisdiction without any minimum contacts analysis); *Hedden v. Isbell*, 792 S.E.2d 571, 574–75 (N.C. Ct. App. 2016) (same); *Manitowoc W. Co. v. Montonen*, 639 N.W.2d 726, 729 & n.3 (Wis. 2002) (same).

corporate officer cannot confer personal jurisdiction over the corporation.[12] Bear in mind, however, the important distinction between a jurisdiction-conferring "tag" on a corporate officer (which some courts reject) and a Rules-compliant service of process on a corporate officer (which Rule 4 approves).[13]

"Tagging" an Unincorporated Entity

The availability of "tag" for acquiring personal jurisdiction over partnerships, limited liability companies, associations, and other unincorporated entities is even less frequently discussed. Some courts permit a jurisdiction-conferring "tag" on such entities' senior employees, perhaps because the company separateness that is a hallmark of corporations may not exist in unincorporated settings; other courts disagree.[14]

Being "Tagged" While Contesting Personal Jurisdiction

A litigant's act of contesting a federal court's personal jurisdiction will not, itself, constitute a waiver of those objections.[15] For similar policy reasons, it would seem that a litigant's personal appearance in court for the purpose of arguing against personal jurisdiction should likewise not compromise those objections by affording the opponent a "tag" opportunity. No case law seems to have squarely confronted this question, perhaps because the answer is so necessarily clear: to allow a jurisdiction-conferring "tag" on the arguing litigant would render illusory the Rules' procedures for how to properly

---

[12]*See, e.g., Martinez v. Aero Caribbean*, 764 F.3d 1062, 1067–70 (9th Cir. 2014); *Nehemiah v. Athletics Cong. of U.S.A.*, 765 F.2d 42, 47 (3d Cir. 1985); *Lewis v. Lewis Elec., LLC*, 2021 WL 6113551, at *4 n.7 (D. Haw. Dec. 27, 2021); *Pastor Enters. v. GKN Driveline N. Am., Inc.*, 2020 WL 5366286, at *4 (D.N.J. Sept. 8, 2020); *C.S.B. Commodities, Inc. v. Urb. Trend (HK) Ltd.*, 626 F. Supp. 2d 837, 851 (N.D. Ill. 2009); *Est. of Ungar v. Palestinian Auth.*, 400 F. Supp. 2d 541, 553 (S.D.N.Y. 2005), *aff'd*, 332 Fed. Appx. 643 (2d Cir. 2009). *But see Northern Light Tech., Inc. v. Northern Lights Club*, 236 F.3d 57, 64 n.10 (1st Cir. 2001) (finding personal jurisdiction over corporate defendant based on the "tag" of its officer).

[13]*See Chan v. Soc'y Expeditions, Inc.*, 39 F.3d 1398, 1404 n.8 (9th Cir. 1994) (personal delivery to corporate officer qualified as proper *service* on defendant corporation, but did not supply tag-based *personal jurisdiction* over corporation). *See generally infra* Authors' Commentary to Rule 4(h) (Rules-based requirements for serving entities).

[14]*Compare First Am. Corp. v. Price Waterhouse LLP*, 154 F.3d 16, 19 (2d Cir. 1998) (New York law "telescopes service and personal jurisdiction into a single inquiry" such that "[i]f valid service is effected on one partner within the state, personal jurisdiction over the partnership is achieved"), *with Nehemiah v. Athletics Cong. of U.S.A.*, 765 F.2d 42, 46–47 (3d Cir. 1985) ("due process considerations preclude effecting personal jurisdiction over an unincorporated association merely by in-state service on its agent"), *and Gibson v. Cowboys Saloon Gainesville, LLC*, 2020 WL 1466412, at *1 (N.D. Fla. Mar. 25, 2020) ("not clear that personal jurisdiction over an LLC's member equals personal jurisdiction over the LLC").

[15]*See supra* § 2.5a (**"Consent By Challenging Personal Jurisdiction"**).

contest personal jurisdiction.[16]

"Tag" and the Legislative Authority Step

Although the constitutionality of "tag" jurisdiction now seems well settled, the first consideration in every personal jurisdiction inquiry—the legislative step—must also be met.[17] Here, a wrinkle emerges. Although some States have expressly codified "tag" jurisdiction as a legislatively authorized means for acquiring jurisdiction,[18] others have not done so—but might still recognize "tag" as a matter of common law.[19] This anomaly in the typical two-step personal jurisdiction inquiry will require careful research by practitioners into the "tag" law of their forum.

§ 2.5c *In Personam* Circumstance #3—Contacts-Based Jurisdiction

CORE CONCEPT

Defendants who neither consent to personal jurisdiction in a State nor are served with original process while there may still be subject to that State's personal jurisdiction if they have adequate "contacts" (or connections) with that State to meet the Constitution's due process mandate. Two types of contacts-based personal jurisdiction exist—specific jurisdiction and general jurisdiction. Each is discussed in turn below.

§ 2.5c1 *In Personam* Circumstance #3—Contacts-Based Jurisdiction—Specific Jurisdiction

CORE CONCEPT

Personal jurisdiction is permitted over a defendant who has

---

[16]*See generally Lamb v. Schmitt*, 285 U.S. 222, 225 (1932) (explaining that common law immunity from service principles rest on theory that "the due administration of justice" is compromised when the spectre of service of process for other lawsuits could "prevent" or "tend to discourage" the "voluntary attendance of those whose presence is necessary or convenient to the judicial administration in the pending litigation").

[17]*See Burnham v. Superior Ct.*, 495 U.S. 604, 627 (1990) ("Nothing we say today prevents individual States from limiting or entirely abandoning the in-state-service basis of jurisdiction.").

[18]*See, e.g.*, N.J. Ct. R. 4:4-4(a)(1) ("primary method" of obtaining personal jurisdiction is personal service "within this State"); N.C. GEN. STAT. § 1-75.4(1)(a) (granting "tag"-based *in personam* jurisdiction over "a natural person present within this State" when served); WIS. STAT. ANN. § 801.05(1)(a) (personal jurisdiction exists in any lawsuit against "a natural person present within this state when served," regardless whether the action arise "within or without" Wisconsin).

[19]*See Roch v. Mollica*, 113 N.E.3d 820, 822–28 (Mass. 2019) (noting absence of Massachusetts statutory grant of "tag" jurisdiction, but acknowledging continued vitality of "tag" as common law principle). *See also Stewart v. Hechtman*, 581 N.W.2d 416, 419–20 (Neb. 1998) (permitting "tag"-based personal jurisdiction in Nebraska, notwithstanding lack of expressly authorizing statute); *Cariaga v. Eighth Jud. Dist. Ct.*, 762 P.2d 886, 887–88 (Nev. 1988) (same, Nevada); *Nutri-W. v. Gibson*, 764 P.2d 693, 694–96 (Wyo. 1988) (same, Wyoming).

certain "minimum contacts" with the forum such that the judge's exercise of judicial power over that defendant would not offend "traditional notions of fair play and substantial justice."[1] This is the Constitution's "case-specific" (or "case-linked" or "conduct-linked") brand of personal jurisdiction.[2] It exists only where the cause of action at issue "aris[es] out of or relate[s] to" the defendant's purposeful actions directed into the forum.[3] A defendant who engages in such purposeful connections with the forum should be able to reasonably foresee that it might be held to account in that forum if its behavior there gives rise to or relates to a cause of action.[4] This prospective predictability thus allows a defendant to make an informed decision whether to engage with the forum (and thereby accept exposure to personal jurisdiction there) or not—an election which affords the defendant with due process.[5] Accordingly, specific jurisdiction implicates two considerations: (a) minimum contacts and (b) traditional notions of fair play and substantial justice (the reasonableness / fairness of the forum).

APPLICATIONS

"Minimum Contacts"

The "minimum contacts" inquiry is not wholly (or even principally) a quantitative one.[6] Even a small number of contacts with the forum (or just one) might be sufficient.[7] Rather than volume, this is really a qualitative assessment.[8] The defendant must have engaged in some behavior through which it "purposefully avail[ed] itself of the privilege of conducting activities within the forum State, thus invoking the benefits

---

[1]*See Int'l Shoe Co. v. Washington*, 326 U.S. 310, 316 (1945).

[2]*See Ford Motor Co. v. Montana Eighth Jud. Dist. Ct.*, 592 U.S. ___, 141 S. Ct. 1017, 1024 (2021) ("case-linked"); *Daimler AG v. Bauman*, 571 U.S. 117, 122 (2014) ("conduct-linked"); *Goodyear Dunlop Tires Ops., S.A. v. Brown*, 564 U.S. 915, 927 (2011) ("case-specific").

[3]*See Ford Motor Co. v. Montana Eighth Jud. Dist. Ct.*, 592 U.S. ___, 141 S. Ct. 1017, 1025 (2021); *Daimler AG v. Bauman*, 571 U.S. 746, 751 & 754 (2014); *Helicopteros Nacionales de Colombia, S.A. v. Hall*, 466 U.S. 408, 414 (1984).

[4]*See World-Wide Volkswagen Corp. v. Woodson*, 444 U.S. 286, 297 (1980).

[5]*See World-Wide Volkswagen Corp. v. Woodson*, 444 U.S. 286, 297 (1980).

[6]*See Int'l Shoe Co. v. Washington*, 326 U.S. 310, 319 (1945) ("the criteria by which we mark the boundary line . . . cannot be simply mechanical or quantitative," and the test is "not merely" whether the defendant's contacts are "a little more or a little less").

[7]*See Burger King Corp. v. Rudzewicz*, 471 U.S. 462, 475 n.18 (1985) ("So long as it creates a 'substantial connection' with the forum, even a single act can support jurisdiction."); *M-I Drilling Fluids UK Ltd. v. Dynamic Air Ltda.*, 890 F.3d 995, 1001 (Fed. Cir. 2018) (same).

[8]*See Int'l Shoe Co. v. Washington*, 326 U.S. 310, 319 (1945) ("Whether due process is satisfied must depend rather upon the quality and nature of the activity in relation to the fair and orderly administration of the laws which it was the purpose of the due process clause to insure.").

and protections" of that State's laws.[9] If it did so, *and* if the cause of action *arose out of* or *relates to* that behavior, then the defendant is deemed to have been placed on "fair warning" that it could be sued there, thus supplying due process.[10]

- *"Purposeful Availment"*: To qualify as "minimum contacts," the connection must be *purposeful*, *with the forum*, and *by the defendant*.[11] The contacts must be "the defendant's own choice" and "show that the defendant deliberately 'reached out beyond' its home—by, for example, 'exploi[ting] a market' in the forum State or entering a contractual relationship centered there."[12] A defendant's purposeful availment of the forum is understood as a "privilege" which, when enjoyed, invokes the "benefits and protections" of that forum's laws,[13] which, in turn, triggers a reciprocal obligation to return there to litigate a related dispute.[14] Accordingly, contacts that are "random," "fortuitous," or "attenuated" will not suffice,[15] nor will the unilateral acts of someone other than the defendant.[16]
  - *Physical Contacts Not Always Necessary:* The connection needed to satisfy the "minimum contacts" test need not always be an in-person, physical one.[17] For example, contracting in a manner that deliberately "reaches out" to create "continuing relationships and obligations" with another State's citizens might suffice, even in the absence

---

[9]*See Hanson v. Denckla*, 357 U.S. 235, 253 (1958).

[10]*See Ford Motor Co. v. Montana Eighth Jud. Dist. Ct.*, 592 U.S. __, 141 S. Ct. 1017, 1030 (2021); *Burger King Corp. v. Rudzewicz*, 471 U.S. 462, 472–73 (1985).

[11]*See Walden v. Fiore*, 571 U.S. 277, 283–86 (2014).

[12]*See Ford Motor Co. v. Montana Eighth Jud. Dist. Ct.*, 592 U.S. __, 141 S. Ct. 1017, 1025 (2021). *See also Burger King Corp. v. Rudzewicz*, 471 U.S. 462, 475 (1985) ("where the contacts proximately result from actions by the defendant *himself* that create a 'substantial connection' with the forum State").

[13]*See J. McIntyre Mach., Ltd. v. Nicastro*, 564 U.S. 873, 880 (2011); *Goodyear Dunlop Tires Ops.s, S.A. v. Brown*, 564 U.S. 915, 924 (2011).

[14]*See Int'l Shoe Co. v. Washington*, 326 U.S. 310, 319 (1945). *See also Ford Motor Co. v. Montana Eighth Jud. Dist. Ct.*, 592 U.S. __, 141 S. Ct. 1017, 1029–30 (2021) (enjoying benefits and protections "creates reciprocal obligations"); *CFA Inst. v. Inst. of Chartered Fin. Analysts of India*, 551 F.3d 285, 293 (4th Cir. 2009) ("minimum contacts" inquiry "is premised on the concept that a corporation that enjoys the privilege of conducting business within a state bears the reciprocal obligation of answering to legal proceedings there").

[15]*See Walden v. Fiore*, 571 U.S. 277, 286 (2014); *Burger King Corp. v. Rudzewicz*, 471 U.S. 462, 472–73 (1985).

[16]*See Burger King Corp. v. Rudzewicz*, 471 U.S. 462, 475 (1985); *Hanson v. Denckla*, 357 U.S. 235, 253 (1958).

[17]*See Walden v. Fiore*, 571 U.S. 277, 283 (2014); *Burger King Corp. v. Rudzewicz*, 471 U.S. 462, 476 (1985).

of physical presence.[18]

○ *Contracting with a Forum Resident:* The mere existence of a contract with a forum resident cannot, alone, fulfill the purposeful availment obligation.[19] Nor will the mere inclusion in that contract of a choice-of-law clause (which selects a particular forum's substantial law to apply).[20] Instead, courts look behind the fact of contracting to assess whether the agreement's negotiations, its terms, its contemplated future consequences, and the parties' actual course of dealing reveal that the defendant purposefully availed itself of the forum.[21]

○ *Placing Products in the "Stream of Commerce":* The Supreme Court has twice considered whether, and under what circumstances, the act of placing products into the "stream of commerce" can supply the purposeful availment needed to satisfy specific jurisdiction. Both times, the Court was unable to produce a majority opinion.[22] Three views divided the Court. Under the first view, specific jurisdiction would require that the defendant not only place the product in the stream of commerce but also undertake additional conduct revealing "an intent or purpose to serve the market in the forum state."[23] Under the second view, a defendant's placement of the product in the stream of commerce would alone suffice for specific jurisdiction, provided the defendant was "aware that the final product is being marketed in the forum State."[24] Under the third view, purposeful availment would be assessed by examining the volume, value, and hazardous character

[18] *See Burger King Corp. v. Rudzewicz*, 471 U.S. 462, 473–76 (1985).

[19] *See Burger King Corp. v. Rudzewicz*, 471 U.S. 462, 478–79 (1985).

[20] *See Sayers Constr., L.L.C. v. Timberline Constr., Inc.*, 976 F.3d 570, 574 (5th Cir. 2020) ("While such clauses can be probative of purposeful availment, they're never dispositive.").

[21] *See Burger King Corp. v. Rudzewicz*, 471 U.S. 462, 478–79 (1985) ("highly realistic" analysis "that recognizes that a 'contract' is 'ordinarily but an intermediate step serving to tie up prior business negotiations with future consequences which themselves are the real object of the business transaction' ") (citation omitted).

[22] *See J. McIntyre Machinery, Ltd. v. Nicastro*, 564 U.S. 873, 881–84 (2011) (plurality opinion: must not only be aware that product is being sold in the forum but must also intend to serve that market); *Asahi Metal Industry Co. v. Superior Ct.*, 480 U.S. 102, 112 (1987) (plurality opinion: same).

[23] *See Asahi Metal Indus. Co. v. Superior Ct.*, 480 U.S. 102, 112 (1987) (O'Connor, J., for the plurality) (sometimes called "awareness-plus" or "stream-of-commerce-plus" test).

[24] *See Asahi Metal Indus. Co. v. Superior Ct.*, 480 U.S. 102, 117 (1987) (Brennan, J., concurring) (sometimes called "mere awareness" test).

of the products.[25] In the Court's most recent (albeit unsuccessful) try, the decisive fifth and sixth votes skirted the issue by emphasizing that, at a minimum, "stream" theory could not rest on "a single, isolated sale."[26] Because there is no definitive ruling from the Supreme Court on "stream" theory, its formulation varies by circuit.[27]

○ *Contacts with the Forum by the Plaintiff:* The "minimum contacts" inquiry focuses on whether the *defendant* has purposefully availed itself of the forum and, for that reason, is now exposed to personal jurisdiction there. There is no companion requirement that the *plaintiff* also have "minimum contacts" with the forum[28] (nor should there be, as the plaintiff consents to the judge's jurisdiction by choosing to file there).[29] Nor does the fact that a plaintiff *has* meaningful contacts with the forum mean that specific personal jurisdiction will necessarily exist there.[30] Obviously, though, a plaintiff's location in the forum is not irrelevant: a defendant who purposefully reaches into the plaintiff's home forum in order to engage with that plaintiff there is the quintessential example of specific jurisdiction.[31]

○ *Entire Nation as the Forum:* In cases where the 5th Amendment Due Process Clause applies, the relevant forum for the purposeful availment inquiry may be the Nation; thus, all of a defendant's contacts with, and throughout, the United States

---

[25] *See Asahi Metal Indus. Co. v. Superior Ct.*, 480 U.S. 102, 122 (1987) (Stevens, J., concurring).

[26] *See J. McIntyre Mach., Ltd. v. Nicastro*, 564 U.S. 873, 888 (2011) (Breyer, J., concurring, with Alito, J.) ("None of our precedents finds that a single isolated sale, even if accompanied by the kind of sales effort indicated here, is sufficient. Rather, this Court's previous holdings suggest the contrary.").

[27] *See, e.g., J.S.T. Corp. v. Foxconn Interconnect Tech. Ltd.*, 965 F.3d 571, 576 (7th Cir. 2020) (following Brennan's "mere awareness" approach); *Parker v. Winwood*, 938 F.3d 833, 840 (6th Cir. 2019) (following O'Connor's "awareness-plus" approach); *Shuker v. Smith & Nephew, PLC*, 885 F.3d 760, 780 (3d Cir. 2018) (concluding that Supreme Court has "rejected" stream theory); *AFTG-TG, LLC v. Nuvoton Tech. Corp.*, 689 F.3d 1358, 1362–65 (Fed. Cir. 2012) (finding no need to decide among views).

[28] *See Keeton v. Hustler Mag., Inc.*, 465 U.S. 770, 779 (1984).

[29] *See Adam v. Saenger*, 303 U.S. 59, 67–68 (1938). *See also United States v. Swiss Am. Bank, Ltd.*, 191 F.3d 30, 35 (1st Cir. 1999) ("a plaintiff ordinarily consents to a court's jurisdiction by filing suit").

[30] *See Walden v. Fiore*, 571 U.S. 277, 284–86 (2014).

[31] *See Ford Motor Co. v. Montana Eighth Jud. Dist. Ct.*, 592 U.S. ___, 141 S. Ct. 1017, 1028 (2021) (resident-plaintiff suing global car company, which extensive serves that State's vehicles market, for in-State accident is "illustration—even a paradigm example—of how specific jurisdiction works").

as a whole are tested.[32]

- *"Arises out of"* or *"Relates to"*: Not only must the defendant's contacts with the forum be "purposeful," the pending lawsuit must also "arise out of" or "relate to" that behavior.[33] This ensures the reciprocal nature of specific jurisdiction (*i.e.*, local accountability in exchange for access to local markets).[34] Accordingly, even a robust volume of purposeful contacts, without connectedness to the lawsuit, will not suffice for specific jurisdiction.[35]
  - "*Arises out of*" is satisfied where the lawsuit's claims are causally connected to the defendant's purposeful activities in the forum (*i.e.*, the plaintiff's injury or loss "came about because of the defendant's in-state conduct").[36]
  - "*Relates to*" is less clear—and may be satisfied by something short of a causal connection.[37] But, in its only case thus far to explore the issue, the Supreme Court was quick to emphasize that this "does not mean anything goes": the "relates-to" standard "incorporates real limits, as it must to adequately protect defendants foreign to a

---

[32]*See, e.g., Ayla, LLC v. Alya Skin Pty. Ltd.*, 11 F.4th 972, 979 (9th Cir. 2021) (conducting 5th Amendment inquiry in Rule 4(k)(2) context).

[33]*See Ford Motor Co. v. Montana Eighth Jud. Dist. Ct.*, 592 U.S. __, 141 S. Ct. 1017, 1025 (2021). *See also Goodyear Dunlop Tires Ops., S.A. v. Brown*, 564 U.S. 915, 919 (2011) ("specific jurisdiction is confined to adjudication of 'issues deriving from, or connected with, the very controversy that establishes jurisdiction' ") (citation omitted).

[34]*See Ford Motor Co. v. Montana Eighth Jud. Dist. Ct.*, 592 U.S. __, 141 S. Ct. 1017, 1025 (2021) ("Our decision in *International Shoe* founded specific jurisdiction on an idea of reciprocity between a defendant and a State: When (but only when) a company 'exercises the privilege of conducting activities within a state'—thus 'enjoy[ing] the benefits and protection of [its] laws'—the State may hold the company to account for related misconduct.").

[35]*See Bristol-Myers Squibb Co. v. Superior Ct.*, 582 U.S. __, 137 S. Ct. 1773, 1781 (2017) ("When there is no [arising from/relates to] connection, specific jurisdiction is lacking regardless of the extent of a defendant's unconnected activities in the State."). *See also Ford Motor Co. v. Montana Eighth Jud. Dist. Ct.*, 592 U.S. __ n.3, 141 S. Ct. 1017, 1027 n.3 (2021) (rejecting view that State courts should have personal jurisdiction over nationwide corporations on any lawsuit, regardless of its unrelatedness to in-State activity: "On that view, for example, a California court could hear a claim against Ford brought by an Ohio plaintiff based on an accident occurring in Ohio involving a car purchased in Ohio. Removing the need for any connection between the case and forum State would transfigure our specific jurisdiction standard as applied to corporations. 'Case-linked' jurisdiction would then become not case-linked at all.") (citation omitted).

[36]*See Ford Motor Co. v. Montana Eighth Jud. Dist. Ct.*, 592 U.S. __, 141 S. Ct. 1017, 1026 (2021).

[37]*See Ford Motor Co. v. Montana Eighth Jud. Dist. Ct.*, 592 U.S. __, 141 S. Ct. 1017, 1026 (2021) ("we have never framed the specific jurisdiction inquiry as always requiring proof of causation").

forum."[38] Accordingly, a plaintiff injured in her home State while using a defendant's product could sue there if that defendant had marketed, sold, and serviced the same product in that State, even if the plaintiff had acquired the product outside the State.[39] But a plaintiff injured in her home State by a defendant's product marketed, sold, and serviced in that State could not sue in a different State merely because other plaintiffs, allegedly injured in the same way by the same product, were suing there.[40]

- *The Internet and "Virtual" Contacts:* The Supreme Court has yet to rule how Internet activities count in a "minimum contacts" analysis.[41] But there seems little urgency for it to do so; the lower federal courts have settled into a fairly stable body of case law on the point:
  - ○ *Mere Accessibility Not Enough:* The courts seem to agree that the ability to view an Internet site or online post from inside the forum State will not, alone, be sufficient to confer specific jurisdiction.[42] That foundational conclusion was essential to the continued vitality of due process as a restraint on the exercise of personal jurisdiction over cyberspace activity: generally speaking, the Internet is everywhere.[43]
  - ○ *"Something More" is Needed:* Appended to their

---

[38] *See Ford Motor Co. v. Montana Eighth Jud. Dist. Ct.*, 592 U.S. __, 141 S. Ct. 1017, 1026 (2021).

[39] *See Ford Motor Co. v. Montana Eighth Jud. Dist. Ct.*, 592 U.S. __, 141 S. Ct. 1017, 1026–32 (2021). *See also LNS Enters. LLC v. Cont'l Motors, Inc.*, 22 F.4th 852, 863 (9th Cir. 2022) (no indication that defendant advertised, sold, or serviced same type of product in State).

[40] *See Bristol-Myers Squibb Co. v. Superior Ct.*, 582 U.S. __, 137 S. Ct. 1773, 1781 (2017) ("What is needed—and what is missing [in such a case]—is a connection between the forum and the specific claims at issue.").

[41] *See Ford Motor Co. v. Montana Eighth Jud. Dist. Ct.*, __ U.S. __, 141 S. Ct. 1017, 1028 n.4 (2021) ("we do not here consider internet transactions, which may raise doctrinal questions of their own"); *Walden v. Fiore*, 571 U.S. 277, 290 (2014) ("[T]his case does not present the very different questions whether and how a defendant's virtual 'presence' and conduct translate into 'contacts' with a particular State. . . . We leave questions about virtual contacts for another day.").

[42] *See, e.g., XMission, L.C. v. Fluent LLC*, 955 F.3d 833, 845 (10th Cir. 2020) ("mere posting" does not confer personal jurisdiction wherever that post can be viewed); *Plixer Int'l, Inc. v. Scrutinizer GmbH*, 905 F.3d 1, 8 (1st Cir. 2018) ("One baseline principle has emerged: a website operator does not necessarily purposefully avail itself of the benefits and protections of every state in which its website is accessible.").

[43] *See ALS Scan, Inc. v. Digital Serv. Consultants, Inc.*, 293 F.3d 707, 712 (4th Cir. 2002) (if merely placing information on the Internet suffices wherever that information is accessed, "then the defense of personal jurisdiction, in the sense that a State has geographically limited judicial power, would no longer exist").

rejection of "mere accessibility" has been what the courts have called: "something more."[44] Although courts have used different terminology ("aiming," "targeting," "directing," "intentionality"), this predicate "something more" tends to be met by a defendant's deliberate, purposeful electronic reaching into the specific forum.[45]

- ○ *Ordinary Purposeful Availment Inquiry:* Whether worded traditionally or specially, courts have otherwise applied familiar "minimum contacts" elements and reasoning to assessing Internet-based personal jurisdiction.[46]
- ○ *The Fading Relevance of "Sliding Scale" Analysis:* Early Internet personal jurisdiction cases found value in applying a "sliding scale" to measure a website's passivity/interactivity, as innovated by a

---

[44] *See Motus, LLC v. CarData Consultants, Inc.*, 23 F.4th 115, 125 (1st Cir. 2022) ("To establish specific jurisdiction, there must be more," such as "specific targeting of forum residents" and "substantial revenue from forum residents" through website); *Young v. New Haven Advoc.*, 315 F.3d 256, 263 (4th Cir. 2002) ("Something more than posting and accessibility is needed to 'indicate that the [newspapers] purposefully (albeit electronically) directed [their] activity in a substantial way to the forum state' ") (citation omitted).

[45] *See, e.g., Curry v. Revolution Lab'ys, LLC*, 949 F.3d 385, 400 (7th Cir. 2020) (767 Internet-based sales into forum sufficient to show purposeful exploitation of local market); *Mavrix Photo, Inc. v. Brand Techs., Inc.*, 647 F.3d 1218, 1231 (9th Cir. 2011) (when website having national viewership and scope "appeals to, and profits from, an audience in a particular state, the site's operators can be said to have 'expressly aimed' at that state). *See generally Advanced Tactical Ordnance Sys., LLC v. Real Action Paintball, Inc.*, 751 F.3d 796, 802–03 (7th Cir. 2014) (" '[o]ur inquiry boils down to this: has [defendant] purposefully exploited the [Indiana] market' beyond simply operating an interactive website accessible in the forum state and sending emails to people who may happen to live there? Has the defendant, in brief, targeted Indiana somehow?").

[46] *Compare Admar Int'l, Inc. v. Eastrock, L.L.C.*, 18 F.4th 783, 786 (5th Cir. 2021) (Internet personal jurisdiction inquiry "should not be different at its most basic level from any other personal jurisdiction case"), *and Curry v. Revolution Lab'ys, LLC*, 949 F.3d 385, 398 (7th Cir. 2020) (declining to fashion Internet-specific jurisdictional test, relying instead on "traditional due process inquiry"), *and Plixer Int'l, Inc. v. Scrutinizer GmbH*, 905 F.3d 1, 8 (1st Cir. 2018) ("extremely reluctant to fashion any general guidelines beyond those that exist in law"), *with ALS Scan, Inc. v. Digital Serv. Consultants, Inc.*, 293 F.3d 707, 714 (4th Cir. 2002) ("a State may, consistent with due process, exercise judicial power over a person outside of the State when that person (1) directs electronic activity into the State, (2) with the manifested intent of engaging in business or other interactions within the State, and (3) that activity creates, in a person within the State, a potential cause of action cognizable in the State's courts."). *See generally Pervasive Software Inc. v. Lexware GmbH & Co. KG*, 688 F.3d 214, 226–27 (5th Cir. 2012) (Internet-based personal jurisdiction analysis "should not be different at its most basic level from any other personal jurisdiction case") (citation omitted).

federal trial judge in Pennsylvania.[47] As the sophistication of online presences has grown, courts have found this blunt approach increasingly less useful.[48]

○ *At the Margins:* With the Supreme Court's recent approval of specific jurisdiction premised on non-causal in-forum activities that "relate to" a cause of action,[49] the cases at the Internet margins may start to become less predictable. For example, using a locally-accessible online portal to make reservations for an out-of-forum event where injury or loss later results may have now come closer to a constitutionally tolerable ground for exercising specific jurisdiction, especially if that portal contains features like a "drop-down" menu that includes the forum locality.[50]

"Traditional Notions of Fair Play and Substantial Justice" (*Reasonableness / Fairness Factors*)

The second of the two specific jurisdiction inquiries considers whether the judge's exercise of jurisdiction would be so unreasonable or unfair as to "offend traditional notions of fair play and substantial justice."[51] This inquiry is separate and *in addi-*

---

[47]*See Zippo Mfg. Co. v. Zippo Dot Com, Inc.*, 952 F. Supp. 1119, 1124 (W.D. Pa. 1997) (describing slide scale as "consistent with well developed [circa 1997] personal jurisdiction principles").

[48]*See, e.g., UMG Recordings, Inc. v. Kurbanov*, 963 F.3d 344, 353 (4th Cir. 2020) (Internet has evolved; attaching too much focus today on "interactivity" may be counterproductive); *Louis Vuitton Malletier, S.A. v. Mosseri*, 736 F.3d 1339, 1355 n.10 (11th Cir. 2013) (noting criticisms of sliding scale).

[49]*See Ford Motor Co. v. Montana Eighth Jud. Dist. Ct.*, 592 U.S. __, 141 S. Ct. 1017 (2021) (approving specific jurisdiction based on non-causal contacts that "relate to" pending lawsuit). *See also id.* at 1028 n.4 (finding no need to resolve hypothetical involving a retired person in Maine carves decoys that he sells through an Internet site: "Can he be sued in any state if some harm arises from the decoy?").

[50]*See Fidrych v. Marriott Int'l, Inc.*, 952 F.3d 124, 139–43 (4th Cir. 2020) (pre-*Ford*, rejecting specific jurisdiction: "South Carolina's inclusion in a list of every other state in the country (and every other country in the world) shows that Marriott was willing to accept reservations from South Carolina residents, but it does not show that Marriott was targeting South Carolina residents through its website. To the contrary, the list of options confirms that the website was accessible to all but targeted at no one in particular."). *Cf. Noboa v. Barcelo Corporacion Empresarial, SA*, 812 F.3d 571, 572–73 (7th Cir. 2016) (rejecting specific jurisdiction in death case brought on behalf of guest who used Orbitz website to book hotel stay and, after arriving, was fatally injured during excursion) (relying on *OBB Personenverkehr AG v. Sachs*, 577 U.S. 27 (2015) (construing Foreign Sovereign Immunities Act, holding that injury was not "based upon" Internet sale of railway's sale that occurred in U.S., but on railway's conduct in Austria)).

[51]*See Burnham v. Superior Ct.*, 495 U.S. 604, 609 (1990); *Int'l Shoe Co. v. Washington*, 326 U.S. 310, 316 (1945).

tion to the "minimum contacts" assessment discussed above.[52] Thus, even if a defendant has qualifying "minimum contacts" with the forum, it would still be improper to exercise specific jurisdiction if doing so would prove so unreasonable or unfair, "so gravely difficult and inconvenient," that traditional notions of fair play and substantial justice would be offended.[53] The Supreme Court has supplied a non-exhaustive list of factors[54] for use in conducing this reasonableness / fairness assessment:

(1) The defendant's burden in litigating in the forum court;
(2) The forum State's interest in having the litigation in its own courts;
(3) The plaintiff's interest in litigating in its chosen forum;
(4) The interstate judicial system's interest in the most effective resolution of the litigation; and
(5) The shared several States' interest in furthering substantive social policies.[55]

In lawsuits involving foreign nationals, the Court added the further precaution that "[g]reat care and reserve should be exercised when extending our notions of personal jurisdiction into the international field."[56]

Burdens of Proof

It is the duty of the party invoking specific jurisdiction (usually the plaintiff) to demonstrate that each defendant has the qualifying "minimum contacts" with the forum to support specific jurisdiction.[57] Particularly in the absence of an evidentiary hearing, that burden can be met simply by a prima facie

[52]*See Burger King Corp. v. Rudzewicz*, 471 U.S. 462, 476 (1985) ("Once it has been decided that a defendant purposefully established minimum contacts within the forum State, these contacts may be considered in light of other factors to determine whether the assertion of personal jurisdiction would comport with 'fair play and substantial justice.' ").

[53]*See Burger King Corp. v. Rudzewicz*, 471 U.S. 462, 478 & 483–84 (1985) ("inconvenience may at some point become so substantial as to achieve *constitutional* magnitude," such as when it makes litigation "so gravely difficult and inconvenient" as to unfairly place that party at a "severe disadvantage"). *See also Asahi Metal Indus. Co. v. Superior Ct.*, 480 U.S. 102, 114 (1987) ("When minimum contacts have been established, often the interests of the plaintiff and the forum in the exercise of jurisdiction will justify even the serious burdens placed on the alien defendant."); *id.* at 116 (Brennan, J., concurring) (finding specific jurisdiction absent, even after first concluding that minimum contacts exist); *Hood v. Am. Auto Care, LLC*, 21 F.4th 1216, 1222 (10th Cir. 2021) (even when minimum contacts exist, "the defendant can still escape jurisdiction by establishing that it would be incompatible with traditional notions of fair play and substantial justice").

[54]*See World-Wide Volkswagen Corp. v. Woodson*, 444 U.S. 286, 292 (1980). *Accord Asahi Metal Indus. Co. v. Superior Ct.*, 480 U.S. 102, 113–14 (1987); *Burger King Corp. v. Rudzewicz*, 471 U.S. 462, 476–77 (1985).

[55]*See World-Wide Volkswagen Corp. v. Woodson*, 444 U.S. 286, 292 (1980).

[56]*See Asahi Metal Indus. Co. v. Superior Ct.*, 480 U.S. 102, 115 (1987).

[57]*See infra* Authors' Commentary to Rule 12(b)(2) ("**Burden of Proof**").

showing.[58] (Even when that prima facie case is opposed, courts typically resolve all factual disputes in favor of the plaintiff.)[59] If the court is satisfied that a defendant is shown to have had sufficient "minimum contacts" with the forum, the burden typically then shifts to the defendant to make "a compelling case" demonstrating why the court's exercise of personal jurisdiction would be unreasonable / unfair.[60] Such proof is unlikely to exist often.[61]

§ 2.5c2 *In Personam* Circumstance #3—Contacts-Based Jurisdiction—General Jurisdiction

CORE CONCEPT

Unlike specific jurisdiction, general jurisdiction is *not* conduct-linked or case-specific. Quite the contrary, to satisfy general jurisdiction, a defendant's contacts need not have any linkage whatsoever to the cause of action.[1] When general jurisdiction exists over a defendant in a particular forum, that forum may hear and rule upon any claim against that defendant wherever it may have arisen.[2] For this reason, general jurisdiction has been dubbed "all-purpose" jurisdiction.[3] But this "sweeping" adjudicative breadth carries with it "a correlative limit."[4] General jurisdiction may only be exercised in a forum where a defendant's contacts are so "continuous and systematic," "so constant and pervasive,"

---

[58] *See infra* Authors' Commentary to Rule 12(b)(2) ("**Burden of Proof**" & "**Legal Test**").

[59] *See infra* Authors' Commentary to Rule 12(b)(2) ("**Legal Test**").

[60] *See Burger King Corp. v. Rudzewicz*, 471 U.S. 462, 477 (1985). *See also Ayla, LLC v. Alya Skin Pty. Ltd.*, 11 F.4th 972, 979 (9th Cir. 2021) (plaintiffs bear burden on purposeful availment and connectedness, then defendant must produce compelling case of unreasonableness).

[61] *See Compania de Inversiones Mercantiles, S.A. v. Grupo Cementos de Chihuahua S.A.B. de C.V.*, 970 F.3d 1269, 1289 (10th Cir. 2020) ("instances where the exercise of personal jurisdiction offends fair play and substantial justice are 'rare' "); *Managed Care Advisory Grp., LLC v. CIGNA Healthcare, Inc.*, 939 F.3d 1145, 1158 (11th Cir. 2019) (when nationwide service is permitted, "only in highly unusual cases" will inconvenience "rise to a level of constitutional concern"). *See also Republic of Panama v. BCCI Holdings (Luxembourg) S.A.*, 119 F.3d 935, 946, 948 (11th Cir. 1997) (litigation must be "so gravely difficult and inconvenient" as to create a "severe disadvantage" in relation to opponent).

[1] *See Ford Motor Co. v. Montana Eighth Jud. Dist. Ct.*, 592 U.S. __, 141 S. Ct. 1017, 1024 (2021) (encompasses "any and all claims" against a defendant, which "need not relate to the forum State or the defendant's activity there" but may instead "concern events and conduct anywhere in the world").

[2] *See Bristol-Myers Squibb Co. v. Superior Ct.*, 582 U.S. __, 137 S. Ct. 1773, 1780 (2017) ("A court with general jurisdiction may hear *any* claim against that defendant, even if all the incidents underlying the claim occurred in a different State.").

[3] *See Goodyear Dunlop Tires Ops., S.A. v. Brown*, 564 U.S. 915, 919 (2011).

[4] *See Ford Motor Co. v. Montana Eighth Jud. Dist. Ct.*, 592 U.S. __, 141 S. Ct. 1017, 1024 (2021).

as "to render [the defendant] essentially at home" there.[5] This test invites an inquiry into more than just the magnitude of a defendants contacts with a forum; it instead compels "an appraisal of a corporation's activities in their entirety, nationwide and worldwide."[6] Due to its narrow availability, this brand of personal jurisdiction has come to play "a reduced role" in contemporary litigation.[7] Nonetheless, general jurisdiction persists to achieve one very important objective: to ensure that plaintiffs always have "at least one clear and certain forum" where they can sue any defendant.[8]

APPLICATIONS

"At Home"

The Supreme Court has offered what it has characterized as the "paradigm forum[s]" for general jurisdiction. For individuals, that place is the person's domicile; for corporations, it is the entity's place of incorporation and principal place of business.[9] The Court has not offered an equivalent descriptive paradigm for unincorporated entities (such as partnerships, limited liability companies, and associations). Extrapolating from the Court's existing paradigms, lower courts have often sited the general jurisdiction of an unincorporated entity by locating its "domicile,"[10] ordinarily the place where it was organized and where it maintains its principal place of business.[11] Some courts, borrowing from subject-matter jurisdiction principles, have also, or instead, considered the citizenship of the entity's members to be potential general jurisdiction

---

[5] *See Daimler AG v. Bauman*, 571 U.S. 117, 122 (2014); *Goodyear Dunlop Tires Ops, S.A. v. Brown*, 564 U.S. 915, 919 (2011).

[6] *See Daimler AG v. Bauman*, 571 U.S. 117, 139 n.20 (2014) ("A corporation that operates in many places can scarcely be deemed at home in all of them.").

[7] *See Daimler AG v. Bauman*, 571 U.S. 117, 128 (2014) ("reduced role"); *id.* at 133 ("less dominant place").

[8] *See Daimler AG v. Bauman*, 571 U.S. 117, 139 (2014).

[9] *See Ford Motor Co. v. Montana Eighth Jud. Dist. Ct.*, — U.S. —, 141 S. Ct. 1017, 1024 (2021); *BNSF Ry. Co. v. Tyrrell*, 581 U.S. —, 137 S. Ct. 1549, 1558 (2017).

[10] *See Frank v. P N K (Lake Charles) L.L.C.*, 947 F.3d 331, 337 n.10 (5th Cir. 2020) (because a business's domicile is general jurisdiction's "guidepost", the particular type of business entity is "not germane"; "instead it is the company's domicile that merits attention").

[11] *See, e.g., Waldman v. Palestine Liberation Org.*, 835 F.3d 317, 332–35 (2d Cir. 2016) (non-sovereign government and foreign agent: "no reason to invent a different test for general personal jurisdiction depending on whether the defendant is an individual, a corporation, or another entity"); *Aldrich v. Nat'l Collegiate Athletic Ass'n*, 484 F. Supp. 3d 779, 790–94 (N.D. Cal. 2020) (association); *Garcia Hamilton & Assocs., L.P. v. RBC Cap. Markets, LLC*, 466 F. Supp. 3d 692, 698 n.5 & 698–99 (S.D. Tex. 2020) (limited liability company); *In re Packaged Seafood Prod. Antitrust Litig.*, 338 F. Supp. 3d 1118, 1139 n.14 (S.D. Cal. 2018) (limited partnership and limited liability partnership). *See generally* Susan Gilles & Angela Upchurch, Finding A "Home" for Unincorporated Entities Post-Daimler Ag v. Bauman, 20 NEV. L.J. 693 (2020).

locations.[12]

"Essentially" At Home

Defendants can (at least theoretically) be "essentially" at home in a location other than their actual home. The Court cites its 1952 decision in *Perkins v. Benquet Consolidated Mining Co.* as "the textbook case" of such an instance.[13] In *Perkins*, wartime necessity required a Philippine mining company to cease its home operations and conduct all its business activities in Ohio. Although the cause of action in that case had nothing to do with Ohio, the Court ruled that the company could be sued there under what we know now to be general jurisdiction.[14] Today, the Court's essentially-at-home measuring stick seems to be how closely (or not) a case's facts mirror those in *Perkins*.[15] This essentially-at-home option has been discussed only tepidly by the Court—as a "possibility," not "foreclose[d]," preserved for some "exceptional case."[16] Conducting that inquiry, the Court has rebuffed every recent attempt at asserting general jurisdiction against a company at locations other than its place of incorporation or principal place of business.[17] And when it rejects general jurisdiction, the Court has done so dismissively.[18] In one especially telling ruling, the Court held the State of Montana lacked general jurisdiction (under the *Perkins* essentially-at-home option) over a railroad that maintained 2,000 miles of permanent rail track secured into the Montana earth and that engaged 2,100 employees in Montana.[19]

---

[12]*See Allen v. IM Sols., LLC*, 83 F. Supp. 3d 1196, 1204 (E.D. Okla. 2015). *But see Aldrich v. Nat'l Collegiate Athletic Ass'n*, 484 F. Supp. 3d 779, 793–94 (N.D. Cal. 2020) (rejecting that approach).

[13]*See Goodyear Dunlop Tires Ops, S.A. v. Brown*, 564 U.S. 915, 927–28 (2011) (discussing *Perkins v. Benguet Consol. Min. Co.*, 342 U.S. 437 (1952)).

[14]*See Perkins v. Benguet Consol. Min. Co.*, 342 U.S. 437, 438–49 (1952).

[15]*See BNSF Ry. Co. v. Tyrrell*, 581 U.S. __, 137 S. Ct. 1549, 1558 (2017) ("exemplified" by *Perkins*); *Daimler AG v. Bauman*, 571 U.S. 117, 129–31 (2014) (*Perkins* is "textbook" example); *Goodyear Dunlop Tires Ops, S.A. v. Brown*, 564 U.S. 915, 929 (2011) ("Unlike the defendant in *Perkins* . . ."); *Helicopteros Nacionales de Colombia, S.A. v. Hall*, 466 U.S. 408, 415–16 (1984) (whether activities resemble those "found to exist in *Perkins*").

[16]*See Daimler AG v. Bauman*, 571 U.S. 117, 139 n.19 (2014).

[17]*See Daimler AG v. Bauman*, 571 U.S. 117, 136 (2014) ("Daimler's slim contacts with the State hardly render it at home there"); *Goodyear Dunlop Tires Ops, S.A. v. Brown*, 564 U.S. 915, 929 (2011) ("petitioners are in no sense at home in North Carolina;" "[t]heir attenuated connections to the State fall far short" of what is necessary).

[18]*See Daimler AG v. Bauman*, 571 U.S. 117, 138–39, 134 S. Ct. 746, 187 L. Ed. 2d 624 (2014) (doing business, permanently and in substantial volume, in forum not sufficient); *Goodyear Dunlop Tires Ops, S.A. v. Brown*, 564 U.S. 915, 929, 131 S. Ct. 2846, 180 L. Ed. 2d 796 (2011) (delivering tens of thousands of tires into forum not sufficient); *Helicopteros Nacionales de Colombia, S.A. v. Hall*, 466 U.S. 408, 415, 104 S. Ct. 1868, 80 L. Ed. 2d 404 (1984) (mere purchases, even at regular intervals, and training sessions in forum not sufficient).

[19]*See BNSF Ry. Co. v. Tyrrell*, 581 U.S. __, 137 S. Ct. 1549, 1559 (2017).

No "Traditional Notions of Fair Play" Inquiry

Unlike in specific jurisdiction cases, there is no second-stage reasonableness/fairness inquiry for general jurisdiction. The "traditional notions of fair play and substantial justice" are deemed immaterial to this type of jurisdiction. Because general jurisdiction exists only where a defendant is "essentially at home," inquiring whether it would be fair and reasonable to expect the defendant to litigate there is discounted at "superfluous."[20]

The Internet and "Virtual" Contacts

As with specific jurisdiction, the Supreme Court has yet to rule whether Internet activities would necessitate a different type or scope of inquiry in general jurisdiction cases. It would seem safe to suppose that if an Internet actor was domiciled, incorporated, or headquartered in the forum (*i.e.*, actually "at-home" there), that party would be amenable to that forum's general jurisdiction. In the essentially-at-home context, the lower federal courts seem to be resolving Internet cases in a manner faithful to that standard's exacting nature, sometimes even finding the need to overrule past precedents that had been decided using the vague, less focused "continuous and systematic" assessment.[21] But some courts have also reserved the possibility that, in some future online case, general jurisdiction based on pervasive virtual presence might be found appropriate under the essentially-at-home standard.[22]

Be Cautious With "Continuous-and-Systematic"

For years, the Court described general jurisdiction as available in those forums where a defendant's activities were "continuous and systematic."[23] That vague formulation seemed to afford practitioners wide berth for creative argument. But that malleability now seems closed off.[24] When used by the Court today, the "continuous and systematic" phrasing is

---

[20] *See Daimler AG v. Bauman*, 571 U.S. 117, 139 n.20 (2014).

[21] *See Erwin-Simpson v. AirAsia Berhad*, 985 F.3d 883, 891–92 (D.C. Cir. 2021) (overruling prior Internet cases that had found general jurisdiction on the basis of "sparse precedent" testing merely for "continuous and systematic" contacts); *Kuan Chen v. United States Sports Acad., Inc.*, 956 F.3d 45, 57–58 (1st Cir. 2020) (defendant not, "in the paradigmatic sense, at home in Massachusetts," nor were Internet contacts with Massachusetts "so unusually substantial as to render [defendant] 'essentially at home' "); *Fidrych v. Marriott Int'l, Inc.*, 952 F.3d 124, 134 (4th Cir. 2020) (though "certainly . . . systematic and continuous," Internet contacts "not substantial enough to 'render [Marriott] essentially at home' ") (citation omitted).

[22] *See Erwin-Simpson v. AirAsia Berhad*, 985 F.3d 883, 891 (D.C. Cir. 2021) ("not preclude the possibility"); *Kuan Chen v. United States Sports Acad., Inc.*, 956 F.3d 45, 57 (1st Cir. 2020) ("not discount the possibility").

[23] *See Helicopteros Nacionales de Colombia, S.A. v. Hall*, 466 U.S. 408, 415 (1984); *Perkins v. Benguet Consol. Min. Co.*, 342 U.S. 437, 438 (1952).

[24] *See Aldrich v. Nat'l Collegiate Athletic Ass'n*, 484 F. Supp. 3d 779, 791 (N.D. Cal. 2020) (before Supreme Court's recent case law, the former and more "simple formulation 'continuous and systematic' was much less stringent").

coupled with the delimiting attribute that those activities must be such as "to render [the defendant] essentially at home."[25] More recently, the Court seems to be distancing itself from the "continuous and systematic" modifier altogether.[26]

Volume Alone Does Not Differentiate General and Specific Jurisdiction

Over the years, courts and scholars occasionally thought of these two types of contacts-based jurisdiction in volume terms (fewer contacts channeled a case towards specific jurisdiction, greater contacts to general jurisdiction). Sometimes, that volume-continuum view was even offered as dictating the outcome of the jurisdictional inquiry (*e.g.*, if a defendant's contacts were not enough to support specific jurisdiction, then they certainly could not be enough to permit general jurisdiction). The Supreme Court's recent case law belies this sort of analysis. Specific (or "conduct-linked") jurisdiction is anchored to *connectedness*—the defendant had to have purposefully availed itself of the forum and, having done so, triggered a reciprocal obligation to defend locally. General (or "all-purpose") jurisdiction is anchored to pinpointing where the defendant is *essentially at home*—the defendant's domicile, place of creation, or principal place of business. The inquiries ask different questions. Accordingly, exercising specific jurisdiction over a defendant might be possible where general jurisdiction is not, just as exercising general jurisdiction over a defendant might be possible where specific jurisdiction is not.[27]

No General / Specific Jurisdiction Mix-and-Match

Embracing similar reasoning, some courts and practitioners had earlier supposed that a middle jurisdictional opportunity lay between specific and general jurisdiction, a conceptual area where a combination of *some connectedness* between contacts

---

[25] *See Daimler AG v. Bauman*, 571 U.S. 117, 138–39 (2014) (proper inquiry "is not whether a foreign corporation's in-forum contacts can be said to be in some sense 'continuous and systematic,' it is whether that corporation's 'affiliations with the State are so 'continuous and systematic' as to render [it] essentially at home in the forum State.' ").

[26] *See Daimler AG v. Bauman*, 571 U.S. 117, 138 (2014) (recounting that phrase "continuous and systematic" was used originally to describe specific jurisdiction, not general jurisdiction). *See also Ford Motor Co. v. Montana Eighth Jud. Dist. Ct.*, __ U.S. __, 141 S. Ct. 1017, 1024 (2021) (describing general jurisdiction as available "only when a defendant is 'essentially at home' in the State," omitting entirely the "continuous and systematic" phrasing).

[27] *Cf. Bristol-Myers Squibb Co. v. Superior Ct.*, 582 U.S. __, 137 S. Ct. 1773, 1778 (2017) (noting general jurisdiction was lacking, then turning to assess specific jurisdiction); *Goodyear Dunlop Tires Ops, S.A. v. Brown*, 564 U.S. 915, 919–20 (2011) (noting specific jurisdiction was lacking, then turning to examine general jurisdiction). *See generally Helicopteros Nacionales de Colombia, S.A. v. Hall*, 466 U.S. 408, 415–16 (1984) (parties concede claims did not arise out of or relate to contacts with the forum, so Court "must explore" whether forum contacts "constitute the kind of continuous and systematic" contacts required for general jurisdiction).

and cause of action (but not enough for specific jurisdiction) and *some heavier volume* of contacts (but not enough for general jurisdiction) could justify a court's exercise of its judicial power. The Supreme Court seemed to reject this possibility as "elid[ing] the essential difference between case-linked (specific) and all-purpose (general) jurisdiction."[28] The Court's recent loosening of the intensity of connectedness required for specific jurisdiction, however, may modestly bridge that gap.[29]

§ 2.6 Acquiring *In Rem* Jurisdiction

CORE CONCEPT

When a judge rests the exercise of personal jurisdiction on authority over property within the court's territory, the judge is invoking either *in rem* or *quasi in rem* personal jurisdiction. In such cases, the resulting judgment is understood as operating directly on the property itself.[1] The difference between these two types of property-based jurisdiction hinges on whom the judgment will affect. A judgment *in rem* generally affects (and binds) the interests of all persons everywhere who might claim an interest in the property.[2] Conversely, a judgment *quasi in rem* affects only the interests of particular persons.[3] *In rem* is discussed in this section; *quasi in rem* in discussed in the next.

APPLICATIONS

Objective of *In Rem* Actions

The goal in *in rem* proceedings is ordinarily to determine the ownership of (*i.e.,* title to) property that is located within the

[28] *See Goodyear Dunlop Tires Ops, S.A. v. Brown*, 564 U.S. 915, 927 (2011). *See also id.* at 919–20 (chiding lower court for "[c]onfusing or blending general and specific jurisdictional inquiries").

[29] *See Ford Motor Co. v. Montana Eighth Jud. Dist. Ct.*, 592 U.S. __, 141 S. Ct. 1017, 1026–32 (2021) ("arise out of or relate to" need not always show causal linkage).

[1] *See Eurasia Int'l, Ltd. v. Holman Shipping, Inc.*, 411 F.3d 578, 584 n.1 (5th Cir. 2005). *See generally California v. Deep Sea Rsch., Inc.*, 523 U.S. 491, 501 (1998) ("a vessel or thing is itself treated as the offender and made the defendant by name or description"); *United States v. Ten Thousand Dollars ($10,000.00) in U.S. Currency*, 860 F.2d 1511, 1513 (9th Cir. 1988) (predicated on "fiction of convenience" that "property is a person against whom suits can be filed and judgments entered").

[2] *See Hanson v. Denckla*, 357 U.S. 235, 246 n.12 (1958) ("A judgment in rem affects the interests of all persons in designated property."); *Becher v. Contoure Labs.*, 279 U.S. 388, 391 (1929) ("A judgment in rem binds all the world . . ."). *See also United States v. Real Prop. Located at 475 Martin Lane, Beverly Hills, CA*, 545 F.3d 1134, 1144 (9th Cir. 2008) ("*In rem* actions are generally considered proceedings 'against all the world,' " in which "the court undertakes to determine all claims that anyone has to a thing in question' ").

[3] *See Shaffer v. Heitner*, 433 U.S. 186, 199 n.17 (1977); *Hanson v. Denckla*, 357 U.S. 235, 246 n.12 (1958).

territory of the court.[4] Such jurisdiction is commonly invoked in admiralty (where a vessel is seized), in bankruptcy (where debtor assets are seized), and in civil condemnation (where instrumentality of a crime is seized).[5]

Limited Effect of *In Rem* Judgments

The effect of a judgment *in rem* is necessarily limited to the property that has been seized and on which the jurisdiction rests.[6] Such a judgment imposes no personal liability on the property's owner (because that owner has not been brought within the court's *in personam* reach).[7] Accordingly, unlike *in personam* judgments, a judgment *in rem* cannot be enforced elsewhere under the Constitution's Full Faith and Credit Clause.[8]

Prerequisites for Exercising *In Rem* Jurisdiction

Although *in rem* case law can often be old and sparse, the following general prerequisites to the exercise of *in rem* jurisdiction appear common:

(1) *Property With Value:* Because jurisdiction cannot be invoked to perform a useless act and because *in rem* jurisdiction is constrained to the value of the property in question, that property must have some value.[9]

(2) *Property Located in the Forum:* A court's *in rem* authority rests on its ability to exercise physical power over the property at issue; consequently, the property in question must lie within the territorial jurisdiction (*i.e.*, within the reach) of the tribunal.[10] The consequence of the property's later removal from the forum, following proper initiation of the *in rem* lawsuit, can be

---

[4] *See In re Matthews*, 395 F.3d 477, 481 (4th Cir. 2005) ("to conclusively determine ownership rights in the seized property," such that " 'it may be transferred to . . . a person who will then hold it free and clear of all claims' ") (citation omitted).

[5] *See, e.g., The Belgenland*, 114 U.S. 355, 366-67 (1885) (admiralty); *Central Virginia Cmty. College v. Katz*, 546 U.S. 356, 359 (2006) (bankruptcy); *United States v. U.S. Coin and Currency*, 401 U.S. 715, 720 (1971) (civil condemnation); 18 U.S.C.A. § 983 (same).

[6] *See United States v. Jantran, Inc.*, 782 F.3d 1177, 1180 (10th Cir. 2015).

[7] *See Shaffer v. Heitner*, 433 U.S. 186, 199 (1977).

[8] *See Nelson v. Miller*, 201 F.2d 277, 280 (9th Cir. 1952).

[9] *See The Jesse Williamson, Jr.*, 108 U.S. 305, 310 (1883) ("[T]his being a suit *in rem* only, the value of the vessel, represented by the stipulation, is all that is in dispute, because that is all the libelant can obtain, or the stipulators can lose, in this suit."); *Martin v. One Bronze Rod*, 2012 WL 13141502, at *3 (M.D. Fla. Apr. 30, 2012) (noting lack of sufficient evidence of "anything of value or historical significance").

[10] *See Hanson v. Denckla*, 357 U.S. 235, 246 (1958). *See also id.* at 250 ("Since a State is forbidden to enter a judgment attempting to bind a person over whom it has no jurisdiction, it has even less right to enter a judgment purporting to extinguish the interest of such a person in property over which the court has no jurisdiction.").

less clear.[11]

(3) *Property Seized By the Court:* The court must acquire effective control of the property in question by a judicial seizure.[12] The timing of this seizure is important: it must occur at the outset of the litigation, since doing so serves the companion goal of ensuring notice to those having a custodial interest in the property.[13] The manner of accomplishing the seizure will depend on the nature of the property seized; actual, physical possession by the court is not always necessary (it may instead be sufficient for the court to effectively interfere with control over the property).[14] For example, seizing a tract of land might be accomplished by a judicial order directing the local land records office to freeze the property's title, pending the outcome of the lawsuit.[15] Seizing intangible property, like shares of stock, might be achieved by an order directing the appropriate authority to halt trading in those shares.[16] Conversely, if the property is jewelry or a vehicle, the court might direct the U.S. Marshal to

---

[11] *See Republic Nat. Bank of Miami v. United States*, 506 U.S. 80, 85–89 (1992) (in civil forfeiture context, removal of property from forum does not divest jurisdiction ("Stasis is not a general prerequisite to the maintenance of jurisdiction"); instead, jurisdiction, once vested, is not ordinarily lost, unless property's departure would make resulting judgment "useless" because "the thing could neither be delivered to the libellants, nor restored to the claimants") (citation omitted). *But cf. United States v. Ten Thousand Dollars ($10,000.00) in U.S. Currency*, 860 F.2d 1511, 1513 (9th Cir. 1988) ("The general rule is that, in an *in rem* action, removal of the *res* ends the jurisdiction of the court. But exceptions exist. If the property is removed by 'an accidental or fraudulent or improper removal' jurisdiction is not destroyed.").

[12] *See United States v. Ursery*, 518 U.S. 267, 277 (1996) ("jurisdiction [is] dependent upon seizure of a physical object"); *Republic Nat. Bank of Miami v. United States*, 506 U.S. 80, 84 (1992) ("a valid seizure of the res is a prerequisite to the *initiation* of an *in rem* civil forfeiture proceeding").

[13] *See Pennoyer v. Neff*, 95 U.S. 714, 727 (1877).

[14] *See United States v. James Daniel Good Real Prop.*, 510 U.S. 43, 57–58 (1993) ("actually or constructively within the reach of the Court' ") (citation omitted); *Cooper v. Reynolds*, 77 U.S. 308, 317 (1870) ("general rule" is "actual seizure and possession of the *res* by the officer of the court," but *in rem* might also "be acquired by acts which are of equivalent import," showing "the dominion of the court over the thing, and in effect subject it to the control of the court").

[15] *See United States v. James Daniel Good Real Prop.*, 510 U.S. 43, 57–58 (1993) ("posting notice on the property and leaving a copy of the process with the occupant"); *Cooper v. Reynolds*, 77 U.S. 308, 317 (1870) ("real estate, which being incapable of removal, and lying within the territorial jurisdiction of the court, is for all practical purposes brought under the jurisdiction of the court by the officer's levy of the writ and return of that fact to the court").

[16] *See Shaffer v. Heitner*, 433 U.S. 186, 191–92 (1977) (stock shares seized "by placing 'stop transfer' orders or their equivalents on the books of the Greyhound Corp.").

take physical custody of the property.[17] Some courts have held that this prerequisite of seizure can be excused with litigants' consent or by waiver.[18]

(4) *Lawful Notice Given:* Proper notice of the seizure must be given.[19] The requisite notice must meet both constitutional requirements (fixed by the Due Process Clause) and service requirements (set by Rule 4). Although, at one time, posting physical notice "upon the thing itself" would likely suffice in most *in rem* cases, the Constitution today is more nuanced—the manner of notice will be examined more particularly to assess "its ability to inform people of the pendency of proceedings that affect their interests."[20]

(5) *Exercise is Constitutionally Proper:* Reasoning that, at base, *in rem* judgments do not really act *against property*, but rather act *against the owner's interest in that property*, the standard for assessing whether an exercise of *in rem* jurisdiction comports with constitutional due process is the same standard used to assess the exercise of jurisdiction over persons and their interests generally—namely, the specific jurisdiction test (discussed above).[21] Because *in rem* lawsuits endeavor to definitively determine the title owner of property that is both located within the court's territory and by then seized by the court, it "would be unusual" for that court to lack such jurisdiction under this standard.[22]

---

[17] *Cf. Hanover Am. Ins. Co. v. Tattooed Millionaire Ent., LLC*, 38 F.4th 501, 508 (6th Cir. 2022) (dispute over $2.5 million not *in rem* because funds not placed within exclusive jurisdiction of court).

[18] *See Leopard Marine & Trading, Ltd. v. Easy St. Ltd.*, 896 F.3d 174, 183–89 (2d Cir. 2018); *Barnes v. Sea Hawaii Rafting, LLC*, 889 F.3d 517, 529 (9th Cir. 2018).

[19] *See Shaffer v. Heitner*, 433 U.S. 186, 206 (1977).

[20] *See Greene v. Lindsey*, 456 U.S. 444, 451–56 (1982) (securely posting notice on door of home will be not only constitutionally adequate but "singularly appropriate and effective," given the law's assumption that owners must watch vigilantly over their property; but because such notices on apartment doors are often removed, such notice was not considered a "reliable means of acquainting interested parties of the fact that their rights are before the courts," especially when other, more reliable means existed).

[21] *See Shaffer v. Heitner*, 433 U.S. 186, 212 (1977). *See also Harrods Ltd. v. Sixty Internet Domain Names*, 302 F.3d 214, 224 (4th Cir. 2002) (minimum contacts test applies in *in rem* cases). *But see United States v. Obaid*, 971 F.3d 1095, 1100–05 (9th Cir. 2020) ("*Shaffer* is limited to *quasi in rem* actions and does not extend to *in rem* actions").

[22] *See Shaffer v. Heitner*, 433 U.S. 186, 207–08 (1977) (claim of interest in forum property may show claimant's expectation of benefits from forum, State has interest in ensuring property's marketability and means to peacefully resolve property disputes, relevant records and witnesses likely located there). *See also Porsche Cars N. Am., Inc. v. Porsche.net*, 302 F.3d 248, 260 (4th Cir. 2002) (in *in rem* action where " 'the property itself is the

Additional Prerequisite for Federal Courts

In addition to the general prerequisites noted above, Rule 4(n) limits the circumstances under which federal courts may exercise *in rem* jurisdiction. Federal courts may invoke *in rem* jurisdiction when some federal statute permits it. In that situation, the appropriate notice to claimants is that set by the applicable statute (or by following the relevant provisions of the federal service of process rule, Rule 4). Otherwise, federal courts may use *in rem* only upon a showing that *in personam* jurisdiction cannot be not obtained in the forum "by reasonable efforts" under Rule 4. In that latter circumstance, *in rem* jurisdiction is obtained by seizing the property "under the circumstances and in the manner" provided by the applicable State law.[23]

No Dueling Exercises of *In Rem* Jurisdiction

If two *in rem* (or *quasi in rem*) actions are filed against the same property, one in State court and the other in federal court, the court first to acquire its jurisdiction or first to assume control of the property is entitled to proceed and the other court must yield.[24] If the first court is federal, it may, if necessary, issue an order restraining the further prosecution of the State proceeding.[25] Relatedly, after one court establishes *in rem* jurisdiction over property, no second court will assume *in rem* jurisdiction over the same property.[26]

§ 2.7 Acquiring *Quasi In Rem* Jurisdiction

CORE CONCEPT

Like *in rem* cases, *quasi in rem* personal jurisdiction rests on the judge's authority over property within his or her territory. Unlike a judgment *in rem*, however, a judgment *quasi in rem* does not bind the whole world but rather only those parties in the lawsuit.[1]

---

source of the underlying controversy between plaintiff and defendant, . . . due process is satisfied' by assigning jurisdiction based on the location of the property").

[23]For a comprehensive treatment of Rule 4(n)'s requirements and operation, *see infra* Rule 4(n) and accompanying authors' commentary.

[24]*See Princess Lida of Thurn & Taxis v. Thompson*, 305 U.S. 456, 466–67 (1939). *See also Chevalier v. Est. of Barnhart*, 803 F.3d 789, 803 (6th Cir. 2015) (confirming continuing vitality of doctrine).

[25]*See Mandeville v. Canterbury*, 318 U.S. 47, 48–49 (1943). It may be that State courts have the right to enjoin later-filed federal proceedings as well. *See Hawthorne Sav. F.S.B. v. Reliance Ins. Co. of Illinois*, 421 F.3d 835, 851 (9th Cir. 2005) ("[T]he only time that state courts can enjoin federal proceedings is when the state courts first acquire in rem or quasi in rem jurisdiction before the federal courts.") (citation omitted).

[26]*See Marshall v. Marshall*, 547 U.S. 293, 311 (2006).

[1]*See Shaffer v. Heitner*, 433 U.S. 186, 199 n.17 (1977); *Tooele Cty. v. United States*, 820 F.3d 1183, 1188 (10th Cir. 2016).

APPLICATIONS

Objective of *Quasi In Rem* Actions

The law recognizes two types of *quasi in rem* lawsuits, each with different goals.

The first type (commonly labeled "***Quasi In Rem* Type #1**") is ordinarily a title fight between competing claimants to the same property, where the litigants each seek to persuade the court that (a) their claim to the property is superior to that of their opponents and (b) their opponents' claims should be declared extinguished.[2] The difference, then, between this first type and *in rem* lawsuits is merely the scope of the resulting judgment (*i.e.*, binds the litigants only *versus* binds the world).[3]

The second type (commonly labeled "***Quasi In Rem* Type #2**") is much different. It involves no competing claims to title, but rather rests on the assurance that the defendant is the one, true, lawful owner of the property in question. A plaintiff's objective in this second type of *quasi in rem* is to win the property in order to satisfy some claim that the plaintiff has against the defendant (a claim which might have no relationship of any kind to the seized property).[4] Functionally, this second *quasi in rem* type is a means for collecting on a debt or other obligation,[5] and had been used principally when the debtor was outside the court's reach but his or her property was not.[6] Today, for constitutional reasons (discussed below), that use is often unavailable. But the strategic value of this second type of *quasi in rem* persists—when available, it may meaningfully encumber a defendant's in-forum assets in a way that could prompt great urgency in seeing to it that the pending lawsuit (or at least the property's seizure) is expeditiously resolved.[7]

Limited Effect of *Quasi in Rem* Judgments

The effect of a judgment *quasi in rem* is limited to the property that has been seized and on which the jurisdiction rests, just as is true with *in rem* judgments. *Quasi in rem* judgments impose no personal liability on the property's owner and will not trigger the Constitution's Full Faith and Credit Clause in a

---

[2]*See Shaffer v. Heitner*, 433 U.S. 186, 199 n.17 (1977); *Hanson v. Denckla*, 357 U.S. 235, 246 n.12 (1958).

[3]*See Hanover Am. Ins. Co. v. Tattooed Millionaire Ent., LLC*, 38 F.4th 501, 509 (6th Cir. 2022).

[4]*See Shaffer v. Heitner*, 433 U.S. 186, 199 n.17 (1977) (in second type, "the plaintiff seeks to apply what he concedes to be the property of the defendant to the satisfaction of a claim against him") (citing *Hanson v. Denckla*, 357 U.S. 235, 246 n.12 (1958)).

[5]*See Cerner Middle E. Ltd. v. iCapital, LLC*, 939 F.3d 1016, 1021–22 (9th Cir. 2019); *Licea v. Curacao Drydock Co.*, 952 F.3d 207, 214–15 (5th Cir. 2015).

[6]*See World Wide Supply OU v. Quail Cruises Ship Mgmt.*, 802 F.3d 1255, 1259–60 (11th Cir. 2015); *Allied Mar., Inc. v. Descatrade SA*, 620 F.3d 70, 74 (2d Cir. 2010).

[7]*See Shaffer v. Heitner*, 433 U.S. 186, 191–92 n.7 (1977) (*quasi in rem* used to seize stock shares belonging to individual officers and directors of corporation, valued collectively at time of seizure in May 1974 at approximately $1.2 million).

way that would allow enforcement elsewhere of any judgment shortfall.[8]

Prerequisites for Exercising *Quasi in Rem* Jurisdiction

The *in rem* discussion above listed five jurisdictional prerequisites, an additional prerequisite when litigating in federal court, and the no-dueling-jurisdiction principle. All apply in *quasi in rem* lawsuits as well.

Nuances in *Quasi In Rem Type* #2 Lawsuits

Lawsuits filed as *in rem* or *quasi in rem type #1* actions proceed similarly. But *quasi in rem type #2* actions are different in nature, which implicates several noteworthy nuances for practice:

(a) *Importance of Defendant's Ownership:* Settled ownership is central to *quasi in rem type #2* lawsuits: whereas *in rem* and *quasi in rem type #1* lawsuits are endeavoring to discern who the rightful owner of the seized property is, *quasi in rem type #2* lawsuits are premised on the assurance that the property owner's identity is already clearly known.[9]

(b) *Importance of the Seized Property's Value:* In most *quasi in rem type #2* lawsuits, the end-game is liquidating the defendant's seized asset to generate funds that will then be used to pay off a debt or obligation owed to the plaintiff. Thus, the convertible value of the seized asset assumes special importance. That importance is accentuated by two attributes of *quasi in rem* litigation: first, the defendant's potential exposure is limited to the value of the seized asset[10] and, as noted above, there is no full-faith-and-credit transferability. Ergo, if a plaintiff's claim is worth, say, $500,000, but the only in-forum asset of the defendant is a $4,000 used car, the attractiveness of *quasi in rem type #2* often diminishes.

(c) *Formidable Constitutional Hurdle:* Some have described *quasi in rem type #2* lawsuits as "basically a

[8]*See CME Media Enters. B.V. v. Zelezny*, 2001 WL 1035138, at *4 (S.D.N.Y. Sept. 10, 2001). *See generally* A.B.A. SEC. LITIG., BUSINESS & COMMERCIAL LITIG. IN FEDERAL COURTS § 55:29 (4th ed. 2020) ("[A] judgment rendered in rem or quasi-in rem will not be enforced against the defendant or its property in other jurisdictions under the Full Faith and Credit Clause.").

[9]*See Shipping Corp. of India v. Jaldhi Overseas Pte Ltd.*, 585 F.3d 58, 69 (2d Cir. 2009) ("depends entirely on the determination that the *res* at issue is the property of the defendant at the moment the *res* is attached[;] . . . If the *res* is not the property of the defendant, then the court lacks jurisdiction.").

[10]*See Shaffer v. Heitner*, 433 U.S. 186, 207 n.23 (1977) (defendant's potential *in rem* liability "is limited by the value of the property"); *Flame S.A. v. Freight Bulk Pte. Ltd.*, 807 F.3d 572, 579 n.2 (4th Cir. 2015) (*quasi in rem* "limits personal jurisdiction over the defendants in the case to the value of the attached vessel").

halfway house between *in rem* and *in personam* jurisdiction"—they are not really actions against the seized property, but in truth are actions against the person of the defendant using the expedient of her in-forum property to acquire an adjudicative power against her that, because of her lack of forum presence, would not otherwise exist.[11] Predictably, then, a *quasi in rem type #2* lawsuit's comportment with constitutional due process is tested using the *International Shoe* specific jurisdiction analysis (discussed earlier).[12] That standard requires that the defendant not only have purposeful contacts with the forum, but also that those purposeful contacts give rise or relate to the lawsuit's claims.[13] This will pose a formidable, often unsurmountable obstacle when the seized property in a *quasi in rem type #2* lawsuit has no connection to the plaintiff's claim.[14]

- *Then, Why Ever Consider Quasi In Rem Type #2?* If property-based *quasi in rem type #2* lawsuits are tested by (and limited by) the same person-based standards as *in personam* lawsuits, why would a litigant ever want to pursue the former if the latter was feasible? After all, *quasi in rem type #2* lawsuits are constrained in ways *in personam* judgments are not—they are limited by the value of the seized asset and non-transferable under full faith and credit principles. Often, litigation strategy supplies the answer to this query: by encumbering an opponent's valuable, in-forum property in a *quasi in rem* proceeding, an opponent (who otherwise may lie outside the court's reach) may be coaxed into consenting to the forum's exercise of *in personam* jurisdiction in or-

[11] *See Ventura Packers, Inc. v. F/V Jeanine Kathleen*, 424 F.3d 852, 860 n.4 (9th Cir. 2005) (citations omitted).

[12] *See Shaffer v. Heitner*, 433 U.S. 186, 212 (1977) ("all assertions of state-court jurisdiction must be evaluated according to the standards set forth in *International Shoe* and its progeny").

[13] *See Ford Motor Co. v. Montana Eighth Jud. Dist. Ct.*, — U.S. —, 141 S. Ct. 1017, 1024–25 (2021).

[14] *See Shaffer v. Heitner*, 433 U.S. 186, 208–09 (1977) (acknowledging that *International Shoe* standard "result[s] in significant change" in *quasi in rem* cases because "the presence of the property alone would not support the State's jurisdiction" and, if other affiliating ties between defendant and forum did not exist, "cases over which the State is now thought to have jurisdiction" could not be brought there). *See also Rush v. Savchuk*, 444 U.S. 320, 328 (1980) ("The ownership of property in the State is *a* contact between the defendant and the forum, and it may suggest the presence of other ties. Jurisdiction is lacking, however, unless there are sufficient contacts to satisfy the fairness standard of *Int'l Shoe*.").

der to have that encumbered property released.[15] As noted above, however, because the *International Shoe* standards govern, the opportunity for such *quasi in rem type #2* lawsuits is far more restricted than before.

- *Not a Hurdle When Merely Enforcing Lawful Judgments:* The *International Shoe* test is not implicated when a plaintiff, who has already fully litigated her claim against the defendant elsewhere in a court of competent jurisdiction, is merely seeking to enforce that out-of-State judgment against the defendant's assets located in the forum. Such enforcement is ensured by the Constitution's Full Faith and Credit Clause; to that use the *International Shoe* test poses no impediment.[16]

(d) *Defendant's Default-or-Submit Dilemma:* Threatened with the loss of its property, a defendant in a *quasi in rem type #2* lawsuit might desire to come into the forum to defend against that claim on its merits, but doing so places the defendant at peril. By appearing in the forum to defend, that defendant may be vulnerable there to being "tagged" with service of process, which would confer *in personam* jurisdiction and expose the defendant to personal liability for the full amount of the claim—and that judgment would be entitled to full-faith-and-credit transferability. Some courts have rescued defendants from this "default-or-submit" dilemma by allowing them to make a "limited appearance" in the forum to defend against the *quasi in rem type #2* claim, immune from "tag" jurisdiction.[17]

§ 2.8 Notice and an Opportunity to Be Heard—Another Prerequisite for Exercising Personal Jurisdiction

CORE CONCEPT

Whether an exercise of personal jurisdiction is theoretically allowable depends on the principles discussed above—consent, tag, forum contacts, and/or property seizure. Then, service of process is the operative event (or "ritual") by which the court's coercive authority over the parties to render a final, binding, and enforce-

[15] *See Shaffer v. Heitner*, 433 U.S. 186, 193 (1977) ("primary purpose" of State's seizure statute was not to hold property pending a title resolution but, "[o]n the contrary, as here employed, . . . to compel the personal appearance of a nonresident defendant to answer and defend a suit brought against him in a court of equity"; once the defendant does so, the seizure is released) (citation omitted).

[16] *See Shaffer v. Heitner*, 433 U.S. 186, 210 & n.36 (1977).

[17] *See United States v. First Nat. City Bank*, 379 U.S. 378, 390 (1965) (surveying case law).

able civil judgment is actually exerted. Notice and an opportunity to be heard is, thus, a precondition to personal jurisdiction.

APPLICATIONS

Notice as a Precondition for Exercising Personal Jurisdiction

Proper notice is considered a prerequisite to the exercise of personal jurisdiction authority.[1] More precisely, proper notice (through service of original process) is the procedural event by which a court asserts its coercive authority over a defending party.[2] This relationship between personal jurisdiction and notice has historical lineage. At common law, a court would acquire personal jurisdiction over a defendant through a writ of *capias ad respondendum*, whereupon the sheriff would take the defendant into custody and bring him before the tribunal.[3] Thus, in a very tangible sense, exercising judicial authority was "grounded" on a court's actual, physical "power over the defendant's person" or the defendant's property.[4] Notice, through service of original process, is "the contemporary counterpart to that writ."[5] Proper personal jurisdiction, then, remains merely inchoate until notice is accomplished: "Accordingly, one becomes a party officially, and is required to take action in that capacity, only upon service of a summons or other authority-asserting measure setting the time within which the party served must appear and defend."[6]

Notice Must, First, Satisfy the U.S. Constitution

The U.S. Constitution's Due Process Clause has long required appropriate notice in civil lawsuits.[7] Notice is considered essential to due process because it facilitates the Constitution's "fundamental requisite" of the defendant's right to an op-

---

[1] *See BNSF Ry. Co. v. Tyrrell*, 581 U.S. —, 137 S. Ct. 1549, 1556 (2017); *Omni Cap. Int'l, Ltd. v. Rudolf Wolff & Co.*, 484 U.S. 97, 104 (1987). *See also Fischer v. Fed. Express Corp.*, 42 F.4th 366, 381 (3d Cir. 2022) ("For a court to exercise personal jurisdiction over a defendant, the defendant must be served process, alerting the defendant to the pendency of the suit and the nature of the claims against her.").

[2] *See Mississippi Pub. Corp. v. Murphree*, 326 U.S. 438, 444–45 (1946); *Morrissey v. Mayorkas*, 17 F.4th 1150, 1156 (D.C. Cir. 2021).

[3] *See Murphy Bros. v. Michetti Pipe Stringing, Inc.*, 526 U.S. 344, 350–51 (1999).

[4] *See Int'l Shoe Co. v. Washington*, 326 U.S. 310, 316 (1945). *See generally McDonald v. Mabee*, 243 U.S. 90, 91 (1917) (Holmes, J.) ("The foundation of jurisdiction is physical power. . .").

[5] *See Murphy Bros. v. Michetti Pipe Stringing, Inc.*, 526 U.S. 344, 350 (1999).

[6] *See Murphy Bros. v. Michetti Pipe Stringing, Inc.*, 526 U.S. 344, 350 (1999).

[7] *See Pennoyer v. Neff*, 95 U.S. 714 (1877) (due process requires "a tribunal competent by its constitution" and, if the personal liability of the defendant is at issue, "he must be brought within its jurisdiction by service of process within the State, or his voluntary appearance"). *See also Mullane v. Cent. Hanover Bank & Tr. Co.*, 339 U.S. 306, 314 (1950) (notice is "[a]n elementary and fundamental requirement of due process in any proceeding which is to be accorded finality").

portunity to be heard: "This right to be heard has little reality or worth unless one is informed that the matter is pending and can choose for himself whether to appear or default, acquiesce or contest."[8]

Interestingly, given the paramount importance it assigns to proper notice, the U.S. Supreme Court has never ruled that *actually* receiving notice is constitutionally indispensable.[9] Sometimes, actual notice may be impractical or even impossible. But "a mere gesture" or idle attempt at notice will violate due process.[10] Instead, the means chosen to impart notice "must be such as one desirous of actually informing the absentee might reasonably adopt to accomplish it," or, in an often recounted phrase: "reasonably calculated, under all the circumstances, to apprise interested parties of the pendency of the action and afford them an opportunity to present their objections."[11]

To meet this standard, the notice method must either "in itself [be] reasonably certain to inform those affected" or, if that is not possible, must not be "substantially less likely to bring home notice than other of the feasible and customary substitutes."[12] Actual, in-hand delivery of written notice to defendants while they are present within the forum "is the classic form of notice" and is "always adequate in any type of proceeding."[13] Whether different means of delivery will satisfy due process will depend on "the practicalities and peculiarities" of each case.[14] Few bright-line constitutional guideposts exist. However, the Court has determined that notice, even if originally proper at the time it was given, may be rendered inadequate if the sender comes to learn the notice failed; in such a case, due process may require a further attempt at notice if, under the circumstances, a further attempt would be

[8] *See Mullane v. Cent. Hanover Bank & Tr. Co.*, 339 U.S. 306, 314 (1950) (citation omitted).

[9] *See Jones v. Flowers*, 547 U.S. 220, 226 (2006); *Dusenbery v. United States*, 534 U.S. 161, 171 (2002). *See also Mullane v. Cent. Hanover Bank & Tr. Co.*, 339 U.S. 306, 317–18 (1950) (acknowledging that class of unknown trust beneficiaries was unlikely to receive actual notice via newspaper publication, but costly and difficult investigations into their identities was not required by due process).

[10] *See Mullane v. Cent. Hanover Bank & Tr. Co.*, 339 U.S. 306, 315 (1950).

[11] *See Mullane v. Cent. Hanover Bank & Tr. Co.*, 339 U.S. 306, 315 (1950).

[12] *See Mullane v. Cent. Hanover Bank & Tr. Co.*, 339 U.S. 306, 315 (1950).

[13] *See Mullane v. Cent. Hanover Bank & Tr. Co.*, 339 U.S. 306, 313 (1950).

[14] *See Mullane v. Cent. Hanover Bank & Tr. Co.*, 339 U.S. 306, 314–15 (1950). *See also Jones v. Flowers*, 547 U.S. 220, 227 (2006) ("the 'notice required will vary with circumstances and conditions' ") (citation omitted). *See generally Mennonite Bd. of Missions v. Adams*, 462 U.S. 791, 799 (1983) (when government is giving notice: "It is true that particularly extensive efforts to provide notice may often be required when the State is aware of a party's inexperience or incompetence."); *Robinson v. Hanrahan*, 409 U.S. 38, 40 (1972) (mailing notice was improper where government knew party was incarcerated at the time).

reasonable.[15]

Notice Must, Second, Also Satisfy the Federal Rules

In addition to being constitutionally adequate, notice in a federal lawsuit must also meet the federal service requirements set out in Rule 4, which are discussed in depth in Part III of this text. Thus, showing that the defendant received actual notice of the lawsuit or that constitutional due process was otherwise met will usually not excuse a failure to satisfy the Rule requirements for proper federal service of process.[16]

Notice Obligation May Be Waived

Because it is intended to safeguard a defendant's interests, a defendant can voluntarily surrender or involuntarily lose an otherwise meritorious challenge to improper service by consent, waiver, or failure to properly and timely assert (and then press) that objection.[17] Indeed, the Rules codify a procedure for formally inviting a defendant to waive formal notice through service of process, in exchange for an extended time to respond to the serving party's complaint.[18]

---

[15] *See Jones v. Flowers*, 547 U.S. 220, 229–30 (2006) (when notice by certified mail is otherwise permitted, more may be required after learning from post office that letter was unclaimed and undelivered: "Deciding to take no further action is not what someone 'desirous of actually informing' [defendant] would do; such a person would take further reasonable steps if any were available.").

[16] *See De Gazelle Grp., Inc. v. Tamaz Trading Establishment*, 817 F.3d 747, 750–51 (11th Cir. 2016) (reliance on actual notice was "misplaced," when service was not compliant with Rule 4); *Freedom Watch, Inc. v. Organization of Petroleum Exporting Countries*, 766 F.3d 74, 81 (D.C. Cir. 2014) (actual notice cannot rescue service that is otherwise defective, absent substantial compliance and "a minor, nonprejudicial defect"); *Crowley v. Bannister*, 734 F.3d 967, 975 (9th Cir. 2013) (actual notice does not confer personal jurisdiction absent complying substantially with Rule 4).

[17] *See generally Murphy Bros. v. Michetti Pipe Stringing, Inc.*, 526 U.S. 344, 350 (1999) ("In the absence of service of process (or waiver of service by the defendant), a court ordinarily may not exercise power over a party the complaint names as defendant."); *Omni Cap. Int'l, Ltd. v. Rudolf Wolff & Co.*, 484 U.S. 97, 104–05 (1987) ("Absent consent, this means there must be authorization for service of summons on the defendant."); Rule 4(d) (waiver by authorization); Rule 12(h)(1) (waiver by forfeiture). *See generally* Authors' Commentary to Rule 12(b)(4)–(5) (**"Timing and Waiver"**).

[18] *See* Rule 4(d) and accompanying Authors' Commentary.

C. SUBJECT-MATTER JURISDICTION

Table of Sections

2.9 Introduction
2.10 Federal Question Jurisdiction
2.11 Diversity Jurisdiction
2.11a —The First Requirement: Complete Diversity of Citizenship
2.11b —The Second Requirement: Amount in Controversy
2.11c —Diversity Jurisdiction in Class Actions and Mass Torts
2.12 Supplemental Jurisdiction

---

§ 2.9 Introduction

CORE CONCEPT

Jurisdiction over persons or things ("personal jurisdiction"), discussed above, defines the limits of a court's reach to require a defendant to appear and defend a lawsuit or the court's reach over property that is the subject of a lawsuit. Subject-matter jurisdiction, by contrast, limits the kind of cases a court may hear, irrespective of where the affected persons or property may be found. Thus, if a person is served with process within the State where a court sits, the court likely has personal jurisdiction over that person. But if the cause of action is of a kind that a federal court cannot hear, the court would still lack subject-matter jurisdiction and the court would lack the constitutional authority to adjudicate the case.

As part of the compromise between states' rights and federal rights, the Constitution established a federal court system with limited subject-matter jurisdiction, only empowered to hear those specific categories of cases authorized in the Constitution.[1] It then permitted Congress to attend to the details of the federal court system, and Congress accordingly enacted a series of federal statutes addressing, among other things, the federal courts' subject-matter jurisdiction. Although there are a number of congressionally-sanctioned subject-matter categories, by far the two most commonly invoked forms of subject-matter jurisdiction are federal question jurisdiction and diversity jurisdiction.[2] Accordingly, this *Handbook* will focus primarily on federal question

---

[1] *See* U.S. Const. art. III, sec. 2.

[2] The statistics vary from year to year, but the official website of the United States courts, on its page titled "Types of Cases" only lists diversity jurisdiction and federal question jurisdiction cases. More granular data are available in the statistical reports on the website. *See* https://www.uscourts.gov/statistics-reports/analysis-reports/statistical-tables-federal-judiciary (last visited on July 11, 2022).

jurisdiction, discussed in Section 2.10, and diversity jurisdiction, discussed in Section 2.11. It will then briefly address some of the less common forms of subject-matter jurisdiction. Before turning to these categories, a few general jurisdictional concepts are important.

APPLICATIONS

Each Claim Must have Subject-Matter Jurisdiction

Subject-matter jurisdiction must be satisfied as to each claim in a case before a federal court will hear that claim.[3]

- *Joined Claims*: The requirement that each claim have a basis for subject-matter jurisdiction applies to joined claims like counterclaims, crossclaims, and third-party claims[4] (although they will often qualify for supplemental jurisdiction, as discussed below). If the complaint is dismissed, the court may continue to adjudicate joined claims for which the court has an independent basis of jurisdiction.[5] Thus, if the court dismisses the complaint, it could retain a counterclaim over which it had diversity or federal question jurisdiction.

Original vs. Supplemental Jurisdiction

In order to bring a case into federal court in the first instance, there must be at least one claim that possesses "original" subject-matter jurisdiction (such as federal question or diversity jurisdiction).[6] Given one claim with original jurisdiction, other claims that are sufficiently related to the claim with original subject-matter jurisdiction may, under appropriate circumstances, be included in the lawsuit through the exercise of "supplemental jurisdiction," even though those other claims might not themselves qualify for original subject-matter jurisdiction.[7]

Constitutional and Statutory Authority

There are two important sources of legal authority for subject-matter jurisdiction, the United States Constitution and federal statutes. To understand and apply subject-matter jurisdiction properly, it is often important to consider both sources of authority; the "nuts and bolts" rules and procedures are imposed by the statutes, but many of the jurisprudential considerations flow from the constitutional limitations on the types of case federal courts may accept.

- *Constitution*: The starting point is the Constitution, which authorizes a federal court system with limited jurisdiction to create a balance between the federal and

---

[3]*See, e.g., Curtis v. GreenPoint Mortg. Funding, Inc.*, 661 F. Supp. 2d 65, 67 (D. Mass. 2009).

[4]*See De Asencio v. Tyson Foods, Inc.*, 342 F.3d 301, 307 (3d Cir. 2003).

[5]*Barefoot Architect, Inc. v. Bunge*, 632 F.3d 822, 836 (3d Cir. 2011).

[6]*Exxon Mobil Corp. v. Allapattah Servs., Inc.*, 545 U.S. 546, 552 (2005).

[7]*See* Section 2.12 for a discussion of supplemental jurisdiction.

state judicial systems. Article III, Section 1 provides that the judicial power of the United States be vested in the Supreme Court and authorizes Congress to create lower courts. Section 2 then lists the types of cases that the federal courts may adjudicate. Essentially, it lists: 1) cases arising under federal laws; 2) cases affecting ambassadors and similar officials; 3) admiralty cases; 4) cases in which the United States is a party; and cases between citizens of different States. Federal courts are only authorized to accept cases falling into at least one of the categories on this list.[8]

- *Federal Statutes*: Congress accepted the invitation in the Constitution to establish the lower courts and created the federal District Courts and the Courts of Appeals (and some specialty courts). Congress then enacted statutes describing the types of cases that these courts were authorized to hear, consistent with the limitations in Article III, Section 2. These statues are primarily found in Title 28 of the United States Code and are explained below. The two most frequently invoked sections are § 1331, titled Federal Question Jurisdiction, and § 1332, which addresses claims between citizens of different States. § 1331 closely tracks the language in Article III. In contrast, § 1332 adds restrictions to the federal courts' diversity jurisdiction that are not found in the Constitution (such as a minimum amount in controversy). Some of the other jurisdictional statutes are discussed below at the end of this section.

Duty to Plead and Demonstrate Jurisdiction

Because they possess only limited subject-matter jurisdiction, federal courts must, at the outset, be persuaded that they have the judicial power to proceed in a pending lawsuit. As a threshold matter, Rule 8(a)(1) requires a plaintiff filing a complaint in federal court to plead, in that complaint, the basis for the court's subject-matter jurisdiction.[9] If subject-matter jurisdiction is challenged or questioned, the burden of demonstrating that the requirements of federal subject-matter jurisdiction are met rests on the party seeking to invoke the court's jurisdiction (the plaintiff when filing a complaint in federal court and a defendant when removing a case from state to federal court).[10]

---

[8] *Powell v. McCormack*, 395 U.S. 486, 512–13 (1969).

[9] *See* Rule 8(a)(1) and accompanying authors' commentary ("**Element 1: Grounds for Jurisdiction**") for a discussion of the manner for pleading subject-matter jurisdiction.

[10] *See G. W. v. Ringwood Bd. of Educ.*, 28 F.4th 465, 468 (3d Cir. 2022) (quoting *Kokkonen v. Guardian Life Insurance Co. of America*, 511 U.S. 375, 377 (1994).

Jurisdiction to Determine Subject-Matter Jurisdiction

A federal court that lacks subject-matter jurisdiction lacks authority to decide a case, and most rulings the court makes before realizing it lacks subject-matter jurisdiction are void.[11] There is one obvious, necessary exception: a federal court is authorized to determine whether it has subject-matter jurisdiction, even if the court ultimately decides that it lacks jurisdiction.[12]

Consent/Waiver

Unlike personal jurisdiction, subject-matter jurisdiction cannot be obtained through consent of the parties.[13] Similarly, subject-matter jurisdiction is not subject to waiver, forfeiture, or estoppel (*e.g.*, failure to raise lack of subject-matter jurisdiction does not result in waiver).[14] The rationale is that the limits on a federal district court's subject-matter jurisdiction are grounded in the constitutional balance of federal and state judicial power, and it is not the prerogative of the parties to enter into agreements that have the effect of upsetting that balance. Moreover, because the parties cannot confer subject-matter jurisdiction on the court by consent, there is no time limit on objections to subject-matter jurisdiction.[15] Instead, lack of subject-matter jurisdiction can be raised at any time, and the court must determine whether it has subject-matter jurisdiction whenever the question arises, either on motion of a party or on its own.[16]

Court's Obligation to Exercise its Subject-Matter Jurisdiction

Except when a jurisdictional statute specifically gives the court discretion to decline to exercise subject-matter jurisdiction, federal courts are normally obligated to hear claims over which they have proper subject-matter jurisdiction.[17]

Additional Grants of Subject-Matter Jurisdiction

Federal question, diversity, and supplemental jurisdiction are the most commonly exercised forms of subject-matter jurisdiction and are explored in depth below. Some of the other jurisdictional statutes are briefly described here.

- *Admiralty*: 28 U.S.C.A. § 1333 authorizes the federal

---

[11] *Mitchell L. Firm, L.P. v. Bessie Jeanne Worthy Revocable Tr.*, 8 F.4th 417, 420 (5th Cir. 2021). *See, e.g., Murray v. Conseco, Inc.*, 467 F.3d 602, 605 (7th Cir. 2006) ("A court that lacks subject matter jurisdiction cannot dismiss a case with prejudice.").

[12] *See United States v. Ruiz*, 536 U.S. 622, 628 (2007); *Republic of Ecuador v. Connor*, 708 F.3d 651, 655–56 (5th Cir. 2013).

[13] *See Insurance Corp. of Ireland, Ltd. v. Compagnie des Bauxites de Guinee*, 456 U.S. 694, 702 (1982); *Nederland Ship. Corp. v. U.S.*, 18 F.4th 115, 122 (3d Cir. 2021).

[14] *Ins. Corp. of Ireland v. Compagnie des Bauxites de Guinee*, 456 U.S. 694, 702 (1982).

[15] *Arbaugh v. Y&H Corp.*, 546 U.S. 500, 506 (2006).

[16] *See Bender v. Williamsport Area School Dist.*, 475 U.S. 534, 541 (1986).

[17] *See Carnegie-Mellon University v. Cohill*, 484 U.S. 343, 356 (1988).

courts to exercise jurisdiction over admiralty, maritime, and prize cases (pertaining to the capture of enemy ships).

- *Bankruptcy*: 28 U.S.C.A. § 1334 vests the federal courts with exclusive jurisdiction over cases arising under the federal bankruptcy laws.
- *Antitrust and Commerce*: 28 U.S.C.A. § 1337 authorizes the federal courts to exercise jurisdiction over claims arising under the federal antitrust laws or under any federal laws governing commerce.
- *Intellectual Property*: 28 U.S.C.A. § 1338 authorizes the federal courts to exercise jurisdiction over claims arising under the federal laws relating to patents, trademarks, and copyrights.
- *Postal Matters*: 28 U.S.C.A. § 1339 authorizes the federal courts to exercise jurisdiction over claims arising under the federal laws relating to the postal service.
- *Internal Revenue and Customs*: 28 U.S.C.A. § 1340 authorizes the federal courts to exercise jurisdiction over claims arising under the federal laws relating to internal revenue and customs.
- *Civil Rights*: 28 U.S.C.A. § 1343 authorizes the federal courts to exercise jurisdiction over claims for deprivation of the civil rights of a United States citizen, as provided by the civil rights laws.
- *United States as a Party*: 28 U.S.C.A. §§ 1345 and 1346 authorize the federal courts to exercise jurisdiction over claims in which the United States is a plaintiff or a defendant. 28 U.S.C.A. § 1361 authorizes the federal courts to exercise jurisdiction over mandamus actions seeking to compel United States officers or employees to perform a duty owed to the plaintiff.

§ 2.10 Federal Question Jurisdiction

CORE CONCEPT

One of the two common forms of federal subject-matter jurisdiction is "federal question jurisdiction" under 28 U.S.C.A. § 1331, which extends to "all civil actions arising under the Constitution, laws, or treaties of the United States." This form of subject-matter jurisdiction is sometimes referred to as "arising under jurisdiction" because the phrase "arising under" appears in both this statute and Article III of the U.S. Constitution and because it captures the concept that the claim must actually be found *in* the federal law, rather than simply loosely depending on the federal law. Federal question jurisdiction typically accounts for under half the civil cases filed in federal courts.[1] The purposes of federal question jurisdiction is to promote the uniform application of federal laws across the country—the interpretation of a federal statute should be the same in Texas and in Maine—and so that the federal judges can develop expertise in applying federal law.[2]

APPLICATIONS

Claims "Arising Under" Federal Law

The vast majority of federal question claims are those that seek a federal remedy for a violation of a right created by a federal statute.[3] In this category of claims, the federal law in question creates a private right of action (that is, the law actually authorizes the plaintiff to bring the sort of claim now pending before the court).[4] For example, 42 U.S.C.A. § 1983 authorizes an action against any person who, under color of law, deprives another person of "any rights, privileges, or immunities secured by the Constitution and laws." If an employee working for a state agency believes that the agency's medical leave policies violate her constitutional rights, she may bring a claim under § 1983 and a federal district court would have federal question jurisdiction over her claim.[5]

- *Constitutional Violations*: Although most federal question cases involve claims arising under a federal statute, a plaintiff can, under the right circumstances, bring a claim simply alleging that the defendant violated the plaintiff's constitutional rights.[6]
- *Claims Arising Under Treaties*: Federal question jurisdiction also extends to claims brought under treaties of the United States,[7] although such claims are even less common than claims arising under the Constitution.
- *Contrast with "Violations" of Federal Laws*: Many federal statutes proscribe the type of conduct that people or companies may or may not engage in, but do not authorize parties to bring claims in court based on violations of the statute. For example, the Federal Food, Drug, and Cosmetic Act (FDCA) dictates how drugs are

---

[1] *See* Admin. Office of the U.S. Courts, Caseload Statistics Data Tables, (Dec. 31, 2021), https://www.uscourts.gov/statistics-reports/caseload-statistics-data-tables.

[2] *Gulf Offshore Co. v. Mobil Oil Corp.*, 453 U.S. 473, 483–84 (1981).

[3] *See Merrell Dow Pharm., Inc. v. Thompson*, 478 U.S. 804, 808 (1986).

[4] *Badgerow v. Walters*, 142 S. Ct. 1310, 1316 (2022).

[5] *See Monell v. Dep't of Soc. Serv. of New York*, 436 U.S. 658 (1978).

[6] *See, e.g., Corr. Servs. Corp. v. Malesko*, 534 U.S. 61, 66 (2001); *Bivens v. Six Unknown Named Agents of Federal Bureau of Narcotics*, 403 U.S. 388, 395–96 (1971).

[7] *See, e.g., Sluss v. United States Dep't of Just., Int'l Prisoner Transfer Unit*, 898 F.3d 1242, 1248–49 (D.C. Cir. 2018).

labeled.[8] It does not authorize a private individual to bring a claim against a drug company alleged to have mislabeled a drug in violation of the FDCA.[9] Thus, a federal court could not exercise federal question jurisdiction over a complaint based on its allegations regarding violations of the FDCA—that complaint would not contain a claim "arising under" the FDCA.[10]

Well-Pleaded Complaint

In general, the basis for original subject-matter jurisdiction must be found in the claims set forth in the complaint.[11] The basis for subject-matter jurisdiction cannot be based on an anticipated federal law defense or matter set forth in the answer or other pleadings.[12] The term "well-pleaded complaint" can be misleading. It is a term of art, and it is not a critique on the drafting skill of the plaintiff. Rather, it simply means that in assessing whether federal subject-matter jurisdiction is present or not, the court will examine only those allegations that would be found in a properly asserted statement of the plaintiff's own claim (and not in some prediction of a defendant's defense or claims).[13]

The effect of the well-pleaded complaint rule is to restrict the scope of federal question jurisdiction. It is always possible, and often happens, that important federal issues will be injected into a lawsuit on the defendant's side of the case (for example, a federal defense to a plaintiff's state law cause of action). Such defendant-triggered federal issues, even if central to the outcome of a case, will not typically confer federal question jurisdiction—not because there is no federal question, but because the federal question arises only in a defense and not in the plaintiff's well-pleaded complaint.[14]

- *Amended Complaints*: When a plaintiff voluntarily amends a complaint, courts look to the amended complaint to determine jurisdiction.[15]
- *Declaratory Judgments*: When applying the well-pleaded complaint rule to a declaratory judgment action, the court aligns the parties as they would be if the case had been brought as a regular claim for relief and not as a declaratory judgment, then applies the well-pleaded complaint concept to that complaint to ensure that the federal question does not arise in a defense or

[8] *See* 21 U.S.C.A. § 301 et seq.

[9] *See Merrell Dow Pharms. Inc. v. Thompson*, 478 U.S. 804, 809 (1986).

[10] *See Merrell Dow Pharms. Inc. v. Thompson*, 478 U.S. 804, 809 (1986).

[11] *See Caterpillar Inc. v. Williams*, 482 U.S. 386, 392 (1987).

[12] *See Aetna Health, Inc. v. Davila*, 542 U.S. 200, 207 (2004).

[13] *See Franchise Tax Bd. v. Construction Laborers Vacation Trust for So. Cal.*, 463 U.S. 1, 27–28 (1983).

[14] *See, e.g., Metropolitan Life Ins. Co. v. Taylor*, 481 U.S. 58, 63 (1987).

[15] *Rockwell Int'l Corp. v. United States*, 549 U.S. 457, 473–74 (2007).

counterclaim.[16]

State Claims That Depend on Federal Law

Although the fundamental premise of federal question jurisdiction is a claim "arising under" a *federal* law, there is also a very narrow category of claims qualifying for federal question jurisdiction: claims where a state remedy is being sought for a violation of a state law but the resolution of that claim will "necessarily turn on some construction of federal law."[17] The mere fact that the court will be required to resolve some federal issue in the course of deciding a plaintiff's state law claims is, alone, not enough to trigger federal question subject-matter jurisdiction.[18] Instead, this scenario presses to "the outer reaches" of federal question jurisdiction, and involves "sensitive judgments about congressional intent, judicial power, and the federal system."[19] When a federal issue is embedded within a state claim, federal question jurisdiction will exist over that state law claim only if the federal issue is:

(1) Necessarily raised by the claim pressed in the plaintiff's lawsuit;
(2) Actually disputed by the parties;
(3) Substantial to the federal system as a whole (and not just substantial in the eyes of the particular parties to the lawsuit); and
(4) Capable of being resolved in federal court without causing a disruption in the federal-state balance approved by Congress (rather than triggering an enormous shift of case volume from state courts into federal court without some clear indication from Congress that such was their intent).[20]

Consequently, while this second type of federal subject-matter jurisdiction exists, it represents a "special and small category."[21]

Federal Civil Rights Statutes

Federal civil rights laws incorporate state wrongful death statutes, so a plaintiff might be able to bring a state-law wrongful death claim in federal court using the court's federal question jurisdiction if the claim qualifies under 28 U.S.C.A. § 1988(a).[22]

---

[16]*See Pressl v. Appalachian Power Co.*, 842 F.3d 299, 302 (4th Cir. 2016). *See also* the coverage of Rule 57 below.

[17]*See Franchise Tax Bd. v. Construction Laborers Vacation Trust for So. Cal.*, 463 U.S. 1, 9 (1983) (cleaned up).

[18]*See Empire Healthchoice Assur., Inc. v. McVeigh*, 547 U.S. 677, 701 (2006).

[19]*Merrell Dow Pharm., Inc. v. Thompson*, 478 U.S. 804, 810 (1986).

[20]*See Gunn v. Minton*, 568 U.S. 251, 256–65 (2013); *Grable & Sons Metal Prods., Inc. v. Darue Eng'g & Mfg.*, 545 U.S. 308, 312–20 (2005).

[21]*Gunn v. Minton*, 568 U.S. 251, 258 (2013).

[22]*Rodgers v. Lancaster Police & Fire Department*, 819 F.3d 205, 208–09 (5th Cir. 2016).

Claims Under Federal Common Law

Where a cause of action is based on federal common law, § 1331 authorizes the use of federal question subject-matter jurisdiction.[23]

Congressionally Chartered Corporations

Most companies incorporated in the United States are created and organized under the law of a particular State. However, a small number of corporations are created through Congressional enactment. The National Railroad Passenger Corporation (Amtrak) is an example. Such federally-created corporations may sue or be sued under § 1331.[24]

Amount in Controversy and Citizenship of the Parties Irrelevant

Federal question jurisdiction does not contain any requirement that the amount in controversy exceed any threshold dollar amount.[25] Thus, if a case arose under the federal civil rights laws and the amount at issue was only ten dollars, the case would still qualify for federal question jurisdiction. Similarly, federal question jurisdiction does not require that the parties have diverse citizenship.[26]

Specific Jurisdictional Statutes

In addition to the broad jurisdictional grant of § 1331, a number of federal statutes establish federal subject-matter jurisdiction over specific categories of federal law claims. For example, 28 U.S.C.A. § 1337 authorizes federal courts to hear civil actions arising under federal laws regulating commerce. In the same fashion, 28 U.S.C.A. § 1338 provides subject-matter jurisdiction over claims arising under federal patent law and 28 U.S.C.A. § 1343 authorizes a federal court to hear claims alleging violations of federally-guaranteed civil rights. When one of those specific jurisdictional grants applies, a plaintiff must bring its action under that section, and all the conditions and limitations of an action under that specific jurisdictional grant will apply.[27]

Exclusive vs. Concurrent Subject-Matter Jurisdiction

Many statutes create exclusive jurisdiction in the federal district courts (specifying that a claim under the statute must be brought in a federal court, sometimes specifying which par-

---

[23] *National Farmers Union Insurance Co. v. Crow Tribe of Indians*, 471 U.S. 845, 850 (1985); *Chase v. Andeavor Logistics, L.P.*, 12 F.4th 864, 871 (8th Cir. 2021).

[24] *Aliotta v. National R.R. Passenger Corp.*, 315 F.3d 756, 758 (7th Cir. 2003).

[25] *Arbaugh v. Y&H Corp.*, 546 U.S. 500, 506 (2006).

[26] *See, e.g., Crosby v. Cooper B-Line, Inc.*, 725 F.3d 795, 797 (7th Cir. 2013).

[27] *See e.g., Shalala v. Illinois Council on Long Term Care, Inc.*, 529 U.S. 1, 4 (2000) (claims under the Medicare Act must be brought under 28 U.S.C.A. § 405(b) and are subject to the limitations of that jurisdictional grant).

ticular federal court).[28] If a federal statute is silent as to whether a claim it creates lies within exclusive federal jurisdiction or instead is subject to the concurrent jurisdiction of federal and state trial courts, the jurisdiction is concurrent (meaning that a claim could be brought in federal or state court), not exclusive.[29]

Attempting to Avoid a Federal Question: Complete Preemption

Ordinarily, the plaintiff has control of the counts in the complaint and may therefore avoid federal question jurisdiction simply by forgoing claims based on federal law.[30] However, in areas where federal law has completely preempted state law, a plaintiff cannot avoid federal question jurisdiction by pleading only state law claims.[31]

Weak Federal Claims

The probability of defeat on the merits does not, by itself, strip a plaintiff's claim of federal question jurisdiction.[32] However, the court will decline to exercise federal question jurisdiction based on a claim arising under a federal law if the claim is "wholly insubstantial and frivolous" or "clearly appears to be immaterial and made solely for the purpose of obtaining jurisdiction."[33]

Original Jurisdiction Only, No Jurisdiction to Review State Court Decisions

The "*Rooker-Feldman* Doctrine" provides that federal question jurisdiction does not authorize a federal court to review a state court judgment even if the state court complaint contained a federal question.[34] Parties who wish to challenge such a judgment may ultimately seek relief from the U.S. Supreme Court, but the original jurisdiction vested in federal district courts by § 1331 does not extend to appellate jurisdiction over state judgments.[35]

§ 2.11 Diversity Jurisdiction

CORE CONCEPT

The second of the common form of federal subject-matter juris-

[28]*See, e.g.*, Section 113(h) of the Comprehensive Environmental Response, Compensation, and Liability Act, 42 U.S.C.A. § 9601 et seq., establishing exclusive jurisdiction in the district court where the site is located.

[29]*Tafflin v. Levitt*, 493 U.S. 455, 458–59 (1990).

[30]*See Caterpillar Inc. v. Williams*, 482 U.S. 386, 394–95 (1987).

[31]*See Beneficial Nat. Bank v. Anderson*, 539 U.S. 1, 8 (2003).

[32]*See Bell v. Hood*, 327 U.S. 678, 682 (1946).

[33]*Steel Co. v. Citizens for a Better Env't*, 523 U.S. 83, 89 (1998); *Oneida Indian Nation of N.Y. State v. Oneida Cty., New York*, 414 U.S. 661, 666 (1974).

[34]*See District of Columbia Court of Appeals v. Feldman*, 460 U.S. 462, 476 (1983); *Rooker v. Fidelity Trust Co.*, 263 U.S. 413, 416 (1923).

[35]*Verizon Maryland, Inc. v. Public Service Com'n of Maryland*, 535 U.S. 635, 644 n.3 (2002).

diction is diversity jurisdiction under 28 U.S.C.A. § 1332.[1] Diversity jurisdiction permits a federal district court to hear state law causes of action if two basic requirements are fulfilled: no plaintiff may be a citizen of the same State as any defendant; and the amount in controversy must exceed $75,000, exclusive of interest and costs. Somewhat over half of the cases in federal court are founded on diversity jurisdiction, and an even larger percentage of jurisdictional complexities arise in this area.

APPLICATIONS

Purpose of Diversity Jurisdiction

The primary original purpose of diversity jurisdiction was to protect out-of-state parties from favoritism by judges toward local parties.[2] For example, suppose a Connecticut company wanted to sue an Alabama company for breach of contract, and, for reasons of personal jurisdiction or venue, had to bring its lawsuit in Alabama. The Connecticut company might fear that the Alabama State court judge might have a relationship with the Alabama company, or perhaps its lawyer, that could influence the course or outcome of the lawsuit. Perhaps the company's CEO and the judge belong to the same social organization. Perhaps the lawyer made a sizeable contribution to the judge's campaign. To foster fair treatment of all citizens, the Constitution authorized the federal courts to hear disputes between citizens of different States, with the idea that federal courts, with appointed federal judges, would provide a "more level playing field" for adjudicating such disputes.

Exceptions for Domestic Relations and Probate Cases

Federal courts routinely do not exercise diversity jurisdiction over cases in which divorce, child custody, or matters of probate are at issue.[3] These exceptions are jurisdictional, and the parties cannot waive them.[4] However, these exceptions to the application of diversity jurisdiction are construed narrowly.[5] Thus, the fact that title to the property that is the subject of the action had earlier been conveyed to one of the parties through a divorce proceeding would not trigger the domestic relations exception.[6]

Diversity Jurisdiction over Claims Arising Under Federal Law

Diversity jurisdiction is not limited to claims arising under state laws—if a claim arises under a federal law but for some

---

[1] *See* Admin. Office of the U.S. Courts, Caseload Statistics Data Tables, (Dec. 31, 2021), https://www.uscourts.gov/statistics-reports/caseload-statistics-data-tables.

[2] *Chick Kam Choo v. Exxon Corp.*, 764 F.2d 1148, 1153 (5th Cir. 1985).

[3] *See Ankenbrandt v. Richards*, 504 U.S. 689, 693 (1992) (domestic matters); *Markham v. Allen*, 326 U.S. 490, 494 (1946) (probate matters).

[4] *Irish v. Irish*, 842 F.3d 736, 740 (1st Cir. 2016).

[5] *Ankenbrandt v. Richards*, 504 U.S. 689, 703 n.6 (1992).

[6] *See, e.g., Matusow v. Trans-Cty. Title Agency, LLC*, 545 F.3d 241, 246 (3d Cir. 2008).

reason does not qualify for federal question jurisdiction, a court may exercise diversity jurisdiction over that claim if it meets all of the requirements.[7]

§ 2.11a The First Requirement: Complete Diversity of Citizenship

CORE CONCEPT

To qualify under § 1332, the parties' diversity must be "complete."[1] Complete diversity means that no plaintiff may be a citizen of the same State as any defendant.[2] Practitioners often think of this as a "versus" test (that is, no one on the left side of the "v." can share the same citizenship with anyone on the right side of the "v."). Complete diversity is evaluated across the complete complaint, and not on a count-by-count or claim-by-claim basis.[3] Thus, in a case where a plaintiff files a two-count complaint against two defendants (the first count against one defendant and the second count against the other defendant), the court will not have diversity jurisdiction over either count unless the plaintiff is not a citizen of the same State as either defendant. The test only compares plaintiffs to defendants, however; there is no requirement that multiple plaintiffs have citizenships different from one another or that defendants have citizenships different from their fellow defendants.[4]

APPLICATIONS

Citizenship of an Individual

An individual is a citizen of an American State if the individual is: (1) an American citizen; and (2) domiciled in the State.[5] A person's domicile is that person's "true, fixed, and permanent home," where the person intends to reside indefinitely, and to where the person intends to return.[6] An individual is a domiciliary, and thus citizen, of only one State at any point in time.[7] If an individual changes residence, the individual's domicile will not change unless the individual intends to reside in the new State indefinitely.[8]

- *Citizenship of Decedents, Infants, and Incompetents*: For

---

[7]*Gottlieb v. Carnival Corp.*, 436 F.3d 335, 340 (2d Cir. 2006) (permitting use of diversity jurisdiction over a claim arising under the Telephone Consumer Protection Act).

[1]*Exxon Mobil Corp. v. Allapattah Servs., Inc.*, 545 U.S. 546, 553 (2005).

[2]*See Lincoln Prop. Co. v. Roche*, 546 U.S. 81, 89 (2005).

[3]*See Exxon Mobil Corp. v. Allapattah Servs., Inc.*, 545 U.S. 546, 553 (2005).

[4]*See, e.g., Harvey v. Grey Wolf Drilling Co.*, 542 F.3d 1077, 1079 (5th Cir. 2008).

[5]*Kantor v. Wellesley Galleries, Ltd.*, 704 F.2d 1088, 1090 (9th Cir. 1983).

[6]*See Vlandis v. Kline*, 412 U.S. 441, 454 (1973).

[7]*See Wachovia Bank v. Schmidt*, 546 U.S. 303, 318 (2006); *Page v. Democratic Nat'l Comm.*, 2 F.4th 630, 635 (7th Cir. 2021).

[8]*See Washington v. Hovensa LLC*, 652 F.3d 340, 345 (3d Cir. 2011);

diversity purposes, parties acting as representatives of decedents' estates, infants, or incompetent persons shall be deemed to take the citizenship of the estate of persons whom they represent.[9]

- *Citizenship of Americans Domiciled Abroad*: Where a citizen of the United States is domiciled outside the United States, that person is not a citizen of any American State and therefore cannot sue or be sued in diversity.[10]
- *Citizenship of Military Personnel*: Persons engaged in military service are presumed to retain the citizenship they had when they entered active service.[11] If, however, they show sufficient evidence of intent to establish a domicile in another State, they may become citizens of that State for diversity purposes.[12]
- *Citizenship of Persons in Prison*: Persons in prison presumptively retain the citizenship that applied to them immediately prior to incarceration.[13]
- *Citizenship in the District of Columbia, Puerto Rico, and U.S. Territories and Possessions*: For purposes of diversity jurisdiction, the District of Columbia, Puerto Rico, the Virgin Islands, Guam, and America's other territories and possessions are treated as American States.[14] Thus, persons domiciled in those places will typically be treated as citizens of those "States" for diversity purposes.[15]

Citizenship of Corporations

A corporation is a citizen of two places: both (1) every State by which it has been incorporated; and (2) the State where it maintains its principal place of business.[16] Generally, modern corporations are only incorporated in one State. A corporation's principal place of business for purposes of diversity jurisdiction is the corporate "nerve center," "the place where a corporation's officers direct, control, and coordinate the corporation's activi-

---

Molinos Valle Del Cibao, C. por A. v. Lama, 633 F.3d 1330, 1341–42 (11th Cir. 2011).

[9] 28 U.S.C.A. § 1332(c)(2); *Gustafson v. zumBrunnen*, 546 F.3d 398, 402 (7th Cir. 2008).

[10] *See, e.g., Louisiana Municipal Police Employees' Retirement System v. Wynn*, 829 F.3d 1048, 1056 (9th Cir. 2016).

[11] *Eckerberg v. Inter-State Studio & Publishing Co.*, 860 F.3d 1079, 1085–86 (8th Cir. 2017).

[12] *Eckerberg v. Inter-State Studio & Publishing Co.*, 860 F.3d 1079, 1086 (8th Cir. 2017).

[13] *Mala v. Crown Bay Marina, Inc.*, 704 F.3d 239, 247 (3d Cir. 2013).

[14] 28 U.S.C.A. § 1332(e).

[15] *See, e.g., Padilla-Mangual v. Pavia Hosp.*, 516 F.3d 29, 30–31 (1st Cir. 2008).

[16] 28 U.S.C.A. § 1332(c); *Navy Fed. Credit Union v. LTD Fin. Servs., LP*, 972 F.3d 344, 356 (4th Cir. 2020); *MacGinnitie v. Hobbs Group, LLC*, 420 F.3d 1234, 1239 (11th Cir. 2005).

ties," typically the corporation's headquarters.[17] Thus, depending on the particular facts of incorporation and the location of business operations, a corporation will typically be a citizen for diversity jurisdiction purposes of one State (if its place of incorporation and principal place of business are the same State), two States (if they are not), or even potentially more than two States (if it chose to incorporate in multiple States). If a corporation has citizenship in more than one jurisdiction, the opposing party must be diverse from all the corporation's citizenships or complete diversity is not established.[18]

- *Citizenship of Close Corporations and Professional Corporations*: Closely held corporations and professional corporations will usually be deemed "corporations" for the purpose of § 1332.[19]
- *Citizenship of Corporations No Longer Conducting Business*: When a corporation is no longer conducting business at the time a lawsuit is commenced, the courts have taken two approaches as to its principal place of business. The first looks to the corporation's most recent place of business to help determine citizenship.[20] The second approach concludes that because a corporation ceased operations before the lawsuit was filed, it has no principal place of business for purposes of diversity jurisdiction.[21]

Citizenship of Unincorporated Associations

For diversity purposes, unincorporated associations such as partnerships, limited liability companies, joint ventures, and labor unions are citizens of every State in which one of its members is a citizen.[22] Thus, for very large unincorporated entities, such as national labor unions with members in every State, diversity of citizenship is unlikely to exist between the labor union and its opponent in a lawsuit.[23] When the case involves class litigation, however, an unincorporated association is treated like a corporation, and is a citizen of the State where it has its principal place of business and the State under

---

[17] *See Hertz Corp. v. Friend*, 559 U.S. 77, 92–93 (2010).

[18] *See, e.g., Panalpina Welttransport GmBh v. Geosource, Inc.*, 764 F.2d 352, 354 (5th Cir. 1985).

[19] *Cote v. Wadel*, 796 F.2d 981, 983 (7th Cir. 1986).

[20] *See, e.g., Harris v. Black Clawson Co.*, 961 F.2d 547, 550–51 (5th Cir. 1992).

[21] *See, e.g., Midlantic Nat. Bank v. Hansen*, 48 F.3d 693, 696 (3d Cir. 1995).

[22] *See Carden v. Arkoma Assocs.*, 494 U.S. 185, 195–96 (1990). *But see Kuntz v. Lamar Corp.*, 385 F.3d 1177, 1183 (9th Cir. 2004) (for purposes of diversity jurisdiction, the Cooperative is to be treated as a corporation simply because it has been incorporated under Idaho law, regardless of the Cooperative's individual structure, purpose, operations, or name.).

[23] *Settlement Funding, L.L.C. v. Rapid Settlements, Limited*, 851 F.3d 530 (5th Cir. 2017).

whose laws it is organized.[24]

Citizenship of Trusts and Trustees

When a trust is the party, the trust is deemed a citizen of every State in which any of its members is a citizen.[25] When the trustee is the party, the trust takes the citizenship of the trustee.[26]

Citizenship of Indian Tribes and Tribal Corporations

Most courts have concluded that Indian tribes are not citizens of a State for the purposes of § 1332.[27] In contrast, tribal corporations are normally treated as equivalent to state corporations for purposes of diversity jurisdiction.[28]

Diversity Jurisdiction when a Party is Not an American Citizen

There are a variety of rules that apply when a case includes parties that are not American citizens:

(1) Complete diversity will exist when the parties on one side are citizens of American States and the opposing parties are citizens or subjects of foreign countries (*e.g.*, P (Cal.) v. D (Egypt));[29]

(2) Complete diversity will exist when the case includes plaintiff(s) and defendant(s) who are American citizens and who satisfy the diversity requirements, and the case also includes additional parties who are citizens or subjects of foreign countries (*e.g.*, P (Cal.) v. D1 (Tex.) + D2 (Egypt));[30]

(3) Complete diversity will exist when a foreign country is a plaintiff suing citizen(s) of American States (*e.g.*, P (Republic of France) v. D (Pa.));[31]

(4) Complete diversity will NOT exist when citizens or subjects of one foreign country are suing citizens or subjects of another foreign country, even if the case includes an American citizen on one side of the "v." (but not on both sides, in which case rule 2 above applies) (*e.g.*, P (England) v. D (Egypt) or P (England) v. D1 (Egypt) + D2 (N.Y.));[32]

(5) Complete diversity will NOT exist when an American

---

[24] 28 U.S.C.A. § 1332(d)(10); *Ferrell v. Express Check Advance of SC LLC*, 591 F.3d 698, 702 (4th Cir. 2010).

[25] *See Americold Realty Trust v. Conagra Foods, Inc.*, 136 S. Ct. 1012, 1017 (2016).

[26] *GBForefront, L.P. v. Forefront Mgmt. Grp., LLC*, 888 F.3d 29, 37 (3d Cir. 2018).

[27] *See, e.g., Wells Fargo Bank, N.A. v. Lake of the Torches Economic Development Corp.*, 658 F.3d 684, 693 (7th Cir. 2011).

[28] *See, e.g., Cook v. AVI Casino Enterprises, Inc.*, 548 F.3d 718, 723 (9th Cir. 2008).

[29] *See JPMorgan Chase Bank v. Traffic Stream (BVI) Infrastructure Ltd.*, 536 U.S. 88, 91 (2002).

[30] *Dresser Indus., Inc. v. Underwriters at Lloyd's of London*, 106 F.3d 494, 498 (3d Cir. 1997).

[31] 28 U.S.C.A. § 1332(a)(4).

[32] *See, e.g., In re DePuy Orthopaedics, Inc. ASR Hip Implant Products Liability Litigation*, 953 F.3d

citizen domiciled abroad is suing or being sued in a federal district court (*e.g.*, P (N.J.) v. D1 (Ohio) + D2 (U.S. citizen domiciled in Turkey));[33]

(6) If an American citizen is also a citizen of a foreign country (i.e., claims "dual" citizenship), the only citizenship that will be evaluated for purposes of diversity jurisdiction is the individual's American citizenship;[34] and

(7) Complete diversity will NOT exist over a suit between a citizen of an American State and a citizen of another country who is a legal resident in the United States (*i.e.*, a green-card holder) and who is domiciled in the same State as the opposing party (*e.g.*, P (N.J.) v. D (citizen of Spain, legal resident and domicile of Fla.)).[35] Likewise, citizens of other countries who are legal residents in the United States and domiciled in different States may not use diversity jurisdiction to sue one another in a district court (*e.g.*, P (citizen of Italy, legal resident and domicile of N.J.) v. D (citizen of Spain, legal resident and domicile of Fla.)).[36]

Suits Against the United States

Section 1332 does not create subject-matter jurisdiction for suits involving the United States.[37] However, 28 U.S.C.A. §§ 1345 and 1346 authorize federal subject-matter jurisdiction when the United States is a plaintiff (§ 1345) or defendant (§ 1346).

Suits Against a State

For purposes of diversity jurisdiction, an American State is not a "citizen."[38] Two results follow from that principle. First, a State cannot be sued to create diversity jurisdiction when the opposing party is a citizen of another State.[39] Second, a State's presence in a suit where diversity jurisdiction is otherwise satisfied will normally not destroy that jurisdiction.[40] For purposes of this aspect of diversity jurisdiction, the District of Columbia, Puerto Rico, the Virgin Islands, Guam, and America's other territories and possessions are treated as American

890 (6th Cir. 2020).

[33]*See Newman-Green, Inc. v. Alfonzo-Larrain*, 490 U.S. 826, 828 (1989).

[34]*Sadat v. Mertes*, 615 F.2d 1176, 1187 (7th Cir. 1980).

[35]*See Tagger v. Strauss Grp. Ltd.*, 951 F.3d 124, 126–27 (2d Cir. 2020).

[36]*Saadeh v. Farouki*, 107 F.3d 52, 61 (D.C. Cir. 1997).

[37]*United States v. Park Place Assocs., Ltd.*, 563 F.3d 907, 919 n.7 (9th Cir. 2009).

[38]*Moor v. County of Alameda*, 411 U.S. 693, 717–18 (1973).

[39]*Moor v. County of Alameda*, 411 U.S. 693, 717–18 (1973).

[40]*Missouri, Kansas & Texas Railway Co. v. Hickman*, 183 U.S. 53, 59 (1901).

States.[41]

Direct Actions against Insurance Companies

In some circumstances, a plaintiff may name the defendant's insurer as an additional defendant or as the only defendant—a "direct action" against the insurer. In such direct actions, the citizenship of both the insured and the insurer are included for purposes of the complete diversity analysis.[42]

Timing of Citizenship

The parties must be diverse at the time the lawsuit is filed.[43] It is irrelevant that the parties may not have been diverse at the time the cause of action arose, or that a party diverse at the time of filing acquires a non-diverse citizenship later on during the course of the lawsuit.[44] Thus, if a citizen of New York seeks to sue another New York citizen in federal district court over a state cause of action, the plaintiff could create diversity of citizenship by making a genuine change of domicile from New York to another jurisdiction prior to filing suit.[45]

- *Timing of Citizenship for Removal*: When a case arrives in federal district court through the process of removal (discussed below), the analysis of jurisdiction, including citizenship, is made as of the date the removal petition was filed.[46] Some courts require that complete diversity have existed at both the time the complaint was filed and at the time the removal petition was filed.[47]

Curing Defects in Diversity

A lack of complete diversity when the case was filed can be cured by dismissal of the non-diverse party under Rule 21.[48] In evaluating whether to dismiss a non-diverse party or to dismiss the entire action, courts will apply the standards from Rule 19 to determine whether proceeding without the non-diverse party will prejudice the rights of the remaining parties.[49] Conversely, if a party who was not diverse at the time the case was filed subsequently changes citizenship and becomes diverse, the original defect in diversity jurisdiction is not cured.[50]

---

[41]*See Barwood, Inc. v. District of Columbia*, 202 F.3d 290, 292 (D.C. Cir. 2000); *Brown v. Francis*, 75 F.3d 860, 865 (3d Cir. 1996).

[42]28 U.S.C.A. § 1332(c); *Kong v. Allied Professional Insurance Co.*, 750 F.3d 1295, 1299 (11th Cir. 2014).

[43]*Grupo Dataflux v. Atlas Glob. Grp., L.P.*, 541 U.S. 567, 571 (2004).

[44]*Mann v. City of Tucson, Dep't of Police*, 782 F.2d 790, 794 (9th Cir. 1986).

[45]*See, e.g.*, *Peterson v. Allcity Ins. Co.*, 472 F.2d 71, 74 (2d Cir. 1972) (motive for change in domicile "is not our concern").

[46]*See Pullman Co. v. Jenkins*, 305 U.S. 534, 537 (1939).

[47]*Kanzelberger v. Kanzelberger*, 782 F.2d 774, 776 (7th Cir. 1986).

[48]*See Caterpillar, Inc. v. Lewis*, 519 U.S. 61, 64 (1996).

[49]*Grice v. CVR Energy, Inc.*, 921 F.3d 966, 969 (10th Cir. 2019).

[50]*See Grupo Dataflux v. Atlas Global Group, L.P.*, 541 U.S. 567, 575 (2004).

Realignment of Parties

The requirement of complete diversity means that the alignment of parties (*i.e.*, as plaintiffs or defendants) may be crucial to a determination of the existence of federal subject-matter jurisdiction. Normally it is a plaintiff who provides the initial alignment of parties in the complaint. However, because a plaintiff is not a disinterested party, the court has authority to re-align the parties to reflect accurately, on the one hand, the parties whose interests coincide and, on the other hand, those parties whose interests conflict with the first group of parties.[51]

Nominal Parties

A court must disregard the citizenship of a nominal party—a party who is not a "real party to the controversy."[52] For example, insurance companies and underwriters are often considered nominal parties when they appear in an action only on behalf of the insured.[53]

"John Doe" Parties

Under certain circumstances, Rule 10 allows a complaint to refer to parties by fictitious names or pseudonyms.[54] The treatment of the citizenship of "John Doe" parties—parties who are unidentified and who many not even exist—depends on the court and the circumstances.

- *Cases Filed in Federal Court*: For cases initially filed in federal court, some courts apply a general rule that diversity jurisdiction is improper if there are John Doe parties because the court cannot confirm its jurisdiction.[55] If the complaint contains enough information to determine the likely citizenship of an unnamed party, some courts will include that party's citizenship in the diversity analysis.[56] Conversely, if the complaint contains little information about the John Doe defendants or the court believes they were included to destroy diversity, some courts will ignore the fictitiously named defendants.[57] Likewise, some courts ignore John Doe parties if it appears that they are "merely nominal parties."[58]
- *Cases Removed to Federal Court*: When a case is initially

[51] *See City of Indianapolis v. Chase Nat'l Bank*, 314 U.S. 63, 69 (1941).

[52] *Navarro Savings Assoc. v. Lee*, 446 U.S. 458, 460 (1980); *Thermoset Corp. v. Bldg. Materials Corp of Am.*, 849 F.3d 1313, 1317 (11th Cir. 2017).

[53] *See, e.g., Broyles v. Bayless*, 878 F.2d 1400, 1402 (11th Cir. 1989).

[54] *See* Rule 10(a) and accompanying authors' commentary ("**Fictitious Name and Pseudonym Litigation**").

[55] *See, e.g., Pain Ctr. of SE Indiana LLC v. Origin Healthcare Sols. LLC*, 893 F.3d 454, 458 (7th Cir. 2018); *Howell by Goerdt v. Trib. Ent. Co.*, 106 F.3d 215, 218 (7th Cir. 1997).

[56] *See, e.g., Abels v. State Farm Fire & Cas. Co.*, 770 F.2d 26, 30–31 (3d Cir. 1985).

[57] *See, e.g., Abels v. State Farm Fire & Cas. Co.*, 770 F.2d 26, 30–31 (3d Cir. 1985).

[58] *See, e.g., DePuy Synthes Sales, Inc. v. OrthoLA, Inc.*, 953 F.3d 469, 479 (7th Cir. 2020); *Pain Ctr. of SE Indiana*

filed in state court and diversity jurisdiction is being evaluated in the context of removal (discussed below), courts disregard parties with fictitious names.[59]

Manipulation of Diversity Jurisdiction

If a party, "by assignment or otherwise," has been "improperly or collusively . . . joined" to invoke jurisdiction, the federal district court will not have jurisdiction.[60] Thus, a plaintiff who wants to sue a defendant in federal court but who is a citizen of the same State as a defendant may not create diversity jurisdiction by collusively assigning the claim to another person who is diverse from the defendant.[61] Conversely, a plaintiff cannot join a nondiverse defendant for the sole purpose of destroying complete diversity, as addressed below in the discussion of removal.[62]

§ 2.11b The Second Requirement: Amount in Controversy

CORE CONCEPT

Diversity jurisdiction requires not only that the parties be citizens of different States, but also that the matter in controversy exceed $75,000, exclusive of interest and costs. The word "exceed" is not extraneous; unless the amount in controversy, exclusive of interests and costs, is $75,000.01 or more, diversity jurisdiction cannot be invoked.[1]

APPLICATIONS

Amount Pleaded in the Complaint: "Legal Certainty" Test

In the ordinary case, a court will accept the amount the plaintiff claims in the complaint unless that amount appears to have been asserted in bad faith[2] or where it is legally certain—based on the liquidated nature of the claim, the manifestly frivolous nature of the prayer for relief, or a statutory limitation on damages recoverable—that the plaintiff cannot recover the jurisdictional amount.[3]

- *Recovery of Less than $75,000.01*: If a plaintiff initially seeks more than $75,000, but ultimately recovers less,

---

LLC v. Origin Healthcare Sols. LLC, 893 F.3d 454, 459 (7th Cir. 2018).

[59] 28 U.S.C. § 1441(a); *Walker v. CSX Transp. Inc.*, 650 F.3d 1392, 1396 (11th Cir. 2011).

[60] 28 U.S.C.A. § 1359; *Kramer v. Caribbean Mills, Inc.*, 394 U.S. 823, 827 (1969).

[61] *Mississippi ex rel. Hood v. AU Optronics Corp.*, 571 U.S. 161, 174 (2014).

[62] *See, e.g., Ticer v. Imperium Ins. Co.*, 20 F.4th 1040, 1044 (5th Cir. 2021).

[1] *Freeland v. Liberty Mut. Fire Ins. Co.*, 632 F.3d 250, 252–53 (6th Cir. 2011).

[2] *See, e.g., Auto-Owners Insurance Co. v. Stevens & Ricci Inc.*, 835 F.3d 388, 395 (3d Cir. 2016).

[3] *St. Paul Mercury Indem. Co. v. Red Cab Co.*, 303 U.S. 283, 289 (1938).

the court's diversity jurisdiction is unaffected.[4] However, the court may deny recovery of costs to the plaintiff and may instead assess costs against the plaintiff based on the small size of the plaintiff's recovery.[5]

Jurisdictional Amount in Equity Cases

Because lawsuits seeking equitable relief typically do not entail monetary damages, a straightforward measurement against the $75,000 threshold is not possible. In general, courts will consider the amount in controversy requirement satisfied if either the benefit to the plaintiff of the equitable relief or the cost to or burden on the defendant to comply with the relief exceeds $75,000.[6] Thus, for example, if a landowner sought an injunction prohibiting a nearby company from discharging pollutants into a stream that was contaminating the landowner's pond and killing the fish, the amount in controversy requirement could be satisfied if the value to the landowner of obtaining the injunction would exceed $75,000 or the burden to the company—perhaps measured by the cost of installing new pollution control equipment—would exceed $75,000.

Aggregation of Claims

If a complaint has more than one claim, questions arise as to whether the value of the claims may be added together to satisfy the amount in controversy requirement. The answer depends on the configuration of the parties and claims.

- *Single Plaintiff v. Single Defendant*: If a plaintiff has multiple claims against the same defendant, the rule is simple and generous; a single plaintiff may aggregate the amount in controversy from all claims against a single defendant, no matter how dissimilar the claims are.[7] Thus, if one plaintiff has two different claims against one defendant, each totaling $40,000, the plaintiff may aggregate those amounts in controversy such that the court may exercise diversity jurisdiction over each claim (assuming the parties are diverse in citizenship). Likewise, if the plaintiff has one claim against a defendant seeking $80,000 and another claim against the same defendant seeking $15,000, the amount in controversy requirement is satisfied for the combined claims. The ability of a single plaintiff to aggregate claims against a single defendant is unaffected by the presence in the lawsuit of additional plaintiffs or

[4] *Auto-Owners Ins. Co. v. Stevens & Ricci Inc.*, 835 F.3d 388, 395–96 (3d Cir. 2016); *Meridian Sec. Ins. Co. v. Sadowski*, 441 F.3d 536, 538 (7th Cir. 2006).

[5] 28 U.S.C.A. § 1332(b).

[6] *See, e.g.*, *Glenwood Light & Water Co. v. Mutual Light, Heat & Power Co.*, 239 U.S. 121, 125–26 (1915); *Phelps Oil & Gas, LLC v. Noble Energy Inc.*, 5 F.4th 1122, 1126 (10th Cir. 2021).

[7] *Snyder v. Harris*, 394 U.S. 332, 335 (1969).

additional defendants.[8] Thus, if one plaintiff sues two defendants and asserts two claims against defendant number 1, the plaintiff may aggregate the amount in controversy from those two claims. Only when a plaintiff tries to aggregate claims against multiple defendants or when multiple plaintiffs try to aggregate their claims does the inquiry become nuanced, as the following two notes illustrate.

- *Single Plaintiff v. Multiple Defendants*: Where a single plaintiff seeks to aggregate the amount in controversy from claims against more than one defendant, aggregation is permitted only if the claims against the defendants involve joint liability.[9] Many tort claims involve such joint liability. For example, if a plaintiff sued two defendants in a three-car pileup, seeking a total of $80,000 and asserting joint and several liability against the defendants, it is quite likely that each defendant's share of liability would be below $75,000 (and thus not satisfy the amount in controversy requirement on its own), and there is a mathematical certainty that both claims could not exceed $75,000. Because the plaintiff has the potential to recover the full $80,000 from either defendant under the principles of joint and several liability, however, the courts consider the amount in controversy requirement satisfied as to both claims.[10]
- *Multiple Plaintiffs*: The circumstances where two or more plaintiffs can aggregate the amount in controversy for their claims to satisfy the jurisdictional amount are even narrower, and do not frequently occur. As a general rule, two plaintiffs may not aggregate their claims to satisfy the jurisdictional amount.[11] Two plaintiffs may aggregate the amount in controversy for their claims only if the claims are truly joint, such as in the case of joint ownership of the property that is the subject of the lawsuit.[12] For example, if two plaintiffs each jointly owned an automobile worth $80,000 and they sued a defendant alleging that the defendant had destroyed the automobile completely, the plaintiffs could aggregate their individual claims to satisfy the jurisdictional amount even though they could not each recover in

[8] *See, e.g., Wolde-Meskel v. Vocational Instruction Project Cmty. Servs., Inc.*, 166 F.3d 59, 62 (2d Cir. 1999) (applying rule despite presence of other parties); *Deajess Med. Imaging, P.C. v. Allstate Ins. Co.*, 344 F. Supp. 2d 907, 913 (S.D.N.Y. 2004) (same).

[9] *LM Ins. Corp. v. Spaulding Enterprises Inc.*, 533 F.3d 542, 548 (7th Cir. 2008).

[10] *See, e.g., Libby, McNeill, & Libby v. City Nat. Bank*, 592 F.2d 504, 510 (9th Cir. 1978); *KR Enterprises, Inc. v. Zerteck Inc.*, 999 F.3d 1044, 1048 (7th Cir. 2021).

[11] *Auto-Owners Ins. Co. v. Stevens & Ricci Inc.*, 835 F.3d 388, 395 (3d Cir. 2016).

[12] *See, e.g., Snyder v. Harris*, 394 U.S. 332, 334 (1969).

excess of $75,000. But if the allegation was that the two plaintiffs each suffered $40,000 in personal injuries when another driver collided with their automobile, they could not aggregate the amount in controversy for their claims because the claims would be seen as distinct—even if the injuries occurred in the same accident.

- *Aggregation of Claims Distinguished from Damages for One Claim*: these aggregation rules only pertain to attempts to aggregate damages from different claims, they do not apply to adding up different elements of damages from one claim. Thus, for example, if the plaintiff was in a car accident with one defendant and sustained both damages to her car and injuries to her body, she would not need to apply aggregation rules—if those damages added up to more than $75,000, her negligence claim would satisfy the amount in controversy requirement on its own. Conversely, if the plaintiff's only harm was $40,000 in damages to her car, she could not seek that same recovery twice, once by alleging a $40,000 loss due to the other driver's negligence and again by alleging the same $40,000 loss due to common law conversion. She would only be entitled to recover the $40,000 one time, so cannot aggregate those amounts.

Enforcement of Arbitration Awards

In cases where district courts are asked to enforce arbitration awards, the courts have adopted three distinct approaches to the amount in controversy requirement: (1) the "award approach," which is based on the amount the claimant was actually awarded, without regard to what the claimant sought;[13] (2) the "demand approach," which focuses the analysis on the amount the claimant sought, not on the amount the claimant was actually awarded;[14] or (3) the "remand approach," which is similar to the "demand approach" and provides that if a party seeks to remand the case to arbitration, the amount in controversy is determined by consideration of the amount claimed in the arbitration.[15]

Burden of Proof

If the amount in controversy is at issue, it is normally the plaintiff's burden to demonstrate that the requirement is met.[16] An exception arises when a plaintiff originally files suit in state court and the defendant removes the case to federal court. In that circumstance, if it is unclear whether the plaintiff's claim meets the amount in controversy requirement, the

---

[13]*See, e.g., Ford v. Hamilton Investments, Inc.*, 29 F.3d 255, 260 (6th Cir. 1994).

[14]*See, e.g., Pershing, L.L.C. v. Kiebach*, 819 F.3d 179, 182 (5th Cir. 2016).

[15]*See, e.g., Karsner v. Lothian*, 532 F.3d 876, 882 (D.C. Cir. 2008).

[16]*Page v. Democratic Nat'l Comm.*, 2 F.4th 630, 634 (7th Cir. 2021); *Abdel-Aleem v. OPK Biotech LLC*, 665 F.3d 38, 41 (1st Cir. 2012).

burden of proving the existence of the jurisdictional amount is shifted to the defendant who removed the case.[17]

§ 2.11c Diversity Jurisdiction in Class Actions and Mass Torts

CORE CONCEPT

The Class Action Fairness Act of 2005 (CAFA)[1] established relaxed requirements for diversity jurisdiction for certain class actions (making it easier to remove class actions filed in state courts). CAFA authorizes diversity jurisdiction if the aggregate amount in controversy exceeds $5 million, there is "nominal diversity" such that at least one member of the class of plaintiffs is a citizen of a different State from at least one defendant, and the class contains at least 100 members. Many mass tort claims receive the same treatment.

APPLICATIONS

Purpose of CAFA

Congress enacted CAFA in response to "numerous problems with our current class action system."[2] One of the key problems identified in CAFA's legislative history was that most class actions were being litigated in state courts with inconsistent application of the rules and inadequate supervision.[3] Sophisticated plaintiff attorneys were filing their claims in state courts with judges who had reputations for readily certifying classes and approving settlements that accomplished little for class members but enriched the plaintiffs' counsel.[4] Accordingly, Congress sought to make it easier for defendants to remove class actions to federal court.[5]

CAFA Requirement #1: Aggregation of Amount in Controversy

Ordinarily, multiple plaintiffs may not aggregate their claims to satisfy the amount-in-controversy requirement. CAFA creates an exception to this general rule, allowing the aggregation of the amounts sought by class members, but establishing a $5,000,000 aggregate requirement, rather than the normal $75,000 requirement.[6] Attorney's fees generally count towards the amount in controversy in class actions.[7]

CAFA Requirement #2: Nominal Diversity of Citizenship

In most circumstances, diversity jurisdiction requires complete diversity of citizenship, such that no plaintiff is a citi-

---

[17] *See McNutt v. General Motors Acceptance Corp.*, 298 U.S. 178, 189 (1936).

[1] 28 U.S.C.A. § 1332(d).

[2] S. REP. 109-14, 3, 2005 U.S.C.C.A.N. 3, 5.

[3] S. REP. 109-14, 3, 2005 U.S.C.C.A.N. 3, 5.

[4] S. REP. 109-14, 3, 2005 U.S.C.C.A.N. 3, 5.

[5] S. REP. 109-14, 3, 2005 U.S.C.C.A.N. 3, 5.

[6] *Verma v. 3001 Castor, Inc.*, 937 F.3d 221, 227 (3d Cir. 2019).

[7] *Verma v. 3001 Castor, Inc.*, 937 F.3d 221, 227 (3d Cir. 2019).

zen of the same State as any defendant. Under CAFA, diversity of citizenship is satisfied if: (a) any member of a class of plaintiffs is a citizen of a State different from any defendant; (b) any member of a class of plaintiffs is a foreign country or a citizen or subject of a foreign country and any defendant is a citizen of an American State; or (c) any member of a class of plaintiffs is a citizen of an American State and any defendant is a foreign country or a citizen or subject of a foreign country.[8]

CAFA Requirement #3: Number of Class Members

CAFA only applies to classes containing at least 100 class members.[9]

CAFA Requirement #4: Defining Class Actions

To qualify for diversity jurisdiction under CAFA, actions filed in federal court must have been filed as putative class actions under Rule 23.[10] If the action was originally filed in a state court and a defendant seeks to remove it to federal court, the action must qualify as a class action under a state statute or rule of judicial procedure analogous to Rule 23.[11]

Original or Removal Jurisdiction

Although one of the primary purposes of CAFA jurisdiction was to facilitate removal of class actions filed in state courts, plaintiffs may also use CAFA jurisdiction to file class actions in federal courts.[12]

Declining Diversity Jurisdiction in Class Actions

Even if a class action has met the requirements for diversity jurisdiction, a federal district court may, in certain circumstances, refrain from hearing it.[13] The court has discretion to decline to exercise diversity jurisdiction when two requirements are met and the court has weighed other prudential considerations. The first of the two requirements is that more than one-third and less than two-thirds of the total membership of a plaintiff class consists of citizens of the State in which the action was originally filed.[14] The second requirement is that the "primary" defendants are citizens of the State in which the action was originally filed.[15] If both those requirements are satisfied, the court must then weigh the following factors in deciding whether to accept or decline jurisdiction:

(a)whether the claims in question involve matters of

---

[8] *See, e.g., Blockbuster, Inc. v. Galeno*, 472 F.3d 53, 58–59 (2d Cir. 2006).

[9] *Serrano v. 180 Connect, Inc.*, 478 F.3d 1018, 1020 (9th Cir. 2007).

[10] 28 U.S.C.A. § 1332(d)(1)(B). *See also Ruhlen v. Holiday Haven Homeowners, Inc.*, 28 F.4th 226, 227 (11th Cir. 2022).

[11] 28 U.S.C.A. § 1332(d)(1)(B). *See also Canela v. Costco Wholesale Corp.*, 971 F.3d 845, 850 (9th Cir. 2020).

[12] *See, e.g., Verma v. 3001 Castor, Inc.*, 937 F.3d 221, 228 (3d Cir. 2019).

[13] *Knepper v. Rite Aid Corp.*, 675 F.3d 249, 260–61 (3d Cir. 2012).

[14] *See, e.g., Hood v. Gilster-Mary Lee Corp.*, 785 F.3d 263, 265 (8th Cir. 2015) (two-thirds requirement is determined as of date of filing original complaint or amended complaint).

[15] 28 U.S.C.A. § 1332(d)(3).

national or interstate interest;

(b) whether the claims will be controlled by the law of the State where the case was originally filed or by the law of another State or States;

(c) whether the plaintiffs have, through artful pleading, sought to avoid federal subject-matter jurisdiction;

(d) whether the action was filed in a court with a clear relationship with the plaintiffs, the underlying events, or the defendants;

(e) whether the number of class plaintiffs who are citizens of the State in which the case was filed is substantially larger than the number of plaintiffs from any other State, and the citizenship of other plaintiffs is dispersed among a significant variety of other States; and

(f) whether during the three years prior to filing the case under consideration, some other class action has been filed asserting similar claims on behalf of the same or other plaintiffs.[16]

- *Local Controversy Exception*: Although the Class Action Fairness Act gives the district court the *discretion* to exercise or decline to exercise subject-matter jurisdiction under the analysis described above, the district court is *required* to decline to exercise jurisdiction if all of the following elements are met: (1) more than two-thirds of class plaintiffs are citizens of the State of original filing;[17] (2) at least one defendant is a citizen of the State where the suit was originally filed and is both a subject of "significant" relief sought by the plaintiff class and a party whose alleged conduct is "a "significant" basis for the plaintiffs' cause of action;[18] (3) principal injuries in the case were incurred in the State of original filing; and (4) there has been no filing of a lawsuit in the last three years based on the same or similar allegations by the same or other plaintiffs against any of the same defendants.[19]
- *Home State Exception*: A district court is also *required* to decline to exercise jurisdiction if: two-thirds or more of the plaintiff class are citizens of the State of original filing; and "primary defendants" are also citizens of that

[16] 28 U.S.C.A. § 1332(d)(3).

[17] *Stewart v. Entergy Corp.*, 35 F.4th 930, 932 (5th Cir. 2022); *Hargett v. RevClaims, LLC*, 854 F.3d 962 (8th Cir. 2017) (explaining distinction between "citizen" and "resident").

[18] *See, e.g., Mason v. Lockwood, Andrews & Newman, P.C.*, 842 F.3d 383, 396–97 (6th Cir. 2016) ("significant basis" does not look to where defendant's actions occurred but rather to comparison of local defendants' conduct with conduct of all defendants).

[19] 28 U.S.C.A. § 1132(d)(4)(A); *In re Sprint Nextel Corp.*, 593 F.3d 669, 672 (7th Cir. 2010).

same State.[20] Courts use a variety of criteria for assessing who the "primary defendants" are, including which defendants stand to lose larger sums of money and which defendants are directly liable (as opposed to secondarily or vicariously liable).[21]

- *Burden of Proving Exceptions*: A plaintiff seeking remand based on one of these exceptions has the burden of demonstrating that the exception applies.[22]

Class Actions Against States

CAFA does not apply to any class action in which the primary defendants are "States, State officials, or other governmental entities against whom the district court may be foreclosed from ordering relief."[23] In other words, plaintiffs cannot use CAFA to circumvent barriers to certain claims against States or state officials such as Eleventh Amendment immunity.[24]

Class Actions Under Certain Securities Laws

CAFA does not apply to any class action that rest "solely" upon a claim arising under certain federal securities laws,[25] the laws of a State involving the internal affairs of corporations or other business entities (provided that the corporation or entity is incorporated or organized in that State), or laws that relate to rights and duties, including fiduciary duties, created by any security or the federal Securities Act of 1933.[26]

Denial of Class Certification

A case properly brought in or removed to federal court under CAFA can remain in federal court even if the case is not ultimately certified as a class action.[27]

Diversity Jurisdiction in Mass Actions

CAFA also provides that certain "mass actions" be deemed class actions removable under CAFA's terms.[28] The definition of a "mass action" is a civil action in which one hundred or more

---

[20] 28 U.S.C.A. § 1132(d)(4)(A); *Madison v. ADT, L.L.C.*, 11 F.4th 325, 327 (5th Cir. 2021); *In re Sprint Nextel Corp.*, 593 F.3d 669, 671 (7th Cir. 2010).

[21] *Madison v. ADT, L.L.C.*, 11 F.4th 325, 327 (5th Cir. 2021); *Vodenichar v. Halcon Energy Properties, Inc.*, 733 F.3d 497, 504 (3d Cir. 2013).

[22] *See Stewart v. Entergy Corp.*, 35 F.4th 930, 932 (5th Cir. 2022); *Benko v. Quality Loan Serv. Corp.*, 789 F.3d 1111, 1116 (9th Cir. 2015) (local controversy exception).

[23] 28 U.S.C.A. § 1332(d)(5)(A); *Woods v. Standard Insurance Co.*, 771 F.3d 1257, 1263 (10th Cir. 2014).

[24] *Woods v. Standard Insurance Co.*, 771 F.3d 1257, 1263 (10th Cir. 2014).

[25] Specifically, § 16(f)(3)1 of the Securities Act of 1933, 15 U.S.C.A. § 78p(f)(3), and § 28(f)(5)(E) of the Securities Exchange Act of 1934, 15 U.S.C.A. § 78bb(f)(5)(E).

[26] 28 U.S.C.A. § 1332(d)(9).

[27] *Coba v. Ford Motor Co.*, 932 F.3d 114, 119 (3d Cir. 2019); *Metz v. Unizan Bank*, 649 F.3d 492, 500 (6th Cir. 2011).

[28] 28 U.S.C. § 1332(d)(11)(A) to (B); *Rainbow Gun Club, Inc. v. Denbury Onshore, L.L.C.*, 760 F.3d 405, 407 (5th Cir. 2014).

persons each seek monetary relief and a joint trial because their claims involve a single event or occurrence that gave rise to the cause of action.[29] All of the terms and conditions for removal of class actions apply except for the aggregation rule; diversity jurisdiction will only exist under CAFA for those plaintiffs in mass actions whose individual claim exceeds $75,000.[30]

Exceptions: Mass Actions Not Covered by CAFA

Mass actions cannot be treated as class actions eligible for removal under CAFA if they fall into any of the four enumerated exceptions.

- *Local Events*: A lawsuit is not a mass action for purposes of CAFA if the claims involved arise from events that occurred in the State where the lawsuit was filed and the injuries from the event are found in that State or contiguous States.[31]
- *Joinder by Defendant*: A lawsuit is not a mass action for purposes of CAFA if the plaintiffs filed their lawsuits as separate actions and the claims were subsequently joined by a motion of a defendant.[32]
- *Public Interest Claims/Private Attorneys General*: Some state laws authorize some lawsuits by private plaintiffs on behalf of the general public (as opposed to asserting claims on their own behalf). When such public interest claims form the entire basis of a lawsuit, the case cannot be a mass action for purposes of CAFA.[33]
- *Consolidation for Pretrial Proceedings Only*: If the cases have been consolidated for pretrial purposes only and will be tried separately, the lawsuit cannot be a mass action within the meaning of CAFA.[34] Rather, the cases must be consolidated through trial, such that the outcome is binding on all of the plaintiffs.[35]
- *Claims for Equitable Relief*: Cases involving claims only for non-monetary equitable relief cannot be treated as

---

[29] *Ramirez v. Vintage Pharmaceuticals, LLC*, 852 F.3d 324, 329 (3d Cir. 2017) (proposal for joint trial may be implicit); *Abraham v. St. Croix Renaissance Group, L.L.P.*, 719 F.3d 270, 272 (3d Cir. 2013) (mass action does not have a class representative, but it does require mass joinder and joint trial).

[30] *Nevada v. Bank of America Corp.*, 672 F.3d 661, 667–68 (9th Cir. 2012).

[31] 28 U.S.C.A. § 1332(d)(11)(B)(ii)(I); *Bonin v. Sabine River Authority of Louisiana*, 961 F.3d 381, 386–87 (5th Cir. 2020).

[32] 28 U.S.C.A. § 1332(d)(11)(B)(ii)(II); *Anderson v. Bayer Corp.*, 610 F.3d 390, 393 (7th Cir. 2010).

[33] 28 U.S.C.A. § 1332(d)(11)(B)(ii)(III); *LG Display Co. v. Madigan*, 665 F.3d 768, 772 (7th Cir. 2011).

[34] 28 U.S.C.A. § 1332(d)(11)(B)(ii)(IV); *Dunson v. Cordis Corp.*, 854 F.3d 551, 554 (9th Cir. 2017).

[35] *Dunson v. Cordis Corp.*, 854 F.3d 551, 555 (9th Cir. 2017).

mass actions under § 1332(d).[36]

CAFA Restrictions on Transfers of Mass Actions

In many circumstances, the federal multidistrict litigation ("MDL") statute, 28 U.S.C.A. § 1407, authorizes transfer of cases involving common questions of fact so that they may be consolidated in a particular district. One unusual feature of CAFA is a provision prohibiting transfer under § 1407 unless a majority of the plaintiffs in an action request such transfer.[37] Thus, in mass actions, it may be possible to remove a case from state court to a federal district court that sits in the same State, but transfer to another federal district court will normally be unavailable to a defendant. This limitation on transfer only applies to mass actions, not to class actions.[38]

CAFA: Statutes of Limitations Following Removal of Mass Actions

The statute of limitations for claims included in a mass action removed under CAFA is tolled for the period that the action is in a federal court.[39]

§ 2.12 Supplemental Jurisdiction

CORE CONCEPT

Once a case is properly in federal court, through an exercise of at least one form of original subject-matter jurisdiction, efficiency may dictate that other related claims—such as counterclaims or crossclaims—be adjudicated at the same time in that same case. Supplemental jurisdiction, authorized by Congress at 28 U.S.C.A. § 1367, permits district courts to exercise subject-matter jurisdiction over certain such related claims. To achieve this objective, supplemental jurisdiction has two threshold requirements. First, there must be at least one claim over which the court has original subject-matter jurisdiction. Second, the claim over which the court is asked to assert supplemental jurisdiction must arise out of the same "case or controversy" as the claim with original jurisdiction.

◆ **NOTE:** 28 U.S.C.A. § 1367, governing supplemental jurisdiction, became effective in December 1990. Prior to that date, the area was governed by two closely related doctrines of case law: pendent jurisdiction and ancillary jurisdiction. In creating supplemental jurisdiction, Congress combined much of those two doctrines.[1] However, Congress also overruled some previously existing features of the case law, so be careful when citing judicial

---

[36] *See Lowery v. Alabama Power Co.*, 483 F.3d 1184, 1202 n.45 (11th Cir. 2007).

[37] 28 U.S.C.A. § 1332(d)(11)(C).

[38] 28 U.S.C.A. § 1332(d)(11)(C)(ii).

[39] 28 U.S.C.A. § 1332(d)(11)(D); *Artis v. District of Columbia*, ___ U.S. ___, 138 S. Ct. 594, 602 n.4 (2018).

[1] *Peacock v. Thomas*, 516 U.S. 349, 355 (1996).

precedent prior to December 1990.

APPLICATIONS

Prerequisite Claim with Original Subject-Matter Jurisdiction

As its name suggests, supplemental jurisdiction is not an independent basis for satisfying the requirements of federal subject-matter jurisdiction. Instead, claims based on supplemental jurisdiction must be able to attach themselves to, or "piggyback off of," some other claim that can satisfy *original* federal subject-matter jurisdiction through federal question jurisdiction, diversity jurisdiction, or the other forms of original jurisdiction that Congress has created.[2]

Same Case or Controversy

Supplemental jurisdiction can only be effective for claims that are "so related" to one another that they "form part of the same case or controversy."[3] Thus, to "piggy-back" into federal court under supplemental jurisdiction, a claim that lacks an independent basis for subject-matter jurisdiction must be deemed part of the same constitutional "case" as some other claim in that lawsuit that does enjoy independent subject-matter jurisdiction. Determining whether that relationship exists focuses on the similarity and overlap between the witnesses and evidence relevant to the respective claims—whether the claims share "a "common nucleus of operative fact."[4]

No Amount in "Controversy Requirement

To qualify for supplemental jurisdiction, a claim need not satisfy any amount in controversy requirement.[5]

Can Apply to Both Joined Claims and Joined (and Intervening) Parties

When its requirements are met, supplemental jurisdiction may be used to bring both new claims[6] and new parties[7] into a federal lawsuit.

Supplemental Jurisdiction's Statutory Disqualifier

Supplemental jurisdiction is subject to a limitation that is designed to prevent clever plaintiffs from circumventing diversity jurisdiction's requirement of complete diversity of citizenship. If an adversary is a citizen of the same State as the

---

[2] *Exxon Mobil Corp. v. Allapattah Servs., Inc.*, 545 U.S. 546, 550 (2005); *Halmekangas v. State Farm Fire & Cas. Co.*, 603 F.3d 290, 293 (5th Cir. 2010).

[3] *Benchmark Ins. Co. v. SUNZ Ins. Co.*, 36 F.4th 766, 771 (8th Cir. 2022); *Price v. Wolford*, 608 F.3d 698, 703 (10th Cir. 2010).

[4] *City of Chicago v. Int'l Coll. of Surgeons*, 522 U.S. 156, 165 (1997); *Benchmark Ins. Co. v. SUNZ Ins. Co.*, 36 F.4th 766, 771 (8th Cir. 2022).

[5] *Espenscheid v. DirectSat USA, LLC*, 688 F.3d 872, 875 (7th Cir. 2012).

[6] *See, e.g., Powers v. United States*, 783 F.3d 570, 576 (5th Cir. 2015) (supplemental jurisdiction over cross-claim).

[7] *Exxon Mobil Corp. v. Allapattah Servs., Inc.*, 545 U.S. 546, 547 (2005).

plaintiff, naming that adversary as a defendant would destroy complete diversity of citizenship. To maneuver around that restriction, a clever plaintiff could name only the diverse adversaries as defendants, hoping that one of those defendants would then implead the non-diverse defendant into the case. The plaintiff could then assert its own claim against that non-diverse third-party defendant under the court's supplemental jurisdiction. Section 1367(b) of the supplemental jurisdiction statute prevents this ploy. It prohibits the exercise of supplemental jurisdiction when *all four* of the following conditions are met:

(1) The claims that independently qualify for federal subject-matter jurisdiction do so *solely* on the basis of diversity jurisdiction (such that if the action includes a claim that qualifies for federal question jurisdiction or some other form of original jurisdiction other than diversity, the disqualifier does not apply[8]); and

(2) The claims that do not independently qualify for federal subject-matter jurisdiction are brought by a plaintiff (*e.g.*, not by a defendant or third-party defendant); and

(3) Those claims are brought either:

 (a) by the original plaintiff, and are asserted against parties joined into the lawsuit under Rule 14 (impleader), Rule 19 (required party joinder), Rule 20 (permissive party joinder), or Rule 24 (intervention); or

 (b) by someone proposing to join into the lawsuit as a co-plaintiff under Rule 19 (required party joinder) or Rule 24 (intervention); and

(4) Exercising supplemental jurisdiction over those claims would be "inconsistent with the jurisdictional requirements" of diversity jurisdiction under section 1332.[9]

- *Inconsistent with the Jurisdictional Requirements:* There is very little case law explaining what this phrase in Section 1367(b) means, but the majority of courts read it to mean that this element bars supplemental jurisdiction unless the claim in question also meets all of the requirements for diversity jurisdiction.[10] Other courts read this phrase to mean that the exception to supplemental jurisdiction applies only if the parties do not have diverse citizenship, without regard to the amount in controversy.[11]
- *Class Actions:* This supplemental jurisdiction exception

[8] *Arroyo v. Rosas*, 19 F.4th 1202, 1210 (9th Cir. 2021); *Clarendon, Ltd. v. State Bank of Saurashtra*, 77 F.3d 631, 637 n.5 (2d Cir. 1996).

[9] 28 U.S.C.A. § 1367(b).

[10] *See, e.g., Griffin v. Lee*, 621 F.3d 380, 386 (5th Cir. 2010); *LM Ins. Corp. v. Spaulding Enterprises Inc.*, 533 F.3d 542, 555 n.5 (7th Cir. 2008).

[11] *See, e.g., RAD Mfg., L.L.C. v.*

does not apply to class actions proceeding in federal court under the Class Action Fairness Act, 28 U.S.C.A. § 1332(d) (discussed above).[12]

Supplemental Jurisdiction's Implied Case Law Disqualifier

In 2005, the Supreme Court considered a purported "drafting gap" in the wording of Section 1367(b).[13] The statute expressly disqualifies for supplemental jurisdiction certain claims by an original plaintiff against a nondiverse *defendant* who was joined permissively to the lawsuit under Rule 20, yet does not disqualify for supplemental jurisdiction a claim by a nondiverse party who proposes to permissively join the lawsuit as a *co-plaintiff* under Rule 20.[14] The Court suggested (but did not expressly hold) that a "contamination theory" view of the complete diversity principle would cure that "drafting gap." Under this analysis, if another plaintiff was added to a complaint over which the court had diversity jurisdiction, as permitted by Rule 20 (for example, by amendment under Rule 15), Section 1367(b) would, due to this "drafting gap," permit the exercise of supplemental jurisdiction over claims by the nondiverse, permissively added Rule 20 plaintiff, but once that joinder was accomplished, the presence of that newly-joined, nondiverse Rule 20 plaintiff would defeat the ability of all of the litigants to satisfy the complete diversity rule. This would in turn either compel the dismissal of the lawsuit entirely or at least the severing (under Rule 21) of the claims involving the newly added, nondiverse plaintiff.

Court's Discretion to Decline Supplemental Jurisdiction

Even if supplemental jurisdiction exists under 28 U.S.C.A. § 1367(a) and (b), the district judge still enjoys discretion to decline to hear supplemental claims in four circumstances listed in the statute.[15] These are the only circumstances in which the court has that discretion—the exercise of supplemental jurisdiction is otherwise mandatory.[16] When a federal court declines to exercise supplemental jurisdiction over a claim, it will typically dismiss the claim without prejudice so that the plaintiff may refile the claim in a state court.[17]

The four circumstances in which a federal court might choose

Advanced Fabrication Servs., Inc., 2017 WL 2653169, at *3 (M.D. Pa. 2017); *Aguayo v. AMCO Ins. Co.*, 59 F. Supp. 3d 1225, 1284 (D.N.M. 2014). *See also Bates Energy Oil & Gas, LLC v. Complete Oil Field Servs., LLC*, 2017 WL 10576036, at *2 n.3 (W.D. Tex. 2017) (noting the uncertainty).

[12] *F5 Cap. v. Pappas*, 856 F.3d 61, 79–82 (2d Cir. 2017).

[13] *See Exxon Mobil Corp. v. Allapattah Servs., Inc.*, 545 U.S. 546, 562–65 (2005).

[14] See 28 U.S.C.A. § 1367(B).

[15] *See* 28 U.S.C.A. § 1367(c); *Carlsbad Tech, Inc. v. HIF Bio, Inc.*, 556 U.S. 635, 639 (2009); *Arroyo v. Rosas*, 19 F.4th 1202, 1210 (9th Cir. 2021).

[16] *See, e.g., Hucul Advertising, LLC v. Charter Township of Gaines*, 748 F.3d 273, 281 (6th Cir. 2014).

[17] *Gregory v. Dillard's, Inc.*, 565 F.3d 464, 477 (8th Cir. 2009).

to decline to exercise supplemental jurisdiction (and, thus, dismiss a claim that otherwise qualifies for supplemental jurisdiction) are:

(1) *Novel or Complex Questions of State Law*: District courts may decline to exercise supplemental jurisdiction if state courts would be better able to untangle a "novel or complex" question of state law.[18] However, federal courts generally employ § 1367(c)(1) only in unusual cases involving the greatest difficulty in applying state law.[19]

(2) *Non-Diverse State Claim Predominates*: The court may decline to exercise supplemental jurisdiction over a state law claim when that claim predominates over the claims which formed the original basis of the court's subject-matter jurisdiction.[20]

(3) *Original Counts Dismissed*: The court may decline to exercise supplemental jurisdiction when it has dismissed all the claims over which it has original jurisdiction.[21] Courts give substantial weight to the point in the case at which the dismissal occurred. If the federal court dismissed the original jurisdiction claims at the outset of the case, it would probably dismiss the supplemental claims immediately.[22] If, however, the federal court proceeded through much of the litigation and had informed itself of the merits of the supplemental claims, then the court would be more likely to retain jurisdiction over the supplemental claims.[23] Some courts hold that the court's discretion must be exercised in favor of dismissal unless "considerations of judicial economy, convenience, and fairness to the parties provide an affirmative justification" for retaining jurisdiction.[24] Under one circumstance, there is no discretion and dismissal becomes mandatory: if the basis for dismissing the claims which the plaintiff

---

[18] 28 U.S.C.A. § 1367(c)(1); *Romero v. Drummond Co., Inc.*, 552 F.3d 1303, 1318 (11th Cir. 2008).

[19] *See, e.g., O'Connor v. State of Nev.*, 27 F.3d 357, 363 (9th Cir. 1994); *Ameritox, Ltd. v. Millennium Lab'ys, Inc.*, 803 F.3d 518, 537 (11th Cir. 2015).

[20] *See, e.g., Ervin v. OS Restaurant Services, Inc.*, 632 F.3d 971, 980 (7th Cir. 2011) ("A simple disparity in numbers [of parties] should not lead a court to the conclusion that a state claim 'substantially predominates' over the [federal] action."); *Borough of W. Mifflin v. Lancaster*, 45 F.3d 780, 789 (3d Cir. 1995) (Section 1367(c)(2)'s authority should be invoked only where there is an important countervailing interest to be served by relegating state claims to the state court. This will normally be the case only where "a state claim constitutes the real body of a case, to which the federal claim is only an appendage").

[21] *Carlsbad Tech., Inc. v. HIF Bio, Inc.*, 556 U.S. 635, 637 (2009).

[22] *See Carnegie-Mellon Univ. v. Cohill*, 484 U.S. 343, 350 (1988).

[23] *See, e.g., Tomaiolo v. Mallinoff*, 281 F.3d 1, 11 (1st Cir. 2002) (discovery closed and motions for summary judgment filed).

[24] *See, e.g., Hedges v. Musco*, 204 F.3d 109, 123 (3d Cir. 2000).

brought under the court's original jurisdiction was a determination that original jurisdiction was lacking, the court is required to dismiss the claims as to which the plaintiff has asserted the court's supplemental jurisdiction too (because the first requirement for supplemental jurisdiction—at least one claim with original jurisdiction—would never have been satisfied).[25]

(4) *Other Exceptional Circumstances*: The court has discretion to dismiss supplemental claims in circumstances not anticipated by Congress,[26] although courts rarely exercise this discretion.[27]

Prohibitions Contained in Other Statutes

Some federal statutes expressly prohibit the exercise of supplemental jurisdiction.[28] Similarly, some state statutes provide that specified claims must be brought in a particular state court, to the exclusion of other courts.[29] Such a state limitation is generally not an obstacle to a federal district court's exercise of supplemental jurisdiction.[30]

When Supplemental Jurisdiction Fails—Tolling a Statute of Limitations

A party's hope to acquire supplemental jurisdiction over a state-law claim may fail; the court could, for example, disagree that § 1367 provides such jurisdiction or the court might believe it best to exercise its discretion not to hear the claim. In such cases, the state-law claim will be dismissed without prejudice, leaving the claimant with the option of refiling the dismissed claim in state court.[31] To preserve that right, the statute of limitations applicable to the dismissed claim is tolled during the time it was pending in federal court[32] and then for a further 30

---

[25] *See Arbaugh v. Y&H Corp.*, 546 U.S. 500, 514 (2006); *Cangemi v. United States*, 13 F.4th 115, 134 (2d Cir. 2021).

[26] *See, e.g., Gregory v. Shelby County, Tenn.*, 220 F.3d 433, 446 (6th Cir. 2000) (State legislature's "clear preference" to have claims tried in state court is exceptional circumstance).

[27] *See Arroyo v. Rosas*, 19 F.4th 1202, 1214 (9th Cir. 2021); *Itar-Tass Russian News Agency v. Russian Kurier, Inc.*, 140 F.3d 442, 448 (2d Cir. 1998).

[28] 28 U.S.C.A. § 1367(a). *See also, e.g.*, 42 U.S.C.A. § 13981(e)(4) (prohibiting use of § 1367 to establish jurisdiction over State law claims seeking divorce, alimony, equitable distribution of marital property, or child custody).

[29] *See, e.g.*, Texas Code Annotated, Government Code § 613.021 (authorizing enforcement against State officials in State court district in which State official holds office).

[30] *Wong v. Minnesota Dep't of Hum. Servs.*, 820 F.3d 922, 931 (8th Cir. 2016).

[31] *Carnegie-Mellon Univ. v. Cohill*, 484 U.S. 343, 350 (1988).

[32] *Varnell v. Dora Consolidated School District*, 756 F.3d 1208, 1217 (10th Cir. 2014) (tolling continues until federal appeal is exhausted).

days following its dismissal by the federal judge.[33]

- *Tolling Stops the Clock*: The tolling provided by 28 U.S.C.A. § 1367(d) holds the state statute of limitations in abeyance for all state law claims pending in federal court and does not merely afford a 30-day grace period to refile a dismissed claim in state court (in other words, the deadline for the plaintiff to refile is the end of the statute of limitations, plus the period of time the case was pending in federal court, plus an additional 30 days).[34]
- *Tolling Other Claims:* The tolling provided by 28 U.S.C.A. § 1367(d) applies to claims that were voluntarily dismissed at the same time as those that were dismissed by the court, so that the plaintiff may choose to refile the entire case in state court.[35]

Claims under Foreign Laws

Claims arising under foreign law are eligible for supplemental jurisdiction.[36]

Supplemental Jurisdiction Does Not Erase Other Jurisprudential Requirements

The existence of supplemental jurisdiction over a claim does not relieve the claiming party from establishing all of the other jurisprudential requirements like standing and ripeness.[37]

Sovereign Immunity

A federal court's authority to exercise supplemental jurisdiction over a claim does not result in a waiver of a claim of sovereign immunity by the federal government[38] or a state government.[39]

***Sua Sponte* Assertion of Supplemental Jurisdiction**

If the claiming party fails to assert supplemental jurisdiction as a basis for the court's subject-matter jurisdiction over a claim, the courts are divided as to whether they may or should invoke their supplemental jurisdiction *sua sponte*.[40]

---

[33]*See* 28 U.S.C. § 1367(d); *Artis v. D.C.*, 138 S. Ct. 594, 598 (2018).

[34]*Artis v. D.C.*, 138 S. Ct. 594, 598 (2018).

[35]28 U.S.C.A. § 1367(d).

[36]*See, e.g., Voda v. Cordis Corp.*, 476 F.3d 887, 894 (Fed. Cir. 2007).

[37]*DaimlerChrysler Corp. v. Cuno*, 547 U.S. 332, 352 (2006).

[38]*See, e.g., San Juan Cty., Utah v. United States*, 503 F.3d 1163, 1182 n.4 (10th Cir. 2007).

[39]*Raygor v. Regents of the University of Minnesota*, 534 U.S. 533, 541 (2002).

[40]*Compare, e.g., U.S. ex rel. Ramseyer v. Century Healthcare Corp.*, 90 F.3d 1514, 1523 n.8 (10th Cir. 1996) (declining to invoke supplemental jurisdiction where plaintiff failed to assert it in complaint), *with Townsquare Media, Inc. v. Brill*, 652 F.3d 767, 774 (7th Cir. 2011) (plaintiff has no affirmative duty to cite § 1367).

D. REMOVAL AND REMAND

Table of Sections

2.13 Removal
2.14 Removal Procedure
2.15 Removal of Class Actions
2.16 Post-Removal Procedures and Remand

---

§ 2.13 Removal

CORE CONCEPT

Removal permits a defendant to override a plaintiff's choice of a state court forum, and to relocate the lawsuit to federal court. The primary statute governing removal is 28 U.S.C.A. § 1441, which authorizes a defendant to remove an action from a state court to federal district court if the federal courts have original subject-matter jurisdiction over the action.[1] Removal has a number of procedural requirements, typically requiring prompt action at the outset of a case. Accordingly, attorneys representing defendants must be vigilant or risk waiving their right to removal. This section describes the circumstances allowing for removal and the next section describes the procedures.

APPLICATIONS

Removal Statutes

Removal is governed by statute (as well as the case law construing those statutes). The most important removal provisions are 28 U.S.C.A. § 1441 (the general statute governing the right to remove) and 28 U.S.C.A. § 1446 (establishing the procedure for accomplishing removal). Additional statutes provide for removal in particular circumstances, such as suits against federal officers or agencies (28 U.S.C.A. §§ 1442, 1442a, and 1444) and suits where a defendant might not be able to assert a federal civil right in a state court (28 U.S.C.A. § 1443). Conversely, 28 U.S.C.A. § 1445 provides that certain kinds of cases (*e.g.,* suits against railroads under the Federal Employers' Liability Act and suits arising under state workers' compensation laws) may not be removed.[2] If a case has been removed, 28 U.S.C.A. §§ 1447–49 establish the procedures a court will follow after removal. Finally, 28 U.S.C.A. § 1453

---

[1]*See Sharma v. HSI Asset Loan Obligation Tr. 2007-1 by Deutsche Bank Natl. Tr. Co.*, 23 F.4th 1167, 1170 (9th Cir. 2022); *Holbein v. TAW Enterprises, Inc.*, 983 F.3d 1049, 1053 (8th Cir. 2020).

[2]*Breuer v. Jim's Concrete of Brevard, Inc.*, 538 U.S. 691, 696 (2003).

governs removal of class actions.

Threshold Removal Requirement: Federal Subject-Matter Jurisdiction Must Exist

Removal is permissible only when at least one claim in the complaint falls within the original subject-matter jurisdiction of the federal district court.[3] When removal is based on federal question jurisdiction, the federal question must be discernable based on a fair reading of the plaintiff's complaint.[4]

- *Timing of Evaluation of Subject-Matter Jurisdiction*: The presence or absence of federal subject-matter jurisdiction is evaluated at the time a notice of removal is filed.[5]
- *Exception—Diversity Jurisdiction*: When diversity jurisdiction is the basis for removal, then technically jurisdiction must exist *both* at the time the State court action was begun *and* at the time the notice of removal was filed, because diversity of citizenship is based on the citizenship of the parties at the time the complaint is filed.[6] This additional timing requirement is rarely significant because removal generally occurs shortly after the complaint is filed. It primarily prevents a defendant from quickly changing domicile to create diversity, then removing. If diversity jurisdiction did not exist when the case was filed but later becomes available through an action of the plaintiff or the court, it may become removable at that time, as discussed in the "After-Acquired" Eligibility for Removal Application in § 2.14, below.
- *Exception—Post-Removal Cures*: If at the time a case is removed, subject-matter jurisdiction is lacking, but the plaintiff subsequently amends the complaint in a way that then establishes valid subject-matter jurisdiction, the defect that existed at the time of removal may be ignored.[7]
- *Burden of Proving Subject-Matter Jurisdiction—Presumption Against Removal*: The party seeking removal carries the burden of establishing that all

---

[3] *Beneficial Nat. Bank v. Anderson*, 539 U.S. 1, 8 (2003); *Bd. of County Commissioners of Boulder County v. Suncor Energy (U.S.A.) Inc.*, 25 F.4th 1238, 1254 (10th Cir. 2022).

[4] *Franchise Tax Board v. Construction Laborers Vacation Trust*, 463 U.S. 1, 10 (1983); *City of Oakland v. BP PLC*, 969 F.3d 895, 903–04 (9th Cir. 2020).

[5] *Caterpillar Inc. v. Lewis*, 519 U.S. 61, 73 (1996); *City of Oakland v. BP PLC*, 969 F.3d 895, 909 (9th Cir. 2020).

[6] *Jerome-Duncan, Inc. v. Auto-By-Tel, L.L.C.*, 176 F.3d 904, 907 (6th Cir. 1999).

[7] *Pegram v. Herdrich*, 530 U.S. 211, 216 n.2 (2000); *Caterpillar Inc. v. Lewis*, 519 U.S. 61, 73 (1996).

jurisdictional requirements for removal are met.[8] The right to remove is narrowly construed;[9] where a doubt exists, a district court will resolve it by remanding the case.[10]

○ *Exception to Presumption Against Removal*: In cases involving the Class Action Fairness Act[11] there is no presumption against removal of a case from a state court to a federal district court.[12]

- *When the State Court Lacks Jurisdiction or Venue*: § 1441(f) permits a federal district court to hear a removed case even if the state court in which the case was originally filed lacked jurisdiction.[13] The statute does not address the state court's lack of venue, but case law indicates that a removed claim must have satisfied the venue rules governing the state court from which it was removed.[14]

Other Removal Limitations

Congress has established other removal constraints that govern this state-to-federal court shifting procedure:

- *Removal Is a Defendant's Option Only*: Only defendants can exercise the option of removal.[15] (Plaintiffs already had their opportunity to make the federal/state forum choice at the time they selected where to file their lawsuit.) Thus, defendants on counterclaims, cross-claims, or third-party impleaders have no right to remove cases from state court.[16]

○ *Exception—Removal by a Foreign State:* 28 U.S.C.A. § 1441(d) authorizes removal of an action asserted against a foreign state by that foreign state, and this provision allows removal by a foreign state brought in as a

[8] *See, e.g., County of San Mateo v. Chevron Corp.*, 32 F.4th 733, 746 (9th Cir. 2022); *Valencia v. Allstate Texas Lloyd's*, 976 F.3d 593, 594–95 (5th Cir. 2020).

[9] *See, e.g., County of San Mateo v. Chevron Corp.*, 32 F.4th 733, 764 (9th Cir. 2022); *Bowling v. U.S. Bank Nat'l Ass'n, As Tr. for C-Bass Mortg. Loan Asset-Backed Certificates, Series 2007-SP2*, 963 F.3d 1030, 1033 (11th Cir. 2020).

[10] *Breuer v. Jim's Concrete of Brevard, Inc.*, 538 U.S. 691, 695–96 (2013) (all doubts to be resolved in favor of removal); *Valencia v. Allstate Texas Lloyd's*, 976 F.3d 593, 595 (5th Cir. 2020.

[11] 28 U.S.C.A. § 1453.

[12] *Dart Cherokee Basin Operating Co., LLC v. Owens*, 574 U.S. 81 (2014). *See Jauregui v. Roadrunner Transportation Services, Inc.*, 28 F.4th 989, 992–93 (9th Cir. 2022).

[13] *See, e.g., Perez v. Does 1–10*, 931 F.3d 641 (8th Cir. 2019).

[14] *See, e.g., PT United Can Co. Ltd. v. Crown Cork & Seal Co., Inc.*, 138 F.3d 65, 72 (2d Cir. 1998) (citing other cases).

[15] 28 U.S.C. § 1441(a).

[16] *Home Depot U.S.A., Inc., v. Jackson*, — U.S. —, 139 S. Ct. 1743 (2019).

third-party defendant.[17]

○ *Removal by the Real Party in Interest:* The courts are divided as to whether an unnamed real party in interest may remove a case.[18]

- *Removal From State Court Only*: Under Congress's general removal statute, the case must have been in state court at the time the removal petition was filed.[19] The statute provides no authority to remove a case from other sorts of tribunals such as a state administrative agency tribunal.[20]
- *Removal to the Local Federal District Court Only*: Removed cases go to only one locale when they arrive into the federal system: to the federal district (or division) encompassing the location where the state court is sitting.[21] Thus, a case removed from a Pennsylvania State trial court in Pittsburgh, Pennsylvania would be sent to the United States District Court for the Western District of Pennsylvania (the federal district court that encompasses the city of Pittsburgh).
- *Forum Selection Clauses*: A valid forum selection clause that limits jurisdiction exclusively to a non-federal court is generally enforceable, notwithstanding that the parties would otherwise be eligible for federal diversity jurisdiction.[22] It is unclear whether that the same result would be reached in a case involving potential federal question jurisdiction (particularly exclusive federal question jurisdiction).
- *Blocking Removal by Careful Claim Selection*: A plaintiff

---

[17] *Davis v. McCourt*, 226 F.3d 506, 509 (6th Cir. 2000).

[18] *Sharma v. HSI Asset Loan Obligation Tr. 2007–1 by Deutsche Bank Natl. Tr. Co.*, 23 F.4th 1167, 1170–71 (9th Cir. 2022) (real party in interest may not remove); *La Russo v. St. George's University School of Medicine*, 747 F.3d 90, 96 (2d Cir. 2014) (real party in interest may remove).

[19] *See, e.g., Yassan v. J.P. Morgan Chase and Co.*, 708 F.3d 963, 968–70 (7th Cir. 2013).

[20] *See, e.g., Porter Trust v. Rural Water Sewer & Solid Waste Management District No. 1*, 607 F.3d 1251, 1253 (10th Cir. 2010); *Oregon Bureau of Labor and Industries ex rel. Richardson v. U.S. West Communications, Inc.*, 288 F.3d 414, 415 (9th Cir. 2002).

[21] 28 U.S.C.A. § 1441(a); *Kerobo v. Southwestern Clean Fuels, Corp.*, 285 F.3d 531, 534 (6th Cir. 2002). *But cf. Peterson v. BMI Refractories*, 124 F.3d 1386, 1394 (11th Cir. 1997) (removal to "wrong" district court is procedural error that is waivable; issue is not jurisdictional in nature).

[22] *See, e.g., Carlyle Investment Management LLC v. Moonmouth Co., SA*, 779 F.3d 214 (3d Cir. 2015); *Atlas Glass & Mirror, Inc. v. Tri-N. Builders, Inc.*, 997 F.3d 367, 375 (1st Cir. 2021). *But cf. Yakin v. Tyler Hill Corp.*, 566 F.3d 72, 76 (2d Cir. 2009) ("[O]bligatory venue language," standing alone limits case to county court only if a federal court was not located in the same county); *Kerobo v. Southwestern Clean Fuels Corp.*, 285 F.3d 531, 534–35 (6th Cir. 2002) (suit in Michigan state court; parties had forum clause selection choosing California venue; holding such a clause could not prevent removal to Michigan federal court).

preferring to litigate in state court can ordinarily foreclose the possibility of removal by electing not to plead claims that would be removal-eligible.[23] In the rare instance that the plaintiff's state law claims are completely preempted by federal law, the lawsuit might still be removable.[24]

Removals Based on Federal Question Jurisdiction

Section 1441 authorizes a defendant to remove any cause of action arising under the Constitution, laws, or treaties of the United States if the federal court has original jurisdiction over the claim.[25] In general, this provision is treated as authorizing removal of cases that could have been filed originally in federal district court pursuant to 28 U.S.C.A. § 1331 (Federal Question Jurisdiction).[26]

- *Removal Based on Federal Question Defense*: A defense that rests on a question of federal law is not grounds for removal.[27] Removal based on a federal question may succeed, if at all, only when the federal question arises on a fair reading of a well-pleaded complaint.[28]

Removal Based on Diversity Jurisdiction

Section 1441(b) also authorizes removal of cases meeting the citizenship and amount-in-controversy requirements of diversity jurisdiction in 28 U.S.C.A. § 1331.

- *Forum-Defendant Exception:* If any defendant who has been properly joined and served is a citizen of the state in which the claim was filed, the action is generally not eligible for removal if the only basis for original subject-matter jurisdiction is diversity jurisdiction.[29] Because this "forum-defendant" exception only applies to defendants who have been served, the exception may sometimes be avoided by a process referred to as "snap removal," under which a defendant removes the action before the forum-defendant has been served.[30] Improper removal due to the forum-defendant rule is a procedural

[23] *See, e.g., Valencia v. Allstate Texas Lloyd's*, 976 F.3d 593, 597 (5th Cir. 2020); *Salzer v. SSM Health Care of Oklahoma, Inc.*, 762 F.3d 1130, 1134 (10th Cir. 2014).

[24] *See Metropolitan Life Ins. Co. v. Taylor*, 481 U.S. 58, 65–66 (1987); *Maglioli v. All. HC Holdings LLC*, 16 F.4th 393, 407 (3d Cir. 2021).

[25] *Rivet v. Regions Bank of Louisiana*, 522 U.S. 470 (1998); *Sharma v. HSI Asset Loan Obligation Tr. 2007-1 by Deutsche Bank Natl. Tr. Co.*, 23 F.4th 1167, 1170 (9th Cir. 2022).

[26] *See, e.g., Eastman v. Marine Mechanical Corp.*, 438 F.3d 544, 549 (6th Cir. 2006).

[27] *Rivet v. Regions Bank of Louisiana*, 522 U.S. 470 (1998); *Mayor and City Council of Baltimore v. BP P.L.C.*, 31 F.4th 178, 197–98 (4th Cir. 2022).

[28] *Caterpillar Inc. v. Williams*, 482 U.S. 386 (1987). *See also The Lamar Co., L.L.C. v. Mississippi Transportation Comm'n*, 976 F.3d 524, 528–29 (5th Cir. 2020).

[29] *Lincoln Property Co. v. Roche*, 546 U.S. 81 (2005); *Tillman v. R.J. Reynolds Tobacco*, 253 F.3d 1302 (11th Cir. 2001).

[30] *See, e.g., Gibbons v. Bristol-Myers Squibb Co.*, 919 F.3d 699 (2d

defect and is waived by a plaintiff when not raised in a motion to remand within 30 days of notice of filing of removal.[31]

- ○ *Class Actions Not Subject to the Forum-Defendant Exception*: The forum-defendant exception does not apply to class actions, which are removable "without regard to whether any defendant is a citizen of the State in which the action is brought."[32]

- *Improper/Fraudulent Joinder*: It is possible that a plaintiff will join a nondiverse defendant for the purpose of preventing removal of claim that would otherwise qualify for diversity jurisdiction. If there is no colorable basis for the claim against the nondiverse defendant, the court will disregard the nondiverse defendant when ruling on a motion for remand challenging the removal.[33] Fraudulent joinder may also be found when a plaintiff engages in "outright fraud" in pleading jurisdictional allegations.[34] A third type of improper joinder arises when the plaintiff's joinder of a nondiverse defendant does not satisfy the requirements for joinder of multiple defendants.[35]
- *Fictitious Names Disregarded*: When the applicable state procedure allows lawsuits against defendants identified by fictitious names (*e.g., General Motors v. John Doe*), the court will disregard the citizenship of such defendants when testing for diversity.[36]
- *Amount In Controversy*: If the complaint states no amount in controversy, the defendant can assert one in its notice of removal, provided it does so plausibly (evidence establishing that assertion is only required if it is challenged).[37]
- *Discovery to Establish Right to Removal*: A district court has discretion to order discovery where some of the jurisdictional facts, like citizenship of the parties, have

---

Cir. 2019); *Encompass Insurance Co. v. Stone Mansion Restaurant, Inc.*, 902 F.3d 147 (3d Cir. 2018).

[31] *Holbein v. TAW Enterprises, Inc.*, 983 F.3d 1049, 1053 (8th Cir. 2020).

[32] 28 U.S.C.A. § 1453(b). *See also Abrego Abrego v. The Dow Chemical Co.*, 443 F.3d 676, 681 (9th Cir. 2006).

[33] *Halsey v. Townsend Corp. of Indiana*, 20 F.4th 1222, 1226 (8th Cir. 2021); *Waste Mgmt., Inc. v. AIG Specialty Ins. Co.*, 974 F.3d 528, 533 (5th Cir. 2020).

[34] *See, e.g., Triggs v. John Crump Toyota, Inc.*, 154 F.3d 1284, 1287 (11th Cir. 1998).

[35] *See, e.g., Williams v. Homeland Ins. Co. of New York*, 18 F.4th 806, 817 (5th Cir. 2021) (applying state joinder procedures); *Crockett v. R.J. Reynolds Tobacco Co.*, 436 F.3d 529, 533 (5th Cir. 2006).

[36] *See, e.g., Weaver v. Metropolitan Life Insurance Co.*, 939 F.3d 618 (5th Cir. 2019).

[37] *See Dart Cherokee Basin Operating Co., LLC v. Owens*, 135 S. Ct. 547, 554 (2014).

not been established.[38]

- *Post-Removal Events Affecting Jurisdiction*: It is unclear whether a case that was properly removed on the basis of diversity jurisdiction must or should be remanded to state court when events occurring after removal would have defeated removal had those events occurred prior to removal.[39]

Waiver of Right to Remove

Some courts hold that a defendant's right to remove a case to federal district court may be waived by taking some course of action that suggests an intention to litigate the merits of the case in state court.[40] However, to be effective, such a waiver must be "clear and unequivocal."[41] Usually, such a waiver will involve acts that are intended to affect an adjudication on the merits of the case.[42] By contrast, an act such as a motion in state court to dismiss for lack of prosecution does not clearly demonstrate an intention to waive a right to seek removal to federal court.[43]

Waiver by Contractual Consent

Parties to a contract may expressly waive their right to remove a case when that agreement is "clear and unequivocal."[44]

Joinder of Both Removable and Non-Removable Claims

Plaintiffs may allege multiple claims, only some of which are removable. When the basis for removal in such a case is the presence of a federal question, the process is clear. Defendants may remove the lawsuit in its entirety. See 28 U.S.C. § 1441(c)(1). Once in federal court, however, the judge must sever all nonremovable claims (those that lack either original or supplemental subject-matter jurisdiction) and then remand those severed claims back to the State court from which they

---

[38] *See, e.g., Platinum-Montaur Life Sciences, LLC v. Navidea Biopharmaceuticals, Inc.*, 943 F.3d 613 (2d Cir. 2019).

[39] *Compare, e.g., Poore v. American-Amicable Life Ins. Co. of Texas*, 218 F.3d 1287, 1290–91 (11th Cir. 2000) (post-removal reduction in amount in controversy does not destroy district court's subject-matter jurisdiction); *Matter of Shell Oil Co.*, 966 F.2d 1130, 1133 (7th Cir. 1992) (jurisdiction valid at time of removal "is unaffected by subsequent acts"); *with, Mayes v. Rapoport*, 198 F.3d 457, 461 (4th Cir. 1999) (post-removal joinder of non-diverse defendant requires remand to state court); *Cobb v. Delta Exports, Inc.*, 186 F.3d 675, 677 (5th Cir. 1999) ("[P]ost-removal joinder of non-diverse defendants pursuant to Fed.R.Civ.P. 19 destroys diversity for jurisdictional purposes and requires remand, even when the newly joined defendants are not indispensable.").

[40] *See, e.g., City of Albuquerque v. Soto Enterprises, Inc.*, 864 F.3d 1089 (10th Cir. 2017); *Yusefzadeh v. Nelson, Mullins, Riley & Scarborough, LLP*, 365 F.3d 1244, 1246 (11th Cir. 2014).

[41] *See, e.g., PR Group, LLC v. Windmill International, Ltd.*, 792 F.3d 1025, 1026 (8th Cir. 2015).

[42] *Tedford v. Warner-Lambert Co.*, 327 F.3d 423 (5th Cir. 2003).

[43] *PR Group, LLC v. Windmill International, Ltd.*, 792 F.3d 1025 (8th Cir. 2015).

[44] *Medtronic Sofamor Danek, Inc. v. Gannon*, 913 F.3d 704, 707 (8th Cir. 2019).

were removed.[45]

By contrast, there is no authority in § 1441(c), or anywhere else, regarding the procedure when an action is removed based on diversity jurisdiction and the action also includes claims over which the court has no basis for subject-matter jurisdiction. Little or no authority exists on the topic, but it appears that in such circumstances the action may be removed under § 1441(b), and the court will dismiss or remand the claims over which it has no jurisdiction.[46]

Removal and Waiver of Eleventh Amendment Immunity

The Eleventh Amendment to the Constitution provides American States with a substantial degree of immunity against lawsuits in federal district courts.[47] There is a substantial amount of uncertainty about whether, when an American State is sued in a state court, the American State waives its Eleventh Amendment immunity if it removes the case to federal court. The federal circuit courts have developed several conflicting approaches to this problem.[48]

Removal and Waiver of Tribal Immunity

If a member of a federally recognized Indian tribe removes a case to federal court, the member does not waive whatever tribal immunity he or she has by doing so.[49]

Suits Against Foreign Countries

Lawsuits against foreign countries or their agents,[50] filed originally in a state court, may be removed regardless of whether the suit was based on a federal question or state law.[51] The right to remove is vested in the foreign country and is substantially unqualified.[52] A removing foreign sovereign does not waive whatever sovereign immunity defenses it may enjoy under federal law.[53]

- *Nonjury Trials Only*: In any suit where removal was based upon a foreign sovereign's removal rights under

---

[45]28 U.S.C.A. § 1441(c)(2). *See, e.g., S J Associated Pathologists, P.L.L.C. v. Cigna Healthcare of Texas, Inc.*, 964 F.3d 369, 374 (5th Cir. 2020).

[46]*See Prolite Bldg. Supply, LLC v. MW Manufacturers, Inc.*, 891 F.3d 256, 259 (7th Cir. 2018).

[47]U.S. Const. Amend. XI.

[48]*See, e.g., Contour Spa at the Hard Rock, Inc. v. Seminole Tribe of Florida*, 692 F.3d 1200, 1205–06 (11th Cir. 2012) (collecting cases).

[49]*Aquinnah/Gay Head Cmty. Ass'n, Inc. v. Wampanoag Tribe of Gay Head (Aquinnah)*, 989 F.3d 72, 83 (1st Cir. 2021); *Bodi v. Shingle Springs Band of Miwok Indians*, 832 F.3d 1011 (9th Cir. 2016).

[50]*Dole Food Co. v. Patrickson*, 538 U.S. 468, 477 (2003) (for a corporation to remove on ground it is instrumentality of foreign state, the foreign state must own a majority of the corporation's shares).

[51]*See, e.g., Hanil Bank v. PT. Bank Negara Indonesia (Persero)*, 148 F.3d 127 (2d Cir. 1998). *See also Davis v. McCourt*, 226 F.3d 506 (6th Cir. 2000) (§ 1441(d) authorizes removal even foreign entity is third-party defendant).

[52]28 U.S.C.A. § 1441(d).

[53]*See, e.g., Rodriguez v. Transnave, Inc.*, 8 F.3d 284, 289 (5th Cir. 1993); *In re Delta American Reinsurance Co.*, 900 F.2d 890, 893 (6th Cir. 1990).

§ 1441(d), the court must try the case without a jury.[54]

Removal of Multiparty, Multidistrict Wrongful Death Actions

Original federal subject-matter jurisdiction extends to certain civil actions arising from a single accident where at least 75 natural persons have died at a discrete location, provided minimal diversity and the other provisions of the Multiparty, Multiforum Jurisdiction statute are satisfied.[55] A defendant may use the federal courts' Multiparty, Multiforum Jurisdiction as the basis for removal.[56]

§ 2.14 Removal Procedure

CORE CONCEPT

Defendants in an action eligible for removal from state court to federal district court may do so by filing a notice of removal with the appropriate federal court within 30 days of notice, whether by a pleading, motion, or otherwise, that the action is eligible for removal. Filing the notice of removal automatically removes the case from the jurisdiction of the state court. If the federal court determines that removal was erroneous, the remedy is remand to the state court from which the case was originally removed.

APPLICATIONS

Notice of Removal—Contents

The notice of removal should contain a concise statement of the grounds upon which removal is based.[1] The notice should be accompanied by copies of "all process, pleadings, and orders served upon" the defendant seeking removal in the state court proceeding.[2]

Notice of Removal—Where Filed

The notice of removal must be filed in the district court that encompasses the territory within which the state lawsuit is pending.[3]

Notice of Removal—Service and Effect

The defendants must give written notice to the state court and to all adverse parties "promptly" after filing the notice of removal.[4] Upon such filing, removal is complete (no motion or

---

[54]*See, e.g., Olympia Exp., Inc. v. Linee Aeree Italiane, S.P.A.*, 509 F.3d 347, 350 (7th Cir. 2007).

[55]28 U.S.C.A. § 1369.

[56]28 U.S.C.A. § 1441(e)(1); *Pettitt v. Boeing Co.*, 606 F.3d 340, 343 (7th Cir. 2010).

[1]*See, e.g., Ticer v. Imperium Ins. Co.*, 20 F.4th 1040, 1045 (5th Cir. 2021); *Strawn v. AT&T Mobility, LLC*, 530 F.3d 293 (4th Cir. 2008).

[2]*See, e.g., Cook v. Randolph County, Ga.*, 573 F.3d 1143 (11th Cir. 2009) (failure to include all state court pleadings and process is not a jurisdictional defect).

[3]*See, e.g., Global Satellite Communication Co. v. Starmill U.K. Ltd.*, 378 F.3d 1269 (11th Cir. 2004).

[4]28 U.S.C.A. § 1446(d).

judicial act is necessary).[5] The state court is immediately divested of its jurisdiction over the lawsuit (and must, in the language of the statute, "proceed no further" on the lawsuit), and jurisdiction is correspondingly immediately invested in the federal court.[6]

Notice of Removal—Unanimous Consent of Defendants

Under the general removal statute, all defendants who have been properly joined and served[7] must "join in or consent to the removal."[8] The courts are split as to whether each defendant must confirm its desire to remove the action or whether one defendant may vouch for the other defendants' consent.[9]

- *Class Actions*: For class actions, *any* defendant may seek removal "without consent of all defendants."[10]
- *Nominal Party Exception*: The requirement for unanimous consent for removal does not include a need to obtain consent of nominal parties, *i.e.*, parties with no immediately apparent stake in the litigation.[11] There is some degree of uncertainty, however, as to how courts should ascertain whether a party is "nominal."[12]

Rule 11

Notices of removal are subject to the provisions of Rule 11, which permits the court to impose sanctions for inappropriate pleadings and motions.[13]

Notice of Removal—Time For Filing

In general, a defendant eligible for removal has 30 days from receipt of the complaint (through formal service or otherwise)

---

[5]28 U.S.C.A. § 1446(d). *See, e.g., Speiser, Krause & Madole P.C. v. Ortiz*, 271 F.3d 884, 887 (9th Cir. 2001); *Yarnevic v. Brink's, Inc.*, 102 F.3d 753, 754 (4th Cir. 1996).

[6]See 28 U.S.C. § 1446(d); *Roman Catholic Archdiocese of San Juan v. Acevedo Feliciano*, 140 S. Ct. 696, 700 (2020).

[7]28 U.S.C.A. § 1446(b)(2)(A). *See also, e.g., Knight v. Mooring Capital Fund, LLC*, 749 F.3d 1180, 1184 (10th Cir. 2014).

[8]28 U.S.C.A. § 1446(a)(2)(A).

[9]*Compare Mayo v. Board of Education of Prince George's County*, 713 F.3d 735, 741 (4th Cir. 2013) (collecting precedent that does not require individual consent), *with Pritchett v. Cottrell, Inc.*, 512 F.3d 1057, 1062 (8th Cir. 2008) (requiring individual consent).

[10]*See Butler v. Denka Performance Elastomer, L.L.C.*, 16 F.4th 427, 436 (5th Cir. 2021); *Greene v. Harley-Davidson, Inc.*, 965 F.3d 767, 775 (9th Cir. 2020). This exception is inapplicable to any class action "solely" involving: (1) a claim concerning a covered security under certain federal securities laws; (2) a claim relating to the internal affairs or governance of a corporation or other business entity arising under the laws of the state that incorporated or organized the enterprise; or (3) a claim relating to the rights and duties, including fiduciary duties, created by the Securities Act of 1933.

[11]*See, e.g., Grace Ranch, L.L.C. v. BP Am. Prod. Co.*, 989 F.3d 301, 309 (5th Cir. 2021) (required parties under Rule 19 cannot be nominal); *Hartford Fire Insurance Co. v. Harleysville Mutual Insurance Co.*, 736 F.3d 255, 259 (4th Cir. 2013).

[12]*See, e.g., Ryan v. State Board of Elections of Illinois*, 661 F.2d 1130, 1134 (7th Cir. 1981).

[13]28 U.S.C.A. § 1446(a).

in which to file a notice of removal.[14] This facially straightforward directive, however, is sometimes mired in complexity. For example, the initial pleading will have been filed in a state court where averments about citizenship diversity or the presence of a federal question may well have been irrelevant and unnecessary; consequently, the initial pleading may not yet contain enough information to confirm whether the lawsuit is truly removable. In other cases, multiple defendants may be named, but not all served at the same time, or the applicable State law might permit a lawsuit to be filed by a "writ," with a complaint to follow sometime later. Notwithstanding these context variants, some timing rules are settled:

- *Notice "By Service or Otherwise"*: Although § 1446 provides that the removal clock is triggered by notice that the case is removable "by service or otherwise," otherwise does not mean informal notice such as emailing a courtesy copy of the complaint to the defendant.[15] Instead, "or otherwise" is intended to encompass the various rules for service of process under state rules of civil procedure that might not constitute service under federal procedure.
- *When Removability is Clear from Service of the Complaint*: If removability is clear from the initial pleading, the 30-day period runs from the defendant's receipt of that pleading.
- *When Removability Is Clear but There Is Only Partial Service*: If, as permitted or required by state law, a summons is served on the defendant, but the complaint is not furnished until a later date, the 30-day period begins to run from the date the defendant received the complaint.[16] If a defendant is served with a summons, but the complaint is filed in court under a state rule that does not mandate service of the complaint, the 30-day period begins to run on the date that the complaint is available to the defendant through filing. If a complaint is filed in state court before any service on the defendant, the 30-day period begins to run from the date of service of the summons on the defendant.[17]
- *When Service Is Waived*: If a defendant has, pursuant to state law, voluntarily waived the formal requirements of service of process, the 30-day period will begin to run

[14] *See McLaren v. UPS Store Inc*, 32 F.4th 232, 236 (3d Cir. 2022); *Par. of Plaquemines v. Chevron USA, Inc.*, 7 F.4th 362, 368 (5th Cir. 2021).

[15] *Murphy Bros., Inc. v. Michetti Pipe Stringing, Inc.*, 526 U.S. 344, 354 (1999).

[16] *Murphy Bros., Inc. v. Michetti Pipe Stringing, Inc.*, 526 U.S. 344, 354 (1999).

[17] *Murphy Bros., Inc. v. Michetti Pipe Stringing, Inc.*, 526 U.S. 344, 354 (1999); *Sikirica v. Nationwide Ins. Co.*, 416 F.3d 214 (3d Cir. 2005).

on the occurrence of some other event,[18] such as the date waiver of service becomes effective.

- *When Multiple Defendants are Named*: In a multi-defendant lawsuit, each defendant has 30 days from that defendant's receipt of notice to file a notice of removal.[19] Thus later-served defendants have a later running time in which to file their notices. Earlier served defendants may consent to the notice of removal filed by a later served defendant, even if the earlier served defendants had not filed timely notices of removal.[20]
- *When Service is Made on an Agent*: Service on an agent that the defendant has designated will start the removal clock.[21] In contrast, when service is made on an agent designated by statute (such as when the local Secretary of State is authorized to be served on defendant's behalf), the 30-day period runs from the date the defendant receives notice that such service has been made.[22]
- *When Removability Is NOT Clear*: If the initial pleading does not disclose a basis for removal, the 30-day period begins to run when the defendant receives "through service or otherwise" information from which, for the first time, the defendant can ascertain that the lawsuit is—or has become—removable.[23] Thus, if the defendant learns about eligibility for removal for the first time from, *e.g.*, an amended pleading, a motion, answers obtained in discovery, or information contained in a post-filing settlement proposal, the 30-day period begins to run on the date of receipt of that information.[24] The defendant generally has no burden to make an independent investigation to assess removability when the right to remove is not apparent from the state court complaint.[25] However, the defendant may support removal with in-

[18] *Murphy Bros., Inc. v. Michetti Pipe Stringing, Inc.*, 526 U.S. 344, 350 (1999).

[19] 28 U.S.C.A. § 1446(b)(2)(B).

[20] 28 U.S.C.A. § 1446(b)(2)(C).

[21] *Anderson v. State Farm Mut. Auto. Ins. Co.*, 917 F.3d 1126, 1128 (9th Cir. 2019).

[22] *See, e.g., Anderson v. State Farm Mutual Automobile Insurance Co.*, 917 F.3d 1126 (9th Cir. 2019).

[23] 28 U.S.C.A. § 1446(b)(3); *McLaren v. UPS Store Inc*, 32 F.4th 232, 234 (3d Cir. 2022).

[24] *See, e.g., Paros Properties LLC v. Colorado Casualty Insurance Co.*, 835 F.3d 1264 (10th Cir. 2016) (email may be paper for purpose of § 1446); *Babasa v. LensCrafters, Inc.*, 498 F.3d 972, 975 (9th Cir. 2007) (letter from opposing counsel identifying amount in controversy is notice of removal eligibility).

[25] *McLaren v. UPS Store Inc*, 32 F.4th 232, 238 (3d Cir. 2022); *Harris v. Bankers Life and Cas. Co.*, 425 F.3d 689, 695 (9th Cir. 2005).

formation that the defendant developed independently.[26]

- *Removal Prior to the 30-Day Period*: If a defendant becomes aware of a lawsuit before the defendant has been served and files a notice of removal, the removal will be timely.[27]
- *Foreign Sovereigns as Defendants*: Where the defendant desiring to remove a case under § 1441(d) is a foreign sovereign within the meaning of the Foreign Sovereign Immunities Act,[28] the court may extend the 30-day time period for removal "for cause shown."[29] It is the defendant's burden to demonstrate good cause for the delay in filing such a petition.[30]

Diversity Cases and Amount in Controversy

In assessing whether a case is removable on the basis of diversity, the general rule is that the amount the plaintiff demands in the initial pleading is considered to be the amount in controversy—so long as it is made in good faith and is not, to a legal certainty, overstated.[31]

- *Nonmonetary Relief*: If the initial pleading seeks only nonmonetary relief, the notice of removal may assert a suitable amount in controversy.[32]
- *Monetary Relief That Is Uncapped or Without Sum-Certain*: If the initial pleading seeks monetary relief but state procedure does not permit a plea for a sum certain or, alternatively, permits recovery of damages greater than the amount sought in the initial pleading, the notice of removal may assert a suitable amount in controversy.[33]
- *Monetary Relief That Qualifies Even When Unpleaded*: If the initial pleading contains a request for monetary relief in an amount less than the jurisdictional requirement, removal may still be appropriate if the district court finds that the amount in controversy is actually satisfied, notwithstanding the apparent shortfall in the initial pleading.
- *Standard of Proof*: If the complaint does not explicitly state an amount in controversy satisfying the requirement for diversity jurisdiction and the defendant seeks to remove the case based on one of the approaches

---

[26]*See, e.g., Pretka v. Kolter City Plaza II, Inc.*, 608 F.3d 744, 759 (11th Cir. 2010).

[27]*See, e.g., Gibbons v. Bristol-Myers Squibb Co.*, 919 F.3d 699, 705 (2d Cir. 2019); *Delgado v. Shell Oil Co.*, 231 F.3d 165, 177 (5th Cir. 2000).

[28]28 U.S.C.A. § 1605.

[29]*See, e.g., Big Sky Network Canada v. Sichuan Provincial Government*, 533 F.3d 1183, 1187 (10th Cir. 2008).

[30]*See, e.g., Big Sky Network Canada, Ltd., v. Sichuan Provincial Government*, 533 F.3d 1183, 1187 (10th Cir. 2008).

[31]28 U.S.C.A. § 1446(c)(2).

[32]28 U.S.C.A. § 1446(c)(2)(A)(i).

[33]28 U.S.C.A. § 1446(c)(2)(A)(ii).

described above, both sides may submit evidence, then the court decides whether the preponderance of the evidence supports a sufficient amount in controversy.[34]

- *Sources of Information to Establish Amount in Controversy*: Where the initial pleading does not disclose a sufficient amount in controversy, the defendant may use information in the state court record or developed in discovery to establish the amount in controversy.[35]

"After-Acquired" Eligibility for Removal

If a case does not qualify for removal at the time of receipt of the original process on a defendant, the defendant will have 30 days to file a notice of removal from service of the amended pleading motion, order, or other paper creating eligibility for removal.[36]

- *Removal Clock Triggered by Service on Defendant:* The 30-day period for removal based on after-acquired eligibility is triggered by service on the defendant of the plaintiff's document or the court's order, not by evidence that the defendant developed independently.[37]
- *One-Year Outside Limit for Removal Based on Diversity Jurisdiction*: If the basis for removal is diversity jurisdiction, the period of time for "after-acquired" eligibility will normally be no more than one year after the commencement of the lawsuit.[38] For purposes of the one-year limitation, courts usually measure "commencement" of the case under the rules governing commencement in the relevant state court.[39]
- *Bad Faith Exception*: The one-year cap does not apply where a plaintiff acted in "bad faith" to prevent a defendant's removal,[40] such as when the plaintiff deliberately failed to disclose the true amount in controversy in order to block removal,[41] or voluntarily dismissed the nondiverse defendant right after the end of the one-year period.[42]
- *Waiver Exception*: The one-year cap is not jurisdictional,

---

[34] *Dart Cherokee Basin Operating Co., LLC v. Owens*, 574 U.S. 81, 88 (2014); *Durbois v. Deutsche Bank Natl. Tr. Co. as Tr. of Holders of AAMES Mortg. Inv. Tr. 20054 Mortg. Backed Notes*, 37 F.4th 1053 (5th Cir. 2022).

[35] 28 U.S.C.A. § 1446(c)(3)(A).

[36] *See, e.g., Skidmore v. Norfolk S. Ry. Co.*, 1 F.4th 206, 210 (4th Cir. 2021); *Durham v. Lockheed Martin Corp.*, 445 F.3d 1247, 1250 (9th Cir. 2006).

[37] *See, e.g., Pretka v. Kolter City Plaza II, Inc.*, 608 F.3d 744, 760 (11th Cir. 2010); *Bosky v. Kroger Texas, LP*, 288 F.3d 208, 211 (5th Cir. 2002).

[38] 28 U.S.C.A. § 1446(c)(1); *Home Depot U. S. A., Inc. v. Jackson*, 139 S. Ct. 1743, 1746 (2019).

[39] *See, e.g., Bush v. Cheaptickets, Inc.*, 425 F.3d 683, 688 (9th Cir. 2005).

[40] 28 U.S.C.A. § 1446(c)(1).

[41] 28 U.S.C.A. § 1446(c)(3)(B).

[42] 28 U.S.C.A. § 1446(c)(1). *See also Hoyt v. Lane Construction Corp.*, 927 F.3d 287 (5th Cir. 2019).

such that if a defendant removes outside the one-year cap and the plaintiff does not object, the removal will be proper.

- *Class Action Exception:* The one-year cap does not apply to class actions.[43]

Amending Notices of Removal

The removing defendant may amend the notice to cure defective allegations of removal jurisdiction.[44] Courts have discretion to permit amendments even after the 30-day time limit for filing a notice of removal has expired.[45] This discretion, however, extends only to amendments seeking to correct allegations in the original notice of removal. If the proposed amendment seeks to raise new allegations, district courts have no discretion to ignore the 30-day time limit. Instead, the court must reject the amendment.[46]

Remedy for Inappropriate Removal

If the federal court determines that removal was improper, it may remand part or all of the case to the state court; dismissal is *not* an appropriate remedy.[47]

§ 2.15 Removal of Class Actions

CORE CONCEPT

Congress enacted the Class Action Fairness Act (CAFA) in 2005. This federal law created greater opportunity for class actions pending in state court to be removed to federal court and, if thereafter remanded back to state court, greater opportunity for appellate review of that decision to remand.

APPLICATIONS

How CAFA Modified the Usual Removal Requirements

The Class Action Fairness Act modified several of the usual requirements and procedures for removal for the class action context. (Note: CAFA assigned special definitions to the terms "class," "class action," "class certification order," and "class members," and those special definitions apply when interpreting the Act.)[1]

- *Diversity of Citizenship:* CAFA relaxes the requirement of complete diversity by permitting the exercise of diversity-based federal subject-matter jurisdiction if any

[43] 28 U.S.C.A. § 1453(b); *McLaren v. UPS Store Inc*, 32 F.4th 232, 236 (3d Cir. 2022); *Braud v. Transport Service Co. of Illinois*, 445 F.3d 801, 806 (5th Cir. 2006).

[44] 28 U.S.C.A. § 1653.

[45] *See, e.g., Wood v. Crane Co.*, 764 F.3d 316, 323 (4th Cir. 2014).

[46] *See, e.g., City of Oakland v. BP PLC*, 969 F.3d 895, 901 (9th Cir. 2020); *Wood v. Crane Co.*, 764 F.3d 316, 323 (4th Cir. 2014).

[47] *See, e.g., University of South Alabama v. American Tobacco Co.*, 168 F.3d 405, 411 (11th Cir. 1999); *Ondis v. Barrows*, 538 F.2d 904, 908 (1st Cir. 1976).

[1] See 28 U.S.C.A. §§ 1332(d), 1453, 1711 to 15.

single class member is diverse from the class opponents.[2]

- *Amount in Controversy:* CAFA also relaxes the amount-in-controversy requirement, by permitting a diversity-based removal if the individual claims of all class members—when aggregated together—exceed $5,000,000, exclusive of interest and costs.[3] Although this figure is obviously larger than the usual more-than-$75,000 threshold, the aggregation effect makes removal more tenable for many classes. (A full summary of all of CAFA's requirements appears with Rule 23 below.)
- *One-Year Limitation on Removal of Diversity Cases:* The one-year outside time limit on after-acquired removability in diversity cases does not apply to class actions under CAFA.[4]
- *Forum-Defendant Rule:* CAFA also lifts the usual prohibition that bars defendants from diversity-based removals when they are citizens of the state where the lawsuit is pending.[5]
- *Unanimous Consent:* CAFA also permits removal on the basis of a single defendant's request; the usual requirement of defendant unanimity is excused.[6]
- *Appellate Review Prohibition:* As explained below, remand decisions are largely immune from appellate review. This bar does not apply to cases removed under the relaxed diversity jurisdiction requirements in CAFA.[7] Instead, CAFA allows appeal from either grants or denials of remand motions, as well as orders issued *sua sponte*, with the following procedures:
    - *Appeal by Permission, Not by Right*: The Courts of Appeal have the discretion, but not the obligation, to hear such an appeal.[8]
    - *10 Days to Apply*: Parties seeking review of a decision granting or denying remand must apply to the appeals court within 10 days of entry of the

[2] 28 U.S.C.A. § 1332(d)(2). *See also Miedema v. Maytag Corp.*, 450 F.3d 1322, 1327 (11th Cir. 2006).

[3] 28 U.S.C.A. § 1332(d). *See also Lizama v. Victoria's Secret Stores, LLC*, 36 F.4th 762, 764 (8th Cir. 2022); *Greene v. Harley-Davidson, Inc.*, 965 F.3d 767, 772 (9th Cir. 2020).

[4] 28 U.S.C.A. § 1446(b). *See, e.g., McLaren v. UPS Store Inc*, 32 F.4th 232, 236 (3d Cir. 2022); *Reece v. Bank of New York Mellon*, 760 F.3d 771, 776 (8th Cir. 2014).

[5] 28 U.S.C.A. § 1453(b).

[6] 28 U.S.C.A. § 1453(b). *See also Bonin v. Sabine River Auth. of Louisiana*, 961 F.3d 381, 387 (5th Cir. 2020); *Farina v. Nokia, Inc.*, 625 F.3d 97, 113 (3d Cir. 2010).

[7] 28 U.S.C.A. § 1453(c)(1); *Dart Cherokee Basin Operating Co., LLC v. Owens*, 574 U.S. 81, 90 (2014); *Chan Healthcare Group, PS v. Liberty Mutual Fire Insurance Co.*, 844 F.3d 1133, 1139 (9th Cir. 2017) (right to appeal limited to diversity class actions).

[8] 28 U.S.C.A. § 1453(c)(1). *See also, e.g., Perdue Pharma, L.P. v. Kentucky*, 704 F.3d 208, 212 (2d Cir. 2013); *Hertz Corp. v. Friend*, 559 U.S. 77, 83 (2010).

order.[9] If the court has denied a motion to remand and the plaintiff files a timely motion to reconsider that adverse decision, the time to appeal starts to run from the date of denial of the motion to reconsider.[10]

- ○ *Appeal of Sua Sponte Remand Orders:* The authorization of an appeal applies to *sua sponte* remand orders.[11]
- ○ *Mass Actions*: The provisions authorizing appeal of remand orders for class actions also apply to "mass actions."[12]

- *60 Days to Rule*: If the appeals court elects to hear the appeal, it must rule within 60 days. The 60-day period begins to run from the date that the appeals court grants the petition to appeal. The period may be extended, however, upon the parties' consent (for "any period of time") or upon court order, issued for good cause shown (for 10 days). If the appeals court fails to rule within the prescribed time, the appeal is deemed denied.

Original Defendants Only

CAFA does not change the established rule that only an original defendant may seek removal.[13] Thus, in most circuits, crossclaim defendants and third-party defendants cannot remove.[14]

Class Actions That Do Not Fall Within CAFA

CAFA excludes from its specially-tailored removal procedures a few categories of class actions: (1) cases "solely" involving claims under federal securities laws;[15] and (2) cases "solely" involving claims arising under state corporate laws governing the internal affairs or governance of state-chartered corporations.[16]

§ 2.16 Post-Removal Procedures and Remand

---

[9] 28 U.S.C.A. § 1453(c)(1).

[10] *See, e.g., Briggs v. Merck Sharp & Dohme*, 796 F.3d 1038, 1046 (9th Cir. 2015).

[11] *See, e.g., Kenny v. Wal-Mart Stores, Inc.*, 881 F.3d 786, 789 (9th Cir. 2018); *Watkins v. Vital Pharmaceuticals, Inc.*, 720 F.3d 1179, 1181 (9th Cir. 2013).

[12] 28 U.S.C.A. § 1 332(d)(11)(A); *Lester v. Exxon Mobil Corp.*, 879 F.3d 582, 591–92 (5th Cir. 2018); *Lowery v. Alabama Power Co.*, 483 F.3d 1184, 1195 (11th Cir. 2007).

[13] *Home Depot U. S. A., Inc. v. Jackson*, 139 S. Ct. 1743, 1751 (2019).

[14] *See, e.g., Palisades Collections LLC v. Shorts*, 552 F.3d 327, 336 (4th Cir. 2008).

[15] *See, e.g., Greenwich Financial Services Distressed Mortgage Fund 3 LLC v. Countrywide Financial Corp.*, 603 F.3d 23, 30 (2d Cir. 2010).

[16] *See, e.g., Dominion Energy, Inc. v. City of Warren Police and Fire Retirement System*, 928 F.3d 325 (4th Cir. 2019) (identifying categories of nonremovable class actions); *Brill v. Countrywide Home Loans, Inc.*, 427 F.3d 446, 450 (7th Cir. 2005).

CORE CONCEPT

Once a case has been removed to a federal district court, the case generally proceeds pursuant to the Federal Rules of Civil Procedure and federal procedural statutes. 28 U.S.C.A. §§ 1447 to 49 contain some additional procedures that apply to removed actions. These procedures authorize the federal court to issue orders and process necessary to effect service on any unserved defendants, to address attempts by plaintiffs to join nondiverse defendants, and to retrieve the State court record.

Additionally, § 1447 contains procedures allowing a court to remand a case—send it back to the state court where it was originally filed,—if the court determines that the removal was improper.

APPLICATIONS

Post-Removal Authority to Issue Orders and Process

At the time of removal, service of process might not yet be complete on all defendants. In such a circumstance, the federal district court is authorized to permit completion of service begun in the state proceeding or, alternatively, to issue its own process to be served on any as-yet-unserved defendants.[1] Defendants who are so served may challenge the removal (by seeking remand, as discussed below).[2] But such post-removal service developments do not ordinarily confer any new rights on plaintiffs.[3]

Post-Removal Joinder of Non-Diverse Defendants

After a case has been removed, the plaintiff may seek to join additional defendants whose presence would destroy the court's subject-matter jurisdiction. In that situation, the court has two options: it may deny the joinder or it may grant the joinder and then remand the lawsuit back to state court.[4] It may not allow the joinder and keep the case in federal court.[5] Factors the district court may weigh include whether the joinder's purpose was to defeat federal jurisdiction, whether the movant has been dilatory in seeking the joinder, whether significant prejudice would follow from denying the joinder, and other case-specific considerations.[6]

Post-Removal Retrieval of the State Court Case Record

The district court is authorized to obtain all the court records of a removed case either by requiring the removing party to provide copies or by issuing a writ of certiorari to the State

[1]*See* 28 U.S.C.A. § 1447(a); *Richards v. Harper*, 864 F.2d 85, 87 (9th Cir. 1988).

[2]*See* 28 U.S.C.A. § 1448; *Murphy Bros. v. Michetti Pipe Stringing*, 526 U.S. 344, 355 n.6 (1999).

[3]*See* 28 U.S.C.A. § 1448; *Lewis v. Rego Co.*, 757 F.2d 66, 69 n.3 (3d Cir. 1985).

[4]*See* 28 U.S.C.A. § 1447(e); *DeMartini v. DeMartini*, 964 F.3d 813, 818 (9th Cir. 2020).

[5]*Cobb v. Delta Exports, Inc.*, 186 F.3d 675, 677 (5th Cir. 1999).

[6]*Hensgens v. Deere & Co.*, 833 F.2d 1179, 1182 (5th Cir. 1987).

court to retrieve the records directly.[7] If the district court orders the removing party to provide the record, that party's failure to comply may permit the federal court to remand the case back to State court.[8] If the State court fails to supply the record following a proper request and payment or tender of proper fees, the district court is authorized to re-create the record "by affidavit or otherwise."[9]

Remand—Generally

Removal occurs immediately (as explained above); it requires no motion or court order, and takes effect upon the filing of the notice of removal.[10] A litigant who believes the removal to be improper must file a motion asking the federal district judge to return the lawsuit to state court by a process known as "remand."[11] Removal is improper (and remand is necessary) if federal subject-matter jurisdiction does not exist over the removed case.[12] Remand also may be required if the procedural requirements for removal were not followed,[13] although such procedural defects may be waived if not properly raised.[14]

Remand—Procedure

A party seeks remand by filing a motion to remand[15] (in contrast to removal, which is accomplished by filing a notice of removal which does not require the judge's approval). The timing for a motion to remand depends on the basis for the request, as explained below.

Remand—On Jurisdictional Grounds

Subject-matter jurisdiction defects cannot be consented to or waived.[16] If federal subject-matter jurisdiction is absent, the removed lawsuit *must* be remanded back to state court.[17] A motion for remand on this basis may be made at any time prior to

---

[7]*See* 28 U.S.C.A. § 1447(b); *Usatorres v. Marina Mercante Nicaraguenses, S.A.*, 768 F.2d 1285, 1287 (11th Cir. 1985).

[8]*See, e.g.*, *Patel v. Moore*, 968 F. Supp. 587, 591 (D. Kan. 1997).

[9]*See* 28 U.S.C.A. § 1449; *Jones v. 24 Hour Fitness USA Inc.*, 2020 WL 1429742, at *3 (S.D. Tex. 2020).

[10]*See* 28 U.S.C.A. § 1446(a); *BP P.L.C. v. Mayor & City Council of Baltimore*, 141 S. Ct. 1532, 1538 (2021).

[11]28 U.S.C.A. § 1447(c); *Powerex Corp. v. Reliant Energy Servs., Inc.*, 551 U.S. 224, 229 (2007).

[12]*Int'l Primate Prot. League v. Administrators of Tulane Educ. Fund*, 500 U.S. 72, 87 (1991); *Ladies Meml. Assn., Inc. v. City of Pensacola, Fla.*, 34 F.4th 988, 993 (11th Cir. 2022).

[13]*City of Yorkville v. Am. S. Ins. Co.*, 654 F.3d 713, 716 (7th Cir. 2011).

[14]*See, e.g.*, *Holbein v. TAW Enterprises, Inc.*, 983 F.3d 1049, 1053 (8th Cir. 2020); *Vasquez v. North County Transit Dist.*, 292 F.3d 1049, 1060 n.5 (9th Cir. 2002).

[15]*See* 28 U.S.C.A. § 1447(c); *Home Depot U. S. A., Inc. v. Jackson*, 139 S. Ct. 1743, 1747 (2019).

[16]*See, e.g.*, *Gonzalez v. Thaler*, 565 U.S. 134, 141 (2012); *Nuevos Destinos, LLC v. Peck*, 999 F.3d 641, 646 (8th Cir. 2021).

[17]*See* 28 U.S.C.A. § 1447(c); *Int'l Primate Prot. League v. Administrators of Tulane Educ. Fund*, 500 U.S. 72, 87 (1991).

final judgment in the case.[18]

- *Remand* Sua Sponte: If the federal district court notices its lack of subject-matter jurisdiction, the court must remand the case on its own initiative.[19] Such action must be taken any time the court notices its lack of subject-matter jurisdiction (up until final judgment).[20]
- *Timing for Jurisdictional Determination:* In general, remand is mandatory if subject-matter jurisdiction was lacking at the time of removal, even if subsequent actions would have conferred subject-matter jurisdiction on the district court had the case been filed then.[21] There is, however, a narrow exception to this rule that occurs when a jurisdictional defect has been cured after removal and the case has been tried in federal court. In such circumstances, the Supreme Court has refused to "wipe out the adjudication postjudgment" so long as there was jurisdiction when the district court entered judgment.[22]

Remand—On Procedural Grounds

When removal is defective for procedural reasons (such as, for example, failure to remove in a timely manner or to have the consent of all defendants), the district court will also remand back to state court—provided a motion for remand is made within 30 days after the filing of the notice of removal.[23]

- *No Remand* Sua Sponte: If the basis for remand is a procedural defect, *sua sponte* remands are improper.[24]
- *Violation of the "Forum-Defendant" Rule:* In diversity cases, the forum-defendant rule prohibits removal when a properly served defendant is a citizen of the State where the lawsuit is then pending.[25] Courts treat removal that violates this forum-defendant bar as a non-jurisdictional defect (which must be raised within 30 days of removal).[26]

---

[18] *See* 28 U.S.C.A. § 1447(c); *Wisconsin Dept. of Corrections v. Schacht*, 524 U.S. 381, 392 (1998); *Hammer v. United States*, 989 F.3d 1, 2 (D.C. Cir. 2021).

[19] *See* 28 U.S.C.A. § 1447(c); *Wis. Dep't of Corr. v. Schacht*, 524 U.S. 381, 389 (1998).

[20] *See Wis. Dep't of Corr. v. Schacht*, 524 U.S. 381, 392 (1998).

[21] *City of Oakland v. BP PLC*, 969 F.3d 895, 909 (9th Cir. 2020).

[22] *Caterpillar Inc. v. Lewis*, 519 U.S. 61, 77 (1996).

[23] *See* 28 U.S.C.A. § 1447(c); *Holbein v. TAW Enterprises, Inc.*, 983 F.3d 1049, 1057 (8th Cir. 2020); *City of Yorkville v. Am. S. Ins. Co.*, 654 F.3d 713, 716 (7th Cir. 2011).

[24] *See, e.g.*, *In re FMC Corp. Packaging Sys. Div.*, 208 F.3d 445, 451 (3d Cir. 2000).

[25] *See* 28 U.S.C.A. § 1441(b)(2); *Gibbons v. Bristol-Myers Squibb Co.*, 919 F.3d 699, 704–05 (2d Cir. 2019).

[26] *See Holbein v. TAW Enterprises, Inc.*, 983 F.3d 1049, 1053 (8th Cir. 2020); *Lively v. Wild Oats Markets, Inc.*, 456 F.3d 933, 940–41 (9th Cir. 2006).

Remand—On Other Grounds

Other grounds justifying remand—ones falling outside this jurisdictional/procedural classification—may exist, such as asking the district court to exercise its discretion to abstain from deciding the dispute.[27] The courts generally hold that such remands need not be sought within the 30-day period following removal.[28]

Burden of Proof, and Resolving Doubts

The burden of proving that removal was appropriate falls on the party who removed the case.[29] Removal statutes are construed strictly,[30] and doubts are usually resolved in favor of remand.[31]

Remanding in Part

Partial remands are required when a lawsuit removed on the basis of federal question jurisdiction also includes nonremovable claims—claims over which the court has no subject-matter jurisdiction.[32] In such instances the district court must sever the claims lacking subject-matter jurisdiction and remand them back to state court.[33] There is no parallel statutory provision addressing removal and remand of a case that contains one claim with diversity jurisdiction and one claim with no form of federal subject-matter jurisdiction.[34] In such circumstances, though, the federal court would not be authorized to exercise jurisdiction over the claim with no form of federal subject-matter jurisdiction and could either remand or dismiss that claim.[35]

Remand Only, No Dismissals

A district court only has authority to remand a case that has been removed improperly; it usually has no authority to dismiss

[27] *See Quackenbush v. Allstate Ins. Co.*, 517 U.S. 706, 712 (1996); *Grace Ranch, L.L.C. v. BP Am. Prod. Co.*, 989 F.3d 301, 311 (5th Cir. 2021).

[28] *See, e.g., Grace Ranch, L.L.C. v. BP Am. Prod. Co.*, 989 F.3d 301, 312 (5th Cir. 2021); *Eastus v. Blue Bell Creameries, L.P.*, 97 F.3d 100, 103 (5th Cir. 1996).

[29] *Rose v. RTN Fed. Credit Union*, 1 F.4th 56, 61 (1st Cir. 2021); *African Methodist Episcopal Church v. Lucien*, 756 F.3d 788, 793 (5th Cir. 2014).

[30] *Ticer v. Imperium Ins. Co.*, 20 F.4th 1040, 1045 (5th Cir. 2021); *Bowling v. U.S. Bank Nat'l Ass'n, As Tr. for C-Bass Mortg. Loan Asset-Backed Certificates, Series 2007–SP2*, 963 F.3d 1030, 1033 (11th Cir. 2020).

[31] *See, e.g., Halsey v. Townsend Corp. of Indiana*, 20 F.4th 1222, 1226 (8th Cir. 2021); *Valencia v. Allstate Texas Lloyd's*, 976 F.3d 593, 595 (5th Cir. 2020).

[32] 28 U.S.C.A. § 1441(c)(2); 28 U.S.C.A. § 1441(c); *Wis. Dep't of Corr. v. Schacht*, 524 U.S. 381, 392 (1998).

[33] 28 U.S.C.A. § 1441(c)(2); *S J Associated Pathologists, P.L.L.C. v. Cigna Healthcare of Texas, Inc.*, 964 F.3d 369, 374 (5th Cir. 2020); *Prolite Bldg. Supply, LLC v. MW Manufacturers, Inc.*, 891 F.3d 256, 259 (7th Cir. 2018).

[34] *Prolite Bldg. Supply, LLC v. MW Manufacturers, Inc.*, 891 F.3d 256, 259 (7th Cir. 2018).

[35] *See Prolite Bldg. Supply, LLC v. MW Manufacturers, Inc.*, 891 F.3d 256, 259 (7th Cir. 2018).

such a case.[36]

Discretion to Impose Costs and Fees Following Remand

When remanding a case back to State court, the district court has the discretion to impose costs and actual expenses, including attorney's fees, incurred as a result of the removal.[37] Fees will generally be awarded when the removing party lacked an objectively reasonable basis for removal.[38] The power to consider a motion for costs and fees continues even if the underlying case has already been remanded to State court.[39]

Remand Logistics

When the district court remands a case, the federal clerk of court will send a certified copy of the remand order to the clerk of the relevant State court.[40] Jurisdiction remains with the district court until that mailing occurs.[41] However, once it occurs, that mailing divests the federal district court of its jurisdiction over the case (other than for limited ancillary functions like awarding costs and fees, as discussed above).[42] If remand is based on a lack of federal subject-matter jurisdiction, the courts are divided as to whether remand becomes effective at the time the order is entered or at the time the order is mailed.[43] Once remand is effective, jurisdiction re-vests in the State court.[44]

Remand—No Appeal or Reconsideration of Most Remand Orders

Subject to a few exceptions, an order by the federal court remanding a lawsuit back to state court for either lack of subject-matter jurisdiction or a procedural defect is not reviewable.[45] This prohibition was designed to reduce the mischief caused by lawsuits ricocheting back and forth between two different court systems.[46] Instead, Congress prescribed that most remand orders are to be made by the district courts and,

---

[36] *Int'l Primate Protection League v. Administrators of Tulane Educ'l Fund*, 500 U.S. 72, 89 (1991); *Hudson Sav. Bank v. Austin*, 479 F.3d 102, 108–09 (1st Cir. 2007).

[37] *See* 28 U.S.C.A. § 1447(c); *Martin v. Franklin Capital Corp.*, 546 U.S. 132, 141 (2005).

[38] *Martin v. Franklin Capital Corp.*, 546 U.S. 132, 141 (2005); *MSP Recovery Claims, Series LLC v. Hanover Ins. Co.*, 995 F.3d 1289, 1296 (11th Cir. 2021).

[39] *Bryant v. Britt*, 420 F.3d 161, 162 (2d Cir. 2005).

[40] *See* 28 U.S.C.A. § 1447(c); *Ball v. City of Indianapolis*, 760 F.3d 636, 640 (7th Cir. 2014).

[41] *Agostini v. Piper Aircraft Corp.*, 729 F.3d 350, 356 (3d Cir. 2013).

[42] *Shapiro v. Logistec USA, Inc.*, 412 F.3d 307, 312 (2d Cir. 2005).

[43] *Compare Bryan v. BellSouth Commc'ns, Inc.*, 492 F.3d 231, 235 n.1 (4th Cir. 2007) (effective immediately) with *Agostini v. Piper Aircraft Corp.*, 729 F.3d 350, 355 (3d Cir. 2013) (effective on mailing), and *Arnold v. Garlock, Inc.*, 278 F.3d 426, 437 (5th Cir. 2001) (same).

[44] *See Arnold v. Garlock, Inc.*, 278 F.3d 426, 438 (5th Cir. 2001).

[45] 28 U.S.C.A. § 1447(d); *Kircher v. Putnam Funds Trust*, 547 U.S. 633, 640 (2006); *Simring v. GreenSky, LLC*, 29 F.4th 1262, 1265 (11th Cir. 2022).

[46] *Powerex Corp. v. Reliant Energy Servs.*, 551 U.S. 224, 237 (2007); *Thomas v. Phoebe Putney Health Sys., Inc*, 972 F.3d 1195, 1201 (11th Cir. 2020).

once made, are final and conclusive.[47] This prohibition is broad—no review is allowed by direct appeal,[48] by writ of mandamus,[49] or even by reconsideration by the issuing trial judges themselves.[50] Review is barred even when the order of remand is "manifestly, inarguably erroneous."[51] This bar may also prevent a second effort at removal by the same parties on similar grounds.[52]

- Notwithstanding the sweeping, seemingly absolutist language of this no-review prohibition, there are exceptions. Some of the most important of these exceptions are:
  - *Denials of Remand:* Only a decision to *grant* remand falls within the prohibition. Orders that deny remand are reviewable on appeal.[53]
  - *Statutory Exceptions:* Congress has enacted two statutory exceptions to its no-review prohibition: remand of removed civil or criminal actions against the United States or its officers or agencies as provided in 28 U.S.C.A. § 1442;[54] and remand of removed civil rights cases as provided in 28 U.S.C.A. § 1443.[55] If a removing defendant asserts removal in part under either of these statutes and the district court remands the case, the entire remand order is reviewable on appeal.[56]
  - *Remand Based on Grounds Other than Subject-Matter Jurisdiction or Timely-Raised Procedural Defect*: When the ground for remand is something other than lack of subject-matter jurisdiction or a timely-raised defect in removal procedure, review of the remand decision may be possible either in the district court that granted it or upon appellate review.[57] Examples of such reviewable grounds for remand include: a remand based on either a motion of a party or the court's own motion that asserts a procedural defect, but does so

[47]*See Ex parte Pa. Co.*, 137 U.S. 451, 454 (1890).

[48]*Kircher v. Putnam Funds Trust*, 547 U.S. 633, 640 (2006).

[49]*Gravitt v. Sw. Bell Tel. Co.*, 430 U.S. 723, 723 (1977).

[50]*Shapiro v. Logistec USA, Inc.*, 412 F.3d 307, 312 (2d Cir. 2005).

[51]*See In re Norfolk Southern Rwy. Co.*, 756 F.3d 282, 287 (4th Cir. 2014).

[52]*See, e.g.*, *Hunt v. Acromed Corp.*, 961 F.2d 1079, 1081–82 (3d Cir. 1992).

[53]*Geruschat v. Ernst Young LLP (In re Seven Fields Dev. Corp.)*, 505 F.3d 237, 245 (3d Cir. 2007).

[54]*See* 28 U.S.C.A. § 1447(d); *Ruppel v. CBS Corp.*, 701 F.3d 1176, 1179 (7th Cir. 2012).

[55]*See* 28 U.S.C.A. § 1447(d); *Kircher v. Putnam Funds Trust*, 547 U.S. 633, 640 n.7 (2006)

[56]*BP P.L.C. v. Mayor & City Council of Baltimore*, 141 S. Ct. 1532, 1538, 209 (2021).

[57]*Quackenbush v. Allstate Ins. Co.*, 517 U.S. 706, 712 (1996).

more than 30 days after removal;[58] a *sua sponte* remand by the district court based only on a procedural defect in removal (not a defect in subject-matter jurisdiction);[59] a remand based on the discretionary authority of the Declaratory Judgment Act;[60] a remand issued by a magistrate judge;[61] a remand based on the district court's authority under 28 U.S.C.A. § 1441(c) to sever and remand claims over which the court lacks subject-matter jurisdiction;[62] a discretionary remand of claims within a district court's supplemental jurisdiction under 28 U.S.C.A. § 1367(c);[63] a remand based on defendants' waiver of their arbitration rights;[64] a remand issued after the district judge erroneously refused to recuse;[65] a remand granted as enforcement of a forum selection clause;[66] an erroneous holding that multiple efforts to remove were barred even where changed circumstances demonstrate that subject-matter jurisdiction has become satisfied;[67] and a district court's decision to abstain from deciding state law questions.[68]

○ *Orders Following Joinder of Non-Diverse Parties:* If a plaintiff seeks to add a non-diverse defendant after removal, the court has the option to allow the joinder and remand the case or disallow the joinder and retain the case. A remand following the joinder of a non-diverse party is considered a jurisdictional ruling and, thus, is non-reviewable.[69] Conversely, if the court decides not

[58]*See, e.g.*, *Mitskovski v. Buffalo & Fort Erie Pub. Bridge Auth.*, 435 F.3d 127, 131–32 (2d Cir. 2006).

[59]*See, e.g.*, *Whole Health Chiropractic & Wellness, Inc. v. Humana Med. Plan, Inc.*, 254 F.3d 1317, 1319 (11th Cir. 2001).

[60]*See, e.g.*, *Snodgrass v. Provident Life & Accident Ins. Co.*, 147 F.3d 1163, 1165 (9th Cir. 1998).

[61]*See, e.g.*, *Vogel v. United States Office Prods. Co.*, 258 F.3d 509, 517–18 (6th Cir. 2001).

[62]*See, e.g.*, *Eastus v. Blue Bell Creameries, L.P.*, 97 F.3d 100, 103 (5th Cir. 1996).

[63]*See, e.g.*, *Carlsbad Tech., Inc. v. HIF Bio, Inc.*, 556 U.S. 635, 640–41 (2009).

[64]*See, e.g.*, *Restoration Pres. Masonry Inc. v. Grove Eur. Ltd.*, 325 F.3d 54, 59 (1st Cir. 2003).

[65]*See, e.g.*, *Republic of Pan. v. Am. Tobacco Co.*, 217 F.3d 343, 345–46 (5th Cir. 2000).

[66]*See, e.g.*, *Yakin v. Tyler Hill Corp.*, 566 F.3d 72, 75 (2d Cir. 2009).

[67]*See, e.g.*, *Benson v. SI Handling Sys., Inc.*, 188 F.3d 780, 783 (7th Cir. 1999).

[68]*See, e.g.*, *Quackenbush v. Allstate Ins. Co.*, 517 U.S. 706, 712 (1996); *City of Fishers, Indiana v. DIRECTV*, 5 F.4th 750, 752 (7th Cir. 2021).

[69]*Powerex Corp. v. Reliant Energy Servs., Inc.*, 551 U.S. 224, 231–32 (2007).

to remand the case, that decision is reviewable.[70]

- ○ *Remands in Class Actions:* A court of appeals has discretion to accept an appeal of a district court's decisions granting or denying remand in class actions.[71] Such appeals must be made within 10 days of entry of the original order.[72]
- ○ *Review of Reviewability*: A court retains the authority to examine whether the basis for remand falls within a non-reviewable category (namely, lack of subject-matter jurisdiction or a timely-raised defect in removal procedure).[73]
- ○ *Review of Fee Awards:* An appeals court may review an award of costs and fees under § 1447(c).[74] In doing so, it may consider the "objective merits" of the remand order to determine the appropriateness of the award (in other words, review of the merits of remand in connection with the fee award does not violate the prohibition on review of remand orders).[75]

---

[70] *See Ingram v. CSX Transp.*, 146 F.3d 858, 863 (11th Cir. 1998).

[71] *See* 28 U.S.C.A. § 1435(c)(1); *Dart Cherokee Basin Operating Co., LLC v. Owens*, 574 U.S. 81, 90 (2014).

[72] *See* 28 U.S.C.A. § 1453(c)(1); *Cutrone v. Mortg. Elec. Registration Sys.*, 749 F.3d 137, 142 (2d Cir. 2014).

[73] *See, e.g., Adkins v. Ill. Cent. R.R. Co.*, 326 F.3d 828, 831 (7th Cir. 2003) (conducting a detailed analysis of whether the court had jurisdiction before concluding it did not).

[74] *See* 28 U.S.C.A. § 1447(c); *MSP Recovery Claims, Series LLC v. Hanover Ins. Co.*, 995 F.3d 1289, 1296 (11th Cir. 2021); *Roxbury Condo. Ass'n v. Anthony S. Cupo Agency*, 316 F.3d 224, 227 (3d Cir. 2003).

[75] *See, e.g., Dahl v. Rosenfeld*, 316 F.3d 1074, 1079 (9th Cir. 2003).

E. VENUE AND *FORUM NON CONVENIENS*

Table of Sections

2.17 Venue
2.17a Venue Transfer and *Forum Non Conveniens*

§ 2.17 Venue

CORE CONCEPT

Venue identifies those federal districts where a plaintiff can sue on a particular claim, based on what Congress deems to be a fair connection between the forum and either the parties or the events in question. Venue requirements are distinct from, and in addition to, subject-matter and personal jurisdictional prerequisites. Thus, it is possible that a federal district court might have personal jurisdiction over a defendant, but the action could still be dismissed for failure to meet venue requirements. For example, a defendant might be served with process within the State where the federal court sits (which would normally satisfy "tag" personal jurisdiction), yet venue might be improper there.

- *Federal "Districts"*: The personal jurisdiction analysis considers whether litigation may proceed within the *State* where the action is pending. In contrast, venue examines whether litigation may proceed in the federal judicial *district* where the action is pending. Districts are established by Congress. In less populous states such as Rhode Island, the entire state may be a single district; more populous states are often divided into from two to four different districts (New York, for example, is divided into the Eastern, Western, Southern, and Northern Districts).
- *Federal "Divisions"*: Sometimes, a federal judicial district will be further divided into smaller geographic areas, called "divisions." For example, the United States District Court for the Eastern District of Virginia is subdivided into four "divisions": the Alexandria Division; the Norfolk Division; the Richmond Division; and the Newport News Division. Local rules of a federal district court might supplement venue statutes by requiring that a case be filed not only in the judicial district with proper venue, but also within the appropriate "division" within that district.[1]

---

[1] *See, e.g., Esurance Ins. Co. v. Hamm*, 387 F. Supp. 3d 1134, 1137 (D. Or. 2019); *Garus v. Rose Acre Farms, Inc.*, 839 F. Supp. 563, 566 n.2 (N.D.

APPLICATIONS

General Venue Options

Congress's general venue statute, Section 1391(b), creates two options for satisfying venue in most cases, plus a third option that may be used if neither of the first two options is available. Keep that limitation in mind: this statute does not ordinarily provide three choices, only two—the third is reserved for only those rare cases where the first two options cannot be used to establish a venue anywhere in the United States.

- *Residence-Based Venue*: If all defendants in the case reside in the same State, then venue lies in any judicial district where any defendant resides.[2] (The meaning of "resides" for venue purposes is discussed below.)
- *Occurrence-Based Venue*: Venue lies in any judicial district in which a substantial part of the events or omissions giving rise to the claim occurred (*e.g.*, in a tort case, where the damage occurred or the wrongful act was done),[3] or where a substantial part of the property that is the subject of the action is found. The analysis of whether events or omissions are "substantial" is qualitative, examining whether there is a "close nexus" between the acts or omissions and the claims.[4] The focus of the occurrence inquiry is on the defendant's activities, not the plaintiff's.[5]
- *Where Any Defendant Is Subject to Personal Jurisdiction*: If, and only if, neither of the above two venue options is available, venue will lie in any judicial district in which any defendant is subject to personal jurisdiction at the time a suit is filed.[6] Because venue lies in any district where a substantial part of the events or omissions occurred, this third catch-all venue provision will only apply when the events that are the subject of the litigation occurred outside the United States.

Defining "Resides"

To apply residence-based venue, Congress had to define "resides" for venue purposes, which it did in 28 U.S.C.A.

Ind. 1993).

[2]*See, e.g., Dr. Robert L. Meinders, D.C., Ltd. v. United Healthcare Servs., Inc.*, 7 F.4th 555, 560 n.6 (7th Cir. 2021); *Courthouse News Serv. v. Schaefer*, 2 F.4th 318, 325 n.3 (4th Cir. 2021).

[3]*See, e.g., Dr. Robert L. Meinders, D.C., Ltd. v. United Healthcare Servs., Inc.*, 7 F.4th 555, 560 n.6 (7th Cir. 2021); *Trois v. Apple Tree Auction Ctr., Inc.*, 882 F.3d 485, 493–94 (5th Cir. 2018).

[4]*Daniel v. Am. Bd. of Emergency Med.*, 428 F.3d 408, 432–34 (2d Cir. 2005).

[5]*See, e.g., Jenkins Brick Co. v. Bremer*, 321 F.3d 1366, 1371–72 (11th Cir. 2003). *But cf., Steen v. Murray*, 770 F.3d 698, 703 (8th Cir. 2014) (a secondary factor can be the effect of the defendant's activities on the plaintiff in the forum.).

[6]*Algodonera De Las Cabezas, S.A. v. American Suisse Capital, Inc.*, 432 F.3d 1343, 1345 (11th Cir. 2005).

§ 1391(c):

- *Residence for Natural Persons*: A natural person's residence is deemed to be the judicial district in which that person is domiciled.[7] A person's domicile is that person's "true, fixed, and permanent home," where the person intends to reside indefinitely, and to where the person intends to return.[8] Typically, a natural person has only one domicile (and thus, for venue purposes, only one residence), notwithstanding that the person in question may actually have homes in several different States.[9] This definition of residence applies to citizens as well as non-citizens lawfully admitted for permanent residence in the United States.[10]
- *Residence for Entities That May Sue or Be Sued in Their Own Names*: Congress provided two different definitions of "resides" for entities that may sue or be sued in their own names (such as corporations, partnerships, etc.):
  - For entities that are defendants, "resides" means any judicial district in which that entity would be subject to the personal jurisdiction of the federal court.[11] But there is a caveat for some corporations:
  - If the defendant is a corporation subject to personal jurisdiction in a particular State and if that State has more than one federal district, the corporation "resides" in that district where its contacts would subject it to personal jurisdiction (had that district been its own state) or, if none, where the corporation has its most significant contacts.[12]
  - Although venue normally turns on the defendants' residences, in certain circumstances it may depend on the plaintiff's residence. For example, as explained below, venue for a claim against the United States is proper in a district where any plaintiff resides. For entities that are plaintiffs, "resides" means the judicial district encompassing the plaintiff's principal place of business.[13]
- *Defendants Not Resident in the United States*: Defen-

---

[7]*See* 28 U.S.C.A. § 1391(c)(1).

[8]*See Vlandis v. Kline*, 412 U.S. 441, 454 (1973).

[9]*See Van Buskirk v. United Grp. of Companies, Inc.*, 935 F.3d 49, 53 (2d Cir. 2019).

[10]28 U.S.C.A. § 1391(c)(1); *In re HTC Corp.*, 889 F.3d 1349, 1359 (Fed. Cir. 2018).

[11]*See* 28 U.S.C.A. § 1391(a) to (c)(2); *TC Heartland LLC v. Kraft Foods Grp. Brands LLC*, 137 S. Ct. 1514, 1517 (2017).

[12]*See* 28 U.S.C.A. § 1391(d); *Jack Henry & Assocs., Inc. v. Plano Encryption Techs. LLC*, 910 F.3d 1199, 1202–06 (Fed. Cir. 2018).

[13]28 U.S.C.A. § 1391(c)(2); *California v. Azar*, 911 F.3d 558, 569 (9th Cir. 2018).

dants not resident in the United States may be sued in any judicial district.[14] Further, if such non-resident defendants are co-defendants with parties who are resident in the United States, only the residence of the United States-based defendants is taken into account in determining the appropriateness of venue.[15] These rules apply to all non-resident defendants, including both non-U.S. citizens and U.S. citizens whose residence is outside the United States.[16]

- *Residence of a State*: If a State is a party, the State has residence for venue purposes in all federal districts within the State.[17]

Specific Statutory Venue Provisions

Some statutory schemes include venue provisions, such as the patent venue statute, 28 U.S.C.A. § 1400(b). In such cases, only the specific statutory provision will apply; the general venue provisions in § 1391 will not be available.[18]

Subject-Matter Jurisdiction, Personal Jurisdiction, and Venue

Subject-matter jurisdiction, personal jurisdiction, and venue are three separate prerequisites for bringing a lawsuit in a federal district court. To proceed in federal court, a plaintiff must satisfy all three of these requirements—satisfying one does not relieve a plaintiff of the obligation to satisfy the others.[19]

Venue Must be Proper for Each Claim in the Complaint

A plaintiff must satisfy venue for each claim in the case.[20] Since residence-based venue only depends on the residences of all of the defendants, it will generally apply or not uniformly as to all claims in the case. In contrast, because occurrence-based venue depends on the location of a substantial portion of the events or omissions in question, the availability of occurrence-based venue in a given district will depend on whether the underlying events occurred in that district, and thus might readily vary from claim to claim. Similar to supplemental jurisdiction, the doctrine of pendent venue may be used to join state-law claims with federal claims.[21]

---

[14] See 28 U.S.C.A. § 1391(c)(3).

[15] 28 U.S.C.A. § 1391(c)(3).

[16] H.R. REP. 112-10, 22, 2011 U.S.C.C.A.N. 576, 580. *See also, e.g., In re HTC Corp.*, 889 F.3d 1349, 1359–60 (Fed. Cir. 2018).

[17] *See, e.g., California v. Azar*, 911 F.3d 558, 569–70 (9th Cir. 2018).

[18] *TC Heartland LLC v. Kraft Foods Grp. Brands LLC*, 137 S. Ct. 1514, 1517 (2017).

[19] *See* 28 U.S.C.A. § 1390(a).

[20] *In re Samsung Elecs. Co., Ltd.*, 2 F.4th 1371, 1377 (Fed. Cir. 2021); *Lamont v. Haig*, 590 F.2d 1124, 1135 (D.C. Cir. 1978).

[21] *See Bredberg v. Long*, 778 F.2d 1285, 1288 (8th Cir. 1985).

Counterclaims and Crossclaims

Generally speaking, only plaintiffs have the burden of satisfying requirements of venue. Counterclaims, crossclaims, and similar actions normally do not raise venue questions.[22] This approach, then, is quite different from the one that applies in jurisdictional analyses, for which every count in a case, no matter if it is brought by a plaintiff or defendant, must satisfy some form of both personal and subject-matter jurisdiction.

Consent to Venue

Venue, like personal jurisdiction, is a waivable protection for defendants against an inconvenient forum. If parties consent to personal jurisdiction in a particular district or state, they may be deemed to have consented to venue there.[23] Moreover, if the plaintiff files suit in a federal judicial district where venue is improper, the court may still hear that case if the defendant does not object to venue.[24] Rule 12(g) and (h), governing timing and waiver of certain motions to dismiss, identify the time and manner in which a defendant must either raise objections to venue or forgo them.[25]

Venue and Removal

If a claim is removed from a state court to a federal district court, the normal venue analysis does not apply. Instead, venue is proper in the federal district encompassing the place where the state court case was pending at the time of removal.[26] Therefore, a party who prefers a different venue for a case that has been removed should seek transfer to the preferred location (as discussed below).[27] If a party does seek transfer, the federal venue statute does apply to evaluating venue in the transferee court.[28] The courts are divided as to whether a party who removed a claim may assert a challenge to the state court's venue after removal.[29]

Remedy for Improper Venue

If the court, on timely objection of a party, finds venue to be improper, the court may dismiss the action, allowing the plaintiff to refile the claim elsewhere if the action is not

---

[22] *See, e.g., Bredberg v. Long*, 778 F.2d 1285, 1288 (8th Cir. 1985).

[23] *See, e.g., Doctor's Associates, Inc. v. Stuart*, 85 F.3d 975, 983 (2d Cir. 1996).

[24] *See, e.g., Leroy v. Great Western United Corp.*, 443 U.S. 173, 180 (1979); *King v. Russell*, 963 F.2d 1301, 1305 (9th Cir. 1992).

[25] *See* the coverage of Rule 12 below.

[26] *See e.g.*, 28 U.S.C.A. § 1441(a); *Polizzi v. Cowles Magazines, Inc.*, 345 U.S. 663, 665 (1953); *Kerobo v. Sw. Clean Fuels, Corp.*, 285 F.3d 531, 534–35 (6th Cir. 2002).

[27] *See Hollis v. Fla. State Univ.*, 259 F.3d 1295, 1298–1300 (11th Cir. 2001).

[28] 28 U.S.C.A. § 1390(c).

[29] *Compare PT United Can Co. v. Crown Cork & Seal Co.*, 138 F.3d 65, 73 (2d Cir. 1998) (challenge not waived), *with Hollis v. Fla. State Univ.*, 259 F.3d 1295, 1298–1300 (11th Cir. 2001) (no venue challenge for a properly removed case).

otherwise barred.[30] This can raise significant statutes of limitations problems for a plaintiff. To mitigate these problems, Congress allows a federal district court, on finding venue to be faulty, to *transfer* a cause of action to a judicial district or division where the case could have originally been filed.[31] The court's discretion to employ this remedy is broad, constrained only by "the interest of justice." The practical consequence of transfer is that the court need not dismiss the action—which means the plaintiff will not run afoul of statutes of limitations.[32]

Special Venue over the United States, its Agencies, and its Officers

Three venue possibilities are available if the United States, a federal agency, or a federal officer acting in an official capacity is a defendant. Caselaw suggests that these venue options apply only to governmental defendants who are part of the executive branch of the federal government (and not to the legislative or judicial branches).[33] These provisions apply to the governmental defendant only; a separate basis for venue must be found as to other defendants.[34] These three venue possibilities are:

(1) *Residence-Based Venue:* Venue will lie in a judicial district where a single defendant in the action resides.[35] Thus, the United States, its agencies, or its officers can be sued in a judicial district where some other defendant resides.[36] That would be true even if the federal officer, for example, did not reside in that district and did no business there; or

(2) *Occurrence-Based Venue:* Venue will lie in a judicial district where "a substantial part of the events or omissions giving rise to the claim occurred, or a substantial part of property that is the subject of the action is situated;"[37] or

(3) *Plaintiff's Residence:* Venue will lie in a judicial district where any plaintiff resides, provided that the cause of action does not involve real property.[38]

- *Nationwide Personal Jurisdiction Over Federal Agencies and Officers:* To ensure that the broad venue authority of for actions involving the United States is not nullified by problems of personal jurisdiction, § 1391(e) also provides that the federal district court shall be able, by

---

[30]*Polizzi v. Cowles Magazines, Inc.*, 345 U.S. 663 (1953); *Lafferty v. St. Riel*, 495 F.3d 72, 79–81 (3d Cir. 2007).

[31]28 U.S.C.A. § 1406.

[32]*See Atlantic Marine Construction Co. v. U.S. District Court for the Western District of Texas*, 571 U.S. 49, 52 (2013) (court should transfer unless extraordinary circumstances unrelated to convenience disfavor transfer).

[33]*See, e.g., King v. Russell*, 963 F.2d 1301, 1303–04 (9th Cir. 1992).

[34]*See* 28 U.S.C.A. § 1391(e); *King v. Russell*, 963 F.2d 1301, 1303 (9th Cir. 1992).

[35]*See* 28 U.S.C.A. § 1391(e).

[36]*See Montgomery v. Barr*, 502 F. Supp. 3d 165, 174 (D.D.C. 2020).

[37]*See, e.g., A.J. Taft Coal Co. v. Barnhart*, 291 F. Supp. 2d 1290, 1308–09 (N.D. Ala. 2003).

[38]*See, e.g., California v. Azar*, 911 F.3d 558, 569 (9th Cir. 2018).

certified mail, to obtain personal jurisdiction over federal agencies and officers not found within the State in which the court sits.

- *Personal Suits Against Federal Officers*: The venue opportunities provided by § 1391(e) as to federal officers are available only when the officers are sued in their official capacities. If they are sued personally for money damages, § 1391(e) is not applicable.[39] In such circumstances the provisions of § 1391(a) or (b), or some other more specific venue statute, would control.

Special Venue Over Foreign Countries

Section 1391(f) prescribes the venue when foreign countries or their agencies are defendants. Four possibilities for venue exist, depending on whether suit is against the foreign sovereign itself, its agency, or its shipping or cargo. These possibilities are:

(1) *Occurrence-Based Venue:* Venue will lie in a judicial district where a substantial portion of the events giving rise to the claim occurred,[40] or where a substantial part of property that is the subject of the claim is located;

(2) *Location of Vessel or Cargo:* Venue will lie in any judicial district where a vessel or cargo belonging to a foreign state is located. This venue possibility is available only if the claim arose under 28 U.S.C.A. § 1605(b), governing suits in admiralty against foreign states; or

(3) *Location of Agency That is Doing Business:* If the defendant is an agency or instrumentality of the foreign state, as described in 28 U.S.C.A. § 1603(b), venue will lie in any judicial district in which the agency is licensed to do business or is doing business.[41] For a corporation to be deemed an "instrumentality" of a foreign state, the foreign state or a political subdivision must be the majority owner—a privately owned corporation will not be considered an instrumentality;[42] or

(4) *Venue in the District of Columbia:* If the defendant is a foreign state itself or a political subdivision of a foreign state, venue may be satisfied in the United States District Court for the District of Columbia.[43]

Special Venue over Admiralty, Maritime, or Prize Cases

The general venue provisions of § 1391, discussed above, do not extend to cases in federal district court arising under

---

[39] *Stafford v. Briggs*, 444 U.S. 527, 542 (1980).

[40] *See, e.g., U.S. Titan, Inc. v. Guangzhou Zhen Hua Shipping Co., Ltd.*, 241 F.3d 135, 153–54 (2d Cir. 2001).

[41] *See Berg v. Kingdom of Netherlands*, 24 F.4th 987, 996 (4th Cir. 2022).

[42] *See, e.g., Singh ex rel. Singh v. Caribbean Airlines Ltd.*, 798 F.3d 1355, 1358 (11th Cir. 2015).

[43] *See, e.g., Telcordia Tech Inc. v. Telkom SA Ltd.*, 458 F.3d 172, 176 (3d Cir. 2006).

federal admiralty or maritime law.[44]

Local or Transitory Actions

Older law restricted certain causes of action dealing with disputes over land to the district in which the land is located.[45] Current law makes no venue distinction for actions that might previously have been deemed "local" or "transitory" in nature.[46]

§ 2.17a Venue Transfer and *Forum Non Conveniens*

CORE CONCEPT

Sometimes, the court where a case has been filed determines that convenience and other prudential considerations dictate that the case should proceed in a different court. There are three different mechanisms a court may use to achieve this result. Congress has enacted two statutes that allow for transfer of venue. 28 U.S.C.A. § 1404 governs transfer when venue was proper in the original court. 28 U.S.C.A. § 1406 governs transfer when venue was not proper in the original court. And finally, when transfer is not possible (such as when the court concludes that the case should proceed in a different country), the *forum non conveniens* doctrine authorizes the court to dismiss the action, requiring the plaintiff to file a new action in the appropriate forum.

APPLICATIONS

Timing For Venue Transfer/*Forum Non Conveniens*

Usually, a defendant will file a motion to transfer to another federal district or to dismiss under the *forum non conveniens* doctrine early in the litigation, and motions filed after substantial proceedings have occurred are unlikely to succeed.[1] Typically, a court will not rule on *forum non conveniens* until it first determines whether its jurisdiction and venue are proper.[2] But that is not an absolute rule; when a *forum non conveniens* analysis will more certainly and expeditiously resolve the question of the most appropriate forum, a court may bypass jurisdiction questions to do so.[3]

- *Sua Sponte Forum Non Conveniens: Forum non conveniens* is ordinarily raised by a party, not by the court on its own initiative. But, provided the court has afforded

---

[44] 28 U.S.C.A. § 1390(b).

[45] *See Eldee-K Rental Properties, LLC v. DIRECTV, Inc.*, 748 F.3d 943, 949 (9th Cir. 2014).

[46] *See Eldee-K Rental Properties, LLC v. DIRECTV, Inc.*, 748 F.3d 943, 949 (9th Cir. 2014).

[1] *See, e.g., Est. of I.E.H. v. CKE Restaurants, Holdings, Inc.*, 995 F.3d 659, 664–65 (8th Cir. 2021) (motion came after the disclose of discovery was too late); *Shi v. New Mighty U.S. Tr.*, 918 F.3d 944, 948–49 (D.C. Cir. 2019).

[2] *See Gulf Oil Corp. v. Gilbert*, 330 U.S. 501, 504 (1947); *Otto Candies, LLC v. Citigroup, Inc.*, 963 F.3d 1331, 1338 (11th Cir. 2020).

[3] *See Sinochem Int'l Co. v. Malaysia Int'l Shipping Corp.*, 549 U.S. 422, 432 (2007).

notice to all parties and an opportunity to be heard, a *sua sponte forum non conveniens* dismissal can be proper.[4]

Transfers to Another Federal District

When the more convenient, appropriate forum is simply a different federal court, the court may transfer the case to a different federal district court in which the case could have been brought or to which all parties have consented, regardless of whether venue is proper in the original court.[5] Because a transferred case is not dismissed, transfer usually creates no statute of limitations problems.[6] Transfer is the standard remedy in cases where it can be applied.[7]

- *Transfers within the Federal Court System Only*: One federal court may only transfer a case to another federal court.[8] If the more convenient, appropriate forum lies outside the United States, the only remedy available is a *forum non conveniens* dismissal of the action, with an opportunity for the plaintiff to file the claim elsewhere.[9]
- *Transfers by Consent*: Parties may consent to venue in a particular district or State.[10] If parties consent to personal jurisdiction in a particular district or state, they may be deemed to have consented to venue there as well.[11]
- *Partial Transfers*: It is uncertain whether a district court may only transfer an entire case or whether a district court may transfer a portion of a case.[12]
- *No Transfers to Certain Territories*: Transfers are not permitted to the district courts for Guam, the Northern Marianas, or the Virgin Islands.[13]

***Forum Non Conveniens*: Overview**

When the court concludes that the current venue is inconvenient but venue transfer is not possible, *forum non conveniens* authorizes a court to dismiss an action so that the plaintiff can

---

[4]*See Wong v. PartyGaming Ltd.*, 589 F.3d 821, 830 (6th Cir. 2009).

[5]*See Sinochem International Co. v. Malaysia International Shipping Corp.*, 549 U.S. 422, 430 (2007); *In re Samsung Elecs. Co., Ltd.*, 2 F.4th 1371, 1375–76 (Fed. Cir. 2021).

[6]*See Ferens v. John Deere Co.*, 494 U.S. 516, 526 (1990); *Lafferty v. St. Riel*, 495 F.3d 72, 81 (3d Cir. 2007).

[7]*See Sinochem Intern. Co. Ltd. v. Malaysia Intern. Shipping Corp.*, 549 U.S. 422, 430 (2007); *Quackenbush v. Allstate Ins. Co.*, 517 U.S. 706, 722 (1996).

[8]*See Atlantic Marine Const. Co. v. U.S. Dist. Court for W. Dist. of Texas*, 571 U.S. 49, 60 (2013); *Nandjou v. Marriott Int'l, Inc.*, 985 F.3d 135, 140–41 (1st Cir. 2021).

[9]*See Quackenbush v. Allstate Ins. Co.*, 517 U.S. 706, 722 (1996); *Nandjou v. Marriott Int'l, Inc.*, 985 F.3d 135, 141 (1st Cir. 2021).

[10]*See* 28 U.S.C. § 1404(a).

[11]*Doctor's Assocs., Inc. v. Stuart*, 85 F.3d 975, 983 (2d Cir. 1996).

[12]*See, e.g., D'Jamoos v. Pilatus Aircraft, Ltd.*, 566 F.3d 94, 110 (3d Cir. 2009) (collecting authority).

[13]*See* 28 U.S.C. § 1404(d).

refile it in the more appropriate forum.[14] In contrast to venue transfer, *forum non conveniens* is a court-made doctrine, not a creature of statute.[15] Dismissal for *forum non conveniens* is only granted in "exceptional circumstances," and defendants bear a "heavy burden in opposing the plaintiff's chosen forum" under this doctrine.[16]

Forum Non Conveniens: Requirement of an Adequate Alternative Forum

A trial court may not dismiss a case on *forum non conveniens* grounds unless it has determined that an adequate alternative forum exists.[17] The defendant has the burden of demonstrating the availability of such a forum.[18] Even if the plaintiff's choice of forum seems strained, the court will retain the case (assuming no problems with jurisdiction and venue) unless the trial court identifies an available alternative forum.[19]

- *Adequacy of an Alternative Forum:* Evaluating the adequacy of an alternative forum requires a determination as to whether the defendants are subject to service of process in the alternative forum and whether the alternative forum addresses the types of claims the plaintiff has brought.[20] For other American courts, this analysis tends to focus on the existence of personal jurisdiction over the defendant.[21]
- *Foreign Alternative Forums:* A non-American forum is probably not adequate if that forum's laws do not provide an appropriate remedy,[22] or where distinctions in procedural law preclude a reasonable opportunity for the plaintiff to present a case.[23] If the claim would be time-barred in the alternative forum, it will not be

---

[14]*Sinochem Intern. Co. Ltd. v. Malaysia Intern. Shipping Corp.*, 549 U.S. 422, 435 (2007); *American Dredging Co. v. Miller*, 510 U.S. 443, 453 (1994).

[15]*Nandjou v. Marriott Int'l, Inc.*, 985 F.3d 135, 140–41 (1st Cir. 2021); *Sierra Frac Sand, L.L.C. v. CDE Global Limited*, 960 F.3d 200, 203 (5th Cir. 2020).

[16]*Shi v. New Mighty U.S. Tr.*, 918 F.3d 944, 947 (D.C. Cir. 2019).

[17]*Gulf Oil Corp. v. Gilbert*, 330 U.S. 501, 506–07 (1947); *Nandjou v. Marriott Int'l, Inc.*, 985 F.3d 135, 140–41 (1st Cir. 2021); *Galustian v. Peter*, 591 F.3d 724, 731 (4th Cir. 2010) (requirement for *forum non coveniens* dismissal is that alternative forum is available for *all defendants*).

[18]*See, e.g., Curtis v. Galakatos*, 19 F.4th 41, 47 (1st Cir. 2021); *Otto Candies, LLC v. Citigroup, Inc.*, 963 F.3d 1331, 1338 (11th Cir. 2020).

[19]*Piper Aircraft Co. v. Reyno*, 454 U.S. 235, 255 (1981); *Curtis v. Galakatos*, 19 F.4th 41, 48 (1st Cir. 2021).

[20]*See, e.g., Curtis v. Galakatos*, 19 F.4th 41, 47–48 (1st Cir. 2021).

[21]*Piper Aircraft Co. v. Reyno*, 454 U.S. 235, 255 n.22 (1981).

[22]*See, e.g., Instituto Mexicano del Seguro Soc. v. Zimmer Biomet Holdings, Inc.*, 29 F.4th 351, 358 (7th Cir. 2022); *Associacao Brasileira de Medicina de Grupo v. Stryker Corp.*, 891 F.3d 615, 621 (6th Cir. 2018).

[23]*See, e.g., Lacey v. Cessna Aircraft Co.*, 932 F.2d 170, 185 n.12 (3d Cir. 1991). *But see Stroitelstvo Bulgaria Ltd. v. Bulgarian-American Enterprise Fund*, 589 F.3d 417, 484 (7th Cir. 2009) (foreign forum's four percent filing fee does not render that forum inade-

adequate.[24] A foreign court might be deemed inadequate based on evidence of corruption, but the level of corruption must be extreme.[25] The probability that a foreign court will not apply American substantive law is usually not weighed heavily in determining the adequacy of an alternative forum.[26]

- *Waiver of Defenses to Alternative Forum:* A defendant seeking transfer can waive objections or defenses to the proposed new forum, thereby rendering it adequate.[27]

Forum Non Conveniens: Deference to the Plaintiff's Choice of Forum

Normally, the court will give substantial deference to a plaintiff's choice of forum.[28] Thus, for a defendant to prevail on a *forum non conveniens* motion, the defendant must demonstrate that the plaintiff's choice of forum was significantly inappropriate, notwithstanding the existence of satisfactory jurisdiction and venue. This deference means that when the court is weighing the public and private interests discussed below, the plaintiff's choice of forum will not be defeated by a mere preponderance of interests favoring dismissal.[29] In most cases, the *forum non conveniens* motion will not be granted unless the factors discussed below "weigh heavily in favor of trial in the alternative forum."[30]

- *Exception—Defendant Seeks to Enforce Valid Forum Selection Clause:* If a defendant asserts a valid forum selection clause in opposition to a plaintiff's choice of forum, the plaintiff's choice of forum is not entitled to

---

quate); *Alpha Therapeutic Corp. v. Nippon Hoso Kyokai*, 199 F.3d 1078, 1090 (9th Cir. 1999) (fact that Japan's civil procedure rules "are not friendly to plaintiffs" did not render it an inadequate forum); *Alfadda v. Fenn*, 159 F.3d 41, 48 (2d Cir. 1998) (inability of plaintiff to use materials obtained through U.S. discovery in a French court is a relevant factor, but not necessarily dispositive).

[24] *Chang v. Baxter Healthcare Corp.*, 599 F.3d 728, 736 (7th Cir. 2010).

[25] *See, e.g., Jones v. IPX Int'l Equatorial Guinea, S.A.*, 920 F.3d 1085, 1091 (6th Cir. 2019); *In re Arbitration between Monegasque de Reassurances, S.A.M. v. Nak Naftogaz of Ukraine*, 311 F.3d 488, 489 (2d Cir. 2002).

[26] *See, e.g., Piper Aircraft Co. v. Reyno*, 454 U.S. 235, 247 (1981); *Lewis v. Liberty Mut. Ins. Co.*, 953 F.3d 1160, 1168–69 (9th Cir. 2020).

[27] *See, e.g., Curtis v. Galakatos*, 19 F.4th 41, 46 (1st Cir. 2021); *Lewis v. Liberty Mut. Ins. Co.*, 953 F.3d 1160, 1168–69 (9th Cir. 2020); *Shi v. New Mighty U.S. Tr.*, 918 F.3d 944, 950 (D.C. Cir. 2019).

[28] *Koster v. (American) Lumbermens Mut. Cas. Co.*, 330 U.S. 518, 524 (1947); *Gulf Oil Corp. v. Gilbert*, 330 U.S. 501, 508 (1947); *Glob. Commodities Trading Grp., Inc. v. Beneficio de Arroz Choloma, S.A.*, 972 F.3d 1101, 1112 (9th Cir. 2020).

[29] *Cf., Atlantic Marine Construction Co. v. U.S. District Court for the Western District of Texas*, 571 U.S. 49 (2013); *Nandjou v. Marriott Int'l, Inc.*, 85 F.3d 135, 141–42 (1st Cir. 2021).

[30] *Sinochem Int'l Co. v. Malaysia Int'l Shipping Corp.*, 549 U.S. 422, 430 (2007).

any weight.[31]

- *Exception—Plaintiff Does Not Reside in District:* If the plaintiff does not reside in the judicial district where the case was filed, the plaintiff's choice of forum receives less deference.[32]
- *Exception—Non-American Plaintiffs:* American plaintiffs receive substantially more deference in their forum choices than do non-American plaintiffs.[33] However, less deference is not the same as no deference at all, and a foreign plaintiff's choice of forum is still entitled to some respect.[34] Additionally, a foreign plaintiff may be entitled to somewhat greater deference if it can establish that the selected forum is highly convenient.[35]
- *Exception—Certain Declaratory Judgment Plaintiffs:* If the plaintiff who has chosen the forum has sought relief in the form of a declaratory judgment, with a "bad faith" motive of taking advantage of the true plaintiff in a race to the forum, the declaratory judgment plaintiff's choice of forum is not entitled any deference.[36]
- *Exception—Plaintiff is Forum Shopping:* A plaintiff who improperly forum shops (as opposed to merely selecting the most advantageous forum) is entitled to less deference in the initial choice of forum.[37]
- *Exception—Identical Suits in Different Venues:* If an unusual case involves identical lawsuits that were filed in different venues, there is no deference to either plaintiff's choice of forum.[38]

Forum Non Conveinens: Judicial Discretion in Weighing Factors

Once a trial court has identified an adequate alternative forum where the case could be brought, it is authorized to

---

[31] *Atlantic Marine Construction Co. v. U.S. District Court for the Western District of Texas*, 571 U.S. 49, 63–64 (2013); *Turner v. Costa Crociere S.p.A.*, 9 F.4th 1341, 1347–48 (11th Cir. 2021); *D & S Consulting, Inc. v. Kingdom of Saudi Arabia*, 961 F.3d 1209, 1212–13 (D.C. Cir. 2020).

[32] *See, e.g., Ayco Farms, Inc. v. Ochoa*, 862 F.3d 945, 950 (9th Cir. 2017).

[33] *Piper Aircraft Co. v. Reyno*, 454 U.S. 235, 256 (1981); *Instituto Mexicano del Seguro Soc. v. Stryker Corp.*, 28 F.4th 732, 737 (6th Cir. 2022); *Shi v. New Mighty U.S. Tr.*, 918 F.3d 944, 949 (D.C. Cir. 2019). *See also Pollux Holding Ltd. v. Chase Manhattan Bank*, 329 F.3d 64, 73 (2d Cir. 2003) (reduced deference even when treaty provides court access to foreign plaintiffs).

[34] *See, e.g., Aenergy, S.A. v. Republic of Angola*, 31 F.4th 119, 132 (2d Cir. 2022); *Lacey v. Cessna Aircraft Co.*, 862 F.2d 38, 45–46 (3d Cir. 1988).

[35] *See, e.g., Lony v. E.I. Du Pont de Nemours & Co.*, 886 F.2d 628, 634 (3d Cir. 1989).

[36] *See, e.g., Hyatt Intern. Corp. v. Coco*, 302 F.3d 707, 718 (7th Cir. 2002).

[37] *See, e.g, Aenergy, S.A. v. Republic of Angola*, 31 F.4th 119, 129 (2d Cir. 2022); *Ayco Farms, Inc. v. Ochoa*, 862 F.3d 945, 950 (9th Cir. 2017).

[38] *See, e.g., Research Automation, Inc. v. Schrader-Bridgeport International, Inc.*, 626 F.3d 973, 979 (7th Cir. 2010).

weigh, on a case by case basis,[39] the important factors of public and private interest in determining whether to grant a defendant's *forum non conveniens* motion.[40] In doing so, the court enjoys significant discretion, including the power to impose conditions on its decisions.[41] However, failure to weigh all the factors of public or private interest that arise in a particular case may be abuse of discretion.[42]

***Forum Non Conveinens:* Public Interest Factors**

The public interest factors may differ somewhat from one case to another, but they include: (1) having local disputes settled locally; (2) avoiding problems of applying foreign law; and (3) avoiding burdening jurors with cases that have no impact on their community.[43] In some cases there may also be questions about the enforceability of a judgment that the court would render if it retained the case.

- *Local Disputes:* The desire to settle local disputes locally (or, alternatively, the desire to avoid imposing distant disputes on a local court) takes into account questions such as the parties' connection to the local forum, where the injury occurred, local court congestion, and burdens on jurors.[44]
- *Application of Foreign Law*: Courts may be reluctant to take cases in which they will be obligated to apply the law of another jurisdiction. However, in a weighing of factors related to *forum non conveniens*, this consideration normally carries only limited weight.[45]
- *Burdening Jurors with Cases of No Local Interest:* This factor contains two parts: whether local citizens should have to carry the burden of trying a case unrelated to their community and whether the citizenry of another

[39] *Van Cauwenberghe v. Biard*, 486 U.S. 517, 529 (1988).

[40] *See, e.g., Instituto Mexicano del Seguro Soc. v. Zimmer Biomet Holdings, Inc.*, 29 F.4th 351, 357 (7th Cir. 2022); *Nandjou v. Marriott Int'l, Inc.*, 85 F.3d 135, 141 (1st Cir. 2021).

[41] *See, e.g., Ayco Farms, Inc. v. Ochoa*, 862 F.3d 945, 948 (9th Cir. 2017); *Compania Naviera Joanna SA v. Koninklijke Boskalis Westminster NV*, 569 F.3d 189, 202–03 (4th Cir. 2009).

[42] *See, e.g., Curtis v. Galakatos*, 19 F.4th 41, 56 (1st Cir. 2021); *EFCO Corp. v. Aluma Systems USA, Inc.*, 268 F.3d 601, 603 (8th Cir. 2001).

[43] *See Instituto Mexicano del Seguro Soc. v. Zimmer Biomet Holdings, Inc.*, 29 F.4th 351, 360 (7th Cir. 2022); *Kolawole v. Sellers*, 863 F.3d 1361, 1372 (11th Cir. 2017).

[44] *Gulf Oil Corp. v. Gilbert*, 330 U.S. 501, 508–09 (1947); *Hefferan v. Ethicon Endo-Surgery Inc.*, 828 F.3d 488, 500 (6th Cir. 2016).

[45] *See, e.g., Curtis v. Galakatos*, 19 F.4th 41, 50 (1st Cir. 2021); *Boosey & Hawkes Music Publishers, Ltd. v. Walt Disney Co.*, 145 F.3d 481, 492 (2d Cir. 1998). *But cf., Volodarskiy v. Delta Airlines, Inc.*, 784 F.3d 349, 353 (7th Cir. 2015) ("One good reason to dismiss a case based on *forum non conveniens* is to avoid the administration or legal complications of interpreting and applying a foreign country's law.").

area has a greater interest in the outcome of a case.[46]

- *Enforceability of a Judgment:* If enforcement of a prospective judgment could require further litigation outside the United States, the court may weigh that factor in determining whether the case should be heard in the United States in the first instance.[47] This consideration would carry particular weight if there is a significant possibility that the judgment would be unenforceable, thus potentially reducing the American judicial proceeding to a waste of time and judicial resources. However, this "enforceability" factor normally plays no role in *forum non conveniens* determinations if enforcement will occur in the United States, because the Full Faith and Credit clause of the Constitution generally requires an American court to enforce the final judgment of another American court.
- *Public Policy:* In unusual cases, courts may retain a particular lawsuit because public policy favors an American forum for such a suit.[48]
- *Pending Litigation in Another Forum*: The existence of concurrent litigation in another court is *not* necessarily a factor arguing in favor of dismissing a case on *forum non conveniens* grounds,[49] although it may be significant if the court believes the plaintiff is engaged in forum shopping.[50]

Private Interest Factors

Private interest factors include: (1) ease of access to evidence;[51] (2) the cost for witnesses to attend trial;[52] (3) the availability of compulsory process;[53] and (4) other factors that might shorten trial or make it less expensive.[54] For the most part, these factors revolve around the impact of forum selection on the ability of parties to prove their case. If a plaintiff's choice of

---

[46] *Gulf Oil Corp. v. Gilbert*, 330 U.S. 501, 508–09 (1947); *Shi v. New Mighty U.S. Tr.*, 918 F.3d 944, 952 (D.C. Cir. 2019).

[47] *Gulf Oil Corp. v. Gilbert*, 330 U.S. 501, 508 (1947).

[48] *See, e.g., Wiwa v. Royal Dutch Petroleum Co.*, 226 F.3d 88, 105 (2d Cir. 2000).

[49] *See, e.g., Adelson v. Hananel*, 510 F.3d 43, 54 (1st Cir. 2007).

[50] *Aenergy, S.A. v. Republic of Angola*, 31 F.4th 119, 129 n.45 (2d Cir. 2022).

[51] *See, e.g., Instituto Mexicano del Seguro Soc. v. Zimmer Biomet Holdings, Inc.*, 29 F.4th 351, 359 (7th Cir. 2022); *Fresh Results, LLC v. ASF Holland, B.V.*, 921 F.3d 1043, 1049–52 (11th Cir. 2019).

[52] *See, e.g., Curtis v. Galakatos*, 19 F.4th 41, 48 (1st Cir. 2021) (the cost of obtaining attendance of willing, witnesses); *Kolawole v. Sellers*, 863 F.3d 1361, 1372 (11th Cir. 2017).

[53] *See, e.g., Aenergy, S.A. v. Republic of Angola*, 31 F.4th 119, 133 (2d Cir. 2022); *Est. of I.E.H. v. CKE Restaurants, Holdings, Inc.*, 995 F.3d 659, 663 (8th Cir. 2021).

[54] *Hefferan v. Ethicon Endo-Surgery Inc.*, 828 F.3d 488, 498–500 (6th Cir. 2016); *Guidi v. Inter-Continental Hotels Corp.*, 224 F.3d 142, 147 (2d Cir. 2000).

forum—or the defendant's proposed alternative—substantially affects a party's ability to put forward witnesses and evidence, the court will be inclined to weigh that consideration heavily.[55]

Court Has No Duty to Identify Other Possible Forums

A court considering a possible transfer or dismissal has no duty to investigate on its own other possible sites for the litigation. The burden to identify suitable alternative forums falls on the party seeking the alternative forum.[56]

Forum Selection Clauses

When the parties' contract contains a forum selection clause designating a court to which transfer is not possible (such as a court outside the United States), courts will dismiss for *forum non conveniens* to enforce the clause.[57] When the parties' contract contains a forum selection clause designating a court within the United States to which transfer is possible, the court will ordinarily transfer to the forum designated in the clause.[58]

Foreign Blocking Statutes

Some countries, apparently concerned about the use of *forum non conveniens* in United States courts, have enacted legislation providing that if one of their citizens files a suit in a United States court, the courts of the plaintiff's home country are closed to that plaintiff on that cause of action.[59] Some courts hold that such foreign blocking statutes render the courts of that country not available.[60]

Conditional Dismissal

When the court believes that another forum would be more appropriate but still retains some concern over whether the case will actually be heard in the alternative forum, the judge may include a clause in the dismissal order providing that parties may return to the dismissing court to resume their case in the event the case cannot proceed in the alternative forum.[61]

---

[55] *Piper Aircraft Co. v. Reyno*, 454 U.S. 235, 242 (1981). *See Curtis v. Galakatos*, 19 F.4th 41, 48 (1st Cir. 2021).

[56] *See, e.g., Danziger & DeLlano, LLP v. Morgan Verkamp LLC*, 948 F.3d 124, 132 (3d Cir. 2020).

[57] *Atlantic Marine Construction Co. v. U.S. District Court for the Western District of Texas*, 571 U.S. 49, 60 (2013); *Don't Look Media LLC v. Fly Victor Ltd.*, 999 F.3d 1284, 1295–96 (11th Cir. 2021); *D & S Consulting, Inc. v. Kingdom of Saudi Arabia*, 961 F.3d 1209, 1213 (D.C. Cir. 2020) (only in unusual cases will the public factors overcome a forum selection clause).

[58] *Atlantic Marine Construction Co. v. U.S. District Court for the Western District of Texas*, 571 U.S. 49, 62 (2013); *In re Becker*, 993 F.3d 731, 732 (9th Cir. 2021).

[59] *See, e.g.,* Costa Rica Codigo Procesal Civil Art. 31 (CCP 31).

[60] *See, e.g., Canales Martinez v. Dow Chemical Co.*, 219 F. Supp. 2d 719, 728 (E.D. La. 2002) (treating Costa Rican courts as not available).

[61] *See, e.g., Chavez v. Occidental Chem. Corp.*, 8 F.4th 91, 95 (2d Cir. 2021); *Vasquez v. Bridgestone/Firestone, Inc.*, 325 F.3d 665, 675 (5th Cir. 2003).

F. THE *ERIE* DOCTRINE

Table of Sections

2.18 Introduction
2.18a —The Namesake: *Erie R.R. Co. v. Tompkins* and its Progeny
2.18b —*Erie* Today, and the Sources of Federal Procedure
2.18c —Identifying the Law to Apply
2.18d —A Residue of Federal Common Law

§ 2.18 Introduction

CORE CONCEPT

Federal district courts hear disputes arising under federal law—that is, under some provision of the U.S. Constitution, a federal statute, or a treaty to which the United States of America is a signatory.[1] When they do so, the law those courts will apply is obviously federal.

But frequently,[2] the federal district courts are also called upon to hear State law disputes—disputes arising under a State's constitution, statutes, or common law. This occurs most often when litigants invoke diversity-of-citizenship[3] or supplemental[4] federal subject-matter jurisdiction. In such cases, the federal court serves as a sort of substitute State tribunal.[5] When a federal court is confronted with a State law dispute, what substantive law should it apply: federal or State? In navigating those lawsuits towards resolution, should federal or State procedural rules apply?

Efforts to determine when federal or State substantive or procedural law applies in State law disputes have bewitched federal courts almost since the founding of the Republic. The body of law used to answer these haunting questions is known today, somewhat inartfully, as "the *Erie* doctrine."

---

[1] 28 U.S.C.A. § 1331 ("federal question" jurisdiction).

[2] Currently, more than twice as many diversity-based federal lawsuits are commenced each year than federal question-based ones. *See* ADMIN. OFFICE OF U.S. COURTS, TABLE C-2—U.S. DISTRICT COURTS-CIVIL FEDERAL JUDICIAL CASELOAD STATISTICS (Mar. 31, 2021), https://www.uscourts.gov/statistics/table/c-2/federal-judicial-caseload-statistics/2021/03/31.

[3] 28 U.S.C.A. § 1332.

[4] 28 U.S.C.A. § 1367. While the original *Erie* doctrine developed in the diversity context, it now seems settled that it also applies in supplemental jurisdiction cases involving non-diverse State claims. *See Felder v. Casey*, 487 U.S. 131, 151 (1988).

[5] *See Guar. Tr. Co. v. York*, 326 U.S. 99, 108–09 (1945) ("a federal court adjudicating a state-created right solely because of the diversity of citizenship of the parties is for that purpose, in effect, only another court of the State").

APPLICATIONS

What the *Erie* Doctrine is Not

Identifying the appropriate law a federal district court should apply to a State dispute is *not* a matter of jurisdiction. Before a court reaches the question of which law to apply, it usually will have addressed and resolved jurisdictional issues in the case. If the court lacks jurisdiction to hear a case, it will dismiss or transfer it. When that happens, the court need not concern itself with identifying the law that would have otherwise been applied. Thus, the *Erie* doctrine inquiry usually only occurs if the district court has the authority to hear and resolve a State law dispute.

The Sources for the *Erie* Inquiry

The *Erie* doctrine derives from one constitutional provision and two federal statutes. The first statute was enacted by the first Congress in 1789 as it formed the lower federal courts; the second was enacted by Congress in 1934 to authorize the drafting of the Federal Rules of Civil Procedure. Each source plays an important role in how we understand the *Erie* doctrine to work today:

- *U.S. Constitution's Supremacy Clause (1788):* directs that the federal Constitution and all laws made pursuant to its authority "shall be the supreme Law of the Land; and the Judges in every State shall be bound thereby, any Thing in the Constitution or Law of any State to the Contrary notwithstanding."[6]
- *Rules of Decision Act (1789):* instructs federal judges that "the laws of the several States shall be regarded as rules of decision in civil actions" tried in federal court, unless federal law provides otherwise.[7] The phrase "rules of decision" means those principles of law that will be applied to determine the outcome of a dispute—in other words, *substantive* law. Federal law "otherwise" provides when the Constitution, an Act of Congress, or a treaty "preempts" State substantive law by establishing some superseding national standard.[8]
- *Rules Enabling Act (1934):* authorizes the U.S. Supreme Court to establish "general rules of practice and procedure and rules of evidence" for lawsuits pending in federal court.[9] But this statute constrains the Court's rule-making authority to rules of *procedure* only ("Such rules shall not abridge, enlarge or modify any substan-

---

[6] U.S. CONST. Art. VI, cl. 2.

[7] 28 U.S.C.A. § 1652.

[8] *See, e.g., Riegel v. Medtronic, Inc.*, 552 U.S. 312, 322–25 (2008) (finding federal statutory preemption of manufacturing standards for medical devices).

[9] 28 U.S.C.A. §§ 2071–72.

tive right.").[10]

§ 2.18a The Namesake: *Erie R.R. Co. v. Tompkins* and its Propgeny

CORE CONCEPT

The *Erie* doctrine explores the primacy of, and limits on, federal law. It rests generally on two guiding premises: (1) in State law disputes, a claimant should not be encouraged to "shop" for a federal forum in the hope that doing so might cause the federal judge to apply a different, outcome-altering law than a State tribunal would use; and (2) in State law disputes, federal courts may not craft a body of common law principles independent of what State courts would apply. Understanding the doctrine begins with the *Erie R.R. Co. v. Tompkins* case[1] itself.

APPLICATIONS

The *Erie* Lawsuit

The *Erie* case arose out of an injury that 26-year-old Harry J. Tompkins suffered from a passing freight train. It was about 2:30 a.m. in late July 1934. Tompkins was walking towards his home down a two-foot-wide dirt clearing that ran alongside railroad tracks. He saw and heard an approaching Erie Railroad Co. freight train but, believing a foot or so was a safe enough distance from the tracks, he kept walking. As the train passed him, a protruding dark object (possibly an unlatched, swinging door on a train car) hit him in the head, rendering him unconscious. As he fell to the ground, his right arm extended over the tracks and was amputated by the wheels of the passing train. Tompkins was a Pennsylvania citizen; the incident occurred in Hughestown, Pennsylvania.[2]

At the time, Pennsylvania had no statutory (enacted) law setting the duty of care owed by a railroad to persons on the railroad's right-of-way. But Pennsylvania's Supreme Court had recently announced a common law rule deeming such persons to be trespassers, to whom a railroad owned only a minimal duty (namely, to avoid wantonly or willfully causing injury). That standard posed a daunting challenge to Tompkins's chances for success in a personal injury lawsuit. After all, a Pennsylvania State court would almost certainly apply this foreboding "trespasser" standard.

So, rather than filing in a Pennsylvania State court, Tompkins filed his personal injury lawsuit in a federal court in New York (the State where the railroad was incorporated). Although

---

[10] 28 U.S.C.A. § 2072(a).

[1] *Erie R.R. Co. v. Tompkins*, 304 U.S. 64 (1938).

[2] *See Tompkins v. Erie R. Co.*, 90 F.2d 603, 603–04 (2d Cir. 1937), *rev'd*, 304 U.S. 64 (1938). *See generally* Edward A. Purcell, Jr., *The Story of* Erie*: How Litigants, Lawyers, Judges, Politics, and Social Change Reshape the Law*, in CIVIL PROCEDURE STORIES 35–38 (Kevin M. Clermont ed., 2d ed. 2008).

the 1789 Rules of Decision Act obligated federal judges to apply a State's substantive laws ("rules of decision"), a nearly hundred-year-old U.S. Supreme Court precedent[3] allowed Tompkins to urge the federal judge to ignore Pennsylvania's case law because it was merely judge-made and, thus, not entitled to the deference the Rules of Decision Act afforded to a State's enacted laws.[4] Indeed, Tompkins argued, in the absence of any *enacted* Pennsylvania law on point, a New York federal judge should feel free to exercise his own, independent judgment as to what the law ought to be (that is, to create judge-made federal common law setting the railroad's duty of care). The federal judge accepted the invitation and ruled that when, as here, a right-of-way was in open and notorious long use by the public, railroads owed an ordinary duty of care (*i.e.*, negligence standard) to passersby. Applying this freshly announced law, a New York federal jury found the railroad breached its duty to Tompkins and awarded Tompkins damages.[5]

The U.S. Supreme Court reversed. It began by not just overruling its earlier precedent, but declaring that precedent unconstitutional.[6] The earlier ruling, explained the Court, "introduced grave discrimination by noncitizens against citizens" by affording those who could access the federal courts' diversity-of-citizenship jurisdiction a possible escape from a State's laws that would otherwise govern a civil dispute in that State's courts.[7] Federal judges, pronounced the Court, may not craft general common law.[8] Instead, when presiding over a State law dispute in diversity, they must apply the same State law that a State court hearing that dispute would have used—

---

[3]*See Swift v. Tyson*, 41 U.S. 1 (1938).

[4]As the *Erie* Court explained the *Swift v. Tyson* precedent, the "unwritten law of the state as declared by its highest court" was not "positive" law and, thus, not implicated by the Rules of Decision Act. *Erie R.R. Co. v. Tompkins*, 304 U.S. 64, 71–72 (1938). Seven years later, the Court explained that, during the age of *Swift*: "Law was conceived as a 'brooding omnipresence' of Reason, of which decisions were merely evidence and not themselves the controlling formulations. Accordingly, federal courts deemed themselves free to ascertain what Reason, and therefore Law, required wholly independent of authoritatively declared State law, even in cases where a legal right as the basis for relief was created by State authority . . . ." *Guar. Tr. Co. v. York*, 326 U.S. 99, 102 (1945). *See also id.* at 103 ("State court decisions were not 'the law' but merely someone's opinion").

[5]*See Tompkins v. Erie R. Co.*, 90 F.2d 603 (2d Cir. 1937), *rev'd*, 304 U.S. 64 (1938).

[6]*See Erie R.R. Co. v. Tompkins*, 304 U.S. 64, 79–80 (1938) ("an unconstitutional assumption of powers by the Courts of the United States" by which "this Court and the lower courts have invaded rights which in our opinion are reserved by the Constitution to the several states").

[7]*See Erie R.R. Co. v. Tompkins*, 304 U.S. 64, 74–75 (1938) (prior precedent "rendered impossible equal protection of the law").

[8]*See Erie R. Co. v. Tompkins*, 304 U.S. 64, 78 (1938) ("There is no federal general common law.").

including State case law.[9]

As later authority would explain it, the decision in *Erie* rested on two principles (later coined "the twin aims of *Erie*"): (1) claimants should not be encouraged to "shop" for a federal forum in the hope of escaping a body of unfavorable local common law; and (2) laws should be applied equitably—whether the courthouse was a State one or a federal one.[10]

Immediate Impact of the *Erie* Ruling

The impact of *Erie* was immediate and lasting. Federal courts would, in the future, now be tasked to apply not just enacted State law, but that State's common law as well.[11] This dampened the temptation to engage in forum shopping. Once federal general common law ceased, litigants lost an important motivation to file in federal district courts (*i.e.,* the hope to obtain different substantive law than a State court would apply was now gone). A corollary to this new approach was that federal courts, unlike their State counterparts, would no longer have authority to recognize new State law causes of action where no State legislature has created them.[12]

As the Supreme Court and other federal tribunals began to apply *Erie*, new and knotty problems emerged in the decision's wake.[13]

---

[9] *See Erie R.R. Co. v. Tompkins*, 304 U.S. 64, 71 (1938). *See also Rodriguez v. Fed. Deposit Ins. Corp.*, ___ U.S. ___, 140 S. Ct. 713, 717 (2020) ("Judicial lawmaking in the form of federal common law plays a necessarily modest role under a Constitution that vests the federal government's 'legislative Powers' in Congress and reserves most other regulatory authority to the States. As this Court has put it [in *Erie*], there is 'no federal general common law.' "); *Cooper v. Toyko Electric Power Co. Holdings, Inc.*, 960 F.3d 549 (9th Cir. 2020) (*Erie* requires application of either State or foreign substantive law).

[10] *See Hanna v. Plumer*, 380 U.S. 460, 467–68 (1965).

[11] *See, e.g., Liberty Synergistics, Inc. v. Microflo, Ltd.*, 718 F.3d 138, 142 n.2 (2d Cir. 2013) (federal court must use State substantive law, whether legislation or common law).

[12] *See Alexander v. Sandoval*, 532 U.S. 275 (2001). *See also Nestle USA, Inc. v. Doe*, 593 U.S. ___, 141 S. Ct. 1931, 1938 (2021) (federal courts may be precluded from recognizing new causes of action involving aliens); *Hernandez v. Mesa*, 589 U.S. ___, 140 S. Ct. 735, 742 (2020) (in light of *Erie*, "federal courts today cannot fashion new claims in the way that they could before 1938"); *City of Milwaukee v. Illinois & Michigan*, 451 U.S. 304, 312 (1981) ("Federal courts, unlike state courts, are not general common-law courts and do not possess a general power to develop and apply their own rules of decision."). *See generally Forbes v. BB&S Acquisition Corp.*, 22 F.4th 22, 25 (1st Cir. 2021) ("Where a state's highest court has not spoken directly, federal courts are restrained. The plaintiff, who made a deliberate choice to sue in federal court rather than in a Massachusetts state court, is not in a position to ask us to blaze a new trail that the Massachusetts courts have not invited.") (cleaned up).

[13] *See Shady Grove Orthopedic Assocs., P.A. v. Allstate Ins. Co.*, 559 U.S. 393, 398 (2010) (noting "*Erie*'s murky waters").

The "Murky" Substantive v. Procedural Law Divide

A harbinger of the "murky"[14] problems to come in the aftermath of *Erie* can be found in the decision's brief concurring opinion from Justice Reed. He agreed with the central holding of *Erie*, *i.e.*, that federal general common law should be abolished and that federal district courts should apply State substantive law. But he offered a prescient comment, noting that the line dividing procedural law from substantive law is "hazy", though he expressed confidence that "no one doubts federal power over procedure"—even in diversity cases.[15] But what seemed obvious to him when *Erie* was decided proved to be less clear as time passed.

The distinction between substantive law ("rules of decision") and procedural law is pivotal in an *Erie* analysis. Congress's 1789 Rules of Decision Act compels federal courts to apply State *substantive* law, absent a federal preemption, but says nothing on the question of *procedural* law. And courts have long identified the difference between the two. Substantive law is the body of legal principles that will determine whether a party has a claim cognizable in a court and whether a legal defense exists that bars such a claim on the merits—what the Supreme Court, in this context, once called "rights and obligations."[16] For example, if a plaintiff were sued on a claim of negligence, most States would permit recovery only if the plaintiff could prove that: (1) the defendant owed the plaintiff a duty of care; (2) the defendant breached that duty; and (3) the breach proximately caused injury to the plaintiff or damage to the plaintiff's property. Those are the ordinary substantive elements of a State law tort claim of negligence. In a State that recognized the defense of contributory negligence, a defendant could defeat the claim by demonstrating that the plaintiff had been contributorily negligent in the event that led to the plaintiff's injury. This assertion of contributory negligence is a substantive defense.

By contrast, procedural law does not address whether the plaintiff has a cause of action or whether the defendant has a merits defense. Instead, procedure governs the way in which both plaintiff and defendant must present their sides of the case to the court—what the Supreme Court, in this context, once called "the manner and means" by which rights and obliga-

[14]*See Shady Grove Orthopedic Assocs., P.A. v. Allstate Ins. Co.*, 559 U.S. 393, 398 (2010) (discussing when courts must "wade into *Erie*'s murky waters").

[15]*Erie R.R. Co. v. Tompkins*, 304 U.S. 64, 90 (1938) (Reed, J., concurring) ("No one doubts federal power over procedure."). But cf., Jinks v. Richland County, S.C., 538 U.S. 456 (2003) (implying that courts cannot always easily untangle the relationship between substance and procedure, no matter what the purpose may be for trying to do so).

[16]*See Byrd v. Blue Ridge Rural Elec. Co-op., Inc.*, 356 U.S. 525, 535 (1958) ("federal courts in diversity cases must respect the definition of state-created rights and obligations by the state courts").

tions are enforced.[17] Thus, procedural law will control, at its simplest level, what pleadings are permitted, how electronic filing is performed, and allowable font sizes and page lengths. More complex problems arise over procedure regulating the joining of additional parties, the conduct of discovery, and the admissibility of evidence. Broadly speaking, procedural rules help direct the course and logistics of a lawsuit. But there is no denying that procedural requirements can influence—and, indeed, even dictate—the outcome of a lawsuit[18] (*e.g.*, a failure to meet a procedural timing deadline can result in default). Thus, while it is true that procedure laws do not endeavor to supply the operative legal standard that will decide the substantive merits of a claim or defense, procedural requirements can have a practical substantive effect on a claim or defense.

Consequently, the availability of a certain federal procedure or a certain State procedure could still encourage litigants to forum-shop to obtain a perceived advantage. For example, some States forbid entirely or meaningfully restrict discovery from an opponent's expert witnesses; in federal court, expert depositions are both available and robust. Conversely, some States tolerate sweeping discovery of electronically stored information; in federal court, such discovery is bounded by evolving proportionality concerns. Thus, the motivation to pursue a federal tribunal in order to obtain a procedural advantage persists.

The *Erie* Progeny—Outcome Determination

After *Erie*, the question of substantive law was clear—in hearing State law disputes, federal courts must apply State substantive law (including the State's common law) unless preempted by federal constitutional, statutory, or treaty-based law. But when State procedural law must be applied by a federal judge proved more elusive.

Just a few years after *Erie*, the early case of *Guaranty Trust Co. v. York*[19] required the Court to choose between application of a federal doctrine limiting the time in which a case had to be filed or a State statute of limitations that set a different time limit. Under the State statute, the plaintiff's claim was barred; under the federal doctrine, the plaintiff's case could proceed.

Guaranty Trust involved an issue that appeared quite arguably procedural. There could be no question that federal courts

---

[17]*See Guar. Tr. Co. of N.Y. v. York*, 326 U.S. 99 (1945) (whether law "concerns merely the manner and the means by which a right to recover, as recognized by the State, is enforced"). *See also Byrd v. Blue Ridge Rural Elec. Co-op., Inc.*, 356 U.S. 525, 536 (1958) ("merely a form and mode" of enforcing right).

[18]*See Byrd v. Blue Ridge Rural Elec. Co-op., Inc.*, 356 U.S. 525, 536–37 (1958) (noting that even State rules as to form and mode "may bear substantially on the question whether the litigation would come out one way in the federal court and another way in the state court if the federal court failed to apply a particular local rule").

[19]*Guaranty Trust Co. of N.Y. v. York*, 326 U.S. 99 (1945).

were authorized to apply their own procedure when a cause of action arises out of federal law. Thus, an approach that would compel federal judges to apply, in all cases, the procedure of the State in which that federal court sits would mean the procedure applied to federal questions would differ from one State to another. The result would be an unacceptable lack of uniformity in the way federal claims were heard across the United States. Likewise, an approach that directed federal courts to apply federal procedure when hearing federal claims and State procedure when hearing State claims would prove unmanageable. In the first place, that approach would require federal judges to learn, and apply, two different bodies of procedure on a regular basis. Secondly, when cases appeared on the federal docket involving both federal and State claims, an attempt to apply federal procedure to those portions of the lawsuit involving federal claims and State procedure to those portions involving State claims would end up mired in confusion. Consider, for example, what would happen if federal rules of evidence treated a certain trial exhibit as inadmissible, while State rules of evidence would allow that exhibit.

Mindful of these variables, *Guaranty Trust* provided useful guidance. It began by rejecting a facile reckoning of the substantive/procedural divide: how a law is characterized by the State would not, alone, be dispositive on the point.[20] Rather, the Court in *Guaranty Trust* counseled a more searching inquiry that must be guided by the underlying goals of *Erie*. The intent of *Erie*, explained the Court, "was to insure that, in all cases where a federal court is exercising jurisdiction solely because of the diversity of citizenship of the parties, the outcome of the litigation in the federal court should be substantially the same, so far as legal rules determine the outcome of a litigation, as it would be if tried in a State court." Or, more colorfully, "[t]he nub of the policy that underlies *Erie R. Co. v. Tompkins* is that for the same transaction the accident of a suit by a non-resident litigant in a federal court instead of in a State court a block away, should not lead to a substantially different result."[21] And thus emerged the "outcome determination" approach to the *Erie* doctrine.

As applied to the facts of *Guaranty Trust*, this approach meant that the federal court should use the State statute of limitations.[22] The reasoning was that under the State rule, the plaintiff's claim was time barred. Application of the federal

---

[20]*See Guar. Tr. Co. of N.Y. v. York*, 326 U.S. 99, 109 (1945) ("it therefore immaterial whether statutes of limitation are characterized either as 'substantive' or 'procedural' in State court opinions in any use of those terms unrelated to the specific issue before us," since "*Erie R. Co. v. Tompkins* was not an endeavor to formulate scientific legal terminology").

[21]*See Guar. Tr. Co. of N.Y. v. York*, 326 U.S. 99, 109–10 (1945).

[22]This result still applies in the context of statutes of limitations. *See Jinks v. Richland County, S.C.*, 538 U.S. 456 (2003) (dicta) ("For *Erie* purposes . . .statutes of limitation are treated as substantive;" citing *Guaranty Trust*). *See also Shady Grove Orthopedic Associates, P.A. v. Allstate*

limitation period would permit the plaintiff to pursue the claim. While it was still possible that the plaintiff might lose the case on the merits, the difference between certain defeat for the plaintiff under the State law and a possibility of victory under the federal law was a sufficient difference in outcome to justify barring the use of federal procedure.

The *Erie* Progeny—Moderating Outcome Determination

The underpinning of *Guaranty Trust* reprised the concern that a sufficiently consequential potential difference in outcome from applying federal procedure would create unacceptable levels of forum shopping of the kind that *Erie* originally sought to prevent. This linkage between outcome determination and forum shopping was an important concern in extending the *Erie* doctrine to procedural issues. But a rigid fixation on "outcome determination" as the basis for choosing between federal procedure and State procedure proved too blunt an analysis.[23] In any given case, even the most modest differences in an unquestionably procedural requirement—for example, page limitations on the length of briefs—can cause a difference in outcome (conforming to page limits might force an attorney to abandon arguments of value). Moreover, because sensible lawyers will litigate only issues that could have a bearing on the outcome of a case, a test that considered only outcome determination might require application of State procedure for almost every State claim filed in federal court—including claims filed in conjunction with federal causes of action.

For that reason, the continuing evolution of the *Erie* doctrine identified other factors to weigh in choosing between State or federal procedure. In *Byrd v. Blue Ridge Rural Electric Cooperative, Inc.*,[24] the Court was called upon to determine whether, in a worker's compensation case, the injured plaintiff was an employee of the defendant, and then who, a jury or a judge, should decide that question. Under State procedure, a judge was authorized to make that decision, while the established federal practice was to leave the question to the jury.

The Supreme Court acknowledged that if the only *Erie* measurement was outcome determination, State procedure (*i.e.*, judge decides, not a jury) might well be compelled—after all, the nature of the decisionmaker could meaningfully impact any dispute.[25] But so sweeping a view, noted the Court, would obvi-

---

Insurance Co., 559 U.S. 393 (2010) (Stevens, J., concurring) (some state procedure is applicable because it is part of state's "substantive rights and remedies").

[23] *Schipani v. McLeod*, 541 F.3d 158, 164–65 (2d Cir. 2008) ("[S]tate law governs the award of prejudgment interest [but] postjudgment interest is governed by federal statute.").

[24] *Byrd v. Blue Ridge Rural Elec. Co-op., Inc.*, 356 U.S. 525 (1958).

[25] *See Byrd v. Blue Ridge Rural Elec. Co-op., Inc.*, 356 U.S. 525, 537 (1958) ("Concededly the nature of the tribunal which tries issues may be important in the enforcement of the parcel of rights making up a cause of action or defense, and bear significantly upon achievement of uniform

ously disrupt the operation of the federal judiciary.[26] The federal courts represent "an independent system for administering justice to litigants who properly invoke its jurisdiction," an "essential characteristic" of which is the right to a trial by jury.[27] And State law should not routinely "disrupt or alter the essential character or function of a federal court."[28] So, the appropriate *Erie* inquiry must be more nuanced, given these "affirmative countervailing considerations": before deciding whether to apply a disruptive State procedure, the federal judge must assess whether that State procedure is "an integral part" of the State's law—that is, a procedure "intended" by the State "to be bound up with the definition of the rights and obligations of the parties"—or, instead, is "merely a form and mode" of litigation.[29]

The decision in *Byrd*, then, requires consideration of the competing State and federal interests in applying State and federal procedure, respectively. These considerations, along with an evaluation of the possibility that application of federal procedure might significantly affect the outcome of the case, are to be weighed to determine whether State or federal procedure should control.[30] In other words, a strong State interest in application of State procedure would weigh in favor of applying State procedure, while a weak State interest would tilt against using State procedure. A strong federal interest in applying federal procedure would support use of federal procedure, while a weak federal interest would diminish the argument for using federal procedure. And, throughout this weighing, the likelihood of federal procedure significantly affecting the outcome of the case must be considered.[31]

While mitigating a blunt use of "outcome determination," *Byrd* also injected new uncertainties into the *Erie* inquiry. How

---

enforcement of the right. It may well be that in the instant personal-injury case the outcome would be substantially affected by whether the issue of immunity is decided by a judge or a jury. Therefore, were 'outcome' the only consideration, a strong case might appear for saying that the federal court should follow the state practice.").

[26] *See Byrd v. Blue Ridge Rural Elec. Co-op., Inc.*, 356 U.S. 525, 538 (1958) ("It cannot be gainsaid that there is a strong federal policy against allowing state rules to disrupt the judge-jury relationship in the federal courts.").

[27] *See Byrd v. Blue Ridge Rural Elec. Co-op., Inc.*, 356 U.S. 525, 537–38 (1958).

[28] *See Byrd v. Blue Ridge Rural Elec. Co-op., Inc.*, 356 U.S. 525, 539 (1958).

[29] *See Byrd v. Blue Ridge Rural Elec. Co-op., Inc.*, 356 U.S. 525, 536 (1958).

[30] *See Byrd v. Blue Ridge Rural Elec. Co-op., Inc.*, 356 U.S. 525, 533–39 (1958).

[31] *See Byrd v. Blue Ridge Rural Elec. Co-op., Inc.*, 356 U.S. 525, 539–40 (1958) ("there is not present here the certainty that a different result would follow, or even the strong possibility that this would be the case"; "We do not think the likelihood of a different result is so strong as to require the federal practice of jury determination of disputed factual issues to yield to the state rule in the interest of uniformity of outcome.).

are the competing State and federal interests to be identified?[32] Once identified, how are they weighed? How certain must an outcome-altering result be before federal procedures are supplanted?[33] The Supreme Court has offered few clues to these questions.

The *Erie* Progeny—Federal Rules of Civil Procedure

Only a few years before the Supreme Court decided *Erie*, Congress enacted the Rules Enabling Act, creating a process by which federal procedural rules could be enacted without necessarily involving direct participation in each rule by Congress. The Rules Enabling Act was the source of, *inter alia,* the current Federal Rules of Civil Procedure, which are so important to the processing of civil cases in federal courts.

Interplay between the *Erie* doctrine and federal rules developed under the authority of the Rules Enabling Act was inevitable. For example, in a case where State procedure required a plaintiff to post a bond before proceeding with a suit, but Federal Rule of Civil Procedure 23.1 required no bond, the Court had to decide whether the State bond requirement prevailed over a federal rule that otherwise appeared to govern the case.[34] In another case, State procedure provided that an applicable statute of limitations continued to run until the defendant was served. By contrast, Federal Rule of Civil Procedure 3 provides that a federal case is "commenced" by filing a complaint with the federal district court. A possible construc-

[32]This suggestion is not meant to indicate that thorough research alone will yield an answer upon which diligent attorneys may confidently rely. Indeed, continuing developments in the Supreme Court indicate that *Byrd* does not identify a single true path with the clarity and precision of a laser. In *Gasperini v. Center for Humanities, Inc.*, 518 U.S. 415 (1996), a jury awarded a large verdict to the plaintiff. Under New York law, a state appellate court has authority to order a new trial when the jury's verdict "deviates materially" from reasonable compensation. Federal procedure differs from that standard in two important respects. First, a federal district judge normally has less discretion to modify a jury's verdict than the New York law allows. Second, New York vests this power in an appellate court. By contrast, the Seventh Amendment to the United States constitution normally imposes much stricter limits on the authority of federal appellate courts to modify jury verdicts.

The Supreme Court grappled with this cluster of problems in the following manner. First, in diversity cases federal district courts—not circuit courts—will apply the New York statute's standard for modifying jury verdicts. This practice, of course, is not directly consistent with the New York mandate to provide such review in appellate courts. Second, in a bow to the Seventh Amendment, federal circuit courts will review the district court's application of the New York law under the existing federal standard for circuit courts, *i.e.,* an abuse of discretion.

[33]*See, e.g., Esfeld v. Costa Crociere, S.P.A.*, 289 F.3d 1300, 1306–09 (11th Cir. 2002) (noting that "vast majority" of federal appellate courts use federal law of forum non conveniens; holding that while forum non conveniens will often be outcome-determinative, federal interest in controlling its own process in a way that is uniform across the country outweighed the outcome-determinative factor; holding that federal law of forum non conveniens should control; citing other cases).

[34]*Cohen v. Beneficial Indus. Loan Corp.*, 337 U.S. 541 (1949).

tion of Rule 3 is that once the case is filed, the statute of limitations is tolled. The case before the Supreme Court was one in which the plaintiff had filed the complaint in federal district court before the statute of limitations had expired, but service of process on the defendant did not occur until after the statute of limitations would have expired.[35] Under State procedure, therefore, the plaintiff's suit was untimely. Under the apparent literal language of Federal Rule 3, the plaintiff's filing was timely, and the case could proceed.

In both cases, the Supreme Court concluded that the applicable procedure was State procedure, but the reasoning was insufficiently persuasive to lay to rest concerns about the impact of the *Erie* doctrine on cases involving rules of procedure developed under the authority of the Rules Enabling Act. Some, but by no means all, of this uneasiness was laid to rest when the Supreme Court decided *Hanna v. Plumer*.[36]

In *Hanna* a plaintiff served the defendant by leaving a copy of the summons and complaint with the defendant's spouse at the defendant's residence. This was lawful service under Federal Rule of Civil Procedure 4. However, under State procedure, service was not satisfactory unless the defendant was served personally. The Supreme Court re-examined its growing body of precedent under the *Erie* doctrine and concluded that service was satisfactory because Rule 4 applied, not the State procedure.[37]

The reasoning of the Court's majority was that the relation of *Erie* to the Rules Enabling Act required a two-step analysis of the possible application of a Federal Rule of Civil Procedure to a State cause of action. The first step was to determine if the rule at issue could lawfully be made. Because the Rules Enabling Act only permitted creation of federal rules which were purely procedural, and which did not endeavor to alter substantive rights, the first inquiry was to determine if the rule in question in a particular case was procedural. In the case at bar Rule 4, governing the means of making service of process on a defendant, affected no substantive rights and clearly passed this "pure procedure" requirement.

The second step was to determine if the federal rule at issue could be harmonized with State procedure, or whether the federal and State procedures were locked in conflict. The Court explained that if the two could be harmonized because, *e.g.*, they did not address the same concerns, no choice between them was necessary. However, if they actually collided, then a federal rule of civil procedure lawfully created under the Rules Enabling Act should be applied over the State procedure.[38]

The literal rule of *Hanna* appears to be that if a Federal Rule of Civil Procedure is a lawful exercise of rule-making

---

[35] *Ragan v. Merchants Transfer & Warehouse Co.*, 337 U.S. 530 (1949).

[36] *Hanna v. Plumer*, 380 U.S. 460 (1965).

[37] *See Hanna v. Plumer*, 380 U.S. 460, 462 (1965).

[38] *See Hanna v. Plumer*, 380 U.S. 460, 468 (1965).

power under the Rules Enabling Act, and the rule conflicts directly with State procedure, the federal rule applies.[39] That approach appears to leave little room for considerations of outcome determination, which had been so important to the Supreme Court in both *Erie* and *Guaranty Trust*.[40]

A concurring opinion in *Hanna* proposed a modification to explain the interplay between the Federal Rules of Civil Procedure and concerns about outcome determination under *Erie*. While agreeing with the result in *Hanna* (application of Rule 4 over conflicting State procedure), Justice Harlan added that a determination of the applicability of a federal rule to a case arising under State law should also take into account whether the possible application of federal procedure would have influenced an attorney's decision to choose the federal court in order to avoid the application of State procedure.[41] Where such a decision might reasonably have been made, and where the application of federal procedure would impinge on a significant State policy, Justice Harlan believed the State procedure should apply—even if, under the majority's test, State procedure conflicted with a valid federal rule of procedure.[42] If applied, Justice Harlan's approach would refine the "outcome-determinative" test for procedure. In essence, Justice Harlan sought to avoide the possibility that a difference in procedure could always determine the outcome by concentrating his analysis on the estimated importance of procedure at the time an attorney was choosing the court in which the case would be heard. Put another way, if a reasonable attorney, upon noticing that federal procedure offered a significant advantage not available under State procedure, would choose the federal court in order to obtain the benefit of federal procedure, the federal procedure would be sufficiently outcome determinative to justify displacing it with State procedure. While Justice Harlan made these observations in the context of federal rule of procedure (and without apparent assent from a majority of his colleagues on the Court), they appear to have applicability also to the circumstances governed by *Byrd, i.e.,* situations in which federal procedure arising purely from case law may conflict with State procedure.

Understanding *Hanna* can be difficult enough. However, the

---

[39]*Shady Grove Orthopedic Associates, P.A. v. Allstate Insurance Co.*, 559 U.S. 393, 405–06 (2010) (plurality opinion) (state law prohibiting class litigation as to particular cause of action "flatly contradict(s)" Rule 23, which authorizes class actions if certain requirements are met; holding Rule 23 controls; also noting "we have rejected every statutory challenge to a Federal Rule that has come before us"). *See also Tompkins v. Crown Corr, Inc.*, 726 F.3d 830, 845 n.4 (6th Cir. 2013) (federal court sitting in diversity uses federal standard for summary judgment).

[40]*See, e.g., Morel v. Daimler-Chrysler AG*, 565 F.3d 20, 24 (1st Cir. 2009) (in situation controlled by *Hanna*, the approaches of both *Erie* and *Guaranty Trust* are inapplicable).

[41]*Hannah v. Plumer*, 380 U.S. 460, 464 (1965) (Harlan, J., concurring).

[42]*Id.*

difficulty is sometimes compounded when *Hanna* is applied in particular cases. In *Walker v. Armco Steel Corp.*,[43] for example, the Supreme Court returned to a question it had originally addressed a generation earlier. *Walker* involved a plaintiff who had sued on a State claim in federal district court. The claim was filed before the statute of limitations expired, but the complaint was not served on the defendant until after the statute would have expired. Applicable State law provided that the statute continued to run until service on the defendant. The plaintiff argued that Federal Rule of Civil Procedure 3, describing an action as "commenced" when filed with the district court, meant that the statute of limitations was tolled by the plaintiff's timely filing with the clerk's office.

Walker was a reprise of *Ragan v. Merchants Transfer & Warehouse Co.*,[44] in which the Court had held that State procedure controlled, and Rule 3 did not apply. Many observers believed that the intervening decision in *Hanna* had nullified the result in *Ragan*. A unanimous Supreme Court, applying *Hanna*, concluded otherwise. The Court recognized that under the *Hanna* analysis, Rule 3 was a lawful rule of procedure, enacted within the authority of the Rules Enabling Act. However, the Court also concluded that Rule 3, at least in diversity cases, was not intended to toll State statutes of limitations. The Court was a bit vague as to the precise purpose of Rule 3 when State claims were before a federal district court.[45] However, its conclusion was that State procedure for tolling a statute of limitation (service on the defendant) controlled because there was "no direct conflict" between the State law and Rule 3.[46] Thus, the requirement of *Hanna* that, before a lawful federal rule can apply to a diversity case it must first be in direct conflict with State procedure was not met, and State law applied.

Walker suggests that there can be grave uncertainty as to the circumstances when a federal rule conflicts to a substantial degree with State procedure. To that extent, *Walker* casts doubt on the predictability of the *Hanna* test as it applies to cases concerning the applicability of federal rules of procedure enacted under the Rules Enabling Act. The Supreme Court appears to be sensitive to this problem, and in the aftermath of *Walker* the Court emphasized that the analysis enunciated in *Hanna* continues to govern in most circumstances.[47] Nevertheless, *Walker* serves as a caution to attorneys that, before assuming a federal rule of procedure displaces State procedure, one must first establish not only that the federal rule is autho-

[43] *Walker v. Armco Steel Corp.*, 446 U.S. 740 (1980).

[44] *Ragan v. Merchants Transfer & Warehouse Co.*, 337 U.S. 530 (1949).

[45] *Walker*, 446 U.S. at 750 ("Rule 3 governs the date from which various timing requirements of the Federal Rules begin to run, but does not affect state statutes of limitations.").

[46] *Id.* at 751, 100 S. Ct. at 1986.

[47] *See, e.g., Burlington Northern R. Co. v. Woods*, 480 U.S. 1 (1987) (applying Hanna test, finding Federal Rule of Appellate Procedure 38 applicable in place of state procedure).

rized by the Rules Enabling Act, but also that the federal rule truly clashes with otherwise applicable State procedure.

The *Erie* Progeny—Congress's Procedural Statutes

Although Congress enacted the Rules Enabling Act to authorize a process for creating rules of procedure in which Congress itself did not have to be the principal scrivener, Congress has also created other important procedural provisions independent of the Rules Enabling Act. These provisions are codified at Title 28 of the United States Code.

When one of these statutory procedures is arguably applicable in a diversity case, considerations related to *Erie* arise again. In this circumstance, as with case law controlled by *Byrd* or rules of procedure controlled by *Hanna*, the federal district court must decide whether federal statutory procedure may be applied, or whether it must defer to State procedure. The Supreme Court explored this question in *Stewart Organization, Inc. v. Ricoh Corp.*[48] *Stewart* addressed whether a motion to transfer a case pursuant to a contractual forum selection clause was enforceable under 28 U.S.C.A. § 1404(a) or unenforceable because State procedure disfavored such clauses.

The Supreme Court held that the standards for transfer of venue under the federal statute controlled. In a straightforward opinion the Court concluded that federal courts are bound to apply procedure enacted by Congress, provided only that Congress was within its constitutional authority and that the statute "covers the point in dispute" before the district court.[49] *Stewart* may have left some modest room for questioning when an attorney can be certain that the federal statutory procedure controls. However, it appears that this question can be answered with somewhat more confidence than the question posed by *Hanna* when a federal rule is at issue, *i.e.,* does the rule conflict sufficiently with State procedure?

§ 2.18b *Erie* Today, and the Sources of Federal Procedure

CORE CONCEPT

The contours of *Erie* and its progeny remain "murky," particularly at the margins. In its foreboding density, it represents civil procedure's analog to property law's rule-against-perpetuities.[1] But, as this recounting demonstrates, the doctrine does possess some discerning attributes. Preliminarily, *Erie* has no relevance when a federal court is hearing a lawsuit premised in federal law; in such cases, the choice is clear—federal substantive and procedural law applies. Thus, the only

[48] *Stewart Organization, Inc. v. Ricoh Corp.*, 487 U.S. 22 (1988).

[49] *Id.* at 26, 108 S. Ct. at 2242.

[1] *See Briseno v. Henderson*, 998 F.3d 1014, 1029 (9th Cir. 2021) ("Every year, tens of thousands of first year law students learn about *Erie R. Co. v. Tompkins*, and, soon after that, they become second-and-third-year law students with poor understanding of the doctrine. Some of these students take the bar exam, fail, and try again or do other things. Others pass and become attorneys who still do not understand *Erie*.").

time practitioners need to "wade into *Erie*'s murky waters" is when the federal court is hearing a State law dispute—in diversity cases and with supplemental jurisdiction claims. In those categories of cases, how *Erie* applies will depend on the context in which it arises.

APPLICATIONS

Substantive Law

Substantive law (the "rules of decision") establishes the parties' rights, obligations, and remedies.[2] Federal courts must apply State substantive law (the "rules of decision"), unless the U.S. Constitution, an Act of Congress, or a U.S. treaty otherwise supplants ("preempts") that State law.[3] And federal courts may not craft "general" federal common law that ignores a State's substantive law merely because it is judge-made common law. Ergo, when applying a State's substantive law, *all* of it must be applied by the federal courts (constitutional law, statutory law, decisional law).[4] So, absent federal "preemption," the substantive law answer is settled today—State substantive law governs in diversity cases.

Procedural Law, Generally

Procedural law establishes the manner-and-means, or form-and-mode, of litigating a civil lawsuit.[5] Although federal courts represent a separate, independent path for civil dispute resolution, sometimes they may be obligated to apply a State's procedures. When that is necessary depends on the relationship between the applicable State and federal procedural laws.

Procedural Law—Unavoidable Clash Between a State Procedural Law and a Federal Rule of Civil Procedure

By their terms, the Federal Rules of Civil Procedure govern in mostly all civil actions filed in federal court.[6] A Federal Rule of Civil Procedure (or Federal Rule of Evidence) will always apply in place of a State procedure if, using the *Hanna* two-step inquiry discussed above, the federal rule at issue (1) unavoidably conflicts with State procedure and (2) the federal rule is valid (namely, a lawful exercise of rule-making power under the Rules Enabling Act and the U.S. Constitution).[7]

A federal rule and a State procedure unavoidably conflict if they cannot coexist or be harmonized, if choosing to apply one necessarily requires rejecting the other.[8]

A federal rule is valid if it was properly promulgated under

---

[2]*See infra* Part II, § 2.18a (**"The 'Murky' Substantive v. Procedural Law Divide"**).

[3]*See* Rules of Decision Act, 28 U.S.C. § 1652 (1789).

[4]*See Erie R.R. Co. v. Tompkins*, 304 U.S. 64, 77–78 (1938).

[5]*See infra* Part II, § 2.18a (**"The 'Murky' Substantive v. Procedural Law Divide"**).

[6]*See* Rule 1.

[7]*See infra* Part II, § 2.18a (**"The *Erie* Progeny—Federal Rules of Civil Procedure"**).

[8]*See Shady Grove Orthopedic Assocs., P.A. v. Allstate Ins. Co.*, 559 U.S. 393, 398 (2010) (whether the federal rule "answers the question in

both the Rules Enabling Act and the U.S. Constitution. Under the Rules Enabling Act, Congress only authorized the crafting of federal rules that were genuinely procedural (that is, which did not alter substantive rights). Under Article III of the U.S. Constitution, Congress was permitted to set the practice and procedure for federal litigation. Both validity tests reduce to a single, essential inquiry: is the contested rule "really regulating procedure" (*i.e.*, the "manner and means" / "form and mode" of litigating), or is it procedural in appearance but containing a hidden substantive objective?[9] The Federal Rules are considered presumptively valid,[10] with the Court never having found any to fail this validity test.[11]

Procedural Law—Unavoidable Clash Between State Procedural Law and a Federal Statute

Congress delegated rulemaking authority to the U.S. Supreme Court, but Congress may also enact procedural laws directly. When it does so, the *Erie* path is similarly straightforward. Federal courts are bound to apply the procedural law enacted by Congress, provided that Congress acted within its constitutional authority and its law is squarely implicated in the issue before the district court.[12]

Procedural Law—Unavoidable Clash Between State Procedural Law and Federal Case Law, or No Unavoidable Clash At All

If federal procedural *case law* conflicts with State procedures, or if there is no inescapable conflict such that federal and State procedures might both be applied harmoniously together, the

---

dispute"); *Burlington N. R. Co. v. Woods*, 480 U.S. 1, 4–5 (1987) ("initial step" asks whether, "when fairly construed, the scope of [federal rule] is 'sufficiently broad' to cause a 'direct collision' with the state law or, implicitly, to 'control the issue' before the court, thereby leaving no room for the operation of that law"). *Cf. Hamilton v. Wal-Mart Stores, Inc.*, 39 F.4th 575, 583–86 (9th Cir. 2022) (because State enforcement actions and federal class actions serve different purposes, they are "fully compatible and do not conflict for purposes of the first step of an *Erie* analysis"). *See generally infra* Part II, § 2.18a ("**The *Erie* Progeny—Federal Rules of Civil Procedure**").

[9] *See Shady Grove Orthopedic Assocs., P.A. v. Allstate Ins. Co.*, 559 U.S. 393, 407 (2010) ("The [validity] test is not whether the [federal] rule affects a litigant's substantive rights; most procedural rules do. What matters is what the rule itself regulates: If it governs only "the manner and means" by which the litigants' rights are "enforced," it is valid; if it alters "the rules of decision by which [the] court will adjudicate [those] rights," it is not.") (plurality; citations omitted). *See also id.* at 472 ("rationally capable of classification" as procedural)).

[10] *See Burlington N. R.R. Co. v. Woods*, 480 U.S. 1, 6 (1987); *Albright v. Christensen*, 24 F.4th 1039, 1048 n.1 (6th Cir. 2022).

[11] *See Hanna v. Plumer*, 380 U.S. 460, 468 (1965). *See also Martin v. Pierce Cnty.*, 34 F.4th 1125, 1132 (9th Cir. 2022) (noting rejection of every challenge to Federal Rules as violative of Rules Enabling Act).

[12] *See Stewart Org., Inc. v. Ricoh Corp.*, 487 U.S. 22, 26 (1988).

Erie choice is at its murkiest.[13] Here, the analysis seems to require a three-part inquiry:

First, the federal court must inquire whether applying the State law could be "outcome determinative"[14]—to achieve the central goal that the outcome in diversity cases tried in a federal court should be "substantially the same, so far as legal rules determine the outcome of a litigation," as they would be if they were tried in a State court.[15] If the choice would be outcome-affecting, the proper inquiry seems to continue on to the next step. (If the choice would not be outcome-affecting, the federal court will presumably apply its own procedure because whether it does so or not would seemingly have no effect on the lawsuit's outcome.)

Second, the court must next assess whether the "twin aims" of *Erie* are implicated by the choice—that is, whether choosing to apply (or not apply) that State law would encourage forum shopping or cause an inequitable administration of the law.[16] If it would, then the analysis seems to continue on to a final step. (If the "twin aims" of *Erie* are not implicated, the federal court will presumably apply its own procedure.)

Third, the court must assess how likely it is that applying federal procedure rather than State procedure would alter the outcome of the lawsuit, and then weigh the competing interests of the federal and State forums.[17] Although the Supreme Court has never given much guidance as to how this third and final inquiry is performed, a weak (or nonexistent) State interest might cause the federal court to ignore the State procedure at issue, while a strong State interest—that is, one "bound up" with "State-created rights and obligations"—may weigh heavily in favor of applying that State procedure—especially if the State's law can be applied in a manner "without disrupting the federal system" (*i.e.*, the two procedures can be accommodated

---

[13]*See Shady Grove Orthopedic Assocs., P.A. v. Allstate Ins. Co.*, 559 U.S. 393, 398 (2010) (Scalia, J.) ("We do not wade into *Erie*'s murky waters unless the federal rule is inapplicable or invalid."); *Albright v. Christensen*, 24 F.4th 1039, 1048–49 (6th Cir. 2022) ("We invoke *Erie* only if no on-point, valid Federal Rule of Civil or Appellate Procedure exists."). *See also Ellis v. Salt River Project Agric. Improvement & Power Dist.*, 24 F.4th 1262, 1270–71 (9th Cir. 2022) ("Because there is no conflict between the state law and the federal rule, we proceed to determine whether the state law applies in federal court under the *Erie* doctrine.").

[14]*See Guaranty Trust Co. of N.Y. v. York*, 326 U.S. 99, 109 (1945). *See also infra* Part II, § 2.18a (**"The *Erie* Progeny—Outcome Determination"**).

[15]*See Guaranty Tr. Co. v. York*, 326 U.S. 99 (1945) ("nub" of *Erie* policy is that "the accident of a suit by a nonresident litigant in a federal court instead of in a State court a block away, should not lead to a substantially different result").

[16]*See Gasperini v. Ctr. for Humans., Inc.*, 518 U.S. 415, 428 (1996). *See also infra* Part II, § 2.18a (**"The *Erie* Lawsuit"**).

[17]*See Byrd v. Blue Ridge Rural Elec. Co-op., Inc.*, 356 U.S. 525, 533–39 (1958). *See also infra* Part II, § 2.18a (**"The *Erie* Progeny—Moderating Outcome Determination"**).

harmoniously,[18] or if, on closer inspection, the court finds that there is no true conflict between the two laws[19]).

§ 2.18c Identifying the Law to Apply

CORE CONCEPT

When a federal court must apply State law on an issue, an obvious threshold task is discerning the content of that law. As *Erie* made plain, the federal judge's chore "is to ascertain what the state law is, not what it ought to be."[1] Although federal judges hear many cases where State law is implicated, they still lack the experience with State law that State judges will typically have. Moreover, when a State judge decides a difficult question of State law, a party has the ability to seek review of that decision by State appellate judges, who presumably are also experienced in State law. By contrast, if a federal district judge applies State law in a potentially erroneous way, the challenge to that decision is heard by other federal judges. Those federal appellate judges, in turn, may not even be from the State whose law is at issue. To address the difficulties presented by this situation, several distinct approaches have evolved.

APPLICATIONS

The Definitive Choice

If the relevant State supreme court has addressed the matter clearly, its word on State law is normally final.[2] In those cases, the federal court's task in locating the governing law is simple.

The Abstention Option

If a definitive pronouncement from the State's highest court is unavailable, the federal court may be inclined to abstain from hearing the case, concluding that difficult questions of State law are best handled in the State court system. This approach has the advantage of forestalling the risk of an errant federal "guess" about the content of State law, but it also ignores "the virtually unflagging obligation of the federal courts to exercise the jurisdiction given them."[3] It also imposes on the parties all the delay and additional expense involved in re-starting the case in State court.

---

[18]*See Gasperini v. Ctr. for Humans., Inc.*, 518 U.S. 415, 436–38 (1996).

[19]*See Walker v. Armco Steel Corp.*, 446 U.S. 740, 751 (1980).

[1]*Klaxon Co. v. Stentor Electric Mfg. Co.*, 313 U.S. 487, 497 (1941). *See also Guijarro v. Enter. Holdings, Inc.*, 39 F.4th 309, 317 (5th Cir. 2022) ("As a federal court sitting in diversity, our job is not to weigh in on the wisdom of the state rule but to faithfully apply it.").

[2]*See C.I.R. v. Bosch's Est.*, 387 U.S. 456, 465 (1967); *West v. American Tel. & Tel. Co.*, 311 U.S. 223, 236 (1940). *See also Q Clothier New Orleans, L.L.C. v. Twin City Fire Ins. Co.*, 29 F.4th 252, 257 (5th Cir. 2022) (courts look first to final decisions from State's highest court).

[3]*See Colorado River Water Conservation Dist. v. United States*, 424 U.S. 800, 817 (1976). *See also id.*

For these reasons and others, federal courts have not employed the abstention option frequently.[4]

The Certification Option

The federal court might choose to ask for assistance from the highest court of the State whose law is at issue using a process known as "certification". Certification is rarely obligatory,[5] but its use can obviate the need for a federal "guess" on the content of State law and, thus, may "greatly simplify an ultimate adjudication in federal court."[6] Certification also offers a path to a clear answer from a definitive source. But the promise of certification has always been limited by some real-world obstacles.

Not all States have certification statutes, and those that do may not obligate their State's high court (often itself overburdened) to agree to supply the requested certification.[7] When it is available, federal courts do not often invoke the procedure.[8] When invoked, certification is an expensive process, obligating litigants to brief and argue the State law issue before yet another court. It also often causes delay, with the federal litigation often held in abeyance as the State court ponders the certified question.[9] And, even when available, invoked, and accepted, certification does not guarantee that the particular advice supplied by the State's high court will precisely match the federal case's needs.[10] Thus, while certification is more accessible than abstention, it,

---

at 813 (abstaining "is the exception, not the rule," reserved only for "exceptional circumstances").

[4]*See Colorado River Water Conservation Dist. v. United States*, 424 U.S. 800, 813 (1976) (abstaining "is the exception, not the rule"); *Meredith v. City of Winter Haven*, 320 U.S. 228, 234, 64 S. Ct. 7, 11, 88 L. Ed. 9 (1943) (abstention should be employed only in "exceptional circumstances"). *See also Minot v. Eckardt-Minot*, 13 F.3d 590, 593 (2d Cir. 1994) (in some limited circumstances, abstention may be appropriate basis to remand case previously removed to federal court, but "courts should be wary of using judicially-crafted abstention doctrines to deny out-of-state litigants a federal forum that they prefer").

[5]*See Lehman Bros. v. Schein*, 416 U.S. 386, 390–91 (1974) (not obligatory, but can help build cooperative judicial federalism). *But cf. McKesson v. Doe*, __ U.S. __,141 S. Ct. 48, 50–51 (2020) (although not obligatory, certification is "advisable" is exceptional circumstances to avoid addressing constitutional issue; vacating and remanding for certification to highest state court).

[6]*See Arizonans for Off. Eng. v. Arizona*, 520 U.S. 43, 79(1997) (cleaned up).

[7]*See generally* Geri J. Yonover, *A Kinder, Gentler* Erie*: Reining in the Use of Certification*, 47 ARK. L. REV. 305, 314–16 (1994) (most but not all jurisdictions have certification statutes).

[8]*See McKesson v. Doe*, __ U.S. __, 141 S. Ct. 48, 50 (2020) ("Federal courts have only rarely resorted to state certification procedures, which can prolong the dispute and increase the expenses incurred by the parties.").

[9]*See, e.g., West American Ins. Co. v. Bank of Isle of Wight*, 673 F. Supp. 760, 764 (E.D. Va. 1987) (certification imposes on time and resources of both state supreme court and parties).

[10]*See, e.g., Valentine v. Sugar Rock, Inc.*, 745 F.3d 729, 735 (4th Cir. 2014) (agreeing to certify question to state supreme court, but acknowledg-

too, offers an imperfect alternative in the quest to obtaining a reliable, definitive answer to a hard question of State law.

The *Erie* "Guess"

The option followed most frequently in the federal courts is the one most burdened by uncertainty: federal courts will endeavor to "predict" what the State high court would do, were the question to be presented to that tribunal[11]—always vigilant to ensure that they are applying State law, not creating, reformulating, or extending it.[12] In doing so, federal courts may consult a variety of sources: other case law or enacted law from that same State that offer clues as to what the State would do; trends in neighboring States and majority views; and even legal scholarship.[13] This path for discerning the content of State law, while frequently used, is also obviously the one fraught with the greatest risk for error. And were the federal court to "predict" incorrectly, the litigants are often bound forever by the result. Thus, for example, if a federal court "predicts" that a State high court would resolve a question in a certain way, that judgment is likely to be final—even if the State's highest court later, in a different case involving different parties, definitively resolves the very same question

ing that state supreme court may choose to "reformulate" question).

[11] *See Camacho v. Ford Motor Co.*, 993 F.3d 308, 311 (5th Cir. 2021) ("In applying Texas law, we are bound by the Texas Supreme Court's decisions. But if that Court has not considered an issue, we make an '*Erie* guess' about how it would rule.").

[12] *See Klaxon Co. v. Stentor Elec. Mfg. Co.*, 313 U.S. 487, 497 (1941) ("the proper function of the . . . federal court is to ascertain what the state law is, not what it ought to be"). *See also Doe v. Trustees of Boston College*, 942 F.3d 527 (1st Cir. 2019) (care should be taken "not to extend state law beyond its well-marked borderline"); *SMI Owen Steel Co. v. Marsh USA, Inc.*, 520 F.3d 432, 442 (5th Cir. 2008) (per curiam) ("When making an *Erie* guess, 'our task is to attempt to predict state law, not to create or modify it.' "); *David v. Tanksley*, 218 F.3d 928, 930 (8th Cir. 2000) ("[O]ur duty is to 'ascertain and apply' Arkansas law, 'not to formulate the legal mind of the state.' ").

[13] *See Guilbeau v. Hess Corp.*, 854 F.3d 310, 312 n.4 (5th Cir. 2017) (sources include: decisions from the high court in analogous cases; rationales and analyses employed by that court on related issues; that court's dicta; lower state court decisions; the "general rule" followed on the question; the rulings of courts of other states; treatises and legal commentaries). *See also SodexoMAGIC, LLC v. Drexel Univ.*, 24 F.4th 183, 204 (3d Cir. 2022) (in making prediction, "the decisions of intermediate Pennsylvania appellate courts receive significant weight in the absence of an indication that the highest state court would rule otherwise") (cleaned up); *Terry Black's Barbecue, L.L.C. v. State Auto. Mut. Ins. Co.*, 22 F.4th 450, 454 (5th Cir. 2022) ("An *Erie* guess must be based on: (1) decisions of the Texas Supreme Court in analogous cases, (2) the rationales and analyses underlying Texas Supreme Court decisions on related issues, (3) dicta by the Texas Supreme Court, (4) lower state court decisions, (5) the general rule on the question, (6) the rulings of courts of other states to which Texas courts look when formulating substantive law, and (7) other available sources, such as treatises and legal commentaries.").

in the opposite manner.[14]

Using the Law the State Court Would Use.

The heart of *Erie* is a rule directing federal district courts to apply the substantive law that a State court would use. In *Erie* itself, application of that rule meant that a federal district court sitting in New York would apply the same substantive law that a New York State trial court would use.

That application may seem straightforward enough, but it contains a subtle distinction. *Erie* does not direct a federal district court sitting in New York to use New York states's substantive law in every case controlled by *Erie*. Instead, it directs the federal district court to defer to the State courts in two different ways: first, to use the same substantive law that the State court would use; and second, to use the same system for determining which State's substantive law the State court would actually apply.[15] The second point is complicated, but can be illustrated using *Erie* itself as an example.

The injury to Tompkins that gave rise to the *Erie* case occurred in Pennsylvania. Tompkins filed his lawsuit in a federal district court in New York. If the case had been heard in a State court in New York, that State court would have had to decide whether to use New York substantive law (the law of the State where the case was heard), Pennsylvania substantive law (the law of the State where the incident took place), or the substantive law of some other State (perhaps, the law of the State where the train had been designed, manufactured, or assembled). On the facts of *Erie*, it was clear at the time the case was heard that a New York State court would have applied the substantive law of Pennsylvania on the ground that the accident giving rise to the suit occurred in Pennsylvania.[16] Because a New York State court would have used Pennsylvania law, the duty of the federal district court in New York under the *Erie* doctrine—to apply the same law that a State court would use—was also to use Pennsylvania law.

An entire body of law (called "conflict of laws" or "choice of law") is devoted to determining when a State trial court should use its own law or the law of another State. While the study of conflict of laws is not immediately within the scope of *Erie*, it is probably apparent how important conflict of laws can be for cases to which the *Erie* doctrine applies.

---

[14]*See Deweerth v. Baldinger*, 38 F.3d 1266, 1274 (2d Cir. 1994).

[15]*See Klaxon Co. v. Stentor Elec. Mfg. Co.*, 313 U.S. 487, 496–97 (1941) (*Erie* compels application of conflict of law principles of forum state).

[16]This point was so thoroughly settled at the time of *Erie* that the discussion of applicable law centered solely on whether federal general common law or Pennsylvania law controlled the case. There was, in short, no suggestion that a federal district court in New York would apply New York substantive law to the facts of *Erie*. That same result might not be quite as clear today, but it was eminently clear when *Erie* was decided.

§ 2.18d A Residue of Federal Common Law

CORE CONCEPT

Although *Erie* abolished federal general common law, another form of federal common law continues to exist on the margin of *Erie*—a "residue" now known as "specialized" federal common law.[1] The Supreme Court has held that such common law may apply to cases nominally involving State law, in which the United States has such a strong interest in a uniform body of law applied across the country, but as to which Congress has not yet acted. In a colorful tutorial by the Second Circuit, this specialized brand of federal common law "functions much like legal duct tape — it is a 'necessary expedient' that permits federal courts to address issues of national concern until Congress provides a more permanent solution."[2] Thus, this is not akin to the federal general common law authority that *Swift v. Tyson* abolished for most State causes of action in federal courts.[3] At the same time, this surviving residue of federal common law can be substantive law, notwithstanding *Erie*. For example, in *Clearfield Trust Co. v. United States,*[4] the Supreme Court concluded that federal law controlled whether the federal government was liable to an innocent party that had cashed a stolen federal payroll check. The need for uniform treatment of federal checks throughout the country was held to require the application of federal common law on this substantive issue.[5]

The number of circumstances in which federal common law may, notwithstanding *Erie*, displace State substantive law are few,[6] limited to a narrow, defined set of categories.[7] They fall basically into two groups: "those in which a federal rule of decision

---

[1]*See City of New York v. Chevron Corp.*, 993 F.3d 81, 89 (2d Cir. 2021) ("*Erie* was not a death knell to all federal common law").

[2]*See City of New York v. Chevron Corp.*, 993 F.3d 81, 90 (2d Cir. 2021).

[3]*Cf., American Electric Power Co. v. Connecticut*, 564 U.S. 410 (2011) (more recent, "keener" understanding of *Erie* recognizes limited existence of federal common law where Congress has directed or where "basic scheme of the Constitution so demands;" Holding that environmental protection falls within Congressional legislative reach, and courts may fill in statutory interstices).

[4]*Clearfield Trust Co. v. U.S.*, 318 U.S. 363 (1943).

[5]*Clearfield Trust Co. v. United States*, 318 U.S. 363, 365 (1943). *But see American Electric Power Co. v. Connecticut*, 564 U.S. 410 (2011) (acknowledging cases like Clearfield, but holding that where Congress actually displaced federal common law, *e.g.*, where environmental legislation has been enacted to authorize containment of carbon dioxide emissions, federal common law is no longer applicable; result holds even if regulatory agency (EPA) has not yet created statutorily authorized regulations).

[6]*See Atherton v. F.D.I.C.*, 519 U.S. 213, 218 (1997) ("cases in which judicial creation of a special federal rule would be justified . . . are . . . 'few and restricted' "); *Wheeldin v. Wheeler*, 373 U.S. 647, 651 (1963) (same).

[7]*See, e.g., Hinderlider v. La Plata River & Cherry Creek Ditch Co.*, 304 U.S. 92 (1938) (disputes between states); *Florida v. Georgia*, __ U.S. __, 138 S. Ct. 2502 (2018) (disputes involv-

is necessary to protect uniquely federal interests, and those in which Congress has given the courts the power to develop substantive law."[8] Such circumstances arise infrequently, as one might expect. The Supreme Court has explained why: "Judicial lawmaking in the form of federal common law plays a necessarily modest role under a Constitution that vests the federal government's 'legislative Powers' in Congress and reserves most other regulatory authority to the States."[9] Accordingly, this specialized federal common law is not central to an understanding of the problems often raised by *Erie*. However, in the occasional case where precedent like *Clearfield Trust* may displace *Erie*, an awareness of the continuing vitality of this pocket of surviving federal common law can be crucial.[10]

---

ing interstate bodies of water); *Banco Nacional de Cuba v. Sabbatino*, 376 U.S. 398 (1964) (disputes involving foreign nations); *Oneida Cty. v. Oneida Indian Nations of N.Y. State*, 470 U.S. 226 (1985) (disputes by Native Americans to sue to enforce aboriginal land rights); *Boyle v. United Technologies Corp.*, 487 U.S. 500 (1988) (disputes involving federal contractors and civil liability of federal officials); *Rodriguez v. FDIC, __, U.S. __*, 140 S. Ct. 713 (2020) (disputes in admiralty). *Sosa v. Alvarez-Machain*, 542 U.S. 692 (2004) (disputes under the federal Alien Tort Statute); *Cf. Empire Healthchoice Assur., Inc. v. McVeigh*, 547 U.S. 677 (2006) (acknowledging Clearfield as "a pathmarking precedent on the authority of federal courts to fashion uniform federal common law on issues of national concern," but noting that such common law is still unusual).

[8] *See Tex. Indus., Inc. v. Radcliff Materials, Inc.*, 451 U.S. 630, 640 (1981).

[9] *See Rodriguez v. FDIC, __, U.S. __*, 140 S. Ct. 713, 717 (2020).

[10] *See, e.g., American Insurance Association v. Garamendi*, 539 U.S. 396, 401 (2003) (federal foreign affairs doctrine mandates dismissal of state law claims that might interfere with U.S. foreign relations); *American Electric Power Co. v. Connecticut*, 564 U.S. 410 (2011) (environmental protection is a federal responsibility, and therefore an area where federal courts may fill in gaps in statutory law or even 'fashion federal law' "); *Illinois v. City of Milwaukee*, 406 U.S. 91 (1972) (acknowledging nonexistence of federal general common law; but ambient or interstate aspects of air and water are proper areas for federal common law). *See also Banco Nacional de Cuba v. Sabbatino*, 376 U.S. 398 (1964) (federal act of state doctrine precludes state law challenge to property expropriation by Cuba); *Revock v. Cowpet Bay West Condominium Association*, 853 F.3d 96 (3d Cir. 2017) (federal common law governs survival of federal claim); *Mujica v. Air Scan, Inc.*, 771 F.3d 580 (9th Cir. 2014) (federal law of international comity applies to diversity case).

G. PRECLUSION (RES JUDICATA AND COLLATERAL ESTOPPEL)

Table of Sections

2.19 Introduction
2.20 Claim Preclusion (Res Judicata—)
2.21 Issue Preclusion (*Collateral Estoppel*)

§ 2.19 Introduction

CORE CONCEPT

Claim preclusion (res judicata) and issue preclusion (collateral estoppel) are companion doctrines that the law has recognized for nearly a thousand years.[1] They address the consequences of an entry of judgment in one lawsuit on subsequent, related cases.[2] At their broadest level, and subject to various exceptions, these doctrines establish the rule that once a case has reached a final judgment, certain claims or issues resolved during that case will be treated as forever decided and, thus, foreclosed from re-litigation. Thus, when claim preclusion (res judicata) applies, a plaintiff who lost a lawsuit will likely be foreclosed from later raising claims which were raised (or perhaps, which could have been raised) in that lawsuit. When issue preclusion (collateral estoppel) applies, an issue squarely resolved in an earlier litigation may be treated as already decided—without further proof—in a subsequent litigation involving that same issue.

The policies behind these related doctrines are grounded in judicial economy and litigation finality. As the U.S. Supreme Court wrote nearly a century ago: "Public policy dictates that there be an end of litigation; that those who have contested an issue shall be bound by the result of the contest; and that matters once tried shall be considered forever settled as between the

[1] *See Minerva Surgical, Inc. v. Hologic, Inc.*, ___ U.S. ___, 141 S. Ct. 2298, 2319 (2021) (Barrett, J., dissenting) (citing authorities tracing doctrines back to "early 1100s" with roots in Roman law).

[2] Importantly, it is the second court — not the court that first heard the case and entered a judgment — that will decide the applicability of the first judgment to other cases. *See Phillips Petroleum Co. v. Shutts*, 472 U.S. 797, 805, 105 S. Ct. 2965, 86 L. Ed. 2d 628 (1985) ("[A] court adjudicating a dispute may not be able to predetermine the res judicata effect of its own judgment."); *Migra v. Warren City Sch. Dist. Bd. of Educ.*, 465 U.S. 75, 81 (1984) ("a federal court must give to a state-court judgment the same preclusive effect as would be given that judgment under the law of the State in which the judgment was rendered").

parties."[3] Enforcing the two preclusion principles serves to "relieve parties of the cost and vexation of multiple lawsuits, conserve judicial resources, and, by preventing inconsistent decisions, encourage reliance on adjudication."[4]

These doctrines can present substantial litigating risks and opportunities for parties.

APPLICATIONS

Terminology

The doctrines—claim preclusion and issue preclusion—have often been mired in an imprecise, varying use of terminology, leaving confusion in its wake. That confusion emanates from several sources.

First, although they enjoy ancient lineage, the traditional terms "res judicata" and "collateral estoppel" are not especially descriptive. More recent case law and scholarship has endeavored to solve that unhelpful nomenclature by replacing the term "claim preclusion" for res judicata and "issue preclusion" for collateral estoppel.[5] Doing so has the obvious advantage of readily orienting the reader to *what*, precisely, is being precluded (an entire claim or just an issue). This new language has received a mixed[6] but largely favorable review, and seems destined to stay.

Second, an exasperating former practice used "res judicata" as an umbrella term to encompass preclusion doctrines generally, leaving the reader to sift through context in order to discern which of the preclusion types (or both) was being discussed.[7] Although this practice seems less common today, it persists[8] and practitioners must be watchful for "res judicata"

---

[3] *See Baldwin v. Iowa State Traveling Men's Ass'n*, 283 U.S. 522, 525–26 (1931). *See also B & B Hardware, Inc. v. Hargis Indus., Inc.*, 575 U.S. 138, 148 (2015) (Court "regularly turns" to Second Restatement of Judgments for ordinary elements of issue preclusion).

[4] *See Allen v. McCurry*, 449 U.S. 90, 94 (1980).

[5] *See, e.g., Yeager v. U.S.*, 557 U.S. 110, 119 n.4 (2009) ("Currently, the more descriptive term 'issue preclusion' is often used in lieu of 'collateral estoppel.' "); *Taylor v. Sturgell*, 553 U.S. 880, 892 n.5 (2008) (new terms "have replaced a more confusing lexicon"); *Kircher v. Putnam Funds Tr.*, 547 U.S. 633, 647 n.14 (2006) ("Modern usage calls for the descriptive term, 'issue preclusion,' in place of 'collateral estoppel.' ").

[6] *See Kircher v. Putnam Funds Tr.*, 547 U.S. 633, 647 n.14 (2006) (using "collateral estoppel" because "we are backsliders out of pity for the tired reader").

[7] *See, e.g., Taylor v. Sturgell*, 553 U.S. 880, 892 n.5 (2008) ("The preclusive effect of a judgment is defined by claim preclusion and issue preclusion, which are collectively referred to as 'res judicata'."); *Covert v. LVNV Funding, LLC*, 779 F.3d 242, 246 (4th Cir. 2015) (res judicata encompasses both claim preclusion and issue preclusion) *Graham v. R.J. Reynolds Tobacco Co.*, 611 F.3d 1324, 1331–32 (11th Cir. 2010) (res judicata can refer to claim preclusion or issue preclusion or both).

[8] *See Brownback v. King*, 592 U.S. —, 141 S. Ct. 740, 747 n.3 (2021) ("The terms res judicata and claim preclusion often are used interchangeably.");

used in this non-specific, categorical way.[9]

Third, the law recognizes other doctrines that, though preclusive in effect, apply in different settings and are governed by different requirements—such as double jeopardy,[10] equitable estoppel,[11] judicial estoppel,[12] and law-of-the-case.[13]

The preclusion doctrines owe their existence almost entirely to development in judge-made common law.[14] Legislative influence on these doctrines is limited, and constitutional considerations arise only in circumstances where claim preclusion or issue preclusion might have the potential to limit the due process right of an interested party to a fair hearing.[15] Thus, invoking preclusion principles to bar a claim by a party who had not yet had a fair opportunity to be heard in court will often run afoul of constitutional due process.[16]

These and other terminology challenges counsel great care in researching these doctrines. A quick, superficial scan of "preclusion" case law is an unreliable substitute for a careful, targeted search into claim preclusion and/or issue preclusion case law.

Lucky Brand Dungarees, Inc. v. Marcel Fashions Grp., Inc., 590 U.S. __, 140 S. Ct. 1589, 1594 (2020) (res judicata "now comprises two distinct doctrines regarding the preclusive effect of prior litigation").

[9]*See Migra v. Warren City Sch. Dist. Bd. of Educ.*, 465 U.S. 75, 77 n.1 (1984) (noting "varying and, at times, seemingly conflicting terminology"; choosing "claim preclusion" to "avoid confusion resulting from the two uses of 'res judicata' ").

[10]*See Currier v. Virginia*, 585 U.S. __, 138 S. Ct. 2144, 2152 (2018) ("any effort to transplant civil preclusion principles into the Double Jeopardy Clause would quickly meet trouble").

[11]*See Wells Cargo, Inc. v. Wells Cargo, Inc.*, 606 F.2d 961, 964 (C.C.P.A. 1979) (while equitable estoppel and res judicata are "closely related," equitable estoppel may be asserted in contexts where res judicata cannot).

[12]*See New Hampshire v. Maine*, 532 U.S. 742, 749 (2001) (judicial estoppel is doctrine "distinct" from res judicata, and may preclude litigant from prevailing on argument in one setting and attempting to prevail on contradictory argument in later setting).

[13]*See Arizona v. California*, 460 U.S. 605, 618 (1984) (unlike res judicata, "law of the case is an amorphous concept" which "posits that when a court decides upon a rule of law, that decision should continue to govern the same issues in subsequent stages in the same case").

[14]*See Taylor v. Sturgell*, 553 U.S. 880, 891 (2008) ("The preclusive effect of a federal-court judgment is determined by federal common law."). *See generally San Remo Hotel, L.P. v. City & Cnty. of San Francisco, Cal.*, 545 U.S. 323, 336 n.17 (2005) ("The authority of the *res judicata*, with the limitations under which it is admitted, is derived by us from the Roman law and the Canonists," quoting Washington, Alexandria, & Georgetown Steam-Packet Co. v. Sickles, 65 U.S. (24 How.) 333, 341 (1861)).

[15]*See, e.g., B & B Hardware, Inc. v. Hargis Indus., Inc.*, 575 U.S. 138, 150 (2015) (Seventh Amendment right to jury trial "does not negate the issue-preclusive effect of a judgment, even if that judgment was entered by a juryless tribunal," citing *Parklane Hosiery Co. v. Shore*, 439 U.S. 322, 337 (1979)).

[16]*See, e.g., South Central Bell Telephone Co. v. Alabama*, 526 U.S. 160, 168 (1999) (due process prevents application of res judicata to bar litigation by parties who did not participate in prior action, either personally, through concept of privity, or through membership in a class).

Common Law (Case Law) Doctrine

Because claim preclusion and issue preclusion are not constitutional in nature, the national import of U.S. Supreme Court precedent on these doctrines is limited. The Court can and does establish the standards for these two doctrines when they are used in federal courts, but the States are free to accept or reject federal approaches to these doctrines (except to the extent of constitutional encroachment). U.S. Supreme Court case law may therefore be an important influence on the development and application of these doctrines in State courts, but such decisions are not necessarily the final word.[17]

Both claim preclusion (res judicata) and issue preclusion (collateral estoppel) are listed as affirmative defenses in the Federal Rules of Civil Procedure.[18] Like all affirmative defenses, the party asserting them defensively bears the burden of pleading and proving them.[19] Failure to properly assert these defenses can result in their waiver or forfeiture.[20] When these preclusion theories are asserted offensively (for example, by a claimant), the burden of pleading and proving likely shifts to that asserting party.[21]

Must Be Asserted as Affirmative Defense

Relationship to Full Faith and Credit

The U.S. Constitution's Full Faith and Credit Clause obligates each State to honor (thus enforce) the competently

---

[17]Because state courts often develop their own case law in this area, federal courts hearing diversity claims must sometimes determine whether to apply state procedure or federal procedure. In other words, federal courts must make an analysis under the rule of *Erie v. Tompkins*, discussed in § 2.18. As a general rule, federal courts have concluded that where state and federal views of res judicata differ, state views should be applied in a diversity case. See, e.g., *Xantech Corp. v. Ramco Industries, Inc.*, 159 F.3d 1089, 1092 (7th Cir. 1998) ("[W]e look to the law of Indiana in this diversity action to determine whether the claims that [the plaintiff] makes in this suit are barred on res judicata grounds.").

[18]*See* Rule 8(c)(1) ("estoppel"; "res judicata"). *See also Taylor v. Sturgell*, 553 U.S. 880, 907 (2008); *Blonder-Tongue Lab'ys, Inc. v. Univ. of Illinois Found.*, 402 U.S. 313, 350 (1971)

[19]*See Taylor v. Sturgell*, 553 U.S. 880, 907 (2008). *See also Blonder-Tongue Lab'ys, Inc. v. Univ. of Illinois Found.*, 402 U.S. 313, 350 (1971) ("The purpose of such pleading is to give the opposing party notice of the plea of estoppel and a chance to argue, if he can, why the imposition of an estoppel would be inappropriate."). *See generally infra* Authors' Commentary to Rule 8(c).

[20]*See Arizona v. California*, 530 U.S. 392, 410 (2000). *See also Burton v. Ghosh*, 961 F.3d 960, 964–72 (7th Cir. 2020) (exhaustive discussion of res judicata waiver principles). *See generally infra* Authors' Commentary to Rule 8(c) (**"Waiver (Forfeiture)"**). *But cf. Shurick v. Boeing Co.*, 623 F.3d 1114, 1116 n.2 (11th Cir. 2010) (permitting court to raise claim preclusion *sua sponte* "in the interest of judicial economy where both actions were brought before the same court").

[21]*See In re Dunston*, 146 B.R. 269, 277 (D. Colo. 1992) ("the party using offensive collateral estoppel bears the burden of proving that the elements of issue preclusion have been met").

rendered[22] final judgments of every other State to the same extent as the rendering State's courts would.[23] A federal full faith and credit statute imposes a similar obligation on federal courts.[24] The result of these full faith and credit mandates is to give the rendering State's judgment "nationwide force."[25] Thus, if the rendering State would give preclusive effect to that judgment, all other State and federal courts will as well.[26]

§ 2.20 Claim Preclusion (*Res Judicata*)

CORE CONCEPT

Claim preclusion (res judicata) terminates a litigant's right to sue entirely. It applies when litigants attempt to re-try the same dispute that they had litigated before. Ordinarily, litigants are allowed only "one bite" at the "litigation apple" with their claim. Once they've had their bite, their litigation rights are exhausted and cannot be re-asserted (subject, of course, to their right to argue in post-trial motions or on appeal that something erroneous occurred *during* that "one bite", necessitating that the case be re-tried).[1] Historically, this principle was known as "merger" and "bar" (the litigant's entire claim is deemed to *merge* into the final judgment, which *bars* the reassertion of that now exhausted claim).[2] For claim preclusion to apply, three elements must be met: claim identity, party identity, and a final, valid judgment on the merits. Each element is examined in turn below.

A helpful claim preclusion (res judicata) spotting tool is this: there must have been a prior litigation. That is the irreducible

---

[22] *Cf. Phillips Petroleum Co. v. Shutts*, 472 U.S. 797, 805 (1985) ("a judgment issued without proper personal jurisdiction over an absent party is not entitled to full faith and credit elsewhere and thus has no res judicata effect as to that party").

[23] *See* U.S. Const. Art. IV, § 1 ("Full Faith and Credit shall be given in each State to the public Acts, Records, and judicial Proceedings of every other State."). *See also Baker by Thomas v. Gen. Motors Corp.*, 522 U.S. 222, 233 (1998) (requirement is "exacting": "A final judgment in one State, if rendered by a court with adjudicatory authority over the subject matter and persons governed by the judgment, qualifies for recognition throughout the land."). *See generally Milwaukee County v. M.E. White Co.*, 296 U.S. 268, 277 (1935) (Clause's purpose was "to alter the status of the several states as independent foreign sovereignties, each free to ignore obligations created under the laws or by the judicial proceedings of the others").

[24] *See* 28 U.S.C.A. § 1738.

[25] *See Baker by Thomas v. Gen. Motors Corp.*, 522 U.S. 222, 233 (1998). *See also Riley v. New York Tr. Co.*, 315 U.S. 343, 349 (1942) (through full faith and credit, "the local doctrines of res judicata, speaking generally, become a part of national jurisprudence").

[26] *See Marrese v. Am. Acad. of Orthopaedic Surgeons*, 470 U.S. 373, 380 (1985); *Kremer v. Chemical Constr. Corp.*, 456 U.S. 461, 466 (1982).

[1] *See Richards v. Jefferson Cty.*, 517 U.S. 793, 797 n.4 (1996) ("The doctrine of *res judicata* rests at bottom upon the ground that the party to be affected, or some other with whom he is in privity, has litigated or had an opportunity to litigate the same matter in a former action in a court of competent jurisdiction.").

[2] *See Lucky Brand Dungarees, Inc. v. Marcel Fashions Grp., Inc.*, 590 U.S. —, 140 S. Ct. 1589, 1595 (2020).

prerequisite for claim preclusion. While the existence of a prior litigation does not necessarily trigger claim preclusion in a later case, the absence of a prior litigation means that claim preclusion cannot possibly apply.[3]

APPLICATIONS

Element #1: Identical Claims

To trigger claim preclusion, a party must be attempting to re-litigate the same claim that the party had litigated before.[4] Obviously, then, if the claims at issue now bear no relationship to claims litigated earlier, the present claims cannot be barred by claim preclusion. If, for example, a plaintiff now suing a defendant for breaching a business contract six weeks ago had previously sued that same defendant three years ago in an entirely unrelated automobile collision case, claim preclusion could not apply — the "claims" in the two cases are different. But if the plaintiff in the auto collision lawsuit had sued the defendant for injuries to the palm of his left hand, it is likely that the same plaintiff could not now sue the same defendant for injuries to the back of his left hand in a later lawsuit. Even though the first lawsuit had not actually sought back-hand injury damages, the "claim" in both lawsuits—auto collision personal injury—would almost certainly be considered the same. Because the plaintiff could have—and, indeed, should have—asserted the back-hand injury at the same time as he litigated his palm injury, he will have lost the right to litigate that injury now.[5]

Claims need not overlap one another completely to trigger claim preclusion. In the example above, the back-hand lawsuit and palm injury lawsuit share much in common, but each would still likely implicate proofs that the other would not (*e.g.*, palm injury prevents plaintiff from grabbing utensils, while back-hand injury prevents plaintiff from sleeping restfully). Nonetheless, claim preclusion would likely still apply.

Over the years, courts struggled to develop rules to assess when two claims share enough in common to satisfy claim preclusion's claim identity requirement.[6] One early approach, now largely abandoned, tested whether the two claims raised the same or different theories of recovery. Another approach

---

[3]*Cf. Lalowski v. City of Des Plaines*, 789 F.3d 784 (7th Cir. 2015) (res judicata inapplicable to claims raised in same suit).

[4]*See New Hampshire v. Maine*, 532 U.S. 742, 748 (2001) (forecloses re-litigation of "the very same claim").

[5]*See Lucky Brand Dungarees, Inc. v. Marcel Fashions Grp., Inc.*, 590 U.S. __, 140 S. Ct. 1589, 1594–95 (2020) ("claim preclusion prevents parties from raising issues that could have been raised and decided in a prior action—even if they were not actually litigated. If a later suit advances the same claim as an earlier suit between the same parties, the earlier suit's judgment 'prevents litigation of all grounds for, or defenses to, recovery that were previously available to the parties, regardless of whether they were asserted or determined in the prior proceeding.' ")

[6]*See generally Carter v. Hinkle*, 52 S.E.2d 135, 138 (Va. 1949) (discussing early theories of claim identity).

asked whether the legal right allegedly invaded in the first claim was the same as or different from the legal right allegedly invaded in the second claim. Still another approach inquired whether the two claims had arisen from the same allegedly wrongful act.

Today, many courts have migrated towards the view that claims are identical for claim preclusion purposes if their "underlying facts are 'related in time, space, origin, or motivation, whether they form a convenient trial unit, and whether their treatment as a unit conforms to the parties' expectations or business understanding or usage.' "[7] Put another way, two claims are identical for claim preclusion purposes if they arise from the "same transaction" or share a "common nucleus of operative fact."[8] This more recent formulation borrows from familiar, existing language that appears in the joinder and supplemental jurisdiction contexts. In performing this inquiry, courts often focus on whether the two claims would require substantially overlapping items of proof.[9] Conversely, if the transactions or events at issue took place at significantly different points in time, claims arising from those different times will generally not be treated as identical.[10] Thus, in a circumstance where ship pilots had sued to recover fees owed by a shipping company under a State statute, the judgment in that case would not preclude subsequent claims for fees arising from voyages that had not yet taken place at the time of the first litigation.[11]

Note, however, that the same transaction/common nucleus approach to claim preclusion has not achieved a universal following. Other formulations exist. One newer alternative

---

[7] *See Interoceanica Corp. v. Sound Pilots, Inc.*, 107 F.3d 86, 90 (2d Cir. 1997) (quoting RESTATEMENT (SECOND) OF JUDGMENTS § 24(b) (1982)).

[8] *See Brownback v. King*, 592 U.S. —, 141 S. Ct. 740, 747 n.3 (2021) (arises from same transaction or involves "common nucleus of operative facts"); *Lucky Brand Dungarees, Inc. v. Marcel Fashions Grp., Inc.*, 590 U.S. —, 140 S. Ct. 1589, 1594 (2020) ("Suits involve the same claim . . . when they arise from the same transaction, or involve a common nucleus of operative facts") (cleaned up); *Apparel Art Intern., Inc. v. Amertex Enterprises Ltd.*, 48 F.3d 576, 583 (1st Cir. 1995) ("a set of facts which can be characterized as a single transaction or a series of related transactions").

[9] *See, e.g., N.L.R.B. v. United Technologies Corp.*, 706 F.2d 1254, 1260 (2d Cir. 1983) (for res judicata, test is whether "same evidence is needed to support both claims, and [whether] the facts essential to the second were present in the first").

[10] *See Lucky Brand Dungarees, Inc. v. Marcel Fashions Grp., Inc.*, 590 U.S. —, 140 S. Ct. 1589, 1596 (2020) (claim preclusion generally does not bar claims based on events postdating initial complaint). *See also S.E.C. v. First Jersey Securities, Inc.*, 101 F.3d 1450, 1464 (2d Cir. 1996) ("If the second litigation involved different transactions, and especially subsequent transactions, there generally is no claim preclusion;" presence of same parties or even overlapping facts need not be dispositive to prove "identical" claims).

[11] *See, e.g., Interoceanica Corp. v. Sound Pilots, Inc.*, 107 F.3d 86, 91 (2d Cir. 1997) ("While the subsequent voyages represent wrongs that are the 'same' in legal theory, they are not related in time, space, or origin to the wrongs litigated [earlier].").

involves weighing of four factors: whether the two lawsuits rest on the same nucleus of facts; whether rights established in the first lawsuit could be impaired if the second lawsuit is allowed to proceed; whether the lawsuits relate to infringement of the same underlying right; and whether essentially the same evidence will be litigated in both actions.[12]

Element #2: Identical Parties

The second requirement for claim preclusion is that the parties in the second action must be identical to, or in privity with, the parties in the first action.[13] It is for this reason that claim preclusion cannot bar the lawsuit of one pedestrian injured by a negligently swerving motorist simply because a second pedestrian, also injured by that same negligently swerving motorist, filed suit earlier and prevailed. Although the claims of the two pedestrians share an obvious transactional relatedness and arise from a nucleus of operative facts that is incontestably common, they remain different people. They are not, in the language of the law, "identical" parties.[14]

For purposes of this second requirement for claim preclusion, parties who are literally the same persons or business entities are clearly "identical." But identity can also be satisfied by those in privity with the earlier litigants. In general, there are several circumstances in which someone not actually a party to the first action may nevertheless be treated as in privity with a person or entity that was a party: (1) where the nonparty succeeded to the interest of a party (for example, by purchasing whatever interest the party may have had after completion of the first litigation); (2) where the nonparty, though technically not participating in the first suit, nevertheless controlled one party's litigation in that suit[15] (for example, where the nonparty is an insurance company for a party); (3) where the nonparty shares a property interest with the party;[16] (4) where the party and nonparty have an agent-principal relationship; (5) where the party otherwise "adequately represented" the interest of

---

[12]*See, e.g., Garity v. APWU National Labor Org.*, 828 F.3d 848 (9th Cir. 2016).

[13]*See Parklane Hosiery Co. v. Shore*, 439 U.S. 322, 327 n.5 (1979) ("Under the doctrine of res judicata, a judgment on the merits in a prior suit bars a second suit involving the same parties or their privies based on the same cause of action.").

[14]*See Cooper v. Harris*, 581 U.S. __, 137 S. Ct. 1455, 1467 (2017) ("one person's lawsuit generally does not bar another's, no matter how similar they are in substance").

[15]*But cf., Taylor v. Sturgell*, 553 U.S. 880, 895–96 (2008) (claim preclusion does not extend to virtual representation).

[16]*See, e.g., Hart v. Yamaha-Parts Distributors, Inc.*, 787 F.2d 1468, 1472 (11th Cir. 1986) (citing these examples). *See also, e.g., Nero v. Ferris*, 222 Va. 807, 813, 284 S.E.2d 828, 831 (1981) ("[P]rivity generally involves a party so identical in interest with another that he represents the same legal right [but making this determination requires] a careful examination into the circumstances of each case.").

the nonparty;[17] or (6) where a person agrees to be bound by the outcome of a case.[18]

While these categories may appear superficially straightforward, nuances and inconsistencies abound when actual party identity is missing. For example, where one entity holds a twenty percent interest in another entity's lawsuit, the two interests were deemed "completely identical" with one another and the entities were held to be in privity.[19] However, defendants sued individually may not be in privity with their employers.[20]

Element #3: Valid, Final Judgment on the Merits

The third element for claim preclusion is that the first litigation proceeded to a valid, final judgment on the merits of that case.

A judgment is **valid** for claim preclusion purposes if it was entered by a court jurisdictionally competent to do so.[21] When a court erroneously hears a case over which it lacks jurisdiction, a timely and proper challenge to the resulting judgment may render that judgment a nullity.[22] If, however, a judgment has become final, either because no appeal was taken or because appeals have been exhausted, claim preclusion will normally bar consideration of any later challenge to the judgment, without regard to whether the court that originally heard the case did so erroneously.[23] The circumstances in which claim preclusion does not prevail over a belated jurisdictional challenge are narrow.[24] Additionally, a belief (even if well founded) that the judgment is wrongly decided on its merits is not

---

[17]*See Howell Hydrocarbons, Inc. v. Adams*, 897 F.2d 183, 188 (5th Cir. 1990).

[18]*See Taylor v. Sturgell*, 553 U.S. 880, 893–95 (2008).

[19]*Virginia Sur. Co. v. Northrop Grumman Corp.*, 144 F.3d 1243, 1247 (9th Cir. 1998).

[20]*See, e.g., Willner v. Budig*, 848 F.2d 1032, 1034 (10th Cir. 1988) ("Res judicata does not bar [plaintiff's] claims against the defendants in their individual capacities because the defendants are not in privity with the University."); *Headley v. Bacon*, 828 F.2d 1272, 1277–79 (8th Cir. 1987) (distinguishing privity between principal and agent from privity between a governmental entity and officials sued in their individual capacities).

[21]*See In re Atlanta Retail, Inc.*, 456 F.3d 1277, 1285 (11th Cir. 2006) ("the prior judgment must be valid in that it was rendered by a court of competent jurisdiction and in accordance with the requirements of due process"). *See generally Brownback v. King*, 592 U.S. __, 141 S. Ct. 740, 749 (2021) ("Ordinarily, a court cannot issue a ruling on the merits 'when it has no jurisdiction' because 'to do so is, by very definition, for a court to act ultra vires.' "); *Sinochem Int'l Co. v. Malaysia Int'l Shipping Corp.*, 549 U.S. 422, 431 (2007) ("Without jurisdiction the court cannot proceed at all in any cause . . .").

[22]For a comprehensive discussion of some of the more significant kinds of jurisdictional requirements applicable to federal district courts *see infra* §§ 2.1 to 2.12 of this text.

[23]*Kontrick v. Ryan*, 540 U.S. 443, 456 n.9 (2007) ("Even subject-matter jurisdiction . . . may not be attacked collaterally.").

[24]*Travelers Indemnity Co. v. Bailey*, 557 U.S. 137, 153 (2009) (subject to narrow exceptions judgments are protected from collateral attack by res judicata; collecting some excep-

enough to deprive it of validity for purposes of claim preclusion, so long as the deciding court possessed the judicial power to rule.[25]

A judgment is **final** for claim preclusion purposes when a trial judge enters that judgment, thus placing the litigants in a position to enforce or appeal the court's ruling.[26] By contrast, courts have held that the dismissal of lawsuit following settlement will not constitute a final judgment for preclusion purposes, absent a contractual commitment to bar future litigation. The result may be different, however, if the parties seek to have their settlement entered by the court as a judgment or decree. Such action may convert a settlement into a final judgment, which therefore may qualify as preclusive in subsequent litigation.[27] Similarly, claim preclusion also may not apply to situations in which a judge renders a decision that has reverberating, dispositive, practical effects, but remains something less than a final judgment. For example, in a case in which plaintiffs seek certification of their lawsuit as a class action, denial of such certification may not necessarily be a final judgment, even though the reality of the situation is that denial of class status is often a punishing blow to the parties seeking certification.[28]

- *Comparison with Finality for Purpose of Appeal:* Courts and attorneys often use the word "finality" to describe a prerequisite for either filing an appeal or for application of principles of claim preclusion. However, finality has different meanings for these two different purposes. When finality is used as a threshold requirement for an appeal,[29] it is a more rigorous requirement than that imposed when finality is required for purposes of apply-

tions).

[25]*See B & B Hardware, Inc. v. Hargis Indus., Inc.*, 575 U.S. 138, 157–58 (2015). *See also City of Arlington v. F.C.C.*, 569 U.S. 290, 297 (2013) ("even an erroneous judgment is entitled to res judicata effect" because "a jurisdictionally proper but substantively incorrect judicial decision is not ultra vires").

[26]*See Clay v. U.S.*, 537 U.S. 522, 527 (2003) ("[A] federal judgment becomes final for appellate review and claim preclusion purposes when the district court disassociates itself from the case, leaving nothing to be done at the court of first instance save execution of the judgment.").

[27]*See, e.g., Richardson v. Alabama State Bd. of Educ.*, 935 F.2d 1240, 1244 (11th Cir. 1991) ("We specifically have held that res judicata applies to Title VII consent decrees."). *But cf. Keith v. Aldridge*, 900 F.2d 736, 740 (4th Cir. 1990) (where parties consent to resolution of one portion of a case but expressly reserve right to continue litigating other claims, res judicata will not block continuation of unresolved litigation).

[28]*See, e.g., In re General Motors Corp. Pick-Up Truck Fuel Tank Products Liability Litigation*, 134 F.3d 133, 146 (3d Cir. 1998) ("Denial of class certification is not a 'judgment' for the purposes of the Anti-Injunction Act while the underlying litigation remains pending."). *See also Quality Associates, Inc. v. Proctor & Gamble Distributing LLC*, 949 F.3d 283 (6th Cir. 2020) (interlocutory decisions prior to final judgment do not have res judicata effect).

[29]*See, e.g.,* 28 U.S.C.A. § 1291.

ing claim preclusion.[30]

A judgment is **on the merits** for claim preclusion purposes if it "actually passes directly on the substance of a particular claim before the court."[31] Litigation that concludes with a final judgment following a jury verdict obviously meets this requirement. So, too, will a litigation that terminates with a merits-based dismissal under Federal Rule of Civil Procedure 12(b)(6).[32] By contrast, cases dismissed for lack of jurisdiction or improper service of process have preclusive effect only to the extent that the jurisdictional or service issue is now considered foreclosed. If the claimant subsequently files a second suit in an appropriate forum or cures a failed service process on the defendant, the original dismissal will normally not foreclose the second suit because the earlier dismissal was not on the merits of the case.[33]

There are even situations where a final judgment on the merits may not have claim preclusion effect because application of the doctrine would conflict with some other, more important, legal principle. For example, if a district court heard a case involving legal and equitable claims with common facts, and erroneously dismissed all the legal claims, entry of a final ruling on the equitable claims might have no claim preclusion effect. Instead, if the equitable ruling rested on findings of facts that were common to both legal and equitable claims, the equitable ruling would be vacated, because the parties have a right under the Constitution's Seventh Amendment to a jury determination of facts relating to legal claims.[34] At the same time, however, it should be noted that this analysis applies to a relatively uncommon situation, and most equitable decisions are entitled to claim preclusion effect even if later changes in facts might otherwise permit the district court to modify its own equitable decree.

---

[30]*See, e.g., Bell v. Taylor*, 827 F.3d 699 (7th Cir. 2016) (for res judicata purposes, finality requirement is more relaxed; citing cases).

[31]*See Brownback v. King*, 592 U.S. __, 141 S. Ct. 740, 748 (2021); *Semtek Int'l Inc. v. Lockheed Martin Corp.*, 531 U.S. 497, 501-02 (2001).

[32]*Federated Dept. Stores, Inc. v. Moitie*, 452 U.S. 394, 399 n. 3, 101 S. Ct. 2424, 69 L. Ed. 2d 103 (1981) (dismissal under Rule 12(b)(6) is final judgment for purposes of res judicata). *Cf., New Haven Inclusion Cases*, 399 U.S. 392, 481, 90 S. Ct. 2054, 26 L. Ed. 2d 691 (1970) (failure to appeal adverse decision makes that decision a matter of res judicata).

[33]*Semtek Intern. Inc. v. Lockheed Martin Corp.*, 531 U.S. 497 (2001) (judgment "on the merits" does not always trigger application of claim preclusion in subsequent lawsuit). *See, e.g., Ritzen Grp., Inc. v. Jackson Masonry, LLC*, __ U.S. __, 140 S. Ct. 582, 590 (2020) (dismissal for lack of personal jurisdiction leaves plaintiff free to file elsewhere); *Dalton v. NPC Int'l, Inc.*, 932 F.3d 693, 696 (8th Cir. 2019) (dismissals for lack of subject-matter jurisdiction must be without prejudice); *Umbenhauer v. Woog*, 969 F.2d 25, 30 (3d Cir. 1992) (same, for lack of proper service).

[34]*Lytle v. Household Mfg., Inc.*, 494 U.S. 545, 555–56 (1990).

Scope of Claim Preclusion

When it applies, claim preclusion's reach can be quite broad. As discussed above, it acts to bar re-litigation of a "claim"—which includes not just those arguments, theories, and remedy demands that were actually litigated, but also those that *could have been* litigated in a prior lawsuit.[35] This scope of claim preclusion differs significantly from the requirement for issue preclusion (which can apply only to issues which were actually litigated—not issues that could have been litigated but were not).

By contrast, if a claim could not have been raised in the first lawsuit, assertion of that claim in later litigation is not barred by claim preclusion. Thus, if the first court lacked jurisdiction to hear a particular kind of claim, that claim may be asserted later in a court of competent jurisdiction.[36] This circumstance most commonly arises when a plaintiff has both a State cause of action and a federal claim which lies within the exclusive subject-matter jurisdiction of a federal court. If the plaintiff files the first claim in a State court, the outcome of that case will not serve as a bar, under claim preclusion, to a subsequent filing on the federal claim in a federal court. However, if the plaintiff filed first in a federal district court which had jurisdiction (either diversity or supplemental jurisdiction) over the State claim, failure to file both claims at once would probably prevent the unasserted claim from being raised in later litigation.

Special Litigation Settings

The preclusion doctrines can be treated in the case law uniquely in different litigation settings, and practitioners should research whether the doctrines are available at all and, if so, in what manner in the context pertinent to their particular litigation. Some special litigation setting highlights are addressed below:

- *Counterclaims:* Traditionally, federal courts might not have applied claim preclusion to a party's unasserted counterclaims, reasoning that Element #2 (party identity) required not only that the parties in the two

---

[35]*See Brownback v. King*, 592 U.S. __, 141 S. Ct. 740, 747 n.3 (2021) (forecloses re-litigation of same claim "even if certain issues were not litigated in the prior action"); *Lucky Brand Dungarees, Inc. v. Marcel Fashions Grp., Inc.*, 590 U.S. __, 140 S. Ct. 1589, 1594–95 (2020) ("prevents parties from raising issues that could have been raised and decided in a prior action—even if they were not actually litigated"); *Cromwell v. Sac County*, 94 U.S. 351 (1876) (same). *See also Kremer v. Chemical Construction Corp.*, 456 U.S. 461 n.22 (1982) ("invocation of res judicata [presupposes] full and fair opportunity to litigate" in first lawsuit).

[36]*Marrese v. American Academy of Orthopaedic Surgeons*, 470 U.S. 373, 382 (1985) ("With respect to matters that were not decided in the state proceedings . . . claim preclusion generally does not apply where 'the plaintiff was unable to . . . seek a remedy because of the limitations on the subject matter jurisdiction of the courts.' ").

lawsuits be the same but also that they be aligned in the same way (*i.e.*, plaintiff in the first case must be plaintiff in the second case). When a party who was a defendant in the first lawsuit later files a new lawsuit (now, as a plaintiff) asserting what could have been a counterclaim earlier, this identity of alignment obviously is not present. The federal compulsory counterclaim rule fills this gap.[37] By operation of that rule (and perhaps not through claim preclusion principles), a defendant who fails to assert a compulsory counterclaim loses the right to bring that claim later.[38] In those State court systems that have no comparable compulsory counterclaim rule, the practice may vary significantly.

- *"Defense Preclusion":* The U.S. Supreme Court has rejected the notion of a freestanding category of "defense preclusion" that could operate independently of the elements of claim preclusion and issue preclusion (and, in addition, has questioned (but did not decide) whether preclusion principles could have any application to defenses).[39]
- *Federal Government Parties:* The preclusion doctrines "unquestionably" may apply against the United States, federal agencies, and federal officers.[40]
- *Decisions of Administrative Agencies:* Either preclusion doctrine may apply to a decision of an administrative agency if the agency was acting in a judicial capacity.[41] Obviously the essential elements of the pertinent preclusion doctrine must be present.
- *Military Tribunals:* In general, judgments of military courts-martial are entitled to the same claim preclusion treatment as would be applied if the original case was decided in a civilian proceeding.[42]
- *Non-American Judgments:* The principles of claim preclusion do not normally require American courts to enforce non-American judgments.[43] However, it is a common, but not universal, practice in American courts to

---

[37] *See* Rule 13(a).

[38] *See, e.g.*, *New York Life Ins. Co. v. Deshotel*, 142 F.3d 873, 882 (5th Cir. 1998) ("It is well settled that a failure to plead a compulsory counterclaim bars a party from bringing a later independent action on that claim.").

[39] *See Lucky Brand Dungarees, Inc. v. Marcel Fashions Grp., Inc.*, 590 U.S. __, 140 S. Ct. 1589, 1594–95 (2020).

[40] *See Alaska Dep't of Env't Conservation v. E.P.A.*, 540 U.S. 461, 490 n.14 (2004); *Montana v. United States*, 440 U.S. 147 (1979).

[41] *See B & B Hardware, Inc. v. Hargis Indus., Inc.*, 575 U.S. 138, 147–60 (2015) (agency decision may be entitled to issue preclusion); *United States v. Utah Construction & Mining Co.*, 384 U.S. 394, 421 (1966) (collecting precedent).

[42] *See Ortiz v. United States*, 585 U.S. __, 138 S. Ct. 2165 (2018). *See also Schlesinger v. Councilman*, 420 U.S. 738 (1975).

[43] *See, e.g.*, *Diorinou v. Mezitis*, 237 F.3d 133 (2d Cir. 2001).

enforce such judgments through the application of comity.[44]

§ 2.21 Issue Preclusion (Collateral Estoppel)

CORE CONCEPT

Issue preclusion (*collateral estoppel*) forecloses a party's ability to re-litigate an issue of fact or law that had been actually, fully, and fairly litigated to a final resolution earlier.[1] Like claim preclusion, it follows from the same "one bite" at the "litigation apple" economy/finality principle.[2] But it is considerably more narrow. Unlike claim preclusion, issue preclusion does not bar an entire lawsuit, only an issue (or issues) within that lawsuit that had been litigated before. Nor does it bar issues that could have been, but actually were not, litigated earlier. If issue preclusion applies, the precluded issue is considered as having been already established for the purposes of the later lawsuit, with no further proof needed on the point.

The elements of issue preclusion have varied among jurisdictions more significantly than have the elements of claim preclusion, as the discussion below recounts. But several elements have been applied consistently throughout the United States: issue identity, vigorous actual prior litigation, essentiality, and a final, valid judgment on the merits. Each element is examined in turn below. The question of *who* may raise issue preclusion and *against whom* implicates the "mutuality" rule on which jurisdictions also differ. That, too, is discussed below. Note that the elements of claim preclusion and issue preclusion have overlap, and both have potentially preclusive effect on later litigation. But while related, the two doctrines are distinct, triggered differently, and have different scope and reach.

Like claim preclusion, an obvious threshold doctrine-spotting prerequisite for issue preclusion is a prior litigation. While the existence of a prior litigation does not necessarily trigger issue

---

[44]*See Gamble v. United States*, 587 U.S. __, 139 S. Ct. 1960 (2019) (noting common practice of enforcement of non-American judgments based on principles of comity, but also noting exceptions still exist). *See also Block v. InterOil Corp.*, 373 F.Supp.3d 683 (N.D. Tex. 2019) (explaining elements of comity).

[1]*See Herrera v. Wyoming*, 587 U.S. __, 139 S. Ct. 1686, 1697 (2019). *See also Brownback v. King*, 592 U.S. __, 141 S. Ct. 740, 747 n.3 (2021) ("precludes a party from relitigating an issue actually decided in a prior case and necessary to the judgment"); *Lucky Brand Dungarees, Inc. v. Marcel Fashions Grp., Inc.*, 590 U.S. __, 140 S. Ct. 1589, 1594 (2020) (same).

[2]*See B & B Hardware, Inc. v. Hargis Indus., Inc.*, 575 U.S. 138, 147 (2015) ("The idea is straightforward: Once a court has decided an issue, it is forever settled as between the parties, thereby protecting against the expense and vexation attending multiple lawsuits, conserving judicial resources, and fostering reliance on judicial action by minimizing the possibility of inconsistent verdicts") (cleaned up); *Astoria Fed. Sav. & Loan Assn. v. Solimino*, 501 U.S. 104, 107 (1991) ("a losing litigant deserves no rematch after a defeat fairly suffered").

preclusion in a later case, the absence of a prior litigation means that issue preclusion cannot possibly apply.

APPLICATIONS

Element #1: Identical Issues

The two preclusion theories are quite different on this first identity element. Claim preclusion had required that there be identical "claims" between the first and second lawsuits. In contrast, issue preclusion requires only that one or more "issues" be identical between the original and later lawsuits.[3] An "issue" for this purpose is "a right, question, or fact distinctly put in issue and directly determined."[4] The issue may be one of fact or one of law.[5] For example, assume a county music festival show injures four people when a guitar amplifier short-circuits and starts a fire. All four injured people file separate lawsuits. For claim preclusion purposes, all are separate claims. But there is at least one "*issue*" that will prove to be identical in all four lawsuits—the cause of the amplifier short-circuiting.

Testing for issue identity can sometimes prove difficult, but it usually examines the degree of overlap in the evidence and arguments, whether new evidence or argument involves the application of the same rule of law, whether pretrial preparation in the first action reasonably could be expected to embrace the matter in the later case, and, perhaps, how closely the two claims relate to one another.[6] But once the requisite overlap for issue identity is found to exist, it will usually be unimportant whether the *claims* in one case bear a significant relationship to claims in another case.[7]

Element #2: Actual, Vigorous Prior Litigation of that Issue

Issue preclusion will not bar litigation of any issue that was not actually raised in a prior proceeding, regardless of whether the issue could have been raised.[8] Thus, for example, a plaintiff who litigates the meaning of one clause in a contract is not

[3]See, e.g., *U.S. v. Shanbaum*, 10 F.3d 305, 311 (5th Cir. 1994) ("[T]he issue under consideration in a subsequent action must be identical to the issue litigated in a prior action.").

[4]*See Southern Pacific R.R. v. U.S.*, 168 U.S. 1, 48 (1897).

[5]*See Herrera v. Wyoming*, 587 U.S. __, 139 S. Ct. 1686, 1697 (2019); *New Hampshire v. Maine*, 532 U.S. 742, 748–749 (2001). *See also Montana v. U. S.*, 440 U.S. 147, 162 (1979) (normal rules of collateral estoppel apply to questions of law, provided that both lawsuits involve substantially related claims).

[6]*See* RESTATEMENT (SECOND) OF JUDGMENTS § 27 cmt. c (1982). *See generally B & B Hardware, Inc. v. Hargis Indus., Inc.*, 575 U.S. 138, 154 (2015) (issues not identical "if the second action involves application of a different legal standard, even though the factual setting of both suits may be the same") (citation omitted).

[7]*See U.S. v. Shanbaum*, 10 F.3d 305, 311 (5th Cir. 1994) ("[U]nder issue preclusion, unlike claim preclusion, the subject matter of the later suit need not have any relationship to the subject matter of the prior suit.").

[8]*See Regions Hosp. v. Shalala*, 522 U.S. 448, 463–64 (1998) ("Absent actual and adversarial litigation about [a certain issue], principles of issue

barred by issue preclusion from litigating the meaning of a different clause in a later lawsuit. An even simpler example would arise if, in the first suit, the defendant chose to default and not enter any defense.[9]

Moreover, the issue in question must have been litigated with vigor.[10] Thus, if an issue was raised in a casual, passing way that did not significantly engage the attention of the litigants, the issue may not be precluded in later litigation because it was not contested with the requisite intensity. To permit issue preclusion to apply to issues raised in such a casual manner—perhaps because their importance to subsequent litigation was not yet foreseen—would produce unfair surprise for litigants.[11] The same could also be true if the stakes in the first litigation pale in relation to those in the later litigation.[12] To hold otherwise might inject needless complexity on the first litigation, as parties jockeyed to ensure that they would not be precluded in subsequent litigation.

Element #3: Issue Squarely Decided, in a Manner Essential to the Judgment

Issue preclusion will not apply unless the issue in question was actually decided by the court,[13] and then only if that deci-

---

preclusion do not hold fast."); *Cromwell v. County of Sac*, 94 U.S. 351, 353 (1877) (judgment in prior lawsuit "operates as an estoppel only as to those matters in issue or points controverted . . .. [T]he inquiry must always be as to the point or question actually litigated."). *But see In re Hill*, 957 F.3d 704 (6th Cir. 2020) (noting that law of some State permits application of issue preclusion to issues that could have affected a default judgment).

[9] *See Cromwell v. Sac County*, 94 U.S. 351 (1876) (default judgments not eligible for collateral estoppel).

[10] *See, e.g., United States v. Bala*, 948 F.3d 948 (8th Cir. 2020). *See also Pike v. Hester*, 891 F.3d 1131, 1144–45 (9th Cir. 2018) (highlighting importance of litigant's incentive in first lawsuit to "litigate vigorously," noting that every circuit assesses "one's incentive to litigate" in issue preclusion contexts). *But cf., In re Hill*, 957 F.3d 704 (6th Cir. 2020) (noting that some States permit application of issue preclusion to interlocutory orders).

[11] *Cromwell v. County of Sac*, 94 U.S. 351, 356 (1877) ("Various considerations, other than the actual merits, may govern a party in bringing forward grounds of recovery or defence in one action, which may not exist in another action upon a different demand, such as the smallness of the amount or the value of the property in controversy, the difficulty of obtaining the necessary evidence, the expense of the litigation, and his own situation at the time."). *But cf., Community Bank of Homestead v. Torcise*, 162 F.3d 1084 (11th Cir.1998) (observing that this requirement does not examine the quality or quantity of evidence or argument presented, only that fair opportunity to present the issue arose in a context where party understood potential adverse consequences).

[12] *See B & B Hardware, Inc. v. Hargis Indus., Inc.*, 575 U.S. 138, 159 (2015) ("Issue preclusion may be inapt if the amount in controversy in the first action was so small in relation to the amount in controversy in the second that preclusion would be plainly unfair. After all, few litigants would spend $50,000 to defend a $5,000 claim.") (cleaned up; citations omitted).

[13] *See Brownback v. King*, 592 U.S. __, 141 S. Ct. 740, 747 n.3, 209 L. Ed. 2d 33 (2021) ("precludes a party from relitigating an issue actually decided

sion was essential to that judgment.[14] Consider, for example, a three-vehicle collision. Driver #1 sues Driver #2 and Driver #3 in a State that follows the pure contributory negligence rule (*i.e.*, any negligence by plaintiff defeats recovery). Assume the jury returns with a verdict finding all three of the drivers negligent. So, Driver #1 has lost his lawsuit. Later, Driver #2 sues Driver #3. Driver #3 cannot use the result in the earlier lawsuit for to preclude the re-litigation of the issue of Driver #2's own negligence—the jury's finding that Driver #2 and Driver #3 were both negligent was not necessary or essential to that judgment. As soon as the jury ruled that Driver #1 was negligent, that case was over.[15] Similarly, if a jury finds for a plaintiff without explaining which (or both) of two distinct grounds is the basis for its verdict, a defendant may retain the right to challenge those same grounds if they arise as issues in subsequent litigation.[16] Conversely, if a jury expressly finds for a plaintiff on two distinct grounds, both of which were vigorously litigated and both of which were decided in the plaintiff's favor, both may be treated as eligible for issue preclusion in subsequent lawsuits.[17]

In sum, issue preclusion is inapplicable if a later court cannot discern whether the particular issue litigated earlier was necessary and essential to the prior outcome.

Element #4: Valid, Final Judgment on the Merits

This element tracks its matching claim preclusion element, and seems to be applied in the same way by the courts. Thus, a judgment is "valid" if it was entered by a court jurisdictionally competent to do so, "final" when a trial judge enters it and places the litigants in a position to enforce or appeal the court's ruling, and "on the merits" if it actually, directly passes on the

---

in a prior case and necessary to the judgment").

[14] *See B & B Hardware, Inc. v. Hargis Indus., Inc.*, 575 U.S. 138, 148 (2015) (earlier determination of issue as "essential to the judgment" listed as among "ordinary elements" of issue preclusion). *Cf. Yeager v. U.S.*, 557 U.S. 110, 122 (2009) ("consideration of hung counts has no place in the issue-preclusion analysis."); *Arizona v. California*, 530 U.S. 392 (2000) (while settlements entered by court as judgment can have res judicata effect, such settlements normally do not have collateral estoppel effect).

[15] *See Rios v. Rios*, 373 S.W.2d 386, 388–39 (Tex. Ct. Civ. App. 1963). Note, however, that not all jurisdictions are clear on whether essentiality is needed in their state formulations of collateral estoppel. *See Metro. Edison Co. v. Pennsylvania Pub. Util. Comm'n*, 767 F.3d 335, 351 n.20 (3d Cir. 2014).

[16] *Cf., e.g.*, Matter of Caton, 157 F.3d 1026, 1029 (5th Cir. 1998) ("We only require that the record introduced have sufficient detail to allow the use of collateral estoppel.").

[17] *But cf., National Satellite Sports, Inc. v. Eliadis, Inc.*, 253 F.3d 900, 909–10 (6th Cir. 2001) (if prior decision involved resolution of two issues, either of which could have supported prior decision, prior judgment is not conclusive as to either issue standing alone; collecting substantial authority on both sides of question).

issue in question.[18]

Against Whom May Issue Preclusion Be Invoked

As a general rule, issue preclusion may not be asserted against anyone who did not appear in the prior action to actually, vigorously litigate the contested issue.[19] Indeed, constitutional due process forbids applying issue preclusion against anyone who never was afforded that opportunity.[20]

Who May Invoke Issue Preclusion

This question is quite a bit more nuanced. Recall that, to trigger the companion doctrine of claim preclusion, the parties in the second lawsuit must be identical to (or in privity with) parties in the first lawsuit. At one time, a similar requirement of party identity also applied in issue preclusion, a requirement known widely as the "mutuality" rule. Under this view, issue preclusion could never apply unless it did so mutually to all parties—in other words, unless all parties stood at the same risk of victory or loss in both lawsuits.[21] The practice of rigidly applying "mutuality" to all issue preclusion cases has eroded over the years,[22] and today, most (but not all)[23] jurisdictions have substantially abandoned an absolutist approach towards "mutuality." In its place, many courts have turned to assessing the fairness, under the particular circumstances of a lawsuit, of permitting application of "non-mutual" issue preclusion.

The terminology of this area can be awkward and off-putting, but courts persist in using the terms in describing, differentiating, and applying collateral estoppel in various settings. Accordingly, understanding this lexicon is important to practitioners:

---

[18]*See supra* § 2.19 (discussing attributes in claim preclusion context). *See also Transaero, Inc. v. La Fuerza Aerea Boliviana*, 162 F.3d 724, 731 (2d Cir. 1998) ("[T]he service of process and personal jurisdiction issues were necessary to support the D.C. Circuit's final judgment—indeed, these issues were the subject of that judgment.").

[19]*See Taylor v. Sturgell*, 553 U.S. 880, 892–95 (2008) (noting general rule, and six exceptions—non-parties may be precluded if they agreed to be bound, if pre-existing substantive legal relationships justify being bound, if their interests were represented in the prior action, if they assumed control over the prior litigation, if they litigated via proxy, or if so required by special statutory scheme).

[20]*See Blonder-Tongue Lab'ys, Inc. v. Univ. of Illinois Found.*, 402 U.S. 313, 329 (1971).

[21]*See Blonder-Tongue Lab'ys, Inc. v. Univ. of Illinois Found.*, 402 U.S. 313, 325 (1971) (discussing reasoning supporting mutuality rule).

[22]*See Blonder-Tongue Lab'ys, Inc. v. Univ. of Illinois Found.*, 402 U.S. 313, 318–26 (1971).

[23]*See, e.g., State Farm Fire & Cas. Co. v. Mabry*, 255 Va. 286, 289, 497 S.E.2d 844, 846 (1998) (imposing requirement that parties in current litigation be identical with parties in prior litigation or in privity with such parties). It should also be noted that collateral estoppel may be invoked against the federal government when the United States is a party to litigation and the elements of collateral estoppel (including requirements of mutuality) are established. *U.S. v. Stauffer Chemical Co.*, 464 U.S. 165 (1984). However, it is also settled that nonmutual collateral estoppel may not be invoked against the federal government. *U.S. v. Mendoza*, 464 U.S. 154 (1984).

- *Mutuality Rule:* as noted above, means the view (now frequently rejected) that a court will not apply issue preclusion unless the parties in the second action are identical to (or in privity with) the parties in the original case.
- *Non-Mutuality Rule:* is the opposite, meaning that a court will not reflexively deny application of issue preclusion simply because the parties in the second lawsuit are not identical to those in the first lawsuit. Ergo, "non-mutual issue preclusion" means that a court found issue preclusion appropriate even though all parties in both lawsuits were not identical.
- *Defensive Non-Mutual Issue Preclusion:* means a request by a defendant to use a plaintiff's loss on an issue suffered during an earlier lawsuit as a shield to ward off a new litigation attack by that same plaintiff; the request is non-mutual because that defendant was not a party to the plaintiff's earlier lawsuit.
- *Offensive Non-Mutual Issue Preclusion:* means a request by a plaintiff to use a defendant's loss on an issue suffered during an earlier lawsuit as a sword to defeat that defendant on that issue in a new litigation; the request is non-mutual because the plaintiff was not a party to the defendant's earlier lawsuit.

With those definitions in mind, the *who-may-invoke-issue-preclusion* question can come into clearer focus—

Defensive Nonmutual Issue Preclusion

"Defensive" nonmutual issue preclusion is an attempt to use the doctrine as a shield—defensively—to repel a claimant's attack. For example, suppose P sues D1 for patent infringement, and suppose that D1's defense is that P's patent is legally invalid. If D1 wins on that ground (patent invalidity), the lawsuit is over as between the two parties and cannot be relitigated (claim preclusion would prevent it).

But assume P later files a second lawsuit against a different defendant, D2, asserting that D2 had also infringed the same patent. Many courts will permit D2 to invoke issue preclusion defensively, thereby foreclosing P's ability to assert in P v. D2 that the patent was valid. Even though the parties are not identical (that is, there is no "mutuality"), this "defensive" use of issue preclusion is generally considered fair because the party who is being precluded had a full and fair opportunity to litigate the patent validity issue in the first lawsuit.[24]

In permitting defensive non-mutual issue preclusion in just such a patent case, the U.S. Supreme Court explained that its calculus included the obvious impact in time, money, and judicial administration, and whether a second roll of the dice

---

[24] *See, e.g., Blonder-Tongue Labs., Inc. v. Univ. of Ill. Found.*, 402 U.S. 313 (1971).

was worth those costs: "Permitting repeated litigation of the same issue as long as the supply of unrelated defendants holds out reflects either the aura of the gaming table or 'a lack of discipline and of disinterestedness on the part of the lower courts, hardly a worthy or wise basis for fashioning rules of procedure.' "[25]

Offensive Nonmutual Issue Preclusion

A more nettlesome use of nonmutual issue preclusion arises when a party seeks to use the rule offensively in an action. A landmark U.S. Supreme Court case illustrates why.

In *Parklane Hosiery Co., Inv. v. Shore,*[26] the defendants had previously been sued by the U.S. Securities and Exchange Commission for making false proxy statements. The Commission sought an injunction, and the defendants lost that lawsuit. Subsequently a class of shareholders sued the defendants on the same grounds and sought issue preclusion for the previous court's finding that the proxy statements had been false and misleading. In contrast to its defensive nonmutual use (where issue preclusion would be used as a shield to ward off a subsequent claim by a plaintiff who had lost a prior lawsuit), this case was an attempt to use the defendants' prior loss as a sword with which to produce a second unfavorable result for those defendants.

The Supreme Court concluded that, at least sometimes, nonmutual issue preclusion could be used offensively as well. However, before doing so, the Court admonished federal judges to examine all the circumstances of a case to ensure that application of the doctrine was fair. Specifically, the Court suggested that judges examine: (1) whether the plaintiff seeking offensive non-mutual issue preclusion could have participated in the previous suit; (2) whether the defendant had a fair chance to litigate the issue with knowledge of the fact that the same issue might arise in subsequent litigation; (3) whether the judgment in the litigation for which issue preclusion is sought was inconsistent with results in any litigation which had taken place still earlier;[27] and (4) whether, in the previous suit, procedural limitations had prevented the defendant from offering some evidence or otherwise defending himself in ways now open in the later litigation.[28]

Non-Mutuality and the United States

Although the United States is as vulnerable as any party to the application of issue preclusion when the requirement of

---

[25]*See Blonder-Tongue Labs., Inc. v. Univ. of Ill. Found.*, 402 U.S. 313, 329 (1971) (citation omitted).

[26]*Parklane Hosiery Co., Inc. v. Shore*, 439 U.S. 322 (1979).

[27]For example, a certain product might be suspected of causing an inhalation injury to human beings. The first ten plaintiffs who sued the manufacturer for product liability all lose, but the eleventh plaintiff wins. Should the manufacturer's loss in the eleventh litigation preclude it from contesting the product's injury-causing capacity thereafter in future lawsuits?

[28]*See Parklane Hosiery Co., Inc. v. Shore*, 439 U.S. 322, 329–33 (1979).

mutuality is satisfied, it is now seems settled that non-mutual issue preclusion (defensive or offensive) may not be applied against the United States.[29]

Exceptions to Issue Preclusion

Even in situations where all the requirements of issue preclusion are satisfied, additional considerations may make application of the doctrine unfair in a particular case. For example, issue preclusion may be inappropriate if "there is reason to doubt the quality, extensiveness, or fairness of procedures followed in prior litigation."[30] Courts are reluctant to impose issue preclusion in circumstances where the affected party might not reasonably have appreciated the risk of issue preclusion in subsequent cases. Additionally, if the law or facts of a situation undergo material change between the first lawsuit and the second one, it might be unfair to impose the doctrine on issues decided in the first suit.[31] Issue preclusion will also typically be inapplicable to situations where a district court judgment is not appealable.[32]

---

[29]*See U.S. v. Mendoza*, 464 U.S. 154, 162 (1984).

[30]*See Montana v. U. S.*, 440 U.S. 147, 164 n.11 (1979). *See also B & B Hardware, Inc. v. Hargis Indus., Inc.*, 575 U.S. 138, 159 (2015) (doctrine "accounts for those 'rare' cases where a 'compelling showing of unfairness' can be made").

[31]*See Herrera v. Wyoming*, 587 U.S. __, 139 S. Ct. 1686, 1697 (2019); *Montana v. U. S.*, 440 U.S. 147, 159 (1979); *C.I.R. v. Sunnen*, 333 U.S. 591, 601 (1948).

[32]*See Kircher v. Putnam Funds Trust*, 547 U.S. 633, 645–47 (2006) (28 U.S.C.A. § 1447(d) makes unreviewable, as a matter of law, many district court decisions to remand removed cases; in such cases there is no collateral estoppel result barring a state court from re-examining the reasoning underlying the decision of the district court-even though the state court should treat the remand decision itself as final).

PART III-A
AN ORIENTATION TO YEARS OF MAJOR RULE AMENDMENTS

The Federal Rules of Civil Procedure have undergone significant revisions during the past several decades, as summarized below. This edition of the *Handbook* contains the current, as-amended language of each Rule. Discussions of how particular amendments impacted federal practice are incorporated into the *Authors' Commentary* that follows each affected Rule.

* * *

Diversity Disclosure and Social Security Amendments (2022). Effective December 1, 2022, Rule 7.1 is amended to require party citizenship disclosures in federal diversity cases, and a concise set of new Supplemental Rules are added for Social Security cases.

Organizational Deponent Amendments (2020). Effective December 1, 2020, Rule 30(b)(6) was amended to impose on parties the duty to confer in good faith about the matters for examination before or promptly after requesting to depose an organization.

Electronic Filing & Service, Class Action Procedure, and Stay-of-Proceedings Amendments (2018). Effective December 2018, Rule 5 was amended to compel electronical filing by most attorneys and to permit electronic service through the courts' e-filing system. Rule 23 was amended to revise certain notice, court approval, and appeal procedures in class actions. Rule 62 was amended to enlarge the length of the post-judgment automatic stay to 30 days. Rule 65.1 was amended to broaden the source of security providers.

General Housekeeping Amendments (2016 & 2017). Effective December 2016 and 2017, technical, ambiguity-clearing amendments were made to Rule 4 (Summons) and Rule 82 (Jurisdiction and Venue Unaffected). Rule 6 was amended to eliminate the adding of 3 days for a response following *electronic* service.

Discovery Amendments (2015). Effective December 2015, the discovery rules were substantially revised. To emphasize proportionality, the benefit/burden balancing language was repositioned from a limitation on discovery into the core definition of the scope of discovery. Relatedly, courts are now expressly authorized to shift the costs of responding to the requesting party. The procedures for document requests were modified in several aspects. Parties are authorized to serve document requests earlier than other discovery techniques in order to promote early discussion and resolution of potential problems. Objections to document requests must now be stated with particularity, and responding parties must specify whether they are withholding any documents on the basis of their objections. Responding parties are also authorized to produce copies instead of making the responsive documents available for inspection. Finally, new provisions address the preservation and loss of electronically stored information. Preservation is now a listed topic for the parties' discovery conference, and a comprehensive scheme for sanctions for spoliation of electronically stored information was added, tying the severity of the sanction to listed factors.

General Housekeeping Amendments (2014 & 2015). One technical, conforming amendment was made in 2014. In addition to the discovery amendments, a number of other Rules were amended in 2015. Rule 1 was amended to emphasize the parties' obligation to apply the Rules cooperatively and proportionally. Rule 4 was amended to tighten the time for service of process, and Rule 16 was amended to accelerate the issuance of the initial scheduling order. Rule 16 also was amended to authorize, but not require, the court to direct that before moving for an order relating to discovery, the movant must request a conference with the court. And Rule 84, sanctioning the federal forms, was abrogated—with only the two forms pertaining to waiver of service of process surviving.

Subpoena Amendments (2013). Effective December 2013, the federal subpoena power was adjusted and Rule 45 reorganized. The amendments changed the identity of the subpoena-issuing court, expanded the scope of service, authorized transfers of motions to quash or enforce, and added clarity to other subpoena practices.

Summary Judgment Amendments (2010). Effective December 2010, Rule 56 was entirely rebuilt. Although the summary judgment standard remains essentially unchanged (*i.e.*, no genuine dispute as to any material fact and entitled to judgment as a matter of law), the revised Rule 56 now: (a) restores the verb "shall" to the summary judgment command; (b) sets out the manner in which matters can be factually supported; (c) approves declarations, as well as affidavits, in introducing that support; (d) permits objections to improper support; (e) elaborates on the district judge's discretion when positions lack support; (f) verifies that motions can be filed immediately; (g) deletes national "default" time periods for opposition and reply briefs; (h) confirms that only the formal summary judgment record must be considered in making rulings; (i) explicitly allows "partial" summary judgments; (j) codifies the court's right to enter judgment in favor of the *non-moving* party, on grounds not requested, and *sua sponte*; (k) emphasizes the trial judge's discretion in treating facts as established for purposes of trial; (l) requires trial courts to explain the reasons for rulings; and (m) expands the available discretionary sanctions for bad faith affidavits and declarations.

Expert Amendments (2010). Also effective December 2010, the Rules governing disclosure and discovery of experts were altered. Rule 26(b)(4)(B) now protects draft expert reports from disclosure as trial preparation material. Rule 26(b)(4)(C) broadens the trial-preparation-material protection for communications between counsel and expert witnesses unless the communications pertain to expert compensation, or to facts, data, or assumptions provided by counsel which the experts considered in forming their opinions. Rule 26(a)(2)(C) requires that, for testifying experts who are not specially retained, parties must now disclose the subject matter of their expected testimony and a summary of the facts and opinions on which they are expected to testify.

Time Computation Amendments (2009). Effective December 2009, the procedures for computing time were adjusted and varying time periods were normalized. No time period was shortened. Most time periods were standardized into multiples of 7 (except those 30 days or longer). The "*less-than-11-day*" rule was eliminated. New hourly time period procedures were added, as were procedures for how time periods begin and end. Most post-trial motion periods were expanded from 10 to 28 days.

"Restyling" Amendments (2007). Effective December 2007, the Rules were all "restyled". This complete, top-to-bottom rewrite was not intended to effect any substantive change in the Rules or their operation, but to clean up the text. Some Rule subparts were repositioned. Language inconsistencies were removed, antiquated and unnecessary references were pruned, needless prose "intensifiers" were deleted, passive voice was rephrased, sentences were simplified, and graphically orienting restructurings (new labels, headings, indentations) was added.

Privacy Amendments (2007). Effective December 2007, the Rules implemented the E-Government Act of 2002 by the adoption of new Rule 5.2 which directs the redaction of certain personal-identifying information, and permits the redaction of other such information filings under seal.

Discovery of Electronic Data Amendments (2006). Effective December 2006, the Rules formalized disclosure and discovery of electronically-stored information, through amendments to the Rules governing pretrial conferences (Rule 16), initial disclosures (Rule 26), interrogatories (Rule 33), document requests (Rule 34), subpoenas (Rule 45), and sanctions (Rule 37). The amendments prescribed the form in which electronic data is to be produced, with attendant procedures for objections and motion practice regarding producing electronic data from particularly burdensome sources or in particularly onerous forms. The amendments also created a safe harbor for electronic data destroyed during routine computer operations.

New Rules. New **Rule 5.1** was adopted in 2006 to gather in a single place the provisions requiring notice, certification, and a right of intervention for constitutional challenges to federal or state laws. New **Rule 7.1** was adopted in 2002 to require the filing of a disclosure statement by nongovernmental corporate parties.

PART III
FEDERAL RULES OF CIVIL PROCEDURE WITH COMMENTARY AND PRACTICE POINTERS

Rules Effective September 16, 1938

Including Amendments Effective December 1, 2022

Research Note

Rule requirements, case law applications, commentary, and references to treatises and law reviews are available in Wright, Miller, et al., Federal Practice and Procedure, *Volumes 4 to 20.*

Use WESTLAW ® *to find cases citing or applying rules.* WESTLAW *may also be used to search for terms in court rules or to update court rules. See the US-RULES and US-ORDERS SCOPE screens for detailed descriptive information and search tips.*

Table of Rules

I. SCOPE OF RULES—FORM OF ACTION

Rule

1. Scope and Purpose.
2. One Form of Action.

II. COMMENCING AN ACTION; SERVICE OF PROCESS, PLEADINGS, MOTIONS, AND ORDERS

3. Commencing An Action.
4. Summons.
4.1. Serving Other Process.
5. Serving and Filing Pleadings and Other Papers.
5.1. Constitutional Challenge to a Statute—Notice, Certification, and Intervention.
5.2. Privacy Protection for Filings Made With the Court.
6. Computing and Extending Time; Time for Motion Papers.

III. PLEADINGS AND MOTIONS

7. Pleadings Allowed; Form of Motions and Other Papers.
7.1. Disclosure Statement.
8. General Rules of Pleading.
9. Pleading Special Matters.
10. Form of Pleadings.
11. Signing Pleadings, Motions, and Other Papers; Representations to Court; Sanctions.
12. Defenses and Objections: When and How Presented; Motion for Judgment on the Pleadings; Consolidating Motions; Waiving Defenses; Pretrial Hearing.
13. Counterclaim and Crossclaim.

14. Third-Party Practice.
15. Amended and Supplemental Pleadings.
16. Pretrial Conferences; Scheduling; Management.

IV. PARTIES

17. Plaintiff and Defendant; Capacity; Public Officers.
18. Joinder of Claims.
19. Required Joinder of Parties.
20. Permissive Joinder of Parties.
21. Misjoinder and Nonjoinder of Parties.
22. Interpleader.
23. Class Actions.
23.1. Derivative Actions By Shareholders.
23.2. Actions Relating to Unincorporated Associations.
24. Intervention.
25. Substitution of Parties.

V. DEPOSITIONS AND DISCOVERY

26. Duty to Disclose; General Provisions Governing Discovery.
27. Depositions to Perpetuate Testimony.
28. Persons Before Whom Depositions May Be Taken.
29. Stipulations About Discovery Procedure.
30. Depositions By Oral Examination.
31. Depositions By Written Questions.
32. Using Depositions in Court Proceedings.
33. Interrogatories to Parties.
34. Producing Documents, Electronically Stored Information, and Tangible Things, or Entering Onto Land, for Inspection and Other Purposes.
35. Physical and Mental Examinations.
36. Requests for Admission.
37. Failure to Make Disclosures or to Cooperate In Discovery; Sanctions.

VI. TRIALS

38. Right to a Jury Trial; Demand.
39. Trial By Jury or By the Court.
40. Scheduling Cases for Trial.
41. Dismissal of Actions.
42. Consolidation; Separate Trials.
43. Taking Testimony.
44. Proving an Official Record.
44.1. Determining Foreign Law.
45. Subpoena.
46. Objecting to a Ruling or Order.
47. Selecting Jurors.
48. Number of Jurors; Verdict.
49. Special Verdict; General Verdict and Questions.
50. Judgment as a Matter of Law In a Jury Trial; Related Motion for a New Trial; Conditional Ruling.
51. Instructions to the Jury; Objections; Preserving a Claim of Error.
52. Findings and Conclusions By the Court; Judgment on Partial Findings.

53. Masters.

VII. JUDGMENT

54. Judgment; Costs.
55. Default; Default Judgment.
56. Summary Judgment.
57. Declaratory Judgment.
58. Entering Judgment.
59. New Trial; Altering Or Amending a Judgment.
60. Relief From a Judgment Or Order.
61. Harmless Error.
62. Stay of Proceedings to Enforce a Judgment.
62.1 Indicative Ruling on a Motion for Relief That is Barred by a Pending Appeal
63. Judge's Inability to Proceed.

VIII. PROVISIONAL AND FINAL REMEDIES

64. Seizing a Person Or Property.
65. Injunctions and Restraining Orders.
65.1. Proceedings Against a Surety.
66. Receivers.
67. Deposit Into Court.
68. offer of Judgment.
69. Execution.
70. Enforcing a Judgment for a Specific Act.
71. Enforcing Relief for Or Against a Nonparty.

IX. SPECIAL PROCEEDINGS

71.1. Condemning Real Or Personal Property.
72. Magistrate Judges; Pretrial Orders.
73. Magistrate Judges; Trial By Consent and Appeal.
74. Method of Appeal From Magistrate to District Judge Under Title 28, U.S.C. § 636(C)(4) and 73(D).
75. Proceedings on Appeal From Magistrate to District Judge Under Rule 73(D).
76. Judgment of the District Judge on the Appeal Under Rule 73(D) and Costs.

X. DISTRICT COURTS AND CLERKS

77. Conducting Business; Clerk's Authority; Notice of An Order Or Judgment.
78. Hearing Motions; Submission on Briefs.
79. Records Kept By the Clerk.
80. Stenographic Transcript as Evidence.

XI. GENERAL PROVISIONS

81. Applicability of the Rules In General; Removed Actions.
82. Jurisdiction and Venue Unaffected.
83. Rules By District Courts; Judge's Directives.
84. Forms [Abrogated].
85. Title.
86. Effective Dates.

I. SCOPE OF RULES; FORM OF ACTION

RULE 1
SCOPE AND PURPOSE

These rules govern the procedure in all civil actions and proceedings in the United States district courts, except as stated in Rule 81. They should be construed, administered, and employed by the court and the parties to secure the just, speedy, and inexpensive determination of every action and proceeding.

[Amended December 29, 1948, effective October 20, 1949; February 28, 1966, effective July 1, 1966; April 22, 1993, effective December 1, 1993; April 30, 2007, effective December 1, 2007; April 29, 2015, effective December 1, 2015.]

AUTHORS' COMMENTARY ON RULE 1

PURPOSE AND SCOPE

The story of the Federal Rules of Civil Procedure is a fascinating one, briefly recounted in Part I of this text. Rule 1 has two objectives—to set the reach for the Rules and to install an overarching philosophy for the Rules' use. The reach of the Rules is well-cabined: they apply in almost all civil cases litigated in federal district courts (not in criminal cases, tax cases, or appeals). The philosophy for the Rules is memorialized in the Rule 1 "touchstones": to pursue the "just, speedy, and inexpensive determination" of all federal civil cases. Those touchstones have been often cited by courts and litigants in interpreting and applying the Rules.

APPLICATIONS

Creation, Status, and Validity of the Federal Rules

Under the authority vested by the Rules Enabling Act of 1934,[1] the United States Supreme Court promulgated the original Federal Rules of Civil Procedure in December 1937. The original Rules became effective in September 1938, superseding inconsistent statutes enacted prior to their effective date. They have been amended on numerous occasions since. The

[1] Act of June 19, 1934, ch. 651, 48 Stat. 1064, codified in current form at 28 U.S.C.A. §§ 2071 to 77.

Rules have the force and effect of a federal statute.[2]

The Rules enjoy "presumptive validity."[3] Nevertheless, although promulgated by the Supreme Court, a Rule may still be challenged as inconsistent with either the rulemaking power delegated by Congress to the Supreme Court under the Rules Enabling Act or the U.S. Constitution.[4] To date, no Rule has ever been declared invalid.[5]

The Advisory Committee and Its Committee Notes

To help draft the original Federal Rules of Civil Procedure, the Supreme Court appointed an Advisory Committee on Rules comprising a panel of judges, attorneys, and law professors. This consultative tradition continues today, in the form of the Judicial Conference of the United States' Advisory Committee on Civil Rules, which considers and recommends amendments to the Rules. The members of the Advisory Committee have included federal and State judges, practicing attorneys (private and governmental), and law professors.[6]

Both the original Advisory Committee and its successors have published "Notes" as an aid in construing and interpreting the drafting purpose underlying each Rule and each amendment. The Committee Notes are only guides; the Notes neither are a part of the Rules nor have they been approved by the Supreme Court. Nonetheless, the Notes have, in practice, assumed the force of a veritable legislative history to the Rules and their amendments. The Notes can therefore be cited as formidable (though non-binding) authority for construing the Rules.[7]

---

[2]*See Sibbach v. Wilson & Co.*, 312 U.S. 1, 13, 61 S. Ct. 422, 85 L. Ed. 479 (1941); *STC.UNM v. Intel Corp.*, 767 F.3d 1351, 1359 (Fed. Cir. 2014).

[3]*See Burlington Northern R. Co. v. Woods*, 480 U.S. 1, 6, 107 S. Ct. 967, 94 L. Ed. 2d 1 (1987); *Gil de Rebollo v. Miami Heat Assocs., Inc.*, 137 F.3d 56, 65 (1st Cir. 1998).

[4]*See Mississippi Pub. Corp. v. Murphree*, 326 U.S. 438, 444, 66 S. Ct. 242, 246, 90 L. Ed. 185 (1946) ("The fact that this Court promulgated the rules as formulated and recommended by the Advisory Committee does not foreclose consideration of their validity, meaning or consistency"). *See also Hanna v. Plumer*, 380 U.S. 460, 471, 85 S. Ct. 1136, 1143, 14 L. Ed. 2d 8 (1965) (when situation is covered by Federal Rules, court must apply them unless "the Rule in question transgresses [ ] the terms of the [Rules] Enabling Act [or the Constitution]").

[5]*See Shady Grove Orthopedic Assocs., P.A. v. Allstate Ins. Co.*, 559 U.S. 393, 407, 130 S. Ct. 1431, 1442, 176 L. Ed. 2d 311 (2010) ("we have rejected every statutory challenge to a Federal Rule that has come before us"). *See also Martin v. Pierce Cnty.*, 34 F.4th 1125, 1132 (9th Cir. 2022) ("no reason to doubt the validity" of Rule 3); *Pledger v. Lynch*, 5 F.4th 511, 520–21 (4th Cir. 2021) (same, Rules 8, 9, 11, and 12); *Interfaith Cmty. Org. v. Honeywell Int'l, Inc.*, 726 F.3d 403, 408–11 (3d Cir. 2013) (rejecting Rules Enabling Act challenge to Rule 68).

[6]The procedure for amending the Federal Rules is more specifically described in Part I of this text.

[7]The original and subsequent amending Notes, along with a survey of case law discussing the Notes' weight and effect, appear in Part VIII

Where the Rules Apply

Rule 1 implements Article III, Section 2 of the Constitution which extends the judicial power of the United States "to all Cases, in Law and Equity, arising under this Constitution, the Laws of the United States, and [its] Treaties . . . [and] to all Cases of admiralty and maritime Jurisdiction."[8] The Rules apply to all civil cases[9] in all district courts of the United States, and "automatically" so.[10] By special congressional enactments, the Rules have been extended to the United States District Court for the District of Columbia,[11] and to the territorial and insular courts of Guam,[12] the Northern Mariana Islands,[13] Puerto Rico,[14] and the Virgin Islands.[15] Because it is not a "district court", the Rules do not apply to the United States Tax Court.[16] Unless a Rule requires or permits the application of State procedure, the federal courts do not apply State procedures that conflict with the Rules,[17] nor do the Rules apply retroactively to govern procedural matters that occurred in a State court prior to a case's removal to federal court.[18]

But the Rules are Not All-Encompassing

The Rules set out many of the powers of federal trial courts,

---

of this text.

[8]*See Vodusek v. Bayliner Marine Corp.*, 71 F.3d 148, 153 (4th Cir. 1995) (citing U.S. Const. art. III, § 2).

[9]*See Ashcroft v. Iqbal*, 556 U.S. 662, 684, 129 S. Ct. 1937, 1953, 73 L. Ed. 2d 868 (2009).

[10]*See Shady Grove Orthopedic Assocs., P.A. v. Allstate Ins. Co.*, 559 U.S. 393, 400, 130 S. Ct. 1431, 1438, 176 L. Ed. 2d 311 (2010).

[11]*See* 28 U.S.C.A. § 88 (officially confirming that the District of Columbia is a judicial district of the United States). *See also* Rule 81(d)(2) (applying law of District of Columbia, where appropriate, when word "state" is used).

[12]*See* 48 U.S.C.A. § 1424 (creating district court of Guam and vesting it with the jurisdiction of a district court of the United States).

[13]*See* 48 U.S.C.A. §§ 1821 & 1822 (creating district court of the Northern Mariana Islands and vesting it with the jurisdiction of a district court of the United States).

[14]*See* 28 U.S.C.A. § 119 (creating Puerto Rico as a judicial district).

[15]*See* 48 U.S.C.A. §§ 1611 & 1612 (creating district court of the Virgin Islands and vesting it with the jurisdiction of a district court of the United States).

[16]*See Organic Cannabis Found., LLC v. C.I.R.*, 962 F.3d 1082, 1088 (9th Cir. 2020). *See also Michaels v. C.I.R.*, 144 F.3d 495, 497 (7th Cir. 1998) (though not binding, Rules "provide a source of persuasive authority to that court in filling any gaps in" tax procedures). *See generally* 26 U.S.C.A. § 7453 (authorizing promulgation of Tax Court rules); Tax Ct. R. 1(b) (directing that Tax Court rules pursue "just, speedy, and inexpensive" determinations).

[17]*See Shady Grove Orthopedic Assocs., P.A. v. Allstate Ins. Co.*, 559 U.S. 393, 398, 130 S. Ct. 1431, 1437, 176 L. Ed. 2d 311 (2010) (if Federal Rule answers procedural question in issue, "it governs" unless it is invalid); *Gasperini v. Ctr. for Humanities, Inc.*, 518 U.S. 415, 427 n.7, 116 S. Ct. 2211, 135 L. Ed. 2d 659 (1996) (declaring it "settled" that a valid, on-point Federal Rule "applies regardless of contrary state law"). For an extended discussion of the *Erie* doctrine, see Part II, § 2.18 of this text.

[18]*See Taylor v. Bailey Tool Mfg. Co.*, 744 F.3d 944, 946–47 (5th Cir. 2014).

but an absence from the Rules of the grant of some specific authority does not necessarily foreclose that authority.[19] Rather, courts enjoy the "inherent power" to respond reasonably to "problems and needs" arising in the course of administering justice (provided that power is not exercised in a manner contrary to an express grant or constraint found in a Rule or statute).[20]

Civil Rules and the Courts of Appeals

By their terms the Federal Rules of Civil Procedure apply only to the federal District Courts.[21] But the policies underlying the Rules may influence procedures followed in the Courts of Appeals.[22]

Civil Rules and Criminal Cases

Likewise, the Federal Rules of Civil Procedure apply only in civil disputes, and do not govern criminal cases.[23]

Specialized Proceedings

Specialized proceedings are governed by the Rules,[24] unless Rule 81 or an act of Congress otherwise provides.[25] Under Rule 81, for example, the Rules apply in bankruptcy proceedings, but only to the extent prescribed by the Federal Rules of Bankruptcy Procedure.[26] Although the Rules apply generally to admiralty proceedings,[27] they do *not* apply to prize proceedings in admiralty.[28] In the absence of federal law providing otherwise, the Rules also apply to, among other proceedings: admission to citizenship proceedings[29] (but not to the Board of Immigration Appeals and deportation proceedings[30]), habeas corpus and quo warranto proceedings,[31] federal arbitrations, proceedings to review orders by the Secretaries of Agriculture

---

[19] *See Sanchez v. City of Chicago*, 880 F.3d 349, 360–61 (7th Cir. 2018).

[20] *See Dietz v. Bouldin*, 579 U.S. 40, 45–48, 136 S. Ct. 1885, 1891–93, 195 L. Ed. 2d 161 (2016); *Degen v. United States*, 517 U.S. 820, 823–824, 116 S. Ct. 1777, 135 L. Ed. 2d 102 (1996).

[21] *See Cooter & Gell v. Hartmarx Corp.*, 496 U.S. 384, 406, 110 S. Ct. 2447, 110 L. Ed. 2d 359 (1990); *Sheldon v. Khanal*, 502 Fed.Appx. 765, 773 (10th Cir. 2012).

[22] *See Newman-Green, Inc. v. Alfonzo-Larrain*, 490 U.S. 826, 832, 109 S. Ct. 2218, 2223, 104 L. Ed. 2d 893 (1989); *Rosenfeld v. Oceania Cruises, Inc.*, 682 F.3d 1320, 1332 n.14 (11th Cir. 2012).

[23] *See U.S. v. Arrington*, 763 F.3d 17, 22 (D.C. Cir. 2014); *United States v. McCalister*, 601 F.3d 1086, 1087–88 (10th Cir. 2010).

[24] *See S.J. v. Issaquah Sch. Dist. No. 411*, 470 F.3d 1288, 1292 (9th Cir. 2006) (citing Rule 1 to reject claim that IDEA actions, because of their "appellate flavor", are not controlled by the Rules).

[25] *See Fed. Energy Regulatory Comm'n v. City Power Mktg., LLC*, 199 F. Supp. 3d 218, 231 (D.D.C. 2016) (Congress can prescribe separate procedures for certain types of actions).

[26] *See* Rule 81(a)(2).

[27] *See Blanchard v. Cortes-Molina*, 453 F.3d 40, 44 (1st Cir.2006).

[28] *See* Rule 81(a)(1).

[29] *See* Rule 81(a)(3).

[30] *See Poole v. Mukasey*, 522 F.3d 259, 263 (2d Cir. 2008).

[31] *See* Rule 81(a)(4).

and Interior, proceedings to enforce National Labor Relations Board orders and Longshore and Harbor Workers' Compensation Act compensation orders, reviewing orders denying a certificate of clearance, and reviewing railway labor dispute arbitration awards.[32]

Likewise, the Rules also apply generally to de novo immigration proceedings,[33] certain civil contempt proceedings,[34] civil actions for forfeiture and penalty actions by the United States,[35] patent cases, removed cases,[36] and proceedings to compel compliance with a subpoena to testify or to produce documents, as issued by an officer or agency of the United States pursuant to federal statute.[37]

Rules to be Harmonized Together

The Rules were designed to be "interdependent."[38] Thus, in interpreting them, courts seek to "harmonize" the Rules with one another, and will only allow one Rule to take precedence over another where a truly irreconcilable conflict arises.[39]

"Just", "Speedy", and "Inexpensive" Mandate

Aside from defining when the Rules apply, Rule 1 also fixes the broad objectives of the Federal Rules of Civil Procedure: they are to be construed, administered, and employed so as to achieve the "just, speedy, and inexpensive determination of every action."[40] This admonition applies also to Local Rules promulgated to supplement the national Rules.[41]

Often cited, these goals have been heralded by the Supreme Court as "the touchstones of federal procedure"[42] and as a "paramount command."[43] Others have written that no part of the Rules is more important than this Rule 1 mandate.[44] The text of Rule 1 emphasizes the trial courts' affirmative duty to exercise the procedural authority the Rules bestow so as to

---

[32] *See* Rule 81(a)(6).

[33] *See Alvear v. Kirk*, 87 F. Supp. 2d 1241, 1243 (D.N.M. 2000) (holding that Rules 12 and 56 governed de novo immigration proceedings pursuant to 8 U.S.C.A. § 1421(c)).

[34] *See United States v. Perez*, 752 F.3d 398, 404 (4th Cir. 2014).

[35] *Cf. U.S. v. Mosavi*, 138 F.3d 1365, 1366 (11th Cir. 1998) (Rules do not apply to criminal forfeitures).

[36] *See* Rule 81(c)(1).

[37] *See* Rule 81(a)(5).

[38] *See Weiss v. Regal Collections*, 385 F.3d 337, 342 (3d Cir. 2004).

[39] *See Weiss v. Regal Collections*, 385 F.3d 337, 342 (3d Cir. 2004).

[40] *See Wood v. GCC Bend, LLC*, 422 F.3d 873, 882–83 (9th Cir. 2005) (noting that the "first of the Federal Rules of Civil Procedure mandates construing the rest" to achieve the Rule 1 touchstones).

[41] *See Stevo v. Frasor*, 662 F.3d 880, 887 (7th Cir. 2011).

[42] *Brown Shoe Co. v. U.S.*, 370 U.S. 294, 306, 82 S. Ct. 1502, 1513, 8 L. Ed. 2d 510 (1962). *See In re Bayer AG*, 146 F.3d 188, 189 (3d Cir. 1998) (commenting that the Rules and Rule 1's touchstones "initiated a revolution in the litigation process in the federal courts in this country" and, ultimately, influenced foreign litigation as well).

[43] *See Dietz v. Bouldin*, 579 U.S. ___, 136 S. Ct. 1885, 1891, 195 L. Ed. 2d 161 (2016).

[44] *See Trevino v. Celanese Corp.*, 701 F.2d 397, 405 (5th Cir. 1983).

resolve civil litigation fairly and without undue cost or delay.[45] This affirmative duty is shared by practicing attorneys, as officers of the court.[46] To realize Rule 1's goals of "just, speedy, and inexpensive" determinations of federal cases, the parties are expected to work diligently to follow the Rules and the courts are called upon to resolutely enforce the Rules, otherwise the Rules—and the laudable objectives they seek—will become illusory.[47] Broadly understood, the Rules encourage the "cooperative and proportional" use of procedure, and discourage "overuse, misuse, and abuse of procedural tools that increase costs and result in delay."[48] They favor decisions on the merits, rather than ones based on mere technicalities.[49]

Courts have quoted these touchstones often as guidance for construing and interpreting the Rules. In finding a Rule's meaning, the touchstones of Rule 1 disfavor any interpretation that will cause confusion[50] or which "lays traps for the unwary."[51] So pervasive is the Rule 1 mission that it has been cited as authority for preventing a litigant from flouting the "spirit" of the Rules, even where the litigant's conduct might otherwise comport with the Rule's literal meaning.[52]

Examples of the judiciary's reliance on Rule 1 to achieve these objectives are legion. A few samples are illustrative. The U.S. Supreme Court cited Rule 1's mandate to justify a broadening of the long-cramped reach of the summary judgment rule.[53] The U.S. Courts of Appeals have cited Rule 1 to permit the

---

[45] *See* Rule 1 advisory committee notes (1993). *See also Johnson v. Board of County Com'rs for County of Fremont*, 868 F. Supp. 1226, 1230 (D. Colo. 1994) (public interest demands seemly, efficient use of judicial resources to achieve Rule 1 goals, and courts are obligated to raise perceived dangers to these objectives even if parties do not).

[46] *See* Rule 1 advisory committee note (2015). *See generally Reebok Int'l Ltd. v. Sebelen*, 959 F. Supp. 553, 558 n. 1 (D.P.R. 1997) (citing Herman Melville's fable, *Bartleby the Scrivener*, as a valuable reminder that "the lawyer's role extends beyond filing motions and be an unquestioning mouthpiece for his client. His role is to engage in the adversarial process in good faith and in accordance with" the precepts of Rule 1).

[47] *See Mused v. U.S. Dept. of Agriculture Food & Nutrition Service*, 169 F.R.D. 28, 35 (W.D. N.Y. 1996).

[48] Rule 1 advisory committee note (2015).

[49] *Schiavone v. Fortune*, 477 U.S. 21, 27, 106 S. Ct. 2379, 2383, 91 L. Ed. 2d 18 (1986); *Foman v. Davis*, 371 U.S. 178, 181, 83 S. Ct. 227, 229, 9 L. Ed. 2d 222 (1962).

[50] *See Rodriguez v. Our Lady of Lourdes Med. Ctr.*, 552 F.3d 297, 302 (3d Cir. 2008).

[51] *See U.S. ex rel. Russell v. Epic Healthcare Mgmt. Group*, 193 F.3d 304, 307–08 (5th Cir. 1999).

[52] *See U.S. v. High Country Broad. Co.*, 3 F.3d 1244, 1245 (9th Cir. 1993). *But see Bank of Hope v. Miye Chon*, 938 F.3d 389, 396 (3d Cir. 2019) (courts have no authority to police the "spirit" of the Rules by restricting speech); *Central States, Southeast & Southwest Areas Pension Fund v. Central Cartage Co.*, 69 F.3d 1312, 1314–15 (7th Cir. 1995) ("the need to consider the objectives in Fed.R.Civ.P. 1 when construing all of the rules does not justify disregarding limitations explicitly built into them").

[53] *See Celotex Corp. v. Catrett*, 477 U.S. 317, 327, 106 S. Ct. 2548, 2555,

promulgation of "standing orders" as case management devices,[54] but yet also to eschew an "unduly rigid application" of local rules,[55] to overrule prior precedent that had inflexibly commanded at least one chance to amend a dismissed complaint (even where no such leave was sought),[56] to approve the "filing" *instanter* of a pleading attached to a motion for leave but never separately filed,[57] to afford judges the discretion (but not the obligation) to convene a hearing when ruling on personal jurisdiction motions,[58] to justify entertaining late-filed dismissal motions[59] or successive summary judgment motions,[60] to issue mandamus to unwind an improper severance and transfer,[61] to require a trial judge's explanation for declining to exercise supplemental jurisdiction a week before the scheduled trial of a short, simple, and long-pending dispute,[62] in determining whether to stay discovery pending a ruling on a potentially dispositive motion,[63] to forbid the "ambushing" of a trial court with belatedly raised objections,[64] and in allowing partial jury verdicts in civil cases.[65]

Likewise, the U.S. District Courts have cited Rule 1 in crafting, during the global Coronavirus pandemic, special protocols for deposing medical witnesses[66] and for permitting remote video depositions,[67] in permitting "predictive coding" while preparing responses to discovery production requests,[68] in disapproving the practice of redacting irrelevant portions of relevant

---

91 L. Ed. 2d 265 (1986) (commenting how summary judgment constitutes an integral role in implementing the Federal Rules' task of just, speedy, and inexpensive resolutions).

[54]*See Mortgage Grader, Inc. v. First Choice Loan Servs. Inc.*, 811 F.3d 1314, 1320–21 (Fed. Cir. 2016).

[55]*See Mitskovski v. Buffalo & Fort Erie Public Bridge Auth.*, 435 F.3d 127, 133 (2d Cir. 2006).

[56]*See Wagner v. Daewoo Heavy Indus. America Corp.*, 314 F.3d 541, 542–43 (11th Cir. 2002).

[57]*See A. Bauer Mech., Inc. v. Joint Arbitration Bd. of Plumbing Contractors' Ass'n & Chicago Journeymen Plumbers' Local Union 130*, 562 F.3d 784, 791 (7th Cir. 2009).

[58]*See Grayson v. Anderson*, 816 F.3d 262, 268–69 (4th Cir. 2016).

[59]*See In re Apple Iphone Antitrust Litig.*, 846 F.3d 313, 317–19 (9th Cir. 2017).

[60]*See Hoffman v. Tonnemacher*, 593 F.3d 908, 911 (9th Cir. 2010).

[61]*See Defense Distributed v. Bruck*, 30 F.4th 414, 427 (5th Cir. 2022).

[62]*See Catzin v. Thank You & Good Luck Corp.*, 899 F.3d 77, 86 (2d Cir. 2018).

[63]*See Henson v. Dep't of Health & Human Servs.*, 892 F.3d 868, 874–75 (7th Cir. 2018).

[64]*See Celle v. Filipino Reporter Enters. Inc.*, 209 F.3d 163, 175–76 (2d Cir. 2000) (rejecting maneuver that "would permit a losing party to lead a trial court into error and then to profit on appeal from the misguidance").

[65]*See Sanchez v. City of Chicago*, 880 F.3d 349, 360–61 (7th Cir. 2018).

[66]*See DeVine v. XPO Logistics Freight*, 446 F. Supp. 3d 332, 333–36 (N.D. Ill. 2020).

[67]*See Rouviere v. DePuy Orthopaedics, Inc.*, 471 F. Supp. 3d 571, 576–77 (S.D.N.Y. 2020) (actually enhances counsel's ability to observe witness's demeanor, since deposition would otherwise occur masked).

[68]*See Moore v. Publicis Groupe*, 287 F.R.D. 182, 182–83 (S.D.N.Y. 2012), *adopted by*, 2012 WL 1446534

documents in response to production requests,[69] in approving the use of "phased" discovery,[70] in allowing subpoena delivery by means other than personal service,[71] in refusing to tolerate deposition errata sheets that alter the substance of a witness' testimony (rather than merely correct transcription errors),[72] in regulating "Rambo"-style litigation tactics,[73] and in limiting the number of testifying experts[74] and setting the timing for rebuttal expert reports.[75]

In the words of one court, this "simple" Rule is a reminder that form should not be exalted over substance.[76] Yet, the Rules' flexibility is certainly not unbounded. Rule 1's touchstones cannot be cited, for example, to contort a claim into something that it obviously is not, under the banner of liberality.[77]

Additional Research References

Wright & Miller, *Federal Practice and Procedure* §§ 1011 to 1040

C.J.S., Federal Civil Procedure §§ 5 et seq.; Federal Courts § 284

West's Key Number Digest, Federal Civil Procedure ⚷21; ⚷31 to 44; Federal Courts ⚷522

(S.D.N.Y. Apr. 26, 2012).

[69]*See Doe v. Trump*, 329 F.R.D. 262, 275–76 (W.D. Wash. 2018).

[70]*See U.S. E.E.O.C. v. PMT Corp.*, 124 F. Supp. 3d 904, 910–17 (D. Minn. 2015).

[71]*See Sec. & Exch. Comm'n v. Pence*, 322 F.R.D. 450, 454 (S.D.N.Y. 2017).

[72]*See E.I. du Pont de Nemours & Co. v. Kolon Indus., Inc.*, 277 F.R.D. 286, 297–98 (E.D.Va. 2011).

[73]*See In re Amezaga*, 195 B.R. 221, 228 (Bankr. D. P.R. 1996) ("Rambo Litigation" is not tolerated because, although it may project zealous advocacy, it does not promote Rule 1's goals); *Applied Telematics, Inc. v. Sprint Corp.*, 1995 WL 79237 (E.D. Pa. 1995) (decrying counsel's "Rambo Litigation" deposition defense tactics as failing to promote goals of Rule 1).

[74]*See Planned Parenthood of Cent. New Jersey v. Verniero*, 22 F. Supp. 2d 331, 339 (D.N.J. 1998).

[75]*See U.S. Bank, N.A. v. Glogowski L. Firm, PLLC*, 339 F.R.D. 579, 580–81 (W.D. Wash. 2021).

[76]*See Hall v. Sullivan*, 229 F.R.D. 501, 504 (D. Md. 2005).

[77]*See Lee v. MBNA Long Term Disability & Benefit Plan*, 136 Fed. Appx. 734, 746 (6th Cir. 2005) (although Rule 1 directs liberal construction of pleadings, it will not justify finding a State claim in a complaint pleaded as an ERISA case).

RULE 2
ONE FORM OF ACTION

There is one form of action—the civil action.

[Amended April 30, 2007, effective December 1, 2007.]

AUTHORS' COMMENTARY ON RULE 2

PURPOSE AND SCOPE

English law long recognized a tribunal difference between law and equity. The English *law courts* would hear "actions" where juries (sometimes) would resolve disputes that sought a remedy at law (often compensatory money damages) based on principles of common law. The English *courts of equity* (or "chancery") would hear "suits" or "bills" where chancellors would, without a jury, resolve disputes that sought equitable relief (often injunctions) based on flexible principles of general fairness. These two types of tribunals co-existed under English law, but evolved with separate sets of rules and procedures. This distinction between law and equity was imported into American jurisprudence during our colonial period, and then preserved in the U.S. Constitution.

Among the many innovations ushered in by the Federal Rules of Civil Procedure was the "merger" of law and equity for procedural purposes. Rule 2 abolished, for the federal judiciary, "law courts" and "equity courts," "chancellors in equity," and "legal procedures" and "equity procedures." By virtue of Rule 2, federal courts were authorized to hear one, unified "form of action"—a "civil action"—and, in resolving that dispute, federal judges were authorized to award legal remedies, equitable remedies, or both in the same proceeding.

APPLICATIONS

Merger of Law and Equity Courts

With the arrival of Rule 2, "actions" at law and "suits" and "bills" in equity were merged together in the federal courts, with only one "form of action" remaining — the "civil action".[1]

[1]*See Petrella v. Metro-Goldwyn-Mayer, Inc.*, 572 U.S. 663, 678, 134 S. Ct. 1962, 1973, 188 L. Ed. 2d 979 (2014); *Crystallex Int'l Corp. v. Bolivarian Republic of Venezuela*, 24 F.4th 242, 253 (3d Cir. 2022).

Civil Action Defined

The term "civil action" means a federal civil lawsuit,[2] regardless of how that lawsuit might be labeled or titled.[3] The term encompasses all component "claims" and "cases" within that lawsuit.[4] But to qualify as a civil action, the proceeding must actually have been commenced.[5]

Joinder of All Claims and Defenses

Without a separate "law-side" and "equity-side" to the federal courts, a party may now join all claims and defenses (legal and equitable) against all opposing parties in the same one action.[6] Note, however, that the Rules—and certain judiciary title statutes—may limit such joinder.[7]

Determining Form of Action

Although the federal courts no longer recognize a distinction in procedure between cases on the "law-side" and suits in "equity", this distinction remains significant when federal courts are called upon to discern the substantive form of a litigation.[8] For example, the court may have to decide a litigation's form to assess its eligibility for a jury trial[9] or, in diversity cases, to properly apply a State law that retains the law/

---

[2]*See Raplee v. United States*, 842 F.3d 328, 332 (4th Cir. 2016).

[3]*See Wade v. Ogden*, 2009 WL 2423535, at *3 (D.Utah Aug. 4, 2009) (rejecting argument that "petition" is distinguishable from "suit" or "complaint").

[4]*See Brown v. Megg*, 857 F.3d 287, 290 (5th Cir. 2017); *Nolan v. Boeing Co.*, 919 F.2d 1058, 1066 (5th Cir. 1990) (ruling that "case" and "action" refer to the same thing—the entirety of a civil proceeding, including third party claims). *See also Fogg v. Ashcroft*, 254 F.3d 103, 107 (D.C. Cir. 2001) (citing Rule 2 as support for holding that statutory cap on damages in "an action brought" under the Civil Rights Act of 1964 applies to entire lawsuit, not just to individual claims within lawsuit).

[5]*See Berroa v. Sumner*, 2018 WL 555242, at *2 (D.N.J. Jan. 25, 2018) (litigation hold notice filed with court was not a civil action); *Tropeano v. Rutland Pharmacy*, 2013 WL 414217, at *2 (D.Vt. Feb. 1, 2013) (injunction motion, filed without complaint, was not a civil action).

[6]*See Johnson v. Spencer*, 950 F.3d 680, 702 (10th Cir. 2020) (rejecting view that relief from judgment is only available to proceedings that are equitable in nature, given the Rules' merger of law and equity); *U.S. ex rel. Rahman v. Oncology Assocs., P.C.*, 198 F.3d 502, 508 (4th Cir. 1999) (mandamus request not improper when made in course of civil lawsuit, given "the modern trend in civil pleading . . . to encourage that all claims for relief be brought in a single suit").

[7]*See, e.g.*, 28 U.S.C.A. § 1367 (enumerating the federal court's supplemental jurisdiction over state law claims); Rule 18 (joinder of claims and remedies); Rule 19 (joinder of parties); Rule 82 (satisfying Rule requirements does not ensure jurisdiction or venue authority).

[8]*See Burlington Northern R. Co. v. Nebraska Public Power Dist.*, 931 F. Supp. 1470, 1479 (D. Neb. 1996).

[9]*See Wooddell v. Int'l Bhd. of Elec. Workers, Local 71*, 502 U.S. 93, 97, 112 S. Ct. 494, 497, 116 L. Ed. 2d 419 (1991) (to decide whether a particular lawsuit would resolve "legal" rights, and thus entitle the litigants to a trial by jury, the courts: (1) compare the action to 18th Century claims brought in English law courts; and (2) determine whether the remedy sought is legal or equitable in nature).

equity distinction.

Equity Principles Applicable

Although the Rules have fused law and equity into a single procedural framework, the federal courts still apply equity principles in appropriate cases.[10]

Complete Relief

When granting final judgment, a court may grant all the relief to which a party is entitled (legal and equitable), regardless of the relief demanded in the pleadings.[11] Note, however, that many judicial districts require parties to list in a pretrial memorandum the specific relief they intend to seek and, thereafter, to remain bound by that listing at trial.[12]

Additional Research References

Wright & Miller, *Federal Practice and Procedure* §§ 1041 to 1050
C.J.S., Federal Civil Procedure § 4, §§ 37 et seq.
West's Key Number Digest, Federal Civil Procedure ⚷5 to 7; ⚷71 to 73; ⚷81 to 87

---

[10]*See Petrella v. Metro-Goldwyn-Mayer, Inc.*, 572 U.S. 663, 678, 134 S. Ct. 1962, 1973, 188 L. Ed. 2d 979 (2014) (laches "was, and remains," a defense to equitable claims for which a legislature has not set a limitation period); *Stainback v. Mo Hock Ke Lok Po*, 336 U.S. 368, 382, 69 S. Ct. 606, 93 L. Ed. 741 (1949) (Rules' merger of law and equity did not affect the substantive principles of equity); *Matter of U.S. Brass Corp.*, 110 F.3d 1261, 1267 (7th Cir. 1997) (since law and equity were merged in the federal courts, judges have freely imported equitable defenses into suits at law).

[11]*See* Rule 54(c).

[12]*See, e.g.*, E.D. Pa. Loc. R. 16.1(c)(3) & (d)(2)(b)(3) (requiring party seeking relief to identify the precise monetary and non-monetary relief requested).

II. COMMENCING AN ACTION; SERVICE OF PROCESS, PLEADINGS, MOTIONS, AND ORDERS

RULE 3
COMMENCING AN ACTION

A civil action is commenced by filing a complaint with the court.

[Amended April 30, 2007, effective December 1, 2007.]

AUTHORS' COMMENTARY ON RULE 3

PURPOSE AND SCOPE

A civil action is considered "commenced" on the date a complaint is filed. This dating function may be important for several purposes, including discerning whether an action is timely under the applicable statute of limitations. In some (but not all) contexts, commencement may toll a limitations period while service of process is being accomplished.

APPLICATIONS

Action "Commences" When Complaint is Filed

An action "commences" within the meaning of the Rules when the complaint is delivered for filing to a court officer authorized to receive it.[1] Without a filing, there is no commencement (and, consequently, no authority for a federal district court to act in the dispute).[2] Similarly, filing a paper other than

[1] *See Farley v. Koepp*, 788 F.3d 681, 684–86 (7th Cir. 2015). *See also U.S. v. $8,221,877.16 in U.S. Currency*, 330 F.3d 141, 159 (3d Cir. 2003) ("commence" is term of art with only one unambiguous meaning—it does not "encompass broad concepts, but rather requires 'invocation of the judicial process' "). *See generally Local Union No. 38, Sheet Metal Workers' Intern. Ass'n, AFL-CIO v. Pelella*, 350 F.3d 73, 82 (2d Cir. 2003) (an action is instituted in federal court when "a plaintiff files a complaint as that constitutes the first step invoking the judicial process").

[2] *See S.E.C. v. Ross*, 504 F.3d 1130, 1140–41 (9th Cir. 2007) (court would not proceed on motion for disgorgement of gains without complaint naming motion's respondent as party); *Adair v. England*, 193 F. Supp. 2d 196, 200 (D.D.C. 2002) (if no complaint filed, federal court lacks jurisdiction to hear petition for injunctive relief).

a complaint will not trigger commencement,[3] unless the court can properly treat the filed paper as a complaint.[4]

Service Often Not Required for "Commencement"

Service of process is generally not a prerequisite for the lawsuit to "commence."[5] So long as service is completed within 90 days after the complaint is filed with the court, the litigants become "plaintiff" and "defendant" when the complaint is filed, not when it is served.[6]

State-Imposed Pre-Filing Chores Often Not Required for "Commencement"

Most recent decisions hold that various pre-filing tasks imposed by State law need not be performed for a federal civil action to "commence."[7]

Filing Fees Often Not Required for "Commencement"

Many court have ruled that the payment of filing fees is required for a lawsuit to commence (and toll the limitations period), but a division among the courts persists on this issue.[8] Prudent practitioners should therefore ensure that all fees are properly paid at the time the complaint is delivered to the

[3]*See Radin v. Jersey City Med. Ctr.*, 375 Fed. Appx. 205, 206–07 (3d Cir. 2010) (per curiam) (filing blank piece of paper containing only a caption did not qualify as "commencement"); *Autoridad de Carreteras y Transportacion v. Transcore Atl., Inc.*, 128 F. Supp. 3d 485, 486 (D.P.R. 2015) (filing a counterclaim did not qualify as "commencement" under terms of forum selection clause because it is not a "complaint"); *Greene v. Philadelphia Housing Auth.*, 789 F. Supp. 2d 582, 585 (E.D.Pa. 2011) (filing motion for TRO, without also filing complaint, did not qualify as "commencement").

[4]*See Muhammad v. Wiles*, 841 Fed. Appx. 681, 686 (5th Cir. 2021) (treating "memorandum" as a complaint); *Woodyard v. Harper*, 162 F. Supp. 3d 3, 4 (D.D.C. 2016) (treating pro se affidavit as a complaint).

[5]*See KLS Diversified Master Fund, L.P. v. McDevitt*, 507 F. Supp. 3d 508, 542–43 (S.D.N.Y. 2020) (filed complaint that has not yet been properly served is still "commenced" and "pending").

[6]*See Howell by Goerdt v. Tribune Entertainment Co.*, 106 F.3d 215, 217 (7th Cir. 1997). *See also Clay v. U.S.*, 199 F.3d 876, 880 (6th Cir. 1999) ("A person becomes 'a party' only by beginning a lawsuit, Fed. R. Civ. P. 3, or by being joined as a party after a suit has been instituted").

[7]*See Martin v. Pierce Cnty.*, 34 F.4th 1125, 1129–32 (9th Cir. 2022) (Washington State's pre-filing arbitration election not required to "commence" in federal court); *Albright v. Christensen*, 24 F.4th 1039, 1046–47 (6th Cir. 2022) (Michigan State's pre-filing medical malpractice notice not required to "commence" in federal court).

[8]*See Morrison v. Nielsen*, 325 F. Supp. 3d 62, 66 (D.D.C. 2018). *See also Searcy v. County of Oakland*, 735 F. Supp. 2d 759, 765–68 (E.D.Mich. 2010) (finding weight of authority favors view that payment is not required for commencement). *Compare Robinson v. America's Best Contacts and Eyeglasses*, 876 F.2d 596, 598 (7th Cir. 1989) (in Rule 4 context, construing local rule to require payment of fee as prerequisite for filing) *with McDowell v. Delaware State Police*, 88 F.3d 188, 191 (3d Cir. 1996) (filing fee is not jurisdictional; complaint is deemed constructively filed when Clerk receives it, so long as plaintiff ultimately pays fee or is granted leave to proceed *in forma pauperis*).

court.

"Commencement" is Provisional—Without Service, Action Dismissible After 90 Days

Although an action becomes "pending" when the complaint is delivered for filing, Rule 4(m) authorizes the district court to dismiss the action, without prejudice, if service of process is not made within 90 days of commencement (unless good cause is shown why service was not accomplished during that period).[9]

"Commencement" is Provisional — Action Dismissible for Later Lack of Diligent Prosecution

Once a plaintiff files the complaint, the plaintiff must prosecute the action with due diligence. Rule 3 does not relieve plaintiffs of their obligation to prosecute the complaint after filing. The court may dismiss any action for lack of due diligence in proceeding with the lawsuit.[10]

Uses of Rule 3's Dating Function

Rule 3's function of "dating" the commencement of a lawsuit as of the day the complaint is filed with the court is useful in many contexts. This dating function may be used to evaluate:

- The timeliness of the action, under the applicable statute of limitations and/or laches (see discussions below);
- Standing, Ripeness, and Mootness;[11]
- Diversity Jurisdiction, which generally vests at the time an action is commenced;[12]
- Venue, which likewise is generally assessed as of the date the action is commenced;[13]
- Competing Jurisdiction Issues, when complaints involving the same parties and issues are filed in two different courts and the governing law provides that the first court to obtain jurisdiction should proceed and the

---

[9]*See* Rule 4(m). *See also Rogers v. Amalgamated Transit Union Local 689*, 115 F. Supp. 3d 76, 78 (D.D.C. 2015). Note, however, that Rule 4(m) does not apply to service within a foreign country, *see* Rule 4(m) (referencing Rule 4(f)); or to service upon a foreign state and its political subdivisions, agencies, and instrumentalities, *see* Rule 4(m) (referencing Rule 4(j)(1)).

[10]*See* Rule 41(b).

[11]*See United States Parole Comm'n v. Geraghty*, 445 U.S. 388, 397, 100 S. Ct. 1202, 63 L. Ed. 2d 479 (1980).

[12]*See Freeport-McMoRan, Inc. v. K N Energy, Inc.*, 498 U.S. 426, 428, 111 S. Ct. 858, 859, 112 L. Ed. 2d 951 (1991) (if diversity jurisdiction exists at time lawsuit is filed, jurisdiction will not be divested by subsequent events). *Cf. Stevens v. Nichols*, 130 U.S. 230, 231–32, 9 S. Ct. 518, 518–19, 32 L. Ed. 914 (1889) (case may be removed to federal court only if diversity exists both at time action is commenced and at time removal is sought).

[13]*See Daughetee v. CHR Hansen, Inc.*, 2011 WL 1113868, at *3–*4 (N.D. Iowa Mar. 25, 2011) (collecting cases showing division on issue, but noting that majority view tests venue as of time of filing).

second court should dismiss or abstain;[14] and

- Litigation of Claims Accruing After the Filing of the Complaint, where new claims usually cannot be litigated in the same case absent an amendment or supplement to the complaint.[15]

"Commencement" in Federal Question Cases

In cases invoking the court's federal question jurisdiction, commencement alone will ordinarily toll the applicable statute of limitations (even though service of process will likely not yet have been accomplished).[16] An exception exists—where the federal question is based on a statute that, itself, contains a separate "commencement" provision, the terms of that provision will control. Where the federal law lacks a specific statute of limitations and the applicable limitations period is "borrowed" either from another federal law[17] or from State law,[18] the filing of the complaint will alone generally toll the limitations period.

- *Special Federal Prerequisites:* Certain federal statutes contain special prerequisites for commencing a civil action, such as receiving a right-to-sue letter or exhausting administrative remedies.[19] Thus, merely filing a complaint pursuant to Rule 3 might not toll the statute of limitations if such prerequisites are not met.

"Commencement" in Diversity Cases

In cases invoking the court's diversity of citizenship jurisdiction, the date of commencement will be used to access uniquely federal issues, such as the presence or absence of diverse citizenship and the computation of time under the Rules.[20]

However, commencement alone will not always toll the limi-

---

[14]*See Wakaya Perfection, LLC v. Youngevity Int'l, Inc.*, 910 F.3d 1118, 1124 (10th Cir. 2018).

[15]*See* Rule 15. *See also Altseimer v. Bell Helicopter Textron Inc.*, 919 F. Supp. 340, 342–43 (E.D. Cal. 1996) (citing Rule 3's "commencement" dating function in refusing to apply new federal statute to existing civil action, where new Act expressly did not apply to lawsuits "commenced" before the date of the Act's enactment).

[16]*See Henderson v. U.S.*, 517 U.S. 654, 657 n.2, 116 S. Ct. 1638, 1641 n.2, 134 L. Ed. 2d 880 (1996). *See also Iran Air v. Kugelman*, 996 F.2d 1253, 1257 (D.C. Cir. 1993) (applying Rule 3 to toll statute of limitations on federally-created right even though service not accomplished until after period had expired).

[17]*See West v. Conrail*, 481 U.S. 35, 35, 107 S. Ct. 1538, 95 L. Ed. 2d 32 (1987) (in action under Railway Labor Act, which lacked specific statute of limitations or commencement period, Rule 3 tolled the applicable statute of limitations upon filing).

[18]*See Sain v. City of Bend*, 309 F.3d 1134, 1135–38 (9th Cir. 2002) (joining other federal circuits in ruling that Rule 3 provides tolling function for limitations period borrowed from State law in Section 1983 case).

[19]*See, e.g., Truitt v. County of Wayne*, 148 F.3d 644, 646 (6th Cir.1998) (discussing EEOC right-to-sue letter procedure).

[20]*See Jenkins v. Village of Maywood*, 506 F.3d 622, 624 (7th Cir. 2007) (although federal courts borrow statute of limitations and coordinate

tations period governing the State law claims. The *Erie* doctrine and its progeny[21] compels that, where State law provides a contrary tolling requirement or tolling limitation, Rule 3 cannot be permitted to give the State law cause of action a longer life in a federal court than it would otherwise have in the State courts.[22] Thus, if under State law the limitations period would not be tolled until service is accomplished or the filing fee is paid, Rule 3 will not act to toll the limitations period merely upon filing.[23] Similarly, where State law requires the issuance of a summons before the applicable statute of limitations is tolled, the federal courts will honor that requirement: until the summons is issued, the limitations period will continue to run.[24]

"Commencement" in Supplemental Jurisdiction Cases

In cases invoking the court's supplemental jurisdiction over an otherwise non-qualifying State law claim, the courts will likely follow the same rules as they do in diversity cases. Rule 3 will not give the State law cause of action longer life in a federal forum than that same cause of action would enjoy in State court.[25]

"Commencement" and Removed Cases

Ordinarily, a case is not considered "re"-commenced if it is removed to federal court. Instead, the general federal approach holds that a lawsuit is deemed "commenced" at one, discrete moment in time—typically, when the original lawsuit is filed in

---

tolling rules from State, federal procedural rules determine when action was voluntarily dismissed).

[21]*See Erie R. Co. v. Tompkins*, 304 U.S. 64, 78, 58 S. Ct. 817, 82 L. Ed. 1188 (1938). The *Erie* doctrine may obligate the federal courts to apply State law in diversity cases. For an extended discussion of the *Erie* doctrine, see *supra* Part II § 2.18 of this text.

[22]*See Walker v. Armco Steel Corp.*, 446 U.S. 740, 740, 100 S. Ct. 1978, 64 L. Ed. 2d 659 (1980); *Ragan v. Merchants Transfer & Warehouse Co.*, 337 U.S. 530, 69 S. Ct. 1233, 93 L. Ed. 1520 (1949).

[23]*See Henderson v. U.S.*, 517 U.S. 654, 657 n. 2, 116 S. Ct. 1638, 1641 n. 2, 134 L. Ed. 2d 880 (1996) (in federal court action upon a right created by State law, plaintiff must serve process before statute of limitations has expired, if law of that State so requires); *Walker v. Armco Steel Corp.*, 446 U.S. 740, 740, 100 S. Ct. 1978, 64 L. Ed. 2d 659 (1980) (Oklahoma law, which tolls statute of limitations only upon service, supersedes Rule 3's tolling effect); *Ragan v. Merchants Transfer & Warehouse Co.*, 337 U.S. 530, 533, 69 S. Ct. 1233, 93 L. Ed. 1520 (1949) (same conclusion under Kansas law); *Habermehl v. Potter*, 153 F.3d 1137, 1139 (10th Cir. 1998) (case was time-barred under Wyoming law, where limitations periods are only tolled 60 days for service, and service was not completed in time). *But cf. Hart v. Bates*, 897 F. Supp. 710, 716 (E.D. N.Y. 1995) (applying federal, rather than Pennsylvania, time limitation for proper service of process where Pennsylvania did not condition "commencement" of civil action upon effective service, and did not deem service as integral to tolling of its statute of limitations).

[24]*See Eades v. Clark Distributing Co., Inc.*, 70 F.3d 441, 442 (6th Cir. 1995).

[25]*See Anderson v. Unisys Corp.*, 47 F.3d 302, 309 (8th Cir. 1995) (affirming dismissal of State law claims where, under Minnesota law, an action is not "commenced" until the initial process is served).

a court of competent jurisdiction.[26] Nevertheless, if an applicable State law requires effective service as a prerequisite to "commencement," the lawsuit might be considered ineligible for removal until the defendant is successfully served.[27]

"Commencement" and Proper Pleading

There is some authority for the proposition that a complaint which is defectively pleaded may not qualify as a proper "commencement" under Rule 3 (and, therefore, may not serve to toll an applicable limitations period).[28]

"Commencement" and Amended Complaints

Often, amendments do not trigger a commencement because they merely enhance or adjust a claim that is then already pending.[29] However, amendments may also add new claims or claims against new parties. In those settings, and when the amendment requires court permission,[30] many courts have ruled that such amendments are deemed filed for commencement (and, perhaps, limitations) purposes at least[31] as of the date that a motion for leave to amend is filed.[32] Practitioners should rely on this principle with great care, however. Whether this treatment applies to all cases (or just those where an earlier amendment was made impossible by circumstances), whether this treatment applies where the motion neither attaches the proposed amended complaint nor properly describes it, and whether this treatment has any effect where the leave is denied, are each unclear.

"Commencement" and Counterclaims

Only complaints are "commenced" (and, thus, implicated by Rule 3). A counterclaim is not a "civil action" and, therefore, is typically not deemed to "commence" within the meaning of

---

[26]*See Wakaya Perfection, LLC v. Youngevity Int'l, Inc.*, 910 F.3d 1118, 1124 (10th Cir. 2018). *But see Wasserman v. Rodacker*, 557 F.3d 635, 639 (D.C.Cir. 2009) (removed actions are "commenced" when removal is effected and clerk receives complaint).

[27]*See, e.g., Dinkel v. General Motors Corp.*, 400 F. Supp. 2d 289, 293 (D. Me. 2005).

[28]*See Male v. Tops Friendly Markets*, 2008 WL 1836948 (W.D. N.Y. 2008) (because contested complaint failed to satisfy the *Twomby* pleading standard, it did not "commence" an action under Rule 3, which denied a later amendment's claim for relation-back status, thus rendering the amending claims untimely).

[29]*See Gerber v. MTC Elec. Techs. Co.*, 329 F.3d 297, 310 (2d Cir. 2003) ("Amending the complaint, even to add additional plaintiffs, did not create a new action."); *Lamb v. Millennium Challenge Corp.*, 573 F. Supp. 3d 346, 360–61 (D.D.C. Sept. 27, 2021).

[30]*See* Rule 15.

[31]If the doctrine of relation-back applies to the amendment, the operative commencement date could be the filing of the original pleading. *See* Rule 15(c).

[32]*See, e.g., Rothman v. Gregor*, 220 F.3d 81, 96 (2d Cir. 2000); *Mayes v. AT & T Information Systems, Inc.*, 867 F.2d 1172, 1173 (8th Cir. 1989). *See also Nett v. Bellucci*, 437 Mass. 630, 630–47, 774 N.E.2d 130, 130–42 (2002) (on certified question from the First Circuit Court of Appeals, citing cases, and extensively discussing "commencement" effect of motion for leave to amend).

Rule 3.[33]

Filing By Mail

The "mailbox" rule generally will not apply in Rule 3 circumstances. If original papers are mailed to the Clerk's Office for filing, filing is only complete—and the lawsuit only "commences"—upon the Clerk's receipt of the complaint.[34]

Filing By Electronic Means

When a complaint is filed through proper electronic means, "commencement" ordinarily occurs once the filing process is complete, regardless of whether the system experiences an electronic glitch[35] or the filing fee is not yet paid.[36]

Filing After Business Hours

Rule 77 prescribes that the District Courts are "always open." Accordingly, a complaint might be deemed to be filed as of the moment it was delivered to the Clerk's Office, even if delivered after business hours.[37]

Pauper and Prisoner Plaintiffs

The federal courts follow an *in forma pauperis* procedure which can allow a federal judge, upon request, to authorize the commencement of a lawsuit without a payment of filing fees.[38] Some courts will even consider a lawsuit conditionally commenced upon the simultaneous[39] filing of a complaint and a motion to proceed *in forma pauperis*[40] (provided that, if the motion is later denied, filing fees are promptly paid);[41] this conditional commencement might also toll the applicable limitations

---

[33]*See Jonathan H. v. Souderton Area Sch. Dist.*, 562 F.3d 527, 529–30 (3d Cir. 2009); *Local Union No. 38, Sheet Metal Workers' Int'l Ass'n, AFL-CIO v. Pelella*, 350 F.3d 73, 82 (2d Cir. 2003).

[34]*See McIntosh v. Antonino*, 71 F.3d 29, 36–37 (1st Cir. 1995); *Cooper v. City of Ashland*, 871 F.2d 104, 105 (9th Cir. 1989).

[35]*See Farley v. Koepp*, 788 F.3d 681, 684–86 (7th Cir. 2015).

[36]*See Searcy v. County of Oakland*, 735 F. Supp. 2d 759, 761 (E.D.Mich. 2010).

[37]*See Turner v. City of Newport*, 887 F. Supp. 149, 150 (E.D. Ky. 1995) (complaint timely filed when delivered to Clerk's post office box, after office had closed, on last day before statute of limitations ran). *But cf.* Rule 6(a)(4).

[38]*See* 28 U.S.C. § 1915(a).

[39]Some courts go further, and conditionally commence an unpaid lawsuit if the *in forma pauperis* motion is later filed within a reasonable time. *See Murray v. Dosal*, 150 F.3d 814, 816 n.4 (8th Cir. 1998); *Robinson v. Yellow Freight Sys.*, 892 F.2d 74 (4th Cir. 1989) (unpublished text available at 1989 WL 152510, at *2).

[40]*See Coleman v. Labor & Indus. Review Comm'n of Wis.*, 860 F.3d 461, 467 (7th Cir. 2017). *See also Powell v. Jacor Commc'ns Corp.*, 320 F.3d 599, 602–03 (6th Cir. 2003) (complaint, which would have been timely filed under Kentucky law had acceptance of complaint not been delayed by *in forma pauperis* petition, was deemed timely filed under Rule 3).

[41]*See Coleman v. Labor & Indus. Rev. Comm'n of Wisc.*, 860 F.3d 461, 467 (7th Cir. 2017).

period.[42] Other courts reject the notion of conditional commencement.[43]

In complaints prepared by *pro se* prisoner plaintiffs, the courts have often followed a variation of the "mailbox" rule that deems a lawsuit as "commenced" upon delivery of the complaint to appropriate prison officials.[44]

Additional Research References

Wright & Miller, *Federal Practice and Procedure* §§ 1051 to 57
C.J.S., Federal Civil Procedure § 3
West's Key Number Digest, Federal Civil Procedure ⚷4

---

[42]*See Mondy v. Sec'y of the Army*, 845 F.2d 1051, 1058 n.2 (D.C. Cir. 1988). *See also Truitt v. County of Wayne*, 148 F.3d 644, 647–48 (6th Cir.1998) (pauper litigant must pay filing fee within applicable limitations period, as tolled during the pendency of the *in forma pauperis* application); *Williams-Guice v. Board of Educ. of City of Chicago*, 45 F.3d 161, 162–64 (7th Cir. 1995) (limitations period resumes running once *in forma pauperis* application is denied).

[43]*See Brown v. Sage*, 941 F.3d 655, 662 (3d Cir. 2019).

[44]*See Cooper v. Brookshire*, 70 F.3d 377, 379–80 (5th Cir.1995); *Dory v. Ryan*, 999 F.2d 679, 682 (2d Cir. 1993). *Cf. Houston v. Lack*, 487 U.S. 266, 108 S. Ct. 2379, 101 L. Ed. 2d 245 (1988) (notice of appeal is "filed" within meaning of Federal Rules of Appellate Procedure when delivered by *pro se* prisoner to prison authorities). *But see Jackson v. Nicoletti*, 875 F. Supp. 1107, 1109–12 (E.D. Pa. 1994) (refusing to extend *Houston v. Lack* appeal-period mailbox rule to *pro se* prisoner's lawsuit under Rule 3; lawsuit dismissed as time-barred where complaint not delivered to clerk within two years after prisoner's claim accrued).

RULE 4
SUMMONS

(a) Contents; Amendments.

(1) *Contents.* A summons must:

(A) name the court and the parties;

(B) be directed to the defendant;

(C) state the name and address of the plaintiff's attorney or—if unrepresented—of the plaintiff;

(D) state the time within which the defendant must appear and defend;

(E) notify the defendant that a failure to appear and defend will result in a default judgment against the defendant for the relief demanded in the complaint;

(F) be signed by the clerk; and

(G) bear the court's seal.

(2) *Amendments.* The court may permit a summons to be amended.

(b) Issuance. On or after filing the complaint, the plaintiff may present a summons to the clerk for signature and seal. If the summons is properly completed, the clerk must sign, seal, and issue it to the plaintiff for service on the defendant. A summons—or a copy of a summons that is addressed to multiple defendants—must be issued for each defendant to be served.

(c) Service.

(1) *In General.* A summons must be served with a copy of the complaint. The plaintiff is responsible for having the summons and complaint served within the time allowed by Rule 4(m) and must furnish the necessary copies to the person who makes service.

(2) *By Whom.* Any person who is at least 18 years old and not a party may serve a summons and complaint.

(3) *By a Marshal or Someone Specially Appointed.* At the plaintiff's request, the court may order

that service be made by a United States marshal or deputy marshal or by a person specially appointed by the court. The court must so order if the plaintiff is authorized to proceed in forma pauperis under 28 U.S.C. § 1915 or as a seaman under 28 U.S.C. § 1916.

(d) Waiving Service.

(1) *Requesting a Waiver.* An individual, corporation, or association that is subject to service under Rule 4(e), (f), or (h) has a duty to avoid unnecessary expenses of serving the summons. The plaintiff may notify such a defendant that an action has been commenced and request that the defendant waive service of a summons. The notice and request must:

(A) be in writing and be addressed:

(i) to the individual defendant; or

(ii) for a defendant subject to service under Rule 4(h), to an officer, a managing or general agent, or any other agent authorized by appointment or by law to receive service of process;

(B) name the court where the complaint was filed;

(C) be accompanied by a copy of the complaint, 2 copies of the waiver form appended to this Rule 4, and a prepaid means for returning the form;

(D) inform the defendant, using the form appended to this Rule 4, of the consequences of waiving and not waiving service;

(E) state the date when the request is sent;

(F) give the defendant a reasonable time of at least 30 days after the request was sent—or at least 60 days if sent to the defendant outside any judicial district of the United States—to return the waiver; and

(G) be sent by first-class mail or other reliable means.

(2) *Failure to Waive.* If a defendant located within the United States fails, without good cause, to sign and return a waiver requested by a plaintiff

located within the United States, the court must impose on the defendant:

(A) the expenses later incurred in making service; and

(B) the reasonable expenses, including attorney's fees, of any motion required to collect those service expenses.

(3) *Time to Answer After a Waiver.* A defendant who, before being served with process, timely returns a waiver need not serve an answer to the complaint until 60 days after the request was sent—or until 90 days after it was sent to the defendant outside any judicial district of the United States.

(4) *Results of Filing a Waiver.* When the plaintiff files a waiver, proof of service is not required and these rules apply as if a summons and complaint had been served at the time of filing the waiver.

(5) *Jurisdiction and Venue Not Waived.* Waiving service of a summons does not waive any objection to personal jurisdiction or to venue.

(e) Serving an Individual Within a Judicial District of the United States. Unless federal law provides otherwise, an individual—other than a minor, an incompetent person, or a person whose waiver has been filed—may be served in a judicial district of the United States by:

(1) following state law for serving a summons in an action brought in courts of general jurisdiction in the state where the district court is located or where service is made; or

(2) doing any of the following:

(A) delivering a copy of the summons and of the complaint to the individual personally;

(B) leaving a copy of each at the individual's dwelling or usual place of abode with someone of suitable age and discretion who resides there; or

(C) delivering a copy of each to an agent authorized by appointment or by law to receive service of process.

(f) Serving an Individual in a Foreign Country.

Unless federal law provides otherwise, an individual—other than a minor, an incompetent person, or a person whose waiver has been filed—may be served at a place not within any judicial district of the United States:

(1) by any internationally agreed means of service that is reasonably calculated to give notice, such as those authorized by the Hague Convention on the Service Abroad of Judicial and Extrajudicial Documents;

(2) if there is no internationally agreed means, or if an international agreement allows but does not specify other means, by a method that is reasonably calculated to give notice:

(A) as prescribed by the foreign country's law for service in that country in an action in its courts of general jurisdiction;

(B) as the foreign authority directs in response to a letter rogatory or letter of request; or

(C) unless prohibited by the foreign country's law, by:

(i) delivering a copy of the summons and of the complaint to the individual personally; or

(ii) using any form of mail that the clerk addresses and sends to the individual and that requires a signed receipt; or

(3) by other means not prohibited by international agreement, as the court orders.

(g) Serving a Minor or an Incompetent Person. A minor or an incompetent person in a judicial district of the United States must be served by following state law for serving a summons or like process on such a defendant in an action brought in the courts of general jurisdiction of the state where service is made. A minor or an incompetent person who is not within any judicial district of the United States must be served in the manner prescribed by Rule 4(f)(2)(A), (f)(2)(B), or (f)(3).

(h) Serving a Corporation, Partnership, or Association. Unless federal law provides otherwise or the defendant's waiver has been filed, a domestic or foreign corporation, or a partnership or other unincorporated association that is subject to suit under a common name, must be served:

(1) in a judicial district of the United States:

(A) in the manner prescribed by Rule 4(e)(1) for serving an individual; or

(B) by delivering a copy of the summons and of the complaint to an officer, a managing or general agent, or any other agent authorized by appointment or by law to receive service of process and—if the agent is one authorized by statute and the statute so requires—by also mailing a copy of each to the defendant; or

(2) at a place not within any judicial district of the United States, in any manner prescribed by Rule 4(f) for serving an individual, except personal delivery under (f)(2)(C)(i).

(i) Serving the United States and Its Agencies, Corporations, Officers, or Employees.

(1) *United States.* To serve the United States, a party must:

(A) (i) deliver a copy of the summons and of the complaint to the United States attorney for the district where the action is brought—or to an assistant United States attorney or clerical employee whom the United States attorney designates in a writing filed with the court clerk—or

(ii) send a copy of each by registered or certified mail to the civil-process clerk at the United States attorney's office;

(B) send a copy of each by registered or certified mail to the Attorney General of the United States at Washington, D.C.; and

(C) if the action challenges an order of a nonparty agency or officer of the United States, send a copy of each by registered or certified mail to the agency or officer.

(2) *Agency; Corporation; Officer or Employee Sued in an Official Capacity.* To serve a United States agency or corporation, or a United States officer or employee sued only in an official capacity, a

party must serve the United States and also send a copy of the summons and of the complaint by registered or certified mail to the agency, corporation, officer, or employee.

(3) *Officer or Employee Sued Individually.* To serve a United States officer or employee sued in an individual capacity for an act or omission occurring in connection with duties performed on the United States' behalf (whether or not the officer or employee is also sued in an official capacity), a party must serve the United States and also serve the officer or employee under Rule 4(e), (f), or (g).

(4) *Extending Time.* The court must allow a party a reasonable time to cure its failure to:

(A) serve a person required to be served under Rule 4(i)(2), if the party has served either the United States attorney or the Attorney General of the United States; or

(B) serve the United States under Rule 4(i)(3), if the party has served the United States officer or employee.

(j) Serving a Foreign, State, or Local Government.

(1) *Foreign State.* A foreign state or its political subdivision, agency, or instrumentality must be served in accordance with 28 U.S.C. § 1608.

(2) *State or Local Government.* A state, a municipal corporation, or any other state-created governmental organization that is subject to suit must be served by:

(A) delivering a copy of the summons and of the complaint to its chief executive officer; or

(B) serving a copy of each in the manner prescribed by that state's law for serving a summons or like process on such a defendant.

(k) Territorial Limits of Effective Service.

(1) *In General.* Serving a summons or filing a waiver of service establishes personal jurisdiction over a defendant:

(A) who is subject to the jurisdiction of a court of

general jurisdiction in the state where the district court is located;

(B) who is a party joined under Rule 14 or 19 and is served within a judicial district of the United States and not more than 100 miles from where the summons was issued;

(C) when authorized by a federal statute.

(2) *Federal Claim Outside State-Court Jurisdiction.* For a claim that arises under federal law, serving a summons or filing a waiver of service establishes personal jurisdiction over a defendant if:

(A) the defendant is not subject to jurisdiction in any state's courts of general jurisdiction; and

(B) exercising jurisdiction is consistent with the United States Constitution and laws.

(*l*) Proving Service.

(1) *Affidavit Required.* Unless service is waived, proof of service must be made to the court. Except for service by a United States marshal or deputy marshal, proof must be by the server's affidavit.

(2) *Service Outside the United States.* Service not within any judicial district of the United States must be proved as follows:

(A) if made under Rule 4(f)(1), as provided in the applicable treaty or convention; or

(B) if made under Rule 4(f)(2) or (f)(3), by a receipt signed by the addressee, or by other evidence satisfying the court that the summons and complaint were delivered to the addressee.

(3) *Validity of Service; Amending Proof.* Failure to prove service does not affect the validity of service. The court may permit proof of service to be amended.

(m) Time Limit for Service. If a defendant is not served within 90 days after the complaint is filed, the court—on motion or on its own after notice to the plaintiff—must dismiss the action without prejudice against that defendant or order that service be made within a specified time. But if the plaintiff shows good cause for the failure, the court must extend the time for service for an appropriate period. This subdivision (m) does not apply to service in a foreign country under Rule 4(f), 4(h)(2), or 4(j)(1) or to service of a notice under Rule 71.1(d)(3)(A).

(n) Asserting Jurisdiction over Property or Assets.

(1) *Federal Law.* The court may assert jurisdiction over property if authorized by a federal statute. Notice to claimants of the property must be given as provided in the statute or by serving a summons under this rule.

(2) *State Law.* On a showing that personal jurisdiction over a defendant cannot be obtained in the district where the action is brought by reasonable efforts to serve a summons under this rule, the court may assert jurisdiction over the defendant's assets found in the district. Jurisdiction is acquired by seizing the assets under the circumstances and in the manner provided by state law in that district.

Official Forms to Accompany Rule 4—Summons

Rule 4 Waiver Request Form:

Notice of a Lawsuit and Request to Waive Service of Summons

(Caption)

To (*name the defendant or — if the defendant is a corporation, partnership, or association — name an officer or agent authorized to receive service*):

Why are you getting this?

A lawsuit has been filed against you, or the entity you represent, in this court under the number shown above. A copy of the complaint is attached.

This is not a summons, or an official notice from the court. It is a request that, to avoid expenses, you waive formal service of a summons by signing and returning the enclosed waiver. To avoid these expenses, you must return the signed waiver within (*give at least 30 days or at least 60 days if the defendant is outside any judicial district of the United States*) from the date shown below, which is the date this notice was sent. Two copies of the waiver form are enclosed, along with a stamped, self-addressed envelope

or other prepaid means for returning one copy.
You may keep the other copy.

What happens next?

If you return the signed waiver, I will file it with the court. The action will then proceed as if you had been served on the date the waiver is filed, but no summons will be served on you and you will have 60 days from the date this notice is sent (see the date below) to answer the complaint (or 90 days if this notice is sent to you outside any judicial district of the United States).

If you do not return the signed waiver within the time indicated, I will arrange to have the summons and complaint served on you. And I will ask the court to require you, or the entity you represent, to pay the expenses of making service.

Please read the enclosed statement about the duty to avoid unnecessary expenses.

I certify that this request is being sent to you on the date below.
Date: ________________

____
(Signature of the attorney or unrepresented party)

____
(Printed name)

____
(Address)

____
(E-mail address)

____
(Telephone number)

Rule 4 Waiver Form:

Waiver of the Service of Summons

(Caption)

To (*name the plaintiff's attorney or the unrepresented plaintiff*):

I have received your request to waive service of a summons in this action along with a copy of the complaint, two copies of this waiver form, and a prepaid means of returning one signed copy of the form to you.

I, or the entity I represent, agree to save the expense of serving a summons and complaint in this case.

I understand that I, or the entity I represent, will keep all defenses or objections to the lawsuit, the court's jurisdiction, and the venue of the action, but that I waive any objections to the absence of a summons or of service.

I also understand that I, or the entity I represent, must file and serve an answer or a motion under Rule 12 within 60 days from, the date when this request was sent (or 90 days if it was sent outside the United States). If I fail to do so, a default judgment will be entered against me or the entity I represent.

Date: ______________

____

(Signature of the attorney or unrepresented party)

____

(Printed name)

____

(Address)

____

(E-mail address)

____

(Telephone number)

____

(Attach the following)

Duty to Avoid Unnecessary Expenses of Serving a Summons

Rule 4 of the Federal Rules of Civil Procedure requires certain defendants to cooperate in saving unnecessary expenses of serving a summons and complaint. A defendant who is located in the United States and who fails to return a signed waiver of service requested by a plaintiff located in the United States will be required to pay the expenses of service, unless the defendant shows good cause for the failure.

"Good cause" does not include a belief that the lawsuit is groundless, or that it has been brought in an improper venue, or that the court has no jurisdiction over this matter or over the defendant or the defendant's property.

If the waiver is signed and returned, you can still make these and all other defenses and objections, but you cannot object to the absence of a summons or of service.

If you waive service, then you must, within the time specified on the waiver form, serve an answer or a motion under Rule 12 on the plaintiff and file a copy with the court. By signing and returning the waiver form, you are allowed more time to respond than if a summons had been served.

[Amended January 21, 1963, effective July 1, 1963; February 28, 1966, effective July 1, 1966; April 29, 1980, effective August 1, 1980; amended by Pub.L. 97-462, § 2, January 12, 1983, 96 Stat. 2527, effective 45 days after January 12, 1983; amended March 2, 1987, effective August 1, 1987; April 22, 1993, effective December 1, 1993; April 17, 2000, effective December 1, 2000; April 30, 2007, effective December 1, 2007; April 29, 2015, effective December 1, 2015; April 28, 2016, effective December 1, 2016.]

AUTHORS' COMMENTARY ON RULE 4

PURPOSE AND SCOPE

Rule 4 sets the procedure for service of process—the task of notifying defendants and impleaded defendants that a federal civil lawsuit has been filed against them. This notification duty has both constitutional and Rule-based attributes. Rule 4 is concerned principally with the latter; it does not, therefore, address whether a chosen method of service is constitutionally sound[1] or whether the defendant is amenable to the forum's personal jurisdiction.[2] Instead, Rule 4 establishes the approved procedures for delivering notice *on the assumption* that the defendant can be constitutionally haled before the forum federal court. Bear in mind, however, that, absent consent or waiver, a proper, constitutionally sound service of process is required to invest the court with personal jurisdiction over each defendant in the lawsuit.

Rule 4 is lengthy but its organization is easily understood. First, Rules 4(a), (b), (c), (d), (*l*), and (m) establish procedures of **general applicability**. Federal notice requires the simultaneous delivery ("service") of a court-issued summons and a complaint (together, often labeled "original process").[3] The delivery must be performed by someone other than a party to the lawsuit who is age 18 or older, and must be successfully accomplished within a fixed time window after the lawsuit is begun (90 days, in most cases, absent an extension). Sometimes, a court may (or must) appoint a U.S. Marshal to perform that delivery. Once delivery has been completed, the court must be so informed. Plaintiffs

[1] For an extended discussion of the constitutional notice requirements, see *supra* Part II § 2.8 of this text.

[2] For an extended discussion of personal jurisdiction, see *supra* Part II §§ 2.2 to 2.8 of this text.

[3] Historically, the term "original process" may technically have referred just to the summons, writ, or other instrument that compelled an appearance or response in court. More colloquially, the phrase "original process" is now often understood as the beginning proceedings in a civil action—the summons and complaint together. *See Silbaugh v. Chao*, 942 F.3d 911, 914 (9th Cir. 2019) ("process" is "commonly understood" in at least certain contexts to refer to summons and complaint). *See generally* Black's Law Dictionary 1399 (10th ed. 2014) ("The term 'process' is not limited to 'summons.' ") (citations omitted).

may, in many instances, invite a defendant to "waive" this formalized delivery by following a certain requesting procedure; when so invited, defendants are usually obligated to comply with the request or risk having the costs of performing formal delivery shifted onto them.

Rules 4(e), (f), (g), (h), (i), and (j) each set **category-specific delivery instructions**: how to notify individuals found within the United States or found abroad, how to notify minors and incompetent persons, how to notify companies and other entities, how to notify the federal government and its various actors, and how to notify foreign governments and State governments. Thus, for most defendants, the practitioner's chore is to identify the particular category of defendant being notified and then to simply follow the specific instructions set out for that category (while abiding by Rule 4's procedures of general applicability).

Rule 4(k) establishes **the judicial reach for federal courts**. In most cases, federal courts will borrow the same personal jurisdiction reach as their local State courts. However, Congress can grant federal courts additional reach by statute, and federal courts may also hale in any additional Rule 13 impleaded parties and Rule 19 required parties who can be served within 100 miles from the federal courthouse. Finally, federal courts may exercise "national-contacts" jurisdiction over defendants who, though not amenable to the personal jurisdiction of any individual State, have qualifying contacts with the United States as a nation and are being sued on a matter arising under federal law.

Rule 4(n) sets the procedures for exercising **property-based jurisdiction** (*in rem* and *quasi in rem*) in a federal lawsuit.

GENERAL COMMENTARY ON SERVICE

"Constitutional" *versus* "Rule 4" Service

The U.S. Constitution's Due Process Clause requires that service be completed in a manner that is "reasonably calculated," under the circumstances, to apprise the defendant of the pending lawsuit and to afford a reasonable opportunity to make a defense.[4] Meeting this constitutional standard, however, is not alone sufficient.[5] The manner of service must *also* comport with the procedural requirements set by Rule 4.[6] The objective of these requirements is to facilitate reasonable

---

[4] *See Jones v. Flowers*, 547 U.S. 220, 226 (2006); *Mullane v. Cent. Hanover Bank & Tr. Co.*, 339 U.S. 306, 314 (1950). For a fuller discussion of the Constitution's notice requirements, see *supra* Part II § 2.8.

[5] "The due process clause does not require ideal or even very good procedures. It only prohibits procedures that are very bad." LUTHER L. MCDOUGAL ET AL., AMERICAN CONFLICTS LAW 78 (5th ed. 2001).

[6] *See Williams v. GEICO Corp.*, 792 F. Supp. 2d 58, 65 (D.D.C. 2011) (satisfying constitutional requirements for notice does not necessarily satisfy the notice requirements imposed by the Rules). *See also Omni*

notice of the lawsuit to adversaries so that they might fairly respond to allegations against them.[7] Service also achieves the further purpose of formally marking the federal court's assertion of its judicial power over the served defendant.[8]

Actual Notice Is Not *Required*

The mere fact that a defendant did not receive actual notice of the lawsuit does not necessarily render service of process defective or personal jurisdiction improper.[9] So long as the constitutional "reasonably calculated" standard is satisfied, lack of actual notice does not offend the Due Process Clause.[10] However, if a plaintiff comes to learn that an attempted service failed to reach the intended defendant, additional efforts to reattempt service might be required when it is reasonable under the circumstances to do so.[11]

Actual Notice Alone is Not *Enough*

Although the core goal of service is to ensure that the defendants are aware of the lawsuit pending against them, simply proving their actual, subjective awareness of the pending lawsuit is unlikely to be sufficient. Actual receipt of notice likely will satisfy the Constitution's due process requirements,[12] but formal compliance with Rule 4 is required as well.[13] However, if actual notice occurred, Rule 4 may be given a liberal construction.[14]

Capital Int'l, Ltd. v. Rudolf Wolff & Co., Ltd., 484 U.S. 97, 104 (1987); *S.E.C. v. Ross*, 504 F.3d 1130, 1140 (9th Cir. 2007); *Albra v. Advan, Inc.*, 490 F.3d 826, 828 (11th Cir. 2007).

[7] *See Henderson v. U.S.*, 517 U.S. 654, 672 (1996).

[8] *See Mann v. Castiel*, 681 F.3d 368, 372 (D.C.Cir.2012). *See generally Omni Capital Int'l, Ltd. v. Rudolf Wolff & Co., Ltd.*, 484 U.S. 97, 104, 108 S. Ct. 404, 98 L. Ed. 2d 415 (1987).

[9] *See Jones v. Flowers*, 547 U.S. 220, 226 (2006) ("Due process process does not require that a property owner receive actual notice before the government may take his property."); *Dusenbery v. United States*, 534 U.S. 161, 171 (2002) (Court has never required actual notice (*i.e.*, receipt of notice) as inexorable requirement for satisfying due process).

[10] *See Jones v. Flowers*, 547 U.S. 220, 226 (2006); *Mullane v. Cent. Hanover Bank & Tr. Co.*, 339 U.S. 306, 314 (1950).

[11] *See Jones v. Flowers*, 547 U.S. 220, 226–39 (2006).

[12] *See United Student Aid Funds, Inc. v. Espinosa*, 559 U.S. 260, 272 (2010) (actual notice satisfies due process rights to notice).

[13] *See De Gazelle Grp., Inc. v. Tamaz Trading Establishment*, 817 F.3d 747, 750–51 (11th Cir. 2016) (reliance on actual notice was "misplaced," when service was not compliant with Rule 4); *Freedom Watch, Inc. v. Organization of Petroleum Exporting Countries*, 766 F.3d 74, 81 (D.C.Cir. 2014) (actual notice cannot rescue service that is otherwise defective, absent substantial compliance and "a minor, nonprejudicial defect"); *Crowley v. Bannister*, 734 F.3d 967, 975 (9th Cir. 2013) (actual notice does not confer personal jurisdiction absent complying substantially with Rule 4).

[14] *See Direct Mail Specialists, Inc. v. Eclat Computerized Techs., Inc.*, 840 F.2d 685, 688 (9th Cir. 1988); *Armco, Inc. v. Penrod-Stauffer Bldg. Sys., Inc.*, 733 F.2d 1087, 1089 (4th Cir. 1984). *See generally Attkisson v. Holder*, 925 F.3d 606, 628 (4th Cir. 2019) ("Absent

Distinguishing *Service* from *Jurisdiction* and *Venue*

Service of the summons and complaint (or waiver of service) is a prerequisite to the district court's exercise of jurisdiction over a defendant.[15] But complying with the federal service rules does not mean that proper jurisdiction and proper venue exists.[16] Though impacted by service,[17] those concepts (jurisdiction and venue) are distinct from service and must be separately satisfied.[18] All of these requirements — proper service, proper jurisdiction, and proper venue — are prerequisites to the exercise of federal judicial power. They concern whether *this court* could have lawful authority to exercise its coercive judicial power over *these litigants* in *this lawsuit*. A brief practitioner's orientation to personal jurisdiction, subject-matter jurisdiction, and venue appears earlier in this text,[19] followed in turn by more thorough treatments of each of those three requirements.[20]

Service of process is the event by which a court asserts its judicial authority over parties in a lawsuit.[21] Ordinarily, that formality is not required as to plaintiffs because plaintiffs are the ones invoking, and thus consenting to, the court's exercise of power over them.[22] But the formality is required as to all those parties who are being haled involuntarily before the court (defendants).[23] Service of process thus accomplishes two objectives: it asserts the court's exercise of its authority over nonconsenting parties to a lawsuit and it is the means by which those nonconsenting parties are notified of both the pendency of

---

waiver or consent, a failure to obtain proper service on the defendant deprives the court of personal jurisdiction over the defendant.") (citation omitted)..

[15]*See BNSF Ry. Co. v. Tyrrell*, 581 U.S. __, 137 S. Ct. 1549, 1556 (2017); *Omni Capital Intern., Ltd. v. Rudolf Wolff & Co., Ltd.*, 484 U.S. 97, 103 (1987).

[16]*See Torres v. Gaines*, 130 F. Supp. 3d 630, 634–35 (D. Conn. 2015) (challenges to personal jurisdiction and service of process are distinct).

[17]*See Mississippi Publishing Corp. v. Murphree*, 326 U.S. 438, 444–45 (1946) ("service of summons is the procedure by which a court having venue and jurisdiction of the subject matter of the suit asserts jurisdiction over the person of the party served").

[18]*See Henderson v. U.S.*, 517 U.S. 654, 670 (1996). *See generally Prewitt Enters., Inc. v. Org. of Petroleum Exporting Countries*, 353 F.3d 916, 925 n.15 (11th Cir. 2003) ("Personal jurisdiction is a composite notion of two separate ideas: amenability to jurisdiction . . . and notice to the defendant through valid service of process.") (citation omitted).

[19]*See supra* Part II, § 2.1.

[20]*See supra* Part II, §§ 2.2 to 2.8.

[21]*See Mississippi Pub. Corp. v. Murphree*, 326 U.S. 438, 444–45 (1946).

[22]*See Adam v. Saenger*, 303 U.S. 59, 67–68 (1938).

[23]*See Int'l Shoe Co. v. Washington*, 326 U.S. 310, 316 (1945) (historically, exercising judicial authority was "grounded" on court's actual, physical, "de facto power" over a defendant's person or property); *Murphy Bros. v. Michetti Pipe Stringing, Inc.*, 526 U.S. 344, 350 (1999) (notice, via service of process, is "the contemporary counterpart" of that exercise of physical power).

the lawsuit and their need to appear and mount a defense.[24]

Immunity from Service

Under certain circumstances, a nonresident defendant who enters a jurisdiction may be considered immune from service of process while physically present there. This sort of immunity from service will generally apply only where that defendant is not otherwise subject to personal jurisdiction under the jurisdiction's long-arm statutes.[25] Such immunity from service is governed by federal case law, and exists where the due administration of justice demands it.[26] Whether to confer such immunity is vested in the discretion of the district court; the purpose of the immunity is *not* primarily to protect the defendant who is seeking to avoid service, but instead to aid the court in its judicial administration.[27]

Persons are generally immune from service when they are present in the jurisdiction to attend court, give a deposition, or conduct settlement discussions in connection with another, unrelated lawsuit, or when they enter the jurisdiction to participate in a legislative or administrative hearing process.[28] This immunity generally encompasses not only the time when the person is actually present in court or attending other formal proceedings, but also typically extends for a reasonable period before and after the proceedings to allow the person to enter and then freely leave the jurisdiction.[29]

Persons may also be immune from service when they are lured by fraud or trickery into the jurisdiction by the plaintiff who then attempts to serve them.[30] Indeed, some courts have even adopted a bright line rule for in-State negotiations: these courts hold that when a plaintiff invites defendants to enter the foreign jurisdiction for settlement discussions, the plaintiff may not, during those discussions, serve the defendants with process unless those defendants are either cautioned that they

[24]*See supra* Part II, § 2.8.

[25]*See Cont'l Indus. Grp., Inc. v. Altunkilic*, 633 Fed. Appx. 61, 62 (2d Cir. 2016).

[26]*See Stewart v. Ramsay*, 242 U.S. 128, 37 S. Ct. 44, 61 L. Ed. 192 (1916). *See also ARW Exploration Corp. v. Aguirre*, 45 F.3d 1455 (10th Cir.1995) (immunity from service is a procedural, not substantive, rule, and *Erie* concerns do not dictate that State law apply).

[27]*See Northern Light Technology, Inc. v. Northern Lights Club*, 236 F.3d 57, 62 (1st Cir. 2001); *Estate of Ungar v. Palestinian Authority*, 396 F. Supp. 2d 376, 381 (S.D. N.Y. 2005).

[28]*See Lamb v. Schmitt*, 285 U.S. 222 (1932); *Page Co. v. MacDonald*, 261 U.S. 446 (1923). *See also Haan Corp. Korea v. Sparkling Drink Sys. Innovation Ctr. Hong Kong*, 2017 WL 8186998, at *2 n.1 (N.D. Ill. Dec. 15, 2017) (immunity not refused merely because first court proceeding (where service occurred) has ended).

[29]*See Cabiri v. Assasie-Gyimah*, 921 F. Supp. 1189, 1193 (S.D. N.Y. 1996).

[30]*See Fitzgerald & Mallory Const. Co. v. Fitzgerald*, 137 U.S. 98, 104, 11 S. Ct. 36, 34 L. Ed. 608 (1890); *Gudavadze v. Kay*, 556 F. Supp. 2d 299, 304 (S.D. N.Y. 2008); *Henkel Corp. v. Degremont, S.A.*, 136 F.R.D. 88, 91 (E.D. Pa. 1991).

may be served while present or, after having entered the jurisdiction, are first given an opportunity to depart immediately after the discussions fail.[31]

Immunity from service can be waived. A defendant who fails to timely assert immunity may be deemed to have waived it.[32] Likewise, a defendant who is immune for the purposes of attending court or a deposition may waive the immunity by arriving in the jurisdiction early, by conducting other business while in the jurisdiction, or by failing to leave the jurisdiction promptly.[33] Some courts have held that defendants may also lack immunity if they enter the forum to defend against criminal charges,[34] to attend proceedings as a mere "spectator" with no obligation to be there,[35] or when the service involves the same case or a case arising out of or involving the same subject matter as the one for which the defendants are already appearing.[36]

Service in Removed Cases

Once a case has been removed from State court to federal court, service of process can be completed (or, if defective, new process can issue) as though the lawsuit had been filed originally in federal court.[37] Prior to removal, the applicable State laws will typically govern the propriety of service and process; following removal, the federal Rules will govern.[38]

---

[31] *See May Dept. Stores Co. v. Wilansky*, 900 F. Supp. 1154, 1164–65 (E.D. Mo. 1995) (collecting cases).

[32] *See Republic Productions, Inc v. American Federation of Musicians of U.S. and Canada*, 173 F. Supp. 330, 333–34 (S.D. N.Y. 1959). *See also Fitzgerald & Mallory Const. Co. v. Fitzgerald*, 137 U.S. 98, 104, 11 S. Ct. 36, 34 L. Ed. 608 (1890) (noting opportunity for a motion challenging service, but observing that no such motion had been filed).

[33] *See Uniroyal, Inc. v. Sperberg*, 63 F.R.D. 55, 58 (S.D. N.Y. 1973) (applying the "dual purpose rule", which forfeits service immunity when person, present in jurisdiction for purpose of administration of justice, engages in unrelated business dealings or social activity). *Cf. Fun-Damental Too, Ltd. v. Hwung*, 1997 WL 289712 (S.D. N.Y. 1997) (immunity not waived where nonresident defendant traveled to forum for deposition and, on night before his deposition, visited a showroom for one hour and had dinner; such activities were "trivial and insubstantial"). *See generally Willbros Int'l, Inc. v. Hydrodive Int'l, Ltd.*, 2008 WL 4178339, at *2 (S.D.Tex. Sept. 5, 2008) (waiver view is "not widely recognized", and is based not on whether other activities occurred but their degree and proportion).

[34] *See Garibay v. Sullivan*, 2010 WL 4509826, at *2 (D.Ariz. Oct. 28, 2010).

[35] *See Northern Light Technology, Inc. v. Northern Lights Club*, 236 F.3d 57, 63 (1st Cir. 2001). *But see Norex Petroleum Ltd. v. Access Indus., Inc.*, 620 F. Supp. 2d 587, 590 (S.D.N.Y. 2009) (voluntary or involuntary character of witness' appearance should not govern availability of privilege).

[36] *See ARW Exploration Corp. v. Aguirre*, 45 F.3d 1455, 1460 (10th Cir. 1995); *Cabiri v. Assasie-Gyimah*, 921 F. Supp. 1189, 1193–94 (S.D. N.Y. 1996).

[37] *See* 28 U.S.C.A. § 1448.

[38] *See Hines v. Regions Bank*, 782 Fed. Appx. 853, 854 (11th Cir. 2019); *Norsyn, Inc. v. Desai*, 351 F.3d 825,

Service When "Federal Law Provides Otherwise"

Congress has, on occasion, written laws that contain their own, particular service of process provisions.[39] In such contexts, various parts of Rule 4 confirm that service of process can be accomplished on individuals, corporations, associations, and other non-governmental entities by following those law-specific provisions.[40]

Service by *Pro Se* Litigants

The fact that litigants are proceeding *pro se* ordinarily will not excuse their failure to accomplish service properly or their mistaken understanding of the service Rules.[41]

Burden of Proving Service of Process

The party attempting service generally bears the burden of establishing that the service is proper[42] (though that burden is ordinarily not implicated until the service is challenged).[43] The ultimate burden may shift, however, if the opposing party does not promptly move to challenge the purported service. If a default judgment is entered against such a party, that party may bear the burden of proving that the purported service was defective.[44]

RULE 4(a)—CONTENTS OF AND AMENDING SUMMONS

CORE CONCEPT

The form of summons for use in federal civil complaints is now

829 n.4 (8th Cir. 2003); *Moore v. McCalla Raymer, LLC*, 916 F. Supp. 2d 1332, 1339 (N.D.Ga. 2013).

[39]*See, e.g.,* 28 U.S.C.A. §§ 1369 & 1697 (when federal Multiparty, Multiforum Jurisdiction applies, service may be made anywhere within the U.S. or, if otherwise permitted, anywhere outside the U.S.).

[40]*See* Rule 4(e) (permitting service on individuals within the United States with a federal law that "provides otherwise"); Rule 4(f) (same, for individuals in a foreign country); Rule 4(h) (same, for corporations and associations). *But see* Rule 4(g) (service on infants and incompetents contains no such provision); Rule 4(i) (same, for United States, its agencies, corporations, officers, or employees); Rule 4(j) (same, for foreign, state, or local governments).

[41]*See Thrasher v. City of Amarillo*, 709 F.3d 509, 512 (5th Cir. 2013); *Albra v. Advan, Inc.*, 490 F.3d 826, 829 (11th Cir.2007).

[42]*See Mann v. Castiel*, 681 F.3d 368, 372 (D.C.Cir. 2012); *Dickerson v. Napolitano*, 604 F.3d 732, 752 (2d Cir. 2010).

[43]*See Connolly v. Shaw's Supermarkets, Inc.*, 355 F. Supp. 3d 9, 14 (D. Mass. 2018) (defendant bears initial burden of raising challenge, then once adequately challenged, burden shifts to plaintiff to show proper service). *See also Prem Sales, LLC v. Guangdong Chigo Heating & Ventilation Equip. Co.*, 494 F. Supp. 3d 404, 410 (N.D. Tex. 2020) (serving party bears burden once form or method of service is challenged). *See generally* Rule 12(b)(5) (characterizing insufficient service as a defense).

[44]*See S.E.C. v. Internet Sols. for Bus. Inc.*, 509 F.3d 1161, 1165 (9th Cir. 2007) (recounting majority view). *But see Oldfield v. Pueblo de Bahia Lora, S.A.*, 558 F.3d 1210, 1217 (11 Cir. 2009) (minority view: burden remains with plaintiff).

standardized.[45] The prior practice of permitting the use of State forms of summons has been abolished.

APPLICATIONS

Purpose of Summons

The purpose of the summons is to alert the defendants that a lawsuit is pending against them and to caution them that they have only a limited time in which to respond.[46] The summons is not expected to provide advice to defendants on response options.[47]

Required Content for a Summons

A proper federal summons for use with a civil complaint must meet the following prerequisites:

- *Be issued from the Clerk*, bearing the clerk's signature and seal;
- *Identify the Case*, by listing the court, the parties, and the name and address of the plaintiff's attorney (or plaintiff, if unrepresented);
- *Be Directed to the Defendant*, specifically;
- *Note the Deadline to Appear and Defend*; and
- *Warn Against Default*, by cautioning that the defendant's failure to appear and defend will result in entry of a default judgment for the relief requested.

Invalid Summons

A summons that has not been issued, signed, and sealed by the clerk of court is a nullity and cannot confer personal jurisdiction over the defendant; this defect is usually considered fundamental and, ordinarily, cannot be waived.[48]

Defects, Liberality, and Amending a Summons

Courts have ruled that, in considering whether to dismiss due to a summons' defects, the summons requirements should be construed liberally, provided the recipient is given sufficient

---

[45] A user-ready template for preparing a *Summons in a Civil Action* is available for download from the Administrative Office of the U.S. Courts. *See* Form AO 440 — Summons in a Civil Action, http://www.uscourts.gov/forms/notice-lawsuit-summons-subpoena/summons-civil-action.

[46] *See U.S. v. Perez*, 752 F.3d 398, 405 (4th Cir. 2014).

[47] *See Frye v. Bowman, Heintz, Boscia, Vician, P.C.*, 193 F. Supp. 2d 1070, 1080 (S.D. Ind. 2002) (noting "inherent difficulties in attempting to provide all potentially helpful information in a summons").

[48] *See Ayres v. Jacobs & Crumplar, P.A.*, 99 F.3d 565, 568–70 (3d Cir. 1996). *See also Silbaugh v. Chao*, 942 F.3d 911, 914–16 (9th Cir. 2019) (valid summons, signed by clerk, necessary for personal jurisdiction); *Harper v. City of New York*, 424 Fed. Appx. 36, 40 (2d Cir. 2011) (summons improper when not issued by clerk and lacking court's seal); *Doyle v. YMCA of New Hampshire*, 560 F. Supp. 3d 499, 502–03 (D.N.H. 2021) (though nonprejudicial because defendant received actual notice, court still lacks discretion to ignore misnaming of defendant and lack of clerk's signature and court seal).

notice and not otherwise prejudiced.[49] Even still, a defendant has the right to receive a compliant summons.[50] Thus, if the summons omits one of the technical requirements for proper form, but otherwise generally complies with the Rule's fundamental[51] requirements, the court may choose not to dismiss the lawsuit but to instead permit an amendment to the summons[52] or grant some other cure.[53] For example, a summons that incorrectly names a defendant,[54] fails to name all defendants,[55] supplies a wrong defendant address,[56] or contains some other comparatively inconsequential defect[57] might not be dismissed for that misstep. However, if the summons more fundamentally fails to comply with the Rule, prejudices a defendant, or shows flagrant disregard for proper procedure,[58] the court may dismiss,[59] permit an amendment to the summons,[60] or quash and

[49]*See, e.g., United Food & Com. Workers Union v. Alpha Beta Co.*, 736 F.2d 1371, 1382 (9th Cir. 1984); *Marquez v. Starrett City Assocs.*, 406 F. Supp. 3d 197, 204 (E.D.N.Y. 2017).

[50]*See Fields v. Norfolk & S. Ry. Co.*, 924 F. Supp. 2d 702, 709 (S.D.W. Va. 2012).

[51]Occasionally, courts have applied this liberality even to fundamental summons errors. *See Gorbaty v. Mitchell Hamline Sch. of Law*, 2020 WL 2769148, at *2 (D. Minn. May 28, 2020) (although lacking Clerk's signature and Court's seal, defendant law school could "deduce" summons and was not prejudiced); *Clark v. Goodwill Indus. of Hawaii, Inc.*, 2009 WL 3050277, at *4-*5 (D.Haw. Sept. 21, 2009) (although "not perfect", service of summons lacking clerk's signature and seal was still in "substantial compliance" with Rule 4).

[52]*See United Food & Com. Workers Union v. Alpha Beta Co.*, 736 F.2d 1371, 1382 (9th Cir. 1984); *Wills v. Hariohm P'ship*, 2020 WL 6119922, at *2 (M.D. Tenn. Oct. 16, 2020); *Marquez v. Starrett City Assocs.*, 406 F. Supp. 3d 197, 204 (E.D.N.Y. 2017).

[53]*See RG Abrams Ins. v. L. Offs. of C.R. Abrams*, 2021 WL 6752232, at *4 (C.D. Cal. Oct. 27, 2021) (pronouncing judicial substitution of "P.C." designation for complaint's errant LLC designation); *Gallan v. Bloom Bus. Jets, LLC*, 480 F. Supp. 3d 1173, 1178–79 (D. Colo. 2020) (granting *nunc pro tunc* permission for out-of-time correction to summons).

[54]*See Fields v. Norfolk & S. Ry. Co.*, 924 F. Supp. 2d 702, 708–09 (S.D.W. Va. 2012) (allowing amendment to summons to cure name error, where defendant received actual notice and asserted no prejudice).

[55]*See Moser v. Lifewatch Inc.*, 2020 WL 1849664, at *4 (S.D. Cal. Apr. 13, 2020).

[56]*See Spiess v. Meyers*, 483 F. Supp. 2d 1082, 1093 (D. Kan. 2007); *Sullivan v. Potter*, 2006 WL 785289, at *2 (D.D.C. 2006).

[57]*See Doe v. Constant*, 354 Fed.Appx. 543, 546 (2d Cir. 2009) (where defendant received actual notice, summons' defects (misstating full business name, labeling party as "commander") were "purely clerical"); *WB Music Corp. v. Futuretoday, Inc.*, 2018 WL 4156589, at *2 (C.D. Cal. Aug. 28, 2018) (spacing error in listing defendant's name did not warrant relief).

[58]*See Soos v. Niagara Cty.*, 195 F. Supp. 3d 458, 463–64 (W.D.N.Y. 2016).

[59]*See Blockchange Ventures I GP, LLC. v. Blockchange, Inc.*, 2021 WL 308277, at *1-*2 (S.D.N.Y. Jan. 29, 2021) (dismissing where served summons was neither signed nor sealed by clerk); *Schroeder v. Kochanowski*, 311 F. Supp. 2d 1241, 1256 (D. Kan. 2004) (dismissing where served summons was copy, lacking court seal, and omitted plaintiff's name and address).

[60]*See Fields v. Norfolk & S. Ry. Co.*, 924 F. Supp. 2d 702, 709 (S.D.W.

allow a corrected service with a proper summons.[61]

RULE 4(b)—ISSUANCE OF SUMMONS

CORE CONCEPT

Once the complaint is filed, the plaintiff is responsible for preparing the summons in an appropriate form, and submitting it to the clerk of court for signing and sealing. If the plaintiff's summons is proper, the clerk will sign and seal the form, and issue it to the plaintiff for service. Copies of the summons must be issued for each defendant.

APPLICATIONS

Plaintiffs' Obligation

It is plaintiffs' obligation to prepare a properly completed summons and then present it to the clerk for signature and the court's seal.[62]

Issuance of Summons Liberally Examined

Courts liberally construe the issuance requirements of Rule 4(b).[63] If the summons is sufficiently accurate to provide proper notice, and any alleged defect in issuance has not prejudiced the defendant, a defect in the form of summons as issued might be discounted as harmless and the plaintiff afforded an opportunity to amend the summons to cure the error.[64]

Photocopies of Summons in Multi-Defendant Cases

An original summons—containing a raised seal-of-the-court and a pen-signed signature of the clerk—may not be necessary in cases involving multiple defendants. In such cases, copies of the original summons (that bear the name of each served defendant) may be used.[65] But each defendant in a multi-defendant case must receive both a summons and complaint, or the service will ordinarily[66] fail.[67]

Va. 2012).

[61] *See Silbaugh v. Chao*, 942 F.3d 911, 915-16 (9th Cir. 2019); *Rose v. Bersa*, 327 F.R.D. 628, 633 (S.D. Ohio 2018).

[62] *See* Rule 4(b) advisory committee note (1993). *See also Trupei v. United States*, 304 Fed. Appx. 776, 780 (11th Cir. 2008).

[63] *But cf. Authors' Commentary to Rule 4(a) supra,* "**Invalid Summons**".

[64] *See Coleman v. Bank of New York Mellon*, 969 F. Supp. 2d 736, 744–45 (N.D. Tex. 2013) (improper issuance overlooked where no prejudice shown).

[65] *See New York Transp., Inc. v. Naples Transp., Inc.*, 116 F. Supp. 2d 382, 386 (E.D. N.Y. 2000).

[66] *Cf. Coleman v. Bank of New York Mellon*, 969 F. Supp. 2d 736, 744 (N.D. Tex. 2013) (in absence of prejudice, mistakenly naming parties in summons as, entity LLP, rather than as individual parties, did not warrant dismissal).

[67] *See Dixon v. Blanc*, 796 Fed. Appx. 684, 688 (11th Cir. 2020); *Watson v. Mylan Pharm.*, 795 Fed. Appx. 584, 587–88 (10th Cir. 2019). *See generally Gant v. Kant*, 314 F. Supp. 2d 532, 533 (D. Md. 2004) ("Each defendant, whether there be one or many, and whether they be members of the same family or strangers, must be served as

RULE 4(c)—SERVICE

CORE CONCEPT

A summons and complaint are served together. The plaintiff is responsible for effective service. A U.S. Marshal will serve process, but only if ordered to do so by the court.

APPLICATIONS

Both Summons and Complaint Must Be Served

In order for Rule 4 service to be proper, the summons and complaint must be served together. Neglecting either one entitles the defendant to a dismissal for improper service.[68] Serving an incomplete copy of the complaint[69] or one missing its exhibits[70] is likewise vulnerable to a dismissal.

Plaintiff Selects the Process Server

Except in certain cases (such as those involving pauper plaintiffs or seamen plaintiffs), the plaintiff generally is responsible for selecting an appropriate person to serve all defendants with copies of the summons and complaint. Typically, the plaintiff appoints a commercial process server who accomplishes the service task for a fee.[71]

Service Only by Adult Non-Party

Any person age 18 or older who is not a party to the lawsuit may serve original process. Because they are "parties" to the lawsuit, plaintiffs may not serve process themselves.[72] This prohibition extends to mailed service; in those cases where mailed service is permitted, the plaintiffs themselves cannot perform the act of mailing.[73] (This bar may apply even if a plaintiff serves pursuant to a State service law that would otherwise permit it.)[74] Service by attorneys for the parties,

---

provided by statute or rule").

[68] *See Cardenas v. City of Chicago*, 646 F.3d 1001, 1005–06 (7th Cir. 2011); *Albra v. Advan, Inc.*, 490 F.3d 826, 828 (11th Cir. 2007).

[69] *See Cherry v. Spence*, 249 F.R.D. 226, 228–29 (E.D. N.C. 2008) (delivering only first page of complaint is failure of service: "defendants cannot admit or deny each allegation in the complaint when they only possess one page of it").

[70] *See Doe #1 v. Am. Fed'n of Gov't Emps.*, 554 F. Supp. 3d 75, 124 (D.D.C. 2021) (citing cases showing division among courts on whether missing exhibits constitutes improper service).

[71] *See Byrd v. Stone*, 94 F.3d 217, 219 (6th Cir. 1996).

[72] *See Thrasher v. City of Amarillo*, 709 F.3d 509, 510 & n.1 (5th Cir. 2013); *Kornea v. J.S.D Mgmt., Inc.*, 366 F. Supp. 3d 660, 668 & n.27 (E.D. Pa. 2019).

[73] *See Constien v. United States*, 628 F.3d 1207, 1213–17 (10th Cir. 2010); *Albra v. Advan, Inc.*, 490 F.3d 826, 829 (11th Cir. 2007); *Norton v. Columbus Cty. Bd. of Elections*, 493 F. Supp. 3d 450, 458 (E.D.N.C. 2020), *aff'd*, 834 Fed. Appx. 54 (4th Cir. 2021).

[74] *See Johnson-Richardson v. Univ. of Phoenix*, 334 F.R.D. 349, 353–57 (D.D.C. 2020) (bar applies, holding, after lengthy discussion, that Rule 4(c)(2) prevails even when service made under Rule 4(e)(1)). *But cf. Follum v. N. Carolina State Univ.*, 2009 WL 2869927, at *1-*2 (E.D.N.C.

though not forbidden, is also not preferred.[75]

Service by Commercial Courier Service

When service of process is attempted via a commercial courier service (like FedEx, United Parcel Service, or DHL), it remains unclear whether such a delivery can qualify as "mail" service,[76] as delivery made "personally" or at a "dwelling",[77] or otherwise.

Service by U.S. Marshal or Others Specially Appointed

The court, upon a plaintiff's request, may direct that the U.S. Marshal or some other specially-appointed person serve process. (Such court-appointed service is required in the cases of pauper plaintiffs[78] or seamen plaintiffs.[79]) When such appointments are officially and properly made, the plaintiff is permitted to rely on the Marshal to complete service (provided plaintiff cooperated and supplied accurate service information).[80] It is unclear how much, if any, independent investigatory work the Marshal must perform in completing service.[81]

Service Must Occur *After* the Complaint is Filed

Service is not effective unless the complaint that is served has first been filed with the court. Thus, the practice of informally presenting an adversary with a courtesy copy of a complaint before it is filed with the clerk of court will not satisfy the requirements for service of process under Rule 4.[82]

2009) (bar may not apply, suggesting that Rule 4(e)(1) would "override" Rule 4(c)(2)), *aff'd*, 370 Fed. Appx. 405 (4th Cir. 2010).

[75]*See Trustees of Local Union No. 727 Pension Fund v. Perfect Parking, Inc.*, 126 F.R.D. 48, 51–52 (N.D. Ill. 1989). *Accord Commodity Futures Trading Com'n v. American Metals Exchange Corp.*, 693 F. Supp. 168, 186 (D.N.J. 1988).

[76]*See Audio Enters., Inc. v. B & W Loudspeakers of America*, 957 F.2d 406, 409 (7th Cir. 1992) (FedEx found not to be "first-class mail"); *Cichocki v. Massachusetts Bay Cmty. Coll.*, 174 F. Supp. 3d 572, 576–77 (D. Mass. 2016) (express mail not authorized service method).

[77]*See Cambridge Holdings Group, Inc. v. Federal Ins. Co.*, 489 F.3d 1356, 1362 (D.C. Cir. 2007) (noting, but failing to rule upon this "novel and unlikely theory"); *Ilaw v. Dep't of Justice*, 309 F.R.D. 101, 104–05 (D.D.C. 2015) (FedEx does not qualify as service by personal "delivery").

[78]28 U.S.C.A. § 1915(c). *See Meade v. Reynolds*, 810 Fed. Appx. 86, 88–89 (3d Cir. 2020); *Williams v. Werlinger*, 795 F.3d 759, 759–61 (7th Cir. 2015).

[79]28 U.S.C.A. § 1916.

[80]*See Robinson v. Clipse*, 602 F.3d 605, 608 (4th Cir. 2010) (time for service should be tolled while trial court considers whether to order Marshal service); *Olsen v. Mapes*, 333 F.3d 1199, 1204–05 (10th Cir. 2003) (plaintiffs not culpable for failing to comply with Rules or court orders when they relied on Marshal to serve).

[81]*Compare Williams v. Werlinger*, 795 F.3d 759, 759–61 (7th Cir. 2015) (must check certain records) *with Allen v. Ryan*, 2015 WL 3960880, at *3 (D. Ariz. June 29, 2015) (only limited obligation to investigate).

[82]*See J.O. Alvarez, Inc. v. Rainbow Textiles, Inc.*, 168 F.R.D. 201, 202–03 (S.D. Tex. 1996) (default judgment not proper against defendants who failed to answer complaint served before it

Service When a Complaint Has Been Amended

Ordinarily, formal service of process is required only for the original complaint; later pleadings (including amended complaints) are served under the less rigorous procedures of Rule 5.[83] There are exceptions, however. If the original complaint is amended before formal service of process has been accomplished with the original (now superseded) complaint, proper service must deliver the revised pleading rather than the original one.[84] Other circumstances may require formal service of the amended complaint, such as where the revised pleading asserts claims against new parties or materially alters the claims against existing parties, where service on the attorney is unlikely to ensure notice to the represented party, or where due process otherwise demands.[85]

RULE 4(d)—WAIVING SERVICE

CORE CONCEPT

The formality of service of process is costly. To reduce the expense of federal litigation, claimants may invite most defending parties to "waive" formal service, and upon a proper request, those defending parties are duty-bound to assent or else they must (with a few exceptions) reimburse the claimants for the costs of formal service and related motion practice.

APPLICATIONS

Former "Service-By-Mail" Rule Abolished

Rule 4 had previously authorized "service by mail" in limited circumstances, though that procedure was troubled by certain "sandbagging" and "blindsiding" risks.[86] It was abolished in 1993, and replaced with the current waiver-of-service procedure of Rule 4(d). Federal service may no longer be accomplished through the mails unless permitted by special federal statute[87] or by applicable State law.[88]

Constitutionality

The constitutionality of the waiver-of-service rule has been

---

was filed; defendants' actual or constructive notice of lawsuit does not satisfy Rule 4 service requirements).

[83]*See Employee Painters' Trust v. Ethan Enterprises, Inc.*, 480 F.3d 993, 999 (9th Cir. 2007); *Mach v. Florida Casino Cruise, Inc.*, 187 F.R.D. 15, 17 (D. Mass. 1999).

[84]*See Rivera Otero v. Amgen Mfg. Ltd.*, 317 F.R.D. 326, 328–29 (D.P.R. 2016).

[85]*See Brait Builders Corp. v. Massachusetts, Div. of Capital Asset Mgmt.*, 644 F.3d 5, 9–10 (1st Cir. 2011); *Employee Painters' Trust v. Ethan Enterprises, Inc.*, 480 F.3d 993, 999 (9th Cir. 2007). *See also infra* Authors' Commentary to Rule 5(a) (**"Pleadings Asserting Claims Against Existing Parties"**).

[86]*See Carimi v. Royal Carribean Cruise Line, Inc.*, 959 F.2d 1344, 1348 (5th Cir. 1992).

[87]*See, e.g.*, Rule 4(e).

[88]*See, e.g.*, Rule 4(e)(1). *See generally Bufkin v. Scottrade, Inc.*, 812 Fed. Appx. 838, 844 (11th Cir. 2020); *Ingram Barge Co., LLC v. Musgrove*, 2019 WL 1226818, at *5 (M.D. Tenn. Mar. 8, 2019), *adopted*, 2019 WL 1212094 (M.D. Tenn. Mar. 14, 2019).

addressed only cursorily (and upheld).[89]

Who May Invoke the Waiver-of-Service Procedure

By its terms, the waiver-of-service procedure is only available for serving individuals, corporations, partnerships, and associations.[90] The procedure may be used to waive service on such parties whether they be located in the United States or in a foreign country.[91] The waiver-of-service procedure is not ordinarily available for serving: (1) the United States Government;[92] (2) agencies, corporations, or officers of the United States;[93] (3) other governments and government-related entities;[94] or (4) minors and incompetent persons.[95] Note, however, that although federal officers are ineligible for waiver-of-service when sued in their official capacities, they are *not* exempt when sued in their individual capacities.[96]

Plaintiff's Choice

A plaintiff is not required to seek a waiver of service. The plaintiff may choose to seek a waiver, or may immediately proceed to traditional formal service of process.[97] But a plaintiff who does *both* simultaneously (seek a waiver and formally serve) will likely lose the right to recover service costs.[98]

---

[89]*See U.S. v. Jones*, 2013 WL 6408639, at *2 (E.D.N.Y. Dec. 9, 2013); *U.S. v. Hafner*, 421 F. Supp. 2d 1220, 1224 (D.N.D. 2006).

[90]*See* Rule 4(d)(1) (citing Rule 4(e), (f), (h)).

[91]*See* Rule 4(d) advisory committee rule (noting cost-saving nature of waiver procedure for defendants who otherwise would be served under international service of process convention, which costs might include "the sometimes substantial expense of translation that may be wholly unnecessary for defendants fluent in English"). *See also Lozano v. Bosdet*, 693 F.3d 485, 488 (5th Cir. 2012).

[92]*See Constien v. United States*, 628 F.3d 1207, 1213 (10th Cir. 2010). *See also Robinson v. Turner*, 886 F. Supp. 1460, 1465 (S.D. Ind. 1995) (commenting that unreliability caused United States to be exempted from Rule 4(d) waiver provisions).

[93]*See Emuchay v. Catron*, 2000 WL 303223, at *2 (D. Conn. 2000) (Rule does not authorize waiver of service in lawsuits against federal employees sued in their official capacities).

[94]*See Frone v. City of Riverdale*, 521 Fed.Appx. 789, 792 (11th Cir. 2013) (not applicable to cities); *Libertarian Party v. Dardenne*, 595 F.3d 215, 218–19 (5th Cir. 2010) (not applicable to State officials sued in official capacity); *Lepone-Dempsey v. Carroll County Com'rs*, 476 F.3d 1277, 1281 (11th Cir. 2007) (not applicable to local governments); *Chapman v. New York State Div. for Youth*, 227 F.R.D. 175, 180 (N.D. N.Y. 2005) (not applicable to State, State agency, or State official).

[95]*See* Rule 4(d)(1).

[96]*See Mosley v. Douglas County Correctional Center*, 192 F.R.D. 282, 283 (D. Neb. 2000). *See also* Rule 4(i)(3) (federal officers and employees sued in their individual capacity are served in the manners prescribed by Rule 4(e), (f), or (g)). *See also* Rule 4(i)(2) advisory committee notes (2000) ("Invocation of the individual service provisions of subdivisions (e), (f), and (g) invokes also the waiver-of-service provisions of subdivision (d)").

[97]*See Budget Rent A Car System Inc. v. Miles*, 2005 WL 1106335, at *3 (S.D. Ohio 2005).

[98]*See Kumaran v. Vision Fin.*

Defendant's Response Options

The Rule does not *require* the defendant to waive,[99] although the defendant may confront financial consequences for failing to waive (see below). If the defendant refuses to waive or otherwise ignores the request, the plaintiff must proceed with formal service under another provision of Rule 4.[100] Until plaintiff accomplishes formal service, the defendant has no obligation to answer the lawsuit.[101]

Incentives for Waiving

By agreeing to waive formal service of process, a defendant's time for responding to the complaint is nearly tripled—from 21 days (following most personal service) to 60 days (following request for waiver).[102] For defendants who are addressed outside the United States, the extension is even longer — a defendant waiving from outside the United States has 90 days to respond to the complaint.[103] Importantly, this 90-day period is triggered not by a defendant's foreign citizenship, but by the mailing of the waiver forms to an address outside the United States.[104]

Consequences of Not Waiving

If the defendant lacks "good cause" for refusing to waive service, the court must tax expenses against the defendant.[105] These expenses include the costs incurred in formally serving process on the defendant, as well as a reasonable attorney's fee for any motion practice required to collect those service costs.[106] Before any expenses will be taxed, the prescribed time for the

---

Markets, LLC, 338 F.R.D. 17, 19 (S.D.N.Y. 2021); *Koellen v. Pollard*, 2010 WL 2330270, at *2 (E.D. Wis. June 7, 2010).

[99]*See Khan v. Hemosphere Inc.*, 825 Fed. Appx. 762, 768 (Fed. Cir. 2020); *Fitzpatrick v. Bank of New York Mellon*, 580 Fed.Appx. 690, 694 (11th Cir. 2014).

[100]*See Cambridge Holdings Group, Inc. v. Federal Ins. Co.*, 489 F.3d 1356, 1362 (D.C. Cir. 2007); *Lepone-Dempsey v. Carroll County Com'rs*, 476 F.3d 1277, 1281 (11th Cir. 2007).

[101]*See Vega v. Hastens Beds, Inc.*, 339 F.R.D. 210, 219 (S.D.N.Y. 2021).

[102]*See* Rule 4(d)(3). One district court extended the 60-day period to 63 days, citing the 3-day addition for mailed service under Rule 6(d), formerly Rule 6(e). *See Petrousky v. Civil Air Patrol, Inc.*, 1998 WL 213726 (N.D. N.Y. 1998).

[103]*See* Rule 4(d)(3).

[104]*See Tire Hanger Corp. v. My Car Guy Concierge Services Inc.*, 2014 WL 2511282, at *3 (C.D. Cal. June 4, 2014) (when waiver form is sent to foreign national who is in the United States, response period is 60 days, not 90 days).

[105]*See Rollin v. Cook*, 466 Fed.Appx. 665, 667 (9th Cir. 2012); *Marcello v. Maine*, 238 F.R.D. 113, 115 (D. Me. 2006). *See also Mathon v. Marine Midland Bank, N.A.*, 875 F. Supp. 986, 986–91 (E.D. N.Y. 1995) (effect of Rule 4(d) is to shift cost of service to defendant who refuses to agree to waive formal service).

[106]*See* Rule 4(d)(2). *See Tann v. Fisher*, 276 F.R.D. 190, 192 (D.Md. 2011) (expenses include reasonable attorney's fees for preparing motion); *Graves v. Church of the Lord Jesus Christ of the Apostalic Faith, Inc.*, 2003 WL 21659168, at *1 (E.D. Pa. 2003) (costs for process server, courier, photocopying, motion expenses).

defendant to waive service must first have expired.[107] Ordinarily, no expenses can be taxed against a non-waiving defendant located outside the United States.[108]

"Good Cause" Defined: The "good cause" necessary for refusing to waive formal service of process will be rare.[109] This "good cause" test is not satisfied by a belief that the claim is unmeritorious or unjust or that the court lacks jurisdiction,[110] or by counsel's claim that he or she was busy or otherwise preoccupied,[111] or by incidental, nonprejudicial waiver form defects.[112] However, failing to invoke the waiver procedure,[113] non-receipt of the waiver request,[114] a failure to otherwise comply with all the requirements of Rule 4(d),[115] a good faith belief that, as a matter of law, the

---

[107] *See Andrew v. Clark*, 561 F.3d 261, 271–72 (4th Cir. 2009).

[108] *See* Rule 4(d)(2). *See also Campinha-Bacote v. Hudson*, 627 Fed. Appx. 508, 510 (6th Cir. 2015). Note that at least one district court has rejected the argument that a foreign defendant should be considered "located" in the United States within the meaning of Rule 4(d) when that defendant has such significant contacts with the forum that it is susceptible to personal jurisdiction in the United States. *See Hoffman-La Roche, Inc. v. Invamed, Inc.*, 183 F.R.D. 157, 160 (D.N.J. 1998).

[109] *See* Rule 4(d) advisory committee note (1993). *See also Neal v. Cochran, Cherry, Givens & Smith, P.C.*, 589 F. Supp. 2d 1363, 1364 (N.D.Ga. 2008).

[110] *See Cho v. JS Autoworld 1 Ltd.*, 97 F. Supp. 3d 351, 359 (E.D.N.Y. 2015) ("good cause" not present from disagreement over claim's merits); *Marcello v. Maine*, 238 F.R.D. 113, 115–16 (D. Me. 2006) (rejecting "good cause" claim that lawsuit was frivolous, motion was premature, and pending motion to dismiss would require cost shift in other direction).

[111] *See D'Agostine v. United Hosp. Supply Corp.*, 1996 WL 417266, at *5 (E.D. Pa. 1996) (rejecting as "good cause" counsel's assertion that "he was in the process of relocating his practice and was in the middle of various litigations").

[112] *See Neal v. Cochran, Cherry, Givens & Smith, P.C.*, 589 F. Supp. 2d 1363, 1365 (N.D.Ga. 2008) (non-misleading error in stating defendant's business name is not good cause).

[113] *See Wooten v. BNSF Ry. Co.*, 387 F. Supp. 3d 1078, 1117 (D. Mont. 2019), *aff'd*, 819 Fed. Appx. 483 (9th Cir. 2020).

[114] *See Owens v. Benton*, 190 Fed. Appx. 762, 764 (11th Cir.2006) (no expenses when unclear that correct parties had been served with waiver forms); *Hy Cite Corp. v. badbusinessbureau.com, L.L.C.*, 418 F. Supp. 2d 1142, 1153–54 (D. Ariz. 2005) (no expenses where defendant never mailed request for waiver, even if defendant informed plaintiff that process was futile). *But see Double S Truck Line, Inc. v. Frozen Food Exp.*, 171 F.R.D. 251, 253–54 (D. Minn. 1997) (service costs taxed against defendant, notwithstanding defendant's claim that it did not receive sufficient time to respond to waiver form; form had been delivered to defendant's agent but was delayed in reaching defendant because agent lacked defendant's accurate address).

[115] *See McGann v. State of N.Y.*, 77 F.3d 672, 674–75 (2d Cir. 1996) (procedure not effective where plaintiff failed to include acknowledgment form along with mailed summons and complaint); *Jones v. Int'l Ass'n of Bridge Structural Ornamental & Reinforcing Iron Workers*, 864 F. Supp. 2d 760, 775–76 (E.D. Wis. 2012) (failed since waiver form lacked plaintiff's signature and contact information); *Perez v. County of Westchester*, 83 F. Supp. 2d 435, 441 (S.D. N.Y. 2000), aff'd, 242 F.3d 367

waiver-of-service provisions would not apply,[116] an illiteracy in English, or proceeding with formal service before the waiver period expires[117] will each likely satisfy the "good cause" test.

Procedure for Seeking Waiver-of-Service

To use the waiver-of-service procedure, claimants must formally and unequivocally[118] request a defendant to waive service, and must do so by complying with six requirements. A failure to meet each requirement may result in a failed service[119] and/or refusal by the court to impose any penalties for a defendant's failure to waive.[120] The party invoking the waiver-of-service procedure bears the burden of proving compliance with the requirements.[121] The mere fact that the defendants come to learn that a complaint has been filed against them will not excuse compliance with the requirements,[122] nor will an informally expressed willingness to waive which is then never formalized.[123] (However, when the parties agree to a waiver independently of the provisions of Rule 4(d), the requirements need not be met).[124]

To qualify under Rule 4(d), the waiver request must:

(2d Cir. 2000) (denying reimbursement where notice and request were not addressed directly to defendant, not accompanied by copy of complaint, and lacked prepaid means for compliance in writing).

[116]*See Mosley v. Douglas County Correctional Center*, 192 F.R.D. 282, 283 (D. Neb. 2000) (finding good cause for failure to waive service because no legal authority addressed whether employees of a municipal corporation were susceptible to procedure).

[117]*See Cobalt Multifamily Investors I, LLC v. Arden*, 2014 WL 3798183, at *3 (S.D.N.Y. July 31, 2014); *Koellen v. Pollard*, 2010 WL 2330270, at *2 (E.D. Wis. June 7, 2010).

[118]*See Mann v. Castiel*, 681 F.3d 368, 373 (D.C.Cir. 2012).

[119]*See Larsen v. Mayo Medical Center*, 218 F.3d 863, 868–69 (8th Cir. 2000) (where Rule 4(d) provisions not complied with strictly, waiver not satisfied and personal service must be obtained); *McGann v. State of N.Y.*, 77 F.3d 672, 674–75 (2d Cir. 1996) (waiver not effective where plaintiff failed to include acknowledgment form along with mailed summons and complaint).

[120]*See Frone v. City of Riverdale*, 521 Fed.Appx. 789, 792 (11th Cir. 2013) (denying reimbursement, where waiver form was not included); *Kumaran v. Vision Fin. Markets, LLC*, 338 F.R.D. 17, 19 (S.D.N.Y. 2021) (denying reimbursement because defendant given less than 30 days to respond and because emailed request lacked prepaid means for return); *Perez v. County of Westchester*, 83 F. Supp. 2d 435, 441 (S.D. N.Y. 2000), aff'd, 242 F.3d 367 (2d Cir. 2000) (denying reimbursement, where notice and request were not addressed directly to defendant, not accompanied by copy of complaint, and lacked prepaid means for compliance).

[121]*See Hopper v. Wyant*, 502 Fed.Appx. 790, 791–92 (10th Cir. 2012); *Flores v. Sch. Bd. of DeSoto Parish*, 116 Fed.Appx. 504, 508 (5th Cir.2004).

[122]*See Mann v. Castiel*, 681 F.3d 368, 373 (D.C.Cir. 2012).

[123]*See Kogan v. Facebook, Inc.*, 334 F.R.D. 393, 398–401 (S.D.N.Y. 2020).

[124]*See US Bank Nat. Ass'n v. Budnick*, 626 Fed. Appx. 438, 440 (5th Cir. 2015).

- *Be in Writing*;[125]
- *Be Addressed to the Individual Defendant or the Entity Defendant's Officer, Managing or General Agent, or Other Authorized Agent*;[126]
    - ○ Note, sending a "blind" mailing simply to a business address is insufficient, as is sending the request to a party's attorney (unless the attorney has been authorized to receive the mailing).[127]
- *Give the Defendant a Reasonable Time to Return the Signed Waiver* (at least 30 days, or 60 days if mailed to a foreign country);[128]
- *List the Return Date, the Presiding Court, the Date the Request is Sent, and the Consequences of Waiving (or Not Waiving) Service*;[129]
    - ○ Note, the official notice form language appears at the end of Rule 4's text.
- *Be Accompanied By*: (1) a copy of the complaint, (2) two copies of the official waiver form, and (3) a prepaid means for returning the form;[130] and
    - ○ Note, the official waiver form language appears at the end of Rule 4's text.
- *Actually Be Sent, by either first-class mail or "other reli-*

[125]*See* Rule 4(d)(1)(A). *Cf. Kopacz v. Hopkinsville Surface & Storm Water Utility*, 2010 WL 2541170, at *1 (W.D. Ky. June 18, 2010) ("verbal" waiver not effective).

[126]*See* Rule 4(d)(1)(A). *See also Henderson v. Republic of Texas*, 672 Fed. Appx. 383, 385–86 (5th Cir. 2016) (failure to address waiver request to corporation's officer or agent rendered request ineffective).

[127]*See Smith v. Bradley Pizza, Inc.*, 314 F. Supp. 3d 1017, 1026 (D. Minn. 2018).

[128]*See* Rule 4(d)(1)(F). *See also Beepot v. JP Morgan Chase Nat. Corp. Servs., Inc.*, 626 Fed. Appx. 935, 937 (11th Cir. 2015). *Cf. Andrew v. Clark*, 561 F.3d 261, 271–72 (4th Cir. 2009) (30-days might not be sufficiently "reasonable", if circumstances suggest that waiver might yet have been returned).

[129]*See* Rule 4(d)(1)(B), (D), (E), & (F); Rule 4 Notice of a Lawsuit and Request to Waive Service of Summons Form (appended following Rule 4). *Cf. Shell v. American Family Rights Ass'n*, 2009 WL 3837890, at *2 (D.Colo. Nov. 13, 2009) (notice effective even though date-sent was missing from form); *Trevino v. D.H. Kim Enterprises, Inc.*, 168 F.R.D. 181, 182–83 (D. Md. 1996) (notice effective even though plaintiffs did not use the official Notice form, but did advise of consequences); *Dymits v. American Brands, Inc.*, 1996 WL 751111 (N.D. Cal. 1996) (notice effective even though plaintiff omitted small portion of official form warning).

[130]*See* Rule 4(d)(1)(C); Rule 4 Waiver of the Service of Summons Form (appended following Rule 4). *See also Cammack New Liberty, LLC v. Int'l Greetings USA, Inc.*, 2009 WL 4807401, at *1–*2 (E.D.Ky. Dec. 5, 2009) (improper because complaint not included); *McGann v. State of N.Y.*, 77 F.3d 672 (2d Cir. 1996) (not effective where plaintiff failed to include an acknowledgment form); *Mason Tenders Dist. Council Pension Fund v. Messera*, 1997 WL 221200, at *6 (S.D. N.Y. 1997) (defective where plaintiffs failed to stamp the return envelope).

able means".[131]

- ○ Note, this may include private hand delivery or fax.[132]

When a Waiver-of-Service Becomes Effective

Service is not considered waived merely because a plaintiff requests it.[133] Rather, waivers-of-service are effective only if the defendant actually signs and returns the waiver form[134] and, then, only when the signed form is filed with the court[135] (there is some authority that a defendant can self-initiate a waiver, by filing one without ever receiving a request from the plaintiff).[136] Neither a generalized (but uneffectuated) willingness to waive[137] nor an oral waiver[138] qualifies. This effective date becomes especially relevant for those States where limitations periods are tolled only upon service, and not mere commencement.[139]

- *Impact on Defendant's Response Time:* This waiver-effective date does not set the time for defendant's response. Instead, that period begins to run earlier, from the date the *request* for waiver was *sent*, and it then expires 60 days later (90 days if the waiver request was mailed to a foreign country).[140]
- *Impact on Rule 4(m) and Limitations Periods:* After a waiver request is sent and while the defendant ponders whether to waive or not, the 90-day window for completing service (Rule 4(m)) and, perhaps, the statute of limi-

---

[131] *See* Rule 4(d)(1)(G). *See also Hy Cite Corp. v. badbusinessbureau.com, L.L.C.*, 418 F. Supp. 2d 1142, 1153–54 (D. Ariz. 2005) (defendant cannot be ordered to pay Rule 4(d) expenses if he was never mailed a request for waiver, even if defendant informed plaintiff that the process was futile).

[132] *See* Rule 4(d)(1)(G). *See also* Rule 4(d) advisory committee note (describing availability of and procedure for electronic communications, such as facsimile transmission).

[133] *See Vega v. Hastens Beds, Inc.*, 339 F.R.D. 210, 219 (S.D.N.Y. 2021).

[134] *See Sun v. Mashantucket Pequot Gaming Enter.*, 309 F.R.D. 157, 164–65 (D. Conn. 2015); *Placide Ayissi-Etoh v. Mae*, 49 F. Supp. 3d 9, 12 (D.D.C. 2014).

[135] *See* Rule 4(d)(4). *See also Davis v. Liese*, 353 Fed.Appx. 95, 98 (10th Cir. 2009); *Moss v. Wyeth, Inc.*, 872 F. Supp. 2d 154, 161–62 (D.Conn. 2012).

[136] *See Greer v. Tennessee Dep't of Correction*, 2022 WL 163692, at *4 (M.D. Tenn. Jan. 18, 2022), *adopted*, 2022 WL 481239 (M.D. Tenn. Feb. 16, 2022); *Cutler v. Green*, 2017 WL 2957817, at *4 n.7 (E.D. Pa. July 11, 2017), *aff'd*, 754 Fed. Appx. 96 (3d Cir. 2018); *Valido-Shade v. Wyeth, LLC*, 875 F. Supp. 2d 474, 477 (E.D. Pa. 2012), *aff'd*, 14-4608 (3d Cir. 2015). *See generally Watson v. Mylan Pharms.*, 795 Fed. Appx. 584, 587 n.5 (10th Cir. 2019) (noting that "sparse authority" on issue favors right of unilateral waiver).

[137] *See Kogan v. Facebook, Inc.*, 334 F.R.D. 393, 398–401 (S.D.N.Y. 2020);

[138] *See Kopacz v. Hopkinsville Surface & Storm Water Utility*, 2010 WL 2541170, at *1 (W.D. Ky. June 18, 2010).

[139] *See* Rule 4(d)(4) advisory committee note (1993). *See also, e.g., Corporex Cos., LLC v. Proskauer Rose, LLP*, 713 F. Supp. 2d 678, 688 (E.D.Ky. 2010) (under Kentucky law, limitations tolled only upon issuance of summons).

[140] *See* Rule 4(d)(3).

tations, will continue to run. Neither is tolled simply because the plaintiff has requested a service waiver.[141] Prudent plaintiffs should bear this impact in mind when considering whether to seek a waiver or to proceed directly to formal service.[142]

Motion to Recover Service Expenses

Where a waiver-eligible defendant refuses, without good cause, to waive formal service of process, a motion to collect the costs and expenses of actual service can be filed promptly after the actual, formal service is completed. The plaintiff need not wait until the bill of costs process at the litigation's end.[143] A defendant's obligation to reimburse these costs is *not* affected by who eventually becomes the prevailing party in the litigation; rather, this obligation remains even if the defendant is otherwise entitled to its bill of costs at the end of the case.[144] Reimbursable expenses may include a reasonable attorney's fee for prosecuting the motion to collect costs, but may *not* include any attorney's fee associated with arranging for formal service after the defendant's refusal to waive.[145] Attorney's fees might not be reimbursed when the plaintiff proceeds *pro se*.[146] The courts scrutinize carefully the requested fees and costs to guard against overreaching by counsel in their requests for reimbursement.[147]

Venue and Jurisdiction Defenses Preserved

A defendant who waives formal service of process does not

---

[141] *See* Rule 4(d) advisory committee note (1993). *See also Weldon v. Electronic Data Systems Corp.*, 138 Fed. Appx. 136, 138 (11th Cir. 2005) (per curiam) (refusing to apply equitable tolling to claim that plaintiff was "misled" by defendant's failure to timely respond to request for waiver of service).

[142] *See generally Larsen v. Mayo Medical Ctr.*, 218 F.3d 863, 868–69 (8th Cir. 2000) (where Rule 4(d) provisions not satisfied, waiver not effective and formal service must be made).

[143] *See Double S Truck Line, Inc. v. Frozen Food Exp.*, 171 F.R.D. 251, 253–54 (D. Minn. 1997).

[144] *See Estate of Darulis v. Garate*, 401 F.3d 1060, 1063–64 (9th Cir. 2005) (Rule 4(d)'s policy "would be undermined if a defendant who creates unnecessary costs can gamble that he or she will be able to sidestep Rule 4(d)(2) via Rule 54(d)(1)"). *See also Chegup v. Ute Indian Tribe of Uintah & Ouray Rsrv.*, 28 F.4th 1051, 1071 (10th Cir. 2022) (dismissal with prejudice does not preclude court's ability to rule on costs motion).

[145] *See Graves v. Church of the Lord Jesus Christ of the Apostalic Faith, Inc.*, 2003 WL 21659168, at *1 (E.D. Pa. 2003) (denying reimbursement for attorney's fees spent arranging formal service after waiver was refused).

[146] *See Prousalis v. Jamgochian*, 38 Fed. Appx. 903, 905 (4th Cir. 2002); *Stern v. Regency Towers, LLC*, 886 F. Supp. 2d 317, 328 (S.D.N.Y. 2012).

[147] *See, e.g.*, *Spring v. Bluestem Brands, Inc.*, 2021 WL 1269118, at *2-*4 (D. Nev. Apr. 6, 2021) (following meticulous computation and analysis, reducing requested $1,420 reimbursement down to $395); *Equity Partners HG, LLC v. Samson, Inc.*, 2019 WL 4773988, at *3-*4 (D.S.D. Sept. 30, 2019) (reducing $3,097.55 request to $1,617.55, due to duplication and excessiveness in local market).

lose the right to contest venue and jurisdiction.[148] The defendant does, however, waive any objection to the sufficiency of either the summons or the method of service,[149] though objections to the timeliness of service might still be proper.[150]

U.S. Marshal's Use of Waiver-of-Service Procedure

When the Rules authorize service by the U.S. Marshal, the Marshal may mail the waiver-of-service forms to the defendants, prior to attempting to serve process personally.[151]

RULE 4(e)—SERVING INDIVIDUALS WITHIN A JUDICIAL DISTRICT OF THE UNITED STATES

CORE CONCEPT

Original process may be served upon any competent, adult individual found within the United States in any of the following manners:

(1) ***Specific Federal Law***: In any manner elsewhere authorized by federal law; or

(2) ***Waiver***: Under the waiver-of-service provisions of Rule 4(d); or

(3) ***State Law***: In the manner authorized either by the State in which the district court sits or by the State in which the service is to be accomplished; or

(4) ***Personal Delivery***: By personally delivering the summons and complaint to the individual being served; or

(5) ***Left at Dwelling***: By leaving the summons and complaint at the individual's dwelling or usual place of abode with a person of suitable age and discretion who is residing there; or

(6) ***Agent***: By delivering the summons and complaint to an agent appointed by the individual to receive service or to an agent authorized by law to receive service.

APPLICATIONS

Service Upon Individuals, Generally

This Rule applies whenever service is made within the United States on a party who is a natural person. Accordingly, it encompasses service on a natural person who conducts his or her unincorporated business under a trade name.[152]

---

[148]*See* Rule 4(d)(5). *See also Don't Look Media LLC v. Fly Victor Ltd.*, 999 F.3d 1284, 1294 (11th Cir. 2021); *Mann v. Castiel*, 681 F.3d 368, 373 (D.C.Cir. 2012).

[149]*See* Rule 4(d) advisory committee note (1993) ("The only issues eliminated are those involving the sufficiency of the summons or the sufficiency of the method by which it is served.").

[150]*See Small v. Georgia*, 446 F. Supp. 3d 1352, 1356–58 (S.D. Ga. 2020).

[151]*See Baez v. Connelly*, 478 Fed. Appx. 674, 676 (1st Cir. 2012); *Banks v. Trammell*, 2014 WL 320075, at *2–*5 (E.D. Mich. Jan. 29, 2014).

[152]*See, e.g., Bridgeport Music, Inc. v. Rhyme Syndicate Music*, 376 F.3d

"Otherwise" Provided Federal Law Service

The service procedures set out in Rule 4(e) may be supplemented by, or replaced with, different procedures that Congress may enact.[153]

State Law Service Generally

The Rules permit service in any manner authorized by *either* the State in which the district court sits *or* the State in which the service is to be accomplished.[154] If service is accomplished in accordance with either of those State's service laws, Rule 4(e) is satisfied.[155] (But this State law option addresses the *manner* of service, not necessarily *who* may perform that service.)[156]

State Law Service—Serving by Mail

The Rules do not nationally authorize service by mail domestically.[157] (Although the Rules permit the mailing of *requests* for waivers-of-service, those requests do not themselves qualify as valid service.)[158] But if the laws of either the federal district's host State or the State of delivery permit mailed service (and many do), serving by mail in a manner that complies with either of those States' mailing laws will be proper.[159]

State Law Service—Serving at Place of Business

The Rules do not nationally authorize service by leaving a copy of the summons and complaint at an individual's place of

---

615, 624–25 (6th Cir. 2004) (service on "Carrumba Music, the d/b/a for Jorge Hinojosa").

[153]*See, e.g., Commodity Futures Trading Com'n v. Worldwide Commodity Corp.*, 366 F. Supp. 2d 276, 280 (E.D. Pa. 2005) (because Commodities Exchange Act has its own specific service provisions, statute governs proper execution of service of summons); *Green v. William Mason & Co.*, 996 F. Supp. 394, 395–96 (D.N.J. 1998) (ERISA permits breach of fiduciary duty claims to be served in any district court where defendants reside or may be found).

[154]*See* Rule 4(e)(1). *See also Calderon Serra v. Banco Santander Puerto Rico*, 747 F.3d 1, 8 (1st Cir. 2014); *Colleton Preparatory Academy, Inc. v. Hoover Universal, Inc.*, 616 F.3d 413, 421 n.9 (4th Cir. 2010).

[155]*See Vax-D Medical Technologies, LLC v. Texas Spine Medical Center*, 485 F.3d 593, 596 (11th Cir. 2007) (service complied with Texas case law regarding individuals who conduct business under assumed name); *Homer v. Jones-Bey*, 415 F.3d 748, 754 (7th Cir. 2005) (effectiveness of service in such circumstances turns on relevant provisions of State law).

[156]*See Johnson-Richardson v. Univ. of Phoenix*, 334 F.R.D. 349, 353–57 (D.D.C. 2020) (Rule 4(c)(2) prevails even when service made under Rule 4(e)(1)). *But cf. Follum v. N. Carolina State Univ.*, 2009 WL 2869927, at *1-*2 (E.D.N.C. Sept. 2, 2009) (surmising that Rule 4(e)(1) would "override" Rule 4(c)(2)), *aff'd*, 370 Fed. Appx. 405 (4th Cir. 2010).

[157]*See Patterson v. Whitlock*, 392 Fed. Appx. 185, 188 (4th Cir. 2010). *Cf.* Rule 4(f) (permitting some mailed service to parties located outside the United States).

[158]*See supra* Rule 4(d) and accompanying authors' commentary (**"When a Waiver-of-Service Becomes Effective"**).

[159]*See, e.g., Wallace v. Federal Employees of U.S. District Court, EDPA*, 325 Fed. Appx. 96, 100–01 (3d Cir. 2009) (Pennsylvania law); *Izen v. Catalina*, 256 F.3d 324, 327 (5th Cir. 2001) (Oklahoma law).

business.[160] But if the laws of either the federal district's host State or the State of delivery permit such service, serving in a manner that complies with either of those States' laws will be proper.[161]

State Law Service—Serving by Publication

The Rules do not nationally authorize service by publication.[162] But if the laws of either the federal district's host State or the State of delivery permit service by publication, serving in a manner that complies with either of those States' laws will be proper.[163]

State Law Service—Serving by E-Mail or Social Media

The Rules do not nationally authorize service by e-mail or through social media portals. But if the laws of either the federal district's host State or the State of delivery permit such service, serving in a manner that complies with either of those States' laws will be proper.[164] Some courts have approved social media portals as a redundant method of notice, to supplement service made through other court-approved means (such as by e-mail), but courts seem wary of approving social media as the exclusive service method, especially without compelling evi-

---

[160]*See Torres v. Gaines*, 130 F. Supp. 3d 630, 635 (D. Conn. 2015); *Klayman v. Obama*, 125 F. Supp. 3d 67, 78 & 90 (D.D.C. 2015). *See also Boateng v. Inter American Univ. of P.R.*, 188 F.R.D. 26, 28 (D.P.R. 1999) (place of employment is not "dwelling place" or "usual place of abode").

[161]*See* Rule 4(e)(1). *See also Golub v. U.S.*, 593 Fed. Appx. 546, 549 (7th Cir. 2014) (service defective, because under applicable State law service must be made at location where defendant actually works); *Gustavia Home, LLC v. Hoyer*, 362 F. Supp. 3d 71, 88–89 (E.D.N.Y. 2019) (service proper under N.Y. law, when made at defendant's actual place of business). *But cf. Ortiz v. Wagstaff*, 523 F. Supp. 3d 347, 356 (W.D.N.Y. Feb. 26, 2021) (no allowance for service by delivery to individual's former employer).

[162]*See Indian Hills Holdings, LLC v. Frye*, 337 F.R.D. 293, 297 (S.D. Cal. 2020). *See generally Boddie v. Connecticut*, 401 U.S. 371, 382 (1971) (noting that publication is "the method of notice least calculated to bring to a potential defendant's attention the pendency of judicial proceedings").

[163]*See Indian Hills Holdings, LLC v. Frye*, 337 F.R.D. 293, 297 (S.D. Cal. 2020). *See also Jes Solar Co. Ltd. v. Tong Soo Chung*, 725 Fed. Appx. 467, 470 (9th Cir. 2018) (denying service by publication because Arizona law would not permit it); *Tatum v. Liberty Hous. Co.*, 701 F.2d 744, 745-46 (8th Cir. 1983) (same, Iowa law); *U.S. Nat'l Bank Ass'n v. Hernandez Galarza*, 291 F. Supp. 3d 238, 241 (D.P.R. 2018) (same, Puerto Rico law).

[164]*See Hulett v. Babb*, 2021 WL 4721907, at *2 (D. Or. Sept. 16, 2021) (Oregon law, approving service by Facebook messaging and name-tagging, supplemented by certified postal mail); *Reflex Media, Inc. v. Richard Easton Ltd.*, 2021 WL 24687, at *1–*2 (D. Nev. Jan. 4, 2021) (Nevada law, approving service by e-mail upon showing of substantial efforts to otherwise locate and serve defendants and confirmation (through test e-mails) of active e-mail address use). *See also* TEX. R. CIV. P. 106(b)(2) (eff. Dec. 31, 2020) (granting courts authority to permit electronic service "by social media, email, or other technology").

dence of the user's identity and regularity of site access.[165]

Service by Personal Delivery

Personal delivery may not always require that the recipient walk away from the encounter clutching the summons and complaint. The service documents must be "tendered" to the recipient. If the recipient is physically confronted with service, but refuses to take personal possession of the service documents, service by personal delivery may still, under certain circumstances, be accomplished by leaving the documents near the recipient (such as on a nearby table or on the floor near the person).[166] Many courts have held that "personal delivery" cannot be accomplished through the mails, including certified mail.[167]

Service at Individual's Dwelling or Usual Abode

An individual can be served with process by delivering the summons and complaint to a "person of suitable age and discretion" residing at the defendant's dwelling or usual place of abode. In such cases, the process need not be handed directly to the served defendant,[168] but it still must be delivered personally to someone residing there.[169] Moreover, the recipient need not necessarily be an adult, so long as the court reaches the case-by-case, fact-specific determination that the recipient was of "suitable age and discretion." Nevertheless, the recipient ordinarily must be "residing" at the home;[170] service upon a non-resident maid will likely be ineffective.[171] Serving permanent staff is less clear: serving an apartment building's

---

[165]*See Doe v. Hyassat*, 337 F.R.D. 12, 15–16 (S.D.N.Y. 2020) (surveying cases, noting due process concerns from courts' inability to confirm whether Facebook profiles bearing defendant's name are truly used by defendant).

[166]*See Norris v. Causey*, 869 F.3d 360, 370 (5th Cir. 2017) (proper to leave service documents in close proximity to uncooperative defendant); *Travelers Cas. & Sur. Co. of America v. Brenneke*, 551 F.3d 1132, 1136 (9th Cir. 2009) (leaving papers in immediate proximity of defendant); *Novak v. World Bank*, 703 F.2d 1305, 1310 n.14 (D.C. Cir. 1983) (leaving papers "on a table or on the floor, near that person"); *Republic Credit Corp. I v. Rance*, 172 F. Supp. 2d 1178, 1181 (S.D. Iowa 2001) (leaving papers at front gate: "This Court has no interest in forcing process servers to chase down defendants and jam court papers into their hands in order to effect personal service, as depicted on television").

[167]*See Thorpe v. Dumas*, 788 Fed. Appx. 644, 648 (11th Cir. 2019) (collecting cases).

[168]*See United States v. Wen-Bing Soong*, 650 Fed. Appx. 425, 428–29 (9th Cir. 2016) (delivery to resident adult son of defendants).

[169]*See German Am. Fin. Advisors & Trust Co. v. Rigsby*, 623 Fed. Appx. 806, 808 (7th Cir. 2015) (taping package to door of the residence is not sufficient).

[170]*See Boissier v. Katsur*, 676 Fed. Appx. 260, 263 (5th Cir. 2017) (service proper on defendant's apartment cotenant); *U.S. v. Rose*, 437 F. Supp. 2d 1166, 1172–73 (S.D. Cal. 2006) (dwelling-house service requires that address be defendant's usual place of abode *and* that papers be left with someone actually residing there).

[171]*Compare Franklin America, Inc. v. Franklin Cast Products, Inc.*, 94 F.R.D. 645, 647 (E.D. Mich. 1982) (service on part-time housekeeper deemed

concierge might qualify as proper service on an apartment resident,[172] while serving the complex's security guard may not.[173]

- *Transient Defendants:* Service at a "dwelling" or "usual place of abode" may not always be an available option. In certain circumstances, there may be no acceptable "dwelling" service location for transient defendants, such as those living aboard ships or those who are homeless, living on the streets or in shelters.[174]
- *Traveling Defendants:* An individual engaged in prolonged travel (for example, a lengthy work assignment away from home) retains the same "usual place of abode" for service purposes, even though that person may be often away.[175]
- *Hotels and Motels:* In certain circumstances, particularly during long, extended stays, service can be appropriate at a hotel or motel where the defendant is residing.[176]
- *Multiple "Usual Abodes":* A person may have two or more "usual places of abode" (and may be properly served at any one of them), so long as each contains sufficient indicia of the permanence of the person's residence there.[177]
- *Relatives, Family, and Friends:* Unless it is also the defendant's dwelling or usual place of abode, service on the home of the defendant's relatives, family, or friends is usually not sufficient.[178]

---

insufficient), *with Barclays Bank of New York v. Goldman*, 517 F. Supp. 403, 413–14 (S.D. N.Y. 1981) (service on resident maid deemed sufficient). *See also Jaffe and Asher v. Van Brunt*, 158 F.R.D. 278, 280 (S.D. N.Y. 1994) (although defendant was not staying at his parents' home when service was made there, service ruled proper where defendant resided at that address when in the area, maintained private bedroom, clothes, phone line, and fax there, received mail there (which mother forwarded to him), and represented to plaintiff that this was his residence); *TRW, Inc. v. Derbyshire*, 157 F.R.D. 59, 60 (D. Colo. 1994) (service on defendant's mother, at address defendant represented to be his current forwarding address, was proper).

[172]*See Rana v. Islam*, 305 F.R.D. 53, 63 (S.D.N.Y. 2015).

[173]*See Kolker v. Hurwitz*, 269 F.R.D. 119, 123–24 (D.P.R. 2010).

[174]*See Cox v. Quigley*, 141 F.R.D. 222, 224–25 (D. Me. 1992) (young college graduate, who left home and was serving on board a ship, had no "dwelling house" or "usual place of abode", other than his ship); *see id.* at 226 ("The last shelter at which a homeless person slept will often not furnish reasonable assurance that process will reach the defendant. For such defendants service at the dwelling house or place of abode is unavailable; personal service may be a plaintiff's only option then, no matter how difficult").

[175]*See S.E.C. v. Marino*, 29 Fed. Appx. 538, 540-41 (10th Cir. 2002).

[176]*See Howard Johnson Intern., Inc. v. Wang*, 7 F. Supp. 2d 336 (S.D. N.Y. 1998), aff'd, 181 F.3d 82 (2d Cir. 1999) (finding hotel to be defendant's dwelling place or usual place of abode).

[177]*See Norris v. Causey*, 869 F.3d 360, 369 (5th Cir. 2017); *National Development Co. v. Triad Holding Corp.*, 930 F.2d 253, 257–58 (2d Cir. 1991).

[178]*See Levine v. Duchacova*, 2010 WL 4941951, at *2 (S.D.Cal. Nov. 30,

Service on Individual's Agent

An individual (including a non-resident person not otherwise present in the forum) may be served with process by serving that individual's in-forum agent for service (which, presumably, encompasses foreign defendants who have domestic, in-forum agents.)[179] The recipient "agent", however, must be authorized to accept service either by appointment or by operation of law.[180] This ordinarily requires appointment for the express purpose of receiving process.[181] Some States have provided, by statute, that service on non-residents (who are otherwise amenable to jurisdiction within the State) may be accomplished by serving the secretary of state, the director of the department of motor vehicles, or some similar State law official.[182] But "delivery" to an agent is not likely accomplished through the mails, including certified mail.[183]

Service on Implied-in-Fact Agents

Courts have, in appropriate contexts, permitted service upon "implied" agents where the factual circumstances support that implication.[184]

Service on Individual's Attorney

Service upon an individual is proper by serving the individual's attorney *only* when the attorney has been specifically authorized to accept service on the individual's behalf.[185]

2010) (even if defendant occasionally visits or vacations there). Compare *Howard v. Shelton*, 277 F.R.D. 168, 170 (S.D.Miss. 2011) (finding apartment of boyfriend to be a usual place of abode).

[179]*See Phoenix Process Equip. Co. v. Capital Equip. & Trading Corp.*, 250 F. Supp. 3d 296, 299–301 (W.D. Ky. 2017).

[180]*See* Rule 4(e)(2)(C). *See also Cardenas v. City of Chicago*, 646 F.3d 1001, 1005–06 (7th Cir. 2011) (agent must be shown to be authorized). *Compare Nazareth Nat'l Bank & Trust Co. v. E.A. Intern. Trust*, 1999 WL 549036 (W.D. Pa. 1999) (service proper on a specified security guard at defendant's residence who was " 'instructed by [defendant] to accept service' "), *with Staudinger v. Hoelscher, Inc.*, 166 F. Supp. 2d 1335, 1339 (D. Kan. 2001) (service improper because plant manager (on whom service was made) was not authorized by virtue of that position to accept service for president and owner of plant).

[181]*See Nyholm v. Pryce*, 259 F.R.D. 101, 104 (D.N.J. 2009) (describing criteria for assessing appointment).

[182]*See, e.g., Goktepe v. Lawrence*, 220 F.R.D. 8, 8–12 (D. Conn. 2004) (Connecticut statute).

[183]*See Thorpe v. Dumas*, 788 Fed. Appx. 644, 648 (11th Cir. 2019).

[184]*See, e.g., U.S. v. Ziegler Bolt and Parts Co.*, 111 F.3d 878, 881 (Fed.Cir. 1997); *U.S. v. Balanovski*, 236 F.2d 298, 303 (2d Cir. 1956). *See also In re Focus Media Inc.*, 387 F.3d 1077, 1082–83 (9th Cir. 2004) (recognizing implied authority to receive service in bankruptcy context). *But cf. United States v. Mednansky*, 615 Fed. Appx. 894, 895 (9th Cir. 2015) (service proper on attorney in related case who signed and acknowledged receipt).

[185]*See United States v. Ziegler Bolt & Parts Co.*, 111 F.3d 878, 881 (Fed. Cir.1997); *Santos v. State Farm Fire & Cas. Co.*, 902 F.2d 1092, 1094 (2d Cir. 1990).

RULE 4(f)—SERVING INDIVIDUALS IN A FOREIGN COUNTRY

CORE CONCEPT

Original process may be served upon any competent, adult defendant outside the United States, who is both amenable to service and subject to the court's personal jurisdiction, as follows:

(1) ***Specific Federal Law***: In any manner elsewhere authorized by federal law; or

(2) ***Waiver***: Under the waiver-of-service provisions of Rule 4(d), if not prohibited by the law of the foreign country of service;[186] or

(3) ***International Agreement — 4(f)(1)***: Where Congress has not established otherwise, service may be completed in any internationally agreed upon manner that is reasonably calculated to give notice, such as the *Hague Convention on the Service Abroad of Judicial and Extrajudicial Documents in Civil or Commercial Matters ("Hague Service Convention")*;[187] or

(4) ***Other Reasonable Methods — 4(f)(2)***: Where Congress has not established otherwise, and where no international agreement exists (or, if one exists, it merely allows but does not specify the means of service), service may be completed through any method that is reasonably calculated to give notice, as set out below; or

  (a) ***Foreign Law***: In the manner prescribed by that country for local service in an action in its courts of general jurisdiction; or

  (b) ***Letters Rogatory***: In the manner directed by that country in response to a letter rogatory or letter of request; or

  (c) ***Personal Delivery/Mail Delivery***: Unless prohibited by that foreign country's law, by either (i) personally delivering the summons and complaint to the individual or (ii) using any form of mail that the clerk addresses and sends, and that requires a signed receipt.

(5) ***Court Order — 4(f)(3)***: In any other manner directed by the court, so long as the chosen method is not prohibited by international agreement.

APPLICATIONS

Applies to Foreign Service, Not Foreign Citizenship

The provisions of Rule 4(f) are not triggered by a defendant's

---

[186] *See R. Griggs Group Ltd. v. Filanto Spa*, 920 F. Supp. 1100, 1103 (D. Nev. 1996).

[187] Nov. 15, 1965, 20 U.S.T. 361, T.I.A.S. No. 6638, 658 U.N.T.S. 163. The text of the Convention on the Service Abroad of Judicial and Extrajudicial Documents in Civil or Commercial Matters is reprinted in the Supplement to 28 U.S.C.A. following Rule 4 (WESTLAW: USCA database, **ci(frcp/2 4) & treaties**).

citizenship, but rather by the place of service. Thus, foreign nationals living, traveling, or conducting business within the United States generally may be served with process domestically under Rule 4(e), just as any other individual may.[188] Conversely, when the defendant (whether an American citizen or a national of another country) is served outside the United States, the provisions of this Rule 4(f) apply.[189]

Domestic Service Might Still Be Possible

When serving an individual located in a foreign country, a plaintiff may invoke one of the foreign country service methods of Rule 4(f), or, if the defendant has a presence in or authorized agent in the United States, service may also be proper on that agent (if one exists),[190] at a dwelling,[191] or by following the applicable State's service law,[192] all as permitted by Rule 4(e).

Serving Minors / Incompetent Persons Abroad

By its terms, the three service methods approved in Rule 4(f) do not apply to serving minors or incompetent persons.[193]

"Otherwise" Provided Federal Law Service

The service procedures set out in Rule 4(f) may be supplemented by, or replaced with, different procedures that Congress may enact.[194]

Rule 4(f)(1): International Agreement — Requirement of Hague Service

The Supreme Court has ruled that service abroad in accordance with the *Hague Service Convention* is mandatory, wherever that *Convention* applies[195] (although some courts have interpreted this precedent as still permitting court-ordered service, even when *Convention* service could be possible).[196] The *Convention* obviously will not apply when the receiving Nation

---

[188]*See generally Volkswagenwerk Aktiengesellschaft v. Schlunk*, 486 U.S. 694, 707–08, 108 S. Ct. 2104, 100 L. Ed. 2d 722 (1988) ("the Due Process Clause does not require an official transmittal of documents abroad every time there is service on a foreign national").

[189]*See Stars' Desert Inn Hotel & Country Club, Inc. v. Hwang*, 105 F.3d 521, 524 (9th Cir. 1997).

[190]*See Volkswagenwerk Aktiengesellschaft v. Schlunk*, 486 U.S. 694, 707–08, 108 S. Ct. 2104, 100 L. Ed. 2d 722 (1988); *Silvious v. Pharaon*, 54 F.3d 697, 701 (11th Cir.1995) (per curiam).

[191]*See United States v. Wen-Bing Soong*, 650 Fed. Appx. 425, 428–29 (9th Cir. 2016).

[192]*See United States v. Wen-Bing Soong*, 650 Fed. Appx. 425, 428–29 (9th Cir. 2016).

[193]*See Brown-Thomas v. Hynie*, 367 F. Supp. 3d 452, 468 (D.S.C. 2019). Serving minors and incompetent persons is addressed by Rule 4(g).

[194]*See, e.g.*, Foreign Sovereign Immunities Act, 28 U.S.C.A. §§ 1601 to 11; International Organizations Immunities Act, 22 U.S.C.A. §§ 288 to 288l.

[195]*See Volkswagenwerk Aktiengesellschaft v. Schlunk*, 486 U.S. 694 (1988). *See also Noco Co. v. CF Grp. SZKMS Co.*, 571 F. Supp. 3d 862, 867–68 (N.D. Ohio 2021).

[196]*See Nagravision SA v. Gotech Int'l Tech. Ltd.*, 882 F.3d 494, 498 (5th Cir. 2018); *Paushok v. Ganbold*, 487 F.

is not a signatory to that treaty,[197] nor will it apply if the signatory Nation refuses to comply with the treaty's provisions,[198] where the defendant's address is unknown,[199] or where service can be effected inside the United States.[200] Service under the *Convention* may require the federal court to issue a formal request for service directly to the receiving Nation's designated authority.[201] Alternatively, service by mail under the *Convention* may be proper.[202]

Rule 4(f)(1): International Agreement — Local Service Details

Process served pursuant to an international agreement must comport with all specific, peculiar requirements imposed by the host country, such as the translation of process into the local language.[203]

Rule 4(f)(2): Other Reasonable Methods — Generally

When no international agreement exists, or when an existing agreement is merely permissive without specifying service methods, four means of service are expressly approved (so long as they are reasonably calculated to give notice).[204] That one or more of these might be available to accomplish service does not necessarily preclude the judge's approval pursuant to Rule 4(f)(3) of a specially tailored method by court order instead.[205] These four methods will often be, in application, very nation-specific:

- *Foreign Law:* This service method borrows the proce-

Supp. 3d 243, 245 (S.D.N.Y. 2020). *See generally Rio Props., Inc. v. Rio Int'l Interlink*, 284 F.3d 1007, 1014–15 (9th Cir. 2002).

[197] *See, e.g., Freedom Watch, Inc. v. Organization of Petroleum Exporting Countries*, 766 F.3d 74, 79 (D.C.Cir. 2014) (Austria); *Nuance Commc'ns, Inc. v. Abbyy Software House*, 626 F.3d 1222, 1237–38 (Fed. Cir. 2010) (Russia).

[198] *See In re Potash Antitrust Litig.*, 667 F. Supp. 2d 907, 929–30 (N.D.Ill. 2009).

[199] *See Braverman Kaskey, P.C. v. Toidze*, 599 Fed.Appx. 448, 452 (3d Cir. 2015); *U.S. v. Real Property Known As 200 Acres of Land Near FM 2686 Rio Grande City, Tex.*, 773 F.3d 654, 659 (5th Cir. 2014).

[200] *See Volkswagenwerk Aktiengesellschaft v. Schlunk*, 486 U.S. 694, 707–08 (1988).

[201] *See Tracfone Wireless, Inc. v. Bequator Corp., Ltd.*, 717 F. Supp. 2d 1307, 1308 (S.D.Fla. 2010).

[202] *See infra* Authors' Commentary to Rule 4(f) (**"Service Internationally Through the Mails"**).

[203] *See Friedman v. Israel Labour Party*, 1997 WL 379181 (E.D. Pa. 1997) (service improper on Israeli defendant where plaintiff failed to send complaint directly to Israeli Director of Courts, as Israel required in its adoption of the Hague Service Convention); *Pennsylvania Orthopedic Ass'n v. Mercedes-Benz A.G.*, 160 F.R.D. 58, 60 (E.D. Pa. 1995) (service attempted under the Hague Convention on a German corporate defendant was ineffective because the complaint had not been translated into German).

[204] *See* Rule 4(f)(2)(A), (2)(B), 2(C)(i), 2(C)(ii).

[205] *See Rio Props., Inc. v. Rio Int'l Interlink*, 284 F.3d 1007, 1014–15 (9th Cir. 2002) (there is no service "hierarchy" that requires use of Rule 4(f)(2)'s options before resorting to a Rule 4(f)(3) court order).

dures "prescribed" by the local country's law for service in its general jurisdiction courts.[206]

- *Letters Rogatory:* This service method is cast in terms of compliance with a case-specific directive from the local country's officials.
- *Personal Delivery/Mail Service:* Unlike the first two Rule 4(f)(2) service methods, service under these last two options does not require affirmative authorization from the local law, but merely the absence of an affirmative local law prohibition (as least under the majority view).[207] This method of mailed service, when applicable, must be made by the clerk of court;[208] if mailed by the parties or someone else, it will likely fail.[209]

Rule 4(f)(3): Court Order — Generally

So long as the method of service is not prohibited by "international agreement,"[210] the plaintiff can request and the district court can order a means of service specifically tailored to achieve service upon individuals in a foreign country.[211] Ordinarily, such service cannot precede the issuance of a valid court order,[212] although there is some authority for allowing an order to be issued with retroactive effect, *nunc pro tunc*.[213]

This type of "court-ordered" service has been particularly useful to the courts when encountering elusive international defendants (especially those striving to evade service of process)[214] or where efforts to use the *Hague Service Convention*

---

[206] *See Artec Grp., Inc. v. Klimov*, 186 F. Supp. 3d 1002, 1012–14 (N.D. Cal. 2016) (such service must comply with local laws, here UAE).

[207] *See SignalQuest, Inc. v. Tien-Ming Chou*, 284 F.R.D. 45, 48–50 (D.N.H. 2012) (discussing majority and minority views, and following majority approach). *But cf. Lagayan v. Odeh*, 318 F.R.D. 208, 209–10 (D.D.C. 2016) (authorizing personal service by judicial order).

[208] *See Ghostbed, Inc. v. Casper Sleep, Inc.*, 315 F.R.D. 689, 692–93 (S.D. Fla. 2016).

[209] *See Rosen v. Netsaits*, 294 F.R.D. 524, 527–28 (C.D. Cal. 2013); *Intelsat Corp. v. Multivision TV LLC*, 736 F. Supp. 2d 1334, 1341–42 (S.D. Fla. 2010). *See generally Brockmeyer v. May*, 383 F.3d 798, 806–08 (9th Cir. 2004) (provision should not be interpreted to permit ordinary mail service).

[210] *See Compania de Inversiones Mercantiles, S.A. v. Grupo Cementos de Chihuahua S.A.B. de C.V.*, 970 F.3d 1269, 1294 (10th Cir. 2020) (relevant Rule 4(f)(3) inquiry is not whether international agreement "affirmatively endorses" proposed service, but whether agreement "prohibit[s]" it); *Densys Ltd. v. 3Shape Trios A/S*, 336 F.R.D. 126, 130–31 (W.D. Tex. 2020) (same).

[211] *See Freedom Watch, Inc. v. Organization of Petroleum Exporting Countries*, 766 F.3d 74, 80 (D.C.Cir. 2014) (special service permitted only if plaintiff affirmatively seeks, and obtains, such a court order).

[212] *See De Gazelle Grp., Inc. v. Tamaz Trading Establishment*, 817 F.3d 747, 750–51 (11th Cir. 2016).

[213] *Compare Marks v. Alfa Group*, 615 F. Supp. 2d 375, 379–80 (E.D.Pa. 2009) (permitting *nunc pro tunc* order), *with Brockmeyer v. May*, 383 F.3d 798, 806 (9th Cir.2004) (denying *nunc pro tunc* order).

[214] *See AngioDynamics, Inc. v.*

have proved unsuccessful.[215] Few restrictions restrain the district court's creativity in crafting an alternate means of service.[216] So long as the alternative service is (1) ordered by the court, (2) not prohibited by applicable international agreement, and (3) reasonably calculated, under the circumstances, to apprise the defendant of the pendency of the action and afford an opportunity to respond,[217] the courts enjoy wide discretion.[218] Indeed, this "court-ordered" service option may even be employed where service could otherwise be accomplished through the various options set forth in Rule 4(f)(2).[219] Although this judicial discretion is broad, some courts have engrafted a threshold common law requirement that special court-ordered service will only issue upon a showing that (a) service otherwise has reasonably been attempted on the defendant and (b) circumstances now make a special court order necessary.[220]

The "court-ordered" service option has been applied by the courts to authorize service by publication,[221] ordinary postal mail,[222] facsimile transmission and telex,[223] e-mail,[224] texting or

Biolitec AG, 780 F.3d 420, 429 (1st Cir. 2015). *See also Rio Properties, Inc. v. Rio Intern. Interlink*, 284 F.3d 1007, 1018 (9th Cir. 2002) (justifying alternate service because plaintiff was "faced with an international e-business scofflaw, playing hide-and-seek with the federal court"); *Smith v. Islamic Emirate of Afghanistan*, 2001 WL 1658211, at *3 (S.D. N.Y. 2001) (permitting alternative service on Osama Bin Laden and Al Qaeda terrorist network).

[215] *See Strabala v. Zhang*, 318 F.R.D. 81, 114 (N.D. Ill. 2016).

[216] *See Rio Props., Inc. v. Rio Int'l Interlink*, 284 F.3d 1007, 1016 (9th Cir. 2002) (listing alternative service authorizations by other courts).

[217] *See Rio Properties, Inc. v. Rio Intern. Interlink*, 284 F.3d 1007, 1014–18 (9th Cir. 2002); *Ghostbed, Inc. v. Casper Sleep, Inc.*, 315 F.R.D. 689, 693–94 (S.D. Fla. 2016).

[218] *See Freedom Watch, Inc. v. Organization of Petroleum Exporting Countries*, 766 F.3d 74, 80 (D.C.Cir. 2014). *But see Rio Properties, Inc. v. Rio Int'l Interlink*, 284 F.3d 1007, 1014 (9th Cir. 2002) (discussing whether discretion to craft alternative service includes methods in violation of foreign country's internal laws).

[219] *See AngioDynamics, Inc. v. Biolitec AG*, 780 F.3d 420, 429 (1st Cir. 2015); *Nuance Commc'ns, Inc. v. Abbyy Software House*, 626 F.3d 1222, 1239 (Fed. Cir. 2010). *See also Rio Properties, Inc. v. Rio Intern. Interlink*, 284 F.3d 1007, 1014–15 (9th Cir. 2002) (expressly rejecting argument that Rule creates "a hierarchy of preferred methods of service of process").

[220] *See CKR L. LLP v. Anderson Invs. Int'l, LLC*, 525 F. Supp. 3d 518, 523–24 (S.D.N.Y. 2021) (courts "ordinarily" permit alternative service "only" upon these showings, designed to deter litigants from "whimsically" seeking alternative service). *See also Noco Co. v. CF Grp. SZKMS Co.*, 571 F. Supp. 3d 862, 867–68 (N.D. Ohio 2021) (same effect).

[221] See *Hausler v. JP Morgan Chase Bank, N.A.*, 141 F. Supp. 3d 248, 252 (S.D.N.Y. 2015) (permitting service by publication and mail); *Smith v. Islamic Emirate of Afghanistan*, 2001 WL 1658211, at *3 (S.D.N.Y. 2001) (permitting service on Osama Bin Laden and Al Qaeda by publication in Afghani newspapers, Pakistani newspaper where Bin Laden published Fatwahs, and broadcast advertising on local television networks).

[222] *See Hausler v. JP Morgan Chase Bank, N.A.*, 141 F. Supp. 3d 248, 252

messaging,[225] social media,[226] delivery to certain members of the defendant's family,[227] delivery to an affiliated business address,[228] delivery to the defendant's attorney[229] or registered agent,[230] and via private overnight courier.[231]

Rule 4(f)(3): Court Order — Service by E-Mail

Courts disagree as to whether the *Hague Service Convention* tolerates court-ordered e-mail service.[232] Some courts, albeit cautiously, have ordered alternative service of process by e-mail in cases involving international defendants with a known e-mail address, who engage in Internet activities, and who attempt to evade service by other means.[233] Noting the many complications with e-mail service (*e.g.*, an inability to confirm actual receipt of an e-mail message, system compatibility issues, possible failure of attachments (such as exhibits) to transmit, be received, or be "opened" in comprehensible form, etc.), courts have granted e-mail service only on a case-by-case basis, upon a proper balancing of these limitations against the corre-

---

(S.D.N.Y. 2015).

[223] *See Studio A. Entm't, Inc. v. Active Distribs., Inc.*, 2008 WL 162785, at *4 (N.D. Ohio 2008) (collecting cases approving service by fax).

[224] *See supra* Authors' Commentary to Rule 4(f) ("**Rule 4(f)(3): Court Order—Service by E-Mail**").

[225] *See CKR L. LLP v. Anderson Invs. Int'l, LLC*, 525 F. Supp. 3d 518, 523–25 (S.D.N.Y. 2021) (permitting WhatsApp messaging).

[226] *See St. Francis Assisi v. Kuwait Fin. House*, 2016 WL 5725002, at *1–*2 (N.D. Cal. Sept. 30, 2016) (service by Twitter); *F.T.C. v. PCCare247 Inc.*, 2013 WL 841037, at *1–*6 (S.D.N.Y. Mar. 7, 2013) (service by Facebook and email).

[227] *See U.S. v. Padilla*, 2002 WL 471838, at *1 (E.D. Cal. 2002) (service via delivery to both daughter and attorney of defendant, with letter requesting that recipients forward to defendant, and offering to send copies directly to defendant's residence if the recipients provided the address).

[228] *See Rio Props., Inc. v. Rio Int'l Interlink*, 284 F.3d 1007, 1016 (9th Cir. 2002) (service on local affiliate); *Guifu Li v. A Perfect Day Franchise, Inc*, 281 F.R.D. 373, 388–89 (N.D.Cal. 2012) (service on franchise).

[229] *See Compania de Inversiones Mercantiles, S.A. v. Grupo Cementos de Chihuahua S.A.B. de C.V.*, 970 F.3d 1269, 1295 (10th Cir. 2020); *Rio Props., Inc. v. Rio Int'l Interlink*, 284 F.3d 1007, 1016 (9th Cir. 2002).

[230] *See TracFone Wireless, Inc. v. Washington*, 290 F.R.D. 686, 688 (M.D. Fla. 2013); *Brown v. China Integrated Energy, Inc.*, 285 F.R.D. 560, 564–66 (C.D. Cal. 2012).

[231] *See TracFone Wireless, Inc. v. Washington*, 290 F.R.D. 686, 687–88 (M.D. Fla. 2013) (FedEx); *Russell Brands, LLC v. GVD Int'l Trading, SA*, 282 F.R.D. 21, 26 (D.Mass. 2012) (same).

[232] *Compare Grp. One Ltd. v. GTE GmbH*, 523 F. Supp. 3d 323, 342–44 (E.D.N.Y. 2021) (Germany's objection to postal mail service does not necessarily foreclose e-mail service) *and Sulzer Mixpac AG v. Medenstar Indus. Co.*, 312 F.R.D. 329, 331 (S.D.N.Y. 2015) (same, per China), *with Prem Sales, LLC v. Guangdong Chigo Heating & Ventilation Equip. Co.*, 494 F. Supp. 3d 404, 416-17 (N.D. Tex. 2020) (China's objection to postal mail service forecloses e-mail service), *and Facebook, Inc. v. 9 Xiu Network (Shenzhen) Tech. Co.*, 480 F. Supp. 3d 977, 982-87 (N.D. Cal. 2020) (same).

[233] *See Rio Properties, Inc. v. Rio Intern. Interlink*, 284 F.3d 1007, 1017–18 (9th Cir. 2002).

sponding benefits of such service in particular circumstances.[234] Among the conditions they may impose, courts that approve e-mail service will likely require that the e-mail address be shown to be an authentic means of reaching the recipient[235] and that the e-mail, once transmitted, did not generate a return "bounce-back" or similar failed-delivery message.[236] Recently, courts have shown greater liberality in permitting e-mail service.[237]

Service Internationally through the Postal Mails

Serving original process via international postal delivery may be accomplished in several ways:

- *First*, many Nations are signatories to the *Hague Service Convention*, and service by international mail is permitted in *Convention*-signatory Nations so long as (a) they have not objected to service by mail and (b) mailed service is allowed in the American forum.[238]
- *Second*, apart from the *Convention*, international mail service is often also proper if the receiving Nation does not forbid it[239] *so long as* it is dispatched by the American clerk of court with a signed receipt required *and* there is no applicable international agreement in place (*e.g.*, the receiving Nation is not a *Convention* signatory) or, if in place, any agreement permits such service.[240] Exacting compliance with these requirements is essential: such mailed service is *not* effective if it is performed by someone other than the court clerk[241] or if the serving party fails to prove affirmatively that service

[234] *See Rio Properties, Inc. v. Rio Intern. Interlink*, 284 F.3d 1007, 1017–18 (9th Cir. 2002) (discussing e-mail option, and finding that e-mail service was perhaps most likely method to notify defendant of summons and complaint); *Sulzer Mixpac AG v. Medenstar Indus. Co.*, 312 F.R.D. 329, 331–32 (S.D.N.Y. 2015) (weighing risks and uncertainties, and ordering email service in China).

[235] *See Grp. One Ltd. v. GTE GmbH*, 523 F. Supp. 3d 323, 342–47 (E.D.N.Y. 2021); *CKR L. LLP v. Anderson Invs. Int'l, LLC*, 525 F. Supp. 3d 518, 524–25 (S.D.N.Y. 2021).

[236] *See FTC v. Cottelli*, 854 Fed. Appx. 837, 838–39 (9th Cir. 2021).

[237] *See, e.g., Microsoft Corp. v. Buy More, Inc.*, 703 Fed. Appx. 476, 480 (9th Cir. 2017); *Lexmark Int'l, Inc. v. Ink Techs. Printer Supplies, LLC*, 295 F.R.D. 259, 261–62 (S.D. Ohio 2013). *But see Anova Applied Elecs., Inc. v. Hong King Grp., Ltd.*, 334 F.R.D. 465, 470–72 (D. Mass. 2020) (ruling that Hague Convention does not authorize e-mail service); *Graphic Styles/Styles Int'l LLC v. Men's Wear Creations*, 99 F. Supp. 3d 519, 523–24 (E.D. Pa. 2015) (same).

[238] *See Water Splash, Inc. v. Menon*, 581 U.S. __, 137 S. Ct. 1504, 1508–13 (2017).

[239] *Cf. Ure v. Oceania Cruises, Inc.*, 122 F. Supp. 3d 1351, 1354 (S.D. Fla. 2015) (finding Ecuadorian law does not permit mail service).

[240] *See* Rule 4(f)(2)(C)(ii). *See also Brockmeyer v. May*, 383 F.3d 798, 806–08 (9th Cir. 2004) (discussing such service); *SignalQuest, Inc. v. Tien-Ming Chou*, 284 F.R.D. 45, 47–48 (D.N.H. 2012) (same).

[241] *See Rosen v. Netsaits*, 294 F.R.D. 524, 527–28 (C.D. Cal. 2013); *Hyundai Merchant Marine Co. Ltd. v. Grand China Shipping (Hong Kong) Co.*, 878

by mail is not prohibited by the foreign country's law.[242]

- *Third*, such service may be expressly ordered by the American court, provided, too, that it is not forbidden by the Nation of service *and* there is no applicable international agreement that forbids it.[243]
- *Fourth*, the Rule broadly permitting service in a manner "prescribed by the law of the foreign country for service in that country" probably will not suffice to authorize international mail service.[244]

Return of Service

Once service abroad is complete, the proof of service can be made in the manner provided by an applicable treaty,[245] by Rule 4(*l*),[246] by the law of the foreign country, or by order of court.[247] If service was accomplished by mail, the proof of service should include a signed return receipt.

Effect of Foreign Service

Foreign countries are not parties to the U.S. Constitution's Full Faith and Credit Clause, and thus the enforcement abroad of a judgment entered by an American federal court is dependent on comity and international treaties.[248] Moreover, in certain foreign countries, failure to adhere to the host nation's service regulations could even subject the unwary process

---

F. Supp. 2d 1252, 1256–57 (S.D.Ala. 2012).

[242]*See Nabulsi v. Nahyan*, 2008 WL 1924235, at *4 (S.D. Tex. 2008). *See also S.E.C. v. Alexander*, 248 F.R.D. 108, 111–14 (E.D. N.Y. 2007).

[243]*See* Rule 4(f)(3). *See also Brockmeyer v. May*, 383 F.3d 798, 806–08 (9th Cir. 2004) (discussing such service).

[244]*See* Rule 4(f)(2)(A). *See also Brockmeyer v. May*, 383 F.3d 798, 806–08 (9th Cir. 2004) (rejecting mail service to United Kingdom under this provision); *Prewitt Enterprises, Inc. v. Organization of Petroleum Exporting Countries*, 353 F.3d 916, 925 (11th Cir. 2003) (same, mail to Austria); *Hyundai Merchant Marine Co. Ltd. v. Grand China Shipping (Hong Kong) Co.*, 878 F. Supp. 2d 1252, 1257 (S.D.Ala. 2012) (same, FedEx to Hong Kong).

[245]*See Northrup King Co. v. Compania Productora Semillas Algodoneras Selectas, S.A.*, 51 F.3d 1383, 1389 (8th Cir. 1995) (certificate of service prepared by Central Authority of *Hague Convention* signatory Nation is "prima facie evidence" of Convention-compliant service); *Unite Nat'l Ret. Fund v. Ariela, Inc.*, 643 F. Supp. 2d 328, 334–35 (S.D.N.Y. 2008) (same). *But see Winston v. Walsh*, 829 Fed. Appx. 448, 452 (11th Cir. 2020) (need not defer to Central Authority's certificate of service where delivery was made to address known to be incorrect).

[246]*See Voice Tele Servs., Inc. v. Zee Telecoms Ltd.*, 338 F.R.D. 200, 204 (S.D.N.Y. 2021) (process server's sworn statement of service creates presumption that service occurred as stated).

[247]*See Tracfone Wireless, Inc. v. Bequator Corp., Ltd.*, 717 F. Supp. 2d 1307, 1309–10 (S.D.Fla. 2010) (authorizing filing of FedEx proof-of-signature as return of service).

[248]*See Phoenix Process Equip. Co. v. Capital Equip. & Trading Corp.*, 250 F. Supp. 3d 296, 309 (W.D. Ky. 2017) (if service method fails to comply with Russian law, enforcing any resulting judgment in Russia may be affected).

server to criminal penalties.[249]

RULE 4(g)—SERVING MINORS AND INCOMPETENT PERSONS

CORE CONCEPT

Original process may be served upon any minor or incompetent person in the following manners:

- ***Service Inside the United States:*** In any manner authorized for the service of process on minors or incompetent persons by the State in which service is to be made.
- ***Service Outside the United States:*** In any manner: (1) prescribed by the law of the foreign country; (2) directed in response to a letter rogatory or letter of request; or (3) by such other means as the court may direct.

APPLICATIONS

State Law Sets Domestic Service Procedures

For domestic service of process to be effective upon a minor or incompetent person, the service must comply with the requirements for such service as promulgated by the State in which service is attempted.[250]

Waiver-of-Service and Minors / Incompetents

For obvious capacity reasons, minors and incompetent persons are not expected to waive formal service.[251]

RULE 4(h)—SERVING CORPORATIONS, PARTNERSHIPS, AND ASSOCIATIONS

CORE CONCEPT

Original process may be served upon any domestic or foreign corporation, partnership, or unincorporated association subject to suit under a common name, in the following manners:

(1) ***Specific Federal Law***: In any manner elsewhere authorized by federal law; or

(2) ***Waiver***: Under the waiver-of-service provisions of Rule 4(d); or

---

[249]*See Volkswagenwerk Aktiengesellschaft v. Schlunk*, 486 U.S. 694 (1988) (discussing possible adverse consequences of failing to comply with applicable international treaties). *See generally* Joseph F. Weis, Jr., *The Federal Rules and the Hague Conventions: Concerns of Conformity and Comity*, 50 U. Pitt. L. Rev. 903 (1989).

[250]*See United States v. Malhas*, 2020 WL 6318720, at *3 (N.D. Cal. Oct. 28, 2020) (rejecting service on incompetent person for failure to comply with California law); *Seibels, Bruce & Co. v. Nicke*, 168 F.R.D. 542, 545 (M.D.N.C. 1996) (rejecting service on minor for failure to comply with Indiana law).

[251]*See* Rule 4(d) advisory committee note (1993) ("Infants or incompetent persons likewise are not called upon to waive service because, due to their presumed inability to understand the request and its consequences, they much generally be served through fiduciaries.").

(3) ***SERVICE INSIDE THE UNITED STATES***:
   (a) ***State Law***: In the manner authorized either by the State in which the district court sits or by the State in which the service is to be accomplished; or
   (b) ***Officer, Managing Agent, or General Agent***: By delivering the summons and complaint to an officer, managing agent, or general agent; or
   (c) ***Other Authorized Agent***: By delivering the summons and complaint to an agent appointed to receive service or authorized by law to receive service; and if required by statute, by also mailing the summons and complaint to the defendant; or
(4) ***SERVICE OUTSIDE THE UNITED STATES***:
In any manner provided for service upon individuals in a foreign country, except personal service.

APPLICATIONS

Service on Officer, or Managing or General Agent

To effectively serve a corporation, partnership, or association through an officer, managing agent, or general agent, the summons and complaint must be directed and delivered to such a person. Simply addressing mail to the company generally, or to its legal department, will usually not suffice.[252] Whether the served individual qualifies as an officer, managing agent, or general agent is a highly fact-specific inquiry,[253] often hinging on the person's authority within the organization.[254] The burden of proving that status lies with the serving party.[255] Persons qualifying for this status typically hold positions of executive responsibility.[256] Thus, delivering service papers to some random employee or representative of the company may not constitute proper service, unless some other provision of federal or State law permits it. Accordingly, service on one of the company's owners,[257] board members,[258] office managers,[259] at-

[252] *See Larsen v. Mayo Medical Center*, 218 F.3d 863, 868 (8th Cir. 2000) (papers mailed to "Medical/Legal Department, Mayo Clinic" was ineffective service under Rule 4(h)).

[253] *See Egan v. Tenet Health Care*, 193 F. Supp. 3d 73, 83–84 (D. Mass. 2016); *Cooney v. Barry Sch. of Law*, 994 F. Supp. 2d 268, 270 (E.D.N.Y. 2014).

[254] *See Egan v. Tenet Health Care*, 193 F. Supp. 3d 73, 83–84 (D. Mass. 2016); *Lopes v. JetsetDC, LLC*, 994 F. Supp. 2d 135, 144 (D.D.C. 2014). *See also Waldman v. Palestine Liberation Org.*, 835 F.3d 317, 328 (2d Cir. 2016) ("overwhelming competent evidence" showed recipient to be "general agent" of PLO).

[255] *See Egan v. Tenet Health Care*, 193 F. Supp. 3d 73, 84 (D. Mass. 2016).

[256] *See Gottlieb v. Sandia Am. Corp.*, 452 F.2d 510, 513 (3d Cir. 1971).

[257] *See Reynolds Innovations, Inc. v. E-CigaretteDirect, LLC*, 851 F. Supp. 2d 961, 963 (M.D.N.C. 2012).

[258] *See Romand v. Zimmerman*, 881 F. Supp. 806, 810 (N.D.N.Y. 1995).

[259] *See Ayers v. Jacobs & Crumplar, P.A.*, 99 F.3d 565, 567–68 (3d Cir. 1996); *Cooney v. Barry Sch. of Law*,

torneys[260] or law department,[261] corporate subsidiaries,[262] insurance reps,[263] or receptionists or secretaries[264] may not, without more, qualify as proper service. Service on a qualifying individual need not occur at the company's headquarters; service might be proper wherever the officer, managing agent, or general agent can be found.[265]

Service on Authorized Agent

Corporations, partnerships, and associations can also be served by delivering the summons and complaint to any other agent specially authorized to receive service, either by appointment or by operation of law.[266] Such person or entity must have been actually (or impliedly) appointed or authorized to receive service of process on the entity's behalf,[267] and the serving party bears the burden of establishing that fact.[268] The fact that a governmental Internet site lists a person or entity as authorized agent is not necessarily depositive on the issue.[269]

"Otherwise" Provided Federal Law Service

The service procedures set out in Rule 4(h) may be supplemented by, or replaced with, different procedures that Congress may enact.[270]

Service Pursuant to State Law

A corporation, partnership, or unincorporated association may also be served in any manner authorized by *either* the State in which the district court sits *or* the State in which the

994 F. Supp. 2d 268, 270–71 (E.D.N.Y. 2014). *But see Vax-D Med. Techs., LLC v. Texas Spine Med. Ctr.*, 485 F.3d 593, 596 (11th Cir. 2007) (service sufficient).

[260] *See Malcolm v. Honeoye Falls-Lima Educ. Ass'n ("HFLEA")*, 684 Fed. Appx. 87, 89 (2d Cir. 2017); *Deptula v. Rosen*, 558 F. Supp. 3d 73, 87 (S.D.N.Y. 2021).

[261] *See Arora v. Buckhead Family Dentistry, Inc.*, 263 F. Supp. 3d 121, 133 (D.D.C. 2017).

[262] *See Mandawala v. Ne. Baptist Hosp.*, 16 F.4th 1144, 1156 (5th Cir. 2021).

[263] *See Schollenberger v. Sears, Roebuck & Co.*, 876 F. Supp. 153, 156 (E.D. Mich. 1995).

[264] *See Smith v. Womans Hosp.*, 671 Fed. Appx. 884, 887 (5th Cir. 2016); *Williams v. GEICO Corp.*, 792 F. Supp. 2d 58, 65 (D.D.C. 2011).

[265] *See Mommaerts v. Hartford Life and Acc. Ins. Co.*, 472 F.3d 967, 967–68 (7th Cir. 2007); *Winston & Strawn LLP v. Law Firm of John Arthur Eaves*, 47 F. Supp. 3d 68, 74 (D.D.C. 2014) (service at home proper).

[266] *See* Rule 4(h)(1)(B).

[267] *See Villanueva v. Account Discovery Sys., LLC*, 77 F. Supp. 3d 1058, 1068 (D.Colo. 2015). *See also Adams v. Sunlighten Inc.*, 328 F.R.D. 477, 482 (W.D. Mich. 2018) (exercising dutifully delegated authority to accept service qualifies as authorized agent); *U.S. ex rel. Thomas v. Siemens AG*, 708 F. Supp. 2d 505, 519 (E.D.Pa. 2010) (mere delivery not sufficient, nor is service on parent automatically proper as service on subsidiary).

[268] *See Nature's First Inc. v. Nature's First Law, Inc.*, 436 F. Supp. 2d 368, 372–73 (D. Conn. 2006).

[269] *See Vazquez-Robles v. CommoLoCo, Inc.*, 757 F.3d 1, 6–9 (1st Cir. 2014).

[270] *See, e.g., D.R.T.G. Builders, L.L.C. v. Occupational Safety & Health Rev. Comm'n*, 26 F.4th 306, 311 (5th Cir. 2022) (Rule 4(h) does not apply to OSHA notifications because Congress enacted different notice method).

service is to be accomplished.[271]

Service at Company Headquarters

The Rules do *not* specifically authorize service by leaving a copy of the summons and complaint at the company's headquarters.[272] This type of service, however, might still be proper if permitted by the operative State law (which Rule 4(h) borrows).[273] For example, some States permit service on corporations by certified mail[274] and others forgive service on the wrong corporate person so long as service is made at the corporate offices following the instructions of corporate employees found there.[275]

Service Made Outside the United States

Service on either a foreign or domestic entity can be accomplished outside the United States by serving that corporation, partnership, or association in any manner authorized by Rule 4(f) for serving individuals outside the United States[276] *except* personal service.[277] Failure to comply with the provisions of that Rule will render the service ineffective.[278] (Note: foreign corporations, partnerships, or associations may also be served inside the United States just like domestic corporations, if one of their officers, managing agents, general agents, or autho-

---

[271] *See Puckett v. Ramirez*, 826 Fed. Appx. 716, 718–20 (11th Cir. 2020) (service ineffective under Texas statute allowing service on secretary of state without evidence of diligent effort to service registered agent); *In re Newbrook Shipping Corp.*, 498 F. Supp. 3d 807, 814 (D. Md. 2020) (under Maryland law, if "good faith effort" to serve resident agent, president, secretary, or treasurer fails, service allowed on "other person expressly or impliedly authorized to receive service").

[272] *See Melkaz Intern. Inc. v. Flavor Innovation Inc.*, 167 F.R.D. 634, 636 (E.D. N.Y. 1996).

[273] *See* Rule 4(h)(1)(A) (incorporating Rule 4(e)(1)).

[274] *See Alfa Corp. v. Alfagres, S.A.*, 385 F. Supp. 2d 1230, 1238 (M.D. Ala. 2005) (Alabama law).

[275] *See M'Baye v. World Boxing Ass'n*, 429 F. Supp. 2d 652, 656–57 (S.D. N.Y. 2006) (New York law). *See also Dailey v. R & J Commercial Contracting*, 2002 WL 484988, at *3 (S.D.Ohio 2002) ("When a corporation holds itself out to the public as receiving mail at a particular address, it must take some minimal steps to insure that when certified mail service is directed to that address, it receives actual notice"); *Battie v. Freeman Decorating*, 2001 WL 1345927, at *1 (E.D. La. 2001) (delivery of summons and complaint to corporation's receptionist may be sufficient service).

[276] *See Compania de Inversiones Mercantiles, S.A. v. Grupo Cementos de Chihuahua S.A.B. de C.V.*, 970 F.3d 1269, 1295 (10th Cir. 2020); *De Gazelle Grp., Inc. v. Tamaz Trading Establishment*, 817 F.3d 747, 749 (11th Cir. 2016). *See also Ganpat v. E. Pac. Shipping, PTE, LTD.*, 553 F. Supp. 3d 324, 328–34 (E.D. La. 2021) (conducting detailed analysis of Singapore civil law in confirming proper service on business).

[277] *See Freedom Watch, Inc. v. Organization of Petroleum Exporting Countries*, 766 F.3d 74, 80 (D.C.Cir. 2014). *But see Nuance Commc'ns, Inc. v. Abbyy Software House*, 626 F.3d 1222, 1238 (Fed. Cir. 2010) (personal delivery may be appropriate if made pursuant to applicable foreign law).

[278] *See Emery v. Wood Indus., Inc.*, 2001 WL 274747, at * 3 (D.N.H. 2001) (hand-delivery of complaint and summons to Assistant Manager in Taiwan failed to comply).

rized agents can be properly served here.[279])

RULE 4(i)—SERVING THE UNITED STATES, ITS AGENCIES, CORPORATIONS, AND OFFICERS

CORE CONCEPT

To properly serve the United States, its agencies, corporations, or officers with original process, the summons and complaint must often be served at multiple locations.

APPLICATIONS

Multiple Service Is Mandatory, Not Discretionary

The purpose of the obligation to serve both the head of the U.S. Department of Justice (the attorney general) and that Department's local representative (the territory's U.S. Attorney) is to ensure that the federal government receives that level of notice necessary to allow the raising of a defense that conforms with the government's broader goals.[280] In cases where a federal officer, employee, or agency is sued, the obligation to complete this multiple-service on the United States ensures that the lawyers responsible for litigating the defense (namely, the Department of Justice) are properly notified.[281] This multiple-service regime is complicated, even confusing to those unfamiliar with it, but it is mandatory. Failing to comply with these obligations will defeat proper service and prevent the court from acquiring jurisdiction over the federal defendants,[282] and may even cause claimants to lose their right to sue if the applicable limitations period has expired in the interim.[283]

Applicability of the Waiver-of-Service Procedure

The Rule 4(d) waiver-of-service procedure is *not* authorized for serving the United States or its agencies[284] or, courts seem to agree, for serving federal personnel sued in their official

---

[279] *See Bazarian Int'l Fin. Associates, L.L.C. v. Desarrollos Aerohotelco, C.A.*, 168 F. Supp. 3d 1, 13–16 (D.D.C. 2016); *U.S. ex rel. Thomas v. Siemens AG*, 708 F. Supp. 2d 505, 519 (E.D.Pa. 2010). *But see Freedom Watch, Inc. v. Org. of Petroleum Exporting Countries*, 107 F. Supp. 3d 134, 137 (D.D.C. 2015) (cannot served foreign entity by a delivery made within the U.S.).

[280] *See Morrissey v. Mayorkas*, 17 F.4th 1150, 1156 (D.C. Cir. 2021).

[281] *See Morrissey v. Mayorkas*, 17 F.4th 1150, 1156 (D.C. Cir. 2021).

[282] *See Felicetty-Stamm v. Secretary Dep't of Homeland Sec.*, 558 Fed. Appx. 189, 191 (3d Cir. 2014); *Walker v. Donahoe*, 528 Fed. Appx. 439, 440–41 (6th Cir. 2013).

[283] *See Morrissey v. Mayorkas*, 17 F.4th 1150, 1153–64 (D.C. Cir. 2021) (trial judges have no obligation to extend service time in such cases merely because of expiring statute of limitations).

[284] *See* Rule 4(d) advisory committee note (1993) ("The United States is not expected to waive service . . . . The same principle is applied to agencies, corporations, and officers of the United States . . . ."); Rule 4(i) advisory committee note (1993) (Rule 4(i) "does not authorize the use of the Notice and Request procedure of revised subdivision (d) when the United States is the defendant").

capacities.[285] Courts are divided whether waiver-of-service can be used in lawsuits suing federal personnel in their individual capacities.[286]

The United States as Defendant

Original process must be served upon the United States as follows:

(1) ***United States Attorney***: By *either* (a) personally delivering the summons and complaint to the United States Attorney for the judicial district in which the action is brought, or her/his designee, *or* (b) sending the summons and complaint by registered or certified mail to the "civil process clerk" at the office of that United States Attorney; *and*

- *Warning:* If service is made under option (b), the mailing has to be addressed to the "Civil Process Clerk" and not the U.S. Attorney; misaddressing the mailed service in this manner renders the service improper.[287]

(2) ***Attorney General***: By *also* sending a copy of the summons and complaint by registered or certified mail to the U.S. Attorney General in Washington, D.C.; *and*

(3) ***Federal Officer or Agency***: In lawsuits attacking the validity of an order of a non-party officer or agency of the United States, by *also* sending a copy of the summons and complaint by registered or certified mail to such officer or agency.

Federal Officers, Agencies, or Corporations as Defendants

Original process may be served upon an officer, agency, or corporation of the United States as follows:

(1) ***United States***: By serving the United States (see above); *and*

(2) ***Federal Officer, Agency, or Corporation***: By *also* sending a copy of the summons and complaint by registered or certified mail to the federal officer, agency, or corporation named as a defendant.[288]

---

[285] *See Marcello v. Maine*, 238 F.R.D. 113, 116 n.3 (D. Me. 2006); *Emuchay v. Catron*, 2000 WL 303223, at *2 (D. Conn. Jan. 27, 2000).

[286] *Compare Libretti v. Courtney*, 2015 WL 12927890, at *3 (D. Wyo. Apr. 17, 2015) (waiver use available) *and Tajeddini v. Gluch*, 942 F. Supp. 772, 778 (D. Conn. 1996) (same) *with Northrop v. United States*, 2008 WL 4681640, at *1 (D. Conn. Oct. 20, 2008) (waiver not available) *and Brown v. Nalley*, 2007 WL 433139, at *2 (D. Colo. Feb. 5, 2007) (same). *See generally* Rule 4(i) advisory committee note (2000) (individual-capacity lawsuits must use Rule 4(e), (f), or (g), which "invokes also the waiver-of-service provisions of subdivision (d)").

[287] *See Vargas v. Potter*, 792 F. Supp. 2d 214, 217 (D.P.R. 2011).

[288] *See* Rule 4(i)(2). *See also Morrissey v. Mayorkas*, 17 F.4th 1150, 1156 (D.C. Cir. 2021) (official-capacity

Federal Officers or Employees Sued in their Individual Capacities

In certain instances, federal officers and employees may be sued in their individual capacities.[289] In such cases, the type of service required will depend on the allegations of the pleading:

- *On-the-Job Claims:* If the federal officers or employees are sued in their individual capacities for acts or omissions occurring in connection with the performance of their federal duties, then proper service requires (1) service upon the United States *and* (2) service upon the officer or employee under Rule 4(e), (f), or (g).[290]
- *Claims Unrelated to the Job:* If the federal officers or employees are sued in their individual capacities for any other acts or omissions (that is, for conduct unrelated to the performance of their federal duties), then proper service requires only service under Rule 4(e), (f), or (g). Service on the United States is not required.[291]

These procedures apply to former federal officers and employees, as well as current personnel.[292] Until this complete service is accomplished, the officers or employees are not properly before the court as defendants.[293]

If the plaintiff intends to sue the federal officials in *both* their individual and official capacities, the plaintiff must: (1) individually serve the officials under Rule 4(e), (f), or (g); *and* (2) serve the United States as well under Rule 4(i).[294] The plaintiff generally does not need to serve the official twice

---

claims against Homeland Security Secretary dismissed for failure to serve United States); *Golub v. United States*, 593 Fed. Appx. 546, 549 (7th Cir. 2014) (official-capacity claims against Homeland Security officer properly dismissed because certified mail receipt contained no signature).

[289] *See Bivens v. Six Unknown Named Agents of Federal Bureau of Narcotics*, 403 U.S. 388, 91 S. Ct. 1999, 29 L. Ed. 2d 619 (1971) (permitting action for money damages against federal officers acting under color of their official authority for injuries caused by unconstitutional conduct).

[290] *See* Rule 4(i)(3). *See also Edwards v. Hillman*, 849 Fed. Appx. 23, 25–26 (3d Cir. 2021) (individual-capacity claims against federal judge properly dismissed because he was never served); *Bernier v. Trump*, 299 F. Supp. 3d 150, 152 (D.D.C. 2018) (individual-capacity claims against prison physician dismissed because he was never served at work, likely because he was no longer employed there).

[291] *See* Rule 4(i)(2)(B) advisory committee note (2000) ("Many actions are brought against individual federal officers or employees of the United States for acts or omissions that have no connection whatever to their government roles. There is no reason to require service on the United States in these actions").

[292] *See* Rule 4(i)(2)(B) advisory committee notes (2000) (action against former federal personnel "is covered by paragraph (2)(B) in the same way as an action against a present officer or employee").

[293] *See Johnson v. Veterans Affairs Med. Ctr.*, 133 F. Supp. 3d 10, 16 (D.D.C. 2015).

[294] *See McCaslin v. Cornhusker State Industries*, 952 F. Supp. 652, 658–59 (D. Neb. 1996) (construing Rule 4(j), holding that service delivered directly to government employees conferred jurisdiction over them only

personally (*i.e.*, one service for each capacity).[295]

To "Send" a "Copy" to Certain Defendants

The requirement to "send" a "copy" of service papers to certain federal defendants may possibly be met by photocopies of those originals,[296] but the papers must be sent by either certified or registered mail with delivery confirmed.[297]

Careful! Name the Correct Federal Defendant

Practitioners should take special care to ensure that the proper defendant is named. A lawsuit may be dismissed if it mistakenly names a federal officer or agency as a defendant when the proper defendant is the United States, or mistakenly names the United States as a defendant when the proper defendant is a federal agency or officer, or mistakenly names federal officers as defendants in their official rather than individual capacities.[298]

Curing Incomplete Service on Federal Defendants

In view of the complexity of these multiple service obligations, Rule 4(i) establishes a "cure" for incomplete service in cases requiring service on officers, agencies, or federal corporations. So long as a prescribed degree of partial service has been made, the court must allow a plaintiff a reasonable period of time to fulfill the multiple service obligations at all other locations.[299]

- *"Cure" is Opportunity for Extension, Not an Excuse of Obligation:* The "cure" provision in Rule 4(i) does not excuse or forgive an incomplete service. To the contrary, the "cure" provision only authorizes an extension of time to complete the plaintiff's obligations—the full, required

---

in their individual capacities; to sue the government itself, service on the chief executive officer or the State attorney general's office was required).

[295]*See* Rule 4(i)(2) advisory committee notes (2000) (amendments intended "to ensure that no one would read the seemingly independent provisions of paragraphs 2(A) and 2(B) to mean that service must be made twice both on the United States and on the United States employee when the employee is sued in both official and individual capacities"). *See also Buttler v. Keller*, 169 F.R.D. 9, 10 (N.D. N.Y. 1996) (under applicable State law, a single service upon an individual, named in both his individual and representative capacities, suffices to confer jurisdiction).

[296]*See Marmolejos v. United States*, 283 F.R.D. 63, 66–67 (D.P.R. 2012).

[297]*See Fuqua v. Turner*, 996 F.3d 1140, 1155–56 (11th Cir. 2021) (certified mail requires proof of delivery effective only if return-receipts are properly signed by addressee or authorized agent); *Shepard v. United States Dep't of Veterans Affs.*, 819 Fed. Appx. 622, 623-24 (10th Cir. 2020) (Federal Express does not qualify as "certified" or "registered" mail). *See generally Republic of Sudan v. Harrison*, 587 U.S. —, 139 S. Ct. 1048, 1057, 203 L. Ed. 2d 433 (2019) (describing "certified mail" as including "a signed returned receipt" which must be received by authorized subordinate).

[298]*See, e.g.*, 28 U.S.C.A. § 2671 (under Federal Torts Claims Act, actions to recover for the torts of a federal agency must name the United States as a defendant).

[299]Rule 4(i)(4).

service under Rule 4(i) must still be accomplished.[300]

- *"Cure" in Federal Agency, Corporation, & Official Capacity Lawsuits:* If the plaintiff succeeds in serving either the United States Attorney or the Attorney General in a lawsuit asserting Rule 4(i)(2) claims (claims against a federal agency or corporation, or official capacity claims against federal officers of employees), but the plaintiff neglects to serve other required parties, the courts will allow the plaintiff a "reasonable time" to perfect proper service.[301] Note, however, that this "cure" provision applies *only* when proper service has already been achieved on the United States Attorney or the Attorney General.[302]
- *"Cure" in On-the-Job Individual Capacity Lawsuits:* In a lawsuit against federal officers or employees sued for Rule 4(i)(3) claims (individual capacity, "on-the-job" claims), a plaintiff who successfully serves the officer or employee will be granted a "reasonable time" to serve the United States as well.[303]
- *"Cure" Not General Extension of Time:* The extension is not unlimited; the "cure" must be accomplished within a "reasonable time" after the original, incomplete service was made.[304]
- *Other Avenues for "Cure":* The "cure" options of Rule 4(i)(4) are in addition the court's general authority to grant extensions under Rules 4(m) and 6(b).[305]

RULE 4(j)—SERVING FOREIGN, STATE, OR LOCAL GOVERNMENTS

CORE CONCEPT

The methods for serving process on a foreign, State, or local

---

[300]*See McMasters v. U.S.*, 260 F.3d 814, 817–18 (7th Cir. 2001).

[301]*See* Rule 4(i)(4)(A). *See also Silbaugh v. Chao*, 942 F.3d 911, 915-16 (9th Cir. 2019).

[302]*See Morrissey v. Wolf*, 333 F.R.D. 1, 2–3 (D.D.C. 2019), *aff'd*, 17 F.4th 1150 (D.C. Cir. 2020). *But see Gargano v. I.R.S.*, 207 F.R.D. 22, 23 (D. Mass. 2002) (some courts, confronted by a failure to serve the U.S. Attorney or Attorney General, "see room for a grant of equitable relief where overly strict adherence to the literal wording of the Rule appears to elevate form over substance," and have applied a four-part analysis that could grant such relief where: (1) all necessary governmental parties have actual notice of lawsuit; (2) government has suffered no prejudice from service defect; (3) plaintiff had justifiable excuse for failure to make proper service; and (4) plaintiff would be severely prejudiced by dismissal).

[303]*See* Rule 4(i)(4)(B).

[304]*See Kurzberg v. Ashcroft*, 619 F.3d 176, 184–86 (2d Cir. 2010) (cure not reasonable where plaintiffs failed to serve during 120-day period after being notified of deficient service by defendant); *Tuke v. U.S.*, 76 F.3d 155, 158 (7th Cir. 1996) (cure not reasonable where plaintiff failed to serve "for months" and, after being notified by the United States of the deficiency, failed to act promptly or properly).

[305]*See Martello v. United States*, 133 F. Supp. 3d 338, 344–47 (D. Mass. 2015). *See also Morrissey v. Wolf*, 333 F.R.D. 1, 2–3 (D.D.C. 2019), *aff'd*, 17 F.4th 1150 (D.C. Cir. 2020) (considering, but rejecting, Rule 4(m) extension).

government vary depending upon the type of government served and the application of other laws.

APPLICATIONS

Applicability of the Waiver-of-Service Procedure

The Rule 4(d) waiver-of-service procedure is *not* authorized for serving foreign, State, or local governments.[306] Whether the waiver procedure may be used to serve employees of a foreign, State, or local government in their official capacities remains unclear.[307]

Foreign Sovereign Immunities Act, Generally

Original process on foreign governments or their political subdivisions, agencies, or instrumentalities must be served in accordance with the federal Foreign Sovereign Immunities Act (FSIA).[308] The FSIA permits four types of service, listed in order of required preference (*i.e.*, the plaintiff must use method one, unless it is unavailable, in which case the plaintiff must use method two, unless it is unavailable, and so on).[309] The provisions of the Act demand "strict adherence."[310]

Serving Foreign Governments

The four permitted methods for serving a foreign government, as prescribed by the FSIA, are, in descending order of preference:

(1) ***Agreed-Method:*** In any manner arranged between the plaintiff and the foreign State, but if not then:

(2) ***International Agreement:*** In accordance with an applicable international treaty or convention, such as the *Hague Convention on the Service Abroad of Judicial and Extrajudicial Documents in Civil or Commercial*

---

[306] *See* Rule 4(d)(1) (Rule 4(j) defendants absent from list of permitted waiver defendants). *See also Moore v. Hosemann*, 591 F.3d 741, 747 (5th Cir. 2009); *Lepone-Dempsey v. Carroll Cnty. Comm'rs*, 476 F.3d 1277, 1281 (11th Cir. 2007). *But see Ecret v. Diamond*, 2007 WL 2743432, at *2–*3 (W.D. Wash. 2007) (though not authorized by Rule 4(j), waiver that was sought and then granted by local government enforced by court).

[307] *Compare Cupe v. Lantz*, 470 F. Supp. 2d 136, 138 (D. Conn. 2007) (Rule 4(d) inapplicable to state employees sued in their official capacities), *with Marcello v. Maine*, 238 F.R.D. 113, 115 (D. Me. 2006) (serving public employees in their official capacities is done through Rule 4(e) which, in turn, permits Rule 4(d) waiver-of-service procedure).

[308] 28 U.S.C.A. § 1608. *See generally Argentine Republic v. Amerada Hess Shipping Corp.*, 488 U.S. 428, 434, 109 S. Ct. 683, 102 L. Ed. 2d 818 (1989).

[309] *See Angellino v. Royal Family Al-Saud*, 688 F.3d 771, 773 (D.C. Cir. 2012).

[310] *See Kumar v. Republic of Sudan*, 880 F.3d 144, 154 (4th Cir. 2018); *Barot v. Embassy of the Republic of Zambia*, 785 F.3d 26, 27 (D.C.Cir. 2015). *But cf. Transaero, Inc. v. La Fuerza Aerea Boliviana*, 30 F.3d 148, 153–54 (D.C. Cir. 1994) (duty may be less strict when defendant is foreign agency or instrumentality, rather than foreign state itself).

Matters,[311] but if not then:

- *Treaty Language:* In interpreting the *Hague Convention*, courts begin with its text, which, if clear, cannot be altered, amended, or added to, whether the contemplated adjustment is "great or small, important or trivial."[312]

(3) ***Ministry of Foreign Affairs:*** By the clerk of court mailing a copy of the summons and complaint and a notice of suit, along with translations thereof, in a manner requiring a signed receipt, to the head of the ministry of foreign affairs,[313] but if such service is not available within 30 days, then:

(4) ***Special Consular Services:*** By the clerk of court mailing a copy of the summons and complaint and a notice of suit, along with translations thereof, in a manner requiring a signed receipt, to the United States Director of Special Consular Services, for transmittal to the foreign State through diplomatic channels.

Serving Foreign Governmental Entities

The permitted methods for serving foreign agencies and instrumentalities, as prescribed by the FSIA, are, in descending order of preference:

(1) ***Agreed-Method:*** By serving process in any manner arranged between the plaintiff and the foreign agency or instrumentality,[314] but if not then:

(2) ***Agent or International Agreement:*** *Either* (a) by delivering process to an officer, managing agent, or general agent of the foreign agency or instrumentality, or to an agent appointed by the foreign agent or instrumentality to receive service of process or authorized by law to receive such service; *or* (b) by serving process in accordance with an applicable international treaty or convention, such as the *Hague Convention on the Service Abroad of Judicial and Extrajudicial Docu-*

---

[311] Nov. 15, 1965, 20 U.S.T. 361, T.I.A.S. No. 6638, 658 U.N.T.S. 163. The text of the Convention on the Service Abroad of Judicial and Extrajudicial Documents in Civil or Commercial Matters is reprinted in the Supplement to 28 U.S.C.A. following Fed.R. Civ.P. 4 (WESTLAW: USCA database, **ci(frcp/2 4) & treaties).**

[312] *See Saint-Gobain Performance Plastics Eur. v. Bolivarian Republic of Venezuela*, 23 F.4th 1036, 1040 (D.C. Cir. 2022) (citing and quoting array of U.S. Supreme Court precedent).

[313] *See Karcher v. Islamic Republic of Iran*, 249 F. Supp. 3d 557, 559 (D.D.C. 2017). Courts are divided on whether that mailing must be delivered in the foreign Nation, rather than to the Nation's embassy in the United States. *See Kumar v. Republic of Sudan*, 880 F.3d 144, 152–60 (4th Cir. 2018) (discussing circuit split).

[314] *See Matter of Arbitration Between Trans Chem. Ltd. & China Nat. Machinery Import & Export Corp.*, 978 F. Supp. 266, 274 (S.D. Tex. 1997), aff'd, 161 F.3d 314 (5th Cir. 1998) (service upon foreign agency was proper because it was made in accordance with the terms of the contract between the agency and the plaintiff).

ments in Civil or Commercial Matters,[315] but if not then:

(3) ***Letter Rogatory, Clerk Mailing, or Court Order:*** In one of the following manners: (a) by delivering process (together with a translation thereof) as directed in response to a letter rogatory or letter of request; *or* (b) by the clerk of court mailing process (along with translations thereof) in a manner requiring a signed receipt, to the agency or instrumentality; *or* (c) by order of court consistent with the law of the place where service is to be accomplished.

Serving State and Local Governments, Generally

A State, municipal corporation, or other State-created government organization may be served with original process in either of two ways, service under either of which is sufficient:[316]

(1) ***Chief Executive Officer:*** By personally delivering the summons and complaint to the chief executive officer of the State, municipal corporation, or governmental organization[317] (note that "delivery," in this provision, has been interpreted to exclude service by mail[318] or commercial courier,[319] but to include agents of the chief executive officer who represent themselves to be authorized recipients of service[320]); or

(2) ***State Law:*** By serving the summons and complaint in the manner authorized by the State in which the service is to be accomplished (which may permit

[315] Nov. 15, 1965, 20 U.S.T. 361, T.I.A.S. No. 6638, 658 U.N.T.S. 163. The text of the Convention on the Service Abroad of Judicial and Extrajudicial Documents in Civil or Commercial Matters is reprinted in the Supplement to 28 U.S.C.A. following Fed.R. Civ.P. 4 (WESTLAW: USCA database, **ci(frcp/2 4) & treaties).**

[316] *See Lawver v. Department of Corrections, State of Neb.*, 2007 WL 3376742, at *4 (D. Neb. 2007) (successful delivery under first method qualified as proper service, even though that delivery would have been found to be improper under second method).

[317] *See Coleman v. Milwaukee Bd. of School Directors*, 290 F.3d 932, 933–34 (7th Cir. 2002) (where school board had no "chief executive officer", only option for plaintiff was to serve as prescribed by State law); *McCaslin v. Cornhusker State Industries*, 952 F. Supp. 652, 658–59 (D. Neb. 1996) (service delivered directly to government employees conferred jurisdiction over them only in their individual capacities; to sue government itself, service on chief executive officer or State attorney general's office was required).

[318] *See Yates v. Baldwin*, 633 F.3d 669, 672 (8th Cir. 2011); *Paul v. Didizian*, 292 F.R.D. 151, 154–56 (D.D.C. 2013).

[319] *See Cichocki v. Massachusetts Bay Cmty. Coll.*, 174 F. Supp. 3d 572, 577 (D. Mass. 2016).

[320] *See Nashville Cmty. Bail Fund v. Gentry*, 446 F. Supp. 3d 282, 298–300 (M.D. Tenn. 2020). *See also Carrasquillo-Serrano v. Municipality of Canovanas*, 991 F.3d 32, 41–42 (1st Cir. 2021) (noting local Puerto Rico law's allowance for service on designees).

mailing).[321] Note, the phrase "that state's law" refers to the State where the served entity is physically located and of which it is a citizen.[322] Some State laws require service on *multiple* officials in order to be proper.[323] Personal service on an official while traveling outside the State or local territory is unlikely to confer jurisdiction on the official's government.[324]

Serving State and Local Government Employees

A lawsuit against State or local government personnel in their official capacities is ordinarily considered a lawsuit against the government itself.[325] Accordingly, service should be proper upon serving that government.[326] Individual capacity lawsuits, however, require service that complies with Rule 4(e).[327]

Serving State and Local Governments, Eleventh Amendment Concerns

The Eleventh Amendment to the U.S. Constitution restricts the authority of the federal courts to hear lawsuits against States.[328] Additionally, individual State and municipal sovereign immunity laws limit the federal courts' ability to enter awards against States, municipalities, and governmental entities.

---

[321] *See Patterson v. Whitlock*, 392 Fed.Appx. 185, 188 n.7 (4th Cir. 2010) (noting State law option, and that North Carolina law permits mailing); *Paul v. Didizian*, 292 F.R.D. 151, 154–56 (D.D.C. 2013) (District of Columbia permits certain mailed service).

[322] *See Rocky Mountain Chipseal, LLC v. Sherman County*, 841 F. Supp. 2d 1224, 1228 (D.Colo. 2012).

[323] *See Peak v. District of Columbia*, 236 F.R.D. 13, 16 (D.D.C. 2006) (proper service upon District of Columbia requires service on both District's Attorney General and Mayor).

[324] *See Rocky Mountain Chipseal, LLC v. Sherman County*, 841 F. Supp. 2d 1224, 1228–30 (D.Colo. 2012) (serving Kansas county commissioner while in Colorado for personal reasons did not vest Colorado with jurisdiction over Kansas county).

[325] *See Will v. Michigan Dep't. of State Police*, 491 U.S. 58, 72 (1989); *Soper v. Hoben*, 195 F.3d 845, 853 (6th Cir. 1999).

[326] *See Johnson v. Marlar*, 807 Fed. Appx. 791, 796 (10th Cir. 2020); *Libertarian Party of Ohio v. Wilhem*, 417 F. Supp. 3d 982, 984–86 (S.D. Ohio 2019). *But cf. Pemberton v. Patton*, 673 Fed. Appx. 860, 864 (10th Cir. 2016) (Rule 4(j)(2)(A) is "inapplicable" for serving individual state correctional officers in constitutional rights lawsuit).

[327] *See Xiu Jian Sun v. Cuomo*, 2019 WL 5307359, at *2 (N.D.N.Y. Oct. 21, 2019); *Kriston v. Peroulis*, 2010 WL 1268087, at *4–5 (D. Colo. Mar. 29, 2010), *aff'd*, 500 Fed. Appx. 744 (10th Cir. 2012).

[328] *See Pennhurst State School & Hosp. v. Halderman*, 465 U.S. 89, 104 S. Ct. 900, 79 L. Ed. 2d 67 (1984) (Eleventh Amendment prevents federal courts from hearing suits for damages filed by citizens against States, unless the defending State first consents). *See also Florida Dept. of State v. Treasure Salvors, Inc.*, 458 U.S. 670, 102 S. Ct. 3304, 73 L. Ed. 2d 1057 (1982) (Eleventh Amendment extends to bar suits by citizens against their own State of residence, in the absence of that State's consent to suit).

RULE 4(k)—TERRITORIAL LIMITS OF EFFECTIVE SERVICE

CORE CONCEPT

The mechanics of service of process (and waiver of service) are prescribed in the various other subparts of Rule 4. This subpart establishes when, upon compliance with those mechanics, a federal court may acquire personal jurisdiction over the served (or waiving) parties.

APPLICATIONS

Exercise of Federal Personal Jurisdiction

There is no broad, general federal long-arm statute,[329] but Rule 4(k) functions like a grant of personal jurisdiction.[330] It provides that, upon effective service of process or a filed waiver of formal service, federal courts acquire personal jurisdiction over a defendant in four circumstances:

- *State Long-Arm Statutes:* If the defendant is amenable to suit in the State where the district court is sitting in accordance with the provisions of that State's jurisdictional statutes;[331] or
- *100-Mile "Bulge" Rule:* If the defendant is (a) joined as an impleaded third-party or required party and (b) served within 100 miles of the place where the summons issues;[332] or
  - *Note:* The bulge rule does *not* apply to service on the original parties to the lawsuit,[333] nor (when it applies) does it require forum-related minimum contacts on the part of the bulge party.[334]
- *Federal Long-Arm Statutes:* If the defendant is amenable to suit in the district court pursuant to the terms of some particular federal statute;[335] or
- *National-Contacts Jurisdiction:* If the defendant meets the prerequisites for national-contacts jurisdiction

[329] *See S.E.C. v. Ross*, 504 F.3d 1130, 1138 (9th Cir. 2007).

[330] *See, e.g., Lyngaas v. Ag*, 992 F.3d 412, 422 (6th Cir. 2021) ("acts as a sort of federal long-arm statute"); *AMA Multimedia, LLC v. Wanat*, 970 F.3d 1201, 1207 (9th Cir. 2020) ("known as the 'federal long-arm statute' ").

[331] Rule 4(k)(1)(A). *See Daimler AG v. Bauman*, 571 U.S. 117, 125 (2014). *See generally Walden v. Fiore*, 571 U.S. 277, 283 (2014) (in "most cases" federal court's personal jurisdiction is "linked" to Rule 4(k)(1)(A) service).

[332] Rule 4(k)(1)(B). *See Fitzgerald v. Wal-Mart Stores East, LP*, 296 F.R.D. 392, 393–94 (D. Md. 2013).

[333] *See Bromfield-Thompson v. Am. Univ. of Antigua/Manipal Educ. Americas LLC*, 2020 WL 6048902, at *4 n.6 (S.D.N.Y. Oct. 13, 2020).

[334] *See Scott v. United States*, 2020 WL 6134890, at *3 (S.D. Ill. Oct. 19, 2020).

[335] Rule 4(k)(1)(C). *See generally Canaday v. Anthem Cos., Inc.*, 9 F.4th 392, 398–99 (6th Cir. 2021) (surveying federal statutes that provide for nationwide service and personal jurisdiction).

(discussed below).

Reminder—Exercise Must *Also* Be Constitutional

Satisfying one of the criteria in the Rule 4(k) schedule means that the federal court's exercise of jurisdiction comports with the Rules, not necessarily that it comports with the U.S. Constitution's Due Process Clause.[336] That separate inquiry must be conducted as well.[337]

Rule 4(k)(2) National-Contacts Jurisdiction—Generally

A federal court may have personal jurisdiction over non-resident defendants who, being sued under federal law, have sufficient contacts with the Nation to warrant the exercise of a federal court's jurisdiction, even though they lack the contacts with any particular State needed to satisfy a State long-arm statute.[338] This "national-contacts" option was created to fill a perceived gap in the reach of federal authority.[339] Because of its exacting requirements, this path to jurisdiction is unlikely to apply frequently,[340] but that is not to say it is disfavored.[341]

Rule 4(k)(2)—Asserting National-Contacts Jurisdiction

To qualify for national-contacts jurisdiction, three conditions (in addition to proper service or waiver of service[342]) are required:[343]

(1) Federal Claims: Plaintiff's claims against the defendant must arise under federal law;[344]

(2) No Conventional Jurisdiction Possible: The defendant must be beyond the jurisdictional reach of any individual State court and no situation-specific federal statute

---

[336]*See* Rule 82 (noting that Rules "do not extend or limit the jurisdiction of the district courts").

[337]*See, e.g.*, *Trois v. Apple Tree Auction Ctr., Inc.*, 882 F.3d 485, 488 (5th Cir. 2018); *Friedman v. Bloomberg L.P.*, 884 F.3d 83, 90 (2d Cir. 2017). *See also Fitzgerald v. Wal-Mart Stores East, LP*, 296 F.R.D. 392, 394–95 (D. Md. 2013) (even if defendant lies within the bulge region, due process must still be examined).

[338]*See* Rule 4(k)(2). *See also Omni Capital Intern., Ltd. v. Rudolf Wolff & Co., Ltd.*, 484 U.S. 97, 108 S. Ct. 404, 413, 98 L. Ed. 2d 415 (1987).

[339]*See Adams v. Unione Mediterranea Di Sicurta*, 364 F.3d 646, 651 (5th Cir. 2004); *In re SSA Bonds Antitrust Litig.*, 420 F. Supp. 3d 219, 240 (S.D.N.Y. 2019).

[340]*See Lyngaas v. Ag*, 992 F.3d 412, 422 (6th Cir. 2021) ("defendants rarely have the requisite relationship with the United States as a whole, but not with any individual state"); *Compania de Inversiones Mercantiles, S.A. v. Grupo Cementos de Chihuahua S.A.B. de C.V.*, 970 F.3d 1269, 1282 (10th Cir. 2020) (in "limited circumstances").

[341]*See Ayla, LLC v. Alya Skin Pty. Ltd.*, 11 F.4th 972, 978 n.1 (9th Cir. 2021) (rarely exercised because unusual for defendant to have U.S.-qualifying contacts but lack State-qualifying contacts).

[342]*See Merial Ltd. v. Cipla Ltd.*, 681 F.3d 1283, 1295 (Fed.Cir. 2012).

[343]*See Genetic Veterinary Scis., Inc. v. LABOKLIN GmbH & Co. KG*, 933 F.3d 1302, 1309 (Fed. Cir. 2019) (listing requirements); *Plixer Int'l, Inc. v. Scrutinizer GmbH*, 905 F.3d 1, 6 (1st Cir. 2018) (same).

[344]*See Getz v. The Boeing Co.*, 654 F.3d 852, 858-60 (9th Cir. 2011) (describing "substantive federal law" requirement, and surveying case law).

applies to confer jurisdiction;[345] *and*

(3) *Exercise of Personal Jurisdiction is Constitutional:* The exercise of personal jurisdiction over the defendant would not offend the Constitution or other federal law.[346] This inquiry implicates the 5th Amendment (not the 14th Amendment) Due Process Clause.[347] To date, neither the U.S. Supreme Court nor the majority of federal circuits has discerned a meaningful difference between those two clauses.[348] However, in assessing whether a defendant's contacts are sufficient for national-contacts personal jurisdiction, courts examine all of the defendant's contacts with, and throughout, the United States as a whole.[349] In doing so, courts may conduct the traditional general (*all-purpose*) jurisdiction[350] and specific (*case-linked*) jurisdiction inquiries.[351] General jurisdiction under Rule 4(k)(2) is unlikely because that type of jurisdiction can only be exercised constitutionally in a forum where the defendant is "essentially at home" (and a foreign defendant meeting that standard in the United States will probably also be amenable to some State's long-arm statute).[352] Specific jurisdiction under Rule 4(k)(2) is more tenable

---

[345] *See Merial Ltd. v. Cipla Ltd.*, 681 F.3d 1283, 1294 (Fed.Cir. 2012); *Fraser v. Smith*, 594 F.3d 842, 848–49 (11th Cir. 2010).

[346] *See Unspam Techs., Inc. v. Chernuk*, 716 F.3d 322, 330 (4th Cir. 2013); *Abelesz v. OTP Bank*, 692 F.3d 638, 660 (7th Cir. 2012).

[347] *See Atchley v. AstraZeneca UK Ltd.*, 22 F.4th 204, 232 (D.C. Cir. 2022); *Lyngaas v. Ag*, 992 F.3d 412, 422 (6th Cir. 2021). For a discussion of the two Clauses, see *supra* Part II—*General Concepts in Federal Civil Practice* § 2.4 (**"Two Different Due Process Clauses"**).

[348] *See Bristol-Myers Squibb Co. v. Superior Ct.*, 582 U.S. __, 137 S. Ct. 1773, 1783–84, 198 L. Ed. 2d 395 (2017) ("leav[ing] open the question" whether 5th Amendment and 14th Amendment "impose[] the same restrictions on the exercise of personal jurisdiction"). *See also Atchley v. AstraZeneca UK Ltd.*, 22 F.4th 204, 232 (D.C. Cir. 2022) ("inquiries are generally analogous," apart from forum scope and federalism concerns); *Lyngaas v. Ag*, 992 F.3d 412, 422 (6th Cir. 2021) ("same" requirements under both Clauses). *But cf. Douglass v. Nippon Yusen Kabushiki Kaisha*, 996 F.3d 289, 293–99 (5th Cir. 2021), *reh'g en banc granted, opinion vacated*, 2 F.4th 525 (5th Cir. 2021) (finding persuasive (because of absence of inter-State federalism concerns), but not adopting, new approach for 5th Amendment cases).

[349] *See Ayla, LLC v. Alya Skin Pty. Ltd.*, 11 F.4th 972, 979 (9th Cir. 2021); *Hetronic Int'l, Inc. v. Hetronic Germany GmbH*, 10 F.4th 1016, 1031 (10th Cir. 2021), *petition for cert. pending*, No. 21-1043 (U.S. Jan. 26, 2022).

[350] *See Livnat v. Palestinian Auth.*, 851 F.3d 45, 56 (D.C. Cir. 2017) (general jurisdiction absent under Rule 4(k)(2) where defendant was not essentially at home in the U.S.).

[351] *See Livnat v. Palestinian Auth.*, 851 F.3d 45, 56 (D.C. Cir. 2017) (either general or specific jurisdiction "can suffice" for Rule 4(k)(2) purposes). For a discussion of these jurisdiction types, see *supra* Part II, § 2.5c1 (**"Specific Jurisdiction"**) and § 2.5c2 (**"General Jurisdiction"**).

[352] *See Livnat v. Palestinian Auth.*, 851 F.3d 45, 56 (D.C. Cir. 2017) (general jurisdiction absent under Rule 4(k)(2) where defendant was not essentially at home in the U.S.).

as it may be exercised on the basis of contacts aimed purposefully towards the United States that give rise or relate to the pending lawsuit,[353] without an unyielding obligation to show actual, physical contacts here.[354] Indeed, in the Rule 4(k)(2) context, one court has even ruled that the specific jurisdiction connectedness inquiry in this context is a "lenient" one.[355]

Rule 4(k)(2)—Burden of Proof for National-Contacts Jurisdiction

The plaintiff bears the burden of establishing the prerequisites for Rule 4(k)(2) national-contacts jurisdiction,[356] and limited jurisdictional discovery may be granted to help with that burden.[357] The courts are divided, however, on how that burden is discharged. The majority approach requires the plaintiff to make three prima facia showings: (1) the claim arises under federal law; (2) no situation-specific federal statute confers jurisdiction; and (3) the defendant's contacts with the United States nationally satisfy due process concerns.[358] Once the plaintiff makes these showings, the burden then shifts to the defendant to show whether some specific State does indeed possess jurisdiction.[359] If the defendant does so, the plaintiff may (a) seek a transfer to that State, (b) discontinue

---

[353]*See, e.g.*, *Atchley v. AstraZeneca UK Ltd.*, 22 F.4th 204, 233–38 (D.C. Cir. 2022) (specific jurisdiction under Rule 4(k)(2) existed, where drug company reached into U.S. to contract with, and serve as exclusive agent for, manufacturer to serve Iraqi clients); *M-I Drilling Fluids UK Ltd. v. Dynamic Air Ltda.*, 890 F.3d 995, 1001 (Fed. Cir. 2018) (same, where company installed and operated allegedly patent-infringing systems on U.S. flagged ships).

[354]*See Mwani v. bin Laden*, 417 F.3d 1, 12 (D.C. Cir. 2005).

[355]*See Lyngaas v. Ag*, 992 F.3d 412, 423 (6th Cir. 2021) ("lenient", "not so stringent," and met if "operative facts are at least marginally related to the alleged contacts").

[356]*See U.S. v. Swiss American Bank, Ltd.*, 191 F.3d 30, 38 (1st Cir. 1999). *See also Erwin-Simpson v. AirAsia Berhad*, 985 F.3d 883, 889 n.1 (D.C. Cir. 2021) (plaintiffs forfeited Rule 4(k)(2) as jurisdictional basis by failing to timely raise it).

[357]*See Toys "R" Us, Inc. v. Step Two, S.A.*, 318 F.3d 446, 458 (3d Cir. 2003) (allowing jurisdictional discovery on limited issue of defendant's business activities in United States); *Dardana Ltd. v. Yuganskneftegaz*, 317 F.3d 202, 208 (2d Cir. 2003) (remanding for jurisdictional discovery). *But cf. In re SSA Bonds Antitrust Litig.*, 420 F. Supp. 3d 219, 241 (S.D.N.Y. 2019) (jurisdictional discovery denied because no "actual plan" for it was proposed and allegations of link to U.S. were conclusory and devoid of any specific facts).

[358]*See ISI Int'l, Inc. v. Borden Ladner Gervais LLP*, 256 F.3d 548, 552 (7th Cir. 2001). *See also Lyngaas v. Ag*, 992 F.3d 412, 422 (6th Cir. 2021) (joining majority approach); *Compania de Inversiones Mercantiles, S.A. v. Grupo Cementos de Chihuahua S.A.B. de C.V.*, 970 F.3d 1269, 1282 (10th Cir. 2020) (joining Fifth, Seventh, Ninth, Eleventh, D.C., and Federal Circuits in majority approach).

[359]*See CGC Holding Co., LLC v. Hutchens*, 974 F.3d 1201, 1208–09 (10th Cir. 2020) (federal court entitled to invoke Rule 4(k)(2) if defendant contests jurisdiction in forum state but refuses to identify other forum possessing jurisdiction); *Haines v. Selendang Ayu M/V*, 403 Fed.Appx. 194,

the lawsuit and re-file it there, or (c) contest the defendant's assertions.[360] This burden-shifting technique invests the defendant with the ability to "knock out" Rule 4(k)(2) by actually conceding personal jurisdiction in some other State.[361] Conversely, failing to do so permits the federal court to proceed with the Rule 4(k)(2) analysis without the accompanying burden of a tedious 50-State constitutional analysis.[362]

The minority approach adds a fourth requirement to the majority's list of showings: that the plaintiff also certify, based on information available to party and counsel, that the defendant is not subject to the jurisdiction of any U.S. State.[363] This requires the type of 50-State constitutional analysis that the majority approach rejects, and, until the plaintiff satisfies all four showings, the defendant has no burden to carry.[364]

Rule 4(k)(2)—Default Judgments

In denying relief from a default judgment, a court may consider whether personal jurisdiction could have been proper under Rule 4(k)(2), even though jurisdiction had been errantly premised on other grounds originally.[365] Moreover, a defaulting defendant will not be relieved of a default entered in a Rule 4(k)(2) case by asserting that some State had jurisdiction over it[366] or that it *ex post facto* consents to some State's

195 (9th Cir. 2010) (Rule 4(k)(2) unavailable because defendants concede amenability in Alaska).

[360] *See ISI Intern., Inc. v. Borden Ladner Gervais LLP*, 256 F.3d 548, 552 (7th Cir. 2001).

[361] *See Zvelo, Inc. v. Check Point Software Techs., Ltd.*, 418 F. Supp. 3d 664, 672 (D. Colo. 2019) (defendant's acknowledgement that it can be sued in California "amounts to consent to personal jurisdiction" there, warranting dismissal of Rule 4(k)(2) lawsuit filed in Colorado).

[362] *See Hetronic Int'l, Inc. v. Hetronic Germany GmbH*, 10 F.4th 1016, 1031 (10th Cir. 2021), *petition for cert. pending*, No. 21-1043 (U.S. Jan. 26, 2022) (defendants concede that no individual State has jurisdiction if they fail to point out which does, since trial court not obligated to independently consider all 50 States); *Merial Ltd. v. Cipla Ltd.*, 681 F.3d 1283, 1294 (Fed.Cir. 2012) (avoids "saddl[ing] the plaintiff with an extraordinary challenge"); *ISI Intern., Inc. v. Borden Ladner Gervais LLP*, 256 F.3d 548, 552 (7th Cir. 2001) ("This procedure makes it unnecessary to traipse through the 50 states, asking whether each could entertain the suit").

[363] *See Motus, LLC v. CarData Consultants, Inc.*, 23 F.4th 115, 127 (1st Cir. 2022). *See also Base Metal Trading, Ltd. v. OJSC "Novokuznetsky Aluminum Factory,"* 283 F.3d 208, 215 (4th Cir.2002) (applying First Circuit approach); *In re SSA Bonds Antitrust Litig.*, 420 F. Supp. 3d 219, 240 (S.D.N.Y. 2019) (same). *But see Automobili Lamborghini S.P.A. v. Lamborghini Latino Am. USA*, 400 F. Supp. 3d 471, 478 n.6 (E.D. Va. 2019) (applying Seventh Circuit test, where Fourth Circuit "has not specifically addressed the issue").

[364] *See Motus, LLC v. CarData Consultants, Inc.*, 23 F.4th 115, 127 (1st Cir. 2022).

[365] *See Merial Ltd. v. Cipla Ltd.*, 681 F.3d 1283, 1296–98 (Fed.Cir. 2012).

[366] *See Nagravision SA v. Gotech Int'l Tech. Ltd.*, 882 F.3d 494, 498–99 (5th Cir. 2018).

jurisdiction.[367]

RULE 4(*l*)—PROVING SERVICE

CORE CONCEPT

Where formal service has not been waived, the process server must present proof of service to the court.

APPLICATIONS

Effect of Proof of Service

A filed proof of service is recognized as prima facie evidence that service was properly accomplished.[368] But, the presumption of validity is rebuttable.[369] Accordingly, an affidavit from the recipient specifically denying his or her authority to accept service may be sufficient to rebut the presumption,[370] though a mere denial of service, devoid of evidentiary support, will probably not suffice.[371] If the presumption is rebutted, the burden of proving proper service of process returns to the plaintiff.[372]

Nature of Proof

The proof of service should contain sufficient facts to confirm that valid service has been accomplished (*e.g.*, the specific place where process was left, the name of the recipient), but ordinarily need not supply a substantive description of the person served or the details of how the service was made.[373] Where service was made by someone other than a U.S. Marshal, an affidavit of service is required,[374] although proof by other means may, under proper circumstances, be acceptable.[375]

Service Outside the United States

If service is made under a treaty or other international

---

[367]*See Merial Ltd. v. Cipla Ltd.*, 681 F.3d 1283, 1294–95 (Fed.Cir. 2012).

[368]*See Blair v. City of Worcester*, 522 F.3d 105, 111 (1st Cir. 2008); *O'Brien v. R.J. O'Brien & Associates, Inc.*, 998 F.2d 1394, 1398 (7th Cir. 1993).

[369]*See Carrasquillo-Serrano v. Municipality of Canovanas*, 991 F.3d 32, 41 (1st Cir. 2021). *See also Gottlieb v. Sandia Am. Corp.*, 452 F.2d 510, 514 (3d Cir. 1971) (return from U.S. Marshal "is not conclusive on the question of service on an agent, it will stand in the absence of proof to the contrary").

[370]*See Blair v. City of Worcester*, 522 F.3d 105, 112 (1st Cir. 2008) (collecting cases).

[371]*See Economy Stone Midstream Fuel, LLC v. M/V A.M. THOMPSON*, 2009 WL 973441, at *1 (N.D.Miss. Apr. 9, 2009).

[372]*See Blair v. City of Worcester*, 522 F.3d 105, 112 (1st Cir. 2008).

[373]*See Williams v. Martinez*, 192 F. Supp. 3d 1, 4 (D.D.C. 2016).

[374]*See* Rule 4(*l*)(1) ("proof must be made by the server's affidavit"). *Cf. Mallett v. Holiday Inn*, 2020 WL 1558113, at *1 (E.D. Tenn. Mar. 31, 2020) (bill and text messages from process server do not qualify as affidavit); *Henderson v. Los Angeles County*, 2013 WL 6255610, at *1 (E.D.N.C. Dec. 4, 2013) (post office receipts not acceptable substitutes for affidavits).

[375]*See Udoinyion v. Guardian Sec.*, 440 Fed.Appx. 731, 735 (11th Cir. 2011) (unsworn statement under penalty of perjury permitted); *TracFone Wireless, Inc. v. Unlimited PCS Inc.*, 279 F.R.D. 626, 631 (S.D.Fla. 2012) (copy of FedEx proof-of-signature form permitted in Rule 4(f)(2) international service case).

agreement, proof of service must be in accordance with that treaty or agreement.[376] If service is made in any other manner, proof of service must include a receipt signed by the addressee or other satisfactory evidence of delivery.[377]

Failure to Present Proof of Service

The plaintiff "must" make a proof of service to the court.[378] But a failure to perform that filing chore will not negate a service of process that had been otherwise properly accomplished.[379] Thus, a defendant cannot claim a postponement of its duty to respond to a complaint merely because no proof of service has yet been filed or, if filed, is somehow flawed in form.[380] This liberality in proving a successful service does not, of course, excuse the obligation to actually accomplish a proper, timely service of process.[381] A failure to prove service may still have some consequences, however. Unless the court has other grounds for finding that service has been properly accomplished, the failure to file a proof of service will likely defeat the court's ability to enter a default judgment.[382]

Amendment to Proof of Service

Where an amendment would cure the defect in the proof of service, the courts generally will grant leave to so amend.[383]

---

[376] *See Northrup King Co. v. Compania Productora Semillas Algodoneras Selectas, S.A.*, 51 F.3d 1383, 1389 (8th Cir. 1995) (certificate of service prepared by Central Authority of *Hague Convention* signatory Nation is "prima facie evidence" of Convention-compliant service); *Ackourey v. Noblehouse Custom Tailors*, 2013 WL 6061365, at *4 (E.D. Pa. Nov. 15, 2013) (in *Hague Convention* service by postal mail, defendants' written acknowledgement of receipt deemed sufficient). *Cf. Burda Media, Inc. v. Viertel*, 417 F.3d 292, 300–02 (2d Cir. 2005) (accepting substitute for formal certificate when defendant suffered no prejudice).

[377] *See Atlantis Marine Towing Salvage & Servs., Inc. v. Escapade Marine Ventures*, 2020 WL 7427023, at *3 (S.D. Fla. Dec. 1, 2020) (FedEx proof of signature can be sufficient for Rule 4(f)(3) service).

[378] *See Mann v. Castiel*, 681 F.3d 368, 373 (D.C.Cir. 2012).

[379] *See* Rule 4(*l*)(3). *See also McLean v. Wayside Outreach Dev. Inc.*, 624 Fed. Appx. 44, 44–45 (2d Cir. 2015) (if defendant actually served, failure to file affidavit was not prejudicial); *Gusler v. City of Long Beach*, 823 F. Supp. 2d 98, 123 (E.D.N.Y. 2011) (belated filing of proof of service did not affect validity of service).

[380] *See Mann v. Castiel*, 681 F.3d 368, 373 (D.C. Cir. 2012).

[381] *See* Rule 4(m). *See also Chhaparwal v. West Virginia University Hospitals, Inc.*, 2008 WL 2543429, at *3 (N.D. W. Va. 2008).

[382] *See Thomas v. Abebe*, 833 Fed. Appx. 551, 555 (5th Cir. 2020); *Smith v. Okla. ex rel. Tulsa Cty. Dist. Att'y Office*, 798 Fed. Appx. 319, 321 (10th Cir. 2020).

[383] *See Hawbecker v. Hall*, 88 F. Supp. 3d 723, 726 (W.D. Tex. 2015) (allowing amendment to correct name appearing on proof of service); *Nolan v. City of Yonkers*, 168 F.R.D. 140, 143 (S.D. N.Y. 1996) (request to amend proof of service should rarely be refused, and then granting leave to do so).

RULE 4(m)—TIME LIMIT FOR SERVICE

CORE CONCEPT

The summons and complaint must be served within 90 days after the complaint is filed, unless the plaintiff is able to show "good cause" why process could not be served within that time. If "good cause" is not shown, the district court must either dismiss the lawsuit without prejudice or, in its discretion, direct that service be accomplished within a new specified time.

APPLICATIONS

Timely Service — The 90-Day Service Period

A federal lawsuit is "commenced" by filing the complaint,[384] and then remains pending for 90 days to enable the claimant to accomplish a valid service of process upon (or obtain a waiver from) each defendant. Failure to complete service within that 90-day window exposes the lawsuit to dismissal.

- *Shortened Period:* This current 90-day period took effect in 2015, reducing the former 120-day period to help trim litigation time.[385] With that shortening, it was anticipated that "good cause" for extensions may occur more often (for example, after a refused waiver request, when a particular defendant proves difficult to serve, or if service is to be made by the U.S. Marshal).[386]
- *Applies to Pro Se / In Forma Pauperis Litigants:* Although their submissions are generally examined with liberality, the 90-day service window still applies to all *pro se*[387] and *in forma pauperis*[388] litigants. Some courts have ruled, however, that the 90-day period will not start running until a pending motion to proceed *in forma pauperis* is granted or, if denied, the filing is otherwise perfected (*i.e.*, filing fee is paid).[389]

Dismissals for Failing to Serve Within 90 Days

Dismissals under this Rule for failure to timely serve process are made without prejudice.[390] If, however, a re-filed complaint would be beyond the applicable statute of limitations, the Rule 4(m) dismissal "without prejudice" will not defeat an

---

[384] *See* Rule 3.

[385] Rule 4(m) advisory committee's note (2015).

[386] *Id.*

[387] *See DiCesare v. Stuart*, 12 F.3d 973, 980 (10th Cir. 1993); *Chrisp v. Univ. of N. Carolina-Chapel Hill*, 471 F. Supp. 3d 713, 715–16 (M.D.N.C. 2020).

[388] *See Evans v. Staples, Inc.*, 375 F. Supp. 3d 117, 121–22 (D. Mass. 2019) (accepting that Rule 4(m) applies, but granting extension); *Matthews v. Marten Transp., Ltd.*, 354 F. Supp. 2d 899, 901–02 (W.D. Wis. 2005) (same, and finding service timely made).

[389] *See Robinson v. Clipse*, 602 F.3d 605, 608–09 (4th Cir. 2010); *Richardson v. Johnson*, 598 F.3d 734, 739 (11th Cir. 2010).

[390] *See Mack v. Dillon*, 594 F.3d 620, 622 (8th Cir. 2010); *Lemoge v. U.S.*, 587 F.3d 1188, 1195–98 (9th Cir. 2009).

affirmative defense asserting time-bar.[391] Moreover, a Rule 4(m) dismissal is generally considered an abandoned claim, and is accorded no interruptive effect on the running of the statute of limitations; thus, the dismissal is the equivalent (for these purposes) of the claim having never been filed at all.[392]

Distinction: Mandatory *versus* Permissive Extensions

Under the pre-1993 version of Rule 4,[393] unless the plaintiff could demonstrate "good cause" for failing to timely serve process, the district court had no alternative but to dismiss the lawsuit without prejudice. Now, under current Rule 4(m), courts distinguish between justified delay ("good cause") and excusable neglect.[394] As to the former (justified delay), the district court *must* grant a plaintiff an extension for "an appropriate period."[395] When "good cause" is not shown, the district court has the option of either dismissing the lawsuit without prejudice or, in the exercise of its discretion, excusing the delay by issuing an order that directs that service be completed within a specified additional period of time.[396]

Mandatory "Good Cause" Extensions

The plaintiff bears the burden of proving that "good cause" exists to excuse a delay in service of process.[397] No fixed guidelines define "good cause,"[398] and it remains an exercise of discretion.[399] But the burden of showing "good cause" is heavy.[400] It typically requires a showing of both diligence on the server's

---

[391]*See Conover v. Lein*, 87 F.3d 905, 908–09 (7th Cir. 1996) (dismissals "without prejudice" under Rule 4(m) are not necessarily dismissals "without consequence," if the pertinent statutes of limitations have run); *Hawkins v. McHugh*, 46 F.3d 10, 12 (5th Cir.1995) (dismissal does not interrupt prescription or toll the prescription period). *See also Cardenas v. City of Chicago*, 646 F.3d 1001, 1008 (7th Cir. 2011) (although ordinarily without prejudice, Rule 4(m) dismissals may be made with prejudice if limitations period has expired).

[392]*See Cruz v. Louisiana ex rel. Dept. of Public Safety and Corrections*, 528 F.3d 375, 379 (5th Cir. 2008).

[393]The prior practice, former Rule 4(j), provided: "If a service of the summons and complaint is not made upon a defendant within 120 days after the filing of the complaint and the party on whose behalf such service was required cannot show good cause why such service was not made within that period, the action shall be dismissed as to that defendant without prejudice upon the court's own initiative with notice to such party or upon motion."

[394]*See Coleman v. Milwaukee Bd. of School Directors*, 290 F.3d 932, 934 (7th Cir. 2002).

[395]*See Morrissey v. Mayorkas*, 17 F.4th 1150, 1156 (D.C. Cir. 2021); *Davis v. Samuels*, 962 F.3d 105, 116 (3d Cir. 2020).

[396]*See Gelin v. Shuman*, 35 F.4th 212, 218–20 (4th Cir. 2022); *Morrissey v. Mayorkas*, 17 F.4th 1150, 1156 (D.C. Cir. 2021).

[397]*See Lepone-Dempsey v. Carroll County Com'rs*, 476 F.3d 1277, 1281 (11th Cir. 2007); *Nafziger v. McDermott Intern., Inc.*, 467 F.3d 514, 521 (6th Cir. 2006).

[398]*See Kurka v. Iowa County*, 628 F.3d 953, 957 (8th Cir. 2010).

[399]*See Zapata v. City of New York*, 502 F.3d 192, 197 (2d Cir. 2007); *Byrd v. Stone*, 94 F.3d 217, 219 (6th Cir. 1996).

[400]*See Kogan v. Facebook, Inc.*, 334 F.R.D. 393, 401–02 (S.D.N.Y. 2020); *Ashbourne v. Hansberry*, 302 F. Supp.

part[401] and a valid reason for the delay.[402] In an appropriate circumstance, courts may also balance whether the delay has caused prejudice to the defendant.[403] Accordingly, a service-evading defendant,[404] difficulty in obtaining defendant-identifying information,[405] a pending bankruptcy stay,[406] a sudden illness or natural catastrophe,[407] or some similarly intruding external factor[408] may justify a finding of "good cause". The "good cause" standard is, thus, applied narrowly to protect only those litigants who have exercised meticulous care in attempting to complete service.[409] Inadvertence or negligence by counsel is not enough,[410] nor is the mere absence of "bad" faith.[411] As one court aptly warned: "The lesson to the federal plaintiff's lawyer is not to take any chances. Treat the [Rule 4(m) time limit] with the respect reserved for a time bomb."[412] After all, the disserved litigants are usually not left without a remedy: they likely acquire a professional malpractice claim against

3d 338, 345 (D.D.C. 2018).

[401]*See Gelin v. Shuman*, 35 F.4th 212, 218 (4th Cir. 2022); *Jewell v. BestBus Co.*, 319 F. Supp. 3d 323, 325 (D.D.C. 2018). *See generally In re Ohio Execution Protocol Litig.*, 370 F. Supp. 3d 812, 816 (S.D. Ohio 2019) (" 'half-hearted efforts' do not constitute good cause").

[402]*See Mann v. Castiel*, 681 F.3d 368, 375 (D.C. Cir. 2012). *See also Kurka v. Iowa Cty.*, 628 F.3d 953, 957 (8th Cir. 2010) (requires good faith and reasonable basis for noncompliance with service rules).

[403]*See Haidon v. Budlong & Budlong, LLC*, 318 F. Supp. 3d 568, 576 (W.D.N.Y. 2018).

[404]*See Mann v. Castiel*, 681 F.3d 368, 374 (D.C.Cir. 2012); *Coleman v. Milwaukee Bd. of Sch. Dtrs.*, 290 F.3d 932, 934 (7th Cir. 2002).

[405]*See In re Ohio Execution Protocol Litig.*, 370 F. Supp. 3d 812, 819–20 (S.D. Ohio 2019); *Strike 3 Holdings, LLC v. Doe*, 337 F. Supp. 3d 246, 258 (W.D.N.Y. 2018).

[406]*See De Tie v. Orange County*, 152 F.3d 1109, 1111–12 (9th Cir. 1998).

[407]*See Matasareanu v. Williams*, 183 F.R.D. 242, 246 (C.D. Cal. 1998); *Gambino v. Village of Oakbrook*, 164 F.R.D. 271, 274 (M.D. Fla. 1995).

[408]*See Gelin v. Shuman*, 35 F.4th 212, 218 (4th Cir. 2022); *Bilal v. Geo Care, LLC*, 981 F.3d 903, 919 (11th Cir. 2020).

[409]*See Despain v. Salt Lake Area Metro Gang Unit*, 13 F.3d 1436, 1438 (10th Cir. 1994). *Cf. Gelin v. Shuman*, 35 F.4th 212, 218 (4th Cir. 2022) (single, failed search for defendants' addresses followed by 10 months delay before seeking extension does not qualify as "good cause").

[410]*See Kogan v. Facebook, Inc.*, 334 F.R.D. 393, 401-02 (S.D.N.Y. 2020); *Estate of Goodwin by & through Alvarado v. Connell*, 376 F. Supp. 3d 1133, 1153 (D. Colo. 2019). *Cf. Lepone-Dempsey v. Carroll County Com'rs*, 476 F.3d 1277, 1282 (11th Cir. 2007) (relying on defendant's assertion that he would sign waiver form was not "good cause") *and Matasareanu v. Williams*, 183 F.R.D. 242, 246 (C.D. Cal. 1998) (lack of legal training and attorney guidance does not constitute "good cause") *and Braithwaite v. Johns Hopkins Hosp.*, 160 F.R.D. 75, 77–78 (D. Md. 1995) (delay resulting from the psychological distress caused by the murder of plaintiff's only daughter during service period did not constitute "good cause").

[411]*See Collins v. Thornton*, 782 Fed. Appx. 264, 267 (4th Cir. 2019).

[412]*Braxton v. U.S.*, 817 F.2d 238, 241 (3d Cir. 1987) (quoting *Siegel, Practice Commentary on Amendment of Federal Rule 4 (Eff. Feb. 26, 1983) with Special Statute of Limitations Precautions*, 96 F.R.D. 88, 103 (1983)).

their counsel.[413]

- *"Good Cause" and U.S. Marshal Delays:* The court may order service by the U.S. Marshal (and must do so for *in forma pauperis* plaintiffs).[414] In such circumstances, "good cause" extensions may be granted when service is delayed due to issues fairly attributable to the Marshal.[415] But such extensions are not guaranteed in all cases:[416] the plaintiff must have properly cooperated with the Marshal (by, for example, supplying an accurate service address)[417] and may even be expected to monitor the efforts of the Marshal or seek a pre-expiration extension.[418] A delay caused by plaintiff's own errors may not merit a "good faith" extension.[419]

Permissive Extensions

When "good cause" is not shown, the decision whether to dismiss or grant a further extension is committed to the district court's discretion;[420] essentially, plaintiffs throw themselves "on the mercy of the district court."[421] Indeed, appellate review is so deferential that any reasoned, principled decision by the trial court is likely to be affirmed.[422]

Although Rule 4(m) lists no criteria for making this determination,[423] the district court is nevertheless still obligated to consider whether circumstances exist to warrant an extension

---

[413]*See Kogan v. Facebook, Inc.*, 334 F.R.D. 393, 407 (S.D.N.Y. 2020).

[414]*See* Rule 4(c)(3) and accompanying Authors' Commentary.

[415]*See Wright v. First Student, Inc.*, 710 F.3d 782, 783–84 (8th Cir. 2013); *Mann v. Castiel*, 681 F.3d 368, 374–75 (D.C.Cir. 2012).

[416]*See Evans v. Staples, Inc.*, 375 F. Supp. 3d 117, 120 (D. Mass. 2019).

[417]*See Brooks v. Johnson*, 924 F.3d 104, 120–21 (4th Cir. 2019); *Fields v. Oklahoma State Penitentiary*, 511 F.3d 1109, 1113 (10th Cir. 2007).

[418]*See Murphy v. City of Tulsa*, 556 Fed. Appx. 664, 668 (10th Cir. 2014) (noting division among courts, and ruling against "good cause"); *Meilleur v. Strong*, 682 F.3d 56, 63 (2d Cir. 2012).

[419]*See Hobbs v. Oklahoma State Penitentiary*, 673 Fed. Appx. 837, 839 (10th Cir. 2016); *Brown v. Davis*, 656 Fed. Appx. 920, 921 (11th Cir. 2016). *See also Brooks v. Johnson*, 924 F.3d 104, 120–21 (4th Cir. 2019) (belated delivery on improper Marshal form did not negate good faith).

[420]*See Jones v. Ramos*, 12 F.4th 745, 749 (7th Cir. 2021); *Davis v. Samuels*, 962 F.3d 105, 116 (3d Cir. 2020). *But see Harris v. South Charlotte Pre-Owned Auto Warehouse, LLC*, 2015 WL 1893839, at *3–*5 (W.D.N.C. Apr. 27, 2015) (recounting split within Fourth Circuit as to whether any extensions are permitted absent good cause).

[421]*See U.S. v. McLaughlin*, 470 F.3d 698, 700 (7th Cir. 2006).

[422]*See Kurka v. Iowa County*, 628 F.3d 953, 959–60 (8th Cir. 2010) (although factors "favored" extension, no abuse of discretion to deny one); *Coleman v. Milwaukee Bd. of School Directors*, 290 F.3d 932, 934 (7th Cir. 2002) (although most judges "would exercise lenity and allow a late service," no abuse of discretion to deny it). *Compare U.S. v. McLaughlin*, 470 F.3d 698, 701 (7th Cir. 2006) (where service delay causes "zero prejudice" to any party or the court, granting permissive extension "cannot be an abuse of discretion").

[423]*See U.S. v. McLaughlin*, 470 F.3d 698, 700 (7th Cir. 2006).

of the 90-day service period.[424] (Although encouraged to do, the Rule does not require district judges to detail the reasoning for their rulings.[425]) In making this evaluation, the court may examine, among other factors, the length of and reasons for the delay, good faith, whether the delay was within the plaintiff's control, prejudice to the defendants, whether the applicable statute of limitations would bar a re-filing, whether the failure to timely serve was due to a difficulty in serving government officials, whether the offending party is proceeding *pro se*, whether the unserved defendant has been evading service or concealing a defect in service, and whether service was eventually accomplished and, if so, how far beyond the 90-day period.[426] Moreover, a defendant's admission of liability will prove an important factor tilting in favor of granting a permissive extension.[427]

- *Time-Bar Impact:* Although the effect of the applicable statute of limitations may be considered by the court in evaluating whether to grant a permissive extension,[428] this does not mean that a permissive extension is mandatory whenever a dismissal would result in a time-bar.[429] Instead, the district court must assess all circumstances, including the litigants' behavior as time-bar approached, in deciding whether a permissive extension is warranted.[430]

Substantive State Law Can Impact 90-Day Period

The substantive laws of some States provide that merely filing a complaint does not toll the applicable statutes of limitations. In those instances, Rule 4(m) will not prevent a cause of action from becoming time-barred during the 90-day

[424] *See Bilal v. Geo Care, LLC*, 981 F.3d 903, 919 (11th Cir. 2020); *Panaras v. Liquid Carbonic Industries Corp.*, 94 F.3d 338, 341 (7th Cir. 1996).

[425] *See Jones v. Ramos*, 12 F.4th 745, 749 (7th Cir. 2021).

[426] *See, e.g., Cardenas v. City of Chicago*, 646 F.3d 1001, 1006 (7th Cir. 2011); *Kurka v. Iowa County*, 628 F.3d 953, 959 (8th Cir. 2010).

[427] *See U.S. v. McLaughlin*, 470 F.3d 698, 701 (7th Cir. 2006).

[428] *See In re Cutuli*, 13 F.4th 1342, 1348 (11th Cir. 2021); *Jones v. Ramos*, 12 F.4th 745, 749 (7th Cir. 2021).

[429] *See Morrissey v. Mayorkas*, 17 F.4th 1150, 1159–60 & 1162 (D.C. Cir. 2021); *Jones v. Ramos*, 12 F.4th 745, 750–51 (7th Cir. 2021). *But cf. Millan v. USAA General Indem. Co.*, 546 F.3d 321, 326 (5th Cir. 2008) (if timebar would result, court may only dismiss upon clear record of delay or contumacious conduct by plaintiff, the absence of a lesser but better sanction, *and* presence of aggravating factor (*e.g.*, delay by client not lawyer, actual prejudice to defendant, delay caused intentionally)).

[430] *See Kogan v. Facebook, Inc.*, 334 F.R.D. 393, 404–07 (S.D.N.Y. 2020) (denying extension, even with time-bar, where plaintiff knew of looming deadline, was reminded about it by defendants, and still made no effort to serve or seek extension); *Morrissey v. Wolf*, 333 F.R.D. 1, 3 (D.D.C. 2019), *aff'd*, 17 F.4th 1150 (D.C. Cir. 2020) (denying extension, even with time-bar, where plaintiff was not *pro se* and received notice from court about Rule 4(m) obligation two weeks before deadline).

service period, if State law would so dictate.[431]

Defendants Can Waive 90-Day Period

Although Rule 4(m) contains mandatory-sounding dismissal language, defendants may still waive the 90-day service period by (among other ways) failing to raise that objection in any Rule 12 motion that is filed.[432]

Sua Sponte Dismissals and Extensions

When service has not been effected within the 90-day service period, the court need not wait for a party's motion to act. On its own initiative, the court may dismiss the action[433] or may order that service be completed within some new, specified time.[434] Either *sua sponte* action requires prior "notice to the plaintiff."[435]

Foreign Service and the 90-Day Period

The 90-day service rule does not apply when service is made outside the United States on an individual, corporation, partnership, or unincorporated association[436] or on a foreign state and its political subdivisions, agencies, and instrumentalities.[437] However, the time allowable for accomplishing foreign service is not necessarily unlimited, as district courts must retain the ability to control their dockets.[438] Some courts have conditioned this foreign service "exemption"

---

[431] *See Whidbee v. Pierce Cty.*, 857 F.3d 1019, 1022–25 (9th Cir. 2017) (Rule 4(m) did not preserve claims that were barred under Washington State limitations period before case was removed); *Larsen v. Mayo Med. Ctr.*, 218 F.3d 863, 868 (8th Cir. 2000) (not preserved when time-barred under Minnesota law); *Habermehl v. Potter*, 153 F.3d 1137, 1139 (10th Cir. 1998) (same, under Wyoming law). *See also* Authors' Commentary to Rule 3 ("**Diversity Jurisdiction Cases**" and "**Supplemental Jurisdiction Cases**").

[432] *See Cabrera v. CMG Dev. LLC*, 717 Fed. Appx. 841, 845 (11th Cir. 2017); *McCurdy v. American Bd. of Plastic Surgery*, 157 F.3d 191, 195 (3d Cir. 1998) (citing cases).

[433] *See* Rule 4(m).

[434] *See Cable v. Coyne-Fague*, 438 F. Supp. 3d 143, 147 (D.R.I. 2020).

[435] *See Meilleur v. Strong*, 682 F.3d 56, 61 (2d Cir. 2012); *Sanders v. Southwestern Bell Tel., L.P.*, 544 F.3d 1101, 1111 (10th Cir. 2008). *See also Walker v. Pa. Dep't of Transp.*, 812 Fed. Appx. 93, 94–95 (3d Cir. 2020) (abuse of discretion to grant *sua sponte* dismissal without prior notice).

[436] *See* Rule 4(m) (referencing Rule 4(f) (serving individuals in foreign country) and Rule 4(h)(2) (serving corporations, partnerships, and unincorporated associations in foreign country). *See Brown-Thomas v. Hynie*, 367 F. Supp. 3d 452, 461 & 467 (D.S.C. 2019); *Rose v. Bersa*, 327 F.R.D. 628, 636 (S.D. Ohio 2018). *See generally Sang Young Kim v. Frank Mohn A/S*, 909 F. Supp. 474, 479–80 (S.D. Tex. 1995) (exclusion of foreign service from time limit "helps to counterbalance the complex and time-consuming nature of foreign service of process").

[437] *See* Rule 4(m) (referencing Rule 4(j)(1)) (serving foreign States and their political subdivisions, agencies, and instrumentalities). *See also Barot v. Embassy of the Republic of Zambia*, 785 F.3d 26, 29 (D.C.Cir. 2015).

[438] *See Nylok Corp. v. Fastener World Inc.*, 396 F.3d 805, 807 (7th Cir. 2005); *Mumford v. Carnival Corp.*, 5 F. Supp. 3d 1365, 1366–67 (S.D. Fla. 2014). *But see Lucas v. Natoli*, 936 F.2d 432, 432–33 (9th Cir.1991) (window for foreign service is unbounded).

on a showing that good faith attempts were made to serve within the 90-day period; if no such attempts were made, these courts hold that the exemption will not apply and the passage of 90 days can justify a dismissal.[439] Other courts have applied a more encompassing "flexible due diligence" standard to decide if a post-90 day foreign service ought to be allowed.[440]

Removed Cases and the 90-Day Period

In removed cases, the 90-day service period runs from the date of removal as to parties who have not yet been served at all, on whom service has not been perfected, or on whom an attempted service proves to be defective.[441]

Amended Complaints and the 90-Day Period

Amending a complaint does not usually "reset" the 90-day service period.[442] However, if the amendment adds new parties to the lawsuit, the 90-day period to serve those new parties begins to run from the date of the amendment.[443] Such an amendment does not usually extend the time for serving the original defendants.[444]

RULE 4(n)—ASSERTING JURISDICTION OVER PROPERTY OR ASSETS

CORE CONCEPT

If authorized by federal statute, the district court may exercise jurisdiction over property. Otherwise, the district court may exercise jurisdiction over a defendant's property only if the property is found within the court's federal district and, then, only when personal (*in personam*) jurisdiction over that defendant cannot be reasonably obtained; in such cases, jurisdiction is acquired by seizing the property as permitted under State law.

APPLICATIONS

Procedure For Property-Based Jurisdiction

A federal court may exercise *in-rem* or *quasi-in-rem* juris-

[439] *See USHA (India), Ltd. v. Honeywell Intern., Inc.*, 421 F.3d 129, 134 (2d Cir. 2005); *Allstate Ins. Co. v. Funai Corp.*, 249 F.R.D. 157, 161–62 (M.D. Pa. 2008).

[440] *See Harris v. Orange S.A.*, 636 Fed. Appx. 476, 485–86 (11th Cir. 2015); *Lozano v. Bosdet*, 693 F.3d 485, 488–89 (5th Cir. 2012).

[441] *See* 28 U.S.C.A. § 1448. *See also UWM Student Ass'n v. Lovell*, 888 F.3d 854, 858 (7th Cir. 2018); *Whidbee v. Pierce Cty.*, 857 F.3d 1019, 1023 (9th Cir. 2017).

[442] *See UWM Student Ass'n v. Lovell*, 888 F.3d 854, 859 (7th Cir. 2018); *Lee v. Airgas Mid-S., Inc.*, 793 F.3d 894, 898 (8th Cir. 2015).

[443] *See City of Merced v. Fields*, 997 F. Supp. 1326, 1338 (E.D. Cal. 1998); *Del Raine v. Carlson*, 153 F.R.D. 622, 628 (S.D. Ill. 1994), rev'd in part on other grounds, 77 F.3d 484 (7th Cir. 1996) (Table).

[444] *See Lindley v. City of Birmingham*, 452 Fed.Appx. 878, 880 (11th Cir. 2011); *Brait Builders Corp. v. Mass. Div. of Capital Asset Mgmt.*, 644 F.3d 5, 9 (1st Cir. 2011).

diction[445] over tangible and intangible[446] property located within its geographic district,[447] but only in two circumstances:

- *Federal Statute:* when a federal statute permits it;[448] in such cases, the required notice to claimants of the property must either conform to the statute's requirements[449] or be accomplished by serving a summons under this Rule 4; or
- *State Law:* when a defendant's assets are found in the district, but only upon a showing that personal jurisdiction over the defendant cannot be obtained there by reasonable efforts to serve a summons under this Rule 4;[450] in such cases, jurisdiction is acquired by seizing the assets under circumstances and in a manner provided by the local State law.

In addition to satisfying these Rule 4(n) requirements, the court's exercise of property-based jurisdiction must, of course, also meet constitutional due process standards.[451]

Effect

A judgment in a *quasi-in-rem* or *in-rem* lawsuit acts only upon the seized property; it has no *in personam* effect. Thus, a plaintiff cannot enforce a *quasi-in-rem* or *in-rem* judgment against property of the defendant located outside the forum State.[452]

Amount in Controversy

A judgment in a *quasi-in-rem* or *in-rem* action only permits execution of the seized property; the courts, however, are divided on the proper method for computing the amount in controversy in diversity cases—either by the value of the seized property or the sum stated in the complaint's demand clause.[453]

Note: If the plaintiff's claim exceeds the value of seized

---

[445]For a discussion of *in rem* and *quasi in rem* jurisdiction, see *supra* Part II §§ 2.6–2.7.

[446]*See Office Depot Inc. v. Zuccarini*, 596 F.3d 696, 700 (9th Cir. 2010) (citing *Harris v. Balk*, 198 U.S. 215 (1905)).

[447]*See Office Depot Inc. v. Zuccarini*, 596 F.3d 696, 700 (9th Cir. 2010).

[448]*See, e.g.*, 28 U.S.C.A. § 1655.

[449]*See United States v. Bank Acct. No. 3200335471*, 538 F. Supp. 2d 463, 467 (D.P.R. 2008) (in accord with federal civil forfeiture statute); *Cable News Network L.P., L.L.L.P. v. CNNews.com*, 162 F. Supp. 2d 484, 494 (E.D. Va. 2001), *aff'd in part, vacated in part on other grounds*, 56 Fed. Appx. 599 (4th Cir. 2003) (in accord with federal anticybersquatting consumer protection act).

[450]*See* Rule 4(n)(2) advisory committee note (1993) (Rule language limits use to "rare" occasions and "exigent circumstances," given both the liberalized availability of personal jurisdiction and due process constraints).

[451]*See Shaffer v. Heitner*, 433 U.S. 186, 207–12, 97 S. Ct. 2569, 53 L. Ed. 2d 683 (1977); *Office Depot Inc. v. Zuccarini*, 596 F.3d 696, 700 (9th Cir. 2010).

[452]*See Shaffer v. Heitner*, 433 U.S. 186, 207 n.23, 97 S. Ct. 2569, 53 L. Ed. 2d 683 (1977) (liability of *in rem* defendant limited to value of property).

[453]*See Great Am. Ins. Co. v. Louis Lesser Enterprises, Inc.*, 353 F.2d 997, 1007–08 (8th Cir. 1965) (noting dis-

property, the plaintiff is free to sue elsewhere for the remaining, unrecovered amount of the claim.[454]

Additional Research References

Wright & Miller, *Federal Practice and Procedure* §§ 1061 to 1137
C.J.S., Federal Civil Procedure §§ 187 to 223
West's Key Number Digest, Process ⚷1 to 47, ⚷48 to 150, ⚷151 to 167

---

agreement among courts).

[454]*See generally U. S. Indus., Inc. v. Gregg*, 58 F.R.D. 469, 475 n.23 (D. Del. 1973) ("A quasi-in-rem judgment does not have a *res judicata* effect on a subsequent action on the same claim, and collateral estoppel does not apply even as to issues actually litigated as long as the judgment is against the property and not the person.").

RULE 4.1
SERVING OTHER PROCESS

(a) In General. Process—other than a summons under Rule 4 or a subpoena under Rule 45—must be served by a United States marshal or deputy marshal or by a person specially appointed for that purpose. It may be served anywhere within the territorial limits of the state where the district court is located and, if authorized by a federal statute, beyond those limits. Proof of service must be made under Rule 4(*l*).

(b) Enforcing Orders: Committing for Civil Contempt. An order committing a person for civil contempt of a decree or injunction issued to enforce federal law may be served and enforced in any district. Any other order in a civil-contempt proceeding may be served only in the state where the issuing court is located or elsewhere in the United States within 100 miles from where the order was issued.

[Adopted April 22, 1993, effective December 1, 1993; April 30, 2007, effective December 1, 2007.]

AUTHORS' COMMENTARY ON RULE 4.1

PURPOSE AND SCOPE

Rule 4.1 sets the procedure for service of types of process other than a civil summons or a subpoena. Such process is served either by a U.S. Marshal or by an individual specially appointed by the court.

APPLICATIONS

What Is "Other Process"

Service of original process is governed by Rule 4, and service of a subpoena is governed by Rule 45. Any "other process" is governed by this Rule 4.1. Such "other process" includes execution orders,[1] orders of civil commitment,[2] orders to show cause,[3] garnishment orders,[4] and certain orders for injunctions, attachments, arrests, and judicial sales.[5] Note, however, that service of process is generally *not* required for decrees and injunctions issued upon existing parties (those who have already been served with original process).[6] Rule 4.1 does not apply to orders of criminal commitment. But the Rule does contemplate a bench warrant for civil contempt of a decree of injunction issued to enforce a federal law.[7]

Process Server

"Other process" must be served either by the U.S. Marshal, a deputy Marshal, or some other person specially appointed for the purpose by the court.[8] A private process server may be so appointed.[9] (Whether to appoint a Marshal or some other person is left to the court's discretion, unless the plaintiff is a pauper or seaman.[10]) Service performed by anyone else is defective.[11] To date, the only case law exception to this requirement appears in the context of process to enforce a judgment for the payment of money. Such enforcement proceedings are governed by Rule 69(a), which provides that the "procedure on execution" must follow State practice. At least one court has held that, notwithstanding the broad, general language of Rule 4.1, the provisions of Rule 69(a) compel that State practice govern the service of process in execution proceedings.[12]

Limits of Service

"Other process" may be served either within the State in which the district court is sitting or as otherwise provided by

---

[1]*See Schneider v. National R.R. Passenger Corp.*, 72 F.3d 17, 20 (2d Cir. 1995).

[2]*See Spectacular Venture, L.P. v. World Star Intern., Inc.*, 927 F. Supp. 683, 685–86 (S.D. N.Y. 1996) (applying Rule 4.1 to civil contempt orders).

[3]*See Fidelity Nat'l Fin., Inc. v. Friedman*, 2010 WL 960420, at *6 (D.Ariz. Mar. 15, 2010).

[4]*See Macro Elecs. Corp. v. Biotech Restorations, L.L.C.*, 2022 WL 1912559, at *1 (M.D. Fla. June 3, 2022).

[5]*See First Sw. Fin. Servs., LLC v. Dennis Waters Constr., LLC*, 2019 WL 1782123, at *2–*3 (S.D. Ga. Apr. 23, 2019); *JTH Tax Inc. v. Lee*, 2007 WL 1320505, at *2 n.2 (C.D. Ill. 2007).

[6]*See U.S. v. Elmes*, 532 F.3d 1138, 1144 (11th Cir. 2008).

[7]*See United States v. Phillips*, 834 F.3d 1176, 1181 (11th Cir. 2016).

[8]*See Fidelity Nat'l Fin., Inc. v. Friedman*, 2010 WL 960420, at *6 (D.Ariz. Mar. 15, 2010).

[9]*See Sumner v. Garner*, 2019 WL 6716193, at *1-*2 (M.D. Fla. Dec. 9, 2019).

[10]*See JTH Tax Inc. v. Lee*, 2007 WL 1320505, at *2 (C.D. Ill. 2007).

[11]*See Schneider v. National R.R. Passenger Corp.*, 72 F.3d 17, 19–20 (2d Cir.1995) (State sheriff who "seized" Amtrak locomotives in course of executing upon $1.8 million plaintiff's personal injury judgment was not Marshal, deputy Marshal, or specially appointed process server, and thus process was defective under Rule 4.1 and sheriff was not entitled to service fee for executing upon trains).

[12]*See Apostolic Pentecostal Church v. Colbert*, 169 F.3d 409, 414 (6th Cir. 1999). *See also Hilao v. Estate of Ferdinand E. Marcos*, 95 F.3d 848, 851–53 (9th Cir. 1996).

federal statute.[13] Special procedures, however, guide serving and enforcing orders of civil commitment. Proper service and enforcement in those proceedings will depend on whether the law to be enforced is federal or State. If federal law, the order may be served and enforced in any federal district. If State law (as in diversity cases), the order may be served only within the State of the issuing court or elsewhere in the United States within 100 miles of where the order was issued.[14] Courts have, by order, approved service of civil commitment orders via forcible entry into premises where the parties in question were reasonably believed to be found, after other service attempts had failed.[15]

Proof of Service

The process server—the U.S. Marshal, deputy Marshal, or specially appointed person—must file a proof of service with the court as provided in Rule 4(*l*).[16]

---

[13]*See Hoult v. Hoult*, 373 F.3d 47, 53 (1st Cir. 2004). *See also United States ex rel. Bunk v. Gosselin Worldwide Moving, N.V.*, 2017 WL 4476846, at *8–*9 (E.D. Va. Aug. 22, 2017) (service of garnishment writ in Belgium not authorized).

[14]*See Dissolved Air Flotation Corp. v. Kothari*, 2019 WL 3017108, at *3 (E.D. Wis. July 10, 2019); *SD Protection, Inc. v. Del Rio*, 587 F. Supp. 2d 429, 435 (E.D.N.Y. 2008).

[15]*See KCI Auto Auction, Inc. v. Ephrem*, 2020 WL 5572775, at *1-*2 (D. Kan. Sept. 15, 2020).

[16]*See* Rule 4.1(a).

RULE 5
SERVING AND FILING PLEADINGS AND OTHER PAPERS

(a) Service: When Required.

(1) *In General.* Unless these rules provide otherwise, each of the following papers must be served on every party:

(A) an order stating that service is required;

(B) a pleading filed after the original complaint, unless the court orders otherwise under Rule 5(c) because there are numerous defendants;

(C) a discovery paper required to be served on a party, unless the court orders otherwise;

(D) a written motion, except one that may be heard ex parte; and

(E) a written notice, appearance, demand, or offer of judgment, or any similar paper.

(2) *If a Party Fails to Appear.* No service is required on a party who is in default for failing to appear. But a pleading that asserts a new claim for relief against such a party must be served on that party under Rule 4.

(3) *Seizing Property.* If an action is begun by seizing property and no person is or need be named as a defendant, any service required before the filing of an appearance, answer, or claim must be made on the person who had custody or possession of the property when it was seized.

(b) Service: How Made.

(1) *Serving an Attorney.* If a party is represented by an attorney, service under this rule must be made on the attorney unless the court orders service on the party.

(2) *Service in General.* A paper is served under this rule by:

(A) handing it to the person;

(B) leaving it:

(i) at the person's office with a clerk or other person in charge or, if no one is in charge, in a conspicuous place in the office; or

(ii) if the person has no office or the office is closed, at the person's dwelling or usual place of abode with someone of suitable age and discretion who resides there;

(C) mailing it to the person's last known address—in which event service is complete upon mailing;

(D) leaving it with the court clerk if the person has no known address;

(E) sending it to a registered user by filing it with the court's electronic-filing system or sending it by other electronic means that the person consented to in writing—in either of which events service is complete upon filing or sending, but is not effective if the filer or sender learns that it did not reach the person to be served; or

(F) delivering it by any other means that the person consented to in writing—in which event service is complete when the person making service delivers it to the agency designated to make delivery.

(3) *Using Court Facilities.* [Abrogated (Apr. 26, 2018, eff. Dec. 1, 2018.)]

(c) Serving Numerous Defendants.

(1) *In General.* If an action involves an unusually large number of defendants, the court may, on motion or on its own, order that:

(A) defendants' pleadings and replies to them need not be served on other defendants;

(B) any crossclaim, counterclaim, avoidance, or affirmative defense in those pleadings and replies to them will be treated as denied or avoided by all other parties; and

(C) filing any such pleading and serving it on the plaintiff constitutes notice of the pleading to all parties.

(2) *Notifying Parties.* A copy of every such order

must be served on the parties as the court directs.

(d) Filing.

(1) *Required Filings; Certificate of Service.*

(A) *Papers after the Complaint.* Any paper after the complaint that is required to be served must be filed no later than a reasonable time after service. But disclosures under Rule 26(a)(1) or (2) and the following discovery requests and responses must not be filed until they are used in the proceeding or the court orders filing: depositions, interrogatories, requests for documents or tangible things or to permit entry onto land, and requests for admission.

(B) *Certificate of Service.* No certificate of service is required when a paper is served by filing it with the court's electronic-filing system. When a paper that is required to be served is served by other means:

(i) if the paper is filed, a certificate of service must be filed with it or within a reasonable time after service; and

(ii) if the paper is not filed, a certificate of service need not be filed unless filing is required by court order or by local rule.

(2) *Nonelectronic Filing.* A paper not filed electronically is filed by delivering it:

(A) to the clerk; or

(B) to a judge who agrees to accept it for filing, and who must then note the filing date on the paper and promptly send it to the clerk.

(3) *Electronic Filing and Signing.*

(A) *By a Represented Person—Generally Required; Exceptions.* A person represented by an attorney must file electronically, unless nonelectronic filing is allowed by the court for good cause or is allowed or required by local rule.

(B) *By an Unrepresented Person—When Allowed or Required.* A person not represented by an attorney:

(i) may file electronically only if allowed by court order or by local rule; and

(ii) may be required to file electronically only by court order, or by a local rule that includes reasonable exceptions.

(C) *Signing.* A filing made through a person's electronic-filing account and authorized by that person, together with that person's name on a signature block, constitutes the person's signature.

(D) *Same as a Written Paper.* A paper filed electronically is a written paper for purposes of these rules.

(4) *Acceptance by the Clerk.* The clerk must not refuse to file a paper solely because it is not in the form prescribed by these rules or by a local rule or practice.

[Amended January 21, 1963, effective July 1, 1963; March 30, 1970, effective July 1, 1970; April 29, 1980, effective August 1, 1980; March 2, 1987, effective August 1, 1987; April 30, 1991, effective December 1, 1991; April 22, 1993, effective December 1, 1993; April 23, 1996, effective December 1, 1996; April 17, 2000, effective December 1, 2000; April 23, 2001, effective December 1, 2001; April 12, 2006, effective December 1, 2006; April 30, 2007, effective December 1, 2007; April 26, 2018, effective December 1, 2018.)

AUTHORS' COMMENTARY ON RULE 5

PURPOSE AND SCOPE

Rule 5 addresses what Rule 4 does not — the service and filing requirements for papers *after* the original complaint. Those requirements are less rigorous than the procedures governing service of original process. But service and filing of subsequent papers in a federal civil lawsuit are important for two obvious reasons: to ensure that each party receives a copy of all documents formally used by their co-parties in prosecuting and defending the case and to create a complete, rationally-assembled record with the clerk. Other Rules establish specialized service requirements for particular circumstances (*e.g.*, Rule 45(b), governing service of subpoenas), and many district courts have local rules that impose other service and filing duties.

Rule 5 describes which other papers (after the original complaint) must be served in a lawsuit; most papers will fall within that obligation. Exceptions are made for parties who default.

Typically, service is made on a party's attorney, not on the party directly (assuming the party is represented). Rule 5 sets out the allowable means for accomplishing that delivery. Rule 5 then establishes filing obligations for legal papers. Parties represented by an attorney must file their papers electronically, unless the court or a local rule permits otherwise. Unrepresented parties may not file electronically, unless the court or a local rule allows it. Neither the clerk of court nor its automated filing system may refuse to accept a filing because of a defect in the paper's form.

RULE 5(a)—SERVICE REQUIRED

CORE CONCEPT

Unless specifically excused by the court, every party who has entered an appearance must be served with a copy of:

- *All Orders required by their terms to be served* (*i.e.*, Rule 77(d) notices of entry of orders);
- *All Pleadings After the Original Complaint*, including amended complaints;
- *All Discovery Papers*;
- *All Written Motions* (except *ex parte* motions); and
- *Other Legal Papers* (such as written notices, appearances, demands, offers of judgment,[1] arbitration awards,[2] and similar papers).

APPLICATIONS

Broadly Construed

Courts expansively construe Rule 5's inventory of legal papers that must be served.[3]

Pleadings Asserting Claims Against New Parties

Pleadings asserting claims against new parties (*e.g.*, third-party claims) constitute "original process" and must be served pursuant to Rule 4.[4] (Rule 5 service is not sufficient.)

Pleadings Asserting Claims Against Existing Parties

Pleadings modifying pending claims or asserting new claims against existing parties (*i.e.*, by amending an original pleading) may usually be served under the less rigorous Rule 5 proce-

---

[1] *See Magnuson v. Video Yesteryear*, 85 F.3d 1424, 1429 (9th Cir. 1996) (service of Rule 68 offers must comply with Rule 5).

[2] *See Hone v. Wal-Mart Stores E., LP*, 2016 WL 6208267, at *3 (D.N.J. Oct. 24, 2016).

[3] *See, e.g., Almy v. Kickert Sch. Bus Line, Inc.*, 2013 WL 80367, at *5 (N.D.Ill. Jan. 7, 2013) (briefs, though not explicitly noted in Rule 5(a), must be served), *aff'd*, 722 F.3d 1069 (7th Cir. 2013).

[4] *See* Rule 14(a)(1). *See also In re Tax Indebtedness of Townley*, 2002 WL 32026154, at *2 (E.D.Wash. Nov. 15, 2002).

dures,[5] provided service of original process has already been accomplished.[6] However, formal Rule 4 service (or, at least, service on the party directly) may be required if:

- New claims are asserted against parties who have defaulted;[7]
- The attorney no longer represents the party or other circumstances show that service on an attorney is unlikely to ensure notice to the party;[8] or
- Fairness or due process concerns compel it (such as where the nature of the claims has changed so fundamentally that the original basis for exercising personal jurisdiction is now in doubt).[9]

Pleadings / Other Papers Against Defaulting Parties

Once proper service of original process is accomplished under Rule 4, it is expected that the served party will appear and defend the case. If, instead, that party defaults, future pleadings and other papers in the lawsuit ordinarily do not need to be served on that party.[10] This encompasses amended complaints.[11] To this rule, there is one exception and one clarification. If a later pleading asserts a new claim for relief against the non-appearing party, that later pleading[12] must be served upon the non-appearing party pursuant to Rule 4, *as original process*.[13] This is intended to ensure that a party, once served, is able to make a fully informed decision, mindful of all

---

[5]*See Vax-D Medical Technologies, LLC v. Texas Spine Medical Center*, 485 F.3d 593, 597 (11th Cir. 2007); *Employee Painters' Trust v. Ethan Enterprises, Inc.*, 480 F.3d 993, 995–99 (9th Cir. 2007).

[6]If it has not, Rule 4 service would be required. *See Kaden v. Chamisa Arts, Inc.*, 2016 WL 7616692, at *3 (W.D. Tex. July 15, 2016); *PNC Bank, N.A. v. Twin Tier Dev. Grp., Inc.*, 2010 WL 5300819, at *1 (M.D. Pa. Dec. 20, 2010).

[7]*See* Rule 5(a)(2). *See also Employee Painters' Trust v. Ethan Enters., Inc.*, 480 F.3d 993, 999 (9th Cir. 2007). *See infra* Authors' Commentary to Rule 5(a) (**"Pleadings/ Other Papers Against Defaulting Parties"**).

[8]*See SEC v. Everest Mgmt. Corp.*, 87 F.R.D. 100, 102 (S.D.N.Y. 1980).

[9]*See, e.g.*, 4B CHARLES ALAN WRIGHT, ARTHUR R. MILLER, ADAM N. STEINMAN, FEDERAL PRACTICE AND PROCEDURE § 1146, at 459–62 (2015) (falling within this category may be cases where bases for personal jurisdiction supporting original filing do not encompass those needed for amended filing).

[10]*See* Rule 5(a)(2). *See also Belkin v. Islamic Republic of Iran*, 667 F. Supp. 2d 8, 19–20 (D.D.C. 2009); *Trustees of the St. Paul Elec. Const. Industry Fringe Benefit Funds v. Martens Elec. Co.*, 485 F. Supp. 2d 1063, 1066 (D. Minn. 2007).

[11]*See In re Chinese Manufactured Drywall Prod. Liab. Litig.*, 742 F.3d 576, 593–94 (5th Cir. 2014); *Blair v. City of Worcester*, 522 F.3d 105, 109 (1st Cir. 2008).

[12]*See Peterson v. Islamic Republic of Iran*, 627 F.3d 1117, 1130 n.5 (9th Cir. 2010) (exception applies only to new claims asserted in pleading (not in motions)).

[13]*See In re Chinese Mfd. Drywall Prods. Liab. Litig.*, 742 F.3d 576, 593 (5th Cir. 2014); *Peterson v. Islamic Republic of Iran*, 627 F.3d 1117, 1130 n.5 (9th Cir. 2010).

consequences, about whether to answer or default.[14] A claim is considered "new" when it differs substantially from the original pleading.[15] Even when the revisions are insubstantial, some courts have still been reluctant to allow a default to be entered against a defendant on the basis of an unserved, amended pleading.[16]

General Exceptions to the Service Requirement

The service requirements set by Rule 5 do *not* apply to the service of:

- *Original complaints* (governed by Rule 4);
- *Ex parte motions*;[17]
- *Pleadings between numerous defendants* (if service is excused by court order under Rule 5(c));
- *Papers governed by special service procedures.*[18]

Effect of Unserved Pleadings and Other Papers

A pleading or other paper that must be served (either under Rule 4 or Rule 5) but is not served will ordinarily be given no legal effect.[19] Thus, amended complaints that are filed but not served are ineffective and usually will not supersede the original,[20] and motion exhibits that are filed but not served may not be relied upon to support or oppose the motion.[21]

- *Case Law Exception:* In the unusual instance where a non-defaulting party is not properly served with a pleading or other paper that must be served, but that party

---

[14] *See Blair v. City of Worcester*, 522 F.3d 105, 109 (1st Cir. 2008); *Varnes v. Local 91, Glass Bottle Blowers Ass'n of U.S. and Canada*, 674 F.2d 1365, 1368 (11th Cir. 1982).

[15] *Compare Fetty v. Louisiana State Bd. of Private Sec. Examiners*, __ F. Supp. 3d __, 2020 WL 520026, at *8 (M.D. La. 2020) ("new", where complaint shifted from official-capacity claims to individual-capacity claims), *with De Curtis v. Ferrandina*, 529 Fed. Appx. 85, 86 (2d Cir. 2013) (not "new", where amendment merely clarified basis for liability); *and Belkin v. Islamic Republic of Iran*, 667 F. Supp. 2d 8, 20 (D.D.C. 2009) (not "new", where causes of action essentially same only new source of remedy added).

[16] *See IBEW Local 595 Health & Welfare Trust Fund v. Givens Elec., Inc.*, 2011 WL 2414346, at *1-*2 (N.D.Cal. June 15, 2011); *O'Callaghan v. Sifre*, 242 F.R.D. 69, 73 (S.D.N.Y. 2007). *But see De Curtis v. Ferrandina*, 529 Fed. Appx. 85, 86 (2d Cir. 2013) (permitting entry of judgment against defaulting party based on unserved amended complaint because it "merely clarified the basis" for liability).

[17] But the basis for entering such an *ex parte* motion must be provided. *See Johnson v. Lamas*, 2011 WL 2982692, at *3 n.4 (E.D.Pa. July 21, 2011).

[18] *See, e.g.*, Rule 45(b) (service procedures for subpoenas); *Gates v. Syrian Arab Republic*, 646 F.3d 2, 5–6 (D.C.Cir. 2011) (when specific federal statute sets service procedures, statute likely supersedes Rule 5(a)).

[19] *See McNally v. O'Flynn*, 2010 WL 891151, at *2 (W.D.N.Y. Mar. 10, 2010) (failure to serve on every party prompts dismissal without prejudice).

[20] *See International Controls Corp. v. Vesco*, 556 F.2d 665, 669 (2d Cir. 1977) (amended complaint remains inchoate until served under Rule 5(a)).

[21] *See Thorne v. Steubenville Police Officer*, 463 F. Supp. 2d 760, 770 (S.D. Ohio 2006).

nonetheless receives actual notice of it through other means and is not prejudiced by the service failure, a court may accept and act on the unserved paper.[22]

Seizure Actions

Actions begun by the seizure of property (arrest, attachment, garnishment) are subject to Rule 5. In these cases, any paper required to be served before filing an answer, claim, or appearance must be served on the person with custody or possession of the property at the time of seizure.

RULE 5(b)—METHOD OF SERVICE

CORE CONCEPT

Service of papers under this Rule is made ordinarily on a party's attorney, not on the party directly (unless that party is unrepresented or the court otherwise orders), in any of the following ways:

- *By Personal Delivery:*
  - (1) Directly, by handing it to the recipient; or
  - (2) At Work, by leaving it at the recipient's office with the person "in charge" or, if no one so qualifies, in a conspicuous place in that office; or
  - (3) At Home, if the recipient has no office or if that office is closed, by delivery to the recipient's dwelling or usual place of abode with someone of suitable age or discretion residing there; or
- *By Mail*, sent to the recipient's last known address; or
- *By Electronic Means*, as prescribed by the court's e-filing system or other electronic means to which the recipient consented; or
- *By Other Agreed-Upon Means*, as consented to in writing; or
- *By Leaving It With the Court Clerk*, if the recipient has no known address.

APPLICATIONS

Service on Attorney, Not Party

Pleadings and other papers generally must be served on the party's attorney, and not on the party directly.[23] However, service may be made on the party directly if a specific Rule so

---

[22]*See McKinnie v. Roadway Express, Inc.*, 341 F.3d 554, 557–59 (6th Cir. 2003) (where party is not properly served with summary judgment motion, but has actual notice of the motion prior to disposition, a court's decision to grant the motion will not be reversed on appeal for this reason unless the affected party demonstrates a genuine issue of material fact that would defeat summary judgment). *But see Magnuson v. Video Yesteryear*, 85 F.3d 1424, 1431 (9th Cir. 1996) (rejecting actual notice view, absent "exceptional good cause").

[23]*See Rai v. WB Imico Lexington Fee, LLC*, 802 F.3d 353, 361 (2d Cir. 2015).

requires, if the party is unrepresented,[24] or if the court so orders.

Parties Represented by Multiple Attorneys

Service is complete upon serving one attorney for each represented party. If a party is represented by multiple counsel, multiple service is ordinarily not required.[25]

Actual Notice Is Not Always Sufficient, or Even Necessary

The fact that a party received actual notice of a legal paper will not necessarily excuse a failure to properly serve that party under Rule 5.[26] Nor will a failure to receive actual notice invalidate service, so long as Rule 5 is followed faithfully and the service, as attempted, was "reasonably calculated, under all circumstances, to apprise interested parties of the pendency of the action and afford them an opportunity to present their objections."[27]

Service at an Office

Service may be completed at the served person's office, by "handing" it to the served person directly or by "leaving" it with "a clerk," with some "other person in charge," or if there is no one in charge, "in a conspicuous place in the office."[28]

Service At Home

Service can be accomplished at the served person's home, if hand delivery or office service are unavailable.[29] Presumably, this Rule will be interpreted by the courts in the same manner as Rule 4. Thus, the recipient of service need not necessarily be an adult, so long as the court reaches the case-by-case, factual determination that the recipient is of "suitable age and discretion."[30] Generally, service must be made on a person "residing" at the home; service on a non-resident (like a part-

---

[24]*See Cent. Illinois Carpenters Health & Welfare Trust Fund v. Con-Tech Carpentry, LLC*, 806 F.3d 935, 937 (7th Cir. 2015).

[25]*See EMW Women's Surgical Ctr., P.S.C. v. Friedlander*, 978 F.3d 418, 447 (6th Cir. 2020); *Buchanan v. Sherrill*, 51 F.3d 227, 228 (10th Cir. 1995).

[26]*See Southern California Darts Ass'n v. Zaffina*, 762 F.3d 921, 928 (9th Cir. 2014) (even with actual notice, serving party must show "exceptional good cause" for not complying with Rule 5(b)).

[27]*See Lightspeed Media Corp. v. Smith*, 761 F.3d 699, 704 (7th Cir. 2014) (quoting *Mullane v. Central Hanover Bank & Trust Co.,* 339 U.S. 306, 314, 70 S. Ct. 652, 94 L. Ed. 865 (1950)). *See also Southern California Darts Ass'n v. Zaffina*, 762 F.3d 921, 928 (9th Cir. 2014) (properly performed service is "not deficient even if it is assumed that, for some reason, the motion was not ultimately conveyed" to intended recipient).

[28]*See* Rule 5(b)(2)(B)(i). *See also Southern Cal. Darts Ass'n v. Zaffina*, 762 F.3d 921, 928 (9th Cir. 2014); *Lightspeed Media Corp. v. Smith*, 761 F.3d 699, 704 (7th Cir. 2014).

[29]*See* Rule 5(b)(2)(B).

[30]*See Stepp v. Rexnord Indus., Inc.*, 2014 WL 3866135, at *3 (S.D. Ind. Aug. 5, 2014) (service failed when papers left unattended on recipient's porch, and not physically handed to

time maid) might well be ineffective.[31]

Service by Mail

Service by mail may usually be made to the served person's last known address,[32] and that service is complete at the moment a properly posted envelope is deposited with the Post Office[33] (though some courts have seemed to view "complete-upon-mailing" as merely a rebuttable presumption[34]). The Post Office's failure to postmark the envelope on the day of deposit does not alter this effect.[35] Non-receipt or non-acceptance usually does not affect the validity of service.[36]

- *Note:* Rule 6(d) gives the recipient of postal-mailed service 3 extra days to respond in certain contexts.

Service By Electronic Transmission

Two methods for electronic service are permitted. *First*, if the server and served person are both registered users of the court's e-filing facilities, a document filed electronically can also be served electronically through that system.[37] No separate consent is required. *Second*, the parties can separately consent to electronic transmission through other means (like ordinary e-mail), so long as they do so in writing.[38] Such consent usually cannot be implied from conduct[39] (*e.g.*, an e-mail address printed on the letterhead,[40] routinely e-mailing one another,[41] objector's own reliance on using e-mail,[42] or failing to

---

resident).

[31] *See supra* Authors' Commentary to Rule 4(e) ("**Service at Individual's Dwelling**") (discussing service on maid and landlady).

[32] *See Trade Well Int'l v. United Cent. Bank*, 825 F.3d 854, 860 (7th Cir. 2016).

[33] *See* Rule 5(b)(2)(C). *See also U.S. v. Clingman*, 288 F.3d 1183, 1185 (10th Cir. 2002); *U.S. v. Novaton*, 271 F.3d 968, 1015–16 (11th Cir. 2001).

[34] *See Wallin v. Sygma Network*, 850 Fed. Appx. 615, 617 (10th Cir. 2021); *Hanna v. Sec'y of U.S. Dep't of Agric.*, 812 Fed. Appx. 104, 105 (3d Cir. 2020).

[35] *See Larez v. Holcomb*, 16 F.3d 1513, 1515 (9th Cir. 1994) (document placed in the mail on last day for service was timely served, even though Post Office did not postmark envelope until next day).

[36] *Dunlap v. Transamerica Occidental Life Ins. Co.*, 858 F.2d 629, 632–33 (11th Cir.1988).

[37] *See* Rule 5(b) advisory committee note (2018). *See also Trevino v. City of Fort Worth*, 944 F.3d 567, 571–72 (5th Cir. 2019).

[38] *See* Rule 5(b) advisory committee note (2018). *See also Dalla-Longa v. Magnetar Cap. LLC*, 33 F.4th 693, 696 (2d Cir. 2022); *O'Neal Constructors, LLC v. DRT Am., LLC*, 991 F.3d 1376, 1379-80 (11th Cir. 2021).

[39] *See* Rule 5(b)(2)(D) advisory committee note (2001). *See also O'Neal Constructors, LLC v. DRT Am., LLC*, 991 F.3d 1376, 1379-80 (11th Cir. 2021) (being party to arbitration agreement did not qualify as express consent); *RFR Industries, Inc. v. Century Steps, Inc.*, 477 F.3d 1348, 1352 (Fed. Cir. 2007) (rejecting argument that "exceptional good cause" could excuse noncompliance with consent-in-writing requirement).

[40] *See* Rule 5(b)(2)(D) advisory committee note (2001) (Changes Made After Publication and Comments).

[41] *See Martin v. Deutsche Bank Sec. Inc.*, 676 Fed. Appx. 27, 29 (2d Cir.

earlier object[43]). Consenting parties should reach specific written agreement on the scope of their consent (*e.g.*, desired recipient, transmission address, format for attachments, duration of consent).[44] Absent an agreement otherwise, and even when consent has been obtained, parties may still serve traditionally through the mail.[45]

Service by electronic transmission is considered complete when: (a) a registered user files a paper with the court's e-filing system for transmission to another registered user; *or* (b) a sender transmits electronically to a recipient using an agreed upon method.[46] But if the server learns that the transmission did not reach the recipient, the service can no longer be considered effective and the server is required to take further actions to make effective service.[47] (The court is not responsible for notifying users of a failed e-filing system transmission.[48]) A failed transmission can be a mechanical one (*e.g.*, an "incomplete" or "failed" fax message) or one relating to a change in the recipient's profile (*e.g.*, original counsel consents to the court's e-filing system, but a change in counsel renders this consent ineffective).[49] However, a recipient's failure to see a successfully transmitted message due to a glitch in the recipient's own computer software or e-mail filters is unlikely to undermine the validity of service.[50]

- *Amendment Note:* These electronic service procedures were revised and broadened in 2018. Earlier caselaw interpreting the less fulsome approach of the pre-amended text should be cited with caution.

Service By "Other Means"

Service by some "other means" is also approved, provided that the served party has consented, in writing, to the alterna-

---

2017); *O'Neal Constructors, LLC v. DRT Am., LLC*, 440 F. Supp. 3d 1396, 1402 (N.D. Ga. 2020), *aff'd*, 991 F.3d 1376 (11th Cir. 2021).

[42] *See Thomas v. Anderson*, 2020 WL 1042517, at *3 (C.D. Ill. Mar. 4, 2020) (no requirement in Rule 5(b) that consent to electronic service be reciprocal).

[43] *See Ortiz-Moss v. New York City Dep't of Transp.*, 623 F. Supp. 2d 404, 407 (S.D.N.Y. 2008).

[44] *See* Rule 5(b)(2)(D) advisory committee note (2001).

[45] *See Wolters Kluwer Fin. Servs., Inc. v. Scivantage*, 564 F.3d 110, 116 (2d Cir. 2009).

[46] *See* Rule 5(b)(2)(E). *See generally Am. Boat Co. v. Unknown Sunken Barge*, 567 F.3d 348, 350 (8th Cir. 2009) (presumption of delivery and receipt applies to e-mails sent using court's e-filing system).

[47] *See* Rule 5(b)(2)(E).

[48] *See* Rule 5(b) advisory committee note (2018).

[49] *See McKinnie v. Roadway Express, Inc.*, 341 F.3d 554, 557 (6th Cir. 2003).

[50] *See Rollins v. Home Depot USA*, 8 F.4th 393, 396–97 (5th Cir. 2021). *See also Kruskal v. Martinez*, 859 Fed. Appx. 336, 337 (10th Cir. 2021) (for service purposes, "doesn't matter" when recipient read e-mail, "only when he received" it).

tive method of service.[51] When permitted, such service by "other means" is deemed complete when the person making the service delivers the document to the entity engaged to make the delivery.[52]

Service via the Clerk of Court

Though permitted, accomplishing service of a paper by "leaving it with the court clerk" is a narrowly restricted path for service. It may only be used when original service of process (or service waiver) under Rule 4 has already been accomplished and, then, only when the current address of the once-served recipient is unknown.[53]

Private Overnight Courier Services

Private overnight courier services (such as FedEx, UPS, or DHL) are not the Post Office, and they do not provide "mail" service. Thus, service through a private courier might not constitute service by "mail" pursuant to Rule 5(b)(2)(C) and, therefore, service is unlikely considered completed upon the courier's taking possession of the document.[54] Rather, service by a private courier is more likely to be deemed a type of personal service, complete only upon the courier's actual delivery of the document to the ultimate recipient.[55] If, however, service by private courier has been consented to, it can qualify as effective service by "other means".[56] (Overnight delivery services provided by the U.S. Post Office are likely still considered "mail" service.[57])

---

[51] *See* Rule 5(b)(2)(F).

[52] *See* Rule 5(b)(2)(F).

[53] *See Reid v. Dan Yant, Inc.*, 2018 WL 8014197, at *1–*3 (E.D.N.Y. Oct. 25, 2018); *Cryer v. UMass Med. Corr. Health*, 2011 WL 841248, at *1–*2 (D. Mass. 2011).

[54] *See Transco Leasing Corp. v. U.S.*, 992 F.2d 552, 554 (5th Cir. 1993) (commenting, without deciding, that service by overnight courier might not qualify as service by mail under Rule 5). *Compare Schudel v. General Elec. Co.*, 120 F.3d 991, 993–94 (9th Cir. 1997) (personal delivery or delivery to U.S. Postal Service could have satisfied service requirement, but delivery to Federal Express did not), *and Magnuson v. Video Yesteryear*, 85 F.3d 1424, 1430–31 (9th Cir. 1996) (delivery by Federal Express is not "mail", noting drafters in 1937 could not have intended to authorize service by private delivery services), *and Audio Enterprises, Inc. v. B & W Loudspeakers of America, a Div. of Equity Intern. Inc.*, 957 F.2d 406, 409 (7th Cir. 1992) (Federal Express is not first class mail within meaning of Rule 4), *and Prince v. Poulos*, 876 F.2d 30, 32 (5th Cir. 1989) (in construing Federal Rule of Appellate Procedure 25, the court held Federal Express is not "public authority" and not form of "mail"), *with U.S. v. Certain Real Property and Premises Known as 63-29 Trimble Road, Woodside, N.Y.*, 812 F. Supp. 332, 334 (E.D. N.Y. 1992) (service via Federal Express "mail" is valid because Rule 5(b) does not require that "mailing" occur through U.S. Postal Service).

[55] *See Edmond v. U.S. Postal Serv.*, 727 F. Supp. 7, 11 (D.D.C. 1989), *aff'd in part and rev'd in part*, 949 F.2d 415 (D.C. Cir. 1991).

[56] *See* Rule 5(b)(2)(F).

[57] *See Danger v. Wachovia Corp.*, 2011 WL 1743763, at *3 (S.D.Fla. May 6, 2011).

Prisoner Plaintiffs

For documents served by *pro se* prisoners, the courts generally recognize a "mailbox" rule that deems documents as served upon their delivery to the prison officials.[58]

RULE 5(c)—SERVING NUMEROUS DEFENDANTS

CORE CONCEPT

Where an unusually large number of defendants are sued, the court may order that the defendants need not serve every other defendant with pleadings and responses, and that crossclaims, counterclaims, and affirmative defenses be deemed automatically denied or avoided as among the numerous defendants.

APPLICATIONS

Court Order

Rule 5(c) is seldom used. It is effective only upon court order,[59] which must be served on all parties.

Court Filing Still Required

Rule 5(c) also does not excuse the pleader's obligation to *file* the pleading with the Court.[60]

Plaintiff Must Always Serve and Be Served

Rule 5(c) does not excuse service *on the plaintiff* of all papers, nor does it excuse service *by the plaintiff* of all papers. Even if the action involves a large number of plaintiffs (*e.g.,* a mass tort case), each plaintiff must still serve each defendant with every Rule 5(a) paper, and each defendant must still serve each plaintiff with every Rule 5(a) paper.

Only Defendants' Pleadings/Responses

This limitation applies only to defendants' pleadings and certain responses thereto; all other papers must still be served.

RULE 5(d)—FILING WITH THE COURT

CORE CONCEPT

Any paper required to be served must also be filed with the court within a reasonable time after service (except for most discovery papers, which are exempted). Represented parties must usually file electronically; unrepresented parties may file electronically only as permitted. Any nonelectronic filing is made with the clerk of court, unless the court permits filing with the judge personally. The clerk of court may not refuse to

---

[58] *See Schroeder v. McDonald*, 55 F.3d 454, 459 (9th Cir.1995) (incarcerated *pro se* litigants effect service under Rule 5(b) by submitting their documents to prison authorities); *cf.* Fed.R.App.P. 4(c) (document deemed "filed" by prisoner when deposited into prison's internal mail system).

[59] *See Kuklachev v. Gelfman*, 2009 WL 497576, at *4 n.5 (E.D.N.Y. Feb. 26, 2009) (parties may not rely on Rule 5(c) in absence of court order).

[60] *See U.S. v. Atlas Lederer Co.*, 282 F. Supp. 2d 687, 701–03 (S.D. Ohio 2001).

accept a paper for filing simply because the paper does not conform to these Rules or the district's local rules.

APPLICATIONS

Electronic Filing - Required of Most Attorneys

Parties who are represented by attorneys must make all their filings electronically using the court's e-filing system.[61] This requirement may be excused only by court order (issued for good cause) or by local rule.[62] Unrepresented parties may not file electronically absent a court order unless a local rule requires (with reasonable exceptions) or permits it.[63] An electronically-filed document is treated the same as a written paper, and is deemed signed when made through an e-filing account, authorized by the filer, and accompanied by the filer's name in a signature block.[64] Filing is complete upon a successful, compliant transmission.[65]

- *Amendment Note:* These filing procedures (including the addition of the now-mandatory e-filing obligation) were revised in 2018. Earlier caselaw interpreting the less fulsome approach of the pre-amended text should be cited with caution.

Nonelectronic Filing - Procedures

When permitted to file nonelectronically, a party may do so in two ways. *First*, the party may physically deliver the document to the clerk of court for filing.[66] Such documents are considered filed when they arrive into the clerk's possession,[67] not the date they are mailed to the clerk[68] (except for prisoner plaintiffs)[69] or slipped, after hours, under the clerk's office door.[70] However, placing a document into the clerk's designated after-

[61]*See* Rule 5(d)(3)(A). An anomaly appears in the amending notes, implying that this requirement is imposed only upon those attorneys who have registered for e-filing. *See* Rule 5(d) advisory committee note (2018) (amendment "recognizes electronic service through the court's transmission facilities as to any registered user" and, further: "a party who registers will be subject to service through the court's facilities unless the court provides otherwise"). The text of as-amended Rule, however, makes no mention of this caveat.

[62]*See* Rule 5(d)(3)(A). *But cf. Pierce v. Ocwen Loan Servicing, LLC*, 987 F.3d 577, 579–80 (6th Cir. 2021) (failing to file electronically as local rules required did not vitiate timeliness).

[63]*See* Rule 5(d)(3)(B).

[64]*See* Rule 5(d)(3)(C)–(D). *See also Scott-Ortiz v. CBRE Inc.*, 501 F. Supp. 3d 717, 721 (D. Ariz. 2020).

[65]*See Farley v. Koepp*, 788 F.3d 681, 684–86 (7th Cir. 2015). *Cf. Klein v. Olson*, 728 Fed. Appx. 846, 848 (10th Cir. 2018) (document not filed where user uploaded document, paid fee, but failed to complete final step of electronically submitting it).

[66]*See* Rule 5(d)(2)(A).

[67]*See Rosas v. Berry Plastics (Pliant LLC)*, 649 Fed. Appx. 3, 4 (2d Cir. 2016); *Riordan v. State Farm Mut. Auto. Ins. Co.*, 589 F.3d 999, 1003 (9th Cir. 2009).

[68]*See In re Robertson*, 774 Fed. Appx. 453, 457 (10th Cir. 2019); *Jacobs v. Clayton Cty. Solicitor Gen. Office*, 685 Fed. Appx. 824, 826–27 (11th Cir. 2017).

[69]*See infra* Authors' Commentary to Rule 5(d) ("**Prisoner Plaintiffs**").

hours depository should qualify as an effective filing.[71] The filing date is not ordinarily delayed pending the typing of the document into the official case docket[72] or awaiting a court decision on a motion to seal;[73] the date of the clerk's possession suffices. *Second*, but only when the judge so permits,[74] papers may be filed with the judge personally, after which the judge is tasked to promptly transmit the papers to the clerk's office.[75]

"Reasonable" Time For Filing

Filing must be accomplished no later than a "reasonable time" after service (if not performed simultaneously).[76] Whether the span between service and filing is "reasonable" is a matter left to the discretion of the district court.[77] Consequently, practitioners should file their papers simultaneously with service or as soon thereafter as possible. Moreover, this Rule only sets the ordinary procedure to be followed. Where, for example, the court fixes a specific time for filing a particular paper, that order (not the more general "reasonable time" standard of Rule 5(d)) must be obeyed.[78]

---

[70] *See Casalduc v. Diaz*, 117 F.2d 915, 916 (1st Cir. 1941).

[71] *See* Rule 77(a) ("When Court Is Open"). *See also Pierce v. Ocwen Loan Servicing, LLC*, 987 F.3d 577, 579 (6th Cir. 2021) (court may not treat use of its official drop box "as a trespass or a non-event"); *Greenwood v. State of N.Y., Office of Mental Health (OMH)*, 842 F.2d 636, 639 (2d Cir. 1988) (document deemed filed when time-stamped and placed in Clerk's Office night depository box); *Turner v. City of Newport*, 887 F. Supp. 149, 151 (E.D. Ky. 1995) (complaint timely filed when placed in Clerk's post office box at 11:30 p.m. on final day of statute of limitations).

[72] *See Han Tak Lee v. Houtzdale SCI*, 798 F.3d 159, 163 (3d Cir. 2015).

[73] *See Demaree v. Pederson*, 887 F.3d 870, 877–78 (9th Cir. 2018).

[74] *See Riordan v. State Farm Mut. Auto. Ins. Co.*, 589 F.3d 999, 1003 (9th Cir. 2009). *See also Tran v. Minnesota Dept. of Transp.*, 2006 WL 2917037, at *2 (D. Minn. 2006), aff'd, 259 Fed. Appx. 901 (8th Cir. 2008) (noting that no judge is under an obligation to permit a filing in this way).

[75] *See Life Ins. Co. of North America v. Von Valtier*, 116 F.3d 279, 282–83 (7th Cir. 1997) (disapproving of trial judge's delay in transmitting motion to the clerk's office, noting that "the system will break down unless the judge scrupulously follows the directions to note the date and transmit the documents immediately to the clerk. Less than perfect adherence to these instructions will mean that actual filing dates will become as uncertain as the former dates of service were, and something as important as the jurisdictional time limit for taking an appeal will once again be subject to factual disputes").

[76] *See* Rule 5(d)(1)(A).

[77] *See Chesson v. Jaquez*, 986 F.2d 363, 365 (10th Cir. 1993) (filing within six days after service is "reasonable", particularly because a weekend fell within that period); *Baldwin v. United States*, 823 F. Supp. 2d 1087, 1110 (D.N.Mar.I. 2011) (filing within five days of service deemed reasonable); *Biocore Medical Technologies, Inc. v. Khosrowshahi*, 181 F.R.D. 660, 668 (D. Kan. 1998), *aff'd*, 348 F.3d 1163 (10th Cir. 2003) (courts have decided that documents filed up to six days after service are filed within a "reasonable time" under Rule 5(d); holding that filing almost two months after service is not "reasonable").

[78] *See Raymond v. Ameritech Corp.*, 442 F.3d 600, 605–06 (7th Cir. 2006).

More Requirements for Effective Filing

Other Rules, the district's local rules, and individual judges' chambers rules may prescribe additional filing duties (though local and chambers rules may do so only so long as what is prescribed is not inconsistent with the Rules).[79] Nationally, other procedural requirements exist:

- *Certificate of Service:* A party's certificate of service must accompany (or be filed within a reasonable time after the service of) every nonelectronically filed document,[80] and should identify the document served, the date of service, and the manner of delivery.[81] A proper certificate raises the presumption of receipt.[82] Because the purpose of the certificate is to verify for the court that proper service has been accomplished, the court may[83] (but is not required to[84]) overlook a missing certificate, provided proper service is uncontested. No certificate of service is needed when a document is filed electronically.[85]
- *Document Itself Must Be Filed:* A document will not be deemed "filed" unless it is separately and formally filed with the court. Thus, attaching a document as an exhibit to another paper will not constitute a "filing" of the attachment.[86]
- *Paying Filing Fees:* Most courts accept a filing as effective, even if the requisite filing fees have not yet been paid (provided they are promptly paid thereafter).[87]

---

[79] *See* Rule 83(a)(1). *See also Weitzner v. Cynosure, Inc.*, 802 F.3d 307, 313–14 (2d Cir. 2015) ("very strongly recommend[ing]" district judges to avoid procedures that delay timely filing).

[80] *See* Rule 5(d)(1)(B)(i) (eff. Dec. 1, 2018). *See also Horowitch v. Diamond Aircraft Indus., Inc.*, 645 F.3d 1254, 1258–59 (11th Cir. 2011) (certificate must be supplied at time of filing, not service).

[81] *See Golden v. McCaughtry*, 915 F. Supp. 77, 79 (E.D. Wis. 1995) (noting certificate of service filing obligation).

[82] *See In re Cendant Corp. Prides Litig.*, 311 F.3d 298, 304 (3d Cir. 2002).

[83] *See Russell v. City of Milwaukee*, 338 F.3d 662, 665–67 (7th Cir. 2003) (failure to include certificate of service with suggestion of death did not defeat court's finding that service had, in fact, been made); *Ives v. Guilford Mills, Inc.*, 3 F. Supp. 2d 191, 194–95 (N.D. N.Y. 1998) (an invalidation under such circumstances "would seem to serve no purpose except to fruitlessly extend the length of this litigation").

[84] *See Leggett v. Lafayette*, 608 Fed.Appx. 187, 191 (5th Cir. 2015).

[85] *See* Rule 5(d)(1)(B).

[86] *See Orsini v. Kugel*, 9 F.3d 1042, 1045 (2d Cir. 1993) (a stipulation had not been "filed" merely because it was attached as an exhibit to another court paper). *But see A. Bauer Mech., Inc. v. Joint Arbitration Bd. of Plumbing Contractors' Ass'n & Chicago Journeymen Plumbers' Local Union 130*, 562 F.3d 784, 791 (7th Cir. 2009) (approving the deemed "filing" *instanter* of pleading attached to motion for leave but never separately filed).

[87] *See Chambers v. HSBC Bank USA, N.A.*, 796 F.3d 560, 566–67 (6th Cir. 2015) (filing proper, but court may dismiss if fees remain unpaid);

Successful Filing, But With Procedural Irregularities

Procedural flaws in the paper will usually not prevent the "filing".[88] Although the clerk of court (and its computer system[89]) may not refuse to file a paper that does not conform to the Rules or to the district's local rules,[90] the clerk may advise the filing party or attorney of a paper's deficiencies. A local rule may also instruct the clerk to inform the judge of the paper's defect (and a judge can order that the paper be refused).[91] The task of enforcing rules concerning procedure and form are reserved exclusively for the district judge.[92] Sanctions of a lesser nature can be imposed for local rule violations.[93]

Unsuccessful, Absent, or Untimely Filing

Ordinarily, in the absence of contumacious behavior, a failure to timely file a properly-served pleading will often be remedied by an order compelling the filing, and not with a dismissal.[94] Practitioners should be wary of over-relying on such liberality; it is not assured by the Rules and, predictably, is unlikely to apply when a litigant's duty was a timely *filing* and not merely a timely *service*.

Discovery Papers

To conserve the spatial resources of the clerk's office and federal courthouses, discovery requests and discovery responses are *not* to be filed with the court unless and until (a) they are actually "used" in court proceedings or (b) the trial court so orders.[95] This prohibition applies to requests, responses, and objections made under the Rules governing depositions, interrogatories, admissions, production demands, and entry upon land demands,[96] as well as to deposition transcripts.[97] Local rules prescribing different filing requirements are superseded

---

Escobedo v. Applebees, 787 F.3d 1226, 1232–34 (9th Cir. 2015) (filing proper, even if *in forma pauperis* petition remains outstanding).

[88]*See Han Tak Lee v. Houtzdale SCI*, 798 F.3d 159, 164 (3d Cir. 2015); *Farley v. Koepp*, 788 F.3d 681, 683–85 (7th Cir. 2015).

[89]*See Shuler v. Garrett*, 715 F.3d 185, 185–87 (6th Cir. 2013) (listing wrong docket number on electronic filing); *Royall v. Nat'l Ass'n of Letter Carriers*, 548 F.3d 137, 141 (D.C. Cir. 2008) ("glitch" in ECF system delayed proper entry on electronic docket).

[90]*See Pierce v. Ocwen Loan Servicing, LLC*, 987 F.3d 577, 580 (6th Cir. 2021); *Pettaway v. Nat'l Recovery Sols., LLC*, 955 F.3d 299, 303 (2d Cir. 2020); *Vince v. Rock County*, 604 F.3d 391, 392 (7th Cir. 2010).

[91]*See United States v. Yepiz*, 844 F.3d 1070, 1081 n.2 (9th Cir. 2016).

[92]*See Jones v. Warden of Stateville Correctional Center*, 918 F. Supp. 1142, 1151 (N.D. Ill. 1995).

[93]*See Klemm v. Astrue*, 543 F.3d 1139, 1143 (9th Cir. 2008).

[94]*See Betty K Agencies, Ltd. v. M/V MONADA*, 432 F.3d 1333, 1340 (11th Cir. 2005).

[95]*See* Rule 5(d)(1). *See also Doe v. Baum*, 282 F. Supp. 3d 972, 984 (E.D. Mich. 2017) (granting leave to file deposition transcripts claimed to correct oral argument statements). *See generally* Rule 5(d) advisory committee (2000) (discussing resource conservation objective).

[96]*See* Rule 5(d) advisory committee note (2000).

by this uniform, national approach.[98] Inappropriately filed discovery materials will likely be stricken from the official court docket.[99] There is, therefore, no implied right of public access to this sort of unfiled discovery.[100]

The phrase "used in the proceeding" is interpreted broadly to include those discovery materials used in connection with motions, pretrial conferences, and otherwise.[101] However, a party who uses discovery materials while interrogating witnesses during depositions usually need not later file those materials with the court.[102] Moreover, if a party uses only a portion of a voluminous discovery document, only the used portion usually need be filed with the court (although any other party would be free to file other relevant portions used).[103]

Prisoner Plaintiffs

As with service under Rule 5(b), a *pro se* prisoner's papers are usually deemed "filed" under Rule 5(d) upon delivery of those documents to the prison officials.[104]

Additional Resource Sources

Wright & Miller, *Federal Practice and Procedure* §§ 1141 to 53
C.J.S., Federal Civil Procedure § 261, § 349
West's Key Number Digest, Federal Civil Procedure ⚷664, ⚷665

---

[97] *See Rohrbough v. Harris*, 549 F.3d 1313, 1318 (10th Cir. 2008).

[98] *See* Rule 5(d) advisory committee note (2000).

[99] *See City of Greenville v. Syngenta Crop Protection, LLC*, 764 F.3d 695, 698 (7th Cir. 2014).

[100] *See Bond v. Utreras*, 585 F.3d 1061, 1076 (7th Cir. 2009); *Ryder v. Union Pac. R.R. Co.*, 315 F.R.D. 186, 189 n.31 (M.D. La. 2016). *See generally Haidon v. Town of Bloomfield*, 552 F. Supp. 3d 265, 272–74 (D. Conn. 2021) (summarizing case law, noting dissenting views).

[101] *See* Rule 5(d) advisory committee note (2000). *See also Allen v. Hays*, 812 Fed. Appx. 185, 191-93 (5th Cir. 2020) (includes video shown by parties to judge during scheduling conference).

[102] *See* Rule 5(d) advisory committee note (2000).

[103] *See* Rule 5(d) advisory committee note (2000).

[104] *See Gibson v. City Municipality of New York*, 692 F.3d 198, 201 n.3 (2d Cir. 2012); *Trepanier v. City of Blue Island*, 364 Fed.Appx. 260, 261–62 (7th Cir. 2010). *Cf. Houston v. Lack*, 487 U.S. 266, 108 S. Ct. 2379, 101 L. Ed. 2d 245 (1988) (*pro se* prisoner's notice of appeal was "filed" within meaning of Federal Rules of Appellate Procedure when notice was delivered to prison authorities).

RULE 5.1
CONSTITUTIONAL CHALLENGE TO A STATUTE—NOTICE, CERTIFICATION, AND INTERVENTION

(a) Notice by a Party. A party that files a pleading, written motion, or other paper drawing into question the constitutionality of a federal or state statute must promptly:

(1) file a notice of constitutional question stating the question and identifying the paper that raises it, if:

(A) a federal statute is questioned and the parties do not include the United States, one of its agencies, or one of its officers or employees in an official capacity; or

(B) a state statute is questioned and the parties do not include the state, one of its agencies, or one of its officers or employees in an official capacity; and

(2) serve the notice and paper on the Attorney General of the United States if a federal statute is questioned—or on the state attorney general if a state statute is questioned—either by certified or registered mail or by sending it to an electronic address designated by the attorney general for this purpose.

(b) Certification by the Court. The court must, under 28 U.S.C. § 2403, certify to the appropriate attorney general that a statute has been questioned.

(c) Intervention; Final Decision on the Merits. Unless the court sets a later time, the attorney general may intervene within 60 days after the notice is filed or after the court certifies the challenge, whichever is earlier. Before the time to intervene expires, the court may reject the constitutional challenge, but may not enter a final judgment holding the statute unconstitutional.

(d) No Forfeiture. A party's failure to file and serve the notice, or the court's failure to certify, does not forfeit a constitutional claim or defense that is otherwise timely asserted.

[Adopted April 12, 2006, effective December 1, 2006; amended April 30, 2007, effective December 1, 2007.]

AUTHORS' COMMENTARY ON RULE 5.1

PURPOSE AND SCOPE

Rule 5.1 is designed to ensure that an affected federal or State government is given notice and the opportunity to intervene in a case that contests the constitutionality of one of its statutes. The Rule compels a party challenging a statute's constitutionality to promptly notify the appropriate attorney general, and directs the district court to also make a certification of the challenge to the same official.

RULE 5.1(a)—NOTICE BY A PARTY

CORE CONCEPT

Any party who draws into question the constitutionality of a federal or State statute must ensure that the appropriate attorney general is informed of the pending litigation challenge.

APPLICATIONS

Goal of Certification

The goal of the certification requirement is to protect the public interest by ensuring that the executive branch of the affected government is alerted any time one of its laws is challenged constitutionally and afforded the opportunity to make its views heard on the challenge.[1] A government has standing to defend its laws' constitutionality.[2]

Applies Only When Statutes are Challenged

By its terms, the Rule 5.1 notice and certification obligation is implicated only by constitutional challenges to federal or State *statutes* (and not to other types of laws[3] or to allegations

[1] *See Oklahoma ex rel Edmondson v. Pope*, 516 F.3d 1214, 1216 (10th Cir. 2008); *Virginia ex rel. Cuccinelli v. Sebelius*, 702 F. Supp. 2d 598, 605–06 & 606 n.4 (E.D.Va. 2010), *rev'd on other grounds*, 656 F.3d 253 (4th Cir. 2011).

[2] *See Diamond v. Charles*, 476 U.S. 54, 62, 106 S. Ct. 1697, 90 L. Ed. 2d 48 (1986).

[3] *See Peruta v. County of San*

that government actors behaved unconstitutionally[4]).

Applies Only to Constitutional Challenges

Similarly, by its terms, the notice and certification obligation is triggered only by challenges to the statute's *constitutionality*, and not merely where its applicability or interpretation is at issue.[5] Moreover, a challenge only under the Supremacy Clause may, likewise, fall outside the notice and certification obligation.[6]

Notice and Service by a Party

With one exception (see below), Rule 5.1(a) requires a party who files a writing (a pleading, written motion, or other paper) that challenges the constitutionality of a federal or State statute to file a notice of the challenge with the district court. The contents of the notice must state the nature of the challenge and identify the document that contains it. It also needs to be filed separately from the complaint or other implicated pleading.[7] Both the notice and the challenge document must then be served on the affected attorney general (federal or State).[8]

- *Exception:* If a federal or State statute is challenged, but the United States or the affected State is already a party itself or through agencies or officers sued in an official capacity, the special notice requirement of Rule 5.1(a) would be redundant and unnecessary, and therefore is

---

Diego, 771 F.3d 570, 574 (9th Cir. 2014) (inapplicable to county policy), *overturned on en banc reh'g on other grounds*, 824 F.3d 919, 924 (9th Cir. 2016); *Healy v. Attorney General Pennsylvania*, 563 Fed. Appx. 139, 143 (3d Cir. 2014) (inapplicable to ethics rule); *Odonnell v. Harris Cty.*, 227 F. Supp. 3d 706, 741 n.23 (S.D. Tex. 2016) (inapplicable to court rules), *aff'd in part, rev'd in part on other grounds*, 892 F.3d 147 (5th Cir. 2018). *But cf. Spirit of Aloha Temple v. Cty. of Maui*, 322 F. Supp. 3d 1051, 1069–70 (D. Haw. 2018) (noting statute-only scope, but ordering notice to State of constitutional challenge to administrative rule).

[4] *See Reese-Bey v. Ochoa*, 2021 WL 7184971, at *8 (C.D. Cal. Dec. 29, 2021), *adopted*, 2022 WL 577257 (C.D. Cal. Feb. 9, 2022).

[5] *See Pyle v. Woods*, 874 F.3d 1257, 1265 (10th Cir. 2017); *Marquez v. KBMS Hosp. Corp.*, 492 F. Supp. 3d 1058, 1066 (C.D. Cal. 2020). *Cf. Smith v. City of Oakland*, __ F. Supp. 3d __, 2020 WL 2517857, at *11 n.9 (N.D. Cal. 2020) (duty not triggered by claim that State law is federally preempted); *Rodriguez v. Providence Cmty. Corr., Inc.*, 191 F. Supp. 3d 758, 769 (M.D. Tenn. 2016) (duty not triggered when facially constitutional statute is challenged as being unconstitutionally applied). *See generally United States v. Lynch*, 137 U.S. 280, 285, 11 S. Ct. 114, 34 L. Ed. 700 (1890) ("The validity of a statute is not drawn in question every time rights claimed under such statute are controverted, nor is the validity of an authority every time an act done by such authority is disputed.").

[6] *See United States v. Zadeh*, 820 F.3d 746, 752–55 (5th Cir. 2016) (so noting, adding that notice to attorney general "is the better practice").

[7] *See Bezingue v. Steuben Lakes Reg'l Waste Dist.*, 507 F. Supp. 3d 1021, 1028 (N.D. Ind. 2020).

[8] *See* Rule 5.1(a)(1).

not required.[9]

Method of Service

Service of the notice on the affected federal or State attorney general must be made via certified or registered mail, or by electronic service through any electronic address established by the attorney general for this purpose.[10]

Timing of Notification

The Rule sets no specific time for the party to make its notification, beyond prescribing that it must do so "promptly."[11]

Prior Precedent

The language of Rule 5.1 closely tracks the text of the now abrogated last three sentences of Rule 24(c), which, in 2006, it replaced. Precedent interpreting that prior text may influence the construction of Rule 5.1, except where the current language differs from the former.

- *Language Change:* The former language had limited the notify-and-serve obligation to situations in which the constitutional challenge to a statute affected the public interest. Rule 5.1(a) expresses no similar textual limitation.[12]

No New Claim or Right

This Rule is not intended to create a new or independent cause of action or basis for relief; it is, instead, merely a vehicle to help ensure that notice to the affected federal or State attorney general will occur.[13]

RULE 5.1(b)—CERTIFICATION BY THE COURT

CORE CONCEPT

The district court must, additionally, certify to the appropriate

[9]*See* Rule 5.1(a)(1)(A)–(1)(B). *See also Nashville Cmty. Bail Fund v. Gentry*, 446 F. Supp. 3d 282, 296–98 (M.D. Tenn. 2020) (no notification required in lawsuit suing clerk of criminal courts in his official capacity); *Shah v. Danberg*, 855 F. Supp. 2d 215, 225 (D.Del. 2012) (no notification required in lawsuit suing department of corrections commissioner in his official capacity). *But see National Ass'n of Mfrs. v. S.E.C.*, 956 F. Supp. 2d 43, 74–75 (D.D.C. 2013), *aff'd in part and rev'd in part on other grounds*, 748 F.3d 359 (D.C. Cir. 2014) (S.E.C.'s status as a party-defendant did not discharge Rule 5.1 notice obligation).

[10]*See* Rule 5.1(a)(2).

[11]*See Pyle v. Woods*, 874 F.3d 1257, 1265 (10th Cir. 2017) (in assessing promptness, court considers whether any prejudice resulted); *Nashville Cmty. Bail Fund v. Gentry*, 446 F. Supp. 3d 282, 295 (M.D. Tenn. 2020) ("only prompt, not immediate, notice" is required); *White v. Universal Fid., LP*, 2018 WL 2347073, at *2 (E.D. Ky. May 23, 2018) (30 days was acceptable).

[12]*See* Rule 5.1 advisory committee note (2006) ("It is better to assure, through notice, that the attorney general is able to determine whether to seek intervention on the ground that the act or statute affects a public interest.").

[13]*See Burruel v. Bonta*, 2022 WL 1323144, at *5–*6 (E.D. Cal. May 3, 2022); *Wopshall v. Travelers Home & Marine Ins. Co.*, 2021 WL 4189852, at *4 (S.D. Fla. Sept. 14, 2021).

federal or State attorney general that a constitutional challenge is pending. This requirement supplements a party's duty as described in Rule 5.1(a).

APPLICATION

Court's Duty to Certify

The district court, independent of and in addition to the duties of notice and service imposed on parties by Rule 5.1(a), must certify to the affected federal or State attorney general that a party has made a constitutional challenge to a federal or State statute.[14]

Goal of Certification

This certification obligation, imposed on the court by 28 U.S.C.A. § 2403, has a single goal, guided by two concerns. First, if the constitutional challenge was not raised by a party, the court's certification ensures that the interested federal or State attorney general will still receive notice of the challenge.[15] Second, because Rule 5.1(d) prohibits a forfeiture of a properly asserted constitutional claim or defense for a party's failure to serve the required notice[16] (and judicial precedent derived from old Rule 24(c) seems to hold that no lesser sanction exists),[17] the judicial certification requirement can backstop a party's tepid motivation to give the notice.

Timing of Certification

The Rule establishes no specific time period for the discharge of the court's certification duty, beyond the prohibition that no final adjudication of unconstitutionality may be entered prior to certification or notice.[18]

RULE 5.1(c)—INTERVENTION; FINAL DECISION ON THE MERITS

CORE CONCEPT

Rule 5.1(c) creates a right of intervention for the federal or State attorney general potentially affected by a constitutional

[14]*See* Rule 5.1(b).

[15]*See* Rule 5.1 advisory committee note (2006) ("The court's certification obligation remains, and is the only notice" when the challenge was not raised in a manner identified in Rule 5.1(a)).

[16]*See* Rule 5.1(d).

[17]*See, e.g., Tonya K. by Diane K. v. Board of Educ. of City of Chicago*, 847 F.2d 1243, 1247 (7th Cir. 1988) (failure to notify is not a jurisdictional defect); *Merrill v. Town of Addison*, 763 F.2d 80, 83 (2d Cir. 1985) ("Absent indication of harm, or prejudice to the government's opportunity to fully present its views, belated certification, while not ideal, is sufficient to honor the purpose of section 2403."). *Cf. In re Young*, 82 F.3d 1407, 1412 (8th Cir. 1996) (temporarily removing case from argument calendar so that appellate court can certify constitutional question and give United States time to intervene).

[18]*See National Ass'n of Mfrs. v. S.E.C.*, 956 F. Supp. 2d 43, 75 (D.D.C. 2013), *aff'd in part and rev'd in part on other grounds*, 748 F.3d 359 (D.C. Cir. 2014); *Hartman v. United Bank Card, Inc.*, 291 F.R.D. 591, 600 (W.D.Wash. 2013).

challenge. It also establishes the rather flexible time limits within which the affected attorney general must act. Rule 5.1(c) also provides that the court may, while the attorney general is considering intervention, proceed forward with a case, but may not, during this period, enter a final judgment holding a statute unconstitutional.

APPLICATIONS

Time to Intervene

An attorney general may intervene as of right within 60 days of filing of the notice of constitutional challenge or certification of the challenge, whichever is earlier. However, the court is authorized to extend the 60-day limit.[19] Such an extension may be granted by motion or the court's *sua sponte* act.[20]

Other Activity

While an attorney general is contemplating intervention, Rule 5.1 envisions that most of the routine activity of the court will continue in the case.[21]

Intervention Only Permitted, Not Required

The attorney general is not *required* to exercise the right to intervene; the decision whether to intervene or not is a matter left to the attorney general's discretion.[22] Thus, an attorney general's choice not to intervene does not preclude an opposition to a constitutional challenge raised in a later case.[23]

Court Rulings While Intervention Periods Are Pending

Until the time for intervention expires, a court may not enter a final judgment declaring a federal or State law unconstitutional; it may, however, reject the constitutional challenge at any time.[24] In practice, courts tend to either postpone a ruling on constitutionality until the government intervenes[25] or, if obviously unmeritorious, deny the constitutional challenge with a right of reconsideration (should the government intervene to

---

[19] *See* Rule 5.1(c).

[20] *See* Rule 5.1 advisory committee note (2006) ("The court may extend the 60-day period on its own or on motion.").

[21] *See* Rule 5.1 advisory committee note (2006) ("Pretrial activities may continue without interruption during the intervention period, and the court retains authority to grant interlocutory relief.").

[22] *See Richmond v. Peraino*, 128 F. Supp. 3d 415, 416 n.1 (D. Mass. 2015).

[23] *See Flying J, Inc. v. Van Hollen*, 597 F. Supp. 2d 848, 855 (E.D.Wis. 2009), *rev'd on other grounds*, 621 F.3d 658 (7th Cir. 2010). *See also Estate of Kunkel v. U.S.*, 689 F.2d 408, 420 (3d Cir.1982) (Becker, J., concurring) (such a construction is "plainly wrong").

[24] *See* Rule 5.1(c). *See also Falkner v. City of Chicago*, 150 F. Supp. 3d 973, 978–80 (N.D. Ill. 2015); *Burghart v. Corrections Corp. of America*, 2008 WL 820178, at *1 n.* (W.D. Okla. 2008); *Delaplaine v. United Airlines, Inc.*, 518 F. Supp. 2d 1275, 1278 n.3 (W.D. Wash. 2007).

[25] *See Hunter v. Hamilton County Bd. of Elections*, 850 F. Supp. 2d 795, 842 (S.D.Ohio 2012).

object).[26]

RULE 5.1(d)—NO FORFEITURE

CORE CONCEPT

Failure by a party or a court to fulfill the requirements of Rule 5.1 does not work a forfeiture of any constitutional claim or defense that is asserted in a timely manner.

APPLICATIONS

Other Consequences for a Failure to Notify or Certify

Although a forfeiture of a constitutional claim or defense is prohibited,[27] the Rule and its predecessor are silent as to other consequences of a party's failure to notify or a court's failure to certify. Such failures have not been considered a jurisdictional defect.[28] But, to allow time for the executive branch's views to be aired and considered, courts have ordered parties to make the required notice,[29] removed cases from an oral argument calendar[30] or otherwise postponed making a ruling,[31] permitted post-oral argument notification and an accompanying permission to intervene,[32] and vacated and remanded to facilitate a trial-level opportunity to intervene.[33] Likewise, the remedy for a belatedly issued notice or certification may, provided no prejudice befalls the executive branch, merely be an invitation for rehearing.[34] Of course, if the court denies the constitutional challenge, the failure to notify and/or certify likely is rendered

---

[26] *See Satkar Hospitality Inc. v. Cook County Bd. of Rev.*, 2011 WL 4431029, at *2 (N.D.Ill. Sept. 21, 2011); *Postell v. Woods*, 2011 WL 3417137, at *2–*3 (W.D.Mich. Aug. 4, 2011).

[27] *See* Rule 5.1(d). *See also Bezingue v. Steuben Lakes Reg'l Waste Dist.*, 507 F. Supp. 3d 1021, 1028 (N.D. Ind. 2020); *Cotto Lopez v. Union de Trabajadores de la Industria Electrica y Riego*, 392 F. Supp. 3d 263, 278 (D.P.R. 2019). *But see Mincey v. Jefferson Capital Sys., LLC*, 2019 WL 4686766, at *7 (D.N.J. Sept. 26, 2019) (declining to entertain constitutional challenge, then dismissing complaint); *Falkner v. City of Chicago*, 150 F. Supp. 3d 973, 978–80 (N.D. Ill. 2015) (dismissing complaint); *Jones v. U-Haul Co. of Massachusetts & Ohio Inc.*, 16 F. Supp. 3d 922, 941 (S.D. Ohio 2014) (refusing to consider constitutional arguments).

[28] *See Tonya K. by Diane K. v. Board of Educ. of City of Chicago*, 847 F.2d 1243, 1247 (7th Cir. 1988); *National Ass'n of Mfrs. v. S.E.C.*, 956 F. Supp. 2d 43, 75 (D.D.C. 2013), *aff'd in part and rev'd in part on other grounds*, 748 F.3d 359 (D.C. Cir. 2014).

[29] *See Castle v. Cobb Cnty.*, 2022 WL 1569705, at *2 (N.D. Ga. May 18, 2022).

[30] *See In re Young*, 82 F.3d 1407, 1412–13 (8th Cir. 1996).

[31] *See Kurtenbach v. Jackley*, 2018 WL 1542499, at *13 (D.S.D. Mar. 29, 2018) (reserving further consideration until compliance).

[32] *See Merrill v. Town of Addison*, 763 F.2d 80, 83 (2d Cir. 1985).

[33] *See Oklahoma ex rel Edmondson v. Pope*, 516 F.3d 1214, 1216 (10th Cir. 2008).

[34] *See National Ass'n of Mfrs. v. S.E.C.*, 956 F. Supp. 2d 43, 75 (D.D.C. 2013), *aff'd in part and rev'd in part on other grounds*, 748 F.3d 359 (D.C. Cir. 2014); *Hartman v. United Bank Card, Inc.*, 291 F.R.D. 591, 600 (W.D.Wash. 2013).

immaterial.[35]

---

[35]*See Bezingue v. Steuben Lakes Reg'l Waste Dist.*, 507 F. Supp. 3d 1021, 1028–29 (N.D. Ind. 2020).

RULE 5.2
PRIVACY PROTECTION FOR FILINGS MADE WITH THE COURT

(a) Redacted Filings. Unless the court orders otherwise, in an electronic or paper filing with the court that contains an individual's social-security number, taxpayer-identification number, or birth date, the name of an individual known to be a minor, or a financial-account number, a party or nonparty making the filing may include only:

(1) the last four digits of the social-security number and taxpayer-identification number;

(2) the year of the individual's birth;

(3) the minor's initials; and

(4) the last four digits of the financial-account number.

(b) Exemptions from the Redaction Requirement. The redaction requirement does not apply to the following:

(1) a financial-account number that identifies the property allegedly subject to forfeiture in a forfeiture proceeding;

(2) the record of an administrative or agency proceeding;

(3) the official record of a state-court proceeding;

(4) the record of a court or tribunal, if that record was not subject to the redaction requirement when originally filed;

(5) a filing covered by Rule 5.2(c) or (d); and

(6) a pro se filing in an action brought under 28 U.S.C.A. §§ 2241, 2254, or 2255.

(c) Limitations on Remote Access to Electronic Files; Social-Security Appeals and Immigration Cases. Unless the court orders otherwise, in an action for benefits under the Social Security Act, and in an action or proceeding relating to an order of removal, to relief from removal, or to immigration benefits or detention, access to an electronic file is authorized as follows:

(1) the parties and their attorneys may have remote electronic access to any part of the case file, including the administrative record;

(2) any other person may have electronic access to the full record at the courthouse, but may have remote electronic access only to:

(A) the docket maintained by the court; and

(B) an opinion, order, judgment, or other disposition of the court, but not any other part of the case file or the administrative record.

(d) Filings Made Under Seal. The court may order that a filing be made under seal without redaction. The court may later unseal the filing or order the person who made the filing to file a redacted version for the public record.

(e) Protective Orders. For good cause, the court may by order in a case:

(1) require redaction of additional information; or

(2) limit or prohibit a nonparty's remote electronic access to a document filed with the court.

(f) Option for Additional Unredacted Filing Under Seal. A person making a redacted filing may also file an unredacted copy under seal. The court must retain the unredacted copy as part of the record.

(g) Option for Filing a Reference List. A filing that contains redacted information may be filed together with a reference list that identifies each item of redacted information and specifies an appropriate identifier that uniquely corresponds to each item listed. The list must be filed under seal and may be amended as of right. Any reference in the case to a listed identifier will be construed to refer to the corresponding item of information.

(h) Waiver of Protection of Identifiers. A person waives the protection of Rule 5.2(a) as to the person's own information by filing it without redaction and not under seal.

[Adopted April 30, 2007, effective December 1, 2007.]

AUTHORS' COMMENTARY ON RULE 5.2

PURPOSE AND SCOPE

The vulnerability of electronically-accessible court files to privacy and security mischief prompted the adoption in 2007 of Rule 5.2. The Rule presumptively protects four categories of personal information (social-security numbers, birth dates, names of minors, and financial account information) by requiring a redacted display of that data, absent an exemption or court order otherwise. Filers may intentionally or inadvertently waive this protection by including unredacted personal information in their own filings. Special access restrictions are also imposed in social-security appeals and immigration cases. Additional protections—including further redactions, sealed filings, and protective orders—may be ordered by the court.

CORE CONCEPT

From many categories of court filings, parties may redact or seal certain personal data identifiers. In social security and immigration cases (where such identifiers are likely to be both especially relevant and peculiarly vulnerable), the redaction right does not generally apply, but electronic access to those files is restricted. For good cause, parties may seek enhanced protections beyond those set forth in Rule 5.2. The right to claim these protections (and the duty of doing so) lies with parties and their counsel.

APPLICATIONS

Privacy and Security Objectives

Rule 5.2 is the federal courts' implementation of the E-Government Act of 2002.[1] It is intended to protect the privacy and security interests implicated by electronic filing of (and the consequent public access to) court papers.[2]

The Rule's Odd "May-Include-Only" Syntax

Rule 5.2(a) is oddly worded. It advises parties and nonparties that they "may include only" redacted versions of certain information. This ambiguous syntax supports two different interpretations: either the granting of a choice (*i.e.*, a filer has been given an non-obligatory option to redact)[3] or the imposing of a prohibition (*i.e.*, a filer has been forbidden from doing

---

[1]Pub.L. No. 107-347, § 205(c)(3), 116 Stat. 2899, 2914 (2002) (codified at 44 U.S.C.A. § 3501 note, as amended 2004).

[2]*See* Rule 5.2 advisory committee note (2006).

[3]As in: In ordering my baseball ticket package for the year, I may or-

anything other than redacting).[4] To date, the courts resoundingly have assumed the latter, that Rule 5.2(a) establishes a mandatory redaction obligation (albeit one that can be waived).[5] The administration of the U.S. Courts appears to concur.[6]

The Redaction Right

Both parties and nonparties who are making a filing with the court must follow these redaction protocols with those court filings:

- *Social Security Number / Taxpayer ID Number:* In lieu thereof, the filer may include only the last four digits of those numbers;
- *Birth Year:* The filer may include only a person's birth year, omitting the birth month and day;
- *Minor's Name:* In lieu thereof, the filer may include only the minor's initials (and, potentially, the initials of the minor's parents[7]); and
- *Financial Account Numbers:* In lieu thereof, the filer may include only the last four digits of those numbers.[8]

In order to facilitate the ready use of the redacted information, the filer may, if he or she wishes, choose among two alternatives. The filer may supplement the redacted version of the materials with an unredacted copy filed under seal.[9] Or the filer may supplement the redacted version by filing, under seal,

---

der the full season's games, or I instead *may include only* those ten games I most want to watch.

[4]As in: In mailing in that ticket order, a fan *may include only* a check or credit card information; never cash.

[5]*See, e.g., M.A.C. v. Gildner*, 853 Fed. Appx. 207, 210 (10th Cir. 2021) ("requires" initials for minors, absent court order); *Mitze v. Saul*, 968 F.3d 689, 693 (7th Cir. 2020) (redaction of personal identifying information "is required"); *Integon Nat'l Ins. Co. v. Reece*, 423 F. Supp. 3d 831, 835 n.3 (E.D. Cal. 2019), *aff'd*, 831 Fed. Appx. 274 (9th Cir. 2020) (including minors' full names "ignores the requirements"); *Offor v. Mercy Med. Ctr.*, 167 F. Supp. 3d 414, 445–46 (E.D.N.Y. 2016) ("requires a party . . . to redact").

[6]*See Doe ex rel. Doe v. Kamehameha Schools / Bernice Pauahi Bishop Estate*, 625 F.3d 1182, 1184 (9th Cir. 2010) (Kozinski, C.J., dissenting) (describing operation of federal judiciary's electronic filing system: "[A]ll who log in are required to check a box indicating that they have read, understand and will comply with the following notice: 'IMPORTANT NOTICE OF REDACTION RESPONSIBILITY: All filers must redact: Social Security or taxpayer-identification numbers; dates of birth; names of minor children; financial account numbers; and, in criminal cases, home addresses, in compliance with Fed.R.Civ.P. 5.2 or Fed.R.Crim.P. 49.1. This requirement applies to all documents, including attachments.' ").

[7]*See S.F. v. Archer Daniels Midland Co.*, 594 Fed.Appx. 11, 12 n.1 (2d Cir. 2014) ("this rule extends to the child's parents"); *A.S. v. Harrison Tp. Bd. of Educ.*, 66 F. Supp. 3d 539, 544 n.3 (D.N.J. 2014) (assuming same). *But cf. E.A. v. Gardner*, 929 F.3d 922, 926 (7th Cir. 2019) (redaction permits use of minors' initials, not fictitious names).

[8]*See* Rule 5.2(a).

[9]*See* Rule 5.2(f). *See also Crossman v. Astrue*, 714 F. Supp. 2d 284, 289 (D.Conn. 2009).

a "reference list" that decodes the redactions.[10]

The Sealing Right

In addition to the sealing options to which a filer is entitled as a supplement to redacted filings, the court may, in its discretion,[11] withdraw the right of redaction in favor of a filing under seal, which the court may later unseal or order a replacement redaction.[12] This sealing/unsealing authority persists in the district court even after an appeal is taken.[13]

Applies to Paper Filings (and Trial Exhibits), As Well As Electronic Filings

Rule 5.2 applies broadly to all filings, whether made electronically or in paper form. Many judicial districts scan materials filed in paper form into their electronic case files, thus rendering those materials electronically accessible to the public in much the same way as they would had they been filed electronically in the first instance.[14] Trial exhibits, if filed with the court, fall similarly within the reach of Rule 5.2.[15]

Unfiled Materials Not Protected

Although other Rules may authorize confidentiality protections in other contexts, Rule 5.2 likely has no application where the materials at issue are not filed.[16]

Exceptions to the Redaction Right

The right of redaction does *not* apply in the following circumstances: (a) when the court orders otherwise,[17] (b) in a forfeiture proceeding, if the financial account number identifies property claimed to be subject to forfeiture,[18] (c) to the record of an administrative or agency proceeding,[19] (d) to the official record of a State court proceeding,[20] (e) to the record of a court or tribunal where the record was not subject to the redaction requirement when originally filed,[21] (f) to social security and immigration cases,[22] (g) to cases where the court orders that fil-

---

[10] *See* Rule 5.2(g).

[11] *See Skky, LLC v. Facebook, Inc.*, 191 F. Supp. 3d 977, 980 (D. Minn. 2016).

[12] *See* Rule 5.2(d).

[13] *See United States v. Seugasala*, 670 Fed. Appx. 641, 641–42 (9th Cir. 2016).

[14] *See* Rule 5.2 advisory committee note (2006) ("It is electronic availability, not the form of the initial filing, that raises the privacy and security concerns addressed in the E-Government Act.").

[15] *See* Rule 5.2 advisory committee note (2006).

[16] *See Kremen v. Cohen*, 2012 WL 2277857, at *2 (N.D.Cal. June 18, 2012) (protection applies only to publically filed materials, not subpoenas).

[17] *See* Rule 5.2(a). *See also Dawn L. v. Greater Johnstown Sch. Dist.*, 586 F. Supp. 2d 332, 339 n.3 (W.D.Pa. 2008) (because minor's birth date is necessary to case, general redaction requirement is exempted).

[18] *See* Rule 5.2(b)(1).

[19] *See* Rule 5.2(b)(2).

[20] *See* Rule 5.2(b)(3).

[21] *See* Rule 5.2(b)(4).

[22] *See* Rule 5.2(b)(5).

ings not be redacted but, instead, be filed under seal,[23] and (h) to *pro se* filings in actions brought under 28 U.S.C.A. §§ 2241, 2254, or 2255.[24] There is unlikely to be an exception to the redaction duty merely because the document or information might be elsewhere publicly accessible.[25]

The Burden of Redacting / Sealing

The burden of exercising this right of redaction or sealing rests with the filer of the materials, and not with the courts or otherwise.[26] Consequently, if a party intends to take advantage of the privacy and security benefits of this right, either the party or counsel must remember to perform the redaction or seek the sealing. The drafters urged counsel to remind their clients that personal data identifiers that could have been, but were not, protected will be publicly accessible over the Internet.[27] The court may, however, order a redaction or sealing *sua sponte*.[28]

Intended (and Inadvertent) Waivers

Parties may intentionally (balancing costs against benefits)[29] or inadvertently (oversight or carelessness)[30] waive their entitlement to Rule 5.2's protection by filing their information without redaction and not under seal. A minor's guardian can waive the redaction protections on behalf of the represented child.[31] An inadvertent failure to redact or seal may be remedied upon motion to the court.[32]

---

[23] *See* Rule 5.2(b)(5).

[24] *See* Rule 5.2(b)(6).

[25] *See Coleman v. Zaccari*, 2011 WL 2607941, at *1 (D.N.H. June 30, 2011).

[26] *See* Rule 5.2(h). *See also* Rule 5.2 advisory committee note (2006). *See also Crossman v. Astrue*, 714 F. Supp. 2d 284, 290 (D.Conn. 2009).

[27] *See* Rule 5.2 advisory committee note (2006) ("Parties must remember that any personal information not otherwise protected by sealing or redaction will be made available over the internet. Counsel should notify clients of this fact so that an informed decision may be made on what information is to be included in a document filed with the court.").

[28] *See Online Payment Solutions Inc. v. Svenska Handelsbanken AB*, 638 F. Supp. 2d 375, 383 n.4 (S.D.N.Y. 2009).

[29] *See* Rule 5.2(h). *See also* Rule 5.2 advisory committee note (2006) ("One may wish to waive the protection if it is determined that the costs of redaction outweigh the benefits to privacy."). *See also United States v. Seugasala*, 670 Fed. Appx. 641, 642 (9th Cir. 2016); *Evans v. Larchmont Baptist Church Infant Care Ctr., Inc.*, 956 F. Supp. 2d 695, 706 n.6 (E.D.Va. 2013).

[30] *See Holt v. Target Corp.*, 2021 WL 2389476, at *2 n.4 (M.D. Tenn. May 6, 2021), *adopted*, 2021 WL 2386124 (M.D. Tenn. June 10, 2021); *Evans v. Larchmont Baptist Church Infant Care Ctr., Inc.*, 956 F. Supp. 2d 695, 706 n.6 (E.D. Va. 2013).

[31] *See Lyons v. Does*, 2022 WL 329268, at *2 (S.D.N.Y. Feb. 3, 2022); *Khabbaz v. Costco Wholesale Corp.*, 2017 WL 10186279, at *1 n.1 (E.D.N.Y. Mar. 15, 2017).

[32] *See* Rule 5.2 advisory committee note (2006) ("If a person files an unredacted identifier by mistake, that person may seek relief from the court."). *See also J.W. v. D.C.*, 318

Additional Privacy / Security Protections

The denomination in Rule 5.2 of certain categories of personal data identifiers is not intended to give rise to a negative presumption that *only* those categories of data are entitled to protection or that the abbreviated identifiers (*e.g.*, last four digits, minor's initials) are not themselves, in an appropriate case, entitled to be shielded further.[33] For "good cause," the court may grant protective orders allowing the redaction of additional information, or either limiting or barring remote electronic access by a nonparty to a filed document.[34] In doing so, courts must balance privacy concerns against the presumptive open access to court records.[35]

Social Security and Immigration Cases

Citing the "prevalence of sensitive information and the volume of filings," the drafters singled out certain social security and immigration cases for special treatment.[36] These cases are *not* entitled to the automatic right of redaction.[37] Although parties and their counsel enjoy unrestricted access to such filings, nonparties are entitled to remote electronic access only to case docket numbers and court disposition documents; to gain full access to the files, nonparties must access them in-person at the courthouse (and may do so, at the courthouse, electronically).[38]

No New Claim or Right

This Rule does not create a new or independent claim or

F.R.D. 196, 199 n.2 (D.D.C. 2016).

[33]*See* Rule 5.2 advisory committee note (2006) (in certain cases, all parts of account number or social security number may need protection, or that protection should extend to other identifiers, like driver's license numbers and alien registration numbers).

[34]*See* Rule 5.2(e). *See also Buster v. Bd. of Cnty. Cmrs. for Lincoln Cnty.*, 2022 WL 1689387, at *1 (D.N.M. May 26, 2022) (home address); *Scheffler v. City of New Hope*, 2018 WL 6012181, at *2 (D. Minn. Nov. 16, 2018) (home addresses of defendant judges); *Goodman v. J.P. Morgan Inv. Mgmt., Inc.*, 301 F. Supp. 3d 759, 784 (S.D. Ohio 2018), *aff'd*, 954 F.3d 852 (6th Cir. 2020) (other financial information); *Fazzio v. Standard Exam'r*, 2018 WL 2336113, at *2 & n.1 (D. Utah May 23, 2018) (minor's photograph); *J.W. v. D.C.*, 318 F.R.D. 196, 197–202 (D.D.C. 2016) (names of minor's parents); *Macias v. Cleaver*, 2016 WL 3549257, at *6 (E.D. Cal. June 30, 2016) (driver's license number).

[35]*See In re Roman Catholic Archbishop of Portland*, 661 F.3d 417, 425–26 (9th Cir. 2011) (refusing to fashion a presumptively-protected approach for personnel records); *Privacy Matters v. U.S. Dep't of Educ. Doe*, 2016 WL 6436658, at *4 (D. Minn. Oct. 27, 2016) (sealing granted); *United States ex rel. Graves v. Internet Corp. for Assigned Names & Numbers, Inc.*, 398 F. Supp. 3d 1307, 1313 (N.D. Ga. 2019) (sealing/redacting denied).

[36]*See* Rule 5.2 advisory committee note (2006). *See also Crossman v. Astrue*, 714 F. Supp. 2d 284, 288–89 (D.Conn. 2009). This Rule applies to actions for benefits under the Social Security Act, and actions or proceedings relating to orders of removal, relief from removal, or immigration benefits or detention. *See* Rule 5.2(c).

[37]*See* Rule 5.2(b)(5).

[38]*See* Rule 5.2(c). *See also Crossman v. Astrue*, 714 F. Supp. 2d 284, 288–90 (D.Conn. 2009).

right of action for its violation.[39]

Enforcement and Sanctions

Courts enforce the redaction obligations by orders that compel the redaction,[40] permanently seal an offending filing,[41] temporarily seal[42] or withdraw[43] unredacted filings pending substitution, judicially alter unredacted filings to accomplish the redaction,[44] strike or ignore unredacted filings,[45] limit document access to parties only,[46] order a re-training of attorneys and their staff,[47] publicly admonish,[48] and, in appropriate cases, issue sanction awards of many varieties.[49] In considering whether to impose sanctions, courts have been influenced by the degree of counsel's vigilance and the unintentional nature of the misstep.[50] A bargained-for agreement to further seal court documents is, alone, unlikely to defeat that presumption.[51]

Privacy Protection and "Particularized" Pleading

Certain federal claims require enhanced detail in pleading (such as fraud, governed by Rule 9(b)), and the redaction/ sealing procedures may be used to properly balance privacy

---

[39] *See Good v. Khosrowshahi*, 296 Fed.Appx. 676, 680 (10th Cir.2008); *Carmax Auto Superstores, Inc. v. Sibley*, 194 F. Supp. 3d 392, 403 (D. Md. 2016).

[40] *See State Farm Mut. Auto. Ins. Co. v. Lawson*, 543 F. Supp. 3d 260, 266 (M.D.N.C. 2021); *Preuss v. Kolmar Labs., Inc.*, 970 F. Supp. 2d 171, 179 n.11 (S.D.N.Y. 2013).

[41] *See State Farm Mut. Auto. Ins. Co. v. Lawson*, 543 F. Supp. 3d 260, 266 (M.D.N.C. 2021); *Struve v. Gardner*, 2021 WL 2004177, at *2 (S.D. Ind. Apr. 9, 2021).

[42] *See Freeman v. Fayetteville Police Dep't*, 2013 WL 2456553, at *2 n.2 (E.D.N.C. June 6, 2013).

[43] *See Smith v. Houston Pilots*, 2013 WL 1787782, at *1 (S.D.Tex. Apr. 25, 2013).

[44] *See Adams v. Andrews*, 2021 WL 2372209, at *2 n.1 (E.D. Va. May 4, 2021), *adopted*, 2021 WL 2366232 (E.D. Va. June 9, 2021).

[45] *See Garcia v. City of E. Chicago Common Council*, 2017 WL 1325429, at *1 (N.D. Ind. Apr. 10, 2017).

[46] *See Brock v. City of New York*, 2021 WL 1600098, at *5 (S.D.N.Y. Apr. 19, 2021).

[47] *See Carpenters' Dist. Council of Greater St. Louis & Vicinity v. Neier Servs. Co.*, 2015 WL 3971070, at *2 (E.D. Mo. June 30, 2015).

[48] *See C.M. ex rel. P.M. v. Syosset Cent. Sch. Dist.*, 2013 WL 5799908, at *5 n.6 (E.D.N.Y. Oct. 25, 2013) (describing "remarkable" failure to comply with Rules), *adopted*, 2013 WL 6157188 (E.D.N.Y. Nov. 22, 2013); *Hanks v. Shinseki*, 2010 WL 3000835, at *4 (N.D.Tex. July 28, 2010) (admonishing, rather than sanctioning, where error caught within one business day and corrected within hours).

[49] *See Reed v. AMCO Ins. Co.*, 2012 WL 846475, at *3 (D.Nev. Mar. 9, 2012) (awarding attorney fees related to motion to seal and sanctions motion); *Weakley v. Redline Recovery Servs., LLC*, 2011 WL 1522413, at *2 (S.D.Cal. Apr. 20, 2011) (imposing costs for 5 years of credit monitoring, and noting potential for later damages lawsuit); *Engeseth v. County of Isanti, Minn.*, 665 F. Supp. 2d 1047, 1048 (D. Minn. 2009) (imposing costs for credit reports and credit monitoring, notice to all affected persons, and charitable donation).

[50] *See Saunders v. Vinton*, 554 Fed. Appx. 36, 39 (2d Cir. 2014); *Alberth v. S. Lakes Plumbing & Heating, Inc.*, 2020 WL 533728, at *2 (E.D. Wis. Feb. 3, 2020).

[51] *See Bernsten v. O'Reilly*, 307 F. Supp. 3d 161, 168 (S.D.N.Y. 2018).

with this command for additional pleading specificity.[52]

---

[52]*See Exergen Corp. v. Wal-Mart Stores, Inc.*, 575 F.3d 1312, 1329 n.6 (Fed.Cir. 2009) (noting Rule 5.2's value in Rule 9(b) fraud cases, where courts endeavor to protect defendants against reputational harm).

RULE 6
COMPUTING AND EXTENDING TIME; TIME FOR MOTION PAPERS

(a) Computing Time. The following rules apply in computing any time period specified in these rules, in any local rule or court order, or in any statute that does not specify a method of computing time.

(1) *Period Stated in Days or a Longer Unit.* When the period is stated in days or a longer unit of time:

(A) exclude the day of the event that triggers the period;

(B) count every day, including intermediate Saturdays, Sundays, and legal holidays; and

(C) include the last day of the period, but if the last day is a Saturday, Sunday, or legal holiday, the period continues to run until the end of the next day that is not a Saturday, Sunday, or legal holiday.

(2) *Period Stated in Hours.* When the period is stated in hours:

(A) begin counting immediately on the occurrence of the event that triggers the period;

(B) count every hour, including hours during intermediate Saturdays, Sundays, and legal holidays; and

(C) if the period would end on a Saturday, Sunday, or legal holiday, the period continues to run until the same time on the next day that is not a Saturday, Sunday, or legal holiday.

(3) *Inaccessibility of the Clerk's Office.* Unless the court orders otherwise, if the clerk's office is inaccessible:

(A) on the last day for filing under Rule 6(a)(1), then the time for filing is extended to the first accessible day that is not a Saturday, Sunday, or legal holiday; or

(B) during the last hour for filing under Rule

6(a)(2), then the time for filing is extended to the same time on the first accessible day that is not a Saturday, Sunday, or legal holiday.

(4) *"Last Day" Defined.* Unless a different time is set by a statute, local rule, or court order, the last day ends:

(A) for electronic filing, at midnight in the court's time zone; and

(B) for filing by other means, when the clerk's office is scheduled to close.

(5) *"Next Day" Defined.* The "next day" is determined by continuing to count forward when the period is measured after an event and backward when measured before an event.

(6) *"Legal Holiday" Defined.* "Legal holiday" means:

(A) the day set aside by statute for observing New Year's Day, Martin Luther King Jr.'s Birthday, Washington's Birthday, Memorial Day, Independence Day, Labor Day, Columbus Day, Veterans' Day, Thanksgiving Day, or Christmas Day;

(B) any day declared a holiday by the President or Congress; and

(C) for periods that are measured after an event, any other day declared a holiday by the state where the district court is located.

(b) Extending Time.

(1) *In General.* When an act may or must be done within a specified time, the court may, for good cause, extend the time:

(A) with or without motion or notice if the court acts, or if a request is made, before the original time or its extension expires; or

(B) on motion made after the time has expired if the party failed to act because of excusable neglect.

(2) *Exceptions.* A court must not extend the time to act under Rules 50(b) and (d), 52(b), 59(b), (d), and (e), and 60(b).

(c) Motions, Notices of Hearing, and Affidavits.

(1) *In General.* A written motion and notice of the

hearing must be served at least 14 days before the time specified for the hearing, with the following exceptions:

(A) when the motion may be heard ex parte;

(B) when these rules set a different time; or

(C) when a court order—which a party may, for good cause, apply for ex parte—sets a different time.

(2) *Supporting Affidavit.* Any affidavit supporting a motion must be served with the motion. Except as Rule 59(c) provides otherwise, any opposing affidavit must be served at least 7 days before the hearing, unless the court permits service at another time.

(d) Additional Time After Certain Kinds of Service. When a party may or must act within a specified time after being served and service is made under Rule 5(b)(2)(C) (mail), (D) (leaving with the clerk), or (F) (other means consented to), 3 days are added after the period would otherwise expire under Rule 6(a).

[Amended effective March 19, 1948; July 1, 1963; July 1, 1966; July 1, 1968; July 1, 1971; August 1, 1983; August 1, 1985; August 1, 1987; December 1, 1999; April 23, 2001, effective December 1, 2001; April 25, 2005, effective December 1, 2005; April 30, 2007, effective December 1, 2007; March 26, 2009, effective December 1, 2009; April 28, 2016, effective December 1, 2016.]

AUTHORS' COMMENTARY ON RULE 6

PURPOSE AND SCOPE

Rule 6 sets the procedure for computing the passage of time under the Rules. Although other Rules prescribe the length of allowable time for such acts as answering pleadings, filing motions, or responding to discovery, Rule 6 dictates how those defined time periods are to be calculated by establishing counting rules for periods stated in hours, days, or longer intervals. Rule 6 also invests the district courts with authority to extend certain time periods (but not others), sets deadlines for motions, hearing notices, and supporting affidavits, and grants automatic extensions following certain types of service.

RULE 6(a)—COMPUTING OF TIME

CORE CONCEPT

All time periods set by the Rules, by local rules, by court orders, or by statutes are governed by the computation methods of Rule 6(a), unless the source itself specifies a different method (or sets a time-certain). Time periods computed using Rule 6 cannot end on a weekend or legal holiday (or, with filing deadlines, on a day when the courthouse is inaccessible). In such instances, a brief, automatic extension is supplied.

APPLICATIONS

No Effect on Dates-Certain or Times-Certain

When the court sets a "date-certain" (*e.g.*, by April 14) or a "time-certain" (*e.g.*, by 1:00 p.m. on April 14) for filing or some other act, Rule 6(a) will *not* automatically extend that date if it falls on a Saturday, Sunday, or holiday[1] (although a court may still grant such extensions in its discretion).[2]

Periods Set in Days or Longer

In counting periods stated in units of time measured in days or longer (*e.g.*, days, months, or years), the day that triggers the period is excluded and then every following day is included. If the period ends on a weekend or a legal holiday, the period is extended to the end of the next day that is not a weekend or legal holiday. (For filing deadlines, the period is also extended past days that the courthouse is inaccessible.) Thus, for example, if a Rule period was due to expire on Saturday, February 21 (and assuming Monday, February 23 was Washington's Birthday), that Rule period would expire at the end of the day on Tuesday, February 24.[3]

- *Triggering Event:* What starts a time period running will depend on the implicated statute, rule, regulation, or other law.[4]
- *When A Day "Ends":* Unless otherwise specified, a day "ends" for electronic filing at midnight in the court's time zone, and for all non-electronic filings when the

---

[1]*See* Rule 6(a) advisory committee note (2009) ("They do not apply when a fixed time to act is set."). *See also Violette v. P.A. Days, Inc.*, 427 F.3d 1015, 1016–20 (6th Cir. 2005); *Ortiz v. Wagstaff*, 523 F. Supp. 3d 347, 355 (W.D.N.Y. 2021). *But cf. Equal Emp. Opportunity Comm'n v. Publix Super Markets, Inc.*, 481 F. Supp. 3d 684, 690–91 (M.D. Tenn. 2020) (noting potential for confusion; forgiving 2-day delay resulting from Monday filing).

[2]*See Design Basics, LLC v. Best Built, Inc.*, 223 F. Supp. 3d 825, 829–30 (E.D. Wis. 2016); *Scanlon v. Greenberg Traurig, LLP*, 778 F. Supp. 2d 56, 59 (D.D.C. 2011).

[3]*See, e.g., Hall v. Sec'y, Dep't of Corr.*, 921 F.3d 983, 986 n.3 (11th Cir. 2019) (demonstrating computation).

[4]*See Tiberio v. Allergy Asthma Immunology of Rochester*, 664 F.3d 35, 37–38 (2d Cir. 2011) (EEOC 90-day limitations period begins on date right-to-sue letter is received by *either* claimant or counsel).

clerk's office is scheduled to close.[5]

- *Counting Months:* The length of our months vary. When a time period is set in "months," one court chose to count the period as starting after the triggering day and then running to the eve of the same calendar date as the starting day in the next month.[6]

Periods Set in Hours

In counting periods stated in units of time measured in hours, the period begins immediately upon the triggering event and includes every hour thereafter. If the period ends on a weekend or a legal holiday, the period is extended to the same time on the next day that is not a weekend or legal holiday. (For filing deadlines, the period is also similarly extended past days that the courthouse is inaccessible.)

- *Inaccessible Final "Hour":* No extensions are automatically provided on days when the clerk's office is inaccessible *unless* that inaccessibility continues into the final hour of the hourly time period.[7]
- *No Rounding-Up:* There is no "rounding" of hourly time periods. They will expire at the precise minute that the computation method produces (*e.g.,* 2:17 p.m.), and not be "rounded-up" to the next whole hour.[8]
- *Crossing Daylight Savings Time:* Because *every* hour is counted, an hourly time period that straddles the shift between daylight savings time and standard time will not produce an extra hour of time.[9]

Legal Holidays — Federal

The term "legal holiday" includes any day so declared by the President or Congress. There are currently ten standing federal holidays:

1. New Year's Day
2. Dr. Martin Luther King, Jr.'s Birthday
3. Washington's Birthday
4. Memorial Day
5. Independence Day

---

[5]*See* Rule 6(a)(4). *See also Justice v. Town of Cicero*, 682 F.3d 662, 664–65 (7th Cir. 2012) (late-night electronic filing accessibility does not excuse failure to e-file before 11:59 p.m. on due-date: "A document entered into the electronic system at 12:01 AM on a Thursday has been filed on Thursday, not on 'virtual Wednesday.' ").

[6]*See Stevens v. Jiffy Lube Int'l, Inc.*, 911 F.3d 1249, 1252 (9th Cir. 2018) (September 14th was triggering day (and, thus, excluded), so September 15th was Day #1; "month" period ended on eve of that first date a month later - October 14th (span of 30 days); next "month" began October 15th, and ended on the same day's eve a month later, November 14th (span of 31 days)).

[7]*See* Rule 6(a)(3) advisory committee note (2009).

[8]*See* Rule 6(a)(2) advisory committee note (2009).

[9]*See* Rule 6(a)(2) advisory committee note (2009).

6. Labor Day
7. Columbus Day
8. Veterans' Day
9. Thanksgiving Day
10. Christmas Day

Legal Holidays — State

A special rule governs holidays that are declared by States. For "forward-looking" time periods (*i.e.*, acts to be taken within a time *after* a triggering event), State holidays are considered "legal holidays" under Rule 6(a). Time periods typically cannot end on such days. However, for "backward-looking" time periods (*i.e.*, acts to be taken no less than a certain time *before* an event), State holidays are *not* considered "legal holidays" under Rule 6(a). In such instances (like with Rule 26(f), which requires an attorney's meeting at least 21 days before a scheduling conference), the 21st day *can* fall on a State holiday and that day will *not* be excluded from the computation.

Legal Holidays — Identifying When There Is One

From time to time, special federal holidays have been recognized.[10] Likewise, States are free to recognize their own holidays, even if the federal judiciary is otherwise open.[11] Occasionally, identifying whether a particular day qualifies as a "legal holiday" under Rule 6(a) can prove difficult. On those occasions, courts note that the Rule provides "reasonable flexibility" and is intended to abate the "hardship" of permitting "days of rest to shorten already tight deadlines."[12] One court has adopted a "simplicity" rule, which holds that any day the President closes the federal government for celebratory or commemorative reasons, a snow emergency, a terrorist act, or some other *force majeure*, creates a rebuttable presumption that a federal holiday was declared.[13] When the local district orders

---

[10] *See, e.g., Reyes-Cardona v. J. C. Penney Co., Inc.*, 690 F.2d 1, 1 (1st Cir. 1982) (legal holiday in Puerto Rico honoring Eugenio Maria de Hostos was properly excluded from computation of time under Rule 6(a)).

[11] *See Rich v. Shrader*, 823 F.3d 1205 n.3, 2016 WL 2994736, at *3 n.3 (9th Cir. 2016) (Cesar Chavez Day a legal holiday in California); *Yepremyan v. Holder*, 614 F.3d 1042, 1044 (9th Cir. 2010) (day after Thanksgiving a legal holiday in California); *Tamez v. Manthey*, 589 F.3d 764, 769 (5th Cir. 2009) (Texas Independence Day a legal holiday in Texas); *Dietrich v. John Ascuaga's Nugget*, 548 F.3d 892, 896 n.3 (9th Cir. 2008) (Nevada Day a legal holiday in Nevada); *Wright v. Trinity Catering, Inc.*, 2007 WL 2155728, at *1–*3 (E.D. La. 2007) (Mardi Gras a legal holiday in Louisiana, implemented parish by parish); *Seacor by Seacor v. Secretary of Dept. of Health and Human Services*, 34 Fed. Cl. 141, 143–44 (1995) (Patriot's Day a legal holiday in Massachusetts).

[12] *See Mashpee Wampanoag Tribal Council, Inc. v. Norton*, 336 F.3d 1094, 1098–99 (D.C. Cir. 2003) (recognizing Christmas Eve 2001 as qualifying holiday for federal litigators, where President gave all Executive Branch employees that day off).

[13] *See Hart v. Sheahan*, 396 F.3d 887, 891 (7th Cir. 2005).

its clerk's office closed, the answer is less certain.[14]

Clerk's Office Inaccessibility

What causes the clerk's office to be considered "inaccessible" is not defined by the Rules,[15] although the drafters emphasize that bad weather is not the only qualifying cause (an "outage" of the clerk's electronic filing system is given as one example).[16] The Rule contemplates that "inaccessibility" will continue to evolve through caselaw.[17] To date, that caselaw has found "inaccessibility" when the clerk's office is closed *officially* for any reason[18] (including inclement weather closures[19] and, perhaps, courthouse holidays[20]), when local weather conditions near the courthouse make traveling to the clerk's office dangerous, difficult, or impossible,[21] or when other circumstances make the courthouse inaccessible as a practical matter.[22] But this "practi-

---

[14]*Compare Garcia-Velazquez v. Frito Lay Snacks Caribbean*, 358 F.3d 6, 9–11 (1st Cir. 2004) (New Year's Eve not excluded, even though Chief Judge declared clerk's office closed), *and In re Cascade Oil Co.*, 848 F.2d 1062, 1064 (10th Cir. 1988) (day after Thanksgiving not excluded, same reasoning), *with Randall v. Allbaugh*, 662 Fed. Appx. 571, 573 n.4 (10th Cir. 2016) (extension to Monday because court "is traditionally closed" on day after Thanksgiving), *and Jones v. U.S.*, 934 F. Supp. 2d 284, 291–92 (D.D.C. 2013) (Thanksgiving Friday excluded when Chief Judge ordered clerk's office closed). *Cf. Keyser v. Sacramento City Unified Sch. Dist.*, 265 F.3d 741, 747 (9th Cir.2001) (day after Thanksgiving qualified as a legal holiday under the Federal Appellate Rules).

[15]*See Organic Cannabis Found., LLC v. Comm'r of Internal Revenue*, 962 F.3d 1082, 1088 (9th Cir. 2020) (omission of definition was intentional).

[16]*See* Rule 6(a)(3) advisory committee note (2009). *Accord Chao Lin v. U.S. Attorney Gen.*, 677 F.3d 1043, 1045 (11th Cir. 2012).

[17]*See* Rule 6(a)(3) advisory committee note (2009). *See also Organic Cannabis Found., LLC v. Comm'r of Internal Revenue*, 962 F.3d 1082, 1088 (9th Cir. 2020). *See generally* William G. Phelps, *When is office of clerk of court inaccessible due to weather or other conditions for purpose of computing time period for filing papers under Rule 6(a) of Federal Rules of Civil Procedure*, 135 A.L.R. Fed. 259.

[18]*See Circuitronix, LLC v. Kinwong Elec. (Hong Kong) Co.*, 993 F.3d 1299, 1304 (11th Cir. 2021).

[19]*See Holden v. Serco Inc.*, 2022 WL 101403, at *5–*6 (E.D. La. Jan. 11, 2022) (to address Hurricane Ida disruptions, time periods extended by general court order for 30 days). *See also Telephone & Data Systems, Inc. v. Amcell F Atlantic City, Inc.*, 20 F.3d 501, 501–02 (D.C. Cir. 1994) (clerk's office is "inaccessible" within the meaning of Rule 6(a) when inclement weather forces office to close, notwithstanding that clerk's office's 24-hour "drop box" was still available).

[20]*See Perry v. Strategic Realty Capital, LLC*, 2019 WL 384000, at *4–*5 (M.D. La. Jan. 30, 2019) (day after Christmas).

[21]The courthouse need not be physically closed in order for the clerk's office to be deemed "inaccessible". *See U.S. Leather, Inc. v. H & W Partnership*, 60 F.3d 222, 222–26 (5th Cir. 1995) ("An ice storm that temporarily knocks out an area's power and telephone service and makes travelling dangerous, difficult or impossible, thereby rendering the federal courthouse inaccessible to those in the area of the courthouse, is enough to come within Rule 6(a)'s weather exception").

[22]*See Organic Cannabis Found., LLC v. Comm'r of Internal Revenue*, 962 F.3d 1082, 1088 (9th Cir. 2020) (not only when clerk's office is "impos-

cal" inaccessibility standard has been applied in an often unyielding way. The requisite inaccessibility, for example, must persist for a "sufficient period of time" leading up to and including the clerk's office scheduled closing time.[23] Thus, inclement weather which renders a courthouse inaccessible during the early morning hours, thus preventing a pre-10:30 a.m. FedEx delivery, would not qualify for an inaccessibility extension if FedEx could have accomplished (but did not attempt) a redelivery when the courthouse was re-opened later that morning.[24] Similarly, an individual's own, personal weather-related or other logistical difficulties, which do not also cause the clerk's office to close, close early, or be otherwise dangerous to reach, generally will not qualify for this extension.[25]

- *Inaccessibility and Electronic Filings:* If the clerk's office is *physically* inaccessible, at least one court has ruled that an inaccessibility extension is warranted *even if* the filing could have been accomplished electronically.[26]

Former Approach: Time Periods of Less than 11 Days

Previously, Rule 6(a) provided that time periods of 11 days or less were to be computed by excluding intervening weekends and holidays. That approach was abrogated in 2009.[27]

Effect on Time Periods Set by Private Contracts

Ordinarily, the Rule 6 computation procedures do *not* apply to time periods set in private contracts.[28]

Effect on Federal Statutes

The Rule 6(a) computation methods apply to "any statute"

---

sible" to reach, but also when, though "technically open," it is unreachable absent "heroic measures"); *Chao Lin v. U.S. Att'y Gen.*, 677 F.3d 1043, 1045 (11th Cir. 2012) (same).

[23] *See Organic Cannabis Found., LLC v. Comm'r of Internal Revenue*, 962 F.3d 1082, 1090 (9th Cir. 2020).

[24] *See Chao Lin v. U.S. Atty. Gen.*, 677 F.3d 1043, 1045–46 (11th Cir. 2012). *See also Organic Cannabis Found., LLC v. Comm'r of Internal Revenue*, 962 F.3d 1082, 1088-90 (9th Cir. 2020) (unsuccessful FedEx delivery due to momentary construction blockage or police action did not qualify: "A temporary obstacle that is encountered *earlier* in the day does not, without more, render the clerk's office 'inaccessible' on 'the last *day* for filing.' ").

[25] *See Chung v. Lamb*, 794 Fed. Appx. 773, 776 (10th Cir. 2019) (counsel's personal difficulties accessing court's e-filing system did not render system "inaccessible"); *McElveen v. Westport Recovery Corp.*, 310 F. Supp. 3d 1374, 1377–79 (S.D. Fla. 2018) (court not inaccessible after hurricane impact had passed).

[26] *See Circuitronix, LLC v. Kinwong Elec. (Hong Kong) Co.*, 993 F.3d 1299, 1304 (11th Cir. 2021) (notwithstanding recent amendments requiring e-filing by all attorneys, "outage" of court's e-filing system "is not a necessary condition of inaccessibility").

[27] *See Yost v. Stout*, 607 F.3d 1239, 1241 n.3 (10th Cir. 2010) (less-than-11-day procedure had made calculating deadlines "unnecessarily complicated" and caused "counterintuitive results").

[28] *See J. Aron & Co., Inc. v. S/S Olga Jacob*, 527 F.2d 416, 417 (5th Cir. 1976).

that does not specify a different approach.[29] Previously, the courts were divided as to whether Rule 6(a) would extend a statutory deadline (especially a limitations deadline) that otherwise expired on a weekend or legal holiday (or, for filing deadlines, a day when the courthouse was inaccessible).[30] It now seems clear that Rule 6(a) applies to all federal statutes[31] (absent a different computation method prescribed in the statute itself).[32]

Effect on Federal Court Orders and Rules

The Rule 6(a) computation methods govern federal court orders (except those setting dates-certain or times-certain[33]) and both national and local court rules.[34]

Effect on State Statutes of Limitation

The Rule 6(a) computation methods may govern in applying State limitations periods, provided the State statute of limitations does not establish a contrary computation method.[35]

Effect on Removed Cases

Several courts have held that Rule 6(a) applies to compute

---

[29] *See* Rule 6(a).

[30] *Compare Bartlik v. U.S. Dept. of Labor*, 62 F.3d 163, 166 (6th Cir. 1995) (en banc) (majority view: holding that Rule 6 counting procedures apply), *with Scanio v. U.S.*, 37 F.3d 858, 860–61 (2d Cir. 1994) (minority view: holding that Rule 6 counting procedures do not apply), *See also Union Nat. Bank of Wichita, Kan. v. Lamb*, 337 U.S. 38, 40–41, 69 S. Ct. 911, 93 L. Ed. 1190 (1949) (holding that a petition for review of State supreme court decision filed on Monday—the ninety-first day of the statutory ninety-day filing period, was timely filed: "[s]ince [Rule 6(a)] had the concurrence of Congress and since no contrary policy is expressed in the statute governing this review, we think that the considerations of liberality and leniency which find expression in Rule 6(a) are equally applicable").

[31] *See, e.g., United States v. Vargas-Soto*, 35 F.4th 979, 992 n.4 (5th Cir. 2022) (federal habeas); *ASARCO, LLC v. Union Pacific R. Co.*, 765 F.3d 999, 1007–08 (9th Cir. 2014) (CERCLA); *Elliot-Leach v. N.Y. City Dep't of Educ.*, 201 F. Supp. 3d 238, 242–43 (E.D.N.Y. 2016) (removal statute).

[32] *See* Rule 6(a) advisory committee note (2009) ("does not apply when computing a time period set by a statute if the statute specifies a method of computing time."). *See also Windland v. Quarterman*, 578 F.3d 314, 317 (5th Cir. 2009) (Rule 6(a)'s general approach supplanted when statute provides different direction); *Milburn v. Zurich Am. Ins. Co.*, 334 F.R.D. 190, 192 (E.D. Mo. 2020) (if period is "jurisdictional", then Rule 6(a) does not apply; otherwise, it does).

[33] *See Destra v. Demings*, 725 Fed. Appx. 855, 859 (11th Cir. 2018).

[34] *See* Rule 6(a).

[35] *See Silo Rest. Inc. v. Allied Prop. & Cas. Ins. Co.*, 420 F. Supp. 3d 562, 579 (W.D. Tex. 2019) (federal courts apply Rule 6(a) in diversity cases only when doing so does not conflict with State practices). *See also Walker v. Armco Steel Corp.*, 446 U.S. 740, 744–53, 100 S. Ct. 1978, 64 L. Ed. 2d 659 (1980) (in diversity case, applying State computation rules that required service before limitations period is tolled); *Fullman v. City of Philadelphia*, 722 Fed. Appx. 242, 245 (3d Cir. 2018) (in civil rights case, applying State computation rules which authorized extension past period-ending weekend days). *But see Matter of Hoffman*, 955 F.3d 440, 444 n.2 (5th Cir. 2020) (summarily applying Rule 6(a) to Texas State limitations statute).

case-filing time periods in removed cases, rejecting a narrower reading of Rule 81(c)'s direction that the Rules apply only "after" removal.[36]

Time-Extending Effects Must be Claimed

The various time-broadening effects of Rule 6's computation methods must be raised and claimed, otherwise they may be deemed forfeited by inaction.[37]

RULE 6(b)—EXTENDING TIME

CORE CONCEPT

The district courts may extend many of the time periods established in the Rules (but not all: most post-trial motion deadlines cannot be extended). Extensions sought before a time period expires may be granted for "good cause". Extensions sought after a time period expires may be granted only "on motion" and only if both "good cause" and "excusable neglect" are proven.

APPLICATIONS

Automatic Extensions Addressed Elsewhere

Automatic extensions (those supplied without a court order) are addressed by other subparts of this Rule;[38] this subpart only concerns extensions available upon court order.

No Stipulated Extensions

Ordinarily, parties may not extend the time periods set in the Rules by simply stipulating to the extension.[39] Court approval is required.[40] Sometimes, however, extensions are pre-approved by these Rules[41] or a district's local rules[42] for certain circumstances, and, in all events, courts anticipate the civility and mutual respect among members of the bar that ought to encourage attorney consent to one another's reasonable, non-

---

[36]*See Milburn v. Zurich Am. Ins. Co.*, 334 F.R.D. 190, 191–92 (E.D. Mo. 2020); *Froehlich v. CACH, LLC*, 289 F.R.D. 454, 455 (S.D. Ohio 2013).

[37]*See Robinson v. Norling*, 25 F.4th 1061, 1062–63 (8th Cir. 2022) (discretion to resurrect forfeited Rule 6(a) timing arguments is not unbounded, but permitting rescue where court raised issue *sua sponte* and effect both was beyond doubt and required no further supporting evidence or argument).

[38]*See* Rule 6(a)(1)(C) & Rule 6(a)(2)(C) (extensions when time periods would end on weekends or legal holidays); Rule 6(a)(3)(A)–(B) (extensions when time periods would end on day courthouse is inaccessible); Rule 6(d) (extensions after being served by mail, by special consent, or by delivery to clerk).

[39]*See Orange Theatre Corp. v. Rayherstz Amusement Corp.*, 130 F.2d 185, 186–87 (3d Cir. 1942); *Rashid v. Delta State Univ.*, 306 F.R.D. 530, 533 (N.D.Miss. 2015).

[40]*See Gray v. Lewis & Clark Expeditions, Inc.*, 12 F. Supp. 2d 993, 995 (D. Neb. 1998); *Allstate Ins. Co. v. Administratia Asigurarilor De Stat*, 163 F.R.D. 196, 199 (S.D. N.Y. 1995).

[41]*See* Rule 29(b) (parties may stipulate to certain discovery deadline extensions)

[42]*See, e.g.,* M.D. Ga. Loc. R. 6.2 (clerk may grant one 14-day extension to file briefs); D.S.D. Loc. R. 12.1 (parties may stipulate to 21-day extension to plead).

prejudicial, good faith extension requests.[43]

***Sua Sponte* Extensions**

Courts may extend time deadlines *sua sponte*, so long as such extensions are permitted *and* the courts act prior to the time period expiring.[44] Once the time period expires, however, extensions may only be granted "on motion."[45] (Occasionally, courts have navigated around this motion-only requirement by inviting parties to file a motion or treating another submission as if it were a motion.[46])

Extensions Before the Time Period Expires

If the extension request is made *before* the time period expires, the district court, in its discretion,[47] may grant an extension for "good cause."[48] Neither notice to the adversary nor a formal motion is required by the Rule, although applicable local rules may establish a more specific extension procedure. "Good cause" is not an especially rigorous standard,[49] and has been interpreted broadly[50] and liberally.[51] But "good cause" still requires at least a reasonable explanation why, despite the party's diligence, an approaching deadline cannot be met.[52] When sought in good faith and without prejudicing the adversary, pre-expiration extensions have been routinely granted.[53] Nonetheless, the court's discretion in ruling remains

---

[43]*See Ahanchian v. Xenon Pictures, Inc.*, 624 F.3d 1253, 1263 (9th Cir. 2010).

[44]*See* Rule 6(b)(1)(A).

[45]*See* Rule 6(b)(1)(B). *See also Lujan v. Nat'l Wildlife Fed'n*, 497 U.S. 871, 896 n.5, 110 S. Ct. 3177, 111 L. Ed. 2d 695 (1990); *Drippe v. Tobelinski*, 604 F.3d 778, 782–85 (3d Cir. 2010).

[46]*See E.M. v. Shady Grove Reprod. Sci. Ctr. P.C.*, 496 F. Supp. 3d 338, 362 n.5 (D.D.C. 2020) (treating counsel's letter as motion to extend, when court then granted).

[47]*See Ott v. Federal Home Loan Mortg. Corp.*, 535 Fed. Appx. 488, 489 (6th Cir. 2013) (noting that extensions are not required (even with good cause), but remain discretionary).

[48]*See Lujan v. National Wildlife Federation*, 497 U.S. 871, 896, 110 S. Ct. 3177, 111 L. Ed. 2d 695 (1990) (cause must be shown before enlargement of time is granted).

[49]*See Alexander v. Saul*, 5 F.4th 139, 154 (2d Cir. 2021) ("non-rigorous standard"); *United States v. Navarro*, 800 F.3d 1104, 1109 (9th Cir. 2015) (same). *But see Utah Republican Party v. Herbert*, 678 Fed. Appx. 697, 700 (10th Cir. 2017) ("good cause" compels a "greater showing" than "excusable neglect").

[50]*See Ahanchian v. Xenon Pictures, Inc.*, 624 F.3d 1253, 1259 (9th Cir. 2010); *Andrews v. Daughtry*, 994 F. Supp. 2d 728, 734–35 (M.D.N.C. 2014).

[51]*See Rachel v. Troutt*, 820 F.3d 390, 394 (10th Cir. 2016).

[52]*See Albright as Next Friend of Doe v. Mountain Home Sch. Dist.*, 926 F.3d 942, 951 (8th Cir. 2019); *Utah Republican Party v. Herbert*, 678 Fed. Appx. 697, 700–01 (10th Cir. 2017). *Cf. Ott v. Fed. Home Loan Mortg. Corp.*, 535 Fed. Appx. 488, 489 (6th Cir. 2013) (merely stating that "the Fourth of July holiday caused an inability to file" was not sufficient); *McGuire v. Nielsen*, 448 F. Supp. 3d 1213, 1259 (D.N.M. 2020) ("rules are not unfettered grants to do justice without reference to their text").

[53]*See Alexander v. Saul*, 5 F.4th 139, 154 (2d Cir. 2021); *Rachel v. Troutt*,

quite broad.[54] When useful, the court may convene an evidentiary hearing to explore the issues of good faith and prejudice.[55]

Extensions After the Time Period Expires

If the extension request is made *after* the time period expires, the district court's discretion is more restricted (though still afforded great deference).[56] The district court may grant such an extension if: (1) "good cause" is shown (discussed above), *and* (2) the failure to act was the result of "excusable neglect."[57] The Supreme Court has characterized excusable neglect as the greater of these two obstacles to a post-expiration extension.[58]

The courts have tested carefully a litigant's claim of excusable neglect; general unfamiliarity with the Rules or a busy professional schedule will not constitute excusable neglect,[59] nor will a delay taken for strategic reasons.[60] Ergo, demonstrating excusable neglect is not easy, nor was it intended to be.[61] As one court aptly wrote: "When parties wait until the last minute to comply with a deadline, they are playing with fire."[62] A formal request for an excusable neglect extension is required; trial courts abuse their discretion in granting such relief in the absence of a motion by the affected litigant.[63]

The Supreme Court has noted that excusable neglect is a "somewhat elastic concept," grounded in equity, not limited exclusively to omissions caused by circumstances outside the moving party's control, but which must be assessed in view of all relevant circumstances surrounding the omission.[64] A show-

---

820 F.3d 390, 394 (10th Cir. 2016).

[54]*See Tindall v. First Solar Inc.*, 892 F.3d 1043, 1048 (9th Cir. 2018) (no abuse of discretion in finding absence of good cause); *Yancick v. Hanna Steel Corp.*, 653 F.3d 532, 537–39 (7th Cir. 2011) (no abuse of discretion in refusing late filing of attorney who waited until last minute).

[55]*See Ahanchian v. Xenon Pictures, Inc.*, 624 F.3d 1253, 1260 (9th Cir. 2010).

[56]*See Lujan v. Nat'l Wildlife Fed'n*, 497 U.S. 871, 895, 110 S. Ct. 3177, 111 L. Ed. 2d 695 (1990) (Rule's text "specifically confers" discretion). *But cf. Kucera v. Cent. Intelligence Agency*, 429 F. Supp. 3d 970, 972 (D.N.M. 2019) ("a higher burden than good cause"); *King v. United States Dep't of Justice*, 292 F. Supp. 3d 182, 186 (D.D.C. 2017) (tested under "less generous" standard than good cause).

[57]*See Cohen v. Bd. of Trustees of Univ. of D.C.*, 819 F.3d 476, 479 (D.C. Cir. 2016); *Murphy v. Eddie Murphy Productions, Inc.*, 611 F.3d 322, 324 (7th Cir. 2010).

[58]*Lujan v. National Wildlife Federation*, 497 U.S. 871, 897, 110 S. Ct. 3177, 111 L. Ed. 2d 695 (1990).

[59]*See Ragguette v. Premier Wines & Spirits*, 691 F.3d 315, 317–33 (3d Cir. 2012); *Keeton v. Morningstar, Inc.*, 667 F.3d 877, 882–84 (7th Cir. 2012).

[60]*See Huggins v. FedEx Ground Package Sys., Inc.*, 592 F.3d 853, 856–57 (8th Cir. 2010).

[61]*See Thompson v. E.I. DuPont de Nemours & Co., Inc.*, 76 F.3d 530, 534 (4th Cir. 1996).

[62]*Spears v. City of Indianapolis*, 74 F.3d 153, 157 (7th Cir. 1996).

[63]*See supra* Authors' Commentary to Rule 6(b) ("***Sua Sponte* Extensions**").

[64]*See Pioneer Inv. Services Co. v.*

ing of "faultlessness" is not always required,[65] and indeed negligent oversight (if that oversight is deemed excusable) is encompassed in this standard.[66] For example, an attorney's inexplicable failure to read and apply "crystal clear" legal rules will not be deemed excusable neglect, but an attorney's "plausible misinterpretation" of an ambiguous legal rule may be.[67] Likewise, an inadvertent, good faith, understandable, minimal, and non-prejudicial calendaring error may qualify,[68] though unexceptional, ordinary calendaring oversights[69] or a crowded work schedule[70] likely will not. Malfunctioning of the court's electronic filing systems will likely qualify,[71] but technical difficulties experienced in counsel's law office might not.[72] The fact that the error lies with the attorney, and not with the attorney's client, is *not* dispositive on whether "excusable neglect" exists. Clients are held responsible for the omissions of their attorneys, even if the clients are not separately culpable for the error.[73]

In testing whether the neglect was excusable, courts have considered the following factors:

1. The prejudice to the opponent (which must encompass something more than the chore of having to now re-

---

Brunswick Associates Ltd. Partnership, 507 U.S. 380, 390–95, 113 S. Ct. 1489, 123 L. Ed. 2d 74 (1993) (construing excusable neglect in the context of Bankruptcy Rule 9006(b), which was patterned after Rule 6(b)). *See also Cohen v. Bd. of Trustees of Univ. of D.C.*, 819 F.3d 476, 479 (D.C. Cir. 2016) (excusable neglect is a totality of circumstances inquiry).

[65] *See Cohen v. Bd. of Trustees of Univ. of D.C.*, 819 F.3d 476, 479 (D.C. Cir. 2016).

[66] *See Mommaerts v. Hartford Life and Acc. Ins. Co.*, 472 F.3d 967, 968 (7th Cir. 2007) (quoting *Pioneer Inv. Services Co. v. Brunswick Associates Ltd. Partnership*, 507 U.S. 380, 395, 113 S. Ct. 1489, 123 L. Ed. 2d 74 (1993)).

[67] *See L.A. Pub. Ins. Adjusters, Inc. v. Nelson*, 17 F.4th 521, 525 (5th Cir. 2021); *Lewis v. School Dist. #70*, 523 F.3d 730, 740 (7th Cir. 2008).

[68] *See Kirkland v. Guardian Life Ins. Co.*, 352 Fed.Appx. 293, 295 (11th Cir. 2009) (counsel calendared proper date, but then filed notice of removal a day earlier than planned); *Adejola v. Barr*, 439 F. Supp. 3d 120, 125 (W.D.N.Y. 2020) (non-prejudicial delay spanning one business day excused).

[69] *See Ragguette v. Premier Wines & Spirits*, 691 F.3d 315, 317–33 (3d Cir. 2012) (no excusable neglect for busy calendar, imprecise instructions to subordinates, inaction by subordinates).

[70] *See Miller v. Chicago Transit Auth.*, 20 F.4th 1148, 1153 (7th Cir. 2021); *Albright as Next Friend of Doe v. Mountain Home Sch. Dist.*, 926 F.3d 942, 951–52 (8th Cir. 2019).

[71] *See Salts v. Epps*, 676 F.3d 468, 474–75 (5th Cir. 2012).

[72] *See Schoenman v. F.B.I.*, 857 F. Supp. 2d 76, 78–83 (D.D.C. 2012) ("malfunctioning scanner" not sufficient); *Phillips v. Seattle Times Co.*, 818 F. Supp. 2d 1277, 1281–82 (W.D.Wash. 2011) (lightning strike that disabled internet connection might excuse 1-day delay but not 3).

[73] *See L.A. Pub. Ins. Adjusters, Inc. v. Nelson*, 17 F.4th 521, 525 (5th Cir. 2021); *Allen v. Murph*, 194 F.3d 722, 724 (6th Cir. 1999). *See generally Pioneer Inv. Servs. Co. v. Brunswick Assocs. Ltd. P'ship*, 507 U.S. 380, 396–97, 113 S. Ct. 1489, 1499, 123 L. Ed. 2d 74 (1993) (parties choose their counsel and are accountable for counsel's acts and omissions).

spond to and litigate an otherwise untimely filing);[74]

2. The length of the delay and its potential impact on the course of the judicial proceedings;
3. The causes for the delay, and whether those causes were within the reasonable control of the moving party; and
4. The moving party's good faith;[75]

On occasion, courts have also tested for other equitable criteria, such as:

5. Whether the omission reflected professional incompetence, such as an ignorance of the procedural rules;
6. Whether the omission reflected an easily manufactured excuse that the court could not verify;
7. Whether the moving party had failed to provide for a consequence that was readily foreseeable; and
8. Whether the omission constituted a complete lack of diligence.[76]

Courts have often ranked reason-for-delay[77] and delay length[78] as especially important considerations. Thus, a party's failure to offer any explanation for a missed deadline[79] or an explanation offered only in vague, nonspecific terms[80] will likely doom most requests to extend an expired deadline. Courts are unlikely to approve new extensions if prior extensions have been granted and ignored.[81] On appeal, the district court's substantial discretion is respected, but a ruling that ignores a material factor, weighs an improper factor, or commits a serious error while weighing correct factors may merit reversal.[82]

No Extensions to Most Post-Trial Motions

The end of a civil trial is often followed by the filing of post-

---

[74]*See Kimberg v. Univ. of Scranton*, 411 Fed. Appx. 473, 479 (3d Cir. 2010).

[75]*See Pioneer Inv. Servs. Co. v. Brunswick Assocs. Ltd. P'ship*, 507 U.S. 380, 395, 113 S. Ct. 1489, 123 L. Ed. 2d 74 (1993); *Miller v. Chicago Transit Auth.*, 20 F.4th 1148, 1153 (7th Cir. 2021); *Spirit Lake Tribe v. Jaeger*, 5 F.4th 849, 854–55 (8th Cir. 2021).

[76]*See See Ragguette v. Premier Wines & Spirits*, 691 F.3d 315, 325–26 (3d Cir. 2012) (discussing factors in appellate extension context, citing national case authorities).

[77]*See Miller v. Chicago Transit Auth.*, 20 F.4th 1148, 1153 (7th Cir. 2021) (can be "immensely persuasive"); *Tubens v. Doe*, 976 F.3d 101, 105 (1st Cir. 2020); *Perez v. El Tequila, LLC*, 847 F.3d 1247, 1253 (10th Cir. 2017).

[78]*See Agee v. City of McKinney*, 593 Fed.Appx. 311, 314 (5th Cir. 2014) (88-day delay refused); *Laboy v. Ontario County*, 56 F. Supp. 3d 255, 258 (W.D.N.Y. 2014) (1-day late filing excused).

[79]*See Bowman v. Korte*, 962 F.3d 995, 997–98 (7th Cir. 2020).

[80]*See Miller v. Chicago Transit Auth.*, 20 F.4th 1148, 1153–54 (7th Cir. 2021).

[81]*See Spears v. City of Indianapolis*, 74 F.3d 153 (7th Cir.1996) (no abuse of discretion where the district court refused to grant a 24-hour extension, after having previously granted earlier extensions); *McIntosh v. Antonino*, 71 F.3d 29 (1st Cir.1995) (no abuse of discretion in court's "exasperated denial" of a third extension).

[82]*See Tubens v. Doe*, 976 F.3d 101, 104 (1st Cir. 2020).

trial motions. The deadlines for filing such motions "must not" be extended by the court.[83] This prohibition is intended to help ensure that the finality of federal judgments (and, with it, appealability) is not inappropriately postponed.[84] For years, the prohibition haunted practitioners, who were confronted by a dishearteningly brief 10-day period for filing post-trial motions. In 2009, those time periods were enlarged to their current, sensible length of 28 days. The prohibition on timing extensions remains unchanged, however. District judges may not extend the deadline for filing post-trial motions seeking:

(1) A judgment as a matter of law, under Rule 50(b);
(2) A new trial, under Rules 50(d), 59(b), or 59(d);
(3) An amendment or expansion of a court's findings in a non-jury (bench) trial, under Rule 52(b); or
(4) An alteration or amendment to, or relief from, a judgment, under Rules 59(e) or 60(b).[85]

This prohibitory language notwithstanding, two nuances in the caselaw merit practitioner attention. First, the prohibition is viewed by many courts as a non-jurisdictional "claim-processing" rule, which means it can be forfeited if not timely invoked.[86] Thus, while district judges are prohibited by Rule 6(b)(2) from doing so, if they inadvertently overlook the prohibition and grant a post-trial motion extension, adversaries must properly object to that misstep or their right to do so is lost.[87] (Note one further trap for the unwary: untimely-filed post-trial motions will *not* suspend the time for taking an appeal.)[88]

Second, an old case law exemption held that in "unique cir-

---

[83] *See Browder v. Director, Dept. of Corrections of Illinois*, 434 U.S. 257, 261–62, 98 S. Ct. 556, 54 L. Ed. 2d 521 (1978). *See also Truthout v. Department of Justice*, 968 F. Supp. 2d 32, 36 (D.D.C. 2013) (no extension, even though deadline missed by just 16 minutes).

[84] *See* Rule 6(b) advisory committee note (1946).

[85] Although not listed specifically as a non-extending Rule, the courts have construed Rule 71A as prohibiting extensions of time to answer in a condemnation proceeding.

[86] *See Legg v. Ulster Cty.*, 979 F.3d 101, 112 (2d Cir. 2020); *Advanced Bodycare Solutions, LLC v. Thione Int'l, Inc.*, 615 F.3d 1352, 1359 n.15 (11th Cir. 2010). *See also Eberhart v. U.S.*, 546 U.S. 12, 19, 126 S. Ct. 403, 163 L. Ed. 2d 14 (2005) (applying "nonjurisdictional claim processing" rule concept in context of Federal Rules of Criminal Procedure).

[87] *See Legg v. Ulster Cty.*, 979 F.3d 101, 112 (2d Cir. 2020); *Advanced Bodycare Sols., LLC v. Thione Int'l, Inc.*, 615 F.3d 1352, 1359 n.15 (11th Cir. 2010). *Cf. Dill v. General American Life Ins. Co.*, 525 F.3d 612, 619 (8th Cir. 2008) (objection timely, even if not raised immediately, provided it is raised prior to court's ruling).

[88] *See* Fed. R. App. P. 4(a)(4)(A). *See also id.* advisory committee note (2016) (appeal time not re-started by untimely motion, even if district court had extended the due date or disposed of motion without explicit reliance on untimeliness, or if opponent consents or fails to object). *See generally infra* Part VI, § 6.3 ("**Extensions — By Filing Post-Trial Motions**"). Previously, the majority view among the courts of appeals had migrated towards the same conclusion. *Compare, e.g., Lizardo v. United States*, 619 F.3d 273, 275-80 (3d Cir. 2010) (majority: appeal forfeited), *with Nat'l Ecological Found. v. Alexander*, 496 F.3d 466, 476 (6th

cumstances" these periods could be extended, provided there was a genuine ambiguity in the Rule language to begin with and the district court took action that gave the parties the specific assurance (albeit improperly) that an extension had been granted.[89] The validity of this exemption has been often questioned and always limited tightly,[90] with the Supreme Court rejecting its application in a related context.[91]

In addition to these express prohibitions, one court has inferred that Rule 6(b) extensions also cannot be granted following entry of a final judgment to, for example, allow a post-judgment amendment to a complaint.[92]

Take Care in Drafting Extension Language

The language of a party's proposed extension order should be chosen carefully. An order extending the time for a defendant to "answer" the complaint does not necessarily extend the time for "moving" to dismiss the complaint. Therefore, broad language is advised: *e.g.*, requesting an extension to "answer, move, or otherwise plead."

Time Periods Set by Statute

The pre-2007 language was clear that extensions under Rule 6(b) could only be granted to time periods set by the Rules themselves or by court orders.[93] Statutory time periods could not be extended under Rule 6(b).[94] The restyled version of Rule 6(b) omits this expressly limiting language.[95] Although the 2007 changes to Rule 6 were "intended to be stylistic only,"[96] the effect of this restyling omission remains uncertain. The few

---

Cir. 2007) (minority: appeal preserved).

[89]*See Eady v. Foerder*, 381 F.2d 980 (7th Cir. 1967). *Accord Mobley v. C.I.A.*, 806 F.3d 568, 577–78 (D.C. Cir. 2015) (applying exemption). *See generally Varhol v. National R.R. Passenger Corp.*, 909 F.2d 1557 (7th Cir. 1990) (equally divided en banc court considered but refused to overrule *Eady*).

[90]*See Robinson v. City of Harvey*, 489 F.3d 864, 870–71 (7th Cir. 2007).

[91]*See Bowles v. Russell*, 551 U.S. 205, 213–14, 127 S. Ct. 2360, 2366, 168 L. Ed. 2d 96 (2007) (denouncing doctrine as "illegitimate", overruling prior case law, and emphasizing "that the timely filing of a notice of appeal in a civil case is a jurisdictional requirement").

[92]*See Auto. Alignment & Body Serv., Inc. v. State Farm Mut. Auto. Ins. Co.*, 953 F.3d 707, 720–21 (11th Cir. 2020) (to allow post-judgment amendments would circumvent time deadlines set in Rules 59 and 60). *See also Klayman v. Jud. Watch, Inc.*, 6 F.4th 1301, 1310 n.2 (D.C. Cir. 2021) (district court may not vacate final judgment to provide more time for party to file post-trial motion).

[93]*See* Fed. R. Civ. P. 6(b) (pre-restyling) ("When by these rules or by a notice given thereunder or by order of court an act is required or allowed to be done at or within a specified time, the court" may grant an enlargement).

[94]*See Kreutzer v. Bowersox*, 231 F.3d 460, 463 n.2 (8th Cir. 2000) ("Rule 6(b), by its own terms, only applies to time limits set by the Federal Rules of Civil Procedure, or to limits set by the court. . . It cannot be used to extend a statutory limit.").

[95]*See* Rule 6(b) ("When an act may or must be done within a specified time, the court may, for good cause, extend the time . . . ").

[96]*See* Rule 6 advisory committee

courts that have addressed the issue have ruled that restyled Rule 6(b), like its predecessor, does not authorize extensions to statutory time periods.[97]

Other Time Extension Rules

Several other Rules authorize the district court to grant extensions of time in particular circumstances.[98]

RULE 6(c)—MOTIONS, NOTICES OF HEARING, AFFIDAVITS

CORE CONCEPT

A written motion and notice of hearing must be served on the non-moving party at least 14 days before a motion hearing date, unless the district court specifies otherwise.

APPLICATIONS

Motion Days

This 14-day notice procedure applies to those district courts with "motion days" or the equivalent (where motions are heard orally). The Rule provides that the non-moving party must be served with notice of all motions at least 14 days before the hearing day, unless the court directs otherwise.[99] This requirement does not apply to motions heard *ex parte*.[100] It is intended to ensure adequate response times and avoid undue prejudice.[101]

Special Timing

This 14-day notice requirement is a default rule of general application. Any Rule that contains a specific, different time period supersedes this default rule, as does any court order fixing a different time period.[102]

Motion Affidavits

When a motion is supported with affidavits, the supporting

---

note (2007).

[97] *See Sherrod v. Breitbart*, 720 F.3d 932, 937–38 (D.C.Cir. 2013); *Sibalich v. Nationwide Ins. Co.*, 2018 WL 4519311, at *2 (D.N.J. Sept. 4, 2018), *adopted*, 2018 WL 4510263 (D.N.J. Sept. 19, 2018).

[98] *See, e.g.*, Rule 4(m) (extensions to serve summons and complaint); Rule 30(d)(1) (extensions for oral depositions); Rule 31(a)(5) (extensions for depositions on written interrogatories); Rule 33(b)(2) (extensions to answer interrogatories); Rule 34(b)(2) (extensions to respond to production requests); Rule 36(a)(3) (extensions to answer requests for admission); Rule 39(b) (extensions to demand jury trial); Rule 59(c) (extensions to submit affidavits in opposition to new trial motion).

[99] *See Stewart Title Guar. Co. v. Cadle Co.*, 74 F.3d 835, 837 (7th Cir. 1996) (district adopted different schedule by local rule, permitting written motions to be filed two days before hearing).

[100] *See* Rule 6(c)(1)(A).

[101] *See Branch Banking & Tr. Co. v. Camco Mgmt., LLC*, 704 Fed. Appx. 826, 830 (11th Cir. 2017).

[102] *See Rosas v. Roman Catholic Archdiocese of Chicago*, 748 Fed. Appx. 64, 66 (7th Cir. 2019) (different time periods set by local rules); *Ciena Corp. v. Jarrard*, 203 F.3d 312, 319–20 (4th Cir. 2000) (different time periods with interlocutory injunctions).

affidavits must be served simultaneously with the motion. When an opposition to a motion is supported with affidavits, the opposing affidavits must be served not less than 7 days before the hearing. Affidavits submitted in support of reply briefs are not addressed by the Rule[103] (although courts are likely to accept them if they are filed along with the reply briefs and constitute proper rebuttal[104]). The purpose of this Rule is to restrain a moving party from belatedly "springing new facts" on an opponent.[105] The district court has discretion in enforcing this Rule,[106] and may modify these service requirements.[107] Untimely affidavits may be stricken.[108]

- *Exception:* Affidavits opposing a motion for new trial must be served within 14 days after service of the motion.[109]

Time Period May Be Extended

This 14-day period may be extended if the requisites for extension in Rule 6(b) are satisfied.[110]

RULE 6(d)—ADDITIONAL TIME AFTER CERTAIN KINDS OF SERVICE

CORE CONCEPT

If a party must perform an act within a specified period after *service* of a document, that specified period is extended by 3 days if the party was served the document by mail, by specially pre-agreed other means, or by leaving it with the court clerk (if permitted).

APPLICATIONS

Purpose

Other Rules permit service of papers, under certain circumstances, to be made by mail, by other, specially pre-agreed means, and by leaving the papers with the court clerk (when

---

[103]*See Martinez v. Palmer*, 2022 WL 1091456, at *2 (D. Idaho Apr. 12, 2022); *McGinnis v. Southeast Anesthesia Associates, P.A.*, 161 F.R.D. 41, 42 (W.D. N.C. 1995).

[104]*See Key v. Shelby County*, 551 Fed. Appx. 262, 264 (6th Cir. 2014). *See also Parker v. Healthcare Inv. Grp., Inc.*, 272 F. Supp. 3d 1303, 1317–19 (N.D. Ala. 2017) (reply affidavits accepted as proper rebuttal).

[105]*See Lovelace v. Lee*, 472 F.3d 174, 204 (4th Cir. 2006); *Peters v. Lincoln Elec. Co.*, 285 F.3d 456, 476 (6th Cir. 2002).

[106]*See Martin v. Bimbo Foods Bakeries Distrib., Inc.*, 2014 WL 2439954, at *8 (E.D.N.C. May 30, 2014).

[107]*See Orsi v. Kirkwood*, 999 F.2d 86, 91–92 (4th Cir. 1993) (enlargements should generally be granted only if cause or excusable neglect is shown).

[108]*See IPFS Corp. v. Carrillo*, 2014 WL 3002087, at *2 (D. Nev. June 27, 2014); *S.D. v. St. Johns County Sch. Dist.*, 632 F. Supp. 2d 1085, 1100 n.15 (M.D.Fla. 2009).

[109]*See* Rule 59.

[110]*See Fox v. Ritz-Carlton Hotel Co., LLC*, 2022 WL 2158709, at *5–*6 (S.D. Fla. June 15, 2022); *Pontones v. San Jose Rest. Inc.*, 2020 WL 6438395, at *4 (E.D.N.C. Nov. 2, 2020).

serving parties with no known address).[111] Such service is generally considered complete (and the time for any response begins to run) at the time of mailing, transmission, or delivery to the clerk; completed service does *not* await actual receipt by the served party. To compensate for time lapses caused by delivery delay, Rule 6(d) adds 3 extra days when service is made using any of these three methods — by mail, by leaving with the clerk of court, or by other pre-agreed means.[112]

- *No 3-Day Extension for Electronic Service:* Maturing technologies and widespread user skills have reduced the risk of service delays caused by suspended or failed electronic transmissions.[113] Thus, no automatic 3-day extensions follow electronic service (in circumstances when electronic service is permitted), though discretionary extensions could still be granted when the electronic service prejudices the recipient (*e.g.*, when service is made after-hours or before/during a weekend or holiday).[114]

Applies to "After-Service" Deadlines Only

This 3-day extension applies only to responses due within a certain time after "service" of a preceding document.

No 3-Day Extension to "After-Filing" Deadlines

There is *no* 3-day extension when responses are due within a prescribed time after the "filing" of a document, even if that document was served through the mails, by pre-agreed means, or left with the clerk.[115] Nor is a 3-day extension self-acquired by the act of mailing a document that must otherwise be filed by a particular date.[116]

- *Post-Trial Motions Caution:* Because most post-trial motions must be "*filed*" (not "served") within 28-days "after the entry of judgment" or "after the jury was discharged," there are *no* 3-day extensions to these periods.[117]

---

[111] *See* Rule 5(b)(2)(C), (D), (F).

[112] *See* Rule 6(d) (as amended 2016) (referencing Rule 5(b)(2)(C) (mail), (D) (clerk), and (F) (other means)). *See generally Dandino, Inc. v. U.S. Dep't of Transp.*, 729 F.3d 917, 921 (9th Cir. 2013) (assuming first-class mail arrives within 3 days to destinations within the contiguous U.S.).

[113] Rule 6(d) advisory committee note (2016).

[114] Rule 6(d) advisory committee note (2016).

[115] *See Lorenzo v. Prime Commc'ns, L.P.*, 806 F.3d 777, 783 (4th Cir. 2015); *Williams v. Illinois*, 737 F.3d 473, 475–76 (7th Cir. 2013). *Compare Green Tree Servicing LLC v. Dillard*, 88 F. Supp. 3d 399, 400 n.2 (D.N.J. 2015) (refusing to add 3-days to 30-day removal time because it is an "after-filing" period), *with N.J. Dep't of Envt'l Prot. v. Exxon Mobil Corp.*, 381 F. Supp. 2d 398, 402 (D.N.J.2005) (adding 3 days to 30-day removal period if notice was served by mail).

[116] *See Johnson v. McBride*, 381 F.3d 587, 589 (7th Cir. 2004).

[117] *See* Rules 50(b), 50(d), 52(b), 59(b), 59(d), 59(e), 60(c)(1). *See also Williams v. Illinois*, 737 F.3d 473, 475–76 (7th Cir. 2013).

No 3-Day Extension to "After-Receipt" Deadlines

There generally is also *no* 3-day extension where responses are due within a prescribed period after actual "receipt" of a document.[118] However, a party may receive additional time when a party receives notice that the delivery of a letter was attempted, unsuccessfully, and is now ready to be picked up. In such cases, the courts may choose to extend the time period so as to allow that party a few extra days to retrieve the letter.[119]

No 3-Day Extension to "Date-Certain" Deadlines

There is no 3-day extension for date-specific deadlines fixed by the court.[120]

No 3-Day Extension to Most Statutes of Limitation

The prevailing view among the courts is that the 3-day extension period does not apply to extend statutes of limitation.[121]

Applies to Objections to Magistrate Judge Rulings

A district judge may direct a magistrate judge to consider and decide nondispositive pretrial matters, and to consider and submit a recommendation on dispositive motions.[122] The parties, thereafter, have 14 days from service to file objections to the magistrate judge's order or recommendation.[123] If the magistrate judge's order or recommendation is served upon the parties by mail, the additional 3-day period of Rule 6(d) applies to extend this 14-day objection period.[124]

Former Less-Than–11–Days Rule

The *less-than-11-days* federal time computation rule which prevailed until 2009 created uncertainty as to how (and when) the 3-added-days extension period should properly be applied. That uncertainty is now resolved; the former approach was abrogated in 2009.[125]

---

[118] *See Begay v. St. Joseph's Indian School*, 922 F. Supp. 270, 272–73 (D.S.D. 1996) (no additional 3-days for responses to mailed right-to-sue letter, where response period begins to run only from date of receipt of letter).

[119] *See Zillyette v. Capital One Financial Corp.*, 179 F.3d 1337, 1341–42 (11th Cir. 1999); *Sousa v. N.L.R.B.*, 817 F.2d 10, 11 (2d Cir. 1987).

[120] *See Sec. & Exch. Comm'n v. Harman Wright Grp., LLC*, 777 Fed. Appx. 276, 277–78, 2019 WL 2484465, at *2 (10th Cir. 2019). *See also Bacon v. Stiefel Labs., Inc.*, 714 F. Supp. 2d 1186, 1189 n.1 (S.D.Fla. 2010) (ruling Rule 6(d) inapplicable, but granting extension to accept late filing).

[121] *See Velez-Diaz v. U.S.*, 507 F.3d 717, 719–20 (1st Cir. 2007) (noting prevailing rule).

[122] *See* 28 U.S.C.A. § 636(b)(1); Rule 72(a) to (b).

[123] *See* 28 U.S.C.A. § 636(b)(1); Rule 72(a) to (b). *Note:* formerly this period was 10 days, but was enlarged to 14 days in 2009.

[124] *See* Rule 72(b) advisory committee's note (1983). *See also Daker v. Comm'r, Georgia Dep't of Corr.*, 820 F.3d 1278, 1286 (11th Cir. 2016).

[125] *See supra* Authors' Commentary to Rule 6(a) ("**Former Approach: Time Periods of Less than 11**

Additional Research References

Wright & Miller, *Federal Practice and Procedure* §§ 1161 to 71

C.J.S., Federal Civil Procedure § 194, § 250, § 302, § 331, §§ 354 to 369, §§ 394 to 436, § 569, § 571§ 701, § 732, §§ 764 to 789 et seq., §§ 933 to 934; Time §§ 2 to 17 et seq.

West's Key Number Digest, Federal Civil Procedure ⚷611.4, ⚷624, ⚷734 to 735, ⚷824, ⚷865, ⚷868, ⚷956, ⚷1051, ⚷1143, ⚷1342 to 1343, ⚷1612, ⚷1679 to 1680, ⚷1701 to 1705, ⚷1991 to 1998; Time ⚷2 to 15

Days").

III. PLEADINGS AND MOTIONS

RULE 7
PLEADINGS ALLOWED; FORM OF MOTIONS AND OTHER PAPERS

(a) Pleadings. Only these pleadings are allowed:

(1) a complaint;

(2) an answer to a complaint;

(3) an answer to a counterclaim designated as a counterclaim;

(4) an answer to a crossclaim;

(5) a third-party complaint;

(6) an answer to a third-party complaint; and

(7) if the court orders one, a reply to an answer.

(b) Motions and Other Papers.

(1) *In General.* A request for a court order must be made by motion. The motion must:

(A) be in writing unless made during a hearing or trial;

(B) state with particularity the grounds for seeking the order; and

(C) state the relief sought.

(2) *Form.* The rules governing captions and other matters of form in pleadings apply to motions and other papers.

[Amended effective March 19, 1948; July 1, 1963; August 1, 1983; April 30, 2007, effective December 1, 2007.]

AUTHORS' COMMENTARY ON RULE 7

PURPOSE AND SCOPE

Rule 7 lists the pleadings permitted in federal court, and sets the general requirements for the form of motions. The provisions of this Rule are often supplemented extensively by local rules and chambers rules, which practitioners should consult carefully.

RULE 7(a)—PLEADINGS

CORE CONCEPT

Rule 7(a) lists six types of pleadings that may be, and routinely are, filed in federal court: (1) a complaint; (2) an answer to a complaint; (3) an answer to a counterclaim, if the counterclaim is so designated; (4) an answer to a crossclaim; (5) a third-party complaint; and (6) a third-party answer. A seventh pleading—a reply to any answer—is permitted, but rarely and only by court order.

APPLICATIONS

Not Pleadings

The list in Rule 7(a) is exhaustive.[1] Assuming no counterclaim or crossclaim is filed,[2] the pleadings in a typical case are considered closed once a complaint and the answer(s) have been filed.[3] Consequently, the following documents—which do not appear in the Rule 7(a) list—are *not* "pleadings": a petition or writ,[4] a "freestanding" or "stand-alone" counterclaim or crossclaim not pleaded in an answer,[5] a "counter-complaint,"[6] a notice of removal,[7] a motion to dismiss,[8] a motion for summary judgment[9] (or summary judgment "statement"[10]), a motion to supplement,[11] a motion for reconsideration,[12] a motion for sanctions,[13] a motion for attorney's fees,[14] a motion to stay,[15] an "in-

---

[1]*See ISC Holding AG v. Nobel Biocare Fin. AG*, 688 F.3d 98, 112 (2d Cir. 2012); *A. Bauer Mech., Inc. v. Joint Arbitration Bd. of Plumbing Contractors' Ass'n & Chicago Journeymen Plumbers' Local Union 130*, 562 F.3d 784, 790 (7th Cir. 2009).

[2]*See Perez v. Wells Fargo N.A.*, 774 F.3d 1329, 1336 (11th Cir. 2014) (if counterclaim asserted, pleadings close after it is answered).

[3]*See Fernandez v. Clean House, LLC*, 883 F.3d 1296, 1299 (10th Cir. 2018).

[4]*See Evans v. McConnell*, 2009 WL 1560192, at *2 n.1 (W.D. Pa. June 3, 2009).

[5]*See Hatcher v. HCP Prairie Vill. KS OPCO LLC*, 515 F. Supp. 3d 1152, 1163 (D. Kan. 2021) (freestanding counterclaims); *Keralink Int'l, Inc. v. Stradis Healthcare, LLC*, 2020 WL 2490110, at *3 (D. Md. May 14, 2020) (standalone crossclaims).

[6]*See U.S. ex rel. Martin Marietta Materials, Inc. v. Nelson, Inc.*, 286 F.R.D. 327, 331 (W.D. Tenn. 2012).

[7]*See A.S. ex rel. Miller v. SmithKline Beecham Corp.*, 769 F.3d 204, 213 (3d Cir. 2014).

[8]*See Richardson v. Stanley Works, Inc.*, 597 F.3d 1288, 1297 (Fed.Cir. 2010).

[9]*See Principal Health Care of Louisiana, Inc. v. Lewer Agency, Inc.*, 38 F.3d 240, 244 (5th Cir. 1994); *CX Reinsurance Co. Ltd. v. Johnson*, 325 F.R.D. 132, 135 (D. Md. 2018).

[10]*See DeSouza v. EGL Eagle Global Logistics LP*, 596 F. Supp. 2d 456, 459 (D.Conn. 2009).

[11]*See United States v. Rogers*, 657 Fed. Appx. 735, 739 (10th Cir. 2016).

[12]*See Schneller v. Fox Subacute at Clara Burke*, 368 Fed.Appx. 275, 278 (3d Cir. 2010); *Nyambal v. Alliedbarton Sec. Servs., LLC*, 344 F. Supp. 3d 183, 188 (D.D.C. 2018).

[13]*See Phinney v. Paulshock*, 181 F.R.D. 185, 207 (D.N.H. 1998), aff'd, 199 F.3d 1 (1st Cir. 1999).

[14]*See Freeman v. Rice*, 548 Fed. Appx. 594, 596 (11th Cir. 2013).

[15]*See Nanosolutions, LLC v. Prajza*, 793 F. Supp. 2d 46, 52 (D.D.C. 2011).

formative" motion,[16] a motion to enforce a settlement,[17] a response to a motion,[18] a "suggestion" under Rule 12(h)(3) of a lack of subject-matter jurisdiction, a brief or memorandum,[19] a reply brief or memorandum,[20] a supplemental brief,[21] exhibits to briefs,[22] affidavits,[23] declarations,[24] discovery papers,[25] expert reports and testimony,[26] court-ordered "reports,"[27] certificates of merit,[28] jury instructions or verdict forms,[29] and notices of appeal.[30]

Definitions

(1) *Complaint:* A complaint is the document that sets out the initial plaintiff's claim for relief. There can be only one operative version of a complaint in a federal civil action; amended complaints supplant their predecessors.[31]

(2) *Answer:* An answer is the document that sets out a party's defenses, objections, and responses (including counterclaims and crossclaims) to the complaint.[32] Affirmative defenses are asserted in the answer (thus, not a separate pleading).[33]

(3) *Counterclaim:* A counterclaim is that portion of an an-

---

[16]*See Colon v. Blades*, 268 F.R.D. 143, 146 (D.P.R. 2010).

[17]*See Vikas WSP, Ltd. v. Econ. Mud Prod. Co.*, 23 F.4th 442, 454 n.7 (5th Cir. 2022).

[18]*See Oyekwe v. Rsch. Now Grp., Inc.*, 542 F. Supp. 3d 496, 504 (N.D. Tex. 2021).

[19]*See Swanigan v. City of Chicago*, 775 F.3d 953, 963 n.7 (7th Cir. 2015).

[20]*See Lewis v. Sec'y of Health & Human Servs.*, 370 F. Supp. 3d 267, 270 (D. Mass. 2019).

[21]*See Pueblo of Pojoaque v. State*, 233 F. Supp. 3d 1021, 1103–04 (D.N.M. 2017).

[22]*See United States ex rel. Jefferson v. Roche Holding AG*, 489 F. Supp. 3d 418, 426 (D. Md. 2020); *Chavez v. Credit Nation Auto Sales, Inc.*, 966 F. Supp. 2d 1335, 1344 (N.D. Ga. 2013).

[23]*See Ojeda v. Louisville Ladder Inc.*, 410 Fed.Appx. 213, 216 (11th Cir. 2010) *Palmer Holdings & Invs., Inc. v. Integrity Ins. Co.*, 505 F. Supp. 3d 842, 862–63 (S.D. Iowa 2020).

[24]*See Granger v. Gill Abstract Corp.*, 566 F. Supp. 2d 323, 334–35 (S.D. N.Y. 2008).

[25]*See Carlson v. Reed*, 249 F.3d 876, 878 n.1 (9th Cir. 2001) (interrogatories are not pleadings).

[26]*See Saiyed v. Council on Am.-Islamic Relations Action Network, Inc.*, 321 F.R.D. 455, 458–59 (D.D.C. 2017).

[27]*See Burns v. Lawther*, 53 F.3d 1237, 1241 (11th Cir.1995) (in prisoner civil rights case, special, pre-answer reports).

[28]*See Liggon-Redding v. Estate of Sugarman*, 659 F.3d 258, 265 n.5 (3d Cir. 2011).

[29]*See Eclipse Packaging, Inc. v. Stewarts of Am., Inc.*, 731 Fed. Appx. 168, 169–70 (4th Cir. 2018).

[30]*See Adkins v. Safeway, Inc.*, 985 F.2d 1101, 1102 (D.C. Cir. 1993).

[31]*See, e.g., Bosarge v. Mississippi Bureau of Narcotics*, 796 F.3d 435, 440 (5th Cir. 2015); *Pintando v. Miami-Dade Hous. Agency*, 501 F.3d 1241, 1243 (11th Cir. 2007).

[32]*See* Rule 8(b)–(c); Rule 13; Rule 14. *See generally LeBoeuf, Lamb, Greene & MacRae, L.L.P. v. Worsham*, 185 F.3d 61, 66–67 (2d Cir. 1999) (responsive pleading (an answer) is required to a complaint).

[33]*See United States ex rel. Patzer v. Sikorsky Aircraft Corp.*, 382 F. Supp. 3d 860, 865–66 (E.D. Wis. 2019).

swer[34] that sets out a defending party's offensive claims against the suing party.

(4) *Crossclaim:* A crossclaim is that portion of an answer that sets out a defending party's claims against a co-plaintiff or co-defendant (that is, someone aligned on the same side of the "v."), often seeking indemnification or contribution.

(5) *Answers to Counterclaims/Crossclaims*: Only answers to counterclaims and crossclaims are considered to be pleadings (the counterclaims and crossclaims themselves are *not* considered pleadings because they are asserted in a party's answer, not as separate, freestanding filings).[35]

- *Note:* Answers occasionally include an averment designated as a "counterclaim" but which is actually just an affirmative defense. Although responses are only required to bona fide counterclaims, practitioners should answer all labeled "counterclaims"—whether they appear facially proper or not—to avoid any risk that the averments might be deemed admitted.

(6) *Reply:* A reply is the pleading by which a party responds to an answer, a counterclaim answer, a crossclaim answer, or a third-party answer.[36] Replies are not permitted as of right; a court order is required before a party may file a reply.[37] New matter pleaded in an answer (to which a reply might otherwise respond) is deemed by the Rules to be automatically denied or avoided unless a reply is ordered.[38]

Motion to Permit or Compel a Reply

Filing a reply is not permitted as of right; it must be authorized by the court.[39] To be granted leave to file a reply, or to compel such a filing by another litigant, the moving party must make a clear and convincing showing of substantial reasons or extraordinary circumstances that require a reply.[40] A frequent example of such court-ordered replies arises in federal civil rights cases, where a court can direct plaintiffs to file specific

---

[34] *See Equitrans, L.P. v. 0.56 Acres More or Less of Permanent Easement Located in Marion Cty., W. Va.*, 145 F. Supp. 3d 622 (N.D. W. Va. 2015); *Bern Unlimited, Inc. v. Burton Corp.*, 25 F. Supp. 3d 170, 177 (D. Mass. 2014).

[35] *See In re Cessna Distrib'ship Antitrust Litig.*, 532 F.2d 64, 67 (8th Cir. 1976); *Equitrans, L.P. v. 0.56 Acres More or Less of Permanent Easement Located in Marion Cty., W. Va.*, 145 F. Supp. 3d 622 (N.D. W. Va. 2015).

[36] *See* Rule 7(a)(7). *See also* Rule 7 advisory committee note (2007).

[37] *See, e.g., Mihos v. Swift*, 358 F.3d 91, 106 (1st Cir. 2004); *U.S. v. Shanbaum*, 10 F.3d 305, 312 n.4 (5th Cir. 1994); *Martinez v. Naranjo*, 328 F.R.D. 581, 597 (D.N.M. 2018).

[38] *See* Rule 8(b)(6). *See also Osberry v. Slusher*, 750 Fed. Appx. 385, 389 (6th Cir. 2018); *Yankton v. Epps*, 652 Fed. Appx. 242, 248 n.35 (5th Cir. 2016).

[39] *See Mills v. Jones*, 2022 WL 993066, at *1 (E.D. Cal. Apr. 1, 2022); *Martinez v. Naranjo*, 328 F.R.D. 581, 597 (D.N.M. 2018).

[40] *See Mills v. Jones*, 2022 WL 993066, at *1 (E.D. Cal. Apr. 1, 2022); *Moviecolor Limited v. Eastman Kodak Co.*, 24 F.R.D. 325, 326 (S.D. N.Y. 1959).

and particularized responses to a public official's immunity defense.[41]

RULE 7(b)—MOTIONS AND OTHER PAPERS

CORE CONCEPT

Rule 7(b) sets the broad, national procedures for motion practice in the federal courts.

APPLICATIONS

Motion Defined

A motion is a request to the court for an order.[42] Letters to a judge ordinarily do not qualify.[43]

Reminder — Check All Local Rules and Procedures

Each federal district and many individual district judges have promulgated local rules, chambers rules, standing orders, and/or case-specific orders that supplement this Rule.[44] Those procedures may significantly impact the logistics of local motion practice (*e.g.*, timing, briefing form, page limits, font size, reply briefs, courtesy copies for chambers, oral arguments, etc.). These local procedures are ordinarily accessible on the district court's official website.

Rules Governing Pleading Form Apply

The Rules that govern the styling of captions and the form of pleadings also apply to motions.[45]

Formal Requirements for Motions

All motions must be in writing, unless they are presented

---

[41]*See Crawford-El v. Britton*, 523 U.S. 574, 118 S. Ct. 1584, 140 L. Ed. 2d 759 (1998) (trial court may order a reply, compelling plaintiff to aver "specific, nonconclusory factual allegations"); *Arnold v. Williams*, 979 F.3d 262, 267 (5th Cir. 2020) (when qualified immunity first raised in an answer, court may direct filing of a reply from plaintiff); *Reyes v. Sazan*, 168 F.3d 158, 161 (5th Cir. 1999) (with "sparse details" of official wrongdoing, "trial courts ought routinely require plaintiffs to file a reply").

[42]*See United States v. Vargas*, 961 F.3d 566, 577 (2d Cir. 2020); *U.S. ex rel. Atkins v. McInteer*, 470 F.3d 1350, 1361 (11th Cir. 2006).

[43]*See Mortensen v. Nevens*, 2011 WL 772885, at *1 (D.Nev. Feb. 25, 2011). *See also Keith v. Mayes*, 2010 WL 3339041, at *2 n.2 (S.D.Ga. Aug. 23, 2010) ("This is a Court of record, not a pen pal. Such requests must be made by motion."). *But cf. Spirit Realty, L.P. v. GH&H Mableton, LLC*, 319 F.R.D. 474, 476 (S.D.N.Y. 2017) (local rules permit certain types of letter-motions).

[44]*See* Rule 83(a)(1) (authorizing district courts to promulgate local rules of practice, provided those rules are consistent with, and not duplicative of, the national Rules and applicable federal statutes).

[45]This directive is not a license for creative lawyering designed to evade either the requirements of other Rules or the express instructions of the court. *See Swanson v. U.S. Forest Service*, 87 F.3d 339, 345 (9th Cir. 1996) (when court denied counsel right to file an overlength motion brief, counsel could not escape this ruling by relying on Rule 7(b)(2) to justify "incorporation by reference" under Rule 10(c) of additional 69 pages of argument contained in earlier filings).

during a hearing or trial.[46] A written "notice of hearing" on the motion will satisfy this requirement.

- *Form:* Written motions must comply with the requirements of Rule 10—they must include a caption listing the name of the court, the title of the action, the docket number, and the title of the motion.
- *Content Particularity:* Written motions must set forth "with particularity" the grounds for seeking the order and the relief sought.[47] This particularity requirement ensures that the court and the adversary receive ample notice of both the relief requested and the moving party's reasoning, so that the court fully understands the motion and the adversary has a meaningful opportunity to respond.[48] The Rule is given a liberal application;[49] "ritualistic detail" is not required[50] and supporting memoranda may be examined in testing a motion's adequacy[51] (though courts will not consult materials submitted after the filing period, as that would defeat the Rule's notice goal).[52] Nonetheless, courts expect reasonable particularity in motions.[53] In making this particularity assessment, the court will consider whether any party is prejudiced by the motion's form and whether it can rule fairly on the motion.[54] Requests for relief made in a passing comment, a stray sentence to a brief, or a footnote are likely to fail the particularity test.[55]

    ○ *Consequences:* A motion that lacks particularity

---

[46]*See Contech Const. Prods., Inc. v. Heierli*, 764 F. Supp. 2d 96, 106 (D.D.C. 2011).

[47]*See Carroll v. Lawton Indep. Sch. Dist. No. 8*, 805 F.3d 1222, 1231 (10th Cir. 2015).

[48]*See Rodríguez-Miranda v. Benin*, 829 F.3d 29, 39 (1st Cir. 2016); *Nordock, Inc. v. Sys. Inc.*, 803 F.3d 1344, 1359–60 (Fed. Cir. 2015).

[49]*See Hinz v. Neuroscience, Inc.*, 538 F.3d 979, 983 (8th Cir. 2008); *Intera Corp. v. Henderson*, 428 F.3d 605, 612–14 (6th Cir. 2005). *See also Hopkins v. Bowen*, 850 F.2d 417, 420 (8th Cir. 1988) (memorandum considered a "motion" for summary judgment where it described grounds and prayed for specific relief, provided opponent suffered no prejudice); *Williams v. E.I. du Pont de Nemours & Co.*, 154 F. Supp. 3d 407, 426 (M.D. La. 2015) (formal motion not always required, if relief and grounds for seeking it set forth with particularity).

[50]*See Kelly v. Moore*, 376 F.3d 481, 484 (5th Cir. 2004). *See also Elustra v. Mineo*, 595 F.3d 699, 707–08 (7th Cir. 2010) (handwritten note, reading: "I never aggred [sic] to settlement vacate order Dec 11-08 and reinstate case", though simple, complied with each requirement of Rule 7(b)).

[51]*See Fort James Corp. v. Solo Cup Co.*, 412 F.3d 1340, 1347 (Fed. Cir. 2005); *Lac Du Flambeau Band of Lake Superior Chippewa Indians v. State of Wis.*, 957 F.2d 515, 516 (7th Cir. 1992).

[52]*See Hinz v. Neuroscience, Inc.*, 538 F.3d 979, 983 (8th Cir. 2008).

[53]*See Nordock, Inc. v. Sys. Inc.*, 803 F.3d 1344, 1359 (Fed. Cir. 2015); *Allender v. Raytheon Aircraft Co.*, 439 F.3d 1236, 1240 (10th Cir. 2006).

[54]*See Cambridge Plating Co., Inc. v. Napco, Inc.*, 85 F.3d 752, 760 (1st Cir. 1996).

[55]*See Anderson v. Bank of the West*, 23 F.4th 1056, 1061 (8th Cir. 2022) ("passing mention" in opposition filing was improper); *Brooks v. Mentor Worldwide LLC*, 985 F.3d 1272,

may be dismissed or denied,[56] with perhaps devastating ramifications.[57]

- *Motions to Amend:* When a party submits a motion to amend, the particularity requirement may require the party to attach to the motion a copy of the proposed amended pleading, unless the motion sets forth the substance of or otherwise adequately describes the contemplated revision.[58] Informal amendment requests—unaccompanied by the proposed amended pleading itself or a summary of its substance—do not conform to Rule 7(b) and may be refused for that reason.[59]

- *Supporting Memorandum or Brief:* Rule 7 does not expressly require a party to submit a supporting memorandum or brief along with motions or oppositions to motions,[60] although many districts impose that obligation by local or chambers rule. A reasonable delay in filing a motion's supporting memorandum or brief may be excused when the motion itself was timely-filed and properly particularized.[61]
- *Form of Order:* Many local rules obligate the moving party to attach a form of order to the motion which, if signed and entered, would grant the relief requested in the motion. Similarly, the party opposing a motion may be required to attach a form of order which would deny the requested relief.

1282–83 (10th Cir. 2021) (one-sentence request at end of motion response); *Cozzarelli v. Inspire Pharms. Inc.*, 549 F.3d 618, 630–31 (4th Cir. 2008) (request in footnote and final sentence). *See generally Frees v. Duby*, 2010 WL 4923535, at *2 (W.D.Mich. Nov. 29, 2010) ("Judges are not like pigs, hunting for truffles buried in briefs.") (quotation omitted).

[56]*See, e.g., Carroll v. Lawton Indep. Sch. Dist. No. 8*, 805 F.3d 1222, 1231 (10th Cir. 2015); *Evans v. Pearson Enterprises, Inc.*, 434 F.3d 839, 853 (6th Cir. 2006).

[57]*See Elustra v. Mineo*, 595 F.3d 699, 707 (7th Cir. 2010) (improperly skeletal post-trial motions do not postpone time for taking an appeal); *Moore v. American Family Mut. Ins. Co.*, 576 F.3d 781, 785 (8th Cir. 2009) (insufficiently particularized post-trial motion preserves nothing for appellate review).

[58]*See Carvelli v. Ocwen Fin. Corp.*, 934 F.3d 1307, 1332 n.17 (11th Cir. 2019); *DelRio-Mocci v. Connolly Props. Inc.*, 672 F.3d 241, 251 (3d Cir. 2012).

[59]*See Brooks v. Mentor Worldwide LLC*, 985 F.3d 1272, 1282–83 (10th Cir. 2021) (one-sentence request at end of motion response); *In re City of Detroit*, 841 F.3d 684, 702 (6th Cir. 2016) (single sentence request, lacking proposing amendment or other particularity, ruled improper); *Benoit v. U.S. Dep't of Agriculture*, 608 F.3d 17, 21 (D.C.Cir. 2010) (unwritten, one-sentence, conditional suggestion not sufficient).

[60]*See Star Mark Mgmt., Inc. v. Koon Chun Hing Kee Soy & Sauce Factory, Ltd.*, 682 F.3d 170, 176–77 (2d Cir. 2012) (noting that "motion" is different than a memorandum).

[61]*See Sturgis Motorcycle Rally, Inc. v. Rushmore Photo & Gifts, Inc.*, 908 F.3d 313, 321 (8th Cir. 2018) (timely, proper post-trial motion not defeated by belated briefing caused by court's delay in docketing trial's transcript).

- *Attaching Affidavits and Other Exhibits:* A party may support a motion with affidavits or other materials (but doing so can have serious procedural ramifications).[62]
- *Signing:* The written motion must be signed in accordance with Rule 11 by the party's counsel or, if unrepresented, by the party herself. If the motion is not signed after the omission is called to the attention of the party or the party's counsel, the court may strike the document.[63]
- *Service:* A signed copy of the motion or "notice of hearing" must be served upon counsel for represented parties or, if unrepresented, upon the party herself. Unless the court directs otherwise, service must be accomplished not later than 14 days prior to the hearing on the motion.[64]
- *Certificate of Service:* Unless filed electronically, the motion must contain a certificate of service verifying service.[65]
- *Filing:* If the motion is served before it is filed, it (or any "notice of hearing") must be filed no later than "a reasonable time" after service.[66]

Opposing Written Motions

Rule 7 contains no requirement that an opponent file an "answer" to any motion and, absent a local or chambers rule to the contrary, a motion can be opposed solely by filing a brief or memorandum. The form, signing, filing, and service requirements for motions are applicable to oppositions as well.

Withdrawing Written Motions

A written motion should be withdrawn with the same formality with which it was filed. Consequently, written motions should be withdrawn in writing.[67]

Hearings and Arguments on Written Motions

The court may, in its discretion, schedule a motion for a hearing or oral argument. Neither is expressly required under the Rules, although local rule provisions may specify additional hearing and argument requirements. Hearings held *ex parte* (without notice to the opponent) are generally discouraged and are permitted only in exceptional circumstances, such as applications for temporary restraining orders.[68]

---

[62] *See, e.g.,* Rule 12(d) (if matters outside the pleadings are presented to, and considered by, the court on a Rule 12(b)(6) motion to dismiss or Rule 12(c) motion for judgment on the pleadings, court must convert motion into Rule 56 motion for summary judgment).

[63] *See* Rule 11(a).

[64] *See* Rule 5 & Rule 6(c).

[65] *See* Rule 5(d)(1)(B).

[66] *See* Rule 5(d)(1)(A).

[67] *See United Coin Meter Co., Inc. v. Seaboard Coastline RR.*, 705 F.2d 839, 843 (6th Cir. 1983).

[68] *See* Rule 65(b).

Oral Motions

Oral motions are permitted if made during a hearing or trial (and, perhaps, during a conference with the court[69]), so long as they are raised in open court at the hearing or trial.[70] This presentation will satisfy the writing requirement of Rule 7 if the oral motion is transcribed or otherwise recorded.[71] The writing requirement for oral motions functions to ensure that the motion is accurately memorialized.[72] Oral motions must also meet the obligation of stating, with particularity, the moving party's grounds for the relief sought.[73]

Amendments to Motions

Neither Rule 7 nor any other Rule expressly provides for amendments to motions. Because motions are not "pleadings," the amendment procedures of Rule 15 do not apply.[74] Nonetheless, federal courts are vested with those inherent powers reasonably needed to manage their affairs and "achieve the orderly and expeditious disposition of cases," provided the exercise of such powers will not contravene any express Rule or statute.[75] Consequently, courts possess broad discretion to permit amendments and supplements to motions when doing so will enable the case to be resolved justly, fairly, and without prejudicing others.[76] Practitioners may choose to seek leave of court to amend a filed motion, rather than file a new one, when a new filing would be out of time or otherwise improper.[77]

---

[69] *See Dynamic CRM Recruiting Sols., L.L.C. v. UMA Educ., Inc.*, 31 F.4th 914, 924 (5th Cir. 2022) (motion deemed adequate, when made "on the record" during pretrial conference).

[70] *See Meriwether v. Coughlin*, 879 F.2d 1037, 1042 (2d Cir. 1989) (because oral motion was asserted in open court, written document not required). *See also Kerry Steel, Inc. v. Paragon Industries, Inc.*, 106 F.3d 147, 154 (6th Cir. 1997) (Rules allow motions at hearings, refusing to hold as significant attorney's omission of utterance: "I move").

[71] *See Atchison, Topeka & Santa Fe Ry. Co. v. California State Bd. of Equalization*, 102 F.3d 425, 427 (9th Cir. 1996); *People of State of Ill. ex rel. Hartigan v. Peters*, 871 F.2d 1336, 1341 (7th Cir. 1989). *See also Trask v. Olin Corp.*, 298 F.R.D. 244, 261–62 (W.D. Pa. 2014) (deeming oral motion proper when made during transcribed telephone status conference, following prior notice to opponent).

[72] *See Taragan v. Eli Lilly and Co., Inc.*, 838 F.2d 1337, 1340–41 (D.C. Cir. 1988) (requirement of adequate opportunity to prepare and respond satisfied by oral motions if they are germane to hearing or trial).

[73] *See Ruiz v. Wing*, 991 F.3d 1130, 1143 (11th Cir. 2021).

[74] *See Caceres v. Scottsdale Ins. Co.*, 2020 WL 977840, at *1 (S.D. Fla. Feb. 28, 2020); *Nyambal v. Alliedbarton Sec. Servs., LLC*, 344 F. Supp. 3d 183, 188 (D.D.C. 2018).

[75] *See Dietz v. Bouldin*, 579 U.S. 40, 45, 136 S. Ct. 1885, 1891–92, 195 L. Ed. 2d 161 (2016).

[76] *See Caceres v. Scottsdale Ins. Co.*, 2020 WL 977840, at *1-*2 (S.D. Fla. Feb. 28, 2020); *United States v. Gordon*, 2019 WL 6640289, at *5 (W.D. Ky. Dec. 5, 2019); *Aracely, R. v. Nielsen*, 319 F. Supp. 3d 110, 132–33 (D.D.C. 2018).

[77] *See, e.g.,* Rule 12(g) and 12(h) (certain defenses deemed waived if not asserted in original Rule 12(b) motion). *See also Wiggins v. Jedson Eng'g, Inc.*, 2020 WL 6993840, at *1 (E.D. Tenn. Apr. 29, 2020) (courts possess

Additional Research References

Wright & Miller, *Federal Practice and Procedure* §§ 1181 to 1200

C.J.S., Federal Civil Procedure § 124, §§ 247 to 280 et seq., §§ 301 to 319 et seq., §§ 363 to 375 et seq.

West's Key Number Digest, Federal Civil Procedure ⚷295, ⚷621 to 665, ⚷671 to 680, ⚷731 to 745, ⚷771 to 786, ⚷903, ⚷611.1 to 612.7

---

discretion to allow amendment to Rule 12(b) motion to include omitted defense).

RULE 7.1
DISCLOSURE STATEMENT*

(a) Who Must File; Contents.

(1) ***Nongovernmental Corporations.*** A nongovernmental corporate party or a nongovernmental corporation that seeks to intervene must file a statement that:

(A) identifies any parent corporation and any publicly held corporation owning 10% or more of its stock; or

(B) states that there is no such corporation.

(2) ***Parties or Intervenors in a Diversity Case.*** In an action in which jurisdiction is based on diversity under 28 U.S.C. § 1332(a), a party or intervenor must, unless the court orders otherwise, file a disclosure statement. The statement must name—and identify the citizenship of—every individual or entity whose citizenship is attributed to that party or intervenor:

(A) when the action is filed in or removed to

---

*The Supreme Court of the United States promulgated amendments to Rule 7.1 on April 11, 2022, to take effect as of December 1, 2022 unless Congress acts on the amendments prior to that date. The text of Rule 7.1, incorporating those amendments, is printed here. The advisory committee note to the amendments appears in Part VIII of this Handbook. The specific language of Rule 7.1 affected by these amendments is set out below, with new matter italicized and omitted matter struck through; ellipsis shows where text continues without further alteration:

(a) Who Must File; Contents.

(1) Nongovernmental Corporations. A nongovernmental corporate party *or a nongovernmental corporation that seeks to intervene* must file two copies of a disclosure statement that:

(A) identifies any parent corporation and any publicly held corporation owning 10% or more of its stock; or

(B) states that there is no such corporation.

(2) Parties or Intervenors in a Diversity Case. *In an action in which jurisdiction is based on diversity under 28 U.S.C. § 1332(a), a party or intervenor must, unless the court orders otherwise, file a disclosure statement. The statement must name—and identify the citizenship of—every individual or entity whose citizenship is attributed to that party or intervenor:*

(A) when the action is filed in or removed to federal court, and

(B) when any later event occurs that could affect the court's jurisdiction under § 1332(a).

(b) **Time to File; Supplemental Filing.** A party, *intervenor, or proposed intervenor* must * * * federal court, and

(B) when any later event occurs that could affect the court's jurisdiction under § 1332(a).

(b) Time to File; Supplemental Filing. A party, intervenor, or proposed intervenor must:

(1) file the disclosure statement with its first appearance, pleading, petition, motion, response, or other request addressed to the court; and

(2) promptly file a supplemental statement if any required information changes.

[Added April 29, 2002, effective December 1, 2002; Amended April 30, 2007, effective December 1, 2007; April 11, 2022, effective December 1, 2022.]

AUTHORS' COMMENTARY ON RULE 7.1

PURPOSE AND SCOPE

Rule 7.1 imposes two disclosure obligations on certain civil litigants. First, most corporate litigants (including proposed intervenors, but excluding government corporations) must disclose the identity of any parent corporation or publicly-held corporation owning 10% or more of their stock. Second, all litigants in an action invoking the court's diversity-based jurisdiction must disclose the citizenship of all persons and entities whose citizenship is attributed to the disclosing party.

CORE CONCEPT

Rule 7.1 combines two, distinct disclosure obligations. The corporate ownership disclosure assists the presiding district judges in deciding whether they need to disqualify themselves from a case due to a personal, financial interest. The citizenship disclosure aids judges in promptly assessing whether complete diversity of citizenship exists in those lawsuits that invoke federal diversity subject-matter jurisdiction.

APPLICATIONS

2022 Amendments to Rule 7.1 (*eff. Dec. 1, 2022*)

Rule 7.1 was amended to extend the corporate disclosure obligation to intervenors (not just existing parties), and to add the citizenship disclosure obligation for diversity cases.

Corporate Ownership Disclosures

The corporate disclosure is imposed to supply federal judges with appropriate information necessary to allow them to make certain informed recusal decisions.[1] The Rule is not designed to cover all circumstances that might call for a district judge's recusal.[2] Rather, the Rule has a narrow reach, targeting only information that would trigger a judge's automatic financial interest disqualification.[3] The Rule should be construed broadly to achieve its purpose of full disclosure of this type of information.[4]

- *Automatic Financial Interest Recusals:* Under the automatic financial interest disqualification rule, federal judges must recuse when they (individually, as fiduciaries, or their immediate household families) have a financial interest in the subject matter of the pending dispute or in one of the litigants, or any other interest that might be substantially affected by the litigation's outcome.[5]
- *Who Must Disclose:* This disclosure obligation applies to nongovernmental corporate litigants—whether original parties or intervenors (as well as those who propose to intervene).[6] But persons or entities that are not parties to the litigation,[7] are not corporations,[8] or lack the requisite stock ownership interests[9] have no corporate ownership disclosure duty.
- *What Must Be Disclosed:* Disclosing parties must file with

[1] *See* Rule 7.1 advisory committee note (2002) (strikes balance between adequate amount of financial information and level of detail that would be difficult, unnecessarily burdensome, and problematic). *See also* *Moyal v. Munsterland Gruppe GmbH & Co. KG*, __ F. Supp. 3d __ n.2, 2021 WL 1963899, at *3 (S.D.N.Y. 2021); *Rubio v. BNSF Railway Co.*, 548 F. Supp. 2d 1220, 1227 (D.N.M. 2008).

[2] *See* Rule 7.1 advisory committee note (2002).

[3] *See* Rule 7.1 advisory committee note (2002). *See generally* *Domain Prot., L.L.C. v. Sea Wasp, L.L.C.*, 23 F.4th 529, 542 (5th Cir. 2022).

[4] *See* *Obesity Research Inst., LLC v. Fiber Research Int'l, LLC*, 2016 WL 739795, at *1 (S.D. Cal. Feb. 25, 2016); *Best Odds Corp. v. iBus Media Ltd.*, 2014 WL 5687730, at *1 (D.Nev. Nov. 4, 2014).

[5] *See* Rule 7.1 advisory committee note (2002). *See also* Code of Conduct for United States Judges at Canon 3C(1)(c) ("A judge shall disqualify himself or herself in a proceeding in which the judge's impartiality might reasonably be questioned, including but not limited to instances in which . . . (c) the judge knows that the judge, individually or as a fiduciary, or the judge's spouse or minor child residing in the judge's household, has a financial interest in the subject matter in controversy or in a party to the proceeding, or any other interest that could be affected substantially by the outcome of the proceeding").

[6] *See* Rule 7.1(a)(1) & 7.1(b) (eff. Dec. 1, 2022).

[7] *See* *Birch v. Lombardo*, 2017 WL 6063068, at *4 (D. Nev. Dec. 6, 2017); *Godhart v. Sharr*, 2012 WL 4359075, at *2 (D.Ariz. Sept. 21, 2012).

[8] *See, e.g.*, *de Borja v. Razon*, 336 F.R.D. 620, 646 (D. Or. 2020) (no duty on unincorporated trusts); *SBFO Operator No. 3, LLC v. Onex Corp.*, 2020 WL 2850249, at *1 (E.D. Mo. June 2, 2020) (no duty on LLPs); *Bardfield v. Chisholm Properties Circuit Events, LLC*, 2010 WL 2278461, at *5 (N.D. Fla. May 4, 2010), *adopted*, 2010 WL 2278459 (N.D. Fla. June 4, 2010) (no duty on individuals).

[9] *See, e.g.*, *Domain Prot., L.L.C. v. Sea Wasp, L.L.C.*, 23 F.4th 529, 542 (5th Cir. 2022) (no duty to reveal creditor relationships).

the court a written statement that either (1) identifies each parent corporation and publicly held corporation owning 10% or more of their stock, *or* (2) states that no such corporation exists.[10] The Rule imposes no further corporate ownership disclosure requirements.[11]

Citizenship Disclosures

The citizenship disclosure is imposed only in those lawsuits where federal subject-matter jurisdiction is based on diversity of citizenship under 28 U.S.C. § 1332(a).[12] The disclosure is intended to better equip judges to make an early assessment whether the complete diversity requirement is satisfied, thereby reducing the risk of a belatedly uncovered jurisdictional defect that then squanders federal judicial resources.[13]

- *Who Must Disclose:* Plaintiffs and all other parties (including intervenors and proposed intervenors) must make this disclosure if the basis for the lawsuit's federal subject-matter jurisdiction is § 1332(a).[14]
    - *Other Diversity Statutes:* The Rule does not expressly address whether disclosure is required when jurisdiction is based on a different diversity statute, such as federal interpleader or the Class Action Fairness Act.[15]
- *What Must Be Disclosed:* The disclosure must state the citizenship of every person or entity whose citizenship is attributed to the disclosing party. For many types of parties, such disclosure is straightforward: for individuals, their domiciles;[16] for corporations, their place(s) of incorporation and principal place of business;[17] and for legal representatives, the citizenship of their estate's decedent, their infant, or their incompetent person.[18] But unincorporated entities—like partnerships, LLCs, and associations—assume the citizenship of each of their

[10]*See* Rule 7.1(a).

[11]*See, e.g., Lath v. BMS CAT*, 2018 WL 3468700, at *2 n.2 (D.N.H. July 17, 2018) (no obligation to list corporate subsidiaries); *Obesity Research Inst., LLC v. Fiber Research Int'l, LLC*, 2016 WL 739795, at *2 (S.D. Cal. Feb. 25, 2016) (no obligation to list members of LLC).

[12]*See* Rule 7.1(a)(2) (eff. Dec. 1, 2022).

[13]*See* Rule 7.1(a)(2) advisory committee note (2022). *See generally Owen Equip. & Erection Co. v. Kroger*, 437 U.S. 365, 373 (1978) ("diversity jurisdiction does not exist unless *each* defendant is a citizen of a different State from *each* plaintiff") (emphasis in original, citing *Strawbridge v. Curtiss*, 7 U.S. 267, 3 Cranch 267 (1806)).

[14]*See* Rule 7.1(a)(2) & advisory committee note (2022).

[15]*See* 28 U.S.C.A. § 1332(d) (Class Action Fairness Act); 28 U.S.C.A. § 1335(a)(1) (federal interpleader).

[16]*See Smith v. Marcus & Millichap, Inc.*, 991 F.3d 1145, 1149 (11th Cir. 2021); *Adams v. W. Marine Prod., Inc.*, 958 F.3d 1216, 1221 (9th Cir. 2020).

[17]*See* 28 U.S.C.A. § 1332(c)(1).

[18]*See* 28 U.S.C.A. § 1332(c)(2).

owners for diversity jurisdiction purposes.[19] Thus, all of those attributing citizenships must be disclosed.[20]

- *Citizenship Timing:* The disclosure must supply those citizenships as they existed when the action was filed in, or removed to, federal court, as well as when any later, jurisdiction-affecting event occurs.[21]
- *Information-and-Belief:* The drafters predict that disclosures made on "information and belief" will likely be acceptable at the pleadings stage if identifying citizenship in such cases proves difficult; and the drafters also noted that post-disclosure discovery may, in some cases, be appropriate to test those jurisdictional facts.[22]
- *Proper Pleading Still Required:* This disclosure obligation is in addition to, not instead of, a pleader's obligation to allege the grounds for the court's federal subject-matter jurisdiction.[23]

When Disclosures Must Be Made

Disclosures are due when a party, intervenor, or potential intervenor files its first appearance, pleading, petition, motion, response, or other request addressed to the court.[24] Timeliness can sometimes be influenced by circumstances, however.[25]

Supplementing the Disclosure

Parties are also obligated under the Rule to "promptly" file a supplemental disclosure when any change in the required information occurs.[26]

Serving Disclosures on Other Parties

The Rule is silent as to whether the statement must be served on other parties. At least one court has ruled that service is not required.[27]

Sealed Disclosures

Under appropriate circumstances, after balancing carefully

---

[19]*See Carden v. Arkoma Assocs.*, 494 U.S. 185, 195–96 (1990) ("diversity jurisdiction in a suit by or against [an unincorporated] entity depends on the citizenship of 'all the members,' 'the several persons composing such association,', 'each of its members').

[20]*See* Rule 7.1(a)(2) & advisory committee note (2022).

[21]*See* Rule 7.1(a)(2)(A)–(2)(B) (eff. Dec. 1, 2022).

[22]*See* Rule 7.1(a)(2) advisory committee note (2022).

[23]*See* Rule 7.1(a)(2) advisory committee note (2022) (citing Rule 8(a)(1)).

[24]*See* Rule 7.1(b)(1).

[25]*See Cain v. J.P. Morgan Chase Bank, Nat'l Ass'n*, 2021 WL 1588936, at *1 (E.D.N.Y. Apr. 23, 2021) (unique bankruptcy-appeal procedural posture).

[26]*See* Rule 7.1(b)(2).

[27]*See Plotzker v. Lamberth*, 2008 WL 4706255, at *12 (W.D.Va. 2008) (service is not required because statements are only "intended to be used by judges in determining whether disqualification is necessary").

the public's interest in disclosure,[28] the court may order disclosures to be made under seal in a manner that both serves this Rule's objectives and avoids collateral mischief.[29]

More Extensive Disclosures Under Local Rules

Local rules may require additional disclosures.[30]

Consequence of Delinquent or Non-Filing

The Rule prescribes no particular ramification for failing to file (or timely file). The disclosure obligation has not been construed as an inflexible precondition for filing a motion or brief in a lawsuit,[31] and courts have excused a failure to file (or timely file) if no prejudice occurs and the oversight is promptly corrected.[32] A typical remedial response by the courts has been an order directing the delinquent party to make its filing.[33] When, however, the omission is persistent (especially after the court presses for the filing), the failure to file can result in contempt,[34] monetary penalties,[35] dismissal,[36] striking appearances and jury demands,[37] or other sanctions.[38]

Collateral Uses of Ownership Disclosures

Both litigants and the courts have used corporate owner-

---

[28]*See Steel Erectors, Inc. v. AIM Steel Int'l, Inc.*, 312 F.R.D. 673, 675 (S.D. Ga. 2016) (weighing interest, and denying sealing).

[29]*See Best Odds Corp. v. iBus Media Ltd.*, 2014 WL 5687730, at *2–*3 (D.Nev. Nov. 4, 2014). *See generally* Rule 7.1(a)(2) advisory committee note (2022).

[30]*See* Rule 7.1 advisory committee note (2002). *See, e.g.*, D. Nev. Loc. R. 7.1-1(a) (directing parties to also disclose anyone who has "a direct, pecuniary interest in the outcome of the case").

[31]*See Feller v. Indymac Mortg. Servs.*, 2010 WL 342187, at *2 (W.D.Wash. Jan. 26, 2010).

[32]*See Urrego v. Samuel I. White, P.C.*, 2018 WL 4524106, at *10 n.10 (E.D. Va. July 3, 2018), *adopted*, 2018 WL 3586316 (E.D. Va. July 26, 2018); *Greenspan v. IAC/Interactivecorp*, 2016 WL 4548050, at *2 (N.D. Cal. Aug. 31, 2016). *See also Knowyourmeme.com Network v. Nizri*, 2021 WL 4441523, at *2 (S.D.N.Y. Sept. 28, 2021) (appeal pending) (refusing to hold removal defective for failure to file Rule 7.1 statement).

[33]*See Am. Builders Ins. Co. v. Adams Homes, LLC*, 2018 WL 4264599, at *3 (S.D. Ala. Sept. 6, 2018); *Hartman v. Charter Commc'ns, Inc.*, 2015 WL 1457468, at *2 (W.D.N.C. Mar. 30, 2015).

[34]*See American Gen. Life Ins. Co. v. Lawson Bros. Trucking Co.*, 2008 WL 4899425, at *1 (S.D.Ill. 2008) (holding attorney-of-record in contempt and directing $100 per day fine until disclosure statement filed).

[35]*See Jacovetti Law, P.C. v. Shelton*, 2020 WL 1491320, at *1-*7 (E.D. Pa. Mar. 27, 2020) (imposing array of monetary and non-monetary sanctions (including ethical/client reporting) for repeated failure to disclose).

[36]*See Medmarc Cas. Ins. Co. v. Sterling & Dowling PC*, 2010 WL 3747754, at *1 (S.D.Ill. Sept. 20, 2010) (threatening non-compliant party with dismissal).

[37]*See Hanratty v. Watson*, 2010 WL 3522996, at *1 (S.D.Ill. Sept. 2, 2010) (threatening non-compliant party with these strikes).

[38]*See Zagaruyka & Assocs. v. HealthSmart Benefit Sols. Inc.*, 2020 WL 4606707, at *3 (W.D. Okla. Aug. 10, 2020) (imposing monetary sanction, formal reprimand, and CLE attendance order).

ship disclosures and the information they contain for various collateral purposes. Content from the disclosures has been offered for the court's consideration in ruling on motions to dismiss,[39] to remand,[40] or to seek other rulings.[41] One court used a disclosure to resolve a dispute concerning a draft settlement agreement,[42] and another court ordered that a plaintiff be judicially estopped from substituting a party-plaintiff due, in part, to confusion created by a delinquent disclosure.[43] But other courts have been more reluctant to give disclosures broad collateral use, refusing to consider the disclosure to be a discovery device (capable of triggering discovery sanctions for noncompliance),[44] to rely on it for the substitution of parties or an amendment to a complaint,[45] or to view it as the discloser's consent to removal.[46]

---

[39] *See Modern Indus. Firebrick Corp. v. Shenango Inc.*, 2012 WL 2405236, at *2 (W.D.N.Y. June 25, 2012); *Mazzolin v. Lehman Bros. Real Estate Fund III, L.P.*, 2011 WL 4435649, at *2 (N.D.Ill. Sept. 23, 2011).

[40] *See Phantomalert, Inc. v. Google Inc.*, 2015 WL 8648669, at *4 (N.D. Cal. Dec. 14, 2015); *Little v. Stock Bldg. Supply, LLC*, 2011 WL 5149145, at *7 (E.D.N.C. Oct. 28, 2011).

[41] *See Rockwell Mining, LLC v. Pocahontas Land LLC*, 2020 WL 7489758, at *3 (S.D.W. Va. Dec. 21, 2020) (citing Statement as basis for denying motion to clarify citizenship for diversity jurisdiction purposes).

[42] *See Ha v. Deutsche Bank New Jersey Services, Inc.*, 2005 WL 589408, at *2 (S.D. N.Y. 2005).

[43] *See Engines Southwest, Inc. v. Kohler Co.*, 2006 WL 1896071, at *8 (W.D. La. 2006).

[44] *See Lath v. BMS CAT*, 2018 WL 3468700, at *2 (D.N.H. July 17, 2018).

[45] *See Gebhart v. Raytheon Aircraft Co.*, 2004 WL 1212047, at *2 (D. Kan. 2004).

[46] *See Hornady Mfg. Co., Inc. v. Green Ramp LLC*, 2021 WL 5867725, at *3 (D. Neb. Dec. 3, 2021), *adopted*, 2021 WL 5895631 (D. Neb. Dec. 10, 2021); *Royal v. Fontenot*, 2010 WL 4068868, at *3–*4 (W.D.La. Oct. 14, 2010).

RULE 8
GENERAL RULES OF PLEADING

(a) Claim for Relief. A pleading that states a claim for relief must contain:

(1) a short and plain statement of the grounds for the court's jurisdiction, unless the court already has jurisdiction and the claim needs no new jurisdictional support;

(2) a short and plain statement of the claim showing that the pleader is entitled to relief; and

(3) a demand for the relief sought, which may include relief in the alternative or different types of relief.

(b) Defenses; Admissions and Denials.

(1) *In General.* In responding to a pleading, a party must:

(A) state in short and plain terms its defenses to each claim asserted against it; and

(B) admit or deny the allegations asserted against it by an opposing party.

(2) *Denials—Responding to the Substance.* A denial must fairly respond to the substance of the allegation.

(3) *General and Specific Denials.* A party that intends in good faith to deny all the allegations of a pleading—including the jurisdictional grounds—may do so by a general denial. A party that does not intend to deny all the allegations must either specifically deny designated allegations or generally deny all except those specifically admitted.

(4) *Denying Part of an Allegation.* A party that intends in good faith to deny only part of an allegation must admit the part that is true and deny the rest.

(5) *Lacking Knowledge or Information.* A party that lacks knowledge or information sufficient to form a belief about the truth of an allegation must so

state, and the statement has the effect of a denial.

(6) *Effect of Failing to Deny.* An allegation—other than one relating to the amount of damages—is admitted if a responsive pleading is required and the allegation is not denied. If a responsive pleading is not required, an allegation is considered denied or avoided.

(c) Affirmative Defenses.

(1) *In General.* In responding to a pleading, a party must affirmatively state any avoidance or affirmative defense, including:

- accord and satisfaction;
- arbitration and award;
- assumption of risk;
- contributory negligence;
- duress;
- estoppel;
- failure of consideration;
- fraud;
- illegality;
- injury by fellow servant;
- laches;
- license;
- payment;
- release;
- res judicata;
- statute of frauds;
- statute of limitations; and
- waiver.

(2) *Mistaken Designation.* If a party mistakenly designates a defense as a counterclaim, or a counterclaim as a defense, the court must, if justice requires, treat the pleading as though it were correctly designated, and may impose terms for doing so.

(d) Pleading to Be Concise and Direct; Alternative Statements; Inconsistency.

(1) *In General.* Each allegation must be simple, concise, and direct. No technical form is required.

(2) *Alternative Statements of a Claim or Defense.* A party may set out two or more statements of a claim or defense alternatively or hypothetically, either in a single count or defense or in separate ones. If a party makes alternative statements, the pleading is sufficient if any one of them is sufficient.

(3) *Inconsistent Claims or Defenses.* A party may state as many separate claims or defenses as it has, regardless of consistency.

(e) Construing Pleadings. Pleadings must be construed so as to do justice.

[Amended effective July 1, 1966; August 1, 1987; April 30, 2007, effective December 1, 2007; April 28, 2010 effective December 1, 2010.]

AUTHORS' COMMENTARY ON RULE 8

PURPOSE AND SCOPE

Rule 8 establishes the "notice" pleading protocol for the federal courts. It sets the basic requirements for pleading claims: an averment of jurisdiction, a showing of a claim entitled to a remedy, and a demand for relief—all to be expressed in short, plain, simple, concise, and direct terms. It also sets the three options for counter-pleading (admit, deny, or lack of knowledge), cautioning that what is not denied will be considered admitted. Defenses (including affirmative defenses) must be raised, also in short and plain terms. Rule 8 concludes by approving the inclusion of alternative, hypothetical, or inconsistent claims or defenses, and admonishes that all pleadings are to be construed to "do justice."

RULE 8(a)—CLAIMS FOR RELIEF

CORE CONCEPT

In a "short" and "plain" statement, a party asserting a claim must include: (1) the grounds for the court's jurisdiction; (2) a statement of a claim showing that the pleader is entitled to relief; and (3) a demand for relief.

APPLICATIONS

Element 1: Grounds for Jurisdiction

A party filing a claim for relief in a complaint, counterclaim, crossclaim, or third-party complaint must state in short and plain terms the basis for the court's subject-matter jurisdiction for each count.[1] When tested for adequacy, the pleading's jurisdictional allegations are examined in their entirety and holistically.[2]

- *"Plausibly" Pleading Jurisdiction:* The courts are unsettled whether the "plausibility" pleading standard established in the U.S. Supreme Court's *Twombly*[3] decision should govern the pleading of jurisdiction,[4] though the sounder view would reject such an application.[5]
- *Diversity Jurisdiction:* When jurisdiction is based on diversity of citizenship,[6] the plaintiff should allege: (1) an amount in controversy that exceeds $75,000 exclusive of interest and costs; and (2) the diverse citizenship of the parties.[7] When, however, the full details of citizenship are not reasonably accessible to the pleader, but a good faith basis exists for believing the parties to be diverse, some courts permit a less detailed allegation.[8]
  - *Mandatory Disclosure, Too:* The claimant must also file a separate citizenship disclosure, stating the citizenships of every person or entity whose

---

[1] For a discussion of the subject-matter jurisdiction of the federal courts, *see supra* Part II, §§ 2.9 to 2.12. *See generally McNutt v. General Motors Acceptance Corp. of Indiana*, 298 U.S. 178, 189, 56 S. Ct. 780, 80 L. Ed. 1135 (1936) (pleader "must allege in his pleading the facts essential to show jurisdiction").

[2] *See DeRoy v. Carnival Corp.*, 963 F.3d 1302, 1311 (11th Cir. 2020) ("the facts and substance of the claims alleged, not the jurisdictional labels attached," determine court's authority); *Rote v. Zel Custom Mfg. LLC*, 816 F.3d 383, 397 (6th Cir. 2016) (examination not confined to complaint section labeled "Jurisdiction and Venue").

[3] *See infra* Authors' Commentary to Rule 8(a)(2) (*"Plausible" Pleadings*).

[4] *See Stifel, Nicolaus & Co. v. Lac du Flambeau Band of Lake Superior Chippewa Indians*, 980 F. Supp. 2d 1078, 1084 n.3 (W.D. Wis. 2013) (discussing division). *See also Cavalieri v. Avior Airlines C.A.*, 25 F.4th 843, 850 (11th Cir. 2022) (plausible averments required); *Ghedi v. Mayorkas*, 16 F.4th 456, 463–64 (5th Cir. 2021) (same); *SM Kids, LLC v. Google LLC*, 963 F.3d 206, 210 (2d Cir. 2020) (same).

[5] *See* 5 CHARLES ALAN WRIGHT & ARTHUR R. MILLER, FEDERAL PRACTICE AND PROCEDURE § 1206 (2021 Supp.) ("A subset of judges has compounded the error by extending Twombly-Iqbal's plausibility standard to Rule 8(a)(1), but this ignores the absence of Rule 8(a)(2)'s 'showing' requirement in Rule 8(a)(1), which contributed to the holdings of Twombly and Iqbal.") (footnotes omitted).

[6] 28 U.S.C.A. § 1332.

[7] This means: *for individuals*, their State of citizenship; *for corporations*, their States of incorporation *and* principal place of business; *for unincorporated associations*, all States of their members' citizenship. *See generally Mikelson v. Conrad*, 839 Fed. Appx. 275, 277 (10th Cir. 2021).

[8] *See Lincoln Ben. Life Co. v. AEI Life, LLC*, 800 F.3d 99, 106–10 (3d Cir. 2015) (permitting plaintiff, following reasonable inquiry, to allege that none of defendant LLC's members are plaintiff's fellow citizens); *Carolina Cas. Ins. Co. v. Team Equip., Inc.*, 741 F.3d 1082, 1085–87 (9th Cir. 2014) (same). *See also Worthington Fed. Bank v. Everest Nat. Ins. Co.*, 110 F. Supp. 3d 1211, 1216–18 (N.D. Ala. 2015) (citizenship not properly alleged, but circumstances satisfied court that diversity was present).

citizenship is attributed to the claimant.[9]

- *Special Diversity Jurisdiction:* When jurisdiction is based on a special type of diversity, the pleader must properly allege those prerequisites.[10]
- *Federal Question Jurisdiction:* When jurisdiction is based on the presence of a federal question,[11] the plaintiff should identify the constitutional, statutory, or treaty basis conferring such jurisdiction.[12] However, a failure to cite the specific federal statute conferring jurisdiction is not necessarily fatal, so long as a proper factual basis for jurisdiction is found.[13]
- *Admiralty Jurisdiction:* Parties intending to proceed under the rules governing admiralty or maritime claims must include a statement in their complaint declaring the action as an admiralty or maritime claim.[14]
- *Supplemental Jurisdiction:* When jurisdiction is based on the court's supplemental jurisdiction,[15] courts are divided on whether, and if so how, parties must plead that intent.[16] A more cautious pleader will explicitly allege how the claim qualifies under the federal supplemental jurisdiction statute.
- *Exception—Jurisdiction Already Acquired:* No statement of jurisdictional grounds is required if the court has already acquired subject-matter jurisdiction.[17] The safer practice is for claimants to always allege jurisdiction.
- *Remedy for Failure:* Omitting a statement of jurisdictional grounds can result in dismissal.[18]
- *Personal Jurisdiction:* Courts have often held that personal jurisdiction need not be alleged in a complaint

---

[9] *See* Rule 7.1(a)(2) (eff. Dec. 1, 2022).

[10] *See, e.g.*, 28 U.S.C.A. § 1332(d)(2) (Class Action Fairness Act diversity); 28 U.S.C.A. § 1335(a) (statutory interpleader diversity).

[11] 28 U.S.C.A. § 1331.

[12] *See Celli v. Shoell*, 40 F.3d 324, 327 (10th Cir. 1994) ("Federal courts are courts of limited jurisdiction, and the presumption is that they lack jurisdiction unless and until a plaintiff pleads sufficient facts to establish it.").

[13] *See Andrus v. Charlestone Stone Prods. Co.*, 436 U.S. 604, 608 n.6, 98 S. Ct. 2002, 56 L. Ed. 2d 570 (1978); *Rote v. Zel Custom Mfg. LLC*, 816 F.3d 383, 396–97 (6th Cir. 2016).

[14] *See* 28 U.S.C.A. § 1333. *See infra* Authors' Commentary to Rule 9(h).

[15] 28 U.S.C.A. § 1367.

[16] *See, e.g., Holland v. Red River Trucking, LLC*, 2011 WL 2417129, at *6 n.8 (E.D. Ky. June 10, 2011) (noting division); *Woodard v. Andrus*, 2010 WL 3704610, at *4 (W.D. La. Sept. 10, 2010) (noting obligation, but finding omission excusable).

[17] *See Bejar v. Gibson*, 2014 WL 3557636, at *5 (D. Kan. July 18, 2014), *aff'd*, 601 Fed. Appx. 628 (10th Cir. 2015) (not required for certain amended complaints); *Essex Ins. Co. v. Sheppard & Sons Const., Inc.*, 2013 WL 5305748, at *2 (W.D. Okla. Sept. 19, 2013) (not required for certain counterclaims); *Dunlop-McCullen v. Pascarella*, 2002 WL 31521012, at *23 (S.D.N.Y. Nov. 13, 2002) (not required for third-party complaints).

[18] *See Travaglio v. Am. Exp. Co.*, 735 F.3d 1266, 1268–69 (11th Cir. 2013).

(though choosing to do so is not improper).[19] This differentiation among jurisdiction types is not unsound: unlike personal jurisdiction, subject-matter jurisdiction is structural (not a convenience based defense), does not depend on being contested by a defendant (but can be raised by anyone at any time), and cannot be conferred by consent, waiver, or forfeiture (but must instead be confirmed independently by the court).[20] Thus, there is sense in requiring a complaint to plead only subject-matter jurisdiction, while awaiting a motion or an answer to contest personal jurisdiction. A minority of courts, nonetheless, hold that alleging personal jurisdiction is a claimant's pleading obligation.[21]

- *Venue:* Courts have ruled that venue—a waivable defense like personal jurisdiction—also need not ordinarily be alleged in a complaint (though doing so is not improper).[22]

Element 2: Short and Plain Statement of the Claim

The pleader must next state, in short and plain terms, a claim showing an entitlement to relief. This requires pleaders to give their opponents fair notice of their claim and the grounds upon which it rests.[23] Intricately detailed factual allegations are not necessary,[24] nor need pleaders factually allege a prima facie case[25] or even identify their precise legal theory[26] (indeed, even asserting an incorrect legal theory might not

---

[19]*See, e.g., Motus, LLC v. CarData Consultants, Inc.*, 23 F.4th 115, 123 (1st Cir. 2022); *Curry v. Revolution Labs.,LLC*, 949 F.3d 385, 392 (7th Cir. 2020); *Caribbean Broad. Sys., Ltd. v. Cable & Wireless P.L.C.*, 148 F.3d 1080, 1090 (D.C. Cir. 1998); *Stirling Homex Corp. v. Homasote Co.*, 437 F.2d 87, 88 (2d Cir. 1971). *See generally* 5 CHARLES A. WRIGHT & ARTHUR R. MILLER, FEDERAL PRACTICE AND PROCEDURE § 1206, at 121 (2004).

[20]*See supra* Part II, § 2.1 (comparing personal and subject-matter jurisdiction).

[21]*See, e.g., Creative Calling Sols., Inc. v. LF Beauty Ltd.*, 799 F.3d 975, 979 (8th Cir. 2015); *United Techs. Corp. v. Mazer*, 556 F.3d 1260, 1274 (11th Cir. 2009). *See also Kenshoo, Inc. v. Aragon Advert., LLC*, — F. Supp. 3d —, 2022 WL 504189, at *6 (E.D.N.Y. 2022) ("little doubt" same plausibility standard applies to jurisdictional allegations); *In re Zantac (Ranitidine) Prod. Liab. Litig.*, — F. Supp. 3d —, 2020 WL 6907056, at *2 (S.D. Fla. Nov. 24, 2020).

[22]*See Myers v. Am. Dental Ass'n*, 695 F.2d 716, 732 (3d Cir. 1982); *Uni-Top Asia Inv. Ltd. v. Sinopec Int'l Petroleum Expl. & Prod. Corp.*, — F. Supp. 3d —, 2022 WL 1202482, at *3 (D.D.C. 2022) (appeal pending).

[23]*See Tellabs, Inc. v. Makor Issues & Rights, Ltd.*, 551 U.S. 308, 319, 127 S. Ct. 2499, 168 L. Ed. 2d 179 (2007); *Erickson v. Pardus*, 551 U.S. 89, 93, 127 S. Ct. 2197, 167 L. Ed. 2d 1081 (2007) (per curiam).

[24]*See Ashcroft v. Iqbal*, 556 U.S. 662, 678, 129 S. Ct. 1937, 173 L. Ed. 2d 868 (2009); *Bell Atlantic Corp. v. Twombly*, 550 U.S. 544, 555 & 555 n.3, 127 S. Ct. 1955, 167 L. Ed. 2d 929 (2007).

[25]*See Swierkiewicz v. Sorema*, 534 U.S. 506, 510–13, 122 S. Ct. 992, 152 L. Ed. 2d 1 (2002); *Safe Streets All. v. Hickenlooper*, 859 F.3d 865, 878 (10th Cir. 2017).

[26]*See Skinner v. Switzer*, 562 U.S. 521, 530, 131 S. Ct. 1289, 179 L. Ed.

always be fatal,[27] provided the allegations otherwise impart fair notice of a cognizable claim.[28]) The Rules rely usually on discovery and summary judgment, rather than pleadings, to flesh out the disputed facts and cull unmeritorious cases.[29] Nor need magic words be incanted by the pleader.[30] Thus, the Rules generally[31] impose a more lenient pleading obligation than do many State courts.[32]

Although encouraging brevity, the federal pleading duty is still far from trivial; the pleading must contain "enough" to give defendants fair notice of a complaint's claims and the grounds for them.[33] The pleaded claim must be facially "plausible" — that is, it must allege sufficient factual content to permit the reasonable inference that the defendant is liable for unlawful conduct.[34] Obviously, this implicates a highly context-specific

---

2d 233 (2011) ("a complaint need not pin plaintiff's claim for relief to a precise legal theory"). *But cf. Ruivo v. Wells Fargo Bank, N.A.*, 766 F.3d 87, 90 (1st Cir. 2014) (plaintiffs must still identity the nature of claims, thus legal allegations remain important).

[27]*See Stanton v. Elliott*, 25 F.4th 227, 237–38 (4th Cir. 2022); *Beaton v. SpeedyPC Software*, 907 F.3d 1018, 1023 (7th Cir. 2018). *See generally Johnson v. City of Shelby*, 574 U.S. 10, 11, 135 S. Ct. 346, 190 L. Ed. 2d 309 (2014) (per curiam) (Rules "do not countenance dismissal of a complaint for imperfect statement of the legal theory supporting the claim asserted").

[28]*See Adams v. Am. Family Mut. Ins. Co.*, 813 F.3d 1151, 1154 (8th Cir. 2016) (theory of liability that was not alleged or even suggested in complaint should be dismissed).

[29]*See Swierkiewicz v. Sorema N. A.*, 534 U.S. 506, 512, 122 S. Ct. 992, 152 L. Ed. 2d 1 (2002).

[30]*See King v. Rubenstein*, 825 F.3d 206, 222 (4th Cir. 2016).

[31]Note, however, that this liberality is qualified in certain cases (see *Enhanced Pleading Exceptions*, below).

[32]*See Dura Pharmaceuticals, Inc. v. Broudo*, 544 U.S. 336, 347, 125 S. Ct. 1627, 161 L. Ed. 2d 577 (2005) ("ordinary pleading rules are not meant to impose a great burden upon a plaintiff"). *See generally Ryan v. Blackwell*, 979 F.3d 519, 524 (6th Cir. 2020) (pleading standard "generally construed quite liberally"). *Smith v. Clark/Smoot/Russell LLC*, 796 F.3d 424, 433 (4th Cir. 2015) (notice pleading is "relatively low" standard).

[33]*See Tellabs, Inc. v. Makor Issues & Rights, Ltd.*, 551 U.S. 308, 319, 127 S. Ct. 2499, 168 L. Ed. 2d 179 (2007) ("must say enough to give the defendant 'fair notice of what the plaintiff's claim is and the grounds upon which it rests' "); *Dura Pharmaceuticals, Inc. v. Broudo*, 544 U.S. 336, 346–47, 125 S. Ct. 1627, 161 L. Ed. 2d 577 (2005) ("ordinary pleading rules are not meant to impose a great burden upon a plaintiff", but allegations must still give fair notice); *Parker v. Landry*, 935 F.3d 9, 13-14 (1st Cir. 2019) ("Although there is no need to spell out endless details, the complaint must do more than merely parrot the contours of a cause of action."); *Amron v. Morgan Stanley Inv. Advisors Inc.*, 464 F.3d 338, 343–44 (2d Cir. 2006) ("we stop well short of saying that Plaintiffs bear no burden at the pleading stage", because they must allege "those facts *necessary* to a finding of liability").

[34]*See Ashcroft v. Iqbal*, 556 U.S. 662, 678, 129 S. Ct. 1937, 173 L. Ed. 2d 868 (2009); *Urquilla-Diaz v. Kaplan Univ.*, 780 F.3d 1039, 1051 (11th Cir. 2015). *See also Ocasio-Hernandez v. Fortuno-Burset*, 640 F.3d 1, 13 (1st Cir. 2011) (proper plausibility inquiry is "the reasonableness of the inference of liability that the plaintiff is asking the court to draw from the facts alleged in the complaint"); *Sepulveda-Villarini v. Dep't of Educ. of Puerto Rico*, 628 F.3d 25, 30 (1st Cir. 2010) (Souter, J.) ("A plausible but inconclusive inference

inquiry.[35] A "plausible" auto collision case may be very concisely pleaded, whereas a "plausible" antitrust or business fraud case may demand a far more robust factual presentation.[36]

The mandate, then, for pleaders is to allege "**sufficient facts**"—enough to move beyond the level of speculation, to "nudge[] their claims across the line from conceivable to plausible."[37] When will pleaded facts be "sufficient"? Zeroing in more exactly on that target has proven practically and conceptually elusive.[38] And judicial direction from the lower courts has not always been clear. Some courts have emphasized a distinction between pleading a "claim" (which is required) and pleading facts that correspond to each element of a legal theory (which, in the view of some courts, is not required).[39] Other courts have cautioned that legal allegations do not "go unscrutinized;" pleaders must still discharge their "responsibility for identifying the nature of [their] claim."[40]

While doctrinal imprecision abounds, some useful guiding markers seem settled. The "plausibility" standard is an objective target, not a subjective one.[41] It does not require that, as

---

from pleaded facts will survive a motion to dismiss . . .").

[35]*See Ashcroft v. Iqbal*, 556 U.S. 662, 679, 129 S. Ct. 1937, 173 L. Ed. 2d 868 (2009).

[36]*See Brooks v. Mentor Worldwide LLC*, 985 F.3d 1272, 1281 (10th Cir. 2021) (degree of required specificity "depends on the context and the type of case"); *Freeman v. Metro. Water Reclamation Dist. of Greater Chicago*, 927 F.3d 961, 965 (7th Cir. 2019) ("some theories of recovery require more detail than others in order to give the required notice"); *Swanson v. Citibank, N.A.*, 614 F.3d 400, 404–05 (7th Cir. 2010) (in "many straightforward cases" the pleading burden is no different than before, though more complex cases "will require more detail" to give notice and to show how the pleading theory's "dots should be connected").

[37]*See Bell Atlantic Corp. v. Twombly*, 550 U.S. 544, 570, 127 S. Ct. 1955, 167 L. Ed. 2d 929 (2007).

[38]*See Bilek v. Fed. Ins. Co.*, 8 F.4th 581, 586 (7th Cir. 2021) ("the required level of specificity is not easily quantified") (cleaned-up).

[39]*See Kaminski v. Elite Staffing, Inc.*, 23 F.4th 774, 777 (7th Cir. 2022) (claim "need not allege facts aligning with . . . claim's every element"); *Bot M8 LLC v. Sony Corp. of Am.*, 4 F.4th 1342, 1352 (Fed. Cir. 2021) (not proper to require pleading of every element of every claim). *But see Delker v. MasterCard Int'l, Inc.*, 21 F.4th 1019, 1024 (8th Cir. 2022) ("complaint must contain either direct or inferential allegations respecting all the material elements necessary to sustain recovery under some viable legal theory") (cleaned up). *See generally Sanchez Oil & Gas Corp. v. Crescent Drilling & Prod., Inc.*, 7 F.4th 301, 309 (5th Cir. 2021) (though litigants should specify breached contract provisions, "Rule 8 does not require that level of granularity").

[40]*See Ruivo v. Wells Fargo Bank, N.A.*, 766 F.3d 87, 90 (1st Cir. 2014).

[41]*See Adams v. City of Indianapolis*, 742 F.3d 720, 728–29 (7th Cir. 2014) (that defense counsel had, during discovery, "figured out" the claims would not obviate an objective pleading failure — such a contention "completely misunderstands the concept of 'notice' pleading"); *Paylor v. Hartford Fire Ins. Co.*, 748 F.3d 1117, 1127 (11th Cir. 2014) ("[W]hy should parties wait until discovery to identify, with precision, the subject of the litigation? That is exactly backward. Civil pleadings are supposed to mark the boundaries

pleaded, the claims appear "likely" or "probably" true."[42] But pleading the "sheer possibility" of a claim[43] will not suffice, nor will a conjectural "pyramid[ing] [of] speculative inference upon speculative inference."[44] A mere "thread-bare" or "formulaic" recital of elements, naked legal conclusions, and unadorned, "the-defendant-unlawfully-harmed-me" accusations will also not be enough.[45] Similarly, offering only equivocal factual allegations — ones equally consistent with either culpable or innocent conduct — fails to raise the required reasonable inference of "plausibility."[46] Instead, the pleaded allegations must be factual (not conclusory) and suggestive (not neutral).[47] Thus, proffering a conclusory inference without supporting facts will not do.[48] In the end, a claim's allegations must "possess enough heft" to show an entitlement to relief (thus justifying that the costly process of litigation continue).[49]

- *"Plausible" Pleadings:* In *Bell Atlantic Corp. v. Twom-*

---

for discovery; discovery is not supposed to substitute for definite pleading.").

[42]*See Ashcroft v. Iqbal*, 556 U.S. 662, 696, 129 S. Ct. 1937, 173 L. Ed. 2d 868 (2009); *Bell Atlantic Corp. v. Twombly*, 550 U.S. 544, 556, 127 S. Ct. 1955, 167 L. Ed. 2d 929 (2007).

[43]*See Ashcroft v. Iqbal*, 556 U.S. 662, 678, 129 S. Ct. 1937, 173 L. Ed. 2d 868 (2009).

[44]*See Jane Doe No. 1 v. Backpage. com, LLC*, 817 F.3d 12, 25 (1st Cir. 2016). *See also In re Google Inc. Cookie Placement Consumer Privacy Litig.*, 806 F.3d 125, 142 (3d Cir. 2015) (dismissal proper when "defendant's plausible alternative explanation is so convincing that plaintiff's explanation is *im*—plausible").

[45]*See Ashcroft v. Iqbal*, 556 U.S. 662, 678, 129 S. Ct. 1937, 173 L. Ed. 2d 868 (2009); *Bell Atlantic Corp. v. Twombly*, 550 U.S. 544, 555, 127 S. Ct. 1955, 167 L. Ed. 2d 929 (2007). *See also Cruz-Arce v. Mgmt. Admin. Servs. Corp.*, 19 F.4th 538, 543 (1st Cir. 2021) ("Although this is a low bar, it still requires more than a cascade of conclusory allegations . . ."); *Landers v. Quality Commc'ns, Inc.*, 771 F.3d 638, 640–41 (9th Cir. 2014) (pre-*Twombly*/*Iqbal* practice of merely pleading elements is gone); *Anderson v. U.S. Dep't of Housing & Urban Dev't*, 554 F.3d 525, 528–29 (5th Cir. 2008) (complaint must do more than name laws allegedly violated).

[46]*See Ashcroft v. Iqbal*, 556 U.S. 662, 678, 129 S. Ct. 1937, 173 L. Ed. 2d 868 (2009). *See also id.* at 678 (allegations that are "merely consistent" with (and not "plausibly suggestive" of) liability do not suffice); *Morman v. Campbell Cty. Mem'l Hosp.*, 632 Fed. Appx. 927, 932 (10th Cir. 2015) (plausibility absent when allegations encompass "wise swath of conduct, much of it innocent"). *But see Hamilton v. Palm*, 621 F.3d 816, 819 (8th Cir. 2010) (dismissal improper where complaint raises plausible inferences both supporting and rejecting liability).

[47]*See Bell Atl. Corp. v. Twombly*, 550 U.S. 544, 557 n.5, 127 S. Ct. 1955, 167 L. Ed. 2d 929 (2007).

[48]*See Brooks v. Mentor Worldwide LLC*, 985 F.3d 1272, 1281 (10th Cir. 2021).

[49]*See Bell Atlantic Corp. v. Twombly*, 550 U.S. 544, 557, 127 S. Ct. 1955, 167 L. Ed. 2d 929 (2007). *See also id.* at 558–59 (noting enormous costs of modern discovery). *See also Pension Ben. Guar. Corp. ex rel. St. Vincent Catholic Med. Ctrs. Ret. Plan v. Morgan Stanley Inv. Mgmt. Inc.*, 712 F.3d 705, 719 (2d Cir. 2013) (citing goal of "prevent[ing] settlement extortion," noting conclusory allegations, standing alone, "are a danger sign that the plaintiff is engaged in a fishing expedition") (citations omitted).

bly,[50] the Supreme Court announced the "plausibility" pleading standard (discussed above). In so doing, the Court expressly overruled the oft-quoted, very forgiving pleading mantra from its 1957 decision in *Conley v. Gibson* (namely, that no complaint should be dismissed for failing to properly state a claim "unless it appears beyond doubt that the plaintiff can prove no set of facts in support of his claim which could entitle him to relief").[51] The *Conley* language, wrote the Court, "earned its retirement" because it might, incorrectly, preserve a conclusorily pleaded claim on the mere theoretical chance that it might later find support.[52] The Court has confirmed that *Twombly*'s "plausibility" standard is not limited only to antitrust cases (as *Twombly* was),[53] and that notice pleading remains the broad objective.[54] But precisely how this "plausibility" line is to be drawn remains uncertain,[55] and it can impose a foreboding burden on those pleaders who sue just on the basis of a

[50]550 U.S. 544, 127 S. Ct. 1955, 167 L. Ed. 2d 929 (2007).

[51]*See Bell Atlantic Corp. v. Twombly*, 550 U.S. 544, 554–63, 127 S. Ct. 1955, 167 L. Ed. 2d 929 (2007) (abrogating language in *Conley v. Gibson*, 355 U.S. 41, 45–46, 78 S. Ct. 99, 2 L. Ed. 2d 80 (1957)). This abrogation was not new rulemaking, but rather an interpretation of the existing language. *See In re Ins. Brokerage Antitrust Litig.*, 618 F.3d 300, 320 (3d Cir. 2010). Moreover, it is likely that *Conley*'s language had already been effectively abandoned in practice. *See Khalik v. United Air Lines*, 671 F.3d 1188, 1194 n.4 (10th Cir. 2012) (commenting that "[e]ven before *Twombly/Iqbal*, cases that survived a motion to dismiss showed a higher level of detail"); *U.S. ex rel. Garst v. Lockheed-Martin Corp.*, 328 F.3d 374, 378 (7th Cir. 2003) (sufficient pleading requires that judges and parties "need not try to fish a gold coin from a bucket of mud"); *Mann v. Boatright*, 477 F.3d 1140, 1148 (10th Cir. 2007) (not court's job "to stitch together cognizable claims for relief from the wholly deficient pleading").

[52]*See Bell Atlantic Corp. v. Twombly*, 550 U.S. 544, 562–63, 127 S. Ct. 1955, 167 L. Ed. 2d 929 (2007). *See also Moss v. U.S. Secret Serv.*, 572 F.3d 962, 968 (9th Cir. 2009) (*Conley*, "read literally, set the bar too low").

[53]*See Ashcroft v. Iqbal*, 556 U.S. 662, 684, 129 S. Ct. 1937, 173 L. Ed. 2d 868 (2009).

[54]*See Ashcroft v. Iqbal*, 556 U.S. 662, 678–79, 129 S. Ct. 1937, 173 L. Ed. 2d 868 (2009) ("Rule 8 marks a notable and generous departure from the hyper-technical, code-pleading regime of a prior era, but it does not unlock the doors of discovery for a plaintiff armed with nothing more than conclusions."); *Erickson v. Pardus*, 551 U.S. 89, 93, 127 S. Ct. 2197, 167 L. Ed. 2d 1081 (2007) ("need only "give the defendant fair notice of what the . . . claim is and the grounds upon which it rests.' "). *See also HDC, LLC v. City of Ann Arbor*, 675 F.3d 608, 614 (6th Cir. 2012) ("inaccurate" to read Supreme Court's cases "so narrowly as to be the death of notice pleading"); *Khalik v. United Air Lines*, 671 F.3d 1188, 1191 (10th Cir. 2012) ("Rule 8(a)(2) still lives. There is no indication the Supreme Court intended a return to the more stringent pre-Rule 8 pleading requirements").

[55]*See Pruell v. Caritas Christi*, 678 F.3d 10, 14 (1st Cir. 2012) ("Adequacy is not always a clear line"); *Khalik v. United Air Lines*, 671 F.3d 1188, 1191 (10th Cir. 2012) (uncertainty whether "plausibility" signals "minimal change" or "significantly heightened fact-pleading standard"); *Starr v. Baca*, 652 F.3d 1202, 1215 (9th

suspicion or surmise (given that their access to discovery, of course, comes only if the complaint survives).[56] It is clear that the standard lies somewhere between fact pleading and conclusory recitations of elements,[57] between mere possibility and probability.[58] As summarized by one court, "plausibility" requires that the pleader supply those case details necessary "to present a story that holds together," and that courts ask only "*could* these things have happened, not *did* they happen."[59]

- *"Information-and-Belief" Pleading:* The viability of pleading upon information and belief remains unclear in the "plausibility" era. Such pleading may remain proper where the facts lie only in the defendants' possession or where the belief is premised on factual information that makes an inference of liability plausible.[60]
- *"Short and Plain":* Each statement of claim must be "short and plain," a directive interpreted to mean: with brevity and clarity.[61] Excessive verbosity may, in an extreme case, warrant dismissal for failure to honor this constraint.[62]
- *Pleading With Excessive Factual Detail:* Practitioners debate the wisdom of pleading with more detail than the

---

Cir. 2011) ("perplexing" difficulty in discerning how to apply standard).

[56]*See Khalik v. United Air Lines*, 671 F.3d 1188, 1191 (10th Cir. 2012); *New Albany Tractor, Inc. v. Louisville Tractor, Inc.*, 650 F.3d 1046, 1050 (6th Cir. 2011).

[57]*See Khalik v. United Air Lines*, 671 F.3d 1188, 1191 (10th Cir. 2012).

[58]*See Dean v. Warren*, 12 F.4th 1248, 1256 (11th Cir. 2021); *Keys v. Humana, Inc.*, 684 F.3d 605, 610 (6th Cir. 2012).

[59]*Swanson v. Citibank, N.A.*, 614 F.3d 400, 404 (7th Cir. 2010) (emphasis in original).

[60]*See Arista Records, LLC v. Doe 3*, 604 F.3d 110, 120 (2d Cir. 2010); *United States v. One Palmetto State Armory PA-15 Machinegun Receiver / Frame, Unknown Caliber, Serial No. LW001804*, 115 F. Supp. 3d 544, 576 (E.D. Pa. 2015), aff'd, 2016 WL 2893670 (3d Cir. 2016).

[61]*See Freeman v. Metro. Water Reclamation Dist. of Greater Chicago*, 927 F.3d 961, 966 (7th Cir. 2019).

[62]*See Kensu v. Corizon, Inc.*, 5 F.4th 646, 653 (6th Cir. 2021) (pleading standard is liberal, but "infinite patience" not required; claimants "must not append so many limbs and outward flourishes to a pleading that neither court nor defendant can easily identify the soul of the claim"). *See also, e.g., Barmapov v. Amuial*, 986 F.3d 1321, 1324–25 (11th Cir. 2021) (affirming dismissal, with prejudice, of 92-page, 440-paragraphed second amended complaint as forbidden "shotgun" pleading); *Knapp v. Hogan*, 738 F.3d 1106, 1109 (9th Cir. 2013) (Rule 8 can be violated both when a pleading "says too little" and when it "says too much"); *Cafasso, U.S. ex rel. v. General Dynamics C4 Sys., Inc.*, 637 F.3d 1047, 1058–59 (9th Cir. 2011) (dismissal without leave to amend proper because "district courts are busy enough without having to penetrate a tome approaching the magnitude of *War and Peace* to discern a plaintiff's claims and allegations"). *But see Hearns v. San Bernardino Police Dept.*, 530 F.3d 1124, 129–133 (9th Cir. 2008) (claim will not be dismissed solely for excessive length, but may be if otherwise improper); *U.S. ex rel. Garst v. Lockheed-Martin Corp.*, 328 F.3d 374, 378 (7th Cir. 2003) (surplusage in "windy but understandable" pleadings should be ignored).

Rules require.[63] Some believe that added detail helps educate the judge and lay a favorable early impression. Others reject that view as unrealistic. In any event, an unnecessarily detailed pleading is risky. It invites a pre-answer motion to dismiss premised on the very detail so gratuitously supplied,[64] and could unhelpfully impact the lawsuit's scope of discovery and effective case management.

- *Sua Sponte Dismissals*: In those rare instances of complaints so confused, vague, or unintelligible as to defy comprehension, *sua sponte* dismissals may be proper.[65]
- *Enhanced Pleading Exceptions:* In certain types of claims, these Rules or the underlying law itself impose on the pleader an enhanced obligation of additional claim detail. For example, claims must be alleged with particularity when: (1) pleading fraud and mistake, under Rule 9(b); (2) pleading demand futility in a shareholder derivative action, under Rule 23.1; and (3) pleading scienter under the Private Securities Litigation Reform Act of 1995, 15 U.S.C.A. § 78U-4(b).[66] Moreover, where those special categories are inseparably intertwined with the essential allegations of other elements of a claim, those elements might be held to this "particularity" requirement as well.[67]
- *RICO Case Statements:* Many Districts require that pleaders alleging violations of the federal Racketeer Influenced and Corrupt Organizations Act ("RICO") submit "RICO Case Statements," to flesh out the factual predicates and legal theory underlying such claims.[68] Such Statements have been approved, unless they would

[63] *See, e.g., Chaveriat v. Williams Pipe Line Co.*, 11 F.3d 1420, 1430 (7th Cir. 1993) (noting increasing trend toward greater specificity in complaints).

[64] *See, e.g., Tamayo v. Blagojevich*, 526 F.3d 1074, 1086 (7th Cir. 2008) (party may plead itself out of court by alleging facts that establish impenetrable defenses); *Jackson v. Marion County*, 66 F.3d 151, 153–54 (7th Cir. 1995) ("[w]e have expressed our puzzlement that lawyers insist on risking dismissal by filing prolix complaints").

[65] *See Amin-Bey v. U.S.*, 583 Fed.Appx. 37, 38 (3d Cir. 2014).

[66] *See Kanter v. Barella*, 489 F.3d 170, 175–76 (3d Cir. 2007) (listing exceptions). *See also Eternity Global Master Fund Ltd. v. Morgan Guar. Trust Co. of N.Y.*, 375 F.3d 168, 177 (2d Cir. 2004) (notice pleading provides standard for judging complaints, except in claims for fraud and mistake, which Rule 9(b) requires be pleaded with particularity); *Credit Suisse First Boston Corp., In re*, 431 F.3d 36, 46 (1st Cir. 2005) (PSLRA imposed pleading obligations beyond Rule 8(a)).

[67] *See Lachmund v. ADM Investor Services, Inc.*, 191 F.3d 777, 783 (7th Cir. 1999) (holding that general allegations of agency do not suffice where the substantive fraud allegations offered by plaintiff are necessary to establish the agency relationship).

[68] *See Northland Ins. Co. v. Shell Oil Co.*, 930 F. Supp. 1069, 1074 (D.N.J. 1996). Many judicial districts require, by Standing Order, chambers policy, or otherwise, that the pleader

obligate the pleader to allege more information than Rule 8(a) and Rule 9(b) would otherwise require.[69]

- *Case Law Exceptions:* Although courts occasionally have tried to impose more elaborate pleading standards in certain categories of cases, it now appears settled that the only permissible exceptions to the "notice" pleading standard of Rule 8(a) are those contained in other Rules or statutes.[70]
- *Admiralty/Maritime Cases:* The "plausibility" standard governs the pleading of admiralty and maritime cases.[71]
- *Pleading in Anticipation of Defenses:* Ordinarily, a pleader need not anticipate defenses, nor preemptively include averments to "plead around" an expected defense.[72]

Element 3: Demand for Relief

The pleader must also make a demand for judgment that identifies the remedies desired and the parties against whom relief is sought.[73] This does not require enormous specificity.[74] For example, most courts do not require complaints to contain a demand for a particular amount of damages,[75] and demanding an improper remedy will not necessarily foreclose the

answer a series of questions that supplement the RICO allegations of the complaint. *See, e.g.*, *National Organization for Women, Inc. v. Scheidler*, 510 U.S. 249, 249, 114 S. Ct. 798, 127 L. Ed. 2d 99 (1994) (noting local rule). This pleading obligation is especially important where the facts noted in the RICO Case Statement are deemed to be pleading averments, properly considered in ruling upon a motion to dismiss. *See Glessner v. Kenny*, 952 F.2d 702, 712 (3d Cir. 1991) (collecting cases so holding).

[69] *See Wagh v. Metris Direct, Inc.*, 363 F.3d 821, 826–28 (9th Cir. 2003).

[70] *See, e.g.*, *Swierkiewicz v. Sorema N. A.*, 534 U.S. 506, 512–15, 122 S. Ct. 992, 152 L. Ed. 2d 1 (2002) (no enhanced "prima facie case of discrimination" standard in employment discrimination cases); *Leatherman v. Tarrant County Narcotics Intelligence & Coordination Unit*, 507 U.S. 163, 113 S. Ct. 1160, 122 L. Ed. 2d 517 (1993) (no "heightened pleading standard" in civil rights cases); *Pratt v. Tarr*, 464 F.3d 730, 731 (7th Cir. 2006) (now "emphatically clear" that courts may not supplement Rule 9(b)'s list of claims that must be pleaded with particularity). *Cf. Mayle v. Felix*, 545 U.S. 644, 655, 125 S. Ct. 2562, 162 L. Ed. 2d 582 (2005) (statutory standards for pleading habeas petition "more demanding" than Rule 8(a)).

[71] *See Bensch v. Est. of Umar*, 2 F.4th 70, 75–79 (2d Cir. 2021).

[72] *See Perry v. Merit Sys. Prot. Bd.*, — U.S. —, 137 S. Ct. 1975, 1986 n.9, 198 L. Ed. 2d 527 (2017); *Siefert v. Hamilton Cty.*, 951 F.3d 753, 761 (6th Cir. 2020).

[73] *See, e.g.*, *Goldsmith v. City of Atmore*, 996 F.2d 1155, 1161 (11th Cir. 1993) (requirement of demand for judgment easily met by identifying requested remedies and parties from whom remedies are sought).

[74] *See Dieffenbach v. Barnes & Noble, Inc.*, 887 F.3d 826, 828 (7th Cir. 2018); *Sheet Metal Workers Local 19 v. Keystone Heating & Air Conditioning*, 934 F.2d 35, 40 (3d Cir. 1991).

[75] *See, e.g.*, *Burlington v. News Corp.*, 2015 WL 3439149, at *11 (E.D. Pa. May 27, 2015); *Alexander v. Se. Wholesale Corp.*, 978 F. Supp. 2d 615, 624 (E.D. Va. 2013). *See also Sawabeh Info. Servs. Co. v. Brody*, 832 F. Supp. 2d 280, 305 & 309 (S.D.N.Y. 2011) ("damaged in an amount to be determined at trial" suffices).

recovery of a proper one.[76] But this flexibility is not unbounded; the complaint must demand relief of some sort[77] and what is demanded must be relief the law allows.[78]

- *"Plausibly" Pleading Relief:* The courts are unsettled whether the *Twombly* "plausibility" pleading standard[79] should govern the pleading of a demand for relief,[80] though the sounder view would reject such an application.[81]
- *Diversity of Citizenship Cases:* In cases based upon diversity of citizenship jurisdiction, a claimant must demand an amount in excess of $75,000, exclusive of interest and costs.[82] [In federal question cases, no such monetary limit is generally required.]
- *Pleading Damages:* Although pleaders are not required to do more than state "the relief sought," the Rules *do* require pleaders to identify the type of relief they seek.[83] Thus, a pleading for equitable relief without any damages demand might foreclose the ability to press for damages later.[84]
- *Pleading Unliquidated Damages:* By local rule, certain Districts expressly forbid a plaintiff to demand a specific sum of unliquidated damages; instead, the pleader in

---

[76] *See Dingxi Longhai Dairy, Ltd. v. Becwood Tech. Grp. L.L.C.*, 635 F.3d 1106, 1108 (8th Cir. 2011).

[77] *See Covarrubias v. Trujillo*, 2020 WL 6541997, at *5 (C.D. Cal. Sept. 17, 2020) (failing to demand any relief violates Rule 8(a)(3)). *See generally Sholty v. Cavalry Portfolio Servs., LLC*, 2019 WL 4394735, at *3 (C.D. Ill. Sept. 13, 2019) ("A complaint without a prayer for relief is nothing more than a essay.").

[78] *See Dunlap v. Illinois Dep't of Corr.*, 2020 WL 3412991, at *2 n.1 (S.D. Ill. June 22, 2020) (seeking "retribution" is improper); *Driskell v. Homosexuals*, 533 B.R. 281, 282 (D. Neb. 2015) (seeking court to declare a "sin" is improper).

[79] *See supra* Authors' Commentary to Rule 8(a)(2) (*"Plausible" Pleadings*).

[80] *See Dotson v. Avon Prods., Inc.*, 2011 WL 891863, at *6 (D.S.C. Feb. 8, 2011), *adopted*, 2011 WL 891858 (D.S.C. Mar. 14, 2011) (noting uncertainty). *Compare Nevada DeAnza Fam. Ltd. P'ship v. Tesoro Ref. & Mktg. LLC*, 474 F. Supp. 3d 1087, 1096 (N.D. Cal. 2020) (implying that *Twombly* does apply), *with Chaleplis v. Karloutsos*, ___ F. Supp. 3d ___, 2022 WL 2304418, at *5 (E.D. Pa. 2022) (ruling that *Twombly* does not apply).

[81] *Cf.* 5 CHARLES ALAN WRIGHT & ARTHUR R. MILLER, FEDERAL PRACTICE AND PROCEDURE § 1206 (2021 Supp.) (noting that judges who apply *Twombly* to other pleading duties under Rule 8 are "ignore[ing] the absence of Rule 8(a)(2)'s 'showing' requirement [in those other duties], which contributed to the holdings of Twombly and Iqbal.") (footnotes omitted).

[82] *See St. Paul Mercury Indem. Co. v. Red Cab Co.*, 303 U.S. 283, 58 S. Ct. 586, 82 L. Ed. 845 (1938).

[83] *See* Rule 8(a)(3). *See also Seven Words LLC v. Network Solutions*, 260 F.3d 1089, 1098 (9th Cir. 2001) ("Surely a simple request 'for damages' would satisfy the notice requirement without imposing any undue burden on the drafter").

[84] *See Seven Words LLC v. Network Solutions*, 260 F.3d 1089, 1098 (9th Cir. 2001) (where damages claim was made years into litigation, after various representations that only declaratory and injunctive relief was sought, court declines to read a damages claim into complaint).

those jurisdictions is permitted only to demand unliquidated damages generally.[85]

- *Equitable and Declaratory Relief:* A party seeking equitable relief should plead the specific act to be prohibited or compelled; a party seeking declaratory relief should plead the specific declaration sought.[86]
- *Special Damages:* A claimant must plead special damages with specificity, as provided by Rule 9(g).
- *Remedy for Failure:* Some courts have ruled that omitting a proper demand for relief is not necessarily fatal to a claim's survival,[87] while others hold that such an omission justifies dismissal.[88]
- *Default Judgment:* In cases of default judgment, a claimant is limited to the specific amount of the demand, as provided by Rule 54(c).
- *Jury Demand:* A jury demand may be included as part of the original pleading. Rule 38 controls the circumstances in which a party may request (or waive) a trial by jury.[89]
- *Alternative, Hypothetical, and Inconsistent Demands:* A party may assert all demands for legal or equitable relief alternatively, hypothetically, and/or inconsistently.[90] Rule 8 protects a party's right to plead inconsistently; under this Rule, portions of a pleading cannot be offered as admissions against other portions containing inconsistent or alternative averments.[91]

Rule 8's Rules Supplant Inconsistent State Rules

Some States impose by statute specialized pleading obliga-

---

[85] *See, e.g.*, D. Del. Loc. R. 9.4 ("A pleading which sets forth a claim for relief in the nature of unliquidated money damages shall state in the ad damnum clause a demand specifying the nature of the damages claimed, e.g., 'compensatory,' 'punitive,' or both, but shall not claim any specific sum"); E.D. Pa. Loc. R. 5.1.1 ("No pleading asserting a claim for unliquidated damages shall contain any allegation as to the specific dollar amount claimed").

[86] *Cf. Johnson v. Paragon Sys., Inc.*, 305 F. Supp. 3d 139, 148 n.7 (D.D.C. 2018) (complaint improper for seeking "declaratory" and "injunctive" relief, without specifying form of either).

[87] *See Dingxi Longhai Dairy, Ltd. v. Becwood Tech. Grp. L.L.C.*, 635 F.3d 1106, 1108 (8th Cir. 2011); *Bontkowski v. Smith*, 305 F.3d 757, 762 (7th Cir. 2002).

[88] *See Griffin v. Blum*, 2020 WL 122988, at *3 (E.D.N.Y. Jan. 9, 2020); *Snyder v. DIMA VIII, Inc.*, 2014 WL 2925448, at *2 (D. Del. June 26, 2014).

[89] *See Thomas v. Home Depot USA, Inc.*, 661 Fed. Appx. 575, 577–78 (11th Cir. 2016) (if jury demanded in original complaint, demand is not lost when omitted from amendment).

[90] *See Shaffer v. George Washington Univ.*, 27 F.4th 754, 768–69 (D.C. Cir. 2022); *Moyle v. Liberty Mut. Ret. Ben. Plan*, 823 F.3d 948, 962 (9th Cir. 2016). *See generally infra* Authors' Commentary to Rule 8(d) ("**Alternative, Hypothetical, and Inconsistent Pleadings**").

[91] *See Rodriguez-Suris v. Montesinos*, 123 F.3d 10, 20 (1st Cir. 1997); *Independent Enterprises Inc. v. Pittsburgh Water and Sewer Authority*, 103 F.3d 1165, 1175 (3d Cir. 1997).

tions for the courts in their jurisdiction. Where such pleading provisions conflict with Rule 8, those inconsistent State requirements will not apply in the federal courts of that State.[92]

Pleadings from *Pro Se* Litigants

Pleadings filed by *pro se* litigants are held to a less stringent standard than those prepared by attorneys.[93] Nevertheless, although construed liberally, *pro se* pleadings are not relieved of the obligation to allege sufficient facts to support a proper legal claim,[94] and to do so under the "plausibility" standard.[95]

RULE 8(b)—DEFENSES; ADMISSIONS AND DENIALS

CORE CONCEPT

To respond to a pleading, parties must state their defenses (in short and plain terms) and admit or deny the allegations asserted against them. Denials must fairly respond to the substance of the allegations. If a responsive pleading is required, parties are deemed to have admitted all allegations they do not deny (except for allegations relating to the amount of damages).

APPLICATIONS

Impact of 2007 "Restyling" Amendments

In 2007, the content of former Rules 8(b) and 8(d) were combined together to form current Rule 8(b).

"Notice" Pleading of Defenses

Rule 8(b) contemplates that defenses, like claims for relief under Rule 8(a), must be short and concise[96] and provide fair notice to the adversary (and the court) of the allegations that the defending party proposes to place in issue.[97] Courts are divided on what effect *Twombly* and the Rule 8(a) "plausible"

---

[92]*See, e.g., Gallivan v. United States*, 943 F.3d 291, 293–94 (6th Cir. 2019) (Ohio law requiring affidavit of merit in medical negligence cases does not apply in federal court); *Cohen v. Office Depot, Inc.*, 184 F.3d 1292, 1299 (11th Cir. 1999) (Florida statute requiring leave of court before pleading punitive damages does not apply in federal court), opinion vacated in part, 204 F.3d 1069, 1072 (11th Cir. 2000) (Rule 8(a) discussion expressly reaffirmed); *Est. of Prasad ex rel. Prasad v. Cnty. of Sutter*, 958 F. Supp. 2d 1101, 1121 (E.D. Cal. 2013) (California law requiring court approval for certain punitive damages claims does not apply in federal court, but noting split of authority).

[93]*See Erickson v. Pardus*, 551 U.S. 89, 94, 127 S. Ct. 2197, 167 L. Ed. 2d 1081 (2007) (per curiam); *Estelle v. Gamble*, 429 U.S. 97, 106, 97 S. Ct. 285, 50 L. Ed. 2d 251 (1976).

[94]*See Requena v. Roberts*, 893 F.3d 1195, 1205 (10th Cir. 2018); *Taylor v. Books A Million, Inc.*, 296 F.3d 376, 378 (5th Cir. 2002).

[95]*See Atherton v. District of Columbia Office of Mayor*, 567 F.3d 672, 681–82 (D.C.Cir. 2009).

[96]*See* Rule 8(b)(1)(A). *See also Montgomery v. Wyeth*, 580 F.3d 455, 467–68 (6th Cir. 2009) (no "heightened" pleading for defense, only "short and plain" response required).

[97]*See Bell v. Taylor*, 827 F.3d 699, 705 (7th Cir. 2016); *Edwards v. CSXT Transp., Inc.*, 338 F.R.D. 590, 594 (E.D.N.C. 2021).

pleading mandate may have on defenses.[98] Some courts have ruled that defenses (like claims) must be asserted with sufficient detail to be "plausible," while others reject that view.[99]

Responsive Pleading Options

When an allegation has been asserted against them, and a responsive pleading is required, pleaders have only three options: (1) admit, (2) deny, or (3) state a lack of knowledge or information necessary to admit or deny.[100] The Rules do not approve or permit other types of responses, and choosing to answer in other ways is a dangerous practice (as shown below).

Denials Must Fairly Respond to the Substance

The purpose of a responsive pleading is to identify for both the opponent and the court those allegations which are contested, as distinct from those which are conceded.[101] Thus, when responsively pleading, parties are obligated to "fairly" respond to the "substance" of an allegation.[102] Each portion of each allegation must be addressed (any portion not denied is considered admitted),[103] and pleaders may not do so in a manner that equivocates or confuses the issues.[104] Ergo, offering an antiquated reply that evades a fair and substantive response is improper.[105] For this reason, refusing to substantively respond because the allegation is "a conclusion of law,"[106] or is a

---

[98]*See Francisco v. Verizon South, Inc.*, 2010 WL 2990159, at *6–*9 (E.D. Va. July 29, 2010) (surveying split). *See generally* William M. Janssen, *The Odd State of Twiqbal Plausibility in Pleading Affirmative Defenses*, 70 WASH. & LEE L. REV. 1573 (2013) (noting division on affirmative defenses).

[99]*See Montgomery v. Wyeth*, 580 F.3d 455, 467–68 (6th Cir. 2009) (no heightened pleading standard applies to defenses). *Compare Francisco v. Verizon South, Inc.*, 2010 WL 2990159, at *6–*9 (E.D. Va. July 29, 2010) (applying "plausibility" to defenses) *with Edwards v. CSXT Transp., Inc.*, 338 F.R.D. 590, 592–93 (E.D.N.C. 2021) (refusing to demand more of answers than "short and plain").

[100]*See Edwards v. CSXT Transp., Inc.*, 338 F.R.D. 590, 594 (E.D.N.C. 2021); *Martinez v. Naranjo*, 328 F.R.D. 581, 598–99 (D.N.M. 2018).

[101]*See Bommarito v. Equixfax Info. Servs., LLC*, 340 F.R.D. 566, 569 (E.D. Mich. 2022); *Edwards v. CSXT Transp., Inc.*, 338 F.R.D. 590, 594 (E.D.N.C. 2021).

[102]*See* Rule 8(b)(2).

[103]*See Cutino v. Nightlife Media, Inc.*, 575 Fed. Appx. 888, 891 (Fed. Cir. 2014). *See also Gross v. Weinstein, Weinburg & Fox, LLC*, 123 F. Supp. 3d 575, 581–82 (D. Del. 2015) (finding responses insufficient, but forebearing from default with final chance of correction).

[104]*See Satco Prod., Inc. v. Seoul Semiconductor Co.*, 551 F. Supp. 3d 1329, 1333–36 (N.D. Ga. 2021) (deeming evasive answers to be admissions); *Reis Robotics USA, Inc. v. Concept Industries, Inc.*, 462 F. Supp. 2d 897, 907–08 (N.D. Ill. 2006) (striking improperly qualified answer, and ordering repleading).

[105]*See Edwards v. CSXT Transp., Inc.*, 338 F.R.D. 590, 594 (E.D.N.C. 2021).

[106]*See Bommarito v. Equixfax Info. Servs., LLC*, 340 F.R.D. 566, 569 (E.D. Mich. 2022) (must not keep court and opponents "in the dark" and "guessing" whether conclusion is being disputed); *Martinez v. Naranjo*, 328 F.R.D. 581, 599 (D.N.M. 2018) (must

characterization of a document which "speaks for itself,"[107] or is a contention that fails to state a cognizable claim for relief,[108] or is an averment that is neither admitted nor denied because the party "demands strict proof thereof"[109] are all examples of evading, rather than fairly responding, to the substance of a pleaded allegation. Counter-pleading in this manner can have case-devastating consequences[110] (though courts may sometimes overlook these evasive practices when they are coupled with an unambiguous denial).[111] Likewise, filing a motion for summary judgment, in lieu of any responsive pleading at all, is worrisome because it is not an option expressly authorized by the Rules.[112]

---

plead to legal conclusions); *Gracedale Sports and Entertainment, Inc. v. Ticket Inlet, LLC*, 1999 WL 618991 (N.D. Ill. 1999) ("flies in the face of the established doctrine that legal conclusions are a proper part of federal pleading, to which Rule 8(b) also compels a response"); *Saldana v. Riddle*, 1998 WL 373413 (N.D. Ill. 1998) ("nonsense" that legal conclusions need not be admitted or denied).

[107]*See Chicago Dist. Council of Carpenters Pension Fund v. Balmoral Racing Club, Inc.*, 2000 WL 876921, at *1 (N.D. Ill. 2000) (rejecting "speaks for itself" responses: "[t]his Court has been attempting to listen to such written materials for years (in the forlorn hope that one will indeed give voice)—but until some such writing does break its silence, this Court will continue to require pleaders to employ one of the three alternatives that are permitted by Rule 8(b)"). *See also Bommarito v. Equixfax Info. Servs., LLC*, 340 F.R.D. 566, 569–70 (E.D. Mich. 2022) (not permitted response); *Martinez v. Naranjo*, 328 F.R.D. 581, 599 (D.N.M. 2018) (improper response). *But cf. Scott v. Harris*, 550 U.S. 372, 378 n.5, 127 S. Ct. 1769, 167 L. Ed. 2d 686 (2007) ("happy to allow the videotape to speak for itself").

[108]*See Bailey v. Gibson Hotel Mgmt., Inc.*, 2018 WL 5815548, at *4 (E.D. Tenn. Nov. 6, 2018) (response inappropriate, permitting defendant to amend answer).

[109]*See Sun Life Assurance Co. of Canada v. Great Lakes Business Credit LLC*, 968 F. Supp. 2d 898, 904 (N.D. Ill. 2013) (improper, meaningless, and clearly violates Rule); *King Vision Pay Per View, Ltd. v. J.C. Dimitri's Restaurant, Inc.*, 180 F.R.D. 332, 333 (N.D. Ill. 1998) (improper).

[110]*See Chicago Dist. Council of Carpenters Pension Fund v. Balmoral Racing Club, Inc.*, 2000 WL 876921, at *1–*2 (N.D. Ill. June 26, 2000) (striking responses, ordering re-pleading, and forbidding counsel from billing client for "correcting" the "counsel's errors"); *King Vision Pay Per View, Ltd. v. J.C. Dimitri's Rest., Inc.*, 180 F.R.D. 332, 334 (N.D. Ill. 1998) (deeming "strict proof" responses to be admissions, commenting that "this action will proceed on that basis").

[111]*See Kane Cty. v. United States*, 772 F.3d 1205 (10th Cir. 2014) ("conclusion-of-law" denial *coupled with* a lack-of-information denial was compliant); *Edwards v. CSXT Transp., Inc.*, 388 F.R.D. 590, 594–95 (E.D.N.C. 2021) (improper responses rescued by global denial); *Martinez v. Naranjo*, 328 F.R.D. 581, 599 (D.N.M. 2018) (improper no-response-required saved by alternative denial); *Keller v. Enhanced Recovery Co., LLC*, 2018 WL 5650036, at *2 (N.D. Ind. Oct. 31, 2018) (same).

[112]*But cf. Pepper v. Vill. of Oak Park*, 430 F.3d 805, 812 (7th Cir. 2005) (no admission, because motion revealed lack of claim as a matter of law); *Trotter v. Jack Anderson Enters., Inc.*, 818 F.2d 431, 436 (5th Cir. 1987) (no admission, because motion gave plain notice of matters to be litigated); *Jurdi v. United States*, 485 F. Supp. 3d 83, 99 (D.D.C. 2020) (no admission, because effect deemed same as Rule

Types of Proper Denials

The Rules permit a party to deny an opponent's allegations in a pleading in several ways, provided the method chosen comports with Rule 11:

- *General Denials:* deny all allegations of a pleading (including those asserting the court's jurisdiction).[113] No magic language is required for a general denial, so long as that intent is clear.[114] But because such sweeping, categorical denials of everything alleged will infrequently comport with Rule 11, they are uncommon.[115]
- *Qualified General Denials:* deny all allegations of a pleading (or a grouped cluster of allegations) except for certain specified ones.
- *Specific Denials:* deny particular paragraphs, one at a time. It is the most common form of pleading denials. (Practitioners who opt for specific denials often begin or end them with a precautionary, catch-all, qualified general denial.[116])
- *Partial Denials:* deny a portion of particular allegation, with a companion response that either admits the remaining portions or states, due to lack of knowledge, that those cannot be either admitted or denied.

Failure to Deny Factual Allegations

A failure to deny the factual allegations of a complaint,[117] amended complaint,[118] or counterclaim/crossclaim[119] will deem them admitted—as may the use of unauthorized responsive pleading options (discussed above). However, courts are unlikely to deem as admitted those facts that were not well pleaded,[120] or statements that constitute mere conclusions of

12(d)-converted pre-answer motion to dismiss).

[113]*See National Restaurant Ass'n Educ. Found. v. Shain*, 287 F.R.D. 83, 87 (D.D.C. 2012).

[114]*See In re Sterten*, 546 F.3d 278, 283 (3d Cir. 2008).

[115]*See U.S. v. $34,796.49, more or less, in U.S. Currency*, 2015 WL 1643582, at *3 (S.D.Ala. Apr. 13, 2015).

[116]*See Aguilar v. PNC Bank, N.A.*, 853 F.3d 390, 403 n.16 (8th Cir. 2017) (approving, as proper federal pleading, use of catch-all statement that "denies each and every allegation" not specifically admitted); *Dawley v. Acme Block & Brick, Inc.*, 335 F.R.D. 122, 124–25 (M.D. Tenn. 2020) (same).

[117]*See Perez v. El Tequila, LLC*, 847 F.3d 1247, 1254 (10th Cir. 2017); *Guggenheim Capital, LLC v. Birnbaum*, 722 F.3d 444, 445 (2d Cir. 2013).

[118]*See Ashley v. Jaipersaud*, 544 Fed. Appx. 827, 828–29 (11th Cir. 2013). *But see Edelman v. Belco Title & Escrow, LLC*, 754 F.3d 389, 393–95 (7th Cir. 2014) (no admissions, where defendant had answered earlier complaint and amended pleading changed no allegations against it).

[119]*See L.A. Pub. Ins. Adjusters, Inc. v. Nelson*, 17 F.4th 521, 527 (5th Cir. 2021) (counterclaim); *Starlight Bldg., Ltd. v. Bazemore*, 2017 WL 6403110, at *5 (E.D. Tex. Sept. 28, 2017) (crossclaim).

[120]*See Nishimatsu Const. Co. v. Houston Nat'l Bank*, 515 F.2d 1200, 1206 (5th Cir. 1975); *Wecosign, Inc. v. IFG Holdings, Inc.*, 845 F. Supp. 2d

law.[121] Nor will courts enter judgment against a defaulting party based on deemed-admitted facts without first testing whether those facts actually state a cognizable claim for relief.[122]

Failure to Deny Amount of Damages

Although a failure to deny usually causes that allegation to be deemed admitted, this result does not occur with allegations relating to the amount of damages.[123]

Denials Based Upon Lack of Knowledge or Information

(1) *Substance of Denial:* A party may deny by pleading a lack of knowledge or information. But to do so, the party must plead *both* lack of knowledge *and* lack of information.[124] In certain circumstances, lack of information may be asserted where the information at issue may exist but has proven to be difficult to uncover.[125] A party pleading lack of knowledge and information is also bound by the obligation of honesty in pleading; an allegation that is obviously within the responding party's knowledge or information cannot be avoided, and averring lack of knowledge or information in such circumstances may have the unintended effect of *admitting* the allegation.[126] However, if the requisite information is accessible to the responding party, but not during the brief responsive-pleading time window, a response invoking lack of knowledge or information may be proper.[127]

(2) *Duty of Investigation:* A party denying based upon a lack of knowledge and information has the duty to reasonably investigate whether the information exists and how difficult it would be to find.[128]

(3) *Effect:* A response properly based upon a lack of knowl-

1072, 1078 (C.D.Cal. 2012).

[121] *See Thompson v. DeWine*, 976 F.3d 610, 616 n.5 (6th Cir. 2020); *Marshall v. Baggett*, 616 F.3d 849, 852 (8th Cir. 2010).

[122] *See Marshall v. Baggett*, 616 F.3d 849, 852 (8th Cir. 2010); *Ryan v. Homecomings Fin. Network*, 253 F.3d 778, 780 (4th Cir. 2001). *See also Ohio Cent. R. Co. v. Central Trust Co.*, 133 U.S. 83, 91, 10 S. Ct. 235, 33 L. Ed. 561 (1890).

[123] *See* Rule 8(b)(6). *See also Vevelstad v. Flynn*, 230 F.2d 695, 703 (9th Cir. 1956); *Int'l Ass'n of Sheet Metal, Air, Rail & Transportation Workers, Loc. Union No. 71 v. Lovejoy Metals, Inc.*, 495 F. Supp. 3d 174, 184 (W.D.N.Y. 2020).

[124] *See Bobbitt v. Freeman Companies*, 2000 WL 1131948 (N.D. Ill. 2000).

[125] *See Clay v. District of Columbia*, 831 F. Supp. 2d 36, 46–47 (D.D.C. 2011).

[126] *See Harvey Aluminum (Inc.) v. N.L.R.B.*, 335 F.2d 749, 757 (9th Cir. 1964); *Bommarito v. Equixfax Info. Servs., LLC*, 340 F.R.D. 566, 567–69 (E.D. Mich. 2022).

[127] *See Bommarito v. Equixfax Info. Servs., LLC*, 340 F.R.D. 566, 567–59 (E.D. Mich. 2022).

[128] *See Bommarito v. Equixfax Info. Servs., LLC*, 340 F.R.D. 566, 568 (E.D. Mich. 2022); *U.S. v. 1866.75 Board Feet, 11 Doors And Casings, More of Less of Dipteryx Panamensis Imported from Nicaragua*, 2008 WL 839792, at *3 (E.D. Va. 2008).

edge and information eludes the effect of a deemed-admission, and thus operates like a denial.[129]

Duty to Re-Assert Denials to Amended Pleadings

When a pleading is one to which a response is required, and it is later amended, the opponent is obligated to timely respond to the amended pleading, with either a motion to dismiss or an answer.[130] The most prudent, safest path to do so is by filing a new document (motion or answer) addressed specifically to the amended pleading. Nonetheless, where the allegations against the responding party have not materially changed and were all previously addressed in a motion or answer to the original pleading, a court might, in an appropriate circumstance, excuse a failure to file a new document and treat the earlier motion or answer as an acceptable response to the now-amended pleading.[131]

No Duty to Respond to Answers, Generally

Unless it contains a counterclaim or crossclaim,[132] or the court orders a reply,[133] pleaders need not—and may not—respond to an answer.[134] All new matter and affirmative defenses contained in an answer are considered denied or avoided automatically.[135]

No Duty to Respond to Allegations Against Others

The 2007 amendments to Rule 8(b) seem to make express what was long understood in practice, namely that a pleader need not responsively plead to allegations directed solely at someone else.[136] If, however, the allegations directly or inferentially target the responsive pleader, a response is

---

[129] *See Bommarito v. Equixfax Info. Servs., LLC*, 340 F.R.D. 566, 568 (E.D. Mich. 2022).

[130] *See* Rule 15(a)(3); *Bern Unlimited, Inc. v. Burton Corp.*, 25 F. Supp. 3d 170, 177 (D. Mass. 2014). *See also Montgomery-Smith v. La. Dep't of Health & Hosps.*, 299 F. Supp. 3d 790, 798–99 (E.D. La. 2018) (in responding to amended pleadings, time to file motion is different from time to file answer).

[131] *See KST Data, Inc. v. DXC Tech. Co.*, 980 F.3d 709, 715–16 (9th Cir. 2020); *Vandewarker v. Cont'l Res., Inc.*, 917 F.3d 626, 630–31 (8th Cir. 2019). *See also Jordan v. City of Philadelphia*, 66 F. Supp. 2d 638, 641 n.1 (E.D. Pa. 1999) (pending motion to dismiss need not be re-filed when amended complaint suffers from same defects as original pleading).

[132] *See* Rule 7(a)(3)–(a)(4).

[133] *See* Rule 7(a)(7).

[134] *See* Rule 7(a) ("[o]nly these pleadings are allowed"). *See also Osberry v. Slusher*, 750 Fed. Appx. 385, 389–90 (6th Cir. 2018).

[135] *See* Rule 8(b)(6) ("If a responsive pleading is not required, an allegation is considered denied or avoided.").

[136] *See* Rule 8(b)(1)(B) (in a counterpleading, party must "admit or deny the allegations asserted *against it* by an opposing party") (emphasis added). *See also United States Sec. & Exch. Comm'n v. Collector's Coffee Inc.*, ___ F. Supp. 3d ___, 2022 WL 1567460, at *7 (S.D.N.Y. 2022) ("it would make no sense to interpret Rule 8(b) to require (or permit) a party to a lawsuit that is named in some claims but not others to present defenses or respond to allegations pertaining to claims in which it was not named"); *City Select Auto Sales, Inc. v. David/Randall Assocs.*,

required.[137]

Special Matters

Rule 9 requires that certain matters be denied more specifically, such as the capacity of a party to sue or be sued, the legal existence of a party, the authority of a party to sue or be sued in a representative capacity, the occurrence or performance of conditions precedent, the issuance of a judgment, or the legality of a document or act.[138]

Fifth Amendment

Where an answer would subject a party to criminal charges or be used as evidence or a link in the evidence in a criminal proceeding, the pleader may refuse to answer by claiming the privilege to be free from self-incrimination, founded in the Fifth Amendment to the United States Constitution.[139]

RULE 8(c)—AFFIRMATIVE DEFENSES

CORE CONCEPT

An affirmative defense is any fact or argument asserted by the respondent that vitiates all or a part of the opposing party's claim. Rule 8(c) provides for the pleading of affirmative defenses, and also directs that misdesignated counterclaims be treated as affirmative defenses. A party must raise all affirmative defenses or risk waiving them.

APPLICATIONS

Definition of Affirmative Defense

An affirmative defense (or "avoidance," a common law companion term)[140] is a defensive assertion of new facts or arguments that, if true, would defeat (or reduce) the asserted claim even if the claim's allegations are proven.[141] By contrast, an allegation that merely shows why a plaintiff cannot meet its

---

Inc., 96 F. Supp. 3d 403, 427 (D.N.J. 2015) ("no obligation" to admit or deny).

[137] *See Griffin v. Fairman*, 1989 WL 153556, at *1 (N.D. Ill. 1989) ("Though a party is of course excused from responding to a separate claim brought only against other parties to the litigation, there is simply no room for the quoted nonresponse to an allegation made in the midst of a claim that does target the responsive pleader.").

[138] *See* Rule 9(a), (c), (d), & (e).

[139] *See, e.g., LaSalle Bank Lake View v. Seguban*, 54 F.3d 387, 389–91 (7th Cir. 1995) (cannot be deemed admitted when defendant invokes Fifth Amendment; complainant must produce evidence to support allegations); *In re Enron Corp. Secs., Derivative & Erisa Litig.*, 762 F. Supp. 2d 942, 961 (S.D.Tex. 2010) (proper, timely invocation of privilege precludes deemed-admission).

[140] *See Germain v. US Bank Nat'l Ass'n as Tr. for Morgan Stanley Mortg. Loan Tr. 2006-7*, 920 F.3d 269, 273–74 (5th Cir. 2019) (technically, "avoidance" admits allegations while suggesting reasons why no recovery is permitted; "affirmative defense" introduces matters outside plaintiff's prima facie case ill-suited for simple denial).

[141] *See Utica Mut. Ins. Co. v. Munich Reinsurance Am., Inc.*, 7 F.4th 50, 63 (2d Cir. 2021); *Emergency One, Inc. v. American Fire Eagle Engine Co., Inc.*, 332 F.3d 264, 271 (4th Cir. 2003). *See also Estate of Hamilton v.*

burden of proof[142] or that purports to merely reserve the right to assert additional defenses later[143] is not an affirmative defense. In diversity cases, State law fixes what qualifies as an affirmative defense.[144]

Burden of Proving Affirmative Defenses

The party raising an affirmative defense has the burden of proving it.[145]

Burden of Pleading Affirmative Defenses

The party proposing to prove an affirmative defense also has the burden of pleading it by asserting it in response to the relevant pleading.[146] The goal of this requirement, consistent with federal pleading practice generally, is to provide notice to the opponent, avoid surprise and undue prejudice, and afford the opponent a chance to argue, if able, why the defense is unfounded.[147]

Properly Pleading Affirmative Defenses

The pleaders' duty is to "affirmatively state" their avoidances and affirmative defenses in their responsive pleading.[148] Prudence dictates that such averments be labeled as affirmative defenses/avoidances and pleaded in separate paragraphs.

Unlike claims (which are governed by Rule 8(a)), Rule 8(c) does not require that affirmative defenses or avoidances make an entitlement "showing."[149] This difference in syntax has caused a division among the courts on whether the *Twombly* "plausibility" standard governs the pleading of affirmative defenses.[150] In a debate that remains largely at the district

---

City of New York, 627 F.3d 50, 57 (2d Cir. 2010) (when defendants wish to make point about something that is not element of claim, they must plead it as affirmative defense).

[142]*See Utica Mut. Ins. Co. v. Munich Reinsurance Am., Inc.*, 7 F.4th 50, 63 (2d Cir. 2021); *Zivkovic v. So. Cal. Edison Co.*, 302 F.3d 1080, 1088 (9th Cir. 2002).

[143]*See U.S. Bank Nat'l Ass'n v. Gerber*, 380 F. Supp. 3d 429, 440 (M.D. Pa. 2018).

[144]*See Racher v. Westlake Nursing Home Ltd. P'ship*, 871 F.3d 1152, 1161–67 (10th Cir. 2017); *LSREF2 Baron, L.L.C. v. Tauch*, 751 F.3d 394, 398 (5th Cir. 2014).

[145]*See Taylor v. Sturgell*, 553 U.S. 880, 907, 128 S. Ct. 2161, 171 L. Ed. 2d 155 (2008); *Petrobras Am., Inc. v. Samsung Heavy Indus. Co., Ltd.*, 9 F.4th 247, 254 (5th Cir. 2021).

[146]*See Taylor v. Sturgell*, 553 U.S. 880, 907 128 S. Ct. 2161, 171 L. Ed. 2d 155 (2008); *John R. Sand & Gravel Co. v. U.S.*, 552 U.S. 130, 133, 128 S. Ct. 750, 169 L. Ed. 2d 591 (2008).

[147]*See Blonder-Tongue Laboratories, Inc. v. University of Illinois Foundation*, 402 U.S. 313, 350, 91 S. Ct. 1434, 28 L. Ed. 2d 788 (1971). *See also Rogers v. McDorman*, 521 F.3d 381, 385 (5th Cir. 2008) (defendants should not be allowed to "lie behind a log" and "ambush" plaintiffs).

[148]*See* Rule 8(c)(1).

[149]*Cf.* Rule 8(a)(2). Depending upon whether Rule 8(c) is properly read as an elaboration of, or wholly independent from, Rule 8(b)(1)(A), it may also be that even a "short and plain" statement is not required for affirmative defenses.

[150]*See* William M. Janssen, *The Odd State of Twiqbal Plausibility in*

court level,[151] some courts have ruled that affirmative defenses (like claims) must be asserted with sufficient detail to be "plausible,"[152] while others reject that view[153] (with some courts imposing a duty of factual "fair notice").[154] The only court of appeals to weigh in squarely on this debate did so in early 2019, announcing that "plausibility" should apply to pleading affirmative defenses,[155] but that opinion's spare reasoning has not, to date, persuaded many out-of-circuit trial courts to follow its lead.[156] In contrast, the trial courts seem increasingly to view "plausibility" battles over affirmative defenses to be useless docket clutter,[157] and, regardless of the proper standard, it seems clear that each link in an affirmative defense's legal reasoning need not be alleged.[158]

But attentive pleading of affirmative defenses remains advisable. While a very austere averment might, given the cir-

---

Pleading Affirmative Defenses, 70 WASH. & LEE L. REV. 1573 (2013) (collecting and cataloguing cases).

[151]*See Herrera v. Churchill McGee, LLC*, 680 F.3d 539, 547 n.6 (6th Cir. 2012) (sidestepping the issue, and "express[ing] no view" on impact of *Twombly* and *Iqbal* on affirmative defenses). *Cf. Kohler v. Flava Enters., Inc.*, 779 F.3d 1016, 1019 (9th Cir. 2015) (standard is "fair notice," which "only requires describing the defense in 'general terms' "); *LSREF2 Baron, L.L.C. v. Tauch*, 751 F.3d 394, 398 (5th Cir. 2014) (impart "fair notice" of defenses); *Montgomery v. Wyeth*, 580 F.3d 455, 467–68 (6th Cir. 2009) (no heightened pleading standard applies to defenses).

[152]*See, e.g., In re Volkswagen "Clean Diesel" Mktg., Sales Pracs., & Prod. Liab. Litig.*, 517 F. Supp. 3d 994, 998 (N.D. Cal. 2021); *VeroBlue Farms USA, Inc. v. Wulf*, 465 F. Supp. 3d 633, 657–58 (N.D. Tex. 2020).

[153]*See, e.g., Edwards v. CSXT Transp., Inc.*, 338 F.R.D. 590, 593 (E.D.N.C. 2021); *Birren v. Royal Caribbean Cruises, Ltd.*, 336 F.R.D. 688, 692–93 (S.D. Fla. 2020).

[154]*See Balon v. Enhanced Recovery Co.*, 316 F.R.D. 96, 104–05 (M.D. Pa. 2016).

[155]*See GEOMC Co. v. Calmare Therapeutics Inc.*, 918 F.3d 92, 97–98 (2d Cir. 2019) (but also noting that brief time for defensive pleading informs the "degree of rigor" in testing adequacy of affirmative defenses).

[156]*See United States ex rel. Patzer v. Sikorsky Aircraft Corp.*, 382 F. Supp. 3d 860, 863–68 (E.D. Wis. 2019) (robust analysis demonstrating why "plausibility" is incorrect standard for pleading affirmative defenses). *See also Spencer v. Carlson*, 2022 WL 902854, at *1 n.3 (E.D. Cal. Mar. 28, 2022) (rejecting Second Circuit's holding, noting difference in Rule 8(a)(2) language); *Aylin & Ramtin, LLC v. Doe*, 2022 WL 658786, at *1–*3 (N.D. Ill. Mar. 4, 2022) (majority of courts "rightly" reject Second Circuit's view); *Maker's Mark Distillery, Inc. v. Spalding Grp., Inc.*, 2020 WL 1430610, at *2 (W.D. Ky. Mar. 23, 2020) (still "no reason" to apply heightened standard); *Whetstone Indus., Inc. v. Yowie Grp., Ltd.*, 2019 WL 5102817, at *1 (M.D. Fla. Oct. 11, 2019) ("remains in the 'no' camp"). *But see Red Label Music Publ'g, Inc. v. Chila Prods.*, 388 F. Supp. 3d 975, 982–83 (N.D. Ill. 2019) (Second Circuit's approach "persuasive").

[157]*See United States ex rel. Patzer v. Sikorsky Aircraft Corp.*, 382 F. Supp. 3d 860, 867 (E.D. Wis. 2019) (explaining how "plausibility" challenges clog, not clear, court dockets); *Martinez v. Naranjo*, 328 F.R.D. 581, 592 (D.N.M. 2018) (noting reluctance to encourage motions to strike defenses "which do not advance the ball in a case").

[158]*See Nicholson v. Biomet, Inc.*, 363 F. Supp. 3d 931, 935 (N.D. Iowa 2019).

cumstances, impart the requisite notice of an affirmative defense,[159] a laundry list of bald, boilerplate affirmative defenses can be vulnerable in some jurisdictions.[160]

But No Duty to Respond to Affirmative Defenses

Although the party asserting them must plead affirmative defenses, there is no duty (absent a court order) on the party opposing affirmative defenses to counter-plead to them. Instead, the Rules deem affirmative defenses automatically denied or avoided.[161]

Enumerated Affirmative Defenses

Rule 8(c) contains a *non-exhaustive*[162] list of defenses that must be pleaded affirmatively: accord and satisfaction, arbitration and award, assumption of risk, contributory negligence, duress, estoppel, failure of consideration, fraud, illegality, injury by fellow servant, laches, license, payment, release, res judicata, statute of frauds, statute of limitations, and waiver.[163]

Unenumerated Affirmative Defenses

A particular defense's absence from the Rule 8(c) list does not necessarily mean it will not be considered an affirmative defense for purposes of this Rule.[164] In fact, whether a defense is an affirmative one or not can sometimes be quite unclear.

---

[159] *See Long v. Howard Univ.*, 550 F.3d 21, 24 (D.C.Cir. 2008) ("claims are barred by the applicable statute of limitations" is sufficient); *Birren v. Royal Caribbean Cruises, Ltd.*, 336 F.R.D. 688, 693 (S.D. Fla. 2020) (alleging that plaintiff's "negligence contributed" to incident and injuries "sufficiently apprises" pleader of comparative fault defense); *Blount v. Johnson Controls, Inc.*, 328 F.R.D. 146, 149–50 (S.D. Miss. 2018) ("simply naming the defense may sometimes suffice").

[160] *See Shechter v. Comptroller of City of New York*, 79 F.3d 265, 270 (2d Cir.1996); *United States ex rel. Patzer v. Sikorsky Aircraft Corp.*, 382 F. Supp. 3d 860, 868 (E.D. Wis. 2019). *See also Nippon Sigmax Co., Ltd. v. Kranos Corp., Inc.*, 2021 WL 2634823, at *2-*5 (C.D. Cal. June 25, 2021) (applying "plausibility" to strike all 31 affirmative defenses as "nothing more" than conclusory statements).

[161] *See Yankton v. Epps*, 652 Fed. Appx. 242, 248 (5th Cir. 2016). *See also* Rule 7(a) (absent court order, there is no duty to counter-plead to an answer, the place where affirmative defenses are typically contained); Rule 8(b)(6) ("If a responsive pleading is not required, an allegation is considered denied or avoided.").

[162] *See Jones v. Bock*, 549 U.S. 199, 212, 127 S. Ct. 910, 166 L. Ed. 2d 798 (2007) (list is nonexhaustive).

[163] "Discharge in bankruptcy" was removed from this list in 2010 to avoid confusion, since such discharges void the underlying judgment. *See* Rule 8(c)(1) advisory committee note (2010).

[164] *See, e.g., Reed v. Columbia St. Mary's Hosp.*, 915 F.3d 473, 477 (7th Cir. 2019) (statutory exemption from Americans with Disabilities Act is an affirmative defense); *In re ZAGG Inc. S'holder Derivative Action*, 826 F.3d 1222, 1231 (10th Cir. 2016) (corporate director exculpation is an affirmative defense); *Dollar v. Smithway Motor Xpress, Inc.*, 710 F.3d 798, 807–08 (8th Cir. 2013) (failure to mitigate is an affirmative defense); *Proctor v. Fluor Enterprises, Inc.*, 494 F.3d 1337, 1350 (11th Cir. 2007) (borrowed servant doctrine is affirmative defense under State law); *Ringuette v. City of Fall River*, 146 F.3d 1, 4 (1st Cir.1998) (qualified immunity is an affirmative defense); *Gray v. Bicknell*, 86 F.3d 1472, 1480 (8th Cir. 1996) (merger is an affirmative defense).

Resolving that question involves a circumstance-dependent, fact-specific inquiry,[165] for which the courts have developed several different tests: whether that defense would bar the right to relief even if the plaintiff's allegations were admitted or proven true[166] (perhaps the most familiar, classical definition); whether the defendant would bear the burden of proving that defense;[167] whether that defense involves an element necessary or extrinsic to plaintiff's cause of action[168] or would merely controvert the plaintiff's proof;[169] or whether a failure to plead it affirmatively would deprive the plaintiff of an opportunity to rebut the defense[170] or adjust litigation strategy to meet it.[171]

Special Matters

When asserting an affirmative defense that raises the capacity of a party to sue or be sued, fraud or mistake, the performance of conditions precedent, the authority of a party to sue or be sued in a representative capacity, the legal existence of a party, the legality of an official document or act, or the issuance of a judgment, the party must plead as required by Rule 9.[172]

Misdesignated Affirmative Defenses

An affirmative defense mislabeled as a counterclaim will be treated as an affirmative defense, and vice versa.[173] An affirmative defense mislabeled as a mere denial will be treated as an affirmative defense (and not be deemed waived) if doing so will promote a disposition of the case on the merits and will not prejudice the adverse parties.[174] Where, however, the claimed error is more than a mere mislabeling and instead proposes to assert a new claim, the party may seek leave to amend.[175]

Waiver (Forfeiture)

An affirmative defense that is not timely pleaded may be

---

[165]*See LSREF2 Baron, L.L.C. v. Tauch*, 751 F.3d 394, 398 (5th Cir. 2014).

[166]*See Wolf v. Reliance Standard Life Ins. Co.*, 71 F.3d 444, 449 (1st Cir. 1995).

[167]*See Reed v. Columbia St. Mary's Hosp.*, 915 F.3d 473, 478 (7th Cir. 2019); *National Market Share, Inc. v. Sterling Nat. Bank*, 392 F.3d 520, 526–27 (2d Cir. 2004).

[168]*See Ingraham v. U.S.*, 808 F.2d 1075, 1079 (5th Cir.1987).

[169]*See Winforge, Inc. v. Coachmen Indus., Inc.*, 691 F.3d 856, 869 (7th Cir. 2012).

[170]*See In re ZAGG Inc. S'holder Derivative Action*, 826 F.3d 1222, 1231 (10th Cir. 2016).

[171]*See In re Sterten*, 546 F.3d 278, 285 (3d Cir. 2008); *National Market Share, Inc. v. Sterling Nat. Bank*, 392 F.3d 520, 526–27 (2d Cir. 2004).

[172]*See* Rule 9(a), (c), (d), & (e).

[173]*See Rundgren v. Washington Mut. Bank, FA*, 760 F.3d 1056, 1063 (9th Cir. 2014); *Hatco Corp. v. W.R. Grace & Co. Conn.*, 59 F.3d 400, 411 n.8 (3d Cir. 1995).

[174]*See Reiter v. Cooper*, 507 U.S. 258, 113 S. Ct. 1213, 122 L. Ed. 2d 604 (1993).

[175]*See Rocheux Int'l of N.J., Inc. v. U.S. Merchants Fin. Group, Inc.*, 741 F. Supp. 2d 651, 660 (D.N.J. 2010).

deemed lost[176] (or, as is often phrased, "waived" or "forfeited").[177] But waiver does not follow inexorably.[178] Waiver may be excused where the unpleaded affirmative defense is later raised without bad faith or dilatory motive and without prejudice to any other party[179] ("prejudice" means that delayed assertion of the defense caused some unfairness apart from that defense's potential merits),[180] where it is included in a pretrial order,[181] where it is actually tried with the parties' implied consent,[182] or where the law on the topic at issue remains unsettled.[183] Waiver may also be excused where "peculiar facts" and the "interests of justice" so warrant,[184] and where the defense was raised at a "pragmatically sufficient time"[185] (*e.g.,* when the defense's applicability was not reasonably known at the time the answer was filed).[186] Thus, for example, in an appropriate case, an affirmative defense asserted for the first time by motion for summary judgment may be considered by the court a motion to amend the defendant's answer, which would prevent waiver.[187] Notwithstanding this general liberality, the trial courts enjoy

---

[176]*See, e.g., Day v. McDonough*, 547 U.S. 198, 202, 126 S. Ct. 1675, 164 L. Ed. 2d 376 (2006); *Utica Mut. Ins. Co. v. Munich Reinsurance Am., Inc.*, 7 F.4th 50, 63 (2d Cir. 2021).

[177]The use of the term "waiver" here, though longstanding by many courts, is imprecise. Classically, "waiver" refers to an intentional relinquishment, while "forfeiture" means a failure to timely assert. *See Hamer v. Neighborhood Hous. Servs. of Chi.*, 583 U.S. ___, 138 S. Ct. 13, 17 n.1, 199 L.Ed.2d 249 (2017). Neglecting to plead an affirmative defense without a conscious intent to surrender it would, thus, be a forfeiture, not a waiver. *See Maalouf v. Islamic Republic of Iran*, 923 F.3d 1095, 1107 (D.C. Cir. 2019) (not pleading affirmative defenses is failure to timely assert). Nonetheless, because the case law persists in using the term "waiver" imprecisely in this context, this text will as well to avoid confusion.

[178]*See Crutcher v. MultiPlan, Inc.*, 22 F.4th 756, 765–66 (8th Cir. 2022); *Reed v. Columbia St. Mary's Hosp.*, 915 F.3d 473, 478 (7th Cir. 2019).

[179]*See Clews v. Cnty. of Schuylkill*, 12 F.4th 353, 358 (3d Cir. 2021); *O'Brien v. Town of Bellingham*, 943 F.3d 514, 527-28 (1st Cir. 2019).

[180]*See Burton v. Ghosh*, 961 F.3d 960, 966 (7th Cir. 2020).

[181]*See Burke v. Regalado*, 935 F.3d 960, 1041 (10th Cir. 2019); *Dollar v. Smithway Motor Xpress, Inc.*, 710 F.3d 798, 808 (8th Cir. 2013).

[182]*See Society of the Holy Transfiguration Monastery, Inc. v. Archbishop Gregory*, 754 F. Supp. 2d 219, 228 (D.Mass. 2010).

[183]*See Pasco ex rel. Pasco v. Knoblauch*, 566 F.3d 572, 577 (5th Cir. 2009).

[184]*See Shell Rocky Mountain Production, LLC v. Ultra Resources, Inc.*, 415 F.3d 1158, 1164 (10th Cir. 2005).

[185]*See Smith v. Travelers Cas. Ins. Co. of Am.*, 932 F.3d 302, 308–09 (5th Cir. 2019). *See also Garofalo v. Village of Hazel Crest*, 754 F.3d 428, 436–37 (7th Cir. 2014) (defense "obvious" throughout case, briefed, and opposed).

[186]*See Burton v. Ghosh*, 961 F.3d 960, 965 (7th Cir. 2020); *O'Brien v. Town of Bellingham*, 943 F.3d 514, 527–28 (1st Cir. 2019).

[187]*See Garcia v. Salvation Army*, 918 F.3d 997, 1008–09 (9th Cir. 2019); *Sompo Japan Ins. Co. of Am. v. Norfolk S. Ry. Co.*, 762 F.3d 165, 176 (2d Cir. 2014). *But cf. Gilbert v. Napolitano*, 670 F.3d 258, 260–61 (D.C.Cir. 2012) (raising affirmative defense in motion to dismiss ruled to be too late); *Litsinger v. Forest River, Inc.*, 536 F. Supp. 3d 334, 348–49 (N.D. Ind. 2021) (raising

broad discretion, and their decisions will likely not be disturbed unless they are entirely unreasonable.[188] In exercising their discretion, the courts remain vigilant to protect the plaintiff against being "ambushed" by an unpleaded affirmative defense.[189] For this reason, waiver is likely to be found where a pleader unexplainably delays in asserting a known or knowable affirmative defense for an untenably long period,[190] or until discovery had closed[191] or an appeal taken.[192] Waiver is also likely if the defense was never asserted expressly, and some contentless "failure-to-state-a-claim" is now being argued as having preserved it.[193] If waived, an affirmative defense ordinarily cannot be later revived by asserting it during subsequent motion practice.[194]

Raising Affirmative Defenses *Sua Sponte*

Some courts have held that certain affirmation defenses—such as res judicata and collateral estoppel—may, in certain instances, be raised by the court *sua sponte*, mindful of the strong public interest in conserving scarce judicial resources by avoiding improper relitigations.[195] Otherwise, courts will usually resist raising affirmative defenses *sua sponte*.[196]

---

affirmative defense in summary judgment filing 2 years into case too late).

[188] *See Old Line Life Ins. Co. of America v. Garcia*, 418 F.3d 546, 550 (6th Cir. 2005); *Castro v. Chicago Housing Authority*, 360 F.3d 721, 735 (7th Cir. 2004). *But see Pasco ex rel. Pasco v. Knoblauch*, 566 F.3d 572, 577 (5th Cir. 2009) (district court erred in simply presuming prejudice from 52-month delay in asserting defense).

[189] *See Reed v. Columbia St. Mary's Hosp.*, 915 F.3d 473, 478–79 (7th Cir. 2019) (forfeiture occurs only when adversary is harmed by delay); *U.S. ex rel. Kraxberger v. Kansas City Power & Light Co.*, 756 F.3d 1075, 1082 (8th Cir. 2014) (failure to plead not fatal where defense is asserted in a way "that does not result in unfair surprise").

[190] *See Burton v. Ghosh*, 961 F.3d 960, 965–72 (7th Cir. 2020) (six years).

[191] *See Reed v. Columbia St. Mary's Hosp.*, 915 F.3d 473, 482 (7th Cir. 2019).

[192] *See Warner Bros. Entm't v. X One X Prods.*, 840 F.3d 971, 980 (8th Cir. 2016).

[193] *See Garcia v. Salvation Army*, 918 F.3d 997, 1008 (9th Cir. 2019); *Saks v. Franklin Covey Co.*, 316 F.3d 337, 350 (2d Cir. 2003).

[194] *See Wood v. Milyard*, 566 U.S. 463, 470, 132 S. Ct. 1826, 1832, 182 L. Ed. 2d 733 (2012) ("affirmative defense, once forfeited, is 'exclu[ded] from the case' ").

[195] *See Shurick v. Boeing Co.*, 623 F.3d 1114, 1116 n.2 (11th Cir. 2010); *In re Colonial Mortgage Bankers Corp.*, 324 F.3d 12, 16 (1st Cir. 2003). *See also U.S. v. Bendolph*, 409 F.3d 155, 164–65 (3d Cir. 2005) (same, statute of limitation defenses).

[196] *See Maalouf v. Islamic Republic of Iran*, 923 F.3d 1095, 1109–12 (D.C. Cir. 2019); *Burgess v. United States*, 874 F.3d 1292, 1296 (11th Cir. 2017). *See also Arizona v. California*, 530 U.S. 392, 412–13, 120 S. Ct. 2304, 2317–18, 147 L. Ed. 2d 374 (2000) (cautioning that *sua sponte* consideration of statute of limitations defenses should be allowed sparingly because doing so erodes principle of party-presentation essential to Nation's adversary-based system of adjudication).

RULE 8(d)—PLEADING TO BE CONCISE AND DIRECT; ALTERNATIVE STATEMENTS; INCONSISTENCY

CORE CONCEPT

Parties must plead claims and defenses in a simple, direct, and concise manner consistent with the federal notice pleading standard. They may do so alternatively, hypothetically, and inconsistently (subject to their Rule 11 duty to do so honestly). No technical pleading forms are necessary.

APPLICATIONS

Impact of 2007 "Restyling" Amendments

In 2007, the content of former Rule 8(b) and 8(d) were combined together in current Rule 8(b). Former Rule 8(e) was moved up and now is current Rule 8(d).

Simple, Concise, and Direct

All pleaded allegations must be simple, concise, and direct. While mere verbosity or excessive length is unlikely, alone, to prompt a dismissal,[197] a pleading may be dismissed (or an amendment required) if the pleading is so convoluted that a court cannot discern a meritorious claim or defense.[198] If the convoluted pleading is not thereafter remedied, it can be dismissed with prejudice and without further right of re-pleading.[199]

Alternative, Hypothetical, and Inconsistent Pleadings

Statements of claims or defenses may be asserted in the alternative, hypothetically, and even inconsistently.[200] Such inconsistent pleading may occur when legitimate doubt as to the true facts exists[201] (every pleading, including alternative, hypothetical, and inconsistent ones, must still abide by the obliga-

---

[197]*See Hearns v. San Bernardino Police Dep't*, 530 F.3d 1124, 1131–32 (9th Cir. 2008) (collecting cases).

[198]*See Embree v. Wyndham Worldwide Corp.*, 779 Fed. Appx. 658, 663-64 (11th Cir. 2019) (affirming dismissal with prejudice for repeated violations of "simple, concise, and direct"); *Barone v. Wells Fargo Bank, N.A.*, 709 Fed. Appx. 943, 951 (11th Cir. 2017) (affirming dismissal of shotgun pleading as noncompliant). *See generally Knapp v. Hogan*, 738 F.3d 1106, 1109 (9th Cir. 2013) (Rule 8 can be violated both when a pleading "says too little" and when it "says too much"); *See generally supra* Authors' Commentary to Rule 8(b) (**"Element 2: Short and Plain Statement of Claim** - *'Short and Plain'* ").

[199]*See California Coal. for Families & Children v. San Diego Cty. Bar Ass'n*, 657 Fed. Appx. 675, 677–78 (9th Cir. 2016); *Plumhoff v. Cent. Mortg. Co.*, 286 F. Supp. 3d 699, 702–04 (D. Md. 2017).

[200]*See* Rule 8(d)(2) to (d)(3). *See also Cleveland v. Policy Management Systems Corp.*, 526 U.S. 795, 805, 119 S. Ct. 1597, 143 L. Ed. 2d 966 (1999) ("Our ordinary Rules recognize that a person may not be sure in advance upon which legal theory she will succeed, and so permit parties to 'set forth two or more statements of a claim or defense alternately or hypothetically,' and to 'state as many separate claims or defenses as the party has regardless of consistency' ").

[201]*See American Int'l Adjustment Co. v. Galvin*, 86 F.3d 1455, 1461 (7th Cir. 1996); *Chambers v. NASA Fed.*

tions set in Rule 11).[202] Thus, for example, a claimant may allege an unjust enrichment claim as a fall-back alternative to a breach of contract claim,[203] unless the existence of a valid, enforceable contract is uncontested[204] or the equity claim is foreclosed for other reasons.[205] Similarly, a defendant can both deny all liability and yet, alternatively, seek contribution from others in the event some liability is found.[206] This Rule's liberality applies into the summary judgment stage as well.[207] At trial, though, a party cannot recover on inconsistent theories.[208] Moreover, the court must be able to readily identify claims or defenses that are pleaded alternatively, hypothetically, or inconsistently.[209] Although no "magic words" are required, it must be reasonably obvious from the pleading itself that these types of claims or defenses are being asserted.[210] While separate inconsistent *claims* and *defenses* are permitted under the Rules, the factual allegations *within* each claim or defense cannot be inconsistent with the alleged right of recovery, or else the claim or defense could defeat itself.[211] Finally, although pleaders may plead in the alternative, they may not, in the

---

Credit Union, 222 F. Supp. 3d 1, 16 (D.D.C. 2016).

[202]*See Harris v. Koenig*, 722 F. Supp. 2d 44, 54 (D.D.C. 2010); *Diamond Triumph Auto Glass, Inc. v. Safelite Glass Corp.*, 344 F. Supp. 2d 936, 944 (M.D. Pa. 2004).

[203]*See Cooper v. Charter Commc'ns Entm'ts. I, LLC*, 760 F.3d 103, 112 (1st Cir. 2014); *Stockton East Water Dist. v. United States*, 583 F.3d 1344, 1368 (Fed.Cir. 2009).

[204]*See Gunther v. Capital One, N.A.*, 703 F. Supp. 2d 264, 276 (E.D.N.Y. 2010).

[205]*See Sivak v. United Parcel Serv. Co.*, 28 F. Supp. 3d 701, 713–14 (E.D.Mich. 2014) (factual support for equity claim is unpleaded).

[206]*See United Fire & Cas. Co. v. Prate Roofing & Installations, LLC*, 7 F.4th 573, 584–85 (7th Cir. 2021).

[207]*See Zeranti v. United States*, 358 F. Supp. 3d 244, 260 n.10 (W.D.N.Y. 2019).

[208]*See Student A v. Liberty Univ., Inc.*, — F. Supp. 3d —, 2022 WL 1423617, at *7 (W.D. Va. 2022); *In re Santa Fe Nat. Tobacco Co. Mktg. & Sales Practices & Prod. Liab. Litig.*, 288 F. Supp. 3d 1087, 1259 (D.N.M. 2017).

[209]*See NewSpin Sports, LLC v. Arrow Elecs., Inc.*, 910 F.3d 293, 307 (7th Cir. 2018); *Sun Life Assurance Co. of Canada v. Imperial Premium Fin., LLC*, 904 F.3d 1197, 1213 n.16 (11th Cir. 2018).

[210]*See Holman v. Indiana*, 211 F.3d 399, 407 (7th Cir. 2000) ("must use a formulation from which it can be reasonably inferred that this is what they were doing").

[211]*See In re Livent, Inc. Noteholders Securities Litigation*, 151 F. Supp. 2d 371, 407 (S.D. N.Y. 2001) (does not "grant[] plaintiffs license to plead inconsistent assertions of facts within the allegations that serve as the factual predicates for an independent, unitary claim. Internally conflicting factual assertions that constitute integral components of a claim must be distinguished from a permissible alternative statement embodying a theory of a whole sufficient claim") (citation omitted). *See also In re Zantac (Ranitidine) Prod. Liab. Litig.*, 510 F. Supp. 3d 1141, 1164–65 (S.D. Fla. 2020); *Thomas v. Kamtek, Inc.*, 143 F. Supp. 3d 1179, 1189 (N.D. Ala. 2015). *See generally Aetna Cas. and Sur. Co. v. Aniero Concrete Co., Inc.*, 404 F.3d 566, 585–86 (2d Cir. 2005) (claim that is "at war with itself" cannot survive summary judgment).

pithy admonishment of one court, "plead in the ambiguous."[212] At least one[213] of the alternative allegations must meet the requisite pleading standards.[214]

Inconsistent Pleadings As Admissions

Because Rule 8(d) protects a party's right to plead inconsistent claims and defenses, statements made in claims or defenses cannot generally be offered as admissions against other claims or defenses within the same pleading that contain inconsistent or alternative averments.[215] However, unequivocal averments of fact, made *within* a particular claim or defense, may constitute judicial admissions that conclusively bind the pleader throughout the litigation.[216] Additionally, if the positions taken by the pleader are accepted by the court, the pleader may be foreclosed by judicial estoppel from taking an inconsistent, contrary position in later proceedings.[217]

RULE 8(e)—CONSTRUING PLEADINGS

CORE CONCEPT

Courts must construe pleadings "so as to do justice." Consequently, so long as a pleading provides the adverse party with proper notice of claims and defenses, it will not be construed hypertechnically.

APPLICATIONS

Impact of 2007 "Restyling" Amendments

The content of current Rule 8(e) contains what formerly was Rule 8(f).

All Pleadings Construed Liberally

One fundamental philosophy of the Rules is liberality over technicality.[218] Because Rule 8(e) requires the courts to construe pleadings "as to do justice," all pleadings are construed

---

[212] *See Joe Hand Promotions, Inc. v. Creative Entm't, LLC*, 978 F. Supp. 2d 1236, 1240 (M.D. Fla. 2013).

[213] *See Elf-Man, LLC v. Brown*, 996 F. Supp. 2d 1056, 1059 (E.D. Wash. 2014) (for multiple claims asserted alternatively, a legal deficiency in one does not doom the others).

[214] *See Brown v. Rawson-Neal Psychiatric Hosp.*, 840 F.3d 1146, 1152 (9th Cir. 2016); *U.S. Bank Nat'l Ass'n v. San Antonio Cash Network*, 252 F. Supp. 3d 714, 720 (D. Minn. 2017).

[215] *See Aholelei v. Department of Public Safety*, 488 F.3d 1144, 1149 (9th Cir. 2007); *Rodriguez-Suris v. Montesinos*, 123 F.3d 10, 20 (1st Cir. 1997). *See also American Intern. Adjustment Co. v. Galvin*, 86 F.3d 1455, 1460 (7th Cir. 1996) (in pleading context, Rules abolish doctrine of election of remedies).

[216] *See El Paso Natural Gas Co. v. U.S.*, 750 F.3d 863, 876–77 (D.C. Cir. 2014).

[217] *See Gabarick v. Laurin Maritime (America) Inc.*, 753 F.3d 550, 554 (5th Cir. 2014). *Cf. Montrose Medical Group Participating Savings Plan v. Bulger*, 243 F.3d 773, 782 (3d Cir. 2001) (judicial estoppel will not apply to assertion of contrary positions in different proceedings when initial claim was never accepted or adopted by court).

[218] *See Minger v. Green*, 239 F.3d 793, 799 (6th Cir. 2001).

liberally.[219] Form is never exalted over substance,[220] and courts are watchful that drafting mistakes alone do not deny a party justice.[221] Each pleading is examined as a whole.[222] In testing federal pleadings, the familiar contract law principle of construing documents against their drafters is not applied.[223] Courts will not rely solely on the labels used by the pleader to describe claims or defenses, but may reach deeper and seek out the true substance of the allegations.[224] Where those allegations, so construed, would state a cognizable claim or defense, the requirements of Rule 8 may be satisfied.

But No Unwarranted Constructions

Although pleadings are liberally construed, the court must still "do justice." A pleading will not be given so unwarrantedly generous a reading that it prejudices another party or denies a party fair notice of a claim or defense.[225] Courts are, thus, not obligated to invent for the pleader a claim or defense not fairly included within the pleading,[226] grant a pleader a type of relief not fairly demanded within the pleading (where to do so will cause prejudice),[227] or tolerate a persistent failure to remedy a

---

[219]*See, e.g.*, *Skaff v. Meridien North America Beverly Hills, LLC*, 506 F.3d 832, 839 (9th Cir. 2007); *Rodriguez v. Doral Mortg. Corp.*, 57 F.3d 1168, 1171 (1st Cir. 1995).

[220]*See Phillips v. Girdich*, 408 F.3d 124, 128 (2d Cir. 2005).

[221]*See Carter v. Ford Motor Co.*, 561 F.3d 562, 566 (6th Cir. 2009)

[222]*See Cahoo v. SAS Analytics Inc.*, 912 F.3d 887, 895 n.3 (6th Cir. 2019).

[223]*See Miller v. Philadelphia Geriatric Center*, 463 F.3d 266, 272 (3d Cir. 2006) ("Pleadings need not be construed most strongly against the pleader, rather we should make a determined effort to understand what she is attempting to set forth.").

[224]*See Stanton v. Elliott*, 25 F.4th 227, 238 (4th Cir. 2022) (claims need not be put "under a special heading, quote the statute, or use magic words"); *Mead Corp. v. ABB Power Generation, Inc.*, 319 F.3d 790, 795 (6th Cir. 2003) (courts do "not rely solely on labels", but "probe deeper and examine the substance of the complaint"). *See also Minger v. Green*, 239 F.3d 793, 799 (6th Cir. 2001) (construing claim labeled as "negligent misrepresentation" (which would be barred) as one for intentional misrepresentation (which could go forward)).

[225]*See Zokari v. Gates*, 561 F.3d 1076, 1084–88 (10th Cir. 2009); *Sadid v. Vailas*, 943 F. Supp. 2d 1125, 1139 (D.Idaho 2013). *See generally Stanard v. Nygren*, 658 F.3d 792, 800 (7th Cir. 2011) (court has no obligation "to sift through a complaint to extract some merit when the attorney who drafted it has failed to do so himself.").

[226]*See Smith v. Aztec Well Servicing Co.*, 462 F.3d 1274, 1284 (10th Cir. 2006). *See generally United States v. Sineneng-Smith*, 590 U.S. __, 140 S. Ct. 1575, 1579, 206 L. Ed. 2d 866 (2020) ("party presentation" principle of U.S. adversarial system of adjudication relies on litigants "to frame the issues for decision," and courts ought not "sally forth each day looking for wrongs to right" but instead must decide only questions parties present) (citations omitted).

[227]*See Seven Words LLC v. Network Solutions*, 260 F.3d 1089, 1098 (9th Cir. 2001) (where damages claim was made years into litigation, after various representations that only declaratory and injunctive relief was sought, court declines to read a damages claim into complaint).

pleading's defects.[228]

Pleadings Drafted by Laypersons

Courts generally apply less stringent standards to pleadings drafted by laypersons, such as *pro se* habeas corpus petitions and social security applications,[229] but nothing in this liberality obliges the court to redraft a *pro se* pleading.[230]

Additional Research References

Wright & Miller, *Federal Practice and Procedure* §§ 1201 to 1290
C.J.S., Federal Civil Procedure §§ 252 to 280 et seq., §§ 301 to 308
West's Key Number Digest, Federal Civil Procedure ⚷631 to 653, ⚷654 to 657, ⚷671 to 680, ⚷731 to 745, ⚷751 to 759

---

[228] *See Kensu v. Corizon, Inc.*, 5 F.4th 646, 653 (6th Cir. 2021) ("infinite patience" not required; claimants "must not append so many limbs and outward flourishes to a pleading that neither court nor defendant can easily identify the soul of the claim").

[229] *See Erickson v. Pardus*, 551 U.S. 89, 94, 127 S. Ct. 2197, 167 L. Ed. 2d 1081 (2007) (per curiam); *Estelle v. Gamble*, 429 U.S. 97, 106, 97 S. Ct. 285, 50 L. Ed. 2d 251 (1976).

[230] *See Snow v. DirecTV, Inc.*, 450 F.3d 1314, 1320 (11th Cir. 2006). *See generally supra* Authors' Commentary to Rule 8(a) ("**Pleadings from *Pro Se* Litigants**").

RULE 9
PLEADING SPECIAL MATTERS

(a) Capacity or Authority to Sue; Legal Existence.

(1) *In General.* Except when required to show that the court has jurisdiction, a pleading need not allege:

(A) a party's capacity to sue or be sued;

(B) a party's authority to sue or be sued in a representative capacity; or

(C) the legal existence of an organized association of persons that is made a party.

(2) *Raising Those Issues.* To raise any of those issues, a party must do so by a specific denial, which must state any supporting facts that are peculiarly within the party's knowledge.

(b) Fraud or Mistake; Conditions of Mind. In alleging fraud or mistake, a party must state with particularity the circumstances constituting fraud or mistake. Malice, intent, knowledge, and other conditions of a person's mind may be alleged generally.

(c) Conditions Precedent. In pleading conditions precedent, it suffices to allege generally that all conditions precedent have occurred or been performed. But when denying that a condition precedent has occurred or been performed, a party must do so with particularity.

(d) Official Document or Act. In pleading an official document or official act, it suffices to allege that the document was legally issued or the act legally done.

(e) Judgment. In pleading a judgment or decision of a domestic or foreign court, a judicial or quasi-judicial tribunal, or a board or officer, it suffices to plead the judgment or decision without showing jurisdiction to render it.

(f) Time and Place. An allegation of time or place is material when testing the sufficiency of a pleading.

(g) Special Damages. If an item of special damage is claimed, it must be specifically stated.

(h) Admiralty or Maritime Claim.

(1) *How Designated.* If a claim for relief is within the admiralty or maritime jurisdiction and also within the court's subject-matter jurisdiction on some other ground, the pleading may designate the claim as an admiralty or maritime claim for purposes of Rules 14(c), 38(e), and 82 and the Supplemental Rules for Admiralty or Maritime Claims and Asset Forfeiture Actions. A claim cognizable only in the admiralty or maritime jurisdiction is an admiralty or maritime claim for those purposes, whether or not so designated.

(2) *Designation for Appeal.* A case that includes an admiralty or maritime claim within this subdivision (h) is an admiralty case within 28 U.S.C. § 1292(a)(3).

[Amended effective July 1, 1966; July 1, 1968; July 1, 1970; August 1, 1987, April 11, 1997, effective December 1, 1997; April 12, 2006, effective December 1, 2006; April 30, 2007, effective December 1, 2007.]

AUTHORS' COMMENTARY ON RULE 9

PURPOSE AND SCOPE

Rule 9 establishes *additional* pleading procedures that *supplement* the primary pleading obligations set out in Rule 8. An enhanced pleading duty is imposed for fraud, mistake, and special damages, as well as for contesting a party's capacity / authority to sue or be sued or for challenging the occurrence or performance of conditions precedent. Rule 9 also allows pleaders, in appropriate cases, to invoke the special procedures available for admiralty and maritime cases.

RULE 9(a)—CAPACITY OR AUTHORITY TO SUE; LEGAL EXISTENCE

CORE CONCEPT

Unless necessary to establish the court's subject-matter jurisdiction, a pleading need not aver capacity or authority to sue, or an association's legal existence. A defendant may challenge these issues, but must do so by specific denial in a responsive pleading or motion.

APPLICATIONS

Pleading Capacity Only When Jurisdictional

The capacity of a person (or entity) to sue or be sued is ordinarily resolved under State law.[1] However, pleaders usually need not allege a party's capacity or authority to sue or be sued or an association's legal existence (though plaintiffs may not rely on this liberality to blithely change their capacity theories at a whim).[2] When, however, capacity, authority, or legal existence is necessary to show the court's subject-matter jurisdiction, these attributes must be averred.[3]

Procedure For *Challenging* Capacity

Ordinarily, a litigant seeking to challenge (a) a party's legal existence, (b) a party's capacity to sue or be sued, or (c) a party's authority to sue or be sued in a representative capacity must raise the issue by specific denial in a responsive pleading[4] or pre-answer motion to dismiss.[5] The required "specific denial" does not always obligate the pleader to spell out in detail what is lacking;[6] but the pleader must include specific facts that are peculiarly within that party's knowledge.[7] The purpose of this pleading duty is to place the adversary on appropriate notice of the defense.[8] Once pleaded, there is no further duty on the challenging party to file an early dispositive motion on the contested issue.[9]

- *Note:* Prior to the 2007 amendments, Rule 9(a) used the language "specific negative averment" in place of the

---

[1]*See* Rule 17(b). *See also Owens v. Baltimore City State's Att'ys Off.*, 767 F.3d 379, 393 (4th Cir. 2014).

[2]*See Robinson v. Hunt Cty.*, 921 F.3d 440, 446 (5th Cir. 2019).

[3]*See Lang v. Texas & P. Ry. Co.*, 624 F.2d 1275, 1277 (5th Cir. 1980). *See also Moore v. City of Harriman*, 272 F.3d 769, 772–74 (6th Cir. 2001) (noting Circuit division on whether Eleventh Amendment requires that capacity be pleaded in civil rights cases).

[4]*See De Saracho v. Custom Food Mach., Inc.*, 206 F.3d 874, 878 (9th Cir. 2000); *Wagner Furniture Interiors, Inc. v. Kemner's Georgetown Manor, Inc.*, 929 F.2d 343, 345 (7th Cir. 1991).

[5]Although Rule 12(b) does not expressly authorize dismissal motions for lack of capacity, courts may permit that defense to be raised in a pre-answer Rule 12(b)(6) motion where the capacity defect appears on the face of the complaint. *See Doe v. Mckesson*, 945 F.3d 818, 824 n.2 (5th Cir. 2019); *Kaupthing ehf. v. Bricklayers & Trowel Trades Int'l Pension Fund Liquidation Portfolio*, 291 F. Supp. 3d 21, 27–29 (D.D.C. 2017).

[6]*See Pugh v. Kobelco Const. Mach. America, LLC*, 413 Fed.Appx. 134, 136 (11th Cir. 2011).

[7]*See* Rule 9(a)(2). *See also DDR Hendon Nassau Park II LP v. RadioShack Corp.*, 2010 WL 723776, at *6 (N.D.Ohio Feb. 24, 2010) (facts are "peculiarly within a party's knowledge" when only that party knows them).

[8]*See AmeriPride Servs., Inc. v. Valley Indus. Serv., Inc.*, 2008 WL 5068672, at *5 (E.D.Cal. Nov. 25, 2008).

[9]*See AmeriPride Servs., Inc. v. Valley Indus. Serv., Inc.*, 2008 WL 5068672, at *5 (E.D.Cal. Nov. 25, 2008).

current (and simpler) "specific denial."

Liberal Construction

Under appropriate circumstances, courts have given Rule 9(a)'s pleading duty a liberal interpretation. Thus, a pleader who mislabels a capacity defense as a challenge to standing may be forgiven.[10]

But Challenges Are Waived if Unpleaded

The defense of lack of either capacity or authority to sue or be sued, or an association's legal existence, is usually waived if not timely and specifically pleaded.[11] Waiver may be excused if the defense is affirmatively apparent from the face of the complaint and a specific denial is found to be unnecessary,[12] where the defense (though late) was raised at the pragmatically earliest time,[13] where the court finds a lack of prejudice under the circumstances of the delay,[14] or where the parties consented to actually trying it.[15] If, however, the defense affects the court's subject-matter jurisdiction, a party may assert that defense at any time or the court may raise it *sua sponte*.[16]

RULE 9(b)—FRAUD, MISTAKE, CONDITIONS OF MIND

CORE CONCEPT

A party must plead fraud and mistake with particularity, but other conditions of the mind (such as malice, intent, and knowledge) may be pleaded generally.

APPLICATIONS

Goal of Pleading With Particularity

Some claims—like fraud—may have an *in terrorem* or stigmatizing effect on defendants and their reputations,[17] and are often easily fabricated (because the evidence is frequently

---

[10]*See Masood v. Saleemi*, 2007 WL 2069853, at *4 (W.D. Wash. 2007).

[11]*See, e.g., RK Co. v. See*, 622 F.3d 846, 849 n.2 (7th Cir. 2010); *De Saracho v. Custom Food Machinery, Inc.*, 206 F.3d 874, 878 (9th Cir. 2000).

[12]*See Brown v. Williamson*, 134 F. Supp. 2d 1286, 1291 (M.D. Ala. 2001). *But cf. Srock v. U.S.*, 2006 WL 2460769, at *4–*5 (E.D. Mich. 2006) (collecting cases and scholarship on late assertion of Rule 9(a) defenses, and ruling that these defenses should be subject to an early waiver rule).

[13]*See Plate v. Johnson*, 339 F. Supp. 3d 759, 765–66 (N.D. Ohio 2018).

[14]*See AmeriPride Servs., Inc. v. Valley Indus. Serv., Inc.*, 2008 WL 5068672, at *5–*8 (E.D.Cal. Nov. 25, 2008).

[15]*See Sturgis Motorcycle Rally, Inc. v. Rushmore Photo & Gifts, Inc.*, 908 F.3d 313, 342 (8th Cir. 2018).

[16]*See E.R. Squibb & Sons, Inc. v. Accident & Cas. Ins. Co.*, 160 F.3d 925, 935–36 (2d Cir. 1998) (if party with capacity defense is strategically not asserting it in order to preserve federal jurisdiction, court may assess the capacity of the parties *sua sponte*).

[17]*See Irving Firemen's Relief & Ret. Fund v. Uber Techs., Inc.*, 998 F.3d 397, 404 (9th Cir. 2021); *Cornielsen v. Infinium Capital Mgmt., LLC*, 916 F.3d 589, 598 (7th Cir. 2019).

circumstantial).[18] The courts expect pleaders to perform a greater pre-complaint investigation in such cases,[19] to ensure that any such claim is "responsible and supported, rather than defamatory and extortionate."[20] This practice also allows an early and informed response from the party defending against such accusations,[21] and guards against lawsuits filed in the unsubstantiated hope of discovering an unknown wrong[22] (*i.e.*, to disincentivize a "sue first, ask questions later" strategy).[23] It helps to ensure that only viable claims of fraud or mistake are permitted to proceed to discovery.[24] Thus, requiring that such claims be pleaded with particularity (1) ensures that the defendants have fair notice of the plaintiff's claim, (2) helps safeguard the defendants against spurious accusations and resulting reputational harm, (3) reduces the possibility that a meritless fraud claim can remain in the case, by ensuring that the full and complete factual allegation is not postponed until discovery, and (4) protects defendants against "strike" suits.[25]

Amount of Particularity Required

The amount of particularity or specificity required for pleading fraud or mistake will differ from case to case,[26] and there is no fixed checklist of the minimum, necessary detail.[27] Generally, the expected detail will depend on the amount of access the pleader has to the specific facts[28] (from prediscovery evi-

---

[18] *See Bennett v. MIS Corp.*, 607 F.3d 1076, 1101 (6th Cir. 2010).

[19] *See Irving Firemen's Relief & Ret. Fund v. Uber Techs., Inc.*, 998 F.3d 397, 404 (9th Cir. 2021); *Foisie v. Worcester Polytechnic Inst.*, 967 F.3d 27, 51 (1st Cir. 2020)..

[20] *See Borsellino v. Goldman Sachs Group, Inc.*, 477 F.3d 502, 507 (7th Cir. 2007). *See generally Grubbs v. Kanneganti*, 565 F.3d 180, 190 (5th Cir. 2009) (describing Rule 9(b) inquiry as "what is required for a ticket to the federal discovery apparatus").

[21] *See Maguire Fin., LP v. PowerSecure Int'l, Inc.*, 876 F.3d 541, 546 (4th Cir. 2017); *United States v. United Healthcare Ins. Co.*, 848 F.3d 1161, 1180 (9th Cir. 2016).

[22] *See United States ex rel. Anita Silingo v. WellPoint, Inc.*, 904 F.3d 667, 677 (9th Cir. 2018); *Maguire Fin., LP v. PowerSecure Int'l, Inc.*, 876 F.3d 541, 546 (4th Cir. 2017).

[23] *See Cornielsen v. Infinium Capital Mgmt., LLC*, 916 F.3d 589, 598 (7th Cir. 2019).

[24] *See United States ex rel. Presser v. Acacia Mental Health Clinic, LLC*, 836 F.3d 770, 776–77 (7th Cir. 2016); *In re BP Lubricants USA Inc.*, 637 F.3d 1307, 1310 (Fed.Cir. 2011).

[25] *See, e.g., Katz v. Belveron Real Est. Partners, LLC*, 28 F.4th 300, 308 (1st Cir. 2022); *IAS Servs. Grp., L.L.C. v. Jim Buckley & Assocs., Inc.*, 900 F.3d 640, 647 (5th Cir. 2018). The term "strike suit" is "professional slang" to refer to litigation that is not brought to redress genuine wrongs, but to inflict a nuisance upon the defendant. *See Cohen v. Beneficial Indus. Loan Corp.*, 337 U.S. 541, 548, 69 S. Ct. 1221, 93 L. Ed. 1528 (1949).

[26] *See IAS Servs. Grp., L.L.C. v. Jim Buckley & Assocs., Inc.*, 900 F.3d 640, 647 (5th Cir. 2018); *United States ex rel. Chorches for Bankr. Estate of Fabula v. Am. Med. Response, Inc.*, 865 F.3d 71, 81 (2d Cir. 2017).

[27] *See Hagerty ex rel. United States v. Cyberonics, Inc.*, 844 F.3d 26, 31 (1st Cir. 2016).

[28] *See, e.g., Ebeid ex rel. U.S. v. Lungwitz*, 616 F.3d 993, 999 (9th Cir.

dence or otherwise),[29] considering the complexity of the claim, the relationship of the parties, the context in which the alleged fraud or mistake occurs,[30] and the amount of specificity necessary for the adverse party to prepare a responsive pleading.[31] The particularity requirement of Rule 9 is not, however, intended to abrogate or mute the Rule 8 "notice" pleading standard that applies in federal courts, and the two Rules must be read in harmony with one another.[32] Plaintiffs are still obligated to plead only "notice" of a fraud or mistake claim (viewed, as are all claims, through the *Twombly* "plausibility" lens).[33] Neither "absolute particularity" nor a showing of evidentiary proofs is needed.[34] But Rule 9(b) plainly compels a higher degree of notice.[35] Thus, in fraud and mistake claims, pleaders usually must supply the "newspaper-first-paragraph"[36] — the "who, what, when, where, and how" of the alleged scheme or mistake.[37] This requirement is not to be applied with excessive rigidity — so long as precision and substantiation are somehow

---

2010) (relaxed where evidence exclusively within defendant's possession); *In re Rockefeller Ctr. Props., Inc. Secs. Litig.*, 311 F.3d 198, 216 (3d Cir. 2002) (relaxed where requisite factual information is peculiarly within defendant's knowledge or control).

[29]*See Edmonson v. Eagle Nat'l Bank*, 922 F.3d 535, 553 (4th Cir. 2019).

[30]*See, e.g., Craftmatic Secs. Litig. v. Kraftsow*, 890 F.2d 628, 645 (3d Cir. 1989) ("[I]n the case of corporate fraud, plaintiff cannot be expected to have personal knowledge of the details of corporate internal affairs."). *See also In re GlenFed, Inc. Secs. Litig.*, 60 F.3d 591, 593 (9th Cir. 1995) (in corporate fraud cases, where misinformation conveyed by prospectus, filing statements, press releases, etc., "reasonable to presume that these are collective actions of the officers;" plaintiffs satisfy Rule 9(b) "by pleading the misrepresentations with particularity and where possible the roles of the individual defendants in the misrepresentations.").

[31]*See Dudley v. Southeastern Factor & Finance Corp.*, 446 F.2d 303, 308 (5th Cir. 1971).

[32]*See IAS Servs. Grp., L.L.C. v. Jim Buckley & Assocs., Inc.*, 900 F.3d 640, 647 (5th Cir. 2018); *Star City Sch. Dist. v. ACI Bldg. Sys., LLC*, 844 F.3d 1011, 1016 (8th Cir. 2017).

[33]*See infra* Authors' Commentary to Rule 9(b) (**"Rule 9(b) Particularity and *Twombly* 'Plausibility'"**).

[34]*See Benavidez v. Cty. of San Diego*, 993 F.3d 1134, 1145 (9th Cir. 2021); *Foisie v. Worcester Polytechnic Inst.*, 967 F.3d 27, 50–51 (1st Cir. 2020). *See also United States v. Molina Healthcare of Ill., Inc.*, 17 F.4th 732, 741 (7th Cir. 2021) (requires specificity, not "that a plaintiff literally prove his case in the complaint").

[35]*See United States ex rel. Bookwalter v. UPMC*, 946 F.3d 162, 176 (3d Cir. 2019) ("must go well beyond Rule 8's threshold of plausibility" and "mere plausible inference of illegality"); *Schaller Tel. Co. v. Golden Sky Sys., Inc.*, 298 F.3d 736, 746 (8th Cir. 2002) ("must contain 'a higher degree of notice' ").

[36]*See United States ex rel. Bookwalter v. UPMC*, 946 F.3d 162, 176 (3d Cir. 2019); *United States ex rel. Berkowitz v. Automation Aids, Inc.*, 896 F.3d 834, 839 (7th Cir. 2018).

[37]*See United States ex rel. Taylor v. Boyko*, 39 F.4th 177, 189 (4th Cir. 2022); *Omnipol, A.S. v. Multinational Def. Servs., LLC*, 32 F.4th 1298, 1307 (11th Cir. 2022). *See also Ezell v. Lexington Ins. Co.*, 926 F.3d 48, 51 (1st Cir. 2019) (Souter, Rtd. J.).

injected into the pleading.[38] "Omniscience" is not required,[39] but nor is conclusory pleading acceptable.[40] The particularity requirement must be met in the pleading itself; generally, courts will not consider after-the-fact elaborations in briefs and memoranda when testing particularity.[41]

Rule 9(b) Particularity and *Twombly* "Plausibility"

Pleaders alleging fraud or mistake must not only do so with particularity, they must also meet the general threshold of Rule 8(a): all allegations must be pleaded in a manner that shows a "plausible" claim for relief.[42]

Fraud

Pleaders are obligated to place fraud defendants on notice of the "precise misconduct" with which they are accused.[43] Each of the circumstances of the alleged fraud must be pleaded with particularity;[44] more is required than mere conclusory allegations of plans or schemes or bald recitations of the technical elements of fraud,[45] or facts that show only that a fraud could have been possible.[46] Many courts require the pleader to allege (1) the time, place, and contents of the false representations or omissions, and explain how they were fraudulent, (2) the identity of the person making the misrepresentations, (3) how the misrepresentations misled the plaintiff, and (4) what the speaker gained from the fraud.[47] In the end, the pleaded facts may need to give rise to a "strong inference" of fraud to comport

---

[38] *See United States v. Molina Healthcare of Ill., Inc.*, 17 F.4th 732, 739 (7th Cir. 2021). *But cf. United States v. Walgreen Co.*, 846 F.3d 879, 881 (6th Cir. 2017) (courts have "no more authority to 'relax' the [Rule 9(b)] pleading standard . . . than . . . to increase it").

[39] *See Williams v. Duke Energy Int'l, Inc.*, 681 F.3d 788, 803 (6th Cir. 2012).

[40] *See OmegaGenesis Corp. v. Mayo Found. for Med. Educ. & Research*, 851 F.3d 800, 807 (8th Cir. 2017).

[41] *See Frederico v. Home Depot*, 507 F.3d 188, 201–02 (3d Cir. 2007).

[42] *See United States ex rel. Taylor v. Boyko*, 39 F.4th 177, 189 (4th Cir. 2022); *United States ex rel. Vermont Nat'l Tel. Co. v. Northstar Wireless, LLC*, 34 F.4th 29, 38 (D.C. Cir. 2022). *See generally Universal Health Servs., Inc. v. United States*, 579 U.S. 176, 195 n.6, 136 S. Ct. 1989, 2004 n.6, 195 L. Ed. 2d 348 (2016).

[43] *See Xia Bi v. McAuliffe*, 927 F.3d 177, 184–85 (4th Cir. 2019); *United States ex rel. Anita Silingo v. WellPoint, Inc.*, 904 F.3d 667, 677 (9th Cir. 2018).

[44] *See Shuker v. Smith & Nephew, PLC*, 885 F.3d 760, 778 (3d Cir. 2018); *Vexol, S.A. de C.V. v. Berry Plastics Corp.*, 882 F.3d 633, 637 (7th Cir. 2018). *See also Xia Bi v. McAuliffe*, 927 F.3d 177, 184–85 (4th Cir. 2019) (circumstances of fraud include reasonable, detrimental reliance).

[45] *See Arkansas Pub. Emps. Ret. Sys. v. Bristol-Myers Squibb Co.*, 28 F.4th 343, 353 (2d Cir. 2022); *Ambassador Press, Inc. v. Durst Image Tech. U.S., LLC*, 949 F.3d 417, 421 (8th Cir. 2020).

[46] *See United States ex. rel. Kelly v. Novartis Pharm. Corp.*, 827 F.3d 5, 13 (1st Cir. 2016).

[47] *See Thayer v. Planned Parenthood of Heartland, Inc.*, 11 F.4th 934, 939 (8th Cir. 2021); *Smith v. Gen. Motors LLC*, 988 F.3d 873, 883 (6th Cir. 2021). *Cf. Olson v. Major League Baseball*, 29 F.4th 59, 71 (2d Cir. 2022) (similar but modestly different elements).

with Rule 9(b).[48] (Ordinarily, however, it is only the *circumstances* of the fraud that must be pleaded with particularity; as for all other facts, the less demanding standard of Rule 8 applies.[49]) Any fraud averment that does not meet this standard may be stricken or dismissed.[50]

- *Claims "Grounded" in Fraud:* The "particularity" requirement of Rule 9(b) applies not only to claims expressly denominated as "fraud" but also to claims that are "grounded" in or "sound" in fraud[51] (which hinges on the applicable substantive law),[52] including misrepresentation (but only when it "sounds" in fraud),[53] forgery,[54] breach of fiduciary duty involving fraud,[55] fraudulent inducement,[56] fraudulent concealment,[57] aiding and abetting a fraud,[58] and other claims involving deceptive conduct.[59] If the claim does not "sound" in fraud, it need not be alleged with particularity, even if it asserts an exacerbated level of misconduct.[60]
- *Federal Statutory Fraud Claims:* Generally, the "particularity" requirement of Rule 9(b) applies equally to both

[48] *See United States ex rel. Bookwalter v. UPMC*, 946 F.3d 162, 176 (3d Cir. 2019); *Nakahata v. New York-Presbyterian Healthcare Sys., Inc.*, 723 F.3d 192, 198 (2d Cir. 2013).

[49] *See Winter ex rel. United States v. Gardens Reg'l Hosp. & Med. Ctr.*, 953 F.3d 1108, 1122 (9th Cir. 2020) (scienter may be pleaded generally).

[50] *See In re Galectin Therapeutics, Inc. Sec. Litig.*, 843 F.3d 1257, 1269 (11th Cir. 2016).

[51] *See Katz v. Belveron Real Est. Partners, LLC*, 28 F.4th 300, 308 (1st Cir. 2022); *Bakery & Confectionary Union & Indus. Int'l Pension Fund v. Just Born II, Inc.*, 888 F.3d 696, 705 (4th Cir. 2018).

[52] *See Olin v. Dakota Access, LLC*, 910 F.3d 1072, 1075–76 (8th Cir. 2018).

[53] *See Matter of Life Partners Holdings, Inc.*, 926 F.3d 103, 118–19 (5th Cir. 2019); *Republic Bank & Trust Co. v. Bear Stearns & Co.*, 683 F.3d 239, 247–48 (6th Cir. 2012). *Cf. Wilding v. DNC Servs. Corp.*, 941 F.3d 1116, 1127-28 (11th Cir. 2019) (applies to negligent misrepresentation, if claim "sound in fraud" under applicable State law).

[54] *See Johnson v. Pushpin Holdings, LLC*, 821 F.3d 871, 876 (7th Cir. 2016).

[55] *See Cornielsen v. Infinium Capital Mgmt., LLC*, 916 F.3d 589, 604 (7th Cir. 2019); *Krys v. Pigott*, 749 F.3d 117, 129 (2d Cir. 2014).

[56] *See FCS Advisors, LLC v. Missouri*, 929 F.3d 618, 620 (8th Cir. 2019).

[57] *See Squires-Cannon v. Forest Pres. Dist. of Cook Cty.*, 897 F.3d 797, 805 (7th Cir. 2018).

[58] *See Quintero Cmty. Ass'n Inc. v. F.D.I.C.*, 792 F.3d 1002, 1010 (8th Cir. 2015).

[59] *See United States v. Molina Healthcare of Ill., Inc.*, 17 F.4th 732, 742 (7th Cir. 2021) (implied false certification); *In re Trib. Co. Fraudulent Conv. Litig.*, 10 F.4th 147, 159 (2d Cir. 2021) (intentional fraudulent conveyance); *Exergen Corp. v. Wal-Mart Stores, Inc.*, 575 F.3d 1312, 1326–27 (Fed.Cir. 2009) ("inequitable conduct" claim in patent litigation).

[60] *See, e.g., Benson v. Fannie May Confections Brands, Inc.*, 944 F.3d 639, 646 (7th Cir. 2019) (not to unfair conduct claims); *Bayerische Landesbank, N.Y. Branch v. Aladdin Capital Mgmt. LLC*, 692 F.3d 42, 64 (2d Cir. 2012) (not to gross negligence and breach of contract claims).

federal statutory fraud and common law fraud,[61] and may be enhanced by Congress still further, as it has been with federal securities fraud claims.[62]

- *State Law Fraud Claims:* The "particularity" requirement applies to both federal and State-law fraud claims.[63]
- *Fraud As An Alternative Claim:* If the pleader alleges both fraud and non-fraud claims, only the fraud claims need to satisfy the particularity requirement (unless the same facts form the basis for both claims).[64]

Mistake

A party must also plead mistake with particularity. This obligates the pleader to plead with particularity the circumstances constituting the mistake — the "who, what, when, where, and how" of the mistake,[65] which may include the precise nature of the mistake, who made the mistake, and when.[66]

No Common Law Additions to Rule 9(b)'s List

Rule 9(b) requires that only fraud and mistake be pleaded with particularity. It is now "emphatically clear" that courts are not permitted to add to this list and require, by case-made edict, that other claims be pleaded with particularity.[67]

Malice, Intent, Knowledge, and Conditions of Mind

A party may allege malice, intent, knowledge, and condition

---

[61]*See Newman v. Metro. Life Ins. Co.*, 885 F.3d 992, 998 (7th Cir. 2018). *See also Smith v. Clark / Smoot / Russell*, 796 F.3d 424, 432 (4th Cir. 2015) (federal False Claims Act lawsuits); *H & Q Props., Inc. v. Doll*, 793 F.3d 852, 855–56 (8th Cir. 2015) (federal RICO lawsuits).

[62]*See Neiman v. Bulmahn*, 854 F.3d 741, 746 (5th Cir. 2017) (PSLRA "raised the pleading bar even higher"); *Schueneman v. Arena Pharm., Inc.*, 840 F.3d 698, 705 (9th Cir. 2016) (PSLRA "ups the ante").

[63]*See Irving Firemen's Relief & Ret. Fund v. Uber Techs., Inc.*, 998 F.3d 397, 404 (9th Cir. 2021); *Hoffman v. L & M Arts*, 838 F.3d 568, 576 (5th Cir. 2016).

[64]*See Kearns v. Ford Motor Co.*, 567 F.3d 1120, 1124 (9th Cir. 2009); *Liquidation Com'n of Banco Intercontinental, S.A. v. Renta*, 530 F.3d 1339, 1355–56 (11th Cir. 2008).

[65]*See Illinois Nat'l Ins. Co. v. Wyndham Worldwide Operations, Inc.*, 653 F.3d 225, 232–33 (3d Cir. 2011); *Sherwin-Williams Co. v. SUSE, LLC*, 2015 WL 10990185, at *6 (D. Utah Oct. 23, 2015).

[66]*See Barber v. America's Wholesale Lender*, 542 Fed. Appx. 832, 837–38 (11th Cir. 2013); *Strauss v. Centennial Precious Metals, Inc.*, 291 F.R.D. 338, 340–41 (D. Neb. 2013). *But see Bankers Trust Co. v. Old Republic Ins. Co.*, 959 F.2d 677, 683 (7th Cir. 1992) (questioning, as a "mystery", why allegations of mistake ought to warrant particularization).

[67]*See Swierkiewicz v. Sorema N. A.*, 534 U.S. 506, 512–15, 122 S. Ct. 992, 152 L. Ed. 2d 1 (2002); *Leatherman v. Tarrant County Narcotics Intelligence & Coordination Unit*, 507 U.S. 163, 168, 113 S. Ct. 1160, 122 L. Ed. 2d 517 (1993). *See also Gallivan v. United States*, 943 F.3d 291, 293-94 (6th Cir. 2019) (not to medical negligence claims); *Concord Assocs., L.P. v. Entm't Props. Trust*, 817 F.3d 46, 52 (2d Cir. 2016) (not to antitrust claims).

of mind generally, as with any ordinary allegation under Rule 8.[68] But this concept of tolerable "generality" is a relative one. Although the enhanced pleading obligations of Rule 9(b) do not apply, the Rule 8 requirements of *Twombly* "plausibility" still do,[69] and the pleaded allegations must give rise to an inference of the requisite state of mind.[70]

Pleading Tensions Between Fraud and Intent

There is some internal tension between Rule 9(b)'s requirement that fraud—which ordinarily requires an intent to deceive—be pleaded with particularity, and Rule 9(b)'s companion provision that intent itself may be pleaded generally. Courts usually resolve this apparent inconsistency by requiring that when the claim is based upon allegations of fraud, the party has a duty to follow the requirement to plead fraud with particularity, and then intent[71] and knowledge[72] generally. But the facts, as pleaded, must give rise to a "strong inference of fraudulent intent."[73]

Group Pleading in Fraud Cases

The particularized pleading requirement is designed to notify each defendant of his, her, or its purported role in the alleged misconduct.[74] Lumping multiple defendants together in a group pleading (*e.g.*, "defendants misled the plaintiff by stating . . .") may defeat this notice objective and, thus, may be found

---

[68]*See Nelson Auto Ctr., Inc. v. Multimedia Holdings Corp.*, 951 F.3d 952, 958 (8th Cir. 2020); *U.S. v. Bollinger Shipyards, Inc.*, 775 F.3d 255, 260 (5th Cir. 2014). *See generally Kaplan v. Lebanese Canadian Bank, SAL*, 999 F.3d 842, 864 (2d Cir. 2021) (unrealistic to expect plaintiff to allege defendant's actual state of mind).

[69]*See Ashcroft v. Iqbal*, 556 U.S. 662, 686–87, 129 S. Ct. 1937, 173 L. Ed. 2d 868 (2009). *See also id.* ("Rule 8 does not empower [a pleader] to plead the bare elements of his cause of action, affix the label 'general allegation,' and expect his complaint to survive a motion to dismiss."). *See also United States ex rel. Taylor v. Boyko*, 39 F.4th 177, 189 (4th Cir. 2022); *OmegaGenesis Corp. v. Mayo Found. for Med. Educ. & Research*, 851 F.3d 800, 804 (8th Cir. 2017).

[70]*See Kaplan v. Lebanese Canadian Bank, SAL*, 999 F.3d 842, 2021 WL 2345642, at *17 (2d Cir. 2021) (alleged facts / events must give rise to inference of knowledge); *United States v. Strock*, 982 F.3d 51, 66 (2d Cir. 2020) (strong inference required).

[71]*See Winter ex rel. United States v. Gardens Reg'l Hosp. & Med. Ctr.*, 953 F.3d 1108, 1122 (9th Cir. 2020); *Biro v. Conde Nast*, 807 F.3d 541, 544–45 (2d Cir. 2015). *See also Chill v. General Elec. Co.*, 101 F.3d 263, 267 (2d Cir. 1996) (speaker's intent need not be pleaded with specificity because plaintiff realistically cannot be held to allege a defendant's actual state of mind).

[72]*See United States ex rel. Mamalakis v. Anesthetix Mgmt. LLC*, 20 F.4th 295, 301 (7th Cir. 2021); *United States ex rel. Anita Silingo v. WellPoint, Inc.*, 904 F.3d 667, 679–80 (9th Cir. 2018).

[73]*See Loreley Fin. (Jersey) No. 3 Ltd. v. Wells Fargo Sec., LLC*, 797 F.3d 160, 176–77 (2d Cir. 2015); *Heinrich v. Waiting Angels Adoption Servs, Inc.*, 668 F.3d 393, 406 (6th Cir. 2012).

[74]*See United States ex rel. Anita Silingo v. WellPoint, Inc.*, 904 F.3d 667, 677 (9th Cir. 2018); *Rocha v. Rudd*, 826 F.3d 905, 911 (7th Cir. 2016).

to be improper under Rule 9(b).[75] Although the courts might not always require a pleader to parse each fact and attribute every false statement to a particular defendant (especially in cases where defendants are accused of performing the exact same role in the fraud),[76] the pleader will be obligated to at least notify each defendant as to how he or she is alleged to have participated in the fraud.[77]

Pleading on Information and Belief

Although Rule 9(b) generally prohibits allegations made on mere information and belief,[78] pleading in this fashion may be permitted if the pleader can show both that the essential information is exclusively within another party's control and specific facts upon which the information-and-belief is based.[79] This relaxation of Rule 9(b) may reflect the practical inability of a pleader to allege factual details that are not accessible prior to discovery.[80] Nonetheless, mindful of the often *in terrorem* effect of such claims, this approach never grants the pleader a license to speculate[81] or offer conclusory, boilerplate averments.[82]

Counterclaims and Affirmative Defenses

When asserting fraud or mistake in counterclaims or affirmative defenses, the pleader must assert fraud or mistake there

---

[75]*See Irving Firemen's Relief & Ret. Fund v. Uber Techs., Inc.*, 998 F.3d 397, 408 (9th Cir. 2021); *Cornielsen v. Infinium Capital Mgmt., LLC*, 916 F.3d 589, 599 (7th Cir. 2019). *But see Phillips v. Scientific-Atlanta, Inc.*, 374 F.3d 1015, 1018–19 (11th Cir. 2004) (permissive "group pleading doctrine" in securities cases allows presumption of group responsibility for statements and omissions).

[76]*See United States ex rel. Anita Silingo v. WellPoint, Inc.*, 904 F.3d 667, 677 (9th Cir. 2018).

[77]*See Streambend Props. II, LLC v. Ivy Tower Minneapolis, LLC*, 781 F.3d 1003, 1013 (8th Cir. 2015); *United States v. Corinthian Colleges*, 655 F.3d 984, 998 (9th Cir. 2011). *Cf. Lerner v. Colman*, 26 F.4th 71, 85 (1st Cir. 2022) (alleging person "participated in the scheme" is insufficient).

[78]*See United States ex rel. Mamalakis v. Anesthetix Mgmt. LLC*, 20 F.4th 295, 301 (7th Cir. 2021); *Ambassador Press, Inc. v. Durst Image Tech. U.S., LLC*, 949 F.3d 417, 421 (8th Cir. 2020).

[79]*See Alix v. McKinsey & Co.*, 23 F.4th 196, 209 (2d Cir. 2022), *petition for cert. filed*, No. 21-1608 (U.S. June 29, 2022); *United States ex rel. Cimino v. Int'l Bus. Machines Corp.*, 3 F.4th 412, 424 (D.C. Cir. 2021).

[80]*See, e.g., In re Rockefeller Ctr. Props., Inc. Secs. Litig.*, 311 F.3d 198, 216 (3d Cir. 2002) (rigidity of pleading requirements may be relaxed where requisite factual information is peculiarly within defendant's knowledge or control); *Corley v. Rosewood Care Ctr., Inc.*, 142 F.3d 1041, 1051 (7th Cir. 1998) (requirement "must be relaxed where the plaintiff lacks access to all facts necessary to detail his claim").

[81]*See Tuchman v. DSC Commc'ns Corp.*, 14 F.3d 1061, 1068 (5th Cir. 1994).

[82]*See United States ex rel. Berkowitz v. Automation Aids, Inc.*, 896 F.3d 834, 841 (7th Cir. 2018); *In re Rockefeller Ctr. Props., Inc. Secs. Litig.*, 311 F.3d 198, 216 (3d Cir. 2002). *See also U.S. ex rel. Karvelas v. Melrose-Wakefield Hosp.*, 360 F.3d 220, 226 (1st Cir. 2004) (relaxed pleading must later be amended, following discovery, with details).

with particularity.[83]

Non-Party Fraud or Mistake

Where fraud or mistake was committed by non-parties[84] or when alleging that non-parties were defrauded,[85] a party may plead fraud or mistake more generally.

Opposing an Insufficiently Particular Pleading

A party may challenge a pleading that fails to plead fraud or mistake with particularity by filing a Rule 12(e) motion for a more definite statement,[86] a Rule 12(f) motion to strike, or a Rule 12(b) motion to dismiss.[87] Often, parties assert these motions in the alternative. The Rule 9(b) particularity requirement is ordinarily not testable later at the summary judgment stage, since by that time the requirement's goal (supplying the detail necessary for the opponent to frame an informed defense) has likely become mooted.[88]

Granting Leave to Amend

Where a complaint is dismissed for failing to allege with particularity, leave to amend will usually be granted freely,[89] unless the amendment is futile and would not cure the particularity deficiency.[90]

Constitutionality of Enhanced Pleading

Any enhanced pleading duty necessarily carries with it the risk that, on occasion, it might cause the dismissal of a valid claim which, had the claim been permitted to reach discovery, could have found sound evidentiary support. The Supreme Court considered this possibility and, citing the authority of

---

[83] *See Bakery & Confectionary Union & Indus. Int'l Pension Fund v. Just Born II, Inc.*, 888 F.3d 696, 705 (4th Cir. 2018); (affirmative defenses); *Exergen Corp. v. Wal-Mart Stores, Inc.*, 575 F.3d 1312, 1325–31 (Fed. Cir. 2009) (counterclaims).

[84] *United States ex. rel. Kelly v. Novartis Pharm. Corp.*, 827 F.3d 5, 13 (1st Cir. 2016).

[85] *See, e.g., Segal v. Gordon*, 467 F.2d 602, 607 (2d Cir. 1972) ("When the pleader is asserting that third persons have been defrauded, he may be unable to detail the claim and less specificity should be required.").

[86] *See, e.g., Coffey v. Foamex L.P.*, 2 F.3d 157, 162 (6th Cir. 1993) (approving use of Rule 12(e) to force correction of complaint defective under Rule 9(b)).

[87] *See, e.g., United States ex rel. Taylor v. Boyko*, 39 F.4th 177, 189 (4th Cir. 2022) (failure to comply with Rule 9(b) "is treated as failure to state a claim under Rule 12(b)(6)"); *Kowal v. MCI Commc'ns Corp.*, 16 F.3d 1271, 1279 (D.C. Cir. 1994) (affirming dismissal under Rule 12(b)(6) for failure to meet requirements of Rule 9(b)).

[88] *See Fulghum v. Embarq Corp.*, 785 F.3d 395, 416–17 (10th Cir. 2015); *McCarthy v. Ameritech Pub., Inc.*, 763 F.3d 469, 478 n.2 (6th Cir. 2014).

[89] *See U.S. ex rel. Estate of Cunningham v. Millennium Labs. of Cal., Inc.*, 713 F.3d 662, 676 (1st Cir. 2013); *United States v. Corinthian Colleges*, 655 F.3d 984, 998 (9th Cir. 2011). *See also U.S. ex rel. Williams v. Bell Helicopter Textron Inc.*, 417 F.3d 450, 454–55 (5th Cir. 2005) (reversing dismissal with prejudice as improperly circumventing one purpose of Rule 9(b)—avoiding unnecessary, preliminary litigation).

[90] *See Chill v. General Elec. Co.*, 101 F.3d 263, 271–72 (2d Cir. 1996).

Congress and the Rules' drafters to adopt special pleading procedures, found no Seventh Amendment (jury right) impediment.[91]

Sealing or Redacting, to Further Protect Reputations

Because reputational harm is one concern of Rule 9(b), courts may require that fraud pleadings be filed under seal, be redacted of individual names, or otherwise safeguarded.[92]

Rule 9(b) and *Pro Se* Pleaders

Pleadings by *pro se* litigants are examined under a less stringent lens, but this leniency gives the court no license to redraft a Rule 9(b)-failing pleading in order to rescue it.[93]

RULE 9(c)—CONDITIONS PRECEDENT

CORE CONCEPT

Where applicable to the cause of action pleaded (such as in contract cases and in certain exhaustion contexts), a plaintiff may aver *generally* that all conditions precedent have been performed or have occurred. Conversely, a defense alleging that a requisite condition precedent has *not* been performed or has *not* occurred must be set forth with particularity.

APPLICATIONS

Applies to Both Contractual and Statutory Conditions

The pleading practice set forth in Rule 9(c) for conditions precedent applies whether the conditions precedent are contractual or statutory in nature.[94]

Duty to Plead Conditions Precedent At All

Courts are divided on what pleading duty Rule 9(c) imposes. Some interpret Rule 9(c) as imposing no affirmative duty to allege the performance of conditions precedent at all.[95] Those courts view Rule 9(c) as simply setting forth the procedure for alleging such performance if the pleader chooses to do so.[96] Other courts read Rule 9(c) as affirmatively imposing a duty to plead such performance, albeit in a general fashion.[97] When the pleading of the performance of conditions precedent is required

---

[91] *See Tellabs, Inc. v. Makor Issues & Rights, Ltd.*, 551 U.S. 308, 327 n.9, 127 S. Ct. 2499, 168 L. Ed. 2d 179 (2007).

[92] *See Exergen Corp. v. Wal-Mart Stores, Inc.*, 575 F.3d 1312, 1329 n.6 (Fed.Cir. 2009).

[93] *See Odion v. Google Inc.*, 628 Fed. Appx. 635, 637 (11th Cir. 2015).

[94] *See Walton v. Nalco Chemical Co.*, 272 F.3d 13, 21 n.13 (1st Cir. 2001).

[95] *See Walton v. Nalco Chem. Co.*, 272 F.3d 13, 21–22 (1st Cir. 2001); *Kiernan v. Zurich Cos.*, 150 F.3d 1120, 1123–24 (9th Cir. 1998).

[96] *See Kiernan v. Zurich Cos.*, 150 F.3d 1120, 1123–24 (9th Cir. 1998); *Mendez v. Bank of America Home Loans Servicing, LP*, 840 F. Supp. 2d 639, 647–48 (E.D.N.Y. 2012).

[97] *See POSCO Energy Co. v. FuelCell Energy, Inc.*, 560 F. Supp. 3d 747, 753–55 (S.D.N.Y. 2021); *Wanjiku v. Johnson Cty.*, 173 F. Supp. 3d 1217, 1236 (D. Kan. 2016). *See also Jackson v. Seaboard C.L.R. Co.*, 678 F.2d 992,

(whether by so interpreting Rule 9(c) or by dictate of some other law), a failure to so plead may prompt a dismissal.[98]

General Allegations Sufficient To *Plead* Conditions

When performance of conditions precedent is pleaded, that pleading need not allege in detail how each condition was performed; the allegations are usually sufficient if they aver generally that all conditions precedent have been performed.[99] Such a pleading may sometimes be very brief, simply tracking the text of Rule 9(c).[100] But other courts require more, such as pleading those facts from which an inference arises that all conditions precedent have been performed.[101]

- *"Plausibility" Pleading:* Courts are also divided on whether *Twombly* plausibility[102] applies to Rule 9(c). Some courts hold that it does,[103] while others allow very general averments to suffice.[104]
- *Applies to All Claimants:* The "allege generally" right likely applies to all claimants, including counterclaim, crossclaim, and third-party pleaders.[105]
- *Allegation Can Support a Dismissal:* If a pleader elects to do more than plead generally, the additional factual specificity the pleader includes can be used, where appropriate, to justify the claim's dismissal.[106]

Specific Allegations Necessary To *Deny* Conditions

Where a defendant seeks to challenge a plaintiff's allegation that a condition precedent has been fulfilled, the denial must be pleaded with specificity and particularity.[107] A failure to so plead deems admitted the allegation that conditions precedent

---

1010 (11th Cir.1982).

[98] *See POSCO Energy Co. v. FuelCell Energy, Inc.*, 560 F. Supp. 3d 747, 753–55 (S.D.N.Y. 2021). *See also Blount v. Kay*, 2016 WL 698146, at *5 (S.D. Miss. Feb. 19, 2016) (with prejudice dismissal).

[99] *See, e.g., Wyatt v. Terhune*, 315 F.3d 1108, 1118 n.12 (9th Cir. 2003); *Walton v. Nalco Chemical Co.*, 272 F.3d 13, 22 (1st Cir. 2001).

[100] *See Gress v. Freedom Mortg. Corp.*, 386 F. Supp. 3d 455, 467 (M.D. Pa. 2019); *Residential Funding Co., LLC v. Embrace Home Loans, Inc.*, 59 F. Supp. 3d 935, 950 (D. Minn. 2014).

[101] *See Beecham v. JC Penney Distrib'n Ctr.*, 2019 WL 2924842, at *3–*4 (D. Kan. July 8, 2019); *Floorcoverings, Intern., Ltd v. Swan*, 2000 WL 528480 (N.D. Ill. 2000).

[102] *See supra* Authors' Commentary to Rule 8(a)(2) (*"Plausible" Pleadings*).

[103] *See POSCO Energy Co. v. FuelCell Energy, Inc.*, 560 F. Supp. 3d 747, 753 (S.D.N.Y. 2021) (*Twombly* applies to Rule 9(c)).

[104] *See Hildebrand v. Allegheny County*, 757 F.3d 99, 112 (3d Cir. 2014); *E.E.O.C. v. Bass Pro Outdoor World, LLC*, 884 F. Supp. 2d 499, 521–22 (S.D.Tex. 2012). *See generally Chesapeake Square Hotel, LLC v. Logan's Roadhouse, Inc.*, 995 F. Supp. 2d 512, 515–19 (E.D. Va. 2014) (providing broad analysis of *Twombly* issue).

[105] *See, e.g., Appalachian Power Co. v. Wagman Heavy Civil, Inc.*, 2019 WL 6188303, at *5 (W.D. Va. Nov. 20, 2019); *John v. Key Energy Servs., Inc.*, 2006 WL 2266262, at *8 (S.D. Tex. Aug. 8, 2006).

[106] *See Business Payment Sys., LLC v. National Processing Co.*, 2012 WL 6020400, at *11 (W.D.Ky. Dec. 3, 2012).

[107] *See E.E.O.C. v. Serv. Temps Inc.*,

were satisfied.[108] and precludes the defendant from later raising conditions precedent as a claim-barring defense.[109] Courts may, however, construe a defendant's attempt at denial leniently, and accept an imperfect denial if it imparts fair notice and imposes no unfair prejudice.[110] Once a condition precedent has been adequately contested by the pleading, the burden returns to plaintiff to prove that the condition precedent contested by the defendant has been met.[111]

- *Denial by Motion:* Some courts permit a specific denial by either an early motion or an answer.[112]

RULE 9(d)—OFFICIAL DOCUMENT OR ACT

CORE CONCEPT

A party pleading the existence or legality of an official document need only assert that the official document was issued legally or the official act was performed legally.

APPLICATIONS

Pleading Official Document or Act

In a claim involving an official document or official act, the pleader need only allege that the document was issued legally or the act was done legally.[113] A defendant who wishes to contest that contention should do so by a specific denial in the responsive pleading.[114] This Rule does not address the admissibility of the document or act.[115]

RULE 9(e)—JUDGMENT

CORE CONCEPT

When pleading any judgment or decision, a party need not allege the jurisdictional authority of the tribunal rendering the

---

679 F.3d 323, 331 (5th Cir. 2012); *Myers v. Central Fla. Invs., Inc.*, 592 F.3d 1201, 1224 (11th Cir. 2010).

[108]*See Myers v. Central Fla. Invs., Inc.*, 592 F.3d 1201, 1224 (11th Cir. 2010).

[109]*See L.A. Pub. Ins. Adjusters, Inc. v. Nelson*, 17 F.4th 521, 526 (5th Cir. 2021).

[110]*See Life Plans, Inc. v. Sec. Life of Denver Ins. Co.*, 800 F.3d 343, 352 n.2 (7th Cir. 2015) (finding pleading, read as a whole, made clear the nature of the denial); *Odyssey Reinsurance Co. v. Cal-Regent Ins. Servs. Corp.*, 123 F. Supp. 3d 343, 353–54 (D. Conn. 2015) (noting leniency approach, accepting argument as motion to amend).

[111]*See Myers v. Central Fla. Invs., Inc.*, 592 F.3d 1201, 1224 (11th Cir. 2010); *Runnemede Owners, Inc. v. Crest Mortg. Corp.*, 861 F.2d 1053, 1057–58 (7th Cir. 1988).

[112]*See Associated Mech. Contractors, Inc. v. Martin K. Eby Constr. Co.*, 271 F.3d 1309, 1317 (11th Cir. 2001); *EEOC v. Klingler Elec. Corp.*, 636 F.2d 104, 107 (5th Cir.1981). *But see L.A. Pub. Ins. Adjusters, Inc. v. Nelson*, 17 F.4th 521, 526 (5th Cir. 2021) (denial could not be included in summary judgment motion filed years after answer was due); *Fox v. Safeco Ins. Co. of Illinois*, 2017 WL 8341728, at *1–*2 n.1 (M.D. Fla. Dec. 4, 2017) (denial cannot be by motion).

[113]*See Shaw v. T-Mobile*, 2020 WL 4334993, at *5 (D. Kan. July 28, 2020).

[114]*See Shaw v. T-Mobile*, 2020 WL 4334993, at *5 (D. Kan. July 28, 2020).

[115]*See Shaw v. T-Mobile*, 2020 WL 4334993, at *5 (D. Kan. July 28, 2020).

judgment.

APPLICATIONS

Pleading Judgments and Decisions

In pleading a judgment or decision, a party need not show that the issuing tribunal had jurisdiction to act (at least absent some separate law requiring otherwise).[116] But the pleader should specify the identity of the body issuing the judgment or decision, the date of the judgment or decision, the parties participating in the proceeding, and the character or effect of the judgment or decision. A party resisting such a pleading should do so specifically, by alleging the particular claimed defect in the ruling.[117]

RULE 9(f)—TIME AND PLACE

CORE CONCEPT

Time and place averments are material allegations and can, if appropriate, support a dismissal of a claim or defense.

APPLICATIONS

Specificity *Not* Required, But If Supplied, Averments Are Material

Rule 9(f) does *not* require that time and place be pleaded[118] (though such averments may be separately required by the substantive law of the underlying claim or defense).[119] Instead, Rule 9(f) simply confirms that, if pleaded, averments of time and place are material and can be considered in testing the sufficiency of a pleading.[120] Thus, if the averments of time and place establish an obvious defense (such as time-bar), the inclusion of those averments can support a dismissal,[121] or, in an appropriate case, a motion for a more definite statement.[122]

---

[116]To enforce a judgment entered by a foreign Nation, the enforcing party seems obligated to make a prima facie showing that the rendering court did not lack jurisdiction. *See Ackermann v. Levine*, 788 F.2d 830, 842 n.12 (2d Cir. 1986); *Kaupthing ehf. v. Bricklayers & Trowel Trades Int'l Pension Fund Liquidation Portfolio*, 291 F. Supp. 3d 21, 32–33 (D.D.C. 2017).

[117]*See* 5A CHARLES A. WRIGHT, ARTHUR R. MILLER, & A. BENJAMIN SPENCER, FEDERAL PRACTICE AND PROCEDURE § 1307 (2018).

[118]*See PTP OneClick, LLC v. Avalara, Inc.*, 413 F. Supp. 3d 1050, 1066 (W.D. Wash. 2019); *Hawkins v. Bd. of Cty. Commrs. of Coffey Cty.*, 376 F. Supp. 3d 1200, 1211 n.8 (D. Kan. 2019).

[119]*See Cantu v. Guerra*, 2021 WL 2652933, at *14 (W.D. Tex. June 28, 2021) (discussing issue).

[120]*See Grosz v. Museum of Modern Art*, 772 F. Supp. 2d 473, 477 (S.D.N.Y. 2010); *In re Maxim Integrated Prods., Inc. Secs. Litig.*, 639 F. Supp. 2d 1038, 1051 (N.D.Cal. 2009).

[121]*See Hidalgo v. Johnson & Johnson Consumer Companies, Inc.*, 148 F. Supp. 3d 285, 294 (S.D.N.Y. 2015); *Stinnett v. U.S.*, 891 F. Supp. 2d 858, 862–63 (M.D.Tenn. 2012).

[122]*See Meyer v. United Airlines, Inc.*, 624 F. Supp. 2d 923, 932 (N.D.Ill. 2008).

RULE 9(g)—SPECIAL DAMAGES

CORE CONCEPT

Special damages must be pleaded specifically.

APPLICATIONS

Purpose

The obligation to plead special damages with specificity is designed to alert the defending parties to the nature of those damages (thus avoiding trial surprise by the extent or character of the claim).[123]

Defined

Identifying special damages is not always clear.[124] "General" damages are the usual, ordinary, natural, direct, and proximate consequences of a defendant's conduct, and thus are inferable from the conduct alleged. By contrast, "special" damages are those that, though perhaps natural and not unexpected, are not necessarily the predictable, inevitable consequences of a defendant's conduct, and thus are not obviously inferable.[125] Special damages depend on the peculiar context of the dispute.[126] For example, in a trespass action, general damages encompass injury to the land itself whereas special damages might include impacts on plaintiff's intended plans for that land.[127] Because they are not obviously inferable, an intent to pursue special damages might not come to the defendant's attention unless pleaded with specificity.[128] Emotional distress damages,[129] defamation damages,[130] business destruction and loss of good will,[131] and damages flowing from trade disparage-

---

[123] *See Carnell Const. Corp. v. Danville Redev't & Housing Auth.*, 745 F.3d 703, 725–26 (4th Cir. 2014); *Bowles v. Osmose Utilities Services, Inc.*, 443 F.3d 671, 675 (8th Cir. 2006).

[124] *See 44 Liquormart, Inc. v. State of R.I.*, 940 F. Supp. 437, 438–39 (D.R.I. 1996).

[125] For a general orientation to the distinction between general and special damages, see *McAfee v. Boczar*, 738 F.3d 81, 91 n.9 (4th Cir. 2013); *National Hispanic Circus, Inc. v. Rex Trucking, Inc.*, 414 F.3d 546, 549 (5th Cir. 2005); *Kerman v. City of New York*, 374 F.3d 93, 125 (2d Cir. 2004). *See generally Roberts v. Graham*, 73 U.S. 578, 579-80, 18 L. Ed. 791 (1867).

[126] *See Weyerhaeuser Co. v. Brantley*, 510 F.3d 1256, 1266 (10th Cir. 2007).

[127] *See Weyerhaeuser Co. v. Brantley*, 510 F.3d 1256, 1266 (10th Cir. 2007).

[128] *See, e.g., Weyerhaeuser Co. v. Brantley*, 510 F.3d 1256, 1267 (10th Cir. 2007); *LINC Finance Corp. v. Onwuteaka*, 129 F.3d 917, 922 (7th Cir. 1997).

[129] *See Blackard v. Hercules, Inc.*, 17 F. Supp. 3d 576, 580 (S.D. Miss. 2014).

[130] *See Smith v. Clinton*, 886 F.3d 122, 128 (D.C. Cir. 2018); *Muzikowski v. Paramount Pictures Corp.*, 322 F.3d 918, 924–27 (7th Cir. 2003).

[131] *See Nestle USA, Inc. v. Crest Foods, Inc.*, 2017 WL 3267665, at *15 (C.D. Cal. July 28, 2017); *Carnell Const. Corp. v. Danville Redev't & Housing Auth.*, 2013 WL 101687, at *11–*12 (W.D.Va. Jan. 8, 2013).

ment[132] are usually deemed special damages and, thus, must be pleaded with specificity. Attorney's fees have traditionally been categorized as special damages,[133] although some courts distinguish between fees recoverable as an element of the underlying substantive claim (likely to be special damages) and fees recoverable under a cost-shifting regimen (likely to not be).[134] Whether punitive damages[135] or prejudgment interest[136] are items of special damages is unclear. Liquidated damages typically are not special damages.[137] In diversity cases, what constitutes special damages is defined by the pertinent State's law.[138]

Level of Required Specificity

A party must "specifically state" items of special damages, but that statement might not need be expressed "with particularity" as certain other allegations must.[139] This pleading obligation is not "reducible to formula," and will depend on the nature of the claim at issue, the alleged injury, and the causal connection between the two.[140] Averments must be sufficiently specific to allow the opponent to meaningfully respond.[141] Consequently, vague, conclusory catch-all allegations (such as "damaged,"

---

[132]*See KBT Corp., Inc. v. Ceridian Corp.*, 966 F. Supp. 369, 375 (E.D. Pa. 1997).

[133]*See, e.g., United Industries, Inc. v. Simon-Hartley, Ltd.*, 91 F.3d 762 (5th Cir. 1996); *Atlantic Purchasers, Inc. v. Aircraft Sales, Inc.*, 705 F.2d 712, 716 n.4 (4th Cir. 1983).

[134]*See, e.g., Wiley v. Portfolio Recovery Assocs., LLC*, ___ F. Supp. 3d ___, 2022 WL 903207, at *6 (D. Minn. 2022) (appeal pending); *Route Triple Seven Ltd. P'ship v. Total Hockey, Inc.*, 127 F. Supp. 3d 607, 613–16 (E.D. Va. 2015).

[135]*Compare Johnson v. Rapid Sheet Metal, LLC*, 2020 WL 6120477, at *3 (D.N.H. Oct. 16, 2020) (surveying national case law, and following majority approach that punitive damages are not governed by Rule 9(g)) *and Hanson v. McBride*, 2020 WL 419334, at *1 n.1 (M.D. Tenn. Jan. 27, 2020) (same result), *with Seirus Innovative Accessories, Inc. v. Cabela's Inc.*, 2011 WL 10968420, at *5 (S.D. Cal. Oct. 5, 2011) (applies to punitive damages), *and A.H. ex rel. Hohe v. Knowledge Learning Corp.*, 2011 WL 2084143, at *2 (D. Kan. May 24, 2011) (same).

[136]*See U.S. v. All Meat and Poultry Products Stored at Lagrou Cold Storage*, 470 F. Supp. 2d 823, 834–35 (N.D. Ill. 2007) (noting, but not resolving, question).

[137]*See Local 705 Bhd. of Teamsters Pension Fund v. Special Serv. Co.*, 2009 WL 1956720, at *2 (N.D.Ill. July 8, 2009).

[138]*See Carnell Const. Corp. v. Danville Redev't & Housing Auth.*, 745 F.3d 703, 725–26 (4th Cir. 2014).

[139]*See ADT LLC v. Vivant Smart Home, Inc.*, 2021 WL 4478932, at *3 (S.D. Fla. Sept. 30, 2021) (contrasting Rules 9(g) and 9(b)); *Leavitt v. Cole*, 291 F. Supp. 2d 1338, 1343–45 (M.D. Fla. 2003) (same). *But cf. Browning v. Clinton*, 292 F.3d 235, 245–46 (D.C. Cir. 2002) (must allege damages "with 'particularity' ").

[140]*See Marseilles Hydro Power, LLC. v. Marseilles Land & Water Co.*, 2003 WL 259142, at *6–*7 (N.D. Ill. 2003). *See also Pippen v. NBCUniversal Media, LLC*, 734 F.3d 610, 614 (7th Cir. 2013) ("hard to know how specific is specific enough").

[141]*See In re U.S. Office of Pers. Mgmt. Data Sec. Breach Litig.*, 928 F.3d 42, 66 (D.C. Cir. 2019). *See generally Suarez Matos v. Ashford Presbyterian Community Hosp., Inc.*, 4 F.3d 47,

business "curtailed,"[142] or "diminution in value"[143]) are risky, as are rounded figures and generalized dollar amounts.[144] A safer statement of special damages would include an estimate of the total damages, a listing of the specific items that comprise that sum, and facts showing the damages to be the natural consequence of the claimed conduct.[145]

Consequences of Failing to Plead Special Damages

A party's failure to plead special damages with specificity may bar that party's recovery of those damages.[146] However, because there is no timing requirement in the Rule, a party can often seek leave from the court to amend to include items of special damages in a pleading.[147] Moreover, because the goal is to protect against unfair surprise, the court may excuse (or at least liberally[148] construe) a weakly pleaded special damages allegation if those damages were not an essential element of the underlying claim[149] or where the opponent was not prejudiced by the absence of further specificity.[150]

RULE 9(h)—ADMIRALTY AND MARITIME CLAIMS

CORE CONCEPT

A pleader wishing to proceed under the special rules governing admiralty and maritime claims must designate the claim as an admiralty or maritime one.

APPLICATIONS

Election to Proceed in Admiralty/Maritime

In 1966, the procedures formerly governing suits in

---

52 (1st Cir. 1993) ("the more natural are the damages, the less the pleading is needed.").

[142] *See Artista Records, Inc. v. Flea World, Inc.*, 356 F. Supp. 2d 411, 428 (D.N.J. 2005).

[143] *See Marseilles Hydro Power, LLC. v. Marseilles Land & Water Co.*, 2003 WL 259142, at *6–*7 (N.D. Ill. Feb. 4, 2003).

[144] *See Ebrahimian v. Nationwide Mut. Fire Ins. Co.*, 960 F. Supp. 2d 405, 418 (E.D.N.Y. 2013). *But see ADT LLC v. Vivant Smart Home, Inc.*, 2021 WL 4478932, at *2–*3 (S.D. Fla. Sept. 30, 2021) (alleging lost "sales, profits, and goodwill" sufficient); *Luxpro Corp. v. Apple, Inc.*, 658 F. Supp. 2d 921, 935–36 (W.D.Ark. 2009) (does not always require pleader to allege specific dollar amount).

[145] *See Browning v. Clinton*, 292 F.3d 235, 245–46 (D.C. Cir. 2002) (specify facts showing damages to be natural, direct of claimed conduct); *US Dominion, Inc. v. Powell*, 554 F. Supp. 3d 42, 74 (D.D.C. 2021) ("precise nature" of losses and how they resulted from defendant's action); *City and County of San Francisco v. Tutor-Saliba Corp.*, 2005 WL 645389, at *17 (N.D. Cal. Mar. 17, 2005) ("not just the total lump sum," but "specific items which make up the lump sum").

[146] *See, e.g., Nunes v. Cable News Network, Inc.*, 31 F.4th 135, 147 (2d Cir. 2022); *Lott v. Levitt*, 556 F.3d 564, 570 (7th Cir. 2009).

[147] *See Jones v. Krautheim*, 208 F. Supp. 2d 1173, 1178 (D. Colo. 2002).

[148] *See Energy Consumption Auditing Servs., LLC v. Brightergy, LLC*, 49 F. Supp. 3d 890, 905 (D.Kan. 2014).

[149] *See Adams v. United States*, 823 F. Supp. 2d 1074, 1086 (D.Idaho 2011).

[150] *See Bowles v. Osmose Utilities Services, Inc.*, 443 F.3d 671, 675 (8th Cir. 2006).

admiralty were fused into the Federal Rules of Civil Procedure, but this unification retained several admiralty-specific procedures that today offer plaintiffs litigating options.[151] So, in filing an admiralty or maritime claim, a plaintiff may have a choice to make—to proceed using those specific admiralty and maritime procedures[152] or not.

When the only available basis for federal subject-matter jurisdiction is admiralty jurisdiction,[153] there is no need for an election; admiralty procedures apply automatically.[154] When an admiralty dispute also has another basis for federal jurisdiction (*e.g.*, diversity), the claimant has a right to elect how to proceed (either under the admiralty rules or not).[155] This right of election is determined claim-by-claim; non-admiralty claims are not converted into admiralty claims merely by being joined with admiralty claims,[156] nor will a claim cognizable in both admiralty and diversity jurisdiction lose its ability to proceed in diversity merely by being joined with an admiralty-only claim (provided that claim has invoked only a non-admiralty basis for jurisdiction).[157] An admiralty election is not necessarily irrevocable; a claimant can request leave to amend (on such a motion, the court will consider whether the claimant took unfair advantage of the original election or otherwise prejudiced other parties).[158]

Significance of Election: Admiralty Procedures

An announced intent to proceed in admiralty or maritime jurisdiction is not, of course, dispositive of the question whether such jurisdiction exists,[159] nor does it necessarily determine whether admiralty or maritime law governs.[160] Rather, choosing to proceed in admiralty is merely the means by which pleaders claim access to those special procedures that have, histori-

---

[151] *See Bensch v. Est. of Umar*, 2 F.4th 70, 76 (2d Cir. 2021); *Caron v. NCL (Bahamas), Ltd.*, 910 F.3d 1359, 1365–66 (11th Cir. 2018).

[152] The full text of the *Supplemental Rules For Certain Admiralty And Maritime Claims* appears at the end of Part III of this text.

[153] *See* 28 U.S.C.A. § 1333.

[154] *See DeRoy v. Carnival Corp.*, 963 F.3d 1302, 1312-13 (11th Cir. 2020); *Garanti Finansal Kiralama A.S. v. Aqua Marine & Trading Inc.*, 697 F.3d 59, 70 (2d Cir. 2012).

[155] *See Poincon v. Offshore Marine Contractors, Inc.*, 9 F.4th 289, 294–95 (5th Cir. 2021); *DeRoy v. Carnival Corp.*, 963 F.3d 1302, 1312 (11th Cir. 2020).

[156] *See Maersk, Inc. v. Neewra, Inc.*, 687 F. Supp. 2d 300, 340 (S.D.N.Y. 2009).

[157] *See Luera v. M/V Alberta*, 635 F.3d 181, 189–93 (5th Cir. 2011).

[158] *See Buccina v. Grimsby*, 889 F.3d 256, 262 (6th Cir. 2018); *Luera v. M/V Alberta*, 635 F.3d 181, 187 (5th Cir. 2011).

[159] *See Jerome B. Grubart, Inc. v. Great Lakes Dredge & Dock Co.*, 513 U.S. 527, 533-34, 115 S.Ct. 1043, 130 L.Ed.2d 1024 (1995) (claim within federal admiralty jurisdiction if incident occurred on navigable waterway, could disrupt maritime commerce, and bears substantial relationship to traditional maritime activity).

[160] *See Corley v. Long-Lewis, Inc.*, 965 F.3d 1222, 1235 (11th Cir. 2020).

cally, attached to actions in admiralty.[161]

Significance of Election: No Jury Trial

Ordinarily, choosing to proceed in admiralty means that the claims in the case are decided by the court, and not by a jury.[162] It defeats a defendant's ability to demand a jury trial for that proceeding.[163] Beyond these bright-line principles, the availability of a jury trial in admiralty proceedings is "unduly complex."[164] The U.S. Supreme Court has ruled that while the Seventh Amendment does not compel jury trials in admiralty cases, neither does it (or any other constitutional provision) prohibit them.[165] The ramifications of that conclusion can be far-reaching. For example, if a plaintiff demands a jury trial in a case that invoked jurisdiction both in admiralty and on a second basis, that jury demand will be honored (so long as the plaintiff is not found to have elected to proceed in admiralty).[166] When a plaintiff joins two claims (an admiralty-only one with a non-admiralty one), convening a jury trial for the entire proceeding is not improper if the claims "arise out of one set of facts" and splitting them would prove "cumbersome, confusing, and time consuming."[167] When a counterclaim is asserted against an original claim that had invoked admiralty jurisdiction, the result is less certain: courts are divided on whether the plaintiff's admiralty election deprives the counterclaim of its right to a jury trial.[168] If the counterclaim's jury demand is honored, it is also possible that the effect of that ruling could force even the original admiralty claim into a jury trial.[169] Other

---

[161]*See Corley v. Long-Lewis, Inc.*, 965 F.3d 1222, 1235 (11th Cir. 2020); *Buccina v. Grimsby*, 889 F.3d 256, 261 (6th Cir. 2018).

[162]*See* Rule 38(e). *See also Caron v. NCL (Bahamas), Ltd.*, 910 F.3d 1359, 1366 (11th Cir. 2018); *Luera v. M/V Alberta*, 635 F.3d 181, 188 (5th Cir. 2011). *See generally Boston Ship Repair, LLC v. Starr Indem. & Liability Co.*, 997 F. Supp. 2d 118, 120 n.1 (D. Mass. 2014) (discussing historical context of nonjury procedure).

[163]*See Great Lakes Reinsurance (UK) SE v. Herzig*, 413 F. Supp. 3d 177, 186 (S.D.N.Y. 2019).

[164]*See Marquette Transp. Co. Gulf-Inland, LLC v. Navigation Mar. Bulgare*, 491 F. Supp. 3d 160, 172 (E.D. La. 2020).

[165]*See Fitzgerald v. U. S. Lines Co.*, 374 U.S. 16, 20, 83 S. Ct. 1646, 10 L. Ed. 2d 720 (1963).

[166]*See Apache Corp. v. Global SantaFe Drilling Co.*, 832 F. Supp. 2d 678, 698 (W.D. La. 2010); *Muhs v. River Rats, Inc.*, 586 F. Supp. 2d 1364, 1371 (S.D. Ga. 2008).

[167]*See Fitzgerald v. U. S. Lines Co.*, 374 U.S. 16, 20-21, 83 S. Ct. 1646, 10 L. Ed. 2d 720 (1963).

[168]*Compare St. Paul Fire & Marine Ins. Co. v. Lago Canyon, Inc.*, 561 F.3d 1181, 1186–89 (11th Cir. 2009) (counterclaim loses jury right) *and Great Lakes Ins. SE v. Andersson*, 525 F. Supp. 3d 205, 206–10 (D. Mass. 2021) (same), *with Wilmington Tr. v. U.S. Dist. Ct. for Dist. of Hawaii*, 934 F.2d 1026, 1029–32 (9th Cir. 1991) (counterclaim retains jury right, discussing saving-to-suitors clause: 28 U.S.C. § 1333(2)) *and In re Lockheed Martin Corp.*, 503 F.3d 351, 360 (4th Cir. 2007) (same).

[169]*See Wilmington Tr. v. U.S. Dist. Ct. for Dist. of Hawaii*, 934 F.2d 1026, 1029-32 (9th Cir. 1991) (if claims closely related factually, entire case

joinder contexts invite still more uncertainties.[170] It also seems that parties can, by agreement, consent to a jury trial that would not otherwise exist in an admiralty proceeding.[171] The lesson for practitioners is to robustly research local law on the particular jury context presented.

Type of Designation Required

The purpose of the designation requirement is to alert the court and fellow parties that the plaintiff intends to proceed under the admiralty rules.[172] To do so, the plaintiff must include an affirmative statement in the pleadings expressing the intent to have the lawsuit proceed as an admiralty or maritime case..[173] Obviously, merely announcing a Rule 9(h) election will not convert a non-admiralty claim into an admiralty claim,[174] though *failing* to make the designation will mean that the claim is not proceeding in admiralty (provided another basis for jurisdiction exists).[175] A plaintiff need not specifically cite to Rule 9(h), although that is certainly the preferred practice; instead, a simple statement invoking the right to proceed in admiralty or maritime is sufficient.[176] When the plaintiff's intent is unclear (*e.g.*, affirmatively asserting both admiralty and another basis for jurisdiction), courts examine the totality of circumstances to assess intent.[177] The inclusion (or absence) of a jury demand can prove a useful, though non-dispositive clue.[178] Some courts will honor the admiralty designation notwithstand-

---

may be tried before jury; if claims are not closely related, then separate trials may be ordered). *But cf. Great Lakes Ins. SE v. Andersson*, 525 F. Supp. 3d 205, 209 n.5 (D. Mass. 2021) ("silence" by First Circuit "cautions against" following this view).

[170]*See Marquette Transp. Co. Gulf-Inland, LLC v. Navigation Mar. Bulgare*, 491 F. Supp. 3d 160, 170-72 (E.D. La. 2020) (plaintiff's original jury demand honored, even after plaintiff invoked admiralty jurisdiction over its new third-party complaint in response to defendant's counterclaim).

[171]*See Buland v. NCL (Bahamas) Ltd*, 992 F.3d 1143, 1147 (11th Cir. 2021) (citing Rule 39(c)(2)).

[172]*See Buccina v. Grimsby*, 889 F.3d 256, 260–61 (6th Cir. 2018); *Greenwell v. Aztar Indiana Gaming Corp.*, 268 F.3d 486, 493 (7th Cir. 2001).

[173]*See Fedorczyk v. Caribbean Cruise Lines, Ltd.*, 82 F.3d 69, 73 (3d Cir. 1996).

[174]*See Moreno v. Ross Island Sand & Gravel Co.*, 2015 WL 5604443, at *16 (E.D. Cal. Sept. 23, 2015).

[175]*See DeRoy v. Carnival Corp.*, 963 F.3d 1302, 1312 (11th Cir. 2020).

[176]*See Poincon v. Offshore Marine Contractors, Inc.*, 9 F.4th 289, 294 (5th Cir. 2021) (explicit cite not required, if "simple statement" invokes admiralty jurisdiction); *Foulk v. Donjon Marine Co., Inc.*, 144 F.3d 252, 256 (3d Cir. 1998) (direct citation to Rule 9(h) is unambiguous and may be preferable, but is not required); *Concordia Co., Inc. v. Panek*, 115 F.3d 67, 72 (1st Cir. 1997) (preferred technique is to expressly invoke Rule 9(h), but phrase "In Admiralty", with no accompanying demand for jury trial, sufficient).

[177]*See Poincon v. Offshore Marine Contractors, Inc.*, 9 F.4th 289, 294–95 (5th Cir. 2021).

[178]*See Poincon v. Offshore Marine Contractors, Inc.*, 9 F.4th 289, 294–95 & n.3 (5th Cir. 2021); *Concordia Co., Inc. v. Panek*, 115 F.3d 67, 72 (1st Cir. 1997); *Vargas v. APL Ltd.*, — F. Supp. 3d —, 2022 WL 757082, at *6 (E.D.N.Y. 2022).

ing an ambiguity.[179]

Appellate Review

Interlocutory orders that determine the rights and liabilities of parties to an admiralty case enjoy a right of immediate appeal.[180]

Additional Research References

Wright & Miller, *Federal Practice and Procedure* §§ 1291 to 1320
C.J.S., Federal Civil Procedure §§ 252 to 257 et seq.
West's Key Number Digest, Federal Civil Procedure ⚷633 to 640

---

[179] *See Luera v. M/V Alberta*, 635 F.3d 181, 188–89 (5th Cir. 2011); *Travelers Prop. Cas. Co. of Am. v. Ocean Reef Charters LLC*, 324 F. Supp. 3d 366, 372–73 (W.D.N.Y. 2018). *But cf. Miles v. M/V HANSA CALEDONIA*, 245 F. Supp. 2d 1261, 1263 (S.D. Ga. 2002) (noting division among courts on question in jury context).

[180] *See* 28 U.S.C.A. § 1292(a)(3). *See generally Williamson v. Recovery Ltd. P'ship*, 731 F.3d 608, 617–20 (6th Cir. 2013) (outlining division among Circuits on scope of admiralty's interlocutory review).

RULE 10
FORM OF PLEADINGS

(a) Caption; Names of Parties. Every pleading must have a caption with the court's name, a title, a file number, and a Rule 7(a) designation. The title of the complaint must name all the parties; the title of other pleadings, after naming the first party on each side, may refer generally to other parties.

(b) Paragraphs; Separate Statements. A party must state its claims or defenses in numbered paragraphs, each limited as far as practicable to a single set of circumstances. A later pleading may refer by number to a paragraph in an earlier pleading. If doing so would promote clarity, each claim founded on a separate transaction or occurrence—and each defense other than a denial—must be stated in a separate count or defense.

(c) Adoption by Reference; Exhibits. A statement in a pleading may be adopted by reference elsewhere in the same pleading or in any other pleading or motion. A copy of a written instrument that is an exhibit to a pleading is a part of the pleading for all purposes.

[Amended April 30, 2007, effective December 1, 2007.]

AUTHORS' COMMENTARY ON RULE 10

PURPOSE AND SCOPE

Rule 10 establishes the form generally required for pleadings and motions. Pleadings and motions must contain a caption. Claims and defenses must be set forth in numbered paragraphs. When doing so would promote clarity, separate counts must be pleaded for each claim or defense premised on a separate transaction or occurrence. Earlier paragraphs may be adopted by reference to avoid repetition, and exhibits may be attached.

RULE 10(a)—CAPTION; NAMES OF PARTIES

CORE CONCEPT

Every pleading and motion must contain a caption.

APPLICATIONS

Contents of Caption

Captions must contain: (a) the name of the court; (b) the title of the action; (c) the file or docket number; and (d) the document's designation (*e.g.*, complaint, answer).

Party Names

The title of every lawsuit must list the names of the parties. In the complaint, the listing must be comprehensive: all parties must be included.[1] Persons and entities not listed there usually are not considered parties to that lawsuit.[2] But being listed does not necessarily confer "party" status for all purposes.[3]

- *Actual Names:* The actual, true names of the parties must be supplied. Descriptive titles (without names) may be appropriate, but only when they clearly identify the party.[4] "Alias" names are not permitted, and pleading with them can justify dismissal.[5]
- *After the Complaint:* In all pleadings (and motions) subsequent to the complaint, the caption can be short-

---

[1]*See Myles v. U.S.*, 416 F.3d 551, 551 (7th Cir. 2005) ("to make someone a party the plaintiff must specify him in the caption and arrange for service of process"). *Cf. Belanger v. BNY Mellon Asset Mgmt., LLC*, 307 F.R.D. 55, 58 n.4 (D.Mass. 2015) (information must appear in caption itself, not merely in attached exhibit).

[2]*See Abraugh v. Altimus*, 26 F.4th 298, 303 (5th Cir. 2022) (courts give captions "considerable weight" when assessing who plaintiffs are, since plaintiffs drafted them); *United States ex rel. Little v. Triumph Gear Sys., Inc.*, 870 F.3d 1242, 1249–50 (10th Cir. 2017) (lawsuit not considered "commenced" against unnamed persons); *Smith v. Eovaldi*, 112 F. Supp. 3d 779, 782 (S.D. Ill. 2015) (persons not listed in caption are not defendants). *But cf. Williams v. Bradshaw*, 459 F.3d 846, 849 (8th Cir. 2006) (caption entitled to "considerable weight," but not determinative as to who are parties to lawsuit).

[3]*See, e.g., Felders v. Bairett*, 885 F.3d 646, 653 (10th Cir. 2018) (no legal consequence until person/entity served with process); *Liberty Mut. Fire Ins. Co. v. EZ-FLO Int'l, Inc.*, 877 F.3d 1081, 1085 (9th Cir. 2017) (same).

[4]*See Mitchell v. Maynard*, 80 F.3d 1433, 1441 (10th Cir. 1996) (party not properly named in caption may still be deemed in case if complaint makes plain that party is intended defendant, although simply mentioning party's name in brief will not suffice). *Compare Abelesz v. Magyar Nemzeti Bank*, 692 F.3d 661, 661 (7th Cir. 2012) ("Holocaust Victims of Bank Theft" was insufficient identification of plaintiffs and improperly "presume[d]" merits of their claims), *and OTR Drivers at Topeka Frito-Lay, Inc.'s Distribution Center v. Frito-Lay, Inc.*, 988 F.2d 1059, 1061 (10th Cir. 1993) ("Over-The-Road Drivers" was insufficient identification of plaintiffs in lawsuit), *with Dean v. Barber*, 951 F.2d 1210, 1216 (11th Cir.1992) ("Chief Deputy of County Jail" was sufficient identification of defendant).

[5]*See Zocaras v. Castro*, 465 F.3d 479, 481–84 (11th Cir. 2006) ("A trial is not a masquerade party nor is it a game of judicial hide-n-seek where the plaintiff may offer the defendant the added challenge of uncovering his real name.").

ened to include only the names of the first plaintiff and first defendant, followed (where necessary) by an indication that others are parties to the case (*e.g.*, "et al.").[6]

- *Notices of Appeal:* All parties should be listed again in a notice of appeal. Omitting names (for example, with "et al.") may fail to perfect the appeal as to anyone whose intent to appeal is not objectively clear.[7]
- *Errors in Caption:* Captioning errors may be overlooked (or cured by an amendment) if the court determines they caused no prejudice and did not compromise the goal of adequate notice.[8]

Fictitious Name and Pseudonym Litigation

Parties have a limited entitlement to the redaction of certain "personal data identifiers."[9] Minors, for example, are permitted by right to litigate using only their initials, instead of their full names.[10] Parties may also seek protective orders to grant the redaction of additional personally identifying information when "good cause" exists.[11]

Beyond these redaction paths, pseudonym litigation is not otherwise expressly authorized.[12] However, in unusual, extraordinary circumstances, courts permit parties to identify themselves throughout the lawsuit by a fictitious name or pseudonym (*e.g.* "Jane Doe").[13] This practice is considered disfavored,[14] the exception (not the rule),[15] and is often denied even in cases involving issues of great intimacy and sensitivity.[16] Pseudonym

---

[6]*See Spivey v. Board of Church Extension and Home Mission of Church of God*, 160 F.R.D. 660, 662 (M.D. Fla. 1995) (requesting counsel to use short form captioning of case in all future court documents).

[7]*See* Fed.R.App.P. 3(c) (modifying *Torres v. Oakland Scavenger Co.*, 487 U.S. 312, 108 S. Ct. 2405, 101 L. Ed. 2d 285 (1988) (use of "et al." phrase did not constitute effective appeal as to parties not specifically named)).

[8]*See Kanuszewski v. Michigan Dep't of Health & Human Servs.*, 927 F.3d 396, 406 n.4 (6th Cir. 2019); *CNX Gas Co. v. Lloyd's of London*, 410 F. Supp. 3d 746, 752 (W.D. Pa. 2019).

[9]*See* Rule 5.2, and Authors' Commentary to Rule 5.2.

[10]*See* Rule 5.2(a)(3).

[11]*See* Rule 5.2(e).

[12]*See Lindsey v. Dayton-Hudson Corp.*, 592 F.2d 1118, 1125 (10th Cir. 1979) ("has no explicit sanction in the federal rules"). *See also* Rule 17(a)(1) (federal civil actions "must be prosecuted in the name of the real party in interest").

[13]*See B.R. v. F.C.S.B.*, 17 F.4th 485, 496 (4th Cir. 2021) ("extraordinary circumstances"); *Doe v. Public Citizen*, 749 F.3d 246, 273 (4th Cir. 2014) ("exceptional circumstances"; "rare dispensation"); *Doe v. Megless*, 654 F.3d 404, 408 (3d Cir. 2011) ("exceptional" circumstances). *See generally Richardson v. Johnson*, 598 F.3d 734, 738 (11th Cir. 2010) ("As a general matter, fictitious-party pleading is not permitted in federal court.").

[14]*See Doe v. Vill. of Deerfield*, 819 F.3d 372, 376–77 (7th Cir. 2016).

[15]*See United States v. Pilcher*, 950 F.3d 39, 45 (2d Cir. 2020).

[16]*See, e.g., Doe v. Skyline Automobiles Inc.*, 375 F. Supp. 3d 401, 404–05 (S.D.N.Y. 2019) (denying pseudonym status to alleged victim of sexual assault, harassment, and discrimination); *Doe v. Mckesson*, 322 F.R.D. 456, 457–58 (M.D. La. 2017)

litigation conflicts with the public's right to open access to the judiciary,[17] a concern of constitutional dimension,[18] and with the right of private litigants to confront their accusers.[19] Some courts have written that a presumption exists against such pseudonym pleading,[20] with others emphasizing that parties in civil cases, bringing lawsuits of their own volition to vindicate their own interests, must be prepared to stand publicly behind their allegations.[21] Nonetheless, pseudonym litigation is not categorically improper nor does it likely deprive a lawsuit of its constitutional case-or-controversy status to be heard in federal court.[22]

There are no "hard and fast" rules that courts apply in judging whether to permit pseudonym litigation.[23] Instead, courts balance the plaintiff's interest in anonymity against the public's interest in disclosure and the prejudice that may befall the defendant.[24] In performing this balance, courts have weighed various factors. Some courts have considered: (1) whether anonymity is genuinely based on a desire to preserve privacy in a sensitive, highly personal matter, or merely to avoid the annoy-

---

(denying pseudonym status to police officer who claimed fear of violent attack); *Doe H. v. Haskell Indian Nations Univ.*, 266 F. Supp. 3d 1277, 1287–90 (D. Kan. 2017) (denying pseudonym status to student suing university following sexual assault); *Rose v. Beaumont Indep. School Dist.*, 240 F.R.D. 264, 265–66 (E.D. Tex. 2007) (denying pseudonym status for young girl concerning involvement in school sex club); *Doe v. Bell Atlantic Business Systems Services, Inc.*, 162 F.R.D. 418, 422 (D. Mass. 1995) (denying pseudonym status to alleged victim of sexual harassment who claimed her traditional Chinese family would react negatively if the allegations became public). *See also Doe v. Cabrera*, 307 F.R.D. 1, 10 (D.D.C. 2014) (if case proceeds to trial, pseudonym must be replaced to avoid subliminal impression that court inferentially agrees with accusations).

[17]*See B.R. v. F.C.S.B.*, 17 F.4th 485, 496 (4th Cir. 2021); *United States v. Pilcher*, 950 F.3d 39, 42 (2d Cir. 2020); *Doe v. Vill. of Deerfield*, 819 F.3d 372, 376–77 (7th Cir. 2016). *See also Doe v. Frank*, 951 F.2d 320, 324 (11th Cir. 1992) ("[l]awsuits are public events").

[18]*See Rose v. Beaumont Indep. School Dist.*, 240 F.R.D. 264, 265–66 (E.D. Tex. 2007); *Doe v. Del Rio*, 241 F.R.D. 154, 156 (S.D. N.Y. 2006).

[19]*See Doe v. Megless*, 654 F.3d 404, 409 (3d Cir. 2011); *Plaintiff B v. Francis*, 631 F.3d 1310, 1315 (11th Cir. 2011).

[20]*See In re Sealed Case*, 931 F.3d 92, 96 (D.C. Cir. 2019); *Plaintiff B v. Francis*, 631 F.3d 1310, 1315 (11th Cir. 2011).

[21]*See Rose v. Beaumont Indep. School Dist.*, 240 F.R.D. 264, 267–68 (E.D. Tex. 2007); *Doe v. Bell Atlantic Business Systems Services, Inc.*, 162 F.R.D. 418, 422 (D. Mass. 1995).

[22]*See B.R. v. F.C.S.B.*, 17 F.4th 485, 490–97 (4th Cir. 2021). *But see National Commodity & Barter Ass'n v. Gibbs*, 886 F.2d 1240, 1245 (10th Cir. 1989) (ruling otherwise, followed by two unpublished circuit decisions: *Capers v. Nat'l R.R. Passenger Corp.*, 673 Fed. Appx. 591, 594–95 (8th Cir. 2016) (per curiam); *Citizens for a Strong Ohio v. Marsh*, 123 Fed. Appx. 630, 636–37 (6th Cir. 2005)).

[23]*See Freedom From Religion Found., Inc. v. Emanuel Cty. Sch. Sys.*, 109 F. Supp. 3d 1353, 1357 (S.D.Ga. 2015).

[24]*See B.R. v. F.C.S.B.*, 17 F.4th 485, 496 (4th Cir. 2021); *United States v. Pilcher*, 950 F.3d 39, 42 (2d Cir. 2020); *In re Sealed Case*, 931 F.3d 92, 96 (D.C. Cir. 2019).

ance, criticism, or embarrassment that the litigation might trigger; (2) whether loss of anonymity poses a risk of retaliatory physical or mental harm to the litigant or to non-parties; (3) the ages of those seeking anonymity; (4) whether their opponent is a governmental or a private party; and (5) the risk of unfairness to that opponent if anonymity were permitted.[25] Other courts have endorsed different criteria in addition to, or in place of, these factors.[26] But, in any event, most lists seem non-exhaustive in nature,[27] with trial judges discouraged from engaging mechanically in "a wooden exercise" of box-checking.[28] To proceed by pseudonym, the party will likely have to petition the court for permission.[29] Specific procedures for doing so vary among the Circuits.[30] Permission, if granted, may be accompanied by a requirement that the true names of the parties be disclosed to the defendants and the court, even if sealed to the general public.[31]

- *Immediate Interlocutory Appeal:* Several Circuits have recognized that the collateral order exception to the finality rule may allow an immediate appeal from an order denying pseudonym treatment.[32]

Temporary Fictitious Naming

At the outset of litigation, a party often may temporarily identify an opponent with a fictitious name so long as the identities of the opponents are clear and their actual names will be uncovered through discovery.[33]

---

[25]*See In re Sealed Case*, 931 F.3d 92, 97 (D.C. Cir. 2019); *Doe v. Pub. Citizen*, 749 F.3d 246, 273 (4th Cir. 2014). *See also Doe v. Garland*, 341 F.R.D. 116, 117–18 (S.D. Ga. 2021) (risk of embarrassment "is not enough").

[26]*See Doe v. Megless*, 654 F.3d 404, 408–12 (3d Cir. 2011) (discussing different approaches); *Sealed Plaintiff v. Sealed Defendant*, 537 F.3d 185, 188–90 (2d Cir. 2008) (listing 10 non-exhaustive factors). *See also Doe v. Kamehameha Schs./Bernice Pauahi Bishop Estate*, 596 F.3d 1036, 1042–46 (9th Cir. 2010) (weighing: severity of threatened harm; reasonableness of fears; vulnerability to retaliation; prejudice to opponent; public interest).

[27]*See, e.g., United States v. Pilcher*, 950 F.3d 39, 42 (2d Cir. 2020) ("non-exhaustive"); *Plaintiff B v. Francis*, 631 F.3d 1310, 1316 (11th Cir. 2011) (must carefully review all circumstances of case).

[28]*See In re Sealed Case*, 931 F.3d 92, 97 (D.C. Cir. 2019).

[29]*See United States ex rel. Little v. Triumph Gear Sys., Inc.*, 870 F.3d 1242, 1249–50 (10th Cir. 2017); *Doe v. City of Miami Gardens*, 389 F. Supp. 3d 1118, 1121 n.1 (S.D. Fla. 2019). *But cf. Doe v. UNUM Life Ins. Co. of Am.*, 164 F. Supp. 3d 1140, 1145 (N.D. Cal. 2016) (rejecting need for pre-filing permission, if permission later sought).

[30]*See Doe v. Megless*, 654 F.3d 404, 408–12 (3d Cir. 2011) (discussing different approaches); *E.E.O.C. v. ABM Industries Inc.*, 249 F.R.D. 588, 592 (E.D. Cal. 2008) (describing procedural variations).

[31]*See W.N.J. v. Yocom*, 257 F.3d 1171, 1172 (10th Cir. 2001).

[32]*See Doe v. Vill. of Deerfield*, 819 F.3d 372, 376 (7th Cir. 2016) (so ruling, and collecting cases).

[33]*See Dean v. Barber*, 951 F.2d 1210, 1216 (11th Cir.1992).

Alterations to the Caption

Beyond the shortening of party names in filings after the complaint,[34] other immaterial alterations to the caption, such as changes in capitalization, fonts, or typefaces, are generally not improper and will not require remedy by the court.[35]

Pro Se Pleadings

In reviewing *pro se* pleadings, courts may scavenge the documents with greater vigor to discern whether the identities of parties are clear from the text of the allegations (if not so in the captions),[36] but even in those instances, if the identities of the intended parties are not clear, the pleading is subject to dismissal.[37]

Same Form for Motions

Rule 10's prescriptions for captions and formatting apply as well to motions and other legal papers.[38]

RULE 10(b)—PARAGRAPHS; SEPARATE STATEMENTS

CORE CONCEPT

Pleadings must set out both claims and defenses in separate, numbered paragraphs, each of which, as far as practicable, should contain a single set of circumstances. Pleadings should contain separate counts for claims arising from different transactions or occurrences, if doing so adds clarity. Defenses (other than denials) should be set forth in separate counts as well.

APPLICATIONS

Paragraphing a Pleading's Allegations

As far as practicable, a party should set forth each distinct allegation of fact in a separate paragraph, and each paragraph should be numbered.[39] Later pleadings may refer back to an earlier pleading's allegations by their paragraph numbers. The purpose of this requirement is to ensure the pleading imparts fair notice and is easily understood by both the opponent and the court.[40]

---

[34] *See supra* Authors' Commentary to Rule 10(a) ("*After the Complaint*").

[35] *See Jaeger v. Dubuque County*, 880 F. Supp. 640, 643–44 (N.D. Iowa 1995) (no Rule 10 violation by capitalization of party names or other alterations of fonts, type faces, ink types, printer types, or printing methods).

[36] *See Shariff v. United States*, 689 Fed. Appx. 18, 19–20 (2d Cir. 2017).

[37] *See Trackwell v. U.S. Government*, 472 F.3d 1242, 1243–44 (10th Cir. 2007).

[38] *See* Rule 7(b)(2).

[39] *See Politico v. Promus Hotels, Inc.*, 184 F.R.D. 232, 234 (E.D. N.Y. 1999) (as far as possible, complaint should avoid multiple allegations per paragraph); *Bieros v. Nicola*, 851 F. Supp. 683, 687 (E.D. Pa. 1994) (each factual allegation should be pleaded in a separate paragraph).

[40] *See Cincinnati Life Ins. Co. v. Beyrer*, 722 F.3d 939, 946 (7th Cir. 2013); *City of Fort Lauderdale v. Scott*, 773 F. Supp. 2d 1355, 1358–59 (S.D.Fla. 2011). *See also O'Donnell v. Elgin, J. & E. Ry. Co.*, 338 U.S. 384, 392, 70 S. Ct. 200, 205, 94 L. Ed. 187 (1949)

"Group" Pleading

"Group" pleading allegations (*e.g.*, accusing the "defendants" generally of engaging in certain misconduct, without particularizing which defendant committed what act) are often inappropriate. Such "group" pleading techniques may defeat the clarity objectives of the separate-paragraph requirement by failing to specify what each party is alleged to have done wrong.[41] This is particularly true with claims that must be alleged with particularity.[42]

Pleading in Separate Counts

A party may include in a single count all theories of recovery, so long as those theories are all premised on the same facts.[43] The more common practice is to plead distinct claims and theories in separate counts[44] (a practice the Rule permits, but does not require).[45] In any event, where the claims and theories rest on different facts[46] or where clarity otherwise requires it,[47] distinct claims and theories must be pleaded in separate

---

(chastising that "unfortunately prolonged course" of trial was due, in part, to failure to separate issues in pleading, preparation, and thinking).

[41] *See Weiland v. Palm Beach Cty. Sheriff's Office*, 792 F.3d 1313, 1323 (11th Cir. 2015) (listing imprecise group allegations as last of four types of improper "shotgun" pleading). *Cf. In re GlenFed, Inc. Securities Litigation*, 60 F.3d 591, 592–93 (9th Cir. 1995) ("group" pleading might be appropriate if complaint alleged that outside directors either participated in day-to-day activities of business, or had special relationship with business, such as participating in preparing or communicating group information).

[42] *See supra* Authors' Commentary to Rule 9(b) ("**Group Pleading**").

[43] *See Motley v. Taylor*, 451 F. Supp. 3d 1251, 1264–65 (M.D. Ala. 2020), *aff'd*, 2022 WL 1506971 (11th Cir. May 12, 2022); *Smith v. Computer Task Group, Inc.*, 568 F. Supp. 2d 603, 612 n.6 (M.D. N.C. 2008).

[44] *See Stone Mountain Game Ranch, Inc. v. Hunt*, 746 F.2d 761, 763 n.1 (11th Cir. 1984) (faulting pleader for "inartfully" having "mixed" contract and tort concepts into a single count); *Anderson Living Trust v. WPX Energy Prod., LLC*, 312 F.R.D. 620, 658 (D.N.M. 2015) (common practice is "consistently . . . required" by federal courts). *But see Bartholet v. Reishauer A.G. (Zurich)*, 953 F.2d 1073, 1078 (7th Cir. 1992) (though common, practice is not required by Rules, which should instead be read as discouraging it).

[45] *See Zavala v. Kruse-W., Inc.*, 398 F. Supp. 3d 731, 739 (E.D. Cal. 2019); *Zurbriggen v. Twin Hill Acquisition Co.*, 338 F. Supp. 3d 875, 882 (N.D. Ill. 2018).

[46] *See Laber v. Long View R.V., Inc.*, 454 F. Supp. 3d 158, 171 (D. Conn. 2020); *Resolution Trust Corp. v. Hess*, 820 F. Supp. 1359, 1370–71 (D. Utah 1993). *See also In re Zantac (Ranitidine) Prod. Liab. Litig.*, 2021 WL 76433, at *13 (S.D. Fla. Jan. 8, 2021) (directing claimants to assert regulatory pre-approval and post-approval design defect claims in separate counts).

[47] *See Pelletier v. Zweifel*, 921 F.2d 1465, 1479 n.29 (11th Cir. 1991) (pendent State claim discounted where no separate court was pleaded); *Dodge v. Susquehanna University*, 796 F. Supp. 829, 831 (M.D. Pa. 1992) (because failure to separate into distinct counts gave defendant impression that no breach of contract claim was being pressed, belatedly asserted breach of contract theory was dismissed). *But cf. Manzanales v. Krishna*, 113 F. Supp. 3d 972, 981 (N.D. Ill. 2015) (separate counts not required when doing so

counts.[48] Separate counts help to ensure that the pleadings achieve their goals of framing the issues, providing a platform for informed pretrial proceedings and discovery management, and facilitating evidentiary admissibility decisions at trial.[49] The practice also enables a court to grant dispositive relief with respect to an entire count, and not just part of one.[50] Thus, the dictates of Rule 10 are not intended to be exceptions to the federal practice against technical forms of pleading, but instead provide the guidelines that help ensure that pleadings are "simple, concise, and direct."[51]

Violations and Remedy

Improper paragraph numbering or lack of conciseness will usually not defeat a pleading, unless the violations interfere with the ability to understand the claims or defenses or otherwise cause prejudice.[52] However, when a party's pleading provides insufficient notice of the claims because of its confusing structure, improper adoption of earlier allegations, failure to separate out counts, or group pleading,[53] the opposing party may move for a more definite statement,[54] to strike the pleading,[55] or for dismissal.[56] Dismissals should be ordered only where it is "virtually impossible" to connect an allegation with the claim it is intended to support.[57] All such motions should be made before counter-pleading. The typical, initial remedy is an

---

would not promote clarity).

[48]*See Bautista v. Los Angeles County*, 216 F.3d 837, 840–41 (9th Cir. 2000). *See generally Weiland v. Palm Beach Cty. Sheriff's Office*, 792 F.3d 1313, 1323 (11th Cir. 2015) (noting "sin of not separating into a different count each cause of action or claim for relief").

[49]*See Davis v. Coca-Cola Bottling Co. Consol.*, 516 F.3d 955, 980 n.57 (11th Cir. 2008); *Bautista v. Los Angeles County*, 216 F.3d 837, 840–41 (9th Cir. 2000).

[50]*See Kole v. Village of Norridge*, 941 F. Supp. 2d 933, 941–42 (N.D.Ill. 2013).

[51]*See Phillips v. Girdich*, 408 F.3d 124, 128 (2d Cir. 2005).

[52]*See Williamson v. Travelport, LP*, 953 F.3d 1278, 1299 (11th Cir. 2020); *Phillips v. Girdich*, 408 F.3d 124, 128 (2d Cir. 2005).

[53]*See Weiland v. Palm Beach Cty. Sheriff's Office*, 792 F.3d 1313, 1320–23 (11th Cir. 2015) (cataloging 4 types of improper "shotgun" pleading sins).

[54]*See U.S. ex rel. Estate of Cunningham v. Millennium Labs. of Cal., Inc.*, 713 F.3d 662, 664 n.2 (1st Cir. 2013).

[55]*See Stock v. Braswell*, 2017 WL 3279059, at *1 n.3 (E.D. Pa. Aug. 2, 2017); *Jackson v. New York State*, 381 F. Supp. 2d 80, 86 (N.D.N.Y. 2005).

[56]*See Jackson v. Bank of Am., N.A.*, 898 F.3d 1348, 1356–59 (11th Cir. 2018) (tolerating "shotgun pleadings" is "toleration of obstruction of justice"); *Cincinnati Life Ins. Co. v. Beyrer*, 722 F.3d 939, 947 (7th Cir. 2013) (dismissal appropriate where court is presented with "a bucket of mud"). *See also Rogler v. U.S. Dep't of Health & Human Servs.*, 620 F. Supp. 2d 123, 128 (D.D.C. 2009) (dismissing complaint as "too long, too convoluted, and too confusing to require" response).

[57]*See Weiland v. Palm Beach Cty. Sheriff's Office*, 792 F.3d 1313, 1325 (11th Cir. 2015); *Afogho as next friends of A.A. v. Illinois Cent. Sch. Dist. 104 Bd. of Educ.*, 421 F. Supp. 3d 585, 597 (S.D. Ill. 2019).

order to replead (or a dismissal with leave to amend).[58] Multiple repleadings may be refused when prior attempts at amendment fail to cure persisting deficiencies.[59]

RULE 10(c)—ADOPTION BY REFERENCE; EXHIBITS

CORE CONCEPT

A party may adopt by reference statements from the same pleading, or from a different pleading or motion filed in the same case. A party may also attach exhibits to a pleading, thereby making those part of the pleading for all purposes.

APPLICATIONS

Adopting Paragraphs by Reference

By specifically cross-referencing earlier paragraphs, a party may incorporate the allegations contained there without having to repeat them. But this practice must be used with care. Rotely adopting wholesale prior sections of a pleading, including portions not germane to the count being pleaded, violates this Rule.[60]

Adopting Documents or Pleadings by Reference

A party may adopt documents or pleadings by reference (in whole or in part) so long as the adopted document or pleading is expressly named. Generally, this practice is limited to documents and pleadings that are already before the court. Documents or pleadings filed in another lawsuit usually cannot be adopted by reference,[61] nor may parts of an abandoned pleading.[62]

Attaching Exhibits

A party may (but is not required to) attach to a pleading copies of "written instruments," such as contracts, notes, legal documents, and other writings on which a claim or defense is based.[63]

- *Unusual Attachments:* Exhibits that are especially lengthy or that contain evidentiary matter (such as deposition transcripts) may not qualify for attachment.[64] Similarly, newspaper articles, commentaries, and car-

---

[58] *See, e.g., Vibe Micro, Inc. v. Shabanets*, 878 F.3d 1291, 1295–96 (11th Cir. 2018); *Phillips v. Girdich*, 408 F.3d 124, 128 (2d Cir. 2005).

[59] *See Lee v. Ne. Illinois Reg'l Commuter R.R. Corp.*, 912 F.3d 1049, 1053 (7th Cir. 2019).

[60] *See Weiland v. Palm Beach Cty. Sheriff's Office*, 792 F.3d 1313, 1320–23 (11th Cir. 2015) (listing such adoptions as among list of improper "shotgun" pleadings).

[61] *See Constellation Energy Commodities Group Inc. v. Transfield ER Cape Ltd.*, 801 F. Supp. 2d 211, 223 (S.D.N.Y. 2011).

[62] *See Galloway v. City of Abbeville*, 871 F. Supp. 2d 1298, 1304–05 (M.D.Ala. 2012).

[63] *See Lynch v. City of New York*, 952 F.3d 67, 79 (2d Cir. 2020); *Banneker Ventures, LLC v. Graham*, 798 F.3d 1119, 1133 (D.C. Cir. 2015).

[64] *See Rose v. Bartle*, 871 F.2d 331, 340 n.3 (3d Cir. 1989).

toons,[65] cryptic memo notes,[66] photographs and x-rays,[67] investigative reports,[68] expert reports,[69] affidavits,[70] and copies of superseded pleadings[71] may also not qualify. However, emails,[72] text messages,[73] video recordings,[74] briefs,[75] and judicial rulings[76] may be proper.

- *Attachments by Opponent:* If the pleader does *not* attach, but instead merely refers to, a written instrument in the pleading, the opponent may usually then attach that instrument to its responsive pleading, so long as the instrument is indisputably authentic and "central" to the original pleader's claim.[77] The same result may follow where the unattached exhibit is not referenced by the original pleader, but is unquestionably integral to the dispute.[78]

Effect of Attaching Exhibits

Exhibits attached to a pleading are made a part of that

---

[65]*See Perkins v. Silverstein*, 939 F.2d 463, 467 (7th Cir. 1991); *Boykin v. Gray*, 895 F. Supp. 2d 199, 205 n.5 (D.D.C. 2012). *But cf. Geinosky v. City of Chicago*, 675 F.3d 743, 745 & n.1 (7th Cir. 2012) (permitting party opposing a dismissal motion to "elaborate on his factual allegations", which may include, in a proper case, referencing a newspaper story).

[66]*See Lynch v. City of New York*, 952 F.3d 67, 79 (2d Cir. 2020).

[67]*See Nkemakolam v. St. John's Military Sch.*, 876 F. Supp. 2d 1240, 1246–47 (D.Kan. 2012) (stricken because they were not included to be assertions of fact). *But see Spoon v. Bayou Bridge Pipeline, LLC*, 335 F.R.D. 468, 471 (M.D. La. 2020) (not stricken because Rule 10(c) is to be interpreted expansively).

[68]*See Dichter-Mad Family Partners, LLP v. U.S.*, 707 F. Supp. 2d 1016, 1019 (C.D.Cal. 2010) (factual allegations and decisions in report by SEC inspector general not properly incorporated). *But see Sewell v. Monroe City Sch. Bd.*, 974 F.3d 577, 582 (5th Cir. 2020) (board of education report attached to complaint deemed incorporated into pleading); *Stewart v. City of Chicago*, 513 Fed.Appx. 619, 619–20 (7th Cir. 2013) (same, police report).

[69]*See Irizarry v. Abbott Lab'ys*, 833 Fed. Appx. 947, 950 (3d Cir. 2020).

[70]*See generally Smith v. Hogan*, 794 F.3d 249, 254 (2d Cir. 2015) (describing division among courts regarding affidavits); *Occupy Columbia v. Haley*, 738 F.3d 107, 116–17 (4th Cir. 2013) (same).

[71]*See Hinton v. Trans Union, LLC*, 654 F. Supp. 2d 440, 446–48 (E.D.Va. 2009) (rejecting attempt by amended complaint to incorporate original complaint), *aff'd*, 382 Fed. Appx. 256 (4th Cir. 2010).

[72]*See Krakow Bus. Park v. Locke Lord, LLP*, 135 F. Supp. 3d 770, 775 (N.D. Ill. 2015).

[73]*See Brach v. Conflict Kinetics Corp.*, 221 F. Supp. 3d 743, 745 n.1 (E.D. Va. 2016).

[74]*See Howell by Goerdt v. Tribune Entertainment Co.*, 106 F.3d 215, 218–19 (7th Cir. 1997) (treating videotape as "appended"). *See generally Gersbacher v. City of New York*, 134 F. Supp. 3d 711, 720 (S.D.N.Y. 2015) (surveying national treatment of video recordings).

[75]*See Dye v. Hofbauer*, 546 U.S. 1, 4, 126 S. Ct. 5, 163 L. Ed. 2d 1 (2005).

[76]*See Ross v. Williams*, 950 F.3d 1160, 1168-69 (9th Cir. 2020).

[77]*See Goines v. Valley Cmty. Servs. Bd.*, 822 F.3d 159, 166 (4th Cir. 2016); *U.S. v. Ritchie*, 342 F.3d 903, 908 (9th Cir. 2003).

[78]*See Goines v. Valley Cmty. Servs. Bd.*, 822 F.3d 159, 166 (4th Cir. 2016); *L-7 Designs, Inc. v. Old Navy, LLC*, 647 F.3d 419, 422 (2d Cir. 2011).

pleading for all purposes.[79]

- *Ruling on Motions to Dismiss:* The court may consider a pleading's attachments in ruling on dismissal motions[80] and motions for judgment on the pleadings,[81] and if an inconsistency exists between the attachment and the pleaded allegations, the attachment will usually control[82] (unless the pleaded allegations are specific, well-pleaded, and contradict statements in the exhibit that are merely conclusory).[83] Similarly, where an attachment reveals a "built-in" defense that bars recovery as a matter of law, the court may grant a dismissal.[84]
- *"Plausibility" and Particularity:* The court may consult attachments in evaluating whether an allegation is "plausible" (Rule 8)[85] and, if fraud or mistake, "stated with particularity" (Rule 9(b)).[86]
- *"Vouching" Risk:* By adopting by reference a portion of an attached document, the pleader does not necessarily "vouch" for the truth of all the contents of the document. The attached document will be read in conjunction with the pleading that adopts it.[87] Thus, a defamation plaintiff may safely attach an allegedly libelous writing without being deemed to have admitted as true all the asserted libels contained in the writing, just as a commercial plaintiff, alleging the non-receipt of goods, may attach an allegedly forged receipt without admitting that the document truthfully recounts that the goods were received.[88] An aggrieved litigant can attach a copy of an appealed-from ruling without being deemed to have

---

[79]*See Quadvest, L.P. v. San Jacinto River Auth.*, 7 F.4th 337, 345 (5th Cir. 2021); *Kiesling v. Holladay*, 859 F.3d 529, 533 (8th Cir. 2017).

[80]*See Tellabs, Inc. v. Makor Issues & Rights, Ltd.*, 551 U.S. 308, 322, 127 S. Ct. 2499, 168 L. Ed. 2d 179 (2007); *Matthew N. Fulton, D.D.S., P.C. v. Enclarity, Inc.*, 962 F.3d 882, 890 (6th Cir. 2020).

[81]*See Moderwell v. Cuyahoga Cty.*, 997 F.3d 653, 657 n.2 (6th Cir. 2021); *Z View Enters., LLC v. Giant Eagle, Inc.*, 834 Fed. Appx. 709, 712 (3d Cir. 2020).

[82]*See Quadvest, L.P. v. San Jacinto River Auth.*, 7 F.4th 337, 345 (5th Cir. 2021); *Comparelli v. Republica Bolivariana De Venezuela*, 891 F.3d 1311, 1316 n.1 (11th Cir. 2018); *Williamson v. Curran*, 714 F.3d 432, 435–36 (7th Cir. 2013).

[83]*See Gill as Next Friend of K.C.R. v. Judd*, 941 F.3d 504, 514–15 (11th Cir. 2019) ("The rule is specific over speculative, concrete over conclusory.").

[84]*See Gill as Next Friend of K.C.R. v. Judd*, 941 F.3d 504, 511–12 (11th Cir. 2019).

[85]*See PHL Variable Ins. Co. v. Town of Oyster Bay*, 929 F.3d 79, 89 (2d Cir. 2019); *Hillesheim v. Myron's Cards & Gifts, Inc.*, 897 F.3d 953, 957 (8th Cir. 2018).

[86]*See Abels v. Farmers Commodities Corp.*, 259 F.3d 910, 921 (8th Cir. 2001); *Adams Respiratory Therapeutics, Inc. v. Perrigo Co.*, 255 F.R.D. 443, 446 (W.D. Mich. 2009).

[87]*See Otis v. Demarasse*, 886 F.3d 639, 646–47 (7th Cir. 2018).

[88]*See Banneker Ventures, LLC v. Graham*, 798 F.3d 1119, 1133–34 (D.C. Cir. 2015); *Guzell v. Hiller*, 223 F.3d 518, 519 (7th Cir. 2000) (giving ex-

thereby "vouched" for the very reasoning or result that litigant is challenging.[89]

Adopting by Reference in Motions

Portions of pleadings may be adopted by reference in a motion, but nothing in the Rule expressly permits the adoption of motions (or portions of motions) into another motion.[90]

Additional Research References

Wright & Miller, *Federal Practice and Procedure* §§ 1321 to 1330
C.J.S., Federal Civil Procedure § 251
West's Key Number Digest, Federal Civil Procedure ⚷625 to 629

---

amples). *See also Jones v. City of Cincinnati*, 521 F.3d 555, 561 (6th Cir. 2008) (attaching interview transcript may vouch that statements were made, but not that they were true); *Pinder v. Knorowski*, 660 F. Supp. 2d 726, 736 (E.D.Va. 2009) (same).

[89]In fact, one Court of Appeals harshly derided this sort of "vouching" argument as "beyond nonsensical" and "unworthy" of the attorneys who asserted it. *See Carroll v. Yates*, 362 F.3d 984, 986 (7th Cir. 2004) ("The logic of the . . . argument is that an appellant, required by the appellate rules to append to his brief the decision of the district court or administrative agency that he is appealing, . . . by doing so kills the appeal because appending amounts to vouching for the truth of the propositions in the appended decision. The argument if accepted would do wonders for our workload, but is beyond nonsensical and unworthy of the office of the Attorney General of Illinois."). The Court, then, directed the filing attorneys to show cause why they should not be sanctioned for briefing "frivolous argumentation". *Id.*

[90]*See Wilson v. Pauling*, 457 F. Supp. 3d 978, n.2 (D. Colo. 2020); *D'Agnese v. Novartis Pharms. Corp.*, 952 F. Supp. 2d 880, 885 (D.Ariz. 2013).

RULE 11
SIGNING PLEADINGS, MOTIONS, AND OTHER PAPERS; REPRESENTATIONS TO THE COURT; SANCTIONS

(a) Signature. Every pleading, written motion, and other paper must be signed by at least one attorney of record in the attorney's name—or by a party personally if the party is unrepresented. The paper must state the signer's address, e-mail address, and telephone number. Unless a rule or statute specifically states otherwise, a pleading need not be verified or accompanied by an affidavit. The court must strike an unsigned paper unless the omission is promptly corrected after being called to the attorney's or party's attention.

(b) Representations to the Court. By presenting to the court a pleading, written motion, or other paper—whether by signing, filing, submitting, or later advocating it—an attorney or unrepresented party certifies that to the best of the person's knowledge, information, and belief, formed after an inquiry reasonable under the circumstances:

(1) it is not being presented for any improper purpose, such as to harass, cause unnecessary delay, or needlessly increase the cost of litigation;

(2) the claims, defenses, and other legal contentions are warranted by existing law or by a nonfrivolous argument for extending, modifying, or reversing existing law or for establishing new law;

(3) the factual contentions have evidentiary support or, if specifically so identified, will likely have evidentiary support after a reasonable opportunity for further investigation or discovery; and

(4) the denials of factual contentions are warranted on the evidence or, if specifically so identified, are reasonably based on belief or a lack of

information.

(c) Sanctions.

(1) *In General.* If, after notice and a reasonable opportunity to respond, the court determines that Rule 11(b) has been violated, the court may impose an appropriate sanction on any attorney, law firm, or party that violated the rule or is responsible for the violation. Absent exceptional circumstances, a law firm must be held jointly responsible for a violation committed by its partner, associate, or employee.

(2) *Motion for Sanctions.* A motion for sanctions must be made separately from any other motion and must describe the specific conduct that allegedly violates Rule 11(b). The motion must be served under Rule 5, but it must not be filed or be presented to the court if the challenged paper, claim, defense, contention, or denial is withdrawn or appropriately corrected within 21 days after service or within another time the court sets. If warranted, the court may award to the prevailing party the reasonable expenses, including attorney's fees, incurred for the motion.

(3) *On the Court's Initiative.* On its own, the court may order an attorney, law firm, or party to show cause why conduct specifically described in the order has not violated Rule 11(b).

(4) *Nature of a Sanction.* A sanction imposed under this rule must be limited to what suffices to deter repetition of the conduct or comparable conduct by others similarly situated. The sanction may include nonmonetary directives; an order to pay a penalty into court; or, if imposed on motion and warranted for effective deterrence, an order directing payment to the movant of part or all of the reasonable attorney's fees and other expenses directly resulting from the violation.

(5) *Limitations on Monetary Sanctions.* The court must not impose a monetary sanction:

(A) against a represented party for violating Rule 11(b)(2); or

(B) on its own, unless it issued the show-cause order under Rule 11(c)(3) before voluntary dismissal or settlement of the claims made by or against the party that is, or whose attorneys are, to be sanctioned.

(6) *Requirements for an Order.* An order imposing a sanction must describe the sanctioned conduct and explain the basis for the sanction.

(d) Inapplicability to Discovery. This rule does not apply to disclosures and discovery requests, responses, objections, and motions under Rules 26 through 37.

[Amended April 28, 1983, effective August 1, 1983; March 2, 1987, effective August 1, 1987; April 22, 1993, effective December 1, 1993; April 30, 2007, effective December 1, 2007.]

AUTHORS' COMMENTARY ON RULE 11

PURPOSE AND SCOPE

Rule 11 establishes the standards attorneys and parties must meet when filing pleadings, motions, or other documents in court. It directs that every pleading, written motion, and other paper submitted during litigation be signed by an attorney of record or the party personally (if unrepresented). The act of presenting such a paper to the court (by signing it, filing it, submitting it, or advocating it) carries with it a certification that, to the best of the presenter's knowledge, information, and belief, as formed after reasonable inquiry, the paper is supportable in law and in fact and is not presented for an improper purpose. Violations of this certification can give rise to sanctions.

RULE 11(a)—SIGNATURE

CORE CONCEPT

Rule 11(a) requires that all federal pleadings, written motions, and other papers be signed by an attorney or, if the litigant is not represented by counsel, by the litigant. An unsigned filing "must" be stricken by the court unless that omission is corrected promptly. The signer's ethical obligations are triggered by this act of signing.

APPLICATIONS

Purpose and Reach of Rule 11

The purposes of Rule 11 are to deter baseless filings and

other attorney and litigant misconduct[1] and to "streamline the administration and procedure of the federal courts."[2] By its terms, Rule 11 applies to every pleading, written motion, or other paper filed or served in the course of litigation,[3] as well as to advocacy of documents previously filed.[4] It does not apply to misconduct unrelated to signed documents[5] or to documents filed in state court.[6] Sanctions for violating Rule 11 are intended to facilitate case management, not to increase the judiciary's caseload by requiring a district court to analyze the reasonableness of legal and factual contentions that it would otherwise not have to ascertain.[7]

Signature of Attorney

If a party has retained counsel, at least one attorney must sign the document and provide the attorney's mailing address, e-mail address and telephone number.[8] Rule 11 requires that an individual attorney must sign the document. A signature that purports to be on behalf of an entire law firm does not satisfy the signature requirement of Rule 11.[9] Use of an attorney's e-filing login and password to electronically file a document constitutes the signature of that attorney on that document for purposes of Rule 11.[10]

Signature of Party

A party must sign the document if the party is not represented by counsel.[11] The party must also provide an address and telephone number, if any. Although courts may be more lenient with pro se litigants, they are not immune from Rule

[1]*See, e.g., Vallejo v. Amgen, Inc.*, 903 F.3d 733, 748–49 (8th Cir. 2018).

[2]*Cooter & Gell v. Hartmarx Corp.*, 496 U.S. 384, 393 (1990).

[3]*See, e.g., Antonious v. Spalding & Evenflo Companies, Inc.*, 281 F.3d 1258, 1261 (Fed. Cir. 2002).

[4]*See, e.g., Tejero v. Portfolio Recovery Associates, L.L.C.*, 955 F.3d 453, 460 (5th Cir. 2020) (letter is not a filing or other paper subject to Rule 11 but could be if incorporated into a pleading); *O'Brien v. Alexander*, 101 F.3d 1479, 1489 (2d Cir. 1996) (oral advocacy flowing directly from documents filed with court fall within scope of Rule 11; other oral statements are not controlled by Rule 11).

[5]*See, e.g., Ali v. Tolbert*, 636 F.3d 622, 626-27 (D.C. Cir. 2011); *Lamboy-Ortiz v. Ortiz-Velez*, 630 F.3d 228, 245 (1st Cir. 2010).

[6]*See, e.g., Bisciglia v. Kenosha Unified School Dist. No. 1*, 45 F.3d 223, 226–27 (7th Cir. 1995). *See also Edwards v. General Motors Corp.*, 153 F.3d 242, 245 (5th Cir. 1998) (Rule 11 inapplicable to filing made in state court before case was removed to federal court; sanctions may be imposed on post-removal filings).

[7]*CQ Intern. Co., Inc. v. Rochem Intern., Inc., USA*, 659 F.3d 53, 62 (1st Cir. 2011).

[8]*See, e.g., In re Lothian Oil Inc.*, 650 F.3d 539, 544 (5th Cir. 2011); *Duran v. Carris*, 238 F.3d 1268, 1271 (10th Cir. 2001) (failure to disclose that brief submitted by allegedly pro se party was actually ghostwritten by attorney is violation of Rule 11(a)).

[9]*Pavelic & LeFlore v. Marvel Entertainment Group*, 493 U.S. 120 (1989).

[10]*Barcomb v. Gen. Motors LLC*, 978 F.3d 545, 550–51 (8th Cir. 2020).

[11]*Maxwell v. Snow*, 409 F.3d 354, 356 (D.C. Cir. 2005).

11 sanctions.[12] Some courts have interpreted Rule 11 to prohibit a represented party from acting on his own behalf unless the district court first enters an order of substitution.[13]

Verification and Affidavits

Rule 11 arguably abolishes requirements of verification and affidavits for documents filed or served in the course of litigation, except where such a requirement is expressly preserved by another rule or statute.[14]

Rule 11(a) supersedes verification or affidavit requirements imposed by state law.[15] Occasionally, however, a federal rule or statute may require verification. For example, Rule 33 requires that interrogatory responses be verified and Rule 23.1, governing derivative actions by shareholders, requires verification of a plaintiff-shareholder's complaint.

Failure to Sign

Except as permitted by the e-filing protocols, the Rule does not permit typed signatures.[16] If a document subject to Rule 11 is not signed, the court has power to strike the document unless the proponent signs it promptly upon notification of the missing signature.[17] A prompt correction of the failure to sign an original complaint, filed within the statute of limitations, allows the complaint to remain timely, even if the signature is submitted after the limitations period expired.[18]

Applies Even After Subject-Matter Jurisdiction Dismissal

Rule 11 applies even in cases where it is subsequently determined that the district court lacked subject-matter jurisdiction.[19]

Applies Even After Rule 41 Voluntary Dismissal

A district court retains jurisdiction to impose Rule 11 sanctions even after a case has been voluntarily dismissed without prejudice under Rule 41.[20]

---

[12] *Maxwell v. Snow*, 409 F.3d 354, 356 (D.C. Cir. 2005); *Warren v. Guelker*, 29 F.3d 1386, 1390 (9th Cir. 1994).

[13] *Ruiz v. Wing*, 991 F.3d 1130, 1144 (11th Cir. 2021).

[14] *See, e.g., Cobell v. Norton*, 391 F.3d 251 (D.C. Cir. 2004) (subject to exceptions, Rule 11 eliminates the need for verification).

[15] *Pledger v. Lynch*, 5 F.4th 511, 520 (4th Cir. 2021).

[16] *Becker v. Montgomery*, 532 U.S. 757, 764 (2001).

[17] *See, e.g., Marcure v. Lynn*, 992 F.3d 625, 630 (7th Cir. 2021) (Rule is not discretionary; an unsigned motion must be stricken unless it is signed promptly after the omission is called to the party's attention).

[18] *McGraw v. Gore*, 31 F.4th 844, 853 (4th Cir. 2022).

[19] *Willy v. Coastal Corp.*, 503 U.S. 131, 137–38 (1992); *Hyde v. Irish*, 962 F.3d 1306 (11th Cir. 2020).

[20] *See, e.g., Cooter & Gell v. Hartmarx Corp.*, 496 U.S. 384, 396–97 (1990); *Adams v. USAA Casualty Insurance Company*, 863 F.3d 1069, 1077, 1079–80 (8th Cir. 2017).

Rule 11 and Appellate Courts

In general, Rule 11 is applicable only district courts.[21] Federal Rule of Appellate Procedure 38 usually controls sanctions for groundless filings in the federal courts of appeals.[22] Rule 11 does apply to the notice of appeal, which is filed in district court and then commences the appeal.[23]

Inapplicable in Administrative Litigation

Normally Rule 11 is not applicable in proceedings before administrative agencies. Application of Rule 11 occurs in such cases only when the case becomes a lawsuit in a federal court.[24]

No Rule 11 "Actions" Against Own Attorney

Rule 11 does not authorize actions in favor of a party against the party's attorney.[25]

RULE 11(b)—REPRESENTATIONS TO COURT

CORE CONCEPT

The act of "presenting" to the court any pleading, written motion, or other paper (which includes signing it, filing it, submitting it, or later advocating it) triggers a series of "certifications" that the presenter is deemed to be making to the judge: namely, that the presentation has a proper purpose, that it has proper legal support and factual support, and that any denials are factually justified.

APPLICATIONS

Starting Point—The Continuing Obligation to Make a Reasonable Inquiry

All persons who sign, file, submit, or later advocate documents are deemed to be certifying to the court that the document or advocacy is: (a) based upon the person's best knowledge, information, or belief; which is in turn (b) based upon an inquiry that was reasonable under the circumstances of the particular case.[26]

The Rule 11 certification applies throughout the pendency of the litigation,[27] and an attorney operates under a "continuous

[21] *See Fengling Liu*, 664 F.3d 367, 373 n.5 (2d Cir. 2011) and Fed. R. Civ. P. 1.

[22] *See, e.g., CFE Group, LLC v. Firstmerit Bank, N.A.*, 809 F.3d 346 (7th Cir. 2015).

[23] *Becker v. Montgomery*, 532 U.S. 757, 764 (2001).

[24] *See, e.g., Santa Maria v. Pacific Bell*, 202 F.3d 1170, 1179 (9th Cir. 2000).

[25] *See, e.g., Mark Industries, Ltd. v. Sea Captain's Choice, Inc.*, 50 F.3d 730, 732 (9th Cir. 1995).

[26] *See, e.g., Collins v. Daniels*, 916 F.3d 1302 (10th Cir. 2019); *City of Livonia Employees' Retirement System and Local 295/Local 851 v. Boeing Co.*, 711 F.3d 754, 762 (7th Cir. 2013).

[27] *See, e,g., McGreal v. Village of Orland Park*, 928 F.3d 556 (7th Cir. 2019).

obligation to make inquiries."[28] While an attorney may rely on information provided by a client, such information must be the product of a reasonable inquiry.[29] The duty of reasonable inquiry applies to both unrepresented parties as well as represented parties and their attorneys, and establishes an objective standard of reasonable under the circumstances.[30] The duty to inquire is not minimized merely because the attorney files hundreds of claims simultaneously.[31] The unwillingness of a party's opponent to cooperate in a pre-litigation examination of facts might not rescue a party's failure to undertake a reasonable inquiry.[32] Moreover, a failure to inform the court of relevant facts can justify Rule 11 sanctions; the Rule does not apply only to affirmative representations.[33]

Representation #1—No Improper Purpose

By presenting a document or arguing on its behalf, the proponent certifies that the presentation has no improper purpose, such as harassment or undue delay or expense. This language is intended to regulate bad faith filings.[34] How this improper purpose standard is applied may depend on whether the accused is an attorney or party,[35] and whether the possibility of sanctions is instigated by a party or *sua sponte* by the court.[36] An improper purpose is tested by objective standards.[37]

The prevailing standard has been framed in different ways: whether the attorney was careful and honest in court filings and representations;[38] whether the legal position at issue had "no chance of success" or was supported by "no reasonable argu-

---

[28] *Gulisano v. Burlington, Inc.*, 34 F.4th 935 (11th Cir. 2022); *Battles v. City of Ft. Myers*, 127 F.3d 1298, 1300 (11th Cir. 1997).

[29] *In re Taylor*, 655 F.3d 274, 284 (3d Cir. 2011).

[30] *Business Guides, Inc. v. Chromatic Communications Enterprises, Inc.*, 498 U.S. 533, 551–54 (1991).

[31] *In re Engle Cases*, 767 F.3d 1082, 1115–16 (11th Cir. 2014).

[32] *Compare View Engineering, Inc. v. Robotic Vision Systems, Inc.*, 208 F.3d 981, 986 (Fed. Cir. 2000) (an opponent "is not required to allow pre-litigation discovery" and lack of such an opportunity is not a defense to sanctions for failure to make reasonable inquiry), *with Amgen Inc. v. Hospira, Inc.*, 866 F.3d 1355, 1362 (Fed. Cir. 2017) (reasonable inquiry met where claimants sought information from opponent prior to litigation, but were rejected).

[33] *See, e.g., Bell v. Vacuforce, LLC*, 908 F.3d 1075 (7th Cir. 2018).

[34] *See, e.g., Cuna Mut. Ins. Soc. v. Office and Professional Employees Intern. Union, Local 39*, 443 F.3d 556, 561 (7th Cir. 2006); *American Intern. Adjustment Co. v. Galvin*, 86 F.3d 1455 (7th Cir. 1996).

[35] *In re Nosek*, 609 F.3d 6, 9 (1st Cir. 2010).

[36] *See, e.g.*, *Adams v. USAA Casualty Insurance Company*, 863 F.3d 1069, 1077 (8th Cir. 2017); *ATSI Communications, Inc. v. Shaar Fund, Ltd.*, 579 F.3d 143, 150–152 (2d Cir. 2009).

[37] *R.P. v. Prescott Unified Sch. Dist.*, 631 F.3d 1117, 1124–25 (9th Cir. 2011).

[38] *See, e.g., Young v. Smith*, 905 F.3d 229 (3d Cir. 2018).

ment";[39] whether the pleading or contention was culpably careless;[40] whether a reasonable attorney in similar circumstances would not have believed his or her actions legally justified;[41] whether the arguments were unequivocally frivolous or show objective unreasonableness;[42] whether the actions "compromise standards of professional integrity and competence";[43] and whether the actions are "akin to contempt"[44] or lie somewhere between "gross negligence" and "outright fraud."[45] A claim is considered frivolous for Rule 11 purposes when it is not well-grounded in fact or not warranted either by existing law or a good faith argument for extending, modifying or reversing existing law.[46]

The filing of contradictory pleadings is not a necessarily a violation of Rule 11 unless the court also finds bad faith was involved,[47] and isolated overstatements do not generally rise to the level of sanctionable litigation misconduct under Rule 11.[48] Rule 11 liability, however, may be found where an attorney files frivolous pleadings despite warning from the court,[49] files multiple identical claims rather than one suit against multiple parties,[50] repackages a prior unsuccessful lawsuit under a different cause of action,[51] or files a motion for attorney's fees claiming to be the prevailing party after settlement of a case.[52]

A writing filed for any improper purpose may be sanctionable even if it is supported by the facts and the law[53] (and even if the court discounts bad motive as irrelevant in determining whether a violation has occurred, motive could still be germane

---

[39]*See Petrella v. Metro-Goldwyn-Mayer, Inc.*, 695 F.3d 946, 957 (9th Cir. 2012).

[40]*Roger Edwards, LLC v. Fiddes & Son Ltd.*, 437 F.3d 140, 142 (1st Cir. 2006) ("To support a finding of frivolousness, some decree of fault is required, but the fault need not be a wicked or subjectively reckless state of mind; rather an individual 'must, at the very least, be culpably careless to commit a violation,' ").

[41]*See, e.g., Vallejo v. Amgen, Inc.*, 903 F.3d 733 (8th Cir. 2018); *Burns v. George Basilikas Trust*, 599 F.3d 673, 677 (D.C. Cir. 2010).

[42]*See, e.g., Woods v. DeAngelo Marine Exhaust, Inc.*, 692 F.3d 1272, 1288 (Fed. Cir. 2012).

[43]*See In re Crescent City Ests., LLC*, 588 F.3d 822, 831 (4th Cir. 2009).

[44]*See Lucas v. Duncan*, 574 F.3d 772, 775 (D.C. Cir. 2009).

[45]*See, e.g., Young v. Smith*, 905 F.3d 229 (3d Cir. 2018).

[46]*In re Ames*, 993 F.3d 27, 34 (1st Cir. 2021).

[47]*Hourani v. Mirtchev*, 796 F.3d 1, 17 (D.C. Cir. 2015); *PAE Government Services, Inc. v. MPRI, Inc.*, 514 F.3d 856, 859-60 (9th Cir. 2007).

[48]*See, e.g., Gaymar Industries, Inc. v. Cincinnati Sub-Zero Products, Inc.*, 790 F.3d 1369 (Fed. Cir. 2015) (collecting cases).

[49]*Royce v. Michael R. Needle P.C.*, 950 F.3d 939, 958 (7th Cir. 2020).

[50]*See, e.g., Havensight Capital LLC v. Nike, Inc.*, 891 F.3d 1167, 1174 (9th Cir. 2018); *De Dios v. International Realty & Investments*, 641 F.3d 1071, 1076 (9th Cir. 2011).

[51]*Meyer v. U.S. Bank Nat. Ass'n*, 792 F.3d 923 (8th Cir. 2015).

[52]*See, e.g., Bell v. Vacuforce, LLC*, 908 F.3d 1075 (7th Cir. 2018).

[53]*See Whitehead v. Food Max of Mississippi, Inc.*, 332 F.3d 796 (5th Cir. 2003).

to the issue of sanctions if a violation is found).[54]

Note, however, that while bad faith or a mischievous purpose can warrant the imposition of sanctions under this "improper purpose" standard, less malevolently culpable behavior (such as innocent but careless lawyering) can still trigger sanctions under this and other Rules.[55]

Representation #2—Proper Support in the Law

Rule 11 sanctions are reserved only for correcting litigation abuse[56] and should not be "applied to adventuresome, though responsible, lawyering which advocates creative legal theories."[57]

Rule 11(b)(2) provides that by presenting a document or arguing on its behalf, a person certifies that the arguments in the document are either justified by existing law or are "nonfrivolous" arguments for alteration in existing law.[58] Rule 11(b)(2) is a change from the previous version of Rule 11, and is intended to be a lesser burden on an advocate than the former standard of "good faith" arguments.[59] Courts apply an objective standard, inquiring whether "a reasonable attorney in like circumstances could have believed the actions to be legally justified."[60]

Courts have observed that tension may exist between Rule 11 and Rule 13, which requires a party to assert all compulsory counterclaims, or risk waiving such claims altogether.[61]

A represented party may not be held personally responsible for a violation of Rule 11(b)(2) by the attorney.[62]

Representation #3—Proper Support in the Facts

A person signing a document or arguing on its behalf also certifies that the factual contentions have "evidentiary support" or, when specifically so stated, will likely have evidentiary support after a reasonable opportunity for further investigation or discovery. This sets a lesser standard than

[54] *Hourani v. Mirtchev*, 796 F.3d 1, 17 (D.C. Cir. 2015).

[55] *See, e.g., MAO-MSO Recovery II, LLC v. State Farm Mutual Automobile Insurance Company*, 935 F.3d 573, 584 (7th Cir. 2019) ("even honest mistakes can be sanctionable"); *Purchasing Power, LLC v. Bluestem Brands, Inc.*, 851 F.3d 1218 n.4 (11th Cir. 2017) (comparing bad-faith requirement for sanctions under court's inherent powers).

[56] *Ario v. Underwriting Members of Syndicate 53 at Lloyds for 1998 Year of Account*, 618 F.3d 277, 297 (3d Cir. 2010).

[57] *Mary Ann Pensiero, Inc. v. Lingle*, 847 F.2d 90, 94 (3d Cir. 1988). *See also MAO-MSO Recovery II, LLC v. State Farm Mutual Automobile Ins. Co.*, 935 F.3d 573, 584 (7th Cir. 2019).

[58] *See, e.g., Van Hoven v. Buckles & Buckles, P.L.C.*, 947 F.3d 889, 896 (6th Cir. 2020); *Kim v. Kimm*, 884 F.3d 98, 106–107 (2d Cir. 2018).

[59] *See, e.g., Independent Lift Truck Builders Union v. NACCO Materials Handling Group, Inc.*, 202 F.3d 965, 968 (7th Cir. 2000).

[60] *Lokhova v. Halper*, 30 F.4th 349, 354 (4th Cir. 2022).

[61] *Spark Connected, LLC v. Semtech Corp.*, 502 F. Supp. 3d 1131, 1141 (E.D. Tex. 2020).

[62] *Lokhova v. Halper*, 30 F.4th 349, 358 (4th Cir. 2022).

that the allegations be "well grounded" in fact.[63] Sanctions generally may not be imposed against an attorney if there is evidence to support the lawyer's assertions;[64] however, mere speculation and conclusory allegations coupled with general carelessness may warrant sanctions.[65] There is no specific requirement under Rule 11 that the attorney distinguish for the court fact from inference.[66] The court errs when it disregards pleaded allegations as implausible based merely on the court's intuition.[67] The court should use Rule 11 to test factual allegations in pleadings rather than striking them[68] or issuing a sweeping pretrial order.[69]

Representation #4—Foundation for Denials

Lastly, a person who denies factual contentions certifies that those denials are warranted by the evidence, unless the person specifically identifies the denial as one reasonably based upon belief or a lack of information.[70]

Conduct That Is Not Considered a "Representation" to the Court

Conduct not involving a document submitted to the court, including the failure to submit a document, is not sanctionable under Rule 11.[71] Thus, disregard of a court order,[72] attorney misconduct during trial,[73] oral statements made during argument that are not included in written submissions to the court,[74] and most out-of-court conduct[75] does not typically fall under Rule 11.

Representations Apply to Portions of Presentations, as Well as the Whole

Portions of a document might be in violation of Rule 11, even though other portions of the same document are ethically

---

[63] *Rotella v. Wood*, 528 U.S. 549, 560–61 (2000).

[64] *See, e.g., Kiobel v. Millson*, 592 F.3d 78, 81 (2d Cir. 2010).

[65] *See, e.g., Kennedy v. Schneider Electric*, 893 F.3d 414, 421 (7th Cir. 2018).

[66] *See Lucas v. Duncan*, 574 F.3d 772, 777 (D.C. Cir. 2009).

[67] *In re Mortgages Ltd.*, 771 F.3d 623, 631-632 (9th Cir. 2014).

[68] *Chambers v. NASCO, Inc.*, 501 U.S. 32, 50 (1991).

[69] *Ringgold-Lockhart v. County of Los Angeles*, 761 F.3d 1057, 1065 (9th Cir. 2014).

[70] *But see, e.g., Attwood v. Singletary*, 105 F.3d 610, 613 (11th Cir. 1997) (actions based on arguably good faith belief are sanctionable where party failed to make reasonable inquiry into accuracy of information).

[71] *Ali v. Tolbert*, 636 F.3d 622, 626–27 (D.C. Cir. 2011) (citing cases).

[72] *Metz v. Unizan Bank*, 655 F.3d 485, 491 (6th Cir. 2011) (Rule 11 does not directly cover the disregard of court orders).

[73] *See, e.g., Balerna v. Gilberti*, 708 F.3d 319, 323 (1st Cir. 2013); *Lamboy-Ortiz v. Ortiz-Velez*, 630 F.3d 228, 245 (1st Cir. 2010).

[74] *See, e.g., In re Bees*, 562 F. 3d 284, 288–89 (4th Cir. 2009).

[75] *Auto-Owners Insurance Company v. Summit Park Townhome Association*, 886 F.3d 852, 858–59 (10th Cir. 2018).

compliant.[76]

Simply Failing to Prevail Is Not a Violation

To be sanctionable under Rule 11, something more than merely failing to win is required.[77] Rule 11 is not a strict liability provision, and a violation may be found only when some significant carelessness is identified.[78]

Improper Rule 11 Motions Can Also Violate Rule 11

Attorneys (and unrepresented parties) may assert that an opponent has violated Rule 11 in a written—and signed—motion, which itself is subject to review under Rule 11 and can, itself, be subject to accusations of violations of Rule 11.[79]

Standard for Attorney's Motion v. Judicial Show Cause Order

The procedures for a Rule 11 issue differ depending on whether an attorney or the court raises the issue. An attorney or party seeking a sanction under Rule 11 must first comply with the "safe harbor" requirement of Rule 11(c), while a judicially initiated "show cause" order need not. However, it is less clear whether the standard for imposition of a Rule 11 sanction also differs depending on whether the issue arises from an attorney's motion or a judge's order.[80]

RULE 11(c)—SANCTIONS

CORE CONCEPT

The "signing" obligation of Rule 11(a) and the presenter "representations" of Rule 11(b) are the foundations for the remedies that appear in Rule 11(c). An attorney or unrepresented party may be punished with sanctions for violating a representation made to the court through the act of signing, filing, submitting, or advocating a pleading, written motion, or other paper, and this subpart sets that procedure. An inquiry to assess

[76] *See, e.g., Ledford v. Peeples*, 568 F.3d 1258, 1307 (11th Cir. 2009) (error for court to fail to isolate claims of each plaintiff in determining whether securities fraud claims were frivolous); *Perez v. Posse Comitatus*, 373 F.3d 321, 325 (2d Cir. 2004) ("the fact that a claim is properly asserted against one defendant does not mean that the same claim may properly be asserted against a different defendant.").

[77] *See, e.g., Morris v. Wachovia Securities, Inc.*, 448 F.3d 268, 278 (4th Cir. 2006).

[78] *Citibank Global Markets, Inc. v. Rodriguez Santana*, 573 F.3d 17 (1st Cir. 2009).

[79] Advisory Committee Note Rule 11. *See, e.g., Smith v. Psychiatric Solutions, Inc.*, 750 F.3d 1253, 1260 (11th Cir. 2014).

[80] *See, e.g., Adams v. USAA Casualty Insurance Company*, 863 F.3d 1069, 1077 (8th Cir. 2017) (rule applies with strictness where sanctions imposed on court's initiative (omitting cited cases)). *See also In re Pennie & Edmonds LLP*, 323 F.3d 86, 90–93 (2d Cir. 2003) (standard is analogous to contempt of court standard). *But see Young v. City of Providence ex rel. Napolitano*, 404 F.3d 33, 39 (1st Cir. 2005) (specifically rejecting foregoing precedent; holding that standard is the same for sanctions sought by attorney or initiated by judge).

whether behavior is sanctionable can be initiated by motion from a party or by the court itself. The goal of any sanction is deterrence.

APPLICATIONS

Applicability to Rule 11(a)

By its terms, Rule 11(c) applies only to violations of Rule 11(b), not Rule 11(a). It is unnecessary to apply Rule 11(c) to Rule 11(a) because the last sentence of Rule 11(a) contains its own sanction—striking of an unsigned paper.

Persons Sanctioned

Rule 11(c) provides that in appropriate circumstances the court may sanction attorneys, law firms, or parties.[81] In evaluating whether to impose sanctions on counsel, courts must balance the role of an attorney as an officer of the court and the duty to represent a client in a zealous and rigorous manner.[82]

Rule 11 allows for sanctions on any attorney who violates the rule <u>or</u> is responsible for a violation. If an attorney agrees to have his or her name placed on a document, the attorney is subject to Rule 11 sanctions.[83] Sanctions against a client are appropriate if the client has made a knowing factual misrepresentation or is the "mastermind" behind the improper conduct.[84]

"Snapshot Rule"

Rule 11 liability is determined at the time a document is filed.[85] However, Rule 11 also imposes a duty of continuing diligence, and is violated when a party continues to maintain a position despite discovery or other evidence that the position has no merit.[86]

Sovereign Immunity

Government attorneys and their clients are subject to sanctions, including monetary sanctions, notwithstanding considerations of sovereign immunity.[87]

---

[81] *See, e.g., Union Planters Bank v. L & J Development Co., Inc.*, 115 F.3d 378, 384 (6th Cir. 1997) ("Rule 11 explicitly allows for the imposition of sanctions upon a party responsible for the rule's violation, provided that a represented party is not sanctioned for a violation of subsection (b)(2) involving unwarranted legal contentions."). *See also Holgate v. Baldwin*, 425 F.3d 671, 677 (9th Cir. 2005) (even lawyer who withdraws from case due to conflict of interest is not immune from Rule 11 sanctions for conduct prior to withdrawal).

[82] *McMillan v. Rodriguez*, 337 F.R.D. 27, 29 (D.P.R. 2020), report and recommendation adopted, (D.P.R. Oct. 23, 2020).

[83] *King v. Whitmer*, 556 F. Supp. 3d 680, 699 (E.D. Mich. 2021).

[84] *Johnson v. 27th Ave. Caraf, Inc.*, 9 F.4th 1300, 1315 (11th Cir. 2021).

[85] *See, e.g., CQ Intern. Co., Inc. v. Rochem Intern., Inc., USA*, 659 F.3d 53, 63 (1st Cir. 2011); *Marlin v. Moody Nat. Bank, N.A.*, 533 F.3d 374, 380 (5th Cir. 2008).

[86] *See, e.g., B & H Medical, L.L.C. v. ABP Admin., Inc.*, 526 F.3d 257, 269 (6th Cir. 2008).

[87] *See, e.g., Mattingly v. U.S.*, 939 F.2d 816, 817–18 (9th Cir. 1991). *Cf.*,

Magistrate Judges

The courts are divided as to whether magistrate judges have the authority to impose Rule 11 sanctions.[88]

Judicial Discretion

All aspects of a district court's Rule 11 determination are reviewed under the abuse-of-discretion standard.[89] Some courts of appeals, however, hold that if a district court finds that Rule 11 was violated, the district court has no discretion and must impose sanctions.[90] In close cases, the district court should provide an explanation of its reasons for imposing or denying sanctions,[91] and a circuit may remand close questions regarding a motion for sanctions where a district court denies sanctions without explanation.[92]

Procedures for Rule 11 Sanctions

Rule 11 contemplates two procedural paths for sanctions. First, a party can file a motion seeking sanctions. Second, the court can trigger the sanctions process *sua sponte*. Both paths are discussed below

Motion for Sanctions: Separate and Specific

Motions for sanctions under Rule 11(c) must be made separately from other motions[93] and must allege with specificity the alleged violation of Rule 11(b).[94]

Motion for Sanctions: Service and Due Process

Motions for sanctions must be served as required under Rule 5. Anyone who may potentially be subjected to Rule 11 sanctions has a due process right to present a defense before any sanction is imposed.[95] In practice, the quality and nature of hearings is controlled by the specific factual circumstances in which the alleged Rule 11 violation occurs.[96]

Motion for Sanctions: "Safe Harbor"

Rule 11 contains a "safe harbor" procedure designed to

King v. Cooke, 26 F.3d 720, 722 (7th Cir. 1994) (noting with approval imposition of Rule 11 sanctions on Indiana Office of the Attorney General, without discussion of sovereign immunity).

[88]*See, e.g., Rajaratnam v. Moyer*, 47 F.3d 922, 923 (7th Cir. 1995) (not allowed). *But see, Maisonville v. F2 America, Inc.*, 902 F.2d 746 (9th Cir. 1990) (allowed).

[89]*Cooter & Gell v. Hartmarx Corp.*, 496 U.S. 384, 405, 110 S. Ct. 2447, 110 L. Ed. 2d 359 (1990).

[90]*Gulisano v. Burlington, Inc.*, 34 F.4th 935 (11th Cir. 2022).

[91]*See, e.g., Willhite v. Collins*, 459 F.3d 866, 870 (8th Cir. 2006).

[92]*See, e.g., Fidrych v. Marriott International, Inc.*, 952 F.3d 124, 147 (4th Cir. 2020).

[93]*See also Star Mark Management, Inc. v. Koon Chun Hing Kee Soy & Sauce Factory, Ltd*, 682 F.3d 170, 179 (2d Cir. 2012); *Nisenbaum v. Milwaukee County*, 333 F.3d 804 (7th Cir. 2003).

[94]*See, e.g., Johnson v. Cherry*, 422 F.3d 540, 551–52 (7th Cir. 2005).

[95]*See, e.g., Marlin v. Moody Nat. Bank, N.A.*, 533 F.3d 374, 380 (5th Cir. 2008); *Perpetual Securities, Inc. v. Tang*, 290 F.3d 132, 141 (2d Cir. 2002).

[96]*See, e.g., Spiller v. Ella Smithers Geriatric Center*, 919 F.2d 339, 346 (5th Cir. 1990).

provide parties with an opportunity to cure a Rule 11 violation before the issue is presented to the court. Rule 11(c)(2) does not permit a sanctions motion to be filed with the court until 21 days after service of the motion, or within any other time frame the court provides.[97] A request for sanctions that fails to follow the proper procedures will be denied.[98] The majority of circuits addressing the issue have required service of the actual motion as opposed to a letter or other informal notice to satisfy the "safe harbor" requirement.[99] If the document challenged by the sanctions motion is withdrawn or corrected within that time frame, the motion may not be filed with the court, and thus no sanctions will be imposed.[100]

Motions for Sanctions: Timing

The duty to offer an offending party a "safe harbor" may preclude an injured party from moving for sanctions after a case has ended,[101] or where the offending attorney has withdrawn from the case.[102] While a party must file before the conclusion of the case, the court may retain jurisdiction to decide the Rule 11 motion after the conclusion of the principal matter.[103] A district court also retains jurisdiction to impose Rule 11 sanctions after the case has been remanded to state court.[104]

Motion for Sanctions: Costs of Presenting or Opposing Sanctions Motion

Rule 11(c)(2) provides the court with discretion to award costs, including attorney's fees, associated with presenting or opposing a sanctions motion.[105] The court should explain the basis for any fee award and specify who, as between the parties

---

[97]*See, e.g., Winterrowd v. American General Annuity Insurance Co.*, 556 F.3d 815, 826 (9th Cir. 2009); *Rector v. Approved Federal Sav. Bank*, 265 F.3d 248, 252–53 (4th Cir. 2001) (sanctioned party's failure to enter timely objection to movant's untimely service waives issue).

[98]*Milman v. Fieger & Fieger, P.C.*, 542 F. Supp. 3d 604, 612 (E.D. Mich. 2021).

[99]See, e.g., *McGreal v. Village of Orland Park*, 928 F.3d 556 (7th Cir. 2019) (allowing informal notice, but noting that no other circuits follow this approach); *Penn, LLC v. Prosper Bus. Dev. Corp.*, 773 F.3d 764, 767–69 (6th Cir. 2014) (requiring formal service of a motion).

[100]*See, e.g., Lawrence v. Richman Group of CT LLC*, 620 F.3d 153 (2d Cir. 2010).

[101]*See, e.g., ResQNet.com, Inc. v. Lansa, Inc.*, 594 F.3d 860, 875 (Fed. Cir. 2010); *Roth v. Green*, 466 F.3d 1179, 1193 (10th Cir. 2006).

[102]*Peer v. Lewis*, 606 F.3d 1306, 1315 (11th Cir. 2010).

[103]*Cooter & Gell v. Hartmarx Corp.*, 496 U.S. 384, 395 (1990); *Matrix IV, Inc. v. American National Bank and Trust Co. of Chicago*, 649 F.3d 539, 553 (7th Cir. 2011) ("Postjudgment motions for sanctions are permissible so long as the moving party substantially complies with Rule 11's safe-harbor requirement.").

[104]*Barlow v. Colgate Palmolive Co.*, 772 F.3d 1001, 1009 (4th Cir. 2014).

[105]*See, e.g., Blixseth v. Yellowstone Mountain Club, LLC*, 854 F.3d 626 (9th Cir. 2017).

and their lawyers, is to pay the award.[106]

Motion for Sanctions: Non-Parties

In general, persons who are not parties to litigation have no standing to bring a Rule 11 motion.[107] Exceptions to that general rule arise in narrow circumstances where a non-party is affected directly by otherwise sanctionable conduct, such as when a person has been named in a proposed amended complaint or a complaint that has not yet been served.[108]

***Sua Sponte* Sanctions: Show Cause Order**

When the court believes there may have been a violation of Rule 11(b), it may initiate the sanction process without waiting for a party to make a motion.[109] To do so, the court issues an order directing the attorney, law firm, or party to show cause why it has not violated Rule 11(b). The show cause order should identify the potentially offending conduct with reasonable specificity.[110] *Sua Sponte* show cause orders are less common than motions for sanctions, and some courts will only issue them in circumstances analogous to contempt of court.[111]

***Sua Sponte* Sanctions: No "Safe Harbor"**

The *sua sponte* sanctions procedure contains no "safe harbor" provision analogous to that applying to a motion for sanctions, although the court in its discretion may afford an offending party an opportunity to cure the violation.[112]

***Sua Sponte* Sanctions: Due Process**

The show cause order guarantees an affected party both notice and an opportunity to explain their conduct and otherwise defend against the proposed sanction.[113]

---

[106] *Boim v. Holy Land Foundation for Relief and Development*, 511 F.3d 707, 749–50 (7th Cir. 2007).

[107] *See, e.g., New York News, Inc. v. Kheel*, 972 F.2d 482, 488–89 (2d Cir. 1992).

[108] *See, e.g., Nyer v. Winterthur Intern.*, 290 F.3d 456 (1st Cir. 2002) (proposed amended complaint); *Greenberg v. Sala*, 822 F.2d 882 (9th Cir.1987) (frivolous complaint not yet served).

[109] *See, e.g., Bell v. Vacuforce, LLC*, 908 F.3d 1075 (7th Cir. 2018); *Muhammad v. Walmart Stores East, L.P.*, 732 F.3d 104, 108 (2d Cir. 2013) (sanctions initiated by court "rarer").

[110] *See, e.g., Clark v. United Parcel Service, Inc.*, 460 F.3d 1004, 1007–1009 (8th Cir. 2006).

[111] *See, e.g., Kaplan v. DaimlerChrysler, A.G.*, 331 F.3d 1251, 1255 (11th Cir. 2003) (Because Rule 11(c)(1)(B) does not provide safe harbor, court must provide notice and opportunity to be heard and "a higher standard ('akin to contempt') than in the case of party-initiated sanctions."). *See also Lucas v. Duncan*, 574 F.3d 772, 775 (D.C.Cir. 2009) (acknowledging "the unusual position of the trial court in such circumstances, serving at once as both prosecutor and judge" but declining to choose between the "akin to contempt" and "objective reasonableness" standards, as both had been violated in that case).

[112] *See, e.g., Elliott v. Tilton*, 64 F.3d 213, 216 (5th Cir. 1995).

[113] *See, e.g., Mitchell v. Nobles*, 873 F.3d 869, 875 (11th Cir. 2017); *Marlin v. Moody Nat. Bank, N.A.*, 533 F.3d 374, 378 (5th Cir. 2008).

Sua Sponte Sanctions: Timing

The court may impose Rule 11 sanctions at any time, even after dismissal.

The court must issue its show cause order before the parties have voluntarily dismissed or settled the action if the court wants to impose monetary sanctions.[114]

Nature of Sanctions: Deterrence Not Punishment

Sanctions for violations of Rule 11(b) are to be imposed to deter similar violations by the offender or others similarly situated, not to compensate another party.[115] This policy represents a substantial change from previous versions of Rule 11, which included a substantially stronger interest in compensating parties who had been damaged by Rule 11 violations.[116]

Sanctions Available

The court is authorized to issue nonmonetary orders,[117] to require payment of a penalty into court, to require payment of some or all of an opposing party's attorney's fees[118] and expenses, or any combination thereof.[119] Payment to an opposing party requires a motion by a party,[120] and is unlikely to occur unless the court believes such payment serves a deterrent purpose.[121] Generally, any monetary sanction must flow directly from the conduct described in the Rule 11 motion. All of the monetary sanctions listed in Rule 11(c)(4) are subject to additional significant limitations, discussed below.

Attorney's Fees

If a sanction includes payment of an opposing party's attorney's fees or associated costs, courts generally use a "lodestar" method of calculating the appropriate amount. "The lodestar is determined by multiplying the number of hours reasonably expended by the reasonable hourly rate."[122] The amount of fees recoverable from the offending party is limited to fees

---

[114] *See, e.g., Wolfington v. Reconstructive Orthopaedic Associates II PC*, 935 F.3d 187, 208 (3rd Cir. 2019) (while the court may impose sanctions following dismissal of an action based on a party's motion, it may not do so *sua sponte).*

[115] *See, e.g., Ringgold-Lockhart v. County of Los Angeles*, 761 F.3d 1057, 1065 (9th Cir. 2014); *DiPaolo v. Moran*, 407 F.3d 140 (3d Cir. 2005).

[116] *Gurary v. Nu-Tech Bio-Med, Inc.*, 303 F.3d 212, 221–22 (2d Cir. 2002).

[117] Nonmonetary sanctions may include dismissal of the action, *see, e.g., Liggon-Redding v. Estate of Sugarman*, 659 F.3d 258, 263 (3d Cir. 2011), or injunctions governing future filings, *Anderson v. Wells Fargo Bank, N.A.*, 953 F.3d 311, 315–16 (5th Cir. 2020).

[118] *See, e.g., Eon-Net LP v. Flagstar Bancorp.*, 653 F.3d 1314, 1320 (Fed. Cir. 2011).

[119] *See, e.g., Riccard v. Prudential Ins. Co.*, 307 F.3d 1277, 1295 (11th Cir. 2002).

[120] *See, e.g., Tejero v. Portfolio Recovery Associates, L.L.C.*, 955 F.3d 453, 458 (5th Cir. 2020).

[121] *See Barber v. Miller*, 146 F.3d 707 (9th Cir.1998).

[122] *View Engineering, Inc. v. Robotic Vision Systems, Inc.*, 208 F.3d 981, 987 (Fed. Cir. 2000). *Skidmore Energy, Inc. v. KPMG*, 455 F.3d 564, 568 (5th Cir. 2006).

incurred as a direct result of the violation.[123] Fees for government attorneys are calculated on the same basis as prevailing rates in the private sector.[124]

The court may not award attorney's fees under Rule 11 when sanctions are imposed *sua sponte*, but may award attorney's fees under its inherent powers if the person being sanctioned has acted in bad faith.[125]

Nonmonetary Sanctions

Nonmonetary sanctions include dismissal unfavorable to the offender,[126] court-ordered pro bono service,[127] reprimands,[128] referrals to bar associations,[129] and suspension.[130]

Sanctions are Not Damages

Sanctions are intended to deter future misbehavior and are not to be used to enforce or collect a judgment,[131] or to make the plaintiff whole,[132] as a substitute for tort damages,[133] or to award punitive damages.[134]

Financial Status of Offender

In assessing monetary sanctions, courts may take into account the financial status of the offender.[135] However, if the offender wants the court to know of the offender's limited ability to pay sanctions, the burden is on the offender to bring the relevant facts before the court.[136]

Alternative Remedies

Rule 11 is in addition to, and not exclusive of, other sources

---

[123] *Divane v. Krull Elec. Co., Inc.*, 200 F.3d 1020, 1030 (7th Cir. 1999).

[124] *See, e.g., King v. Fleming*, 899 F.3d 1140 (10th Cir. 2018) (court could find no reason to use state employee's salary rather than prevailing market rates in determining attorney's fees).

[125] *Schlafly v. Eagle F.*, 970 F.3d 924, 938 (8th Cir. 2020); *Willhite v. Collins*, 459 F.3d 866, 869–870 (8th Cir. 2006).

[126] *See, e.g., King v. Fleming*, 899 F.3d 1140 (10th Cir. 2018) (five factor test for imposing "extreme sanction "of dismissal with prejudice"); *Liggon-Redding v. Estate of Sugarman*, 659 F.3d 258, 263 (3d Cir. 2011).

[127] *Reinhardt v. Gulf Ins. Co.*, 489 F.3d 405, 416 (1st Cir. 2007).

[128] *In re Rodriguez*, 891 F.3d 576, 577 (5th Cir. 2018).

[129] *Collins v. Daniels*, 916 F.3d 1302 (10th Cir. 2019); *Teaford v. Ford Motor Co.*, 338 F.3d 1179 (10th Cir. 2003).

[130] *See, e.g., Matter of Dragoo*, 186 F.3d 614, 615–16 (5th Cir. 1999). *But see, Hutchinson v. Pfeil*, 208 F.3d 1180, 1186 (10th Cir. 2000) (sanctions should not be used to drive attorneys out of practice).

[131] *Universitas Educ., LLC v. Nova Group, Inc.*, 784 F.3d 99, 103 (2d Cir. 2015).

[132] *See, e.g., Showan v. Pressdee*, 922 F.3d 1211 (11th Cir. 2019).

[133] *Bus. Guides, Inc. v. Chromatic Commc'ns Enters., Inc.*, 498 U.S. 533, 553–54 (1991).

[134] *See, e.g., Showan v. Pressdee*, 922 F.3d 1211 (11th Cir. 2019).

[135] *See, e.g., Star Mark Management, Inc. v. Koon Chun Hing Kee Soy & Sauce Factory, Ltd*, 682 F.3d 170, 179 (2d Cir. 2012); *Shales v. General Chauffeurs, Sales Drivers and Helpers Local Union*, 557 F.3d 746, 748–49 (7th Cir. 2009).

[136] *See, e.g., Young v. Smith*, 905 F.3d 229 (3d Cir. 2018).

of sanctioning authority.[137]

Duty to Mitigate

A party seeking attorney's fees or other damages under Rule 11 must have made reasonable efforts to mitigate its losses.[138]

Monetary Sanctions: Frivolous Arguments of Law

Rule 11(c)(5)(A) explicitly prohibits application of monetary sanctions against a represented party for violations of the certification that legal arguments be supported by existing law or by a nonfrivolous argument for changing the law.[139] This limitation is consistent with the requirement that sanctions support deterrence—sanctioning a party for legal arguments is unlikely to deter future improper legal arguments by that party.

Order Imposing Sanctions

If the court imposes sanctions, it should describe the offending conduct and explain the basis for the sanction the court imposed.[140]

Appellate Procedure

An attorney who wishes to appeal the imposition of Rule 11 sanctions cannot rely on the client's notice of appeal, and instead must file a separate notice of appeal.[141] A district court's decision on a post-judgment Rule 11 motion is a separate judgment that requires the filing of a separate notice of appeal.[142]

Rule 11(d)—INAPPLICABILITY TO DISCOVERY

CORE CONCEPT

Rules 26 through 37, governing the discovery process, control the circumstances when sanctions may be imposed for inappropriate behavior in discovery. For that reason, Rule 11(d) provides that Rule 11(a), (b) and (c) have no applicability to discovery issues.[143]

---

[137] *See, e.g., Thomas v. Tenneco Packaging Co., Inc.*, 293 F.3d 1306 (11th Cir. 2002); *U.S. Express Lines Ltd. v. Higgins*, 281 F.3d 383, 393 (3d Cir. 2002).

[138] *See, e.g., Andretti v. Borla Performance Industries, Inc.*, 426 F.3d 824, 834 (6th Cir. 2005); *Pollution Control Industries of America, Inc. v. Van Gundy*, 21 F.3d 152, 156 (7th Cir. 1994).

[139] *See, e.g., Marlin v. Moody Nat. Bank, N.A.*, 533 F.3d 374, 378 (5th Cir. 2008).

[140] *See, e.g., Fidrych v. Marriott International, Inc.*, 952 F.3d 124, 147 (4th Cir. 2020). *But cf., McLane, Graf, Raulerson & Middleton, P.A. v. Rechberger*, 280 F.3d 26, 44–45 (1st Cir. 2002) (district court encouraged, but not required, to give reasons for denying sanctions).

[141] *See Halim v. Great Gatsby's Auction Gallery, Inc.*, 516 F.3d 557, 564 (7th Cir. 2008).

[142] *Keck Garrett & Associates, Inc. v. Nextel Communications, Inc.*, 517 F.3d 476, 488 (7th Cir. 2008).

[143] *See, e.g., Patelco Credit Union v. Sahni*, 262 F.3d 897, 913 (9th Cir. 2001); *DR Distributors, LLC v. 21 Century Smoking, Inc.*, 513 F. Supp.

Additional Research References

Wright & Miller, *Federal Practice and Procedure* §§ 1331 to 39
C.J.S. Federal Civil Procedure § 260
West's Key Number Digest, Federal Civil Procedure ⚷660 to 661, ⚷2750 to 2848

3d 839, 950 (N.D. Ill. 2021).

RULE 12
DEFENSES AND OBJECTIONS: WHEN AND HOW PRESENTED; MOTION FOR JUDGMENT ON THE PLEADINGS; CONSOLIDATING MOTIONS; WAIVING DEFENSES; PRETRIAL HEARING

(a) Time to Serve a Responsive Pleading.

(1) *In General.* Unless another time is specified by this rule or a federal statute, the time for serving a responsive pleading is as follows:

(A) A defendant must serve an answer:

(i) within 21 days after being served with the summons and complaint; or

(ii) if it has timely waived service under Rule 4(d), within 60 days after the request for a waiver was sent, or within 90 days after it was sent to the defendant outside any judicial district of the United States.

(B) A party must serve an answer to a counterclaim or crossclaim within 21 days after being served with the pleading that states the counterclaim or crossclaim.

(C) A party must serve a reply to an answer within 21 days after being served with an order to reply, unless the order specifies a different time.

(2) *United States and Its Agencies, Officers, or Employees Sued in an Official Capacity.* The United States, a United States agency, or a United States officer or employee sued only in an official capacity must serve an answer to a complaint, counterclaim, or crossclaim within 60 days after service on the United States attorney.

(3) *United States Officers or Employees Sued in an Individual Capacity.* A United States officer or employee sued in an individual capacity for an act or omission occurring in connection with

duties performed on the United States' behalf must serve an answer to a complaint, counterclaim, or crossclaim within 60 days after service on the officer or employee or service on the United States attorney, whichever is later.

(4) *Effect of a Motion.* Unless the court sets a different time, serving a motion under this rule alters these periods as follows:

(A) if the court denies the motion or postpones its disposition until trial, the responsive pleading must be served within 14 days after notice of the court's action; or

(B) if the court grants a motion for a more definite statement, the responsive pleading must be served within 14 days after the more definite statement is served.

(b) How to Present Defenses. Every defense to a claim for relief in any pleading must be asserted in the responsive pleading if one is required. But a party may assert the following defenses by motion:

(1) lack of subject-matter jurisdiction;
(2) lack of personal jurisdiction;
(3) improper venue;
(4) insufficient process;
(5) insufficient service of process;
(6) failure to state a claim upon which relief can be granted; and
(7) failure to join a party under Rule 19.

A motion asserting any of these defenses must be made before pleading if a responsive pleading is allowed. If a pleading sets out a claim for relief that does not require a responsive pleading, an opposing party may assert at trial any defense to that claim. No defense or objection is waived by joining it with one or more other defenses or objections in a responsive pleading or in a motion.

(c) Motion for Judgment on the Pleadings. After the pleadings are closed—but early enough not to delay trial—a party may move for judgment on the pleadings.

(d) Result of Presenting Matters Outside the

Pleadings. If, on a motion under Rule 12(b)(6) or 12(c), matters outside the pleadings are presented to and not excluded by the court, the motion must be treated as one for summary judgment under Rule 56. All parties must be given a reasonable opportunity to present all the material that is pertinent to the motion.

(e) Motion for a More Definite Statement. A party may move for a more definite statement of a pleading to which a responsive pleading is allowed but which is so vague or ambiguous that the party cannot reasonably prepare a response. The motion must be made before filing a responsive pleading and must point out the defects complained of and the details desired. If the court orders a more definite statement and the order is not obeyed within 14 days after notice of the order or within the time the court sets, the court may strike the pleading or issue any other appropriate order.

(f) Motion to Strike. The court may strike from a pleading an insufficient defense or any redundant, immaterial, impertinent, or scandalous matter. The court may act:

(1) on its own; or

(2) on motion made by a party either before responding to the pleading or, if a response is not allowed, within 21 days after being served with the pleading.

(g) Joining Motions.

(1) *Right to Join.* A motion under this rule may be joined with any other motion allowed by this rule.

(2) *Limitation on Further Motions.* Except as provided in Rule 12(h)(2) or (3), a party that makes a motion under this rule must not make another motion under this rule raising a defense or objection that was available to the party but omitted from its earlier motion.

(h) Waiving and Preserving Certain Defenses.

(1) *When Some Are Waived.* A party waives any defense listed in Rule 12(b)(2) to (5) by:

(A) omitting it from a motion in the circumstances

described in Rule 12(g)(2); or

(B) failing to either:

(i) make it by motion under this rule; or

(ii) include it in a responsive pleading or in an amendment allowed by Rule 15(a)(1) as a matter of course.

(2) *When to Raise Others.* Failure to state a claim upon which relief can be granted, to join a person required by Rule 19(b), or to state a legal defense to a claim may be raised:

(A) in any pleading allowed or ordered under Rule 7(a);

(B) by a motion under Rule 12(c); or

(C) at trial.

(3) *Lack of Subject-Matter Jurisdiction.* If the court determines at any time that it lacks subject-matter jurisdiction, the court must dismiss the action.

(i) Hearing Before Trial. If a party so moves, any defense listed in Rule 12(b)(1) to (7)—whether made in a pleading or by motion—and a motion under Rule 12(c) must be heard and decided before trial unless the court orders a deferral until trial.

[Amended December 27, 1946, effective March 19, 1948; January 21, 1963, effective July 1, 1963; February 28, 1966, effective July 1, 1966; March 2, 1987, effective August 1, 1987; April 22, 1993, effective December 1, 1993; April 17, 2000, December 1, 2000; April 30, 2007, effective December 1, 2007; March 26, 2009, effective December 1, 2009.]

AUTHORS' COMMENTARY ON RULE 12

PURPOSE AND SCOPE

Among the most frequently invoked of the Federal Rules of Civil Procedure, Rule 12 pursues an important adjudicative principle: if there is a problem with the pleadings or with the court's ability to preside over a lawsuit, that problem should be addressed early so as not to waste the parties' or the court's time unnecessarily. That objective begins with Rule 12(a), which establishes the varying deadlines for parties to respond to a complaint, counterclaim, crossclaim, or third-party claim. Most deadlines are quite short.

Then, Rule 12(b) requires that all defenses be asserted in a responsive pleading ("answer"), though the Rule permits one alternative to immediate counter-pleading: the filing of a pre-answer motion challenging any of 7 threshold defenses and objections (lack of subject-matter jurisdiction, personal jurisdiction, or proper venue; insufficient process or service of process; failure to state a cognizable claim for relief; and failure to join a required party). The proper, timely filing of such a pre-answer motion suspends the time for counter-pleading until the court resolves the motion. Rule 12(i) allows a party to request that the court consider and rule upon the pending motion before trial (although the court has discretion to defer).

Whether to pose a pre-answer motion challenge or, instead, to proceed directly to a counter-pleading is the responding party's prerogative. But the choice comes with consequences. If a Rule 12 motion is filed, Rule 12(g) requires the movant to include in a single, omnibus motion all then-available Rule 12 defenses and objections that the party wishes to assert. Omitting a challenge to personal jurisdiction, venue, process, or service of process forfeits those objections for the duration of the case, as Rule 12(h) cautions. Challenges for failing to state a cognizable claim or neglecting to join a required party are preserved, but only until time of trial. A defect in subject-matter jurisdiction is never forfeit and can be raised at any time. (The same consolidation/waiver principles apply when a party chooses not to file a pre-answer motion: that party's answer must plead all desired Rule 12 defenses and objections—failing to include personal jurisdiction, venue, process, or service of process challenges forfeits them.)

Rule 12(e) permits a party to request the court to compel a claimant to more clearly plead its claim, when the claim's vagueness or ambiguity renders a proper response impossible. Rule 12(f) permits a party to invite the court to strike redundant, immaterial, impertinent, or scandalous matter from the pleading, as well as strike any insufficient defenses. These motions, like those made under Rule 12(b), are encompassed in the Rule 12(g) consolidation mandate and subject to the Rule 12(h) waiver risk. Both motions are viewed by the courts with disfavor and granted only sparingly.

Finally, Rule 12(c) allows a party to move for judgment on the pleadings, once the pleadings are closed. Such motions can be used to challenge the adequacy of the pleaded allegations or to obtain a final merits ruling when the face of the pleaded allegations allow for a conclusive disposition.

The defense of failure to state a cognizable claim, authorized by Rule 12(b)(6), is a frequent threshold challenge in federal practice. It may be asserted in a pre-answer motion to dismiss or a post-answer motion for judgment on the pleadings. In either event, the challenge is treated as a pleadings-based attack and resolved principally on the face of the pleaded allegations. If extrinsic materials are considered, the court must convert the challenge to a summary judgment motion and proceed under those procedures.

RULE 12(a)—TIME FOR SERVING RESPONSIVE PLEADINGS

CORE CONCEPT

Answers to complaints must ordinarily be served within 21 days after service, except when service is waived (then 60 days if waived from the U.S. or 90 days if waived from abroad) or when serving the federal government, its agencies, or certain of its officers or employees (then 60 days). Answers to counterclaims and crosscLaims, as well as court-ordered replies to an answer, must be served within 21 days.

APPLICATIONS

Answers and Replies

Unless a Rule 12 motion is filed, a party usually must serve an answer within 21 calendar days after being served with a summons and complaint (including a third-party complaint[1]), a counterclaim, or a crossclaim. A party must serve a reply within 21 calendar days after being served with a court order directing a reply. If no responsive pleading is required, defenses and objections can be asserted at trial.[2]

- *Calculated from Service:* By their terms, these time periods run from (and to) the dates of *service*, not the dates of *filing*.
- *Service Made Abroad:* These response periods apply when service of process is accomplished in a foreign country (the 90-day response period applies only when service is waived from outside the U.S.).[3]
- *Time for Pre-Answer Motions:* The Rules do not expressly set the time for filing pre-answer motions, but cautious practitioners will assume the deadlines mirror those governing the service of answers.[4]
- *Time Computation Amendments:* The time period governing most responsive pleadings was extended in 2009 from 20 days to 21 days.

Exception: When Formal Service of Process is Waived

Waiving formal service of process is encouraged by gener-

---

[1] *See AMF Holdings, LLC v. Elie*, 2016 WL 10540637, at *1 (N.D. Ga. Sept. 6, 2016) (Rule 12 timing applied to third-party complaints). *See also* Rule 14(a)(2)(A) (third-party defendant "must assert any defense against the third-party plaintiff's claim *under Rule 12*") (emphasis added).

[2] *See* Rule 12(b).

[3] *See Leon v. Cont'l AG*, 176 F. Supp. 3d 1315, 1319 (S.D. Fla. 2016).

[4] *See infra* Authors' Commentary to Rule 12(b) ("**Time for Making Motion**").

ous extensions of these response times. A defendant who agrees to waive formal service receives 60 days to respond (if the waiver request was mailed to a U.S. address) and 90 days to respond (if mailed to an address outside the U.S.). These extensions apply only to service of original process. The time periods run from the date the waiver request was sent.[5]

Exception: Serving the United States, Its Officers and Agencies

Responsive pleadings must be served within 60 days by the United States, by its agencies, and by those federal officers and employees who are *either* sued in their "official" capacities or sued in their "individual" capacities for acts or omissions occurring in connection with the performance of their federal duties.[6] In "individual" capacity, "on-the-job" lawsuits against federal personnel, this 60-day period begins to run when the individual is served or when the U.S. Attorney is served, whichever is later.[7] In all other cases (lawsuits against the United States, a federal agency, or a federal officer or employee sued in an official capacity), the 60-day period begins to run when the U.S. Attorney is served.[8] This pleading timetable applies to both current and former federal officers and employees.[9]

Note: When a pleading names as defendants both a governmental party and a non-governmental party, only the governmental party receives 60 days to serve a responsive pleading. The non-governmental party's time for serving a responsive pleading is unaffected.

Exception: Extensions by the Court or the Parties

The time for serving responsive pleadings may be extended by court order[10] or by stipulation of the parties once approved by the court.[11]

Exception: Tolling Effect of Rule 12(b) Motion

Rule 12(b) motions to dismiss and Rule 12(e) motions for more definite statement must be filed before a responsive pleading (because, by their nature, the remedy they seek is preanswer relief).[12] The act of serving either motion ordinarily

[5] *See* Rule 4(d); *infra* Authors' Commentary to Rule 4(d).

[6] *See* Rule 12(a)(2).

[7] *See* Rule 12(a)(3).

[8] *See* Rule 12(a)(2)(A).

[9] *See* Rule 12(a)(3) advisory committee notes (2000).

[10] *See* Rule 12(a)(4); Rule 6(b). *See generally Woods-Early v. Corning Inc.*, 330 F.R.D. 117, 126–27 (W.D.N.Y. 2019) (denying motion, directing answer within 30 days).

[11] *See Orange Theatre Corp. v. Rayherstz Amusement Corp.*, 130 F.2d 185, 187 (3d Cir. 1942) (though "commendable as professional comity," extensions of pleading time need court approval). *See also* D.S.C. Civ. R. 12.01 (authorizing one stipulated extension); D. Colo. Civ. R. 6.1(a) (same).

[12] *See* 12(b) (Rule 12(b) motions "must be made before pleading if a responsive pleading is allowed").

suspends the party's time for serving a responsive pleading,[13] and that tolling usually continues to run until the court has ruled on the pending motion.[14] Thereafter, the time for filing the postponed responsive pleading is:

- If the court's order on the motion denies relief or postpones resolving the motion until trial: within 14 days after "notice" of the court's action.[15]
- If the court's order resolves a motion for more definite statement by requiring a clearer claim: the responsive pleading to the more definite statement must be served within 14 days after service of that new statement.[16]
- 3 extra days are added to these periods if service is made on the party by mail, by leaving with the clerk, or by special consent.[17]
- Courts may deviate from these time periods by establishing special schedules for a case, which then control.[18]

Exceptions to Tolling Effect Rule

The tolling effect of a pending Rule 12(b) motion may be altered (or eliminated completely) in the following circumstances:

- *Motion by Other Defendant:* The tolling effect of a pending Rule 12(b) motion does not inure to the benefit of all defendants; only those defendants who file a Rule 12(b) motion receive the tolling.[19]
- *Motions Filed Against Amended Pleadings:* It is not clear whether a party who files a Rule 12(b) motion to an amended pleading is entitled automatically to a new

---

[13] *See* Rule 12(a)(4).

[14] *See Butler v. Broward County Cent. Examining Bd.*, 367 Fed.Appx. 991, 992 (11th Cir. 2010); *Bonilla v. City of Allentown*, 359 F. Supp. 3d 281, 296 (E.D. Pa. 2019). *But cf. Hill v. Blue Cross and Blue Shield of Michigan*, 237 F.R.D. 613, 616–17 (E.D. Mich. 2006) (to resolve longstanding delays in case, court strikes motion to dismiss, without prejudice, and orders defendant to file its answer).

[15] *See* Rule 12(a)(4)(A). Neither the Advisory Committee Notes nor published case law have described when a party is deemed to have received "notice" of such a court order within the meaning of Rule 12(a)(4)(A) (*e.g.*, when the order is docketed, when it arrives at counsel's office or the party's home, when counsel or the party actually sees it, etc.). The sparse case law references to this section either offer no substantive guidance at all or use language that appears directly inconsistent with the plain terms of the Rule itself. *See, e.g., U.S. v. $57,960.00 in U.S. Currency*, 58 F. Supp. 2d 660, 668 (D.S.C. 1999) (dated from "being served" with denial order); *Ziegler v. Ziegler*, 28 F. Supp. 2d 601, 620 (E.D. Wash. 1998) (dated from "after receipt" of denial order); *U.S. v. Ware*, 172 F.R.D. 458, 459 (D. Kan. 1997) (dated from "after the court's denial" of motion); *Johnson-Medland v. Bethanna*, 1996 WL 612467 (E.D. Pa. 1996) (dated from "the date of this order").

[16] *See* Rule 12(a)(4)(B).

[17] *See* Rule 6(d).

[18] *See* 12(a)(4). *See also U.S. v. Elmes*, 532 F.3d 1138, 1145–46 (11th Cir. 2008) (alternate time set by court order prevails over general time period).

[19] *See Hanley v. Volpe*, 48 F.R.D. 387, 387–88 (E.D. Wis. 1970).

Rule 12(a) tolling period. Some authority rejects such a tolling as a misreading of Rule 12(a);[20] others acknowledge the tolling.[21]

- *Motions to Strike:* The tolling effect of a freestanding Rule 12(f) motion is not expressly addressed, and little caselaw confronts the question.[22] Some scholars doubt that tolling applies.[23] Prudent practitioners seeking such a tolling should request it from the court.[24]
- *Summary Judgment Motions:* Rule 12(b) motions receive the tolling effect; Rule 56 motions might not. Thus, filing an early summary judgment in lieu of either a Rule 12 motion or an answer might *not* toll the running of the 21-day response period (and, thus, risks admitting all pleaded allegations).[25]
- *Motions Converted to Summary Judgment Motions:* When materials outside the pleadings are presented with a Rule 12(b) motion (and not excluded by the court), the Rule 12(b) motion generally must be converted to a Rule 56 motion for summary judgment.[26] The tolling effect may still apply to such converted motions.[27]
- *Partial Motions:* A party may file a partial Rule 12 mo-

---

[20]*See General Mills, Inc. v. Kraft Foods Global, Inc.*, 487 F.3d 1368, 1376–77 (Fed. Cir. 2007), *clarified by*, 495 F.3d 1378, 1378–81 (Fed. Cir. 2007).

[21]*See, e.g., Castillo v. Sch. Bd. of Broward Cty.*, 645 Fed. Appx. 966, 966–67 (11th Cir. 2016) (default not warranted, since motion timely filed from service of amended complaint); *Farmer v. Las Vegas Metro. Police Dep't*, 423 F. Supp. 3d 1008, 1015–16 (D. Nev. 2019) (tolling applied when original and amended complaints served together).

[22]*See Skaggs v. Subway Real Estate Corp.*, 2006 WL 1042337, at *5 (D. Conn. Apr. 19, 2006) (presuming, without discussion, tolling applies).

[23]*See* 5B CHARLES A. WRIGHT & ARTHUR R. MILLER, FEDERAL PRACTICE AND PROCEDURE § 1346, at 46–47 (2004) (and 2020 Supp. § 1346, at 8-9).

[24]*See Talarico v. Port Auth. of N.Y. & N.J.*, 367 F. Supp. 3d 161, 165 n.1 (S.D.N.Y. 2019) (granting motion to postpone answer until motion to strike resolved).

[25]*Compare Modrowski v. Pigatto*, 712 F.3d 1166, 1170 (7th Cir. 2013) (Rule 56 motion does not toll time for filing answers); *with Wavecom Sols. Corp. v. Verizon Hawaii Int'l Inc.*, 2011 WL 5374428, at *5 (D. Haw. Nov. 7, 2011) (Rule 56 motion tolls time for filing answer). *Compare also Pena v. City of Rio Grande City*, 398 F. Supp. 3d 127, 143 (S.D. Tex. 2019), *rev'd on other grounds*, 2020 WL 3053964 (5th Cir. June 8, 2020) (most courts reject view that pre-answer Rule 56 motion constitutes a default); *and Parker v. U.S. Dep't of Justice*, 214 F. Supp. 3d 79, 85 (D.D.C. 2016) (refusing to deem unaddressed facts as admitted); *with Pesce v. City of Des Moines*, 439 F. Supp. 3d 1101, 1107-09 (S.D. Iowa 2020) (refusing default as to facts contested by Rule 56 motion, but deeming as admitted unaddressed facts from pleading). *See also Mann v. Lee*, 2009 WL 5178095, at *2-*3 (N.D. Cal. Dec. 22, 2009) (noting case law uncertainty and granting extension of time to answer until motion is decided). *See generally* 10A CHARLES A. WRIGHT, ARTHUR R. MILLER, & MARY K. KANE, FEDERAL PRACTICE AND PROCEDURE § 2718, at 329–30 (2016) (advocating for analogous tolling for pre-answer Rule 56 motions).

[26]*See* Rule 12(d).

[27]*See Marquez v. Cable One, Inc.*,

tion (*e.g.*, seeking the dismissal of counts I, III, and VI of the complaint). The substantial majority of courts favor a complete tolling in such cases, with the partial motion suspending that party's responsive pleading obligations to all unchallenged counts.[28] A minority and some commentary would demand an interim, partial answer to the unchallenged counts.[29]

- *Appellate Remands:* It is not clear how much time a defendant has to responsively plead if an appellate court reverses a Rule 12(b) motion the trial court had granted.

Manipulative Motions and Tolling Effect

Courts will not tolerate the use of this Rule 12 tolling feature in attempts to frivolously manipulate the time period for responsive pleading (for example, by deliberately mislabeling summary judgment as a Rule 12 motion or by filing a patently frivolous motion just to obtain the tolling effect).[30]

State Court Rules Do Not Apply

Federal procedure governs the time for responding to a federal complaint, answer (if a response is ordered), counterclaim, or crossclaim. This is true even if a State law that would

---

463 F.3d 1118, 1120–21 (10th Cir. 2006).

[28] *See Ideal Instruments, Inc. v. Rivard Instruments, Inc.*, 434 F. Supp. 2d 598, 637–40 (N.D. Iowa 2006) (following majority approach, holding that motion to dismiss suspends time for responding to all portions of complaint, even unchallenged ones). *Accord, e.g., In re Am. Express Anti-Steering Rules Antitrust Litig.*, 343 F. Supp. 3d 94, 98 (E.D.N.Y. 2018); *Maass v. Lee*, 189 F. Supp. 3d 581, 587–88 (E.D. Va. 2016); *Betz v. First Credit Servs., Inc.*, 139 F. Supp. 3d 451, 456 n.4 (D.D.C. 2015); *Abbott v. Rosenthal*, 2 F. Supp. 2d 1139, 1142–43 (D. Idaho 2014); *Finnegan v. University of Rochester Medical Center*, 180 F.R.D. 247, 249–50 (W.D. N.Y. 1998); *Brocksopp Engineering, Inc. v. Bach-Simpson Ltd.*, 136 F.R.D. 485, 486–87 (E.D. Wis. 1991); *Baker v. Universal Die Casting, Inc.*, 725 F. Supp. 416, 420–21 (W.D. Ark. 1989); *Business Incentives Co., Inc. v. Sony Corp. of America*, 397 F. Supp. 63, 70 (S.D. N.Y. 1975).

[29] *See Gerlach v. Michigan Bell Tel. Co.*, 448 F. Supp. 1168, 1174 (E.D. Mich. 1978) (responsive pleading was required to unchallenged counts, refusing to enter default, but awarding plaintiffs attorney fees for filing for default). *See also 19 Recordings Ltd. v. Sony Music Entm't*, 97 F. Supp. 3d 433, 447 (S.D.N.Y. 2015) (directing either responsive pleading to remaining courts or explanation why those are not admitted); *Okaya (USA), Inc. v. U.S.*, 27 Ct. Int'l Trade 1509, 2003 WL 22284567 (2003) (motion to dismiss part of a complaint did not extend time to answer remainder). *See generally* Scott L. Cagan, *A "Partial" Motion to Dismiss Under Federal Rule of Civil Procedure 12: You Had Better Answer*, 39 Fed.B.J. 202 (1992) (advocating same result). *But see Tingley Systems, Inc. v. CSC Consulting, Inc.*, 152 F. Supp. 2d 95, 122 (D. Mass. 2001) ("no court has relied on [*Gerlach*'s] reasoning or followed its ruling" and "one court explicitly rejected its reasoning").

[30] *See Ricke v. Armco, Inc.*, 158 F.R.D. 149, 150 (D. Minn. 1994) ("Such an attempt to manipulate the Federal Rules of Civil Procedure should not be condoned or encouraged by the Court"); *Resolution Trust Corp. v. Ruggiero*, 994 F.2d 1221, 1227 (7th Cir. 1993) (frivolous motion under Rule 12 buys movant no additional time within which to serve responsive pleading).

have provided a longer response period.[31]

RULE 12(b)—DEFENSES AND OBJECTIONS

CORE CONCEPT

All legal and factual defenses to a claim for relief must be asserted in the responsive pleading to the claim. However, seven enumerated defenses may alternatively be asserted by motion served before the responsive pleading is due.

APPLICATIONS

Obligation to Assert Defenses and Objections

All defenses to a claim for relief must be asserted in a responsive pleading (if a responsive pleading is required). If no responsive pleading is required, that party may ordinarily assert its defenses, for the first time, at trial.[32] If a responsive pleading is required, the pleader is given a choice: the following seven enumerated defenses and objections may be asserted *either* in a responsive pleading *or* by pre-answer motion:

- Lack of Subject-Matter Jurisdiction, Rule 12(b)(1).
- Lack of Personal Jurisdiction, Rule 12(b)(2).
- Improper Venue, Rule 12(b)(3).
- Insufficient Process, Rule 12(b)(4).
- Insufficient Service of Process, Rule 12(b)(5).
- Failure to State a Claim for which Relief Can Be Granted, Rule 12(b)(6).
- Failure to Join a Party Under Rule 19 (persons needed for just adjudication), Rule 12(b)(7).

Motion Permitted, Not Compelled

No pleader is *compelled* to file a pre-answer motion, even if one would be proper. Pleaders may instead proceed directly to a responsive pleading and raise their defenses and objections there.[33]

Waiver Risks with Defenses and Objections

The act of asserting a particular defense or objection will not result in a waiver of other, perhaps inconsistent defenses or objections asserted along with it.[34] But neglecting to assert it may: if a party chooses to file a Rule 12 motion which includes no objection to personal jurisdiction, venue, process, or service, those omitted objections are deemed waived and ordinarily

---

[31] *See Young v. United States*, 942 F.3d 349, 351 (7th Cir. 2019); *Beller & Keller v. Tyler*, 120 F.3d 21, 25–26 (2d Cir. 1997).

[32] *See Multiquimica Dominicana v. Chemo Int'l, Inc.*, 707 Fed. Appx. 692, 693 n.4 (11th Cir. 2017); *BCC Merch. Sols., Inc. v. Jet Pay, LLC*, 129 F. Supp. 3d 440, 454 n.14 (N.D. Tex. 2015).

[33] *See C&C Inv. Props., L.L.C. v. Trustmark Nat'l Bank*, 838 F.3d 655, 660 (5th Cir. 2016).

[34] *See Fowler v. Sprint Spectrum L.P.*, 2018 WL 8333422, at *2 n.1 (C.D. Cal. Sept. 26, 2018); *JP Morgan Chase Bank, N.A. v. Horvath*, 862 F. Supp. 2d 744, 753 (S.D. Ohio 2012).

cannot be raised later in a pleading, a motion, or at trial.[35]

Time for Making Motion

The Rules do not prescribe a deadline for filing pre-answer motions (beyond requiring that they be made before responsively pleading).[36] Consequently, the safest filing windows for pre-answer motions are the responsive pleading deadlines set in Rule 12(a). Nonetheless, some courts, citing the absence of an explicit motions deadline, have allowed Rule 12(b) motions to be filed after the normal responsive pleading time so long as the filing occurs before an answer—though this liberality can carry serious risks.[37] This view of motion timing might, in an appropriate case, permit an amendment to a pending motion to add a previously omitted defense.[38]

Form of Motion

Rule 12 provides only sparse guidance on the form and procedure for federal motion practice.[39] Other Rules provide some additional detail. For example, Rule 7 requires that motions generally be in writing, include a caption, state with particularity the basis for the motion, and request specific relief.[40] Rule 11 mandates that all motions be signed and be presented for only proper, legally-warranted, factually-warranted purposes.[41] Rule 5 requires that motions be served upon each party to the litigation and be filed with the court within a reasonable time after service.[42] Rule 78 provides for the hearing and disposition of motions, and provides that the district court, by rule or order, may permit motions to be submitted and determined on the written submissions only, without oral argument.[43]

Most other details of federal motion practice and procedure are governed by local court rules and chambers policies, and

---

[35] *See* Rule 12(h). *See also infra* Authors' Commentary to Rule 12(h).

[36] *See* Rule 12(b).

[37] *See Hedeen Int'l, LLC v. Zing Toys, Inc.*, 811 F.3d 904, 905–06 (7th Cir. 2016) (personal jurisdiction defense not automatically waived when motion filed before a past-due answer, but noting default and other waiver risks if delay is unapproved); *Bechtel v. Liberty Nat. Bank*, 534 F.2d 1335, 1340–41 (9th Cir. 1976) (same effect). *See also Luv N' Care, Ltd. v. Babelito,S. A.*, 306 F. Supp. 2d 468, 471–72 (S.D.N.Y. 2004) (motion not waived where filing delay explained by settlement discussions and service complications). *But see Farmers Elevator Mut. Ins. Co. v. Carl J. Austad & Sons, Inc.*, 343 F.2d 7, 12 (8th Cir. 1965) (responsive pleading time dictates motion deadline).

[38] *See Bechtel v. Liberty Nat. Bank*, 534 F.2d 1335, 1341 n.8 (9th Cir. 1976); *Wiggins v. Jedson Eng'g, Inc.*, 2020 WL 6993840, at *1 (E.D. Tenn. Apr. 29, 2020). *See generally supra* Authors' Commentary to Rule 7(b) ("**Amendments to Motions**").

[39] *See, e.g.*, Rule 12 (enumerating types of pre-answer motions; requiring motion before answer; permitting extrinsic materials to be submitted on converted motions).

[40] *See* Rule 7(b)(1).

[41] *See* Rule 11.

[42] *See* Rule 5(a)-(b) (duty to serve); Rule 5(d) (duty to file).

[43] *See* Rule 78.

may vary greatly from court to court.[44] For example:

- *Pre-Filing Consultation:* Some districts require that the moving party meet and confer with the adversary prior to filing any motion, and then certify that good faith attempts to resolve the motion before filing have failed.[45]
- *Form of Order:* Some districts require that the moving party include with the motion a proposed blank form of order.[46]
- *Legal Memorandum:* Some districts require that a brief or memorandum accompany the motion.[47]
- *Page Limits:* Many districts set page limits that must be followed strictly, unless leave of court is sought and granted for the filing of a longer document.[48]
- *Oral Argument:* Some districts establish a formal procedure for seeking oral argument on a motion.[49]
- *Miscellaneous Requirements:* Local rules provide a myriad of other requirements, varying from district to district.[50]

Because significant differences abound, practitioners must carefully consult their district's local rules before engaging in motion practice.

Responses to Motions

The Federal Rules also provide very little guidance on the practice and procedure for responding to motions. This detail is also almost always governed by the district's local rules of practice, which may establish requirements regarding:

- *Time for Responding:* Many districts require non-moving parties to file their opposition papers within a certain number of days after *either* the filing of or service of the motion.[51]
- *Forms of Order:* Some districts require that the non-

[44]*See* Rule 83(a) (authorizing districts to establish local rules of practice).

[45]*See, e.g.*, E.D. Mich. Loc. R. 7.1(a) (duty to seek concurrence in motion); D. Or. Loc. R. 7.1(a) (good faith certification requirement).

[46]*See, e.g.*, D. Idaho Loc. R. 7.1(a)(1) (requiring proposed order under certain circumstances); W.D. Pa. Loc. R. 7.1(B) (motion improper if proposed order is not included).

[47]*See, e.g.*, E.D. Pa. Loc. R. 7.1(c); D.R.I. Loc. R. 7(a).

[48]*See, e.g.*, M.D. Pa. Loc. R. 7.8(b) (requiring double-spaced briefs limited to 15 pages); D.S.C. Loc. R. 7.05(B)(1) (35 page limit for initial brief).

[49]*See, e.g.*, D.Az. Loc. R. 7.2(f) (request made by notation directly on motion or response); D.S.D. Loc. R. 7.1 (request made either in conclusion of motion or by separate pleading); D. Utah Loc. R. 7.1(f) (oral argument only granted for "good cause shown").

[50]*See, e.g.*, M.D. Pa. Loc. R. 7.8(a) (memoranda must state legal question presented); D.S.C. Loc. R. 7.05(a)(1) (memoranda must contain "concise summary of the nature of the case").

[51]*See, e.g.*, Alaska Loc. R. 7.1(e) (opposition due within 15 days after service of motion); E.D. Tenn. Loc. R. 7.1(a) (opposition to dispositive motion due within 21 days of service).

moving party include a proposed form of order.[52]

- *Page Limits:* Many districts establish page limits for opposition papers.[53]
- *Reply Briefs:* Some districts permit the moving party to file a reply brief, so long as the reply is filed within a prescribed period.[54] Local rules may also set reply brief page limits.[55]

Because these response provisions vary so greatly from judicial district to judicial district, non-moving parties must take care to consult the district's local rules before responding to a pending motion.

Liberal Reading of Motions

Liberality applies to motions to dismiss. A motion to dismiss will generally not be rejected merely because it fails to cite which particular Rule it invokes.[56] But practitioners are wise to ensure that the precise nature of their motion is always clear.

Preliminary Motions Not Listed in Rule 12

Rule 12 does not provide an exhaustive list of all possible preliminary motions.[57] For example, motions for extensions of time, to amend a pleading, to intervene, to substitute parties, or for the entering of a stay or an order commanding the posting of security may all be raised as preliminary motions.

Amended Pleadings

An amended complaint supersedes its predecessor.[58] Although a responsive pleader cannot ordinarily use the filing of such an amendment to revive defenses or objections that could have been asserted to the original complaint earlier, but were

---

[52]*See, e.g.*, E.D. Pa. Loc. R. 7.1(a); W.D. Tenn. Loc. R. 7.2(a)(2).

[53]*See, e.g.*, D. Az. Loc. R. 7.2(e) (opposition brief limited to 15 pages); M.D. Fla. Loc. R. 3.01(b) (opposition brief limited to 20 pages); D. Vt. Loc. R. 7(a)(4) (opposition to dispositive motions limited to 25 pages).

[54]*See, e.g.*, D. Neb. Loc. R. 7.0.1(c) (reply briefs must be filed within 7 days after opposition brief is filed and served); D.S.C. Loc. R. 7.07 (reply briefs are "discouraged", but may be filed within 7 days after service of the opposition). *But see* M.D. Fla. Loc. R. 3.01(b) (no reply briefs permitted absent leave of court); D.N.H. Loc. R. 7.1(e)(2) (no reply briefs to nondispositive motions).

[55]*See, e.g.*, E.D. Mich. Loc. R. 7.1(c) (reply briefs limited to 5 pages); N.D. Tex. Loc. R. 7.2(c) (reply briefs limited to 10 pages).

[56]*See Travel All Over the World, Inc. v. Kingdom of Saudi Arabia*, 73 F.3d 1423, 1429 (7th Cir. 1996).

[57]*See Custom Vehicles, Inc. v. Forest River, Inc.*, 464 F.3d 725, 727 (7th Cir. 2006) ("Motions may be proper despite the lack of a specific rule"); *International Ass'n of Entrepreneurs of America v. Angoff*, 58 F.3d 1266, 1271 (8th Cir. 1995) (although Rule 12(b) ostensibly enumerates available pre-answer motions, courts have discretion to permit other, unenumerated pre-answer motions).

[58]*See Palakovic v. Wetzel*, 854 F.3d 209, 220 (3d Cir. 2017); *Neubauer v. FedEx Corp.*, 849 F.3d 400, 403 (8th Cir. 2017).

not and are now waived,[59] if the amended complaint adds new theories or alters the lawsuit's scope, the defendant is usually free to file a new answer (which could include new defenses and counterclaims).[60]

RULE 12(b)(1)—DISMISSAL FOR LACK OF SUBJECT-MATTER JURISDICTION

CORE CONCEPT

A case must be dismissed if the court lacks jurisdictional authority over the subject-matter of the dispute.

APPLICATIONS

Types of Challenges

A Rule 12(b)(1) motion challenging subject-matter jurisdiction questions the very power of the court to hear the case.[61] Such challenges may be made either *facially* ("technically") or *substantively* ("factually").[62] On a *facial* challenge, the defendant contests the sufficiency of the pleader's allegations of subject-matter jurisdiction.[63] A pleader is required to adequately aver the basis for the court's jurisdiction; if the pleader fails to do so, the lawsuit can be dismissed.[64] On a *substantive* challenge, the defendant disputes the underlying truth of the pleader's alleged jurisdictional facts.[65] In such a challenge, the pleading itself may have adequately alleged the presence of federal subject-matter jurisdiction, but the actual facts and allegations before the court may belie that averment, confirming that federal jurisdiction is absent and, thus, compelling the case's dismissal.[66]

Legal Test

The existence of subject-matter jurisdiction is tested as of the date the lawsuit was filed[67] or, in removed cases, on the

---

[59] *See Sohns v. Dahl*, 392 F. Supp. 1208, 1220 (W.D. Va. 1975).

[60] *See Heckler & Koch, Inc. v. German Sport Guns GmbH*, 976 F. Supp. 2d 1020, 1028–29 (S.D. Ind. 2013).

[61] *See Morrison v. Nat'l Australia Bank Ltd.*, 561 U.S. 247, 254, 130 S. Ct. 2869, 177 L. Ed. 2d 535 (2010). For a detailed discussion of federal subject-matter jurisdiction, see *supra* Part II, §§ 2.9 to 2.12.

[62] *See Lindke v. Tomlinson*, 31 F.4th 487, 490 n.1 (6th Cir. 2022); *Harty v. W. Point Realty, Inc.*, 28 F.4th 435, 441 (2d Cir. 2022).

[63] *See Laufer v. Looper*, 22 F.4th 871, 875 (10th Cir. 2022); *Meland v. WEBER*, 2 F.4th 838, 843 (9th Cir. 2021).

[64] *See* Rule 8(a)(1); *Gibbs v. Buck*, 307 U.S. 66, 77, 59 S. Ct. 725, 83 L. Ed. 1111 (1939).

[65] *See Lindke v. Tomlinson*, 31 F.4th 487, 490 n.1 (6th Cir. 2022); *Cebollero-Bertran v. Puerto Rico Aqueduct & Sewer Auth.*, 4 F.4th 63, 69 (1st Cir. 2021).

[66] *See Gibbs v. Buck*, 307 U.S. 66, 59 S. Ct. 725, 83 L. Ed. 1111 (1939); *Silha v. ACT, Inc.*, 807 F.3d 169, 173 (7th Cir. 2015).

[67] *See Grupo Dataflux v. Atlas Global Group, L.P.*, 541 U.S. 567, 574, 124 S. Ct. 1920, 158 L. Ed. 2d 866 (2004); *Conolly v. Taylor*, 27 U.S. 556,

date of removal[68] (or, perhaps, *both* the dates of original filing *and* removal).[69] In diversity cases, a post-filing dismissal of a non-diverse party may rescue deficient jurisdiction,[70] though a post-filing change in a party's citizenship will not.[71]

The legal test used to conduct the subject-matter jurisdiction assessment depends on the type of challenge:

- *Facial (or "Technical") Challenges:* In examining facial (or technical) challenges to federal subject-matter jurisdiction, the court will construe the complaint liberally, accept all uncontroverted, well-pleaded factual allegations as true, and view all reasonable inferences in plaintiff's favor.[72] But legal conclusions (even those couched as factual allegations) will not be assumed true.[73] The court will view the allegations as a whole; if a conclusory averment of subject-matter jurisdiction is contradicted by other allegations in the pleading, the case may be dismissed.[74] This approach mirrors the procedure (and safeguards for the nonmoving party) of Rule 12(b)(6).[75] The adequacy of the pleading will be tested under the "short and plain" standard of Rule 8(a)(1), with some courts applying the "plausibility" lens established in *Twombly* to conduct the inquiry.[76]
- *Substantive (or "Factual") Challenges:* In substantive (or factual) subject-matter jurisdiction attacks, the court will *not* presume that plaintiff's controverted factual al-

7 L. Ed. 518 (1829) (Marshall, C.J.).

[68]*See Koenigsberger v. Richmond Silver Mining Co.*, 158 U.S. 41, 49–50, 15 S. Ct. 751, 39 L. Ed. 889 (1895).

[69]Only some Circuits have expressly adopted this dual requirement. *See, e.g., Strotek Corp. v. Air Transp. Ass'n. of Am.*, 300 F.3d 1129, 1131 (9th Cir. 2002); *Ryan ex rel. Ryan v. Schneider Nat. Carriers, Inc.*, 263 F.3d 816, 819 (8th Cir. 2001).

[70]*See Newman-Green, Inc. v. Alfonzo-Larrain*, 490 U.S. 826, 832, 109 S. Ct. 2218, 104 L. Ed. 2d 893 (1989).

[71]*See Grupo Dataflux v. Atlas Glob. Grp., L.P.*, 541 U.S. 567, 575, 124 S. Ct. 1920, 158 L. Ed. 2d 866 (2004).

[72]*See Scheuer v. Rhodes*, 416 U.S. 232, 234–37, 94 S. Ct. 1683, 40 L. Ed. 2d 90 (1974); *Lacewell v. Off. of Comptroller of Currency*, 999 F.3d 130, 140 (2d Cir. 2021).

[73]*See Daniel v. Univ. of Texas Sw. Med. Ctr.*, 960 F.3d 253, 256 (5th Cir. 2020); *Rote v. Zel Custom Mfg. LLC*, 816 F.3d 383, 387 (6th Cir. 2016).

[74]*See Gibbs v. Buck*, 307 U.S. 66, 59 S. Ct. 725, 83 L. Ed. 1111 (1939); *New Mexicans for Bill Richardson v. Gonzales*, 64 F.3d 1495, 1499 (10th Cir. 1995).

[75]*See Glob. Tech., Inc. v. Yubei (XinXiang) Power Steering Sys. Co.*, 807 F.3d 806, 810 (6th Cir. 2015); *Branson Label, Inc. v. City of Branson*, 793 F.3d 910, 914 (8th Cir. 2015).

[76]*See Cavalieri v. Avior Airlines C.A.*, 25 F.4th 843, 850 (11th Cir. 2022); *Ghedi v. Mayorkas*, 16 F.4th 456, 463–64 (5th Cir. 2021); *SM Kids, LLC v. Google LLC*, 963 F.3d 206, 210 (2d Cir. 2020). *See also Brownback v. King*, 592 U.S. __, 141 S. Ct. 740, 749 n.8, 209 L. Ed. 2d 33 (2021) (implying *Twombly* applies). *But see Maya v. Centex Corp.*, 658 F.3d 1060, 1068 (9th Cir. 2011) (*Twombly* not proper approach for testing jurisdictional questions of standing). For an in-depth discussion of the *Twombly* standard, see Authors' Commentary to Rule 8(a) *supra* and Rule 12(b)(6) *infra*.

legations are true,[77] but may instead weigh the evidence and find the facts,[78] so long as this factfinding does not involve the merits of the dispute.[79] In doing so, the court enjoys broad discretion. The court may rule on the basis of undisputed record facts,[80] may receive and consider extrinsic evidence,[81] or may convene an evidentiary hearing or plenary trial to resolve disputed jurisdictional facts.[82] Whether to convene such a hearing will depend on whether the parties have requested one[83] and on the circumstances (including whether the parties have received notice and a fair opportunity to be heard).[84] If a material fact concerning jurisdiction is disputed, a plenary hearing may be necessary to resolve the contested issue.[85]

- *"Intertwined" Merits:* If the merits are so intertwined with the jurisdiction issue that the two cannot be separated,[86] the ultimate resolution of the court's subject-matter jurisdiction may need to await trial.[87] In such instances, several courts apply summary judgment principles, inquiring whether a genuine dispute exists over material jurisdiction facts; if so, the lawsuit must proceed to trial for the factfinder's determination of those facts.[88] Other courts differ in their approach.[89]

---

[77]*See Boim v. Am. Muslims for Palestine*, 9 F.4th 545, 558 (7th Cir. 2021); *Long v. Se. Pa. Transp. Auth.*, 903 F.3d 312, 320 (3d Cir. 2018).

[78]*See Bolivarian Republic of Venezuela v. Helmerich & Payne Int'l Drilling Co.*, 581 U.S. __, 137 S. Ct. 1312, 1316, 197 L. Ed. 2d 663 (2017); *Arbaugh v. Y&H Corp.*, 546 U.S. 500, 514, 126 S. Ct. 1235, 163 L. Ed. 2d 1097 (2006). *But see Edison v. United States*, 822 F.3d 510, 517 (9th Cir. 2016) (factual disputes must be resolved in plaintiff's favor).

[79]*See Arbaugh v. Y&H Corp.*, 546 U.S. 500, 514, 126 S. Ct. 1235, 163 L. Ed. 2d 1097 (2006).

[80]*See Moore v. Bryant*, 853 F.3d 245, 248 (5th Cir. 2017);

[81]*See infra* Authors' Commentary to Rule 12(b)(1) ("**Extrinsic Materials**").

[82]*See Saleh v. Sulka Trading Ltd.*, 957 F.3d 348, 353 (2d Cir. 2020); *Buckler v. United States*, 919 F.3d 1038, 1044 (8th Cir. 2019).

[83]*See Molina v. Aurora Loan Servs., LLC*, 635 Fed. Appx. 618, 627 (11th Cir. 2015); *McCann v. Newman Irrevocable Trust*, 458 F.3d 281, 290 (3d Cir. 2006).

[84]*See Johnson v. U.S.*, 534 F.3d 958, 964 (8th Cir. 2008); *McCann v. Newman Irrevocable Trust*, 458 F.3d 281 (3d Cir. 2006).

[85]*See Lincoln Ben. Life Co. v. AEI Life, LLC*, 800 F.3d 99, 105 (3d Cir. 2015).

[86]*See Odyssey Marine Expl., Inc. v. Unidentified Shipwrecked Vessel*, 657 F.3d 1159, 1169–70 (11th Cir. 2011) (defining "intertwined"); *Paper, Allied-Industrial, Chem. & Energy Workers Int'l Union v. Continental Carbon Co.*, 428 F.3d 1285, 1292 (10th Cir. 2005) (same).

[87]*See Arbaugh v. Y&H Corp.*, 546 U.S. 500, 514, 126 S. Ct. 1235, 1244, 163 L. Ed. 2d 1097 (2006); *Buckler v. United States*, 919 F.3d 1038, 1044 (8th Cir. 2019).

[88]*See PDVSA US Litig. Tr. v. Lukoil Pan Americas, LLC*, 991 F.3d 1187, 1191–92 (11th Cir. 2021); *Croyle by & through Croyle v. United States*, 908 F.3d 377, 380 (8th Cir. 2018).

Burden of Proof

When challenged, the party invoking the court's subject-matter jurisdiction bears the burden of establishing it.[90] On a facial challenge, the party bears only a pleading burden, not an evidentiary one.[91] On a substantive challenge (and, later, at trial), the party assumes a merits burden which must be carried by a preponderance of the evidence.[92] In federal question cases, the party must demonstrate a non-frivolous claim based on federal law[93] (not an especially onerous burden),[94] and must meet all other statutory prerequisites for litigating the federal claim (such as exhaustion of administrative remedies and compliance with all claims-filing limitations and requirements).[95] In diversity cases, the party must demonstrate complete diversity of citizenship[96] and a claim that in good faith exceeds $75,000 exclusive of interest and costs.[97] In all cases, the party must demonstrate constitutional standing[98]

---

[89] *See S.R.P. ex rel. Abunabba v. United States*, 676 F.3d 329, 344 & n.7 (3d Cir. 2012) (noting approach, and disagreement among Circuits). *See also Al Shimari v. CACI Premier Tech., Inc.*, 758 F.3d 516, 532 (4th Cir. 2014) (when inextricably intertwined with merits, factual disputes resolved "only after appropriate discovery").

[90] *See Thomson v. Gaskill*, 315 U.S. 442, 446, 62 S. Ct. 673, 86 L. Ed. 951 (1942); *Lujan v. Defenders of Wildlife*, 504 U.S. 555, 561, 112 S. Ct. 2130, 119 L. Ed. 2d 351 (1992).

[91] *See Lacewell v. Off. of Comptroller of Currency*, 999 F.3d 130, 140 (2d Cir. 2021); *Hutton v. Nat'l Bd. of Examiners in Optometry, Inc.*, 892 F.3d 613, 620–21 (4th Cir. 2018).

[92] *See Collins v. United States*, 996 F.3d 102, 108 (2d Cir. 2021); *In re S. Recycling, L.L.C.*, 982 F.3d 374, 379 (5th Cir. 2020).

[93] *See Neitzke v. Williams*, 490 U.S. 319, 327, 109 S. Ct. 1827, 104 L. Ed. 2d 338 (1989); *Hagans v. Lavine*, 415 U.S. 528, 536–37, 94 S. Ct. 1372, 39 L. Ed. 2d 577 (1974); *Bell v. Hood*, 327 U.S. 678, 682–83, 66 S. Ct. 773, 90 L. Ed. 939 (1946). *Cf. Holloway v. Pagan River Dockside Seafood, Inc.*, 669 F.3d 448, 452 (4th Cir. 2012) (Rule 12(b)(1) dismissal for deficient federal case is proper only if claim is insubstantial, implausible, precedentially foreclosed, or otherwise completely devoid of merit). Allegations that fail to meet the "frivolous" test warranting dismissal under Rule 12(b)(1) may still be dismissed under Rule 12(b)(6) for failing to state a cognizable claim for relief.

[94] *See Metro Hydroelectric Co., LLC v. Metro Parks*, 541 F.3d 605, 610 (6th Cir. 2008).

[95] *See Hart v. Dep't of Labor ex rel. U.S.*, 116 F.3d 1338, 1340–41 (10th Cir. 1997) (analyzing under Rule 12(b)(1) the defense that plaintiff failed to file timely claim with proper agency as required by the Federal Tort Claims Act).

[96] *See City of Indianapolis v. Chase Nat'l Bank of New York*, 314 U.S. 63, 69, 62 S. Ct. 15, 86 L. Ed. 47 (1941); *Lincoln Ben. Life Co. v. AEI Life, LLC*, 800 F.3d 99, 104 (3d Cir. 2015).

[97] *See St. Paul Mercury Indem. Co. v. Red Cab Co.*, 303 U.S. 283, 289, 58 S. Ct. 586, 82 L. Ed. 845 (1938) (dismissal proper only when it appears claim is not made in good faith or that, to a "legal certainty," it is over-valued). *See also Dart Cherokee Basin Operating Co., LLC v. Owens*, 574 U.S. 81, 87–89, 135 S. Ct. 547, 190 L. Ed. 2d 495 (2014) (on removal, defendant's value should be similarly accepted, unless it is contested).

[98] *See Spokeo, Inc. v. Robins*, 578 U.S. 330, 337–38, 136 S. Ct. 1540, 1547, 194 L. Ed. 2d 635 (2016); *Lujan v. Defs. of Wildlife*, 504 U.S. 555, 560–61, 112 S. Ct. 2130, 2136, 119 L.

and a live "case or controversy" subject to the federal courts' judicial power under Article III of the Constitution.[99]

Timing and Waiver

Challenges to subject-matter jurisdiction may be raised at any time, by any party, or by the court.[100] Such challenges can even be raised after final judgment is entered.[101] A party cannot waive or forfeit the requirement of subject-matter jurisdiction,[102] nor can the parties consent to have a case heard in federal court where subject-matter jurisdiction is absent.[103]

- *But Preclusion Can Apply:* A party who loses a challenge to subject-matter jurisdiction in the district court may appeal, but res judicata principles ordinarily bar that party from challenging the ruling collaterally[104] (indeed, this same bar may even apply where the party had the *opportunity* to contest subject-matter jurisdiction but failed to do so).[105]

Extrinsic Materials

The appropriate role for extrinsic materials depends on the type of Rule 12(b)(1) challenge the parties make. In a facial (or technical) attack, the court is limited to considering the complaint alone[106] (supplemented, perhaps, by its attached exhibits[107] and any facts that are uncontested[108] or subject to judicial

---

Ed. 2d 351 (1992). *See generally Lexmark Int'l, Inc. v. Static Control Components, Inc.*, 572 U.S. 118, 128 n.4, 134 S. Ct. 1377, 188 L. Ed. 2d 392 (2014) (only constitutional standing, not statutory ("prudential") standing, implicates subject-matter jurisdiction).

[99]*See, e.g., Davis v. Anthony, Inc.*, 886 F.3d 674, 676–77 (8th Cir. 2018) (mootness challenges reviewed under Rule 12(b)(1)); *Bateman v. City of West Bountiful*, 89 F.3d 704, 706 (10th Cir. 1996) (ripeness challenges are examined under Rule 12(b)(1)).

[100]*See Arena v. Graybar Elec. Co.*, 669 F.3d 214, 223 (5th Cir. 2012); *American Telecom Co., L.L.C. v. Republic of Lebanon*, 501 F.3d 534, 539 (6th Cir. 2007).

[101]*See Arbaugh v. Y&H Corp.*, 546 U.S. 500, 506, 126 S. Ct. 1235, 163 L. Ed. 2d 1097 (2006). *See also* Rule 60(b)(4). *But cf. Grupo Dataflux v. Atlas Glob. Grp., L.P.*, 541 U.S. 567, 571, 124 S. Ct. 1920, 1924, 158 L. Ed. 2d 866 (2004) ("at any time prior to final judgment"); Authors' Commentary to Rule 12(h) ("**Objections to Subject-Matter Jurisdiction**" — "*Asserted At Any Time*") (noting possible bar on collateral attacks).

[102]*See Arbaugh v. Y&H Corp.*, 546 U.S. 500, 514, 126 S. Ct. 1235, 163 L. Ed. 2d 1097 (2006).

[103]*See Neirbo Co. v. Bethlehem Shipbuilding Corporation*, 308 U.S. 165, 60 S. Ct. 153, 84 L. Ed. 167 (1939).

[104]*See Ins. Corp. of Ireland v. Compagnie des Bauxites de Guinee*, 456 U.S. 694, 702 n.9, 102 S. Ct. 2099, 72 L. Ed. 2d 492 (1982); *Chicot Cnty. Drainage Dist. v. Baxter State Bank*, 308 U.S. 371, 375–78, 60 S. Ct. 317, 319–20, 84 L. Ed. 329 (1940).

[105]*See Corbett v. MacDonald Moving Servs., Inc.*, 124 F.3d 82, 88–89 (2d Cir. 1997).

[106]*See Thomas v. TOMS King (Ohio), LLC*, 997 F.3d 629, 634 (6th Cir. 2021); *Walker v. Beaumont Indep. Sch. Dist.*, 938 F.3d 724, 734 (5th Cir. 2019).

[107]*See Davis v. Anthony, Inc.*, 886 F.3d 674, 679 (8th Cir. 2018); *Carter v. HealthPort Techs., LLC*, 822 F.3d 47, 56 (2d Cir. 2016).

notice[109]). In a substantive (or factual) attack, the court may consider affidavits and other materials submitted the parties,[110] as well as matters of public record[111] and facts subject to judicial notice.[112] Considering such extrinsic materials in this way does not require the court to convert the motion into one for summary judgment.[113] However, if a Rule 12(b)(1) attack is coupled with a Rule 12(b)(6) merits attack, the extrinsic evidence can only be consulted to rule on subject-matter jurisdiction (absent a summary judgment conversion).[114]

Allowing Pre-Ruling Jurisdictional Discovery

When a defendant moves to dismiss for lack of subject-matter jurisdiction, discovery of the factual issues implicated by the motion may be permitted.[115] This is especially true where the discovery seeks information peculiarly within the knowledge of the adversary.[116] The party seeking the discovery bears the burden of showing its need,[117] and failing to make such a showing justifies a denial of jurisdictional discovery.[118] The trial judge enjoys broad discretion in resolving such requests.[119]

Mislabeled Motions

Provided no prejudice is caused, courts often excuse a mislabeling of a Rule 12(b)(1) motion as a Rule 12(b)(6) failure to state a claim motion, and *vice versa*, and simply apply the appropriate Rule's test.[120] Summary judgment motions that

---

[108] *See Flores v. Pompeo*, 936 F.3d 273, 276 (5th Cir. 2019).

[109] *See Hyatt v. Yee*, 871 F.3d 1067, 1071 n.15 (9th Cir. 2017);

[110] *See Bolivarian Republic of Venezuela v. Helmerich & Payne Int'l Drilling Co.*, 581 U.S. __, 137 S. Ct. 1312, 1316, 197 L. Ed. 2d 663 (2017); *Kennedy v. Floridian Hotel, Inc.*, 998 F.3d 1221, 1230 (11th Cir. 2021).

[111] *See White v. Lee*, 227 F.3d 1214, 1242 (9th Cir. 2000).

[112] *See Ctr. for Biological Diversity, Inc. v. BP Am. Prod. Co.*, 704 F.3d 413, 423 (5th Cir. 2013).

[113] *See Am. Diabetes Ass'n v. U.S. Dep't of Army*, 938 F.3d 1147, 1151 (9th Cir. 2019); *Buckler v. United States*, 919 F.3d 1038, 1044 (8th Cir. 2019). *But cf. Baker v. USD 229 Blue Valley*, 979 F.3d 866, 872 (10th Cir. 2020) (no conversion *unless* resolving question is intertwined with merits).

[114] *See United States ex rel. Customs Fraud Investigations, LLC. v. Victaulic Co.*, 839 F.3d 242, 251 (3d Cir. 2016).

[115] *See Breakthrough Mgmt. Group, Inc. v. Chukchansi Gold Casino & Resort*, 629 F.3d 1173, 1189 (10th Cir. 2010); *Skwira v. U.S.*, 344 F.3d 64, 71–72 (1st Cir. 2003).

[116] *See Gualandi v. Adams*, 385 F.3d 236, 244 (2d Cir. 2004).

[117] *See Breakthrough Mgmt. Group, Inc. v. Chukchansi Gold Casino & Resort*, 629 F.3d 1173, 1189 n.11 (10th Cir. 2010); *Freeman v. U.S.*, 556 F.3d 326, 341–42 (5th Cir. 2009).

[118] *See In re S. Recycling, L.L.C.*, 982 F.3d 374, 385–86 (5th Cir. 2020); *Broidy Capital Mgmt. LLC v. Benomar*, 944 F.3d 436, 446–47 (2d Cir. 2019).

[119] *See In re S. Recycling, L.L.C.*, 982 F.3d 374, 386 (5th Cir. 2020); *Broidy Capital Mgmt. LLC v. Benomar*, 944 F.3d 436, 446 (2d Cir. 2019).

[120] *See Doermer v. Oxford Fin. Grp., Ltd.*, 884 F.3d 643, 646 (7th Cir. 2018) (treating Rule 12(b)(1) motion as Rule 12(b)(6) challenge); *Corrie v. Caterpillar, Inc.*, 503 F.3d 974, 980 (9th Cir. 2007) (treating Rule 12(b)(6) motion as Rule 12(b)(1) challenge).

contest subject-matter jurisdiction may likewise be re-framed.[121]

Hearing on Motion

Although a court must afford the plaintiff an opportunity to be heard before dismissing under Rule 12(b)(1), an evidentiary or oral hearing is not always necessary.[122]

***Sua Sponte* Dismissals**

Verifying its subject-matter jurisdiction is a federal court's "first duty" in every case;[123] indeed, courts have an independent obligation to confirm their subject-matter jurisdiction, whether an objection is made by the litigants or not.[124] Accordingly, *sua sponte* dismissals on this basis may be ordered by the trial court or by a subsequent appeals court.[125]

Sequence of Rulings

Attacks on a court's jurisdiction must be considered and resolved before addressing other motions that implicate a claim's merits.[126]

Ruling Deferred

Although the question of subject-matter jurisdiction is resolved by the court, not the jury, the court may defer ruling on the challenge until after further materials are presented, after discovery is conducted, or after evidence is received at trial.[127] The court may *not*, however, defer ruling upon a subject-matter jurisdictional challenge in order to rule instead upon a simpler dispositive motion attacking the underlying merits of the lawsuit.[128]

---

[121] *See Hakki v. Sec'y, Dep't of Veterans Affs.*, 7 F.4th 1012, 1023 (11th Cir. 2021).

[122] *See Kennedy v. Floridian Hotel, Inc.*, 998 F.3d 1221, 1232 (11th Cir. 2021); *In re Eckstein Marine Serv. L.L.C.*, 672 F.3d 310, 319–20 (5th Cir. 2012).

[123] *See McCready v. White*, 417 F.3d 700, 702 (7th Cir. 2005).

[124] *See Arbaugh v. Y&H Corp.*, 546 U.S. 500, 514, 126 S. Ct. 1235, 163 L. Ed. 2d 1097 (2006).

[125] *See Arbaugh v. Y&H Corp.*, 546 U.S. 500, 506, 126 S. Ct. 1235, 163 L. Ed. 2d 1097 (2006).

[126] *See Steel Co. v. Citizens for a Better Env't*, 523 U.S. 83, 101, 118 S. Ct. 1003, 140 L. Ed. 2d 210 (1998) (rejecting process of assuming jurisdiction in order to dispose of a case by way of a less muddled merits principle: "Hypothetical jurisdiction produces nothing more than a hypothetical judgment—which comes to the same thing as an advisory opinion, disapproved by this Court from the beginning."). But courts may bypass subject-matter jurisdiction to dismiss for lack of personal jurisdiction, *see Ruhrgas AG v. Marathon Oil Co.*, 526 U.S. 574, 578, 119 S. Ct. 1563, 143 L. Ed. 2d 760 (1999) ("no unyielding jurisdictional hierarchy" among types of jurisdiction); and may bypass to dismiss on the basis of other "threshold grounds for denying audience to a case on the merits," *see Sinochem Int'l Co. v. Malaysia Int'l Shipping Corp.*, 549 U.S. 422, 431, 127 S. Ct. 1184, 167 L. Ed. 2d 15 (2007) (forum non conveniens dismissal).

[127] *See Land v. Dollar*, 330 U.S. 731, 67 S. Ct. 1009, 91 L. Ed. 1209 (1947); *Valentin v. Hospital Bella Vista*, 254 F.3d 358, 364 n.3 (1st Cir. 2001).

[128] *See supra* Authors' Commentary

Remedy

Generally, the court will permit a party to amend unless it is clear that subject-matter jurisdiction cannot be truthfully averred.[129] When the court lacks subject-matter jurisdiction, it must dismiss the case in its entirety,[130] unless a transfer to a different federal court would cure the jurisdictional defect.[131]

Prejudice on Dismissal

A dismissal for lack of subject-matter jurisdiction is not a decision on the merits (nor could it be since the dismissal confirms the court's lack of authority to act on the merits).[132] Accordingly, such dismissals ordinarily will not preclude plaintiffs from re-filing their claims in courts that have the right to hear their disputes.[133] However, where the requirements for pleading a claim overlap entirely with the requirements for pleading its subject-matter jurisdiction, a dismissal may qualify as a merits ruling.[134]

Dismissal's Effect on Supplemental Jurisdiction

If a lawsuit's federal claims are dismissed for lack of subject-matter jurisdiction, then all supplemental jurisdiction claims will ordinarily be dismissed as well.[135]

Revisiting an Earlier Motion's Denial

A court may deny a motion to dismiss for lack of jurisdiction (for example, upon a facial (or technical) challenge to the face of the pleading), and later discover that jurisdiction is factually defective. In such instances, the court must re-

---

to Rule 12(b)(1) ("**Sequence of Rulings**").

[129] *See Leaf v. Supreme Court of State of Wis.*, 979 F.2d 589, 595 (7th Cir. 1992) (leave to amend defective allegations of subject-matter jurisdiction should be freely given).

[130] *See Arbaugh v. Y&H Corp.*, 546 U.S. 500, 514, 126 S. Ct. 1235, 163 L. Ed. 2d 1097 (2006).

[131] *See* 28 U.S.C.A. § 1631 (authorizing intra-court transfers to cure want of jurisdiction); *Holmes Grp., Inc. v. Vornado Air Circulation Sys., Inc.*, 535 U.S. 826, 834, 122 S. Ct. 1889, 1895, 153 L. Ed. 2d 13 (2002) (directing transfer from Federal Circuit to Tenth Circuit).

[132] *See Green v. Dep't of Educ. of City of New York*, 16 F.4th 1070, 1074 (2d Cir. 2021); *Dalton v. NPC Int'l, Inc.*, 932 F.3d 693, 696 (8th Cir. 2019). *See generally Frederiksen v. City of Lockport*, 384 F.3d 437, 438 (7th Cir. 2004) ("A suit dismissed for lack of jurisdiction cannot *also* be dismissed 'with prejudice'; that's a disposition on the merits, which only a court with jurisdiction may render. . . . 'No jurisdiction' and 'with prejudice' are mutually exclusive.").

[133] *See Wesco Ins. Co. v. Roderick Linton Belfance, LLP*, 39 F.4th 326, 334 (6th Cir. 2022); *Mitchell v. Bailey*, 982 F.3d 937, 944 (5th Cir. 2020). *See also Harty v. W. Point Realty, Inc.*, 28 F.4th 435, 444–45 (2d Cir. 2022) (denying leave to amend is not dismissal with prejudice; it merely forces plaintiff to re-file).

[134] *See Brownback v. King*, 592 U.S. —, 141 S. Ct. 740, 749–50 & n.8, 209 L. Ed. 2d 33 (2021).

[135] *See Cohen v. Postal Holdings, LLC*, 873 F.3d 394, 399 (2d Cir. 2017); *Arena v. Graybar Elec. Co.*, 669 F.3d 214, 223–24 (5th Cir. 2012).

examine its ruling either on motion or *sua sponte*.[136]

Appealability

A dismissal premised upon a lack of subject-matter jurisdiction is ordinarily considered an immediately appealable final order,[137] absent leave to amend.[138] However, denying a motion to dismiss for lack of subject-matter jurisdiction generally is interlocutory and not immediately appealable.[139]

RULE 12(b)(2)—DISMISSAL FOR LACK OF PERSONAL JURISDICTION

CORE CONCEPT

A particular defendant may be dismissed from the lawsuit if personal jurisdiction over that defendant is absent.

APPLICATIONS

In Personam and *In Rem* Actions

Motions under this Rule may be used to challenge any asserted personal jurisdiction by the court, whether *in personam*, *in rem*, or *quasi in rem*.[140]

Special Appearances

The Rules have abandoned the concepts of "special" and "general" appearances.[141] Now, a defendant can assert jurisdictional defenses, venue defenses, and even substantive defenses under Rule 12 without impliedly consenting to the court's personal jurisdiction.[142]

Burden of Proof

The party inviting the court's exercise of personal jurisdiction—ordinarily, the plaintiff[143] or third-party plaintiff[144]—bears the burden of demonstrating that it is both statutorily autho-

---

[136] *See Mastafa v. Chevron Corp.*, 770 F.3d 170, 186–87 (2d Cir. 2014).

[137] *See Attias v. Carefirst, Inc.*, 865 F.3d 620, 624 (D.C. Cir. 2017); *Whisnant v. United States*, 400 F.3d 1177, 1180 (9th Cir. 2005).

[138] *See Attias v. Carefirst, Inc.*, 865 F.3d 620, 624 (D.C. Cir. 2017). *Cf. Cooper v. Ramos*, 704 F.3d 772, 776–77 (9th Cir. 2012) (merely casting dismissal as "without prejudice" did not defeat finality, absent leave to amend).

[139] *See Ashmore v. CGI Grp., Inc.*, 860 F.3d 80, 85 (2d Cir. 2017); *Harrison v. Nissan Motor Corp. in U.S.A.*, 111 F.3d 343, 347–48 (3d Cir. 1997).

[140] *See Newhard, Cook & Co. v. Inspired Life Centers, Inc.*, 895 F.2d 1226, 1228 (8th Cir. 1990).

[141] *See In re Hijazi*, 589 F.3d 401, 413 (7th Cir. 2009); *S.E.C. v. Ross*, 504 F.3d 1130, 1149 (9th Cir. 2007). *See also Orange Theatre Corp. v. Rayherstz Amusement Corp.*, 139 F.2d 871, 874 (C.C.A. 3d Cir. 1944) (defendants are "no longer required at the door of the federal courthouse to intone that ancient abracadabra of the law, de bene esse, in order by its magic power himself to remain outside even while he steps within").

[142] *See In re Hijazi*, 589 F.3d 401, 413 (7th Cir. 2009).

[143] *See Eighteen Seventy, LP v. Jayson*, 32 F.4th 956, 964 (10th Cir. 2022); *Danziger & De Llano, L.L.P. v. Morgan Verkamp, L.L.C.*, 24 F.4th 491, 495 (5th Cir. 2022).

[144] *See Stranahan Gear Co. v. NL Indus., Inc.*, 800 F.2d 53, 58 (3d Cir. 1986); *Royal & Sun All. Ins. PLC v.*

rized and constitutionally permissible,[145] and must do so as to each claim[146] against each resisting opponent.[147] The *nature* of that burden changes (and may shift), depending on the type of personal jurisdiction being invoked.[148] The *weight* of that burden changes as well, depending on the way the challenge is made.[149] Precisely when this burden is triggered seems to now divide the courts. For some courts, the burden is triggered by the act of filing a claim for relief (under this view, alleging personal jurisdiction is a pleading obligation);[150] for other courts, the burden is triggered once a resisting defendant contests the court's exercise of personal jurisdiction by filing a motion to dismiss.[151]

- *Further Trial Burden:* If properly raised and preserved, an objection to personal jurisdiction can obligate the invoking party to prove at trial, by a preponderance of the evidence, all salient jurisdictional facts.[152]

Types of Challenges

A defendant can challenge personal jurisdiction theoretically or factually (or both). Theoretical challenges contest the plaintiff's theory of jurisdiction (*e.g.*, that the defendant subjected itself to jurisdiction in the forum by engaging in a

---

UPS Supply Chain Sols., Inc., 2018 WL 1888483, at *2 (S.D.N.Y. Apr. 5, 2018).

[145] *See Motus, LLC v. CarData Consultants, Inc.*, 23 F.4th 115, 121 (1st Cir. 2022); *Charles Schwab Corp. v. Bank of Am. Corp.*, 883 F.3d 68, 82 (2d Cir. 2018). For a detailed discussion of personal jurisdiction, including the role of both Rule 4(k) and the Constitution's Due Process Clause, see *supra* Part II, §§ 2.2 to 2.8.

[146] *See Dental Dynamics, LLC v. Jolly Dental Grp., LLC*, 946 F.3d 1223, 1228 (10th Cir. 2020).

[147] *See Bristol-Myers Squibb Co. v. Superior Ct.*, 582 U.S. —, 137 S. Ct. 1773, 1783, 198 L. Ed. 2d 395 (2017) (specific jurisdiction "must be met as to each defendant"); *Beydoun v. Wataniya Rests. Holding, Q.S.C.*, 768 F.3d 499, 504 (6th Cir. 2014) (burden to establish jurisdiction "over each defendant independently").

[148] *Compare SPV Osus Ltd. v. UBS AG*, 882 F.3d 333, 343 (2d Cir. 2018) (for general jurisdiction, plaintiff must show such continuous and systematic in-forum contacts by defendant as to render that defendant "essentially at home" in forum), *with Carmona v. Leo Ship Mgmt., Inc.*, 924 F.3d 190, 193 (5th Cir. 2019) (for specific jurisdiction, plaintiff must show defendant had minimum contacts with forum that relate or give rise to plaintiff's claim; if so, then burden shifts to defendant to make a "compelling case" of unfairness). The various substantive alternatives for exercising personal jurisdiction are discussed in Part II, *supra*, §§ 2.2 to 2.8.

[149] *See infra* Authors' Commentary to Rule 12(b)(2) ("**Legal Test**").

[150] *See* Authors' Commentary to Rule 8(a)(1) ("*Personal Jurisdiction*").

[151] *See Motus, LLC v. CarData Consultants, Inc.*, 23 F.4th 115, 123 (1st Cir. 2022) ("Even though a plaintiff need not plead facts that suffice to ground the exercise of in personam jurisdiction, it must — if challenged — ensure that the record contains such facts."); *Rogers v. City of Hobart, Indiana*, 996 F.3d 812, 818 (7th Cir. 2021) (burden arises "once" defendant moves to dismiss); *UMG Recordings, Inc. v. Kurbanov*, 963 F.3d 344, 350 (4th Cir. 2020) (burden "following" defendant's challenge).

[152] *See infra* Authors' Commentary to Rule 12(b)(2) ("**'Renewed' Motion at Trial**").

particular set of actions). If the court determines that those facts, if proven to be true, would subject the defendant to personal jurisdiction in the forum, no hearing or factual resolution is required and the theoretical challenge fails.[153] Alternatively (or additionally), the defendant may challenge personal jurisdiction factually by disputing jurisdictional facts the plaintiff has averred. When jurisdiction is challenged factually, the court or the factfinder must resolve (at least provisionally) the resulting factual dispute.[154]

Legal Test

How a court performs the Rule 12(b)(2) inquiry, and the weight borne by the party invoking the court's personal jurisdiction, hinges on whether the challenge is a theoretical one or a factual one:[155]

- *Theoretical (Facial) Challenges:* If the motion rests on the allegations alone, the plaintiff only has to present a *prima facie* showing of jurisdiction[156] (tested, it seems, under the *Twombly* plausibility standard)[157]—namely, that those factual allegations, as set out in the complaint, motion papers, memoranda, and affidavits,[158] are sufficient, if credited by the factfinder, to confer personal jurisdiction.[159] No differential factfinding is performed;[160] instead, the uncontroverted allegations in the complaint are accepted as true and factual disputes are resolved in the pleader's favor.[161] For these reasons, this burden on

---

[153]*See XMission, L.C. v. Fluent LLC*, 955 F.3d 833, 839 (10th Cir. 2020); *In re Magnetic Audiotape Antitrust Litigation*, 334 F.3d 204, 206 (2d Cir. 2003).

[154]*See AcryliCon USA, LLC v. Silikal GmbH*, 985 F.3d 1350, 1364 (11th Cir. 2021); *Credit Lyonnais Securities (USA), Inc. v. Alcantara*, 183 F.3d 151, 153 (2d Cir. 1999).

[155]*See Dorchester Fin. Secs., Inc. v. Banco BRJ, S.A.*, 722 F.3d 81, 84-85 (2d Cir. 2013); *Oldfield v. Pueblo De Bahia Lora, S.A.*, 558 F.3d 1210, 1219 n.19 (11th Cir. 2009).

[156]*See Eighteen Seventy, LP v. Jayson*, 32 F.4th 956, 964 (10th Cir. 2022); *Danziger & De Llano, L.L.P. v. Morgan Verkamp, L.L.C.*, 24 F.4th 491, 495 (5th Cir. 2022).

[157]*See Frost v. LG Elecs., Inc.*, 801 Fed. Appx. 496, 498 (9th Cir. 2020); *Dudnikov v. Chalk & Vermilion Fine Arts, Inc.*, 514 F.3d 1063, 1070 (10th Cir. 2008). *See generally Hawkins v. i-TV Digitalis Tavkozlesi zrt.*, 935 F.3d 211, 226 (4th Cir. 2019) (prima facie analysis resembles *Twombly* plausibility inquiry). Note, the *Twombly* standard is discussed in the Authors' Commentary to Rule 8(a) *supra* and Rule 12(b)(6) *infra*.

[158]*See Grayson v. Anderson*, 816 F.3d 262, 267–68 (4th Cir. 2016). *But cf. Creative Calling Sols., Inc. v. LF Beauty Ltd.*, 799 F.3d 975, 979 (8th Cir. 2015) (if court receives and relies on affidavits, motion becomes in substance one for summary judgment).

[159]*See Eighteen Seventy, LP v. Jayson*, 32 F.4th 956, 964–65 (10th Cir. 2022); *Motus, LLC v. CarData Consultants, Inc.*, 23 F.4th 115, 121 (1st Cir. 2022).

[160]*See AcryliCon USA, LLC v. Silikal GmbH*, 985 F.3d 1350, 1364–65 (11th Cir. 2021); *Baskin-Robbins Franchising LLC v. Alpenrose Dairy, Inc.*, 825 F.3d 28, 34 (1st Cir. 2016).

[161]*See Eighteen Seventy, LP v.*

plaintiff is considered "relatively slight."[162] Note, however, that neither legal conclusions and argumentative inferences[163] nor allegations expressly contradicted by affidavit[164] will be presumed true, and any undisputed facts offered by the defendant may also be considered.[165] In this posture, the plaintiff's burden is only a preliminary one; if the jurisdictional challenge is renewed, the plaintiff will later have to prove the jurisdictional facts at trial by a preponderance of the evidence.[166]

- *Factual Challenges:* If the defendant goes beyond a theoretical challenge and contests the underlying truth of plaintiff's jurisdictional allegations (or when the court otherwise finds it unfair to make merely a preliminary ruling), the court may conduct an evidentiary hearing,[167] from which it can find the jurisdictional facts.[168] There, the plaintiff may no longer rest on mere allegations, but must evidentially demonstrate the court's jurisdiction.[169] At the hearing (which may or may not involve live testimony), the court must allow the parties a fair opportunity to present their jurisdictional evidence and

Jayson, 32 F.4th 956, 964 (10th Cir. 2022); *Apple Inc. v. Zipit Wireless, Inc.*, 30 F.4th 1368, 1374 (Fed. Cir. 2022). *See also Ayla, LLC v. Alya Skin Pty. Ltd.*, 11 F.4th 972, 978 (9th Cir. 2021) ("We may not assume the truth of allegations in a pleading which are contradicted by affidavit, but factual conflicts between dueling affidavits must be resolved in the plaintiff's favor.") (cleaned up).

[162] *See Ingram Barge Co., LLC v. Zen-Noh Grain Corp.*, 3 F.4th 275, 278 (6th Cir. 2021). *See also Johnson v. Arden*, 614 F.3d 785, 794 (8th Cir. 2010) ("minimal" showing). *But cf. AMA Multimedia, LLC v. Wanat*, 970 F.3d 1201, 1207 (9th Cir. 2020) (*prima facie* inquiry is "not toothless"); *Massachusetts Sch. of Law at Andover, Inc. v. American Bar Ass'n*, 142 F.3d 26, 34 (1st Cir. 1998) (need not credit conclusory allegations or draw "far-fetched inferences").

[163] *See Lin v. TipRanks, Ltd.*, 19 F.4th 28, 33 (1st Cir. 2021); *UMG Recordings, Inc. v. Kurbanov*, 963 F.3d 344, 350 (4th Cir. 2020).

[164] *See Kuan Chen v. United States Sports Acad., Inc.*, 956 F.3d 45, 56 (1st Cir. 2020); *XMission, L.C. v. Fluent LLC*, 955 F.3d 833, 836 (10th Cir. 2020). *But cf. AMA Multimedia, LLC v. Wanat*, 970 F.3d 1201, 1207 (9th Cir. 2020) (conflicting affidavits must be resolved in plaintiff's favor, unless plaintiff's allegations are not evidentially supported); *Malone v. Stanley Black & Decker, Inc.*, 965 F.3d 499, 505–06 (6th Cir. 2020) (conflicting affidavit "was irrelevant" in *prima facie* inquiry).

[165] *See Kuan Chen v. United States Sports Acad., Inc.*, 956 F.3d 45, 54 (1st Cir. 2020).

[166] *See AcryliCon USA, LLC v. Silikal GmbH*, 985 F.3d 1350, 1364-65 (11th Cir. 2021); *Mullins v. TestAmerica, Inc.*, 564 F.3d 386, 399 (5th Cir. 2009).

[167] *See Kuan Chen v. United States Sports Acad., Inc.*, 956 F.3d 45, 51 (1st Cir. 2020); *Grayson v. Anderson*, 816 F.3d 262, 268 (4th Cir. 2016). *Cf. Sneha Media & Entm't, LLC v. Associated Broad. Co. P Ltd.*, 911 F.3d 192, 197 n.* (4th Cir. 2018) (following full discovery, court may sometimes decide issue without need for hearing).

[168] *See Walk Haydel & Associates, Inc. v. Coastal Power Production Co.*, 517 F.3d 235, 241–42 (5th Cir. 2008).

[169] *See Malone v. Stanley Black & Decker, Inc.*, 965 F.3d 499, 504 (6th Cir. 2020).

supporting legal arguments.[170] Throughout the process, the plaintiff bears the full preponderance burden.[171]

- *"Intertwined" Merits:* If such factfinding would prove to be intertwined with the merits, courts may defer a final jurisdictional ruling until trial, allowing the jury to resolve the implicated factual dispute (for both jurisdictional and merits purposes).[172] Other courts prefer an intermediate approach, permitting an evidentiary hearing with limited factfinding to predict the probable likelihood of personal jurisdiction which, if found, then allows the case to proceed but again postpones until trial the ultimate determination of jurisdiction.[173]
- *A Middle Course:* Sometimes, a court can opt for a middle course. If the defendant submits affidavits or other evidence opposing jurisdiction but no evidentiary hearing is held, the plaintiff must respond with affirmative evidence of its own showing jurisdiction but its burden remains a *prima facie* one. In such instances, the court resolves factual disputes revealed by the filings in plaintiff's favor.[174]
- *No Implied "Companion" Motions:* Personal jurisdiction, venue, and service of process may each be challenged together, but only if done expressly; moving on one ground does not imply (or avoid a waiver of) an unexpressed challenge on another ground.[175]

Timing and Waiver

Challenges to personal jurisdiction are waived unless raised by pre-answer motion (if there is one) or in the responsive pleading.[176] Even if properly raised, the defense may later be deemed forfeited if the defendant fails to seasonably press for a

---

[170] *See Grayson v. Anderson*, 816 F.3d 262, 268 (4th Cir. 2016).

[171] *See AcryliCon USA, LLC v. Silikal GmbH*, 985 F.3d 1350, 1364 (11th Cir. 2021); *Malone v. Stanley Black & Decker, Inc.*, 965 F.3d 499, 505 (6th Cir. 2020).

[172] *See Dorchester Fin. Secs., Inc. v. Banco BRJ, S.A.*, 722 F.3d 81, 87 (2d Cir. 2013); *Walk Haydel & Associates, Inc. v. Coastal Power Production Co.*, 517 F.3d 235, 242 (5th Cir. 2008).

[173] *See Kuan Chen v. United States Sports Acad., Inc.*, 956 F.3d 45, 52 (1st Cir. 2020).

[174] *See AMA Multimedia, LLC v. Wanat*, 970 F.3d 1201, 1207 (9th Cir. 2020); *Matlin v. Spin Master Corp.*, 921 F.3d 701, 705 (7th Cir. 2019). *Cf. Sneha Media & Entm't, LLC v. Associated Broad. Co. P Ltd.*, 911 F.3d 192, 197 n.* (4th Cir. 2018) (following full discovery, court may sometimes decide issue without need for hearing).

[175] *See, e.g., Hemispherx Biopharma, Inc. v. Johannesburg Consol. Investments*, 553 F.3d 1351, 1361 (11th Cir. 2008) (personal jurisdiction objection does not preserve service challenge); *Safety Equip. Inst. v. Signature Lacrosse, LLC*, 438 F. Supp. 3d 685, 686–88 (E.D. Va. 2020) (venue objection does not preserve personal jurisdiction challenge).

[176] *See* Rule 12(h)(1). *See also Ins. Corp. of Ireland v. Compagnie des Bauxites de Guinee*, 456 U.S. 694, 703, 102 S. Ct. 2099, 72 L. Ed. 2d 492 (1982).

ruling on the objection,[177] conducts itself as though jurisdiction exists,[178] or misbehaves during jurisdictional discovery.[179] But there usually is no waiver when a defendant, having properly preserved its objection to personal jurisdiction, also includes a responsive claim for affirmative relief (*e.g.*, counterclaim, crossclaim, third-party claim),[180] nor is a party who consented to personal jurisdiction in an earlier case foreclosed from objecting to it in a later one.[181]

Waiting for Default to Raise Personal Jurisdiction Objections

Ordinarily, defendants must raise objections to personal jurisdiction either in their Rule 12 motion or in their answer (if no Rule 12 motion is filed).[182] But defendants have one further option: they may default and then resist the resulting judgment collaterally. But defendants choose this strategy at their peril; if their collateral attack on jurisdiction fails, they almost certainly will be held to have abandoned their right to defend on the merits.[183]

"Renewed" Motion at Trial

Motions to dismiss for lack of personal jurisdiction are usually resolved before trial.[184] However, the court's ruling on the motion can be tentative and preliminary (especially when made under the predictive *prima facie* standard). At trial, the defendant can insist that the plaintiff affirmatively prove, by a preponderance of the evidence, all the alleged jurisdictional facts.[185] The defendant must renew the motion to do so.[186]

- *Sua Sponte Revisits:* The trial judge is permitted to re-

---

[177] *See Estate of Klieman by & through Kesner v. Palestinian Auth.*, 923 F.3d 1115, 1120–22 (D.C. Cir. 2019); *H-D Michigan, LLC v. Hellenic Duty Free Shops S.A.*, 694 F.3d 827, 847–48 (7th Cir. 2012).

[178] *See In re Asbestos Prod. Liab. Litig. (No. VI)*, 921 F.3d 98, 104–08 (3d Cir. 2019) ("words alone are insufficient" to preserve defense, where conduct shows voluntary or involuntary forfeiture); *Boulger v. Woods*, 917 F.3d 471, 477–78 (6th Cir. 2019) (inquiry is more art than science, hinging on whether defendant's behavior shows voluntary submission to court's jurisdiction).

[179] *See Brown v. Lockheed Martin Corp.*, 814 F.3d 619, 625 (2d Cir. 2016).

[180] *See S.E.C. v. Ross*, 504 F.3d 1130, 1149 (9th Cir. 2007); *Rates Technology Inc. v. Nortel Networks Corp.*, 399 F.3d 1302, 1307–08 (Fed. Cir. 2005). *See also Bayou Steel Corp. v. M/V Amstelvoorn*, 809 F.2d 1147, 1151 (5th Cir. 1987) (discussing divergent views; adopting majority approach).

[181] *See Charles Schwab Corp. v. Bank of Am. Corp.*, 883 F.3d 68, 88–89 (2d Cir. 2018).

[182] *See* Rule 12(g)–(h).

[183] *See Ins. Corp. of Ireland, Ltd. v. Compagnie des Bauxites de Guinee*, 456 U.S. 694, 706, 102 S. Ct. 2099, 72 L. Ed. 2d 492 (1982); *Baldwin v. Iowa State Traveling Men's Ass'n*, 283 U.S. 522, 525, 51 S. Ct. 517, 75 L. Ed. 1244 (1931).

[184] *See* Rule 12(i). *See also Acryli-Con USA, LLC v. Silikal GmbH*, 985 F.3d 1350, 1364 (11th Cir. 2021).

[185] *See Sneha Media & Entm't, LLC v. Associated Broad. Co. P Ltd.*, 911 F.3d 192, 196–97 (4th Cir. 2018); *Mullins v. TestAmerica, Inc.*, 564 F.3d 386, 399 (5th Cir. 2009).

examine an earlier personal jurisdiction ruling, and if it does so, it usually may apply a mere reconsideration standard (essentially, revisiting the same forgiving *prima facie* analysis performed earlier).[187]

Summary Judgment Challenges

The appropriate procedural vehicle for contesting personal jurisdiction is generally a motion to dismiss under Rule 12(b)(2). Courts are divided on whether personal jurisdiction may properly be resolved on summary judgment.[188]

Extrinsic Materials

The parties may submit affidavits, interrogatories, depositions, oral testimony (if an evidentiary hearing is convened), and other materials to support their positions on personal jurisdiction.[189]

Allowing Pre-Ruling Jurisdictional Discovery

Access to jurisdictionally-targeted discovery may be made available to the parties,[190] and courts may grant that access prior to ruling on a pending Rule 12(b)(2) motion.[191] Whether, and under what constraints, to permit jurisdictional discovery are matters typically reserved for the trial judge's discretion.[192] Jurisdictional discovery may be allowed where a "colorable" case for jurisdiction has been made, where the material facts that bear on jurisdiction are controverted, where a more satisfactory development of those facts is necessary, and where plaintiff has demonstrated that discovery will permit a supplementation of the jurisdictional allegations.[193] Conversely, such discovery may be properly refused when it is untimely

---

[186]*See Mullins v. TestAmerica, Inc.*, 564 F.3d 386, 399 & 399 n.7 (5th Cir. 2009) (absent special circumstances, failure to renew forecloses defendant's right to insist on preponderance burden at trial or waives defense entirely).

[187]*See Northern Laminate Sales, Inc. v. Davis*, 403 F.3d 14, 23 (1st Cir. 2005).

[188]*Compare Marten v. Godwin*, 499 F.3d 290, 295 n.2 (3d Cir. 2007) (summary judgment is inappropriate vehicle), *with Creative Calling Sols., Inc. v. LF Beauty Ltd.*, 799 F.3d 975, 979 (8th Cir. 2015) (when affidavits considered, motion becomes summary judgment), *and Dorchester Fin. Sec., Inc. v. Banco BRJ, S.A.*, 722 F.3d 81, 85 (2d Cir. 2013) (proper to consider on summary judgment).

[189]*See Kuan Chen v. United States Sports Acad., Inc.*, 956 F.3d 45, 56 (1st Cir. 2020); *Pederson v. Frost*, 951 F.3d 977, 979 (8th Cir. 2020).

[190]*See Oppenheimer Fund, Inc. v. Sanders*, 437 U.S. 340, 351, 98 S. Ct. 2380, 57 L. Ed. 2d 253 (1978) ("discovery is available to ascertain the facts bearing on [jurisdictional] issues").

[191]*See U.S. v. Swiss American Bank, Ltd.*, 274 F.3d 610, 625 (1st Cir. 2001) ("timely and properly supported" motion for jurisdictional discovery "merits solicitous attention"). *See, e.g., GTE New Media Services Inc. v. BellSouth Corp.*, 199 F.3d 1343, 1351–52 (D.C. Cir. 2000).

[192]*See Motus, LLC v. CarData Consultants, Inc.*, 23 F.4th 115, 128 (1st Cir. 2022) (unlike website videos, "jurisdictional discovery is not available on demand"); *AMA Multimedia, LLC v. Wanat*, 970 F.3d 1201, 1207 (9th Cir. 2020).

[193]*See Motus, LLC v. CarData Consultants, Inc.*, 23 F.4th 115, 128

sought,[194] where the request is improperly supported[195] or supported by mere hunches and conjecture,[196] where the claim is "attenuated" and based on bare allegations that are specifically denied,[197] where a colorable case for jurisdiction has not been made,[198] where the plaintiff's claim is "clearly frivolous"[199] or otherwise based on alleged facts that, even if true, would not support jurisdiction,[200] or where the plaintiff lacks a good faith belief that such discovery could support the jurisdictional allegations.[201] Jurisdictional discovery into whether an entity defendant has qualifying contacts with the forum may be granted more liberally[202] than such discovery of an individual[203]

(1st Cir. 2022); *Nuance Cmmc'ns, Inc. v. Abbyy Software House*, 626 F.3d 1222, 1235–36 (Fed.Cir. 2010). *See also Eurofins Pharma US Holdings v. BioAlliance Pharma SA*, 623 F.3d 147, 157 (3d Cir. 2010) (permitted upon showing with reasonable particularity that jurisdiction exists).

[194] *See Platten v. HG Bermuda Exempted Ltd.*, 437 F.3d 118, 139–40 (1st Cir. 2006); *Massachusetts School of Law at Andover, Inc. v. American Bar Ass'n*, 142 F.3d 26, 37 (1st Cir. 1998).

[195] *See Motus, LLC v. CarData Consultants, Inc.*, 23 F.4th 115, 128 (1st Cir. 2022) ("contained no indication of what facts might be developed through discovery"); *Carefirst of Maryland, Inc. v. Carefirst Pregnancy Centers, Inc.*, 334 F.3d 390, 402–03 (4th Cir. 2003) ("only speculation or conclusory assertions about contacts with a forum state").

[196] *See Viasystems, Inc. v. EBM-Papst St. Georgen GmbH & Co., KG*, 646 F.3d 589, 598 (8th Cir. 2011); *Nuance Cmmc'ns, Inc. v. Abbyy Software House*, 626 F.3d 1222, 1236 (Fed.Cir. 2010). *See also Eurofins Pharma US Holdings v. BioAlliance Pharma SA*, 623 F.3d 147, 157 (3d Cir. 2010) (no fishing expeditions).

[197] *See Unspam Techs., Inc. v. Chernuk*, 716 F.3d 322, 330 n.* (4th Cir. 2013); *Getz v. The Boeing Co.*, 654 F.3d 852, 860 (9th Cir. 2011).

[198] *See Livnat v. Palestinian Auth.*, 851 F.3d 45, 57 (D.C. Cir. 2017); *Negron-Torres v. Verizon Communications, Inc.*, 478 F.3d 19, 27 (1st Cir. 2007).

[199] *See Massachusetts School of Law at Andover, Inc. v. American Bar Ass'n*, 107 F.3d 1026, 1042 (3d Cir. 1997).

[200] *See Estate of Klieman by & through Kesner v. Palestinian Auth.*, 923 F.3d 1115, 1126–27 (D.C. Cir. 2019); *Viasystems, Inc. v. EBM-Papst St. Georgen GmbH & Co., KG*, 646 F.3d 589, 598 (8th Cir. 2011).

[201] *See Caribbean Broadcasting System, Ltd. v. Cable & Wireless P.L.C.*, 148 F.3d 1080, 1090 (D.C. Cir. 1998) (discussing good faith belief requirement). *See also Kelly v. Syria Shell Petroleum Development B.V.*, 213 F.3d 841, 855–56 (5th Cir. 2000) (denied where discovery sought could not have added any significant facts); *Terracom v. Valley Nat. Bank*, 49 F.3d 555, 562 (9th Cir. 1995) (denied where plaintiff failed to demonstrate how further discovery could establish jurisdiction).

[202] *See Massachusetts School of Law at Andover, Inc. v. American Bar Ass'n*, 107 F.3d 1026, 1042 (3d Cir. 1997) (jurisdictional discovery often relates to "doing business" inquiry). *See also Metcalfe v. Renaissance Marine, Inc.*, 566 F.3d 324, 336 (3d Cir. 2009) (such discovery "particularly appropriate" where defendant is corporation).

[203] *See Massachusetts School of Law at Andover, Inc. v. American Bar Ass'n*, 107 F.3d 1026, 1042 (3d Cir. 1997) (presumption in favor of jurisdictional discovery is reduced when defendant is an individual).

or a foreign sovereign.[204]

- *Foreign Discovery:* Generally, a party may (but is not necessarily obligated to) pursue foreign discovery through the Hague Evidence Convention.[205] When personal jurisdiction over the foreign party is contested, the courts are divided as to whether discovery can proceed simply under the Rules or whether Convention discovery is required until the question of jurisdiction is resolved.[206]

Sua Sponte Dismissals

Several Circuits forbid *sua sponte* dismissals for lack of personal jurisdiction, reasoning that the objection is a waivable defense that must be properly asserted or else it is lost.[207] Other Circuits permit those *sua sponte* dismissals, provided plaintiffs are afforded an opportunity to contest the issue and to introduce new supporting evidence (sometimes as late as on appeal).[208] Still others permit (or require) *sua sponte* examinations of personal jurisdiction when defendants have not appeared to defend and a default judgment against them is being sought.[209]

Ruling Deferred

The court may defer ruling on the challenge until after further materials are presented or after jurisdictional discovery is conducted,[210] or even, in appropriate circumstances, until trial.[211] But a court generally must resolve personal jurisdiction

---

[204]*See Alpha Therapeutic Corp. v. Nippon Hoso Kyokai*, 199 F.3d 1078, 1087–88 (9th Cir. 1999) (discussing the circumspection under which jurisdictional discovery from foreign sovereign should be ordered).

[205]Hague Convention on the Taking of Evidence Abroad in Civil or Commercial Matters, opened for signature, Mar. 18, 1970, 23 U.S.T. 2555, T.I.A.S. No. 7444, *reprinted in* 28 U.S.C.A. § 1781 Note. *See Societe Nationale Industrielle Aerospatiale v. U.S. Dist. Court for Southern Dist. of Iowa*, 482 U.S. 522, 533–36, 107 S. Ct. 2542, 96 L. Ed. 2d 461 (1987) (first resort to Convention discovery is not required).

[206]*See In re Automotive Refinishing Paint Antitrust Litigation*, 358 F.3d 288, 299–305 (3d Cir. 2004) (ruling that Convention discovery is not required, but citing case law split).

[207]*See, e.g., City of New York v. Mickalis Pawn Shop, LLC*, 645 F.3d 114, 133 (2d Cir. 2011); *Pakootas v. Teck Cominco Metals, Ltd.*, 452 F.3d 1066, 1076 (9th Cir. 2006).

[208]*See Hazim v. Schiel & Denver Book Publishers*, 647 Fed. Appx. 455, 457–58 (5th Cir. 2016); *Buchanan v. Manley*, 145 F.3d 386, 388–89 (D.C. Cir. 1998). *Cf. Trujillo v. Williams*, 465 F.3d 1210, 1217 (10th Cir. 2006) (*sua sponte* rulings on personal jurisdiction are proper under 28 U.S.C.A. § 1915 where defense is obvious and no further factual record is necessary).

[209]*See, e.g., Sinoying Logistics Pte Ltd. v. Yi Da Xin Trading Corp.*, 619 F.3d 207, 213 (2d Cir. 2010); *Mwani v. bin Laden*, 417 F.3d 1, 6 (D.C.Cir. 2005).

[210]*See Theunissen v. Matthews*, 935 F.2d 1454 (6th Cir.1991); *Data Disc, Inc. v. Systems Technology Associates, Inc.*, 557 F.2d 1280, 1285 (9th Cir. 1977).

[211]*See supra* Authors' Commentary to Rule 12(b)(2) (**"Legal Test - *'Inter-***

issues before reaching merits issues.[212]

Effect of Denial of Motion

If a party's Rule 12(b)(2) motion is denied, that party's active participation in the ensuing trial will not constitute a waiver of *either* the party's ability to renew the motion at time of trial *or* the right to contest personal jurisdiction on appeal.[213]

Remedy

If a court determines that it lacks the ability to exercise personal jurisdiction in a dispute, it may either dismiss the lawsuit or transfer it to any federal court where it could have been brought.[214]

Prejudice on Dismissal

A dismissal for lack of personal jurisdiction generally does not preclude the plaintiff from refiling the lawsuit against the defendant in a forum where that defendant is amenable to jurisdiction.[215]

Appealability

A dismissal as to all defendants for lack of personal jurisdiction is generally considered an appealable final order.[216] Conversely, a dismissal as to less than all defendants[217] or a denial of the motion to dismiss[218] is not yet a final order and ordinarily cannot be immediately appealed. If a court revisits an earlier personal jurisdiction ruling following a "renewed"

---

twined Merits' ").

[212]*See In re Lipitor Antitrust Litig.*, 855 F.3d 126, 151 (3d Cir. 2017); *Glob. Gold Min., LLC v. Ayvazian*, 612 Fed. Appx. 11, 16 (2d Cir. 2015). *Cf. Chudasama v. Mazda Motor Corp.*, 123 F.3d 1353, 1367–68 (11th Cir. 1997) (courts should rule on dismissal motions before enlarging scope of discovery). *See generally Steel Co. v. Citizens for a Better Env't*, 523 U.S. 83, 118 S. Ct. 1003, 140 L. Ed. 2d 210 (1998) (rejecting so-called "hypothetical" or "assumed" jurisdiction theory); *Ruhrgas AG v. Marathon Oil Co.*, 526 U.S. 574, 119 S. Ct. 1563, 143 L. Ed. 2d 760 (1999) (there is no "unyielding hierarchy" *among* jurisdictional requirements, and courts are free to resolve simpler personal jurisdiction challenges before reaching potentially more difficult questions of subject-matter jurisdiction).

[213]*See Northern Laminate Sales, Inc. v. Davis*, 403 F.3d 14, 23 (1st Cir. 2005). *See also Mullins v. TestAmerica, Inc.*, 564 F.3d 386, 398–99 (5th Cir. 2009).

[214]*See Herman v. Cataphora, Inc.*, 730 F.3d 460, 466 (5th Cir. 2013). *See also* 28 U.S.C.A. § 1631 (authorizing intra-court transfers to cure want of jurisdiction); *Franco v. Mabe Trucking Co., Inc.*, 3 F.4th 788, 792–95 (5th Cir. 2021) (noting Circuit agreement that Section 1631 applies to lack of personal jurisdiction).

[215]*See Ritzen Grp., Inc. v. Jackson Masonry, LLC*, 589 U.S. __, 140 S. Ct. 582, 590, 205 L. Ed. 2d 419 (2020); *Nafziger v. McDermott Int'l, Inc.*, 467 F.3d 514, 520 (6th Cir. 2006).

[216]*See Ritzen Grp., Inc. v. Jackson Masonry, LLC*, 589 U.S. __, 140 S. Ct. 582, 590, 205 L. Ed. 2d 419 (2020); *Carteret Sav. Bank, F.A. v. Shushan*, 919 F.2d 225, 230 (3d Cir. 1990).

[217]*See Morton Int'l., Inc. v. A.E. Staley Mfg. Co.*, 460 F.3d 470, 476 (3d Cir. 2006).

[218]*See CGC Holding Co. v. Broad & Cassel*, 773 F.3d 1076, 1098 (10th Cir. 2014); *Northern Laminate Sales, Inc. v. Davis*, 403 F.3d 14, 23 (1st Cir. 2005).

motion at or after trial, appealing the later ruling may be necessary to preserve the issue for appeal.[219]

RULE 12(b)(3)—DISMISSAL FOR IMPROPER VENUE

CORE CONCEPT

A case will be dismissed or transferred if venue is improper in the chosen forum.

APPLICATIONS

Proper Scope of Rule 12(b)(3)

Venue protects defendants against the risk of an unfair or unduly inconvenient place for trial.[220] But Rule 12(b)(3) is the proper vehicle for seeking a dismissal only when venue in the chosen forum is *improper* under the federal venue statutes[221] (though the court retains the discretion to transfer, rather than dismiss, were it to find venue improper).[222] Rule 12(b)(3) is not the proper tool for seeking a convenience transfer[223] or a dismissal or transfer pursuant to a forum selection clause[224] or mandatory arbitration clause.[225] However, if a mis-labeled motion's true intent is clear and no prejudice would result, a court might reframe the motion and rule on it using the appropriate analysis.[226]

Burden of Proof

In its motion, a party opposing venue must first articulate why venue is improper.[227] Courts are divided on who, then, must carry the ultimate burden in a Rule 12(b)(3) contest.

---

[219]*See AcryliCon USA, LLC v. Silikal GmbH*, 985 F.3d 1350, 1366 (11th Cir. 2021).

[220]*See Leroy v. Great W. United Corp.*, 443 U.S. 173, 183–84, 99 S. Ct. 2710, 61 L. Ed. 2d 464 (1979). For a detailed discussion of venue and the federal venue statutes, see *supra* Part II, §§ 2.17 to 2.17a.

[221]*See Atlantic Marine Const. Co. v. U.S. Dist. Court for Western Dist. of Texas*, 571 U.S. 49, 55, 134 S. Ct. 568, 187 L. Ed. 2d 487 (2013).

[222]*See infra* Authors' Commentary to Rule 12(b)(3) (**"Remedy"**).

[223]*See* 28 U.S.C.A. § 1404 (authorizing transfer to more convenient district).

[224]*See Atlantic Marine Const. Co. v. U.S. Dist. Court for Western Dist. of Texas*, 571 U.S. 49, 55–60, 134 S. Ct. 568, 187 L. Ed. 2d 487 (2013) (proper vehicle is either motion to transfer under 28 U.S.C.A. § 1404(a)—and transfer should be ordered, absent "extraordinary circumstances unrelated to the convenience of the parties"—or *forum non conveniens* dismissal).

[225]*See Boykin v. Fam. Dollar Stores of Michigan, LLC*, 3 F.4th 832, 837–38 (6th Cir. 2021) (so holding, but noting earlier Circuit split). *See generally Scherk v. Alberto-Culver Co.*, 417 U.S. 506, 519, 94 S. Ct. 2449, 2457, 41 L. Ed. 2d 270 (1974) ("An agreement to arbitrate before a specified tribunal is, in effect, a specialized kind of forum-selection clause . . .").

[226]*See Dr. Robert L. Meinders, D.C., Ltd. v. United Healthcare Servs., Inc.*, 7 F.4th 555, 561 (7th Cir. 2021); *Don't Look Media LLC v. Fly Victor Ltd.*, 999 F.3d 1284, 1296 (11th Cir. 2021).

[227]*See Exelon Generation Co., LLC v. Grumbles*, 380 F. Supp. 3d 1, 9 (D.D.C. 2019) (must present facts that defeat assertion of venue). *See also Fed. Trade Comm'n v. BINT Operations LLC*, __ F. Supp. 3d __, 2022 WL 990276, at *8 (E.D. Ark. 2022) (burden

Under the majority view, the party asserting venue (ordinarily, the plaintiff) must bear that burden.[228] Under the minority view, the party opposing venue (the movant) must demonstrate that it is improper.[229] As with personal jurisdiction challenges, the weight of the burden changes, depending on the way the challenge is made.[230]

Legal Test

The procedure for resolving a Rule 12(b)(3) motion is the same as the procedure used for testing challenges to personal jurisdiction.[231] The court may resolve the motion on the basis of the written submissions alone, or may convene an evidentiary hearing.[232]

With written submissions alone (without a hearing), a venue challenge is generally defeated if the plaintiff makes a *prima facie* showing of venue[233] by setting forth sufficient facts which, if proven true, would confer venue.[234] (It is unclear when *Twombly* "plausibility" ought to govern this obligation.[235]) Under this standard, plaintiff's well-pleaded factual allegations regarding venue are accepted as true;[236] all reasonable inferences and factual conflicts are also resolved in plaintiff's favor.[237] No such deference, however, will be given to unsupported inferences[238] or legal conclusions.[239] In ruling, the court may take judicial notice of appropriate public records.[240]

Once the plaintiff's venue allegations are controverted by

---

lies with plaintiff "[o]nce a defendant raises the issue of proper venue by motion").

[228] *See, e.g., Deb v. SIRVA, Inc.*, 832 F.3d 800, 810 (7th Cir. 2016); *Gulf Ins. Co. v. Glasbrenner*, 417 F.3d 353, 355 (2d Cir. 2005).

[229] *See Myers v. American Dental Ass'n*, 695 F.2d 716, 724 (3d Cir. 1982); *Doshier v. Twitter, Inc.*, 417 F. Supp. 3d 1171, 1174 (E.D. Ark. 2019).

[230] *See infra* Authors' Commentary to Rule 12(b)(3) (**"Legal Test"**).

[231] *See Gulf Ins. Co. v. Glasbrenner*, 417 F.3d 353, 355 (2d Cir. 2005); *Carney v. Horion Invs. Ltd.*, 107 F. Supp. 3d 216, 222 (D.Conn. 2015).

[232] *See Hancock v. Am. Tel. & Tel. Co.*, 701 F.3d 1248, 1261 (10th Cir. 2012); *Centerville ALF, Inc. v. Balanced Care Corp.*, 197 F. Supp. 2d 1039, 1046 (S.D. Ohio 2002).

[233] *See Mitrano v. Hawes*, 377 F.3d 402, 405 (4th Cir. 2004); *Tour Tech. Software, Inc. v. RTV, Inc.*, 377 F. Supp. 3d 195, 200 (E.D.N.Y. 2019).

[234] *See Slyce Acquisition Inc. v. Syte—Visual Conception Ltd.*, 422 F. Supp. 3d 1191, 1198 (W.D. Tex. 2019); *Langton v. Cbeyond Communication, L.L.C.*, 282 F. Supp. 2d 504, 508 (E.D. Tex. 2003).

[235] *See Walsh v. Bank of Am. NA*, 113 F. Supp. 3d 108, 112 (D.D.C. 2015) (seeming to assume it should). Note: the *Twombly* standard is discussed in the Authors' Commentary to Rule 8(a) *supra* and Rule 12(b)(6) *infra*.

[236] *See Deb v. SIRVA, Inc.*, 832 F.3d 800, 809 (7th Cir. 2016); *N-N v. Mayorkas*, 540 F. Supp. 3d 240, 251 (E.D.N.Y. 2021).

[237] *See Jackson v. Payday Fin., LLC*, 764 F.3d 765, 773 (7th Cir. 2014); *Petersen v. Boeing Co.*, 715 F.3d 276, 279 (9th Cir. 2013).

[238] *See Herbert v. Sebelius*, 925 F. Supp. 2d 13, 17 (D.D.C. 2013).

[239] *See Black Lives Matter D.C. v. Trump*, 544 F. Supp. 3d 15, 28 (D.D.C. 2021).

[240] *See Ross v. Davis*, 74 F. Supp. 3d 231, 235 (D.D.C. 2014).

the opponent (by affidavit or otherwise), those allegations will no longer be presumed true,[241] and plaintiff must go beyond the pleadings by offering affirmative evidence in support of the forum's venue.[242] Contested facts are resolved in the plaintiff's favor.[243]

Finally, if the court convenes an evidentiary hearing, the allegations are not presumed true, the preponderance of the evidence standard applies,[244] and the court may assess credibility and find the facts[245] (though it ought to avoid factfinding that encroaches into the merits of the case).[246]

- *No Implied "Companion" Motions:* Personal jurisdiction, venue, and service of process may each be challenged together, but only if done expressly; moving on one ground does not imply (or avoid a waiver of) an unexpressed challenge on another ground.[247]

Timing and Waiver

Venue challenges are waived unless raised by motion (if there is one) or in the responsive pleading.[248] A defaulting defendant, thus, generally is deemed to have waived any objections to venue.[249] When properly asserted and preserved, a venue objection is unlikely to be deemed waived merely because the objecting defendant also asserts a counterclaim.[250] Because venue defenses may be waived, some (but not all) courts hold that *sua sponte* venue dismissals are usually improper.[251]

Cases Involving Multiple Defendants or Claims

Where a case involves more than one defendant, or more

---

[241] *See Deb v. SIRVA, Inc.*, 832 F.3d 800, 809 (7th Cir. 2016); *Hancock v. Am. Tel. & Tel. Co.*, 701 F.3d 1248, 1260 (10th Cir. 2012).

[242] *See Allstate Life Ins. Co. v. Stanley W. Burns, Inc.*, 80 F. Supp. 3d 870, 875 (N.D.Ill. 2015).

[243] *See Scott v. Buckner Co.*, 388 F. Supp. 3d 1320, 1324 (D. Colo. 2019).

[244] *See Gulf Ins. Co. v. Glasbrenner*, 417 F.3d 353, 355 (2d Cir. 2005).

[245] *See Symbology Innovations, LLC v. Lego Sys., Inc.*, 282 F. Supp. 3d 916, 924–25 (E.D. Va. 2017).

[246] *See Belcher-Robinson, L.L.C. v. Linamar Corp.*, 699 F. Supp. 2d 1329, 1333–34 (M.D.Ala. 2010).

[247] *See, e.g., Safety Equip. Inst. v. Signature Lacrosse, LLC*, 438 F. Supp. 3d 685, 686–88 (E.D. Va. 2020) (venue objection does not preserve personal jurisdiction challenge).

[248] *See* Rule 12(h)(1). *See also Wachovia Bank v. Schmidt*, 546 U.S. 303, 316, 126 S. Ct. 941, 163 L. Ed. 2d 797 (2006); *Automobile Mechanics Local 701 Welfare and Pension Funds v. Vanguard Car Rental USA, Inc.*, 502 F.3d 740, 746 (7th Cir. 2007).

[249] *See Union Planters Bank, N.A. v. EMC Mortg. Corp.*, 67 F. Supp. 2d 915, 920 (W.D. Tenn. 1999).

[250] *See Hillis v. Heineman*, 626 F.3d 1014, 1016–19 (9th Cir. 2010).

[251] *Compare Automobile Mechanics Local 701 Welfare & Pension Funds v. Vanguard Car Rental USA, Inc.*, 502 F.3d 740, 746–47 (7th Cir. 2007) (noting and following majority rule); *and Gomez v. USAA Fed. Sav. Bank*, 171 F.3d 794, 796 (2d Cir. 1999) (not absent "extraordinary circumstances"); *with Moler v. Wells*, 18 F.4th 162, 167 n.8 (5th Cir. 2021) (district court may *sua sponte* transfer case for improper venue); *and Stjernholm v. Peterson*, 83 F.3d 347, 349 (10th Cir. 1996) (until defendants waive it, courts *sua sponte* may raise defective venue, provided parties given opportunity to be heard).

than one claim against a defendant, venue must be proper as to each defendant and as to each claim.[252] However, some courts may apply pendent or ancillary venue principles to hear claims that arise out of a common nucleus of operative facts with a pending, properly venued claim.[253]

Extrinsic Materials

The parties may submit affidavits and other materials to support their positions on improper venue.[254]

Pre-Ruling Venue Discovery

The court may, in its discretion,[255] permit limited discovery to aid in resolving the motion,[256] provided the requesting party makes a detailed showing of the discovery it proposes to conduct or the results it expects that discovery to supply.[257]

Remedy

Ordinarily, a court may either dismiss for improper venue or transfer to a forum where venue would be proper,[258] or, if appropriate, retain jurisdiction over claims for which venue is proper and sever the remainder.[259]

Sequence in Ruling

Although courts ordinarily resolve pending personal jurisdictional challenges first, they have discretion, in appropriate circumstances, to dismiss or transfer on venue grounds without sorting through a more nettlesome jurisdictional dispute.[260]

Ruling Deferred

The court may defer ruling on a venue challenge pending

---

[252]*See Harrison Prosthetic Cradle Inc. v. Roe Dental Lab'y, Inc.*, — F. Supp. 3d —, 2022 WL 2203770, at *2 (N.D. Ohio 2022); *Polytek Dev. Corp. v. 'Doc' Johnson Enters.*, 532 F. Supp. 3d 243, 250 n.2 (E.D. Pa. 2021).

[253]*See Smith v. Swaffer*, 566 F. Supp. 3d 791, 803 (N.D. Ohio 2021).

[254]*See Deb v. SIRVA, Inc.*, 832 F.3d 800, 809–10 (7th Cir. 2016); *Petersen v. Boeing Co.*, 715 F.3d 276, 279 (9th Cir. 2013).

[255]*See Kaia Foods, Inc. v. Bellafiore*, 70 F. Supp. 3d 1178, 1182 (N.D.Cal. 2014).

[256]*See Oppenheimer Fund, Inc. v. Sanders*, 437 U.S. 340, 351 n.13, 98 S. Ct. 2380, 57 L. Ed. 2d 253 (1978) ("discovery is available to ascertain the facts bearing on [venue]"). *See also Centerville ALF, Inc. v. Balanced Care Corp.*, 197 F. Supp. 2d 1039, 1046 (S.D. Ohio 2002).

[257]*See Uni-Top Asia Inv. Ltd. v. Sinopec Int'l Petroleum Expl. & Prod. Corp.*, — F. Supp. 3d —, 2022 WL 1202482, at *4 (D.D.C. 2022) (appeal pending).

[258]*See In re HTC Corp.*, 889 F.3d 1349, 1352 n.2 (Fed. Cir. 2018); *Smith v. Swaffer*, 566 F. Supp. 3d 791, 802 (N.D. Ohio 2021).

[259]*See Get In Shape Franchise, Inc. v. TFL Fishers, LLC*, 167 F. Supp. 3d 173, 195 (D. Mass. 2016).

[260]*See Leroy v. Great W. United Corp.*, 443 U.S. 173, 180, 99 S. Ct. 2710, 61 L. Ed. 2d 464 (1979); *Oldham v. Pa. State Univ.*, 507 F. Supp. 3d 637, 643-44 (M.D.N.C. 2020) (collecting cases). *See also Goldlawr, Inc. v. Heiman*, 369 U.S. 463, 466-67, 82 S. Ct. 913, 8 L. Ed. 2d 39 (1962) (court lacking personal jurisdiction may still transfer to new venue).

further factual development.[261]

"Renewed" Motion at Trial

Although rarely discussed, it is likely that a pretrial rejection of a venue challenge does not foreclose a renewed challenge at trial or relieve the plaintiff of its obligation to establish the requisite venue facts at trial by a preponderance of the evidence.[262]

Prejudice on Dismissal

A dismissal for improper venue generally does not preclude the plaintiff from re-filing the claim in a forum where venue is proper.[263]

Appealability

Ordinarily, a dismissal for improper venue is immediately appealable as a "final order."[264] Conversely, a denial of a motion to dismiss for lack of venue is interlocutory and not immediately appealable.[265]

RULES 12(b)(4) and (b)(5)—DISMISSAL FOR (OR QUASHING OF) INSUFFICIENT PROCESS OR SERVICE

CORE CONCEPT

Improper process, or improper service of that process, can be quashed or cause the lawsuit to be dismissed.

APPLICATIONS

Insufficient Process—Rule 12(b)(4)

The process (summons and complaint) may be insufficient if the forms are technically deficient[266] (*e.g.*, wrong name[267] or not sealed by the clerk[268]). Because dismissals for defects in the forms of summons are generally disfavored, courts often overlook minor technical defects (particularly where they can be

---

[261] *See Tenpenny v. U.S.*, 285 F.2d 213 (6th Cir. 1960).

[262] *See Long John Silver's, Inc. v. DIWA III, Inc.*, 650 F. Supp. 2d 612, 619 (E.D. Ky. 2009) (discussing principle in context of personal jurisdiction challenge).

[263] *See Johnson v. Western & Southern Life Ins. Co.*, 598 Fed.Appx. 454, 456 (7th Cir. 2015); *In re Hall, Bayoutree Associates, Ltd.*, 939 F.2d 802, 804 (9th Cir. 1991).

[264] *See Ritzen Grp., Inc. v. Jackson Masonry, LLC*, 589 U.S. __, 140 S. Ct. 582, 590, 205 L. Ed. 2d 419 (2020).

[265] *See Hohn v. U.S.*, 524 U.S. 236, 248, 118 S. Ct. 1969, 1976, 141 L. Ed. 2d 242 (1998); *Brickstructures, Inc. v. Coaster Dynamix, Inc.*, 952 F.3d 887, 890 (7th Cir. 2020). *But cf. In re HTC Corp.*, 889 F.3d 1349, 1352–61 (Fed. Cir. 2018) (in proper instance, mandamus may be proper).

[266] *See Grp. One Ltd. v. GTE GmbH*, 523 F. Supp. 3d 323, 332 n.8 (E.D.N.Y. 2021); *Gallan v. Bloom Bus. Jets, LLC*, 480 F. Supp. 3d 1173, 1178 (D. Colo. 2020). *See also Vega v. Hastens Beds, Inc.*, 339 F.R.D. 210, 218 n.6 (S.D.N.Y. 2021) (noting some courts analyze failure to translate documents served abroad under Rule 12(b)(4), other courts use 12(b)(5)).

[267] *See Naranjo v. Universal Sur. of America*, 679 F. Supp. 2d 787, 795 (S.D.Tex. 2010).

[268] *See Ayres v. Jacobs & Crumplar, P.A.*, 99 F.3d 565, 569 (3d Cir. 1996).

cured), unless the complaining party is able to demonstrate actual prejudice.[269]

Insufficient Service—Rule 12(b)(5)

Service of the process may be insufficient if, for example, the mode of delivery is invalid,[270] service is made on an improper person,[271] or delivery is either never accomplished or not accomplished within 90 days after commencement.[272]

Distinguishing Between Rules 12(b)(4) and 12(b)(5)

Courts have noted that, although distinct,[273] the differences between motions under Rules 12(b)(4) and 12(b)(5) have not always been clear or observed in practice.[274] A mislabeling of a Rule 12(b)(4) or 12(b)(5) motion, particularly if no one is prejudiced, may be overlooked by the courts.[275]

Consequence

Service of process is a prerequisite for personal jurisdiction. Courts generally cannot exercise adjudicating power over a defendant who has not properly been served with (or waived service of) process.[276]

Legal Test

A motion to dismiss under these two Rules must be made with specificity, by describing how the process or service failed and why that failure prejudiced the defendant.[277] Once a proper motion is made, the plaintiff must make a *prima facie* demon-

---

[269] *See Doyle v. YMCA of New Hampshire*, 560 F. Supp. 3d 499, 502 (D.N.H. 2021) (in absence of any showing of prejudice, ordering new service (rather than dismissal) to cure misnamed defendant, lack of clerk's signature, and missing court seal); *Gallan v. Bloom Bus. Jets, LLC*, 480 F. Supp. 3d 1173, 1179 (D. Colo. 2020) (allowing *nunc pro tunc* service extension where "nominally deficient" summons, which caused no prejudice, was quickly remedied).

[270] *See Gallan v. Bloom Bus. Jets, LLC*, 480 F. Supp. 3d 1173, 1178 (D. Colo. 2020); *Sunset Homeowners Ass'n, Inc. v. DiFrancesco*, 386 F. Supp. 3d 299, 303 (W.D.N.Y. 2019).

[271] *See Hardy v. Joseph I. Sussman, P.C.*, 953 F. Supp. 2d 102, 106 n.1 (D.D.C. 2013); *Naranjo v. Universal Sur. of America*, 679 F. Supp. 2d 787, 795 (S.D.Tex. 2010).

[272] *See Jones v. Mirza*, 230 F. Supp. 3d 339, 341 (D. Del. 2017); *John v. City of Bridgeport*, 309 F.R.D. 149, 153–54 (D. Conn. 2015).

[273] *See Vega v. Hastens Beds, Inc.*, 339 F.R.D. 210, 215 (S.D.N.Y. 2021); *Doyle v. YMCA of New Hampshire*, 560 F. Supp. 3d 499, 502 (D.N.H. 2021).

[274] *See Almont Ambulatory Surgery Ctr., LLC v. UnitedHealth Group, Inc.*, 99 F. Supp. 3d 1110, 1126 (C.D.Cal. 2015).

[275] *See Haidon v. Budlong & Budlong, LLC*, 318 F. Supp. 3d 568, 575 (W.D.N.Y. 2018); *Boulger v. Woods*, 306 F. Supp. 3d 985 (S.D. Ohio 2018), *aff'd*, 917 F.3d 471 (6th Cir. 2019).

[276] *See Murphy Bros. v. Michetti Pipe Stringing, Inc.*, 526 U.S. 344, 350, 119 S. Ct. 1322, 143 L. Ed. 2d 448 (1999); *Omni Capital Int'l, Ltd. v. Rudolf Wolff & Co.*, 484 U.S. 97, 104, 108 S.Ct. 404, 98 L.Ed.2d 415 (1987). *See also Doe #1 v. Am. Fed'n of Gov't Emps.*, 554 F. Supp. 3d 75, 122 (D.D.C. 2021) (failure to properly serve is "fatal jurisdictional defect") (cleaned up).

[277] *See O'Brien v. R.J. O'Brien & Associates, Inc.*, 998 F.2d 1394, 1400 (7th Cir. 1993); *Photolab Corp. v.*

stration of proper process and service through specific factual averments and other supporting materials; conclusory statements will usually not overcome a defendant's sworn representation controverting good service.[278] (But, likewise, a defendant's motion comprised of only conclusory, unsworn assertions is unlikely to overcome a process server's affidavit.[279]) The plaintiff will usually be given the benefit of any factual doubts in resolving a service challenge,[280] and the requisites for Rule 4 service are liberally construed.[281] Courts may resolve any disputed questions of fact by considering affidavits, depositions, and oral testimony.[282] The adequacy of service accomplished after removal is tested under these Rules (not State law).[283]

- *No Implied "Companion" Motions:* Personal jurisdiction, venue, and service of process may be challenged together, but only if done expressly; moving on one ground does not imply (or avoid a waiver of) an intended but unfiled challenge on the other ground.[284]
- *No Summary Judgment Option:* Process and service objections ordinarily cannot be raised in summary judgment motions. Such motions will instead likely be treated as requests for a ruling on a pleaded defense (assuming the objections were preserved in the party's responsive pleading).[285]

Burden of Proof

Once a party resisting service raises a credible challenge,[286] the burden then shifts, in the view of most[287] courts, to the serving party to show that the court's personal jurisdiction is

---

Simplex Specialty Co., 806 F.2d 807, 810 (8th Cir. 1986).

[278]*See TAGC Mgmt., LLC v. Lehman*, 842 F. Supp. 2d 575, 580–81 (S.D.N.Y. 2012).

[279]*See U.S. v. Jost*, 9 F. Supp. 3d 303, 307 (W.D.N.Y. 2014).

[280]*See United States v. Park*, 389 F. Supp. 3d 561, 567 (N.D. Ill. 2019); *Wanjiku v. Johnson Cty.*, 173 F. Supp. 3d 1217, 1228 (D. Kan. 2016).

[281]*See Morgan Stanley v. Babu*, 448 F. Supp. 3d 497, 504 & 509 (D. Md. 2020); *Richardson v. Roberts*, 355 F. Supp. 3d 367, 370 (E.D.N.C. 2019).

[282]*See Travelers Cas. & Sur. Co. of America v. Telstar Const. Co., Inc.*, 252 F. Supp. 2d 917, 923 (D. Ariz. 2003); *Mende v. Milestone Technology, Inc.*, 269 F. Supp. 2d 246, 251 (S.D. N.Y. 2003).

[283]*See Egan v. Tenet Health Care*, 193 F. Supp. 3d 73, 79 (D. Mass. 2016).

[284]*See Hemispherx Biopharma, Inc. v. Johannesburg Consol. Invs.*, 553 F.3d 1351, 1360–61 (11th Cir. 2008).

[285]*See King v. Taylor*, 694 F.3d 650, 657 n.2 (6th Cir. 2012); (discussing Rule 12(i) conversion of such motions); *Rose v. Bersa*, 327 F.R.D. 628, 630 (S.D. Ohio 2018).

[286]*See Cheeks v. Belmar*, 331 F.R.D. 499, 504 (E.D. Mo. 2019) (after "plausible challenge" made to sufficiency of service); *Connolly v. Shaw's Supermarkets, Inc.*, 355 F. Supp. 3d 9, 14 (D. Mass. 2018) (defendant bears "initial burden" of showing insufficiency).

[287]*But see Molinelli-Freytes v. Univ. of Puerto Rico*, 727 F. Supp. 2d 60, 63 (D.P.R. 2010) (party seeking dismissal bears burden of showing failed service).

properly exercised.[288] The process server's return is *prima facie* evidence of good service;[289] but such proof is not conclusive,[290] and can be overcome by strong and convincing evidence to the contrary.[291] A conclusory representation that the defendant was properly served will not overcome a defendant's sworn affidavit otherwise.[292] A similar burden-shifting analysis likely applies when the motion challenges the form of process, rather than its service.[293]

- *Further Trial Burden:* If properly raised and preserved, an objection to process or to service of process can obligate the serving party to prove at trial, by a preponderance of the evidence, all salient facts necessary to establish proper service.[294]

Timing and Waiver

Challenges to either the form of process or the adequacy of service are waived unless raised in the pre-answer motion (if there is one) or in the responsive pleading (if no motion is filed).[295] Consequently, a defendant generally may not move for a dismissal under these Rules *after* filing an answer that omitted that defense[296] or *after* filing a pre-answer Rule 12 motion that omitted that defense.[297] Waiver can also follow when a defendant makes a motion to transfer for improper venue (under 28 U.S.C. § 1406) which neglects to include that

---

[288] *See Scott v. Maryland State Dep't of Labor*, 673 Fed. Appx. 299, 304 (4th Cir. 2016); *Cardenas v. City of Chicago*, 646 F.3d 1001, 1005 (7th Cir. 2011); *Dickerson v. Napolitano*, 604 F.3d 732, 752 (2d Cir. 2010).

[289] *See Blair v. City of Worcester*, 522 F.3d 105, 111–12 (1st Cir. 2008); *Yueh-Lan Wang by & through Winston Wen-Young Wong v. New Mighty U.S. Tr.*, 322 F.R.D. 11, 30 (D.D.C. 2017).

[290] *See Gottlieb v. Sandia Am. Corp.*, 452 F.2d 510, 514 (3d Cir. 1971); *Raynor v. D.C.*, 296 F. Supp. 3d 66, 69–70 (D.D.C. 2017).

[291] *See O'Brien v. R.J. O'Brien & Assocs.*, 998 F.2d 1394, 1398 (7th Cir. 1993); *Yueh-Lan Wang by & through Winston Wen-Young Wong v. New Mighty U.S. Tr.*, 322 F.R.D. 11, 30 (D.D.C. 2017).

[292] *See Raynor v. D.C.*, 296 F. Supp. 3d 66, 69–70 (D.D.C. 2017); *Blau v. Allianz Life Ins. Co. of N. Am.*, 124 F. Supp. 3d 161, 173 (E.D.N.Y. 2015).

[293] *See Boring v. Pattillo Indus. Real Estate*, 426 F. Supp. 3d 1341, 1345 (N.D. Ga. 2019); *Xie v. Sklover & Co., LLC*, 260 F. Supp. 3d 30, 38 (D.D.C. 2017). *But see Oliver v. New York State Police*, 2019 WL 453363, at *5 (W.D.N.Y. Feb. 5, 2019) (discussing opposite-burden minority view).

[294] *See generally Kornea v. J.S.D Mgmt., Inc.*, 366 F. Supp. 3d 660, 667 (E.D. Pa. 2019).

[295] *See King v. Taylor*, 694 F.3d 650, 656 (6th Cir. 2012); *Williams v. Jones*, 11 F.3d 247, 251 (1st Cir. 1993).

[296] *See* Rule 12(h)(1)(B). A litigant's right to contest objections to service or process may be foreclosed if an answer is filed before the motion. *See Green v. City of Bessemer, Alabama*, 202 F. Supp. 2d 1272, 1273–74 (N.D. Ala. 2002) (Rule 12(b)(5) motion untimely when filed three days after party answered the complaint).

[297] *See Chute v. Walker*, 281 F.3d 314, 319 (1st Cir. 2002) (because defendant omitted Rule 12(b)(5) defense from Rule 12(b)(6) motion to dismiss, it was waived).

defendant's alternative challenge to process and/or service.[298] Of course, defendants will not waive these defenses by appearing in court to assert them,[299] or by not supplying plaintiffs with advance notice of an intent to raise them.[300] But the defenses may still be forfeited—even if properly asserted originally—if the movant fails to timely press for a ruling or otherwise participates in the litigation in a manner that belies those defenses.[301]

Waiting for Default to Raise Service Objections

Defendants do not waive process or service objections by failing to timely assert them if, due to the process or service failure, those defendants never learned about the attempted service in time to object.[302] In such circumstances, the defendants should be permitted to raise their objections when the purported service comes to their attention or even by collateral attack on any ensuing judgment.[303] Less certain is whether defendants who actually know of the attempted service may properly withhold their objections to it and wait to assert them in a later collateral attack.[304] In any collateral attack, defendants likely will bear the burden of proving the process or ser-

---

[298]*See Rodriguez v. Pan Am. Health Org.*, 502 F. Supp. 3d 200, 231–33 (D.D.C. 2020) (equating Section 1406 motions with Rule 12(b)(4)/(b)(5) motions).

[299]*See Mattiaccio v. DHA Group, Inc.*, 20 F. Supp. 3d 220, 227 (D.D.C. 2014).

[300]*See Davis v. Mara*, 587 F. Supp. 2d 422, 428–29 (D.Conn. 2008) ("No Rule specifies any duty of a defendant to notify a plaintiff of its intention to raise either of these defenses").

[301]*See King v. Taylor*, 694 F.3d 650, 658 (6th Cir. 2012). *See generally Broadcast Music, Inc. v. M.T.S. Enters., Inc.*, 811 F.2d 278, 281 (5th Cir. 1987) (service objections waived when parties gave impression of having been served then, later, tried to "pull failure of service out of the hat like a rabbit").

[302]*See generally* 5C CHARLES A. WRIGHT & ARTHUR R. MILLER, FEDERAL PRACTICE AND PROCEDURE § 1391, at 521 (2004) ("if a party is never served at all, he or she cannot be held to have waived the right to object to a lack of jurisdiction over the person by nonassertion within [21] days; due process would preclude the result and the rules themselves prevent it").

[303]*See generally Ins. Corp. of Ireland v. Compagnie des Bauxites de Guinee*, 456 U.S. 694, 706, 102 S. Ct. 2099, 72 L. Ed. 2d 492 (1982) ("A defendant is always free to ignore the judicial proceedings, risk a default judgment, and then challenge that judgment on jurisdictional grounds in a collateral proceeding."); *Baldwin v. Traveling Men's Assn.*, 283 U.S. 522, 525, 51 S.Ct. 517, 75 L.Ed. 1244 (1931) (same).

[304]*Compare Leab v. Streit*, 584 F. Supp. 748, 760 (S.D.N.Y. 1984) (permitting collateral attack) *and Radiation Tech., Inc. v. S. Rad, Inc.*, 68 F.R.D. 296, 300 & 304 (N.D. Ga. 1975) (same) *with Corestates Leasing, Inc. v. Wright-Way Exp., Inc.*, 190 F.R.D. 356, 358 (E.D. Pa. 2000) (finding waiver). *See generally* 5C CHARLES A. WRIGHT & ARTHUR R. MILLER, FEDERAL PRACTICE AND PROCEDURE § 1391, at 522 (2004) ("If the defendant is merely arguing that there is no jurisdiction because service of process or the content of the papers was defective or improper and thus did not effectuate jurisdiction over this person, then the objection is not of a constitutional dimension and Rule 12(h)(1) waiver principles clearly should apply.").

vice deficiency.[305]

Sua Sponte Motions

Most courts generally refuse to allow *sua sponte* challenges to process or service.[306]

Extrinsic Materials

The parties may produce affidavits and other materials to support their positions on insufficient process or service.[307] The court may properly receive and consider such materials[308] (as well as those of which it may take judicial notice[309]) in deciding the motion, and may even convene an evidentiary hearing[310]—all without converting the motion to dismiss into a motion for summary judgment.[311]

Remedy

A party may request that the case be dismissed under these Rules or, alternatively, that service be quashed and re-attempted.[312] The court, too, has discretion. If process or service is found to be defective, the court may either quash or dismiss,[313] but will likely choose to quash if there is some reasonable prospect that the defendant can be properly served with sufficient process,[314] so long as doing so does not prejudice the

[305] *See "R" Best Produce, Inc. v. DiSapio*, 540 F.3d 115, 126 (2d Cir. 2008).

[306] *See Nuance Commc'ns, Inc. v. Abbyy Software House*, 626 F.3d 1222, 1240–41 (Fed. Cir. 2010); *Chute v. Walker*, 281 F.3d 314, 319–20 & 320 n.6 (1st Cir. 2002) (collecting cases). *But see Cardenas v. City of Chicago*, 646 F.3d 1001, 1005 (7th Cir. 2011) (suggesting court may dismiss on its own motion).

[307] *See Vega v. Hastens Beds, Inc.*, 339 F.R.D. 210, 215 (S.D.N.Y. 2021); *Torres v. Gaines*, 130 F. Supp. 3d 630, 634–35 (D. Conn. 2015).

[308] *See Grp. One Ltd. v. GTE GmbH*, 523 F. Supp. 3d 323, 332 (E.D.N.Y. 2021); *Paulsen v. Abbott Labs.*, 368 F. Supp. 3d 1152, 1163 (N.D. Ill. 2019).

[309] *See Warden v. DirecTV, LLC*, 92 F. Supp. 3d 1140, 1143 (D.N.M. 2015).

[310] *See SignalQuest, Inc. v. Tien-Ming Chou*, 284 F.R.D. 45, 46 (D.N.H. 2012).

[311] *See Boulger v. Woods*, 306 F. Supp. 3d 985, 993 (S.D. Ohio 2018), *aff'd*, 917 F.3d 471 (6th Cir. 2019); *Winston & Strawn LLP v. Law Firm of John Arthur Eaves*, 47 F. Supp. 3d 68, 71–72 (D.D.C. 2014). *But see Cubero Valderama v. Delta Air Lines, Inc.*, 931 F. Supp. 119, 120 (D.P.R. 1996) (because court considered documents filed by party challenging service of process, it applied summary judgment standards to motion).

[312] *See DiFillippo v. Special Metals Corp.*, 299 F.R.D. 348, 353 (N.D.N.Y 2014); *TAGC Mgmt., LLC v. Lehman*, 842 F. Supp. 2d 575, 580–81 (S.D.N.Y. 2012). *See generally R. Griggs Group Ltd. v. Filanto Spa*, 920 F. Supp. 1100, 1102 (D. Nev. 1996) (federal courts possess the authority to quash improper service of process, rather than dismissing the complaint, even though the Rules technically do not provide for a "Motion to Quash").

[313] *See Cardenas v. City of Chicago*, 646 F.3d 1001, 1005 (7th Cir. 2011); *Vega v. Hastens Beds, Inc.*, 339 F.R.D. 210, 217 & 222 (S.D.N.Y. 2021).

[314] *See Umbenhauer v. Woog*, 969 F.2d 25, 30–31 (3d Cir. 1992); *Pell v. Azar Nut Co., Inc.*, 711 F.2d 949, 950 (10th Cir. 1983).

defendant.[315]

Ruling Deferred

It may be proper to sidestep a pending challenge to service of process, in order to dismiss on the merits on a separately pending Rule 12(b)(6) motion.[316]

Prejudice on Dismissal

A dismissal for insufficient process or service is generally without prejudice and will not usually preclude the plaintiff from attempting to re-serve properly.[317] Where, however, the applicable limitations period has expired, it likely is not error to grant an insufficient process or service dismissal with prejudice.[318]

Appealability

Because dismissals for insufficient process or service are generally without prejudice and interlocutory, they are not immediately appealable as final orders unless the running of the applicable limitations period has caused a time-bar.[319]

RULE 12(b)(6)—DISMISSAL FOR FAILURE TO STATE A CLAIM UPON WHICH RELIEF CAN BE GRANTED

CORE CONCEPT

A motion to dismiss for failure to state a claim is the modern day descendant of the common law demurrer.[320] It tests the sufficiency of a pleader's claim for relief. The Rule allows trial courts to terminate lawsuits "that are fatally flawed in their legal premises and destined to fail, and thus to spare litigants the burdens of unnecessary pretrial and trial activity."[321]

APPLICATIONS

Legal Test

Rule 12(b)(6) motions test whether the pleaders accom-

---

[315] *See Cassano v. Altshuler*, 186 F. Supp. 3d 318, 323 (S.D.N.Y. 2016); *Gonzalez v. Ritz Carlton Hotel Co. of Puerto Rico*, 241 F. Supp. 2d 142, 147–48 (D.P.R. 2003).

[316] *See Taylor v. Westor Capital Group*, 943 F. Supp. 2d 397, 399–400 (S.D.N.Y. 2013) (collecting cases).

[317] *See Umbenhauer v. Woog*, 969 F.2d 25, 30 (3d Cir. 1992); *Marine Wholesale & Warehouse Co. v. United States*, 315 F. Supp. 3d 498, 509 (D.D.C. 2018).

[318] *See Cardenas v. City of Chicago*, 646 F.3d 1001, 1007–08 (7th Cir. 2011).

[319] *See Mid S. Carbon Corp. v. TriCamp Capital, LLC*, 622 Fed. Appx. 223, 224 (4th Cir. 2015); *Umbenhauer v. Woog*, 969 F.2d 25, 30 n.6 (3d Cir. 1992).

[320] *See De Sole v. U.S.*, 947 F.2d 1169, 1178 (4th Cir. 1991); *Inv'rs Syndicate of Am., Inc. v. City of Indian Rocks Beach*, 434 F.2d 871, 876 (5th Cir. 1970).

[321] *Advanced Cardiovascular Systems, Inc. v. Scimed Life Systems, Inc.*, 988 F.2d 1157, 1160 (Fed. Cir. 1993). *See also Foley v. Wells Fargo Bank, N.A.*, 772 F.3d 63, 72 (1st Cir. 2014) ("weed out" cases that plaintiffs "could never win"); *Port Authority of New York & New Jersey v. Arcadian Corp.*, 189 F.3d 305, 312 (3d Cir. 1999) ("screen out cases" where no relief could possibly be granted).

plished what they were obligated to do under the federal pleading rules (Rules 8 and 9).[322] A claim will fail this inspection if it asserts a legal theory that is not cognizable as a matter of law[323] or if the factual tale it alleges is ruled to be implausible.[324]

When a claim is challenged under Rule 12(b)(6), the court presumes that all well-pleaded allegations are true, resolves all reasonable doubts and inferences in the pleader's favor, and views the pleading in the light most favorable to the non-moving party.[325] No claim will be dismissed merely because the trial judge disbelieves the allegations or feels that recovery is remote or unlikely.[326] Neither "detailed factual allegations"[327] nor evidentiary-level factual showings[328] are required of pleaders, and pleaders enjoy "the benefit of imagination."[329]

Yet, although encouraging brevity,[330] the federal pleading

---

[322] *See Int'l Energy Ventures Mgmt., L.L.C. v. United Energy Grp., Ltd.*, 818 F.3d 193, 203 (5th Cir. 2016) ("the one and only method for testing" whether pleading standards set by Rules 8 and 9 have been met); *Hefferman v. Bass*, 467 F.3d 596, 599–600 (7th Cir. 2006) ("does not stand alone", but implicates Rules 8 and 9). *See generally supra* Authors' Commentary to Rule 8(a) and Rule 9.

[323] *See Neitzke v. Williams*, 490 U.S. 319, 326–27, 109 S. Ct. 1827, 104 L. Ed. 2d 338 (1989). *See also Beckington v. Am. Airlines, Inc.*, 926 F.3d 595, 604 (9th Cir. 2019) (dismissal proper if complaint lacks a "cognizable legal theory"). *But cf. Davison v. Randall*, 912 F.3d 666, 691 (4th Cir. 2019) (dismissals disfavored when claim proposes "a novel and colorable legal theory" best assessed after further factual development).

[324] *See Bell Atlantic Corp. v. Twombly*, 550 U.S. 544, 555 & 570, 127 S. Ct. 1955, 167 L. Ed. 2d 929 (2007).

[325] *See Fitzgerald v. Barnstable Sch. Comm.*, 555 U.S. 246, 249, 129 S. Ct. 788, 172 L. Ed. 2d 582 (2009); *Tellabs, Inc. v. Makor Issues & Rights, Ltd.*, 551 U.S. 308, 322, 127 S. Ct. 2499, 168 L. Ed. 2d 179 (2007); *Bell Atlantic Corp. v. Twombly*, 550 U.S. 544, 555, 127 S. Ct. 1955, 167 L. Ed. 2d 929 (2007).

[326] *See Bell Atlantic Corp. v. Twombly*, 550 U.S. 544, 555–56, 127 S. Ct. 1955, 167 L. Ed. 2d 929 (2007); *Swierkiewicz v. Sorema N. A.*, 534 U.S. 506, 508, 122 S. Ct. 992, 152 L. Ed. 2d 1 (2002); *Neitzke v. Williams*, 490 U.S. 319, 327, 109 S. Ct. 1827, 104 L. Ed. 2d 338 (1989). *See also George v. SI Grp., Inc.*, 36 F.4th 611, 619 (5th Cir. 2022) ("tests the sufficiency of the pleadings, not the merits of the case"); *Doe v. Baum*, 903 F.3d 575, 581 (6th Cir. 2018) ("If it is at all plausible (beyond a wing and a prayer) that a plaintiff would succeed if he proved everything in his complaint, the case proceeds.").

[327] *See Ashcroft v. Iqbal*, 556 U.S. 662, 678, 129 S. Ct. 1937, 173 L. Ed. 2d 868 (2009); *Bell Atlantic Corp. v. Twombly*, 550 U.S. 544, 555, 127 S. Ct. 1955, 167 L. Ed. 2d 929 (2007).

[328] *See Cortes-Ramos v. Martin-Morales*, 956 F.3d 36, 41 (1st Cir. 2020) (pleader need not prove elements of claim); *Harbourt v. PPE Casino Resorts Maryland, LLC*, 820 F.3d 655, 658 (4th Cir. 2016) (pleading need not "forecast" evidence); *Connelly v. Lane Const. Corp.*, 809 F.3d 780, 788–89 (3d Cir. 2016) (pleading need not show prima facie case, since that sets evidentiary (not pleading) obligation).

[329] *See Dagi v. Delta Airlines, Inc.*, 961 F.3d 22, 27 (1st Cir. 2020). *But cf. Schillinger v. Kiley*, 954 F.3d 990, 994 (7th Cir. 2020) (claim does not proceed "merely because some set of facts can be imagined that would entitle a plaintiff to relief").

[330] *See Ashcroft v. Iqbal*, 556 U.S. 662, 678–79, 129 S. Ct. 1937, 173 L.

duty is still far from trivial.[331] The pleading must contain "enough" information to give defendants fair notice of both the complaint's claims and the grounds on which they rest.[332] Specifically, federal pleaders must demonstrate that their allegations "possess enough heft" to *show* an *entitlement to relief* (and, thus, are sufficient to allow the costly process of litigation to continue).[333] Pleaders must allege enough facts to raise their claims beyond the level of speculation,[334] by "nudg[ing] their claims across the line from conceivable to plausible."[335] A successful pleader, therefore, is expected to do more than merely incant labels, conclusions, and the formulaic elements of a cause of action.[336]

In testing for comportment with Rule 12(b)(6), courts typically perform a two-step[337] inquiry — first, legal conclusions are isolated, so as to uncover the pleading's purely factual allegations, and second, those factual allegations are presumed true and then examined for plausibility.[338] Only a pleading's *facts* are presumed true at this stage; its speculation and conjecture is not,[339] nor are its bald assertions, conclusions, or inferences,[340]

Ed. 2d 868 (2009) (generous departure from hyper-technical pleading regime); *Tellabs, Inc. v. Makor Issues & Rights, Ltd.*, 551 U.S. 308, 319, 127 S. Ct. 2499, 168 L. Ed. 2d 179 (2007) (encouraging brevity).

[331]*See Ashcroft v. Iqbal*, 556 U.S. 662, 678–79, 129 S. Ct. 1937, 173 L. Ed. 2d 868 (2009) (Rule 8 "does not unlock the doors of discovery for a plaintiff armed with nothing more than conclusions"). *See also Amron v. Morgan Stanley Inv. Advisors Inc.*, 464 F.3d 338, 343–44 (2d Cir. 2006) ("we stop well short of saying that Plaintiffs bear no burden at the pleading stage"); *Doyle v. Hasbro, Inc.*, 103 F.3d 186, 190 (1st Cir. 1996) ("real", "not entirely a toothless tiger").

[332]*See Tellabs, Inc. v. Makor Issues & Rights, Ltd.*, 551 U.S. 308, 319, 127 S. Ct. 2499, 168 L. Ed. 2d 179 (2007); *Dura Pharmaceuticals, Inc. v. Broudo*, 544 U.S. 336, 346–47, 125 S. Ct. 1627, 161 L. Ed. 2d 577 (2005).

[333]*See Bell Atlantic Corp. v. Twombly*, 550 U.S. 544, 557, 127 S. Ct. 1955, 167 L. Ed. 2d 929 (2007). *See also Rios-Campbell v. U.S. Dep't of Commerce*, 927 F.3d 21, 24 (1st Cir. 2019) ("screening mechanism designed to weed out cases that do not warrant either discovery or trial"); *Bissessur v. Indiana Univ. Bd. of Trustees*, 581 F.3d 599, 604 (7th Cir. Sept. 2009) (allowing pure conclusory pleadings "would sanction a fishing expedition costing both parties, and the court, valuable time and resources").

[334]*See Ashcroft v. Iqbal*, 556 U.S. 662, 678, 129 S. Ct. 1937, 173 L. Ed. 2d 868 (2009); *Bell Atlantic Corp. v. Twombly*, 550 U.S. 544, 555, 127 S. Ct. 1955, 167 L. Ed. 2d 929 (2007).

[335]*See Bell Atlantic Corp. v. Twombly*, 550 U.S. 544, 570, 127 S. Ct. 1955, 167 L. Ed. 2d 929 (2007).

[336]*See Ashcroft v. Iqbal*, 556 U.S. 662, 678, 129 S. Ct. 1937, 173 L. Ed. 2d 868 (2009); *Bell Atlantic Corp. v. Twombly*, 550 U.S. 544, 555, 127 S. Ct. 1955, 167 L. Ed. 2d 929 (2007).

[337]*See In re Montreal, Maine & Atl. Ry., Ltd.*, 888 F.3d 1, 6 (1st Cir. 2018) (courts "choreograph a two-step pavane").

[338]*See Ashcroft v. Iqbal*, 556 U.S. 662, 678–79, 129 S. Ct. 1937, 173 L. Ed. 2d 868 (2009). *Cf. Oakwood Lab'ys LLC v. Thanoo*, 999 F.3d 892, 903–04 (3d Cir. 2021) (adopting three-step inquiry, starting with additional first step: taking note of elements plaintiff must plead).

[339]*See Taha v. Int'l Bhd. of Teamsters, Local 781*, 947 F.3d 464, 469 (7th Cir. 2020); *Jane Doe No. 1 v.*

legal conclusions "couched" or "masquerading" as facts,[341] unwarranted deductions of fact,[342] or averments contradicted by its own exhibits or other materials of which the court may take proper notice.[343]

A claim is facially "plausible" when it alleges sufficient factual content to permit the reasonable inference that the defendant is liable for unlawful conduct,[344] thus giving rise to a "reasonably founded hope that the discovery process will reveal relevant evidence" to support the claims.[345] Determining whether a claim crosses the "plausibility" line is a "context-specific task" that draws on the deciding court's "judicial experience and common sense."[346] To reach the "realm of plausible liability," a pleader's allegations must be factual (not conclusory) and suggestive (not neutral).[347] Pleaders must meet this pleading burden for each element required for a recovery under some actionable theory[348] (although when tested, a pleading is not parsed, part by part, but is read as a whole).[349] Pleadings that

Backpage.com, LLC, 817 F.3d 12, 25 (1st Cir. 2016).

[340]*See Ashcroft v. Iqbal*, 556 U.S. 662, 678–79, 129 S. Ct. 1937, 173 L. Ed. 2d 868 (2009). *See also Brooks v. Mentor Worldwide LLC*, 985 F.3d 1272, 1281 (10th Cir. 2021) (allegations are conclusory when they pose an inference without supplying underlying facts or are otherwise "devoid of any factual enhancement"); *Bissessur v. Indiana Univ. Bd. of Trustees*, 581 F.3d 599, 603 (7th Cir. 2009) ("A plaintiff may not escape dismissal on a contract claim, for example, by stating that he had a contract with the defendant, gave the defendant consideration, and the defendant breached the contract. What was the contract? The promises made? The consideration? The nature of the breach?"); *Aulson v. Blanchard*, 83 F.3d 1, 3 (1st Cir. 1996) (deferential standard does not obligate court "to swallow the plaintiff's invective hook, line, and sinker").

[341]*See Bell Atlantic Corp. v. Twombly*, 550 U.S. 544, 555, 127 S. Ct. 1955, 167 L. Ed. 2d 929 (2007) (quoting *Papasan v. Allain*, 478 U.S. 265, 286, 106 S. Ct. 2932, 92 L. Ed. 2d 209 (1986)).

[342]*See In re SuperValu, Inc.*, 925 F.3d 955, 962 (8th Cir. 2019); *Attkisson v. Holder*, 925 F.3d 606, 619–20 (4th Cir. 2019).

[343]*See Produce Pay, Inc. v. Izguerra Produce, Inc.*, 39 F.4th 1158, 1161 (9th Cir. 2022). *See infra* Authors' Commentary to Rule 12(b)(6) ("**Extrinsic Materials**" — *Exhibit Contradictions*").

[344]*See Ashcroft v. Iqbal*, 556 U.S. 662, 678, 129 S. Ct. 1937, 173 L. Ed. 2d 868 (2009). *Cf. Lampon-Paz v. Department of Homeland Sec.*, 612 Fed.Appx. 73, 75 (3d Cir. 2015) (allegations of victimization by "brain-mapping, subliminal messaging, and other methods to control his mind and harm his body" ruled not plausible).

[345]*See Bell Atlantic Corp. v. Twombly*, 550 U.S. 544, 559, 127 S. Ct. 1955, 167 L. Ed. 2d 929 (2007) (citations omitted).

[346]*See Ashcroft v. Iqbal*, 556 U.S. 662, 679, 129 S. Ct. 1937, 173 L. Ed. 2d 868 (2009).

[347]*See Bell Atl. Corp. v. Twombly*, 550 U.S. 544, 557 n.5, 127 S. Ct. 1955, 167 L. Ed. 2d 929 (2007). *See generally Costabile v. New York City Health & Hosps. Corp.*, 951 F.3d 77, 81 (2d Cir. 2020) (courts will not "invent factual allegations" claimant hasn't pleaded).

[348]*See Allen v. Walmart Stores, L.L.C.*, 907 F.3d 170, 178 (5th Cir. 2018); *Pension Benefit Guar. Corp. v. Findlay Indus., Inc.*, 902 F.3d 597, 605 (6th Cir. 2018).

[349]*See Meardon v. Reg.*, 994 F.3d 927, 934 (8th Cir. 2021); *Jane Doe No.*

are unable to "show" the requisite plausible entitlement to relief are thereby exposed by Rule 12(b)(6) at an early stage in the litigation so as to minimize the costs of time and money by the litigants and the courts.[350]

How *Twombly* "Plausibility" Impacts Rule 12(b)(6)

The Supreme Court announced the "plausibility" pleading standard in *Bell Atlantic Corp. v. Twombly*, a 2007 antitrust case.[351] In so doing, the Court expressly overruled the oft-quoted, very forgiving pleading mantra from its 1957 decision in *Conley v. Gibson* (namely, that no complaint should be dismissed for failing to state a claim "unless it appears beyond doubt that the plaintiff can prove no set of facts in support of his claim which could entitle him to relief").[352] The *Conley* language, wrote the Court, "earned its retirement" because it might preserve an insufficient, conclusorily-pleaded claim on the mere theoretical chance that it might later find support.[353] Two years later, the Court in *Ashcroft v. Iqbal* confirmed that this "plausibility" examination was not reserved just for antitrust cases (like *Twombly*).[354]

The boundary-setting that *Twombly* requires is not always easily discerned,[355] with some courts suggesting that *Twombly*

---

1 v. Backpage.com, LLC, 817 F.3d 12, 24 (1st Cir. 2016). *See generally Tellabs, Inc. v. Makor Issues & Rts., Ltd.*, 551 U.S. 308, 322–23, 127 S. Ct. 2499, 2509, 168 L. Ed. 2d 179 (2007).

[350]*See Bell Atlantic Corp. v. Twombly*, 550 U.S. 544, 558, 127 S. Ct. 1955, 167 L. Ed. 2d 929 (2007) (citations omitted).

[351]*Bell Atlantic Corp. v. Twombly*, 550 U.S. 544, 127 S. Ct. 1955, 167 L. Ed. 2d 929 (2007). *See generally supra* Authors' Commentary to Rule 8(a) ("**Element 2: Short and Plain Statement of the Claim**").

[352]*See Bell Atlantic Corp. v. Twombly*, 550 U.S. 544, 554–63, 127 S. Ct. 1955, 167 L. Ed. 2d 929 (2007) (abrogating language in *Conley v. Gibson*, 355 U.S. 41, 45–46, 78 S. Ct. 99, 2 L. Ed. 2d 80 (1957)). It is likely that *Conley*'s language had already been effectively abandoned in practice. *See U.S. ex rel. Garst v. Lockheed-Martin Corp.*, 328 F.3d 374, 378 (7th Cir. 2003) (sufficient pleading requires that judges and parties "need not try to fish a gold coin from a bucket of mud"); *Mann v. Boatright*, 477 F.3d 1140, 1148 (10th Cir. 2007) (not court's job "to stitch together cognizable claims for relief from the wholly deficient pleading").

[353]*See Bell Atlantic Corp. v. Twombly*, 550 U.S. 544, 562–63, 127 S. Ct. 1955, 167 L. Ed. 2d 929 (2007). *See also Moss v. U.S. Secret Serv.*, 572 F.3d 962, 968 (9th Cir. 2009) (*Conley*, "read literally, set the bar too low"); *McGovern v. City of Philadelphia*, 554 F.3d 114, 121 n.5 (3d Cir. 2009) (assertion that discovery be permitted to marshal facts necessary to support alleged theory is "misguided" understanding of federal pleading).

[354]*See Ashcroft v. Iqbal*, 556 U.S. 662, 684, 129 S. Ct. 1937, 173 L. Ed. 2d 868 (2009).

[355]*See Irrera v. Humpherys*, 859 F.3d 196, 198 (2d Cir. 2017) ("courts have struggled to draw the line"); *Runnion ex rel. Runnion v. Girl Scouts of Greater Chicago & NW. Ind.*, 786 F.3d 510, 520 (7th Cir. 2015) ("considerable uncertainty and variation"); *Courie v. Alcoa Wheel & Forged Prods.*, 577 F.3d 625, 630 (6th Cir. 2009) ("Exactly how implausible is "implausible" remains to be seen . . . ").

might still not even apply in all contexts.[356] Courts have generally read the decision as effecting a meaningful[357] (though perhaps not seismic)[358] change in direction in federal pleading (prompted principally, it is believed, by the burgeoning costs of discovery).[359] In any event, the post-*Twombly* "notice" pleading standard is (at least theoretically) quite different from *Conley*'s stated, forgiving directive that a complaint should not be dismissed unless a court is able to positively confirm that the pleader has no possible claim for relief.[360]

But under this new regime, much of the pre-*Twombly* pleading mandate survives. The basic "notice" pleading standard remains the rule in federal courts,[361] and it often is not an onerous burden.[362] The pleading of tediously detailed factual allega-

---

[356]*See Smith v. Duffey*, 576 F.3d 336, 340 (7th Cir. 2009) (Posner, J.) (musing that standard might not govern where case imposes low pretrial discovery burden); *Gunasekera v. Irwin*, 551 F.3d 461, 466 (6th Cir. 2009) (same effect). Indeed, some courts continue to incant the now-retired *Conley* language. *See, e.g., Boquist v. Courtney*, 32 F.4th 764, 782 (9th Cir. 2022); *Meriwether v. Hartop*, 992 F.3d 492, 498 (6th Cir. 2021).

[357]*See Khalik v. United Air Lines*, 671 F.3d 1188, 1191–92 (10th Cir. 2012) (*Twombly* is a "middle ground" between heightened pleading and mere labels, and notice pleading regime of Rule 8(a) "still lives"); *Phillips v. Bell*, 365 Fed.Appx. 133, 138 (10th Cir. 2010) (plausibility test overrules prior Circuit precedent that complaint with only conclusory allegations could survive); *Courie v. Alcoa Wheel & Forged Prods.*, 577 F.3d 625, 629–30 (6th Cir. 2009) ("while this new *Iqbal/Twombly* standard screens out the 'little green men' cases just as *Conley* did, it is designed to also screen out cases that, while not utterly impossible, are 'implausible.'); *Tamayo v. Blagojevich*, 526 F.3d 1074, 1083 (7th Cir. 2008) (*Twombly* "retooled federal pleading standards").

[358]*See In re Insurance Brokerage Antitrust Litig.*, 618 F.3d 300, 319 n.17 (3d Cir. 2010) (although originally believing the plausibility standard "repudiated" earlier Supreme Court precedent, now "we are not so sure"); *Arista Records, LLC v. Doe 3*, 604 F.3d 110, 119 (2d Cir. 2010) (*Twombly* opinion itself "belied" the notion that a heightened pleading standard is required); *Bissessur v. Indiana Univ. Bd. of Trustees*, 581 F.3d 599, 603 (7th Cir. 2009) ("Our system operates on a notice pleading standard; *Twombly* and its progeny do not change this fact."). *See generally* William M. Janssen, *Iqbal "Plausibility" in Pharmaceutical and Medical Device Litigation*, 71 LA. L. REV. 541 (2011) (discussing impact across pharmaceutical and medical device litigation sector).

[359]*See Pension Ben. Guar. Corp. ex rel. St. Vincent Catholic Med. Ctrs. Ret. Plan v. Morgan Stanley Inv. Mgmt. Inc.*, 712 F.3d 705, 719 (2d Cir. 2013). Judge Posner's eloquent assessment of this motivation is noteworthy. *See Swanson v. Citibank, N.A.*, 614 F.3d 400, 411–12 (7th Cir. 2010) (Posner, J., dissenting).

[360]*See Tamayo v. Blagojevich*, 526 F.3d 1074, 1084 (7th Cir. 2008) (opining that *Twombly* inverted *Conley* approach—complaint now must do more than merely *avoid foreclosing* all possible bases for recovery, but must instead affirmatively *suggest* entitlement to relief).

[361]*See Sylvia v. Wisler*, 875 F.3d 1307, 1326 (10th Cir. 2017); *United States ex rel. Hanna v. City of Chicago*, 834 F.3d 775, 779 (7th Cir. 2016).

[362]*See Diedrich v. Ocwen Loan Servicing, LLC*, 839 F.3d 583, 589 (7th Cir. 2016); *Johnson v. Riverside Healthcare System, LP*, 534 F.3d 1116, 1122 (9th Cir. 2008). *See also Leal v. McHugh*, 731 F.3d 405, 410 (5th Cir. 2013) (Rule 12(b)(6) motions "viewed

tions is still not required,[363] nor is the pleading of every fact necessary to sustain the plaintiff's merits burden.[364] Nor will a claim be dismissed because the factual allegations do not support the pleader's chosen legal theory, if those allegations would provide for relief under another viable theory.[365] It is still not the courts' role to weigh whether the pleader's ultimate success on the merits is probable or unlikely,[366] or to choose between competing allegations that are both plausible.[367] The requisite "plausibility," therefore, is *not* measured by a likelihood of success.[368] But, though "plausibility" does not require a showing of "probability," it also is not satisfied upon a showing of mere "possibility."[369] Thus, allegations that are "merely consistent" with (and not "plausibly suggestive" of) liability are not enough.[370] And this "plausibility" must appear affirmatively, on the face of the pleading.[371]

In the end, precisely how *Twombly* applies will depend on context:[372] a "plausible" auto accident case may be very concisely pleaded, whereas a "plausible" antitrust or RICO case (often

---

with disfavor").

[363]*See Ashcroft v. Iqbal*, 556 U.S. 662, 678, 129 S. Ct. 1937, 678 173 L. Ed. 2d 868 (2009); *Bell Atlantic Corp. v. Twombly*, 550 U.S. 544, 555 & n.3, 127 S. Ct. 1955, 167 L. Ed. 2d 929 (2007).

[364]*See Carrero-Ojeda v. Autoridad de Energia Electrica*, 755 F.3d 711, 718 (1st Cir. 2014).

[365]*See Johnson v. City of Shelby*, 574 U.S. 10, 11–12, 135 S. Ct. 346, 190 L. Ed. 2d 309 (2014); *Topchian v. JPMorgan Chase Bank, N.A.*, 760 F.3d 843, 849 (8th Cir. 2014).

[366]*See Bell Atlantic Corp. v. Twombly*, 550 U.S. 544, 556, 127 S. Ct. 1955, 167 L. Ed. 2d 929 (2007).

[367]*See Doe v. Princeton Univ.*, 30 F.4th 335, 344 (3d Cir. 2022); *VoteVets Action Fund v. U.S. Dep't of Veterans Affs.*, 992 F.3d 1097, 1104 & 1106 (D.C. Cir. 2021). *But see Doe v. Samford Univ.*, 29 F.4th 675, 689 (11th Cir. 2022) (ruling that plaintiff's allegations of sexual discrimination "permit obvious alternative explanations" which render claim implausible).

[368]*See Melendez v. McAleenan*, 928 F.3d 425, 427 (5th Cir. 2019).

[369]*See Ashcroft v. Iqbal*, 556 U.S. 662, 678, 129 S. Ct. 1937, 173 L. Ed. 2d 868 (2009) ("The plausibility standard is not akin to a 'probability requirement,' but it asks for more than a sheer possibility that a defendant has acted unlawfully. Where a complaint pleads facts that are 'merely consistent with' a defendant's liability, it 'stops short of the line between possibility and plausibility of 'entitlement to relief.' ' ").

[370]*See Ashcroft v. Iqbal*, 556 U.S. 662, 678, 129 S. Ct. 1937, 173 L. Ed. 2d 868 (2009); *Bell Atl. Corp. v. Twombly*, 550 U.S. 544, 557, 127 S. Ct. 1955, 167 L. Ed. 2d 929 (2007).

[371]*See Bell Atl. Corp. v. Twombly*, 550 U.S. 544, 570, 127 S. Ct. 1955, 1974, 167 L. Ed. 2d 929 (2007) (requiring "enough facts to state a claim to relief that is plausible on its face"). *See also Neubauer v. FedEx Corp.*, 849 F.3d 400, 404–05 (8th Cir. 2017) (courts need not "mine" lengthy complaints "searching for nuggets that might refute obvious pleading deficiencies"); *Morales-Tanon v. Puerto Rico Elec. Power Auth.*, 524 F.3d 15, 18 (1st Cir. 2008) (view that pleaders need only to plead enough facts for *courts* to frame some cognizable claim is now "simply wrong").

[372]*See Ashcroft v. Iqbal*, 556 U.S. 662, 679, 129 S. Ct. 1937, 173 L. Ed. 2d 868 (2009) (assessing plausibility is "context-specific task"). *See also Brooks v. Mentor Worldwide LLC*, 985 F.3d 1272, 1281 (10th Cir. 2021) (required degree of specificity "depends on the context and the type of case").

built on inferences from facts that might be either innocent or culpable) may demand a fuller factual presentation.[373]

Using Rule 12(b)(6) With Enhanced Pleading Failures

Several Rules and some federal statutes obligate parties to plead certain claims or defenses with enhanced detail.[374] A pleading that lacks that required additional detail constitutes a failure to state a cognizable claim, remedied through a Rule 12(b)(6) motion to dismiss.[375]

Burden of Proof

The burden of proving that the pleader has failed to state a claim lies with the moving party.[376] Accordingly, dismissal is not warranted merely because a non-moving party fails to oppose the motion; courts must independently assess the challenged pleading against the pleading standards.[377]

Timing and Waiver

The defense of failure to state a claim may be asserted pre-answer, by motion filed before any responsive pleading.[378] Courts disagree whether multiple such pre-answer challenges are technically proper[379] and, if so, whether a later pre-answer motion may raise arguments that existed but were not asserted

---

[373]*See Kansas Penn Gaming, LLC v. Collins*, 656 F.3d 1210, 1215 (10th Cir. 2011) (required nature and specificity of claim "will vary based on context"); *In re Insurance Brokerage Antitrust Litig.*, 618 F.3d 300, 319 n.18 (3d Cir. 2010) ("Some claims will demand relatively more factual detail to satisfy this standard, while others require less."). This shifting-scale view of Rule 8(a)'s demands may well have predated *Twombly*. *See Tyco Fire Prods. LP v. Victaulic Co.*, 777 F. Supp. 2d 893, 989 (E.D.Pa. 2011) (noting pre-*Twombly* precedent that "the more substantively complex the cause of action, the greater the mandate for detail under [Rule 8(a)].").

[374]*See, e.g.*, Rule 9(b) (fraud and mistake must be pleaded "with particularity"); Rule 9(c) (denying conditions precedent must be done "with particularity"); Rule 9(g) (special damages must be pleaded "specifically"); 15 U.S.C.A. § 78u-4 (Private Securities Litigation Reform Act requires securities fraud elements to be pleaded with particularity).

[375]*See Vess v. Ciba-Geigy Corp. USA*, 317 F.3d 1097, 1107 (9th Cir. 2003) (motion to dismiss for Rule 9(b) pleading failure is "functional equivalent" of Rule 12(b)(6) motion); *Harrison v. Westinghouse Savannah River Co.*, 176 F.3d 776, 783 n.5 (4th Cir. 1999) (noncompliance with Rule 9(b) "is treated as" failure to state claim under Rule 12(b)(6)).

[376]*See Marcure v. Lynn*, 992 F.3d 625, 631 (7th Cir. 2021); *Raymond v. Avectus Healthcare Sols., LLC*, 859 F.3d 381, 383 (6th Cir. 2017).

[377]*See Marcure v. Lynn*, 992 F.3d 625, 631–33 (7th Cir. 2021); *Servicios Azucareros de Venezuela, C.A. v. John Deere Thibodeaux, Inc.*, 702 F.3d 794, 806 (5th Cir. 2012). *But see Cohen v. Bd. of Trustees of Univ. of D.C.*, 819 F.3d 476, 481–83 (D.C. Cir. 2016) (surveying Circuits, but following minority approach).

[378]*See* Rule 12(b). *See also Patrick v. Rivera-Lopez*, 708 F.3d 15, 18 (1st Cir. 2013).

[379]*Compare In re Apple iPhone Antitrust Litig.*, 846 F.3d 313, 318 (9th Cir. 2017) (not proper), *with Ennenga v. Starns*, 677 F.3d 766, 773 (7th Cir. 2012) (proper).

earlier[380] (courts may tolerate successive motions when, under the circumstances, doing so serves the interests of justice).[381] The defense may also be asserted in the answer, or post-answer, in a Rule 12(c) motion for judgment on the pleadings or a Rule 56 motion for summary judgment.[382] A mislabeled post-answer Rule 12(b)(6) motion may be treated as a Rule 12(c) motion, if no prejudice results.[383] Finally, the defense may also be raised during trial, but is waived if not asserted at least by that time.[384]

Extrinsic Materials

In ruling on a Rule 12(b)(6) motion, the court focuses principally on the complaint itself, but often may[385] also consider a small category of additional materials: exhibits attached to the complaint (unless their authenticity is questioned);[386] documents that the complaint incorporates by reference;[387] documents that, though not attached to the complaint, accompany the dismissal motion, are integral to and relied upon in the complaint, and are not contested as inauthentic;[388] information subject to judicial notice;[389] matters of public rec-

---

[380]*See Leyse v. Bank of Am. Nat. Ass'n*, 804 F.3d 316, 319–22 (3d Cir. 2015) (surveying division among courts). *Compare Doe v. Columbia-Brazoria Indep. Sch. Dist.*, 855 F.3d 681, 686 (5th Cir. 2017) (proper), *with In re Apple Iphone Antitrust Litig.*, 846 F.3d 313, 317–18 (9th Cir. 2017) (improper).

[381]*See In re Apple Iphone Antitrust Litig.*, 846 F.3d 313, 318-19 (9th Cir. 2017); *Albers v. Bd. of Cty. Comm'rs of Jefferson Cty.*, 771 F.3d 697, 703–04 (10th Cir. 2014).

[382]*See* Rule 12(h)(2)(B) (under Rule 12(c)); Rule 12(d) (under Rule 56).

[383]*See Patrick v. Rivera-Lopez*, 708 F.3d 15, 18 (1st Cir. 2013); *MacDonald v. Grace Church Seattle*, 457 F.3d 1079, 1081 (9th Cir. 2006).

[384]*See* Rule 12(h)(2). *See also Arbaugh v. Y&H Corp.*, 546 U.S. 500, 507 126 S. Ct. 1235, 163 L. Ed. 2d 1097 (2006) (Rule 12(b)(6) objection "endures up to, but not beyond, trial on the merits").

[385]At least one court has confirmed expressly that the district court is not reflexively *required* to consider extrinsic evidence in its Rule 12(b)(6) ruling, but may do so in the exercise of its discretion. *See Davis v. HSBC Bank Nevada, N.A.*, 691 F.3d 1152, 1159–60 (9th Cir. 2012).

[386]*See Rivera v. Kress Stores of Puerto Rico, Inc.*, 30 F.4th 98, 102 (1st Cir. 2022); *United States ex rel. Foreman v. AECOM*, 19 F.4th 85, 106 (2d Cir. 2021). For a discussion of permissibly attached exhibits to pleadings, see *supra* Authors' Commentary to Rule 10(c) ("**Attaching Exhibits**").

[387]*See Tellabs, Inc. v. Makor Issues & Rights, Ltd.*, 551 U.S. 308, 322, 127 S. Ct. 2499, 168 L. Ed. 2d 179 (2007). *But see Khoja v. Orexigen Therapeutics, Inc.*, 899 F.3d 988, 1002–03 (9th Cir. 2018) (discussing practical limits of "incorporation-by-reference" doctrine).

[388]*See Mendoza v. Amalgamated Transit Union Int'l*, 30 F.4th 879, 884 (9th Cir. 2022); *Doe v. Princeton Univ.*, 30 F.4th 335, 342 (3d Cir. 2022). *See generally Schmidt v. Skolas*, 770 F.3d 241, 249–50 (3d Cir. 2014) (explaining rationale for exception).

[389]*See Tellabs, Inc. v. Makor Issues & Rights, Ltd.*, 551 U.S. 308, 322, 127 S. Ct. 2499, 168 L. Ed. 2d 179 (2007). *See also Basic Cap. Mgmt., Inc. v. Dynex Cap., Inc.*, 976 F.3d 585, 588–89 (5th Cir. 2020) (describing judicial notice process).

ord;[390] and concessions by plaintiffs made in their response to the motion.[391] Some courts may even consider additional facts set out in briefs (for illustrative purposes only, and only so long as they are consistent with the pleadings).[392] When the content of foreign law is at issue, the court may also consider extrinsic materials proposing to prove such law.[393]

The parties *may* submit (and the court *may* consider) further materials, but with a consequence—the motion will be re-cast. If the court, in its discretion,[394] considers such additional extrinsic evidence, the motion must be converted into a Rule 56 request for summary judgment.[395]

- *Exhibit v. Pleading Inconsistencies:* Extrinsic evidence that is properly consulted by a court can materially impact its Rule 12(b)(6) ruling. Courts have sometimes written casually on this point, occasionally in sweeping, categorical terms.[396] When actually explored, however, the matter is revealed to be more nuanced.[397] A pleading's claim may be rendered implausible if its factual allegations are "utterly discredited" by an attached exhibit,[398] warranting a grant of the motion and a dismissal.[399] But this inquiry must remain consistent with the pleadings-only nature of this motion.[400] Thus, if a properly consulted exhibit contradicts general, conclusory allega-

[390] *See Cruz-Arce v. Mgmt. Admin. Servs. Corp.*, 19 F.4th 538, 543 (1st Cir. 2021); *Simko v. U.S. Steel Corp*, 992 F.3d 198, 201 n.1 (3d Cir. 2021).

[391] *See Breiding v. Eversource Energy*, 939 F.3d 47, 49 (1st Cir. 2019).

[392] *See Geinosky v. City of Chicago*, 675 F.3d 743, 745 n.1 (7th Cir. 2012) (in Seventh Circuit practice, party opposing Rule 12(b)(6) motion "may submit materials outside the pleadings to illustrate the facts the party expects to be able to prove," to add "weight behind the pleadings the court must evaluate," but for only "illustrative purposes").

[393] *See de Fontbrune v. Wofsy*, 838 F.3d 992, 998–1000 (9th Cir. 2016).

[394] *See Trans-Spec Truck Service, Inc. v. Caterpillar Inc.*, 524 F.3d 315, 321 (1st Cir. 2008); *Pueschel v. U.S.*, 369 F.3d 345, 353 n.3 (4th Cir. 2004).

[395] For more discussion of this conversion process, see *infra* Authors' Commentary to Rule 12(d).

[396] *See, e.g., Quadvest, L.P. v. San Jacinto River Auth.*, 7 F.4th 337, 345 (5th Cir. 2021) ("the exhibit and not the allegation controls"); *Kaplan v. Univ. of Louisville*, 10 F.4th 569, 576 (6th Cir. 2021) (exhibit "trumps").

[397] *See Khoja v. Orexigen Therapeutics, Inc.*, 899 F.3d 988, 1003 (9th Cir. 2018) ("what inferences a court may draw from an incorporated document should also be approached with caution").

[398] *See Cagayat v. United Collection Bureau, Inc.*, 952 F.3d 749, 755–56 (6th Cir. 2020).

[399] *See Gen. Guar. Ins. Co. v. Parkerson*, 369 F.2d 821, 825 (5th Cir. 1966) ("This complaint is plagued not by what it lacks, but by what it contains. All of the paths to relief which the pleading suggests are blocked by the allegations and the attached documents themselves, without more."). *See generally Hoefling v. City of Miami*, 811 F.3d 1271, 1277 (11th Cir. 2016) ("The classic example is when a plaintiff attaches a document to his complaint but his allegations about what the document is or says contradict the document itself.").

[400] *See Khoja v. Orexigen Therapeutics, Inc.*, 899 F.3d 988, 1003 (9th Cir. 2018) (courts are prohibited from resolving factual disputes at

tions in a pleading, those allegations might not be credited and the exhibit may control.[401] Conversely, if a pleading's specific, well-pleaded allegations either do not appear in a properly consulted exhibit or are contradicted by merely conclusory statements in the exhibit, the pleading's allegations will likely be credited.[402]

"Clarifying" the Complaint with Briefs/Oral Argument

Although the factual averments in the *pleading* are deemed true on a motion to dismiss, statements offered in a legal memorandum or brief are collateral to the pleadings and are ordinarily not entitled to that presumption of truth.[403] Nevertheless, so long as they are consistent with the pleadings,[404] the pleader's memorandum or brief can be used to "clarify" allegations of the pleading,[405] as can "factual elaborations" supplied by pleaders[406] and statements made by the pleaders during oral argument.[407] When such extrinsic enhancements introduce new facts not alleged in the pleadings, however, the motion must be converted to a summary judgment proceeding.[408]

Pleading in Anticipation of Affirmative Defenses

Ordinarily, plaintiffs need not anticipate the defendants' likely affirmative defenses,[409] nor attempt to preemptively "plead around" them in the complaint.[410] Whether the complaint states a claim upon which relief can be granted is gener-

---

pleadings stage, thus all well-pleaded facts are assumed true and all reasonable inferences are drawn in pleader's favor).

[401]*See Gill as Next Friend of K.C.R. v. Judd*, 941 F.3d 504, 514 (11th Cir. 2019). *See also Tritz v. U.S. Postal Serv.*, 721 F.3d 1133, 1135 n.1 (9th Cir. 2013) ("we need not accept as true conclusory allegations that are contradicted by documents referred to in the complaint").

[402]*See Gill as Next Friend of K.C.R. v. Judd*, 941 F.3d 504, 514 (11th Cir. 2019). *See also Khoja v. Orexigen Therapeutics, Inc.*, 899 F.3d 988, 1003 (9th Cir. 2018) ("it is improper to assume the truth of an incorporated document if such assumptions only serve to dispute facts stated in a well-pleaded complaint").

[403]*See E.I. du Pont de Nemours & Co. v. Kolon Indus., Inc.*, 637 F.3d 435, 449 (4th Cir. 2011); *Dorsey v. Portfolio Equities, Inc.*, 540 F.3d 333, 338 (5th Cir. 2008).

[404]*See Peterson v. Wexford Health Sources, Inc.*, 986 F.3d 746, 752 n.2 (7th Cir. 2021). *Cf. Epstein v. Epstein*, 843 F.3d 1147, 1151 n.5 (7th Cir. 2016) (rejecting entirely new assertion, since "this latitude is not unlimited").

[405]*See Pegram v. Herdrich*, 530 U.S. 211, 229, 120 S. Ct. 2143, 147 L. Ed. 2d 164 (2000); *Vance v. Rumsfeld*, 653 F.3d 591, 602 n.6 (7th Cir. 2011).

[406]*See Kuebler v. Vectren Corp.*, 13 F.4th 631, 636 (7th Cir. 2021).

[407]*See Maio v. Aetna, Inc.*, 221 F.3d 472, 485 (3d Cir. 2000).

[408]*See Demarais v. Gurstel Chargo, P.A.*, 869 F.3d 685, 696 n.2 (8th Cir. 2017). *See generally infra* Authors' Commentary to Rule 12(d). *Cf. Kuebler v. Vectren Corp.*, 13 F.4th 631, 636 (7th Cir. 2021) (extrinsic evidence offered to "illustrate allegations" in pleading requires no conversion).

[409]*See Perry v. Merit Sys. Prot. Bd.*, 582 U.S. __, 137 S. Ct. 1975, 1987 n.9, 198 L. Ed. 2d 527 (2017); *O'Gorman v. City of Chicago*, 777 F.3d 885, 889 (7th Cir. 2015).

[410]*See Perry v. Merit Sys. Prot. Bd.*, 582 U.S. __, 137 S. Ct. 1975, 1987 n.9, 198 L. Ed. 2d 527 (2017); *Xechem, Inc.*

ally not dependent on whether the defendant has a defense.[411]

Dismissing "Built-In" Affirmative Defenses

The court will dismiss for failing to state a claim where the face of the complaint reveals patent, "built-in" affirmative defenses, such as statute of limitations, preclusion, preemption, exhaustion of administrative remedies, or statute of frauds.[412] Parties can, in this manner, essentially "plead themselves out of court" in two ways. First, they can allege facts that establish (perhaps inadvertently) an affirmative defense[413] or demonstrate that success on the merits is otherwise not possible.[414] Second, they can attach extrinsic materials to their pleadings that reveal the presence of the same sort of "built-in" defenses.[415] "Built-in" defense dismissals are proper only where the damning facts are readily ascertainable from the face[416] of the complaint, its attachments, the public record, or other allowable sources of judicial notice, *and* those facts conclusively demonstrate the defense.[417]

- *Best Resolved Under Rule 12(c):* Although courts have dismissed claims based on "built-in" defenses, the preferred practice is to seek a judgment on the pleadings under Rule 12(c) once the pleadings have closed.[418]

Sua Sponte Motions

The trial court may, on its own initiative, and without an adversary's motion, dismiss a pleading for failing to state a

---

v. Bristol-Myers Squibb Co., 372 F.3d 899, 901 (7th Cir. 2004).

[411] *See U.S. v. Northern Trust Co.*, 372 F.3d 886, 888 (7th Cir. 2004).

[412] *See, e.g., Bell v. Eagle Mountain Saginaw Indep. Sch. Dist.*, 27 F.4th 313, 320–26 (5th Cir. 2022) (copyright fair use); *Stevens v. St. Tammany Par. Gov't*, 17 F.4th 563, 571 (5th Cir. 2021) (res judicata); *Whiteside v. Hover-Davis, Inc.*, 995 F.3d 315, 319 (2d Cir. 2021) (limitations); *Marshall's Locksmith Serv. Inc. v. Google, LLC*, 925 F.3d 1263, 1267 (D.C. Cir. 2019) (federal preemption); *Doe v. Mckesson*, 922 F.3d 604, 609 n.3 (5th Cir. 2019) (lack of capacity); *Miller v. BAC Home Loans Servicing, L.P.*, 726 F.3d 717, 726 (5th Cir. 2013) (statute of frauds); *Bryant v. Rich*, 530 F.3d 1368, 1380 n.2 (11th Cir. 2008) (exhaustion).

[413] *See Orgone Capital III, LLC v. Daubenspeck*, 912 F.3d 1039, 1043–44 (7th Cir. 2019); *Lupian v. Joseph Cory Holdings LLC*, 905 F.3d 127, 130–31 (3d Cir. 2018).

[414] *See San Geronimo Caribe Project, Inc. v. Acevedo-Vila*, 687 F.3d 465, 492 (1st Cir. 2012); *Trudeau v. Federal Trade Com'n.*, 456 F.3d 178, 193 (D.C. Cir. 2006). *See also Knapp v. Hogan*, 738 F.3d 1106, 1109 (9th Cir. 2013) (Rule 8 can be violated both when a pleading "says too little" and when it "says too much").

[415] *See Sams v. Yahoo! Inc.*, 713 F.3d 1175, 1179 (9th Cir. 2013); *Burke v. 401 N. Wabash Venture, LLC*, 714 F.3d 501, 505 (7th Cir. 2013). *See generally supra* Authors' Commentary to Rule 12(b)(6) ("**Extrinsic Materials**").

[416] *See Boquist v. Courtney*, 32 F.4th 764, 774 (9th Cir. 2022); *Bell v. Eagle Mountain Saginaw Indep. Sch. Dist.*, 27 F.4th 313, 320 (5th Cir. 2022).

[417] *See Dagi v. Delta Airlines, Inc.*, 961 F.3d 22, 27 (1st Cir. 2020); *Parungao v. Cmty. Health Sys., Inc.*, 858 F.3d 452, 457 (7th Cir. 2017).

[418] *See Gunn v. Cont'l Cas. Co.*, 968 F.3d 802, 806 (7th Cir. 2020).

claim upon which relief may be granted.[419] Such dismissals are "strong medicine, and should be dispensed sparingly."[420] Generally, the trial court must first notify the pleader of its intention to grant a *sua sponte* dismissal and permit an opportunity to amend or otherwise respond.[421] A *sua sponte* dismissal entered without forewarning to the plaintiff may still be affirmed if doing so would not, under the circumstances, prejudice an opponent[422] or where the pleading's allegations are "patently meritless" and without any hope of cure.[423] In such a case, the party defending the dismissal carries the burden of demonstrating that the allegations, drawn most favorably to the pleader, are beyond all hope.[424]

***Pro Se* Litigants**

Courts are particularly cautious while inspecting pleadings prepared by plaintiffs who lack counsel and are proceeding *pro se*. Often inartful, and rarely composed to the standards expected of practicing attorneys, *pro se* pleadings are viewed with considerable liberality and are held to less stringent standards than those expected of pleadings drafted by lawyers[425] (a relaxation that persists after *Twombly*).[426] Nevertheless, unrepresented plaintiffs are not relieved of their obligation to allege sufficient facts to support a cognizable legal claim.[427] Indeed, *in forma pauperis* claims may be dismissed if found legally frivolous.[428] Moreover, courts usually may not give *pro se* litigants legal advice, lest the courts' impartiality be called

---

[419] *See Robertson v. Anderson Mill Elementary Sch.*, 989 F.3d 282, 290–91 (4th Cir. 2021); *Century Sur. Co. v. Blevins*, 799 F.3d 366, 372 (5th Cir. 2015). *But cf. Blue Cross & Blue Shield of Alabama v. Sanders*, 138 F.3d 1347, 1354 (11th Cir. 1998) (because "failure to state a claim" is not a jurisdictional issue, court may not *sua sponte* decide the question unless plaintiff has preserved it).

[420] *See Garayalde-Rijos v. Municipality of Carolina*, 747 F.3d 15, 22 (1st Cir. 2014). *See also Knight v. Mooring Capital Fund, LLC*, 749 F.3d 1180, 1190 (10th Cir. 2014) (disfavored).

[421] *See Hager v. DBG Partners, Inc.*, 903 F.3d 460, 464 (5th Cir. 2018); *Reed v. Lieurance*, 863 F.3d 1196, 1207 (9th Cir. 2017).

[422] *See Robertson v. Anderson Mill Elementary Sch.*, 989 F.3d 282, 290–91 (4th Cir. 2021).

[423] *See Rollins v. Wackenhut Services, Inc.*, 703 F.3d 122, 127 (D.C.Cir. 2012); *Christiansen v. West Branch Cmty. Sch. Dist.*, 674 F.3d 927, 938 (8th Cir. 2012).

[424] *Martinez-Rivera v. Sanchez Ramos*, 498 F.3d 3, 7 (1st Cir. 2007).

[425] *See Erickson v. Pardus*, 551 U.S. 89, 94, 127 S. Ct. 2197, 167 L. Ed. 2d 1081 (2007) (per curiam); *Estelle v. Gamble*, 429 U.S. 97, 106, 97 S. Ct. 285, 50 L. Ed. 2d 251 (1976); *Haines v. Kerner*, 404 U.S. 519, 520–21, 92 S. Ct. 594, 30 L. Ed. 2d 652 (1972).

[426] *See Bowman v. Iddon*, 848 F.3d 1034, 1039 (D.C. Cir. 2017); *Luis v. Zang*, 833 F.3d 619, 626 (6th Cir. 2016).

[427] *See Ottah v. Fiat Chrysler*, 884 F.3d 1135, 1141 (Fed. Cir. 2018); *Chhim v. Univ. of Texas at Austin*, 836 F.3d 467, 469 (5th Cir. 2016).

[428] *See* 28 U.S.C.A. § 1915(e)(2)(B); 28 U.S.C.A. § 1915A. *See also Neitzke v. Williams*, 490 U.S. 319, 109 S. Ct. 1827, 104 L. Ed. 2d 338 (1989) (describing standards for dismissals of *in forma pauperis* pleadings as frivolous).

into question.[429] Dismissals of *pro se* pleaders are ordinarily accompanied by leave to replead (unless it is clear that the best possible case has been pleaded).[430]

Oral Argument

The trial judge may, but is not obligated to, convene oral argument on a Rule 12(b)(6) motion to dismiss.[431]

Postponing Discovery

Some courts permit a postponement of discovery after a Rule 12(b)(6) motion is filed, and then continuing for so long as it remains pending.[432] Because such motions challenge pleading (and not evidentiary) sufficiency, pleaders are ordinarily not allowed to engage in discovery to rescue deficient allegations.[433]

Voluntary Dismissals While Motion is Pending

Plaintiffs may voluntarily dismiss a lawsuit at any time prior to the point where their adversaries serve an answer or a motion for summary judgment.[434] Consequently, plaintiffs are generally permitted to voluntarily dismiss their lawsuits while a pre-answer motion to dismiss is pending (and that privilege likely persists even when the defendant attaches extrinsic materials to its motion, which would otherwise command a conversion to summary judgment procedures—provided the court has not yet converted the motion).[435]

Manner of Ruling

Although no detailed written opinion is required, the practice preferred by appellate courts is that a dismissal be accompanied by some explanation for the decision, so as to supply both the parties and a reviewing court with the benefit of

---

[429] *See Bilal v. Geo Care, LLC*, 981 F.3d 903, 911 (11th Cir. 2020); *Rothman v. United States*, 508 F.2d 648, 653 n.8 (3d Cir.1975).

[430] *See Modrall v. Corker*, 654 Fed. Appx. 1021, 1022 (11th Cir. 2016); *Hale v. King*, 642 F.3d 492, 503 (5th Cir. 2011).

[431] *See* Rule 78 ("By rule or order, the court may provide for submitting and determining motions on briefs, without oral hearings."); *Greene v. WCI Holdings Corp.*, 136 F.3d 313, 316 (2d Cir. 1998) ("Every circuit to consider the issue has determined that the 'hearing' requirements of Rule 12 . . . do not mean that an oral hearing is necessary, but only require that a party be given the opportunity to present its views to the court").

[432] *See City of Oakland v. BP PLC*, 969 F.3d 895, 910 (9th Cir. 2020) (designed to allow defendants to challenge pleading sufficiency without being subject to sometimes "prohibitive" costs of discovery); *Cortes-Ramos v. Martin-Morales*, 956 F.3d 36, 45 (1st Cir. 2020) (resolving Rule 12(b)(6) "generally does not require discovery").

[433] *See Ashcroft v. Iqbal*, 556 U.S. 662, 686, 129 S. Ct. 1937, 173 L. Ed. 2d 868 (2009). *See also Gonzalez v. Google LLC*, 2 F.4th 871, 906-07 (9th Cir. 2021) (plaintiffs may not rely on "anticipated discovery" to meet pleading obligations).

[434] *See* Rule 41(a)(1)(A)(i).

[435] *See In re Bath and Kitchen Fixtures Antitrust Litigation*, 535 F.3d 161, 166 (3d Cir. 2008); *Swedberg v. Marotzke*, 339 F.3d 1139, 1142–45 (9th Cir. 2003).

the trial court's reasoning.[436]

Ruling Deferred

Where circumstances persuade the court that claims should not be dismissed until further factual development is accomplished, the court may deny the Rule 12(b)(6) motion and revisit the merits of claims on a Rule 12(c) motion for judgment on the pleadings or a Rule 56 motion for summary judgment.[437] But pre-ruling discovery is not, as a matter of course, necessarily available to all litigants resisting a motion to dismiss.[438]

Remedy and Post-Ruling Amendments

A claim that is not legally cognizable or not factually plausible will be dismissed, though piecemeal dismissals of parts of a claim are not proper.[439] If dismissed, the court will generally permit the pleader one post-dismissal opportunity to amend,[440] even when the court doubts that the pleading defects can be overcome,[441] unless the court concludes that any amendment would be futile or inequitable.[442]

- *Failing to Request Leave to Amend:* Although courts may grant leave to amend a dismissed complaint even when it is not requested,[443] neglecting to seek such leave is risky. Trial courts generally do not abuse their discretion by failing to allow an amendment opportunity that the pleader did not request[444] or requested only alternatively or in passing.[445]
- *Duty to Explain Proposed Amendments*: When a replead-

[436]*See Metzler Inv. GMBH v. Corinthian Colleges, Inc.*, 540 F.3d 1049, 1061 n.5 (9th Cir. 2008).

[437]*See Wright v. North Carolina*, 787 F.3d 256, 263 (4th Cir. 2015) ("novel" claims, falling outside prior case law, and best assessed after further factual development, may merit refusing early dismissal).

[438]*See Bell Atlantic Corp. v. Twombly*, 550 U.S. 544, 556–57, 127 S. Ct. 1955, 167 L. Ed. 2d 929 (2007); *Lister v. Bank of America, N.A.*, 790 F.3d 20, 23–24 (1st Cir. 2015); *Zink v. Lombardi*, 783 F.3d 1089, 1105–06 (8th Cir. 2015).

[439]*See Bilek v. Fed. Ins. Co.*, 8 F.4th 581, 587 (7th Cir. 2021).

[440]*See O'Brien v. Vill. of Lincolnshire*, 955 F.3d 616, 628 (7th Cir. 2020); *Loreley Fin. (Jersey) No. 3 Ltd. v. Wells Fargo Sec., LLC*, 797 F.3d 160, 191 (2d Cir. 2015).

[441]*See Ostrzenski v. Seigel*, 177 F.3d 245, 252–53 (4th Cir. 1999).

[442]*See Nowlin v. Pritzker*, 34 F.4th 629, 635–36 (7th Cir. 2022); *Knowles v. TD Ameritrade Holding Corp.*, 2 F.4th 751, 758 (8th Cir. 2021).

[443]*See Schmitt v. Kaiser Found. Health Plan of Wash.*, 965 F.3d 945, 960 (9th Cir. 2020); *Estate of Lagano v. Bergen County Prosecutor's Office*, 769 F.3d 850, 861 (3d Cir. 2014).

[444]*See Nunes v. Cable News Network, Inc.*, 31 F.4th 135, 147 n.7 (2d Cir. 2022) (contention that court abused discretion in not granting amendment when none was requested "is frivolous"); *Blackburn v. Shire US Inc*, 18 F.4th 1310, 1318 (11th Cir. 2021) (court not required to grant counseled claimant leave to amend *sua sponte*). *But cf. Mullin v. Balicki*, 875 F.3d 140, 151 (3d Cir. 2017) (general rule modified in civil rights cases, where amendment required unless inequitable or futile).

[445]*See Squeri v. Mount Ida Coll.*, 954 F.3d 56, 74 (1st Cir. 2020); *Chaidez v. Ford Motor Co.*, 937 F.3d 998,

ing appears futile, courts may insist (prior to any amendment) that the plaintiffs first explain how a subsequent revision would cure their pleading deficiency.[446]

- *Appealing, Rather Than Amending*: A plaintiff who is otherwise entitled to file an amended complaint following a Rule 12(b)(6) dismissal may choose instead to stand on the original complaint and appeal the dismissal.[447]
- *Amendments After Entry of Judgment:* The generous post-dismissal amendment practice changes once the trial court enters its judgment. At that point, post-judgment relief (under Rules 59 or 60) is necessary, though a timely submitted, credible post-dismissal amendment will likely be considered carefully.[448]

Prejudice on Dismissal

Unless the ruling is premised on mere technical pleading defects or the court directs otherwise (or permits an amended pleading),[449] a dismissal for failing to state a claim is deemed to be a ruling on the merits, and, once final, is accorded full res judicata effect.[450] Conversely, an order denying dismissal under Rule 12(b)(6) does not conclusively resolve anything,[451] nor does it somehow forecast who will prevail at trial (or even whether the case can survive summary judgment).[452]

1007-08 (7th Cir. 2019).

[446]*See Noto v. 22nd Century Grp., Inc.*, 35 F.4th 95, 107–08 (2d Cir. 2022); *Matter of Life Partners Holdings, Inc.*, 926 F.3d 103, 125–26 (5th Cir. 2019). *See generally Toone v. Wells Fargo Bank, N.A.*, 716 F.3d 516, 524 (10th Cir. 2013) ("The district court is not required to imagine all possible amendments and determine whether any would state a claim.").

[447]*See Alston v. Parker*, 363 F.3d 229, 235 (3d Cir. 2004) ("If the plaintiff does not desire to amend, he may file an appropriate notice with the district court asserting his intent to stand on the complaint, at which time an order to dismiss the action would be appropriate"). *See also Arduini v. Hart*, 774 F.3d 622, 636 (9th Cir. 2014) (plaintiffs commonly amend after a dismissal, but are not required to do so); *Massuda v. Panda Exp., Inc.*, 759 F.3d 779, 784 (7th Cir. 2014) (choosing to stand on dismissed complaint usually deprives party of post-appeal amendment); *WMX Technologies, Inc. v. Miller*, 104 F.3d 1133, 1136 (9th Cir. 1997) (holding that plaintiff must obtain final judgment from district court before "standing" on original complaint and taking immediate appeal).

[448]*See NewSpin Sports, LLC v. Arrow Elecs., Inc.*, 910 F.3d 293, 310–11 (7th Cir. 2018).

[449]*See Cohen v. Bd. of Trustees of Univ. of D.C.*, 819 F.3d 476, 484 (D.C. Cir. 2016) (technical inadequacy dismissals should be without prejudice); *Claudio-De Leon v. Sistema Universitario Ana G. Mendez*, 775 F.3d 41, 49–50 (1st Cir. 2014) (forum selection clause dismissals should be without prejudice).

[450]*See Brownback v. King*, 592 U.S. —, 141 S. Ct. 740, 748, 209 L. Ed. 2d 33 (2021); *Federated Dept. Stores, Inc. v. Moitie*, 452 U.S. 394, 399, 101 S. Ct. 2424, 69 L. Ed. 2d 103 (1981).

[451]*See PA Prison Soc. v. Cortes*, 622 F.3d 215, 247 (3d Cir. 2010).

[452]*See Martinez v. Novo Nordisk Inc.*, 992 F.3d 12, 19–20 (1st Cir. 2021) (denial does not preclude later summary judgment); *Abbas v. Foreign Policy Group, LLC*, 783 F.3d 1328,

Appealability

Whether Rule 12(b)(6) rulings are appealable (immediately or otherwise) can be a challenging inquiry and merits careful study. A ruling that grants a Rule 12(b)(6) motion in its entirety and with prejudice, thus terminating the litigation, will almost certainly be a final order and immediately appealable.[453] However, the ruling might not be immediately appealable if it grants the motion but allows repleading[454] (unless the pleader elects to stand on the dismissed pleading[455]) or if it grants the motion only in part.[456] If the ruling denies the motion, the ruling is likely not immediately appealable,[457] or, if the plaintiff has prevailed at trial, appealable at all.[458] But exceptions exist. For example, a ruling that denies a dismissal on certain immunity grounds may be immediately appealed,[459] as may denials that are "inextricably intertwined" with another order that is immediately appealable.[460]

RULE 12(b)(7)—DISMISSAL FOR FAILURE TO JOIN A RULE 19 PARTY

CORE CONCEPT

A case may be dismissed if there is an absent party without whom complete relief cannot be granted or whose interest in the dispute is of such a nature that to proceed without that party could prejudice either that absent party or an existing party.

APPLICATIONS

Purpose

The purpose of Rule 19 is to facilitate the joinder, into a single lawsuit, of all parties who are inseparably interested in

---

1334 (D.C. Cir. 2015) (same).

[453] *See ALA, Inc. v. CCAIR, Inc.*, 29 F.3d 855, 859–60 (3d Cir.1994). *See also Borden v. Allen*, 646 F.3d 785, 812 (11th Cir. 2011) (Rule 12(b)(6) is a ruling on the merits).

[454] *See Goode v. Cent. Va. Legal Aid Soc'y, Inc.*, 807 F.3d 619, 623 (4th Cir. 2015).

[455] *See Bing v. Brivo Sys., LLC*, 959 F.3d 605, 615 & n.7 (4th Cir. 2020); *Alston v. Parker*, 363 F.3d 229, 235 (3d Cir. 2004).

[456] Such partial grants might be made immediately appealable upon court order. *See, e.g.*, Rule 54(b); 28 U.S.C.A. § 1292(b).

[457] *See Ridpath v. Board of Governors Marshall University*, 447 F.3d 292, 304 (4th Cir. 2006); *Hill v. City of New York*, 45 F.3d 653, 659 (2d Cir. 1995).

[458] *See ClearOne Commc'ns, Inc. v. Biamp Systems*, 653 F.3d 1163, 1172 (10th Cir. 2011) (no right to appeal from Rule 12(b)(6) ruling; appeal must be from motion for judgment as a matter of law); *Bennett v. Pippin*, 74 F.3d 578, 585 (5th Cir.1996) (same).

[459] *See, e.g., Puerto Rico Aqueduct and Sewer Authority v. Metcalf & Eddy, Inc.*, 506 U.S. 139, 113 S. Ct. 684, 121 L. Ed. 2d 605 (1993) (denial of Eleventh Amendment immunity); *Mitchell v. Forsyth*, 472 U.S. 511, 105 S. Ct. 2806, 86 L. Ed. 2d 411 (1985) (denial of qualified immunity); *Zamani v. Carnes*, 491 F.3d 990, 994 (9th Cir. 2007) (denial of anti-SLAPP motion); *Goldstein v. City of Long Beach*, 481 F.3d 1170, 1172 (9th Cir. 2007) (denial of absolute immunity motion).

[460] *See Angelotti Chiropractic, Inc. v. Baker*, 791 F.3d 1075, 1086 (9th Cir. 2015).

a dispute, to protect their interests and the interests of the existing parties, as well as and to shield the courts against a squandering of judicial resources.[461]

Legal Test

The courts are hesitant to dismiss for failure to join absent parties, and will not do so on a vague possibility that unjoined persons may have an interest affected by the litigation.[462] The test is not mechanically formalistic, but hinges on the peculiar factual circumstances and practicalities each case presents.[463] When a Rule 12(b)(7) motion is filed, the court will conduct a two-step assessment. The court, first, will determine if someone absent from the lawsuit qualifies as a "required" party within the meaning of Rule 19(a) and, second, if so, whether joining that party into the lawsuit is feasible (and, if not, how best to proceed under Rule 19(b)).[464] The court conducts this inquiry on the basis of the pleadings as they appear at the time the joinder is proposed,[465] and while State law may prove relevant to assessing the interests of the respective parties, the Rule 12(b)(7) issue remains ultimately a question of federal law.[466] The court will accept all of the pleader's well-pleaded factual allegations as true, and will draw all reasonable inferences in the pleader's favor.[467] However, legal conclusions and conclusorily-supported "threadbare recitals" of elements will not be accepted as true.[468] The ultimate decision is committed to the trial court's sound discretion.[469]

Timing and Waiver

An objection to the absence of a Rule 19 indispensable party

---

[461] *See Nanko Shipping, USA v. Alcoa, Inc.*, 850 F.3d 461, 464 (D.C. Cir. 2017); *Askew v. Sheriff of Cook Cty.*, 568 F.3d 632, 634 (7th Cir. 2009).

[462] *See Nanko Shipping, USA v. Alcoa, Inc.*, 850 F.3d 461, 464 (D.C. Cir. 2017); *Fort Yates Pub. Sch. Dist. No. 4 v. Murphy ex rel. C.M.B.*, 786 F.3d 662, 671 (8th Cir. 2015).

[463] *See Provident Tradesmens Bank & Trust Co. v. Patterson*, 390 U.S. 102, 118, 88 S. Ct. 733, 19 L. Ed. 2d 936 (1968); *Gunvor SA v. Kayablian*, 948 F.3d 214, 219 (4th Cir. 2020).

[464] *See Dine Citizens Against Ruining Our Env't v. Bureau of Indian Affairs*, 932 F.3d 843, 851 (9th Cir. 2019); *Delgado-Caraballo v. Hosp. Pavia Hato Rey, Inc.*, 889 F.3d 30, 37 (1st Cir. 2018). *See also Union Pac. R.R. Co. v. City of Palestine*, 517 F. Supp. 3d 609, 619 (E.D. Tex. 2021) (when court is asked to interpret a contract, contracting parties must generally be joined). *See generally infra* Authors' Commentary to Rule 19.

[465] *See Register v. Cameron & Barkley Co.*, 467 F. Supp. 2d 519, 530 (D.S.C. 2006).

[466] *See Provident Tradesmens Bank & Trust Co. v. Patterson*, 390 U.S. 102, 125 n.22, 88 S. Ct. 733, 19 L. Ed. 2d 936 (1968).

[467] *See Dine Citizens Against Ruining Our Env't v. Bureau of Indian Affairs*, 932 F.3d 843, 851 (9th Cir. 2019); *Butler v. City of New York*, 559 F. Supp. 3d 253, 264 (S.D.N.Y. 2021).

[468] *See Pittsburgh Logistics Sys., Inc. v. C.R. England, Inc.*, 669 F. Supp. 2d 613, 618 (W.D.Pa. 2009).

[469] *See Fort Yates Pub. Sch. Dist. No. 4 v. Murphy ex rel. C.M.B.*, 786 F.3d 662, 671–72 (8th Cir. 2015); *Am. Trucking Ass'n, Inc. v. N.Y. State Thruway Auth.*, 795 F.3d 351, 356 (2d Cir. 2015).

may be asserted by motion filed before a responsive pleading, in the responsive pleading itself, by motion for judgment on the pleadings, or during the trial on the merits.[470] But the trial judge has the discretion to reject a motion as untimely if the motion is found to have been submitted intentionally late to serve a litigant's own strategic purposes, rather than to protect interests relating to an absent party.[471]

Burden of Proof

The burden lies with the person seeking the dismissal.[472] Some courts, however, shift the burden to the party opposing joinder once a *prima facie* case of required party status has been made.[473]

Motions by Non-Parties

It is unclear whether non-parties may move for a Rule 19 dismissal, though courts often treat such motions as mislabeled intervention requests or suggestions for *sua sponte* Rule 19 rulings.[474]

***Sua Sponte* Motions**

Although the absence of a Rule 19 party is not a jurisdictional defect, the court may, on its own initiative, raise the absence of a Rule 19 party.[475]

Remedy

The court will, if possible, order that an absent Rule 19(a) required party be joined in the lawsuit. If joinder is not possible, the court will consider whether in equity and good conscience the lawsuit should continue without the absent party.[476] Dismissals are disfavored, however,[477] and will be granted only when the defect cannot be cured and some serious prejudice or

---

[470] *See* Rule 12(h)(2). *See also Legal Aid Soc'y v. City of New York*, 114 F. Supp. 2d 204, 219 (S.D. N.Y. 2000) (failure to join indispensable party is not "threshold defense", and may be raised through end of trial).

[471] *See, e.g., Stooksbury v. Ross*, 528 Fed.Appx. 547, 556 (6th Cir. 2013); *Fireman's Fund Ins. Co. v. Nat'l Bank of Coops.*, 103 F.3d 888, 896 (9th Cir. 1996).

[472] *See Am. Gen. Life & Accident Ins. Co. v. Wood*, 429 F.3d 83, 92 (4th Cir. 2005); *Citizen Band Potawatomi Indian Tribe of Oklahoma v. Collier*, 17 F.3d 1292, 1293 (10th Cir. 1994).

[473] *See Hood ex rel. Mississippi v. City of Memphis*, 570 F.3d 625, 628 (5th Cir. 2009). *See generally Advanced Cardiology Ctr. Corp. v. Rodriguez*, 675 F. Supp. 2d 245, 250 (D.P.R. 2009) (surveying case law).

[474] *See MasterCard Int'l Inc. v. Visa Int'l Serv. Ass'n, Inc.*, 471 F.3d 377, 382 (2d Cir. 2006) (only parties can make 12(b)(7) motions); *Deschutes River All. v. Portland Gen. Elec. Co.*, 323 F. Supp. 3d 1171, 1176–77 (D. Or. 2018) (same); *Johnson v. Qualawash Holdings, L.L.C.*, 990 F. Supp. 2d 629, 635–36 (W.D. La. 2014) (noting uncertainty and *sua sponte* option).

[475] *See Republic of Philippines v. Pimentel*, 553 U.S. 851, 861, 128 S. Ct. 2180, 171 L. Ed. 2d 131 (2008); *Provident Tradesmens Bank & Trust Co. v. Patterson*, 390 U.S. 102, 111, 88 S. Ct. 733, 19 L. Ed. 2d 936 (1968).

[476] *See* Rule 19(b).

[477] *See Delgado-Caraballo v. Hosp. Pavia Hato Rey, Inc.*, 889 F.3d 30, 37 (1st Cir. 2018); *Fort Yates Public Sch.*

inefficiency would follow.[478]

Extrinsic Materials

The parties may produce affidavits and other materials to support their positions on the absence of a Rule 19 party.[479] The court may also consider evidence that is properly subject to judicial notice.[480] The courts differ on the legal effect of such extrinsic materials. Some courts hold that those materials can be considered freely without converting the motion into a summary judgment analysis,[481] while others hold that a conversion is required.[482]

Ruling Deferred

The court may defer ruling on the challenge until after discovery is conducted.[483]

Prejudice on Dismissal

A dismissal for lack of a Rule 19 party generally does not preclude the plaintiff from re-instituting the claim in a court that can join the absent party.[484]

Appealability

The district court's denial of a Rule 12(b)(7) motion is usually interlocutory and not immediately appealable.[485]

RULE 12(c)—JUDGMENT ON THE PLEADINGS

CORE CONCEPT

A party can move for judgment on the pleadings once the pleadings are closed.

Dist. No. 4 v. Murphy ex rel. C.M.B., 786 F.3d 662, 671 (8th Cir. 2015).

[478] *See Am. Trucking Ass'n, Inc. v. New York State Thruway Auth.*, 795 F.3d 351, 357 (2d Cir. 2015).

[479] *See Davis Companies v. Emerald Casino, Inc.*, 268 F.3d 477, 480 n.4 (7th Cir. 2001); *Citizen Band Potawatomi Indian Tribe of Oklahoma v. Collier*, 17 F.3d 1292, 1293 (10th Cir. 1994).

[480] *See Auto-Owners Ins. Co. v. Morris*, 191 F. Supp. 3d 1302, 1304 (N.D. Ala. 2016).

[481] *See Tinoco v. San Diego Gas & Elec. Co.*, 327 F.R.D. 651, 657 (S.D. Cal. 2018); *Auto-Owners Ins. Co. v. Morris*, 191 F. Supp. 3d 1302, 1304 (N.D. Ala. 2016).

[482] *See Raytheon Co. v. Continental Cas. Co.*, 123 F. Supp. 2d 22, 32 (D. Mass. 2000); *Steward v. Gwaltney of Smithfield, Ltd.*, 954 F. Supp. 1118, 1121 (E.D. Va. 1996), aff'd, 103 F.3d 120 (4th Cir. 1996).

[483] *See Raytheon Co. v. Continental Cas. Co.*, 123 F. Supp. 2d 22, 32 (D. Mass. 2000); *Mije Associates v. Halliburton Services*, 552 F. Supp. 418, 419 (S.D. N.Y. 1982).

[484] *See University of Pittsburgh v. Varian Med. Sys., Inc.*, 569 F.3d 1328, 1332 (Fed.Cir. 2009); *Dredge Corp. v. Penny*, 338 F.2d 456, 463–64 (9th Cir. 1964). *See De Wit v. Firstar Corp.*, 879 F. Supp. 947, 992 (N.D. Iowa 1995) (dismissals with prejudice appropriate only where court orders joinder of party and joinder is not accomplished).

[485] *See Alto v. Black*, 738 F.3d 1111, 1130 (9th Cir. 2013) (not within collateral order doctrine); *PepsiCo., Inc. v. F. T. C.*, 472 F.2d 179, 185 (2d Cir. 1972) (not a "final order").

APPLICATIONS

Purpose

Rule 12(c) can be used to achieve either of two separate objectives.[486] First, a Rule 12(c) motion can be used to seek a substantive, merits disposition of the underlying dispute on grounds that are exposed by an examination of all the pleadings.[487] Second, a Rule 12(c) motion can alternatively be used to press, *post-answer*, three of the Rule 12 defenses: failure to state a claim, to state a legal defense, or to join a Rule 19(b) required party.[488] Neither type of motion is ripe until the pleadings have formally closed.[489] Regardless of the type of use, a Rule 12(c) motion remains a pleadings-based attack, with its inquiry limited principally to the pleadings themselves.[490]

Legal Test

Because the motion represents a challenge at an embryonic stage in the litigation,[491] the court will construe the pleadings liberally[492] and will not resolve contested facts.[493] Instead, the court will accept all well-pleaded material allegations of the nonmoving party as true, and view all facts and inferences in a light most favorable to the pleader.[494] (Thus, when the *plaintiff* is the moving party, denials and other averments pleaded in the defendant's answer are presumed true and all reasonable inferences are drawn in the defendant's favor.[495]) But legal conclusions will not be presumed true,[496] and no unwarranted factual inferences will be drawn to aid a pleader.[497] In ruling, a court may consider whether claims have been undermined by pleaded allegations[498] or by properly considered extrinsic facts

---

[486] *See Alexander v. City of Chicago*, 994 F.2d 333, 340 (7th Cir. 1993) (Crabb, J., concurring).

[487] *See Hale v. Metrex Research Corp.*, 963 F.3d 424, 427 (5th Cir. 2020).

[488] *See* Rule 12(h)(2)(B).

[489] *See infra* Authors' Commentary to Rule 12(c) (**"Timing and Waiver"**).

[490] *See Barany-Snyder v. Weiner*, 539 F.3d 327, 332 (6th Cir. 2008). *See also infra* Authors' Commentary to Rule 12(c) (**"Extrinsic Materials"**).

[491] *See Perez-Acevedo v. Rivero-Cubano*, 520 F.3d 26, 29 (1st Cir. 2008).

[492] *See U.S. v. 0.073 acres of land, more or less, situate in Parishes of Orleans & Jefferson*, 705 F.3d 540, 543 (5th Cir. 2013).

[493] *See Pit River Tribe v. Bureau of Land Mgmt.*, 793 F.3d 1147, 1158 (9th Cir. 2015); *Perez v. Wells Fargo N.A.*, 774 F.3d 1329, 1335 (11th Cir. 2014).

[494] *See Wearry v. Foster*, 33 F.4th 260, 265 (5th Cir. 2022); *Conner v. Cleveland Cnty.*, 22 F.4th 412, 416 (4th Cir. 2022), *petition for cert. pending*, No. 21-1538 (U.S. June 8, 2022).

[495] *See Lively v. WAFRA Inv. Advisory Grp., Inc.*, 6 F.4th 293, 305 (2d Cir. 2021).

[496] *See Barber v. Charter Twp. of Springfield*, 31 F.4th 382, 387 (6th Cir. 2022); *Garza v. Escobar*, 972 F.3d 721, 727 (5th Cir. 2020).

[497] *See Barber v. Charter Twp. of Springfield*, 31 F.4th 382, 387 (6th Cir. 2022); *Massey v. Ojaniit*, 759 F.3d 343, 353 (4th Cir. 2014).

[498] *See Buchanan-Moore v. County of Milwaukee*, 570 F.3d 824, 827 (7th Cir. 2009).

or materials.[499]

The courts have articulated different tests for deciding Rule 12(c) motions, depending on the motion's purpose. When the motion seeks a merits disposition of the dispute, the test tracks the summary judgment inquiry and asks whether—informed by the averments and responses in the pleadings—the movant is entitled to a judgment as a matter of law because no genuine dispute exists as to any material fact.[500] Unlike summary judgment motions, however, this type of Rule 12(c) motion considers only the face of the pleadings and a few other modest categories of extrinsic materials.[501] Alternatively, when the motion seeks only to press a Rule 12 defense, the test tracks the Rule 12(b)(6) inquiry[502] and asks whether the contested pleading succeeded in alleging a "plausible" claim for relief[503] or in stating a legal defense.[504] A few courts follow a hybrid test that cites the Rule 12(b)(6) test as controlling but adds the "no-material-factual-dispute" inquiry as well.[505]

- *Post-Discovery Motions:* One court has suggested that the operative legal test might differ depending on whether the motion is filed during or after discovery.[506]
- *Cross-Motions:* When both parties file motions for judgment on the pleadings, the court treats each motion separately (*i.e.,* with each motion, accepting the non-movant's allegations of fact as true and drawing reasonable inferences in that party's favor).[507]
- *No Implied Trial Admissions:* Although Rule 12(c) presumes the pleaders' facts as true for motion purposes, the moving party is free, if its motion is denied, to

---

[499] *See infra* Authors' Commentary to Rule 12(c) ("**Extrinsic Materials**"—"*Exhibit Contradictions*").

[500] *See In Re Gaddy*, 977 F.3d 1051, 1055 (11th Cir. 2020); *Mid-Am. Salt, LLC v. Morris Cty. Coop. Pricing Council*, 964 F.3d 218, 226 (3d Cir. 2020).

[501] *See Corn v. Mississippi Dep't of Pub. Safety*, 954 F.3d 268, 277 n.6 (5th Cir. 2020). *See also infra* Authors' Commentary to Rule 12(c) ("**Extrinsic Materials**").

[502] *See Wearry v. Foster*, 33 F.4th 260, 265 (5th Cir. 2022); *Barber v. Charter Twp. of Springfield*, 31 F.4th 382, 386 (6th Cir. 2022).

[503] *See Vengalattore v. Cornell Univ.*, 36 F.4th 87, 102 (2d Cir. 2022); *Templeton v. Jarmillo*, 28 F.4th 618, 621 (5th Cir. 2022). For a discussion of the *Twombly* "plausibility" standard, see *supra* Authors' Commentary to Rule 12(b)(6) ("**Legal Test**" and "**How *Twombly* 'Plausibility' Impacts Rule 12(b)(6)**").

[504] *See* Rule 12(h)(2)(B).

[505] *See Moderwell v. Cuyahoga Cty.*, 997 F.3d 653, 659 (6th Cir. 2021); *Wolfington v. Reconstructive Orthopaedic Assocs. II PC*, 935 F.3d 187, 195 (3d Cir. 2019).

[506] *See Grajales v. Puerto Rico Ports Auth.*, 682 F.3d 40, 44–46 (1st Cir. 2012) (musing that it is an "obvious anomaly" to test for plausibility in a pleading (so as to avoid unwarranted, costly discovery) when discovery has occurred).

[507] *See U.S. Sec. & Exch. Comm'n v. Hui Feng*, 935 F.3d 721, 728 (9th Cir. 2019); *Mercury Sys., Inc. v. S'holder Representative Servs., LLC*, 820 F.3d 46, 51 (1st Cir. 2016).

disprove or contradict those facts at trial.[508]

Any Party May File Motion

Rule 12(c) motions may be filed by any party,[509] with the requisite inquiry reconfigured accordingly. Thus, if a plaintiff moves for judgment on the pleadings, all well-pleaded factual allegations in the answer are presumed true and all reasonable inferences are drawn in the defendant's favor.[510]

Timing and Waiver

A motion for judgment on the pleadings is premature if filed before the pleadings have closed.[511] Thus, the motion is not ripe if the complaint[512] (and any counterclaims, crossclaims, or third-party claims[513]) have not yet been answered. However, motions need not be postponed until the period for amendments as-of-right to the pleadings has passed[514] or until discovery is completed.[515] Courts may treat an out-of-time (post-answer) Rule 12(b)(6) motion to dismiss as though it were filed as a Rule 12(c) motion.[516] Rule 12(c) contains no explicit outer time limit on filing, beyond the admonition that all such motions must be filed "early enough not to delay trial."[517] Thus, the fact that discovery has already begun does not necessarily render

---

[508] *See Wyman v. Wyman*, 109 F.2d 473, 474 (C.C.A. 9th Cir. 1940).

[509] *See Lively v. WAFRA Inv. Advisory Grp., Inc.*, 6 F.4th 293, 305 (2d Cir. 2021) ("both plaintiffs and defendants can move"); *Dist. No. 1, Pac. Coast Dist., Marine Engineers Beneficial Ass'n, AFL-CIO v. Liberty Mar. Corp.*, 933 F.3d 751, 760 (D.C. Cir. 2019) ("either party").

[510] *See Lively v. WAFRA Inv. Advisory Grp., Inc.*, 6 F.4th 293, 305 (2d Cir. 2021). *See also Beal v. Missouri Pac. R. R. Corp.*, 312 U.S. 45, 51, 61 S. Ct. 418, 421, 85 L. Ed. 577 (1941).

[511] *See Barber v. Charter Twp. of Springfield*, 31 F.4th 382, 386 (6th Cir. 2022); *Lively v. WAFRA Inv. Advisory Grp., Inc.*, 6 F.4th 293, 301 (2d Cir. 2021).

[512] *See Lillian B. ex rel. Brown v. Gwinnett Cty. Sch. Dist.*, 631 Fed. Appx. 851, 852–53 (11th Cir. 2015); *Doe v. U.S.*, 419 F.3d 1058, 1061 (9th Cir. 2005). However, the courts may agree to choose to treat premature, pre-answer Rule 12(c) motions as motions to dismiss under Rule 12(b)(6).

[513] *See Mandujano v. City of Pharr*, 786 Fed. Appx. 434, 436 (5th Cir. 2019); *Perez v. Wells Fargo N.A.*, 774 F.3d 1329, 1336–37 (11th Cir. 2014). *But cf. NanoMech, Inc. v. Suresh*, 777 F.3d 1020, 1023 (8th Cir. 2015) ("technically" improper decision to consider premature Rule 12(c) may be harmless error).

[514] *See Rezende v. Ocwen Loan Servicing, LLC*, 869 F.3d 40, 43 n.3 (1st Cir. 2017)).

[515] *See Lively v. WAFRA Inv. Advisory Grp., Inc.*, 6 F.4th 293, 301 (2d Cir. 2021). *See also Carlson v. Reed*, 249 F.3d 876, 878 n.1 (9th Cir. 2001) (rejecting as "frivolous" that Rule 12(c) motion was granted prematurely where discovery had not yet been completed).

[516] *See Villeneuve v. Avon Prod., Inc.*, 919 F.3d 40, 49 (1st Cir. 2019); *Brokers' Choice of Am., Inc. v. NBC Universal, Inc.*, 861 F.3d 1081, 1102 (10th Cir. 2017).

[517] *See Hindel v. Husted*, 875 F.3d 344, 346 (6th Cir. 2017); *Am. Trucking Associations, Inc. v. New York State Thruway Auth.*, 238 F. Supp. 3d 527 (S.D.N.Y. 2017), *aff'd*, 886 F.3d 238 (2d Cir. 2018).

the motion untimely.[518] But this time window is not unbounded. Motions filed too long after the pleadings are closed may be refused as untimely.[519] Rule 12(c) cannot be used to revive defenses and objections that a party waived by failing to assert in a pre-answer Rule 12(b) motion or responsive pleading,[520] and waivable defenses not included in a party's Rule 12(c) motion are also likely lost (even though they may have been preserved in that party's answer).[521] When Rule 12(c) and Rule 56 motions are both pending, the court need not necessarily rule on the Rule 12(c) motion first.[522]

Dismissing "Built-In" Affirmative Defenses

As in Rule 12(b)(6) practice, the court may grant judgment on the pleadings when the allegations (or the content of properly-considered extrinsic materials) reveal an affirmative defense that fatally defeats the pleader's claim.[523] In fact, some courts hold that "built-in" affirmative defenses are only properly raised by Rule 12(c) (or Rule 56) motions, and not under Rule 12(b)(6).[524]

Civil Rights and *Pro Se* Cases

Several courts view Rule 12(c) motions as "disfavored" in civil rights cases,[525] and hold that such motions should be applied with "particular strictness"[526] and in a manner that tests pleadings under a "very lenient, even de minimis" standard.[527] Likewise, complaints filed *pro se* are tested liberally, though a

---

[518]*See PDX N., Inc. v. Comm'r New Jersey Dep't of Lab. & Workforce Dev.*, 978 F.3d 871, 880 (3d Cir. 2020) (motion filed shortly after pleadings closed but after party submitted all of its discovery was not untimely, especially because no trial date had yet been set).

[519]*See* Rule 12(c) (motion must be made "[a]fter the pleadings are closed" yet "early enough not to delay trial"). *See General Elec. Co. v. Sargent & Lundy*, 916 F.2d 1119, 1131 (6th Cir. 1990) (reversing "timeliness" denial of Rule 12(c) motion where no allegation of prejudice was pressed and where prejudice was not articulated).

[520]*See Kearney v. Goord*, 2011 WL 1303296, at *2 (W.D.N.Y. Mar. 14, 2011), *adopted*, 2011 WL 1213099 (W.D.N.Y. Mar. 31, 2011). *See generally Albers v. Bd. of Cty. Comm'rs of Jefferson Cty.*, 771 F.3d 697, 701 (10th Cir. 2014) (litigant loses waivable defenses if omitted from prior Rule 12 motion). *But cf. Patel v. Contemporary Classics of Beverly Hills*, 259 F.3d 123, 126 (2d Cir. 2001) (Rule 12(c) can be used to resolve a non-waivable defense brought after the close of pleadings).

[521]*See infra* Authors' Commentary to Rule 12(h) ("**Waiver By Post-Answer Rule 12(c) Motion Omission**").

[522]*See S.E.C. v. Wolfson*, 539 F.3d 1249, 1264–65 (10th Cir. 2008).

[523]*See Jardin De Las Catalinas Ltd. P'ship v. Joyner*, 766 F.3d 127, 132 (1st Cir. 2014). *See also supra* Authors' Commentary to Rule 12(b)(6) ("**Dismissing "Built-In" Affirmative Defenses**").

[524]*See United States v. Rogers Cartage Co.*, 794 F.3d 854, 860–61 (7th Cir. 2015).

[525]*See McGlone v. Bell*, 681 F.3d 718, 728 (6th Cir. 2012).

[526]*See Cleveland v. Caplaw Enters.*, 448 F.3d 518, 521 (2d Cir. 2006); *Irish Lesbian & Gay Organization v. Giuliani*, 143 F.3d 638, 644 (2d Cir. 1998).

[527]*See Deravin v. Kerik*, 335 F.3d 195, 200 (2d Cir. 2003).

plausible claim for relief must nevertheless be stated.[528]

Extrinsic Materials

In ruling on a Rule 12(c) motion, the court will of course consider the pleaded allegations,[529] but may[530] also consider: exhibits attached to, or incorporated by reference in,[531] the complaint[532] or answer[533] (provided those exhibits qualify for attachment[534] and are undisputed and central to the claim[535]); matters of public record;[536] facts subject to judicial notice;[537] and motion exhibits that are integral to the pleadings and authentic.[538]

Other types of extrinsic evidence may be presented by the parties on a Rule 12(c) motion, but doing so comes with a consequence. If the court, in its discretion, considers (or does not exclude) such evidence,[539] the court must convert the motion into a request for summary judgment under Rule 56.[540] And defending parties cannot sidestep this conversion by appending such other evidence as exhibits to their answers.[541] Yet, given the liberality of federal amendments, courts might allow certain

---

[528]*See Hogan v. Fischer*, 738 F.3d 509, 516 (2d Cir. 2013).

[529]*See Velarde v. GW GJ, Inc.*, 914 F.3d 779, 781 n.1 (2d Cir. 2019); *Bosarge v. Mississippi Bureau of Narcotics*, 796 F.3d 435, 440 (5th Cir. 2015).

[530]Attaching any of these limited categories of allowable extrinsic materials is an option for the moving party, not a requirement. *See Cooke v. Jackson Nat'l Life Ins. Co.*, 919 F.3d 1024, 1028 (7th Cir. 2019).

[531]*See Lively v. WAFRA Inv. Advisory Grp., Inc.*, 6 F.4th 293, 305–06 (2d Cir. 2021); *Webb v. Trader Joe's Co.*, 999 F.3d 1196, 1201 (9th Cir. 2021).

[532]*See Buckley v. Hennepin Cnty.*, 9 F.4th 757, 760 (8th Cir. 2021); *Lively v. WAFRA Inv. Advisory Grp., Inc.*, 6 F.4th 293, 305–06 (2d Cir. 2021).

[533]*See Lively v. WAFRA Inv. Advisory Grp., Inc.*, 6 F.4th 293, 305 (2d Cir. 2021). *See generally* Rule 10(c) (written instruments attached as exhibits to "a pleading" considered part of that pleading "for all purposes").

[534]*See supra* Authors' Commentary to Rule 10(c) ("**Attaching Exhibits**").

[535]*See Horsley v. Feldt*, 304 F.3d 1125, 1134–35 (11th Cir. 2002); *Massey v. Ojaniit*, 759 F.3d 343, 347–48 (4th Cir. 2014).

[536]*See Wolfington v. Reconstructive Orthopaedic Assocs. II PC*, 935 F.3d 187, 195 (3d Cir. 2019); *MyMail, Ltd. v. ooVoo, LLC*, 934 F.3d 1373, 1378–79 (Fed. Cir. 2019).

[537]*See Lively v. WAFRA Inv. Advisory Grp., Inc.*, 6 F.4th 293, 305–6 (2d Cir. 2021); *Webb v. Trader Joe's Co.*, 999 F.3d 1196, 1201 (9th Cir. 2021).

[538]*See Wolfington v. Reconstructive Orthopaedic Assocs. II PC*, 935 F.3d 187, 195 (3d Cir. 2019); *MyMail, Ltd. v. ooVoo, LLC*, 934 F.3d 1373, 1378–79 (Fed. Cir. 2019).

[539]There is a division among the Circuits as to when the conversion obligation is triggered. There are three approaches. Some courts require conversion anytime extrinsic evidence is not expressly excluded, others require conversion only if the court "considers" the extrinsic evidence, and still others require conversion only if, after considering the extrinsic evidence, the court chooses to "rely" on it. *See Max Arnold & Sons, LLC v. W.L. Hailey & Co., Inc.*, 452 F.3d 494, 502–03 (6th Cir. 2006) (collecting cases, and electing first approach).

[540]*See* Rule 12(d). *See also Lively v. WAFRA Inv. Advisory Grp., Inc.*, 6 F.4th 293, 305–06 (2d Cir. 2021); *Clark v. Stone*, 998 F.3d 287, 296 (6th Cir. 2021). For a more extensive discussion of this conversion process, see *infra* Authors' Commentary to Rule 12(d).

[541]*See Horsley v. Feldt*, 304 F.3d 1125, 1134–35 (11th Cir. 2002) ("Other-

extrinsic materials generated during pre-ruling discovery to fill gaps in a pleading[542] or affirm an otherwise improper Rule 12(c) consideration of extrinsic materials when doing so is harmless error.[543]

- *Exhibit v. Pleading Inconsistencies:* Although the court normally accepts as true all of the nonmoving party's well-pleaded allegations when ruling on a Rule 12(c) motion, the court need not accept allegations that are utterly discredited by extrinsic materials properly attached to the pleadings or subject to judicial notice.[544] The operation of this principle seems to track its Rule 12(b)(6) analogue.[545]

Remedy

If the Rule 12(c) motion is granted, the prevailing parties obtain a final judgment in their favor.[546]

Entry of a Partial Judgment

Unlike summary judgment, Rule 12(c) contains no express grant of authority for a district court to issue a partial judgment, and at least one Circuit has suggested that such authority does not exist.[547]

Prejudice on Entry

Granting a Rule 12(c) motion for judgment on the pleadings will ordinarily terminate the case with prejudice,[548] but a court may permit a post-ruling leave to amend (unless it is clear that no amendment could save the pleading).[549]

---

wise, the conversion clause of Rule 12(c) would be too easily circumvented and disputed documents attached to an answer would have to be taken as true at the pleadings stage.").

[542] *See Ideal Steel Supply Corp. v. Anza*, 652 F.3d 310, 324–26 (2d Cir. 2011). *See also Bishop v. Air Line Pilots Ass'n, Int'l*, 900 F.3d 388, 399 n.2 (7th Cir. 2018) (nonmovant has greater flexibility, and may submit additional materials that are "consistent with the pleadings").

[543] *See Federated Mut. Ins. Co. v. Coyle Mech. Supply Inc.*, 983 F.3d 307, 313–14 (7th Cir. 2020); *Ginsburg v. InBev NV/SA*, 623 F.3d 1229, 1236 (8th Cir. 2010).

[544] *See, e.g., Massey v. Ojaniit*, 759 F.3d 343, 347 (4th Cir. 2014) (courts need not accept as true allegations that contradict exhibit); *Chandavong v. Fresno Deputy Sheriff's Ass'n*, ___ F. Supp. 3d ___, 2022 WL 1215182, at *1 (E.D. Cal. 2022) (same); *Friends of Trumbull v. Chicago Bd. of Educ.*, 123 F. Supp. 3d 990, 992–93 (N.D. Ill. 2015) ("exhibit takes precedence").

[545] *See supra* Authors' Commentary to Rule 12(b)(6) (**"Extrinsic Materials"** — *"Exhibit v. Pleading Inconsistencies"*).

[546] *See Republic Steel Corp. v. Pennsylvania Eng'g Corp.*, 785 F.2d 174, 177 n.2 (7th Cir. 1986) (Rule 12(c) motions are directed towards obtaining final judgments on the merits).

[547] *See BBL, Inc. v. City of Angola*, 809 F.3d 317, 325 (7th Cir. 2015).

[548] *See Jorgensen v. Larsen*, 930 F.2d 922 (10th Cir. 1991) (becomes final judgment on merits); *Chandler v. Forsyth Tech. Cmty. Coll.*, 294 F. Supp. 3d 445, 452 (M.D.N.C. 2018), *aff'd*, 739 Fed. Appx. 203 (4th Cir. 2018) (same).

[549] *See Harris v. County of Orange*, 682 F.3d 1126, 1131 (9th Cir. 2012).

Appealability

For the same reasons noted in Rule 12(b)(6)'s discussion of appealability, practitioners must proceed with care in analyzing appeals from Rule 12(c) motions for judgment on the pleadings.[550] Generally, a decision granting such a motion is considered a "final order," and thus immediately appealable, but a decision denying such a motion is deemed "interlocutory" and must await a final disposition on the merits.[551]

RULE 12(d)—PRESENTING MATTERS OUTSIDE THE PLEADINGS

CORE CONCEPT

Motions under Rule 12(b)(6) and Rule 12(c) are designed to test the content of pleadings. Consequently, with only a few exceptions, a court may not consider content beyond the pleadings when ruling on these motions, unless it converts the pending motion into one seeking summary judgment and proceeds according to Rule 56.

APPLICATIONS

Purpose

Rule 12(d) respects the essential attribute of Rule 12(b)(6) and Rule 12(c) motions by requiring that such motions be recast into summary judgment requests when materials outside the pleadings are examined, thereby ensuring that the distinct policies of pleadings challenges (*i.e.*, testing the pleaded allegations) and factual challenges (*i.e.*, testing the existence of supporting evidence) are honored.[552]

Mechanics of "Conversion"

When, while considering a Rule 12(b)(6) or 12(c) motion, a court is presented with materials outside the pleadings, and does not exclude them, the court is obligated to "convert" the pleadings challenge into a summary judgment motion.[553] To do so, the court must give all parties notice of the conversion and an opportunity to both be heard and to present further materi-

[550]*See supra* Authors' Commentary to Rule 12(b)(6) ("**Appealability**").

[551]*See Occupy Columbia v. Haley*, 738 F.3d 107, 115 (4th Cir. 2013) (denials normally interlocutory, but immunity-based denials are appealable collateral orders); *Paskvan v. City of Cleveland Civil Service Com'n*, 946 F.2d 1233, 1235 (6th Cir. 1991). *But see Estate of Drayton v. Nelson*, 53 F.3d 165, 166 (7th Cir. 1994) (order granting judgment on pleadings was not final, appealable order because lawsuit remained pending against other defendants).

[552]*See Bruni v. City of Pittsburgh*, 824 F.3d 353, 360–61 (3d Cir. 2016); *Glob. Network Commc'ns, Inc. v. City of New York*, 458 F.3d 150, 155 (2d Cir. 2006).

[553]*See George v. SI Grp., Inc.*, 36 F.4th 611, 619 n.4 (5th Cir. 2022); *United States ex rel. Foreman v. AECOM*, 19 F.4th 85, 106 (2d Cir. 2021).

als in support of their positions on the now-converted motion.[554] Following conversion, and upon a proper request by the parties, the court typically ensures that the parties have a reasonable opportunity for discovery prior to ruling on the converted motion.[555] (Ordinarily, conversion (and the consideration of extrinsic materials) is not appropriate when discovery has not yet occurred.[556]) The court then proceeds to evaluate the motion as a request for summary judgment under Rule 56.[557]

Triggering "Conversion"

Although this conversion procedure is mandatory, not discretionary,[558] conversion does not occur automatically.[559] The court retains the discretion to ignore any extra-pleading materials that the parties have submitted, in which case no conversion is necessary.[560] In fact, even when the court fails to expressly exclude extra-pleading materials, a conversion may not be necessary if the materials were, in fact, ignored by the court.[561]

Type of Required Notice of "Conversion"

The required notice of conversion may be either actual or constructive.[562] The former is more obvious and transparent, and thus to be preferred.[563] But actual, formal notice might not be necessary if the non-moving party should have reasonably

---

[554] *See George v. SI Grp., Inc.*, 36 F.4th 611, 619 n.4 (5th Cir. 2022); *Federated Mut. Ins. Co. v. Coyle Mech. Supply Inc.*, 983 F.3d 307, 316 (7th Cir. 2020). *See also Snider v. L-3 Commc'ns Vertex Aerospace, L.L.C.*, 946 F.3d 660, 667 (5th Cir. 2019) (10 days' notice required).

[555] *See Hurd v. D.C., Gov't*, 864 F.3d 671, 687 (D.C. Cir. 2017); *SBRMCOA, LLC v. Bayside Resort, Inc.*, 707 F.3d 267, 272–73 (3d Cir. 2013).

[556] *See Zak v. Chelsea Therapeutics Int'l, Ltd.*, 780 F.3d 597, 606 (4th Cir. 2015); *Foley v. Wells Fargo Bank, N.A.*, 772 F.3d 63, 73–74 (1st Cir. 2014).

[557] *See infra* Authors' Commentary to Rule 56.

[558] *See Nakahata v. New York-Presbyterian Healthcare Sys., Inc.*, 723 F.3d 192, 203 (2d Cir. 2013).

[559] *See Sorace v. U.S.*, 788 F.3d 758, 767 (8th Cir. 2015); *Swedberg v. Marotzke*, 339 F.3d 1139, 1142–45 (9th Cir. 2003).

[560] *See Albright v. Christensen*, 24 F.4th 1039, 1043 (6th Cir. 2022); *Federated Mut. Ins. Co. v. Coyle Mech. Supply Inc.*, 983 F.3d 307, 313 (7th Cir. 2020). *See also Bates v. Green Farms Condo. Ass'n*, 958 F.3d 470, 484 (6th Cir. 2020) (court must "expressly" reject extrinsic materials).

[561] There is a division among the Circuits as to when the conversion obligation is triggered. There are three approaches. Some courts require conversion anytime extrinsic evidence is not expressly excluded, others require conversion if the court "considers" the extrinsic evidence, and still others require conversion only if, after considering the extrinsic evidence, the court chooses to "rely" on it in ruling. *See Max Arnold & Sons, LLC v. W.L. Hailey & Co., Inc.*, 452 F.3d 494, 502–03 (6th Cir. 2006) (collecting cases, and electing first approach).

[562] *See Barron ex rel. D.B. v. South Dakota Bd. of Regents*, 655 F.3d 787, 791–92 (8th Cir. 2011).

[563] *See Snider v. L-3 Commc'ns Vertex Aerospace, L.L.C.*, 946 F.3d 660, 667 (5th Cir. 2019) ("better practice"); *Wolfington v. Reconstructive Orthopaedic Assocs. II PC*, 935 F.3d 187, 198 (3d Cir. 2019) ("easy" and "removes ambiguities").

anticipated the conversion, was not taken by surprise, and was not deprived of a reasonable opportunity to respond to those materials.[564] Thus, a court's neglect in providing formal notice may be excused, for example, where the moving party dual-labeled its motion to dismiss as a motion for summary judgment "in the alternative,"[565] where the non-movants had submitted extra-pleading materials of their own,[566] or where the non-movants failed to show that factual materials existed which controvert the moving party's contentions.[567]

Exceptions to the "Conversion" Requirement

Various exceptions to the conversion procedure have been recognized. First, no conversion is ordinarily[568] required when the court considers exhibits attached to the complaint (unless their authenticity is questioned), documents that the complaint incorporates by reference or are otherwise integral to the claim (provided they are undisputed), information subject to judicial notice, or matters of public record (including orders and other materials in the record of the case).[569] Note, however, parties cannot escape the conversion rule simply by attaching to their answer whatever extrinsic materials might be helpful to their later motion.[570]

Second, no conversion is usually required if the moving party merely submits the omitted portions of a document that had already been attached, in excerpted form, to the complaint.[571]

Third, a party may waive any objection to a failure to properly convert by failing to timely contest it.[572]

Fourth, even if not waived, a failure to properly convert may

---

[564]*See Thompson v. Cope*, 900 F.3d 414, 425–26 (7th Cir. 2018); *Foley v. Wells Fargo Bank, N.A.*, 772 F.3d 63, 72 (1st Cir. 2014).

[565]*See Hearing v. Minnesota Life Ins. Co.*, 793 F.3d 888, 892 (8th Cir. 2015); *Miller v. Herman*, 600 F.3d 726, 733 (7th Cir. 2010). *But cf. Sahu v. Union Carbide Corp.*, 548 F.3d 59, 69 (2d Cir. 2008) (noting principle, but finding notice inadequate on facts).

[566]*See Trinity Marine Products, Inc. v. United States*, 812 F.3d 481, 487 (5th Cir. 2016); *Hearing v. Minnesota Life Ins. Co.*, 793 F.3d 888, 892 (8th Cir. 2015). *But cf. Sahu v. Union Carbide Corp.*, 548 F.3d 59, 69 (2d Cir. 2008) (noting principle, but finding notice inadequate on facts).

[567]*See U.S. v. Rogers Cartage Co.*, 794 F.3d 854, 860 (7th Cir. 2015); *Russell v. Harman Int'l Indus., Inc.*, 773 F.3d 253, 257 (D.C. Cir. 2014).

[568]*But see Occupy Columbia v. Haley*, 738 F.3d 107, 116–17 (4th Cir. 2013) (surveying Circuit split on whether affidavits attached as exhibits may be considered).

[569]*See supra* Authors' Commentary to Rule 12(b)(6) ("**Extrinsic Materials**"); to Rule 12(c) ("**Extrinsic Materials**").

[570]*See Horsley v. Feldt*, 304 F.3d 1125, 1134–35 (11th Cir. 2002) ("Otherwise, the conversion clause of Rule 12(c) would be too easily circumvented and disputed documents attached to an answer would have to be taken as true at the pleadings stage.").

[571]*See Cooper v. Pickett*, 137 F.3d 616, 622–23 (9th Cir. 1997); *In re Stac Electronics Securities Litigation*, 89 F.3d 1399, 1405 (9th Cir. 1996).

[572]*See Berera v. Mesa Med. Group, PLLC*, 779 F.3d 352, 358 n.7 (6th Cir. 2015); *Thulin v. Shopko Stores Operating Co., LLC*, 771 F.3d 994, 997–98 (7th Cir. 2014).

be deemed harmless if the non-moving party had an adequate opportunity to respond and was not otherwise prejudiced[573] or if the court's ruling either hinged in no way on the extrinsic materials[574] or was otherwise defensibly grounded on some independent basis.[575]

Notifying *Pro Se* Litigants of Conversion

Because they are unlikely to appreciate the consequence of a conversion to summary judgment procedures, *pro se* litigants will ordinarily be entitled to notice of that conversion and its meaning.[576]

Reverse "Conversions"

At least one Circuit has rejected the possibility of *reverse* "conversions": treating a summary judgment motion as a Rule 12(b)(6) motion to dismiss in order to assess the pleading's adequacy under the *Twombly* "plausibility" standard.[577]

RULE 12(e)—MOTION FOR MORE DEFINITE STATEMENT

CORE CONCEPT

If a pleading is so vague or ambiguous that a responsive pleading cannot be prepared, the responding party need not counterplead, but may instead move the court for an order directing the pleader to serve a more definite statement.

APPLICATIONS

Distinct from Rule 12(b)(6) Motions

Motions to dismiss and motions for more definite statements are not interchangeable. A motion to dismiss under Rule 12(b)(6) attacks a pleading for failing to allege a cognizable claim eligible for some type of relief. In contrast, a Rule 12(e) motion for more definite statement attacks pleadings that may or may not be capable of stating cognizable legal claims, but are so unintelligibly unclear in their present form that drafting a response to them is impossible.[578]

- *Mislabeled Motions:* A motion to dismiss under Rule

---

[573] *See Bates v. Green Farms Condo. Ass'n*, 958 F.3d 470, 484 (6th Cir. 2020); *Demarais v. Gurstel Chargo, P.A.*, 869 F.3d 685, 696 n.2 (8th Cir. 2017).

[574] *See Bates v. Green Farms Condo. Ass'n*, 958 F.3d 470, 484 (6th Cir. 2020).

[575] *See Standing Akimbo, LLC v. United States through Internal Revenue Serv.*, 955 F.3d 1146, 1155–56 (10th Cir. 2020); *Wolfington v. Reconstructive Orthopaedic Assocs. II PC*, 935 F.3d 187, 199 (3d Cir. 2019).

[576] *See Parada v. Banco Industrial De Venezuela, C.A.*, 753 F.3d 62, 68 (2d Cir. 2014); *Renchenski v. Williams*, 622 F.3d 315, 339–41 (3d Cir. 2010).

[577] *See Feliciano-Munoz v. Rebarber-Ocasio*, 970 F.3d 53, 60–62 (1st Cir. 2020). *See also Rios-Campbell v. U.S. Dep't of Com.*, 927 F.3d 21, 25 (1st Cir. 2019) ("Just because a cucumber can be turned into a pickle does not mean that a pickle can be turned into a cucumber. . .").

[578] *See Swierkiewicz v. Sorema N.A.*, 534 U.S. 506, 514, 122 S.Ct. 992, 152

12(b)(6) that, more correctly, is a motion for a more definite statement may be so converted by the court in its discretion.[579]

- *Filing Both Motions:* A party may file a motion to dismiss and a motion for more definite statement in the alternative.[580] In an appropriate case, the court may consider the motion for more definite statement first and hold the motion to dismiss in abeyance.[581]

Disfavored Motion

The Rules require the pleader to serve only a short, plain statement showing an entitlement to relief.[582] Due to these liberal pleading requirements in federal court, motions for a more definite statement are disfavored[583] and granted only sparingly.[584] They are not a substitute for discovery,[585] and ordinarily will not be granted where the level and nature of the detail sought is more properly a role for discovery.[586]

Legal Test

Motions for a more definite statement target unintelligibility, not a mere lack of detail.[587] They are proper only when a pleading is so hopelessly vague or ambiguous that a defendant cannot understand the allegations and, therefore, cannot fairly be expected to frame a response or denial, at least not without risking prejudice.[588] Such motions are particularly ill-suited to situations where the information sought is already within the defendant's knowledge and the motion merely seeks the formality of the recital of known facts.[589] Nevertheless, courts continue to grant these motions, even though disfavored, when the

---

L.Ed.2d 1 (2002) (when pleadings fail to provide sufficient notice, motion for more definite statement may be sought before counter-pleading).

[579]*See Verizon Washington, D.C., Inc. v. United States*, 254 F. Supp. 3d 208, 218 (D.D.C. 2017); *Luna-Reyes v. RFI Const., LLC*, 57 F. Supp. 3d 495, 504 (M.D.N.C. 2014).

[580]*See Adobe Sys. Inc. v. A & S Elecs., Inc.*, 153 F. Supp. 3d 1136, 1147 (N.D. Cal. 2015).

[581]*See Thomas v. Independence Tp.*, 463 F.3d 285, 301 (3d Cir. 2006).

[582]*See* Rule 8(a)(2).

[583]*See Boudreaux v. Axiall Corp.*, 564 F. Supp. 3d 488, 506 (W.D. La. 2021); *Jolly v. Hoegh Autoliners Shipping AS*, 546 F. Supp. 3d 1105, 1119 (M.D. Fla. 2021).

[584]*See Ames v. Dep't of Marine Res. Com'r*, 256 F.R.D. 22, 26 (D. Me. 2009); *N.Y. v. Cedar Park Concrete Corp.*, 665 F. Supp. 238, 248 (S.D.N.Y. 1987).

[585]*See Jolly v. Hoegh Autoliners Shipping AS*, 546 F. Supp. 3d 1105, 1119 (M.D. Fla. 2021); *La. State Conf. of Nat'l Ass'n for Advancement of Colored People v. Louisiana*, 490 F. Supp. 3d 982, 1024 (M.D. La. 2020).

[586]*See Middaugh v. InterBank*, 528 F. Supp. 3d 509, 534 (N.D. Tex. 2021); *State v. Exxon Mobil Corp.*, 406 F. Supp. 3d 420, 480 (D. Md. 2019).

[587]*See Student A v. Liberty Univ., Inc.*, __ F. Supp. 3d __, 2022 WL 1423617, at *3 (W.D. Va. 2022); *CoorsTek Korea Ltd. v. Loomis Prod. Co.*, __ F. Supp. 3d __, 2022 WL 493419, at *5 (E.D. Pa. 2022).

[588]*See CoorsTek Korea Ltd. v. Loomis Prod. Co.*, __ F. Supp. 3d __, 2022 WL 493419, at *5 (E.D. Pa. 2022); *Middaugh v. InterBank*, 528 F. Supp. 3d 509, 534 (N.D. Tex. 2021).

[589]*See Babcock & Wilcox Co. v. McGriff, Seibels & Williams, Inc.*, 235

federal notice pleading standards are not met.[590] Just as Rule 12(e) motions are not legitimate substitutes for discovery, discovery is not a fair substitute for proper pleading.[591] Both the court and the litigants are entitled to know, at the pleading stage, who is being sued, why, and for what.[592] Whether to grant or deny a Rule 12(e) motion is committed to the district judge's sound discretion.[593] Courts have found Rule 12(e) particularly useful in several contexts:

- *Special Pleading Obligations:* To seek facts that must be specially pleaded, such as fraud, mistake, and special damages.[594]
- *Threshold Defenses:* To seek (in certain particular situations only) facts necessary to determine whether threshold defenses exist, such as immunity from suit (what motivated the conduct),[595] statute of limitations (when claim arose), or statute of frauds (whether contract was written or oral, term for performance).[596]
- *Rule 10 Violations:* To seek a re-pleading of a complaint or claim that is confusingly consolidated in a single

---

F.R.D. 632, 633 (E.D. La. 2006).

[590]*See Swierkiewicz v. Sorema N. A.*, 534 U.S. 506, 512, 122 S. Ct. 992, 998, 152 L. Ed. 2d 1 (2002) (if pleading "fails to specify the allegations in a manner that provides sufficient notice", defendant can move for more definite statement before responding). *See also Thomas v. Independence Twp.*, 463 F.3d 285, 301 (3d Cir. 2006); *O'Boyle v. Sweetapple*, 187 F. Supp. 3d 1365, 1369–70 (S.D. Fla. 2016).

[591]*Cf. Eisenach v. Miller-Dwan Medical Center*, 162 F.R.D. 346, 348 (D. Minn. 1995) ("any current view that the deficiencies in pleading may be cured through liberalized discovery is at increasingly mounting odds with the public's dissatisfaction with exorbitantly expansive discovery, and the impact that the public outcry has had upon our discovery Rules").

[592]*See Fant v. City of Ferguson*, 107 F. Supp. 3d 1016, 1027 (E.D. Mo. 2015). *See generally McHenry v. Renne*, 84 F.3d 1172, 1179–80 (9th Cir. 1996) ("[p]rolix, confusing complaints such as the ones plaintiffs filed in this case impose unfair burdens on litigants and judges. As a practical matter, the judge and opposing counsel, in order to perform their responsibilities, cannot use a complaint such as the one plaintiffs filed, and must prepare outlines to determine who is being sued for what. . . . The judge wastes half a day in chambers preparing the 'short and plain statement' which Rule 8 obligated plaintiffs to submit. He then must manage the litigation without knowing what claims are made against whom. This leads to discovery disputes and lengthy trials, prejudicing litigants in other case who follow the rules, as well as defendants in the case in which the prolix pleading is filed.").

[593]*See Apothio, LLC v. Kern Cnty.*, — F. Supp. 3d —, 2022 WL 1215259, at *8 (E.D. Cal. 2022); *Wingard v. Louisiana through Dep't of Pub. Safety & Corr.*, — F. Supp. 3d —, 2022 WL 969769, at *1 n.7 (M.D. La. 2022).

[594]*See* Rule 9. *See also Wagner v. First Horizon Pharmaceutical Corp.*, 464 F.3d 1273, 1280 (11th Cir. 2006); *Allstate Indem. Co. v. Dixon*, 304 F.R.D. 580, 582 (W.D.Mo. 2015).

[595]*See Crawford-El v. Britton*, 523 U.S. 574, 598, 118 S. Ct. 1584, 140 L. Ed. 2d 759 (1998); *Thomas v. Independence Tp.*, 463 F.3d 285, 289 (3d Cir. 2006).

[596]*See Lewis v. Bellows Falls Congregation of Jehovah's Witnesses*, 95 F. Supp. 3d 762, 777 (D.Vt. 2015) (use in seeking potentially dispositive threshold information such as critical dates).

count (when multiple counts would be proper), lacks numbered paragraphs, or otherwise violates the presentation dictates of Rule 10.[597]

- *Changing Circumstances:* To update facts when changed circumstances or the passage of time makes the lawsuit's viability clouded.[598]
- *RICO Case Statements*: To compel the filing of "RICO Case Statements," required in many judicial districts to flesh out the factual predicates and legal theory underlying federal civil racketeering claims.[599]

Burden of Proof

The burden lies with the moving party to demonstrate that the challenged pleading is too vague or ambiguous to permit a response. The moving party must identify the deficiencies in the pleading, list the details sought to be provided, and assert an inability to frame a response.[600] The motion must be made formally and properly.[601]

Timing and Waiver

Obviously, a motion for more definite statement must be filed before the party serves a response to the pleading that the party is claiming is so vague and ambiguous that responding is impossible.[602] Additionally, the moving party should appreciate the consequence of moving for Rule 12(e) relief: once any Rule 12 motion is made (which includes Rule 12(e)), any waivable defense that could have been joined in that motion—but was omitted—will be considered lost.[603] To abate the harshness of this result, the court may permit the moving party to withdraw

---

[597] *See Weiland v. Palm Beach Cty. Sheriff's Office*, 792 F.3d 1313, 1321 n.10 (11th Cir. 2015).

[598] *See Thorp v. District of Columbia*, 309 F.R.D. 88, 90 (D.D.C. 2015).

[599] *See Northland Ins. Co. v. Shell Oil Co.*, 930 F. Supp. 1069, 1074 (D.N.J. 1996). Where claims are asserted under the federal Racketeer Influenced and Corrupt Organizations Act ("RICO"), 18 U.S.C.A. §§ 1961 to 68, many judicial districts now require, by Standing Order, chambers policy, or otherwise, that the pleader answer a series of questions that supplement the RICO allegations of the complaint. *See, e.g.*, S.D. Cal. Rule 11.1; W.D. N.Y. Rule 5.1; *National Organization for Women, Inc. v. Scheidler*, 510 U.S. 249, 249, 114 S. Ct. 798, 800, 127 L. Ed. 2d 99 (1994) (noting local rule in force in Northern District of Illinois). This pleading obligation is especially important where the facts noted in the RICO Case Statement are deemed to be pleading averments, properly considered in ruling upon a motion to dismiss. *See Glessner v. Kenny*, 952 F.2d 702, 712 (3d Cir. 1991) (collecting cases so holding).

[600] *See Apothio, LLC v. Kern Cnty.*, _ F. Supp. 3d _, 2022 WL 1215259, at *8 (E.D. Cal. 2022); *Weems Indus., Inc. v. Teknor Apex Co.*, 540 F. Supp. 3d 839, 847 (N.D. Iowa 2021).

[601] *See Holley v. Gilead Scis., Inc.*, 379 F. Supp. 3d 809, 834 (N.D. Cal. 2019) (denying Rule 12(e) motion, in part, because it was raised only in footnote).

[602] *See Marx v. Gumbinner*, 855 F.2d 783, 792 (11th Cir. 1988); *Powell v. Subaru of Am., Inc.*, 502 F. Supp. 3d 856, 898 (D.N.J. 2020).

[603] *See* Rules 12(g) & 12(h). *See also Caldwell-Baker Co. v. Southern Illinois Railcar Co.*, 225 F. Supp. 2d 1243, 1259, (D. Kan. 2002) (party moving for

the Rule 12(e) motion so as to permit a more fulsome Rule 12 filing.[604]

Tolling Effect

While the motion is pending, the party's time for serving a response to the challenged pleading is postponed.[605] If the motion is granted and a more definite statement is prepared, the response to that new pleading must be served within 14 days after service of the more definite statement (unless the court orders otherwise).[606] If the motion is denied, the responsive pleading must be served with 14 days after notice of the court's ruling (unless the court orders otherwise).[607]

Applies only to Pleadings

By its terms, Rule 12(e) is available to compel more definite statements only in pleadings. It cannot be used to require added detail in motions.[608]

Use By Claimants

When an answer pleads an unintelligible defense, some courts permit claimants to invoke Rule 12(e) to force a repleading of that defense.[609] Other courts reject that use, reasoning that, because claimants are usually not required to counterplead to an answer, Rule 12(e)—by its terms—is inapplicable.[610]

Sua Sponte Motions

The district court may, on its own initiative, strike a deficient pleading and direct the pleader to file a more definite statement.[611] This *sua sponte* option is especially valuable to resolve "shotgun pleading" deficiencies,[612] or when a motion to dismiss is pending but the more appropriate relief is re-

---

more definite statement may not later assert by motion another Rule 12(b) defense that was then available).

[604] *See Caldwell-Baker Co. v. Southern Illinois Railcar Co.*, 225 F. Supp. 2d 1243, 1259 (D. Kan. 2002) (party's withdrawal of Rule 12(e) motion abated possible waiver of motion to dismiss for lack of personal jurisdiction).

[605] *See* Rule 12(a)(4).

[606] *See* Rule 12(a)(4)(B).

[607] *See* Rule 12(a)(4)(A).

[608] *See Brown v. F.B.I.*, 793 F. Supp. 2d 368, 382 (D.D.C. 2011); *Marcello v. Maine*, 489 F. Supp. 2d 82, 85 (D. Me. 2007).

[609] *See Construction Industry Laborers Pension Fund v. Explosive Contractors, Inc.*, 2013 WL 3984371, at *4 (D.Kan. Aug. 1, 2013); *Exhibit Icons, LLC v. XP Cos., LLC*, 609 F. Supp. 2d 1282, 1300 (S.D. Fla. 2009).

[610] *See* Rule 12(e) (permitting motions for more definite statements only for those pleadings "to which a responsive pleading is allowed"). *See also United States ex rel. Patzer v. Sikorsky Aircraft Corp.*, 382 F. Supp. 3d 860, 865 (E.D. Wis. 2019) (Rules provide no Rule 12(e)-similar mechanism for plaintiffs seeking more definite statements about affirmative defenses); *Armstrong v. Snyder*, 103 F.R.D. 96, 100 (E.D.Wis. 1984) (same result).

[611] *See Green v. Sec'y, Dep't of Corr.*, 28 F.4th 1089, 1159 (11th Cir. 2022).

[612] *See Weiland v. Palm Beach Cty. Sheriff's Office*, 792 F.3d 1313, 1321 n.10 (11th Cir. 2015).

pleading with a more definite statement.[613]

Remedy

To comply with a Rule 12(e) order for a more definite statement, the pleader must amend the pleading to add sufficient detail to satisfy the court.[614] If the pleader fails to serve a more definite statement, fails to serve it timely, or fails to include a meaningful enhancement to deficiently pleaded allegations, the court may strike the pleading or make such other order as it deems just,[615] including a dismissal with prejudice.[616]

Appealability

Rulings on motions for a more definite statement are ordinarily considered interlocutory and not immediately appealable.[617]

RULE 12(f)—MOTION TO STRIKE

CORE CONCEPT

On its own initiative or upon motion, the court may strike from a pleading any insufficient defense or any redundant, immaterial, impertinent, or scandalous matter.

APPLICATIONS

Purpose

Both insufficient defenses and redundant, immaterial, impertinent, or scandalous matter may be stricken from a pleading in order to avoid the time, effort, and expense necessary to litigate spurious issues.[618] Such motions may be granted when necessary to clean up the pleadings, streamline the litigation, or sidestep unnecessary effort on immaterial issues.[619] But this remedy is considered a "drastic" one,[620] and is never permitted for idle ends.[621] The motion generally cannot be used to purposelessly cull pleadings of "inappropriately hyperbolic

---

[613] *See Thomas v. Independence Tp.*, 463 F.3d 285, 289 (3d Cir. 2006).

[614] *See Godfrey v. Upland Borough*, 246 F. Supp. 3d 1078, 1086 (E.D. Pa. 2017); *Chennareddy v. Dodaro*, 282 F.R.D. 9, 14 (D.D.C. 2012).

[615] *See Weiland v. Palm Beach Cty. Sheriff's Office*, 792 F.3d 1313, 1321 n.10 (11th Cir. 2015); *Chennareddy v. Dodaro*, 282 F.R.D. 9, 14 (D.D.C. 2012).

[616] *See Shuhaiber v. Illinois Dep't of Corr.*, 980 F.3d 1167, 1170–71 (7th Cir. 2020); *Jackson v. Bank of Am., N.A.*, 898 F.3d 1348, 1358 (11th Cir. 2018).

[617] *See Mitchell v. E-Z Way Towers, Inc.*, 269 F.2d 126, 131 (5th Cir. 1959).

[618] *See Operating Eng'rs Local 324 Health Care Plan v. G & W Const. Co.*, 783 F.3d 1045, 1050 (6th Cir. 2015); *Whittlestone, Inc. v. Handi-Craft Co.*, 618 F.3d 970, 973 (9th Cir. 2010).

[619] *See Boscov's Dep't Store, Inc. v. Am. Guarantee & Liab. Ins. Co.*, 546 F. Supp. 3d 354, 361 (E.D. Pa. 2021) (appeal pending); *Corning Inc. v. Shenzhen Xinhao Photoelectric Tech. Co.*, 546 F. Supp. 3d 204, 218 (W.D.N.Y. 2021).

[620] *See Donelson v. Ameriprise Fin. Servs., Inc.*, 999 F.3d 1080, 1091–92 (8th Cir. 2021); *E.S. v. Best W. Int'l, Inc.*, 510 F. Supp. 3d 420, 425-26 (N.D. Tex. 2021).

[621] *See Payne v. Tri-State Careflight, LLC*, 327 F.R.D. 433, 445 (D.N.M. 2018) (often "purely cosmetic" or "time wast-

allegations, ill-conceived attempts at levity, and other similar manifestations of bad judgment in drafting."[622]

General Test

Motions to strike are disfavored by the courts[623] and rarely granted,[624] especially so when they delay the litigation with little corresponding benefit.[625] In considering a motion to strike, courts will generally apply the same test used to determine a Rule 12(b)(6) motion[626]—the courts will deem as admitted all of the non-moving party's well-pleaded facts, draw all reasonable inferences in the pleader's favor, and resolve all doubts in favor of denying the motion to strike.[627] But the court will not accept as true the non-moving party's conclusions of law.[628] If disputed questions of fact or law remain as to the challenged material or defense, the motion to strike must be denied.[629] Likewise, if any doubt remains as to the potential later relevance of the contested allegations, the motion will be denied.[630] Beyond these legal constraints, the decision to strike or not is committed to the district judge's discretion.[631]

Burden of Proof

The burden lies with the party moving to strike.[632] Given the disfavored nature of the relief, the burden on the moving party is formidable.[633] The moving party must state the basis for the motion with particularity and identify specifically the

---

ers"); *Eagle View Techs., Inc. v. Xactware Sols., Inc.*, 325 F.R.D. 90, 95 (D.N.J. 2018) ("dilatory tactic").

[622] *See Saylavee LLC v. Hockler*, 228 F.R.D. 425, 426 (D. Conn. 2005).

[623] *See Donelson v. Ameriprise Fin. Servs., Inc.*, 999 F.3d 1080, 1092 (8th Cir. 2021); *Hemlock Semiconductor Operations, LLC v. SolarWorld Indus. Sachsen GmbH*, 867 F.3d 692, 697 (6th Cir. 2017).

[624] *See Operating Eng'rs Local 324 Health Care Plan v. G & W Const. Co.*, 783 F.3d 1045, 1050 (6th Cir. 2015); *Zurich Am. Life Ins. Co. v. Nagel*, 538 F. Supp. 3d 396, 399 (S.D.N.Y. 2021).

[625] *See Manning v. Boston Med. Ctr. Corp.*, 725 F.3d 34, 59 (1st Cir. 2013); *Rosales v. Cty. of San Diego*, 511 F. Supp. 3d 1070, 1083 (S.D. Cal. 2021).

[626] *See Johnson Outdoors Inc. v. Navico, Inc.*, 774 F. Supp. 2d 1191, 1195 (M.D.Ala. 2011); *Starnes Family Office, LLC v. McCullar*, 765 F. Supp. 2d 1036, 1047 (W.D.Tenn. 2011).

[627] *See Petrie v. Electronic Game Card, Inc.*, 761 F.3d 959, 965 (9th Cir. 2014); *Figueroa v. Kern Cty.*, 506 F. Supp. 3d 1051, 1056 (E.D. Cal. 2020).

[628] *See Dodson v. Strategic Restaurants Acquisition Co. II, LLC*, 289 F.R.D. 595, 603 (E.D.Cal. 2013); *U.S. v. Rohm and Haas Co.*, 939 F. Supp. 1142, 1151 (D.N.J. 1996).

[629] *See Edwards v. Juan Martinez, Inc.*, 506 F. Supp. 3d 1061, 1077 (D. Nev. 2020); *Spoon v. Bayou Bridge Pipeline, LLC*, 335 F.R.D. 468, 470 (M.D. La. 2020).

[630] *See Saroya v. Univ. of Pac.*, 503 F. Supp. 3d 986, 993 (N.D. Cal. 2020); *Spoon v. Bayou Bridge Pipeline, LLC*, 335 F.R.D. 468, 471 (M.D. La. 2020).

[631] *See Donelson v. Ameriprise Fin. Servs., Inc.*, 999 F.3d 1080, 1091 (8th Cir. 2021); *Royce v. Michael R. Needle P.C.*, 950 F.3d 939, 952 (7th Cir. 2020).

[632] *See Iovino v. Michael Stapleton Assocs., Ltd.*, — F. Supp. 3d —, 2022 WL 1213278, at *4 (W.D. Va. 2022); *Roamingwood Sewer & Water Ass'n v. Nat'l Diversified Sales, Inc.*, 509 F. Supp. 3d 198, 204 (M.D. Pa. 2020).

[633] *See United States ex rel. Dildine v. Pandya*, 389 F. Supp. 3d 1214, 1223 (N.D. Ga. 2019); *Gates v. District of*

relief sought.[634] The moving party must show at least that the allegations bear no possible relation to the controversy.[635] Many courts require, also, a showing of prejudice were the allegations to remain unstricken.[636] But this prejudice requirement remains controversial. Rule 12(f) does not, by its terms, require a showing of prejudice, and for this reason some courts have refused to impose that obligation on the movant.[637] The seeming majority of courts, however, test for prejudice, often citing, as support, the disfavor with which Rule 12(f) relief is viewed.[638] If considered, the requisite prejudice will exist when the contested allegation would confuse the issues or, by its length and complexity, place an undue burden on the respondent, inject the possibility of unnecessarily extensive and burdensome discovery, improperly increase the time, expense, and complexity of the trial, or otherwise unduly burden the moving party.[639]

Test For Striking Defenses

A motion to strike is the claimant's parallel to a Rule 12(b)(6) motion to dismiss. The court may strike any defense that is legally insufficient either as a matter of pleading or as a matter of law.[640] Defenses that are insufficiently pleaded are those that fail to impart the level of notice required by Rules 8 and 9[641] (courts are divided whether affirmative defenses must satisfy the *Twombly* "plausibility" standard; some impose the *Twombly* standard and some do not[642]). Thus, naked, conclusory defenses may be ruled insufficient and stricken.[643]

Defenses are insufficient as a matter of law if they are not

Columbia, 66 F. Supp. 3d 1, 27 (D.D.C. 2014).

[634]*See Anderson v. Davis Polk & Wardwell LLP*, 850 F. Supp. 2d 392, 409 (S.D.N.Y. 2012); *Credit General Ins. Co. v. Midwest Indem. Corp.*, 916 F. Supp. 766, 771 (N.D. Ill. 1996).

[635]*See MirTech Inc. v. AgroFresh Inc.*, 561 F. Supp. 3d 447, 459 (D. Del. 2021); *United States v. Mariner Health Care, Inc.*, 552 F. Supp. 3d 938, 954 (N.D. Cal. 2021).

[636]*See MirTech Inc. v. AgroFresh Inc.*, 561 F. Supp. 3d 447, 459 (D. Del. 2021); *Birren v. Royal Caribbean Cruises, Ltd.*, 336 F.R.D. 688, 691–93 (S.D. Fla. 2020).

[637]*See Guardant Health, Inc. v. Natera, Inc.*, 580 F. Supp. 3d 691, 713 (N.D. Cal. 2022); *Van v. LLR, Inc.*, 523 F. Supp. 3d 1077, 1081 (D. Alaska 2021). *See generally Lane v. Page*, 272 F.R.D. 581, 598–600 (D.N.M. 2011) (discussing controversy).

[638]*See, e.g., Campaign Legal Ctr. v. Iowa Values*, 573 F. Supp. 3d 243, 252 (D.D.C. 2021); *Kantsevoy v. LumenR LLC*, 301 F. Supp. 3d 577, 611 (D. Md. 2018).

[639]*See Capri Sun GmbH v. Am. Beverage Corp.*, 414 F. Supp. 3d 414, 435 (S.D.N.Y. 2019); *LeSEA, Inc. v. LeSEA Broad. Corp.*, 379 F. Supp. 3d 732, 742 (N.D. Ind. 2019).

[640]*See GEOMC Co. v. Calmare Therapeutics Inc.*, 918 F.3d 92, 95 (2d Cir. 2019) (may be stricken because no supporting facts are pleaded or because defense is legally insufficient).

[641]*See Unigestion Holding, S.A. v. UPM Tech., Inc.*, 305 F. Supp. 3d 1134, 1140 (D. Or. 2018); *Haley Paint Co. v. E.I. Du Pont De Nemours & Co.*, 279 F.R.D. 331, 335–36 (D.Md. 2012).

[642]*See supra* Authors' Commentary to Rule 8(c) ("**Properly Pleading Affirmative Defenses**").

[643]*See Crumpton v. Octapharma Plasma, Inc.*, 513 F. Supp. 3d 1006, 1012 (N.D. Ill. 2021); *Westchester Gen.*

recognized defenses to the pleaded claim,[644] could otherwise not succeed under any circumstances[645] (that is, no evidence in support of those defenses would be admissible at trial),[646] or might confuse the issues in the lawsuit.[647] The objective of such strikes is to eliminate irrelevant and frivolous defenses, the trial of which would otherwise unnecessarily waste time and money.[648] Thus, to strike a defense, the moving party must generally show there is no question of fact or law which might allow the challenged defense to succeed (and, in some courts, prejudice if the defense remains in the case).[649] In conducting this analysis, the court will construe the pleadings liberally in favor of the defendant (the non-moving party).[650] Ordinarily, if the motion has merit, the court will strike the insufficient defense in its entirety, and will not attempt to carve the defense in portions.[651] If the defense is stricken, the pleader will generally be granted leave to file an amended answer unless the amendment would be futile.[652]

- *Strikes Seeking Merits Dispositions:* Motions to strike are generally inappropriate to challenge the substantive merits of a pleaded defense.[653]
- *Strikes Involving Inference-Drawing*: Defenses will not be stricken if the court would be required to draw factual inferences or decide disputed questions of fact in a man-

---

Hosp., Inc. v. Evanston Ins. Co., 333 F.R.D. 594, 596–97 (S.D. Fla. 2019).

[644] *See Birren v. Royal Caribbean Cruises, Ltd.*, 336 F.R.D. 688, 691 (S.D. Fla. 2020) ("patently frivolous" or "clearly invalid"); *Nicholson v. Biomet, Inc.*, 363 F. Supp. 3d 931, 936 (N.D. Iowa 2019) ("foreclosed" by "controlling" law).

[645] *See Hemlock Semiconductor Operations, LLC v. SolarWorld Indus. Sachsen GmbH*, 867 F.3d 692, 697 (6th Cir. 2017); *U.S. v. Renda*, 709 F.3d 472, 479 (5th Cir. 2013).

[646] *See Butcher v. City of Marysville*, 398 F. Supp. 3d 715, 728 (E.D. Cal. 2019); *Openshaw v. Cohen, Klingenstein & Marks, Inc.*, 320 F. Supp. 2d 357, 364 (D. Md. 2004).

[647] *See Waste Mgmt. Holdings, Inc. v. Gilmore*, 252 F.3d 316, 347 (4th Cir. 2001); *U.S. v. Honeywell Int'l, Inc.*, 841 F. Supp. 2d 112, 113 (D.D.C. 2012).

[648] *See Van v. LLR, Inc.*, 523 F. Supp. 3d 1077, 1080–81 (D. Alaska 2021); *Strobel v. Rusch*, 431 F. Supp. 3d 1315, 1324-25 (D.N.M. 2020).

[649] *See Badar v. Swissport USA, Inc.*, 492 F. Supp. 3d 54, 58–59 (E.D.N.Y. 2020); *Progressive Express Ins. Co. v. Star Painting & Waterproofing, Inc.*, 333 F.R.D. 600, 601 (S.D. Fla. 2019).

[650] *See E.E.O.C. v. Product Fabricators, Inc.*, 873 F. Supp. 2d 1093, 1097 (D.Minn. 2012); *Employers Ins. Co. of Wausau v. Crouse-Community Center, Inc.*, 489 F. Supp. 2d 176, 179 (N.D. N.Y. 2007).

[651] *See Stowe Woodward, L.L.C. v. Sensor Products, Inc.*, 230 F.R.D. 463, 468–69 (W.D. Va. 2005).

[652] *See Hartford Underwriters Ins. Co. v. Kraus USA, Inc.*, 313 F.R.D. 572, 575 (N.D. Cal. 2016); *U.S. v. Green*, 33 F. Supp. 2d 203, 212 (W.D. N.Y. 1998).

[653] *See Red Label Music Publ'g, Inc. v. Chila Prods.*, 388 F. Supp. 3d 975, 982 (N.D. Ill. 2019) (may only strike "insufficient" defense, not one that is colorable but arguably "a loser on the merits"); *Neveu v. City of Fresno*, 392 F. Supp. 2d 1159, 1185 (E.D. Cal. 2005) (merits arguments not appropriate on motion to strike).

ner that favors the moving party.[654]

- *Strikes Involving Substantial and Disputed Questions:* Motions to strike are generally not intended to resolve substantial and disputed questions of law: legal issues on which courts are divided, confused or unsettled legal areas, or issues involving close or new questions of law.[655]
- *Strikes Involving Admissibility:* Motions to strike are ordinarily improper tools for requesting anticipatory evidentiary and admissibility rulings.[656]
- *Strikes Before Discovery:* Although motions to strike must generally be filed before a responsive pleading is served, some courts have noted their reluctance to strike defenses where there has been no significant discovery.[657]

Test For Striking Redundant, Immaterial, Impertinent, or Scandalous Matter

Absent a strong reason for doing so, courts will generally "not tamper with pleadings."[658] A court will not strike such matter unless it bears no possible relation to the parties' dispute or could confuse the issues.[659] Thus, facts supplying important context and background, though not strictly relevant to a claim's elements, should not be stricken.[660] Moreover, mere redundancy, immateriality, impertinence, or scandalousness is not sufficient to justify striking an allegation—the allegation must also generally be shown to be prejudicial to the moving party.[661] (This prejudice requirement seems likely to dim any Rule 12(f) motion's chance for success if the trial is to proceed non-jury.) If any doubt exists whether the contested matter should be stricken, the motion should be denied.[662] Consequently, to prevail on such a motion, the moving party must es-

[654]*See Augustus v. Board of Public Instruction of Escambia County, Fla.*, 306 F.2d 862, 868 (5th Cir. 1962); *Newborn Bros. Co. v. Albion Eng'g Co.*, 299 F.R.D. 90, 93–94 (D.N.J. 2014).

[655]*See Koch v. White*, 134 F. Supp. 3d 158, 164–65 (D.D.C. 2015); *Karpov v. Karpov*, 307 F.R.D. 345, 348 (D.Del. 2015). *See also Canadian St. Regis Band of Mohawk Indians ex rel. Francis v. New York*, 278 F. Supp. 2d 313, 324 (N.D. N.Y. 2003) (otherwise, courts would risk "offering an advisory opinion on an abstract and hypothetical set of facts").

[656]*See Aoki v. Benihana, Inc.*, 839 F. Supp. 2d 759, 764 (D.Del. 2012).

[657]*See Canadian St. Regis Band of Mohawk Indians ex rel. Francis v. New York*, 278 F. Supp. 2d 313, 324–25 (N.D. N.Y. 2003).

[658]*See Westwide Winery, Inc. v. SMT Acquisitions, LLC*, 511 F. Supp. 3d 256, 264 (E.D.N.Y. 2021); *Bey v. Washington Metro. Area Transit Auth.*, 341 F. Supp. 3d 1, 11 (D.D.C. 2018).

[659]*See Lipsky v. Commonwealth United Corp.*, 551 F.2d 887, 893 (2d Cir.1976); *Saroya v. Univ. of Pac.*, 503 F. Supp. 3d 986, 993 (N.D. Cal. 2020).

[660]*See Stanbury L. Firm v. I.R.S.*, 221 F.3d 1059, 1063 (8th Cir. 2000); *Nunes v. Lizza*, 486 F. Supp. 3d 1267, 1299 (N.D. Iowa 2020).

[661]*See Dionisio v. Ultimate Images & Designs, Inc.*, 391 F. Supp. 3d 1187, 1191 (S.D. Fla. 2019); *Greenwich Ins. Co. v. Rodgers*, 729 F. Supp. 2d 1158, 1162 (C.D.Cal. 2010).

[662]*See Southwestern Bell Telephone, L.P. v. Missouri Public Service Com'n*, 461 F. Supp. 2d 1055,

tablish that: (1) no evidence in support of the contested allegations would be admissible at trial; (2) the allegations have no bearing on the relevant issues in the case; and (3) denying the strike would prejudice the moving party.[663] A court will not permit use of the motion to strike a complaint's claims.[664]

If granted, the court's order will typically describe in detail the precise matter that must be stricken.[665]

- *Redundant Matter:* A redundant allegation is a needless repetition of other averments.[666]
- *Immaterial Matter:* Immaterial allegations are those that either bear no essential or important relationship to the pleader's claim for relief or contain a statement of unnecessary particulars,[667] or when no evidence to support them would be admissible at trial.[668]
- *Impertinent Matter:* An impertinent allegation is an averment that does not pertain to, or is unnecessary to, the issues in dispute.[669] If the pleader would not be permitted to offer evidence at trial in support of the allegation, the allegation is likely impertinent.[670]
- *Scandalous Matter:* Scandalous matter does not merely offend someone's sensibilities; it must cast a person or entity in an improperly derogatory light.[671] Such matter will not be stricken if it describes acts or events relevant

---

1064 (E.D. Mo. 2006), aff'd, 530 F.3d 676 (8th Cir. 2008).

[663] *See Torre v. Charter Commc'ns, Inc.*, 493 F. Supp. 3d 276, 290 (S.D.N.Y. 2020).

[664] *See Olagues v. Timken*, 908 F.3d 200, 204–05 (6th Cir. 2018); *Roamingwood Sewer & Water Ass'n v. Nat'l Diversified Sales, Inc.*, 509 F. Supp. 3d 198, 204 (M.D. Pa. 2020).

[665] *See Salahuddin v. Cuomo*, 861 F.2d 40, 43 (2d Cir. 1988) (court would strike only so much of pleading as is redundant or immaterial).

[666] *See Greys Ave. Partners, LLC v. Theyers*, 484 F. Supp. 3d 895, 906 (D. Haw. 2020); *Spoon v. Bayou Bridge Pipeline, LLC*, 335 F.R.D. 468, 470 (M.D. La. 2020). *See also Sorosky v. Burroughs Corp.*, 826 F.2d 794, 802 (9th Cir. 1987) (where no arguments were presented in support of theory, it was vulnerable to dismissal as redundant). *But cf. Dethmers Mfg. Co., Inc. v. Automatic Equipment Mfg. Co.*, 23 F. Supp. 2d 974, 1008–09 (N.D. Iowa 1998) (mere duplicative remedies do not necessarily make claims "redundant" if those claims require proof of different elements, but claim that simply recasts same elements under the guise of different theory may be stricken as redundant).

[667] *See Petrie v. Electronic Game Card, Inc.*, 761 F.3d 959, 967 (9th Cir. 2014); *Roamingwood Sewer & Water Ass'n v. Nat'l Diversified Sales, Inc.*, 509 F. Supp. 3d 198, 204 (M.D. Pa. 2020).

[668] *See Holmes v. Fischer*, 764 F. Supp. 2d 523, 532 (W.D.N.Y. 2011); *Johnson v. M & M Communications, Inc.*, 242 F.R.D. 187, 189 (D. Conn. 2007).

[669] *See Whittlestone, Inc. v. Handi-Craft Co.*, 618 F.3d 970, 974 (9th Cir. 2010); *Nunes v. Lizza*, 486 F. Supp. 3d 1267, 1299 (N.D. Iowa 2020).

[670] *See Fantasy, Inc. v. Fogerty*, 984 F.2d 1524, 1527 (9th Cir. 1993), rev'd on other grounds, 510 U.S. 517, 114 S. Ct. 1023, 127 L. Ed. 2d 455 (1994); *Zurich Am. Life Ins. Co. v. Nagel*, 538 F. Supp. 3d 396, 399 (S.D.N.Y. 2021).

[671] *See United States v. Coney*, 689 F.3d 365, 379-80 (5th Cir. 2012) (mere risk of offending someone's sensibilities does not justify a strike, if plead-

to the parties' dispute, unless the descriptions contain unnecessary detail.[672] Notably, some case law suggests that the typical disfavor with which courts approach Rule 12(f) motions does not govern when the contested allegations are scandalous and also immaterial or impertinent.[673]

Striking Prayers For Relief

The courts are divided on when (or if) prayers for relief may be stricken under Rule 12(f). Some courts permit such motions to argue that a type of relief is categorically unavailable,[674] while others do not.[675]

Striking Improper Jury Demands

Rule 12(f) is a proper vehicle for striking an improper demand for trial by jury.[676]

Striking Class Action Allegations

Rule 12(f) is theoretically available to strike class action allegations, but only in the rare instance where it is obvious from the pleadings that class treatment would not be proper.[677]

---

ings are directly relevant and supported). *See also Alvarado-Morales v. Digital Equip. Corp.*, 843 F.2d 613, 617–18 (1st Cir. 1988) ("impugned" character of defendant); *Roamingwood Sewer & Water Ass'n v. Nat'l Diversified Sales, Inc.*, 509 F. Supp. 3d 198, 204 (M.D. Pa. 2020) (casts derogatory light, uses repulsive language, or detracts from dignity of court); *Righthaven LLC v. Democratic Underground, LLC*, 791 F. Supp. 2d 968, 977 (D. Nev. 2011) (casts person in "cruelly derogatory light"); *Global View Ltd. Venture Capital v. Great Central Basin Exploration, L.L.C.*, 288 F. Supp. 2d 473, 481 (S.D. N.Y. 2003) ("amounts to nothing more than name calling, and does not contribute to [the] . . .substantive claims"). *See generally Arunachalam v. Int'l Bus. Machines Corp.*, 989 F.3d 988, 999 n.14 (Fed. Cir. 2021) (discussing various definitions for "scandalous" used by courts).

[672] *See Talbot v. Robert Matthews Distributing Co.*, 961 F.2d 654, 664–65 (7th Cir. 1992) (matter is "scandalous" if it bears no possible relation to the controversy); *Sirois v. E. W. Partners, Inc.*, 285 F. Supp. 3d 1152, 1162 n.8 (D. Haw. 2018) (if relevant, facts that are derogatory or unpleasant not stricken).

[673] *See Brown v. Maxwell*, 929 F.3d 41, 52 n.42 (2d Cir. 2019).

[674] *See Wiegand v. Royal Caribbean Cruises Ltd.*, 473 F. Supp. 3d 1348, 1351 (S.D. Fla. 2020); *Doe v. Indyke*, 457 F. Supp. 3d 278, 284–89 (S.D.N.Y. 2020).

[675] *See Whittlestone, Inc. v. Handi-Craft Co.*, 618 F.3d 970, 974 (9th Cir. 2010).

[676] *See Red Hawk Fire & Sec., LLC v. Siemens Indus. Inc.*, 449 F. Supp. 3d 449 (D.N.J. 2020); *Starnes Family Office, LLC v. McCullar*, 765 F. Supp. 2d 1036, 1055 (W.D.Tenn. 2011).

[677] *See Manning v. Boston Med. Ctr. Corp.*, 725 F.3d 34, 59 (1st Cir. 2013); *Pilgrim v. Universal Health Card, LLC*, 660 F.3d 943, 949 (6th Cir. 2011). *See generally Donelson v. Ameriprise Fin. Servs., Inc.*, 999 F.3d 1080, 1092 (8th Cir. 2021) (surveying Circuit split).

Striking Counterclaims

Although defensive in nature, counterclaims are not "defenses" and, thus, ordinarily cannot be attacked under Rule 12(f).[678]

Striking Portions of Judicial Opinion

Rule 12(f) cannot ordinarily be invoked to strike a portion of a court's judicial decision.[679]

Striking Documents Other Than Pleadings

As defined in Rule 12(f), motions to strike are directed to "pleadings" only. Consequently, these motions are technically not available to strike material contained in motions, briefs, affidavits, or other non-pleadings.[680] Nonetheless, some courts have considered Rule 12(f) challenges to non-pleadings,[681] or construed them as mislabeled invitations to adjudicate the admissibility of the contested materials,[682] often reasoning that Rule 12(f) offers the only viable vehicle for challenging the materiality and pertinence of the documents under attack.[683]

---

[678]*See GEOMC Co. v. Calmare Therapeutics Inc.*, 918 F.3d 92, 101 (2d Cir. 2019) (instead, proper bases would be Rules 12(b)(6), 12(c), or 56).

[679]*See Act Now to Stop War and End Racism Coalition v. District of Columbia*, 286 F.R.D. 117, 125 & 132 (D.D.C. 2012).

[680]*See Bunn v. Perdue*, 966 F.3d 1094, 1099 (10th Cir. 2020) (not for motions, briefs, and memoranda); *Palmer Holdings & Invs., Inc. v. Integrity Ins. Co.*, 505 F. Supp. 3d 842, 862 (S.D. Iowa 2020) (not for affidavits); *F.E.I. Co. v. United States*, 409 F. Supp. 3d 305, 318 n.5 (M.D. Pa. 2019) (not for proposed findings of fact and conclusions of law); *Lewis v. Sec'y of Health & Human Servs.*, 370 F. Supp. 3d 267, 270 (D. Mass. 2019) (not for sur-reply briefs); *Bey v. Washington Metro. Area Transit Auth.*, 341 F. Supp. 3d 1, 12–13 (D.D.C. 2018) (not for deposition transcripts or interrogatory answers); *Saiyed v. Council on Am.-Islamic Relations Action Network, Inc.*, 321 F.R.D. 455, 458–59 (D.D.C. 2017) (not for expert reports); *Stillwagon v. City of Delaware*, 175 F. Supp. 3d 874, 889–90 (S.D. Ohio 2016) (not for reply brief); *Kennedy v. Gish, Sherwood & Friends, Inc.*, 143 F. Supp. 3d 898, 905 (E.D. Mo. 2015) (not for statement of uncontroverted facts); *Hagen v. Siouxland Obstetrics & Gynecology, P.C.*, 934 F. Supp. 2d 1026, 1042–43 (N.D. Iowa 2013) (not for appendix); *Albertson v. Fremont County*, 834 F. Supp. 2d 1117, 1123 n.3 (D.Idaho 2011) (not for exhibits to motion response).

[681]*See, e.g., Barnes v. D.C.*, 289 F.R.D. 1, 6 (D.D.C. 2012) (Rule 12(f) proper for expert reports); *Henok v. Chase Home Fin., LLC*, 925 F. Supp. 2d 46, 53 n.2 (D.D.C. 2013) (Rule 12(f) proper for affidavits/declarations in support of pleadings). *See also Stephenson v. Fam. Sols. of Ohio, Inc.*, 499 F. Supp. 3d 467, 475 (N.D. Ohio 2020) (district court can invoke its "inherent power" over docket control to consider motion to strike).

[682]*See Snadon v. SEW-Eurodrive Inc.*, 421 F. Supp. 3d 1360, 1364 (N.D. Ga. 2019); *Natural Resources Defense Council v. Kempthorne*, 539 F. Supp. 2d 1155, 1161–61 (E.D. Cal. 2008). *See also Palmer Holdings & Invs., Inc. v. Integrity Ins. Co.*, 505 F. Supp. 3d 842, 862–63 (S.D. Iowa 2020) (construing motion as challenge to significance/weight of extrinsic material).

[683]*See U.S. Equal Employment Opportunity Comm'n v. Dimensions Healthcare Sys.*, 188 F. Supp. 3d 517, 522 n.5 (D. Md. 2016); *Wane v. Loan Corp.*, 926 F. Supp. 2d 1312, 1317 (M.D.Fla. 2013).

But, as highlighted above, many other courts reject this view.[684] Note, some federal districts have authorized a separate motion to "strike" for non-compliance with local rules.[685]

Timing and Waiver

A motion to strike must be made before a responsive pleading is served or, if no responsive pleading is required, within 21 days after service of the preceding pleading.[686] In view of the court's authority to strike on its own initiative, this 21-day period is often not applied strictly when the proposal to strike has merit.[687] Parties should appreciate the consequence of moving to strike under Rule 12(f)—only one, pre-answer Rule 12 motion is permitted, and if one is filed, any waivable defense that could have been joined with—but was omitted from—the Rule 12(f) motion will be considered lost.[688] Accordingly, movants should take care to ensure that all pre-answer motions they intend to make, and especially their waivable defenses, are asserted together with their Rule 12(f) motion to strike in an omnibus motion.

***Sua Sponte* Strikes**

The court may, on its own initiative, strike matter from a pleading.[689] Thus, the court may properly consider a party's untimely motion or "suggestion" under Rule 12(f) to strike matter from the pleading.[690]

Extrinsic Materials

Generally, the court will not consider extrinsic materials on a motion to strike.[691] Instead, the grounds supporting the motion to strike must be readily apparent from the face of the

---

[684]*See Johnson v. Gestamp Alabama, LLC*, 946 F. Supp. 2d 1180, 1192 (N.D.Ala. 2013) (discussing differing views, and rejecting use of motion to strike); *Martin v. Town of Westport*, 558 F. Supp. 2d 228, 230–31 (D. Conn. 2008) (recounting, and adopting, view that Rule 12(f) should not be used for documents other than pleadings).

[685]*See Bunn v. Perdue*, 966 F.3d 1094, 1099 (10th Cir. 2020); *Young v. Hartford Cas. Ins. Co.*, 503 F. Supp. 3d 1125, 1170–71 (D.N.M. 2020).

[686]*See U.S. v. $38,000.00 Dollars in U.S. Currency*, 816 F.2d 1538, 1547 (11th Cir. 1987); *Culinary and Service Employees Union, AFL-CIO Local 555 v. Hawaii Employee Ben. Admin., Inc.*, 688 F.2d 1228, 1232 (9th Cir. 1982). *See also Martinez v. Naranjo*, 328 F.R.D. 581, 596 (D.N.M. 2018) (denying tardy motion as out-of-time).

[687]*See Balon v. Enhanced Recovery Co.*, 316 F.R.D. 96, 99 (M.D. Pa. 2016); *Newborn Bros. Co. v. Albion Eng'g Co.*, 299 F.R.D. 90, 95–96 (D.N.J. 2014).

[688]*See Williams & Cochrane, LLP v. Quechan Tribe of Fort Yuma Indian Reservation*, 329 F.R.D. 247, 254–55 (S.D. Cal. 2018) (discussing effect of Rules 12(g) and 12(h) on motions to strike).

[689]*See Arunachalam v. Int'l Bus. Machines Corp.*, 989 F.3d 988, 999 n.14 (Fed. Cir. 2021); *Delta Consulting Group, Inc. v. R. Randle Const., Inc.*, 554 F.3d 1133, 1141 (7th Cir. 2009).

[690]*See U.S. v. Lot 65 Pine Meadow*, 976 F.2d 1155, 1157 (8th Cir. 1992); *In re Complaint of Rationis Enterprises, Inc. of Pananma*, 210 F. Supp. 2d 421, 424–25 (S.D. N.Y. 2002).

[691]*See Giuliani v. Polysciences, Inc.*, 275 F. Supp. 3d 564, 572 (E.D. Pa. 2017); *Drew v. Quest Diagnostics*, 992

pleadings at issue,[692] from materials incorporated within them by reference, or from content of which the court may take judicial notice.[693] If the court does consider extrinsic materials, the motion to strike must ordinarily be converted into a motion for summary judgment.[694]

Mislabeled Rule 12(f) Motions

The appropriate vehicle for testing the factual sufficiency of a pleading is usually not a motion to strike, but a Rule 12(b)(6) motion to dismiss or a Rule 12(c) motion for judgment on the pleadings.[695] Ordinarily, a mislabeled motion to strike that challenges factual sufficiency will simply be treated as a motion to dismiss.[696]

Prejudice on Dismissal

Where an allegation or defense is stricken as technically deficient, the dismissal is generally without prejudice to refile with a technically correct pleading.[697]

Appealability

Although scant case law exists on the point, rulings on motions to strike are usually considered interlocutory and not immediately appealable.[698]

RULE 12(g)—JOINING MOTIONS

CORE CONCEPT

A defending party may file a pre-answer motion (which usually postpones the obligation to file an answer) in order to press defenses and objections listed in Rule 12. If a defending party elects

---

F. Supp. 2d 1177, 1182 (N.D. Ala. 2014). *See also Diamond Scientific Co. v. Ambico, Inc.*, 848 F.2d 1220, 1226 (Fed. Cir. 1988) (although extrinsic materials are generally not considered on a motion to strike, they may be accepted by the court where they present uncontested factual matters). *But see Fantasy, Inc. v. Fogerty*, 984 F.2d 1524, 1528–29 (9th Cir. 1993), rev'd on other grounds, 510 U.S. 517, 114 S. Ct. 1023, 127 L. Ed. 2d 455 (1994).

[692] *See Sirois v. E. W. Partners, Inc.*, 285 F. Supp. 3d 1152, 1159 (D. Haw. 2018); *Balon v. Enhanced Recovery Co.*, 316 F.R.D. 96, 98 (M.D. Pa. 2016).

[693] *See Petrie v. Electronic Game Card, Inc.*, 761 F.3d 959, 966 (9th Cir. 2014); *Sirois v. E. W. Partners, Inc.*, 285 F. Supp. 3d 1152, 1159 (D. Haw. 2018).

[694] *See Liberty Mut. Ins. Co. v. Precision Valve Corp.*, 402 F. Supp. 2d 481, 484 (S.D. N.Y. 2005).

[695] *See Herrera v. Di Meo Bros., Inc.*, 529 F. Supp. 3d 819, 833 (N.D. Ill. 2021); *Williams v. County of Alameda*, 26 F. Supp. 3d 925, 948–49 (N.D. Cal. 2014).

[696] *See Koch v. White*, 134 F. Supp. 3d 158, 165 (D.D.C. 2015). *See also Haynish v. Bank of Am., N.A.*, 284 F. Supp. 3d 1037, 1053 (N.D. Cal. 2018) (not meant to duplicate Rule 12(b)(6) or Rule 56).

[697] *See Cisco Sys., Inc. v. Beccela's Etc., LLC*, 403 F. Supp. 3d 813, 823 (N.D. Cal. 2019); *Haley Paint Co. v. E.I. Du Pont De Nemours & Co.*, 279 F.R.D. 331, 336 (D. Md. 2012). *Cf.*. *Westchester Gen. Hosp., Inc. v. Evanston Ins. Co.*, 333 F.R.D. 594, 597 (S.D. Fla. 2019) (dismissed with prejudice if insufficient as matter of law, without-prejudice if technically deficient).

[698] *See Shultz v. Mfrs. & Traders Trust Co.*, 103 F.2d 771, 771 (2d Cir. 1939).

to do so, that party may include all of its Rule 12 defenses and objections then available in a single, omnibus motion. Rule 12(g) must be read in conjunction with Rule 12(h), concerning waiver of certain omitted defenses.

APPLICATIONS

Rule and Its Consequences

Any Rule 12 motion may be joined with any other Rule 12 motion.[699] This consolidation mandate produces four consequences once a Rule 12 motion is made. *First*, a party is generally permitted to make only one Rule 12 motion; thus, a party who intends to have the court resolve *any* Rule 12 defense or objection at the pre-answer motion stage must simultaneously present to the court every *other* Rule 12 defense or objection the party intends to then raise.[700] *Second*, including all such Rule 12 defenses and objections together at once causes no forfeiture of those that are inconsistent with one another.[701] *Third*, omitting from any Rule 12 pre-answer motion an objection to personal jurisdiction, venue, process, or service of process waives that objection.[702] *Fourth*, omitting other, non-waivable Rule 12 defenses and objections could be deemed as surrendering the party's right to have those matters considered at the pre-answer stage, thus relegating the party to having to wait until later in the case to assert them.[703] The intent behind these consequences is to avoid piecemeal litigating tactics, where defendants seek dismissal on one ground, lose there, and then seek dismissal anew on a different ground.[704]

Exception—Applies Only If Defenses Were "Available"

A party is required to assert in an omnibus motion only those defenses and objections "available" to that party.[705] Thus, if the legal basis for a particular defense or objection does not yet exist or if it would be futile based on current, controlling precedent, that defense or objection need not be included in the

[699]*See* Rule 12(g)(1).

[700]*See* Rule 12(g)(2). *See McCurdy v. American Bd. of Plastic Surgery*, 157 F.3d 191, 194 (3d Cir. 1998).

[701]*See Mattiaccio v. DHA Group, Inc.*, 20 F. Supp. 3d 220, 227 (D.D.C. 2014). *See also Duro Textiles, LLC v. Sunbelt Corp.*, 12 F. Supp. 3d 221, 224–25 (D. Mass. 2014) (improper to "reserve" on raising defenses in fear that raising them will forfeit others).

[702]*See* Rule 12(h)(1). *See also infra* Authors' Commentary to Rule 12(h)(1) ("**Basic Rule: Waived Defenses and Objections**").

[703]*See Jaffer v. Standard Chartered Bank*, 301 F.R.D. 256, 259 (N.D. Tex. 2014); *Negron v. School Dist. of Philadelphia*, 994 F. Supp. 2d 663, 666–67 (E.D. Pa. 2014).

[704]*See Leyse v. Bank of Am. Nat. Ass'n*, 804 F.3d 316, 320 (3d Cir. 2015); *Ennenga v. Starns*, 677 F.3d 766, 773 (7th Cir. 2012). *See generally Moser v. Benefytt, Inc.*, 8 F.4th 872, 877 (9th Cir. 2021) (to "allow the court to do a reasonably complete job") (cleaned up).

[705]*See Moser v. Benefytt, Inc.*, 8 F.4th 872, 877–79 (9th Cir. 2021); *In re Micron Tech., Inc.*, 875 F.3d 1091, 1097 (Fed. Cir. 2017).

omnibus motion.[706] For example, a party is not obliged to assert an objection to untimely service while the time permitted for timely service has not yet expired.[707] Accordingly, new defenses and objections may be later asserted if they are triggered by an alteration to the pleadings,[708] by a change in the law occurring while the motion is pending,[709] or by other interim developments.[710] But parties must act promptly. An unnecessarily lengthy delay in asserting a latent Rule 12 objection may, itself, be deemed a waiver.[711]

Exception—Amended Complaints

Because an amended complaint supersedes its predecessor, a second Rule 12 motion directed to new content contained in that amended pleading should generally be proper.[712] If, however, the second motion raises as new objections those which were, or could have been, earlier asserted against the original pleading, the courts' views are divided. Some courts permit such later motions;[713] others do not.[714]

---

[706] *See Cruson v. Jackson Nat'l Life Ins. Co.*, 954 F.3d 240, 250 (5th Cir. 2020) (citing national precedent).

[707] *See Boulger v. Woods*, 917 F.3d 471, 476–77 (6th Cir. 2019); *Teamsters Local 639 Employers, Health Trust v. Hileman*, 988 F. Supp. 2d 18, 25 (D.D.C. 2013).

[708] *See infra* Authors' Commentary to Rule 12(e) ("**Exception—Amended Complaints**"). *Compare YETI Coolers, LLC v. Walmart Inc.*, 2018 WL 5304119, at *2 (W.D. Tex. Oct. 25, 2018) (Rule 12(e) motion improper because argument was previously available), *with In re Fosamax Prod. Liab. Litig.*, 2013 WL 6669706, at *2–*3 (S.D.N.Y. Dec. 18, 2013) (Rule 12(e) motion proper because argument was not previously available).

[709] *See In re Micron Tech., Inc.*, 875 F.3d 1091, 1097 (Fed. Cir. 2017) (not waived by change in law); *Gucci America, Inc. v. Weixing Li*, 768 F.3d 122, 135–36 (2d Cir. 2014) (same). *See generally Holzsager v. Valley Hospital*, 646 F.2d 792, 796 (2d Cir. 1981) (courts will not demand clairvoyance from litigants; parties not deemed to have waived defenses or objections not then known to them). *Compare Am. Fid. Assur. Co. v. Bank of New York Mellon*, 810 F.3d 1234, 1241–42 (10th Cir. 2016) (waived, no true change in law) *with Practice Mgmt. Support Servs., Inc. v. Cirque du Soleil, Inc.*, 301 F. Supp. 3d 840, 862–64 (N.D. Ill. 2018) (not waived due to change in law).

[710] *See Cruson v. Jackson Nat'l Life Ins. Co.*, 954 F.3d 240, 249–50 (5th Cir. 2020) (order certifying class); *Prod. Source Int'l, LLC v. Foremost Signature Ins. Co.*, 234 F. Supp. 3d 619, 625 n.4 (D.N.J. 2017) (subsequent settlement of other lawsuit); *Allstate Ins. Co. v. Elzanaty*, 929 F. Supp. 2d 199, 215 (E.D.N.Y. 2013) (new arbitration developments).

[711] *See Strauss v. Credit Lyonnais, S.A.*, 175 F. Supp. 3d 3, 13 (E.D.N.Y. 2016); *Gilmore v. Palestinian Interim Self-Gov't Auth.*, 8 F. Supp. 3d 9, 12–17 (D.D.C. 2014).

[712] *See Negron v. Sch. Dist. of Phila.*, 994 F. Supp. 2d 663, 666–67 (E.D. Pa. 2014). *But cf. Stoffels ex rel., SBC Concession Plan v. SBC Commc'ns, Inc.*, 430 F. Supp. 2d 642, 648 (W.D. Tex. 2006) (Rule 12(g) applies to amended complaints if "defense was available when the first 12(b)(6) motion was made"). *See generally supra* Authors' Commentary to Rule 12(g) ("**Exception—Applies Only If Defenses Were 'Available'**").

[713] *See Brokers' Choice of Am., Inc. v. NBC Universal, Inc.*, 861 F.3d 1081, 1101–02 (10th Cir. 2017); *In re Mylan N.V. Sec. Litig.*, 379 F. Supp. 3d 198, 210 n.7 (S.D.N.Y. 2019).

Exception—Prior Abstention Motions

Some courts have ruled that the bar against successive Rule 12 motions to dismiss will not apply where the preceding motion to dismiss or to stay was based on an abstention principle.[715]

Exception—Successive Rule 12(b)(6) Motions

A pre-answer motion may challenge a complaint under Rule 12(b)(6) for failing to state a claim upon which relief can be granted. But Rule 12(b)(6) is accorded special treatment under Rule 12(g)'s consolidation mandate. The *defense* of failure-to-state-a-claim is not waived if omitted from a pre-answer Rule 12 motion; to the contrary, that *defense* may be raised in a later pleading, a Rule 12(c) motion for judgment on the pleadings, or at trial.[716] Less clear, however, is whether that *defense* can be raised in a second or subsequent *pre-answer* motion, or must it wait until later. Some courts have interpreted this Rule to tolerate successive pre-answer Rule 12(b)(6) motions (at least absent prejudice or adverse impact on judicial economy).[717] Other courts disagree, reading the Rule as rendering improper the filing of successive pre-answer motions to dismiss (especially where they raise arguments that could have been asserted earlier).[718] Those courts, however, then often forgive this technical misstep as harmless error.[719]

"Amending" a Rule 12 Motion

To avoid waiving Rule 12 defenses that were omitted inadvertently from a Rule 12 motion, parties may seek leave of court to amend or supplement their Rule 12 motions to include omitted defenses or objections.[720] In considering such amendments, the court may examine whether the amendment request

---

[714] *See Albany Ins. Co. v. Almacenadora Somex, S.A.*, 5 F.3d 907, 909 (5th Cir. 1993); *Gilmore v. Shearson / American Exp. Inc.*, 811 F.2d 108, 112 (2d Cir. 1987). *See also Pruco Life Ins. Co. v. Wilmington Trust Co.*, 616 F. Supp. 2d 210, 214–16 (D.R.I. 2009) ("in law, as in life, do-overs are a rare commodity, and Rule 12 does not provide one here").

[715] *See Aetna Life Ins. Co. v. Alla Medical Services, Inc.*, 855 F.2d 1470, 1475 (9th Cir. 1988); *Ciolli v. Iravani*, 625 F. Supp. 2d 276, 290 n.7 (E.D.Pa. 2009).

[716] *See* Rule 12(h)(2).

[717] *See Doe v. Columbia-Brazoria Indep. Sch. Dist. by & through Bd. of Trustees*, 855 F.3d 681, 686 (5th Cir. 2017); *Ennenga v. Starns*, 677 F.3d 766, 773 (7th Cir. 2012). *See also Boothe Farms, Inc. v. Dow Chem. Co.*, 487 F. Supp. 3d 758, 759–60 (E.D. Ark. 2020) (refusing to hear motion would prompt Rule 12(c) filing on same grounds: "More paper is not what this case needs."); *Cross v. Ciox Health, LLC*, 438 F. Supp. 3d 572, 581–82 (E.D.N.C. 2020) (allowing Rule 12(b)(6) motion filed 4 minutes after Rule 12(b)(1) motion because foreclosing it would not serve scope and purpose of Rules).

[718] *See In re Apple Iphone Antitrust Litig.*, 846 F.3d 313, 317–18 (9th Cir. 2017); *Leyse v. Bank of Am. Nat. Ass'n*, 804 F.3d 316, 321–22 & n.5 (3d Cir. 2015).

[719] *See In re Apple Iphone Antitrust Litig.*, 846 F.3d 313, 317–18 (9th Cir. 2017); *Leyse v. Bank of Am. Nat. Ass'n*, 804 F.3d 316, 321 (3d Cir. 2015).

[720] *See Chatman-Bey v. Thorn-*

was filed before the Rule 12 motion was heard, the time interval between the original Rule 12 motion and the attempted correction, the moving party's good faith, and the likelihood that the omission was intentional and tactical, or merely inadvertent.[721]

Applies Only to Same Moving Party

The consolidation obligation is only triggered when the same party attempts to make a later Rule 12 motion. Thus, a Rule 12 filing by one co-defendant does not foreclose a later Rule 12 filing by a different co-defendant,[722] even when they share the same counsel.[723] Similarly, a government officer who moves to dismiss claims filed against him in his official capacity is likely not foreclosed from later asserting Rule 12 defenses to claims filed against him in his individual capacity.[724]

Applies to All Rule 12 Motions

This omnibus consolidation requirement applies to all Rule 12 motions, including the Rule 12(b) defenses as well as Rule 12(e) motions for more definite statements and Rule 12(f) motions to strike.[725] Thus, for example, a motion seeking only a more definite statement will likely have the effect of waiving any motion to strike as well as challenges to personal jurisdiction, venue, process, and service.[726]

Applies Only to Rule 12 Motions

This consolidation provision applies only to Rule 12 motions and only to defenses that may be asserted under Rule 12.[727] It

---

burgh, 864 F.2d 804, 813 (D.C. Cir. 1988); *Glater v. Eli Lilly & Co.*, 712 F.2d 735, 738 (1st Cir. 1983).

[721] *See Thomas v. Bank*, 2009 WL 481349, at *1 (M.D.Ga. Feb. 25, 2009) (denying amendment sought tactically); *Nycal Corp. v. Inoco PLC*, 949 F. Supp. 1115, 1119–20 (S.D. N.Y. 1997) (same). *See also Maxtena, Inc. v. Marks*, 2012 WL 113386, at *11 (D.Md. Jan. 12, 2012) (rejecting, seemingly categorically, such amendments as "an end run around both Rule 12(g)(2) and settled law).

[722] *See Muhammed v. Bernstein*, 2013 WL 3177864, at *4 (D.Md. June 21, 2013) (co-defendant have no obligation to file joint Rule 12 motions).

[723] *See Schnabel v. Lui*, 302 F.3d 1023, 1034 (9th Cir. 2002).

[724] *See King v. Taylor*, 694 F.3d 650, 656–57 (6th Cir. 2012).

[725] *See Gables Ins. Recovery v. United Healthcare Ins. Co.*, 39 F. Supp. 3d 1377, 1391 n.10 (S.D. Fla. 2013) (applies to Rule 12(f) motions); *BAC Home Loans Servicing LP v. Fall Oaks Farm LLC*, 848 F. Supp. 2d 818, 824 (S.D. Ohio 2012) (applies to Rule 12(e) motions).

[726] *See, e.g., Apothio, LLC v. Kern Cnty.*, __ F. Supp. 3d __, 2022 WL 1215259, at *23 (E.D. Cal. 2022) (filing motions to dismiss/more definite statement waived motion to strike).

[727] Thus, the consolidation mandate applies to motions to transfer for *improper* venue, because those are remedied under Rule 12(b)(3). *See Rodriguez v. Pan Am. Health Org.*, 502 F. Supp. 3d 200, 231–33 (D.D.C. 2020), *aff'd*, 29 F.4th 706 (D.C. Cir. 2022). But it does not apply to motions to transfer venue for *convenience* of witnesses or parties, because those do not implicate Rule 12(b)(3). *See Yavuz v. 61 MM, Ltd.*, 576 F.3d 1166, 1173 (10th Cir. 2009) (not to forum non conveniens motions); *Perrigo Co. v. Merial Ltd.*, 215 F. Supp. 3d 1329, 1335–36 (N.D. Ga. 2016) (not to 28 U.S.C. § 1406 motions).

does not apply to motions allowed under other Rules or laws,[728] nor does it apply to affirmative defenses (which remain preserved, even after a Rule 12 motion, if timely asserted in the responsive pleading).[729]

Later Rule 12(c) Motion on Same Grounds

A party enjoys the right to press a failure to state a claim defense in a post-answer Rule 12(c) motion for judgment on the pleadings.[730] Most courts construe this right broadly, permitting its use even where the party could have, or actually did, press this same defense in its earlier pre-answer motion.[731] Other courts, though permitting such motions, have questioned whether such a use comports with Rule 12(g)'s "consolidation" policy.[732]

RULE 12(h)—WAIVING AND PRESERVING CERTAIN DEFENSES

CORE CONCEPT

Rule 12(h) lists the defenses and objections that are waived if not timely asserted.

APPLICATIONS

Early Waivable Defenses and Objections

Four defenses and objections—lack of personal jurisdiction (Rule 12(b)(2)), improper venue (Rule 12(b)(3)), insufficient process (Rule 12(b)(4)), and insufficient service (Rule 12(b)(5))—are waived unless they are:

- *Asserted by Pre-Answer Motion*, if a pre-answer Rule 12 motion is filed, or
- *Asserted in the Answer*, if no pre-answer Rule 12 motion is filed (though raising a waivable defense in the answer *after* omitting it from a pre-answer Rule 12 motion will

[728] *See Conrad v. Phone Directories Co.*, 585 F.3d 1376, 1383 n.2 (10th Cir. 2009) (not to motion to compel arbitration under FAA); *Aetna Life Ins. Co. v. Alla Med. Servs., Inc.*, 855 F.2d 1470, 1474–75 (9th Cir. 1988) (not to motions to stay); *Gray v. United States*, 556 F. Supp. 3d 832, 860 n.20 (W.D. Tenn. 2021) (not to motion for summary judgment); *Wright v. Linebarger Googan Blair & Sampson, LLP*, 782 F. Supp. 2d 593, 614–16 (W.D.Tenn. 2011) (not to motions under Rule 17 challenging real party in interest status); *American Med. Ass'n v. United Healthcare Corp.*, 588 F. Supp. 2d 432, 439 (S.D.N.Y. 2008) (not to motions to amend).

[729] *See Brent v. Wayne Cty. Dep't of Human Servs.*, 901 F.3d 656, 693 (6th Cir. 2018); *Amgen Inc. v. Sandoz Inc.*, 877 F.3d 1315, 1324 (Fed. Cir. 2017).

[730] *See* Rule 12(g)(2) (failure to state claim is exception to bar on later motions); Rule 12(h)(2)(B) (permitting failure to state a claim to be raised on later Rule 12(c) motion).

[731] *See Abecassis v. Wyatt*, 7 F. Supp. 3d 668, 670 (S.D. Tex. 2014); *Alexander v. City of Greensboro*, 801 F. Supp. 2d 429, 434 (M.D. N.C. 2011).

[732] *See Juliana v. United States*, 339 F. Supp. 3d 1062, 1076 n.4 (D. Or. 2018); *Sprint Telephony PCS, L.P. v. County of San Diego*, 311 F. Supp. 2d 898, 904–05 (S.D. Cal. 2004).

not rescue it).[733]

Judicial economy underlies this waiver provision. Waiver is designed to prevent the delaying effect of the piecemeal assertion of Rule 12 objections and defenses through multiple motions, and to permit the early dismissal of inappropriate claims before the court devotes unnecessary time and resources to adjudication.[734]

Waiver Only If Defenses Were "Available"

The waiver provision of Rule 12(h) will apply only to bar unasserted defenses and objections that were "available" at the time of the party's Rule 12 motion or responsive pleading.[735]

Waiver is Mandatory, Not Discretionary

The waiver provision of Rule 12(h) seems to impose a mandatory, not discretionary, obligation.[736]

Waiver By Improper Assertion

A Rule 12(h) waivable defense may be lost not merely by a failure to assert it at all, but also by asserting it untimely,[737] incompletely,[738] or obscurely or indirectly.[739]

Waiver (or "Forfeiture") By Implication

By the very act of suing, a plaintiff impliedly waives any personal jurisdiction and venue objections.[740] Defendants, too, by their conduct, may impliedly relinquish objections to personal jurisdiction, venue, insufficient process, or insufficient service of process, even though those defenses were originally

---

[733] *See Vallone v. CJS Sols. Grp., LLC*, 9 F.4th 861, 864 (8th Cir. 2021); *Quinn v. Specialized Loan Servicing, LLC*, 414 F. Supp. 3d 1122, 1124 (N.D. Ill. 2019).

[734] *See Ennenga v. Starns*, 677 F.3d 766, 773 (7th Cir. 2012); *Flory v. U.S.*, 79 F.3d 24, 25 (5th Cir. 1996).

[735] *See* Rule 12(h)(1)(A) (waiver by omission from motion "in the circumstances described in Rule 12(g)(2)"); Rule 12(g)(2) (barring second motion asserting defense or objection "available" at time of original motion). *See generally supra* Authors' Commentary to Rule 12(g) (**"Exception—Applies Only If Defenses Were 'Available'"**).

[736] *See Pusey v. Dallas Corp.*, 938 F.2d 498, 501 n.4 (4th Cir.1991) (trial court *prohibited* from dismissing on basis of waived defense); *Pardazi v. Cullman Med. Ctr.*, 896 F.2d 1313, 1316–17 (11th Cir. 1990) (same).

[737] *See Ramer v. U.S.*, 620 F. Supp. 2d 90, 102 (D.D.C. 2009) (defense waived when asserted in motion reply brief, not opening brief).

[738] *See Crispin-Taveras v. Municipality of Carolina*, 647 F.3d 1, 7 (1st Cir. 2011) (objection to manner of service waived when party earlier objected only to service timeliness); *Columbia Sportswear N. Am., Inc. v. Seirus Innovative Accessories, Inc.*, 265 F. Supp. 3d 1196, 1202 (D. Or. 2017) (vague venue reference did not preserve all types of venue objections).

[739] *See, e.g., Hemispherx Biopharma, Inc. v. Johannesburg Consol. Invs.*, 553 F.3d 1351, 1360–61 (11th Cir. 2008) (personal jurisdiction challenge does not imply a companion (but unasserted) service challenge). *Cf. Vallone v. CJS Sols. Grp., LLC*, 9 F.4th 861, 864–65 (8th Cir. 2021) (no waiver, even though "personal jurisdiction" phrase not used, where pleading's intent was unambiguous).

[740] *See Adam v. Saenger*, 303 U.S. 59, 67–68, 58 S. Ct. 454, 82 L. Ed. 649 (1938).

asserted properly. Such a forfeiture may follow when the contesting defendant fails to promptly press the court for a dispositive ruling on its objections,[741] behaves during the litigation in a manner that effectively submits to the court's jurisdiction,[742] or is sanctioned for noncompliance with court orders.[743]

- *No Waiver by Early Filings:* A defendant who files documents during the pre-answer/pre-motion period will ordinarily not trigger this forfeiture-by-implication doctrine.[744]
- *No Waiver by Asserting Affirmative Claims:* Although some contrary authority persists,[745] many courts hold that a party does *not* waive a properly asserted objection to personal jurisdiction by pressing an affirmative claim for relief[746] or by filing ancillary motions (*e.g.*, for stay or injunction pending appeal) premised on the asserted jurisdictional defense.[747] This view construes such affirmative claims for relief as simply contingent on the court's denial of the party's jurisdictional objections.[748]
- *No Waiver While Motion is Pending:* A defendant, who properly moves for a dismissal, usually does not waive that motion by participating in court processes while its motion is pending.[749]
- *No Waiver After Motion Loss:* A defendant who properly asserts a waivable defense, presses for dismissal on that basis, but loses, will ordinary not waive the pressed

---

[741]*See In re Micron Tech., Inc.*, 875 F.3d 1091, 1100–02 (Fed. Cir. 2017); *King v. Taylor*, 694 F.3d 650, 658 (6th Cir. 2012).

[742]*See In re Asbestos Prod. Liab. Litig. (No. VI)*, 921 F.3d 98, 105–08 (3d Cir. 2019); *Barnes v. Sea Hawaii Rafting, LLC*, 889 F.3d 517, 529–30 (9th Cir. 2018).

[743]*See Brown v. Lockheed Martin Corp.*, 814 F.3d 619, 625 (2d Cir. 2016).

[744]*See Blessing v. Chandrasekhar*, 988 F.3d 889, 894–99 (6th Cir. 2021) (filing notice of appearance does not, alone, waive personal jurisdiction); *White v. Christian*, 474 F. Supp. 3d 1196, 1199 (D. Colo. 2020) (filing for extension of time to answer and for leave to attend scheduling conference telephonically, and participating in drafting of proposed CMO, did not waive personal jurisdiction); *J.R. v. Walgreens Boots All., Inc.*, 470 F. Supp. 3d 534, 546–47 (D.S.C. 2020) (participating in preliminary injunction hearing did not waive personal jurisdiction, when extended time to answer complaint had not yet passed).

[745]*See Frank's Casing Crew & Rental Tools, Inc. v. PMR Technologies, Ltd.*, 292 F.3d 1363, 1372 (Fed. Cir. 2002) (non-resident defendant waived personal jurisdiction objection when it filed class action counterclaim asserting unrelated infringements).

[746]*See Hillis v. Heineman*, 626 F.3d 1014, 1017–19 (9th Cir. 2010); *Rates Tech. Inc. v. Nortel Networks Corp.*, 399 F.3d 1302, 1307–08 (Fed.Cir. 2005).

[747]*See PaineWebber Inc. v. Chase Manhattan Private Bank (Switzerland)*, 260 F.3d 453, 461 (5th Cir. 2001) (defendant did not waive personal jurisdiction defense by filing motion for stay and injunction premised on the jurisdictional defense).

[748]*See Bayou Steel Corp. v. M/V Amstelvoorn*, 809 F.2d 1147, 1149 (5th Cir. 1987).

[749]*See In re Atrium Med. Corp. C-Qur Mesh Prod. Liab. Litig. (MDL No. 2753)*, 299 F. Supp. 3d 324, 329 (D.N.H. 2017).

defense by continuing to participate in defending the case.[750]

Waiver By Pre-Answer Summary Judgment Omission

A party cannot escape waiver by jumping ahead of the answer / pre-answer motion to dismiss stage and filing an early motion for summary judgment. Defenses (like personal jurisdiction) that could have, but were not, raised in such a summary judgment motion may result in waiver as well.[751]

Waiver By Post-Answer Rule 12(c) Motion Omission

A waivable defense that has been preserved in a party's answer may still yet be waived if that defense is omitted from a post-answer motion for judgment on the pleadings.[752]

Waiver Not Avoided By Others' Motions

In a multi-party lawsuit, one defendant's preservation of a defense or objection will not necessarily preserve that same defense or objection for other parties.[753]

Avoiding Waiver By Answering Only (No Motion)

Notwithstanding a language anomaly in Rule 12,[754] parties have the option of asserting their defenses *either* by motion *or* in their responsive pleading.[755] Thus, unless a waiver (or "forfeiture") by implication later occurs (see above), parties who elect not to file a Rule 12 motion at all still preserve their defenses and objections by asserting them in their responsive pleading,[756] and may thereafter challenge them on a Rule 12(c) motion for judgment on the pleadings.[757]

Avoiding Waiver By Amending an Answer

A party who chooses not to file a pre-answer Rule 12 motion

---

[750] *See Shatsky v. Palestine Liberation Org.*, 955 F.3d 1016, 1032–34 (D.C. Cir. 2020).

[751] *See Casares v. Agri-Placements Int'l, Inc.*, 12 F. Supp. 3d 956, 965–66 (S.D. Tex. 2014).

[752] *See Boulger v. Woods*, 306 F. Supp. 3d 985, 994–95 (S.D. Ohio 2018), *aff'd*, 917 F.3d 471 (6th Cir. 2019) (although included in party's answer, service objections vulnerable to waiver when omitted from Rule 12(c) motion); *Mississippi ex rel. Hood v. Entergy Mississippi, Inc.*, 2017 WL 2973998, at *2 (S.D. Miss. July 11, 2017) (although included in party's answer, personal jurisdiction objection waived when omitted from Rule 12(c) motion); *Broussard v. Texas Dep't of Criminal Justice*, 2006 WL 1517532, at *8 (S.D. Tex. May 30, 2006) (same). *But cf.* 5C CHARLES A. WRIGHT & ARTHUR R. MILLER, FEDERAL PRACTICE AND PROCEDURE § 1385 (2004) (explaining how Rule operates to foreclose "successive *pre-answer* motions") (emphasis added). *But see Index Fund, Inc. v. Hagopian*, 107 F.R.D. 95, 102 (S.D.N.Y. 1985) (Rule 12(c) motion does not trigger waiver provisions of Rule 12(h)(1)).

[753] *See In re: Howmedica Osteonics Corp.*, 867 F.3d 390, 398 n.3 (3d Cir. 2017).

[754] *See Pope v. Elabo GmbH*, 588 F. Supp. 2d 1008, 1012–13 (D.Minn. 2008) (noting anomaly).

[755] *See* Rule 12(h)(1)(B).

[756] *See Argentine Republic v. National Grid Plc*, 637 F.3d 365, 367 (D.C.Cir. 2011); *Coons v. Industrial Knife Co.*, 620 F.3d 38, 41 (1st Cir. 2010).

[757] *See Adami v. Cardo Windows, Inc.*, 299 F.R.D. 68, 88 (D.N.J. 2014).

will lose any waivable defenses and objections which that party omits from its answer *or any amendment to its answer allowed "as a matter of course."*[758] This "matter-of-course" amendment window is narrow, encompassing only one amendment and only if it is done either (a) within 21 days after service of the original answer or (b) if a response to that original answer was required, within 21 days after service of the responsive pleading or responsive Rule 12(b), (e), or (f) motion.[759] Although amendments beyond this brief time window are "freely" given "when justice so requires,"[760] those are not "matter-of-course" amendments, but depend on leave of court, and thus cannot rescue an omitted waivable defense or objection.[761]

Avoiding Waiver By "Amending" a Motion

A party who chose to file a pre-answer Rule 12 motion but omitted from that filing a waivable defense may request the court to exercise its discretion to allow that party to amend or supplement its pending motion.[762]

Preserved But Waivable Defenses and Objections

Defenses and objections to a failure to state a claim upon which relief can be granted (Rule 12(b)(6)), failure to join an indispensable party (Rule 12(b)(7)), and failure to state a legal defense (Rule 12(f)) are waived *only* if not asserted before the close of trial.[763] These defenses, though generally preserved throughout the lawsuit, may not be raised for the first time in post-trial motions or on appeal.[764]

- *Only One Pre-Answer Rule 12(b)(6) Motion:* Some (but not all) courts have ruled that successive, pre-answer Rule 12(b)(6) motions are prohibited by Rule 12(g)'s requirement that all Rule 12 defenses (including failure to state a claim) be raised in a single, omnibus, pre-answer motion—if the party chooses to file a motion.[765]
- *Non-Waiver Applies to Rule 19(b) Parties Only:* Rule 12(h) preserves only the defense of dismissal for failing to join a required party whose joinder is not feasible.

---

[758] *See* Rule 12(h)(1)(B)(ii).

[759] *See* Rule 15(a)(1).

[760] *See* Rule 15(a)(2).

[761] *See Ellibee v. Leonard*, 226 Fed. Appx. 351, 358 (5th Cir. 2007); *Glater v. Eli Lilly & Co.*, 712 F.2d 735, 738 (1st Cir. 1983); *Konigsberg v. Shute*, 435 F.2d 551, 552 (3d Cir. 1970). *See generally McCurley v. Royal Seas Cruises, Inc.*, 2019 WL 3006469, at *4 (S.D. Cal. July 10, 2019) ("By negative implication, a party may not use Rule 15(a)(2) to resurrect a waived defense.").

[762] *See supra* Authors' Commentary to Rule 12(g) (**"'Amending' a Rule 12 Motion"**).

[763] *See Arbaugh v. Y&H Corp.*, 546 U.S. 500, 507, 126 S. Ct. 1235, 163 L. Ed. 2d 1097 (2006); *Ennenga v. Starns*, 677 F.3d 766, 773 (7th Cir. 2012).

[764] *See Brown v. Trustees of Bos. Univ.*, 891 F.2d 337, 357 (1st Cir. 1989). *See generally Arbaugh v. Y&H Corp.*, 546 U.S. 500, 507, 126 S. Ct. 1235, 163 L. Ed. 2d 1097 (2006) ("endures up to, but not beyond, trial on the merits").

[765] *See supra* Authors' Commentary to Rule 12(g) (**"Exception—Successive Rule 12(b)(6) Motions"**).

The failure to join a Rule 19(a) required party who could be feasibly joined is waived if omitted from a pre-answer Rule 12 motion, if one is filed, or from the responsive pleading, if one is not.[766]

- *Preserved in Multi-Case Litigations:* A defendant sued in multiple lawsuits does not waive Rule 12(b) defenses in later cases by having failed to assert similar defenses in earlier cases.[767]

Objections to Subject-Matter Jurisdiction

Because objections to the court's subject-matter jurisdiction concern the court's structural authority to hear and decide the parties' dispute, no one can waive such an objection, be estopped from raising the objection, or cure such a problem by consenting to jurisdiction where none exists.[768]

- *Asserted At Any Time:* Objections to subject-matter jurisdiction may be made in the omnibus Rule 12 motion, in the responsive pleading, in subsequent pretrial motions, in a motion for relief from final judgment, or on appeal.[769]
- *But Not Collaterally:* A party who loses a challenge to subject-matter jurisdiction in the district court may appeal, but res judicata principles ordinarily bar that party from challenging the ruling collaterally[770] (indeed, this same bar may even apply where the party had the *opportunity* to contest subject-matter jurisdiction but failed to do so).[771]
- *Styling of Post-Answer Motions:* Although a Rule 12(b)(1) motion to dismiss for lack of subject-matter jurisdiction is technically untimely if filed after the pleadings are closed, the courts will typically treat such a belated fil-

---

[766] *See Citibank, N.A. v. Oxford Props. & Fin. Ltd.*, 688 F.2d 1259, 1262 n.4 (9th Cir. 1982); *Buddy's Plant Plus Corp. v. CentiMark Corp.*, 2014 WL 1317578, at *6-*7 (W.D. Pa. Mar. 31, 2014), *aff'd,* 604 Fed. Appx. 134 (3d Cir. 2015).

[767] *See In re Cathode Ray Tube (CRT) Antitrust Litig.*, 27 F. Supp. 3d 1002, 1008–09 (N.D. Cal. 2014).

[768] *See Gonzalez v. Thaler*, 565 U.S. 134, 141, 132 S. Ct. 641, 181 L. Ed. 2d 619 (2012) (can never be waived or forfeited); *Commodity Futures Trading Comm'n v. Schor*, 478 U.S. 833, 851, 106 S. Ct. 3245, 92 L. Ed. 2d 675 (1986) (cannot be conferred by consent). *See also Wye Oak Tech., Inc. v. Republic of Iraq*, 24 F.4th 686, 698–99 (D.C. Cir. 2022) ("hard to accept" that subject-matter jurisdiction can be foreclosed by law-of-the-case doctrine).

[769] *See Henderson ex rel. Henderson v. Shinseki*, 562 U.S. 428, 434–35, 131 S. Ct. 1197, 179 L. Ed. 2d 159 (2011); *Arbaugh v. Y&H Corp.*, 546 U.S. 500, 506, 126 S. Ct. 1235, 163 L. Ed. 2d 1097 (2006).

[770] *See Ins. Corp. of Ireland v. Compagnie des Bauxites de Guinee*, 456 U.S. 694, 702 n.9, 102 S. Ct. 2099, 72 L. Ed. 2d 492 (1982); *Chicot Cnty. Drainage Dist. v. Baxter State Bank*, 308 U.S. 371, 375–78, 60 S. Ct. 317, 319–20, 84 L. Ed. 329 (1940).

[771] *See Corbett v. MacDonald Moving Servs., Inc.*, 124 F.3d 82, 88–89 (2d Cir. 1997).

ing as a Rule 12(c) motion,[772] a "Rule 12(h)(3) motion,"[773] or a "suggestion" to the court that it lacks subject-matter jurisdiction,[774] and will then apply the Rule 12(b)(1) standards.[775]

- *Raised By Court:* The trial court and the court of appeals have an obligation to examine for subject-matter jurisdiction on their own initiative.[776]

Waiting for Default, Then Collaterally Attacking

Although the Rules require defendants to raise their objections to process, service, and personal jurisdiction in either an omnibus Rule 12 motion or the answer (if no motion is filed), these defenses are not necessarily lost where the defendants neither appear nor defend, but default.[777] In that instance, the constitutional protections of due process may permit those defendants to raise some objections in opposition to the motion for default[778] or collaterally.[779] But defendants act at their peril if they actually receive notice of the pending lawsuit and choose to ignore it, in reliance on their own, untested belief that process, service, or personal jurisdiction was faulty. Minimally, they must guess correctly. If they've guessed wrong, they likely forfeit their right to defend on the merits.[780] Conversely, if they timely raise these objections (and thus avoid a default), they

---

[772]*See Cruz v. AAA Carting & Rubbish Removal, Inc.*, 116 F. Supp. 3d 232, 238 n.3 (S.D.N.Y. 2015).

[773]*See Anson v. United States*, 294 F. Supp. 3d 144, 156 (W.D.N.Y. 2018).

[774]*See S.J. v. Hamilton County, Ohio*, 374 F.3d 416, 418 n.1 (6th Cir. 2004).

[775]*See Thompson v. Alabama*, 293 F. Supp. 3d 1313, 1317 (M.D. Ala. 2017) (Rule 12(h)(3) motions); *Cruz v. AAA Carting & Rubbish Removal, Inc.*, 116 F. Supp. 3d 232, 239 (S.D.N.Y. 2015) (Rule 12(c) motions).

[776]*See Henderson ex rel. Henderson v. Shinseki*, 562 U.S. 428, 434, 131 S. Ct. 1197, 179 L. Ed. 2d 159 (2011); *Insurance Corp. of Ireland, Ltd. v. Compagnie des Bauxites de Guinee*, 456 U.S. 694, 704, 102 S. Ct. 2099, 72 L. Ed. 2d 492 (1982).

[777]*See Wong v. PartyGaming Ltd.*, 589 F.3d 821, 826 n.3 (6th Cir. 2009) (party does not waive Rule 12(b) defense simply by failing to respond timely). *Cf. In re Teknek, LLC*, 512 F.3d 342, 346 (7th Cir. 2007) (party not properly served who chooses to appear, without raising personal jurisdiction defense, waives it).

[778]*See Stinecipher v. U.S.*, 239 F.R.D. 282, 283 (D.D.C. 2006) (unless proper service is satisfied, court lacks power to assert personal jurisdiction). *See also Trustees of the St. Paul Elec. Const. Industry Fringe Benefit Funds v. Martens Elec. Co.*, 485 F. Supp. 2d 1063, 1065 (D. Minn. 2007) (defendants who are not properly served are protected against default).

[779]*See Insurance Corp. of Ireland, Ltd. v. Compagnie des Bauxites de Guinee*, 456 U.S. 694, 706, 102 S. Ct. 2099, 72 L. Ed. 2d 492 (1982) ("A defendant is always free to ignore the judicial proceedings, risk a default judgment, and then challenge that judgment on jurisdictional grounds in a collateral proceeding."); *Baldwin v. Iowa State Traveling Men's Ass'n*, 283 U.S. 522, 525, 51 S. Ct. 517, 75 L. Ed. 1244 (1931) (defendant objecting to personal jurisdiction has "the election not to appear at all," and then to attack collaterally).

[780]*See* Rule 12(h)(1) (if court *has* jurisdiction, failure to properly assert process, service, and personal jurisdiction defense waives them); Rule 8(b)(6) (any allegation not timely denied is admitted, if response was required).

have assented to the forum's jurisdiction to determine its own jurisdiction, and are thereafter barred from attacking collaterally and must appeal.[781]

- *Actual Notice:* Defendants who seek to object on service grounds, but who received actual notice of the lawsuit, may be found to have waived their service objections[782] or to have had their objections otherwise materially limited.[783]
- *Appearing to Defend Post Default:* Appearing to participate following entry of default will likely waive service and personal jurisdiction objections, unless, upon appearing, the defaulting party promptly asserts them.[784]
- *Appearing and Abandoning:* Likewise, those objections may also be waived if the defendant begins to assert them but then abandons them.[785]
- *Burden of Proof:* In a direct challenge, the party invoking the court's jurisdiction bears the burden of proving it; in a collateral challenge, the party contesting the original court's jurisdiction has the burden of disproving it.[786]

RULE 12(i)—HEARING BEFORE TRIAL

CORE CONCEPT

Unless the court orders that such motions are deferred until trial, the court may schedule Rule 12(b) defenses and Rule 12(c) motions for a pretrial hearing and resolution.

APPLICATIONS

Impact of 2007 "Restyling" Amendments

Rule 12(i) was repositioned in 2007. The current content of Rule 12(i) was formerly found in Rule 12(d).

---

[781]*See Philos Techs., Inc. v. Philos & D, Inc.*, 645 F.3d 851, 856 (7th Cir. 2011).

[782]*See Corestates Leasing, Inc. v. Wright-Way Exp., Inc.*, 190 F.R.D. 356, 358 (E.D. Pa. 2000); *see also O'Meara v. Waters*, 464 F. Supp. 2d 474, 476 (D. Md. 2006) (if defendants receive actual notice, failure to comply strictly with Rule 4 might be excused and service deemed valid). *See generally* 5C CHARLES A. WRIGHT & ARTHUR R. MILLER, FEDERAL PRACTICE AND PROCEDURE § 1391, at 522 (2004) ("If the defendant is merely arguing that there is no jurisdiction because service of process or the content of the papers was defective or improper and thus did not effectuate jurisdiction over this person, then the objection is not of a constitutional dimension and Rule 12(h)(1) waiver principles clearly should apply.").

[783]*See Burda Media, Inc. v. Viertel*, 417 F.3d 292, 299 (2d Cir. 2005) (where defaulting defendant had actual knowledge of proceeding, but delayed challenging service of process, that defendant will, in motion to vacate default, bear burden of proving that contested service did *not* occur).

[784]*See Democratic Republic of Congo v. FG Hemisphere Associates, LLC*, 508 F.3d 1062, 1064–65 (D.C. Cir. 2007).

[785]*See City of New York v. Mickalis Pawn Shop, LLC*, 645 F.3d 114, 134–36 (2d Cir. 2011).

[786]*See Philos Techs., Inc. v. Philos & D, Inc.*, 645 F.3d 851, 856–57 (7th Cir. 2011).

Rule 12(b) Defenses Asserted by Motion

When a Rule 12(b) defense or objection is asserted by motion, the moving papers themselves should include a "notice of hearing" or similar reference compliant with the district's local rules. A motion filed post-answer, however styled, may be treated as a Rule 12(i) request for a pretrial ruling.[787]

Rule 12(b) Defenses Asserted by Responsive Pleading

When a Rule 12(b) defense or objection is asserted only in the responsive pleading (*i.e.*, where no pre-answer Rule 12(b) motion is filed), a Rule 12(i) application for preliminary hearing is the vehicle used to obtain a pretrial determination from the court on those defenses and objections[788] (and such an application may be essential to save the party from forfeiting those defenses and objections[789]).

When Pretrial Determinations are Proper

Even in the presence of a genuine factual dispute, the court may nevertheless decide, *pretrial*, challenges affecting subject-matter jurisdiction, personal jurisdiction, standing, venue, and certain threshold defenses (like preclusion).[790] In deciding whether these types of issues should be determined preliminarily, or should instead await resolution at trial, the court weighs the need to test these defenses and the litigants' interest in having the objections resolved promptly against the expense and delay of a preliminary hearing, the court's difficulty in deciding the issues preliminarily, and the likelihood that the issues will become so interconnected with the merits that deferring them until trial would be preferable.[791]

On Motion or *Sua Sponte*

A hearing may be ordered upon a party's request or by the court *sua sponte*.[792]

Oral Argument and Hearing

The moving party is generally not *entitled* to oral argument or an evidentiary hearing on the motion; instead, the right of "hearing" is ordinarily satisfied upon affording a party the opportunity to, in some manner, present its views and arguments

---

[787] *See King v. Taylor*, 694 F.3d 650, 657 n.2 (6th Cir. 2012).

[788] *See generally Rivera-Gomez v. de Castro*, 900 F.2d 1, 2 (1st Cir. 1990) (Rule is "perhaps too infrequently invoked and too often overlooked"; but can "be an excellent device for conserving time, expenses, and scarce judicial resources by targeting early resolution of threshold issues").

[789] *See supra* Authors' Commentary to Rule 12(h) ("**Waiver (or 'Forfeiture') By Implication**").

[790] *See Cameron v. Children's Hosp. Medical Center*, 131 F.3d 1167, 1170 (6th Cir. 1997).

[791] *See Cameron v. Children's Hosp. Medical Center*, 131 F.3d 1167, 1170–71 (6th Cir. 1997).

[792] *See Beltre v. Lititz Healthcare Staffing Solutions LLC*, 757 F. Supp. 2d 373, 376 (S.D.N.Y. 2010).

to the court.[793] Moreover, the court enjoys discretion on what type of hearing to allow: a hearing only on briefs, an oral argument,[794] or a full evidentiary hearing.[795]

When Pretrial Determinations are Properly Deferred

A district court's *pretrial* review and disposition of Rule 12(b) defenses and Rule 12(c) motions is discretionary, not mandatory.[796] In appropriate cases, involving peculiarly complicated factual and legal issues, or where further factual development is necessary, the court may defer resolving Rule 12(b) defenses until time of trial.[797]

Additional Research References

C.J.S., Federal Civil Procedure § 302, §§ 376 to 409 et seq., §§ 413 to 440 et seq., §§ 796 et seq., §§ 842 et seq.

West's Key Number Digest, Federal Civil Procedure ⚷734 to 735, ⚷941 to 1020, ⚷1041 to 1068, ⚷1101 to 1150, ⚷1721 to 1843

---

793 *See Greene v. WCI Holdings Corp.*, 136 F.3d 313, 316 (2d Cir. 1998). *See also In re Eckstein Marine Serv. L.L.C.*, 672 F.3d 310, 319–20 (5th Cir. 2012); *Odyssey Marine Exploration, Inc. v. Unidentified Shipwrecked Vessel*, 657 F.3d 1159, 1170 (11th Cir. 2011).

794 *See Obert v. Republic Western Ins. Co.*, 398 F.3d 138, 143 (1st Cir. 2005).

795 *See Kregler v. City of New York*, 646 F. Supp. 2d 570, 578 (S.D.N.Y. 2009), *vacated on other grounds*, 2010 WL 1740806 (2d Cir. May 3, 2010).

796 *See AcryliCon USA, LLC v. Silikal GmbH*, 985 F.3d 1350, 1364 (11th Cir. 2021).

797 *See Chavez v. T & B Mgmt., LLC*, 286 F. Supp. 3d 742, 745 (M.D.N.C. 2017); *Nissim Corp. v. ClearPlay, Inc.*, 351 F. Supp. 2d 1343, 1346 (S.D. Fla. 2004).

RULE 13
COUNTERCLAIM AND CROSSCLAIM

(a) Compulsory Counterclaim.

(1) *In General.* A pleading must state as a counterclaim any claim that—at the time of its service—the pleader has against an opposing party if the claim:

(A) arises out of the transaction or occurrence that is the subject matter of the opposing party's claim; and

(B) does not require adding another party over whom the court cannot acquire jurisdiction.

(2) *Exceptions.* The pleader need not state the claim if:

(A) when the action was commenced, the claim was the subject of another pending action; or

(B) the opposing party sued on its claim by attachment or other process that did not establish personal jurisdiction over the pleader on that claim, and the pleader does not assert any counterclaim under this rule

(b) Permissive Counterclaim. A pleading may state as a counterclaim against an opposing party any claim that is not compulsory.

(c) Relief Sought in a Counterclaim. A counterclaim need not diminish or defeat the recovery sought by the opposing party. It may request relief that exceeds in amount or differs in kind from the relief sought by the opposing party.

(d) Counterclaim Against the United States. These rules do not expand the right to assert a counterclaim—or to claim a credit—against the United States or a United States officer or agency.

(e) Counterclaim Maturing or Acquired After Pleading. The court may permit a party to file a supplemental pleading asserting a counterclaim that matured or was acquired by the party after serving an earlier pleading.

(f) [Abrogated]

(g) Crossclaim Against a Coparty. A pleading may state as a crossclaim any claim by one party against a coparty if the claim arises out of the transaction or occurrence that is the subject matter of the original action or of a counter-claim, or if the claim relates to any property that is the subject matter of the original action. The crossclaim may include a claim that the coparty is or may be liable to the crossclaimant for all or part of a claim asserted in the action against the crossclaimant.

(h) Joining Additional Parties. Rules 19 and 20 govern the addition of a person as a party to a counterclaim or crossclaim.

(i) Separate Trials; Separate Judgments. If the court orders separate trials under Rule 42(b), it may enter judgment on a counterclaim or crossclaim under Rule 54(b) when it has jurisdiction to do so, even if the opposing party's claims have been dismissed or otherwise resolved.

[Amended effective March 19, 1948; July 1, 1963; July 1, 1966; August 1, 1987; April 30, 2007, effective December 1, 2007; March 26, 2009, effective December 1, 2009.]

AUTHORS' COMMENTARY ON RULE 13

PURPOSE AND SCOPE

In order to facilitate the resolution of all related claims at one time, the Rules allow a variety of additional claims to be joined to the action after the plaintiffs commence it. Rule 13 authorizes two such claims—counterclaims and crossclaims—in order to achieve resolution in a single suit of all disputes arising out of common matters.[1]

Rule 13 authorizes persons who are already parties to an action to assert counterclaims against an opposing party. To facilitate judicial economy, Rule 13 authorizes defending parties (typically defendants) to assert any and all claims they have against claiming parties (typically plaintiffs). Some counterclaims are compulsory—these must be raised in pending litigation or they

[1] *MWK Recruiting Inc. v. Jowers*, 833 Fed. Appx. 560, 563 (5th Cir. 2020).

will be waived. Other counterclaims are permissive—these may either be raised in the pending litigation or retained for subsequent litigation. Rule 13 also controls the circumstances in which one defending party may assert a crossclaim against another co-defending party.

RULE 13(a)—COMPULSORY COUNTERCLAIM

CORE CONCEPT

Subject to some exceptions discussed below, compulsory counterclaims are those counterclaims arising from the same transaction or occurrence that gave rise to the plaintiff's complaint. Such counterclaims are so closely related to claims already raised by a plaintiff that it would be inefficient to litigate them in separate actions. Consequently, compulsory counterclaims generally must be asserted in the pending litigation or they are waived.

APPLICATIONS

Procedure

A defending party asserts a compulsory counterclaims by asserting it in the answer to the pleading asserting claims against the defending party (typically, asserted by the defendant in the answer to the complaint).[2] Counterclaims should be pleaded under the same plausibility standard established in Rule 8 and in *Twombly* and *Iqbal*,[3] as discussed in detail in the Rule 8(a)(2) coverage above.

Same Transaction or Occurrence

Courts generally agree that this standard for identifying compulsory counterclaims should be construed liberally, to further the goal of judicial economy.[4] However, courts differ in the way they actually apply the standard to specific facts. One test is: (1) whether the issues of law and fact in the various claims are essentially the same; (2) whether, in the absence of the compulsory counterclaim rule, res judicata would bar a subsequent suit on the counterclaim; (3) whether the same evidence could be used to support or refute the claim and counterclaim; and (4) whether a logical relationship exists between claim and counterclaim.[5] Not all the questions need be answered affirmatively before a counterclaim may be deemed compulsory.[6]

Other courts sometimes find a compulsory counterclaim

---

[2] *See, e.g., Shelter Mut. Ins. Co. v. Public Water Supply Dist. No. 7 of Jefferson County, Mo.*, 747 F.2d 1195 (8th Cir. 1984).

[3] *GEOMC Co. v. Calmare Therapeutics Inc.*, 918 F.3d 92, 99 (2d Cir. 2019).

[4] *See, e.g., In re Rearden LLC*, 841 F.3d 1327 (Fed. Cir. 2016).

[5] *See Equitrans, L.P. v. Moore*, 725 Fed. Appx. 221, 224 (4th Cir. 2018); *ABS Global, Inc. v. Inguran, LLC*, 914 F.3d 1054 (7th Cir. 2019).

[6] *See, e.g., Equitrans, L.P. v. Moore*, 725 Fed. Appx. 221, 224 (4th Cir. 2018).

when there is any significant logical relationship between the plaintiff's claim and the counterclaim.[7] To determine whether a logical relationship exists, courts examine whether the same operative facts serve as the basis of both claims or if the core facts in the original claim activate additional legal rights, otherwise dormant, in the defendant.[8] Thus, if a plaintiff sued on a contract, and the defendant had a counterclaim resting on an assertion that the contract was a violation of federal antitrust law, the "logical relationship" test would probably treat the counterclaim as compulsory.[9]

Other, less broad, applications of the standard may require substantial overlap in all elements of the claims before a counterclaim is deemed compulsory.[10] Some courts require the compulsory counterclaim to arise from the same underlying facts.[11]

Exceptions to "Same Transaction" Standard

A counterclaim is not compulsory unless it arises from the same transaction or occurrence as one of the claims filed by an opposing party. However, the converse—that counterclaims arising from the same transaction or occurrence are compulsory—is not always true. Listed below are the circumstances in which a counterclaim need not be asserted even though it shares the same transaction or occurrence as a claim filed by an opposing party.[12]

- *Immature Claims:* A counterclaim that does not mature until after the party has served a pleading is not a compulsory counterclaim, even if it arises from the same transaction or occurrence as a claim filed by an opposing party.[13] Rule 13(e) provides that such a claim may be asserted as a permissive counterclaim by filing a supplemental pleading, as provided by Rule 15(d), or it may be retained for future litigation, at the discretion of the party who holds the claim.

Similarly, claims not asserted during a bankruptcy filing, although technically ripe, may not be compulsory if the lender

[7]*See, e.g., Mitchell v. CB Richard Ellis Long Term Disability Plan*, 611 F.3d 1192 (9th Cir. 2010); *In re Eldercare Properties, Ltd.*, 568 F.3d 506, 519 (5th Cir. 2009).

[8]*Shenzhen Kinwong Elec. Co. v. Kukreja*, 574 F. Supp. 3d 1191, 1209 (S.D. Fla. 2021).

[9]*See, e.g., Berrey v. Asarco Inc.*, 439 F.3d 636, 645–46 (10th Cir. 2006).

[10]*See, e.g., Mattel, Inc v. MGA Entertainment, Inc.*, 705 F.3d 1108, 1110 (9th Cir. 2013) (in determining whether counterclaim is compulsory court looks to facts rather than legal theory).

[11]*Hammervold v. Blank*, 3 F.4th 803, 810 (5th Cir. 2021).

[12]*See, e.g., Kane v. Magna Mixer Co.*, 71 F.3d 555, 561–62 (6th Cir. 1995).

[13]*See, e.g., Karum Holdings LLC v. Lowe's Companies, Incorporated*, 895 F.3d 944 (7th Cir. 2018); *Pace v. Timmermann's Ranch and Saddle Shop Inc.*, 795 F.3d 748 (7th Cir. 2015).

has reason to believe the debtor may pay without litigation.[14]

- *Counterclaims Only Become Compulsory when a Responsive Pleading is Filed:* Even if a counterclaim arises from the same transaction or occurrence as a plaintiff's claim, it does not become a compulsory counterclaim until the time when the party holding the counterclaim is required to file a responsive pleading.[15] Thus, if a defendant initially filed a motion to dismiss under Rule 12(b), that rule provides that no pleading need be filed until the court decides the Rule 12(b) motion. If the court granted the motion to dismiss, the defendant never had an obligation to file a responsive pleading. In that circumstance, any claim the defendant had against the plaintiff would not be deemed a compulsory counterclaim and would be preserved for assertion in subsequent litigation. Similarly, if a plaintiff and defendant settle the plaintiff's claim before the defendant files an answer, any counterclaim the defendant has is not compulsory.[16]
- *Lack of Jurisdiction Over Necessary Parties:* If a counterclaim requires joinder of an additional person not subject to the court's jurisdiction, the counterclaim will not be deemed compulsory, irrespective of the amount of overlap it shares with the plaintiff's claim.[17] It does not follow that if the district court could have acquired jurisdiction of a non-party, a later claim against that "non-party" although based on the same facts as the original action, will be considered barred as a compulsory claim.[18]
- *Pending Lawsuits:* A counterclaim is not compulsory if it has already been asserted in other litigation. Thus, if one person filed suit in a state court, and the opponent of that claim then sued in federal court, the original state claim would not be a compulsory counterclaim in federal court because it is already the subject of pending litigation.[19]
- *Quasi in Rem / In Rem Jurisdiction:* Where the plaintiff's complaint rests on the court's quasi in rem or in rem

[14] *See, e.g., Greene v. U.S. Dept. of Educ.*, 770 F.3d 667, 669 (7th Cir. 2014).

[15] *Cf., e.g., Tyler v. DH Capital Management, Inc.*, 736 F.3d 455, 459 (6th Cir. 2013) ("Where the adverse party has no opportunity to file a pleading, it has no opportunity to assert its counterclaim, and thus its claim will not be barred.").

[16] *See, e.g., Bluegrass Hosiery, Inc. v. Speizman Industries, Inc.*, 214 F.3d 770 (6th Cir. 2000); *Carteret Sav. & Loan Ass'n v. Jackson*, 812 F.2d 36, 38 (1st Cir. 1987).

[17] *See, e.g., Landmark Bank v. Machera*, 736 F. Supp. 375, 379 (D. Mass. 1990).

[18] *Pace v. Timmermann's Ranch and Saddle Shop Inc.*, 795 F.3d 748 (7th Cir. 2015).

[19] *See, e.g., Canon Latin America, Inc. v. Lantech (CR), S.A.*, 508 F.3d 597, 602 (11th Cir. 2007); *In re Piper Aircraft Corp.*, 244 F.3d 1289, 1296 (11th Cir. 2001).

jurisdiction, a counterclaim will not be compulsory,[20] so long as the defendant refrains from raising any counterclaims under Rule 13. If, however, the defendant raises a Rule 13 counterclaim, then all other counterclaims that fall within the same transaction or occurrence as the plaintiff's claim—and not exempted by other exceptions, discussed above—are compulsory counterclaims and must be asserted.

- *Injunction/Declaratory Judgment Actions:* In some circumstances, defendants who have been sued only on equity claims may not be required to assert claims for money damages as counterclaims.[21]

Who Constitutes an "Opposing Party"

Rule 13(a) requires assertion of compulsory counterclaims against an "opposing party." Precedent on the issue is not plentiful, but in general it appears that the term "opposing party" is read rather broadly. Thus, a person who is sufficiently closely related to a plaintiff who should have been sued on a compulsory counterclaim in previous litigation may be able to argue that the defendant waived the counterclaim as to that person as well as to the actual plaintiff.[22]

Subject-Matter Jurisdiction

Compulsory counterclaims must satisfy subject-matter jurisdiction. The party asserting a counterclaim must include allegations demonstrating that subject-matter jurisdiction is satisfied.[23] Because compulsory counterclaims must arise from the same transaction or occurrence as the plaintiff's claim, however, counterclaims virtually always meet the "same case or controversy" requirement for supplemental jurisdiction.[24]

Under the doctrine of ancillary jurisdiction, a district court retains the authority to decide compulsory counterclaims even after it has resolved the plaintiff's original claims, regardless of

[20] *Baker v. Gold Seal Liquors, Inc.*, 417 U.S. 467, 469, 94 S. Ct. 2504, 2506, 41 L. Ed. 2d 243 (1974).

[21] *See, e.g., Allan Block Corp. v. County Materials Corp.*, 512 F.3d 912, 916 (7th Cir. 2008) (declaratory judgment exception to res judicata is consistent with Rule 13 as rule is "in effect a procedural implementation of" the doctrine of res judicata); *Duane Reade, Inc. v. St. Paul Fire and Marine Ins. Co.*, 600 F.3d 190, 197 (2nd Cir. 2010) (where prior actions involved both declaratory relief and breach of contract claims, the declaratory judgment exception to Rule 13 was not available); *U.S. v. Snider*, 779 F.2d 1151, 1156 (6th Cir. 1985).

[22] *See, e.g., Transamerica Occidental Life Ins. Co. v. Aviation Office of America, Inc.*, 292 F.3d 384 (3d Cir. 2002) (successor in interest to party in prior litigation is "opposing party" under Rule 13(a)); *Pace v. Timmermann's Ranch and Saddle Shop Inc.*, 795 F.3d 748 (7th Cir. 2015) (employees of company would likely not have been considered as parties).

[23] *McNutt v. General Motors Acceptance Corp. of Indiana*, 298 U.S. 178, 189 (1936).

[24] *Baker v. Gold Seal Liquors, Inc.*, 417 U.S. 467, 468–69 (1974); *Barefoot Architect, Inc. v. Bunge*, 632 F.3d 822, 826 (3d Cir. 2011).

whether the court would have original jurisdiction over the counterclaims.[25]

Personal Jurisdiction Over Plaintiffs

By instituting an action, a plaintiff has generally consented to the court's personal jurisdiction to adjudicate related claims,[26] and by definition, a compulsory counterclaim is closely related to the plaintiff's claim.

Venue

Compulsory counterclaims need not satisfy venue requirements.[27]

Failure to Assert a Compulsory Counterclaim

Defendants who do not assert compulsory counterclaims are usually barred from raising the counterclaims in subsequent litigation.[28] Rule 13(a) is limited by Rule 15(a), which permits a party to amend a pleading once as of right within certain designated time frames. Thus, a party who failed to include a compulsory counterclaim within an initial answer might be able to use Rule 15(a) to amend the answer of right or, if the time in which to amend of right has already passed, to seek leave of opposing counsel or leave of court to amend. However, once judgment is entered on a plaintiff's claim, compulsory counterclaims that were not raised are effectively barred.[29]

- *Class Actions:* The normal requirement that a compulsory counterclaim must be timely raised is generally inapplicable to claims held by class action defendants.[30]

Mislabelled Counterclaims

Parties sometimes mistakenly identify counterclaims as crossclaims, and *vice versa*. They may also mislabel a counterclaim as a defense. Courts usually attach no significance to such errors, unless somehow they unfairly prejudice an opposing party.[31]

Statutes of Limitations

Most courts agree that if the counterclaim was within the statute of limitations at the time the complaint was filed, the limitation period on the counterclaim is tolled by the filing of

---

[25]*Vikas WSP, Ltd. v. Econ. Mud Prod. Co.*, 23 F.4th 442, 451 (5th Cir. 2022).

[26]*Adam v. Saenger*, 303 U.S. 59 (1938); *Schnabel v. Lui*, 302 F.3d 1023, 1037 (9th Cir. 2002).

[27]*See, e.g., Schoot v. U.S.*, 664 F. Supp. 293, 295 (N.D. Ill. 1987).

[28]*Baker v. Gold Seal Liquors, Inc.*, 417 U.S. 467, 469 (1974).

[29]*See e.g., Mali v. Federal Ins. Co.*, 720 F.3d 387 (2d Cir. 2013).

[30]*See, e.g., Allapattah Services, Inc. v. Exxon Corp.*, 333 F.3d 1248 (11th Cir. 2003), aff'd, 545 U.S. 546, 125 S. Ct. 2611, 162 L. Ed. 2d 502 (2005) (normal practice is to wait until liability is established and individual class members file damage claims; at that point setoffs and counterclaims can properly be adjudicated on an individual basis).

[31]*Reiter v. Cooper*, 507 U.S. 258, 262 (1993).

the complaint (for example, while a motion to dismiss is adjudicated).[32] Although the statute of limitations is tolled for compulsory counterclaims, it may not be tolled for permissive counterclaims, which are regarded as independent causes of action.[33]

Counterclaims to Amended or Supplemented Pleadings

If the plaintiff files an amended complaint, some courts hold that a counterclaim to the original complaint is no longer operative unless it is repleaded in the answer to the amended complaint. Other courts have permitted a defendant to pursue a counterclaim, even if not reasserted in an amended answer, unless the plaintiff shows that the failure to replead it caused prejudice.[34]

If the plaintiff files a supplemental complaint, the defendant must file any compulsory counterclaims that newly arise from supplemental allegations, but is not required to replead counterclaims that arose from claims in the original pleading.[35]

- *Asserting New Counterclaims in Amended Answers:* If a defending party seeks to assert new counterclaims in an amended answer, the court may be less inclined to allow new counterclaims that expand the scope of the litigation by introducing new factual or legal issues—particularly at a later stage of the litigation.[36]

RULE 13(b)—PERMISSIVE COUNTERCLAIM

CORE CONCEPT

Permissive counterclaims are any counterclaims that are not compulsory, including counterclaims arising out of the same transaction or occurrence as the opposing party's claims, but which fall within one or more of the exceptions to Rule 13(a) compulsory counterclaims, discussed above. Permissive counterclaims may be filed in the pending action but may also be asserted in a separate action. Because permissive counterclaims generally will not qualify for supplemental jurisdiction, they generally require a basis for original subject-matter jurisdiction (such as diversity or federal question jurisdiction).

APPLICATIONS

Procedure

A defending party asserts a permissive counterclaim by as-

---

[32] *Connecticut Gen. Life Ins. Co. v. BioHealth Lab'ys, Inc.*, 988 F.3d 127, 135 (2d Cir. 2021).

[33] *See MirTech Inc. v. AgroFresh Inc.*, 561 F. Supp. 3d 447, 458 (D. Del. 2021).

[34] *Sinclair Wyoming Ref. Co. v. A & B Builders, Ltd.*, 989 F.3d 747, 776 (10th Cir. 2021).

[35] *Z View Enterprises, LLC v. Giant Eagle, Inc.*, 834 Fed. Appx. 709, 712 (3d Cir. 2020).

[36] *See, e.g., GEOMC Co. v. Calmare Therapeutics, Inc.*, 918 F.3d 92 (2d Cir. 2019) (taking restrictive view of appropriate scope of late arising amended counterclaims).

serting it in the answer to the pleading asserting claims against the defending party (typically, asserted by the defendant in the answer to the complaint).[37] Counterclaims should be pleaded under the same plausibility standard established in Rule 8 and in *Twombly* and *Iqbal*,[38] as discussed in detail in the Rule 8(a)(2) coverage above.

Definition: Any Counterclaim that is Not Compulsory

Rule 13(b) defines a permissive counterclaim as any counterclaim that is not compulsory. Thus, the "same transaction or occurrence test" discussed above in the coverage of Rule 13(a) determines whether a counterclaim is compulsory or permissive.[39] Additionally, counterclaims that arise out of the same transaction or occurrence as the claim asserted against the defending party but qualify for one of the exceptions discussed above (such as claims that are not yet ripe or that are already the subject of pending litigation) are also permissive counterclaims.[40]

Subject-Matter Jurisdiction

Permissive counterclaims must satisfy requirements for subject-matter jurisdiction.[41] The party asserting a counterclaim must include allegations demonstrating that subject-matter jurisdiction is satisfied.[42] Because permissive counterclaims typically do not arise from the same transaction or occurrence as the plaintiff's claim, however, counterclaims often do not meet the "same case or controversy" requirements for supplemental jurisdiction, and must qualify for some form of original subjedt-matter júrisdiction (such as diversity or federal question jurisdiction).[43]

Personal Jurisdiction: Waiver of Defense

Filing a permissive counterclaim may constitute a waiver of any objection to personal jurisdiction, even where the defendant objected to personal jurisdiction in a motion to dismiss or responsive pleading.[44]

Venue

It is unclear whether permissive counterclaims must satisfy

---

[37]*See, e.g., Shelter Mut. Ins. Co. v. Public Water Supply Dist. No. 7 of Jefferson County, Mo.*, 747 F.2d 1195 (8th Cir. 1984).

[38]*GEOMC Co. v. Calmare Therapeutics Inc.*, 918 F.3d 92, 99 (2d Cir. 2019).

[39]*See, e.g., Warshawsky & Co. v. Arcata Nat. Corp.*, 552 F.2d 1257, 1261 (7th Cir. 1977).

[40]*See Karum Holdings LLC v. Lowe's Companies, Incorporated*, 895 F.3d 944 (7th Cir. 2018).

[41]*Asilonu v. Asilonu*, 550 F. Supp. 3d 282, 297 (M.D.N.C. 2021).

[42]*McNutt v. General Motors Acceptance Corp. of Indiana*, 298 U.S. 178, 189 (1936).

[43]*See, e.g., Oak Park Trust and Sav. Bank v. Therkildsen*, 209 F.3d 648, 651 (7th Cir. 2000); *Unique Concepts, Inc. v. Manuel*, 930 F.2d 573, 574 (7th Cir. 1991).

[44]*See* Author's Commentary to Rule 12 (h), *supra*, "Implied Waiver."

venue requirements.[45]

Failure to Assert a Permissive Counterclaim

No sanction attaches if a party holding a permissive counterclaim chooses not to assert it in pending litigation; the claim is not treated as barred, and may be asserted at a later date.[46]

Mislabeled Counterclaims

Parties sometimes mistakenly identify counterclaims as crossclaims, and *vice versa.* They may also mislabel a counterclaim as a defense. Courts usually attach no significance to such errors, unless somehow they unfairly prejudice an opposing party.[47]

Statutes of Limitations

The filing of a complaint does not toll the statute of limitations for a permissive counterclaim.[48] (in contrast to a compulsory counterclaim, as discussed above under Rule 13(a)).

Separate Trials

Permissive counterclaims not arising from the same transaction or occurrence as the opposing party's claim may contain substantial potential for confusing the trier of fact or delaying adjudication of the original claims. Thus, Rule 13(i) authorizes the court to order separate proceedings.

RULE 13(c)—RELIEF SOUGHT IN A COUNTERCLAIM

CORE CONCEPT

Rule 13(c) provides that: (1) counterclaims may be for any amount, irrespective of whether the amount sought in the counterclaim exceeds the amount sought in the other party's claim;[49] and (2) counterclaims may seek kinds of relief not sought in the opposing party's claim.[50] For example, if the opposing party's claim sought money damages only, the counterclaim could seek either money damages, equitable relief, or both money damages and equitable relief.

RULE 13(d)—COUNTERCLAIM AGAINST THE UNITED STATES

CORE CONCEPT

As a general rule, the United States and its officers and agen-

---

[45]*See, e.g., Hansen v. Shearson/American Exp., Inc.*, 116 F.R.D. 246, 251 (E.D. Pa. 1987) (suggesting that "in some circumstances" permissive counterclaims must satisfy venue requirements).

[46]*See, e.g., U.S. Philips Corp. v. Sears Roebuck & Co.*, 55 F.3d 592, 599 (Fed. Cir. 1995).

[47]*Reiter v. Cooper*, 507 U.S. 258, 262 (1993).

[48]*See, e.g., Employers Ins. of Wausau v. U.S.*, 764 F.2d 1572, 1576 (Fed. Cir. 1985).

[49]*In re S. Scrap Material Co., L.L.C.*, 713 F. Supp. 2d 568, 583 (E.D. La. 2010).

[50]*Fisher v. Blue Cross & Blue Shield of Texas*, 879 F. Supp. 2d 581, 590 (N.D. Tex. 2012).

cies are immune from suits in federal courts unless the United States waives its sovereign immunity. Rule 13(d) expressly provides that the counterclaim provisions of Rule 13(a) and (b) do not alter the law of sovereign immunity.[51]

APPLICATIONS

Filing a Complaint is Not a Waiver of Immunity

By filing a complaint, the United States generally does not waive sovereign immunity as to counterclaims for amounts above those sums for which the United States is suing, even if the counterclaims arise from the same transaction or occurrence as the complaint brought by the United States.[52] By contrast, a State which voluntarily joins litigation waives sovereign immunity for all compulsory counterclaims.[53]

Setoffs

Some courts have permitted counterclaims against the United States where the claim and counterclaim arise from the same transaction or occurrence and the money sought in the counterclaim is a setoff against the government's claim that will only reduce the government's recovery.[54]

RULE 13(e)—COUNTERCLAIM MATURING OR ACQUIRED AFTER PLEADING

CORE CONCEPT

If counterclaims mature or are acquired after a party has pleaded, the party may seek leave to assert them in a supplemental pleading, subject to the court's discretion.

APPLICATIONS

Procedure

A party seeking to assert a Rule 13(e) counterclaim must file a motion and supporting materials explaining the circumstances in which the counterclaim matured or was acquired.[55] The determination of whether a counterclaim matured or was acquired after the serving of the pleading is case specific.[56]

Supplemental Counterclaims are Permissive

Rule 13(e) is permissive in nature, even if the supplemental

---

[51] *See, e.g., In re Armstrong*, 206 F.3d 465, 473 (5th Cir. 2000); *U.S. ex rel. Fallon v. Accudyne Corp.*, 921 F. Supp. 611 (W.D. Wis. 1995).

[52] *See, e.g., U.S. v. Johnson*, 853 F.2d 619, 621 (8th Cir. 1988). Of course, the right to counterclaim does not expand any waiver of sovereign immunity by the United States. *See United States v. $4,480,466.16 in Funds Seized from Bank of America Account Ending in 2653*, 942 F.3d 655, 666 n.10 (5th Cir. 2019).

[53] *Gardner v. New Jersey*, 329 U.S. 565, 574 (1947).

[54] *See, e.g., Berrey v. Asarco Inc.*, 439 F.3d 636, 643 (10th Cir. 2006); *U.S. v. Forma*, 42 F.3d 759, 765 (2d Cir. 1994).

[55] *See, e.g., All West Pet Supply Co. v. Hill's Pet Products Div., Colgate-Palmolive Co.*, 152 F.R.D. 202, 204 (D. Kan. 1993).

[56] *In re Rearden LLC*, 841 F.3d 1327 (Fed. Cir. 2016).

counterclaim arises out of the same transaction or occurrence as the opposing party's claim. Thus, a party holding a counterclaim of the kind controlled by Rule 13(e) may seek leave to assert it, but is under no obligation to do so.[57]

Judicial Discretion to Hear Rule 13(e) Counterclaim

If a party seeks to raise a Rule 13(e) counterclaim, the court has discretion to refuse to hear the counterclaim in the pending action.[58] Generally, courts permit Rule 13(e) counterclaims where they will not confuse the trier of fact or where they will not unfairly prejudice other parties, particularly through excessively delaying the litigation.[59] The court's discretion to dismiss a Rule 13(e) does not depend on whether the counterclaim would have been compulsory or permissive if available at the time of the original responsive pleading.[60]

Jurisdiction

Rule 13(e) counterclaims must meet one of the bases of subject-matter jurisdiction, such as federal question jurisdiction, diversity jurisdiction, or supplemental jurisdiction. If the Rule 13(e) counterclaim arises out of the same transaction or occurrence as the original claim, then it will likely satisfy supplemental jurisdiction. If not, the counterclaim will need an independent basis of jurisdiction.

Venue

There is no venue requirement for Rule 13(e) counterclaims.

RULE 13(f) — OMITTED COUNTERCLAIM PROVISION (DELETED)

Rule 13(f) provided for filing of a counterclaim omitted through "oversight, inadvertence, or excusable neglect, or when justice requires." The subsection was deleted from the Rules in 2009. The Civil Rules Advisory Committee of the Judicial Conference concluded that this subsection potentially conflicted with Rule 15 and was, in any case, redundant. The filing of an omitted counterclaim is now governed by Rule 15.[61]

RULE 13(g)—CROSSCLAIM AGAINST COPARTY

CORE CONCEPT

Rule 13(g) permits persons who are already parties to a suit to

[57] *Stone v. Department of Aviation*, 453 F.3d 1271, 1280 (10th Cir. 2006).

[58] *See, e.g., U.S. ex rel. Westrick v. Second Chance Body Armor, Inc.*, 893 F. Supp. 2d 258, 263 (D.D.C. 2012).

[59] *See, e.g., Residential Credit Opportunities Tr. v. Poblete*, 245 F. Supp. 3d 91, 97 (D.D.C. 2017).

[60] *See American Home Assur. Co. v. Pope*, 487 F.3d 590, 604 n.6 (8th Cir. 2007).

[61] Civil Rules Advisory Committee Meeting, April 7–8 2008, Congressional Information Service Records of the U.S. Judicial Conference, p. 36; Civil Rules Advisory Committee Meeting, April 19–20, 2007, Congressional Information Service Records of the U.S. Judicial Conference, p.2; Civil Rules Advisory Committee Meeting, September 7–8, 2006, Congressional Information Service Records of the U.S. Judicial Conference, p.3.

bring related claims against persons on the same side of the litigation. This rule is almost always used by defendants, since plaintiffs rarely file crossclaims against each other. An essential difference between a crossclaim and a counterclaim is that crossclaims are suits against persons who had not, until the crossclaim was filed, been opponents of the person asserting the crossclaim. Counterclaims, by contrast, are suits against persons who have already sued the person asserting the counterclaim.

APPLICATIONS

Procedure

Crossclaims are typically raised in a responsive pleading.

Crossclaims Are Always Permissive

Unlike compulsory counterclaims under Rule 13(a), Rule 13(g) does not create a category of compulsory crossclaims. Instead, all crossclaims are permissive, and may therefore be asserted in the pending litigation or in a separate action.[62]

Same Transaction or Occurrence

Crossclaims must arise out of the same transaction or occurrence as the original action, or relate to the same property that is in dispute in the original action.[63] In this important sense crossclaims, though permissive, are fundamentally different from permissive counterclaims, which may arise from a transaction or occurrence that is different from the one pleaded in the original action. The standard for "same transaction or occurrence" varies from court to court. The most liberal interpretation requires a logical relation between the crossclaim and the original action.[64] Other courts look to the degree of overlap between the evidence to be used in the crossclaim and the evidence relevant to the original action.[65]

Crossclaims Against Coparties

Rule 13(g) provides that crossclaims may be brought only if at least one crossclaim defendant is a person already party to an action.[66] There is some uncertainty, however, as to whether the crossclaim defendant must be a coparty or whether the crossclaim defendant need only be a party who is not on a side of the case that is in opposition to the crossclaim plaintiff.[67]

Comparison With Impleader

A key difference between Rule 13(g) and Rule 14 impleader

---

[62] *See, e.g., U.S. v. Confederate Acres Sanitary Sewage and Drainage System, Inc.*, 935 F.2d 796, 799 (6th Cir. 1991).

[63] *See, e.g., Federal Land Bank of St. Louis v. Cupples Bro.*, 116 F.R.D. 63, 65 (E.D. Ark. 1987).

[64] *See, e.g., Seattle Audubon Soc. v. Lyons*, 871 F. Supp. 1286, 1290 (W.D. Wash. 1994).

[65] *See, e.g., Danner v. Anskis*, 256 F.2d 123 (3d Cir.1958).

[66] *See, e.g., In re Oil Spill by Amoco Cadiz off Coast of France on March 16, 1978*, 699 F.2d 909, 913 (7th Cir. 1983).

[67] *See, e.g., Luyser v. Textron, Inc.*, 266 F.R.D. 54 (S.D.N.Y. 2010) (explaining split and collecting diverging opinions).

is that Rule 13(g) requires that at least one crossclaim defendant already be a party. Rule 14, by contrast, provides a means of joining persons who were not previously parties to a pending suit.[68] Additionally, Rule 14 requires a claim asserting that the third-party defendant is liable, in whole or in part, for the liabilities asserted against the third-party plaintiff (sometimes called "derivative liability" or contribution). Rule 13(g) requires only that the crossclaim arise out of the same transaction or occurrence; the liability asserted need not be derivative.

Affirmative Relief or Derivative Liability

A crossclaimant may seek either affirmative relief or contribution toward liability the crossclaimant may have as a result of claims already filed against the crossclaimant.

Additional Rule 18 Claims

Once a party has asserted one crossclaim that qualifies under Rule 13(g)—a claim that is transactionally related—the party may then assert any other claims it has against the crossclaim defendant, even if entirely unrelated, under Rule 18(a).

Subject-Matter Jurisdiction

Crossclaims must satisfy some form of subject-matter jurisdiction. Moreover, the party asserting a counterclaim must include allegations demonstrating subject-matter jurisdiction.[69] However, subject-matter jurisdiction is usually not a problem with crossclaims; because Rule 13(g) requires that crossclaims arise out of the same transaction or occurrence as the original action, crossclaims will usually satisfy the "same case or controversy" requirement for supplemental jurisdiction.[70] Additional claims joined pursuant to Rule 18(a) might not, though—such claims will need a form of original subject-matter jurisdiction, such as diversity or federal question jurisdiction.

Personal Jurisdiction

Crossclaims must meet the requirements of personal jurisdiction. If the court in the original action has already acquired personal jurisdiction over the parties, it will normally also have jurisdiction over the parties for purposes of a crossclaim. If, however, jurisdiction is defective in the original action, it is possible that the crossclaim will suffer from similar jurisdictional defects.

---

[68] *See, e.g., Ambraco, Inc. v. Bossclip B.V.*, 570 F.3d 233, 242 (5th Cir. 2009) (claim properly brought under Rule 14 impleader rather than Rule 13(g) when crossclaimant had been dismissed as a party to the underlying suit before crossclaim under Rule 13(g) had been asserted).

[69] *McNutt v. General Motors Acceptance Corp. of Indiana*, 298 U.S. 178, 189 (1936).

[70] *See, e.g., Ryan ex rel. Ryan v. Schneider Nat. Carriers, Inc.*, 263 F.3d 816, 819, (8th Cir. 2001).

Venue

Crossclaims need not satisfy venue requirements.[71]

Mislabeled Crossclaims

Parties sometimes mistakenly identify crossclaims as counterclaims, and *vice versa*. Courts usually attach no significance to such errors, unless they somehow unfairly prejudice an opposing party.[72]

Statutes of Limitations

Crossclaims seeking "affirmative and independent relief" generally do not relate back to the original complaint—and thus are evaluated under the applicable statute of limitations base on the date the crossclaim was filed. By contrast, crossclaims "in the nature of recoupment, indemnity, or contribution" will typically enjoy the benefit of relation back to the date of the filing of the original action.[73]

RULE 13(h)—JOINING ADDITIONAL PARTIES

CORE CONCEPT

Rule 13(h) provides that, if it is desirable or necessary to add an additional nonparty to a counterclaim or crossclaims, Rules 19 and 20, governing joinder of persons, apply.

APPLICATIONS

Procedure

Although the law is not entirely settled, it appears that when counterclaimants or crossclaimants seek to join additional parties under Rule 13(h), they may simply name the new parties in their pleadings and then make appropriate service on the parties to be joined; there appears to be no need to file a motion requesting leave to join the parties.[74]

Prerequisite of One Party

Rule 13(a), (b), and (g) provide that counterclaims and crossclaims cannot brought unless at least one person defending the claim is already a party to the action. However, once one such person is named in a counterclaim or crossclaim, Rule 13(h) permits joinder of other persons on that counterclaim or

---

[71] *See, e.g., Bredberg v. Long*, 778 F.2d 1285, 1288 (8th Cir. 1985).

[72] *See, e.g., Schwab v. Erie Lackawanna R. Co.*, 438 F.2d 62, 64 (3d Cir. 1971).

[73] *See, e.g., Kansa Reinsurance Co., Ltd. v. Congressional Mortg. Corp. of Texas*, 20 F.3d 1362, 1367–68 (5th Cir. 1994).

[74] *See, e.g., Northfield Ins. Co. v. Bender Shipbuilding & Repair Co., Inc.*, 122 F.R.D. 30 (S.D. Ala. 1988) (1966 amendment to Rule 13(h) eliminated requirement to obtain judicial approval for joinder); *but see Mountain States Sports, Inc. v. Sharman*, 353 F. Supp. 613, 618 (D. Utah 1972), aff'd, 548 F.2d 905 (10th Cir. 1977) (general practice is to seek an order joining additional parties).

crosssclaim, subject to the authority of Rules 19 and 20.[75]

Subject-Matter Jurisdiction

Rule 13(h) claims must satisfy one form of subject-matter jurisdiction.[76]

(1) *Claims by Original Plaintiff*: If the counterclaim or crossclaim is part of a case based solely on diversity of citizenship, and was filed by someone who was a plaintiff on the original claim, supplemental jurisdiction is not available as to new parties joined under either Rule 19 or Rule 20.[77]

Personal Jurisdiction

Additional parties may be joined under Rule 13(h) only if they are subject to the personal jurisdiction of the court.[78]

Venue

Venue requirements do not apply to counterclaims or crossclaims in which Rule 13(h) joinder is sought.[79]

RULE 13(i)—SEPARATE TRIALS; SEPARATE JUDGMENTS

CORE CONCEPT

Because additional claims added to a case through Rule 13(a), (b), and (g) have substantial potential for confusing the trier of fact or delaying adjudication of the original claims, Rule 13(i) authorizes the court to hold separate hearings, as provided by Rule 42(b), and/or enter separate judgments, as provided by Rule 54(b).

APPLICATIONS

Judicial Discretion

Courts have substantial discretion to order separate trials and enter separate judgments.[80]

Additional Research References

Wright & Miller, *Federal Practice and Procedure* §§ 1401 to 37
C.J.S., Federal Civil Procedure §§ 309 to 319 et seq.
West's Key Number Digest, Federal Civil Procedure ⚷771 to 786

---

[75] *See, e.g., Asset Allocation and Management Co. v. Western Employers Ins. Co.*, 892 F.2d 566, 574 (7th Cir. 1989) (noting interplay of Rules 13(h) and 20).

[76] *Federal Deposit Ins. Corp. v. La Rambla Shopping Center, Inc.*, 791 F.2d 215, 220 (1st Cir. 1986); *Rayman v. Peoples Sav. Corp.*, 735 F. Supp. 842, 854 (N.D. Ill. 1990).

[77] 28 U.S.C.A. § 1367(b).

[78] *See, e.g., Cordner v. Metropolitan Life Ins. Co.*, 234 F. Supp. 765, 769 (S.D.N.Y. 1964).

[79] *See, e.g., Schoot v. United States*, 664 F. Supp. 293, 296 (N.D. Ill. 1987).

[80] *See, e.g., McLaughlin v. State Farm Mut. Auto. Ins. Co.*, 30 F.3d 861, 870 (7th Cir. 1994).

RULE 14
THIRD-PARTY PRACTICE

(a) When a Defending Party May Bring in a Third Party.

(1) *Timing of the Summons and Complaint.* A defending party may, as third-party plaintiff, serve a summons and complaint on a nonparty who is or may be liable to it for all or part of the claim against it. But the third-party plaintiff must, by motion, obtain the court's leave if it files the third-party complaint more than 14 days after serving its original answer.

(2) *Third-Party Defendant's Claims and Defenses.* The person served with the summons and third-party complaint—the "third-party defendant":

(A) must assert any defense against the third-party plaintiff's claim under Rule 12;

(B) must assert any counterclaim against the third-party plaintiff under Rule 13(a), and may assert any counterclaim against the third-party plaintiff under Rule 13(b) or any crossclaim against another third-party defendant under Rule 13(g);

(C) may assert against the plaintiff any defense that the third-party plaintiff has to the plaintiff's claim; and

(D) may also assert against the plaintiff any claim arising out of the transaction or occurrence that is the subject matter of the plaintiff's claim against the third-party plaintiff.

(3) *Plaintiff's Claims Against a Third-Party Defendant.* The plaintiff may assert against the third-party defendant any claim arising out of the transaction or occurrence that is the subject matter of the plaintiff's claim against the third-party plaintiff. The third-party defendant must then assert any defense under Rule 12 and any counterclaim under Rule 13(a), and may assert any counterclaim under Rule 13(b) or any cross-

claim under Rule 13(g).

(4) *Motion to Strike, Sever, or Try Separately.* Any party may move to strike the third-party claim, to sever it, or to try it separately.

(5) *Third-Party Defendant's Claim Against a Nonparty.* A third-party defendant may proceed under this rule against a nonparty who is or may be liable to the third-party defendant for all or part of any claim against it.

(6) *Third-Party Complaint In Rem.* If it is within the admiralty or maritime jurisdiction, a third-party complaint may be in rem. In that event, a reference in this rule to the "summons" includes the warrant of arrest, and a reference to the defendant or third-party plaintiff includes, when appropriate, a person who asserts a right under Supplemental Rule C(6)(a)(i) in the property arrested.

(b) When a Plaintiff May Bring in a Third Party. When a claim is asserted against a plaintiff, the plaintiff may bring in a third party if this rule would allow a defendant to do so.

(c) Admiralty or Maritime Claim.

(1) *Scope of Impleader.* If a plaintiff asserts an admiralty or maritime claim under Rule 9(h), the defendant or a person who asserts a right under Supplemental Rule C(6)(a)(i) may, as a third-party plaintiff, bring in a third-party defendant who may be wholly or partly liable—either to the plaintiff or to the third-party plaintiff—for remedy over, contribution, or otherwise on account of the same transaction, occurrence, or series of transactions or occurrences.

(2) *Defending Against a Demand for Judgment for the Plaintiff.* The third-party plaintiff may demand judgment in the plaintiff's favor against the third-party defendant. In that event, the third-party defendant must defend under Rule 12 against the plaintiff's claim as well as the third-party plaintiff's claim; and the action proceeds as if the plaintiff had sued both the third-party defendant and the third-party

plaintiff.

[Amended effective March 19, 1948; July 1, 1963; July 1, 1966; August 1, 1987; April 17, 2000, effective December 1, 2000; April 12, 2006, effective December 1, 2006; April 30, 2007, effective December 1, 2007; March 26, 2009, effective December 1, 2009.]

AUTHORS' COMMENTARY ON RULE 14

PURPOSE AND SCOPE

Rule 14 permits defendants to join other persons, not yet parties, who may be obligated to reimburse the defendant for some or all of that party's liability. The decision to seek joinder, or to hold the claim for assertion in later litigation, belongs to the party defending on the claim: Rule 14 contains no requirement similar to Rule 13(a), which makes compulsory the assertion of certain counterclaims. One common situation for using Rule 14 impleader is when a nonparty, as a guarantor of some transaction, has an obligation to indemnify a party if the party is forced to pay on a claim. Third-party practice is also commonly employed when the plaintiff names some, but not all, of the potential tortfeasors in the complaint, and one of the named defendants seeks contribution from one of the unnamed tortfeasors. Rule 14 also describes the rights of persons who are joined as third-party defendants to claim and defend against the original plaintiffs and defendants, as well as to join still other persons who may be liable to the third parties.

NOTE: The labels necessitated by Rule 14 are superficially complex, but follow a consistent pattern. A party who seeks to join another person under Rule 14 is called a third-party plaintiff. The person joined is called a third-party defendant. Thus, if a defendant in a pending action sought to join someone not yet a party under Rule 14, the defendant would carry the additional title of third-party plaintiff, and the person joined would be a third-party defendant. If the third-party defendant sought, in turn, to join someone else, the person joined would be a fourth-party defendant, and the third-party defendant would carry the additional title of fourth-party plaintiff.

RULE 14(a)—A DEFENDING PARTY MAY BRING IN THIRD PARTY

CORE CONCEPT

Rule 14(a) describes the power of defendants to implead third parties. The Rule also describes the defenses available to third-party defendants, as well as the circumstances in which third-party defendants may claim against plaintiffs and defendants.

Finally, Rule 14(a) authorizes third-party defendants to implead potential fourth-party defendants who may be liable for some or all of any claim the third-party defendants might have to pay.

APPLICATIONS

Purpose

The purpose of Rule 14 is to permit additional parties whose rights may be affected by the decision in the original action to be joined so as to expedite the final determination of the rights and liabilities of all the interested parties in one suit.[1] District courts should allow impleader on any colorable claim of derivative liability that will not unduly delay, complicate, or prejudice the proceedings.[2]

Third-Party Plaintiff's Discretion

A party's right to implead under Rule 14 is optional; there is no obligation to implead third parties.[3]

Who May Be Impleaded

Only persons not already parties may be impleaded.[4] This provision of Rule 14 stands in contrast to provisions of Rule 13, governing counterclaims and crossclaims, in which at least one of the persons sued on a counterclaim or crossclaim must already be a party to the case.

Procedure

A third-party defendant is joined upon service of a summons and third-party complaint.[5] For purposes of impleader under Rule 14, Rule 4(k) permits service on a third-party defendant found within 100 miles of the place from where the summons issued-without regard to whether such service takes place within another state.[6] This is a small but sometimes crucial expansion of personal jurisdiction in the context of Rule 14.

Time: Leave of Court

Rule 14(a) permits service of a third-party complaint "at any time." However, a party may file a third-party complaint without obtaining leave of court only in the fourteen-day period

---

[1] *See, e.g., American Zurich Ins. Co. v. Cooper Tire & Rubber Co.*, 512 F.3d 800, 805 (6th Cir. 2008). *See also Arch Ins. Co. v. Harleysville Worcester Ins. Co.*, 56 F. Supp. 3d 576, 583 (S.D.N.Y. 2014) (Rule 14 is a rule of judicial economy).

[2] *Marolda v. Tisbury Towing & Transportation Co.*, 518 F. Supp. 3d 544, 548 (D. Mass. 2021).

[3] *See, e.g., Fernandez v. Corporacion Insular De Seguros*, 79 F.3d 207 (1st Cir.1996).

[4] *See, e.g., Cutting Underwater Technologies USA, Inc. v. Eni U.S. Operating Co.*, 671 F.3d 512, 514, n.2 (5th Cir. 2012); *Mauney v. Imperial Delivery Services, Inc.*, 865 F. Supp. 142, 153 (S.D. N.Y. 1994).

[5] *See, e.g., Jackson v. Southeastern Pennsylvania Transp. Authority*, 727 F. Supp. 965, 966 (E.D. Pa. 1990).

[6] Rule 4(k).

following that party's service of an answer to a claim,[7] or by such other deadline established by the court. Thereafter, a third-party complaint may be filed only upon motion, served on all parties, and after obtaining leave of court.[8] Numerous factors guide the court's discretion to grant a request to file a third-party complaint: (1) potential prejudice to existing parties; (2) whether the impleader will add new issues that may complicate the case or delay trial; (3) whether there was unreasonable delay in filing the third party complaint; and (4) whether the third party complaint fails to state a claim.[9] Generally, courts permit assertion of impleader claims unless they are raised so late in a pending suit that they unreasonably prejudice persons who are already parties.[10]

Derivative Liability

Rule 14(a) explicitly provides that claims against third-party defendants must be derivative of claims pending against the third-party plaintiff—the third-party plaintiff must assert that the third-party defendant is liable for some or all of the liability asserted against the third-party plaintiff.[11] Rule 14(a) provides no authorization to assert claims against third-party plaintiffs that not are derivative of claims already pending.[12] It is not enough that the third-party claim simply arises from the same transaction or occurrence as the original claim; rather, the nonparty's liability must be in the nature of contribution to the third-party plaintiff's liability.[13] The third-party claim need not have accrued in order for a third-party plaintiff to seek indemnification; a third-party plaintiff need not wait until it has been found liable to implead a third-party defendant.[14] If the claims in the original, underlying action are settled, a court may dismiss the Rule 14 claim.[15]

Affirmative Relief from a Third-Party Defendant; Rule 18

Once a defendant/third-party plaintiff has properly im-

[7]*See, e.g., Smith v. Local 819 I.B.T. Pension Plan*, 291 F.3d 236 (2d Cir. 2002).

[8]*See, e.g., Raytheon Aircraft Credit Corp. v. Pal Air Intern., Inc.*, 923 F. Supp. 1408 (D. Kan. 1996).

[9]*Millers Cap. Ins., Co. v. Hydrofarm, Inc.*, 340 F.R.D. 198, 210 (D.D.C. 2022).

[10]*See, e.g., Lexington Insurance Co. v. S.H.R.M. Catering Services, Inc.*, 567 F.3d 182, 187 (5th Cir. 2009); *Marseilles Hydro Power, LLC v. Marseilles Land and Water Co.*, 299 F.3d 643, 650 (7th Cir. 2002).

[11]*See, e.g., Watson v. Cartee*, 817 F.3d 299 (6th Cir. 2016).

[12]*See, e.g., American Zurich Ins. Co. v. Cooper Tire & Rubber Co.*, 512 F.3d 800, 805 (6th Cir. 2008); *Cordova v. FedEx Ground Package Systems, Inc.*, 104 F. Supp. 3d 1119 (D. Or. 2015).

[13]*Produce Pay, Inc. v. Agrosale, Inc.*, 533 F. Supp. 3d 1140, 1144 (S.D. Fla. 2021).

[14]*Millers Cap. Ins., Co. v. Hydrofarm, Inc.*, 340 F.R.D. 198, 213 (D.D.C. 2022).

[15]*American Zurich Ins. Co. v. Cooper Tire & Rubber Co.*, 512 F.3d 800, 805–06 (6th Cir. 2008).

pleaded a third-party defendant under Rule 14 by asserting a claim seeking derivative liability, the third-party plaintiff may then assert any other claims it has against the third-party defendant—even claims completely unrelated to the claims in the original complaint—under Rule 18.[16] If the Rule 18 claims do not relate to the claims in the original complaint, however, they would not qualify for supplemental jurisdiction and would therefore need their own basis of federal subject-matter jurisdiction.

Defenses Available

Third-party defendants are entitled to raise their own defenses against the third-party plaintiff.[17] The explicit language of Rule 14(a) also authorizes third-party defendants to assert defenses that the third-party plaintiff may have against the original claim.[18] A third-party defendant asserts its defenses by pleading them in its answer or in a motion to dismiss.[19]

Counterclaims by Third-Party Defendants

Rule 14(a) authorizes third-party defendants to file claims against third-party plaintiffs,[20] consistent with the requirements of Rule 13. Applying Rule 13 to such claims means that, when the counterclaims satisfy the requirements of Rule 13(a), governing compulsory counterclaims, they must be filed in the pending action or they are waived.

Crossclaims by Third-Party Defendants

If more than one third-party defendant has been impleaded, Rule 14(a) authorizes the third-party defendants to file claims against one another, subject to the requirements of Rule 13(g). Because Rule 13(g) is permissive, such claims may be filed or may be retained for subsequent litigation. Additionally, because Rule 13(g) only permits crossclaims that arise out of the same transaction or occurrence as the original claims, third-party claims must relate to the transaction or occurrence underlying the original claims by the third-party plaintiff.

Claims Against Plaintiffs

Rule 14(a) permits a third-party defendant to make claims

[16]*See King Fisher Marine Serv., Inc. v. 21st Phoenix Corp.*, 893 F.2d 1155, 1166 (10th Cir. 1990); *Federalpha Steel LLC Creditors' Tr. v. Fed. Pipe & Steel Corp.*, 245 F.R.D. 615, 619 (N.D. Ill. 2007).

[17]*See, e.g., Coons v. Industrial Knife Co.*, 620 F.3d 38, 43 (1st Cir. 2010).

[18]Fed.R.Civ.P. 14(a); *Tonge v. Doctors' Ctr. Hosp.*, 531 F. Supp. 3d 491, 505 (D.P.R. 2021) (third-party plaintiff cannot file a third-party complaint against alleged joint tortfeasors if original plaintiff's claims against such third-party defendant is time barred).

[19]*See Tonge v. Doctors' Ctr. Hosp.*, 531 F. Supp. 3d 491, 498 (D.P.R. 2021).

[20]*Cf., Thomas v. Barton Lodge II, Ltd.*, 174 F.3d 636 (5th Cir. 1999) (observing that some courts prohibit third-party defendants' suits against original defendants who are not third-party plaintiffs; concluding that such prohibitions are erroneous, and permitting such claims).

against an original plaintiff that arise out of the same transaction or occurrence as the claims originally filed by the plaintiff. Such claims are permissive, in that they may either be raised or retained for subsequent litigation. Note, however, that if an original plaintiff has already sued the third-party defendant in the litigation, the third-party defendant's claims against the plaintiff may be compulsory counterclaims subject to Rule 13(a). In such a circumstance, a third-party defendant's claims against a plaintiff are not permissive.

Plaintiffs' Claims Against Third-Party Defendants

Rule 14(a) also permits plaintiffs to sue persons joined as third-party defendants, provided that the claim arises out of the same transaction or occurrence as the original claims against the defendants.[21] The language of Rule 14(a) makes clear that assertion of such claims is discretionary, and a plaintiff may choose to retain the claims for subsequent litigation.[22]

Third-Party Defendants' Counterclaims Against Plaintiffs

If a plaintiff sues a third-party defendant, any counterclaims the third-party defendant may have are governed by Rule 13.

Third-Party Defendants' Crossclaims Upon Suit by Plaintiffs

Just as Rule 14(a) permits third-party defendants to crossclaim against one another after being joined by a third-party plaintiff, the Rule also permits third-party defendants to crossclaim against one another if one or more third-party defendants is sued by a plaintiff. Rule 14(a) expressly provides that such crossclaims are regulated by Rule 13.

Third-Party Counterclaim Defendant Not Entitled to Remove

Although original defendants may have a right to remove cases based on the claims in the complaint, they cannot remove cases based on counterclaims asserted against them by third-party defendants.[23]

Severance; Separate Trials

Third-party practice has obvious potential for complexity and for confusing a trier of fact. Rule 14(a) therefore provides that *any* party to the litigation may move to strike or sever the claims. Courts have substantial discretion when deciding such

[21] *U.S. ex rel. S. Prawer and Co. v. Fleet Bank of Maine*, 24 F.3d 320, 328 (1st Cir. 1994).

[22] *See, e.g., Luera v. M/V Alberta*, 635 F.3d 181, 185 n.3 (5th Cir. 2011); *Atchison, Topeka and Santa Fe Ry. Co. v. Hercules Inc.*, 146 F.3d 1071, 1073 (9th Cir. 1998).

[23] *Home Depot U.S.A., Inc. v. Jackson*, — U.S. —, 139 S. Ct. 1743, 1747–48 (2019).

motions.[24] Courts weigh numerous factors in determining whether third-party claims should be severed.[25]

Fourth-Party Practice

Rule 14(a) grants third-party defendants the same power to implead as is enjoyed by the defendants. Thus, third-party defendants may join persons not yet parties who may be liable to the third-party defendants for part or all of the liability the third-party defendants may have to the third-party plaintiffs.

Rights of Fourth-Party Defendants

Although not explicitly addressed in Rule 14(a), it seems settled that fourth-party defendants enjoy all the rights and authority the Rule provides to third-party defendants, including availability of defenses, counterclaims, crossclaims, and impleader of additional persons.[26]

Admiralty and Maritime Cases; In Rem Jurisdiction

Rule 14(a) provides that third-party complaints arising under the admiralty jurisdiction of the court may be in rem actions against maritime property. In such cases, the summons used in conventional litigation may be supplanted by admiralty process, and the terminology for third-party plaintiffs and defendants may conform to admiralty practice.

Subject-Matter Jurisdiction

Every third-party claim must fall within the court's subject-matter jurisdiction. Because third-party claims of necessity are closely related to the original claims between the plaintiff and defendant, subject-matter jurisdiction can usually be obtained under supplemental jurisdiction.[27] However, an important exception to that generalization exists for claims asserted by original plaintiffs against third-party defendants. 28 U.S.C.A. § 1367(b), governing restrictions on supplemental jurisdiction, provides that when the original claims in the case are based solely on diversity jurisdiction, suits by plaintiffs against persons made parties under Rule 14 may not be founded on supplemental jurisdiction[28] (as discussed in more detail in the General Concepts section in Part II).

---

[24]*See, e.g., United States v. Cacace*, 796 F.3d 176 (2d Cir. 2015); *First Nat. Bank of Nocona v. Duncan Sav. and Loan Ass'n*, 957 F.2d 775, 777 (10th Cir. 1992).

[25]*See United States v. Cacace*, 796 F.3d 176 (2d Cir. 2015); *Oklahoma ex rel. Edmondson v. Tyson Foods, Inc.*, 237 F.R.D. 679, 681 (N.D. Okla. 2006) (listing factors).

[26]*See, e.g., Garnay, Inc. v. M/V Lindo Maersk*, 816 F. Supp. 888 (S.D. N.Y. 1993).

[27]*See, e.g., Watson v. Cartee*, 817 F.3d 299 (6th Cir. 2016); *Kemper/Prime Indus. Partners v. Montgomery Watson Americas, Inc.*, 487 F.3d 1061, 1063 (7th Cir. 2007).

[28]*See, e.g., State Nat. Ins. Co. Inc. v. Yates*, 391 F.3d 577, 579 (5th Cir. 2004); *Grimes v. Mazda North American Operations*, 355 F.3d 566, 572 (6th Cir. 2004).

Personal Jurisdiction; Service of Process

Every third-party claim must also satisfy requirements of personal jurisdiction.[29] For service of process on parties joined under Rule 14, a special provision in Rule 4(k)(1)(B) provides a sometimes useful extension of normal limits on service to include service anywhere within 100 miles of the place where the summons is issued.[30]

Venue

Requirements of venue do not apply to claims asserted under Rule 14.[31]

RULE 14(b)—WHEN A PLAINTIFF MAY BRING IN A THIRD PARTY

CORE CONCEPT

If a plaintiff is the subject of a counterclaim, the plaintiff may join third parties who may be liable for part or all of that claim, in the same manner that Rule 14(a) authorizes defendants to join third parties.

APPLICATIONS

Counterclaim Prerequisite

A plaintiff may not join persons under Rule 14 until a counterclaim has been asserted against the plaintiff, and the plaintiff must assert that the third-party defendants are liable for some or all of the plaintiff's liability under the counterclaim.[32]

Applicability of Rule 14(a) to Plaintiff's Third-Party Claims

If a plaintiff files a third-party complaint after having been served with a counterclaim, all of the procedures in Rule 14(a) apply.[33]

Subject-Matter Jurisdiction: Restraints on Supplemental Jurisdiction

A Rule 14(b) claim must fall within the court's subject-matter jurisdiction. Although Rule 14(b) claims will often qualify for supplemental jurisdiction, an important exception applies to Rule 14(b) claims: 28 U.S.C.A. § 1367(b) provides that when the original claims in the case are based solely on diversity jurisdiction, suits by plaintiffs against persons made parties under Rule 14 may not be founded on supplemental

---

[29] *See, e.g., Rodd v. Region Const. Co.*, 783 F.2d 89 (7th Cir. 1986).

[30] *See, e.g., ESAB Group, Inc. v. Centricut, Inc.*, 126 F.3d 617, 622 (4th Cir. 1997).

[31] *See, e.g., Gundle Lining Const. Corp. v. Adams County Asphalt, Inc.*, 85 F.3d 201 (5th Cir. 1996).

[32] *See, e.g., International Fidelity Ins. Co. v. Sweet Little Mexico Corp.*, 665 F.3d 671, 675 (5th Cir. 2011).

[33] *See, e.g., Powell, Inc. v. Abney*, 83 F.R.D. 482, 485 (S.D. Tex. 1979).

jurisdiction[34] (as discussed in more detail in the General Concepts section in Part II).

Personal Jurisdiction

A plaintiff's third-party claims must satisfy requirements of personal jurisdiction.

RULE 14(c)—ADMIRALTY OR MARITIME CLAIM

CORE CONCEPT

When the original cause of action arises under the court's admiralty jurisdiction, the defendant may join third persons by alleging either that: they are liable to reimburse the defendant for some or all of the defendant's liability, or that the third persons are liable directly to the plaintiff.[35] This expands the general practice of impleader under Rule 14(a), where a defendant may implead only to establish that the person joined is liable to the defendant, and may not implead by alleging that the person to be joined is liable directly to the plaintiff.[36] The practical result of this feature of Rule 14(c) is that the third person becomes a co-defendant in the original action, rather than a third-party defendant.[37]

APPLICATIONS

Demand for Judgment

In order to designate an impleaded third-party defendant as a defendant to the plaintiff's original complaint, the literal language of Rule 14(c) appears to require that the third-party complaint "demand judgment against the third-party defendant in favor of the plaintiff." While there is some authority indicating that the third-party complaint must specifically demand judgment in that precise way, the greater weight of authority is that the requirement of Rule 14(c) should be liberally construed. Thus, clear language intending to implead third-party defendants as co-defendants to the original complaint satisfies the requirement of Rule 14(c).[38]

Applicability of Rule 14(a)

Beyond the special provision of Rule 14(c) that may make the third party a co-defendant, Rule 14(c) impleader actions

---

[34] *See, e.g., State Nat. Ins. Co. Inc. v. Yates*, 391 F.3d 577, 579 (5th Cir. 2004); *Grimes v. Mazda North American Operations*, 355 F.3d 566, 572 (6th Cir. 2004).

[35] *Afunday Charters, Inc. v. ABC Ins. Co.*, 997 F.3d 390, 392 (1st Cir. 2021).

[36] *See, e.g., Duval v. Northern Assur. Co. of America*, 722 F.3d 300, 305–06 (5th Cir. 2013); *Spring City Corp. v. American Bldgs. Co.*, 193 F.3d 165, 169 (3d Cir. 1999).

[37] *See, e.g., Afunday Charters, Inc. v. ABC Ins. Co.*, 997 F.3d 390, 391 (1st Cir. 2021); *Mike Hooks Dredging Co., Inc. v. Marquette Transp. Gulf-Inland, L.L.C.*, 716 F.3d 886, 894–95 (5th Cir. 2013).

[38] *See, e.g., Royal Ins. Co. of America v. Southwest Marine*, 194 F.3d 1009, 1018 (9th Cir. 1999) (collecting cases).

generally proceed under the relevant provisions of Rule 14(a).[39]

Prerequisite of Rule 9(h)

Rule 14(c) is available only when the original plaintiff has asserted a claim "within the meaning of Rule 9(h)."[40] A claim is deemed to have been brought in admiralty under Rule 9(h) if it is *only* cognizable within the court's admiralty jurisdiction, regardless of whether the plaintiff has designated it as an admiralty claim.[41]

Subject-Matter Jurisdiction

Persons impleaded under Rule 14(c) will generally be subject to the admiralty jurisdiction of the court.[42]

Personal Jurisdiction

Persons impleaded under Rule 14(c) must be within either the personal jurisdiction, quasi in rem jurisdiction, or in rem jurisdiction of the court. Because in rem jurisdiction is generally available in admiralty practice, however, jurisdictional requirements may usually be satisfied without difficulty.

Venue

Venue requirements do not generally apply to claims asserted under Rule 14.[43]

Additional Research References

Wright & Miller, *Federal Practice and Procedure* §§ 1441 to 65
C.J.S., Federal Civil Procedure §§ 117 to 126 et seq., § 318
West's Key Number Digest, Federal Civil Procedure ⚷281 to 297

---

[39] *See, e.g., Rosario v. American Export-Isbrandtsen Lines, Inc.*, 531 F.2d 1227, 1231–32 (3d Cir. 1976), (noting that apart from special provision, Rule 14(c) does not operate exclusive of Rule 14(a)).

[40] *See, e.g., Ambraco, Inc. v. Bossclip B.V.*, 570 F.3d 233, 243 (5th Cir. 2009); *Vargas v. APL Ltd.*, — F. Supp. 3d —, 2022 WL 757082, at *5 (E.D.N.Y. 2022).

[41] *Marolda v. Tisbury Towing & Transportation Co.*, 518 F. Supp. 3d 544, 549 (D. Mass. 2021).

[42] *See, e.g., Harrison v. Glendel Drilling Co.*, 679 F. Supp. 1413, 1417 (W.D. La. 1988).

[43] *See, e.g., Gundle Lining Const. Corp. v. Adams County Asphalt, Inc.*, 85 F.3d 201, 209 (5th Cir. 1996).

RULE 15
AMENDED AND SUPPLEMENTAL PLEADINGS

(a) Amendments Before Trial.

(1) *Amending as a Matter of Course.* A party may amend its pleading once as a matter of course within:

(A) 21 days after serving it, or

(B) if the pleading is one to which a responsive pleading is required, 21 days after service of a responsive pleading or 21 days after service of a motion under Rule 12(b), (e), or (f), whichever is earlier.

(2) *Other Amendments.* In all other cases, a party may amend its pleading only with the opposing party's written consent or the court's leave. The court should freely give leave when justice so requires.

(3) *Time to Respond.* Unless the court orders otherwise, any required response to an amended pleading must be made within the time remaining to respond to the original pleading or within 14 days after service of the amended pleading, whichever is later.

(b) Amendments During and After Trial.

(1) *Based on an Objection at Trial.* If, at trial, a party objects that evidence is not within the issues raised in the pleadings, the court may permit the pleadings to be amended. The court should freely permit an amendment when doing so will aid in presenting the merits and the objecting party fails to satisfy the court that the evidence would prejudice that party's action or defense on the merits. The court may grant a continuance to enable the objecting party to meet the evidence.

(2) *For Issues Tried by Consent.* When an issue not raised by the pleadings is tried by the parties'

express or implied consent, it must be treated in all respects as if raised in the pleadings. A party may move—at any time, even after judgment—to amend the pleadings to conform them to the evidence and to raise an unpleaded issue. But failure to amend does not affect the result of the trial of that issue.

(c) Relation Back of Amendments.

(1) *When an Amendment Relates Back.* An amendment to a pleading relates back to the date of the original pleading when:

(A) the law that provides the applicable statute of limitations allows relation back;

(B) the amendment asserts a claim or defense that arose out of the conduct, transaction, or occurrence set out—or attempted to be set out—in the original pleading; or

(C) the amendment changes the party or the naming of the party against whom a claim is asserted, if Rule 15(c)(1)(B) is satisfied and if, within the period provided by Rule 4(m) for serving the summons and complaint, the party to be brought in by amendment:

(i) received such notice of the action that it will not be prejudiced in defending on the merits; and

(ii) knew or should have known that the action would have been brought against it, but for a mistake concerning the proper party's identity.

(2) *Notice to the United States.* When the United States or a United States officer or agency is added as a defendant by amendment, the notice requirements of Rule 15(c)(1)(C)(i) and (ii) are satisfied if, during the stated period, process was delivered or mailed to the United States attorney or the United States attorney's designee, to the Attorney General of the United States, or to the officer or agency.

(d) Supplemental Pleadings. On motion and reasonable notice, the court may, on just terms, permit a party to serve a supplemental pleading setting out any transaction, occurrence, or event that happened after the date of the pleading to be supplemented. The court may permit supplementation even though the original pleading is defective in stating a claim or defense. The court may order that the opposing party plead to the supplemental pleading within a specified time.

[Amended January 21, 1963, effective July 1, 1963; February 28, 1966, effective July 1, 1966; March 2, 1987, effective August 1, 1987; April 30, 1991, effective December 1, 1991; amended by Pub.L. 102-198, § 11, December 9, 1991, 105 Stat. 1626; amended April 22, 1993, effective December 1, 1993; April 30, 2007, effective December 1, 2007; March 26, 2009, effective December 1, 2009.]

AUTHORS' COMMENTARY ON RULE 15

PURPOSE AND SCOPE

Rule 15 governs the circumstances in which parties who have already pleaded in a case will be permitted to amend their pleadings. The Rule also addresses whether a claim asserted in an amended pleading will be timely if the statute of limitations has run. Finally, the Rule provides the circumstances in which parties will be allowed to supplement their pleadings to describe events that have occurred since the original pleadings were filed.

RULE 15(a)—AMENDMENTS BEFORE TRIAL

CORE CONCEPT

Rule 15(a)(1) provides an automatic right to amend a pleading a single time within 21 days after serving it. Alternatively, if the pleading is one that requires a responsive pleading, the pleading may be amended of right once within "21 days after service of either a responsive pleading or a motion under Rule 12(b), (e), or (f), whichever is earlier."[1]

If a party's right to amend has lapsed, Rule 15(a)(2) authorizes parties to file a motion seeking leave to amend from the court or to file an amended pleading with written consent from opposing parties.

NOTE: Although an amended pleading might be timely under Rule 15(a), that does not mean the *claims asserted* in the pleading are timely—that issue is controlled. by Rule 15(c).

---

[1] *Vanguard Outdoor, LLC v. City of Los Angeles*, 648 F.3d 737 (9th Cir. 2011).

APPLICATIONS

Amendment of Right

A party may amend a pleading one time[2] without leave of court or consent of opposing parties, under either of two circumstances. First, a pleading may be amended of right if the amendment is filed within 21 days after serving it.[3] Alternatively, if the pleading to be amended requires a responsive pleading, it may be amended of right within 21 days of service of a responsive pleading or 21 days after service of a motion under Rule 12(b), (e), or (f) (whichever is earlier).[4] If timely, a party may use the right to amend the complaint once as a matter of course even if it has previously amended its complaint pursuant to a motion filed under Rule 15(a)(2).[5]

Amendment by Motion

In addition to the right to amend as a matter of course under Rule 15(a)(1), Rule 15(a)(2) authorizes parties to seek leave to amend by motion. Attempts to amend a pleading through some other mechanism, such as by request in a brief, run a high risk of rejection by the district court.[6]

- *Attaching the Proposed Amended Pleading as an Exhibit:* When a party submits a motion to amend, many courts require the party to attach to the motion a copy of the proposed amended pleading, unless the motion adequately describes the contemplated revision.[7] Attaching the proposed amended pleading is a best practice.

Liberal Amendment Policy

Rule 15(a)(2) directs the court to grant leave to amend "when justice so requires." The policy is intended to facilitate resolution on the merits, rather than technical pleading requirements. A district court possesses broad discretion in its decision whether to grant leave to amend a pleading.[8] Generally, leave to amend is granted unless a weighing of several factors suggests that leave would be inappropriate: (1) futility;

---

[2]*See, e.g., Nichols v. Alabama State Bar*, 815 F.3d 726, 733 n.5 (11th Cir. 2016); *Daulatzai v. Maryland*, 338 F.R.D. 587, 589 (D. Md. 2021) (amendment in state court prior to removal counts).

[3]*Hamric v. Wilderness Expeditions, Inc.*, 6 F.4th 1108, 1115 (10th Cir. 2021).

[4]*See Simio, LLC v. FlexSim Software Prod., Inc.*, 983 F.3d 1353, 1366 n.9 (Fed. Cir. 2020); *Savignac v. Jones Day*, 341 F.R.D. 120, 122 (D.D.C. 2022) (Rules 15(a)(1)(A) and (B) are mutually exclusive; under Rule 15(a)(1)(B), "the time to amend begins when the *pleading* is served and ends 21 days after the *response* is served").

[5]*Gilman & Bedigian, LLC v. Sackett*, 337 F.R.D. 113, 115 (D. Md. 2020).

[6]*See, e.g., Crosby v. Twitter, Inc.*, 921 F.3d 617 (6th Cir. 2019); *United States ex rel. Petratos v. Genentech, Inc.*, 855 F.3d 481, 493–94 (3d Cir. 2017).

[7]*See, e.g., U.S. ex rel. Atkins v. McInteer*, 470 F.3d 1350, 1362 (11th Cir. 2006).

[8]*Olivarez v. T-mobile USA, Inc.*, 997 F.3d 595, 602 (5th Cir. 2021).

(2) undue delay; (3) prejudice; or (4) bad faith.[9] In practice, the burden is usually on the party opposing the amendment to demonstrate why the amendment should not be permitted.[10]

- *Prejudice to Opposing Parties:* If leave to amend is denied, it will often occur because an amendment would cause unfair prejudice to another party.[11] Prejudice is most commonly found when there has been substantial unjustified delay in moving to amend that creates an unfair disadvantage for an opposing party.[12] Some courts hold that mere delay in seeking leave to amend, absent a showing of bad faith or undue prejudice, does not provide a basis for a district court to deny leave to amend.[13] However, while Rule 15(a) imposes no time limits on motions for leave to amend pleadings, substantial unexplained and unjustified delays in seeking leave to amend generally reduce the prospects for obtaining leave to amend.[14] By contrast, no unfair prejudice exists simply because a party has to defend against new or better pleaded claims.[15]
- *Futility:* If the claims or defenses in an amended pleading would be legally insufficient—subject to a motion to dismiss or a motion for judgment on the pleadings—the court can deem the amendment "futile" and deny leave to amend on that basis.[16]
- *Repeat Amendments:* A court's normally liberal approach to granting leave to amend may be circumscribed if the pleading has already been the subject of previous amendments.[17]
- *Failure to Attach Proposed Amended Pleading:* A failure to attach the proposed amended pleading to the motion

---

[9] *L. Offs. of David Freydin, P.C. v. Chamara*, 24 F.4th 1122, 1133 (7th Cir. 2022). *Cf., U.S. ex rel. Lee v. SmithKline Beecham, Inc.*, 245 F.3d 1048, 1052 (9th Cir. 2001) (factors do not get equal weight; futility of amendment, by itself, can be ground for denying leave to amend).

[10] *See, e.g., C.F. v. Capistrano Unified School District*, 654 F.3d 975, 985 (9th Cir. 2011) (policy should be applied with " 'extreme liberality' ").

[11] *See, e.g., DLJ Mortg. Cap., Inc. v. Sheridan*, 975 F.3d 358, 369 (3d Cir. 2020); *Kreg Therapeutics, Inc. v. VitalGo, Inc.*, 919 F.3d 405 (7th Cir. 2019) (unforeseeable change in critical legal theory at last minute may be unfair prejudice).

[12] *See, e.g., Jin v. Metropolitan Life Ins. Co.*, 295 F.3d 335 (2d Cir. 2002); *Pittman v. Experian Information Solutions, Inc.*, 901 F.3d 619 (6th Cir. 2018) (burden of showing undue prejudice declines as length of unexplained delay increases).

[13] *Allianz Glob. Invs. GmbH v. Bank of Am. Corp.*, 473 F. Supp. 3d 361 (S.D.N.Y. 2020).

[14] *Krupski v. Costa Crociere, S.p.A.*, 560 U.S. 538, 553 (2010).

[15] *See, e.g., Popp Telcom v. American Sharecom, Inc.*, 210 F.3d 928, 943 (8th Cir. 2000).

[16] *See, e.g., Adhikari v. Kellogg, Brown & Root, Inc.*, 845 F.3d 184 (5th Cir. 2017); *Rodriguez v. United States*, 286 F.3d 972, 980 (7th Cir. 2002).

[17] *See, e.g., Ascon Properties, Inc. v. Mobil Oil Co.*, 866 F.2d 1149, 1160 (9th Cir. 1989).

is reason enough to deny leave to amend.[18]

- *Ability to Cure:* At least some courts hold that where a complaint's deficiency could be cured by an amendment, leave to amend must be given—and where a party has not sought such leave, district courts are expected to notify parties of the opportunity to amend.[19]
- *Civil Rights Cases:* The liberal amendment policy is particularly potent in civil rights cases.[20]
- *Attempts to Add Non-diverse Parties After Removal*: Pursuant to 28 U.S.C.A. § 1447(e), courts must scrutinize a motion to amend that would join non-diverse parties in cases previously removed to federal court.[21] When a claimant amends the complaint as a matter of right under Rule 15(a) to join non-diverse parties who would destroy diversity jurisdiction, some debate exists between district courts as to whether 28 U.S.C.A. § 1447(e) applies or whether a fraudulent joinder analysis applies.[22]

No Sua Sponte Authority to Amend or Duty to Suggest

The court has no authority to enter an amendment sua sponte.[23] Likewise, the court does not have a duty to invite a party to amend a pleading.[24]

No Authority for Nonparties to Seek Amendment

Only parties may amend a pleading; nonparties have no authority to seek an amendment.[25]

Pleadings Only

Rule 15 authorizes the amendment of pleadings only, as defined by Rule 7. Motions are not pleadings, and therefore may not be amended pursuant to Rule 15.

Effect of Amendment on Pending Motions

If an amended pleading is properly entered in the case, it

---

[18] *Far E. Aluminium Works Co. v. Viracon, Inc.*, 27 F.4th 1361, 1367 (8th Cir. 2022); *Axline v. 3M Co.*, 8 F.4th 667, 676 (8th Cir. 2021).

[19] *Shane v. Fauver*, 213 F.3d 113 (3d Cir. 2000). *But see Myles v. U.S.*, 416 F.3d 551 (7th Cir. 2005) (no need for district judge to tell *pro se* plaintiff "he *ought* to amend; even *pro se* litigants are masters of their own complaints. . .. Fomenting litigation is not part of the judicial function.").

[20] *LaSpina v. SEIU Pennsylvania State Council*, 985 F.3d 278, 291 (3d Cir. 2021).

[21] *Sparta Surgical Corp. v. National Association of Securities Dealers, Inc.*, 159 F.3d 1209, 1213 (9th Cir. 2009); *Shargian v. Shargian*, ___ F. Supp. 3d ___, 2022 WL 819732, at *3 (E.D. La. 2022).

[22] *Mayes v. Rapoport*, 198 F.3d 457, 461 (4th Cir. 1999); *McDermott v. CareAllies, Inc.*, 503 F. Supp. 3d 225, 229 (D.N.J. 2020).

[23] *See e.g., Miccosukee Tribe of Indians of Florida v. United States*, 716 F.3d 535, 559 (11th Cir. 2013).

[24] *See, e.g., Gomez v. Wells Fargo Bank, N.A.*, 676 F.3d 655, 665 (8th Cir. 2012).

[25] *United States ex rel. Little v. Triumph Gear Systems, Inc.*, 870 F.3d 1242 (10th Cir. 2017).

has the effect of nullifying motions that were directed at the original pleading; if the moving party wishes to attack the amended pleading, it must file a new motion.[26]

Sequence of Amendments

Typically, if a party seeks to amend a pleading more than once, the party will first try to amend as a matter of course under Rule 15(a)(1). Usually, a party will try to amend pursuant to Rule 15(a)(2) only when amendment of course is unavailable.[27] However, this sequence is not mandatory; where a party first properly amends under Rule 15(a)(2), the party will retain the right to amend once pursuant to Rule 15(a)(1).[28]

Termination of Right to Amend

Many courts hold that once the court has entered an order of final judgment, the parties' ability to amend of right terminates.[29] Thus if the court grants a motion to dismiss, and enters judgment, the dismissed party does not have a right to amend.[30] A party seeking to file an amended complaint post-judgment must first have the judgment vacated or set aside pursuant to Rule 59(e) or 60(b).[31] To amend a pleading after dismissal of a case, a party must first move to reopen the case and then move for leave to amend.[32]

Multiple Opposing Parties

If some opposing parties have already filed responsive pleadings and others have not, courts generally hold that the original pleading may be amended as of right, at least as to those parties who have not yet pleaded.[33]

Relation to Joinder Rules

When a party seeks to amend a complaint under Rule 15(a) to join additional claims or parties, the joinder will not be permitted simply because the requirements of Rule 15 have been met. In addition, the applicable joinder rules must also be

---

[26]*See, e.g., Dykes v. Portfolio Recovery Associates, LLC*, 306 F.R.D. 529, 530 (E.D. Va. 2015).

[27]*See, e.g., Ramirez v. County of San Bernardino*, 806 F.3d 1002, 1007 (9th Cir. 2015).

[28]*See, e.g., Ramirez v. County of San Bernadino*, 806 F.3d 1002, 1007 (9th Cir. 2015).

[29]*See, e.g., Jacobs v. Tempur-Pedic International, Inc.*, 626 F.3d 1327,1344 (11th Cir. 2010). *Cf., Geier v. Missouri Ethics Commission*, 715 F.3d 674, 677 (8th Cir. 2013) (right to amend terminates after case is dismissed, but leave to amend may still be available). *But cf., Tate v. SCR Medical Transportation*, 809 F.3d 343, 346 (7th Cir. 2015) ("serious mistake" if court dismisses case prior to expiration of 21-day period for right to amend).

[30]*See, e.g., Gates v. Syrian Arab Republic*, 646 F.3d 1 (D.C. Cir. 2011).

[31]*Metzler Inv. Gmbh v. Chipotle Mexican Grill, Inc.*, 970 F.3d 133, 142 (2d Cir. 2020).

[32]*Brooks v. Mentor Worldwide LLC*, 985 F.3d 1272 (10th Cir. 2021).

[33]*See, e.g., Williams v. Board of Regents of University System of Georgia*, 441 F.3d 1287, 1296 (11th Cir. 2006).

satisfied.[34]

Relation to Rule 16

If the deadline for amending pleadings in a case management order has expired, the movant must demonstrate good cause to modify the scheduling order under Rule 16(b) before the more liberal standard of Rule 15(a) applies to the district court's decision to grant or deny leave.[35]

Amendments Dismissing Part of an Action: Relation to Rule 41(a)

Courts differ as to the proper procedural mechanism for voluntarily dismissing part of an action. Some courts require a motion to amend pursuant to Rule 15(a).[36] Other courts allow voluntary dismissal of part of an action by notice pursuant to Rule 41.[37]

Motion to Amend Following Rule 56 Motion

If a party seeks to amend a pleading after a motion for summary judgment has been filed, the court will normally take a closer look at the proposed amendment before granting it.[38]

Amendment Following Removal to Comply with Federal Pleading Standards

If a case is removed from state court, it is possible that a party will be ordered under Rule 81(c) to file a repleading that conforms to federal practice. Generally, such a mandated repleading will not deprive a party of a one-time right to amend that may be available under Rule 15(a).[39]

Adverse Party's Consent

If a party's proposed amendment falls outside the time limits described above, a party may still amend without leave of court with the opposing party's consent.[40] When their duties to their own clients are not at issue, attorneys often cooperate in such matters as a matter of professional courtesy, and/or because they recognize that withholding consent will only force

---

[34] *See, e.g., Hinson v. Norwest Financial South Carolina, Inc.*, 239 F.3d 611, 618 (4th Cir. 2001). *But see Bibbs v. Early*, 541 F.3d 267, 275 n.39 (5th Cir. 2008) (if a party seeks to amend a pleading to drop or add parties, Rule 15 takes precedence over Rule 21).

[35] *Olivarez v. T-mobile USA, Inc.*, 997 F.3d 595, 602 (5th Cir. 2021).

[36] *See Dynamic CRM Recruiting Sols., L.L.C. v. UMA Educ., Inc.*, 31 F.4th 914, 924 (5th Cir. 2022); *Perry v. Schumacher Grp. of Louisiana*, 891 F.3d 954, 958 (11th Cir. 2018).

[37] *See Bowers v. National Collegiate Athletic Ass'n*, 346 F.3d 402, 413 (3d Cir. 2003); *Commercial Space Mgmt. Co., Inc. v. Boeing Co., Inc.*, 193 F.3d 1074, 1079 (9th Cir. 1999).

[38] *See, e.g., Parish v. Frazier*, 195 F.3d 761, 764 (5th Cir. 1999); *Squyres v. Heico Companies, L.L.C.*, 782 F.3d 224, 239 (5th Cir. 2015).

[39] *See, e.g., Kuehl v. F.D.I.C.*, 8 F.3d 905, 907 (1st Cir. 1993) (but where party engages in dilatory conduct in meeting Rule 81(c) requirements, Rule 15(a) right to amend may be treated as exhausted).

[40] *See, e.g., American States Ins. Co. v. Dastar Corp.*, 318 F.3d 881, 888 (9th Cir. 2003).

the party trying to amend to seek leave of court. Rule 15(a) requires that consent of other parties be in writing.[41]

Termination of Leave to Amend; Rules 59 and 60

Some courts hold that once a case has been dismissed—with or without prejudice—leave to file subsequent amendments to pleadings lapses.[42] The situation may change if a plaintiff can meet the requirements of Rule 59(e)[43] (governing motions to alter or amend judgments) or Rule 60(b) (governing motions to vacate judgments).[44] Furthermore, some courts treat dismissal without prejudice, by itself, as an opportunity to amend a defective pleading.[45]

Explanation of Denial of Leave to Amend

Failure by the district court to explain its reasons for denying leave to amend may by itself be abuse of the court's discretion, unless the reason for the court's decision is apparent on the record.[46]

Imposition of Costs

As a condition of granting leave to amend, a court may require an amending party to pay the opponent's costs caused by the amendment.[47]

Effect of Amendment

An amended pleading displaces the earlier pleading.[48] If a party filing an amendment wishes to preserve some portions of the original pleading, the party should incorporate those portions by specific reference in the amended pleading or file a supplemental pleading under Rule 15(d).

Responding to Amended Pleadings

Rule 15(a) provides that if the pleading amended is one to which a responsive pleading is appropriate, the opposing party

---

[41]*See, e.g., Minter v. Prime Equipment Co.*, 451 F.3d 1196, 1204 (10th Cir. 2006). *But cf., Mooney v. City of New York*, 219 F.3d 123 (2d Cir. 2000) (plaintiff's response on merits to defense raised on motion rather than by responsive pleading is construed "as an implied grant of leave to amend the answer").

[42]*See, e.g., Feliciano-Hernandez v. Pereira-Castillo*, 663 F.3d 527, 538 (1st Cir. 2011); *Williams v. Citigroup, Inc.*, 659 F.3d 208, 213 (2d Cir. 2011).

[43]*Cf., Leisure Caviar, LLC v. United States Fish & Wildlife Service*, 616 F.3d 612, 616 (6th Cir. 2010) (for post judgment motions to amend, evaluation under Rule 15 or Rule 59(e) is the same).

[44]*See, e.g., Summers v. Earth Island Institute*, 555 U.S. 488, 129 S. Ct. 1142, 1153, 173 L. Ed. 2d 1, 13 (2009).

[45]*Wilcox v. Georgetown Univ.*, 987 F.3d 143, 146 (D.C. Cir. 2021).

[46]*Foman v. Davis*, 371 U.S. 178, 182 (1962). *See also Aatrix Software, Inc. v. Green Shades Software, Inc.*, 882 F.3d 1121, 1126 (Fed. Cir. 2018)

[47]*See, e.g., Van Buskirk v. United Group of Companies, Inc.*, 935 F.3d 49 (2d Cir. 2019).

[48]*See, e.g., In re Wireless Telephone Federal Cost Recovery Fees Litigation*, 396 F.3d 922, 928 (8th Cir. 2005). *See also Rockwell International Corp. v. United States*, 549 U.S. 457 (2007) (voluntarily amended complaint controls determination of jurisdiction).

will have either the time remaining before a response to the unamended version was due, or fourteen days from service of the amended pleading—whichever is longer—to respond.[49] The court has authority to alter those time limits as may be appropriate in the circumstances of the case.[50] Rule 15(a)(3) does not render a prior response to a prior pleading moot, such that a defendant may not be required to file a new answer when the allegations in the amended complaint do not change the scope or theory of the case.[51]

Amendment at or Following Trial: Relationship to Rule 15(b)

Technically, a motion for leave of court to amend a pleading may be made at any time under Rule 15(a). However, if a suit has advanced to trial or post-trial motions, Rule 15(b), pertaining to amendments to conform to the evidence, is probably a more appropriate vehicle for amending the pleadings. However, the difference between Rule 15(a) and (b) is not a bright line, and generally courts are liberal in granting permission for substantive amendments under either provision provided that no unfair prejudice thereby accrues to other parties.[52]

Relationship to Rule 15(c)

The analyses for leave to amend under Rule 15(a) and for "relation back" under Rule 15(c) are independent. A court may deny a motion for leave to amend even if the proposed amendment would, if filed, relate back.[53] Likewise, an amendment may be proper under Rule 15(a) but a new claim in the amended pleading may be untimely under Rule 15(c).

RULE 15(b)—AMENDMENTS DURING AND AFTER TRIAL

CORE CONCEPT

Rule 15(b) permits amendments to pleadings in two circumstances. The first situation arises when an issue not raised in the original pleadings is tried by consent of, or without objection by, the parties.[54] The second occurs when an issue not raised in the pleadings is objected to, but the proposed amendment will either not create unfair prejudice, or such prejudice as may result can be cured by other judicial action. Notwithstanding the reference in Rule 15 to a "trial," pleadings may be deemed amended to

[49]*See, e.g., General Mills, Inc. v. Kraft Foods Global, Inc.*, 495 F.3d 1378, 1379 (Fed. Cir. 2007).

[50]*See also California Public Employees' Retirement System v. Chubb Corp.*, 394 F.3d 126 (3d Cir. 2004).

[51]*KST Data, Inc. v. DXC Tech. Co.*, 980 F.3d 709, 715 (9th Cir. 2020).

[52]*See, e.g., U.S. for Use and Benefit of Seminole Sheet Metal Co. v. SCI, Inc.*, 828 F.2d 671 (11th Cir. 1987).

[53]*Se. Pennsylvania Transportation Auth. v. Orrstown Fin. Servs. Inc.*, 12 F.4th 337, 349 (3d Cir. 2021).

[54]*Cf., Marsh v. Butler County, Ala.*, 268 F.3d 1014, 1024 n.4 (11th Cir. 2001).

conform to the evidence presented at hearings before a district judge.[55]

APPLICATIONS

Timing; Relationship to Rule 15(a)

Motions to amend under Rule 15(b) may theoretically be made at any time. The language of the Rule, however, speaks to matters raised at trial, suggesting that the Rule should not generally be used at earlier stages of litigation.[56] Instead, early in the litigation it is more appropriate to seek to amend a pleading under the authority of Rule 15(a). Generally speaking, motions to amend under Rule 15(b) are made at trial or in the immediate aftermath of a trial.[57] However, some courts apply Rule 15(b) to some pre-trial situations "to address discrepancies."[58]

Rule 15(a) and 15(b) apply a similar presumption in favor of granting leave to amend, absent significant prejudice to the opposing party.[59] Leave to amend will be denied under both sections if amendment would be futile.[60]

Claims for Relief

Rule 15(b) may be employed to assert claims for affirmative relief, even after a trial is ended. Thus, for example, a counterclaim may be asserted through a Rule 15(b) amendment where the evidence on the counterclaim was heard at trial.[61] The purpose of Rule 15(b) is to bring the pleadings in line with issues actually tried.[62]

Failure to Object: Implied Consent

Rule 15(b) provides that an opposing party's consent to an amendment may be express or implied.[63] The issue of implied consent arises in two circumstances: 1) where a new claim is

---

[55] *Gov't Emps. Ret. Sys. of Virgin Islands v. Gov't of Virgin Islands*, 995 F.3d 66, 82 n.11 (3d Cir. 2021).

[56] *See, e.g., Cook v. City of Bella Villa*, 582 F.3d 840, 852 (8th Cir. 2009). *But see Desertrain v. City of Los Angeles*, 754 F.3d 1147, 1154 (9th Cir. 2014) (amendment under Rule 15(b) permissible in motion for summary judgment); *Ahmad v. Furlong*, 435 F.3d 1196, 1203 (10th Cir. 2006) (noting extensive split of authority as to whether Rule 15(b) should be applied to issues raised in a motion for summary judgment on the eve of trial; collecting cites).

[57] *See, e.g., United States v. 5443 Suffield Terrace*, 607 F.3d 504 (7th Cir. 2010). *See also Oneida Indian Nation v. County of Oneida*, 617 F.3d 114, 142 n.3 (2d Cir. 2010).

[58] *See, e.g., Liberty Lincoln-Mercury, Inc. v. Ford Motor Co.*, 676 F.3d 318, 327 n.7 (3d Cir. 2012) (not deciding issue, but collecting conflicting authorities).

[59] *See, e.g., Shields v. Illinois Department of Corrections*, 746 F.3d 782, 798 (7th Cir. 2014).

[60] *United States ex rel. Raffington v. Bon Secours Health Sys., Inc.*, 567 F. Supp. 3d 429, 448 (S.D.N.Y. 2021).

[61] *See, e.g., In re Meyertech Corp.*, 831 F.2d 410, 421 (3d Cir. 1987).

[62] *Perea v. Ed. Cultural, Inc.*, 13 F.4th 43, 49 (1st Cir. 2021).

[63] *See, e.g., Brand v. National Union Fire Insurance Co. of Pittsburgh, Pa.*, 934 F.3d 799 (8th Cir. 2019) (implied consent applies when parties understand that evidence applied to

introduced outside the complaint, for example in an interrogatory answer or in a pretrial memorandum, and is treated by the opposing party as having been pleaded; or 2) where during trial, a party acquiesces to the introduction of evidence which is relevant only to the new claim.[64] Courts consider three factors in determining whether an issue was litigated by implied consent: (1) whether the parties recognized that the unpleaded issue entered the case; (2) whether the evidence supporting it was introduced without objection; and (3) whether a finding of consent prejudiced the opposing party's opportunity to respond.[65] Introduction of evidence that is arguably relevant to pleaded issues does not give a party fair notice that new issues are entering the case, and a failure to object to such evidence does not constitute implied consent under Rule 15(b).[66] If the court finds implied consent, the court will deem the pleadings amended to reflect the issues actually litigated.[67]

Deemed Amendments and Motions to Amend

Rule 15(b) expressly provides that if parties are found to have consented to the litigation of issues outside the original pleadings, there is no requirement that a formal amended pleading be filed. Instead, the result in the case will stand and the pleadings will be deemed to be amended to conform to the evidence in the record.[68] However, if an opposing party objects to evidence outside the pleadings, the party seeking relief under Rule 15(b) must make a motion to amend.[69] Such amendments may be permitted on either of two grounds: the absence of unfair prejudice to the objecting party,[70] or the ability of the court to cure such prejudice.[71]

Grounds for Denying Rule 15(b) Amendments

Courts deny Rule 15(b) amendments on any of four grounds: bad faith; undue delay; unfair prejudice to an opponent; or

---

impleaded issue). *But see Ryan v. Editions Limited West, Inc.*, 786 F.3d 754, 767 n.5 (9th Cir. 2015) (no consent where issue is only "inferentially suggested by incidental evidence in the record").

[64]*Katz v. Belveron Real Est. Partners, LLC*, 28 F.4th 300, 309 (1st Cir. 2022)

[65]*Gov't Emps. Ret. Sys. of Virgin Islands v. Gov't of Virgin Islands*, 995 F.3d 66, 81–82 (3d Cir. 2021).

[66]*Doe #6 v. Miami-Dade Cty.*, 974 F.3d 1333 (11th Cir. 2020); *Sasse v. U.S. Dept. of Labor*, 409 F.3d 773, 781 (6th Cir. 2005).

[67]*See, e.g., House of Flavors, Inc. v. TFG Michigan, L.P.*, 643 F.3d 35, 41 (1st Cir. 2011).

[68]*See, e.g., People for Ethical Treatment of Animals v. Doughney*, 263 F.3d 359, 367 (4th Cir. 2001); *Creative Demos, Inc. v. Wal-Mart Stores, Inc.*, 142 F.3d 367, 371–72 (7th Cir. 1998).

[69]*See, e.g., Green Country Food Market, Inc. v. Bottling Group, LLC*, 371 F.3d 1275, 1281 (10th Cir. 2004).

[70]*See, e.g., New York State Elec. & Gas Corp. v. Secretary of Labor*, 88 F.3d 98 (2d Cir. 1996).

[71]*See, e.g., Green Country Food Market, Inc. v. Bottling Group, LLC*, 371 F.3d 1275, 1280 (10th Cir. 2004).

futility of a proposed amendment.[72] If an issue is tried with the express or implied consent of the parties, however, the district court must accept the amended pleading.[73]

- *Unfair Prejudice*: Determinations of unfair prejudice are highly fact specific. The most likely circumstance in which such prejudice will be found occurs when the objecting party is surprised by the evidence and has no reasonable opportunity to meet it.[74] Courts are rarely receptive to "trial by ambush" tactics and reject last-ditch efforts to alter or amend liability theories at the close of trial.[75]
- *Curing Unfair Prejudice*: If the source of unfair prejudice is surprise, courts may attempt to cure the problem by using their authority under Rule 15(b) to grant a continuance, so that the objecting party can prepare for the new evidence.[76] Such an order may include re-opening discovery.

Statute of Limitations for New Claims: Relationship to Rule 15(c)

If a new claim is asserted through a pleading amended pursuant to Rule 15(b), there may still be questions about the timeliness of the claim. While Rule 15(b) may permit the amended pleading, Rule 15(c) controls whether the amended pleading is deemed to have been filed on the date of the original pleading or the date of the amendment. The distinction is significant when questions of statutes of limitations are raised.

Issues Decided on Summary Judgment

Rule 15(b) questions usually arise in situations where a case has gone to trial and a dispute has arisen as to whether an issue or claim has been "tried by express or implied consent." Whether the principles underlying Rule 15(b) apply to an issue outside the pleadings that was decided on summary judgment appears to be an open question.[77]

RULE 15(c)—RELATION BACK OF AMENDMENTS

CORE CONCEPT

When an amended pleading adds a new claim, questions may arise about whether the new claim was brought within the statute of limitations. Depending on when the limitations period

---

[72] *See, e.g., FilmTec Corp. v. Hydranautics*, 67 F.3d 931, 935 (Fed. Cir. 1995).

[73] *But cf., Kehoe Component Sales, Inc. v. Best Lighting Products, Inc.*, 796 F.3d 576 (6th Cir. 2015); *Net Moneyin, Inc. v. VeriSign, Inc.*, 545 F.3d 1359, 1372 (Fed. Cir. 2008).

[74] *See, e.g., Walton v. Nalco Chemical Co.*, 272 F.3d 13, 20 (1st Cir. 2001).

[75] *Vital Pharms., Inc. v. Monster Energy Co.*, 553 F. Supp. 3d 1180, 1238 (S.D. Fla. 2021).

[76] *See, e.g., Menendez v. Perishable Distributors, Inc.*, 763 F.2d 1374, 1379 (11th Cir. 1985).

[77] *Canada v. Samuel Grossi & Sons, Inc.*, 476 F. Supp. 3d 42, 57 (E.D. Pa. 2020) (recognizing circuit split).

ended, it may be critical to determine whether the new claim is deemed to have been filed on the date of the original pleading or on the date of the amended pleading. Rule 15(c) answers that question. It establishes two different tests—one for an amendment that adds a claim between existing parties to the litigation and one for an amendment that adds a claim against a new defendant.

APPLICATIONS

Relation Back for Amendments that Add a Claim

If an amended pleading adds a claim among existing parties, the new claim will relate back to the date of the original pleading if: 1) the law that provides the statute of limitations governing the cause of action permits relation back; or 2) the claim in the amended pleading arose from the same transaction or occurrence as that set forth in the original pleading.[78]

- *Statute of Limitations*: If the statute of limitations governing a particular cause of action permits relation back of amended pleadings, relation back is permitted. Thus, if the law governing the statute of limitations is more generous regarding relation back, the court will apply that law.[79] Alternatively, if Rule 15(c) more generously allows relation back, the court will apply it.[80]
- *Same Transaction or Occurrence*: The courts have adopted various standards for determining whether two claims arise out of the same transaction or occurrence. The assessment is very specific to the facts of the particular case, but in general this requirement is satisfied if there is a substantial logical relationship between the transactions or occurrences at issue.[81] The "same transaction or occurrence" test also appears in Rule 13 and Rule 14, and courts construe it the same way throughout the joinder rules.[82] See the discussion of this issue in Rule 13 for more detail.

Relation Back for Amendments That Add or Change a Party

If an amended pleading adds a party or changes the name of a party, a claim in the amended pleading will relate back to the date of the original pleading if: 1) the law that provides the statute of limitations governing the cause of action permits relation back; or 2) it arises from the same transaction or occur-

---

[78] *Mayle v. Felix*, 545 U.S. 644, 656 (2005).

[79] *See, e.g., Morel v. Daimler-Chrysler AG*, 565 F.3d 20, 26 (1st Cir. 2009).

[80] *See, e.g., Butler v. National Community Renaissance of California*, 766 F.3d 1191 (9th Cir. 2014); *Morel v. Daimler-Chrysler AG*, 565 F.3d 20, 26 (1st Cir. 2009).

[81] *See, e.g., United Mine Workers of America v. Gibbs*, 383 U.S. 715, 724 (1996); *Scott v. Chipotle Mexican Grill, Inc.*, 954 F.3d 502 (2d Cir. 2020).

[82] *See, e.g., In re EMC Corp.*, 677 F.3d 1351, 1357 (Fed. Cir. 2012).

rence as the original pleading and within the 90-day period after filing of the original pleading[83] that Rule 4(m) provides for service of process, the party named in the amended pleading received sufficient notice of the pendency of the action so as not to be prejudiced in preparing a defense and knew or should have known that but for a mistake of identity the party would have been named in the original pleading. Thus, the test for relation back under Rule 15(c) for amendments that add new parties includes the requirement for relation back of amendments that add new claims among the existing parties, then imposes an additional requirement that the new parties have fair and timely notice of the claims being asserted against them.

- *Notice:* Rule 15(c) only requires notice that, in the particular circumstances of a case, ensures that the party joined is not unfairly prejudiced by an amended pleading that relates back to an earlier date.[84] The notice may be actual or constructive.[85] If a party to be joined in an amended complaint learned of a suit within the 90-day period provided by Rule 4(m) for service of the original complaint,[86] or any "good cause" extensions provided under Rule 4(m),[87] the notice generally will be satisfied.[88] In some circumstances, the court will presume notice. For example, a parent corporation may be deemed to have received notice of an action served on its subsidiary.[89] Similarly, if the proposed change merely corrects a "misnomer" in the party's name, the party will be deemed to have received notice.[90] In determining whether a party has received notice, the court may consider relevant extrinsic evidence, and is not confined to examination of the pleadings themselves.[91]
- *Knowledge of Mistaken Identity*: Before an amended

---

[83] *See, e.g., Lee v. Airgas Mid-South, Inc.*, 793 F.3d 894 (8th Cir. 2015) (time starts to run from date of serving original complaint; adding new party starts time limit for new party, but not for existing parties).

[84] *See, e.g., Glover v. F.D.I.C.*, 698 F.3d 139, 146 (3d Cir. 2012); *Garvin v. City of Philadelphia*, 354 F.3d 215, 222 (3d Cir. 2003).

[85] *See, e.g., Force v. City of Memphis*, 101 F.3d 702, 884 (6th Cir. 1996) (constructive notice may be found in, *inter alia*, the following factors: "the relationship of the new defendants to the defendant(s) originally named, whether the same attorney represented both [the] original and new defendants, and whether the new defendants are officials of the original defendant").

[86] *See, e.g., Jones v. Bernanke*, 557 F.3d 670, 675 (D.C. Cir. 2009).

[87] *McGraw v. Gore*, 31 F.4th 844, 849 (4th Cir. 2022).

[88] *See, e.g., Singletary v. Pennsylvania Dept. of Corrections*, 266 F.3d 186, 189 (3d Cir. 2001).

[89] *See, e.g., Krupski v. Costa Crociere, S.p.A.*, 560 U.S. 538, 554 (2010).

[90] *See, e.g., Datskow v. Teledyne, Inc., Continental Products Div.*, 899 F.2d 1298, 1301–02 (2d Cir. 1990).

[91] *See, e.g., Silbaugh v. Chao*, 942 F.3d 911 (9th Cir. 2019); *Wilkins v. Montgomery*, 751 F.3d 214, 225 (4th

pleading may relate back, the proponent of the pleading must also establish that within the 90-day period provided by Rule 4(m), the person to be joined knew, or should have known, that the person would have been sued under the original pleading but for some mistake in identity.[92] Thus, if a subsidiary corporation was sued when the claim should have been against its parent, and was served within the period provided by Rule 4(m), the parent might be charged with timely knowledge of the fact that the proper defendant should have been the parent.[93] With natural persons, the requirement may be satisfied when the name of the proper defendant is similar to the name of the person originally designated as a defendant, *and* the proper defendant knew of the mistake within the time limit established by Rule 4(m).[94] It is unclear whether the mistake may be one of either fact or law,[95] but in other respects this requirement has been construed rather strictly.[96] A common mistake is naming the wrong entity when there is a complex corporate structure.[97] Naming a "John Doe" defendant indicates uncertainty about the defendant's identity, rather than a "mistake" within the meaning of Rule 15(c).[98]

Undue Delay and Relation Back

Under Rule 15(a), a court may sometimes properly deny leave to amend a pleading when a party has delayed excessively and without good cause in seeking leave.[99] However, undue delay plays no role in relation back under Rule 15(c).[100]

Relation to Laches and Statutes of Repose

Laches is a case law doctrine that may be raised by a defendant where the plaintiff unreasonably delays in bringing a lawsuit, and thereby unfairly harms the defendant. Rule 15(c) governs circumstances where application of the Rule might avoid unfairness arising from strict application of a statute of limitations. Because laches applies, if at all, only in the

---

Cir. 2014).

[92] *Krupski v. Costa Crociere, S.p.A.*, 560 U.S. 538, 548 (2010).

[93] *Krupski v. Costa Crociere, S.p.A.*, 560 U.S. 538, 554 (2010).

[94] *See, e.g., Brown v. Shaner*, 172 F.3d 927, 933 (6th Cir. 1999).

[95] *Compare, e.g., Woods v. Indiana University-Purdue University at Indianapolis*, 996 F.2d 880, 887 (7th Cir. 1993) (indicating that mistake may be of fact or law), *with Rendall-Speranza v. Nassim*, 107 F.3d 913, 918 (D.C. Cir. 1997) (amendment permitted, if at all, only for mistake of fact).

[96] *Krupski v. Costa Crociere S.p.A.*, 560 U.S. 538 (2010); *Ceara v. Deacon*, 916 F. 3d 208 (2d Cir. 2018).

[97] *Leonard v. Gen. Motors L.L.C.*, 504 F.Supp.3d 73, 90–91 (D. Conn. 2020).

[98] *Herrera v. Cleveland*, 8 F.4th 493, 495 (7th Cir. 2021).

[99] *Krupski v. Costa Crociere, S.p.A.*, 560 U.S. 538, 553 (2010).

[100] *Krupski v. Costa Crociere, S.p.A.*, 560 U.S. 538, 553 (2010).

absence of a relevant statute of limitations, Rule 15 "has no controlling force where . . . a defendant's remedy is provided by the equitable doctrine of laches."[101]

A statute of repose gives defendants protection from suit after a certain amount of time, and is slightly different from a statute of limitations, which is subject to considerations such as equitable tolling. At least one court has concluded that Rule 15(c) permits relation back after the repose period.[102]

Relation Back is Distinct from Right to Amend

Rule 15(c) deals only with whether the filing date of an amendment relates back to the date the original pleading was filed. That issue is completely distinct from whether a party may amend its pleading.[103]

Inapplicability to Separate Actions

Rule 15(c) applies, if at all, only to proposed amendments to existing pleadings. It is inapplicable to a situation where a party has filed a new lawsuit and seeks "relation back" status for the claim in that case.[104]

Right to Amend Not Restricted to "Pleadings"

Although Rule 15(c) itself refers only to amendments of pleadings, it is also appropriately applied to amendments of some other documents filed in district court.[105] However, Rule 15(c) does not permit relation back of an untimely notice of appeal.[106]

Relation Back to Correct Defects in Pleadings

There is no discussion in Rule 15(c) of the possibility of applying relation back to permit correction of formal defects in a pleading. However, such a correction will usually relate back.[107]

Removed Cases

The relation back standard in Rule 15(c) applies to amendments in a case removed to federal court, even where relation back would not be available under state law.[108]

Adding Plaintiffs: Relation Back and Rule 17

In general Rule 15(c)(1)(C) does not address the question of

---

[101] *Brzozowski v. Correctional Physician Services, Inc.*, 360 F.3d 173, 182 (3d Cir. 2004).

[102] *SEPTA v. Orrstown Fin. Servs. Inc.*, 12 F.4th 337, 349 (3d Cir. 2021).

[103] *See, e.g., Campbell v. Air Jamaica, Ltd.*, 760 F.3d 1165, 1175–76 (11th Cir. 2014); *Williams v. Lampe*, 399 F.3d 867 (7th Cir. 2005).

[104] *See, e.g., Farris v. United States*, 333 F.3d 1211, 1215 (11th Cir. 2003).

[105] *Scarborough v. Principi*, 541 U.S. 401, 416–18 (2004) (applying Rule 15(c) to application for award of attorney fees).

[106] *See, e.g., Cruz v. International Collection Corp.*, 673 F.3d 991, 1002 (9th Cir. 2012).

[107] *See, e.g., In re IFC Credit Corp.*, 663 F.3d 315, 321 (7th Cir. 2011) (lawyer inadvertently failed to sign document).

[108] *Robinson v. Se. Pennsylvania Transportation Auth.*, 572 F. Supp. 3d 136, 144 (E.D. Pa. 2021).

whether the addition of a plaintiff through an amended pleading will relate back to the date of the original pleading. Although the case law is not unanimous on the point, it appears that a proposed addition of a plaintiff that otherwise meets the standards of Rule 15 will be allowed to relate back.[109]

At the same time, Rule 17(a), governing requirements to prosecute a case in the name of the real party in interest, expressly provides that joinder or substitution of the real party in interest automatically relates back to the original filing date, apparently without regard to the requirements of Rule 15. Although the matter is not free of doubt, it appears that in such circumstances Rule 17(a), and not Rule 15, should control.[110]

Relation Back and the "First to File" Rule

Under the first-to-file doctrine, a district court may choose to transfer, stay, or dismiss an action where a similar complaint has been filed in another district court. Some courts have found that the filing of a complaint triggers the first-filed rule regardless of whether the plaintiff later amends the complaint. Other courts, however, consider a later action to become "first filed" if the claims relate back to an original complaint that was chronologically filed first.[111]

Relation Back Against the United States

Rule 15(c) applies when the United States is added as a defendant. The requirements of timely notice of the action and knowledge of a mistake in identity are satisfied if the original pleading was served on the United States Attorney (or designee), the Attorney General, or an agency or officer who would have been a proper defendant if named in the original complaint.[112] This express provision cuts through much of what might otherwise have been substantial technical obstacles to use of relation back against the United States.[113] However, even when the United States is a defendant, the amended

---

[109]*See, e.g., Freight Drivers & Helpers Local Union No. 557 Pension Fund v. Penske Logistics LLC*, 784 F.3d 210, 219 (4th Cir. 2015); *In re Community Bank of Northern Virginia*, 622 F.3d 275, 297 (3d Cir. 2010).

[110]*See, e.g., Scheufler v. General Host Corp.*, 126 F.3d 1261, 1271 (10th Cir. 1997) (noting uncertainty; applying relation-back provisions of Rule 17(a)). *But cf., Plubell v. Merck & Co.*, 434 F.3d 1070, 1072 (8th Cir. 2006) (acknowledging that Rule 15(c) does not "expressly" address issues of changing amendments, but concluding that Rule 15(c) applies to such situations by analogy); *Cliff v. Payco General American Credits, Inc.*, 363 F.3d 1113, 1132 (11th Cir. 2004) (concluding that use of Rule 15(c)(1)(C) "rests on solid ground;" no discussion of Rule 17); *Crocheron v. State Farm Fire & Cas. Co.*, 621 B.R. 659, 664–65 (E.D. Mich. 2020) (courts have used Rule 15(c) in conjunction with Rule 17(a) to enable an amendment substituting the real party in interest to relate back to the time the original action was filed).

[111]*SMIC, Americas v. Innovative Foundry Techs. LLC*, 473 F. Supp. 3d 1021, 1025 (N.D. Cal. 2020).

[112]*See, e.g., Roman v. Townsend*, 224 F.3d 24, 28 (1st Cir. 2000).

[113]*See, e.g., Delgado-Brunet v. Clark*, 93 F.3d 339, 344 (7th Cir. 1996).

pleading must still arise out of the same transaction or occurrence as the original pleading, and service of the original pleading upon the federal officers must occur within the 90-day period provided by Rule 4(m).

RULE 15(d)—SUPPLEMENTAL PLEADINGS

CORE CONCEPT

Rule 15(d) governs circumstances in which parties are permitted to supplement previous pleadings to encompass events that have occurred since the earlier pleadings were filed.[114]

APPLICATIONS

Leave of Court

There is no unqualified right to file a supplemental pleading.[115] Authority to file a supplemental pleading is obtained by filing a motion.[116] Courts freely grant such leave when the supplemental pleadings will not unfairly prejudice other parties.[117]

Party's Discretion

Supplemental pleadings are optional. Thus, if a party acquires a claim as a result of facts arising after the original pleading was filed and the requirements of Rule 15(d) are satisfied, there is an opportunity, but not a duty, to file a supplemental pleading asserting the claim.[118]

Same Transaction or Occurrence

If the issues addressed in a proposed supplemental pleading are related to the transaction or occurrence that gave rise to the original pleadings, and no other considerations of fairness weigh against hearing the supplemental pleading, courts generally permit the supplemental pleading.[119] A supplemental pleading may be permitted even if it arises from a separate transaction, but totally unrelated supplemental pleadings are disfavored.

However, in the infrequent circumstance where a supplemental pleading is rejected on the ground that it states a distinct cause of action, the plaintiff may simply file a separate action

---

[114] *See, e.g., T Mobile Northeast LLC v. City of Wilmington*, 913 F.3d 311 (3d Cir. 2019).

[115] *Howard v. City of Coos Bay.*, 871 F.3d 1032 (9th Cir. 2017).

[116] *See, e.g., Bornholdt v. Brady*, 869 F.2d 57, 68 (2d Cir. 1989). *But see Cabrera v. City of Huntington Park*, 159 F.3d 374, 382 (9th Cir. 1998) (per curiam) (Plaintiff's "failure formally to plead a malicious prosecution claim either in an amended or supplemental pleading does not preclude the district court from considering the claim.").

[117] *See, e.g., Galen Hosp. Alaska, Inc. v. Azar*, 474 F. Supp. 3d 214, 223 (D.D.C. 2020); *Quaratino v. Tiffany & Co.*, 71 F.3d 58, 66 (2d Cir. 1995).

[118] *See, e.g., Lundquist v. Rice Memorial Hosp.*, 238 F.3d 975, 977 (8th Cir. 2001).

[119] *City of Hawthorne v. Wright*, 493 U.S. 813 (1989); *Weeks v. New York State (Div. of Parole)*, 273 F.3d 76, 88 (2d Cir. 2001).

and then move to consolidate the new action with the pending case pursuant to Rule 42(a).[120]

Standard

To be permitted, the facts to be added in the supplemental pleading must have arisen after "the date of the pleading to be supplemented."[121] Judicial decisions to grant or deny Rule 15(d) motions to supplement pleadings are generally based on the same factors of fairness courts weigh when considering motions to amend pleadings under Rule 15(a).[122] There is a split of authority about whether a party must meet the "good cause" standard in Rule 16(b) to supplement the pleadings after a case management deadline.[123]

Time to File

In general, Rule 15(d) contains no restriction on the time in which a supplemental pleading may be filed. However, the court may consider inappropriate delay in attempting to assert supplemental claims as grounds for refusing to grant permission to file the supplemental pleading.[124] Additionally, a supplemental pleading is normally inappropriate if it attempts to introduce a new and distinct cause of action after the original case has gone to final judgment.[125]

Scope of Supplemental Pleadings

Supplemental pleadings should be restricted to events occurring since initiation of the suit.[126] If the issues raised predate the original pleadings, supplemental pleadings are not the appropriate mechanism for raising them. Instead, a party should seek to amend the pleadings pursuant to Rule 15(a) or (b).[127]

Intervening Judicial Decisions

Intervening judicial decisions that change the applicable law are not the sort of "occurrences or events" that might implicate Rule 15(d).[128]

Additional Parties

In general, supplemental pleadings may join additional parties, subject to the normal requirements of jurisdiction. However, where such joinder might confuse the trier of fact or unduly distract attention from the original claims, proposals to

---

[120] *See, e.g., Predator International, Inc. v. Gamo Outdoor USA, Inc.*, 793 F.3d 1177, 1187 (10th Cir. 2015).

[121] Fed.R.Civ.P. 15(d). *See also Mattox v. Edelman*, 851 F.3d 583, 591 (6th Cir. 2017).

[122] *See, e.g., Glatt v. Chicago Park Dist.*, 87 F.3d 190 (7th Cir. 1996).

[123] *Desio v. State Farm Mut. Auto. Ins. Co.*, 339 F.R.D. 632, 642 (D. Nev. 2021).

[124] *See, e.g., Quaratino v. Tiffany & Co.*, 71 F.3d 58, 66 (2d Cir. 1995).

[125] *Summers v. Earth Island Institute*, 555 U.S. 488 (2009).

[126] *See Haggard v. Bank of the Ozarks, Inc.*, 668 F.3d 196, 202 (5th Cir. 2012).

[127] *See, e.g., Flaherty v. Lang*, 199 F.3d 607, 613 (2d Cir. 1999).

[128] *See, e.g., United States v. Hicks*, 283 F.3d 380, 385 (D.C. Cir. 2002).

add new parties may reduce the prospects for obtaining permission from the court to file a supplemental pleading.[129]

Relationship to Original Pleadings

Unlike amended pleadings, supplemental pleadings usually do not displace the original pleadings. Thus, there is no necessity to incorporate portions of the original pleadings in a supplemental pleading, although it may be convenient to incorporate portions of original pleadings and avoid duplication.

Mislabeled Pleadings

If a party inadvertently mislabels a supplemental pleading as an amended pleading, the court will disregard the error if it does not unfairly prejudice an opposing party.[130]

Defective Original Pleadings

Rule 15(d) explicitly provides that defects in the original pleadings have no effect on a party's ability to file a supplemental pleading.[131] Thus, even an uncorrectable defect in the original pleading, requiring dismissal of the counts that pleading contains, does not necessarily bar filing of a supplemental pleading, if the supplemental pleading itself is free from substantial defects.

Responses to Supplemental Pleadings

Rule 15(d) does not create either a right or duty to respond to a supplemental pleading. Instead, the Rule vests the court with authority to order a response when appropriate in the circumstances of a case. Typically, an opportunity to respond will be permitted when the supplemental pleading asserts a new cause of action.

Relation Back of Supplemental Pleadings

Because supplemental pleadings address only events that have occurred since the original pleadings were filed, no question normally arises as to whether supplemental pleadings relate back to the date the original pleadings were filed.[132] However, where relation back is important to the supplemental pleadings, courts tend to apply the standards of Rule 15(c) to determine whether relation back should be permitted.[133]

---

[129] *See, e.g., Planned Parenthood of Southern Arizona v. Neely*, 130 F.3d 400, 402 (9th Cir. 1997).

[130] *See, e.g., Cabrera v. City of Huntington Park*, 159 F.3d 374, 382 (9th Cir. 1998).

[131] *Mathews v. Diaz*, 426 U.S. 67, n.8 (1976); *TMobile Ne. LLC v. City of Wilmington, Delaware*, 913 F.3d 311 (3d Cir. 2019).

[132] *But see Innovative Therapies, Inc. v. Kinetic Concepts, Inc.*, 599 F.3d 1377, 1384 (Fed. Cir. 2010) (Rule 15(c) "does not treat events that post-date the original pleading as if they had occurred at an earlier time.").

[133] *See, e.g., F.D.I.C. v. Knostman*, 966 F.2d 1133, 1138 (7th Cir. 1992). *Cf., T Mobile Northeast LLC v. City of Wilmington*, 913 F.3d 311 (3d Cir. 2019) (allowed supplemental complaint will be treated as relating back to original complaint).

Subject-Matter Jurisdiction and Standing

There is authority for permitting the use of Rule 15(d) to cure at least some defects in subject-matter jurisdiction (such as exhaustion of administrative remedies).[134] Rule 15(d) may also be used to correct standing defects if a supplemental pleading alleges facts that arose after the original complaint was filed.[135]

Additional Research References

Wright & Miller, *Federal Practice and Procedure* §§ 1471 to 1510
C.J.S., Federal Civil Procedure §§ 322 to 356 et seq.
West's Key Number Digest, Federal Civil Procedure ⚷821 to 853, ⚷861 to 852

---

[134] *Mathews v. Diaz*, 426 U.S. 67, 75 (1976); *Saddozai v. Davis*, 35 F.4th 705, 706 (9th Cir. 2022).

[135] *See, e.g., Scahill v. District of Columbia*, 909 F.3d 1177 (D.C. Cir. 2018).

RULE 16
PRETRIAL CONFERENCES; SCHEDULING; MANAGEMENT

(a) Purposes of a Pretrial Conference. In any action, the court may order the attorneys and any unrepresented parties to appear for one or more pretrial conferences for such purposes as:

(1) expediting disposition of the action;

(2) establishing early and continuing control so that the case will not be protracted because of lack of management;

(3) discouraging wasteful pretrial activities;

(4) improving the quality of the trial through more thorough preparation; and

(5) facilitating settlement.

(b) Scheduling.

(1) *Scheduling Order.* Except in categories of actions exempted by local rule, the district judge—or a magistrate judge when authorized by local rule—must issue a scheduling order:

(A) after receiving the parties' report under Rule 26(f); or

(B) after consulting with the parties' attorneys and any unrepresented parties at a scheduling conference.

(2) *Time to Issue.* The judge must issue the scheduling order as soon as practicable, but unless the judge finds good cause for delay, the judge must issue it within the earlier of 90 days after any defendant has been served with the complaint or 60 days after any defendant has appeared.

(3) *Contents of the Order.*

(A) *Required Contents.* The scheduling order must limit the time to join other parties, amend the pleadings, complete discovery, and file motions.

(B) *Permitted Contents.* The scheduling order may:

(i) modify the timing of disclosures under Rules 26(a) and 26(e)(1);

(ii) modify the extent of discovery;

(iii) provide for disclosure, discovery, or preservation of electronically stored information;

(iv) include any agreements the parties reach for asserting claims of privilege or of protection as trial-preparation material after information is produced, including agreements reached under Federal Rule of Evidence 502;

(v) direct that before moving for an order relating to discovery, the movant must request a conference with the court;

(vi) set dates for pretrial conferences and for trial; and

(vii) include other appropriate matters.

(4) *Modifying a Schedule.* A schedule may be modified only for good cause and with the judge's consent.

(c) Attendance and Matters for Consideration at a Pretrial Conference.

(1) *Attendance.* A represented party must authorize at least one of its attorneys to make stipulations and admissions about all matters that can reasonably be anticipated for discussion at a pretrial conference. If appropriate, the court may require that a party or its representative be present or reasonably available by other means to consider possible settlement.

(2) *Matters for Consideration.* At any pretrial conference, the court may consider and take appropriate action on the following matters:

(A) formulating and simplifying the issues, and eliminating frivolous claims or defenses;

(B) amending the pleadings if necessary or desirable;

(C) obtaining admissions and stipulations about facts and documents to avoid unnecessary proof, and ruling in advance on the admissibility of evidence;

(D) avoiding unnecessary proof and cumulative evidence, and limiting the use of testimony under Federal Rule of Evidence 702;

(E) determining the appropriateness and timing of summary adjudication under Rule 56;

(F) controlling and scheduling discovery, including orders affecting disclosures and discovery under Rule 26 and Rules 29 through 37;

(G) identifying witnesses and documents, scheduling the filing and exchange of any pretrial briefs, and setting dates for further conferences and for trial;

(H) referring matters to a magistrate judge or a master;

(I) settling the case and using special procedures to assist in resolving the dispute when authorized by statute or local rule;

(J) determining the form and content of the pretrial order;

(K) disposing of pending motions;

(L) adopting special procedures for managing potentially difficult or protracted actions that may involve complex issues, multiple parties, difficult legal questions, or unusual proof problems;

(M) ordering a separate trial under Rule 42(b) of a claim,

counterclaim, crossclaim, third-party claim, or particular issue;

(N) ordering the presentation of evidence early in the trial on a manageable issue that might, on the evidence, be the basis for a judgment as a matter of law under Rule 50(a) or a judgment on partial findings under Rule 52(c);

(O) establishing a reasonable limit on the time allowed to present evidence; and

(P) facilitating in other ways the just, speedy, and inexpensive disposition of the action.

(d) Pretrial Orders. After any conference under this rule, the court should issue an order reciting the action taken. This order controls the course of the action unless the court modifies it.

(e) Final Pretrial Conference and Orders. The court may hold a final pretrial conference to formulate a trial plan, including a plan to facilitate the admission of evidence. The conference must be held as close to the start of trial as is reasonable, and must be attended by at least one attorney who will conduct the trial for each party and by any unrepresented party. The court may modify the order issued after a final pretrial conference only to prevent manifest injustice.

(f) Sanctions.

(1) *In General.* On motion or on its own, the court may issue any just orders, including those authorized by Rule 37(b)(2)(A)(ii)-(vii), if a party or its attorney:

(A) fails to appear at a scheduling or other pretrial conference;

(B) is substantially unprepared to participate—or does not participate in good faith—in the conference; or

(C) fails to obey a scheduling or other pretrial order.

(2) *Imposing Fees and Costs.* Instead of or in addition to any other sanction, the court must order the party, its attorney, or both to pay the reasonable expenses—including attorney's fees—incurred because of any noncompliance with this rule, unless the noncompliance was substantially justified or other circumstances make an award of expenses unjust.

[Amended April 28, 1983, effective August 1, 1983; March 2, 1987, effective August 1, 1987; April 22, 1993, effective December 1, 1993; April 12, 2006, effective December 1, 2006; April 30, 2007, effective December 1, 2007; April 29, 2015, effective December 1, 2015.]

AUTHORS' COMMENTARY ON RULE 16

PURPOSE AND SCOPE

Rule 16 empowers the district court to exercise active control over its docket to expedite disposition, avoid waste, and promote settlement. The court has discretion to hold pretrial conferences and Rule 16 *requires* the court to issue a scheduling order setting procedures for discovery and trial in most cases. If the court does hold a pretrial conference, Rule 16 requires the court to issue a pretrial order after such a pretrial conference detailing the action at the conference and establishing the course of action to be followed. The order is binding unless subsequently modified by the court.

RULE 16(a)—PRETRIAL CONFERENCES

CORE CONCEPT

Rule 16(a) outlines the parameters and objectives for the court's pretrial conferences with the parties. When preparing for a pretrial conference, the litigants should consult both Rule 16(c) and the local rules concerning the subjects to be discussed at a pretrial conference.

APPLICATIONS

Pretrial Conferences

(1) *Initial or First Conference:* The court may convene the first pretrial conference as soon as all of the parties have been served with the complaint. Typically, the court will delay the pretrial conference until after an answer is filed or preliminary motions to dismiss are resolved.[1] The first pretrial conference permits the parties to familiarize the court with the issues in the case and to propose a discovery schedule. After the conference, the court will issue an order detailing the decisions reached and action taken. Typically, the initial conference will address issues of scope and timing of discovery, filing of parties' pretrial narrative statements, the timing for filing of motions, alternative dispute resolution, and possibly an anticipated date for trial.

(2) *Subsequent and Final Pretrial Conferences:* Ordinarily, the court holds a final pretrial conference after the close of discovery, after ruling on dispositive pretrial motions and after the filing of the pretrial narrative statements.[2] At this conference, the court sets a trial date, seeks to further clarify the is-

---

[1] *Ndoromo v. Barr*, 486 F. Supp. 3d 388, 395 (D.D.C. 2020), aff'd, 2021 WL 2525717 (D.C. Cir. 2021).

[2] *But see Mizwicki v. Helwig*, 196 F.3d 828, 833 (7th Cir. 1999) (there is no requirement that the court conduct

sues, discusses any extraneous matters, sets a schedule for any remaining motions, and encourages settlement discussions.[3]

(3) *Other Pretrial Conferences:* Local rule may require the court to hold one pretrial conference, but the court may hold as many pretrial conferences as it deems necessary to apprise the court of the progress of the case.

Pretrial Orders

If, as is normally the case, the court orders a conference, Rule 16(d) provides that the court "should" issue an order describing any action taken.[4]

Court's Discretion

Although pretrial conferences occur frequently, they are apparently not mandatory. Instead, the court has discretion as to whether to hold such a conference in a particular case or, if a conference is held, to issue an order.[5] If an order is issued, the court may modify it later "to prevent manifest injustice."[6]

Who Must Attend

Rule 16(a) authorizes the court to order attorneys and unrepresented parties to attend pretrial conferences,[7] and makes no reference to represented parties. Courts have held that represented parties (in contrast to their attorneys) may also be directed to attend.[8] Additionally, at least one court has held that the judge must also attend, and cannot delegate that function to a law clerk.[9]

Motion for Pretrial Conference

Generally, the court will set the time for pretrial conferences. However, the parties may seek a pretrial conference either by informal request or by motion.[10] The court has discretion to order additional pretrial conferences.

RULE 16(b)—SCHEDULING

CORE CONCEPT

After receiving the discovery report required under Rule 26(f) or after conducting a scheduling conference under Rule 16(a), the court will issue a scheduling order setting timetables for pretrial

a final pretrial conference).

[3] *Cf., Colon-Cabrera v. Esso Standard Oil Co. (Puerto Rico), Inc.*, 723 F.3d 82, 89–90 (1st Cir. 2013).

[4] Rule 16(d).

[5] Rule 16(d) and (e).

[6] Rule 16(e). *See also, e.g., Morgan v. City of Chicago*, 822 F.3d 317 (7th Cir. 2016).

[7] *Royal Palace Hotel Associates, Inc. v. International Resort Classics, Inc.*, 178 F.R.D. 595, 597 (M.D. Fla. 1998).

[8] *See, e.g., Matter of Sargeant Farms, Inc.*, 224 B.R. 842, 845 (Bankr. M.D. Fla. 1998) (requiring attendance of party representative with settlement authority).

[9] *Connolly v. National School Bus Service, Inc.*, 177 F.3d 593 (7th Cir. 1999).

[10] *See, e.g., Garcia-Perez v. Hospital Metropolitano*, 597 F.3d 6, 9 (1st Cir. 2010).

matters.[11] This scheduling order must be issued within 60 days after the appearance of a defendant and within 90 days of the service of the complaint.[12] District courts have broad discretion to enforce scheduling order deadlines.[13]

APPLICATIONS

Mandatory Topics

Rule 16(b) requires the court's order to include time limits for: joining parties[14] and amending pleadings;[15] filing motions;[16] and completing discovery.[17]

Optional Topics

At the court's discretion, the scheduling order may also include: modifications of time limits for disclosures under Rule 26(a) and (e)(1) and of the amount of discovery parties shall be permitted; the disclosure or discovery of electronic data; provisions for recalling privileged documents after production; dates for pretrial conferences and for trial; treatment of electronically stored information; a requirement that parties seek a conference with the court before filing a discovery motion;[18] and other matters the court deems appropriate.[19]

Modification of Scheduling Order Deadlines: Good Cause

For good cause shown, the court may grant a motion modifying or enlarging the deadlines in the scheduling order.[20] Courts consider the following factors: (1) the explanation for the failure to complete discovery on time, (2) the importance of the amendment, (3) the potential prejudice in allowing the amendment, and (4) the availability of a continuance to cure such prejudice.[21] The primary measure of Rule 16's "good cause"

[11] *See, e.g., In re Swift Transportation Co., Inc.*, 830 F.3d 913 (9th Cir. 2016).

[12] The Advisory Committee Note to the 2015 Amendment to Rule 16(b)(2).

[13] *Batiste v. Lewis*, 976 F.3d 493, 500 (5th Cir. 2020).

[14] *Johnson v. Mammoth Recreations, Inc.*, 975 F.2d 604, 608 (9th Cir. 1992) (noting mandatory nature of Rule 16(b) as to time limit on party joinder).

[15] *See, e.g., Millennium Partners, L.P. v. Colmar Storage, LLC*, 494 F.3d 1293 (11th Cir. 2007); *AmerisourceBergen Corp. v. Dialysist West, Inc.*, 445 F.3d 1132, 1141 (9th Cir. 2006).

[16] *Rosario-Diaz v. Gonzalez*, 140 F.3d 312 (1st Cir.1998).

[17] *Suntrust Bank v. Blue Water Fiber, L.P.*, 210 F.R.D. 196, 199 (E.D. Mich. 2002).

[18] Rule 16(b)(3)(c)(B)(v).

[19] *Does I thru XXIII v. Advanced Textile Corp.*, 214 F.3d 1058, 1068 (9th Cir. 2000) (the court may use its powers under Rule 16 to address a party's need for anonymity).

[20] *Seale v. Peacock*, 32 F.4th 1011, 1031 (10th Cir. 2022); *Hussain v. Nicholson*, 435 F.3d 359, 368 (D.C. Cir. 2006) (attorney error generally does not constitute good cause, but may in extreme circumstances).

[21] *Omega Hosp., LLC v. United Healthcare of Louisiana, Inc.*, 566 F. Supp. 3d 543, 548 (M.D. La. 2021).

standard is the moving party's diligence.[22] Good cause exists when the schedule cannot reasonably be met despite the diligence of the party seeking the extension.[23] Courts also consider possible prejudice to the party opposing the modification.[24]

Rule 16 Deadlines for Amending Pleadings: Relation to Rule 15

Rule 15 governs amended and supplemental pleadings. The relationship between Rule 15 and Rule 16(b) is complex, partly because the two rules can be entangled at different points in a case.[25] If a party seeks to amend a pleading before the district court enters a Rule 16(b) scheduling order or before the time limit of a scheduling order expires, the proposed amended pleading will be evaluated under the liberal amendment standard of Rule 15(a). However, once the date for amending pleadings in the court's Rule 16 scheduling order has passed, a party must demonstrate good cause to amend a pleading.[26]

Rule 15(b)—pertaining to amending pleadings to conform to the evidence—has a different relationship with Rule 16(b) than is described above for Rule 15(a). Almost by definition, a pleading amended pursuant to Rule 15(b) will be amended well after the time limit set by a district court's scheduling order under Rule 16(b) has expired. Accordingly, Rule 15(b) is applied notwithstanding the expiration of time limits for amendments imposed by Rule 16(b).[27]

Although there is a split of authority, the majority position is that a motion to supplement under Rule 15(d) filed after a deadline to amend triggers the Rule 16(b) "good cause" analysis.[28]

Rule 16 Discovery Deadlines: Relation to Rule 26 Deadlines

Rule 26(a) establishes a variety of default deadlines for various discovery activities. If the court's scheduling order provides a different date for any of these activities, a party must show "good cause" for failure to comply with that date.[29]

---

[22] *Helena Agri-Enterprises, LLC v. Great Lakes Grain, LLC*, 988 F.3d 260, 272 (6th Cir. 2021).

[23] Advisory Committee Notes to Rule 16 (1983 amendments). *See also Husky Ventures, Inc. v. B55 Investments, Ltd.*, 911 F.3d 1000 (10th Cir. 2018).

[24] *Garza v. Lansing Sch. Dist.*, 972 F.3d 853, 879 (6th Cir. 2020).

[25] *See Sacerdote v. New York Univ.*, 9 F.4th 95, 115 (2d Cir. 2021) (describing three sets of standards intertwined in Rule 15 and Rule 16).

[26] *See, e.g., MidAmerica C2L Inc. v. Siemens Energy Inc.*, 25 F.4th 1312, 1335 (11th Cir. 2022); *Branch Banking & Trust Co. v. D.M.S.I., LLC*, 871 F.3d 751 (9th Cir. 2017).

[27] *See, e.g., Clark v. Martinez*, 295 F.3d 809, 815 (8th Cir. 2002).

[28] *Desio v. State Farm Mut. Auto. Ins. Co.*, 339 F.R.D. 632, 639 (D. Nev. 2021).

[29] *Kumar v. Frisco Indep. Sch. Dist.*, 476 F. Supp. 3d 439, 468 (E.D. Tex. 2020).

RULE 16(c)—ATTENDANCE AND MATTERS FOR CONSIDERATION AT PRETRIAL CONFERENCES

CORE CONCEPT

Rule 16(c) contains a list of topics that the court may consider at Rule 16 conferences. Rule 16(c) also allows for the consideration of any other matters that may facilitate the "just, speedy, and inexpensive disposition of the action."

APPLICATIONS

Topics for Conferences

During a pretrial conference, the court may seek to define and simplify the contested facts, theories, and issues,[30] determine the preclusive effect of prior litigation,[31] eliminate frivolous claims or defenses,[32] determine whether an amendment of the pleadings is necessary,[33] address disclosure and discovery issues,[34] seek the admission or denial of facts or documents, make advance rulings on the admissibility of evidence[35] and the appropriateness of expert witnesses,[36] require parties to file lists identifying witnesses[37] and documents, entertain requests to limit witnesses,[38] govern the order of proof at trial, adopt special procedures for complex issues or cases,[39] and discuss pretrial narrative statements, pending motions, stipulations limiting the issues for trial,[40] and scheduling matters. The court may consider stays, consolidations, or separate trials.[41] The court may also require parties to schedule presentation of evidence so that, if judgment as a matter of law or judgment on partial findings is appropriate, the court may

---

[30] *See, e.g., Lassiter v. City of Philadelphia*, 716 F.3d 53, 55 (3d Cir. 2013).

[31] *See, e.g., In re Engles Cases*, 767 F.3d 1082, 1090 (11th Cir. 2014).

[32] *See, e.g., MacArthur v. San Juan County*, 495 F.3d 1157, 1161–62 (10th Cir. 2007). *But cf., Rogan v. Menino*, 175 F.3d 75 (1st Cir. 1999) (district court cannot ignore procedural safeguards of Rule 56 summary judgment by dismissing defendants at pretrial conference).

[33] *See, e.g., Lassiter v. City of Philadelphia*, 716 F.3d 53, 55 (3d Cir. 2013).

[34] *See, e.g., Arias v. DynCorp*, 752 F.3d 1011, 1014 (D.C. Cir. 2014).

[35] *Skydive Arizona, Inc. v. Quattrocchi*, 673 F.3d 1105, 1113 (9th Cir. 2012).

[36] *See, e.g., Avila v. Willits Environmental Remediation Trust*, 633 F.3d 828, 833–34 (9th Cir. 2011).

[37] *Hollander v. Sandoz Pharmaceuticals Corp.*, 289 F.3d 1193 (10th Cir. 2002).

[38] *Planned Parenthood of Cent. New Jersey v. Verniero*, 22 F. Supp. 2d 331, 339 (D.N.J. 1998).

[39] *See, e.g., Adinolfe v. United Technologies Corp.*, 768 F.3d 1161, 1167 (11th Cir. 2014).

[40] *In re Air Crash Over Taiwan Straits on May 25, 2002*, 331 F. Supp. 2d 1176, 1194 (C.D. Cal. 2004) (discussing the split in authority over whether a court can require a party to stipulate as to uncontested facts); *Briggs v. Dalkon Shield*, 174 F.R.D. 369, 373 (D. Md. 1997) (the trial court may have "authority to order one party to accept a stipulation offered by the opposing party.").

[41] *See, e.g., Afunday Charters, Inc. v. ABC Ins. Co.*, 997 F.3d 390 (1st Cir. 2021) (separate trials authorized by Rule 16(c)(2)(M)).

reach those questions early in the trial. The court will also likely pursue the potential for settlement.[42] At the pretrial conference in a non-jury case, the court may decide to refer certain matters to another district judge, a magistrate judge, or a master.

Authority of Representatives

At the appropriate pretrial conference, which is usually the final pretrial conference, an attorney or party representative with the authority to enter stipulations and make admissions must be present.[43] Rule 16(c) also authorizes the court, if appropriate, to require that an attorney or party representative with authority to settle the case be present or available by telephone.

Memorializing Pretrial Conference

A court reporter generally will be present whenever the court expects to discuss and rule on issues at pretrial conference. In unusual circumstances, parties may bring their own stenographers if the court does not order a court reporter.

Settlement

The court may order parties to attend a conference where settlement will be discussed[44] but may not coerce those parties into settlement.[45] The court cannot mandate that the conference be open to the public.[46]

Rulings on Motions

At the pretrial conference, the court may rule on discovery motions, jurisdictional challenges, Rule 12(b) defenses preserved under Rule 12(g) and 12(h), other Rule 12 motions if those motions were not decided previously, motions for summary judgment,[47] or motions in limine.[48]

---

[42]*F.T.C. v. Freecom Communications, Inc.*, 401 F.3d 1192, 1208 (10th Cir. 2005) (the court may require that a party or its representative be present or available by telephone in order to consider settlement); *Sloan v. State Farm Mut. Auto. Ins. Co.*, 360 F.3d 1220, 1227 (10th Cir. 2004) (while settlement is an appropriate topic for a pretrial conference, some cases cannot be settled and the parties' desire for a trial must be respected).

[43]*See, e.g., In re University of Michigan*, 936 F.3d 460 (6th Cir. 2019) (acknowledging court's authority to compel attendance in most cases; but in situations where government official is involved (particularly an official who lacks authority to make final decision), district court does not normally have authority to compel attendance of particular public officer).

[44]*In re Patenaude*, 210 F.3d 135, 144 (3d Cir. 2000).

[45]*Goss Graphics Systems, Inc. v. DEV Industries, Inc.*, 267 F.3d 624, 627 (7th Cir. 2001).

[46]*See, e.g., In re University of Michigan*, 936 F.3d 460 (6th Cir. 2019); *Goodyear Tire & Rubber Co. v. Chiles Power Supply Inc.*, 332 F.3d 976 (6th Cir. 2003).

[47]*Pine Ridge Coal Co. v. Local 8377, United Mine Workers of America*, 187 F.3d 415, 419 (4th Cir. 1999); *but see Rogan v. Menino*, 175 F.3d 75, 80 (1st Cir. 1999) (court may not deprive a party of the procedural protections of Rule 56 by granting summary judg-

Binding Effect of Statements at Pretrial Conference

A party is held at trial to admissions and stipulations made at a pretrial conference.[49] However, the court may permit a party in certain circumstances to withdraw its stipulations.

Pretrial Memorandum or Narrative Statement

(1) *Time:* At the first pretrial conference and in its scheduling order the court will usually provide a date on which the parties must file a pretrial memorandum or pretrial narrative statement. The court usually orders the plaintiff's pretrial narrative statement to be filed several weeks after the close of discovery and the defendant's pretrial narrative statement several weeks after the filing of the plaintiff's statement.

(2) *Contents:* Local rule or court order will define the information parties are required to include in their pretrial narrative statements. Ordinarily, the parties must state their legal theories or defenses, provide a list of witnesses and documents to be presented at trial, detail the intended use of expert witnesses, and describe any exceptional legal or evidentiary questions that will be asserted at trial.

(3) *Effect and Amendment of:* The pretrial narrative statements are generally binding on the parties at trial, and failure to raise a legal issue may constitute waiver of that issue.[50] However, the court may permit the amendment of a pretrial narrative statement to include evidence not available at the time of filing the statement or for other legitimate reasons.[51]

(4) *Failure to File:* When a party fails to file a pretrial narrative statement required by local rule or court order, the court may impose sanctions under Rule 16(f).

RULE 16(d)—PRETRIAL ORDERS

CORE CONCEPT

Rule 16(d) requires the court to issue a pretrial order memorializing the action taken at any pretrial conference.[52] Once a pretrial order has been entered,[53] it supersedes all pleadings and controls the subsequent course of the case.[54] A pretrial order may

---

ment under Rule 16).

[48] *Tucker v. Ohtsu Tire & Rubber Co., Ltd.*, 49 F. Supp. 2d 456, 462–63 (D. Md. 1999).

[49] *Cf., Scahill v. District of Columbia*, 909 F.3d 1177 (D.C. Cir. 2018) (final pretrial order "supercede[s] all prior pleadings").

[50] *See McLean Contracting Co. v. Waterman Steamship Corp.*, 277 F.3d 477 (4th Cir. 2002).

[51] *Payne v. S. S. Nabob*, 302 F.2d 803, 807 (3d Cir. 1962).

[52] *Athridge v. Rivas*, 141 F.3d 357, 362 (D.C. Cir. 1998).

[53] *Wall v. County of Orange*, 364 F.3d 1107, 1111 (9th Cir. 2004) (a pretrial order that was lodged but not entered is not controlling).

[54] *Rockwell Intern. Corp. v. U.S.*, 549 U.S. 457 (2007).

include amendments to the pleadings,[55] stipulations, a statement of the issues for trial, the defenses available, the date for the filing of pretrial narrative statements, evidentiary or witness lists, and the date set for trial. The court may order a party to draft the order on the court's behalf.

APPLICATIONS

Pretrial Order Binding on Parties

All matters mentioned in the pretrial order are binding on the parties at trial.[56] Evidence or legal theories that are not at least implicitly raised in the pretrial order will be barred at trial unless admitted without objection.[57] Pretrial orders may not, however, be binding in retrials of the matter[58] or in subsequent litigation.[59] Because the purpose of Rule 16 is to clarify the real nature of the dispute,[60] a claim or theory not raised in the pretrial order should not be considered by the factfinder.[61] The court may impose sanctions under Rule 16(f) for a party's failure to comply with the order.

Objection to Pretrial Order and Preservation of Right to Appeal

In order to preserve a party's rights on appeal, a party should object to a pretrial order at the time it is issued or at the commencement of trial by asserting a motion to amend the order.

Modification of Pretrial Order

Where its modification will not unduly prejudice the opposing party, the court has discretion to modify a pretrial order to prevent manifest injustice.[62] The court may also modify a pretrial order when evidence not raised in the pretrial statement is discovered after the pretrial order has been issued,[63] or is introduced at trial.[64]

---

[55] *Deere v. Goodyear Tire and Rubber Co.*, 175 F.R.D. 157, 164–65 (N.D. N.Y. 1997).

[56] *Friedman & Friedman, Ltd. v. Tim McCandless, Inc.*, 606 F.3d 494 (8th Cir. 2010).

[57] *Caradigm USA LLC v. PruittHealth, Inc.*, 964 F.3d 1259, 1279 (11th Cir. 2020).

[58] *Johns Hopkins University v. CellPro, Inc.*, 152 F.3d 1342, 1357 (Fed. Cir. 1998).

[59] *Atchison, Topeka and Santa Fe Ry. Co. v. Hercules Inc.*, 146 F.3d 1071, 1074 (9th Cir. 1998).

[60] *See, e.g., Doe v. Tangipahoa Parish School Bd.*, 478 F.3d 679 (5th Cir. 2007); *Myrick v. Husqvarna Pro. Prod., Inc.*, 508 F.Supp.3d 846, 860 (D. Kan. 2020).

[61] *See, e.g., Kona Technology Corp. v. Southern Pacific Transp. Co.*, 225 F.3d 595, 604 (5th Cir. 2000).

[62] *Galdamez v. Potter*, 415 F.3d 1015, 1020 (9th Cir. 2005) (setting forth a four-part test for determination of whether to modify a pretrial order); *In re El Paso Refinery, L P*, 171 F.3d 249, 255 (5th Cir. 1999).

[63] *Ross v. Garner Printing Co.*, 285 F.3d 1106, 1114 (8th Cir. 2002).

[64] *See United Phosphorus, Ltd. v. Midland Fumigant, Inc.*, 205 F.3d 1219, 1236 (10th Cir. 2000).

Appeal of Pretrial Order

Prior to the entry of judgment, a party has no right to a direct appeal from a pretrial order.[65] Ultimately, the pretrial order will be reviewed for abuse of discretion.[66]

RULE 16(e)—FINAL PRETRIAL CONFERENCE AND ORDERS

CORE CONCEPT

The court will usually conduct the final pretrial conference after the pretrial narrative statements have been filed and as close to trial as possible.[67] At the final pretrial conference, the court will make a schedule for any remaining motions and set a trial date. Stipulations and admissions made at this last pretrial conference are normally binding.[68]

An attorney who will conduct the trial or an unrepresented party must attend the conference with the authority to enter stipulations and make admissions.

Standard for Modifying Final Pretrial Order

Final pretrial orders are not easily modifiable. The general standard for a modification or amendment is prevention of "manifest injustice."[69] Manifest injustice generally cannot be shown where a party requests to amend based on evidence that the party knew about at the time of the pretrial conference.[70] As applied in the context of damages, late pretrial amendments have been permitted where no surprise would result and the change was already supported by evidence in the record.[71] It is unsettled whether the focus is on manifest injustice to the moving party or the nonmoving party.[72]

Relation to Rule 36(b)

Rule 36 governs request for admissions.[73] Rule 36(b) governs circumstances in which an admission previously made may be

---

[65] *Bradley v. Milliken*, 468 F.2d 902 (6th Cir. 1972).

[66] *Harper v. Albert*, 400 F.3d 1052, 1063 (7th Cir. 2005); *Koch v. Koch Industries, Inc.*, 203 F.3d 1202, 1222 (10th Cir. 2000).

[67] *See Matter of Rhone-Poulenc Rorer Pharmaceuticals, Inc.*, 138 F.3d 695, 697 (7th Cir. 1998).

[68] *See, e.g., Pittman by Hamilton v. County of Madison*, 863 F.3d 734 (7th Cir. 2017).

[69] Rule 16(e). *See also, e.g., Rodriguez-Garcia v. Miranda-Marin*, 610 F.3d 756 (1st Cir. 2010).

[70] *Jordan v. Maxfield & Oberton Holdings, L.L.C.*, 977 F.3d 412, 421 (5th Cir. 2020).

[71] *See, e.g., United States ex rel. Concilio De Salud Integral De Loiza, Inc. v. J.C. Remodeling, Inc.*, 962 F.3d 34 (1st Cir. 2020). *Cf., e.g., Quick Techs, Inc. v. Sage Group PLC*, 313 F.3d 338 (5th Cir. 2002) (rejecting proposed amended pretrial order adding new claim for distinguishable damages).

[72] *McBroom v. Ethicon, Inc.*, 341 F.R.D. 40, 43 (D. Ariz. 2022) (focusing on the moving party, but recognizing opposing authority).

[73] Rule 36.

withdrawn or amended.[74] Rule 36(b) expressly states that the standard for permitting such a change is found in Rule 16(e).[75]

RULE 16(f)—SANCTIONS

CORE CONCEPT

Upon motion or on the court's own initiative, the court will impose sanctions to force parties to comply with scheduling and pretrial orders and to compensate parties for expenses caused by an opposing party's noncompliance.[76] Sanctions may also attach to incorrect or incomplete pretrial statements,[77] or the failure to participate in a settlement conference in good faith.[78]

APPLICATIONS

Procedural and Substantive Errors

When a party commits a procedural error, courts generally will not impose sanctions that compromise the merits of the case.[79] Instead the court should impose costs and fees. When a party commits a substantive error, the court may impose sanctions which compromise the merits of a party's case.[80]

Sanctions Imposed on Party's Motion

A party may file a motion for sanctions when a party or a party's attorney does not obey a scheduling[81] or pretrial order, when a party does not appear at a pretrial conference,[82] when a party is unprepared at a pretrial conference, or when a party does not act in good faith at a pretrial conference. The motion should be asserted as soon as possible after the sanctionable activity. Unless made during a hearing or trial, a party must file a written motion stating the reasons for the sanctions with particularity and the relief or order sought.

Sanctions Imposed Sua Sponte

When the court seeks to impose sanctions on its own initiative, the court must first provide notice and an opportunity to

---

[74] Rule 36(b).

[75] Rule 16(e). *See, e.g., Tate & Lyle Americas, LLC v. Glatt Air Techniques, Inc*, 863 F.3d 569 (7th Cir. 2017).

[76] *Garlepied v. Main*, 2001 WL 305264, at *1 (E.D. La. 2001).

[77] *Bronk v. Ineichen*, 54 F.3d 425, 10 A.D.D. 143 (7th Cir. 1995).

[78] *Smith v. Northwest Financial Acceptance, Inc.*, 129 F.3d 1408, 1419 (10th Cir. 1997); *Landmark Legal Foundation v. E.P.A.*, 272 F. Supp. 2d 70, 88 (D.D.C. 2003).

[79] *Rice v. City of Chicago*, 333 F.3d 780, 786 (7th Cir. 2003).

[80] *See, e.g., Lucien v. Breweur*, 9 F.3d 26, 29 (7th Cir. 1993). *But see, Ball v. City of Chicago*, 2 F.3d 752, 758 (7th Cir. 1993) (punishing a lawyer through monetary sanctions preferable to punishing plaintiff through dismissal when fault lies with lawyer).

[81] *Lucas Automotive Engineering, Inc. v. Bridgestone/Firestone, Inc.*, 275 F.3d 762 (9th Cir. 2001) (sanctioning a party for failing to appear for a scheduled mediation).

[82] *Templet v. HydroChem Inc.*, 367 F.3d 473, 481 (5th Cir. 2004).

be heard to the sanctionable party.[83]

Purposes of Sanctions

Sanctions may be assessed to punish for improper conduct,[84] for purposes of deterrence,[85] or to compensate the party injured by the improper conduct.

Finding of Sanctionable Activity

The court will examine the record and any materials submitted by the parties. The court must make a specific finding of sanctionable activity. When it finds that a party has committed sanctionable activities, the court has discretion to impose sanctions, even in the absence of bad faith.[86] However, sanctions may be imposed under Rule 16(f) only where the allegedly violated order is unambiguous.[87] The court will not impose sanctions when the party can substantially justify its violation[88] or where the award of expenses would be unjust.

(1) *Against Whom:* The court may impose sanctions against the party and/or any attorney of the party.[89] Where a represented party has no knowledge of the sanctionable activity, the court may order sanctions against the attorney alone and preclude reimbursement from the client.

(2) *Notice and Hearing:* Before imposing sanctions, the court must provide the alleged sanctionable party with notice and an opportunity to be heard either orally or in writing.[90]

Nature of Sanctions

The court have considerable discretion to design a sanction that appropriately matches the violation.[91] The court can impose any sanctions it deems appropriate,[92] including but not

---

[83]*Ford v. Alfaro*, 785 F.2d 835 (9th Cir. 1986); *Newton v. A.C. & S., Inc.*, 918 F.2d 1121 (3d Cir. 1990).

[84]*U.S. v. Samaniego*, 345 F.3d 1280, 1284 (11th Cir. 2003).

[85]*See, e.g., Media Duplication Services, Ltd. v. HDG Software, Inc.*, 928 F.2d 1228, 1242 (1st Cir. 1991).

[86]*Rice v. Barnes*, 201 F.R.D. 549, 551 (M.D. Ala. 2001); *Martin Family Trust v. Heco/Nostalgia Enterprises Co.*, 186 F.R.D. 601, 604 (E.D. Cal. 1999).

[87]*See, e.g., Act Now to Stop War and End Racism Coalition v. District of Columbia*, 846 F.3d 391, 414–15 (D.C. Cir. 2017).

[88]*Firefighter's Institute for Racial Equality ex rel. Anderson v. City of St. Louis*, 220 F.3d 898, 902 (8th Cir. 2000).

[89]*Nick v. Morgan's Foods, Inc.*, 270 F.3d 590, 597 (8th Cir. 2001); *Republic of Philippines v. Westinghouse Elec. Corp.*, 43 F.3d 65 (3d Cir. 1994).

[90]*Tellado v. IndyMac Mortgage Services*, 707 F.3d 275, 282 (3d Cir. 2013) (absence of notice requires reversal of sanctions order).

[91]*Liebowitz v. Bandshell Artist Mgmt.*, 6 F.4th 267, 290 (2d Cir. 2021); *Republic of Philippines v. Westinghouse Elec. Corp.*, 43 F.3d 65 (3d Cir. 1994).

[92]*Young v. Gordon*, 330 F.3d 76 (1st Cir. 2003); *Arnold v. Krause, Inc.*, 233 F.R.D. 126, 129 (W.D. N.Y. 2005) (Rule 16(f) allows the court to impose sanctions it deems just).

limited to the following:[93]

(1) *Discovery Sanctions:* Rule 16(f) incorporates the discovery sanctions found in Rule 37(b)(2)(B),[94] (C),[95] and (D), such as refusing to allow a party to support or oppose designated claims or defenses,[96] striking pleadings or parts thereof, precluding witnesses not properly disclosed,[97] or treating the conduct as contempt of court.[98]

(2) *Reasonable Expenses:* The court must require the sanctionable person to pay reasonable expenses,[99] including attorney fees caused by noncompliance with Rule 16, unless the court finds that the noncompliance was "substantially justified" or that an award of expenses would be "unjust."[100] These expenses may be the only sanctions ordered or in addition to another sanction.

(3) *Court Costs:* The court may impose court costs on a party who causes court expense by the sanctionable activities.

(4) *Fines and Disciplinary Action:* In lieu of or in addition to other sanctions, the court may impose a fine[101] upon or seek disciplinary action against the sanctionable party.[102]

(5) *Dismissal:* The court may even dismiss a case[103] or enter default judgment[104] for failure to obey pretrial orders.[105] However, a trial court must apply lesser sanctions than dismissal except in an extreme situation where there is a clear record of delay or disobedience.[106] Some pertinent factors considered by the courts are the severity of the violation, the legitimacy of the party's excuse, repetition of violations, the deliberateness of the misconduct, mitigating excuses, prejudice

---

[93] *Nick v. Morgan's Foods, Inc.*, 270 F.3d 590, 595–96 (8th Cir. 2001).

[94] *Velez v. Awning Windows, Inc.*, 375 F.3d 35, 44 (1st Cir. 2004).

[95] *In re Orthopedic "Bone Screw" Products Liability Litigation*, 132 F.3d 152, 154 (3d Cir. 1997).

[96] *Velez v. Awning Windows, Inc.*, 375 F.3d 35, 42 (1st Cir. 2004).

[97] *See, e.g., Amplatz v. Country Mutual Insurance Co.*, 823 F.3d 1167 (8th Cir. 2016).

[98] *Trilogy Communications, Inc. v. Times Fiber Communications, Inc.*, 109 F.3d 739, 745 (Fed. Cir. 1997); *Bronk v. Ineichen*, 54 F.3d 425, 10 A.D.D. 143 (7th Cir. 1995).

[99] *See, e.g., Tracinda Corp. v. DaimlerChrysler AG*, 502 F.3d 212, 214 (3d Cir. 2007); *Former Employees of Tyco Electronics, Fiber Optics Div. v. U.S. Dept. of Labor*, 27 Ct. Int'l Trade 380, 259 F. Supp. 2d 1246 (2003) (attorney's fees can be reduced even if reasonable for the tasks at issue).

[100] *Richardson v. Nassau County*, 184 F.R.D. 497 (E.D. N.Y. 1999).

[101] *Nick v. Morgan's Foods, Inc.*, 270 F.3d 590, 595–96 (8th Cir. 2001).

[102] *See Legault v. Zambarano*, 105 F.3d 24, 28–29 (1st Cir. 1997).

[103] *See, e.g., Nascimento v. Dummer*, 508 F.3d 905, 909 (9th Cir. 2007).

[104] *ChromaDex, Inc. v. Elysium Health, Inc.*, 535 F. Supp. 3d 906, 912 (C.D. Cal. 2021) (entering default is appropriate only where a court finds that the party's conduct demonstrates willfulness, fault, or bad faith).

[105] *Bay Fireworks, Inc. v. Frenkel & Co., Inc.*, 359 F. Supp. 2d 257, 262 (E.D. N.Y. 2005).

[106] *Tower Ventures, Inc. v. City of Westfield*, 296 F.3d 43, 45–46 (1st Cir. 2002).

to the court or opponent, and the adequacy of lesser sanctions.[107]

Additional Research References

Wright & Miller, *Federal Practice and Procedure* §§ 1521 to 1540
C.J.S., Federal Civil Procedure §§ 905 to 914
West's Key Number Digest, Federal Civil Procedure ⚷1921 to 1943

---

[107] *Gripe v. City of Enid, Okl.*, 312 F.3d 1184, 1188 (10th Cir. 2002); *Ehrenhaus v. Reynolds*, 965 F.2d 916, 921 (10th Cir. 1992).

IV. PARTIES

RULE 17
PLAINTIFF AND DEFENDANT; CAPACITY; PUBLIC OFFICERS

(a) Real Party in Interest.

(1) *Designation in General.* An action must be prosecuted in the name of the real party in interest. The following may sue in their own names without joining the person for whose benefit the action is brought:

(A) an executor;

(B) an administrator;

(C) a guardian;

(D) a bailee;

(E) a trustee of an express trust;

(F) a party with whom or in whose name a contract has been made for another's benefit; and

(G) a party authorized by statute.

(2) *Action in the Name of the United States for Another's Use or Benefit.* When a federal statute so provides, an action for another's use or benefit must be brought in the name of the United States.

(3) *Joinder of the Real Party in Interest.* The court may not dismiss an action for failure to prosecute in the name of the real party in interest until, after an objection, a reasonable time has been allowed for the real party in interest to ratify, join, or be substituted into the action. After ratification, joinder, or substitution, the action proceeds as if it had been originally commenced by the real party in interest.

(b) Capacity to Sue or Be Sued. Capacity to sue or be sued is determined as follows:

(1) for an individual who is not acting in a representative capacity, by the law of the individual's domicile;

(2) for a corporation, by the law under which it was organized; and

(3) for all other parties, by the law of the state where the court is located, except that:

(A) a partnership or other unincorporated association with no such capacity under that state's law may sue or be sued in its common name to enforce a substantive right existing under the United States Constitution or laws; and

(B) 28 U.S.C. §§ 754 and 959(a) govern the capacity of a receiver appointed by a United States court to sue or be sued in a United States court.

(c) Minor or Incompetent Person.

(1) *With a Representative.* The following representatives may sue or defend on behalf of a minor or an incompetent person:

(A) a general guardian;

(B) a committee;

(C) a conservator; or

(D) a like fiduciary.

(2) *Without a Representative.* A minor or an incompetent person who does not have a duly appointed representative may sue by a next friend or by a guardian ad litem. The court must appoint a guardian ad litem—or issue another appropriate order—to protect a minor or incompetent person who is unrepresented in an action.

(d) Public Officer's Title and Name. A public officer who sues or is sued in an official capacity may be designated by official title rather than by name, but the court may order that the officer's name be added.

[Amended effective March 19, 1948; October 20, 1949; July 1, 1966; August 1, 1987; August 1, 1988; November 18, 1988; April 30, 2007, effective December 1, 2007.]

AUTHORS' COMMENTARY ON RULE 17

PURPOSE AND SCOPE

Rule 17 controls the determination of who may prosecute or defend against an action in federal court. The primary purposes of the Rule are to ensure that the parties have a significant interest in the litigation and to protect the defendant against a subsequent action by the party actually entitled to recover.[1]

RULE 17(a)—REAL PARTY IN INTEREST

CORE CONCEPT

The only parties on whose behalf suits may be initiated are those persons whose interests will be materially affected by the outcome;[2] the "real party in interest."[3] The real party in interest is the person who is entitled to enforce the right asserted under the governing substantive law.[4] Such persons must be the named plaintiffs unless one of the exceptions applies. This requirement is imposed on plaintiffs so that defendants will only have to face one suit over the same interest.[5]

APPLICATIONS

Naming the Interested Party

Subject to exceptions discussed below, the suit must be commenced not only on behalf of the real party in interest but also in the name of the real party in interest.[6] Thus, the real party in interest generally must be named in the caption.[7] For example, a claim by a corporation must be brought in the corporation's name, not the name of its principal owner.[8] In rare instances, compelling concerns relating to personal privacy or confidentiality may warrant some degree of anonymity in judicial proceedings, including the use of a pseudonym.[9]

---

[1] *Russ v. Jackson Cty. Sch. Bd.*, __ F. Supp. 3d __, 613 n.1 (N.D. Fla. 2021).

[2] *See, e.g., United HealthCare Corp. v. American Trade Ins. Co., Ltd.*, 88 F.3d 563, 569 (8th Cir. 1996).

[3] *Abraugh v. Altimus*, 26 F.4th 298, 304 (5th Cir. 2022).

[4] *Wilmington Tr., Nat'l Ass'n as Tr. for Holders of UBS Com. Mortg. Tr. 2018-C10, Com. Mortg. Pass-Through Certificates, Series 2018-C10 v. 410 S. Main St. LLC*, 584 F. Supp. 3d 689, 701 (N.D. Ind. 2022); *Cahoo v. Fast Enterprises LLC*, 528 F. Supp. 3d 719 (E.D. Mich. 2021).

[5] *See, e.g., Curtis Lumber Co. v. Louisiana Pacific Corp.*, 618 F.3d 762, 771 (8th Cir. 2010); *Marina Management Services, Inc. v. Vessel My Girls*, 202 F.3d 315, 318 (D.C. Cir. 2000).

[6] *United States v. Aetna Casualty & Surety Co.*, 338 U.S. 366, 380–81 (1949) (if insurer pays entire loss to insured, insurer is real party in interest; if insurer pays only part of loss, both insured and insurer are real parties in interest); *Abraugh v. Altimus*, 26 F.4th 298, 304 (5th Cir. 2022). *But cf., Sealed Plaintiff v. Sealed Defendant*, 537 F.3d 185, 191 n.3 (2d Cir. 2008) (use of pseudonym does not conflict with Rule 17(a)).

[7] *Lincoln Property Co. v. Roche*, 546 U.S. 81 (2005).

[8] *Bryant v. BMW of N. Am. LLC*, __ F. Supp. 3d __, 2022 WL 432501, at *2 (E.D. Wis. 2022).

[9] *Doe v. Regents of Univ. of Colorado*, __ F. Supp. 3d __, 2022 WL

Remedy

The preferred remedy when the complaint names the wrong party as a plaintiff is to allow the party an opportunity to amend so that the action can be prosecuted by the real party in interest.[10] Dismissal is a disfavored remedy for violation of the requirement to name the real party in interest as plaintiff.[11] Before a court grants a motion to dismiss, it must allow a real party in interest a reasonable opportunity to correct the defect by joining the action, or, if permitted as an exception to Rule 17(a), to ratify continuation of the action in the name of the original plaintiff.[12] If the real party in interest takes such action, it is effective as if the joinder or ratification had occurred at the onset of the litigation.[13]

- *Ratification:* Rule 17(a) explicitly allows the real party in interest to ratify an action brought in someone else's name by: (1) authorizing continuation of the action and (2) agreeing to be bound by its result.[14]

No Mandatory Joinder of All Potential Plaintiffs: Rule 19

Rule 17(a) requires that the plaintiff must generally be a real party in interest. It does not require the joinder of all persons who are real parties in interest with similar claims.[15] To determine whether an unnamed person should have been joined, see Rule 19.[16]

Rule 17(a) Does Not Apply to the Naming of Defendants

Rule 17(a) governs the identity of the plaintiffs in an action; it does not address the identity of the defendants.[17]

1210429, *4 (D. Colo. 2022); *Student "B" v. Howard Cty. Cmty. Coll.*, 512 F. Supp. 3d 610, 613 n.1 (D. Md. 2021).

[10] *See, e.g.*, *Esposito v. U.S.*, 368 F.3d 1271, 1272 (10th Cir. 2004); *Dunmore v. U.S.*, 358 F.3d 1107, 1112 (9th Cir. 2004).

[11] *See, e.g.*, *Wieburg v. GTE Southwest Inc.*, 272 F.3d 302, 308–09 (5th Cir. 2001); *Intown Properties Management, Inc. v. Wheaton Van Lines, Inc.*, 271 F.3d 164, 170 (4th Cir. 2001).

[12] *Harrison v. Forde*, ___ F. Supp. 3d ___, 2022 WL 898742, at *2 (S.D. Ala. 2022).

[13] *See, e.g.*, *Scheufler v. General Host Corp.*, 126 F.3d 1261, 1270 (10th Cir. 1997); *O'Hara v. District No. 1-PCD*, 56 F.3d 1514, 1519 (D.C. Cir. 1995).

[14] *Cahoo v. Fast Enterprises LLC*, 528 F. Supp. 3d 719, 745 (E.D. Mich. 2021).

[15] *See, e.g.*, *Moss v. Princip*, 913 F.3d 508 (5th Cir. 2019); *Excimer Associates, Inc. v. LCA Vision, Inc.*, 292 F.3d 134, 140 (2d Cir. 2002).

[16] *See, e.g.*, *Tifford v. Tandem Energy Corp.*, 562 F.3d 699, 707 (5th Cir. 2009).

[17] *Lincoln Property Co. v. Roche*, 546 U.S. 81, 90 (2005).

Raising a Rule 17(a) Defense

The manner in which a defendant may invoke Rule 17(a) is not clear.[18] Some courts indicate that the appropriate way to raise Rule 17 is through a pleading,[19] while other authority indicates it might be the appropriate subject of a motion.[20]

Invoking Rule 17(a) *Sua Sponte*

Most courts hold that the district court, as well as the parties, may raise a Rule 17(a) issue.[21]

Timing; Waiver

Rule 17(a) does not provide an express time limit within which an objection must be made. However, if the objection is not made with reasonable promptness, it may be waived.[22]

Exceptions to Naming Interested Party

Rule 17(a) explicitly exempts certain categories of persons from the general principle that the named party be the real party in interest. The most important of these enumerated exceptions are executors, administrators, guardians, trustees,[23] persons who have made contracts on behalf of third parties,[24] and circumstances where a statute authorizes suit in the name of a representative party.[25]

Suits in the Name of the United States

If a statute allows the United States to sue on behalf of a real party in interest, Rule 17(a) also permits the United States to be the named plaintiff.

Relation to Rule 15

If an existing party must be replaced for failure to meet the requirements of Rule 17, the real party in interest would normally join the litigation through the amendment process of Rule 15. If a party is properly joined under Rule 17, any evalu-

[18] *Whelan v. Abell*, 953 F.2d 663, 672 n.7 (D.C. Cir. 1992).

[19] *See, e.g., Addax Energy SA v. M/V Yasa H. Mulla*, 987 F.3d 80, 85 (4th Cir. 2021) (Rule 17 may be raised as affirmative defense).

[20] *See, e.g., In re Signal Intern., LLC*, 579 F.3d 478, 490 n.8 (5th Cir. 2009); *Lans v. Digital Equipment Corp.*, 252 F.3d 1320 (Fed. Cir. 2001).

[21] *See, e.g., Weissman v. Weener*, 12 F.3d 84 (7th Cir. 1993).

[22] *See, e.g., DaVita, Inc. v. Marietta Mem'l Hosp. Emp. Health Benefit Plan*, 978 F.3d 326 (6th Cir. 2020).

[23] *See, e.g., Revitalizing Auto Communities Env't Response Tr. v. Nat'l Grid USA*, 10 F.4th 87, 97 (2d Cir. 2021); *Lenon v. St. Paul Mercury Ins. Co.*, 136 F.3d 1365, 1370 n.2 (10th Cir. 1998).

[24] *See, e.g., Local 538 United Broth. of Carpenters and Joiners of America v. U.S. Fidelity and Guar. Co.*, 70 F.3d 741, 743 (2d Cir. 1995).

[25] *See, e.g., Wilson v. Dollar General Corp.*, 717 F.3d 337 (4th Cir. 2013) (in bankruptcy cases, Chapter 7 trustee has standing, not debtor; but in Chapter 13 cases, both trustee and debtor may have standing); *U.S. ex rel. Long v. SCS Business & Technical Institute, Inc.*, 173 F.3d 870 (D.C. Cir. 1999) (False Claims Act).

ation of the joinder under Rule 15 will not be rigorous.[26] There is disagreement about whether a court may entertain a motion filed by a plaintiff who lacks standing to amend a complaint to substitute a party who does have standing.[27]

Intervenors under Rule 24

If a person seeks to intervene in an action under Rule 24 in order to assert a claim, that potential party must meet the requirements of Rule 17(a).[28]

Relation to Rule 25

Rule 17 controls who may be named as a plaintiff at the time of the commencement of the suit, while Rule 25(c) controls events occurring after the suit is filed.[29]

Citizenship of the Plaintiff for Purposes of Diversity Jurisdiction

Although Rule 17(a) dictates the identity of the named plaintiff, separate rules determine whose citizenship must be considered for purpose of evaluating diversity jurisdiction.[30] For example, Rule 17(a) permits an executor of a decedent's estate to be a named plaintiff. However, § 1332(c)(2) provides that for purposes of diversity jurisdiction in an action brought on behalf of a decedent, the relevant citizenship is that of the deceased. Thus, under Rule 17(a), the executor may initiate the suit, but diversity is dependent on the citizenship of the decedent.[31]

Article III Standing v. Real Party in Interest

While the requirements of standing and Rule 17(a) may differ in some respects,[32] both share the requirement that the

---

[26]*See, e.g., Intown Properties Management, Inc. v. Wheaton Van Lines, Inc.*, 271 F.3d 164, 170 (4th Cir. 2001); *Scheufler v. General Host Corp.*, 126 F.3d 1261, 1270 (10th Cir. 1997).

[27]*Compare Yan v. ReWalk Robotics Ltd.*, 973 F.3d 22 (1st Cir. 2020) (motion to substitute allowed); *with Crocheron v. State Farm Fire & Cas. Co.*, 621 B.R. 659, 662 (E.D. Mich. 2020) (where the original plaintiff has no standing to bring the action, she has no standing to make a motion to substitute the real party in interest).

[28]*See, e.g., Ross v. Marshall*, 426 F.3d 745, 757 (5th Cir. 2005).

[29]*See, e.g., F.D.I.C. v. Deglau*, 207 F.3d 153, 159 (3d Cir. 2000); *Kumaran v. Nat'l Futures Ass'n*, ___ F. Supp. 3d ___, 2022 WL 1749133, at *4 (S.D.N.Y. 2022).

[30]*Wilmington Tr., Nat'l Ass'n as Tr. for Holders of UBS Com. Mortg. Tr. 2018-C10, Com. Mortg. Pass-Through Certificates, Series 2018-C10 v. 410 S. Main St. LLC*, ___ F. Supp. 3d ___, 2022 WL 355779, at *5 (N.D. Ind. 2022).

[31]*See, e.g., Airlines Reporting Corp. v. S and N Travel, Inc.*, 58 F.3d 857, 862 (2d Cir. 1995).

[32]*See, e.g, Abraugh v. Altimus*, 26 F.4th 298, 304 (5th Cir. 2022) (Rule 17(a) requires that case be prosecuted in name of real party in interest, while constitutional standing requires: (1) injury in fact; (2) connection between injury and defendant's conduct; and (3) redressability); *Rawoof v. Texor Petroleum Co.*, 521 F.3d 750, 756 (7th Cir. 2008).

plaintiff has a personal interest in the case.[33] A key difference between Rule 17(a) and Article III standing is that an affirmative defense under Rule 17(a) can be waived, while Article III standing is a constitutional requirement that cannot be waived.[34]

RULE 17(b)—CAPACITY TO SUE OR BE SUED

CORE CONCEPT

This provision chooses the law that will govern the capacity of a person to prosecute or defend a suit in federal court.

APPLICATIONS

Natural Persons

For individuals, the law of their domicile determines their capacity to sue or be sued.[35] Domicile is generally defined as the jurisdiction where a person has established a physical presence and has the intent to remain for an indefinite period.[36]

Natural Persons as Representatives of Others

For natural persons suing on behalf of another, such as guardians or executors of estates, the law of the state in which the court sits determines their capacity to sue or be sued.[37]

Corporations

The capacity of a corporation to sue or be sued is governed by the law of the jurisdiction in which the corporation is incorporated.[38]

Unincorporated Associations

If the cause of action is based on a federal question, an unincorporated association like a partnership may sue or be sued to enforce a right under the United States Constitution or laws.[39] By contrast, if the cause of action is founded on state law, the capacity of an unincorporated association to sue or be sued is governed by state law.[40]

Governmental Entities

Governmental entities may be sued only if a governing state

---

[33] *See, e.g., APCC Services, Inc. v. Sprint Communications Co.*, 418 F.3d 1238 (D.C. Cir. 2005).

[34] *RK Co. v. See*, 622 F.3d 846 (7th Cir. 2010).

[35] *See, e.g., Johns v. County of San Diego*, 114 F.3d 874 (9th Cir.1997).

[36] *See, e.g., Stifel v. Hopkins*, 477 F.2d 1116, 1120 (6th Cir. 1973).

[37] *See, e.g., Revitalizing Auto Communities Env't Response Tr. v. Nat'l Grid USA*, 10 F.4th 87, 97 (2d Cir. 2021); *Crozier for A.C. v. Westside Cmty. Sch. Dist.*, 973 F.3d 882, 887 (8th Cir. 2020).

[38] *See, e.g., Pappas v. Philip Morris, Inc.*, 915 F.3d 889 (2d Cir. 2019).

[39] *Fort Lauderdale Food Not Bombs v. City of Fort Lauderdale*, 11 F.4th 1266, 1280 (11th Cir. 2021); *Fund Liquidation Holdings LLC v. Bank of Am. Corp.*, 991 F.3d 370, 382 (2d Cir. 2021).

[40] *See, e.g., Doe v. McKesson*, 922 F.3d 604 (5th Cir. 2019).

law authorizes such a suit.[41] It is unclear whether the capacity of a wholly owned corporation of the United States, such as the Tennessee Valley Authority, to sue or be sued should be determined under state or federal law.[42]

Receivers

The capacity of receivers appointed by a federal judge to litigate in a federal court is governed by 28 U.S.C.A. §§ 754 (appointment of receivers in different federal judicial districts) and 959(a) (suits against receivers).

Capacity Distinguished from Real Party in Interest

There are two important differences between capacity (Rule 17(b)) and real parties in interest (Rule 17(a)) and the concerns they address. The first is that satisfying real party in interest requirements is the duty of those who file claims, most typically plaintiffs. Capacity, by contrast, measures the ability of both plaintiffs and defendants to participate in a suit, even if the defendant has not filed a counterclaim or a crossclaim. The second difference is in the concepts underlying the respective provisions of Rule 17. Individuals may, because they are individuals, have capacity to sue. Capacity alone, however, does not permit those individuals to initiate a suit or to defend one. Unless they also have a material interest in the outcome of a cause of action, they may not bring a suit (or defend against a suit) because they are not also the real parties in interest.[43] Thus, to bring a suit, a party must have both "capacity," under the applicable law chosen by Rule 17(b), as well as a real stake in the outcome, as defined by Rule 17(a). To be sued, a defendant need only satisfy the law of capacity selected by Rule 17(b).

RULE 17(c)—MINOR OR INCOMPETENT PERSONS

CORE CONCEPT

Rule 17(c) requires that infants and other persons unable to represent their own interests must be represented in suits in federal court.[44] The provisions apply irrespective of whether the infant or incompetent person is participating in the suit as a plaintiff or defendant.

---

[41] *See, e.g., Smith v. Munday*, 848 F.3d 248, 256–57 (4th Cir. 2017) (state law does not permit suit against police department); *Connelly v. Cook Cnty. Assessor's Off.*, __ F. Supp. 3d __, 2022 WL 294764, at *2 (N.D. Ill. 2022).

[42] *Waterhouse v. Tennessee Valley Auth.*, 475 F. Supp. 3d 817, 823 (E.D. Tenn. 2020), aff'd, 2021 WL 1230371 (6th Cir. 2021).

[43] *See, e.g., Revitalizing Auto Communities Env't Response Tr. v. Nat'l Grid USA*, 10 F.4th 87, 98 (2d Cir. 2021); *Lans v. Digital Equipment Corp.*, 252 F.3d 1320 (Fed. Cir. 2001).

[44] *See, e.g., Baloco ex rel. Tapia v. Drummond Co.*, 640 F.3d 1338, 1350 (11th Cir. 2011).

APPLICATIONS

Infants and Incompetents Already Represented

Where persons unable to care for their own interests already have others charged with the duty to care for them outside of litigation, such as guardians, Rule 17(c) grants such guardians authority to sue on behalf of the persons in their care.[45]

Infants and Incompetents Not Already Represented

Where persons unable to care for their own interests are not already within the legal authority of others, the court has power to appoint guardians *ad litem* (persons who will represent the interest of others in litigation), and to make other orders consistent with the best interests of infants and incompetents in litigation.[46] Unlike Rule 17(b), Rule 17(c) does not defer to state standards for appointment; instead Rule 17(c) directs the district court to look to the best interests of the infant.[47]

In the absence of "actual documentation or testimony by a mental health professional, a court of record, or a relevant public agency," the district court has no duty to make a sua sponte inquiry into a pro se party's lack of mental capacity.[48]

However, if an unrepresented party is an infant or an incompetent person, the district court normally has an affirmative duty to appoint a guardian *ad litem* or to take other appropriate action.[49] If a district court receives "verifiable evidence of incompetence," it is required to make a *sua sponte* inquiry.[50]

Absence of Interest in Case

If a person has no interest in a case that could have been

---

[45] *See, e.g., Kile v. United States*, 915 F.3d 682 (10th Cir. 2019): *Fernandez-Vargas v. Pfizer*, 522 F.3d 55, 67 (1st Cir. 2008).

[46] *See, e.g., Berrios v. New York City Housing Authority*, 564 F.3d 130, 134 (2d Cir. 2009); *Wenger v. Canastota Cent. School Dist.*, 146 F.3d 123 (2d Cir. 1998); *but see Bunn v. Perdue*, 966 F.3d 1094, 1100 (10th Cir. 2020) (party cannot evade rules about attorney representation by naming person as his non-attorney representative under Rule 17 without a showing of incompetence).

[47] *See, e.g., Gibbs ex rel. Gibbs v. Carnival Cruise Lines*, 314 F.3d 125, 135-36 (3d Cir. 2002); *but see Rideau v. Keller Independent School District*, 819 F.3d 155, 163 (5th Cir. 2016) (permitting use of state law for Rule 17(c) issues where Rule 17(b) calls for application of state law in analogous situations).

[48] *See, e.g., Naruto v. Slater*, 888 F.3d 418 (9th Cir. 2018); *Ferrelli v. River Manor Health Care Center*, 323 F.3d 196, 202 (2d Cir. 2003).

[49] *See, e.g., Sanchez v. R.G.L.*, 761 F3d. 495, 507–08 (5th Cir. 2014); *Ferrelli v. River Manor Health Care Center*, 323 F.3d 196, 202 (2d Cir. 2003) (Rule 17(c) inquiry is mandatory "if there has been an adjudication of incompetence by an appropriate court of record or a relevant public agency").

[50] *See, e.g., Powell v. Symons*, 680 F.3d 301, 307 (3d Cir. 2012) (bizarre behavior of a prison inmate, standing alone, will not trigger evaluation of competence); *Mayorga v. Ronaldo*, 491 F. Supp. 3d 840, 858 (D. Nev. 2020).

protected by a guardian *ad litem*, the court is not required to evaluate the person's competence prior to dismissal.[51]

Comparing Standing with Lack of Capacity

Standing is a jurisdictional requirement. Where standing is lacking, it cannot be waived or cured. Lack of capacity, by contrast, is not jurisdictional, and a defect in appointment of a guardian can be cured if there is a timely objection and notice of the defect.[52]

Standing of "Next Friend"

Rule 17 (c) imposes no requirement that a next friend have standing to sue in the same case on the next friend's own behalf.[53]

Substituted Real Party in Interest: Statute of Limitations

If a case requires substitution of a real party in interest, the claim of the substituted party relates back to the date of the original filing.[54]

Liberal Standard for Substitution

If substitution is only formal and will not alter the substance of the case, substitution should be liberally allowed.[55] The result should obviously be different if the proposed substitution is made in bad faith or would otherwise be unjust to the opposing party.[56]

Prior Determination of Incompetence

There is no prerequisite that a state authority determine incompetence before a district court appoints a guardian *ad litem*.[57]

Incompetence: Delay of Trial

A criminal defendant who suffers from significant mental impairment may be entitled to a delay in trial proceedings until the impairment eases. However, in civil litigation mental incompetence may not have the same result. Instead, the court may employ Rule 17(c) to appoint a guardian *ad litem*.[58]

---

[51] *See, e.g., Harris v. Magnum*, 863 F.3d 1133 (9th Cir. 2017).

[52] *See, e.g., Lewis v. Ascension Parish School Board*, 662 F.3d 343, 347 (5th Cir. 2011).

[53] *See, e.g., In re Asacol Antitrust Litigation*, 907 F.3d 42 (1st Cir. 2018).

[54] *See, e.g., Klein ex rel. Qlik Technologies, Inc. v. Qlik Technologies, Inc.*, 906 F.3d 215 (2d Cir. 2018).

[55] *See, e.g., Klein ex rel. Qlik Technologies, Inc. v. Qlik Technologies, Inc.*, 906 F.3d 215 (2d Cir. 2018). *But see National Credit Union Administration Board v. U.S. Bank National Association*, 898 F.3d 243 (2d Cir. 2018) (untimely motion to substitute may be denied).

[56] *See, e.g., Klein ex rel. Qlik Technologies, Inc. v. Qlik Technologies, Inc.*, 906 F.3d 215 (2d Cir. 2018).

[57] *See, e.g., Fonner v. Fairfax County*, 415 F.3d 325 (4th Cir. 2005).

[58] *See, e.g., United States v. Mandycz*, 351 F.3d 222, 225 n.1 (6th Cir. 2003).

Authority of Representative

When a representative is appointed under Rule 17(c), that person has most of the authority that a competent client would have. However, Rule 17(c) does not by itself give the appointed person the right to serve as legal counsel for the infant or incompetent person.[59]

Other Orders

Section 17(c) expressly authorizes the district court to issue other orders necessary to protect infants and incompetents.[60] This authority includes the power to determine rates of compensation for guardians *ad litem* and to determine which party shall bear the cost of such expenses.[61]

RULE 17(d)—PUBLIC OFFICER'S TITLE AND NAME

CORE CONCEPT

Rule 17(d) allows suit by or against a public officer under either that person's official title or personal name. The court may add the individual's name in cases where the official title alone has been used. The primary advantage of suing a public officer by title, rather than individual name, is that departure of the person from office thereby does not require consideration of a substitution of names under Rule 25.[62]

Additional Research References

Wright & Miller, *Federal Practice and Procedure* §§ 1541 to 73
C.J.S., Federal Civil Procedure §§ 46 to 62 et seq.
West's Key Number Digest, Federal Civil Procedure ⚷111, ⚷131 to 149

---

[59] *See, e.g., Tindall v. Poultney High School Dist.*, 414 F.3d 281 (2d Cir. 2005) (right to proceed *pro se* does not apply to non-attorney parents who are guardians *ad litem* of minor children). *But cf. Machadio v. Apfel*, 276 F.3d 103, 106 (2d Cir. 2002) (acknowledging general rule, but noting statutory exception permitting, *inter alia,* non-lawyer parents to bring Social Security claims on behalf of their children).

[60] *See, e.g., Robidoux v. Rosengren*, 638 F.3d 1177, 1181 (9th Cir. 2011).

[61] *Gaddis v. U.S.*, 381 F.3d 444, 453 (5th Cir. 2004) (court may apportion guardian *ad litem* fees as court costs).

[62] *See, e.g, Tanvir v. Tanzin*, 894 F.3d 449 n.7 (2d Cir. 2018).

RULE 18
JOINDER OF CLAIMS

(a) In General. A party asserting a claim, counterclaim, crossclaim, or third-party claim may join, as independent or alternative claims, as many claims as it has against an opposing party.

(b) Joinder of Contingent Claims. A party may join two claims even though one of them is contingent on the disposition of the other; but the court may grant relief only in accordance with the parties' relative substantive rights. In particular, a plaintiff may state a claim for money and a claim to set aside a conveyance that is fraudulent as to that plaintiff, without first obtaining a judgment for the money.

[Amended effective July 1, 1966; August 1, 1987; April 30, 2007, effective December 1, 2007.]

AUTHORS' COMMENTARY ON RULE 18

PURPOSE AND SCOPE

Although Rule 18 is short, it is one of the linchpins of the scheme of joinder rules designed to foster efficient use of the courts. Rule 18(a) provides that, if one party has already asserted a claim, counterclaim, crossclaim, or third-party claim against another party, the claiming party may also assert any other claims it has against that defending party, whether or not they are related in any way to the first claim. For example, Rule 13(g) provides that a defendant may assert a crossclaim against a codefendant if the crossclaim is transactionally related to the plaintiff's claim against the defendant. Once the defendant has asserted one such transactionally related crossclaim, Rule 18 authorizes the defendant to assert any other claims against the codefendant, even if not transactionally related. This rule thus promotes efficiency—once two parties are in court on one claim, they might as well have the option to litigate all of their disputes. Of course, as with all claims, the court must have subject-matter jurisdiction over claims brought under Rule 18, and any unrelated Rule 18 claims will not qualify for supplemental jurisdiction and will need their own original jurisdiction.

Rule 18(b) authorizes a party to assert claims that are contingent on resolution of other claims in the same action. For example, a plaintiff may bring a personal injury claim and also include a claim alleging that the defendant fraudulently transferred assets to the defendant's spouse to shield the assets from any judgment ensuing on the personal injury claim. The second claim is only potentially relevant if the plaintiff succeeds on the first claim, but the plaintiff may maintain both claims in the same action.

CORE CONCEPT

Rule 18(a) allows parties who have already asserted one proper claim against a defending party to assert any other claims against that same defendant, regardless of whether the various claims are related in any way (legally or factually).[1]

APPLICATIONS

Parties Who May Join Claims

The right to join claims is available to any claimant who is a party to the case (not just plaintiffs), irrespective of whether the claims filed will be counterclaims, crossclaims, third-party claims, or original claims filed by the plaintiff.[2]

Rule 18(a) is Permissive, Not Compulsory

A party choosing not to bring unrelated claims is free to file them in separate actions.[3] This assumes the claim is not otherwise barred by considerations such as a statute of limitations. For claims related to a claim included in the pleadings, though, attempts to assert the claims in subsequent actions may be subject to res judicata or collateral estoppel.[4]

Prerequisite of One Valid Claim

Rule 18 does not authorize the bringing of the first claim in an action. Rather, it authorizes joining—or including—additional claims once one proper claim has been pleaded. Thus, with respect to crossclaims, a defendant must first assert one proper crossclaim under Rule 13(g), and only then may use Rule 18(a) to bring any other claims it has against the crossclaim defendant.[5] Likewise, to assert an impleader claim against a nonparty, a third-party plaintiff must first comply with the requirements of Rule 14(a), and then may use Rule

---

[1] *See, e.g., Vodusek v. Bayliner Marine Corp.*, 71 F.3d 148, 154 (4th Cir. 1995); *Deajess Medical Imaging, P.C. v. Allstate Ins. Co.*, 381 F. Supp. 2d 307, 310 (S.D. N.Y. 2005).

[2] *See, e.g., Horia v. Nationwide Credit & Collection, Inc.*, 944 F.3d 970 (7th Cir. 2019).

[3] *See, e.g., Perkins v. Board of Trustees of University of Illinois*, 116 F.3d 235 (7th Cir. 1997).

[4] *See, e.g., Garity v. APWU National Labor Organization*, 828 F.3d 848, 895 n.5 (9th Cir. 2016).

[5] Rule 18(a). *See also First National Bank of Cincinnati v. Pepper*, 454 F.2d 626 (2d Cir. 1972).

18(a) to include other claims against the third-party defendant.[6]

Relation to Rule 15

Rule 18 identifies the circumstances in which a party may, in the party's original pleading, join more than one claim against other parties. However, if a party seeks to assert an additional claim after filing the original pleading, the party must also meet the requirements of Rule 15, governing amendments to pleadings.[7]

Joinder of Additional Parties: Relation to Rule 20

Rule 18 only governs joinder of *claims*, not joinder of *parties*.[8] Thus, while Rule 18 is quite broad in allowing parties to assert all of their claims against other parties, determining whether all of the parties are properly included in an action requires analysis of the party joinder rules. If claims are to be asserted by or against multiple parties, Rule 20 governs the requirements to be met for the inclusion of the various parties.[9] In most situations the court will first inquire as to the applicability of Rule 20 before considering the applicability of Rule 18.[10] The reason for this approach is that Rule 20 contains limitations not found in Rule 18.[11]

Separate Trials

Even though Rule 18(a) authorize the joinder of wholly unrelated claims, the trial court may exercise its discretion to order separate trials on different claims pursuant to Rule 42(b).[12]

Jurisdiction and Venue

Joinder under Rule 18(a) does not excuse satisfaction of jurisdiction and venue requirements.[13]

RULE 18(b)—JOINDER OF CONTINGENT CLAIMS

CORE CONCEPT

Rule 18(b) permits joining two claims in a single action, even if one of the claims is dependent on the outcome of the other. Rule 18(b) is only infrequently applied, most often when one of the claims alleges a fraudulent conveyance designed to

[6] *Lehman v. Revolution Portfolio L.L.C.*, 166 F.3d 389, 394 (1st Cir. 1999); *Amason & Assocs., Inc. v. Core Tuscaloosa 519-611 Red Drew, LLC*, 472 F. Supp. 3d 1116, 1121 (N.D. Ala. 2020).

[7] *Carver v. Atwood*, 18 F.4th 494, 497 (5th Cir. 2021).

[8] *See, e.g., Intercon Research Associates, Ltd., v. Dresser Industries, Inc.*, 696 F.2d 53, 56-57 (7th Cir. 1982); *Bradbury Co., Inc. v. Teissier-duCros*, 231 F.R.D. 413, 415 (D. Kan. 2005).

[9] *See, e.g., Pace v. Timmermann's Ranch and Saddle Shop, Inc.*, 795 F.3d 748 n.10 (7th Cir. 2015).

[10] *See, e.g., Pace v. Timmermann's Ranch and Saddle Shop, Inc.*, 795 F.3d 748, 755 n.10 (7th Cir. 2015).

[11] *See, e.g., UWM Student Association v. Lovell*, 888 F.3d 854 (7th Cir. 2018).

[12] *See, e.g., Parmer v. National Cash Register Co.*, 503 F.2d 275, 277 (6th Cir. 1974).

[13] *See, e.g., King Fisher Marine Service, Inc. v. 21st Phoenix Corp.*, 893 F.2d 1155, 1158 (10th Cir. 1990).

hide assets from any judgment entered on another claim (with Rule 18(b) eliminating the need to defer the fraudulent conveyance claim until judgment has been entered in another claim).[14]

Additional Research References

Wright & Miller, *Federal Practice and Procedure* §§ 1581 to 94
C.J.S., Federal Civil Procedure §§ 40 to 41, § 301;
Fraudulent Conveyances § 331, § 494
West's Key Number Digest, Federal Civil Procedure ⇐81 to 87

---

[14] *See, e.g., Huntress v. Huntress' Estate*, 235 F.2d 205, 207–08 (7th Cir. 1956); *PCS Nitrogen, Inc. v. Ross Dev. Corp.*, 127 F. Supp. 3d 568, 593 (D.S.C. 2015).

RULE 19
REQUIRED JOINDER OF PARTIES

(a) Persons Required to Be Joined if Feasible.

(1) *Required Party.* A person who is subject to service of process and whose joinder will not deprive the court of subject-matter jurisdiction must be joined as a party if:

(A) in that person's absence, the court cannot accord complete relief among existing parties; or

(B) that person claims an interest relating to the subject of the action and is so situated that disposing of the action in the person's absence may:

(i) as a practical matter impair or impede the person's ability to protect the interest; or

(ii) leave an existing party subject to a substantial risk of incurring double, multiple, or otherwise inconsistent obligations because of the interest.

(2) *Joinder by Court Order.* If a person has not been joined as required, the court must order that the person be made a party. A person who refuses to join as a plaintiff may be made either a defendant or, in a proper case, an involuntary plaintiff.

(3) *Venue.* If a joined party objects to venue and the joinder would make venue improper, the court must dismiss that party.

(b) When Joinder Is Not Feasible. If a person who is required to be joined if feasible cannot be joined, the court must determine whether, in equity and good conscience, the action should proceed among the existing parties or should be dismissed. The factors for the court to consider include:

(1) the extent to which a judgment rendered in the person's absence might prejudice that person or the existing parties;

(2) the extent to which any prejudice could be lessened or avoided by:

(A) protective provisions in the judgment;
(B) shaping the relief; or
(C) other measures;

(3) whether a judgment rendered in the person's absence would be adequate; and

(4) whether the plaintiff would have an adequate remedy if the action were dismissed for nonjoinder.

(c) Pleading the Reasons for Nonjoinder. When asserting a claim for relief, a party must state:

(1) the name, if known, of any person who is required to be joined if feasible but is not joined; and

(2) the reasons for not joining that person.

(d) Exception for Class Actions. This rule is subject to Rule 23.

[Amended effective July 1, 1966; August 1, 1987; April 30, 2007, effective December 1, 2007.]

AUTHORS' COMMENTARY ON RULE 19

PURPOSE AND SCOPE

The general rule for civil actions in federal courts is that the plaintiff may choose whom to sue and whom not to sue. Thus, for example, if a plaintiff believes he was injured by a lawnmower containing a defectively manufactured blade, the plaintiff may sue the lawnmower manufacturer, blade manufacturer, or both, depending on practical and strategic considerations. If the plaintiff chooses only to sue the lawnmower manufacturer, neither defendant is unfairly disadvantaged; the blade manufacturer is happy to be left off the caption, and the lawnmower manufacturer has the option to implead the blade manufacturer as a third-party defendant (under Rule 14) or to defend by itself, then bring a contribution claim in a separate action against the blade manufacturer if the plaintiff succeeds.

Sometimes, however, the plaintiff's decision to omit a potential defendant creates problems. For example, if a plaintiff seeks to recover from a limited fund that the defendant controls and a nonparty also has a claim against that fund, the rights of the defendant or the nonparty might be impaired by a ruling in favor of the plaintiff if the case proceeds without the nonparty. If the plaintiff's claim exhausts the fund, and the nonparty subsequently establishes a claim against the fund as well, either the nonparty will be harmed because the fund has been depleted or the defendant will be exposed to liabilities exceeding the fund.

Rule 19(a) governs whether an absent party is a "required party." It requires joinder, when feasible (taking into account jurisdiction and venue), of nonparties if proceeding in their absence would either materially reduce the likelihood that the court can provide justice for the existing parties or protect the existing parties from conflicting or double exposure, or would impair the ability of the absent nonparties to protect their interests.

Rule 19(b) directs the court how to proceed if a required party cannot be joined for reasons of jurisdiction or venue. It provides the court with discretion to dismiss the case or to proceed without the required party, and provides factors for exercising that discretion.

Analysis under Rule 19 entails three steps. First, the court will determine whether a nonparty is a required party. Second, if so, the court will determine whether the party can be joined, from a jurisdictional and venue perspective. If the required party can be joined, the court will order the required party's joinder. Third, if the required party cannot be joined, the court must determine whether to dismiss the case or proceed without the required party. In order to facilitate consideration of required parties, Rule 19 imposes an obligation on the plaintiff to identify potentially interested parties in the complaint. A defendant may file a motion to dismiss for failure to include a required party under Rule 12(b)(7).

RULE 19(a)—PERSONS REQUIRED TO BE JOINED IF FEASIBLE

CORE CONCEPT

When feasible, nonparties must be joined when their absence will either materially reduce the likelihood that the court can provide justice for those already parties or be detrimental to the nonparties themselves.

NOTE: More than most Rules, the application of Rule 19 is highly practical and fact specific.[1] When the court addresses questions of impairment of interest, the court will pragmatically examine both legal and actual, real-world, impairment.[2]

APPLICATIONS

Joinder of Required Parties When Feasible

The court may order that required parties be joined, if

---

[1] *Merrill Lynch, Pierce, Fenner & Smith, Inc. v. Flanders-Borden*, 11 F.4th 12, 17 (1st Cir. 2021).

[2] *McKiver v. Murphy-Brown, LLC*, 980 F.3d 937, 951 (4th Cir. 2020).

feasible, in the following circumstances:

(1) The court identifies a nonparty in whose absence complete relief cannot be granted to those already parties to the case.[3] In this circumstance, courts focus only on whether they can grant complete relief to the existing parties without regard to what effect a decision may have on absent parties.[4] For example, when an Indian group sues a state for exclusive fishing rights, and does not join other competing Indian groups, complete relief cannot be granted.[5]

(2) The court identifies a party whose interest may be impaired either practically or legally without the participation of a nonparty.[6] The interest of the nonparty must be a legally protected interest and not merely some stake in the outcome.[7] For example, when a plaintiff seeks to recover from a limited fund controlled by the defendant, and a nonparty has a claim against the fund, the court may join the nonparty so as to protect that person's possibility of sharing in the fund before it is exhausted.[8] By contrast, when the interests of an absent group are adequately represented by existing parties, the absent group need not be joined.[9]

(3) Several persons, including a nonparty, have overlapping interests in a defendant's property and there is a possibility of inconsistent obligations. For example, if a tenant seeks an injunction to enforce a lease against a landlord, complications can arise if the property is also subject to a potentially conflicting lease held by another person. In that circumstance, joinder of the second tenant will prevent there is a risk that the landlord will be subject to inconsistent duties to the two tenants.[10] It should be noted, however, that a party will not be required unless there is a risk of inconsistent obligations, and not merely a theoretical possibility.[11]

- *Joinder required when "Feasible"*: Rule 19(a) requires joinder of a required nonparty when that joinder is

---

[3]*See, e.g., Disabled Rights Action Committee v. Las Vegas Events, Inc.*, 375 F.3d 861 (9th Cir. 2004).

[4]*PECO Energy Co. v. Nationwide Mut. Ins. Co.*, __ F. Supp. 3d __, 2022 WL 507438, at *6 (E.D. Pa. 2022).

[5]*See, e.g., Citizen Potawatomi Nation v. Norton*, 248 F.3d 993, 998 (10th Cir. 2001); *Manybeads v. U.S.*, 209 F.3d 1164, 1165 (9th Cir. 2000).

[6]*Samantar v. Yousuf*, 560 U.S. 305, 324 (2010); *International Paper Co. v. Denkmann Associates*, 116 F.3d 134, 137 (5th Cir. 1997).

[7]*Jamul Action Comm. v. Simermeyer*, 974 F.3d 984, 996 (9th Cir. 2020).

[8]*See, e.g., In re Torcise*, 116 F.3d 860, 865 (11th Cir. 1997); *Angst v. Royal Maccabees Life Ins. Co.*, 77 F.3d 701, 705 (3d Cir. 1996).

[9]*See, e.g., Salt River Project Agricultural Improvement & Power District v. Lee*, 672 F.3d 1176, 1180 (9th Cir. 2012) (listing factors for assessing adequate representation).

[10]*See, e.g., Dawavendewa v. Salt River Project Agr. Imp. and Power Dist.*, 276 F.3d 1150, 1157–58 (9th Cir. 2002).

[11]*See, e.g., Massachusetts v. Wampanoag Tribe of Gay Head (Aquinnah)*, 853 F.3d 618, 624 (1st Cir. 2017).

feasible, taking into account subject-matter jurisdiction, personal jurisdiction, and venue.[12] A party's joinder is not feasible if that party is entitled to Eleventh Amendment immunity.[13]

- *Forecast of Future Events:* Application of Rule 19(a) will often require a district court to forecast future procedural developments and other events, placing a special burden on the court.[14]
- *Parties to Contracts:* As a general rule, courts construing contracts often require that all parties to the contract be joined.[15]
- *Shareholder Derivative Suits:* A shareholder's derivative suit against a corporation typically makes the corporation itself a required party.[16]
- *Third-Party Indemnitors:* In general, an entity does not become a required party simply because it may have to indemnify a named party.[17]
- *Injunctive Relief:* When the plaintiff seeks injunctive relief, all the persons or entities who would be subject to the injunction are required parties.[18]

Requirement for "Reasoned Analysis"

If the court determines that absent persons cannot feasibly be joined, the court must provide an explanation for why that is so.[19] Under Rule 19(a), the court must identify the absent party's interests and potential prejudice; under Rule 19(b), the court must weigh the risk of prejudice along with other equitable factors to determine whether the case should be dismissed.[20] The court may consider facts outside the pleadings.[21]

---

[12]*See, e.g., PaineWebber, Inc. v. Cohen*, 276 F.3d 197, 200 (6th Cir. 2001); *Keweenaw Bay Indian Community v. State*, 11 F.3d 1341, 1347 (6th Cir. 1993).

[13]*Gensetix, Inc. v. Bd. of Regents of Univ. of Texas Sys.*, 966 F.3d 1316 (Fed. Cir. 2020).

[14]*See, e.g., Home Buyers Warranty Corp. v. Hanna*, 750 F.3d 427, 434 (4th Cir. 2014).

[15]*See, e.g., Dawavendewa v. Salt River Project Agr. Imp. and Power Dist.*, 276 F.3d 1150, 1156–57 (9th Cir. 2002). *But see Alpha Painting & Construction Co. v. Delaware River Port Authority of Pennsylvania and New Jersey*, 853 F.3d 671, 688 (3d Cir. 2017) (successful second lowest bidder is not necessary party to unsuccessful lowest bidder's challenge to award of contract).

[16]*See Ravenswood Investment Co. L.P., v. Avalon Correctional Services*, 651 F.3d 1219, 1225 (10th Cir. 2011); *Gabriel v. Preble*, 396 F.3d 10, 13 (1st Cir. 2005).

[17]*See, e.g., Gardiner v. Virgin Islands Water &Power Authority*, 145 F.3d 635, 641 (3d Cir. 1998).

[18]*Donald J. Trump for President, Inc. v. Boockvar*, 493 F. Supp. 3d 331, 374 (W.D. Pa. 2020).

[19]*See, e.g., Delgado-Caraballo v. Hospital Pavia Hato Rey, Inc.*, 889 F.3d 30 (1st Cir. 2018).

[20]*De Csepel v. Republic of Hungary*, 27 F.4th 736, 747 (D.C. Cir. 2022).

[21]*Rook v. First Liberty Ins. Corp.*, 2022 WL 794983, at *1 (N.D. Fla.

Procedure

Typically, if the plaintiff fails to name a required party, a defendant raises the issue by filing a motion to dismiss the claim under Rule 12(b)(7), governing dismissals for failure to join a person who is a required party under Rule 19.[22] Only a party may make a Rule 12(b)(7) motion, but the court may raise the issue *sua sponte*.[23] Typically, the court will either: (1) order the person joined and deny the motion to dismiss; (2) refuse to order joinder and deny the motion to dismiss; or (3) acknowledge that the person crucial to the action cannot (for reasons of jurisdiction or venue) be joined and grant the motion to dismiss.

Service on Nonparties

If the court determines that a nonparty should be joined in pending litigation, it will direct that service be made upon that nonparty.[24] Such service may properly employ the "bulge" provision of Rule 4(k), permitting service within 100 miles of the place where the service issued without regard to normal limitations that may be imposed by otherwise applicable law.[25]

Burden of Proof

The initial burden for the party advocating joinder requires only a showing of the possibility that an unjoined party is required. If an initial appraisal of the facts indicates that a possibly necessary party is absent, the burden shifts to the party who opposes joinder.[26]

Prerequisite that Nonparty to be Joined as Defendant be Subject to Cause of Action

The courts are divided as to whether the person whose joinder as a defendant is sought must, as a prerequisite to joinder, be subject to a cause of action.[27]

Time

Rule 19 contains no express time limit within which a party must file a Rule 19 motion. However, undue delay in filing can

2022).

[22]*See, e.g., HS Resources, Inc. v. Wingate*, 327 F.3d 432, 438–39 (5th Cir. 2003) (describing relationship of Rule 12(b)(7) to Rule 19).

[23]*Republic of Philippines v. Pimentel*, 553 U.S. 851 (2008).

[24]*See, e.g., PaineWebber, Inc. v. Cohen*, 276 F.3d 197, 200 (6th Cir. 2001).

[25]Rule 4(k). *See also Quinones v. Pennsylvania General Ins. Co.*, 804 F.2d 1167, 1173–74 (10th Cir. 1986).

[26]*Lee v. Learfield Commc'ns, LLC*, 486 F. Supp. 3d 1041, 1047 (E.D. La. 2020).

[27]*Compare, e.g., Vieux Carre Property Owners, Residents & Associates, Inc. v. Brown*, 875 F.2d 453, 457 (5th Cir. 1989) ("[I]t is implicit in Rule 19(a) itself that before a party . . . will be joined as a defendant the plaintiff must have a cause of action against it."), *with E.E.O.C. v. Peabody Western Coal Co.*, 400 F.3d 774, 783 (9th Cir. 2005) (permitting joinder notwithstanding lack of cause of action against third person where joinder will help effect complete relief between parties).

be grounds for denying a motion,[28] particularly if absent persons will not be prejudiced by nonjoinder.[29]

Joinder of Plaintiffs

When a nonparty should join as a plaintiff but refuses to do so, the court may join the person as an involuntary plaintiff or as a defendant.[30]

Relation to Intervention Under Rule 24

Rule 24(a)(2) governs many circumstances in which a person not a party seeks voluntarily to intervene in a case as a party. In that sense, Rule 24(a) is the flip side of Rule 19, which addresses involuntary joinder. Both Rules 19 and 24 require that the non-joined person possess an interest relating to the pending action.[31] As a practical matter, an interest that would satisfy Rule 24(a)(2) will also satisfy Rule 19(a).[32] If an absent party does not seek to intervene under Rule 24, the court may infer that it lacks an interest relating to the subject-matter of the action, such that its joinder is not necessary under Rule 19.[33]

Joinder in Diversity Cases

In diversity cases joining an additional party may destroy complete diversity of citizenship. Courts have limited ability to avoid the problem, depending on whether the person to be joined should be joined as a plaintiff or a defendant. If the person to be joined could be made either an involuntary plaintiff or a defendant, the court may preserve jurisdiction simply by aligning the joined person in a way that maintains diversity.[34] However, if the person can only be joined as a defendant and that joinder would destroy diversity, the court has no room to maneuver. In this situation, the court must apply Rule 19(b) to determine whether to proceed without the non-joined party.[35]

---

[28] *See, e.g., National Association of Chain Drug Stores v. New England Carpenters Health Benefit Fund*, 582 F.3d 30, 43 (1st Cir. 2009); *Northeast Drilling, Inc. v. Inner Space Services, Inc.*, 243 F.3d 25, 36–37 (1st Cir. 2001).

[29] *See, e.g., Sierra Club v. Hathaway*, 579 F.2d 1162, 1166 (9th Cir. 1978).

[30] *Independent Wireless Telegraph Co. v. Radio Corporation of America*, 269 U.S. 459 (1926).

[31] *Klamath Irrigation Dist. v. United States Bureau of Reclamation*, 489 F. Supp. 3d 1168, 1180 (D. Or. 2020) (questions of adequate representation under Rules 19 and 24 are parallel).

[32] *See, e.g., United Keetoowah Band of Cherokee Indians of Oklahoma v. United States*, 480 F.3d 1318, 1324 n.3 (Fed Cir. 2007).

[33] *Union Pac. R.R. Co. v. City of Palestine*, 517 F. Supp. 3d 609, 620 (E.D. Tex. 2021).

[34] *Helm v. Zarecor*, 222 U.S. 32 (1911). *Cf., Mayes v. Rapoport*, 198 F.3d 457, 462 (4th Cir. 1999).

[35] *Cf., Cobb v. Delta Exports, Inc.*, 186 F.3d 675, 677 (5th Cir. 1999); *see also Ravenswood Investment Co., v. Avalon Correctional Services*, 651 F.3d 1219, 1225 (10th Cir. 2011).

RULE 19(b)—WHEN JOINDER IS NOT FEASIBLE

CORE CONCEPT

Rule 19(b) governs whether the court should proceed without persons who should be joined, but who cannot be joined because their joinder would defeat jurisdiction or venue. In other words, the Rule 19(b) factors determine whether the party is merely required to be joined in the litigation if possible or is indispensable.[36] The court has substantial discretion to determine, under the considerations listed in Rule 19(b), whether to continue the litigation without the person or to dismiss the action because a party cannot be joined.[37]

NOTE: In most cases under Rule 19(b), the court attempts to continue the suit rather than dismiss it.[38] Thus a defendant who has filed a motion under Rule 12(b)(7) should contemplate ways to reach a compromise with the court and opposing counsel that continues the suit on terms more favorable to the defendant. Shaping appropriate remedies is one area that might offer particularly good prospects for such terms.

At the same time, cases can and do arise in which a court simply cannot join a defendant whose presence is essential to a just outcome. In that situation, harsh as the result may be, the court is authorized (and sometimes obligated) to dismiss the case notwithstanding that the plaintiff will therefore be unable to obtain a just hearing.[39]

APPLICATIONS

Only for Required Parties

If joinder is not required under Rule 19(a), the court will proceed without joinder. In such cases, the court does not have to evaluate the applicability of Rule 19(b).[40]

Who May Raise Rule 19(b)

The parties may raise Rule 19 issues. Additionally, the court may raise Rule 19(b) issues *sua sponte*.[41]

Factors

Rule 19(b) lists the following factors for the court to consider when deciding whether to allow a case to proceed without a

---

[36] *GE Oil & Gas, LLC v. Waguespack*, 523 F. Supp. 3d 926, 937 (W.D. La. 2021).

[37] *Gensetix, Inc. v. Bd. of Regents of Univ. of Texas Sys.*, 966 F.3d 1316, 1325 (Fed. Cir. 2020); *Provident Tradesmens Bank & Trust Co. v. Patterson*, 390 U.S. 102, 119 (1968).

[38] *See, e.g., McKiver v. Murphy-Brown, LLC*, 980 F.3d 937 (4th Cir. 2020); *Delgado-Caraballo v. Hospital Pavia Hato Rey, Inc.*, 889 F.3d 30 (1st Cir. 2018).

[39] *Florida Wildlife Federation, Inc. v. United States Army Corps of Engineers*, 859 F.3d 1306 (11th Cir. 2017); *Republic of Philippines v. Pimentel*, 553 U.S. 851 (2008).

[40] *See, e.g., Snap-on Tools Corp. v. Mason*, 18 F.3d 1261, 1267 (5th Cir. 1994).

[41] *See, e.g., Manning v. Energy Conversion Devices, Inc.*, 13 F.3d 606, 609 (2d Cir. 1994).

required party or to dismiss the case because a required party cannot be joined:

(1) *Adverse Consequences of Proceeding Without a Person:* The court will examine whether adverse consequences such as legal or practical damage may result by proceeding without a party.[42] For example, persons already parties may be damaged if there is a potential for inconsistent judgments or they will need to initiate a separate lawsuit.[43] Similarly, a person not joined may be harmed if the suit proceeds to judgment and exhausts a fund from which compensation might otherwise have been anticipated.[44] Finally, if there is a risk of collateral estoppel for the absent person, that factor weighs in favor of dismissing the action.[45] By contrast, if a potential party shows no interest in a case, its interests probably are not significantly affected by the outcome of the case.[46]

If the interest at risk is that of the absent party and that interest is adequately represented by someone already in the case, a court might consider the risk of impairment to be ameliorated.[47] Courts are less likely to find prejudice to an absent party when its interests are aligned in all respects with a participating party.[48]

(2) *Avoiding Adverse Consequences:* The second consideration directs the court to determine if means are available to the court for minimizing potential damage. For example, if a tenant sought injunctive relief against a landlord and the tenant agreed to a damage remedy rather than an injunction, the risk to the landlord of mutually inconsistent injunctions involving other tenants is minimized and the case may be allowed to proceed.[49]

(3) *Adequacy of a Judgment:* This consideration addresses

---

[42] *Cf., HB General Corp. v. Manchester Partners, L.P.*, 95 F.3d 1185, 1193 (3d Cir. 1996).

[43] *See, e.g., Estate of Alvarez v. Donaldson Co., Inc.*, 213 F.3d 993 (7th Cir. 2000); *National Union Fire Ins. Co. of Pittsburgh, PA v. Rite Aid of South Carolina, Inc.*, 210 F.3d 246, 252 (4th Cir. 2000).

[44] *See, e.g., In re Torcise*, 116 F.3d 860, 865 (11th Cir. 1997).

[45] *See, e.g., Schulman v. J.P. Morgan Inv. Management, Inc.*, 35 F.3d 799, 806 (3d Cir. 1994).

[46] *See, e.g., Gardiner v. Virgin Islands Water & Power Authority*, 145 F.3d 635 (3d Cir.1998). *But cf., Tell v. Trustees of Dartmouth College*, 145 F.3d 417 (1st Cir.1998) (fact that potential party is silent is a different situation from where potential party disclaimed an interest).

[47] *See, e.g., Hooper v. Wolfe*, 396 F.3d 744, 749 (6th Cir. 2005); *Dainippon Screen Mfg. Co., Ltd. v. CFMT, Inc.*, 142 F.3d 1266 (Fed. Cir. 1998) (presence of parent corporation in suit assures adequate representation of absent subsidiary).

[48] *De Csepel v. Republic of Hungary*, 27 F.4th 736, 748 (D.C. Cir. 2022).

[49] *See, e.g., Smith v. United Brotherhood of Carpenters & Joiners of America*, 685 F.2d 164, 166 (6th Cir. 1982); *Jota v. Texaco, Inc.*, 157 F.3d 153, 162 (2d Cir. 1998). *But see Laker Airways, Inc. v. British Airways, PLC*, 182 F.3d 843, 849 (11th Cir. 1999) (although plaintiff no longer seeks injunctive relief, prejudice to absent entity would still be significant because finding in favor of plaintiff would still require court to find that absent entity acted improperly).

"adequacy" primarily from the point of view of the public interest in efficient and final disposition of legal disputes.[50] Thus a judgment in a person's absence that will leave related claims by or against that person undecided may be deemed an "inadequate" judgment.[51]

(4) *Availability of Another Forum:* The court will examine whether another forum is available in which the claimant may sue existing defendants as well as the person who cannot be joined.[52] When another forum is not available to the claimant, the court in most cases will proceed with the action.[53]

If, however, a required person or entity is not available because the person or entity is immune from suit, the availability (or not) of an alternative forum will normally not be a significant factor.[54]

- *Relative Weight of Factors:* The considerations listed in Rule 19(b) are factors to be weighed, so that in a given case one might be more important than others.[55] Every consideration need not be satisfied before dismissal is ordered, or before the case may proceed.[56] Additionally, it is possible that in a particular case other factors not listed in Rule 19(b) could be important.[57]

Public Interest Exception

In some cases where a public right is to be litigated but some persons cannot be joined, courts have fashioned a "public interest exception" to Rule 19. When applicable, this exception means that such absent persons are not deemed crucial, without regard to whatever a Rule 19 analysis might have concluded. The scope of this exception is narrow.[58]

---

[50] *See, e.g., Home Buyers Warranty Corp. v. Hanna*, 750 F.3d 427 (4th Cir. 2014); *Muscogee (Creek) Nation v. Poarch Band of Creek Indians*, 525 F. Supp. 3d 1359, 1370 (M.D. Ala. 2021).

[51] *Republic of Philippines v. Pimentel*, 553 U.S. 851 (2008); *Estate of Alvarez v. Donaldson Co., Inc.*, 213 F.3d 993 (7th Cir. 2000).

[52] *Cf., City of Marietta v. CSX Transp., Inc.*, 196 F.3d 1300, 1307 (11th Cir. 1999); *Laker Airways, Inc. v. British Airways, PLC*, 182 F.3d 843, 849 (11th Cir. 1999).

[53] *But see Republic of Philippines v. Pimentel*, 553 U.S. 851 (2008) (dismissal under Rule 19(b) can sometimes occur even when plaintiffs have no alternative forum).

[54] *See, e.g., Davis ex rel. Davis v. United States*, 343 F.3d 1282, 1293–94 (10th Cir. 2003).

[55] *See, e.g., Delgado v. Plaza Las Americas, Inc.*, 139 F.3d 1 (1st Cir. 1998).

[56] *See, e.g., Universal Reinsurance Co., Ltd. v. St. Paul Fire and Marine Ins. Co.*, 312 F.3d 82, 88–89 (2d Cir. 2002); *Rhone-Poulenc Inc. v. International Ins. Co.*, 71 F.3d 1299, 1301 (7th Cir. 1995).

[57] *See, e.g., Gardiner v. Virgin Islands Water & Power Authority*, 145 F.3d 635, 640 (3d Cir. 1998).

[58] *National Licorice Co. v. National Labor Relations Board*, 309 U.S. 350, 363 (1940); *Kickapoo Tribe of Indians of Kickapoo Reservation in Kansas v.*

Failure to Seek Intervention

If a person who would practically be affected by a judgment has not sought to intervene, a court might not weigh that person's interests as heavily,[59] but may still take that person's interests into account in determining whether to proceed in the person's absence.[60]

Nonparties Who May be Impleaded

If a nonparty can be added by impleader under Rule 14, dismissal under Rule 19(b) is not available.[61]

Removed Cases

Following removal, the inability of a district court to join a required person due to, *e.g.*, that person's effect on diversity jurisdiction, may not inevitably force the court to choose between dismissal and continuation of the case without the absent person. Instead, the court has discretion to permit joinder, followed by remand to the state court.[62]

Effect of Dismissal: Relation to Rule 41(b)

Rule 41 governs the effects of dismissals. In cases that have been dismissed for failure to join a party under Rule 19, Rule 41(b) provides that the dismissal is without prejudice to refiling unless the order of dismissal provides otherwise.[63]

RULE 19(c)—PLEADING THE REASONS FOR NONJOINDER

CORE CONCEPT

Rule 19(c) places an affirmative duty on parties seeking relief to identify in their pleadings potentially interested persons who have not been joined and to provide the reason that such persons were not joined. The defendant may use the names provided by the plaintiff as a basis for a motion to dismiss the action for failure to join required parties under Rule 12(b)(7). Likewise, the court may use this information to notify these persons, so that they may join on their own initiative.

RULE 19(d)—EXCEPTION FOR CLASS ACTIONS

CORE CONCEPT

When Rule 19 and Rule 23, governing class actions, both apply to a case and they are in conflict, Rule 23 controls.

Babbitt, 43 F.3d 1491 (D.C. Cir. 1995).

[59]*Thunder Basin Coal Co. v. Southwestern Public Service Co.*, 104 F.3d 1205, 1208 (10th Cir. 1997).

[60]*See, e.g., Shields v. Wilkinson*, 790 F.3d 469, (8th Cir. 2015); *Kickapoo Tribe of Indians of Kickapoo Reservation in Kansas v. Babbitt*, 43 F.3d 1491 (D.C. Cir. 1995).

[61]*See, e.g., EEOC v. Peabody Western Coal Co.*, 610 F.3d 1070 (9th Cir. 2010) (collecting authority).

[62]28 U.S.C.A. § 1447(e). *See, e.g., Bailey v. Bayer CropScience L.P.*, 563 F.3d 302, 308 (8th Cir. 2009).

[63]Rule 41(b). *See also U.S. ex rel. May v. Purdue Pharma, L.P.*, 737 F.3d 908, 914 (4th Cir. 2013).

Additional Research References

Wright & Miller, *Federal Practice and Procedure* §§ 1601 to 26
C.J.S., Federal Civil Procedure §§ 95 to 112 et seq.
West's Key Number Digest, Federal Civil Procedure ⚷201 to 233

RULE 20
PERMISSIVE JOINDER OF PARTIES

(a) Persons Who May Join or Be Joined.

(1) *Plaintiffs.* Persons may join in one action as plaintiffs if:

(A) they assert any right to relief jointly, severally, or in the alternative with respect to or arising out of the same transaction, occurrence, or series of transactions or occurrences; and

(B) any question of law or fact common to all plaintiffs will arise in the action.

(2) *Defendants.* Persons—as well as a vessel, cargo, or other property subject to admiralty process in rem—may be joined in one action as defendants if:

(A) any right to relief is asserted against them jointly, severally, or in the alternative with respect to or arising out of the same transaction, occurrence, or series of transactions or occurrences; and

(B) any question of law or fact common to all defendants will arise in the action.

(3) *Extent of Relief.* Neither a plaintiff nor a defendant need be interested in obtaining or defending against all the relief demanded. The court may grant judgment to one or more plaintiffs according to their rights, and against one or more defendants according to their liabilities.

(b) Protective Measures. The court may issue orders—including an order for separate trials—to protect a party against embarrassment, delay, expense, or other prejudice that arises from including a person against whom the party asserts no claim and who asserts no claim against the party.

[Amended effective July 1, 1966; August 1, 1987; April 30, 2007, effective December 1, 2007.]

AUTHORS' COMMENTARY ON RULE 20

PURPOSE AND SCOPE

Rule 20 describes the circumstances in which multiple plaintiffs or multiple defendants may be joined in a single action. The provisions for multiple plaintiffs and multiple defendants are parallel—both require claims that arise out of the same transaction or occurrence or series of transactions or occurrences, and both require at least one issue of law or fact common to each plaintiff or each defendant. Rule 20 is permissive only, allowing joinder in many situations, but not requiring it.[1] Rule 20 also gives the court authority to sever claims for separate trials. In addition, Rule 21 provides that a court may, in appropriate circumstances, dismiss parties joined under Rule 20.[2]

RULE 20(a)—PERSONS WHO MAY JOIN OR BE JOINED

CORE CONCEPT

Joinder of parties is generally allowed in the interest of judicial economy, subject to fulfillment of two prerequisites: the persons who join as plaintiffs or who are joined as defendants must be interested in claims that arise out of the same transaction or occurrence, or series of transactions or occurrences; and all the parties joined must share in common at least one question of law or fact.[3]

APPLICATIONS

"Same Transaction or Occurrence" Test

The courts have adopted various standards for determining whether two claims arise out of the same transaction or occurrence. The assessment is very specific to the facts of the particular case, but in general this requirement is satisfied if there is a substantial logical relationship between the transactions or occurrences at issue.[4] The "same transaction or occurrence" test also appears in Rule 13 and Rule 14, and courts construe it the same way throughout the joinder rules.[5] See the discussion of this issue in Rule 13 for more detail. The only difference is that Rule 20 broadens the test by allowing for joinder of multiple plaintiffs or defendants when the claims involving

---

[1] *See, e.g., Applewhite v. Reichhold Chemicals, Inc.*, 67 F.3d 571, 574 (5th Cir. 1995).

[2] *Preston v. Wiegand*, 573 F. Supp. 3d 1299, 1305 (N.D. Ill. 2021).

[3] *Epic Systems Corp. v. Lewis*, __ U.S. __, 138 S. Ct. 1612, 1613 n.3 (2018).

[4] *See, e.g., United Mine Workers of America v. Gibbs*, 383 U.S. 715, 724 (1996); *Scott v. Chipotle Mexican Grill, Inc.*, 954 F.3d 502 (2d Cir. 2020).

[5] *See, e.g., In re EMC Corp.*, 677 F.3d 1351, 1357 (Fed. Cir. 2012).

them arise out of the same "series" of transactions or occurrences.[6]

Common Question of Law or Fact

The text of Rule 20(a) requires only that the joined parties share "any" common question of fact or law.[7] Some courts, however, require a substantial overlap such that considerations of judicial economy and fairness dictate that all the issues be resolved in one lawsuit.[8] For example, defendants who are allegedly jointly liable will almost invariably be subject to Rule 20 joinder.[9]

- *Handling Cases with Minimal Commonalities:* Courts possess a variety of case management tools to manage discovery and resolution of claims and defenses that have minimal common issues of law or fact.[10]

Court Discretion on Rule 20 Questions

Rule 20(a) is intended to afford broad opportunities for joinder of parties who have—or are the subject of—substantially related claims. However, the trial court retains substantial discretion to deny joinder in circumstances where joinder might produce jury confusion or undue delay in resolving a case.[11]

- *Duty to Explain Analysis:* The court should explain its analysis of the "same transaction or occurrence" test when ruling on a Rule 20(a) issue.[12]

Admiralty Actions

Under Rule 20(a) a party may join parties, vessels, and other property subject to admiralty jurisdiction.[13]

Right to Relief Judged Separately

Notwithstanding joinder, parties receive judgment according to the respective merits of their individual cases. In other words, the victory of one of the joined parties in a case does not necessarily guarantee victory (or defeat) to another joined

---

[6]*See, e.g., Hanley v. First Invs. Corp.*, 151 F.R.D. 76, 79 (E.D. Tex. 1993).

[7]*Lee v. Cook County*, 635 F.3d 969, 971 (7th Cir. 2011).

[8]*See, e.g., Am. Transit Ins. Co. v. Bilyk*, 514 F. Supp. 3d 463 (E.D.N.Y. 2021).

[9]*See, e.g., In re EMC Corp.*, 677 F.3d 1351, 1356 (Fed. Cir. 2012).

[10]*Preston v. Wiegand*, 573 F. Supp. 3d 1299, 1307 (N.D. Ill. 2021).

[11]*See, e.g., Chavez v. Illinois State Police*, 251 F.3d 612 (7th Cir. 2001) (affirming denial of rule 20 joinder when discovery had already been terminated two years earlier and defendants would be unfairly prejudiced by need to reopen discovery); *Thompson v. Boggs*, 33 F.3d 847, 858 (7th Cir. 1994) (in civil rights case against police officer, joinder of second party properly denied where the circumstances would create jury confusion).

[12]*Moore v. Rohm & Haas Co.*, 446 F.3d 643, 647 (6th Cir. 2006).

[13]*See, e.g., Luera v. M/V Alberta*, 635 F.3d 181, 194 (5th Cir. 2011) (Rule 20 permits "hybrid proceedings," involving admiralty and non-admiralty claims).

party.[14]

Jurisdiction and Venue

Satisfying Rule 20 does not relieve the plaintiff of the obligation to satisfy subject-matter jurisdiction, personal jurisdiction, and venue; these are all separate requirements.[15]

Amended Pleadings: Relation to Rule 15

Rule 15 generally governs the circumstances when a party may amend a pleading, including amendments to add new parties. Thus, if an amended pleading would include multiple plaintiffs or defendants, it must meet the requirements of both Rules 15 and 20.[16]

Relation to Rules 13, 14 and 18

Each of the joinder rules performs a different function, and individual situations may require the application of two or more of the joinder rules. Rule 20(a) only governs when two or more plaintiffs or defendants may be included in the same action. Joinder of claims is controlled by Rules 13 and 18. Joinder of third-parties is governed by Rule 14.

Remedy for Misjoinder

If a pleading does not comply with Rule 20, Rule 21 allows a court, on motion or *sua sponte*, to add or drop a party or to sever claims to address the misjoinder.[17]

RULE 20(b)—PROTECTIVE MEASURES

CORE CONCEPT

Although Rule 20(a) may permit plaintiffs to join together, or to join several defendants together, the court retains discretion to order separate trials or other proceedings if necessary in the interest of justice.

APPLICATIONS

Embarrassment, Expense, or Delay

Primary factors considered by the court in determining whether to order separate trials are unreasonable embarrassment, expense or delay. The considerations in Rule 20(b) are implicated by a motion to add new claims against new defendants late in a case.[18] The rule's language is construed to be

---

[14] *See, e.g., Triggs v. John Crump Toyota, Inc.*, 154 F.3d 1284, 1290 (11th Cir. 1998).

[15] *See, e.g., Merrill Lynch & Co. Inc. v. Allegheny Energy, Inc.*, 500 F.3d 171, 179 (2d Cir. 2007).

[16] *Carver v. Atwood*, 18 F.4th 494, 497 (5th Cir. 2021).

[17] *See, e.g., Coalition to Defend Affirmative Action, Integration and Immigrant Rights and Fight for Equality By Any Means Necessary v. Regents of University of Michigan*, 701 F.3d 466, 489 (6th Cir. 2012).

[18] *Kris v. Dusseault Fam. Revocable Tr.*, — F. Supp. 3d —, 2022 WL 867989, at *3 (D.N.H. 2022).

broad enough to permit separation when injustice would occur.[19] These broad standards afford the trial court significant discretion in determining whether to separate the parties.

Additional Research References

Wright & Miller, *Federal Practice and Procedure* §§ 1651 to 60
C.J.S., Federal Civil Procedure §§ 94 to 116
C.J.S., Federal Civil Procedure § 318, § 917, § 918
West's Key Number Digest, Federal Civil Procedure ⚷241 to 267

---

[19]*See, e.g., Coleman v. Quaker Oats Co.*, 232 F.3d 1271, 1296 (9th Cir. 2000).

RULE 21
MISJOINDER AND NONJOINDER OF PARTIES

Misjoinder of parties is not a ground for dismissing an action. On motion or on its own, the court may at any time, on just terms, add or drop a party. The court may also sever any claim against a party.

[April 30, 2007, effective December 1, 2007.]

AUTHORS' COMMENTARY ON RULE 21

PURPOSE AND SCOPE

Rule 21 contains the remedy for misjoinder or nonjoinder that violates other Rules governing multiparty litigation. It ensures that inappropriate joinder of a party, or failure to join a party that should have been joined, need not result in dismissal of the action. It also provides the court with discretion to sever claims against a party for separate trials, or to order separate trials for joined parties,[1] even if the joinder was otherwise appropriate.

APPLICATIONS

What Constitutes Inappropriate Joinder

Joinder may be inappropriate for a variety of reasons, including situations in which joinder of parties produces defects in jurisdiction or venue.[2] Additionally, joinder that does not meet the requirements of Rule 20(a) may necessitate the use of Rule 21.[3]

Severance: Factors to Weigh

A request to sever claims under Rule 21 will normally lead a court to weigh several factors in making its decision: "(1) whether the claims arise out of the same transaction or occur-

[1] *Parchman v. SLM Corp.*, 896 F.3d 728, 733 (6th Cir. 2018).

[2] *See, e.g., Whitaker v. American Telecasting, Inc.*, 261 F.3d 196, 206–07 (2d Cir. 2001).

[3] *See, e.g., Coalition to Defend Affirmative Action, Integration and Immigrant Rights and Fight for Equality By Any Means Necessary v. Regents of University of Michigan*, 701 F.3d 466, 489 (6th Cir. 2012); *Acevedo v. Allsup's Convenience Stores, Inc.*, 600 F.3d 516, 521 (5th Cir. 2010).

rence; (2) whether the claims present some question of law or fact; (3) whether settlement of the claims or judicial economy would be facilitated; (4) whether prejudice would be avoided if severance were granted; and (5) whether different witnesses and documentary proof are required for the separate claims."[4] Rule 21 permits a court to sever claims at any time, even without a finding of improper joinder.[5]

Procedure Following Severance

If a claim is severed from an action and is not dismissed, the severed claim will normally proceed as a separate and independent cause of action.[6]

Inappropriate Joinder: Consequences

The consequence of an inappropriate joinder will not be dismissal of the entire action.[7] Instead, the court will order the inappropriately joined party dismissed so that the remainder of the action may continue.[8]

Failure to Join

If a party should have been joined but was not, the court will simply order appropriate service of process.[9]

Amendments Adding a New Party: Relationship to Rule 15

If parties seek to add a party under Rule 21, courts generally use the standard of Rule 15, governing amendments to pleadings, to determine whether to allow the addition.[10]

Dropping a Required Party: Relation to Rule 19

When the court is considering dropping a party who qualifies as a "required party" under Rule 19, the court should apply the factors in Rule 19(b).[11] Additionally, Rule 21 cannot be used to create diversity by substituting a diverse party for a non-

---

[4] *Morris v. Northrop Grumman Corp.*, 37 F. Supp. 2d 566, 580 (E.D.N.Y. 1999).

[5] *DJ's Tree Serv. & Logging, Inc. v. Bandit Indus., Inc.*, 557 F. Supp. 3d 511, 522 (D. Vt. 2021).

[6] *See, e.g., Herklotz v. Parkinson*, 848 F.3d 894, 898 (9th Cir. 2017).

[7] *See, e.g., Alvarez v. City of Chicago*, 605 F.3d 445, 450 (7th Cir. 2010) ("[M]isjoinder of parties is never a ground for dismissing an action.").

[8] *Newman-Green, Inc. v. Alfonzo-Larrain*, 490 U.S. 826, 832 (1989). *But cf., DirecTV, Inc. v. Leto*, 467 F.3d 842, 846 (3d Cir. 2006) ("Although a district court has discretion to choose either severance or dismissal in remedying misjoinder, it is permitted under Rule 21 to opt for the latter only if 'just' - that is, if doing so 'will not prejudice any substantial right.' ").

[9] *See, e.g., Melendres v. Arpaio*, 784 F.3d 1254, 1260 (9th Cir. 2015).

[10] *See, e.g., Galustian v. Peter*, 591 F.3d 724, 730 (4th Cir. 2010) (acknowledging that some courts do not use Rule 15(a), but concluding that most courts do); *Waite v. UMG Recordings, Inc.*, 477 F. Supp. 3d 265, 269 (S.D.N.Y. 2020).

[11] *See, e.g., Ravenswood Investment Co. v. Avalon Correctional Services*, 651 F.3d 1219, 1225 (10th Cir. 2011).

diverse party.[12]

Substitution of Parties: Relation to Rule 25

Rule 25 governs substitution of parties in any of the specific sections addressed by that Rule. By contrast, Rule 21 governs substitution "in the discretion of the court in situations not covered by Rule 25."[13]

Separation of Claims: Relation to Rule 42(b)

When a claim is severed under Rule 21, it ceases to be part of the same suit.[14] By contrast, if an issue is separated under Rule 42(b), it will be tried separately but remain part of the same lawsuit. The most important result of this distinction is that severed proceedings under Rule 21 become final as each proceeding goes to judgment, and may be appealed individually. Separate trials under Rule 42(b), by contrast, are typically not ready for appeal until all claims and issues are decided.[15]

Timing

The court may order dismissal or the addition of a party at any time in the action, subject only to the need to protect all parties from unfair prejudice.[16] When the court orders joinder of a party, plaintiffs must comply with the requirements of Rules 3 and 4 relating to the issuance of a summons and service on the added party.[17] A dispensable nondiverse party may be dismissed from a suit at any time, even after judgment has been entered.[18]

Motion

Adding or dropping a party may be done upon motion of someone already a party, or upon the court's own initiative, although a court does not abuse its discretion by declining to take these actions on its own initiative without input from the parties about the consequences of such an action.[19]

Preserving Diversity Jurisdiction

Even where a party is appropriately joined, circumstances can arise where the court can apply Rule 21 to drop a party. A

---

[12] *See, e.g., Salazar v. Allstate Texas Lloyd's, Inc.*, 455 F.3d 571, 573 (5th Cir. 2006); *Northern Trust Co. v. Bunge Corp.*, 899 F.2d 591, 597 (7th Cir. 1990).

[13] *Mathis v. Bess*, 761 F. Supp. 1023, 1026 (S.D. N.Y. 1991).

[14] *See, e.g., Rice v. Sunrise Express, Inc.*, 209 F.3d 1008, 1013 (7th Cir. 2000).

[15] *See, e.g., Acevedo-Garcia v. Monroig*, 351 F.3d 547, 559–60 (1st Cir. 2003).

[16] *Newman-Green, Inc. v. Alfonzo-Larrain*, 490 U.S. 826, 832 (1989). *But cf., Summers v. Earth Island Institute*, 555 U.S. 488, 500 (2009) (Rule 21 does not permit joinder *"after the trial is over, judgment has been entered, and a notice of appeal has been filed."*) (emphasis in original).

[17] *Mullen v. Tiverton Sch. Dist.*, 504 F. Supp. 3d 21, 34, n.6 (D.R.I. 2020).

[18] *Graham v. Mentor Worldwide LLC*, 998 F.3d 800, 803 (8th Cir. 2021).

[19] *Democratic Party of Wisconsin v. Vos*, 966 F.3d 581, 587 (7th Cir. 2020).

notable example arises when a court dismisses a nondiverse party in order to obtain diversity jurisdiction over the remaining parties.[20]

Severance to Create Diversity Jurisdiction

To remove a case based on diversity of citizenship, the removing party must ordinarily demonstrate complete diversity among the parties properly joined in the State court action. If a non-diverse defendant is improperly or fraudulently joined (*i.e.*, there is no possibility of recovery against that defendant), however, the court can disregard the citizenship of that defendant in evaluating its jurisdiction. In the absence of fraudulent joinder, federal courts should not use Rule 21 to drop the non-diverse defendants and thus create diversity jurisdiction.[21]

Severance in the Interest of Justice

Even if parties or claims have been appropriately joined, the court may nonetheless order separate trials in the interest of justice.[22]

Transfer and Severance

Section 1404(a) of Title 28 of the United States Code provides district courts with broad authority to transfer litigation to another district court.[23] In a circumstance where only part of an action could be transferred, Rule 21 complements § 1404 by authorizing severance of the case so that portions eligible for transfer may be transferred.[24] However, the court must carefully weigh the inefficiencies and inconvenience of splitting the suit against the advantages to be gained from a partial transfer.[25]

Additional Research References

Wright & Miller, *Federal Practice and Procedure* §§ 1681 to 89

C.J.S., Federal Civil Procedure §§ 117 to 126 et seq., §§ 171 to 177 et seq., §§ 318, §§ 343, §§ 803 to 809

West's Key Number Digest, Federal Civil Procedure ⚷87, ⚷384 to 386, ⚷387 to 388

---

[20] *See, e.g., Newman-Green, Inc. v. Alfonzo-Larrain*, 490 U.S. 826, 832–33 (1989); *Louisiana Municipal Police Employees' Retirement System v. Wynn*, 829 F.3d 1048, 1057 (9th Cir. 2016).

[21] *Williams v. Homeland Ins. Co. of New York*, 18 F.4th 806, 816 (5th Cir. 2021).

[22] *See, e.g., Rice v. Sunrise Express, Inc.*, 209 F.3d 1008, 1016 (7th Cir. 2000).

[23] 28 U.S.C.A. § 1404(a).

[24] *See, e.g., In re Nintendo of America, Inc.*, 756 F.3d 1363, 1364–65 (Fed. Cir. 2014).

[25] *Def. Distributed v. Bruck*, 30 F.4th 414, 428 (5th Cir. 2022).

RULE 22
INTERPLEADER

(a) Grounds.

(1) *By a Plaintiff.* Persons with claims that may expose a plaintiff to double or multiple liability may be joined as defendants and required to interplead. Joinder for interpleader is proper even though:

(A) the claims of the several claimants, or the titles on which their claims depend, lack a common origin or are adverse and independent rather than identical; or

(B) the plaintiff denies liability in whole or in part to any or all of the claimants.

(2) *By a Defendant.* A defendant exposed to similar liability may seek interpleader through a crossclaim or counterclaim.

(b) Relation to Other Rules and Statutes. This rule supplements—and does not limit—the joinder of parties allowed by Rule 20. The remedy this rule provides is in addition to—and does not supersede or limit—the remedy provided by 28 U.S.C. §§ 1335, 1397, and 2361. An action under those statutes must be conducted under these rules.

[Amended effective October 20, 1949; August 1, 1987; April 30, 2007, effective December 1, 2007.]

AUTHORS' COMMENTARY ON RULE 22

PURPOSE AND SCOPE

When one party holds an asset and multiple other parties claim some right to or interest in the asset, the party holding the asset potentially faces considerable risk. Say, for example, the administrator of a fund is aware of claims against the fund that exceed the total value of the fund. If the administrator starts paying out claims in the order they arrive, or in any other order, there may come a time when the fund is exhausted but some of the claims remain unsatisfied. Alternatively, the administrator might start prorating the payments and later discover that some of the claims were not valid. In either event, the unhappy claimants might bring actions against the administrator. Another common application of Rule 22 occurs when there are competing claims by beneficiaries to insurance proceeds.

Federal procedure provides two options for the holder of an asset or "stake" subject to competing claims. Both of these options are referred to as "interpleader," where the stakeholder interpleads or deposits the stake into the court to let the claimants vie for the asset through judicial proceedings, thereby mitigating the stakeholder's risk of being sued by the unsatisfied claimants. One of these options is Rule 22 interpleader and the other is "statutory interpleader" under 28 U.S.C.A. §§ 1335, 1397, and 2361. These forms of interpleader have some differences that make one or the other more advantageous in a given situation, and are concurrent, such that the stakeholder may choose either if both are available. This section will explain both options.

RULE 22(a)—GROUNDS

CORE CONCEPT

Interpleader allows a stakeholder to join multiple, mutually inconsistent claimants in a single action, and thereby determine all of the competing rights in the asset (the "stake") at one time.

APPLICATIONS

Claims Against the Stake

The only requirement under Rule 22 is that the interpleader plaintiff plead that the competing claims are at least partly inconsistent with one another, *e.g.*, where the claims against a fund exceed the value of the fund.[1] Interpleader actions need not be based on identical competing claims, or claims with a common origin, nor must the claims be totally incompatible with one another.

- *Good Faith Belief*: To file an interpleader action under Rule 22 the stakeholder need not be certain that the claims will exceed the value of the stake, and instead must only have a "good faith" belief in the existence of colorable competing claims against the stake.[2]

Stakeholder as Claimant

The interpleader plaintiff may also be a claimant, as for

---

[1] *See, e.g., Hussain v. Boston Old Colony Ins. Co.*, 311 F.3d 623, 634 (5th Cir. 2002); *Rhoades v. Casey*, 196 F.3d 592, 600 (5th Cir. 1999).

[2] *See, e.g., Michelman v. Lincoln National Life Insurance Co.*, 685 F.3d 887, 894 (9th Cir. 2012) (standard is not high); *Auto Parts Manufacturing Mississippi, Inc. v. King Construction of Houston, L.L.C.*, 782 F.3d 186, 192 (5th Cir. 2015).

example where a limited insurance fund is subject to claims exceeding the value of the fund.[3] The insurance company may in appropriate circumstances be permitted to initiate the interpleader action, and then to participate as a claimant if it contends that the other claims against the insurance fund are without merit. Interpleader is proper whenever there are, or may be, competing claims and is available even if the plaintiff denies liability in whole or in part to any or all of the claimants.[4]

Defendants May Employ Interpleader

Sometimes a stakeholder will already have been sued by a claimant, but other claimants are not parties to the action. In such circumstances the stakeholder is entitled to initiate the interpleader action through a counterclaim or cross-claim, and then join the other claimants in the action.[5]

Subject-Matter Jurisdiction

Rule 22 does not create jurisdiction in interpleader actions. Instead, it only authorizes interpleader *if* jurisdictional requirements in the federal courts are met.[6] If the underlying cause of action is a federal question, subject-matter jurisdiction for an interpleader is usually satisfied without difficulty. More commonly, however, the interpleader will arise from a state cause of action, and then the standard requirements for diversity jurisdiction must also be satisfied. The citizenship of the stakeholder must be diverse from that of the claimants,[7] and the amount in controversy must exceed $75,000. The claimants need not be diverse among themselves.[8] Statutory interpleader, discussed below, has less stringent requirements for diversity jurisdiction and a lower amount-in-controversy requirement.[9]

Personal Jurisdiction

Interpleader actions are against individuals, not against the asset, and so must satisfy requirements of personal jurisdiction. This means that service of process on claimants must satisfy Rule 4 service requirements as well as constitutional Due Process protections discussed in the section on

[3] *Cf.*, *Nationwide Mut. Fire Ins. Co. v. Eason*, 736 F.2d 130, 133 (4th Cir. 1984).

[4] *AmGuard Ins. Co. v. SG Patel & Sons II LLC*, 999 F.3d 238, 245 (4th Cir. 2021).

[5] *Grubbs v. General Elec. Credit Corp.*, 405 U.S. 699 (1972); *Weaver v. Metropolitan Life Insurance Col.*, 939 F.3d 618 (5th Cir. 2019).

[6] *See, e.g., Federated Mutual Insurance Co. v. Moody Station and Grocery*, 821 F.3d 973 (8th Cir. 2016); *Arnold v. KJD Real Estate, LLC*, 752 F.3d 700, 704 (7th Cir. 2014).

[7] *See, e.g., Weaver v. Metropolitan Life Insurance Co.*, 939 F.3d 618 (5th Cir. 2019).

[8] *Gold-Fogel v. Fogel*, 16 F.4th 790, 799 (11th Cir. 2021); *Commercial Union Ins. Co. v. U.S.*, 999 F.2d 581, 584 (D.C. Cir. 1993).

[9] *See Wells Fargo Bank, N.A. v. Mesh Suture, Inc.*, 31 F.4th 1300, 1306 (10th Cir. 2022); *Arnold v. KJD Real Estate, LLC*, 752 F.3d 700, 704 (7th Cir. 2014).

personal jurisdiction.[10]

Venue Requirements

Rule 22 interpleader actions are subject to the general venue requirements contained in 28 U.S.C.A. § 1391.[11]

Payment into Court: Relation to Rule 67

Rule 22 does not require that the stakeholder turn the asset in dispute over to the custody of the court.[12] However, in practice, payment into court occurs in many Rule 22 cases.[13] The original stakeholder may then be discharged from the case.[14] Rule 67, which authorizes a party, with leave of court, to pay a sum of money in dispute into court pending the outcome of the case, is sometimes the mechanism cited for payment of the stake into court in Rule 22 cases.[15]

Inconsistent Individual Actions: No Injunctions

Rule 22 interpleader contains no authority for the court to enjoin individual actions brought by claimants against the stakeholder. This is one of the important disadvantages of Rule 22 interpleader[16] as compared with statutory interpleader.

Costs and Attorney's Fees

In Rule 22 interpleader cases the district court has power to award both costs and attorney's fees.[17]

RULE 22(b)—RELATION TO OTHER RULES AND STATUTES

CORE CONCEPT

Rule 22 explicitly states that interpleader under the Rule exists alongside and complements, rather than supersedes, statutory interpleader.[18]

---

[10] *See, e.g., Metropolitan Life Ins. Co. v. Chase*, 294 F.2d 500, 502 (3d Cir. 1961).

[11] *See, e.g., Leader Nat. Ins. Co. v. Shaw*, 901 F. Supp. 316, 320 (W.D. Okla. 1995).

[12] *See, e.g., State Farm Life Insurance Co. v. Jonas*, 775 F.3d 867, 869 (7th Cir. 2014).

[13] *See, e.g., Matter of Bohart*, 743 F.2d 313, 317 (5th Cir. 1984); *Kurland v. U.S.*, 919 F. Supp. 419 (M.D. Fla. 1996).

[14] *Prudential Ins. Co. of Am. v. McFadden*, 504 F. Supp. 3d 627, 638 (E.D. Ky. 2020).

[15] *See, e.g., Southtrust Bank of Florida, N.A. v. Wilson*, 971 F. Supp. 539, 542 (M.D. Fla. 1997).

[16] If the Rule 22 interpleader action has gone to judgment, a district court has authority to issue an injunction to protect the integrity of the judgment. *See, e.g., New York Life Ins. Co. v. Deshotel*, 142 F.3d 873 (5th Cir. 1998) (if judgment has been entered in interpleader case, court may act under authority of All Writs Statute, 28 U.S.C.A. § 1651). This authority, however, falls short of the authority federal courts enjoy in statutory interpleader cases to enjoin litigation that may compete with a pending interpleader action.

[17] *See, e.g., Sun Life Assurance Co. of Canada v. Sampson*, 556 F.3d 6, 8 (1st Cir. 2009).

[18] *See, e.g., Lee v. West Coast Life Insurance Co.*, 688 F.3d 1004, 1008

Additional Research References
Wright & Miller, *Federal Practice and Procedure* §§ 1701 to 21

STATUTORY INTERPLEADER

PURPOSE AND SCOPE

The sections of 28 U.S.C.A. that together comprise the federal interpleader statute share much in common with Rule 22. Like the Rule, the interpleader statute permits a stakeholder plaintiff to file an action against two or more adverse claimants to a stake that the plaintiff holds.[19] Once joined, the statute also contemplates that the claimants will then litigate against one another to determine the best disposition of the stake. However, the federal statute differs significantly from Rule 22 in a number of important respects. Thus, there may be circumstances where both sources of interpleader authority should be employed, or where only one source and not the other will suffice.

The three specific sections of 28 U.S.C.A. that govern statutory interpleader are §§ 1335, 1397, and 2361. Section 1335 establishes the elements of a statutory interpleader action. Section 1397 establishes the special venue provisions governing statutory interpleader. Section 2361 establishes the broad personal jurisdiction of a court hearing an interpleader action, and also authorizes the court to enjoin other federal or state judicial actions that may interfere with the interpleader.

28 U.S.C.A. § 1335. INTERPLEADER

CORE CONCEPT

The interpleader statute allows a stakeholder to join multiple, mutually inconsistent claims of various parties, and thereby determine rights in the asset (the "stake") in a single proceeding.

APPLICATIONS

Claims Against the Stake

Like Rule 22, the only requirement for statutory interpleader is that the interpleader plaintiff plead that the competing claims are at least partly inconsistent with one another, *e.g.*, where the claims against a fund exceed the value of the

(9th Cir. 2012); *Metropolitan Life Ins. Co. v. Price*, 501 F.3d 271, 275 (3d Cir. 2007).

[19] *Cf.*, *AmGuard Ins. Co. v. SG Patel & Sons II LLC*, 999 F.3d 238, 244 (4th Cir. 2021); *Airborne Freight Corp. v. U.S.*, 195 F.3d 238, 240 (5th Cir. 1999).

fund.[20] Interpleader actions need not be based on identical competing claims, or claims with a common origin, nor must the claims be totally incompatible with one another.[21]

- *Good Faith Belief:* To file a statutory interpleader action, the stakeholder need not be certain that the claims will exceed the value of the stake, and instead must only have a "good faith" belief in the existence of colorable competing claims against the stake.[22]

Stakeholder as Claimant

The interpleader plaintiff may also be a claimant,[23] as is the case with Rule 22 interpleader.

Inconsistent Claims v. Unrelated Transactions

A stakeholder may not force a general creditor to participate in an interpleader action when the general creditor's claim is unrelated to the underlying stake.[24]

General Claims Against Unrelated Assets

Interpleader may be used only to regulate claims against the stake itself. If the claims held by a creditor do not implicate the interpleader asset, relief through use of interpleader is not available as to those claims.[25]

Defendants May Employ Interpleader

Unlike Rule 22, the federal interpleader statute contains no *explicit* authority for defendants to initiate interpleader actions through a counterclaim or crossclaim. However, case law establishes that defendants may employ the interpleader statute in a manner parallel to that explicitly authorized by Rule 22.[26]

Subject-Matter Jurisdiction

As with Rule 22, a federal court must have subject-matter jurisdiction before it can hear statutory interpleader claims.[27] However, in diversity cases the requirements for subject-matter jurisdiction in statutory interpleader are considerably more relaxed when compared to those which Rule 22 actions must satisfy. In diversity cases, statutory interpleader actions satisfy subject-matter jurisdiction if the stake at issue is worth $500

[20] *See, e.g., Rhoades v. Casey*, 196 F.3d 592, 600 (5th Cir. 1999).

[21] *See, e.g., Metropolitan Property and Cas. Ins. Co. v. Shan Trac, Inc.*, 324 F.3d 20, 23 (1st Cir. 2003).

[22] *See, e.g., Michelman v. Lincoln National Life Insurance Co.*, 685 F.3d 887, 894 (9th Cir. 2012).

[23] *State Farm Fire & Cas. Co. v. Tashire*, 386 U.S. 523, 533 (1967); *AmGuard Ins. Co. v. SG Patel & Sons II LLC*, 999 F.3d 238, 244 (4th Cir. 2021).

[24] *See, e.g., Airborne Freight Corp. v. United States*, 195 F.3d 238, 239 (5th Cir. 1999).

[25] *See, e.g., In re Millenium Multiple Employer Benefit Plan,* 772 F.3d 634, 643 (10th Cir. 2014).

[26] *See, e.g., Ellis Nat. Bank of Jacksonville v. Irving Trust Co.*, 786 F.2d 466, 467 (2d Cir. 1986).

[27] *Metropolitan Life Ins. Co. v. Price*, 501 F.3d 271, 275 (3d Cir. 2007).

or more[28] and if the citizenship of only one of the claimants is diverse from that of any other claimant (not including the stakeholder).[29] Interpleader cases involving federal questions are unusual, but not unheard of.[30]

- *Supplemental Jurisdiction over Additional Claims:* In cases where the subject-matter jurisdiction requirements for interpleader are satisfied, additional claims that meet the requirements for supplemental jurisdiction may also be heard.[31]
- *Timing of Jurisdiction:* Jurisdiction in interpleader cases is determined at the time the interpleader action is instituted.[32]

Payment Into Court

The interpleader statute requires that the plaintiff deposit the asset at issue with the court.[33] This requirement is relaxed only if the plaintiff provides a bond in an amount subject to the court's discretion.[34] There is no similar explicit requirement for a bond in a Rule 22 action, but courts often require similar performance by plaintiffs in Rule 22 cases anyway.

Costs and Attorney's Fees

In statutory interpleader cases the district court has power to award both costs and attorney's fees.[35]

28 U.S.C.A. § 1397. INTERPLEADER

CORE CONCEPT

Section 1397 provides that venue in a statutory interpleader action may be found in any judicial district in which one of the claimants resides.[36] This requirement differs from the traditional

[28] *State Farm Fire & Casualty Co. v. Tashire*, 386 U.S. 523 (1967); *AmGuard Ins. Co. v. SG Patel & Sons II LLC*, 999 F.3d 238, 245 (4th Cir. 2021).

[29] *See, e.g., AmGuard Ins. Co. v. SG Patel & Sons II LLC*, 999 F.3d 238, 245 (4th Cir. 2021); *First Trust Corp. v. Bryant*, 410 F.3d 842, 852 (6th Cir. 2005).

[30] Cf., *Metropolitan Life Ins. Co. v. Price*, 501 F.3d 271, 276 (3d Cir. 2007).

[31] *See, e.g., Benchmark Ins. Co. v. SUNZ Ins. Co.*, 36 F.4th 766, 771 (8th Cir. 2022); *Watson v. Cartee*, 817 F.3d 299 (6th Cir. 2016).

[32] *See, e.g., Wells Fargo Bank, N.A. v. Mesh Suture, Inc.*, 31 F.4th 1300, 1308 (10th Cir. 2022); *Walker v. Pritzker*, 705 F.2d 942, 944 (7th Cir. 1983).

[33] *Republic of Philippines v. Pimentel*, 553 U.S. 851 (2008); *Acuity v. Rex, LLX*, 929 F.3d 995 (2d Cir. 2019) (full amount in dispute must be deposited).

[34] *See e.g., U.S. Fire Ins. Co. v. Asbestospray, Inc.*, 182 F.3d 201, 210 (3d Cir. 1999).

[35] *See, e.g., Sun Life Assurance Co. of Canada v. Sampson*, 556 F.3d 6, 8 (1st Cir. 2009) (acknowledging that § 1335 contains no express authority, but holding that authority has long been part of court's equity power in interpleader cases).

[36] *See, e.g., First Trust Corp. v. Bryant*, 410 F.3d 842, 853 n.7 (6th Cir. 2005).

federal court venue requirements for Rule 22 interpleader.[37]

28 U.S.C.A. § 2361. PROCESS AND PROCEDURE

CORE CONCEPT

Section 2361 provides substantially expanded personal jurisdiction over the claimants. These powers often provide the plaintiff with a major advantage over analogous provisions governing Rule 22 actions. Section 2361 also authorizes the district court to enter final judgment discharging the stakeholder from further liability, thereby making the injunction permanent.[38]

APPLICATIONS

Process and Personal Jurisdiction

Statutory interpleader provides for nationwide personal jurisdiction and service of process.[39] Rule 22 actions, by contrast, must satisfy standard requirements for personal jurisdiction and service of process.

Relief for Disinterested Stakeholders

When the district court is satisfied that interpleader has been invoked properly, § 2361 expressly authorizes the district court, in appropriate circumstances, to discharge a disinterested stakeholder.[40] The scope of such a discharge, however, extends to potential liability arising from multiple claims relating to distribution of the property in dispute. Unless all parties have received adequate notice and an opportunity to be heard, the discharge will not normally extend to the stakeholder's potential liability for, e.g., damage to the property while the stakeholder had custody.[41]

Stakeholder Relief Not Automatic

The stakeholder's obligations do not terminate automatically upon deposit of the funds with the court. Instead, the stakeholder is not relieved of responsibility until the court acts.[42]

---

[37] *See* 28 U.S.C.A. § 1391; *Wells Fargo Bank, N.A. v. Mesh Suture, Inc.*, 31 F.4th 1300, 1306 n.3 (10th Cir. 2022).

[38] *AmGuard Ins. Co. v. SG Patel & Sons II LLC*, 999 F.3d 238, 245 (4th Cir. 2021).

[39] *AmGuard Ins. Co. v. SG Patel & Sons II LLC*, 999 F.3d 238, 245 (4th Cir. 2021); *NYLife Distributors, Inc. v. Adherence Group, Inc.*, 72 F.3d 371, 375 (3d Cir. 1995). *But cf., Acuity v. Rex, LLC*, 929 F.3d 995 (8th Cir. 2019) (relaxed personal jurisdiction requirement for interpleader actions only effective as long as interpleader count exists).

[40] *See, e.g., Auto Parts Manufacturing Mississippi, Inc. v. King Construction of Houston, L.L.C.*, 782 F.3d 186, 192 (5th Cir. 2015); *In re Millenium Multiple Employer Welfare Benefit Plan*, 772 F.3d 634, 639 (10th Cir. 2014).

[41] *U.S. v. High Technology Products, Inc.*, 497 F.3d 637, 643–44 (6th Cir. 2007).

[42] *See, e.g., In re T.S.C. Seiber Services, L.C.*, 771 F.3d 246, 252 (5th Cir. 2014).

Injunctive Powers

In statutory interpleader cases, the federal court has authority to enjoin other federal or state proceedings that may affect the assets that are the subject of the interpleader action.[43] No comparable authority exists in Rule 22 actions, although the court might use other authority to issue an injunction, such as the All Writs Statute.[44]

All Appropriate Orders: Attorney's Fees

The crucial powers conferred by § 2361 — to serve process nationwide and to enjoin conflicting actions — are reinforced by an additional provision authorizing the court to "make all appropriate orders to enforce its judgment." This provision has been construed to authorize awards of costs and attorney's fees.[45]

Additional Research References

Wright & Miller, *Federal Practice and Procedure* §§ 1701 to 21
C.J.S., Interpleader §§ 2 to 52, §§ 53 to 57
West's Key Number Digest, Interpleader ⚷1 to 43

---

[43] *See, e.g., Lorillard Tobacco Co. v. Chester*, 589 F.3d 835, 844 (6th Cir. 2009).

[44] *See, New York Life Ins. Co. v. Deshotel*, 142 F.3d 873, 879 (5th Cir. 1998).

[45] *See, e.g., Sun Life Assurance Co. of Canada v. Sampson*, 556 F.3d 6, 8 (1st Cir. 2009).

RULE 23
CLASS ACTIONS

(a) Prerequisites. One or more members of a class may sue or be sued as representative parties on behalf of all members only if:

(1) the class is so numerous that joinder of all members is impracticable;

(2) there are questions of law or fact common to the class;

(3) the claims or defenses of the representative parties are typical of the claims or defenses of the class; and

(4) the representative parties will fairly and adequately protect the interests of the class.

(b) Types of Class Actions. A class action may be maintained if Rule 23(a) is satisfied and if:

(1) prosecuting separate actions by or against individual class members would create a risk of:

(A) inconsistent or varying adjudications with respect to individual class members that would establish incompatible standards of conduct for the party opposing the class; or

(B) adjudications with respect to individual class members that, as a practical matter, would be dispositive of the interests of the other members not parties to the individual adjudications or would substantially impair or impede their ability to protect their interests;

(2) the party opposing the class has acted or refused to act on grounds that apply generally to the class, so that final injunctive relief or corresponding declaratory relief is appropriate respecting the class as a whole; or

(3) the court finds that the questions of law or fact common to class members predominate over any questions affecting only individual members, and that a class action is superior to other available methods for fairly and efficiently adjudicating the controversy. The matters pertinent to these findings include:

(A) the class members' interests in individually controlling the prosecution or defense of separate actions;

(B) the extent and nature of any litigation concerning the controversy already begun by or against class members;

(C) the desirability or undesirability of concentrating the litigation of the claims in the particular forum; and

(D) the likely difficulties in managing a class action.

(c) Certification Order; Notice to Class Members; Judgment; Issues Classes; Subclasses.

(1) *Certification Order.*

(A) *Time to Issue.* At an early practicable time after a person sues or is sued as a class representative, the court must determine by order whether to certify the action as a class action.

(B) *Defining the Class; Appointing Class Counsel.* An order that certifies a class action must define the class and the class claims, issues, or defenses, and must appoint class counsel under Rule 23(g).

(C) *Altering or Amending the Order.* An order that grants or denies class certification may be altered or amended before final judgment.

(2) *Notice.*

(A) *For (b)(1) or (b)(2) Classes.* For any class certified under Rule 23(b)(1) or (b)(2), the court may direct appropriate notice to the class.

(B) *For (b)(3) Classes.* For any class certified under Rule 23(b)(3)—or upon ordering notice under Rule 23(e)(1) to a class proposed to be certified for purposes of settlement under Rule 23(b)(3)—the court must direct to class members the best notice that is practicable under the circumstances, including individual notice to all members who can be identified through reasonable effort. The notice may be by one or more of the following: United States mail, electronic means, or other appropriate means. The notice must clearly and concisely state in plain, easily understood language:

(i) the nature of the action;

(ii) the definition of the class certified;

(iii) the class claims, issues, or defenses;

(iv) that a class member may enter an appearance through an attorney if the member so desires;

(v) that the court will exclude from the class any member who requests exclusion;

(vi) the time and manner for requesting exclusion; and

(vii) the binding effect of a class judgment on members under Rule 23(c)(3).

(3) *Judgment.* Whether or not favorable to the class, the judgment in a class action must:

(A) for any class certified under Rule 23(b)(1) or (b)(2), include and describe those whom the court finds to be class members; and

(B) for any class certified under Rule 23(b)(3), include and specify or describe those to whom the Rule 23(c)(2) notice was directed, who have not requested exclusion, and whom the court finds to be class members.

(4) *Particular Issues.* When appropriate, an action may be brought or maintained as a class action with respect to particular issues.

(5) *Subclasses.* When appropriate, a class may be divided into subclasses that are each treated as a class under this rule.

(d) Conducting the Action.

(1) *In General.* In conducting an action under this rule, the court may issue orders that:

(A) determine the course of proceedings or prescribe measures to prevent undue repetition or complication in presenting evidence or argument;

(B) require—to protect class members and fairly conduct the action—giving appropriate notice to some or all class members of:

(i) any step in the action;

(ii) the proposed extent of the judgment; or

(iii) the members' opportunity to signify whether they consider the representation fair and adequate, to intervene and present claims or defenses, or to otherwise come into the action;

(C) impose conditions on the representative parties or on intervenors;

(D) require that the pleadings be amended to eliminate allegations about representation of absent persons and that the action proceed accordingly; or

(E) deal with similar procedural matters.

(2) *Combining and Amending Orders.* An order under Rule 23(d)(1) may be altered or amended from time to time and may be combined with an order under Rule 16.

(e) **Settlement, Voluntary Dismissal, or Compromise.** The claims, issues, or defenses of a certified class—or a class proposed to be certified for purposes of settlement—may be settled, voluntarily dismissed, or compromised only with the court's approval. The following procedures apply to a proposed settlement, voluntary dismissal, or compromise:

(1) *Notice to the Class.*

(A) *Information That Parties Must Provide to the Court.* The parties must provide the court with information sufficient to enable it to determine whether to give notice of the proposal to the class.

(B) *Grounds for a Decision to Give Notice.* The court must direct notice in a reasonable manner to all class members who would be bound by the proposal if giving notice is justified by the parties' showing that the court will likely be able to:

(i) approve the proposal under Rule 23(e)(2); and

(ii) certify the class for purposes of judgment on the proposal.

(2) *Approval of the Proposal.* If the proposal would bind class members, the court may approve it only after a hearing and only on finding that it is fair, reasonable, and adequate after considering whether:

(A) the class representatives and class counsel have adequately represented the class;

(B) the proposal was negotiated at arm's length;

(C) the relief provided for the class is adequate, taking into account:

(i) the costs, risks, and delay of trial and appeal;

(ii) the effectiveness of any proposed method of distributing relief to the class, including the method of processing class-member claims;

(iii) the terms of any proposed award of attorney's fees, including timing of payment; and

(iv) any agreement required to be identified under Rule 23(e)(3); and

(D) the proposal treats class members equitably relative to each other.

(3) *Identifying Agreements.* The parties seeking approval must file a statement identifying any agreement made in connection with the proposal.

(4) *New Opportunity to Be Excluded.* If the class action was previously certified under Rule 23(b)(3), the court may refuse to approve a settlement unless it affords a new opportunity to request exclusion to individual class members who had an earlier opportunity to request exclusion but did not do so.

(5) *Class-Member Objections.*

(A) *In General.* Any class member may object to the proposal if it requires court approval under this subdivision (e). The objection must state whether it applies only to the objector, to a specific subset of the class, or to the entire class, and also state with specificity the grounds for the objection.

(B) *Court Approval Required for Payment in Connection with an Objection.* Unless approved by the court after a hearing, no payment or other consideration may be provided in connection with:

(i) forgoing or withdrawing an objection, or

(ii) forgoing, dismissing, or abandoning an appeal from a judgment approving the proposal.

(C) *Procedure for Approval.* After an Appeal. If approval under Rule 23(e)(5)(B) has not been obtained before an appeal is docketed in the court of appeals, the procedure of Rule 62.1 applies while the appeal remains pending.

(f) Appeals. A court of appeals may permit an appeal from an order granting or denying class-action certification under this rule, but not from an order under Rule 23(e)(1). A party must file a petition for permission to appeal with the circuit clerk within 14 days after the order is entered, or within 45 days after the order is entered if any party is the United States, a United States agency, or a United States officer or employee sued for an act or omission occurring in connection with duties performed on the United States' behalf. An appeal does not stay proceedings in the district court unless the district judge or the court of appeals so orders.

(g) Class Counsel.

(1) *Appointing Class Counsel.* Unless a statute provides otherwise, a court that certifies a class must appoint class counsel. In appointing class counsel, the court:

(A) must consider:

(i) the work counsel has done in identifying or investigating potential claims in the action;

(ii) counsel's experience in handling class actions, other complex litigation, and the types of claims asserted in the action;

(iii) counsel's knowledge of the applicable law; and

(iv) the resources that counsel will commit to representing the class;

(B) may consider any other matter pertinent to counsel's ability to fairly and adequately represent the interests of the class;

(C) may order potential class counsel to provide information on any subject pertinent to the appointment and to propose terms for attorney's fees and nontaxable costs;

(D) may include in the appointing order provisions about the award of attorney's fees or nontaxable costs under Rule 23(h); and

(E) may make further orders in connection with the appointment.

(2) *Standard for Appointing Class Counsel.* When one applicant seeks appointment as class counsel, the court may appoint that applicant only if the applicant is adequate under Rule 23(g)(1) and (4). If more than one adequate applicant seeks appointment, the court must appoint the applicant best able to represent the interests of the class.

(3) *Interim Counsel.* The court may designate interim counsel to act on behalf of a putative class before determining whether to certify the action as a class action.

(4) *Duty of Class Counsel.* Class counsel must fairly and adequately represent the interests of the class.

(h) **Attorney's Fees and Nontaxable Costs.** In a certified class action, the court may award reasonable attorney's fees and nontaxable costs that are authorized by law or by the parties' agreement. The following procedures apply:

(1) A claim for an award must be made by motion under Rule 54(d)(2), subject to the provisions of this subdivision (h), at a time the court sets. Notice of the motion must be served on all parties and, for motions by class counsel, directed to class members in a reasonable manner.

(2) A class member, or a party from whom payment is sought, may object to the motion.

(3) The court may hold a hearing and must find the facts and state its legal conclusions under Rule 52(a).

(4) The court may refer issues related to the amount of the award to a special master or a magistrate judge, as provided in Rule 54(d)(2)(D).

[Amended Feb. 28, 1966, eff. July 1, 1966; March 2, 1987, eff. Aug. 1, 1987; April 24, 1998, eff. Dec. 1, 1998; March 27, 2003, eff. Dec. 1, 2003; April 30, 2007, eff. Dec. 1, 2007; March 26, 2009, eff. Dec. 1, 2009; Apr. 26, 2018, eff. Dec. 1, 2018.]

AUTHORS' COMMENTARY ON RULE 23

PURPOSE AND SCOPE

Rule 23 authorizes class actions as a means of joining parties in situations where the number of parties is sufficiently large so that it is impractical or inefficient for the parties to pursue their claims individually or through more conventional methods of joinder. Rule 23 contemplates the class of litigants will be represented both by counsel and by "class representatives," *i.e.,* active members of the class who make many decisions on behalf of the entire class.

Rule 23(a) establishes four prerequisites for maintaining a class action, and every class action must satisfy all four. The first is numerosity—the members of the class must be so numerous as to make individual actions impracticable. The second is commonality—there must be common issues of law or fact among the class members' claims. The third is typicality—the claims of the class representatives must be typical of the claims of the other class members. The fourth is adequacy of representation—the class representatives and class counsel must both adequately protect the interests of the class.

In addition to satisfying all four Rule 23(a) prerequisites, every class action must fit within at least one of the four approved categories of class action described in Rule 23(b), designed to ensure that a class action is a sensible way to proceed. The first category authorizes a class action where prosecuting individual actions could result in varying adjudications that could establish inconsistent standards of conduct for the defendant. The second category authorizes a class action to protect against adjudications of individual class members that could dispose of, impair, or impede other members' interests who are not parties to the individual action. The third category authorizes classes where the action involves injunctive or declaratory relief to protect the class opponent from, for example, conflicting injunctions from individual proceedings. The fourth and final category authorizes a class action where the court determines that those questions of law or fact common to the members of the class predominate over other questions, and a class action is a superior method for resolving the claims.

Class actions do not proceed at the whim of the class representatives. Rather, the court must "certify" that the "putative class" is appropriate to proceed as a class action. Once the court certifies the class, there is potential for enriching the representatives and the lawyers at the expense of the absent class members who are not representatives and who therefore do not fully participate in many decisions. Class actions also present special problems of case management for the courts. Accordingly, the court is charged with the obligation to carefully monitor the litigation process and progress, including approval of settlements and attorney's fees.

RULE 23(a)—PREREQUISITES

CORE CONCEPT

The specialized purpose of class actions—handling large numbers of litigants through class representatives[1]—makes necessary four requirements intended to ensure that the opportunity to bring a class action is not misused or abused. Two of these requirements have developed under the common law, and others are listed in Rule 23(a). *All* requirements, whether in Rule 23(a) or developed in case law, must be satisfied before the court will certify a case as a class action.[2] Once the requirements are satisfied, the court is authorized to certify a class action without regard to whether state law attempts to impose additional requirements or prohibit class litigation.[3]

NOTE: In addition to the common law and Rule 23(a) requirements, a class action will not be certified unless it also fits within some provision of Rule 23(b).[4] Class actions must also meet the requirements of both personal jurisdiction and federal subject-matter jurisdiction, which apply somewhat differently to class actions. Thus, while Rule 23(a) must be satisfied, meeting the requirements of Rule 23(a) alone will not produce a court-certified class action. Except for Rule 23(b), discussed separately, the ad-

---

[1] *See Taylor v. Sturgell*, 553 U.S. 880, 894, 128 S. Ct. 2161, 171 L. Ed. 2d 155 (2008).

[2] *See Wal-Mart Stores, Inc. v. Dukes*, 564 U.S. 338, 350–51, 131 S. Ct. 2541, 180 L. Ed. 2d 374 (2011).

[3] *See Shady Grove Orthopedic Assocs., P.A. v. Allstate Ins. Co.*, 559 U.S. 393, 432, 130 S. Ct. 1431, 176 L. Ed. 2d 311 (2010).

[4] *See Wal-Mart Stores, Inc. v. Dukes*, 564 U.S. 338, 345, 131 S. Ct. 2541, 180 L. Ed. 2d 374 (2011); *Shady Grove Orthopedic Assocs., P.A. v. Allstate Ins. Co.*, 559 U.S. 393, 398, 130 S. Ct. 1431, 176 L. Ed. 2d 311 (2010); *A. B. v. Hawaii State Dep't of Educ.*, 30 F.4th 828, 834 (9th Cir. 2022).

ditional prerequisites not mentioned in Rule 23(a), including case law requirements, venue, and special questions of jurisdiction, are discussed immediately below. Additionally, even if a proposed class meets all the requirements mentioned above, the district court retains discretion not to certify the class action.

APPLICATIONS

Rule 23(a) Prerequisites for a Class, Generally

In order for a class to be certified under Rule 23(a), plaintiffs must satisfy four requirements: (1) numerosity — the class must be "so numerous that joinder of all members is impracticable;" (2) commonality — there must be common questions of law or fact among class members; (3) typicality — the claims or defenses of the class representative must be typical of the claims of the class members; and (4) adequacy of representation — the class representative must fairly and adequately protect the class's interests.[5] A likelihood of the moving party's success on the merits is not among Rule 23(a)'s requirements.[6] Courts consider questions related to the merits only to the extent required to determine whether Rule 23(a)'s requirements are satisfied.[7]

General Pleading Requirements

A plaintiff must affirmatively demonstrate that the requirements of Rule 23 have been satisfied with evidentiary proof[8] and cannot summarily plead that the proposed class meets the requirements.[9]

Prerequisites: Numerosity, Commonality, Typicality, and Adequacy of Representation

(1) *Numerosity:* Rule 23(a)(1) requires the members of the class to be sufficiently large to warrant class treatment because the alternative of joinder is "impracticable."[10] When a class's membership changes over time, this factor weighs in favor of

---

[5]*See* Rule 23(a)(1)–(4). *See also Wal-Mart Stores, Inc. v. Dukes*, 564 U.S. 338, 349, 131 S. Ct. 2541, 180 L. Ed. 2d 374 (2011); *Cleven v. Mid-Am. Apartment Communities, Inc.*, 20 F.4th 171, 175–76 (5th Cir. 2021); *Simpson v. Dart*, 23 F.4th 706, 711 (7th Cir. 2022).

[6]*See Amgen Inc. v. Conn. Ret. Plans & Tr. Funds*, 568 U.S. 455, 466, 133 S. Ct. 1184, 185 L. Ed.2d 308 (2013) ("Rule 23 grants courts no license to engage in free-ranging merits inquiries at the certification stage."); *Simpson v. Dart*, 23 F.4th 706, 711 (7th Cir. 2022).

[7]*See Amgen Inc. v. Conn. Ret. Plans & Tr. Funds*, 568 U.S. 455, 466, 133 S. Ct. 1184, 185 L. Ed.2d 308 (2013); *Simpson v. Dart*, 23 F.4th 706, 711 (7th Cir. 2022).

[8]*See Comcast Corp. v. Behrend*, 569 U.S. 27, 33, 133 S. Ct. 1426, 185 L. Ed.2d 515 (2013); *In re Zetia (Ezetimibe) Antitrust Litig.*, 7 F.4th 227, 234 (4th Cir. 2021).

[9]*See Wal-Mart Stores, Inc. v. Dukes*, 564 U.S. 338, 350, 131 S. Ct. 2541, 180 L. Ed.2d 374 (2011); *Olean Wholesale Grocery Coop., Inc. v. Bumble Bee Foods LLC*, 31 F.4th 651, 664 (9th Cir. 2022); *In re Zetia (Ezetimibe) Antitrust Litig.*, 7 F.4th 227, 234 (4th Cir. 2021).

[10]*See Cent. States Se. & Sw. Areas Health & Welfare Fund v. Merck-Medco*

practicability of joinder.[11] When addressing numerosity, Rule 23(a)(1) does not impose absolute limitations, so courts must examine the specifics facts of each case.[12] There is no threshold number of class members guaranteed to satisfy the "numerosity" requirement of Rule 23(a).[13] A class comprised of several hundreds or thousands of members will almost always meet this test.[14] While declining to create any bright-line rule, the Supreme Court has stated that a class with only fifteen members "would be too small to meet the numerosity requirement."[15] Accordingly, a class of ten litigants or less will usually not meet this test[16] and will instead be consigned to joinder under Rule 20. Several circuits apply a rebuttable presumption that a class of forty members satisfies the numerosity threshold.[17]

If part of a claim is assigned to a second party, it is possible that assignee may be counted as an additional member of the class for purposes of numerosity[18] unless the district court finds that the purpose of partial assignment is to inflate the number of class members to satisfy the numerosity requirement.[19]

When determining numerosity, a court's consideration of future class members is not unusual or objectionable because their claims will be ripe upon becoming members of the class.[20] A sufficient estimate of future members is all that is needed for a court to assess what weight to give to this factor.[21]

While the numerosity requirement is fact specific, the

Managed Care, L.L.C., 504 F.3d 229, 244–45 (2d Cir. 2007); *A. B. v. Hawaii State Dep't of Educ.*, 30 F.4th 828, 835 (9th Cir. 2022). *See also In re Zetia (Ezetimibe) Antitrust Litig.*, 7 F.4th 227, 236 (4th Cir. 2021) (vacating lower court's denial of class certification based on erroneous application of Rule 23(a) that focused on impracticality of "individual suits rather than joinder").

[11] *See A. B. v. Hawaii State Dep't of Educ.*, 30 F.4th 828, 838 (9th Cir. 2022).

[12] *See A. B. v. Hawaii State Dep't of Educ.*, 30 F.4th 828, 835 (9th Cir. 2022); *General Tel. Co. of the NW., Inc. v. EEOC*, 446 U.S. 318, 330, 100 S. Ct. 1698, 64 L. Ed.2d 319 (1980).

[13] *See Anderson v. Weinert Enterprises, Inc.*, 986 F.3d 773, 777 (7th Cir. 2021) (key inquiry is not number of class members alone, but practicality of joinder); *Trevizo v. Adams*, 455 F.3d 1155, 1162 (10th Cir. 2006).

[14] *See Bacon v. Honda of Am. Mfg., Inc.*, 370 F.3d 565, 570 (6th Cir. 2004).

[15] *See Gen. Tel. Co. of the Nw. v. Equal Emp. Opportunity Comm'n*, 446 U.S. 318, 330, 100 S. Ct. 1698, 64 L. Ed. 2d 319 (1980).

[16] *See Nat'l Ass'n of Gov't Emps. v. City Pub. Serv. Bd. of San Antonio, Tex.*, 40 F.3d 698, 715 (5th Cir. 1994); *Gen. Tel. Co. of the Nw. v. Equal Emp. Opportunity Comm'n*, 446 U.S. 318, 330, 100 S. Ct. 1698, 64 L. Ed. 2d 319 (1980).

[17] *See Jin v. Shanghai Original, Inc.*, 990 F.3d 251, 263 (2d Cir. 2021); *Mielo v. Steak 'n Shake Operations, Inc.*, 897 F.3d 467, 486 (3d Cir. 2018).

[18] *See In re Modafinil Antitrust Litig.*, 837 F.3d 238, 252 (3d Cir. 2016).

[19] *See In re Modafinil Antitrust Litig.*, 837 F.3d 238, 252 (3d Cir. 2016).

[20] *See A. B. v. Hawaii State Dep't of Educ.*, 30 F.4th 828, 834 (9th Cir. 2022).

[21] *See A. B. v. Hawaii State Dep't of Educ.*, 30 F.4th 828, 838 (9th Cir. 2022).

requirement of impracticability of joinder must be affirmatively and specifically addressed in the certification motion.[22] It is not necessary that joinder of all parties be impossible, only that the difficulty or inconvenience posed by the joining of all parties make a class action appropriate.[23]

(2) *Commonality*: Under Rule 23(a)(2), a plaintiff must establish that there questions or law or fact common to the class.[24] A common question must be capable of classwide resolution, meaning that its truth or falsity will resolve a central issue relating to the validity of one of the claims.[25] The existence of shared legal issues with divergent factual predicates is sufficient.[26] By contrast, an "individual" question will require class members to present evidence that varies from "member to member."[27] To satisfy the requirement of Rule 23(a)(2), the common questions need not predominate, though courts have recognized an overlap of Rule 23(b)(3)'s predominance requirements with Rule 23(a), requiring plaintiffs to prove there are questions of law or fact common to the class that can be determined in "one stroke"[28] in order to prove such common questions predominate under Rule 23(b)(3).[29] Historically, courts have approached this requirement with a liberal attitude, and close questions as to the existence of sufficient commonality have tended to be resolved in favor of finding common questions.[30] However, failure to meet the commonality requirement of Rule 23(a)(2) is, by itself, a sufficient ground to deny

---

[22]*See Golden v. City of Columbus*, 404 F.3d 950, 965 (6th Cir. 2005).

[23]*See A. B. v. Hawaii State Dep't of Educ.*, 30 F.4th 828, 834 (9th Cir. 2022); *Robidoux v. Celani*, 987 F.2d 931, 935 (2d Cir. 1993) (" 'Impractability' does not mean 'impossibility,' but only the difficulty or inconvenience of joining all members of the class."). *See also Novella v. Westchester Cnty.*, 661 F.3d 128, 143 (2d Cir. 2011).

[24]*See* Fed. R. Civ. P. 23(a)(2). *See Olean Wholesale Grocery Coop., Inc. v. Bumble Bee Foods LLC*, 31 F.4th 651, 663 (9th Cir. 2022).

[25]*See Wal-Mart Stores, Inc. v. Dukes*, 564 U.S. 338, 350, 131 S. Ct. 2541, 180 L. Ed. 2d 374 (2011); *Olean Wholesale Grocery Coop., Inc. v. Bumble Bee Foods LLC*, 31 F.4th 651, 663 (9th Cir. 2022).

[26]*See Gonzalez v. U.S. Immigr. & Customs Enf't*, 975 F.3d 788, 807 (9th Cir. 2020).

[27]*See Tyson Foods, Inc. v. Bouaphakeo*, 577 U.S. 442, 453, 136 S. Ct. 1036, 194 L. Ed.2d 124 (2016); *Olean Wholesale Grocery Coop., Inc. v. Bumble Bee Foods LLC*, 31 F.4th 651, 663 (9th Cir. 2022).

[28]*See Wal-Mart Stores, Inc. v. Dukes*, 564 U.S. 338, 349, 131 S. Ct. 2541, 180 L. Ed. 2d 374 (2011); *Ross v. Gossett*, 33 F.4th 433, 437 (7th Cir. 2022); *Olean Wholesale Grocery Coop., Inc. v. Bumble Bee Foods LLC*, 31 F.4th 651, 664 (9th Cir. 2022).

[29]*See Tyson Foods, Inc. v. Bouaphakeo*, 577 U.S. 442, 453–54, 136 S. Ct. 1036, 194 L. Ed.2d 124 (2016); *Olean Wholesale Grocery Coop., Inc. v. Bumble Bee Foods LLC*, 31 F.4th 651, 664 (9th Cir. 2022).

[30]*See Stewart v. Abraham*, 275 F.3d 220, 227 (3d Cir. 2001); *Mullen v. Treasure Chest Casino, LLC*, 186 F.3d 620, 625 (5th Cir. 1999). *But cf.*, *Wal-Mart Stores v. Dukes*, 564 U.S. 338, 350, 131 S. Ct. 2541, 180 L. Ed. 2d 374 (2011).

certification.[31] Moreover, mere allegations that class members have suffered common injuries are not enough to satisfy the commonality requirement.[32]

Particularly in class actions involving fraud, there is now somewhat greater harmony between commonality for purposes of Rule 23(a) and the more stringent requirements for pleading fraud with particularity under Rule 9(b). For example, in securities cases controlled by the Private Securities Litigation Reform Act of 1995, it is settled that a plaintiff seeking to serve as a class representative must plead with particularity sufficient to satisfy the requirements of Rule 9(b).[33]

In class actions based on allegations of employment discrimination, there are at least two ways by which a plaintiff may successfully assert that a class of claimants shares a common question of law or fact with the named class representative.[34] The first is to demonstrate that some sort of testing procedure applicable to the group unfairly prejudices the group in hiring or promotion.[35] The second means of satisfying Rule 23(a)(2) is to provide significant evidence that the defendant has a general policy of discrimination.[36]

> **NOTE:** Although Rule 23(a) may be satisfied even if the common questions of law or fact do not predominate in the case, predominance becomes a required showing if the class seeks certification under Rule 23(b)(3). The interplay between Rule 23(a) and Rule 23(b) is discussed further below.

(3) *Class Representatives' Claims Must Be Typical:* Claims are typical under Rule 23(a)(3) when other members have the same or similar injury as the class representative, when the claim is based on conduct that is not unique to the class representative, and when the class has been injured by the same course of conduct.[37] Rule 23(a)(3) requires that the claims of class representatives be typical of the class as a whole, not merely some portion thereof.[38] Generally the class representatives need not have claims identical in all respects with other

---

[31] *See Wal-Mart Stores, Inc. v. Dukes*, 564 U.S. 338, 350, 131 S. Ct. 2541, 180 L. Ed. 2d 374 (2011).

[32] *See Olean Wholesale Grocery Coop., Inc. v. Bumble Bee Foods LLC*, 31 F.4th 651, 664 (9th Cir. 2022).

[33] *See Berger v. Compaq Computer Corp.*, 257 F.3d 475, 478 (5th Cir. 2001).

[34] *See Wal-Mart Stores, Inc. v. Dukes*, 564 U.S. 338, 353, 131 S. Ct. 2541, 180 L. Ed. 2d 374 (2011); *Simpson v. Dart*, 23 F.4th 706, 711 (7th Cir. 2022).

[35] *See Wal-Mart Stores, Inc. v. Dukes*, 564 U.S. 338, 353, 131 S. Ct. 2541, 180 L. Ed. 2d 374 (2011); *Simpson v. Dart*, 23 F.4th 706, 711 (7th Cir. 2022).

[36] *See Wal-Mart Stores, Inc. v. Dukes*, 564 U.S. 338, 353, 131 S. Ct. 2541, 180 L. Ed. 2d 374 (2011).

[37] *See A. B. v. Hawaii State Dep't of Educ.*, 30 F.4th 828, 839 (9th Cir. 2022); *Boley v. Universal Health Servs., Inc.*, 36 F.4th 124, 133 (3d Cir. 2022).

[38] *See McFields v. Dart*, 982 F.3d 511, 518 (7th Cir. 2020); *Rector v. City and Cnty. of Denver*, 348 F.3d 935, 950 (10th Cir. 2003).

members of the class.[39] Substantial commonality appears to be sufficient, even if differences among the claims (*e.g.*, issues of damages) also exist.[40] This requirement is intended to ensure that class representatives will represent the best interests of class members who take a less active part in managing the litigation.[41] It also considerably overlaps with the common law requirement that class representatives be members of the class they seek to represent.[42]

NOTE: Commonality versus Typicality The commonality and typicality requirements of Rule 23(a) share some characteristics,[43] but they retain important differences. One point of divergence is that commonality addresses the relation of the entire class's claims, whereas typicality focuses on the individual claims of class representatives.[44]

(4) *Representatives Must Fairly Protect the Class:* Because class actions vest the class representatives with decision-making authority that impacts the interests of absent, passive class members, Rule 23(a)(4) requires the court to ensure that class representatives fully meet their responsibilities.[45] To be an adequate representative, the class representative(s) must be a member of the class and must have the same interest and injury as the class members.[46] Courts examine two factors to determine the class representative's adequacy: (1) the class representative must not have interests that conflict with the members of the class; and (2) the class representative must appear willing and able to present the case with the support of counsel.[47] The "adequacy" requirement does not necessarily mean that *all* class representatives must be adequate. If there is more than one named representative, the requirement may

[39] *See Gonzalez v. United States Immigr. & Customs Enf't*, 975 F.3d 788, 809 (9th Cir. 2020) (typicality looks at the nature of the claim of the class representative not the specific facts); *Lightbourn v. Cnty. of El Paso, Tex.*, 118 F.3d 421, 426, 22 A.D.D. 618 (5th Cir. 1997).

[40] *See Ball v. Union Carbide Corp.*, 376 F.3d 554, 569 (6th Cir. 2004) (requirements of Rule 23(a)(2) and (3) "tend to merge"); *Alpern v. UtiliCorp United, Inc.*, 84 F.3d 1525, 1540 (8th Cir. 1996).

[41] *See Howard v. Cook Cnty. Sheriff's Off.*, 989 F.3d 587, 605 (7th Cir. 2021).

[42] *See Robinson v. Sheriff of Cook Cnty.*, 167 F.3d 1155, 1157 (7th Cir. 1999).

[43] *See Custom Hair Designs by Sandy v. Cent. Payment Co., LLC*, 984 F.3d 595, 604 (8th Cir. 2020); *J.D. v. Azar*, 925 F.3d 1291 (D.C. Cir. 2019).

[44] *See* Fed. R. Civ. P. 23(a)(2), (3).

[45] *See In re Suboxone (Buprenorphine Hydrochlorine & Naloxone) Antitrust Litig.*, 967 F.3d 264, 272 (3d Cir. 2020).

[46] *See Santiago v. City of Chicago*, 19 F.4th 1010, 1018 (7th Cir. 2021).

[47] *See J.D. v. Azar*, 925 F.3d 1291, 1313 (D.C. Cir. 2019); *Denney v. Deutsche Bank AG*, 443 F.3d 253, 268 (2d Cir. 2006). *See also Slade v. Progressive Security Ins. Co.*, 856 F.3d 408 (5th Cir. 2017) (assessing (1) zeal and competence of class counsel; (2) ability of class representatives to take active role and to protect interests of entire class; and (3) potential conflicts interests between class and class representatives).

be satisfied when one representative is adequate.[48]

Only conflicts that are fundamental and impact the heart of the litigation are sufficient to defeat the adequacy requirement.[49] A fundamental conflict arises where some party members claim to be harmed by the same conduct that benefitted other members of the class.[50] Minor differences of interest between the class representative and the members of the class will not defeat certification.[51] The court may avoid some intraclass conflicts by certifying subclasses with separate representation[52] or appointing a new representative.[53]

Courts tend to be particularly sensitive to the adequacy requirement.[54] Class representatives can be disqualified when fundamental conflicts of interest exist[55] and when the proposed class representative lacks integrity.[56] If, in the course of litigation, the trial court finds that class representatives previously approved have become inadequate, the court retains authority to order appointment of new representatives.[57] Mootness of a named plaintiff's claim does not, per se, render the class representative inadequate.[58]

- *Adequacy of Counsel:* Rule 23(a)(4) contains no express language addressing the issue of whether it authorizes the court to examine the ability of the class's legal counsel to represent the class.[59] Instead, Rule 23(g) expressly grants a district court the right and responsibility to appoint suitable counsel.[60] However, courts often cite Rule 23(a)(4) as authority to evaluate adequacy of class counsel.[61] Furthermore, a determination that class counsel is adequate does not compensate for inadequate

---

[48]*See Chambers v. Whirlpool Corp.*, 980 F.3d 645, 671 (9th Cir. 2020).

[49]*See In re Equifax Inc. Customer Data Sec. Breach Litig.*, 999 F.3d 1247, 1275 (11th Cir. 2021); *Ward v. Dixie Nat. Life Ins. Co.*, 595 F.3d 164, 180 (4th Cir. 2010) ("[F]or conflict of interest to defeat the adequacy requirement, 'that conflict must be fundamental.'").

[50]*See In re Equifax Inc. Customer Data Sec. Breach Litig.*, 999 F.3d 1247, 1275 (11th Cir. 2021).

[51]*See In re Equifax Inc. Customer Data Sec. Breach Litig.*, 999 F.3d 1247, 1275 (11th Cir. 2021).

[52]*See Howard v. Cook Cty. Sheriff's Off.*, 989 F.3d 587, 610 (7th Cir. 2021); *Santiago v. City of Chicago*, 19 F.4th 1010, 1018 (7th Cir. 2021).

[53]*See Santiago v. City of Chicago*, 19 F.4th 1010, 1018 (7th Cir. 2021).

[54]*See J.D. v. Azar*, 925 F.3d 1291 (D.C. Cir. 2019); *Stirman v. Exxon Corp.*, 280 F.3d 554, 563 (5th Cir. 2002).

[55]*See In re Equifax Inc. Customer Data Sec. Breach Litig.*, 999 F.3d 1247, 1275 (11th Cir. 2021).

[56]*See also Stampley v. Alton Transp., Inc.*, 958 F.3d 580, 585 (2d Cir. 2020); *Savino v. Computer Credit, Inc.*, 164 F.3d 81, 87 (2d Cir. 1998).

[57]*See Binta B. ex rel. S.A. v. Gordon*, 710 F.3d 608, 618 (6th Cir. 2013).

[58]*See Sosna v. Iowa*, 419 U.S. 393, 399–401, 403, 95 S. Ct. 553, 42 L. Ed.2d 532 (1975); *Cohen v. Brown Univ.*, 16 F.4th 935, 946–47 (1st Cir. 2021) (collecting cases)

[59]*See* Rule 23(a)(4).

[60]*See* Rule 23(g).

[61]*See Ortiz v. Fibreboard Corp.*,

class representatives.[62]

- *The "Most Sophisticated" Investor:* When a class action also falls within the scope of the Private Securities Litigation Reform Act of 1995, this requirement is modified; in that context, the court is obligated to appoint the "most adequate plaintiff" who is most capable of representing the class as the class representative.[63] This requirement, however, has been held not to require that the chosen person possess unique advantages of experience, expertise, wealth, or intellect.[64]

General Considerations

(1) *Diversity-Based Lawsuits*: In most class actions, federal subject-matter jurisdiction based on diversity of citizenship is now governed by special provisions applicable only to class actions under § 1332(d). Subject to a few exceptions, § 1332(d)(2) provides that the amount in controversy requirement for class actions is a sum that exceeds $5,000,000, exclusive of interest and costs.[65] This requirement is often easier to meet than the standard for non-class litigation of more than $75,000 for each plaintiff, exclusive of interest and costs.[66] The reason is that the figure of more than $5,000,000 may be met by adding all the claims of the class members together,[67] whereas the amount of more than $75,000 is normally a requirement that each plaintiff must satisfy.[68]

Section 1332(d)(2) permits the requirement of diversity of citizenship in most class actions to be met in any of three ways: (A) a single member of the class may be a citizen of an American state that is different from the citizenship of any defendant; (B) a single member of the class may be a citizen or subject of a foreign state and any defendant is a citizen of an American state; or (C) a single member of a class may be a citizen of an American state and any defendant is either a foreign state or a

527 U.S. 815, 857, 119 S. Ct. 2295, 144 L. Ed. 2d 715 (1999) (recognizing that "the adequacy of representation enquiry is also concerned with the competency and conflicts of class counsel"); *Slade v. Progressive Sec. Ins. Co.*, 856 F.3d 408, 412 (5th Cir. 2017); *See Dewey v. Volkswagen Aktiengesellschaft*, 681 F.3d 170 (3d Cir. 2012).

[62] *See Irvin v. Harris*, 944 F.3d 63, 71 (2d Cir. 2019).

[63] *See Berger v. Compaq Computer Corp.*, 279 F.3d 313, 313 (5th Cir. 2002). *See also In re Cavanaugh*, 306 F.3d 726, 729 (9th Cir. 2002).

[64] *See Berger v. Compaq Computer Corp.*, 279 F.3d 313, 313 (5th Cir. 2002). *See also In re Cavanaugh*, 306 F.3d 726, 729 (9th Cir. 2002) (party with largest financial stake in litigation presumptively is most adequate party and, assuming requirements of Rule 23 are met, will typically be lead plaintiff).

[65] *See* 28 U.S.C.A. § 1332(d)(2). *See also, e.g., Frazier v. Pioneer Americas LLC*, 455 F.3d 542, 545 (5th Cir. 2006).

[66] *See* 28 U.S.C.A. § 1332(a).

[67] *See* 28 U.S.C.A. § 1332(d)(6). *See also, e.g., Frazier v. Pioneer Americas LLC*, 455 F.3d 542, 547 n.10 (5th Cir. 2006).

[68] *See* 28 U.S.C.A. § 1332(a).

citizen or subject of a foreign state.[69] This requirement permits the diversity of citizenship requirement to be satisfied even where some members of the class might not be of diverse citizenship from one or more defendants, which is a very different standard from the requirement for diverse citizenship in non-class litigation.[70]

Section 1332(d) also contains several exceptions to the special jurisdictional standards for class actions. Together, however, these exceptions constitute a relatively small proportion of the total number of class actions that are now otherwise jurisdictionally eligible to be filed in federal district court. The first potential exception arises when more than one-third, but less than two-thirds, of the class members as well as the primary defendants are citizens of the same state in which the action was originally filed. In that circumstance, § 1332(d) affords the district court discretion to decline to exercise its jurisdiction, after considering six factors: whether the claims involve matters of national or interstate interest; whether the claims will be subject to the law of the forum state or the laws of other states; whether the original pleading in the class action was pleaded in a manner intended to avoid federal jurisdiction; whether the action was filed in a forum with a "distinct" nexus with the class, the alleged wrong, or the defendants; whether the forum is the place of citizenship of a disproportionate number of class members, and the remaining class members are dispersed among a substantial number of other states; and whether, during the previous three years, other class actions asserting similar claims were filed on behalf of the same persons.[71]

Another exception, found in 28 U.S.C.A. § 1332(d)(4), requires the district court to decline jurisdiction if the following elements are met: more than two-thirds of the class members are citizens of the forum state; at least one significant defendant is a citizen of the forum state; principal injuries giving rise to the cause of action occurred in the forum state; and during the previous three years, no similar class action involving essentially the same parties has been filed.[72]

Additionally, the more generous jurisdictional standards of § 1332(d) do not apply if the primary defendants are states, state agencies, or state officials, or if the membership of the proposed class is less than one hundred.[73] Finally, these jurisdictional standards do not apply to three distinct categories of class actions: lawsuits arising under designated federal securities laws; lawsuits relating to the internal affairs of

[69] *See* 28 U.S.C.A. § 1332(d)(2)(A) to (C).

[70] *See Evans v. Walter Indus., Inc.*, 449 F.3d 1159, 1163 (11th Cir. 2006); *Abrego Abrego v. Dow Chem. Co.*, 443 F.3d 676, 680 (9th Cir. 2006).

[71] *See* 28 U.S.C.A. § 1332(d)(3).

[72] *See* 28 U.S.C.A. § 1332(d)(4).

[73] *See* 28 U.S.C.A. § 1332(d)(5).

corporations arising under the laws of the states where such corporations are incorporated; and lawsuits relating to the rights, duties, and obligations pursuant to a security as defined by federal law.[74]

Where § 1332(d) does not apply, the general standards for determining diversity jurisdiction apply. In such circumstances, diversity of citizenship is likely satisfied if the class representatives are diverse from the party opposing the class.[75] Additionally, the amount in controversy requirement for class actions that do not fall within the more generous jurisdictional provisions of § 1332(d) is probably still controlled by the standard for non-class litigation. However, this standard has been loosened considerably, as is discussed under *Supplemental Jurisdiction*, immediately below.

There is an important exception to the general rule that conventional jurisdictional standards apply to a case if § 1332(d) does not apply. If a case was properly removed from state court, but class certification is later denied, the district court nevertheless retains jurisdiction of such a case.[76]

For purposes of § 1332(d), an unincorporated association is deemed a citizen of the state in which its principal place of business is located as well as the state in which it was organized.[77] This provision differs from the treatment of unincorporated associations in non-class litigation.

Under § 1332(d)(11), most mass actions will, for jurisdictional purposes, be treated in a manner like the way other provisions of § 1332(d) address most class actions.

2) *Supplemental Jurisdiction*: The Supreme Court resolved substantial uncertainty as to whether members of a Rule 23 class must satisfy the amount in controversy requirement individually.[78] The Court held that when Congress enacted 28 U.S.C.A. § 1367 (governing supplemental jurisdiction), it effectively provided that if a single member of the class meets the amount in controversy requirement for diversity jurisdiction, all other members whose claims fall short of the requirement amount may nonetheless qualify for supplemental jurisdiction if the other elements of § 1367 are satisfied.[79] This holding is applicable to classes governed by Rule 23 but usually not to

---

[74] *See* 28 U.S.C.A. § 1332(d)(9).

[75] *See Supreme Tribe of Ben Hur v. Cauble*, 255 U.S. 356, 366, 41 S. Ct. 338, 65 L. Ed. 673 (1921) (overruled in part on other grounds by Toucey v. New York Life Ins. Co., 314 U.S. 118, 62 S. Ct. 139, 86 L. Ed. 100 (1941)).

[76] *See United Steel, Paper & Forestry, Rubber, Mfg., Energy, Allied Indus. & Serv. Workers Int'l Union, AFL-CIO, CLC v. Shell Oil Co.*, 602 F.3d 1087, 1091 (9th Cir. 2010); *Cunningham Charter Corp. v. Learjet, Inc.*, 592 F.3d 805, 806–07 (7th Cir. 2010); *Vega v. T-Mobile USA, Inc.*, 564 F.3d 1256, 1268 n.12 (11th Cir. 2009).

[77] *See* 28 U.S.C.A. § 1332(d)(10).

[78] *See Exxon Mobil Corp. v. Allapattah Servs., Inc.*, 545 U.S. 546, 558–59, 125 S. Ct. 2611, 162 L. Ed. 2d 502 (2005).

[79] *See Exxon Mobil Corp. v. Allapattah Servs., Inc.*, 545 U.S. 546, 558–59, 125 S. Ct. 2611, 162 L. Ed. 2d 502

parties intervening in a class pursuant to Rule 24. Section 1367 is discussed in greater detail elsewhere in this text.

(3) *Federal Question-Based Lawsuits:* Federal courts have subject-matter jurisdiction over class actions involving federal questions in the same manner as conventional litigation.[80]

(4) *Personal Jurisdiction:* Jurisdiction over a defendant in a class action is obtained in the same manner, and subject to the same requirements, as jurisdiction over any defendant in conventional litigation.[81] However, personal jurisdiction requirements only apply to the class representative — a district court is not required to have personal jurisdiction over absent class members' claims against a defendant.[82]

- *Due Process for Plaintiffs:* Although plaintiff class members have due process rights as well, they differ from the defendant's due process rights that are protected in the personal jurisdiction "minimum contacts" analysis.[83] Plaintiffs' due process rights are ensured with measures like notice and an opportunity to opt out, addressed in other portions of Rule 23.[84]

(5) *Venue:* Venue in class actions does not generally differ from venue in conventional litigation. However, if venue is based on the residence of the class, the residences of the class representatives are examined, not those of the entire class.[85]

(6) *Choice of Law:* In class actions based on state law, the court can only apply the law of a jurisdiction that has a sufficient relationship with an individual litigant.[86] Thus, individual litigants from states other than the forum may be entitled to have the law of some other state applied to their claims.[87] In a class action, therefore, it is possible that the court may have to apply the laws of a variety of states to different class members.[88]

(7) *Defendant Classes:* While most class actions involve a plaintiff class, courts may certify a defendant class.[89] The provisions of Rule 23 apply in much the same fashion as they apply

---

(2005).

[80]*See Blevins v. Aksut*, 849 F.3d 1016, 1020 (11th Cir. 2017).

[81]*See Mussat v. IQVIA, Inc.*, 953 F.3d 441, 447–48 (7th Cir. 2020).

[82]*See Mussat v. IQVIA, Inc.*, 953 F.3d 441, 443–49 (7th Cir. 2020).

[83]*See Phillips Petroleum Co. v. Shutts*, 472 U.S. 797, 808–09, 105 S. Ct. 2965, 86 L. Ed. 2d 628 (1985); *In re Hyundai and Kia Fuel Econ. Litig.*, 926 F.3d 539, 566 (9th Cir. 2019).

[84]*See Phillips Petroleum Co. v. Shutts*, 472 U.S. 797, 812, 105 S. Ct. 2965, 86 L. Ed. 2d 628 (1985).

[85]*See Mussat v. IQVIA, Inc.*, 953 F.3d 441 (7th Cir. 2020).

[86]*See Phillips Petroleum Co. v. Shutts*, 472 U.S. 797, 816–23, 105 S. Ct. 2965, 86 L. Ed. 2d 628 (1985).

[87]*See Phillips Petroleum Co. v. Shutts*, 472 U.S. 797, 816–23, 105 S. Ct. 2965, 86 L. Ed. 2d 628 (1985).

[88]*See Phillips Petroleum Co. v. Shutts*, 472 U.S. 797, 816–23, 105 S. Ct. 2965, 86 L. Ed. 2d 628 (1985).

[89]*See Consolidated Rail Corp. v. Town of Hyde Park*, 47 F.3d 473, 483 (2d Cir. 1995). *But see Henson v. E. Lincoln Twp.*, 814 F.2d 410, 415–17

to plaintiff classes.[90] A potential distinction between a plaintiff class and a defendant class is heightened concern to ensure that the representatives of a defendant class adequately represent the interests of the class because, at least initially, the representatives of a defendant class are chosen by the plaintiff who is suing the class.[91]

(8) Federal Power Over State Class Actions: Nothing in Rule 23 authorizes district courts to enjoin state courts from certifying state class actions.[92]

Burden of Proof: Discovery

The party who is seeking certification has the burden of proving that the requirements for class certification are satisfied.[93] The standard of proof is preponderance of the evidence.[94] Given the existence of this burden, it follows that in many cases, there will be a need for some early discovery.[95]

Pro Se Classes

Pro se class actions are discouraged.[96]

Defining a Class

A prerequisite to class certification is the existence of a class that can be defined with reasonable particularity.[97] The class must also be ascertainable by being defined in a way that membership is capable of determination.[98]

Class Representative Must Be Class Member

At least initially, the class representative must be a member of the class.[99] The purpose of this requirement is part of the courts' determination that class representatives will reflect the

---

(7th Cir. 1987) (defendant classes may not be certified under Rule 23(b)(2)); *Bazemore v. Friday*, 751 F.2d 662, 669–700 (4th Cir. 1984), *affirmed in relevant part,* 478 U.S. 385, 387 (1986) (Rule 23(b)(2) defendant classes generally prohibited, except where there is a challenge to "a statewide [government] rule or practice so that relief is available if the rule or practice is invalid").

[90] *See Consolidated Rail Corp. v. Town of Hyde Park*, 47 F.3d 473, 483–84 (2d Cir. 1995).

[91] *See Ameritech Ben. Plan Comm. v. Commc'n Workers of Am.*, 220 F.3d 814, 819 (7th Cir. 2000).

[92] *See Smith v. Bayer Corp.*, 564 U.S. 299, 302, 131 S. Ct. 2368, 180 L. Ed. 2d 341 (2011).

[93] *See Halliburton Co. v. Erica P. John Fund, Inc.*, 573 U.S. 258, 134 S. Ct. 2398 (2014); *J.D. v. Azar*, 925 F.3d 1291, 1317 (D.C. Cir. 2019); *1988 Tr. for Allen Child. Dated 8/8/88 v. Banner Life Ins. Co.*, 28 F.4th 513, 521 (4th Cir. 2022).

[94] *See Novella v. Westchester Cnty.*, 661 F.3d 128, 148–49 (2d Cir. 2011).

[95] *See Priddy v. Health Care Serv. Corp.*, 870 F.3d 657, 660 (7th Cir. 2017).

[96] *See Fymbo v. State Farm Fire & Cas. Co.*, 213 F.3d 1320, 1321 (10th Cir. 2000).

[97] *See Rensel v. Centra Tech, Inc.*, 2 F.4th 1359, 1369 (11th Cir. 2021); *See McKeague v. TMBC, LLC*, 847 F.3d 992 (8th Cir. 2017); *Young v. Nationwide Mut. Ins. Co.*, 693 F.3d 532, 538 (6th Cir. 2012).

[98] *See Rensel v. Centra Tech, Inc.*, 2 F.4th 1359, 1369 (11th Cir. 2021)

[99] *See E. Texas Motor Freight Sys. Inc. v. Rodriguez*, 431 U.S. 395, 403, 97 S. Ct. 1891, 52 L. Ed. 2d 453 (1977);

interests of the class.[100] If a class representative was once a member but ceases to be a member of the class, the proper remedy is to select a new, suitable member of the class as a replacement representative.[101]

Standing for Class Members

Absent, passive members of a class need not meet standing requirements,[102] provided that the class representatives satisfy standing.[103] This settled view applies equally to settlement classes and non-settlement classes.[104]

Arbitration Versus Class Actions

In general, contractual provisions that require arbitration of disputes are enforceable under the Federal Arbitration Act.[105] In the context of class actions, an arbitration provision precluding class arbitration or class litigation is enforceable, notwithstanding state law to the contrary.[106]

Relation of EEOC Claims to Rule 23

In general, actions initiated by the Equal Employment Opportunity Commission are not subject to the requirements of Rule 23.[107]

Other State Bars to Federal Class Actions

Notwithstanding state laws unrelated to arbitration (discussed above) that purport to prohibit class actions, district courts may certify such actions under Rule 23.[108]

Relation to Rule 68

Rule 68 governs offers of judgment. Circuit courts have identified at least two points of overlap between Rule 23 and

---

Santiago v. City of Chicago, 19 F.4th 1010, 1018 (7th Cir. 2021).

[100]*See Santiago v. City of Chicago*, 19 F.4th 1010, 1018 (7th Cir. 2021).

[101]*See Holmes v. Pension Plan of Bethlehem Steel Corp.*, 213 F.3d 124, 135-36 (3d Cir. 2000). *But see Kifer v. Ellsworth*, 346 F.3d 1155, 1156 (7th Cir. 2003) ("but the mooting of the class representative's personal claim does not bar him from continuing to represent the class, . . . as otherwise defendants might delay the grant of relief in class actions indefinitely by buying off the class representatives in succession.").

[102]*See Flecha v. Medicredit, Inc.*, 946 F.3d 762, 769 (5th Cir. 2020).

[103]*See Denney v. Deutsche Bank, AG*, 443 F.3d 253, 263–64 (2d Cir. 2006); *Flecha v. Medicredit, Inc.*, 946 F.3d 762, 769 (5th Cir. 2020).

[104]*See Neale v. Volvo Cars of N. Am., LLC*, 794 F.3d 353, 362 (3d Cir. 2015).

[105]*See* 9 U.S.C.A. § 2. *See also Am. Exp. Co. v. Italian Colors Rest.*, 570 U.S. 228, 233, 133 S. Ct. 2304, 186 L. Ed. 2d 417 (2013).

[106]*See AT&T Mobility LLC v. Concepcion*, 563 U.S. 333, 341, 131 S. Ct. 1740, 179 L. Ed. 2d 742 (2011). *See also Lamps Plus, Inc. v. Varela, 587 U.S.*___, 139 S. Ct. 1407, 1415, 203 L. Ed. 2d 636 (2019) (ambiguous agreement cannot be basis for compelling class arbitration).

[107]*See Gen. Tel. Co. of the Nw. v. Equal Emp. Opportunity Comm'n*, 446 U.S. 318, 324, 100 S. Ct. 1698, 64 L. Ed. 2d 319 (1980).

[108]*See Shady Grove Orthopedic Assocs., P.A. v. Allstate Ins. Co.*, 559 U.S. 393, 402, 130 S. Ct. 1431, 176 L. Ed. 2d 311 (2010); *See Am. Copper & Brass, Inc. v. Lake City Indus. Prod., Inc.*, 757 F.3d 540, 546 (6th Cir. 2014).

Rule 68.

The first issue can arise when a defendant makes an offer of judgment for the full amount that a plaintiff may lawfully collect if the plaintiff's claim prevails on the merits. This situation usually occurs when there is a statutory cap on the plaintiff's claim. When such an offer of judgment is made, courts normally apply Rule 68 to end the litigation without regard to any preference the plaintiff may have.[109] Whatever merit this approach may have in ordinary civil litigation, it can produce a complication in a case that has been or may be certified as a class action. For example, if a defendant makes an offer of judgment to an individual litigant for a full statutory amount, a court's decision to use a default judgment to effectively force a settlement of the case could preclude litigation of issues that were appropriate for treatment as a class action. It is now resolved, however, that a Rule 68 offer of judgment to an individual plaintiff cannot be used to render a putative class action moot.[110]

The second issue arises when a proper offer of judgment is made under Rule 68, which requires to the court to enter judgment.[111] Rule 23, by contrast, affords the court substantial authority to review and approve or reject a proposed settlement of a class action.[112] Courts have resolved this apparent conflict by treating the authority of a district court under Rule 23 as an exception to the general requirement of Rule 68, controlling most offers of judgment outside the context of class litigation.[113]

Binding Effect of Class Actions: Collateral Attack

In general, members of a class who are not excluded from the class by, e.g., opt-out provisions such as Rule 23(c)(2), are bound by the judgment in the case.[114] However, there is an important exception to that general rule if a court finds the class was not adequately represented by the class representatives and class counsel. The court will make two inquiries to

---

[109] *See McCauley v. Trans Union, L.L.C.*, 402 F.3d 340, 341–42 (2d Cir. 2005) (where plaintiff rejects such offer, proper remedy is to enter default judgment for full dollar amount, plus costs).

[110] *See Campbell-Ewald Co. v. Gomez*, 577 U.S. 153, 162, 136 S. Ct. 663, 193 L. Ed. 571 (2016); *Radha Geismann, M.D., P.C. v. ZocDoc, Inc.*, 909 F.3d 534, 541 (2d Cir. 2018).

[111] *See* Fed. R. Civ. P. 68. *See Webb v. James*, 147 F.3d 617, 621 (7th Cir. 1998).

[112] *See Ramming v. Nat. Gas Pipeline Co. of Am.*, 390 F.3d 366, 371 (5th Cir. 2004) (duty of court to review settlement of class actions under Rule 23 provides potential exception to Rule 68; same result when case involves plea for injunctive relief); *Gordon v. Gouline*, 81 F.3d 235, 239–40 (D.C. Cir. 1996) (collecting cases where court held fairness hearings prior to entering judgment on Rule 68 offers); *Minner v. Off. Depot, Inc.*, 336 F.R.D. 213, 215–16 (D. Colo. 2020) (collecting cases demonstrating that application of Rule 68 offers in putative class action context is unsettled).

[113] *See Ramming v. Nat. Gas Pipeline Co. of Am.*, 390 F.3d 366, 371 (5th Cir. 2004).

[114] *See Richardson v. Wells Fargo Bank, N.A.*, 839 F.3d 442, 450 (5th Cir. 2016).

determine the possible existence of a lack of adequate representation: (1) did the court reach a correct conclusion as to the adequacy of representation the class received from its representatives and counsel; and (2) did the representatives and counsel "vigorously and tenaciously" protect the class?[115] If the answer to both questions is in the affirmative, then the Due Process clauses of the Constitution do not ban the application of preclusion principles.[116]

Statutes of Limitation: Equitable Tolling

In a case based on federal question jurisdiction, institution of the class action tolls applicable statutes of limitations for the class.[117] The statute remains in suspension until the district court denies certification.[118] If the statute resumes running, it does so from the point at which it was tolled.[119] This protection applies to parties who subsequently seek to intervene in the suit after certification has been denied.[120] However, it apparently does not apply to circumstances in which plaintiffs file their actions *before* class certification has been denied.[121] Further, if the class was certified under Rule 23(b)(3) and some members of the class exercise their right to opt out of the class under Rule 23(c)(2), the statute remains tolled as to those individuals until they exercise the right to opt out.[122] This protection applies even to members of the class who were unaware of the pendency of the class litigation.[123] Moreover, equitable tolling applies to "all members of the putative class until class certification has been denied."[124]

The equitable considerations that are the foundation for tolling statutes of limitations, in some circumstances, do not generally apply to situations in which an individual litigant is faced

---

[115]*See Richardson v. Wells Fargo Bank, N.A.*, 839 F.3d 442, 454 (5th Cir. 2016).

[116]*See Richardson v. Wells Fargo Bank, N.A.*, 839 F.3d 442 (5th Cir. 2016).

[117]*See Am. Pipe & Const. Co. v. Utah*, 414 U.S. 538, 550–51, 94 S. Ct. 756, 38 L. Ed. 2d 713 (1974); *Crown, Cork & Seal Co. v. Parker*, 462 U.S. 345, 353–54, 103 S. Ct. 2392, 76 L. Ed. 2d 628 (1983); *Potter v. Comm'r of Soc. Sec.*, 9 F.4th 369, 377 (6th Cir. 2021).

[118]*See Taylor v. United Parcel Serv., Inc.*, 554 F.3d 510, 519 (5th Cir. 2008) (an appeal of the denial of class certification does not extend the tolling period.).

[119]*See Am. Pipe & Const. Co. v. Utah*, 414 U.S. 538, 542–43, 94 S. Ct. 756, 38 L. Ed. 2d 713 (1974).

[120]*See Am. Pipe & Const. Co. v. Utah*, 414 U.S. 538, 553, 94 S. Ct. 756, 38 L. Ed. 2d 713 (1974).

[121]*See Stein v. Regions Morgan Keegan Select High Income Fund, Inc.*, 821 F.3d 780, 788–89 (6th Cir. 2016).

[122]*See Am. Pipe & Const. Co. v. Utah*, 414 U.S. 538, 550–51, 94 S. Ct. 756, 38 L. Ed. 2d 713 (1974).

[123]*See Am. Pipe & Const. Co. v. Utah*, 414 U.S. 538, 551, 94 S. Ct. 756, 38 L. Ed. 2d 713 (1974); *Sawyer v. Atlas Heating & Sheet Metal Works, Inc.*, 642 F.3d 560, 561 (7th Cir. 2011).

[124]*See Crown, Cork & Seal Co., Inc. v. Parker*, 462 U.S. 345, 354, 103 S. Ct. 2392, 76 L. Ed. 2d 628 (1983). *But cf., China Agritech, Inc. v. Resh*, *__ U.S.__*, 138 S. Ct. 1800, 1802, 201 L. Ed. 2d 123 (2018) (benefit of equitable tolling does not extend to second, untimely filed class action).

with the barrier of a statute of repose. In that circumstance, the Supreme Court has held that a statute of repose will prevail over an attempt to toll the running of the statute.[125]

It is uncertain whether plaintiffs who file individual actions while a motion to certify is pending should get the benefit of tolling.[126] Attorneys will need to consult local precedent and practice.

This doctrine of equitable tolling, though applicable to cases based on federal question jurisdiction, applies to class actions arising from state claims only when state law also provides for equitable tolling.[127]

Equitable Tolling Opportunities Restricted to Unnamed Class Members

The application of equitable tolling in class action cases cannot be used to extend the time in which plaintiffs named in the original suit may file new claims.[128] This rule applies to both new class actions and new individual claims by named members of the original class.[129]

Relation of Class Actions to Fair Labor Standards Act

Under certain circumstances, the Fair Labor Standards Act[130] provides employees with an opportunity to file a collective action against their employers. However, the procedures for filing such a claim differ in some respects from the requirements for filing a class action.[131] Nevertheless, it appears that, notwithstanding the differences between the two bodies of law, a single complaint may nevertheless contain causes of action that seek relief under either or both of those provisions.[132]

RULE 23(b)—TYPES OF CLASS ACTIONS

CORE CONCEPT

Before a class action will be certified, federal jurisdiction must exist, and the Rule 23(a) prerequisites must all be satisfied. In addition, a class will not be certified unless it fits within at least

---

[125] *See California Pub. Employees' Ret. Sys. v. ANZ Sec., Inc.*, __U.S.__, 137 S. Ct. 2042, 2050, 198 L. Ed. 2d 584 (2017).

[126] *Compare In re Hanford Nuclear Rsrv. Litig.*, 534 F.3d 986, 1009 (9th Cir. 2008) (permitting tolling) *and In re WorldCom Sec. Litig.*, 496 F.3d 245, 256 (2d Cir. 2007) (denial of tolling might force individual into inappropriate early decision on individual lawsuit versus class action) *with Wyser-Pratte Mgmt. Co., Inc. v. Telxon Corp.*, 413 F.3d 553, 569 (6th Cir. 2005) (purpose of tolling is undercut by premature individual lawsuit prior to class certification decision).

[127] *See, e.g., Wade v. Danek Med., Inc.*, 182 F.3d 281, 286–87 (4th Cir. 1999).

[128] *See China Agritech, Inc. v. Resh*, __U.S.__, , 138 S. Ct. 1800, 1806, 201 L. Ed. 2d 123 (2018).

[129] *See China Agritech, Inc. v. Resh*, __U.S.__, , 138 S. Ct. 1800, 1806, 201 L. Ed. 2d 123 (2018).

[130] 29 U.S.C.A. § 201 *et seq.*

[131] *See Calderone v. Scott*, 838 F.3d 1101, 1103–04 (11th Cir. 2016).

[132] *See Calderone v. Scott*, 838 F.3d 1101, 1104 (11th Cir. 2016).

one of the categories of classes described in Rule 23(b).[133] Unlike the requirement that all Rule 23(a) prerequisites be satisfied, Rule 23(b) is met if any one of the Rule 23(b) categories applies,[134] though there are sometimes advantages to satisfying more than one category.

APPLICATIONS

Rule 23(b)(1)(A): Risk of Inconsistent Standards of Conduct for the Defendant

A class may be certified if the opposing party will otherwise be placed at risk of being subjected to inconsistent standards of conduct.[135] Rule 23(b)(1)(A) is reserved for that subset of cases in which the different adjudicatory outcomes would put the defendant in a true bind, for example, where a plan administrator is obligated to treat each member the same.[136]

Rule 23(b)(1)(B): Risk of Practical Impairment of Non-Parties' Interests

A class may be certified if piecemeal litigation involving individual class members may dispose of, impair, or impede the interests of individuals who are not parties to the individual litigation.[137] Under Rule 23(b)(1)(B), the class does not depend on the degree of individual proof required for individual plaintiffs to recover, but instead rests on the recognition that deciding a plaintiff's claim might result in other plaintiffs being unable to bring their own claims separately.[138] One of the most common applications of Rule 23(b)(1)(B) occurs when numerous claimants seek relief from a limited fund and, in the absence of class certification, individual lawsuits might deplete the fund before all worthy claimants had a chance to obtain a share of the fund.[139] However, to obtain certification under Rule 23(b)(1)(B) in such circumstances, it is settled that the "limited" fund must be "limited by more than the agreement of the parties."[140]

- *"Inconsistent Standards of Conduct" Contrasted with*

---

[133]*See Puffer v. Allstate Ins. Co.*, 675 F.3d 709, 716 (7th Cir. 2012); *Messner v. Northshore Univ. HealthSystem*, 669 F.3d 802, 811 (7th Cir. 2012).

[134]*See Messner v. Northshore Univ. Health Sys.*, 669 F.3d 802, 811 (7th Cir. 2012).

[135]*See, e.g., In re Integra Realty Res., Inc.*, 354 F.3d 1246, 1263–64 (10th Cir. 2004).

[136]*See Boley v. Universal Health Servs., Inc.*, 337 F.R.D. 626, 638 (E.D. Pa. 2021); *Gaston v. LexisNexis Risk Sols., Inc.*, 483 F. Supp. 3d 318, 341 (W.D.N.C. 2020).

[137]*See In re Integra Realty Res., Inc.*, 354 F.3d 1246, 1264 (10th Cir. 2004). *But cf., Tilley v. TJX Companies, Inc.*, 345 F.3d 34, 42 (1st Cir. 2003) (certification under Rule 23(b)(1)(B) "cannot rest solely on an anticipated stare decisis effect").

[138]*See Boley v. Universal Health Servs., Inc.*, 36 F.4th 124, 136 (3d Cir. 2022).

[139]*See Gaston v. LexisNexis Risk Sols., Inc.*, 483 F. Supp. 3d 318, 341 (W.D.N.C. 2020).

[140]*See Ortiz v. Fibreboard Corp.*, 527 U.S. 815, 821, 119 S. Ct. 2295, 144 L. Ed. 2d 715 (1999).

"Risk of Practical Impairment": Rule 23(b)(1)(A) has the primary purpose of protecting the opponent of the class from the possibility of creating inconsistent standards of conduct.[141] In a situation where Rule 23(b)(1)(A) is suitable, there is less concern about the potential class members, because even if no class is certified, individual members of the class can still bring their claims individually without loss to themselves. In a Rule 23(b)(1)(B) situation involving potential "practical impairment;" however, failure to certify a class creates the probability that individual members will not be able to share recovery in limited resources in a proportional manner, fair to all.[142]

Rule 23(b)(2): Classes Seeking Injunctive or Declaratory Relief

A class may be certified where the primary relief sought is injunctive or declaratory in nature.[143] Rule 23(b)(2) applies only when a single injunction or declaratory judgment would provide relief to the class as a whole.[144] Accordingly, if class members would be entitled to different injunctions or declaratory judgments, a class cannot be certified.[145] Rule 23(b)(2) does not require, however, that the relief to each class member be identical.[146]

There are two elements to satisfy before a class may be certified under Rule 23(b)(2): the class must share a general claim against the opposing party,[147] and the class must seek either final injunctive or declaratory relief.[148] Some courts have permitted preliminary injunctive relief under Rule 23(b)(2), stating that the plain language of the Rule does not restrict prelimi-

---

[141] *See In re Integra Realty Res., Inc.*, 354 F.3d 1246, 1263–64 (10th Cir. 2004).

[142] *See Ortiz v. Fibreboard Corp.*, 527 U.S. 815, 834, 119 S. Ct. 2295, 144 L. Ed. 2d 715 (1999).

[143] *See Wal-Mart Stores, Inc. v. Dukes*, 564 U.S. 338, 365, 131 S. Ct. 2541, 180 L. Ed. 2d 374 (2011) (Rule 23(b)(2) addresses only injunctive relief, not other equitable relief such as back pay); *Barrows v. Becerra*, 24 F.4th 116, 132 (2d Cir. 2022).

[144] *See Jennings v. Rodriguez*, — U.S. —, 138 S. Ct. 830, 852, 200 L. Ed. 2d 122 (2018); *Barrows v. Becerra*, 24 F.4th 116, 132 (2d Cir. 2022) (injunctive or declaratory relief is appropriate when it applies to the class as a whole).

[145] *See Barrows v. Becerra*, 24 F.4th 116, 132 (2d Cir. 2022).

[146] *See Barrows v. Becerra*, 24 F.4th 116, 132 (2d Cir. 2022).

[147] *See Gates v. Rohm & Haas Co.*, 655 F.3d 255, 264 (3d Cir. 2011); *Heffner v. Blue Cross & Blue Shield of Alabama, Inc.*, 443 F.3d 1330, 1344 (11th Cir. 2006).

[148] *See Wal-Mart Stores, Inc. v. Dukes*, 564 U.S. 338, 360, 131 S. Ct. 2541, 180 L. Ed. 2d 374 (2011); *Vallario v. Vandehey*, 554 F.3d 1259, 1268 (10th Cir. 2009). *But cf., J.D. v. Azar*, 925 F.3d 1291, 1319 (D.C. Cir. 2019) ((b)(2) class may proceed even if some class members are ideologically opposed to suit; no need to provide dissenters with opt-out option).

nary injunctions.[149]

Unlike claims for which class certification is sought under, *e.g.*, Rule 23(b)(3), a determination to certify a class under Rule 23(b)(2) does not rest on considerations of manageability or judicial economy.[150] Furthermore, instead of requiring common issues, Rule 23(b)(2) requires common behavior by the defendant toward the class.[151] Race and gender discrimination class actions, seeking an alteration in the future behavior of the opponent of the class, are typical of the class actions certified under Rule 23(b)(2).[152]

- *Obtaining Damages in Rule 23(b)(2) Class Actions*: Certification of a class under Rule 23(b)(2) requires that the relief sought in the case is primarily declaratory or injunctive in nature. It may not always be disabling to attach a plea for damages to a Rule 23(b)(2) certification, but seeking damages in a Rule 23(b)(2) case could impair the prospects for certification under that provision.[153] Some courts avoid due process concerns by issuing a "divided certification," i.e., certifying the damages claims under Rule 23(b)(3) while certifying the injunctive relief under 23(b)(2).[154]

NOTE: If damages are more important in the case than equitable remedies, it is likely that the suit will be certified under some provision other than Rule 23(b)(2) or not certified at all.[155] Alternatively, if a class is certified based on the predominance of common legal or factual questions under Rule 23(b)(3), substantial difficulties could follow. Rule 23(b)(3) class representatives may be burdened with substantial expenses in notifying other class members of the litigation. Thus, in seeking damages

---

[149] *See Meyer v. Portfolio Recovery Assocs., LLC*, 707 F.3d 1036, 1043 (9th Cir. 2012) ("The plain language of FRCP 23(b)(2) does not restrict class certification to instances when final injunctive relief issues; it only requires that final injunctive relief be appropriate."). *But cf., Kartman v. State Farm Mut. Auto. Ins. Co.*, 634 F.3d 883 (7th Cir. 2011) (Rule 23(b)(2) contains requirement that injunctive relief be final).

[150] *See Rodriguez v. Hayes*, 578 F.3d 1032, 1051 (9th Cir. 2010) (citing other cases). *But see Kartman v. State Farm Mut. Auto. Ins. Co.*, 634 F.3d 883, 893 (7th Cir. 2011) (denying certification where injunction would be "administratively challenging," requiring a judge "to write an insurance-adjustment code").

[151] *See Prantil v. Arkema Inc.*, 986 F.3d 570, 580 (5th Cir. 2021).

[152] *See Vallario v. Vandehey*, 554 F.3d 1259, 1269 (10th Cir. 2009).

[153] *See Wal-Mart Stores, Inc. v. Dukes*, 564 U.S. 338, 362, 131 S. Ct. 2541, 180 L. Ed. 2d 374 (2011) (absence of procedural protections of notice and right to opt out that are found in Rule 23(b)(3) are reasons to curtail use of Rule 23(b)(2) in cases involving monetary claims); *See Kanter v. Warner-Lambert Co.*, 265 F.3d 853, 860 (9th Cir. 2001) ("In Rule 23(b)(2) cases, monetary damage requests are generally allowable only if they are merely incidental to the litigation.").

[154] *See Spegele v. USAA Life Ins. Co.*, 336 F.R.D. 537, 558 (W.D. Tex. 2020).

[155] *See Wal-Mart Stores, Inc. v. Dukes*, 564 U.S. 338, 131 S. Ct. 2541, 180 L. Ed. 2d 374 (2011).

in a Rule 23(b)(2) class, the benefits of obtaining damages should be weighed against the possibility that the case might be certified under Rule 23(b)(3). If notification expenses in a particular case are likely to be substantial, it is prudent to consider whether the class should seek damages at all.[156] Notification duties for a Rule 23(b)(3) class are discussed in Rule 23(c)(2), below. For other notification obligations the court may impose, see Rule 23(d)(2) and (e).

- *Ascertainability of Members of Rule 23(b)(2) Classes*: In class actions governed by Rule 23(b)(2), there is no requirement that individual class members be ascertainable.[157]
- *Hybrid Certification*: Because money damages are not usually available in classes certified under Rule 23(b)(2), courts have sometimes considered certification under some combined application of Rule 23(b)(2) and (3). Under this approach, a court might certify a class under Rule 23(b)(2) for the purpose of liability and then consider certification under Rule 23(b)(3) to determine damages.[158] Whether this approach, which could be viewed as an attempt to circumvent the general proscription on money damages in Rule 23(b)(2) cases while also easing the burden of meeting the "predominance and superiority" requirements of Rule 23(b)(3), will survive Supreme Court scrutiny is currently an unresolved issue.
- *No "Predominance" Requirement in Rule 23(b)(2)*: Technically, Rule 23(b)(2) contains no requirement that questions common to the class must predominate over non-common questions, as required when certifying a class under Rule 23(b)(3). However, the requirement for cohesiveness in Rule 23(b)(2) classes — such as an issue of race or gender — will involve a closer bond between members of a (b)(2) class than typically exists in a (b)(3) class.[159]
- *Supervisory Problems*: Certification under Rule 23(b)(2)

[156] *Cf., Allen v. Int'l Truck & Engine Corp.*, 358 F.3d 469, 470 (7th Cir. 2004) (suggesting that when case involving both equitable relief and money damages is certified under Rule 23(b)(2), notice and right to opt out may still be required for damages issues).

[157] *See Cole v. City of Memphis*, 839 F.3d 530, 542 (6th Cir. 2016).

[158] *See Ebert v. Gen. Mills, Inc.*, 823 F.3d 472, 477 (8th Cir. 2016).

[159] *See Donelson v. Ameriprise Fin. Servs., Inc.*, 999 F.3d 1080, 1093 (8th Cir. 2021); *See Prantil v. Arkema Inc.*, 986 F.3d 570, 580 (5th Cir. 2021); *Ahmad v. City of St. Louis*, 995 F.3d 635, 644 (8th Cir. 2021) (because unnamed class members are bound without an opportunity to opt out, a Rule 23(b)(2) class requires even greater cohesiveness than a damages class). *But see J.D. v. Azar*, 925 F.3d 1291, 1319 (D.C. Cir. 2019) (Rule 23(b)(2) class may proceed even if some class members are ideologically opposed to suit; no need to provide dissenters with opt-out provision).

may be denied because the injunctive relief necessary would place an undue administrative burden on the court.[160]

- *Rule 23(b)(2) and Jury Trials*: The Seventh Amendment to the United States Constitution normally provides a right to trial by jury in federal district courts in civil litigation where money damages are sought.[161] At the same time, in class actions certified under Rule 23(b)(2), the case must be based primarily on claims, which do not normally qualify to be heard by a jury. When the occasional Rule 23(b)(2) class action also contains a plea for money damages, issues relating to damages alone or to both damages and injunctive or declaratory relief may require trial by jury, but issues going to the injunctive or declaratory claims alone should be heard by the judge.[162]

Rule 23(b)(3): Predominance of Common Legal or Factual Questions

A class may be certified where questions of law or fact common to the members of the class predominate over other questions.[163] Rule 23(b)(3) certification is often a last resort for classes that cannot be certified under any other portion of Rule 23(b).[164] Two special mandatory requirements exist for Rule 23(b)(3) classes. First, common questions must *predominate* over individual interests.[165] Resolution of the "predominance" analysis is heavily fact-dependent.[166] To determine predominance, courts ask if common issues in the case are more important or prevalent than individual issues.[167] Common questions of law or fact will typically be answered by using the same evidence to make a generalized showing of proof, while

[160]*See Kartman v. State Farm Mut. Auto. Ins. Co.*, 634 F.3d 883, 893 (7th Cir. 2011) (denying certification where injunctive relief would be "administratively challenging" requiring a judge "to write an insurance-adjustment code").

[161]*See Beacon Theatres, Inc. v. Westover*, 359 U.S. 500, 510, 79 S. Ct. 948, 3 L. Ed. 2d 988 (1959).

[162]*See Allen v. Int'l Truck & Engine Corp.*, 358 F.3d 469, 471 (7th Cir. 2004).

[163]*See* Rule 23(b)(3).

[164]*See DeBoer v. Mellon Mortg. Co.*, 64 F.3d 1171, 1175 (8th Cir. 1995); *Murray v. GMAC Mortg. Corp.*, 434 F.3d 948, 953 (7th Cir. 2006).

[165]*See Amgen Inc. v. Connecticut Ret. Plans & Tr. Funds*, 568 U.S. 455, 460, 133 S. Ct. 1184, 185 L. Ed. 2d 308 (2013) (if an issue's resolution will cause class to win or lose case, Rule 23(b)(3) predominance test is satisfied); *Amchem Prod., Inc. v. Windsor*, 521 U.S. 591, 623, 117 S. Ct. 2231, 138 L. Ed. 2d 689 (1997) (predominance not satisfied if there are a number of significant questions peculiar to different categories within class or to individuals within class).

[166]*See Tyson Foods, Inc. v. Bouaphakeo*, 577 U.S. 442, 467, 136 S. Ct. 1036, 194 L. Ed. 2d 124 (2016).

[167]*See Johannessohn v. Polaris Indus. Inc.*, 9 F.4th 981, 984 (8th Cir. 2021). *See also Santiago v. City of Chicago*, 19 F.4th 1010, 1016 (7th Cir. 2021) ("The guiding principle behind predominance is whether the proposed class's claims arise from a common nucleus of operative facts and issues.").

individual questions require the presentation of evidence that varies by class member.[168] The district court must evaluate evidence to determine whether a common question predominates without weighing that evidence to determine whether the plaintiff class will ultimately prevail on the merits.[169]

When one or more common issues are said to predominate, the predominance requirement can be satisfied even though other matters need to be tried separately, such as determining individual damages.[170]

A well-defined class may inevitably contain some individuals who have suffered no harm, but the percentage must be de minimis.[171]

The party seeking certification must prove that the predominance requirement is met.[172]

In other Rule 23(b) classes, by contrast, because the classes themselves will necessarily be more cohesive than a class certified under Rule 23(b)(3),[173] there is only the requirement, stated in Rule 23(a)(2), that common questions of law or fact exist among the class members, with no requirement that the common questions predominate.[174]

- *Certification Requirements for Classes Where Common Questions Predominate: Superiority*: The second requirement for certification under Rule 23(b)(3) is a finding that a class action is the superior means of adjudicating

168 *See Ross v. Gossett*, 33 F.4th 433, 439 (7th Cir. 2022); *Johannessohn v. Polaris Indus. Inc.*, 9 F.4th 981, 984 (8th Cir. 2021).

169 *See In re Allstate Corp. Sec. Litig.*, 966 F.3d 595, 603 (7th Cir. 2020). *See also Santiago v. City of Chicago*, 19 F.4th 1010, 1016 (7th Cir. 2021) ("common questions predominate where the case claims the existence of a widespread or uniform practice").

170 *See Tyson Foods, Inc. v. Bouaphakeo*, 577 U.S. 442, 439, 136 S. Ct. 1036, 194 L. Ed. 2d 124 (2016) (predominance satisfied, even when damages or affirmative defenses must be tried separately); *Ross v. Gossett*, 33 F.4th 433, 439 (7th Cir. 2022). *But cf., Ibe v. Jones*, 836 F.3d 516 (5th Cir. 2016) (noting that absence of method to make mathematical calculations of individual damages may render class treatment unsuitable).

171 *See In re Rail Freight Fuel Surcharge Antitrust Litig.*, 934 F.3d 619, 624–25 (D.C. Cir. 2019) (finding lack of predominance when 12.7% of class members suffered no harm).

172 *See Comcast Corp. v. Behrend*, 569 U.S. 27, 30, 133 S. Ct. 1426, 185 L. Ed. 2d 515 (2013); *Wal-Mart Stores, Inc. v. Dukes*, 564 U.S. 338, 351, 131 S. Ct. 2541, 2551, 180 L. Ed. 2d 374 (2011). *But cf., Halliburton Co. v. Erica P. John Fund, Inc.*, 563 U.S. 804 (2014) (requirement in stock fraud class actions that every plaintiff prove direct reliance on defendant's misrepresentation would make certification under Rule 23(b)(3) practically impossible).

173 *See Avritt v. Reliastar Life Ins. Co.*, 615 F.3d 1023, 1035 (8th Cir. 2010); *Holmes v. Continental Can Co.*, 706 F.2d 1144, 1155 n.8 (11th Cir. 1983).

174 *See Amchem Prod., Inc. v. Windsor*, 521 U.S. 591, 623, 117 S. Ct. 2231, 2249, 138 L. Ed. 2d 689 (1997); *Prantil v. Arkema Inc.*, 986 F.3d 570 (5th Cir. 2021).

the controversy.[175] A finding that common questions predominate will have significant additional influence on the court's determination of superiority, for the existence of predominant common issues will often support a conclusion that a class action is a superior means of adjudicating individual claims.[176] In reaching the "superiority" determination, a court is required to make the following findings set forth in Rule 23(b)(3): the class members' interest in pursuing individual actions; the nature and extent of similar pending litigation; the desire to concentrate claims in a certain forum; and the difficulty in managing the class.[177] The court may also address other issues that, in particular cases, are relevant to determining whether certification of a class action is the best way to proceed.[178] The court's determination of superiority is a serious one that, like predominance, must be thoroughly examined.[179]

- *Individual Interests in Separate Actions*: The court will evaluate the desire, if any, of individual litigants to pursue their own separate actions, and the net balance of interests between such individuals and the class as a whole.[180] Because individual litigants who feel the need to control their own cases may exercise their right under Rule 23(c) to "opt out" of a Rule 23(b)(3) class, it is usually possible to certify the class and still accommodate most of the needs of such individuals. Harmonizing individual interests can be more difficult if it is likely that so many individuals would opt out that the "class" no longer contains the bulk of its potential members. In that circumstance, the evidence of such strong interest in individual litigation would argue strongly against certifying a Rule 23(b)(3) class.
- *Pending Litigation*: The court will also consider the effects of any other pending litigation on the proposed class action. If individual class members have already

[175]*See Amchem Prod., Inc. v. Windsor*, 521 U.S. 591, 615, 117 S. Ct. 2231, 138 L. Ed. 2d 689 (1997); *Gregory v. Finova Cap. Corp.*, 442 F.3d 188, 191 n.3 (4th Cir. 2006).

[176]*See McFields v. Dart*, 982 F.3d 511, 519 (7th Cir. 2020); *Gintis v. Bouchard Transp. Co.*, 596 F.3d 64, 67–68 (1st Cir. 2010).

[177]*See* Rule 23(b)(3)(A)–(D).

[178]*See In re Vivendi, S.A. Sec. Litig.*, 838 F.3d 223, 263–64 (2d Cir. 2016) (court may consider whether foreign courts will give preclusive effect to judgment); *Castano v. Am. Tobacco Co.*, 84 F.3d 734, 749 (5th Cir.1996) (court may consider whether class action will preserve judicial resources).

[179]*See Gintis v. Bouchard Transp. Co.*, 596 F.3d 64, 68 (1st Cir. 2010).

[180]*See Zinser v. Accufix Rsch. Inst., Inc.*, 253 F.3d 1180, 1191 (9th Cir. 2001). *See also, Heaven v. Trust Co. Bank*, 118 F.3d 735, 738 (11th Cir. 1997) (counterclaims against individual class members is a factor to consider in evaluating whether, under Rule 23(b)(3)(A), individual members might have interest in controlling their own cases).

initiated their own cases, it may be difficult to justify certification of a Rule 23(b)(3) class on grounds of judicial economy.[181]

- *Progress in Class Litigation*: If the court hearing the class action has already invested enough resources in the case so that dismissal or refusal to certify the action would be inefficient, a strong argument exists in favor of certifying the class so that the action can be concentrated in the chosen forum.[182]
- *Geography*: Another consideration that may bear on the wisdom of proceeding with the class action in the chosen forum is geography. If the case is being heard in an area of the country where the class or the evidence is concentrated, this can support an argument for continuing in the chosen forum.[183]
- *Difficulties in Managing a Class Action*: Courts can refuse to certify if too many administrative difficulties exist in class actions.[184] In exercising this discretion, courts consider a wide variety of factors affecting ease of administration of a case. Examples of problems in managing a class include internal disputes within a class and problems of notification of class members,[185] as well as the impact that state law variations can have on management in a multi-state case.[186]
- *Rule 23(b)(3)*: *Ascertainability*: Floating within a court's evaluation of a motion to certify a class under Rule 23(b)(3) is a need to determine whether a class is ascertainable.[187] This inquiry places a burden on a plaintiff class representative to demonstrate that the

---

[181]*See City of Inglewood v. City of Los Angeles*, 451 F.2d 948, 952 n.4 (9th Cir. 1971). *But cf., Hanlon v. Chrysler Corp.*, 150 F.3d 1011 (9th Cir.1998) (no bar to class certification where only a few pending lawsuits may be difficult to merge into class action).

[182]*See In re Mid-Atl. Toyota Antitrust Litig.*, 564 F. Supp. 1379, 1390, n.18 (D. Md. 1983).

[183]*See Zinser v. Accufix Rsch. Inst., Inc.*, 253 F.3d 1180, 1192 (9th Cir. 2001); *Langley v. Coughlin*, 715 F. Supp. 522, 561 (S.D. N.Y. 1989).

[184]*See* Rule 23(b)(3)(D).

[185]*See Zinser v. Accufix Research Institute, Inc.*, 253 F.3d 1180, 1192 (9th Cir. 2001).

[186]*See Webb v. Exxon Mobile Corp.*, 856 F.3d 1150, 1157 (8th Cir. 2017). *But cf., Cherry v. Dometic Corp.*, 986 F.3d 1296, 1304 (11th Cir. 2021) (administrative feasibility is not a requirement for certification under Rule 23); *Sullivan v. DB Investments, Inc.*, 667 F.3d 273, 301 (3d Cir. 2011) (differences in laws of fifty states do not, *ipso facto*, prevent class certification); *Mullen v. Treasure Chest Casino, LLC*, 186 F.3d 620, 627 (5th Cir. 1999) (superiority requirement satisfied by: lack of complex choice-of-law or *Erie* problems; modest number of class members; bifurcated-trial plan; and likelihood that trial would focus on secondhand smoke as both result of poor ventilation and cause of illnesses). *Cf., Cruson v. Jackson Nat. Life Ins. Co.*, 954 F.3d 240 (5th Cir. 2020) (failure to assess differences in state law in case involving national class is ground for decertification).

[187]*See Rensel v. Centra Tech, Inc.*, 2 F.4th 1359, 1369 (11th Cir. 2021).

proposed class is identifiable and that the members of the proposed class are encompassed by the definition of the class.[188] Ascertainability is an implied prerequisite that must be satisfied first because a clear class definition is necessary for the court to analyze the factors enumerated in Rule 23.[189]

- *Affirmative Defenses:* A defendant's possible affirmative defenses against claims by individual class members will not, of themselves, prevent the parties seeking class certification from meeting the requirement.[190]
- *Antitrust Litigation:* Antitrust plaintiffs must establish Article III standing as well as "antitrust standing," which is critically important for evaluating "predominance" under Rule 23(b)(3).[191] To survive a claim under Section 1 of the Sherman Act, each antitrust class member must prove individual injury, known as "antitrust impact."[192] Establishing antitrust standing at the class certification stage requires antitrust plaintiffs to "demonstrate that the element of antitrust impact is capable of proof at trial through evidence that is common to the class rather than individual to its members."[193] If damages to the class cannot be demonstrated through common proof, establishing liability for each class member defeats Rule 23(b)(3) predominance.[194] Accordingly, it is common (and appropriate) to prove antitrust impact by the use of class-wide averages.[195]

"Fail-Safe" Classes Disapproved

A "fail-safe" class is one in which the class is defined to include only persons who are entitled to relief.[196] Such a class, in theory, would permit class members to win their case without risk that

[188] *See Byrd v. Aaron's, Inc.*, 784 F.3d 154, 163 (3d Cir. 2015); *Shelton v. Bledsoe*, 775 F.3d 554, 560 (7th Cir. 2015); *Rensel v. Centra Tech, Inc.*, 2 F.4th 1359, 1369 (11th Cir. 2021).

[189] *See Cherry v. Dometic Corp.*, 986 F.3d 1296, 1302 (11th Cir. 2021).

[190] *See Tyson Foods, Inc. v. Bouaphakeo*, 577 U.S. 442, 439, 136 S. Ct. 1036, 194 L. Ed. 2d 124 (2016) (predominance satisfied, even when damages or affirmative defenses must be tried separately); *See Smilow v. Sw. Bell Mobile Sys., Inc.*, 323 F.3d 32, 39–40 (1st Cir. 2003).

[191] *See In re Zetia (Ezetimibe) Antitrust Litig.*, 7 F.4th 227, 238 (4th Cir. 2021).

[192] *See In re Hydrogen Peroxide Antitrust Litig.*, 552 F.3d 305, 311 (3d Cir. 2008), *as amended* (Jan. 16, 2009).

[193] *See In re Hydrogen Peroxide Antitrust Litig.*, 552 F.3d 305, 311–12 (3d Cir. 2008), *as amended* (Jan. 16, 2009).

[194] *See In re Hydrogen Peroxide Antitrust Litig.*, 552 F.3d 305, 311–12 (3d Cir. 2008), *as amended* (Jan. 16, 2009). *See also Bell Atl. Corp. v. AT & T Corp.*, 339 F.3d 294, 302 (5th Cir. 2003).

[195] *See In re Zetia (Ezetimibe) Antitrust Litig.*, 7 F.4th 227, 238 (4th Cir. 2021).

[196] *See Orduno v. Pietrzak*, 932 F.3d 713, 716 (8th Cir. 2019).

they might be bound by an adverse judgment.[197] Courts seem to universally reject certification of such classes.[198] Similarly, the "rule against one-way intervention" may lead a court to refuse to issue a pre-certification ruling on the merits of a plaintiff's claim because the named plaintiff could opt not to seek class certification if the plaintiff receives an unfavorable pre-certification ruling.[199]

RULE 23(c)—CERTIFICATION ORDER; NOTICE TO CLASS MEMBERS; JUDGMENT; ISSUES CLASSES; SUBCLASSES

CORE CONCEPT

Once a lawsuit is shown to be eligible for class action treatment, the court will determine whether to formally certify the case as a class action. The court may do so *sua sponte* or upon motion, but such determinations should be made at "an early practicable time." If the court authorizes class treatment, the certified class needs to be defined (including whether to divide the class into subclasses), class counsel must be appointed, and the question of notice must be considered. These procedures establish class action logistics but impose no new *sub silentio* class action prerequisites.[200]

APPLICATIONS

Motion or Court Initiative

A party may seek certification by motion, or the court may on its own initiative make the certification decision.[201] The lack of a motion to certify does not relieve the district court of its duty to make this determination, and the lack of such a motion cannot be the basis for denial of class certification.[202] In deciding whether certification is appropriate, the district court will normally treat the factual allegations contained in the complaint as true.[203]

Timing

Rule 23(c) provides no rigid timetable for resolving the certification issue, but courts are directed to make the decision "at

---

[197] *See Young v. Nationwide Mut. Ins. Co.*, 693 F.3d 532, 538 (6th Cir. 2012).

[198] *See Randleman v. Fidelity Nat. Title Ins. Co.*, 646 F.3d 347 (6th Cir. 2011). *See also Orduno v. Pietrzak*, 932 F.3d 710 (8th Cir. 2019).

[199] *See Spring House Tavern, Inc. v. Am. Fire & Cas. Co.*, 337 F.R.D. 371, 375 (E.D. Pa. 2020).

[200] *See Cherry v. Dometic Corp.*, 986 F.3d 1296, 1304 (11th Cir. 2021).

[201] *See Trevizo v. Adams*, 455 F.3d 1155, 1161 (10th Cir. 2006); *McGowan v. Faulkner Concrete Pipe Co.*, 659 F.2d 554, 559 (5th Cir. 1981).

[202] *See Trevizo v. Adams*, 455 F.3d 1155, 1161 (10th Cir. 2006); *McGowan v. Faulkner Concrete Pipe Co.*, 659 F.2d 554, 559 (5th Cir. 1981).

[203] *See Vallario v. Vandehey*, 554 F.3d 1259, 1265 (10th Cir. 2009).

an early practicable time."[204] District courts have discretion to set deadlines for when parties must move for class certification.[205]

Preemptive Motion to Deny Certification

There is apparently no provision that would prevent the opponent of a class from moving to deny certification, even where the proponent of a class has not yet sought certification.[206] Motions to strike, however, are disfavored and the defendant must definitively establish that a class action cannot be maintained consistent with the class allegations.[207]

Conditional Certification

In the past, Rule 23(c)(1) permitted the court to make certification conditional upon later developments in the case. However, Rule 23(c)(1) was amended in 2003 to remove the language authorizing conditional certification.[208]

Defining Claims, Issues, or Defenses

If a class is certified, Rule 23(c)(1)(B) directs the district court to define the class, *i.e.*, to include in the certification order a clear and complete summary of the claims, issues, and defenses subject to class treatment.[209] The definition should describe the class in a way that makes clear what the scope of the litigation and the breadth of the res judicata effect may be.[210] However, district courts do not always fulfill this requirement completely, requiring remand for a more specific and deliberate treatment of the class issues, claims, and defenses.[211]

Amending a Certification Order

Rule 23(c)(1)(C) authorizes a district court to alter or amend its original certification order at any time prior to final judg-

---

[204] *See Danny B. ex rel. Elliott v. Raimondo*, 784 F.3d 825, 837 (1st Cir. 2015); *Kerkhof v. MCI WorldCom, Inc.*, 282 F.3d 44, 55 (1st Cir. 2002) (post-judgment certification should usually be discouraged because it would frustrate the opt-out mechanisms for Rule 23(b)(3)).

[205] *See Davidson v. O'Reilly Auto Enterprises, LLC*, 968 F.3d 955, 962 (9th Cir. 2020).

[206] *See Kasalo v. Harris & Harris, Ltd.*, 656 F.3d 557, 563 (7th Cir. 2011).

[207] *See Dowding v. Nationwide Mut. Ins. Co.*, 490 F. Supp. 3d 1291, 1298 (N.D. Ill. 2020).

[208] *See Hohider v. United Parcel Serv., Inc.*, 574 F.3d 169, 202 (3d Cir. 2009).

[209] *See Lewis v. City of Chicago*, 702 F.3d 958, 962 (7th Cir. 2012); *Simpson v. Dart*, 23 F.4th 706, 713 (7th Cir. 2022) (observing that under Rule 23(c)(1)(B), class certification "may be appropriate as to some of the class's claims but not others.").

[210] *See Spano v. Boeing Co.*, 633 F.3d 574, 584 (7th Cir. 2011). *See also Mullen v. Treasure Chest Casino, LLC*, 186 F.3d 620, 624 n.1 (5th Cir. 1999) (class of employees alleging illness caused by defective ventilation system is not deficient because allegation of defective system or injury from it has yet to be proven on merits).

[211] *See Wachtel ex rel. Jesse v. Guardian Life Ins. Co. of Am.*, 453 F.3d 179, 184 (3d Cir. 2006).

ment on the merits.[212] The heightened motion-for-reconsideration standard does not apply.[213] District courts have the authority to decertify a class *sua sponte* at any time before final judgment is entered if they find that the class no longer meets the requirements of Rule 23.[214]

Notice

Rule 23(c)(2) establishes various notice options or requirements for cases certified under Rule 23. For classes certified pursuant to Rule 23(b)(1) or (2), Rule 23(c)(2)(A) authorizes—but does not require—the district court to order notice to such classes.[215] This authority is intended to supplement the court's already existing power under Rule 23(d)(2) to issue notice in some circumstances to class members.[216] Courts will be cautious in their use of notice to Rule 23(b)(1) and (2) classes so as not to burden the class representatives with unnecessary costs of notice.[217]

Because absent class members in a Rule 23(b)(2) class do not receive notice and are not permitted to opt out of the class,[218] such class members cannot challenge certification of the class.[219] This apparently harsh result is mitigated by other authority permitting absent class members to challenge imposition of res judicata or collateral estoppel. The alternative grounds for such a challenge would be either inadequate representation in the prior litigation[220] or lack of constitutionally required notice.[221]

Rule 23(c)(2) also establishes special requirements for notifying class members of pending Rule 23(b)(3) actions.[222] The reason for this provision arises from the special nature of Rule 23(b)(3) suits, in which common questions must predominate, and the class suit must be superior to alternative methods of

---

[212] *See White v. Nat'l Football League*, 756 F.3d 585, 594 (8th Cir. 2014) (court may decertify class *sua sponte,* even at the appellate level); *Voss v. Rolland*, 592 F.3d 242, 251 (1st Cir. 2010).

[213] *See Hargrove v. Sleepy's LLC*, 974 F.3d 467, 470 (3d Cir. 2020).

[214] *See Jin v. Shanghai Original, Inc.*, 990 F.3d 251, 261 (2d Cir. 2021).

[215] *See Randall v. Rolls-Royce Corp.*, 637 F.3d 818, 820 (7th Cir. 2011).

[216] *See* Rule 23(c)(2) advisory committee notes to 2003 amendments. *See also Eubanks v. Billington*, 110 F.3d 87, 96 (D.C. Cir. 1997).

[217] *See* Rule 23(c)(2) advisory committee notes to 2003 amendments; *Rahman v. Chertoff*, 530 F.3d 622, 626 (7th Cir. 2008).

[218] *See Lewis v. City of Chicago*, 702 F.3d 958, 962 (7th Cir. 2012). *But cf., Johnson v. Meriter Health Servs. Emp. Ret. Plan*, 702 F.3d 364, 370 (7th Cir. 2012) (Rule 23(c)(2)(A) gives district court authority to require notice to (b)(2) class members).

[219] *See Ticor Title Ins. Co. v. Brown*, 511 U.S. 117, 121, 114 S. Ct. 1359, 128 L. Ed. 2d 33 (1994).

[220] *See Hansberry v. Lee*, 311 U.S. 32, 42–43, 61 S. Ct. 115, 85 L. Ed. 22 (1940).

[221] *See Wal-Mart Stores, Inc. v. Dukes*, 564 U.S. 338, 362–63, 131 S. Ct. 2541, 180 L. Ed. 2d 374 (2011).

[222] *See* Fed. R. Civ. P. 23(c)(2)(B).

adjudication.[223] To ensure proper notice to the class, Rule 23(c)(2) provides that individual members must receive the "best notice practicable," which includes individual notice to members who can be reasonably identified.[224] The Federal Judicial Center has determined that notice plans that reach between 70 and 95 percent of the class are reasonable.[225]

Finally, Rule 23(c)(2) also requires that if a class action requires certification under both Rule 23(b)(2) and (b)(3), the usually more burdensome notice requirements in a (b)(3) class must be satisfied for the (b)(2) class.[226]

Non-Expert and Expert Evidence

If, in seeking class certification, a party tries to introduce expert testimony over an opposing party's objection, the district court must evaluate such evidence according to established standards for admission of expert evidence developed in the context of non-class litigation.[227] There is currently a circuit split relating to whether evidence used to determine class certification must be admissible at the class certification stage.[228]

Certification and the Merits

The analysis necessary for certification may often properly overlap with assessment of the merits of the plaintiffs' claim.[229] However, courts cannot engage in "free-ranging merits" inquiries — questions relating to the merits may only be considered to the extent relevant to determine if class certification is appropriate under Rule 23.[230] In that vein, if an expert witness's evidence is "critical to class certification," the district court

---

[223] *See* Fed. R. Civ. P. 23(b)(3).

[224] *See Briseno v. ConAgra Foods, Inc.*, 844 F.3d 1121, 1129 (9th Cir. 2017) (standard is best practicable notice, not necessarily actual notice); *Schwarzschild v. Tse*, 69 F.3d 293, 295 (9th Cir. 1995) (in general, Rule 23(c)(2) requires notice to class members before merits are adjudicated; in unusual case where summary judgment is granted prior to certification, plaintiff no longer has duty of notification). *Cf., Mirfasihi v. Fleet Mortg. Corp.*, 356 F.3d 781, 786 (7th Cir. 2004) ("When individual notice is infeasible, notice by publication in a newspaper of national circulation . . . is an acceptable substitute.").

[225] *See In re Restasis (Cyclosporine Ophthalmic Emulsion) Antitrust Litig.*, 527 F. Supp. 3d 269, 273 (E.D.N.Y. 2021).

[226] *See* Rule 23(c)(2) advisory committee notes to 2003 amendments.

[227] *See Prantil v. Arkema Inc.*, 986 F.3d 570, 576 (5th Cir. 2021); *In re Blood Reagents Antitrust Litig.*, 783 F.3d 183, 187 (3d Cir. 2015).

[228] *See Allen v. Ollie's Bargain Outlet, Inc.*, 37 F.4th 890, 906–09 (3d Cir. 2022) (collecting cases from various circuits and explaining reasoning behind each circuit's holdings).

[229] *See Comcast Corp. v. Behrend*, 569 U.S. 27, 33–34, 133 S. Ct. 1426, 185 L. Ed. 2d 515 (2013) ("class determination generally involves considerations that are enmeshed in the factual and legal issues"); *Amgen Inc. v. Connecticut Ret. Plans & Tr. Funds*, 568 U.S. 455, 465–66, 133 S. Ct. 1184, 185 L. Ed. 2d 308 (2013); *Olean Wholesale Grocery Coop., Inc. v. Bumble Bee Foods LLC*, 31 F.4th 651, 667 (9th Cir. 2022).

[230] *See Amgen Inc. v. Connecticut Ret. Plans & Tr. Funds*, 568 U.S. 455, 466, 133 S. Ct. 1184, 185 L. Ed. 2d 308 (2013); *Olean Wholesale Grocery Coop., Inc. v. Bumble Bee Foods LLC*, 31 F.4th 651, 667 (9th Cir. 2022).

must rule on challenges to the expert's qualifications or conclusions prior to deciding a motion for certification.[231] A finding on the merits for purposes of certification does not bind a fact-finder that later addresses issues of facts for purposes of a judgment in the case.[232]

Extension of Rule 23(c)(2) to Rule 23(e)(1) situations

The notice requirements for Rule 23(b)(3) classes also apply to classes that might be certified for purposes of settlement under Rule 23(e)(1).

Elements of Notice to Rule 23(b)(3) Classes

Rule 23(c)(2) specifies that notification will include the following: (1) "the nature of the action, (2) the definition of the class certified, (3) the class claims, issues, or defenses," (4) the right of individual members of the class to appear through counsel if they choose, (5) the right to opt out of the class and not be bound by any judgment,[233] (6) "the time and manner for requesting exclusion,"[234] and (7) the binding effect of a class judgment on members of the class who do not opt out.[235]

Opting Out of Rule 23(b)(1) and (b)(2) Classes

The opt-out provision of Rule 23(c)(2) literally applies to Rule 23(b)(3) classes only.[236] However, a district court has discretionary authority to permit opting out of Rule 23(b)(1) and (b)(2) classes.[237]

Means of Notice: Expenses

Notice to Rule 23(b)(3) may be provided by first class mail or, in appropriate circumstances, by electronic means or other appropriate means.[238] The plaintiffs may seek to have the defendant provide the notice.[239]

No Requirement to "Opt In"

There is no provision in Rule 23(c) requiring class members

---

[231] *See Am. Honda Motor Co. v. Allen*, 600 F.3d 813, 815–16 (7th Cir. 2010).

[232] *See Sali v. Corona Reg'l Med. Ctr.*, 909 F.3d 996, 1004 (9th Cir. 2018).

[233] *See Abbott Lab'ys v. CVS Pharmacy, Inc.*, 290 F.3d 854, 859 (7th Cir. 2002).

[234] *See* Rule 23(c)(2)(B)(ii).

[235] *See generally Eisen v. Carlisle & Jacquelin*, 417 U.S. 156, 94 S. Ct. 2140, 40 L. Ed. 2d 732 (1974). *See also In re Citizens Bank, N.A.*, 15 F.4th 607, 612 (3d Cir. 2021).

[236] *See* Fed. R. Civ. P. 23(c)(2).

[237] *See McReynolds v. Richards-Cantave*, 588 F.3d 790, 800 (2d Cir. 2009); *Penson v. Terminal Transp. Co., Inc.*, 634 F.2d 989, 993 (5th Cir. 1981). *But see Senegal on behalf of a class v. JPMorgan Chase Bank, N.A.*, 939 F.3d 878, 880 (7th Cir. 2019) (no opting out of (b)(2) class because relief is "indivisible"). *Rahman v. Chertoff*, 530 F.3d 622, 626 (7th Cir. 2008) ("Members of a Rule 23(b)(2) class . . . can't opt out.").

[238] *See Schneider v. Chipotle Mexican Grill, Inc.*, 336 F.R.D. 588, 596 (N.D. Cal. 2020) (approving notice by extensive digital media plan); *Weeks v. Matrix Absence Mgmt. Inc.*, 494 F. Supp. 3d 653, 659 (D. Ariz. 2020) (notice by email).

[239] *See Oppenheimer Fund, Inc. v. Sanders*, 437 U.S. 340, 356–59, 98 S. Ct. 2380, 57 L. Ed. 2d 253 (1978).

to "opt in" to participate.[240] Rule 23(c) contains only an "opt out" provision.[241] Rule 23(c)'s "opt-out" provision is in "sharp contrast" to the Fair Labor Standards Act's opt-in requirement.[242]

Parties Bound by Judgment

Rule 23(c)(3) affords the court substantial discretion to determine the binding effect of a class action. Class actions certified under either Rule 23(b)(1) or (b)(2) bind whomever the court finds to be within the membership of the class[243] and contain no requirement that the class members receive notice of the action.[244] Conversely, Rule 23(b)(3) actions bind class members who did not opt out under Rule 23(c)(2) and whom the court defines as members.[245] Thus it is possible that persons in a (b)(3) class might not get actual notice under Rule 23(c)(2) because their names and/or addresses are unknown yet be bound because the court found them to be members of the class. If a class action is not certified, its result is not binding on nonparties.[246]

Issue Classes and Subclasses

Rule 23(c)(4) permits an "issue class" to be maintained as a class action;[247] however, Rule 23(a)'s prerequisites and a showing that the action is maintainable under one of Rule 23(b)'s provisions is required.[248] The Rule authorizes the court to create subclasses only as to particular issues.[249] The American Law Institute adopted certain factors for courts to consider when faced with Rule 23(c)(4) motions to certify, which some

---

[240]*See Phillips Petroleum Co. v. Shutts*, 472 U.S. 797, 812, 105 S. Ct. 2965, 86 L. Ed. 2d 628(1985). *See also N. Sound Cap. LLC Merck & Co.*, 938 F.3d 482, 493 (3d Cir. 2019) (person does not become party "until the time to opt out has lapsed").

[241]*See* Fed. R. Civ. P. 23(c)(2).

[242]*See In re Citizens Bank, N.A.*, 15 F.4th 607, 612 (3d Cir. 2021).

[243]*See Taylor v. Sturgell*, 553 U.S. 880, 894, 128 S. Ct. 2161, 171 L. Ed. 2d 155 (2008).

[244]*See Langbecker v. Elec. Data Sys. Corp.*, 476 F.3d 299, 306 (5th Cir. 2007); *Payne v. Travenol Lab'ys, Inc.*, 673 F.2d 798, 812 (5th Cir. 1982).

[245]*See Eisen v. Carlisle & Jacquelin*, 417 U.S. 156, 176, 94 S. Ct. 2140, 2152, 40 L. Ed. 2d 732 (1974); *In re Citizens Bank, N.A.*, 15 F.4th 607, 612 (3d Cir. 2021).

[246]*See Smith v. Bayer Corp.*, 564 U.S. 299, 305 n.4, 131 S. Ct. 2368, 180 L. Ed. 2d 341 (2011); *Faber v. Ciox Health, Inc.*, 944 F.3d 593, 603 (6th Cir. 2019) (granting of summary judgment in defendant's favor after class certification but prior to notice of certification to absent class members did not bind absent members).

[247]*See* Rule 23(c)(4). *See also Russell v. Educ. Comm'n for Foreign Med. Graduates*, 15 F.4th 259, 266 (3d Cir. 2021).

[248]*See Russell v. Educ. Comm'n for Foreign Med. Graduates*, 15 F.4th 259, 266–67 (3d Cir. 2021).

[249]*See Castano v. Am. Tobacco Co.*, 84 F.3d 734, 745 n.21 (5th Cir. 1996). *But cf., McMahon v. LVNV Funding, Inc.*, 807 F.3d 872 (7th Cir. 2015) (if case requires findings of individual causation and/or damages, court may employ use of Rule 23(c)(4).

courts have incorporated.[250]

Rule 23(c)(5) authorizes the court to create subclasses within an action.[251] If subclasses are certified, each subclass is treated as an independent class for purposes of the action.

The circumstances in which the court is most likely to create subclasses occur when the class members share a cause of action against a class opponent but also experience differing interests among themselves.[252] The most common use of subclasses is to help simplify the manageability of the primary class action.[253] Occasionally, however, subclasses can help the overarching class meet the certification requirements of Rule 23. Rule 23(c)(4) permits certification of subclasses even where predominance has not been satisfied for the cause of action as a whole.[254] For example, a class may be certified for liability purposes only.[255]

Classes for Settlement

Courts are authorized to certify classes created for purposes of settlement only. When a court considers certification of a settlement class, it must first ensure that all the relevant elements of Rule 23 are met, but need not inquire whether the case, if tried, would present intractable management problems.[256]

If a court considers certification of a settlement class, it may notify class members of the possibility of class certification at the time the court notifies class members of the proposed settlement.[257]

Persons who may wish to contest settlements in class actions are generally free to intervene.[258]

Courts have refused to broaden the concept of a settlement class to include approval of a "negotiation class."[259]

---

[250]*See Russell v. Educ. Comm'n for Foreign Med. Graduates*, 15 F.4th 259, 268 & n.3 (3d Cir. 2021) (listing nine factors).

[251]*See In re Visa Check/MasterMoney Antitrust Litig.*, 280 F.3d 124, 141 (2d Cir. 2001).

[252]*See Ortiz v. Fibreboard Corp.*, 527 U.S. 815, 119 S. Ct. 2295, 144 L. Ed. 2d 715 (1999); *Hawkins v. Comparet-Cassani*, 251 F.3d 1230 (9th Cir. 2001).

[253]*Peters v. Aetna Inc.*, 2 F.4th 199, 243 (4th Cir. 2021) (when "theories depend on distinct proof or legal questions common to some but not all class members, then subclasses may be created for purposes of case management.").

[254]*See Cahoo v. Fast Enterprises LLC*, 508 F. Supp. 3d 138, 161 (E.D. Mich. 2020).

[255]*See Felps v. Mewbourne Oil Co., Inc.*, 336 F.R.D. 664, 669 (D.N.M. 2020).

[256]*See Amchem Prod., Inc. v. Windsor*, 521 U.S. 591, 620, 117 S. Ct. 2231, 2248, 138 L. Ed. 2d 689 (1997); *In re Nat'l Prescription Opiate Litig.*, 976 F.3d 664, 674 (6th Cir. 2020).

[257]*See In re Gen. Motors Corp. Pick-Up Truck Fuel Tank Prod. Liab. Litig.*, 55 F.3d 768, 778 (3d Cir. 1995).

[258]*See Crawford v. Equifax Payment Servs., Inc.*, 201 F.3d 877, 881 (7th Cir. 2000).

[259]*See In re Nat'l Prescription Opiate Litig.*, 976 F.3d 664, 673 (6th

RULE 23(d)—CONDUCTING THE ACTION

CORE CONCEPT

Courts possess authority to craft orders governing class actions. Central to class actions is a need to protect the interests of absent class members who are less involved than persons engaged in more conventional litigation. At the same time, the potential administrative complexity of class actions requires that courts have tools to ensure the litigation remains manageable.

APPLICATIONS

District Court's Duty, Broad Authority, and Discretion

Due to the potential for abuse in the class action context, district courts have a duty, broad authority, and wide (but not unbounded) discretion to control the litigation and enter appropriate orders to govern the conduct of the attorneys and the parties.[260]

Orders to Streamline Litigation

Courts are authorized under Rule 23(d)(1)(A) to enter such orders to streamline the litigation.[261] Courts may also create subclasses to improve manageability of the action.[262] Rule 23(d) explicitly vests the court with broad discretion to limit cumulative or repetitive evidence or argument.[263]

Relation to Rule 16

Rule 23(d)(2) contains two provisions. First, it authorizes alteration or amendment of any order previously issued under Rule 23(d)(1). Second, it provides that such an alteration or amendment may be combined with a pretrial order issued under Rule 16. When the court combines orders under Rules 16 and 23(d)(2), applications to modify the orders will be judged by a less exacting standard under Rule 23(d)(2) rather than the stringent requirements for relief from a pretrial order under Rule 16.[264]

Orders to Require Notice to Class Members

Rule 23(d)(1)(B) allows the court to require notice to class members as the court deems necessary.[265] The court's authority under this provision is very broad and encompasses discretion

---

Cir. 2020).

[260] *See Gulf Oil Co. v. Bernard*, 452 U.S. 89, 100, 101 S. Ct. 2193, 68 L. Ed. 2d 693 (1981); *In re Equifax Inc. Customer Data Sec. Breach Litig.*, 999 F.3d 1247, 1266 (11th Cir. 2021).

[261] *See Peters v. Aetna Inc.*, 2 F.4th 199, 243–44 (4th Cir. 2021) ("district court could limit the common questions to eliminate or streamline those without proven commonality.").

[262] *See Peters v. Aetna Inc.*, 2 F.4th 199, 243–44 (4th Cir. 2021) (Rule 23(d) authorizes court to create subclasses and expedite resolution of the case by segregating distinct legal issues).

[263] *See* Rule 23(d)(1)(A). *See also In re Equifax Inc. Customer Data Sec. Breach Litig.*, 999 F.3d 1247, 1266 (11th Cir. 2021).

[264] *See* Rule 23 advisory committee note (2007).

[265] *See S. Ute Indian Tribe v. Amoco Prod. Co.*, 2 F.3d 1023, 1026 n.2 (10th

to order notice to the class of almost any important event in the litigation.[266] The court may use its power in a variety of circumstances, including: notice of any step in the action, the proposed extent of a judgment, and the opportunity for members to express whether they consider representation fair and adequate.[267]

Orders to Impose Conditions on Class Representatives and Intervenors

Rule 23(d)(1)(C) provides explicit authority for the court to monitor class representatives and intervenors[268] and supports both fair representation for the class and expeditious processing of the entire case.[269]

- *Communications Directed to Class Members:* District courts have authority to safeguard class members from unauthorized or misleading communications from the parties, non-parties, or counsel who threaten or interfere with a class action.[270] Abusive communications include anything related to the class that poses a serious threat to the fairness of the litigation process, adequacy of representation, or the administration of justice.[271] Before exercising this discretion, courts must weigh the need to protect the class against the right to free speech under the First Amendment and must carefully craft orders restricting speech as little as possible.[272] Orders restricting communications should demonstrate a likelihood of serious abuse and be based on a clear record with specific findings.[273]

Cir.1993).

[266]*See Jefferson v. Ingersoll Intern. Inc.*, 195 F.3d 894, 898 (7th Cir. 1999). *But see Cobell v. Kempthorne*, 455 F.3d 317, 324 (D.C. Cir. 2006) (Rule 23(d)(2) authorizes orders affecting notice of procedural matters, but provides no authority to issue orders relating to substantive relief); *Cruz v. Am. Airlines, Inc.*, 356 F.3d 320, 331 (D.C. Cir. 2004) (expressing doubt that Rule 23(d)(2) grants authority to order notice to a class that has not been certified).

[267]*See Cobell v. Kempthorne*, 455 F.3d 317, 324 (D.C. Cir. 2006).

[268]*See In re Equifax Inc. Customer Data Sec. Breach Litig.*, 999 F.3d 1247, 1266 (11th Cir. 2021); *In re Auto. Parts Antitrust Litig., End-Payor Actions*, 33 F.4th 894, 906 (6th Cir. 2022) ("[I]ntervenors still are subject to the court's power under Rule 23(d)(1)(C) to impose conditions on their participation in the action.").

[269]*But see Cobell v. Kempthorne*, 455 F.3d 317, 323 (D.C. Cir. 2006) (Rule 23(d)(3) cannot be used to impose a condition on non-class defendant).

[270]*See Fox v. Saginaw Cnty., Michigan*, 35 F.4th 1042, 1047 (6th Cir. 2022); *Lloyd v. Covanta Plymouth Renewable Energy, LLC*, 532 F. Supp. 3d 259, 261 (E.D. Pa. 2021).

[271]*See Fox v. Saginaw Cnty., Michigan*, 35 F.4th 1042, 1047 (6th Cir. 2022) (abusive communications "could be sharing misleading information, misrepresenting the nature of the class action, or coercing prospective class members to opt out of a class.").

[272]*See Gulf Oil Co. v. Bernard*, 452 U.S. 89, 102, 101 S. Ct. 2193, 2201, 68 L. Ed. 2d 693 (1981); *Fox v. Saginaw Cnty., Michigan*, 35 F.4th 1042, 1047 (6th Cir. 2022).

[273]*See Fox v. Saginaw Cnty., Michigan*, 35 F.4th 1042, 1047 (6th Cir. 2022) (finding party's communications abusive when (1) party distorted facts sur-

Orders to Reject Class Certification

Rule 23(d)(1)(D) allows the court to enter an order striking the class allegations.[274] Because Rule 23 contains an explicit vehicle for eliminating class allegations from the complaint, courts apply Rule 23 rather than Rule 12(f) to motions to strike class allegations.[275] This provision is typically employed when the court has already refused, under Rule 23(c)(1), to certify the case as a class action. It may also be used if the court originally certified a class, but later altered its decision and refused certification. In either circumstance, Rule 23(d)(1)(D) contemplates that a suit denied class certification may still proceed as conventional litigation, assuming that the requirements of such litigation are satisfied.

Orders Regarding Other Procedural Matters

Rule 23(d)(1)(E) makes explicit that the authority of the court to issue orders to process a class suit expeditiously and fairly is not limited to the other provisions of Rule 23(d).[276] In so doing, Rule 23(d)(1)(E) re-emphasizes the broad discretion a trial court enjoys in class litigation.[277] Courts have broad discretion to use their power to redress Rule 23(d) transgressions in a variety of circumstances.[278]

Orders Altering or Amending Prior Orders

As a practical matter, Rule 23(d)'s declaration that the court may alter prior orders as necessary to the conduct of the suit means the court is not bound by its own interlocutory decisions in class actions. Thus, the court enjoys almost complete flexibility to adjust class litigation as events may require.

---

rounding claims process and (2) party engaged class members and then encouraged them to opt out of the class based on a one-sided presentation of facts).

[274] *See Free v. Allstate Indem. Co.*, 541 F. Supp. 3d 767, 770 (E.D. Tex. 2021).

[275] *See Texas Hill Country Landscaping, Inc. v. Caterpillar, Inc.*, 522 F. Supp. 3d 402, 410 (N.D. Ill. 2021).

[276] *See Molski v. Gleich*, 318 F.3d 937, 947 (9th Cir. 2003) (even with class certified under rule 23(b)(2), "a district court may require notice and the right to opt-out under its discretionary authority provided in Rule 23(d)[(1)(C)]").

[277] *See Davidson v. O'Reilly Auto Enterprises, LLC*, 968 F.3d 955, 963–64 (9th Cir. 2020) (observing that a district court may abuse its discretion if it unreasonably applies rules in a way that deprives a party of an opportunity to present class allegations or a motion for class certification).

[278] *See Chen-Oster v. Goldman, Sachs & Co.*, 449 F. Supp. 3d 216, 271 (S.D.N.Y. 2020) ("Courts have variously exercised their discretion to redress Rule 23(d) transgressions with measures that range from voiding arbitration clauses altogether, to ordering notice and opportunity for class members to opt out of arbitration and remain in the class action (or vice-versa), to merely warning parties to refrain from specified future activity.").

RULE 23(e)—SETTLEMENT, VOLUNTARY DISMISSAL, OR COMPROMISE

CORE CONCEPT

Voluntary dismissal or compromise of a class action requires court approval, and proposals to settle the case must also be submitted to the entire class for approval. The district court acts as a fiduciary on behalf of the class to ensure the settlement is "fair, reasonable, and adequate."[279] Proposed settlement agreements warrant special scrutiny when the record suggests that the settlement is driven by counsel fees.[280] This requirement of court supervision recognizes the fact that class actions are especially vulnerable to the possibility that the class representatives or the class attorneys may be placed in circumstances where their personal interests conflict with the interests of absent, passive class members. The risk of inappropriate collaboration between class representatives, or class counsel, and the class opponent is probably greatest when questions of settlement or voluntary dismissal are at issue.[281] Rule 23(e) attempts to contain the mischief of such conflicts by imposing a series of obligations on both the court and the parties seeking approval of the proposed settlement.

APPLICATIONS

Authority to Settle: Judicial Approval

Rule 23(e)(1)(A) expressly authorizes class representatives to settle claims, issues, or defenses as appropriate.[282] However, this authority is subject to other provisions in Rule 23(e) that give the power to approve the settlement to the district court,[283] which in turn must consider the views of class members before making its decision.[284] Additionally, in many circumstances, a district court's approval of a settlement is subject to challenge on appeal by nonnamed class members.[285] However, persons who are not class members lack standing to challenge a class

[279] *See Robinson v. Nat'l Student Clearinghouse*, 14 F.4th 56, 59 (1st Cir. 2021); *In re Equifax Inc. Customer Data Sec. Breach Litig.*, 999 F.3d 1247, 1265 (11th Cir. 2021).

[280] *See Briseno v. Henderson*, 998 F.3d 1014, 1024 (9th Cir. 2021).

[281] *See In re Vitamins Antitrust Class Actions*, 215 F.3d 26, 30 (D.C. Cir. 2000).

[282] *See* Rule 23(e)(1)(A) advisory committee notes (2003).

[283] *See In re Equifax Inc. Customer Data Sec. Breach Litig.*, 999 F.3d 1247, 1264 (11th Cir. 2021) ("[T]he parties' decision to settle a class action is not consummated until the district court actually approves it.").

[284] *See McAdams v. Robinson*, 26 F.4th 149, 157 (4th Cir. 2022) (quoting *Phillips Petroleum Co. v. Shutts*, 472 U.S. 797, 811–12, 105 S. Ct. 2965, 86 L. Ed. 2d 628 (1985)) ("The [absent class member] must receive notice plus an opportunity to be heard.").

[285] *See Devlin v. Scardelletti*, 536 U.S. 1, 1, 122 S. Ct. 2005, 153 L. Ed. 2d 27 (2002); *Fidel v. Farley*, 534 F.3d 508, 513 (6th Cir. 2008).

settlement.[286] Although the exact process a district court should follow when presented with a settlement class is not prescribed by Rule 23, some circuits require the court to determine that the settlement class meets the requirements for class certification under Rule 23(a) and (b), and then separately determine that the settlement is fair to that class.[287]

Protection of Class Opponents

The duty of the district court under Rule 23(e) to protect the interests of class members does not extend to parties (usually defendants) who are not members of the class.[288]

Comparison With Conventional Litigation

Rule 23(e) is an exception to the standard practice that parties may normally settle their disputes without the approval of the court.[289]

All Class Actions

Rule 23(e) applies to all actions certified under any portion of Rule 23(b).[290]

Elements of Settlement

The power to approve a settlement lies within the discretion of a district court, and such decisions are infrequently disturbed on appeal.[291] However, some important considerations may restrict that discretion. These include a requirement that there be a hearing if the proposed settlement would bind class members.[292] Additionally, the hearing must lead to a conclusion that the settlement would be "fair, reasonable, and adequate" to meet the interests of the class.[293]

To reach that conclusion, amended Rule 23(e)(2) requires that the court consider whether: class representatives and class counsel adequately represented the class; negotiations with

---

[286] *See* Rule 23(c)(5)(A). *See also Douglas v. The W. Union Co.*, 955 F.3d 662, 665 (7th Cir. 2020) ("only a 'class member' may object to a class settlement").

[287] *See Sourovelis v. City of Philadelphia*, 515 F. Supp. 3d 343, 351 (E.D. Pa. 2021).

[288] *See In re Deepwater Horizon*, 739 F.3d 790, 820 (5th Cir. 2014) (defendant is expected to protect its own interests).

[289] *See In re Equifax Inc. Customer Data Sec. Breach Litig.*, 999 F.3d 1247, 1264 (11th Cir. 2021) (class action may be settled only with court's approval); *Robinson v. Nat'l Student Clearinghouse*, 14 F.4th 56, 59 (1st Cir. 2021); *In re Cendant Corp. Litig.*, 264 F.3d 201, 231 (3d Cir. 2001); *In re Painewebber Ltd. Partnerships Litig.*, 147 F.3d 132, 137 (2d Cir. 1998).

[290] *See Grimes v. Vitalink Commc'ns Corp.*, 17 F.3d 1553, 1557 (3d Cir. 1994). *But cf., White v. Nat'l Football League*, 756 F.3d 585, 591–93 (8th Cir. 2014) (requirements of Rule 23(e) inapplicable to claim outside scope of certified class).

[291] *See Robinson v. Nat'l Student Clearinghouse*, 14 F.4th 56, 59 (1st Cir. 2021) ("court enjoys considerable range in approving or disapproving a class action settlement").

[292] *See* Rule 23(e)(2).

[293] *See* Rule 23(e)(2). *See also Hanlon v. Chrysler Corp.*, 150 F.3d 1011 (9th Cir. 1998); *Robinson v. Nat'l Student Clearinghouse*, 14 F.4th 56, 59 (1st Cir. 2021).

non-class parties took place at arm's length; the proposed relief for the class is adequate; and whether individual members of the class are treated fairly among themselves.[294] The Advisory Committee has explained that the first of these two factors are procedural in nature, and the latter two factors are substantive in nature.[295] The proponents of a proposed settlement or voluntary dismissal are obligated to disclose any agreements that have been made that relate to the proposal.[296]

In reaching a determination of adequacy, the court is instructed to inquire about: costs, risks and delay of the trial and appeal; effectiveness of proposed methods of distributing relief; attorneys' fees; and disclosure of agreements related to the proposed settlement.[297] The precise itemization of additional factors for consideration varies by circuit. One circuit examines five additional factors: the strength of the merits; difficulty of proving the case or strong defenses likely to be encountered during trial; the expected length and expense of additional litigation; the defendant's solvency; and opposition to the settlement.[298] Another circuit considers the following factors: (1) possibility of fraud; (2) complexity and expense; (3) amount of discovery undertaken; (4) likelihood of success; (5) views of lawyers on both sides; (6) views of class members; and (7) the public interest.[299] The most important of these facts is the probability of success on the merits.[300]

In a nationwide settlement of class claims, there is no need to consider differences in state law.[301]

Pre-Certification and Decertified Class Settlements

The notice requirement of Rule 23(e) applies even in some situations where the class was decertified or never certified at

---

[294] *See* Rule 23(e)(2)(A)–(D). *See Cohen v. Brown Univ.*, 16 F.4th 935, 943 (1st Cir. 2021) (explaining the first two factors are "procedural" in nature "looking to the conduct of the litigation.

[295] *See Cohen v. Brown Univ.*, 16 F.4th 935, 943–44 (1st Cir. 2021) (quoting 2018 Advisory Committee note: first two factors look to "the conduct of the litigation and of the negotiations leading up to the proposed settlement; last two factors guide a " 'substantive review' of the terms of the proposed settlement").

[296] *See* Rule 23(e)(2) advisory committee notes (2003). *But see Caligiuri v. Symantec Corp.*, 855 F.3d 860 (8th Cir. 2017) (court need not know final amount received by class before approving settlement).

[297] *See* Rule 23(e)(2)(A)–(D). *See also* Rule 23(e)(3); *McAdams v. Robinson*, 26 F.4th 149, 157 (4th Cir. 2022); *Rawa v. Monsanto Co.*, 934 F.3d 862 (8th Cir. 2019) (most important factor in determining adequacy is balancing strength of plaintiff's case against terms of settlement).

[298] *See McAdams v. Robinson*, 26 F.4th 149, 157 (4th Cir. 2022) (citing *In re Jiffy Lube Sec. Litig.*, 927 F.2d 155, 159 (4th Cir. 1991)).

[299] *See Poplar Creek Dev. Co. v. Chesapeake Appalachia, L.L.C.*, 636 F.3d 235, 244 (6th Cir. 2011).

[300] *See Poplar Creek Dev. Co. v. Chesapeake Appalachia, L.L.C.*, 636 F.3d 235, 244 (6th Cir. 2011).

[301] *See Rawa v. Monsanto Co.*, 934 F.3d 862 (8th Cir. 2019).

all.[302] Settlements occurring prior to certification are subject to a high procedural standard due to the heightened possibility for collusion.[303] Collusion is not always evident on the face of the settlement agreement, so courts are required to search for "subtle signs" to determine if class counsel have put their own interests above the interest of the class.[304] Courts have recognized several potential signs of collusion: a large fee with little to no monetary relief for the class;[305] a "clear sailing" provision under which a defendant agrees not to object to attorneys' fees;[306] and an agreement that fees not awarded will revert to the defendant instead of the class.[307] When these signs of collusion exist, they are not an automatic "death knell," but courts are required to examine the record to assure that the requested attorneys' fees are not unreasonably high.[308]

Simultaneous Certification and Settlement

In a situation where parties seek simultaneous class certification and approval of settlement, courts are obligated to look even more closely at the fairness of the settlement proposal.[309]

Effect on Individual Claims

The power of the court to approve or reject settlements of class litigation does not extend to individual claims which members of the class may possess separate from the class claims. By its terms, the approval power of Rule 23(e)(1)(A) is limited to class litigation only.[310]

Notice of Proposed Settlement

A decision to give notice of a proposed settlement to the

---

[302] *See Culver v. City of Milwaukee*, 277 F.3d 908, 914–15 (7th Cir. 2002). *See also Doe v. Lexington-Fayette Urb. Cnty. Gov't*, 407 F.3d 755, 761 (6th Cir. 2005) (noting that *Culver's* requirement of notice to all classes is clear majority rule). *Cf., Shelton v. Pargo, Inc.*, 582 F.2d 1298, 1315 (4th Cir. 1978) (no automatic requirement of notice to non-certified class members in the absence of collusion or unfair prejudice).

[303] *See Kim v. Allison*, 8 F.4th 1170, 1179 (9th Cir. 2021) ("Because these early, pre-certification settlements are so open to abuse and so little subject to scrutiny at the time by the district court, the court is required to search for "subtle signs" that plaintiff's counsel has subordinated class relief to self-interest."); *In re Bluetooth Headset Prod. Liab. Litig.*, 654 F.3d 935, 946–47 (9th Cir. 2011) (collecting cases from sister circuits).

[304] *See Kim v. Allison*, 8 F.4th 1170, 1179 (9th Cir. 2021); *In re Bluetooth Headset Prod. Liab. Litig.*, 654 F.3d 935, 947 (9th Cir. 2011).

[305] *See Murray v. GMAC Mortg. Corp.*, 434 F.3d 948, 952 (7th Cir. 2006); *Kim v. Allison*, 8 F.4th 1170, 1179 (9th Cir. 2021).

[306] *See Kim v. Allison*, 8 F.4th 1170, 1179 (9th Cir. 2021); *Weinberger v. Great N. Nekoosa Corp.*, 925 F.2d 518, 524 (1st Cir. 1991).

[307] *See Mirfasihi v. Fleet Mortg. Corp.*, 356 F.3d 781, 785 (7th Cir. 2004); *Kim v. Allison*, 8 F.4th 1170, 1179 (9th Cir. 2021).

[308] *See Kim v. Allison*, 8 F.4th 1170, 1180 (9th Cir. 2021); *In re Bluetooth Headset Prod. Liab. Litig.*, 654 F.3d 935, 947 (9th Cir. 2011).

[309] *See Halley v. Honeywell Int'l, Inc.*, 861 F.3d 481, 488 (3d Cir. 2017).

[310] *See* Rule 23(e)(1)(A) advisory committee notes (2003).

entire class rests with the court.[311] However, the burden rests on the parties to provide the court with sufficient information on which to base a decision.[312] The court will provide notice if the parties are able to demonstrate that the court would be likely to approve the settlement under the standards established by proposed amended Rule 23(e)(2) and could also certify the class (if certification has not already occurred) for purposes of judgment on the proposed settlement.[313]

While Rule 23(e) does not specify what a notice must include, to comport with constitutional and procedural due process and bind absent class members, the notice to the class must inform class members of the pendency of the action and provide an opportunity for class members to present objections.[314] The notice must also apprise the class members of the terms of the proposed settlement and the options available to them in connection with the case.[315] The notice requirement for Rule 23(e)(1) will usually satisfy the notice requirement Rule 23(c)(2)(B) imposes on classes to be certified under Rule 23(b)(3).[316]

Rule 23(e)(1) expressly requires the district court to hold a hearing and make findings before approving a class settlement or voluntary dismissal.[317] The findings must include a determination that the proposed course of resolution for the class action is "fair, reasonable, and adequate."[318]

If a class action is resolved on the merits, there is no requirement of notice to class members.[319]

Material Changes to Settlement: Notice Requirement

A material change in an existing settlement will normally require a new round of notice and a hearing.[320] Some courts have allowed non-material modifications without requiring new

[311] *See* Rule 23(e)(1)(B) advisory committee note (2018).

[312] *See* Rule 23(e)(1)(A) advisory committee note (2018).

[313] *See* Rule 23(e)(1)(B) advisory committee note (2018).

[314] *See McAdams v. Robinson*, 26 F.4th 149, 157–58 (4th Cir. 2022); *Mullane v. Cent. Hanover Bank & Tr. Co.*, 339 U.S. 306, 313, 70 S. Ct. 652, 94 L. Ed. 865 (1950).

[315] *See McAdams v. Robinson*, 26 F.4th 149, 157–58 (4th Cir. 2022) *Wal-Mart Stores, Inc. v. Visa U.S.A., Inc.*, 396 F.3d 96, 114 (2d Cir. 2005).

[316] *See* Rule 23(e) advisory committee note (2018).

[317] *See In re Syncor ERISA Litig.*, 516 F.3d 1095, 1097 (9th Cir. 2008).

[318] *See McAdams v. Robinson*, 26 F.4th 149, 157–58 (4th Cir. 2022); *Does 1–2 v. Déjà Vu Services, Inc.*, 925 F.3d 886 (6th Cir. 2019) (most important factor is probability of success on the merits). *See also Int'l Union, United Auto., Aerospace, & Agr. Implement Workers of Am. v. Gen. Motors Corp.*, 497 F.3d 615, 629 (6th Cir. 2007) (no requirement that proposed settlement offer pro rata distribution to individual members of class; settlement need only be fair, reasonable and adequate).

[319] *See Lewis v. City of Chicago*, 702 F.3d 958, 962–63 (7th Cir. 2012).

[320] *See Pearson v. Target Corp., NBTY, Inc.*, 893 F.3d 980, 986 (7th Cir. 2018); *In re Baby Prods. Antitrust Litig.*, 708 F.3d 163, 175 & n.10 (3d Cir. 2013).

notice.[321]

Other Factors

While the court is authorized to determine whether the settlement is fair to passive, absent members of the class,[322] the court must still give substantial deference to a consensus of class members on the wisdom of the settlement.[323] Second, while the court must pass on the fairness of the proposal, it may not rewrite the settlement to make it conform to the court's view of a satisfactory settlement.[324] Third, notwithstanding a request from both sides of a lawsuit, a district court has no authority under Rule 23(e) to take up the task of distributing residual funds.[325] Fourth, the court's duty is primarily to the members of the class,[326] and it is fiduciary in nature.[327] If persons have previously opted out of the class, the court has no power or duty to use the settlement process to address their interests.[328] Fifth, at least in class actions affected by fee shifting provisions in civil rights cases, the court has the authority and duty to review waivers of attorney's fees that are part of a proposed settlement.[329] Finally, the court's authority to certify a class created for purposes of settlement and to approve the proposed settlement is subject to a determination that the proposed class meets the requirements of Rule 23(a) and (b).[330]

---

[321] *See Friske v. Bonnier Corp.*, 543 F. Supp. 3d 543, 545 (E.D. Mich. 2021) (collecting cases).

[322] *See Robinson v. Nat'l Student Clearinghouse*, 14 F.4th 56, 59 (1st Cir. 2021); *Hanlon v. Chrysler Corp.*, 150 F.3d 1011, 1026 (9th Cir. 1998).

[323] *See Cnty. of Suffolk v. Alcorn*, 266 F.3d 131, 135 (2d Cir. 2001); *Poplar Creek Dev. Co. v. Chesapeake Appalachia, L.L.C.*, 636 F.3d 235, 244 (6th Cir. 2011).

[324] *See Evans v. Jeff D.*, 475 U.S. 717, 726, 106 S. Ct. 1531, 89 L. Ed. 2d 747 (1986); *In re Wireless Tel. Fed. Cost Recovery Fees Litig.*, 396 F.3d 922, 934 (8th Cir. 2005).

[325] *See In re Lupron Mktg. & Sales Pracs. Litig.*, 677 F.3d 21, 38 (1st Cir. 2012). *Cf., Roes, 1–2 v. SFBSG Mgmt., LLC*, 944 F.3d 1035, 1049 (9th Cir. 2019) (provision providing for unclaimed funds to revert to defendants is disfavored because it creates incentive to set up obstacles to recovery by class members).

[326] *See In re Cendant Corp. Litig.*, 264 F.3d 286, 295 (3d Cir. 2001); *Tennessee Ass'n of Health Maint. Organizations, Inc. v. Grier*, 262 F.3d 559, 566 (6th Cir. 2001).

[327] *See Kim v. Allison*, 8 F.4th 1170, 1178 (9th Cir. 2021) ("The district court must act as a ficuciary, protecting the interests of the absent class members by scrutinizing the settlement's fairness in light of well-established factors.").

[328] *See In re Vitamins Antitrust Class Actions*, 215 F.3d 26, 30 (D.C. Cir. 2000). *But see In re Heritage Bond Litig.*, 546 F.3d 667, 677 (9th Cir. 2008) (in litigation controlled by Private Securities Litigation Reform Act, if a settlement satisfies the requirements of Rule 23(e)(2) but is rejected by some defendants, district court has authority to impose prohibition on non-settling defendants' future claims for contribution and indemnity).

[329] *See Evans v. Jeff D.*, 475 U.S. 717, 728, 106 S. Ct. 1531, 89 L. Ed. 2d 747 (1986).

[330] *See Amchem Prod., Inc. v. Windsor*, 521 U.S. 591, 593, 117 S. Ct. 2231, 138 L. Ed. 2d 689 (1997). *See also Ortiz v. Fibreboard Corp.*, 527 U.S. 815, 849, 119 S. Ct. 2295, 144 L. Ed. 2d 715 (1999) (fairness hearing

Court's Duty to Ensure that Settlement is Actually Paid

When a district court retains jurisdiction over a settlement agreement, it has a duty to ensure that the terms of the settlement are followed.[331]

Protection against Loss by Class Members

Congress provided district courts with authority to approve a proposed settlement involving a payment by members of the class to class counsel that would be a net loss to the class members. However, that authority is restricted to cases in which the court, by a written finding, concludes that nonmonetary benefits to the class "substantially" outweigh the monetary loss.[332] This provision of § 1713 is not restricted to cases involving "coupon" settlements, and appears to apply to class action settlements generally.

Protection against Geographic Discrimination

Congress has prohibited approval of proposed settlements in which some members of the class receive greater amounts of value than others based "solely" on their closer geographic ties to the location of the court hearing the case.[333] This provision appears to apply not only to "coupon" settlements but to class action settlements generally.

Additional Opportunity to Opt Out of Class

Rule 23(e)(4) provides members of classes previously certified under Rule 23(b)(3) with an additional opportunity to opt out of the proposed settlement or voluntary dismissal.[334] The notification obligations attendant on this opportunity will be the same as those required for initial certification of a Rule 23(b)(3) class under Rule 23(c)(2)(B). There are some restrictions on this new opportunity to opt out. First, it applies only to classes certified under Rule 23(b)(3). Second, only individual class members may exercise the option to opt out if they choose. No one has standing to attempt to opt out for other members of the class.[335]

Special Provisions for "Coupon" Settlements

In 2005, Congress enacted numerous provisions under the Class Action Fairness Act ("CAFA") that are effective in class actions in which some or all members of the class will receive an award in the form of coupons.[336] If a settlement is considered a "coupon" settlement, CAFA imposes additional restrictions to

---

under Rule 23(e) cannot adequately substitute for failure of class certification movants to demonstrate that certification requirements of Rule 23(a) and (b) are met).

[331]*See Managed Care Advisory Grp., LLC v. CIGNA Healthcare, Inc.*, 939 F.3d 1145, 1162 (11th Cir. 2019).

[332]*See* 28 U.S.C.A. § 1713.

[333]28 U.S.C.A. § 1714.

[334]*See Moulton v. U.S. Steel Corp.*, 581 F.3d 344, 354 (6th Cir. 2009).

[335]*See* Rule 23(e)(3) advisory committee notes to 2003 amendments.

[336]*See* 28 U.S.C.A. § 1712.

the approval process.[337]

CAFA does not define "coupon," so federal appellate courts have developed standards to determine if the award to the class constitutes "coupon" relief.[338] Courts typically use three factors to guide this inquiry: whether class members have to spend more money to take advantage of a credit; whether the credit is valid only for certain services or products; and the flexibility of the credit, including expiration and transferability.[339]

Courts are required to apply heightened scrutiny, and when the attorney receives a contingency fee based on the value of the coupons, the fee shall be based on the value of the coupons that are redeemed by class members.[340] The effect of this provision is to reduce potential disparities between the award of contingency fees to class counsel and the nominal value of coupons to class members.[341]

Additionally, if a proposed settlement will provide the class with coupons, but the attorney's fee is not measured solely as a contingency award, § 1712(b) provides that the additional portion of the attorney's fee shall be based on the reasonable amount of time the lawyer expended on the case.[342]

The foregoing provisions are subject to review and approval by the court.[343] They include authorization for an appropriate fee in cases involving equitable relief.[344] Moreover, in making calculations as to the appropriate amount to be awarded as an attorney's fee, § 1712 expressly authorizes (but does not require) the use of a lodestar/multiplier method of determining fees,[345] discussed at greater length below.

If the proposed settlement contains both coupons and equitable relief, § 1712(c) provides that § 1712(a) shall govern the calculation of that portion of the attorney's fees applicable to

---

[337] *See* 28 U.S.C.A. § 1712. *See also McKinney-Drobnis v. Oreshack*, 16 F.4th 594, 602 (9th Cir. 2021).

[338] *See In re: Lumber Liquidators Chinese-Manufactured Flooring Prod. Mktg., Sales Pracs. & Prod. Liab. Litig.*, 952 F.3d 471, 489 (4th Cir. 2020); *In re Easysaver Rewards Litig.*, 906 F.3d 747, 755 (9th Cir. 2018).

[339] *In re Easysaver Rewards Litig.*, 906 F.3d 747, 755 (9th Cir. 2018); *In re: Lumber Liquidators Chinese-Manufactured Flooring Prod. Mktg., Sales Pracs. & Prod. Liab. Litig.*, 952 F.3d 471, 489 (4th Cir. 2020). *See also In re Sw. Airlines Voucher Litig.*, 799 F.3d 701, 706 (7th Cir. 2015) (summarizing additional factors, including whether "the coupons have modest value compared to the new purchase for which they must be used," and whether "the coupons expire soon, are not transferable, and/or cannot be aggregated").

[340] 28 U.S.C.A. § 1712(a). *See also McKinney-Drobnis v. Oreshack*, 16 F.4th 594, 602 (9th Cir. 2021)

[341] *See McKinney-Drobnis v. Oreshack*, 16 F.4th 594, 602 (9th Cir. 2021) (quoting *In re Easysaver Rewards Litig.*, 906 F.3d 747, 755 (9th Cir. 2018)) ("By requiring courts to use the redemption-rate value of the coupons instead of the face value, CAFA 'ensures that class counsel benefit[s] only from coupons that provide actual relief to the class.'").

[342] *See* 28 U.S.C.A. § 1712(b)(1).

[343] *See McKinney-Drobnis v. Oreshack*, 16 F.4th 594, 602 (9th Cir. 2021).

[344] *See* 28 U.S.C.A. § 1712(b)(2).

[345] *See* 28 U.S.C.A. § 1712(b)(2).

the award of coupons, and § 1712(b) shall govern the calculation of that portion of the attorney's fee attributable to considerations other than the award of coupons.[346]

Section 1712(d) provides the court with authority, upon motion of one of the parties, to obtain expert testimony on the issue of the actual value to class members of the coupons that are redeemed.[347] This provision appears to be relevant not only to calculation of an attorney's fee but also to the value and appropriateness of the settlement to the class. Judicial review of the appropriateness of a settlement to the class is discussed elsewhere in the analysis of Rule 23 and related material.

Finally, § 1712(e) authorizes the court to require that a portion of the value of unclaimed coupons be distributed to charitable or governmental organizations, as the parties choose. Such a distribution, however, cannot be used to calculate attorney's fees under § 1712.[348]

Class Settlements and *Cy Pres*

Cy Pres is a doctrine that originated in the context of charitable trusts and distributions. Historically, it has been applied when the terms of a charitable gift cannot be fulfilled. In that situation, rather than treating the gift as having failed, courts sometimes apply *cy pres* to re-direct the gift to a deserving third party to achieve a purpose somewhat similar to the original intent of the gift.

In the context of class action settlements, *cy pres* provisions have been developed as a tool to address unclaimed or non-distributable funds.[349] *Cy pres* is normally applied when the award can be strongly linked with the underlying law and the interest of passive class members.[350] *Cy pres* has sometimes been applied to distribute excess settlement funds when, e.g., the identity or location of class members is unknown or some other reason prevents distribution to class members.[351]

Courts have recognized several potential options for distributing unclaimed or non-distributable funds.[352] One option is to allow the funds to escheat to the government.[353] Courts have also allowed additional pro rata distributions to class members

[346]*See* 28 U.S.C.A. § 1712(c).

[347]*See* 28 U.S.C.A. § 1712(d).

[348]*See* 28 U.S.C.A. § 1712(e).

[349]*See In re Google Inc. St. View Elec. Commc'ns Litig.*, 21 F.4th 1102, 1110 (9th Cir. 2021).

[350]*See In re Google Referrer Header Privacy Litig.*, 869 F.3d 737 (9th Cir. 2017).

[351]*See In re Baby Prod. Antitrust Litig.*, 708 F.3d 163, 172 (3d Cir. 2013); *In re Google Inc. St. View Elec. Commc'ns Litig.*, 21 F.4th 1102, 1110 (9th Cir. 2021). *But cf., Klier v. Elf Atochem N. Am., Inc.*, 658 F.3d 468, 479 (5th Cir. 2011) (where distribution to class is realistic, *cy pres* is inapplicable).

[352]*See In re Google Inc. St. View Elec. Commc'ns Litig.*, 21 F.4th 1102, 1110 (9th Cir. 2021).

[353]*See In re Google Inc. St. View Elec. Commc'ns Litig.*, 21 F.4th 1102, 1110 (9th Cir. 2021) (citing *Hodgson v. YB Quezada*, 498 F.2d 5, 6 (9th Cir. 1974)).

who have claimed funds,[354] and in exceptional circumstances have even permitted funds to revert to the defendant.[355] In approving the recipients of a *cy pres* distribution, a court is expected to carefully examine any conflict of interest between any of the *cy pres* recipients and any party to the case.[356]

Objections to Proposed Settlement; Payments

Any class member may object to a proposed settlement. But, so as to enable the parties to respond and the court to evaluate them, objections must specify their grounds and to whom they apply.[357] Additionally, payment may not be made without court approval in connection with an action to refrain from raising or pursuing an objection on appeal.[358] Courts are aware of the phenomenon of "objector blackmail," in which class members object to a class action settlement in the hope of extracting a side payment.[359] District courts may grant an objector the right to conduct discovery to enable the court to determine the objection's merit.[360]

NOTE: Limitations on the court's discretion notwithstanding, judicial control of settlements in class litigation is still far-reaching.[361]

Relation to Rule 62.1

Rule 62.1 governs indicative rulings that a district court may issue while a case is pending on appeal.[362] Rule 23(e)(5)(C) provides that while an undecided motion for payment is before the district court while an appeal is pending, the procedure under Rule 62.1 applies as long as the appeal remains pending.[363]

Legislative Expansion of Notice Requirements for Settlement

Congress enacted notice requirements for proposed settlements of class actions. Within ten days of the filing of a proposed settlement with the district court, each defendant

[354]*See In re Google Inc. St. View Elec. Commc'ns Litig.*, 21 F.4th 1102, 1110–11 (9th Cir. 2021); *Klier v. Elf Atochem N. Am., Inc.*, 658 F.3d 468, 473 (5th Cir. 2011).

[355]*See In re Google Inc. St. View Elec. Commc'ns Litig.*, 21 F.4th 1102, 1111 (9th Cir. 2021) (citing *Hodgson v. YB Quezada*, 498 F.2d 5, 6 (9th Cir. 1974)).

[356]*See In re Google Inc. Cookie Placement Consumer Priv. Litig.*, 934 F.3d 316, 327 (3d Cir. 2019).

[357]Fed. R. Civ. P. 23(e)(5). *See also 1988 Tr. for Allen Child. Dated 8/8/88 v. Banner Life Ins. Co.*, 28 F.4th 513, 520 (4th Cir. 2022).

[358]Fed. R. Civ. P. 23(e)(5).

[359]*See Pearson v. Target Corp.*, 968 F.3d 827, 829 (7th Cir. 2020).

[360]*See 1988 Tr. for Allen Child. Dated 8/8/88 v. Banner Life Ins. Co.*, 28 F.4th 513, 521 (4th Cir. 2022).

[361]*See In re BankAmerica Corp. Sec. Litig.*, 350 F.3d 747, 751 (8th Cir. 2003); *1988 Tr. for Allen Child. Dated 8/8/88 v. Banner Life Ins. Co.*, 28 F.4th 513, 521 (4th Cir. 2022) (Rule 23(e) makes district court "fiduciary" and "guardian" of rights of passive members of class).

[362]Fed. R. Civ. P. 62.1.

[363]Fed. R. Civ. P. 23(e)(5)(C).

participating in the proposed settlement must serve notice of the proposed settlement, to include the following documents on both the appropriate federal official and the appropriate state official in each state in which any class member resides: (1) the complaint, amended complaint (if any), and material filed with such pleadings (unless such documents are available electronically, in which case an appropriate explanation of access to the documents will suffice); (2) notice of any scheduled hearing in the case; (3) notice of any proposed or final notification to class members of their right to seek exclusion from the case, or a statement that no such right exists, as well as a copy of the proposed settlement; (4) a copy of the final settlement; (5) a copy of any contemporaneous agreement reached between class counsel and defendants' counsel; (6) any final judgment or notice of dismissal; (7) if feasible, names of the class members residing in each state and an estimate of the proportion of the settlement likely to be distributed in each state, or if that information is not reasonably available, a reasonable estimate of such information; and (8) any written judicial opinions relating to items three through six.[364]

For purposes of this provision, the appropriate federal official is the Attorney General of the United States. The appropriate state official is that person with primary regulatory authority over the business in which the defendant engages. If there is no such person, the appropriate state official is the state attorney general. If the defendant is a federal or state depositary institution, a foreign bank, or a subsidiary of any such institution, the appropriate federal official is not the Attorney General, but the person who has primary federal regulatory authority over such an entity. The appropriate state official also becomes the corresponding state official with similar regulatory authority when a defendant is a state financial institution.[365]

Presumably so that appropriate federal or state officials may participate in the settlement process, § 1715(d) provides that a final order approving a settlement may not issue until at least 90 days after the latest date of notification to federal or state officials required under § 1715(b).[366] If a class member is able to establish that the requirements of § 1715(b) were not met, the class member has the option to refuse to comply with the settlement agreement. No such option exists if the defendants have complied with § 1715(b).[367]

RULE 23(f)—APPEALS

CORE CONCEPT

Although ordinarily litigants must wait until entry of a final

[364] 28 U.S.C.A. § 1715(b).

[365] 28 U.S.C.A. § 1715(a).

[366] 28 U.S.C.A. § 1715(d).

[367] 28 U.S.C.A. § 1715(e).

judgment to appeal interlocutory orders, an exception exists for class actions. Because of the threshold (often dispositive) significance of class treatment, the courts of appeals are permitted to allow an immediate appeal from a district court decision that grants or denies class certification. But the time window for seeking such review is brief. If granted, such appeals do not stay the proceedings below unless either the district court or the appeals court so orders.

APPLICATIONS

Discretionary, Not Mandatory

Permitting an appeal from an order granting or denying class certification rests in the discretion of the court of appeals.[368] The Rule sets no express parameters for the exercise of this discretion, with case law expected to refine when immediate appeals are appropriate.[369] Indeed, though this discretion is considered largely unfettered,[370] allowing such immediate appeals is not expected to be a commonplace event.[371]

Circumstances where immediate review may be proper tend to fall within a few categories. First, if a denial of class certification would likely preclude any realistic chance that individual claims could be prosecuted, and the district court's decision was questionable, circuits are inclined to grant review.[372] Second, if a district court's grant of class certification puts substantial pressure on a defendant to settle without regard to the merits of a case, and the certification grant is questionable, review is appropriate.[373] Third, review may be appropriate when the implicated issues will help develop law regarding class

---

[368]*See* Rule 23(f) ("A court *may* permit an appeal from an order granting or denying class-action certification . . . .") (emphasis added). *See also Moser v. Benefytt, Inc.*, 8 F.4th 872, 875 (9th Cir. 2021).

[369]*See* Rule 23(f) comm. Notes; *Laudato v. EQT Corp.*, 23 F.4th 256, 260 (3d Cir. 2022).

[370]*See Microsoft Corp. v. Baker*, 582 U.S. __, 137 S. Ct. 1702, 1709, 198 L. Ed. 2d 132 (2017).

[371]*See In re Lorazepam & Clorazepate Antitrust Litig.*, 289 F.3d 98, 105 (D.C. Cir. 2002); *Waste Mgmt. Holdings, Inc. v. Mowbray*, 208 F.3d 288, 294 (1st Cir. 2000). *But see Laudato v. EQT Corp.*, 23 F.4th 256, 260 (3d Cir. 2022) (quoting *Rodriguez v. Nat'l City Bank*, 726 F.3d 372, 376–77 (3d Cir. 2013)) ("Contrary to the more limited approaches some other circuits utilize, [the Third Circuit] exercises [its] 'very broad discretion' using a more liberal standard.").

[372]*See Sumitomo Copper Litig. v. Credit Lyonnais Rouse, Ltd.*, 262 F.3d 134, 140 (2d Cir. 2001). *See also Chamberlan v. Ford Motor Co.*, 402 F.3d 952, 957 (9th Cir. 2005) (death knell can apply to either plaintiffs or defendant; for plaintiff, because individual damages are too small to justify piecemeal litigation, or defendant, if certification will force defendant to settle rather than incur costs and run risk of "potentially ruinous liability"); *Marisol A. v. Giuliani*, 126 F.3d 372, 375 (2d Cir. 1997) (appellate court exercises "even greater deference when the district court has certified a class than when it has declined to do so.").

[373]*See Tardiff v. Knox Cnty.*, 365 F.3d 1, 3 (1st Cir. 2004); *Laudato v. EQT Corp.*, 23 F.4th 256, 260 (3d Cir. 2022) (appellate review is appropriate "when class certification risks plac[e] inordinate . . .pressure on defendants to settle").

actions.[374] (For this last possibility to apply, some courts do not require that there be evidence of some error by the district court,[375] but other courts have imposed additional caveats that the development of law must be both important to the pending litigation and to class action law generally, as well as unlikely to be subject to meaningful review at the termination of the case in the district court.[376])

- *District Court's Role:* Once a district court has granted or denied class certification, its role under Rule 23(f) becomes minor. The district court's entry of its order on class certification starts the running of the brief 14-day period during which a Rule 23(f) application to appeal must ordinarily be filed.[377] But, unlike in Section 1292(b) appeals, the district court is not required by Rule 23(f) to approve the immediate appeal or certify that a controlling question of uncertain law exists which, if resolved, would materially advance the litigation.[378] Such certifications—a precondition for Section 1292(b) appeals—do not exist in the Rule 23(f) context.[379] Nevertheless, if shared, the district court's views on whether an immediate appeal is desirable may provide cogent insights that the courts of appeals would value.[380]

Appeals for Clear Error

If a party can demonstrate that the district court's certification decision is clearly erroneous, review under Rule 23(f) may be appropriate.[381] In that circumstance, some circuits have held that review should normally occur without regard to whether other factors, such as those discussed immediately above, are

---

[374] *See In re Allstate Corp. Sec. Litig.*, 966 F.3d 595, 614 (7th Cir. 2020); *Laudato v. EQT Corp.*, 23 F.4th 256, 260 (3d Cir. 2022); *Chamberlan v. Ford Motor Co.*, 402 F.3d 952, 957 (9th Cir. 2005).

[375] *See Blair v. Equifax Check Servs., Inc.*, 181 F.3d 832, 835 (7th Cir. 1999).

[376] *See, e.g, Vallario v. Vandehey*, 554 F.3d 1259, 1263 (10th Cir. 2009) (noting narrowness of this category: "a certification decision must involve an unresolved issue of law relating to class actions that is likely to evade end-of-case review, and this issue must be significant to the case at hand, as well as to class action cases generally").

[377] *See* Rule 23(f). As discussed below, this time window is 45 days when the federal government or one of its official actors is a party.

[378] *Cf.* 28 U.S.C.A. § 1292(b). *See generally infra* Authors' Commentary to Part VI, § 6.2 ("**Discretionary Interlocutory Appeals**").

[379] *See* Rule 23(f) advisory committee note (1998) (contrasting § 1292(b)). *See also Microsoft Corp. v. Baker*, 582 U.S. __, 137 S. Ct. 1702, 1709, 198 L. Ed. 2d 132 (2017) (Rule 23(f) "departs from the § 1292(b) model," citing advisory committee notes). Likewise, Rule 23(f) requires no partial-finality determination from the district court, as would a Rule 54(b) appeal. *See Gelboim v. Bank of Am. Corp.*, 574 U.S. 405, 409 n.1, 135 S. Ct. 897, 190 L. Ed. 2d 789 (2015) (contrasting Rule 23(f) with Rule 54(b)).

[380] *See* Rule 23(f) advisory committee note (1998).

[381] *See Chamberlan v. Ford Motor Co.*, 402 F.3d 952, 957 (9th Cir. 2005); *Laudato v. EQT Corp.*, 23 F.4th 256, 260 (3d Cir. 2022).

present.[382]

Some courts that emphasize the appropriateness of appellate review in the circumstance of clear error have also adopted a slightly different characterization of the factors that other courts have used. Instead of identifying the three independent circumstances in which appellate review may be appropriate, these circuits have melded the factors together in a way that weighs all of them, plus one or two others. In such circuits, Rule 23(f) petitions may be granted if consideration of these factors—taken together, not independently—justify review: (1) the "death knell" consideration, discussed above; (2) potential abuse of discretion by the district court in making its certification decision;[383] (3) whether the appeal presents an unsettled legal question of general importance and importance in the instant litigation that might not be susceptible to review at a later point in the case; (4) the status of the case in the district court, including consideration of progress in discovery, other unresolved motions, and the passage of time since initiation of the case; and (5) the possibility that at some future time it will be clear that prompt review now was appropriate.[384] Courts that follow this approach weigh most heavily the presence of manifest error in the district court's decision.[385] When such error is found, it may be unnecessary for the appellate court to find that the other factors favor review before granting a Rule 23(f) petition.[386]

Finally, the failure of a district court to adequately explain the reasons for its decision will often be grounds for a remand.[387]

Brief Time Window

An application for a Rule 23(f) immediate appeal must be

[382]*See Prado-Steiman ex rel. Prado v. Bush*, 221 F.3d 1266, 1275 (11th Cir. 2000). *Cf.*, *Carnegie v. Household Intern., Inc.*, 376 F.3d 656 (7th Cir. 2004) ("the more novel the issue presented by the appeal and so the less likely that the district court's resolution of it will stand . . .the stronger the case for allowing the appeal").

[383]*Cf., Driver v. AppleIllinois, LLC*, 739 F.3d 1073, 1076 (7th Cir. 2014).

[384]*See Prado-Steiman ex rel. Prado v. Bush*, 221 F.3d 1266, 1274–75 (11th Cir. 2000); *Lienhart v. Dryvit Sys., Inc.*, 255 F.3d 138, 145 (4th Cir. 2001).

[385]*See Prado-Steiman ex rel. Prado v. Bush*, 221 F.3d 1266, 1274–75 (11th Cir. 2000); *Lienhart v. Dryvit Sys., Inc.*, 255 F.3d 138, 145 (4th Cir. 2001).

[386]*See Lienhart v. Dryvit Sys., Inc.*, 255 F.3d 138, 146 (4th Cir. 2001); *Prado-Steiman ex rel. Prado v. Bush*, 221 F.3d 1266, 1275 (11th Cir. 2000).

[387]*See Beck v. Maximus, Inc.*, 457 F.3d 291, 297 (3d Cir. 2006); *Simpson v. Dart*, 23 F.4th 706, 713–14 (7th Cir. 2022) (explaining that a "one size (or one claim) approach is at odds with the rigorous analysis required at the certification stage;" instead, a "district court should begin by identifying the elements of the plaintiff's various claims: only by properly circumscribing the claims and breaking them down into their constituent elements can a district court decide which issues are common, individual, and predominant") (internal quotations omitted); *Santiago v. City of Chicago*, 19 F.4th 1010, 1017 (7th Cir. 2021) (vacating and remanding class certification order where the district court "analyzed the proposed classes under each provision [of Rule 23], but never made clear which claims the analyses refer to.").

made to the court of appeals within 14 days after the district court has entered its order granting or denying class certification.[388] If any party seeking permission to appeal is the United States, one of its agencies, or an employee acting in an official capacity, the time for filing is extended from 14 days to 45 days.[389] The computation of time for an appeal under Rule 23(f) is governed by Rule 6(a).[390] The filing period runs from the original order granting or denying class certification, and a later order that does not change the status quo will not revive the time limit.[391] However, filing a motion for reconsideration within the time window may toll the running of the Rule 23(f) time limit.[392] The time period is rule-based, and, thus, non-jurisdictional and subject to waiver or forfeiture, but it is not amenable to equitable tolling.[393]

Issues for and Scope of Immediate Review

The possibility of immediate appellate review is limited to the district court's class certification decision.[394] Partial denial of class certification can trigger grounds to appeal under Rule 23(f).[395] While appellate courts are permitted to review anything the district court properly includes in its order certifying the class,[396] courts must limit their review to whether the district court correctly selected and applied the criteria set forth under Rule 23 and should not engage in merits inquiries that are not

---

[388]*See Gutierrez v. Johnson & Johnson*, 523 F.3d 187, 192 (3d Cir. 2008); *Gary v. Sheahan*, 188 F.3d 891, 892 (7th Cir. 1999) (failure to seek appellate review within time limit of Rule 23(f) means "appeal must wait until the final judgment"). *See also In re Wholesale Grocery Prod. Antitrust Litig.*, 849 F.3d 761 (8th Cir. 2017) (district court's refusal to reconsider denial of class certification does not trigger new time limit for application of Rule 23(f); collecting authority).

[389]*See* Rule 23(f) (as amended 2018).

[390]*See Delta Airlines v. Butler*, 383 F.3d 1143, 1145 (10th Cir. 2004); *In re Veneman*, 309 F.3d 789, 793 (D.C. Cir. 2002).

[391]*See Strange On Behalf of Strange v. Islamic Republic of Iran, Int. Section*, 964 F.3d 1190, 1201 (D.C. Cir. 2020).

[392]*See Shin v. Cobb Cnty. Bd. of Educ.*, 248 F.3d 1061, 1064–65 (11th Cir. 2001). *But cf. Gary v. Sheahan*, 188 F.3d 891, 893 (7th Cir. 1999) (late or successive motions to reconsider the district court's certification decision do not toll the time limits of Rule 23(f)).

[393]*See Nutraceutical Corp. v. Lambert*, __ U.S. __, 139 S. Ct. 710, 714–15, 209 L. Ed. 43 (2019).

[394]*See In re Wholesale Grocery Prod. Antitrust Litig.*, 849 F.3d 761, 766 (8th Cir. 2017) ("By its clear terms Rule 23(f) has no application in the absence of 'an order granting or denying class-action certification,' "). *See also Asher v. Baxter Intern. Inc.*, 505 F.3d 736, 738 (7th Cir. 2007) ("Rule 23(f) does not allow interlocutory appeals from orders designating (or not designating) lead plaintiffs.").

[395]*See Mussat v. IQVIA, Inc.*, 953 F.3d 441, 444–45 (7th Cir. 2020); *Driver v. AppleIllinois, LLC*, 739 F.3d 1073, 1076 (7th Cir. 2014).

[396]*See Moser v. Benefytt, Inc.*, 8 F.4th 872, 875 (9th Cir. 2021) (explaining "[a]nything that properly enters the determination whether to certify a class is bound up with the order, which a court of appeals may then review under Rule 23(f)). *See also BP P.L.C. v. Mayor & City Council of Baltimore*, __*U.S.*__, 141 S. Ct. 1532, 1540, 209 L. Ed. 2d 631 (2021) (because *order* is appealable, court of appeals may address any issues fairly included within it).

related to certification.[397] The courts of appeals may consider standing and subject-matter jurisdiction on a Rule 23(f) appeal.[398]

Multiple Appeals

Courts may authorize multiple Rule 23(f) appeals.[399]

Stay of District Court Proceedings

If the circuit court allows an appeal under Rule 23(f), the appeal does not automatically stay proceedings in the district court.[400] Instead, a party seeking such a stay must apply to either the district court or the court of appeals.[401] Rule 23(f) contemplates infrequent stays and was drafted with the purpose of avoiding delay.[402]

Alternatives to Rule 23(f)

If a party is dissatisfied with the district court's ruling, the party may forego the option offered by Rule 23(f) and litigate the existing uncertified non-class action on the merits to the point of final judgment,[403] at which time an appeal of the decision (including an appeal of class certification) would be appropriate under standard procedure.[404] Parties who are denied both class certification and an immediate Rule 23(f) appeal may not, however, voluntarily dismiss their claims to manufac-

---

[397] *See Moser v. Benefytt, Inc.*, 8 F.4th 872, 875 (9th Cir. 2021); *Alcantar v. Hobart Serv.*, 800 F.3d 1047, 1053 (9th Cir. 2015) (quoting *Eisen v. Carlisle & Jacquelin*, 417 U.S. 156, 177, 94 S. Ct. 2140, 2152, 40 L. Ed. 2d 732 (1974)) ("In determining the propriety of a class action, the question is not whether the plaintiff or plaintiffs have stated a cause of action or will prevail on the merits, but rather whether the requirements of Rule 23 are met."). *See also Stockwell v. City & Cnty. of San Francisco*, 749 F.3d 1107, 1113 (9th Cir. 2014) ("Rule 23(f) applies *only* to class certification decisions, merits inquiries unrelated to certification exceed our limited Rule 23(f) jurisdiction").

[398] *See Rivera v. Wyeth-Ayerst Lab'ys*, 283 F.3d 315, 319 (5th Cir. 2002) (standing); *Lindsay v. Gov't Emps. Ins. Co.*, 448 F.3d 416, 420 (D.C. Cir. 2006) (subject-matter jurisdiction).

[399] *See Goldman Sachs Grp., Inc. v. Arkansas Tchr. Ret. Sys.*, ___ U.S. ___, 141 S. Ct. 1951, 1960, 210 L. Ed. 2d 347 (2021).

[400] *See Prado-Steiman ex rel. Prado v. Bush*, 221 F.3d 1266, 1273 (11th Cir. 2000).

[401] *See Prado-Steiman ex rel. Prado v. Bush*, 221 F.3d 1266, 1273 (11th Cir. 2000).

[402] *See Earl v. Boeing Co.*, 21 F.4th 895, 898, 900 (5th Cir. 2021); *Blair v. Equifax Check Servs., Inc.*, 181 F.3d 832, 835 (7th Cir. 1999) ("a stay would depend on a demonstration that the probability of error in the class certification decision is high enough that the costs of pressing ahead in the district court exceed the costs of waiting."); *Prado-Steiman ex rel. Prado v. Bush*, 221 F.3d 1266, 1273 n.8 (11th Cir. 2000) ("Rule 23(f) contemplates that in most cases discovery, (at the very least, merits discovery) will continue [despite] an appeal of the class certification order.").

[403] *See Microsoft Corp. v. Baker*, 582 U.S. ___, 137 S. Ct. 1702, 1711, 198 L. Ed. 2d 132 (2017).

[404] 28 U.S.C.A. § 1291. *See also Microsoft Corp. v. Baker*, 582 U.S. ___, 137 S. Ct. 1702, 1708–15, 198 L. Ed. 2d 132 (2017).

ture finality for appeal.[405]

RULE 23(g)—CLASS COUNSEL

CORE CONCEPT

Rule 23(g) governs the way a court appoints and supervises counsel to represent the class.

APPLICATIONS

Prerequisite: Certification of a Class

A decision to appoint class counsel should not occur until the court first certifies a class.[406] A district court may, however, designate interim counsel to act on behalf of a putative class before determining whether to certify it.[407]

Applicable Standards

Rule 23(g) identifies four factors the court must evaluate in appointing class counsel:[408] the work an attorney has already done on the case; the attorney's experience in other class actions and complex litigation;[409] the attorney's familiarity with law applicable to the case; and resources.[410]

At the end of its evaluation, the court should select class counsel who will "fairly and adequately represent the interests of the class."[411] Class counsel's duty to the class under Rule 23(g)(4) continues through the entry of final judgment.[412] A court has a duty to monitor class proceedings and reassess rulings as the case progresses, which includes the duty to monitor class counsel to ensure the interests of the class are being protected.[413] A class may be decertified by the court *sua sponte* if the court finds that class counsel is no longer satisfying its duty under Rule 23(g)(4).[414] Instead of decertifying the class, the court may consider other measures, such as disciplinary ac-

---

[405]*See Microsoft Corp. v. Baker*, 582 U.S. —, 137 S. Ct. 1702, 1711, 198 L. Ed. 2d 132 (2017).

[406]*See In re Samsung Top-Load Washing Mach. Mktg., Sales Pracs. & Prod. Liab. Litig.*, 997 F.3d 1077, 1087–88 (10th Cir. 2021) (quoting *Sheinberg v. Sorensen*, 606 F.3d 130, 132 (3d Cir. 2010)).

[407]*Troy Stacy Enterprises Inc. v. Cincinnati Ins. Co.*, 337 F.R.D. 405, 409 (S.D. Ohio 2021).

[408]*See* Rule 23(g)(1)–(4). *See also Sheinberg v. Sorensen*, 606 F.3d 130, 132 (3d Cir. 2010).

[409]*See* Rule 23(g). *See also Sheinberg v. Sorensen*, 606 F.3d 130, 132 (3d Cir. 2010).

[410]*See* Rule 23(g)(1)(C) and (E). *See Eubank v. Pella Corp.*, 753 F.3d 718, 724 (7th Cir. 2014); *Northstar Fin. Advisors, Inc. v. Schwab Invs.*, 779 F.3d 1036, 1048 (9th Cir. 2015).

[411]*See* Rule 23(g)(1), (2), & (4). *See In re Samsung Top-Load Washing Mach. Mktg., Sales Pracs. & Prod. Liab. Litig.*, 997 F.3d 1077, 1088 (10th Cir. 2021).

[412]*See In re Samsung Top-Load Washing Mach. Mktg., Sales Pracs. & Prod. Liab. Litig.*, 997 F.3d 1077, 1088 (10th Cir. 2021).

[413]*See In re Samsung Top-Load Washing Mach. Mktg., Sales Pracs. & Prod. Liab. Litig.*, 997 F.3d 1077, 1088 (10th Cir. 2021) (quoting *Jin v. Shanghai Original, Inc.*, 990 F.3d 251, 262 (2d Cir. 2021)).

[414]*See Jin v. Shanghai Original, Inc.*, 990 F.3d 251, 262 (2d Cir. 2021).

tion against class counsel.[415] In this process, the court may consider the costs and fees a proposed attorney expects to get from the case.[416]

Ultimately, the court has a duty to select from among the potential attorneys the lawyer(s) who will best represent the class."[417] Courts may broadly consider any factor relevant to counsel's ability and character.[418]

Reverse Auctions

Historically, courts have discouraged reverse auctions, "the practice whereby the defendant in a series of class actions picks the most ineffectual class lawyers to negotiate a settlement with the hope that the district court will approve a weak settlement that will preclude other claims against the defendant."[419] Reverse auctions require "mendacity" and "underhanded activity" and typically fail to satisfy the "adequate representation" requirement.[420] Rule 23(g)(1)(C)(iii) and (g)(2)(C) now provide the court with express authority to examine and propose appropriate terms for compensation and to include those requirements as part of the order appointing class counsel. The result should be to control attorney's fees and costs while ensuring that the class opponent is not able to choose, unilaterally, the lawyers who will cost the least and who may not do the best work. These portions of Rule 23(g) harmonize closely with Rule 23(h), governing awards of attorney's fees.

RULE 23(h)—ATTORNEY'S FEES AND NONTAXABLE COSTS

CORE CONCEPT

In class actions, courts may award fees authorized by law or the parties' agreement. If no contractual or statutory basis for awarding fees exists, courts may rely on the common fund doctrine and award reasonable attorney's fees from the common fund obtained for the benefit of the class. Courts may also employ the lodestar method, which measures the cumulative lodestar of

---

[415] *See In re Samsung Top-Load Washing Mach. Mktg., Sales Pracs. & Prod. Liab. Litig.*, 997 F.3d 1077, 1088 (10th Cir. 2021) (citing *Sheinberg v. Sorensen*, 606 F.3d 130, 134 (3d Cir. 2010)).

[416] *See* Rule 23(g)(1)(C) to (D). *See Sheinberg v. Sorensen*, 606 F.3d 130, 133 n.1 (3d Cir. 2010).

[417] *See* Rule 23(g)(2). *But cf., Martin v. Blessing*, 571 U.S. 1040, 1044–45, 134 S. Ct. 402, 187 L. Ed. 2d 446 (2013) (district court's broad discretion to evaluate matters pertinent to certification does not extend to consideration of race and gender of class counsel).

[418] *See Schumacher v. Inslee*, 526 F. Supp. 3d 878, 883–84 (W.D. Wash. 2021) (rejecting proposed class counsel who purchased stolen information and engaged in a conspiracy with a former client that led to client's criminal conviction).

[419] *See Reynolds v. Beneficial Nat. Bank*, 288 F.3d 277, 282 (7th Cir. 2002). *See also In re Cendant Corp. Litig.*, 264 F.3d 201 (3d Cir. 2001).

[420] *See Swinton v. SquareTrade, Inc.*, 960 F.3d 1001, 1005 (8th Cir. 2020); *Negrete v. Allianz Life Ins. Co. of N. Am.*, 523 F.3d 1091, 1099 (9th Cir. 2008).

all attorney time invested against the total recovery. Rule 23(h) also establishes a procedure by which a fee application may be made and objections to that application may be heard.

APPLICATIONS

Independent Assessment

An existing agreement between the parties may form the basis of the district court's assessment of a fee award.[421] However, a court's duty to assess the reasonableness of an award of fees is an independent obligation,[422] even where parties have reached agreement on a dollar amount.[423] A "reasonable" fee is one that attracts competent counsel but does not result in a windfall for the attorneys.[424]

Court's "Fiduciary" Obligation

In a class action, the need for a court to closely monitor closely requests for fees and expenses is acute because, at the fee-setting stage, class members and attorneys for the class will typically have adversarial relationships.[425]

Methods of Calculation

Measurement of the appropriate amount of a fee is usually determined through one of two methods: the percentage-of-the-recovery method or the lodestar method.[426] Typically, district courts can choose the method it deems appropriate based on its judgment and the nature of the case.[427] Some courts use the percentage-of-the-recovery method and the lodestar method as a discretionary "cross-check" to ensure reasonableness of the fee.[428]

In common fund settlements, courts may award the lawyers a fee based on a reasonable percentage of the fund obtained for the class.[429] To determine reasonableness of the fee in common fund cases, courts commonly apply a number of relevant factors

---

[421] *See, e.g., Rodriguez v. Disner*, 688 F.3d 645, 653 (9th Cir. 2012). *See also In re Equifax Inc. Customer Data Sec. Breach Litig.*, 999 F.3d 1247, 1278 (11th Cir. 2021) (court may award reasonable fees authorized by parties' agreement).

[422] *See In re Optical Disk Drive Prod. Antitrust Litig.*, 959 F.3d 922, 929 (9th Cir. 2020) (court's duty exists without regard to objections from class members).

[423] *See In re: Bluetooth Headset Prod. Liab. Litig.*, 654 F.3d 935, 941 (9th Cir. 2011).

[424] *In re Home Depot Inc.*, 931 F.3d 1065, 1082 (11th Cir. 2019) (quoting *Perdue v. Kenny A. ex rel. Winn*, 559 U.S. 542, 552, 130 S. Ct. 1662, 1672, 176 L. Ed. 2d 494 (2010)).

[425] *See In re Optical Disk Drive Prod. Antitrust Litig.*, 959 F.3d 922, 930 (9th Cir. 2020).

[426] *See McAdams v. Robinson*, 26 F.4th 149, 162 (4th Cir. 2022); *In re Life Time Fitness, Inc., Tel. Consumer Prot. Act (TCPA) Litig.*, 847 F.3d 619, 622 (8th Cir. 2017).

[427] *See McAdams v. Robinson*, 26 F.4th 149, 162 (4th Cir. 2022).

[428] *See In re Equifax Inc. Customer Data Sec. Breach Litig.*, 999 F.3d 1247, 1281 (11th Cir. 2021).

[429] *See Blum v. Stenson*, 465 U.S. 886, 900, 104 S. Ct. 1541, 79 L. Ed. 2d 891 (1984) (approving calculation based on percentage of fund); *In re Equifax Inc. Customer Data Sec.*

known as the *Johnson* factors.[430] These factors include: time and labor required; novelty and difficulty of questions involved; skill required to properly perform required services; preclusion of other employment due to acceptance of the case; customary fee; whether fee is fixed or contingent; time limitations imposed by the client or circumstances; amount involved and results obtained; experience, reputation, and ability of attorneys; "undesirability" of the case; nature and length of professional relationship with the client; and awards in similar cases.[431] Courts have allowed attorney's fee awards ranging from 19 to 45% of the settlement fund.[432]

In circumstances where the court believes another approach is appropriate or where no fund is available, *e.g.*, where the class seeks injunctive relief, courts typically measure the appropriate fee through a "lodestar" approach.[433] Courts have recognized the "strong presumption" that the lodestar figure is reasonable,[434] particularly in fee-shifting cases.[435] In the context of a class action, district courts have made their lodestar calculation based only on the reasonable hourly rate multiplied by the reasonable number of hours devoted to the case.[436] Finally, factors such as difficulty of the case, quality of legal

---

Breach Litig., 999 F.3d 1247, 1281 (11th Cir. 2021) (approving counsel fee of 20% of common fund as reasonable and using lodestar as a cross-check).

[430] *See In re Equifax Inc. Customer Data Sec. Breach Litig.*, 999 F.3d 1247, 1278 (11th Cir. 2021) (citing *Johnson v. Georgia Highway Exp., Inc.*, 488 F.2d 714, 717–19 (5th Cir. 1974)).

[431] *See In re Equifax Inc. Customer Data Sec. Breach Litig.*, 999 F.3d 1247, 1278 n.22 (11th Cir. 2021) (quoting *Johnson v. Georgia Highway Exp., Inc.*, 488 F.2d 714, 717–19 (5th Cir. 1974)).

[432] *See McAdams v. Robinson*, 26 F.4th 149, 162 (4th Cir. 2022) (quoting *In re SmithKline Beckman Corp. Sec. Litig.*, 751 F. Supp. 525, 533 (E.D. Pa. 1990)). *See also In re Equifax Inc. Customer Data Sec. Breach Litig.*, 999 F.3d 1247, 1281 (11th Cir. 2021) (collecting cases with common fund awards ranging between 20 to 30% and finding 20.36 percent is "well within the percentages permitted in other common fund cases, and even in other megafund cases.").

[433] *See* 28 U.S.C.A. § 1712(b) (expressly authorizing, but not mandating, use of lodestar method to calculate attorney's fees). *See also McAdams v. Robinson*, 26 F.4th 149, 162 (4th Cir. 2022) ("court may choose method it deems appropriate based on its judgment and the facts of the case."); *In re Life Time Fitness, Inc., Tel. Consumer Prot. Act (TCPA) Litig.*, 847 F.3d 619, 622 (8th Cir. 2017) (court may choose between methods); *In re Synthroid Mktg. Litig.*, 264 F.3d 712, 718 (7th Cir. 2001) ("We have held repeatedly that, when deciding on appropriate fee levels in common-fund cases, courts must do their best to award counsel the market price for legal services, in light of the risk of nonpayment and the normal rate of compensation in the market at the time."); *In re Cendant Corp. PRIDES Litig.*, 243 F.3d 722, 732 (3d Cir. 2001) (lodestar applicable when anticipated relief is too small to justify use of percentage-of-recovery method but case still has potential social benefit).

[434] *See McAdams v. Robinson*, 26 F.4th 149, 162 (4th Cir. 2022) (quoting *Perdue v. Kenny A. ex rel. Winn*, 559 U.S. 542, 554, 130 S. Ct. 1662, 176 L. Ed. 2d 494 (2010)).

[435] *See In re Home Depot Inc.*, 931 F.3d 1065, 1082 (11th Cir. 2019).

[436] *See In re Equifax Inc. Customer Data Sec. Breach Litig.*, 999 F.3d 1247, 1279 n.23 (11th Cir. 2021); *City of Burlington v. Dague*, 505 U.S. 557,

work, risk of failure, etc., may be used in some cases to modify the result (up or down) reached by the simple multiplication of hours and rates.[437] Because the lodestar amount is presumptively reasonable, the use of a "risk multiplier" is only used in rare and exceptional circumstances, such as when the lodestar does not reflect the true value of the attorney's work.[438] To obtain a multiplier, the attorney must produce "specific evidence" demonstrating that an enhancement is necessary to produce a reasonable fee.[439] The Supreme Court has recognized three examples that may warrant a multiplier: where the method used to calculate an hourly rate does not reflect the attorney's true market value; where counsel incurs an extraordinary amount of expenses; and where there is "exceptional delay in the payment of fees."[440]

Fees in "Megafund" and Common Fund Cases

In general, courts recognize that an approval of fees in a case involving a particularly large fund—a megafund—should consider the size of the fund.[441] However, courts have recognized that requiring a court to consider the economies of scale to limit fees in megafund cases "lack rigor" and could result in perverse incentives for counsel to settle quickly for less.[442] Courts tend to be averse to defining a "megafund" but remain confident they recognize a megafund when they see it.[443] Attorney's fees in megafund cases typically range between 20% to 30%.[444]

Counsel in common fund cases may recover expenses that

565–66 (1992); *Pierce v. Visteon Corp.*, 791 F.3d 782 (7th Cir. 2015).

[437] *See Gunter v. Ridgewood Energy Corp.*, 223 F.3d 190, 195 n.1 (3d Cir. 2000); *Goldberger v. Integrated Res., Inc.*, 209 F.3d 43, 53 (2d Cir. 2000).

[438] *See In re Home Depot Inc.*, 931 F.3d 1065, 1082 (11th Cir. 2019); (citing *Perdue v. Kenny A. ex rel. Winn*, 559 U.S. 542, 554, 130 S. Ct. 1662, 176 L. Ed. 2d 494 (2010)).

[439] *See In re Home Depot Inc.*, 931 F.3d 1065, 1082 (11th Cir. 2019) (citing *Perdue v. Kenny A. ex rel. Winn*, 559 U.S. 542, 553, 130 S. Ct. 1662, 176 L. Ed. 2d 494 (2010)).

[440] *See In re Home Depot Inc.*, 931 F.3d 1065, 1082 (11th Cir. 2019) (quoting *Perdue v. Kenny A. ex rel. Winn*, 559 U.S. 542, 554–56, 130 S. Ct. 1662, 176 L. Ed. 2d 494 (2010)).

[441] *See In re Optical Disk Drive Prod. Antitrust Litig.*, 959 F.3d 922, 931 (9th Cir. 2020) (benchmark of twenty-five percent of little use in a case involving a megafund); *Wal-Mart Stores, Inc. v. Visa U.S.A. Inc.*, 396 F.3d 96, 122 (2d Cir. 2005) (economies of scale can create undeserved windfall in megafund cases).

[442] *See In re Equifax Inc. Customer Data Sec. Breach Litig.*, 999 F.3d 1247, 1280 (11th Cir. 2021) (rejecting to consider the economies of scale to determine reasonableness of fee and finding that an "economies of scale" factor lacks rigor because it provides "no direction to courts about when to start decreasing the percentage award, nor by how much.").

[443] *See In re Optical Disk Drive Prod. Antitrust Litig.*, 959 F.3d 922 (9th Cir. 2020).

[444] *See In re Equifax Inc. Customer Data Sec. Breach Litig.*, 999 F.3d 1247, 1281 (11th Cir. 2021) (collecting cases).

would normally be charged to a fee-paying client.[445]

Motion Required

An application for attorney's fees must be made by motion, subject to Rule 54(d).[446] The fee petition must be filed before the date the court sets for objections pertaining to fees.[447] Class counsel, who typically recover the common fund for the class, are entitled to attorney's fees; however, other lawyers and firms that provide a substantial and independent benefit to the class may also recover fees from the common fund.[448]

Notice

The motion for fees must be served on all parties.[449] If the motion is made by class counsel, as it typically will be, it must also be directed to class members "in a reasonable manner."[450]

Incentive Awards for Class Representatives

Courts have routinely granted incentive awards, also known as service awards, to named class representatives for the time and effort sacrificed to prosecute the claims and benefit the class.[451] However, some circuits have recently rejected the use of incentive awards, relying on two Supreme Court cases from the 1880s.[452]

When drafting motions to approve a settlement agreement, it is important to avoid making the settlement contingent upon the district court's approval of an incentive award because doing so may invalidate the entire settlement.[453]

---

[445]*See Bekker v. Neuberger Berman Grp. 401(k) Plan Inv. Comm.*, 504 F. Supp. 3d 265, 271 (S.D.N.Y. 2020).

[446]*See In re Mercury Interactive Corp. Sec. Litig.*, 618 F.3d 988, 993–94 (9th Cir. 2010).

[447]*See Johnson v. NPAS Sols., LLC*, 975 F.3d 1244, 1252 (11th Cir. 2020).

[448]*See Arkin v. Pressman, Inc.*, 38 F.4th 1001 (11th Cir. 2022); *In re Volkswagen "Clean Diesel" Mktg., Sales Pracs., & Prods. Liab. Litig.*, 914 F.3d 623, 641 (9th Cir. 2019) ("Various courts, including our own, have determined that even non-class counsel can be entitled to attorneys' fees.").

[449]*See In re Delphi Corp. Sec., Derivative & "ERISA" Litig.*, 248 F.R.D. 483, 506 (E.D. Mich. 2008)

[450]*See In re Delphi Corp. Sec., Derivative & "ERISA" Litig.*, 248 F.R.D. 483, 506 (E.D. Mich. 2008).

[451]*See In re Equifax Inc. Customer Data Sec. Breach Litig.*, 999 F.3d 1247, 1281 (11th Cir. 2021) (recognizing incentive awards are "commonplace in modern class-action litigation").

[452]*See In re Equifax Inc. Customer Data Sec. Breach Litig.*, 999 F.3d 1247, 1281–82 (11th Cir. 2021) (citing *Johnson v. NPAS Sols., LLC*, 975 F.3d 1244, 1259 (11th Cir. 2020) and holding that incentive awards "are prohibited as a matter of law" in the Eleventh Circuit). *See also In re Dry Max Pampers Litig.*, 724 F.3d 713, 722 (6th Cir. 2013) (neither approving nor disapproving of incentive awards in general, but recognizing the 6th Circuit's sensible "fear that incentive awards may lead named plaintiffs to expect a bounty for bringing suit or to compromise the interest of the class for personal gain.").

[453]*Compare In re Equifax Inc. Customer Data Sec. Breach Litig.*, 999 F.3d 1247, 1281 (11th Cir. 2021) (reversing lower court's decision *only* for the purpose of vacating incentive award where approval of settlement was not contingent upon approval of incentive award) *with Radcliffe v.*

Objections, Hearing, and Findings

Both class members and the party who may have to pay the fees have standing to object to the motion.[454] The court has discretion—but not an obligation[455]—to hold a hearing on the motion. The court must make findings of fact and conclusions of law in a manner consistent with the requirements of Rule 52(a) (governing the court's duty in such matters when issues are tried to the court).[456]

If the court approves a lump-sum attorney's fee, it may be appropriate to permit attorneys to divide the fee among themselves by agreement.[457]

Special Masters and Magistrate Judges

Rule 23(h) permits the district court to refer matters relating to fees to special masters or magistrate judges.[458]

Protection against Loss by Class Members

In 28 U.S.C.A. § 1713, Congress provided the district court with authority to approve a proposed settlement involving a payment by members of the class to class counsel that would be a net loss to the class members. However, that authority is restricted to cases in which the court, by a written finding, concludes that nonmonetary benefits to the class "substantially" outweigh the monetary loss.[459] This provision of § 1713 is not restricted to cases involving "coupon" settlements, and appears to apply to class action settlements generally.

Additional Research References

Wright & Miller, *Federal Practice and Procedure* §§ 1751 to 1805
C.J.S., Federal Civil Procedure §§ 63 to 92, § 170
West's Key Number Digest, Federal Civil Procedure ⚷161 to 189
5 Newberg and Rubenstein on Class Actions § 15:80 (6th ed.)

Experian Info. Sols. Inc., 715 F.3d 1157, 1164–67 (9th Cir. 2013) (invalidating settlement that "explicitly condition[ed] the incentive awards on the class representatives' support for the settlement").

[454] *Cf.*, *Stetson v. Grissom*, 821 F.3d 1157 (9th Cir. 2016).

[455] *But cf.*, *In re High Sulfur Content Gasoline Prod. Liab. Litig.*, 517 F.3d 220, 231–32 (5th Cir. 2008) (while district court is not required to hold hearing on motion for attorney's fees in class action, a determination to hold such a hearing triggers requirements of notice and opportunity to be heard; rejecting *ex parte* hearing).

[456] *See* Fed. R. Civ. P. 52(a).

[457] *See In re Life Time Fitness, Inc., Tel. Consumer Prot. Act (TCPA) Litig.*, 847 F.3d 619, 623–24 (8th Cir. 2017); *In re High Sulfur Content Gasoline Prod. Liability Litig.*, 517 F.3d 220, 234 (5th Cir. 2008).

[458] *See In re Volkswagen and Audi Warranty Extension Litig.*, 692 F.3d 4, 10 n.3 (1st Cir. 2012).

[459] 28 U.S.C.A. § 1713.

RULE 23.1
DERIVATIVE ACTIONS

(a) Prerequisites. This rule applies when one or more shareholders or members of a corporation or an unincorporated association bring a derivative action to enforce a right that the corporation or association may properly assert but has failed to enforce. The derivative action may not be maintained if it appears that the plaintiff does not fairly and adequately represent the interests of shareholders or members who are similarly situated in enforcing the right of the corporation or association.

(b) Pleading Requirements. The complaint must be verified and must:

(1) allege that the plaintiff was a shareholder or member at the time of the transaction complained of, or that the plaintiff's share or membership later devolved on it by operation of law;

(2) allege that the action is not a collusive one to confer jurisdiction that the court would otherwise lack; and

(3) state with particularity:

(A) any effort by the plaintiff to obtain the desired action from the directors or comparable authority and, if necessary, from the shareholders or members; and

(B) the reasons for not obtaining the action or not making the effort.

(c) Settlement, Dismissal, and Compromise. A derivative action may be settled, voluntarily dismissed, or compromised only with the court's approval. Notice of a proposed settlement, voluntary dismissal, or compromise must be given to shareholders or members in the manner that the court orders.

[Added effective July 1, 1966; amended effective August 1, 1987; April 30, 2007, effective December 1, 2007.]

AUTHORS' COMMENTARY ON RULE 23.1

PURPOSE AND SCOPE

A shareholder derivative lawsuit is a civil action filed by a shareholder (or member) of a corporation or unincorporated association. It alleges that the shareholder's (or member's) company has been injured or possesses some other right that the company's leadership is not pursuing. In effect, the shareholder (or member) is suing to protect the company from harm due to the inaction of its officers, directors, or comparable leaders. Often, the shareholder derivative lawsuit is aimed at the officers, directors, or other leaders for alleged misbehavior or inattention. These types of lawsuits can help vindicate a company's rights for the best interests of all shareholders. But these lawsuits also risk disrupting and distracting the company's leadership, diverting energy, talent, and resources to wasteful concerns, and potentially harassing the company's leaders into an unmeritorious settlement that degrades the company's assets (and thus harms the very shareholders whose interests the lawsuit should be protecting). Rule 23.1 imposes a series of procedural requirements—not normally present in other civil actions—to help preserve the benefit of shareholder derivative lawsuits while containing their risks.

RULE 23.1(a)—DERIVATIVE ACTION

CORE CONCEPT

Shareholders or members of a corporation may bring an action on behalf of a corporation that the corporation has not asserted.[1] Only persons who will fairly and adequately represent the interests of other similarly situated shareholders or members may enforce the corporation's rights.

APPLICATIONS

Applicability

For the requirements of Rule 23.1 to apply to a case, a plaintiff must be a "shareholder" or "member"[2] seeking to enforce a right of a corporation or unincorporated association.[3] While brought by shareholders or members, derivative suits

[1] *Cf., e.g., Kokocinski on behalf of Medtronic, Inc. v. Collins*, 850 F.3d 354 (8th Cir. 2017).

[2] *See In re Facebook, Inc., Initial Pub. Offering Derivative Litig.*, 797 F.3d 148, 157 (2d Cir. 2015).

[3] *See Lefkovitz v. Wagner*, 395 F.3d 773, 776 (7th Cir. 2005) (a derivative suit can be brought on behalf of a partnership or other unincorporated form).

are assets of the corporation or association.[4] Other types of derivative claims need not meet the standards of Rule 23.1.[5]

Aligning Corporation / Association Based on Its Interests

Typically, the corporation or association is initially named as a defendant in a Rule 23.1 case to ensure its presence in the case as a Rule 19(a) required party (formerly, an "indispensable" party) to the lawsuit.[6] The corporation or association is then aligned based on its actual interests.[7] If the corporation's interests are antagonistic to the plaintiff, such as when fraud or malfeasance is alleged, then it will remain a defendant.[8] However, if the corporation's interests are in line with the plaintiff, such as when the plaintiff is a majority shareholder, the corporation or association will be as a plaintiff.[9]

Subject-Matter Jurisdiction

If the cause of action is based exclusively on state law, the requirements of diversity jurisdiction must be satisfied.[10] Because the corporation is treated as a required party needed for just adjudication,[11] aligning the corporate entity as a plaintiff or defendant can have significant consequences for jurisdiction.[12] Diversity jurisdiction is not solely determined by the pleadings' identification of parties as plaintiffs or defendants.[13] Instead, courts look to the pleadings to determine whether the corporation is antagonistic to the litigating share-

---

[4]*See Seafarers Pension Plan on behalf of Boeing Co. v. Bradway*, 23 F.4th 714, 719 (7th Cir. 2022); *Lefkovitz v. Wagner*, 395 F.3d 773, 776 (7th Cir. 2005).

[5]*Daily Income Fund, Inc. v. Fox*, 464 U.S. 523, 528 (1984) (Rule 23.1 applies only when "a shareholder claims a right that could have been, but was not, 'asserted' by the corporation."); *Lefkovitz v. Wagner*, 395 F.3d 773, 776 (7th Cir. 2005) (shareholder or member can sue "[w]hen a corporation is injured by a wrongful act but the board of directors refuses to seek legal relief"). *See also Kayes v. Pac. Lumber Co.*, 51 F.3d 1449, 1462–63 (9th Cir. 1995) (Rule 23.1 applies narrowly; it is not applicable to "plan beneficiaries" seeking "to enforce the right of the plan against its fiduciaries").

[6]*See Liddy v. Urbanek*, 707 F.2d 1222, 1224 (11th Cir. 1983); *Grgurev v. Licul*, 229 F. Supp. 3d 267, 282 (S.D.N.Y. 2017).

[7]*See Liddy v. Urbanek*, 707 F.2d 1222, 1224 (11th Cir. 1983); *Grgurev v. Licul*, 229 F. Supp. 3d 267, 282 (S.D.N.Y. 2017).

[8]*See Liddy v. Urbanek*, 707 F.2d 1222, 1224 (11th Cir. 1983).

[9]*See Liddy v. Urbanek*, 707 F.2d 1222, 1224–25 (11th Cir. 1983).

[10]*See* 28 U.S.C.A. § 1332.

[11]*See Liddy v. Urbanek*, 707 F.2d 1222, 1224–25 (11th Cir. 1983); *Hildebrand v. Lewis*, 281 F. Supp. 2d 837, 845 (E.D. Va. 2003).

[12]*See Reilly Mortg. Grp., Inc. v. Mount Vernon Sav. & Loan Ass'n*, 568 F. Supp. 1067, 1073 (E.D. Va. 1983) (citing *Liddy v. Urbanek*, 707 F.2d 1222 (11th Cir. 1983) and explaining that an antagonistic corporation "will be realigned as a defendant, even if diversity of citizenship among the parties is thereby defeated."). *See also Hildebrand v. Lewis*, 281 F. Supp. 2d 837, 845 (E.D. Va. 2003).

[13]*See Am. Motorists Ins. Co. v. Trane Co.*, 657 F.2d 146, 149 (7th Cir. 1981).

holder[14] and may also look beyond the pleadings and consider the nature of the dispute to assess the parties' interests.[15] Subsequent events, such as a change in strategy, generally will not be considered.[16] Instead, the facts forming the basis for alignment must be in existence at the time the action is commenced.[17] Courts have aligned the corporation in ways that defeat diversity[18] and in ways that maintain it.[19]

Personal Jurisdiction

Personal jurisdiction over defendants who are natural persons is obtained in derivative suits in the same manner as in other litigation.[20] However, for corporations aligned as defendants, Congress has enacted a special service of process provision that allows plaintiffs in shareholder derivative suits to serve process on such corporate defendants "in any district where [they are] organized or licensed to do business or . . . doing business."[21]

Venue

Congress has also enacted a special statute for derivative suits that provides the plaintiff may sue in any judicial district where the corporation might have sued the same defendants,[22] supplementing the ordinary array of venue options available in federal litigation.[23]

RULE 23.1(b)—PLEADING REQUIREMENTS

CORE CONCEPT

Special pleading requirements apply for derivative actions

---

[14]*See Smith v. Sperling*, 354 U.S. 91, 97, 77 S. Ct. 1112, 1 L. Ed. 2d 1205 (1957); *Hildebrand v. Lewis*, 281 F. Supp. 2d 837, 845 (E.D. Va. 2003); *Reilly Mortg. Grp., Inc. v. Mount Vernon Sav. & Loan Ass'n*, 568 F. Supp. 1067, 1074 (E.D. Va. 1983).

[15]*See Am. Motorists Ins. Co. v. Trane Co.*, 657 F.2d 146, 149 (7th Cir. 1981); *Hildebrand v. Lewis*, 281 F. Supp. 2d 837, 845 (E.D. Va. 2003) (quoting *Smith v. Sperling*, 354 U.S. 91, 95, 77 S. Ct. 1112, 1 L. Ed. 2d 1205 (1957)) (courts look at "pleadings and the nature of the dispute").

[16]*See Am. Motorists Ins. Co. v. Trane Co.*, 657 F.2d 146, 149 (7th Cir. 1981); *Reilly Mortg. Grp., Inc. v. Mount Vernon Sav. & Loan Ass'n*, 568 F. Supp. 1067, 1074 (E.D. Va. 1983) (recognizing that if a court were to allow a corporation's change in strategy to defeat jurisdiction, "the court would hazard the venerable principle that jurisdiction is established at the commencement of the action, and, once established, cannot be ousted by later events.").

[17]*See Am. Motorists Ins. Co. v. Trane Co.*, 657 F.2d 146, 149 (7th Cir. 1981).

[18]*See Frank v. Hadesman and Frank, Inc.*, 83 F.3d 158 (7th Cir. 1996); *Liddy v. Urbanek*, 707 F.2d 1222, 1224–25 (11th Cir. 1983).

[19]*See Reilly Mortg. Grp., Inc. v. Mount Vernon Sav. & Loan Ass'n*, 568 F. Supp. 1067, 1074 (E.D. Va. 1983).

[20]*See Young v. Colgate-Palmolive Co.*, 790 F.2d 567, 569 (7th Cir. 1986) ("federal district court has personal jurisdiction over a party in a diversity suit only if a court of the state in which it sits would have such jurisdiction.").

[21]*See* 28 U.S.C.A. § 1695.

[22]*See* 28 U.S.C.A. § 1401.

[23]*See* 28 U.S.C.A. § 1391.

governed by Rule 23.1, including the obligation to verify the complaint.

Verification of Complaint

Complaints that initiate shareholders' derivative actions must be sworn to and notarized. This is a departure from the general practice in federal civil procedure, which usually imposes no federal requirement for verification of a complaint.[24] In appropriate circumstances, verifiers may rely, in signing, on competent information obtained from other, qualified sources.[25]

Standing: Continuous Ownership Requirement

Under Rule 23.1(b)(1), the complaint must state that the derivative suit is initiated on behalf of a person who: (1) was a shareholder at the time the cause of action arose or became a shareholder by operation of law from someone who had been a shareholder at that time;[26] and (2) remained a shareholder at the time the suit was filed.[27] If the plaintiff is divested of ownership while the suit is pending, the suit will usually be dismissed.[28] The plaintiff must also meet the "contemporaneous ownership rule," *i.e.*, demonstrate possession of an ownership interest in the company contemporaneous with the conduct for which it seeks recovery.[29] In diversity suits, it is unsettled whether these standing requirements of Rule 23.1 will apply if state law is less strict.[30]

---

[24]*See generally W. Run Student Hous. Assocs., LLC v. Huntington Nat. Bank*, 712 F.3d 165, 173 n.4 (3d Cir. 2013) (although federal complaints are ordinarily not verified, they must still comply with Rule 11's ethical obligations).

[25]*See Surowitz v. Hilton Hotels Corp.*, 383 U.S. 363, 364–74, 86 S. Ct. 845, 15 L. Ed. 2d 807 (1966). *See also Lewis v. Curtis*, 671 F.2d 779, 788 (3d Cir. 1982) (reliance on Wall Street Journal article satisfies requirement).

[26]*Cf., e.g., In re Facebook, Inc., Initial Pub. Offering Derivative Litig.*, 797 F.3d 148 (2d Cir. 2015).

[27]*See In re Bank of New York Derivative Litig.*, 320 F.3d 291, 298 (2d Cir. 2003) (requiring plaintiff to own stock "*throughout* the course of the activities that constitute the *primary basis* of the complaint"); *Rosenbaum v. MacAllister*, 64 F.3d 1439, 1443 (10th Cir. 1995) (identifying one exception to those requirements).

[28]*See, e.g., Johnson v. United States*, 317 F.3d 1331, 1333–34 (Fed. Cir. 2003) (plaintiff who loses shareholder status through bankruptcy proceeding while instant lawsuit was pending loses standing upon cancellation of shares); *Schilling v. Belcher*, 582 F.2d 995, 999 (5th Cir. 1978) ("It is generally held that the ownership requirement continues throughout the life of the suit and that the action will abate if the plaintiff ceases to be a shareholder before the litigation ends.").

[29]*In re Bank of New York Derivative Litig.*, 320 F.3d 291, 296 (2d Cir. 2003); *Rubenstein on Behalf of Jefferies Fin. Grp. Inc. v. Adamany*, 532 F. Supp. 3d 154, 163 (S.D.N.Y. 2021).

[30]*See Kona Enterprises, Inc. v. Est. of Bishop*, 179 F.3d 767, 769 (9th Cir. 1999) (holding that standing requirement of Rule 23.1 "is procedural in nature and thus applicable in diversity actions"); *Fagin v. Gilmartin*, 432 F.3d 276, 285 (3d Cir. 2005) ("The question of whether the plaintiff is a 'shareholder' is determined by state law.").

Collusive Attempts to Invoke Federal Jurisdiction

Rule 23.1(b)(2) requires the plaintiff to swear that a shareholder derivative suit based on diversity jurisdiction was not brought to manufacture federal court jurisdiction on behalf of the corporation.[31] Collusive joinder might occur where the director's neglect or refusal to take action is manufactured.[32] If the shareholders and the corporation are not truly adverse or antagonistic, the court will realign the parties, potentially destroying diversity jurisdiction.[33] Antagonism is found when management refuses to take action to undo a business transaction or when it approves the transaction in a way that any demand to undo it would be futile.[34] Antagonistic claims usually involve fraud, breach of trust, or illegality.[35] Antagonism may also be found where the corporate managers are opposed to the lawsuit.[36]

Pleading With Particularity

Rule 23.1 requires that certain allegations of the shareholder derivative complaint be pleaded with particularity.[37] This standard differs substantially from ordinary notice pleading and means that the plaintiff must provide additional factual detail.[38] The requirement of particularity is usually satisfied by plaintiffs who explain the facts behind their conclusory allegations.[39]

- *Explanation of Efforts to Encourage Corporation to Protect Its Own Interest*: Rule 23.1 requires that a plaintiff allege in the complaint, "with particularity," the following facts: (1) the efforts plaintiff made, if any,

---

[31] *Austar Int'l Ltd. v. AustarPharma LLC*, 425 F. Supp. 3d 336, 352–53 (D.N.J. 2019) (requirement does not apply to federal question claims); *Wesolek v. Layton*, 914 F. Supp. 2d 853, 863 (S.D. Tex. 2012).

[32] *See Smith v. Sperling*, 354 U.S. 91, 95–96 n.4, 77 S. Ct. 1112, 1 L. Ed. 2d 1205 (1957).

[33] *See Smith v. Sperling*, 354 U.S. 91, 95–96 n.3, 77 S. Ct. 1112, 1 L. Ed. 2d 1205 (1957); *In re Digimarc Corp. Derivative Litig.*, 549 F.3d 1223, 1234 (9th Cir. 2008).

[34] *See Reilly Mortg. Grp., Inc. v. Mount Vernon Sav. & Loan Ass'n*, 568 F. Supp. 1067, 1073 (E.D. Va. 1983).

[35] *See Smith v. Sperling*, 354 U.S. 91, 95, 77 S. Ct. 1112, 1 L. Ed. 2d 1205 (1957); *In re Kauffman Mut. Fund Actions*, 479 F.2d 257, 268 (1st Cir. 1973).

[36] *See Swanson v. Traer*, 354 U.S. 114, 116 (1957). *Cf., In re Digimarc Corp. Derivative Litig.*, 549 F.3d 1223, 1235 (9th Cir. 2008) (antagonism exists where complaint alleges that defendants who control corporation are engaged in fraud or malfeasance).

[37] *See Carpenters' Pension Fund of Illinois v. Neidorff*, 30 F.4th 777, 784 (8th Cir. 2022) (heightened pleading standard "requires that the complaint . . .allege the facts that will enable a federal court to decide whether such a demand requirement has been satisfied").

[38] *See Carpenters' Pension Fund of Illinois v. Neidorff*, 30 F.4th 777, 784 (8th Cir. 2022); *In re Cardinal Health, Inc. Derivative Litig.*, 518 F. Supp. 3d 1046, 1063 (S.D. Ohio 2021).

[39] *See Halebian v. Berv*, 590 F.3d 195, 206 n.7 (2d Cir. 2009); *In re Abbott Lab'ys Derivative S'holders Litig.*, 325 F.3d 795, 804 (7th Cir. 2003); *Canty v. Day*, 13 F. Supp. 3d 333, 341 (S.D.N.Y. 2014).

to encourage those who control the corporation—shareholders, officers and/or directors—to take action;[40] and (2) the reasons why the efforts were unsuccessful, or reasons why no effort was made.[41]

- *Demand: Futility*: Rule 23.1 requires the plaintiff to make a demand on the corporate officers to pursue the suit.[42] The facts of this demand must be pleaded with particularity.[43] The purpose of this requirement is to give the corporation's directors an opportunity to exercise their reasonable business judgment.[44] The requirement that the plaintiff demand that the corporation bring the lawsuit may be waived, however, if it is clear from the facts of a case that such a demand would be clearly futile. Rule 23.1 requires the plaintiff to plead with particularity the facts establishing futility[45] to enable a court to determine if the demand requirement has been satisfied.[46] The standard by which the facts are evaluated is a matter of state law.[47] However, plaintiffs are not entitled to discovery to establish the particular facts underlying an allegation of futility.[48]

Special Litigation Committees

When officers of a business entity are faced with a lawsuit where demand is deemed futile, the corporation may respond by appointing a special litigation committee to investigate the

[40] *See Star v. TI Oldfield Dev., LLC*, 962 F.3d 117, 127 n.10 (4th Cir. 2020).

[41] *See Gomes v. Am. Century Cos., Inc.*, 710 F.3d 811, 815 (8th Cir. 2013); *Stepak v. Addison*, 20 F.3d 398, 402 (11th Cir. 1994).

[42] *See Star v. TI Oldfield Dev., LLC*, 962 F.3d 117, 134 (4th Cir. 2020); *F5 Cap. v. Pappas*, 856 F.3d 61, 82 (2d Cir. 2017) (shareholder demand requirement includes duty to exhaust "intra-corporate" remedies).

[43] *See Dorvit on behalf of Power Sols. Int'l, Inc. v. Winemaster*, 950 F.3d 984, 988 (7th Cir. 2020) (absent showing of futility, failure to make demand disposes of case); *In re Abbott Lab'ys Derivative S'holders Litig.*, 325 F.3d 795, 804 (7th Cir. 2003).

[44] *See Dorvit on behalf of Power Sols. Int'l, Inc. v. Winemaster*, 950 F.3d 984, 988 (7th Cir. 2020); *Rop v. Fed. Hous. Fin. Agency*, 485 F. Supp. 3d 900, 926 (W.D. Mich. 2020).

[45] *See Carpenters' Pension Fund of Illinois v. Neidorff*, 30 F.4th 777, 784 (8th Cir. 2022); *Espinoza v. Dimon*, 797 F.3d 229, 236 (2d Cir. 2015); *Westmoreland Cnty. Emp. Ret. Sys. v. Parkinson*, 727 F.3d 719, 722 (7th Cir. 2013).

[46] *See Carpenters' Pension Fund of Illinois v. Neidorff*, 30 F.4th 777, 784 (8th Cir. 2022) (recognizing heightened pleading requirement and explaining "where shareholders do not make demand on the board, those shareholders must plead with particularity the reasons why such demand would have been futile and should therefore be excused.").

[47] *Kamen v. Kemper Fin. Servs., Inc.*, 500 U.S. 90, 108–09, 111 S. Ct. 1711, 114 L. Ed. 2d 152 (1991); *Lowinger v. Oberhelman*, 924 F.3d 360, 366 (7th Cir. 2019); *Carpenters' Pension Fund of Illinois v. Neidorff*, 30 F.4th 777, 784 (8th Cir. 2022) (applying Delaware state law to Delaware corporation to assess demand futility).

[48] *See In re Merck & Co., Inc. Sec., Derivative & ERISA Litig.*, 493 F.3d 393, 400 (3d Cir. 2007).

matter.[49] In that circumstance courts will usually grant a request to stay proceedings in the derivative action until the committee can make a report recommending a course of action, *e.g.*, terminate the litigation, take it over, or authorize the original plaintiff to continue it. The court has authority to accept or reject the recommendation.[50]

Adequacy of Representation

The plaintiff in a shareholder derivative suit must be a person who will adequately represent the best interests of those on whose behalf the suit is prosecuted—the corporation and other shareholders.[51] Perhaps because Rule 23.1 derivative suits present fewer of the case management problems associated with Rule 23 class actions, the courts seem less concerned in derivative suits with the quality and experience of the plaintiff's counsel.[52]

RULE 23.1(c)—SETTLEMENT, DISMISSAL, AND COMPROMISE

CORE CONCEPT

Rule 23.1(c) provides that any settlement of a derivative action is subject to the court's approval. It also establishes a notice requirement for such settlements.[53]

Settlement Subject to Court Approval

Derivative suits may not be dismissed or settled without prior judicial approval.[54] The district court enjoys broad, but not totally unfettered, discretion to evaluate a proposed

---

[49]*See Joy v. North*, 692 F.2d 880, 888 (2d Cir. 1982); *Strougo on Behalf of Brazil Fund, Inc. v. Padegs*, 986 F. Supp. 812, 814 (S.D. N.Y. 1997).

[50]*See Strougo on Behalf of Brazil Fund, Inc. v. Padegs*, 986 F. Supp. 812, 814 (S.D. N.Y. 1997).

[51]*But see Powers v. Eichen*, 229 F.3d 1249, 1254 (9th Cir. 2000) (concluding that Rule 23.1 does not offer as much protection as Rule 23; "Unlike . . . Rule 23, in shareholder derivative suits under Rule 23.1, a preliminary affirmative determination that the named plaintiffs will fairly and adequately represent the interests of the other class members is not a prerequisite to the maintenance of the action.").

[52]*Cf., In re Sonus Networks, Inc. S'holder Derivative Litig.*, 422 F. Supp. 2d 281, 292 (D. Mass. 2006), aff'd, 499 F.3d 47 (1st Cir. 2007) (inadequate representation, including fraud or collusion, will vitiate attempt to impose res judicata; however, allegation of mere failure to raise additional facts does not, by itself, constitute inadequate representation).

[53]*See In re UnitedHealth Grp. S'holder Derivative Litig.*, 631 F.3d 913, 917 (8th Cir. 2011) (noting that notice requirements for class actions are usually more extensive than notice requirements under Rule 23.1(c)).

[54]*See Burks v. Lasker*, 441 U.S. 471, 485 n.16 (1979); *In re Sonus Networks, Inc, S'holder Derivative Litig.*, 499 F.3d 47, 65 (1st Cir. 2007) (noting that "some involuntary dismissals have been held to be the functional equivalent of a voluntary dismissal and thus are subject to the notice-before-dismissal requirement.").

settlement.[55] In determining whether to approve a settlement, courts usually apply the same factors used to determine the fairness of a settlement in a class action under Rule 23.[56] These factors include the adequacy of representation by the class representative and class counsel, arm's length negotiations, the adequacy of the relief provided for the class, and the equitable treatment of class members.[57] The court may consider the response of other shareholders who will be affected by the outcome of the case.[58]

The main factor courts consider when determining the fairness of a settlement is the extent of the benefit the corporation will derive from the settlement.[59] In theory, the court should not rewrite a proposed settlement, but should limit itself to approving or disapproving the proposal.[60] In practice, courts have substantial ability to influence the contents of a settlement by indicating what the court deems a satisfactory compromise. In any event, persons who wish to oppose a proposed settlement or appeal a settlement must first intervene in the case.[61] Objectors to a derivative action settlement are entitled to attorney's fees from the settlement fund if their objections increase the common fund or otherwise result in a substantial benefit.[62]

Notice of Settlement

Rule 23.1 requires the court to order notice of voluntary dismissals or proposed settlements to interested persons.[63] The court has substantial discretion within the circumstances of the particular case to determine the manner in which notification will occur.[64]

If the dismissal is involuntary, there is no notice

[55]*See McDannold v. Star Bank, N.A.*, 261 F.3d 478, 488 (6th Cir. 2001); *Shlensky v. Dorsey*, 574 F.2d 131, 147 (3d Cir. 1978) (district court has "wide discretion" in determining fairness of settlement, "as long as the court takes into account all of the relevant factors.").

[56]*See Shlensky v. Dorsey*, 574 F.2d 131, 147 (3d Cir. 1978). *See also Girsh v. Jepson*, 521 F.2d 153, 157 (3d Cir. 1975) (listing nine factors courts consider when determining fairness of class action settlement, and additional nonexclusive factors as later expanded by *In re Prudential Ins. Co. Am. Sales Prac. Litig. Agent Actions*, 148 F.3d 283, 323 (3d Cir. 1998)). *See also* Rule 23(e)(2).

[57]*See* Rule 23(e)(2).

[58]*See Bell Atl. Corp. v. Bolger*, 2 F.3d 1304, 1311 (3d Cir.1993).

[59]*See Shlensky v. Dorsey*, 574 F.2d 131, 147 (3d Cir. 1978).

[60]*See United Founders Life Ins. Co. v. Consumers Nat. Life Ins. Co.*, 447 F.2d 647, 655 (7th Cir. 1971) ("The business judgment of the court is not to be substituted for that of the parties.").

[61]*See Robert F. Booth Trust v. Crowley*, 687 F.3d 314, 318 (7th Cir. 2012) (intervention should be granted freely).

[62]*In re Wells Fargo & Co. S'holder Derivative Litig.*, 523 F. Supp. 3d 1108, 1111 (N.D. Cal. 2021).

[63]*See Robert F. Booth Trust v. Crowley*, 687 F.3d 314, 318 (7th Cir. 2012).

[64]*See Kyriazi v. W. Elec. Co.*, 647 F.2d 388, 395 (3d Cir. 1981).

requirement.[65]

Bond Requirements

Many states require that plaintiffs in derivative suits post bonds from which the defendants will be compensated for litigation expenses if the defendants prevail. Rule 23.1 contains no such requirement. In diversity suits, however, federal courts will enforce security requirements established under state law.[66]

Numerosity Requirements

Under Rule 23.1's plain text, the plaintiff must fairly and adequately represent the interests of shareholders or members who are similarly situated.[67] However, Rule 23.1 does not require that the plaintiff represent any particular number of similarly situated persons. Thus, it will often be to the advantage of a shareholder who is one among a small group of similarly situated people to file a derivative action rather than try to file a class action, which may require a greater number of plaintiffs under Rule 23(a)(1).

Additional Research References

Wright & Miller, *Federal Practice and Procedure* §§ 1821 to 41
C.J.S., Corporations §§ 397 to 413
Corporations and Business Organizations ⚩2020 to 2065, ⚩2020 to 2115, ⚩2120 to 2165, ⚩2170 to 2212, ⚩2220 to 2244

---

[65]*See Arduini v. Hart*, 774 F.3d 622, 637 (9th Cir. 2014).

[66]*See Cohen v. Beneficial Indus. Loan Corp.*, 337 U.S. 541 (1949); *Fagin v. Gilmartin*, 432 F.3d 276, 285 (3d Cir. 2005).

[67]*See* Rule 23.1(a).

RULE 23.2
ACTIONS RELATING TO UNINCORPORATED ASSOCIATIONS

Rule 23.2 applies to an action brought by or against the members of an unincorporated association as a class by naming certain members as representative parties. The action may be maintained only if it appears that those parties will fairly and adequately protect the interests of the association and its members. In conducting the action, the court may issue any appropriate orders corresponding with those in Rule 23(d), and the procedure for settlement, voluntary dismissal, or compromise must correspond with the procedure in Rule 23(e).

[Added effective July 1, 1966; April 30, 2007, effective December 1, 2007.]

AUTHORS' COMMENTARY ON RULE 23.2

PURPOSE AND SCOPE

Both class actions (under Rule 23) and shareholder derivative actions (under Rule 23.1) permit plaintiffs to litigate in a representative capacity, seeking a remedy that could benefit both them and others who are similarly interested in the case's outcome but are not present before the court as parties. Because such actions could significantly impact the rights and obligations of absent persons, courts must be more vigilant in overseeing the litigation. Rule 23.2 extends some of the procedural protections of class actions and shareholder derivative lawsuits to members of unincorporated associations who are sued through representatives, or on whose behalf representatives have initiated suit. Rule 23.2 is devoted to ensuring that representatives of the unincorporated association adequately represent the interest of the entire membership of that association.

NOTE: Rule 23.2 does not *create* a right for representatives of an unincorporated association to sue or be sued. Rather, it governs such a suit when the applicable state or federal law provides a cause of action by or against the unincorporated association, but does not permit suit by or against the association as an entity.[1]

APPLICATIONS

Requirement of Membership in Unincorporated Association: Rule 17

Before a plaintiff may represent the interests of an unincorporated association, the plaintiff must prove that an association exists and the plaintiff is a member. Rule 17(b) provides that the legal existence of an unincorporated association is controlled by the law of the forum state.[2]

Fair and Adequate Representation

The court's first concern is to ascertain whether the interests of the unincorporated association's representatives conflict with those of the association or its membership. However, the case law is divided as to whether an association's representatives in a Rule 23.2 case must meet the standards developed for adequate class representation in Rule 23(a), governing class actions.[3]

Orders Regulating Proceedings

Rule 23.2 explicitly incorporates Rule 23(d), governing the court's power to issue orders in the course of class action litigation. Because the court's authority under Rule 23(d) is broad, the effect of this incorporation is to give the trial court greater discretion to issue orders ensuring both the efficient processing of the case and substantial protection for passive members of the unincorporated association. Elements of Rule 23(d) should therefore also be consulted in the course of applying Rule 23.2.

Approval of Settlement

Rule 23.2 also explicitly incorporates Rule 23(e), which provides a court substantial authority to approve or disapprove

---

[1] *See Northbrook Excess & Surplus Ins. Co. v. Med. Malpractice Joint Underwriting Ass'n of Massachusetts*, 900 F.2d 476, 478 (1st Cir. 1990) ("Rule 23.2 provides a mechanism by which an association may sue or be sued through a representative where state law prevents the association from doing so in its own name."). *Cf.*, *Benn v. Seventh-Day Adventist Church*, 304 F. Supp. 2d 716, 723 (D. Md. 2004) (most courts hold that where state law permits suit by unincorporated association as an entity, "Rule 23.2 is unavailable."). *But see Curley v. Brignoli, Curley & Roberts Assocs.*, 915 F.2d 81, 87 (2d Cir. 1990) (collecting cases rejecting restrictive interpretation and reasoning that if drafters of Rule 23.2 intended availability of 23.2 suit to turn on state capacity laws, the drafters could have so provided in the text of the rule).

[2] *See* Rule 17(b).

[3] *Compare Gravenstein v. Campion*, 96 F.R.D. 137, 140 (D. Alaska 1982) (Rule 23 requirements applied to Rule 23.2 lawsuit) *with Curley v. Brignoli, Curley & Roberts Assocs.*, 915 F.2d 81, 86 (2d Cir. 1990) (requirements of Rule 23(a) do not apply to cases proceeding under Rule 23.2).

settlements in class actions. As a practical matter, the effect is to require not only consultation of Rule 23(e), but also strong consideration of the possibility of inviting the trial judge to participate in settlement discussions whenever the discussions have advanced sufficiently to make participation practicable.

Numerosity

Rule 23.2 contains no requirement that the membership of the unincorporated association rise above some minimum number.[4]

Citizenship for Diversity Jurisdiction

Where an unincorporated association may sue or be sued through representatives, courts determine diversity by examining the citizenship of the representatives.[5] Thus, an unincorporated association often can create diversity jurisdiction by selecting a representative who is a citizen of a different state from the defendants (provided that the amount in controversy exceeds $75,000, exclusive of interest and costs).

Amount in Controversy

The amount in controversy is determined by examining the individual claims of the membership of the unincorporated association. This approach creates a substantial hurdle to achieving diversity jurisdiction. Thus, if an unincorporated association has a claim for $1,000,000, the claim would appear to exceed the more-than-$75,000 requirement by a safe margin. If, however, the association has 10,000 members, and each member has an equal share in the aggregate claim of $1,000,000, the value of the suit to each member is only one hundred dollars—well short of the threshold for diversity jurisdiction.

Additional Research References

Wright & Miller, *Federal Practice and Procedure* § 1861
C.J.S., Associations § 8, §§ 40 to 48, §§ 51 to 53; Federal Civil Procedure §§ 76 to 93
West's Key Number Digest, Associations ⚷20(1); Federal Civil Procedure ⚷186.5

---

[4] *See Curley v. Brignoli, Curley & Roberts Assocs.*, 915 F.2d 81, 86 (2d Cir. 1990) (numerosity and other prerequisites of Rule 23(a) inapplicable in Rule 23.2 case).

[5] *See Aetna Cas. & Sur. Co. v. Iso-Tex, Inc.*, 75 F.3d 216, 218 (5th Cir. 1996).

RULE 24
INTERVENTION

(a) Intervention of Right. On timely motion, the court must permit anyone to intervene who:

(1) is given an unconditional right to intervene by a federal statute; or

(2) claims an interest relating to the property or transaction that is the subject of the action, and is so situated that disposing of the action may as a practical matter impair or impede the movant's ability to protect its interest, unless existing parties adequately represent that interest.

(b) Permissive Intervention.

(1) *In General.* On timely motion, the court may permit anyone to intervene who:

(A) is given a conditional right to intervene by a federal statute; or

(B) has a claim or defense that shares with the main action a common question of law or fact.

(2) *By a Government Officer or Agency.* On timely motion, the court may permit a federal or state governmental officer or agency to intervene if a party's claim or defense is based on:

(A) a statute or executive order administered by the officer or agency; or

(B) any regulation, order, requirement, or agreement issued or made under the statute or executive order.

(3) *Delay or Prejudice.* In exercising its discretion, the court must consider whether the intervention will unduly delay or prejudice the adjudication of the original parties' rights.

(c) Notice and Pleading Required. A motion to intervene must be served on the parties as provided in Rule 5. The motion must state the grounds for intervention and be accompanied by a pleading that sets out the claim or defense for which intervention is sought.

[Amended effective March 19, 1948; October 20, 1949; July 1, 1963; July 1, 1966; August 1, 1987; December 1, 1991; April 12, 2006, effective December 1, 2006; April 30, 2007, effective December 1, 2007.]

AUTHORS' COMMENTARY ON RULE 24

PURPOSE AND SCOPE

Plaintiffs are generally considered the "masters" of their lawsuits, choosing whom to sue and what claims to assert. Indeed, Rule 20 provides plaintiffs substantial discretion to name fellow plaintiffs and fellow defendants. This Rule 24 constrains that choice. It permits persons and entities who have not been named as parties to seek to enter or "intervene" in a lawsuit. The Rule imposes no obligation on such persons or entities to make that request. Instead, those persons retain a choice—try to enter this pending lawsuit or wait to pursue their interests in some other way. But if such persons or entities decide to try to intervene in an existing suit, Rule 24 establishes the procedures for doing so. The Rule divides intervenors into two groups: those seeking intervention as of right under Rule 24(a); and those who seek the court's permission to intervene under Rule 24(b).

RULE 24(a)—INTERVENTION OF RIGHT

CORE CONCEPT

Rule 24(a) identifies two distinct circumstances in which a person may be entitled to intervene in pending litigation: where a federal statute confers a right to intervene; and where the intervenor is able to satisfy all elements for intervention as of right: timeliness; a legally protectable interest; impairment of that interest; and inadequate representation of interest by existing parties.[1] Failure to satisfy any single requirement is a basis to deny a motion for intervention as of right.[2] As a practical matter the questions of existence of an interest and impairment of that interest are frequently so interwoven as to be hard to discuss as separate factors.[3] While the burden of proof under Rule 24(a) is on the movant, the Rule is construed liberally.[4]

[1] *See Kalbers v. United States Dep't of Just.*, 22 F.4th 816, 822 (9th Cir. 2021); *United States v. Segal*, 938 F.3d 898, 908 (7th Cir. 2019).

[2] *See Victim Rts. L. Ctr. v. Rosenfelt*, 988 F.3d 556, 560 (1st Cir. 2021).

[3] *See Tri-State Generation & Transmission Ass'n, Inc. v. New Mexico Pub. Regul. Comm'n*, 787 F.3d 1068, 1071 (10th Cir. 2015) (citing *Nat. Res. Def. Council, Inc. v. U.S. Nuclear Regul. Comm'n*, 578 F.2d 1341, 1345 (10th Cir. 1978)).

[4] *See Kalbers v. United States*

APPLICATIONS

Intervenor's Choice

There is no obligation to intervene. If the requirements of intervention are met, the decision to intervene rests with the potential intervenor.[5]

Intervention by Statutory Right

The first basis for intervention of right under Rule 24(a)(1) depends on the applicability of some federal statute that confers on the prospective intervenor an unconditional right to intervene in the pending litigation.[6] If applicants satisfy this statutory intervention right, they need not also show an interest-impairment based right under Rule 24(a)(2); the two bases operate independently.[7] But statutory intervention rights are construed narrowly.[8] As a practical result, persons seeking to intervene under Rule 24(a) should routinely consider arguing for intervention under the "interest" test of Rule 24(a)(2)—even in circumstances where they believe they might qualify for intervention as a statutory right under Rule 24(a)(1).[9]

Even where a right to intervene exists under a federal statute, the court may impose conditions on the intervention as appropriate.[10]

Intervention by Showing Impaired Interest or Impeded, Generally

The right to intervene under Rule 24(a)(2) exists when the court finds that the applicant has met three prerequisites: (1) an interest in the subject matter of the pending litigation; (2) a substantial risk that, in the intervenor's absence, the litigation will, as a practical matter, impair or impede that interest; and (3) the existing litigants do not adequately represent that interest.[11] By the terms of the Rule, a fourth prerequisite—

Dep't of Just., 22 F.4th 816, 822 (9th Cir. 2021); *Kane Cnty., Utah v. United States*, 928 F.3d 877, 890 (10th Cir. 2019); *Adam Joseph Res. v. CNA Metals Ltd.*, 919 F.3d 856, 864 (5th Cir. 2019).

[5] *See Martin v. Wilks*, 490 U.S. 755, 763, 109 S. Ct. 2180, 104 L. Ed. 2d 835 (1989) (Rule 24 does not require intervention; it is permissive, not mandatory; drawing contrast with Rule 19). *See also Westchester Fire Ins. Co. v. Mendez*, 585 F.3d 1183, 1187 (9th Cir. 2009) (citing *Kourtis v. Cameron*, 419 F.3d 989, 998 (9th Cir. 2005)) ("There is no duty of mandatory intervention imposed upon nonparties, and the decision not to intervene thus does not expose a nonparty to the earlier proceedings' preclusive effects.").

[6] *See* Rule 24(a)(1). *See also Ruiz v. Estelle*, 161 F.3d 814, 828 (5th Cir. 1998).

[7] *See Ruiz v. Estelle*, 161 F.3d 814, 828 (5th Cir. 1998).

[8] *See Phar-Mor, Inc. v. Coopers & Lybrand*, 22 F.3d 1228, 1232 (3d Cir. 1994).

[9] *See, e. g., In re Fin. Oversight & Mgmt. Board for Puerto Rico*, 872 F.3d 57, 62–63 (1st Cir. 2017).

[10] *See In re Fin. Oversight & Mgmt. Board for Puerto Rico*, 872 F.3d 57, 64 (1st Cir. 2017).

[11] *See* Rule 24(a)(2). *See Cooper v. Newsom*, 26 F.4th 1104, 1106 (9th Cir. 2022); *In re Auto. Parts Antitrust*

timeliness—must also be shown.[12] Each prerequisite is discussed below. If intervention is granted, the intervening party must continue to meet these requirements throughout the duration of the litigation or be subject to being dismissed from the case.

Prerequisite #1—Interest in Subject Matter

The type of "interest" that will satisfy Rule 24(a)(2) is fact-dependent.[13] To be cognizable under the Rule, the interest must be direct, substantial, and legally protectable.[14] A person who has an interest that alone would qualify as a case or controversy will likely meet this requirement.[15] However, it is not necessary that the intervenor be a party with the right to bring the cause of action independently or establish Article III standing. An actual economic interest in the subject matter of the action will generally be adequate to satisfy the Rule.[18] The asserted economic interest must be "ripe."[19] However, non-property interests which are "concrete, personalized, and legally protectable" will also suffice.[20] Non-property interests found to satisfy this requirement include a religious liberty interest,[21] an environmental conservation interest,[22] a likelihood of being legally bound by the judgment in the pending litigation,[23] and an interest in the employment practices of the intervenor.[24] A desire to present an additional or varied argument[25] or merely

---

Litig., End-Payor Actions, 33 F.4th 894, 900 (6th Cir. 2022).

[12]*See* Rule 24(a)(2). *See Cooper v. Newsom*, 26 F.4th 1104, 1106 (9th Cir. 2022); *In re Auto. Parts Antitrust Litig., End-Payor Actions*, 33 F.4th 894, 900 (6th Cir. 2022).

[13]*See Wal-Mart Stores, Inc. v. Texas Alcoholic Beverage Comm'n*, 834 F.3d 562, 566 (5th Cir. 2016); *Utahns for Better Transp. v. U.S. Dept. of Transp.*, 295 F.3d 1111, 1115 (10th Cir. 2002).

[14]*In re New York City Policing During Summer 2020 Demonstrations*, 27 F.4th 792, 799 (2d Cir. 2022); *Cooper v. Newsom*, 13 F.4th 857, 865 (9th Cir. 2021) (protectable interest exists if protected by law and there is a relationship between the interest and the claim at issue and interest "will suffer a practical impairment in the pending litigation.").

[15]*See Aurora Loan Servs., Inc. v. Craddieth*, 442 F.3d 1018, 1022 (7th Cir. 2006).

[18]*See, e. g., Texas v. United States*, 805 F.3d 653, 658 (5th Cir. 2015) (a property interest is "the most elementary right" protected by the Rule; therefore, "property interests are almost always adequate").

[19]*See United States v. Segal*, 938 F.3d 898, 909 (7th Cir. 2019).

[20]*See Texas v. United States*, 805 F.3d 653, 658 (5th Cir. 2015). *See also State v. City of Chicago*, 912 F.3d 979 (7th Cir. 2019).

[21]*See Commonwealth of Pennsylvania v. President United States of Am.*, 888 F.3d 52, 58 (3d Cir. 2018).

[22]*See W. Energy All. v. Zinke*, 877 F.3d 1157, 1164, 1165 (10th Cir. 2017).

[23]*See Stauffer v. Brooks Bros., Inc.*, 619 F.3d 1321, 1328–29 (Fed. Cir. 2010); *City of Emeryville v. Robinson*, 621 F.3d 1251, 1259 (9th Cir. 2010).

[24]*See Bridgeport Guardians, Inc. v. Delmonte*, 602 F.3d 469, 473–74 (2d Cir. 2010).

[25]*See Sec. & Exch. Comm'n v. LBRY, Inc.*, 26 F.4th 96, 99 (1st Cir. 2022).

add to the factual record[26] has been found insufficient.

Prerequisite #2—Impairment of Interest

A qualifying risk of impairment to an applicant's interest may include legal impairment, such as a risk that principles of stare decisis may apply.[27] But other practical consequences of litigation may also satisfy the "impairment" element. For example, even though a party may not, through res judicata or collateral estoppel, be bound by the judgment, a substantial risk of practical impairments can sometimes constitute sufficient risk of "impairment" to a party seeking to intervene.[28]

Courts distinguish between a possibility of future injury and concrete harm that is real and definite to establish an injury in fact.[29]

In a recent case involving an action brought by the North Carolina State Conference of the NAACP against North Carolina's governor and State Board of Elections, the Supreme Court recognized that States may organize themselves in many ways, and when a State chooses to allocate authority between officials that are not required to answer to each other, different interests and perspectives may emerge.[30] Accordingly, federal courts should "rarely question that a State's interests will be practically impaired or impeded if its duly authorized representatives are excluded from participating in federal litigation challenging state law."[31]

In challenges to administrative agency actions, the D.C. Court of Appeals has found "significant injury in fact" where the agency's action is challenged in court proceedings, and a party which would benefit from the action seeks to intervene in the challenge.[32] Where a challenge to a county's concealed-carry licensing procedure amounted to a challenge to the constitutionality of the State's regulation of firearms, the State had a sig-

---

[26] *See Brandt v. Gooding*, 636 F.3d 124, 131 (4th Cir. 2011).

[27] *See United States. v. City of Los Angeles, Cal.*, 288 F.3d 391, 401 (9th Cir. 2002) (potential impairment is sufficient); *Sierra Club v. Espy*, 18 F.3d 1202, 1207 (5th Cir. 1994).

[28] *See Comm'r, Alabama Dep't of Corr. v. Advance Loc. Media, LLC*, 918 F.3d 1161, 1170–71 (11th Cir. 2019); *City of Chicago v. Fed. Emergency Mgmt. Agency*, 660 F.3d 980, 986 (7th Cir. 2011).

[29] *See Liddell v. Special Admin. Bd. of Transitional Sch. Dist. of City of St. Louis*, 894 F.3d 959, 965 (8th Cir. 2018).

[30] *See Berger v. N. Carolina State Conf. of the NAACP*, __U.S.__, , 142 S. Ct. 2191, 2201 (2022).

[31] *See Berger v. N. Carolina State Conf. of the NAACP*, __U.S.__, , 142 S. Ct. 2191, 2201 (2022) (collecting two Supreme Court opinions stating the same and reasoning, "where a State chooses to divide its sovereign authority among different officials and authorize their participation in a suit challenging state law, a full consideration of the State's practical interests may require the involvement of different voices with different perspectives.").

[32] *See Crossroads Grassroots Pol'y Strategies v. Fed. Election Comm'n*, 788 F.3d 312, 316–317 (D.C. Cir. 2015).

nificant interest in intervening.[33] Where an environmental group sought to intervene on the side of a township to defend the legality of an anti-fracking ordinance following entry of a consent decree, the group's rights were not affected by the consent decree and so they did not have the impairment of interest necessary to intervene.[34]

Prerequisite #3—Adequate Representation by Existing Parties

Even if the person seeking intervention demonstrates that the elements of "interest" and "impairment" are satisfied, intervention under Rule 24(a)(2) will be denied if the interest at risk is represented adequately by persons already parties to the action.[35] The district court must undertake a searching, contextual comparison of the absentee's interests and the interests of existing parties.[36]

The U.S. Supreme Court recently clarified the test courts should apply when determining if an existing defendant "adequately represents" the same interests a proposed intervenor seeks to uphold.[37] The Court ruled that a lower court had improperly applied a "presumption" that an existing party (Board of Elections) would adequately represent the intervenor's (legislative leaders) interests, and that this presumption had not been overcome.[38] The Supreme Court stated that, in cases where a prospective intervenor's interests are *identical* to the existing party, it may be appropriate to apply such a presumption.[39] However, in cases where the intervenor's interest is *similar* to, but not *identical* with, the existing party, a presumption of adequate representation is typically improper.[40]

In situations involving "similar" interests, the burden of establishing inadequate representation is on the applicant for

[33]*See Peruta v. Cnty. of San Diego*, 824 F.3d 919, 940 (9th Cir. 2016).

[34]*See Seneca Res. Corp. v. Twp. of Highland, Elk Cnty., Pennsylvania*, 863 F.3d 245, 257–58 (3d Cir. 2017). *Cf. W. Energy All. v. Zinke*, 877 F.3d 1157, 1164, 1167–68 (10th Cir. 2017) (conservation group's environmental concern and preserving reforms it had worked to implement were each protectable interests).

[35]*See Daggett v. Comm'n on Governmental Ethics & Election Pracs.*, 172 F.3d 104, 111 (1st Cir. 1999); *Clark v. Putnam Cnty.*, 168 F.3d 458, 461 (11th Cir. 1999).

[36]*See Driftless Area Land Conservancy v. Huebsch*, 969 F.3d 742, 748 (7th Cir. 2020); *Crossroads Grassroots Pol'y Strategies v. Fed. Election Comm'n*, 788 F.3d 312, 320 (D.C. Cir. 2015).

[37]*See, Berger v. N. Carolina State Conf. of the NAACP*, __U.S.__, , 142 S. Ct. 2191, 2201 (2022).

[38]*See, Berger v. N. Carolina State Conf. of the NAACP*, __U.S.__, , 142 S. Ct. 2191, 2203 (2022).

[39]*See, Berger v. N. Carolina State Conf. of the NAACP*, __U.S.__, , 142 S. Ct. 2191, 2204 (2022).

[40]*See, Berger v. N. Carolina State Conf. of the NAACP*, __U.S.__, , 142 S. Ct. 2191, 2204 (2022) (citing *Trbovich v. United Mine Workers of Am.*, 404 U.S. 528, 538, 92 S. Ct. 630, 636, 30 L. Ed. 2d 686 (1972)).

intervention, but it is generally minimal.[41] This minimal burden permits intervention to those who bear an interest that may be practically impeded or impaired unless an existing party adequately represents the same interest.[42] The minimal burden has been met when, for example, the existing party has a greater incentive to compromise a claim than the proposed intervenor.[43]

Intervention on appeal has been permitted where the intervenor had a "unique interest in the subject matter of the case," which interest was adequately represented by the federal government throughout litigation, but the government declined to appeal.[44]

Lack of adequate representation is most easily demonstrated if the interest is not currently represented at all, or if the persons already parties have positions clearly adverse to those of the intervention applicant.[45] Moreover, a difference in tactics does not of itself necessarily indicate a lack of adequate representation.[46]

Adequate representation is generally presumed where an existing party is charged with the responsibility of representing the intervenor's interest.[47] This is commonly seen where a State represents its citizens, citizens seek to intervene as of right, and the state shares the same interest as the citizens. However, where the narrower interest of the prospective intervenor would require that the government "shirk its duty" to the general

---

[41]*See Berger v. N. Carolina State Conf. of the NAACP*, __U.S.__, , 142 S. Ct. 2191, 2204 (2022); *Trbovich v. United Mine Workers of Am.*, 404 U.S. 528, 538 n.10, 92 S. Ct. 630, 636, 30 L. Ed. 2d 686 (1972); *Barnes v. Sec. Life of Denver Ins. Co.*, 953 F.3d 704, 705–06 (10th Cir. 2020); *Entergy Gulf States Louisiana, L.L.C. v. E.P.A.*, 817 F.3d 198, 203 (5th Cir. 2016) (applicant need only show that representation of interest "may be" inadequate).

[42]*See Berger v. N. Carolina State Conf. of the NAACP*, __U.S.__, , 142 S. Ct. 2191, 2204 (2022) (citing *Trbovich v. United Mine Workers of Am.*, 404 U.S. 528, 92 S. Ct. 630, 636, 30 L. Ed. 2d 686 (1972)).

[43]*See Tech. Training Assocs., Inc. v. Buccaneers Ltd. P'ship*, 874 F.3d 692, 697 (11th Cir. 2017) (existing party with statute of limitations issues more likely to settle than intervenor with no statute of limitations concerns).

[44]*See United States v. Osage Wind, LLC*, 871 F.3d 1078, 1085-86 (10th Cir. 2017).

[45]*See Entergy Gulf States Louisiana, L.L.C. v. E.P.A.*, 817 F.3d 198, 203 (5th Cir. 2016); *City of Chicago v. Fed. Emergency Mgmt. Agency*, 660 F.3d 980, 986–87 (7th Cir. 2011).

[46]*See Sec. & Exch. Comm'n v. LBRY, Inc.*, 26 F.4th 96, 100 (1st Cir. 2022); *See Swinton v. SquareTrade, Inc.*, 960 F.3d 1001, 1005 (8th Cir. 2020); *U.S. v. City of Miami*, 278 F.3d 1174, 1179 (11th Cir. 2002).

[47]*See Oakland Bulk & Oversized Terminal, LLC v. City of Oakland*, 960 F.3d 603, 620 (9th Cir. 2020); *Planned Parenthood of Wisconsin, Inc. v. Kaul*, 942 F.3d 793, 799 (7th Cir. 2019). *But see Commonwealth of Pennsylvania v. President United States of Am.*, 888 F.3d 52, 58 (3d Cir. 2018) (Catholic charitable group permitted to intervene to defend religious exemption to contraceptive mandate of Affordable Care Act as government/defendant might not adequately protect that interest).

public, there is no presumption of adequate representation.[48]

There must continue to be a lack of adequate representation by other parties throughout the litigation or the intervenor risks being dismissed from the case.[49]

Prerequisite #4—Timeliness

Rule 24(a) explicitly imposes a "timeliness" requirement on motions to intervene.[50] However, unlike timing elements in other Rules, a fixed period of days is not prescribed.[51] The timeliness of a motion to intervene is highly "contextual,"[52] and courts are generally reluctant to dispose of a motion to intervene based on timeliness issues.[53] Typically, courts weigh several factors[54] in determining timeliness: (1) length of delay in seeking intervention;[55] (2) prejudicial impact of such delay on existing parties;[56] (3) prejudice to intervenor if intervention is denied;[57] (4) the stage of the litigation;[58] (5) other factors af-

---

[48]*See North Dakota ex rel. Stenehjem v. United States*, 787 F.3d 918, 921 (8th Cir. 2015). *See also W. Energy All. v. Zinke*, 877 F.3d 1157, 1164, 1169 (10th Cir. 2017) (conservation group permitted to intervene where government's interest in protecting land might conflict with executive order directive for "review of agency regulations that potentially burden the development of oil and gas resources").

[49]*See Coal. to Defend Affirmative Action, Integration & Immigrant Rts. & Fight for Equal. By Any Means Necessary v. Regents of Univ. of Michigan*, 701 F.3d 466, 490 (6th Cir. 2012).

[50]*See Associated Builders & Contractors, Inc. v. Herman*, 166 F.3d 1248, 1257 (D.C. Cir. 1999).

[51]*See Heaton v. Monogram Credit Card Bank of Georgia*, 297 F.3d 416 (5th Cir. 2002); *U.S. v. State of Wash.*, 86 F.3d 1499, 1503 (9th Cir. 1996).

[52]*See Wal-Mart Stores, Inc., v. Texas Alcoholic Beverage Comm'n*, 834 F.3d 562, 565 (5th Cir. 2016).

[53]*See Wallach v. Eaton Corp.*, 837 F.3d 356, 371–72 (3d Cir. 2016).

[54]Although substantially the same, the factors are sometimes stated differently. *See Ali v. City of Chicago*, 34 F.4th 594, 599 (7th Cir. 2022); *See Adam Joseph Res. v. CNA Metals Ltd.*, 919 F.3d 856, 865, 866 (5th Cir. 2019) ("unusual circumstance" found when existing parties attempted to hide settlement from intervenor); *W. Energy All. v. Zinke*, 877 F.3d 1157 (10th Cir. 2017) (consolidating factors into three considerations).

[55]*See Ali v. City of Chicago*, 34 F.4th 594, 599 (7th Cir. 2022); *Kalbers v. United States Dep't of Just.*, 22 F.4th 816, 823 (9th Cir. 2021); *See United States v. Ritchie Special Credit Invs., Ltd.*, 620 F.3d 824, 831 (8th Cir. 2010).

[56]*See Comm'r, Alabama Dep't of Corr. v. Advance Loc. Media, LLC*, 918 F.3d 1161, 1171 (11th Cir. 2019) (most important factor in assessing timeliness is prejudice to existing party); *Effjohn Int'l Cruise Holdings, Inc. v. A&L Sales, Inc.*, 346 F.3d 552, 561 (5th Cir. 2003) (inquiry is whether other parties were prejudiced *by the delay*, not whether they would be prejudiced *by the intervention of the party*). *See also Kalbers v. United States Dep't of Just.*, 22 F.4th 816, 825 (9th Cir. 2021); *In re Auto. Parts Antitrust Litig., End-Payor Actions*, 33 F.4th 894, 905 (6th Cir. 2022).

[57]*See Ali v. City of Chicago*, 34 F.4th 594, 599 (7th Cir. 2022).

[58]*See Kalbers v. United States Dep't of Just.*, 22 F.4th 816, 826 (9th Cir. 2021); *United Food & Com. Workers Union, Loc. No. 663 v. United States Dep't of Agric.*, 36 F.4th 777, 780 (8th Cir. 2022).

fecting fairness in an individual case,[59] and requests for intervention during the pendency of the case from post-judgment or post-settlement requests.[60] The determination of timeliness should focus on prejudice to existing parties and not be used as "a tool of retribution to punish the tardy would-be intervenor.[61] The timeliness of a motion to intervene is frequently measured from the time the petitioner should have known his interest was not adequately represented.[62] This point in time may occur when the intervenor learns that an existing party will not appeal,[63] when a party files a stipulation of dismissal,[64] or when the intervenor "seeks to make a legal argument not pursued by a named party."[65]

In this analysis, courts frequently distinguish intervention during a district court case from intervention on appeal.[66] A change in circumstances can justify an otherwise untimely motion to intervene.[67]

- *"Collateral Purpose" Exception*: Some courts modify the timeliness requirement of Rule 24(a) when the purpose of the intervention application is only to modify, e.g., an existing protective order.[68] This view has not been adopted in all circuits.[69]

---

[59]*See Adam Joseph Res. v. CNA Metals Ltd.*, 919 F.3d 856 (5th Cir. 2019) (attempt to hide settlement from law firm with contingent fee interest constituted "unusual circumstances' that justified intervention on appeal; any prejudice to existing parties "was of their own making").

[60]*See Lopez-Aguilar v. Marion Cnty. Sheriff's Dep't*, 924 F.3d 375, 389 (7th Cir. 2019) (citing cases from sister circuits that have similarly held fact that motion to intervene was filed within time limit for filing notice of appeal is entitled to significant weight). *Sommers v. Bank of Am., N.A.*, 835 F.3d 509, 513 (5th Cir. 2016) (attempt to intervene after dismissal of case "is a factor weighing against timeliness").

[61]*See, e.g., Adam Joseph Res. v. CNA Metals Ltd.*, 919 F.3d 856, 865 (5th Cir. 2019).

[62]*See Kalbers v. United States Dep't of Just.*, 22 F.4th 816, 823 (9th Cir. 2021) ("Delay is measured from the date the proposed intervenor should have been aware that its interests would no longer be protected adequately by the parties, *not the date it learned of the litigation*."); *See St. Bernard Par. v. Lafarge N. Am., Inc.*, 914 F.3d 969, 974 (5th Cir. 2019).

[63]*See United States v. Osage Wind, LLC*, 871 F.3d 1078, 1084–86 (10th Cir. 2017); *Food Mktg. Inst. v. Argus Leader Media*, __U.S.__, , 139 S. Ct. 2356, 2362, 204 L. Ed. 2d 742 (2019).

[64]*See In re Brewer*, 863 F.3d 861, 872 (D.C. Cir. 2017).

[65]*See Akiachak Native Cmty. v. United States Dep't of Interior*, 827 F.3d 100, 109 (D.C. Cir. 2016).

[66]*See generally Marino v. Ortiz*, 484 U.S. 301, 304 (1988); *Pub. Serv. Co. of New Mexico v. Barboan*, 857 F.3d 1101, 1113 (10th Cir. 2017).

[67]*See Peruta v. Cnty. of San Diego*, 824 F.3d 919, 940–41 (9th Cir. 2016).

[68]*See United Nuclear Corp. v. Cranford Ins. Co.*, 905 F.2d 1424, 1427 (10th Cir. 1990). *See also Pansy v. Borough of Stroudsburg*, 23 F.3d 772, 780 n.9 (3d Cir. 1994).

[69]*See Empire Blue Cross & Blue Shield v. Janet Greeson's A Place For Us, Inc.*, 62 F.3d 1217, 1221 (9th Cir. 1995); *Banco Popular de Puerto Rico v. Greenblatt*, 964 F.2d 1227, 1230–34 (1st Cir. 1992).

Burden of Proof

While an applicant seeking to intervene as of right has the burden to show that requirements for intervention are met, those requirements are broadly interpreted in favor of intervention at the district court level but only permit it on appeal in exceptional cases for imperative reasons.[70]

Conditional Intervention

It appears that if a court permits intervention as of right, it may impose conditions on such intervention (such as barring the intervenor from asserting new claims) to ensure the fair, efficacious, and prompt resolution of the litigation.[71]

Subject-Matter Jurisdiction

When a person seeks to intervene as of right, subject-matter jurisdiction may be established either through an independent basis of original jurisdiction (such as diversity jurisdiction[72] or federal question jurisdiction[73]) or through supplemental jurisdiction.[74] However, in circumstances where the basis for subject-matter jurisdiction in the underlying case is diversity of citizenship, and the intervening person is not diverse from the parties on one side of the case, the availability of supplemental jurisdiction depends on whether the would-be intervenor will be aligned as a plaintiff or a defendant. If the intervenor will be a plaintiff, it is probable that the intervenor will not be able to employ supplemental jurisdiction.[75] If, on the other hand, the intervenor will be aligned as a defendant, supplemental jurisdiction will normally be available.[76] Where a party who is dispensable under Rule 19 and is also nondiverse seeks to intervene under Rule 24, diversity jurisdiction is not necessar-

---

[70] *See Pub. Serv. Co. of New Mexico v. Barboan*, 857 F.3d 1101, 1113 (10th Cir. 2017). *See also Kalbers v. United States Dep't of Just.*, 22 F.4th 816, 823 (9th Cir. 2021) (noting court favors intervention); *Wal-Mart Stores, Inc. v. Texas Alcoholic Beverage Comm'n*, 834 F.3d 562, 565 (5th Cir. 2016) ("Rule 24 is to be liberally construed.").

[71] *See In re Fin. Oversight & Mgmt. Bd. for Puerto Rico for Puerto Rico*, 872 F.3d 57, 64 (1st Cir. 2017); *Salvors, Inc. v. Unidentified Wrecked & Abandoned Vessel*, 861 F.3d 1278, 1290–91 (11th Cir. 2017).

[72] *See* 28 U.S.C.A. § 1332.

[73] *See* 28 U.S.C.A. § 1331.

[74] *See* 28 U.S.C.A. § 1367.

[75] *See* 28 U.S.C.A. § 1367(b) (in cases where original basis of jurisdiction is diversity and person intervening under Rule 24 will be aligned as a plaintiff, supplemental jurisdiction is not available). *See Exxon Mobil Corp. v. Allapattah Servs., Inc.*, 545 U.S. 546, 560 (2005) ("Section 1367(b) withholds supplemental jurisdiction over the claims of plaintiffs who seek to intervene pursuant to Rule 24."). *But cf., Aurora Loan Servs., Inc. v. Craddieth*, 442 F.3d 1018, 1025 (7th Cir. 2006) (in diversity cases supplemental jurisdiction normally not available to intervenor plaintiffs; but prohibition on use of supplemental jurisdiction inapplicable where a person is "forced to intervene to protect an interest that arose during the course of a federal litigation in which he had no stake at the outset").

[76] *See Exxon Mobil Corp. v. Allapattah Servs., Inc.*, 545 U.S. 546, 560 (2005) (noting that 28 U.S.C.A. § 1367(b) does not prohibit use of supplemental jurisdiction in such circumstances).

ily defeated.[77]

Where the original basis for jurisdiction in the underlying case is a federal question, supplemental jurisdiction is routinely available without regard to the intervenor's status as a plaintiff or defendant.[78]

If the court does not have competent jurisdiction, intervention cannot be used as a cure because Rule 24 does not provide a basis for jurisdiction.[79] However, a "curative approach" has been recognized that allows the court to treat the pleading of an intervenor as a separate action even if the underlying claim is jurisdictionally deficient where the intervention is sought before any action has been taken by the defendants.[80]

Personal Jurisdiction

When a person attempts to intervene under Rule 24, that person submits to the jurisdiction of the court.[81] However, where the would-be intervenor simultaneously objects to personal jurisdiction, the court may find that the intervenor has not consented.[82]

Amicus Curiae Are Not Intervenors

There is a superficial similarity between the process of intervention and the opportunity to file an amicus curiae brief. Courts do not equate amicus status with the rights and respon-

---

[77] *See In re Olympic Mills Corp.*, 477 F.3d 1, 12 (1st Cir. 2007) (in bankruptcy case, court reviewed case law and concluded "the weight of authority holds that claims launched by necessary but dispensable, nondiverse defendant-intervenors do not defeat the original jurisdiction (diversity) that obtained at the commencement of the action").

[78] *See Grace United Methodist Church v. City of Cheyenne*, 451 F.3d 643, 672–73 (10th Cir. 2006) (for intervention of right in case originally based on federal question jurisdiction, supplemental jurisdiction is sufficient and no independent basis of jurisdiction is required).

[79] *See Police & Fire Ret. Sys. of City of Detroit v. IndyMac MBS, Inc.*, 721 F.3d 95, 111–12 (2d Cir. 2013) (stating rule and holding that where no named plaintiff in the suit had constitutional standing to bring asserted claims intervention not proper); *Disability Advocs., Inc. v. New York Coal. for Quality Assisted Living, Inc.*, 675 F.3d 149, 160–161 (2d Cir. 2012) (intervention denied six years into litigation and after five week hearing where court found original plaintiff's lacked standing).

[80] *See Miller & Miller Auctioneers, Inc. v. G.W. Murphy Indus., Inc.*, 472 F.2d 893, 895–96 (10th Cir. 1973) (upheld interpleader where intervenor had separate and independent basis for jurisdiction despite lack of jurisdiction for underlying case).

[81] *See Cnty. Sec. Agency v. Ohio Dept. of Com.*, 296 F.3d 477, 483 (6th Cir. 2002) (refusing to permit reservation of objections to jurisdiction made by petitioning intervenor; "a motion to intervene is fundamentally incompatible with an objection to personal jurisdiction").

[82] *See S.E.C. v. Ross*, 504 F.3d 1130, 1149–50 (9th Cir. 2007) (reviewing cases and acknowledging that courts have generally concluded that a party who intervenes consents to jurisdiction as a matter of law but declines to find such consent where intervenor objected to court's exercise of personal jurisdiction, sufficiency of process, and venue).

sibilities of a party joined through intervention.[83] The ability for a party to present its view in an amicus brief may be a reason to deny intervention.[84]

Standing of Intervenor

Intervenors of right must have Article III standing to pursue any relief that may differ from the relief sought by the original party with standing.[85]

Dismissal of Original Party

In some cases, an intervenor with an independent basis of jurisdiction may be allowed to continue the suit after the original party is dismissed.[86] The requirements for continuing the suit in such a circumstance appear to be the existence of an independent basis for jurisdiction and a recognition that dismissal of the intervenor would result in unnecessary delay.[87]

Impact of Dismissal

Generally, it is impossible to intervene in a case that no longer exists.[88] However, some circuits have allowed intervention when an intervenor seeks status as a party to appeal.[89] The reason for allowing intervention in this circumstance is because, although final judgment is entered, if an appellate court concludes the lower court erred in denying intervention, and the prospective intervenor was entitled to intervene, then the intervenor would have standing to appeal that decision.[90]

Class Actions

An absent (non-named) class member seeking intervention as of right must satisfy the same requirements as other

---

[83]*See United States v. City of Los Angeles, Cal.*, 288 F.3d 391, 400 (9th Cir. 2002) ("[A]micus status is insufficient to protect the [petitioner for intervention's] rights because such status does not allow the [petitioner] to raise issues or arguments formally and gives it no right of appeal."); *Coal. of Arizona/New Mexico Ctys. for Stable Econ. Growth v. Dep't of Interior*, 100 F.3d 837, 844 (10th Cir. 1996) ("[T]he right to file a brief as amicus curiae is no substitute for the right to intervene as a party in the action under Rule 24(a)(2).").

[84]*See Victim Rts. L. Ctr. v. Rosenfelt*, 988 F.3d 556, 564 (1st Cir. 2021).

[85]*See Town of Chester v. Laroe Ests., Inc.*, — U.S. —, 137 S. Ct. 1645, 1651, 198 L. Ed. 2d 64 (2017); *Wayne Land & Min. Grp., LLC v. Delaware River Basin Comm'n*, 959 F.3d 569, 570–71 (3d Cir. 2020). *See also Kane Cnty, Utah v. United States*, 950 F.3d 1323, 1325 (10th Cir. 2020) (an intervenor can establish "piggyback standing" when seeking the same relief as an existing party).

[86]*See In re Molasky*, 843 F.3d 1179, 1184–85 (9th Cir. 2016); *Diamond v. Charles*, 476 U.S. 54, 68–69, 106 S. Ct. 1697, 90 L. Ed. 2d 48 (1986).

[87]*See In re Molasky*, 843 F.3d 1179, 1184–85 (9th Cir. 2016); *Diamond v. Charles*, 476 U.S. 54, 68–69, 106 S. Ct. 1697, 90 L. Ed. 2d 48 (1986).

[88]*See DeOtte v. State*, 20 F.4th 1055, 1066 (5th Cir. 2021); *CVLR Performance Horses, Inc. v. Wynne*, 792 F.3d 469, 474 (4th Cir. 2015).

[89]*See DeOtte v. State*, 20 F.4th 1055, 1066 (5th Cir. 2021).

[90]*See DeOtte v. State*, 20 F.4th 1055, 1067 (5th Cir. 2021) (quoting *DBSI/TRI IV Ltd. P'ship v. United States*, 465 F.3d 1031, 1037 (9th Cir. 2006)).

intervenors.[91] But the class nature of the lawsuit does have some unique impacts. In a class action lawsuit, the timeliness clock does not start running until the putative intervenor knows that the class representative will not represent the intervenor's interest.[92] The filing of a class action also tolls the running of the applicable statute of limitations for prospective intervenors; if class treatment is denied by the court, the statute then resumes running so as to allow members of the (former) class action to seek intervention into the lawsuit as named parties.[93]

RULE 24(b)—PERMISSIVE INTERVENTION

CORE CONCEPT

Permissive intervention is not intervention that the court *must* allow, but instead that the court *may* allow in its discretion. Consequently, the requirements are less demanding. It does not require the applicant to demonstrate the sort of interest required for intervention of right. Instead, a court may grant permissive intervention when a timely motion shows that intervention is conditionally authorized by statute or when the applicant has: an independent ground for jurisdiction; a timely motion; and a common question of law or fact.[94] The court's discretion to grant or reject Rule 24(b)(2) intervention applications is far broader than with intervention as of right.[95] Intervention offers parties a streamlined alternative to filing a separate lawsuit and seeking consolidation under Rule 42.[96]

APPLICATIONS

Permissive Intervention by Conditional Statutory Right

Congress can create a statutory right of intervention conditioned on the fulfillment of certain requirements. Intervention under such a statute would be permissive. For example, some statutes accord the court authority to allow intervention by some public official such as the United States Attorney General.[97]

Permissive Intervention by Showing a Common Question of Law or Fact

The bedrock requirement for Rule 24(b)(2) permissive

[91] *See In re Pet Foods Prod. Liab. Litig.*, 629 F.3d 333, 349 (3d Cir. 2010).

[92] *See Wallach v. Eaton Corp.*, 837 F.3d 356, 375–76 (3d Cir. 2016).

[93] *See Am. Pipe & Const. Co. v. Utah*, 414 U.S. 538, 553 (1974).

[94] *See Flynt v. Lombardi*, 782 F.3d 963, 966 (8th Cir. 2015).

[95] *See United States v. Albert Inv. Co., Inc.*, 585 F.3d 1386, 1390 (10th Cir. 2009) (court of appeals reviews the denial of motion to intervene as of right de novo and denial of motion for permissive intervention for abuse of discretion).

[96] *See PrimeSource Bldg. Prod., Inc. v. United States*, 494 F. Supp. 3d 1307, 1334 (Ct. Int'l Trade 2021).

[97] *See* 42 U.S.C.A. § 2000a-3(a); *PrimeSource Bldg. Prod., Inc. v. United States*, 494 F. Supp. 3d 1307, 1328 (Ct. Int'l Trade 2021).

intervention is a demonstration by the person seeking intervention that a common question of law or fact exists between that person's claim or defense and the pending litigation.[98] Intervenors do not share a defense where the plaintiff cannot assert a claim against them.[99] A contingent financial interest in the outcome will not suffice.[100] Many courts dispense with the requirement of a strong nexus of fact or law where a litigant seeks to intervene solely for a collateral purpose, such as to unseal judicial records or modify a protective order.[101] This stretching of the Rule is justified on the basis of judicial economy and because the would-be intervenor is not seeking to litigate on the merits.

Permissive Intervention for Public Officials

Rule 24(b) authorizes intervention by officers or agencies if the pending litigation raises questions of law administered by the officer or agency or questions of regulations issued by the officer or agency.[102]

Judicial Discretion

The district court has broad discretion and may consider almost any factor that is rationally relevant.[103]

Timing

Applications to intervene under Rule 24(b) must be "timely."[104] The determination of what constitutes a timely application rests within the court's discretion in the context of the facts and circumstances in a particular case.[105] Many courts will deny intervention where the existing parties have commenced settlement negotiations.[106] Because Rule 24(b) intervention questions do not typically affect the interests of nonparties as importantly as Rule 24(a) cases, courts tend to hold motions for permissive intervention to a more rigorous standard of timeliness than would be applied to motions for intervention of

---

[98] *See Buck v. Gordon*, 959 F.3d 219, 223 (6th Cir. 2020).

[99] *See N. Am. Interpipe, Inc. v. United States*, 519 F. Supp. 3d 1313, 1334–35 (Ct. Int'l Trade 2021).

[100] *See Crum & Forster Specialty Ins. Co. v. Strong Contractors, Inc.*, 488 F. Supp. 3d 192, 198 (E.D. Pa. 2020).

[101] *See Flynt v. Lombardi*, 782 F.3d 963, 967 (8th Cir. 2015); *Vanda Pharms., Inc. v. Food & Drug Admin.*, 539 F. Supp. 3d 44, 50 (D.D.C. 2021).

[102] *See Harris v. Amoco Prod. Co.*, 768 F.2d 669, 680 (5th Cir. 1985).

[103] *See T-Mobile Ne. LLC v. Town of Barnstable*, 969 F.3d 33, 40 (1st Cir. 2020); *Scholl v. Mnuchin*, 483 F. Supp. 3d 822, 825 (N.D. Cal. 2020) (enumerating factors).

[104] *See* Rule 24(b). *See also Cameron v. EMW Women's Surgical Ctr, P.S.C.*, __U.S.__, , 142 S. Ct. 1002, 1012, 212 L. Ed. 2d 114 (2022).

[105] *See Amador Cnty., Cal. v. U.S. Dep't of the Interior*, 772 F.3d 901, 904–905 (D.C. Cir. 2014); *Cameron v. EMW Women's Surgical Ctr., P.S.C.*, __U.S.__, , 142 S. Ct. 1002, 1012, 212 L. Ed. 2d 114 (2022) (stating most important factor in the case was the fact that the intervenor sought intervention "as soon as it became clear" the intervenor's interests "would no longer be protected").

[106] *See Jones v. Stanford*, 525 F. Supp. 3d 420, 423 (E.D.N.Y. 2021).

right.[107]

Delay or Prejudice

Rule 24(b) expressly authorizes the court to deny permissive intervention if intervention will unduly delay or prejudice the pending litigation.[108] The provision permits denial of intervention if undue delay to existing parties will result even from an arguably timely application which might occur if the complexity added by an intervenor would prolong the litigation excessively.[109] Similarly, inappropriate prejudice to existing parties might occur if the presence of the intervenor might shift the focus of the litigation from the pending issues to those introduced by the intervenor.[110] Permissive intervention is disfavored if the case has already settled[111] or the court has already entered judgment.[112]

To the extent that the claim is duplicative or weak on its merits, the court will be inclined to give greater weight to concerns about delay or prejudice.[113]

Subject-Matter Jurisdiction

Persons attempting to intervene under Rule 24(b)(2) must establish an independent basis for subject-matter jurisdiction. Supplemental jurisdiction is not available to would-be permissive intervenors seeking to intervene as plaintiffs[114] and may not be available for those proposing to enter permissively as fellow defendants.[115] An independent basis of jurisdiction may not be required where a party seeks to intervene to modify a protective order or unseal documents, as these parties are not seeking to litigate on the merits.[116]

---

[107] *See Banco Popular de Puerto Rico v. Greenblatt*, 964 F.2d 1227, 1230 (1st Cir. 1992). *But cf. R & G Mortg. Corp. v. Fed. Home Loan Mortg. Corp.*, 584 F.3d 1, 11 (1st Cir. 2009) (when intervenor seeks both as of right and permissive intervention, a finding of untimeliness with respect to the former normally applies to the latter).

[108] *See* Rule 24(b)(3).

[109] *See, e.g., Tri-State Generation & Transmission Ass'n, Inc. v. New Mexico Pub. Regul. Comm'n*, 787 F.3d 1068, 1075 (10th Cir. 2015) (potential for burdensome or duplicative discovery appropriate consideration in denying permissive intervention).

[110] *See Alaniz v. Tillie Lewis Foods*, 572 F.2d 657, 659 (9th Cir. 1978).

[111] *See Alaniz v. Tillie Lewis Foods*, 572 F.2d 657, 659 (9th Cir. 1978).

[112] *See Bond v. Utreras*, 585 F.3d 1061, 1071 (7th Cir. 2009). *But see Blum v. Merrill Lynch Pierce Fenner & Smith Inc.*, 712 F.3d 1349, 1354 (9th Cir. 2013) (no prejudice where action between original litigants had been settled).

[113] *See Massachusetts v. Microsoft Corp.*, 373 F.3d 1199 (D.C. Cir. 2004).

[114] *See* 28 U.S.C.A. § 1367(b). *See also E.E.O.C. v. Nat'l Children's Ctr., Inc.*, 146 F.3d 1042, 1046 (D.C. Cir. 1998).

[115] *See* 28 U.S.C.A. § 1367(a).

[116] *See Flynt v. Lombardi*, 782 F.3d 963, 967 (8th Cir. 2015).

Use of Rule 24(a) Factors

Courts frequently apply intervention as of right factors to a permissive intervention analysis.[117]

Standing for Non-statutory Permissive Intervention

Although a person seeking intervention under Rule 24(b)(2) need not demonstrate an "interest" within the kinds contemplated by Rule 24(a)(2), the person seeking permissive intervention must nonetheless have a sufficient stake in the litigation to satisfy ordinary requirements for standing.[118] Whether standing is required for permissive intervention may depend on the type of case and the status of the case at the time.[119]

Conditional Permissive Intervention

If intervention is permitted under Rule 24(b), the court has substantial authority to impose conditions on the intervention.[120]

RULE 24(c)—NOTICE AND PLEADING REQUIRED

CORE CONCEPT

Rule 24(c) contains the provisions for notice and service of process of a motion to intervene. It also requires that the motion to intervene be accompanied by a pleading that identifies the claim or defense which is the basis of the attempt to intervene.

APPLICATIONS

Service of Process

The motion to intervene should be filed with the court and served on all persons already parties to the pending litigation

---

[117] *See Tri-State Generation & Transmission Ass'n, Inc. v. New Mexico Pub. Regul. Comm'n*, 787 F.3d 1068, 1075 (10th Cir. 2015) (As to the prospective intervenors' "suggestion that Rule 24(b) does not provide for consideration of adequate representation, we have elsewhere affirmed denial of permissive intervention on such grounds"); *Floyd v. City of New York*, 770 F.3d 1051, 1057 (2d Cir. 2014) (To be granted intervention as of right or by permission, "an applicant must (1) timely file an application, (2) show an interest in the action, (3) demonstrate that the interest may be impaired by the disposition of the action, and (4) show that the interest is not protected adequately by the parties to the action.") *But see Planned Parenthood of Wisconsin, Inc. v. Kaul*, 942 F.3d 793, 804 (7th Cir. 2019). (Rule 24 (a)(2) is not just a repeat of Rule 24 (a)(1); "We have thus cautioned courts not to deny permissive intervention solely because a proposed intervenor failed to prove an element of intervention as of right").

[118] *See Sierra Club v. Entergy Arkansas LLC*, 503 F. Supp. 3d 821, 862 (E.D. Ark. 2020); *N. Am. Interpipe, Inc. v. United States*, 519 F. Supp. 3d 1313, 1329–30 (Ct. Int'l Trade 2021) (noting that evidence required at pleading stage is unclear). *See also Defs. of Wildlife v. Perciasepe*, 714 F.3d 1317, 1327 (D.C. Cir. 2013) (issue of whether standing required for permissive intervention is an open question in D.C. Circuit).

[119] *See Bond v. Utreras*, 585 F.3d 1061, 1069–70 (7th Cir. 2009).

[120] *See League of Women Voters of U.S. v. Newby*, 963 F.3d 130 (D.C. Cir. 2020) (allowed party to intervene for limited purpose of seeking to unseal judicial records); *Beauregard, Inc. v. Sword Servs. L.L.C.*, 107 F.3d 351, 352 (5th Cir. 1997).

as provided in Rule 5.[121]

Service of Proposed Pleading

In addition to the motion to intervene, Rule 24(c) also requires that the applicant for intervention file and serve a proposed pleading explaining the claim or defense that is the purpose of the intervention.[122] This proposed pleading should also be served consistent with the requirements of Rule 5, governing service on persons already parties.

Failure to Meet Rule 24(c) Motion and Pleading Requirements

There is a split of authority as to the consequences an intervenor should experience for failure to meet the motion and pleading requirements of Rule 24(c). An apparent majority of circuits has held that failure to comply with Rule 24(c) should not of itself disqualify the attempt to intervene.[123] A smaller number of circuits has applied the requirements more rigorously.[124]

Additional Research References

Wright & Miller, *Federal Practice and Procedure* §§ 1900 to 23
C.J.S., Federal Civil Procedure §§ 128 to 155
West's Key Number Digest, Federal Civil Procedure ⇔311 to 345

---

[121] *See In re Chinese Manufactured Drywall Prod. Liab. Litig.*, 753 F.3d 521 (5th Cir. 2014).

[122] *See Bridges v. Dep't of Maryland State Police*, 441 F.3d 197, 208 (4th Cir. 2006); *Retired Chicago Police Ass'n v. City of Chicago*, 7 F.3d 584, 595 (7th Cir. 1993).

[123] *See League of Women Voters of Michigan v. Johnson*, 902 F.3d 572 (6th Cir. 2018); *In re Fin. Oversight and Mgmt. Bd. for Puerto Rico for Puerto Rico*, 872 F.3d 57, 65 (1st Cir. 2017).

[124] *See King v. Univ. Healthcare Sys., L.C.*, 645 F.3d 713, 727 (5th Cir. 2011); *Hollywood Mobile Ests. Ltd. v. Seminole Tribe of Florida*, 641 F.3d 1259 (11th Cir. 2011).

RULE 25
SUBSTITUTION OF PARTIES

(a) Death.

(1) *Substitution if the Claim Is Not Extinguished.* If a party dies and the claim is not extinguished, the court may order substitution of the proper party. A motion for substitution may be made by any party or by the decedent's successor or representative. If the motion is not made within 90 days after service of a statement noting the death, the action by or against the decedent must be dismissed.

(2) *Continuation Among the Remaining Parties.* After a party's death, if the right sought to be enforced survives only to or against the remaining parties, the action does not abate, but proceeds in favor of or against the remaining parties. The death should be noted on the record.

(3) *Service.* A motion to substitute, together with a notice of hearing, must be served on the parties as provided in Rule 5 and on nonparties as provided in Rule 4. A statement noting death must be served in the same manner. Service may be made in any judicial district.

(b) Incompetency. If a party becomes incompetent, the court may, on motion, permit the action to be continued by or against the party's representative. The motion must be served as provided in Rule 25(a)(3).

(c) Transfer of Interest. If an interest is transferred, the action may be continued by or against the original party unless the court, on motion, orders the transferee to be substituted in the action or joined with the original party. The motion must be served as provided in Rule 25(a)(3).

(d) Public Officers; Death or Separation from Office. An action does not abate when a public officer who is a party in an official capacity dies, resigns, or otherwise ceases to hold office while the action is pending. The officer's successor is automatically substituted as a party. Later proceedings should be in the substituted party's name, but any misnomer not affecting the parties' substantial rights must be disregarded. The court may order substitution at any time, but the absence of such an order does not affect the substitution.

[Amended effective October 20, 1949; July 19, 1961; July 1, 1963; August 1, 1987; April 30, 2007, effective December 1, 2007.]

AUTHORS' COMMENTARY ON RULE 25

PURPOSE AND SCOPE

Dismissal of federal lawsuits on the basis of a curable technicality is heavily disfavored under the Rules. Rule 25 is designed to address four of those curable defects categories. This Rule must be read in conjunction with Rule 17(a), which instructs that federal civil lawsuits must be prosecuted only in the names of, and for the benefit of, the "real parties in interest." Nonetheless, there are times when the real parties in interest are unable to continue on as litigants—when they die, become incompetent, or depart from public office. In such circumstances, Rule 25 allows for the substitution into the lawsuit of successor parties who will continue the task of prosecuting or defending those lawsuits.

RULE 25(a)—DEATH

CORE CONCEPT

Substitution is permitted when a party dies, provided the applicable substantive law permits the deceased person's claim in litigation to survive.[1]

APPLICATIONS

When Substitution is Permitted

A threshold prerequisite for substitution upon death requires that the claim in litigation must be capable of surviving the death of the party, a matter which is resolved by deferring to the controlling federal or State law. If, under that controlling law, the claim does not survive the death of a party,

[1] *See Figueroa v. Sec'y of Health & Hum. Servs.*, 715 F.3d 1314, 1318–19 (Fed. Cir. 2013). *See also Revock v. Cowpet Bay W. Condo. Ass'n*, 853 F.3d 96, 109 (3d Cir. 2017) (collecting cases where courts have applied a uniform federal rule to determine the issue of survival of a federal claim: "remedial claims survive, but penal claims do not.").

there can be no substitution.[2]

Suggestion of Death Filed and Served

Death of a party is suggested by written notice on the record, which should be filed and served on all parties pursuant to Rule 5.[3] Nonparty representatives of the deceased should be served pursuant to Rule 4.[4]

Procedure for Substitution—Motion for Substitution

Rule 25(a)(1) provides that any party, or the persons affiliated with the deceased party, may make a motion for substitution.[5] Until a motion for substitution has been made and granted, the court has no authority to proceed with the deceased party's case.[6]

- *Service of Motion:* The motion should be filed and served on all parties consistent with the requirements of Rule 5.[7] Nonparty representatives of the deceased should be served with process pursuant to Rule 4.[8] Rule 25(a)(3) authorizes service of such process in any federal judicial district.
- *Hearing:* If there is a dispute as to the appropriateness of the proposed substituted party, the court has a duty to resolve the issue and may hold a hearing before ruling on the motion.[9] The notice of hearing should be filed and served on all parties in the manner provided by Rule 5.[10]
- *Timing:* The time in which the motion for substitution must be made is 90 days from when the death of the party is "suggested" on the record of the case. Thus, a party may have been deceased for a substantial period before a suggestion of death is made, and that fact will

---

[2] *See Grinblat v. Michell Wolf LLC*, 338 F.R.D. 15, 16 (E.D.N.Y. 2021); *Asklar v. Honeywell, Inc.*, 95 F.R.D. 419, 422 (D. Conn. 1982).

[3] *See Barlow v. Ground*, 39 F.3d 231, 233–34 (9th Cir. 1994) (90 days does not start to run until representative of estate is properly served). *See also In re LeFande*, 919 F.3d 554 (D.C. Cir. 2019) (death notice not filed by estate representatives or identifying state representatives does not trigger running of Rule 25 time limit).

[4] *See Barlow v. Ground*, 39 F.3d 231 (9th Cir. 1994) (requiring service on nonparty representatives under Rule 4). *See also Gilmore v. Lockhard*, 936 F.3d 857 (9th Cir. 2019) (service on other parties or nonparty representative of deceased should comply with Rule 25(a).

[5] *See In re Baycol Products Litigation*, 616 F.3d 778, 785 (8th Cir. 2010); *Atkins v. City of Chicago*, 547 F.3d 869, 872 (7th Cir. 2008).

[6] *See Campbell v. Iowa, Third Jud. Dist. Dep't of Corr. Servs.*, 702 F.3d 1140, 1141 (8th Cir. 2013).

[7] *See Sampson v. ASC Indus.*, 780 F.3d 679, 681 (5th Cir. 2015); *Martinez v. Superior HealthPlan, Inc.*, 371 F. Supp. 3d 370, 387 (W.D. Tex. 2019).

[8] *See Giles v. Campbell*, 698 F.3d 153, 158 (3d Cir. 2012); *Snider v. Vertex Aerospace, LLC*, 338 F.R.D. 358, 363 (S.D. Miss. 2021).

[9] *See Escareno v. Noltina Crucible and Refractory Corp.*, 139 F.3d 1456 (11th Cir.1998).

[10] *See Giles v. Campbell*, 698 F.3d 153, 155 (3d Cir. 2012).

have no consequence for the 90-day limitation.[11] However, a party interested in securing substitution under the amended rule should not wait indefinitely because a court may deny substitution if it causes prejudice.[12] The 90-day deadline for a party to move for substitution begins to run upon service of a notice of the death on that party, regardless of whether that notice was also served upon the decedent's successor or representative.[13]

- *Failure to Move for Substitution Within 90 Days:* If more than 90 days elapses following the suggestion of death without a motion for substitution, Rule 25(a)(1) provides that the suit will be dismissed as to the deceased party. However, notwithstanding the apparently mandatory language of the Rule, the cases generally hold that the courts have discretion to extend the time in which a party may move for substitution.[14]

Death Prior to Lawsuit

If a person dies before a lawsuit is filed, Rule 25 is inapplicable. Rule 25(a) is available, if at all, only when the party is alive when the lawsuit begins.[15] This result applies even where a lawsuit can be filed after the death of a potential plaintiff. Substitution remains available after filing and prior to service of a summons.[16]

---

[11] *See Adkins v. City of Chicago*, 547 F.3d 869, 873–74 (7th Cir. 2008).

[12] *See Snider v. Vertex Aerospace, LLC*, 338 F.R.D. 358, 363 (S.D. Miss. 2021) (denying motion to substitute made five years after death, where estate was closed).

[13] *See Kotler v. Jubert*, 986 F.3d 147, 150 (2d Cir. 2021) (noting some contrary decisions in other jurisdictions); *Gilmore v. Lockard*, 936 F.3d 857, 865 (9th Cir. 2019) (recognizing "other circuits have suggested that nonparty successors or representatives of the deceased party must be personally served—or, at a minimum, identified—in order to trigger the 90-day period"); *Fariss v. Lynchburg Foundry*, 769 F.2d 958, 962 (4th Cir. 1985) ("Rule 25(a)(1) directs that both parties and appropriate nonparties be served with the suggestion of death to commence the 90-day substitution period, for the rule seeks to assure the parties to the action and other concerned persons of notice of the death so that they may take appropriate action to make substitution for the deceased party.") (internal quotations and citation omitted).

[14] *See Zanowick v. Baxter Healthcare Corp.*, 850 F.3d 1090, 1094 (9th Cir. 2017). *See also Gilmore v. Lockhard*, 936 F.3d 857, 867 (9th Cir. 2019) (claims against substituted party relate back to date of original filing). *But see, Kaubisch v. Weber*, 408 F.3d 540, 543 (8th Cir. 2005) (acknowledging district court's discretion; but "the misapplication or misreading of the plain language of Rule 25 does not establish excusable neglect").

[15] *See LN Mgmt., LLC v. JPMorgan Chase Bank, N.A.*, 957 F.3d 943 (9th Cir. 2020) (collecting cases).

[16] *Gilmore v. Lockard*, 936 F.3d 857, 864 (9th Cir. 2019) (finding "service *after* substitution would still preserve a party's rights and claims, while ensuring that a court has personal jurisdiction over the new, proper party" and recognizing the "Supreme Court inferred as much more than a century ago, finding 'no reason why the representative of a deceased party should not be brought in by the same

Original Parties Must Have Been Correct Parties

Rule 25 authorizes substitution only when the case was brought by the correct original parties.[17]

Status of Successor

A party who replaces a deceased party receives the status the deceased party possessed at the time of death. For example, if the deceased party had already consented to trial by a magistrate judge, the successor is bound by that consent.[18]

RULE 25(b)—INCOMPETENCY

CORE CONCEPT

Substitution is permitted when a party becomes incompetent during the course of the litigation.

APPLICATIONS

Survival of the Action

Incompetency will not ordinarily extinguish a cause of action.

Procedure for Substitution—Motion for Substitution

The incompetent party's representative must file a motion with the court for substitution. The motion along with a notice of hearing must be filed and served on all parties (in accordance with Rule 5) and any nonparties (in accordance with Rule 4), and service may be made in any federal judicial district.

- *Timing:* Rule 25(b) contains no reference to time limitations for motions to substitute parties, though some courts have imposed a "reasonable" time filing obligation.[19]

RULE 25(c)—TRANSFER OF INTEREST

CORE CONCEPT

When the holder of an interest in litigation transfers that interest to another, the lawsuit may be continued by (or against) the original party. However, the transferee may, upon motion to the court, seek permission to join in the lawsuit or to substitute in place of the original party.

APPLICATIONS

Option to Substitute Parties

Rule 25(c) does not require that the person now holding the

---

procedure, whether the death of a party occur before or after service" when interpreting a similar state procedural rule).

[17]*See Silberman v. Miami Dade Transit*, 927 F.3d 1123, 1131 (11th Cir. 2019).

[18]*See Brook, Weiner, Sered, Kreger & Weinberg v. Coreq, Inc.*, 53 F.3d 851, 852 (7th Cir. 1995).

[19]*See Kuelbs v. Hill*, 615 F.3d 1037, 1042 (8th Cir. 2010).

interest transferred be substituted for the transferor-party.[20] Instead, the action will continue in the name of the transferor unless the court chooses to order substitution or joinder of the transferee.[21] Thus, the case may go to judgment without any substitution of parties having occurred, and the absence of a formal substitution will have no consequence.[22] If it is appropriate in the circumstances of the particular case, both the transferor and transferee will be bound by the court's judgment.[23]

Procedure for Substitution—Motion for Substitution

A transferee who seeks to join or substitute must file a motion with the court. The motion, along with a notice of hearing, must be filed and served on all parties (in accordance with Rule 5) and any nonparties (in accordance with Rule 4). Service may be made in any federal judicial district.

- *Timing:* Rule 25(c) contains no time limit in which substitution must take place.[24]
- *Evidentiary Hearing:* Courts often conduct an evidentiary hearing when considering a Rule 25(c) motion, though there is no express requirement that the court do so.[25]

Subject-Matter Jurisdiction: Relation to Rule 19

Joinder of a nondiverse party under Rule 25(c) does not usually destroy diversity jurisdiction.[26] However, if the joined party was someone who would have been indispensable under Rule 19 at the time the case was filed, joinder will destroy diversity jurisdiction.[27]

Personal Jurisdiction

Courts generally hold that when successors in interest are joined under Rule 25(c), they are subject to the personal jurisdiction of the court simply because they are successors in interest, without regard to whether they had any other minimum

---

[20] *See In re Expert S. Tulsa, LLC*, 842 F.3d 1293 (10th Cir. 2016); *F.D.I.C. v. SLE, Inc.*, 722 F.3d 264, 268 (5th Cir. 2013).

[21] *See Burka v. Aetna Life Ins. Co.*, 87 F.3d 478, 482–83 (D.C. Cir. 1996).

[22] *See Mojave Desert Holdings, LLC v. Crocs, Inc.*, 995 F.3d 969, 977 (Fed. Cir. 2021) (Rule 25(c) is "wholly permissive"); *Arnold Graphics Indus., Inc. v. Indep. Agent Ctr., Inc.*, 775 F.2d 38, 40 (2d Cir. 1985) (enforcing judgment against successor corporation where substitution was made only after judgment).

[23] *See Luxliner P.L. Export, Co. v. RDI/Luxliner, Inc.*, 13 F.3d 69, 71 (3d Cir. 1993).

[24] *Mojave Desert Holdings, LLC v. Crocs, Inc.*, 995 F.3d 969, 977 (Fed. Cir. 2021).

[25] *See Sullivan v. Running Waters Irrigation, Inc.*, 739 F.3d 354, 359–60 (7th Cir. 2014) (particularly true where party did not request hearing or demonstrate need for hearing).

[26] *See Freeport-McMoRan, Inc. v. K N Energy, Inc.*, 498 U.S. 426, 428 (1991); *see also Perez v. Staples Cont. & Com. LLC*, 31 F.4th 560, 567 (7th Cir. 2022) (citing *Freeport*, recognizing the "well-established rule" that "diversity of citizenship is assessed at the time the action is filed" and "may not be divested by subsequent events.").

[27] *Freeport-McMoRan, Inc. v. K N Energy, Inc.*, 498 U.S. 426, 428 (1991).

contacts.[28]

Extinguishing Corporate Causes of Action

Rule 25(c) follows the substantive law on the issue of survival of a cause of action after corporate reorganizations. Thus, if substantive law directs that dissolution of a corporation also extinguishes the corporation's causes of action, Rule 25(c) will not save the cause of action.[29]

When the Transferee Is Bound

For Rule 25(c) to bind a transferee to the same obligations that burdened the transferor, an "interest" must be transferred between the parties.[30] Rule 25(c) does not define an interest and instead relies on substantive law to define "interest."[31] Normally, the mere purchase of assets by a successor entity does not usually bind the successor to the obligations of the transferor.[32]

Status of Successor

A party who enters a case as the legal successor of a corporation receives the status which the predecessor corporation possessed at the time the successor entered the case. For example, if the predecessor corporation had already consented to trial by a magistrate judge, the successor is bound by that consent.[33]

Service of Process

If a motion to substitute parties is made under Rule 25(c), service should meet the requirements established in Rule 25(a) for motions to make substitutions for deceased parties.

---

[28] *See Rodriguez-Miranda v. Benin*, 829 F.3d 29 (1st Cir. 2016).

[29] *See Citibank v. Grupo Cupey, Inc.*, 382 F.3d 29, 32–33 (1st Cir. 2004).

[30] *See Sullivan v. Running Waters Irrigation, Inc.*, 739 F.3d 354, 357 (7th Cir. 2014).

[31] *See Sullivan v. Running Waters Irrigation, Inc.*, 739 F.3d 354, 357 (7th Cir. 2014).

[32] *See Sullivan v. Running Waters Irrigation, Inc.*, 739 F.3d 354, 357–58 (7th Cir. 2014). *But see Upholsterers' Int'l Union Pension Fund v. Artistic Furniture of Pontiac*, 920 F.2d 1323, 1327–29 (7th Cir. 1990) (in ERISA action to recover delinquent pension fund obligation, purchase of assets is transfer of interest under Rule 25(c) that creates binding obligations in transferee entity).

[33] *See Andrews v. Lakeshore Rehabilitation Hosp.*, 140 F.3d 1405, 1408 (11th Cir. 1998) (where transfer of interest occurs prior to trial, Rule 25(c) is not applicable and therefore "does not save plaintiff's amendments from the statute of limitations"); *QSI-Fostoria DC, LLC v. Gen. Elec. Cap.*, 223 F.R.D. 465, 467 (N.D. Ohio 2004). *Brook, Weiner, Sered, Kreger & Weinberg v. Coreq, Inc.*, 53 F.3d 851, 852 (7th Cir. 1995) ("A successor takes over without any other change in the status of the case," and therefore a successor to a corporation is bound by the corporation's previous consent to trial by a magistrate judge).

Effect on Merits

Application of Rule 25(c) does not change the court's evaluation of the merits of the case.[34]

Statute of Limitations

Substitution does not affect the statute of limitations.[35]

Relation to Rule 17

Rule 25(c) governs transfers of interest during the pendency of a case. Rule 17(a), by contrast, governs situations in which an interest is transferred before the suit is filed.[36]

RULE 25(d)—PUBLIC OFFICERS; DEATH OR SEPARATION FROM OFFICE

CORE CONCEPT

Public office holders (e.g., the President, the Director of EPA or FDA, a governor, or a mayor) often sue or are sued in their official capacities. In other words, the lawsuit may be captioned with the officeholder's name ("U.S. Department of Agriculture Secretary Robert Jones, plaintiff" or "Governor Sally Smith, defendant"), even though the lawsuit is actually asserting a claim by or against the office that person occupies. In such official capacity lawsuits, when the named public officer dies, resigns, or otherwise ceases to hold that office, the successor is substituted automatically into the lawsuit and the case continues.

APPLICATIONS

Applies in Official Capacity Lawsuits Only

This automatic substitution procedure applies only when public officers are named as parties in their official capacities. It does not control substitution where those persons (who happen to be public officers) are suing or being sued personally.[37]

Procedure for Substitution—No Motion Necessary

Because the substitution under Rule 25(d) occurs automatically, there is no need to file or serve a motion seeking the

---

[34] *See Rodriguez-Miranda v. Benin*, 829 F.3d 29 (1st Cir. 2016).

[35] *See For Senior Help, LLC v. Westchester Fire Ins. Co.*, 515 F. Supp. 3d 787, 809 (M.D. Tenn. 2021); *Blachy v. Butcher*, 221 F.3d 896, 911 (6th Cir. 2000).

[36] *See F.D.I.C. v. Deglau*, 207 F.3d 153, 159 (3d Cir. 2000). *But see For Senior Help, LLC v. Westchester Fire Ins. Co.*, 515 F. Supp. 3d 787, 809 (M.D. Tenn. 2021) (bankruptcy trustee could be substituted as the real party in interest under Rule 17(a)(3) or Rule 25(c)).

[37] *See Soc'y of Separationists v. Pleasant Grove City*, 416 F.3d 1239, 1241 n.2 (10th Cir. 2005) (absence of claims against defendants personally makes substitution of successors proper, because suit was brought against elected officials in their official capacity). *Cf.*, *Bunn v. Conley*, 309 F.3d 1002, 1009 (7th Cir. 2002) (Bivens claim is suit against government officer in individual (not official) capacity; thus newly appointed officer cannot be substituted for officer originally sued in individual capacity).

substitution.[38]

- *Timing:* For the same reason that no motion is necessary under Rule 25(d), Rule 25(d) imposes no time requirements.

Order of Substitution

The court has discretion to order that a new public officer be substituted for a predecessor but need not do so. Whether the court does so or not, the automatic substitution will have already occurred.[39]

Substitutions in the Style of the Case

Proceedings subsequent to the substitution shall be in the name of the substituted party. However, this directive is usually no more than a formality, for no consequence attaches to the continued erroneous use of the name of the original party—unless such error somehow has an adverse effect on the case.[40]

Effect of Automatic Substitution—Survival of the Action

An action by or against a public officer does not abate when the incumbent officer leaves his or her post and substitution occurs.[41]

Events Prior to Substitution: Stipulations, Admissions, Etc.

The substituted successor official is bound by the results of previous events in the case.[42]

Additional Research References

Wright & Miller, *Federal Practice and Procedure* §§ 1951 to 62
3B J. Moore & J. Kennedy, Moore's Federal Practice ¶ 25.06 (2d ed. 1982)
C.J.S., Federal Civil Procedure §§ 156 to 168 et seq.
West's Key Number Digest, Federal Civil Procedure ⟹351 to 366, 391

---

[38] *Cheney v. U.S. Dist. Court for Dist. of Columbia*, 541 U.S. 913, 916 (2004); *Bilal v. Geo Care, LLC*, 981 F.3d 903, 918 (11th Cir. 2020).

[39] *See Shakman v. Democratic Org. of Cook Cnty.*, 919 F.2d 455, 456 (7th Cir. 1990).

[40] *See Cable v. Ivy Tech State Coll.*, 200 F.3d 467, 475 (7th Cir. 1999); *Presbytery of New Jersey of Orthodox Presbyterian Church v. Florio*, 40 F.3d 1454, 1458 (3d Cir. 1994).

[41] *See Saldana-Sanchez v. Lopez-Gerena*, 256 F.3d 1, 10, (1st Cir. 2001).

[42] *See Morales Feliciano v. Rullan*, 303 F.3d 1, 7–8 (1st Cir. 2002).

V. DISCLOSURES AND DISCOVERY

RULE 26
DUTY TO DISCLOSE; GENERAL PROVISIONS GOVERNING DISCOVERY

(a) **Required Disclosures.**

(1) *Initial Disclosure.*

(A) *In General.* Except as exempted by Rule 26(a)(1)(B) or as otherwise stipulated or ordered by the court, a party must, without awaiting a discovery request, provide to the other parties:

(i) the name and, if known, the address and telephone number of each individual likely to have discoverable information—along with the subjects of that information—that the disclosing party may use to support its claims or defenses, unless the use would be solely for impeachment;

(ii) a copy—or a description by category and location—of all documents, electronically stored information, and tangible things that the disclosing party has in its possession, custody, or control and may use to support its claims or defenses, unless the use would be solely for impeachment;

(iii) a computation of each category of damages claimed by the disclosing party—who must also make available for inspection and copying as under Rule 34 the documents or other evidentiary material, unless privileged or protected from disclosure, on which each computation is based, including materials bearing on the nature and extent of injuries suffered; and

(iv) for inspection and copying as under Rule 34, any insurance agreement under which an insurance business may be liable to satisfy all or part of a possible judgment in the action or to indemnify or reimburse for payments made to satisfy the judgment.

(B) *Proceedings Exempt from Initial Disclosure.* The following proceedings are exempt from initial disclosure:

(i) an action for review on an administrative record;

(ii) a forfeiture action in rem arising from a federal statute;

(iii) a petition for habeas corpus or any other proceeding to challenge a criminal conviction or sentence;

(iv) an action brought without an attorney by a person in the custody of the United States, a state, or a state subdivision;

(v) an action to enforce or quash an administrative summons or subpoena;

(vi) an action by the United States to recover benefit payments;

(vii) an action by the United States to collect on a student loan guaranteed by the United States;

(viii) a proceeding ancillary to a proceeding in another court; and

(ix) an action to enforce an arbitration award.

(C) *Time for Initial Disclosures—In General.* A party must make the initial disclosures at or within 14 days after the parties' Rule 26(f) conference unless a different time is set by stipulation or court order, or unless a party objects during the conference that initial disclosures are not appropriate in this action and states the objection in the proposed discovery plan. In ruling on the objection, the court must determine what disclosures, if any, are to be made and must set the time for disclosure.

(D) *Time for Initial Disclosures—For Parties Served or Joined Later.* A party that is first served or otherwise joined after the Rule 26(f) conference must make the initial disclosures within 30 days after being served or joined, unless a different time is set by stipulation or court order.

(E) *Basis for Initial Disclosure; Unacceptable Excuses.* A party must make its initial disclosures based on the information then reasonably available to it. A party is not excused from making its disclosures because it has not fully investigated the case or because it challenges the sufficiency of another party's disclosures or because another party has not made its disclosures.

(2) *Disclosure of Expert Testimony.*

(A) *In General.* In addition to the disclosures required by Rule 26(a)(1), a party must disclose to the other parties the identity of any witness it may use at trial to present evidence under Federal Rule of Evidence 702, 703, or 705.

(B) *Witnesses Who Must Provide a Written Report.* Unless otherwise stipulated or ordered by the court, this disclosure must be accompanied by a written report—prepared and signed by the witness—if the witness is one retained or specially employed to provide expert testimony in the case or one whose duties as the party's employee regularly involve giving expert testimony. The report must contain:

(i) a complete statement of all opinions the witness will express and the basis and reasons for them;

(ii) the facts or data considered by the witness in forming them;

(iii) any exhibits that will be used to summarize or support them;

(iv) the witness's qualifications, including a list of all publications authored in the previous 10 years;

(v) a list of all other cases in which, during the previous 4 years, the witness testified as an expert at trial or by deposition; and

(vi) a statement of the compensation to be paid for the study and testimony in the case.

(C) *Witnesses Who Do Not Provide a Written Report.* Unless otherwise stipulated or ordered by the court, if the witness is not required to provide a written report, this disclosure must state:

(i) the subject matter on which the witness is expected to present evidence under Federal Rule of Evidence 702, 703, or 705; and

(ii) a summary of the facts and opinions to which the witness is expected to testify.

(D) *Time to Disclose Expert Testimony.* A party must make these disclosures at the times and in the sequence that the court orders. Absent a stipulation or a court order, the disclosures must be made:

(i) at least 90 days before the date set for trial or for the case to be ready for trial; or

(ii) if the evidence is intended solely to contradict or rebut evidence on the same subject matter identified by another party under Rule 26(a)(2)(B) or (C), within 30 days after the other party's disclosure.

(E) *Supplementing the Disclosure.* The parties must supplement these disclosures when required under Rule 26(e).

(3) *Pretrial Disclosures.*

(A) *In General.* In addition to the disclosures required by Rule 26(a)(1) and (2), a party must provide to the other parties and promptly file the following information about the evidence that it may present at trial other than solely for impeachment:

(i) the name and, if not previously provided, the address and telephone number of each witness—separately identifying those the party expects to present and those it may call if the need arises;

(ii) the designation of those witnesses whose

testimony the party expects to present by deposition and, if not taken stenographically, a transcript of the pertinent parts of the deposition; and

(iii) an identification of each document or other exhibit, including summaries of other evidence—separately identifying those items the party expects to offer and those it may offer if the need arises.

(B) *Time for Pretrial Disclosures; Objections.* Unless the court orders otherwise, these disclosures must be made at least 30 days before trial. Within 14 days after they are made, unless the court sets a different time, a party may serve and promptly file a list of the following objections: any objections to the use under Rule 32(a) of a deposition designated by another party under Rule 26(a)(3)(A)(ii); and any objection, together with the grounds for it, that may be made to the admissibility of materials identified under Rule 26(a)(3)(A)(iii). An objection not so made—except for one under Federal Rule of Evidence 402 or 403—is waived unless excused by the court for good cause.

(4) *Form of Disclosures.* Unless the court orders otherwise, all disclosures under Rule 26(a) must be in writing, signed, and served.

(b) **Discovery Scope and Limits.**

(1) *Scope in General.* Unless otherwise limited by court order, the scope of discovery is as follows: Parties may obtain discovery regarding any nonprivileged matter that is relevant to any party's claim or defense and proportional to the needs of the case, considering the importance of the issues at stake in the action, the amount in controversy, the parties' relative access to relevant information, the parties' resources, the importance of the discovery in resolving the issues, and whether the burden or expense of the proposed discovery outweighs its likely benefit. Information within this scope of discovery need

not be admissible in evidence to be discoverable.

(2) *Limitations on Frequency and Extent.*

(A) *When Permitted.* By order, the court may alter the limits in these rules on the number of depositions and interrogatories or on the length of depositions under Rule 30. By order or local rule, the court may also limit the number of requests under Rule 36.

(B) *Specific Limitations on Electronically Stored Information.* A party need not provide discovery of electronically stored information from sources that the party identifies as not reasonably accessible because of undue burden or cost. On motion to compel discovery or for a protective order, the party from whom discovery is sought must show that the information is not reasonably accessible because of undue burden or cost. If that showing is made, the court may nonetheless order discovery from such sources if the requesting party shows good cause, considering the limitations of Rule 26(b)(2)(C). The court may specify conditions for the discovery.

(C) *When Required.* On motion or on its own, the court must limit the frequency or extent of discovery otherwise allowed by these rules or by local rule if it determines that:

(i) the discovery sought is unreasonably cumulative or duplicative, or can be obtained from some other source that is more convenient, less burdensome, or less expensive;

(ii) the party seeking discovery has had ample opportunity to obtain the information by discovery in the action; or

(iii) the proposed discovery is outside the scope permitted by Rule 26(b)(1).

(3) *Trial Preparation: Materials.*

(A) *Documents and Tangible Things.* Ordinarily, a party may not discover documents and tangible things that are prepared in anticipation of litigation or for trial by or for another party or its representative (including the other party's attorney, consultant, surety, indemnitor, insurer, or agent). But, subject to Rule 26(b)(4), those materials may be discovered if:

(i) they are otherwise discoverable under Rule 26(b)(1); and

(ii) the party shows that it has substantial need for the materials to prepare its case and cannot, without undue hardship, obtain their substantial equivalent by other means.

(B) *Protection Against Disclosure.* If the court orders discovery of those materials, it must protect against disclosure of the mental impressions, conclusions, opinions, or legal theories of a party's attorney or other representative concerning the litigation.

(C) *Previous Statement.* Any party or other person may, on request and without the required showing, obtain the person's own previous statement about the action or its subject matter. If the request is refused, the person may move for a court order, and Rule 37(a)(5) applies to the award of expenses. A previous statement is either:

(i) a written statement that the person has signed or otherwise adopted or approved; or

(ii) a contemporaneous stenographic, mechanical, electrical, or other recording—or a transcription of it—that recites substantially verbatim the person's oral statement.

(4) *Trial Preparation: Experts.*

(A) *Deposition of an Expert Who May Testify.* A party may depose any person who has been identified as an expert whose opinions may be presented at trial. If Rule 26(a)(2)(B) requires a report from the expert, the deposition may be conducted only after the report is provided.

(B) *Trial-Preparation Protection for Draft Reports or Disclosures.* Rules 26(b)(3)(A) and (B) protect drafts of any report or disclosure required under Rule 26(a)(2), regardless of the form in which the draft is recorded.

(C) *Trial-Preparation Protection for Communications Between a Party's Attorney and Expert Witnesses.* Rules 26(b)(3)(A) and (B) protect communications between the party's attorney and any witness required to provide a report under Rule 26(a)(2)(B), regardless of the form of the communications, except to the extent that the communications:

(i) relate to compensation for the expert's study or testimony;

(ii) identify facts or data that the party's attorney provided and that the expert considered in forming the opinions to be expressed; or

(iii) identify assumptions that the party's attorney provided and that the expert relied on in forming the opinions to be expressed.

(D) *Expert Employed Only for Trial Preparation.* Ordinarily, a party may not, by interrogatories or deposition, discover facts known or opinions held by an expert who has been retained or specially employed by another party in anticipation of litigation or to prepare for trial and who is not expected to be called as a witness at trial. But a party may do so only:

(i) as provided in Rule 35(b); or

(ii) on showing exceptional circumstances under which it is impracticable for the party to obtain facts or opinions on the same subject by other means.

(E) *Payment.* Unless manifest injustice would result, the court must require that the party seeking discovery:

(i) pay the expert a reasonable fee for time spent in responding to discovery under Rule 26(b)(4)(A) or (D); and

(ii) for discovery under (D), also pay the other party a fair portion of the fees and expenses it reasonably incurred in obtaining the expert's facts and opinions.

(5) *Claiming Privilege or Protecting Trial-Preparation Materials.*

(A) *Information Withheld.* When a party withholds information otherwise discoverable by claiming that the information is privileged or subject to protection as trial-preparation material, the party must:

(i) expressly make the claim; and

(ii) describe the nature of the documents, communications, or tangible things not produced or disclosed—and do so in a manner that, without revealing information itself privileged or protected, will enable other parties to assess the claim.

(B) *Information Produced.* If information produced in discovery is subject to a claim of privilege or of protection as trial-preparation material, the party making the claim may notify any party that received the information of the claim and the basis for it. After being notified, a party must promptly return, sequester, or destroy the specified information and any copies it has; must not use or disclose the information until the claim is resolved; must take reasonable steps to retrieve the information if the party disclosed it before being notified; and may promptly present the information to the court under seal for a determination of the claim. The producing party must preserve the information until the claim is resolved.

(c) **Protective Orders.**

(1) *In General.* A party or any person from whom discovery is sought may move for a protective order in the court where the action is pending—or as an alternative on matters relating to a deposition, in the court for the district where the deposition will be taken. The motion must include a certification that the movant has in good faith conferred or attempted to confer with other affected parties in an effort to resolve the dispute without court action. The court may, for good cause, issue an order to protect a party or person

from annoyance, embarrassment, oppression, or undue burden or expense, including one or more of the following:

(A) forbidding the disclosure or discovery;

(B) specifying terms, including time and place or the allocation of expenses, for the disclosure or discovery;

(C) prescribing a discovery method other than the one selected by the party seeking discovery;

(D) forbidding inquiry into certain matters, or limiting the scope of disclosure or discovery to certain matters;

(E) designating the persons who may be present while the discovery is conducted;

(F) requiring that a deposition be sealed and opened only on court order;

(G) requiring that a trade secret or other confidential research, development, or commercial information not be revealed or be revealed only in a specified way; and

(H) requiring that the parties simultaneously file specified documents or information in sealed envelopes, to be opened as the court directs.

(2) *Ordering Discovery.* If a motion for a protective order is wholly or partly denied, the court may, on just terms, order that any party or person provide or permit discovery.

(3) *Awarding Expenses.* Rule 37(a)(5) applies to the award of expenses.

(d) **Timing and Sequence of Discovery.**

(1) *Timing.* A party may not seek discovery from any source before the parties have conferred as required by Rule 26(f), except in a proceeding exempted from initial disclosure under Rule 26(a)(1)(B), or when authorized by these rules, by stipulation, or by court order.

(2) *Early Rule 34 Requests.*

(A) *Time to Deliver.* More than 21 days after the summons and complaint are served on a party, a request under Rule 34 may be delivered:

(i) to that party by any other party, and

(ii) by that party to any plaintiff or to any other party that has been served.

(B) *When Considered Served.* The request is considered to have been served at the first Rule 26(f) conference.

(3) *Sequence.* Unless the parties stipulate or the court orders otherwise for the parties' and witnesses' convenience and in the interests of justice:

(A) methods of discovery may be used in any sequence; and

(B) discovery by one party does not require any other party to delay its discovery.

(e) **Supplementing Disclosures and Responses.**

(1) *In General.* A party who has made a disclosure under Rule 26(a)—or who has responded to an interrogatory, request for production, or request for admission—must supplement or correct its disclosure or response:

(A) in a timely manner if the party learns that in some material respect the disclosure or response is incomplete or incorrect, and if the additional or corrective information has not otherwise been made known to the other parties during the discovery process or in writing; or

(B) as ordered by the court.

(2) *Expert Witness.* For an expert whose report must be disclosed under Rule 26(a)(2)(B), the party's duty to supplement extends both to information included in the report and to information given during the expert's deposition. Any additions or changes to this information must be disclosed by the time the party's pretrial disclosures under Rule 26(a)(3) are due.

(f) **Conference of the Parties; Planning for Discovery.**

(1) *Conference Timing.* Except in a proceeding exempted from initial disclosure under Rule 26(a)(1)(B) or when the court orders otherwise, the parties must confer as soon as practicable—and in any event at least 21 days before a

scheduling conference is to be held or a scheduling order is due under Rule 16(b).

(2) *Conference Content; Parties' Responsibilities.* In conferring, the parties must consider the nature and basis of their claims and defenses and the possibilities for promptly settling or resolving the case; make or arrange for the disclosures required by Rule 26(a)(1); discuss any issues about preserving discoverable information; and develop a proposed discovery plan. The attorneys of record and all unrepresented parties that have appeared in the case are jointly responsible for arranging the conference, for attempting in good faith to agree on the proposed discovery plan, and for submitting to the court within 14 days after the conference a written report outlining the plan. The court may order the parties or attorneys to attend the conference in person.

(3) *Discovery Plan.* A discovery plan must state the parties' views and proposals on:

(A) what changes should be made in the timing, form, or requirement for disclosures under Rule 26(a), including a statement of when initial disclosures were made or will be made;

(B) the subjects on which discovery may be needed, when discovery should be completed, and whether discovery should be conducted in phases or be limited to or focused on particular issues;

(C) any issues about disclosure, discovery, or preservation of electronically stored information, including the form or forms in which it should be produced;

(D) any issues about claims of privilege or of protection as trial-preparation materials, including—if the parties agree on a procedure to assert these claims after production—whether to ask the court to include their agreement in an order under Federal Rule of Evidence 502;

(E) what changes should be made in the limitations on discovery imposed under these rules or by local rule, and what other limitations should be imposed; and

(F) any other orders that the court should issue under Rule 26(c) or under Rule 16(b) and (c).

(4) *Expedited Schedule.* If necessary to comply with its expedited schedule for Rule 16(b) conferences, a court may by local rule:

(A) require the parties' conference to occur less than 21 days before the scheduling conference is held or a scheduling order is due under Rule 16(b); and

(B) require the written report outlining the discovery plan to be filed less than 14 days after the parties' conference, or excuse the parties from submitting a written report and permit them to report orally on their discovery plan at the Rule 16(b) conference.

(g) **Signing Disclosures and Discovery Requests, Responses, and Objections.**

(1) *Signature Required; Effect of Signature.* Every disclosure under Rule 26(a)(1) or (a)(3) and every discovery request, response, or objection must be signed by at least one attorney of record in the attorney's own name—or by the party personally, if unrepresented—and must state the signer's address, e-mail address, and telephone number. By signing, an attorney or party certifies that to the best of the person's knowledge, information, and belief formed after a reasonable inquiry:

(A) with respect to a disclosure, it is complete and correct as of the time it is made; and

(B) with respect to a discovery request, response, or objection, it is:

(i) consistent with these rules and warranted by existing law or by a nonfrivolous argument for extending, modifying, or reversing existing law, or for establishing new law;

(ii) not interposed for any improper purpose, such as to harass, cause unnecessary delay, or needlessly increase the cost of litigation; and

(iii) neither unreasonable nor unduly burdensome or expensive, considering the needs of the case, prior discovery in the case, the amount in controversy, and the importance of the issues at stake in the action.

(2) *Failure to Sign.* Other parties have no duty to act on an unsigned disclosure, request, response, or objection until it is signed, and the court must strike it unless a signature is promptly supplied after the omission is called to the attorney's or party's attention.

(3) *Sanction for Improper Certification.* If a certification violates this rule without substantial justification, the court, on motion or on its own, must impose an appropriate sanction on the signer, the party on whose behalf the signer was acting, or both. The sanction may include an order to pay the reasonable expenses, including attorney's fees, caused by the violation.

[Amended December 27, 1946, effective March 19, 1948; January 21, 1963, effective July 1, 1963; February 28, 1966, effective July 1, 1966; March 30, 1970, effective July 1, 1970; April 29, 1980, effective August 1, 1980; April 28, 1983, effective August 1, 1983; March 2, 1987, effective August 1, 1987; April 22, 1993, effective December 1, 1993; April 17, 2000, effective December 1, 2000; April 12, 2006, effective December 1, 2006; April 30, 2007, effective December 1, 2007; April 28, 2010, effective December 1, 2010; April 29, 2015, effective December 1, 2015.]

AUTHORS' COMMENTARY ON RULE 26

PURPOSE AND SCOPE

Of all the discovery rules, Rule 26 is the most important—it is the omnibus rule that controls the parameters for all of the discovery devices set forth in the discovery section of the Rules. And maybe the most important provision in Rule 26 is Rule 26(b)(1), which defines the scope of discovery for all the discovery procedures as "any nonprivileged matter that is relevant to any party's claim or defense and proportional to the needs of the case." That one clause clarifies that privileged matter like attorney-client communications are exempt from discovery, requires that matter be relevant to a claim or defense already in the case to be discoverable, and introduces the concept of proportionality—balancing the benefits and burdens of discovery.

In addition to this balancing, Rule 26 establishes a variety of limitations and protections for the participants in discovery. Rule 26(b) limits discovery that is unreasonably cumulative or duplicative, or that can be obtained from another source that is more convenient or less burdensome or expensive. The rule also contains some protections specific to electronically stored information or ESI.

Rule 26(b) also houses a number of provisions relating to information shielded by privilege or related doctrine. Although a party need not provide privileged matter during discovery, the party asserting the privilege must advise the opposing party of the privilege assertion and must describe the circumstances justifying the privilege assertion. This information is typically provided in a "privilege log" that describes details like the author of the privileged document, the recipients, the date of its creation, and the subject matter. These privileges typically come from the applicable body of law governing the claims in the action, but Rule 26(b) also creates a protection for "trial preparation materials," much like the common law work product doctrine, that functions much like a privilege. This protection for trial preparation materials applies to all cases proceeding in federal court, regardless of whether they are governed by federal or State substantive law.

The protections for privileged communications and trial preparation materials are automatic, but Rule 26(c) also contains provisions that authorize the court, in its discretion, to impose other limitations by issuing "protective orders." On motion, and for "good cause," the court may issue a protective order forbidding or limiting the specified discovery, protecting the manner in which sensitive trade secret or confidential information is handled, or shielding a party from the burdens of discovery in a whole host of other manners.

In order to make the discovery process flow more smoothly, Rule 26(f) requires the parties to conduct a discovery conference before they commence discovery. At this conference, the parties discuss a list of topics related to the discovery process, such as the amount of time they will need for discovery, adjustments to the limits on the number of interrogatories and depositions, and potential issues that they anticipate in connection with the discovery of ESI. The parties then prepare a report of their conference and send it to the judge, who uses the report to frame the initial case management order setting the dates and parameters for discovery.

In general, the parties may not commence discovery until they have conducted their discovery conference. After the conference, though, they may conduct discovery in any sequence they choose, and one party is not constrained by the discovery conducted by the other party (meaning that, just because Party A chooses to conduct written discovery first before proceeding to depositions, Party B is not prohibited from starting with depositions right from the outset).

Most discovery occurs pursuant to affirmative request by one party to another, but Rule 26(a) contains three exceptions—stages at which parties must make disclosures automatically, without waiting for a request from another party. The first automatic disclosure occurs at the beginning of a case, when each party must disclose the documents and witnesses the party intends to use to support its own claims or defenses. The second occurs in the middle of the case, when the parties must disclose expert reports describing the opinions their experts will offer. The final automatic disclosure occurs shortly before trial, when each party discloses information related to the trial, like the witnesses and exhibits they intend to offer.

In recognition that all of the information may not be immediately available at the outset of the lawsuit, Rule 26(e) imposes an ongoing obligation to supplement these disclosures and the other discovery responses. This duty to supplement applies to disclosures and responses that the party learns were incomplete or inaccurate when made and also extends to responses that were originally accurate but that have become inaccurate or incomplete over time.

Finally, Rule 26 contains a parallel provision to Rule 11 (which requires that each pleading, motion, brief, and other non-discovery document submitted to the court be signed, certifying that the document is supported by fact and law and is not being filed for an improper purpose). Rule 26(g) requires that each discovery document be signed. It provides that the signature constitutes a certification that: disclosures and discovery responses are complete and correct; that objections are based on existing law or a nonfrivolous argument for modifying the law; that the discovery or response is not intended to harass, delay, or drive up the cost of litigation; and that the discovery is not unreasonable or unduly burdensome or expensive.

NOTE: Rule 26 was substantially revised in 2000, 2006, 2007, 2010, and 2015, so care should be exercised when citing or relying on older decisions pertaining to Rule 26.

RULE 26(a)—REQUIRED DISCLOSURES

CORE CONCEPT

Rule 26(a) requires that parties disclose certain information automatically, without the need for discovery requests, at three points during the litigation. First, all parties must make broad initial disclosures at or shortly after they conduct the discovery meeting under Rule 26(f). Second, all parties must make disclosures about expert testimony 90 days before trial. Third, all parties must make the pretrial disclosures 30 days before trial. These disclosure deadlines are often modified by court order.

RULE 26(a)(1)—INITIAL DISCLOSURE

CORE CONCEPT

At the commencement of discovery, each party must disclose: 1) the identity of individuals with discoverable information that the party may use to support *its own* claims or defenses; 2) a copy of the documents that the party may use to support *its own* claims or defenses or a description of those documents by category and location; 3) a computation of each category of damages with supporting documentation; and 4) insurance information.

APPLICATIONS

Time for Initial Disclosure

Parties must make their initial disclosures at or within 14 days after the discovery meeting required by Rule 26(f), unless a different time is set by court order or stipulation.[1] Parties joined or served after the Rule 26(f) conference must make the initial disclosures within 30 days after being joined or served, unless a different time is set by stipulation or court order.

Thus, Rule 26 establishes the following typical sequence for the early discovery events:

- First, the court may schedule an initial scheduling conference and must issue an initial scheduling order;
- Second, the parties conduct their Rule 26(f) discovery meeting at least 21 days before the court's initial scheduling conference or the due date for the scheduling order and submit a report to the court;
- Third, the parties make their voluntary disclosures by, at the latest, 14 days after their Rule 26(f) discovery meeting;
- Fourth, in cases where the court conducts an initial scheduling conference, the parties meet with the judge for the scheduling conference to discuss the timetable for the balance of the discovery events; and
- Finally, the court issues its initial scheduling order.

Disclosures Automatic

The initial disclosures are automatically required, without any need for a request or demand.[2]

Service and Filing

Initial disclosures are served on the other parties but are not filed unless they are used in the proceedings or the court

---

[1] *Novak v. Board of Trustees of Southern Illinois University*, 777 F.3d 966, 972 (7th Cir. 2015) (disclosure by court set deadline); *R & R Sails, Inc. v. Ins. Co. of Pennsylvania*, 673 F.3d 1240, 1246 (9th Cir. 2012).

[2] *See Higgs v. Costa Crociere S.P.A. Co.*, 969 F.3d 1295, 1305 (11th Cir. 2020).

orders filing.[3]

Content of Initial Disclosure

Rule 26(a)(1) requires automatic initial disclosure of four categories of information:

(i) *Potential Witnesses*: Parties must disclose the name, and if known the address and telephone number,[4] of each individual likely to have discoverable[5] information that the disclosing party may[6] use to support *its own claims or defenses*.[7] Parties must also identify the subjects of such information.[8]

(ii) *Documents*: Parties must provide a copy of, or a description by category and location[9] of, all documents, electronically stored information, and tangible things[10] that the disclosing party may use to support *its own claims or defenses*.[11] Except in cases with very few documents, parties will often disclose categories and locations rather than producing all the documents.[12] Opposing parties who want copies of documents disclosed by description of category and location must request them in discovery.[13] Parties must provide or describe all disclosable documents in

---

[3]*See* Rule 5(d)(1); *Laslovich v. State Farm Fire and Cas. Co.*, 307 F.R.D. 533, 537 (D. Mont. 2015).

[4]*Tamas v. Family Video Movie Club, Inc.*, 304 F.R.D. 543, 545 (N.D. Ill. 2015) (address); *Lawrence v. Hoban Mgmt., Inc.*, 103 F. Supp. 3d 1216, 1218 (S.D. Cal. 2015) (phone number).

[5]*King v. Akima Glob. Servs., LLC*, 323 F.R.D. 403 (S.D. Fla. 2017) (witnesses with hearsay information must be disclosed because the information is discoverable, even if potentially inadmissible).

[6]*Guzman v. Bridgepoint Educ., Inc.*, 305 F.R.D. 594, 605 (S.D. Cal. 2015) (disclosure required of witnesses the party "may" call, not that the party "intends" to call).

[7]*Doe v. Young*, 664 F.3d 727, 734 (8th Cir. 2011); *City of Chicago v. Purdue Pharma L.P.*, 2017 WL 2819948 (N.D. Ill. 2017) (use refers to using the *witness*, not witnesses with *information* the party may use).

[8]*Harriman v. Hancock County*, 627 F.3d 22, 29 (1st Cir. 2010); *McGovern v. George Washington Univ.*, 25 F. Supp. 3d 167, 178 (D.D.C. 2017) (list of topics sufficient).

[9]*Axis Ins. Co. v. Am. Specialty Ins. & Risk Servs., Inc.*, 340 F.R.D. 570, 574 (N.D. Ind. 2021); *Lopez v. Don Herring Ltd.*, 327 F.R.D. 567, 589 (N.D. Tex. 2018) (no obligation to produce the documents if described by category and location).

[10]*Alifax Holding Spa v. Alcor Sci. Inc.*, 404 F. Supp. 3d 552, 566 (D.R.I. 2019); *U.S. United Ocean Serv., LLC v. Powerhouse Diesel Serv., Inc.*, 999 F. Supp. 2d 1235, 1241 (E.D. La. 2013).

[11]*Burdyn v. Old Forge Borough*, 330 F.R.D. 399, 407 (M.D. Pa. 2019); *ArcelorMittal Indiana Harbor LLC v. Amex Nooter, LLC*, 320 F.R.D. 455, 460 (N.D. Ind. 2017) (duty extends to documents to be used in a motion or during discovery, as well as to at trial).

[12]*Ingenco Holdings, LLC v. Ace Am. Ins. Co.*, 921 F.3d 803, 821 (9th Cir. 2019); *City of Chicago v. Purdue Pharma L.P.*, 2017 WL 2819948 (N.D. Ill. 2017) (noting the lack of case law regarding the degree of specificity required).

[13]*Mission Toxicology, LLC v. UnitedHealthcare Ins. Co.*, 499 F. Supp. 3d 338, 344 (W.D. Tex. 2020).

their "possession, custody, or control."[14] See Rule 34 for a discussion of the meaning of that phrase.

(iii) *Damages Computations*: Each party must provide a computation—not just the totals[15] or an estimate[16]—of any category of damages claimed by that party.[17] This requirement typically applies to plaintiffs, but also applies to defendants seeking damages in a counterclaim or crossclaim.[18] The Advisory Committee notes refer to parties claiming "damages or other monetary relief,"[19] but the courts are divided as to whether equitable claims for monetary relief are covered by the initial disclosure requirement.[20] The requirement only applies to damages that are capable of calculation, not to subjective damages like emotional distress or pain and suffering.[21] Each party must also produce the nonprivileged documents supporting the computation, including documents bearing on the nature and extent of injuries suffered.[22] The courts are divided as to whether the disclosure needs to include a computation of attorney's fees.[23]

(iv) *Insurance*: Each party must provide all insurance policies that may provide coverage for part or all of any judgment that might be entered in the action,[24] including reinsurance agreements.[25]

Use Not Limited to Use at Trial

The disclosure of witnesses and documents that a party

[14] *See Merechka v. Vigilant Ins. Co.*, 26 F.4th 776, 788 (8th Cir. 2022).

[15] *Gym Door Repairs, Inc. v. Young Equip. Sales, Inc.*, 331 F. Supp. 3d 221, 237–38 (S.D.N.Y. 2018).

[16] *Foodbuy, LLC v. Gregory Packaging, Inc.*, 987 F.3d 102, 117 (4th Cir. 2021).

[17] *MLC Intell. Prop., LLC v. Micron Tech., Inc.*, 10 F.4th 1358, 1371 (Fed. Cir. 2021); *Karum Holdings LLC v. Lowe's Companies, Inc.*, 895 F.3d 944, 951 (7th Cir. 2018) (disclosure of damages model).

[18] *HCG Platinum, LLC v. Preferred Prod. Placement Corp.*, 873 F.3d 1191, 1201 (10th Cir. 2017) (counterclaim).

[19] The 1993 Amendment to the Advisory Committee Note to Rule 26(a)(1).

[20] *See United States v. Honeywell Int'l Inc.*, 337 F.R.D. 456, 461 (D.D.C. 2020) (disclosure required for unjust enrichment claim); *N. Nat. Gas Co. v. L.D. Drilling, Inc.*, 405 F. Supp. 3d 981, 1002 (D. Kan. 2019) (disclosure not required for claims for disgorgement or civil penalties).

[21] *Williams v. Trader Pub. Co.*, 218 F.3d 481, 487 (5th Cir. 2000).

[22] *Bresler v. Wilmington Trust Co.*, 855 F.3d 178, 209 (4th Cir. 2017) (dissent); *Howe v. City of Akron*, 801 F.3d 718, 747 (6th Cir. 2012).

[23] *See Smith v. AS Am., Inc.*, 829 F.3d 616, 624 (8th Cir. 2016) (no obligation to disclose); *Harner v. USAA Gen. Indem. Co.*, ___ F. Supp. ___, 2022 WL 718489, at *2 (S.D. Cal. 2022) (obligation to disclose).

[24] *Sun River Energy, Inc. v. Nelson*, 800 F.3d 1219, 1222 (10th Cir. 2015).

[25] *See Diamondrock Hospitality Co. v. Certain Underwriters At Lloyd's Of London Subscribing To Policy Numbers Prpna1700847 And Prpna1702387*, 2019 WL 8883540, at *3 (V.I. Super. 2019) (collecting cases).

may "use" to support its claims or defenses is not limited to use at trial—it pertains to use to support a motion, at a pretrial conference, or in discovery as well.[26]

Only Information to Support the Disclosing Party's Claims or Defenses

Rule 26(a)(1) requires disclosure only of information and documents that the disclosing party may use to support its own claims or defenses.[27] This provision dovetails with the exclusionary sanction of Rule 37(c)(1), so that a party may not use information or documents not disclosed initially or by supplement.[28] That does not mean that information that undermines a party's claims or defenses is not discoverable, of course. Rather, to obtain information or documents that do not support a party's claims or defenses, opposing parties must serve affirmative discovery like interrogatories or document requests.[29]

Impeachment

Information and documents that a party may use "solely for impeachment" need not be disclosed.[30]

Electronically Stored Information

Rule 26(a)(1)(A)(ii) specifically requires the disclosure of the "electronically stored information" that a party may use to support its claims or defenses.[31] If electronically stored information is very costly or burdensome to disclose, a party may invoke Rule 26(b)(2) (pursuant to which a party may notify the other parties that it is not collecting and disclosing certain electronically stored information, and then either party may ask the court to determine whether the information need be disclosed).

Excluded Proceedings

Rule 26(a)(1)(B) excludes 9 categories of proceedings from the initial disclosures:

(1) appeals from administrative proceedings;[32]
(2) a forfeiture action in rem arising from a federal statute;[33]
(3) petitions for habeas corpus or like challenges to crimi-

[26]*Higgs v. Costa Crociere S.P.A. Co.*, 969 F.3d 1295, 1305 (11th Cir. 2020).

[27]*Hayes v. SkyWest Airlines, Inc.*, 12 F.4th 1186, 1202 (10th Cir. 2021).

[28]The 2000 Amendment to the Advisory Committee Note to Rule 26(a)(1).

[29]*See Hayes v. SkyWest Airlines, Inc.*, 12 F.4th 1186, 1202 (10th Cir. 2021).

[30]*Olivarez v. GEO Group, Inc.*, 844 F.3d 200, 204–05 (5th Cir. 2016) (discussing the difference between substantive and impeachment evidence); *Vaughn v. Hobby Lobby Stores, Inc.*, 539 F. Supp. 3d 577, 593 (W.D. La. 2021) (evidence that serves both substantive and impeachment functions must be disclosed).

[31]*Merechka v. Vigilant Ins. Co.*, 26 F.4th 776, 788 (8th Cir. 2022).

[32]*Bruce v. Anthem Ins. Companies, Inc.*, 307 F.R.D. 465, 466–67 (N.D. Tex. 2015) (action against an ERISA administrator not exempt from disclosure requirements).

[33]*U.S. v. Real Property Known As 200 Acres of Land Near FM 2686 Rio*

nal convictions or sentences;

(4) pro se prisoner actions;[34]

(5) actions to enforce or quash an administrative summons or subpoena;

(6) actions by the United States to recover benefit payments;

(7) actions by the United States to collect on student loans guaranteed by the United States;

(8) proceedings ancillary to proceedings in other courts;[35] and

(9) actions to enforce arbitration awards.

Disclose Information "Reasonably Available"

The parties must make their initial disclosures based on the information then "reasonably available."[36] Parties and lawyers have a duty to conduct an investigation to determine what disclosable information is reasonably available.[37]

Incomplete Investigation Not an Excuse

A party may not avoid the initial disclosure requirements by claiming that its investigation is not yet complete.[38] The Rules envision that the initial disclosure will often be incomplete, and account for this through the duty to supplement as additional information is encountered.[39]

Failure to Disclose

Failure to make the initial disclosures required by Rule 26(a)(1) may preclude the party from using the undisclosed witness or information as evidence on a motion,[40] at a hearing, or at trial,[41] unless the party failing to make the disclosure can

---

Grande City, Tex., 773 F.3d 654, 661 (5th Cir. 2014) (the exemption renders the disclosures not automatic, but the court may still impose the disclosure requirement).

[34] *Royse v. Walmart Stores, Inc.*, 59 F. Supp. 3d 293 (D. Mass. 2014).

[35] *See Mays v. United Ass'n Local 290 Apprenticeship & Journeymen Training Tr. Fund*, 407 F. Supp. 3d 1121, 1139 (D. Or. 2019).

[36] *Baker Hughes Inc. v. S&S Chem., LLC*, 836 F.3d 554, 568 (6th Cir. 2016) (no duty to disclose information not yet available); *San Francisco Baykeeper v. West Bay Sanitary Dist.*, 791 F. Supp. 2d 719, 733 (N.D. Cal. 2011) (defining "reasonably available").

[37] *Sun River Energy, Inc. v. Nelson*, 800 F.3d 1219, 1223 (10th Cir. 2015).

[38] *Hovanec v. Miller*, 331 F.R.D. 624, 633 (W.D. Tex. 2019); *Cates v. Trustees of Columbia Univ. in City of New York*, 330 F.R.D. 369, 372 (S.D.N.Y. 2019).

[39] *Morris v. BNSF Ry. Co.*, 969 F.3d 753, 765 (7th Cir. 2020).

[40] *Steffek v. Client Servs., Inc.*, 948 F.3d 761, 768 (7th Cir. 2020); *King v. Ford Motor Co.*, 872 F.3d 833, 838 (7th Cir. 2017).

[41] *Wilson v. AM General Corp.*, 167 F.3d 1114 (7th Cir.1999) (rejecting claim that the witnesses were impeachment witnesses and excluding their testimony); *Quesenberry v. Volvo Group North Am., Inc.*, 267 F.R.D. 475, 478 (W.D. Va. 2010) (no need to show that bad faith was the cause of the nondisclosure).

demonstrate[42] that the failure was harmless or there was substantial justification.[43] The court may also impose other measures to cure any prejudice from the failure to disclose.[44] Generally, providing the identity of a witness or producing the documents in discovery will not excuse failure to disclose under Rule 26(a)(1), because that does not put the other party on notice that the producing party may use that witness or those documents to support its claims or defenses.[45] For example, a party may produce a great volume of documents in discovery that it does not intend to offer affirmatively to support its positions, so merely producing a document is not the equivalent of identifying it as a document the party intends to offer.[46] However, if the full substance of the required disclosure has been conveyed in discovery, the matter will not be excluded.[47]

Other Party's Failure to Disclose

A party may not refuse to make the Rule 26(a) disclosures because another party has also failed to do so.[48] Likewise, a party believing that another party's disclosure was not sufficient must nonetheless make its own disclosures.[49] The solutions for those failures is either the automatic exclusion of undisclosed matter under Rule 37(c) or a motion to compel under Rule 37(a).

Stipulations Not to Disclose

The parties may stipulate to the elimination or modification of the initial disclosures unless precluded from doing so by local rule or court order.

Form of Disclosures

The initial disclosures should be in writing, signed, and served on other parties unless otherwise directed by local rule or court order.[50] The signature constitutes a certification that

---

[42]*See C & H Liquor Store, Inc. v. Harleysville Preferred Ins. Co.*, 413 F. Supp. 3d 1238, 1244 (N.D. Ga. 2019) (the burden is on the party seeking to use the undisclosed witness or information).

[43]*See Antrim Pharm. LLC v. Bio-Pharm, Inc.*, 950 F.3d 423, 433 (7th Cir. 2020); *Russell v. Absolute Collection Serv., Inc.*, 763 F.3d 385, 396 (4th Cir. 2014) (court has broad discretion in determining sanctions).

[44]*Foodbuy, LLC v. Gregory Packaging, Inc.*, 987 F.3d 102, 117 (4th Cir. 2021) (ordering a week-long recess to cure failure to disclose damages calculation).

[45]*Morris v. BNSF Ry. Co.*, 969 F.3d 753, 765 (7th Cir. 2020).

[46]*See Benjamin v. B & H Educ., Inc.*, 877 F.3d 1139, 1150 (9th Cir. 2017) (mention of witness in interrogatory response is insufficient).

[47]*Taylor v. Mentor Worldwide LLC*, 940 F.3d 582, 608 (11th Cir. 2019); *Kreg Therapeutics, Inc. v. VitalGo, Inc.*, 919 F.3d 405, 417 (7th Cir. 2019).

[48]*See Jacobsen v. Deseret Book Co.*, 287 F.3d 936, 954 (10th Cir. 2002); *Hovanec v. Miller*, 331 F.R.D. 624, 633 (W.D. Tex. 2019).

[49]Rule 26(a)(1)(E).

[50]*See S.E.C. v. TheStreet.Com*, 273 F.3d 222, 233 (2d Cir. 2001) (initial disclosures under Rule 26(a)(1) are not filed unless ordered by the court or

the disclosure is complete and accurate under Rule 26(g)(1).[51]

Objections to Making the Disclosures

A party believing that Rule 26(a)(1) initial disclosures are "not appropriate in the circumstances of the action" may object during the Rule 26(f) discovery conference. If not resolved, the objection should then be stated in the Rule 26(f) discovery plan filed with the court. Disclosures are not required thereafter except as ordered by the court.[52]

New or Late Served Parties

Parties who have not been joined or served at the time of the initial disclosures or the Rule 26(f) discovery conference must still make initial disclosures. The time for their disclosures will be 30 days from when they are served or joined, unless modified by stipulation or order.

Duty to Supplement

Rule 26(e) requires a party to supplement its Rule 26(a)(1) disclosure if it learns that the information was or has become incomplete or incorrect.[53]

RULE 26(a)(2)—DISCLOSURE OF EXPERT TESTIMONY

CORE CONCEPT

Each party must disclose the identity of its testifying expert witnesses and some information about their testimony. For typical retained experts, parties must disclose a detailed expert report. For non-retained experts such as treating physicians, parties must disclose a summary of the opinions to be offered by the experts.

APPLICATIONS

Which Experts

Rule 26(b)(2) divides experts into three categories. The first category includes the typical expert witness who is engaged to provide expert testimony for purposes of the litigation.[54] It also includes employees of the party who are "specially employed to provide expert testimony in the case" or "whose duties as the party's employee regularly involve giving expert testimony."[55] The second category includes experts who will testify but have

---

used in a subsequent stage of the proceedings).

[51] *Moore v. Publicis Groupe*, 287 F.R.D. 182, 188 (S.D.N.Y. 2012).

[52] The 2000 Amendment to the Advisory Committee Note to Rule 26(a)(1).

[53] *See Birch | Rea Partners, Inc. v. Regent Bank*, 27 F.4th 1245, 1253 (7th Cir. 2022); *Hayes v. SkyWest Airlines, Inc.*, 12 F.4th 1186, 1202 (10th Cir. 2021).

[54] *See, e.g., Walter Int'l Prods., Inc. v. Salinas*, 650 F.3d 1402, 1409 (11th Cir. 2011).

[55] *See, e.g., Torres v. City of Los Angeles*, 548 F.3d 1197, 1212 (9th Cir. 2008); *Prieto v. Malgor*, 361 F.3d 1313, 1318 (11th Cir. 2004).

not been engaged (and are not being paid).[56] These witnesses are sometimes called "hybrid" witnesses because they were typically involved in the underlying events and will present both fact and expert testimony.[57] Treating physicians frequently fall into this category.[58] It also includes other employees of the party who will offer expert testimony, but do not qualify under the first category.[59] Parties must disclose the identity of experts in these first two categories, plus additional information as described below.[60] The final category includes experts who will not testify, such as consulting experts.[61] Parties are generally not required to make disclosures for these non-testifying experts.[62]

- *Experts Who Provide Affidavits for Summary Judgment Motions:* Determining whether a party must disclose an expert who will provide an affidavit in connection with a motion for summary judgment entails consideration of Rule 26(a)(2) and Rule 56(c)(4), which requires that an affidavit submitted in connection with a motion for summary judgment show that the affiant is competent to testify on the matters stated in the affidavit and that the testimony would be admissible. If the expert will testify at trial and the deadline for expert disclosures has passed with no disclosure of the expert, some courts will not consider the expert's affidavit on the theory that the expert would be excluded at trial as undisclosed, and therefore the affidavit does not meet the competency and admissibility requirements of Rule 56(c)(4).[63] Other courts exclude the affidavits of undisclosed experts submitted in connection with a motion for summary judgment without discussing Rule 56(c)(4) or whether the expert could testify *at trial*.[64] If the deadline for expert disclosures has not yet passed, the rules do not,

---

[56]*See, e.g., Downey v. Bob's Disc. Furniture Holdings*, 633 F.3d 1, 6 (1st Cir. 2011).

[57]*See Timpson by & through Timpson v. Anderson Cnty. Disabilities & Special Needs Bd.*, 31 F.4th 238, 253 (4th Cir. 2022).

[58]*See Goodman v. Staples The Office Superstore, LLC*, 644 F.3d 817 (9th Cir. 2011).

[59]*See Tokai Corp. v. Easton Enterprises, Inc.*, 632 F.3d 1358, 1365 (Fed. Cir. 2011); *Prieto v. Malgor*, 361 F.3d 1313, 1318 (11th Cir. 2004).

[60]*Wallace v. Andeavor Corp.*, 916 F.3d 423, 428 (5th Cir. 2019); *Tribble v. Evangelides*, 670 F.3d 753, 758 (7th Cir. 2012).

[61]*See, e.g., R.C. Olmstead, Inc. v. CU Interface, LLC*, 606 F.3d 262, 272 (6th Cir. 2010).

[62]*See Moore v. Napolitano*, 926 F. Supp. 2d 8, 25 n.12 (D.D.C. 2013) (the "plain language of Rule 26(a)(2) limits the rule to experts who may testify at trial.").

[63]*See, e.g., Barry v. Silver*, 2011 WL 13298552, at *2 (M.D. Fla. 2011); *Lenzen v. Workers Comp. Reinsurance Ass'n*, 843 F. Supp. 2d 981, 985 (D. Minn. 2011), aff'd, 705 F.3d 816 (8th Cir. 2013).

[64]*See, e.g., Arizpe v. Principal Life Ins. Co.*, 398 F. Supp. 3d 27, 47 (N.D. Tex. 2019); *Winders v. State Farm Fire & Cas. Co.*, 359 F. Supp. 3d 1274, 1281 (N.D. Ga. 2018).

on their face, require that a party make the Rule 26(a)(2) disclosures for an expert before the party may submit an affidavit from the expert in connection with a motion for summary judgment,[65] although the court would have the authority to require the party to make the disclosures to assess admissibility or competency.

Time for Expert Disclosure

The time for expert disclosures can be set by the court[66] or stipulated by the parties. In the absence of a court order or stipulation, the expert disclosures must be made 90 days before the trial date.[67] If the expert testimony is purely to contradict or rebut testimony disclosed by another party, then the disclosure must be made within 30 days after the disclosure by the other party.[68] Leave may be obtained to disclose an expert report for an expert witness after the time for expert disclosures.[69]

Disclosures Automatic

The expert disclosures are automatically required, without any need for a request or demand.

Form of Disclosures

An expert report must be in writing and signed by the witness. An expert disclosure for a non-retained expert should be in writing and signed by the attorney.[70] The attorney's signature constitutes a certification that the disclosure is complete and accurate, as provided by Rule 26(g)(1).

Service and Filing

Expert disclosures are served on the other parties, but are not filed unless they are used in the proceedings or the court orders filing.[71]

Content of Disclosure

The disclosure must contain the identity of any witness who may provide expert testimony under the Federal Rules of Evi-

---

[65] *See Soukhaphonh v. Hot Topic, Inc.*, 2017 WL 10378493, at *2 n.2 (C.D. Cal. 2017).

[66] *See Optronic Techs., Inc. v. Ningbo Sunny Elec. Co.*, 20 F.4th 466, 488 (9th Cir. 2021); *Gonzalez-Rivera v. Centro Medico Del Turabo, Inc.*, 931 F.3d 23, 27 (1st Cir. 2019).

[67] *Karum Holdings LLC v. Lowe's Companies, Inc.*, 895 F.3d 944, 951 (7th Cir. 2018); *Lutz v. Glendale Union High School*, 403 F.3d 1061, 1071 (9th Cir. 2005) (the 90-day period applies only in the absence of a court established deadline).

[68] *U.S. v. $231,930.00 in U.S. Currency*, 614 F.3d 837, 841 (8th Cir. 2010); *Wegener v. Johnson*, 527 F.3d 687, 690–91 (8th Cir. 2008).

[69] *See Thorncreek Apartments III, LLC v. Mick*, 886 F.3d 626, 636 (7th Cir. 2018) (allowing late report); *Wegener v. Johnson*, 527 F.3d 687, 692 (8th Cir. 2008) (the court has discretion to exclude the untimely report when allowing it would require another continuance of the trial).

[70] *Karum Holdings LLC v. Lowe's Companies, Inc.*, 895 F.3d 944, 951 (7th Cir. 2018).

[71] *S.E.C. v. TheStreet.Com*, 273 F.3d 222, 233 (2d Cir. 2001).

dence governing expert testimony (primarily rules 701–705).[72] In addition to the expert's identity, parties must disclose information about the nature of the anticipated testimony. The form and level of detail required depends on whether the expert was retained or specially employed (the first category described above).

- *Content Disclosure for Retained Experts: Expert Report:* For each retained or specially employed expert, a party must disclose a written expert report[73] signed by the expert[74] (but the lawyers sometimes play a heavy role in the drafting process[75]). The report must contain:
  - ○ a complete statement of all the expert's opinions and the basis and reasons for each opinion;[76]
  - ○ the facts or data considered by the expert,[77] including documents provided by counsel[78] (but note that Rule 26(a)(2) does not require that the documents considered by the expert be attached to the report, just that they are described or disclosed in the report);[79]
  - ○ any exhibits to be used as support for or as a summary of the opinions;[80]
  - ○ the qualifications of the expert and all publications authored by the expert in the past 10 years;[81]

---

[72]*Est. of W. by W. v. Domina L. Grp., PC LLO*, 981 F.3d 652, 654 (8th Cir. 2020); *Hamburger v. State Farm Mut. Auto. Ins. Co.*, 361 F.3d 875, 883 n. 4 (5th Cir. 2004).

[73]*Timpson by & through Timpson v. Anderson Cnty. Disabilities & Special Needs Bd.*, 31 F.4th 238, 253 (4th Cir. 2022); *E.E.O.C. v. AutoZone, Inc.*, 707 F.3d 824, 833 (7th Cir. 2013).

[74]*Neiberger v. Fed Ex Ground Package System, Inc.*, 566 F.3d 1184, 1191 (10th Cir. 2009); *Svanaco, Inc. v. Brand*, 417 F. Supp. 3d 1042, 1051 n.6 (N.D. Ill. 2019) (the report must be signed but need not be sworn).

[75]*Optronic Techs., Inc. v. Ningbo Sunny Elec. Co.*, 20 F.4th 466, 477 (9th Cir. 2021); *U.S. v. Kalymon*, 541 F.3d 624, 638 (6th Cir. 2008).

[76]*Guevara v. NCL (Bahamas) Ltd.*, 920 F.3d 710, 717 (11th Cir. 2019); *U.S. ex rel. Tennessee Valley Authority v. 1.72 Acres of Land In Tennessee*, 821 F.3d 742 (6th Cir. 2016) (requiring "absolute compliance" with this requirement).

[77]*Biestek v. Berryhill*, 139 S. Ct. 1148, 1154 (2019) (expert must produce "all data"); *Guevara v. NCL (Bahamas) Ltd.*, 920 F.3d 710, 717 (11th Cir. 2019).

[78]*Fidelity Nat. Title Ins. Co. of New York v. Intercounty Nat. Title Ins. Co.*, 412 F.3d 745 (7th Cir. 2005) (party must disclose all documents "considered" by the expert, without regard to the expert's document retention policy); *In re Benicar (Olmesartan) Prod. Liab. Litig.*, 319 F.R.D. 139, 140–41 (D.N.J. 2017) (the rule requires the disclosure of all information provided to the expert, including privileged information).

[79]*Vox Mktg. Grp., LLC v. Prodigy Promos L.C.*, 521 F. Supp. 3d 1135, 1145 (D. Utah 2021).

[80]*Bradshaw v. FFE Transp. Serv., Inc.*, 715 F.3d 1104, 1109 (8th Cir. 2013); *Estate of Thompson v. Kawasaki Heavy Industries, Ltd.*, 291 F.R.D. 297, 314 (N.D. Iowa 2013) (disclosure must contain demonstrative exhibits).

[81]*Bazarian Int'l Fin. Assocs., LLC v. Desarrollos Aerohotelco, C.A.*, 315 F. Supp. 3d 101, 116 (D.D.C. 2018) (lack of detail harmless); *Paramount Media*

○ the expert's compensation for the review and testimony;[82] and

○ a list of all other cases in which the expert has testified at trial or at deposition in the past 4 years.[83]

The report itself should contain all the required information with considerable detail,[84] and may not satisfy the requirements of Rule 26(a)(2)(B) by incorporating other material.[85] At the same time, the report does not need to contain every word that the expert will use at trial, and experts are allowed to elaborate on and explain the opinions contained in the report.[86] In evaluating the sufficiency of an expert report, the court will consider the purposes of the disclosure rule—to avoid surprise and minimize the expense of deposing the expert—and the ability of the opposing party to formulate a response.[87]

- *Content Disclosure for Non-Retained Experts:* For experts who were not retained or specially employed, such as a treating physician who will offer expert opinions (the second category described above), the disclosure must contain:
  ○ the subject matter on which the expert is expected to present evidence; and
  ○ a summary of the facts and opinions to which the witness is expected to testify.[88]

Because the expert is not being paid to testify, this disclosure is typically prepared by counsel and does not need to be signed by the expert. Additionally, it can be significantly less detailed

---

Group, Inc. v. Village of Bellwood, 308 F.R.D. 162, 167 (N.D. Ill. 2015) (expert must disclose all publications, not just those deemed relevant to the litigation).

[82]*See Lopez-Ramirez v. Toledo-Gonzalez*, 32 F.4th 87, 92 (1st Cir. 2022); *FF Cosmetics FL Inc. v. City of Miami Beach*, 114 F. Supp. 3d 1257, 1259 (S.D. Fla. 2015) (report should disclose total compensation, not just hourly rate).

[83]*Paramount Media Group, Inc. v. Village of Bellwood*, 308 F.R.D. 162, 166 (N.D. Ill. 2015) (long list of names and chambers of judges inadequate); *Shukh v. Seagate Technology, LLC*, 295 F.R.D. 228, 239 (D. Minn. 2013).

[84]*Walter Intern. Prods., Inc. v. Salinas*, 650 F.3d 1402, 1410 (11th Cir. 2011) (short letter deemed inadequate); *Krischel v. Hennessy*, 533 F. Supp. 2d 790, 797–98 (N.D. Ill. 2008) (the report may not be "sketchy and vague").

[85]*Ingram v. Novartis Pharms. Corp.*, 282 F.R.D. 563, 564–65 (W.D. Okla. 2012) (references to other reports and testimony improper); *U.S. v. Alabama Power Co.*, 274 F. Supp. 2d 686, 691 (N.D. Ala. 2011) (expert cannot rely on documents identified by other experts).

[86]*Landivar v. Celebrity Cruises, Inc.*, 340 F.R.D. 192, 195 (S.D. Fla. 2022).

[87]*Landivar v. Celebrity Cruises, Inc.*, 340 F.R.D. 192, 195 (S.D. Fla. 2022); *Doe by & through Pike v. Pike*, 405 F. Supp. 3d 243, 248 (D. Mass. 2019).

[88]*Timpson by & through Timpson v. Anderson Cnty. Disabilities & Special Needs Bd.*, 31 F.4th 238, 253 (4th Cir. 2022); *Vanderberg v. Petco Animal Supplies Stores, Inc.*, 906 F.3d 698, 702 (8th Cir. 2018).

than an expert report.[89] Some courts require an expert report for non-retained experts whose testimony will go beyond their personal involvement in the events that form the basis of the litigation.[90]

Failure to Disclose

The failure to satisfy the expert disclosure requirements may preclude the party from introducing the testimony at trial, either altogether[91] or as to specific opinions not disclosed in the report.[92] Such sanctions are "automatic and mandatory"[93] unless the party failing to disclose can show the failure was justified or harmless.[94] However, when exclusion of expert testimony equates to dismissal of the action, courts are more reluctant to exclude the testimony.[95] At the same time, a party who believes that an opposing party has made an inadequate disclosure should file a motion to compel a more complete disclosure or a motion to exclude the expert promptly, because waiting until trial to raise the issue may result in waiver.[96] The courts are divided as to whether disclosure of the expert opinions or required information in discovery is a substitute for inclusion in the expert disclosure.[97] Disclosure of the witness as a fact witness is not a substitute for disclosure as an expert witness.[98]

Stipulations Not to Disclose Expert Reports

The parties may stipulate to the elimination or modification of the expert report disclosures unless precluded from doing so

---

[89] *See Gruttemeyer v. Transit Auth.*, 31 F.4th 638, 644 (8th Cir. 2022).

[90] See *Beaton v. SpeedyPC Software*, 338 F.R.D. 232, 236-37 (N.D. Ill. 2021); *White v. City of Greensboro*, 532 F. Supp. 3d 277, 298 (M.D.N.C. 2021).

[91] *Gonzalez-Rivera v. Centro Medico Del Turabo, Inc.*, 931 F.3d 23, 27 (1st Cir. 2019) (disclosure of witness identity is not sufficient); *U.S. ex rel. Tennessee Valley Authority v. 1.72 Acres of Land In Tennessee*, 821 F.3d 742 (6th Cir. 2016).

[92] *Commodores Entm't Corp. v. McClary*, 879 F.3d 1114, 1129 (11th Cir. 2018); *Boston Gas Co. v. Century Indem. Co.*, 529 F.3d 8 (1st Cir. 2008).

[93] *Novak v. Board of Trustees of Southern Illinois University*, 777 F.3d 966, 972 (7th Cir. 2015). *But see S.E.C. v. Jasper*, 678 F.3d 1116, 1124 (9th Cir. 2012) (no error in admitting document prepared by undisclosed expert where the opposing party did not object).

[94] *Martinez v. United States*, 33 F.4th 20 (1st Cir. 2022) (burden to show harmlessness is on the party failing to disclose); *Taylor v. Mentor Worldwide LLC*, 940 F.3d 582, 607 (11th Cir. 2019).

[95] *Martinez v. United States*, 33 F.4th 20 (1st Cir. 2022).

[96] *Rodrick v. Wal-Mart Stores East, L.P.*, 666 F.3d 1093, 1096 (8th Cir. 2012).

[97] *See Walter Intern. Prods., Inc. v. Salinas*, 650 F.3d 1402, 1410 (11th Cir. 2011) (a report is necessary to effectively take an expert deposition); *Smith v. Tenet Healthsystem SL, Inc.*, 436 F.3d 879, 889 (8th Cir. 2006) (expert could rely on x-rays disclosed at the deposition because failure to disclose in the report was harmless); *In re Sulfuric Acid Antitrust Litig.*, 432 F. Supp. 2d 794 (N.D. Ill. 2006) (asking about additional opinions at deposition may open the door for admission of those opinions at trial).

[98] *Karum Holdings LLC v. Lowe's Companies, Inc.*, 895 F.3d 944, 951 (7th Cir. 2018).

by local rule or court order.

Nature of Testimony is Measure, Not Witness Qualification

The expert disclosures are required if the testimony is expert in nature, not factual;[99] expert disclosures are not required if a witness with expertise is being called to give percipient factual testimony.[100]

Party Testifying as an Expert

An individual party who intends to present expert testimony must list him or herself as an expert and disclose the information required by Rule 26(a)(2)(C), but need not produce an expert report.[101]

Treating Physicians

An expert report is generally not required for a treating physician to testify regarding the treatment if the party has not retained the physician as an expert,[102] although a number of courts require an expert report when the treating physician will offer testimony beyond the scope of the treatment rendered.[103] However, parties must disclose the subject matter and a summary of the facts and opinions as to which a treating physician is expected to testify under F.R.E. 702 (pertaining to expert testimony).[104] It is unsettled whether a treating physician's factual description of the treatment constitutes F.R.E. 702 expert testimony or percipient fact testimony.[105] A physician conducting an Independent Medical Examination will generally be considered an expert for purposes of Rule 26(a)(2),[106] but the obligation to produce a report for a physician conducting an examination under Rule 35 is governed by

---

[99] *White v. Hefel*, 875 F.3d 350, 355 (7th Cir. 2017); *Dobbins v. Greyhound Lines, Inc.*, 336 F.R.D. 144, 146 (E.D. Mich. 2020).

[100] *Ryan Development Co., L.C. v. Indiana Lumbermens Mut. Ins. Co.*, 711 F.3d 1165, 1170–71 (10th Cir. 2013) (accountants permitted to testify as percipient witnesses); *Gomez v. Rivera Rodriguez*, 344 F.3d 103, 113 (1st Cir. 2003) (Rule 26(a)(2) does not encompass a percipient witness who happens to be an expert).

[101] *U.S. ex rel. Jones v. Brigham & Women's Hosp.*, 678 F.3d 72, 90 (1st Cir. 2012); *Mem'l Hall Museum, Inc. v. Cunningham*, 455 F. Supp. 3d 347, 363 (W.D. Ky. 2020).

[102] *See Merch. v. Corizon Health, Inc.*, 993 F.3d 733, 739 (9th Cir. 2021). *But see Harvey v. District of Columbia*, 798 F.3d 1042, 1056 (D.C. Cir. 2016).

[103] *See Gruttemeyer v. Transit Auth.*, 31 F.4th 638, 644 (8th Cir. 2022); *Goodman v. Staples The Office Superstore, LLC*, 644 F.3d 817, 820 (9th Cir. 2011).

[104] *See Gruttemeyer v. Transit Auth.*, 31 F.4th 638, 644 (8th Cir. 2022); *Merch. v. Corizon Health, Inc.*, 993 F.3d 733, 739 (9th Cir. 2021).

[105] *See Goodman v. Staples The Office Superstore, LLC*, 644 F.3d 817, (9th Cir. 2011) (discussing the split in authority); *Kaganovich v. McDonough*, 547 F. Supp. 3d 248, 275–78 (E.D.N.Y. 2021).

[106] *Whitney v. U.S.*, 251 F.R.D. 1 (D.D.C. 2008).

Rule 35, not by Rule 26(a)(2).[107] When an attorney has referred a client to the physician, the physician is more likely to be treated as a specially retained expert.[108]

Rebuttal and Impeachment Testimony

Parties must disclose rebuttal expert testimony just like any other expert testimony. The court usually sets the time for disclosure of rebuttal testimony, which is often 30 days after disclosure of the testimony it is rebutting.[109] Rebuttal testimony must explain, repel, counteract, or disprove evidence of the adverse party's expert;[110] courts will not allow parties to use rebuttal expert testimony to advance new arguments or new evidence that should have been part of the party's case-in-chief.[111] The courts are divided about whether expert impeachment evidence must be disclosed.[112]

Objections to Disclosures

Parties may object to expert disclosures they believe to be inadequate.[113] The court's case management order may designate a period for filing objections to the sufficiency of expert disclosures, in which case such objections are waived if not timely raised.[114]

Duty to Supplement

Rule 26(a)(2)(E) explicitly incorporates the duty under 26(e) to supplement an expert disclosure or testimony given during an expert deposition if the party learns that the information provided was incomplete or incorrect.[115] The supplement need not comply with Rule 26(a)(2) independently; rather, the combination of the original disclosure and the supplement will

---

[107] *Diaz v. Con-Way Truckload, Inc.*, 279 F.R.D. 412, 418 (S.D. Tex. 2012).

[108] *Perkins v. U.S.*, 626 F. Supp. 2d 587 (E.D. Va. 2009).

[109] *See Bradshaw v. FFE Transp. Serv., Inc.*, 715 F.3d 1104, 1106 (8th Cir. 2013); *Crawford-Brunt v. Kruskall*, 489 F. Supp. 3d 4, 7 (D. Mass. 2020).

[110] *U.S. Bank, N.A. v. Glogowski L. Firm, PLLC*, 339 F.R.D. 579, 580 (W.D. Wash. 2021); *United States ex rel. Morsell v. NortonLifeLock, Inc.*, 567 F. Supp. 3d 248, 267 (D.D.C. 2021).

[111] *Pandya v. Marriott Hotel Servs., Inc.*, 552 F. Supp. 3d 1364, 1375 (N.D. Ga. 2021); *In re Kind LLC "Healthy & All Natural" Litig.*, 337 F.R.D. 581, 607 (S.D.N.Y. 2021).

[112] *See U.S. v. $231,930.00 in U.S. Currency*, 614 F.3d 837, 841 (8th Cir. 2010) (impeachment evidence need not be disclosed); *Wegener v. Johnson*, 527 F.3d 687, 690–91 (8th Cir. 2008) (impeachment evidence must be disclosed).

[113] *Bradshaw v. FFE Transp. Serv., Inc.*, 715 F.3d 1104, 1108 (8th Cir. 2013); *Saiyed v. Council on Am.-Islamic Relations Action Network, Inc.*, 321 F.R.D. 455, 458–59 (D.D.C. 2017) (proper procedure is a motion to exclude the testimony, not a motion to strike the report).

[114] *Bradshaw v. FFE Transp. Serv., Inc.*, 715 F.3d 1104, 1108 (8th Cir. 2013).

[115] *Est. of W. by W. v. Domina L. Grp., PC LLO*, 981 F.3d 652, 654 (8th Cir. 2020); *Taylor v. Mentor Worldwide LLC*, 940 F.3d 582, 592 (11th Cir. 2019) (duty extends to information in the report or provided at deposition).

be viewed in combination.[116] Parties may not use the supplementation process to circumvent the deadline for expert disclosures and disclose information that should have been included in the original disclosure.[117] Moreover, a party may not cure a deficient expert report by supplementing it with later deposition testimony.[118] Supplemental expert information should be disclosed by the time the pretrial disclosures are made under Rule 26(a)(3), 30 days before trial unless otherwise set by the court.[119]

Social Security Administration Hearings

Expert disclosures are not required for experts testifying in Social Security Administration hearings.[120]

Experts Testifying as to Foreign Law

Expert disclosures are not required for experts testifying as to foreign law under Rule 44.1.[121]

RULE 26(a)(3)—PRETRIAL DISCLOSURES

CORE CONCEPT

Prior to trial, the parties must disclose the witnesses that they may call at trial, the deposition testimony that they may offer at trial, and the exhibits that they may offer at trial.

APPLICATIONS

Time for Pretrial Disclosure

The time for pretrial disclosures is often set by the court. In the absence of a court deadline, the pretrial disclosures must be made 30 days before the trial date.[122]

Disclosures Automatic

The pretrial disclosures are automatically required, without any need for a request or demand.

---

[116] *Microsource, LLC v. Eco World Grp., LLC*, — F. Supp. 3d —, 2022 WL 545034, at *31 (N.D. Iowa 2022).

[117] *In re Complaint of C.F. Bean L.L.C.*, 841 F.3d 365, 371 (5th Cir. 2016); *but see United States v. 4.620 Acres of Land, more or less, in Hidalgo Cnty., Texas*, 576 F. Supp. 3d 467, 486 (S.D. Tex. 2021) (allowing a supplement adding one piece of data that was previously available but inadvertently omitted from the original report).

[118] *Ciomber v. Coop. Plus, Inc.*, 527 F.3d 635, 642 (7th Cir. 2008)

[119] *Taylor v. Mentor Worldwide LLC*, 940 F.3d 582, 610 (11th Cir. 2019); *In re Complaint of C.F. Bean L.L.C.*, 841 F.3d 365, 371 (5th Cir. 2016).

[120] *Biestek v. Berryhill*, 139 S. Ct. 1148, 1154 (2019).

[121] *Clarke v. Marriott Int'l, Inc.*, 403 F. Supp. 3d 474, 480 (D.V.I. 2019).

[122] *Benjamin v. Sparks*, 986 F.3d 332, 342 (4th Cir. 2021); *Amplatz v. Country Mut. Ins. Co.*, 823 F.3d 1167, 1171 (8th Cir. 2016).

Service and Filing

Pretrial disclosures are served on the other parties and, unlike the other automatic disclosures, are also filed.[123]

Content of Pretrial Disclosure

Rule 26(a)(3) requires a pretrial disclosure of the following information:

(A) *Witnesses*: The parties must disclose the name and, unless already disclosed, the address and phone number of each witness that they may call at trial.[124] The disclosure should separately indicate those witnesses the parties *expect* to testify and those they *may call if needed*.[125] The purpose of this distinction is to give the court and the parties a realistic list of the likely witnesses while also allowing parties to protect their right to call other less likely witnesses (by listing them as "may call if needed" witnesses, avoiding the sanction of exclusion of undisclosed witnesses).

(B) *Depositions*: The parties must designate the deposition testimony that they expect to introduce.[126] Although the rule is phrased in terms of the disclosing party's "expectation," the obligation is not measured by the party's subjective expectation at that moment in time—undisclosed deposition testimony will be excluded under the terms of Rule 37(c) regardless of the party's subjective expectations.[127] If the deposition was recorded other than stenographically, then the parties must provide a transcript of the parts of the testimony they intend to introduce.[128]

(C) *Exhibits*: The parties must identify all exhibits, including demonstrative or summary exhibits, that they may use at trial. The disclosure should separately indicate those exhibits that the parties *expect* to introduce and those that they *may introduce if needed*.

Rebuttal Pretrial Disclosures

Rule 26(a)(3) does not mention rebuttal disclosures. Sometimes, these issues are addressed by the court's pretrial order or local rules. In the absence of an order or local rule on point, if an opponent's pretrial disclosure contains an unexpected witness, exhibit, or deposition designation, the best

---

[123] *See* Rule 26(a)(4).

[124] *See Wilson v. Superclub Ibiza, LLC*, 931 F. Supp. 2d 61, 63 (D.D.C. 2013) (exclusion of witness not warranted for failure to disclose address).

[125] *But see Walter Intern. Prods., Inc. v. Salinas*, 650 F.3d 1402, 1415 (11th Cir. 2011) (court may require the parties to submit a list of witnesses they will actually call, not those that they "may" call).

[126] *Benjamin v. Sparks*, 986 F.3d 332, 340-41 (4th Cir. 2021).

[127] *Benjamin v. Sparks*, 986 F.3d 332, 340-41 (4th Cir. 2021).

[128] *Tilton v. Capital Cities/ABC, Inc.*, 115 F.3d 1471, 1478 (10th Cir. 1997).

practice is to bring these issues to the court's attention as soon as possible.

- *Deposition Designations Providing Context:* For deposition testimony needed to provide full context for an opponent's designations, Rule 32(a)(6) allows a party to introduce the testimony at trial (seemingly without the need to advise the court of the designation in advance, although doing so is likely a good idea).[129]

Supplemental Pretrial Disclosures

Rule 26(e) generally requires supplementation of the Rule 26(a) disclosures "in a timely manner," but with Rule 26(a)(3) disclosures typically occurring shortly before trial, supplemental disclosures are potentially prejudicial. Nonetheless, courts may allow supplemental pretrial disclosures of newly discovered evidence or witnesses.[130]

Impeachment

The pretrial disclosure is not required to include documents or testimony to be introduced solely for impeachment.[131]

Failure to Disclose

Any witnesses, deposition testimony, or exhibits not properly disclosed will be excluded from use at trial unless the failure was substantially justified or harmless.[132]

Objections to Deposition Testimony or Exhibits

A party who objects to the use of any portion of a deposition or to the admissibility of a listed exhibit must serve and file a written list of objections within 14 days of the disclosure of the intent to use the deposition testimony or exhibit.[133] The list of objections should state the grounds for the objections. Failure to state an objection is a waiver of the objection,[134] except for objections to relevancy under Rules 402 and 403 of the Federal Rules of Evidence (because those objections depend on the context in which the testimony is offered). The list of objections during the disclosure process is not the same as making the objection at trial, however—a party must still object if the de-

---

[129]*See Fed. Trade Comm'n v. Innovative Designs, Inc.*, 489 F. Supp. 3d 378, 392 n.24 (W.D. Pa. 2020), aff'd, 2021 WL 3086188 (3d Cir. 2021).

[130]*See, e.g., Harrison v. Burlage*, 2009 WL 3048687, at *3 (S.D. Fla. 2009) (noting that the opposing party had reserved the right to supplement its disclosures).

[131]*Sanchez v. City of Chicago*, 700 F.3d 919, 930 (7th Cir. 2012); *Hammel v. Eau Galle Cheese Factory*, 407 F.3d 852, 869 (7th Cir. 2005).

[132]*Benjamin v. Sparks*, 986 F.3d 332, 340–41 (4th Cir. 2021).

[133]*United States v. An Easement & Right-of-way Over 1.58 Acres of Land*, 343 F. Supp. 3d 1321, 1341 (N.D. Ga. 2018).

[134]*Martin v. Harris*, 560 F.3d 210, 219 (4th Cir. 2009); *United States v. An Easement & Right-of-way Over 1.58 Acres of Land*, 343 F. Supp. 3d 1321, 1341 (N.D. Ga. 2018).

position testimony or exhibit is offered at trial.[135]

Discovery Seeking Rule 26(a)(3) Information

Parties will not be required to respond to discovery requests seeking the information covered by Rule 26(a)(3) at an earlier stage in the litigation.[136] Thus, a party does not need to respond substantively to an interrogatory seeking witness names or a document request seeking trial exhibits and can instead respond that the information will be provided by Rule 26(a)(3) disclosure.

RULE 26(a)(4)—FORM OF DISCLOSURES

CORE CONCEPT

The automatic disclosures under Rule 26(a) should be in writing, signed, and served on other parties, unless otherwise directed by local rule or court order.[137] Only the pretrial disclosure under Rule 26(a)(3) must be filed, unless a court order or local rules provide for filing other disclosures.[138] The signature constitutes a certification that the disclosure is complete and accurate, as provided by Rule 26(g)(1).

RULE 26(b)(1)—DISCOVERY SCOPE AND LIMITS—SCOPE IN GENERAL

CORE CONCEPT

In general, any matter that is relevant to the claim or defense of any party in the pending action and is proportional to the needs of the case is discoverable unless it is privileged.[139] Discovery is limited with respect to work product or trial preparation materials, non-testifying expert witnesses, and physical or mental examinations.

APPLICATIONS

"Relevant" Defined

The term "relevant" is not defined by the Rules, but is extremely broad.[140] Courts have defined "relevant" to encompass "any matter that bears on, or that reasonably could lead to other matters that could bear on, any issue that is or may be in the case."[141] Courts also have defined "relevant" as "germane."[142] Courts differ about whether to use the definition of relevance

---

[135] The Advisory Committee Note to the 1993 Amendment to Rule 26.

[136] *See Diaz-Garcia v. Surillo-Ruiz*, 321 F.R.D. 472, 474 (D.P.R. 2017); *In re Steffensen*, 567 B.R. 188, 194 (D. Utah 2016).

[137] *Karum Holdings LLC v. Lowe's Companies, Inc.*, 895 F.3d 944, 951 (7th Cir. 2018).

[138] *See Hartis v. Chicago Title Ins. Co.*, 694 F.3d 935, 942 (8th Cir. 2012).

[139] *Oceana, Inc. v. Ross*, 920 F.3d 855, 865 (D.C. Cir. 2019); *Gov't of Ghana v. ProEnergy Servs., LLC*, 677 F.3d 340, 342 (8th Cir. 2012).

[140] *See Gilmore v. Palestinian Interim Self-Gov't Auth.*, 843 F.3d 958, 968 (D.C. Cir. 2016); *Sherman v. Sheffield Fin., LLC*, 338 F.R.D. 247, 252 (D. Minn. 2021).

[141] *Oppenheimer Fund, Inc. v. Sanders*, 437 U.S. 340, 351 (1978); *Jackson Women's Health Org. v. Dobbs*,

in Rule 401 of the Federal Rules of Evidence.[143]

- *Categories of Evidence Requiring Heightened Showing of Relevance:* Some courts require a heightened or particularized showing of relevance for certain categories of evidence, such as settlement agreements,[144] tax returns,[145] and computer source code.[146]

Relevant to "Any Party's Claim or Defense"

A party may discover any matter that is relevant to any claim, issue, or defense that is pleaded in the case,[147] regardless of which party raised the claim, issue, or defense.[148] Discovery is not permitted to develop new claims or defenses not already pleaded,[149] to identify additional parties,[150] to explore matter that is not presently germane on the theory that it might conceivably become so,[151] or to gather information for use in another proceeding.[152] Discovery is permitted with respect to claims that have been challenged by motion, but if a claim has been dismissed, further discovery that is relevant only to that claim is not allowed.[153]

Relevant vs. Admissible

Evidence need not be admissible to be relevant, and thus discoverable.[154] For example, a settlement agreement between the plaintiff and one defendant might not be admissible at trial

---

945 F.3d 265, 281 (5th Cir. 2019).

[142] *See West Penn Power Co. v. N.L.R.B.*, 394 F.3d 233, 242 (4th Cir. 2005); *Crowley Marine Services, Inc. v. N.L.R.B.*, 234 F.3d 1295, 1297 (D.C. Cir. 2000).

[143] *Compare Carlson v. Colorado Ctr. for Reprod. Med., LLC*, 341 F.R.D. 266, 275 (D. Colo. 2022) (applying Rule 401); *with Hollis v. CEVA Logistics U.S., Inc.*, __ F. Supp. 3d __, 2022 WL 1591731, at *5 (N.D. Ill. 2022) (Rule 401 does not apply).

[144] *See Close v. Acct. Resol. Servs.*, 557 F. Supp. 3d 247, 250 (D. Mass. 2021) (discussing the split on this issue); *Hoerchler v. Equifax Info. Servs., LLC*, 568 F. Supp. 3d 931, 936 (N.D. Ill. 2021).

[145] *See DeMasi v. Weiss*, 669 F.2d 114, 119 (3d Cir. 1982); *Allen v. Banner Life Ins. Co.*, 340 F.R.D. 232, 241 (D.N.J. 2022).

[146] *See LoganTree LP v. Garmin Int'l, Inc.*, 339 F.R.D. 171, 182 (D. Kan. 2021).

[147] *In re Clinton*, 973 F.3d 106, 114 (D.C. Cir. 2020); *Amgen Inc. v. Hospira, Inc.*, 866 F.3d 1355, 1361 (Fed. Cir. 2017).

[148] *See Sentis Group, Inc. v. Shell Oil Co.*, 763 F.3d 919, 925 (8th Cir. 2014); *Target Corp. v. ACE Am. Ins. Co.*, 576 F. Supp. 3d 609, 615-16 (D. Minn. 2021) (one party's theory of the case does not limit an opposing party's discovery).

[149] *See Kennicott v. Sandia Corp.*, 327 F.R.D. 454, 472 (D.N.M. 2018); *Cole's Wexford Hotel, Inc. v. Highmark Inc.*, 209 F. Supp. 3d 810, 822 (W.D. Pa. 2016).

[150] *See In re Williams-Sonoma, Inc.*, 947 F.3d 535, 539–41 (9th Cir. 2020).

[151] *Wall v. Reliance Standard Life Ins. Co.*, 341 F.R.D. 1, 5 (D.D.C. 2022).

[152] *Oppenheimer Fund, Inc. v. Sanders*, 437 U.S. 340, 352 n.17 (1978).

[153] *Oppenheimer Fund, Inc. v. Sanders*, 437 U.S. 340, 351 (1978); *Durand v. Hanover Ins. Grp., Inc.*, 294 F. Supp. 3d 659, 689 (W.D. Ky. 2018).

[154] *Seattle Times Co. v. Rhinehart*, 467 U.S. 20 (1984); *Servotronics, Inc. v. Boeing Co.*, 954 F.3d 209, 215 (4th Cir. 2020).

but might be relevant to determining another defendant's right to a set-off, and would therefore be discoverable.[155] Conversely, admissible evidence is almost always discoverable.[156]

Proportionality

Discovery must be "proportional to the needs of the case"—essentially the expected benefits of the discovery must be in line with the cost and burden of the discovery and the value of the case.[157] Rule 26(b)(1) contains a list of factors for evaluating proportionality: the importance of the issues at stake in the action;[158] the amount in controversy;[159] the parties' relative access to relevant information;[160] the parties' resources;[161] the importance of the discovery in resolving the issues;[162] and whether the burden or expense of the proposed discovery outweighs its likely benefit.[163] The court has broad discretion in considering and weighing these factors.[164] No single factor outweighs the others, and the parties do not need to address each and every factor when briefing proportionality.[165] Under Rule 26(b)(2), the court *must* limit discovery that it determines is not proportional to the needs of the case.[166] Indeed, some courts hold that they have an affirmative duty to assess

---

[155] *See BladeRoom Grp. Ltd. v. Emerson Elec. Co.*, 20 F.4th 1231, 1251 (9th Cir. 2021); *Burke v. Regalado*, 935 F.3d 960, 1048 (10th Cir. 2019) (concurrence).

[156] *Walls v. City of New York*, 502 F. Supp. 3d 686, 692 n.5 (E.D.N.Y. 2020); *Surgery Ctr. at 900 N. Michigan Ave., LLC v. Am. Physicians Assurance Corp., Inc.*, 317 F.R.D. 620, 630 (N.D. Ill. 2016).

[157] *See Helena Agri-Enterprises, LLC v. Great Lakes Grain, LLC*, 988 F.3d 260, 274 (6th Cir. 2021); *Virginia Dep't of Corr. v. Jordan*, 921 F.3d 180, 188 (4th Cir. 2019).

[158] *Waskul v. Washtenaw Cnty. Cmty. Mental Health*, 569 F. Supp. 3d 626, 632 (E.D. Mich. 2021) (civil rights claim raises important issues); *City of Rockford v. Mallinckrodt ARD Inc.*, 326 F.R.D. 489, 495 (N.D. Ill. 2018) (allegations of prescription drug price fixing raise important issues).

[159] *City of Rockford v. Mallinckrodt ARD Inc.*, 326 F.R.D. 489, 495 (N.D. Ill. 2018); *Coffey v. Hartford Life & Accident Ins. Co.*, 318 F.R.D. 320, 325 (W.D. Va. 2017).

[160] *Chelsey Nelson Photography LLC v. Louisville/Jefferson Cnty. Metro Gov't*, 556 F. Supp. 3d 657, 667–68 (W.D. Ky. 2021); *Walls v. City of New York*, 502 F. Supp. 3d 686, 695 (E.D.N.Y. 2020).

[161] *Chelsey Nelson Photography LLC v. Louisville/Jefferson Cnty. Metro Gov't*, 556 F. Supp. 3d 657, 675 (W.D. Ky. 2021); *Garcia Ramirez v. U.S. Immigration & Customs Enf't*, 331 F.R.D. 194, 199 (D.D.C. 2019).

[162] *Koppel v. Moses*, __ F. Supp. 3d __, 2022 WL 1568444, at *2 (D. Mass. 2022); *United States Sec. & Exch. Comm'n v. Collector's Coffee Inc.*, 338 F.R.D. 309, 317 (S.D.N.Y. 2021).

[163] *Virginia Dep't of Corr. v. Jordan*, 921 F.3d 180, 190 n.3 (4th Cir. 2019); *Cazorla v. Koch Foods of Mississippi, L.L.C.*, 838 F.3d 540, 554 n.42 (5th Cir. 2016).

[164] *JP Morgan Chase Bank, N.A. v. DataTreasury Corp.*, 936 F.3d 251, 260 (5th Cir. 2019).

[165] *Wall v. Reliance Standard Life Ins. Compnay*, 341 F.R.D. 1, 5 (D.D.C. 2022); *Lynch v. Experian Info. Sols., Inc.*, __ F. Supp. 3d __, 2022 WL 190753, at *4 (D. Minn. 2022).

[166] *Koppel v. Moses*, __ F. Supp. 3d __, 2022 WL 1568444, at *2 (D. Mass. 2022); *Mir v. L-3 Commc'n Integrated Sys., L.P.*, 319 F.R.D. 220, 225–26 (N.D. Tex. 2016). *See also Vallejo v.*

proportionality, even if the parties do not raise it.[167] The ultimate burden is on the party seeking to resist the discovery to demonstrate that the discovery is not proportional to the needs of the case[168]—typically using affidavits or other evidence[169]—but the practical effect of the rule is that both parties often must submit evidence supporting their positions on proportionality.[170] At the same time, if the discovery is facially overbroad or unduly burdensome, a court might not require evidentiary support for a proportionality objection.[171]

Nonprivileged

Privileged matters are protected from discovery under the language of Rule 26(b)(1).[172] *Confidential* matters, on the other hand, do not enjoy blanket protection from discovery, and instead are frequently the subject of protective orders under Rule 26(c).[173] The procedures for asserting privilege are in Rule 26(b)(5).

Limitations on Discovery

The broad scope of discovery authorized by Rule 26(b)(1) is curtailed by the limitations in other portions of Rule 26(b).[174]

Burden of Demonstrating Discoverability

The party seeking the discovery has the initial burden to demonstrate that the information sought is relevant.[175] Once that showing has been made, the burden shifts to the party resisting the discovery to explain why discovery should not be permitted.[176]

Duty to Preserve

Parties and attorneys have a duty to preserve relevant evidence once litigation has commenced or is reasonably

---

Amgen, Inc., 903 F.3d 733, 742 (8th Cir. 2018) (proportionality a "collective responsibility" of parties and the court).

[167]*See, e.g., Lopez v. Don Herring Ltd.*, 327 F.R.D. 567, 583 (N.D. Tex. 2018); *Noble Roman's, Inc. v. Hattenhauer Distrib. Co.*, 314 F.R.D. 304, 307 and 312 (S.D. Ind. 2016).

[168]*Target Corp. v. ACE Am. Ins. Co.*, 576 F. Supp. 3d 609, 622 (D. Minn. 2021).

[169]*See Vallejo v. Amgen, Inc.*, 903 F.3d 733, 743 (8th Cir. 2018); *Scherer v. FCA US, LLC*, 538 F. Supp. 3d 1002, 1005 (S.D. Cal. 2021).

[170]*See Mir v. L-3 Commc'n Integrated Sys., L.P.*, 319 F.R.D. 220, 226 (N.D. Tex. 2016).

[171]*See Deakin v. Magellan Health, Inc.*, 340 F.R.D. 424, 435 (D.N.M. 2022).

[172]*See Jolivet v. Compass Grp. USA, Inc.*, 340 F.R.D. 7, 17 (N.D. Tex. 2021); *Guo Wengui v. Clark Hill, PLC*, 338 F.R.D. 7, 10 (D.D.C. 2021).

[173]*See Waskul v. Washtenaw Cnty. Cmty. Mental Health*, 569 F. Supp. 3d 626, 640 (E.D. Mich. 2021).

[174]*In re Cooper Tire & Rubber Co.*, 568 F.3d 1180 (10th Cir. 2009); *Mach. Sols., Inc. v. Doosan Infracore Am. Corp.*, 323 F.R.D. 522, 526 (D.S.C. 2018).

[175]*Alexander v. New York City Dep't of Educ.*, 339 F.R.D. 372, 374 (S.D.N.Y. 2021); *Delta T, LLC v. Williams*, 337 F.R.D. 395, 398 (S.D. Ohio 2021).

[176]*Delta T, LLC v. Williams*, 337 F.R.D. 395, 398 (S.D. Ohio 2021); *Thomas v. City of New York*, 336 F.R.D. 1, 2 (E.D.N.Y. 2020).

anticipated.[177] Some courts find this duty arises in part under Rule 26(b)(1).[178]

Jurisdictional Issues

Discovery is allowed with respect to jurisdictional issues.[179] Thus, parties may conduct discovery pertaining to other parties' citizenship, the amount in controversy, or a party's contacts with the forum state.[180]

Location of Evidence

Parties may conduct discovery regarding the location and existence of documents and other evidence[181] and about the identity and location of persons having knowledge of discoverable matters.[182]

Matters Known to Others

A party must provide information and documents it possesses, regardless of who else possesses that information. Thus, it generally is not proper to object on the basis that the party already has the information it is requesting or that information is in the public record[183] or is otherwise available to the party[184] (although the court might curtail such requests as unduly burdensome in some circumstances).

Impeachment

Discovery is generally allowed of matters that the requesting party would use to impeach the responding party's witnesses.[185] Thus, one normally may ask whether the responding party has any criminal convictions and may inquire as to prior statements.[186] It is less clear whether a party may inquire as to what other parties will use for impeachment of the requesting party.

---

[177] *See, e.g., Zubulake v. UBS Warburg LLC*, 220 F.R.D. 212, 217 (S.D.N.Y. 2003).

[178] *See Zbylski v. Douglas County School District*, 154 F. Supp. 3d 1146, 1158 (D. Colo. 2015).

[179] *Oppenheimer Fund, Inc. v. Sanders*, 437 U.S. 340, 351 (1978); *Shuker v. Smith & Nephew, PLC*, 885 F.3d 760, 782, n.20 (3d Cir. 2018).

[180] *Inventus Power v. Shenzhen Ace Battery*, 339 F.R.D. 487, 497 (N.D. Ill. 2021) (discovery as to personal jurisdiction).

[181] *Dauska v. Green Bay Packaging Inc.*, 291 F.R.D. 251, 257 (E.D. Wis. 2013).

[182] *Brooks v. Kerry*, 37 F. Supp. 2d 187, 202–03 (D.D.C. 2014).

[183] *CRST Expedited, Inc. v. Swift Transportation Co. of Arizona, LLC*, 328 F.R.D. 231, 237 (N.D. Iowa 2018); *Mid-Atlantic Recycling Technologies, Inc. v. City of Vineland*, 222 F.R.D. 81 (D.N.J. 2004). *But see Bleecker v. Standard Fire Ins. Co.*, 130 F.Supp.2d 726, 738–39 (E.D.N.C. 2000) (denying motion to compel where information sought was publicly available).

[184] *Abrahamsen v. Trans-State Exp., Inc.*, 92 F.3d 425, 428 (6th Cir. 1996).

[185] *Hickman v. Taylor*, 329 U.S. 495, 511 (1947); *Varga v. Rockwell Intern. Corp.*, 242 F.3d 693, 697 (6th Cir. 2001).

[186] *See Curro v. Watson*, 884 F. Supp. 708 (E.D.N.Y. 1995), aff'd, 100 F.3d 942 (2d Cir. 1996) (limiting impeachment discovery to areas related to expected testimony).

Discovery of Attorneys

Attorneys with discoverable facts not covered by attorney-client privilege or work product protection are subject to discovery despite being retained by one of the parties to represent it in the litigation.[187]

RULE 26(b)(2)—LIMITATIONS ON FREQUENCY AND EXTENT

CORE CONCEPT

Rule 26(b)(2) requires the court, "on motion or on its own,"[188] to limit the frequency or extent of discovery if: the discovery is *unreasonably* cumulative or duplicative;[189] the discovery is obtainable from another source more convenient, less burdensome, or less expensive;[190] or the discovery is outside the scope set forth in Rule 26(b)(1) (*i.e.*, not nonprivileged, relevant to a claim or defense, and proportional to the needs of the case).[191] The court must also limit discovery if the party seeking the discovery has had "ample opportunity" to obtain the information during prior discovery.[192] Rule 26(b)(2)(B) also establishes a procedure for limiting the need to search for and produce electronically stored information if it would be unreasonably burdensome or costly to do so.

APPLICATIONS

Assertion of the Rule 26(b)(2) Limitations

One method of asserting the limitations in Rule 26(b)(2) is by making an objection to a discovery request, such as objecting to an interrogatory or request for production as cumulative or overly burdensome. A party may also make a motion for a protective order under Rule 26(c) seeking broader protection from discovery exceeding the Rule 26(b)(2) limitations.[193]

---

[187] *Gamache v. Hogue*, __ F. Supp. 3d __, 2022 WL 989483, at *3 (M.D. Ga. 2022); *United Phosphorus, Ltd. v. Midland Fumigant, Inc.*, 164 F.R.D. 245 (D. Kan. 1995).

[188] *V5 Techs. v. Switch, Ltd.*, 334 F.R.D. 306, 314 (D. Nev. 2019) (courts have duty to limit discovery that is "outside the scope permitted by Rule 26(b)(1)."); *Shukh v. Seagate Technology, LLC*, 295 F.R.D. 228, 237 (D. Minn. 2013).

[189] *Johnson Tr. of Operating Engineers Local #49 Health & Welfare Fund v. Charps Welding & Fabricating, Inc.*, 950 F.3d 510, 525 (8th Cir. 2020) (duplicative); *Inventus Power v. Shenzhen Ace Battery*, 339 F.R.D. 487, 497 (N.D. Ill. 2021) (limiting the number of depositions on the same topic); *Thomas v. City of New York*, 336 F.R.D. 1, 3 (E.D.N.Y. 2020) (some overlap is permissible).

[190] *Loomis v. Unum Grp. Corp.*, 338 F.R.D. 225, 228 (E.D. Tenn. 2021); *Baumer v. Schmidt*, 423 F. Supp. 3d 393, 410 (E.D. Mich. 2019).

[191] *Koppel v. Moses*, __ F. Supp. 3d __, 2022 WL 1568444, at *2 (D. Mass. 2022); *Loomis v. Unum Grp. Corp.*, 338 F.R.D. 225, 228 (E.D. Tenn. 2021).

[192] *Edwards v. Scripps Media, Inc.*, 331 F.R.D. 116, 122 (E.D. Mich. 2019); *Ball Corp. v. Air Tech of Michigan, Inc.*, 329 F.R.D. 599, 602 (N.D. Ind. 2019).

[193] *See Garcia Ramirez v. U.S. Immigration & Customs Enf't*, 331 F.R.D. 194, 198 (D.D.C. 2019).

Alteration of Limits Established by Other Rules

Other rules place additional limits on discovery, such as the duration of depositions and the number of interrogatories and depositions. Rule 26(a)(2)(A) authorizes the district court to issue orders altering those limits.[194] Additionally, because Rule 36 imposes no limitation on requests for admission, Rule 26(a)(2)(A) authorizes the district courts to limit the number of requests for admission by local rule or case-specific order.[195]

Electronically Stored Information (ESI)

Rule 26(b)(2)(B) limits discovery of electronically stored information from sources that are not "reasonably accessible" because of undue burden or cost, and establishes a procedure for invoking this limitation.[196] The party invoking the protection must identify the sources of information that it is neither searching nor producing with sufficient particularity that the requesting party can evaluate the burden and cost of producing the information.[197] If the requesting party believes that the information should be produced, the parties must confer to see if they can resolve the issue without court intervention.[198] If the informal conference does not resolve the issue, the requesting party may file a motion to compel[199] or the responding party may file a motion for a protective order. In either type of motion, the responding party bears the burden of showing that the information is not reasonably accessible in terms of undue burden or cost.[200] Even following such a showing, the court may require production of the information upon good cause shown.[201] Relevant factors include the specificity of the request, the information that is or should be available from other sources, predictions of the importance of the information, the importance of the issues at stake, and the parties' resources.[202] If it orders discovery of such ESI, it may impose conditions on the produc-

---

[194] *See Merchia v. United States Internal Revenue Serv.*, 336 F.R.D. 396, 400 (D. Mass. 2020); *Republic of Turkey v. Christie's, Inc.*, 326 F.R.D. 402, 405–406 (S.D.N.Y. 2018).

[195] *Koppel v. Moses*, __ F. Supp. 3d __, 2022 WL 1568444, at *2 (D. Mass. 2022).

[196] *See FCA US LLC v. Bullock*, 329 F.R.D. 563, 566 (E.D. Mich. 2019); *U.S. ex rel. Carter v. Bridgepoint Educ., Inc.*, 305 F.R.D. 225, 239 (S.D. Cal. 2015) (backup tapes are per se inaccessible).

[197] The 2006 Amendment to the Advisory Committee Note to Rule 26(b)(2).

[198] The 2006 Amendment to the Advisory Committee Note to Rule 26(b)(2).

[199] *See Black Love Resists In the Rust by & through Soto v. City of Buffalo, N.Y.*, 334 F.R.D. 23, 29 (W.D.N.Y. 2019); *Bagley v. Yale University*, 307 F.R.D. 59, 65–66 (D. Conn. 2015).

[200] *See Thomas v. City of New York*, 336 F.R.D. 1, 2 (E.D.N.Y. 2020); *Cratty v. City of Wyandotte*, 296 F. Supp. 3d 854, 859 (E.D. Mich. 2017).

[201] *Black Love Resists In the Rust by & through Soto v. City of Buffalo, N.Y.*, 334 F.R.D. 23, 29 (W.D.N.Y. 2019); *Bagley v. Yale University*, 307 F.R.D. 59, 65–66 (C. Conn. 2015).

[202] *See Black Love Resists In the Rust by & through Soto v. City of Buffalo, N.Y.*, 334 F.R.D. 23, 29 (W.D.N.Y. 2019); *Disability Rights Council of Greater Washington v.*

tion, such as shifting some or all of the costs to the requesting party.

Burden of Proof

In the context of a contested assertion of the limitations in Rule 26(b)(2)(B), the party asserting the limitation must demonstrate its applicability.[203] Vague, unsupported assertions are generally not sufficient.[204]

RULE 26(b)(3)—TRIAL PREPARATION: MATERIALS

CORE CONCEPT

Rule 26(b)(3) provides limited protection to otherwise discoverable[205] documents and tangible things that a party or its representative prepared in anticipation of litigation. Such "trial preparation materials" must be produced in discovery *only* when the information contained there is not reasonably available from any other source. The protection for "trial preparation materials" in Rule 26(b)(3) is essentially the codification of the "work product" doctrine first announced by the Supreme Court in *Hickman v. Taylor*,[206] and both the courts and this section use both terms.[207]

APPLICATIONS

Documents and Tangible Things (and Intangible Mental Impressions)

The trial preparation materials protection applies to documents and tangible things.[208] Some courts also allow a party to assert the work product protection—the common law doctrine established in *Hickman v. Taylor*—in response to discovery inquiries that seek the party's trial strategy, counsel's mental impressions, or "intangible work product."[209] It is unsettled whether the trial preparation materials protection applies to compilations of documents, such as documents selected for de-

Washington Metropolitan Transit Authority, 242 F.R.D. 139 (D.D.C. 2007).

[203]*See Equal Emp. Opportunity Comm'n v. Heart of CarDon, LLC*, 339 F.R.D. 602, 605 (S.D. Ind. 2021).

[204]Rodriguez v. City of Chicago, 429 F. Supp. 3d 537, 543 (N.D. Ill. 2019).

[205]*Stoffels v. SBC Commc'n, Inc.*, 263 F.R.D. 406, 411–12 (W.D. Tex. 2009) (first step is to determine if materials are attorney-client communications, because work product protection only applies to documents that are otherwise discoverable).

[206]*Hickman v. Taylor*, 329 U.S. 495 (1947); *Adams v. Mem'l Hermann*, 973 F.3d 343, 349 (5th Cir. 2020) (codification).

[207]*Mitchell v. Archer Daniels Midland Co.*, 329 F.R.D. 178, 180 (E.D. Tenn. 2019) (the difference in phrasing between "work product" and "trial preparation materials" is not suggestive of different legal standards).

[208]*In re Professionals Direct Ins. Co.*, 578 F.3d 432, 438 (6th Cir. 2009); *In re Avandia Mktg., Sales Practices & Prod. Liab. Litig.*, 415 F. Supp. 3d 498, 507 (E.D. Pa. 2019).

[209]*Adams v. Mem'l Hermann*, 973 F.3d 343, 349 (5th Cir. 2020); *United States v. Deloitte LLP*, 610 F.3d 129, 136 (D.C. Cir. 2010).

position preparation.[210]

Underlying Facts Not Protected

The trial preparation materials protection does not apply to the *facts* relating to the litigation, which are almost always discoverable,[211] but it does apply to documents prepared in anticipation of litigation that describe or summarize the facts.[212]

Prepared in Anticipation of Litigation

The trial preparation materials protection applies only to documents prepared "in anticipation of litigation."[213] The focus of the analysis is whether the *purpose* for the creation of the document was the anticipation of litigation.[214] The analysis is both subjective and objective, asking whether the party prepared the document based on its *subjective* anticipation of litigation and whether that subjective anticipation was *objectively reasonable*.[215] Some courts ask whether the document was prepared "because of the prospect of litigation."[216] Courts differ as to whether the document must have been prepared for *use* in anticipated litigation.[217] Most courts apply the protection to documents prepared when litigation is expected but has not yet been commenced;[218] the timing of the preparation of the documents is not critical, as long as they were primarily concerned with the litigation.[219] Conversely, the protection does not apply

---

[210] *See In re Grand Jury Subpoenas Dated March 19, 2002 and August 2, 2002*, 318 F.3d 379, 385 (2d Cir. 2003); *Meighan v. TransGuard Ins. Co. of Am., Inc.*, 298 F.R.D. 436, 441 (N.D. Iowa 2014) (compilation of documents protected).

[211] *Adams v. Mem'l Hermann*, 973 F.3d 343, 349 (5th Cir. 2020); *In re Cendant Corp. Sec. Litig.*, 343 F.3d 658, 662 (3d Cir. 2003).

[212] *Am. Civil Liberties Union of N. California v. United States Dep't of Justice*, 880 F.3d 473, 488 (9th Cir. 2018); *Competitive Enter. Inst. v. U. S. Envtl Prot. Agency*, 232 F. Supp. 3d 172 (D.D.C. 2017).

[213] *Am. Civil Liberties Union of N. California v. United States Dep't of Justice*, 880 F.3d 473, 483 (9th Cir. 2018) (employing a "because of" test); *In re Professionals Direct Ins. Co.*, 578 F.3d 432, 439 (6th Cir. 2009) (the court will look at the subjective anticipation and the objective reasonableness of the anticipation); *In re Apollo Group, Inc. Sec. Litig.*, 251 F.R.D. 12, 19 (D.D.C. 2008) ("litigation" includes administrative proceedings).

[214] *Holladay v. Royal Caribbean Cruises, Ltd.*, 333 F.R.D. 588, 591 (S.D. Fla. 2019); *Parneros v. Barnes & Noble, Inc.*, 332 F.R.D. 482, 492 (S.D.N.Y. 2019).

[215] *Pinnacle Sur. Servs., Inc. v. Manion Stigger, LLP*, 370 F. Supp. 3d 745, 755 (W.D. Ky. 2019); *Ohio A. Philip Randolph Inst. v. Smith*, 360 F. Supp. 3d 681, 692 (S.D. Ohio 2018).

[216] *von Kahle v. Cargill, Inc.*, __ F. Supp. 3d __, 2022 WL 1223264, at *3 (S.D.N.Y. 2022).

[217] Compare *United States v. Textron Inc. & Subsidiaries*, 577 F.3d 21, 29 (1st Cir. 2009) (focus is on documents prepared for use in litigation); *with United States v. Adlman*, 134 F.3d 1194, 1198 (2d Cir. 1998) (no need for document purpose to be to assist at trial).

[218] *E.E.O.C. v. Lutheran Social Serv.*, 186 F.3d 959 (D.C. Cir. 1999); *Collardey v. All. for Sustainable Energy, LLC*, 406 F. Supp. 3d 977, 982 (D. Colo. 2019) (likelihood of litigation need not be certain).

[219] *In re Professionals Direct Ins. Co.*, 578 F.3d 432, 439 (6th Cir. 2009)

to documents prepared in the regular course of business,[220] even though litigation was pending.[221] The trend seems to be to apply the protection to documents prepared in anticipation of any litigation, not just the pending action.[222] However, documents designed to make a party better prepared to defend future litigation generally may not qualify as trial preparation materials even though prepared by the party's litigation counsel.[223] A document prepared with dual litigation and non-litigation purposes will be considered to have been prepared in anticipation of litigation if it would not have been created in substantially similar form but for the prospect of litigation.[224] Public relations work is generally treated as a business activity rather than legal work product, even if such work may bear on litigation strategy or is completed by an attorney.[225] However, some documents prepared by public relations consultants that implicitly reflect attorney work product may garner work product protection.[226]

Prepared by Parties and Their Representatives

The trial preparation materials protection applies to documents prepared by parties and their representatives.[227] Rule 26(b)(3) describes "representative" as including a party's attorney, consultant, surety, indemnitor, insurer,[228] or agent. Thus, while an attorney is one form of representative, work

---

(the party must demonstrate that litigation was the "driving force" behind the preparation of the document); *In re Ford Motor Co.*, 110 F.3d 954 (3d Cir. 1997).

[220] *von Kahle v. Cargill, Inc.*, __ F. Supp. 3d __, 2022 WL 1223264, at *3 (S.D.N.Y. 2022); *Regents of the Univ. of Minnesota v. United States*, 340 F.R.D. 293, 304 (D. Minn. 2021).

[221] *Mir v. L-3 Commc'n Integrated Sys., L.P.*, 315 F.R.D. 460, 463 (N.D. Tex. 2016); *Gillespie v. Charter Commc'n*, 133 F. Supp. 3d 1195, 1201 (E.D. Mo. 2015).

[222] *See F.T.C. v. Grolier, Inc.*, 462 U.S. 19, 26 (1983); *Hobley v. Burge*, 433 F.3d 946, 949 (7th Cir. 2006) ("the privilege endures after termination of the proceedings for which the documents were created . . ."); *Truman v. City of Orem*, 362 F. Supp. 3d 1121, 1136 (D. Utah 2019). *But see Williams v. Big Picture Loans, LLC*, 303 F. Supp. 3d 434 (E.D. Va. 2018) ("vague, inchoate threat of future litigation" insufficient).

[223] *See Munguia-Brown v. Equity Residential*, 337 F.R.D. 509, 514 (N.D. Cal. 2021).

[224] *Am. Civil Liberties Union of N. California v. United States Dep't of Justice*, 880 F.3d 473, 485–86 (9th Cir. 2018); *Eastman v. Thompson*, __ F. Supp. 3d __, 2022 WL 894256, at *14 (C.D. Cal. 2022).

[225] *Anderson v. SeaWorld Parks & Entm't, Inc.*, 329 F.R.D. 628, 635 (N.D. Cal. 2019); *Universal Standard Inc. v. Target Corp.*, 331 F.R.D. 80, 93 (S.D.N.Y. 2019).

[226] *Anderson v. SeaWorld Parks & Entm't, Inc.*, 329 F.R.D. 628, 636-639 (N.D. Cal. 2019).

[227] *Rojas v. Fed. Aviation Admin.*, 989 F.3d 666, 676 (9th Cir. 2021); *McKinley v. Board of Governors of Fed. Reserve Sys.*, 647 F.3d 331, 341 (D.C. Cir. 2011) (consultant deemed to be party's agent).

[228] *See F.T.C. v. Boehringer Ingelheim Pharmaceuticals, Inc.*, 778 F.3d 142, 149 (D.C. Cir. 2015).

product does not require any involvement by an attorney;[229] the protection applies to documents prepared by a party or any of its representatives in anticipation of litigation.[230] Thus, the trial preparation materials protection applies to reports prepared by an investigator on behalf of a party.[231] The courts disagree about whether a nonparty witness who prepares a document in anticipation of litigation may assert the work product protection.[232]

Prepared by Experts

Generally, the discoverability of documents prepared by experts or of communications with experts is governed by Rule 26(b)(4)—titled Trial Preparation: Experts—not by the general trial preparation materials protections under Rule 26(b)(3).[233]

Who May Assert

The party or the party's attorney may invoke the trial preparation materials protection.[234]

How the Protection is Asserted

The trial preparations materials protection is typically asserted as an objection to a document request or as part of a privilege log. The asserting party must provide a detailed description of the materials and the basis for the trial preparation materials protection with particularity.[235]

Obtaining Trial Preparation Materials

Trial preparation materials are discoverable if the requesting party makes a sufficient showing of two requirements:

1) that the party cannot, without undue hardship,[236] obtain the same or substantially equivalent information;[237] and
2) that the attorney has a *substantial* need for the

[229] *Shih v. Petal Card, Inc.*, 565 F. Supp. 3d 557, 574 (S.D.N.Y. 2021).

[230] *Parneros v. Barnes & Noble, Inc.*, 332 F.R.D. 482, 492 (S.D.N.Y. 2019); *Kandel v. Brother Intern. Corp.*, 683 F. Supp. 2d 1076, 1084 (C.D. Cal. 2010).

[231] *See In re Grand Jury Subpoena (Mark Torf/Torf Environmental Mgmt.)*, 357 F.3d 900, 907 (9th Cir. 2004); *In re Grand Jury Subpoena Dated Oct. 22, 2001*, 282 F.3d 156, 161 (2d Cir. 2002).

[232] *Compare Duck v. Warren*, 160 F.R.D. 80 (E.D. Va. 1995) (not allowing assertion by nonparty); *with Klosin v. E.I. du Pont de Nemours & Co.*, 561 F. Supp. 3d 343, 352–53 (W.D.N.Y. 2021) (allowing assertion by nonparty).

[233] *Republic of Ecuador v. Mackay*, 742 F.3d 860, 865–71 (9th Cir. 2014); *Republic of Ecuador v. Hinchee*, 741 F.3d 1185, 1189–93 (11th Cir. 2013).

[234] *Hobley v. Burge*, 433 F.3d 946, 949 (7th Cir. 2006); *Banneker Ventures, LLC v. Graham*, 253 F. Supp. 3d 64, 69 (D.D.C. 2017).

[235] *Zenith Ins. Co. v. Texas Inst. for Surgery, L.L.P.*, 328 F.R.D. 153, 162 (N.D. Tex. 2018) (general assertion of protection insufficient); *Hunton & Williams LLP v. U.S. Envtl. Prot. Agency*, 346 F. Supp. 3d 61, 84 (D.D.C. 2018).

[236] *Collardey v. All. for Sustainable Energy, LLC*, 406 F. Supp. 3d 977, 983 (D. Colo. 2019) (the expense of another deposition does not constitute undue hardship).

[237] *Appleton Papers, Inc. v. E.P.A.*, 702 F.3d 1018, 1023 (7th Cir. 2012);

information.[238]

For example, a party may obtain a written witness statement in opposing counsel's files if the witness is no longer available.[239] Similarly, there may be no substitute for photographs taken or records created shortly after an incident.[240] Work product is also discoverable in an action where the work product is directly at issue,[241] such as in an action for legal malpractice[242] or a bad faith insurance claim.[243] As discussed immediately below, however, opinion work product is shielded from discovery even if the opposing party makes the two showings required to obtain fact work product.[244]

Mental and Legal Impressions

The mental impressions and legal evaluations of an attorney, investigator, or claims agent (sometimes referred to as "core" or "opinion" work product[245]) enjoy an almost absolute privilege from disclosure.[246] Opinion or core work product may be obtained only when the mental impressions are at issue in the case and the need for them is compelling.[247] Thus, an attorney may redact statements reflecting mental and legal impressions from trial preparation materials that must be disclosed.[248] Note, however, that the protections for opinion work product do not apply to information requested in interrogatories, which may require the respondent to make legal contentions requiring the application of law to facts (in other words, the responding attorney may not interpose an objection on the basis that such a legal contention is the attorney's core or opinion work product).

United Kingdom v. U.S., 238 F.3d 1312, 1322 (11th Cir. 2001).

[238] *F.T.C. v. Boehringer Ingelheim Pharmaceuticals, Inc.*, 778 F.3d 142, 153–58 (D.C. Cir. 2015); *Republic of Ecuador v. Mackay*, 742 F.3d 860, 866 (9th Cir. 2014).

[239] *McCoo v. Denny's Inc.*, 192 F.R.D. 675 (D. Kan. 2000) (statements from witnesses who failed to appear for their depositions must be produced).

[240] *See Felisberto v. Dumdey*, 541 F. Supp. 3d 142, 152 (D. Mass. 2021); *Le v. Diligence, Inc.*, 312 F.R.D. 245, 247 (D. Mass. 2015).

[241] *United States v. Sanmina Corp.*, 968 F.3d 1107, 1119 (9th Cir. 2020); *New York Times Co. v. United States Dep't of Justice*, 939 F.3d 479, 494 (2d Cir. 2019).

[242] *Windsor Sec., LLC v. Arent Fox LLP*, 273 F. Supp. 3d 512, 518 (S.D.N.Y. 2017); *Rutgard v. Haynes*, 61 F. Supp. 2d 1082 (S.D. Cal. 1999), aff'd, 11 Fed. Appx. 818 (9th Cir. 2001).

[243] *Holmgren v. State Farm Mut. Auto. Ins. Co.*, 976 F.2d 573, 577 (9th Cir. 1992); *Skyline Wesleyan Church v. California Dep't of Managed Health Care*, 322 F.R.D. 571, 587 (S.D. Cal. 2017).

[244] *Truman v. City of Orem*, 362 F. Supp. 3d 1121, 1128 (D. Utah 2019).

[245] *See F.T.C. v. Boehringer Ingelheim Pharmaceuticals, Inc.*, 778 F.3d 142, 151 (D.C. Cir. 2015).

[246] *Upjohn Co. v. United States*, 449 U.S. 383, 400 (1981); *In re Search Warrant Issued June 13, 2019*, 942 F.3d 159, 174 (4th Cir. 2019).

[247] *Jolivet v. Compass Grp. USA, Inc.*, 340 F.R.D. 7, 17 (N.D. Tex. 2021); *McKenzie Law Firm, P.A. v. Ruby Receptionists, Inc.*, 333 F.R.D. 638, 641 (D. Or. 2019).

[248] *See In re EchoStar Commc'n Corp.*, 448 F.3d 1294 (Fed. Cir. 2006).

Statements

- *Statement of a Party:* A party may always obtain a copy of the party's own statement[249] or a statement by the party's agent or representative—an opposing party may not contend that the statement is work product.[250] To obtain a copy of a party's statement, the party does not need to use the document request procedures in Rule 34, but instead may simply make a request under Rule 26(b)(3).[251]
- *Statement of a Nonparty Witness:* Any witness has a right to a copy of the witness's own statement.[252] Parties, in contrast, do not have an absolute right to a copy of a nonparty witness's statement—such statements may be trial preparation materials if they meet the criteria for the protection.[253] Courts generally start with the presumption that recordings of witness interviews by or at the direction of an attorney in anticipation of litigation are not discoverable, regardless of whether they contain attorney mental impressions.[254] Some courts are reluctant to apply the work product protection to clandestine recordings of witness statements.[255] A party can attempt to get a copy of a witness's statement directly from the witness or by making the showing of necessity required to obtain trial preparation materials.[256]
- *Definition of Statement:* A statement can either be a written statement that the witness has signed, adopted, or approved, or a contemporaneous verbatim recording of the witness's oral statement.[257]

---

[249] *Corley v. Rosewood Care Center, Inc.*, 142 F.3d 1041, 1052 (7th Cir. 1998); *Cicel (Beijing) Sci. & Tech. Co. v. Misonix, Inc.*, 331 F.R.D. 218, 233 (E.D.N.Y. 2019).

[250] *Woodard v. Nabors Offshore Corp.*, 2001 WL 13339 (E.D. La. 2001).

[251] *Manske v. UPS Cartage Serv., Inc.*, 798 F. Supp. 2d 213, 214–15 (D. Me. 2011) (discussing the timing for production of a statement under Rule 26(b)(3)); *Rofail v. U.S.*, 227 F.R.D. 53, 55 (E.D.N.Y. 2005).

[252] *Thomas v. Old Town Dental Group, P.A.*, 300 F.R.D. 585, 589 n.3 (S.D. Fla. 2014).

[253] *New York Times Co. v. U.S. Dept. of Justice*, 138 F. Supp. 3d 462, 472 (S.D.N.Y. 2015); *Ott v. City of Milwaukee*, 291 F.R.D. 151, 154 (E.D. Wis. 2013).

[254] *Mitchell v. Archer Daniels Midland Co.*, 329 F.R.D. 178, 181 (E.D. Tenn. 2019).

[255] *See, e.g.*, *Brown v. Praxair, Inc.*, 2018 WL 5116499, at *5 (M.D. La. 2018).

[256] *Garcia v. City of El Centro*, 214 F.R.D. 587, 594–95 (S.D. Cal. 2003) (there is a split as to whether the mere passage of time creates a substantial need for a witness statement).

[257] *See Mitchell v. Archer Daniels Midland Co.*, 329 F.R.D. 178, 179 (E.D. Tenn. 2019) (audio recordings treated as statements); *Stevens v. School City of Hobart*, 306 F.R.D. 609, 610 (N.D. Ind. 2015) (deposition transcript from prior case is a statement).

Not a Privilege

Technically, the protection for work product or trial preparation materials is not a privilege,[258] although it functions much like a qualified privilege.[259] Thus, statutes or rules of evidence that apply to privileges do not necessarily apply to the trial preparation material protection.

Controlling Law

Unlike most privileges, the trial preparation materials doctrine is always controlled by federal common law, even in diversity cases.[260]

Burden of Proof

The party asserting the trial preparation materials doctrine has the burden of demonstrating that the subject documents are trial preparation materials.[261] Satisfying this burden may entail the submission of affidavits or other evidence.[262] The party seeking an opponent's trial preparation materials then has the burden of showing the necessity of obtaining the trial preparation materials and the lack of substantially equivalent evidence elsewhere.[263] The courts vary as to which party has the burden of establishing waiver or nonwaiver.[264]

Waiver

Evaluating waiver of the trial preparation materials doctrine entails an evaluation of F.R.E. 502 as well as Rule 26(b)(3).[265] Generally, disclosure of documents to an adverse party, or in a manner such that an adverse party may see the documents, constitutes a waiver of the trial preparation materials protection with respect to those documents.[266] Disclosure of documents to someone not adverse, such as a third person, a co-defendant, or a consultant, may not constitute a waiver of

---

[258] *Jolivet v. Compass Grp. USA, Inc.*, 340 F.R.D. 7, 17 (N.D. Tex. 2021).

[259] *See United States v. Sanmina Corp.*, 968 F.3d 1107, 1119 (9th Cir. 2020) (describing it as a qualified privilege).

[260] *von Kahle v. Cargill, Inc.*, __ F. Supp. 3d __, 2022 WL 1223264, at *3 (S.D.N.Y. 2022); *Jolivet v. Compass Grp. USA, Inc.*, 340 F.R.D. 7, 17 (N.D. Tex. 2021).

[261] *Biegas v. Quickway Carriers, Inc.*, 573 F.3d 365, 381 (6th Cir. 2009); *von Kahle v. Cargill, Inc.*, __ F. Supp. 3d __, 2022 WL 1223264, at *3 (S.D.N.Y. 2022).

[262] *Jolivet v. Compass Grp. USA, Inc.*, 340 F.R.D. 7, 18 (N.D. Tex. 2021).

[263] *Jolivet v. Compass Grp. USA, Inc.*, 340 F.R.D. 7, 18 (N.D. Tex. 2021); *Klosin v. E.I. du Pont de Nemours & Co.*, 561 F. Supp. 3d 343, 358 (W.D.N.Y. 2021).

[264] *Compare Pilkington N. Am., Inc. v. Mitsui Sumitomo Ins. Co. of Am.*, 341 F.R.D. 10, 13 (S.D.N.Y. 2022) (burden on the party asserting the protection), *with Carlson v. Colorado Ctr. for Reprod. Med., LLC*, 341 F.R.D. 266, 286 (D. Colo. 2022) (burden on the party asserting waiver).

[265] *See Appleton Papers, Inc. v. E.P.A.*, 702 F.3d 1018, 1026 (7th Cir. 2012).

[266] *United States v. Sanmina Corp.*, 968 F.3d 1107, 1121 (9th Cir. 2020); *New York Times Co. v. United States Dep't of Justice*, 939 F.3d 479, 494 (2d Cir. 2019).

the trial preparation materials protection.[267] Disclosure of fact work product to a testifying expert or court appointed expert may constitute waiver.[268] Some courts hold that disclosure to a third-party who does not share a common interest in developing legal theories and analyses of documents results in waiver.[269] This differs from most privileges, which are waived by disclosure to anyone, not just parties.[270] Additionally, some courts hold that, in contrast to the attorney-client privilege, waiver of the trial preparation materials protection applies only to the documents disclosed, not to the entire subject matter.[271] The courts are divided as to which party has the burden of proving waiver.[272]

Recalling Inadvertently Produced Trial Preparation Materials

Rule 26(b)(5)(B) establishes a procedure to recall attorney work product that has already been produced, which is described below.

Use of Trial Preparation Materials at Trial

Documents withheld as trial preparation materials during discovery may not be used at trial.[273]

Crime-Fraud Exception

The crime-fraud exception exempts materials from the attorney-client privilege and the trial preparation materials doctrine if the materials relate to assistance from an attorney in connection with criminal or fraudulent activities.[274]

Protection Survives Termination of the Litigation

Documents that were created in anticipation of litigation

---

[267]*United States v. Sanmina Corp.*, 968 F.3d 1107, 1119 (9th Cir. 2020); *Appleton Papers, Inc. v. E.P.A.*, 702 F.3d 1018, 1021–22 (7th Cir. 2012) (non-testifying expert); *Jolivet v. Compass Grp. USA, Inc.*, 340 F.R.D. 7, 17 (N.D. Tex. 2021) (third person).

[268]*Ecuadorian Plaintiffs v. Chevron Corp.*, 619 F.3d 373, 378 n.8 (5th Cir. 2010); *South Yuba River Citizens League v. National Marine Fisheries Service*, 257 F.R.D. 607, 614 (E.D. Cal. 2009) (emails from counsel contained information considered by the expert, and thus were discoverable).

[269]*See In re Lindsey*, 158 F.3d 1263, 1282 (D.C. Cir. 1998) (the usual rule is that disclosure to a third party waives work product protection); *In re Zofran (Ondansetron) Prod. Liab. Litig.*, 392 F. Supp. 3d 179, 185 (D. Mass. 2019) (disclosure at a public conference is waiver).

[270]*United States v. Sanmina Corp.*, 968 F.3d 1107, 1120–21 (9th Cir. 2020).

[271]*See, e.g.*, *Appleton Papers, Inc. v. E.P.A.*, 702 F.3d 1018, 1025–26 (7th Cir. 2012); *Mir v. L-3 Commc'n Integrated Sys., L.P.*, 315 F.R.D. 460, 467 (N.D. Tex. 2016).

[272]*Compare Pilkington N. Am., Inc. v. Mitsui Sumitomo Ins. Co. of Am.*, 341 F.R.D. 10, 13 (S.D.N.Y. 2022) (burden on the party asserting the protection), *with Carlson v. Colorado Ctr. for Reprod. Med., LLC*, 341 F.R.D. 266, 286 (D. Colo. 2022) (burden on the party asserting waiver).

[273]*Appleton Papers, Inc. v. E.P.A.*, 702 F.3d 1018, 1022–23 (7th Cir. 2012).

[274]*In re Search Warrant Issued June 13, 2019*, 942 F.3d 159, 175 n.15 (4th Cir. 2019); *Drummond Co., Inc. v. Conrad & Scherer, LLP*, 885 F.3d 1324, 1335 (11th Cir. 2018).

remain subject to the work product protections even after the litigation has concluded.[275]

RULE 26(b)(4)—TRIAL PREPARATION: EXPERTS

CORE CONCEPT

Discovery of the typical engaged expert who will testify at trial normally consists of the expert disclosure under Rule 26(a)(2) and a deposition of the expert, and may also include interrogatories or production requests for documents outside the protections in Rule 26(b)(4), which shield draft expert reports and most communications with testifying experts. Only very limited discovery is permitted with respect to non-testifying experts.

APPLICATIONS

Depositions of Testifying Experts

Parties may take the deposition of any expert witness who may testify at trial.[276]

- *Time for Expert Depositions:* If an expert report is to be disclosed for an expert witness, then the deposition of that witness may not occur before the report is disclosed.[277]
- *Supplemental Expert Disclosure*: If an expert issues a supplemental expert report after the expert has been deposed, an opposing party may be entitled to a second deposition to explore the new opinions in the supplemental disclosure.[278]

Testifying Expert Discovery Fees

The court must impose the reasonable expert fees incurred in responding to the discovery[279] on the party taking discovery of an expert who may testify at trial[280] unless manifest injustice would result.[281] For a deposition, the fee normally includes compensation for time testifying, and most courts also award

---

[275]*See F.T.C. v. Grolier Inc.*, 462 U.S. 19, 24–26 (1983); *Klosin v. E.I. du Pont de Nemours & Co.*, 561 F. Supp. 3d 343, 354 (W.D.N.Y. 2021).

[276]*R.C. Olmstead, Inc., v. CU Interface, LLC*, 606 F.3d 262, 272 (6th Cir. 2010).

[277]*Taylor v. Mentor Worldwide LLC*, 940 F.3d 582, 610 (11th Cir. 2019).

[278]*Taylor v. Mentor Worldwide LLC*, 940 F.3d 582, 610 (11th Cir. 2019).

[279]*Stanley v. Cottrell, Inc.*, 784 F.3d 454, 464 (8th Cir. 2015); *Gwin v. Am. River Transp. Co.*, 482 F.3d 969, 975 (7th Cir. 2007) (abuse of discretion not to award fees); *Knight v. Kirby Inland Marine Inc.*, 482 F.3d 347, 356 (5th Cir. 2007) (fees for testimony at a *Daubert* hearing are not recoverable).

[280]*Crabtree v. Experian Info. Sols., Inc.*, 948 F.3d 872, 884 (7th Cir. 2020) (the court is not required to conduct a *Daubert* hearing to determine whether the expert will be allowed to testify before awarding fees).

[281]*Crabtree v. Experian Info. Sols., Inc.*, 948 F.3d 872, 884 (7th Cir. 2020); *Nilssen v. Osram Sylvania, Inc.*, 528 F.3d 1352 (Fed. Cir. 2008) (injustice is not limited to indigence, and can be based on the conduct of the party seeking fees).

preparation time.[282] It does not include other costs associated with an expert deposition, such as fees for the transcript.[283] However, if the expert charges more than a "reasonable" fee, the court only requires the requesting party to pay the "reasonable" rate.[284] Some courts hold that flat fees for depositions are *per se* unreasonable.[285] Courts are split as to whether and when treating physicians are entitled to an expert witness fee.[286] A party seeking to recover the fees its expert incurred in attending a deposition should seek them at the time of the deposition; they may not be recovered as costs after the case concludes.[287]

- *Non-testifying Expert Fees*: If discovery is obtained from non-testifying experts, the court must also require the requesting party to pay a fair share of the expenses the experts incurred to form their opinions, in addition to the experts' time responding to the discovery.[288]

Experts Specially Retained but Not Expected to Testify

A party may not, by interrogatory or deposition, discover the identity of,[289] facts known by, or opinions held by, experts who are not expected to testify, unless the party makes a showing of exceptional circumstances rendering it impracticable to obtain facts or opinions on the same subject by other means.[290] Such further discovery might be allowed when the particular consulting expert was the only expert to examine evidence that is no longer available (such as a blood sample or accident scene).[291] A party may shield an expert from discovery who was previously designated as a testifying expert by re-designating the witness as non-testifying.[292] Conversely, communications with a consulting expert made before the expert was engaged or after the engagement ended will not be shielded from

---

[282]*Phillips v. Tangilag*, 14 F.4th 524, 543 (6th Cir. 2021); *Knight v. Kirby Inland Marine Inc.*, 482 F.3d 347, 356 (5th Cir. 2007) (fees for testimony are mandatory, but fees for other discovery are within the court's discretion).

[283]*Plastronics Socket Partners, Ltd. v. Dong Weon Hwang*, ___ F. Supp. 3d ___, 2020 WL 1324733, at *12 (E.D. Tex. 2020).

[284]*Cohen v. Jaffe, Raitt, Heuer, & Weiss, P.C.*, 322 F.R.D. 298, 302 (E.D. Mich. 2017); *English v. Washington Metro. Area Transit Auth.*, 293 F. Supp. 3d 13, 15 (D.D.C. 2017).

[285]*Mendez-Caton v. Caribbean Fam. Health Ctr.*, 340 F.R.D. 60, 65 (E.D.N.Y. 2022).

[286]*See Wirtz v. Kansas Farm Bureau Services, Inc.*, 355 F. Supp. 2d 1190, 1212–13 (D. Kan. 2005).

[287]See *Abernathy v. E. Illinois R.R. Co.*, 940 F.3d 982, 994 (7th Cir. 2019).

[288]*See Guarantee Trust Life Ins. Co. v. Am. Medical and Life Ins. Co.*, 291 F.R.D. 234, 238 (N.D. Ill. 2013).

[289]*Williams v. Bridgeport Music, Inc.*, 300 F.R.D. 120, 122 (S.D.N.Y. 2014).

[290]*Republic of Ecuador v. Mackay*, 742 F.3d 860, 866 (9th Cir. 2014); *R.C. Olmstead, Inc., v. CU Interface, LLC*, 606 F.3d 262, 272 (6th Cir. 2010).

[291]*See, e.g., Strobl v. Werner Enterprises, Inc.*, 577 F. Supp. 3d 960, 965-67 (S.D. Iowa 2022); *Spearman Industries, Inc. v. St. Paul Fire and Marine Ins. Co.*, 128 F. Supp. 2d 1148 (N.D. Ill. 2001).

[292]*See Benham v. Ozark Materials River Rock, LLC*, 885 F.3d 1267, 1276 (10th Cir. 2018); *Layman v. Junior Players Golf Academy, Inc.*, 314 F.R.D.

discovery.[293] Some courts hold that a non-testifying expert loses the protections from discovery if the expert consults with a testifying expert[294] or provides documents to a testifying expert.[295]

- *Production Requests Pertaining to Consulting Experts*: Rule 26(b)(4) only explicitly shields consulting experts from interrogatories and depositions.[296] Accordingly, production requests regarding consulting experts are not necessarily shielded by Rule 26(b)(4),[297] although some courts shield consulting experts from production requests despite this language,[298] and other courts shield consulting experts from document requests without recognizing the particular scope of the language in Rule 26(b)(4).[299] Documents created by or for a consulting expert for the purpose of or in anticipation of litigation might be shielded by the protections for work product or trial preparation materials under Rule 26(b)(3), even if not shielded by Rule 26(b)(4),[300] although some courts hold that Rule 26(b)(4) is the only rule that governs expert work product.[301]

Discovery of Treating Physician

There is a split of authority as to whether a treating physician is a fact witness or an expert witness for purposes of the provisions of Rule 26(b)(4).[302] See the discussion of Rule 26(a)(2) above for more detail and case law on this topic.

Experts Informally Consulted

No discovery is permitted of experts informally consulted but not retained.[303]

379, 383 (D.S.C. 2016).

[293] *See In re Zofran (Ondansetron) Prod. Liab. Litig.*, 392 F. Supp. 3d 179, 186 (D. Mass. 2019).

[294] *See In re Chevron Corp.*, 633 F.3d 153, 164 n.17 (3d Cir. 2011).

[295] *Ecuadorian Plaintiffs v. Chevron Corp.*, 619 F.3d 373, 378 (5th Cir. 2010).

[296] *Ibrahim v. Dep't of Homeland Sec.*, 669 F.3d 983, 999 (9th Cir. 2012).

[297] *See In re Zofran (Ondansetron) Prod. Liab. Litig.*, 392 F. Supp. 3d 179, 186 (D. Mass. 2019).

[298] *See Lexington Luminance LLC v. Feit Elec. Co., Inc.*, 2020 WL 10052401, at *9 (C.D. Cal. 2020).

[299] *See, e.g., Strobl v. Werner Enterprises, Inc.*, 577 F. Supp. 3d 960, 965-67 (S.D. Iowa 2022); *U.S. Inspection Servs., Inc. v. NL Engineered Sols., LLC*, 268 F.R.D. 614, 617 (N.D. Cal. 2010).

[300] *See, e.g., In re Cendant Corp. Sec. Litig.*, 343 F.3d 658, 665 (3d Cir. 2003) (Rule 26(b)(3) and (b)(4) apply independently).

[301] *See, e.g., Republic of Ecuador v. Hinchee*, 741 F.3d 1185, 1191 (11th Cir. 2013).

[302] *See Patterson v. Avis Rent A Car Systems, Inc.*, 48 F. Supp. 3d 532, 533 (S.D.N.Y. 2014) (treating physician entitled to fees for attending deposition); *Demar v. U.S.*, 199 F.R.D. 617 (N.D. Ill. 2001) (treating physician not entitled to expert fees from the party noticing the physician's deposition).

[303] *Eisai Co., Ltd. v. Teva Pharmaceuticals USA, Inc.*, 247 F.R.D. 440, 442 (D.N.J. 2007); *West Tennessee*

Experts Employed or Generally Retained by a Party

Full discovery is permitted regarding an expert who is a full-time employee of a party or who was retained generally, rather than in connection with pending or anticipated litigation.[304] No expert fees are awarded in connection with such discovery.

Experts Who Witnessed or Participated in Events

Discovery pertaining to an expert who acquired her knowledge and facts through witnessing or participating in the events that form the basis for the complaint is not covered by Rule 26(b)(4), which is limited to information acquired or developed in anticipation of litigation.[305] Thus, full fact discovery is allowed regarding such experts, and no expert fees are awarded.[306]

Party Who Is an Expert

A party cannot avoid discovery or obtain expert fees by claiming to be an expert witness.[307]

Written Discovery Regarding Experts

Rule 26(a)(2) requires disclosures regarding experts who will testify, and Rule 26(b)(4) authorizes depositions of testifying experts and protects certain communications with experts from discovery. Beyond these provisions, the Rules do not explicitly authorize or prohibit other discovery relating to experts. The fact that some documents are protected as expert trial preparation material certainly suggests that other documents are discoverable, and many cases implicitly authorize written discovery relating to experts.[308]

- *Drafts of Expert Reports and Disclosures*: Drafts of expert reports or expert disclosures for testifying experts are not discoverable.[309] In contrast, reports prepared by non-retained experts are not shielded.[310]
- *Communications with Experts*: Communications between

Chapter of Associated Builders and Contractors, Inc. v. City of Memphis, 219 F.R.D. 587, 591 (W.D. Tenn. 2004).

[304] *Dunn v. Sears, Roebuck & Co.*, 639 F.2d 1171, 1174 (5th Cir. 1981); *Essex Builders Group, Inc. v. Amerisure Ins. Co.*, 235 F.R.D. 703 (M.D. Fla. 2006).

[305] *Smith-Bunge v. Wisconsin Cent., Ltd.*, 946 F.3d 420, 422 (8th Cir. 2019); *Battle ex rel. Battle v. Memorial Hosp. at Gulfport*, 228 F.3d 544, 551 (5th Cir. 2000).

[306] *Paquin v. Fed. Nat. Mortg. Ass'n*, 119 F.3d 23, 33 (D.C. Cir. 1997) (denying payment of fees for alleged experts with personal knowledge).

[307] *See Krepps v. NIIT (USA), Inc.*, 297 F.R.D. 579, 580–81 (N.D. Ill. 2013).

[308] *See, e.g., Wardell v. Zimmer, Inc.*, 2019 WL 13135858, at *1 (D. Alaska 2019); *Dyson Tech. Ltd. v. Maytag Corp.*, 241 F.R.D. 247, 251 (D. Del. 2007).

[309] *Rojas v. Fed. Aviation Admin.*, 922 F.3d 907, 922 (9th Cir. 2019); *Hernandez v. The Office of the Comm'r of Baseball*, 335 F.R.D. 45, 48 (S.D.N.Y. 2020) (notes do not constitute a draft report); *Gerke v. Travelers Cas. Ins. Co. of Am.*, 289 F.R.D. 316, 321 (D. Or. 2013) (but, the opposing party is entitled to know if counsel drafted a portion of the expert's report).

[310] *Holladay v. Royal Caribbean Cruises, Ltd.*, 334 F.R.D. 628, 635 (S.D. Fla. 2020).

counsel and experts who are required to provide an expert report (*i.e.*, those retained or specially employed to testify) are protected as trial preparation materials unless they pertain to:

(i) compensation for the expert;

(ii) the facts or data that counsel provided and the expert considered in forming the opinions to be expressed; or

(iii) the assumptions that counsel provided and the expert relied on in forming the opinions to be expressed.[311]

- *Fraud or Other Misconduct:* These protections may yield if there is fraud or other misconduct in connection with the expert testimony.[312] Communications with experts who are not required to provide expert reports (*i.e.*, treating physicians and other experts not retained or specially employed) are not protected under Rule 26(b)(4)[313]— but they may be protected under other doctrines or privileges.[314] Rule 26(b)(4) only references communications between experts and *counsel*, and most courts have declined to apply the protection to communications between experts and non-lawyers.[315] Additionally, the protections only apply to *communications*; an expert's notes to herself may not be protected.[316]
- *Discovery Expanding the Scope of the Rule 26(a)(2) Disclosures*: Rule 26(a)(2) requires the disclosure of very precise information, such as instances in which the expert has testified within the past four years. Some courts hold that an opposing party cannot expand the scope of the expert disclosure by, for example, requesting the identification of instances where the expert has been retained but did not testify or by seeking publications for a period greater than the 10 years specified in Rule 26(a)(2).[317]
- *Subpoenas to Experts*: The scope of discovery permitted

[311]*Republic of Ecuador v. Mackay*, 742 F.3d 860, 866 (9th Cir. 2014); *TrueNorth Companies, L.C. v. TruNorth Warranty Plans of N. Am., LLC*, 353 F. Supp. 3d 788, 798 (N.D. Iowa 2018).

[312]*Taylor v. Mentor Worldwide LLC*, 940 F.3d 582, 611 n.9 (11th Cir. 2019).

[313]*Ramaco Res., LLC v. Fed. Ins. Co.*, 2020 WL 5261320, at *3 (S.D.W. Va. 2020)

[314]Advisory Committee Notes to the 2010 Amendments to Rule 26(b)(4)(C).

[315]*See, e.g., Republic of Ecuador v. Hinchee*, 741 F.3d 1185, 1189 (11th Cir. 2013).

[316]*Hernandez v. The Office of the Comm'r of Baseball*, 335 F.R.D. 45, 49 (S.D.N.Y. 2020) (the protection only applies to communications with counsel, not to the expert's notes).

[317]*D'Souza v. Marmaxx Operating Corp.*, 2017 WL 1322243, at *6 (W.D. Tex. 2017); *Est. of William I. Allison ex rel. Allison v. Vince Scoggins, P.A.*, 2011 WL 650383, at *2 (W.D.N.C. 2011).

by subpoena is the same as scope for party discovery.[318] Accordingly, a party cannot circumvent any of the limits on expert discovery by serving a subpoena on the expert.[319]

Privilege Log

The courts disagree about whether it is necessary to list documents withheld based on Rule 26(b)(4) on a privilege log.[320]

Duty of Attorney to Review Expert's File

Some courts hold that the attorney has a duty to review the expert's files to determine which communications and documents should be disclosed—the attorney cannot rely on the expert to make these discoverability determinations.[321]

Ex Parte Communications with Experts for Another Party

A party should not have *ex parte* communications with an expert for another party.[322]

RULE 26(b)(5)—CLAIMING PRIVILEGE OR PROTECTING TRIAL-PREPARATION MATERIALS

CORE CONCEPT

A party who withholds information based on a claim of privilege or work product/trial preparation materials protection must state the claim expressly and describe the nature of the documents or information so withheld in a manner that will enable other parties to assess the claim of privilege or protection. If privileged information is inadvertently produced in discovery, the producing party may so notify the parties that received the information. The receiving parties must then either return, sequester, or destroy the information, but may ask the court to determine the validity of the privilege assertion.

APPLICATIONS

Asserting Privilege as to a Document

A party asserting a privilege must expressly make the claim with sufficient detail that other parties and the court can assess the privilege assertion, without disclosing the privileged

[318] *Jordan v. Comm'r, Mississippi Dep't of Corr.*, 947 F.3d 1322, 1329 (11th Cir. 2020).

[319] *Cadence Educ., LLC v. Vore*, 2018 WL 2926442, at *4 (D. Kan. 2018); *Marsh v. Jackson*, 141 F.R.D. 431, 433 (W.D. Va. 1992).

[320] *See Strobl v. Werner Enterprises, Inc.*, 577 F. Supp. 3d 960, 967-68 (S.D. Iowa 2022) (no log required); *Est. of William I. Allison ex rel. Allison v. Vince Scoggins, P.A.*, 2011 WL 650383, at *2 (W.D.N.C. 2011) (log required).

[321] *See Gerke v. Travelers Cas. Ins. Co. of Am.*, 289 F.R.D. 316, 322 (D. Or. 2013).

[322] *See Sanderson v. Boddie-Noell Enterprises, Inc.*, 227 F.R.D. 448 (E.D. Va. 2005); *Sewell v. Maryland Dept. of Transp.*, 206 F.R.D. 545 (D. Md. 2002).

information.[323] Many courts require a party asserting a privilege to produce a privilege log describing the documents withheld.[324] The Rules do not specify the time for production of a privilege log, and the case law varies. Some courts hold that the log must be produced at the same time the response to the document request is due[325] and some allow a reasonable time.[326] If a motion regarding the privileges is pending, some courts hold that the respondent may wait until the court rules upon pending objections before generating the privilege log.[327] Privileges may be waived broadly for failure to produce a privilege log,[328] undue delay in producing a privilege log,[329] or failure to produce a sufficiently detailed log,[330] or specifically for any documents omitted from the privilege log.[331] Some courts allow parties to list withheld documents by category, as long as the description of the category contains enough information to allow the receiving party and the court to make a determination about the assertion as to the documents within the category.[332] The courts are divided as to how to handle email chains on a privilege log.[333] Parties often agree not to log communications with trial counsel after the litigation has commenced.[334] Some courts hold that a party does not need to log expert materials shielded from discovery under Rule 26(b)(4), such as draft reports.[335]

---

[323] *Equal Employment Opportunity Comm'n v. BDO USA, L.L.P.*, 856 F.3d 356, 363 (5th Cir. 2017); *N.L.R.B. v. Interbake Foods, LLC*, 637 F.3d 492, 502 (4th Cir. 2011).

[324] *See Stallworth v. Bryant*, 936 F.3d 224, 229 (5th Cir. 2019); *Oceana, Inc. v. Ross*, 920 F.3d 855, 865 (D.C. Cir. 2019).

[325] *See, e.g, S.E.C. v. v. Yorkville Advisors, LLC*, 300 F.R.D. 152, 157 (S.D.N.Y. 2014).

[326] *See Monco v. Zoltek Corp.*, 317 F. Supp. 3d 995, 999 (N.D. Ill. 2018) (log must be produced in a "timely manner."); *Segar v. Holder*, 277 F.R.D. 9, 17 (D.D.C. 2011).

[327] *U.S. v. Philip Morris Inc.*, 314 F.3d 612, 621 (D.C. Cir. 2003).

[328] *Pearlshire Cap. Grp., LLC v. Zaid*, 490 F. Supp. 3d 1299, 1303 (N.D. Ill. 2020); *Tom v. S.B., Inc.*, 280 F.R.D. 603, 614 (D.N.M. 2012).

[329] *RightCHOICE Managed Care, Inc. v. Hosp. Partners, Inc.*, 489 F. Supp. 3d 907, 916 (W.D. Mo. 2020).

[330] *In re Aenergy, S.A.*, 451 F. Supp. 3d 319, 328 (S.D.N.Y. 2020) (ordering submission of a revised log); *Sulaymu-Bey v. City of New York*, 372 F. Supp. 3d 90, 94 (E.D.N.Y. 2019) (same). *But see Progressive Cas. Ins. Co. v. F.D.I.C.*, 298 F.R.D. 417, 421 (N.D. Iowa 2014) (in the absence of bad faith, waiver is not appropriate for technical shortcomings of the log).

[331] *Cicel (Beijing) Sci. & Tech. Co. v. Misonix, Inc.*, 331 F.R.D. 218, 228 (E.D.N.Y. 2019); *Robinson v. Texas Auto. Dealers Ass'n*, 214 F.R.D. 432, 456 (E.D. Tex. 2003).

[332] *In re Actos Antitrust Litig.*, 340 F.R.D. 549, 553 (S.D.N.Y. 2022); *Jolivet v. Compass Grp. USA, Inc.*, 340 F.R.D. 7, 21 (N.D. Tex. 2021).

[333] *See In re Actos Antitrust Litig.*, 340 F.R.D. 549, 553 (S.D.N.Y. 2022); *Muro v. Target Corp.*, 250 F.R.D. 350 (N.D. Ill. 2007).

[334] *Grider v. Keystone Health Plan Central, Inc.*, 580 F.3d 119, 140 n.22 (3d Cir. 2009).

[335] *See Strobl v. Werner Enterprises, Inc.*, 577 F. Supp. 3d 960, 967-68 (S.D. Iowa 2022); *Williams v. Bridgeport*

Asserting Privilege in Response to a Deposition Question, Interrogatory, or RFA

At a deposition, a party may orally raise an objection to an individual question, then refuse to provide the privileged information (by counsel instructing the witness not to answer).[336] In response to interrogatories or requests for admission, a party may make a written objection to an individual question or request and withhold the privileged information. The objection must include sufficient information so that the court and opposing counsel can assess the applicability of the privilege.[337]

Failure to State Claim of Privilege with Sufficient Specificity

If a party withholds information without properly disclosing the basis, the party may have waived the privilege,[338] and may be subject to sanctions.[339]

Challenging Privilege Assertions

A party may challenge the privilege assertion for documents listed on a privilege log by filing a motion to compel, which places the burden on the party asserting the privilege to establish an evidentiary basis, by affidavit, deposition transcript, or other evidence, for each element of the privilege.[340] The court may also, at its discretion, review the challenged documents *in camera* and make its own determinations.[341]

Law Establishing Privileges

The law applicable to privileges in federal court depends upon whether the action involves a state law issue or a federal cause of action. If a court is applying the forum state's substantive laws, that state's laws of privilege also apply,[342] except as to the trial preparation materials (work product) protection, which is governed by Rule 26(b)(3) and federal common law.[343] If the action is governed by federal law, then Rule 501 of the Federal Rules of Evidence applies, which instructs the federal

---

Music, Inc., 300 F.R.D. 120, 122 (S.D.N.Y. 2014).

[336] Fed. R. Civ. P. 30(c)(2).

[337] *Burns v. Imagine Films Entertainment, Inc.*, 164 F.R.D. 589 (W.D.N.Y. 1996).

[338] *Texas Brine Co., LLC & Occidental Chem. Corp.*, 879 F.3d 1224, 1230 n.5 (10th Cir. 2018); *Equal Employment Opportunity Comm'n v. BDO USA, L.L.P.*, 876 F.3d 690, 697 (5th Cir. 2017).

[339] *See Urban 8 Fox Lake Corp. v. Nationwide Affordable Hous. Fund 4, LLC*, 334 F.R.D. 149, 164 (N.D. Ill. 2020); *Jones v. Hernandez*, 322 F.R.D. 411, 416 (S.D. Cal. 2017).

[340] *See N.L.R.B. v. Interbake Foods, LLC*, 637 F.3d 492, 501 (4th Cir. 2011); *Jolivet v. Compass Grp. USA, Inc.*, 340 F.R.D. 7, 21 (N.D. Tex. 2021).

[341] *Carlson v. Colorado Ctr. For Reprod. Med., LLC*, 341 F.R.D. 266, 290 (D. Colo. 2022); *Jolivet v. Compass Grp. USA, Inc.*, 340 F.R.D. 7, 21 (N.D. Tex. 2021).

[342] *See Veracities PBC v. Strand*, ___ F. Supp. 3d ___, 2022 WL 1439039, at *2 (D. Or. 2022); *Total Rx Care, LLC v. Great N. Ins. Co.*, 318 F.R.D. 587, 595 (N.D. Tex. 2017).

[343] *Tompkins v. R.J. Reynolds Tobacco Co.*, 92 F. Supp. 2d 70 (N.D.N.Y. 2000).

courts to develop a body of federal common law privileges.[344] If the action includes both federal law claims and state law claims, federal privilege law applies to evidence relevant to both claims.[345]

Who May Assert

Usually, only the person holding a privilege may assert it. Certainly, a party may not assert a privilege of a nonparty witness or another party. When an attorney is deposed, the privilege technically belongs to the client, but courts allow the attorney to assert the privilege if asked about an attorney-client communication.[346]

Disclosure of Privileged Information

Privileges generally are waived by voluntary disclosure,[347] either during discovery or elsewhere.[348] Thus, caution should be exercised responding to discovery requests pertaining to privileged matters.

Documents Containing Privileged and Nonprivileged Matter

If part of a document contains privileged matter and part does not, a party must provide the nonprivileged matter, but may redact the privileged matter.[349]

Privileged Matter to be Introduced at Trial

A majority of courts hold that a party cannot assert a privilege at the discovery stage, then introduce the privileged matter at trial.[350] Consequently, any matter intended to be introduced at trial should be produced during discovery if requested.

Particular Privileges

A detailed analysis of every potential privilege is beyond the scope of this *Handbook*. The following is an overview of the most commonly asserted privileges:

- *Attorney-Client:* The attorney-client privilege applies to confidential communications between a client and the client's attorney that occur in connection with legal representation or in the process of obtaining legal

[344]*See Veracities PBC v. Strand*, ___ F. Supp. 3d ___, 2022 WL 1439039, at *2 (D. Or. 2022); *Doe v. Old Dominion Univ.*, 289 F. Supp. 3d 744, 749 (E.D. Va. 2018).

[345]*Agster v. Maricopa Cnty.*, 422 F.3d 836, 839 (9th Cir. 2005); *Snipes v. United States*, 334 F.R.D. 548, 551 (N.D. Cal. 2020).

[346]*See Martin Marietta Materials, Inc. v. Bedford Reinforced Plastics, Inc.*, 227 F.R.D. 382, 390 (W.D. Pa. 2005) (privilege belongs to the client, not to the attorney).

[347]*Appleton Papers, Inc. v. E.P.A.*, 702 F.3d 1018, 1024 (7th Cir. 2012).

[348]*See In re Lott*, 424 F.3d 446, 452 (6th Cir. 2005) (attorney-client privilege is waived when the legal advice is placed at issue).

[349]*See Christine Asia Co. v. Alibaba Grp. Holding Ltd.*, 327 F.R.D. 52, 54 (S.D.N.Y. 2018).

[350]*Doe v. Eli Lilly & Co., Inc.*, 99 F.R.D. 126, 127 (D.D.C. 1983).

representation.[351] It applies to communications with an in-house attorney if the attorney is providing legal services.[352] It does not protect documents or other physical evidence provided to the attorney (other than written communications to the attorney), the underlying facts,[353] information or evidence gathered by the attorney from other sources, or notes and memoranda prepared by the attorney (but such notes and memoranda may be protected as trial preparation materials under Rule 26(b)(3)).

- *Self-Incrimination:* The Fifth Amendment to the United States Constitution provides persons (whether or not parties to a litigation) with a privilege against testifying in a manner that would tend to incriminate them.[354] The privilege applies to depositions,[355] interrogatories, requests for admission, and request for production of documents,[356] as well as at trial. Corporations may not assert the privilege, but corporate representatives may assert it if their testimony would incriminate them personally, regardless of whether they are testifying in their individual or representative capacities.[357]
- *Governmental Privileges:* The United States and the individual States must produce all relevant, nonprivileged matter, just as any other party.[358] However, the United States has some extra privileges:
  - *Military or State Secrets:* The United States has a qualified privilege for matters that involve military or state secrets.[359]
  - *Statutory Privilege:* Some statutes require governmental agencies and other entities to file certain documents or reports, and designate those submissions as confidential. A common example is income tax returns. Under the regulation,[360] the United States receives and keeps tax returns, but is not required to produce them to private litigants. Note that the privilege belongs to the United States

---

[351] *Diversified Industries, Inc. v. Meredith*, 572 F.2d 596, 612 (8th Cir. 1977); *Goldstein v. F.D.I.C.*, 494 B.R. 82, 90 (D.D.C. 2013).

[352] *See United States Equal Emp. Opportunity Comm'n v. George Washington Univ.*, 502 F. Supp. 3d 62, 80 (D.D.C. 2020).

[353] *Martin Marietta Materials, Inc. v. Bedford Reinforced Plastics, Inc.*, 227 F.R.D. 382, 392 (W.D. Pa. 2005).

[354] *De Vita v. Sills*, 422 F.2d 1172 (3d Cir.1970).

[355] *In re Folding Carton Antitrust Litig.*, 609 F.2d 867 (7th Cir.1979).

[356] *Gordon v. Fed. Deposit Ins. Corp.*, 427 F.2d 578, 580 (D.C. Cir. 1970); *Merrifield v. Gussman*, 296 F. Supp. 3d 362, 366 (D. Mass. 2017).

[357] *U.S. v. Kordel*, 397 U.S. 1, 8 (1970).

[358] *U. S. v. Procter & Gamble Co.*, 356 U.S. 677, 681 (1958).

[359] *See General Dynamics Corp. v. U.S.*, 563 U.S. 478 (2011).

[360] 26 C.F.R. § 301.6103(a-1)(c)).

only—the individual filing the return may be required to produce it.

  - ○ *Executive Privilege:* The Executive branch of the United States government has a general qualified privilege, grounded in the need for the executive branch to gather information.[361]

- *Other Privileges:* In some states, communications with spouses, physicians, clergy, journalists, accountants, and social workers are privileged.

Burden of Proof

The party raising a privilege has the burden of establishing the existence of the privilege.[362]

Recalling Privileged Information

Rule 26(b)(5)(B) establishes a procedure to recall privileged information that has already been produced in discovery.[363] A party believing that it has produced privileged information may notify the parties who have received the information. The notice should be in writing (unless circumstances do not allow, such as in a deposition)[364] and should be sufficiently detailed to allow the receiving parties to evaluate the claim of privilege.[365] After receiving such a notice, the receiving party must return, sequester, or destroy the specified information and all copies (including taking reasonable steps to retrieve any information that the receiving party had already disclosed to other persons).[366] Some courts hold that an attorney violates Rule 26(b)(5)(B) by reviewing the documents after an opposing party initiates this recall procedure.[367] If the receiving party does not agree with the privilege assertion, it can present the situation to the court for a determination of the privilege claim. During the court's review of the privilege claim, the receiving party is prohibited from using the information and the producing party must preserve it. Alternatively, the parties can propose their

[361]*U.S. v. Nixon*, 418 U.S. 683 (1974).

[362]*Republic of Ecuador v. Hinchee*, 741 F.3d 1185, 1189 (11th Cir. 2013); *Heathman v. U.S. Dist. Court for Central Dist. of California*, 503 F.2d 1032, 1033 (9th Cir. 1974); *Martin Marietta Materials, Inc. v. Bedford Reinforced Plastics, Inc.*, 227 F.R.D. 382, 389 (W.D. Pa. 2005) (party asserting the privilege has the initial burden, then the burden shifts to the opposing party to establish waiver).

[363]*See United States Equal Emp. Opportunity Comm'n v. George Washington Univ.*, 502 F. Supp. 3d 62, 71-78 (D.D.C. 2020) (the procedure does not apply to documents obtained outside the discovery process); *Stewart Title Guar. Co. v. Owlett & Lewis, P.C.*, 297 F.R.D. 232, 240 (M.D. Pa. 2013).

[364]*Lloyds of London Syndicate 2003 v. Fireman's Fund Ins. Co. of Ohio*, 320 F.R.D. 557, 561 (D. Kan. 2017).

[365]The 2006 Amendment to the Advisory Committee Note to Rule 26(b)(5)(B).

[366]*Ground Zero Center for Non-Violent Action v. U. S. Dep't of Navy*, 860 F.3d 1244 (9th Cir. 2017).

[367]*United States Equal Emp. Opportunity Comm'n v. George Washington Univ.*, 502 F. Supp. 3d 62, 71-78 (D.D.C. 2020).

own procedures for privileged information that has inadvertently been produced or disclosed.

- *Waiver of the Privilege for Recalled Information:* Rule 26(b)(5)(B) does not address whether the privilege or protection is preserved or waived for information that was disclosed and then recalled. In other words, the accidental production might or might not have resulted in waiver of the privilege, and the Rule 26(b)(5)(B) recall procedure does not affect that analysis, which instead is controlled by the applicable law on privilege waiver.[368] In cases governed by federal law, waiver is governed by Rule 502(b) of the Federal Rules of Evidence, which provides that disclosure does not constitute waiver if the disclosure was inadvertent, the holder of the privilege took reasonable precautions to prevent disclosure, and the holder promptly attempted to rectify the error, such as by using the recall provisions of Rule 26(b)(5)(B).[369]

RULE 26(c)—PROTECTIVE ORDERS

CORE CONCEPT

The court may enter orders designed to protect the parties and witnesses during the discovery process.

APPLICATIONS

Purposes of Protective Orders

Rule 26(c) specifically instructs the court to limit the frequency or extent of discovery if justice so requires to protect someone from annoyance, embarrassment,[370] oppression,[371] undue burden[372] or expense.[373] Protective orders are also frequently used to limit the frequency or extent of discovery if: (i) the discovery sought is unreasonably cumulative or is obtainable from a more convenient or less burdensome or expensive source; (ii) the party seeking the discovery has had ample opportunity to obtain the information; or (iii) the discovery is outside the scope of discovery set forth in Rule 26(b)(1).[374] Protective orders generally apply to formal discovery, and it is

[368] *Carmody v. Bd. of Trustees of Univ. of Illinois*, 893 F.3d 397, 406 (7th Cir. 2018).

[369] F.R.E. 502(b); *Shaffer v. Pennsbury Sch. Dist.*, 525 F. Supp. 3d 573, 577–78 (E.D. Pa. 2021).

[370] *Seattle Times Co. v. Rhinehart*, 467 U.S. 20, 35 n. 21 (1984) (the rule serves in part to protect parties' privacy interests); *In re Avandia Mktg., Sales Practices & Prod. Liab. Litig.*, 924 F.3d 662, 671 (3d Cir. 2019).

[371] *Nieves v. OPA, Inc.*, 948 F. Supp. 2d 887, 892–93 (N.D. Ill. 2013) (Rule 26(c) is designed to protect a party from harassing discovery).

[372] *In re Ohio Execution Protocol Litig.*, 845 F.3d 231, 240 (6th Cir. 2016); *Jackson v. Allstate Ins. Co.*, 785 F.3d 1193, 1202 (8th Cir. 2015).

[373] *Stagman v. Ryan*, 176 F.3d 986 (7th Cir. 1999).

[374] *NRA Grp., LLC v. Durenleau*, 340 F.R.D. 94, 98 (M.D. Pa. 2021); *United States v. All Assets Held at Bank Julius Baer & Co., Ltd.*, 202 F. Supp. 3d 1, 6 (D.D.C. 2016).

not settled whether courts may limit informal investigations.[375]

Types of Protective Order

Rule 26(c)(1) authorizes the court to protect a person from "annoyance, embarrassment, oppression, or undue burden or expense."[376] The Rule then lists eight categories of protective orders, which are discussed immediately below. The list is not exclusive, however, and the court has broad discretion to make any type of protective order required by justice.[377] The specifically enumerated categories are below.

(1) *Order that Disclosure or Discovery Not be Had:* The court may order that the automatic disclosure or requested discovery not occur.[378]

(2) *Specified Terms and Conditions:* The court can impose terms and conditions on the automatic disclosure or the taking of discovery.[379] The court may designate the time, location, or conditions of a deposition,[380] or the time to respond to discovery requests.[381] The court may order the party seeking discovery to pay the responding party's resulting expenses or may allocate the costs of responding among the parties.[382] The court may set deadlines for the completion of various phases of discovery or order that discovery be conducted in a particular sequence.[383] The court may delay or stay discovery[384]—for example, while a dispositive motion is

---

[375] *See In re Bofi Holding, Inc. Sec. Litig.*, 318 F.R.D. 129, 133 (S.D. Cal. 2016) (courts may not limit informal investigations); *Hirt v. Unified Sch. Dist. No. 287*, 308 F. Supp. 3d 1157, 1183 (D. Kan. 2018) (limiting interviews with non-parties).

[376] *Loomis v. Unum Grp. Corp.*, 338 F.R.D. 225, 228 (E.D. Tenn. 2021); *Sec. & Exch. Comm'n v. Lemelson*, 334 F.R.D. 359, 361 (D. Mass. 2020).

[377] *Seattle Times Co. v. Rhinehart*, 467 U.S. 20, 36 (1984); *Ampong v. Costco Wholesale Corp.*, 550 F. Supp. 3d 136, 139 (S.D.N.Y. 2021).

[378] *Paxton v. Landesk Software, Inc.*, 332 F.R.D. 368, 369 (M.D. Fla. 2019) (prohibiting discovery of the plaintiff's employers); *Estate of Levingston v. County of Kern*, 320 F.R.D. 520, 528 (E.D. Cal. 2017) (prohibiting deposition of "apex" executive).

[379] *Duling v. Gristede's Operating Corp.*, 266 F.R.D. 66, 71 (S.D.N.Y. 2010).

[380] *Reid v. Temple Univ. Hosp., Inc.*, 329 F.R.D. 531, 533 (E.D. Pa. 2019); *McArthur v. Rock Woodfired Pizza & Spirits*, 318 F.R.D. 136, 139 (W.D. Wa. 2016).

[381] *Manske v. UPS Cartage Services, Inc.*, 789 F. Supp. 2d 213, 216–17 (D. Me. 2011).

[382] *Singleton v. Arkansas Hous. Authorities Prop. & Cas. Self-Insured Fund, Inc.*, 934 F.3d 830, 840 (8th Cir. 2019); *George v. Professional Disposables Int'l, Inc.*, 2016 WL 3029936, at *2 (S.D.N.Y. 2016) (shifting costs is the exception).

[383] *Builders Ass'n of Greater Chicago v. City of Chicago*, 170 F.R.D. 435, 437 (N.D. Ill. 1996) (order setting the sequence of discovery appropriate when a potentially dispositive threshold issue has been raised).

[384] *See ProCare Hospice of Nevada, LLC v. OneCare Hospice, LLC*, 340 F.R.D. 174, 176 (D. Nev. 2021); *Oliver v. City of New York*, 540 F. Supp. 3d 434, 435 (S.D.N.Y. 2021).

pending.[385]

(3) *Method of Discovery:* The court may direct that discovery, either generally or as to an individual witness or topic, be taken by a particular method (such as by written discovery only, not by oral deposition).[386] The general principle is that the parties may select their own discovery methods without interference from the court.[387] Thus, most motions to restrict the discovery methods are denied unless the moving party shows special circumstances.[388]

(4) *Limit of Scope or Time:* The court may limit the scope of the automatic disclosures or discovery to specific areas of inquiry[389] or to a specific time period.[390] The court may also limit discovery to a critical or threshold issue.[391] If a jurisdictional dispute exists, the court may restrict discovery to the jurisdictional issues, then permit broad discovery if jurisdiction is found to exist.[392] Similarly, if liability and damages are to be tried separately, the court may restrict discovery to liability issues until the first phase of the case is complete.

(5) *Persons Present:* The court may exclude (or sequester) the public, the press, other witnesses, or other nonparties from a deposition[393] or access to documents produced in discovery.[394] The court generally will not exclude the parties or their attorneys.

(6) *Sealed Transcript:* In general, discovery produced by

---

[385] *Ema Fin., LLC v. Vystar Corp.*, 336 F.R.D. 75, 79 (S.D.N.Y. 2020) (stay disfavored); *Sprint Solutions, Inc. v. Cell Xchange, Inc.*, 49 F. Supp. 3d 1074, 1078 (M.D. Fla. 2014) (before staying discovery, the court should take a "preliminary peek" at the merits to see if the motion seems meritorious and dispositive).

[386] *See Bless v. Cook Cnty. Sheriff's Off.*, 9 F.4th 565, 570–71 (7th Cir. 2021).

[387] *See National Life Ins. Co. v. Hartford Acc. and Indem. Co.*, 615 F.2d 595 (3d Cir. 1980); *Ball Corp. v. Air Tech of Michigan, Inc.*, 329 F.R.D. 599, 603 (N.D. Ind. 2019).

[388] *Nguyen v. Excel Corp.*, 197 F.3d 200, 208–09 (5th Cir. 1999); *Harris v. Clay Cty., Mississippi*, 514 F. Supp. 3d 880, 882 (N.D. Miss. 2021) (order prohibiting depositions disfavored).

[389] *See Liese v. Indian River County Hosp. Dist.*, 701 F.3d 334, 355 (11th Cir. 2012); *Capri Sun GmbH v. Am. Beverage Corp.*, 414 F. Supp. 3d 414, 434 (S.D.N.Y. 2019).

[390] *See Ball Corp. v. Air Tech of Michigan, Inc.*, 329 F.R.D. 599, 603 (N.D. Ind. 2019).

[391] *Vivid Technologies, Inc. v. Am. Science & Engineering, Inc.*, 200 F.3d 795, 804 (Fed. Cir. 1999) (staying discovery on all other issues until critical issue is resolved).

[392] *See Anwar v. Dow Chem. Co.*, 876 F.3d 841, 854 (6th Cir. 2017).

[393] *Oakley, Inc. v. Grangeville Depot LLC*, 336 F.R.D. 191, 193 (D. Idaho 2020).

[394] *Phillips ex rel. Estates of Byrd v. General Motors Corp.*, 307 F.3d 1206 (9th Cir. 2002) (the public generally, and the press in particular, are presumptively entitled to access documents produced in discovery, and good cause must be demonstrated to limit such access); *D.A. v. Meridian Joint School Dist. No. 2*, 289 F.R.D. 614, 634 (D. Idaho 2013).

private litigants is private until it is filed, at which point it becomes public.[395] The court may order a deposition transcript sealed, and thus not part of the public record.[396] Similar orders have been entered with respect to interrogatory answers or documents to be produced,[397] although such orders are not expressly authorized by 26(c).[398] Courts are generally reluctant to seal court papers and do so only for "compelling reasons."[399] Some courts do not apply this heightened standard to records attached to *non-dispositive* motions.[400] Once a sealing order has been entered, parties are prohibited from disclosing to third persons information obtained pursuant to the court order. The prohibition generally does not apply, however, to information already in a party's possession when the order is entered.[401]

(7) *Confidential Information:* The court may enter an order restricting disclosure of private personal information,[402] trade secrets, and confidential research, development, or commercial information[403] obtained during discovery.[404] There is no absolute privilege or protection with respect to such matters.[405] The normal procedure is for the parties to negotiate an agreement as to the

---

[395] *Bond v. Utreras*, 585 F.3d 1061, 1065–66 (7th Cir. 2009); *Suell v. United States*, 32 F. Supp. 3d 1190, 1192 (S.D. Ala. 2014).

[396] *Pintos v. Pacific Creditors Ass'n*, 565 F.3d 1106, 1115 (9th Cir. 2009) (once documents have been attached to a dispositive motion and become part of the public record, having them sealed involves a heightened burden); *In re Estate of Martin Luther King, Jr., Inc. v. CBS, Inc.*, 184 F. Supp. 2d 1353, 1362 (N.D. Ga. 2002) (only the court may seal documents; the parties cannot do so by stipulation).

[397] *Center for Auto Safety v. Chrysler Group, LLC*, 809 F.3d 1092, 1095 (9th Cir. 2016); *Apple Inc. v. Samsung Elec. Co., Ltd.*, 727 F.3d 1214, 1222 (Fed. Cir. 2013).

[398] *Morgan v. U.S. Dept. of Justice*, 923 F.2d 195 (D.C. Cir. 1991).

[399] *Signature Mgmt. Team, LLC v. Doe*, 876 F.3d 831, 836 (6th Cir. 2017); *Kamakana v. City & Cty. of Honolulu*, 447 F.3d 1172, 1178 (9th Cir. 2006).

[400] *See Kamakana v. City & Cty. of Honolulu*, 447 F.3d 1172, 1179 (9th Cir. 2006); *Software Rts. Archive, LLC v. Facebook, Inc.*, 485 F. Supp. 3d 1096, 1113 (N.D. Cal. 2020).

[401] *Seattle Times Co. v. Rhinehart*, 467 U.S. 20, 34 (1984).

[402] *Prado v. Equifax Info. Servs. LLC*, 331 F.R.D. 134, 137 (N.D. Cal. 2019); *Smith v. Yeager*, 322 F.R.D. 96, 98 (D.D.C. 2017).

[403] *R.C. Olmstead, Inc., v. CU Interface, LLC*, 606 F.3d 262, 269 (6th Cir. 2010) (court may decide whether trade secrets are relevant and whether the need for discovery outweighs the harm of production); *Phillips v. General Motors Corp.*, 289 F.3d 1117 (9th Cir. 2002) (the enumerated categories of confidential information are not exclusive, and settlement information can be protected).

[404] *Seattle Times Co. v. Rhinehart*, 467 U.S. 20 (1984).

[405] *Fed. Open Market Comm. of Fed. Reserve Sys. v. Merrill*, 443 U.S. 340 (1979); *In re Violation of Rule 28(D)*, 635 F.3d 1352, 1357 (Fed. Cir. 2011).

handling of confidential information,[406] which is often memorialized in a stipulated confidentiality order signed by the court—this procedure gives the court the ability to enforce the parties' agreement.[407] If the parties cannot agree to a confidentiality stipulation, the responding party can move for a protective order or the party seeking the discovery can move to compel under Rule 37(a). The party seeking the discovery will have the burden of showing that the information is relevant and proportional to the needs of the case.[408] In most cases, the discovery will be allowed, but under restricted conditions regarding further disclosure. The court can fashion any order it sees fit, requiring the information to be filed under seal,[409] limiting how the information may be used, who may see it, etc.[410] The court may also order disclosure of limited portions of confidential information, such as ordering disclosure of the ingredients of a product, but not the formula. The court can also designate an impartial third person to examine the confidential information.

(8) *Simultaneous Exchange:* The court may order the parties to simultaneously file designated documents or information in sealed envelopes, to be opened as directed by the court. This procedure is most common in patent cases, where it can be an advantage to know an opponent's contentions.

Standard—Good Cause

Protective orders are entered for "good cause."[411] The court has almost complete discretion in determining what constitutes good cause.[412] "Good cause" exists when the discovery will cause a clearly defined and serious injury to the party seeking protection,[413] which must be shown with specificity.[414] The proportionality principles from Rule 26(b)(1) will govern the good cause

---

[406] *Suell v. United States*, 32 F. Supp. 3d 1190, 1192 (S.D. Ala. 2014).

[407] *But see Pinnacle Sur. Servs., Inc. v. Manion Stigger, LLP*, 370 F. Supp. 3d 745, 756 (W.D. Ky. 2019) (refusing to sign a stipulated protective order because the parties had not met and conferred about a "dispute").

[408] *In re Cooper Tire & Rubber Co.*, 568 F.3d 1180 (10th Cir. 2009) (the burden then shifts to the party seeking the information to show that it is relevant and necessary); *Bruno & Stillman, Inc. v. Globe Newspaper Co.*, 633 F.2d 583 (1st Cir.1980).

[409] *Fitzhenry-Russell v. Keurig Dr. Pepper Inc.*, 345 F. Supp. 3d 1111, 1120 (N.D. Cal. 2018).

[410] *See Paycom Payroll, LLC v. Richison*, 758 F.3d 1198, 1202–03 (10th Cir. 2014) (attorney's eyes only); *In re Violation of Rule 28(D)*, 635 F.3d 1352, 1357 (Fed. Cir. 2011).

[411] *In re Avandia Mktg., Sales Practices & Prod. Liab. Litig.*, 924 F.3d 662, 671 (3d Cir. 2019); *In re Ohio Execution Protocol Litig.*, 845 F.3d 231, 236 (6th Cir. 2016).

[412] *Seattle Times Co. v. Rhinehart*, 467 U.S. 20 (1984); *IDS Prop. Cas. Ins. Co. v. Gov't Emps. Ins. Co.*, 985 F.3d 41, 50 (1st Cir. 2021).

[413] *Matter of Energetic Tank, Inc.*, 567 F. Supp. 3d 453, 456 (S.D.N.Y.

analysis;[415] the court will balance the need of the party seeking the discovery against the burden on the party responding.[416] Many courts will enter stipulated protective orders without requiring a good cause showing, but some courts independently assess good cause even when the parties have stipulated to the order.[417]

Burden of Proof

The party seeking the protective order generally has the burden of showing that good cause exists by stating particular and specific facts.[418] Broad, general allegations of harm are not sufficient.[419] In some circumstances, the court will shift the burden to the party seeking the discovery, particularly when one party is seeking disfavored discovery like deposing the opposing party's lawyer.[420]

Which Court

Protective orders are obtained by motion filed in the district where the action is pending.[421] When a nonparty is served with a subpoena to testify or produce documents in a district other than the one where the case is pending, the nonparty may file a motion to quash or modify the subpoena in the district where performance is commanded.[422]

Certificate of Conference

A motion for protective order must include a certification that the movant has in good faith conferred or attempted to confer with the other party in an effort to resolve the dispute without court action.[423] Courts will frequently deny motions for protective orders that do not include the meet and confer certificate.[424] Some courts do not require a written certification when the motion for a protective order relates to an oral

---

2021); *Nothstein v. USA Cycling*, 337 F.R.D. 375, 393 (E.D. Pa. 2020).

[414] *In re Avandia Mktg., Sales Practices & Prod. Liab. Litig.*, 924 F.3d 662, 671 (3d Cir. 2019).

[415] *Republic of Turkey v. Christie's, Inc.*, 326 F.R.D. 402, 406 (S.D.N.Y. 2018).

[416] *In re: Chiquita Brands Int'l, Inc.*, 965 F.3d 1238, 1251 (11th Cir. 2020); *Cazorla v. Koch Foods of Mississippi, L.L.C.*, 838 F.3d 540, 555 (5th Cir. 2016).

[417] *See In re: Chiquita Brands Int'l, Inc.*, 965 F.3d 1238, 1249–50 (11th Cir. 2020) (discussing the split).

[418] *Gulf Oil Co. v. Bernard*, 452 U.S. 89, 102 (1981); *In re Nat'l Prescription Opiate Litig.*, 927 F.3d 919, 930 (6th Cir. 2019).

[419] *In re: Chiquita Brands Int'l, Inc.*, 965 F.3d 1238, 1251 (11th Cir. 2020); *Pansy v. Borough of Stroudsburg*, 23 F.3d 772, 786 (3d Cir. 1994).

[420] *Wilcox v. La Pensee Condo. Ass'n, Inc.*, __ F. Supp. 3d __, 2022 WL 1564502, at *2 (S.D. Fla. 2022); *Mannina v. D.C.*, 334 F.R.D. 336, 339 (D.D.C. 2020).

[421] *Sargeant v. Hall*, 951 F.3d 1280, 1284 (11th Cir. 2020).

[422] Rule 45(d)(3).

[423] *Gov't of Ghana v. ProEnergy Serv., LLC*, 677 F.3d 340, 342 (8th Cir. 2012); *Guillen v. B.J.C.R. LLC*, 341 F.R.D. 61, 66 (D. Nev. 2022).

[424] *See, e.g., Gov't of Ghana v. ProEnergy Serv., LLC*, 677 F.3d 340, 342 (8th Cir. 2012); *Quintana v. USAA Life Ins. Co.*, 434 F. Supp. 3d 932, 939

deposition.[425] Likewise, if the motion for a protective order is filed in response to a motion to compel, the court may not require a separate meet and confer for the motion for a protective order.[426]

Timing

There is no set period for filing a motion for a protective order.[427] Normally, the motion must be filed before the discovery is to occur, unless there is no opportunity to do so.[428]

Who May File

A motion may be made by the person or entity whose interests are affected by the subject discovery, which may be a party or a nonparty from whom discovery is sought (typically by subpoena).[429] A party may not move for a protective order to protect the interests of a nonparty, but may move to protect the party's own interests affected by discovery sought from a nonparty.[430]

Depositions vs. Written Discovery

Motions for protective orders are most common in connection with depositions because such motions are the only mechanism for asserting a concern about a deposition issue in advance of the deposition.[431] With written discovery, a party can make objections to individual requests without providing a substantive response (and without the expense and burden of filing a motion and the need to demonstrate good cause). The onus then shifts to the party seeking the discovery to move to compel an answer under Rule 37(a).

Denial of Motion for Protective Order—Order Compelling Discovery

If the court denies a motion for a protective order, it may at the same time issue an order compelling the discovery.[432] Such an order can facilitate obtaining sanctions under Rule 37.

Discovery While Motion for Protective Order Pending

Technically, a motion for protective order does not automati-

---

(W.D. Wash. 2020).

425 *See Abdallah v. Abdel-Rahman*, 2016 WL 4467983, *1 (V.I. Super. Ct. 2016).

426 *See Buie v. D.C.*, 327 F.R.D. 1, 7 (D.D.C. 2018).

427 *Bhasker v. Kemper Cas. Ins. Co.*, 361 F. Supp. 3d 1045, 1119 (D.N.M. 2019); *Benavidez v. Sandia Nat'l Lab.*, 319 F.R.D. 696, 721 (D.N.M. 2017).

428 *Mims v. Central Mfrs. Mut. Ins. Co.*, 178 F.2d 56 (5th Cir.1949); *Benavidez v. Sandia Nat'l Lab.*, 319 F.R.D. 696, 721 (D.N.M. 2017).

429 *Silkwood v. Kerr-McGee Corp.*, 563 F.2d 433 (10th Cir.1977).

430 *See Continuum on S. Beach Condo. V. QBE Ins. Corp.*, 338 F.R.D. 668, 669 (S.D. Fla. 2021); *Eichenwald v. Rivello*, 321 F. Supp. 3d 562, 565 (D. Md. 2018).

431 *See James Lee Constr., Inc. v. Gov't Emps. Ins. Co.*, 339 F.R.D. 562, 568 (D. Mont. 2021); *U.S. v. One Gulfstream G-V Jet Aircraft Displaying Tail Number VPCES*, 304 F.R.D. 10, 12–13 (D.D.C. 2014).

432 *See ProCare Hospice of Nevada, LLC v. OneCare Hospice, LLC*, 340 F.R.D. 174, 179 (D. Nev. 2021).

cally stay the discovery that is the subject of the motion.[433] Thus, for example, a motion for protective order to prevent a deposition should not be filed on the day of the deposition, unless it was not practical to file it sooner. However, some local rules provide for an automatic stay of the discovery that is the subject of the motion.[434]

Expenses and Attorney's Fees

The court must require the party losing a motion for protective order to pay the expenses the opposing party incurred in connection with the motion, including reasonable attorney's fees, unless: 1) the moving party failed to meet and confer;[435] the losing party's position was "substantially justified";[436] or other circumstances make an award unjust.[437]

Motion to Vacate or Modify Protective Order

If circumstances change, a party may move to vacate or modify a protective order.[438] Modification of a protective order requires a similar good cause showing as required for entry of a protective order in the first instance.[439]

RULE 26(d)—TIMING AND SEQUENCE OF DISCOVERY

CORE CONCEPT

With one exception, parties may not conduct discovery prior to their discovery conference under Rule 26(f). The exception is that parties may serve Rule 34 document requests prior to the Rule 26(f) conference to facilitate identification and discussion of potential document production issues, but for purposes of calculating the response date, they are deemed served as of the time of the Rule 26(f) conference. After the Rule 26(f) conference, each party may conduct whatever discovery that party chooses, in any sequence, regardless of the discovery undertaken by other parties, unless the court has issued a protective order dictating the sequence. The various discovery devices may be used in any order or simultaneously.

---

[433] *Creative Solutions Group, Inc. v. Pentzer Corp.*, 199 F.R.D. 443, 444 (D. Mass. 2001) (motion to stay discovery does not stay discovery).

[434] *Ecrix Corp. v. Exabyte Corp.*, 191 F.R.D. 611, 617 (D. Colo. 2000).

[435] *Bark v. Northrop*, 300 F.R.D. 486, 490 (D. Oregon 2014).

[436] *Josendis v. Wall to Wall Residence Repairs, Inc.*, 662 F.3d 1292, 1313 (11th Cir. 2011); *ProCare Hospice of Nevada, LLC v. OneCare Hospice, LLC*, 340 F.R.D. 174, 179 n.10 (D. Nev. 2021).

[437] *Jones v. Dufek*, 830 F.3d 523, 528–29 (D.C. Cir. 2016).

[438] *F.T.C. v. AbbVie Products LLC*, 713 F.3d 54, 66 (11th Cir. 2013) (burden is on the party seeking modification); *In re Teligent, Inc.*, 640 F.3d 53, 58 (2d Cir. 2011) (where there has been reasonable reliance on the protective order, the court should not modify it unless it was improvidently entered or there are compelling circumstances).

[439] *In re: Chiquita Brands Int'l, Inc.*, 965 F.3d 1238, 1250 (11th Cir. 2020) (discussing which party bears the burden of demonstrating good cause).

APPLICATIONS

Commencement of Discovery

Normally, parties may not conduct discovery, other than document requests as discussed immediately below, prior to their discovery conference under Rule 26(f).[440]

- *Early Service of Document Requests:* Document requests may be served before the parties' Rule 26(f) conference on: 1) a plaintiff or 2) a defendant, if it has been more than 21 days since that defendant was served with the summons and complaint.[441] The purpose is not to accelerate the response time, but rather to allow the parties to discuss document production issues at their Rule 26(f) conference and to raise them with the court at an early stage of the proceedings.[442] Accordingly, the requests will be deemed served as of the time of the Rule 26(f) conference and the response will not be due until 30 days after the conference.[443]
- *Excluded Proceedings:* The moratorium on early discovery established by Rule 26(d) does not apply to the proceedings exempted from the initial disclosures and discovery conference process by Rule 26(a)(1)(E).[444]
- *Expedited Discovery:* Parties may conduct expedited discovery—discovery before their Rule 26(f) conference—by court order for good cause shown or by stipulation.[445] One common circumstance where plaintiffs seek expedited discovery is when they need discovery to identify and serve some of the defendants.[446]

No Set Discovery Sequence

Although interrogatories and document production typically precede depositions, each party may conduct discovery in any sequence it chooses.[447] Likewise, the parties may conduct discovery simultaneously; there is no obligation for any party to wait until others have completed their discovery.[448]

---

[440] *Passmore v. Baylor Health Care System*, 823 F.3d 292, 298 (5th Cir. 2016); *Greater Baltimore Center for Pregnancy Concerns, Inc. v. Mayor and City Council of Baltimore*, 721 F.3d 264, 275 n.5 (4th Cir. 2013).

[441] *See Midwest Sign & Screen Printing Supply Co. v. Dalpe*, 386 F. Supp. 3d 1037, 1058 (D. Minn. 2019).

[442] Rule 26 advisory committee's note (2015).

[443] Rule 26(d)(2)(B).

[444] *Durham v. IDA Grp. Ben. Trust*, 276 F.R.D. 259, 262 (N.D. Ind. 2011).

[445] *Mullane v. Almon*, 339 F.R.D. 659, 662 (N.D. Fla. 2021); *Let Them Play MN v. Walz*, 556 F. Supp. 3d 968, 974 (D. Minn. 2021).

[446] *See Strike 3 Holdings, LLC v. Doe*, 964 F.3d 1203, 1207 (D.C. Cir. 2020).

[447] *Doe v. Trump*, 329 F.R.D. 262, 273, n.12 (W.D. Wash. 2018); *Liguria Foods, Inc. v. Griffith Laboratories, Inc.*, 320 F.R.D. 168, 183 (N.D. Iowa 2017).

[448] *George C. Frey Ready-Mixed Concrete, Inc. v. Pine Hill Concrete Mix Corp.*, 554 F.2d 551 (2d Cir.1977); *Gabarick v. Laurin Maritime (Am.),*

Limiting the Discovery Sequence by Protective Order or Stipulation

The court has broad discretion to issue a protective order under Rule 26(c) providing for discovery in a specified sequence or according to a schedule "for the convenience of the parties and witnesses and in the interests of justice."[449] The court may also stay discovery[450] or limit initial discovery to a threshold issue.[451] Such orders are within the broad discretion of the court, but are reserved for unusual circumstances.[452] Additionally, the parties can stipulate to a particular discovery sequence.[453]

Failure to Respond by Another Party Not an Excuse

A party is not excused from responding to discovery because another party has failed to respond to discovery.[454] The proper remedy if another party fails to respond to discovery is a motion to compel under Rule 37(a), not a refusal to comply with valid discovery requests.[455]

No Mutuality

There is no requirement that a party conduct discovery in the same manner or sequence used by other parties. Each party is free to conduct any authorized discovery in any sequence regardless of the discovery conducted by other parties.[456]

RULE 26(e)—SUPPLEMENTING DISCLOSURES AND RESPONSES

CORE CONCEPT

Parties have a duty to supplement automatic disclosures and discovery responses if they were incomplete or incorrect at the time they were made or have become so with the passage of time.[457] This duty is automatic, and does not require a request.

APPLICATIONS

Conditions Requiring Supplemental Responses

The following three conditions require supplemental

Inc., 274 F.R.D. 208, 210 (E.D. La. 2011).

[449] *Crawford-El v. Britton*, 523 U.S. 574, 598 (1998).

[450] *Oliver v. City of New York*, 540 F. Supp. 3d 434, 435 (S.D.N.Y. 2021); *Saunders v. City of Chicago*, 146 F. Supp. 3d 957, 968 (N.D. Ill. 2015).

[451] *Ema Fin., LLC v. Vystar Corp.*, 336 F.R.D. 75, 79 (S.D.N.Y. 2020).

[452] *See Ema Fin., LLC v. Vystar Corp.*, 336 F.R.D. 75, 79 (S.D.N.Y. 2020); *St. Louis Group, Inc. v. Metals and Additives Corp., Inc.*, 275 F.R.D. 236, 239 (S.D. Tex. 2011).

[453] Rule 26(d)(3).

[454] *Mulero-Abreu v. Puerto Rico Police Dept.*, 675 F.3d 88, 92 (1st Cir. 2012); *Infanzon v. Allstate Ins. Co.*, 335 F.R.D. 305, 312 (C.D. Cal. 2020).

[455] *Infanzon v. Allstate Ins. Co.*, 335 F.R.D. 305, 312 (C.D. Cal. 2020).

[456] *See Dauska v. Green Bay Packaging Inc.*, 291 F.R.D. 251, 257 (E.D. Wis. 2013); *Keller v. Edwards*, 206 F.R.D. 412 (D. Md. 2002).

[457] *See, e.g., Rodowicz v. Massachusetts Mut. Life Ins. Co.*, 279 F.3d 36, 45, (1st Cir. 2002).

disclosures or responses:

(1) *Automatic Disclosures:* A party must at reasonable intervals supplement its initial,[458] expert,[459] and pretrial disclosures under Rule 26(a) if the party or its attorney learns that the information disclosed was incomplete or incorrect if the information has not otherwise been made known to the other parties;[460]

(2) *Incorrect Response:* A party must supplement a response to an interrogatory, request for inspection, or request for admission that the party or its attorney[461] learns was incorrect or incomplete if the information has not otherwise been made known to the other parties;[462] and

(3) *Court Order:* The duty to supplement may also arise by court order.[463]

- *Duty to Supplement Dependent on Duty to Disclose or Respond:* The duty to supplement only extends to providing documents or information that were already required to be provided or disclosed—it does not create any independent duties.[464]

Timing of Supplemental Responses

The Rules do not establish a specific time period for the duty to supplement.[465] Instead, supplements are to be made "in a timely manner."[466] "Timely" has been defined as "without undue delay upon discovering the information that is to be provided."[467] The duty to supplement is ongoing,[468] and does not

---

[458] *Birch | Rea Partners, Inc. v. Regent Bank*, 27 F.4th 1245, 1253 (7th Cir. 2022); *HCG Platinum, LLC v. Preferred Prod. Placement Corp.*, 873 F.3d 1191, 1200 n.9 (10th Cir. 2017).

[459] *Guevara v. NCL (Bahamas) Ltd.*, 920 F.3d 710, 718 (11th Cir. 2019); *David E. Watson, P.C. v. U.S.*, 668 F.3d 1008, 1014 (8th Cir. 2012).

[460] *Hernandez v. Results Staffing, Inc.*, 907 F.3d 354, 362 (5th Cir. 2018); *U.S. Commodity Futures Trading Com'n v. Kratville*, 796 F.3d 873, 887–88 (8th Cir. 2015).

[461] *Ritchie Risk-Linked Strategies Trading (Ireland), Ltd. v. Coventry First LLC*, 280 F.R.D. 147, 156 (S.D.N.Y. 2012).

[462] *In re Celexa & Lexapro Mktg. & Sales Practices Litig.*, 915 F.3d 1, 17 (1st Cir. 2019); *Hernandez v. Results Staffing, Inc.*, 907 F.3d 354, 361 (5th Cir. 2018).

[463] *Chevron Corp. v. Salazar*, 275 F.R.D. 437, 449 (S.D.N.Y. 2011).

[464] *L.A. Terminals, Inc. v. United Nat'l Ins. Co.*, 340 F.R.D. 390, 396 (C.D. Cal. 2022).

[465] *See Jama v. City and County of Denver*, 304 F. Supp. 2d 289, 299–300 (D. Col. 2014); *AVX Corp. v. Cabot Corp.*, 252 F.R.D. 70, 77 (D. Mass. 2008) (parties should supplement at appropriate intervals *during the discovery period*).

[466] *Bisig v. Time Warner Cable, Inc.*, 940 F.3d 205, 218, n.7 (6th Cir. 2019); *Allstate Interiors & Exteriors, Inc. v. Stonestreet Const., LLC*, 730 F.3d 67, 75–6 (1st Cir. 2013).

[467] *Fair Isaac Corp. v. Fed. Ins. Co.*, 337 F.R.D. 413, 419 (D. Minn. 2021).

[468] *United States v. Brace*, 334 F.R.D. 472, 478 (W.D. Pa. 2020).

end when discovery ends.[469] Supplements made after the close of discovery, however, may not satisfy the Rules, particularly when the party had the documents or information in its possession, custody, or control prior to the close of discovery.[470] Additionally, local rules[471] or court orders[472] may set time requirements for supplementing.

- *Outer Time Limit for Supplementing Expert Disclosures:* Supplemental expert information must be disclosed, at the latest, by the time the pretrial disclosures are made, 30 days before trial unless otherwise set by the court.[473]

No Request to Supplement Needed

The obligations to supplement are self-effectuating; there is no need to serve a request to supplement or motion to compel.[474] Nonetheless, a party will sometimes serve a request to supplement or a motion to compel if it is concerned that another party has new information that it has not yet disclosed or produced.[475]

After-Acquired Information

The duty to supplement is triggered by information or documents acquired after serving the original disclosure or response, even if the disclosure or response was accurate when made.[476]

Supplementing Expert Discovery

The obligations to supplement described above apply to both expert reports[477] and depositions of testifying experts.[478] A party may not use the supplementing procedure to submit an amended or rebuttal report not based on new information,[479] nor may a party use Rule 26(e) to cure a defective or problematic

---

[469] *L.A. Terminals, Inc. v. United Nat'l Ins. Co.*, 340 F.R.D. 390, 396 (C.D. Cal. 2022); *Fair Isaac Corp. v. Fed. Ins. Co.*, 337 F.R.D. 413, 419 (D. Minn. 2021).

[470] *See Morris v. BNSF Ry. Co.*, 969 F.3d 753, 766 (7th Cir. 2020); *Eldridge v. Gordon Brothers Group, LLC*, 316 F.R.D. 12, 29 (D. Mass. 2016).

[471] *See, e.g., BNJ Leasing, Inc. v. Portabull Fuel Serv., LLC*, __ F. Supp. 3d __, 2022 WL 782561, at *2 (S.D. Miss. 2022).

[472] *See, e.g., Deakin v. Magellan Health, Inc.*, 340 F.R.D. 424, 433 (D.N.M. 2022).

[473] *Guevara v. NCL (Bahamas) Ltd.*, 920 F.3d 710, 718 (11th Cir. 2019); *Bresler v. Wilmington Trust Co.*, 855 F.3d 178, 190 (4th Cir. 2017).

[474] *See Midwestern Pet Foods, Inc. v. Societe des Produits Nestle S.A.*, 685 F.3d 1046, 1056–57 (Fed. Cir. 2012); *Fast v. GoDaddy.com LLC*, 340 F.R.D. 326, 335 (D. Ariz. 2022).

[475] *See Hovanec v. Miller*, 331 F.R.D. 624, 634 (W.D. Tex. 2019).

[476] *See West v. Bell Helicopter Textron, Inc.*, 803 F.3d 56, 71–72 (1st Cir. 2015); *Woods v. DeAngelo Marine Exhaust, Inc.*, 692 F.3d 1272, 1278–83 (Fed. Cir. 2012).

[477] *Crawford v. ITW Food Equip. Grp., LLC*, 977 F.3d 1331, 1341 (11th Cir. 2020); *Guevara v. NCL (Bahamas) Ltd.*, 920 F.3d 710, 718 (11th Cir. 2019).

[478] *Taylor v. Mentor Worldwide LLC*, 940 F.3d 582, 592 (11th Cir. 2019).

[479] *See In re Complaint of C.F. Bean L.L.C.*, 841 F.3d 365, 371 (5th Cir. 2016); *E.E.O.C. v. Freeman*, 778 F.3d 463, 467 n.7 (4th Cir. 2015).

expert report.[480]

Supplementing Contention Interrogatories

A party must supplement its responses to contention interrogatories as its theories and positions evolve.[481]

Supplementing Requests for Admission

Rule 26(e) imposes a duty to supplement a denial or statement of inability to admit or deny if the party learns that the original response is in some material respect incomplete or incorrect, and if the additional or corrective information has not been provided to the other parties in writing or at a deposition.[482] Conversely, a party does not have the unilateral right to change an admission by supplement; rather, a party must file a motion to withdraw or amend its admission under Rule 36(b).[483]

Information Already Provided

A party need not supplement a disclosure or discovery response if the other parties have already received the additional or corrective information during the discovery process or in writing.[484] However, the information received must be complete—for example, the mention of a name in documents or during a deposition does not relieve a party of the obligation to disclose that witness as someone with discoverable information that the party may use to support its claims or defenses.[485] Furthermore, attaching a previously undisclosed document to a brief or motion does not constitute a supplement.[486] It is a far better practice to make a formal supplement, because informal disclosure during discovery will rarely satisfy Rule 26(e).[487]

No Other Duty

The duties described in Rule 26(e) are the only duties to

---

[480] *Petrone v. Werner Enterprises, Inc.*, 940 F.3d 425, 434 (8th Cir. 2019); *Guevara v. NCL (Bahamas) Ltd.*, 920 F.3d 710, 719 (11th Cir. 2019).

[481] *MLC Intell. Prop., LLC v. Micron Tech., Inc.*, 10 F.4th 1358, 1372 (Fed. Cir. 2021); *Woods v. DeAngelo Marine Exhaust, Inc.*, 692 F.3d 1272, 1280 (Fed. Cir. 2012).

[482] *VeroBlue Farms USA Inc. v. Wulf*, __ F.R.D. __, 2021 WL 5176839, at *4 (N.D. Tex. 2021); *House v. Giant of Maryland LLC*, 232 F.R.D. 257, 259 (E.D. Va. 2005).

[483] *Nat'l Union Fire Ins. Co. of Pittsburgh, PA v. PVT Ltd.*, 338 F.R.D. 579, 585–86 (S.D.N.Y. 2021).

[484] *Baker Hughes Inc. v. S&S Chem., LLC*, 836 F.3d 554, 568 (6th Cir. 2016); *Pina v. Children's Place*, 740 F.3d 785, 793 (1st Cir. 2014).

[485] *Am. Steel Erectors v. Local Union No. 7, Intern. Ass'n of Bridge, Structural, Ornamental & Reinforcing Iron Workers*, 815 F.3d 43, 57 n.2 (1st Cir. 2016); *Walsh v. Fusion Japanese Steakhouse, Inc.*, __ F. Supp. 3d __, 2022 WL 395253, at *13 (W.D. Pa. 2022) (documents); *V5 Techs. v. Switch, Ltd.*, 334 F.R.D. 615, 618 (D. Nev. 2020) (deposition testimony).

[486] *United States v. Brace*, 334 F.R.D. 472, 478 (W.D. Pa. 2020); *Malone v. Portfolio Recovery Assoc., LLC*, 308 F.R.D. 518, 522 (W.D. Kent. 2015).

[487] *Webster v. Psychiatric Med. Care, LLC*, 386 F. Supp. 3d 1358, 1365 (D. Mont. 2019) (quoting the advisory committee note).

supplement.[488] Thus, an instruction in a set of interrogatories that the interrogatories are continuing or purporting to impose a duty to supplement greater than or different from the obligation in Rule 26(e) is ineffective.

Sanctions

Failure to supplement a disclosure or discovery response is the equivalent of providing incorrect information in the initial disclosure or response. The court may exclude evidence[489] or claims,[490] may order a continuance and further discovery, or take any other action—or no action—as it deems appropriate[491] (*see* Rule 37 for a more detailed analysis of the available sanctions).

Motion to Compel

A party believing another party has failed to supplement when obligated to do so may file a motion to compel seeking the supplementation and sanctions.[492]

Supplementation Not Necessarily a Cure-All

Supplementing a disclosure or discovery response does not necessarily insulate a party from sanctions if the disclosure or discovery response was improper or incomplete at the time it was made.[493]

RULE 26(f)—CONFERENCE OF THE PARTIES; PLANNING FOR DISCOVERY

CORE CONCEPT

The parties must confer and develop a proposed discovery plan to submit to the court in writing addressing a variety of discovery issues, including the discovery schedule, ESI issues, and any modifications to the limits or scope of discovery.

APPLICATIONS

Time for Conference

The parties must confer "as soon as practicable and in any event at least 21 days before a scheduling conference is held or

[488]*Alvariza v. Home Depot*, 240 F.R.D. 586, 590 (D. Colo. 2007), *aff'd*, 241 F.R.D. 663 (D. Colo. 2007) (no duty to supplement documents informally produced by agreement).

[489]*See HCG Platinum, LLC v. Preferred Prod. Placement Corp.*, 873 F.3d 1191, 1205 (10th Cir. 2017); *Russell v. Absolute Collection Services, Inc.*, 763 F.3d 385, 396–97 (4th Cir. 2014).

[490]*U.S. v. Philip Morris USA, Inc.*, 219 F.R.D. 198, 200–01 (D.D.C. 2004); *Loral Fairchild Corp. v. Victor Co. of Japan, Ltd.*, 911 F. Supp. 76, 80 (E.D.N.Y. 1996).

[491]*Zampierollo-Rheinfeldt v. Ingersoll-Rand de Puerto Rico, Inc.*, 999 F.3d 37, 47-48 (1st Cir. 2021) (broad discretion); *Foodbuy, LLC v. Gregory Packaging, Inc.*, 987 F.3d 102, 117 (4th Cir. 2021) (same).

[492]*Hovanec v. Miller*, 331 F.R.D. 624, 634 (W.D. Tex. 2019).

[493]*Faiella v. Sunbelt Rentals, Inc.*, 341 F.R.D. 553, 567 (D.N.J. 2022).

a scheduling order is due under Rule 16(b)."[494] The timing of the discovery conference may be modified by local rule or court order.[495]

Agenda for Discovery Conference

At the discovery conference, the parties must discuss all of the topics that the discovery plan addresses (listed below). In addition, the parties should discuss the nature and basis of their claims and defenses[496] and the possibilities of prompt settlement or resolution of the case.[497] They must also make or arrange for the initial automatic disclosures required by Rule 26(a)(1) and discuss orders that the court should enter.[498]

Content of Discovery Plan

Many local rules contain a template for the discovery plan the parties must prepare. The discovery plan should indicate the parties' positions or proposals concerning:

(1) *Automatic Disclosures*: Any changes to the timing, form, or requirement for disclosures under Rule 26(a).[499] The plan must explicitly state when the initial disclosures were or are to be made;

(2) *Discovery Scope and Schedule*: The likely subjects of discovery, the completion date for discovery, and any discovery that should be conducted in phases or limited to or focused on particular issues;[500]

(3) *Electronically Stored Information*: Issues relating to the disclosure, production, or preservation of electronically stored information, including the sources of such information, the form in which it should be produced, and the costs of such production;[501]

(4) *Privilege Issues*: Issues relating to claims of privilege

---

[494] *AFT Michigan v. Project Veritas*, 294 F. Supp. 3d 693, 694 (E.D. Mich. 2018) (motion to dismiss does not affect obligation to participate in Rule 26(f) conference); *Manny Film LLC v. Doe Subscriber Assigned IP Address 50.166.88.98*, 98 F. Supp. 3d 693, 694 n.3 (D.N.J. 2015).

[495] *Sai v. Dep't of Homeland Sec.*, 99 F. Supp. 3d 50, 58 (D.D.C. 2015) (Rule 26(f) conference stayed pending resolution of motion to dismiss).

[496] *King v. Taylor*, 694 F.3d 650, 660 n.6 (6th Cir. 2012).

[497] *See Howe v. City of Enter.*, 861 F.3d 1300, 1302 (11th Cir. 2017); *U.S. ex rel. FLFMC, LLC v. TFH Publ'ns., Inc.*, 855 F. Supp. 2d 300, 302 (D.N.J. 2012) (discussion of alternative dispute resolution required by local rules).

[498] *Mallinckrodt, Inc. v. Masimo Corp.*, 254 F. Supp. 2d 1140, 1157 (C.D. Cal. 2003).

[499] *In re Bristol-Myers Squibb Sec. Litig.*, 205 F.R.D. 437, 440–41 (D.N.J. 2002) (the discovery conference should include a discussion of what documents are available in electronic format, and the format to be used for disclosures and production of such documents).

[500] *Beezley v. Fenix Parts, Inc.*, 328 F.R.D. 198, 201 (N.D. Ill. 2018); *Fiber Optic Designs, Inc. v. New England Pottery, LLC*, 262 F.R.D. 586, 599 (D. Colo. 2009).

[501] *See United States v. Brace*, 1 F.4th 137, 140 (3d Cir. 2021); *DR Distributors, LLC v. 21 Century Smoking, Inc.*, 513 F. Supp. 3d 839, 964 (N.D. Ill. 2021).

or work product protection, including any procedures to be used in the event of the inadvertent production of privileged information (to the extent that they differ from the procedures in Rule 26(b)(2)(B));[502]

(5) *Discovery Limits*: Any changes to the discovery limits established by the Rules or by local rule, plus any additional limits; and

(6) *Other Orders*: Any other case management or protective orders proposed for the court's consideration.

Submission of Plan

The parties should submit to the court a written report of the plan within 14 days of the discovery meeting.[503] The court may order that the discovery plan be submitted at a different time or that the plan be submitted orally at the Rule 16 conference with the court.

In-Person Attendance

The rules do not require that the Rule 26(f) conference be conducted in person, and the parties may participate by telephone.[504] However, the court can order the parties to participate in person.

Good Faith Participation

The attorneys (and unrepresented parties) have a good faith obligation to schedule the discovery conference[505] and to attempt to agree on a proposed discovery plan and report.[506]

Excluded Proceedings

A discovery conference and discovery plan are not required in proceedings listed in Rule 26(a)(1)(B) as exempted from initial disclosures.[507] Additionally, the parties may be excused from the discovery conference and plan requirements by court order.

---

[502] See the 2006 Amendment to the Advisory Committee Note to Rule 26(f) for a discussion of possible agreements regarding inadvertently produced privileged material, such as the "quick peek" procedure and the "clawback" procedure.

[503] *See Nat'l Labor Relations Bd. v. Anderson Excavating, Co.*, 925 F.3d 970, 974 n.3 (8th Cir. 2019).

[504] The Advisory Committee Note to the 2000 Amendment to Rule 26(f) expresses a preference for in person meetings, but recognizes that the distances some counsel would have to travel and the resulting expenses may outweigh the benefits of an in-person meeting.

[505] *USA Gymnastics v. Liberty Ins. Underwriters, Inc.*, 27 F.4th 499, 514 (7th Cir. 2022).

[506] *See Siems v. City of Minneapolis*, 560 F.3d 824, 826–27 (8th Cir. 2009) (dismissal based, in part, on failure to participate in the Rule 26(f) conference); *Beezley v. Fenix Parts, Inc.*, 328 F.R.D. 198, 200 (N.D. Ill. 2018).

[507] *See, e.g., Orbe v. True*, 201 F. Supp. 2d 671 (E.D. Va. 2002) (habeas corpus proceedings exempt from Rule 26(f)).

RULE 26(g)—SIGNING DISCLOSURES AND DISCOVERY REQUESTS, RESPONSES, AND OBJECTIONS

CORE CONCEPT

Rule 26(g) requires that parties and lawyers conduct the discovery process in good faith.[508] It requires that every disclosure, request for discovery, and response or objection must be signed by at least one attorney of record. The signature constitutes a certification that to the best of the signer's knowledge, information, and belief, the document is complete and correct and is being served for proper purposes within the Rules.

APPLICATIONS

Signature

Every disclosure, discovery request, response, or objection must be signed by at least one attorney of record (or by the party, if unrepresented).[509] At least one court has held that the "attorney of record" for this purpose must be admitted to practice before the court.[510] The document must also state the address, e-mail address, and telephone number of the signer.[511]

Certification for Initial and Pretrial Disclosures

For the initial disclosure and the pretrial disclosure, the signature constitutes a certification to the best of the signer's knowledge, information, and belief formed after "reasonable inquiry" that the disclosure is complete and correct.[512] Expert disclosures in the form of expert reports signed by the expert are not covered by this Rule.

Certification for Other Discovery Documents

For discovery requests, responses, and objections,[513] the signature constitutes a certification to the best of the signer's knowledge, information, and belief formed after "reasonable inquiry" that:

(A) The document is consistent with the Rules and existing law, or with a nonfrivolous argument for extension, modification, or reversal of existing law, or for establishing new law;[514]

(B) The document is not imposed for any improper purpose,

---

[508] *DR Distributors, LLC v. 21 Century Smoking, Inc.*, 513 F. Supp. 3d 839, 965 (N.D. Ill. 2021).

[509] *U.S. v. Real Property Known As 200 Acres of Land Near FM 2686 Rio Grande City, Tex.*, 773 F.3d 654, 661 (5th Cir. 2014) (objection not signed); *Dugan v. Smerwick Sewerage Co.*, 142 F.3d 398, 407 (7th Cir. 1998).

[510] *Siser North America, Inc. v. Herika G. Inc.*, 325 F.R.D. 200, 208 (E.D. Mich. 2018).

[511] *Lopez v. Don Herring Ltd.*, 327 F.R.D. 567, 576 (N.D. Tex. 2018).

[512] *Olivarez v. GEO Group, Inc.*, 844 F.3d 200, 203 (5th Cir. 2016).

[513] *Younes v. 7-Eleven, Inc.*, 312 F.R.D. 692, 704 (D.N.J. 2015) (certification applies to objections).

[514] *Jackson Women's Health Org. v. Dobbs*, 945 F.3d 265, 281 (5th Cir. 2019); *Lopez v. Don Herring Ltd.*, 327 F.R.D. 567, 584 (N.D. Tex. 2018).

such as to harass, delay, or cause needless expense for an opponent;[515] and

(C) The discovery is not unreasonably or unduly burdensome or expensive, given the nature of the case, the discovery already conducted, the amount in controversy, and the importance of the issues at stake in the litigation.[516]

Certification re Documents Produced in Discovery

An attorney's signature certifies that documents produced during discovery are not fraudulent.[517]

Signer's Duty of Inquiry

The signer of a discovery document is under an obligation to make a reasonable inquiry into the issues covered by the certification before signing the document.[518] An attorney signing a discovery document must make a reasonable effort to assure that the client has provided all of the responsive documents and information.[519]

Unsigned Discovery Documents

If without substantial justification a discovery disclosure, request, response, or objection is unsigned, the unsigned document will be stricken, no party will be obligated to respond to the unsigned document,[520] and the attorney serving the unsigned discovery document may be subject to sanctions.[521]

Sanctions

If a certification is made in violation of Rule 26(g) without a substantial justification,[522] the court must impose an appropriate sanction on the party, the attorney, or both.[523] Although the

---

[515] *Woodward v. Holtzman*, 329 F.R.D. 16, 23 (W.D.N.Y. 2018); *Younes v. 7-Eleven, Inc.*, 312 F.R.D. 692, 704–05 (D.N.J. 2015) (boilerplate objections can violate Rule 26(g)).

[516] *See Legault v. Zambarano*, 105 F.3d 24, 27 (1st Cir. 1997); *Lopez v. Don Herring Ltd.*, 327 F.R.D. 567, 577 (N.D. Tex. 2018).

[517] *SPV-LS, LLC v. Transamerica Life Ins. Co.*, 912 F.3d 1106, 1114 (8th Cir. 2019).

[518] *Green Leaf Nursery v. E.I. DuPont De Nemours and Co.*, 341 F.3d 1292, 1305 (11th Cir. 2003); *DR Distributors, LLC v. 21 Century Smoking, Inc.*, 513 F. Supp. 3d 839, 952 (N.D. Ill. 2021).

[519] *Legault v. Zambarano*, 105 F.3d 24, 28 (1st Cir. 1997); *Fast v. GoDaddy.com LLC*, 340 F.R.D. 326, 355 n.18 (D. Ariz. 2022).

[520] *Johnson v. BAE Systems, Inc.*, 307 F.R.D. 220, 224 (D.D.C. 2013); *Saria v. Massachusetts Mut. Life Ins. Co.*, 228 F.R.D. 536, 539 (S.D.W. Va. 2005).

[521] *Walls v. Paulson*, 250 F.R.D. 48, 52 (D.D.C. 2008).

[522] *Olivarez v. GEO Group, Inc.*, 844 F.3d 200, 205–06 (5th Cir. 2016); *Grider v. Keystone Health Plan Central, Inc.*, 580 F.3d 119, 139–40 (3d Cir. 2009) (sanctions vacated because the court did not expressly consider whether the violators had substantial justification).

[523] *SPV-LS, LLC v. Transamerica Life Ins. Co.*, 912 F.3d 1106, 1113 (8th Cir. 2019); *Rojas v. Town of Cicero*, 775 F.3d 906, 909 (7th Cir. 2015) (sanctions mandatory).

Rule makes sanctions mandatory,[524] some courts have interpreted the Rule to condition the requirement for sanctions on prejudice to another party.[525] The sanction may include expenses incurred because of the violation, including attorney's fees,[526] and may also include substantive sanctions like dismissal.[527] A court may impose sanctions upon motion[528] or *sua sponte*.[529] Unlike many discovery sanctions provisions, Rule 26(g) does not impose a meet and confer prerequisite before seeking sanctions,[530] (although professional courtesy may dictate brining the failure to the attention of opposing counsel and providing an opportunity to cure the failure).

- *Inherent Power to Sanction:* Although courts have inherent powers to sanction parties and lawyers for improper litigation conduct, Rule 26(g) and Rule 37 are the primary mechanisms for sanctioning discovery conduct and the courts should use their inherent authority only for discovery abuses that do not violate Rule 26(g) or Rule 37.[531]

Additional Research References

Wright & Miller, *Federal Practice and Procedure* §§ 2001 to 2052
C.J.S., Federal Civil Procedure §§ 526 to 535
West's Key Number Digest, Federal Civil Procedure ⚷1261 to 1278

---

[524] *SPV-LS, LLC v. Transamerica Life Ins. Co.*, 912 F.3d 1106, 1113 (8th Cir. 2019) (the court has discretion over the nature of the sanctions, but not whether to impose them).

[525] *State v. United States Dep't of Commerce*, 461 F. Supp. 3d 80, 88 (S.D.N.Y. 2020).

[526] *LaJeunesse v. BNSF Ry. Co.*, 333 F.R.D. 649, 675 (D.N.M. 2019); *Heller v. City of Dallas*, 303 F.R.D. 466, 477 (N.D. Tex. 2014).

[527] *Zalaski v. City of Hartford*, 723 F.3d 382, 395 (2d Cir. 2013); *LaJeunesse v. BNSF Ry. Co.*, 333 F.R.D. 649, 672 (D.N.M. 2019).

[528] *See Membreno v. Atlanta Rest. Partners, LLC*, 338 F.R.D. 66, 77 (D. Md. 2021) (delay in filing motion can reduce sanctions).

[529] *Sec. Nat. Bank of Sioux City, IA v. Day*, 800 F.3d 936, 942 (8th Cir. 2015); *DR Distributors, LLC v. 21 Century Smoking, Inc.*, 513 F. Supp. 3d 839, 962 (N.D. Ill. 2021).

[530] *Scott Hutchison Enter., Inc. v. Cranberry Pipeline Corp.*, 318 F.R.D. 44, 51 (S.D.W. Va. 2016).

[531] *Yukos Cap. S.A.R.L. v. Feldman*, 977 F.3d 216, 235-36 (2d Cir. 2020).

RULE 27
DEPOSITIONS TO PERPETUATE TESTIMONY

(a) Before an Action Is Filed.

(1) *Petition.* A person who wants to perpetuate testimony about any matter cognizable in a United States court may file a verified petition in the district court for the district where any expected adverse party resides. The petition must ask for an order authorizing the petitioner to depose the named persons in order to perpetuate their testimony. The petition must be titled in the petitioner's name and must show:

(A) that the petitioner expects to be a party to an action cognizable in a United States court but cannot presently bring it or cause it to be brought;

(B) the subject matter of the expected action and the petitioner's interest;

(C) the facts that the petitioner wants to establish by the proposed testimony and the reasons to perpetuate it;

(D) the names or a description of the persons whom the petitioner expects to be adverse parties and their addresses, so far as known; and

(E) the name, address, and expected substance of the testimony of each deponent.

(2) *Notice and Service.* At least 21 days before the hearing date, the petitioner must serve each expected adverse party with a copy of the petition and a notice stating the time and place of the hearing. The notice may be served either inside or outside the district or state in the manner provided in Rule 4. If that service cannot be made with reasonable diligence on an expected adverse party, the court may order service by publication or otherwise. The court must appoint an attorney to represent persons not served in

the manner provided in Rule 4 and to cross-examine the deponent if an unserved person is not otherwise represented. If any expected adverse party is a minor or is incompetent, Rule 17(c) applies.

(3) *Order and Examination.* If satisfied that perpetuating the testimony may prevent a failure or delay of justice, the court must issue an order that designates or describes the persons whose depositions may be taken, specifies the subject matter of the examinations, and states whether the depositions will be taken orally or by written interrogatories. The depositions may then be taken under these rules, and the court may issue orders like those authorized by Rules 34 and 35. A reference in these rules to the court where an action is pending means, for purposes of this rule, the court where the petition for the deposition was filed.

(4) *Using the Deposition.* A deposition to perpetuate testimony may be used under Rule 32(a) in any later-filed district-court action involving the same subject matter if the deposition either was taken under these rules or, although not so taken, would be admissible in evidence in the courts of the state where it was taken.

(b) Pending Appeal.

(1) *In General.* The court where a judgment has been rendered may, if an appeal has been taken or may still be taken, permit a party to depose witnesses to perpetuate their testimony for use in the event of further proceedings in that court.

(2) *Motion.* The party who wants to perpetuate testimony may move for leave to take the depositions, on the same notice and service as if the action were pending in the district court. The motion must show:

(A) the name, address, and expected substance of the testimony of each deponent; and

(B) the reasons for perpetuating the testimony.

(3) *Court Order.* If the court finds that perpetuating the testimony may prevent a failure or delay of

justice, the court may permit the depositions to be taken and may issue orders like those authorized by Rules 34 and 35. The depositions may be taken and used as any other deposition taken in a pending district-court action.

(c) Perpetuation by an Action. This rule does not limit a court's power to entertain an action to perpetuate testimony.

[Amended effective March 19, 1948; October 20, 1949; July 1, 1971; August 1, 1987; April 25, 2005, effective December 1, 2005; April 30, 2007, effective December 1, 2007; March 26, 2009, effective December 1, 2009.]

AUTHORS' COMMENTARY ON RULE 27

PURPOSE AND SCOPE

Almost all discovery in federal court occurs after the case has been commenced, under timing constraints established generally in Rule 26 and specifically in the rules governing each specific discovery device. Rule 27 is an exception to this general rule. It addresses the situation where someone needs to preserve testimony that is at risk of becoming unavailable (such as by death of the witness), yet the person cannot preserve the testimony in the ordinary way by simply taking a deposition because litigation has not yet been commenced and, for some reason, cannot be commenced, or while an appeal is pending.

Under these circumstances, Rule 27 provides one mechanism for preserving such testimony by taking a deposition. However, because these depositions are such a departure from the normal course, Rule 27 imposes significant restrictions on them. In order to obtain a Rule 27 deposition to preserve testimony, the person seeking the deposition must submit a verified petition demonstrating that the petitioner expects to bring litigation in federal court but is presently unable to commence the action and that the witness's testimony is relevant to the action but in danger of being lost.

RULE 27(a)—BEFORE AN ACTION IS FILED

CORE CONCEPT

Rule 27 is most commonly used to perpetuate testimony when there is a danger that important testimony will be lost, but for some reason a civil action cannot yet be commenced.

APPLICATIONS

Petition

A request to take a Rule 27 deposition is made by petition containing the following:

(1) A statement that the petitioner expects to be a party to an action in federal court,[1] but is presently unable to bring the action (remember, subject-matter jurisdiction is a constitutional limitation on the powers of federal courts. In a normal lawsuit, the complaint must set forth the basis for federal subject-matter jurisdiction. Here, the court does not have a complaint so must use the information in the petition to satisfy itself that it has the constitutional power to rule on the petition);[2]

(2) A description of the subject matter of the anticipated action and the petitioner's relationship to the action;

(3) The facts that the petitioner intends to establish by the testimony, and the petitioner's need for perpetuating the testimony;[3]

(4) The identities and addresses of the persons expected to be adverse parties in the action;[4] and

(5) The identity of the deponent(s) and a detailed description of the substance of their testimony.[5]

The petition must be verified (*i.e.,* accompanied by a statement signed by the petitioner that the factual averments are accurate)[6] and must include a proposed order describing the procedure and scope of the deposition.

- *Subject-Matter Jurisdiction:* A proceeding to perpetuate testimony is not a separate civil action, and does not require its own basis for jurisdiction.[7] However, the petition must demonstrate that the anticipated legal action would have federal subject-matter jurisdiction and would

---

[1]*See Teamsters Local 404 Health Servs. & Ins. Plan v. King Pharm., Inc.*, 906 F.3d 260, 267 (2d Cir. 2018); *In re Obalon Therapeutics, Inc.*, 321 F.R.D. 245, 248 (E.D.N.C. 2017).

[2]*In re Obalon Therapeutics, Inc.*, 321 F.R.D. 245, 248 (E.D.N.C. 2017). *See also In re Rivada Networks Pursuant to 28 U.S.C. § 1782 to Conduct Discovery for Use in a Foreign Proceeding*, 230 F. Supp. 3d 467 (E.D. Va. 2017) (Rule 27 applies to deposition to be taken in federal court in the U.S. in connection with a lawsuit in Mexico).

[3]*In re Obalon Therapeutics, Inc.*, 321 F.R.D. 245, 248 (E.D.N.C. 2017); *In re Yamaha Motor Corp., U.S.A.*, 251 F.R.D. 97, 99 (N.D.N.Y. 2008).

[4]*Norex Petroleum Ltd. v. Access Industries, Inc.*, 620 F. Supp. 2d 587, 590 (S.D.N.Y. 2009) (petition defective because it did not include the witness's address).

[5]*Penn Mut. Life Ins. Co. v. U.S.*, 68 F.3d 1371, 1374, (D.C. Cir. 1995) (Rule 27 requires a "narrowly tailored showing of the substance" of the testimony); *In re Petition of Allegretti*, 229 F.R.D. 93, 97 (S.D.N.Y. 2005).

[6]*In re Obalon Therapeutics, Inc.*, 321 F.R.D. 245, 248 (E.D.N.C. 2017); *In re Chester County Elec., Inc.*, 208 F.R.D. 545, 546–47 (E.D. Pa. 2002).

[7]*Socha v. Pollard*, 621 F.3d 667, 671 (7th Cir. 2010).

be eligible to proceed in federal court.[8]

Preservation of Documents

On its face, Rule 27 only authorizes depositions, not document requests.[9] However, some courts will allow parties to use Rule 27 to preserve documentary evidence that might be lost.[10]

Likelihood of Future Litigation

A party does not need to demonstrate that litigation is absolutely certain in order to prevail on a motion to perpetuate; instead, the court must find the party to be acting in anticipation of litigation.[11]

Risk of Loss of Testimony

To obtain a Rule 27 deposition, a party must show that there is a risk of the testimony or evidence being lost,[12] which might be satisfied when circumstances indicate that memories may fade.[13] In making this determination, the deponent's age alone can present a sufficient risk the deponent will be unable to testify in the future.[14] A party does not need to demonstrate certainty that the testimony will be lost, such as when the deponents are on their deathbeds.

Pre-Litigation Only

Once litigation has been commenced, Rules 30 and 31 addressing depositions in pending actions take over and Rule 27(a) may no longer be used.[15]

---

[8] *Qin v. Deslongchamps*, 31 F.4th 576, 581 (7th Cir. 2022); *Socha v. Pollard*, 621 F.3d 667, 671 (7th Cir. 2010). *But see Application of Deiulemar Compagnia Di Navigazione S.p.A. v. M/V Allegra*, 198 F.3d 473, 479 (4th Cir. 1999) (allowing Rule 27 discovery to preserve evidence for an arbitration); *In re Rivada Networks Pursuant to 28 U.S.C. § 1782 to Conduct Discovery for Use in a Foreign Proceeding*, 230 F. Supp. 3d 467 (E.D. Va. 2017) (Rule 27 applies to deposition to be taken in federal court in the U.S. in connection with a lawsuit in Mexico).

[9] *U.S. v. Van Rossem*, 180 F.R.D. 245, 247 (W.D.N.Y. 1998).

[10] *Application of Deiulemar Compagnia Di Navigazione S.p.A. v. M/V Allegra*, 198 F.3d 473, 478 (4th Cir. 1999) (inspection of ship engine repairs); *In re I-35W Bridge Collapse Site Inspection*, 243 F.R.D. 349, 352 (D. Minn. 2007) (inspection of bridge collapse site).

[11] *Teamsters Local 404 Health Servs. & Ins. Plan v. King Pharm., Inc.*, 906 F.3d 260, 267 (2d Cir. 2018); *Calderon v. U.S. Dist. Court for Northern Dist. of California*, 144 F.3d 618 (9th Cir. 1998).

[12] *Qin v. Deslongchamps*, 31 F.4th 576, 581 (7th Cir. 2022); *Calderon v. U.S. Dist. Court for Northern Dist. of California*, 144 F.3d 618 (9th Cir. 1998).

[13] *State of Arizona v. State of California*, 292 U.S. 341 (1934).

[14] *Penn Mut. Life Ins. Co. v. U.S.*, 68 F.3d 1371, 1375 (D.C. Cir. 1995); *In re Ramirez*, 241 F.R.D. 595 (W.D. Tex. 2006).

[15] *19th Street Baptist Church v. St. Peters Episcopal Church*, 190 F.R.D. 345, 348 (E.D. Pa. 2000).

Inability to Bring Suit

One requirement for petitions to perpetuate testimony is that the movant not be able to bring a lawsuit.[16] One basis for such inability is a lack of sufficient information to draft the complaint under the constraints of Rule 11.[17] However, Rule 27 may not be used to find testimony necessary to file suit,[18] and applies only where known testimony is to be preserved.[19]

Place of Filing

The petition may be filed in the district in which any of the adverse parties resides.[20] If *all* adverse parties are both not American citizens and not residing in the United States, the petition may be filed in any district.

Hearing

The court must hold a hearing on a Rule 27 petition.[21]

Notice and Service

At least 21 days prior to the hearing, the petitioner must send notice and a copy of the petition to all expected adverse parties.[22] The notice may be served in the manner provided under Rule 4. If personal service cannot be made, the court can order service by publication or otherwise. In such cases, the court must appoint an attorney to represent those not personally served.

Standard for Ruling

The court will order the deposition if it is satisfied that the perpetuation of the testimony may prevent a future failure or delay of justice.[23]

Contents of Court Order

The court must designate the deponent(s), the subject matter of the examination, and whether the deposition will be oral

---

[16] *In re Enable Commerce, Inc.*, 256 F.R.D. 527, 532 (N.D. Tex. 2009); *In re Town of Amenia, NY*, 200 F.R.D. 200 (S.D.N.Y. 2001) (party can take a Rule 27 deposition when a declaratory judgment is technically possible but the parties are still negotiating).

[17] *Petition of Alpha Industries, Inc.*, 159 F.R.D. 456 (S.D.N.Y. 1995).

[18] *Application of Deiulemar Compagnia Di Navigazione S.p.A. v. M/V Allegra*, 198 F.3d 473, 485 (4th Cir. 1999); *In re Obalon Therapeutics, Inc.*, 321 F.R.D. 245, 248 (E.D.N.C. 2017).

[19] *In re Ramirez*, 241 F.R.D. 595 (W.D. Tex. 2006); *Petition of Ford*, 170 F.R.D. 504, 507 (M.D. Ala. 1997).

[20] See *In re Obalon Therapeutics, Inc.*, 321 F.R.D. 245, 248 (E.D.N.C. 2017).

[21] *In re I-35W Bridge Collapse Site Inspection*, 243 F.R.D. 349, 351 (D. Minn. 2007).

[22] *In re Petition of Allegretti*, 229 F.R.D. 93, 96 (S.D.N.Y. 2005); *In re Chester County Elec., Inc.*, 208 F.R.D. 545, 546–47 (E.D. Pa. 2002).

[23] *In re Charter Comm'n, Inc., Subpoena Enforcement Matter*, 393 F.3d 771, 784 (8th Cir. 2005); *In re Navy Chaplaincy*, 287 F.R.D. 100, 102 (D.D.C. 2012).

or written.[24]

Conduct of the Deposition

The deposition is taken in accordance with the terms of the court's order and Rules 30 and 31 (governing oral and written depositions).

Scope of Deposition

The scope of a deposition under Rule 27 is often narrower than a typical discovery deposition, and will be governed by the court's order.[25] In general, courts have required that the evidence to be preserved be material and competent, not merely discoverable.[26]

Not Available for Pre-Complaint Fact Discovery

A party lacking sufficient information to draft a complaint may not use Rule 27 to develop the missing information.[27] Rather, Rule 27 only authorizes preservation of known testimony.[28]

Use of the Transcript

A deposition taken pursuant to Rule 27 may be used in any subsequent action in federal court involving the subject matter identified in the petition under the general terms and conditions governing use of depositions in Rule 32(a).[29]

Bankruptcy Proceedings

Rule 27 does not apply in contested matters before a bankruptcy court.[30]

Appeals

A grant or denial of a Rule 27 petition is appealable as a final order.[31]

RULE 27(b)—PENDING APPEAL

CORE CONCEPT

Rule 27 may be used while a case is on appeal, or while the period to appeal is running, to preserve testimony in the event that

---

[24] *Martin v. Reynolds Metals Corp.*, 297 F.2d 49, 55 (9th Cir. 1961).

[25] *State of Nev. v. O'Leary*, 63 F.3d 932, 936 (9th Cir. 1995); *In re Navy Chaplaincy*, 287 F.R.D. 100, 102 (D.D.C. 2012).

[26] *In re Hopson Marine Transp., Inc.*, 168 F.R.D. 560, 565 (E.D. La. 1996).

[27] *Qin v. Deslongchamps*, 31 F.4th 576, 581 (7th Cir. 2022); *Teamsters Local 404 Health Servs. & Ins. Plan v. King Pharm., Inc.*, 906 F.3d 260, 267 (2d Cir. 2018).

[28] *Qin v. Deslongchamps*, 31 F.4th 576, 581 (7th Cir. 2022); *United States v. Cuya*, 964 F.3d 969, 973 (11th Cir. 2020).

[29] *Chevron Oronite Co., L.L.C. v. Jacobs Field Servs. N. Am., Inc.*, 951 F.3d 219, 227–28 (5th Cir. 2020).

[30] *See In re Szadkowski*, 198 B.R. 140, 141 n. 1 (D. Md. 1996). *See also* Fed. R. Bankr. Proc. Rule 9014.

[31] *See Qin v. Deslongchamps*, 31 F.4th 576, 581 (7th Cir. 2022); *Martin v. Reynolds Metals Corp.*, 297 F.2d 49 (9th Cir.1961).

further proceedings are needed.[32] A request for a deposition pending an appeal is made by motion (not petition, in contrast to Rule 27(a)) to the district court where the action proceeded.[33] The motion must include the names and addresses of the deponents, the substance of their testimony, and the reasons for perpetuating their testimony.[34] Otherwise, a motion pursuant to Rule 27(b) is subject to the notice, service, and other requirements and conditions for a petition under Rule 27(a) described above.

RULE 27(c)—PERPETUATION BY AN ACTION

CORE CONCEPT

Rule 27 is not the exclusive method of perpetuating testimony.[35] Thus, for example, a deposition that would be admissible in a subsequent proceeding in state court will also be admissible in federal court, even though the offering party may not have complied with Rule 27. Likewise, a party may preserve testimony under a method authorized by statute.

Additional Research References

Wright & Miller, *Federal Practice and Procedure* §§ 2071 to 2076. Lisnek & Kaufman, *Depositions: Procedure, Strategy and Technique*
C.J.S., Federal Civil Procedure §§ 544 to 547
West's Key Number Digest, Federal Civil Procedure ⚷1291 to 1299

---

[32] *See Schreier v. Weight Watchers Northeast Region, Inc.*, 872 F. Supp. 1 (E.D.N.Y. 1994), aff'd, 57 F.3d 1064 (2d Cir. 1995).

[33] *U.S. v. Van Rossem*, 180 F.R.D. 245, 247 (W.D.N.Y. 1998) (motion to compel Rule 27 discovery denied because need to perpetuate testimony was not demonstrated).

[34] *Foy v. Dicks*, 1996 WL 745501 (E.D. Pa. 1996) (petitioners' Rule 27 motion denied for failure to assert reasons why perpetuation of evidence was necessary).

[35] *See Nissei Sangyo America, Ltd. v. U.S.*, 31 F.3d 435 (7th Cir. 1994) (action to perpetuate foreign bank records).

RULE 28
PERSONS BEFORE WHOM DEPOSITIONS MAY BE TAKEN

(a) **Within the United States.**

(1) *In General.* Within the United States or a territory or insular possession subject to United States jurisdiction, a deposition must be taken before:

(A) an officer authorized to administer oaths either by federal law or by the law in the place of examination; or

(B) a person appointed by the court where the action is pending to administer oaths and take testimony.

(2) *Definition of "Officer."* The term "officer" in Rules 30, 31, and 32 includes a person appointed by the court under this rule or designated by the parties under Rule 29(a).

(b) **In a Foreign Country.**

(1) *In General.* A deposition may be taken in a foreign country:

(A) under an applicable treaty or convention;

(B) under a letter of request, whether or not captioned a "letter rogatory";

(C) on notice, before a person authorized to administer oaths either by federal law or by the law in the place of examination; or

(D) before a person commissioned by the court to administer any necessary oath and take testimony.

(2) *Issuing a Letter of Request or a Commission.* A letter of request, a commission, or both may be issued:

(A) on appropriate terms after an application and notice of it; and

(B) without a showing that taking the deposition in another manner is impracticable or inconvenient.

(3) *Form of a Request, Notice, or Commission.* When a letter of request or any other device is used according to a treaty or convention, it must be captioned in the form prescribed by that treaty or convention. A letter of request may be addressed "To the Appropriate Authority in [name of country]." A deposition notice or a commission must designate by name or descriptive title the person before whom the deposition is to be taken.

(4) *Letter of Request—Admitting Evidence.* Evidence obtained in response to a letter of request need not be excluded merely because it is not a verbatim transcript, because the testimony was not taken under oath, or because of any similar departure from the requirements for depositions taken within the United States.

(c) **Disqualification.** A deposition must not be taken before a person who is any party's relative, employee, or attorney; who is related to or employed by any party's attorney; or who is financially interested in the action.

[Amended December 27, 1946, effective March 19, 1948; January 21, 1963, effective July 1, 1963; April 29, 1980, effective August 1, 1980; March 2, 1987, effective August 1, 1987; April 22, 1993, effective December 1, 1993; April 30, 2007, effective December 1, 2007.]

AUTHORS' COMMENTARY ON RULE 28

PURPOSE AND SCOPE

Rule 28 specifies the type of person who must be present at a deposition to administer the oath and to record the testimony and lists criteria that disqualify candidates from consideration, such as being related to a party.

RULE 28(a)—WITHIN THE UNITED STATES

CORE CONCEPT

In the United States, or a territory or insular possession, depositions may be taken before an officer authorized to administer oaths under federal or state law.[1] Typically, a stenographer is such an officer. A deposition may also be taken before someone appointed by the court or before a person designated by the parties by stipulation pursuant to Rule 29.[2]

RULE 28(b)—IN A FOREIGN COUNTRY

CORE CONCEPT

The procedures for taking depositions in a foreign country depend upon the particular country. Some countries have treaties with the United States that facilitate such depositions. Other countries strictly prohibit such depositions altogether.

NOTE: In some countries, the taking of evidence under unauthorized procedures may subject the interrogator to severe—even criminal—sanctions. Before taking such evidence, a practitioner should consult the Hague Convention and all applicable treaties.[3]

APPLICATIONS

Alternatives

Depending upon the laws of the foreign country, a deposition in a foreign country may be taken:

(1) Pursuant to any applicable treaty or convention (such as the Hague Convention);[4]

(2) Pursuant to a letter request (or letter rogatory), which is a formal communication between the court in which an action is proceeding and another court requesting that the testimony of a foreign witness be taken under the direction of the foreign court;[5]

(3) Upon a notice of deposition by any person authorized to administer oaths either by the laws of the foreign country or the United States;[6] or

(4) Before persons commissioned by the court, who will have power to administer an oath and hear testimony by virtue of their oaths.[7]

Method Optional

A party seeking to depose a witness in a foreign country

---

[1] *Hudson v. Spellman High Voltage*, 178 F.R.D. 29, 32 (E.D.N.Y. 1998).

[2] *Popular Imports, Inc. v. Wong's Intern., Inc.*, 166 F.R.D. 276, 279–80 (E.D.N.Y. 1996).

[3] The Hague Convention on the Taking of Evidence Abroad in Civil or Commercial Matters is reproduced as a note to 28 U.S.C.A. § 1781, and may also be found on WESTLAW in the IEL database, ci(vii-b & text). *See Societe Nationale Industrielle Aerospatiale v. U.S. Dist. Court for Southern Dist. of Iowa*, 482 U.S. 522 (1987).

[4] *See Shi v. New Mighty U.S. Tr.*, 918 F.3d 944, 951 (D.C. Cir. 2019); *Packard v. City of New York*, 326 F.R.D. 66, 68 (S.D.N.Y. 2018).

[5] *See Packard v. City of New York*, 326 F.R.D. 66, 68 (S.D.N.Y. 2018); *Perrigo Co. & Subsidiaries v. United States*, 294 F. Supp. 3d 740, 741–42 (W.D. Mich. 2018).

[6] *See Packard v. City of New York*, 326 F.R.D. 66, 68 (S.D.N.Y. 2018).

[7] *Packard v. City of New York*, 326 F.R.D. 66, 68 (S.D.N.Y. 2018).

may use any of the methods listed in Rule 28(b) allowed by the foreign country's laws and may combine two or more methods.

Issuance of Letter Requests

All courts of the United States are authorized to issue letter requests or letters rogatory,[8] which are typically channeled through the United States Department of State.

Testimony Pursuant to a Letter Request

The evidence taken pursuant to a letter request varies according to the foreign country's laws. Sometimes the foreign judge examines the witness, then makes a written summary of the testimony, which is acknowledged as correct by the witness. The United States court will then decide what weight to give the testimony depending upon the method of recording.

Compelling Attendance of Witness

If the witness is a party, then the witness is subject to the United States court's sanctions if the witness fails to appear as noticed. If the party witness is a United States citizen, then the witness still may be subject to the United States court's subpoena power.[9] However, if the nonparty witness is an alien, then the party will have to rely on a letter request.

RULE 28(c)—DISQUALIFICATION

CORE CONCEPT

The officer at a deposition may not be a relative, employee, or attorney of any of the parties,[10] or an employee or relative of an attorney for a party, or anyone with a financial interest in the action.[11]

APPLICATIONS

Objections

Objections to the officer must be raised before the deposition starts or as soon thereafter as the interest of the officer becomes known or should have become known with due diligence. Otherwise, the objection is waived.[12]

Additional Research References

Wright & Miller, *Federal Practice and Procedure* §§ 2081 to 2084
C.J.S., Federal Civil Procedure § 593

---

[8] *See U.S. v. Reagan*, 453 F.2d 165 (6th Cir. 1971).

[9] *Shi v. New Mighty U.S. Tr.*, 918 F.3d 944, 951 (D.C. Cir. 2019).

[10] *See Schoolcraft v. City of New York*, 296 F.R.D. 231, 239 (S.D.N.Y. 2013) (plaintiff's attorney may not operate the videocamera).

[11] *Ott v. Stipe Law Firm*, 169 F.R.D. 380, 381 (E.D. Okla. 1996) (plaintiff is not permitted to administer oath).

[12] See Rule 32(d)(2).

West's Key Number Digest, Federal Civil Procedure ⚷1371

RULE 29
STIPULATIONS ABOUT DISCOVERY PROCEDURE

Unless the court orders otherwise, the parties may stipulate that:

(a) a deposition may be taken before any person, at any time or place, on any notice, and in the manner specified—in which event it may be used in the same way as any other deposition; and

(b) other procedures governing or limiting discovery be modified—but a stipulation extending the time for any form of discovery must have court approval if it would interfere with the time set for completing discovery, for hearing a motion, or for trial.

[Amended March 30, 1970, effective July 1, 1970; April 22, 1993, effective December 1, 1993; April 30, 2007, effective December 1, 2007.]

AUTHORS' COMMENTARY ON RULE 29

PURPOSE AND SCOPE

The discovery rules set various time limitations, numeric limitations, and other restrictions on discovery. These are just defaults, however, and the parties are free to stipulate to modified discovery procedures. The primary restraint on this ability to modify discovery procedures is that the parties may not enter into a stipulation extending the time for any discovery if the extension would interfere with a hearing or trial date or the court's overall discovery deadline. Thus, the judge controls the overall schedule, but within the framework the judge has established, the parties may agree to their own set of discovery procedures.

APPLICATIONS

Procedures

Stipulations under Rule 29 may be written or oral.[1] They do require clear agreement by both parties; a letter from one party without an acceptance by the other party is not a Rule 29 stipulation.[2] Stipulations are self-effectuating and do not need to receive court approval or even be filed with the court unless they would affect the court's schedule, as discussed below.[3]

Stipulations Regarding Depositions

The parties may designate the person before whom a deposition will occur and the time, location, notice requirements, and method of taking the deposition.[4] Thereafter, a deposition taken in accordance with the stipulation may be used as if taken in accordance with the provisions governing oral and written depositions in Rules 30 and 31.[5]

Stipulations Regarding Discovery Methods other than Depositions

The parties may stipulate to modified procedures regarding discovery other than depositions, such as stipulations: modifying the time to respond to written discovery;[6] modifying the limit on the number of interrogatories; to conduct examinations of a party under Rule 35; specifying procedures for discovery of ESI;[7] or determining the scope or sequence of discovery.[8]

Stipulations Affecting the Court's Schedule

The parties need court approval to modify a discovery date or deadline if the extension would interfere with the court's discovery deadline or with a hearing or trial date.[9] Thus, for example, a court might not enforce a stipulation to conduct a deposition after the court's discovery deadline.[10]

---

[1] *I/P Engine, Inc. v. AOL, Inc.*, 283 F.R.D. 322, 324 n.3 (E.D. Va. 2012).

[2] *Ferring Pharmaceuticals Inc., v. Serenity Pharmaceuticals, LLC*, 331 F.R.D. 75, 79 (S.D.N.Y. 2019).

[3] *In re DFI Proceeds, Inc.*, 441 B.R. 914, 916 (N.D. Ind. 2011).

[4] *In re Angst*, 428 B.R. 776, 781 (N.D. Ohio 2010); *Reder Enter., Inc. v. Loomis, Fargo & Co. Corp.*, 490 F. Supp. 2d 111 (D. Mass. 2007) (parties may stipulate that depositions be taken "at any . . . place").

[5] *See In re Angst*, 428 B.R. 776, 781 (N.D. Ohio 2010).

[6] *Nasreen v. Capitol Petroleum Grp., LLC*, 340 F.R.D. 489, 493 (D.D.C. 2022); *Puerto Rico Medical Emergency Group, Inc. v. Iglesia Episcopal Puertorriqueña, Inc.*, 318 F.R.D. 224, 228 (D.P.R. 2016).

[7] *See In re Actos Antitrust Litig.*, 340 F.R.D. 549, 551 (S.D.N.Y. 2022).

[8] *See, e.g., Silver State Intellectual Technologies, Inc. v. Garmin Intern., Inc.*, 35 F. Supp. 3d 1271, 1274 (D. Nev. 2014).

[9] *See Hassebrock v. Berhoft*, 815 F.3d 334, 338 (7th Cir. 2016); *Laborers' Pension Fund v. Blackmore Sewer Const., Inc.*, 298 F.3d 600, 605–06 (7th Cir. 2002).

[10] *Wyles v. Sussman*, 445 F. Supp. 3d 751, 759 (C.D. Cal. 2020).

Court Override

The court can order that parties perform under the Rules as written, vitiating any stipulations.[11]

Additional Research References

Wright & Miller, *Federal Practice and Procedure* §§ 2091 to 2092
C.J.S., Federal Civil Procedure § 566
West's Key Number Digest, Federal Civil Procedure ⚷1326

---

[11] *In re Westinghouse Elec. Corp.-Uranium Contracts Litig.*, 570 F.2d 899, 902 (10th Cir.1978); *I/P Engine, Inc. v. AOL, Inc.*, 283 F.R.D. 322, 325 (E.D. Va. 2012).

RULE 30
DEPOSITIONS BY ORAL EXAMINATION

(a) **When a Deposition May Be Taken.**

(1) *Without Leave.* A party may, by oral questions, depose any person, including a party, without leave of court except as provided in Rule 30(a)(2). The deponent's attendance may be compelled by subpoena under Rule 45.

(2) *With Leave.* A party must obtain leave of court, and the court must grant leave to the extent consistent with Rule 26(b)(1) and (2):

(A) if the parties have not stipulated to the deposition and:

(i) the deposition would result in more than 10 depositions being taken under this rule or Rule 31 by the plaintiffs, or by the defendants, or by the third-party defendants;

(ii) the deponent has already been deposed in the case; or

(iii) the party seeks to take the deposition before the time specified in Rule 26(d), unless the party certifies in the notice, with supporting facts, that the deponent is expected to leave the United States and be unavailable for examination in this country after that time; or

(B) if the deponent is confined in prison.

(b) **Notice of the Deposition; Other Formal Requirements.**

(1) *Notice in General.* A party who wants to depose a person by oral questions must give reasonable written notice to every other party. The notice must state the time and place of the deposition and, if known, the deponent's name and address. If the name is unknown, the notice must provide a general description sufficient to identify the

person or the particular class or group to which the person belongs.

(2) *Producing Documents.* If a subpoena duces tecum is to be served on the deponent, the materials designated for production, as set out in the subpoena, must be listed in the notice or in an attachment. The notice to a party deponent may be accompanied by a request under Rule 34 to produce documents and tangible things at the deposition.

(3) *Method of Recording.*

(A) *Method Stated in the Notice.* The party who notices the deposition must state in the notice the method for recording the testimony. Unless the court orders otherwise, testimony may be recorded by audio, audiovisual, or stenographic means. The noticing party bears the recording costs. Any party may arrange to transcribe a deposition.

(B) *Additional Method.* With prior notice to the deponent and other parties, any party may designate another method for recording the testimony in addition to that specified in the original notice. That party bears the expense of the additional record or transcript unless the court orders otherwise.

(4) *By Remote Means.* The parties may stipulate—or the court may on motion order—that a deposition be taken by telephone or other remote means. For the purpose of this rule and Rules 28(a), 37(a)(2), and 37(b)(1), the deposition takes place where the deponent answers the questions.

(5) *Officer's Duties.*

(A) *Before the Deposition.* Unless the parties stipulate otherwise, a deposition must be conducted before an officer appointed or designated under Rule 28. The officer must begin the deposition with an on-the-record statement that includes:

(i) the officer's name and business address;

(ii) the date, time, and place of the deposition;

(iii) the deponent's name;

(iv) the officer's administration of the oath or affirmation to the deponent; and

(v) the identity of all persons present.

(B) *Conducting the Deposition; Avoiding Distortion.* If the deposition is recorded nonstenographically, the officer must repeat the items in Rule 30(b)(5)(A)(i)-(iii) at the beginning of each unit of the recording medium. The deponent's and attorneys' appearance or demeanor must not be distorted through recording techniques.

(C) *After the Deposition.* At the end of a deposition, the officer must state on the record that the deposition is complete and must set out any stipulations made by the attorneys about custody of the transcript or recording and of the exhibits, or about any other pertinent matters.

(6) *Notice or Subpoena Directed to an Organization.*[1] In its notice or subpoena, a party may name as the deponent a public or private corporation, a partnership, an association, a governmental agency, or other entity and must describe with reasonable particularity the matters for examination. The named organization must then designate one or more officers, directors, or managing agents, or designate other persons who consent to testify on its behalf; and it may set out the matters on which each person designated will testify. Before or promptly after the notice or

---

[1]Rule 30(b)(6) was amended effective December 1, 2020. The language altered by this amendment is printed here, with additions underlined and deletions struck through:

(6) Notice or Subpoena Directed to an Organization. In its notice or subpoena, a party may name as the deponent a public or private corporation, a partnership, an association, a governmental agency, or other entity and must describe with reasonable particularity the matters for examination. The named organization must ~~then~~ designate one or more officers, directors, or managing agents, or designate other persons who consent to testify on its behalf; and it may set out the matters on which each person designated will testify. Before or promptly after the notice or subpoena is served, the serving party and the organization must confer in good faith about the matters for examination. A subpoena must advise a nonparty organization of its duty to confer with the serving party and to designate each person who will testify. The persons designated must testify about information known or reasonably available to the organization. This paragraph (6) does not preclude a deposition by any other procedure allowed by these rules.

subpoena is served, the serving party and the organization must confer in good faith about the matters for examination. A subpoena must advise a nonparty organization of its duty to confer with the serving party and to designate each person who will testify. The persons designated must testify about information known or reasonably available to the organization. This paragraph (6) does not preclude a deposition by any other procedure allowed by these rules.

(c) Examination and Cross-Examination; Record of the Examination; Objections; Written Questions.

(1) *Examination and Cross-Examination.* The examination and cross-examination of a deponent proceed as they would at trial under the Federal Rules of Evidence, except Rules 103 and 615. After putting the deponent under oath or affirmation, the officer must record the testimony by the method designated under Rule 30(b)(3)(A). The testimony must be recorded by the officer personally or by a person acting in the presence and under the direction of the officer.

(2) *Objections.* An objection at the time of the examination—whether to evidence, to a party's conduct, to the officer's qualifications, to the manner of taking the deposition, or to any other aspect of the deposition—must be noted on the record, but the examination still proceeds; the testimony is taken subject to any objection. An objection must be stated concisely in a nonargumentative and nonsuggestive manner. A person may instruct a deponent not to answer only when necessary to preserve a privilege, to enforce a limitation ordered by the court, or to present a motion under Rule 30(d)(3).

(3) *Participating Through Written Questions.* Instead of participating in the oral examination, a party may serve written questions in a sealed envelope on the party noticing the deposition, who must deliver them to the officer. The officer must ask the deponent those questions and record the answers verbatim.

(d) Duration; Sanction; Motion to Terminate or Limit.

(1) *Duration.* Unless otherwise stipulated or ordered by the court, a deposition is limited to 1 day of 7 hours. The court must allow additional time consistent with Rule 26(b)(1) and (2) if needed to fairly examine the deponent or if the deponent, another person, or any other circumstance impedes or delays the examination.

(2) *Sanction.* The court may impose an appropriate sanction—including the reasonable expenses and attorney's fees incurred by any party—on a person who impedes, delays, or frustrates the fair examination of the deponent.

(3) *Motion to Terminate or Limit.*

(A) *Grounds.* At any time during a deposition, the deponent or a party may move to terminate or limit it on the ground that it is being conducted in bad faith or in a manner that unreasonably annoys, embarrasses, or oppresses the deponent or party. The motion may be filed in the court where the action is pending or the deposition is being taken. If the objecting deponent or party so demands, the deposition must be suspended for the time necessary to obtain an order.

(B) *Order.* The court may order that the deposition be terminated or may limit its scope and manner as provided in Rule 26(c). If terminated, the deposition may be resumed only by order of the court where the action is pending.

(C) *Award of Expenses.* Rule 37(a)(5) applies to the award of expenses.

(e) Review by the Witness; Changes.

(1) *Review; Statement of Changes.* On request by the deponent or a party before the deposition is completed, the deponent must be allowed 30 days after being notified by the officer that the transcript or recording is available in which:

(A) to review the transcript or recording; and

(B) if there are changes in form or substance, to sign a statement listing the changes and the reasons for making them.

(2) *Changes Indicated in the Officer's Certificate.* The officer must note in the certificate prescribed by Rule 30(f)(1) whether a review was requested and, if so, must attach any changes the deponent makes during the 30-day period.

(f) **Certification and Delivery; Exhibits; Copies of the Transcript or Recording; Filing.**

(1) *Certification and Delivery.* The officer must certify in writing that the witness was duly sworn and that the deposition accurately records the witness's testimony. The certificate must accompany the record of the deposition. Unless the court orders otherwise, the officer must seal the deposition in an envelope or package bearing the title of the action and marked "Deposition of [witness's name]" and must promptly send it to the attorney who arranged for the transcript or recording. The attorney must store it under conditions that will protect it against loss, destruction, tampering, or deterioration.

(2) *Documents and Tangible Things.*

(A) *Originals and Copies.* Documents and tangible things produced for inspection during a deposition must, on a party's request, be marked for identification and attached to the deposition. Any party may inspect and copy them. But if the person who produced them wants to keep the originals, the person may:

(i) offer copies to be marked, attached to the deposition, and then used as originals—after giving all parties a fair opportunity to verify the copies by comparing them with the originals; or

(ii) give all parties a fair opportunity to inspect and copy the originals after they are marked—in which event the originals may be used as if attached to the deposition.

(B) *Order Regarding the Originals.* Any party may move for an order that the originals be attached to the deposition pending final disposition of the case.

(3) *Copies of the Transcript or Recording.* Unless otherwise stipulated or ordered by the court, the officer must retain the stenographic notes of a deposition taken stenographically or a copy of the recording of a deposition taken by another method. When paid reasonable charges, the officer must furnish a copy of the transcript or recording to any party or the deponent.

(4) *Notice of Filing.* A party who files the deposition must promptly notify all other parties of the filing.

(g) **Failure to Attend a Deposition or Serve a Subpoena; Expenses.** A party who, expecting a deposition to be taken, attends in person or by an attorney may recover reasonable expenses for attending, including attorney's fees, if the noticing party failed to:

(1) attend and proceed with the deposition; or

(2) serve a subpoena on a nonparty deponent, who consequently did not attend.

[Amended January 21, 1963, effective July 1, 1963; March 30, 1970, effective July 1, 1970; March 1, 1971, effective July 1, 1971; November 20, 1972, effective July 1, 1975; April 29, 1980, effective August 1, 1980; March 2, 1987, effective August 1, 1987; April 22, 1993, effective December 1, 1993; April 17, 2000, effective December 1, 2000; April 30, 2007, effective December 1, 2007; April 29, 2015, effective December 1, 2015; April 27, 2020, effective December 1, 2020.]

AUTHORS' COMMENTARY ON RULE 30

PURPOSE AND SCOPE

Rule 30 is one of four rules that specifically govern depositions: Rules 28, 30, 31, and 32. Rules 30 and Rule 31 address the procedures for and conduct at the actual deposition, with Rule 30 covering oral examination and Rule 31 covering written examination (which is rarely used). Rule 32 then specifies how parties may use a deposition transcript or recording in subsequent stages of the lawsuit. Rule 28 controls who may be the neutral officer who administers a deposition, typically a stenographer or videographer.

Rule 30 covers a broad range of topics relating to the mechanics of depositions, including: limits on the number and duration of depositions; the procedures for "noticing" or scheduling depositions; technical requirements for recording depositions; taking depositions of designated representatives of organizations like corporations; the conduct of direct and cross-examination and the manner of interposing objections; the process for a witness to review the transcript and make changes; and sanctions for failing to attend a properly-noticed deposition.

In addition to the four rules specifically focused on depositions, the general rules governing all discovery also apply to depositions. For example, the scope of inquiry in a deposition is the general scope of discovery in Rule 26(b)(1). A party wishing to limit the duration of a deposition or prevent inquiry into certain topics would file a motion for a protective order under Rule 26(c). And a party believing that an opponent has acted improperly at a deposition would file a motion to compel or for sanctions under Rule 37.

RULE 30(a)—WHEN A DEPOSITION MAY BE TAKEN

CORE CONCEPT

In general, a party may take the deposition of up to 10 witnesses, party or otherwise, at any time after the parties have conducted the discovery conference under Rule 26(f) and before the discovery deadline (typically set in the court's Case Management Order). A party may only depose each witness one time, absent a stipulation, court order, or other unusual circumstance.

APPLICATIONS

Persons Subject to Deposition

Rule 30 authorizes any party to take the deposition of any person, party or not, without leave of court.[2] A party may even take the party's own deposition—which ordinarily would not make sense (there's no real benefit to having a party's lawyer ask the party questions on the record; they can do that privately), but would be warranted if, for example, the party will be unable to attend trial. One may also take the deposition of attorneys, including the attorneys for parties,[3] although the attorney-client privilege may shield most of an attorney's information and many courts subject requests to depose opposing counsel to heightened scrutiny.[4] Depositions are also permitted of the United States, individual States, public officials, and other governmental agencies and subdivisions.[5]

- *Apex Doctrine*: One limitation on this broad right to take depositions is called the "Apex Doctrine," under which some courts hold that high-ranking governmental of-

---

[2]*Sali v. Corona Reg'l Med. Ctr.*, 884 F.3d 1218, 1222 (9th Cir. 2018); *Sherman v. Sheffield Fin., LLC*, 338 F.R.D. 247, 252 (D. Minn. 2021).

[3]*Smith-Bunge v. Wisconsin Cent., Ltd.*, 946 F.3d 420, 423 (8th Cir. 2019).

[4]*Gamache v. Hogue*, — F. Supp. 3d —, 2022 WL 989483, at *3 (M.D. Ga. 2022).

[5]*U. S. v. Procter & Gamble Co.*, 356 U.S. 677 (1958).

ficials or corporate officers cannot be deposed unless the apex individual has firsthand knowledge of relevant facts and those facts cannot be obtained through less intrusive forms of discovery.[6] Some courts extend this protection to all government officials.[7]

- *Compelling Attendance*: A party is compelled to attend a deposition if served with a notice of deposition, discussed below in Rule 30(b)(1). A nonparty is compelled to attend if served with a subpoena, discussed below in Rule 45.[8]

Number of Depositions

The plaintiffs as a group are limited to 10 depositions total, without distinction between written and oral examination, as are the defendants and third-party defendants.[9] Subpoenas to produce documents do not count towards the 10-deposition limit.[10] It is not clear whether expert depositions count toward the limit.[11]

- *Counting Depositions of Rule 30(b)(6) Representatives:* A notice to take the deposition of a corporate representative under Rule 30(b)(6) will count as one deposition toward the 10-deposition limit, regardless of the number of representatives designated to appear and testify.[12]
- *Modifying the Deposition Limit:* The limit on the number of depositions may be increased or decreased by stipulation or by order of court.[13] In ruling on a motion to expand the number of depositions, the court will consider not only the necessity of the additional depositions, but also the depositions already conducted.[14]

Repeat Depositions

Leave of court or a stipulation of the parties is required to depose someone a second time.[15] Leave of court is not required to reconvene and continue a deposition that was suspended or

---

[6]*See United States v. Newman*, 531 F. Supp. 3d 181, 188 (D.D.C. 2021); *Odom v. Roberts*, 337 F.R.D. 359, 363–64 (N.D. Fla. 2020).

[7]*Bless v. Cook Cnty. Sheriff's Off.*, 9 F.4th 565, 571 (7th Cir. 2021).

[8]*Camoco, LLC v. Leyva*, 333 F.R.D. 603, 607 (W.D. Tex. 2019).

[9]*O'Leary v. Accretive Health, Inc.*, 657 F.3d 625, 636 (7th Cir. 2011); *Thykkuttathil v. Keese*, 294 F.R.D. 597, 599 (W.D. Wash. 2013) (depositions are counted per side, not per party).

[10]*Andamiro U.S.A. v. Konami Amusement of Am., Inc.*, 2001 WL 535667 (C.D. Cal. 2001).

[11]*Express One Intern., Inc. v. Sochata*, 2001 WL 363073 (N.D. Tex. 2001).

[12]*Stevens v. CoreLogic, Inc.*, 893 F.3d 648, 661 n.13 (9th Cir. 2018).

[13]*O'Leary v. Accretive Health, Inc.*, 657 F.3d 625, 636 (7th Cir. 2011); *Raniola v. Bratton*, 243 F.3d 610, 628 (2d Cir. 2001).

[14]*Madison v. Jack Link Associates Stage Lighting & Productions, Inc.*, 297 F.R.D. 532, 535 (S.D. Fla. 2013).

[15]*See Spectrum Ass'n Mgmt. of Texas, L.L.C. v. Lifetime HOA Mgmt. L.L.C.*, 5 F.4th 560, 565 (5th Cir. 2021); *Wagner v. Gallup, Inc.*, 788 F.3d 877, 890–91 (8th Cir. 2015).

not completed the first day.[16] Leave to take a repeat deposition is governed by the principles of proportionality in Rule 26(b)(1) and the limitations on discovery in Rule 26(b)(2), such as whether the sought-after information could have been obtained in the first deposition.[17]

- *Rule 30(b)(6) Depositions:* The courts are divided as to how to apply the limitation on repeat depositions of the same individual to depositions of company representatives under Rule 30(b)(6). Some courts have held that it is impermissible to issue a second Rule 30(b)(6) notice without leave of court.[18] Leave of court is generally not required to take the deposition of a witness as a Rule 30(b)(6) representative even if the witness has already been deposed in his or her individual capacity.[19] Courts are divided as to whether leave of court is required to take the deposition of an individual who has already been deposed as a designated representative under Rule 30(b)(6).[20]

Time for Conducting Depositions

Depositions generally may be taken at any time after the Rule 26(f) discovery conference and before the cut-off date for discovery established by the court.[21] Leave of court is generally required to depose someone prior to the time when the parties conduct the discovery conference under Rule 26(f).[22] An exception occurs when the deponent is expected to leave the United States.[23] In such instances, the notice of deposition must contain a certification with the facts supporting the need for the early deposition.[24] Additionally, in proceedings listed in Rule 26(a)(1)(B) as exempt from initial disclosures, there is no

---

[16] *Paige v. Consumer Programs, Inc.*, 248 F.R.D. 272, 275 (C.D. Cal. 2008) (when the party appears but the deposition does not occur, the party may be re-noticed without violating the rule against second depositions).

[17] *VeroBlue Farms USA Inc. v. Wulf*, __ F.R.D. __, 2021 WL 5176839, at *10 (N.D. Tex. 2021) (new information); *Lofgren v. BNSF Ry. Co.*, 231 F. Supp. 3d 322, 323 n.1 (D.N.D. 2017).

[18] See *Ameristar Jet Charter, Inc. v. Signal Composites, Inc.*, 244 F.3d 189 (1st Cir. 2001); *Infernal Tech., LLC v. Epic Games, Inc.*, 339 F.R.D. 226, 230 n.4 (E.D.N.C. 2021).

[19] *See Edwards v. Scripps Media, Inc.*, 331 F.R.D. 116, 121 (E.D. Mich. 2019); *Martin v. Bimbo Foods Bakeries Distribution, LLC*, 313 F.R.D. 1, 9 (E.D.N.C. 2016).

[20] *See Ameristar Jet Charter, Inc. v. Signal Composites, Inc.*, 244 F.3d 189 (1st Cir. 2001); *Nationstar Mortgage, LLC v. Flamingo Trails No. 7 Landscape Maint. Ass'n*, 316 F.R.D. 327, 333 (D. Nev. 2016) (allowing the deposition of the same person as an individual and a Rule 30(b)(6) representative).

[21] *Doe v. Trump*, 329 F.R.D. 262, 274 (W.D. Wash. 2018) (nothing improper about a deposition at the "eleventh hour," right before the close of discovery).

[22] *See Mullane v. Almon*, 339 F.R.D. 659, 662 (N.D. Fla. 2021); *Fed. Trade Comm'n v. Simple Health Plans LLC*, 379 F. Supp. 3d 1346 (S.D. Fla. 2019).

[23] Rule 30(a)(2)(C).

[24] *19th Street Baptist Church v. St. Peters Episcopal Church*, 190 F.R.D. 345, 348 n. 5 (E.D. Pa. 2000).

preliminary waiting period for depositions.

Depositions for Use at Trial

There is no longer any distinction between discovery depositions and depositions for use at trial (sometimes called "*de bene esse* depositions"); any deposition is subject to the limitations in Rule 30 and can be used for any of the purposes authorized in Rule 32.[25]

Post-Judgment Depositions

A judgment creditor is entitled to take depositions of the judgment debtor to inquire into the assets necessary to satisfy the judgment.[26]

Deponent in Prison

Leave of court must be obtained in order to take the deposition of a person confined in prison.[27]

RULE 30(b)(1)—NOTICE OF THE DEPOSITION; OTHER FORMAL REQUIREMENTS: NOTICE IN GENERAL

CORE CONCEPT

A party intending to take a deposition must serve a written notice upon all other parties identifying the deponent and time and location of the deposition. Depositions are only admissible against parties properly noticed or actually represented at the deposition.

APPLICATIONS

Content of Notice

A deposition notice must state the date, time, and place of the deposition[28] and the manner of recording the deposition.[29] It must also state the name and address of the deponent, if known, or a general description sufficient to identify the deponent. The deposition notice does not need to describe the topics to be covered in the deposition (except for a notice to take the deposition of a designated representative of a corporation, discussed below in Rule 30(b)(6)).[30] If a subpoena duces tecum (seeking documents) is to be served under Rule 45, then the notice must include a description of the documents sought.[31]

---

[25] *Manley v. AmBase Corp.*, 337 F.3d 237, 247 (2d Cir. 2003); *Green v. City of Phoenix*, 330 F.R.D. 239, 240 (D. Ariz. 2019).

[26] *Credit Lyonnais, S.A. v. SGC Intern., Inc.*, 160 F.3d 428, 430 (8th Cir. 1998).

[27] *Evans v. Griffin*, 932 F.3d 1043, 1044–45 (7th Cir. 2019); *Smith v. Florida Dept. of Corrections*, 713 F.3d 1059, 1062 n.3 (11th Cir. 2013).

[28] *Huddleston v. Bowling Green Inn of Pensacola*, 333 F.R.D. 581, 587 (N.D. Fla. 2019); *Shockey v. Huhtamaki, Inc.*, 280 F.R.D. 598, 600 (D. Kan. 2012).

[29] *Schoolcraft v. City of New York*, 296 F.R.D. 231, 239 (S.D.N.Y. 2013).

[30] *Libertarian Party of Ohio v. Husted*, 302 F.R.D. 472, 476 (S.D. Ohio 2014) (only depositions of organizations under Rule 30(b)(6) require a list of topics).

[31] *Orleman v. Jumpking, Inc.*,

Service and Filing of Notice

Deposition notices are served on all parties, but are not filed.[32] If a party is represented by more than one attorney, service on any of them is sufficient.[33]

Failure to Serve Notice

If a party does not receive a notice of a deposition and does not appear, or is not represented at the deposition, the testimony cannot be used against that party, even if the party had actual knowledge that the deposition was to occur.[34]

Timing of Notice

Rule 30(b)(1) states that a party must give "reasonable" notice.[35] There is no bright line as to what is reasonable notice, and the determination is extremely discretionary.[36] If the parties cannot agree on a mutually acceptable date, then the reasonableness of the notice may be challenged by a motion for a protective order under Rule 26(c).

Deposition of a Party

A deposition notice compels parties to attend a deposition, without the need for a subpoena.[37] A corporate party is required to produce directors, officers, and managing agents pursuant to a notice of deposition;[38] a subpoena is required for other employees.[39]

Deposition of a Nonparty

A notice of deposition is not binding on a nonparty. Instead, a party must serve a subpoena pursuant to Rule 45 to force a nonparty to attend a deposition.[40] However, the party taking the deposition must still serve a deposition notice upon the

---

2000 WL 1114849 (D. Kan. 2000) (description of documents to be produced must be attached to or included in the notice).

[32] *DeepGulf, Inc. v. Moszkowski*, 330 F.R.D. 600, 606 (N.D. Fla. 2019).

[33] *EMW Women's Surgical Ctr., P.S.C. v. Friedlander*, 978 F.3d 418, 447 (6th Cir. 2020).

[34] *Evans v. Griffin*, 932 F.3d 1043, 1048 (7th Cir. 2019) (witness who did not receive notice cannot be sanctioned for refusing to testify).

[35] *Evans v. Griffin*, 932 F.3d 1043, 1048 (7th Cir. 2019) (1 day notice not reasonable); *Kolon Industries Inc. v. E.I. DuPont de Nemours & Co.*, 748 F.3d 160, 173 (4th Cir. 2014) (5 days notice not reasonable).

[36] *Kolon Industries Inc. v. E.I. DuPont de Nemours & Co.*, 748 F.3d 160, 173 (4th Cir. 2014) (5 days notice not reasonable).

[37] *DeepGulf, Inc. v. Moszkowski*, 330 F.R.D. 600, 605 (N.D. Fla. 2019); *Estate of Levingston v. County of Kern*, 320 F.R.D. 520, 524 (E.D. Cal. 2017).

[38] *Inventus Power v. Shenzhen Ace Battery*, 339 F.R.D. 487, 507 (N.D. Ill. 2021) (listing factors for managing agents); *Sherman v. Sheffield Fin., LLC*, 338 F.R.D. 247, 254 (D. Minn. 2021).

[39] *Calderon v. Experian Information Solutions, Inc.*, 287 F.R.D. 629, 631 (D. Idaho 2012), aff'd, 290 F.R.D. 508 (D. Idaho 2013); *U.S. Fidelity & Guar. Co. v. Braspetro Oil Services Co.*, 2001 WL 43607 (S.D.N.Y. 2001).

[40] *Lefkoe v. Jos. A. Bank Clothiers, Inc.*, 577 F.3d 240, 246 (4th Cir. 2009); *Nationstar Mortgage, LLC v. Flamingo Trails No. 7 Landscape Maint. Ass'n*, 316 F.R.D. 327, 332 (D. Nev. 2016).

other parties.[41]

One Notice Sufficient for All Parties

Each party does not have to serve its own notice in order to examine the witness; all parties are entitled to conduct examination once one party has served a deposition notice on the witness.[42]

Sanctions for Failure to Appear

The sanctions for failure to appear at a deposition depend upon whether the witness is a party. Nonparty witnesses may be held in contempt of court for failure to obey a subpoena.[43] Party witnesses are subject to the sanctions described in Rule 37(d).[44]

Place of Examination

Although the party noticing the deposition sets the location in the notice,[45] the witness or other parties may challenge the location by motion for protective order. For a nonparty witness, the witness must travel up to 100 miles from the place where the witness resides, is employed, or regularly transacts business.[46] For a party deponent, the noticing party may select any location for the deposition, but in general, plaintiffs will be required to travel to the district where the suit is pending for their depositions,[47] whereas defendants can have their depositions taken where they work or live.[48] Also, in general, the deposition of a corporation occurs at its principal place of business.[49] These general principles are just presumptions and will yield in extenuating circumstances, such as a plaintiff who is too sick to travel, and the court has broad discretion in setting the location.[50]

Motion for Protective Order

If a notice of deposition is facially valid, then the witness must attend or file a motion for a protective order pursuant to

[41] *Lefkoe v. Jos. A. Bank Clothiers, Inc.*, 577 F.3d 240, 246 (4th Cir. 2009).

[42] *FCC v. Mizuho Medy Co. Ltd.*, 257 F.R.D. 679, 681–82 (S.D. Cal. 2009).

[43] Rule 45(g); *Blackmer v. United States*, 284 U.S. 421, 435-36 (1932).

[44] *Panzer v. Swiftships, LLC*, 318 F.R.D. 326, 328 (E.D. La. 2016).

[45] *DeepGulf, Inc. v. Moszkowski*, 330 F.R.D. 600, 607 (N.D. Fla. 2019); *Jefferson v. Stinson Morrison Heckler LLP*, 249 F. Supp. 3d 76, 81 (D.D.C. 2017).

[46] *See* Rule 45(c)(1).

[47] *Huddleston v. Bowling Green Inn of Pensacola*, 333 F.R.D. 581, 584 (N.D. Fla. 2019); *Kean v. Board of Trustees of the Three Rivers Regional Library System*, 321 F.R.D. 448, 452 (S.D. Ga. 2017).

[48] *DeepGulf, Inc. v. Moszkowski*, 330 F.R.D. 600, 607 (N.D. Fla. 2019); *Alpha Capital Anstalt v. Real Goods Solar, Inc.*, 323 F.R.D. 177, 178 (S.D.N.Y. 2017).

[49] *Inventus Power v. Shenzhen Ace Battery*, 339 F.R.D. 487, 507 (N.D. Ill. 2021); *Edwards v. Scripps Media, Inc.*, 331 F.R.D. 116, 126 (E.D. Mich. 2019).

[50] *Inventus Power v. Shenzhen Ace Battery*, 339 F.R.D. 487, 507 (N.D. Ill. 2021); *S.E.C. v. Aly*, 320 F.R.D. 116, 118 (S.D.N.Y. 2017).

Rule 26(c).[51] The motion must be made before the time scheduled for the deposition, and must show good cause for the requested protection.

RULE 30(b)(2)—PRODUCING DOCUMENTS

CORE CONCEPT

A witness may be compelled to bring documents to a deposition. The procedures differ depending on whether the witness is a party or a nonparty.

APPLICATIONS

Parties

A party may be compelled to bring documents to a deposition by attaching a Rule 34 request for inspection to the deposition notice. The party to be deposed must be accorded 30 days to interpose objections to the document request[52] (the rationale being that one should not be able to circumvent the 30-day period in the document request rule by issuing a notice of deposition).[53]

Nonparties

A nonparty may be compelled to bring documents to a deposition by describing the documents in a subpoena duces tecum served on the witness under Rule 45(a)(1)(A)(iii) and including a description of the documents in the deposition notice served on other parties.[54]

RULE 30(b)(3)—METHOD OF RECORDING

CORE CONCEPT

The party taking the deposition may have it recorded by audio, audiovisual, or stenographic means, and must specify the means of recording in the deposition notice.[55] Other parties may arrange for additional methods of recording.

APPLICATIONS

Methods Available

The party taking the deposition may choose to have it recorded by audio, audiovisual, or stenographic means, unless

---

[51]*Collins v. Wayland*, 139 F.2d 677 (C.C.A. 9th Cir. 1944); *Panzer v. Swiftships, LLC*, 318 F.R.D. 326, 328 (E.D. La. 2016).

[52]*Dowling v. Cleveland Clinic Foundation*, 593 F.3d 472, 479 (6th Cir. 2010); *Liner v. FCA US LLC*, 333 F.R.D. 122, 125–26 (N.D. Ill. 2019).

[53]*See Duvall v. Heart of CarDon*, — F. Supp. 3d —, 2020 WL 1274992, at *5 (S.D. Ind. 2020); *Canal Barge Co. v. Commonwealth Edison Co.*, 2001 WL 817853 (N.D. Ill. 2001).

[54]*See Liner v. FCA US LLC*, 333 F.R.D. 122, 125 (N.D. Ill. 2019); *Lee v. U.S. Dept. of Justice*, 287 F. Supp. 2d 15, 22 (D.D.C. 2003), aff'd, 413 F.3d 53 (D.C. Cir. 2005).

[55]*Pioneer Drive, LLC v. Nissan Diesel Am., Inc.*, 262 F.R.D. 552, 555, n.2 (D. Mont. 2009).

the court orders otherwise.[56] However, the method of recording must comply with all of the provisions of Rule 30, such as having an officer perform the duties specified in Rule 30(b)(5).[57]

Additional Methods of Recording

Any party may arrange for a method of recording a deposition in addition to that specified in the notice of deposition.[58] The party desiring such additional method of recording must send prior notice to all other parties and to the deponent,[59] and will bear the expense of the additional recording unless otherwise ordered by the court.[60] Some courts allow attorneys to record or videotape depositions for their own use, but such recordings would not be admissible.[61]

Cost of Recording

The party taking the deposition bears the cost of the party's chosen method(s) of recording.[62] If another party arranges for an additional method of recording, that party bears the cost of that additional method.

Transcript

Any party may, at its own expense, arrange for a transcript to be made of a deposition recorded by nonstenographic means.[63]

Use of Nonstenographic Depositions

In order to use a nonstenographically recorded deposition at trial or in connection with a dispositive motion, a party must submit a transcript of the portions to be introduced for the court's use.[64]

---

[56] *Planned Parenthood of Columbia/Willamette, Inc. v. Am. Coalition of Life Activists*, 290 F.3d 1058 (9th Cir. 2002); *Citizens for Responsibility and Ethics in Washington v. Cheney*, 580 F. Supp. 2d 168, 183 (D.D.C. 2008) (videotaping denied when the limited issues before the court made videotape not helpful to the court); *Banks v. Office of the Senate Sergeant-At-Arms*, 241 F.R.D. 370 (D.D.C. 2007) (videotape of deposition not permitted because the party intended to use the tape for publicity, not for proper purposes).

[57] *Alcorn v. City of Chicago*, 336 F.R.D. 440, 442 (N.D. Ill. 2020) (Zoom's recording function is not sufficient); *Rouviere v. DePuy Orthopaedics, Inc.*, 471 F. Supp. 3d 571, 573 (S.D.N.Y. 2020).

[58] *Pioneer Drive, LLC v. Nissan Diesel Am., Inc.*, 262 F.R.D. 552, 555 (D. Mont. 2009).

[59] *Ogden v. Keystone Residence*, 226 F. Supp. 2d 588, 605 (M.D. Pa. 2002).

[60] *See Craftsmen Limousine, Inc. v. Ford Motor Co.*, 579 F.3d 894, 897 (8th Cir. 2009) (discussing when the expenses of a videotaped deposition can be recovered as costs).

[61] *See Schoolcraft v. City of New York*, 296 F.R.D. 231, 240 (S.D.N.Y. 2013).

[62] *Morrison v. Reichhold Chem., Inc.*, 97 F.3d 460, 464 (11th Cir. 1996); *Cherry v. Champion Intern. Corp.*, 186 F.3d 442, 448–49 (4th Cir. 1999) (discussing the recovery of alternative means of recording as costs under 28 U.S.C.A. § 1920).

[63] *Hudson v. Spellman High Voltage*, 178 F.R.D. 29 (E.D.N.Y. 1998).

[64] *Hudson v. Spellman High*

Objections to Manner of Recording

Objections to the manner of recording of a deposition should be raised prior to the commencement of the deposition via a motion for protective order under Rule 26(c) or at the commencement of the deposition under Rule 30(c).[65]

RULE 30(b)(4)—BY REMOTE MEANS

CORE CONCEPT

The parties may stipulate, or move the court for an order, that a deposition be taken by telephone, videoconference, or other remote means.[66] The court may also authorize remote depositions *sua sponte*.[67] Such depositions are deemed to occur in the district where the deponent is located when answering the questions,[68] and the court reporter/officer should be in the presence of the witness, not the attorneys.[69]

APPLICATIONS

COVID-19

Travel restrictions and other complications related to COVID-19 resulted in frequent requests to take depositions remotely. When contested, the courts have generally granted these requests.[70] Courts have generally concluded that advances in technology essentially eliminate the prejudice caused by remote depositions.[71]

Standard

Generally, leave to take depositions by remote means is at the court's discretion,[72] and will be granted liberally.[73] Courts consider both the hardships caused by travel and the potential

---

Voltage, 178 F.R.D. 29 (E.D.N.Y. 1998).

[65] *Fanelli v. Centenary College*, 211 F.R.D. 268 (D.N.J. 2002) (anxiety over videotaping not good cause sufficient to warrant a protective order).

[66] *Caballero v. Fuerzas Armadas Revolucionarias de Colombia*, 562 F. Supp. 3d 867, 886 (C.D. Cal. 2021); *In re Terrorist Attacks on Sept. 11, 2001*, 337 F.R.D. 575, 577-78 (S.D.N.Y. 2020).

[67] *See United States for use & benefit of Chen v. K.O.O. Constr., Inc.*, 445 F. Supp. 3d 1055, 1056 (S.D. Cal. 2020).

[68] *Hudson v. Spellman High Voltage*, 178 F.R.D. 29, 32 (E.D.N.Y. 1998).

[69] *Aquino v. Automotive Service Industry Ass'n*, 93 F. Supp. 2d 922 (N.D. Ill. 2000).

[70] *See, e.g., Rouviere v. DePuy Orthopaedics, Inc.*, 471 F. Supp. 3d 571, 574 (S.D.N.Y. 2020); *Swenson v. GEICO Cas. Co.*, 336 F.R.D. 206, 209 (D. Nev. 2020).

[71] *See, e.g., In re Terrorist Attacks on Sept. 11, 2001* 337 F.R.D. 575, 577–78 (S.D.N.Y. 2020).

[72] *Rouviere v. DePuy Orthopaedics, Inc.*, 471 F. Supp. 3d 571, 574 (S.D.N.Y. 2020); *In re Terrorist Attacks on Sept. 11, 2001*, 337 F.R.D. 575, 578 (S.D.N.Y. 2020).

[73] *Swenson v. GEICO Cas. Co.*, 336 F.R.D. 206, 209 (D. Nev. 2020); *United States for use & benefit of Chen v. K.O.O. Constr., Inc.*, 445 F. Supp. 3d 1055, 1057 (S.D. Cal. 2020) (logistics for exhibits not a bar to remote depositions).

prejudice caused by not having the witness present in person.[74]

Who May Seek

Although motions to take depositions remotely are typically filed by the noticing party seeking to avoid traveling to the witness, they can also be filed by the receiving party seeking to avoid traveling to the location of the deposition.[75]

Remote Depositions of Rule 30(b)(6) Designees

The provisions for remote depositions apply to depositions of party representatives under Rule 30(b)(6) as well as to depositions of specific individuals.[76]

RULE 30(b)(5)—OFFICER'S DUTIES

CORE CONCEPT

Unless the parties stipulate otherwise, a deposition must be conducted before an officer qualified under Rule 28.[77] At the beginning of a deposition, the officer shall place on the record administrative details identifying and describing the deposition. During the deposition, the officer must accurately and neutrally depict the witness's demeanor and appearance in the recording.

APPLICATIONS

Statement at Deposition Beginning

The officer recording the deposition shall begin the record with a statement that includes:

A) the officer's name and business address;
B) the date, time, and place of deposition;
C) the name of the deponent;
D) the administration of the oath or affirmation to the deponent; and
E) an identification of all persons present.[78]

If the deposition is recorded other than stenographically, then each separate tape or unit of recording must begin with: the officer's name and business address; the date, time and place of the deposition; and the deponent's name.

Statement at Deposition End

The officer recording the deposition shall close the record by stating that the deposition is complete and setting forth any

---

[74] *Rouviere v. DePuy Orthopaedics, Inc.*, 471 F. Supp. 3d 571, 574 (S.D.N.Y. 2020); *In re Terrorist Attacks on Sept. 11, 2001*, 337 F.R.D. 575, 578 (S.D.N.Y. 2020).

[75] *See S.E.C. v. Razmilovic*, 738 F.3d 14, 21 (2d Cir. 2013); *Republic of Turkey v. Christie's, Inc.*, 326 F.R.D. 402, 406 (S.D.N.Y. 2018) (ordering the moving party to pay a portion of the non-moving party's travel costs).

[76] *See Estate of Gerasimenko v. Cape Wind Trading Co.*, 272 F.R.D. 385, 390 (S.D.N.Y. 2011).

[77] *Alcorn v. City of Chicago*, 336 F.R.D. 440, 443 (N.D. Ill. 2020) (attorney may not record the deposition); *Rouviere v. DePuy Orthopaedics, Inc.*, 471 F. Supp. 3d 571, 573 (S.D.N.Y. 2020).

[78] *Alcorn v. City of Chicago*, 336 F.R.D. 440, 442 (N.D. Ill. 2020).

administrative stipulations regarding the deposition.

Witness Demeanor

The recording device should accurately and neutrally depict the witness's demeanor and appearance.[79] The camera angle and focus should remain constant, and may not be manipulated to emphasize or de-emphasize certain testimony or otherwise influence viewer perceptions.

RULE 30(b)(6)—NOTICE OR SUBPOENA DIRECTED TO AN ORGANIZATION

CORE CONCEPT

Rule 30(b)(6) allows a party to notice the deposition of a corporation, partnership, association, governmental agency, or other organization and to specify the areas of inquiry. The organization must then designate one or more representatives to testify as to the organization's collective knowledge in the designated areas of inquiry. Designated witnesses' testimony is not limited to their firsthand knowledge, and they must prepare for the deposition so that they can present the entire entity's collective information.

APPLICATIONS

Entitles Subject to Rule 30(b)(6) Depositions

A party may send a Rule 30(b)(6) deposition notice to a corporation,[80] partnership,[81] association, governmental agency,[82] or any other type of organization.[83]

Content of Notice—Deposition Topics

The notice (and the subpoena, for a nonparty) must state that the organization has the duty to designate a representative and must specify the areas of inquiry with reasonable particularity.[84] The topic list is often attached as an exhibit to the notice. Notices that include topics outside the scope of

---

[79] *Alcorn v. City of Chicago*, 336 F.R.D. 440, 442 (N.D. Ill. 2020); *Pioneer Drive, LLC v. Nissan Diesel Am., Inc.*, 262 F.R.D. 552, 555 (D. Mont. 2009).

[80] *See, e.g.*, *Snapp v. United Transportation Union*, 889 F.3d 1088, 1103 (9th Cir. 2018); *Vehicle Mkt. Research, Inc. v. Mitchell Int'l, Inc.*, 839 F.3d 1251, 1255 (10th Cir. 2016).

[81] *Starlight Intern. Inc. v. Herlihy*, 186 F.R.D. 626, 638 (D. Kan. 1999) (Rule 30(b)(6) applies to partnerships and joint ventures).

[82] *Ibrahim v. U.S. Dep't of Homeland Sec.*, 912 F.3d 1147, 1162 (9th Cir. 2019); *United States v. Ancient Coin Collectors Guild*, 899 F.3d 295, 324 (4th Cir. 2018).

[83] Advisory Committee Notes to the 2007 Amendments (the phrase "other entity" is intended to capture any type of organization not specifically listed, such as limited liability companies).

[84] *Fuentes v. Classica Cruise Operator Ltd, Inc.*, 32 F.4th 1311, 1321 (11th Cir. 2022); *Adidas Am., Inc. v. TRB Acquisitions LLC*, 324 F.R.D. 389, 395 (D. Or. 2017) (requiring "painstaking" detail); *McArthur v. Rock Woodfired Pizza & Spirits*, 318 F.R.D. 136, 143 (W.D. Wa. 2016) (case law conflicts on the required level of detail).

discovery in Rule 26(b)(1),[85] list too many topics, or are otherwise too burdensome may not be enforceable.[86]

Notice vs. Subpoena

If the organization is a party, a notice of deposition is all that is needed. If the organization is not a party, then the requesting party must serve a subpoena on the organization and a notice of deposition on all parties.[87] The distance limitations and other protections of Rule 45 apply to subpoenas to take the deposition of a designated representative of a nonparty.[88]

Duty to Confer

The 2020 amendment to Rule 30(b)(6) imposed a new requirement that the party serving the deposition notice or subpoena and the organization to be deposed by designated representative confer about the topics for the deposition before or promptly after service.[89] The objective of this conference is to make the deposition more effective and efficient and to minimize disputes.[90] Ideally, the discussion will lead to clarity and focus for the topics and better selection and preparation of the designated representative(s).

Objections to the Notice

The Rules do not establish a procedure for objecting to a Rule 30(b)(6) deposition notice. While parties sometimes serve formal objections to the notice, the objections do not relieve the party of the obligation to produce a witness or to respond to questions under topics to which the party has objected.[91] The safer procedure (assuming discussions with opposing counsel do not result in agreement) is to move for a protective order under Rule 26(c) if a party believes the Rule 30(b)(6) notice is problematic.[92]

Selection of Representatives

The representative does not have to be an officer or director

---

[85] *Prasad v. George Washington Univ.*, 325 F.R.D. 1, 3 (D.D.C. 2018).

[86] *See Prasad v. George Washington Univ.*, 323 F.R.D. 88 (D.D.C. 2017); *Edelen v. Campbell Soup Co.*, 265 F.R.D. 676, 684 (N.D. Ga. 2010) (40 pages and 120 topics was too burdensome).

[87] *See Mattel, Inc. v. Walking Mountain Productions*, 353 F.3d 792, 797 (9th Cir. 2003); *Cates v. LTV Aerospace Corp.*, 480 F.2d 620 (5th Cir. 1973).

[88] *Wultz v. Bank of China Ltd.*, 293 F.R.D. 677, 679–81 (S.D.N.Y. 2013); *Estate of Klieman v. Palestinian Authority*, 293 F.R.D. 235, 239 (D.D.C. 2013).

[89] *Guinnane v. Dobbins*, 479 F. Supp. 3d 989, 994–955 (D. Mont. 2020).

[90] Rule 30 advisory committee's note (2020).

[91] *See James Lee Constr., Inc. v. Gov't Emps. Ins. Co.*, 339 F.R.D. 562, 568 (D. Mont. 2021); *Ball Corp. v. Air Tech of Michigan, Inc.*, 329 F.R.D. 599, 602 (N.D. Ind. 2019).

[92] *See Guinnane v. Dobbins*, 479 F. Supp. 3d 989, 995 (D. Mont. 2020); *Ball Corp. v. Air Tech of Michigan, Inc.*, 329 F.R.D. 599, 602 (N.D. Ind. 2019).

of the organization, does not need to be the most knowledgeable person about the listed topics,[93] and in fact does not even need to be employed by the organization.[94] Instead, the company has a duty to make a conscientious, good-faith effort to designate a representative capable of testifying regarding the designated topics.[95] Regardless of the status of the representative, however, the representative's testimony will be admissible against the organization[96] and the organization must prepare the representative to testify as to the organization's collective knowledge and information.[97] The organization may name more than one representative.[98] Sometimes, in-house counsel is selected as the organization's representative.[99] The fact that the most logical representative has already been deposed individually does not allow the responding party to object to the Rule 30(b)(6) notice on the basis of the prohibition in Rule 30(a) on deposing the same witness twice.[100] Similarly, taking a Rule 30(b)(6) deposition is not necessarily duplicative of a fact witness deposition[101] even if the same person is being deposed in both instances.[102] If an organization has absolutely no information regarding the listed topics, the organization may so advise the party issuing the notice in lieu of designating a representative.[103]

- *Designation of Prior Testimony:* A party may avoid designating a Rule 30(b)(6) representative if it clearly states its intention for its employees' prior deposition testimony to represent the testimony of the organization

---

[93] *Kartagener v. Carnival Corp.*, 380 F. Supp. 3d 1290, 1294 (S.D. Fla. 2019); *Estate of Rosado-Rosario v. Falken Tire Corp.*, 319 F.R.D. 71, 74 (D.P.R. 2016).

[94] *See Gilead Scis., Inc. v. Merck & Co.*, 888 F.3d 1231, 1244 (Fed. Cir. 2018); *Ecclesiastes 9:10-11-12, Inc. v. LMC Holding Co.*, 497 F.3d 1135, 1146–47 (10th Cir. 2007).

[95] *Ecclesiastes 9:10-11-12, Inc. v. LMC Holding Co.*, 497 F.3d 1135, 1146–47 (10th Cir. 2007) (organization must designate representatives, and cannot use lack of knowledgeable employees as an excuse); *Brazos River Authority v. GE Ionics, Inc.*, 469 F.3d 416, 433 (5th Cir. 2006).

[96] *Edwards v. Scripps Media, Inc.*, 331 F.R.D. 116, 121 (E.D. Mich. 2019).

[97] *Wultz v. Bank of China Ltd.*, 298 F.R.D. 91, 99 (S.D.N.Y. 2014); *Crawford v. George & Lynch, Inc.*, 19 F. Supp. 3d 546, 553–54 (D. Del. 2013).

[98] *Infernal Tech., LLC v. Epic Games, Inc.*, 339 F.R.D. 226, 230 (E.D.N.C. 2021); *Kartagener v. Carnival Corp.*, 380 F. Supp. 3d 1290, 1294 (S.D. Fla. 2019).

[99] *See In re Pioneer Hi-Bred Intern., Inc.*, 238 F.3d 1370, 1376 (Fed. Cir. 2001) (addressing the attorney-client privilege issues when counsel is designated as the corporate representative); *Bhasker v. Kemper Cas. Ins. Co.*, 361 F. Supp. 3d 1045, 1121 (D.N.M. 2019).

[100] *Edwards v. Scripps Media, Inc.*, 331 F.R.D. 116, 121 (E.D. Mich. 2019); *Martin v. Bimbo Foods Bakeries Distribution, LLC*, 313 F.R.D. 1, 9 (E.D.N.C. 2016).

[101] *White v. City of Cleveland*, 417 F. Supp. 3d 896, 909 (N.D. Ohio 2019).

[102] *Ball Corp. v. Air Tech of Michigan, Inc.*, 329 F.R.D. 599, 603–04 (N.D. Ind. 2019); *Edwards v. Scripps Media, Inc.*, 331 F.R.D. 116, 121 (E.D. Mich. 2019).

[103] *Bigsby v. Barclays Capital Real Estate, Inc.*, 329 F.R.D. 78, 81 (S.D.N.Y. 2019).

on all of the topics in the Rule 30(b)(6) notice, such that a Rule 30(b)(6) deposition would be duplicative.[104]

Deposition of Specific Party Representative

To depose a specific officer, director, or managing agent, a party should not use Rule 30(b)(6), which allows the recipient to pick the deponent; rather, a party should serve a notice of deposition indicating that the individual's testimony is sought in the individual's official capacity.[105] The organization is then subject to sanctions if the named representative fails to appear.[106] Such depositions may be subject to the Apex Doctrine, discussed above in the coverage of Rule 30(a).

Failure to Designate and Produce Properly Prepared Representative

If an organization provides a witness who is not adequately prepared to answer questions squarely within the topics listed in a notice of deposition, then the organization has failed to comply with its obligations under the rule and may be subject to sanctions.[107] The organization can also be sanctioned for failing to designate a representative[108] or if the designated representative fails to appear at the deposition.[109]

Scope of Testimony

The scope of testimony in a Rule 30(b)(6) deposition is controlled by two considerations. Like any discovery, the testimony is limited by the scope of discovery considerations in Rule 26(b)(1), such as privilege, relevance to a claim or defense in the case, and proportionality,[110] and the limitations in the remaining subsections of Rule 26(b). Additionally, the scope of testimony is affected by the topics listed in the deposition notice. As to those topics, the representative(s) must testify to all matters known or reasonably available to the organization.[111] Thus, the representative will often testify to matters outside

---

[104] *Woods v. Standard Fire Ins. Co.*, — F. Supp. 3d —, 2022 WL 677567, at *2 (E.D. Ky. 2022); *Edwards v. Scripps Media, Inc.*, 331 F.R.D. 116, 121 (E.D. Mich. 2019).

[105] *Cummings v. General Motors Corp.*, 365 F.3d 944, 953 (10th Cir. 2004); *Calderon v. Experian Information Solutions, Inc.*, 287 F.R.D. 629, 631 (D. Idaho 2013).

[106] *Bon Air Hotel, Inc. v. Time, Inc.*, 376 F.2d 118 (5th Cir. 1967); *Covad Commc'n Co. v. Revonet, Inc.*, 267 F.R.D. 14, 24 (D.D.C. 2010).

[107] *Sciarretta v. Lincoln Nat. Life Ins. Co.*, 778 F.3d 1205, 1212–13 (11th Cir. 2015) (court imposed sanctions sua sponte); *Baker v. St. Paul Travelers Ins. Co.*, 670 F.3d 119, 124 (1st Cir. 2012).

[108] *See Clientron Corp. v. Devon IT, Inc.*, 894 F.3d 568, 572 (3d Cir. 2018); *Ecclesiastes 9:10-11-12, Inc. v. LMC Holding Co.*, 497 F.3d 1135 (10th Cir. 2007) (case dismissed after plaintiff delayed making designation, then the logical representative died).

[109] *Sali v. Corona Reg'l Med. Ctr.*, 884 F.3d 1218, 1223 n.4 (9th Cir. 2018).

[110] See *Virginia Dep't of Corr. v. Jordan*, 921 F.3d 180, 189 (4th Cir. 2019); *James Lee Constr., Inc. v. Gov't Emps. Ins. Co.*, 339 F.R.D. 562, 569 (D. Mont. 2021).

[111] *Fuentes v. Classica Cruise Operator Ltd, Inc.*, 32 F.4th 1311, 1321

the representative's personal knowledge.[112] The courts are divided as to whether the examination of the representative is limited to the areas of inquiry identified in the notice of deposition,[113] but testimony outside the designated topics will not bind the organization.[114]

Contentions, Legal Positions, Theories, and Hypotheticals

The courts are divided about whether a Rule 30(b)(6) deposition notice may include topics regarding the party's legal contentions or facts supporting those contentions.[115] However, many courts are reluctant to allow depositions of opposing counsel, and will closely examine notices under Rule 30(b)(6) that are "back door" attempts to depose opposing counsel.[116] Hypothetical questions are not appropriate for a Rule 30(b)(6) deposition since the deponent will not be able to prepare for them due to the fact that a hypothetical question would require the witness to answer with a personal opinion rather than the entity's position.[117]

Duty to Prepare

The organization has a duty to gather the reasonably available information and prepare the representative(s) so that the representatives can give complete, knowledgeable, and binding testimony.[118] Failure to adequately prepare the representative can result in sanctions.[119]

- *Use of Notes to Testify*: The designated representative is

---

(11th Cir. 2022).

[112]*Fuentes v. Classica Cruise Operator Ltd, Inc.*, 32 F.4th 1311, 1321 (11th Cir. 2022); *Virginia Dep't of Corr. v. Jordan*, 921 F.3d 180, 193 (4th Cir. 2019).

[113]*Doe I v. Exxon Mobil Corp.*, 539 F. Supp. 3d 59, 74 (D.D.C. 2021) ("must generally stick to the noticed topics"); *Mitnor Corp. v. Club Condominiums*, 339 F.R.D. 312, 321 (N.D. Fla. 2021) (not limited); *Crawford v. George & Lynch, Inc.*, 19 F. Supp. 3d 546, 554 (D. Del. 2013) (noting the split).

[114]*Mitnor Corp. v. Club Condominiums*, 339 F.R.D. 312, 321 (N.D. Fla. 2021); *McKinney / Pearl Rest. Partners, L.P. v. Metro. Life Ins. Co.*, 241 F. Supp. 3d 737, 752 (N.D. Tex. 2017).

[115]*See United States v. Ancient Coin Collectors Guild*, 899 F.3d 295, 324 (4th Cir. 2018) (inquiry into party's legal theories improper); *Brazos River Authority v. GE Ionics, Inc.*, 469 F.3d 416, 432 (5th Cir. 2006) (testimony as to subjective beliefs and opinions proper); *Woods v. Standard Fire Ins. Co.*, — F. Supp. 3d —, 2022 WL 677567, at *7 (E.D. Ky. 2022) (noting the split in authority).

[116]*See A.R. ex rel. Root v. Dudek*, 304 F.R.D. 668, 670 (S.D. Fla. 2015) (party could avoid problem by not designating counsel); *Winston & Strawn LLP v. Law Firm of John Arthur Eaves*, 307 F.R.D. 259, 262–63 (D.D.C. 2014).

[117]*Edwards v. Scripps Media, Inc.*, 331 F.R.D. 116, 125–126 (E.D. Mich. 2019); *Schall v. Suzuki Motor of Am., Inc.*, 2017 WL 4050319, at *5 (W.D. Ky. 2017).

[118]*Sciarretta v. Lincoln Nat. Life Ins. Co.*, 778 F.3d 1205, 1213 (11th Cir. 2015); *Brazos River Authority v. GE Ionics, Inc.*, 469 F.3d 416, 433 (5th Cir. 2006).

[119]*Fuentes v. Classica Cruise Operator Ltd, Inc.*, 32 F.4th 1311, 1322 (11th Cir. 2022); *Black Horse Lane Assoc., L.P. v. Dow Chem. Corp.*, 228

not required to memorize all of the entity's information,[120] and may refer to notes when testifying, but may not simply read pre-prepared answers.[121]

Binding Effect of Testimony

Testimony by a Rule 30(b)(6) representative regarding the designated topics is the testimony of the organization, and has the effect of an evidentiary admission by, and is binding on, the organization.[122] Most courts hold that the testimony does not create a judicial admission, however, and thus may be controverted or explained by the party.[123] However, courts will sometimes prevent a party from contradicting its designee to defeat summary judgment, under the "sham affidavit rule."[124] The organization may be prohibited from using information not disclosed during the Rule 30(b)(6) deposition unless the information was unavailable at the time of the deposition.[125]

Compelling Testimony of Representative at Trial

It is unsettled whether one party can compel another party to produce a Rule 30(b)(6) designee to appear and testify at trial.[126] If a Rule 30(b)(6) designee does appear to testify at trial, courts may require the witness to testify to the matters discussed at the deposition (even if outside the witness's personal knowledge), but the rules of evidence will still apply.[127]

Procedures re Duration, Location, and Number of Depositions

The application of the general procedures for duration, location, and number of depositions to Rule 30(b)(6) depositions is addressed in the sections of Rule 30 addressing those topics, and will not be repeated in detail here. In general: the deposition of each designated representative must be conducted in

---

F.3d 275, 301–05 (3d Cir. 2000).

[120] *Fuentes v. Classica Cruise Operator Ltd, Inc.*, 32 F.4th 1311, 1322 (11th Cir. 2022).

[121] *Doe I v. Exxon Mobil Corp.*, 539 F. Supp. 3d 59, 74 (D.D.C. 2021).

[122] *Snapp v. United Transportation Union*, 889 F.3d 1088, 1104 (9th Cir. 2018); *In re Flint Water Cases*, __ F. Supp. 3d __, 2022 WL 409522, at *14 (E.D. Mich. 2022).

[123] *See Mays v. LaRose*, 951 F.3d 775, 790 (6th Cir. 2020); *Calvary Chapel Bible Fellowship v. Cty. of Riverside*, 948 F.3d 1172, 1176 (9th Cir. 2020).

[124] *See Quest Integrity USA, LLC v. Cokebusters USA Inc.*, 924 F.3d 1220, 1226 (Fed. Cir. 2019); *Daubert v. NRA Group, LLC*, 861 F.3d 382, 389 (3d Cir. 2017).

[125] *Donahue v. Republic Nat'l Distrib. Co., LLC*, 489 F. Supp. 3d 455, 464 (E.D. La. 2020); *QBE Ins. Corp. v. Jorda Enters., Inc.*, 277 F.R.D. 676, 690 (S.D. Fla. 2012).

[126] *Compare Hill v. Homeward Residential, Inc.*, 799 F.3d 544, 553 (6th Cir. 2015) (parties may not use Rule 36(b)(6) to compel a representative to testify at trial), *with In re DePuy Orthopaedics, Inc., Pinnacle Hip Implant Prod. Liab. Litig.*, 888 F.3d 753, 784 (5th Cir. 2018) (ordering a 30(b)(6) representative to appear and testify at trial).

[127] *See In re: Taxotere (Docetaxel) Prod. Liab. Litig.*, 26 F.4th 256, 265–66 (5th Cir. 2022); *Brazos River Auth. v. GE Ionics, Inc.*, 469 F.3d 416, 434–35 (5th Cir. 2006).

one seven-hour day; Rule 36(b)(6) depositions are presumptively conducted in the vicinity of the organization's headquarters; and a Rule 30(b)(6) deposition counts as one of the 10 depositions allowed per side (even if the responding party designates more than one representative).

RULE 30(c)—EXAMINATION AND CROSS-EXAMINATION; RECORD OF THE EXAMINATION; OBJECTIONS; WRITTEN QUESTIONS

CORE CONCEPT

In general, the examination of witnesses at a deposition proceeds much like at trial, except that many objections are reserved until the testimony is offered into evidence. Objections to questions must be stated in a non-suggestive and non-argumentative manner.

APPLICATIONS

Oath or Affirmation

The officer before whom the deposition is to be taken (usually the stenographer) will put the witness under oath or affirmation at the beginning of the deposition.

Recording

The officer will arrange to have the testimony recorded, either stenographically or otherwise (as discussed above under Rule 30(b)(3)).

Examination

Examination proceeds as at trial and subject to the Federal Rules of Evidence,[128] with direct examination and cross-examination.[129] Unlike trial, cross-examination is not limited to matters raised on direct, although the admission at trial of the deposition transcript may be limited on that basis. Because no judge is present to rule on objections, the witness answers each question even if there is an objection[130] unless instructed not to answer by counsel (which is only authorized in very narrow circumstances, as described below).

---

[128] *Ferring Pharm. Inc. v. Serenity Pharm., LLC*, 331 F.R.D. 75, 78 (S.D.N.Y. 2019); *Brincko v. Rio Props., Inc.*, 278 F.R.D. 576, 579 (D. Nev. 2011).

[129] *See Ferring Pharm. Inc. v. Serenity Pharm., LLC*, 331 F.R.D. 75, 78 (S.D.N.Y. 2019); *Sperling v. City of Kennesaw Dept.*, 202 F.R.D. 325, 329 (N.D. Ga. 2001) (adverse party entitled to review and use writing used by witness to refresh recollection).

[130] *Ferring Pharm. Inc. v. Serenity Pharm., LLC*, 331 F.R.D. 75, 78 (S.D.N.Y. 2019); *Rangel v. Gonzalez Mascorro*, 274 F.R.D. 585, 594 (S.D. Tex. 2011).

Witness's Rights

At a deposition, witnesses have the same rights as at trial, and may refresh their recollections with former testimony.[131] In general, a witness may not consult with counsel while a question is pending, except to ask about the applicability of a privilege.[132] The extent to which a witness has the right to confer with counsel during breaks is unsettled.[133]

Objections to Questions

Some objections to questions must be raised at the time of the deposition or they are waived, others are reserved until trial. The way to determine whether an objection must be made is to determine whether the examiner could rephrase the question to cure the objection.[134] Thus, parties must object to leading questions in order to give the examiner an opportunity to ask the question in a non-leading fashion. Conversely, parties do not need to raise objections such as relevancy or competency that cannot be cured by rephrasing.

Phrasing of Objections

Objections must be stated in a concise, non-suggestive manner.[135] Attorneys should not use an objection to instruct the witnesses how to answer (or not answer) a question on the record.[136] However, the specific nature of the objection should be stated so that the court later can rule on the objection (*e.g.*, "objection, leading" or "objection, lack of foundation").[137]

Answering after Objections to Questions

After an objection to the nature of a question, the witness answers the question subject to the objection.[138] The court then rules on any objections at the time the testimony is offered into

---

[131] *See Magee v. Paul Revere Life Ins. Co.*, 172 F.R.D. 627, 637 (E.D.N.Y. 1997) (deponent repeatedly consulted his notes to refresh his memory at the deposition).

[132] *See In re Stratosphere Corp. Sec. Litig.*, 182 F.R.D. 614, 620 (D. Nev. 1998); *Hall v. Clifton Precision, a Div. of Litton Systems, Inc.*, 150 F.R.D. 525, 526 (E.D. Pa. 1993).

[133] *Compare In re Stratosphere Corp. Sec. Litig.*, 182 F.R.D. 614, 620 (D. Nev. 1998) (witness permitted to confer during breaks); *Hall v. Clifton Precision, a Div. of Litton Systems, Inc.*, 150 F.R.D. 525, 526 (E.D. Pa. 1993) (witness not permitted to confer during breaks).

[134] *Quiksilver, Inc. v. Kymsta Corp.*, 247 F.R.D. 579, 582 (C.D. Cal. 2007) (objections waived as to errors that could be obviated, removed, or cured).

[135] *Mitnor Corp. v. Club Condominiums*, 339 F.R.D. 312, 316 (N.D. Fla. 2021); *Sec. Nat. Bank of Sioux City, Iowa v. Abbott Laboratories*, 299 F.R.D. 595, 604 (N.D. Iowa 2014).

[136] *Sec. Nat. Bank of Sioux City, Iowa v. Day*, 800 F.3d 936, 942 (8th Cir. 2015); *Mitnor Corp. v. Club Condominiums*, 339 F.R.D. 312, 316–17 (N.D. Fla. 2021).

[137] *Mitnor Corp. v. Club Condominiums*, 339 F.R.D. 312, 316 (N.D. Fla. 2021); *Moloney v. U.S.*, 204 F.R.D. 16, 20–21 (D. Mass. 2001).

[138] *Fashion Exch. LLC v. Hybrid Promotions, LLC*, 333 F.R.D. 302, 307 (S.D.N.Y. 2019); *E.E.O.C. v. Freeman*, 288 F.R.D. 92, 97 (D. Md. 2012).

evidence or otherwise proffered to the court.[139] The only exception to this procedure is if an attorney gives an instruction not to answer a question, as discussed below.

Instruction Not to Answer

An instruction to a witness not to answer a question is only allowed in three narrow circumstances:[140] 1) to assert a privilege (*e.g.*, attorney-client communication);[141] 2) to enforce a court order limiting the scope or length of the deposition;[142] or 3) to suspend the deposition for purposes of a filing a motion under Rule 30(d)(3) to terminate or limit the deposition.[143] Thus, it is inappropriate for counsel to instruct a witness not to answer a question on the basis of relevance,[144] or on the basis that the question has been asked and answered,[145] is harassing,[146] is outside the scope of the expert witness's report,[147] or is outside the areas of inquiry identified in the notice of deposition for a Rule 30(b)(6) deposition of a party representative.[148] If an attorney improperly instructs a witness not to respond to a question, sanctions are available under Rule 30(d)(2).[149]

Refusal to Answer Question

If a witness refuses to answer a question, the examining party may suspend the proceedings to seek an order under Rule 37(a) compelling an answer or may reserve the right to move for an order to compel and proceed to other areas.

Documents Reviewed by the Witness

One common topic at depositions is which documents the witness reviewed in preparation for the deposition. Some courts

---

[139] *See Betker v. City of Milwaukee*, 22 F. Supp. 3d 915 (E.D. Wis. 2014).

[140] *Baker v. St. Paul Travelers Ins. Co.*, 670 F.3d 119, 123 (1st Cir. 2012); *Mitnor Corp. v. Club Condominiums*, 339 F.R.D. 312, 319 (N.D. Fla. 2021).

[141] *Shaffer v. Pennsbury Sch. Dist.*, 525 F. Supp. 3d 573, 580 (E.D. Pa. 2021); *Shvartser v. Lekser*, 292 F. Supp. 3d 272, 276 (D.D.C. 2018); *Green v. Cosby*, 160 F. Supp. 3d 431, 438 (D. Mass. 2016).

[142] *Baker v. St. Paul Travelers Ins. Co.*, 670 F.3d 119, 123 (1st Cir. 2012); *Ollison v. Wexford Health Sources, Inc.*, 337 F.R.D. 165, 171 (C.D. Ill. 2020) (test is objective, not based on a party's subjective understanding of the court's order).

[143] *See VeroBlue Farms USA Inc. v. Wulf*, — F.R.D. —, 2021 WL 5176839, at *11 (N.D. Tex. 2021); *Biovail Laboratories, Inc. v. Anchen Pharmaceuticals, Inc.*, 233 F.R.D. 648, 653 (C.D. Cal. 2006).

[144] *Resolution Trust Corp. v. Dabney*, 73 F.3d 262, 266 (10th Cir. 1995); *VeroBlue Farms USA Inc. v. Wulf*, — F.R.D. —, 2021 WL 5176839, at *10 (N.D. Tex. 2021).

[145] *Brincko v. Rio Props., Inc.*, 278 F.R.D. 576, 581 (D. Nev. 2011); *Athridge v. Aetna Cas. and Sur. Co.*, 184 F.R.D. 200, 208 (D.D.C. 1998).

[146] *Redwood v. Dobson*, 476 F.3d 462, 467–68 (7th Cir. 2007); *Brincko v. Rio Props., Inc.*, 278 F.R.D. 576, 581 (D. Nev. 2011).

[147] *Junger v. Singh*, 514 F. Supp. 3d 579, 602 (W.D.N.Y. 2021).

[148] *See E.E.O.C. v. Freeman*, 288 F.R.D. 92, 97–99 (D. Md. 2012); *Paparelli v. Prudential Ins. Co. of Am.*, 108 F.R.D. 727, 730–31 (D. Mass. 1985).

[149] *Junger v. Singh*, 514 F. Supp. 3d 579, 602 (W.D.N.Y. 2021).

consider the attorney's selection of the important documents for review to be protected attorney work product.[150] Others apply FRE 612, which requires disclosure of documents used to refresh the witness's recollection.[151] Some courts treat this issue differently depending on whether the witness was a corporate representative testifying under Rule 30(b)(6).[152]

Exhibits

Exhibits used during the deposition are appended to the transcript. If there are any objections to an exhibit, it is still appended subject to a subsequent ruling on the objection.

Objections to Procedures

All objections to the qualifications of the officer, to the manner of recording, to the conduct of a party, or to any other procedure must be raised at the deposition or they are waived.[153]

Written Questions

Instead of attending a deposition in person, a party can send written questions to the party taking the deposition, who will then ask the questions to the deponent on the record.[154] This procedure is rarely used.

Attendance by Other Persons

Other witnesses are not automatically excluded from observing a deposition absent a court order under Rule 30(d) and Rule 26(c)(1)(E).[155] Disputes regarding who may be present during a deposition are resolved by motion for protective order under Rule 26(c).[156]

RULE 30(d)—DURATION; SANCTION; MOTION TO TERMINATE OR LIMIT

CORE CONCEPT

A deposition is limited to 7 hours during 1 day, absent a stipulation or court order. If a witness or lawyer engages in unreasonable or vexatious conduct during a deposition, the court may impose appropriate sanctions including the attorney's fees and

---

[150] *See Sporck v. Peil*, 759 F.2d 312, 315 (3d Cir. 1985).

[151] *See Adidas Am., Inc. v. TRB Acquisitions LLC*, 324 F.R.D. 389, 393 (D. Or. 2017); *Northern Natural Gas Co. v. Approximately 9117.53 acres in Pratt, Kingman, and Reno Counties, Kan.*, 289 F.R.D. 644, 650 (D. Kan. 2013).

[152] *See Adidas Am., Inc. v. TRB Acquisitions LLC*, 324 F.R.D. 389, 394 (D. Or. 2017).

[153] *Orlowski v. Bates*, 146 F. Supp. 3d 908, 934 (W.D. Tenn. 2015); *Addison v. CMH Homes, Inc.*, 47 F. Supp. 3d 404, 414 (D.S.C. 2014).

[154] *See U.S. v. One Gulfstream G-V Jet Aircraft Displaying Tail Number VPCES, Its Tools and Appurtenances*, 304 F.R.D. 10, 17 (D.D.C. 2014).

[155] *In re Terra Intern., Inc.*, 134 F.3d 302, 305–06 (5th Cir. 1998) (party moving to exclude witnesses must show good cause); *Stoyanov v. Mabus*, 126 F. Supp. 3d. 531, 552 (D. Md. 2015).

[156] *See D.A. v. Meridian Joint School Dist. No. 2*, 289 F.R.D. 614, 633–34 (D. Idaho 2013) (allowing the witness's psychologist to be present).

other expenses caused by such conduct.

APPLICATIONS

Duration of Depositions

Depositions have presumptive a time limit of 1 day of 7 hours.[157] The time period includes only time spent examining the witness; lunch and other breaks are not counted.[158] The parties can extend or eliminate the time limitation by stipulation,[159] or can file a motion to extend or reduce the time limit (discussed below).

Motion to Extend Time

A party may file a motion to extend the 1 day, 7 hour limitation for specified depositions or for the case in general.[160] The court must allow additional time if needed for a "fair examination" of the witness or if the examination has been impeded or delayed by another person or by circumstances.[161] Examples of situations in which an extended deposition would be warranted include: witnesses who need interpreters;[162] examinations covering long periods of time or numerous and/or lengthy documents (although the Advisory Committee suggests that a prerequisite might be sending the documents to the witness to review prior to the deposition); instances where documents were requested but not produced prior to the deposition; multi-party cases (if the parties have taken measures to avoid duplicative questioning); depositions in which the lawyer for the witness also wants to ask questions; depositions of expert witnesses; depositions interrupted by power outage, health emergency, or other like event; and depositions in which improper objections or other conduct by other attorneys or the witness has impeded the examination.[163] The court is unlikely to order an extended deposition if the extended deposition would be cumulative or unreasonably burdensome.[164] The burden will be on the party moving for an extension to show

---

[157] *Guevara v. NCL (Bahamas) Ltd.*, 920 F.3d 710, 719 n.4 (11th Cir. 2019).

[158] *United States ex rel. Baltazar v. Warden*, 302 F.R.D. 256, 267 (N.D. Ill. 2014).

[159] *Vazquez-Rijos v. Anhang*, 654 F.3d 122, 130 (1st Cir. 2011).

[160] *See JTR Enterprises, LLC v. An Unknown Quantity of Colombian Emeralds, Amethysts and Quartz Crystals*, 297 F.R.D. 522, 531–32 (S.D. Fla. 2013).

[161] *Infernal Tech., LLC v. Epic Games, Inc.*, 339 F.R.D. 226, 231 (E.D.N.C. 2021); *Republic of Turkey v. Christie's, Inc.*, 326 F.R.D. 402, 405 (S.D.N.Y. 2018).

[162] *Republic of Turkey v. Christie's, Inc.*, 326 F.R.D. 402, 405 (S.D.N.Y. 2018).

[163] *Kleppinger v. Texas Dept. of Transp.*, 283 F.R.D. 330, 333 (S.D. Tex. 2012); *LaPlante v. Estano*, 226 F.R.D. 439, 430–40 (D. Conn. 2005) (deposition extended because party and attorney were recalcitrant and uncooperative).

[164] Rule 26(b)(2); *George v. City of Buffalo*, 789 F. Supp. 2d 417, 436 (W.D.N.Y. 2011).

good cause why the extension is warranted.[165]

Motion to Terminate or Limit Deposition

A party may move to limit the time of or terminate a deposition.[166] The motion must be made during the deposition.[167] In order to prevail on a motion to terminate an examination, the moving party must demonstrate that the examination was being conducted in bad faith or in an unreasonably annoying, embarrassing, or oppressive manner.[168] The court can then order the deposition concluded or can limit the time and/or scope of the deposition,[169] and may impose upon the losing party or attorney an appropriate sanction, including the reasonable costs and attorney's fees incurred as a result.[170] A party may make a motion to limit the deposition in advance under Rule 26(c) or can suspend the deposition to seek an order under Rule 30(d).[171]

Rule 30(b)(6) Designated Representatives

If an organization designates more than 1 representative in response to a deposition notice under Rule 30(b)(6), the 1-day, 7-hour limitation will apply separately to each representative,[172] although the court has discretion to reduce or increase the time limit for the depositions.[173]

Sanctions for Impediment or Delay

If a party, attorney, or witnesses engages in conduct that unreasonably impedes, delays, or otherwise frustrates a deposition, the court may, upon motion or *sua sponte*,[174] impose an "appropriate sanction" on the person engaging in the obstructive behavior.[175] A common sanction is a second deposition of

---

[165] *VeroBlue Farms USA Inc. v. Wulf*, — F.R.D. —, 2021 WL 5176839, at *10 (N.D. Tex. 2021).

[166] *United States ex rel. Baltazar v. Warden*, 302 F.R.D. 256, 259 (N.D. Ill. 2014).

[167] *VeroBlue Farms USA Inc. v. Wulf*, — F.R.D. —, 2021 WL 5176839, at *11 (N.D. Tex. 2021).

[168] *VeroBlue Farms USA Inc. v. Wulf*, — F.R.D. —, 2021 WL 5176839, at *10 (N.D. Tex. 2021); *Mirlis v. Greer*, 249 F. Supp. 3d 611, 615 n.9 (D. Conn. 2017).

[169] *Brincko v. Rio Props., Inc.*, 278 F.R.D. 576, 581 (D. Nev. 2011); *Withers v. eHarmony, Inc.*, 267 F.R.D. 316, 321 (C.D. Cal. 2010).

[170] *Otsuka Pharmaceutical Co., Ltd. V. Apotex Corp.*, 310 F.R.D. 256, 261 n.9 (D.N.J. 2015); *Horton v. Maersk Line, Ltd.*, 294 F.R.D. 690, 696–98 (S.D. Ga. 2013).

[171] *See Oakley, Inc. v. Grangeville Depot LLC*, 336 F.R.D. 191, 195 (D. Idaho 2020).

[172] *Infernal Tech., LLC v. Epic Games, Inc.*, 339 F.R.D. 226, 230 (E.D.N.C. 2021); *Buie v. D.C.*, 327 F.R.D. 1, 15 (D.D.C. 2018).

[173] *Buie v. D.C.*, 327 F.R.D. 1, 15 (D.D.C. 2018).

[174] *Sec. Nat. Bank of Sioux City, Iowa v. Day*, 800 F.3d 936, 942 (8th Cir. 2015); *Mitnor Corp. v. Club Condominiums*, 339 F.R.D. 312, 321 (N.D. Fla. 2021).

[175] *Sec. Nat. Bank of Sioux City, Iowa v. Day*, 800 F.3d 936, 942 (8th Cir. 2015); *Doe I v. Exxon Mobil Corp.*, 539 F. Supp. 3d 59, 73 (D.D.C. 2021).

the witness,[176] but the court has broad discretion and may even dismiss the case.[177] The court may also impose the reasonable expenses and attorney's fees caused by the behavior on the offending person.[178] The witness may be sanctioned for evasive or nonresponsive answers.[179] An attorney can be sanctioned for excessive or improper objections,[180] an improper instruction not to answer a question,[181] or for failing to curb improper conduct by the witness.[182] Conversely, asking irrelevant questions of a witness may also constitute harassment.[183]

Which Court for Motion to Terminate

If a deposition is occurring outside the district where the case is pending, a motion to terminate or limit the deposition may be filed either in the court where the case is pending or in the district where the deposition is occurring.[184]

Suspension of Deposition

A party desiring to make a motion to terminate or limit a deposition may suspend the deposition for the period of time necessary to make the motion.[185]

Expenses of Motion to Terminate

In ruling on a motion to terminate or limit the deposition, the court must consider awarding expenses, including attorney's fees, to the prevailing party.[186]

Parallel to Protective Order

A party may seek the same types of protection for a deposition under Rule 30(d) that are available under a protective or-

---

[176]See *Ollison v. Wexford Health Sources, Inc.*, 337 F.R.D. 165, 171 (C.D. Ill. 2020); *AdTrader, Inc. v. Google LLC*, 405 F. Supp. 3d 862, 867 (N.D. Cal. 2019).

[177]*Donelson v. Hardy*, 931 F.3d 565, 569 (7th Cir. 2019); *Barksdale Sch. Portraits, LLC v. Williams*, 339 F.R.D. 341, 345–46 (D. Mass. 2021).

[178]*Ryan v. Astra Tech, Inc.*, 772 F.3d 50, 56–57 (1st Cir. 2014); *Baker v. St. Paul Travelers Ins. Co.*, 670 F.3d 119, 123 (1st Cir. 2012).

[179]*Doe I v. Exxon Mobil Corp.*, 539 F. Supp. 3d 59, 73, at *8–9 (D.D.C. 2021).

[180]*Sec. Nat. Bank of Sioux City, Iowa v. Day*, 800 F.3d 936, 942 (8th Cir. 2015); *Fashion Exch. LLC v. Hybrid Promotions, LLC*, 333 F.R.D. 302, 305 (S.D.N.Y. 2019).

[181]*See Junger v. Singh*, 514 F. Supp. 3d 579, 602 (W.D.N.Y. 2021).

[182]*Doe I v. Exxon Mobil Corp.*, 539 F. Supp. 3d 59, 75 (D.D.C. 2021).

[183]*Prouty v. Thippanna*, 541 F. Supp. 3d 125, 128–29 (D. Mass. 2021) (irrelevant questions about the witness's immigration status were harassment); *V5 Techs. v. Switch, Ltd.*, 334 F.R.D. 306, 313 n.9 (D. Nev. 2019).

[184]Rule 30(d)(3)(A); *VeroBlue Farms USA Inc. v. Wulf*, — F.R.D. —, 2021 WL 5176839, at *11 (N.D. Tex. 2021).

[185]*McClelland v. Blazin' Wings, Inc.*, 675 F. Supp. 2d 1074, 1081 (D. Colo. 2009).

[186]Rule 37(a)(3); *United States ex rel. Baltazar v. Warden*, 302 F.R.D. 256, 267 (N.D. Ill. 2014); *Sec. Nat. Bank of Sioux City, Iowa v. Abbott Lab.*, 299 F.R.D. 595, 598–99 (N.D. Iowa 2014) (awarding sanctions *sua sponte*).

der under Rule 26(c).[187] A motion for a protective order under Rule 26(c) provides similar protection before a deposition begins, at which point Rule 30(d) takes over.

RULE 30(e)—REVIEW BY THE WITNESS; CHANGES

CORE CONCEPT

The opportunity to review and correct the transcript is available upon timely request. Typically, at the end of the deposition, the officer will ask the witness whether the witness wants to read and review the transcript or waive that right.

APPLICATIONS

Request to Review

To obtain an opportunity to review and correct the transcript, the deponent or a party must make a request prior to the completion of the deposition.[188] Typically, the court reporter will ask at the end of a deposition whether the witness wishes to read and sign the transcript or waive signature.

Submission of Changes

If a review is requested, the court reporter will make the deposition transcript available to the witness, typically by sending a copy to the witness to review.[189] The witness must submit an errata statement describing any changes within 30 days of notification that the transcript is available.[190] The statement should state the reasons for the changes and be signed by the witness.[191] The time for submission of changes may be extended by the court upon motion.[192] Any changes that are submitted are attached to the transcript.

Changes in Form—to Correct Transcription Errors

Changes in form, such as transcription errors, are entered into the transcript with an explanation as to the reason for the

[187] *See Wellin v. Wellin*, 211 F. Supp. 3d 793, 800 (D.S.C. 2016); *In re CFS-Related Sec. Fraud Litig.*, 256 F. Supp. 2d 1227, 1240 (N.D. Okla. 2003).

[188] *Hambleton Bros. Lumber Co. v. Balkin Enterprises, Inc.*, 397 F.3d 1217, 1226 (9th Cir. 2005); *Diaz-Casillas v. Doctors' Ctr. Hosp. San Juan*, 342 F. Supp. 3d 218, 225 (D.P.R. 2018).

[189] *Parkland Venture, LLC v. City of Muskego*, 270 F.R.D. 439, 441 (E.D. Wis. 2010) (court reporter not required to send a copy to the witness, can make the copy available at the reporter's office).

[190] *Monge v. RG Petro-Machinery (Group) Co. Ltd.*, 701 F.3d 598, 612 (10th Cir. 2012); *Delaware Valley Floral Group, Inc. v. Shaw Rose Nets, LLC*, 597 F.3d 1374, 1379–81 (Fed. Cir. 2010).

[191] *Nucor Corp. v. Requenez*, 578 F. Supp. 3d. 873, 907 (S.D. Tex. 2022); *Alvarado v. GC Dealer Servs. Inc.*, 511 F. Supp. 3d 321, 330 n.3 (E.D.N.Y. 2021).

[192] *Veolia Water Solutions & Technologies North Am., Inc. v. Aquatech Intern. Corp.*, 123 F. Supp. 3d 695, 704 (W.D. Pa. 2015).

change.[193]

Changes in Substance

The courts vary as to their approach when a witness wants to make changes in the substance of the testimony,[194] which are also entered into the transcript with an explanation as to the reason for the change.[195] With changes in substance, the deposition can be reconvened to explore the basis for the substantive change.[196] A deponent who changes the answers may be impeached with the former answers.[197] Some courts do not allow substantive changes when they view the changes as an attempt to create issues of fact to prevent summary judgment, sometimes referred to as the "sham affidavit" rule.[198]

Failure to Submit Changes

A witness who fails to submit any changes or return the signed errata sheet within the time period allowed waives the right to make corrections to the transcript.[199]

RULE 30(f)—CERTIFICATION AND DELIVERY; EXHIBITS; COPIES OF THE TRANSCRIPT OR RECORDING; FILING

CORE CONCEPT

The officer must certify that the witness was duly sworn and that the deposition transcript was a true record of the testimony given by the deponent.

---

[193] *See Aldapa v. Fowler Packing Co., Inc.*, 323 F.R.D. 316, 333 (E.D. Cal. 2018).

[194] *See Pina v. Children's Place*, 740 F.3d 785, 792 (1st Cir. 2014) (Rule 30(e) authorizes changes in form or substance); *Gonzalez v. Fresenius Medical Care North Am.*, 689 F.3d 470, 480 (5th Cir. 2012) (substantive changes drafted by counsel not proper); *Norelus v. Denny's, Inc.*, 628 F.3d 1270, 1281 (11th Cir. 2010) ("novella-length errata sheet making a slew of material changes to their client's deposition testimony was improper").

[195] *Norelus v. Denny's, Inc.*, 628 F.3d 1270, 1295 (11th Cir. 2010); *Podell v. Citicorp Diners Club, Inc.*, 112 F.3d 98, 103 (2d Cir. 1997).

[196] *See Pina v. Children's Place*, 740 F.3d 785, 791 (1st Cir. 2014); *Norelus v. Denny's, Inc.*, 628 F.3d 1270, 1294 (11th Cir. 2010).

[197] *Thorn v. Sundstrand Aerospace Corp.*, 207 F.3d 383, 388–89 (7th Cir. 2000); *Podell v. Citicorp Diners Club, Inc.*, 112 F.3d 98, 103 (2d Cir.1997) (the changes made do not replace the deponent's original answers; the original information remains part of the record and may be introduced at trial).

[198] *Sinclair Wyoming Ref. Co. v. A & B Builders, Ltd.*, 989 F.3d 747, 785 (10th Cir. 2021); *Thorn v. Sundstrand Aerospace Corp.*, 207 F.3d 383, 389 (7th Cir. 2000).

[199] *Nucor Corp. v. Requenez*, 578 F. Supp. 3d. 873, 908 (S.D. Tex. 2022) (striking errata sheet five days late); *Karpenski v. Am. General Life Co., LLC*, 999 F. Supp. 2d 1218, 1224 (W.D. Wash. 2014) (missing by a day or 2 might not warrant waiver).

APPLICATIONS

Certificate

The officer shall prepare and sign[200] a written certificate to accompany the record of the deposition.[201] The certificate should indicate that the witness was sworn, that the deposition is a true and accurate record of the testimony, and whether review of the record was requested.[202] Rule 30 does not set a deadline for this certification.[203]

Uncertified Transcript

A deposition transcript that is not properly certified is inadmissible.[204]

Original Transcript

The stenographer should supply the original transcript and certification to the party noticing the deposition in a sealed envelope,[205] which should be preserved for use at trial.

Copies of the Transcript

Any party or the deponent can purchase a copy of the recording of the deposition for a reasonable charge.[206] If the deposition was recorded stenographically and has not been transcribed, then the party seeking the transcript will normally have to pay the transcription costs, unless the court orders otherwise.

Exhibits

Upon the request of a party, a document produced or used at a deposition may be marked for identification and annexed to the deposition transcript. A copy of a document may be substituted for the original. If documents are produced at a deposition, any party has a right to inspect and copy them.

Retaining Recording

The officer should retain a copy of the transcript or record-

---

[200] *Hochroth v. Ally Bank*, 461 F. Supp. 3d 986, 998 (D. Haw. 2020) (refusing to consider transcript with unsigned certification).

[201] *Orr v. Bank of Am., NT & SA*, 285 F.3d 764, 774 (9th Cir. 2002); (an affidavit of counsel is not sufficient to authenticate a deposition transcript); *Giulio v. BV CenterCal, LLC*, 815 F. Supp. 2d 1162, 1169 (D. Or. 2011).

[202] *Sweetin v. City of Texas City, Texas*, 568 F. Supp. 3d 789, 794–95 (S.D. Tex. 2021); *Del Toro-Pacheco v. Pereira-Castillo*, 662 F. Supp. 2d 202, 211 (D.P.R. 2009).

[203] *Morgan v. Huntington Ingalls, Inc.*, 879 F.3d 602, 610 (5th Cir. 2018).

[204] *Hochroth v. Ally Bank*, 461 F. Supp. 3d 986, 998 (D. Haw. 2020) (refusing to consider transcript with unsigned certification); *Berbick v. Precinct 42*, 977 F. Supp. 2d 268, 273–74 (S.D.N.Y. 2013) (excerpt of deposition was properly considered in the context of a motion for summary judgment even though signature was not included).

[205] *Alcorn v. City of Chicago*, 336 F.R.D. 440, 442 (N.D. Ill. 2020); *Ratliff v. City of Shannon Hills*, 52 F. Supp. 3d 904, 910 (E.D. Ark. 2014) (only the party noticing the deposition gets the originals).

[206] *Rivera v. DiSabato*, 962 F. Supp. 38, 39–40 (D.N.J. 1997).

ing of the deposition.[207]

RULE 30(g)—FAILURE TO ATTEND A DEPOSITION OR SERVE SUBPOENA; EXPENSES

CORE CONCEPT

The court may award expenses, including attorney's fees, to a party that appears for a deposition that does not occur because either: (1) the party noticing the deposition does not attend;[208] or (2) the party fails to subpoena a witness and that witness does not appear. In both cases, the party noticing the deposition may be ordered to pay the expenses of other parties incurred as a result of appearing for the deposition.

Additional Research References

Wright & Miller, *Federal Practice and Procedure* §§ 2101 to 2120
C.J.S., Federal Civil Procedure §§ 548 to 583 et seq., 600 to 644 et seq.
West's Key Number Digest, Federal Civil Procedure ⚷1311 to 1456

---

[207] *Alcorn v. City of Chicago*, 336 F.R.D. 440, 442 (N.D. Ill. 2020).

[208] *Albee v. Continental Tire North Am., Inc.*, 780 F. Supp. 2d 1005, 1012–13 (E.D. Cal. 2011) (awarding fees based on the cancellation of a deposition the night before, when the witness had already prepared and traveled).

RULE 31
DEPOSITIONS BY WRITTEN QUESTIONS

(a) **When a Deposition May Be Taken.**

(1) *Without Leave.* A party may, by written questions, depose any person, including a party, without leave of court except as provided in Rule 31(a)(2). The deponent's attendance may be compelled by subpoena under Rule 45.

(2) *With Leave.* A party must obtain leave of court, and the court must grant leave to the extent consistent with Rule 26(b)(1) and (2):

(A) if the parties have not stipulated to the deposition and:

(i) the deposition would result in more than 10 depositions being taken under this rule or Rule 30 by the plaintiffs, or by the defendants, or by the third-party defendants;

(ii) the deponent has already been deposed in the case; or

(iii) the party seeks to take a deposition before the time specified in Rule 26(d); or

(B) if the deponent is confined in prison.

(3) *Service; Required Notice.* A party who wants to depose a person by written questions must serve them on every other party, with a notice stating, if known, the deponent's name and address. If the name is unknown, the notice must provide a general description sufficient to identify the person or the particular class or group to which the person belongs. The notice must also state the name or descriptive title and the address of the officer before whom the deposition will be taken.

(4) *Questions Directed to an Organization.* A public or private corporation, a partnership, an association, or a governmental agency may be deposed

by written questions in accordance with Rule 30(b)(6).

(5) *Questions from Other Parties.* Any questions to the deponent from other parties must be served on all parties as follows: cross-questions, within 14 days after being served with the notice and direct questions; redirect questions, within 7 days after being served with cross-questions; and recross-questions, within 7 days after being served with redirect questions. The court may, for good cause, extend or shorten these times.

(b) **Delivery to the Officer; Officer's Duties.** The party who noticed the deposition must deliver to the officer a copy of all the questions served and of the notice. The officer must promptly proceed in the manner provided in Rule 30(c), (e), and (f) to:

(1) take the deponent's testimony in response to the questions;

(2) prepare and certify the deposition; and

(3) send it to the party, attaching a copy of the questions and of the notice.

(c) **Notice of Completion or Filing.**

(1) *Completion.* The party who noticed the deposition must notify all other parties when it is completed.

(2) *Filing.* A party who files the deposition must promptly notify all other parties of the filing.

[Amended March 30, 1970, effective July 1, 1970; March 2, 1987, effective August 1, 1987; April 22, 1993, effective December 1, 1993; April 30, 2007, effective December 1, 2007; April 29, 2015, effective December 1, 2015.]

AUTHORS' COMMENTARY ON RULE 31

PURPOSE AND SCOPE

Rule 31 contains the procedures for taking depositions through written questions. Depositions by written question are rarely used, and their only advantage seems to be that they may be less expensive than depositions by oral question.

RULE 31(a)—WHEN A DEPOSITION MAY BE TAKEN

CORE CONCEPT

Any party may take depositions by serving written questions, which are asked by the deposition officer (typically, the stenographer) and answered orally by the witness. Depositions by written question are rarely used, and their only advantage seems to be that they may be less expensive than depositions by oral question.[1]

APPLICATIONS

Substitute for Oral Deposition

The most common use of depositions by written question may be as a court-ordered alternative for a deposition by oral questions when there is an objection to the oral deposition.[2]

Notice

A party seeking to take a deposition by written questions must serve a notice on all other parties stating the name and address of the deponent, if known, or a general description sufficient to identify the deponent and providing the name or title and address of the stenographer or officer before whom the deposition will be taken.[3]

Timing of Notice

The notice of written deposition may be served at any time after the parties have conducted the discovery conference under Rule 26(f), or earlier with leave of court. In proceedings listed in Rule 26(a)(1)(B) as exempt from initial disclosures, there is no preliminary waiting period for written depositions. The latest time to conduct a deposition upon written questions will be governed by the court's scheduling order.[4]

Subpoenas vs. Deposition Notices

Subpoenas must be used to compel the attendance of nonparty witnesses. Party witnesses and representatives of corporations are compelled to attend by virtue of the deposition notice alone.

Service of Direct-Examination

The written deposition questions for direct examination are

---

[1]*See Brown v. Carr*, 236 F.R.D. 311 (S.D. Tex. 2006) ("If plaintiff is unable to afford to take depositions via telephone, then he may take depositions upon written questions.").

[2]*See Faford v. Grand Trunk W. R.R. Co.*, 335 F.R.D. 503, 504 (E.D. Mich. 2020) (written deposition proposed to address COVID-19 concerns); *Mannina v. D.C.*, 334 F.R.D. 336, 348 (D.D.C. 2020).

[3]*Rahn v. Hawkins*, 464 F.3d 813, 821–22 (8th Cir. 2006).

[4]*See Summerville v. Local 77*, 369 F. Supp. 2d 648, 651 (M.D. N.C. 2005), aff'd, 142 Fed. Appx. 762 (4th Cir. 2005) (written deposition questions are treated like other written discovery, and must be served such that the responses are due before the close of written discovery).

served upon all parties with the notice.[5]

Cross, Redirect, and Recross

Within 14 days of service of the notice and direct examination questions (or such other time set by the court), any other party may serve cross-examination questions.[6] The noticing party may then serve redirect examination questions within 7 days, and the other party may serve re-cross examination questions within 7 more days. The court may shorten or lengthen these time periods upon motion and for cause shown. All questions should be served on all parties.

Number of Depositions

The plaintiffs as a group are limited to 10 depositions total, without distinction between written and oral examination, as are the defendants and the third-party defendants. This number may be increased or decreased by stipulation or by order of court.

Scope of Questions

The scope of the written deposition questions is the same as oral questions, and is controlled by Rule 26.

Persons Subject

Both parties and nonparties are subject to written depositions.[7]

Corporate Representative

A party may require a corporation or organization to designate a representative to respond to the questions, as described in detail above under Rule 30(b)(6).

Repeat Depositions

Leave of court is required to depose someone a second time.[8]

Deponent in Prison

If the deponent is in prison, leave of court is required to take a written deposition.[9]

Objections

Objections to the form of a written question (*e.g.*, because it is leading) must be served in writing upon the party propounding the question within the time for serving succeeding questions and within 7 days of the last questions authorized.[10]

---

[5] *In re Lenders Mortg. Services, Inc.*, 224 B.R. 707, 710 (E.D. Mo. 1997).

[6] *See Jackson v. Russel*, 122 F. Supp. 3d 199, 202 (D. Del. 2015).

[7] *New Hampshire Motor Transport Ass'n v. Rowe*, 324 F. Supp. 2d 231, 237 (D. Me. 2004) (written deposition questions, in contrast to interrogatories, can be served on nonparties).

[8] *Rahn v. Hawkins*, 464 F.3d 813, 821–22 (8th Cir. 2006).

[9] *Whitehurst v. U.S.*, 231 F.R.D. 500, 501 (S.D. Tex. 2005).

[10] *See Rule 32(d)(3)(C); Whitehurst v. U.S.*, 231 F.R.D. 500, 501 (S.D. Tex. 2005).

RULE 31(b)—DELIVERY TO THE OFFICER; OFFICER'S DUTIES

CORE CONCEPT

Once all the questions have been served, the party initiating the deposition provides all the questions to the deposition officer. The officer then promptly takes the deposition by reading the questions and recording the answers.[11] A transcript is then prepared and submitted to the witness as provided in Rule 30 governing oral depositions.

RULE 31(c)—NOTICE OF COMPLETION OR FILING

CORE CONCEPT

When the deposition has been completed, the party who noticed the deposition must provide notice to all other parties. Local rules usually determine whether the officer files a sealed transcript with the court. If so, the party noticing the deposition must promptly give notice of the filing of the transcript to all other parties.

Additional Research References

Wright & Miller, *Federal Practice and Procedure* §§ 2131 to 2133
C.J.S., Federal Civil Procedure §§ 591 to 592
West's Key Number Digest, Federal Civil Procedure ⚿1369 to 1370

[11] *See Sherrod v. Breitbart*, 304 F.R.D. 73, 76 n.3 (D.D.C. 2014) (the witness must be present and testifies live, not by written responses); *Estate of Ungar v. Palestinian Authority*, 451 F. Supp. 2d 607, 612 (S.D.N.Y. 2006).

RULE 32
USING DEPOSITIONS IN COURT PROCEEDINGS

(a) **Using Depositions.**

(1) *In General.* At a hearing or trial, all or part of a deposition may be used against a party on these conditions:

(A) the party was present or represented at the taking of the deposition or had reasonable notice of it;

(B) it is used to the extent it would be admissible under the Federal Rules of Evidence if the deponent were present and testifying; and

(C) the use is allowed by Rule 32(a)(2) through (8).

(2) *Impeachment and Other Uses.* Any party may use a deposition to contradict or impeach the testimony given by the deponent as a witness, or for any other purpose allowed by the Federal Rules of Evidence.

(3) *Deposition of Party, Agent, or Designee.* An adverse party may use for any purpose the deposition of a party or anyone who, when deposed, was the party's officer, director, managing agent, or designee under Rule 30(b)(6) or 31(a)(4).

(4) *Unavailable Witness.* A party may use for any purpose the deposition of a witness, whether or not a party, if the court finds:

(A) that the witness is dead;

(B) that the witness is more than 100 miles from the place of hearing or trial or is outside the United States, unless it appears that the witness's absence was procured by the party offering the deposition;

(C) that the witness cannot attend or testify because of age, illness, infirmity, or imprisonment;

(D) that the party offering the deposition could

not procure the witness's attendance by subpoena; or

(E) on motion and notice, that exceptional circumstances make it desirable—in the interest of justice and with due regard to the importance of live testimony in open court—to permit the deposition to be used.

(5) *Limitations on Use.*

(A) *Deposition Taken on Short Notice.* A deposition must not be used against a party who, having received less than 14 days' notice of the deposition, promptly moved for a protective order under Rule 26(c)(1)(B) requesting that it not be taken or be taken at a different time or place—and this motion was still pending when the deposition was taken.

(B) *Unavailable Deponent; Party Could Not Obtain an Attorney.* A deposition taken without leave of court under the unavailability provision of Rule 30(a)(2)(A)(iii) must not be used against a party who shows that, when served with the notice, it could not, despite diligent efforts, obtain an attorney to represent it at the deposition.

(6) *Using Part of a Deposition.* If a party offers in evidence only part of a deposition, an adverse party may require the offeror to introduce other parts that in fairness should be considered with the part introduced, and any party may itself introduce any other parts.

(7) *Substituting a Party.* Substituting a party under Rule 25 does not affect the right to use a deposition previously taken.

(8) *Deposition Taken in an Earlier Action.* A deposition lawfully taken and, if required, filed in any federal-or state-court action may be used in a later action involving the same subject matter between the same parties, or their representatives or successors in interest, to the same extent as if taken in the later action. A deposition previously taken may also be used as allowed by the Federal Rules of Evidence.

(b) **Objections to Admissibility.** Subject to Rules 28(b) and 32(d)(3), an objection may be made at a hearing or trial to the admission of any deposition testimony that would be inadmissible if the witness were present and testifying.

(c) **Form of Presentation.** Unless the court orders otherwise, a party must provide a transcript of any deposition testimony the party offers, but may provide the court with the testimony in nontranscript form as well. On any party's request, deposition testimony offered in a jury trial for any purpose other than impeachment must be presented in nontranscript form, if available, unless the court for good cause orders otherwise.

(d) **Waiver of Objections.**

(1) *To the Notice.* An objection to an error or irregularity in a deposition notice is waived unless promptly served in writing on the party giving the notice.

(2) *To the Officer's Qualification.* An objection based on disqualification of the officer before whom a deposition is to be taken is waived if not made:

(A) before the deposition begins; or

(B) promptly after the basis for disqualification becomes known or, with reasonable diligence, could have been known.

(3) *To the Taking of the Deposition.*

(A) *Objection to Competence, Relevance, or Materiality.* An objection to a deponent's competence—or to the competence, relevance, or materiality of testimony—is not waived by a failure to make the objection before or during the deposition, unless the ground for it might have been corrected at that time.

(B) *Objection to an Error or Irregularity.* An objection to an error or irregularity at an oral examination is waived if:

(i) it relates to the manner of taking the deposition, the form of a question or answer, the oath or affirmation, a party's conduct, or other matters that might have been corrected at that time; and

(ii) it is not timely made during the deposition.

(C) *Objection to a Written Question.* An objection to the form of a written question under Rule 31 is waived if not served in writing on the party submitting the question within the time for serving responsive questions or, if the question is a recross-question, within 7 days after being served with it.

(4) *To Completing and Returning the Deposition.* An objection to how the officer transcribed the testimony—or prepared, signed, certified, sealed, endorsed, sent, or otherwise dealt with the deposition—is waived unless a motion to suppress is made promptly after the error or irregularity becomes known or, with reasonable diligence, could have been known.

[Amended March 30, 1970, effective July 1, 1970; November 20, 1972, effective July 1, 1975; April 29, 1980, effective August 1, 1980; March 2, 1987, effective August 1, 1987; April 22, 1993, effective December 1, 1993; April 30, 2007, effective December 1, 2007; March 26, 2009, effective December 1, 2009.]

AUTHORS' COMMENTARY ON RULE 32

PURPOSE AND SCOPE

Rules 27, 28, 30, and 31 control the way one arranges for and conducts a deposition. Once the deposition is over and has been transcribed or recorded, Rule 32 dictates how parties may use the deposition transcript or recording. Rule 32 makes a distinction between two types of use: use of the deposition to impeach a witness; and use of the deposition for other purposes, such as to prove the facts that are disputed in the lawsuit.

Because impeachment applies to a witness who is testifying live at trial (and thus available to both parties), Rule 32 broadly allows use of a deposition for impeachment, as long as the deposition was properly noticed and conducted. If a party wants to use a deposition for purposes other than impeachment—generally as a substitute for live testimony—Rule 32 imposes additional restrictions. A deposition may be used for any purpose if the witness was a party and the person seeking to use the deposition is an adverse party, or if the witness is "unavailable," such as dead, incapacitated, or so far away that the witness cannot be subpoenaed to testify live.

Note that the requirements and restrictions in Rule 32 are in addition to those in the Federal Rules of Evidence. Thus, the use deposition testimony must comply with both Rule 32 and the applicable Federal Rules of Evidence.

Rule 32 also contains a provision protecting against the use of a misleading excerpt of a deposition. If one party introduces only part of a deposition, other parties may compel the offering party to also introduce other parts at the same time that, in fairness, should be considered along with the part that was introduced. Thus, the effect of this provision is to alter the timing of the presentation of the other portions of the testimony to the jury—normally, other parties would have to wait until their turn to question the witness, after the first party was finished, to introduce other portions of the deposition it wanted the jury to hear, perhaps after the jury had formed initial impressions that might be difficult to change. Rule 32 prevents that prejudice by allowing the jury to hear the entire context at one time.

Rule 32 also authorizes deposition testimony to be offered in stenographic or nonstenographic form, such as by videorecording. In jury trials, Rule 32 allows a party to require that the nonstenographic form be used if available.

Finally, Rule 32 addresses the manner in which parties may present, and the court will rule on, objections to deposition testimony. It also describes which objections are waived if not properly presented. Keep in mind that Rules 30 and 32 work together to govern depositions, and both regulate the manner of asserting and presenting objections to the procedures and substance of depositions.

RULE 32(a)—USING DEPOSITIONS

CORE CONCEPT

Rule 32 establishes a three-part test for admissibility of deposition testimony that the party seeking to introduce the testimony must satisfy:[1]

1. The party against whom the testimony is offered was present at, represented at, or had reasonable notice of the deposition;
2. The testimony is otherwise admissible under the Federal Rules of Evidence; and
3. The testimony is admissible under the provisions in Rule 32(a)(2)-(8), which allows testimony used for impeachment, testimony of an adverse party, and testimony of an unavailable witness.[2]

---

[1]*Howard v. Gray*, 291 F.R.D. 6, 9–10 (D.D.C. 2013) (burden is on the party seeking to introduce the testimony).

[2]*Walsh v. Fusion Japanese Steakhouse, Inc.*, __ F. Supp. 3d __, 2022 WL

APPLICATIONS

Use for Impeachment

A deposition may always be used to impeach or contradict a witness (if the first 2 general requirements above are met).[3]

Use for Substantive Purposes

A deposition may be used as substantive evidence (to prove or disprove a fact) in two circumstances: when the witness is an adverse party and when the witness is unavailable.

- *Adverse Party*: The deposition of an adverse party may be used as substantive evidence.[4] This principle applies to a party organization's officers, directors, and managing agents,[5] and to representatives designated under Rule 30(b)(6).[6] It is unsettled whether the deposition of a former party (*e.g.,* one who has settled) may be used as substantive evidence.[7]
- *Unavailable Witness*: The deposition of an unavailable nonparty witness may also be used as substantive, non-impeachment evidence if the party seeking to introduce the testimony establishes one of the following five conditions:[8]
  - (A) The witness is dead.[9] However, if the witness dies during the taking of the deposition, so that one party does not have a full opportunity to examine the witness, then the court has discretion as to whether to admit the testimony;
  - (B) The witness is more than 100 miles from the

395253, at *16 (W.D. Pa. 2022); *In re 3M Combat Arms Earplug Prod. Liab. Litig.*, 338 F.R.D. 167, 170 (N.D. Fla. 2021).

[3]*Berkowitz v. Berkowitz*, 817 F.3d 809, 812 (1st Cir. 2016).

[4]*Chevron Oronite Co., L.L.C. v. Jacobs Field Servs. N. Am., Inc.*, 951 F.3d 219, 227 (5th Cir. 2020); *Creative Consumer Concepts, Inc. v. Kreisler*, 563 F.3d 1070, 1080 (10th Cir. 2009) (no need to show that the witness is unavailable when introducing the testimony of a party opponent).

[5]*Shanklin v. Norfolk Southern Ry. Co.*, 369 F.3d 978 (6th Cir. 2004); *Palmer Coal & Rock Company v. Gulf Oil Company*, 524 F.2d 884 (10th Cir. 1975).

[6]*In re 3M Combat Arms Earplug Prod. Liab. Litig.*, 338 F.R.D. 167, 170 (N.D. Fla. 2021); *Gonzalez Production Systems v. Martinrea Int'l Inc.*, 310 F.R.D. 341, 343 (E.D. Mich. 2015) (noting that some courts are reluctant to admit the deposition testimony of a Rule 30(b)(6) designee if the designee is available to testify).

[7]*See Junger v. Singh*, 514 F. Supp. 3d 579 (W.D.N.Y. 2021) (noting lack of authority); *Powertrain, Inc. v. Ma*, 88 F. Supp. 3d 679, 691 (N.D. Miss. 2015) (deposition of former party not admissible).

[8]*Dillard v. Smith*, 558 F. Supp. 3d 308, 316 n.4 (W.D. Va. 2021) (offering party has the burden of demonstrating unavailability); *Powertrain, Inc. v. Ma*, 88 F. Supp. 3d 679, 692 (N.D. Miss. 2015).

[9]*See Chevron Oronite Co., L.L.C. v. Jacobs Field Servs. N. Am., Inc.*, 951 F.3d 219, 227, n.9 (5th Cir. 2020); *Dellwood Farms, Inc. v. Cargill, Inc.*, 128 F.3d 1122, 1128 (7th Cir. 1997).

courthouse[10] (measured "as the crow flies")[11] or outside the United States, unless it appears that the party offering the testimony procured the absence of the witness;[12]

(C) The deponent is unable to attend trial because of age,[13] illness,[14] infirmity, or imprisonment;[15]

(D) The party offering the deposition was unable to procure the deponent's attendance at trial by subpoena,[16] despite the use of reasonable diligence;[17] or

(E) Exceptional other circumstances.[18] For example, the court admitted the deposition testimony of a witness who refused to testify at trial by invoking a privilege.[19] In order to take advantage of the catchall, a party must give notice to the other party of its intent.[20] The general policy favoring live testimony leads to a restrictive reading of this "catchall" clause.[21]

Even if one of these conditions is satisfied, however, the court has discretion as to whether to admit the testimony.[22] For example, when one party represented that a witness would voluntarily appear at trial, the court conditionally held that an-

---

[10] *Spectrum Ass'n Mgmt. of Texas, L.L.C. v. Lifetime HOA Mgmt. L.L.C.*, 5 F.4th 560, 564 (5th Cir. 2021); *Fletcher v. Tomlinson*, 895 F.3d 1010, 1020 (8th Cir. 2018).

[11] *See Rodriguez v. Cty. of Los Angeles*, 891 F.3d 776, 808 (9th Cir. 2018); *Lyman v. St. Jude Med. S.C., Inc.*, 580 F. Supp. 2d 719, 728 n.5 (E.D. Wis. 2008).

[12] *McDowell v. Blankenship*, 759 F.3d 847, 851–52 (8th Cir. 2014) (choice to take a job in a remote location is not procuring absence to affect litigation); *Garcia-Martinez v. City and County of Denver*, 392 F.3d 1187, 1191–92 (10th Cir. 2004).

[13] *U.S. v. Firishchak*, 468 F.3d 1015, 1023 (7th Cir. 2006).

[14] *Whalley v. Blazick*, — F. Supp. 3d —, 2022 WL 304658, at *4 (M.D. Pa. 2022) (party asserting illness should provide objective medical support); *Smith v. Pfizer Inc.*, 714 F. Supp. 2d 845, 853 (M.D. Tenn. 2010).

[15] *Draper v. Rosario*, 836 F.3d 1072, 1081 (9th Cir. 2016); *Delgado v. Pawtucket Police Dept.*, 668 F.3d 42, 46 (1st Cir. 2012) (it is not enough to show the witness is in prison, the party must show that the witness is unavailable because of imprisonment).

[16] *Thomas v. Cook County Sheriff's Dept.*, 604 F.3d 293, 308 (7th Cir. 2009) (knowledge of the witness's location is not dispositive if the party has exercised reasonable efforts to obtain the witness's attendance); *Griman v. Makousky*, 76 F.3d 151, 154 (7th Cir. 1996).

[17] *Kuri v. Folino*, 409 F. Supp. 3d 626, 640 (N.D. Ill. 2019) (court has discretion regarding diligence).

[18] *See McDowell v. Blankenship*, 759 F.3d 847, 851–52 (8th Cir. 2014); *Battle ex rel. Battle v. Memorial Hosp. at Gulfport*, 228 F.3d 544, 554 (5th Cir. 2000) (videotaped deposition of physician allowed).

[19] *Emmi v. DeAngelo*, 261 F. Supp. 3d 556, 560 (E.D. Pa. 2017).

[20] *Hall v. Jaeho Jung*, 819 F.3d 378, 383 n.2 (7th Cir. 2016).

[21] *See McDowell v. Blankenship*, 759 F.3d 847, 851–52 (8th Cir. 2014); *Griman v. Makousky*, 76 F.3d 151, 153 (7th Cir. 1996).

[22] *Hall v. Jaeho Jung*, 819 F.3d 378, 383–84 (7th Cir. 2016).

other party could not offer the witness's testimony for substantive purposes even though the witness was more than 100 miles from the courthouse.[23]

Must Comply with Rules of Evidence

Even if the criteria in Rule 32 for use of a deposition have been satisfied, the deposition must still be admissible under the Federal Rules of Evidence.[24] The rules of evidence are applied as though the deponent were present and testifying.[25] Thus, the effect of Rule 32 is to negate the hearsay objection.[26] Furthermore, as with any evidence, the admission of deposition testimony is subject to the court's discretion.[27]

Use of Part of a Deposition

If a party introduces only part of a deposition, any adverse party may require the offering party to introduce additional parts necessary to clarify the offered text.[28] Such adverse parties have the right to have the additional text introduced immediately following the admission of the offered testimony.[29] The admission of the additional parts is still subject to evidentiary objections.[30]

Deposition Taken in Another Matter

A party may use a deposition transcript from another matter if the other matter involves the same subject matter between the same parties (or persons in privity with the parties),[31] or if the use is otherwise authorized by the Federal Rules of Evidence.[32] The proposed use of the transcript still must comply with the other provisions of Rule 32 and with the Federal Rules of Evidence.[33] Thus, for example, a party may only use the deposition of a nonparty witness taken from an-

[23] *Stevenson v. Holland*, 504 F. Supp. 3d 1107, 1147–1148 (E.D. Cal. 2020).

[24] *Info-Hold, Inc. v. Muzak LLC*, 783 F.3d 1365, 1372 (Fed. Cir. 2015).

[25] *Sara Lee Corp. v. Kraft Foods Inc.*, 276 F.R.D. 500, 502–03 (N.D. Ill. 2011); *S.E.C. v. Franklin*, 348 F. Supp. 2d 1159, 1162 (S.D. Cal. 2004).

[26] *Chevron Oronite Co., L.L.C. v. Jacobs Field Servs. N. Am., Inc.*, 951 F.3d 219, 227 (5th Cir. 2020); *Fletcher v. Tomlinson*, 895 F.3d 1010, 1020–21 (8th Cir. 2018).

[27] *Coletti v. Cudd Pressure Control*, 165 F.3d 767, 773 (10th Cir. 1999).

[28] *Lentomyynti Oy v. Medivac, Inc.*, 997 F.2d 364 (7th Cir.1993); *Saget v. Trump*, 351 F. Supp. 3d 251, 256 (E.D.N.Y. 2019).

[29] *Westinghouse Elec. Corp. v. Wray Equipment Corp.*, 286 F.2d 491, 494 (1st Cir. 1961); *Trepel v. Roadway Exp., Inc.*, 194 F.3d 708, 710 (6th Cir. 1999).

[30] *See Heary Bros. Lightning Protection Co., Inc. v. Lightning Protection Institute*, 287 F. Supp. 2d 1038, 1065 n.10 (D. Ariz. 2003), aff'd in part, rev'd in part, 262 Fed. Appx. 815 (9th Cir. 2008).

[31] *Gamble v. FCA US LLC*, 993 F.3d 534, 538 (7th Cir. 2021); *Alexander v. Casino Queen, Inc.*, 739 F.3d 972, 978 (7th Cir. 2014) (party must have had a similar motive to examine the witness).

[32] *In re 3M Combat Arms Earplug Prod. Liab. Litig.*, 338 F.R.D. 167, 170 (N.D. Fla. 2021).

[33] *Brown v. Vivint Solar, Inc.*, — F. Supp. 3d —, 2020 WL 2513518, at *2 (M.D. Fla. 2020); *Powertrain, Inc. v.*

other matter if the witness is unavailable.[34]

Depositions of Experts

Courts vary as to their approach to requests to present expert testimony by deposition. Some courts allow such use if the expert meets the criteria for being unavailable.[35] Others disallow routine use of expert depositions because most retained experts are technically unavailable.[36]

Documents Attached to Transcript

A document attached to a deposition transcript may be used under the same circumstances as the transcript itself (*i.e.*, within the constraints of Rule 32 and the Federal Rules of Evidence).[37]

Who May Use

Deposition transcripts may be used by any party, regardless of who noticed the deposition.[38]

Use of One's Own Deposition

Parties who know they will be "unavailable" at the time of the trial may take their own depositions and offer the testimony under the provisions of Rule 32(a)(4).[39] The court will evaluate whether the party truly was unavailable.[40]

Presence or Reasonable Notice

The deposition may be used against any party who was present or represented at, or had reasonable notice of, the deposition.[41] A deposition cannot be used against a party who demonstrates that it was unable to obtain counsel to represent it at the deposition despite the exercise of diligence. Likewise, the deposition cannot be used against a party who received less than 14 days' notice and who had filed a motion for a protective order that was pending at the time of the deposition.[42]

Ma, 88 F. Supp. 3d 679, 692 (N.D. Miss. 2015).

[34] *Brown v. Vivint Solar, Inc.*, __ F. Supp. 3d __, 2020 WL 2513518, at *2 (M.D. Fla. 2020); *Powertrain, Inc. v. Ma*, 88 F. Supp. 3d 692, 692 (N.D. Miss. 2015).

[35] See, e.g., *Junger v. Singh*, 514 F. Supp. 3d 579 (W.D.N.Y. 2021).

[36] See, e.g., *Diamond Resorts Int'l, Inc. v. Aaronson*, 378 F. Supp. 3d 1143 (M.D. Fla. 2019).

[37] *Gore v. Maritime Overseas Corp.*, 256 F. Supp. 104, 119 (E.D. Pa. 1966), aff'd in part, rev'd in part, 378 F.2d 584 (3d Cir. 1967).

[38] *Savoie v. Lafourche Boat Rentals, Inc.*, 627 F.2d 722 (5th Cir. 1980).

[39] *Richmond v. Brooks*, 227 F.2d 490 (2d Cir.1955).

[40] *Vevelstad v. Flynn*, 16 Alaska 83, 230 F.2d 695 (9th Cir. 1956).

[41] *Creative Consumer Concepts, Inc. v. Kreisler*, 563 F.3d 1070, 1080 (10th Cir. 2009); *S.E.C. v. Phan*, 500 F.3d 895, 913 (9th Cir. 2007).

[42] *U.S. S.E.C. v. Talbot*, 430 F. Supp. 2d 1029 (C.D. Cal. 2006), rev'd on other grounds, 530 F.3d 1085 (9th Cir. 2008) (amended notice does not trigger the timing provision where the original notice put the party on notice of the date of the deposition).

Discovery Depositions vs. Depositions for Use at Trial

Rule 32 does not draw any distinctions between depositions taken for discovery purposes and those taken "for use at trial."[43]

Motion for Summary Judgment

Deposition transcripts may be used in support of or in opposition to motions for summary judgment.[44] Indeed, some courts treat deposition testimony as equivalent to an affidavit in the context of a summary judgment motion and allow use of deposition testimony even if all of the criteria of Rule 32 are not satisfied.[45] The use of depositions in connection with summary judgment is authorized by Rule 56(c), not Rule 32.[46]

RULE 32(b)—OBJECTIONS TO ADMISSIBILITY

CORE CONCEPT

Deposition testimony may not be introduced if the testimony would not be admissible if the witness were present and testifying live.

APPLICATIONS

Rules of Evidence

A deposition admissible under Rule 32 must also be admissible under the Federal Rules of Evidence.[47] Evidentiary rulings are made as though the deponent were present and testifying.[48]

RULE 32(c)—FORM OF PRESENTATION

CORE CONCEPT

Deposition testimony may be offered in stenographic or nonstenographic form—primarily by videorecording. In jury trials, any party may require that the nonstenographic form be used if available.

APPLICATIONS

Nonstenographic Forms

A party expecting to use a nonstenographic form of deposition testimony at trial must provide other parties with a transcript in advance of trial as part of the Rule 26(a)(3) pre-

---

[43]*Manley v. AmBase Corp.*, 337 F.3d 237, 247 (2d Cir. 2003); *Green v. City of Phoenix*, 330 F.R.D. 239, 240 (D. Ariz. 2019).

[44]*Carmen v. San Francisco Unified School Dist.*, 237 F.3d 1026, 1028 (9th Cir. 2001); *Beiswenger Enterprises Corp. v. Carletta*, 46 F. Supp. 2d 1297 (M.D. Fla. 1999) (allowing the use of a deposition from another action to support a motion for summary judgment).

[45]*Gamble v. FCA US LLC*, 993 F.3d 534, 538–39 (7th Cir. 2021); *Alexander v. Casino Queen, Inc.*, 739 F.3d 972, 978 (7th Cir. 2014) (Rule 32 is primarily a limitation on the use of deposition testimony *at trial*).

[46]*Gamble v. FCA US LLC*, 993 F.3d 534, 538 (7th Cir. 2021).

[47]*Marshall v. Planz*, 145 F. Supp. 2d 1258 (M.D. Ala. 2001).

[48]*Hebert v. Prime Ins. Co.*, 459 F. Supp. 3d 766, 771 (W.D. La. 2020).

trial disclosure. A party offering nonstenographic forms of testimony must also provide a transcript to the court.[49]

Jury Trials

In a jury trial, any party may require that depositions be offered in nonstenographic form if available unless the deposition is being used for impeachment or the court orders otherwise for good cause shown.

RULE 32(d)—WAIVER OF OBJECTIONS

CORE CONCEPT

Objections to the procedures at a deposition must be asserted as soon as practicable or they are waived.

APPLICATIONS

Defects in Procedures

Objections to the notice must be made in writing to the party issuing the notice,[50] unless there was no opportunity to object.[51] Objections as to the manner of the oath or affirmation administered must be made at the time of the deposition or they are waived.[52] Objections to the qualifications of the officer (*e.g.*, stenographer), which are set forth in Rule 28, must be made before the start of the deposition or they are waived. Objections as to the manner of transcription or as to the procedures used in correcting and signing the transcript must be made in the form of a motion to suppress, which must be made with "reasonable promptness" after the defect is discovered or should have been discovered with due diligence, or they are waived.[53]

Objections to Oral Questions

Objections that can be cured by rephrasing the question, such as leading question objections, must be raised at the deposition or they are waived.[54] All other objections, such as relevance,[55] hearsay, capacity, competence,[56] etc., are reserved

---

[49] *Tilton v. Capital Cities/ABC, Inc.*, 115 F.3d 1471, 1479 (10th Cir. 1997) (a party intending to use a videotape deposition must provide a transcript).

[50] *State Farm Mut. Auto. Ins. Co. v. Dowdy ex rel. Dowdy*, 445 F. Supp. 2d 1289, 1293 (N.D. Okla. 2006).

[51] *Oates v. S. J. Groves & Sons Co.*, 248 F.2d 388 (6th Cir. 1957).

[52] *Cabello v. Fernandez-Larios*, 402 F.3d 1148, 1160 (11th Cir. 2005); *VeroBlue Farms USA Inc. v. Wulf*, — F.R.D. —, 2021 WL 5176839, at *10 (N.D. Tex. 2021).

[53] *Sec. Nat. Bank of Sioux City, IA v. Day*, 800 F.3d 936, 943 (8th Cir. 2015).

[54] *SkinMedica, Inc. v. Histogen Inc.*, 727 F.3d 1187, 1213 (Fed. Cir. 2013).

[55] *Rangel v. Gonzalez Mascorro*, 274 F.R.D. 585, 591 (S.D. Tex. 2011); *Quantachrome Corp. v. Micromeritics Instrument Corp.*, 189 F.R.D. 697, 700 (S.D. Fla. 1999).

[56] *VeroBlue Farms USA Inc. v. Wulf*, — F.R.D. —, 2021 WL 5176839, at *10 (N.D. Tex. 2021).

until the testimony is offered.[57]

Objections to Documents

Rule 32(d) does not mention waiver of objections to documents, and some courts have held that such objections are not waived.[58]

Objections to Written Deposition Questions

Objections to the form of a written question (*e.g.*, because it is leading) must be served in writing upon the party propounding the question within the time for serving succeeding questions and within 7 days of the last questions authorized.

Additional Research References

Wright & Miller, *Federal Practice and Procedure* §§ 2142 to 2157
C.J.S., Federal Civil Procedure §§ 544 to 568, 633 to 638 et seq.
West's Key Number Digest, Federal Civil Procedure ⟹1297, 1298, 1334, 1432 to 1440

---

[57] *Klayman v. Judicial Watch, Inc.*, 297 F. Supp. 3d 80, 85 (D.D.C. 2018) (competence); *State Farm Mut. Auto. Ins. Co. v. Dowdy ex rel. Dowdy*, 445 F. Supp. 2d 1289, 1293 (N.D. Okla. 2006) (such objections should not be made at the deposition).

[58] *Klayman v. Judicial Watch, Inc.*, 297 F. Supp. 3d 80, 83 (D.D.C. 2018).

RULE 33
INTERROGATORIES TO PARTIES

(a) **In General.**

(1) *Number.* Unless otherwise stipulated or ordered by the court, a party may serve on any other party no more than 25 written interrogatories, including all discrete subparts. Leave to serve additional interrogatories may be granted to the extent consistent with Rule 26(b)(1) and (2).

(2) *Scope.* An interrogatory may relate to any matter that may be inquired into under Rule 26(b). An interrogatory is not objectionable merely because it asks for an opinion or contention that relates to fact or the application of law to fact, but the court may order that the interrogatory need not be answered until designated discovery is complete, or until a pretrial conference or some other time.

(b) **Answers and Objections.**

(1) *Responding Party.* The interrogatories must be answered:

(A) by the party to whom they are directed; or

(B) if that party is a public or private corporation, a partnership, an association, or a governmental agency, by any officer or agent, who must furnish the information available to the party.

(2) *Time to Respond.* The responding party must serve its answers and any objections within 30 days after being served with the interrogatories. A shorter or longer time may be stipulated to under Rule 29 or be ordered by the court.

(3) *Answering Each Interrogatory.* Each interrogatory must, to the extent it is not objected to, be answered separately and fully in writing under oath.

(4) *Objections.* The grounds for objecting to an interrogatory must be stated with specificity. Any ground not stated in a timely objection is waived

unless the court, for good cause, excuses the failure.

(5) *Signature.* The person who makes the answers must sign them, and the attorney who objects must sign any objections.

(c) **Use.** An answer to an interrogatory may be used to the extent allowed by the Federal Rules of Evidence.

(d) **Option to Produce Business Records.** If the answer to an interrogatory may be determined by examining, auditing, compiling, abstracting, or summarizing a party's business records (including electronically stored information), and if the burden of deriving or ascertaining the answer will be substantially the same for either party, the responding party may answer by:

(1) specifying the records that must be reviewed, in sufficient detail to enable the interrogating party to locate and identify them as readily as the responding party could; and

(2) giving the interrogating party a reasonable opportunity to examine and audit the records and to make copies, compilations, abstracts, or summaries.

[Amended December 27, 1946, effective March 19, 1948; March 30, 1970, effective July 1, 1970; April 29, 1980, effective August 1, 1980; April 22, 1993, effective December 1, 1993; April 12, 2006, effective December 1, 2006; April 30, 2007, effective December 1, 2007; April 29, 2015, effective December 1, 2015.]

AUTHORS' COMMENTARY ON RULE 33

PURPOSE AND SCOPE

Rule 33 sets forth the procedures for interrogatories. Each party is limited to 25 interrogatories, unless the parties or court agree to a different limit. Interrogatories may pose purely factual questions or may ask questions that blend fact and law (sometimes called "contention interrogatories"). Parties have a right to send interrogatories, and do not need to ask for permission from the court.

The recipient must respond within 30 days, although stipulated extensions are common. The response often consists of a mixture of objections and substantive responses. The attorney is responsible for the objections, and the attorney's signature certifies under Rule 26(g) that the objections are made in good faith. The party must sign a verification attesting to the accuracy of the factual responses—this is one of the few places where the federal rules require such a verification.

Sometimes, interrogatories request detailed information that is located in documents held by the responding party. If that is the case, the responding party may refer to the documents instead of drafting a substantive response. However, the responding party may only take advantage of this option if the information is located in the documents and the burden would be substantially the same for either party to analyze the documents and extract the answer.

RULE 33(a)—IN GENERAL

CORE CONCEPT

Any party may serve up to 25 interrogatories or questions on any other party. The scope of interrogatories is the broad discovery available under Rule 26.

APPLICATIONS

Who May Be Served

Interrogatories are limited to parties to the action,[1] although the parties need not be adverse. If the party is a corporation, interrogatories should be addressed to the corporation, not to a corporate officer or the attorney.[2] In class actions, the courts are split as to whether only the named representatives can be served.[3]

Time for Service

Interrogatories can be served after the parties have conducted the discovery conference under Rule 26(f),[4] or earlier with leave of court. In proceedings listed in Rule 26(a)(1)(B) as exempt from initial disclosures, there is no preliminary waiting period for interrogatories. The Rules do not set an outer limit on how late in the case interrogatories may be served, but many local rules or case management orders will set such a limit. Usually, when such a deadline exists, interrogatories must be

---

[1] *U.S. v. Lot 41, Berryhill Farm Estates*, 128 F.3d 1386, 1397 (10th Cir. 1997); *Pegatron Tech. Serv., Inc. v. Zurich Am. Ins. Co.*, 377 F. Supp. 3d 1197, 1203 (D. Or. 2019).

[2] *Holland v. Minneapolis-Honeywell Regulator Co.*, 28 F.R.D. 595 (D.D.C. 1961).

[3] *Brennan v. Midwestern United Life Ins. Co.*, 450 F.2d 999 (7th Cir. 1971) (unnamed members of class required to respond); *Wainwright v. Kraftco Corp.*, 54 F.R.D. 532 (N.D. Ga. 1972) (unnamed members of class not required to respond).

[4] *Krause v. Buffalo and Erie County Workforce Development Consortium, Inc.*, 425 F. Supp. 2d 352 (W.D.N.Y. 2006).

served so that the answers are due before the deadline.[5]

Number

Each party may serve up to 25 interrogatories on each other party.[6] This limit may be adjusted pursuant to a court order or stipulation.[7] Note that parties may coordinate to maximize their allowable interrogatories. For example, in a case with multiple plaintiffs, they may divide up topics, effectively expanding the number of interrogatories that may be served on each defendant. When a party is confronted with what it believes to be an excessive number of interrogatories, the appropriate course of action is to either move for a protective order before answering any interrogatories or answer up to the numerical limit and object to the remainder without answering;[8] answering interrogatories in excess of the numerical limit can constitute waiver of the objection to the number of interrogatories.[9]

- *Subparts*: If an interrogatory has subparts, each subpart may count as a separate interrogatory if it is really a discrete question.[10] The Rules do not define "discrete subparts," but many courts follow the "common theme test" or "related question" approach, which provides that subparts that are logically or factually subsumed within and that are necessarily related to the primary question should not be treated as separate interrogatories.[11] An interrogatory that asks for the factual basis for any denials of requests for admission might be deemed to contain a subpart for each request for admission.[12]

Scope of Questions

The scope of interrogatories is controlled by Rule 26(b).[13] The information sought must be relevant to the claims or defenses in the case and proportional to the needs of the case, but need not be admissible evidence. Privileged information is not

[5]See *Friedman v. Live Nation Merch., Inc.*, 833 F.3d 1180, 1185 n.2 (9th Cir. 2016); *Thomas v. Pacificorp*, 324 F.3d 1176 (10th Cir. 2003).

[6]*Chudasama v. Mazda Motor Corp.*, 123 F.3d 1353, 1357 (11th Cir. 1997); *Mondragon v. Scott Farms, Inc.*, 329 F.R.D. 533, 541 (E.D.N.C. 2019).

[7]*Rates Tech., Inc. v. Mediatrix Telecom, Inc.*, 688 F.3d 742, 748 (Fed. Cir. 2012); *Nat'l Urb. League v. Ross, No.*, 508 F. Supp. 3d 663, 684 (N.D. Cal. 2020).

[8]*Mondragon v. Scott Farms, Inc.*, 329 F.R.D. 533, 541 (E.D.N.C. 2019).

[9]*Mondragon v. Scott Farms, Inc.*, 329 F.R.D. 533, 541–42 (E.D.N.C. 2019).

[10]*Synopsys, Inc. v. ATopTech, Inc*, 319 F.R.D. 293, 295–96 (N.D. Cal. 2016); *Erfindergemeinschaft Uropep GbR v. Eli Lilly and Co.*, 315 F.R.D. 191, 195 (E.D. Tex. 2016).

[11]*Nance-Bush v. Lone Star Coll. Sys. Dist.*, 337 F.R.D. 135, 138 (S.D. Tex. 2021); *Superior Sales W., Inc. v. Gonzalez*, 335 F.R.D. 98, 104 (W.D. Tex. 2020).

[12]*Superior Sales W., Inc. v. Gonzalez*, 335 F.R.D. 98, 104–05 (W.D. Tex. 2020).

[13]*Deakin v. Magellan Health, Inc.*, 340 F.R.D. 424, 431 (D.N.M. 2022); *Gersh v. Anglin*, 341 F.R.D. 55, 59 (D. Mont. 2022).

discoverable, and discovery is limited with respect to expert witnesses and trial preparation materials as discussed in Rule 26(b).

Opinions or Contentions

Rule 33 authorizes interrogatories that seek an opinion or contention that relates to fact or the application of law to fact.[14] However, the court may order that a contention interrogatory not be answered until discovery is complete or until after the pre-trial conference is held.[15] An interrogatory that asks for a pure legal conclusion, without application to the facts, is improper.[16]

Form

Parties have a great deal of latitude in framing interrogatories, as long as the responding party can reasonably determine the information to include in the answer. Only rarely will a question be so ambiguous that it does not require an answer, although the responding party can limit the scope of its answer.

Proceedings Where Interrogatories Available

Rule 33 applies to all civil actions in district court, including post-judgment proceedings (*e.g.*, interrogatories in aid-of-execution). Rule 33 does not apply to habeas proceedings.[17]

RULE 33(b)—ANSWERS AND OBJECTIONS

CORE CONCEPT

The responding party must answer interrogatories separately and in writing within 30 days after service. Objections must be stated with specificity, and objections are waived if not made timely. The responding party must verify the answers and the attorney must sign any objections.

APPLICATIONS

Answers

Each interrogatory must be answered separately and fully[18] in writing,[19] unless an objection is interposed in lieu of an

---

[14] *MLC Intell. Prop., LLC v. Micron Tech., Inc.*, 10 F.4th 1358, 1372 (Fed. Cir. 2021).

[15] *Chelsey Nelson Photography LLC v. Louisville/Jefferson Cnty. Metro Gov't*, 556 F. Supp. 3d 657, 678–79 (W.D. Ky. 2021); *Lopez v. Don Herring Ltd.*, 327 F.R.D. 567, 579–80 (N.D. Tex. 2018).

[16] *Gingerich v. City of Elkhart Probation Dept.*, 273 F.R.D. 532, 537 (N.D. Ind. 2011); *U.S. v. Boyce*, 148 F. Supp. 2d 1069 (S.D. Cal. 2001), aff'd, 36 Fed. Appx. 612 (9th Cir. 2002).

[17] *Harris v. Nelson*, 394 U.S. 286, 293–94 (1969); *Sloan v. Pugh*, 351 F.3d 1319, 1322 (10th Cir. 2003).

[18] *V5 Techs. v. Switch, Ltd.*, 334 F.R.D. 297, 305 (D. Nev. 2019); *Barnes v. District of Columbia*, 289 F.R.D. 1, 6 (D.D.C. 2012).

[19] *Lopez v. Don Herring Ltd.*, 327 F.R.D. 567, 579 (N.D. Tex. 2018); *Vazquez-Fernandez v. Cambridge College, Inc.*, 269 F.R.D. 150, 154 (D.P.R. 2010).

answer.[20] The answer must include all information within the party's possession, custody, or control or known by the party's agents.[21] This includes *facts* in an attorney's possession and information supplied to the party by others.[22] At the same time, a party does not have to obtain publicly available information not in its possession, custody, or control.[23] If the party has no such information within its possession, custody, or control, the answer may so state,[24] although some courts require the responding party to describe the efforts it undertook to locate responsive information.[25] If only some information is available, that information must be provided, and may be prefaced with a statement placing the answer in context. Generally, incorporating the pleadings or other discovery responses will not be sufficient,[26] although the answer to one interrogatory may incorporate information provided in another. Likewise, a reference to a collection of documents is generally not a sufficient response.[27]

Service and Filing

The responding party must serve the answers on all other parties. Interrogatory answers are not filed unless they are the subject of a motion, in which case they can be attached as an exhibit.

Time to Answer

Answers and objections are due within 30 days of service unless the due date is modified by informal agreement or stipulation under Rule 29 or by court order.[28] Extensions of this deadline are quite common, typically by an informal email exchange. Failure to serve a response in a timely manner may constitute a waiver of all objections.[29]

---

[20] *U.S. v. All Assets Held at Bank Julius Baer & Company, Ltd.*, 309 F.R.D. 1, 5 (D.D.C. 2015) (answers must be "true, explicit, responsive, complete, and candid"); *Vazquez-Fernandez v. Cambridge College, Inc.*, 269 F.R.D. 150, 154 (D.P.R. 2010).

[21] *Myhre v. Seventh-Day Adventist Church Reform Movement Am. Union Int'l Missionary Soc'y*, 298 F.R.D. 633, 647 (S.D. Cal. 2014).

[22] *Hickman v. Taylor*, 329 U.S. 495, 504 (1947); *see also Gingerich v. City of Elkhart Probation Dept.*, 273 F.R.D. 532, 541–42 (N.D. Ind. 2011).

[23] *Huthnance v. District of Columbia*, 255 F.R.D. 285, 292 (D.D.C. 2008).

[24] *Hansel v. Shell Oil Corp.*, 169 F.R.D. 303, 305 (E.D. Pa. 1996) (answer should set forth the efforts used to attempt to obtain the requested information).

[25] *United States ex rel. Martino-Fleming v. S. Bay Mental Health Ctr., Inc.*, 332 F.R.D. 1, 6 (D. Mass. 2019).

[26] *V5 Techs. v. Switch, Ltd.*, 334 F.R.D. 297, 305 (D. Nev. 2019); *Lawman v. City of San Francisco*, 159 F. Supp. 3d 1130, 1140 (D.D.C. 2016).

[27] *Chelsey Nelson Photography LLC v. Louisville/Jefferson Cnty. Metro Gov't*, 556 F. Supp. 3d 657, 679 (W.D. Ky. 2021).

[28] *See Rachel v. Troutt*, 820 F.3d 390, 394 (10th Cir. 2016); *Nasreen v. Capitol Petroleum Grp., LLC*, 340 F.R.D. 489, 493 (D.D.C. 2022).

[29] *See Mulero-Abreu v. Puerto Rico Police Dept.*, 675 F.3d 88, 90 (1st Cir. 2012); *CRST Expedited, Inc. v. Swift*

Who Answers

Technically, the party answers the interrogatories,[30] not the party's attorney (although it is common practice for the attorney to draft the answers, and some courts allow the attorney to sign the answers[31]). The attorney interposes the objections.[32] If the party is a corporation or organization, an officer or agent[33] will answer for the corporation.[34] The answering officer or agent need not have first-hand knowledge of the information being provided.[35] However, the responding agent's answers must provide the composite knowledge available to the party.[36] If the party is incompetent, the party's attorney or guardian may answer.[37]

Verification

Interrogatory answers must include a signed verification or affidavit attesting to the accuracy of the answers.[38] When the party is an individual, the party, not the attorney, must sign the verification.[39] This is one of the few exceptions to the general principle under the Federal Rules of Civil Procedure that the attorney may sign all pleadings and papers. A representative of a corporate party may verify interrogatory answers without personal knowledge of every response by furnishing the information available to the corporation.[40] The courts generally allow an attorney to verify interrogatory answers for a corporation.[41] If the responding party makes objections, the at-

---

Transportation Co. of Arizona, LLC, 328 F.R.D. 231, 235 (N.D. Iowa 2018) (court has discretion to consider untimely objections).

[30] *Lopez v. Don Herring Ltd.*, 327 F.R.D. 567, 579 (N.D. Tex. 2018); *Huthnance v. District of Columbia*, 255 F.R.D. 297, 300 (D.D.C. 2008).

[31] *See Assessment Techs. Inst., LLC v. Parkes*, __ F. Supp. 3d __, 2022 WL 1102461, at *4 (D. Kan. 2022).

[32] *Superior Sales W., Inc. v. Gonzalez*, 335 F.R.D. 98, 103 (W.D. Tex. 2020).

[33] *Wilson v. Volkswagen of Am., Inc.*, 561 F.2d 494, 508 (4th Cir. 1977) (attorney may serve as agent).

[34] *General Dynamics Corp. v. Selb Mfg. Co.*, 481 F.2d 1204 (8th Cir. 1973); *Lopez v. Don Herring Ltd.*, 327 F.R.D. 567, 579 (N.D. Tex. 2018).

[35] *Jiminez-Carillo v. Autopart Intern., Inc.*, 285 F.R.D. 668, 670 (S.D. Fla. 2012); *Brown v. White's Ferry, Inc.*, 280 F.R.D. 238, 242–43 (D. Md. 2012).

[36] *Jiminez-Carillo v. Autopart Intern., Inc.*, 285 F.R.D. 668, 670 (S.D. Fla. 2012); *Law v. National Collegiate Athletic Ass'n*, 167 F.R.D. 464, 476 (D. Kan. 1996).

[37] *Hall v. Hague*, 34 F.R.D. 449 (D. Md. 1964).

[38] *United States v. $284,950.00 in U.S. Currency*, 933 F.3d 971, 974 (8th Cir. 2019); *In re World Trade Center Disaster Site Litig.*, 722 F.3d 483, 485 (2d Cir. 2013) (if the signature is not under oath, it does not satisfy Rule 33(b)).

[39] *Lopez v. Don Herring Ltd.*, 327 F.R.D. 567, 579 (N.D. Tex. 2018); *Sprint Commc'n Co. L.P. v. Crow Creek Sioux Tribal Court*, 316 F.R.D. 254, 273 (D.S.D. 2016).

[40] *Suzuki v. Abiomed, Inc.*, 943 F.3d 555, 565 (1st Cir. 2019); *Shepherd v. Am. Broad. Co., Inc.*, 62 F.3d 1469, 1482 (D.C. Cir. 1995).

[41] *Rea v. Wichita Mortg. Corp.*, 747 F.2d 567, 574 n.6 (10th Cir. 1984); *Wood v. Credit One Bank*, 277 F. Supp. 3d 821, 831 (E.D. Va. 2017).

torney must sign the response.[42]

Objections

If the responding party believes that a particular interrogatory is outside the scope of discovery or otherwise improper, the party may object to the question in lieu of answering it or in conjunction with an answer that takes the objection into account.[43] The objection must be made in writing, must state the grounds of the objection with specificity,[44] and must be signed by the attorney for the responding party.[45] Many courts hold that general or boilerplate objections are ineffective.[46] Some common objections are:

- *Overly broad, unduly vague, and ambiguous:* When a question is written so broadly that it extends to information not relevant to the claims or defenses in the matter (such as a question not limited in time to the events relevant to the complaint), the question may be overly broad.[47] When a question is susceptible to numerous meanings, it may be unduly vague and ambiguous. In general, these objections are probably not justification for refusing to answer a question altogether, but the responding party can raise the objection, then expressly limit the scope of the response.
- *Burdensome and oppressive:* In general, the responding party must produce the information available without *undue* effort or expense (recognizing that all discovery responses require some effort and expense). Thus, questions that require extensive research, compilation of data, or evaluation of data may be objectionable.[48] The responding party is not required to prepare the adverse party's case. Likewise, an interrogatory that seeks a

[42] *Superior Sales W., Inc. v. Gonzalez*, 335 F.R.D. 98, 103 (W.D. Tex. 2020).

[43] *Superior Sales W., Inc. v. Gonzalez*, 335 F.R.D. 98, 103 (W.D. Tex. 2020). *But see Gassaway v. Jarden Corp.*, 292 F.R.D. 676, 681–82 (D. Kan. 2013) (holding that a party who objects to and answers an interrogatory waives the objections. Note, however, that this appears to be an outlier position).

[44] *See Mulero-Abreu v. Puerto Rico Police Dept.*, 675 F.3d 88, 93 (1st Cir. 2012) (blanket objection improper); *Delta T, LLC v. Williams*, 337 F.R.D. 395, 399 (S.D. Ohio 2021).

[45] *CRST Expedited, Inc. v. Swift Transportation Co. of Arizona, LLC*, 328 F.R.D. 231, 235 (N.D. Iowa 2018); *Heller v. City of Dallas*, 303 F.R.D. 466, 484 (N.D. Tex. 2014).

[46] *See Nei v. Travelers Home & Marine Ins. Co.*, 326 F.R.D. 652, 656 (D. Mont. 2018); *Siser N. Am., Inc. v. Herika G. Inc.*, 325 F.R.D. 200, 209–10 (E.D. Mich. 2018).

[47] *Jewish Hospital Ass'n of Louisville, Ky. v. Struck Const. Co., Inc.*, 77 F.R.D. 59 (W.D. Ky. 1978).

[48] *IBP, Inc. v. Mercantile Bank of Topeka*, 179 F.R.D. 316, 321 (D. Kan. 1998) (interrogatory asking for every fact and application of law to fact supporting claim held burdensome).

high level of detail may be overly burdensome.[49]

- *Privileged information:* Questions that seek information protected by the attorney-client privilege or by another privilege are objectionable. When privileged information is withheld, the responding party must explicitly state the objection and describe the nature of the information not provided sufficiently to enable other parties to assess the applicability of the privilege. Care should be exercised in responding to such interrogatories, because the privilege may be waived by revealing part or all of the privileged communication.
- *Not proportional to the needs of the case:* A party may object that an interrogatory seeks information that is not proportional to the needs of the case, in light of the factors listed in Rule 26(b)(1).

Failure to Object Is Waiver

All grounds for objection must be specifically stated in a timely response or they are waived.[50] The court may excuse the failure to make timely objections for "good cause."[51]

Objection to Part of Interrogatory

If only some aspects of an interrogatory are objectionable, the responding party must answer the interrogatory to the extent that it is not objectionable.[52] Thus, if an interrogatory is overly broad, the responding party should provide information responsive to the interrogatory as if narrowed so as not to be overly broad.[53] A number of courts have held that the common practice of objecting, then answering "subject to and without waiving" the objections is improper and waives the objections unless the response describes in particularity the information not being provided.[54]

Discretion of Court

The district court has extremely broad discretion in ruling on objections to interrogatories.[55]

---

[49]*See Mach. Sols., Inc. v. Doosan Infracore Am. Corp.*, 323 F.R.D. 522, 528 (D.S.C. 2018) (interrogatory seeking "all facts" was unduly burdensome); *Ritchie Risk-Linked Strategies Trading (Ireland), Ltd. v. Coventry First LLC*, 273 F.R.D. 367, 369 (S.D.N.Y. 2010).

[50]*Friedman v. Live Nation Merch., Inc.*, 833 F.3d 1180, 1185 n.2 (9th Cir. 2016); *In re 650 Fifth Avenue and Related Properties*, 830 F.3d 66, 99 n.30 (2d Cir. 2016).

[51]*Nasreen v. Capitol Petroleum Grp., LLC*, 340 F.R.D. 489, 494 (D.D.C. 2022).

[52]*Mondragon v. Scott Farms, Inc.*, 329 F.R.D. 533, 541 n.2 (E.D.N.C. 2019); *Samsung Elec. Am. Inc. v. Yang Kun "Michael" Chung*, 325 F.R.D. 578, 590 (N.D. Tex. 2017).

[53]*See Walls v. Int'l Paper Co.*, 192 F.R.D. 294 (D. Kan. 2000).

[54]*See Lopez v. Don Herring Ltd.*, 327 F.R.D. 567, 592 (N.D. Tex. 2018); *Heller v. City of Dallas*, 303 F.R.D. 466, 488–90 (N.D. Tex. 2014).

[55]*Mack v. Great Atlantic and Pacific Tea Co., Inc.*, 871 F.2d 179, 186 (1st Cir. 1989).

Rulings on Objections Not Immediately Appealable

The court's rulings on objections to interrogatories are not final orders, and cannot be appealed until the conclusion of the case.

Motion for a Protective Order

As an alternative to making objections to individual questions, the responding party may make a motion for a protective order under Rule 26(c). A motion for a protective order is appropriate when most or all of a set of interrogatories is too burdensome or cumulative. The burden is on the moving party to show good cause for the protective order.[56] Motions for protective orders in response to interrogatories are not common because it is easier and less expensive to interpose objections, and the burden is then on the opposing party to file a motion to compel under Rule 37(a), as discussed below.

Motion to Compel

If the responding party fails to answer sufficiently or objects to an interrogatory, the propounding party may file a motion to compel under Rule 37(a).[57] The burden is on the moving party to demonstrate that the responses were incomplete,[58] and the burden is on the responding party (the non-moving party) to convince the court that the interrogatories were objectionable.[59]

Sanctions for Failure to Answer

If a party files no response to an interrogatory (as opposed to an insufficient response as discussed above), the court may impose the sanctions specified in Rule 37(b)(2), such as deeming certain facts established or refusing to allow the party to oppose or support certain claims.[60]

Sanctions for Untrue Answers

If an answer is untrue, either at the time it was made or subsequently, and is not corrected by supplementation, the court may exclude evidence related to the topic or make whatever order justice requires.[61] The person signing the verification may also be subject to sanctions for making a false verification.

Duty to Supplement

A party must supplement its response to an interrogatory if the party learns that the response is in some material respect

---

[56] *BPP Retail Properties, LLC v. North Am. Roofing Serv., Inc.*, 300 F.R.D. 59, 61 (D.P.R. 2014).

[57] *Nasreen v. Capitol Petroleum Grp., LLC*, 340 F.R.D. 489, 493 (D.D.C. 2022); *Areizaga v. ADW Corp.*, 314 F.R.D. 428, 433 (N.D. Tex. 2016).

[58] *Haynes v. Navy Fed. Credit Union*, 286 F.R.D. 33, 37 (D.D.C. 2012).

[59] *Autoridad de Carreteras y Transportacion v. Transcore Atlantic, Inc.*, 319 F.R.D. 422, 427 (D.P.R 2016); *Areizaga v. ADW Corp.*, 314 F.R.D. 428, 434 (N.D. Tex. 2016).

[60] *See* Rule 37(d).

[61] *Garcia v. Berkshire Life Ins. Co. of Am.*, 569 F.3d 1174, 1180 (10th Cir. 2009) (dismissing the case based on fabrications).

incomplete or incorrect and if the additional or corrective information has not been provided to the other parties in writing or at a deposition.[62] Supplemental responses must be verified just like original responses.[63]

Requests for Documents

Interrogatories may not be used to obtain documents[64] or authorizations.[65] Rather, a document request must be made under Rule 34. However, interrogatories may inquire about the existence of documents and the facts contained in documents. Furthermore, the responding party has the option, under certain circumstances, to produce documents in lieu of answering an interrogatory, as discussed below under Rule 33(d).

RULE 33(c)—USE

CORE CONCEPT

Interrogatory answers are not binding admissions, but generally may be used in the same manner as statements made in court by the party.

APPLICATIONS

Use of Interrogatory Answers at Trial

Answers to interrogatories may be used at trial or in support of a motion. They are treated like any other evidence, and may be offered and admitted into evidence as allowed by the Federal Rules of Evidence.[66] Interrogatory answers are generally not hearsay with respect to the party making the answer because they are party admissions.[67] However, they may be hearsay if offered against another party. Interrogatory answers may be objected to on any other grounds, such as relevance. If only part of an answer is read, the responding party may require that other parts of the answer be admitted at the same time in order to provide the full context for the portion offered.[68]

Answers Not Binding

Interrogatory answers are not binding admissions;[69] a party may take a different position at trial unless it would prejudice

[62]*See Covad Commc'n Co. v. Revonet, Inc.*, 258 F.R.D. 17 (D.D.C. 2009).

[63]*Lopez v. Don Herring Ltd.*, 327 F.R.D. 567, 591 (N.D. Tex. 2018); *Knights Armament Co. v. Optical Systems Technology, Inc.*, 254 F.R.D. 463, 466 (M.D. Fla. 2008).

[64]*Alltmont v. U.S.*, 177 F.2d 971 (3d Cir. 1949).

[65]*Mir v. L-3 Commc'n Integrated Sys., L.P.*, 319 F.R.D. 220, 227 (N.D. Tex. 2016).

[66]*AMCO Ins. Co. v. Inspired Techs., Inc.*, 648 F.3d 875, 881 (8th Cir. 2011); *Heller v. City of Dallas*, 303 F.R.D. 466, 474 (N.D. Tex. 2014).

[67]*Underberg v. U.S.*, 362 F. Supp. 2d 1278, 1283 (D.N.M. 2005).

[68]*Grace & Co. v. City of Los Angeles*, 278 F.2d 771 (9th Cir.1960).

[69]*Bradley v. Allstate Ins. Co.*, 620 F.3d 509, 527 n.21 (5th Cir. 2010).

another party.[70] Opposing parties may then impeach by questioning the reason for the changed answer. Additionally, a party can supplement or amend its answers in ways that materially change them, and is obligated to do so under certain circumstances discussed above under Rule 26(e).

Use of Interrogatory Answers in a Summary Judgment Motion

Interrogatory answers may be used in support of or in opposition to a motion for summary judgment, as provided in Rule 56(c).[71]

RULE 33(d)—OPTION TO PRODUCE BUSINESS RECORDS

CORE CONCEPT

A party may produce business records in lieu of answering an interrogatory when requested information is located in the records and the burden of extracting the requested information would be substantially equal for either party.

APPLICATIONS

Business Records Only

Only business records of the responding party may be used in lieu of interrogatory answers.[72] Thus, a party cannot produce pleadings[73] or deposition transcripts[74] or refer to the administrative record[75] or public sources of information instead of answering an interrogatory.

Records Must Contain the Information

In order to respond to an interrogatory by producing business records, a party must affirmatively state that the records contain the requested information;[76] it is not sufficient to state that the records *may* contain the information.[77]

Identify Specific Records

A party responding to an interrogatory by producing busi-

[70] *Sunshine Heifers, LLC v. Moohaven Dairy, LLC*, 13 F. Supp. 3d 770, 778 (E.D. Mich. 2014).

[71] *Bradley v. Allstate Ins. Co.*, 620 F.3d 509, 527 n. 21 (5th Cir. 2010); *McSparren v. Pennsylvania*, 289 F. Supp. 3d 616, 626 n.3 (M.D. Pa. 2018).

[72] *U.S. ex rel. Landis v. Tailwind Sports Corp.*, 317 F.R.D. 592, 595 (D.D.C. 2016).

[73] *Melius v. National Indian Gaming Com'n*, 2000 WL 1174994 (D.D.C. 2000).

[74] *VeroBlue Farms USA Inc. v. Wulf*, — F.R.D. —, 2021 WL 5176839, at *28 (N.D. Tex. 2021); *U.S. ex rel. Landis v. Tailwind Sports Corp.*, 317 F.R.D. 592, 595 (D.D.C. 2016).

[75] *Mullins v. Prudential Ins. Co. of Am.*, 267 F.R.D. 504, 514 (W.D. Ky. 2010).

[76] *See U.S. ex rel. Landis v. Tailwind Sports Corp.*, 317 F.R.D. 592, 595 (D.D.C. 2016); *Nature's Plus Nordic A/S v. Natural Organics, Inc.*, 274 F.R.D. 437, 440–41 (E.D.N.Y. 2011) (documents in foreign language do not contain the information as contemplated by Rule 32(d)).

[77] *Daiflon, Inc. v. Allied Chem. Corp.*, 534 F.2d 221 (10th Cir. 1976).

ness records must provide sufficient detail so that the propounding party can identify which individual documents contain the information requested.[78] The responding party may not identify a huge volume of documents making it infeasible for the requesting party to determine the answer.[79]

Equal Burden to Derive the Answer

In order to respond to interrogatories by producing business records, the burden of deriving or ascertaining the answer must be substantially equal for the requesting party and the producing party.[80]

Burden of Proof

The responding party bears the initial burden of demonstrating the criteria for producing documents in lieu of answering an interrogatory.[81] If the requesting party challenges the equality of the burden to derive the answer, it will have the burden of establishing that its burden would be greater than the responding party's.[82]

Contention Interrogatories

A number of courts have held that a party may not refer to documents in lieu of responding to contention interrogatories, as the responding party's contentions are not likely to be found in business records.[83]

Privileged Documents

A party cannot elect to identify business records in lieu of responding to an interrogatory and then withhold the records as privileged.[84]

Expense of Compiling Records

In its discretion, the court may, upon motion for a protective order under Rule 26(c), require the requesting party to pay

---

[78] *Alexsam, Inc. v. IDT Corp.*, 715 F.3d 1336, 1344 (Fed. Cir. 2013); *VeroBlue Farms USA Inc. v. Wulf*, — F.R.D. —, 2021 WL 5176839, at *27 (N.D. Tex. 2021).

[79] *VeroBlue Farms USA Inc. v. Wulf*, — F.R.D. —, 2021 WL 5176839, at *27 (N.D. Tex. 2021); *United States ex rel. Martino-Fleming v. S. Bay Mental Health Ctr., Inc.*, 332 F.R.D. 1, 6 (D. Mass. 2019).

[80] *U.S. ex rel. Landis v. Tailwind Sports Corp.*, 317 F.R.D. 592, 594 (D.D.C. 2016); *Lawman v. City of San Francisco*, 159 F. Supp. 3d 1130, 1140 (D.D.C. 2016).

[81] *U.S. S.E.C. v. Elfindepan, S.A.*, 206 F.R.D. 574, 577 (M.D. N.C. 2002).

[82] *United States ex rel. Martino-Fleming v. S. Bay Mental Health Ctr., Inc.*, 332 F.R.D. 1, 6 (D. Mass. 2019).

[83] *United States ex rel. Martino-Fleming v. S. Bay Mental Health Ctr., Inc.*, 332 F.R.D. 1, 9–10 (D. Mass. 2019); *U.S. ex rel. Landis v. Tailwind Sports Corp.*, 317 F.R.D. 592, 594 (D.D.C. 2016); *but see Ayers v. Cont'l Cas. Co.*, 240 F.R.D. 216, 227 (N.D.W. Va. 2007) (allowing the use of Rule 33(d) in response to contention interrogatories).

[84] *Vazquez-Fernandez v. Cambridge College, Inc.*, 269 F.R.D. 150, 158 (D.P.R. 2010).

the responding party's cost of compiling the records.[85]

Motion to Compel

If the requesting party believes that its burden to find the answers from the records is substantially greater than that of the responding party or that the responding party's use of Rule 33(d) is otherwise improper, the requesting party can file a motion to compel an answer.[86] The court may find the burden not substantially the same, yet nonetheless deny the motion to compel if the court finds that the burden on the responding party to answer fully would be excessive or unreasonable.[87]

Additional Research References

Wright & Miller, *Federal Practice and Procedure* §§ 2161 to 2182
C.J.S., Federal Civil Procedure §§ 645 to 695 et seq.
West's Key Number Digest, Federal Civil Procedure ⚷1471 to 1542

---

[85] *See* Rule 26(c) (detail on costs).

[86] *See United States ex rel. Martino-Fleming v. S. Bay Mental Health Ctr., Inc.*, 332 F.R.D. 1, 3 (D. Mass. 2019); *Maxtena, Inc. v. Marks*, 289 F.R.D. 427, 437 (D. Md. 2012).

[87] The Advisory Committee Note to the 1970 amendment of Rule 33(c).

RULE 34
PRODUCING DOCUMENTS, ELECTRONICALLY STORED INFORMATION, AND TANGIBLE THINGS, OR ENTERING ONTO LAND, FOR INSPECTION AND OTHER PURPOSES

(a) **In General.** A party may serve on any other party a request within the scope of Rule 26(b):

(1) to produce and permit the requesting party or its representative to inspect, copy, test, or sample the following items in the responding party's possession, custody, or control:

(A) any designated documents or electronically stored information—including writings, drawings, graphs, charts, photographs, sound recordings, images, and other data or data compilations—stored in any medium from which information can be obtained either directly or, if necessary, after translation by the responding party into a reasonably usable form; or

(B) any designated tangible things; or

(2) to permit entry onto designated land or other property possessed or controlled by the responding party, so that the requesting party may inspect, measure, survey, photograph, test, or sample the property or any designated object or operation on it.

(b) **Procedure.**

(1) *Contents of the Request.* The request:

(A) must describe with reasonable particularity each item or category of items to be inspected;

(B) must specify a reasonable time, place, and manner for the inspection and for performing the related acts; and

(C) may specify the form or forms in which electronically stored information is to be produced.

(2) *Responses and Objections.*

(A) *Time to Respond.* The party to whom the request is directed must respond in writing within 30 days after being served or — if the request was delivered under Rule 26(d)(2) — within 30 days after the parties' first Rule 26(f) conference. A shorter or longer time may be stipulated to under Rule 29 or be ordered by the court.

(B) *Responding to Each Item.* For each item or category, the response must either state that inspection and related activities will be permitted as requested or state with specificity the grounds for objecting to the request, including the reasons. The responding party may state that it will produce copies of documents or of electronically stored information instead of permitting inspection. The production must then be completed no later than the time for inspection specified in the request or another reasonable time specified in the response.

(C) *Objections.* An objection must state whether any responsive materials are being withheld on the basis of that objection. An objection to part of a request must specify the part and permit inspection of the rest.

(D) *Responding to a Request for Production of Electronically Stored Information.* The response may state an objection to a requested form for producing electronically stored information. If the responding party objects to a requested form—or if no form was specified in the request—the party must state the form or forms it intends to use.

(E) *Producing the Documents or Electronically Stored Information.* Unless otherwise stipulated or ordered by the court, these procedures apply to producing documents or electronically stored information:

(i) A party must produce documents as they are kept in the usual course of business or must organize and label them to correspond to the categories in the request;

(ii) If a request does not specify a form for producing electronically stored information, a party must produce it in a form or forms in which it is ordinarily maintained or in a reasonably usable form or forms; and

(iii) A party need not produce the same electronically stored information in more than one form.

(c) **Nonparties.** As provided in Rule 45, a nonparty may be compelled to produce documents and tangible things or to permit an inspection.

[Amended December 27, 1946, effective March 19, 1948; March 30, 1970, effective July 1, 1970; April 29, 1980, effective August 1, 1980; March 2, 1987, effective August 1, 1987; April 30, 1991, effective December 1, 1991; April 22, 1993, effective December 1, 1993; April 12, 2006, effective December 1, 2006; April 30, 2007, effective December 1, 2007; April 29, 2015, effective December 1, 2015.]

AUTHORS' COMMENTARY ON RULE 34

PURPOSE AND SCOPE

Rule 34 sets forth the procedures for obtaining access to documents and tangible things (such as an allegedly defective product) within the "possession, custody, or control" of other parties, and for gaining entry onto other parties' land for inspection. Although the Rule authorizes requests for inspection of tangible things and property, it is most commonly used to obtain access to documents and many attorneys refer to Rule 34 production requests as "document requests" (and this text may use that term).

The scope of document requests, like all discovery generally, is controlled by Rule 26(b)(1), and extends to any nonprivileged matter relevant to a party's claim or defense and proportional to the needs of the case. However, Rule 34 contains another important scope concept; it extends to all documents in the responding party's "possession, custody, or control." This phrase is broadly framed to ensure full access to relevant documents. It essentially means that parties cannot refuse to produce documents in their files by arguing that the documents actually belong to someone else, nor can they shield documents by turning them over to someone else; if the party retains control over the documents (*i.e.*, can get them back by asking), then the party must produce them.

Recognizing the importance of electronic media in modern society, Rule 34 contains a number of provisions addressing the production of "electronically stored information," commonly referred to as "ESI." The Rules are drafted both broadly and in general terms to encompass all forms of electronic data in a world where methods of electronic communication emerge so rapidly that the Rules could not be amended quickly enough to describe them specifically.

Not only is the discovery of ESI important, however, it adds cost and complexity to the process. ESI is typically gathered using computers to search for and select responsive documents, either through search terms or more "intelligent" algorithms. Parties often use computer programs to review and organize the documents that are relevant to the litigation, and the format in which documents are produced becomes important—a program may work better with pdfs, jpegs, or documents in their native format. In some cases, "metadata"—the hidden data that many programs store about files, such as the author, date of creation, date of last modification, etc.—is important, and the manner of producing ESI may affect whether metadata is preserved and produced.

Rule 34 contains a number of provisions to address these ESI complications. It authorizes early service of document requests so that the parties may identify and address ESI problems or disputes in their Rule 26(f) discovery conference or in an early conference with the judge. It also authorizes the requesting party to specify the format in which the responding party should produce the ESI, and allows the responding party to object to that format. Other more general protections relating to ESI are found in Rule 26.

The recipient must respond to document requests within 30 days, although stipulated extensions are common. The response often consists of a mixture of objections and statements regarding whether the responding party has responsive documents. Unlike interrogatory responses, only the attorney signs the response to document requests; the responding party does not sign a verification for responses to document requests. If a party objects to a document request, the response must both: 1) state the objection with specificity; and 2) state whether the responding party is withholding any documents on the basis of the objection. These requirements allow the requesting party to evaluate whether to challenge the objection with a motion to compel under Rule 37(a).

In addition to the written response, the responding party must provide the responsive documents. Rule 34 establishes two options. First, the party may make the documents available for the requesting party to inspect. The requesting party may then arrange for copies as it sees fit. Alternatively, the responding party may simply make copies of the responsive documents and provide them to the requesting party.

Rule 34 also establishes two options for organizing the responsive documents. First, the party may "label them to correspond to the categories in the request." Typically, parties put unique identifying numbers on each page of each document they are producing to create a record of what they have produced. They then use these numbers to inform the requesting party which documents were responsive to each document request. Alternatively, parties may produce documents "as they are kept in the ordinary course of business." Under this approach, a party might allow an opponent to access the party's files to conduct its own search for responsive documents.

NOTE: Rule 34 was substantially revised in 2015 and great care should be exercised when citing decisions pertaining to Rule 34.

RULE 34(a)—IN GENERAL

CORE CONCEPT

A party may serve a document request on another party, which compels the responding party to search for and produce all responsive, nonprivileged documents relevant to any party's claim or defense in its "possession, custody, or control," unless it was prepared in anticipation of litigation, pertains to expert witnesses, or would be disproportionate to the needs of the case or unreasonably burdensome to produce.

APPLICATIONS

Scope

The scope of document requests and other discovery under Rule 34 is the broad discovery available under Rule 26.[1] Generally, any nonprivileged document relevant to any party's claim or defense is discoverable unless it was prepared in anticipation of litigation, it pertains to expert witnesses, or producing it would be disproportional to the needs of the case or unreasonably burdensome to produce.

Documents

"Documents" is broadly defined to include all forms of recorded information. Rule 34(a) specifically lists writings, drawings, graphs, charts, photographs, phonorecords, and other data compilations.[2]

Electronically Stored Information

Rule 34(a) specifically includes "electronically stored information" (commonly referred to as "ESI") among the categories

---

[1] *Hernandez v. Results Staffing, Inc.*, 907 F.3d 354, 361 (5th Cir. 2018).

[2] *Paisley Park Enterprises, Inc. v. Boxill*, 330 F.R.D. 226, 234 (D. Minn. 2019); *Zenith Ins. Co. v. Texas Inst. for Surgery, L.L.P.*, 328 F.R.D. 153, 160 (N.D. Tex. 2018).

of documents and things that must be produced.[3] ESI is intended to be a broad and flexible term encompassing email, electronic files, and information "stored in any medium."[4] For more information about the discovery of ESI, see the Sedona Principles: Best Practices, Recommendations & Principles for Addressing Electronic Document Production, Third Edition,[5] upon which the courts have come to rely.[6]

Metadata

One particular form of electronically stored information that has drawn considerable attention in litigation is metadata (data about data), which describes the data that many programs store about documents created in the program, such as the identity of the author, when the document was created, the identity of those editing the document, and when those edits occurred.[7] Some courts have adopted local rules addressing the production of metadata.[8] Metadata raises a host of issues (including preservation or destruction of metadata and potential attorney-client privilege issues),[9] and should be discussed during the Rule 26(f) conference. A party seeking metadata should specifically request it.[10]

No Duty to Create Documents

Generally, a party is not required to create documents meeting the document requests, only to produce documents already in existence.[11] However, a party may be required to query an

---

[3]*In re Actos Antitrust Litig.*, 340 F.R.D. 549, 551 (S.D.N.Y. 2022); *U.S. ex rel. Carter v. Bridgepoint Educ., Inc.*, 305 F.R.D. 225, 236 (S.D. Cal. 2015).

[4]*See Paisley Park Enterprises, Inc. v. Boxill*, 330 F.R.D. 226, 234 (D. Minn. 2019) (text messages); *In the Matter of the Search of Information Associated with Email Addresses Stored at Premises Controlled by the Microsoft Corp.*, 212 F. Supp. 30 1023, 1035 (D. Kan. 2016).

[5]19 Sedona Conf. J. 1 (2018), available at https://thesedonaconference.org/sites/default/files/publications/The%20Sedona%20Principles%20Third%20Edition.19TSCJ1.pdf.

[6]*See, e.g., John B. v. Goetz*, 531 F.3d 448, 460 (6th Cir. 2008) (referring to the second edition).

[7]*CBT Flint Partners, LLC v. Return Path, Inc.*, 737 F.3d 1320, 1328 n.2 (Fed. Cir. 2013); The Sedona Principles: Best Practices, Recommendations & Principles for Addressing Electronic Document Production, Third Edition, 19 Sedona Conf. J. 1, 169 (2018), available at https://thesedonaconference.org/sites/default/files/publications/The%20Sedona%20Principles%20Third%20Edition.19TSCJ1.pdf.

[8]*See, e.g., Black Love Resists In the Rust by & through Soto v. City of Buffalo, N.Y.*, 334 F.R.D. 23, 30 (W.D.N.Y. 2019).

[9]*See, e.g., U.S. ex rel. Carter v. Bridgepoint Educ., Inc.*, 305 F.R.D. 225, 245–46 (S.D. Cal. 2015); *Southern New England Telephone Co. v. Global NAPs, Inc.*, 251 F.R.D. 82, 89 (D. Conn. 2008).

[10]*See U.S. ex rel. Carter v. Bridgepoint Educ., Inc.*, 305 F.R.D. 225, 245–46 (S.D. Cal. 2015) (most courts only order production of metadata if sought in the initial request); *Covad Commc'n Co. v. Revonet, Inc.*, 267 F.R.D. 14, 18 (D.D.C. 2010).

[11]*Lynch v. Experian Info. Sols., Inc.*, 569 F. Supp. 3d 959, 967 (D. Minn. 2021); *Castleberry v. Camden Cty.*, 331 F.R.D. 559, 564 n.5 (S.D. Ga.

existing database for relevant information.[12]

Tangible Things

Rule 34 allows a party to inspect and copy, test, or sample tangible things relevant to the action (*e.g.*, the allegedly defective product in a products liability case).[13] If the requested testing is destructive, courts balance the burdens of altering the object against the benefits of obtaining the evidence sought, requiring that the information gained from the destructive testing be integral to proving the requesting party's case rather than just strengthening an already established claim or defense.[14] Rule 34 does not state whether the responding party has the right to have a representative present during the inspection, which is left to the court's discretion.[15]

Property

A party has the right to enter onto another party's land to inspect, measure, survey, photograph, test, or sample property or a designated object or operation if relevant to the pending action.[16] The persons conducting the inspection do not have a right to question the representatives of the party whose property is being inspected.[17]

Parties Only

Only parties are obligated to respond to document requests.[18] Documents may be obtained from nonparties by a subpoena under Rule 45.[19]

Documents Within a Party's Possession, Custody, or Control

A party must produce all discoverable documents or things responsive to a request that are in the party's "possession, custody, or control."[20] Control means the legal or practical right

2019). *But see Harris v. Athol-Royalston Regional School District Comm.*, 200 F.R.D. 18 (D. Mass. 2001) (party required to create a handwriting exemplar).

[12] *N. Shore-Long Island Jewish Health Sys., Inc. v. MultiPlan, Inc.*, 325 F.R.D. 36, 51 (E.D.N.Y. 2018).

[13] *Ramos v. Carter Exp. Inc.*, 292 F.R.D. 406, 408 (S.D. Tex. 2013); *Harris v. Athol-Royalston Regional School Dist. Comm.*, 206 F.R.D. 30, 32–33 (D. Mass. 2002) (fingerprint samples may be obtained under either Rule 34 or Rule 35).

[14] *Komar Investments, Inc. v. Zurich Am. Ins. Co.*, 331 F.R.D. 181, 183–184 (S.D. Fla. 2019).

[15] *See Smith v. Nexus RVs, LLC*, 331 F.R.D. 491, 495 (N.D. Ind. 2019).

[16] *Albany Bank & Trust Co. v. Exxon Mobil Corp.*, 310 F.3d 969, 974 (7th Cir. 2002); *DuPonte v. Coyne-Fague*, 384 F. Supp. 3d 225, 227 (D.R.I. 2019).

[17] *U.S. v. Territory of the Virgin Islands*, 280 F.R.D. 232, 236–37 (D. Virgin Islands 2012).

[18] *See Hobley v. Burge*, 433 F.3d 946, 949 (7th Cir. 2006); *Puerto Rico Med. Emergency Group, Inc. v. Iglesia Episcopal Puertorriqueña, Inc.*, 318 F.R.D. 224, 232 (D.P.R. 2016).

[19] *Hobley v. Burge*, 433 F.3d 946, 949 (7th Cir. 2006).

[20] *Kissinger v. Reporters Comm. for Freedom of the Press*, 445 U.S. 136, 166 (1980); *Wiwa v. Royal Dutch Petro-*

to obtain the documents on demand.[21] A party's ability to access the documents in the normal course of business weighs in favor of finding control.[22] Documents held by the party's attorney,[23] expert,[24] insurance company,[25] healthcare provider,[26] accountant,[27] bank,[28] spouse,[29] contractor,[30] officer,[31] or agent[32] are deemed to be within the party's control. Likewise, documents held by a subsidiary, affiliated corporation, or branch office may be within a party's control.[33] Electronic documents on the server of a third-party provider, such as text messages or emails, are within the party's control.[34] Documents held by one governmental agency may be within the control of another agency if the agencies are cooperating in a joint investigation.[35] Documents owned by a third person but possessed by a party are within the party's custody.[36] When documents are located outside the United States, the application of "possession, custody, or control" becomes complex, and may implicate discovery treaties.[37] The courts are divided as to whether a party will be deemed to have possession, custody, or control of documents which the party may release by authorization, such

---

leum Co., 392 F.3d 812, 821 (5th Cir. 2004).

[21] *Thermal Design, Inc. v. Am. Soc'y of Heating Refrigerating and Air-Conditioning Eng'rs, Inc.*, 755 F.3d 832, 839 (7th Cir. 2014); *Robinson v. Moskus*, 491 F. Supp. 3d 359, 360 (C.D. Ill. 2020).

[22] *Bhasker v. Kemper Cas. Ins. Co.*, 361 F. Supp. 3d 1045, 1118 (D.N.M. 2019).

[23] *Cicel (Beijing) Sci. & Tech. Co. v. Misonix, Inc.*, 331 F.R.D. 218, 236 (E.D.N.Y. 2019); *Bhasker v. Kemper Cas. Ins. Co.*, 361 F. Supp. 3d 1045, 1118 (D.N.M. 2019).

[24] *Raimey v. Wright Nat. Flood Ins. Co.*, 76 F. Supp. 3d 452, 456 (E.D.N.Y. 2014).

[25] *Henderson v. Zurn Ind., Inc.*, 131 F.R.D. 560, 567 (S.D. Ind. 1990).

[26] *Landry v. Swire Oilfield Servs., L.L.C.*, 323 F.R.D. 360, 382 (D.N.M. 2018).

[27] *Wardrip v. Hart*, 934 F. Supp. 1282, 1286, 18 A.D.D. 447 (D. Kan. 1996).

[28] *Merchia v. United States Internal Revenue Serv.*, 336 F.R.D. 396, 399 (D. Mass. 2020).

[29] *Monroe's Estate v. Bottle Rock Power Corp.*, 2004 WL 737463 (E.D. La. 2004).

[30] *Mercy Catholic Medical Center v. Thompson*, 380 F.3d 142, 160 (3d Cir. 2004).

[31] *Flagg v. City of Detroit*, 252 F.R.D. 346, 353 (E.D. Mich. 2008).

[32] *Am. Rock Salt Co., LLC v. Norfolk Southern Corp.*, 228 F.R.D. 426, 457 (W.D.N.Y. 2004).

[33] *Equal Emp. Opportunity Comm'n v. Heart of CarDon, LLC*, 339 F.R.D. 602, 606 (S.D. Ind. 2021); *Coventry Capital US LLC v. EEA Life Settlements Inc.*, 334 F.R.D. 68, 73 (S.D.N.Y. 2020).

[34] *See Torrey v. Infectious Diseases Soc'y of Am.*, 334 F.R.D. 79, 85–86 (E.D. Tex. 2019); *Flagg v. City of Detroit*, 252 F.R.D. 346, 352–53 (E.D. Mich. 2008) (text messages are within the party's control).

[35] *United States Sec. & Exch. Comm'n v. Collector's Coffee Inc.*, 337 F.R.D. 70, 75 (S.D.N.Y. 2020).

[36] *Societe Internationale Pour Participations Industrielles Et Commerciales, S. A. v. Rogers*, 357 U.S. 197 (1958); *Pennsylvania v. Navient Corp.*, 348 F. Supp. 3d 394, 398 (M.D. Pa. 2018).

[37] See *In re Barnwell Enterprises Ltd*, 265 F. Supp. 3d 1, 15–16 (D.D.C. 2017).

as medical records.[38] A party must produce all documents in its possession, custody, or control even if it believes that the requesting party already has the documents.[39] The party seeking production bears the burden of establishing the producing party's possession, custody, or control over the documents.[40]

Duty to Search for Documents

A responding party must make a reasonable search of all sources reasonably likely to contain responsive documents.[41]

Documents Available from Another Source

The fact that copies of documents are available from another source, such as public records, is not, by itself, a valid basis for objecting or refusing to produce such documents if they are within the possession, custody, or control of the responding party.[42] Depending on the circumstances, however, the availability of alternative sources for the requested documents may support an objection on the basis of undue burden.[43] A party that does not have the requested records in its possession, custody, or control will not be required to obtain those documents from public sources or third parties.[44]

Proceedings Where Requests Available

Document requests are available in all civil actions in federal court, subject to certain narrow exceptions listed in Rule 81. Document requests are available in bankruptcy proceedings.

Procedures in Aid of Execution

Document requests may be served following the entry of judgment, as part of procedures in aid of execution.[45]

Contractual Agreements

Parties sometimes have previously entered into agreements defining a right to inspect designated documents (such as an

---

[38] *Compare Mir v. L-3 Commc'n Integrated Sys., L.P.*, 319 F.R.D. 220, 227–30 (N.D. Tex. 2016) (party required to sign authorization) with *Vazquez-Fernandez v. Cambridge College, Inc.*, 269 F.R.D. 150, 165 (D.P.R. 2010) (party not required to sign authorization).

[39] *McNair v. D.C.*, 325 F.R.D. 20, 21 (D.D.C. 2018).

[40] *Coventry Capital US LLC v. EEA Life Settlements Inc.*, 334 F.R.D. 68, 73 (S.D.N.Y. 2020); *Meridian Labs., Inc. v. OncoGenerix USA, Inc.*, 333 F.R.D. 131, 135 (N.D. Ill. 2019).

[41] *Sell v. Country Life Ins. Co.*, 189 F. Supp. 3d 925, 932–33 (D. Ariz. 2016); *Heller v. City of Dallas*, 303 F.R.D. 466, 485 (N.D. Tex. 2014).

[42] *Hernandez v. Results Staffing, Inc.*, 907 F.3d 354, 362 n.14 (5th Cir. 2018); *Waskul v. Washtenaw Cnty. Cmty. Mental Health*, 569 F. Supp. 3d 626, 638 (E.D. Mich. 2021). *But see Bleecker v. Standard Fire Ins. Co.*, 130 F. Supp. 2d 726 (E.D.N.C. 2000) (discovery is not required when documents are readily obtainable by the party seeking a motion to compel).

[43] *See Tequila Centinela, S.A. de C.V. v. Bacardi & Co. Ltd.*, 242 F.R.D. 1 (D.D.C. 2007).

[44] *Shcherbakovskiy v. Da Capo Al Fine, Ltd.*, 490 F.3d 130, 138 (2d Cir. 2007); *Raza v. City of New York*, 998 F. Supp. 2d 70, 87 (E.D.N.Y. 2013).

[45] *See* Rule 69.

agreement restricting one party's right to inspect another party's financial records for one year). Such agreements may be upheld by the court, if reasonable.

RULE 34(b)—PROCEDURE

CORE CONCEPT

Any party may serve document requests on any other party, who must respond in writing within 30 days.

APPLICATIONS

Who May Serve

Any party may serve document requests.

Who May Be Served

Document requests are limited to parties to the action, although the recipient need not be an adverse party.[46] If the recipient is a corporation, document requests should be addressed to the corporation, not to a corporate officer or an attorney. In a class action, the courts are split as to whether only the named representatives can be served.[47]

Service and Filing of Document Requests

The party propounding the document requests must serve them on all other parties. Document requests are not filed unless they are the subject of a motion, in which case they can be attached as an exhibit.

Time for Service

Most discovery cannot commence until the parties have conducted their discovery conference under Rule 26(f). Rule 34 creates an exception for document requests. Starting 21 days after a defendant has been served with the summons and complaint, requests to inspect may be served on that party or by that party on a plaintiff or any other defendant who has also been served.[48] The Rules do not set an outer limit on how late document requests may be served, but many local rules or case management orders set such a limit.[49] Usually, when such a deadline exists, document requests must be served so that the response is due before the deadline.[50]

---

[46] *U.S. v. 2121 Celeste Road SW, Albuquerque, N.M.*, 307 F.R.D. 572 (D.N.M. 2015).

[47] *Brennan v. Midwestern United Life Ins. Co.*, 450 F.2d 999 (7th Cir. 1971) (unnamed members of class required to respond); *Wainwright v. Kraftco Corp.*, 54 F.R.D. 532 (N.D. Ga. 1972) (unnamed members of class not required to respond).

[48] *Liguria Foods, Inc. v. Griffith Laboratories, Inc.*, 320 F.R.D. 168, 183 (N.D. Iowa 2017).

[49] *See N. Shore-Long Island Jewish Health Sys., Inc. v. MultiPlan, Inc.*, 325 F.R.D. 36, 44 (E.D.N.Y. 2018) (scheduling order).

[50] *Thomas v. Pacificorp*, 324 F.3d 1176, 1179 (10th Cir. 2003); *Kaplan v. Kaplan*, 903 F. Supp. 2d 1304 (M.D. Fla. 2012), aff'd, 524 F. App'x 547 (11th Cir. 2013).

Number

The Rule contains no limitation on the number of document requests.[51] Some districts have local rules limiting the number of document requests.[52]

Form of Requests

A request for inspection should be a formal document[53] setting forth the items or categories of items[54] to be inspected with "reasonable particularity."[55] Some courts allow informal requests, such as email requests, to be enforced under appropriate circumstances.[56] What constitutes "reasonable particularity" depends on the particular situation; essentially, the test is whether the responding party can determine what documents to produce.[57] The request should also specify a reasonable time, place, and manner for the inspection.[58] The time designated should be after the time to respond has elapsed (30 days). If the request seeks electronically stored information, the request may, but is not required to, specify the form in which the information is to be produced.[59]

Response

A party served with a document request must serve a written response[60] or move for a protective order under Rule 26(c). Otherwise, the party will be subject to the sanctions in Rule 37(d). The response should fairly respond to each request.[61] It may state that the request will be complied with in the manner requested.[62] It may also state that the request will be complied with, but at some other time or place, or in some other manner. The response should specify a reasonable time, place, and man-

---

[51] *Bourguignon v. Spielvogel*, 2004 WL 743668 (D. Conn. 2004).

[52] *See Lurensky v. Wellinghoff*, 258 F.R.D. 27 (D.D.C. 2009).

[53] *Suid v. Cigna Corp.*, 203 F.R.D. 227, 229–29 (D.V.I. 2001) (letters between counsel are not document requests under Rule 34).

[54] *Dauska v. Green Bay Packaging Inc.*, 291 F.R.D. 251, 261 (E.D. Wis. 2013).

[55] *Regan-Touhy v. Walgreen Co.*, 526 F.3d 641, 649–50 (10th Cir. 2008) (all-encompassing requests are not sufficiently particular); *L.A. Terminals, Inc. v. United Nat'l Ins. Co.*, 340 F.R.D. 390, 395 (C.D. Cal. 2022).

[56] *See Westport Ins. Corp. v. Hippo Fleming & Pertile Law Offices*, 319 F.R.D. 214, 218 (W.D. Pa. 2017); *Trask v. Olin Corp.*, 298 F.R.D. 244, 259–60 (W.D. Pa. 2014) (discussing the split of authority on this issue).

[57] *L.A. Terminals, Inc. v. United Nat'l Ins. Co.*, 340 F.R.D. 390, 395 (C.D. Cal. 2022); *VeroBlue Farms USA Inc. v. Wulf*, ___ F.R.D. ___, 2021 WL 5176839, at *6 (N.D. Tex. 2021).

[58] *Mezu v. Morgan State Univ.*, 775 F. Supp. 2d 801, 805 (D. Md. 2011); *Southern Estate Services, Inc. v. Puritan Fin. Services, Inc.*, 2000 WL 1725086 (E.D. La. 2000).

[59] *Mondragon v. Scott Farms, Inc.*, 329 F.R.D. 533, 545 (E.D.N.C. 2019).

[60] *Starcher v. Cor. Medical Systems, Inc.*, 144 F.3d 418, 420–21 (6th Cir. 1998), aff'd, 527 U.S. 198 (1999); *Bibbs v. New River Community and Technical College*, 285 F.R.D. 382, 388 (S.D.W. Va. 2012).

[61] *Mulero-Abreu v. Puerto Rico Police Dept.*, 675 F.3d 88, 93 (1st Cir. 2012).

[62] *Renfrow v. Redwood Fire and Cas. Ins. Co.*, 288 F.R.D. 514, 521 (D. Nev. 2013).

ner for the inspection.[63] The response may also raise objections to some or all of the requests.[64] If the request does not specify the form for production of electronically stored information, or if the responding party has objected to the form specified in the request, then the response must specify the form in which electronically stored information will be produced. Finally, the response may advise that the party has no responsive documents in its possession, custody, or control.[65] The response is generally not required to be verified or under oath, in contrast to interrogatory answers.[66]

Time to Respond

A written response is due within 30 days of service,[67] except that, for document requests served before the parties' Rule 26(f) conference, the responses are due 30 days after the Rule 26(f) conference.[68] The time to respond may be modified by informal agreement or stipulation under Rule 29.[69] If the responding party intends to object to some of the document requests, a stipulation for an extension should specify that the time is extended to answer and serve objections.[70] The period for responding may also be shortened or lengthened by the court, typically upon motion by one of the parties.[71]

Service and Filing of Response

The response must be served upon all parties. The response is not filed unless it is referenced in a motion, in which case the response can be attached as an exhibit.

Objections

If the responding party determines that a particular document request is outside the scope of discovery or otherwise

---

[63]*See Autoridad de Carreteras y Transportacion v. Transcore Atlantic, Inc.*, 319 F.R.D. 422, 434 (D.P.R. 2016) (it is improper to state that documents will be produced at some unspecified time).

[64]*Renfrow v. Redwood Fire and Cas. Ins. Co.*, 288 F.R.D. 514, 521 (D. Nev. 2013).

[65]*See BDI Capital, LLC v. Bulbul Investments LLC*, 446 F. Supp. 3d 1127, 1132 n.6 (N.D. Ga. 2020); *Fishel v. BASF Group*, 175 F.R.D. 525, 531 (S.D. Iowa 1997).

[66]*Napolitano v. Synthes USA, LLC*, 297 F.R.D. 194, 200 (D. Conn. 2014). *But see Vazquez-Fernandez v. Cambridge College, Inc.*, 269 F.R.D. 150, 154 (D.P.R. 2010) (when the answer is something other than an objection or an agreement to produce, it must be verified).

[67]*Nasreen v. Capitol Petroleum Grp., LLC*, 340 F.R.D. 489, 493 (D.D.C. 2022); *Merchia v. United States Internal Revenue Serv.*, 336 F.R.D. 396, 398 (D. Mass. 2020).

[68]*Lopez v. Don Herring Ltd.*, 327 F.R.D. 567, 582 (N.D. Tex. 2018).

[69]*Nasreen v. Capitol Petroleum Grp., LLC*, 340 F.R.D. 489, 493 (D.D.C. 2022); *Lopez v. Don Herring Ltd.*, 327 F.R.D. 567, 582 (N.D. Tex. 2018).

[70]*Coregis Ins. Co. v. Baratta & Fenerty, Ltd.*, 187 F.R.D. 528, 530 (E.D. Pa. 1999).

[71]*Symons Intern. Group, Inc. v. Continental Cas. Co.*, 306 F.R.D. 612, 618 (S.D. Ind. 2014); *Ellsworth Associates, Inc. v. U.S.*, 917 F. Supp. 841, 844 (D.D.C. 1996) (motion for expedited discovery is particularly appropriate with a claim for injunctive relief).

problematic, the party may object to the request in lieu of or in addition to making the documents available for inspection.[72] The objection must be made in writing and must be signed by the attorney for the responding party.[73] The response must state the grounds of the objection with specificity,[74] and a number of courts hold general or boilerplate objections to be ineffective.[75] Additionally, some courts hold that the responding party has a duty to construe discovery requests in a reasonable manner, and should not strain to find objections.[76] Some common objections are:

- *Overly broad, unduly vague, and/or ambiguous:* When a document request is written so broadly that it extends to documents not relevant to the claims or defenses in the matter (such as a request not limited in time to the events relevant to the complaint), the request may be overly broad.[77] When a request is susceptible to numerous meanings, it may be unduly vague and ambiguous. In general, these objections are probably not justification for refusing to provide documents altogether, but the responding party can raise the objection, then expressly limit the scope of the response.
- *Burdensome and oppressive:* In general, the responding party must produce the documents available without undue effort or expense (recognizing that all discovery responses require effort and expense). Thus, requests that require extensive research, compilation, or evaluation of documents may be objectionable.[78] The responding party is not required to prepare the adverse party's case.
- *Privileged information:* Requests that seek documents protected by the attorney-client privilege or by another privilege are objectionable.[79] When privileged documents are withheld, the responding party must explicitly state the objection and describe the nature of the documents

---

[72] *Lurensky v. Wellinghoff*, 258 F.R.D. 27 (D.D.C. 2009) (objections must be to specific requests — general objection that the requests are burdensome is insufficient).

[73] *Frontier-Kemper Constructors, Inc. v. Elk Run Coal Co., Inc.*, 246 F.R.D. 522, 527–28 (S.D. W. Va. 2007).

[74] *Allen v. Banner Life Ins. Co.*, 340 F.R.D. 232, 239 n.4 (D.N.J. 2022); *Nei v. Travelers Home & Marine Ins. Co.*, 326 F.R.D. 652, 656 (D. Mont. 2018).

[75] *Infanzon v. Allstate Ins. Co.*, 335 F.R.D. 305, 308–09 (C.D. Cal.2020); *Siser N. Am., Inc. v. Herika G. Inc.*, 325 F.R.D. 200, 209–10 (E.D. Mich. 2018).

[76] *L.A. Terminals, Inc. v. United Nat'l Ins. Co.*, 340 F.R.D. 390, 396 (C.D. Cal. 2022).

[77] *Westhemeco Ltd. v. New Hampshire Ins. Co.*, 82 F.R.D. 702 (S.D.N.Y. 1979).

[78] *Chambers (Robert) v. Capital Cities/ABC, Burke (Daniel), Callahan (Robert)*, 154 F.R.D. 63 (S.D.N.Y. 1994).

[79] *Merrifield v. Gussman*, 296 F. Supp. 3d 362, 366 (D. Mass. 2017) (Fifth Amendment); *Tequila Centinela, S.A. de C.V. v. Bacardi & Co. Ltd.*, 242 F.R.D. 1 (D.D.C. 2007).

not produced sufficiently to enable other parties to assess the applicability of the privilege.[80] A log of the documents withheld on the basis of privilege should be provided to the requesting party, either at the time of the responses or at a mutually agreeable time.[81] Care should be exercised in responding to such requests, because the privilege may be waived by revealing part or all of the privileged documents.

- *Trial preparation materials (work product):* Rule 26(b)(3) provides that trial preparation materials may be discovered only upon a showing that the party is unable to obtain the equivalent information through other means without undue hardship.[82] Documents withheld as trial preparation materials are typically listed on the privilege log.
- *Not proportional to the needs of the case:* A party may object that a document request seeks information that is not proportional to the needs of the case, in light of the factors listed in Rule 26(b)(1).
- *Form of electronically stored information:* If the requesting party specifies a form for the production of electronically stored information that the responding party believes is burdensome or otherwise objectionable, Rule 34(b) specifically provides for objections to the request.

Statement Regarding Objections and Withheld Documents

A party making an objection to a Rule 34 request must state whether any responsive materials are being withheld on the basis of that objection.[83] The responding party does not need to make a detailed log of each document withheld, and only needs to alert other parties to the fact that documents have been withheld so they can make a more informed decision as to whether to challenge the objection and can conduct an "informed discussion" about what was withheld.[84] An objection that explains the scope of the response will be deemed to satisfy this requirement.[85] For example, if the response objects that the request is overly broad in terms of the time covered by the request, then states that the responding party will produce all responsive documents within the last five years, other parties

[80] *U.S. v. Philip Morris Inc.*, 347 F.3d 951, 954 (D.C. Cir. 2003); *Jones v. Hernandez*, 322 F.R.D. 411, 413 (S.D. Cal. 2017).

[81] *Burlington Northern & Santa Fe Ry. Co. v. U.S. Dist. Court for Dist. of Mont.*, 408 F.3d 1142, 1147 (9th Cir. 2005).

[82] *See* Rule 26(b)(3) (discovery of work product).

[83] *Crozer-Chester Med. Ctr. v. Nat'l Lab. Rels. Bd.*, 976 F.3d 276, 292 (3d Cir. 2020).

[84] *See Crozer-Chester Med. Ctr. v. Nat'l Lab. Rels. Bd.*, 976 F.3d 276, 292 (3d Cir. 2020).

[85] *See Deakin v. Magellan Health, Inc.*, 340 F.R.D. 424, 435 (D.N.M. 2022); *Diaz v. New York Paving Inc.*, 553 F. Supp. 3d 11, 21 (S.D.N.Y. 2021).

will be on notice that the responding party has withheld documents more than five years old.[86]

Failure to Object Is Waiver

In contrast to Rule 33 governing interrogatories, Rule 34 does not contain an explicit provision stating that failure to serve timely objections results in a waiver of those objections.[87] Some courts hold that such waiver is implied.[88] The fact that the 2015 amendments eliminated the discrepancy between Rule 33 and Rule 34 regarding stating objections with particularity, but did not eliminate the discrepancy regarding waiver, may cause the courts to stop inferring waiver in Rule 34. The court can excuse the waiver for good cause shown.[89]

Objection to Part of Request

If only part of a request is objectionable, the responding party must specify the objectionable part and respond to the remaining parts.[90] A number of courts have held that the common practice of objecting, then answering "subject to and without waiving" the objections is improper and waives the objections unless the response describes in particularity the documents not being provided.[91]

Court Rulings on Objections

The district court has extremely broad discretion in ruling on objections to document requests.[92] The court will balance the need for the documents and the burden of producing them, but will generally require production unless the administration of justice would be impeded. The court may allow inspection under specified conditions and may restrict further disclosure of sensitive documents. The court may also privately inspect the documents before ruling.

Motion for a Protective Order

As an alternative to making objections to individual document requests, the responding party may make a motion for a

---

[86]Rule 34 advisory committee's note (2015).

[87]*Liguria Foods, Inc. v. Griffith Lab., Inc.*, 320 F.R.D. 168, 185 (N.D. Iowa 2017) (holding that waiver applies nonetheless); *Samsung Elec. Am., Inc. v. Chung*, 321 F. Supp. 3d 250, 281 (N.D. Tex. 2017) (same).

[88]*See FCA US LLC v. Bullock*, 329 F.R.D. 563, 566 (E.D. Mich. 2019). *But see Ashford v. City of Milwaukee*, 304 F.R.D. 547, 549 (E.D. Wisc. 2015) (the difference in language between Rule 33 and Rule 34 is not accidental).

[89]*United Auto. Ins. Co. v. Veluchamy*, 747 F. Supp. 2d 1021, 1027 (N.D. Ill. 2010).

[90]*Crozer-Chester Med. Ctr. v. Nat'l Lab. Rels. Bd.*, 976 F.3d 276, 292 (3d Cir. 2020); *Mir v. L-3 Commc'n Integrated Sys., L.P.*, 315 F.R.D. 460, 463 (N.D. Tex. 2016).

[91]*See Heller v. City of Dallas*, 303 F.R.D. 466, 488–90 (N.D. Tex. 2014).

[92]*McConnell v. Canadian Pac. Realty Co.*, 280 F.R.D. 188, 192 (M.D. Pa. 2011).

protective order under Rule 26(c).[93] A motion for a protective order is appropriate when most or all of a set of document requests is too burdensome or cumulative. The burden is on the moving party to show hardship or injustice. Motions for protective orders in response to document requests are not common because it is easier and less expensive to interpose objections, and the burden is then on the opposing party to file a motion to compel under Rule 37(a).

Sanctions for Failure to Respond

If a party files no response to a set of document requests, the court may impose sanctions under Rule 37(b)(2), such as deeming certain facts established or refusing to allow the party to oppose or support certain claims.[94] The court may also deem objections to the document request waived by the failure to file a timely response.[95] Furthermore, the court must award reasonable expenses, including attorney's fees, caused by the responding party's failure to answer, unless the court finds that the failure to answer was justified.

Duty to Search for Responsive Documents

The responding party has the duty to conduct a diligent search for responsive documents.[96]

Production of Documents

The responding party has the option of allowing the serving party to inspect, copy, test, or sample[97] the documents or of providing copies of the responsive documents.[98] If the responding party chooses to allow the requesting party to inspect the documents, the responding party may allow access to the documents as they are normally kept (*i.e.,* "There is our file room.").[99] If the responding party provides copies of or access to selected responsive documents, the party must organize and label them to correspond to the categories requested.[100] The requesting party may insist on inspecting an original when a copy would

---

[93] *Simms v. Center for Correctional Health and Policy Studies*, 272 F.R.D. 36, 40 (D.D.C. 2011) (motion for protective order to shift costs of production).

[94] *See Land Ocean Logistics, Inc. v. Aqua Gulf Corp.*, 181 F.R.D. 229, 235 (W.D.N.Y. 1998) (preclusion of evidence is a harsh sanction reserved for exceptional cases).

[95] *Scaturro v. Warren and Sweat Mfg. Co., Inc.*, 160 F.R.D. 44, 46 (M.D. Pa. 1995).

[96] *See BDI Capital, LLC v. Bulbul Investments LLC*, 446 F. Supp. 3d 1127, 1132 n.6 (N.D. Ga. 2020).

[97] *Superior Production Partnership v. Gordon Auto Body Parts Co., Ltd.*, 784 F.3d 311, 322 (6th Cir. 2015).

[98] Rule 34(b)(2)(B).

[99] *Landry v. Swire Oilfield Servs., L.L.C.*, 323 F.R.D. 360, 390 n.22 (D.N.M. 2018) ("usual course" need not be optimal or reasonable, so long as documents are not deliberately jumbled); *Gross v. Lunduski*, 304 F.R.D. 136, 152 (W.D.N.Y. 2014).

[100] *Comite Fiestas De La Calle San Sebastian, Inc. v. Cruz*, 177 F. Supp. 3d 716, 718 n.4 (D.P.R. 2016); *Go v. Rockefeller Univ.*, 280 F.R.D. 165, 169 (S.D.N.Y. 2012).

not reflect the colors or signature on the original.[101]

Production of Electronically Stored Information

The production of electronically stored information raises a host of issues, many of which are discussed in the Sedona Principles: Best Practices, Recommendations & Principles for Addressing Electronic Document Production.[102]

- *Format for Production:* Rule 34(b) allows, but does not require, the requesting party to specify the form or format in which it is requesting electronically stored information (such as pdf, jpeg, tiff, or native format).[103] If the requesting party wants the electronically stored information in a particular format (such as one that is compatible with a particular software application or one that includes metadata), the requesting party should so specify in the request.[104] The responding party can then produce the electronically stored information in that form or object and specify the form in which it will produce the information.[105] If the requesting party does not specify the form, then the responding party must produce the electronically stored information in the form in which it is ordinarily maintained or in a form that is reasonably usable.[106] Unless the responding party is producing the electronically stored information in the form specified by the requesting party, the responding party must specify the form it intends to use for production in its written response to the document request.[107] If the responding party objects to the form stated by the requesting party, or if the requesting party is not satisfied with the form specified by the responding party, then the parties must meet and confer under Rule

[101]*Robinson-Reeder v. Am. Council on Educ.*, 262 F.R.D. 41, 45 (D.D.C. 2009).

[102]The Sedona Principles: Best Practices, Recommendations & Principles for Addressing Electronic Document Production, Third Edition, 19 Sedona Conf. J. 1, 57–147 (2018), available at https://thesedonaconference.org/sites/default/files/publications/The%20Sedona%20Principles%20Third%20Edition.19TSCJ1.pdf. *See also John B. v. Goetz*, 531 F.3d 448, 459 (6th Cir. 2008) (*citing* the Sedona Principles, second edition); *Gross v. Lunduski*, 304 F.R.D. 136, 158 (W.D. N.Y.).

[103]*Star Direct Telecom, Inc. v. Global Crossing Bandwidth, Inc.*, 272 F.R.D. 350, 359 (W.D.N.Y. 2011); *Covad Commc'n Co. v. Revonet, Inc.*, 254 F.R.D. 147, 149 (D.D.C. 2008).

[104]*See Pruess v. Presbyterian Health Plan, Inc.*, 579 F. Supp. 3d 1235, 1243 (D.N.M. 2022); *Landry v. Swire Oilfield Servs., L.L.C.*, 323 F.R.D. 360, 390, 396 (D.N.M. 2018).

[105]*See Pruess v. Presbyterian Health Plan, Inc.*, 579 F. Supp. 3d 1235, 1243 (D.N.M. 2022); *Puerto Rico Med. Emergency Group, Inc. v. Iglesia Episcopal Puertorriqueña, Inc.*, 318 F.R.D. 224, 229 (D.P.R. 2016).

[106]*CBT Flint Partners, LLC v. Return Path, Inc.*, 737 F.3d 1320, 1331 (Fed. Cir. 2013) (encrypted data must be decrypted); *Landry v. Swire Oilfield Servs., L.L.C.*, 323 F.R.D. 360, 390 (D.N.M. 2018) (non-searchable format is not reasonably usable).

[107]The 2006 Amendment to the Advisory Committee Note to Rule 34(b).

37(a)(2)(B).[108] Sometimes, the court's case management order will specify the form for production of ESI.[109] Under any of these scenarios, a party need not produce electronically stored information in more than one form[110] unless ordered to do so by the court.[111]

- *Organization of ESI:* As discussed above, Rule 34 provides the responding party with the choice of organizing and labeling the documents to correspond to the requests or of producing the documents as maintained in the ordinary course of business. Some courts do not require a party to organize and label ESI, recognizing that parties use electronic searching techniques for ESI.[112] At the same time, ESI must be produced in a manner that allows the requesting party, with reasonable effort, to identify and obtain the documents responsive to the requests.[113]
- *Access to Servers or Hard Drives:* Sometimes, the requesting party will seek access to the producing party's servers or hard drives or to have those devices imaged so that the requesting party can conduct its own searches or forensic analysis, but the courts will require that access only when the specific situation warrants.[114]

Redaction

Most courts hold that a party may redact privileged matter from documents it produces, but may not redact portions of the documents that the party deems not relevant.[115]

Time for Production

The responding party must produce the responsive documents at the time specified in the request or at another "reasonable time" specified in the response.[116] Neither the Rule nor the Advisory Committee notes give any guidance as to what would be considered a reasonable time. ESI is subject to the

---

[108] *Ford Motor Co. v. Edgewood Properties, Inc.*, 257 F.R.D. 418 (D.N.J. 2009).

[109] *See In re Actos Antitrust Litig.*, 340 F.R.D. 549, 551 (S.D.N.Y. 2022).

[110] *Lopez v. Don Herring Ltd.*, 327 F.R.D. 567, 578 (N.D. Tex. 2018); *U.S. ex rel. Carter v. Bridgepoint Educ., Inc.*, 305 F.R.D. 225, 244 (S.D. Cal. 2015).

[111] *DR Distributors, LLC v. 21 Century Smoking, Inc.*, 513 F. Supp. 3d 839, 938 (N.D. Ill. 2021) (requiring production in native format and hard copy).

[112] *See Anderson Living Trust v. WPX Energy Prod., LLC*, 298 F.R.D. 514, 515–27 (D.N.M. 2014).

[113] *United States v. Maverick Mktg., LLC*, 427 F. Supp. 3d 1386, 1397 (Ct. Int'l Trade 2020).

[114] *See, e.g., John B. v. Goetz*, 531 F.3d 448, 460 (6th Cir. 2008); *Motorola Sols., Inc. v. Hytera Commc'ns Corp.*, 314 F. Supp. 3d 931, 940 (N.D. Ill. 2018).

[115] *See Christine Asia Co. v. Alibaba Grp. Holding Ltd.*, 327 F.R.D. 52, 54 (S.D.N.Y. 2018).

[116] *Deakin v. Magellan Health, Inc.*, 340 F.R.D. 424, 432–33 (D.N.M. 2022) (requiring an end date for the rolling production); *Waskul v. Washtenaw Cnty. Cmty. Mental Health*, 569 F. Supp. 3d 626, 637 (E.D. Mich. 2021).

same timing rules as production of paper documents,[117] but the process of gathering and producing ESI can be time-consuming such that producing ESI at the time the response is due or shortly thereafter can be difficult.

Use of Produced Documents

Documents produced in response to document requests are treated like any other evidence, and are admissible as allowed by the rules of evidence.[118]

Cost of Gathering and Copying

In general, the producing party bears the cost of searching for and gathering responsive documents.[119] If the responding party makes documents available for inspection, the requesting party must pay for copies of the documents it chooses to have copied.[120] The rules are silent about who pays for copies if the responding party chooses to produce copies of the responsive documents instead of making them available for inspection, and the courts have not yet addressed this issue. The court has the authority to shift some or all of the costs of collecting and producing documents to the requesting party.[121] Cost shifting has become increasingly common with ESI.[122]

Procedures for Inspection, Testing, or Sampling

Procedures for inspection, testing, or sampling, such as who will be present and protocols for the testing or sampling, are set by agreement of the parties or by the court on motion for a protective order or motion to compel.[123] Requests to perform destructive testing or invasive sampling are more likely to draw objection or require court intervention.[124]

Motion to Compel

If the responding party fails to respond to a document request or to allow an inspection, or objects to a document request, the propounding party may file a motion to compel under Rule 37(a), after conducting the required meet and confer

---

[117] *DR Distributors, LLC v. 21 Century Smoking, Inc.*, 513 F. Supp. 3d 839, 939 (N.D. Ill. 2021).

[118] *See Castro v. DeVry University, Inc.*, 786 F.3d 559, 578–79 (7th Cir. 2015).

[119] *S. Ute Indian Tribe v. Amoco Prod. Co.*, 2 F.3d 1023, 1029–30 (10th Cir.1993); *U.S. ex rel. Carter v. Bridgepoint Educ., Inc.*, 305 F.R.D. 225, 237 (S.D. Cal. 2015).

[120] *LightGuard Sys., Inc. v. Spot Devices, Inc.*, 281 F.R.D. 593, 598 (D. Nev. 2012); *Obiajulu v. City of Rochester, Dept. of Law*, 166 F.R.D. 293, 297 (W.D.N.Y. 1996) (plaintiff may bring copying machine or pay the defendant a reasonable copying cost).

[121] *See U.S. ex rel. Carter v. Bridgepoint Educ., Inc.*, 305 F.R.D. 225, 237–40 (S.D. Cal. 2015).

[122] *U.S. ex rel. Carter v. Bridgepoint Educ., Inc.*, 305 F.R.D. 225, 240 (S.D. Cal. 2015).

[123] *See Smith v. Nexus RVs, LLC*, 331 F.R.D. 491, 493 (N.D. Ind. 2019); *Ramos v. Carter Exp. Inc.*, 292 F.R.D. 406, 408–11 (S.D. Tex. 2013).

[124] *See Ramos v. Carter Exp. Inc.*, 292 F.R.D. 406, 408–11 (S.D. Tex. 2013).

with opposing counsel.[125] The burden of persuasion is on the responding party (the nonmoving party) to convince the court that a document request is objectionable[126] or that the withheld documents are privileged.[127]

RULE 34(c)—NONPARTIES

CORE CONCEPT

Although document requests or requests for inspection cannot be served on a nonparty, documents or inspections can be obtained from a nonparty by a subpoena under Rule 45.[128] Furthermore, Rule 34 does not preclude an independent action for production of documents or things or for permission to enter onto land (but such actions may be unnecessary under the expanded subpoena powers in Rule 45).[129]

Additional Research References

Wright & Miller, *Federal Practice and Procedure* §§ 2201 to 2218

C.J.S., Federal Civil Procedure §§ 696 to 740 et seq.

West's Key Number Digest, Federal Civil Procedure ⚿1551 to 1640

---

[125] *Molski v. Franklin*, 222 F.R.D. 433, 435 (S.D. Cal. 2004); *U.S. v. Kattar*, 191 F.R.D. 33, 35–36 (D.N.H. 1999).

[126] *Nei v. Travelers Home & Marine Ins. Co.*, 326 F.R.D. 652, 656 (D. Mont. 2018); *Heller v. City of Dallas*, 303 F.R.D. 466, 483 (N.D. Tex. 2014).

[127] *U.S. v. All Assets Held at Bank Julius Baer & Co., Ltd.*, 142 F. Supp. 3d 37, 41 (D.D.C. 2015); *Felder v. Washington Metro. Area Transit Auth.*, 153 F. Supp. 3d 221, 224 (D.D.C. 2015).

[128] *Hobley v. Burge*, 433 F.3d 946, 949 (7th Cir. 2006); *V5 Techs. v. Switch, Ltd.*, 332 F.R.D. 356, 366 (D. Nev. 2019).

[129] *See Darbeau v. Library of Congress*, 453 F. Supp. 2d 168, 171 (D.D.C. 2006).

RULE 35
PHYSICAL AND MENTAL EXAMINATIONS

(a) **Order for an Examination.**

(1) *In General.* The court where the action is pending may order a party whose mental or physical condition—including blood group—is in controversy to submit to a physical or mental examination by a suitably licensed or certified examiner. The court has the same authority to order a party to produce for examination a person who is in its custody or under its legal control.

(2) *Motion and Notice; Contents of the Order.* The order:

(A) may be made only on motion for good cause and on notice to all parties and the person to be examined; and

(B) must specify the time, place, manner, conditions, and scope of the examination, as well as the person or persons who will perform it.

(b) **Examiner's Report.**

(1) *Request by the Party or Person Examined.* The party who moved for the examination must, on request, deliver to the requester a copy of the examiner's report, together with like reports of all earlier examinations of the same condition. The request may be made by the party against whom the examination order was issued or by the person examined.

(2) *Contents.* The examiner's report must be in writing and must set out in detail the examiner's findings, including diagnoses, conclusions, and the results of any tests.

(3) *Request by the Moving Party.* After delivering the reports, the party who moved for the examination may request—and is entitled to receive—from the party against whom the examination order was issued like reports of all earlier or

later examinations of the same condition. But those reports need not be delivered by the party with custody or control of the person examined if the party shows that it could not obtain them.

(4) *Waiver of Privilege.* By requesting and obtaining the examiner's report, or by deposing the examiner, the party examined waives any privilege it may have—in that action or any other action involving the same controversy—concerning testimony about all examinations of the same condition.

(5) *Failure to Deliver a Report.* The court on motion may order—on just terms—that a party deliver the report of an examination. If the report is not provided, the court may exclude the examiner's testimony at trial.

(6) *Scope.* This subdivision (b) applies also to an examination made by the parties' agreement, unless the agreement states otherwise. This subdivision does not preclude obtaining an examiner's report or deposing an examiner under other rules.

[Amended effective July 1, 1970; August 1, 1987; November 18, 1988; December 1, 1991; April 30, 2007, effective December 1, 2007.]

AUTHORS' COMMENTARY ON RULE 35

PURPOSE AND SCOPE

Rule 35 authorizes a party to request a physical or mental examination of another party if that party's physical or mental condition has been placed "in controversy." Unlike the other discretionary discovery tools, a party does not have a right to a Rule 35 examination, and instead needs a court order or a stipulation from the party to be examined. Furthermore, the burden on the moving party is not the ordinary burden of persuasion, but instead is the heightened "good cause" standard. When a party's physical condition is plainly in controversy, however, stipulations for Rule 35 examinations are common.

Rule 35 also contains provisions requiring the examiner to prepare a written report setting out the examiner's findings. The Rule allows the examined party to request a copy of the report, but invoking that right obligates the examined party to produce copies of any reports it has from examinations for the same condition.

RULE 35(a)—ORDER FOR AN EXAMINATION

CORE CONCEPT

Rule 35 requires a party to submit to a mental or physical examination when the party's mental or physical condition is in controversy in the action. In contrast to most other discovery procedures, mental or physical examinations are available only by consent or motion. To prevail, the moving party must demonstrate "good cause" for the examination, which will generally exist in every case in which the plaintiff is claiming personal injuries.

APPLICATIONS

Consent

In many cases, the circumstances justifying a Rule 35 examination are apparent, and the party to be examined consents to the examination. For example, in a tort action where the plaintiff seeks to recover for personal injuries, many plaintiffs will consent to an examination of the alleged injuries. The consent can be by formal stipulation under Rule 29[1] or by informal agreement.

Motion

Absent consent, a request for examination must be made by motion, with a proposed order attached, served upon the person to be examined and all parties.[2] The motion should specify the time, place, manner, conditions, and scope of the examination and the person or persons by whom it is to be made, as well as the grounds supporting the motion.[3]

- *Duty to Meet and Confer:* Rule 35(a) does not explicitly require the parties to meet and confer before filing a motion for a Rule 35 examination, although some courts consider such efforts in ruling on a Rule 35(a) motion[4] and some courts order the parties to meet and confer regarding Rule 35 examinations.[5]

Order

If the court grants a motion for a Rule 35 examination, it must issue an order that specifies the examiner and the time,

---

[1]*E.E.O.C. v. Grief Bros. Corp.*, 218 F.R.D. 59, 64 (W.D.N.Y. 2003).

[2]*Smith v. Vestavia Hills Board of Educ.*, 218 F. Supp. 3d 1285, 1296 (N.D. Ala. 2016); *Gavin v. Hilton Worldwide, Inc.*, 291 F.R.D. 161, 164 (N.D. Cal. 2013).

[3]*See Ornelas v. Southern Tire Mart, LLC*, 292 F.R.D. 388, 397 (S.D. Tex. 2013).

[4]*See Robinson v. De Niro*, __ F. Supp. 3d __, 2022 WL 1210772, at *2 (S.D.N.Y. 2022).

[5]*See, e.g., Malark v. RBC Cap. Markets, LLC*, 2020 WL 13032695, at *1 (D. Minn. 2020).

place, manner, conditions, and scope of the examination.[6] These topics are discussed individually below. The order may also include protective measures deemed appropriate by the court.[7]

Persons Subject to Examination

In general, only parties are subject to Rule 35 examination.[8] Additionally, a person who is within the control of a party may be subject to examination.[9] Thus, a parent suing on behalf of an injured child may have to produce the child for examination.[10] This principle has also been extended to a spouse when one spouse is suing for injuries to the other.[11] In such case, the party has a duty to make a good faith effort to obtain the presence of the person to be examined.[12]

Condition in Controversy

Examinations for a particular condition are allowed only when that condition is in controversy.[13] The plaintiff's condition is typically placed at issue by the claims in the complaint,[14] but can also be placed at issue by representations made during the litigation or by a defense.[15]

Good Cause

The court will order an examination "for good cause shown."[16] The burden of demonstrating good cause rests with the moving party.[17] The requirement of good cause is not a formality; the court must genuinely balance the need for the

---

[6] *Mager v. Wisconsin Cent. Ltd.*, 924 F.3d 831, 838 (6th Cir. 2019).

[7] *Schaeffer v. Sequoyah Trading & Transp.*, 273 F.R.D. 662, 664 (D. Kan. 2011) (ordering videotaping of the examination); *Favale v. Roman Catholic Diocese of Bridgeport*, 235 F.R.D. 553, 555 (D. Conn. 2006).

[8] *Schlagenhauf v. Holder*, 379 U.S. 104 (1964); *Smith v. Vestavia Hills Board of Educ.*, 218 F. Supp. 3d 1285, 1296 (N.D. Ala. 2016).

[9] *But see Smith v. Vestavia Hills Board of Educ.*, 218 F. Supp. 3d 1285, 1296 n.3 (N.D. Ala. 2016) (employees of a party not subject to examination under Rule 35).

[10] *Sali v. Corona Reg'l Med. Ctr.*, 884 F.3d 1218, 1223 (9th Cir. 2018); *but see Fong Sik Leung v. Dulles*, 226 F.2d 74, 76 (9th Cir. 1955) (a guardian suing on behalf of a child is not subject to examination under Rule 35).

[11] *In re Certain Asbestos Cases*, 112 F.R.D. 427, 434 (N.D. Tex. 1986).

[12] The Advisory Committee Note to the 1970 amendment of Rule 35(a).

[13] *Green v. Branson*, 108 F.3d 1296, 1304 (10th Cir. 1997) (denying motion by the plaintiff to have himself examined where purpose was for the plaintiff, a prisoner, to obtain treatment); *Ashby v. Mortimer*, 329 F.R.D. 650, 653 (D. Idaho 2019).

[14] *In re E.I. du Pont de Nemours & Co. C-8 Pers. Injury Litig.*, 379 F. Supp. 3d 669, 672–73 (S.D. Ohio 2019).

[15] *See Schlagenhauf v. Holder*, 379 U.S. 104, 112 (1964); *Ashby v. Mortimer*, 329 F.R.D. 650, 654 (D. Idaho 2019) (denial of paternity places defendant's DNA in controversy); *Ornelas v. Southern Tire Mart, LLC*, 292 F.R.D. 388, 390 (S.D. Tex. 2013).

[16] *Schlagenhauf v. Holder*, 379 U.S. 104 (1964); *Mager v. Wisconsin Cent. Ltd.*, 924 F.3d 831, 838 (6th Cir. 2019).

[17] *Winstead v. Lafayette County Board of County Comm'r*, 315 F.R.D. 612, 613 (N.D. Fla. 2016); *J.H. v. School Town of Munster*, 38 F. Supp. 3d 986, 988 (N.D. Ind. 2014).

information with the right to privacy and safety of the party.[18] Courts may consider factors like the possibility of obtaining the desired information by other means and whether the plaintiff intends to offer expert testimony to prove the injury or condition at issue.[19] In a tort action where the plaintiff seeks to recover for personal injuries, good cause will almost always be found to exist.[20] It becomes less clear when the party has not put the party's own mental or physical condition at issue.[21]

Time for Filing Motion

There is no time limit on the filing of a motion for an examination, although the court can take the timing of the motion into account in ruling on the motion.[22]

Who Conducts Exam

The examination may be conducted by any suitably licensed or certified examiner or examiners.[23] In general, the court will allow the movant to select the examiner unless the person to be examined raises a valid objection.[24] The court may reject a particular examiner upon a showing of bias[25] or, under certain circumstances, if the examiner is a different gender from the person to be examined. Some local rules have provisions regarding the selection of the examiner.[26] The court order must designate the examiner, and may be invalid if it fails to do so.

Testimony of Examiner

The party conducting the examination may call the examiner to testify as an expert witness (assuming the criteria for expert testimony are satisfied). The courts are split as to

---

[18] *Schlagenhauf v. Holder*, 379 U.S. 104, 118 (1964); *Grogan v. Kumar*, 873 F.3d 273, 280 (5th Cir. 2017).

[19] *Flack v. Nutribullet, L.L.C.*, 333 F.R.D. 508, 513 (C.D. Cal. 2019).

[20] *Schlagenhauf v. Holder*, 379 U.S. 104, 112 (1964); *Flack v. Nutribullet, L.L.C.*, 333 F.R.D. 508, 513 (C.D. Cal. 2019).

[21] *See Ornelas v. Southern Tire Mart, LLC*, 292 F.R.D. 388, 391 (S.D. Tex. 2013); *Bradford Felmly v. Hills*, 222 F.R.D. 257, 258–59 (D.V.I. 2004).

[22] *See Robinson v. De Niro*, ___ F. Supp. 3d ___, 2022 WL 1210772, at *2 (S.D.N.Y. 2022) (motion deemed timely when filed before the deadline for expert discovery); *Arthur v. Dunn*, 195 F. Supp. 3d 1257, 1275 n.18 (M.D. Ala. 2016).

[23] *Merritt v. Stolt Offshore, Inc.*, 2004 WL 224578 (E.D. La. 2004) (holding that the court may order more than one examiner); *Fischer v. Coastal Towing Inc.*, 168 F.R.D. 199, 201 (E.D. Tex. 1996) (vocational-rehabilitation expert deemed a "suitably licensed and/or certified examiner").

[24] *Douponce v. Drake*, 183 F.R.D. 565, 566 (D. Colo. 1998) (allowing the defendant's selected examiner despite allegations of bias); *Lahr v. Fulbright & Jaworski, L.L.P.*, 164 F.R.D. 196, 202–03 (N.D. Tex. 1995).

[25] *See O'Sullivan v. Rivera*, 229 F.R.D. 184 (D.N.M. 2004) (the fact that the expert regularly testifies for defendants does not disqualify the expert under Rule 35); *Nyfield v. Virgin Islands Telephone Corp.*, 2001 WL 378858 (D.V.I. 2001) (absent evidence of bias, defendants allowed their chosen examiner.).

[26] *But see Hunt v. R & B Falcon Drilling USA, Inc.*, 2000 WL 1838327 (E.D. La. 2000) (a motion for a court appointed examiner is more properly brought under Federal Rule of Evidence 706).

whether the party who was examined may call the examiner as an expert.[27]

Type of Examination

The type of examination allowable depends on the circumstances of the case. Examinations can include blood tests, DNA tests,[28] x-rays,[29] electrocardiograms, fingerprint analysis,[30] and other safe, medically accepted tests indicated by the condition at issue.[31] Vocational examinations are also permissible.[32] The burden on the movant to show good cause will be greater if the tests are more invasive, painful, or burdensome, or if repeated examinations are sought.[33] However, a party who objects to a particular test as too painful or invasive may be precluded from offering evidence of the type that would result from the test. The courts are divided as to whether the motion must identify each test to be administered.[34]

Mental Examinations

Mental examinations are allowable if a person's mental condition is at issue.[35] The examination may be conducted by a psychiatrist or psychologist. Many courts are reluctant to order a mental examination based solely on a "garden variety" emotional distress allegation.[36]

Duration of the Examination

Disputes sometimes arise about the duration of the examination. Many courts are reluctant to impose a limit on the duration of the examination below the amount of time that

---

[27]*Rawers v. United States*, 488 F. Supp. 3d 1059, 1079 n.29 (D.N.M. 2020) (discussing the split); *Downs v. River City Group, LLC*, 288 F.R.D. 507, 511–13 (D. Nev. 2013) (requiring special circumstances for the plaintiff to call the examiner).

[28]*Ashby v. Mortimer*, 329 F.R.D. 650, 654 (D. Idaho 2019); *Turk v. Mangum*, 268 F. Supp. 3d 928, 939 (S.D. Tex. 2017).

[29]*Tarte v. U.S.*, 249 F.R.D. 856 (S.D. Fla. 2008) (x-rays and MRIs are routine procedures).

[30]*Harris v. Athol-Royalston Regional School Dist. Comm.*, 206 F.R.D. 30, 32–33 (D. Mass. 2002) (fingerprint samples may be obtained under either Rule 34 or Rule 35).

[31]*See Jefferys v. LRP Publications, Inc.*, 184 F.R.D. 262, 263 (E.D. Pa. 1999) (allowing interview by vocational expert).

[32]*See Ornelas v. Southern Tire Mart, LLC*, 292 F.R.D. 388, 393 (S.D. Tex. 2013); *Storms v. Lowe's Home Centers, Inc.*, 211 F.R.D. 296, 297 (W.D. Va. 2002).

[33]*See Patterson v. Def. POW/MIA Accounting Agency*, 343 F. Supp. 3d 637, 657 (W.D. Tex. 2018) (presumption against disinterment to conduct examination).

[34]*See Robinson v. De Niro*, ___ F. Supp. 3d ___, 2022 WL 1210772, at *2 (S.D.N.Y. 2022) (tests identified in motion); *Ren v. Phoenix Satellite Television (US), Inc.*, 309 F.R.D. 34, 37 (D.D.C. 2015) (describing the split in authority).

[35]*Robinson v. De Niro*, ___ F. Supp. 3d ___, 2022 WL 1210772, at *2 (S.D.N.Y. 2022); *Flores-Febus v. MVM, Inc.*, 299 F.R.D. 338, 340 (D.P.R. 2014).

[36]*See Snipes v. United States*, 334 F.R.D. 667, 669 (N.D. Cal. 2020); *In re E.I. du Pont de Nemours & Co. C-8 Pers. Injury Litig.*, 379 F. Supp. 3d 669, 672 (S.D. Ohio 2019).

the examining expert has requested.[37]

Objections to the Safety of the Examination

In order to oppose a mental or physical exam on the grounds that the exam is unsafe, a party must demonstrate that the proposed test is potentially dangerous. The burden then shifts to the party requesting the examination to show that it is both necessary and safe.[38]

Number of Examinations

If multiple conditions of the plaintiff are at issue, the court can order multiple examinations.[39] When permanent injuries are claimed or under other appropriate circumstances, the court may allow a second examination just before trial.[40] A stronger showing of necessity is usually required for a second examination.[41]

Time and Location

The court will designate the time and location of the examination in the order.[42] Usually, the plaintiff will be required to travel to the district where the action is pending to be examined.[43]

Cost of Examination

The moving party must pay the medical or professional expenses of the examination. The person to be examined is not entitled to compensation for transportation costs[44] or lost time.

Who Is Present at Examination

The court has discretion to determine who may be present at the examination.[45] Some courts allow persons being examined by a doctor to bring their own physician, others do not.[46] It is

---

[37]*See Robinson v. De Niro*, __ F. Supp. 3d __, 2022 WL 1210772, at *2 (S.D.N.Y. 2022); *Ren v. Phoenix Satellite Television (US), Inc.*, 309 F.R.D. 34, 37 (D.D.C. 2015).

[38]*Pena v. Troup*, 163 F.R.D. 352, 353–54 (D. Colo. 1995).

[39]*See Ornelas v. Southern Tire Mart, LLC*, 292 F.R.D. 388, 392 (S.D. Tex. 2013).

[40]*See Galieti v. State Farm Mut. Auto. Ins. Co.*, 154 F.R.D. 262 (D. Colo. 1994).

[41]*Furlong v. Circle Line Statue of Liberty Ferry, Inc.*, 902 F. Supp. 65 (S.D.N.Y. 1995).

[42]*J.H. v. School Town of Munster*, 38 F. Supp. 3d 986, 988 (N.D. Ind. 2014).

[43]*Rodriguez v. Gusman*, 974 F.3d 108, 115 (2d Cir. 2020) (plaintiff not required to travel when legally barred from entering the U.S.).

[44]*McCloskey v. United Parcel Service General Services Co.*, 171 F.R.D. 268, 270 (D. Or. 1997).

[45]*See Tarte v. U.S.*, 249 F.R.D. 856 (S.D. Fla. 2008) (presence of 3rd party or recording device are within the court's discretion); *Bethel v. Dixie Homecrafters, Inc.*, 192 F.R.D. 320 (N.D. Ga.2000).

[46]*See Ren v. Phoenix Satellite Television (US), Inc.*, 309 F.R.D. 34, 36 (D.D.C. 2015) (courts generally do not permit attorneys or other experts to be present); *Favale v. Roman Catholic Diocese of Bridgeport*, 235 F.R.D. 553, 555 (D. Conn. 2006) (Rule 35 does not provide for anyone to be present).

also unsettled whether attorneys have a right to be present.[47]

Audio and Video Recording

The court may, in its discretion, allow the examination to be recorded, but many courts do not allow audio, video, or stenographic recording of the examination absent "special circumstances."[48]

No Inherent Authority to Order Examinations

Rule 35 provides the exclusive mechanism for obtaining an examination of a party. Thus, for example, a court does not have the inherent authority to order a party to submit to a blood test, and must follow the procedures in Rule 35.[49]

Sanctions

If a party fails to comply with the order, most of the sanctions in Rule 37(b)(2)—imposing sanctions for failure to comply with a discovery order—are available, such as deeming certain facts established or refusing to allow the violator to oppose or support certain claims.[50] However, contempt sanctions are not available for failure to submit to the examination.[51] If a person within the control of a party is to be examined, no sanctions apply to that person because the person is not a party. The party's duty is to make a good faith effort to obtain the person's presence, and the party will be subject to sanctions if the party fails to make the requisite good faith effort.[52]

Actions Applicable

Examinations are available in all civil actions in federal court,[53] subject to certain narrow exceptions in Rule 81. The court may also order an examination in connection with a deposition to perpetuate testimony under Rule 27.[54]

Appeal

The courts are split as to whether an order directing or refusing an examination is interlocutory, and thus generally not

[47]*See Ornelas v. Southern Tire Mart, LLC*, 292 F.R.D. 388, 395–96 (S.D. Tex. 2013) (requiring special circumstances for counsel to be present); *Marsch v. Rensselaer County*, 218 F.R.D. 367, 371 (N.D.N.Y. 2003) (Fifth Amendment concerns dictated allowing counsel to be present).

[48]*See Mager v. Wisconsin Cent. Ltd.*, 924 F.3d 831, 836 (6th Cir. 2019) (discussing unauthorized recording); *Robinson v. De Niro*, ___ F. Supp. 3d ___, 2022 WL 1210772, at *2 (S.D.N.Y. 2022) (no good cause to record); *Buckler v. Israel*, 309 F.R.D. 672, 674 (S.D. Fla. 2015) (stenographer not allowed).

[49]*Fong Sik Leung v. Dulles*, 226 F.2d 74, 76 (9th Cir. 1955).

[50]*See Mager v. Wisconsin Cent. Ltd.*, 924 F.3d 831, 836 (6th Cir. 2019).

[51]*Sibbach v. Wilson & Co.*, 312 U.S. 1, 312 U.S. 655 (1941); *Foy v. U.S.*, 285 F.R.D. 407, 408–09 (N.D. Iowa 2012) (Rule 35 applicable in habeas proceedings).

[52]The Advisory Committee Note to the 1970 amendment of Rule 35(a).

[53]*Caban ex rel. Crespo v. 600 E. 21st Street Co.*, 200 F.R.D. 176 (E.D.N.Y. 2001) (Rule 35 governs in diversity cases even in the face of conflicting state rules regarding examinations of parties).

[54]*See* Rules 27(a)(3) and 27(b).

appealable until the end of the action, or may be appealed immediately as a collateral order.[55]

RULE 35(b)—EXAMINER'S REPORT

CORE CONCEPT

Upon request by the party or person examined, the party who moved for the examination must provide a copy of a detailed written report by the examiner, together with any reports of earlier examinations for the same condition. Following the delivery of such a copy, the examined party must provide copies of reports of any other examinations for the same condition, whether conducted before or after the Rule 35 examination.

APPLICATIONS

Report

The examiner must prepare a written report that sets out in detail the examiner's findings, including diagnoses, conclusions, and the results of any tests.[56]

Request for Report

The examined party may obtain a copy of the examiner's report by making a request to the examining party.[57] The examining party is not obligated to disclose the report under the expert disclosure provisions in Rule 26(a)(2)—the Rule 35 process exclusively governs the exchange of Rule 35 reports.[58]

Reports of Examination by Agreement

The report exchanging provisions apply to examinations by agreement unless the agreement expressly provides otherwise.

The Report Limits Testimony by the Examiner

Testimony by the examiner will be limited to the opinions disclosed in the report.[59]

Request for Report Waives Privileges

A request for a report under Rule 35 acts as a waiver of the doctor-patient or psychologist-patient privilege for other examinations for the same condition.[60] Thus, the examined party may not refuse to produce other reports on the basis of privilege once the party has requested a copy of the report of the Rule 35 examination.

Deposing the Examiner

The examined party may take the deposition of the

---

[55] *See Goodman v. Harris County*, 443 F.3d 464, 467–68 (5th Cir. 2006); *O'Malley v. Chrysler Corp.*, 160 F.2d 35 (C.C.A. 7th Cir. 1947).

[56] *Flack v. Nutribullet, L.L.C.*, 333 F.R.D. 508, 513 (C.D. Cal. 2019).

[57] *Flack v. Nutribullet, L.L.C.*, 333 F.R.D. 508, 513 (C.D. Cal. 2019).

[58] *Flack v. Nutribullet, L.L.C.*, 333 F.R.D. 508, 513 (C.D. Cal. 2019).

[59] *Licciardi v. TIG Ins. Group*, 140 F.3d 357 (1st Cir. 1998) (testimony beyond the scope of the report excluded).

[60] *Cunningham v. Connecticut Mut. Life Ins.*, 845 F. Supp. 1403 (S.D. Cal. 1994).

examiner.[61]

Failure to Exchange Reports

If either party fails to provide covered reports, the court can order production or exclude testimony related to the conditions at issue.[62]

Failure to Draft Report

If the examiner fails to prepare or provide a report, the court may exclude the examiner's testimony.[63]

Extraneous Material

If the report contains extraneous or unreasonably prejudicial material, the court can order those portions excised.

Additional Research References

Wright & Miller, *Federal Practice and Procedure* §§ 2231 to 2239
C.J.S., Federal Civil Procedure §§ 752 to 755
West's Key Number Digest, Federal Civil Procedure ⚷1651 to 1664

---

[61]*Tarte v. U.S.*, 249 F.R.D. 856, 859 (S.D. Fla. 2008).

[62]Fed. R. Civ. P. 35(b)(5).

[63]Fed. R. Civ. P. 35(b)(5).

RULE 36
REQUESTS FOR ADMISSION

(a) **Scope and Procedure.**

(1) *Scope.* A party may serve on any other party a written request to admit, for purposes of the pending action only, the truth of any matters within the scope of Rule 26(b)(1) relating to:

(A) facts, the application of law to fact, or opinions about either; and

(B) the genuineness of any described documents.

(2) *Form; Copy of a Document.* Each matter must be separately stated. A request to admit the genuineness of a document must be accompanied by a copy of the document unless it is, or has been, otherwise furnished or made available for inspection and copying.

(3) *Time to Respond; Effect of Not Responding.* A matter is admitted unless, within 30 days after being served, the party to whom the request is directed serves on the requesting party a written answer or objection addressed to the matter and signed by the party or its attorney. A shorter or longer time for responding may be stipulated to under Rule 29 or be ordered by the court.

(4) *Answer.* If a matter is not admitted, the answer must specifically deny it or state in detail why the answering party cannot truthfully admit or deny it. A denial must fairly respond to the substance of the matter; and when good faith requires that a party qualify an answer or deny only a part of a matter, the answer must specify the part admitted and qualify or deny the rest. The answering party may assert lack of knowledge or information as a reason for failing to admit or deny only if the party states that it has made reasonable inquiry and that the information it knows or can readily obtain is insufficient to enable it to admit or deny.

(5) *Objections.* The grounds for objecting to a request

must be stated. A party must not object solely on the ground that the request presents a genuine issue for trial.

(6) *Motion Regarding the Sufficiency of an Answer or Objection.* The requesting party may move to determine the sufficiency of an answer or objection. Unless the court finds an objection justified, it must order that an answer be served. On finding that an answer does not comply with this rule, the court may order either that the matter is admitted or that an amended answer be served. The court may defer its final decision until a pretrial conference or a specified time before trial. Rule 37(a)(5) applies to an award of expenses.

(b) **Effect of an Admission; Withdrawing or Amending It.** A matter admitted under this rule is conclusively established unless the court, on motion, permits the admission to be withdrawn or amended. Subject to Rule 16(e), the court may permit withdrawal or amendment if it would promote the presentation of the merits of the action and if the court is not persuaded that it would prejudice the requesting party in maintaining or defending the action on the merits. An admission under this rule is not an admission for any other purpose and cannot be used against the party in any other proceeding.

[Amended December 27, 1946, effective March 19, 1948; March 30, 1970, effective July 1, 1970; March 2, 1987, effective August 1, 1987; April 22, 1993, effective December 1, 1993; April 30, 2007, effective December 1, 2007.]

AUTHORS' COMMENTARY ON RULE 36

PURPOSE AND SCOPE

Rule 36 authorizes a party to serve another party with requests for admission in two categories: 1) requests to admit facts, the application of law to facts (similar to contention interrogatories), or opinions about either; and 2) the genuineness of any documents (to avoid the need to have a record custodian appear and testify about the documents' authenticity).

Admissions under Rule 36 are more powerful than admissions

obtained by other discovery techniques, like depositions or interrogatories. A party making an admission at a deposition or in response to an interrogatory can attempt to explain away the admission at trial by, for example, claiming to have been confused or to have misunderstood the question—the jury may not believe the explanation, but the party has the opportunity to offer it. An admitted request for admission, in contrast, is binding, and cannot be controverted or explained away at trial.

Requests for admission are a discretionary discovery device—any party may choose to serve them without leave of court. Rule 36 does not limit the number of requests for admission, although some local rules establish a limit. The recipient of requests for admission must serve a response within 30 days. Rule 36 attempts to avoid dodging the request by requiring that, if the response does not admit the request, it must specifically deny it or state in detail that the answering party cannot admit or deny it. The response may include objections as well.

Rule 36 (in conjunction with Rule 37) establishes a number of sanctions associated with requests for admission. The first is self-implementing; if a party does not timely respond to a request, the request is deemed admitted. Second, if a responding party denies a request and the requesting party subsequently proves that the matter was true or the document was authentic, then the requesting party may file a motion seeking its attorney's fees in proving the matter true or the document authentic, and the court must grant the motion unless it finds that the responding party had a reasonable basis to believe it would prevail on the matter.

RULE 36(a)—SCOPE AND PROCEDURE

CORE CONCEPT

Rule 36 establishes a procedure whereby one party serves requests for admission on another party, who must investigate and either admit, deny with specificity, demonstrate an inability to admit or deny, or object to each requested admission. Any request that is not denied in a timely fashion is admitted.

Rule 36 requests may address two topics: 1) facts or the application of law to facts; and 2) the authenticity of documents (to avoid having a records custodian appear to lay a foundation). Rule 36 admissions are particularly valuable in that any matter admitted is conclusively established—and thus may not be countered or explained away at trial. This quality is unique to requests for admission; admissions made in response to interrogatories or at depositions are generally admissible at trial, but are not conclusively established.

APPLICATIONS

Who May Serve

Any party may serve requests for admission.

Who May Be Served

Requests for admission are limited to parties to the action, although the party need not be an adverse party.

Time for Service

Requests for admission can be served after the parties have conducted the discovery conference under Rule 26(f).[1] In proceedings listed in Rule 26(a)(1)(B) as exempt from initial disclosures, there is no preliminary waiting period for requests for admission. The Rules do not set an outer limit on how late in the case requests for admission may be served, and courts are split as to whether requests for admission are discovery devices subject to a general discovery cutoff.[2] However, many local rules or case management orders will set a time limit for requests for admission. Usually, when such a time limit exists, requests for admission must be served so that the response is due before the specified deadline.[3]

Service and Filing of Requests for Admission

Copies of the requests for admission should be served on all parties. The requests are not filed at the time of service, but may be filed as an exhibit to a motion.

Contents and Format of Request

Each fact or matter for which admission is requested should be set forth in a separate paragraph.[4] All facts that are part of the request should be set forth in the request; it is improper to incorporate facts by reference to other text. Requests for admission must be simple, direct, and concise so they may be admitted or denied with little or no explanation or qualification.[5]

Scope and Topics

Requests for admission are subject to the general discovery scope set forth in Rule 26(b)(1) and the limitations on discovery in Rule 26(b)(2).[6] Within that general scope, requests for admission are limited to two categories:

- *Facts, the Application of Law to Fact, or Opinions about*

---

[1] *DIRECTV, Inc. v. DeVries*, 302 F. Supp. 2d 837, 838 (W.D. Mich. 2004).

[2] *Wyles v. Sussman*, 445 F. Supp. 3d 751, 756–57 (C.D. Cal. 2020).

[3] *Laborers' Pension Fund v. Blackmore Sewer Const., Inc.*, 298 F.3d 600, 605 (7th Cir. 2002); *Grondal v. Mill Bay Members Ass'n, Inc.*, 471 F. Supp. 3d 1095, 1124 (E.D. Wash. 2020) (no obligation to respond to untimely requests).

[4] *See Mach. Sols., Inc. v. Doosan Infracore Am. Corp.*, 323 F.R.D. 522, 535 (D.S.C. 2018) (each document should be the subject of a separate request); *Helget v. City of Hays, Kan.*, 300 F.R.D. 496, 499 (D. Kan. 2014) (where request contains multiple compound facts, responding party may deny if any of the facts are not true).

[5] *United Coal v. Powell Construction*, 839 F.2d 958, 967–68 (3d Cir. 1988); *Tamas v. Family Video Movie Club, Inc.*, 301 F.R.D. 346, 347 (N.D. Ill. 2014).

[6] *Inland Empire Waterkeeper v. Corona Clay Co.*, 17 F.4th 825, 837 (9th Cir. 2021); *Holcombe v. Helena Chemical Co.*, 238 F. Supp. 3d 767, 775 (D.S.C. 2017) (request pertaining to dismissed claim disallowed).

Either: Requests for admission may pertain to any issue in the case, including the ultimate facts at issue,[7] the application of law to fact,[8] or jurisdictional issues, but may not seek an admission as to a pure conclusion of law.[9] The purpose of requests for admission is to narrow the issues for trial,[10] not to lead to the discovery of admissible evidence.[11]

- *Authenticity of Documents:* A request may ask that the genuineness or authenticity of a document be admitted.[12] Each request should be limited to a single document and a copy of the document should be attached, unless it has already been provided in discovery.[13]

Opinions and Conclusions

A request for admission is not objectionable because it involves an opinion or contention that relates to fact or the application of law to fact.[14] A request may not seek a pure legal conclusion, with no application to the facts.[15]

Number

Rule 36 contains no limitation on the number of requests for admission. Some districts have local rules limiting the number of requests.

Time to Answer

A written response is due within 30 days of service.[16] The time to answer may be extended by stipulation under Rule 29.[17] Additionally, the court has discretion to lengthen or shorten the time in which a party must respond.[18]

---

[7] *In re Carney*, 258 F.3d 415, 419 (5th Cir. 2001).

[8] *Quasius v. Schwan Food Co.*, 596 F.3d 947, 950 (8th Cir. 2010); *In re Carney*, 258 F.3d 415, 419 (5th Cir. 2001).

[9] *Thompson v. Beasley*, 309 F.R.D. 236, 241 (N.D. Miss. 2015); *P.L.U.S. Brokerage, Inc. v. Jong Eun Kim*, 908 F. Supp. 2d 711, 715 (D. Md. 2012).

[10] *TD Bank N.A. v. Hill*, 928 F.3d 259, 287 (3d Cir. 2019).

[11] *See Thompson v. Beasley*, 309 F.R.D. 236, 241 (N.D. Miss. 2015); *Cutino v. Untch*, 303 F.R.D. 413, 414 (S.D. Fla. 2014).

[12] *Republic of Turkey v. Christie's, Inc.*, 326 F.R.D. 394, 399 (S.D.N.Y. 2018); *Booth Oil Site Administrative Group v. Safety-Kleen Corporation*, 194 F.R.D. 76, 80 (W.D.N.Y. 2000).

[13] *Mach. Sols., Inc. v. Doosan Infracore Am. Corp.*, 323 F.R.D. 522, 535 (D.S.C. 2018).

[14] *Marchand v. Mercy Medical Center*, 22 F.3d 933 (9th Cir.1994); *Woodward v. Holtzman*, 329 F.R.D. 16, 25 (W.D.N.Y. 2018).

[15] *Mach. Sols., Inc. v. Doosan Infracore Am. Corp.*, 323 F.R.D. 522, 534 (D.S.C. 2018); *P.L.U.S. Brokerage, Inc. v. Jong Eun Kim*, 908 F. Supp. 2d 711, 715 (D. Md. 2012).

[16] *Johnson v. Miller*, 363 F. Supp. 3d 806, 811 (E.D. Ky. 2019); *Dillon v. United States*, 357 F. Supp. 3d 49, 55 (D. Mass. 2019).

[17] *Lopez v. Don Herring Ltd.*, 327 F.R.D. 567, 582 (N.D. Tex. 2018); *Edeh v. Equifax Information Services, LLC*, 295 F.R.D. 219, 228 (D. Minn. 2013).

[18] *Manatt v. Union Pacific R. Co.*, 122 F.3d 514, 517 (8th Cir. 1997); *Black Hills Molding, Inc. v. Brandom Holdings, LLC*, 295 F.R.D. 403, 420

Service and Filing of Responses

Copies of the responses should be served on all parties. The responses are not filed at the time of service, but may be filed as an exhibit to a motion.

Form of Response

The response should be in writing and signed by the attorney, or by the party if unrepresented.[19] It should be a single document organized in numbered paragraphs to correspond to the requests.

Responses

The responding party essentially has four possible responses to a request for admission: the party can admit the request (in part or in full); deny the request (in part or in full); set forth reasons why the party cannot admit or deny the request; or object to the request (by a specific objection or by a motion for a protective order under Rule 26(c), as described below).[20]

Denials

A denial must specifically address the substance of the requested admission.[21] The denial may be as simple as the single word "denied,"[22] or may be a longer sentence, but may not sidestep the request or be evasive.[23] If the propounding party feels that the denial is not sufficiently specific, the party can move the court to determine the sufficiency of the denial.[24] If the court deems the denial not sufficiently specific, it can deem the denial an admission or order a more specific answer.

Partial Denials

If the responding party believes that part of a requested admission is accurate and part is not, the proper response is to admit the accurate portion and deny the balance.[25]

Inability to Admit or Deny

If the responding party is genuinely unable to admit or deny the requested admission, the party can so state, but must describe in detail why, after reasonable inquiry, the party can-

---

(D.S.D. 2013) (responses served 1 day late deemed timely).

[19]The Advisory Committee Note to Rule 36(a).

[20]*See Odom v. Roberts*, 337 F.R.D. 347, 351 (N.D. Fla. 2020).

[21]*Helget v. City of Hays, Kan.*, 300 F.R.D. 496, 502 (D. Kan. 2014) (improper to change the wording in the request); *Lynn v. Monarch Recovery Mgmt., Inc.*, 285 F.R.D. 350, 363 (D. Md. 2012).

[22]*Caruso v. Coleman Co.*, 1995 WL 347003 (E.D. Pa. 1995); *Wanke v. Lynn's Transp. Co.*, 836 F. Supp. 587 (N.D. Ind. 1993).

[23]*Asea, Inc. v. Southern Pac. Transp. Co.*, 669 F.2d 1242, 1245 (9th Cir. 1981) (evasive denial may be deemed an admission); *U.S. ex rel. Englund v. Los Angeles County*, 235 F.R.D. 675 (E.D. Cal. 2006) (denial may not be based on an overly-technical reading of the request.).

[24]*See TD Bank N.A. v. Hill*, 928 F.3d 259, 276 n.9 (3d Cir. 2019).

[25]*ATD Corp. v. Lydall, Inc.*, 159 F.3d 534, 549 (Fed. Cir. 1998); *JSM Marine LLC v. Gaughf*, 407 F. Supp. 3d 1358, 1380 (S.D. Ga. 2019).

not admit or deny.[26] Some courts hold that a general statement that the responding party has insufficient information to respond will be treated as an insufficient answer, and upon motion the court will treat the answer as an admission or will order a further answer.[27] Other courts hold that a statement that the responding party has made reasonable inquiry is sufficient, without detail about the nature of the inquiry.[28]

Objections

Objections must be made in writing within the time allowed for answering.[29] Typical grounds for objections to requests for admission are:

- *Privilege:* If a response requires the disclosure of privileged matters, it is objectionable.[30] *See* Rule 26(b)(5) (discussing commonly asserted privileges).
- *Vague or Ambiguous:* A request may be objectionable if it is so vague or ambiguous that the responding party cannot answer it.[31]
- *Seeking a Pure Legal Conclusion:* A request may be objectionable if it seeks a pure legal conclusion, without requiring the application of facts specific to the matter.[32]

Improper Objections

A party cannot refuse to answer a request on the basis that the serving party already knows the answer, that the request calls for an opinion or contention, that the subject matter is within the other party's own knowledge, that it invades the province of the jury, that it addresses a subject for expert testimony, that it presents a genuine issue for trial,[33] that it pertains to the "ultimate facts,"[34] that the document at issue

---

[26] *Yoder & Frey Auctioneers, Inc. v. EquipmentFacts, LLC*, 774 F.3d 1065, 1076 (6th Cir. 2014); *VeroBlue Farms USA Inc. v. Wulf*, — F.R.D. —, 2021 WL 5176839, at *14 (N.D. Tex. 2021).

[27] *Riberio v. Macy's Retail Holdings, Inc.*, 310 F.R.D. 547, 548 (N.D. Ga. 2015); *Erie Ins. Property & Cas. Co. v. Johnson*, 272 F.R.D. 177, 184 (S.D.W. Va. 2010).

[28] *See S.E.C. v. Goldstone*, 300 F.R.D. 505, 523–24 (D.N.M. 2014); *Edeh v. Equifax Information Services, LLC*, 291 F.R.D. 330, 337 (D. Minn. 2013).

[29] *P.L.U.S. Brokerage, Inc. v. Jong Eun Kim*, 908 F. Supp. 2d 711, 716 (D. Md. 2012) (failure to assert objections waives the objections).

[30] *U.S. v. One Tract of Real Property Together With all Bldgs., Improvements, Appurtenances and Fixtures*, 95 F.3d 422, 428 (6th Cir. 1996); *In re Avandia Mktg., Sales Practices & Prod. Liab. Litig.*, 415 F. Supp. 3d 498, 505 (E.D. Pa. 2019).

[31] *See Republic of Turkey v. Christie's, Inc.*, 326 F.R.D. 394, 399 (S.D.N.Y. 2018); *Erie Ins. Property & Cas. Co. v. Johnson*, 272 F.R.D. 177, 185 (S.D.W. Va. 2010).

[32] *Mach. Sols., Inc. v. Doosan Infracore Am. Corp.*, 323 F.R.D. 522, 534 (D.S.C. 2018); *P.L.U.S. Brokerage, Inc. v. Jong Eun Kim*, 908 F. Supp. 2d 711, 715 (D. Md. 2012).

[33] *Woodward v. Holtzman*, 329 F.R.D. 16, 25 n.6 (W.D.N.Y. 2018); *Cumis Ins. Soc'y, Inc. v. Clark*, 318 F. Supp. 3d 199, 215 (D.D.C. 2018).

[34] *Padgett v. Big Sandy Reg'l Det.*

speaks for itself,[35] that the responding party is not the custodian of the document, or that it is more properly directed to another party.[36] Likewise, it is irrelevant who has the burden of proof with respect to the matter for which admission is requested. An improper objection is not the same as an admission, and the proper response to an improper objection is to file a motion to compel a further response.[37]

Duty to Supplement

Rule 26(e) imposes a duty to supplement a denial or statement of inability to admit or deny if the party learns that the original response is in some material respect incomplete or incorrect, and if the additional or corrective information has not been provided to the other parties in writing or at a deposition.[38] Conversely, a party does not have the unilateral right to change an admission by supplement; rather, a party must file a motion to withdraw or amend its admission under Rule 36(b).[39]

Motion for a Protective Order

As an alternative to making objections to individual requests for admission, the responding party may make a motion for a protective order under Rule 26(c). A motion for a protective order is potentially appropriate when most or all of a set of requests is objectionable. Motions for protective orders relating to written discovery are rare, however, because it is easier and less expensive for the responding party to interpose objections, shifting the burden to the requesting party to file a motion to compel.

Failure to Respond

Failure to respond in a timely fashion is deemed an admission.[40]

Serving Untimely Responses

If the allowed time for a response has passed, responding parties sometimes simply serve untimely responses and sometimes move for leave to serve the untimely responses. The court has discretion to allow the receiving party to submit the

Ctr., 424 F. Supp. 3d 506, 509 (E.D. Ky. 2019).

[35]*VeroBlue Farms USA Inc. v. Wulf*, __ F.R.D. __, 2021 WL 5176839, at *13 (N.D. Tex. 2021).

[36]*Harris v. Koenig*, 271 F.R.D. 356, 374 (D.D.C. 2010); *Frontier-Kemper Constructors, Inc. v. Elk Run Coal Co., Inc.*, 246 F.R.D. 522, 531 (S.D.W. Va. 2007).

[37]*See TD Bank N.A. v. Hill*, 928 F.3d 259, 276 n.9 (3d Cir. 2019); *Butler v. Oak Creek-Franklin School Dist.*, 172 F. Supp. 2d 1102, 1122, (E.D. Wis. 2001).

[38]*VeroBlue Farms USA Inc. v. Wulf*, __ F.R.D. __, 2021 WL 5176839, at *4 (N.D. Tex. 2021); *House v. Giant of Maryland LLC*, 232 F.R.D. 257, 259 (E.D. Va. 2005).

[39]*Nat'l Union Fire Ins. Co. of Pittsburgh, PA v. PVT Ltd.*, 338 F.R.D. 579, 585–86 (S.D.N.Y. 2021).

[40]*Batyukova v. Doege*, 994 F.3d 717, 724 (5th Cir. 2021); *Kaliannan v. Liang*, 2 F.4th 727, 736 (8th Cir. 2021).

response.[41] Some courts apply the standard for withdrawing admissions under Rule 36(b) to such late responses,[42] others apply the "good cause" standard from Rule 6(b) to attempts to submit untimely responses to requests for admission,[43] and others apply both.[44]

Motion to Determine Sufficiency/Motion to Compel

If a party believes that a response is insufficient or that an objection is improper, the party can move the court to determine the sufficiency of the answer or objection.[45] "Insufficient" refers to the specificity of the response, not whether the response is correct or in good faith.[46] The burden will be on the party raising an objection to show that the objection was proper.[47] If the court determines that the answer was insufficient, it can deem the answer an admission or can order a more complete answer.[48] The court may also defer ruling until later in the pretrial proceedings.[49]

- *Expenses of Motion to Determine Sufficiency:* The party losing a motion to determine the sufficiency of a response pays the other party's expenses incurred in connection with the motion, including a reasonable attorney's fee, pursuant to Rule 37(a)(5).[50]

Sanctions

The sanctions available depend upon the conduct of the responding party. The sanction for failure to respond is that the requests are deemed admitted.[51] The sanction for improperly denying a request is that the responding party will be required to pay the costs that the other party incurred in proving the matter, including attorney's fees.[52] The sanction for an insufficient answer or improper objection is that the response

---

[41] *U.S. v. Petroff-Kline*, 557 F.3d 285, 293–93 (6th Cir. 2009) (responses 3 days late deemed timely); *U.S. Bank Nat'l Ass'n v. Gunn*, 23 F. Supp. 3d 426, 433 (D. Del. 2014).

[42] *See Estate of Jones by Jones v. City of Martinsburg, W. Virginia*, 961 F.3d 661, 666 (4th Cir. 2020).

[43] *Mason Tenders Dist. Council Welfare Fund v. LJC Dismantling Corp.*, 400 F. Supp. 3d 7, 22 (S.D.N.Y. 2019).

[44] *See C.J. Hughes Constr. Co. Inc. v. EQM Gathering OPCO, LLC*, 358 F. Supp. 3d 486, 489 n.1 (W.D. Pa. 2019).

[45] *See TD Bank N.A. v. Hill*, 928 F.3d 259, 276 n.9 (3d Cir. 2019); *McCarthy v. Ameritech Pub., Inc.*, 763 F.3d 488, 493 (6th Cir. 2014).

[46] *Foretich v. Chung*, 151 F.R.D. 3 (D.D.C. 1993).

[47] *In re Avandia Mktg., Sales Practices & Prod. Liab. Litig.*, 415 F. Supp. 3d 498, 505 (E.D. Pa. 2019).

[48] *VeroBlue Farms USA Inc. v. Wulf*, — F.R.D. —, 2021 WL 5176839, at *4 (N.D. Tex. 2021); *Odom v. Roberts*, 337 F.R.D. 347, 351 (N.D. Fla. 2020).

[49] The Advisory Committee Note to Rule 36(a).

[50] *See McCarthy v. Ameritech Pub., Inc.*, 763 F.3d 488, 493–94 (6th Cir. 2014).

[51] *VeroBlue Farms USA Inc. v. Wulf*, — F.R.D. —, 2021 WL 5176839, at *4 (N.D. Tex. 2021); *Shelton v. Fast Advance Funding, LLC*, 378 F. Supp. 3d 356 (E.D. Pa. 2019).

[52] *McCarthy v. Ameritech Pub., Inc.*, 763 F.3d 488, 491 (6th Cir. 2014); *VeroBlue Farms USA Inc. v. Wulf*, — F.R.D. —, 2021 WL 5176839, at *5

may be deemed an admission, plus if the requesting party filed a motion to compel, the responding party will be liable for the requesting party's expenses in bringing the motion, including a reasonable attorney's fee.[53] Sanctions can be awarded against the party under Rule 37(c) and/or against the attorney under Rule 26(g).[54]

RULE 36(b)—EFFECT OF AN ADMISSION; WITHDRAWING OR AMENDING IT

CORE CONCEPT

An admission is deemed conclusively established unless the court permits withdrawal or amendment of the admission.

APPLICATIONS

Binding Nature of Formal Admissions

A matter formally admitted under Rule 36 is conclusively established and may not be contradicted[55] unless the court allows for the withdrawal or amendment of the admission.[56] In contrast, a statement at a deposition or in an interrogatory answer may be controverted or explained away at trial.[57] Likewise, an informal, extrajudicial admission is admissible evidence, but not conclusive.[58]

Admissions Binding Only in Pending Proceeding

An admission is only binding within the action in which the request was served.[59]

Use of Admissions at Trial or in Motion Practice

An admission may be introduced at trial or in the context of a motion, such as a motion for summary judgment.[60] Additionally, a party may ask the judge to instruct the jury that they must accept the admitted fact as conclusive.[61]

Evidentiary Objections

Admissions are still subject to evidentiary objections at

(N.D. Tex. 2021).

[53]*Lynn v. Monarch Recovery Mgmt., Inc.*, 285 F.R.D. 350, 365 (D. Md. 2012).

[54]*Johnson Intern. Co. v. Jackson Nat. Life Ins. Co.*, 19 F.3d 431 (8th Cir. 1994).

[55]*Inland Empire Waterkeeper v. Corona Clay Co.*, 17 F.4th 825, 837 (9th Cir. 2021); *United Fire & Cas. Co. v. Prate Roofing & Installations, LLC*, 7 F.4th 573, 584 (7th Cir. 2021).

[56]*Pinnacle Advert. & Mktg. Grp., Inc. v. Pinnacle Advert. & Mktg. Grp., LLC*, 7 F.4th 989, 1007 (11th Cir. 2021).

[57]*Berkowitz v. Berkowitz*, 817 F.3d 809, 812 (1st Cir. 2016).

[58]*Murrey v. U.S.*, 73 F.3d 1448, 1455 (7th Cir. 1996); *Hewett v. City of King*, 29 F. Supp. 3d 584, 635 n.34 (M.D.N.C. 2014).

[59]*United Fire & Cas. Co. v. Prate Roofing & Installations, LLC*, 7 F.4th 573, 584 (7th Cir. 2021); *Am. Civil Liberties Union v. The Florida Bar*, 999 F.2d 1486 (11th Cir.1993).

[60]*Sec'y U. S. Dep't of Labor v. Kwasny*, 853 F.3d 87, 91 (3d Cir. 2017); *Quasius v. Schwan Food Co.*, 596 F.3d 947, 950–51 (8th Cir. 2010).

[61]*Inland Empire Waterkeeper v. Corona Clay Co.*, 17 F.4th 825, 837 (9th Cir. 2021).

trial, such as relevance and hearsay.[62] However, adverse parties can use the exception to the hearsay rule for admissions of party opponents.[63]

Use by Party Making Admission

The party making the admission may not introduce it at trial.[64]

Co-parties Not Bound

An admission will only be binding on the admitting party and will not be binding on any co-parties.[65]

Withdrawal

Upon motion,[66] the court may allow withdrawal or amendment of an admission when doing so will aid in the resolution of the matter on the merits and when the party who obtained the admission will not be prejudiced by the amendment or withdrawal.[67] "Prejudice" focuses upon the difficulty a party may face in proving its case due to the sudden need to obtain evidence with respect to issues previously addressed by the admissions.[68] Amendment or withdrawal will not be allowed where prejudice will result to the opponent from reliance on the admission.[69] At the same time, courts generally favor adjudication of claims on the merits, and will allow withdrawal in the absence of prejudice to the opposing party.[70] The court has broad discretion in ruling on motions to withdraw or amend admissions.[71] Notably absent from this test is any mention of the responding party's conduct or reason for seeking the amendment or withdrawal—while the court may consider whether the party seeking withdrawal had good cause, it is not required

---

[62]*Walsh v. McCain Foods Ltd.*, 81 F.3d 722, 726 (7th Cir. 1996); *Harris v. Koenig*, 271 F.R.D. 356, 373 (D.D.C. 2010).

[63]*Walsh v. McCain Foods Ltd.*, 81 F.3d 722, 726 (7th Cir. 1996).

[64]*In re Air Crash*, 982 F. Supp. 1060, 1067 (D.S.C. 1996).

[65]*Kemp v. Hudgins*, 133 F. Supp. 3d 1271, 1275 n.17 (D. Kan. 2015).

[66]*Stine Seed Co. v. A & W Agribusiness, LLC*, 862 F.3d 1094, 1102 (8th Cir. 2017) ("motion" includes court papers that are not formal motions); *Beane v. RPW Legal Servs., PLLC*, 378 F. Supp. 3d 948 (W.D. Wash. 2019) (unilateral withdrawal ineffective); *Nat'l Fire & Marine Ins. Co. v. Wells*, 301 F. Supp. 3d 1082, 1090 (N.D. Ala. 2018) (court may not *sua sponte* withdraw an admission).

[67]*Wells Fargo Bank, N.A. v. Mesh Suture, Inc.*, 31 F.4th 1300, 1313 n.9 (10th Cir. 2022); *Tate & Lyle Americas LLC v. Glatt Air Techniques Inc.*, 863 F.3d 569, 571 (7th Cir. 2017).

[68]*Kerry Steel, Inc. v. Paragon Indus., Inc.*, 106 F.3d 147, 154 (6th Cir. 1997); *Brook Vill. N. Assocs. v. Gen. Elec. Co.*, 686 F.2d 66, 70 (1st Cir. 1982).

[69]*Blow v. Bijora, Inc.*, 855 F.3d 793, 799 (7th Cir. 2017); *Simstad v. Scheub*, 816 F.3d 893, 899 (7th Cir. 2016).

[70]*See Anderson v. Hansen*, __ F. Supp. 3d __, 2022 WL 308577, at *4 (E.D. Wis. 2022); *United States Sec. & Exch. Comm'n v. Collector's Coffee Inc.*, 537 F. Supp. 3d 497, 500 (S.D.N.Y. 2021).

[71]*Foss v. Marvic Inc.*, 994 F.3d 57, 63 (1st Cir. 2021); *Simstad v. Scheub*, 816 F.3d 893, 899 (7th Cir. 2016); *Conlon v. U.S.*, 474 F.3d 616, 621 (9th Cir. 2007).

to do so.[72] Some local rules require parties to meet and confer before filing a motion to withdraw or amend admissions.[73] When a court allows withdrawal or modification of an admission, both responses may be admissible and used to impeach the party.[74]

- *Withdrawal of Deemed Admission:* Courts will sometimes deem a response filed shortly after the due date to be made pursuant to an implied or constructive motion to withdraw the deemed admission[75] (but the safer course is to file a motion to withdraw). The courts are split as to whether an attempt to serve late responses is governed by Rule 36(b),[76] Rule 6(b) (governing extending time periods),[77] or both.[78]

Proof of Admission by Failure to Answer

In order to use the failure to answer as an admission, the offering party must prove service of the requests and the failure to answer.[79] This can be accomplished by filing the requests (with the certificate of service) and an affidavit that no response was received.

Additional Research References

Wright & Miller, *Federal Practice and Procedure* §§ 2251 to 2265
C.J.S., Federal Civil Procedure §§ 756 to 774 et seq.
West's Key Number Digest, Federal Civil Procedure ⚷1671 to 1686

---

[72] *See Friedman v. Live Nation Merchandise, Inc.*, 833 F.3d 1180, 1185 (9th Cir. 2016) (court may consider reason for delay); *In re Durability Inc.*, 212 F.3d 551 (10th Cir. 2000).

[73] *See, e.g., Edeh v. Equifax Information Services, LLC*, 295 F.R.D. 219, 224 (D. Minn. 2013).

[74] *Edwards v. Jolliff-Blake*, 907 F.3d 1052, 1066 (7th Cir. 2018).

[75] *See Estate of Jones by Jones v. City of Martinsburg, W. Virginia*, 961 F.3d 661, 666 (4th Cir. 2020).

[76] *See Estate of Jones by Jones v. City of Martinsburg, W. Virginia*, 961 F.3d 661, 666 (4th Cir. 2020).

[77] *Mason Tenders Dist. Council Welfare Fund v. LJC Dismantling Corp.*, 400 F. Supp. 3d 7, 22 (S.D.N.Y. 2019).

[78] *See C.J. Hughes Constr. Co. Inc. v. EQM Gathering OPCO, LLC*, 358 F. Supp. 3d 486, 489 n.1 (W.D. Pa. 2019).

[79] *Gilbert v. General Motors Corporation*, 133 F.2d 997 (2d Cir. 1943).

RULE 37
FAILURE TO MAKE DISCLOSURES OR TO COOPERATE IN DISCOVERY; SANCTIONS

(a) **Motion for an Order Compelling Disclosure or Discovery.**

(1) *In General.* On notice to other parties and all affected persons, a party may move for an order compelling disclosure or discovery. The motion must include a certification that the movant has in good faith conferred or attempted to confer with the person or party failing to make disclosure or discovery in an effort to obtain it without court action.

(2) *Appropriate Court.* A motion for an order to a party must be made in the court where the action is pending. A motion for an order to a nonparty must be made in the court where the discovery is or will be taken.

(3) *Specific Motions.*

(A) *To Compel Disclosure.* If a party fails to make a disclosure required by Rule 26(a), any other party may move to compel disclosure and for appropriate sanctions.

(B) *To Compel a Discovery Response.* A party seeking discovery may move for an order compelling an answer, designation, production, or inspection. This motion may be made if:

(i) a deponent fails to answer a question asked under Rule 30 or 31;

(ii) a corporation or other entity fails to make a designation under Rule 30(b)(6) or 31(a)(4);

(iii) a party fails to answer an interrogatory submitted under Rule 33; or

(iv) a party fails to produce documents or fails to respond that inspection will be permitted—or fails to permit inspection—as requested under Rule 34.

(C) *Related to a Deposition.* When taking an oral deposition, the party asking a question may complete or adjourn the examination before moving for an order.

(4) *Evasive or Incomplete Disclosure, Answer, or Response.* For purposes of this subdivision (a), an evasive or incomplete disclosure, answer, or response must be treated as a failure to disclose, answer, or respond.

(5) *Payment of Expenses; Protective Orders.*

(A) *If the Motion Is Granted (or Disclosure or Discovery Is Provided After Filing).* If the motion is granted—or if the disclosure or requested discovery is provided after the motion was filed—the court must, after giving an opportunity to be heard, require the party or deponent whose conduct necessitated the motion, the party or attorney advising that conduct, or both to pay the movant's reasonable expenses incurred in making the motion, including attorney's fees. But the court must not order this payment if:

(i) the movant filed the motion before attempting in good faith to obtain the disclosure or discovery without court action;

(ii) the opposing party's nondisclosure, response, or objection was substantially justified; or

(iii) other circumstances make an award of expenses unjust.

(B) *If the Motion Is Denied.* If the motion is denied, the court may issue any protective order authorized under Rule 26(c) and must, after giving an opportunity to be heard, require the movant, the attorney filing the motion, or both to pay the party or deponent who opposed the motion its reasonable expenses incurred in opposing the motion, including attorney's fees. But the court must not order this payment if the motion was substantially justified or other circumstances make an award of expenses unjust.

(C) *If the Motion Is Granted in Part and Denied in Part.* If the motion is granted in part and denied in part, the court may issue any protective order authorized under Rule 26(c) and may, after giving an opportunity to be heard, apportion the reasonable expenses for the motion.

(b) **Failure to Comply with a Court Order.**

(1) *Sanctions in the District Where the Deposition Is Taken.* If the court where the discovery is taken orders a deponent to be sworn or to answer a question and the deponent fails to obey, the failure may be treated as contempt of court. If a deposition-related motion is transferred to the court where the action is pending, and that court orders a deponent to be sworn or to answer a question and the deponent fails to obey, the failure may be treated as contempt of either the court where the discovery is taken or the court where the action is pending.

(2) *Sanctions Sought in the District Where the Action Is Pending.*

(A) *For Not Obeying a Discovery Order.* If a party or a party's officer, director, or managing agent—or a witness designated under Rule 30(b)(6) or 31(a)(4)—fails to obey an order to provide or permit discovery, including an order under Rule 26(f), 35, or 37(a), the court where the action is pending may issue further just orders. They may include the following:

(i) directing that the matters embraced in the order or other designated facts be taken as established for purposes of the action, as the prevailing party claims;

(ii) prohibiting the disobedient party from supporting or opposing designated claims or defenses, or from introducing designated matters in evidence;

(iii) striking pleadings in whole or in part;

(iv) staying further proceedings until the order is obeyed;

(v) dismissing the action or proceeding in whole or in part;

(vi) rendering a default judgment against the disobedient party; or

(vii) treating as contempt of court the failure to obey any order except an order to submit to a physical or mental examination.

(B) *For Not Producing a Person for Examination.* If a party fails to comply with an order under Rule 35(a) requiring it to produce another person for examination, the court may issue any of the orders listed in Rule 37(b)(2)(A)(i)-(vi), unless the disobedient party shows that it cannot produce the other person.

(C) *Payment of Expenses.* Instead of or in addition to the orders above, the court must order the disobedient party, the attorney advising that party, or both to pay the reasonable expenses, including attorney's fees, caused by the failure, unless the failure was substantially justified or other circumstances make an award of expenses unjust.

(c) **Failure to Disclose, to Supplement an Earlier Response, or to Admit.**

(1) *Failure to Disclose or Supplement.* If a party fails to provide information or identify a witness as required by Rule 26(a) or (e), the party is not allowed to use that information or witness to supply evidence on a motion, at a hearing, or at a trial, unless the failure was substantially justified or is harmless. In addition to or instead of this sanction, the court, on motion and after giving an opportunity to be heard:

(A) may order payment of the reasonable expenses, including attorney's fees, caused by the failure;

(B) may inform the jury of the party's failure; and

(C) may impose other appropriate sanctions, including any of the orders listed in Rule 37(b)(2)(A)(i)-(vi).

(2) *Failure to Admit.* If a party fails to admit what is requested under Rule 36 and if the requesting

party later proves a document to be genuine or the matter true, the requesting party may move that the party who failed to admit pay the reasonable expenses, including attorney's fees, incurred in making that proof. The court must so order unless:

(A) the request was held objectionable under Rule 36(a);

(B) the admission sought was of no substantial importance;

(C) the party failing to admit had a reasonable ground to believe that it might prevail on the matter; or

(D) there was other good reason for the failure to admit.

(d) **Party's Failure to Attend Its Own Deposition, Serve Answers to Interrogatories, or Respond to a Request for Inspection.**

(1) *In General.*

(A) *Motion; Grounds for Sanctions.* The court where the action is pending may, on motion, order sanctions if:

(i) a party or a party's officer, director, or managing agent—or a person designated under Rule 30(b)(6) or 31(a)(4)—fails, after being served with proper notice, to appear for that person's deposition; or

(ii) a party, after being properly served with interrogatories under Rule 33 or a request for inspection under Rule 34, fails to serve its answers, objections, or written response.

(B) *Certification.* A motion for sanctions for failing to answer or respond must include a certification that the movant has in good faith conferred or attempted to confer with the party failing to act in an effort to obtain the answer or response without court action.

(2) *Unacceptable Excuse for Failing to Act.* A failure described in Rule 37(d)(1)(A) is not excused on the ground that the discovery sought was objectionable, unless the party failing to act has a pending motion for a protective order under Rule

26(c).

(3) *Types of Sanctions.* Sanctions may include any of the orders listed in Rule 37(b)(2)(A)(i)-(vi). Instead of or in addition to these sanctions, the court must require the party failing to act, the attorney advising that party, or both to pay the reasonable expenses, including attorney's fees, caused by the failure, unless the failure was substantially justified or other circumstances make an award of expenses unjust.

(e) **Failure to Preserve Electronically Stored Information.** If electronically stored information that should have been preserved in the anticipation or conduct of litigation is lost because a party failed to take reasonable steps to preserve it, and it cannot be restored or replaced through additional discovery, the court:

(1) upon finding prejudice to another party from loss of the information, may order measures no greater than necessary to cure the prejudice; or

(2) only upon finding that the party acted with the intent to deprive another party of the information's use in the litigation may:

(A) presume that the lost information was unfavorable to the party;

(B) instruct the jury that it may or must presume the information was unfavorable to the party; or

(C) dismiss the action or enter a default judgment.

(f) **Failure to Participate in Framing a Discovery Plan.** If a party or its attorney fails to participate in good faith in developing and submitting a proposed discovery plan as required by Rule 26(f), the court may, after giving an opportunity to be heard, require that party or attorney to pay to any other party the reasonable expenses, including attorney's fees, caused by the failure.

[Amended December 29, 1948, effective October 20, 1949; March 30, 1970, effective July 1, 1970; April 29, 1980, effective August 1, 1980; amended by Pub.L. 96-481, Title II, § 205(a), October 21, 1980, 94 Stat. 2330, effective October 1, 1981; amended March 2, 1987, effective August 1, 1987; April 22, 1993, effective December 1, 1993; April 17, 2000, effective December 1, 2000; April 12, 2006, effective December 1, 2006; April 30, 2007, effective December 1, 2007; April 16, 2013, effective December 1, 2013; April 29, 2015, effective December 1, 2015.]

AUTHORS' COMMENTARY ON RULE 37

PURPOSE AND SCOPE

Rule 37 provides the policing mechanisms for the discovery process. It addresses two primary functions in that regard: compelling parties to perform as the Rules require and sanctioning parties who fail to do so.

The process for compelling other parties to perform their obligations under the discovery rules is relatively straightforward. A party who believes that another party has not properly performed—such as by failing to submit responses to discovery requests or by submitting responses that are inadequate—may file a motion to compel under Rule 37(a). The court then has broad discretion to grant or deny the motion, as with almost all discovery issues. In connection with the order granting or denying the motion, the court must award attorney's fees to the prevailing party (unless each side wins some of the issues, the losing party's position was "substantially justified," or the court finds circumstances that make an award of attorney's fees "unjust").

The process for sanctions is substantially more complicated because the potential need for sanctions can arise in a multitude of circumstances. Rule 37(b) authorizes a wide variety of sanctions. Some of them relate to the evidence, such as precluding evidence not properly provided during discovery or deeming certain facts established without the need for evidence. Other sanctions involve advising the jury of discovery misconduct. The court may even impose case concluding sanctions like dismissal or judgment in extreme circumstances. Finally, as with the motion to compel, the court will ordinarily award attorney's fees to the prevailing party.

Rule 37(b) authorizes these sanctions for violation of a court order regarding discovery (such as an order entered in response to a motion to compel), but some of the other subparts of Rule 37 incorporate the Rule 37(b) list of sanctions. Virtually all of the Rule 37(b) sanctions are available when a party fails to respond to interrogatories or document requests or fails to appear for a properly noticed deposition.

Some transgressions, however, trigger special sanctions. For example, failure to respond to requests for admission results in the requests being deemed admitted without the need for a motion or any other pretrial action by the party who sent the requests. Likewise, failure to disclose a document required by any of the automatic disclosures in Rule 26(a) results in the exclusion of that document from evidence, again without any pretrial action by an opposing party.

Failure to preserve—or "spoliation" of—electronically stored evidence (ESI) has its own set of sanctioning procedures. Rule 37(e) establishes prerequisites that must be satisfied before any sanction is permissible, then sets two tiers of sanctions. The most severe sanctions— case-concluding sanctions or an "adverse inference" instruction to the jury that it may or must presume that the lost ESI would have been harmful to the party failing to preserve it—are available only if the court finds a party acted with the specific intent to affect the litigation when it failed to preserve the ESI. Lesser sanctions are available if the court finds that another party was prejudiced by the spoliation of the ESI, and are limited to the sanctions necessary to cure the prejudice.

The duty to first "meet and confer" with the other party to attempt to resolve discovery disputes informally before seeking recourse from the court is a theme throughout the discovery enforcement process. A party must meet and confer before filing a motion to compel or a motion for sanctions for failure to respond to interrogatories or document requests. There are certain situations, however, where Rule 37 allows a party to seek sanctions immediately, without meeting and conferring. When a party has failed to comply with an order compelling it to fulfill its discovery obligations, the aggrieved party does not have to conduct a second meet and confer (having already done so as a prerequisite to filing the motion to compel). Likewise, the self-implementing sanctions for undisclosed documents and unanswered requests for admission do not require a meet and confer conference.

Although Rule 37 provides a detailed framework for enforcing the parties' discovery obligations, it is not the only source of sanctioning authority; a court may also use its inherent power to control cases on its docket.[1]

NOTE: Rule 37(e) was substantially revised in 2015, and care should be exercised when citing case law pertaining to Rule 37(e) that predates this amendment.

RULE 37(a)—MOTION FOR AN ORDER COMPELLING DISCLOSURE OR DISCOVERY

CORE CONCEPT

If an opponent fails to perform its obligations under the discovery rules, the first step—after trying to resolve the dispute informally—is to file a motion for an order compelling the discovery sought.

[1] *Chambers v. NASCO, Inc.*, 501 U.S. 32, 50 (1991); *Haeger v. Goodyear Tire & Rubber Co.*, 813 F.3d 1233, 1244–45 (9th Cir. 2015).

APPLICATIONS

Basis for Motion to Compel

A party may file a motion to compel if another party has failed to fulfill its obligations under the discovery rules. Specific situations warranting a motion to compel include when a party: fails to make any of the disclosures required under Rule 26(a); fails to respond or to respond properly to duly served discovery requests;[2] fails to produce documents in response to a document request;[3] interposes improper objections or provides incomplete or insufficient answers to discovery requests;[4] fails to appear for a properly noticed deposition;[5] fails to answer a deposition question;[6] fails to designate a representative to testify at a deposition under Rule 30(b)(6); or fails to exercise good faith efforts to produce its expert for a deposition.[7] A party may also make a motion to compel against a nonparty who has failed to comply with a subpoena.[8]

Procedures

Motions to compel should include the disputed discovery requests and any responses as exhibits,[9] and should contain the meet and confer certification (discussed below).[10] They are served on all parties and filed with the court. There is no set time limit for filing a motion to compel, but the court will consider delay in filing the motion and the procedural posture of the case in deciding whether a motion to compel is timely.[11] The courts differ as to which party has the burden of proof in a motion to compel.[12] The court has broad discretion in ruling on

---

[2]*United States v. $284,950.00 in U.S. Currency*, 933 F.3d 971, 974 (8th Cir. 2019) (an evasive response is treated like no response).

[3]*See, e.g., Carlson v. Colorado Ctr. for Reprod. Med., LLC*, 341 F.R.D. 266 (D. Colo. 2022); *United States v. Newman*, 531 F. Supp. 3d 181, 187 (D.D.C. 2021).

[4]*United States v. $284,950.00 in U.S. Currency*, 933 F.3d 971, 974 (8th Cir. 2019).

[5]*Sali v. Corona Reg'l Med. Ctr.*, 884 F.3d 1218, 1222 (9th Cir. 2018).

[6]*Evans v. Griffin*, 932 F.3d 1043, 1046 (7th Cir. 2019); *Sali v. Corona Reg'l Med. Ctr.*, 884 F.3d 1218, 1222 (9th Cir. 2018).

[7]*Sali v. Corona Reg'l Med. Ctr.*, 884 F.3d 1218, 1222–25 (9th Cir. 2018).

[8]*P.H. Glatfelter Co. v. Windward Prospects Ltd.*, 847 F.3d 452, 455 n.2 (7th Cir. 2017); *In re John Adams Assocs., Inc.*, 255 F.R.D. 7, 7 (D.D.C. 2008).

[9]*Lopez v. Don Herring Ltd.*, 327 F.R.D. 567, 585 (N.D. Tex. 2018).

[10]*Samsung Elec. Am. Inc. v. Yang Kun "Michael" Chung*, 325 F.R.D. 578, 594 (N.D. Tex. 2017).

[11]*PCS Phosphate Co., Inc. v. Norfolk Southern Corp.*, 238 F.R.D. 555, 558 (E.D.N.C. 2006) (close of discovery often considered deadline for motions to compel where no deadline set); *U.S. ex rel. Purcell v. MWI Corp.*, 232 F.R.D. 14, 17 (D.D.C. 2005).

[12]*See Nasreen v. Capitol Petroleum Grp., LLC*, 340 F.R.D. 489, 494 (D.D.C. 2022) (burden is different if the responding party answered at all); *Wall v. Reliance Standard Life Ins. Co.*, 341 F.R.D. 1, 6 (D.D.C. 2022) (moving party must prove relevance, resisting party must establish objections); *Hancock v. Aetna Life Ins. Co.*, 321 F.R.D. 383, 390 (W.D. Wash. 2017)

a motion to compel.[13]

Meet and Confer Certification

The motion to compel must be accompanied by a certification that the movant has in good faith conferred or attempted to confer with the other party or person in an effort to resolve the dispute without court action.[14] Some courts require that the certification describe the efforts to resolve the dispute with particularity so that the court can assess whether the parties' efforts were reasonable.[15] The certification can simply be a statement in the motion. If the moving party attempted unsuccessfully to meet and confer, the certification should describe the party's efforts to meet with the opposing party.[16] In general, courts will deny motions to compel that do not have a meet and confer certificate.[17] The court has discretion to waive the meet and confer requirement,[18] such as when the court has directed one party to file the motion to compel. The court also has discretion to explore whether the parties actually met and conferred in good faith, even if they submitted a certificate.[19]

Which Court

The proper court in which to file a motion to compel depends on the location and status of the person or entity that is the subject of the motion. If the person or entity is a party, then a motion to compel must be filed in the court where the action is pending.[20] If the motion to compel pertains to a subpoena for deposition or to produce documents issued to a nonparty, then a motion to compel should be filed in the district where perfor-

---

(moving party must prove discoverability); *S.C. State Conf. of NAACP v. McMaster*, ___ F. Supp. 3d ___, 2022 WL 425011, at *3 (D.S.C. 2022) (burden is on the party resisting discovery).

[13] *See S.C. State Conf. of NAACP v. McMaster*, ___ F. Supp. 3d ___, 2022 WL 425011, at *3 (D.S.C. 2022); *Prasad v. Nallapati*, ___ F. Supp. 3d ___, 2022 WL 1051293, at *2 (E.D.N.C. Apr. 2022).

[14] *Houston v. C.G. Sec. Services, Inc.*, 820 F.3d 855, 858 (7th Cir. 2016); *Rivera-Almodovar v. Instituto Socioeconomico Comunitario, Inc.*, 730 F.3d 23, 27–28 (1st Cir. 2013); *but see Benavidez v. Sandia Nat'l Lab.*, 319 F.R.D. 696, 725 (D.N.M. 2017) (entertaining a motion despite technically insufficient meet and confer).

[15] *Deakin v. Magellan Health, Inc.*, 340 F.R.D. 424, 445 (D.N.M. 2022) (single letter not sufficient); *LoganTree LP v. Garmin Int'l, Inc.*, 339 F.R.D. 171, 178 (D. Kan. 2021).

[16] *See Acosta v. Austin Elec. Servs. LLC*, 324 F.R.D. 210, 213 (D. Ariz. 2017).

[17] *Smith on behalf of C.M. v. Tacoma Sch. Dist.*, 476 F. Supp. 3d 1112, 1137 (W.D. Wash. 2020); *In re Avandia Mktg., Sales Practices & Prod. Liab. Litig.*, 415 F. Supp. 3d 498, 503–04 (E.D. Pa. 2019).

[18] *V5 Techs. v. Switch, Ltd.*, 334 F.R.D. 297, 302 (D. Nev. 2019); *Cicel (Beijing) Sci. & Tech. Co. v. Misonix, Inc.*, 331 F.R.D. 218, 229 (E.D.N.Y. 2019).

[19] *V5 Techs. v. Switch, Ltd.*, 334 F.R.D. 297, 301–02 (D. Nev. 2019).

[20] *U.S. ex rel. Pogue v. Diabetes Treatment Centers of Am., Inc.*, 444 F.3d 462, 468, (6th Cir. 2006); *Lynn v. Monarch Recovery Mgmt., Inc.*, 285 F.R.D. 350, 355 (D. Md. 2012).

mance was to occur.[21] That court can adjudicate the motion or transfer it to the court where the action is pending.[22]

Expenses

In general, the victorious party in a motion to compel is entitled to recover its expenses in preparing the motion, including reasonable attorney's fees.[23] The movant is also entitled to expenses if the respondent provides a disclosure or discovery response after the motion was filed.[24] The award of expenses by the court is mandatory[25] unless: the movant failed to confer with the respondent in good faith prior to filing the motion;[26] the losing party demonstrates that its conduct was "substantially justified;"[27] or other circumstances render an award of expenses "unjust."[28] The award of sanctions does not depend on a finding of bad faith or willful misconduct by the sanctioned party.[29] As a practical matter, though, many judges are reluctant to award attorney's fees and find a basis to avoid imposing sanctions.

- *Substantially Justified:* To demonstrate substantial justification, the losing party must demonstrate some unsettled issue of law or like circumstance.[30] The test is generally an objective one, and does not turn on the losing party's good faith.[31]
- *Circumstances Rendering an Award Unjust:* Determining whether an award of sanctions would be unjust is a flexible analysis that entails consideration of the nature of the offending party's conduct and the harm or preju-

---

[21]Rule 45(d)(2)(B)(i); *HT S.R.L. v. Velasco*, 125 F. Supp. 3d 211, 219 (D.D.C. 2015).

[22]Rule 45(f).

[23]*Lightspeed Media Corp. v. Smith*, 830 F.3d 500, 507 (7th Cir. 2016) (award should include all expenses incurred as a result of the improper conduct); *Josendis v. Wall to Wall Residence Repairs, Inc.*, 662 F.3d 1292, 1313–14 (11th Cir. 2011).

[24]*See Howard v. City of Albuquerque*, 349 F. Supp. 3d 1137, 1146 (D.N.M. 2018); *Protopapas v. EMCOR Gov't Serv., Inc.*, 251 F. Supp. 3d 249, 257 (D.D.C. 2017).

[25]*Jackson v. Nassau Cnty.*, __ F. Supp. 3d __, 2022 WL 1460241, at *1 (E.D.N.Y. 2022); *Infanzon v. Allstate Ins. Co.*, 335 F.R.D. 305, 311 (C.D. Cal. 2020).

[26]*Vanderberg v. Petco Animal Supplies Stores, Inc.*, 906 F.3d 698, 701 (8th Cir. 2018).

[27]*Shumpert v. City of Tupelo*, 905 F.3d 310, 326 (5th Cir. 2018) (other professional and personal obligations are not substantial justification); *Parsi v. Daioleslam*, 778 F.3d 116, 126–27 (D.C. Cir. 2015).

[28]*Arnold v. ADT Sec. Services, Inc.*, 627 F.3d 716, 721 (8th Cir. 2010); *Rickels v. City of South Bend, Ind.*, 33 F.3d 785 (7th Cir.1994).

[29]*Mason Tenders Dist. Council of Greater New York v. Phase Constr. Serv., Inc.*, 318 F.R.D. 28, 43 (S.D.N.Y. 2016).

[30]*Pierce v. Underwood*, 487 U.S. 552, 565 (1988) (motion is substantially justified if it raises an issue about which there is a genuine dispute or if reasonable people could differ as to the appropriateness of the contested action); *Parsi v. Daioleslam*, 778 F.3d 116, 126–27 (D.C. Cir. 2015).

[31]*Jackson v. Nassau Cnty.*, __ F. Supp. 3d __, 2022 WL 1460241, at *2 (E.D.N.Y. 2022).

dice to the opposing party.[32]

- *Opportunity to be Heard*: The court must provide the non-moving party with an opportunity to be heard, either orally or in writing, before imposing sanctions.[33]
- *Burden of Proof:* The party seeking to avoid sanctions bears the burden of demonstrating that its conduct was substantially justified or that other circumstances render an award of expenses unjust.[34]
- *Who Pays Expenses:* The court may impose the expenses on the party, the attorney, or both.[35]
- *Motion Granted in Part:* If a motion to compel is granted in part and denied in part, the court may apportion the expenses as it sees fit.[36]
- *Nonparties:* A nonparty may be required to pay expenses incurred because of the nonparty's failure to comply with a subpoena.[37]
- *Contingency Fees:* The courts are divided as to whether a party has "incurred" attorney's fees as a result of a motion to compel if the party is being represented under a contingency fee arrangement (such that the party does not actually incur any additional fees as a consequence of the motion to compel).[38]
- *Fees From United States:* Attorney's fees can be awarded against the United States.[39]
- *Reasonableness of Fees:* The court will typically examine the claimed fees and award the fees it determines to be reasonable.[40]
- *Fees for Meeting and Conferring*: The courts are split as to whether the fees incurred in meeting and conferring

[32]*DR Distributors, LLC v. 21 Century Smoking, Inc.*, 513 F. Supp. 3d 839, 961 (N.D. Ill. 2021).

[33]*Hassoun v. Searls*, 524 F. Supp. 3d 101, 109 (W.D.N.Y. 2021); *Big City Dynasty v. FP Holdings, L.P.*, 336 F.R.D. 507, 513 n.10 (D. Nev. 2020).

[34]*White v. Larusch*, 532 F. Supp. 3d 122, 124 (W.D.N.Y. 2021); *Infanzon v. Allstate Ins. Co.*, 335 F.R.D. 305, 311 (C.D. Cal. 2020).

[35]*Infanzon v. Allstate Ins. Co.*, 335 F.R.D. 305, 314 (C.D. Cal. 2020) (fees awarded against attorney); *AngioDynamics, Inc. v. Biolitec AG*, 305 F. Supp. 3d 300 (D. Mass. 2018) (fees awarded jointly against party and attorney).

[36]*Baylor v. Mitchell Rubenstein & Ass., P.C.*, 857 F.3d 939, 951 (D.C. Cir. 2017).

[37]*HT S.R.L. v. Velasco*, 125 F. Supp. 3d 211, 231 (D.D.C. 2015).

[38]*See White v. Larusch*, 532 F. Supp. 3d 122, 124–25 (W.D.N.Y. 2021) (discussing the split).

[39]*U.S. v. Horn*, 29 F.3d 754 (1st Cir. 1994) (fees may be assessed against the United States as a sanction).

[40]*Jackson v. Nassau Cnty.*, — F. Supp. 3d —, 2022 WL 1460241, at *2 (E.D.N.Y. 2022); *Thomas v. Bannum Place of Saginaw*, 421 F. Supp. 3d 494, 496–98 (E.D. Mich. 2019) (denying fee request altogether based on unreasonably high claim).

are recoverable.[41]

- *Magistrate Judges:* Magistrate judges are authorized to award attorney's fees in connection with a motion to compel.[42]
- *Appeal of Fee Award:* An award of attorney's fees is not a final, appealable order.[43]

Motion Denied—Protective Order

If the court denies a motion to compel, it can at the same time enter a protective order under Rule 26(c).[44] The court will award expenses to the party who obtained the protective order.[45]

RULE 37(b)—FAILURE TO COMPLY WITH A COURT ORDER

CORE CONCEPT

Rule 37(b) contains a list of sanctions that become available if a party or deponent fails to obey an order to provide or permit discovery, such as an order compelling discovery under Rule 37(a). Other portions of Rule 37 incorporate the list of sanctions in Rule 37(b), such as Rules 37(c) and (d) which impose sanctions if a party fails altogether to perform certain discovery obligations. The court generally has broad discretion to impose one or more of the listed sanctions or any other sanction it deems appropriate.

APPLICATIONS

Violation of Order Prerequisite

Rule 37(b) does not authorize sanctions unless the court has already issued a discovery order with which a party or deponent has failed to comply.[46] Any discovery order may satisfy this prerequisite,[47] such as an order compelling under Rule 37(a), an order issued in a conference under Rule 16,[48] an order

---

[41] *Infanzon v. Allstate Ins. Co.*, 335 F.R.D. 305, 314 (C.D. Cal. 2020).

[42] *Hangzhou Aoshuang E-Com. Co. v. 008Fashion*, 336 F.R.D. 154, 157 (N.D. Ill. 2020).

[43] *Cunningham v. Hamilton County, Ohio*, 527 U.S. 198, 200 (1999); *Isaacson v. Manty*, 721 F.3d 533, 537 (8th Cir. 2013).

[44] *Bhasker v. Kemper Cas. Ins. Co.*, 361 F. Supp. 3d 1045, 1120 (D.N.M. 2019); *Zenith Ins. Co. v. Texas Inst. for Surgery, L.L.P.*, 328 F.R.D. 153, 161 (N.D. Tex. 2018).

[45] *Zenith Ins. Co. v. Texas Inst. for Surgery, L.L.P.*, 328 F.R.D. 153, 161 (N.D. Tex. 2018); *Rodriquez v. Parsons Infrastructure & Technology Group, Inc.*, 271 F.R.D. 620, 622–23 (S.D. Ind. 2010).

[46] *Confederacion Hipica de Puerto Rico, Inc. v. Confederacion de Jinetes Puertorriquenos, Inc.*, 30 F.4th 306, 317 n.6 (1st Cir. 2022); *Yukos Cap. S.A.R.L. v. Feldman*, 977 F.3d 216, 234 (2d Cir. 2020).

[47] *Sali v. Corona Reg'l Med. Ctr.*, 884 F.3d 1218, 1222 (9th Cir. 2018); *Infanzon v. Allstate Ins. Co.*, 335 F.R.D. 305, 313 (C.D. Cal. 2020).

[48] *Mager v. Wisconsin Cent. Ltd.*, 924 F.3d 831, 837 (6th Cir. 2019). *But see Holmes v. Trinity Health*, 729 F.3d 817, 820–21 (8th Cir. 2013) (preliminary scheduling order not sufficient to support Rule 37(b) sanctions).

requiring an examination under Rule 35,[49] or a standing order of the court pertaining to discovery.[50] Some courts authorize sanctions under Rule 37(b) for violations of protective orders issued under Rule 26(c) if the protective order permitted some discovery.[51] Although Rule 37(b) is limited to violations of court orders, Rules 37(c) and 37(d) authorize the court to impose the sanctions listed under Rule 37(b) for conduct other than violation of a discovery order, as discussed below.

- *Burden of Proof:* The party seeking sanctions has the burden of demonstrating non-compliance with the order.[52]
- *Intent not Required:* The moving party only needs to show a violation of the court's discovery order; the movant does not need to establish bad faith or intent by the violator.[53]
- *Exception to Order Prerequisite Under Courts' Inherent Power:* Courts occasionally impose the sanctions, including those listed in Rule 37(b), in the absence of a violation of an order compelling discovery, using the courts' inherent power to manage cases on their dockets.[54]

Who may be Sanctioned

The court may sanction a party, an officer, director, or managing agent of a party,[55] and/or an attorney[56] who fails to obey an order to permit or provide discovery.

Sanctions

The typical discovery order is issued by the judge presiding over the case. For violations of such orders, Rule 37(b)(2) contains a list of sanctions described below. The court has broad discretion regarding whether to impose sanctions,[57] any if so which sanction or combination of sanctions it deems appropri-

---

[49] *Mager v. Wisconsin Cent. Ltd.*, 924 F.3d 831, 837 (6th Cir. 2019); *Sali v. Corona Reg'l Med. Ctr.*, 884 F.3d 1218, 1223 (9th Cir. 2018).

[50] *SiteLock LLC v. GoDaddy.com LLC*, 562 F. Supp. 3d 283, 318 (D. Ariz. 2022).

[51] *See Smith & Fuller, P.A. v. Cooper Tire & Rubber Co.*, 685 F.3d 486, 489 (5th Cir. 2012) (discussing the split of authority); *Doe I v. Exxon Mobil Corp.*, 539 F. Supp. 3d 59, 72 (D.D.C. 2021).

[52] *Coltrane v. Wilkins*, 340 F.R.D. 476, 480 (D.D.C. 2022); *Syntel Sterling Best Shores Mauritius Ltd. v. TriZetto Grp.*, 328 F.R.D. 100, 119 (S.D.N.Y. 2018).

[53] *e360 Insight, Inc. v. Spamhaus Project*, 658 F.3d 637, 642–43 (7th Cir. 2011); *DR Distributors, LLC v. 21 Century Smoking, Inc.*, 513 F. Supp. 3d 839, 919 (N.D. Ill. 2021).

[54] *See Yukos Cap. S.A.R.L. v. Feldman*, 977 F.3d 216, 235 (2d Cir. 2020); *Life Techs. Corp. v. Govindaraj*, 931 F.3d 259, 267 n.8 (4th Cir. 2019).

[55] *See Life Techs. Corp. v. Govindaraj*, 931 F.3d 259, 267 (4th Cir. 2019); *Sali v. Corona Reg'l Med. Ctr.*, 884 F.3d 1218, 1222 n.4 (9th Cir. 2018).

[56] *Harmon v. City of Santa Clara*, 323 F.R.D. 617, 626 (N.D. Cal. 2018).

[57] *SiteLock LLC v. GoDaddy.com LLC*, 562 F. Supp. 3d 283, 298 (D. Ariz. 2022).

ate,[58] as long as the sanction is "just" and there is a nexus between the sanction and the discovery violation.[59] Some courts limit discovery sanctions to "extreme situations" where the opposing party's violation is due to willfulness, bad faith, or fault.[60] Although courts have generally imposed only the sanctions listed, the court is not limited to the sanctions on the list.[61] The listed sanctions authorize a court to:

- *Deem Facts Established:* The court may deem as established the facts that the moving party was seeking to establish.[62]
- *Give an Adverse Inference Instruction:* Although Rule 37(b) does not specifically refer to it, courts sometimes issue an adverse inference instruction to the jury, allowing or requiring them to presume that lost evidence would have been adverse to the party failing to preserve it.[63]
- *Prohibit Evidence:* The court may refuse to allow the disobedient party to introduce certain matters into evidence or to support or oppose certain claims or defenses.[64]
- *Strike Pleadings:* The court may strike any pleading or portion of a pleading.[65]
- *Issue a Stay:* The court may stay further proceedings until the order is obeyed.[66]
- *Make a Dispositive Ruling:* In extreme situations, typically for repeat offenders where lesser sanctions have proved unsuccessful, the court may dismiss an action or portions of the action[67] or enter judgment against the

[58] *Clientron Corp. v. Devon IT, Inc.*, 894 F.3d 568, 577 (3d Cir. 2018); *Campidoglio LLC v. Wells Fargo & Co.*, 870 F.3d 963, 975 (9th Cir. 2017).

[59] *Klayman v. Jud. Watch, Inc.*, 6 F.4th 1301, 1312 (D.C. Cir. 2021); *The Law Funder, L.L.C. v. Munoz*, 924 F.3d 753, 758 (5th Cir. 2019).

[60] *Fair Hous. of Marin v. Combs*, 285 F.3d 899, 905 (9th Cir. 2002).

[61] *Clientron Corp. v. Devon IT, Inc.*, 894 F.3d 568, 580 (3d Cir. 2018); *S.E.C. v. Razmilovic*, 738 F.3d 14, 25 (2d Cir. 2013).

[62] *Insurance Corp. of Ireland, Ltd. v. Compagnie des Bauxites de Guinee*, 456 U.S. 694 (1982) (deeming personal jurisdiction established); *Clientron Corp. v. Devon IT, Inc.*, 894 F.3d 568, 578 (3d Cir. 2018).

[63] *See Higgs v. Costa Crociere S.P.A. Co.*, 969 F.3d 1295, 1304–07 (11th Cir. 2020); *Flagg v. City of Detroit*, 715 F.3d 165, 177 (6th Cir. 2013).

[64] *Klayman v. Jud. Watch, Inc.*, 6 F.4th 1301, 1312 (D.C. Cir. 2021); *Funk v. Belneftekhim*, 861 F.3d 354, 363–64 (2d Cir. 2017).

[65] *See Clientron Corp. v. Devon IT, Inc.*, 894 F.3d 568, 577 (3d Cir. 2018); *Syntel Sterling Best Shores Mauritius Ltd. v. TriZetto Grp.*, 328 F.R.D. 100, 119 (S.D.N.Y. 2018).

[66] *Houghtaling v. Eaton*, 559 F. Supp. 3d 164, 169 (W.D.N.Y. 2021).

[67] *See Indep. Producers Grp. v. Copyright Royalty Bd.*, 966 F.3d 799, 811 (D.C. Cir. 2020); *Mager v. Wisconsin Cent. Ltd.*, 924 F.3d 831, 837 (6th Cir. 2019). *See also Atchison, Topeka and Santa Fe Ry. Co. v. Hercules Inc.*, 146 F.3d 1071, 1074 (9th Cir. 1998) (court may not dismiss a separate but related action).

disobedient party.[68] In evaluating a request for case-dispositive sanctions, a court will consider whether the violation was willful or in bad faith, prejudice to the nonmoving party, and whether a lesser sanction would ensure compliance with future orders.[69]

- *Hold the Disobedient Party in Contempt:* The court may treat the failure to obey its order as a contempt of court,[70] with the exception of a failure to submit to a mental or physical examination (which is punishable by other sanctions, but not as contempt).[71]

Expenses

In addition to, or instead of, the listed sanctions, the court will require the party not complying with the court order[72] and/or the party's attorney[73] to pay all expenses, including reasonable attorney's fees, incurred by the moving party as a result of the failure to comply.[74] This includes expenses incurred in the motion for sanctions,[75] but not expenses incurred in obtaining the order compelling the discovery (although these expenses may be recoverable under Rule 37(a)).[76] The court must award such expenses[77] unless it finds that the failure was "substantially justified" or that other circumstances exist that would make the award "unjust."[78] A court may not award monetary sanctions in excess of actual expenses.[79] The award of fees is a collateral matter that the court can address even after dismissal of the case.[80]

---

[68]*See Corcamore, LLC v. SFM, LLC*, 978 F.3d 1298, 1307-08 (Fed. Cir. 2020); *Hernandez v. Acosta Tractors Inc.*, 898 F.3d 1301, 1306 (11th Cir. 2018).

[69]*See United States v. Yennie*, — F. Supp. 3d —, 2022 WL 457780, at *3 (D. Minn. 2022); *Hornady v. Outokumpu Stainless USA*, 572 F. Supp. 3d 1162, 1188 (S.D. Ala. 2021).

[70]*Serra Chevrolet, Inc. v. General Motors Corp.*, 446 F.3d 1137 (11th Cir. 2006); *General Ins. Co. of Am. v. Eastern Consol. Utilities, Inc.*, 126 F.3d 215, 220 (3d Cir. 1997) (nonparty held in contempt); *Jones v. J.C. Penney's Dept. Stores, Inc.*, 228 F.R.D. 190, 198 (W.D.N.Y. 2005) (attorney held in contempt).

[71]Rule 37(b)(2)(A)(vii).

[72]*Coltrane v. Wilkins*, 340 F.R.D. 476, 484 (D.D.C. 2022); *Diamond Consortium, Inc. v. Hammervold*, 386 F. Supp. 3d 904, 914 (M.D. Tenn. 2019).

[73]*Rates Technology, Inc. v. Mediatrix Telecom, Inc.*, 688 F.3d 742, 748 (Fed. Cir. 2012).

[74]*McLaughlin v. Phelan Hallinan & Schmieg, LLP*, 756 F.3d 240, 249 (3d Cir. 2014).

[75]*Houston v. C.G. Sec. Services, Inc.*, 820 F.3d 855, 859 (7th Cir. 2016).

[76]*But see Ramgoolie v. Ramgoolie*, 333 F.R.D. 30, 39 (S.D.N.Y. 2019) (awarding expenses for both motions).

[77]*State v. United States Dep't of Commerce*, 461 F. Supp. 3d 80, 94–95 (S.D.N.Y. 2020).

[78]*Sali v. Corona Reg'l Med. Ctr.*, 884 F.3d 1218, 1220 (9th Cir. 2018); *Sik Gaek, Inc. v. Harris*, 789 F.3d 797, 800 (7th Cir. 2015).

[79]*Clientron Corp. v. Devon IT, Inc.*, 894 F.3d 568, 581, n.7 (3d Cir. 2018).

[80]*Diamond Consortium, Inc. v. Hammervold*, 386 F. Supp. 3d 904, 910 (M.D. Tenn. 2019).

Sanctions by Court Where Deposition to Occur

When a deposition is taken outside the district where the case is pending, a judge from that district may issue an order compelling the witness to be sworn in or to answer a question. If the witness fails to comply with such an order, the court issuing the order may treat the failure as a contempt of court.[81] If a motion was filed in the court where the discovery was to occur and that court transferred the motion to the court where the action was pending (see Rule 45), then either court may impose contempt sanction for failure to obey the order.[82]

No Meet and Confer Requirement

In contrast to many of the sanctions provisions, a party does not need to meet and confer with the opposing party before filing a motion for sanctions under Rule 37(b).[83] The rationale for this exception is that the parties would have already met and conferred before obtaining the first discovery order—which the opposing party has then violated—and that a second meet and confer is therefore not warranted.

Magistrate Judges

Magistrate Judges can impose sanctions under Rule 37(b).[84]

Notice and Opportunity to be Heard

Before imposing discovery sanctions, the court should provide the offending party with notice and an opportunity to be heard.[85]

No Contempt for Failure to Produce Another for Examination Under Rule 35

If a party fails to comply with an order to produce another person for a mental or physical examination (such as when the party is the guardian or custodian of the person to be examined), the party is subject to all the sanctions in Rule 37(b)(2) except for contempt, unless the party can show that the party was unable to produce the individual.[86]

Preservation Order

The importance of discovery of electronically stored information has led parties to seek orders requiring opposing par-

---

[81] *See Diamond Consortium, Inc. v. Hammervold*, 386 F. Supp. 3d 904, 914 (M.D. Tenn. 2019).

[82] Rule 37(b)(1).

[83] *Acosta v. Austin Elec. Servs. LLC*, 325 F.R.D. 322, 324 (D. Ariz. 2018); *Scott Hutchison Enter., Inc. v. Cranberry Pipeline Corp.*, 318 F.R.D. 44, 51 (S.D.W. Va. 2016).

[84] *See Moore v. Napolitano*, 723 F. Supp. 2d 167, 171–72 (D.D.C. 2010).

[85] *See McLaughlin v. Phelan Hallinan & Schmieg, LLP*, 756 F.3d 240, 249–50 (3d Cir. 2014); *S.E.C. v. Razmilovic*, 738 F.3d 14, 24 (2d Cir. 2013).

[86] *Societe Internationale Pour Participations Industrielles Et Commerciales, S. A. v. Rogers*, 357 U.S. 197 (1958).

ties to preserve evidence.[87] If a party violates a preservation order by failing to preserve evidence other than ESI, sanctions are available under Rule 37(b).[88] If a party violates a preservation order by failing to preserve ESI, sanctions may be available under both Rules 37(b) and 37(e).[89] A preservation order is not a prerequisite to sanctions for spoliation under Rule 37(e); it just creates an additional source of sanctioning authority (and potentially obviates an argument that the party did not realize it was obligated to preserve the documents in question).

Waiver of Sanctions

A party might be deemed to have waived its rights to sanctions by not strictly enforcing the order, such as by failing to make attempts to schedule a physical examination[90] or by failing to bring a motion for sanctions in a reasonable period of time.[91]

Appeals

Sanctions orders are normally interlocutory orders not immediately appealable, but sometimes may be appealed under the collateral order doctrine.[92]

RULE 37(c)—FAILURE TO DISCLOSE, TO SUPPLEMENT AN EARLIER RESPONSE, OR TO ADMIT

CORE CONCEPT

If a party improperly fails to make the automatic disclosures under Rule 26(a) or makes false or misleading disclosures, or if a party fails to supplement a prior discovery response as required by Rule 26(e)(1), the party generally will not be permitted to use the information or documents not properly provided, and may be subject to a variety of additional sanctions. If a party improperly fails to admit a matter that is subsequently proven to be true, that party must pay the cost the other party incurred in proving the matter.

APPLICATIONS

Exclusion of Matter Not Disclosed

If a party fails to make the automatic disclosures under

---

[87] *See Moore v. CITGO Refining and Chem. Co., L.P.*, 735 F.3d 309, 314 (5th Cir. 2013).

[88] *See Moore v. CITGO Refining and Chem. Co., L.P.*, 735 F.3d 309, 316 (5th Cir. 2013) (dismissing case for failure to preserve critical notes); *Flagg v. City of Detroit*, 715 F.3d 165, 177 (6th Cir. 2013).

[89] *See Ellis v. Hobbs Police Dep't*, 2020 WL 1041688, at *4 (D.N.M. 2020).

[90] *Hinson v. Michigan Mut. Liab. Co.*, 275 F.2d 537 (5th Cir.1960).

[91] *U.S. Fidelity & Guar. Co. v. Baker Material Handling Corp.*, 62 F.3d 24, 29 (1st Cir. 1995); *Tolliver v. Fed. Republic of Nigeria*, 265 F. Supp. 2d 873 (W.D. Mich. 2003).

[92] *Funk v. Belneftekhim*, 861 F.3d 354, 362 (2d Cir. 2017); *U.S. ex rel. Pogue v. Diabetes Treatment Centers of Am., Inc.*, 444 F.3d 462, 472 (6th Cir. 2006).

Rule 26(a) in a timely manner[93] or makes false, incomplete, or misleading disclosures, the party will not be permitted to use the documents,[94] information,[95] expert testimony,[96] damages,[97] or witnesses[98] not properly disclosed unless the party demonstrates that the failure was "substantially justified" or harmless.[99] The party seeking sanctions bears the burden of demonstrating a violation of the disclosure requirements,[100] and the party facing sanctions bears the burden of proving justification or harmlessness.[101] The exclusion of evidence or witnesses not properly disclosed is automatic,[102] and there is no need to meet and confer[103] or file a written motion for sanctions[104] (although parties sometimes do file written motions if they become aware of evidence or witnesses that an opposing party failed to disclose or provide by supplement).[105] The court has discretion as to whether exclusion is an appropriate sanction.[106] Some courts consider exclusion mandatory in the absence of justification or harmlessness,[107] others balance the competing concerns using a list of factors,[108] and others are reluctant to exclude evidence in the absence of willful decep-

---

[93]*Zampierollo-Rheinfeldt v. Ingersoll-Rand de Puerto Rico, Inc.*, 999 F.3d 37, 47 (1st Cir. 2021); *Petrone v. Werner Enterprises, Inc.*, 940 F.3d 425, 434 (8th Cir. 2019).

[94]*Chisolm v. 7-Eleven, Inc.*, 383 F. Supp. 3d 1032, 1044 (S.D. Cal. 2019); *Brown v. AT & T Serv. Inc.*, 236 F. Supp. 3d 1000, 1005 (S.D. Tex. 2017).

[95]*Ingenco Holdings, LLC v. Ace Am. Ins. Co.*, 921 F.3d 803, 821 (9th Cir. 2019); *E.E.O.C. v. Serv. Temps Inc.*, 679 F.3d 323, 334 (5th Cir. 2012).

[96]*MLC Intell. Prop., LLC v. Micron Tech., Inc.*, 10 F.4th 1358, 1369 (Fed. Cir. 2021); *Guevara v. NCL (Bahamas) Ltd.*, 920 F.3d 710, 718 (11th Cir. 2019).

[97]*See Moore v. Equitrans, L.P.*, 27 F.4th 211, 225 (4th Cir. 2022); *MLC Intell. Prop., LLC v. Micron Tech., Inc.*, 10 F.4th 1358, 1371 (Fed. Cir. 2021).

[98]*Doe v. Young*, 664 F.3d 727, 734 (8th Cir. 2011); *Crispin-Taveras v. Municipality Of Carolina*, 647 F.3d. 1, 8 (1st Cir. 2011).

[99]*Sec. & Exch. Comm'n v. GenAudio Inc.*, 32 F.4th 902, 937–38 (10th Cir. 2022); *Merch. v. Corizon Health, Inc.*, 993 F.3d 733, 740 (9th Cir. 2021).

[100]*V5 Techs. v. Switch, Ltd.*, 334 F.R.D. 615 (D. Nev. 2020).

[101]*U.S. ex rel. Tenn. Valley Auth. V. 1.72 Acres of Land in Tenn.*, 821 F.3d 742, 752 (6th Cir. 2016); *Riley v. Tesla, Inc.*, __ F. Supp. 3d __, 2022 WL 1486905, at *3 (S.D. Fla. 2022).

[102]*Merch. v. Corizon Health, Inc.*, 993 F.3d 733, 740 (9th Cir. 2021).

[103]*Vanderberg v. Petco Animal Supplies Stores, Inc.*, 906 F.3d 698, 707 (8th Cir. 2018).

[104]*Karum Holdings LLC v. Lowe's Companies, Inc.*, 895 F.3d 944, 951 (7th Cir. 2018); *Wilkins v. Montgomery*, 751 F.3d 214, 221 (4th Cir. 2014).

[105]*See, e.g., United States ex rel. Morsell v. NortonLifeLock, Inc.*, 567 F. Supp. 3d 248, 269 (D.D.C. 2021).

[106]*Merch. v. Corizon Health, Inc.*, 993 F.3d 733, 740 (9th Cir. 2021); *Taylor v. Mentor Worldwide LLC*, 940 F.3d 582, 593 (11th Cir. 2019).

[107]*NutraSweet Co. v. X-L Eng'g Co.*, 227 F.3d 776, 786 (7th Cir. 2000); *McCoy v. Town of Pittsfield*, 565 F. Supp. 3d 125, 130 (D.N.H. 2021).

[108]*Harriman v. Hancock Cnty.*, 627 F.3d 22, 30 (1st Cir. 2010); *Nicholas v. Pa. State Univ.*, 227 F.3d 133, 148 (3d Cir. 2000).

tion or other bad faith conduct.[109]

- *Harmlessness*: In evaluating harmlessness, courts consider factors such as: the surprise to the party seeking exclusion; the ability to cure that surprise; the extent to which allowing the evidence would disrupt the trial; the explanation for the party's failure to disclose; and the importance of the testimony.[110]
- *Substantial Justification*: A failure to disclose is substantially justified if reasonable people could differ as to whether disclosure was required.[111]
- *When Exclusion is a Dispositive Sanction:* When exclusion of information or documents is effectively dispositive of a claim (such as exclusion of the plaintiff's expert in a case requiring expert testimony), a court may scrutinize the request for sanctions more closely.[112] Some courts place the burden on the party seeking to avoid a dispositive sanction to propose a lesser appropriate sanction.[113]

Exclusion of Matter Not Properly Provided by Supplement

If a party fails to supplement its automatic disclosures or a prior discovery response as required under Rule 26(e), the party will not be permitted to use the documents,[114] information,[115] opinions,[116] damages,[117] or witnesses[118] not properly provided by supplement unless the party can demonstrate that it had "substantial justification" or the failure was harmless.[119] Likewise, matter improperly provided by supplement (such as an untimely supplement or a supplement providing matter

---

[109] *Bergfeld v. Unimin Corp.*, 319 F.3d 350, 355 (8th Cir. 2003); *Meyers v. Pennypack Woods Home Ownership Assn.*, 559 F.2d 894, 905 (3d Cir. 1977) (overruled on other grounds by Goodman v. Lukens Steel Co., 777 F.2d 113 (3d Cir. 1985)).

[110] *Sec. & Exch. Comm'n v. GenAudio Inc.*, 32 F.4th 902, 937–38 (10th Cir. 2022); *Bisig v. Time Warner Cable, Inc.*, 940 F.3d 205, 219 (6th Cir. 2019).

[111] *Diaz v. New York Paving Inc.*, 553 F. Supp. 3d 11, 21–22 (S.D.N.Y. 2021); *Sikkelee v. Precision Airmotive Corp.*, 522 F. Supp. 3d 120, 161 (M.D. Pa. 2021).

[112] *Merch. v. Corizon Health, Inc.*, 993 F.3d 733, 740 (9th Cir. 2021); *Karum Holdings LLC v. Lowe's Companies, Inc.*, 895 F.3d 944, 952–53 (7th Cir. 2018).

[113] *Merch. v. Corizon Health, Inc.*, 993 F.3d 733, 740 (9th Cir. 2021).

[114] *Fast v. GoDaddy.com LLC*, 340 F.R.D. 326, 349 (D. Ariz. 2022); *Doe v. Belmont Univ.*, 367 F. Supp. 3d 732, 742 (M.D. Tenn. 2019).

[115] *See Walsh v. Fusion Japanese Steakhouse, Inc.*, — F. Supp. 3d —, 2022 WL 395253, at *14 (W.D. Pa. 2022); *Photographic Illustrators Corp. v. Orgill, Inc.*, 370 F. Supp. 3d 232, 250 (D. Mass. 2019).

[116] *Guevara v. NCL (Bahamas) Ltd.*, 920 F.3d 710, 718 (11th Cir. 2019); *Air Turbine Technology, Inc. v. Atlas Copco AB*, 410 F.3d 701, 711–12 (Fed. Cir. 2005).

[117] *Eldridge v. Gordon Bros. Grp., L.L.C.*, 863 F.3d 66, 85 (1st Cir. 2017).

[118] *Stella v. Dep't of Educ.*, 367 F. Supp. 3d 235, 263–64 (D. Del. 2019); *Donohue v. New York*, 347 F. Supp. 3d 110, 145 (N.D.N.Y. 2018).

[119] *Eldridge v. Gordon Bros. Grp., L.L.C.*, 863 F.3d 66, 85 (1st Cir. 2017);

that should have been disclosed originally) may be subject to exclusion under Rule 37(c).[120]

Additional Sanctions

In addition to or in lieu of precluding the evidence, upon motion and after an opportunity to be heard,[121] the court may inform the jury of the party's failure to disclose or supplement[122] or impose any of the sanctions listed above under Rule 37(b).[123] The court has broad discretion in awarding sanctions under Rule 37(c).[124]

Expenses

In addition to exclusion or other sanctions, the court may, after providing an opportunity to be heard, order payment of expenses, including reasonable attorney's fees, caused by the failure to disclose or supplement.[125] Expenses and fees under Rule 37(c) may only be awarded against the party, not against the attorney, in contrast to other provisions of Rule 37.[126]

Explanation of Sanctions

The court order must state the basis for its decision to impose sanctions so that the sanctioned party may obtain meaningful appellate review.[127]

Exclusion Applies at Trial, Hearing, or Motion

The information or witnesses not properly disclosed or provided by supplement are most commonly excluded from trial, but also may be excluded from a hearing or motion.[128]

Jackson v. Allstate Ins. Co., 785 F.3d 1193, 1204 (8th Cir. 2015).

[120] *Krause v. Cty. of Mohave*, 459 F. Supp. 3d 1258, 1269 (D. Ariz. 2020); *Redmond-Nieves Okuma Am. Corp.*, 332 F.R.D. 418, 420 (D. Mass. 2019).

[121] *Paladin Associates, Inc. v. Montana Power Co.*, 328 F.3d 1145, 1164–65 (9th Cir. 2003) (the opportunity to submit briefs was an opportunity to be heard).

[122] *See DR Distributors, LLC v. 21 Century Smoking, Inc.*, 513 F. Supp. 3d 839, 958-59 (N.D. Ill. 2021).

[123] *See In re Gravel*, 6 F.4th 503, 515 (2d Cir. 2021); *Dura Automotive Systems of Indiana, Inc. v. CTS Corp.*, 285 F.3d 609, 615–16 (7th Cir. 2002) (sanctions in lieu of evidence exclusion only if the failure to disclose was substantially justified).

[124] *Taylor v. Mentor Worldwide LLC*, 940 F.3d 582, 593 (11th Cir. 2019); *Magnetar Tech. Corp. v. Intamin, Ltd.*, 801 F.3d 1150, 1155 (9th Cir. 2015).

[125] *Brown v. Elliott*, 876 F.3d 637, 645 (4th Cir. 2017).

[126] *Sun River Energy, Inc. v. Nelson*, 800 F.3d 1219, 1225–26 (10th Cir. 2015); *Grider v. Keystone Health Plan Central, Inc.*, 580 F.3d 119, 141 (3d Cir. 2009). *But see A PDX Pro Co., Inc. v. Dish Network Service LLC*, 311 F.R.D. 642, 651 (D. Colo. 2015) (sanctions may be available under Rule 26(g) for signing the disclosure or response).

[127] *Mutual Service Ins. Co. v. Frit Industries, Inc.*, 358 F.3d 1312, 1326 (11th Cir. 2004); *but see Umbenhower v. Copart, Inc.*, 222 F.R.D. 672, 675 (D. Kan. 2004) (court need not make explicit findings regarding substantial justification or harmlessness).

[128] *Sec. & Exch. Comm'n v. GenAudio Inc.*, 32 F.4th 902, 936 (10th Cir. 2022); *Birch | Rea Partners, Inc. v. Regent Bank*, 27 F.4th 1245, 1253 (7th Cir. 2022).

Failure to Admit

If a party fails to admit a matter that another party subsequently proves at trial,[129] the other party can move for its reasonable expenses, including reasonable attorney's fees, incurred in proving the matter.[130] The court then must[131] award expenses unless one of the following four conditions exists:

(1) The request was objectionable;[132]
(2) The admission sought was of no substantial importance, such as when the proof of the matter was trivial;[133]
(3) The party refusing to admit had reasonable grounds to believe that it would be successful on the matter;[134] or
(4) Other good reasons exist for the failure to admit, such as a genuine inability to determine the truth of the matter.[135]

- *Improper Statement of Inability to Admit:* The sanctions in Rule 37(c) apply to an improper statement of inability to admit or deny, as well as to an improper denial.[136]

RULE 37(d)—PARTY'S FAILURE TO ATTEND ITS OWN DEPOSITION, SERVE ANSWERS TO INTERROGATORIES, OR RESPOND TO A REQUEST FOR INSPECTION

CORE CONCEPT

Rule 37(d) provides that upon motion, sanctions are immediately available against a party who fails to appear for the party's deposition after being served with proper notice or fails to serve a written response to properly-served interrogatories or requests to inspect documents or things.

APPLICATIONS

When Available

Sanctions under Rule 37(d) are available when a party fails to appear for the party's deposition after being served with proper notice,[137] fails to answer or object to properly-served in-

---

[129] *McCarthy v. Ameritech Pub., Inc.*, 763 F.3d 488, 492 (6th Cir. 2014); *Odom v. Roberts*, 337 F.R.D. 347, 353 (N.D. Fla. 2020).

[130] *Leonard v. Stemtech Int'l Inc*, 834 F.3d 376, 402 (3d Cir. 2016).

[131] *VeroBlue Farms USA Inc. v. Wulf*, — F.R.D. —, 2021 WL 5176839, at *5 (N.D. Tex. 2021).

[132] *Russo v. Baxter Healthcare Corp.*, 51 F. Supp. 2d 70, 78 (D.R.I. 1999).

[133] *Leonard v. Stemtech Int'l Inc*, 834 F.3d 376, 402 (3d Cir. 2016); *McCarthy v. Ameritech Pub., Inc.*, 763 F.3d 488, 490–91 (6th Cir. 2014).

[134] *Yoder & Frey Auctioneers, Inc. v. EquipmentFacts, LLC*, 774 F.3d 1065, 1075 (6th Cir. 2014); *Mutual Service Ins. Co. v. Frit Industries, Inc.*, 358 F.3d 1312, 1326 (11th Cir. 2004).

[135] *Maynard v. Nygren*, 332 F.3d 462, 470 (7th Cir. 2003).

[136] *Odom v. Roberts*, 337 F.R.D. 347, 353 (N.D. Fla. 2020).

[137] *Lopez v. Whirlpool Corp.*, 989

terrogatories,[138] or fails to serve a written response to a properly-served request to inspect documents or things.[139] A court order is not a prerequisite to sanctions under Rule 37(d).[140] Rule 37(d) does not specify when the motion for sanctions must be filed, but some courts have held that the motion must be filed without "unreasonable delay,"[141] and before the entry of judgment.[142] The court should provide the party to be sanctioned with an opportunity to be heard before imposing sanctions.[143]

- *Incomplete Response to Interrogatories or Document Requests:* Rule 37(d) only applies if the party fails altogether to serve a response to interrogatories or document requests.[144] If the party serves an incomplete or evasive response, the proper procedure is a motion to compel under Rule 37(a), then a motion for sanctions under Rule 37(b) if the party does not comply with the court order.[145] Some courts allow sanctions under Rule 37(d) when the response to the discovery requests is so deficient as to be tantamount to no response at all.[146]

Parties Only

Rule 37(d) applies only to parties; a nonparty's failure to attend a deposition may result in contempt sanctions, but does not result in sanctions under Rule 37(d).[147]

Failures of a Party's Rule 30(b)(6) Representative

A corporation or organization that is a party is subject to the sanctions in Rule 37(d) if its officer, director, managing agent, or person designated to testify under Rule 30(b)(6) fails to appear for a deposition after being properly noticed.[148] Likewise, if a party refuses to designate a representative under

F.3d 656, 665 (8th Cir. 2021); *Evans v. Griffin*, 932 F.3d 1043, 1045 (7th Cir. 2019).

[138]*Roney v. Starwood Hotels & Resorts Worldwide, Inc.*, 236 F.R.D. 346 (E.D. Mich. 2006); *Jayne H. Lee, Inc. v. Flagstaff Industries Corp.*, 173 F.R.D. 651, 653 (D. Md. 1997).

[139]*Alvariza v. Home Depot*, 240 F.R.D. 586, 590 (D. Colo. 2007), aff'd, 241 F.R.D. 663 (D. Colo. 2007) (Rule 37(c) sanctions do not apply to informal agreements to provide documents, only to properly served Rule 34 document requests); *Roney v. Starwood Hotels & Resorts Worldwide, Inc.*, 236 F.R.D. 346 (E.D. Mich. 2006).

[140]*Washington Metropolitan Area Transit Com'n v. Reliable Limousine Service, LLC*, 776 F.3d 1, 7 (D.C. Cir. 2015).

[141]*See Lancaster v. Independent School Dist. No. 5*, 149 F.3d 1228, 1237 (10th Cir. 1998).

[142]*See Mercy v. Suffolk County, New York*, 748 F.2d 52, 55–56 (2d Cir. 1984).

[143]*Lopez v. Whirlpool Corp.*, 989 F.3d 656, 666 (8th Cir. 2021).

[144]*Fast v. GoDaddy.com LLC*, 340 F.R.D. 326, 335 (D. Ariz. 2022); *DR Distributors, LLC v. 21 Century Smoking, Inc.*, 513 F. Supp. 3d 839, 954 (N.D. Ill. 2021).

[145]*Fjelstad v. Am. Honda Motor Co., Inc.*, 762 F.2d 1334 (9th Cir. 1985).

[146]*See Melendez-Garcia v. Sanchez*, 629 F.3d 25, 33, n.5 (1st Cir. 2010).

[147]*Kamps v. Fried, Frank, Harris, Shriver & Jacobson L.L.P.*, 274 F.R.D. 115, 118 (S.D.N.Y. 2011).

[148]*Ecclesiastes 9:10-11-12, Inc. v. LMC Holding Co.*, 497 F.3d 1135, 1147

Rule 30(b)(6), the party will be subject to sanctions under Rule 37(d).[149] In extreme cases, a party who produces an unprepared or inappropriate representative may also be subject to sanctions under Rule 37(d).[150]

Certification of Conference for Written Discovery

A motion for sanctions under Rule 37(d) for failure to respond to interrogatories or requests for inspection must include a certification that the movant has in good faith conferred or attempted to confer with the other party or person in an effort to obtain a response without court action.[151] This requirement does not apply to the failure to appear for a deposition (because the harm already occurred when the noticing party showed up for the deposition and the deponent did not appear, so an agreement during a meet and confer to appear at another date does not cure the harm).[152]

Available Sanctions

Rule 37(d) states that the court may impose whatever sanctions are "just,"[153] including those listed in Rule 37(b)[154] except for contempt of court sanctions (because the party has not violated a court order).[155] The court has broad discretion in deciding what sanction to impose.[156] The court can consider all the circumstances, such as whether the failure was accidental or in bad faith, in determining the sanctions to impose.[157] The sanctions may be imposed on the party, the attorney, or both.[158]

(10th Cir. 2007); *Atlantic Cape Fisheries v. Hartford Fire Ins. Co.*, 509 F.2d 577 (1st Cir. 1975).

[149] *Ferko v. National Ass'n for Stock Car Auto Racing, Inc.*, 218 F.R.D. 125, 133 (E.D. Tex. 2003).

[150] *See Baker v. St. Paul Travelers Ins. Co.*, 670 F.3d 119, 124 (1st Cir. 2012); *Guinnane v. Dobbins*, 479 F. Supp. 3d 989, 995 (D. Mont. 2020).

[151] *Black Horse Lane Assoc., L.P. v. Dow Chem. Corp.*, 228 F.3d 275, 301 (3d Cir. 2000); *Olin Corp. v. Lamorak Ins. Co.*, 517 F. Supp. 3d 161, 177 (S.D.N.Y. 2021).

[152] *Nationstar Mortgage, LLC v. Flamingo Trails No. 7 Landscape Maint. Ass'n*, 316 F.R.D. 327, 335 (D. Nev. 2016); *Grand Oaks, Inc. v. Anderson*, 175 F.R.D. 247, 250 (N.D. Miss. 1997); *but see Simms v. Center for Correctional Health and Policy Studies*, 272 F.R.D. 36, 39 (D.D.C. 2011) (requiring a certification of conference even for failure to attend a deposition).

[153] *In re Hutter*, 207 B.R. 981, 986 (Bankr. D. Conn. 1997), aff'd, 2001 WL 34778750 (D. Conn. 2001).

[154] *Solvay Specialty Polymers USA, LLC v. Zhenguo (Leo) Liu*, 331 F.R.D. 187, 190 (N.D. Ga. 2019); *Gonzalez v. Batmasian*, 319 F.R.D. 403, 405 (S.D. Fla. 2017).

[155] *See Bishop v. First Mississippi Fin. Group, Inc.*, 221 F.R.D. 461 (S.D. Miss. 2004) (dismissal for failure to appear at depositions and respond to motions); *Viswanathan v. Scotland County Bd. of Educ.*, 165 F.R.D. 50 (M.D.N.C. 1995), aff'd, 76 F.3d 377 (4th Cir. 1996).

[156] *Black Horse Lane Assoc., L.P. v. Dow Chem. Corp.*, 228 F.3d 275, 301 (3d Cir. 2000); *Flores v. Entergy Nuclear Operations, Inc.*, 313 F. Supp. 3d 511, 521 (S.D.N.Y. 2018).

[157] *See Karimi v. Golden Gate Sch. of Law*, 361 F. Supp. 3d 956, 969 (N.D. Cal. 2019); *In re Sumitomo Copper Litig.*, 204 F.R.D. 58, 60–61 (S.D.N.Y. 2001).

[158] *Valle v. Wolff*, 627 B.R. 821, 831

Expenses

The court must require that the party failing to participate in discovery and/or the party's attorney pay the resulting expenses of the other party,[159] including reasonable attorney's fees,[160] unless it finds that the failure was "substantially justified"[161] or that other circumstances exist that would make the award "unjust."[162] The award of expenses can be in addition to or instead of other sanctions.

Improper Excuses for Failure to Perform Discovery Obligations

It is not a defense to a motion for sanctions under Rule 37(d) to argue that the discovery request was objectionable.[163] Likewise, a party may not refuse to respond to discovery requests or appear for a deposition because the opposing party has committed discovery violations[164] or failed to respond to discovery.[165] Informal notification that a party will not appear for a deposition, particularly when given shortly before the deposition, will not excuse failure to attend.[166] The proper response to an objectionable discovery request is to serve a response interposing the objections or file a motion for a protective order under Rule 26(c), not to ignore the discovery request.[167] However, even filing a protective order may not be a sufficient basis not to appear at a deposition if the court has

---

(D. Md. 2021); *Flores v. Entergy Nuclear Operations, Inc.*, 313 F. Supp. 3d 511, 521 (S.D.N.Y. 2018).

[159] *John Wiley & Sons, Inc. v. Book Dog Books, LLC*, 298 F.R.D. 145, 149–52 (S.D.N.Y. 2014) (hotel and travel costs and court reporter fees); *Robles v. Green Bay Educ. Ass'n*, 295 F.R.D. 301, 302 (E.D. Wisc. 2013) (room rental, court reporter fees, and mileage).

[160] *Hyde & Drath v. Baker*, 24 F.3d 1162 (9th Cir.1994); *Dubois v. Maritimo Offshore Pty Ltd.*, 422 F. Supp. 3d 545, 563 (D. Conn. 2019) (applying the lodestar method).

[161] *Telluride Mgmt. Solutions, Inc. v. Telluride Inv. Group*, 55 F.3d 463 (9th Cir. 1995) (good faith but incorrect belief that the action had been dismissed was not sufficient to excuse absence from a deposition); *Valle v. Wolff*, 627 B.R. 821, 829 (D. Md. 2021) (inadvertent failure to check email is not sufficient).

[162] *Miller v. Int'l Paper Co.*, 408 F.2d 283, 292–94 (5th Cir. 1969); *Nationstar Mortgage, LLC v. Flamingo Trails No. 7 Landscape Maint. Ass'n*, 316 F.R.D. 327, 335 (D. Nev. 2016) (burden is on party asserting that its conduct was substantially justified or an award would be unjust).

[163] *EMW Women's Surgical Ctr., P.S.C. v. Friedlander*, 978 F.3d 418, 446 (6th Cir. 2020); *Int'l Broth. of Elec. Workers, Local Union No. 545 v. Hope Elec. Corp.*, 380 F.3d 1084, 1106 (8th Cir. 2004).

[164] *John Wiley & Sons, Inc. v. Book Dog Books, LLC*, 298 F.R.D. 145, 148–49 (S.D.N.Y. 2014).

[165] *Mulero-Abreu v. Puerto Rico Police Dept.*, 675 F.3d 88, 92 (1st Cir. 2012); *Infanzon v. Allstate Ins. Co.*, 335 F.R.D. 305, 312 (C.D. Cal. 2020).

[166] *Panzer v. Swiftships, LLC*, 318 F.R.D. 326, 328 (E.D. La. 2016); *John Wiley & Sons, Inc. v. Book Dog Books, LLC*, 298 F.R.D. 145, 149 (S.D.N.Y. 2014).

[167] *Kamps v. Fried, Frank, Harris, Shriver & Jacobson L.L.P.*, 274 F.R.D. 115, 118 (S.D.N.Y. 2011); *Amobi v. District of Columbia Dept. of Corrections*, 257 F.R.D. 8, 10–11 (D.D.C. 2009).

not acted on the motion, particularly if the motion was filed at the last minute.[168]

Court Order

Although a court order is not a prerequisite to a motion for sanctions under Rule 37(d), the motion may still be brought if the party failing to participate in discovery had been ordered to participate[169] (although a motion under Rule 37(b) is usually the better option).

Which Court

A motion for sanctions under Rule 37(d) is filed in the court in which the action is pending.[170]

Refusal to Be Sworn In at Deposition

A party appearing for a deposition at the designated time but who refuses to be sworn in is not generally subject to Rule 37(d) sanctions.[171] Instead, the opposing party should file a motion to compel under Rule 37(a), then seek sanctions under Rule 37(b) if the party still refuses to be sworn in.

Refusal to Answer Specific Questions

A party who appears and is sworn in, but who then refuses to answer a specific question or questions is not subject to sanctions under Rule 37(d).[172] The proper procedure is for the party taking the deposition to move to compel answers under Rule 37(a), then move for sanctions under Rule 37(b) if the party still refuses to answer.[173] The same result is reached with respect to evasive or incomplete answers. However, if the party refuses to answer all or substantially all of the questions, Rule 37(d) may apply.[174]

Continuation of Deposition

Courts differ as to whether Rule 37(d) sanctions apply to a party who fails to appear for the continuation of a deposition.[175]

Compliance After Motion

Once a motion for sanctions has been filed, the non-

---

[168] *EMW Women's Surgical Ctr., P.S.C. v. Friedlander*, 978 F.3d 418, 447 (6th Cir. 2020).

[169] *See Independent Productions Corp. v. Loew's Inc.*, 283 F.2d 730 (2d Cir.1960); *M.B. v. CSX Transp., Inc.*, 299 F.R.D. 341 (N.D.N.Y. 2014).

[170] *Diamond Consortium, Inc. v. Hammervold*, 386 F. Supp. 3d 904, 914 (M.D. Tenn. 2019).

[171] *Aziz v. Wright*, 34 F.3d 587, 589 (8th Cir. 1994).

[172] *See Evans v. Griffin*, 932 F.3d 1043, 1045 (7th Cir. 2019); *Baker v. St. Paul Travelers Ins. Co.*, 670 F.3d 119, 123 (1st Cir. 2012).

[173] *Evans v. Griffin*, 932 F.3d 1043, 1045 (7th Cir. 2019).

[174] *Black Horse Lane Assoc., L.P. v. Dow Chem. Corp.*, 228 F.3d 275, 301 (3d Cir. 2000) (Rule 30(b)(6) representative); *GMAC Bank v. HTFC Corp.*, 248 F.R.D. 182, 185 (E.D. Pa. 2008).

[175] *Miller v. Int'l Paper Co.*, 408 F.2d 283, 292–294 (5th Cir. 1969) (no sanctions if continuation date not set forth in a deposition notice); *John Wiley & Sons, Inc. v. Book Dog Books, LLC*, 298 F.R.D. 145, 149 (S.D.N.Y. 2014) (sanctions where parties had agreed to the continuation date).

participating party cannot avoid sanctions by responding to the discovery request.[176] However, the court can consider that conduct in deciding what sanctions to impose.[177]

RULE 37(e)—FAILURE TO PRESERVE ELECTRONICALLY STORED INFORMATION

CORE CONCEPT

Rule 37(e) contains the provisions for sanctioning a party who fails to take reasonable steps to preserve electronically stored information that it was required to preserve. It does not authorize any sanctions unless the lost information cannot be restored or replaced through additional discovery. If the court finds prejudice to another party from the loss of the information, it may impose only measures no greater than necessary to cure the prejudice. If the court finds that the spoliating party acted with the intent to deprive another party of the information's use in the litigation, the court may impose the more severe sanctions of presuming that the information was unfavorable to the spoliating party, instructing the jury that it may or must presume that the information was unfavorable to the spoliating party, dismissing the action, or entering a default judgment.

APPLICATIONS

Prerequisites for Sanctions

Rule 37(e) authorizes sanctions for failure to preserve ESI only if three prerequisites are met:

(1) There must have been a duty to preserve the ESI at the time the ESI was lost.[178] Rule 37 does not create a duty to preserve; that duty is found in common law or statute and typically arises when litigation has been commenced or is reasonably anticipated and the ESI is reasonably likely to be relevant to a party's claim or defense.[179] Additionally, the court may create or enhance the duty by issuing a preservation order;[180]

(2) The ESI was lost because a party failed to take reasonable steps to preserve it.[181] ESI lost despite reasonable measures to preserve it, such as through the routine operation of a computer system or as a result of dam-

---

[176] *Valle v. Wolff*, 627 B.R. 821, 828 (D. Md. 2021).

[177] *Antico v. Honda of Camden*, 85 F.R.D. 34, 36 (E.D. Pa. 1979).

[178] *Eur. v. Equinox Holdings, Inc.*, __ F. Supp. 3d __, 2022 WL 832027, at *3 (S.D.N.Y. 2022); *Borum v. Brentwood Vill., LLC*, 332 F.R.D. 38, 45 (D.D.C. 2019).

[179] *See Fast v. GoDaddy.com LLC*, 340 F.R.D. 326, 336 (D. Ariz. 2022); *Hollis v. CEVA Logistics U.S., Inc.*, __ F. Supp. 3d __, 2022 WL 1591731, at *5 (N.D. Ill. 2022).

[180] Rule 37 advisory committee's note (2015).

[181] *Eur. v. Equinox Holdings, Inc.*, __ F. Supp. 3d __, 2022 WL 832027, at *3 (S.D.N.Y. 2022); *Borum v. Brentwood Vill., LLC*, 332 F.R.D. 38, 45–46 (D.D.C. 2019).

age to a computer system, will not support sanctions.[182] The court may take into account the party's technical sophistication in evaluating whether measures were reasonable.[183] However, parties and attorneys have an obligation to familiarize themselves with the party's data retention systems to ensure that potentially relevant information is being preserved,[184] and must suspend routine or automatic destruction of ESI;[185] and

(3) The ESI cannot be restored or replaced through additional discovery.[186] ESI often exists in multiple locations, so loss from one location will not support sanctions if the ESI also exists in another location.[187] ESI that might have been deemed inaccessible, such as ESI located on backup tapes—might become discoverable if the accessible versions have been lost.[188] The issue is whether the ESI itself can be restored or replaced—testimony about the contents of the ESI is not sufficient.[189] Note that this prerequisite may preclude Rule 37(e) sanctions even for deliberately, maliciously destroyed ESI if another source of the information is subsequently located.[190]

- *Burden of Proof:* Most courts hold that the party seeking spoliation sanctions bears the burden of establishing these prerequisites.[191]

Sanctions to Cure Prejudice to Another Party

If the court finds the three prerequisites satisfied and finds

---

[182]Rule 37 advisory committee's note (2015).

[183]*Fast v. GoDaddy.com LLC*, 340 F.R.D. 326, 344 (D. Ariz. 2022).

[184]*In re Keurig Green Mountain Single-Serve Coffee Antitrust Litig.*, 341 F.R.D. 474, 495 (S.D.N.Y. 2022); *DR Distributors, LLC v. 21 Century Smoking, Inc.*, 513 F. Supp. 3d 839, 931–33 (N.D. Ill. 2021) (duty to disable autodelete functions).

[185]*Charlestown Cap. Advisors, LLC v. Acero Junction, Inc.*, 337 F.R.D. 47, 61 (S.D.N.Y. 2020); *Johns v. Gwinn*, 503 F. Supp. 3d 452, 468 (W.D. Va. 2020).

[186]*Fast v. GoDaddy.com LLC*, 340 F.R.D. 326, 341 (D. Ariz. 2022); *Oracle Am., Inc. v. Hewlett Packard Enter. Co.*, 328 F.R.D. 543, 552 (N.D. Cal. 2018).

[187]*See Eur. v. Equinox Holdings, Inc.*, __ F. Supp. 3d __, 2022 WL 832027, at *4 (S.D.N.Y. 2022); *Borum v. Brentwood Vill., LLC*, 332 F.R.D. 38, 46 (D.D.C. 2019); *Oracle Am., Inc. v. Hewlett Packard Enter. Co.*, 328 F.R.D. 543, 552 (N.D. Cal. 2018).

[188]*See Freidig v. Target Corp.*, 329 F.R.D. 199, 208 (W.D. Wis. 2018); Rule 37 advisory committee's note (2015).

[189]*Hollis v. CEVA Logistics U.S., Inc.*, __ F. Supp. 3d __, 2022 WL 1591731, at *6 (N.D. Ill. 2022).

[190]*Marquette Transp. Co. Gulf Island, LLC v. Chembulk Westport M/V*, 2016 WL 930946, *3 (E.D. La. 2016).

[191]*Borum v. Brentwood Vill., LLC*, 332 F.R.D. 38, 43 (D.D.C. 2019). *But see Hollis v. CEVA Logistics U.S., Inc.*, __ F. Supp. 3d __, 2022 WL 1591731, at *3 (N.D. Ill. 2022) (party with better access to the information should bear the burden of proof); *DR Distributors, LLC v. 21 Century Smoking, Inc.*, 513 F. Supp. 3d 839, 978–79 (N.D. Ill. 2021) (questioning which party should bear the burden of proving whether reasonable steps were taken).

prejudice to another party from the loss of the information,[192] the court may impose sanctions, but may only impose measures necessary to cure the prejudice.[193] The court has wide discretion in fashioning an appropriate sanction to cure the prejudice,[194] and the measures need not cure every conceivable prejudicial effect.[195] The measures may not include the more severe sanctions in Rule 37(e)(2), however.[196] Examples of appropriate sanctions include forbidding the spoliating party from introducing certain evidence at trial,[197] permitting parties to present evidence and arguments to the jury about the loss of the ESI,[198] giving instructions to the jury to assist it in evaluating such evidence and argument,[199] providing that the trial judge may consider the failure to preserve in reaching a decision in a bench trial,[200] and monetary penalties.[201]

- *Prejudice Defined:* Prejudice has been defined as an impairment to a party's ability to obtain the evidence necessary for its case.[202] The moving party does not need to establish the contents of the missing ESI with certainty, but does need to demonstrate a likelihood that the lost evidence would have assisted it.[203] The rule does not assign the burden of proving prejudice to either party, and it will be up to the court's discretion to assess

---

[192]*Eur. v. Equinox Holdings, Inc.*, __ F. Supp. 3d __, 2022 WL 832027, at *6 (S.D.N.Y. 2022); *Borum v. Brentwood Vill., LLC*, 332 F.R.D. 38, 47 (D.D.C. 2019).

[193]*Boudreau v. Shaw's Supermarkets, Inc.*, 955 F.3d 225, 237 (1st Cir. 2020); *Barbera v. Pearson Educ., Inc.*, 906 F.3d 621, 627 (7th Cir. 2018).

[194]*Eur. v. Equinox Holdings, Inc.*, __ F. Supp. 3d __, 2022 WL 832027, at *3 (S.D.N.Y. 2022); *Johns v. Gwinn*, 503 F. Supp. 3d 452, 474 (W.D. Va. 2020).

[195]*Eur. v. Equinox Holdings, Inc.*, __ F. Supp. 3d __, 2022 WL 832027, at *3 (S.D.N.Y. 2022).

[196]*Eur. v. Equinox Holdings, Inc.*, __ F. Supp. 3d __, 2022 WL 832027, at *4 (S.D.N.Y. 2022); *Borum v. Brentwood Vill., LLC*, 332 F.R.D. 38, 49 (D.D.C. 2019).

[197]*ML Healthcare Servs., LLC v. Publix Super Markets, Inc.*, 881 F.3d 1293, 1308 (11th Cir. 2018); *DR Distributors, LLC v. 21 Century Smoking, Inc.*, 513 F. Supp. 3d 839, 956 (N.D. Ill. 2021).

[198]*Hollis v. CEVA Logistics U.S., Inc.*, __ F. Supp. 3d __, 2022 WL 1591731, at *2 (N.D. Ill. 2022); *Ali v. Dainese USA, Inc.*, 577 F. Supp. 3d 205, 224 (S.D.N.Y. 2021).

[199]*See DR Distributors, LLC v. 21 Century Smoking, Inc.*, 513 F. Supp. 3d 839, 958 (N.D. Ill. 2021).

[200]*DR Distributors, LLC v. 21 Century Smoking, Inc.*, 513 F. Supp. 3d 839, 863 (N.D. Ill. 2021); *Johns v. Gwinn*, 503 F. Supp. 3d 452, 474 (W.D. Va. 2020).

[201]*Charlestown Cap. Advisors, LLC v. Acero Junction, Inc.*, 337 F.R.D. 47, 59 (S.D.N.Y. 2020); *Paisley Park Enterprises, Inc. v. Boxill*, 330 F.R.D. 226, 238 (D. Minn. 2019).

[202]*Fast v. GoDaddy.com LLC*, 340 F.R.D. 326, 336 (D. Ariz. 2022); *Hollis v. CEVA Logistics U.S., Inc.*, __ F. Supp. 3d __, 2022 WL 1591731, at *7 (N.D. Ill. 2022).

[203]*In re Keurig Green Mountain Single-Serve Coffee Antitrust Litig.*, 341 F.R.D. 474, 495 (S.D.N.Y. 2022); *Johns v. Gwinn*, 503 F. Supp. 3d 452, 470 (W.D. Va. 2020).

prejudice.[204] Some courts presume prejudice if the party acted in bad faith or with gross negligence.[205] Some courts submit the issue of prejudice to the jury.[206]

Sanctions for Intent to Affect the Litigation

If the court finds the three prerequisites satisfied and finds that a party acted with the intent to deprive another party of the information's use in the litigation, the court may impose more severe sanctions.[207] The rule does not assign the burden of establishing intent on either party, and some courts require the moving party to prove intent.[208] Although intent may be inferred from circumstantial evidence,[209] gross negligence is insufficient to satisfy the standard of "intent to deprive."[210] In a bench trial, the court may presume that the lost ESI was unfavorable to the party failing to preserve it. In a jury trial, the court may make an adverse inference instruction to the jury that it may or must presume the information was unfavorable to the party failing to preserve it.[211] The court may also impose dispositive sanctions, dismissing the action or entering default judgment for the plaintiff.[212] The court does not need to find prejudice to another party to impose these more severe sanctions.[213] The court also has the discretion to impose lesser sanctions even if the court finds the intent to deprive.[214]

Motion for Sanctions

A party seeks spoliation sanctions under Rule 37(e) by motion. There is no set deadline or timing requirement for fil-

---

[204]*Eur. v. Equinox Holdings, Inc.*, __ F. Supp. 3d __, 2022 WL 832027, at *3 (S.D.N.Y. 2022); *DR Distributors, LLC v. 21 Century Smoking, Inc.*, 513 F. Supp. 3d 839, 981 (N.D. Ill. 2021).

[205]*See, e.g., Fed. Trade Comm'n v. F&G Int'l Grp. Holdings, LLC*, 339 F.R.D. 325, 332 (S.D. Ga. 2021); *Ottoson v. SMBC Leasing & Fin., Inc.*, 268 F. Supp. 3d 570, 581 (S.D.N.Y. 2017).

[206]*See Hollis v. CEVA Logistics U.S., Inc.*, __ F. Supp. 3d __, 2022 WL 1591731, at *8 (N.D. Ill. 2022).

[207]*Auer v. City of Minot*, 896 F.3d 854, 858 (8th Cir. 2018) (intent can be proven indirectly); *Barbera v. Pearson Educ., Inc.*, 906 F.3d 621, 628 (7th Cir. 2018).

[208]*See Hollis v. CEVA Logistics U.S., Inc.*, __ F. Supp. 3d __, 2022 WL 1591731, at *6 (N.D. Ill. 2022); *Eur. v. Equinox Holdings, Inc.*, __ F. Supp. 3d __, 2022 WL 832027, at *3 (S.D.N.Y. 2022).

[209]*Fast v. GoDaddy.com LLC*, 340 F.R.D. 326, 336 (D. Ariz. 2022); *Eur. v. Equinox Holdings, Inc.*, __ F. Supp. 3d __, 2022 WL 832027, at *3 (S.D.N.Y. 2022).

[210]*Borum v. Brentwood Vill., LLC*, 332 F.R.D. 38, 48 (D.D.C. 2019); *Culhane v. Wal-Mart Supercenter*, 364 F. Supp. 3d 768, 772 (E.D. Mich. 2019).

[211]*Paisley Park Enterprises, Inc. v. Boxill*, 330 F.R.D. 226, 236 (D. Minn. 2019); *Moody v. CSX Transportation, Inc.*, 271 F. Supp. 3d 410, 432 (W.D.N.Y. 2017) (adverse inference).

[212]*Coan v. Dunne*, 602 B.R. 429, 737 (D. Conn. 2019); *Culhane v. Wal-Mart Supercenter*, 364 F. Supp. 3d 768, 772 (E.D. Mich. 2019).

[213]*In re Keurig Green Mountain Single-Serve Coffee Antitrust Litig.*, 341 F.R.D. 474, 496 (S.D.N.Y. 2022); *Borum v. Brentwood Vill., LLC*, 332 F.R.D. 38, 48 (D.D.C. 2019).

[214]*Borum v. Brentwood Vill., LLC*, 332 F.R.D. 38, 49 (D.D.C. 2019); *CAT3, LLC v. Black Lineage, Inc.*, 164 F. Supp. 3d 488, 501 (S.D.N.Y. 2016).

ing a motion for spoliation sanctions, but unreasonable delay may result in denial of the motion.[215]

ESI Only

Rule 37(e) only applies to the failure to preserve ESI.[216] The authority for sanctions for spoliating paper documents or other non-ESI evidence comes from the courts' inherent authority over cases on their dockets, or from Rule 37(b) if a party violates a preservation order.[217] However, some courts are using their discretion under that inherent authority to apply the standards in Rule 37(e) to paper documents.[218]

Judge vs. Jury

Although judges have made the factual findings underlying the vast majority of their Rule 37(e) rulings, the judge can submit the Rule 37(e) factual issues to the jury.[219]

Proportionality

Throughout the ESI spoliation analysis, the courts will include proportionality in their analysis.[220] For example, in determining whether a party failed to take "reasonable steps" to preserve ESI, the court will consider the cost of the steps, the value of the case, and the other proportionality factors.[221]

Other Authority for Sanctions

Most courts have held that Rule 37(e) is the court's only sanctioning authority for spoliation of ESI, and that Rule 37(e) forecloses reliance on the court's inherent authority or state law as authority for such sanctions,[222] but some courts view Rule 37(e) as an additional source of sanctioning authority[223] and some courts view Rule 37(e) as only preempting reliance on other sources of sanctioning authority for the harsh sanc-

[215] *Larios v. Lunardi*, 442 F. Supp. 3d 1299, 1305 (E.D. Cal. 2020).

[216] *Black v. Costco Wholesale Corp.*, 542 F. Supp. 3d 750, 752 (M.D. Tenn. 2021) (videotape is ESI); *Moody v. CSX Transportation, Inc.*, 271 F. Supp. 3d 410, 425 (W.D.N.Y. 2017) (although a laptop is a tangible object, failure to preserve it is failure to preserve the ESI on it).

[217] *See Best Payphones, Inc. v. City of New York*, 2016 WL 792396, *3, 5 (E.D.N.Y. 2016).

[218] *See, e.g., Mcqueen v. Aramark Corp.*, 2016 WL 6988820, *4 (D. Utah Nov. 29, 2016).

[219] *See Hollis v. CEVA Logistics U.S., Inc.*, — F. Supp. 3d —, 2022 WL 1591731, at *8 (N.D. Ill. 2022); *Cahill v. Dart*, 2016 WL 7034139, *4 (N.D. Ill. 2016).

[220] Rule 37 advisory committee's note (2015). *See also Certusview Tech., LLC v. S&N Locating Serv., LLC*, 2016 WL 6681181, *2, n.2 (E.D. Va. 2016).

[221] Rule 37 advisory committee's note (2015). *See also Snider v. Danfoss, LLC*, 2017 WL 2973464, *1, n.2 (N.D. Ill. 2017).

[222] *See, e.g., Hollis v. CEVA Logistics U.S., Inc.*, — F. Supp. 3d —, 2022 WL 1591731, at *2 (N.D. Ill. 2022); *Eur. v. Equinox Holdings, Inc.*, — F. Supp. 3d —, 2022 WL 832027, at *3 (S.D.N.Y. 2022).

[223] *See Borum v. Brentwood Vill., LLC*, 332 F.R.D. 38, 43 (D.D.C. 2019) (courts should use Rule 37(e) when feasible); *Ronnie Van Zant, Inc. v. Pyle*, 270 F. Supp. 3d 656, 668, n.16 (S.D.N.Y. 2017).

tions in Rule 37(e)(2).[224] Rule 37(e) does not affect spoliation of evidence other than ESI or the viability of an independent tort claim for spoliation if state law applies and authorizes the claim.[225] Additionally, if the court has issued a preservation order and a party violates that order, sanctions may be available for violation of the court order under Rule 37(b).[226]

Expenses

Unlike most of the provisions in Rule 37, Rule 37(e) makes no mention of an award of expenses or attorney's fees incurred in connection with the Rule 37(e) motion to the prevailing party.[227] The courts disagree about whether it is permissible to award expenses under Rule 37(e).[228]

RULE 37(f)—FAILURE TO PARTICIPATE IN FRAMING A DISCOVERY PLAN

CORE CONCEPT

If a party fails to participate in developing a proposed discovery plan as required by Rule 26(f), the court may, after opportunity for a hearing, require the party failing to participate to pay the expenses of the other party, including reasonable attorney's fees, caused by the failure.

Additional Research References

Wright & Miller, *Federal Practice and Procedure* §§ 2281 to 2293

C.J.S., Federal Civil Procedure §§ 535 to 547, 640 to 644, 694, 695, 748 to 774

West's Key Number Digest, Federal Civil Procedure ⚷1278, 1299, 1451 to 1456, 1537 to 1542, 1636 to 1640, 1663 to 1664, 1685

---

[224] *Burris v. JPMorgan Chase & Co.*, 341 F.R.D. 604, 612 (D. Ariz. 2022) (authority to award attorney's fees not preempted).

[225] Rule 37 advisory committee's note (2015).

[226] *See Ellis v. Hobbs Police Dep't*, 2020 WL 1041688, at *4 (D.N.M. 2020).

[227] *See Paisley Park Enterprises, Inc. v. Boxill*, 330 F.R.D. 226, 237–38 (D. Minn. 2019); *Wal-Mart Stores, Inc. v. Cuker Interactive, LLC*, 2017 WL 239341, *2 (W.D. Ark. 2017).

[228] *See In re Keurig Green Mountain Single-Serve Coffee Antitrust Litig.*, 341 F.R.D. 474, 498 (S.D.N.Y. 2022) (court has the discretion to award fees); *Wal-Mart Stores, Inc. v. Cuker Interactive, LLC*, 2017 WL 239341, *2 (W.D. Ark. 2017) (award of expenses unauthorized).

VI. TRIALS

RULE 38

RIGHT TO A JURY TRIAL; DEMAND

(a) **Right Preserved.** The right of trial by jury as declared by the Seventh Amendment to the Constitution—or as provided by a federal statute—is preserved to the parties inviolate.

(b) **Demand.** On any issue triable of right by a jury, a party may demand a jury trial by:

(1) serving the other parties with a written demand—which may be included in a pleading—no later than 14 days after the last pleading directed to the issue is served; and

(2) filing the demand in accordance with Rule 5(d).

(c) **Specifying Issues.** In its demand, a party may specify the issues that it wishes to have tried by a jury; otherwise, it is considered to have demanded a jury trial on all the issues so triable. If the party has demanded a jury trial on only some issues, any other party may—within 14 days after being served with the demand or within a shorter time ordered by the court—serve a demand for a jury trial on any other or all factual issues triable by jury.

(d) **Waiver; Withdrawal.** A party waives a jury trial unless its demand is properly served and filed. A proper demand may be withdrawn only if the parties consent.

(e) **Admiralty and Maritime Claims.** These rules do not create a right to a jury trial on issues in a claim that is an admiralty or maritime claim under Rule 9(h).

[Amended February 28, 1966, effective July 1, 1966; March 2, 1987, effective August 1, 1987; April 22, 1993, effective December 1, 1993; April 30, 2007, effective December 1, 2007; March 26, 2009, effective December 1, 2009.]

AUTHORS' COMMENTARY ON RULE 38

PURPOSE AND SCOPE

Rule 38 starts the "Trials" section of the Rules. Rule 38 and Rule 39 contain the provisions for obtaining a jury trial, with Rule 38 setting forth the procedures for requesting, or "demanding," a jury trial and Rule 39 controlling whether an action will be tried before a jury or a judge. Recognize at the outset, though, that these Rules do not create the right to a jury trial or define the extent of the right—the Seventh Amendment to the Constitution defines the right to a jury trial. Accordingly, Rule 38(a) states that it "preserves" the rights in the Seventh Amendment.

Although the Seventh Amendment creates the right to a jury trial in certain circumstances, those rights are waivable and require affirmative action to invoke. Rules 38(b), 38(c), and 38(d) control the procedural aspects of making a jury trial demand and the consequences of failing to do so, and for withdrawing a jury trial demand.

NOTE: The right to a jury trial is waived unless a jury trial demand is served within 14 days of the answer or last pleading.

RULE 38(a)—RIGHT PRESERVED

CORE CONCEPT

Rule 38 essentially codifies the Constitution's Seventh Amendment, which provides that the parties have a right to trial by jury for all suits "at common law" with more than $20 in controversy. In general, a suit "at common law" refers to a legal claim—typically seeking money damages—not an equitable claim such as a claim for injunctive relief.

APPLICATIONS

Jury Right Preserved, Not Created

Rule 38 does not *create* a right to a jury trial; that right arises under the Seventh Amendment to the Constitution or under federal statute.[1] Rule 38(a) recognizes that the Federal Rules of Civil Procedure are designed to "*preserve*" that constitutional right.[2]

Sources of Jury Right

The primary source of the right to a jury trial is the Seventh Amendment, which provides that the parties have a right to trial by jury for all suits at common law with more than $20 in

[1] *See Hard Candy, LLC v. Anastasia Beverly Hills, Inc.*, 921 F.3d 1343, 1354 (11th Cir. 2019).

[2] *Macsherry v. Sparrows Point, LLC*, 973 F.3d 212, 227 (4th Cir. 2020).

controversy.[3] The right to a jury trial may also be provided by statute.[4] If a statute contains procedures for invoking or demanding the right to a jury trial, the statutory provisions will control, not Rule 38.[5]

"At Common Law"—Law vs. Equity

Under the Seventh Amendment and Rule 38, the parties generally have a right to a jury in all actions that, in 1791 at the time of the enactment of the Seventh Amendment, would have been tried "at common law," such as tort or breach of contract actions for money damages, but no right to a jury in actions that historically would have been tried in the courts of equity, such as actions for injunctive relief or specific performance.[6] Although there are no longer separate courts of law and equity in the federal court system, the historical distinction remains critical for determining the right to a jury trial.

Counterclaims

The right to a jury trial extends to counterclaims (permissive or compulsory), even if the complaint only contains equitable claims.[7]

Declaratory Judgment Actions

The right to a jury trial is preserved in declaratory judgment actions. If the issues would have been triable by a jury had something other than declaratory relief been sought, a right to a jury trial exists in a declaratory judgment action.[8] For example, if the underlying situation involves an alleged breach of contract, a declaratory judgment regarding whether certain conduct would constitute a breach and result in money damages would implicate a right to a jury trial, but a declaratory judgment action regarding specific performance would not.[9]

---

[3] *Hard Candy, LLC v. Anastasia Beverly Hills, Inc.*, 921 F.3d 1343, 1354 (11th Cir. 2019); *Jones v. United Parcel Serv., Inc.*, 674 F.3d 1187, 1203 (10th Cir. 2012).

[4] *Lindenberg v. Jackson Nat'l Life Ins. Co.*, 912 F.3d 348, 377 (6th Cir. 2018); *Burch v. P.J. Cheese, Inc.*, 861 F.3d 1338, 1347 (11th Cir. 2017).

[5] *Burch v. P.J. Cheese, Inc.*, 861 F.3d 1338, 1347 (11th Cir. 2017).

[6] *See Tull v. U.S.*, 481 U.S. 412, 417 (1987); *Parklane Hosiery Co., Inc. v. Shore*, 439 U.S. 322, 333 (1979).

[7] *See Beacon Theatres, Inc. v. Westover*, 359 U.S. 500, 508 (1959); *Elm Ridge Exploration Co., LLC v. Engle*, 721 F.3d 1199, 1221–22 (10th Cir. 2013).

[8] *See Simler v. Conner*, 372 U.S. 221 (1963); *Beacon Theatres, Inc. v. Westover*, 359 U.S. 500, 509–510 (1959).

[9] *Marseilles Hydro Power, LLC v. Marseilles Land & Water Co.*, 299 F.3d 643, 649 (7th Cir. 2002).

Individual Issues

The right to a jury trial is evaluated claim-by-claim, not for the entire case.[10] If one claim triable at law is present in the case, then the parties have a right to a jury trial on that claim; whether the primary or principal claim is legal or equitable is immaterial.[11] Issues on which a jury trial is not properly demanded may be tried by the court.[12]

Newly Created/Statutory Claims

For claims that did not exist in 1791 at the time of the Seventh Amendment such as statutory claims, courts use a two-pronged analysis to evaluate the right to a jury trial. The court will try to determine the cause of action in existence in 1791 most analogous to the new claim and see whether that claim enjoyed the right to a jury trial, and will consider whether the relief sought is more akin to a legal or equitable remedy, with the latter factor having a greater impact on the outcome.[13]

Policy Favors Jury Trials

There is a strong policy in favor of jury trials, so courts will tend to allow jury trials if it is unclear whether an issue historically would have been triable at law.[14]

Governing Law

Federal law generally governs whether an issue is legal or equitable, not state law.[15] The determination of whether a party has a right to a jury trial is a legal determination made by the judge.[16]

Right Depends on Facts and Claims, Not Labels

The court bases its rulings on the issues raised by the facts and relief alleged in the pleadings, not on the labels used by the parties.[17]

Jury Issues First

When there are jury and nonjury issues or claims present, the jury should first determine the jury trial issues, then the

---

[10] *Smith v. Nexus RVs, LLC*, 572 F. Supp. 3d 550, 556 (N.D. Ind. 2021); *SFF-TIR, LLC v. Stephenson*, 262 F. Supp. 3d 1165, 1199 (N.D. Ok. 2017).

[11] *Beacon Theatres, Inc. v. Westover*, 359 U.S. 500 (1959).

[12] *Carbone v. Cable News Network, Inc.*, 910 F.3d 1345, 1353 (11th Cir. 2018).

[13] *Chauffeurs, Teamsters and Helpers, Local No. 391 v. Terry*, 494 U.S. 558, 565 (1990); *Granfinanciera v. Nordberg*, 492 U.S. 33, 42 (1989).

[14] *Beacon Theatres, Inc. v. Westover*, 359 U.S. 500, 501 (1959); *SFF-TIR, LLC v. Stephenson*, 262 F. Supp. 3d 1165, 1201 (N.D. Ok. 2017).

[15] *Lindenberg v. Jackson Nat'l Life Ins. Co.*, 912 F.3d 348, 377 (6th Cir. 2018); *Simler v. Conner*, 372 U.S. 221 (1963); *Jones v. United Parcel Serv., Inc.*, 674 F.3d 1187, 1206 (10th Cir. 2012).

[16] *Indiana Lumbermens Mut. Ins. Co. v. Timberland Pallet and Lumber Co., Inc.*, 195 F.3d 368, 374 (8th Cir. 1999).

[17] *Dairy Queen, Inc. v. Wood*, 369 U.S. 469, 478–79 (1962); *FN Herstal SA v. Clyde Armory Inc.*, 838 F.3d 1071, 1088 (11th Cir. 2016).

court should resolve any remaining issues, so that the right to a jury trial on the legal claims is not infringed through the judge's prior determination of the equitable claims.[18] Any factual findings made by the jury are then binding on the judge when trying the nonjury issues.[19]

Procedural Posture Irrelevant

The procedural device by which the parties arrive at court is irrelevant; legal issues may be tried by jury even if the claims are brought under the historically equitable joinder provisions such as class actions, derivative actions, and intervention.[20]

RULE 38(b)—DEMAND

CORE CONCEPT

Any party may make assert its right to a jury trial by making a jury trial "demand." The demand then applies to all parties for the duration of the case.

APPLICATIONS

Form of Demand

The jury trial demand should be in writing,[21] and can be part of a pleading[22] or a separate signed document.[23] Rule 38 does not require any particular language or placement, so long as the intent to demand a jury is clear.[24] Although it is better practice to make the demand a separate statement set off from the main body of the pleading, courts are reluctant to find waiver of the right to a jury trial,[25] and will honor a demand that is embedded in the main body of the pleading if it "alerts a careful reader that a jury trial was requested."[26] Thus, a request in the ad damnum paragraph for damages in "such amount as may be awarded by a jury" was sufficient,[27] but a request for

---

[18] *Beacon Theatres, Inc. v. Westover*, 359 U.S. 500 (1959); *Starr Intern. Co., Inc. v. Am. Intern. Group, Inc.*, 623 F. Supp. 2d 497 (S.D.N.Y. 2009).

[19] *Liberty Mut. Fire Ins. Co. v. Woolman*, 913 F.3d 977, 993 (10th Cir. 2019).

[20] *Ross v. Bernhard*, 396 U.S. 531 (1970).

[21] *Solis v. County of Los Angeles*, 514 F.3d 946, 954 n.11 (9th Cir. 2008); *U.S. Leather, Inc. v. Mitchell Mfg. Group, Inc.*, 276 F.3d 782, 790 (6th Cir. 2002) (oral jury demand insufficient).

[22] *Solis v. County of Los Angeles*, 514 F.3d 946, 953 (9th Cir. 2008); *Chen v. Hunan Manor Enter., Inc.*, 340 F.R.D. 85, 88 (S.D.N.Y. 2022).

[23] *Davis v. Nationwide Mut. Fire Ins. Co.*, 783 F. Supp. 2d 825, 839 (E.D. Va. 2011) (jury demand in brief that was filed and served effective).

[24] *Macsherry v. Sparrows Point, LLC*, 973 F.3d 212, 227 (4th Cir. 2020); *Lutz v. Glendale Union High School*, 403 F.3d 1061, 1063 (9th Cir. 2005) (local rule requiring a particular placement is unenforceable).

[25] *Aetna Ins. Co. v. Kennedy to Use of Bogash*, 301 U.S. 389, 393 (1937); *CoxCom, Inc. v. Chaffee*, 536 F.3d 101, 110 (1st Cir. 2008).

[26] *Lutz v. Glendale Union High Sch.*, 403 F.3d 1061, 1064–65 (9th Cir. 2005) (cleaned up).

[27] *Lutz v. Glendale Union High Sch.*, 403 F.3d 1061, 1064-65 (9th Cir. 2005).

relief as awarded by a jury or by the court was not sufficient.[28] To avoid timing problems, many lawyers include the jury trial demand in the complaint or answer. It is probably not sufficient to indicate a jury trial on the civil coversheet or legal backer.[29] Likewise, a jury trial demand in a motion is probably not effective.[30]

Timing of Service and Filing

A party wishing a jury trial for an issue must *serve* a jury trial demand within 14 days after service of the last pleading raising or responding to that issue.[31] Normally, the last pleading is the answer to the pleading raising the issue.[32] The party must also *file* the jury trial demand within a reasonable time, as provided in Rule 5(d).[33] If a jury trial demand is served after the 14th day, the court has discretion to consider the demand.[34] A party waives its right to a jury trial unless it properly serves and files a demand.[35]

No Need for Other Parties to Make Additional Demands

Once one party has made a jury trial demand, the other parties may rely on that demand and do not need to file jury trial demands of their own.[36] A party may not rely on the designation on the docket, however, only upon a proper demand by another party.[37]

Amendments

An amended or supplemental pleading does not restart the jury trial demand clock for issues raised in the original pleading,[38] but would create the right to make a demand for an

---

[28] *Macsherry v. Sparrows Point, LLC*, 973 F.3d 212, 228 (4th Cir. 2020).

[29] *Johnson v. Dalton*, 57 F. Supp. 2d 958, 959 (C.D. Cal. 1999). *But see Wright v. Lewis*, 76 F.3d 57, 59 (2d Cir. 1996) (demand on a civil cover sheet effective if the cover sheet is served).

[30] *Bogosian v. Woloohojian Realty Corp.*, 323 F.3d 55, 62 (1st Cir. 2003).

[31] *Macsherry v. Sparrows Point, LLC*, 973 F.3d 212, 227 (4th Cir. 2020); *T G Plastics Trading Co., Inc. v. Toray Plastics (Am.), Inc.*, 775 F.3d 31, 36 (1st Cir. 2014).

[32] *See U.S. v. California Mobile Home Park Mgmt. Co.*, 107 F.3d 1374, 1378 (9th Cir. 1997) ("last pleading" is the answer to the intervenor's complaint); *Wilburn v. St. Joseph Cty. Juvenile Justice Ctr.*, 353 F. Supp. 3d 736, 742 (N.D. Ind. 2018).

[33] *Solis v. County of Los Angeles*, 514 F.3d 946, 954 n.11 (9th Cir. 2008); *Harrington v. Wilber*, 384 F. Supp. 2d 1321, 1324 (S.D. Iowa 2005).

[34] *Zivkovic v. Southern California Edison Co.*, 302 F.3d 1080 (9th Cir. 2002) (court's discretion is narrow); *Members v. Paige*, 140 F.3d 699 (7th Cir.1998) (judge may require a litigant to offer a reason for not meeting the deadline).

[35] *Macsherry v. Sparrows Point, LLC*, 973 F.3d 212, 227 (4th Cir. 2020).

[36] *U.S. Sec. & Exch. Comm'n v. Jensen*, 835 F.3d 1100, 1107 (9th Cir. 2016).

[37] *KnightBrook Ins. Co. v. Payless Car Rental Sys., Inc.*, 43 F. Supp. 3d 965, 983–84 (D. Ariz. 2014).

[38] *Mega Life and Health Ins. Co. v. Pieniozek*, 585 F.3d 1399, 1404 (11th

altogether new claim.[39] The focus is the issue, not the evidence, legal theory, or remedy.[40] Therefore, if the original complaint seeks damages on the grounds that the plaintiff's firing violated his First Amendment rights and an amended complaint adds a breach of contract claim seeking the same damages, the amended complaint would not trigger a new right to demand a jury trial.[41] An amendment that simply adds a jury trial demand does not cure waiver.[42]

- *Amendments Adding New Parties:* An amendment adding a new party but asserting the same claims and issues as in the original complaint may not necessarily trigger the right for the newly added party to make a jury demand (creating the awkward situation where that party lost the right to a jury trial before being named as a party). Courts sometimes address this inequity by granting the newly added party the right to make a late jury trial demand under Rule 39(b).[43]

Removal

The removing party or the plaintiff may make a jury trial demand within 14 days of filing the removal petition.[44] Others may make demands within 14 days of service of the petition.[45] If a pleading directed to the issue on which a jury trial is sought is filed after the petition, then all parties have 14 days from service of the pleading to file a jury trial demand.[46] If, prior to removal, a party has made a jury trial demand in accordance with state procedures or has made a jury trial demand that would satisfy federal requirements,[47] or if state procedures do not require an express demand, then no jury trial demand is necessary following removal.[48]

Objections to Jury Trial Demand

A party objecting to a jury trial demand may challenge it by

Cir. 2009); *Huff v. Dobbins, Fraker, Tennant, Joy & Perlstein*, 243 F.3d 1086 (7th Cir. 2001).

[39]*Chen v. Hunan Manor Enter., Inc.*, 340 F.R.D. 85, 88 (S.D.N.Y. 2022); *Wilburn v. St. Joseph Cty. Juvenile Justice Ctr.*, 353 F. Supp. 3d 736, 742 (N.D. Ind. 2018).

[40]*California Scents v. Surco Prod., Inc.*, 406 F.3d 1102, 1106 (9th Cir. 2005); *Chen v. Hunan Manor Enter., Inc.*, 340 F.R.D. 85, 88 (S.D.N.Y. 2022).

[41]*Hostrop v. Board of Jr. College Dist. No. 515, Cook and Will Counties and State of Ill.*, 523 F.2d 569 (7th Cir. 1975).

[42]*Macsherry v. Sparrows Point, LLC*, 973 F.3d 212, 220 (4th Cir. 2020).

[43]*See Chen v. Hunan Manor Enter., Inc.*, 340 F.R.D. 85, 88 (S.D.N.Y. 2022).

[44]*Macsherry v. Sparrows Point, LLC*, 973 F.3d 212, 227 (4th Cir. 2020).

[45]*Wilhelm v. Wilhelm*, 662 F. Supp. 2d 424, 426 (D. Md. 2009).

[46]*See Rule 81(c); Lutz v. Glendale Union High School*, 403 F.3d 1061, 1063 (9th Cir. 2005).

[47]*See Macsherry v. Sparrows Point, LLC*, 973 F.3d 212, 227 (4th Cir. 2020); *Lutz v. Glendale Union High School*, 403 F.3d 1061, 1063 (9th Cir. 2005).

[48]Rule 81(c); *Wilhelm v. Wilhelm*, 662 F. Supp. 2d 424, 426 (D. Md. 2009).

filing a motion to strike.[49] The Rules do not specify a time limit for moving to strike a jury trial demand.[50]

Improper Denial of Jury Right

A party who believes that the court has incorrectly denied its right to a jury trial may either seek a writ of mandamus or take an appeal after final judgment.[51]

RULE 38(c)—SPECIFYING ISSUES

CORE CONCEPT

A party may limit a jury trial demand to specific issues.[52] Other parties then have 14 days to make a jury trial demand for remaining issues.[53] A jury trial demand that does not specify individual issues is deemed a demand for a jury trial on all issues that are properly triable to a jury.[54]

RULE 38(d)—WAIVER; WITHDRAWAL

CORE CONCEPT

Failure to serve and file a timely jury trial demand is a waiver of the right.[55]

APPLICATIONS

Presumption Against Waiver

Recognizing that the right to a jury trial is a fundamental constitutional right, courts are reluctant to find waiver.[56]

Inadvertence Not an Excuse

Inadvertence is not a defense to waiver of the right to a jury trial by failure to file a demand.[57] The court may take inadvertence into account when considering a request under Rule 39(b) to order a jury trial despite the absence of a timely demand, although some courts consider inadvertence an inadequate excuse.[58]

---

[49] *See Wilburn v. St. Joseph Cty. Juvenile Justice Ctr.*, 353 F. Supp. 3d 736, 741 (N.D. Ind. 2018).

[50] *Jones-Hailey v. Corp. of Tennessee Valley Authority*, 660 F. Supp. 551, 553 (E.D. Tenn. 1987) (motion to strike jury trial demand allowed one month before trial).

[51] *Dairy Queen, Inc. v. Wood*, 369 U.S. 469 (1962); *California Scents v. Surco Prod., Inc.*, 406 F.3d 1102, 1106 (9th Cir. 2005).

[52] *Outlaw v. City of Hartford*, 884 F.3d 351, 368 (2d Cir. 2018).

[53] *See Outlaw v. City of Hartford*, 884 F.3d 351, 368 (2d Cir. 2018).

[54] *Burch v. P.J. Cheese, Inc.*, 861 F.3d 1338, 1344 (11th Cir. 2017); *Allison v. Citgo Petroleum Corp.*, 151 F.3d 402 (5th Cir. 1998).

[55] *Macsherry v. Sparrows Point, LLC*, 973 F.3d 212, 227 (4th Cir. 2020); *Solis v. County of Los Angeles*, 514 F.3d 946, 955 (9th Cir. 2008) (local rule cannot create additional requirements resulting in waivers).

[56] *Aetna Ins. Co. v. Kennedy to Use of Bogash*, 301 U.S. 389, 393 (1937); *CoxCom, Inc. v. Chaffee*, 536 F.3d 101, 110 (1st Cir. 2008).

[57] *Montanez-Baez v. Puerto Rico Ports Auth.*, 509 F. Supp. 2d 152, 155 (D.P.R. 2007).

[58] *See Andrews v. Columbia Gas Transmission Corp.*, 544 F.3d 618, 632

Waiver by Agreement

Parties may agree—as part of a contract or by representation to the court, for example—to waive their right to a jury trial.[59]

Amendments and Prior Waiver

In the event an amended complaint raises new factual issues, a prior waiver of the right to a jury trial due to a lack of a timely demand does not apply to the newly-raised issues.[60]

Participation in Bench Trial is Waiver

A party waives the right to a jury trial if the party participates in a nonjury trial without objecting.[61]

Withdrawal of Demand

Once a proper jury trial demand has been made, it cannot be withdrawn except with the consent of all parties.[62] The withdrawal may be by written stipulation or orally on the record.[63] This protection applies even following default judgment (such that the plaintiff cannot unilaterally withdraw a jury trial demand for the determination of damages following entry of default).[64] However, if no right to a jury trial existed at the time the demand was made or if the case develops such that the right to a jury trial no longer exists, the court can designate the case as nonjury without the consent of the parties.[65]

RULE 38(e)—ADMIRALTY AND MARITIME CLAIMS

CORE CONCEPT

Rule 38 does not create a right to a jury trial for admiralty or maritime claims.[66] If there are two grounds for subject-matter jurisdiction, one in admiralty or maritime jurisdiction and one under a different form of subject-matter jurisdiction, the plaintiff may elect under Rule 9(h) to proceed in admiralty, precluding the

---

(6th Cir. 2008).

[59] *Hulsey v. West*, 966 F.2d 579, 581 (10th Cir.1992); *Reed v. Ezelle Inv. Properties Inc.*, 353 F. Supp. 3d 1025, 1037 (D. Or. 2018).

[60] *Acosta v. Austin Elec. Servs. LLC*, 348 F. Supp. 3d 944, 947 (D. Ariz. 2018); *Wilburn v. St. Joseph Cty. Juvenile Justice Ctr.*, 353 F. Supp. 3d 736, 742 (N.D. Ind. 2018).

[61] *U.S. v. Resnick*, 594 F.3d 562, 569 (7th Cir. 2010); *Bostic v. Goodnight*, 443 F.3d 1044, 1047 (8th Cir. 2006); *but see U.S. Sec. & Exch. Comm'n v. Jensen*, 835 F.3d 1100, 1107 (9th Cir. 2016) (repeated earlier objections preserved the issue).

[62] *Outlaw v. City of Hartford*, 884 F.3d 351, 368 (2d Cir. 2018); *U.S. Sec. & Exch. Comm'n v. Jensen*, 835 F.3d 1100, 1107 (9th Cir. 2016).

[63] *Smith v. Nexus RVs, LLC*, 572 F. Supp. 3d 550, 556 (N.D. Ind. 2021).

[64] *Snelling v. Tribal Vapors*, __ F. Supp. 3d __, 2021 WL 1227836, at *25 (D.N.M. 2021).

[65] *FN Herstal SA v. Clyde Armory Inc.*, 838 F.3d 1071, 1089 (11th Cir. 2016); *Kramer v. Banc of Am. Sec., LLC*, 355 F.3d 961, 968 (7th Cir. 2004).

[66] *See Fitzgerald v. U. S. Lines Co.*, 374 U.S. 16 (1963); *Buland v. NCL (Bahamas) Ltd*, 992 F.3d 1143, 1147 (11th Cir. 2021).

defendant from exercising the right to a jury trial.[67] However, jury trials in an admiralty claim are not forbidden.[68]

Additional Research References

Wright & Miller, *Federal Practice and Procedure* §§ 2301 to 2322

C.J.S., Admiralty §§ 216 to 218; Federal Civil Procedure §§ 943 to 950; Juries §§ 9, 11, 84 to 113 et seq.

West's Key Number Digest, Admiralty ⚷80; Jury ⚷9 to 37

---

[67] *Great Lakes Ins. SE v. Crabtree*, __ F. Supp. 3d __, 2022 WL 110686, at *2 (S.D. Fla. 2022).

[68] *See Buland v. NCL (Bahamas) Ltd*, 992 F.3d 1143, 1147 (11th Cir. 2021); *Luera v. M/V Alberta*, 635 F.3d 181, 194 (5th Cir. 2011).

RULE 39
TRIAL BY JURY OR BY THE COURT

(a) **When a Demand Is Made.** When a jury trial has been demanded under Rule 38, the action must be designated on the docket as a jury action. The trial on all issues so demanded must be by jury unless:

(1) the parties or their attorneys file a stipulation to a nonjury trial or so stipulate on the record; or

(2) the court, on motion or on its own, finds that on some or all of those issues there is no federal right to a jury trial.

(b) **When No Demand Is Made.** Issues on which a jury trial is not properly demanded are to be tried by the court. But the court may, on motion, order a jury trial on any issue for which a jury might have been demanded.

(c) **Advisory Jury; Jury Trial by Consent.** In an action not triable of right by a jury, the court, on motion or on its own:

(1) may try any issue with an advisory jury; or

(2) may, with the parties' consent, try any issue by a jury whose verdict has the same effect as if a jury trial had been a matter of right, unless the action is against the United States and a federal statute provides for a nonjury trial.

[Amended April 30, 2007, effective December 1, 2007.]

AUTHORS' COMMENTARY ON RULE 39

PURPOSE AND SCOPE

Rule 39 contains the provisions controlling which actions are tried before a jury and which actions are tried before a judge. Its provisions are triggered by a jury trial demand under Rule 38, following which the court will designate the case as a jury action on the docket. The court must then conduct a jury trial unless the parties stipulate to a nonjury trial or the court determines that the parties did not have a right to a jury trial under the

Seventh Amendment or a federal statute. Even if no party makes a proper jury trial demand under Rule 38, however, Rule 39 authorizes the parties to file a motion seeking a jury trial on any issue for which they could have demanded a jury trial.

For actions where no right to a jury trial exists, Rule 39 provides two options for empaneling a jury. First, the court may empanel an advisory jury, whose verdict is not binding on the court—the judge takes the advisory jury verdict into consideration, but has the authority to issue a judgment that differs from the jury's verdict. Second, if the parties consent, the court may conduct a binding jury trial even for issues where no right to a jury trial exists.

RULE 39(a)—WHEN A DEMAND IS MADE

CORE CONCEPT

Once a jury trial has been demanded for a claim, the docket will be so designated and the claim must be tried to a jury unless the parties stipulate otherwise or the court determines that no right to a jury trial exists.[1]

APPLICATIONS

Stipulations

The parties may stipulate to a nonjury trial, even if a timely jury trial demand has been filed.[2] The stipulation to trial by the court may be for the entire case or may be limited to specific issues.[3] The stipulation may also be to submit the case to the court to decide based on briefs and stipulated facts and evidence.[4] The stipulation should be clear and unambiguous,[5] and must be made either:

- in writing and filed with the court;[6] or
- orally in open court and entered in the record.[7]

Striking Improper Jury Demand

When a party has filed a jury trial demand for a claim where no jury right exists, such as an equity claim, the court should

---

[1]*Macsherry v. Sparrows Point, LLC*, 973 F.3d 212, 227 (4th Cir. 2020); *Solis v. County of Los Angeles*, 514 F.3d 946, 954 (9th Cir. 2008).

[2]*Outlaw v. City of Hartford*, 884 F.3d 351, 368 (2d Cir. 2018); *U.S. Sec. & Exch. Comm'n v. Jensen*, 835 F.3d 1100, 1107 (9th Cir. 2016).

[3]*Outlaw v. City of Hartford*, 884 F.3d 351, 368 (2d Cir. 2018); *Gaworski v. ITT Commercial Finance Corp.*, 17 F.3d 1104 (8th Cir. 1994).

[4]*Fernandez v. St. Louis Cty., Missouri*, 538 F. Supp. 3d 888, 893 (E.D. Mo. 2021).

[5]*Hupp v. Siroflex of Am., Inc.*, 159 F.R.D. 29 (S.D. Tex. 1994) (failure to object is not a stipulation).

[6]*Solis v. County of Los Angeles*, 514 F.3d 946, 955 (9th Cir. 2008); *Garcia-Ayala v. Lederle Parenterals, Inc.*, 212 F.3d 638, 645 (1st Cir. 2000).

[7]*Solis v. County of Los Angeles*, 514 F.3d 946, 955 (9th Cir. 2008); *Fuller v. City of Oakland, Cal.*, 47 F.3d 1522 (9th Cir. 1995).

order a nonjury trial, either *sua sponte*[8] or upon motion to strike.[9] A party may file a motion to strike an improper jury trial demand at any time prior to trial.[10]

Jury Verdict Following Demand Binding

If a trial occurs before a jury following a jury trial demand, the verdict is binding and the court may not treat it as advisory.[11]

Contractual Waiver

The enforceability of contractual agreements to waive the right to a jury trial is determined by State law.[12]

Waiver by Participation in Bench Trial

Participating in a bench trial without objection may constitute a waiver of the right to a jury trial, even if a timely demand was filed.[13]

Improper Denial of Jury Demand—Mandamus

If the district court improperly denies a party the right to a jury trial, the party may attempt to challenge that ruling immediately by petitioning for a writ of mandamus in the Court of Appeals.[14]

RULE 39(b)—WHEN NO DEMAND IS MADE

CORE CONCEPT

When no party has filed a timely jury trial demand, the court will hear the trial unless, upon motion, the court orders a jury trial of claims for which a jury trial could properly have been made.

APPLICATIONS

No Jury Without Demand or Motion

The court may not empanel a jury without a demand or mo-

---

[8] *Tegal Corp. v. Tokyo Electron Am., Inc.*, 257 F.3d 1331, 1341 (Fed. Cir. 2001); *Society of Professional Engineering Employees in Aerospace v. Boeing Co.*, 921 F. Supp. 2d 1122 (D. Kan. 2013).

[9] *FN Herstal SA v. Clyde Armory Inc.*, 838 F.3d 1071, 1090 (11th Cir. 2016); *In re County of Orange*, 784 F.3d 520, 525 (9th Cir. 2015).

[10] *FN Herstal SA v. Clyde Armory Inc.*, 838 F.3d 1071, 1090 (11th Cir. 2016).

[11] *See Smith Flooring, Inc. v. Pennsylvania Lumbermens Mut. Ins. Co.*, 713 F.3d 933, 939 (8th Cir. 2013).

[12] *In re County of Orange*, 784 F.3d 520, 527–32 (9th Cir. 2015); *IFC Credit Corp. v. United Business & Indus. Fed. Credit Union*, 512 F.3d 989, 991 (7th Cir. 2008). *See also In re Borowiak IGA Foodliner, Inc.*, 879 F.3d 848, 849 (8th Cir. 2018) (by filing a jury trial demand, the defendant lost its ability to enforce a contractual waiver).

[13] *Solis v. County of Los Angeles*, 514 F.3d 946, 955–56 (9th Cir. 2008); *U.S. v. Rangel de Aguilar*, 308 F.3d 1134, 1138 (10th Cir. 2002); *but see U.S. Sec. & Exch. Comm'n v. Jensen*, 835 F.3d 1100, 1107 (9th Cir. 2016) (repeated earlier objections preserved the issue).

[14] *In re Borowiak IGA Foodliner, Inc.*, 879 F.3d 848, 849 (8th Cir. 2018); *In re County of Orange*, 784 F.3d 520, 525–26 (9th Cir. 2015).

tion,[15] except in an advisory capacity.[16]

Motion for Jury Trial

Upon motion by one of the parties, the court has discretion to order a jury trial of claims for which a jury trial could properly have been made.[17] Courts are split on the standard for granting such motions, with some courts creating a presumption in favor of granting Rule 39(b) motions,[18] some courts creating a balancing test,[19] and some courts holding that the discretion to grant a Rule 39(b) motion is narrow and cannot rest on mere inadvertence.[20]

RULE 39(c)—ADVISORY JURY; JURY TRIAL BY CONSENT

CORE CONCEPT

The judge may impanel an advisory jury if the case will not be tried to a binding jury, and may conduct a binding jury trial of any claim—legal or equitable—if all parties consent.

APPLICATIONS

Procedure for Advisory Jury

The court may empanel an advisory jury on motion or *sua sponte*.[21] The court has broad discretion as to whether to impanel an advisory jury even if the parties do not consent.[22]

Advisory Verdict Non-binding

The judge is the ultimate trier of fact with an advisory jury and has complete discretion to adopt or reject the verdict of the advisory jury.[23]

Court Must Make Findings of Fact and Conclusions of Law

The court must make its own findings of fact and conclusions of law in cases tried with an advisory jury.[24]

---

[15] *Sartin v. Cliff's Drilling Co.*, 2004 WL 551209 (E.D. La. 2004).

[16] *Swofford v. B & W, Inc.*, 336 F.2d 406, 409 (5th Cir. 1964).

[17] *Carbone v. Cable News Network, Inc.*, 910 F.3d 1345, 1353 (11th Cir. 2018); *T G Plastics Trading Co., Inc. v. Toray Plastics (Am.), Inc.*, 775 F.3d 31, 36 (1st Cir. 2014).

[18] *See, e.g., Green Const. Co. v. Kansas Power & Light Co.*, 1 F.3d 1005 (10th Cir. 1993).

[19] *See, e.g., Macsherry v. Sparrows Point, LLC*, 973 F.3d 212, 220 (4th Cir. 2020).

[20] *See, e.g., Pacific Fisheries Corp. v. HIH Cas. & General Ins., Ltd.*, 239 F.3d 1000, 1002 (9th Cir. 2001); *Higgins v. Boeing Co.*, 526 F.2d 1004, 1006 n.2 (2d Cir. 1975).

[21] *Navarro v. Procter & Gamble Co.*, 529 F. Supp. 3d 742, 756 (S.D. Ohio 2021).

[22] *Mala v. Crown Bay Marina, Inc.*, 704 F.3d 239, 249 (3d Cir. 2013); *Schaffart v. ONEOK, Inc.*, 686 F.3d 461, 475 (8th Cir. 2012).

[23] *Reyes v. Garland*, 26 F.4th 516, 521 (1st Cir. 2022); *Schaffart v. ONEOK, Inc.*, 686 F.3d 461, 475 (8th Cir. 2012).

[24] *Reyes v. Garland*, 26 F.4th 516, 521 (1st Cir. 2022); *Kinetic Concepts,*

Binding Jury with Consent

If no claims at law are present, the judge still may impanel a normal, binding jury with the consent (either express, implied,[25] or by failure to object) of *all* parties.[26] The jury verdict in a case tried to a jury by consent has the same binding effects as a jury verdict following a jury trial demand.[27] Consent of the parties does not *require* the judge to empanel a jury, it merely gives the court the discretion to do so.[28] An exception to this rule is that certain statutes prohibit jury trials in specified actions against the United States.[29]

Mixed Jury and Nonjury Issues

In a case in which a jury trial has been demanded as to some of the claims, or if the right to a jury trial exists as to only some of the claims, the court may consider the nonjury claims as being submitted to the jury on an advisory basis.[30]

Advisory Jury with Legal Claims

Rule 39(c) states that a judge may empanel an advisory jury "[i]n an action not triable of right by a jury" and some courts limit the use of advisory juries to actions where the right to a jury trial does not exist.[31] Other courts construe this language broadly to include any action for which the right has not been exercised.[32]

Proceedings on Remand

If a case is reversed and remanded on appeal following a trial before an advisory jury on the grounds that the parties had a right to a binding jury, the district court cannot simply treat the advisory jury as if it had been a binding jury, and instead must conduct a new trial.[33] If a case is reversed and remanded on appeal following a trial before a binding jury upon the consent of the parties, the trial court is free on remand

---

Inc. v. Smith & Nephew, Inc., 688 F.3d 1342, 1357 (Fed. Cir. 2012).

[25] *Hayes v. SkyWest Airlines, Inc.*, 401 F. Supp. 3d 1194, 1206, n.20 (D. Colo. 2019) (submission of jury instructions is implied consent).

[26] *See Full Spectrum Software, Inc. v. Forte Automation Sys., Inc.*, 858 F.3d 666, 674 (1st Cir. 2017); *FN Herstal SA v. Clyde Armory Inc.*, 838 F.3d 1071, 1089 (11th Cir. 2016).

[27] *Harbor Breeze Corp. v. Newport Landing Sportfishing, Inc.*, 28 F.4th 35, 41 (9th Cir. 2022).

[28] *Ed Peters Jewelry Co., Inc. v. C & J Jewelry Co., Inc.*, 215 F.3d 182 (1st Cir.2000).

[29] *See Palischak v. Allied Signal Aerospace Co.*, 893 F. Supp. 341, 342 (D.N.J. 1995).

[30] *See 4 Pillar Dynasty LLC v. New York & Co., Inc.*, 933 F.3d 202, 207 (2d Cir. 2019); *Texas Advanced Optoelectronic Sols., Inc. v. Renesas Elecs. Am., Inc.*, 895 F.3d 1304, 1319 (Fed. Cir. 2018).

[31] *See Jammal v. Am. Family Ins. Co.*, 914 F.3d 449, 452 (6th Cir. 2019); *Ernster v. Luxco, Inc.*, 596 F.3d 1000, 1006 n.5 (8th Cir. 2010) (only actions not triable as of right to a jury may be tried with an advisory jury).

[32] *See Affordable Communities of Missouri v. EF & A Capital Corp.*, 295 F.R.D. 389, 391 (E.D. Mo. 2013).

[33] *Williams v. Centerra Grp., LLC*, 579 F. Supp. 3d 778, 785 (D.S.C. 2022).

to reconsider whether to try the case to a jury.[34]

Additional Research References

Wright & Miller, *Federal Practice and Procedure* §§ 2323 to 2350
C.J.S., Federal Civil Procedure §§ 933, 946, 1028 to 1030; Juries §§ 11, 91 to 98
West's Key Number Digest, Federal Civil Procedure ⚷1991, 2251, 2252; Jury ⚷25(1), 28(6)

---

[34]*Harbor Breeze Corp. v. Newport Landing Sportfishing, Inc.*, 28 F.4th 35, 41 (9th Cir. 2022).

RULE 40
SCHEDULING CASES FOR TRIAL

Each court must provide by rule for scheduling trials. The court must give priority to actions entitled to priority by a federal statute.

[Amended April 30, 2007, effective December 1, 2007.]

AUTHORS' COMMENTARY ON RULE 40

PURPOSE AND SCOPE

Rule 40 delegates the trial scheduling function to individual district courts, who are directed to formulate their own rules for placing cases on the trial calendar.

APPLICATIONS

Individual Judges' Broad Discretion

Individual judges have broad discretion regarding cases on their dockets.[1] They may give precedence to cases of public importance or cases in which delay will cause hardship.[2]

Precedence by Statute

Rule 40 recognizes that some statutes provide for precedence for actions brought under the statute's provisions.[3]

Motion for Continuance

The trial judge has great discretion in ruling on motions to continue a trial date.[4]

Additional Research References

Wright & Miller, *Federal Practice and Procedure* §§ 2351 to 2352
C.J.S., Federal Civil Procedure § 934

---

[1] *Prime Rate Premium Fin. Corp., Inc. v. Larson*, 930 F.3d 759, 766 (6th Cir. 2019).

[2] *See Clinton v. Jones*, 520 U.S. 681, 707–708 (1997) (the court abused its discretion in deferring trial until after president left office).

[3] *See Prime Rate Premium Fin. Corp., Inc. v. Larson*, 930 F.3d 759, 766 (6th Cir. 2019).

[4] *Clinton v. Jones*, 520 U.S. 681, 706–707 (1997).

West's Key Number Digest, Federal Civil Procedure ⚿1993 to 1994

RULE 41
DISMISSAL OF ACTIONS

(a) **Voluntary Dismissal.**

(1) *By the Plaintiff.*

(A) *Without a Court Order.* Subject to Rules 23(e), 23.1(c), 23.2, and 66 and any applicable federal statute, the plaintiff may dismiss an action without a court order by filing:

(i) a notice of dismissal before the opposing party serves either an answer or a motion for summary judgment; or

(ii) a stipulation of dismissal signed by all parties who have appeared.

(B) *Effect.* Unless the notice or stipulation states otherwise, the dismissal is without prejudice. But if the plaintiff previously dismissed any federal-or state-court action based on or including the same claim, a notice of dismissal operates as an adjudication on the merits.

(2) *By Court Order; Effect.* Except as provided in Rule 41(a)(1), an action may be dismissed at the plaintiff's request only by court order, on terms that the court considers proper. If a defendant has pleaded a counterclaim before being served with the plaintiff's motion to dismiss, the action may be dismissed over the defendant's objection only if the counterclaim can remain pending for independent adjudication. Unless the order states otherwise, a dismissal under this paragraph (2) is without prejudice.

(b) **Involuntary Dismissal; Effect.** If the plaintiff fails to prosecute or to comply with these rules or a court order, a defendant may move to dismiss the action or any claim against it. Unless the dismissal order states otherwise, a dismissal under this subdivision (b) and any dismissal not under this rule—except one for lack of jurisdiction, improper venue, or failure to join a party under Rule 19—operates as an adjudication on the merits.

(c) **Dismissing a Counterclaim, Crossclaim, or Third-Party Claim.** This rule applies to a dismissal of any counterclaim, crossclaim, or third-party claim. A claimant's voluntary dismissal under Rule 41(a)(1)(A)(i) must be made:
 (1) before a responsive pleading is served; or
 (2) if there is no responsive pleading, before evidence is introduced at a hearing or trial.

(d) **Costs of a Previously Dismissed Action.** If a plaintiff who previously dismissed an action in any court files an action based on or including the same claim against the same defendant, the court:
 (1) may order the plaintiff to pay all or part of the costs of that previous action; and
 (2) may stay the proceedings until the plaintiff has complied.

[Amended effective March 19, 1948; July 1, 1963; July 1, 1966; July 1, 1968; August 1, 1987; December 1, 1991; April 30, 2007, effective December 1, 2007.]

AUTHORS' COMMENTARY ON RULE 41

PURPOSE AND SCOPE

Rule 41 establishes three procedural mechanisms for obtaining a dismissal: by notice; by stipulation; or by motion. One of the most common situations for using Rule 41 is to dismiss a case that the parties have settled. Rule 41 also authorizes a plaintiff to dismiss a case unilaterally, without consent from the defendant or court permission, so long as the plaintiff dismisses the case early in the proceeding, before the defendant has answered or filed a motion for summary judgment (but note that a Rule 12 motion to dismiss does not terminate the right to voluntary dismissal—if the defendant identifies a flaw in the complaint in an early motion to dismiss, the plaintiff may elect to walk away by dismissing the complaint). If the defendant has already filed an answer or a motion for summary judgment and the defendant will not stipulate to dismissal, a plaintiff may still seek dismissal of the action, but needs court permission.

All of the above types of dismissal are "voluntary dismissals"—dismissals where the plaintiff is voluntarily dismissing the case. Rule 41 also authorizes a defendant to file a motion for "involuntary dismissal." Rule 41 lists three types of conduct by the plaintiff that will potentially support a defendant's motion for involuntary dismissal: failure to prosecute the case (letting it languish); failure to comply with the Federal Rules of Civil Procedure (typically repeated, systematic failure); or failure to comply with the court's orders.

A voluntary dismissal is presumed to be without prejudice—allowing the plaintiff to file another action with the same claims—unless it specifies otherwise. Conversely, an involuntary dismissal is presumed to be with prejudice unless it specifies otherwise. The "Two Dismissal Rule" provides an exception to these general presumptions. If a plaintiff has already dismissed a claim once, the second dismissal of the same claim is deemed to be "on the merits," resulting in a dismissal with prejudice (to prevent a plaintiff from filing and dismissing repeatedly to harass the defendant).

RULE 41(a)(1)—VOLUNTARY DISMISSAL; BY THE PLAINTIFF

CORE CONCEPT

The plaintiff may dismiss an action without consent of the court either by stipulation of all parties or unilaterally if the defendant has not yet filed an answer or motion for summary judgment.

APPLICATIONS

Notice of Dismissal

Dismissal under Rule 41(a)(1) is achieved by filing a "notice of dismissal"; no motion or court order is required.[1] The notice is effective when filed,[2] but must be served on all parties pursuant to Rule 5(a).

Timing of Notice

Unless stipulated to by all parties, a plaintiff may only file a notice of dismissal if the defendant has not yet served an answer or motion for summary judgment.[3] Otherwise, a plaintiff must file a motion under Rule 41(a)(2).[4] Filing an amended complaint does not revive the plaintiff's right to file a notice of dismissal.[5] If some of the defendants have answered and others have not, some courts allow a notice of dismissal as

---

[1] *Frank v. Gaos*, 139 S. Ct. 1041, 1046 (2019).

[2] *Noga v. Fulton Fin. Corp. Emp. Benefit Plan*, 19 F.4th 264, 270 n.2 (3d Cir. 2021); *Anago Franchising, Inc. v. Shaz, LLC*, 677 F.3d 1272, 1277 (11th Cir. 2012).

[3] *Welsh v. Correct Care, L.L.C.*, 915 F.3d 341, 343 (5th Cir. 2019); *PTA-FLA, Inc. v. ZTE USA, Inc.*, 844 F.3d 1299, 1307 (11th Cir. 2016).

[4] *GF Gaming Corp. v. City of Black Hawk, Colo.*, 405 F.3d 876, 887–88 (10th Cir. 2005); *Otey v. City of Fairview Heights*, 125 F. Supp. 3d 874, 881 (S.D. Ill. 2015).

[5] *Welsh v. Correct Care, L.L.C.*, 915 F.3d 341, 344 (5th Cir. 2019).

to the defendants who have not yet answered.[6]

Notice Must be Unconditional

A dismissal must be unconditional[7] and unequivocal[8] in both dismissals by notice and by stipulation, although the parties may privately impose conditions (such as the payment of a sum of money) on their agreement to a stipulation for dismissal.

Absolute Right

The right to voluntarily dismiss an action by notice is generally considered absolute, not requiring assent by the court or opposing parties.[9] Likewise, the court cannot impose conditions in connection with a notice of voluntary dismissal[10] (in contrast to the court's ability to do so in connection with a motion for voluntary dismissal under Rule 41(a)(2)).

Stipulation by All Parties

A stipulation for dismissal of the entire action must be signed by all parties who have appeared in the action.[11] If the dismissal is only as to select parties, only those parties must sign the stipulation.[12] At least one court has held that the requirement for signature by all parties includes defendants who have already settled and been dismissed by nonfinal orders.[13]

Effect of Voluntary Dismissal

A voluntary dismissal leaves the situation as if the lawsuit had never been filed, unless the dismissal is specified as with prejudice.[14] In general, a dismissal under Rule 41(a) deprives the court of any further jurisdiction.[15] If parties want the court to retain jurisdiction (such as to enforce a settlement agreement), they need to ask the court to enter an order to that ef-

---

[6] *See, e.g., Welsh v. Correct Care, L.L.C.*, 915 F.3d 341, 344 (5th Cir. 2019).

[7] *Scam Instrument Corp. v. Control Data Corp.*, 458 F.2d 885 (7th Cir.1972); *Hyde Const. Co. v. Koehring Co.*, 388 F.2d 501, 507 (10th Cir. 1968).

[8] *Carter v. Beverly Hills Sav. and Loan Ass'n*, 884 F.2d 1186 (9th Cir. 1989).

[9] *United States v. UCB, Inc.*, 970 F.3d 835, 849 (7th Cir. 2020); *Wellfount, Corp. v. Hennis Care Ctr. of Bolivar, Inc.*, 951 F.3d 769, 772 (6th Cir. 2020).

[10] *Borzilleri v. Bayer Healthcare Pharms., Inc.*, 24 F.4th 32, 41 (1st Cir. 2022); *Xlear, Inc. v. Focus Nutrition, LLC*, 893 F.3d 1227, 1238 (10th Cir. 2018).

[11] *See Est. of W. v. Smith*, 9 F.4th 1361, 1367 (11th Cir. 2021) (stipulation need not include fictitious defendants); *Garber v. Chicago Mercantile Exch.*, 570 F.3d 1361, 1365 (Fed. Cir. 2009); *but see Role v. Eureka Lodge No. 434, I.A. of M & A.W. AFL-CIO*, 402 F.3d 314, 318 (2d Cir. 2005) (oral stipulation in court and on the record is enforceable).

[12] *Nat'l City Golf Fin. v. Scott*, 899 F.3d 412, 415 n.3 (5th Cir. 2018).

[13] *Everett v. BRP-Powertrain, GmbH & Co. KG*, 282 F. Supp. 3d 1063, 1066 (E.D. Wis. 2017).

[14] *United States v. L-3 Commc'ns EOTech, Inc.*, 921 F.3d 11, 19 (2d Cir. 2019); *Nelson v. Napolitano*, 657 F.3d 586, 587 (7th Cir. 2011).

[15] *Est. of W. v. Smith*, 9 F.4th 1361, 1368 (11th Cir. 2021); *Absolute Activist Value Master Fund Ltd. v. Devine*, 998 F.3d 1258, 1265 (11th Cir. 2021).

fect before the dismissal is filed.[16] A Rule 41(a)(1) dismissal *without prejudice* is not a judgment for purposes of a post-judgment motion under Rule 59,[17] but it is a "proceeding" for purposes of a motion under Rule 60.[18] A voluntary dismissal *with prejudice* can create a final judgment.[19]

Preclusion; Two Dismissal Rule

Dismissals by notice or stipulation are presumed without prejudice unless they specify otherwise.[20] The courts are split as to whether any of the interim rulings entered before the dismissal may be accorded preclusive effect in a subsequent action.[21] A voluntary dismissal that is specified as with prejudice is given the same res judicata/claim preclusion effect as any other judgment.[22]

- *Two Dismissal Rule*: Voluntary dismissals under Rule 41(a)(1)[23] are governed by the Two Dismissal Rule: although the first voluntary dismissal of a given claim is presumed to be without prejudice, the second dismissal acts as a final adjudication on the merits and will preclude a third action asserting a claim that was or could have been asserted in the earlier actions.[24] A party wishing to dismiss a case for the second time but avoid the harsh consequences of the Two Dismissal Rule may enter into a stipulation that expressly provides that the second dismissal is without prejudice[25] or file a motion for voluntary dismissal under Rule 41(a)(2) asking the court to dismiss the action without prejudice.[26]
- *Two Dismissal Rule for Actions in State Court*: The Two Dismissal Rule applies to actions filed in state court on

---

[16] *See Def. Distributed v. United States Dep't of State*, 947 F.3d 870, 872 n.1 (5th Cir. 2020); *Nat'l City Golf Fin. v. Scott*, 899 F.3d 412, 415–16 (5th Cir. 2018).

[17] *Def. Distributed v. United States Dep't of State*, 947 F.3d 870, 873 (5th Cir. 2020); *Galaza v. Wolf*, 954 F.3d 1267, 1270 (9th Cir. 2020).

[18] *Nat'l City Golf Fin. v. Scott*, 899 F.3d 412, 417 (5th Cir. 2018).

[19] *Galaza v. Wolf*, 954 F.3d 1267, 1270 (9th Cir. 2020).

[20] *Noga v. Fulton Fin. Corp. Emp. Benefit Plan*, 19 F.4th 264, 270 (3d Cir. 2021); *Papera v. Pennsylvania Quarried Bluestone Co.*, 948 F.3d 607, 611 (3d Cir. 2020) (intent to dismiss with prejudice must be clear).

[21] See *Harvey Specialty & Supply v. Anson Flowline Equip.*, 434 F.3d 320, 324 (5th Cir. 2005) (no preclusive effect); *Robinette v. Jones*, 476 F.3d 585, 589–590 (8th Cir. 2007) (potential preclusive effect).

[22] *Norfolk Southern Corp. v. Chevron, U.S.A., Inc.*, 371 F.3d 1285 (11th Cir.2004).

[23] *Wellfount, Corp. v. Hennis Care Ctr. of Bolivar, Inc.*, 951 F.3d 769, 772 (6th Cir. 2020) (the Two Dismissal Rule only applies to dismissals under Rule 41(a)(1)).

[24] *Noga v. Fulton Fin. Corp. Emp. Benefit Plan*, 19 F.4th 264, 270 (3d Cir. 2021); *Jian Yang Lin v. Shanghai City Corp*, 950 F.3d 46, 50 (2d Cir. 2020).

[25] *Jian Ying Lin v. Shanghai City Corp*, 329 F.R.D. 36, 41 (S.D.N.Y. 2018).

[26] *VS PR, LLC v. ORC Miramar Corp.*, 34 F.4th 67, 70–71 (1st Cir. 2022); *Wellfount, Corp. v. Hennis Care Ctr. of Bolivar, Inc.*, 951 F.3d 769, 772 (6th Cir. 2020).

the first occasion and in federal court on the second occasion.[27] However, if the second action is filed and dismissed in state court, it will not trigger the Two Dismissal Rule[28] unless the state has a similar rule.[29] Once an action is barred in federal court by the Two Dismissal Rule, it will also be barred in state court.

Statute of Limitations

An action dismissed without prejudice does not toll the statute of limitations.[30]

Rules and Statutes Requiring Court Approval of Dismissals

Rule 41(a)(1) is expressly subject to the provisions of Rule 23(e) (requiring court approval for the dismissal of a class action)[31] and Rule 66 (governing cases in which a receiver has been appointed). Voluntary dismissal under Rule 41(a)(1), without court approval, may not be available as to claims under statutes that require court approval of settlements, such as *qui tam* actions,[32] actions under the Fair Labor Standards Act,[33] and shareholders' derivative actions.[34] Rule 41 does apply to appeals of certain proceedings to a federal court, such as an appeal of a decision by the Board of Veterans' Appeals.[35]

Removal

Rule 41 applies with equal force to cases removed from state court.[36]

Dismissal Following Rule 12(b) Motions to Dismiss

In general, a motion to dismiss pursuant to Rule 12(b) for failure to state a claim or for lack of jurisdiction, proper service of process, or venue does not terminate the plaintiff's unilateral right to dismiss.[37] An exception may arise if the court has held

---

[27] *See Dvorak v. Granite Creek GP Flexcap I, LLC*, 908 F.3d 248, 249 (7th Cir. 2018).

[28] *Rader v. Baltimore & O. R. Co.*, 108 F.2d 980 (7th Cir. 1940).

[29] *See Dvorak v. Granite Creek GP Flexcap I, LLC*, 908 F.3d 248, 249 (7th Cir. 2018); *Manning v. South Carolina Dept. of Highway and Public Transp.*, 914 F.2d 44 (4th Cir. 1990).

[30] *Beck v. Caterpillar Inc.*, 50 F.3d 405 (7th Cir. 1995).

[31] *Frank v. Gaos*, 139 S. Ct. 1041, 1046 (2019).

[32] *See United States v. L-3 Commc'ns EOTech, Inc.*, 921 F.3d 11, 18 (2d Cir. 2019); *Bailey v. Shell Western E&P, Inc.*, 609 F.3d 710, 719 (5th Cir. 2010).

[33] *Samake v. Thunder Lube, Inc.*, 24 F.4th 804, 809–10 (2d Cir. 2022); *Mei Xing Yu v. Hasaki Rest., Inc.*, 944 F.3d 395, 411–12 (2d Cir. 2019).

[34] *Baker v. America's Mortg. Servicing, Inc.*, 58 F.3d 321 (7th Cir. 1995).

[35] *Graves v. Principi*, 294 F.3d 1350 (Fed. Cir. 2002).

[36] *In re Amerijet Intern., Inc.*, 785 F.3d 967, 974 (5th Cir. 2015) (answer filed in state court prevents Rule 41(a)(1) notice).

[37] *Manze v. State Farm Ins. Co.*, 817 F.2d 1062, 1066 (3d Cir. 1987); *Mitchell v. U.S. Bank Nat'l Ass'n for Wells Fargo Asset Sec. Corp. Mortg.*

extensive hearings on the motion[38] or converted the motion to dismiss into a motion for summary judgment.[39]

Dismissal of Part of Action

Courts differ as to the proper procedural mechanism for voluntarily dismissing part of an action. Some courts allow voluntary dismissal of part of an action by notice pursuant to Rule 41.[40] Other courts only allow voluntary dismissal of an entire action,[41] and require dismissal of part of an action to be accomplished by a motion to amend pursuant to Rule 15(a).[42] Some courts allow dismissal of individual *defendants* under Rule 41 but require an amendment to dismiss some, but not all, *claims*.[43] Some courts will deem an improper Rule 41 notice to be a voluntary amendment under Rule 15.[44] A third-party plaintiff may voluntarily dismiss the third-party complaint under Rule 41(a)(1).[45]

Ancillary Jurisdiction: Costs and Fees; Sanctions

Following a voluntary dismissal under Rule 41, the district court retains "ancillary jurisdiction" over the matter to award costs.[46] The defendant is not considered the prevailing party following a voluntary dismissal pursuant to Rule 41(a)(1) for purposes of statutes governing the award of attorney's fees to the prevailing party.[47] Additionally, a court may still impose sanctions for a Rule 11 violation following voluntary dismissal.[48]

Final Appealable Order/Judgment

The courts differ as to whether the first voluntary dismissal

---

Pass-Through Certificates Series 2006-AR4, 293 F. Supp. 3d 209, 213 (D.D.C. 2018).

[38] *Harvey Aluminum, Inc. v. Am. Cyanamid Co.*, 203 F.2d 105 (2d Cir. 1953).

[39] *In re Bath and Kitchen Fixtures Antitrust Litig.*, 535 F.3d 161, 166 (3d Cir. 2008); *Swedberg v. Marotzke*, 339 F.3d 1139 (9th Cir.2003).

[40] *See Bowers v. National Collegiate Athletic Ass'n*, 346 F.3d 402, 413 (3d Cir. 2003); *Commercial Space Mgmt. Co., Inc. v. Boeing Co., Inc.*, 193 F.3d 1074, 1079 (9th Cir. 1999).

[41] *Absolute Activist Value Master Fund Ltd. v. Devine*, 998 F.3d 1258, 1265 (11th Cir. 2021).

[42] *See Perry v. Schumacher Grp. of Louisiana*, 891 F.3d 954, 958 (11th Cir. 2018); *PTA-FLA, Inc. v. ZTE USA, Inc.*, 844 F.3d 1299, 1307 (11th Cir. 2016).

[43] *Dr. Robert L. Meinders, D.C., Ltd. v. United Healthcare Servs., Inc.*, 7 F.4th 555, 559 n.4 (7th Cir. 2021) (but advocating for use of Rule 15); *Williams v. Seidenbach*, 958 F.3d 341, 345 (5th Cir. 2020).

[44] *See Dean v. Kaiser Found. Health Plan, Inc.*, 562 F. Supp. 3d 928, 931 (C.D. Cal. 2022).

[45] *Century Mfg. Co., Inc. v. Central Transport Intern., Inc.*, 209 F.R.D. 647 (D. Mass. 2002).

[46] *Automation Support, Inc. v. Humble Design, L.L.C.*, 982 F.3d 392, 394 (5th Cir. 2020); *Sequa Corp. v. Cooper*, 245 F.3d 1036, 1037 (8th Cir. 2001).

[47] *O.F. Mossberg & Sons, Inc. v. Timney Triggers, LLC*, 955 F.3d 990, 993 (Fed. Cir. 2020); *Xlear, Inc. v. Focus Nutrition, LLC*, 893 F.3d 1227, 1238 (10th Cir. 2018).

[48] *Cooter & Gell v. Hartmarx Corp.*, 496 U.S. 384, 395 (1990); *Absolute Activist Value Master Fund Ltd. v. Devine*, 998 F.3d 1258, 1265 (11th Cir. 2021).

under Rule 41(a)(1) is considered a final appealable order.[49] If the court had already adjudicated some claims, a voluntary dismissal of the remaining claims may convert the earlier interlocutory order into a final order.[50] The second dismissal is a final, appealable order.[51] A voluntary dismissal under Rule 41(a)(1) is not a judgment[52]

RULE 41(a)(2)—BY COURT ORDER; EFFECT

CORE CONCEPT

Except as provided in Rule 41(a)(1) above (authorizing dismissal by stipulation or before an answer or motion for summary judgment has been filed), voluntary dismissal of an action must be by court order.[53]

APPLICATIONS

Discretion of Court

The decision whether to grant or deny the plaintiff's motion for voluntary dismissal is within the sound discretion of the court,[54] although some courts hold that the court has no discretion to deny a motion to dismiss *with prejudice* (reasoning that it is unfair to force an unwilling plaintiff to go to trial).[55] A court should grant a motion for voluntary dismissal unless a defendant can show that it will suffer some plain legal prejudice as a result.[56] Some jurisdictions have factors for the court to consider.[57] In general, courts are more likely to grant motions for voluntary dismissal at earlier stages of the litigation.[58]

Conditions

The court may include terms and conditions in its order granting voluntary dismissal in order to prevent prejudice to the defendant.[59] These conditions may be proposed by the par-

---

[49]*See Love v. Wal-Mart Stores, Inc.*, 865 F.3d 1322, 1325 (11th Cir. 2017) (dismissal appealable); *Williams v. Seidenbach*, 958 F.3d 341, 343 (5th Cir. 2020) (dismissal not appealable).

[50]*Galaza v. Wolf*, 954 F.3d 1267, 1270 (9th Cir. 2020).

[51]*Muzikowski v. Paramount Pictures Corp.*, 322 F.3d 918, 923–24 (7th Cir. 2003).

[52]*Smart Study Co. v. B+Baby Store*, 540 F. Supp. 3d 428, 431 (S.D.N.Y. 2021).

[53]*Tillman v. BNSF Ry. Co.*, 33 F.4th 1024, 1027 (8th Cir. 2022); *Welsh v. Correct Care, L.L.C.*, 915 F.3d 341, 343 (5th Cir. 2019).

[54]*Polansky v. Exec. Health Res. Inc*, 17 F.4th 376, 393 (3d Cir. 2021); *Wellfount, Corp. v. Hennis Care Ctr. of Bolivar, Inc.*, 951 F.3d 769, 774 (6th Cir. 2020).

[55]*Smoot v. Fox*, 340 F.2d 301 (6th Cir.1964).

[56]*United States v. $70,670.00 in U.S. Currency*, 929 F.3d 1293, 1300 (11th Cir. 2019); *United States ex rel. Vaughn v. United Biologics, L.L.C.*, 907 F.3d 187, 196–97 (5th Cir. 2018).

[57]*Tillman v. BNSF Ry. Co.*, 33 F.4th 1024, 1027–28 (8th Cir. 2022).

[58]*See Mullen v. Heinkel Filtering Sys., Inc.*, 770 F.3d 724, 728 (8th Cir. 2014); *Thatcher v. Hanover Ins. Grp., Inc.*, 659 F.3d 1212, 1214 (8th Cir. 2011).

[59]*Frank v. Crawley Petroleum Corp.*, 992 F.3d 987, 998 (10th Cir.

ties or *sua sponte* by the court.[60] The court may impose conditions on voluntary dismissals with or without prejudice.[61] The court has discretion as to whether to impose conditions and, if so, what conditions to impose,[62] but it may be an abuse of discretion to impose sanctions in the absence of prejudice to the defendant.[63] Examples of such conditions include the payment of costs[64] and/or attorney's fees,[65] the payment of costs and fees in the future if the plaintiff subsequently chooses to refile the action,[66] the production of specified documents,[67] making the dismissal with prejudice,[68] requiring that any subsequent action be filed in the same court,[69] providing that discovery from the pending action would carry over to any subsequent actions,[70] and an agreement not to assert specified claims in another action.[71] If the plaintiff is unhappy with the conditions imposed by the court, the plaintiff may decline the dismissal.[72] The court may retain jurisdiction to enforce the conditions.[73]

2021) (purpose of conditions is to prevent prejudice); *Welsh v. Correct Care, L.L.C.*, 915 F.3d 341, 344 (5th Cir. 2019).

[60] *Brown v. Baeke*, 413 F.3d 1121, 1123 (10th Cir. 2005) (some conditions proposed by the plaintiff, and others added by the court).

[61] *Frank v. Crawley Petroleum Corp.*, 992 F.3d 987, 998 (10th Cir. 2021) (conditions are rare when dismissal is with prejudice).

[62] *See Frank v. Crawley Petroleum Corp.*, 992 F.3d 987, 1002 (10th Cir. 2021).

[63] *Frank v. Crawley Petroleum Corp.*, 992 F.3d 987, 1002 (10th Cir. 2021).

[64] *Blaes v. Johnson & Johnson*, 858 F.3d 508, 516 (8th Cir. 2017); *Chavez v. Illinois State Police*, 251 F.3d 612 (7th Cir.2001).

[65] *United States v. $70,670.00 in U.S. Currency*, 929 F.3d 1293, 1304 (11th Cir. 2019) (addressing fee awards against the US); *Paysys Int'l, Inc. v. Atos IT Servs. Ltd.*, 901 F.3d 105, 110 (2d Cir. 2018).

[66] *Sargeant v. Hall*, 951 F.3d 1280, 1285 n.3 (11th Cir. 2020).

[67] *In re Vitamins Antitrust Litig.*, 198 F.R.D. 296 (D.D.C. 2000).

[68] *Michigan Surgery Inv., LLC v. Arman*, 627 F.3d 572, 575 (6th Cir. 2010) (must give the plaintiff notice and an opportunity to withdraw the motion before making dismissal with prejudice); *Elbaor v. Tripath Imaging, Inc.*, 279 F.3d 314, 316 n.1 (5th Cir. 2002) (the court may require the dismissal to be with prejudice to protect the defendant, but not to punish the plaintiff).

[69] *Frank v. Crawley Petroleum Corp.*, 992 F.3d 987, 992 (10th Cir. 2021).

[70] *Frank v. Crawley Petroleum Corp.*, 992 F.3d 987, 992 (10th Cir. 2021).

[71] *See Bechuck v. Home Depot U.S.A., Inc.*, 814 F.3d 287, 298–99 (5th Cir. 2016) (reversing the trial court's imposition of a condition that the plaintiff refile, if at all, in the same court).

[72] *Welsh v. Correct Care, L.L.C.*, 915 F.3d 341, 344 (5th Cir. 2019); *Paysys Int'l, Inc. v. Atos IT Servs. Ltd.*, 901 F.3d 105, 108 (2d Cir. 2018).

[73] *Raab v. City of Ocean City, New Jersey*, 833 F.3d 286, 296 (3d Cir. 2016).

Prejudice

A voluntary dismissal by order of court can be with or without prejudice.[74] A court order granting voluntary dismissal is presumed to be without prejudice unless it explicitly specifies otherwise.[75]

- *Two Dismissal Rule*: The Two Dismissal Rule (described above in Rule 41(a)(1)) does not apply to voluntary dismissals by court order under Rule 41(a)(2).[76]

Dismissal by Motion when Dismissal by Notice is Available

A party may seek dismissal by motion under Rule 41(a)(2) even if the defendant has not yet answered or filed a motion for summary judgment and dismissal by notice is therefore available under Rule 41(a)(1), in order to avoid the Two Dismissal Rule or seek other terms and conditions in the court order dismissing the action.[77]

Defendant as Prevailing Party

For purposes of statutes that award costs or fees to the prevailing party, a defendant can be deemed the prevailing party following a dismissal with prejudice under Rule 41(a)(2).[78]

Counterclaims

If the defendant has filed a counterclaim, then the plaintiff cannot dismiss the action against the defendant's objections unless the counterclaim can remain pending for adjudication.[79] The defendant may dismiss its counterclaim in the same manner that Rule 41 provides for dismissal of a plaintiff's claims.[80]

Dismissal of Part of Action

The plaintiff may dismiss some, but not all, of the defendants under Rule 41(a)(2), but courts differ as to the proper procedural mechanism for voluntarily dismissing some, but not

---

[74] *See, e.g., Carter v. City of Alton*, 922 F.3d 824, 826 (7th Cir. 2019); *Minnesota Mining And Mfg. Co. v. Barr Laboratories, Inc.*, 289 F.3d 775, 779 (Fed. Cir. 2002).

[75] *Wellfount, Corp. v. Hennis Care Ctr. of Bolivar, Inc.*, 951 F.3d 769, 772 (6th Cir. 2020); *United States v. Ponzo*, 913 F.3d 162, 167 (1st Cir. 2019).

[76] *VS PR, LLC v. ORC Miramar Corp.*, 34 F.4th 67, 70–71 (1st Cir. 2022); *Wellfount, Corp. v. Hennis Care Ctr. of Bolivar, Inc.*, 951 F.3d 769, 772 (6th Cir. 2020)

[77] *Wellfount, Corp. v. Hennis Care Ctr. of Bolivar, Inc.*, 951 F.3d 769, 772–73 (6th Cir. 2020).

[78] *Dunster Live, LLC v. LoneStar Logos Mgmt. Co., LLC.*, 908 F.3d 948, 951 (5th Cir. 2018); *K'oyitl'ots'ina, Ltd. v. Gottschalk*, 500 F. Supp. 3d 51, 55 (S.D.N.Y. 2020); *Feliciano Rivera v. Pina Nieves*, 292 F. Supp. 3d 560, 564 (D.P.R. 2018) (dismissal without prejudice is not prevailing).

[79] *See PTA-FLA, Inc. v. ZTE USA, Inc.*, 844 F.3d 1299, 1308 (11th Cir. 2016); *Walter Kidde Portable Equipment, Inc. v. Universal Sec. Instruments, Inc.*, 479 F.3d 1330, 1336 (Fed. Cir. 2007).

[80] *See Auto-Owners Ins. Co. v. Summit Park Townhome Ass'n*, 886 F.3d 852, 857 (10th Cir. 2018); *Morden v. XL Specialty Ins. Co.*, 315 F.R.D. 676, 678 (D. Utah 2016).

all, of the claims.[81] Some courts allow voluntary dismissal by court order pursuant to Rule 41(a)(2).[82] Some courts require a motion to amend pursuant to Rule 15(a).[83]

Enforcement of Settlement Agreement

Normally, a federal court does not retain jurisdiction over an action to enforce the terms of a settlement and stipulated dismissal.[84] In order to vest the district court with such jurisdiction, parties often include in their motion for voluntary dismissal or in their attached proposed order a provision that the court will continue to have jurisdiction to enforce the parties' settlement agreement.[85] The court may, at its discretion, make the parties' compliance with a settlement agreement part of its dismissal order.[86]

Circumvention of Rules or Prior Rulings/Forum Shopping

Courts sometimes prohibit a party from using dismissal without prejudice to circumvent limitations in the Rules, to avoid the effects of prior rulings, or to obtain a more advantageous forum.[87] So, for example, a court might not allow a party to use Rule 41(a)(2) to cure an untimely jury demand (by dismissal, then refiling a new complaint with a jury demand).[88] Likewise, a court might not allow a party to dismiss a claim in order to refile the case with an additional defendant for the purpose of defeating diversity jurisdiction.[89]

Final Appealable Order/Judgment

The courts differ as to whether a plaintiff can appeal the granting or denial of a motion for voluntary dismissal *without*

---

[81] *See Jet, Inc. v. Sewage Aeration Sys.*, 223 F.3d 1360, 1364 (Fed. Cir. 2000) (Rule 41(a)(2) and Rule 15(a) are functionally interchangeable).

[82] *See CDK Glob., LLC v. Tulley Auto. Grp., Inc.*, 489 F. Supp. 3d 282, 297-98 (D.N.J. 2020); *Guzman-Fonalledas v. Hosp. Expanol Auxilio Mutuo*, 289 F. Supp. 3d 331, 333 (D.P.R. 2018).

[83] *Williams v. Seidenbach*, 958 F.3d 341, 360–61 (5th Cir. 2020); *Campbell v. Altec Indus., Inc.*, 605 F.3d 839, 840 n.1 (11th Cir. 2010).

[84] *Solv-Ex Corp. v. Quillen*, 186 F.R.D. 313, 315 (S.D.N.Y. 1999); *Lee v. Runyon*, 18 F. Supp. 2d 649, 653 (E.D. Tex. 1998).

[85] *See Raab v. City of Ocean City, New Jersey*, 833 F.3d 286, 296 (3d Cir. 2016); *Kelly v. Wengler*, 822 F.3d 1085, 1094–95 (9th Cir. 2016).

[86] *Kokkonen v. Guardian Life Ins. Co. of Am.*, 511 U.S. 375, 381 (1994).

[87] *Tillman v. BNSF Ry. Co.*, 33 F.4th 1024, 1028 (8th Cir. 2022); *Blaes v. Johnson & Johnson*, 858 F.3d 508, 512 (8th Cir. 2017).

[88] *Russ v. Standard Ins. Co.*, 120 F.3d 988, 990 (9th Cir. 1997); *but see Hoffmann v. Alside, Inc.*, 596 F.2d 822, 823 (8th Cir. 1979).

[89] *Tillman v. BNSF Ry. Co.*, 33 F.4th 1024, 1029 (8th Cir. 2022); *Blaes v. Johnson & Johnson*, 858 F.3d 508, 512 (8th Cir. 2017); *but see Goodwin v. Reynolds*, 757 F.3d 1216, 1220 (11th Cir. 2014) (allowing dismissal without prejudice so the case could be refiled in State court when the defendant had manipulated jurisdiction).

prejudice.[90] Voluntary dismissal *with prejudice* is a final appealable order,[91] except in the class-action context.[92] The plaintiff may be able to appeal the granting of its own motion to dismiss if the court imposes conditions on the dismissal that prejudice the plaintiff[93] or if the purpose of the dismissal was to expedite appeal of interlocutory rulings.[94] The defendant may appeal an order granting a motion for voluntary dismissal.[95] A voluntary dismissal pursuant to Rule 41(a)(2) can constitute a judgment for purposes of post-judgment rules.[96] A Rule 41(a)(2) order dismissing only part of an action is not a final, appealable order.[97]

RULE 41(b)—INVOLUNTARY DISMISSAL; EFFECT

CORE CONCEPT

Involuntary dismissal is a remedy that a defendant may seek by motion. Rule 41(b) governs two types of involuntary dismissals: dismissal for failure to prosecute and dismissal for failure to comply with other Rules or with a court order.

APPLICATIONS

Disfavored

Involuntary dismissal is within the discretion of the court,[98] but is disfavored and is granted sparingly.[99]

Failure to Prosecute

The court may dismiss for failure to prosecute *sua sponte*[100] or upon motion.[101] Local Rules may specify the conditions for dismissal for failure to prosecute (for example, lack of activity

---

[90]*See Corley v. Long-Lewis, Inc.*, 965 F.3d 1222, 1229 (11th Cir. 2020) (appealable); *Gaddis v. DeMattei*, 30 F.4th 625, 629 (7th Cir. 2022) (not appealable).

[91]*Henson v. Fid. Nat'l Fin., Inc.*, 943 F.3d 434, 440 (9th Cir. 2019); *Paysys Int'l, Inc. v. Atos IT Servs. Ltd.*, 901 F.3d 105, 107 n.2 (2d Cir. 2018).

[92]*Sperring v. LLR, Inc.*, 995 F.3d 680, 682 (9th Cir. 2021); *Langere v. Verizon Wireless Servs., LLC*, 983 F.3d 1115, 1120 (9th Cir. 2020).

[93]*See Corley v. Long-Lewis, Inc.*, 965 F.3d 1222, 1229 (11th Cir. 2020); *Chavez v. Illinois State Police*, 251 F.3d 612 (7th Cir. 2001).

[94]*See Langere v. Verizon Wireless Servs., LLC*, 983 F.3d 1115, 1119 (9th Cir. 2020); *Henson v. Fid. Nat'l Fin., Inc.*, 943 F.3d 434, 440 (9th Cir. 2019).

[95]*Corley v. Long-Lewis, Inc.*, 965 F.3d 1222, 1229 (11th Cir. 2020).

[96]*Henson v. Fid. Nat'l Fin., Inc.*, 943 F.3d 434, 440 (9th Cir. 2019) (Rule 60).

[97]*Corley v. Long-Lewis, Inc.*, 965 F.3d 1222, 1229 (11th Cir. 2020).

[98]*Hildebrand v. Allegheny Cty.*, 923 F.3d 128, 132 (3d Cir. 2019); *Baptiste v. Sommers*, 768 F.3d 212, 216–17 (2d Cir. 2014).

[99]*Hildebrand v. Allegheny Cty.*, 923 F.3d 128, 132 (3d Cir. 2019); *Gates v. Strain*, 885 F.3d 874, 883 (5th Cir. 2018).

[100]*Carver v. Atwood*, 18 F.4th 494, 497 (5th Cir. 2021); *Coleman v. Sweetin*, 745 F.3d 756, 766–67 (5th Cir. 2014).

[101]*Hildebrand v. Allegheny Cty.*, 923 F.3d 128, 129 (3d Cir. 2019); *McMahan v. Deutsche Bank AG*, 892 F.3d 926, 930 (7th Cir. 2018).

for a period of one year).[102] Other courts have developed factors for assessing failure to prosecute.[103] Although courts have discretion in ruling on a dismissal for failure to prosecute,[104] some courts view such dismissals with prejudice as a harsh remedy reserved for extreme situations.[105]

Failure to Comply with Order

The court may dismiss an action based on the plaintiff's failure to comply with a court order *sua sponte* or upon motion.[106]

Failure to Comply with Rules

The court may dismiss an action for failure to comply with the Rules.[107] For example, the plaintiff may risk involuntary dismissal by filing an overly-lengthy and complex complaint that does not comply with Rule 8(a)'s requirement for "a short and plain statement of the claim"[108] (although most courts would not dismiss for failure to comply with the Rules unless the conduct was egregious and ongoing).

- *Discovery Rules:* Rule 37 controls the sanctions for failure to comply with the discovery rules. So, dismissal might be a proper sanction for failure to comply with the discovery rules, but the dismissal would be under Rule 37, not Rule 41.[109]
- *Local Rules:* Technically, Rule 41(b) does not provide for dismissal based on failure to comply with a district's Local Rules, but some courts will dismiss under Rule 41 for failure to comply with Local Rules.[110]

Preclusion: Presumption of Prejudice

Involuntary dismissals under Rule 41 are presumed to be

---

[102] *See Wagner v. Ashcroft*, 214 F.R.D. 78 (N.D.N.Y. 2003).

[103] *See Attkisson v. Holder*, 925 F.3d 606, 625 (4th Cir. 2019); *Hildebrand v. Allegheny Cty.*, 923 F.3d 128, 132 (3d Cir. 2019).

[104] *Mondelli v. Berkeley Heights Nursing & Rehab. Ctr.*, 1 F.4th 145 n.3 (3d Cir. 2021).

[105] *See Hamer v. LivaNova Deutschland GmbH*, 994 F.3d 173, 177 (3d Cir. 2021); *Schafer v. City of Defiance Police Dep't*, 529 F.3d 731, 736 (6th Cir. 2008).

[106] *Slack v. McDaniel*, 529 U.S. 473 (2000); *Auto-Owners Ins. Co. v. Summit Park Townhome Ass'n*, 886 F.3d 852, 858 (10th Cir. 2018) (*sua sponte*).

[107] *Bank of Am., N.A. v. Woodcrest Homeowners Ass'n*, 381 F. Supp. 3d 1280, 1284 (D. Nev. 2019); *Jiggetts v. District of Columbia*, 319 F.R.D. 408, 413 (D.D.C. 2017).

[108] *Hearns v. San Bernardino Police Dep't*, 530 F.3d 1124, 1129 (9th Cir. 2008); *Sessa v. Ancestry.com Operations Inc.*, 561 F. Supp. 3d 1008, 1019 (D. Nev. 2021).

[109] *Mager v. Wisconsin Cent. Ltd.*, 924 F.3d 831, 837 n.3 (6th Cir. 2019); *Reyes v. Dart*, 801 F.3d 879, 881 (7th Cir. 2015). *But see Bonet v. Now Courier, Inc.*, 203 F. Supp. 3d 1195, 1199 (S.D. Fla. 2016) (dismissing under Rule 41 primarily for discovery transgressions).

[110] *See Cornett v. Dobson*, 338 F.R.D. 97, 99 (E.D. Ky. 2021); *Ollison v. Curry Cty. Det. Ctr.*, 429 F. Supp. 3d 920, 922 (D.N.M. 2019).

with prejudice unless the court specifies otherwise.[111]

- *Prejudice for Dismissal Under Other Rules:* Rule 41(b) provides that dismissal under other rules also operates as an adjudication on the merits (and thus may be given preclusive effect)[112] except a dismissal for lack of jurisdiction, improper venue, or failure to join a Rule 19 required party.[113]

Dismissal Under Other Rules

Rule 41(b) governs only the two specified types of involuntary dismissal. Other types of dismissal are addressed elsewhere, such as in Rule 12(b) governing dismissal for reasons like failure to state a claim and lack of jurisdiction.

Dismissal of Part of an Action

In contrast to Rule 41(a), Rule 41(b) expressly authorizes the dismissal of individual claims, as opposed to the entire action.[114]

Final Appealable Order/Judgment

The plaintiff may appeal an involuntary dismissal—with or without prejudice—as a final order.[115] Whether a Rule 41(b) dismissal constitutes a "final judgment" depends on the context.[116]

RULE 41(c)—DISMISSING A COUNTERCLAIM, CROSSCLAIM, OR THIRD-PARTY CLAIM

CORE CONCEPT

The provisions of Rule 41 apply to counterclaims, crossclaims, and third-party claims with equal force.[117]

---

[111] *Lomax v. Ortiz-Marquez*, — U.S. —, 140 S. Ct. 1721, 1725 (2020); *Papera v. Pennsylvania Quarried Bluestone Co.*, 948 F.3d 607, 610 (3d Cir. 2020).

[112] *Ryder v. Hyles*, 27 F.4th 1253, 1258 (7th Cir. 2022); *Beach Blitz Co. v. City of Miami Beach, Fla.*, 13 F.4th 1289, 1299 (11th Cir. 2021).

[113] Rule 41(b); *Rote v. Comm. on Jud. Conduct & Disability of Jud. Conf. of United States*, — F. Supp. 3d —, 2021 WL 6197041, at *20 (D. Or. 2021).

[114] *Williams v. Seidenbach*, 958 F.3d 341, 360 (5th Cir. 2020).

[115] *Applied Underwriters, Inc. v. Lichtenegger*, 913 F.3d 884, 890 (9th Cir. 2019); *Wynder v. McMahon*, 360 F.3d 73, 76 (2d Cir. 2004).

[116] *See, e.g., Krekelberg v. City of Minneapolis*, 991 F.3d 949, 955 (8th Cir. 2021) (dismissals not judgments under the Driver's Protection Privacy Act); *Okafor v. Statebridge Co. LLC*, 311 F.R.D. 24, 25 (D. Mass. 2015) (dismissal reviewable under Rule 60).

[117] *Orca Yachts, L.L.C. v. Mollicam, Inc.*, 287 F.3d 316, 319 (4th Cir. 2002).

RULE 41(d)—COSTS OF A PREVIOUSLY DISMISSED ACTION

CORE CONCEPT

If a plaintiff who has already *voluntarily* dismissed an action commences another action on the same claim,[118] the court, in its discretion, can stay the second action until the plaintiff[119] pays such costs of the first action as the court deems appropriate.[120] In exercising this discretion, the court may consider the plaintiff's motives in dismissing the initial action and whether the plaintiff acted in bad faith.[121] The courts are split as to whether an award of costs under Rule 41(d) may include attorney's fees.[122] The motion for such fees is filed in the court where the second action is filed.[123] Rule 41(d) only applies when the second action is filed in federal court;[124] state rules of civil procedure would control a similar claim when the second action is filed in state court.

Additional Research References

Wright & Miller, *Federal Practice and Procedure* §§ 2361 to 2376

C.J.S., Federal Civil Procedure §§ 486, 775 to 819 et seq., 839 to 869 et seq.

West's Key Number Digest, Federal Civil Procedure ⚷1691 to 1715, 1721 to 1729, 1741, 1758 to 1765, 1821 to 1842

---

[118] *Cotiviti, Inc. v. Deagle*, 501 F. Supp. 3d 243, 255 (S.D.N.Y. 2020) (cases must depend on the same "core showing"); *Garza v. Citigroup Inc.*, 311 F.R.D. 111, 115 (D. Del. 2015).

[119] *Duffy v. Ford Motor Co.*, 218 F.3d 623, 636 (6th Cir. 2000) (Rule 41(d) discusses the imposition of costs upon the plaintiffs, not counsel).

[120] *Garza v. Citigroup Inc.*, 881 F.3d 277, 281 (3d Cir. 2018); *Horowitz v. 148 S. Emerson Assocs. LLC*, 888 F.3d 13, 24 (2d Cir. 2018).

[121] *Cotiviti, Inc. v. Deagle*, 501 F. Supp. 3d 243, 255 (S.D.N.Y. 2020).

[122] *See Garza v. Citigroup Inc.*, 881 F.3d 277, 281 (3d Cir. 2018) (noting the split and determining that attorney's fees may be recovered only when an underlying statute defines costs as including attorney's fees); *Horowitz v. 148 S. Emerson Assocs. LLC*, 888 F.3d 13, 24 (2d Cir. 2018) (court free to award attorney's fees); *Rogers v. Wal-Mart Stores, Inc.*, 230 F.3d 868, 875 (6th Cir. 2000) (fees are not available in the 6th Circuit).

[123] *Sargeant v. Hall*, 951 F.3d 1280, 1286 (11th Cir. 2020).

[124] *Sargeant v. Hall*, 951 F.3d 1280, 1286 (11th Cir. 2020).

RULE 42
CONSOLIDATION; SEPARATE TRIALS

(a) **Consolidation.** If actions before the court involve a common question of law or fact, the court may:

(1) join for hearing or trial any or all matters at issue in the actions;

(2) consolidate the actions; or

(3) issue any other orders to avoid unnecessary cost or delay.

(b) **Separate Trials.** For convenience, to avoid prejudice, or to expedite and economize, the court may order a separate trial of one or more separate issues, claims, crossclaims, counterclaims, or third-party claims. When ordering a separate trial, the court must preserve any federal right to a jury trial.

[Amended effective July 1, 1966; April 30, 2007, effective December 1, 2007.]

AUTHORS' COMMENTARY ON RULE 42

PURPOSE AND SCOPE

Rule 42 allows the court to control the manner in which the cases on its docket are organized; the court may consolidate several actions into a single proceeding—either entirely or for specific phases or activities—or may conduct separate trials of various issues within a single action. The Rule fosters efficiency and fairness. It establishes a threshold requirement for consolidation that the actions have at least one common issue of law or fact—it would be too confusing and wasteful to try two or more completely unrelated cases at the same time. It establishes convenience, prejudice-avoidance, time, and cost as the considerations for ordering separate trials for issues or claims joined in a single action. In general, the trial court has broad discretion regarding consolidation or conducting separate trials.

RULE 42(a)—CONSOLIDATION

CORE CONCEPT

When multiple actions properly pending before one court share common issues of law or fact, the court can consolidate the actions, either completely or for limited proceedings or stages.

APPLICATIONS

Procedure

Consolidation is achieved by motion of any party[1] or by the court *sua sponte.*[2] Local rules may determine to which judge a motion to consolidate should be presented if the matters are pending before different judges.[3] In appropriate circumstances, the court may appoint one lawyer as lead or liaison counsel.[4] The court may also designate a lead plaintiff.[5]

- *Other Orders*: Rule 42(a) authorizes the court to "issue any other orders to avoid unnecessary cost or delay."[6]

Court's Discretion

In deciding whether to consolidate actions, the court should balance the savings to the judicial system against the possible inconvenience, delay, or prejudice to the parties.[7] The court has broad discretion in this balancing process,[8] and does not need the parties' consent.[9] The party seeking consolidation bears the burden of persuading the court that consolidation is appropriate.[10]

Common Issues Necessary

Although the court has broad discretion, it may not consolidate actions that do not share at least one common issue of law or fact.[11] It may consolidate actions that do not have the same parties or claims, however.[12]

---

[1] *In re Stitch Fix, Inc. Sec. Litig.*, 393 F. Supp. 3d 833, 834 (N.D. Cal. 2019).

[2] *Lester v. Exxon Mobil Corp.*, 879 F.3d 582, 592 (5th Cir. 2018).

[3] *Stewart v. O'Neill*, 225 F. Supp. 2d 16, 21 (D.D.C. 2002).

[4] *See, e.g., In re Bemis Co. Sec. Litig.*, 512 F. Supp. 3d 518, 527 (S.D.N.Y. 2021); *In re Snap Inc. Sec. Litig.*, 334 F.R.D. 209, 214 (C.D. Cal. 2019).

[5] *Plymouth Cnty. Ret. Sys. v. Apache Corp.*, 566 F. Supp. 3d 712, 716 (S.D. Tex. 2021).

[6] *United States v. Yale Univ.*, 337 F.R.D. 35, 46 (D. Conn. 2021).

[7] *Campbell v. Boston Sci. Corp.*, 882 F.3d 70, 74 (4th Cir. 2018); *Eghnayem v. Boston Sci. Corp.*, 873 F.3d 1304, 1313 (11th Cir. 2017).

[8] *Eghnayem v. Boston Sci. Corp.*, 873 F.3d 1304, 1313 (11th Cir. 2017); *A.S. ex rel. Miller v. SmithKline Beecham Corp.*, 769 F.3d 204, 212 (3d Cir. 2014).

[9] *Lester v. Exxon Mobil Corp.*, 879 F.3d 582, 592 (5th Cir. 2018); *Connecticut General Life Ins. Co. v. Sun Life Assur. Co. of Canada*, 210 F.3d 771 (7th Cir. 2000).

[10] *Innovation Ventures, L.L.C. v. Custom Nutrition Labs., L.L.C.*, 451 F. Supp. 3d 769, 793 (E.D. Mich. 2020); *Ellis v. Arrowood Indem. Co.*, 115 F. Supp. 3d 869, 872 (E.D. Ky. 2015).

[11] *Scott v. Chipotle Mexican Grill, Inc.*, 954 F.3d 502, 516 n.5 (2d Cir. 2020); *Malcolm v. National Gypsum Co.*, 995 F.2d 346 (2d Cir. 1993).

[12] *Rauch v. Vale S.A.*, 378 F. Supp. 3d 198, 204 (E.D.N.Y. 2019).

Limited Consolidation

The court may consolidate actions for all purposes,[13] for pretrial proceedings only,[14] for specified hearings or issues,[15] or for trial.[16]

Both Actions Must be Properly Pending in the Court

In order to consolidate two or more actions, the actions must be properly pending in the same court.[17]

- *Actions in Different Districts:* Actions in different districts may not be consolidated. However, if actions are pending in different districts that ought to be consolidated, one or more of the actions may be transferred under the venue transfer statute, 28 U.S.C.A. § 1404[18] or under the Multidistrict Litigation (MDL) procedures described in Part V of this Handbook, so that all the actions are then pending in a single district, and may be consolidated.[19]

Actions Remain Separate

In general, consolidated actions retain their separate identity.[20] Thus, the pleadings will remain separate and the court will enter separate judgments in each action.[21] However, the court can merge the cases or order that briefs and rulings apply to all consolidated cases.[22]

Improper Alignment Creating Conflicts of Interest

Consolidation may be improper if it aligns parties who have conflicting interests.[23]

Arbitration

Many courts do not permit consolidation of arbitrations unless there is an express provision in the arbitration agreements

---

[13]*See McCullough v. World Wrestling Ent., Inc.*, 838 F.3d 210, 214, n.6 (2d Cir. 2016).

[14]*See Katz v. Realty Equities Corp.*, 521 F.2d 1354, 1358 (2d Cir. 1975).

[15]*See Window World of Chicagoland, LLC v. Window World, Inc.*, 811 F.3d 900, 903 (7th Cir. 2016).

[16]*See Scott v. Chipotle Mexican Grill, Inc.*, 954 F.3d 502, 516, n.5 (2d Cir. 2020).

[17]*See ACR Energy Partners, LLC v. Polo North Country Club, Inc.*, 309 F.R.D. 193, 194–95 (D.N.J. 2015) (improperly removed case cannot be consolidated); *Thermodyn Corp. v. 3M Co.*, 593 F. Supp. 2d 972, 991 (N.D. Ohio 2008) (court must have jurisdiction over both cases).

[18]*See Desire, LLC v. Manna Textiles, Inc.*, 986 F.3d 1253, 1272 (9th Cir. 2021); *In re Fifth Third Early Access Cash Advance Litig.*, 925 F.3d 265, 272 (6th Cir. 2019).

[19]*In re Korean Air Lines Co., Ltd.*, 642 F.3d 685, 699–700 (9th Cir. 2011).

[20]*See Hall v. Hall*, 138 S. Ct. 1118, 1125 (2018).

[21]*Horizon Asset Mgmt. Inc. v. H & R Block, Inc.*, 580 F.3d 755, 769 (8th Cir. 2009).

[22]*In re Air Crash at Lexington, KY, AUGUST 27, 2006*, 251 F.R.D. 258, 260–61 (E.D. Ky. 2008); *Specht v. Netscape Communications Corp.*, 150 F. Supp. 2d 585, 586, (S.D. N.Y. 2001), aff'd, 306 F.3d 17 (2d Cir. 2002).

[23]*Dupont v. Southern Pac. Co.*, 366 F.2d 193 (5th Cir. 1966); *Atkinson v. Roth*, 297 F.2d 570 (3d Cir.1961).

providing for consolidation.[24]

Appeals

An order granting or denying a motion for consolidation is not appealable as a final judgment,[25] although mandamus may be available under extreme circumstances.[26] A final judgment in one of a group of cases that have been consolidated is immediately appealable even if some of the other cases are not yet resolved.[27]

RULE 42(b)—SEPARATE TRIALS

CORE CONCEPT

The court may conduct separate trials of any claim or issue.[28]

APPLICATIONS

Procedure

The court may order separate trials *sua sponte* or by motion of any party.[29]

Standard

Rule 42(b) lists three circumstances supporting bifurcation—for convenience, to avoid prejudice, or to expedite and economize—and any one of these may support bifurcation.[30] In deciding whether to order separate trials, the court will balance the savings to the judicial system against the possible inconvenience, delay, or prejudice to the parties.[31] The court has broad discretion in this balancing process,[32] and may bifurcate over a party's objection.[33] Many courts hold that bifurcation

[24] *Champ v. Siegel Trading Co., Inc.*, 55 F.3d 269, 274 (7th Cir. 1995); *but see Office & Professional Employees Intern. Union, AFL-CIO v. Sea-Land Service, Inc.*, 210 F.3d 117, 123 (2d Cir. 2000) (district court may consolidate two arbitration proceedings without consideration of whether consolidation was authorized by Rule 42(a)).

[25] *National Ass'n for Advancement of Colored People of Louisiana v. Michot*, 480 F.2d 547, 548 (5th Cir. 1973).

[26] *In re Repetitive Stress Injury Litig.*, 11 F.3d 368 (2d Cir.1993).

[27] *Hall v. Hall*, 138 S. Ct. 1118, 1125 (2018).

[28] *Bridgeport Music, Inc. v. Justin Combs Pub.*, 507 F.3d 470, 481 (6th Cir. 2007); *Aiello v. Geico Gen. Ins. Co.*, 379 F. Supp. 3d 1123, 1128 (D. Nev. 2019).

[29] *Jackson Women's Health Org. v. Dobbs*, 945 F.3d 265, 269 n.4 (5th Cir. 2019) (*sua sponte*); *Barnes v. Sea Hawaii Rafting, LLC*, 889 F.3d 517, 539 (9th Cir. 2018).

[30] *Glover v. Hryniewich*, 341 F.R.D. 36, 38 (E.D. Va. 2022); *Johnson v. Baltimore Police Dep't*, 500 F. Supp. 3d 454, 458 (D. Md. 2020).

[31] *See McKiver v. Murphy-Brown, LLC*, 980 F.3d 937, 974 (4th Cir. 2020); *Allstate Ins. Co. v. Vizcay*, 826 F.3d 1326, 1333 (11th Cir. 2016).

[32] *Nester v. Textron, Inc.*, 888 F.3d 151, 162 (5th Cir. 2018); *In re September 11 Litig.*, 802 F.3d 314, 339 (2d Cir. 2015).

[33] *Jackson Women's Health Org. v. Dobbs*, 945 F.3d 265, 269 n.4 (5th Cir. 2019).

should be the exception, not a routine procedure.[34] Even in situations where bifurcation is more common, like the separation of the liability phase from the damages phase, courts will scrutinize requests for bifurcation.[35]

Burden of Proof

The burden is on the moving party to demonstrate that bifurcation is justified.[36]

Pretrial Proceedings

Rule 42(b) authorizes the court to order separate *trials* of separate issues or claims—the case remains a single action for discovery and other pretrial purposes.[37] However, Rules 1, 16, and 26(c) authorize the court to phase discovery and otherwise structure pretrial procedures to achieve the just, speedy, and inexpensive determination of the action.[38]

Single Action

A separation under Rule 42 separates aspects of the action for trial, but the aspects remain part of a single action, and result in a single judgment.[39] This contrasts with claims that are severed pursuant to Rule 21.[40]

Common Circumstances for Separate Trials

The most common instance of separate trials is when the court first conducts a trial as to liability, then as to damages if necessary.[41] Punitive damages are also sometimes bifurcated.[42] Courts also conduct separate trials of bad faith insurance claims and accompanying breach of contract claims,[43] or where a defendant seeks indemnity from a third-party defendant.[44] Bifurcation may also be appropriate when trial of one issue

[34] *Saunders v. Metro. Prop. Mgmt., Inc.*, 561 F. Supp. 3d 629, 631 (W.D. Va. 2021); *Young v. Mentor Worldwide LLC*, 312 F. Supp. 3d 765, 768 (E.D. Ark. 2018).

[35] *RCHFU, LLC v. Marriott Vacations Worldwide Corp.*, 445 F. Supp. 3d 1327, 1339–40 (D. Colo. 2020).

[36] *McKiver v. Murphy-Brown, LLC*, 980 F.3d 937, 974 (4th Cir. 2020).

[37] *Jimenez v. GEICO Gen. Ins. Co.*, 448 F. Supp. 3d 1108, 1115 (D. Nev. 2020).

[38] *See Edwards Vacuum, LLC v. Hoffman Instrumentation Supply, Inc.*, 556 F. Supp. 3d 1156, 1180 (D. Or. 2021).

[39] *White v. ABCO Engineering Corp.*, 199 F.3d 140, 145 (3d Cir. 1999); *Reid v. General Motors Corp.*, 240 F.R.D. 260, 263 (E.D. Tex. 2007).

[40] *Rice v. Sunrise Express, Inc.*, 209 F.3d 1008, 1014–16 (7th Cir. 2000); *Pinson v. U.S. Department of Justice*, 74 F. Supp. 3d 283 n.7 (D.D.C. 2014).

[41] *See Gafford v. General Elec. Co.*, 997 F.2d 150 (6th Cir. 1993); *Saunders v. Metro. Prop. Mgmt., Inc.*, 561 F. Supp. 3d 629, 631 (W.D. Va. 2021).

[42] *See McKiver v. Murphy-Brown, LLC*, 980 F.3d 937, 974 (4th Cir. 2020); *Nester v. Textron, Inc.*, 888 F.3d 151, 162–63 (5th Cir. 2018).

[43] *Optical Works & Logistics, LLC v. Sentinel Ins. Co., Ltd.*, ___ F. Supp. 3d ___, 2021 WL 928275, at *3 (D.R.I. 2021).

[44] *Glover v. Hryniewich*, 341 F.R.D. 36, 39 (E.D. Va. 2022).

may obviate the need to try another.[45]

Separate Trials for Each Defendant

The court may order separate trials for each defendant, particularly if one is in bankruptcy, as long as the defendants are not required parties under Rule 19.[46]

Jury Trials

The procedures the court employs for separate trials may not affect the parties' rights to a jury trial.[47] Separate trials may be conducted before one jury or different juries.[48] If there are jury and nonjury claims present, the jury claims may have to be tried first, so that the court does not make factual findings that should properly have been made by the jury.[49]

Appeals

An order granting or denying a motion for bifurcation is not appealable as a final judgment, although mandamus may be available under extreme circumstances.[50]

Additional Research References

Wright & Miller, *Federal Practice and Procedure* §§ 2381 to 2392
C.J.S., Federal Civil Procedure §§ 611, 916 to 918
West's Key Number Digest, Federal Civil Procedure ⚷8, 1953 to 1965

---

[45] *Stevenson v. Holland*, 504 F. Supp. 3d 1107, 1127, 1129 (E.D. Cal. 2020) (statute of limitations issue bifurcated); *Castillo v. GEICO Cas. Co.*, 446 F. Supp. 3d 710, 714 (D. Nev. 2020).

[46] *Hecht v. City of New York*, 217 F.R.D. 148, 150 (S.D.N.Y. 2003).

[47] *Shum v. Intel Corp.*, 499 F.3d 1272, 1276 (Fed. Cir. 2007); *Danjaq LLC v. Sony Corp.*, 263 F.3d 942, 961–62 (9th Cir. 2001).

[48] *See Reid v. General Motors Corp.*, 240 F.R.D. 260, 263 (E.D. Tex. 2007) (separate juries should not be allowed to pass on overlapping issues of fact because of the risk of inconsistent verdicts).

[49] *See Dairy Queen, Inc. v. Wood*, 369 U.S. 469, 479 (1962); *Beacon Theatres, Inc. v. Westover*, 359 U.S. 500 (1959).

[50] *See In re Repetitive Stress Injury Litig.*, 11 F.3d 368 (2d Cir. 1993).

RULE 43
TAKING TESTIMONY

(a) **In Open Court.** At trial, the witnesses' testimony must be taken in open court unless a federal statute, the Federal Rules of Evidence, these rules, or other rules adopted by the Supreme Court provide otherwise. For good cause in compelling circumstances and with appropriate safeguards, the court may permit testimony in open court by contemporaneous transmission from a different location.

(b) **Affirmation Instead of an Oath.** When these rules require an oath, a solemn affirmation suffices.

(c) **Evidence on a Motion.** When a motion relies on facts outside the record, the court may hear the matter on affidavits or may hear it wholly or partly on oral testimony or on depositions.

(d) **Interpreter.** The court may appoint an interpreter of its choosing; fix reasonable compensation to be paid from funds provided by law or by one or more parties; and tax the compensation as costs.

[Amended effective July 1, 1966; July 1, 1975; August 1, 1987, December 1, 1996; April 30, 2007, effective December 1, 2007.]

AUTHORS' COMMENTARY ON RULE 43

PURPOSE AND SCOPE

Prior to the enactment of the Federal Rules of Evidence, Rule 43 was entitled "Evidence" and contained evidence provisions that functioned as a very general set of evidence rules. However, in conjunction with the enactment of the Federal Rules of Evidence in 1975, Rule 43 was dramatically scaled back. Today, it contains a grab-bag of minor provisions relating to the taking of testimony. It establishes a preference for live testimony in open court, but authorizes testimony by videoconference or other form of "contemporaneous transmission." Courts have regularly found the issues surrounding COVID-19 to constitute good cause for remote testimony. Rule 43 accords a witness the option of making a "solemn affirmation" to testify truthfully instead of taking an oath (which typically contains a religious reference). It speaks to the manner of submitting evidence to support a motion, allowing submission of affidavits, deposition testimony, or live testimony. Finally, Rule 43 authorizes the court to appoint an interpreter and to determine how the interpreter is paid.

RULE 43(a)—IN OPEN COURT

CORE CONCEPT

There is a preference in federal court for testimony taken in open court. All testimony must be in that form unless otherwise authorized by the Federal Rules of Evidence,[1] federal statute, or stipulation of the parties.[2]

APPLICATIONS

Live Testimony

The Rules place a strong emphasis on live testimony taken in open court.[3]

Remote Testimony

Rule 43(a) allows the transmitting of testimony from a different location.[4] However, the Rules continue to emphasize live testimony in court, and transmitted testimony is permitted only for good cause shown in compelling circumstances.[5] Transmitted testimony might be allowed when unexpected circumstances, such as an accident, illness, or immigration status[6] render a witness unable to appear in court.[7]

- *Appropriate Safeguards*: In cases where remote testimony is to be used, the court must employ appropriate safeguards to protect the procedure and the parties' interests.[8]
- *COVID-19*: Courts have regularly found the issues surrounding COVID-19 to constitute good cause for remote

---

[1] *Kuntz v. Sea Eagle Diving Adventures Corp.*, 199 F.R.D. 665, 667 (D. Haw. 2001); *Saverson v. Levitt*, 162 F.R.D. 407, 408 (D.D.C. 1995).

[2] *In re RFC & ResCap Liquidating Tr. Action*, 444 F. Supp. 3d 967, 970 (D. Minn. 2020).

[3] *Draper v. Rosario*, 836 F.3d 1072, 1081–82 (9th Cir. 2016); *Perotti v. Quinones*, 790 F.3d 712, 723 (7th Cir. 2015).

[4] *United States v. Approximately $299,873.70 Seized From a Bank of Am. Acct.*, 15 F.4th 1332, 1339 (11th Cir. 2021); *Perotti v. Quinones*, 790 F.3d 712, 723 (7th Cir. 2015).

[5] *Benjamin v. Sparks*, 986 F.3d 332, 344 (4th Cir. 2021); *Thomas v. Anderson*, 912 F.3d 971, 977 (7th Cir. 2018).

[6] *United States v. Approximately $299,873.70 Seized From a Bank of Am. Acct.*, 15 F.4th 1332, 1339 (11th Cir. 2021).

[7] *Rodriguez v. Gusman*, 974 F.3d 108, 114 (2d Cir. 2020) (immigration status); *In re RFC & ResCap Liquidating Tr. Action*, 444 F. Supp. 3d 967, 971 (D. Minn. 2020).

[8] *Parkhurst v. Belt*, 567 F.3d 995 (8th Cir. 2009); *VMX-Glob. USA, LLC v. Noble Env't Tech*, 339 F.R.D. 690, 692 (S.D. Fla. 2021).

testimony.[9]

RULE 43(b)—AFFIRMATION INSTEAD OF AN OATH

CORE CONCEPT

A party who, for religious reasons or otherwise, chooses not to take an oath, may make a "solemn affirmation" instead.[10]

RULE 43(c)—EVIDENCE ON A MOTION

CORE CONCEPT

A party may submit affidavits and documentary evidence in support of or in opposition to a motion; an evidentiary hearing is not required.[11] The court, in its discretion, may order oral evidence taken[12] or may request deposition transcripts when a motion is based on facts not of record.[13] The court may also consider a motion solely on the parties' written submissions.[14]

RULE 43(d)—INTERPRETER

CORE CONCEPT

The court may, in its discretion, appoint an interpreter,[15] who then should take an oath or affirmation that the translation will be accurate. If an interpreter is appointed, the court may determine the interpreter's fees. The court may apportion the fees among the parties, and may award the fees as costs after the conclusion of the trial.

Additional Research References

Wright & Miller, *Federal Practice and Procedure* §§ 2401 to 2417

C.J.S., Courts § 1-110; Federal Civil Procedure §§ 368, 373, 935; Witnesses §§ 320 to 326

West's Key Number Digest, Courts ⚷56; Federal Civil Procedure ⚷2011; West's Key Number Digest, Witnesses ⚷227, 228, 230

---

[9] *See, e.g., Steele v. Nat'l R.R. Passenger Corp.*, — F. Supp. 3d —, 2022 WL 1154351, at *3 (W.D. Wash. 2022); *VMX-Glob. USA, LLC v. Noble Env't Tech*, 339 F.R.D. 690, 691 (S.D. Fla. 2021).

[10] *Doe v. Phillips*, 81 F.3d 1204 (2d Cir. 1996); *Robinson v. Alameda County*, 875 F. Supp. 2d 1029, 1034 n.3 (N.D. Cal. 2012).

[11] *Grayson v. Anderson*, 816 F.3d 262, 268 (4th Cir. 2016); *Killer Joe Nevada, LLC v. Does 1-20*, 807 F.3d 908, 913 (8th Cir. 2015).

[12] *Archdiocese of Milwaukee v. Doe*, 743 F.3d 1101, 1109 (7th Cir. 2014) (oral testimony not favored in summary judgment motions because of the temptation to make credibility determinations); *PAR Microsystems, Inc. v. Pinnacle Development Corp.*, 995 F. Supp. 655 (N.D. Tex. 1997) (oral testimony permitted only when a controlling credibility question is presented).

[13] *Smith v. Oakland County Circuit Court*, 344 F. Supp. 2d 1030, 1051 (E.D. Mich. 2004).

[14] *Sunseri v. Macro Cellular Partners*, 412 F.3d 1247, 1248 (11th Cir. 2005).

[15] *Pedraza v. Phoenix*, 1994 WL 177285 (S.D.N.Y. 1994) (no right to a court-ordered translation of pre-trial motions).

RULE 44
PROVING AN OFFICIAL RECORD

(a) **Means of Proving.**

(1) *Domestic Record.* Each of the following evidences an official record—or an entry in it—that is otherwise admissible and is kept within the United States, any state, district, or commonwealth, or any territory subject to the administrative or judicial jurisdiction of the United States:

(A) an official publication of the record; or

(B) a copy attested by the officer with legal custody of the record—or by the officer's deputy—and accompanied by a certificate that the officer has custody. The certificate must be made under seal:

(i) by a judge of a court of record in the district or political subdivision where the record is kept; or

(ii) by any public officer with a seal of office and with official duties in the district or political subdivision where the record is kept.

(2) *Foreign Record.*

(A) *In General.* Each of the following evidences a foreign official record—or an entry in it—that is otherwise admissible:

(i) an official publication of the record; or

(ii) the record—or a copy—that is attested by an authorized person and is accompanied either by a final certification of genuineness or by a certification under a treaty or convention to which the United States and the country where the record is located are parties.

(B) *Final Certification of Genuineness.* A final certification must certify the genuineness of the signature and official position of the attester or of any foreign official whose certificate of genuineness relates to the attestation or is in a chain of certificates of genuineness relating to the attestation. A final certification may be made by a secretary of a United States embassy or legation; by a consul general, vice consul, or consular agent of the United States; or by a diplomatic or consular official of the foreign country assigned or accredited to the United States.

(C) *Other Means of Proof.* If all parties have had a reasonable opportunity to investigate a foreign record's authenticity and accuracy, the court may, for good cause, either:

(i) admit an attested copy without final certification; or

(ii) permit the record to be evidenced by an attested summary with or without a final certification.

(b) **Lack of a Record.** A written statement that a diligent search of designated records revealed no record or entry of a specified tenor is admissible as evidence that the records contain no such record or entry. For domestic records, the statement must be authenticated under Rule 44(a)(1). For foreign records, the statement must comply with (a)(2)(C)(ii).

(c) **Other Proof.** A party may prove an official record—or an entry or lack of an entry in it—by any other method authorized by law.

[Amended effective July 1, 1966; August 1, 1987; December 1, 1991; April 30, 2007, effective December 1, 2007.]

AUTHORS' COMMENTARY ON RULE 44

PURPOSE AND SCOPE

Rule 44 describes methods for authenticating official records of the United States or foreign governments, such as a weather bureau record, a record of conviction, a tax return, or a marriage or birth certificate. A party may prove an official record by introducing an official publication of the record or by submitting a copy of the record accompanied by a certificate from the officer who has custody of the record. A party may prove lack of an official record—*e.g.*, no tax return exists—by introducing a written statement that a diligent search uncovered no record, accompanied by a certificate of the officer who would have custody of the record. Rule 44 is not the only mechanism for proving an official record, and Rule 44 explicitly authorizes proof by another method authorized by law.

RULE 44(a)(1)—MEANS OF PROVING; DOMESTIC RECORD

CORE CONCEPT

An official record kept within the United States is authenticated if it is an official publication or if it is a copy of an official record which is attested to by the legal custodian and accompanied by a certificate made by a judge or public officer with a seal of office.

APPLICATIONS

Official Record

"Official record" is not a defined term, but includes such documents as weather bureau records, records of conviction, tax returns, marriage and birth certificates, and selective service files. "Official" does not mean "public"; the public need not have access to "official records."

Not Summaries

The Rule applies only to the record itself, not to summaries of the contents of the record.

Authentication Only, Not Admissibility

Rule 44 only *authenticates* records. It does not render the records admissible or immune from other objections such as relevance or hearsay (but see the exception to the hearsay rule for official records).[1]

Official Publication

When a document has been printed by government authority, its authenticity is established.

Official Records Kept in the United States

Rule 44 applies to all official federal, state, or local records physically maintained within the United States or within territories subject to United States jurisdiction, not just to United States official records. Thus, it includes foreign government records maintained in the United States.

Attested Copy

A copy of an official record may be attested to by the officer having legal custody of the record or by the officer's deputy.[2]

- *Certificate:* The attested copy must be accompanied by a

[1] *Moreno v. Macaluso*, 844 F. Supp. 736 (M.D. Fla. 1994).

[2] *U.S. v. Estrada-Eliverio*, 583 F.3d 669, 672 (9th Cir. 2009).

certificate that the attesting individual has custody of the record.[3] The certificate may be made by a judge in the district or political subdivision in which the document is kept or by a public official with duties in the district or political subdivision in which the document is kept, provided that the official has a seal of office and authenticates the certificate with that seal.[4]

RULE 44(a)(2)—MEANS OF PROVING; FOREIGN RECORD

CORE CONCEPT

A foreign official record may be authenticated in essentially the same manner as a domestic record (described immediately above), with some minor variations.

APPLICATIONS

Official Publication

As with a domestic official record, official publications of foreign official records are self-authenticating.[5] Under this rule, a document that, on its face, appears to be an official publication will be admissible unless another party can demonstrate that it is not an official publication.[6] Official publications from a foreign government website will be accepted by the court as self-authenticating.[7]

Attested Copy with Certificate

A foreign official record may be attested to by any person authorized by the laws of that country to attest records if the signature is certified by a secretary of embassy or legation, consul general, consul, vice consul or consular agent of the United States, or a diplomatic or consular official of the foreign country assigned or accredited to the United States.[8] The certification will not be necessary if the United States and the foreign country are signatories to a treaty providing for proof of foreign records without a certification and the foreign record is submitted in accordance with the treaty.[9] In particular, see the

---

[3] *U.S. v. Estrada-Eliverio*, 583 F.3d 669, 672 (9th Cir. 2009); *Croy v. Ravalli Cty.*, 472 F. Supp. 3d 877, 887 (D. Mont. 2020).

[4] *Espinoza v. I.N.S.*, 45 F.3d 308 (9th Cir. 1995).

[5] *Rote v. Zel Custom Mfg., LLC*, 383 F. Supp. 3d 779, 785 (S.D. Ohio 2019); *Construction Drilling, Inc. v. Chusid*, 63 F. Supp. 2d 509 (D.N.J. 1999).

[6] *Rote v. Zel Custom Mfg., LLC*, 383 F. Supp. 3d 779, 785 (S.D. Ohio 2019).

[7] *Rote v. Zel Custom Mfg., LLC*, 383 F. Supp. 3d 779, 785 (S.D. Ohio 2019).

[8] *Starski v. Kirzhnev*, 682 F.3d 51, 53 (1st Cir. 2012); *U.S. v. Squillacote*, 221 F.3d 542 (4th Cir. 2000).

[9] *Corovic v. Mukasey*, 519 F.3d 90, 93 n.2 (2d Cir. 2008) (verification by apostille); *U.S. v. Pintado-Isiordia*, 448 F.3d 1155, 1157 (9th Cir. 2006).

Hague Public Documents Convention,[10] and the Convention Abolishing the Requirement of Legalization for Foreign Public Documents.[11]

- *Chain of Certifications:* An attestation may also be certified via a chain of certifications, as long as the chain leads to one of the officials listed above.[12]

Attested Copy Without Certificate

The court has discretion to admit an attested copy of a foreign official record without a certificate if all parties have had a reasonable opportunity to investigate the authenticity and accuracy of the record, or for good cause.[13]

RULE 44(b)—LACK OF A RECORD

CORE CONCEPT

A party may prove the absence of a particular record with a written statement that after diligent search, no record or entry of the specified nature exists. The statement must be authenticated in the same manner as for an official record.

RULE 44(c)—OTHER PROOF

CORE CONCEPT

The methods in Rule 44 are not exclusive.[14] Quite often, an official will testify as to the authenticity of an official record. Similarly, certain documents are self-authenticating under Rules 901 and 902 of the Federal Rules of Evidence.[15] Additionally Rule 902 allows the court to relax the Rule 44 authentication requirements if the party so requesting shows that it was unable to satisfy the Rule's requirements for authentication despite reasonable efforts.[16]

Additional Research References

Wright & Miller, *Federal Practice and Procedure* §§ 2431 to 2437

[10] Reprinted in *Martindale Hubbell*, Int'l Law Digests. *See also Jiang v. Gonzales*, 474 F.3d 25, 29 n. 4 (1st Cir. 2007); *Soonhee Kim v. Ferdinand*, 287 F. Supp. 3d 607, 624 (E.D. La. 2018).

[11] The Convention Abolishing the Requirement of Legalization for Foreign Public Documents may be found on WESTLAW in the IEL database, ci(vii-c & text).

[12] *See U.S. v. Squillacote*, 221 F.3d 542 (4th Cir. 2000).

[13] *Zhanling Jiang v. Holder*, 658 F.3d 1118, 1120 (9th Cir. 2011); *Vatyan v. Mukasey*, 508 F.3d 1179, 1184 (9th Cir. 2007) (only when party unable to satisfy the requirements despite reasonable efforts).

[14] *U.S. v. Lopez*, 747 F.3d 1141, 1150 n.5 (9th Cir. 2014) (FRE 901); *U.S. v. Estrada-Eliverio*, 583 F.3d 669, 672 (9th Cir. 2009).

[15] *See U.S. v. Lopez*, 747 F.3d 1141, 1150 n.5 (9th Cir. 2014).

[16] *Starski v. Kirzhnev*, 682 F.3d 51, 54 (1st Cir. 2012).

C.J.S., Evidence §§ 634 et seq.
West's Key Number Digest, Evidence ⇨366

RULE 44.1
DETERMINING FOREIGN LAW

A party who intends to raise an issue about a foreign country's law must give notice by a pleading or other writing. In determining foreign law, the court may consider any relevant material or source, including testimony, whether or not submitted by a party or admissible under the Federal Rules of Evidence. The court's determination must be treated as a ruling on a question of law.

[Added effective July 1, 1966; amended effective July 1, 1975; August 1, 1987; April 30, 2007, effective December 1, 2007.]

AUTHORS' COMMENTARY ON RULE 44.1

PURPOSE AND SCOPE

When a claim, defense, or other issue that arises under a foreign country's laws is before the court, the judge must determine the contents of that foreign law. Rule 44.1 establishes procedures when a party intends to raise such an issue of foreign law. It requires the party to provide notice of its intent to rely on foreign law, then authorizes the judge to rely on any relevant source of information to determine the foreign law, even if the information would otherwise be inadmissible under the Federal Rules of Evidence. Common methods of proving foreign law include treatises and testimony from lawyers familiar with the foreign law.

APPLICATIONS

Notice of Foreign Law Issue

A party must give written notice to the court and all other parties of its intent to raise an issue concerning foreign law.[1] The notice should specify the issues or claims purportedly governed by foreign law, but need not state the specific provi-

[1] *Azarax, Inc. v. Syverson*, 990 F.3d 648, 652 (8th Cir. 2021); *Malin Intern. Ship Repair & Drydock, Inc. v. Oceanografia, S.A. de C.V.*, 817 F.3d 241, 247 (5th Cir. 2016).

sions of the foreign law.[2] Failure to provide the required notice of intent to raise an issue concerning foreign law can result in a waiver of the right to raise the issue.[3] The notice may be included in a pleading or motion or may be a separate document.[4]

Timing for Notice

Rule 44.1 does not set a specific time for filing the notice.[5] If the notice is a separate document, it should be served as soon as possible to give a reasonable opportunity to all parties to prepare.[6] If not already raised, issues of foreign law are sometimes raised at the pretrial conference.[7] However, unwarranted delay in providing notice can result in waiver.[8]

Party Giving Notice

Notice is normally given by the party whose claim or defense is based on foreign law, but may be raised by any party. If one party has given notice, other parties can rely on that notice and do not need to provide their own notices.[9] If parties believe that a different foreign law applies from the law raised by another party, they should issue separate notices.

Court Determines Foreign Law

The determination of foreign law is a matter of law, not a matter of fact, and is therefore made by the court.[10]

Materials Used by the Court

The court may consider any relevant material or source to determine foreign law,[11] regardless of whether it is admissible.[12] Common methods of proving foreign law are through expert

[2]*See In re Griffin Trading Co.*, 683 F.3d 819, 822 (7th Cir. 2012) (notice only need be reasonable to avoid unfair surprise).

[3]*In re Magnetic Audiotape Antitrust Litig.*, 334 F.3d 204 (2d Cir. 2003); *In re Wachovia Equity Sec. Litig.*, 753 F. Supp. 2d 326, 380 n.49 (S.D.N.Y. 2011) (reservation of right in footnote insufficient notice).

[4]*Vexol, S.A. de C.V. v. Berry Plastics Corp.*, 882 F.3d 633, 635 (7th Cir. 2018) (notice in motion); *In re Griffin Trading Co.*, 683 F.3d 819, 822 (7th Cir. 2012) (notice in complaint); *Local 875 I.B.T. Pension Fund v. Pollack*, 992 F. Supp. 545 (E.D.N.Y. 1998) (notice in reply papers not sufficient).

[5]*Azarax, Inc. v. Syverson*, 990 F.3d 648, 652 (8th Cir. 2021); *Rationis Enterprises Inc. of Panama v. Hyundai Mipo Dockyard Co.*, 426 F.3d 580, 585 (2d Cir. 2005).

[6]*See APL Co. Pte. Ltd. v. UK Aerosols Ltd.*, 582 F.3d 947, 955 (9th Cir. 2009); *Rationis Enterprises Inc. of Panama v. Hyundai Mipo Dockyard Co., Ltd.*, 426 F.3d 580 (2d Cir. 2005); *Club Car, Inc. v. Club Car (Quebec) Import, Inc.*, 362 F.3d 775, 782 (11th Cir. 2004) (notice 2 weeks before trial reasonable).

[7]*Mutual Service Ins. Co. v. Frit Indus., Inc.*, 358 F.3d 1312, 1321 (11th Cir. 2004).

[8]*Azarax, Inc. v. Syverson*, 398 F. Supp. 3d 425, 434 (D. Minn. 2019).

[9]*In re Griffin Trading Co.*, 683 F.3d 819, 823 (7th Cir. 2012).

[10]*Animal Sci. Prod., Inc. v. Hebei Welcome Pharm. Co.*, 138 S. Ct. 1865, 1868 (2018).

[11]*Animal Sci. Prod., Inc. v. Hebei Welcome Pharm. Co.*, 138 S. Ct. 1865, 1868 (2018).

[12]*Animal Sci. Prod., Inc. v. Hebei

testimony or declarations,[13] affidavits from lawyers practicing in the foreign country,[14] case law or other legal materials from the foreign country,[15] and treatises.[16] The court is not limited by the materials that the parties submit,[17] and may also do its own research[18] or seek the aid of an expert witness to help in the interpretation of foreign law,[19] but is under no obligation to do so.[20] The court may also appoint a special master to determine foreign law.[21] A statement by a foreign government regarding the interpretation of its own laws is not binding, but is entitled to "respectful consideration."[22]

- *Hearing:* Even though the determination of foreign law is a matter of law, the court may conduct a hearing and take testimony (as would normally be undertaken for factual determinations).[23]
- *Disclosure of Experts:* Parties are not required to make the Rule 26(a)(2) disclosure of experts who will testify as to foreign law.[24]

Burden of Proof

The party seeking application of foreign law has the burden of proving the applicability and content of the foreign law.[25]

Absence of Proof/Presumption

In the absence of proof of foreign law, the court may presume that the foreign law would be the same as local law.[26]

Welcome Pharm. Co., 138 S. Ct. 1865, 1868 (2018).

[13]*See Fahmy v. Jay-Z*, 891 F.3d 823, 832 n.13 (9th Cir. 2018) (testimony); *de Fontbrune v. Wofsy*, 838 F.3d 992, 994 (9th Cir. 2016) (declarations).

[14]*Mamani v. Sanchez Bustamante*, 968 F.3d 1216, 1245 (11th Cir. 2020); *In re Vitamin C Antitrust Litig.*, 837 F.3d 175, 183 (2d Cir. 2016).

[15]*Clarke v. Marriott Int'l, Inc.*, 403 F. Supp. 3d 474, 481 (D.V.I. 2019).

[16]*See Access Telecom, Inc. v. MCI Telecommunications Corp.*, 197 F.3d 694, 713 (5th Cir. 1999).

[17]*Bugliotti v. Republic of Argentina*, 952 F.3d 410, 414 (2d Cir. 2020).

[18]*Hay Grp. Mgmt., Inc. v. Schneider*, 965 F.3d 244, 249 n.13 (3d Cir. 2020); *Cassirer v. Thyssen-Bornemisza Collection Found.*, 862 F.3d 951, 964 n.12 (9th Cir. 2017).

[19]*Rosales v. Lynch*, 821 F.3d 625, 629 n.12 (5th Cir. 2016).

[20]*Bodum USA, Inc. v. La Cafetiere, Inc.*, 621 F.3d 624, 628 (7th Cir. 2010); *Heng Ren Invs. LP v. Sinovac Biotech Ltd.*, 542 F. Supp. 3d 59, 67 (D. Mass. 2021).

[21]*Henry v. S/S Bermuda Star*, 863 F.2d 1225, 1227–28 & n.3 (5th Cir. 1989); *Bouchillon v. SAME Deutz-Fahr, Grp.*, 268 F. Supp. 3d 890, 906 (N.D. Miss. 2017).

[22]*Animal Sci. Prod., Inc. v. Hebei Welcome Pharm. Co.*, 138 S. Ct. 1865, 1868 (2018)

[23]*Bugliotti v. Republic of Argentina*, 952 F.3d 410, 413 (2d Cir. 2020).

[24]*Clarke v. Marriott Int'l, Inc.*, 403 F. Supp. 3d 474, 480 (D.V.I. 2019).

[25]*G & G Prods. LLC v. Rusic*, 902 F.3d 940, 947 (9th Cir. 2018); *Bel-Ray Co., Inc. v. Chemrite Ltd.*, 181 F.3d 435, 440 (3d Cir.1999).

[26]*MacDonald v. CashCall, Inc*, 883 F.3d 220, 228 (3d Cir. 2018); *but see Bugliotti v. Republic of Argentina*, 952 F.3d 410, 413 (2d Cir. 2020) (encouraging the trial court to make an independent determination of foreign

Motion to Dismiss/Motion for Summary Judgment

Because it is a legal determination, not a factual determination, a court may determine an issue of foreign law in the context of a motion to dismiss[27] or a motion for summary judgment.[28]

Choice of Law

Rule 44.1 is implicated only after the court has determined that a foreign country's laws apply using the forum State's choice of law provisions in diversity actions and federal common law choice of law rules for claims arising under federal statutes.[29]

Appellate Review

A ruling as to foreign law is interlocutory, and cannot be immediately appealed.

Additional Research References

Wright & Miller, *Federal Practice and Procedure* §§ 2441 to 2447
C.J.S., Evidence §§ 12 to 26
West's Key Number Digest, Action ⚷17

---

law).

[27]*de Fontbrune v. Wofsy*, 838 F.3d 992, 996 (9th Cir. 2016).

[28]*See Animal Sci. Prod., Inc. v. Hebei Welcome Pharm. Co.*, 138 S. Ct. 1865, 1868 (2018); *Gonzalez-Segura v. Sessions*, 882 F.3d 127, 130 (5th Cir. 2018) (differences of opinion do not create a genuine dispute of material fact).

[29]*See G & G Prods. LLC v. Rusic*, 902 F.3d 940, 947 (9th Cir. 2018); *Cassirer v. Thyssen-Bornemisza Collection Found.*, 862 F.3d 951, 961 (9th Cir. 2017).

RULE 45
SUBPOENA

(a) **In General.**

(1) *Form and Contents.*

(A) *Requirements—In General.* Every subpoena must:

(i) state the court from which it issued;

(ii) state the title of the action and its civil-action number;

(iii) command each person to whom it is directed to do the following at a specified time and place: attend and testify; produce designated documents, electronically stored information, or tangible things in that person's possession, custody, or control; or permit the inspection of premises; and

(iv) set out the text of Rule 45(d) and (e).

(B) *Command to Attend a Deposition—Notice of the Recording Method.* A subpoena commanding attendance at a deposition must state the method for recording the testimony.

(C) *Combining or Separating a Command to Produce or to Permit Inspection; Specifying the Form for Electronically Stored Information.* A command to produce documents, electronically stored information, or tangible things or to permit the inspection of premises may be included in a subpoena commanding attendance at a deposition, hearing, or trial, or may be set out in a separate subpoena. A subpoena may specify the form or forms in which electronically stored information is to be produced.

(D) *Command to Produce; Included Obligations.* A command in a subpoena to produce documents, electronically stored information, or tangible things requires the responding person to permit inspection, copying, testing, or sampling of the materials.

(2) *Issuing Court.* A subpoena must issue from the court where the action is pending.

(3) *Issued by Whom.* The clerk must issue a subpoena, signed but otherwise in blank, to a party who requests it. That party must complete it before service. An attorney also may issue and sign a subpoena if the attorney is authorized to practice in the issuing court.

(4) *Notice to Other Parties Before Service.* If the subpoena commands the production of documents, electronically stored information, or tangible things or the inspection of premises before trial, then before it is served on the person to whom it is directed, a notice and a copy of the subpoena must be served on each party.

(b) **Service.**

(1) *By Whom and How; Tendering Fees.* Any person who is at least 18 years old and not a party may serve a subpoena. Serving a subpoena requires delivering a copy to the named person and, if the subpoena requires that person's attendance, tendering the fees for 1 day's attendance and the mileage allowed by law. Fees and mileage need not be tendered when the subpoena issues on behalf of the United States or any of its officers or agencies.

(2) *Service in the United States.* A subpoena may be served at any place within the United States.

(3) *Service in a Foreign Country.* 28 U.S.C. § 1783 governs issuing and serving a subpoena directed to a United States national or resident who is in a foreign country.

(4) *Proof of Service.* Proving service, when necessary, requires filing with the issuing court a statement showing the date and manner of service and the names of the persons served. The statement must be certified by the server.

(c) **Place of Compliance.**

(1) *For a Trial, Hearing, or Deposition.* A subpoena may command a person to attend a trial, hearing, or deposition only as follows:

(A) within 100 miles of where the person resides,

is employed, or regularly transacts business in person; or

(B) within the state where the person resides, is employed, or regularly transacts business in person, if the person

(i) is a party or a party's officer; or

(ii) is commanded to attend a trial and would not incur substantial expense.

(2) *For Other Discovery.* A subpoena may command:

(A) production of documents, electronically stored information, or tangible things at a place within 100 miles of where the person resides, is employed, or regularly transacts business in person; and

(B) inspection of premises at the premises to be inspected.

(d) **Protecting a Person Subject to a Subpoena; Enforcement.**

(1) *Avoiding Undue Burden or Expense; Sanctions.* A party or attorney responsible for issuing and serving a subpoena must take reasonable steps to avoid imposing undue burden or expense on a person subject to the subpoena. The court for the district where compliance is required must enforce this duty and impose an appropriate sanction—which may include lost earnings and reasonable attorney's fees—on a party or attorney who fails to comply.

(2) *Command to Produce Materials or Permit Inspection.*

(A) *Appearance Not Required.* A person commanded to produce documents, electronically stored information, or tangible things, or to permit the inspection of premises, need not appear in person at the place of production or inspection unless also commanded to appear for a deposition, hearing, or trial.

(B) *Objections.* A person commanded to produce documents or tangible things or to permit inspection may serve on the party or attorney designated in the subpoena a written objection to inspecting, copying, testing, or sampling any or all of the materials or to inspecting the premises—or to producing electronically stored information in the form or forms requested. The objection must be served before the earlier of the time specified for compliance or 14 days after the subpoena is served. If an objection is made, the following rules apply:

(i) At any time, on notice to the commanded person, the serving party may move the court for the district where compliance is required for an order compelling production or inspection.

(ii) These acts may be required only as directed in the order, and the order must protect a person who is neither a party nor a party's officer from significant expense resulting from compliance.

(3) *Quashing or Modifying a Subpoena.*

(A) *When Required.* On timely motion, the court for the district where compliance is required must quash or modify a subpoena that:

(i) fails to allow a reasonable time to comply;

(ii) requires a person to comply beyond the geographical limits specified in Rule 45(c);

(iii) requires disclosure of privileged or other protected matter, if no exception or waiver applies; or

(iv) subjects a person to undue burden.

(B) *When Permitted.* To protect a person subject to or affected by a subpoena, the court for the district where compliance is required may, on motion, quash or modify the subpoena if it requires:

(i) disclosing a trade secret or other confidential research, development, or commercial information; or

(ii) disclosing an unretained expert's opinion or information that does not describe specific occurrences in dispute and results from the expert's study that was not requested by a party.

(C) *Specifying Conditions as an Alternative.* In the circumstances described in Rule 45(d)(3)(B), the court may, instead of quashing or modifying a subpoena, order appearance or production under specified conditions if the serving party:

(i) shows a substantial need for the testimony or material that cannot be otherwise met without undue hardship; and

(ii) ensures that the subpoenaed person will be reasonably compensated.

(e) **Duties in Responding to a Subpoena.**

(1) *Producing Documents or Electronically Stored Information.* These procedures apply to producing documents or electronically stored information:

(A) *Documents.* A person responding to a subpoena to produce documents must produce them as they are kept in the ordinary course of business or must organize and label them to correspond to the categories in the demand.

(B) *Form for Producing Electronically Stored Information Not Specified.* If a subpoena does not specify a form for producing electronically stored information, the person responding must produce it in a form or forms in which it is ordinarily maintained or in a reasonably usable form or forms.

(C) *Electronically Stored Information Produced in Only One Form.* The person responding need not produce the same electronically stored information in more than one form.

(D) *Inaccessible Electronically Stored Information.* The person responding need not provide discovery of electronically stored information from sources that the person identifies as not reasonably accessible because of undue burden or cost. On motion to compel discovery or for a protective order, the person responding must show that the information is not reasonably accessible because of undue burden or cost. If that showing is made, the court may nonetheless order discovery from such sources if the requesting party shows good cause, considering the limitations of Rule 26(b)(2)(C). The court may specify conditions for the discovery.

(2) *Claiming Privilege or Protection.*

(A) *Information Withheld.* A person withholding subpoenaed information under a claim that it is privileged or subject to protection as trial-preparation material must:

(i) expressly make the claim; and

(ii) describe the nature of the withheld documents, communications, or tangible things in a manner that, without revealing information itself privileged or protected, will enable the parties to assess the claim.

(B) *Information Produced.* If information produced in response to a subpoena is subject to a claim of privilege or of protection as trial-preparation material, the person making the claim may notify any party that received the information of the claim and the basis for it. After being notified, a party must promptly return, sequester, or destroy the specified information and any copies it has; must not use or disclose the information until the claim is resolved; must take reasonable steps to retrieve the information if the party disclosed it before being notified; and may promptly present the information under seal to the court for the district where compliance is required for a determination of the claim. The person who produced the information must preserve the information until the claim is resolved.

(f) **Transferring a Subpoena-Related Motion.** When the court where compliance is required did not issue the subpoena, it may transfer a motion under this rule to the issuing court if the person subject to the subpoena consents or if the court finds exceptional circumstances. Then, if the attorney for a person subject to a subpoena is authorized to practice in the court where the motion was made, the attorney may file papers and appear on the motion as an officer of the issuing court. To enforce its order, the issuing court may transfer the order to the court where the motion was made.

(g) **Contempt.** The court for the district where compliance is required—and also, after a motion is transferred, the issuing court—may hold in contempt a person who, having been served, fails without adequate excuse to obey the subpoena or an order related to it.

[Amended December 27, 1946, effective March 19, 1948; December 29, 1948, effective October 20, 1949; March 30, 1970, effective July 1, 1970; April 29, 1980, effective August 1, 1980; April 29, 1985, effective August 1, 1985; March 2, 1987, effective August 1, 1987; April 30, 1991, effective December 1, 1991; April 25, 2005, effective December 1, 2005; April 12, 2006, effective December 1, 2006; April 30, 2007, effective December 1, 2007; April 16, 2013, effective December 1, 2013.]

AUTHORS' COMMENTARY ON RULE 45

PURPOSE AND SCOPE

Rule 45 governs subpoenas, which are the mechanism for obtaining discovery and testimony from ***nonparties***, as well as for obtaining the testimony of a party at a hearing or trial. Because nonparties typically have no stake in the outcome of the litigation, however, the discovery allowed of nonparties is more limited than discovery of parties. A party may only issue a subpoena to a nonparty to compel two actions: 1) testimony at a deposition, hearing, or trial (sometimes called a subpoena *ad testificandum*); and 2) production of documents (sometimes called a subpoena *duces tecum*) or inspection of property or tangible things—subpoenas cannot compel other discovery like interrogatories or requests for admission.

Issuing a subpoena does not require the judge's involvement, or even permission. Nor does it require assistance from the clerk's office or the U.S. Marshals. Rather, attorneys are authorized to issue subpoenas. Form subpoenas are generally available from court websites, with blanks to be filled in with the pertinent information. They are then served by any nonparty who is over 18 years old. If the subpoena requires attendance (such as at a deposition or hearing), the service must also include one day's attendance fee and mileage.

There are limits on both the location and burdensomeness of the tasks that may be compelled by subpoena. The limits on the location of the tasks are designed to protect the recipient from undue burden. Of course, every subpoena subjects the recipient to burden, so Rule 45 only attempts to minimize that burden, not eliminate it. Accordingly, in many circumstances, a subpoena may only compel performance by a nonparty within 100 miles of where the nonparty resides, is employed, or regularly transacts business in person. In addition, Rule 45 imposes an obligation on a party serving a subpoena to avoid imposing undue burden or expense on the recipient. Rules 45(d) and (e) set forth a variety of protections for subpoena recipients in language that must be included in the subpoena (thus alerting subpoena recipients to their duties and rights).

One particularly powerful protection for recipients of a subpoena to produce documents or permit an inspection is the right to send a written objection to the party serving the subpoena. That objection relieves the recipient of the duty to perform the tasks in the subpoena and shifts the burden to the issuing party to obtain a court order compelling compliance. This objection right is not available to the recipient of a subpoena to testify—to avoid the obligation to appear, the recipient would need to file a motion to quash or modify the subpoena or a motion for a protective order.

Performance of the tasks in the subpoena proceed much like the equivalent discovery tasks. If the subpoena is for a deposition, the deposition proceeds like any other deposition except that, typically, the attorneys for the parties do not represent the witness, and thus generally may not instruct the witness not to answer questions. Sometimes, the nonparty recipient will bring counsel to the deposition, and the witness's counsel may instruct the witness not to answer a question in accordance with the limitations in Rule 30.

If the subpoena requires production of documents, it will include a list of the documents to be produced. The rules for document production in Rule 34 generally apply, such that the subpoena will apply to documents in the recipient's possession, custody, or control that are responsive and within the scope of discovery in Rule 26(b)(1)—nonprivileged matter relevant to any party's claim or defense and proportional to the needs of the case.

RULE 45(a)—IN GENERAL

CORE CONCEPT

Parties to legal proceedings have the power to issue a subpoena compelling a nonparty to: appear and testify at a designated time and location in a deposition, hearing, or trial; produce documents or things, or permit the inspection of premises.

APPLICATIONS

Contents

Every subpoena should:

(1) state the name of the court issuing the subpoena;[1]
(2) contain the caption and civil action number of the case;[2]
(3) command the recipient to appear and give testimony (describing the method of recording if the testimony is to be given at a deposition[3]), to produce for inspection the documents, electronically stored information, or things described in the subpoena or in an attachment thereto,[4] or to permit inspection of premises at a designated time and location;[5] and
(4) recite the language in subsections (c) and (d) of Rule 45.

NOTE: Blank subpoenas generally are available on the uscourts.gov website or at the clerk's office and will include the requisite language.

Scope

Subpoenas are limited to two functions: compelling a witness to testify (in the old days, sometimes called a subpoena *ad testificandum*) and compelling a nonparty to permit the inspection of documents, tangible things, or property (sometimes called a subpoena *duces tecum*). Thus, a party cannot, by subpoena, compel a nonparty to answer interrogatories, answer requests for admission, preserve documents, or submit to a medical examination under Rule 35.[6] The scope of documents or information that can be obtained by subpoena is the same as the scope of discovery generally under Rule 26.[7]

Issuance

Typically, a subpoena is issued by an attorney authorized to practice in the issuing court.[8] This applies equally to attorneys admitted *pro hac vice* (for one matter only). To be effective, the subpoena must be signed by the issuing attorney.[9] A subpoena may also be issued by the clerk of court.[10]

Which Court

All subpoenas are issued from the court where the action is

---

[1] *Morris v. Sequa Corp.*, 275 F.R.D. 562, 565 (N.D. Ala. 2011).

[2] *U.S. v. Patiwana*, 267 F. Supp. 2d 301 (E.D.N.Y. 2003) (enforcing subpoena despite failure to include a civil action number).

[3] *Simon v. FIA Card Servs., N.A.*, 732 F.3d 259, 268 (3d Cir. 2013).

[4] *Insituform Technologies, Inc. v. Cat Contracting, Inc.*, 168 F.R.D. 630, 633 (N.D. Ill. 1996).

[5] *Kinetic Concepts, Inc. v. Convatec Inc.*, 268 F.R.D. 226, 240 (M.D.N.C. 2010).

[6] *Dunlap v. Presidential Advisory Comm'n on Election Integrity*, 319 F. Supp. 3d 70, 102 (D.D.C. 2018) (subpoena cannot compel document preservation).

[7] *Jordan v. Comm'r, Mississippi Dep't of Corr.*, 947 F.3d 1322, 1329 (11th Cir. 2020).

[8] *U.S. S.E.C. v. Hyatt*, 621 F.3d 687, 693 (7th Cir. 2010).

[9] *See Akande v. Philips*, 386 F. Supp. 3d 281, 297 (W.D.N.Y. 2019); *Atlantic Inv. Mgmt., LLC v. Millennium Fund I, Ltd.*, 212 F.R.D. 395, 397 (N.D. Ill. 2002) (lack of signature waived by conduct of recipient).

[10] *U.S. S.E.C. v. Hyatt*, 621 F.3d 687, 693 (7th Cir. 2010).

pending (even for a deposition occurring outside the district or state where the action is pending).[11]

Number

There is no limit on the number of subpoenas in a civil action (but the limits on the number and duration of depositions in Rule 30 will apply to depositions taken pursuant to subpoena).

Time for Service of Subpoenas

The majority of the courts treat subpoenas to testify at depositions or for production of documents as discovery activities that must be issued within the discovery deadlines.[12] Subpoenas for trial testimony may be served at any time.

Subpoenas to Produce Documents

Nonparties may be compelled to produce documents in their possession, custody, or control pursuant to a subpoena *duces tecum*.[13] The provisions of Rule 34(a) governing documents in the responding party's "possession, custody, or control" (described in detail in the coverage of Rule 34(a) above) also apply to subpoenas.[14] The nonparty must produce responsive documents even though many or all of them are likely to also be in the possession, custody, or control of a party.[15] A subpoena for documents may be a stand-alone document or may be combined with a subpoena to testify.[16]

- *Advance Notice of Document Subpoena:* Prior to serving a subpoena for the production of documents, the issuing party must provide notice and a copy of the subpoena to all other parties.[17] The purpose of this requirement is to give other parties an opportunity to object to or challenge the subpoena before the production occurs.[18]
- *Electronically Stored Information:* Rule 45 allows a party to subpoena electronically stored information or ESI.[19] Provisions regarding subpoenas for ESI are set forth in Rule 45(e) below.
- *Asserting Privileges:* The recipient of a subpoena *duces*

[11] *Morrill v. Scott Fin. Corp.*, 873 F.3d 1136, 1146 n.3 (9th Cir. 2017).

[12] *See Buhrmaster v. Overnite Transp. Co.*, 61 F.3d 461, 464 (6th Cir. 1995); *Akande v. Philips*, 386 F. Supp. 3d 281, 298 (W.D.N.Y. 2019).

[13] *Sergeeva v. Tripleton Int'l Ltd.*, 834 F.3d 1194, 1200 (11th Cir. 2016).

[14] *See Acosta v. La Piedad Corp.*, 894 F.3d 947, 951–52 (8th Cir. 2018).

[15] *In re Novo Nordisk Sec. Litig.*, 530 F. Supp. 3d 495, 502 (D.N.J. 2021).

[16] *El Encanto, Inc. v. Hatch Chile Co., Inc.*, 825 F.3d 1161, 1163 (10th Cir. 2016).

[17] *Petrie v. Electronic Game Card, Inc.*, 761 F.3d 959, 967 n.9 (9th Cir. 2014); *Planet Fitness Int'l Franchise v. JEG-United, LLC*, — F. Supp. 3d —, 2022 WL 1444504, at *2 (D.N.H. 2022).

[18] The Advisory Committee Note to the 2013 Amendments to Rule 45 (noting that this requirement already existed but was frequently violated).

[19] *See Lofton v. Verizon Wireless (VAW) LLC*, 308 F.R.D. 276, 290 (N.D. Cal. 2015); *St. Jude Medical S.C., Inc. v. Janssen-Counotte*, 305 F.R.D. 630, 638 (D. Or. 2015).

tecum may refuse to produce privileged documents.[20] Rule 45(e) contains provisions regarding the assertion of privileges. If the issuing party chooses to contest the privilege assertion, that party can move to compel production of the withheld documents pursuant to Rule 37(a) and can request that the court conduct an *in camera* inspection of such documents. Another party may also move to quash a subpoena to protect its privileged documents.[21]

Subpoena to Inspect Property

A subpoena may be used to obtain inspection, testing, or sampling of the real or personal property of a nonparty.[22]

Subpoena for Testimony

A subpoena may be used to compel a nonparty to testify at a deposition[23] (parties are compelled to testify at depositions by deposition notice under Rule 30, without the need for a subpoena). A subpoena may also be used to compel a witness—party or nonparty—to appear and testify at a hearing or trial.[24]

Subpoenas to Parties Unnecessary for Discovery Purposes

A subpoena is not necessary to take the deposition of a party or an officer, director, or managing agent of a party,[25] or to compel a party to produce documents;[26] a notice of deposition pursuant to Rule 30(b) or Rule 31(a) or a document request under Rule 34 is sufficient.[27] A subpoena is necessary for all other employees of corporations or other entities,[28] and to compel parties to appear and testify at hearings or trials.[29]

Organization Representative

Like the procedure for taking the deposition of the representative of a party that is a corporation or other type of organization under Rule 30(b)(6), a party may use a subpoena to

---

[20] *In re Motion to Compel Compliance with Subpoena Directed to Cooke Legal Grp., PLLC*, 333 F.R.D. 291, 294 (D.D.C. 2019); *In re Teligent, Inc.*, 459 B.R. 190, 199–200 (S.D.N.Y. 2011).

[21] *Williams v. Big Picture Loans, LLC*, 303 F. Supp. 3d 434, 440 (E.D. Va. 2018).

[22] *Fitzpatrick v. Arco Marine, Inc.*, 199 F.R.D. 663, 664 (C.D. Cal. 2001) (inspection of a ship).

[23] *Garrett v. Hanson*, 429 F. Supp. 3d 311, 318 (E.D. Tex. 2019).

[24] *See Chao v. Tyson Foods, Inc.*, 255 F.R.D. 556, 557–58 (N.D. Ala. 2009).

[25] *E.I. DuPont de Nemours and Co. v. Kolon Indus., Inc.*, 268 F.R.D. 45, 48 (E.D. Va. 2010) (the law is sketchy as to who is considered a managing agent).

[26] *Dixon v. Ford Motor Credit Co.*, 2000 WL 1182274 (E.D. La. 2000).

[27] *COMSAT Corp. v. National Sci. Found.*, 190 F.3d 269, 278 (4th Cir. 1999); *but see First City, Texas-Houston, N.A. v. Rafidain Bank*, 197 F.R.D. 250, 254 (S.D.N.Y. 2000) (nothing in the Rules prevents issuing a subpoena to a party).

[28] *Memory Bowl v. North Pointe Ins. Co.*, 280 F.R.D. 181, 187 (D.N.J. 2012).

[29] *See Chao v. Tyson Foods, Inc.*, 255 F.R.D. 556, 557–58 (N.D. Ala. 2009).

take the deposition of a representative of a nonparty organization, describing the information sought in the subpoena and requiring the organization to designate a representative qualified to testify about the designated issues.[30]

Subpoenas to Experts

The case law is unsettled as to when it is proper to issue subpoenas to expert witnesses, and if so for what purposes. Some courts hold that it is improper to issue a subpoena to an expert retained by another party because discovery of such experts should proceed through the party who designated the expert pursuant to Rules 26(a)(2) and the protections in Rule 26(b)(4).[31] Other courts, however, do not categorically prohibit such subpoenas.[32] When the expert has not been designated by one of the parties, the protections in Rule 45(d)(3)(B) apply, as discussed below.

United States or States

As a general rule, agencies and representatives of the United States or a State must comply with subpoenas.[33]

RULE 45(b)—SERVICE

CORE CONCEPT

Subpoenas may be served at any place within the United States (nationwide service) by any nonparty at least 18 years old.

APPLICATIONS

Manner of Service

Service is accomplished by "delivery" to the named person.[34] The courts are divided as to whether that delivery must be personal, in-hand service or can be accomplished by delivery to the recipient's residence or place of business.[35] Service upon the witness's lawyer is not sufficient.

- *Serving a Corporation:* Service of a subpoena on a corporation is controlled by Rule 4(h)(1). That Rule authorizes service on a corporation: 1) in the same manner for serving an individual; or 2) by delivering a copy to an officer, managing agent, or agent authorized for

[30]*Price Waterhouse LLP v. First Am. Corp.*, 182 F.R.D. 56, 61 (S.D.N.Y. 1998).

[31]*Sines v. Darling Ingredients, Inc.*, 2022 WL 1554824, *20 (D.N.M. 2022).

[32]*See Profitt v. Highlands Hosp. Corp.*, 2022 WL 409696, at *4 (E.D. Ky. 2022).

[33]*Ott v. City of Milwaukee*, 682 F.3d 552, 557 (7th Cir. 2012) (state agencies); *Yousuf v. Samantar*, 451 F.3d 248, 251–53 (D.C. Cir. 2006) (agencies of the United States).

[34]*SiteLock, LLC v. GoDaddy.com, LLC*, 338 F.R.D. 146, 148 (D. Or. 2021).

[35]*See Ott v. City of Milwaukee*, 682 F.3d 552, 557 (7th Cir. 2012) (personal service not required); *Dyno Nobel, Inc. v. Johnson*, __ F. Supp. 3d __, 2022 WL 507431, at *2 (E.D. Ky. 2022) (majority of courts require personal service); *Castleberry v. Camden Cty.*, 331 F.R.D. 559, 651–62 (S.D. Ga. 2019) (discussing the split authority).

service of process.[36]

Place of Service

A subpoena may be served at any place within the United States.[37] That does not mean that the recipient must travel throughout the United States—limits on the distance that a subpoena may require the recipient to travel are set forth in Rule 45(c). Thus, for example, if a party in a case pending in New York wants to take the deposition of a nonparty residing in California, the party may issue a subpoena from New York, serve it in California on the nonparty, then conduct the deposition within 100 miles of the nonparty's residence.

- *Service on a Corporation or Entity:* There is some authority suggesting that a corporation may only be served where it has minimum contacts.[38]

Who May Serve

A subpoena may be served by any person who is at least 18 years old and who is not a party.[39] The U.S. Marshals may serve subpoenas, which a party may seek by motion to the judge handling the case.[40] Subpoenas are often served by a hired process server.[41]

Tender of Expenses

If the recipient's attendance is commanded, service must be accompanied by the tender of the fees and expenses for a one-day appearance,[42] unless the issuing party is the United States or a United States officer or agency. There is no requirement to tender witness fees and expenses when the subpoena is only for the production of documents.[43] The amount of fees and expenses is controlled by 28 U.S.C.A. § 1821.[44]

Subpoena to Non-US Citizens

A subpoena may be served on someone who is not a citizen or resident of the United States, as long as it is served within the United States.[45] However, the court must have personal

---

[36] *In re Newbrook Shipping Corp.*, 31 F.4th 889, 897 (4th Cir. 2022).

[37] *Managed Care Advisory Grp., LLC v. CIGNA Healthcare, Inc.*, 939 F.3d 1145, 1154 (11th Cir. 2019).

[38] *See Gucci Am., Inc. v. Weixing Li*, 768 F.3d 122, 141 n.20 (2d Cir. 2014).

[39] *Harden v. Hillman*, 993 F.3d 465, 476 (6th Cir. 2021).

[40] *See Harden v. Hillman*, 993 F.3d 465, 476 (6th Cir. 2021).

[41] *See Harden v. Hillman*, 993 F.3d 465, 476 (6th Cir. 2021).

[42] *Hill v. Homeward Residential, Inc.*, 799 F.3d 544, 553 (6th Cir. 2015); *In re Dennis*, 330 F.3d 696, 704–05 (5th Cir. 2003) (mileage need not be precise, only a reasonable estimate).

[43] *U.S. E.E.O.C. v. Laidlaw Waste, Inc.*, 934 F. Supp. 286, 290 n.6 (N.D. Ill. 1996).

[44] 28 U.S.C.A. § 1821 is reprinted in this book. *See also Fisher v. Ford Motor Co.*, 178 F.R.D. 195 (N.D. Ohio 1998).

[45] *Instituto Mexicano del Seguro Soc. v. Zimmer Biomet Holdings, Inc.*, 518 F. Supp. 3d 1258, 1267 (N.D. Ind.

jurisdiction over the recipient in order to enforce the subpoena.[46]

Service in Foreign Countries

Under certain circumstances, a national or resident of the United States subject to the jurisdiction of the court may be in a foreign country. The procedure for issuing a subpoena to compel such a witness to testify at trial is governed by 28 U.S.C.A. § 1783 (the Walsh Act),[47] which provides for the issuance of such a subpoena if the court finds that the witness's testimony or documents are "necessary in the interest of justice," and it is not possible to obtain the testimony or documents by other means. The person serving such a subpoena must advance the recipient's estimated travel expenses.

NOTE: The Walsh Act only governs issuing a subpoena to a trial witness. Rule 30 discusses how and when foreign witnesses may be deposed.

Proof of Service

If necessary, service can be proved by filing a statement of the date and manner of service, certified by the person making service.[48]

Notice to Other Parties

If the subpoena is for a deposition, a notice of deposition and the subpoena must be served on all parties pursuant to Rule 30 or 31. If the subpoena requires the production of documents or inspection of premises, notice must be served upon all parties prior to service on the recipient so that the other parties may assert any privileges or objections and may obtain the same or additional documents.[49]

Arbitrations

The federal courts can enforce subpoenas issued by arbitrators under the provisions of the Federal Arbitration Act, 9 U.S.C.A. § 1 et seq.[50]

RULE 45(c)—PLACE OF COMPLIANCE

CORE CONCEPT

The recipient of a subpoena generally will not be required to travel more than 100 miles from where the recipient resides, works, or regularly transacts business to produce documents or provide deposition testimony. A recipient may be required to

---

2021); *Probulk Carriers Ltd. v. Marvel Int'l Mgmt. and Transportation*, 180 F. Supp. 3d 290, 292 (S.D.N.Y. 2016).

[46] *Leibovitch v. Islamic Republic of Iran*, 852 F.3d 687, 689–90 (7th Cir. 2017).

[47] *Curtis v. Galakatos*, 19 F.4th 41, 50 n.6 (1st Cir. 2021).

[48] *See United States v. Ray*, 337 F.R.D. 561, 575 (S.D.N.Y. 2020).

[49] *Josendis v. Wall to Wall Residence Repairs, Inc.*, 662 F.3d 1292, 1303 n.17 (11th Cir. 2011); *Williams v. Thaler*, 602 F.3d 291, 311 (5th Cir. 2010).

[50] *Managed Care Advisory Grp., LLC v. CIGNA Healthcare, Inc.*, 939 F.3d 1145, 1154 (11th Cir. 2019).

travel anywhere within the state where the person resides, works, or regularly transacts business to give testimony if the person is a party, an officer of a party, or is commanded to testify at trial.

APPLICATIONS

Testimony at Deposition

A subpoena to compel a nonparty to testify at a deposition may require the recipient to travel at most 100 miles from where the recipient resides, is employed, or regularly transacts business in person.[51] Compelling a *party* to give deposition testimony is controlled by Rule 30.

Testimony at Hearing

A subpoena to testify at a hearing may require a nonparty recipient to travel at most 100 miles from where the recipient resides, is employed, or regularly transacts business in person.[52] If the recipient is a party or officer of a party, the recipient may be required to travel up to 100 miles from, or anywhere within the state, where the recipient resides, is employed, or regularly transacts business in person.[53] These limitations also apply to arbitration hearings.[54]

Testimony at Trial

A subpoena to testify at trial may require the recipient to travel up to 100 miles from, or anywhere within the state, where the recipient resides, is employed, or regularly transacts business in person, unless a nonparty witness would incur substantial expense if required to travel from a location that is within the state but more than 100 miles.[55] If a nonparty recipient would incur substantial expense to travel within the state but more than 100 miles, the issuing party can reimburse the recipient for the travel expenses, thereby requiring the recipient to travel within the state.[56]

Remote Testimony

When a witness will provide testimony remotely, the courts are divided as to whether the place of compliance should be deemed to be the location of the hearing or trial or should be the location of the witness.[57]

---

[51] *Planet Fitness Int'l Franchise v. JEG-United, LLC*, — F. Supp. 3d —, 2022 WL 1444504, at *3 (D.N.H. 2022) (vacation property does not constitute residence); *Saget v. Trump*, 351 F. Supp. 3d 251, 253 (E.D.N.Y. 2019).

[52] *Saget v. Trump*, 351 F. Supp. 3d 251, 253 (E.D.N.Y. 2019).

[53] Rule 45(c)(1)(B)(i).

[54] *Broumand v. Joseph*, 522 F. Supp. 3d 8, 21–22 (S.D.N.Y. 2021).

[55] *Good v. BioLife Plasma Servs., L.P.*, — F. Supp. 3d —, 2022 WL 1837071, at *5 (E.D. Mich. 2022); *Garrett v. Hanson*, 429 F. Supp. 3d 311, 318 (E.D. Tex. 2019).

[56] The Advisory Committee Note to the 2013 Amendments to Rule 45.

[57] *See Broumand v. Joseph*, 522 F. Supp. 3d 8, 23 (S.D.N.Y. 2021) (place of hearing); *In re Newbrook Shipping Corp.*, 498 F. Supp. 3d 807, 815 (D. Md. 2020) (place of witness).

Production of Documents, ESI, and Tangible Things

A subpoena to produce documents, ESI, or tangible things may require the recipient to travel at most 100 miles from where the recipient resides, is employed, or regularly transacts business in person.[58] Note that this limitation pertains to the place of production, not the location of the documents—a recipient will have to produce documents within its possession, custody, or control, regardless of the location of the documents.[59] ESI is typically exchanged electronically, rendering distance limitations inapplicable.[60] Likewise, if the responding party can simply mail responsive paper documents, the distance limitation may not apply.[61]

- *Place of Compliance for Corporation or Entity:* A corporation's compliance obligations are measured from its headquarters.[62]

Inspection of Premises

A subpoena to inspect premises is performed at the premises to be inspected.

RULE 45(d)—PROTECTING A PERSON SUBJECT TO A SUBPOENA; ENFORCEMENT

CORE CONCEPT

An attorney has a duty not to issue a subpoena for improper purposes or to impose undue burden on the recipient of the subpoena. Rule 45(d) provides mechanisms to challenge a subpoena that violates these duties.

APPLICATIONS

Duty to Avoid Undue Burden

An attorney issuing a subpoena has a duty to avoid causing undue burden on or expense to the recipient or any other person.[63] Some courts use the proportionality concepts from

[58] *Europlay Capital Advisors, LLC v. Does*, 323 F.R.D. 628, 629 (C.D. Cal. 2018); *Total Rx Care, LLC v. Great N. Ins. Co.*, 318 F.R.D. 587, 592 (N.D. Tex. 2017).

[59] *Sergeeva v. Tripleton Int'l Ltd.*, 834 F.3d 1194, 1200 (11th Cir. 2016); *In re Motion to Compel Compliance with Subpoena Directed to Cooke Legal Grp., PLLC*, 333 F.R.D. 291, 296 (D.D.C. 2019).

[60] *See Planet Fitness Int'l Franchise v. JEG-United, LLC*, — F. Supp. 3d —, 2022 WL 1444504, at *3 (D.N.H. 2022); *Dyno Nobel, Inc. v. Johnson*, — F. Supp. 3d —, 2022 WL 507431, at *3 (E.D. Ky. 2022).

[61] *See Planet Fitness Int'l Franchise v. JEG-United, LLC*, — F. Supp. 3d —, 2022 WL 1444504, at *3 (D.N.H. 2022); *Dyno Nobel, Inc. v. Johnson*, — F. Supp. 3d —, 2022 WL 507431, at *3 (E.D. Ky. 2022).

[62] *See In re Rule 45 Subpoenas Issued to Google LLC & LinkedIn Corp. Dated July 23, 2020*, 337 F.R.D. 639, 646 (N.D. Cal. 2020).

[63] *Virginia Dep't of Corr. v. Jordan*, 921 F.3d 180, 189 (4th Cir. 2019) (duty encompasses burdens on any person); *Legal Voice v. Stormans Inc.*, 738 F.3d 1178, 1185 (9th Cir. 2013).

Rule 26(b)(1) to analyze whether expense or burden is "undue."[64] Many courts also recognize that nonparties, who typically do not have any stake in the outcome of the litigation, should not be subjected to the same burdens as parties.[65] The court *must* enforce this duty and *must* impose an appropriate sanction, which may include attorney's fees and lost wages, on a party or attorney who fails to comply with this duty.[66]

Attendance by Person Producing Documents

A person subpoenaed to produce documents or things or to permit an inspection need not actually appear at the designated time, as long as the person complies with the subpoena.[67]

Objection to Subpoena to Produce Documents

A person subpoenaed to produce documents or things or to permit an inspection may serve an objection to all or part of the subpoena within 14 days after service of the subpoena (or before the time designated in the subpoena, if sooner).[68] Objections to subpoenas are customarily made by letter.[69] Once an objection has been served on the party issuing the subpoena, the subpoena recipient is not obligated to comply with the subpoena.[70] Failure to serve timely objections may constitute a waiver of objections to the subpoena other than objections relating to service,[71] and grounds omitted from the objections are also waived.[72] The objection procedure is optional; a recipient may file a motion to quash or modify (discussed below) instead.[73]

- *Nonparties Only:* Only nonparties may serve objections; parties must contest a subpoena by a motion to quash or modify the subpoena[74] or a motion for protective order.[75] Motions to quash by parties are not governed by the 14-

---

[64]*See Virginia Dep't of Corr. v. Jordan*, 921 F.3d 180, 189 (4th Cir. 2019).

[65]*Rossman v. EN Eng'g, LLC*, 467 F. Supp. 3d 586, 590 (N.D. Ill. 2020).

[66]*See Legal Voice v. Stormans Inc.*, 738 F.3d 1178, 1185 (9th Cir. 2013); *In re Risner*, 338 F.R.D. 380, 382 (S.D. Ohio 2021).

[67]*CresCom Bank v. Terry*, 269 F. Supp. 3d 708, 713 (D.S.C. 2017).

[68]*In re: Modern Plastics Corp.*, 890 F.3d 244, 252 (6th Cir. 2018).

[69]*See Tuite v. Henry*, 98 F.3d 1411, 1416 (D.C. Cir. 1996).

[70]*U.S. S.E.C. v. Hyatt*, 621 F.3d 687, 694 (7th Cir. 2010); *Pamida, Inc. v. E.S. Originals, Inc.*, 281 F.3d 726, 732 (8th Cir. 2002).

[71]*SiteLock, LLC v. GoDaddy.com, LLC*, 338 F.R.D. 146, 155 (D. Or. 2021); *Am. Fed'n of Musicians of the U. S. and Canada v. Skodam Films, LLC*, 313 F.R.D. 39, 43 (N.D. Tex. 2015) (court has discretion to consider untimely objections).

[72]*Ott v. City of Milwaukee*, 682 F.3d 552, 558 (7th Cir. 2012) (reservation of right to assert additional objections ineffective); *In re DG Acquisition Corp.*, 151 F.3d 75, 81 (2d Cir. 1998).

[73]*In re Risner*, 338 F.R.D. 380, 382 (S.D. Ohio 2021); *Sines v. Kessler*, 325 F.R.D. 563, 566 (E.D. La. 2018).

[74]*In re DMCA Subpoena to Reddit, Inc.*, 441 F. Supp. 3d 875, 887 (N.D. Cal. 2020); *Williams v. Big Picture Loans, LLC*, 303 F. Supp. 3d 434, 440 (E.D. Va. 2018).

[75]*S.E.C. v. Goldstone*, 301 F.R.D. 593, 645 (D.N.M. 2014); *Sun Capital*

day limit for objections.[76]

- *Objection Procedure Not Applicable to Subpoena to Testify:* The objection procedure does not apply to testimonial subpoenas; those may only be challenged by a motion to quash or modify the subpoena, as discussed below.[77]
- *Motion to Compel Following Objection:* If a subpoena recipient serves an objection to the subpoena, the serving party may file a motion to compel under Rule 37(a) in the court for the district where compliance is required.[78] The motion must be served on the subpoena recipient as well as all other parties. If the district where compliance is required is different from the district where the case is pending, the moving party would commence an ancillary proceeding to file the motion to compel.[79] The Rule states that an objection may be made "at any time," but a party risks waiver by delaying filing its motion to compel.[80]
- *Significant Expense / Compensation for Respondent:* If the recipient of a subpoena to produce documents or permit inspection serves an objection and the issuing party files a motion to compel, the court must, if it grants the motion, protect the responding person from significant expense resulting from compliance.[81] The compensation may include wages lost because of the subpoena, and may also include attorney's fees.[82]

Motion to Quash or Modify; Mandatory Relief

A subpoena recipient, or another person asserting privilege,[83] may move to quash a subpoena in the court for the district where compliance is required.[84] The motion must be

Partners, Inc. v. Twin City Fire Ins. Co., 303 F.R.D. 673, 678 (S.D. Fla. 2014).

[76] *In re New York City Policing During Summer 2020 Demonstrations*, 563 F. Supp. 3d 84, 88 (S.D.N.Y. 2021).

[77] *See Ceroni v. 4Front Engineered Sols., Inc.*, 793 F. Supp. 2d 1268, 1275 (D. Colo. 2011).

[78] *P.H. Glatfelter Co. v. Windward Prospects Ltd.*, 847 F.3d 452, 455 n.2 (7th Cir. 2017); *Drummond Co., Inc. v. Terrance P. Collingsworth, Conrad & Scherer, LLP*, 816 F.3d 1319, 1322 (11th Cir. 2016).

[79] *See P.H. Glatfelter Co. v. Windward Prospects Ltd.*, 847 F.3d 452, 455 n.2 (7th Cir. 2017).

[80] *V5 Techs. v. Switch, Ltd.*, 332 F.R.D. 356, 361–62 (D. Nev. 2019).

[81] *See In re: Modern Plastics Corp.*, 890 F.3d 244, 252 (6th Cir. 2018); *Legal Voice v. Stormans Inc.*, 738 F.3d 1178, 1184–85 (9th Cir. 2013).

[82] *Voice v. Stormans Inc.*, 757 F.3d 1015, 1016 (9th Cir. 2014); *Mattel, Inc. v. Walking Mountain Productions*, 353 F.3d 792, 814 (9th Cir. 2003).

[83] *Total Rx Care, LLC v. Great N. Ins. Co.*, 318 F.R.D. 587, 593 (N.D. Tex. 2017) (party asserting privilege); *Jee Family Holdings, LLC v. San Jorge Children's Healthcare, Inc.*, 297 F.R.D. 19, 20 (D.P.R. 2014) (nonparty asserting privilege).

[84] *Managed Care Advisory Grp., LLC v. CIGNA Healthcare, Inc.*, 939 F.3d 1145, 1158 (11th Cir. 2019); *Texas Brine Co., LLC & Occidental Chem.*

"timely" filed[85]—the recipient should file the motion before the subpoena date for performance.[86] A party moving to quash or modify a subpoena should file the motion before the subpoena is served.[87] Failure to file a motion to quash may constitute a waiver of objections to the subpoena.[88] The courts vary as to who has the burden in a motion to quash.[89] Some courts and local rules require counsel for the moving party to make a reasonable effort to confer with opposing counsel prior to filing a motion to quash.[90] Rule 45(d)(3) lists situations in which a subpoena *must* be quashed or modified:[91]

(1) *Time to Comply:* the subpoena does not provide reasonable time to comply;[92]

(2) *Distance to Travel:* the subpoena requires a person to travel beyond the limits specified in Rule 45(c)[93] (which vary depending on whether the recipient is a party or nonparty and on the actions compelled by the subpoena);

(3) *Privileged Matters:* the subpoena requires the disclosure of privileged or other protected matters[94] (Rule 45(e)(2) addresses the manner for the recipient to assert a privilege claim); or

(4) *Undue Burden:* the subpoena subjects the recipient to

Corp., 879 F.3d 1224, 1227 (10th Cir. 2018).

[85]*See In re New York City Policing During Summer 2020 Demonstrations*, 563 F. Supp. 3d 84, 88 (S.D.N.Y. 2021) (14-day time limit for objections not applicable); *Sines v. Kessler*, 325 F.R.D. 563, 567 (E.D. La. 2018).

[86]In re DMCA § 512(h) *Subpoena to Twitter, Inc.*, __ F. Supp. 3d __, 2022 WL 2205476, at *2 n.2 (N.D. Cal. 2022).

[87]*United States v. Ray*, 337 F.R.D. 561, 574 (S.D.N.Y. 2020).

[88]*In re Flat Glass Antitrust Litig.*, 288 F.3d 83, 90 (3d Cir. 2002); *In re New York City Policing During Summer 2020 Demonstrations*, 563 F. Supp. 3d 84, 88 (S.D.N.Y. 2021).

[89]*See, e.g., Wiwa v. Royal Dutch Petroleum Co.*, 392 F.3d 812, 818 (5th Cir. 2004) (moving party has burden); *Green v. Cosby*, 314 F.R.D. 164, 169 (E.D. Pa. 2016) (shifting burden).

[90]*See Hill v. Wheatland Waters, Inc.*, 327 F. Supp. 2d 1294, 1298 n.5 (D. Kan. 2004); *In re Bennett Funding Group, Inc.*, 259 B.R. 243, 250 (N.D.N.Y. 2001).

[91]*See Texas Keystone, Inc. v. Prime Natural Res., Inc.*, 694 F.3d 548, 554 (5th Cir. 2012); *Dyno Nobel, Inc. v. Johnson*, __ F. Supp. 3d __, 2022 WL 507431, at *4 (E.D. Ky. 2022) (modifying, not quashing).

[92]*Arkansas State Conf. NAACP v. Arkansas Bd. Of Apportionment*, __ F. Supp. 3d __, 2022 WL 496908, at *3 n.23 (E.D. Ark. 2022) (1 day before hearing not reasonable); *In re Newbrook Shipping Corp.*, 498 F. Supp. 3d 807, 815 (D. Md. 2020) (3 days not reasonable).

[93]*In re Rule 45 Subpoenas Issued to Google LLC & LinkedIn Corp. Dated July 23, 2020*, 337 F.R.D. 639, 646 (N.D. Cal. 2020); *United States v. Brown*, 223 F. Supp. 3d 697, 703 (N.D. Ohio 2016) (motion denied where documents could be mailed).

[94]*Jordan v. Comm'r, Mississippi Dep't of Corr.*, 947 F.3d 1322, 1336 (11th Cir. 2020) (other protected matter); *ML Healthcare Servs., LLC v. Publix Super Markets, Inc.*, 881 F.3d 1293, 1306 (11th Cir. 2018) (only privilege, not inadmissibility, warrants quashing a subpoena).

undue burden.[95] One of the factors that affects undue burden is whether the requested information can be obtained from the parties.[96] This provision is sometimes used as justification for imposing the nonparty's expenses on the party issuing the subpoena to cure the undue burden on the nonparty.[97] Only the subpoena recipient has standing to file a motion to quash based on undue burden—other parties do not.[98]

Motion to Quash or Modify; Permissive Relief upon Demonstration of Substantial Need

Rule 45(d)(3)(B) lists circumstances in which the court has discretion to quash or modify a subpoena. The court also has the option of imposing conditions on the recipient's compliance,[99] if the serving party shows a "substantial need" for the testimony, documents, or inspection and ensures that the recipient will be reasonably compensated.[100] These circumstances are:

(1) *Trade Secrets:* the subpoena requires disclosure of trade secrets or other confidential research, development, or commercial information;[101] or

(2) *Unretained Experts:* the subpoena seeks opinions from experts who have not been retained (so that other parties cannot obtain the experts' testimony by subpoena without paying their fees).[102]

Motion to Compel

Rule 45(d)(2)(B) explicitly authorizes a party to file a motion in the court where compliance is required to compel compliance with a subpoena following objections by the recipient.[103] Even in the absence of objections, however, a motion to compel

---

[95] *Jordan v. Comm'r, Mississippi Dep't of Corr.*, 947 F.3d 1322, 1337 (11th Cir. 2020); *Virginia Dep't of Corr. v. Jordan*, 921 F.3d 180, 189 (4th Cir. 2019) (applying proportionality to the undue burden analysis).

[96] *Fishon v. Peloton Interactive, Inc.*, 336 F.R.D. 67, 69 (S.D.N.Y. 2020).

[97] *See In re: Modern Plastics Corp.*, 890 F.3d 244, 251 (6th Cir. 2018); *Voice v. Stormans Inc.*, 757 F.3d 1015, 1016 (9th Cir. 2014).

[98] *Colonial Funding Network, Inc. v. Genuine Builders, Inc.*, 326 F.R.D. 206, 213–14 (D.S.D. 2018).

[99] *ML Healthcare Servs., LLC v. Publix Super Markets, Inc.*, 881 F.3d 1293, 1306 n.7 (11th Cir. 2018) (condition limiting the disclosure of confidential information).

[100] *Fed. Trade Comm'n v. Trudeau*, 845 F.3d 272, 275 (7th Cir. 2016).

[101] *Jordan v. Comm'r, Mississippi Dep't of Corr.*, 947 F.3d 1322, 1335–36 (11th Cir. 2020) (courts balance the claim to privacy against the need for disclosure); *ML Healthcare Servs., LLC v. Publix Super Markets, Inc.*, 881 F.3d 1293, 1306 n.7 (11th Cir. 2018).

[102] *In re World Trade Center Lower Manhattan Disaster Site Litig.*, 304 F.R.D. 379, 382–83 (S.D.N.Y. 2015); *In re Domestic Drywall Antitrust Litig.*, 300 F.R.D. 234, 239 (E.D. Pa. 2014) (protection does not apply when information sought is factual).

[103] *Fla. State Conf. of Branches & Youth Units of NAACP v. Lee*, 568 F. Supp. 3d 1301, 1304 (S.D. Fla. 2021); *SiteLock, LLC v. GoDaddy.com, LLC*, 338 F.R.D. 146, 151 (D. Or. 2021).

under Rule 37(a) is the proper procedure for asking the court to compel the recipient of a subpoena to perform the obligations commanded by the subpoena.[104]

- *Subpoena Issued by Arbitrator:* The federal courts can enforce subpoenas issued by arbitrators under the provisions of the Federal Arbitration Act, 9 U.S.C.A. § 1 et seq.[105]

Appeal

The courts are divided as to whether rulings quashing or compelling compliance with subpoenas are interlocutory, not subject to immediate appeal, or may be appealed immediately as collateral orders.[106] Some courts require the recipient of a subpoena to refuse to comply, and then appeal the contempt and sanctions order.[107]

RULE 45(e)—DUTIES IN RESPONDING TO A SUBPOENA

CORE CONCEPT

Although Rule 45(e) is broadly titled "duties in responding to a subpoena," its provisions only address the recipient's duties when responding to a subpoena to produce documents. It requires that documents be produced as they are normally kept or may be separated, organized, and labeled to correspond to the requests. When privileges are asserted, the recipient must describe the privilege assertions with enough detail that other parties and the court can assess the privilege assertion.

APPLICATIONS

Production of Documents

The scope of production under a subpoena is the same as the scope for discovery generally under Rule 26—essentially nonprivileged matter[108] relevant to any party's claim or defense and proportional to the needs of the case.[109] The responding party has the option of allowing the serving party to inspect and copy the documents where they are normally kept (*e.g.*,

---

[104]*See In re John Adams Assocs., Inc.*, 255 F.R.D. 7, 7 (D.D.C. 2008).

[105]*Managed Care Advisory Grp., LLC v. CIGNA Healthcare, Inc.*, 939 F.3d 1145, 1154 (11th Cir. 2019).

[106]*See, e.g., Legal Voice v. Stormans Inc.*, 738 F.3d 1178, 1183–84 (9th Cir. 2013) (ruling appealable collateral order); *Ott v. City of Milwaukee*, 682 F.3d 552, 554–55 (7th Cir. 2012) (ruling not appealable until the end of the litigation).

[107]*See, e.g., Ott v. City of Milwaukee*, 682 F.3d 552, 554–55 (7th Cir. 2012); *In re Flat Glass Antitrust Litig.*, 288 F.3d 83, 87–88 (3d Cir. 2002).

[108]*In re Motion to Compel Compliance with Subpoena Directed to Cooke Legal Grp., PLLC*, 333 F.R.D. 291, 294 (D.D.C. 2019).

[109]*Jordan v. Comm'r, Mississippi Dep't of Corr.*, 947 F.3d 1322, 1329 (11th Cir. 2020).

"There is our file room").[110] The responding party may also collect the responsive documents and organize and label them to correspond to the categories requested.[111] The responding party may make copies for the requesting party, but is not obligated to do so.

Electronically Stored Information

Rule 45 expressly allows for the party issuing the subpoena to request to inspect, copy, sample, or test electronically stored information.

- *Form of Electronically Stored Information:* Rule 45(e)(1)(B) allows, but does not require, the requesting party to specify the form in which it is requesting electronically stored information (*i.e.*, pdf, jpeg, tiff, native format, etc.). If the requesting party does not specify the form, then the responding person must produce the electronically stored information in the form in which it is ordinarily maintained or in a form that is reasonably usable.[112] In any event, a person need not produce electronically stored information in more than one form.[113]
- *Undue Burden or Cost:* If the responding person believes that the production of electronically stored information from certain sources will cause undue burden or cost, the person can, in lieu of producing the information, identify those sources.[114] If a motion to compel or quash is filed, the responding person will have the burden of showing that production would cause undue burden or cost.[115] The burden would then shift to the requesting party to show good cause why the electronically stored information should be produced nonetheless.[116] In such cases, the court may specify conditions for the production, such as requiring the requesting party to pay the expenses of the production.[117]

---

[110] *Kinetic Concepts, Inc. v. Convatec Inc.*, 268 F.R.D. 226, 240 (M.D.N.C. 2010); *In re John Adams Associates, Inc.*, 255 F.R.D. 7, 8 (D.D.C. 2008).

[111] *Kinetic Concepts, Inc. v. Convatec Inc.*, 268 F.R.D. 226, 240 (M.D.N.C. 2010).

[112] *Am. Fed'n of Musicians of the United States and Canada v. Skodam Films, LLC*, 313 F.R.D. 39, 43 (N.D. Tex. 2015).

[113] *Am. Fed'n of Musicians of the United States and Canada v. Skodam Films, LLC*, 313 F.R.D. 39, 43 (N.D. Tex. 2015).

[114] *Am. Fed'n of Musicians of the United States and Canada v. Skodam Films, LLC*, 313 F.R.D. 39, 43 (N.D. Tex. 2015); *Guy Chem. Co., Inc. v. Romaco AG*, 243 F.R.D. 310 (N.D. Ind. 2007).

[115] *Guy Chem. Co., Inc. v. Romaco AG*, 243 F.R.D. 310 (N.D. Ind. 2007).

[116] *Am. Fed'n of Musicians of the United States and Canada v. Skodam Films, LLC*, 313 F.R.D. 39, 43 (N.D. Tex. 2015); *Guy Chem. Co., Inc. v. Romaco AG*, 243 F.R.D. 310 (N.D. Ind. 2007) (good cause where no other source exists for the information).

[117] *Guy Chem. Co., Inc. v. Romaco*

Asserting a Privilege

When the subpoena recipient seeks to withhold information that is privileged, the recipient must expressly claim the privilege and describe the nature of the documents, communications, or things not produced in sufficient detail that the court and parties can assess the privilege.[118] The party asserting the privilege should provide a detailed privilege log at the time of asserting the privilege or within a reasonable time thereafter.[119] The court has discretion to excuse the failure to provide a privilege log if the basis for the privilege assertion is apparent.[120] The privilege provisions of Rule 45(e) are similar to the general privilege provisions in Rule 26(b)(5), and attorneys faced with a privilege issue relating to a subpoena may want to consult the commentary and case law relevant to both Rules.[121]

Recalling Privileged Information

Rule 45(e)(2)(B) establishes a procedure to recall privileged information that has already been produced. Anyone believing that a person has produced privileged information in response to a subpoena may provide a notification to the parties who have received the information.[122] After receiving such a notification, the receiving party must return, sequester, or destroy the specified information and all copies (including taking reasonable steps to retrieve any information that the receiving party had already disclosed to other persons). If the receiving party does not agree with the privilege assertion, it can file a motion asking the court for the district where compliance is required for a determination of the privilege claim. During the pendency of the court's review of the privilege claim, the receiving party is prohibited from using the information and the producing party must preserve it.

RULE 45(f)—TRANSFERRING A SUBPOENA-RELATED MOTION

CORE CONCEPT

Motions regarding the scope or validity of a subpoena are filed in the district where performance of the subpoena is to occur. That court can transfer such motions to the court where the action is pending, although such transfers are infrequent. The court where the action is pending then transfers its order back to the

---

AG, 243 F.R.D. 310 (N.D. Ind. 2007).

[118] *Jordan v. Comm'r, Mississippi Dep't of Corr.*, 908 F.3d 1259, 1267 (11th Cir. 2018); *Texas Brine Co., LLC & Occidental Chem. Corp.*, 879 F.3d 1224, 1229 n.5 (10th Cir. 2018) (failure to assert detailed objection constitutes waiver).

[119] *In re Grand Jury Proceedings*, 802 F.3d 57, 67–68 (1st Cir. 2015).

[120] *Jordan v. Comm'r, Mississippi Dep't of Corr.*, 947 F.3d 1322, 1328 n.3 (11th Cir. 2020).

[121] *See Texas Brine Co., LLC & Occidental Chem. Corp.*, 879 F.3d 1224, 1228 n.3 (10th Cir. 2018).

[122] *See Universal Standard Inc. v. Target Corp.*, 331 F.R.D. 80, 83–84 (S.D.N.Y. 2019).

original court for enforcement.

APPLICATIONS

Grounds for Transfer

A court has discretion to transfer a subpoena-related motion to the court where the action is pending if the person subject to the subpoena consents[123] or the court finds "exceptional circumstances."[124] Exceptional circumstances are rare, and the person seeking transfer bears the burden of establishing appropriate grounds.[125] Generally, a court will transfer a motion based on exceptional circumstances only when the potential for disrupting the underlying litigation outweighs the interests of the nonparty subpoena recipient in obtaining local resolution of the motion.[126]

Transfer of Resulting Order

If a subpoena-related motion is transferred to the court where the underlying action is pending, that the court can transfer its order ruling on the motion back to the court for the district where compliance is required if such transfer is necessary to enforce the order.[127]

Admission to the Transferee Court Unnecessary

If a subpoena-related motion is transferred pursuant to Rule 45(f), attorneys authorized to practice in the court where the Rule 45 motion was originally filed may file papers and appear in the court in the transferee court in relation to the motion without seeking admission to practice in the transferee court.[128]

RULE 45(g)—CONTEMPT

CORE CONCEPT

Failure to obey a properly served, valid subpoena or subpoena-related order without adequate excuse is a contempt of the court for the district where compliance is required,[129] and also of the issuing court after transfer of a subpoena-related motion under

---

[123] *Full Circle United, LLC v. Bay Tek Ent., Inc.*, — F. Supp. 3d —, 2022 WL 210855, at *2 (S.D.N.Y. 2022); *In re Braden*, 344 F. Supp. 3d 83, 89 (D.D.C. 2018).

[124] *See Morrill v. Scott Fin. Corp.*, 873 F.3d 1136, 1146 n.3 (9th Cir. 2017).

[125] *In re Braden*, 344 F. Supp. 3d 83, 90 (D.D.C. 2018); *Green v. Cosby*, 216 F. Supp. 3d 560, 565 (E.D. Pa. 2016).

[126] *See Hoog v. PetroQuest, LLC*, 338 F.R.D. 515, 517 (S.D. Fla. 2021); *In re Nonparty Subpoenas Duces Tecum*, 327 F.R.D. 23, 24 (D.D.C. 2018).

[127] *P.H. Glatfelter Co. v. Windward Prospects Ltd.*, 847 F.3d 452, 458 (7th Cir. 2017).

[128] *In re Braden*, 344 F. Supp. 3d 83, 95 (D.D.C. 2018); *CSS, Inc. v. Herrington*, 354 F. Supp. 3d 702, 712 (N.D. Tex. 2017).

[129] *Blackmer v. U.S.*, 284 U.S. 421, 435–36 (1932); *Wallace v. Kmart Corp.*, 687 F.3d 86, 88 (3d Cir. 2012).

Rule 45(f).[130] Contempt is the only sanction for a nonparty's failure to comply with a subpoena.[131]

APPLICATIONS

Standard for Holding Subpoena Recipient in Contempt

To prevail on a request for contempt finding, the moving party must establish by clear and convincing evidence[132] that: (1) a subpoena set forth an unambiguous command;[133] (2) the alleged contemnor violated that command; (3) the violation was significant, meaning the alleged contemnor did not substantially comply with the subpoena; and (4) the alleged contemnor failed to make a reasonable and diligent effort to comply.[134]

Due Process

Before sanctions may be imposed on a person charged with contempt under Rule 45, due process requires that the person receive notice and an opportunity to be heard and that the court have personal jurisdiction over the nonparty to be sanctioned.[135]

Adequate Excuse

Inability to comply is an adequate excuse.[136] The fact that the subpoena would require the recipient to travel greater distances than those listed in Rule 45(c) is also an adequate excuse.[137] Likewise, a timely objection to the subpoena is an adequate excuse.[138] Preferring to work instead of comply with the subpoena is not an adequate excuse.[139]

Appeal

Nonparty witnesses who are held in contempt may immediately appeal the contempt order.[140]

---

[130] *Wultz v. Bank of China Ltd.*, 304 F.R.D. 38, 45–46 (S.D.N.Y. 2014).

[131] *Sali v. Corona Reg'l Med. Ctr.*, 884 F.3d 1218, 1224 (9th Cir. 2018).

[132] *Acosta v. La Piedad Corp.*, 894 F.3d 947, 951 (8th Cir. 2018).

[133] *Acosta v. La Piedad Corp.*, 894 F.3d 947, 951 (8th Cir. 2018).

[134] *See Acosta v. La Piedad Corp.*, 894 F.3d 947, 951 (8th Cir. 2018); *Sprint Solutions, Inc. v. iCell Guru, Inc.*, 310 F.R.D. 563, 569 (N.D. Ill. 2015).

[135] *Gucci Am., Inc. v. Weixing Li*, 768 F.3d 122, 141 (2d Cir. 2014) (court must have personal jurisdiction over nonparty); *U.S. S.E.C. v. Hyatt*, 621 F.3d 687, 694 (7th Cir. 2010).

[136] *Acosta v. La Piedad Corp.*, 894 F.3d 947, 951 (8th Cir. 2018); *Sali v. Corona Reg'l Med. Ctr.*, 884 F.3d 1218, 1224 (9th Cir. 2018).

[137] *See Hillard v. Guidant Corp.*, 76 F. Supp. 2d 566, 570 (M.D. Pa. 1999); *National Property Investors VIII v. Shell Oil Co.*, 917 F. Supp. 324, 328 (D.N.J. 1995).

[138] *Flatow v. The Islamic Republic of Iran*, 196 F.R.D. 203, 208 (D.D.C. 2000).

[139] *Higginbotham v. KCS Intern., Inc.*, 202 F.R.D. 444, 455 (D. Md. 2001).

[140] *U.S. v. Ryan*, 402 U.S. 530, 532–33 (1971); *Wallace v. Kmart Corp.*, 687 F.3d 86, 89 (3d Cir. 2012).

Additional Research References

Wright & Miller, *Federal Practice and Procedure* §§ 2451 to 2463

C.J.S., Federal Civil Procedure §§ 582 to 583 et seq., 644; Witnesses §§ 13 to 27 et seq.

West's Key Number Digest, Federal Civil Procedure 🔑1353 to 1354, 1456; Witnesses 🔑7 to 16, 21

matter at trial.[12]

Additional Research References

Wright & Miller, *Federal Practice and Procedure* §§ 2471 to 2473
C.J.S., Federal Civil Procedure §§ 370 et seq., 941 to 942
West's Key Number Digest, Federal Civil Procedure ⚷2017 to 2019

[12] *Walden v. Georgia-Pacific Corp.*, 126 F.3d 506, 518 (3d Cir. 1997). *See also Inter Medical Supplies, Ltd. v. EBI Medical Sys., Inc.*, 181 F.3d 446, 455 (3d Cir. 1999) (objection unnecessary following motion *in limine* where the court has made a definitive ruling on the issue and is unlikely to reconsider).

RULE 47
SELECTING JURORS

(a) **Examining Jurors.** The court may permit the parties or their attorneys to examine prospective jurors or may itself do so. If the court examines the jurors, it must permit the parties or their attorneys to make any further inquiry it considers proper, or must itself ask any of their additional questions it considers proper.

(b) **Peremptory Challenges.** The court must allow the number of peremptory challenges provided by 28 U.S.C. § 1870.

(c) **Excusing a Juror.** During trial or deliberation, the court may excuse a juror for good cause.

[Amended effective July 1, 1966; December 1, 1991; April 30, 2007, effective December 1, 2007.]

AUTHORS' COMMENTARY ON RULE 47

PURPOSE AND SCOPE

Although many aspects of the jury selection process vary considerably from court to court, there are some consistent components. In general, the clerk's office gathers a large panel of potential jurors, from which the actual jurors are selected. There is usually a process for collecting information from the panel members, often by combination of written questionnaires and oral questioning (often called "voir dire"). This information includes demographic information like age, address, educational background, and occupation, as well as information bearing on potential bias, like relationship or familiarity with the parties or lawyers. In some courts, the lawyers make brief statements and ask questions, and in others the judge or a clerk asks the questions.

Once this information is solicited, the lawyers have an opportunity to strike jurors from the pool. There are two types of strikes—for cause and peremptory. With strikes for cause, a party typically challenges the juror and the judge then decides whether the juror should remain on the panel (sometimes after asking the juror if he or she can issue a verdict based on the evidence or would be swayed by the grounds identified in the challenge). In contrast, lawyers have almost unfettered discretion in exercising peremptory strikes—the only recognized improper grounds for a peremptory strike are race and gender.

Many of these jury selection procedures are set by local rule or individual chambers practices, and Rule 47 only establishes a couple of national principles. It authorizes the court to oversee the examination of jurors to gather information about them and provides the court with broad discretion in how it structures this examination. It also generally describes the processes for striking potential jurors.

RULE 47(a)—EXAMINING OF JURORS

CORE CONCEPT

The court and/or the parties may ask prospective jurors questions in order to determine bias and to enable the parties to exercise their peremptory challenges in a meaningful manner.

APPLICATIONS

Scope of Examinations

The court has broad discretion with respect to the scope of voir dire.[1] It may conduct the examination itself or allow the parties do so.[2] If the court conducts the examination, the parties may submit proposed questions, which the court may ask if it deems appropriate.[3] The court must allow sufficient questioning so that the selection process is meaningful.

Challenges for Cause

Parties can ask the court to exclude individual jurors or the entire panel "for cause." Partiality is the main grounds for such challenges.[4] The party making the challenge has the burden of persuading the court. Parties may also challenge the selection process. All challenges should be made at the time of jury selection, not in a motion for new trial.[5]

Qualifications for Jurors

The qualifications for jurors are governed by the Jury Selection and Service Act of 1968, 28 U.S.C.A. § 1861 et seq. Essentially, jurors must be United States citizens, have resided in the district for at least one year, meet minimum literacy requirements and be fluent in English, be mentally and physi-

---

[1] *Csiszer v. Wren*, 614 F.3d 866, 875 (8th Cir. 2010); *Smith v. Vicorp, Inc.*, 107 F.3d 816, 817 (10th Cir. 1997).

[2] *Csiszer v. Wren*, 614 F.3d 866, 875 (8th Cir. 2010).

[3] *Csiszer v. Wren*, 614 F.3d 866, 875 (8th Cir. 2010); *Smith v. Tenet Healthsystem SL, Inc.*, 436 F.3d 879, 884 (8th Cir. 2006).

[4] *See Swain v. Alabama*, 380 U.S. 202, 220 (1965); *Darbin v. Nourse*, 664 F.2d 1109, 1113 (9th Cir. 1981).

[5] *Atlas Roofing Mfg. Co. v. Parnell*, 409 F.2d 1191 (5th Cir.1969).

cally capable of service, and be free from pending charges or past convictions of crimes punishable by imprisonment for more than 2 years.

Excluded Groups

The Jury Selection and Service Act of 1968 provides for the establishment of certain groups who are precluded or excused from serving. Generally, these include: persons providing vital services (such as members of the armed services and policemen); persons for whom service would be a particular hardship (such as sole proprietors, mothers with young children, persons with gravely ill family members); and those excluded by the court for partiality or because they are likely to be disruptive.

RULE 47(b)—PEREMPTORY CHALLENGES

CORE CONCEPT

Peremptory challenges are challenges that a party makes unilaterally, without the need for court permission or approval. Peremptory challenges are governed by 28 U.S.C.A. § 1870, which provides that each party has 3 peremptory challenges,[6] and generally need not give any explanation for using those challenges. Peremptory challenges are not a constitutionally protected fundamental right, but are merely one means to the constitutional end of an impartial jury and a fair trial.[7] When there are multiple plaintiffs or defendants, the court may require them to exercise the challenges collectively or may allow additional challenges.[8]

APPLICATIONS

Improper Grounds

Although parties have almost unfettered discretion in exercising peremptory strikes, it is improper to use a peremptory challenge to exclude a juror on the basis of race[9] or gender.[10]

---

[6] *Jimenez v. City of Chicago*, 732 F.3d 710, 715 (7th Cir. 2013); *Bryant v. City of Hartford*, — F. Supp. 3d —, 2022 WL 445808, at *7 (D. Conn. 2022).

[7] *Jimenez v. City of Chicago*, 732 F.3d 710, 715 (7th Cir. 2013); *Alaska Rent-A-Car, Inc. v. Avis Budget Group, Inc.*, 709 F.3d 872, 880 (9th Cir. 2013).

[8] *In re Air Crash Disaster*, 86 F.3d 498, 518–519 (6th Cir. 1996); *Bryant v. City of Hartford*, — F. Supp. 3d —, 2022 WL 445808, at *7 (D. Conn. 2022).

[9] *See Flowers v. Mississippi*, 139 S. Ct. 2228, 2241 (2019); *Edmonson v. Leesville Concrete Co., Inc.*, 500 U.S. 614 (1991).

[10] *J.E.B. v. Alabama ex rel. T.B.*, 511 U.S. 127, 129 (1994).

RULE 47(c)—EXCUSING A JUROR

CORE CONCEPT

The court may excuse a juror for reasons of sickness,[11] family emergency, juror misconduct, or for other "good cause shown."[12] A juror's refusal to join the majority is not grounds for excuse.[13]

APPLICATIONS

Considerations for Excusing a Juror

The judge has broad discretion in deciding whether to excuse a juror and whether to question the juror before deciding whether to exclude the juror.[14] The court may scrutinize not only spoken words, but gestures and attitudes in order to ensure the jury's impartiality and competence.[15] The court should not excuse a juror for failing to join in the verdict favored by other jurors, though.[16]

Additional Research References

Wright & Miller, *Federal Practice and Procedure* §§ 2481 to 2485. Bennett & Hirschhorn, Bennett's *Guide to Jury Selection and Trial Dynamics in Civil and Criminal Litigation.*

C.J.S., Juries §§ 208 to 250 et seq., 251 to 285 et seq.

West's Key Number Digest, Jury ⚷83 to 142

---

[11] *Davis v. Velez*, 797 F.3d 192, 208 (2d Cir. 2015).

[12] *See Harris v. Folk Const. Co.*, 138 F.3d 365, 371 (8th Cir. 1998); *Bostick v. State Farm Mut. Auto. Ins. Co.*, 314 F. Supp. 3d 1265, 1272 (M.D. Fla. 2018) (juror was disruptive and refused to follow court instructions).

[13] *See Murray v. Laborers Union Local No. 324*, 55 F.3d 1445, 1450–51 (9th Cir. 1995); *Saint-Jean v. Emigrant Mortg. Co.*, 337 F. Supp. 3d 186, 205 (E.D.N.Y. 2018).

[14] *See United States v. Hodge*, 933 F.3d 468, 481 (5th Cir. 2019).

[15] *Harris v. Folk Const. Co.*, 138 F.3d 365, 371 (8th Cir. 1998); *Bostick v. State Farm Mut. Auto. Ins. Co.*, 314 F. Supp. 3d 1265, 1272 (M.D. Fla. 2018).

[16] *See United States v. Hodge*, 933 F.3d 468, 481 (5th Cir. 2019).

RULE 48
NUMBER OF JURORS; VERDICT; POLLING

(a) **Number of Jurors.** A jury must begin with at least 6 and no more than 12 members, and each juror must participate in the verdict unless excused under Rule 47(c).

(b) **Verdict.** Unless the parties stipulate otherwise, the verdict must be unanimous and must be returned by a jury of at least 6 members.

(c) **Polling.** After a verdict is returned but before the jury is discharged, the court must on a party's request, or may on its own, poll the jurors individually. If the poll reveals a lack of unanimity or lack of assent by the number of jurors that the parties stipulated to, the court may direct the jury to deliberate further or may order a new trial.

[Amended effective December 1, 1991; April 30, 2007, effective December 1, 2007; March 26, 2009, effective December 1, 2009.]

AUTHORS' COMMENTARY ON RULE 48

PURPOSE AND SCOPE

Rule 48 controls the makeup and decisions of a jury. It provides that a jury must consist of 6 to 12 jurors. It provides that the jury's verdict must be unanimous, and gives the parties the right to demand that the jury be polled to verify that the verdict was in fact unanimous. These provisions may be altered by stipulation, such that the parties may agree to a jury smaller than 6 or to a decision by less than a unanimous verdict.

RULE 48(a)—NUMBER OF JURORS

CORE CONCEPT

The court may select any number of jurors from 6 to 12, inclusive.[1] The parties may also stipulate to fewer than 6 jurors.[2]

RULE 48(b)—VERDICT

CORE CONCEPT

Absent a stipulation, verdicts must be unanimous.[3] Verdicts are considered unanimous even if 1 or more jurors reluctantly joins just to reach a verdict.[4]

APPLICATIONS

Excused Jurors

If a juror is excused for illness or other reason, a unanimous verdict among the remaining jurors will be valid if at least 6 jurors remain.[5] If fewer than 6 remain, the parties may consent to allow the trial or deliberations to continue, and then will be bound by the verdict.[6] Otherwise, the court will declare a mistrial.

Stipulations

By stipulation, the parties can agree that a unanimous decision is not necessary, and that the decision of a specified majority will be taken as the decision of the jury.[7] The parties may also stipulate to a jury of less than 6 members.

Further Deliberations Following Deadlock—Allen Charges

If a jury reports being unable to reach a unanimous verdict, the majority of the courts allow an "Allen charge," an instruction to the jury to deliberate further to attempt to break the deadlock.[8]

---

[1] *See Show v. Ford Motor Co.*, 659 F.3d 584, 586 (7th Cir. 2011); *Wolfe v. Fayetteville, Arkansas Sch. Dist.*, 648 F.3d 860, 869 (8th Cir. 2011).

[2] *In re Nat'l Prescription Opiate Litig.*, — F. Supp. 3d —, 2022 WL 668434, at *7 (N.D. Ohio 2022); *Meyers v. Wal-Mart Stores, East, Inc.*, 77 F. Supp. 2d 826, 827 (E.D. Mich. 1999), aff'd, 257 F.3d 625 (6th Cir. 2001).

[3] *Jazzabi v. Allstate Ins. Co.*, 278 F.3d 979, 985 (9th Cir. 2002) (jury must be unanimous as to affirmative defense as well as ultimate verdict); *Robinson v. Cattaraugus County*, 147 F.3d 153, 161 (2d Cir. 1998).

[4] *See Cary v. Allegheny Technologies Inc.*, 267 F. Supp. 2d 442 (W.D. Pa. 2003) (allowing a charge to the jury about the benefits of reaching a verdict—sometimes called an "Allen charge," named after *Allen v. United States*, 164 U.S. 492 (1896)).

[5] *Weaver v. Blake*, 454 F.3d 1087 (10th Cir.2006).

[6] *Meyers v. Wal-Mart Stores, East, Inc.*, 257 F.3d 625, 633 (6th Cir. 2001) (a bench trial is essentially a stipulation to trial before zero jurors).

[7] *Baxter Healthcare Corp. v. Spectramed, Inc.*, 49 F.3d 1575 (Fed. Cir. 1995); *Cook v. Rockwell Intern. Corp.*, 428 F. Supp. 2d 1152, 1154 (D. Colo. 2006).

[8] *Cary v. Allegheny Technologies Inc.*, 267 F. Supp. 2d 442, 446 (W.D.

Alternate Jurors

Alternate jurors are not used in civil trials in federal court.[9]

Advisory Jury

It does not appear that the provisions of Rule 48 regarding unanimity pertain to advisory juries.[10]

RULE 48(c)—POLLING

CORE CONCEPT

After the verdict is read and before the jury is discharged, a party may demand that the jury be polled to verify that the verdict is unanimous and that no juror was coerced into signing the verdict.[11] The court may also poll the jury *sua sponte*. If 1 or more jurors dissents, the court may require the jury to deliberate further or may declare a mistrial. Polling must occur before the verdict is recorded and the jury is discharged.[12] The trial must be conducted in a manner that provides the parties an opportunity to exercise their right to have the jury polled.[13] The right to have the jury polled is not constitutional, however, and can be waived if not timely exercised.[14]

Additional Research References

Wright & Miller, *Federal Practice and Procedure* §§ 2491 to 2492. Bennett & Hirschhorn, Bennett's *Guide to Jury Selection and Trial Dynamics in Civil and Criminal Litigation.*

C.J.S., Federal Civil Procedure §§ 995 et seq.; Juries § 4

West's Key Number Digest, Federal Civil Procedure ⚷2191; Jury ⚷4

Pa. 2003).

[9]*Herbert v. Architect of Capitol*, 920 F. Supp. 2d 33, 47 (D.D.C. 2013).

[10]*N.A.A.C.P. v. Acusport Corp.*, 253 F. Supp. 2d 459 (E.D.N.Y. 2003).

[11]*See Ira Green, Inc. v. Military Sales & Service Co.*, 775 F.3d 12, 24 (1st Cir. 2014) (polling is mandatory upon timely request); *Verser v. Barfield*, 741 F.3d 734, 738 (7th Cir. 2013).

[12]*See Wagner v. Jones*, 928 F. Supp. 2d 1084, 1093 (S.D. Iowa 2013).

[13]*See Smego v. Payne*, 854 F.3d 387, 39–97 (7th Cir. 2017); *Verser v. Barfield*, 741 F.3d 734, 740–41 (7th Cir. 2013).

[14]*Ira Green, Inc. v. Military Sales & Service Co.*, 775 F.3d 12, 25 (1st Cir. 2014).

RULE 49
SPECIAL VERDICT; GENERAL VERDICT AND QUESTIONS

(a) **Special Verdict.**

(1) *In General.* The court may require a jury to return only a special verdict in the form of a special written finding on each issue of fact. The court may do so by:

(A) submitting written questions susceptible of a categorical or other brief answer;

(B) submitting written forms of the special findings that might properly be made under the pleadings and evidence; or

(C) using any other method that the court considers appropriate.

(2) *Instructions.* The court must give the instructions and explanations necessary to enable the jury to make its findings on each submitted issue.

(3) *Issues Not Submitted.* A party waives the right to a jury trial on any issue of fact raised by the pleadings or evidence but not submitted to the jury unless, before the jury retires, the party demands its submission to the jury. If the party does not demand submission, the court may make a finding on the issue. If the court makes no finding, it is considered to have made a finding consistent with its judgment on the special verdict.

(b) **General Verdict with Answers to Written Questions.**

(1) *In General.* The court may submit to the jury forms for a general verdict, together with written questions on one or more issues of fact that the jury must decide. The court must give the instructions and explanations necessary to enable the jury to render a general verdict and answer the questions in writing, and must direct

the jury to do both.

(2) *Verdict and Answers Consistent.* When the general verdict and the answers are consistent, the court must approve, for entry under Rule 58, an appropriate judgment on the verdict and answers.

(3) *Answers Inconsistent with the Verdict.* When the answers are consistent with each other but one or more is inconsistent with the general verdict, the court may:

(A) approve, for entry under Rule 58, an appropriate judgment according to the answers, notwithstanding the general verdict;

(B) direct the jury to further consider its answers and verdict; or

(C) order a new trial.

(4) *Answers Inconsistent with Each Other and the Verdict.* When the answers are inconsistent with each other and one or more is also inconsistent with the general verdict, judgment must not be entered; instead, the court must direct the jury to further consider its answers and verdict, or must order a new trial.

[Amended effective July 1, 1963; August 1, 1987; April 30, 2007, effective December 1, 2007.]

AUTHORS' COMMENTARY ON RULE 49

PURPOSE AND SCOPE

There are a number of different forms the verdict can take, the simplest of which is a "general verdict." With a general verdict, the jury's verdict slip gives the jury the option of marking the slip indicating that they find for the defendant or marking the slip indicating that they find for the plaintiff and designating the amount they award to the plaintiff. One of the limitations with a general verdict is that, if an appellate court finds a legal error by the trial court, no one knows the basis of the jury's ruling; everyone just knows the bottom-line result. Thus, the legal error identified by the appellate court might have been fundamental to the outcome or might have been irrelevant, and that uncertainty often necessitates a new trial.

Rule 49 establishes two alternatives to a general verdict

designed to minimize the likelihood that the court will need to conduct a new trial if an appellate court finds an error in the trial court proceedings. The court may submit a "special verdict" to the jury, which allows the jury to make separate findings as to each issue of material fact.

Alternatively, the court may submit both a general verdict and written questions which obtain the jury's factual findings on the pivotal issues framed by the questions. With sufficient information gathered through a special verdict or written questions, if the court of appeals concludes that the trial court made an error, the trial court may be able to mold the verdict to be consistent with both the jury's factual findings and the law as instructed by the court of appeals, avoiding the need for a new trial.

One of the risks with these alternative approaches is that the jury might return a verdict form that contains inconsistencies—after all, jurors are lay people and the legal process can be confusing. Rule 49 provides the court with options to resolve these inconsistencies.

RULE 49(a)—SPECIAL VERDICT

CORE CONCEPT

The court may require the jury to return special verdicts as to each issue of material fact, instead of a general verdict in favor of one party.

APPLICATIONS

Comparison with General Verdict

A general verdict is a single statement disposing of the entire case (*e.g.*, "We find in favor of the defendant.").[1] Special verdicts ask the jury to decide specific factual questions (*e.g.*, "At the time of the accident, was the vehicle was proceeding at an excessive rate of speed?").[2] The type of verdict, and the applicable rules, are determined by the form of the jury verdict, not the label.[3]

Roles of the Court and the Jury with Special Verdicts

With special verdicts, the jury is not asked to apply the law to the facts of the case and announce the ultimate outcome. Rather, after the jury returns its special verdict responses making factual findings, the court applies the relevant law and

---

[1] *Team Contractors, L.L.C. v. Waypoint Nola, L.L.C.*, 976 F.3d 509, 514 (5th Cir. 2020); *Antrim Pharm. LLC v. Bio-Pharm, Inc.*, 950 F.3d 423, 427 n.1 (7th Cir. 2020).

[2] *See Antrim Pharm. LLC v. Bio-Pharm, Inc.*, 950 F.3d 423, 427 n.1 (7th Cir. 2020); *Frank C. Pollara Group, LLC v. Ocean View Inv. Holding, LLC*, 784 F.3d 177, 190 (3d Cir. 2015).

[3] *Team Contractors, L.L.C. v. Waypoint Nola, L.L.C.*, 976 F.3d 509, 517 (5th Cir. 2020); *Jones v. Treubig*, 963 F.3d 214, 232 n.10. (2d Cir. 2020).

determines the final result.[4]

Scope of Questions

The special verdicts should fairly present the case, and should cover all material factual issues.[5] In contrast to general verdicts, which require the jury to apply the law as described by the judge to the facts that the jury finds, special verdicts should be limited to factual findings.[6]

Form of Questions

Special verdicts may take different forms. Sometimes the questions will require the jury to write a brief answer (such as "yes" or "no"). Sometimes alternative special verdicts will be written out, and the jury need only choose one alternative.

Instructions to Jury

The court must give the jury sufficient instructions so that they can determine each issue before them (as discussed below under Rule 51).[7] However, because special verdicts are limited to factual issues, lengthy instructions on the substantive law should be unnecessary (but instructions on issues like the burden of proof are still appropriate).[8] Conversely, there is no prohibition on the court providing instructions, even if technically unnecessary in light of the questions.[9] If a special verdict involves a mixed question of fact and law, the court must give instructions as to the applicable law.[10]

Court's Discretion to Use Special Verdicts

The court has virtually absolute discretion as to the use of special verdicts.[11] This discretion extends to determining the content and layout of the verdict form and the questions submitted to the jury, provided the questions are reasonably capable of an interpretation that would allow the jury to address all factual issues essential to judgment.[12] Generally,

---

[4]*Team Contractors, L.L.C. v. Waypoint Nola, L.L.C.*, 976 F.3d 509, 514 (5th Cir. 2020).

[5]*Team Contractors, L.L.C. v. Waypoint Nola, L.L.C.*, 976 F.3d 509, 517 (5th Cir. 2020); *Frank C. Pollara Group, LLC v. Ocean View Inv. Holding, LLC*, 784 F.3d 177, 190 (3d Cir. 2015).

[6]*Team Contractors, L.L.C. v. Waypoint Nola, L.L.C.*, 976 F.3d 509, 514 (5th Cir. 2020); *Function Media, L.L.C. v. Google, Inc.*, 708 F.3d 1310, 1328–29 (Fed. Cir. 2013).

[7]*Sprinkle v. AMZ Mfg. Corp.*, 567 Fed.Appx. 163, 165 (3d Cir. 2014).

[8]*See Outlaw v. City of Hartford*, 884 F.3d 351, 368 (2d Cir. 2018); *Flores v. City of Westminster*, 873 F.3d 739, 756 (9th Cir. 2017).

[9]*See Ermini v. Scott*, 937 F.3d 1329, 1336 (11th Cir. 2019).

[10]*Manufacturers Hanover Trust Co. v. Drysdale Sec. Corp.*, 801 F.2d 13, 26 (2d Cir. 1986); *Tights, Inc. v. Acme-McCrary Corp.*, 541 F.2d 1047, 1061 (4th Cir. 1976).

[11]*See Sec. and Exch. Comm'n v. Capital Solutions Monthly Income Fund*, 818 F.3d 346, 354 (8th Cir., 2016); *Ling Nan Zheng v. Liberty Apparel Co. Inc.*, 617 F.3d 182, 186 (2d Cir. 2010).

[12]*E.E.O.C. v. Mgmt. Hospitality of Racine, Inc.*, 666 F.3d 422, 439–40 (7th Cir. 2012); *U.S. v. Real Property*

special verdicts are more appropriate in complex cases.[13] Special verdicts are also valuable when the status of the law is uncertain, so that if the trial court is reversed on the law, the special verdicts may render a new trial unnecessary.[14]

Omission of Issues

If the court submits special verdicts to the jury and omits a question of material fact raised by the pleadings or evidence, a party must object to the omission before the jury retires or that party waives the right to a jury trial on that issue.[15] As to issues not submitted to the jury and not objected to, the court may make the finding.[16] If the court merely enters a judgment based on the jury's special verdicts, the court will be deemed to have ruled in a consistent fashion on issues not submitted to the jury.[17]

Consistency of Special Verdicts

If there is a construction of the special verdicts that renders them consistent, the court will adopt it.[18] Otherwise, the court may require the jury to deliberate further[19] or may declare a mistrial.[20] The court may not, however, enter judgment contrary to the jury's special verdicts[21] or enter a verdict when the jury's special verdicts are inconsistent and the jury has been discharged.[22]

Failure to Make Unanimous Findings

If the jury fails to agree unanimously on some of the answers to special verdicts, the judge can: resubmit the special verdicts to the jury for further deliberations; ask the parties if they would be willing to accept the majority responses; enter judgment on the basis of the unanimous special verdicts if they are dispositive; declare the entire case a mistrial; or order a

---

Located at 20832 Big Rock Drive, Malibu, Cal. 902655, 51 F.3d 1402, 1408 (9th Cir. 1995).

[13] *Dinco v. Dylex Ltd.*, 111 F.3d 964, 969 (1st Cir. 1997).

[14] *See Gourdeau v. City of Newton*, 238 F. Supp. 3d 179, 182–83 (D. Mass. 2017).

[15] *See Flores v. City of Westminster*, 873 F.3d 739, 757 (9th Cir. 2017); *Vojdani v. Pharmsan Labs, Inc.*, 741 F.3d 777, 782 (7th Cir. 2013).

[16] *Raicevic v. Fieldwood Energy, L.L.C.*, 979 F.3d 1027, 1034 (5th Cir. 2020); *Vojdani v. Pharmsan Labs, Inc.*, 741 F.3d 777, 782 (7th Cir. 2013).

[17] *Universal Truckload, Inc. v. Dalton Logistics, Inc.*, 946 F.3d 689, 698 (5th Cir. 2020); *Flores v. City of Westminster*, 873 F.3d 739, 757 (9th Cir. 2017).

[18] *Flores v. City of Westminster*, 873 F.3d 739, 756 (9th Cir. 2017); *Technical Resource Services, Inc. v. Dornier Medical Sys., Inc.*, 134 F.3d 1458, 1464 (11th Cir. 1998).

[19] *Selgas v. Am. Airlines, Inc.*, 858 F. Supp. 316 (D.P.R. 1994).

[20] *Team Contractors, L.L.C. v. Waypoint Nola, L.L.C.*, 976 F.3d 509, 514 (5th Cir. 2020).

[21] *Kinetic Concepts, Inc. v. Smith & Nephew, Inc.*, 688 F.3d 1342, 1359 (Fed. Cir. 2012); *Lore v. City of Syracuse*, 670 F.3d 127, 167 (2d Cir. 2012).

[22] *Team Contractors, L.L.C. v. Waypoint Nola, L.L.C.*, 976 F.3d 509, 514 (5th Cir. 2020).

partial retrial of the issues not unanimously agreed upon.[23]

Failure to Request Special Verdicts

Failure to request special verdicts or to object to the use of a general verdict may constitute waiver of the "general-verdict rule."[24] The "general-verdict rule" provides that a general verdict may be overturned if it could be based on a number of alternative theories or sets of facts, one or more of which subsequently turns out to be legally insufficient or improper.[25] Thus, if a defendant fails to object to the use of a general verdict and one of the plaintiff's theories of liability is determined to be legally or factually unsupported, the defendant cannot appeal if the trial court decides to leave the verdict in place rather than ordering a new trial.[26]

Objections

Objections to the special verdicts should be made before the jury retires.[27] Objections to the jury's responses or to the judgment to be entered based on the jury's responses should be made, if possible, before the jury is discharged. Courts disagree as to whether failure to do so results in a waiver of the objections.[28]

RULE 49(b)—GENERAL VERDICT WITH ANSWERS TO WRITTEN QUESTIONS

CORE CONCEPT

The court may submit a general verdict and written questions or interrogatories about specific factual issues to the jury.[29]

APPLICATIONS

Purpose

Written questions (previously referred to as interrogatories) can serve 2 functions. First, they focus the jury's attention on important factual issues and provide a mechanism to ensure that the general verdict is consistent with the jury's factual findings. Second, if the court is subsequently reversed on a legal issue, a new trial may be avoided if the questions contain

---

[23] *Baxter Healthcare Corp. v. Spectramed, Inc.*, 49 F.3d 1575 (Fed. Cir. 1995).

[24] *Morse v. Fusto*, 804 F.3d 538, 551–52 (2d Cir. 2015).

[25] *See United N.Y. & N.J. Sandy Hook Pilots Ass'n v. Halecki*, 358 U.S. 613, 619 (1959).

[26] *See Morse v. Fusto*, 804 F.3d 538, 551–52 (2d Cir. 2015).

[27] *Cash v. Cnty. of Erie*, 654 F.3d 324, 340 (2d Cir. 2011); *Shcherbakovskiy v. Da Capo Al Fine, Ltd.*, 490 F.3d 130, 141 (2d Cir. 2007).

[28] *See Function Media, L.L.C. v. Google, Inc.*, 708 F.3d 1310, 1328 (Fed. Cir. 2013) (no waiver); *Trainor v. HEI Hospitality, LLC*, 699 F.3d 19, 34 (1st Cir. 2012) (waiver).

[29] *Frank C. Pollara Group, LLC v. Ocean View Inv. Holding, LLC*, 784 F.3d 177, 190 (3d Cir. 2015); *Zhang v. Am. Gem Seafoods, Inc.*, 339 F.3d 1020 (9th Cir. 2003).

sufficient findings.[30]

Court's Discretion to Use Written Questions

As with special verdicts, the court has virtually absolute discretion with respect to the use of written questions to the jury and with respect to the format of the questions.[31] The court also has broad discretion in evaluating the consistency of the answers and the general verdict, and in selecting the remedy for any inconsistencies as described below.[32]

Scope of Questions

Because the jury also returns a general verdict, the scope of the questions is not as critical as with special verdicts—every issue need not be covered.[33]

Instructions to the Jury

The court must give the jury the instructions necessary to render a general verdict and to answer the questions and must direct the jury to do both.[34] In contrast to the instructions for a special verdict, the instructions for a general verdict with questions must advise the jury of the law to apply as well as the process for making factual determinations.[35]

Answers and Verdict Consistent

If the general verdict is consistent with the answers to the questions, then the court will enter judgment accordingly. Ambiguity usually will be resolved in favor of consistency.[36]

Answers and Verdict Not Consistent

If the answers to the questions are internally consistent but not consistent with the general verdict, the court has 3 options: it can order the jury to deliberate further;[37] it can enter judgment based on the answers if they are sufficient;[38] or it can de-

---

[30] *See EMC Corp. v. Pure Storage, Inc.*, 204 F. Supp. 3d 749, 763 (D. Del. 2016).

[31] *Sprinkle v. AMZ Mfg. Corp.*, 567 Fed.Appx. 163, 164 (3d Cir. 2014); *Micrel, Inc. v. TRW, Inc.*, 486 F.3d 866 (6th Cir. 2007).

[32] *Reider v. Philip Morris USA, Inc.*, 793 F.3d 1254, 1259 (11th Cir. 2015); *Radvansky v. City of Olmsted Falls*, 496 F.3d 609, 618 (6th Cir. 2007).

[33] *See Kinetic Concepts, Inc. v. Smith & Nephew, Inc.*, 688 F.3d 1342, 1359 (Fed. Cir. 2012).

[34] *Team Contractors, L.L.C. v. Waypoint Nola, L.L.C.*, 976 F.3d 509, 515 (5th Cir. 2020).

[35] *Team Contractors, L.L.C. v. Waypoint Nola, L.L.C.*, 976 F.3d 509, 520 (5th Cir. 2020).

[36] *See U.S. Equal Employment Opportunity Comm'n v. Consol Energy, Inc.*, 860 F.3d 131, 147 (4th Cir. 2017) (court retains discretion to check for jury confusion); *Reider v. Philip Morris USA, Inc.*, 793 F.3d 1254, 1259 (11th Cir. 2015).

[37] *U.S. Equal Employment Opportunity Comm'n v. Consol Energy, Inc.*, 860 F.3d 131, 147 (4th Cir. 2017); *Jones v. Southpeak Interactive Corp. of Delaware*, 777 F.3d 658, 673–74 (4th Cir. 2015).

[38] *C.B. v. City of Sonora*, 730 F.3d 816, 824 (9th Cir. 2013); *Masters v. UHS of Delaware, Inc.*, 631 F.3d 464, 475 (8th Cir. 2011).

clare a mistrial.[39] The court may not enter judgment based on the general verdict in the face of inconsistent answers (although judgment may be proper if the inconsistent answers go to a different issue or are not necessary for the judgment).[40] If the answers are internally inconsistent and inconsistent with the general verdict, the court can order further deliberations or declare a mistrial, but cannot enter judgment.[41]

Inconsistent Answers

When the answers to the questions are internally inconsistent, the court may order the jury to deliberate further or may order a new trial.[42]

Inconsistent General Verdicts

When general verdicts on different claims are inconsistent, a court may not simply mold one of the two verdicts to be consistent with the other. Faced with inconsistent general verdicts, the court may take one of four approaches: (1) allow the verdicts to stand; (2) attempt to read the verdicts in a manner that will resolve the inconsistencies; (3) resubmit the question to the jury; or (4) order a new trial.[43]

Failure to Object to Inconsistency—Waiver

Failure to object to an inconsistency prior to the jury being excused can result in waiver of the objection, and the court may enter judgment according to the general verdict.[44]

Failure to Request

Failure to request a general verdict with questions or object to the use of a general verdict may constitute waiver of the "general-verdict rule."[45] The "general-verdict rule" provides that a general verdict may be overturned if could be based on a number of alternative theories or sets of facts, one or more of which subsequently turns out on appeal to be legally insufficient or improper.[46] Thus, if a defendant fails to object to the use of a general verdict and one of the plaintiff's theories of li-

---

[39]*See Masters v. UHS of Delaware, Inc.*, 631 F.3d 464, 475 (8th Cir. 2011); *Intermatic Inc. v. Lamson & Sessions Co.*, 273 F.3d 1355, 1369 (Fed. Cir. 2001).

[40]*Christiansen v. Wright Med. Tech., Inc.*, 851 F.3d 1203, 1213 (11th Cir. 2017); *Armstrong ex rel. Armstrong v. Brookdale University Hospital and Medical Center*, 425 F.3d 126, 135 (2d Cir. 2005).

[41]*Innovation Ventures, LLC v. N2G Distributing, Inc.*, 763 F.3d 524, 538 (6th Cir. 2014).

[42]*Christiansen v. Wright Med. Tech., Inc.*, 851 F.3d 1203, 1213 (11th Cir. 2017); *Reider v. Philip Morris USA, Inc.*, 793 F.3d 1254, 1259 (11th Cir. 2015) (court has broad discretion as to which option to select).

[43]*City of Los Angeles v. Heller*, 475 U.S. 796, 805–06 (1986).

[44]*Cont'l Vineyard, LLC v. Vinifera Wine Co., LLC*, 973 F.3d 747, 754 (7th Cir. 2020); *Team Contractors, L.L.C. v. Waypoint Nola, L.L.C.*, 976 F.3d 509, 515 (5th Cir. 2020).

[45]*Morse v. Fusto*, 804 F.3d 538, 551–52 (2d Cir. 2015).

[46]See *United N.Y. & N.J. Sandy Hook Pilots Ass'n v. Halecki*, 358 U.S. 613, 619 (1959).

ability is determined to be legally or factually unsupported, the defendant cannot appeal if the trial court decides to leave the verdict in place rather than ordering a new trial.[47]

Additional Research References

Wright & Miller, *Federal Practice and Procedure* §§ 2501 to 2513. Bennett & Hirschhorn, *Bennett's Guide to Jury Selection and Trial Dynamics in Civil and Criminal Litigation.*

C.J.S., Federal Civil Procedure §§ 1009 to 1027 et seq.

West's Key Number Digest, Federal Civil Procedure ⚷2211 to 2220, 2231 to 2242

---

[47] *See Morse v. Fusto*, 804 F.3d 538, 551–52 (2d Cir. 2015).

RULE 50
JUDGMENT AS A MATTER OF LAW IN A JURY TRIAL; RELATED MOTION FOR A NEW TRIAL; CONDITIONAL RULING

(a) **Judgment as a Matter of Law.**

(1) *In General.* If a party has been fully heard on an issue during a jury trial and the court finds that a reasonable jury would not have a legally sufficient evidentiary basis to find for the party on that issue, the court may:

(A) resolve the issue against the party; and

(B) grant a motion for judgment as a matter of law against the party on a claim or defense that, under the controlling law, can be maintained or defeated only with a favorable finding on that issue.

(2) *Motion.* A motion for judgment as a matter of law may be made at any time before the case is submitted to the jury. The motion must specify the judgment sought and the law and facts that entitle the movant to the judgment.

(b) **Renewing the Motion After Trial; Alternative Motion for a New Trial.** If the court does not grant a motion for judgment as a matter of law made under Rule 50(a), the court is considered to have submitted the action to the jury subject to the court's later deciding the legal questions raised by the motion. No later than 28 days after the entry of judgment—or if the motion addresses a jury issue not decided by a verdict, no later than 28 days after the jury was discharged—the movant may file a renewed motion for judgment as a matter of law and may include an alternative or joint request for a new trial under Rule 59. In ruling on the renewed motion, the court may:

(1) allow judgment on the verdict, if the jury returned a verdict;

(2) order a new trial; or
(3) direct the entry of judgment as a matter of law.

(c) **Granting the Renewed Motion; Conditional Ruling on a Motion for a New Trial.**

(1) *In General.* If the court grants a renewed motion for judgment as a matter of law, it must also conditionally rule on any motion for a new trial by determining whether a new trial should be granted if the judgment is later vacated or reversed. The court must state the grounds for conditionally granting or denying the motion for a new trial.

(2) *Effect of a Conditional Ruling.* Conditionally granting the motion for a new trial does not affect the judgment's finality; if the judgment is reversed, the new trial must proceed unless the appellate court orders otherwise. If the motion for a new trial is conditionally denied, the appellee may assert error in that denial; if the judgment is reversed, the case must proceed as the appellate court orders.

(d) **Time for a Losing Party's New-Trial Motion.** Any motion for a new trial under Rule 59 by a party against whom judgment as a matter of law is rendered must be filed no later than 28 days after the entry of the judgment.

(e) **Denying the Motion for Judgment as a Matter of Law; Reversal on Appeal.** If the court denies the motion for judgment as a matter of law, the prevailing party may, as appellee, assert grounds entitling it to a new trial should the appellate court conclude that the trial court erred in denying the motion. If the appellate court reverses the judgment, it may order a new trial, direct the trial court to determine whether a new trial should be granted, or direct the entry of judgment.

[Amended January 21, 1963, effective July 1, 1963; March 2, 1987, effective August 1, 1987; April 30, 1991, effective December 1, 1991; April 22, 1993, effective December 1, 1993; April 27, 1995, effective December 1, 1995; April 12, 2006, effective December 1, 2006; April 30, 2007, effective December 1, 2007; March 26, 2009, effective December 1, 2009.]

AUTHORS' COMMENTARY ON RULE 50

PURPOSE AND SCOPE

The purpose of a trial is to resolve factual disputes—generally issues where the fact finder must assess witness credibility and decide who to believe. In contrast, legal disputes are resolved by the judge based on legal analysis and precedent, without the need for credibility determinations. Recognizing this function of trials, Rule 50 provides that, once one side has offered all of its evidence on a particular claim, defense, or issue at a jury trial, the other side may then file a motion for judgment as a matter of law, arguing that even if the jury believes every piece of evidence offered by the opposing party, that evidence would not support a ruling in the opposing party's favor.

Motions for judgment as a matter of law are adjudicated under the same standard as motions for summary judgment, discussed in detail below in the coverage for Rule 56, with one nuanced difference; in a jury trial, a court is more likely to conditionally deny a motion for judgment as a matter of law and let the jury decide the case. Then, the judge might grant a renewed motion for judgment as a matter of law if the jury reaches a verdict that the judge believes to be unsupported by the evidence. This approach both accords greater respect to the parties' Seventh Amendment right to a jury trial and reduces the likelihood of needing to conduct a new trial if it turns out on appeal that the judge was wrong in overturning the jury's verdict—the verdict can simply be reinstated. To foster this approach, Rule 50 provides that, if the court denies a motion for judgment as a matter law during trial, it is presumed to have done so subject to the right to revisit the decision following trial in a renewed motion.

A party bringing an unsuccessful Rule 50 motion for judgment as a matter of law during trial must renew the motion again at the conclusion of the trial—failure to follow this two-step process may result in waiver of the grounds that could have been asserted in a Rule 50 motion. Renewed Rule 50 motions are often accompanied by motions for a new trial under Rule 59. Rule 50 addresses the complex relationship between these two options for providing relief from an improper jury verdict.

RULE 50(a)—JUDGMENT AS A MATTER OF LAW

CORE CONCEPT

Rule 50(a) allows the court to take a case away from the jury by entering a judgment as a matter of law if there is not sufficient evidence in the record to raise a genuine factual dispute.

APPLICATIONS

Who May Make Motion

Although motions for judgment as a matter of law are most commonly made by defendants, plaintiffs may also make Rule 50 motions. Thus, if the plaintiff enters evidence sufficient to support each element of the plaintiff's case and that evidence is not contradicted during the defendant's case, the plaintiff will be entitled to a judgment as a matter of law.[1] In addition, some courts hold that the judge may enter judgment as a matter of law *sua sponte*,[2] although other courts hold that judgment as a matter of law may only be made on grounds properly raised by the parties in a Rule 50(a) motion, calling into question the court's ability to issue judgment as a matter of law *sua sponte*.[3]

Content of Motion

A motion for judgment as a matter of law must specify the judgment sought (*i.e.,* the counts or issues upon which judgment is sought) and the law and facts supporting the judgment.[4] Any issue not clearly articulated in this manner may be waived.[5]

Form and Timing of Motion

A motion for judgment as a matter of law may be made orally[6] or in writing, but must be explicitly made on the record.[7] The motion may be made after the opposing party has been fully heard on an issue, at any time before submission of the case to the jury.[8] Such motions are typically made at the close of the plaintiff's case (by the defendant) or at the close of the record.

Subject of Motion

A motion for judgment as a matter of law may seek judgment on entire claims or defenses or on specific issues that are

---

[1] *Hurd v. Am. Hoist and Derrick Co.*, 734 F.2d 495, 499 (10th Cir. 1984); *Walter E. Heller & Co. v. Video Innovations, Inc.*, 730 F.2d 50, 54 (2d Cir. 1984).

[2] *See Santos-Arrieta v. Hosp. Del Maestro*, 14 F.4th 1, 9 (1st Cir. 2021); *Axelson v. Watson*, 999 F.3d 541, 545 (8th Cir. 2021).

[3] *See Santos-Arrieta v. Hosp. Del Maestro*, 14 F.4th 1, 10 (1st Cir. 2021); *Mountain Dudes v. Split Rock Holdings, Inc.*, 946 F.3d 1122, 1131 (10th Cir. 2019).

[4] *Olsen as Tr. for Xurex, Inc. v. Di Mase*, 24 F.4th 1197, 1202 (8th Cir. 2022); *Santos-Arrieta v. Hosp. Del Maestro*, 14 F.4th 1, 8 (1st Cir. 2021).

[5] *Olsen as Tr. for Xurex, Inc. v. Di Mase*, 24 F.4th 1197, 1202 (8th Cir. 2022); *Santos-Arrieta v. Hosp. Del Maestro*, 14 F.4th 1, 8 (1st Cir. 2021).

[6] *See, e.g., Santos-Arrieta v. Hosp. Del Maestro*, 14 F.4th 1, 5 (1st Cir. 2021); *Howell v. Wexford Health Sources, Inc.*, 987 F.3d 647, 652 (7th Cir. 2021).

[7] *Hanover Am. Ins. Co. v. Tattooed Millionaire Ent., LLC*, 974 F.3d 767, 780–83 (6th Cir. 2020); *Ross v. Rhodes Furniture, Inc.*, 146 F.3d 1286, 1289 (11th Cir. 1998).

[8] *Moskos v. Hardee*, 24 F.4th 289, 294 (4th Cir. 2022); *Santos-Arrieta v. Hosp. Del Maestro*, 14 F.4th 1, 8 (1st Cir. 2021).

not wholly dispositive of a claim or defense.[9]

Standard

The standard for a motion for judgment as a matter of law is the same as for a motion for summary judgment (making that substantial body of case law applicable).[10] Judgment as a matter of law is appropriate when the evidence in the record could not properly support a particular verdict.[11] This determination is a matter of law for the court.[12] The court must view all evidence in the light most favorable to the party opposing the motion;[13] it may not make credibility determinations or weigh the evidence.[14] The court must also draw all reasonable inferences from the evidence in favor of the party opposing the motion.[15] However, the court may disregard testimony that is opposed to undisputed physical facts.[16] Moreover, a "mere scintilla" of evidence is not sufficient to avoid judgment as a matter of law.[17] Given the sanctity of the jury process, however, many courts are reluctant to take a case away from a jury.[18]

Opportunity to Cure

A major purpose of the motion is to bring a deficiency in the evidence to the attention of opposing parties so they may cure the defect.[19] The court has a duty to apprise the non-moving party of the materiality of the dispositive fact and provide that party with an opportunity to present any available evidence.[20]

Motion Held Under Consideration

The court is under no obligation to grant a motion for judg-

---

[9] *Ross v. Rhodes Furniture, Inc.*, 146 F.3d 1286, 1289–90 (11th Cir. 1998); *Chesapeake Paper Prod. Co. v. Stone & Webster Engineering Corp.*, 51 F.3d 1229, 1236 (4th Cir. 1995).

[10] *See Gray v. Hudson*, 28 F.4th 87, 95 (9th Cir. 2022); *Surgery Ctr. at 900 N. Michigan Ave., LLC v. Am. Physicians Assurance Corp., Inc.*, 922 F.3d 778, 784 (7th Cir. 2019).

[11] *Weisgram v. Marley Co.*, 528 U.S. 440, 453–54 (2000); *Anderson v. Liberty Lobby, Inc.*, 477 U.S. 242 (1986).

[12] *See Brownstein v. Lindsay*, 742 F.3d 55, 63 (3d Cir. 2014); *Graham Const. Services v. Hammer & Steel Inc.*, 755 F.3d 611, 616 (8th Cir. 2014).

[13] *Galloway v. U.S.*, 319 U.S. 372 (1943); *Cloutier v. GoJet Airlines, LLC*, 996 F.3d 426, 439 (7th Cir. 2021).

[14] *Reeves v. Sanderson Plumbing Prods., Inc.*, 530 U.S. 133, 150 (2000); *ITyX Sols. AG v. Kodak Alaris, Inc.*, 952 F.3d 1, 9 (1st Cir. 2020).

[15] *Johnston v. Borders*, 36 F.4th 1254 (11th Cir. 2022); *Alonso v. Westcoast Corp.*, 920 F.3d 878, 882 (5th Cir. 2019).

[16] *See, e.g., Daddi v. United Overseas Exp. Lines, Inc., Oriental Inventor*, 674 F.2d 175, 177 (2d Cir. 1982).

[17] *A.B. Small Co. v. Lamborn & Co.*, 267 U.S. 248, 254 (1925); *Filipovich v. K & R Exp. Sys., Inc.*, 391 F.3d 859, 863 (7th Cir. 2004).

[18] *Bayer Healthcare LLC v. Baxalta Inc.*, 989 F.3d 964, 979 (Fed. Cir. 2021); *Hernandez v. Boles*, 949 F.3d 251, 256 (6th Cir. 2020).

[19] *See Weisgram v. Marley Co.*, 528 U.S. 440, 454 (2000); *Santos-Arrieta v. Hosp. Del Maestro*, 14 F.4th 1, 9 (1st Cir. 2021).

[20] *Reed v. Lieurance*, 863 F.3d 1196, 1210 (9th Cir. 2017); *Waters v. Young*, 100 F.3d 1437, 1441 (9th Cir. 1996) (the court's duty is especially important when confronted with pro se litigants).

ment as a matter of law even if the record supports the motion.[21] Courts often defer ruling on a Rule 50(a) motion, allowing the jury to reach a verdict in order to minimize the likelihood of needing a new trial.[22] If the jury reaches the same conclusion as the judge, then the judge will take no action. If the jury reaches the opposite conclusion, the judge can enter judgment as a matter of law. Then, if the case is appealed and the appellate court disagrees with the judge, there is no need for a new trial as the trial court can simply reinstate the jury verdict.[23]

Motion Granted

If the court grants a motion for judgment as a matter of law, it will enter the appropriate judgment without involvement of the jury.[24]

Motion Denied—Conditional Submission to the Jury

If the court does not grant the motion for judgment as a matter of law, the court is considered to have submitted the action to the jury subject to the court's later deciding the questions raised by the motion.[25] If it was the defendant's motion that the court denied, the defendant may put on evidence. However, if the plaintiff's case lacked certain evidence and that evidence is brought out during the defendant's case, the deficiency will be cured.[26]

Failure to Make a Rule 50(a) Motion—Prerequisite to Appeal

A motion for judgment as a matter of law before the close of the record is a prerequisite to challenging the sufficiency of the evidence on appeal.[27] Statements by the judge that Rule 50(a) motions are deemed made and denied or are unnecessary may not relieve parties from making a formal motion.[28] The courts are divided as to whether appellate issues other than those relating to the sufficiency of the evidence, such as pure issues of

[21] *Montano v. Orange County, Texas*, 842 F.3d 865, 873 (5th Cir. 2016); *Cornwell Ent., Inc. v. Anchin, Block & Anchin, LLP*, 830 F.3d 18, 20 (1st Cir. 2016).

[22] *See Biogen MA Inc. v. EMD Serono, Inc.*, 976 F.3d 1326, 1330 (Fed. Cir. 2020); *Lexington Ins. Co. v. Horace Mann Ins. Co.*, 861 F.3d 661, 672 (7th Cir. 2017) (recommending that the trial court *always* take Rule 50(a) motions under advisement).

[23] *Colonial Lincoln-Mercury, Inc. v. Musgrave*, 749 F.2d 1092, 1098 (4th Cir. 1984); *U.S. v. Singleton*, 702 F.2d 1159, 1172 (D.C. Cir. 1983).

[24] *See Lexington Ins. Co. v. Horace Mann Ins. Co.*, 861 F.3d 661, 666 (7th Cir. 2017).

[25] *Hanover Am. Ins. Co. v. Tattooed Millionaire Ent., LLC*, 974 F.3d 767, 780 (6th Cir. 2020); *Holder v. Illinois Dept. of Corrections*, 751 F.3d 486, 490 (7th Cir. 2014).

[26] *Trustees of University of Pennsylvania v. Lexington Ins. Co.*, 815 F.2d 890, 903 (3d Cir. 1987); *Peterson v. Hager*, 724 F.2d 851, 854 (10th Cir. 1984).

[27] *Unitherm Food Sys., Inc. v. Swift-Eckrich, Inc.*, 546 U.S. 394 (2006); *Rexing Quality Eggs v. Rembrandt Enterprises, Inc.*, 996 F.3d 354, 370 n.64 (7th Cir. 2021).

[28] *Hanover Am. Ins. Co. v. Tattooed Millionaire Ent., LLC*, 974 F.3d 767, 783 (6th Cir. 2020).

law, are affected.[29] An exception to this principle occurs if the verdict constitutes plain error on the face of the record and a miscarriage of justice would result if the verdict remained in effect.[30]

- *Unavailable Grounds:* A party is not obligated to make a motion raising grounds that did not become available until the jury rendered its verdict.[31] However, if grounds for a Rule 50 motion arise after a party has already made a Rule 50(a) motion but before the case is submitted to the jury, the party must make a second Rule 50(a) motion or risk waiving the new grounds.[32]

Issues Previously Raised in Unsuccessful Summary Judgment Motions

The courts differ as to the extent to which a party must raise issues from an unsuccessful motion for summary judgment in a motion for judgment as a matter of law.[33] Some courts do not require presentation of pure legal issues in the form of a Rule 50 motion.[34] Others require all issues raised in a summary judgment motion to be presented in a Rule 50 motion in order to preserve the issues for appeal.[35] Some courts allow a party to make a Rule 50(a) motion that simply renews the issues advanced in a prior motion for summary judgment.[36] There are also gradations to these approaches.[37] There are also gradations to these approaches.[38] If you are not sure which category your jurisdiction and/or motion falls into, it is good practice to raise summary judgment issues in a Rule 50 motion at the end

[29] *Murphy-Sims v. Owners Ins. Co.*, 947 F.3d 628, 630 (10th Cir. 2020) (motion not required to appeal pure legal issue); *Ji v. Bose Corp.*, 626 F.3d 116, 128 (1st Cir. 2010) (requiring motion for judgment as a matter of law for all issues).

[30] *Alonso v. Westcoast Corp.*, 920 F.3d 878, 884 (5th Cir. 2019); *Stephenson v. Doe*, 332 F.3d 68, 75–76 (2d Cir. 2003).

[31] *See Ridgell v. City of Pine Bluff*, 935 F.3d 633, 636 (8th Cir. 2019).

[32] *Santos-Arrieta v. Hosp. Del Maestro*, 14 F.4th 1, 10 (1st Cir. 2021).

[33] *See Lexington Ins. Co. v. Horace Mann Ins. Co.*, 861 F.3d 661, 670 (7th Cir. 2017) (no need to file Rule 50 motions following successful motion for summary judgment).

[34] *See Kars 4 Kids Inc. v. Am. Can!*, 8 F.4th 209, 217 n.3 (3d Cir. 2021); *Mimms v. CVS Pharmacy, Inc.*, 889 F.3d 865, 869 (7th Cir. 2018).

[35] *See, e.g., Feld Motor Sports, Inc. v. Traxxas, L.P.*, 861 F.3d 591, 596 (5th Cir. 2017); *Varghese v. Honeywell Intern., Inc.*, 424 F.3d 411, 420–23 (4th Cir. 2005).

[36] *See, e.g., Tan Lam v. City of Los Banos*, 976 F.3d 986, 994 (9th Cir. 2020).

[37] *See, e.g., Duban v. Waverly Sales Co.*, 760 F.3d 832, 835 (8th Cir. 2014) (requiring a party to file a Rule 50(a) motion during trial but not a Rule 50(b) renewal in order to preserve a pure legal issue raised on summary judgment).

[38] *See, e.g., Duban v. Waverly Sales Co.*, 760 F.3d 832, 835 (8th Cir. 2014) (requiring a party to file a Rule 50(a) motion during trial but not a Rule 50(b) renewal in order to preserve a pure legal issue raised on summary judgment).

of the other party's case.[39]

Binding Jury Trials Only

Rule 50 applies only to binding jury cases.[40] The appropriate motion in nonjury trials and trials with an advisory jury is a motion for judgment on partial findings under Rule 52(c).[41]

RULE 50(b)—RENEWING THE MOTION AFTER TRIAL; ALTERNATIVE MOTION FOR A NEW TRIAL

CORE CONCEPT

After trial, parties must renew their unsuccessful Rule 50(a) motions for judgment as a matter of law, and the court can enter a judgment that is inconsistent with the jury's verdict if it determines that the verdict was not supported by the evidence.

APPLICATIONS

Scope

Rule 50(b) motions address the sufficiency of the evidence.[42] Some courts hold that Rule 50(b) does not apply to pretrial rulings or other rulings not related to the sufficiency of the evidence.[43] It only applies in cases with binding jury trials, not to cases with bench trials or advisory juries.[44] As described above under Rule 50(a), the courts are divided about whether a party must follow the Rule 50(a)/50(b) sequence to raise legal issues unsuccessfully advanced at the summary judgment stage.[45]

Content of Motion

A renewed motion for judgment after trial must state the grounds for relief,[46] and may include only those grounds raised in the original motion for judgment as a matter of law.[47]

---

[39] *Haberman v. The Hartford Ins. Group*, 443 F.3d 1257 (10th Cir. 2006).

[40] *Stop Illinois Health Care Fraud, LLC v. Sayeed*, 957 F.3d 743, 748 (7th Cir. 2020); *Spartan Concrete Prod., LLC v. Argos USVI, Corp.*, 929 F.3d 107, 112 n.1 (3d Cir. 2019).

[41] *Spartan Concrete Prod., LLC v. Argos USVI, Corp.*, 929 F.3d 107, 112 n.1 (3d Cir. 2019); *4 Pillar Dynasty LLC v. New York & Co., Inc.*, 933 F.3d 202, 209 n.6 (2d Cir. 2019).

[42] *Antrim Pharm. LLC v. Bio-Pharm, Inc.*, 950 F.3d 423, 428 (7th Cir. 2020).

[43] *Antrim Pharm. LLC v. Bio-Pharm, Inc.*, 950 F.3d 423, 428 (7th Cir. 2020).

[44] *4 Pillar Dynasty LLC v. New York & Co., Inc.*, 933 F.3d 202, 209 n.6 (2d Cir. 2019).

[45] *See Osterhout v. Bd. of Cnty. Commissioners of LeFlore Cnty., Oklahoma*, 10 F.4th 978, 984 n.3 (10th Cir. 2021) (Rule 50(b) does not apply to issues not submitted to the jury); *Hanover Am. Ins. Co. v. Tattooed Millionaire Ent., LLC*, 974 F.3d 767, 785 (6th Cir. 2020).

[46] *Andreas v. Volkswagen of Am., Inc.*, 336 F.3d 789 (8th Cir.2003).

[47] *Santos-Arrieta v. Hosp. Del Maestro*, 14 F.4th 1, 8 (1st Cir. 2021) (issue must be "distinctly" articulated); *Ruckh v. Salus Rehab., LLC*, 963 F.3d 1089, 1109 n.12 (11th Cir. 2020) (issues must be "closely related," but "complete identity" not required).

Timing

The motion must be filed not later than 28 days after the *entry* of the judgment[48] (not the *notice* of entry of the judgment). If the jury does not return a verdict, such as with a mistrial, or if the subject of the motion for judgment as a matter of law was an issue not decided by the verdict, the parties have 28 days from the discharge of the jury.[49] Rule 6(b)(2) expressly forbids the court from enlarging the time to file a Rule 50(b) motion.[50] The time limit is not jurisdictional, however, so if an opposing party does not object to a late-filed Rule 50(b) motion, the party waives objections based on the timing of the motion.[51]

Failure to File is Waiver of Appeal

Failure to file a renewed motion under Rule 50(b) limits a party's right to appeal.[52] Likewise, parties waive individual arguments by failing to assert them in support of or in opposition to the Rule 50(b) motion.[53] Some courts do not apply this restriction rigidly,[54] some courts consider the objection waived if not advanced by an opposing party,[55] and others allow review for plain error in the absence of a Rule 50(b) motion.[56] A party who is successful at trial has no obligation to file a post-verdict Rule 50(b) motion, and if an opposing party appeals, the successful party may raise arguments advanced in a Rule 50(a) motion but not renewed.[57]

Standard

A renewed motion for judgment as a matter of law under Rule 50(b) is evaluated under the same standard as the initial motion under Rule 50(a);[58] the motion will be denied if the evidence in the record could properly support the verdict, viewing

---

[48] *Monohon v. BNSF Ry. Co.*, 17 F.4th 773, 779 (8th Cir. 2021); *Hinz v. Neuroscience, Inc.*, 538 F.3d 979, 983 (8th Cir. 2008) (where motion filed timely but brief filed 1 day late, brief could not be considered).

[49] *Mountain Dudes v. Split Rock Holdings, Inc.*, 946 F.3d 1122, 1131 (10th Cir. 2019).

[50] *Circuitronix, LLC v. Kinwong Elec. (Hong Kong) Co.*, 993 F.3d 1299, 1304 (11th Cir. 2021); *Legg v. Ulster Cty.*, 979 F.3d 101, 110 (2d Cir. 2020).

[51] *Legg v. Ulster Cty.*, 979 F.3d 101, 105–06 (2d Cir. 2020); *Escribano v. Travis Cty., Texas*, 947 F.3d 265, 272 (5th Cir. 2020).

[52] *Oritz v. Jordan*, 562 U.S. 180 (2011); *Unitherm Food Sys. v. Swift-Eckrich, Inc.*, 546 U.S. 394, 407 (2006).

[53] *Mountain Dudes v. Split Rock Holdings, Inc.*, 946 F.3d 1122, 1131–32 (10th Cir. 2019); *Promega Corp. v. Life Techs. Corp.*, 875 F.3d 651, 661 (Fed. Cir. 2017).

[54] *See Ortiz v. Jordan*, 562 U.S. 180, 189 (2011); *Minnesota Supply Co. v. Raymond Corp.*, 472 F.3d 524, 535–36 (8th Cir. 2006) (failure to renew the motion not a waiver when the court advised the party that there was no need to renew the motion).

[55] *Mountain Dudes v. Split Rock Holdings, Inc.*, 946 F.3d 1122, 1136 (10th Cir. 2019).

[56] *See Moss v. Princip*, 913 F.3d 508, 522 (5th Cir. 2019); *Parker v. Arkansas Dep't of Correction*, 888 F.3d 396, 398 n.3 (8th Cir. 2018).

[57] *Cox v. Wilson*, 959 F.3d 1249, 1259 (10th Cir. 2020).

[58] *McGinnis v. Am. Home Mortgage Servicing, Inc.*, 817 F.3d 1241, 1254 (11th Cir. 2016); *Connelly v. Metropoli-*

the evidence and all inferences in the light most favorable to the non-moving party.[59] Given the sanctity of the jury process, many courts are reluctant to overturn jury verdicts.[60]

Rule 50(a) Motion During Trial a Prerequisite

A party cannot make a motion for judgment after trial unless it filed a motion for judgment as a matter of law before the case was submitted to the jury,[61] and may not assert grounds unless it raised similar grounds in the Rule 50(a) motion[62] (unless the grounds were not available at that time).[63] Some courts apply a somewhat "fuzzy" approach to this prerequisite, allowing a renewed motion to follow an "ambiguous or inartfully made motion under Rule 50(a),"[64] or when the moving party raised the issues at a conference.[65] Additionally, if the opposing party fails to object to an issue in a Rule 50(b) motion on the grounds that the moving party did not raise the issue in a Rule 50(a) motion, the opposing party waives the objection.[66] If there was no motion for judgment as a matter of law but the evidence does not support the verdict, the court can order a new trial under Rule 59.[67]

Motion for a New Trial

A party may join a motion for a new trial with a motion for judgment after trial or request a new trial in the alternative.[68] A new trial is favored over a judgment contrary to the verdict when it appears that the party could present sufficient evidence to support the verdict at a future date.[69]

---

tan Atlanta Rapid Transit Authority, 764 F.3d 1358, 1363–34 (11th Cir. 2014).

[59] *See Monohon v. BNSF Ry. Co.*, 17 F.4th 773, 779 (8th Cir. 2021); *Tercero v. Texas Southmost Coll. Dist.*, 989 F.3d 291, 299 (5th Cir. 2021).

[60] *See, e.g., Triolo v. Nassau Cnty.*, 24 F.4th 98, 105 (2d Cir. 2022); *VHT, Inc. v. Zillow Grp., Inc.*, 918 F.3d 723, 736 (9th Cir. 2019).

[61] *Hanover Am. Ins. Co. v. Tattooed Millionaire Ent., LLC*, 974 F.3d 767, 780 (6th Cir. 2020); *Moss v. Princip*, 913 F.3d 508, 522 (5th Cir. 2019).

[62] *Hanover Am. Ins. Co. v. Tattooed Millionaire Ent., LLC*, 974 F.3d 767, 780 (6th Cir. 2020); *Puga v. RCX Sols., Inc.*, 922 F.3d 285, 290 (5th Cir. 2019).

[63] *See Abellan v. Lavelo Prop. Mgmt., LLC*, 948 F.3d 820, 827 (7th Cir. 2020); *Ridgell v. City of Pine Bluff*, 935 F.3d 633, 636 (8th Cir. 2019).

[64] *Ericsson Inc. v. TCL Commc'n Tech. Holdings Ltd.*, 955 F.3d 1317, 1324 (Fed. Cir. 2020) (technical noncompliance may be excused); *Williams v. Gaye*, 895 F.3d 1106, 1131 n.20 (9th Cir. 2018).

[65] *McGinnis v. Am. Home Mortgage Servicing, Inc.*, 817 F.3d 1241, 1263 (11th Cir. 2016).

[66] *Mountain Dudes v. Split Rock Holdings, Inc.*, 946 F.3d 1122, 1136 (10th Cir. 2019); *OTR Wheel Eng'g, Inc. v. W. Worldwide Servs., Inc.*, 897 F.3d 1008, 1016 (9th Cir. 2018).

[67] *See Johnson v. New York, N.H. & H.R. Co.*, 344 U.S. 48, 54 (1952); *Texas Advanced Optoelectronic Sols., Inc. v. Renesas Elecs. Am., Inc.*, 895 F.3d 1304, 1311 (Fed. Cir. 2018).

[68] *See Vega v. Chicago Park Dist.*, 954 F.3d 996, 1004 (7th Cir. 2020); *Smith v. City & Cty. of Honolulu*, 887 F.3d 944, 949 (9th Cir. 2018).

[69] *See Cornwell Ent., Inc. v. Anchin, Block & Anchin, LLP*, 830 F.3d 18, 24 (1st Cir. 2016).

Court's Options in Ruling on a Rule 50(b) Motion and a Motion for New Trial

If the jury returned a verdict, the court may allow the verdict to stand, order a new trial (potentially of limited scope), or direct entry of judgment as a matter of law.[70] If no verdict was returned, the court may order a new trial or direct the entry of judgment as a matter of law. When a motion for new trial is joined with a motion for judgment after trial, Rule 50 specifically requires that the court rule on both motions.[71]

Appeals

Rulings on motions for judgment after trial are final, appealable orders.[72] In contrast, an order granting a new trial may not be a final, appealable order.[73]

RULE 50(c)—GRANTING THE RENEWED MOTION; CONDITIONAL RULINGS ON A MOTION FOR A NEW TRIAL

CORE CONCEPT

If the court grants a motion for judgment as a matter of law after trial and a motion for a new trial was also filed, the court must also make a conditional ruling on the motion for a new trial setting forth the reasons for its conditional ruling.[74]

APPLICATIONS

New Trial Ruling Conditional on Appellate Reversal

The trial court's rulings on the motion for a new trial are applicable if the appeals court reverses the granting of the judgment as a matter of law.[75] In that case, the appeals court will enter the original verdict or order a new trial, depending on the trial court's conditional ruling. The appeals court may also review the trial court's conditional ruling on the motion for a new trial.[76]

Granting of Both Motions

If the trial court grants both a motion for judgment notwithstanding the verdict and a motion for a new trial, the

---

[70] *Escribano v. Travis Cty., Texas*, 947 F.3d 265, 270 (5th Cir. 2020); *In re: Cox Enterprises, Inc.*, 871 F.3d 1093, 1096 (10th Cir. 2017).

[71] *See Jennings v. Jones*, 587 F.3d 430, 432 (1st Cir. 2009).

[72] *Escribano v. Travis Cty., Texas*, 947 F.3d 265, 270 (5th Cir. 2020).

[73] *Escribano v. Travis Cty., Texas*, 947 F.3d 265, 270 (5th Cir. 2020); *Binder v. Long Island Lighting Co.*, 57 F.3d 193 (2d Cir. 1995).

[74] *Santos-Arrieta v. Hosp. Del Maestro*, 14 F.4th 1, 12 (1st Cir. 2021) (remanding when the trial court failed to make a conditional ruling); *Network-1 Techs., Inc. v. Hewlett-Packard Co.*, 981 F.3d 1015, 1028 (Fed. Cir. 2020).

[75] *In re Biogen '755 Patent Litig.*, 335 F. Supp. 3d 688, 700 (D.N.J. 2018); *Fioto v. Manhattan Woods Golf Enterprises, LLC.*, 304 F. Supp. 2d 541 (S.D.N.Y. 2004).

[76] *See Cote v. R.J. Reynolds Tobacco Co.*, 909 F.3d 1094, 1109 (11th Cir. 2018).

ruling on the motion for a new trial is automatically deemed conditional.[77]

RULE 50(d)—TIME FOR A LOSING PARTY'S NEW-TRIAL MOTION

CORE CONCEPT

If the court grants a motion for judgment as a matter of law after trial, the party against whom judgment was entered may file a Rule 59 motion for a new trial no later than 28 days after the entry of judgment.[78]

RULE 50(e)—DENYING THE MOTION FOR JUDGMENT AS A MATTER OF LAW; REVERSAL ON APPEAL

CORE CONCEPT

If the losing party appeals the denial of a motion for judgment as a matter of law after trial, the prevailing party may on appeal assert grounds for a new trial in the event that the court reverses the denial of the motion for judgment as a matter of law.[79] If the appellate court does reverse, it may order the entry of judgment, order a new trial, or remand to the trial court to determine whether a new trial is warranted.[80]

Additional Research References

Wright & Miller, *Federal Practice and Procedure* §§ 2521 to 2540
C.J.S., Federal Civil Procedure §§ 958 to 977 et seq.
C.J.S., Federal Civil Procedure § 1034, § 1089, § 1093, §§ 1219 to 1226 et seq.
West's Key Number Digest, Federal Civil Procedure ⚷2111 to 2156, 2601 to 2610

---

[77] *See Smart v. City of Miami Beach, Fla.*, 933 F. Supp. 2d 1366, 1381 (S.D. Fla. 2013).

[78] *See Promega Corp. v. Life Techs. Corp.*, 875 F.3d 651, 664–65 (Fed. Cir. 2017).

[79] *See Bunn v. Oldendorff Carriers GmbH & Co. KG*, 723 F.3d 454, 468 (4th Cir. 2013).

[80] *Sardis v. Overhead Door Corp.*, 10 F.4th 268, 279 (4th Cir. 2021).

RULE 51
INSTRUCTIONS TO THE JURY; OBJECTIONS; PRESERVING A CLAIM OF ERROR

(a) **Requests.**

(1) *Before or at the Close of the Evidence.* At the close of the evidence or at any earlier reasonable time that the court orders, a party may file and furnish to every other party written requests for the jury instructions it wants the court to give.

(2) *After the Close of the Evidence.* After the close of the evidence, a party may:

(A) file requests for instructions on issues that could not reasonably have been anticipated by an earlier time that the court set for requests; and

(B) with the court's permission, file untimely requests for instructions on any issue.

(b) **Instructions.** The court:

(1) must inform the parties of its proposed instructions and proposed action on the requests before instructing the jury and before final jury arguments;

(2) must give the parties an opportunity to object on the record and out of the jury's hearing before the instructions and arguments are delivered; and

(3) may instruct the jury at any time before the jury is discharged.

(c) **Objections.**

(1) *How to Make.* A party who objects to an instruction or the failure to give an instruction must do so on the record, stating distinctly the matter objected to and the grounds for the objection.

(2) *When to Make.* An objection is timely if:

(A) a party objects at the opportunity provided under Rule 51(b)(2); or

(B) a party was not informed of an instruction or action on a request before that opportunity to object, and the party objects promptly after learning that the instruction or request will be, or has been, given or refused.

(d) **Assigning Error; Plain Error.**

(1) *Assigning Error.* A party may assign as error:

(A) an error in an instruction actually given, if that party properly objected; or

(B) a failure to give an instruction, if that party properly requested it and—unless the court rejected the request in a definitive ruling on the record—also properly objected.

(2) *Plain Error.* A court may consider a plain error in the instructions that has not been preserved as required by Rule 51(d)(1) if the error affects substantial rights.

[Amended effective August 1, 1987; March 27, 2003, effective December 1, 2003; April 30, 2007, effective December 1, 2007.]

AUTHORS' COMMENTARY ON RULE 51

PURPOSE AND SCOPE

Rule 51 contains procedures relating to instructing the jury about the law that it is supposed to apply. Typically, the judge will provide the parties with an opportunity to submit proposed instructions. The judge will then advise the parties of the intended instructions, giving them an opportunity to object on the record and outside the jury's presence. Before the jury retires to deliberate, the judge will then read the instructions to the jury, giving the parties another opportunity to object to the as-delivered instructions. The judge may also give the jury additional instructions at any time before the jury is discharged. Failure to properly object to the instructions can result in waiver of the right to appeal based on the content of the instructions.

RULE 51(a)—REQUESTS

CORE CONCEPT

The parties may submit proposed jury instructions to the court. Proposed instructions are submitted at the close of the evidence or at such earlier time as directed by the court.

APPLICATIONS

Timing of Requests

Requests for jury instructions are normally made at the close of the evidence, or earlier if the court so directs.[1] If the court has set a time before the close of evidence for submission of requests for instructions, a party may submit additional requests for instructions after the close of evidence on issues that the party could not have anticipated when it first submitted its requests.[2] Local rules may set the time for making requests for jury instructions. The court, in its discretion, may consider untimely requests.[3]

Form and Content of Requests

Requests normally should be reasonably neutral statements of the law governing the case, and not overly argumentative. Requests should be in writing.[4] The requests should include every issue upon which the party wants the court to instruct the jury, and some courts consider the party's failure to request a particular instruction in their analysis of whether the party has waived objections to the court's failure to give that instruction.[5]

Service

Requests for instruction must be served on every other party.[6]

RULE 51(b)—INSTRUCTIONS

CORE CONCEPT

The court must inform the parties of its proposed instructions before instructing the jury and before the parties' closing arguments to the jury, and must give the parties an opportunity to object on the record and out of the jury's hearing. The judge may also give the jury additional instructions at any time before the judge discharges the jury.

APPLICATIONS

Informing Parties of Proposed Instructions

The court is required to inform the parties of its proposed jury instructions and its rulings on the parties' requests before

---

[1] *Potthast v. Metro-North Railroad Co.*, 400 F.3d 143, 153 (2d Cir. 2005); *Jenkins v. Corizon Health Inc.*, ___ F. Supp. 3d ___, 2022 WL 390554, at *1 (S.D. Ga. 2022).

[2] *Potthast v. Metro-North Railroad Co.*, 400 F.3d 143, 153 (2d Cir. 2005); *Williams v. Dist. of Columbia*, 825 F. Supp. 2d 88, 103 (D.D.C. 2011).

[3] *Morgan v. City of Chicago*, 822 F.3d 317, 341 (7th Cir. 2016).

[4] *Raynor v. G4S Secure Sols. (USA) Inc.*, 327 F. Supp. 3d 925, 943 (W.D.N.C. 2018).

[5] *See, e.g., Rodriguez v. Miami-Dade Cty.*, 339 F. Supp. 3d 1279, 1287 (M.D. Fla. 2018).

[6] Rule 51(a)(1).

the closing arguments and before it instructs the jury[7] so that the counsel may adjust their closings accordingly. Failure to do so, however, will not be grounds for a new trial unless it is prejudicial.[8] Some courts hold that the court need not give the actual instructions to the parties, as long as the court describes the proposed instructions with sufficient detail that the parties understand the nature of the instructions the court proposes to deliver.[9]

Form and Procedure for Instructions

Instructions are given to the jury in open court at any time after trial begins and before the jury is discharged.[10] The judge may repeat portions of the charge or give a supplemental charge at the jury's request, but must afford the parties notice and an opportunity to be present for such additional instructions.[11] The judge may submit a written copy of the instructions to the jury, although it is not commonly done in federal court.

Content of Instructions

If the court is going to use a general verdict, the court should give an instruction on every material legal issue in the case.[12] The instruction should clearly and understandably convey the status of the applicable law.[13] There is no particular wording or order mandated,[14] and the judge need not use the language requested by the parties. Narrowly-tailored instructions are favored over broad statements of the law. If the court is using a special verdict addressing factual questions to the jury, the jury instructions need not address issues of substantive law, but may still address issues like the burden of proof.[15]

Instructions to Deadlocked Jury

The judge may instruct a jury claiming to be deadlocked to make further attempts to reach a verdict (sometimes called an

---

[7]*Denault v. Ahern*, 857 F.3d 76, 89 (1st Cir. 2017) (the rule does not require the court to provide the parties with a written copy of the instructions); *Johnson v. Gen. Bd. of Pension & Health Benefits of the United Methodist Church*, 733 F.3d 722, 732 (7th Cir. 2013).

[8]*Johnson v. Gen. Bd. of Pension & Health Benefits of the United Methodist Church*, 733 F.3d 722, 732 (7th Cir. 2013); *Delano v. Kitch*, 542 F.2d 550 (10th Cir. 1976).

[9]*DeCaro v. Hasbro, Inc.*, 580 F.3d 55, 65 (1st Cir. 2009); *Porter v. City of Philadelphia*, 337 F. Supp. 3d 530, 561 (E.D. Pa. 2018).

[10]*See Dietz v. Bouldin*, __ U.S. __, 136 S. Ct. 1885, 1892 (2016) (court may even recall a discharged jury with proper precautions).

[11]*See Dietz v. Bouldin*, __ U.S. __, 136 S. Ct. 1885, 1892 (2016) (court may even recall a discharged jury with proper precautions).

[12]*See Williams v. Dist. of Columbia*, 825 F. Supp. 2d 88, 91 (D.D.C. 2011).

[13]*See Williams v. Dist. of Columbia*, 825 F. Supp. 2d 88, 91 (D.D.C. 2011).

[14]*Williams v. Dist. of Columbia*, 825 F. Supp. 2d 88, 91 (D.D.C. 2011).

[15]*Outlaw v. City of Hartford*, 884 F.3d 351, 368 (2d Cir. 2018); *Flores v. City of Westminster*, 873 F.3d 739, 756 (9th Cir. 2017).

"Allen charge," named after *Allen v. United States*, 164 U.S. 492 (1896)).[16] The judge may not, however, coerce reluctant jurors to join the majority.

Comments on Evidence

The court, in its discretion, may comment on the evidence and even focus the jury's attention on certain portions of the evidence. If the judge does so, the judge must make it clear to the jury that they, not the judge, are the ultimate fact finders.

Opportunity to Object

The court must give the parties an opportunity to raise objections to the instructions on the record and out of the hearing of the jury before the instructions and closing arguments are delivered.[17] If the court fails to give the parties an opportunity to raise the objections, parties with objections should request an opportunity.[18] If instructions are reread or the jury is given additional instructions, a party may object at that time.[19]

RULE 51(c)—OBJECTIONS

CORE CONCEPT

Objections to the instructions must be made on the record with a statement of the grounds.

APPLICATIONS

Content of Objection

An objection must state "distinctly the matter objected to and the grounds for the objection."[20] Parties must state their objections with sufficient clarity and specificity that the judge can understand the nature of the objection and remedy the problem if the judge agrees.[21] The objection need not conform to any particular formality, so long as the basis is clear.[22] A gen-

---

[16] *Cary v. Allegheny Technologies Inc.*, 267 F. Supp. 2d 442, 446 (W.D. Pa. 2003).

[17] *United States v. Valdes-Ayala*, 900 F.3d 20, 38 n.17 (1st Cir. 2018); *Zia Shadows, L.L.C. v. City of Las Cruces*, 829 F.3d 1232, 1242 (10th Cir. 2016).

[18] *See Johnson v. Gen. Bd. of Pension & Health Benefits of the United Methodist Church*, 733 F.3d 722, 732 (7th Cir. 2013) (counsel objected promptly after the court gave the instructions when the court had not previously provided an opportunity to place objections on the record).

[19] *Barrett v. Orange County Human Rights Com'n*, 194 F.3d 341, 349 (2d Cir. 1999).

[20] *Olsen as Tr. for Xurex, Inc. v. Di Mase*, 24 F.4th 1197, 1204 (8th Cir. 2022); *Sindi v. El-Moslimany*, 896 F.3d 1, 19 (1st Cir. 2018).

[21] *Joseph J. Henderson & Sons, Inc. v. Travelers Prop. Cas. Ins. Co. of Am.*, 956 F.3d 992, 1000 (8th Cir. 2020); *Murray v. S. Route Mar. SA*, 870 F.3d 915, 921 (9th Cir. 2017).

[22] *Coston v. Nangalama*, 13 F.4th 729, 732 (9th Cir. 2021); *Blackorby v. BNSF Ry. Co.*, 936 F.3d 733, 739 (8th Cir. 2019).

eral objection, without specificity, is insufficient.[23] Likewise, tendering an alternative instruction, without objecting to a specific error in the court's instruction, may not be sufficient.[24] Any issue not so raised in an objection is waived, subject only to plain error review under Rule 51(d).[25]

Time of Objections

A party must object to the content of the instructions at the opportunity provided by the court before the instructions and closing arguments are delivered,[26] even if the party has previously raised and attempted to preserve the same objection.[27] If a party was not informed of an instruction or action on a request for an instruction prior to the opportunity to object provided by the court, the party may object promptly upon learning that the instruction was or would be given or refused.[28]

Objection on the Record

Objections to jury instructions must be on the record; objections made off the record in chambers are not effective.[29] Many courts hold that it is not sufficient to have proposed an instruction that the court does not give,[30] although some courts hold that an alternative instruction may be sufficient if it brings the precise nature of the alleged error into focus.[31]

Failure to Object

If a party fails to object to an instruction before the jury

---

[23] *Joseph J. Henderson & Sons, Inc. v. Travelers Prop. Cas. Ins. Co. of Am.*, 956 F.3d 992, 1000 (8th Cir. 2020).

[24] *Olsen as Tr. for Xurex, Inc. v. Di Mase*, 24 F.4th 1197, 1204 (8th Cir. 2022); *but see Coston v. Nangalama*, 13 F.4th 729, 732 (9th Cir. 2021) (alternative instruction may be sufficient if it brings the precise nature of the alleged error into focus).

[25] *Teixeira v. Town of Coventry by & through Przybyla*, 882 F.3d 13, 18 (1st Cir. 2018); *W. Plains, L.L.C. v. Retzlaff Grain Co. Inc.*, 870 F.3d 774, 790 (8th Cir. 2017).

[26] *Covidien LP v. Esch*, 993 F.3d 45, 53 (1st Cir. 2021); *Zia Shadows, L.L.C. v. City of Las Cruces*, 829 F.3d 1232, 1242 (10th Cir. 2016).

[27] *Torres-Rivera v. O'Neill-Cancel*, 406 F.3d 43, 49–50 (1st Cir. 2005) (party must object even if the party previously proposed the instruction that the court declined to give); *Libbey-Owens-Ford Co. v. Ins. Co. of North Am.*, 9 F.3d 422 (6th Cir. 1993) (objections waived even though the trial court told the parties that previously raised objections were preserved); *but see Vicor Corp. v. Vigilant Ins. Co.*, 674 F.3d 1, 8 n.4 (1st Cir. 2012) (reference to earlier overruled objection sufficient).

[28] *See Vista Mktg., LLC v. Burkett*, 812 F.3d 954, 975 (11th Cir. 2016); *Johnson v. Gen. Bd. of Pension & Health Benefits of the United Methodist Church*, 733 F.3d 722, 732 (7th Cir. 2013).

[29] *See Russell v. Anderson*, 966 F.3d 711, 720 (8th Cir. 2020); *Colon-Millin v. Sears Roebuck De Puerto Rico, Inc.*, 455 F.3d 30, 41 (1st Cir. 2006) (judge's statement that the parties could rely on objections asserted earlier in chambers did not relieve them of the obligation to state the objections on the record).

[30] *Olsen as Tr. for Xurex, Inc. v. Di Mase*, 24 F.4th 1197, 1204 (8th Cir. 2022); *Emamian v. Rockefeller Univ.*, 971 F.3d 380, 387 (2d Cir. 2020).

[31] *See Coston v. Nangalama*, 13 F.4th 729, 732 (9th Cir. 2021).

begins deliberations and the court has not already made a definitive ruling on the record regarding the subject instruction,[32] the party waives the objection[33] (subject to plain error review as provided in Rule 52(d)).[34] Some courts will undertake appellate review in the absence of a timely objection if the party never had an opportunity to object,[35] or if the party has already made its position clear to the court and the court has made a definitive ruling[36] or has made it apparent that further attempts to object would be unavailing,[37] but other courts strictly require a timely objection on the record.[38] Similarly, some courts will undertake appellate review in the absence of a timely objection if an objection would have been a pointless formality.[39] Thus, as a general matter, if a party does not make a timely objection, it is limited to objections of plain error under Rule 51(d).[40]

RULE 51(d)—ASSIGNING ERROR; PLAIN ERROR

CORE CONCEPT

A party may base an appeal on an instruction if the party made a proper objection or upon plain error.

APPLICATIONS

Appeal of Issues Preserved by Objection

In general, a party may only raise on appeal issues regarding the instructions that the party properly raised as objections before the trial judge.[41] A party may only raise on appeal an issue regarding an instruction not given if the party made a

---

[32]*See Emamian v. Rockefeller Univ.*, 971 F.3d 380, 387-88 (2d Cir. 2020); *Ray v. Ropes & Gray LLP*, 799 F.3d 99, 109 (1 Cir. 2015) (no need to object again if the court has already ruled on a motion *in limine* on the same point).

[33]*Kaiser v. Johnson & Johnson*, 947 F.3d 996, 1018 (7th Cir. 2020); *United States v. Valdes-Ayala*, 900 F.3d 20, 38 n.17 (1st Cir. 2018).

[34]*Russell v. Anderson*, 966 F.3d 711, 720 (8th Cir. 2020).

[35]*Drumgold v. Callahan*, 707 F.3d 28, 52 (1st Cir. 2013); *Schmitz v. Canadian Pacific Ry. Co.*, 454 F.3d 678 (7th Cir. 2006) (judge changed the instructions without notifying the parties).

[36]*Kaufman v. Microsoft Corp.*, 34 F.4th 1360, 1370 (Fed. Cir. 2022).

[37]*Emamian v. Rockefeller Univ.*, 971 F.3d 380, 387 (2d Cir. 2020).

[38]*See Eller v. Trans Union, LLC*, 739 F.3d 467, 479–80 (10th Cir. 2013); *Shcherbakovskiy v. Da Capo Al Fine, Ltd.*, 490 F.3d 130, 141 n.2 (2d Cir. 2007) (judge's assurance that the movant would be deemed to have made "every motion available" did not preserve objections).

[39]*See Rosa-Rivera v. Dorado Health, Inc.*, 787 F.3d 614, 618 (1st Cir. 2015) (no need to object when the court has already made a definitive ruling on the record); *CollegeNet, Inc. v. ApplyYourself, Inc.*, 418 F.3d 1225 (Fed. Cir. 2005).

[40]*Olsen as Tr. for Xurex, Inc. v. Di Mase*, 24 F.4th 1197, 1204 (8th Cir. 2022); *Rodriguez-Valentin v. Doctors' Ctr. Hosp. (Manati), Inc.*, 27 F.4th 14, 24 (1st Cir. 2022).

[41]*May v. Nationstar Mortgage, LLC*, 852 F.3d 806, 819 (8th Cir. 2017); *Connelly v. Hyundai Motor Co.*, 351 F.3d 535, 544 (1st Cir. 2003) (an objection on one ground does not preserve appellate review of a different ground).

proper request for the instruction[42] and either the court made a definitive ruling on the record rejecting the request[43] or the party made a proper objection regarding the omitted instruction.[44] Many courts hold that the court's failure to give a proposed instruction, without a definitive ruling rejecting the instruction or an objection, is not sufficient to preserve the issue for appeal.[45]

Appeal of Issues Not Preserved by Objection

The appeals court may, under extreme circumstances when justice demands, reverse even if no objections were made when an instruction contains plain error.[46] Additionally, the appeals court may consider an issue not preserved by objection where there has been a supervening change in the law.[47]

Additional Research References

Wright & Miller, *Federal Practice and Procedure* §§ 2551 to 2558. Devitt, Blackmar, Wolff & O'Malley, *Federal Jury Practice and Instructions.*

C.J.S., Federal Civil Procedure §§ 983 to 994 et seq.

West's Key Number Digest, Federal Civil Procedure ⚷2171 to 2185

---

[42] *Microsoft Corp. v. i4i Ltd. P'ship*, 564 U.S. 91, 112 (2011); *Connick v. Thompson*, 563 U.S. 51, 75 (2011).

[43] *Kaufman v. Microsoft Corp.*, 34 F.4th 1360, 1370 (Fed. Cir. 2022).

[44] *Abellan v. Lavelo Prop. Mgmt., LLC*, 948 F.3d 820, 832 (7th Cir. 2020); *United States ex rel. Oberg v. Pennsylvania Higher Educ. Assistance Agency*, 912 F.3d 731, 736 (4th Cir. 2019).

[45] *Skidmore as Tr. for Randy Craig Wolfe Tr. v. Zeppelin*, 952 F.3d 1051, 1072 (9th Cir. 2020) (failure to give a proposed instruction without an objection is not sufficient); *United States ex rel. Oberg v. Pennsylvania Higher Educ. Assistance Agency*, 912 F.3d 731, 736–738 (4th Cir. 2019) (court's statement that it would not "read anybody's instructions" is not a definitive ruling).

[46] *See Wantou v. Wal-Mart Stores Texas, L.L.C.*, 23 F.4th 422, 432 (5th Cir. 2022); *Black v. Wrigley*, 997 F.3d 702, 711 (7th Cir. 2021).

[47] *See Cadena v. Pacesetter Corp.*, 224 F.3d 1203, 1212 (10th Cir. 2000); *Anixter v. Home-Stake Production Co.*, 77 F.3d 1215, 1230–31 (10th Cir. 1996).

RULE 52
FINDINGS AND CONCLUSIONS BY THE COURT; JUDGMENT ON PARTIAL FINDINGS

(a) **Findings and Conclusions.**

(1) *In General.* In an action tried on the facts without a jury or with an advisory jury, the court must find the facts specially and state its conclusions of law separately. The findings and conclusions may be stated on the record after the close of the evidence or may appear in an opinion or a memorandum of decision filed by the court. Judgment must be entered under Rule 58.

(2) *For an Interlocutory Injunction.* In granting or refusing an interlocutory injunction, the court must similarly state the findings and conclusions that support its action.

(3) *For a Motion.* The court is not required to state findings or conclusions when ruling on a motion under Rule 12 or 56 or, unless these rules provide otherwise, on any other motion.

(4) *Effect of a Master's Findings.* A master's findings, to the extent adopted by the court, must be considered the court's findings.

(5) *Questioning the Evidentiary Support.* A party may later question the sufficiency of the evidence supporting the findings, whether or not the party requested findings, objected to them, moved to amend them, or moved for partial findings.

(6) *Setting Aside the Findings.* Findings of fact, whether based on oral or other evidence, must not be set aside unless clearly erroneous, and the reviewing court must give due regard to the trial court's opportunity to judge the witnesses' credibility.

(b) **Amended or Additional Findings.** On a party's motion filed no later than 28 days after the entry of judgment, the court may amend its findings—or make additional findings—and may amend the judgment accordingly. The motion may accompany a motion for a new trial under Rule 59.

(c) **Judgment on Partial Findings.** If a party has been fully heard on an issue during a nonjury trial and the court finds against the party on that issue, the court may enter judgment against the party on a claim or defense that, under the controlling law, can be maintained or defeated only with a favorable finding on that issue. The court may, however, decline to render any judgment until the close of the evidence. A judgment on partial findings must be supported by findings of fact and conclusions of law as required by Rule 52(a).

[Amended December 27, 1946, effective March 19, 1948; January 21, 1963, effective July 1, 1963; April 28, 1983, effective August 1, 1983; April 29, 1985, effective August 1, 1985; April 30, 1991, effective December 1, 1991; April 22, 1993, effective December 1, 1993; April 27, 1995, effective December 1, 1995; April 30, 2007, effective December 1, 2007; March 26, 2009, effective December 1, 2009.]

AUTHORS' COMMENTARY ON RULE 52

PURPOSE AND SCOPE

Rule 52 provides all of the procedures for bench trials analogous to those for jury trials in Rules 47–51. Instead of a verdict reached by the jury at the end of the trial process, in a bench trial the judge makes written findings of fact and conclusions of law. The judge may issue these immediately following trial, but much more often, the judge solicits proposed findings of fact and conclusions of law from the parties, then issues the court's findings and conclusions after reviewing the parties' submissions. The judge also issues findings of fact and conclusions of law following proceedings relating to temporary restraining orders or preliminary injunctions, but is not required to do so when ruling on other motions.

Rule 52(c) establishes the bench-trial equivalent of a Rule 50 motion for judgment as a matter of law. It authorizes the judge to rule against a party on a claim, defense, or issue if the party has already introduced all its evidence on that issue and the court finds the evidence insufficient to support the party's position. The fundamental difference between these two types of motions is that in a Rule 52(c) motion, the judge—as the ultimate fact finder in a bench trial—may make credibility determinations and neither party enjoys any presumptions in its favor.

After the court enters its findings of fact and conclusions of law, the parties have 28 days to point out errors to the court and ask the court to alter or supplement its findings and conclusions. After they are finalized, the court will enter judgment based on the findings and conclusions. If the judgment is appealed, the court of appeals will give great deference to the trial court's findings of fact, and will not disturb them unless they are clearly erroneous. The trial court's conclusions of law, in contrast, are reviewed *de novo*—without deference—by the appellate courts.

RULE 52(a)—FINDINGS AND CONCLUSIONS

CORE CONCEPT

After a bench trial, the trial judge must explicitly state findings of fact and conclusions of law upon which the judge bases the judgment.

APPLICATIONS

Findings and Conclusions Mandatory and Automatic

The requirement that the judge make findings of fact and conclusions of law is mandatory and automatic;[1] the parties do not need to request findings.

Form of Findings

The findings of fact and conclusions of law must be on the record.[2] They may be a separate document[3] or may be included in an order[4] or opinion.[5] The court may also make its findings orally as long as it does so on the record.[6] If the court makes separate findings, then on appeal those findings control over any contradictory factual statements in an opinion.[7] The court should make separate findings of fact and conclusions of law.[8]

---

[1] *See UGI Sunbury LLC v. A Permanent Easement for 1.7575 Acres*, 949 F.3d 825, 837 (3d Cir. 2020); *Richard v. Reg'l Sch. Unit 57*, 901 F.3d 52, 59 (1st Cir. 2018).

[2] *Compulife Software Inc. v. Newman*, 959 F.3d 1288, 1308 (11th Cir. 2020).

[3] *See, e.g.*, *Harmony Haus Westlake, LLC v. Parkstone Prop. Owners Ass'n, Inc.*, 440 F. Supp. 3d 654 (W.D. Tex. 2020).

[4] *Reetz v. Hartford Life & Accident Ins. Co.*, 294 F. Supp. 3d 1068, 1070 n.3 (W.D. Wash. 2018); *Doe v. Trump*, 288 F. Supp. 3d 1045, 1055 n.3 (W.D. Wash. 2017).

[5] *U.S. Bank Nat. Ass'n v. Verizon Communications, Inc.*, 761 F.3d 409, 433 (5th Cir. 2014); *Attorney General of Oklahoma v. Tyson Foods, Inc.*, 565 F.3d 769, 782 (10th Cir. 2009).

[6] *Fed. Trade Comm'n v. On Point Cap. Partners LLC*, 17 F.4th 1066, 1080 (11th Cir. 2021); *Dexia Credit Local v. Rogan*, 602 F.3d 879, 884–85 (7th Cir. 2010).

[7] *Snow Machines, Inc. v. Hedco, Inc.*, 838 F.2d 718, 727 (3d Cir. 1988).

[8] *Reyes v. Garland*, 26 F.4th 516, 521 (1st Cir. 2022); *Colchester v. Lazaro*, 16 F.4th 712, 727 (9th Cir. 2021).

Content of Findings and Conclusions

The findings must be sufficient to indicate the factual basis for the ultimate judgment[9] and permit meaningful appellate review,[10] but need not be extensive[11] or address all the evidence presented at trial.[12] Findings that are conclusory and do not adequately explain the basis for the decision are not sufficient.[13] The court need not make findings on uncontested or stipulated facts.[14]

Credibility Determinations and Inferences

When making findings of fact, the court makes credibility determinations, accepting or rejecting the testimony of witnesses and drawing any inferences it deems appropriate.[15]

Proposed Findings and Conclusions

The court may require the parties to submit proposed findings of fact and conclusions of law,[16] although the court's wholesale adoption of the prevailing party's submission is discouraged.[17]

Proceedings Requiring Findings Under Rule 52

The court must make findings of fact and conclusions of law in nonjury trials,[18] in trials with advisory juries,[19] in proceedings for preliminary or permanent injunctions,[20] for an award of attorney's fees in a class action,[21] and when the court grants a motion for judgment after the plaintiff has presented evi-

---

[9] *Colchester v. Lazaro*, 16 F.4th 712, 727 (9th Cir. 2021); *Realogy Holdings Corp. v. Jongebloed*, 957 F.3d 523, 530 (5th Cir. 2020).

[10] *Fed. Trade Comm'n v. On Point Cap. Partners LLC*, 17 F.4th 1066, 1080 (11th Cir. 2021); *Ramos v. Banner Health*, 1 F.4th 769, 777 (10th Cir. 2021).

[11] *Fed. Trade Comm'n v. On Point Cap. Partners LLC*, 17 F.4th 1066, 1080 (11th Cir. 2021).

[12] *Colchester v. Lazaro*, 16 F.4th 712, 727 (9th Cir. 2021); *Eli Lilly & Co. v. Arla Foods, Inc.*, 893 F.3d 375, 385 (7th Cir. 2018).

[13] *UGI Sunbury LLC v. A Permanent Easement for 1.7575 Acres*, 949 F.3d 825, 837 (3d Cir. 2020).

[14] *Simeonoff v. Hiner*, 249 F.3d 883, 891 (9th Cir. 2001).

[15] *See Spartan Concrete Prod., LLC v. Argos USVI, Corp.*, 929 F.3d 107, 112 n.1 (3d Cir. 2019); *Diesel Props S.r.l. v. Greystone Business Credit II LLC*, 631 F.3d 42, 52 (2d Cir. 2011).

[16] *Am. River Transp. Co. v. Kavo Kaliakra SS*, 148 F.3d 446, 449 (5th Cir. 1998) (proposed findings adopted by the court are entitled to the same deference).

[17] *McLennan v. Am. Eurocopter Corp., Inc.*, 245 F.3d 403, 409 (5th Cir. 2001); *Counihan v. Allstate Ins. Co.*, 194 F.3d 357, 365 (2d Cir. 1999).

[18] *Eni US Operating Co., Inc. v. Transocean Offshore Deepwater Drilling, Inc.*, 919 F.3d 931, 935 (5th Cir. 2019).

[19] *OCI Wyoming, L.P. v. PacifiCorp*, 479 F.3d 1199, 1203 (10th Cir. 2007); *Kolstad v. Am. Dental Ass'n*, 108 F.3d 1431, 1440 (D.C. Cir. 1997).

[20] *See Georgia Advoc. Off. v. Jackson*, 4 F.4th 1200, 1208 (11th Cir. 2021); *Eli Lilly & Co. v. Arla Foods, Inc.*, 893 F.3d 375, 385 (7th Cir. 2018).

[21] *Fessler v. Porcelana Corona De Mexico, S.A. DE C.V.*, 23 F.4th 408, 417 (5th Cir. 2022).

dence pursuant to Rule 52(c).[22] Findings are not required for motions for summary judgment,[23] motions to dismiss under Rule 12(b),[24] or any other motions.[25] Findings may be required for actions before administrative agencies that submit reports and recommendations to the district court.[26] In bankruptcy proceedings, the bankruptcy court issues proposed findings of fact and conclusions of law that are then reviewed by the district court under the standard set forth in Rule 52(a)(6), as described below.[27]

No Findings in Jury Trials

Rule 52 generally does not apply to binding jury trials.[28] Rule 52 does apply to cases tried before an advisory jury.[29] If a case contains some claims at law tried to a jury and some equitable claims to be decided by the judge, the judge must make findings of fact and conclusions of law for the equitable claims.[30]

Interlocutory Injunctions

Findings of fact and conclusions of law are required for interlocutory injunctions (*i.e.*, preliminary injunctions or TROs),[31] but not necessarily at the same level of detail as for other matters.[32] Findings are not required in ruling on a motion to dissolve an injunction.[33]

---

[22] *Nieto v. Kapoor*, 268 F.3d 1208, 1217 (10th Cir. 2001).

[23] *Barry v. Moran*, 661 F.3d 696, 702 n.9 (1st Cir. 2011).

[24] *Stewart v. Norcold, Inc.*, 24 F.4th 1183, 1185 (8th Cir. 2022); *Jones v. Dufek*, 830 F.3d 523, 528 (D.C. Cir. 2016).

[25] *Quincy Bioscience, LLC v. Ellishbooks*, 957 F.3d 725 (7th Cir. 2020) (default judgment); *Gov't of Province of Manitoba v. Zinke*, 849 F.3d 1111, 1118 (D.C. Cir. 2017) (Rule 60 motion); *W.G. v. Senatore*, 18 F.3d 60 (2d Cir. 1994) (motion for attorney's fees); *but see Kelly v. Golden*, 352 F.3d 344, 352 (8th Cir. 2003) (when awarding attorney's fees, the court must make findings).

[26] *LabMD, Inc. v. Fed. Trade Comm'n*, 894 F.3d 1221 n.33 (11th Cir. 2018); *Muller v. First Unum Life Ins. Co.*, 341 F.3d 119, 124 (2d Cir. 2003).

[27] *See Exec. Benefits Ins. Agency v. Arkison*, 573 U.S. 25, 30 (2014); *Matter of Russell*, 941 F.3d 199, 204 (5th Cir. 2019).

[28] *Sturgis Motorcycle Rally, Inc. v. Rushmore Photo & Gifts, Inc.*, 908 F.3d 313, 343 (8th Cir. 2018); *Dresser-Rand Co. v. Virtual Automation Inc.*, 361 F.3d 831, 847 (5th Cir. 2004).

[29] *Reyes v. Garland*, 26 F.4th 516, 521 (1st Cir. 2022); *OCI Wyoming, L.P. v. PacifiCorp*, 479 F.3d 1199, 1203 (10th Cir. 2007).

[30] *Texas Advanced Optoelectronic Sols., Inc. v. Renesas Elecs. Am., Inc.*, 895 F.3d 1304, 1319 (Fed. Cir. 2018).

[31] *Murata Mach. USA v. Daifuku Co., Ltd.*, 830 F.3d 1357, 1363 (10th Cir. 2001); *H-D Michigan, LLC v. Hellenic Duty Free Shops S.A.*, 694 F.3d 827, 845 (7th Cir. 2012).

[32] *Murata Mach. USA v. Daifuku Co., Ltd.*, 830 F.3d 1357, 1363 (10th Cir. 2001); *Osthus v. Whitesell Corp.*, 639 F.3d 841, 845 (8th Cir. 2011).

[33] *Baltimore & O. R. Co. v. Chicago River & I. R. Co.*, 170 F.2d 654 (7th Cir. 1948).

Master's Findings

Findings in a master's report and recommendation are considered the court's findings if the court adopts them.[34]

Challenges to the Sufficiency of the Evidence

If the court makes findings of fact that a party believes not to be supported by the evidence in the record, Rule 52(a)(5) authorizes challenges to the findings.[35] This procedure differs from the procedure for jury trials, where Rule 50 requires a motion challenging the sufficiency of the evidence *during trial*.[36] This authority is limited to challenging the findings that the court actually made, and does not allow parties to inject new issues after the conclusion of trial.[37]

Appeals of Findings

Rule 52(a)(6) sets the standard for appellate review of the trial court's factual findings, and provides that they will not be set aside unless clearly erroneous.[38] This deference is not limited to oral testimony—Rule 52(a)(6) explicitly requires appellate courts to give "due regard" to the trial court's credibility determinations[39]—but also to other evidence like documents.[40] Damage awards are factual findings governed by the clear error standard.[41] In contrast, the trial court's conclusions of law are reviewed *de novo*.[42] For mixed questions of law or fact, the standard depends on whether the issue is primarily legal or factual.[43]

RULE 52(b)—AMENDED OR ADDITIONAL FINDINGS

CORE CONCEPT

Upon motion, the court may amend or supplement its findings and/or judgment.

---

[34]Rule 52(a)(4).

[35]*Advanced Fluid Sys., Inc. v. Huber*, 958 F.3d 168, 187 (3d Cir. 2020).

[36]*Schaub v. VonWald*, 638 F.3d 905, 924 (8th Cir. 2011).

[37]*Advanced Fluid Sys., Inc. v. Huber*, 958 F.3d 168, 187 (3d Cir. 2020).

[38]*June Med. Servs. L. L. C. v. Russo*, __ U.S. __, 140 S. Ct. 2103, 2121 (2020); *Teva Pharmaceuticals USA, Inc. v. Sandoz, Inc.*, __ U.S. __, 135 S. Ct. 831, 836–37 (2015) (rule applies to both subsidiary and ultimate facts).

[39]*June Med. Servs. L. L. C. v. Russo*, __ U.S. __, 140 S. Ct. 2103, 2121 (2020).

[40]*Chesnut v. United States*, 15 F.4th 436, 441 (6th Cir. 2021); *Atl. Specialty Ins. Co. v. Coastal Envtl. Grp. Inc.*, 945 F.3d 53, 63 (2d Cir. 2019).

[41]*United States for Use & Benefit of Am. Civ. Constr., LLC v. Hirani Eng'g & Land Surveying, PC*, 26 F.4th 952, 959 (D.C. Cir. 2022).

[42]*Chesnut v. United States*, 15 F.4th 436, 441 (6th Cir. 2021); *C. L. v. Del Amo Hosp., Inc.*, 992 F.3d 901, 909 (9th Cir. 2021).

[43]*See, e.g., U.S. Bank Nat. Ass'n ex rel. CWCapital Asset Mgmt. LLC v. Vill. at Lakeridge, LLC*, 138 S. Ct. 960, 967 (2018).

APPLICATIONS

Timing

Motions to amend the findings must be filed no later than 28 days after entry of *final* judgment.[44] This time period is absolute, and cannot be enlarged by the court.[45] The motion may be filed before entry of judgment.

Grounds

Proper grounds for a motion to amend include newly discovered evidence,[46] a change in the law, or a manifest error of fact or law by the trial court.[47] A motion to amend should not merely relitigate old issues, reargue the merits of the case,[48] or raise arguments that could have been raised prior to the issuance of judgment.[49] A party may move to amend the findings of fact even if the modified or additional findings in effect reverse the judgment.[50] Once a motion to amend has been filed, the court can amend any findings it deems appropriate; it is not limited to the issues raised in the motion.[51]

Conclusions of Law

Rule 52(b) specifically authorizes a court to amend its "findings," which technically refers to the findings of fact, not the conclusions of law. Some courts construe Rule 52(b) as impliedly authorizing amendment of the court's conclusions of law as well.[52]

Failure to File—Limited Waiver

In contrast to Rule 50, a party is not required to file a Rule 52(b) motion to preserve most issues for appeal, but some courts hold that failure to file a Rule 52(b) motion waives challenges

---

[44]*Golden Blount, Inc. v. Robert H. Peterson Co.*, 438 F.3d 1354, 1358 (Fed. Cir. 2006); *Hakeem v. Lamar*, __ F. Supp. 3d __, 2020 WL 7711860, at *7 n.2 (D.N.M. 2020) (time limit not triggered by interlocutory orders).

[45]F.R.C.P. 6(b)(2); *Martin v. Monumental Life Ins. Co.*, 240 F.3d 223, 237–38 (3d Cir. 2001).

[46]*See Parada v. Anoka Cnty.*, 555 F. Supp. 3d 663, 681 (D. Minn. 2021) (evidence that was merely not offered into evidence does not support a motion to amend); *Gutierrez v. Johnson & Johnson*, 743 F. Supp. 2d 418, 422 (D.N.J. 2010).

[47]*Paleteria La Michoacana, Inc. v. Productos Lacteos Tocumbo S.A. De C.V.*, 247 F. Supp. 3d 76, 91 (D.D.C. 2017); *Gutierrez v. Johnson & Johnson*, 743 F. Supp. 2d 418, 422 (D.N.J. 2010).

[48]*In re Busch*, 369 B.R. 614, 621 (B.A.P. 10th Cir. 2007); *In re Sanctuary Belize Litig.*, 528 F. Supp. 3d 390, 394 (D. Md. 2021).

[49]*Perrier-Bilbo v. United States*, 954 F.3d 413, 435 (1st Cir. 2020); *Diocese of Winona v. Interstate Fire & Cas. Co.*, 89 F.3d 1386, 1397 (9th Cir. 1996).

[50]*Golden Blount, Inc. v. Robert H. Peterson Co.*, 438 F.3d 1354, 1358 (Fed. Cir. 2006).

[51]*Golden Blount, Inc. v. Robert H. Peterson Co.*, 438 F.3d 1354, 1358 (Fed. Cir. 2006).

[52]*U.S. Gypsum Co. v. Schiavo Bros.*, 668 F.2d 172, 180 & n.9 (3d Cir. 1981); *Advanced Fluid Sys., Inc. v. Huber*, 381 F. Supp. 3d 362 (M.D. Pa. 2019).

to the specificity of the court's findings.[53]

Tolling of Time for Appeals

The filing of a motion to amend the findings tolls the running of the time to file an appeal.[54] The appeal clock starts over when the court enters an order granting or denying the motion to amend.[55] If a party files a notice of appeal while a Rule 52(b) motion is pending, the district court retains jurisdiction to rule on the motion.[56]

RULE 52(c)—JUDGMENT ON PARTIAL FINDINGS

CORE CONCEPT

At any time in a nonjury trial after a party has presented all its evidence with respect to a particular issue, the court may enter judgment against that party on that issue if the evidence failed to persuade the judge.

APPLICATIONS

Nonjury Trials Only

Rule 52(c) applies only in nonjury trials.[57] The parallel for jury trials is a motion for judgment as a matter of law under Rule 50(a).[58] However, the court has the ability to treat a motion filed under Rule 50 as a Rule 52(c) motion.[59]

Timing of Motion

A Rule 52(c) motion may be made at any time after all the evidence has been presented on a particular topic;[60] although motions for judgment on partial findings are typically made at the close of the opposing party's case,[61] the movant technically does not need to wait until the opposing party has rested.[62] In fact, the court can grant a Rule 56(c) motion even though the

---

[53]*Paraflon Investments, Ltd. v. Fullbridge, Inc.*, 960 F.3d 17, 32 (1st Cir. 2020); *Irving Tanning Co. v. Kaplan*, 876 F.3d 384, 390, 393 n.8 (1st Cir. 2017).

[54]*Mondis Tech. Ltd. v. LG Elecs. Inc.*, 6 F.4th 1379, 1384 (Fed. Cir. 2021); *Conille v. Council 93, Am. Fed'n of State, Cty. & Mun. Employees*, 935 F.3d 1, 6 (1st Cir. 2019).

[55]*See Conille v. Council 93, Am. Fed'n of State, Cty. & Mun. Employees*, 935 F.3d 1, 6 (1st Cir. 2019).

[56]*United States v. Young*, __ F. Supp. 3d __, 2021 WL 534869, at *20 (D.N.M. 2021); *Hakeem v. Lamar*, __ F. Supp. 3d __, 2020 WL 7711860, at *5 (D.N.M. 2020).

[57]*Fillmore v. Page*, 358 F.3d 496, 502–03 (7th Cir. 2004); *Northeast Drilling, Inc. v. Inner Space Services, Inc.*, 243 F.3d 25, 35 (1st Cir. 2001).

[58]*Federal Ins. Co. v. HPSC, Inc.*, 480 F.3d 26, 32 (1st Cir. 2007); *M & M Poultry, Inc. v. Pilgrim's Pride Corp.*, 281 F. Supp. 3d 610, 619 (N.D.W. Va. 2017).

[59]*Williams v. Sake Hibachi Sushi & Bar Inc.*, 574 F. Supp. 3d 395, 401 (N.D. Tex. 2021).

[60]*DLJ Mortg. Cap., Inc. v. Sheridan*, 975 F.3d 358, 366 (3d Cir. 2020); *Stop Illinois Health Care Fraud, LLC v. Sayeed*, 957 F.3d 743, 748 (7th Cir. 2020).

[61]*See, e.g., Pinkston v. Madry*, 440 F.3d 879, 885–86 (7th Cir. 2006); *Pub. Patent Found., Inc. v. GlaxoSmithKline Consumer Healthcare, L.P.*, 801 F. Supp. 2d 249, 255 (S.D.N.Y. 2011).

[62]*DLJ Mortg. Cap., Inc. v. Sheridan*, 975 F.3d 358, 366 (3d Cir.

opposing party has represented that it has additional evidence on the topic if the court determines that the additional evidence would have little or no probative value or would not affect the court's decision.[63]

Standard for Granting

The trial judge rules on motions for judgment on partial findings as a final factfinder, reviewing all evidence presented thus far without presumptions in favor of either party.[64] The judge grants the motion if, upon the evidence already presented, the judge would find in favor of the moving party.[65]

Scope of Judgment

If the judge grants the motion, the judge will enter judgment on the claim or issue that is the subject of the motion and on any claim, issue, counterclaim, crossclaim, or third-party claim that is determined by the outcome of the issue that is the subject of the motion.[66]

Findings of Fact and Conclusions of Law

If the judge grants a motion for judgment on partial findings, the judge must make findings of fact and conclusions of law pursuant to Rule 52(a).[67]

Deferred Ruling

The judge has discretion to defer ruling until all evidence has been presented.[68] If the judge defers ruling on a motion for judgment on partial findings and either party enters additional evidence regarding the subject of the motion, the judge will consider all the evidence when ultimately ruling.[69]

Additional Research References

Wright & Miller, *Federal Practice and Procedure* §§ 2571 to 2591
C.J.S., Federal Civil Procedure §§ 1036 to 1056 et seq.
West's Key Number Digest, Federal Civil Procedure ⚷2261 to 2293

2020).

[63]*DLJ Mortg. Cap., Inc. v. Sheridan*, 975 F.3d 358, 366 (3d Cir. 2020).

[64]*See DLJ Mortg. Cap., Inc. v. Sheridan*, 975 F.3d 358, 366 (3d Cir. 2020); *Stop Illinois Health Care Fraud, LLC v. Sayeed*, 957 F.3d 743, 748 (7th Cir. 2020).

[65]*See Brotherston v. Putnam Investments, LLC*, 907 F.3d 17, 30 (1st Cir. 2018).

[66]*See Cantwell & Cantwell v. Vicario*, 464 B.R. 776, 783 (N.D. Ill. 2011).

[67]*DLJ Mortg. Cap., Inc. v. Sheridan*, 975 F.3d 358, 372 (3d Cir. 2020); *Stop Illinois Health Care Fraud, LLC v. Sayeed*, 957 F.3d 743, 748 (7th Cir. 2020).

[68]*DLJ Mortg. Cap., Inc. v. Sheridan*, 975 F.3d 358, 372 (3d Cir. 2020).

[69]*S.E.C. v. Razmilovic*, 822 F. Supp. 2d 234, 257–58 (E.D.N.Y. 2011); *TransCanada Pipelines Ltd. v. USGen New England, Inc.*, 458 B.R. 195, 214–15 (D. Md. 2011).

RULE 53
MASTERS

(a) **Appointment.**

(1) *Scope.* Unless a statute provides otherwise, a court may appoint a master only to:

(A) perform duties consented to by the parties;

(B) hold trial proceedings and make or recommend findings of fact on issues to be decided without a jury if appointment is warranted by:

(i) some exceptional condition; or

(ii) the need to perform an accounting or resolve a difficult computation of damages; or

(C) address pretrial and posttrial matters that cannot be effectively and timely addressed by an available district judge or magistrate judge of the district.

(2) *Disqualification.* A master must not have a relationship to the parties, attorneys, action, or court that would require disqualification of a judge under 28 U.S.C. § 455, unless the parties, with the court's approval, consent to the appointment after the master discloses any potential grounds for disqualification.

(3) *Possible Expense or Delay.* In appointing a master, the court must consider the fairness of imposing the likely expenses on the parties and must protect against unreasonable expense or delay.

(b) **Order Appointing a Master.**

(1) *Notice.* Before appointing a master, the court must give the parties notice and an opportunity to be heard. Any party may suggest candidates for appointment.

(2) *Contents.* The appointing order must direct the master to proceed with all reasonable diligence and must state:

(A) the master's duties, including any investigation or enforcement duties, and any limits on the master's authority under Rule 53(c);

(B) the circumstances, if any, in which the master may communicate ex parte with the court or a party;

(C) the nature of the materials to be preserved and filed as the record of the master's activities;

(D) the time limits, method of filing the record, other procedures, and standards for reviewing the master's orders, findings, and recommendations; and

(E) the basis, terms, and procedure for fixing the master's compensation under Rule 53(g).

(3) *Issuing.* The court may issue the order only after:

(A) the master files an affidavit disclosing whether there is any ground for disqualification under 28 U.S.C. § 455; and

(B) if a ground is disclosed, the parties, with the court's approval, waive the disqualification.

(4) *Amending.* The order may be amended at any time after notice to the parties and an opportunity to be heard.

(c) **Master's Authority.**

(1) *In General.* Unless the appointing order directs otherwise, a master may:

(A) regulate all proceedings;

(B) take all appropriate measures to perform the assigned duties fairly and efficiently; and

(C) if conducting an evidentiary hearing, exercise the appointing court's power to compel, take, and record evidence.

(2) *Sanctions.* The master may by order impose on a party any noncontempt sanction provided by Rule 37 or 45, and may recommend a contempt sanction against a party and sanctions against a nonparty.

(d) **Master's Orders.** A master who issues an order must file it and promptly serve a copy on each party. The clerk must enter the order on the docket.

(e) **Master's Reports.** A master must report to the court as required by the appointing order. The master must file the report and promptly serve a copy on each party, unless the court orders otherwise.

(f) **Action on the Master's Order, Report, or Recommendations.**

(1) *Opportunity for a Hearing; Action in General.* In acting on a master's order, report, or recommendations, the court must give the parties notice and an opportunity to be heard; may receive evidence; and may adopt or affirm, modify, wholly or partly reject or reverse, or resubmit to the master with instructions.

(2) *Time to Object or Move to Adopt or Modify.* A party may file objections to—or a motion to adopt or modify—the master's order, report, or recommendations no later than 21 days after a copy is served, unless the court sets a different time.

(3) *Reviewing Factual Findings.* The court must decide de novo all objections to findings of fact made or recommended by a master, unless the parties, with the court's approval, stipulate that:

(A) the findings will be reviewed for clear error; or

(B) the findings of a master appointed under Rule 53(a)(1)(A) or (C) will be final.

(4) *Reviewing Legal Conclusions.* The court must decide de novo all objections to conclusions of law made or recommended by a master.

(5) *Reviewing Procedural Matters.* Unless the appointing order establishes a different standard of review, the court may set aside a master's ruling on a procedural matter only for an abuse of discretion.

(g) **Compensation.**

(1) *Fixing Compensation.* Before or after judgment, the court must fix the master's compensation on the basis and terms stated in the appointing order, but the court may set a new basis and terms after giving notice and an opportunity to be heard.

(2) *Payment.* The compensation must be paid either:

(A) by a party or parties; or

(B) from a fund or subject matter of the action within the court's control.

(3) *Allocating Payment.* The court must allocate payment among the parties after considering the nature and amount of the controversy, the parties' means, and the extent to which any party is more responsible than other parties for the reference to a master. An interim allocation may be amended to reflect a decision on the merits.

(h) **Appointing a Magistrate Judge.** A magistrate judge is subject to this rule only when the order referring a matter to the magistrate judge states that the reference is made under this rule.

[Amended February 28, 1966, effective July 1, 1966; April 28, 1983, effective August 1, 1983; March 2, 1987, effective August 1, 1987; April 30, 1991, effective December 1, 1991; April 22, 1993, effective December 1, 1993; March 27, 2003, effective December 1, 2003; April 30, 2007, effective December 1, 2007; March 26, 2009, effective December 1, 2009.]

AUTHORS' COMMENTARY ON RULE 53

PURPOSE AND SCOPE

If a judge is faced with an issue that would be unusually burdensome or time consuming to handle or that requires an expertise that the judge lacks, such as a complicated damages calculation or an accounting of the finances of a business, the judge may appoint a "master" to assist the judge. Rule 53 generally affords the court broad discretion in the appointment of masters, but it requires the judge to consider both the imposition of the expense of the master on the parties and the likely delay caused by the appointment.

The procedure for the use of a master starts with notice to the parties, providing them an opportunity to express their positions on the use of a master and to propose candidates. Rule 53 places few restrictions on who the judge may select as a master, so long as the master does not have a close relationship to the parties, lawyers, or cause of action. The judge may appoint a magistrate judge to serve as a master, although actions by a magistrate judge do not come under the ambit of Rule 53 unless the district judge so specifies.

If the judge decides to appoint a master, the judge issues an order identifying the master, describing the master's duties, setting any limits on the master's authority, and specifying the manner in which the master may communicate with the parties. The order also establishes the time limits for the master's tasks and submissions to the judge, including any materials the master should preserve and include. Finally, the order addresses the master's rate of compensation and the allocation of the compensation among the parties.

Once appointed, a master has most—but not all—of the powers of the trial judge. The master may issue orders, hold evidentiary hearings with witness testimony and documentary evidence, and impose sanctions on misbehaving parties. A master does not have contempt powers, though, and instead may recommend that the judge hold a party in contempt.

Typically, a master submits a "report" or "report and recommendation" to the court at the end of the process. The parties then have 21 days to file written objections. Normally, the court then reviews the master's procedures, factual determinations, and conclusions of law de novo—with no deference—unless the parties stipulate to be bound by the master's factual findings. The judge may then adopt, modify, or reject the master's report.

RULE 53(a)—APPOINTMENT

CORE CONCEPT

The court may appoint a master to conduct trials in limited circumstances and to conduct certain pretrial and post-trial functions.

APPLICATIONS

Functions Performed by Master

Rule 53 defines three categories of functions that a master may perform. A master may:

- Perform duties consented to by the parties;[1]
- Hold trial proceedings and make recommended findings of fact on nonjury issues if the appointment is warranted by an exceptional condition or by the need to perform an accounting or resolve a difficult computation of damages;[2] or
- Address pretrial or post-trial matters if they cannot be addressed effectively and timely by the court.[3]

---

[1]*See In re Amtrak Train Derailment in Philadelphia, Pennsylvania on May 12, 2015*, 268 F. Supp. 3d 739, 750 (E.D. Pa. 2017); *Gulf States Reorganization Grp., Inc. v. Nucor Corp.*, 822 F. Supp. 2d 1201, 1205 (N.D. Ala. 2011).

[2]*See Howe v. City of Akron*, 801 F.3d 718, 756 (6th Cir. 2015); *Zaki Kulaibee Establishment v. McFliker*, 771 F.3d 1301, 1315 (11th Cir. 2014).

[3]*See Shakman v. Clerk of Cook Cty.*, 994 F.3d 832, 839 (7th Cir. 2021) (master appointed to monitor compliance with the court's order); *Rohrbough v. Harris*, 549 F.3d 1313, 1318 (10th Cir. 2008) (master attended depositions to rule on objections).

Jury Trials

The court may not appoint a master in matters to be tried to a jury unless the parties consent.[4]

Ineligible Persons

A person cannot be a master if related to the parties, the action, or the court under the same standards that govern disqualification of a judge set forth in 28 U.S.C.A. § 455.[5] The clerk of court and the clerk's deputies are also ineligible. The parties can waive this restriction with the court's approval.[6]

Court's Discretion—Expense and Delay

The court has discretion as to whether to refer a matter to a master,[7] but reference should be the exception, not the rule.[8] In determining whether to appoint a master, the court must consider the fairness of imposing the cost of the master's compensation on the parties and the effects of delay.[9] The court has discretion to refuse to appoint a master even if the parties have consented.[10]

Magistrate Judges

The court may appoint a United States Magistrate Judge to serve as a master.[11] The provisions regarding compensation do not apply when a United States Magistrate Judge is designated to serve as a master.

Multiple Masters

The court may appoint more than one person to serve as master in a case.[12]

Common References

References are most common in patent, trademark, and copyright actions.[13] They are also used occasionally to supervise

---

[4] The Advisory Committee Note to the 2003 Amendments to Rule 53.

[5] *Moore as Next Friend to Moore v. Tangipahoa Par. Sch. Bd.*, 912 F.3d 247, 251 (5th Cir. 2018); *U.S. v. Apple Inc.*, 787 F.3d 131, 138 (2d Cir. 2015).

[6] *See In re Deepwater Horizon*, 824 F.3d 571, 579 (5th Cir. 2016); *Paycom Payroll, LLC v. Richison*, 758 F.3d 1198, 1208 (10th Cir. 2014).

[7] *Middle Tennessee News Co., Inc. v. Charnel of Cincinnati, Inc.*, 250 F.3d 1077 (7th Cir.2001); *U.S. v. State of Wash.*, 157 F.3d 630, 660 (9th Cir. 1998).

[8] *U.S. v. State of Washington*, 135 F.3d 618, 646 (9th Cir. 1998); *Richardson v. Trump*, 496 F. Supp. 3d 165, 190 (D.D.C. 2020).

[9] *See Gaddis v. U.S.*, 381 F.3d 444, 462 (5th Cir. 2004); *Taylor v. Islamic Republic of Iran*, 811 F. Supp. 2d 1, 17 (D.D.C. 2011).

[10] The Advisory Committee Note to the 2003 Amendments to Rule 53.

[11] *S.E.C. v. AMX, Intern., Inc.*, 872 F. Supp. 1541 (N.D. Tex. 1994).

[12] *United States v. United States Bd. of Water Commissioners*, 893 F.3d 578, 597 (9th Cir. 2018) (appointing the California Control Board); *N. Nat. Gas Co. v. L.D. Drilling*, 862 F.3d 1221, 1227, n.7 (10th Cir. 2017) (appointing a three-person commission).

[13] *See Absolute Software, Inc. v. Stealth Signal, Inc.*, 659 F.3d 1121, 1131 (Fed. Cir. 2011).

or facilitate discovery[14] (and increasingly frequently with e-discovery), to determine damages following summary judgment on liability when the damages are difficult to calculate, and to oversee compliance with injunctions or other court orders.[15]

RULE 53(b)—ORDER APPOINTING A MASTER

CORE CONCEPT

A master is appointed by an order setting forth the duties and parameters of the reference.

APPLICATIONS

Notice and Opportunity to Be Heard

The court must give notice of the proposed appointment of a master to the parties and provide an opportunity to be heard before appointing the master.[16] Written submissions will provide an "opportunity to be heard" unless the circumstances require live testimony.[17]

Party Proposals of Candidates for Appointment

A party may suggest candidates for appointment as master.[18]

Contents of Order

The order appointing a master must:

- Direct the master to proceed with all reasonable diligence;[19]
- State the master's duties and any limits on the master's authority;[20]
- State the circumstances, if any, in which the master may communicate *ex parte* with the court or a party;[21]
- State the nature of the materials to be preserved and filed as the record of the master's activities;[22]
- State the time limits, methods of filing the record, other procedures, and standards for reviewing the master's

[14] *Pearlshire Cap. Grp., LLC v. Zaid*, 490 F. Supp. 3d 1299, 1302 n.1 (N.D. Ill. 2020) (appointment of special master to conduct *in camera* review of 800 documents).

[15] *See Shakman v. Clerk of Cook Cty.*, 994 F.3d 832, 839 (7th Cir. 2021); *U.S. v. Microsoft Corp.*, 147 F.3d 935, 954 (D.C. Cir. 1998).

[16] *In re Deepwater Horizon*, 824 F.3d 571, 579 (5th Cir. 2016).

[17] The Advisory Committee Note to the 2003 Amendment to Rule 53.

[18] *Arkansas Teacher Ret. Sys. v. State St. Bank and Trust Co.*, 232 F. Supp. 3d 189, 195 (D. Mass. 2017).

[19] Rule 53(b)(2).

[20] *See Sibley v. Sprint Nextel Corp.*, 298 F.R.D. 683, 685 (D. Kan. 2014).

[21] *See C.D.S., Inc. v. Zetler*, 254 F. Supp. 3d 625, 632–33 (S.D.N.Y. 2017); *U.S. v. Apple Inc.*, 787 F.3d 131, 138 (2d Cir. 2015).

[22] *In re Deepwater Horizon*, 824 F.3d 571, 580 (5th Cir. 2016).

orders, findings, and recommendations;[23] and
- State the basis, terms, and procedures for determining the master's compensation under Rule 53(g).[24]

The order may also address other procedural issues that the court deems appropriate.[25]

Affidavit re Grounds for Disqualification

Before the court can enter the order appointing the master, the master must file an affidavit disclosing whether there is any ground for disqualification under 28 U.S.C.A. § 455.[26] If a ground for disqualification is disclosed, the court may not enter the order unless the parties have consented to waive the disqualification.[27]

Amendment of Order

The order appointing the master may be amended at any time after notice to the parties and an opportunity to be heard.[28]

Challenging Reference

The proper method for contesting a reference is a motion to amend, vacate, or revoke the reference.[29] Failure to make such a motion may be deemed a consent or waiver.[30] If the motion to vacate is denied, the disgruntled party may attempt to compel the court to vacate by a writ of mandamus.[31] Orders of reference are interlocutory and may not be appealed directly,[32] but may be appealed at the conclusion of the district court proceedings.[33]

RULE 53(c)—MASTER'S AUTHORITY

CORE CONCEPT

Absent specific limitations in the order appointing the master, the master has all powers necessary to perform the referred matters, including regulating the proceedings, ruling on evidentiary

---

[23] *Sibley v. Sprint Nextel Corp.*, 298 F.R.D. 683, 687 (D. Kan. 2014).

[24] *Sibley v. Sprint Nextel Corp.*, 298 F.R.D. 683, 688 (D. Kan. 2014); *In re Holocaust Victim Assets Litig.*, 528 F. Supp. 2d 109, 119, (E.D.N.Y. 2007).

[25] *See United States ex rel. Int'l Bhd. of Elec. Workers Local Union No. 98 v. Farfield Co.*, 438 F. Supp. 3d 348, 357 (E.D. Pa. 2020).

[26] *See Dolby Labs. Licensing Corp. v. Adobe Inc.*, 402 F. Supp. 3d 855, 876 (N.D. Cal. 2019); *Arkansas Teacher Ret. Sys. v. State St. Bank and Trust Co.*, 232 F. Supp. 3d 189, 194 (D. Mass. 2017).

[27] *Dolby Labs. Licensing Corp. v. Adobe Inc.*, 402 F. Supp. 3d 855, 876 (N.D. Cal. 2019); *In re Deepwater Horizon*, 824 F.3d 571, 579 (5th Cir. 2016).

[28] Rule 53(b)(4).

[29] *Fajardo Shopping Center, S.E. v. Sun Alliance Ins. Co. of Puerto Rico, Inc.*, 167 F.3d 1, 6 (1st Cir. 1999).

[30] *See In re K-Dur Antitrust Litig.*, 686 F.3d 197, 207 n.5 (3d Cir. 2012); *Fajardo Shopping Center, S.E. v. Sun Alliance Ins. Co. of Puerto Rico, Inc.*, 167 F.3d 1, 6 (1st Cir. 1999).

[31] *La Buy v. Howes Leather Co.*, 352 U.S. 249, 254–55 (1957); *U.S. v. Microsoft Corp.*, 147 F.3d 935 (D.C. Cir. 1998).

[32] *Shakman v. Clerk of Cook Cty.*, 994 F.3d 832, 839 (7th Cir. 2021).

[33] *Sierra Club v. Clifford*, 257 F.3d 444 (5th Cir.2001).

issues, placing witnesses under oath, examining witnesses, and sanctioning parties.[34] The master has discretion as to what procedures to employ, with the only requirement being that when the master determines that a hearing is necessary, the master must make a record of the evidence offered and excluded in the same manner and subject to the same limitations as provided in the Federal Rules of Evidence for a nonjury trial.[35] The court has the duty to oversee the master's performance of the master's duties to ensure that they are appropriately discharged.[36]

APPLICATIONS

Authority to Impose Sanctions

The master may impose any non-contempt sanction on a party provided by Rule 37 or 45. The master may also recommend that the judge impose contempt sanctions on a party and sanctions on a nonparty.

Evidentiary Hearings

Unless otherwise limited by the order appointing the master, the master may exercise the powers of the court to compel (by subpoena under Rule 45), take, and record evidence.[37]

RULE 53(d)—MASTER'S ORDERS

CORE CONCEPT

A master who makes an order must file the order with the clerk and promptly serve a copy on each party. The clerk must enter the order on the docket.

RULE 53(e)—MASTER'S REPORTS

CORE CONCEPT

A master must prepare reports as directed by the order of appointment. The master must file all reports with the clerk and promptly serve a copy upon each party unless the court directs otherwise.[38]

APPLICATIONS

Supporting Materials

The master should provide the court with all portions of the record that the master deems relevant to a report. The parties may seek to designate additional materials from the record,

---

[34] *In Re J.T. Thorpe, Inc.*, 870 F.3d 1121, 1134 (9th Cir. 2017); *N. Nat. Gas Co. v. L.D. Drilling*, 862 F.3d 1221, 1226 n.7 (10th Cir. 2017).

[35] *U.S. v. Clifford Matley Family Trust*, 354 F.3d 1154, 1159 (9th Cir. 2004).

[36] *Cordoza v. Pacific States Steel Corp.*, 320 F.3d 989, 999 (9th Cir. 2003).

[37] *N. Nat. Gas Co. v. L.D. Drilling*, 862 F.3d 1221, 1227 n.7 (10th Cir. 2017).

[38] *See Schaefer Fan Co., Inc. v. J & D Mfg.*, 265 F.3d 1282, 1289 (Fed. Cir. 2001).

and may seek to supplement the record. The court may require that additional materials from the record be filed.[39]

Sealed Report

Sealing of the report from public access may be appropriate, particularly with respect to pretrial and post-trial matters. A report detailing a continuing or failed settlement effort is one example of a report that might be sealed.[40]

RULE 53(f)—ACTION ON THE MASTER'S ORDER, REPORT, OR RECOMMENDATIONS

CORE CONCEPT

Rule 53(f) sets forth the procedures for the court to act on the master's report and the standards by which the court should review the report.

APPLICATIONS

Actions by the Parties

A party may file objections to the master's order, report, or recommendations no later than 21 days from the time the order, report, or recommendation is served, unless the court sets a different time.[41] A party may also file a motion to adopt or modify the order, report, or recommendations in the same timeframe.[42] This time period is not jurisdictional, and the court has the authority to consider a late objection or motion.[43]

Actions by the Court

When considering an order, report, or recommendation from a master, the court may adopt or affirm, modify, reject or reverse in whole or in part, or resubmit to the master with instructions.[44]

Opportunity to be Heard

Before acting on an order, report, or recommendation from a master, the court must provide the parties with an opportunity to be heard.[45] Written submissions will provide an opportunity to be heard, but court has discretion to consider

---

[39] *In re Deepwater Horizon*, 824 F.3d 571, 580 (5th Cir. 2016).

[40] The Advisory Committee Note to the 2003 Amendment to Rule 53.

[41] *See In re Actos (Pioglitazone) Prod. Liab. Litig.*, 274 F. Supp. 3d 485, 550 n.94 (W.D. La. 2017) (shortening the period to 10 days); *Sibley v. Sprint Nextel Corp.*, 298 F.R.D. 683, 687 n.12 (D. Kan. 2014).

[42] *See Barry v. Islamic Republic of Iran*, 437 F. Supp. 3d 15, 52 (D.D.C. 2020).

[43] *See Wallace v. Skadden, Arps, Slate, Meagher & Flom, LLP*, 362 F.3d 810, 816 (D.C. Cir. 2004); *Petties v. District of Columbia*, 291 F.R.D. 1, 3 (D.D.C. 2013).

[44] *Consejo de Salud de la Comunidad de la Playa de Ponce, Inc. v. Gonzalez-Feliciano*, 695 F.3d 83, 99 (1st Cir. 2012); *Arkansas Tchr. Ret. Sys. v. State St. Bank & Tr. Co.*, — F. Supp. 3d —, 2021 WL 951307, at *9 (D. Mass. 2021) (modifying report).

[45] *Barry v. Islamic Republic of Iran*, 437 F. Supp. 3d 15, 52 n.45 (D.D.C. 2020); *In re Actos (Pioglitazone) Prod. Liab. Litig.*, 274 F. Supp. 3d 485, 550

additional evidence in connection with its review of the master's report.[46]

Review of Master's Findings of Fact

Absent a stipulation otherwise,[47] the court must decide *de novo* all objections to findings of fact made or recommended by a master.[48] The court may also review *de novo* findings of fact made or recommended by a master in the absence of an objection.[49] In its *de novo* review, the court may, but is not required to, receive evidence.[50] The parties may stipulate, with the court's consent, that the master's findings of fact will only be reviewed for clear error,[51] or that the court will review the master's findings of fact on the record, without taking new evidence or considering the master's credibility determinations.[52] The parties may also stipulate, with the court's consent, that the master's findings of fact will be final if the master was appointed by consent or was appointed to address pretrial or post-trial matters.[53] The court may withdraw its consent to a stipulation for clear error review or finality, and may reopen the opportunity for the parties to object.[54]

Review of Master's Conclusions of Law

The court must decide *de novo* all objections to conclusions of law made or recommended by a master.[55]

Review of Master's Procedural Rulings

In the absence of a different standard set by the order of appointment, the court reviews a master's rulings on procedural matters for abuse of discretion.[56]

Appeals

The report of the master is not appealable until adopted by

---

n.94 (W.D. La. 2017).

[46] *Commissariat à l'Energie Atomique v. Samsung Electronics Co.*, 245 F.R.D. 177, 179 (D. Del. 2007).

[47] *See T.B. v. San Diego Unified Sch. Dist.*, 293 F. Supp. 3d 1177, 1185 (S.D. Cal. 2018); *AgGrow Oils, L.L.C. v. National Union Fire Ins. Co. of Pittsburgh, PA*, 276 F. Supp. 2d 999, 1005 (D.N.D. 2003).

[48] *N. Nat. Gas Co. v. L.D. Drilling*, 862 F.3d 1221, 1227 n.7 (10th Cir. 2017); *Arkansas Tchr. Ret. Sys. v. State St. Bank & Tr. Co.*, 527 F. Supp. 3d 40, 54 (D. Mass. 2021).

[49] The Advisory Committee Note to the 2003 Amendment to Rule 53.

[50] *Kaplan v. Hezbollah*, 213 F. Supp. 3d 27, 42–43 (D.D.C. 2016).

[51] Rule 53(f)(3)(A). *See also* The Advisory Committee Note to the 2003 Amendment to Rule 53; *Grace v. City of Detroit*, 341 F. Supp. 2d 709, 714 (E.D. Mich. 2004), aff'd, 216 Fed. Appx. 485 (6th Cir. 2007).

[52] *See United States ex rel. Int'l Bhd. of Elec. Workers Local Union No. 98 v. Farfield Co.*, 438 F. Supp. 3d 348, 357, 362 (E.D. Pa. 2020).

[53] *Dunn v. Dunn*, 318 F.R.D. 652, 683 (M.D. Ala. 2016).

[54] The Advisory Committee Note to the 2003 Amendment to Rule 53.

[55] *N. Nat. Gas Co. v. L.D. Drilling*, 862 F.3d 1221, 1227 n.7 (10th Cir. 2017).

[56] *Midwest Athletics & Sports All. LLC v. Xerox Corp.*, 545 F. Supp. 3d 16, 19 (W.D.N.Y. 2021); *Rover Pipeline LLC v. 1.23 Acres of Land*, 419 F. Supp. 3d 1010, 1013 n.1 (E.D. Mich. 2019).

the court. Only issues that are raised in objections to the master's report are preserved for appeal.[57]

RULE 53(g)—COMPENSATION

CORE CONCEPT

The court sets the compensation for a master. The master's compensation will be allocated among the parties or taken from the subject matter of the litigation.

APPLICATIONS

Amount of Compensation

The court establishes the compensation for a master in the order of appointment.[58] The court may require the posting of a bond to secure payment of the fee or require the payment of the fee into escrow.[59] The court may revise the compensation basis and terms after notice to the parties and an opportunity to be heard.[60]

Who Pays the Master's Compensation

The court may impose the master's fee upon any party or may apportion it among the parties.[61] In assigning responsibility for the master's fee, the court should consider the nature and amount of the controversy, the parties' financial means, and the extent to which any party is more responsible for the reference to the master.[62] The court may make an interim allocation and may adjust the interim allocation later to reflect the decision on the merits.[63] The court may also direct that the fee be paid from any fund or subject matter of the action in the custody of the court.[64]

Collection of Compensation

The master may obtain a writ of execution against a party not paying its share of the master's fee. The master may not withhold the report to obtain payment.

---

[57] *Absolute Software, Inc. v. Stealth Signal, Inc.*, 659 F.3d 1121, 1131 (Fed. Cir. 2011).

[58] *Gaddis v. U.S.*, 381 F.3d 444, 462 (5th Cir. 2004); *Cordoza v. Pacific States Steel Corp.*, 320 F.3d 989, 999 (9th Cir. 2003).

[59] *Allapattah Services, Inc. v. Exxon Corp.*, 157 F. Supp. 2d 1291, 1325 (S.D. Fla. 2001).

[60] *Moore v. Tangipahoa Parish School Board*, 843 F.3d 198, 202 (5th Cir. 2016).

[61] *See United States v. 269 Acres, More or Less, Located in Beaufort Cty. S.C.*, 995 F.3d 152, 170–71 (4th Cir. 2021); *Netsphere, Inc. v. Baron*, 703 F.3d 296, 313 (5th Cir. 2012).

[62] *United States v. 269 Acres, More or Less, Located in Beaufort Cty. S.C.*, 995 F.3d 152, 171 (4th Cir. 2021) (court has broad discretion); *Zaki Kulaibee Establishment v. McFliker*, 771 F.3d 1301, 1315 n.26 (11th Cir. 2014).

[63] Rule 53(g)(3). *See also Chevron Corp. v. Donziger*, 990 F.3d 191, 205 (2d Cir. 2021).

[64] *See Peterson v. Islamic Republic of Iran*, 224 F. Supp. 3d 17, 21 (D.D.C. 2016); *Six L's Packing Co., Inc. v. Post & Taback, Inc.*, 132 F. Supp. 2d 306, 309 (S.D.N.Y. 2001).

RULE 53(h)—APPOINTING A MAGISTRATE JUDGE

CORE CONCEPT

The provisions of Rule 53 do not pertain to matters referred to magistrate judges unless the order of reference specifically states that it is made pursuant to Rule 53.[65]

Additional Research References

Wright & Miller, *Federal Practice and Procedure* §§ 2601 to 2615

C.J.S., Federal Civil Procedure §§ 890 to 904; United States Commissioners § 3

West's Key Number Digest, Federal Civil Procedure ⚷1871 to 1908; United States Magistrates ⚷14

---

[65] *See Wallace v. Skadden, Arps, Slate, Meagher & Flom, LLP*, 362 F.3d 810, 814–16 (D.C. Cir. 2004).

VII. JUDGMENT

RULE 54
JUDGMENT; COSTS

(a) Definition; Form. "Judgment" as used in these rules includes a decree and any order from which an appeal lies. A judgment should not include recitals of pleadings, a master's report, or a record of prior proceedings.

(b) Judgment on Multiple Claims or Involving Multiple Parties. When an action presents more than one claim for relief—whether as a claim, counterclaim, crossclaim, or third-party claim—or when multiple parties are involved, the court may direct entry of a final judgment as to one or more, but fewer than all, claims or parties only if the court expressly determines that there is no just reason for delay. Otherwise, any order or other decision, however designated, that adjudicates fewer than all the claims or the rights and liabilities of fewer than all the parties does not end the action as to any of the claims or parties and may be revised at any time before the entry of a judgment adjudicating all the claims and all the parties' rights and liabilities.

(c) Demand for Judgment; Relief to Be Granted. A default judgment must not differ in kind from, or exceed in amount, what is demanded in the pleadings. Every other final judgment should grant the relief to which each party is entitled, even if the party has not demanded that relief in its pleadings.

(d) Costs; Attorney's Fees.

(1) *Costs Other Than Attorney's Fees.* Unless a federal statute, these rules, or a court order provides otherwise, costs—other than attorney's fees—should be allowed to the prevailing party. But costs against the United States, its officers, and its agencies may be imposed only to the

extent allowed by law. The clerk may tax costs on 14 days' notice. On motion served within the next 7 days, the court may review the clerk's action.

(2) *Attorney's Fees.*

(A) *Claim to Be by Motion.* A claim for attorney's fees and related nontaxable expenses must be made by motion unless the substantive law requires those fees to be proved at trial as an element of damages.

(B) *Timing and Contents of the Motion.* Unless a statute or a court order provides otherwise, the motion must:

(i) be filed no later than 14 days after the entry of judgment;

(ii) specify the judgment and the statute, rule, or other grounds entitling the movant to the award;

(iii) state the amount sought or provide a fair estimate of it; and

(iv) disclose, if the court so orders, the terms of any agreement about fees for the services for which the claim is made.

(C) *Proceedings.* Subject to Rule 23(h), the court must, on a party's request, give an opportunity for adversary submissions on the motion in accordance with Rule 43(c) or 78. The court may decide issues of liability for fees before receiving submissions on the value of services. The court must find the facts and state its conclusions of law as provided in Rule 52(a).

(D) *Special Procedures by Local Rule; Reference to a Master or a Magistrate Judge.* By local rule, the court may establish special procedures to resolve fee-related issues without extensive evidentiary hearings. Also, the court may refer issues concerning the value of services to a special master under Rule 53 without regard to the limitations of Rule 53(a)(1), and may refer a motion for attorney's fees to a magistrate judge under Rule 72(b) as if it were a dispositive pretrial matter.

(E) *Exceptions.* Subparagraphs (A)–(D) do not apply to claims for fees and expenses as sanctions for violating these rules or as sanctions under 28 U.S.C. § 1927.

[Amended December 27, 1946, effective March 19, 1948; April 17, 1961, effective July 19, 1961; March 2, 1987, effective August 1, 1987; April 22, 1993, effective December 1, 1993; amended April 29, 2002, effective December 1, 2002; March 27, 2003, effective December 1, 2003; April 30, 2007, effective December 1, 2007; March 26, 2009, effective December 1, 2009.]

AUTHORS' COMMENTARY ON RULE 54

PURPOSE AND SCOPE

Discerning whether a particular court ruling qualifies as a "judgment" is important in federal civil practice: it determines whether an enforceable, final obligation has been imposed from which an immediate appeal may be taken.

Rule 54(a) addresses this definitional, finality question. Ordinarily, an order is a "judgment" if it closes out proceedings in the case and opens the opportunity for disgruntled parties to file an appeal. Conversely, most interim rulings the court will enter during the life of a civil lawsuit—*e.g.,* orders to amend pleadings, to permit special service of process, to allow additional depositions, to resolve a challenge to a proposed expert witness, to extend times for filing briefs—will not qualify as "judgments."

Rule 54(b) allows the district court to enter a *partial* "judgment" when one of its interim rulings resolves—completely and with finality—either one of the lawsuit's multiple claims for relief or the rights and liabilities of one of the lawsuit's multiple parties. This authority is discretionary, not mandatory (and supplements other avenues for appealability established by statute or caselaw).[1]

Rule 54(c) directs the district court to grant parties all relief to which they are entitled, even if that relief was not expressly demanded (except where judgment is entered by default).

Lastly, Rule 54(d) provides that the lawsuit's prevailing party is usually entitled to a reimbursement of statutorily-defined "costs," though the awarding of "costs" remains vested in the district judge's discretion. Rule 54(d) also sets the procedures and time deadlines for pursuing both reimbursable "costs" and, when elsewhere permitted by law, non-"cost" litigation expenses and attorney's fees.

---

[1] For fuller discussion of the attributes that can make a district court ruling appealable, see *infra* Part VI, § 6.2 ("**Step One: Appealability**").

RULE 54(a)—DEFINITION AND FORM OF "JUDGMENT"

CORE CONCEPT

A judgment usually is any appealable decree or order.

APPLICATIONS

Definition

To be a "judgment" within the meaning of Rule 54(a), the court's order or decree ordinarily must be a ruling from which an appeal can be taken.[2] In the federal courts, appeals may be taken from *final decisions* by district courts and from a limited category of other, non-final, interlocutory rulings.[3] Although no particular wording or form is prescribed,[4] a ruling qualifies as a "final decision" (and, thus, a "judgment") if it clearly shows the district judge's intention that the order serve as his or her final act in the case[5] (or, with appealable interlocutory rulings, his or her final act on the motion).[6] Conversely, most non-final, interim orders do not qualify as "judgments"[7] and are not appealable unless another Rule or statute provides otherwise.[8]

Appears Alone (and May Even Be Oral)

To reduce confusion and uncertainty about what is (and is not) a "judgment", it should appear alone. It should not include recitals of the pleadings, a master's report, or a record of prior proceedings.[9] But this admirable directive is complicated with non-final interlocutory orders, which may be immediately ap-

---

[2]*See Labertew v. Langemeier*, 846 F.3d 1028, 1033 (9th Cir. 2017); *In re Metropolitan Gov't of Nashville & Davidson County, Tenn.*, 606 F.3d 855, 860 (6th Cir. 2010). *But cf. Keith Mfg. Co. v. Butterfield*, 955 F.3d 936, 940 (Fed. Cir. 2020) ("judgment" is term "often congruent" with but not equivalent to final order; some voluntary dismissals qualify).

[3]*See infra* Part VI, § 6.2 (**"Step One: Appealability"**).

[4]*See United States v. Hark*, 320 U.S. 531, 534, 64 S. Ct. 359, 88 L. Ed. 290 (1944). The Administrative Office of the U.S. Courts has developed an approved recommended form of judgment. *See* Judgment in a Civil Case, A.O. Form 450 (available at http://www.uscourts.gov/sites/default/files/ao450.pdf).

[5]*See United States v. F. & M. Schaefer Brewing Co.*, 356 U.S. 227, 232–34, 78 S. Ct. 674, 2 L. Ed. 2d 721 (1958). *See generally Hall v. Hall*, 584 U.S. ___, 138 S. Ct. 1118, 1123–24, 200 L. Ed. 2d 399 (2018) ("ends the litigation on the merits and leaves nothing for the court to do but execute the judgment"). *See generally Wilcox v. Georgetown Univ.*, 987 F.3d 143, 146–47 (D.C. Cir. 2021) (contrasting dismissal of complaints without prejudice (often non-final) with dismissal of actions (usually presumed final)).

[6]*See Ueckert v. Guerra*, 38 F.4th 446, 450–51 (5th Cir. 2022).

[7]*See Auto Servs. Co. v. KPMG, LLP*, 537 F.3d 853, 856 (8th Cir. 2008); *DeJohn v. Temple University*, 537 F.3d 301, 307 (3d Cir. 2008).

[8]*See, e.g.*, Rule 54(b); 28 U.S.C. § 1292.

[9]*See Cooke v. Jackson Nat'l Life Ins. Co.*, 882 F.3d 630, 631 (7th Cir. 2018) (should state who won what relief, and omit reasons why). *See generally supra* Authors' Commentary to

pealable (and, thus, "judgments") even when they are issued by the judge orally from the bench.[10]

RULE 54(b)—JUDGMENT ON MULTIPLE CLAIMS OR INVOLVING MULTIPLE PARTIES

CORE CONCEPT

A judgment entered as to fewer than all claims or all parties in a lawsuit is ordinarily not immediately appealable. Instead, the appeal must generally await the entry of judgment as to all remaining claims and parties. However, the district court can make its adjudication of discrete claims or parties "final," and immediately appealable, if no just reason exists to delay that ruling's appeal.

APPLICATIONS

Purpose

When they first took effect, the Federal Rules of Civil Procedure liberalized the possibilities for joining multiple claims and multiple parties into a single lawsuit.[11] But routinely permitting separate, piecemeal appeals from various rulings as they resolved parts of a multi-claim, multi-party lawsuit would be inefficient and contrary to the historic federal policy favoring one appeal on all issues at the conclusion of the lawsuit.[12] Nonetheless, compelling litigants to wait out the disposition of all parts of such a lawsuit could, occasionally, prove unduly harsh or unjust; for those instances, Rule 54(b) supplied an alternative—partial final judgments.[13]

The Ordinary Practice (No Immediate Appeal)

Absent a Rule 54(b) partial-judgment determination, interim rulings that do not end the litigation in its entirely are interlocutory, usually not immediately appealable, and subject to revision by the district judge.[14] This right of revision is

---

Rule 58(a) (discussing "separate document" requirement for judgments).

[10] *See Ueckert v. Guerra*, 38 F.4th 446, 450–51 (5th Cir. 2022).

[11] *See Sears, Roebuck & Co. v. Mackey*, 351 U.S. 427, 432-33, 76 S. Ct. 895, 100 L. Ed. 1297 (1956).

[12] *See Curtiss-Wright Corp. v. General Elec. Co.*, 446 U.S. 1, 8, 100 S. Ct. 1460, 64 L. Ed. 2d 1 (1980). *See also Rowland v. S. Health Partners, Inc.*, 4 F.4th 422, 425 (6th Cir. 2021) (with narrow exceptions, federal courts follow a one-case/one-appeal approach).

[13] *See Gelboim v. Bank of America Corp.*, 574 U.S. 405, 409-10, 135 S. Ct. 897, 190 L. Ed. 2d 789 (2015); *Dickinson v. Petroleum Conversion Corp.*, 338 U.S. 507, 511, 70 S. Ct. 322, 94 L. Ed. 299 (1950).

[14] *See Williams v. Seidenbach*, 958 F.3d 341, 346–47 (5th Cir. 2020); *Spring Creek Expl. & Prod. Co., LLC v. Hess Bakken Inv., II, LLC*, 887 F.3d 1003, 1023–24 (10th Cir. 2018). *See generally In re Domestic Airline Travel Antitrust Litig.*, 3 F.4th 457, 459 (D.C. Cir. 2021) (judgments are "final" when they dispose of all claims and all parties); *Williams v. Seidenbach*, 958 F.3d 341, 343 (5th Cir. 2020) (en banc) ("there is no final decision as to one defendant until there is a final decision as to all defendants").

broad,[15] but not limitless; it is cabined in by other doctrines, including law-of-the-case.[16] Rule 54(b) represents an exception to this ordinary practice.

Three Prerequisites to Rule 54(b) Partial Judgments

In evaluating whether to grant a Rule 54(b) determination, the district courts function like "dispatchers."[17] They may "dispatch" a portion of the lawsuit for immediate appeal, but only if: (1) at least one claim or the rights and liabilities of at least one party have become fully resolved; (2) there is no just reason to delay the appeal; *and* (3) a partial final judgment is directed to be entered on the docket.

Prerequisite #1: Claim or Party Fully Resolved

An adjudication must *either* (a) finally resolve at least one claim or (b) finally resolve the rights and liabilities of at least one party, such that nothing more is left to do on that claim or with that party but await the conclusion of the remaining portions of the litigation.[18] This limitation is a pivotal one. Rule 54(b) does not alter the normal rules of appellate finality for individual claims, and no appeal may be taken from district court rulings on any particular claim until the court finally resolves that claim.[19] Thus, for example, where a portion of a claim is resolved, but the amount of damages, the question of insurance coverage, or affirmative defenses remain to be decided, that claim has not been finally resolved (even if all other issues are completely adjudicated), and a Rule 54(b) determination is not appropriate.[20]

- *Multiple Claims:* An appeal from one dismissed claim (when other claims still remain) is possible only when that claim is resolved entirely and as to all parties.[21] Thus, Rule 54(b) is inapplicable where the lawsuit

---

[15]*See Austin v. Kroger Texas, L.P.*, 864 F.3d 326, 336 (5th Cir. 2017); *Cobell v. Jewell*, 802 F.3d 12, 25–26 (D.C. Cir. 2015).

[16]*See U.S. Tobacco Coop. Inc. v. Big S. Wholesale of Virginia, LLC*, 899 F.3d 236, 256–57 (4th Cir. 2018).

[17]*See Curtiss-Wright Corp. v. General Elec. Co.*, 446 U.S. 1, 8, 100 S. Ct. 1460, 64 L. Ed. 2d 1 (1980); *Sears, Roebuck & Co. v. Mackey*, 351 U.S. 427, 435, 76 S. Ct. 895, 100 L. Ed. 1297 (1956).

[18]*See Curtiss-Wright Corp. v. General Elec. Co.*, 446 U.S. 1, 7, 100 S. Ct. 1460, 64 L. Ed. 2d 1 (1980).

[19]*See Sears, Roebuck & Co. v. Mackey*, 351 U.S. 427, 437, 76 S. Ct. 895, 100 L. Ed. 1297 (1956). *See also Kinsale Ins. Co. v. JDBC Holdings, Inc.*, 31 F.4th 870, 873 (4th Cir. 2022) (preserves finality, as "ultimate disposition of an individual claim" entered in multi-claim lawsuit); *Attias v. CareFirst, Inc.*, 969 F.3d 412, 416 (D.C. Cir. 2020) (does not abandon finality, it just allows it to be assessed ruling by ruling).

[20]*See Linde v. Arab Bank, PLC*, 882 F.3d 314, 322–23 (2d Cir. 2018); *Alfred E. Mann Found. for Sci. Research v. Cochlear Corp.*, 841 F.3d 1334, 1347 (Fed. Cir. 2016). *See generally Liberty Mut. Ins. Co. v. Wetzel*, 424 U.S. 737, 744, 96 S. Ct. 1202, 1206, 47 L. Ed. 2d 435 (1976).

[21]*See Tetra Techs., Inc. v. Continental Ins. Co.*, 755 F.3d 222, 228 (5th Cir. 2014).

involves either a single claim only or multiple claims that have already been resolved to finality.[22] Claims that have been severed or separated from the original claim, and which are thereafter proceeding independently, may themselves be eligible for an appeal once dismissed.[23]

- *"Claim" Defined*: The term "claim" is not defined in the Rule nor well explained in Supreme Court precedent; as a result, the concept proves sometimes elusive in application.[24] No universal, bright-line rules aid in the defining task.[25] A "claim" is, at base, an enforceable right arising from a set of facts.[26] Beyond that generality, the law-drawing becomes more indefinite. A simple variation in legal theory alone will not suffice to create a separate "claim,"[27] nor will the mere fact that the allegations were pleaded separately.[28] Rather, this assessment implicates practical concerns. Multiple claims might exist where each claim is factually independent,[29] where each claim could be enforced separately,[30] where each claim seeks to vindicate a different legal right,[31] where there is more than one potential recovery, or where different types of relief are requested.[32] If, however, only one recovery is possible (even though several legal theo-

---

[22]*See Gelboim v. Bank of America Corp.*, 574 U.S. 405, 416, 135 S. Ct. 897, 190 L. Ed. 2d 789 (2015); *Liberty Mut. Ins. Co. v. Wetzel*, 424 U.S. 737, 742–44, 96 S. Ct. 1202, 47 L. Ed. 2d 435 (1976). *But cf. Williams v. Seidenbach*, 958 F.3d 341, 343-48 (5th Cir. 2020) (en banc) (court may invoke Rule 54(b) to permit appeal of a ruling even after plaintiffs voluntarily dismiss all other defendants).

[23]*See Brooks v. District Hosp. Partners, L.P.*, 606 F.3d 800, 805–06 (D.C. Cir. 2010).

[24]*See In re Fifth Third Early Access Cash Advance Litig.*, 925 F.3d 265, 273 (6th Cir. 2019) ("trickier than it sounds"; "term of art"); *Pakootas v. Teck Cominco Metals, Ltd.*, 905 F.3d 565, 574–75 (9th Cir. 2018) (not well defined; Supreme Court's "judicial crumbs" have not led to consensus among lower courts).

[25]*See Johnson v. Ocwen Loan Servicing, L.L.C.*, 916 F.3d 505, 508 (5th Cir. 2019); *Planned Parenthood Sw. Ohio Region v. DeWine*, 696 F.3d 490, 500 (6th Cir. 2012).

[26]*See In re Fifth Third Early Access Cash Advance Litig.*, 925 F.3d 265, 273 (6th Cir. 2019); *Pakootas v. Teck Cominco Metals, Ltd.*, 905 F.3d 565, 575 (9th Cir. 2018).

[27]*See Marseilles Hydro Power, LLC v. Marseilles Land and Water Co.*, 518 F.3d 459, 464 (7th Cir. 2008).

[28]*See EJS Props., LLC v. City of Toledo*, 689 F.3d 535, 538 (6th Cir. 2012).

[29]*See Seatrain Shipbuilding Corp. v. Shell Oil Co.*, 444 U.S. 572, 579-84, 100 S. Ct. 800, 63 L. Ed. 2d 36 (1980); *Nat'l Credit Union Admin. Bd. v. Jurcevic*, 867 F.3d 616, 623–24 (6th Cir. 2017).

[30]*See Acumen Re Mgmt. Corp. v. General Sec. Nat. Ins. Co.*, 769 F.3d 135, 141 (2d Cir. 2014). *Cf. General Acquisition, Inc. v. GenCorp, Inc.*, 23 F.3d 1022, 1028 (6th Cir. 1994) (if action seeks to vindicate only one legal right, but alleges several elements of damage, only one claim presented).

[31]*See United States ex rel. Ibanez v. Bristol-Myers Squibb Co.*, 874 F.3d 905, 913–14 (6th Cir. 2017).

[32]*See Marseilles Hydro Power, LLC v. Marseilles Land and Water Co.*, 518 F.3d 459, 464 (7th Cir. 2008); *Advanced Magnetics, Inc. v. Bayfront Partners, Inc.*, 106 F.3d 11, 16 (2d Cir. 1997).

ries are offered to support that recovery) or if alternative recoveries either substantially overlap or are mutually exclusive, the partial adjudication will not be eligible for immediate appeal under Rule 54(b).[33] Put another way, if the claim in question so overlaps the claims that remain for trial that an appeal at the end of the case on the retained claims would compel the court to retrace the same ground it would have addressed had the first claim received a Rule 54(b) determination, Rule 54(b) treatment is inappropriate.[34] But this "overlap" inquiry is performed with care; the mere existence of some factual overlap will not, alone, defeat the possibility of multiple claims.[35] Counterclaims[36] and claims in consolidated cases[37] are assessed using this same inquiry.

- *Multiple Parties:* An appeal by one dismissed party (when claims by other parties still remain) is possible only when that one party's rights and interests are resolved entirely and the district court so signifies.[38] Rule 54(b) is not just limited to defendants. If the criteria for Rule 54(b) is satisfied, the dismissal of any party (plaintiff or defendant) may be appealed.[39] A named but unserved, nonappearing defendant will not be considered a "party" for the purpose of applying this Rule,[40] unless the court contemplates further action as to that defendant.[41]

Prerequisite #2: No Just Reason For Delay

The district court must state, in clear and unmistakable language, there is no just reason to delay the appeal of the

---

[33]*See Peerless Network, Inc. v. MCI Commc'ns Servs., Inc.*, 917 F.3d 538, 543 (7th Cir. 2019); *Pakootas v. Teck Cominco Metals, Ltd.*, 905 F.3d 565, 575 (9th Cir. 2018).

[34]*See Rankins v. Sys. Sols. of Kentucky, LLC*, 40 F.4th 589, 591–93 (7th Cir. 2022); *Outdoor Cent., Inc. v. GreatLodge.com, Inc.*, 643 F.3d 1115, 1119 (8th Cir. 2011). *See also Kinsale Ins. Co. v. JDBC Holdings, Inc.*, 31 F.4th 870, 874 (4th Cir. 2022) (mandatory 5-factor inquiry: relationship among claims; possibility that need for appeal may become mooted; potential for need to revisit issues; set-off risks posed by claims or counterclaims; delay/economy).

[35]*See Pakootas v. Teck Cominco Metals, Ltd.*, 905 F.3d 565, 575 (9th Cir. 2018); *Intellectual Ventures I LLC v. Capital One Fin. Corp.*, 850 F.3d 1332, 1336 (Fed. Cir. 2017).

[36]*See Curtiss-Wright Corp. v. General Elec. Co.*, 446 U.S. 1, 9, 100 S. Ct. 1460, 64 L. Ed 2d 1 (1980); *MCI Constructors, LLC v. City of Greensboro*, 610 F.3d 849, 855 n.5 (4th Cir. 2010).

[37]*See Florida Wildlife Fed'n, Inc. v. Administrator, U.S. E.P.A.*, 737 F.3d 689, 692–93 (11th Cir. 2013).

[38]*See Brooks v. District Hosp. Partners, L.P.*, 606 F.3d 800, 805 n.2 (D.C. Cir. 2010).

[39]*See Brooks v. District Hosp. Partners, L.P.*, 606 F.3d 800, 805 n.2 (D.C.Cir. 2010).

[40]*See Charles v. Atkinson*, 826 F.3d 841, 842 (5th Cir. 2016); *Cambridge Holdings Group, Inc. v. Federal Ins. Co.*, 489 F.3d 1356, 1360–61 (D.C. Cir. 2007).

[41]*See Kaplan v. Cent. Bank of the Islamic Republic of Iran*, 896 F.3d 501, 506–07 (D.C. Cir. 2018).

adjudicated claim or the adjudicated rights and liabilities of a party. This determination requires a weighing of both the equities in the case and the judicial administrative interests (especially the interest in avoiding piecemeal appeals).[42] Ordinarily, this weighing will favor an immediate appeal only where delay in appealing presents some risk of hardship or injustice that would be avoided by an immediate review, where a plaintiff could be prejudiced by a delay in recovering a monetary judgment, or where an expensive, duplicative trial could be avoided by reviewing a dismissed claim promptly before the remaining claims reach trial.[43] Conversely, where multiple claims, even if separate, could again be subject to yet another review in a later appeal,[44] or where the claims, though discrete, are so interrelated as to form a single factual unit,[45] an immediate appeal would be improper. Whether "just cause" exists is a determination made on a case-by-case basis.[46] Certain nonexhaustive[47] criteria guide a court's consideration:

- The relationship between adjudicated and unadjudicated claims;
- The possibility that the need for appellate review might be mooted by future developments in the district court;
- The possibility that the district court might be obligated to consider the same issue on a later occasion;
- The presence (or absence) of a claim or counterclaim that could result in a set-off against the judgment now sought to be made final and appealed; and
- Other factors, including delay, economic and solvency concerns, shortening of trial time, frivolity of competing claims, and expense.[48]

A Rule 54(b) determination is likely to be improper where the litigation itself—and the contested claim's resolution—is routine and would inevitably return to the trial court on es-

---

[42] *See Attias v. CareFirst, Inc.*, 969 F.3d 412, 417 (D.C. Cir. 2020); *In re Fifth Third Early Access Cash Advance Litig.*, 925 F.3d 265, 275 (6th Cir. 2019).

[43] *See Nystedt v. Nigro*, 700 F.3d 25, 30 (1st Cir. 2012); *Taco John's of Huron, Inc. v. Bix Produce Co.*, 569 F.3d 401, 402 (8th Cir. 2009).

[44] *See Transport Workers Union of America, Local 100, AFL-CIO v. New York City Transit Authority*, 505 F.3d 226, 230 (2d Cir. 2007).

[45] *See Attias v. CareFirst, Inc.*, 969 F.3d 412, 417 (D.C. Cir. 2020); *Novick v. AXA Network, LLC*, 642 F.3d 304, 311 (2d Cir. 2011).

[46] *See Sears, Roebuck & Co. v. Mackey*, 351 U.S. 427, 76 S. Ct. 895, 100 L. Ed. 1297 (1956); *McAdams v. McCord*, 533 F.3d 924, 928 (8th Cir. 2008). *See also Doe v. City of Chicago*, 360 F.3d 667, 673 (7th Cir. 2004) (ruling that there was "just reason for delay" and, thus, Rule 54(b) relief was not available, where factual development of certain claim was necessary).

[47] *See U.S. Citizens Ass'n v. Sebelius*, 705 F.3d 588, 596 (6th Cir. 2013).

[48] *See Rowland v. S. Health Partners, Inc.*, 4 F.4th 422, 427 (6th Cir. 2021); *Downing v. Riceland Foods, Inc.*, 810 F.3d 580, 585 (8th Cir. 2016).

sentially the same set of facts.[49]

Prerequisite #3: Entry of Partial Judgment Directed

In clear and unmistakable language, the district court must direct that judgment be entered as to at least one claim or one party.[50]

Use of "Magic Language"

Immediate appealability hinges on the district court "expressly" determining that there is no just reason for delay[51] and then directing entry of a partial final judgment.[52] A court's failure to incant this exact language may be overlooked, however, so long as the trial judge's intent to proceed under Rule 54(b) is otherwise unmistakably clear[53] (though not all courts embrace this liberality).[54] In any event, however it is communicated, the determination must always be made "expressly"[55] and the intent "unmistakable".[56]

- *Abandoned Claims*: A district court's judgment that resolves some open claims, but leaves others unaddressed, may still be deemed to be final (even without the inclusion of the "magic language"), if the unaddressed claims were abandoned[57] or otherwise terminated by subsequent events.[58]
- *Subsequent Determination*: An order lacking the Rule 54(b) specifics may be cured by a supplemental order,[59]

[49] *See Wood v. GCC Bend, LLC*, 422 F.3d 873, 878 (9th Cir. 2005). *See also Credit Francais Intern., S.A. v. Bio-Vita, Ltd.*, 78 F.3d 698, 707 (1st Cir. 1996) (early appeal is particularly suspect when the appellants remain litigants before the trial court).

[50] *See CBX Res., L.L.C. v. ACE Am. Ins. Co.*, 959 F.3d 175, 177 (5th Cir. 2020) (intention must be "unmistakable"); *Blackman v. District of Columbia*, 456 F.3d 167, 175–76 (D.C. Cir. 2006) (must be an express direction for entry of judgment). *But cf. Rowland v. S. Health Partners, Inc.*, 4 F.4th 422, 426-27 (6th Cir. 2021) (does not require district court to enter partial final judgment in its Rule 54(b) determination, only that it "recognize" such entry has been made).

[51] *See United States v. Gila Valley Irrigation Dist.*, 859 F.3d 789, 797–98 (9th Cir. 2017); *HSBC Bank USA, N.A. v. Townsend*, 793 F.3d 771, 778 (7th Cir. 2015).

[52] *See In re Methyl Tertiary Butyl Ether ("MTBE") Prod. Liab. Litig.*, 859 F.3d 178, 187–88 (2d Cir. 2017).

[53] *See Doe v. Vigo Cty.*, 905 F.3d 1038, 1042 (7th Cir. 2018); *Crostley v. Lamar County*, 717 F.3d 410, 420 (5th Cir. 2013).

[54] *See Schrock v. Wyeth, Inc.*, 727 F.3d 1273, 1278–79 (10th Cir. 2013); *Joint Venture 1 v. Weyand*, 649 F.3d 310, 319–20 (5th Cir. 2011).

[55] *See New Mexico v. Trujillo*, 813 F.3d 1308, 1316 (10th Cir. 2016); *Nystedt v. Nigro*, 700 F.3d 25, 30 (1st Cir. 2012).

[56] *See CBX Res., L.L.C. v. ACE Am. Ins. Co.*, 959 F.3d 175, 177 (5th Cir. 2020).

[57] *See DIRECTV, Inc. v. Budden*, 420 F.3d 521, 525–26 (5th Cir. 2005).

[58] *See Schippers v. U.S.*, 715 F.3d 879, 884–85 (11th Cir. 2013).

[59] *See Intellectual Ventures I LLC v. Capital One Fin. Corp.*, 850 F.3d 1332, 1336 & n.3 (Fed. Cir. 2017); *Glover v. F.D.I.C.*, 698 F.3d 139, 144 n.5 (3d Cir. 2012).

including one issued upon remand from an appeal.[60]

Explanation by the District Court

Detailed statements of reasons are not necessary.[61] But in its order entering a Rule 54(b) judgment, the district court must clearly and cogently explain why it has concluded that an immediate appellate review of the order is advisable,[62] or those reasons must be readily apparent from the record.[63] The district court should not simply reprint, in boilerplate, the formula of the Rule[64] or autograph a defendant's Rule 54(b) request.[65] The court of appeals may, in the absence of a written explanation, dismiss the appeal as inappropriately allowed under Rule 54(b)[66] or subject the determination to special scrutiny.[67] Although dismissal of the appeal is permitted (and perhaps even likely) without a corresponding explanation from the trial court, dismissal is not compulsory; the failure to offer a written explanation is not a jurisdictional defect that *compels* the appeal's dismissal.[68]

Duty of Counsel in Explanation Requirement

In moving for a Rule 54(b) determination, the courts expect counsel, as officers of the court and advocates for an immediate appeal, to assist the district judge by making appropriate submissions that express the reasons for and basis of a Rule

---

[60]*See Rollins v. Mortgage Elec. Regis. Sys., Inc.*, 737 F.3d 1250, 1253–54 (9th Cir. 2013).

[61]*See Johnson v. Ocwen Loan Servicing, L.L.C.*, 916 F.3d 505, 509 (5th Cir. 2019); *Doe v. Vigo Cty.*, 905 F.3d 1038, 1042 (7th Cir. 2018).

[62]*See Kinsale Ins. Co. v. JDBC Holdings, Inc.*, 31 F.4th 870, 874 (4th Cir. 2022) ("should state" findings); *Adams v. C3 Pipeline Constr. Inc.*, 30 F.4th 943, 957 n.3 (10th Cir. 2021) ("should clearly articulate" reasons and "make careful statements based on the record"); *Novick v. AXA Network, LLC*, 642 F.3d 304, 310 (2d Cir. 2011) (reasoned, even if brief, explanation required).

[63]*See Johnson v. Ocwen Loan Servicing, L.L.C.*, 916 F.3d 505, 509 (5th Cir. 2019); *Doe v. Vigo Cty.*, 905 F.3d 1038, 1042 (7th Cir. 2018).

[64]*See iLOR, LLC v. Google, Inc.*, 550 F.3d 1067, 1072 (Fed.Cir. 2008); *Akers v. Alvey*, 338 F.3d 491, 495 (6th Cir. 2003).

[65]*See Boston Prop. Exchange Transfer Co. v. Iantosca*, 720 F.3d 1, 7–8 (1st Cir. 2013); *Williams v. County of Dakota*, 687 F.3d 1064, 1068 (8th Cir. 2012).

[66]*See New Mexico v. Trujillo*, 813 F.3d 1308, 1316–17 (10th Cir. 2016); *Adler v. Elk Glenn, LLC*, 758 F.3d 737, 738 (6th Cir. 2014).

[67]*See Williams v. County of Dakota*, 687 F.3d 1064, 1068 (8th Cir. 2012). *See also Kinsale Ins. Co. v. JDBC Holdings, Inc.*, 31 F.4th 870, 874 (4th Cir. 2022) (lack of findings/reasoning nullifies normal appellate deference).

[68]*See Jewel v. Nat'l Sec. Agency*, 810 F.3d 622, 628 (9th Cir. 2015); *Brown v. Eli Lilly & Co.*, 654 F.3d 347, 355 (2d Cir. 2011). *See also Smith ex rel. Smith v. Half Hollow Hills Cent. School Dist.*, 298 F.3d 168, 171 (2d Cir. 2002) (under rare circumstances, reason for certification may be sufficiently obvious that no explanation is required and court of appeals is able to provide meaningful review without explanation from trial judge of why certification was deemed appropriate).

54(b) determination.[69] In fact, if the trial judge fails to offer a detailed explanation for the Rule 54(b) determination, the reasons offered by counsel can assume special significance.[70] But counsel cannot, by agreement that they exist, create the Rule 54(b) prerequisites if they are absent.[71]

Burden of Proof

The moving party bears the burden of establishing that a partial judgment should be entered under Rule 54(b).[72]

Procedure and Timing for Rule 54(b) Determinations

The Rule establishes no fixed procedure for obtaining a Rule 54(b) determination.[73] Case law tends to confirm that trial judges may make such determinations *sua sponte*[74] or upon motion by a party.[75] Some courts have set a narrow time window for Rule 54(b) motions,[76] while others refuse to endorse any rigid, judicially-crafted deadline.[77] In any event, prudent practitioners are wise to move promptly under Rule 54(b) lest their "thumb-twiddling" itself be deemed evidence of their tolerance for an ordinary, non-immediate, end-of-case appeal.[78]

Discretion of District Judge

The court is not *required* to enter a final judgment in an action involving multiple claims or parties where the court resolves claims involving less than all parties or less than all

---

[69] *See Federal Home Loan Mortgage Corp. v. Scottsdale Ins. Co.*, 316 F.3d 431, 441–42 (3d Cir. 2003).

[70] *See Williams v. County of Dakota*, 687 F.3d 1064, 1067–68 (8th Cir. 2012).

[71] *See Williams v. County of Dakota*, 687 F.3d 1064, 1067 (8th Cir. 2012).

[72] *See Braswell Shipyards, Inc. v. Beazer East, Inc.*, 2 F.3d 1331, 1335 (4th Cir. 1993); *Anthuis v. Colt Industries Operating Corp.*, 971 F.2d 999, 1003 (3d Cir. 1992).

[73] *See DaSilva v. Indiana*, 30 F.4th 671, 673 (7th Cir. 2022) (although Rules are otherwise "chock full of time limits," Rules 54(b) contains none).

[74] *See U.S. Citizens Ass'n v. Sebelius*, 705 F.3d 588, 593–97 (6th Cir. 2013); *Intergraph Corp. v. Intel Corp.*, 253 F.3d 695, 699 (Fed. Cir. 2001).

[75] *See Cincinnati Ins. Co. v. All Plumbing, Inc.*, 812 F.3d 153, 158 (D.C. Cir. 2016).

[76] *See King v. Newbold*, 845 F.3d 866, 868 (7th Cir. 2017) (absent "extreme hardship," Rule 54(b) determinations cannot be made beyond 30 days from entry of contested order).

[77] *See Est. of Beauford v. Correct Care Sols., LLC*, 2021 WL 50873, at *3 (D. Colo. Jan. 5, 2021), *rev'd on other grounds*, 35 F.4th 1248 (10th Cir. 2022) (Rule 54(b) text "imposes no time limit"; rejecting court-crafted deadlines as "based on policy considerations and the Rule's text"); *Miami Tribe of Oklahoma v. United States*, 2006 WL 3848949, at *4 (D. Kan. Dec. 29, 2006) (adopting no specific period, but 10 months delay too long); *Bank of N.Y. v. Hoyt*, 108 F.R.D. 184, 185 (D.R.I. 1985) (court "eschews any such inflexible criterion").

[78] *See Bank of N.Y. v. Hoyt*, 108 F.R.D. 184, 185–86 (D.R.I. 1985). *See also Birkes v. Tillamook Cty.*, 2012 WL 2178964, at *3 n.1 (D. Or. June 13, 2012). *See generally DaSilva v. Indiana*, 30 F.4th 671, 673 (7th Cir. 2022) ("When the party seeking to appeal takes too much time to request a Rule 54(b) judgment, that creates delay and undermines the function of a partial final judgment.").

claims.[79] To the contrary, whether to enter a judgment under Rule 54(b) is reserved for the sound discretion of the district judge.[80] Because such judgments are contrary to the historic federal policy against piecemeal appeals,[81] Rule 54(b) orders are not granted routinely,[82] or merely with the hope of avoiding a trial,[83] or as an accommodation to counsel.[84] Instead, the district court must carefully balance the needs of the parties for an immediate appeal against the interest of efficient management of the litigation.[85] Rule 54(d) determinations are the exceptions, not the rule.[86]

- *No "Tag-Along" Partial Appeals:* A decision to permit an immediate appeal of one ruling is not, alone, sufficient justification to grant Rule 54(b) relief for other rulings.[87]

Warning: Effect of Rule 54(b) Judgments

Once a Rule 54(b) judgment is entered, the time for appeal on that judgment begins to run,[88] as does post-judgment interest.[89] Consequently, failing to file an appeal timely after entry of the Rule 54(b) judgment may forever forfeit the right

---

[79] *See generally Ruiz v. Blentech Corp.*, 89 F.3d 320, 323 (7th Cir. 1996) (court has two options in placing into final form individual orders in multi-party cases: Rule 54(b) finality order or final order disposing of all claims respecting all parties).

[80] *See Curtiss-Wright Corp. v. General Elec. Co.*, 446 U.S. 1, 100 S. Ct. 1460, 64 L. Ed. 2d 1 (1980). *See generally Sears, Roebuck & Co. v. Mackey*, 351 U.S. 427, 437, 76 S. Ct. 895, 900, 100 L. Ed. 1297 (1956) (discretion lies primarily with the district court "as the one most likely to be familiar with the case and with any justifiable reasons for delay").

[81] *See Reiter v. Cooper*, 507 U.S. 258, 263, 113 S. Ct. 1213, 122 L. Ed. 2d 604 (1993); *Curtiss-Wright Corp. v. General Elec. Co.*, 446 U.S. 1, 8, 100 S. Ct. 1460, 64 L. Ed. 2d 1 (1980).

[82] *See Curtiss-Wright Corp. v. General Elec. Co.*, 446 U.S. 1, 10, 100 S. Ct. 1460, 64 L. Ed. 2d 1 (1980) (sound judicial administration does not require that Rule 54(b) requests be granted routinely).

[83] *See Credit Francais Intern., S.A. v. Bio-Vita, Ltd.*, 78 F.3d 698, 706 (1st Cir. 1996) (possibility of avoiding a trial is "rarely, if ever, a self-sufficient basis for a Rule 54(b) certification").

[84] *See Jones v. W. Plains Bank & Trust Co.*, 813 F.3d 700, 703 (8th Cir. 2015); *Nystedt v. Nigro*, 700 F.3d 25, 29 (1st Cir. 2012).

[85] *See In re Fifth Third Early Access Cash Advance Litig.*, 925 F.3d 265, 275 (6th Cir. 2019).

[86] *See Kinsale Ins. Co. v. JDBC Holdings, Inc.*, 31 F.4th 870, 876 (4th Cir. 2022); *Elliott v. Archdiocese of New York*, 682 F.3d 213, 220 (3d Cir. 2012). *See also L.B. Foster Co. v. America Piles, Inc.*, 138 F.3d 81, 86 (2d Cir. 1998) (reserved for "the infrequent harsh case" where danger exists for hardship or injustice through delay, which could be alleviated by immediate appeal).

[87] *See King v. Newbold*, 845 F.3d 866, 868 (7th Cir. 2017) (absent "extreme hardship," Rule 54(b) determinations cannot be made beyond 30 days from entry of contested order).

[88] *See Johnson v. Ocwen Loan Servicing, L.L.C.*, 916 F.3d 505, 508 (5th Cir. 2019); *Kolawole v. Sellers*, 863 F.3d 1361, 1367 (11th Cir. 2017). *See also Brown v. Eli Lilly & Co.*, 654 F.3d 347, 354 (2d Cir. 2011) (appeal time began and ended, while counsel relied on errant conclusion that appeal right had not yet ripened).

[89] *See* 28 U.S.C.A. § 1961; *Hooks v. Washington Sheraton Corp.*, 642 F.2d 614, 616 (D.C. Cir. 1980).

of appeal.[90] Moreover, some courts have ruled that the time for appeal following a Rule 54(b) determination can begin to run even earlier—on the date the order granting Rule 54(b) relief was signed and mailed to the parties.[91] Litigants who neglect to appeal in this accelerated time window might be able to collaterally attack the trial court's Rule 54(b) determination, but that strategy is not free from doubt.[92]

Effect of Non-Rule-54(b) Partial Rulings

Unless the court enters a separate judgment under Rule 54(b), litigants in a multi-party case who are dismissed technically remain in the case until the final resolution of all claims as to all parties. Dismissed litigants are, however, usually entitled to rely on the dismissal until notified that they have been rejoined as parties. Thus, until notified otherwise, dismissed litigants need not participate in discovery, in pretrial proceedings, or in the trial itself.[93]

"Certification" Nomenclature

Often in the case law, the Rule 54(b) determination procedure is described as a "certification", a "misnomer born of confusion."[94] The term "certification" describes the procedure for seeking immediate appellate review of interlocutory orders under 28 U.S.C.A. § 1292(b).[95] Conversely, a Rule 54(b) determination, if granted, effectively severs what becomes a *final* judgment (albeit as to one or more but fewer than all claims or parties) from the remaining claims and parties in the case.[96]

Appeals—Denials of Rule 54(b) Requests

Rule 54(b) operates to create an exception to the settled federal policy disfavoring piecemeal appeals. Unsurprisingly,

---

[90] *See Vermont Ry., Inc. v. Town of Shelburne*, 918 F.3d 82, 87 (2d Cir. 2019); *Johnson v. Ocwen Loan Servicing, L.L.C.*, 916 F.3d 505, 508 (5th Cir. 2019).

[91] *See Silivanch v. Celebrity Cruises, Inc.*, 333 F.3d 355, 364–65 (2d Cir. 2003) ("[t]here is no requirement that such a certification be docketed in order for it to become effective", and thus the order became effective, and the appeal period began to run, when the order "was signed and mailed to the parties"). *But cf. Brown v. Mississippi Valley State University*, 311 F.3d 328, 331–32 (5th Cir. 2002) (for purposes of Rule 4 of the Federal Rules of Appellate Procedure, judgment becomes final on the date Rule 54(b) determination is entered).

[92] *See Johnson v. Ocwen Loan Servicing, L.L.C.*, 916 F.3d 505, 508 (5th Cir. 2019) (discussing national case law).

[93] *See Bennett v. Pippin*, 74 F.3d 578, 587 (5th Cir. 1996).

[94] *See James v. Price Stern Sloan, Inc.*, 283 F.3d 1064, 1067–68 n. 6 (9th Cir. 2002).

[95] For a discussion of Section 1292(b) certification appeals, see *infra* Part VI § 6.2 ("**Discretionary Interlocutory Appeals**").

[96] *See James v. Price Stern Sloan, Inc.*, 283 F.3d 1064, 1067–68 n. 6 (9th Cir. 2002) ("Referring to a Rule 54(b) severance order as a 'certification' misleadingly brings to mind the kind of rigorous judgment embodied in the section 1292(b) certification process. In reality, issuance of a Rule 54(b) order is a fairly routine act that is reversed only in the rarest instances").

courts have rebuffed attempts to immediately appeal denials of Rule 54(b) determinations as premature until a final ruling is entered on the merits.[97]

Appeals — Improper Grants of Rule 54(b) Requests

The court of appeals will examine an appealed-from order's eligibility under Rule 54(b),[98] even if the propriety of the Rule 54(b) determination is not contested by the litigants.[99] If the appeals court finds that the district court's Rule 54(b) determination was given or prepared improperly, appellate jurisdiction is lost.[100] But counsel should be very careful before relying on their own conclusions in this regard; if the court of appeals disagrees or, finding an impropriety, overlooks it, a litigant's failure to have filed an appeal could prove disastrous, since appellate courts are not bound by counsel's views on the question.[101]

Appeals — Prematurely Filed

If an appeal is taken before the district court issues a Rule 54(b) determination, many Circuits have ruled that a belated determination "ripens" the otherwise premature appeal, so long as the determination is issued prior to the date the court of appeals considers the appeal.[102]

Appeals — Scope of "Determination"

On appeal following a Rule 54(b) determination, the court of appeals will confine its review only to those specific claims or parties regarding which the determination was granted (including all merged interlocutory orders). Other aspects of the still-ongoing lawsuit will not be examined during the appeal.[103]

RULE 54(c)—DEMAND FOR JUDGMENT; RELIEF TO BE GRANTED

CORE CONCEPT

The district court generally must grant all the relief to which the prevailing party is entitled, whether or not such relief was

[97]*See United Industries, Inc. v. Eimco Process Equipment Co.*, 61 F.3d 445, 448 (5th Cir. 1995).

[98]*See HSBC Bank USA, N.A. v. Townsend*, 793 F.3d 771, 778 (7th Cir. 2015); *Noel v. Hall*, 568 F.3d 743, 747 (9th Cir. 2009). *See generally Kinsale Ins. Co. v. JDBC Holdings, Inc.*, 31 F.4th 870, 873–74 (4th Cir. 2022) (label district court attaches to its order "does not control").

[99]*See United States ex rel. Ibanez v. Bristol-Myers Squibb Co.*, 874 F.3d 905, 913 (6th Cir. 2017).

[100]*See EJS Props., LLC v. City of Toledo*, 689 F.3d 535, 538 (6th Cir. 2012); *Elliott v. Archdiocese of New York*, 682 F.3d 213, 220 & 224 (3d Cir. 2012).

[101]*See Brown v. Eli Lilly & Co.*, 654 F.3d 347, 355 (2d Cir. 2011).

[102]*See, e.g., HCG Platinum, LLC v. Preferred Prod. Placement Corp.*, 873 F.3d 1191, 1199 n.7 (10th Cir. 2017); *Patterson v. Aker Sols. Inc.*, 826 F.3d 231, 233 n.1 (5th Cir. 2016).

[103]*See Gonzalez v. Mid-Continent Cas. Co.*, 969 F.3d 554, 562 (5th Cir. 2020); *Monsanto Co. v. McFarling*, 363 F.3d 1336, 1343 n.1 (Fed. Cir. 2004).

formally requested in the pleadings. In default judgments, however, the district court may not award relief beyond that sought in the complaint.

APPLICATIONS

Default Judgments

Defendants don't always default by accident or neglect. Sometimes, defendants default deliberately, perhaps reasoning that the relief the claimant's pleading seeks is not worth the fight to resist. Consequently, because a litigant may be relying on the pleaded demand in choosing to default,[104] a claimant may not receive a default judgment that differs either in "kind" or in "amount" from what was sought in the pleadings.[105] Among the sparse exceptions to this rule are where the defendant originally appeared in the action and was placed on proper notice of a possible expanded relief[106] and where the complaint fairly identified the nature of the claimed loss and placed the defendant on notice that the value of that loss would continue to accrue during the litigation.[107]

- *"Defaulting" Party:* A party defaults within the meaning of Rule 54(c) by either failing to appear at all or defaulting following an appearance.[108]
- *Differing in "Kind":* Whether relief on default differs in "kind" hinges on whether the pleadings afforded adequate notice of that relief.[109]
- *Boilerplate Language:* In determining (for default purposes) what remedies have been pleaded, courts are disinclined to expand the available remedies on the basis of vague, boilerplate, catch-all language in a pleading.[110]
- *Post-Restyling Impacts*: The post-2007 "restyled" language of Rule 54(c) may have inadvertently broadened

---

[104] *See Hooper-Haas v. Ziegler Holdings, LLC*, 690 F.3d 34, 40 (1st Cir. 2012); *Silge v. Merz*, 510 F.3d 157, 160 (2d Cir.2007).

[105] *See Hooper-Haas v. Ziegler Holdings, LLC*, 690 F.3d 34, 39–40 (1st Cir. 2012); *Silge v. Merz*, 510 F.3d 157, 160 (2d Cir. 2007).

[106] *See Silge v. Merz*, 510 F.3d 157, 161 n.5 (2d Cir. 2007).

[107] *See Boland v. Yoccabel Const. Co., Inc.*, 293 F.R.D. 13, 18–19 (D.D.C. 2013); *Finkel v. Triple A Group, Inc.*, 708 F. Supp. 2d 277, 282 (E.D.N.Y. 2010).

[108] *See Hooper-Haas v. Ziegler Holdings, LLC*, 690 F.3d 34, 40 n.4 (1st Cir. 2012).

[109] *See ExxonMobil Oil Corp. v. Black Stone Petroleum Inc.*, 221 F. Supp. 3d 755, 766–69 (E.D. Va. 2016); *Belizaire v. RAV Investigative & Sec. Servs. Ltd.*, 61 F. Supp. 3d 336, 345–46 (S.D.N.Y. 2014). *See also Maalouf v. Islamic Republic of Iran*, 514 F. Supp. 4th 280, 288 n.4 (D.D.C. 2021) (denying punitive damages and prejudgment interest since both were omitted from fourth amended complaint).

[110] *See Emory v. United Air Lines, Inc.*, 720 F.3d 915, 921 n.10 (D.C. Cir. 2013); *Silge v. Merz*, 510 F.3d 157, 160 (2d Cir. 2007). *But cf. Alutiiq Int'l Sols., LLC v. OIC Marianas Ins. Corp.*, 149 F. Supp. 3d 1208, 1213–14 (D. Nev. 2016) (allowing larger sum, where pleading alleged "not less than" amount, with "the exact amount to be proven at trial").

the scope of relief that a litigant can receive against a defaulting party, forbidding now relief that differs from the "pleadings" rather than the former, more restrictive language of "demand for judgment."[111]

Non-Default Judgments

Where the defendant has answered or otherwise appeared to defend the lawsuit, a plaintiff may receive a judgment for an amount greater than that sought in the complaint,[112] as well as types of relief not mentioned in the complaint's demand clause.[113] It is generally the court's duty to grant all appropriate relief.[114] Pleadings serve as "guides" to the nature of the case, but the lawsuit is ultimately measured by what is pleaded and proven, not merely by what was demanded.[115] Defendants, likewise, may benefit from Rule 54(c)'s liberality.[116]

- *Types of Unpleaded Relief Permitted:* Courts have permitted litigants to recover punitive damages,[117] nominal damages,[118] alternative damages,[119] attorney's fees,[120] prejudgment interest,[121] accruing ERISA damages,[122] and

---

[111]*See Hooper-Haas v. Ziegler Holdings, LLC*, 690 F.3d 34, 40–41 (1st Cir. 2012) (discussing possible substantive impact). *But see Cooper v. Gen. Am. Life Ins. Co.*, 827 F.3d 729, 732 n.2 (8th Cir. 2016) (amendment intended to be "stylistic only").

[112]*See Avitia v. Metropolitan Club of Chicago, Inc.*, 49 F.3d 1219, 1229 (7th Cir. 1995) (except for "special damages" under Rule 9(g), plaintiffs are not obligated to itemize their damages in their complaints).

[113]*See Holt Civic Club v. City of Tuscaloosa*, 439 U.S. 60, 65–66, 99 S. Ct. 383, 387–388, 58 L. Ed. 2d 292 (1978) (courts should not dismiss meritorious constitutional claims because pleadings specify one remedy, rather than another). *See also Doe v. Purdue Univ.*, 928 F.3d 652, 666–67 (7th Cir. 2019); *People for Ethical Treatment of Animals, Inc. v. Gittens*, 396 F.3d 416, 420–21 (D.C. Cir. 2005).

[114]*See Felce v. Fiedler*, 974 F.2d 1484, 1501 (7th Cir. 1992) (Rule 54(c) to be liberally construed and court must grant whatever relief is appropriate). *See Feldman v. Philadelphia Housing Authority*, 43 F.3d 823, 832 (3d Cir. 1994) (nature of relief is "determined by the merits of the case, not by the pleadings").

[115]*See Minyard Enters., Inc. v. Southeastern Chem. & Solvent Co.*, 184 F.3d 373, 386 (4th Cir. 1999); *Baker v. John Morrell & Co.*, 266 F. Supp. 2d 909, 929 (N.D. Iowa 2003), *aff'd*, 382 F.3d 816, 831 (8th Cir. 2004).

[116]*See Portillo v. Cunningham*, 872 F.3d 728, 734–35 (5th Cir. 2017) (permitting dismissal on basis not raised explicitly in answer).

[117]*See Bowles v. Osmose Utilities Services, Inc.*, 443 F.3d 671, 675 (8th Cir. 2006); *Jennings v. Town of Stratford*, 263 F. Supp. 3d 391, 408 (D. Conn. 2017).

[118]*See Jackson v. Hill*, 569 Fed.Appx. 697, 699 (11th Cir. 2014).

[119]*See United States v. Cardaci*, 856 F.3d 267, 270 n.1 (3d Cir. 2017) (rental payments, rather that sale proceeds).

[120]*See Sea-Land Service, Inc. v. Murrey & Son's Co. Inc.*, 824 F.2d 740, 745 (9th Cir. 1987); *Black v. O'Haver*, 567 F.2d 361, 370–71 (10th Cir. 1977).

[121]*See, e.g., RK Co. v. See*, 622 F.3d 846, 853–54 (7th Cir. 2010); *Rathborne Land Co., L.L.C. v. Ascent Energy, Inc.*, 610 F.3d 249, 262 (5th Cir. 2010). *But see Silge v. Merz*, 510 F.3d 157, 160 (2d Cir.2007) (award of prejudgment interest not permitted).

[122]*See Boland v. Yoccabel Const. Co., Inc.*, 293 F.R.D. 13, 18–19 (D.D.C.

even declaratory[123] and injunctive relief[124] where those remedies were not expressly sought in the complaints, in appropriate cases. Moreover, a pleader's decision to seek relief later found to be unavailable will not defeat the pleader's ability to receive other relief to which she or he might be entitled.[125]

Limitations on Awarding Additional Relief

The Rule's liberality is intended to protect against the risk that clumsy drafting or technical missteps could deprive the pleader of a deserved recovery.[126] But the courts' ability to award unpleaded relief is not unbounded. The courts' remedy-awarding authority remains tethered to the lawsuit.[127] While the demand clause does not rigidly constrain the relief options available to a court, a fair reading of the entire pleading does.[128] The Rule does not countenance "trial-by-ambush."[129]

Thus, the Rule will not permit a recovery on issues or claims that were not actually litigated,[130] nor will it revive relief lost in the pleadings or through a failure of proof.[131] It will not allow relief against a defendant from whom no relief has been sought,[132] or force upon the litigants a remedy none of them

2013).

[123] *See San Diego Unified Port Dist. v. Monsanto Co.*, __ F. Supp. 3d __, 2020 WL 1479071, at *15 (S.D. Cal. 2020).

[124] *See Whole Woman's Health v. Hellerstedt*, 579 U.S. __, 136 S. Ct. 2292, 2307, 195 L. Ed. 2d 665 (2016). *See also Doe v. Purdue Univ.*, 928 F.3d 652, 666–67 (7th Cir. 2019) (unpleaded expungement of academic record). *But see Peterson v. Bell Helicopter Textron, Inc.*, 788 F.3d 384, 389–90 (5th Cir. 2015) (unpleaded injunctive relief may not be awarded if result would be prejudicial).

[125] *See Saint Anthony Hosp. v. Eagleson*, 40 F.4th 492, 513 (7th Cir. 2022); *Rollerson v. Brazos River Harbor Navigation Dist. of Brazoria Cnty.*, 6 F.4th 633, 646 (5th Cir. 2021).

[126] *See USX Corp. v. Barnhart*, 395 F.3d 161, 165 (3d Cir. 2004); *Ohio A. Phillip Randolph Inst. v. Husted*, 350 F. Supp. 3d 662, 673 (S.D. Ohio 2018).

[127] *See Knight v. Alabama*, 476 F.3d 1219, 1229 n.19 (11th Cir. 2007).

[128] *See JTH Tax, Inc. v. Aime*, 984 F.3d 284, 290–91 (4th Cir. 2021).

[129] *See Peterson v. Bell Helicopter Textron, Inc.*, 806 F.3d 335, 340–41 (5th Cir. 2015).

[130] *See Abrams v. Nucor Steel Marion, Inc.*, 694 Fed. Appx. 974, 983–84 (6th Cir. 2017) (no relief on unpleaded factual allegation); *Town of Portsmouth v. Lewis*, 813 F.3d 54, 61–62 (1st Cir. 2016) (no relief on remedy that party conditioned on theory it lost); *Old Republic Ins. Co. v. Employers Reinsurance Corp.*, 144 F.3d 1077, 1080–81 (7th Cir. 1998) (no relief on unasserted theory). *See generally Rodriguez v. Doral Mortg. Corp.*, 57 F.3d 1168, 1173 (1st Cir. 1995) (Rule's thesis is "hollow at its core" as it permits no relief premised on unlitigated issues).

[131] *See Gilbane Bldg. Co. v. Fed. Reserve Bank of Richmond*, 80 F.3d 895, 904 (4th Cir. 1996) (relief permitted only where factfinder reaches predicate factual conclusions); *Rodriguez v. Doral Mortg. Corp.*, 57 F.3d 1168, 1173 (1st Cir. 1995) (relief lost by failure of pleading or proof).

[132] *See Powell v. National Bd. of Medical Examiners*, 364 F.3d 79, 86 (2d Cir. 2004); *N.A.A.C.P., Jefferson County Branch v. U.S. Sugar Corp.*, 84 F.3d 1432, 1438 (D.C. Cir. 1996).

desires.[133] Litigants will be held bound to representations made during a pretrial conference or in a pretrial order that outlined the claims and relief in the case.[134] In short, this Rule will not permit an additional award that would be unfairly prejudicial or unjust.[135] Thus, pleaders may not manipulatively "cap" their claims to achieve some tactical advantage, and then receive under this Rule the very relief they earlier shunned,[136] or belatedly press for damages after an injunction-only demand becomes moot.[137]

RULE 54(d)—COSTS AND ATTORNEY'S FEES

CORE CONCEPT

The prevailing party in a lawsuit is presumptively entitled to the reimbursement of "costs" (a term defined by statute), which may be taxed by the clerk upon 14 days' notice, subject to later judicial review on timely motion. When permitted by law, the reimbursement of other litigation expenses—attorney's fees and expenditures not qualifying as statutory "costs"—must be sought by motion filed not later than 14 days from entry of judgment, unless those sums were established at trial as an element of damages compensable under the controlling substantive law.

APPLICATIONS

Governing Law

Federal law governs the availability and scope of allowable costs, even in diversity cases[138] and even if State law would dictate a different result.[139]

For Whom May Costs Be Taxed (*Prevailing Party*)

Costs should be taxed in favor of the prevailing party, un-

---

[133]*See Minyard Enterprises, Inc. v. Southeastern Chemical & Solvent Co.*, 184 F.3d 373, 386 (4th Cir. 1999).

[134]*See Walker v. Anderson Elec. Connectors*, 944 F.2d 841, 844 (11th Cir. 1991) (limiting plaintiff to relief demanded at pretrial conference). *See also Seven Words LLC v. Network Solutions*, 260 F.3d 1089, 1098 (9th Cir. 2001) (where damages claim was made years into litigation, after representations that only declaratory and injunctive relief was sought, after motion to dismiss, and only days before oral argument on appeal, court declines to read damages claim into complaint).

[135]*See Portillo v. Cunningham*, 872 F.3d 728, 735 (5th Cir. 2017); *Cooper v. Gen. Am. Life Ins. Co.*, 827 F.3d 729, 732 (8th Cir. 2016). *See also Cullen v. Saddler*, 668 Fed. Appx. 656, 658 (7th Cir. 2016) (refusing to grant $2 million punitive request when pleadings and discovery sought only $350).

[136]*See Morgan v. Gay*, 471 F.3d 469, 476–77 (3d Cir. 2006), (construing Class Action Fairness Act of 2005); *De Aguilar v. Boeing Co.*, 47 F.3d 1404, 1410 (5th Cir. 1995) (construing removal jurisdiction).

[137]*See Medici v. City of Chicago*, 856 F.3d 530, 532–33 (7th Cir. 2017).

[138]*See Humann v. KEM Elec. Co-op., Inc.*, 497 F.3d 810, 813 (8th Cir. 2007); *Gobbo Farms & Orchards v. Poole Chemical Co., Inc.*, 81 F.3d 122, 123 (10th Cir. 1996).

[139]*See Stender v. Archstone-Smith Operating Tr.*, 958 F.3d 938, 940–47 (10th Cir. 2020).

less a Rule or federal statute directs otherwise.[140] A prevailing plaintiff is one who succeeds on some significant issue in the litigation and thereby achieves some of the benefit sought in filing the lawsuit.[141] A plaintiff, thus, "prevails" by obtaining a judgment on the merits or a court-order consent decree,[142] by obtaining an award of monetary damages (even nominal damages),[143] or by obtaining some other relief that materially alters the parties' legal relationship by modifying the behavior of the defendant in a way that directly benefits the plaintiff.[144] A party who loses the judgment, but whose litigation nonetheless prompts the opponent to change its behavior in some way[145] or can otherwise cite to some "moral victory"[146] is likely *not* a prevailing party. Similarly, a settlement, even one brokered by the court or prompted by a court's comments on the case's merits, will likely produce a "prevailing party" only if it results in a consent decree.[147]

A prevailing defendant is one who defeats the litigation and obtains a denial of relief. Thus, a dismissal, with prejudice and on the merits, of all claims against a defendant will generally make that defendant a prevailing party,[148] as well as dismissals that include without-prejudice dismissals of companion State law claims over which the court has declined to exercise supplemental jurisdiction.[149]

A litigant need not succeed on all issues to qualify as a

---

[140] *See* Rule 54(d)(1). *See also Green v. Mercy Hous., Inc.*, 991 F.3d 1056, 1057 (9th Cir. 2021).

[141] *See Baker v. Lindgren*, 856 F.3d 498, 502 (7th Cir. 2017); *Shum v. Intel Corp.*, 629 F.3d 1360, 1367 (Fed.Cir. 2010). *Cf. Texas State Teachers Ass'n v. Garland Indep. Sch. Dist.*, 489 U.S. 782, 791–92, 109 S. Ct. 1486, 103 L. Ed. 2d 866 (1989).

[142] *See Xlear, Inc. v. Focus Nutrition, LLC*, 893 F.3d 1227, 1236–37 (10th Cir. 2018); *Carter v. Inc. Vill. of Ocean Beach*, 759 F.3d 159, 163 (2d Cir. 2014). *See generally Buckhannon Bd. & Care Home, Inc. v. W. Virginia Dep't of Health & Human Res.*, 532 U.S. 598, 604, 121 S. Ct. 1835, 149 L. Ed. 2d 855 (2001) (explaining "prevailing party" in other context).

[143] *See Farrar v. Hobby*, 506 U.S. 103, 111–13, 113 S. Ct. 566, 121 L. Ed. 2d 494 (1992); *Barber v. T.D. Williamson, Inc.*, 254 F.3d 1223, 1234 (10th Cir. 2001).

[144] *See Buckhannon Bd. and Care Home, Inc. v. West Virginia Dept. of Health and Human Resources*, 532 U.S. 598, 605, 121 S. Ct. 1835, 149 L. Ed. 2d 855 (2001); *Farrar v. Hobby*, 506 U.S. 103, 111–13, 113 S. Ct. 566, 121 L. Ed. 2d 494 (1992).

[145] *See Carter v. Incorporated Village of Ocean Beach*, 759 F.3d 159, 163 (2d Cir. 2014). *See also Buckhannon Bd. & Care Home, Inc. v. W. Va. Dep't of Health & Human Res.*, 532 U.S. 598, 600–10 (2001) (rejecting, in another context, "catalyst theory" of prevailing party status).

[146] *See Richardson v. City of Chicago*, 740 F.3d 1099, 1102 (7th Cir. 2014).

[147] *See Xlear, Inc. v. Focus Nutrition, LLC*, 893 F.3d 1227, 1236–39 (10th Cir. 2018).

[148] *See Keith Mfg. Co. v. Butterfield*, 955 F.3d 936, 939–40 (Fed. Cir. 2020); *Donelson v. Hardy*, 931 F.3d 565, 570 (7th Cir. 2019). *See also B.E. Tech., L.L.C. v. Facebook, Inc.*, 940 F.3d 675, 677–79 (Fed. Cir. 2019) (dismissal for mootness qualifies because it "rebuffed" plaintiff's claim).

[149] *See Thompson v. Kanabec Cty.*, 958 F.3d 698, 709 (8th Cir. 2020); *Allen*

prevailing party.[150] For example, a counterclaiming defendant may be deemed a prevailing party by defeating the larger primary claim even if losing on the smaller counterclaim.[151] Some courts hold that there can be only one prevailing party,[152] though, in mixed judgment outcomes, that status might be assigned claim-by-claim.[153]

Generally, there are no prevailing parties if the case is dismissed for lack of jurisdiction[154] or *forum non conveniens*.[155] Similarly, if certain parties prevail originally, but later lose under a subsequent ruling at the trial court or on appeal, their status, and their entitlement to costs, changes.[156] Where a lawsuit ends in a "dead heat" or "tie," it is also possible that neither party will qualify as "prevailing."[157]

A litigant who is deemed a "prevailing party" for purposes of awarding attorney's fees is likewise a "prevailing party" for purposes of taxing costs.[158]

Against Whom May Costs Be Taxed

Under Rule 54(d), costs may be taxed only against the nonprevailing party; costs may not be taxed under this Rule against counsel for a litigant.[159] When taxed in a multiple-lawsuit proceeding, costs should be allocated among the various cases.[160]

Types of Taxable Costs

Litigation expenses fall broadly into three categories—taxable "costs", nontaxable expenses, and attorney's fees. Congress

---

v. Lang, 738 Fed. Appx. 934, 944–47 (10th Cir. 2018).

[150] *See SSL Servs., LLC v. Citrix Sys., Inc.*, 769 F.3d 1073, 1086 (Fed. Cir. 2014); *Maker's Mark Distillery, Inc. v. Diageo North America, Inc.*, 679 F.3d 410, 425 (6th Cir. 2012). *See also Fireman's Fund Ins. Co. v. Tropical Shipping and Const. Co., Ltd.*, 254 F.3d 987, 1012–13 (11th Cir. 2001) (noting precedent awarding costs where prevailing party obtains a judgment "on even a fraction" of claims).

[151] *See Ira Green, Inc. v. Military Sales & Serv. Co.*, 775 F.3d 12, 28 (1st Cir. 2014); *Haynes Trane Serv. Agency, Inc. v. American Standard, Inc.*, 573 F.3d 947, 967 (10th Cir. 2009).

[152] *See Royal Palm Props., LLC v. Pink Palm Props., LLC*, 38 F.4th 1372, 1378–79 (11th Cir. 2022); *Shum v. Intel Corp.*, 629 F.3d 1360, 1366–70 (Fed.Cir. 2010).

[153] *See Williams v. Gaye*, 895 F.3d 1106, 1133 (9th Cir. 2018).

[154] *See Miles v. State of California*, 320 F.3d 986, 988 (9th Cir. 2003).

[155] *See Dattner v. Conagra Foods, Inc.*, 458 F.3d 98, 101 (2d Cir. 2006).

[156] *See Peterson v. Nelnet Diversified Sols., LLC*, 15 F.4th 1033, 1049 (10th Cir. 2021); *Ace Partners, LLC v. Town of E. Hartford*, 883 F.3d 190, 203 (2d Cir. 2018).

[157] *See Royal Palm Props., LLC v. Pink Palm Props., LLC*, 38 F.4th 1372, 1378–81 (11th Cir. 2022); *E. Iowa Plastics, Inc. v. PI, Inc.*, 832 F.3d 899, 906–07 (8th Cir. 2016).

[158] *See Dattner v. Conagra Foods, Inc.*, 458 F.3d 98, 101 (2d Cir. 2006); *Tunison v. Continental Airlines Corp., Inc.*, 162 F.3d 1187, 1189–90 (D.C. Cir. 1998).

[159] *See In re Cardizem CD Antitrust Litigation*, 481 F.3d 355, 359–60 (6th Cir. 2007); *Wilder v. GL Bus Lines*, 258 F.3d 126, 127–31 (2d Cir. 2001).

[160] *See Winter v. Novartis Pharms. Corp.*, 739 F.3d 405, 411–12 (8th Cir. 2014).

set the categories of taxable "costs" by statute,[161] and they are deliberately[162] modest, usually representing only a fraction of total litigation expenses[163] (though parties may, by contract, alter this standard[164]). Although limited, taxable costs can nevertheless still be substantial.[165] These statutorily permitted taxable costs are:

1. Clerk and U.S. Marshal fees,[166] which might include *pro hac vice* admission fees;[167]
2. Transcript fees, for *both*[168] printed or electronically recorded transcripts, so long as they were "necessarily obtained for use in the case" (including transcripts received into evidence or otherwise "necessary" for trial preparation,[169] but not for transcripts taken solely for discovery purposes, as a mere convenience to counsel or the court, or of witnesses withdrawn or precluded);[170] court reporter attendance fees,[171] and, if allowed, real-time transcript feeds,[172] videotape depositions[173] (though at-trial setup and playback costs are less

---

[161] *See* 28 U.S.C.A. § 1920. *See also* 28 U.S.C.A. §§ 1911 to 31 (defining costs provisions generally). In addition, the Rules allow costs to be taxed in other instances: when an attorney violates Rule 11, conducts discovery improperly in violation of Rule 37, or rejects unwisely an offer of settlement under Rule 68.

[162] *Stender v. Archstone-Smith Operating Tr.*, 958 F.3d 938, 941 (10th Cir. 2020) (recounting history of Congress's restraint on "costs" awards).

[163] *See Taniguchi v. Kan Pacific Saipan, Ltd.*, 566 U.S. 560, 573, 132 S. Ct. 1997, 182 L. Ed. 2d 903 (2012).

[164] *See Yellow Pages Photos, Inc. v. Ziplocal, LP*, 846 F.3d 1159, 1166 (11th Cir. 2017).

[165] *See In re Online DVD-Rental Antitrust Litig.*, 779 F.3d 914, 925 (9th Cir. 2015) (reviewing award of $710,194 in costs against non-prevailing plaintiff); *In re Williams Secs. Litig.-WCG Subclass*, 558 F.3d 1144, 1147 (10th Cir. 2009) (affirming award of more than $600,000 in costs against non-prevailing plaintiff).

[166] *See Winniczek v. Nagelberg*, 400 F.3d 503, 504–05 (7th Cir. 2005) (allowing docketing fee to be taxed).

[167] *See Craftsmen Limousine, Inc. v. Ford Motor Co.*, 579 F.3d 894, 898 (8th Cir. 2009).

[168] *See Stanley v. Cottrell, Inc.*, 784 F.3d 454, 465–67 (8th Cir. 2015).

[169] *See Barcomb v. Gen. Motors LLC*, 978 F.3d 545, 551 (8th Cir. 2020); *Dullmaier v. Xanterra Parks & Resorts*, 883 F.3d 1278, 1296 (10th Cir. 2018). *See also Smith v. Tenet Healthsystem SL, Inc.*, 436 F.3d 879, 889 (8th Cir. 2006) (taxable if necessary, even if not introduced at trial).

[170] *See In re Williams Secs. Litig.-WCG Subclass*, 558 F.3d 1144, 1147–48 (10th Cir. 2009); *Marmo v. Tyson Fresh Meats, Inc.*, 457 F.3d 748, 763 (8th Cir. 2006).

[171] *See Harney v. City of Chicago*, 702 F.3d 916, 927–28 (7th Cir. 2012).

[172] *See Dindinger v. Allsteel, Inc.*, 853 F.3d 414, 431 (8th Cir. 2017).

[173] *See U.S. ex rel. Long v. GSDMIdea City, L.L.C.*, 807 F.3d 125, 130–31 (5th Cir. 2015); *Craftsmen Limousine, Inc. v. Ford Motor Co.*, 579 F.3d 894, 897–98 (8th Cir. 2009). *But cf. Cherry v. Champion Intern. Corp.*, 186 F.3d 442, 448–49 (4th Cir. 1999) (prevailing party must make a showing why *both* the transcript and the video deposition were "necessary").

clear[174]), and perhaps even the stenographic transcription of those videotapes.[175]

3a. Printing fees;

3b. Witness fees and witnesses' travel and subsistence expenses, where the witnesses' testimony was material, relevant, and reasonably necessary to the case[176] (including officers/directors of a corporate party, provided they are not personally also parties),[177] including subpoena expenses;[178]

4a. Fees to "exemplify" materials (which may include reimbursement for many methods of illustration, including models, charts, graphs, and perhaps computerized presentation systems,[179] but likely not electronically-stored information processing expenses[180] or ancillary document gathering or other preparatory costs[181]);

4b. Fees to print copies of "any materials" necessary for use in the case[182] (which likely includes copying documents for discovery,[183] and also likely encompasses, in an electronic data environment, the "functional equivalent" of making copies (*e.g.*, scanning, format conversion, and maybe imaging) but likely excludes other preparatory ESI expenses (*e.g.*, searching, gathering,

---

[174] *See Zastrow v. Houston Auto M. Imports Greenway, Ltd.*, 695 Fed. Appx. 774, 780 (5th Cir. 2017).

[175] *See Little v. Mitsubishi Motors North America, Inc.*, 514 F.3d 699, 701–02 (7th Cir. 2008); *Tilton v. Capital Cities/ABC, Inc.*, 115 F.3d 1471, 1478 (10th Cir. 1997).

[176] *See* 28 U.S.C.A. § 1821(b). *See also Marmo v. Tyson Fresh Meats, Inc.*, 457 F.3d 748, 763 (8th Cir.2006); *Baisden v. I'm Ready Prods., Inc.*, 793 F. Supp. 2d 970, 976–85 (S.D.Tex. 2011).

[177] *See Stevens v. CoreLogic, Inc.*, 893 F.3d 648, 660–61 (9th Cir. 2018).

[178] *See Smith W. Texas Props., Ltd. v. Allied Prop. & Cas. Ins. Co.*, 555 F. Supp. 3d 342, 348 (W.D. Tex. 2021).

[179] *See Cefalu v. Village of Elk Grove*, 211 F.3d 416, 427–28 (7th Cir. 2000) (affirming reimbursement for cost of computerized, multi-media system used to present exhibits to jury). *But cf. Kohus v. Toys R Us, Inc.*, 282 F.3d 1355, 1357–61 (Fed. Cir. 2002) (reversing award of $12,950 for video model/animation as unauthorized under federal law); *Arcadian Fertilizer, L.P. v. MPW Indus. Services, Inc.*, 249 F.3d 1293, 1297 (11th Cir. 2001) (refusing reimbursement for videotape exhibits and computer animation).

[180] *See Country Vintner of North Carolina, LLC v. E. & J. Gallo Winery, Inc.*, 718 F.3d 249, 261–62 (4th Cir. 2013); *Race Tires America, Inc. v. Hoosier Racing Tire Corp.*, 674 F.3d 158, 168–72 (3d Cir. 2012).

[181] *See CBT Flint Partners, LLC v. Return Path, Inc.*, 737 F.3d 1320, 1328 (Fed. Cir. 2013).

[182] *See Little v. Mitsubishi Motors North America, Inc.*, 514 F.3d 699, 701 (7th Cir. 2008); *BDT Products, Inc. v. Lexmark Intern., Inc.*, 405 F.3d 415, 419–20 (6th Cir. 2005).

[183] *See Johnson Tr. of Operating Eng'rs Local #49 v. Charps Welding & Fabricating, Inc.*, 950 F.3d 510, 527 (8th Cir. 2020); *U.S. ex rel. Long v. GSDMIdea City, L.L.C.*, 807 F.3d 125, 129 (5th Cir. 2015).

culling));[184] in seeking reimbursement, a copy-by-copy tracking or itemization may not be necessary, so long as a reasonably accurate calculation is supplied;[185]

5. Certain docket fees;[186] and
6. Fees for court-appointed experts (which often include guardians and special masters)[187] and interpreters (though limited to oral interpreters, not translators of written work).[188]

Litigation Expenses That Ordinarily Cannot Be Taxed

Litigation-related expenses that fall outside the scope of "costs" may not be taxed under Rule 54(d) unless authorized by agreement, other statute, or court rule.[189] Thus, courts ordinarily will not tax as "costs" the fees and expenses of expert witnesses (beyond the modest travel and subsistence expenses noted above for witnesses generally);[190] computer-assisted legal research;[191] trial consultants who prepared computer animations, videos, powerpoint slides, and graphic illustrations;[192] postage, overnight courier, and similar messenger or delivery

[184] *See United States v. Halliburton Co.*, 954 F.3d 307, 311–12 (D.C. Cir. 2020) (encompasses "digital equivalent of a law-firm associate photocopying documents to be produced to opposing counsel," but excludes other e-discovery charges); *Race Tires Am., Inc. v. Hoosier Racing Tire Corp.*, 674 F.3d 158, 171 (3d Cir. 2012) (no Congressional intent to shift all e-discovery expenses). *But see Colosi v. Jones Lang LaSalle Americas, Inc.*, 781 F.3d 293, 296–98 (6th Cir. 2015) (permitting recovery of costs to "image" computer's hard-drive, rejecting "overly restrictive" construction of "costs").

[185] *See United States ex rel King v. Solvay Pharm., Inc.*, 871 F.3d 318, 336 (5th Cir. 2017); *In re Williams Secs. Litig.-WCG Subclass*, 558 F.3d 1144, 1148 (10th Cir. 2009).

[186] *See BDT Products, Inc. v. Lexmark Intern., Inc.*, 405 F.3d 415, 419–20 (6th Cir. 2005). *See also Zastrow v. Houston Auto M. Imports Greenway, Ltd.*, 695 F. App'x 774, 780 (5th Cir. 2017) (noting uncertainty whether PACER fees are always, never, or sometimes awardable).

[187] *See Doe v. Kidd*, 656 Fed. Appx. 643, 659 (4th Cir. 2016); *Gaddis v. United States*, 381 F.3d 444, 451 (5th Cir. 2004).

[188] *See Taniguchi v. Kan Pacific Saipan, Ltd.*, 566 U.S. 560, 564-75, 132 S. Ct. 1997, 182 L. Ed. 2d 903 (2012).

[189] *See Arlington Cent. School Dist. Bd. of Educ. v. Murphy*, 548 U.S. 291, 301, 126 S. Ct. 2455, 165 L. Ed. 2d 526 (2006).

[190] *See Arlington Cent. School Dist. Bd. of Educ. v. Murphy*, 548 U.S. 291, 301, 126 S. Ct. 2455, 165 L. Ed. 2d 526 (2006); *West Virginia University Hospitals, Inc. v. Casey*, 499 U.S. 83, 102, 111 S. Ct. 1138, 113 L. Ed. 2d 68 (1991); *Crawford Fitting Co. v. J. T. Gibbons, Inc.*, 482 U.S. 437, 439, 107 S. Ct. 2494, 96 L. Ed. 2d 385 (1987).

[191] *But compare Stender v. Archstone-Smith Operating Tr.*, 958 F.3d 938, 942 (10th Cir. 2020) ("crystal clear" not taxable); *and Smith W. Texas Props., Ltd. v. Allied Prop. & Cas. Ins. Co.*, 555 F. Supp. 3d 342, 349 (W.D. Tex. 2021) (not taxable); *with Dindinger v. Allsteel, Inc.*, 853 F.3d 414, 432 (8th Cir. 2017) (could be taxable under certain conditions); *with Little v. Mitsubishi Motors N. Am., Inc.*, 514 F.3d 699, 701 (7th Cir. 2008) (categorically taxable).

[192] *See Summit Technology, Inc. v. Nidek Co., Ltd.*, 435 F.3d 1371, 1374–75 (Fed. Cir. 2006). *But see Marmo v. Tyson Fresh Meats, Inc.*, 457 F.3d 748, 763 (8th Cir.2006) (taxing as "copying and exemplication" costs the expenses

services;[193] telephone calls;[194] facsimile transmissions;[195] paralegal expenses;[196] travel, lodging, transportation, and parking;[197] mediation;[198] or post-trial / pre-appeal costs (like supersedeas bond premiums).[199] Courts are divided on whether the costs of private process servers are taxable.[200]

Attorney's Fees as Costs

In the absence of a federal statute to the contrary, attorney's fees may not be taxed as costs beyond the modest provisions set forth in 28 U.S.C.A. § 1923.[201]

Exceptions: Attorney's fees, however, may be taxed against a common fund generated in a class action or shareholders' derivative action,[202] and where a party instituted, defended, or conducted litigation in bad faith.[203]

Burden of Proof

The burden of proving the amount of compensable costs lies with the party seeking those costs.[204] Once the prevailing party demonstrates the amount of its costs and that they fall within an allowable category of taxable costs, the prevailing party enjoys a strong presumption that its costs will be awarded in

---

for graphic and visual aids, and other materials for electronic display).

[193] *See U.S. ex rel. Long v. GSDMIdea City, L.L.C.*, 807 F.3d 125, 133 (5th Cir. 2015); *Smith v. Tenet Healthsystem SL, Inc.*, 436 F.3d 879, 889–90 (8th Cir. 2006); *Smith W. Texas Props., Ltd. v. Allied Prop. & Cas. Ins. Co.*, 555 F. Supp. 3d 342, 349 (W.D. Tex. 2021).

[194] *See Smith W. Texas Props., Ltd. v. Allied Prop. & Cas. Ins. Co.*, 555 F. Supp. 3d 342, 348 (W.D. Tex. 2021); *O'Bryhim v. Reliance Standard Life Ins. Co.*, 997 F. Supp. 728, 737–38 (E.D. Va. 1998), aff'd, 188 F.3d 502 (4th Cir. 1999).

[195] *See O'Bryhim v. Reliance Standard Life Ins. Co.*, 997 F. Supp. 728, 737–38 (E.D. Va. 1998), *aff'd*, 188 F.3d 502 (4th Cir. 1999); *Garshman Co., Ltd. v. General Elec. Co., Inc.*, 993 F. Supp. 25, 29 (D. Mass. 1998), *aff'd*, 176 F.3d 1, 7 (1st Cir. 1999).

[196] *See Thomas v. Treasury Management Ass'n, Inc.*, 158 F.R.D. 364, 372 (D. Md. 1994).

[197] *See Stender v. Archstone-Smith Operating Tr.*, 958 F.3d 938, 942 (10th Cir. 2020) ("crystal clear" not taxable); *Smith W. Texas Props., Ltd. v. Allied Prop. & Cas. Ins. Co.*, 555 F. Supp. 3d 342, 349 (W.D. Tex. 2021).

[198] *See Brisco-Wade v. Carnahan*, 297 F.3d 781, 782 (8th Cir. 2002).

[199] *See Republic Tobacco Co. v. North Atlantic Trading Co., Inc.*, 481 F.3d 442, 447–48 (7th Cir. 2007).

[200] *See Francisco v. Verizon South, Inc.*, 272 F.R.D. 436, 441–42 (E.D.Va. 2011) (discussing divided case law).

[201] *See Alyeska Pipeline Service Co. v. Wilderness Society*, 421 U.S. 240, 95 S. Ct. 1612, 44 L. Ed. 2d 141 (1975). *See also Marx v. General Revenue Corp.*, 568 U.S. 371, 381–82, 133 S. Ct. 1166, 185 L. Ed. 2d 242 (2013) (noting "bedrock principle" of "American Rule" where litigants each pay own attorney's fees).

[202] *See Mills v. Electric Auto-Lite Co.*, 396 U.S. 375, 90 S. Ct. 616, 24 L. Ed. 2d 593 (1970).

[203] *See Chambers v. NASCO, Inc.*, 501 U.S. 32, 111 S. Ct. 2123, 115 L. Ed. 2d 27 (1991).

[204] *See In re Williams Secs. Litig.-WCG Subclass*, 558 F.3d 1144, 1148 (10th Cir. 2009). *Cf. Smith W. Texas Props., Ltd. v. Allied Prop. & Cas. Ins. Co.*, 555 F. Supp. 3d 342, 348 (W.D. Tex. 2021) (reducing "miscellaneous costs" entry because claimant failed to carry burden of adequate description).

full measure.[205] The party opposing the award of costs bears the burden (an "uphill battle")[206] of demonstrating that the award would be improper.[207]

Discretion of District Court

Rule 54(d) provides that costs "should" be taxed.[208] This mandate creates a presumption in favor of the award of costs to the prevailing party,[209] but reserves for the district judge the discretion to deny costs in appropriate circumstances.[210] A "sound basis" is needed to overcome this presumption,[211] since denying costs is essentially a "penalty" that deprives a litigant of an entitlement.[212] If the court chooses not to award costs to a prevailing party, the court must explain its good reasons for not doing so[213] (although a formal written opinion is not required when costs are awarded[214] or denied entirely[215]). An implicit justification will ordinarily be insufficient to sustain the denial on appeal,[216] unless the reasons for denying costs are clear.[217]

---

[205] *See infra* Authors' Commentary to Rule 54(d) ("**Discretion of District Court**"). *See generally Richardson v. Chicago Transit Auth.*, 926 F.3d 881, 893 (7th Cir. 2019) (presumption "is difficult to overcome"); *Yellow Pages Photos, Inc. v. Ziplocal, LP*, 846 F.3d 1159, 1166 (11th Cir. 2017) (presumption is "strong").

[206] *See Crosby v. City of Chicago*, 949 F.3d 358, 363 (7th Cir. 2020). *See also Lange v. City of Oconto*, 28 F.4th 825, 845 (7th Cir. 2022) ("difficult to overcome").

[207] *See Lange v. City of Oconto*, 28 F.4th 825, 845 (7th Cir. 2022); *Thompson v. Kanabec Cty.*, 958 F.3d 698, 709 (8th Cir. 2020).

[208] *See Stafford Invs., LLC v. Vito*, 2009 WL 1362513, at *11 (E.D.Pa. May 14, 2009), *aff'd*, 375 Fed. Appx. 221 (3d Cir. 2010) (noting 2007 Restyling Amendments revision of syntax "as of course" to "should" retained preamendment meaning).

[209] *See Marx v. General Revenue Corp.*, 568 U.S. 371, 377, 133 S. Ct. 1166, 185 L. Ed. 2d 242 (2013); *Delta Air Lines, Inc. v. August*, 450 U.S. 346, 352, 101 S. Ct. 1146, 67 L. Ed. 2d 287 (1981).

[210] *See Marx v. General Revenue Corp.*, 568 U.S. 371, 377, 133 S. Ct. 1166, 185 L. Ed. 2d 242 (2013); *Crawford Fitting Co. v. J. T. Gibbons, Inc.*, 482 U.S. 437, 107 S. Ct. 2494, 96 L. Ed. 2d 385 (1987); *Farmer v. Arabian Am. Oil Co.*, 379 U.S. 227, 85 S. Ct. 411, 13 L. Ed. 2d 248 (1964).

[211] *See Yellow Pages Photos, Inc. v. Ziplocal, LP*, 846 F.3d 1159, 1166 (11th Cir. 2017); *U.S. ex rel. Long v. GSDMIdea City, L.L.C.*, 807 F.3d 125, 128 (5th Cir. 2015). *See also Goldberg v. Pacific Indem. Co.*, 627 F.3d 752, 755 n.4 (9th Cir. 2010) ("limited discretion" to refuse to tax costs); *Utah Animal Rights Coalition v. Salt Lake County*, 566 F.3d 1236, 1245 (10th Cir. 2009) ("valid reason").

[212] *See Debord v. Mercy Health System of Kansas, Inc.*, 737 F.3d 642, 659 (10th Cir. 2013).

[213] *See Lange v. City of Oconto*, 28 F.4th 825, 845 (7th Cir. 2022); *Edwards v. 4JLJ, L.L.C.*, 976 F.3d 463, 466–67 (5th Cir. 2020).

[214] *See In re Online DVD-Rental Antitrust Litig.*, 779 F.3d 914, 932 (9th Cir. 2015); *Craftsmen Limousine, Inc. v. Ford Motor Co.*, 579 F.3d 894, 896–97 (8th Cir. 2009).

[215] *See Reger v. Nemours Found., Inc.*, 599 F.3d 285, 289 (3d Cir. 2010).

[216] *See Holton v. City of Thomasville School Dist.*, 425 F.3d 1325, 1355–56 (11th Cir. 2005).

[217] *See McLaughlin v. Hagel*, 767 F.3d 113, 120 (1st Cir. 2014).

Mandatory Reasons for Denying Costs

The district court must deny costs if another Rule or a federal statute so commands.[218] Statutory displacement can occur when Congress imposes conditions on or installs an alternative standard for awarding costs (whether or not the statute recites an intent to displace Rule 54(d)).[219] But statutory silence usually leaves the ordinary Rule 54(d) approach in place.[220]

- *Effect of Rule 68 Offers:* When implicated, Rule 68 compels even a prevailing party to pay an opponent's costs if the victory is less favorable than an unaccepted offer of judgment.[221] The consensus view among courts is that Rule 68 thus "reverses" Rule 54(d).[222]

Discretionary Reasons for Denying Costs

The proper exercise of a trial court's discretion to deny costs may hinge on whether the costs paid for materials necessarily obtained for use in the case.[223] Costs may be denied, for example, where both parties partially prevail in the litigation,[224] where the prevailing party's recovery was only nominal or substantially less than what was sought[225] (or where costs would be disproportionate to the litigation's result),[226] where a party prevailed only after the opponent had first obtained a modicum of relief,[227] where the prevailing party needlessly prolonged the litigation or otherwise behaved in bad faith,[228] where the losing party is indigent or would become indigent by paying,[229] or where there is some other injustice in taxing

---

[218] *See Marx v. Gen. Revenue Corp.*, 568 U.S. 371, 377, 133 S. Ct. 1166, 185 L. Ed. 2d 242 (2013). *See also Lange v. City of Oconto*, 28 F.4th 825, 846 (7th Cir. 2022) (detailing required analysis).

[219] *See Marx v. Gen. Revenue Corp.*, 568 U.S. 371, 377–78, 133 S. Ct. 1166, 185 L. Ed. 2d 242 (2013).

[220] *See Marx v. Gen. Revenue Corp.*, 568 U.S. 371, 377–88, 133 S. Ct. 1166, 185 L. Ed. 2d 242 (2013); *Faludi v. U.S. Shale Sols., L.L.C.*, 950 F.3d 269, 276 (5th Cir. 2020).

[221] *See* Rule 68. *See infra* Authors' Commentary to Rule 68.

[222] *See Stanczyk v. City of New York*, 752 F.3d 273, 280–82 (2d Cir. 2014) (discussing and then embracing consensus approach).

[223] *See Allison v. Bank One-Denver*, 289 F.3d 1223, 1248 (10th Cir. 2002).

[224] *See Farrar v. Hobby*, 506 U.S. 103, 115–16, 113 S. Ct. 566, 121 L. Ed. 2d 494 (1992) (having considered the amount and nature of the plaintiff's success on the merits, district courts may award modest fees or no fees at all). *See also Baker v. Lindgren*, 856 F.3d 498, 502 (7th Cir. 2017); *Ira Green, Inc. v. Military Sales & Serv. Co.*, 775 F.3d 12, 28 (1st Cir. 2014).

[225] *See Debord v. Mercy Health System of Kansas, Inc.*, 737 F.3d 642, 660 (10th Cir. 2013); *Champion Produce, Inc. v. Ruby Robinson Co., Inc.*, 342 F.3d 1016, 1022–23 (9th Cir. 2003).

[226] *See Dunne v. Res. Converting, LLC*, 991 F.3d 931, 941–42 (8th Cir. 2021).

[227] *See Knology, Inc. v. Insight Commc'ns Co., L.P.*, 460 F.3d 722, 727–28 (6th Cir. 2006).

[228] *See Dunne v. Res. Converting, LLC*, 991 F.3d 931, 941–42 (8th Cir. 2021); *Edwards v. 4JLJ, L.L.C.*, 976 F.3d 463, 466–67 (5th Cir. 2020).

[229] *See Marx v. Gen. Revenue Corp.*, 568 U.S. 371, 387 n.9, 133 S. Ct. 1166, 185 L. Ed. 2d 242 (2013).

costs.[230] Other discretionary criteria leave the courts divided. Some courts have rested a refusal to tax costs on a plaintiff's good faith in litigating,[231] financial disparity,[232] the case's complexity, difficulty, or closeness,[233] its public interest,[234] and whether taxing costs might chill future litigation.[235] Other courts reject such grounds for denying costs.[236]

Taxing Costs For or Against the United States

The United States may be awarded costs in the same manner as any prevailing party.[237] Costs may be taxed against the United States in accordance with the list set forth in 28 U.S.C.A. § 1920,[238] except that in non-tort actions, the district court may refuse to tax costs upon a finding that the United States' position was substantially justified or where special circumstances make an award of costs unjust.[239]

Taxing Costs Against States

Some courts have construed the Eleventh Amendment to the United States Constitution as prohibiting a district court's right to tax costs against a State.[240]

Costs in Pauper Actions

The district court may, in its discretion, permit a civil litigant, criminal defendant, or appellant to proceed without the prepayment of costs upon receiving an affidavit showing an inability to pay costs.[241]

Procedure & Timing:[242] Non-Attorney's Fee Costs

To obtain an award of costs, the prevailing party must file a "Bill of Costs" with the clerk (the district court may have a preprinted form for this purpose). The Bill of Costs must be

[230] *See Debord v. Mercy Health System of Kansas, Inc.*, 737 F.3d 642, 660 (10th Cir. 2013) (costs unreasonably high or unnecessary); *Cherry v. Champion Intern. Corp.*, 186 F.3d 442, 446 (4th Cir. 1999).

[231] *See Singleton v. Smith*, 241 F.3d 534, 539 (6th Cir.2001).

[232] *See Escriba v. Foster Poultry Farms, Inc.*, 743 F.3d 1236, 1247–48 (9th Cir. 2014).

[233] *See Draper v. Rosario*, 836 F.3d 1072, 1087–88 (9th Cir. 2016).

[234] *See Draper v. Rosario*, 836 F.3d 1072, 1087–88 (9th Cir. 2016).

[235] *See Draper v. Rosario*, 836 F.3d 1072, 1087–89 (9th Cir. 2016).

[236] *See, e.g., Reger v. Nemours Found., Inc.*, 599 F.3d 285, 289 (3d Cir. 2010) (rejecting wealth disparity and chilling effect); *Pacheco v. Mineta*, 448 F.3d 783, 794–95 (5th Cir. 2006) (rejecting good faith); *Rodriguez v. Whiting Farms, Inc.*, 360 F.3d 1180, 1190 (10th Cir. 2004) (rejecting closeness); *Mitchell v. City of Moore*, 218 F.3d 1190, 1204 (10th Cir. 2000) (rejecting public interest).

[237] *See U.S. E.E.O.C. v. W&O, Inc.*, 213 F.3d 600, 620 (11th Cir. 2000); *U.S. v. Lynd*, 349 F.2d 785, 790 (5th Cir. 1965).

[238] *See* 28 U.S.C.A. § 1920.

[239] *See* 28 U.S.C.A. § 2412.

[240] *See Alyeska Pipeline Service Co. v. Wilderness Society*, 421 U.S. 240, 269 n. 44, 95 S. Ct. 1612, 44 L. Ed. 2d 141 (1975).

[241] *See* 28 U.S.C.A. § 1915.

[242] In 2009, the two Rule 54(d)(1) time periods, which had long been set at 1-day and 5-days, were enlarged to 14-days and 7-days.

verified by affidavit. The clerk may tax costs on 14-days notice. Within 7 days thereafter, a disappointed party may seek court review of the clerk's assessment. Some courts have ruled that a failure to seek review within this period waives the losing party's right to challenge the award.[243] Other courts have noted that the time period is not jurisdictional and untimely objections may, in the trial court's discretion, be considered.[244] In any event, a party is not usually expected to file a Bill of Costs until that party has "prevailed."[245] The district court is authorized to conduct a *de novo* review of the clerk's assessments.[246] Costs may be taxed against multiple losing parties either in allocated amounts or jointly and severally.[247] The time for filing a Bill of Costs is typically regulated by local court rule, but usually is set after the court has rendered its decision in the case.[248]

Procedure & Timing: Attorney's Fees & Nontaxable Expenses

Where an award of attorney's fees and related nontaxable expenses is appropriate, Rule 54(d)(2) fixes the procedure for obtaining such an award.[249] This procedure does *not* apply to attorney's fees recoverable as an element of damages (if the substantive law requires those fees to be proven at trial as an element of damages) or to fees and expenses awarded as sanctions.[250] Courts are cautioned against permitting fee requests to spur a "second major litigation".[251] The procedure follows:

1. *Motion Required:* The prevailing party must apply by motion for such an award. The motion must: (a) specify

[243]*See Fid. & Deposit Co. of Md. v. Edward E. Gillen Co.*, 926 F.3d 318, 328 (7th Cir. 2019); *Mendiola-Martinez v. Arpaio*, 836 F.3d 1239, 1262 (9th Cir. 2016).

[244]*See Debord v. Mercy Health System of Kansas, Inc.*, 737 F.3d 642, 659 (10th Cir. 2013); *Corwin v. Walt Disney Co.*, 475 F.3d 1239, 1254 (11th Cir. 2007).

[245]*See E.E.O.C. v. AutoZone, Inc.*, 707 F.3d 824, 845 (7th Cir. 2013).

[246]*See In re Paoli R.R. Yard PCB Litigation*, 221 F.3d 449, 453 (3d Cir. 2000).

[247]*In re Paoli R.R. Yard PCB Litigation*, 221 F.3d 449, 449 (3d Cir. 2000).

[248]*See S.A. Healy Co. v. Milwaukee Metropolitan Sewerage Dist.*, 60 F.3d 305, 307 (7th Cir. 1995) (because Rule 54(d) specifies no uniform national deadline for filing Bills of Costs, such timing is typically governed by local court rules).

[249]*See, e.g., Sinkler v. Berryhill*, 932 F.3d 83, 86–90 (2d Cir. 2019) (Rule 54(d) applies to fee awards in social security ruling challenge). *See generally supra* Authors' Commentary to Rule 54(d) ("**Litigation Expenses That Ordinarily Cannot Be Taxed**").

[250]*See Taurus IP, LLC v. DaimlerChrysler Corp.*, 726 F.3d 1306, 1342-43 (Fed.Cir. 2013); *Carolina Power & Light Co. v. Dynegy Marketing and Trade*, 415 F.3d 354, 358–59 (4th Cir. 2005). *See also Richardson v. Wells Fargo Bank, N.A.*, 740 F.3d 1035, 1036–40 (5th Cir. 2014) (in appropriate cases, attorney's fees are recoverable under Rule 54(d) as collateral costs of litigation, even though authorized by contract term). *See generally* Rule 54(d)(2) advisory committee note (1993).

[251]*See Hensley v. Eckerhart*, 461 U.S. 424, 437, 103 S. Ct. 1933, 76 L. Ed. 2d 40 (1983).

the judgment; (b) identify the legal source authorizing such an award of fees and/or expenses; and (c) state the amount, or a fair estimate of the amount, of the requested award.[252]

- *Court-Implemented Settlements:* In cases where a settlement must be implemented by the court, the district court may also require that the motion disclose any fee agreement affecting the litigation.

2. *Time for Filing:* Unless provided otherwise by statute,[253] court order,[254] or local court rule,[255] motions must be filed with the court no later than 14 days after entry of judgment.[256] This time trigger assumes a qualifying judgment (which encompasses preliminary injunctions[257] and, also, will usually require compliance with the separate document rule).[258] Failure to file within this allotted time constitutes a waiver of a party's right to recover such fees or expenses.[259] This deadline helps both to ensure that the opponent receives proper notice of the claim and to promote a prompt ruling from the district court, thus facilitating simultaneous appellate review of both the merits and the fees/expenses award.[260] The deadline also forecloses the revival of disputes that adversaries reasonably thought were closed.[261] Most courts agree that this 14-day period does not begin to run until post-trial motions under Rules 50(b), 52(b), or 59 are resolved.[262]

- *Early Filing:* Motions filed before the 14-day pe-

[252] *See* Rule 54(d)(2)(A) to (2)(B). *See also Spirit Lake Tribe v. Jaeger*, 5 F.4th 849, 853 (8th Cir. 2021); *In re Ferrell*, 539 F.3d 1186, 1192 (9th Cir. 2008).

[253] Rule 54(b) has been interpreted to apply broadly. *See, e.g., Walker v. Astrue*, 593 F.3d 274, 274–80 (3d Cir. 2010) (noting Circuit split, but finding Rule 54(d) applies to certain fee petitions under Social Security Act).

[254] *See Hayes v. Comm'r of Soc. Sec.*, 895 F.3d 449, 452–53 (6th Cir. 2018); *Small Justice LLC v. Xcentric Ventures LLC*, 873 F.3d 313, 327 (1st Cir. 2017).

[255] *See Hayes v. Comm'r of Soc. Sec.*, 895 F.3d 449, 453 (6th Cir. 2018).

[256] *See Xlear, Inc. v. Focus Nutrition, LLC*, 893 F.3d 1227, 1234 (10th Cir. 2018) (Rule 54(d) is inapplicable if there was no judgment).

[257] *See Spirit Lake Tribe v. Jaeger*, 5 F.4th 849, 853-54 (8th Cir. 2021) (motions filed more than 14 days after entry of preliminary injunctions are untimely because injunctions are orders "from which an appeal lies").

[258] *See CX Reinsurance Co. Ltd. v. Johnson*, 977 F.3d 306, 308-14 (4th Cir. 2020); *Villoldo v. Castro Ruz*, 821 F.3d 196, 204 (1st Cir. 2016).

[259] *See Zimmerman v. City of Austin*, 969 F.3d 564, 569-70 (5th Cir. 2020). *See also Lauth v. Covance, Inc.*, 863 F.3d 708, 718 (7th Cir. 2017) (waiver can even be imposed *sua sponte*); *Perfect 10, Inc. v. Giganews, Inc.*, 847 F.3d 657, 676 (9th Cir. 2017) (though not jurisdictional, missing time deadline justifies denial, absent compelling showing).

[260] *See United Industries, Inc. v. Simon-Hartley, Ltd.*, 91 F.3d 762, 766 (5th Cir. 1996).

[261] *See Robinson v. City of Harvey*, 617 F.3d 915, 918–19 (7th Cir. 2010) ("Litigation must have its end.").

[262] *See CX Reinsurance Co. Ltd. v.*

riod begins may be proper, since the Rule appears to set only a deadline, not a filing window.[263]

- *Amended Judgments:* Amended judgments are "judgments" just the same, and the 14-day period will run from them as well.[264]
- *Local Rules & Standing Orders:* Several Districts have promulgated local rules or standing orders that modify the length of the 14-day filing period.[265]
- *Extensions:* Because the time period is not jurisdictional, courts seem able to grant extensions.[266]

3. *Time for Serving:* Motions for attorney's fees and nontaxable costs must be served in accordance with Rule 5(a).[267]
4. *Opponent's Response:* Upon request, the court must provide the opponent with the opportunity to present evidence in opposition to the requested award.[268]
5. *Hearings:* Neither an evidentiary hearing nor an oral argument is required;[269] instead, motions are typically resolved on affidavits alone.[270]
6. *Court's Delegation:* The court may enlist the help of a Special Master for setting the proper valuation for attorney services. The court may also refer the entire motion to a magistrate judge for a Report & Recommendation.
7. *Court's Ruling:* In ruling on a Rule 54(d)(2) motion, the court must issue findings of fact and conclusions of law as required under Rule 52(a), and must issue a separate judgment as required under Rule 58. The court may, at its option, bifurcate its consideration of the motion to resolve liability issues first, before considering the

---

Johnson, 977 F.3d 306, 314–15 (4th Cir. 2020); *Bailey v. County of Riverside*, 414 F.3d 1023, 1024 (9th Cir. 2005).

[263]*See Radtke v. Caschetta*, 822 F.3d 571, 573–74 (D.C. Cir. 2016). *But see Brown & Pipkins, LLC v. Serv. Employees Int'l Union*, 846 F.3d 716, 730–31 (4th Cir. 2017) (motions not proper until judgment is entered).

[264]*See Radtke v. Caschetta*, 822 F.3d 571, 573–74 (D.C. Cir. 2016); *Quigley v. Rosenthal*, 427 F.3d 1232, 1236–37 (10th Cir. 2005).

[265]*See, e.g.*, *Hayes v. Comm'r of Soc. Sec.*, 895 F.3d 449, 452–53 (6th Cir. 2018); *Planned Parenthood of Cent. N.J. v. Attorney Gen. of New Jersey*, 297 F.3d 253, 259–61 (3d Cir. 2002).

[266]*See Tancredi v. Metro. Life Ins. Co.*, 378 F.3d 220, 227 (2d Cir. 2004); *Green v. Administrators of Tulane Educ. Fund*, 284 F.3d 642, 664 (5th Cir. 2002).

[267]*See* Rule 54(d)(2)(B) advisory committee note (2002) (noting deletion of 14-day service requirement "to establish a parallel with Rules 50, 52, and 59. Service continues to be required under Rule 5(a)").

[268]*See Sloane v. Equifax Information Services, LLC*, 510 F.3d 495, 507 (4th Cir. 2007).

[269]*See Killer Joe Nevada, LLC v. Does 1–20*, 807 F.3d 908, 913 (8th Cir. 2015) (no oral argument); *Miller v. Dugan*, 764 F.3d 826, 830 (8th Cir. 2014) (no evidentiary hearing).

[270]*See Menchise v. Akerman Senterfitt*, 532 F.3d 1146, 1153 (11th Cir. 2008).

amount of an appropriate award.

8. *Additional Procedures By Local Rule:* Rule 54(d)(2) permits the district courts to promulgate local rules to govern procedures for claims without the need for extensive evidentiary hearings.[271]

Procedure: Costs Bonds

Collateral to the authority to award costs, courts also have the authority to require litigants to post a bond to safeguard against dissipation of funds needed to reasonably cover anticipated taxable costs. Cost bonds are not sanctions, and may not be imposed upon indigent parties in a manner that functionally denies them access to the federal courts.[272]

Effect of an Attorney's Fees Motion on "Finality"

The filing of a Rule 54(d)(2) motion for an award of attorney's fees does not ordinarily affect the finality of the underlying judgment.[273] However, when a *timely* motion for fees is made, and so long as no notice of appeal has yet been filed (or become effective), the district court may enter an order directing that the fees motion be deemed to have the same effect as a timely Rule 59 motion and, thereby, toll the time for taking an appeal until after the motion is resolved.[274] In such an instance, a single appeal is thereafter permitted (to challenge the merits ruling, the fees ruling, or both).[275] This tolling option applies only to fees motions, not to the taxation of costs.[276] If, however, the district court does not issue a tolling order, the time for taking an appeal from the fees ruling runs separately from the time for appealing the merits judgment, and usually does not begin until the district court has entirely completed its work in resolving the fees issues.[277]

---

[271] The advisory committee notes suggest that, by local rule, the district courts may even adopt schedules listing customary attorney's fees or factors that affect attorney's fees within a particular legal community. *See* Rule 54(d)(2)(D) advisory committee note (1998). *See, e.g.*, C.D. Cal. R. 55-3; D. Md. R. App'x B.

[272] *See Gay v. Chandra*, 682 F.3d 590, 594–95 (7th Cir. 2012).

[273] *See* Rule 58(e). *See also Moody Nat. Bank of Galveston v. GE Life & Annuity Assur. Co.*, 383 F.3d 249, 250 (5th Cir. 2004).

[274] *See* Rule 58(e). *See also Nutrition Distribution LLC v. IronMag Labs, LLC*, 978 F.3d 1068, 1071-75 (9th Cir. 2020) (en banc) (to toll appeal time, court must timely order that motion be so treated).

[275] *See JPMorgan Chase Bank, N.A. v. Winget*, 920 F.3d 1103, 1107 (6th Cir. 2019).

[276] *See Moody Nat. Bank of Galveston v. GE Life and Annuity Assur. Co.*, 383 F.3d 249, 253 (5th Cir. 2004).

[277] *See JPMorgan Chase Bank, N.A. v. Winget*, 920 F.3d 1103, 1106–08 (6th Cir. 2019); *Mayer v. Wall Street Equity Grp., Inc.*, 672 F.3d 1222, 1224 (11th Cir. 2012).

Additional Research References

Wright & Miller, *Federal Practice and Procedure* §§ 2651 to 79

C.J.S., Federal Civil Procedure §§ 1105 to 1120 et seq., 1236; Federal Courts § 293(17)

West's Key Number Digest, Federal Civil Procedure ⚷2391 to 2399, 2571 to 2587, 2721 to 2742.5; Federal Courts ⚷660

RULE 55
DEFAULT; DEFAULT JUDGMENT

(a) Entering a Default. When a party against whom a judgment for affirmative relief is sought has failed to plead or otherwise defend, and that failure is shown by affidavit or otherwise, the clerk must enter the party's default.

(b) Entering a Default Judgment.

(1) *By the Clerk.* If the plaintiff's claim is for a sum certain or a sum that can be made certain by computation, the clerk—on the plaintiff's request, with an affidavit showing the amount due—must enter judgment for that amount and costs against a defendant who has been defaulted for not appearing and who is neither a minor nor an incompetent person.

(2) *By the Court.* In all other cases, the party must apply to the court for a default judgment. A default judgment may be entered against a minor or incompetent person only if represented by a general guardian, conservator, or other like fiduciary who has appeared. If the party against whom a default judgment is sought has appeared personally or by a representative, that party or its representative must be served with written notice of the application at least 7 days before the hearing. The court may conduct hearings or make referrals—preserving any federal statutory right to a jury trial—when, to enter or effectuate judgment, it needs to:

(A) conduct an accounting;

(B) determine the amount of damages;

(C) establish the truth of any allegation by evidence; or

(D) investigate any other matter.

(c) Setting Aside a Default or a Default Judgment. The court may set aside an entry of default for good cause, and it may set aside a final default judgment under Rule 60(b).

(d) Judgment Against the United States. A default judgment may be entered against the United States, its officers, or its agencies only if the claimant establishes a claim or right to relief by evidence that satisfies the court.

[Amended effective August 1, 1987; April 30, 2007, effective December 1, 2007; March 26, 2009, effective December 1, 2009; April 29, 2015, effective December 1, 2015.]

AUTHORS' COMMENTARY ON RULE 55

PURPOSE AND SCOPE

Rule 55 sets the procedure for defaults and default judgments in the federal courts. Because non-merits judgments are not favored (since they run counter to the strong federal policy preferring decisions on the merits), Rule 55 also establishes the procedure for setting aside defaults and default judgments.

RULE 55(a)—ENTERING A DEFAULT

CORE CONCEPT

The clerk of court must enter a default against a party who has failed to plead or otherwise defend.

APPLICATIONS

Distinguished From Default Judgment

The clerk's entry of a party's default is the official recognition that a defending party is delinquent in its duty to plead or otherwise defend.[1] The entry of default is a prerequisite for the entry of judgment upon that default.[2] It is, in effect, akin to a finding of liability with the entry of final judgment yet to come.[3] Thus, there are two stages in a default proceeding—the establishment of the default itself, followed by the entry of a default judgment.[4]

- *Default as Sanction:* It is not clear whether this same

---

[1] *See City of New York v. Mickalis Pawn Shop, LLC*, 645 F.3d 114, 128 (2d Cir. 2011); *New York Life Ins. Co. v. Brown*, 84 F.3d 137, 141 (5th Cir. 1996).

[2] *See infra* Authors' Commentary to Rule 55(b) ("**Prerequisites to Judgment by Default**").

[3] *See Alameda v. Secretary of Health, Ed. and Welfare*, 622 F.2d 1044, 1048 (1st Cir. 1980).

[4] *See Fidrych v. Marriott Int'l, Inc.*, 952 F.3d 124, 130 (4th Cir. 2020); *VLM Food Trading Int'l, Inc. v. Illinois Trading Co.*, 811 F.3d 247, 255 (7th Cir. 2016).

two-stage process is required when default is entered by the court as a sanction against a misbehaving party.[5]

Who May Seek Entry of Default

Although used most familiarly against delinquent defendants, the default procedure can be applied equally against any defending party having an unmet obligation to counter-plead or otherwise defend (including any litigant defending counterclaims, crossclaims, or third-party claims).[6]

Prerequisites to Entry of Default

A motion for entry of default must be made promptly[7] and properly.[8] The party against whom default is being sought must be subject to the court's jurisdiction.[9] Additionally, the clerk of court must be satisfied, by the movant's affidavit or otherwise, that the delinquent party was properly served with process[10] and has thereafter failed to plead or otherwise defend.[11] Courts have interpreted the phrase "otherwise defend" broadly, permitting entries of default for persistent lack of pretrial diligence or discovery misbehavior, failure to appear at an adjourned trial's resumption, dismissing counsel without an appointed replacement, and abandonment of an active defense.[12]

- *2007 "Restyling" Impact:* In 2007, the phrase "as

---

[5]*Compare United States v. Di Mucci*, 879 F.2d 1488, 1490–95 (7th Cir. 1989) (suggesting Rule 55(a) applies in discovery sanctions); *with Hoxworth v. Blinder, Robinson & Co.*, 980 F.2d 912, 919 (3d Cir. 1992) (noting Rule 55(a) and Rule 37 represent separate paths for default sanctions); *with Fifth Third Bank v. KCII Insure Servs., LLC*, 2012 WL 718898, at *2 n.1 (D. Kan. Mar. 5, 2012) (Rule 55(a)'s "preliminary step is unnecessary" when default judgment entered as discovery sanction).

[6]*See Commerce Bank & Trust Co. v. Ria LLC*, 314 F.R.D. 338, 339–41 (D. Mass. 2016) (default on unanswered crossclaim); *Viveros v. Nationwide Janitorial Ass'n, Inc.*, 200 F.R.D. 681, 684 (N.D. Ga. 2000) (default on unanswered counterclaim). *See also* Rule 55 advisory committee note (2007) (applies to "any party against whom a judgment for affirmative relief is requested").

[7]*See Harvey v. United States*, 685 F.3d 939, 946 (10th Cir. 2012) (actively litigating for more than two years before seeking default for 1-day late filing forfeited timeliness objection).

[8]*See Fox v. United States Postal Serv.*, 2019 WL 8619622, at *3 (6th Cir. Oct. 30, 2019) (unpublished) (verbal requests insufficient). *But cf. Oppenheimer v. City of Madeira*, 336 F.R.D. 559, 563–64 (S.D. Ohio 2020) (recasting improperly labeled motion to strike as motion for entry of default).

[9]*See Thomas v. Bank of Am., N.A.*, 557 Fed. Appx. 873, 875 (11th Cir. 2014) (without personal jurisdiction, good cause exists to set aside entry of default).

[10]*See Colclough v. Gwinnett Pub. Sch.*, 734 Fed. Appx. 660, 662 (11th Cir. 2018); *Barrett v. Tri-Coast Pharmacy, Inc.*, 518 F. Supp. 3d 810, 822 (D.N.J. 2021).

[11]*See New York Life Ins. Co. v. Brown*, 84 F.3d 137, 141 (5th Cir. 1996); *Mid-Gulf Shipping Co. Inc. v. Energy Subsea LLC*, 472 F. Supp. 3d 318, 322 (E.D. La. 2020).

[12]*See City of New York v. Mickalis Pawn Shop, LLC*, 645 F.3d 114, 129–30 (2d Cir. 2011) (collecting cases). *See also, e.g., Arwa Chiropractic, P.C. v. Med-Care Diabetic & Med. Supplies, Inc.*, 961 F.3d 942, 948 (7th Cir. 2020) (corporation's failure to timely replace withdrawing counsel); *United States v.*

provided by these rules" was stricken from Rule 55(a), confirming that an evinced "intent to defend" is sufficient to avoid a default even if it is manifested in a manner that does not comport strictly with the Rules.[13]

Entry of Default is Mandatory

If a party is found to have failed to plead or otherwise defend, entry of default is mandatory, not discretionary.[14] Indeed, a delinquent party is considered already to be default, even if the formal entry of default has not yet been docketed.[15]

Entry by Clerk or Court

Although entry of default is typically a ministerial act undertaken by the clerk, the district judges themselves possess the power to enter default as well.[16]

Contested Motions for Entry of Default

Where a motion for entry of default is opposed by a party who has entered an appearance, the courts may, in considering the contested motion, apply the criteria guiding motions to set aside a default.[17]

Effect of Entry of Default

The entry of default provides formal notice to litigants that they are in default (that is, delinquent on the obligation to "plead or otherwise defend").[18] Upon entry, a defaulting party is deemed to have admitted all well-pleaded allegations of the complaint (except for the amount of damages);[19] allegations that are not well-pleaded, as well as conclusions of law, are not deemed admitted.[20] This greatly limits that party's ability to defend against the claim. A defaulting party is ordinarily foreclosed from raising any defenses other than a challenge to

---

$23,000 in U.S. Currency, 356 F.3d 157, 163 (1st Cir. 2004) (refusal to file verified statement required by admiralty and maritime rules); *Curtis v. Illumination Arts, Inc.*, 33 F. Supp. 3d 1200, 1210 (W.D. Wash. 2014) (as sanction for persistent discovery misbehavior).

[13]*See In re Clark*, 2010 WL 2639842, at *3 (W.D.Wash. June 28, 2010).

[14]*See Bricklayers and Allied Craftworkers Local 2, Albany, N.Y. Pension Fund v. Moulton Masonry & Const., LLC*, 779 F.3d 182, 186 (2d Cir. 2015); *Perez v. Wells Fargo N.A.*, 774 F.3d 1329, 1337 (11th Cir. 2014).

[15]*See Siegler v. Sorrento Therapeutics, Inc.*, 2021 WL 3046590, at *12 (Fed. Cir. 2021); *Perez v. Wells Fargo N.A.*, 774 F.3d 1329, 1337 (11th Cir. 2014).

[16]*See City of New York v. Mickalis Pawn Shop, LLC*, 645 F.3d 114, 128 (2d Cir. 2011); *Betz v. First Credit Servs., Inc.*, 139 F. Supp. 3d 451, 455 (D.D.C. 2015).

[17]*See* Rule 55(c). *See also Schmir v. Prudential Ins. Co. of America*, 220 F.R.D. 4, 5 (D. Me. 2004) (applying Rule 55(c) factors). *See also Finley v. Kondaur Capital Corp.*, 909 F. Supp. 2d 969, 983–84 (W.D.Tenn. 2012).

[18]*See Tweedy v. RCAM Title Loans, LLC*, 611 F. Supp. 2d 603, 605 (W.D.Va. 2009).

[19]*See Equal Emp. Opportunity Comm'n v. Roark-Whitten Hosp. 2, LP*, 28 F.4th 136, 157 (10th Cir. 2022); *Burkhart v. Grigsby*, 886 F.3d 434, 438 (4th Cir. 2018).

[20]*See Escalante v. Lidge*, 34 F.4th 486, 492–93 (5th Cir. 2022); *Martinizing Int'l, LLC v. BC Cleaners, LLC*,

the legal sufficiency of the pleading to support a cognizable judgment, the adequacy of service of process, and the propriety of the court's jurisdiction.[21] Default is not, however, an absolute confession of liability and of the opponent's right to recover,[22] and the court may examine the pleaded allegations to confirm that they do, in fact, state a cognizable cause of action.[23]

Appealability

Entry of default is an interlocutory order, from which an immediate appeal ordinarily cannot be taken.[24] However, in an appeal from entry of a default judgment, the appeals court may review both the interlocutory entry of default as well as the ensuing entry of default judgment.[25]

RULE 55(b)—ENTERING A DEFAULT JUDGMENT

CORE CONCEPT

Where the defendant has been defaulted for failing to appear and the moving party has submitted evidence by affidavit establishing damages in a sum certain or in a sum that can be made certain by computation, the clerk of court will enter a default judgment upon motion. In all other cases, the *court* (and *not* the clerk) may enter a default judgment.

APPLICATIONS

Effect of a Default Judgment

A default judgment transforms the delinquent party's admissions (which occur upon entry of the default) into a final judgment; it usually terminates the litigation by producing an enforceable, final award in favor of the pleader.[26]

Prerequisites to Judgment by Default

Before a default judgment may be granted, a "default" under Rule 55(a) must first have been entered.[27] The request for a

855 F.3d 847, 850 (8th Cir. 2017).

[21] *See VLM Food Trading Int'l, Inc. v. Illinois Trading Co.*, 811 F.3d 247, 255 (7th Cir. 2016); *Tyco Fire & Sec., LLC v. Alcocer*, 218 Fed. Appx. 860, 863–64 (11th Cir. 2007).

[22] *See CapitalKeys, LLC v. Democratic Republic of Congo*, 278 F. Supp. 3d 265, 285 (D.D.C. 2017); *Evans v. Larchmont Baptist Church Infant Care Ctr., Inc.*, 956 F. Supp. 2d 695, 702–03 (E.D.Va. 2013).

[23] *See Escalante v. Lidge*, 34 F.4th 486, 492–93 (5th Cir. 2022); *Sampson v. Lambert*, 903 F.3d 798, 805–06 (8th Cir. 2018). *See generally City of New York v. Mickalis Pawn Shop, LLC*, 645 F.3d 114, 137 n.23 (2d Cir. 2011) (collecting cases).

[24] *See City of New York v. Mickalis Pawn Shop, LLC*, 645 F.3d 114, 128 n. 15 (2d Cir. 2011); *Symantec Corp. v. Global Impact, Inc.*, 559 F.3d 922, 923 (9th Cir. 2009).

[25] *See City of New York v. Mickalis Pawn Shop, LLC*, 645 F.3d 114, 129 (2d Cir. 2011).

[26] *See City of New York v. Mickalis Pawn Shop, LLC*, 645 F.3d 114, 128 (2d Cir. 2011).

[27] *See Giddens v. Lawson*, 734 Fed. Appx. 706, 711 (11th Cir. 2018); *Heard v. Caruso*, 351 F. App'x 1, 15–16 (6th Cir. 2009). *See also In re Hansmeier*, 581 B.R. 605, 609 (D. Minn. 2017) (grant of default judgment before

default judgment must be made promptly.[28] The entering court must confirm that it has subject-matter jurisdiction over the dispute,[29] and also may (some Circuits hold "must") confirm that it possesses personal jurisdiction over the defaulting parties.[30] The court must then determine whether the now-admitted facts constitute a proper cause of action[31] and a legitimate basis for entry of a judgment.[32] (Although defaulting parties are precluded from contesting facts now deemed admitted, they may always challenge whether those admitted facts establish a cognizable claim for relief.[33]) Some courts have characterized this inquiry as akin to a "reverse" motion to dismiss—confirming judicially that the pleaded allegations plausibly suggest an entitlement to the default remedy sought,[34] with all well-pleaded factual allegations accepted as true and all reasonable inferences drawn in the moving party's favor.[35] If damages are awarded, their amount must be fixed.[36] The court must respect the due process rights of the defaulting party,[37] which requires minimally the 7-day notice to appearing defendants (see below) and the opportunity to be heard on the details and

---

entry of default is reversible error). *But see La Barbera v. Fed. Metal & Glass Corp.*, 666 F. Supp. 2d 341, 347 (E.D.N.Y. 2009) (court may excuse failure to obtain entry of default before seeking default judgment).

[28]*See Harvey v. United States*, 685 F.3d 939, 946 (10th Cir. 2012) (actively litigating for more than two years before seeking a default judgment for a 1-day late filing forfeited the timeliness objection).

[29]*See Jennifer Matthew Nursing & Rehab. Ctr. v. U.S. Dep't of Health & Human Servs.*, 607 F.3d 951, 955 (2d Cir.2010); *Warmbier v. Democratic People's Republic of Korea*, 356 F. Supp. 3d 30, 42 (D.D.C. 2018).

[30]*See Bixler v. Foster*, 596 F.3d 751, 761 (10th Cir. 2010); *Mwani v. bin Laden*, 417 F.3d 1, 6 (D.C. Cir. 2005). *See generally City of New York v. Mickalis Pawn Shop, LLC*, 645 F.3d 114, 133 (2d Cir. 2011) (surveying views on obligation to inquire).

[31]*See Bixler v. Foster*, 596 F.3d 751, 762 (10th Cir. 2010); *Murray v. Lene*, 595 F.3d 868, 871 (8th Cir. 2010).

[32]*See Escalante v. Lidge*, 34 F.4th 486, 489 (5th Cir. 2022) (defaulting defendant admits factual allegations "but the district court still may inquire whether those allegations demonstrate legal liability"); *Purzel Video GmbH v. Martinez*, 13 F. Supp. 3d 1140, 1145 (D. Colo. 2014).

[33]*See Wooten v. McDonald Transit Assocs., Inc.*, 788 F.3d 490, 496 (5th Cir. 2015); *Marshall v. Baggett*, 616 F.3d 849, 852 (8th Cir. 2010). *See also Ohio Cent. R. Co. v. Central Trust Co.*, 133 U.S. 83, 10 S. Ct. 235, 33 L. Ed. 561 (1890) (defaulting defendant "is not precluded from contesting the sufficiency of the bill, or from insisting that the averments contained in it do not justify the decree").

[34]*See Surtain v. Hamlin Terrace Found.*, 789 F.3d 1239, 1245–48 (11th Cir. 2015); *Auctus Fund, LLC v. MJ Biotech, Inc.*, 544 F. Supp. 3d 190, 193 (D. Mass. 2021). *Cf. Wooten v. McDonald Transit Assocs., Inc.*, 788 F.3d 490, 498 n.3 (5th Cir. 2015) (disavowing *Twombly*-like inquiry, then seemingly conducting one).

[35]*See Finkel v. Romanowicz*, 577 F.3d 79, 84 (2d Cir. 2009).

[36]*See Fidrych v. Marriott Int'l, Inc.*, 952 F.3d 124, 130–31 (4th Cir. 2020) (until amount of damages is fixed, order operates only as entry of default, not default judgment).

[37]*See City of New York v. Mickalis Pawn Shop, LLC*, 645 F.3d 114, 132–33 (2d Cir. 2011).

nature of the resulting default judgment.[38]

The "Appearance" 7-Day Rule

If a default judgment is being sought against a party who has "appeared" (as that term is used in Rule 55(b)), that party must be served with *written* notice of the application for a default judgment at least 7 days[39] before the hearing.[40] Such an appearance, obviously, must have occurred *before* the default judgment is entered in order to trigger the entitlement to written notice.[41] The entitlement to notice can be waived if an objection is not timely raised.[42]

Defining a Party's "Appearance"

A party "appears" in the action by making some presentation or submission to the court (*e.g.*, filing an entry of appearance, serving a responsive pleading, serving a Rule 12 motion to dismiss, or having counsel attend a conference on the client's behalf).[43] Some courts have taken an even wider view,[44] ruling that "appearing" within the meaning of Rule 55(b) is not necessarily limited to a formal event in court.[45] For example, informal acts such as correspondence or telephone calls between counsel might constitute the requisite appearance,[46] as might engaging in settlement negotiations.[47] Given the judicial philosophy disfavoring default judgments, the courts may search to find

[38] *See City of New York v. Mickalis Pawn Shop, LLC*, 645 F.3d 114, 132 (2d Cir. 2011).

[39] The Rule 55(b) time period, which had long been set at 3-days, was enlarged to 7-days by the 2009 amendments to the Rules.

[40] *See* Rule 55(b)(2).

[41] *See Jenkens & Gilchrist v. Groia & Co.*, 542 F.3d 114, 118 n.2 (5th Cir. 2008).

[42] *See U.S. v. Varmado*, 342 Fed. Appx. 437, 439–40 (11th Cir. 2009) (unpublished opinion).

[43] *See Sun Bank of Ocala v. Pelican Homestead and Sav. Ass'n*, 874 F.2d 274, 276 (5th Cir. 1989) (filing motion to dismiss constitutes "appearing"); *Hudson v. State of North Carolina*, 158 F.R.D. 78, 80 (E.D. N.C. 1994).

[44] *See New York v. Green*, 420 F.3d 99, 105 (2d Cir. 2005) (noting division among the Circuits on the issue).

[45] *See Silverman v. RTV Communications Group, Inc.*, 2002 WL 483421, at *3 (S.D. N.Y. 2002) (appearance "is broadly defined and is not limited to a formal court filing"). *See also Rogers v. Hartford Life and Acc. Ins. Co.*, 167 F.3d 933, 936–37 (5th Cir. 1999) (court does not construe "appeared" as requiring filing of responsive papers or actual in-court actions by defendant). *But see Zuelzke Tool & Engineering Co., Inc. v. Anderson Die Castings, Inc.*, 925 F.2d 226, 230 (7th Cir. 1991) (rejecting informal contacts approach); *Town and Country Kids, Inc. v. Protected Venture Inv. Trust #1, Inc.*, 178 F.R.D. 453, 455 (E.D. Va. 1998) (parties "appear" in action only where they make presentation or submission to court).

[46] *See Sun Bank of Ocala v. Pelican Homestead and Sav. Ass'n*, 874 F.2d 274, 276–77 (5th Cir. 1989); *Johnson v. Orkin, LLC*, 286 F.R.D. 337, 338–39 (N.D.Ill. 2012). *See generally New York v. Green*, 420 F.3d 99, 106 (2d Cir.2005) (noting prevailing view, that informal contacts, like telephone calls, may suffice provided there is "clear intention to defend").

[47] *See S.E.C. v. Getanswers, Inc.*, 219 F.R.D. 698, 700 (S.D. Fla. 2004).

that an appearance has occurred.[48] Nevertheless, merely accepting or waiving service of process will usually not qualify as "appearing" within the meaning of this Rule.[49]

Entry of Default Judgment by Clerk

The clerk may only enter a default judgment where the following three prerequisites are met:

1. A defendant was defaulted because of a failure to appear; *and*
2. The defendant is not a minor or incompetent person;[50] *and*
3. The moving party submits an affidavit establishing that the amount due is either a sum certain or a sum that can be made certain by computation.

- *"Sum Certain" Defined:* A claim is not a "sum certain" under Rule 55 unless there is no doubt as to the amount that must be awarded,[51] that the amount due is beyond question (such as actions on money judgments or negotiable instruments).[52] This standard is not met where some portion of damages, such as "reasonable" attorney's fees or punitive damages, still needs to be determined.[53]

Entry of Default Judgment by Court

In all other circumstances, the court may enter the default judgment:

1. Where the party has "appeared", in which case the appearing party must be served with written notice of the application for default judgment at least 7 days before any hearing on the application;[54] or
2. Where the party is a minor or incompetent person, in which case a default judgment may be entered only if

---

[48]*See Franchise Holding II, LLC. v. Huntington Restaurants Group, Inc.*, 375 F.3d 922, 927 (9th Cir. 2004).

[49]*See Rogers v. Hartford Life & Acc. Ins. Co.*, 167 F.3d 933, 936–37 (5th Cir. 1999).

[50]*See Barrett v. Tri-Coast Pharmacy, Inc.*, 518 F. Supp. 3d 810, 822 (D.N.J. 2021) (affirmation made upon counsel's "information and belief" that defaulted party is not minor/incompetent suffices).

[51]*See Franchise Holding II, LLC. v. Huntington Restaurants Group, Inc.*, 375 F.3d 922, 928–29 (9th Cir. 2004); *KPS & Associates, Inc. v. Designs By FMC, Inc.*, 318 F.3d 1, 19–20 (1st Cir. 2003).

[52]*See KPS & Associates, Inc. v. Designs By FMC, Inc.*, 318 F.3d 1, 19–20 (1st Cir. 2003). *See also Snelling v. Tribal Vapors*, 2021 WL 1227836, at *47–*48 (D.N.M. 2021) ("sum certain" not satisfied merely by demanding specific dollar amount).

[53]*See Dailey v. R & J Comm'l Contracting*, 2002 WL 484988, at *3 (S.D. Ohio 2002) (error for clerk to enter requested judgment involving punitive damages).

[54]*See Canal Ins. Co. v. Ashmore*, 61 F.3d 15, 17 (8th Cir. 1995) (abuse of discretion to fail to set aside default judgment where defendant never received notice); *D.B. v. Bloom*, 896 F. Supp. 166, 170 (D.N.J. 1995) (court must be satisfied that party received notice of motion).

the minor or incompetent is represented;[55] or

3. Where the amount due is not certain[56] or the relief sought is noneconomic;[57] or
4. Where the party has been defaulted for a reason other than a failure to appear. For example, in appropriate circumstances, a default judgment can be entered as a sanction against a misbehaving litigant.[58]

Fashioning the Default Judgment

When the damages amount is not a sum certain, the court may convene an evidentiary hearing[59] or simply rely on affidavits or other documentary evidence.[60] Convening an evidentiary hearing may not be mandatory in all cases;[61] so long as a proper factual basis supports the court's award,[62] whether (and how) to conduct hearings is often left to the trial judge's discretion.[63] The Rule expressly approves of hearings when needed for an accounting or a determination of damage amounts, to receive evidence on allegations, or to otherwise investigate.[64] Although the entry of default deprives the defaulting party of the right to contest most of the complaint's factual allegations (unless the default is set aside),[65] the defaulting party may contest the amount of damages.[66] Thus, all the well-pleaded facts in the complaint (except those relating to the amount of damages) are presumed true,[67] but the moving party

---

[55] *See Andrade v. Arby's Rest. Grp., Inc.*, 225 F. Supp. 3d 1115, 1127 (N.D. Cal. 2016).

[56] *See Campbell v. Humphries*, 353 F. App'x 334, 337 (11th Cir. 2009).

[57] *See Nevada Gen. Ins. Co. v. Anaya*, 326 F.R.D. 685, 690 (D.N.M. 2018) (declaratory judgment relief).

[58] *See Fanning v. Wegco, Inc.*, 5 F. Supp. 2d 1, 4 (D.D.C. 2013).

[59] *See Wooten v. McDonald Transit Assocs., Inc.*, 788 F.3d 490, 496 (5th Cir. 2015); *Finkel v. Romanowicz*, 577 F.3d 79, 87 (2d Cir. 2009).

[60] *See Ling Chen v. Asian Terrace Rest., Inc.*, 507 F. Supp. 3d 430, 433 (E.D.N.Y. 2020); *Argonaut Ins. Co. v. Lynchburg Steel & Specialty Co.*, 308 F. Supp. 3d 218, 221 (D.D.C. 2018).

[61] *See Giovanno v. Fabec*, 804 F.3d 1361, 1366 (11th Cir. 2015); *Greathouse v. JHS Sec. Inc.*, 784 F.3d 105, 116–17 (2d Cir. 2015). *But cf. Quincy Bioscience, LLC v. Ellishbooks*, 957 F.3d 725, 729 n.25 (7th Cir. 2020) (default judgment may not be entered without hearing unless sum-certain or sum-ascertainable from definite figures in evidence or affidavits); *UnitedHealthcare Ins. Co. v. Holley*, 724 F. App'x 285, 289 (5th Cir. 2018) (same).

[62] *See AngioDynamics, Inc. v. Biolitec AG*, 780 F.3d 429, 436–37 (1st Cir. 2015); *Marcus Food Co. v. DiPanfilo*, 671 F.3d 1159, 1172 (10th Cir. 2011).

[63] *See Grant v. Pottinger-Gibson*, 725 F. App'x 772, 774 (11th Cir. 2018); *Cement & Concrete Workers Dist. Council Welfare Fund, Pension Fund, Annuity Fund, Educ. & Training Fund & Other Funds v. Metro Found. Contractors Inc.*, 699 F.3d 230, 233 (2d Cir. 2012).

[64] *See* Rule 55(b)(2)(A)-(2)(D).

[65] *See supra* Authors' Commentary to Rule 55(a) ("**Effect of Entry of Default**").

[66] *See Finkel v. Romanowicz*, 577 F.3d 79, 83 n.6 (2d Cir. 2009); *Cotton v. Mass. Mut. Life Ins. Co.*, 402 F.3d 1267, 1278 (11th Cir. 2005).

[67] *See Arwa Chiropractic, P.C. v. Med-Care Diabetic & Med. Supplies,*

must prove damages[68] with reasonable certainty[69] and the court must independently determine them.[70] Moreover, although proximate cause (when properly pleaded) is irrefutably established upon the defendant's default, the moving party must still show that the compensation requested relates to damages flowing naturally from the loss alleged.[71] An evidentiary basis must support the damages sought.[72] However, all doubts[73] and reasonable inferences from the evidence are drawn in the moving party's favor.[74] The court enjoys "considerable latitude" in fashioning relief.[75]

- *Jury Right:* Although a right to a jury is expressly preserved for post-default hearings *if granted by federal statute*,[76] most courts that have passed on the question have ruled that defaulting parties have no Seventh Amendment jury right in such hearings.[77]

Default in Multiple Defendant Cases

Where the plaintiff alleges joint liability against multiple defendants or the defendants have closely related defenses, the default of one defendant usually will not result in a judgment against another defendant. Instead, the court will allow the lawsuit to proceed as to the other, non-defaulting defendants. The result in the litigation (*e.g.*, judgment for plaintiff or judgment for defendants) will then simply be entered as to the

---

Inc., 961 F.3d 942, 948 (7th Cir. 2020); *Finkel v. Romanowicz*, 577 F.3d 79, 84 (2d Cir. 2009).

[68] *See Cement & Concrete Workers Dist. Council Welfare Fund, Pension Fund, Annuity Fund, Educ. & Training Fund & Other Funds v. Metro Found. Contractors Inc.*, 699 F.3d 230, 234 (2d Cir. 2012); *Rubicon Glob. Ventures, Inc. v. Chongqing Zongshen Grp. Imp./Exp. Corp.*, 226 F. Supp. 3d 1141, 1148 (D. Or. 2016).

[69] *See In re Catt*, 368 F.3d 789, 793 (7th Cir. 2004); *Credit Lyonnais Sec. (USA), Inc. v. Alcantara*, 183 F.3d 151, 155 (2d Cir. 1999).

[70] *See Int'l Ass'n of Sheet Metal, Air, Rail & Transportation Workers, Loc. Union No. 71 v. Lovejoy Metals, Inc.*, 495 F. Supp. 3d 174, 184 (W.D.N.Y. 2020); *Cong. Hunger Ctr. v. Gurey*, 308 F. Supp. 3d 223, 228 (D.D.C. 2018).

[71] *See Greyhound Exhibitgroup, Inc. v. E.L.U.L. Realty Corp.*, 973 F.2d 155, 159 (2d Cir. 1992).

[72] *See Cement & Concrete Workers Dist. Council Welfare Fund, Pension Fund, Annuity Fund, Educ. & Training Fund & Other Funds v. Metro Found. Contractors Inc.*, 699 F.3d 230, 233 (2d Cir. 2012); *Malluk v. Berkeley Highlands Prods., LLC*, ___ F. Supp. 3d ___, 2020 WL 1033339, at *2 (D. Colo. 2020).

[73] *See Enron Oil Corp. v. Diakuhara*, 10 F.3d 90, 96 (2d Cir.1993); *Jackson v. Beech*, 636 F.2d 831, 836 (D.C.Cir.1980).

[74] *See Finkel v. Romanowicz*, 577 F.3d 79, 84 (2d Cir. 2009); *Pleitez v. Carney*, 594 F. Supp. 2d 47, 48–49 (D.D.C. 2009).

[75] *See Fanning v. Seneca One Realty LLC*, 265 F. Supp. 3d 31, 33 (D.D.C. 2017).

[76] *See* Rule 55(b)(2). *See also Olcott v. Del. Flood Co.*, 327 F.3d 1115, 1124 (10th Cir. 2003).

[77] *See KD v. Douglas Cty. Sch. Dist. No. 001*, 1 F.4th 591, 601–02 (8th Cir. 2021); *Olcott v. Del. Flood Co.*, 327 F.3d 1115, 1124 (10th Cir. 2003). *But cf. Snelling v. Tribal Vapors*, 2021 WL 1227836, at *51 (D.N.M. 2021) (if jury trial properly demanded pre-default, consent of all parties needed before demand can be withdrawn).

defaulting defendant as well.[78]

Defaulting Defendants in the Military

The federal Soldiers' and Sailors' Civil Relief Act of 1940[79] prohibits the entry of any federal or State judgment by default against absent military defendants, unless the court first appoints counsel to represent the absent defendants' interests. Often, the court may simply stay a lawsuit against the absent military defendants until their return.

Note: In seeking a default judgment, a plaintiff ordinarily must, by factual averment or affidavit, attest that the defaulting defendant is not in the military.[80]

Limitation on Default Judgments

No judgment by default can be greater in amount or different in kind from the demand contained in the complaint.[81]

Discretion of District Court

Judgments by default are disfavored and are never granted as a matter of right.[82] Whether to enter a judgment by default is a decision entrusted to the sound discretion of the district court.[83] Thus, a party's default does not entitle the plaintiff to an automatic default judgment,[84] nor need the judge presume that the pleader's allegations constitute a valid cause of action.[85] Before exercising their discretion and entering a default judgment, courts may examine: the standards for setting aside a

---

[78]*See Frow v. De La Vega*, 82 U.S. 552, 21 L. Ed. 60 (1872). *But see Whelan v. Abell*, 953 F.2d 663, 674–75 (D.C. Cir. 1992) (construing *Frow* narrowly to hold that a default order that is inconsistent with a judgment on the merits must be set aside only where the liability is actually "joint" (i.e., where the theory of recovery would render all defendants (even the defaulting defendant) liable if any one of the defendants is liable)). *See generally Arwa Chiropractic, P.C. v. Med-Care Diabetic & Med. Supplies, Inc.*, 961 F.3d 942, 951 (7th Cir. 2020) (separate judgments proper where liability is joint-and-several, and not merely joint (or vicarious)); *Martin v. Coughlin*, 895 F. Supp. 39, 43 (N.D. N.Y. 1995) (same, and noting Second Circuit view that it is "most unlikely" that *Frow* principle survived promulgation of Rule 54(b)).

[79]50 U.S.C.A.App. § 3931.

[80]*See Barrett v. Tri-Coast Pharmacy, Inc.*, 518 F. Supp. 3d 810, 822 (D.N.J. 2021) (affidavit supported by "necessary facts" required).

[81]*See* Rule 54(c).

[82]*See Surtain v. Hamlin Terrace Found.*, 789 F.3d 1239, 1244–45 (11th Cir. 2015); *Belcourt Pub. Sch. Dist. v. Davis*, 786 F.3d 653, 661 (8th Cir. 2015).

[83]*See Belcourt Pub. Sch. Dist. v. Davis*, 786 F.3d 653, 661 (8th Cir. 2015); *Greathouse v. JHS Sec. Inc.*, 784 F.3d 105, 116–17 (2d Cir. 2015). *See also Serv. Employees Int'l Union Local 32BJ, Dist. 36 v. Shamrock-Clean, Inc.*, 325 F. Supp. 3d 631, 634–35 (E.D. Pa. 2018) (disputes involving large sums should not be decided by default judgments "if it can reasonably be avoided").

[84]*See Escalante v. Lidge*, 34 F.4th 486, 492 (5th Cir. 2022); *Bricklayers & Allied Craftworkers Local 2, Albany, N.Y. Pension Fund v. Moulton Masonry & Const., LLC*, 779 F.3d 182, 186 (2d Cir. 2015).

[85]*See Finkel v. Romanowicz*, 577 F.3d 79, 84 (2d Cir. 2009).

default;[86] whether a responsive pleading has since (though belatedly) been received;[87] whether the deemed-admitted allegations are contrary to judicially-noticed facts or other uncontroverted material in the case file;[88] and a myriad of other factors, such as the federal policy favoring decisions on the merits, the presence of excusable neglect, the clarity of the grounds for default, the adequacy of notice, the size of the claim, the facts in dispute, and prejudice to either party.[89] Nevertheless, and notwithstanding the preference for decisions on the merits,[90] where the inquiry satisfies the court that a default judgment is proper, it will be entered.[91] Unresponsive litigants should not be allowed to halt the adversary process, and diligent parties should be protected against undue delay and uncertainty.[92]

Appealability

An entry of judgment by default constitutes a final order,[93] provided it is not conditional and does not contemplate any further proceedings.[94] Whether it is appealable can be less clear. Some courts require, as a prerequisite to appealability, that the losing party first file a motion with the district judge requesting that the default judgment be vacated; others do not so require.[95] A refusal to enter judgment by default is considered interlocutory, generally appealable only when the case's final order is entered.[96]

---

[86]*See Guggenheim Cap., LLC v. Birnbaum*, 722 F.3d 444, 454–55 (2d Cir. 2013); *Travelers Cas. & Sur. Co. of Am. v. Perlman*, 351 F. Supp. 3d 930, 932 (E.D. Pa. 2019). *See generally infra* Authors' Commentary to Rule 55(c).

[87]*See Davila v. Marshall*, 649 Fed. Appx. 977, 980 (11th Cir. 2016); *Andrade v. Arby's Rest. Grp., Inc.*, 225 F. Supp. 3d 1115, 1127 (N.D. Cal. 2016).

[88]*See Escalante v. Lidge*, 34 F.4th 486, 493 (5th Cir. 2022).

[89]*See, e.g., NewGen, LLC v. Safe Cig, LLC*, 840 F.3d 606, 616 (9th Cir. 2016) (listing various factors); *Belcourt Pub. Sch. Dist. v. Davis*, 786 F.3d 653, 661 (8th Cir. 2015) (same).

[90]*See Belcourt Pub. Sch. Dist. v. Davis*, 786 F.3d 653, 661 (8th Cir. 2015).

[91]*See Fanning v. Wellman Dynamics Corp.*, 113 F. Supp. 3d 172, 174 (D.D.C. 2015); *Swarna v. Al-Awadi*, 607 F. Supp. 2d 509, 527–29 (S.D.N.Y. 2009).

[92]*See Cong. Hunger Ctr. v. Gurey*, 308 F. Supp. 3d 223, 227 (D.D.C. 2018); *Jones v. Marquis Props., LLC*, 212 F. Supp. 3d 1010, 1015 (D. Colo. 2016).

[93]*See also Dreith v. Nu Image, Inc.*, 648 F.3d 779, 789 n.1 (9th Cir. 2011) (same principle applies to defaults entered as Rule 37 sanctions).

[94]*See Swarna v. Al-Awadi*, 622 F.3d 123, 140 (2d Cir. 2010).

[95]*See Prime Rate Premium Fin. Corp., Inc. v. Larson*, 930 F.3d 759, 768 (6th Cir. 2019) (recounting circuit split). *Compare Stelly v. Duriso*, 982 F.3d 403, 407 (5th Cir. 2020) (not required) *with Consorzio Del Prosciutto Di Parma v. Domain Name Clearing Co., LLC*, 346 F.3d 1193, 1195 (9th Cir. 2003) (required).

[96]*See Garrett v. Richardson*, 773 Fed. Appx. 717, 718 (4th Cir. 2019); *Bird v. Reese*, 875 F.2d 256, 256 (9th Cir. 1989). *See also Watson v. Mylan Pharm., Inc.*, 701 Fed. Appx. 729, 731 n.1 (10th Cir. 2017) (denial may be appealed with final judgment). *But cf. FirstBank Puerto Rico v. Jaymo Props.,*

RULE 55(c)—SETTING ASIDE DEFAULT OR A DEFAULT JUDGMENT

CORE CONCEPT

The court may set aside the entry of default for good cause, and may vacate a judgment by default in accordance with Rule 60(b) (which governs the grounds upon which a party may seek relief from a judgment).

APPLICATIONS

Policy and Liberality

Defaults and default judgments are disfavored, since they are inconsistent with the federal courts' preference for resolving disputes on their merits.[97] This preference is reflected in the two-step default process (default first, default judgment later), which affords two opportunities to appear and seek to avoid the effects of default.[98] Motions for relief from both defaults and default judgments are considered liberally[99] and are often granted.[100] Where only a default has been entered (without an ensuing default judgment), the standard for lifting the default is especially generous.[101]

Setting Aside a Default

Rule 55(c) authorizes the district courts, "for good cause", to set aside the entry of a default. Not susceptible to a precise definition, "good cause" has been labeled a liberal and "mutable" standard, one anchored in equity[102] that varies from situation to situation.[103] It is a standard applied generously since a judgment will not have yet been entered upon that default.[104] Ergo,

---

LLC, 379 Fed. Appx. 166, 168–69 (3d Cir. 2010) (nonfinal denials of default judgment immediately appealable if collateral order doctrine applies).

[97] *See Sindhi v. Raina*, 905 F.3d 327, 331 (5th Cir. 2018); *Harvey v. United States*, 685 F.3d 939, 946 (10th Cir. 2012). *But see O'Brien v. R.J. O'Brien & Assoc., Inc.*, 998 F.2d 1394, 1401 (7th Cir.1993) ("this circuit no longer follows the earlier doctrine disfavoring defaults").

[98] *See Fanning v. AMF Mech. Corp.*, 326 F.R.D. 11, 14-15 (D.D.C. 2018).

[99] *See Colleton Preparatory Academy, Inc. v. Hoover Universal, Inc.*, 616 F.3d 413, 417 (4th Cir. 2010); *United States v. $22,050.00 U.S. Currency*, 595 F.3d 318, 322 (6th Cir. 2010).

[100] *See Indigo America, Inc. v. Big Impressions, LLC*, 597 F.3d 1, 6 (1st Cir. 2010); *California Trout v. F.E.R.C.*, 572 F.3d 1003, 1027 n.1 (9th Cir. 2009).

[101] *See Colleton Preparatory Academy, Inc. v. Hoover Universal, Inc.*, 616 F.3d 413, 418 (4th Cir. 2010); *U.S. v. Signed Personal Check No. 730 of Yubran S. Mesle*, 615 F.3d 1085, 1091 n.1 (9th Cir. 2010).

[102] *See Gilmore v. Palestinian Interim Self-Gov't Auth.*, 843 F.3d 958, 966 (D.C. Cir. 2016).

[103] *See Perez v. Wells Fargo N.A.*, 774 F.3d 1329, 1338 n.7 (11th Cir. 2014); *Commerce Bank & Trust Co. v. Ria LLC*, 314 F.R.D. 338, 340 (D. Mass. 2016).

[104] *See Colleton Preparatory Academy, Inc. v. Hoover Universal, Inc.*, 616 F.3d 413, 420 (4th Cir. 2010); *Johnson v. New York Univ.*, 324 F.R.D.

entries of default are often set aside.[105] The requisite "good cause," however, is not good cause for the defendant's delinquency, but rather good cause justifying the court's intervention to set the default aside.[106] An absence of jurisdiction will obviously qualify.[107]

Otherwise, in testing for "good cause", the courts generally consider the following three factors:[108] (1) whether the default is proven to have not been willful or culpable (which typically requires more than mere inaction or negligence);[109] (2) whether a meritorious defense exists (usually not a heavy burden, requiring only the alleging of sufficient facts that, if true, would constitute a defense);[110] and (3) whether the opponent would be prejudiced were the default lifted (which means not mere litigation delay or the chore of having to prove the merits,[111] but some loss of evidence, unavailability of witnesses, or other impairment of the ability to litigate).[112] Some courts also include, as a leading factor, an inquiry into the swiftness of the action taken to remedy the default.[113]

In addition to these leading factors, courts have often considered other equitable criteria as well, including: (a) whether the default resulted from a good faith mistake in following a rule of procedure;[114] (b) the nature of the defendant's explanation for defaulting;[115] (c) any history of dilatory con-

---

65, 69 (S.D.N.Y. 2018).

[105]*See California Trout v. F.E.R.C.*, 572 F.3d 1003, 1027 n.1 (9th Cir. 2009).

[106]*See Sims v. EGA Products, Inc.*, 475 F.3d 865, 868 (7th Cir. 2007).

[107]*See Trade Well Int'l v. United Cent. Bank*, 825 F.3d 854, 859 (7th Cir. 2016); *Strabala v. Zhang*, 318 F.R.D. 81, 89 (N.D. Ill. 2016).

[108]*See Khochinsky v. Republic of Poland*, 1 F.4th 1, 7 (D.C. Cir. 2021); *Courser v. Allard*, 969 F.3d 604, 624 (6th Cir. 2020); *Johnson v. Leonard*, 929 F.3d 569, 573 (8th Cir. 2019).

[109]*See Bricklayers & Allied Craftworkers Local 2, Albany, N.Y. Pension Fund v. Moulton Masonry & Const., LLC*, 779 F.3d 182, 186–87 (2d Cir. 2015); *A.P. Moller-Maersk A/S, Trading v. Safewater Lines (I) PVT, Ltd.*, 322 F.R.D. 255, 258 (S.D. Tex. 2017).

[110]*See U.S. v. Signed Personal Check No. 730 of Yurban S. Mesle*, 615 F.3d 1085, 1094 (9th Cir. 2010); *Indigo America, Inc. v. Big Impressions, LLC*, 597 F.3d 1, 6 (1st Cir. 2010). *See also Khochinsky v. Republic of Poland*, 1 F.4th 1, 7 (D.C. Cir. 2021) ("even a hint of a suggestion which, if proven, would constitute a complete defense" may suffice).

[111]*See Colleton Preparatory Academy, Inc. v. Hoover Universal, Inc.*, 616 F.3d 413, 417 & 419 n.6 (4th Cir. 2010); *U.S. v. Signed Personal Check No. 730 of Yurban S. Mesle*, 615 F.3d 1085, 1092 (9th Cir. 2010).

[112]*See East Coast Exp., Inc. v. Ruby, Inc.*, 162 F.R.D. 37, 39 (E.D. Pa. 1995); *Mathon v. Marine Midland Bank, N.A.*, 875 F. Supp. 986, 992 (E.D.N.Y. 1995).

[113]*See Arwa Chiropractic, P.C. v. Med-Care Diabetic & Med. Supplies, Inc.*, 961 F.3d 942, 949 (7th Cir. 2020); *Perez v. Wells Fargo N.A.*, 774 F.3d 1329, 1338 n.7 (11th Cir. 2014).

[114]*See Indigo America, Inc. v. Big Impressions, LLC*, 597 F.3d 1, 3 (1st Cir. 2010).

[115]*See Indigo America, Inc. v. Big Impressions, LLC*, 597 F.3d 1, 3 (1st Cir. 2010).

duct;[116] (d) the amount in controversy;[117] (e) the availability of effective alternative sanctions;[118] (f) whether entry of a default would produce a harsh or unfair result;[119] and (g) various other factors.[120] For many courts, each particular consideration need not be satisfied,[121] and this list of criteria is non-exhaustive.[122] For those courts, motions to set aside default are made in a "practical, commonsense manner, without rigid adherence to, or undue reliance upon, a mechanical formula."[123] Other courts take a more unyielding approach, treating the leading factors as mandatory, with a failure to meet any one sufficient, alone, to justify denying the motion.[124]

- *Note:* This "good cause" test is more lenient than the Rule 60(b) standards for lifting a default judgment.[125] Thus, circumstances that would warrant lifting a default judgment likely suffice as "good cause" to set aside a default.

Vacating a Final Judgment by Default

Once a final judgment is entered upon a party's default, the task of vacating it becomes more difficult.[126] The court may vacate a default judgment if the defaulting party satisfies one of the Rule 60(b) reasons for vacating a judgment (*i.e.*, mistake,

---

[116] *See Colleton Preparatory Academy, Inc. v. Hoover Universal, Inc.*, 616 F.3d 413, 417 (4th Cir. 2010).

[117] *See Indigo America, Inc. v. Big Impressions, LLC*, 597 F.3d 1, 3 (1st Cir. 2010); *Compania Interamericana Export-Import, S.A. v. Compania Dominicana de Aviacion*, 88 F.3d 948, 951 (11th Cir. 1996).

[118] *See Colleton Preparatory Academy, Inc. v. Hoover Universal, Inc.*, 616 F.3d 413, 417 (4th Cir. 2010); *Agnew v. E*Trade Secs. LLC*, 811 F. Supp. 2d 1177, 1183 (E.D.Pa. 2011).

[119] *See Richardson v. Nassau County*, 184 F.R.D. 497, 501 (E.D. N.Y. 1999); *Canfield v. VSH Restaurant Corp.*, 162 F.R.D. 431, 433 (N.D. N.Y. 1995).

[120] *See Perez v. Wells Fargo N.A.*, 774 F.3d 1329, 1338 n.7 (11th Cir. 2014) (public interest; significance of defendant's financial loss); *In re Chinese-Mfd. Drywall Prods. Liab. Litig.*, 753 F.3d 521, 545 (5th Cir. 2014) (same).

[121] *See Gilmore v. Palestinian Interim Self-Gov't Auth.*, 843 F.3d 958, 966 (D.C. Cir. 2016); *In re Chinese-Mfd. Drywall Prods. Liab. Litig.*, 753 F.3d 521, 545 (5th Cir. 2014).

[122] *See Koerner v. CMR Constr. & Roofing, L.L.C.*, 910 F.3d 221, 225 (5th Cir. 2018); *Indigo America, Inc. v. Big Impressions, LLC*, 597 F.3d 1, 3 (1st Cir. 2010).

[123] *See KPS & Associates, Inc. v. Designs By FMC, Inc.*, 318 F.3d 1, 12 (1st Cir. 2003).

[124] *See See, e.g., Koerner v. CMR Constr. & Roofing, L.L.C.*, 910 F.3d 221, 225 (5th Cir. 2018) (finding of willfulness "ends the inquiry"); *United States v. Certain Real Prop. commonly known as 21105 116TH St. Bristol, Wis.*, 845 F. Supp. 2d 961, 964 (E.D. Wis. 2012) ("the default will stand" if claimant cannot show all three). *Cf. Brandt v. American Bankers Ins. Co.*, 653 F.3d 1108, 1111–12 (9th Cir. 2011) (if any of leading factors is absent, court may—but is not compelled to—deny relief).

[125] *See JMB Mfg., Inc. v. Child Craft, LLC*, 799 F.3d 780, 792 (7th Cir. 2015); *Colleton Preparatory Academy, Inc. v. Hoover Universal, Inc.*, 616 F.3d 413, 420–21 (4th Cir. 2010).

[126] *See Arwa Chiropractic, P.C. v. Med-Care Diabetic & Med. Supplies, Inc.*, 961 F.3d 942, 948–49 (7th Cir. 2020); *Grant v. City of Blytheville*, 841 F.3d 767, 772 (8th Cir. 2016).

inadvertence, surprise, excusable neglect; newly discovered evidence; misconduct by an adverse party; void judgment; satisfied or discharged judgment; other extraordinary circumstances).[127] Frequently, Rule 60(b)(1) is the chosen subrule for such motions,[128] and courts there typically apply the same leading factors used in considering whether to set aside entry of a default (*e.g.*, willfulness, meritorious defense, lack of prejudice, and, perhaps, quick filing),[129] though the factors may be examined more demandingly since a judgment has now been entered.[130]

Default judgments are "the biggest weapon in the district court's armory" and may be useful in reining in recalcitrant parties or penalizing prejudicial tactics,[131] but they generally will not be appropriate where the misstep does not prejudice the adversary or costs the erring party an otherwise certain victory.[132] Rather, vacating a default judgment is an equitable inquiry that considers all relevant circumstances.[133] The time for filing such motions is that applicable to the particular subrule of Rule 60(b) chosen by the moving party.[134]

- *Applies Only When Judgment Is Final:* The more demanding Rule 60(b) inquiry applies only after damages have been determined and a final, appealable judgment has been entered; until that time, the more forgiving "good cause" standard governs.[135]

Burden of Proof

The burden of demonstrating that either a default or default judgment should be lifted lies with the moving party.[136]

Discretion of District Court

Because it clashes with the federal courts' preference for decisions on the merits, defaulting a party is viewed as a drastic step and extreme sanction, and ought to be reserved for only

---

[127] *See* Rule 60(b)(1)–(b)(6).

[128] *See* Rule 60(b)(1) ("mistake, inadvertence, surprise, or excusable neglect").

[129] *See United States v. Welsh*, 879 F.3d 530, 533 (4th Cir. 2018); *Acosta v. DT & C Glob. Mgmt., LLC*, 874 F.3d 557, 560 (7th Cir. 2017). *See also Brandt v. Am. Bankers Ins. Co.*, 653 F.3d 1108, 1111 (9th Cir. 2011) (acknowledging that factors are the same).

[130] *See Am. Transit Ins. Co. v. Bilyk*, 546 F. Supp. 3d 192, 197 (E.D.N.Y. 2021) (same factors, but "applied more rigorously").

[131] *See Mommaerts v. Hartford Life and Acc. Ins. Co.*, 472 F.3d 967, 967–69 (7th Cir. 2007).

[132] *See Mommaerts v. Hartford Life and Acc. Ins. Co.*, 472 F.3d 967, 969–69 (7th Cir. 2007).

[133] *See Brandt v. American Bankers Ins. Co.*, 653 F.3d 1108, 1112 (9th Cir. 2011).

[134] *See* Rule 60(c).

[135] *See* Rule 55(c) advisory committee note (2015). *See also Arwa Chiropractic, P.C. v. Med-Care Diabetic & Med. Supplies, Inc.*, 961 F.3d 942, 948–49 (7th Cir. 2020); *Sindhi v. Raina*, 905 F.3d 327, 332–33 & n.3 (5th Cir. 2018).

[136] *See Sindhi v. Raina*, 905 F.3d 327, 332 (5th Cir. 2018); *Indigo America, Inc. v. Big Impressions, LLC*, 597 F.3d 1, 4 (1st Cir. 2010).

rare occasions.[137] Accordingly, at least the "good cause" criteria are applied forgivingly,[138] with doubts resolved in favor of lifting the default.[139] Whether to set aside the entry of default or vacate a default judgment is left to the discretion of the district judge.[140]

Sua Sponte Set Asides

Although defaults and default judgments are set aside usually upon motion of a party, the district courts may do so *sua sponte*.[141]

RULE 55(d)—DEFAULT JUDGMENT AGAINST THE UNITED STATES

CORE CONCEPT

No default judgment may be entered against the United States or any federal agency or officer, unless the plaintiff establishes, by evidence satisfactory to the court, a claim or right to relief.

APPLICATIONS

Impact of 2007 "Restyling" Amendments

The 2007 amendments repositioned the content of former Rule 55(e) to its current location, in Rule 55(d). The former content of Rule 55(d) was deleted as unnecessary.

Policy

The entry of default judgments against the United States is especially disfavored.[142] The courts reason that federal taxpayers (on whom the burden of paying the default judgment would ultimately fall) should not be called upon to pay a penalty imposed as the consequence of the neglect of some government official, if to do so would cause a windfall to the litigant.[143] Thus, Rule 55(d) is intended to prevent the entry of default judgments against the United States for mere procedural

---

[137] *See U.S. v. Signed Personal Check No. 730 of Yurban S. Mesle*, 615 F.3d 1085, 1091 (9th Cir. 2010); *Stewart v. Astrue*, 552 F.3d 26, 28 (1st Cir. 2009). *See also Martin v. Coughlin*, 895 F. Supp. 39, 42 (N.D. N.Y. 1995) (default judgment is "a weapon of last, and not first, resort").

[138] *See United States v. $22,050.00 U.S. Currency*, 595 F.3d 318, 322 (6th Cir. 2010).

[139] *See Khochinsky v. Republic of Poland*, 1 F.4th 1, 7 (D.C. Cir. 2021); *Courser v. Allard*, 969 F.3d 604, 624 (6th Cir. 2020).

[140] *See Koerner v. CMR Constr. & Roofing, L.L.C.*, 910 F.3d 221, 225 (5th Cir. 2018); *Doe v. Hesketh*, 828 F.3d 159, 174–75 (3d Cir. 2016).

[141] *See Judson Atkinson Candies, Inc. v. Latini-Hohberger Dhimantec*, 529 F.3d 371, 385–86 (7th Cir. 2008) (approving *sua sponte* set asides of default; collecting cases); *AGCO Fin., LLC v. Littrell*, 320 F.R.D. 45, 49 (D. Minn. 2017).

[142] *See Harvey v. United States*, 685 F.3d 939, 946 (10th Cir. 2012); *Payne v. Barnhart*, 725 F. Supp. 2d 113, 116 (D.D.C. 2010).

[143] *See Compania Interamericana Export-Import, S.A. v. Compania Dominicana de Aviacion*, 88 F.3d 948, 951 (11th Cir. 1996); *ABI Inv. Group v. F.D.I.C.*, 860 F. Supp. 911, 914 (D.N.H. 1994).

missteps.[144] Consequently, such defaults are frequently denied outright or set aside.[145] This "presumption-against-defaulting" the government is especially strong when the movant is seeking criminal habeas relief.[146]

Applies Only to Default Judgments, Not Defaults

Although default judgments may not be entered summarily against the United States, the default itself may be.[147]

Plaintiff's High Burden

To obtain a default judgment against the United States or federal officers or agencies, plaintiffs must carry the heavy burden of establishing a claim or right-to-relief.[148] They must do so by evidence that is satisfactory to the court.[149] This inquiry does not necessarily require a hearing, or either more or different evidence than might otherwise be received.[150] (However, at least one court has ruled that the burden for default against the United States requires a demonstration of an evidentiary basis that is legally sufficient for a reasonable jury to find for the plaintiff.[151]) Instead, the courts assume a flexible approach in determining the procedures necessary to conduct this inquiry.[152] If uncontroverted, a plaintiff's *evidence* may be accepted as true,[153] but if the government comes forward with a meritorious defense and a willingness to litigate, the default judgment will likely be refused.[154]

Foreign Governments

By statute, Congress requires that this same "satisfies-the-court" standard be applied in actions against foreign governments, foreign political subdivisions, and foreign agencies and instrumentalities.[155]

---

[144]*See Arevalo v. U.S.*, 2008 WL 3874795, at *6 (E.D. Pa. 2008).

[145]*See Payne v. Barnhart*, 725 F. Supp. 2d 113, 116 (D.D.C. 2010).

[146]*See U.S. v. Dill*, 555 F. Supp. 2d 514, 521 (E.D. Pa. 2008).

[147]*See Alameda v. Secretary of Health, Ed. and Welfare*, 622 F.2d 1044, 1048 (1st Cir. 1980) (default may be entered, commenting that exemption from default judgments "heightens" United States' obligation to cooperate with court). *See also Washington v. Astrue*, 2009 WL 1916238, at *1 (S.D.Fla. June 30, 2009).

[148]*See Campbell v. U.S.*, 375 Fed. Appx. 254, 261 (3d Cir. 2010); *Willever v. United States*, 775 F. Supp. 2d 771 (D.Md. 2011).

[149]*See Sims v. Lee*, 651 Fed. Appx. 570, 571 (9th Cir. 2016); *Harvey v. United States*, 685 F.3d 939, 946–56 (10th Cir. 2012).

[150]*See Commercial Bank of Kuwait v. Rafidain Bank*, 15 F.3d 238, 242 (2d Cir. 1994).

[151]*See Smith ex rel. Smith v. Islamic Emirate of Afghanistan*, 262 F. Supp. 2d 217, 223–24 (S.D. N.Y. 2003).

[152]*See Jin v. Ministry of State Security*, 557 F. Supp. 2d 131, 139–40 (D.D.C. 2008); *Gadoury v. U.S.*, 187 B.R. 816, 822 (D.R.I. 1995).

[153]*See Estate of Botvin ex rel. Ellis v. Islamic Republic of Iran*, 772 F. Supp. 2d 218, 227 (D.D.C. 2011).

[154]*See Stewart v. Astrue*, 552 F.3d 26, 28–29 (1st Cir. 2009).

[155]*See* 28 U.S.C.A. § 1608(e). *See also Owens v. Republic of Sudan*, 864

Additional Research References

Wright & Miller, *Federal Practice and Procedure* §§ 2681 to 2702
C.J.S., Federal Civil Procedure §§ 1122 to 1134 et seq.
West's Key Number Digest, Federal Civil Procedure ⚷2411 to 2455

F.3d 751, 785 (D.C. Cir. 2017).

RULE 56
SUMMARY JUDGMENT

(a) Motion for Summary Judgment or Partial Summary Judgment. A party may move for summary judgment, identifying each claim or defense—or the part of each claim or defense—on which summary judgment is sought. The court shall grant summary judgment if the movant shows that there is no genuine dispute as to any material fact and the movant is entitled to judgment as a matter of law. The court should state on the record the reasons for granting or denying the motion.

(b) Time to File a Motion. Unless a different time is set by local rule or the court orders otherwise, a party may file a motion for summary judgment at any time until 30 days after the close of all discovery.

(c) Procedures.

(1) *Supporting Factual Positions.* A party asserting that a fact cannot be or is genuinely disputed must support the assertion by:

(A) citing to particular parts of materials in the record, including depositions, documents, electronically stored information, affidavits or declarations, stipulations (including those made for purposes of the motion only), admissions, interrogatory answers, or other materials; or

(B) showing that the materials cited do not establish the absence or presence of a genuine dispute, or that an adverse party cannot produce admissible evidence to support the fact.

(2) *Objection That a Fact Is Not Supported by Admissible Evidence.* A party may object that the material cited to support or dispute a fact cannot be presented in a form that would be admissible in evidence.

(3) *Materials Not Cited.* The court need consider

only the cited materials, but it may consider other materials in the record.

(4) *Affidavits or Declarations.* An affidavit or declaration used to support or oppose a motion must be made on personal knowledge, set out facts that would be admissible in evidence, and show that the affiant or declarant is competent to testify on the matters stated.

(d) When Facts Are Unavailable to the Nonmovant. If a nonmovant shows by affidavit or declaration that, for specified reasons, it cannot present facts essential to justify its opposition, the court may:

(1) defer considering the motion or deny it;

(2) allow time to obtain affidavits or declarations or to take discovery; or

(3) issue any other appropriate order.

(e) Failing to Properly Support or Address a Fact. If a party fails to properly support an assertion of fact or fails to properly address another party's assertion of fact as required by Rule 56(c), the court may:

(1) give an opportunity to properly support or address the fact;

(2) consider the fact undisputed for purposes of the motion;

(3) grant summary judgment if the motion and supporting materials—including the facts considered undisputed—show that the movant is entitled to it; or

(4) issue any other appropriate order.

(f) Judgment Independent of the Motion. After giving notice and a reasonable time to respond, the court may:

(1) grant summary judgment for a nonmovant;

(2) grant the motion on grounds not raised by a party; or

(3) consider summary judgment on its own after identifying for the parties material facts that may not be genuinely in dispute.

(g) Failing to Grant All the Requested Relief. If

the court does not grant all the relief requested by the motion, it may enter an order stating any material fact—including an item of damages or other relief—that is not genuinely in dispute and treating the fact as established in the case.

(h) Affidavit or Declaration Submitted in Bad Faith. If satisfied that an affidavit or declaration under this rule is submitted in bad faith or solely for delay, the court—after notice and a reasonable time to respond—may order the submitting party to pay the other party the reasonable expenses, including attorney's fees, it incurred as a result. An offending party or attorney may also be held in contempt or subjected to other appropriate sanctions.

[Amended effective March 19, 1948; July 1, 1963; August 1, 1987; April 30, 2007, effective December 1, 2007; March 26, 2009, effective December 1, 2009; April 28, 2010, effective December 1, 2010.]

The 2010 Summary Judgment Amendments

In 2010, the federal summary judgment Rule underwent its most extensive revision since it was first adopted in 1938. The current version of Rule 56 appears above. Because courts, practitioners, and academics occasionally need to consult the prior language, the pre-amendment version of Rule 56 is reprinted below in reduced font.

[Former text of Rule 56:]

Rule 56. Summary Judgment

(a) By a Claiming Party. A party claiming relief may move, with or without supporting affidavits, for summary judgment on all or part of the claim.

(b) By a Defending Party. A party against whom relief is sought may move, with or without supporting affidavits, for summary judgment on all or part of the claim.

(c) Time for a Motion, Response, and Reply; Proceedings.

(1) These times apply unless a different time is set by local rule or the court orders otherwise:

(A) a party may move for summary judgment at any time until 30 days after the close of all discovery;

(B) a party opposing the motion must file a response within 21 days after the motion is served or a responsive pleading is due, whichever is later; and

(C) the movant may file a reply within 14 days after the response is served.

(2) The judgment sought should be rendered if the pleadings, the discovery and disclosure materials on file, and any affidavits show that there is no genuine issue as to any material fact and that the movant is entitled to judgment as a matter of law.

(d) Case Not Fully Adjudicated on the Motion.

(1) *Establishing Facts.* If summary judgment is not rendered on the whole

action, the court should, to the extent practicable, determine what material facts are not genuinely at issue. The court should so determine by examining the pleadings and evidence before it and by interrogating the attorneys. It should then issue an order specifying what facts—including items of damages or other relief—are not genuinely at issue. The facts so specified must be treated as established in the action.

(2) *Establishing Liability.* An interlocutory summary judgment may be rendered on liability alone, even if there is a genuine issue on the amount of damages.

(e) Affidavits; Further Testimony.

(1) *In General.* A supporting or opposing affidavit must be made on personal knowledge, set out facts that would be admissible in evidence, and show that the affiant is competent to testify on the matters stated. If a paper or part of a paper is referred to in an affidavit, a sworn or certified copy must be attached to or served with the affidavit. The court may permit an affidavit to be supplemented or opposed by depositions, answers to interrogatories, or additional affidavits.

(2) *Opposing Party's Obligation to Respond.* When a motion for summary judgment is properly made and supported, an opposing party may not rely merely on allegations or denials in its own pleading; rather, its response must—by affidavits or as otherwise provided in this rule—set out specific facts showing a genuine issue for trial. If the opposing party does not so respond, summary judgment should, if appropriate, be entered against that party.

(f) When Affidavits Are Unavailable. If a party opposing the motion shows by affidavit that, for specified reasons, it cannot present facts essential to justify its opposition, the court may:

(1) deny the motion;

(2) order a continuance to enable affidavits to be obtained, depositions to be taken, or other discovery to be undertaken; or

(3) issue any other just order.

(g) Affidavit Submitted in Bad Faith. If satisfied that an affidavit under this rule is submitted in bad faith or solely for delay, the court must order the submitting party to pay the other party the reasonable expenses, including attorney's fees, it incurred as a result. An offending party or attorney may also be held in contempt.

AUTHORS' COMMENTARY ON RULE 56

PURPOSE AND SCOPE

Summary judgment is proper in federal court when there is no true disagreement as to any material fact and, on that record, one party is entitled by law to prevail. In such circumstances, there is no factual dispute to sort out and, consequently, no valuable service for a factfinder to perform. A trial would be a squandering, meaningless exercise.

But summarily entering a judgment must be done with care. Judges may not assess credibility of witnesses, weigh the evidence, or choose between competing reasonable inferences; those functions are all the province of a factfinder. The sole question to be answered in resolving a summary judgment motion is whether there is a genuine, evidence-based dispute requiring submission to a factfinder. Motions for summary judgment thus test the parties' evidence (not just their pleaded allegations, as a Rule 12(b) motion does), and are governed by the same legal standard as Rule 50 judgments as a matter of law—the difference being timing: summary judgment is predictive (before trial), while JMOL assesses the full evidentiary record as actually tried.

Rule 56(a) establishes the legal standard governing federal summary judgment, and encourages trial judges to explain the reasons for granting or denying such motions.

Rule 56(b) sets an alterable default time schedule for filing a motion (it may be filed "at any time," but ordinarily not later than 30 days after the close of discovery).

Rule 56(c)(1) and (c)(4) advises parties on how to support or oppose such motions. Rule 56(c)(2) permits objections to an opponent's use of inadmissible supporting materials, and Rule 56(h) authorizes the imposition of sanctions for any summary judgment affidavit or declaration submitted in bad faith or solely for purposes of delay. If the non-moving party is not yet ready to file its opposition to a pending motion, Rule 56(d) sets a procedure for requesting a forbearance while discovery ensues.

In ruling on summary judgment motions, courts are directed by Rule 56(c)(3) to examine those portions of the record cited by the parties. When confronted by a party's inadequate presentation, courts are afforded an array of options by Rule 56(e). If full or partial summary judgment is proper, courts "shall" grant it, as instructed by Rule 56(a). If it is not, Rule 56(g) allows courts to declare certain facts as "established" for the duration of the case, if their canvass of the record supports that finding.

Finally, Rule 56(f) authorizes a court to grant summary judgment *sua sponte*, on grounds not raised by the parties, or in favor of the non-moving party—provided the court first supplies the parties with adequate notice and an appropriate opportunity to respond.

COMPARISONS WITH OTHER ADJUDICATION RULES

Dismissals / Judgments on the Pleadings: Motions to dismiss (under Rule 12(b)(6)) and for judgment on the pleadings (under Rule 12(c)) are *as-alleged* challenges. They test whether a pleading's averments of law and fact, if proven true, would be legally sufficient to sustain a claim or defense.[1] In contrast, motions for summary judgment are *as-provable* challenges. They test whether, irrespective of the allegations,

[1] *See supra* Authors' Commentary to Rule 12(b)(6) ("**Legal Test**") and Rule 12(c) ("**Legal Test**").

evidence exists to establish a genuine factual dispute.[2]

Judgments as a Matter of Law (JMOL): Motions for judgments as a matter of law (under Rule 50) are *as-proven* challenges — the federal equivalent of directed verdict and JNOV motions. They test whether, informed by the evidence actually presented at trial, a reasonable jury could return a verdict for the non-moving party. In this respect, both summary judgment motions and JMOL motions use the same lens of the reasonable factfinder to test a party's claim or defense.[3] The difference is timing. Summary judgment assessments are made pre-trial, and are supported by pleadings, discovery, affidavits, and other "cold" evidence. JMOL assessments are made during or after trial, with the judge having listened to the live testimony and evidentiary presentation. Thus, Rule 50 motions for JMOL ask whether there is any need for the trial—then underway—to continue on to the jury deliberation stage, whereas Rule 56 motions for summary judgment ask whether there is any need to convene a trial in the first place.

RULE 56(a) — MOTION FOR SUMMARY JUDGMENT OR PARTIAL SUMMARY JUDGMENT

CORE CONCEPT

Parties may move to summarily terminate a claim, defense, or entire lawsuit. If the court determines that an actual trial before a factfinder is unnecessary (because there is no true, material factual dispute for a factfinder to resolve), the court shall grant summary judgment.

APPLICATIONS

2010 Amendments — Amended Rule 56(a)

In 2010, the summary judgment rule was restructured. Current Rule 56(a) now contains the standards for granting summary judgment (repositioned, but substantively unchanged from prior practice)[4] and new provisions expressly allowing "partial" summary judgment and directing trial courts to

---

[2]*See Celotex Corp. v. Catrett*, 477 U.S. 317, 324, 106 S. Ct. 2548, 91 L. Ed. 2d 265 (1986) (Rule 56 "requires the nonmoving party to go beyond the pleadings" and, with affidavits or otherwise, "designate 'specific facts showing that there is a genuine issue for trial' "). *See also United States ex rel. Greenfield v. Medco Health Sols., Inc.*, 880 F.3d 89, 98 n.7 (3d Cir. 2018) (evidentiary burden in opposing summary judgment is "significantly greater" than opposing dismissal).

[3]*See Anderson v. Liberty Lobby, Inc.*, 477 U.S. 242, 250–51, 106 S. Ct. 2505, 91 L. Ed. 2d 202 (1986) (summary judgment standard "mirrors the standard for a directed verdict under Federal Rule of Civil Procedure 50(a), which is that the trial judge must direct a verdict if, under the governing law, there can be but one reasonable conclusion as to the verdict"). *See also Reeves v. Sanderson Plumbing Prods., Inc.*, 530 U.S. 133, 150, 120 S. Ct. 2097, 147 L. Ed. 2d 105 (2000) (Rule 50 and 56 as "analogous" contexts with "mirror[ing]" standards and the "same" inquiry).

[4]*See Burton v. Teleflex Inc.*, 707 F.3d 417, 425 n.6 (3d Cir. 2013); *Newell Rubbermaid, Inc. v. Raymond Corp.*, 676 F.3d 521, 533 (6th Cir. 2012). *See*

explain their reasons when ruling on motions. Deleted (apparently as surplusage[5]) was former text that had noted expressly that such motions could be filed by any party.

Motions by Claiming Parties

Summary judgment is not only a defensive tool; claimants can move for summary judgment on their own claims as well.[6] They bear a heavier burden when doing so, however.[7]

Motions by Defending Parties

Defending parties may move for summary judgment.[8] The case law is divided on whether filing a pre-answer summary judgment motion will have the effect of tolling the time for filing a responsive pleading (as a pre-answer Rule 12(b) motion would).[9] In any event, it is clear that filing an answer is not a prerequisite for filing a summary judgment motion.[10]

Motions by Both Parties (Cross-Motions)

Both parties may seek summary judgment in the same action, with "cross-motions" under Rule 56.[11]

Motions by Others

Summary judgment is available only to parties—those who have filed claims or who are defending against filed claims.[12]

Motions by *Pro Se* Litigants

Courts construe a *pro se* litigant's submissions liberally and interpret them in a manner to raise the strongest arguments they suggest.[13] Additionally, some courts require special advance notice to *pro se* litigants before summary judgment may be entered against them.[14]

---

generally Rule 56 advisory committee note (2010) ("The standard for granting summary judgment remains unchanged.").

[5]*See* Rule 56(a) (current text prescribes broadly that "[a] party" may seek summary judgment).

[6]*See Alexander v. CareSource*, 576 F.3d 551, 557–58 (6th Cir. 2009).

[7]*See Barnes v. Sea Hawaii Rafting, LLC*, 889 F.3d 517, 538 (9th Cir. 2018). *See generally infra* Authors' Commentary to Rule 56(a) (**"Burdens of Proof"**).

[8]*See Jefferson v. Chattanooga Pub. Co.*, 375 F.3d 461, 463 (6th Cir. 2004).

[9]*See supra* Authors' Commentary to Rule 12(a) (**"Exceptions to the Tolling Effect Rule** — *Summary Judgment Motions*").

[10]*See HS Resources, Inc. v. Wingate*, 327 F.3d 432, 440 (5th Cir. 2003).

[11]*See infra* Authors' Commentary to Rule 56(a) (**"Cross-Motions"**).

[12]*See Scottsdale Ins. Co. v. Knox Park Const., Inc.*, 488 F.3d 680, 685 (5th Cir. 2007).

[13]*See Williams v. Annucci*, 895 F.3d 180, 187 (2d Cir. 2018).

[14]*See infra* Authors' Commentary to Rule 56(e) (**"Motions Involving *Pro Se* Litigants"**).

Purpose

The purpose of summary judgment is to isolate, and then terminate, claims and defenses that are factually unsupported.[15] It is not a disfavored technical shortcut, but rather an integral component of the Rules.[16] Summary judgment motions must be resolved with regard not only for the rights of those asserting claims and defenses to have their positions heard by a factfinder, but also for the rights of persons opposing such claims and defenses to demonstrate, under this Rule and *before* trial, that the claims or defenses have no factual basis.[17] Thus, a party moving for summary judgment forces the opponent to come forward with at least one sworn averment of fact essential to the contested portion(s) of that opponent's claims or defenses, before the time-consuming process of litigation will be permitted to continue.[18]

Legal Test

Summary judgment shall be granted if the summary judgment record shows that: (1) there is no genuine dispute, (2) as to any material fact, and (3) the moving party is entitled to judgment.[19]

- *Genuine Dispute:*[20] A "genuine dispute" exists when a rational factfinder, considering the evidence in the summary judgment record, could find in favor of the nonmoving party.[21] Ergo, a dispute is "genuine" if it has a

---

[15] *See Celotex Corp. v. Catrett*, 477 U.S. 317, 323–24, 106 S. Ct. 2548, 91 L. Ed. 2d 265 (1986).

[16] *See Celotex Corp. v. Catrett*, 477 U.S. 317, 327, 106 S. Ct. 2548, 91 L. Ed. 2d 265 (1986). *See generally Little v. Liquid Air Corp.*, 37 F.3d 1069, 1075 (5th Cir. 1994) (explaining prevailing pre-1986 view that summary judgment was disfavored).

[17] *See Celotex Corp. v. Catrett*, 477 U.S. 317, 327, 106 S. Ct. 2548, 91 L. Ed. 2d 265 (1986). *See generally Murray v. Kindred Nursing Ctrs. W. LLC*, 789 F.3d 20, 24–25 (1st Cir. 2015) ("avoid[s] full-dress trials in unwinnable cases, thereby freeing courts to utilize scarce judicial resources in more beneficial ways").

[18] *See Lujan v. National Wildlife Federation*, 497 U.S. 871, 888–89, 110 S. Ct. 3177, 3188–89, 111 L. Ed. 2d 695 (1990).

[19] *See Beard v. Banks*, 548 U.S. 521, 529, 126 S. Ct. 2572, 165 L. Ed. 2d 697 (2006); *Department of Commerce v. U.S. House of Representatives*, 525 U.S. 316, 327, 119 S. Ct. 765, 142 L. Ed. 2d 797 (1999); *Nebraska v. Wyoming*, 507 U.S. 584, 589, 113 S. Ct. 1689, 123 L. Ed. 2d 317 (1993); *Celotex Corp. v. Catrett*, 477 U.S. 317, 322, 106 S. Ct. 2548, 91 L. Ed. 2d 265 (1986).

[20] The 2010 Amendments replaced the phrase "genuine issue" with "genuine dispute," reasoning that it better reflected the focus of the Rule 56 determination. *See* Rule 56(a) advisory committee note (2010). *See also Rodriguez v. Village Green Realty, Inc.*, 788 F.3d 31, 39 n.9 (2d Cir. 2015).

[21] *See Ricci v. DeStefano*, 557 U.S. 557, 586, 129 S. Ct. 2658, 174 L. Ed. 2d 490 (2009); *Scott v. Harris*, 550 U.S. 372, 380, 127 S. Ct. 1769, 167 L. Ed. 2d 686 (2007); *Anderson v. Liberty Lobby, Inc.*, 477 U.S. 242, 247–252, 106 S. Ct. 2505, 91 L. Ed. 2d 202 (1986); *Matsushita Elec. Indus. Co., Ltd. v. Zenith Radio Corp.*, 475 U.S. 574, 586–587, 106 S. Ct. 1348, 89 L. Ed. 2d 538 (1986).

real basis in the evidentiary record.[22] It is not created by a mere "scintilla" of favorable evidence, or by evidence that is only "colorable" or insufficiently probative.[23] It is also not created by positing a factual scenario that is definitively contradicted by incontestable evidence in the summary judgment record.[24] When a claim or defense is factually improbable, a more persuasive record may be needed to show a genuine dispute.[25] The court will test for a "genuine dispute" through the lens of the quantum of proof applicable to the substantive claim or defense at issue (*e.g.*, if the claim or defense must be established by clear and convincing proof, the court will assess whether the proffered evidence could lead a reasonable factfinder to conclude that such a quantum of evidence is present).[26]

- *Material Fact:* A fact is "material" if it might affect the outcome of the case.[27] Whether a fact qualifies as "material" hinges on the substantive law at issue.[28] Disputes (even if "genuine") over irrelevant or unnecessary facts will not defeat a motion for summary judgment.[29]
- *Appropriate As A Matter Of Law:* Judgment is appropriate "as a matter of law" when the moving party should prevail because the non-moving party has failed to make an adequate showing on an essential element of its case, as to which that party has the burden of proof.[30] Thus, the mere fact that the moving party's summary judg-

---

[22]*See Melton v. Abston*, 841 F.3d 1207, 1219 (11th Cir. 2016).

[23]*See Anderson v. Liberty Lobby, Inc.*, 477 U.S. 242, 247–252, 106 S. Ct. 2505, 91 L. Ed. 2d 202 (1986).

[24]*See Scott v. Harris*, 550 U.S. 372, 380, 127 S. Ct. 1769, 167 L. Ed. 2d 686 (2007) (court should not adopt plaintiff's version of high-speed auto chase that was "blatantly contradicted" by unchallenged videotape) evidence). *Accord Intel Corp. Inv. Policy Comm. v. Sulyma*, 589 U.S. —, 140 S. Ct. 768, 779, 206 L. Ed. 2d 103 (2020). *See also Coble v. City of White House*, 634 F.3d 865, 868–69 (6th Cir. 2011) (the *Scott* principle—no need to credit "visible fiction"—applies not just to conflicting videotape but to all types of objective conflicting evidence).

[25]*See Matsushita Elec. Indus. Co., Ltd. v. Zenith Radio Corp.*, 475 U.S. 574, 587, 106 S. Ct. 1348, 89 L. Ed. 2d 538 (1986).

[26]*See Anderson v. Liberty Lobby, Inc.*, 477 U.S. 242, 254, 106 S. Ct. 2505, 91 L. Ed. 2d 202 (1986).

[27]*See Anderson v. Liberty Lobby, Inc.*, 477 U.S. 242, 248, 106 S. Ct. 2505, 91 L. Ed. 2d 202 (1986). *See also Wright ex rel. Trust Co. of Kansas v. Abbott Laboratories, Inc.*, 259 F.3d 1226, 1231–32 (10th Cir. 2001) ("material" if, under substantive law, fact is "essential to the proper disposition of the claim").

[28]*See Anderson v. Liberty Lobby, Inc.*, 477 U.S. 242, 248, 106 S. Ct. 2505, 91 L. Ed. 2d 202 (1986).

[29]*See Anderson v. Liberty Lobby, Inc.*, 477 U.S. 242, 248, 106 S. Ct. 2505, 91 L. Ed. 2d 202 (1986). *See also Scott v. Harris*, 550 U.S. 372, 380, 127 S. Ct. 1769, 167 L. Ed. 2d 686 (2007).

[30]*See Cleveland v. Policy Management Systems Corp.*, 526 U.S. 795, 804, 119 S. Ct. 1597, 143 L. Ed. 2d 966 (1999); *Celotex Corp. v. Catrett*, 477 U.S. 317, 323, 106 S. Ct. 2548, 91 L. Ed. 2d 265 (1986).

ment record is uncontested,[31] or even unresponded to,[32] is not enough.

Burdens of Proof

The party moving for summary judgment bears the initial burden of showing the absence of a genuine, material dispute and an entitlement to judgment[33]—a *prima facie* obligation that will "put the ball in play."[34] This showing does not obligate the moving party to disprove the opponent's claims or defenses.[35] Instead, this burden may often be discharged simply by pointing out for the court an absence of evidence to support the non-moving party's claims or defenses.[36] Although a "modest threshold,"[37] this burden remains a real one; it requires more than an empty, unparticularized assertion that the opponent has produced no evidence.[38] This *prima facie* burden is heavier when the moving party is the one having the ultimate burden of persuasion at trial, requiring that party to show not only that it can carry its burden of proving all essential elements of its claim or defense,[39] but also that no reasonable jury would disbelieve that evidence.[40] If the movant fails to meet its *prima facie* burden, the summary judgment motion can be dismissed or denied,[41] treated as a mere pleadings challenge

---

[31] *See Edwards v. Aguillard*, 482 U.S. 578, 595, 107 S. Ct. 2573, 96 L. Ed. 2d 510 (1987).

[32] *See Torres-Rosado v. Rotger-Sabat*, 335 F.3d 1, 9 (1st Cir. 2003).

[33] *See Celotex Corp. v. Catrett*, 477 U.S. 317, 323, 106 S. Ct. 2548, 91 L. Ed. 2d 265 (1986).

[34] *See Evans Cabinet Corp. v. Kitchen In'l, Inc.*, 593 F.3d 135, 140 (1st Cir. 2010).

[35] *See Edwards v. Aguillard*, 482 U.S. 578, 595, 107 S. Ct. 2573, 96 L. Ed. 2d 510 (1987); *Celotex Corp. v. Catrett*, 477 U.S. 317, 323, 106 S. Ct. 2548, 91 L. Ed. 2d 265 (1986).

[36] *See Celotex Corp. v. Catrett*, 477 U.S. 317, 106 S. Ct. 2548, 91 L. Ed. 2d 265 (1986). *See also Spierer v. Rossman*, 798 F.3d 502, 508 (7th Cir. 2015) (burden is often just "one of demonstration rather than production).

[37] *See Irobe v. U.S. Dep't of Agric.*, 890 F.3d 371, 377 (1st Cir. 2018).

[38] *See Nick's Garage, Inc. v. Progressive Cas. Ins. Co.*, 875 F.3d 107, 114–17 (2d Cir. 2017). *See also Fret v. Melton Truck Lines, Inc.*, 706 Fed. Appx. 824, 828 (5th Cir. 2017) (mere conclusory statement does not satisfy movant's burden).

[39] *See Barnes v. Sea Hawaii Rafting, LLC*, 889 F.3d 517, 537–38 (9th Cir. 2018); *Hotel 71 Mezz Lender LLC v. Nat'l Ret. Fund*, 778 F.3d 593, 601 (7th Cir. 2015). *See also Ouellette v. Beaupre*, 977 F.3d 127, 135 (1st Cir. 2020) (when defendant seeks summary judgment on affirmative defense, its evidence on issue must be "conclusive").

[40] *See Leone v. Owsley*, 810 F.3d 1149, 1153–54 (10th Cir. 2015); *Rich v. Sec'y, Fla. Dep't of Corr.*, 716 F.3d 525, 530 (11th Cir.2013). *Cf. Hunt v. Cromartie*, 526 U.S. 541, 553, 119 S. Ct. 1545, 143 L. Ed. 2d 731 (1999) ("Summary judgment in favor of the party with the burden of persuasion, however, is inappropriate when the evidence is susceptible of different interpretations or inferences by the trier of fact.").

[41] *See Nick's Garage, Inc. v. Progressive Cas. Ins. Co.*, 875 F.3d 107, 114–17 (2d Cir. 2017) (dismissed as facially deficient).

governed by the forgiving Rule 12(b)(6) standards,[42] or perhaps deferred pending supplementation by the movant.[43]

If the moving party meets its *prima facie* burden, then the burden of going forward shifts to the non-moving party to show, by affidavit or otherwise, that a genuine dispute of material fact remains for the factfinder to resolve.[44] The non-moving party's burden here is not especially onerous, but nor is it trifling.[45] Indeed, a summary judgment motion brings with it "put up or shut up" time for the non-moving party.[46] Once this stage arrives, the non-moving party is not saved by mere allegations or denials,[47] assertions in legal memoranda or argument,[48] speculation,[49] conclusory statements,[50] empty rhetoric,[51] characterizations of disputed facts,[52] suspicion,[53] or simply recounting the generous notice-pleading standards of the federal courts.[54] Nor will an "earnest hope" to discover evidence suffice,[55] or a promise to come forward later with proof,[56] a hope to discredit the opponent's evidence at trial,[57] or the possibility

---

[42] *See Air-Con, Inc. v. Daikin Applied Latin Am., LLC*, 21 F.4th 168, 177 (1st Cir. 2021).

[43] *See* Rule 56(e). *See also Nick's Garage, Inc. v. Progressive Cas. Ins. Co.*, 875 F.3d 107, 116 n.4 (2d Cir. 2017).

[44] *See Celotex Corp. v. Catrett*, 477 U.S. 317, 106 S. Ct. 2548, 91 L. Ed. 2d 265 (1986). *See also Beard v. Banks*, 548 U.S. 521, 529, 126 S. Ct. 2572, 165 L. Ed. 2d 697 (2006).

[45] *See Burton v. Kohn Law Firm*, 934 F.3d 572, 579 (7th Cir. 2019).

[46] *See Harney v. Speedway SuperAmerica, LLC*, 526 F.3d 1099, 1104 (7th Cir. 2008); *Berckeley Inv. Group, Ltd. v. Colkitt*, 455 F.3d 195, 201 (3d Cir. 2006). *See also Kreg Therapeutics, Inc. v. VitalGo, Inc.*, 919 F.3d 405, 416 (7th Cir. 2019) ("Summary judgment is no time for half-hearted advocacy."); *Sommerfield v. City of Chicago*, 863 F.3d 645, 649 (7th Cir. 2017) (parties required "to put their evidentiary cards on the table").

[47] *See California v. Texas*, 593 U.S. __, 141 S. Ct. 2104, 2117, 210 L. Ed. 2d 230 (2021); *First Nat. Bank of Ariz. v. Cities Service Co.*, 391 U.S. 253, 289, 88 S. Ct. 1575, 20 L. Ed. 2d 569 (1968).

[48] *See Acker v. Gen. Motors, L.L.C.*, 853 F.3d 784, 788 (5th Cir. 2017); *Berckeley Inv. Group, Ltd. v. Colkitt*, 455 F.3d 195, 201 (3d Cir. 2006).

[49] *See Canaan Christian Church v. Montgomery Cnty.*, 29 F.4th 182, 192 (4th Cir. 2022); *Moon v. Olivarez*, 26 F.4th 220, 226 (5th Cir. 2022).

[50] *See Reddy v. Buttar*, 38 F.4th 393, 403 (4th Cir. 2022); *Johnson v. Johnson*, 23 F.4th 136, 141 (1st Cir. 2022).

[51] *See Rosaura Bldg. Corp. v. Municipality of Mayaguez*, 778 F.3d 55, 61 (1st Cir. 2015).

[52] *See Alman v. Reed*, 703 F.3d 887, 895–96 (6th Cir. 2013); *Carroll v. Lynch*, 698 F.3d 561, 565 (7th Cir. 2012).

[53] *See Genzer v. James River Ins. Co.*, 934 F.3d 1156, 1160 (10th Cir. 2019).

[54] *See Tucker v. Union of Needletrades, Industrial and Textile Employees*, 407 F.3d 784, 788 (6th Cir. 2005).

[55] *See Balser v. Int'l Union of Elec., Elec., Salaried, Mach. & Furniture Workers (IUE) Local 201*, 661 F.3d 109, 118 (1st Cir. 2011).

[56] *See Cutting Underwater Techs. USA, Inc. v. Eni U.S. Operating Co.*, 671 F.3d 512, 517 (5th Cir. 2012); *Island Software & Computer Serv., Inc. v. Microsoft Corp.*, 413 F.3d 257, 261–62 (2d Cir. 2005).

[57] *See Robbins v. Becker*, 794 F.3d 988, 993 (8th Cir. 2015); *Nunes v. Massachusetts Dep't of Correction*, 766

that a jury could disbelieve the moving party's evidence.[58] While circumstantial evidence may properly be considered,[59] it must lead to more than speculation to ward off summary judgment.[60] In sum, "hope" and "brash conjecture" are not enough.[61] "Evidence, not contentions, avoids summary judgment,"[62] and non-moving parties must arrive brandishing more than "a cardboard sword."[63]

Accordingly, a non-moving party must "go beyond the pleadings,"[64] and show adequately probative evidence creating a triable controversy.[65] A party does not meet this burden by offering evidence which is merely colorable[66] or which implies some metaphysical factual doubt,[67] or by simply theorizing a "plausible scenario" in support of the party's claims, especially when that proffered scenario conflicts with direct, contrary evidence.[68] Rather, the non-moving party must identify specific[69] record evidence and explain how that material defeats summary judgment.[70] (And if the non-moving party has the ultimate burden of persuasion (*e.g.*, as a claimant), it must do so as to each contested, essential element on which it bears that burden.)[71] At bottom, the Rule imposes a "relatively lenient

---

F.3d 136, 142 (1st Cir. 2014).

[58]*See Hinson v. Bias*, 927 F.3d 1103, 1115–16 (11th Cir. 2019).

[59]*See Davenport v. Edward D. Jones & Co., L.P.*, 891 F.3d 162, 167 (5th Cir. 2018); *Castro v. DeVry U., Inc.*, 786 F.3d 559, 564–65 (7th Cir. 2015).

[60]*See Geness v. Cox*, 902 F.3d 344, 357 (3d Cir. 2018).

[61]*See Balser v. Int'l Union of Elec., Elec., Salaried, Mach. & Furniture Workers (IUE) Local 201*, 661 F.3d 109, 118 (1st Cir. 2011).

[62]*See Al-Zubaidy v. TEK Industries, Inc.*, 406 F.3d 1030, 1036 (8th Cir. 2005).

[63]*See Calvi v. Knox County*, 470 F.3d 422, 426 (1st Cir. 2006).

[64]*See Celotex Corp. v. Catrett*, 477 U.S. 317, 324, 106 S. Ct. 2548, 91 L. Ed. 2d 265 (1986). *See also Theriault v. Genesis HealthCare LLC*, 890 F.3d 342, 348 (1st Cir. 2018) (motion's role is "to pierce the pleadings" and probe the proof). *Cf. Rios-Campbell v. U.S. Dep't of Commerce*, 927 F.3d 21, 24–25 (1st Cir. 2019) (rejecting notion of "reverse-conversion," where summary judgment motion is examined under Rule 12(b)(6) pleading-based inquiry).

[65]*See Robbins v. Becker*, 794 F.3d 988, 993 (8th Cir. 2015); *Kenney v. Floyd*, 700 F.3d 604, 608 (1st Cir. 2012).

[66]*See Horror Inc. v. Miller*, 15 F.4th 232, 240–41 (2d Cir. 2021); *Rocky Mountain Prestress, LLC v. Liberty Mut. Fire Ins. Co.*, 960 F.3d 1255, 1259 (10th Cir. 2020).

[67]*See Matsushita Elec. Indus. Co., Ltd. v. Zenith Radio Corp.*, 475 U.S. 574, 586, 106 S.Ct. 1348, 89 L.Ed.2d 538 (1986).

[68]*See Scott v. Harris*, 550 U.S. 372, 380, 127 S. Ct. 1769, 167 L. Ed. 2d 686 (2007); *Swanson v. Leggett & Platt, Inc.*, 154 F.3d 730, 733 (7th Cir. 1998).

[69]*See Lewis v. Casey*, 518 U.S. 343, 358, 116 S. Ct. 2174, 2183, 135 L. Ed. 2d 606 (1996); *Lucas v. S.C. Coastal Council*, 505 U.S. 1003, 1012 n.3, 112 S. Ct. 2886, 2891, 120 L. Ed. 2d 798 (1992).

[70]*See Diaz v. Kaplan Higher Educ., L.L.C.*, 820 F.3d 172, 176 (5th Cir. 2016); *Denn v. CSL Plasma, Inc.*, 816 F.3d 1027, 1032 (8th Cir. 2016).

[71]*See KD v. Douglas Cty. Sch. Dist. No. 001*, 1 F.4th 591, 597 (8th Cir. 2021).

standard" to survive the motion and continue on to trial[72]—if, on the evidence presented, a fair-minded jury could return a verdict for the nonmoving party, summary judgment will be denied.[73]

How the parties may marshal their evidence to meet their respective summary judgment obligations is addressed elsewhere in the Rule.[74]

Ruling on the Motion, Generally

If the moving party fails to carry its initial *prima facie* burden of showing the absence of a genuine, material dispute or its entitlement to judgment, the court will deny the motion.[75] If, however, the moving party carries its initial burden, the court "shall" grant summary judgment for that party if the non-moving party's response fails to show a genuine, material dispute.[76] Conversely, if the non-moving party succeeds in showing a genuine, material dispute (or otherwise demonstrates why the moving party is not entitled to a judgment), the court must deny the motion.[77] In ruling, the court must consider the record evidence as a whole.[78]

"Shall": Court's Discretion in Ruling on the Motion

Controversy has swirled over Rule 56(a)'s use of the verb "shall" and the resulting breadth of discretion district courts enjoy in ruling on summary judgment motions.[79] Certainly, there is no discretion to decide motions on the basis of clearly erroneous findings of fact, an erroneous legal standard, or an

---

[72]*See Amgen Inc. v. Connecticut Ret. Plans & Trust Funds*, 568 U.S. 455, 479–80, 133 S. Ct. 1184, 185 L. Ed. 2d 308 (2013). *See also Ellis v. Fid. Mgmt. Tr. Co.*, 883 F.3d 1, 7 (1st Cir. 2018) ("not a high bar to clear").

[73]*See Anderson v. Liberty Lobby, Inc.*, 477 U.S. 242, 248, 106 S. Ct. 2505, 91 L. Ed. 2d 202 (1986).

[74]*See* Rule 56(c). *See also infra* Authors' Commentary to Rule 56(c) (**"Procedure #1: Supporting Factual Positions"**).

[75]*See Hotel 71 Mezz Lender LLC v. Nat'l Ret. Fund*, 778 F.3d 593, 601–02 (7th Cir. 2015) (if movant fails to carry this burden, court is obligated to deny motion).

[76]*See Beard v. Banks*, 548 U.S. 521, 529, 126 S. Ct. 2572, 165 L. Ed. 2d 697 (2006). *See generally infra* Authors' Commentary to Rule 56(a) (**" 'Shall': Court's Discretion in Ruling on the Motion"**).

[77]*See Ortiz v. Jordan*, 562 U.S. 180, 188, 131 S. Ct. 884, 178 L. Ed. 2d 703 (2011). *See generally* Rule 56 advisory committee note (2007).

[78]*See Lesiv v. Illinois Cent. R.R. Co.*, 39 F.4th 903, 911 (7th Cir. 2022) (as "whole," instead of "asking whether any particular piece of evidence proves the case by itself"); *Dowden, Tr. of Est. of Hugh Dana Huchingson v. Cornerstone Nat'l Ins. Co.*, 11 F.4th 866, 872 (8th Cir. 2021). *See generally infra* Authors' Commentary to Rule 56(c) (**"Procedure #3: Content of Summary Judgment Record"**).

[79]After many decades as "shall", this verb was changed to "should" during the 2007 "restyling" amendments. *See* Rule 56(c) advisory committee note (2007). The 2010 Amendments originally considered changing it again to "must" but decided instead to restore it back to the original "shall" in fear of inadvertently altering the prevailing summary judgment standard. *See* Rule 56(a) advisory committee note (2010).

improper application of the law.[80] Nor is there discretion to grant summary judgment where a genuine, material dispute remains.[81] In all other contexts, the proper measure of a court's discretion is less clear. Some case precedent suggests that very little discretion exists.[82] But other precedent suggests differently.[83] For example, some courts hold that summary judgment may be denied where the factual records are "disturbingly thin" or "contain gaps" that could be resolved by readily obtainable evidence,[84] where the court concludes that a fuller factual development is necessary,[85] or where there is some particular reason to believe that the wiser course would be to proceed to trial.[86] In a non-jury / bench trial, the district judge may have more discretion still.[87]

Doubts and Inferences

In ruling on a motion for summary judgment, the court will never weigh the evidence or choose between competing facts.[88] Instead, the court's role under Rule 56 is narrowly limited to assessing the threshold issue of whether a genuine dispute exists as to material facts requiring a trial.[89] Thus, the evidence of the non-moving party will be believed as true, all evidence will be construed in the light most favorable to the non-moving party, and all doubts and reasonable inferences will be drawn in the non-moving party's favor.[90] Of course, this generous treatment applies only to the non-moving party's *evidence*; as

[80]*See In re Brown*, 342 F.3d 620, 633 (6th Cir. 2003).

[81]*See Ortiz v. Jordan*, 562 U.S. 180, 188, 131 S. Ct. 884, 178 L. Ed. 2d 703 (2011).

[82]*See Beard v. Banks*, 548 U.S. 521, 529, 126 S. Ct. 2572, 165 L. Ed. 2d 697 (2006) (if non-moving party fails to show genuine issue of material fact, "the law requires entry of judgment"); *Celotex Corp. v. Catrett*, 477 U.S. 317, 322, 106 S. Ct. 2548, 91 L. Ed. 2d 265 (1986) ("plain language of Rule 56(b) mandates the entry of summary judgment); *Oviedo v. Washington Metro. Area Transit Auth.*, 948 F.3d 386, 396 n.7 (D.C. Cir. 2020) ("shall" reinforces that courts have "no discretion" where movant meets its burden and nonmovant does not); *Fox v. Transam Leasing, Inc.*, 839 F.3d 1209, 1219 (10th Cir. 2016) (court "required" to grant summary judgment when non-moving party failed to meet evidentiary burden).

[83]*See* Rule 56 advisory committee note (2007) (citing *Kennedy v. Silas Mason Co.*, 334 U.S. 249, 256–57, 68 S. Ct. 1031, 92 L. Ed. 1347 (1948)).

[84]*See Spratt v. Rhode Island Dept. Of Corrections*, 482 F.3d 33, 43 (1st Cir. 2007).

[85]*See Kennedy v. Silas Mason Co.*, 334 U.S. 249, 68 S. Ct. 1031, 92 L. Ed. 1347 (1948).

[86]*See Anderson v. Liberty Lobby, Inc.*, 477 U.S. 242, 255, 106 S. Ct. 2505, 91 L. Ed. 2d 202 (1986).

[87]*See Lyles v. Medtronic Sofamor Danek, USA, Inc.*, 871 F.3d 305, 311 (5th Cir. 2017) (may have greater inference-drawing leeway).

[88]*See Anderson v. Liberty Lobby, Inc.*, 477 U.S. 242, 255, 106 S. Ct. 2505, 91 L. Ed. 2d 202 (1986).

[89]*See Anderson v. Liberty Lobby, Inc.*, 477 U.S. 242, 249, 106 S. Ct. 2505, 91 L. Ed. 2d 202 (1986).

[90]*See Tolan v. Cotton*, 572 U.S. 650, 651 & 656–57, 134 S. Ct. 1861, 188 L. Ed. 2d 895 (2014); *Crawford v. Metropolitan Gov't of Nashville & Davidson County*, 555 U.S. 271, 274 n.1, 129 S. Ct. 846, 172 L. Ed. 2d 650 (2009); *Beard v. Banks*, 548 U.S. 521,

noted above, unsupported contentions or speculation cannot ward off summary judgment.[91] The court also may credit those portions of the moving party's evidence, from disinterested sources, that are uncontradicted and unimpeached.[92]

The boundary dividing reasonable inferences from impermissible speculation is "often thin," though certainly consequential.[93] "Reasonable" inferences are those fairly drawn from all the facts then before the court, after sifting through the array of possible inferences the facts could support. "Reasonable" inferences need not be necessarily more probable or likely than other inferences that might tilt in the moving party's favor. Instead, so long as more than one reasonable inference can be drawn, and one such inference creates a genuine dispute of material fact, the trier of fact is entitled to decide which inference to believe and summary judgment on that ground is not appropriate.[94]

Conversely, an inference is an unreasonable one if it is strained,[95] supported only by acrimonious invective[96] or speculation and conjecture,[97] posits vacantly that "something must have existed,"[98] or rests only on barebones and conclusory assertions.[99]

530–31, 126 S. Ct. 2572, 165 L. Ed. 2d 697 (2006); *Reeves v. Sanderson Plumbing Prods., Inc.*, 530 U.S. 133, 150–51, 120 S. Ct. 2097, 147 L. Ed. 2d 105 (2000); *Hunt v. Cromartie*, 526 U.S. 541, 550–55, 119 S. Ct. 1545, 143 L. Ed. 2d 731 (1999); *Eastman Kodak Co. v. Image Technical Services, Inc.*, 504 U.S. 451, 456, 112 S. Ct. 2072, 119 L. Ed. 2d 265 (1992); *Anderson v. Liberty Lobby, Inc.*, 477 U.S. 242, 255, 106 S. Ct. 2505, 91 L. Ed. 2d 202 (1986); *Adickes v. S. H. Kress & Co.*, 398 U.S. 144, 157–59, 90 S. Ct. 1598, 26 L. Ed. 2d 142 (1970).

[91] *See Prosper v. Martin*, 989 F.3d 1242, 1252 (11th Cir. 2021).

[92] *See Reeves v. Sanderson Plumbing Prods., Inc.*, 530 U.S. 133, 151, 120 S. Ct. 2097, 147 L. Ed. 2d 105 (2000). *Cf. Little v. Liquid Air Corp.*, 37 F.3d 1069, 1075 (5th Cir. 1994) (resolving doubts in favor of non-moving party is triggered only when parties have submitted evidence of contradictory facts).

[93] *See Halsey v. Pfeiffer*, 750 F.3d 273, 287 (3d Cir. 2014) (cleaned up).

[94] *See Hunt v. Cromartie*, 526 U.S. 541, 552–53, 119 S. Ct. 1545, 143 L. Ed. 2d 731 (1999). *Cf. Dukes v. Deaton*, 852 F.3d 1035, 1042 (11th Cir. 2017) (inferences "must be plausible" to be credited).

[95] *See Fox v. Amazon.com, Inc.*, 930 F.3d 415 (6th Cir. 2019).

[96] *See Alston v. Int'l Ass'n of Firefighters, Loc. 950*, 998 F.3d 11, 24 (1st Cir. 2021).

[97] *See GeoMetWatch Corp. v. Behunin*, 38 F.4th 1183, 1200–01 (10th Cir. 2022); *Lavite v. Dunstan*, 932 F.3d 1020, 1029 (7th Cir. 2019).

[98] *See SportFuel, Inc. v. PepsiCo, Inc.*, 932 F.3d 589, 601 (7th Cir. 2019) ("[T]he time to pursue this idea was during discovery.").

[99] *See Fed. Trade Commn. v. Moses*, 913 F.3d 297, 305 (2d Cir. 2019) (conclusory averments/denials are "not evidence"); *Mancini v. City of Providence by and through Lombardi*, 909 F.3d 32, 44 (1st Cir. 2018) ("hornbook law" that conclusory allegations cannot avoid summary judgment). *See generally Daugherty v. Page*, 906 F.3d 606, 611 (7th Cir. 2018) ("Summary judgment is not a time to be coy: '[c]onclusory statements not grounded in specific facts' are not enough.").

Credibility Questions

The proper inquiry in a summary judgment motion is not which side has the most evidence, but merely whether enough evidence favors the nonmoving party to support a decision for that party.[100] For this reason, courts will not decide the credibility of witnesses or other evidence in ruling on a motion for summary judgment.[101] Evaluating credibility, weighing evidence, and drawing factual inferences are all functions reserved for the jury.[102] However, simply lobbing broad, conclusory attacks on a witness's credibility is not enough to defeat summary judgment.[103]

State of Mind Questions

Summary judgment is not automatically foreclosed merely because a person's state of mind (such as motive, knowledge, intent, good faith or bad faith, malice, fraud, conspiracy, or consent) is at issue.[104] But such cases will seldom lend themselves to a summary disposition because questions of credibility will ordinarily abound.[105] Thus, summary judgment is used "sparingly" and "seldom granted" in cases involving peculiarly intensive state of mind questions such as employment discrimination actions,[106] antitrust cases,[107] racial gerry-

---

[100]*See Ziccarelli v. Dart*, 35 F.4th 1079, 1083 (7th Cir. 2022); *Sears v. Roberts*, 922 F.3d 1199, 1207 (11th Cir. 2019).

[101]*See Tolan v. Cotton*, 572 U.S. 650, 656, 134 S. Ct. 1861, 188 L. Ed. 2d 895 (2014); *Anderson v. Liberty Lobby, Inc.*, 477 U.S. 242, 255, 106 S. Ct. 2505, 91 L. Ed. 2d 202 (1986).

[102]*See Reeves v. Sanderson Plumbing Prods., Inc.*, 530 U.S. 133, 150–51, 120 S. Ct. 2097, 147 L. Ed. 2d 105 (2000); *Anderson v. Liberty Lobby, Inc.*, 477 U.S. 242, 255, 106 S. Ct. 2505, 91 L. Ed. 2d 202 (1986).

[103]*See Deville v. Marcantel*, 567 F.3d 156, 165 (5th Cir. 2009); *Levesque v. Doocy*, 560 F.3d 82, 87 (1st Cir. 2009); *Island Software and Computer Service, Inc. v. Microsoft Corp.*, 413 F.3d 257, 261–62 (2d Cir. 2005).

[104]*See United States ex rel. Gugenheim v. Meridian Senior Living, LLC*, 36 F.4th 173, 178–79 (4th Cir. 2022) (scienter under False Claims Act); *Tolbert v. Smith*, 790 F.3d 427, 435 (2d Cir. 2015) (employment discrimination); *In re Online DVD-Rental Antitrust Litig.*, 779 F.3d 914, 921 (9th Cir. 2015) (antitrust). *See also Little v. Liquid Air Corp.*, 37 F.3d 1069, 1075 n.14 (5th Cir. 1994) (renouncing prior view that certain types of cases are inappropriate for Rule 56).

[105]*See Hutchinson v. Proxmire*, 443 U.S. 111, 99 S. Ct. 2675, 61 L. Ed. 2d 411 (1979). *See also Taite v. Bridgewater State Univ., Bd. of Trustees*, 999 F.3d 86, 93 (1st Cir. 2021) ("proceed with caution and restraint" when pretext, motive, and intent involved); *Graham v. Long Island R.R.*, 230 F.3d 34, 38 (2d Cir. 2000) (used "sparingly" where intent and state of mind are implicated).

[106]*See Lounds v. Lincare, Inc.*, 812 F.3d 1208, 1220–21 (10th Cir. 2015) (no summary judgment "mini-trials" into a defendant's "state of mind"); *Tolbert v. Smith*, 790 F.3d 427, 434 (2d Cir. 2015) ("caution" needed in such cases); *Peterson v. Scott County*, 406 F.3d 515, 521 (8th Cir. 2005) ("seldom" granted in such cases).

[107]*See Smith Wholesale Co., Inc. v. R.J. Reynolds Tobacco Co.*, 477 F.3d 854, 862 (6th Cir. 2007) (disfavored, but not precluded, in antitrust litigation); *Ashley Creek Phosphate Co. v. Chevron USA, Inc.*, 315 F.3d 1245, 1253 (10th Cir. 2003) ("sparingly" in

mandering claims,[108] and certain intellectual property disputes.[109]

Predominantly Legal Disputes

Summary judgment is often appropriate in cases where the disputes are primarily legal, rather than factual in nature.[110]

Stipulated Facts

If the parties stipulate to the facts, obviously no genuine dispute as to material facts then exists for a factfinder to resolve.[111] Nevertheless, the summary judgment standard remains the same. The court must draw inferences from the stipulated facts, and resolve those inferences in favor of the non-moving party.[112]

Cross-Motions

Cross-motions for summary judgment are also examined under the usual Rule 56 standards.[113] Each cross-motion must be evaluated on its own merits,[114] with the court viewing all facts and reasonable inferences in the light most favorable to

---

antitrust cases). *But cf. In re Wholesale Grocery Prods. Antitrust Litig.*, 752 F.3d 728, 732–33 & 733 n.4 (8th Cir. 2014) (neither favored nor disfavored in antitrust cases, but governed by same standard as all other cases); *In re Publ'n Paper Antitrust Litig.*, 690 F.3d 51, 61 (2d Cir. 2012) (favored in antitrust cases, serving a "vital function" by avoiding a chilling effect on pro-competitive market forces).

[108] *See Hunt v. Cromartie*, 526 U.S. 541, 553 n.9, 119 S. Ct. 1545, 143 L. Ed. 2d 731 (1999).

[109] *See Zobmondo Entm't, LLC v. Falls Media, LLC*, 602 F.3d 1108, 1113 (9th Cir. 2010) ("disfavored in the trademark arena"); *Latimer v. Roaring Toyz, Inc.*, 601 F.3d 1224, 1232 (11th Cir. 2010) ("historically viewed . . . as inappropriate in the copyright infringement context").

[110] *See, e.g., In re Energy Future Holdings Corp.*, 990 F.3d 728, 737 (3d Cir. 2021) (interpretation of unambiguous contracts); *Evans v. Fed. Bureau of Prisons*, 951 F.3d 578, 584 (D.C. Cir. 2020) (most FOIA cases); *Cooper Indus., Ltd. v. Nat'l Union Fire Ins. Co.*, 876 F.3d 119, 128 (5th Cir. 2017) (insurance policy interpretation); *Thomas v. Metro. Life Ins. Co.*, 631 F.3d 1153, 1160 (10th Cir. 2011) (statutory interpretation).

[111] *See Cincom Sys., Inc. v. Novelis Corp.*, 581 F.3d 431, 435 (6th Cir. 2009); *Centennial Ins. Co. v. Ryder Truck Rental, Inc.*, 149 F.3d 378, 382 (5th Cir.1998).

[112] *See Leebaert v. Harrington*, 332 F.3d 134, 138–39 (2d Cir. 2003); *Luden's Inc. v. Local Union No. 6 of Bakery, Confectionery and Tobacco Workers' Intern. Union of America*, 28 F.3d 347, 353 (3d Cir. 1994). *But see United Paperworkers Intern. Union Local 14, AFL-CIO-CLC v. International Paper Co.*, 64 F.3d 28, 31 (1st Cir. 1995) (summary judgment standard may be modified where dispute arrives as "case stated"; in that instance, trial judge is free to engage in certain factfinding, including drawing of inferences). *But see also U.S. Fidelity and Guar. Co. v. Planters Bank & Trust Co.*, 77 F.3d 863, 866 (5th Cir. 1996) (recognizing a "hint of a distinction" between standard applied in jury cases and arguably more lenient standard in certain non-jury cases).

[113] *See In re Fin. Oversight & Mgmt. Bd. for Puerto Rico*, 37 F.4th 746, 759 (1st Cir. 2022); *Reform Am. v. City of Detroit*, 37 F.4th 1138, 1147 (6th Cir. 2022).

[114] *See Reform Am. v. City of Detroit*, 37 F.4th 1138, 1147 (6th Cir. 2022); *B-21 Wines, Inc. v. Bauer*, 36 F.4th 214, 221 (4th Cir. 2022).

the nonmoving party.[115] Thus, the mere fact that cross-motions have been filed does not, by itself, necessarily justify the entry of a summary judgment,[116] nor will the denial of one cross-motion compel the grant of the other cross-motion.[117]

Partial Motions

Motions may seek summary judgment as to the entire claim or defense, or just parts of a claim or defense.[118]

Trial Court's Duty to Explain

Rule 56(a) directs trial judges to set forth, "on the record," the reasons for their disposition of summary judgment motions, although the particular form and content of that explanation is left to the court's discretion.[119] This requirement facilitates both subsequent trial-level proceedings and appeals.[120] But trial courts are ordinarily not expected to pen "elaborate essays using talismanic phrases," unless doing so is necessary to dispel appellate concerns that material facts were overlooked or a wrong legal standard was applied.[121]

Effect of Ruling—"Law Of The Case"

The "law of the case" doctrine holds that when a court decides upon a rule of law, that decision should generally control the same issues throughout the subsequent stages in the same case.[122] It is based on the sound, salutary policy of judicial finality—that all litigation should come to an end.[123] This is a prudential doctrine; it guides and influences the court's exercise of discretion, but it does not limit the court's jurisdiction or power.[124] It may not apply where intervening controlling authority warrants a revisiting of an earlier

[115] *See CANarchy Craft Brewery Collective, L.L.C. v. Texas Alcoholic Beverage Comm'n*, 37 F.4th 1069, 1074 (5th Cir. 2022); *Shea v. Millett*, 36 F.4th 1, 6 (1st Cir. 2022).

[116] *See Reform Am. v. City of Detroit*, 37 F.4th 1138, 1147 (6th Cir. 2022); *Marcatante v. City of Chicago*, 657 F.3d 433, 438–39 (7th Cir. 2011).

[117] *See Christian Heritage Academy v. Oklahoma Secondary School Activities Ass'n*, 483 F.3d 1025, 1030 (10th Cir. 2007).

[118] *See Ford v. Marion Cty. Sheriff's Office*, 942 F.3d 839, 849 (7th Cir. 2019); *Lehr v. City of Sacramento*, 624 F. Supp. 2d 1218, 1222–23 (E.D.Cal. 2009). *See generally* Rule 56(a) advisory committee note (2010) (2010 amendments "make clear" that motions may seek summary judgment as to entire claim or defense, or just part).

[119] *See* Rule 56(a) advisory committee note (2010). *See also D'Onofrio v. Vacation Publications, Inc.*, 888 F.3d 197, 210 n.13 (5th Cir. 2018).

[120] *See* Rule 56(a) advisory committee note (2010).

[121] *See Jackson v. Federal Exp.*, 766 F.3d 189, 196–97 (2d Cir. 2014).

[122] *See Arizona v. California*, 460 U.S. 605, 618, 103 S. Ct. 1382, 75 L. Ed. 2d 318 (1983).

[123] *See Lyons v. Fisher*, 888 F.2d 1071, 1074 (5th Cir. 1989). *See also Gindes v. U.S.*, 740 F.2d 947, 949 (Fed. Cir. 1984) (doctrine rests upon important public policy litigants do not enjoy right to cover same ground twice, hoping that passage of time or changes in court's composition will alter outcome).

[124] *See Pepper v. United States*, 562 U.S. 476, 506–07, 131 S. Ct. 1229, 1250–51, 179 L. Ed. 2d 196 (2011); *Arizona v. California*, 460 U.S. 605, 618, 103 S. Ct. 1382, 75 L. Ed. 2d 318

decision.[125] Because *denials* of summary judgment generally do nothing more than acknowledge that a genuine issue of material fact remains for trial, such denials are typically not accorded any preclusive effect nor do they become "law of the case."[126] The same is true for other interlocutory rulings that preceded the entry of summary judgment.[127]

Constitutionality of Summary Judgment

Only once has the Supreme Court examined the constitutionality of summary judgment, on a claim that the procedure deprives defeated claimants of their Seventh Amendment rights to a trial by jury. The Court rejected this argument, reasoning that any time summary judgment is granted, it is only because there *is* no triable issue for the jury.[128] No lower federal court has ever declared summary judgment unconstitutional.

Appealability

The general rule is that an order granting summary judgment is appealable when it constitutes the "final order" in the case[129] or, if non-final (such as partial summary judgments), if the district court permits a proper interlocutory appeal under Rule 54(b)[130] or 28 U.S.C. § 1292(b),[131] or perhaps if all remaining claims in the lawsuit are thereafter dismissed *with*

(1983).

[125] *See Marable v. Nitchman*, 511 F.3d 924, 930 n.11 (9th Cir. 2007).

[126] *See Switzerland Cheese Ass'n, Inc. v. E. Horne's Market, Inc.*, 385 U.S. 23, 25, 87 S. Ct. 193, 17 L. Ed. 2d 23 (1966); *Cangemi v. United States*, 13 F.4th 115, 140 (2d Cir. 2021). *But see Federal Ins. Co. v. Scarsella Bros., Inc.*, 931 F.2d 599, 601 (9th Cir. 1991) (doctrine not amenable to broad generalizations, and may apply to summary judgment denials when trial court intends to resolve definitively legal questions in issue).

[127] *See Graves v. Lioi*, 930 F.3d 307, 318 (4th Cir. 2019) (inconsistent Rule 12(b)(6) dismissal rulings); *Gander Mountain Co. v. Cabela's, Inc.*, 540 F.3d 827, 830–31 (8th Cir. 2008) (arguably inconsistent discovery rulings).

[128] *See Fidelity & Deposit Co. v. U.S.*, 187 U.S. 315, 319–21, 23 S. Ct. 120, 47 L. Ed. 194 (1902). *See also Jefferson v. Sewon Am., Inc.*, 891 F.3d 911, 919–20 (11th Cir. 2018) (constitutionality attack is "[n]onsense"); *J.R. Simplot v. Chevron Pipeline Co.*, 563 F.3d 1102, 1117 (10th Cir. 2009) (declaring Seventh Amendment question "well-settled"). *But see* Suja A. Thomas, *Why Summary Judgment is Unconstitutional*, 93 VA. L. REV. 139 (2007) (arguing why Rule 56 violates the Seventh Amendment).

[129] *See Fraternal Order of Police, Lodge 1 v. City of Camden*, 842 F.3d 231, 237 (3d Cir. 2016); *Santaella v. Metropolitan Life Ins. Co.*, 123 F.3d 456, 461 (7th Cir. 1997). *Cf. Liberty Mut. Ins. Co. v. Wetzel*, 424 U.S. 737, 96 S. Ct. 1202, 47 L. Ed. 2d 435 (1976) (grant of partial summary judgment not an appealable final order); *Underwood v. Bank of Am. Corp.*, 996 F.3d 1038, 1049 n.6 (10th Cir. 2021) (not appealable final order if counterclaim remains, unless effect of ruling moots counterclaims).

[130] *See Frye v. CSX Transp., Inc.*, 933 F.3d 591, 601 (6th Cir. 2019); *Pakootas v. Teck Cominco Metals, Ltd.*, 905 F.3d 565, 576 (9th Cir. 2018).

[131] *See Swinomish Indian Tribal Cmty. v. BNSF Ry. Co.*, 951 F.3d 1142, 1151 (9th Cir. 2020); *Ermini v. Scott*, 937 F.3d 1329, 1339 n.5 (11th Cir. 2019).

prejudice.[132]

The appealability of an order denying summary judgment is less simple. If the denial is based on the presence of genuinely disputed facts, that order decides merely that the case must continue on; it neither finally settles nor even tentatively resolves anything else about the merits.[133] For this reason, it is ordinarily not immediately appealable[134] (unless the effect of the denial, in the peculiar circumstances of that case, results in entry of a final judgment).[135] Several courts hold that, once a trial on the merits occurs, the denial order can never be reviewed on appeal, because the "prediction" that denial represented has been rendered moot by the actual introduction of evidence at trial.[136] Other courts recognize an exception to this general prohibition, and permit a summary judgment denial to be reviewed on appeal if the denial was based on the interpretation of a pure question of law.[137] Other courts narrow that exception still further, permitting review when the denial was based on a pure question of law and the judge was the fact-finder (non-jury, bench trial).[138] Other courts hold that, although such review is generally denied, an appeal might be tolerated were "extraordinary circumstances" to exist.[139] Still other courts permit appellate review of a denial of summary judgment when a companion ruling granting summary judgment is simultaneously appealed.[140] Mindful of the variety of these approaches and the uncertainty they introduce, prudent practitioners

[132]*See Gaddis v. DeMattei*, 30 F.4th 625, 630 (7th Cir. 2022); *Noga v. Fulton Fin. Corp. Emp. Benefit Plan*, 19 F.4th 264, 271 (3d Cir. 2021). *See also SodexoMAGIC, LLC v. Drexel Univ.*, 24 F.4th 183, 203 (3d Cir. 2022) (partial summary judgment and partial dismissal to proceed in arbitration).

[133]*See Switzerland Cheese Ass'n, Inc. v. E. Horne's Market, Inc.*, 385 U.S. 23, 25, 87 S. Ct. 193, 17 L. Ed. 2d 23 (1966).

[134]*See Plumhoff v. Rickard*, 572 U.S. 765, 771, 134 S. Ct. 2012, 188 L. Ed. 2d 1056 (2014); *Ortiz v. Jordan*, 562 U.S. 180, 188, 131 S. Ct. 884, 178 L. Ed. 2d 703 (2011).

[135]*See Henderson v. Glanz*, 813 F.3d 938, 947 (10th Cir. 2015); *Karuk Tribe of Cal. v. U.S. Forest Serv.*, 640 F.3d 979, 987 (9th Cir. 2011).

[136]*See Kreg Therapeutics, Inc. v. VitalGo, Inc.*, 919 F.3d 405, 416 (7th Cir. 2019); *New York Marine & General Ins. Co. v. Continental Cement Co., LLC*, 761 F.3d 830, 838 (8th Cir. 2014). *Cf. Travelers Cas. & Sur. Co. v. Ins. Co. of N. America*, 609 F.3d 143, 167 n.32 (3d Cir. 2010) (court need not decide whether case presented "one of those rare instances" which permitted review of summary judgment denial following merits trial).

[137]*See SRI Intl., Inc. v. Cisco Sys., Inc.*, 930 F.3d 1295, 1302 n.5 (Fed. Cir. 2019). *See generally New York Marine & General Ins. Co. v. Continental Cement Co., LLC*, 761 F.3d 830, 838-39 (8th Cir. 2014) (surveying divided case law; permitting appeal).

[138]*See Becker v. Tidewater, Inc.*, 586 F.3d 358, 365 n.4 (5th Cir. 2009).

[139]*See Pahuta v. Massey-Ferguson, Inc.*, 170 F.3d 125, 132 (2d Cir. 1999). *See also Vanderklok v. United States*, 868 F.3d 189, 196 (3d Cir. 2017) (review may be permitted under collateral order doctrine).

[140]*See McKeen-Chaplin v. Provident Sav. Bank, FSB*, 862 F.3d 847, 850 (9th Cir. 2017); *Quik Payday, Inc. v. Stork*, 549 F.3d 1302, 1306 n.1 (10th Cir. 2008). *See also Stilwell v. Am. Gen. Life Ins. Co.*, 555 F.3d 572,

should always renew summary judgment motions with a Rule 50 motion for judgment as a matter of law at the close of the evidence (and, if rejected, again after the trial has concluded).[141]

- *Exceptions:* Exceptions exist. For example, if the motion asserts questions of immunity from suit, a denial of summary judgment may be immediately appealable.[142]

RULE 56(b) — TIME TO FILE A MOTION

CORE CONCEPT

Parties may move for summary judgment at any time until 30 days after the close of all discovery, absent a local rule or court order directing otherwise. The time for responding to motions is left undefined, to be set by local rule or court order.

APPLICATIONS

Time for Filing

A national timing procedure governs summary judgment motions, permitting their filing at any time "until 30 days after the close of discovery."[143] This procedure is only a "default" provision, however, and can be modified freely by local rule or court order.[144] Indeed, because a time deadline specially tailored to the needs of the particular case will often "work better," this national default timeframe is likely to be replaced "in most cases" by case-specific scheduling orders, periods proposed by the parties, case staging regimes, or local rules.[145] Under a former version of the Rule, a claimant had to wait 20-days after commencing the action before becoming eligible to file for summary judgment; that restriction, deemed "outmoded" by the

---

576 (7th Cir. 2009) (denial of one cross-motion may be appealed along with grant of other cross-motion).

[141]*See HOK Sport, Inc. v. FC Des Moines, L.C.*, 495 F.3d 927, 942 (8th Cir. 2007); *Chemetall GMBH v. ZR Energy, Inc.*, 320 F.3d 714, 718–19 (7th Cir. 2003).

[142]*See Plumhoff v. Rickard*, 572 U.S. 765, 771–72, 134 S. Ct. 2012, 188 L. Ed. 2d 1056 (2014); *Ortiz v. Jordan*, 562 U.S. 180, 188, 131 S. Ct. 884, 178 L. Ed. 2d 703 (2011). *See also Black v. Dixie Consumer Prod. LLC*, 835 F.3d 579, 584 (6th Cir. 2016) (defense in the nature of an immunity).

[143]*See* Rule 56(b). *See also Colclough v. Gwinnett Pub. Sch.*, 734 Fed. Appx. 660, 662 (11th Cir. 2018) (period encompasses any discovery extension court orders); *Savage v. Azar*, 317 F. Supp. 3d 438, 440 (D.D.C. 2018) (denying out-of-time motion). *Note:* the syntax of this Rule includes the ambiguous use of the word "until". Because "until" could connote the last of the permitted days, or the first of the forbidden days, this word choice is not ideal. When read in conjunction with the 2009 amendments to Rule 6(a)(1)(C) and Rule 6(a)(4), however, the most reasonable reading seems to be that this "until" period runs to the close of the 30th day after the end of discovery.

[144]*See Cioni v. Globe Specialty Metals, Inc.*, 617 Fed.Appx. 42, 45 n.2 (3d Cir. 2015). *See generally Hoffman v. Tonnemacher*, 593 F.3d 908, 911 (9th Cir. 2010) (case-specific, tailored scheduling orders "are likely to work better than default rules").

[145]*See* Rule 56(c)(1) advisory committee notes (2009). *See also Moss v. Wyeth, Inc.*, 872 F. Supp. 2d 154, 160 (D.Conn. 2012) (motion timely if comports with scheduling order).

drafters, was deleted in 2009.[146] In current practice, motions for summary judgment are timely even if filed before an answer or dismissal motion.[147] Less clear is whether such pre-answer motions serve to toll a defending party's responsive pleading obligations.[148]

Quick Motions (Filed Before / During Discovery)

Early summary judgment motions (those filed at the time the lawsuit is commenced or otherwise before, or during, discovery) are clearly permitted, unless foreclosed by local rules or scheduling orders.[149] Such early filings, though consistent with some prior case law,[150] seem at odds with the Supreme Court's admonition in 1986 that summary judgment should be granted only after the nonmoving party has had an "adequate time for discovery."[151] Recent opinions continue to incant this assurance.[152] The drafters of the 2009 and 2010 amendments to the Rule addressed this issue obliquely, noting that motions filed at commencement, though permitted, may prove premature[153] and, if so, courts may readily extend the response time.[154] Seeking a deferral of a ruling pending further discovery always remains an option for the nonmoving party.[155] In any event, in practice, pre-discovery summary judgment motions are the

---

146*See* Rule 56(c)(1) advisory committee notes (2009).

147*See infra* Authors' Commentary to Rule 56(a) (**"Quick Motions (Filed Before / During Discovery)"**).

148*See supra* Authors' Commentary to Rule 12(a) (**"Exceptions to Tolling Effect Rule**—*Summary Judgment Motions*").

149*See MDK Sociedad De Responsabilidad Limitada v. Proplant Inc.*, 25 F.4th 360, 366 (5th Cir. 2022); *Crawford v. Tilley*, 15 F.4th 752, 764 n.3 (6th Cir. 2021); *Smith v. OSF HealthCare Sys.*, 933 F.3d 859, 864 (7th Cir. 2019). *See also Estate of Todashev by Shibly v. United States*, 815 Fed. Appx. 446, 450 (11th Cir. 2020) (no "blanket prohibition" on pre-discovery motions); *Foley v. Wells Fargo Bank, N.A.*, 772 F.3d 63, 72 (1st Cir. 2014) (waiting until discovery ends sometimes is "an asinine exercise"). *See generally* Rule 56(b) advisory committee note (2010).

150*See, e.g., Alholm v. American Steamship Co.*, 144 F.3d 1172, 1177 (8th Cir. 1998) (Rule 56 does not require that discovery be closed before motion can be heard); *Brill v. Lante Corp.*, 119 F.3d 1266, 1275 (7th Cir. 1997) ("a party can file a motion for summary judgment at any time, indeed, even before discovery has begun").

151*Celotex Corp. v. Catrett*, 477 U.S. 317, 322, 106 S. Ct. 2548, 91 L. Ed. 2d 265 (1986).

152*See, e.g., Bailey v. KS Mgmt. Servs., L.L.C.*, 35 F.4th 397, 401 (5th Cir. 2022) (summary judgment appropriate only after "full opportunity to conduct discovery"); *Goodman v. Diggs*, 986 F.3d 493, 500 (4th Cir. 2021) (summary judgment often vacated when granted before adequate discovery, because nonmovant is otherwise forced into fencing match without sword or mask).

153*See* Rule 56(b) advisory committee note (2010).

154*See* Former Rule 56(c)(1) advisory committee note (2009).

155*See* Rule 56(d). *See also Jeffries v. Barr*, 965 F.3d 843, 848 (D.C. Cir. 2020) (deferral requests can abate surprise and "death knell" of early-filed motions).

exception, not the norm.[156]

Multiple Motions

Consistent with this timing liberality,[157] a district court may permit a second motion for summary judgment,[158] especially where there has been an intervening change in the controlling law, where new evidence has become available or the factual record has otherwise expanded through discovery, or where a clear need arises to correct a manifest injustice.[159]

Time for Responding

The Rules set no national time period for responding to summary judgment motions.[160] Following longstanding practice, this response period is instead addressed by local rule in the applicable District or by chambers order.[161]

RULE 56(c) — PROCEDURES

CORE CONCEPT

Several summary judgment procedures are nationally defined: the manner for factually supporting motions and oppositions; the method for objecting to improper support for motions or oppositions; the content of the summary judgment record; and the requirements for supporting or opposing affidavits and declarations. Other summary judgment procedures are imposed by local rule or case law.

---

[156]*See Jeffries v. Barr*, 965 F.3d 843, 848 (D.C. Cir. 2020) (motions "typically" follow at least some discovery); *Haynes v. D.C. Water & Sewer Auth.*, 924 F.3d 519, 530 (D.C. Cir. 2019) (usually premature without full opportunity to conduct discovery); *Assn. of Car Wash Owners Inc. v. City of New York*, 911 F.3d 74, 83 (2d Cir. 2018) (should be granted "[o]nly in the rarest of cases").

[157]*See Cioni v. Globe Specialty Metals, Inc.*, 618 Fed. Appx. 42, 45 n.2 (3d Cir. 2015).

[158]*See Hoffman v. Tonnemacher*, 593 F.3d 908, 910–12 (9th Cir. 2010); *Narducci v. Moore*, 572 F.3d 313, 324 (7th Cir.2009).

[159]*See Brown v. City of Syracuse*, 673 F.3d 141, 147 n.2 (2d Cir. 2012) (where factual record has expanded); *Enlow v. Tishomingo County, Miss.*, 962 F.2d 501, 506 (5th Cir. 1992) (when new facts were presented by amended pleading); *Williamsburg Wax Museum, Inc. v. Historic Figures, Inc.*, 810 F.2d 243, 251 (D.C. Cir. 1987) (premised upon expanded record); *Geneva Int'l Corp. v. Petrof, Spol, S.R.O.*, 608 F. Supp. 2d 993, 997–98 (N.D.Ill. 2009) (upon intervening change in controlling law, new evidence or expanded factual record, or need to correct a clear error or prevent manifest injustice).

[160]In 2009, a national 21-day response period had been adopted, but it was rescinded in 2010. *See* Former Rule 56(c)(1)(B) (amended 2009; deleted 2010).

[161]*See* Rule 56(b) advisory committee note (2010) ("Scheduling orders or other pretrial orders can regulate timing to fit the needs of the case."). Historically, many courts, relying on the Rule's former language, had required at least a 10-day response period, although that requirement was subject to being lifted if a shortened period would cause no prejudice. *See* Former Rule 56(c) (rescinded 2007) ("The motion shall be served at least 10 days before the time fixed for the hearing."). *See also Celestine v. Petroleos de Venezuella SA*, 266 F.3d 343, 350 (5th Cir. 2001) (describing preamendment practice).

APPLICATIONS

2010 Amendments — Amended Rule 56(c)

The current content of Rule 56(c) includes affidavit requirements (formerly in Rule 56(e)(1)), a recasting of the opposition requirements (formerly in Rule 56(e)(2) and as described in the Supreme Court's *Celotex* decision), and two new provisions addressing objections to improper factual support and the content of the summary judgment record. Formerly, Rule 56(c) had also contained the legal standard for granting summary judgment (now repositioned to Rule 56(a)).

Procedure #1: Supporting Factual Positions

The burdens on parties moving for, and resisting, summary judgment are discussed above.[162] The procedure begins when the moving parties "identify" each claim, defense, or part thereof on which they seek summary judgment.[163] They thus isolate the battleground for the summary judgment contest (and, consequently, the nonmoving parties generally need not offer contesting evidence on issues and points not raised by the moving papers).[164] Once the contours of the contest are set, parties moving for, or resisting, summary judgment may factually support their positions in either of two ways:

- *Option A:* They may cite the court to the summary judgment record (which may contain depositions, documents, electronically stored information, affidavits or declarations, stipulations, admissions, interrogatory answers, and other materials). In doing so, their citations must be specific and to "particular parts" of the record materials;[165] *or*
- *Option B:* They may show either (a) that the materials cited by their opponent do not establish the absence or presence of a genuine dispute or (b) that the opponent cannot produce admissible evidence to support a claimed fact.[166] Note, however, that where the party moving for summary judgment is the one bearing the ultimate burden of proof (*e.g.*, the claimant), the road to summary

[162] *See supra* Authors' Commentary to Rule 56(a) (**"Legal Test"** and **"Burdens of Proof"**).

[163] *See* Rule 56(a).

[164] *See U.S. v. King-Vassel*, 728 F.3d 707, 711–12 (7th Cir. 2013). *But cf. infra* Authors' Commentary to Rule 56(f)(2) (**"Summary Judgment on Unrequested Grounds"**).

[165] *See* Rule 56(c)(1)(A). *See also Clapper v. Amnesty Int'l USA*, 568 U.S. 398, 411–12, 133 S. Ct. 1138, 185 L. Ed. 2d 264 (2013); *Erickson v. Nationstar Mortg., LLC*, 31 F.4th 1044, 1048 (8th Cir. 2022); *In re StockX Customer Data Sec. Breach Litig.*, 19 F.4th 873, 882 (6th Cir. 2021). *See generally* Rule 56(c)(1)(A) advisory committee note (2010). *But cf. Beenick v. LeFebvre*, 684 Fed. Appx. 200, 206 (3d Cir. 2017) (failure to cite to specific parts overlooked where source was before the court and not voluminous).

[166] *See* Rule 56(c)(1)(B). *See also In re Louisiana Crawfish Producers*, 852 F.3d 456, 462 (5th Cir. 2017). *See generally* Rule 56(c)(1)(A) advisory committee note (2010).

judgment is steeper and *Option B* has less relevance: such a movant may not merely point to an absence of support for the non-movant's positions but must also come forward with such affirmative support on each issue material to its case that no reasonable factfinder could rule otherwise.[167]

Because summary judgment, when entered, obviates the need for a trial, facts forming the basis for such a ruling must be (1) material, (2) undisputed, and (3) admissible in evidence.[168] In addition to the parties' submissions, the court may, in an appropriate circumstance, also consider evidence of which it may take judicial notice,[169] even court filings and discovery in another lawsuit, so long as those materials are made part of the summary judgment record.[170]

- *Additional Local Rule Requirements:* Many districts have promulgated local rules imposing additional submission obligations. For example, some districts require parties moving for summary judgment to file a listing of material facts they claim to be undisputed,[171] which the court, then, may treat as admitted unless the non-moving party properly responds with specific evidence to the contrary.[172]

Procedure #2: Objecting to Improper Support

Materials offered to support or oppose a fact during summary judgment briefing must be capable of being offered at trial in an admissible form.[173] (Ordinarily, this does not mean that, at the briefing stage, the submitted facts be presented in

---

[167] *See Barnes v. Sea Hawaii Rafting, LLC*, 889 F.3d 517, 537–38 (9th Cir. 2018); *United States v. Donovan*, 661 F.3d 174, 185 (3d Cir. 2011). *See also Access Mediquip L.L.C. v. UnitedHealthcare Ins. Co.*, 662 F.3d 376, 378 (5th Cir. 2011), *adhered to on reh'g en banc*, 698 F.3d 229 (5th Cir. 2012) (same procedure when defendant moves on affirmative defense).

[168] *See Boyer-Liberto v. Fontainebleau Corp.*, 752 F.3d 350, 355 (4th Cir. 2014).

[169] *See Spaine v. Community Contacts, Inc.*, 756 F.3d 542, 545 (7th Cir. 2014).

[170] *See Fuqua v. Turner*, 996 F.3d 1140, 1148–49 (11th Cir. 2021); *Alexander v. Casino Queen, Inc.*, 739 F.3d 972, 978–79 (7th Cir. 2014).

[171] *See, e.g.*, M.D. Pa. Loc. R. 56.1 ("Upon any motion for summary judgment pursuant to Fed.R.Civ.P. 56, there shall be filed with the motion a separate, short and concise statement of the material facts, in numbered paragraphs, as to which the moving party contends there is no genuine issue to be tried. The papers opposing a motion for summary judgment shall include a separate, short and concise statement of the material facts, responding to the numbered paragraphs set forth in the statement required in the foregoing paragraph, as to which it is contended that there exists a genuine issue to be tried."). *See also* D. Conn. Loc. R. 56(a) (same effect); M.D. Ga. Loc. R. 56 (same effect).

[172] *See Hinterberger v. City of Indianapolis*, 966 F.3d 523, 525–30 (7th Cir. 2020); *Jackson v. Fed. Exp.*, 766 F.3d 189, 194–95 (2d Cir. 2014).

[173] *See* Rule 56(c)(2). *See also Standish v. Jackson Hole Mountain Resort Corp.*, 997 F.3d 1095, 1107 (10th Cir. 2021); *Igasaki v. Illinois Dep't of Fin. & Pro. Regul.*, 988 F.3d 948, 955-56 (7th Cir. 2021).

an admissible form, only that an admissible form exists by which those facts may be later introduced at trial).[174] A party may object that the opponent has supported a position (either seeking or opposing summary judgment) by material that cannot be presented at trial in a form that would be admissible.[175] This right of objection has supplanted the former practice, approved by some courts, of moving to "strike" improper summary judgment support.[176]

Objections under this Rule function like trial objections to evidence, but tailored to the pretrial setting.[177] Objections must specifically explain what particular exhibit is improper and why[178] (for example, demonstrating that the proffered evidence would be inadmissible hearsay)[179] Once made, the objection shifts the burden to the opponent to defend the contested material as admissible in its current form or to explain some other anticipated form by which it may be later admitted.[180] Failure to make an objection under this Rule does not forfeit a later objection to admissibility at time of trial,[181] but the absence of an objection invites the court to accept the evidence's admissibility as uncontested for the limited purpose of ruling on the summary judgment motion.[182] In considering objections under this Rule, the trial judge may rule explicitly or implicitly, so long as the record clearly supports the apparent

---

[174]*See Sandoval v. Cty. of San Diego*, 985 F.3d 657, 666 (9th Cir. 2021) (focus at summary judgment stage is not on *form* of proffered evidence, but on its *content*). *See generally infra* Authors' Commentary to Rule 56(c)(4) ("**Procedure #4: Content of Affidavits / Declarations** - *Specific Admissible Facts*"). Indeed, the most frequently submitted support on a summary judgment motion—affidavits—will rarely (if ever) be admissible at trial in the absence of the affiant.

[175]*See* Rule 56(c)(2). *Cf. Wi-LAN Inc. v. Sharp Elecs. Corp.*, 992 F.3d 1366, 1372 (Fed. Cir. 2021) (declaration not acceptable unless declarant available to testify at trial).

[176]*See Villeneuve v. Avon Prod., Inc.*, 919 F.3d 40, 45 n.4 (1st Cir. 2019) ("no need to make a separate motion to strike"); *Horn v. Med. Marijuana, Inc.*, 383 F. Supp. 3d 114, 126 (W.D.N.Y. 2019) (same).

[177]*See Tolar v. Marion Bank & Tr., Co.*, 378 F. Supp. 3d 1103, 1108 (N.D. Ala. 2019), *aff'd*, 997 F.3d 1280 (11th Cir. 2021); *Wi-LAN Inc. v. Sharp Elecs. Corp.*, 362 F. Supp. 3d 226, 234 (D. Del. 2019).

[178]*See Mercado-Reyes v. City of Angels, Inc.*, 320 F. Supp. 3d 344, 348 (D.P.R. 2018); *Halebian v. Berv*, 869 F. Supp. 2d 420, 443 n. 24 (S.D.N.Y. 2012).

[179]*See Loomis v. Cornish*, 836 F.3d 991, 996–97 (9th Cir. 2016); *Spring Street Partners-IV, L.P. v. Lam*, 730 F.3d 427, 441–42 (5th Cir. 2013).

[180]*See* Rule 56(c)(2) advisory committee note (2010). *See also Campos v. Steves & Sons, Inc.*, 10 F.4th 515, 521–22 (5th Cir. 2021) ("precondition" for considering improper-form evidence is showing possibility that it can be presented in admissible form for trial); *Steffek v. Client Servs., Inc.*, 948 F.3d 761, 769 (7th Cir. 2020).

[181]*See* Rule 56(c)(2) advisory committee note (2010).

[182]*See Maurer v. Independence. Town*, 870 F.3d 380, 384–85 (5th Cir. 2017); *Bird v. W. Valley City*, 832 F.3d 1188, 1194 n.1 (10th Cir. 2016).

determination.[183] In either event, in ruling, the judge may consider objected-to materials only after determining that their facts would be admissible at trial.[184]

How this Rule harmonizes with certain elements of prior practice remains unclear. For example, formerly, a party objecting to summary judgment materials on other grounds (*e.g.*, that an affiant lacked personal knowledge or was incompetent) was *compelled* to object in a timely fashion or risk forfeiting the objection.[185] This procedure developed, wrote one court, to avoid the objecting party playing the game of "dog-in-the-manger" — fighting the summary judgment motion on its merits and only later, if unsuccessful, unveiling technical objections as a hidden "ace".[186] Additionally, in those districts permitting motions to strike improper summary judgment support,[187] a body of guiding case law admonished courts, in ruling on those motions, to use "a scalpel, not a butcher knife" so as to strike off only offending portions.[188]

Procedure #3: Content of Summary Judgment Record

The summary judgment record is generally understood as comprised of those materials filed with the judge—via briefs, exhibits, and appendices—in support of or in opposition to a pending summary judgment motion.[189] Although tasked to consider the summary judgment record as a "whole,"[190] judges are only obliged to consider those particular materials *cited* by the parties in support of or in opposition to their respective positions.[191] Judges are not required to "scour the record" independently, beyond those portions cited by the parties, in search

[183] *See Campbell v. Shinseki*, 546 Fed. Appx. 874, 878–79 (11th Cir. 2013).

[184] *See Steffek v. Client Servs., Inc.*, 948 F.3d 761, 769 (7th Cir. 2020); *Jacoby v. Keers*, 779 Fed. Appx. 676, 679 (11th Cir. 2019).

[185] *See MSK EyEs Ltd. v. Wells Fargo Bank, Nat'l Ass'n*, 546 F.3d 533, 543 n.6 (8th Cir. 2008).

[186] *See Desrosiers v. Hartford Life and Acc. Co.*, 515 F.3d 87, 91–92 (1st Cir. 2008).

[187] *See Campbell v. Shinseki*, 546 Fed. Appx. 874, 879 (11th Cir. 2013) (describing pre-2010 practice and 2010 amendments' effect). *See also supra* Authors' Commentary to Rule 12(f) ("**Striking Documents Other Than Pleadings**").

[188] *See Perez v. Volvo Car Corp.*, 247 F.3d 303, 315–16 (1st Cir. 2001). *See also Ondo v. City of Cleveland*, 795 F.3d 597, 604–05 (6th Cir. 2015).

[189] *See Alexander v. Casino Queen, Inc.*, 739 F.3d 972, 978–79 (7th Cir. 2014). *See generally Celotex Corp. v. Catrett*, 477 U.S. 317, 322–23, 106 S. Ct. 2548, 91 L. Ed. 2d 265 (1986) (describing categories of materials that may be consulted).

[190] *See Williamson v. Brevard Cty.*, 928 F.3d 1296, 1304 (11th Cir. 2019); *de Lima Silva v. Dept. of Corr.*, 917 F.3d 546, 559 (7th Cir. 2019). *See also Torry v. City of Chicago*, 932 F.3d 579, 584 (7th Cir. 2019) (materials properly considered in support of motion, even though submitted in opposition to adversary's motion).

[191] *See Flynn v. FCA US LLC*, 39 F.4th 946, 953 (7th Cir. 2022) ("the rule assigns to the parties the responsibility to 'cit[e] to particular parts of materials in the record' when asserting that genuine factual disputes preclude summary judgment"); *Vasquez v. Hong Kong & Shanghai Banking Corp., Ltd.*, 477 F. Supp. 3d 241, 261

of record material pertinent to the pending summary judgment motion.[192] Such a separate, judicial canvass of the full record, though not forbidden,[193] is also not required,[194] and judges are admonished, if they do canvass, to do so warily, mindful of their roles as neutral arbiters, not partisan advocates.[195]

- *"Lodged", Not Filed Documents:* Documents attached to a submission that a court refuses to accept, although perhaps contained in the court clerk's official file, are not part of the summary judgment record.[196]
- *First Amendment Claims:* Some courts had earlier adopted a caselaw-based caveat, directing trial judges to perform an independent record search in First Amendment and other sensitive case types[197] (whether this mandate survived the adoption of Rule 56(c)(3) remains unclear).

Procedure #4: Content of Affidavits / Declarations

Affidavits or declarations may be used to support or oppose a motion for summary judgment if they meet four prerequisites: (1) sworn or otherwise subscribed as true under a risk of perjury; (2) made on personal knowledge; (3) set out facts that would be admissible in evidence; and (4) show that the maker is competent to testify on the matters expressed.[198] A court generally will not consider affidavits and declarations failing these prerequisites,[199] though a submission may be received in part if a portion is admissible even if other portions are not.[200]

(S.D.N.Y. 2020) (because party did not cite declaration in opposition, court was "at liberty on that ground alone not to consider it").

[192]*See Waggel v. George Washington Univ.*, 957 F.3d 1364, 1377 n.4 (D.C. Cir. 2020); *Torry v. City of Chicago*, 932 F.3d 579, 584 (7th Cir. 2019). *See also Rodgers v. City of Des Moines*, 435 F.3d 904, 908 (8th Cir.2006) ("Without some guidance, we will not mine a summary judgment record searching for nuggets of factual disputes to gild a party's arguments."); *United States v. Dunkel*, 927 F.2d 955, 956 (7th Cir. 1991) ("Judges are not like pigs, hunting for truffles buried in briefs.").

[193]*See Flynn v. FCA US LLC*, 39 F.4th 946, 953 (7th Cir. 2022); *Perkins v. Hastings*, 915 F.3d 512, 522 n.3 (8th Cir. 2019).

[194]*See Flynn v. FCA US LLC*, 39 F.4th 946, 953 (7th Cir. 2022); *Durant v. D.C. Gov't*, 875 F.3d 685, 699 (D.C. Cir. 2017).

[195]*See In re Rumsey Land Co., LLC*, 944 F.3d 1259, 1280 (10th Cir. 2019).

[196]*See Nicholson v. Hyannis Air Serv., Inc.*, 580 F.3d 1116, 1127 & 1127 n.5 (9th Cir. 2009).

[197]*See 303 Creative LLC v. Elenis*, 6 F.4th 1160, 1171 (10th Cir. 2021); *Clear Channel Outdoor, Inc. v. City of New York*, 594 F.3d 94, 103 (2d Cir. 2010).

[198]*See* Rule 56(c)(4).

[199]*See Wi-LAN Inc. v. Sharp Elecs. Corp.*, 992 F.3d 1366, 1372 (Fed. Cir. 2021); *In re: Green*, 968 F.3d 516, 523 (5th Cir. 2020). *But see Ruby v. Springfield R-12 Public School Dist.*, 76 F.3d 909, 912 (8th Cir. 1996) (absent motion to strike or other timely objection, judge may consider document which fails to conform to formal requirements).

[200]*See Ondo v. City of Cleveland*, 795 F.3d 597, 604 (6th Cir. 2015).

- *Sworn:* An affidavit must be sworn[201] and a declaration must be made under penalty of perjury[202] to qualify. Thus, verified complaints (ordinarily not required under the Rules) likely suffice,[203] while a party's unsworn statements and emails[204] and an attorney's representations at oral argument[205] generally will not.
- *Personal Knowledge*: The affidavit or declaration must be made upon personal knowledge,[206] though the basis for that personal knowledge need not be stated if it is clear or inferable from the context.[207] Statements based on "information and belief" — facts the maker *believes* are true, but does not *know* are true — are not proper.[208] Likewise, inferences and opinions must be premised on first-hand observations or personal experience.[209] A statement will not be rejected merely because it is a self-serving recitation by the party[210] or one uncorrobo-

---

[201] *See Adickes v. S. H. Kress & Co.*, 398 U.S. 144, 158 n.17, 90 S. Ct. 1598, 26 L. Ed. 2d 142 (1970). *See also Adams v. C3 Pipeline Constr. Inc.*, 30 F.4th 943, 975 (10th Cir. 2021) (unsigned affidavits are not proper summary judgment evidence). *Cf. Collins v. Seeman*, 462 F.3d 757, 760 n.1 (7th Cir. 2006) (rejecting unsworn written witness summaries); *Watts v. Kroger Co.*, 170 F.3d 505, 508 (5th Cir. 1999) (same, for handwritten statements); *Chaiken v. VV Pub. Corp.*, 119 F.3d 1018, 1033 (2d Cir. 1997) (same, for unsworn letters).

[202] *See* Rule 56(c)(4) advisory committee note (2010) (formal affidavits are "no longer required," and declarations under penalty of perjury pursuant to 28 U.S.C.A. § 1746 are sufficient). *See also Mann v. Mohr*, 802 Fed. Appx. 871, 877 (6th Cir. 2020); *United States ex rel. Doe v. Heart Sol., PC*, 923 F.3d 308, 315–16 (3d Cir. 2019).

[203] *See Porter v. Pennsylvania Dep't of Corr.*, 974 F.3d 431, 443 (3d Cir. 2020); *Taylor v. Stevens*, 946 F.3d 211, 220 n.12 (5th Cir. 2019). *But cf. Lantec, Inc. v. Novell, Inc.*, 306 F.3d 1003, 1019 (10th Cir. 2002) (court properly refused to consider verified complaint as summary judgment affidavit where allegations were merely conclusory).

[204] *See United States ex rel. Doe v. Heart Sol., PC*, 923 F.3d 308, 315–16 (3d Cir. 2019); *Banks v. Deere*, 829 F.3d 661, 667–68 (8th Cir. 2016).

[205] *See Lane v. Dep't of Interior*, 523 F.3d 1128, 1140 (9th Cir. 2008).

[206] *See Boykin v. Fam. Dollar Stores of Michigan, LLC*, 3 F.4th 832, 841-42 (6th Cir. 2021); *Endy v. Cty. of Los Angeles*, 975 F.3d 757, 763 (9th Cir. 2020).

[207] *See Garza-Flores v. Mayorkas*, 38 F.4th 440, 445 (5th Cir. 2022); *Garcia-Garcia v. Costco Wholesale Corp.*, 878 F.3d 411, 418–19 (1st Cir. 2017).

[208] *See Automatic Radio Mfg. Co. v. Hazeltine Research*, 339 U.S. 827, 831, 70 S. Ct. 894, 94 L. Ed. 1312 (1950); *USA Gymnastics v. Liberty Ins. Underwriters, Inc.*, 27 F.4th 499, 513 (7th Cir. 2022).

[209] *See Briggs v. Potter*, 463 F.3d 507, 512 (6th Cir. 2006); *Argo v. Blue Cross and Blue Shield of Kansas, Inc.*, 452 F.3d 1193, 1200 (10th Cir. 2006). *See also Payne v. Pauley*, 337 F.3d 767, 772 (7th Cir. 2003) (personal knowledge may include reasonable inferences grounded in observation or other first-hand experience; they may not be "flights of fancy, speculations, hunches, intuitions, or rumors about matters remote from that experience").

[210] *See Great Am. Ins. Co. v. Emps. Mut. Cas. Co.*, 18 F.4th 486, 493 n.7 (5th Cir. 2021); *Janny v. Gamez*, 8 F.4th 883, 900 (10th Cir. 2021).

rated by other evidence[211] (indeed, it would make little sense for a party to submit one that was not self-serving). But the self-serving affirmations must be more than mere conclusions or unsupported inferences; in other words, such statements must aver specific facts and otherwise satisfy the requirements of this Rule.[212]

- *Specific Admissible Facts:* The affidavit or declaration must also contain specific facts[213] which, in turn, must be admissible in evidence at time of trial.[214] It is not necessary that the evidence be submitted in a *form* that would be admissible at trial (indeed, most summary judgment motions are supported and opposed by affidavit evidence), so long as the offered evidence may ultimately be presented at trial in an admissible form.[215] Thus, hearsay statements,[216] conclusory averments,[217] unfounded self-serving declarations,[218] ambiguous statements,[219] speculation or conjecture,[220] inadmissible settle-

---

[211]*See Great Am. Ins. Co. v. Emps. Mut. Cas. Co.*, 18 F.4th 486, 493 n.7 (5th Cir. 2021); *United States v. Stein*, 881 F.3d 853, 858 (11th Cir. 2018) (en banc).

[212]*See Guzman v. Allstate Assurance Co.*, 18 F.4th 157, 160–61 (5th Cir. 2021); *Boykin v. Fam. Dollar Stores of Michigan, LLC*, 3 F.4th 832, 841-42 (6th Cir. 2021).

[213]*See Camara v. Mastro's Restaurants LLC*, 952 F.3d 372, 374–75 (D.C. Cir. 2020); *Howard v. Kansas City Police Dep't*, 570 F.3d 984, 997 (8th Cir. 2009).

[214]*See Burton v. Kohn Law Firm*, 934 F.3d 572, 583–84 (7th Cir. 2019); *Crews v. Monarch Fire Protection Dist.*, 771 F.3d 1085, 1092 (8th Cir. 2014).

[215]*See Poincon v. Offshore Marine Contractors, Inc.*, 9 F.4th 289, 299 n.4 (5th Cir. 2021); *Klayman v. Jud. Watch, Inc.*, 6 F.4th 1301, 1315 (D.C. Cir. 2021). *See also Campos v. Steves & Sons, Inc.*, 10 F.4th 515, 521–22 (5th Cir. 2021) ("precondition" for considering improper-form evidence is showing possibility that it can be presented in admissible form for trial); *Sandoval v. Cty. of San Diego*, 985 F.3d 657, 666 (9th Cir. 2021) (focus at summary judgment stage is not on *form* of proffered evidence, but on its *content*). *See generally Celotex Corp. v. Catrett*, 477 U.S. 317, 324, 106 S. Ct. 2548, 91 L. Ed. 2d 265 (1986) (parties need not depose their own witnesses).

[216]*See Stanton v. Elliott*, 25 F.4th 227, 237 n.7 (4th Cir. 2022); *Eaton v. J. H. Findorff & Son, Inc.*, 1 F.4th 508, 512 n.3 (7th Cir. 2021).

[217]*See Greene v. Westfield Ins. Co.*, 963 F.3d 619, 627 (7th Cir. 2020); *D'Onofrio v. Vacation Publications, Inc.*, 888 F.3d 197, 208 (5th Cir. 2018). *See also Lujan v. National Wildlife Federation*, 497 U.S. 871, 888, 110 S. Ct. 3177, 111 L. Ed. 2d 695 (1990) (object of Rule 56 is not to replace conclusory averments in a pleading with conclusory allegations in an affidavit).

[218]*See Manley v. Rowley*, 847 F.3d 705, 711 (9th Cir. 2017); *Evans v. Technologies Applications & Service Co.*, 80 F.3d 954, 962 (4th Cir. 1996). *See also Delange v. Dutra Const. Co., Inc.*, 183 F.3d 916, 921 (9th Cir. 1999) (when nonmoving party relies only on own affidavit to oppose summary judgment, his affidavit may not be conclusory or unsupported).

[219]*See Archuleta v. Wal-Mart Stores, Inc.*, 543 F.3d 1226, 1234 (10th Cir. 2008).

[220]*See D'Onofrio v. Vacation Publications, Inc.*, 888 F.3d 197, 208–09 (5th Cir. 2018); *Matherly v. Andrews*, 859 F.3d 264, 280 (4th Cir. 2017).

ment materials,[221] or inadmissible expert opinions[222] are generally improper in summary judgment affidavits and declarations. A party's promise that he or she has certain unidentified "additional evidence," which will be produced at trial, is also insufficient.[223] Nor will the hope of a devastating cross-examination of the affiant suffice,[224] at least not without specific, credibility-undermining evidence.[225] But the specific-facts obligation does not require an affiant to prove a negative; a summary denial that an event occurred, made by an affiant with personal knowledge, can be proper.[226]

- *Competence:* The affidavit or declaration must demonstrate that the maker is competent to testify as to the facts contained in the document.[227] Competence to testify may be inferred from the documents themselves.[228] Ordinarily, statements of counsel in a memorandum of law are not competent to support or oppose that litigant's own summary judgment position.[229]
- *"Acquired" Competence:* In appropriate circumstances, the makers of affidavits and declarations can "acquire" competence and personal knowledge they otherwise lack by research and a proper review of records.[230]
- *Impact of Rule 26(a)(2) Expert Disclosures:* Some courts have ruled that an expert may not be "competent" (nor the expert's affidavit "admissible") within the meaning

---

[221] *See Coutard v. Mun. Credit Union*, 848 F.3d 102, 113–14 (2d Cir. 2017).

[222] *See Felkins v. City of Lakewood*, 774 F.3d 647, 651–53 (10th Cir. 2014); *Ruffin v. Shaw Industries, Inc.*, 149 F.3d 294, 295 (4th Cir. 1998).

[223] *See Angelex, Ltd. v. United States*, 907 F.3d 612, 620 (D.C. Cir. 2018); *Geske & Sons, Inc. v. N.L.R.B.*, 103 F.3d 1366, 1376 (7th Cir. 1997).

[224] *See United States v. 3234 Washington Ave. N.*, 480 F.3d 841, 845 (8th Cir. 2007).

[225] *See Waldon v. Wal-Mart Stores, Inc.*, 943 F.3d 818, 823 (7th Cir. 2019); *Nationwide Prop. & Cas. Ins. Co. v. Faircloth*, 845 F.3d 378, 382 (8th Cir. 2016).

[226] *See Boykin v. Fam. Dollar Stores of Michigan, LLC*, 3 F.4th 832, 842 (6th Cir. 2021); *S. Katzman Produce Inc. v. Yadid*, 999 F.3d 867, 877–78 (2d Cir. 2021).

[227] *See Ondo v. City of Cleveland*, 795 F.3d 597, 604–05 (6th Cir. 2015); *Boyer-Liberto v. Fontainebleau Corp.*, 752 F.3d 350, 355 (4th Cir. 2014).

[228] *See Barthelemy v. Air Lines Pilots Ass'n*, 897 F.2d 999, 1018 (9th Cir. 1990) (affiant's competence could be inferred from position with the company).

[229] *See Orson, Inc. v. Miramax Film Corp.*, 79 F.3d 1358, 1372 (3d Cir. 1996) (legal memoranda and oral argument are not evidence and cannot independently create genuine issue of disputed fact sufficient to preclude summary judgment).

[230] *See Cocroft v. HSBC Bank USA, N.A.*, 796 F.3d 680, 686 (7th Cir. 2015) (affidavit by records custodian); *Nader v. Blair*, 549 F.3d 953, 963 (4th Cir. 2008) (affidavit from witness familiar with record-keeping practices). *But cf. Hernandez-Santiago v. Ecolab, Inc.*, 397 F.3d 30, 35 (1st Cir. 2005) (affidavit that represented merely "review of relevant manufacturing and sales records" not sufficient, where affiant did not attest that he conducted or supervised review or had personal knowledge of results of review).

of Rule 56(c)(4) if the proffering party had a duty of pretrial disclosure regarding the expert which that party failed to discharge.[231]

Affidavits and Declarations to Authenticate Summary Judgment Documents and Exhibits

Documents (even documents obtained through discovery) might not automatically become part of a summary judgment record merely because they are cited in a supporting memorandum.[232] Many courts long required that every document used to support or oppose a summary judgment motion be authenticated through an affidavit or declaration, which must be made upon personal knowledge and must both identify and authenticate the offered document.[233] Documents that failed to satisfy this authentication requirement could be disregarded by the court in resolving the pending motion.[234] It remains unclear whether the 2010 Amendments altered this practice.[235] The drafters had deleted earlier Rule language on which this authentication practice may have been based,[236] but

---

[231] *See Barry v. Silver*, 2011 WL 13298552, at *2 (M.D. Fla. Feb. 28, 2011) ("competent to testify" requires having satisfied Rule 26(a)(2) expert disclosure obligations). *See also Norwood v. E. Allen Cty. Sch.*, 2018 WL 4680008, at *10 n.10 (N.D. Ind. Sept. 28, 2018) (excluding expert's opinion as inadmissible in part because of party's non-disclosure of expert); *Lenzen v. Workers Comp. Reins. Ass'n*, 843 F. Supp. 2d 981, 985 (D. Minn. 2011), *aff'd*, 705 F.3d 816 (8th Cir. 2013) (same). *But cf. Soukhaphonh v. Hot Topic, Inc.*, 2017 WL 10378493, at *2 n.2 (C.D. Cal. Sept. 14, 2017) (questioning whether testifying expert's Rule 56 submission must satisfy Rule 26(a)(2)'s disclosure requirements, and also noting that time to disclose expert reports "has not yet passed"). *See generally supra* Authors' Commentary to Rule 26(a)(2) (**"Which Experts**—*Expert Affidavits for Summary Judgment Motions"*).

[232] *See Hoffman v. Applicators Sales and Serv., Inc.*, 439 F.3d 9, 15 (1st Cir. 2006).

[233] *See DG&G, Inc. v. FlexSol Packaging Corp. of Pompano Beach*, 576 F.3d 820, 825–26 (8th Cir. 2009); *Alexander v. CareSource*, 576 F.3d 551, 558–59 (6th Cir. 2009). *But see H. Sand & Co. v. Airtemp Corp.*, 934 F.2d 450, 454 (2d Cir.1991) (motion exhibit authentication only required when authenticity is challenged).

[234] *See Scott v. Edinburg*, 346 F.3d 752, 759–60 n.7 (7th Cir. 2003); *Citizens for Better Forestry v. U.S. Dept. of Agriculture*, 341 F.3d 961, 972 n.7 (9th Cir. 2003).

[235] Some courts hold that the 2010 amendments changed this practice. *See Glasser v. Hilton Grand Vacations Co.*, 948 F.3d 1301, 1313 (11th Cir. 2020) (requirement eliminated in 2010); *Garcia-Garcia v. Costco Wholesale Corp.*, 878 F.3d 411, 418 n.11 (1st Cir. 2017) ("authentication" no longer required after 2010); *Maurer v. Independence. Town*, 870 F.3d 380, 384 (5th Cir. 2017) (evidence need not be authenticated). Other courts disagree. *See Steffek v. Client Servs., Inc.*, 948 F.3d 761, 769 (7th Cir. 2020) (authentication required at summary judgment stage); *Edwards v. Hiland Roberts Dairy, Co.*, 860 F.3d 1121, 1127 (8th Cir. 2017) (no error in excluding consideration of unauthenticated exhibit).

[236] *See* Rule 56(e)(1) (rescinded 2010) ("If a paper or part of a paper is referred to in an affidavit, a sworn or certified copy must be attached to or served with the affidavit.").

did so for apparently unrelated reasons.[237] Moreover, the 2010 drafters had earlier emphasized that the Rule 56(c) amendments were not intended to dislodge prevailing local practices on submission form.[238]

"Vouching" Risk with Summary Judgment Affidavits

At least one court has ruled that a party offering a summary judgment affidavit or declaration effectively concedes that it qualifies for consideration (that is, that the statements made are sworn, made upon personal knowledge, factually specific and admissible, and competent). The court may properly deny a party's later, pretrial *in limine* motion to strike testimony that the same party had earlier itself offered in support of a summary judgment brief.[239]

Contradictory Sworn Evidence from Same Party

Most courts have embraced the "sham affidavit" rule, which ordinarily prevents a party[240] from defeating summary judgment by simply denying, in an affidavit or declaration, a fact that the party had earlier admitted in a sworn statement.[241] To create a genuine dispute for trial sufficient to defeat summary judgment, such a party must, in addition to the denial itself, offer an explanation for the inconsistency that the district court finds adequate to allow a reasonable juror to *both* accept the current denial and yet still assume either the truth of, or the party's good faith belief in, the earlier sworn statement.[242] Thus, courts may allow subsequent, contradicting affidavits where

[237] *See* Rule 56(c)(4) advisory committee notes (2010) ("The requirement that a sworn or certified copy of a paper referred to in an affidavit or declaration be attached to the affidavit or declaration is omitted as unnecessary given the requirement . . . that a statement or dispute of fact be supported by materials in the record.").

[238] *See* Rule 56(c)(1) advisory committee notes (2010) (noting amended Rule 56(c)(1) "does not address the form for providing the required support," and "[d]ifferent courts and judges have adopted different forms").

[239] *See Williams v. Trader Pub. Co.*, 218 F.3d 481, 485 (5th Cir. 2000) (in employment case, party offered affidavits of certain male employees to support its summary judgment position, then later attempted to argue that testimony of same male employees was inadmissible because the male employees were not in situations "nearly identical" to plaintiff; court ruled testimony was properly admitted because defendant, by introducing same evidence at summary judgment stage, contended evidence would be relevant and admissible at trial).

[240] *See Foster v. City of Indio*, 908 F.3d 1204, 1213 (9th Cir. 2018) (sham affidavit rule applies only to parties, not non-party witnesses).

[241] *See Perez v. Staples Cont. & Com. LLC*, 31 F.4th 560, 569–70 (7th Cir. 2022); *Boykin v. Fam. Dollar Stores of Mich., LLC*, 3 F.4th 832, 842-43 (6th Cir. 2021). *See generally James v. Hale*, 959 F.3d 307, 315–16 (7th Cir. 2020) (every federal circuit permits judges to disregard affidavits that contradict prior testimony, citing cases).

[242] *See Cleveland v. Policy Mgmt. Sys. Corp.*, 526 U.S. 795, 804, 119 S. Ct. 1597, 143 L. Ed. 2d 966 (1999). *See also Asalde v. First Class Parking Sys. LLC*, 898 F.3d 1136, 1143 (11th Cir. 2018) (second affidavit identifying valet ticket's source, submitted after first affidavit denied knowing source, was not sham when actual ticket was found in interim).

the original statement was demonstrably mistaken[243] or genuinely ambiguous and the later affidavit supplies a mere clarification or supplementation,[244] or where the affidavit contains newly discovered evidence.[245]

Form of Motion / Local Rule Requirements

Motions for summary judgment generally must be in writing.[246] Local rules may prescribe supplemental briefing requirements for summary judgment motions,[247] and such requirements have been enforced strictly.[248]

Hearings and Oral Argument

Although the district court may, in its discretion, convene a hearing or oral argument on the Rule 56 motion, neither is required.[249] Receiving live oral testimony in conjunction with a summary judgment motion is both rare and problematic. Because the summary judgment procedure is intended to offer a speedy resolution when the material facts are undisputed, and because the court may not resolve facts that remain disputed, oral testimony in summary judgment proceedings is granted "sparingly" and "with great care."[250]

Miscellaneous Other Procedures

Over time, federal courts embraced various other local procedures for summary judgment practice, some local rule-based and some purely common law. Several follow:

- *Party Admissions:* Admissions by a party—whether express (intentional acknowledgment) or through default (*e.g.*, where a party fails to deny Rule 36 requests for admission)—are considered conclusive as to the matters admitted, cannot be contradicted by affidavit or other-

---

[243]*See Perez v. Staples Cont. & Com. LLC*, 31 F.4th 560, 569–70 (7th Cir. 2022).

[244]*See Perez v. Staples Cont. & Com. LLC*, 31 F.4th 560, 569–70 (7th Cir. 2022); *Boykin v. Fam. Dollar Stores of Mich., LLC*, 3 F.4th 832, 842-43 (6th Cir. 2021). *See generally Reich v. City of Elizabethtown*, 945 F.3d 968, 976 (6th Cir. 2019) (definition of "contradiction" is relatively narrow).

[245]*See Perez v. Staples Cont. & Com. LLC*, 31 F.4th 560, 569–70 (7th Cir. 2022).

[246]*See National Fire Ins. v. Bartolazo*, 27 F.3d 518, 520 (11th Cir. 1994); *Hanson v. Polk County Land, Inc.*, 608 F.2d 129, 131 (5th Cir. 1979).

[247]*See, e.g., supra* Authors' Commentary to Rule 56(c)(1) ("**Procedure #1: Supporting Factual Positions**"—*Additional Local Rule Requirements*) (undisputed-facts statements).

[248]*See Hinterberger v. City of Indianapolis*, 966 F.3d 523, 525–30 (7th Cir. 2020); *Jackson v. Fed. Exp.*, 766 F.3d 189, 194 (2d Cir. 2014). *See generally Hollingsworth v. Perry*, 558 U.S. 183, 191, 130 S. Ct. 705, 175 L. Ed. 2d 657 (2010) (per curiam) (district court local rules have "force of law").

[249]*See* Rule 78(b) (authorizing determination of motions without oral argument). *See also Jones v. Secord*, 684 F.3d 1, 6 (1st Cir. 2012); *Johnson v. U.S.*, 460 F.3d 616, 620 (5th Cir. 2006).

[250]*See Seamons v. Snow*, 206 F.3d 1021, 1025–26 (10th Cir. 2000).

wise, and can support a grant of summary judgment.[251]

- *Briefs:* The court may consider concessions in a party's brief or during oral argument in gauging whether a genuine issue of material fact exists; otherwise, however, the parties' briefs are not evidence.[252]
- *New Evidence in Reply:* If the moving party introduces new evidence in a reply brief or memoranda, the trial court will usually not accept and consider the new evidence without first affording the non-moving party an opportunity to respond.[253]

RULE 56(d)—WHEN FACTS ARE UNAVAILABLE TO THE NONMOVANT

CORE CONCEPT

Once a motion for summary judgment is filed, the non-moving party must show to the court that a genuine, material factual dispute exists to defeat summary judgment. If the non-moving party is still conducting productive discovery or for some other reason is not yet ready or able to make that showing, the party may file an affidavit or declaration explaining why a ruling on summary judgment should be postponed. The court, in its discretion, may grant a temporary reprieve.

APPLICATIONS

2010 Amendments — Amended Rule 56(d)

Current Rule 56(d) contains the content of former Rule 56(f), without change in substance.[254] Former Rule 56(d), which authorized courts that were unable to grant summary judgment to declare material facts as established for purposes of trial, has been revised and repositioned to current Rule 56(g).

Purpose

Rule 56(d) affords diligent litigants a "safety valve" designed to abate a premature swing of the "summary judgment axe."[255] The procedure it establishes as a condition for granting relief helps ensure both that the Rule's protections are being invoked

[251]*See In re Carney*, 258 F.3d 415, 420 (5th Cir. 2001).

[252]*See Orson, Inc. v. Miramax Film Corp.*, 79 F.3d 1358, 1372 (3d Cir. 1996) (legal memoranda and oral argument are not evidence and cannot create factual dispute that prevents summary judgment); *American Title Ins. Co. v. Lacelaw Corp.*, 861 F.2d 224, 226–27 (9th Cir. 1988) (court, may consider statements of fact in summary judgment briefing as party admissions for Rule 56 purposes).

[253]*See Mirando v. U.S. Dep't of Treasury*, 766 F.3d 540, 549 (6th Cir. 2014); *Beaird v. Seagate Technology, Inc.*, 145 F.3d 1159, 1163–65 (10th Cir. 1998).

[254]*See* Rule 56(d) advisory committee note (2010). *See also Burns v. Town of Palm Beach*, 999 F.3d 1317, 1331 n.3 (11th Cir. 2021) (so noting, and observing that pre-2010 case precedents remains "fully applicable" to current rule).

[255]*See Rivera-Torres v. Rey-Hernandez*, 502 F.3d 7, 10–11 (1st Cir. 2007).

in good faith and that the district judge is afforded the showing needed to assess the merits of the request for a delay.[256]

Requirement #1: Formal Request

A party seeking Rule 56(d) relief must make that request specifically by, for example, plainly asking the trial court to deny the pending motion or to defer it until discovery is completed.[257] But the denial/deferral request need not necessarily be made by motion; indeed, the submission of an affidavit or some other sworn declaration alone may be sufficient.[258] However, neglecting to seek relief at all[259] or making passing mention in a footnote to a brief[260] will not trigger the protection of this Rule.

Requirement #2: Affidavit or Declaration

Some courts will not consider a Rule 56(d) request unless it is accompanied by a sworn affidavit or proper declaration.[261] Other courts accept representations of counsel (as officers of the court) as sufficient[262] or, in appropriate circumstances, may excuse the failure to submit a formal affidavit where all necessary information has been otherwise supplied.[263]

Requirement #3: Showing of Reasons / Existence

Although relief under this Rule is often and liberally granted,[264] it does not come automatically.[265] Before the courts will postpone a summary judgment ruling pending further discovery, the courts will generally require a Rule 56(d) mov-

---

[256] *See Harrods Ltd. v. Sixty Internet Domain Names*, 302 F.3d 214, 244 (4th Cir. 2002); *Pastore v. Bell Tel. Co.*, 24 F.3d 508, 511 (3d Cir. 1994).

[257] *See Jones v. Secord*, 684 F.3d 1, 6 (1st Cir. 2012) ("[C]ourts, like the deity, tend to help those who help themselves, and Rule 56(d) is not self-executing. A party must invoke it.").

[258] *See Shelton v. Bledsoe*, 775 F.3d 554, 566–68 (3d Cir. 2015).

[259] *See Rocky Mountain Prestress, LLC v. Liberty Mut. Fire Ins. Co.*, 960 F.3d 1255, 1264 (10th Cir. 2020); *Meadows v. Latshaw Drilling Co., L.L.C.*, 866 F.3d 307, 313 (5th Cir. 2017). *See also Faiella v. Fed. Nat'l Mortg. Ass'n*, 928 F.3d 141, 146 (1st Cir. 2019) (failure to invoke Rule 56(d) "relinquishes any right to challenge" entry of summary judgment on grounds that facts were insufficiently developed).

[260] *See Allen v. Sybase, Inc.*, 468 F.3d 642, 662 (10th Cir. 2006).

[261] *See Rocky Mountain Prestress, LLC v. Liberty Mut. Fire Ins. Co.*, 960 F.3d 1255, 1264 (10th Cir. 2020); *1077 Madison St., LLC v. Daniels*, 954 F.3d 460, 464 (2d Cir. 2020).

[262] *See Baron Servs., Inc. v. Media Weather Innovations LLC*, 717 F.3d 907, 912 n.8 (Fed.Cir. 2013); *Snook v. Trust Co. of Ga. Bank of Savannah, N.A.*, 859 F.2d 865, 871 (11th Cir. 1988).

[263] *See Goodman v. Diggs*, 986 F.3d 493, 501 (4th Cir. 2021); *Unan v. Lyon*, 853 F.3d 279, 293 (6th Cir. 2017).

[264] *See McClure v. Ports*, 914 F.3d 866, 875 (4th Cir. 2019); *Jacked Up, L.L.C. v. Sara Lee Corp.*, 854 F.3d 797, 816 (5th Cir. 2017). *But see U.S. ex rel. Folliard v. Government Acquisitions, Inc.*, 764 F.3d 19, 26–27 (D.C.Cir. 2014) (judges must, however, still weigh the requirements).

[265] *See Nat'l Union Fire Ins. Co. of Pittsburgh v. Dish Network, LLC*, 17 F.4th 22, 34 (10th Cir. 2021); *United States ex rel. Booker v. Pfizer, Inc.*, 847 F.3d 52, 61 (1st Cir. 2017).

ant to show: (1) what particular discovery the movant intends to seek; (2) how that discovery would preclude the entry of summary judgment; and (3) why this discovery had not been or could not have been obtained earlier.[266] Some courts require a further showing of a plausible basis for believing that the sought-after facts exist.[267] In assessing the adequacy of the nonmovant's opportunity for discovery, the court will consider the time spanning through the date of its *ruling* on the summary judgment motion, not merely the time that elapsed before the filing of that motion.[268]

Although the affidavit or declaration need not contain evidentiary facts,[269] the showings made must be specific[270]—vague or baldly conclusory statements will not suffice.[271] Nor will a vacant hope that discovery will yield helpful evidence[272] or the mere assertion that critical evidence could lie in the opponent's possession.[273] The Rule does not countenance a "fishing expedition."[274] Moreover, the affidavit or declaration containing these showings must be authoritative (that is, it must be taken by someone with first-hand knowledge of the statements made).[275]

Burden on the Movant

The party moving to postpone the summary judgment ruling bears the burden of demonstrating the requisite basis for

---

[266] Though the Circuits describe the criteria variously, their essence seeks these same three, core showings. *See, e.g., Adams v. C3 Pipeline Constr. Inc.*, 30 F.4th 943, 968 (10th Cir. 2021); *Binh Hoa Le v. Exeter Fin. Corp.*, 990 F.3d 410, 413 (5th Cir. 2021); *Helena Agri-Enters., LLC v. Great Lakes Grain, LLC*, 988 F.3d 260, 273 (6th Cir. 2021). *Cf. Emigrant Residential LLC v. Pinti*, 37 F.4th 717, 725 (1st Cir. 2022) (five-element showing: "authoritativeness, timeliness, good cause, utility, and materiality").

[267] *See Yassin v. Weyker*, 39 F.4th 1086, 1091 (8th Cir. 2022); *Bailey v. KS Mgmt. Servs., L.L.C.*, 35 F.4th 397, 401 (5th Cir. 2022); *Doe v. Brown Univ.*, 943 F.3d 61, 71 (1st Cir. 2019).

[268] *See Burns v. Town of Palm Beach*, 999 F.3d 1317, 1335 (11th Cir. 2021) (with extensions, 10 months of discovery permitted between motion's filing and its disposition).

[269] *See Price ex rel. Price v. Western Resources, Inc.*, 232 F.3d 779, 783–84 (10th Cir. 2000).

[270] *See Adams v. C3 Pipeline Constr. Inc.*, 30 F.4th 943, 969 (10th Cir. 2021); *Burns v. Town of Palm Beach*, 999 F.3d 1317, 1334 (11th Cir. 2021).

[271] *See Bailey v. KS Mgmt. Servs., L.L.C.*, 35 F.4th 397, 401 (5th Cir. 2022); *Burns v. Town of Palm Beach*, 999 F.3d 1317, 1334 (11th Cir. 2021).

[272] *See MAO-MSO Recovery II, LLC v. State Farm Mut. Auto. Ins. Co.*, 994 F.3d 869, 877 (7th Cir. 2021); *Trans-W. Petroleum, Inc. v. United States Gypsum Co.*, 830 F.3d 1171, 1175 (10th Cir. 2016).

[273] *See Alphonse Hotel Corp. v. Tran*, 828 F.3d 146, 151 (2d Cir. 2016); *Anzaldua v. Northeast Ambulance & Fire Protection Dist.*, 793 F.3d 822, 837 (8th Cir. 2015).

[274] *See Hamric v. Wilderness Expeditions, Inc.*, 6 F.4th 1108, 1119 (10th Cir. 2021); *Johnson v. Moody*, 903 F.3d 766, 772 (8th Cir. 2018).

[275] *See C.B. Trucking, Inc. v. Waste Management, Inc.*, 137 F.3d 41, 44 n.2 (1st Cir. 1998).

relief under Rule 56(d).[276]

Timing

A Rule 56(d) motion to postpone a summary judgment ruling must be made in a timely fashion, which at least generally means before the party files a response to the pending motion or, in any event, prior to any scheduled oral argument on the motion.[277] In other words, a party cannot hold off seeking a Rule 56(d) postponement and oppose the motion on its merits, with the strategy of unfurling a later Rule 56(d) request if that merits opposition fails.[278]

When Rule 56(d) Requirements Might Be Relaxed

A failure to satisfy the ordinary Rule 56(d) requirements—a formal request, an affidavit, and a showing of reasons—may be relaxed or excused if summary judgment is sought before the nonmoving parties (through no fault of their own) have had an opportunity for discovery.[279] *Pro se* litigants, too, might be forgiven for irregularities in the formality of a postponement request.[280] But practitioners are cautioned against relying on this liberality: courts "hasten" to remind parties that they ignore Rule 56(d)'s requirements "at their peril."[281]

Postponing Very Early Filed Motions for Summary Judgment

When a summary judgment motion is filed very early in the litigation, before a realistic opportunity for discovery, courts generally grant Rule 56(d) postponements freely.[282] Courts disagree whether parties are *entitled* to an opportunity for

---

[276] *See Burns v. Town of Palm Beach*, 999 F.3d 1317, 1334 (11th Cir. 2021); *Atay v. Cty. of Maui*, 842 F.3d 688, 698 (9th Cir. 2016).

[277] *See In re PHC, Inc. Shareholder Litig.*, 762 F.3d 138, 144 (1st Cir. 2014); *Blough v. Holland Realty, Inc.*, 574 F.3d 1084, 1091 n.5 (9th Cir. 2009).

[278] *See Bormuth v. Cty. of Jackson*, 870 F.3d 494, 502 (6th Cir. 2017); *Nieves-Romero v. U.S.*, 715 F.3d 375, 381 (1st Cir. 2013).

[279] *See Nader v. Blair*, 549 F.3d 953, 961 (4th Cir. 2008). *See infra* Authors' Commentary to Rule 56(d) (**"Postponing Very Early Filed Motions for Summary Judgment"**).

[280] *See Goodman v. Diggs*, 986 F.3d 493, 501 (4th Cir. 2021); *Dewitt v. Corizon, Inc.*, 760 F.3d 654, 659 (7th Cir. 2014). *But see Crowley v. Bannister*, 734 F.3d 967, 978–79 (9th Cir. 2013) (trial court has no obligation to specially notify *pro se* litigants of Rule 56(d) function).

[281] *See Harrods Ltd. v. Sixty Internet Domain Names*, 302 F.3d 214, 246 & n.19 (4th Cir. 2002) (making comment, and "reiterat[ing] that our court expects full compliance" with Rule). *See also Bradley v. U.S.*, 299 F.3d 197, 207 (3d Cir. 2002) ("strong presumption against a finding of constructive compliance" with Rule).

[282] *See Hamric v. Wilderness Expeditions, Inc.*, 6 F.4th 1108, 1119 (10th Cir. 2021); *Jacobson v. U.S. Dep't of Homeland Sec.*, 882 F.3d 878, 883 (9th Cir. 2018). *See also Emigrant Residential LLC v. Pinti*, 37 F.4th 717, 724 (1st Cir. 2022) (when movant has not yet had full and fair opportunity for discovery, "strong presumption" favors Rule 56(d) relief).

discovery prior to a ruling on summary judgment.[283] In any event, summary judgment is often refused on early motions,[284] with exceptions permitted in only rare instances.[285] With such early filed motions, the courts recognize that the Rule 56(d) affiant or declarant may not be capable of framing a postponement request with great specificity.[286] Nevertheless, even with very early motions, Rule 56(d) relief may still be denied where the supporting affidavit or declaration is vague or conclusory[287] or where additional discovery could not make a factual or legal difference to the outcome.[288]

District Court's Discretion / Options in Ruling

Although relief under this Rule is often and liberally granted,[289] it does not come automatically.[290] Whether to grant or deny a Rule 56(d) postponement is committed to the district court's wide discretion.[291] In ruling, the district court must balance the moving party's need for the requested discovery against the burden the discovery and delay will place on the opposing party.[292] Ergo, a fulsome showing of all requirements

---

[283] *Compare Nader v. Blair*, 549 F.3d 953, 961 (4th Cir. 2008) (court "must refuse" summary judgment where nonmovant has not had opportunity to discover information essential to its position), *with Reflectone, Inc. v. Farrand Optical Co.*, 862 F.2d 841, 843 (11th Cir. 1989) (per curiam) (though not general rule, no "blanket prohibition" on pre-discovery grant of summary judgment). *See generally supra* Authors' Commentary to Rule 56(b) ("**Quick Motions (Filed Before / During Discovery**").

[284] *See Anderson v. Liberty Lobby, Inc.*, 477 U.S. 242, 250 n.5, 106 S. Ct. 2505, 91 L. Ed. 2d 202 (1986).

[285] *See CenTra, Inc. v. Estrin*, 538 F.3d 402, 420–21 (6th Cir. 2008); *Miller v. Wolpoff & Abramson, L.L.P.*, 321 F.3d 292, 303–04 (2d Cir. 2003).

[286] *See Burlington Northern Santa Fe R. Co. v. Assiniboine and Sioux Tribes of Fort Peck Reservation*, 323 F.3d 767, 773–74 (9th Cir. 2003) (affiant cannot be expected to frame motion with great specificity as to nature of discovery likely to develop useful information because ground for such specificity has not yet been laid).

[287] *See Trans-W. Petroleum, Inc. v. United States Gypsum Co.*, 830 F.3d 1171, 1175–76 (10th Cir. 2016).

[288] *See GEICO Cas. Co. v. Isaacson*, 932 F.3d 721, 726–27 (8th Cir. 2019) (where evidence sought was not type that courts could consider in ruling); *United States v. Supreme Court of New Mexico*, 824 F.3d 1263, 1278–79 (10th Cir. 2016) (where only purely legal questions raised).

[289] *See Nat'l Union Fire Ins. Co. of Pittsburgh v. Dish Network, LLC*, 17 F.4th 22, 34 (10th Cir. 2021); *Pledger v. Lynch*, 5 F.4th 511, 526 (4th Cir. 2021). *See also Doe v. City of Memphis*, 928 F.3d 481, 490–91 (6th Cir. 2019) ("granted almost as a matter of course"). *But cf. U.S. ex rel. Folliard v. Government Acquisitions, Inc.*, 764 F.3d 19, 26–27 (D.C.Cir. 2014) (judges must, however, still weigh the requirements).

[290] *See Nat'l Union Fire Ins. Co. of Pittsburgh v. Dish Network, LLC*, 17 F.4th 22, 34 (10th Cir. 2021); *United States ex rel. Booker v. Pfizer, Inc.*, 847 F.3d 52, 61 (1st Cir. 2017).

[291] *See Emigrant Residential LLC v. Pinti*, 37 F.4th 717, 727 (1st Cir. 2022); *Smith v. OSF HealthCare Sys.*, 933 F.3d 859, 865 (7th Cir. 2019).

[292] *See Harbert Intern., Inc. v. James*, 157 F.3d 1271, 1280 (11th Cir. 1998).

raises a strong presumption in favor of relief,[293] especially when coupled with a showing that much of the sought-after information lies within the control of an adversary (particularly a recalcitrant one).[294] Conversely, a failure to make a properly-supported motion may well lead the court to deny the requested postponement and proceed to rule on the merits of the pending summary judgment motion.[295] A movant's lack of diligence in beginning or pursuing discovery (which includes failing to press timely to challenge any improper discovery delays or other mischief[296]) also bodes poorly for the movant.[297] After all, "Rule 56(d) is meant to minister to the vigilant, not to those who sleep upon perceptible rights."[298]

On the basis of a party's meritorious Rule 56(d) showings, the district court may: (1) deny the motion for summary judgment; (2) grant a continuance to allow affidavits to be prepared and submitted; (3) permit discovery; or (4) make any other order as is just.[299] Conversely, if the court denies the Rule 56(d) motion, an explicit explanation is not necessary unless the evidence sought is relevant to a summary judgment ruling.[300] The court should rule promptly on Rule 56(d) motions (for obvious fairness and efficiency reasons),[301] and ordinarily should resolve any pending Rule 56(d) motion before proceeding on to decide the underlying summary judgment motion itself.[302]

Appealability

Rules 56(d) rulings implicate the typical constraints governing the appealability of interlocutory rulings.[303] An added wrinkle is introduced if the Rule 56(d) motion was referred to a

[293]*See In re PHC, Inc. Shareholder Litig.*, 762 F.3d 138, 144 (1st Cir. 2014).

[294]*See In re Avandia Mktg., Sales & Prod. Liab. Litig.*, 945 F.3d 749, 761 (3d Cir. 2019); *In re PHC, Inc. Shareholder Litig.*, 762 F.3d 138, 144-45 (1st Cir. 2014).

[295]*See Burns v. Town of Palm Beach*, 999 F.3d 1317, 1334 (11th Cir. 2021); *United States ex rel. Booker v. Pfizer, Inc.*, 847 F.3d 52, 61–62 (1st Cir. 2017). *See also Cervantes v. Jones*, 188 F.3d 805 (7th Cir. 1999) (affirming denial of motion where excuse for failing to conduct deposition earlier was desire to refrain from beginning discovery in order to "foster an atmosphere conducive to settlement").

[296]*See MAO-MSO Recovery II, LLC v. State Farm Mut. Auto. Ins. Co.*, 994 F.3d 869, 877–78 (7th Cir. 2021).

[297]*See Lillie v. Off. of Fin. Institutions State of La.*, 997 F.3d 577, 586–87 (5th Cir. 2021); *Pina v. Children's Place*, 740 F.3d 785, 795 (1st Cir. 2014).

[298]*See Pina v. Children's Place*, 740 F.3d 785, 794–95 (1st Cir. 2014).

[299]*See In re Avandia Mktg., Sales & Prod. Liab. Litig.*, 945 F.3d 749, 761 (3d Cir. 2019); *Meadows v. Latshaw Drilling Co., L.L.C.*, 866 F.3d 307, 313 (5th Cir. 2017).

[300]*See Stevens v. Corelogic, Inc.*, 899 F.3d 666, 677 (9th Cir. 2018).

[301]*See Smith v. OSF HealthCare Sys.*, 933 F.3d 859, 868 n.3 (7th Cir. 2019).

[302]*See In re Avandia Mktg., Sales & Prod. Liab. Litig.*, 945 F.3d 749, 761–62 (3d Cir. 2019).

[303]*See Sullivan v. Wells*, 428 Fed. Appx. 240, 241 (4th Cir. 2011) (order denying Rule 56(f), now re-labeled as Rule 56(d), is not immediately appealable interlocutory order). *See generally In re Flint Water Cases*, 960 F.3d 820, 829 (6th Cir. 2020) (discovery orders

magistrate judge for disposition: in such cases, the disappointed party's ability to appeal that ruling will also depend on whether that party first properly objected to the magistrate judge's disposition at the district court level.[304]

RULE 56(e) — FAILING TO PROPERLY SUPPORT OR ADDRESS A FACT

CORE CONCEPT

When a party fails to properly support or oppose a motion for summary judgment, the court has several options. It may grant summary judgment (but only when doing so is appropriate, never merely because a party is procedurally delinquent). It may grant the delinquent party a further opportunity to show its support or opposition. It may treat the unaddressed fact as undisputed for the purpose of the motion. Or it may issue some other appropriate order.

APPLICATIONS

2010 Amendments — Amended Rule 56(e)

Former Rule 56(e) prescribed the requirements for a proper summary judgment affidavit and set out the opposing party's burden to respond. These provisions have been repositioned: the affidavit requirements to amended Rule 56(c)(4) and the responding obligations to amended Rule 56(c)(1).

No Summary Judgments by "Default"

Summary judgment may not be entered automatically, upon the non-moving party's failure to respond at all or to respond properly.[305] Likewise, summary judgment may not be denied automatically simply because the moving party failed to reply properly to the opponent's response.[306] Instead, summary judgment should be granted if, but only if, it is appropriate to do so.[307] Consequently, although it is treacherously unwise to fail to oppose a summary judgment motion, even entirely uncontested motions must be examined carefully by the district court to determine whether the record confirms that no genuine dispute of material fact remains and that judgment is appropri-

---

generally are non-final and not immediately appealable); *Drummond Co. v. Terrance P. Collingsworth, Conrad & Scherer, LLP*, 816 F.3d 1319, 1322 (11th Cir. 2016) (same).

[304] *See MAO-MSO Recovery II, LLC v. State Farm Mut. Auto. Ins. Co.*, 994 F.3d 869, 877 (7th Cir. 2021); *Williams v. Wells Fargo Bank, N.A.*, 901 F.3d 1036, 1042 (8th Cir. 2018).

[305] *See Perez v. El Tequila, LLC*, 847 F.3d 1247, 1254–55 (10th Cir. 2017); *Winston & Strawn, LLP v. McLean*, 843 F.3d 503, 505 & 507–08 (D.C. Cir. 2016). *See also United States v. One Piece of Real Prop. Located at 5800 SW 74th Ave., Miami, Fla.*, 363 F.3d 1099, 1101 (11th Cir. 2004) (district court cannot base entry of summary judgment on mere fact that motion was unopposed, but must consider motion's merits). *See generally* Rule 56(e) advisory committee note (2010).

[306] *See* Rule 56(e) advisory committee note (2010).

[307] *See* Rule 56(a) (summary judgment entered only if no genuine dispute of material facts exists *and* movant is entitled to judgment).

ate as a matter of law[308] (which includes confirming that the proffered legal theory is sound).[309]

District Court's Options If Support Is Improper

When confronting an improperly supported motion or opposition, the court has several options in how to respond:

- *Another Chance:* The court may (or may not, in its discretion[310]) permit the delinquent party a further opportunity to file a proper motion or response, with Rule 56(c)-qualifying support.[311] It is presumed that this choice will be a court's likely "preferred first step."[312]
- *"Deemed" Undisputed:* A fact improperly supported or improperly contested may be treated by the court as undisputed.[313] The court is not compelled to do so, however,[314] and should not do so if the summary judgment record reveals the fact at issue to be genuinely disputed.[315] (This does not compel the court to canvass the full record, but to at least review those materials cited in the motion papers.[316]) If the court does treat the fact as undisputed, that consequence is limited to the summary judgment motion only; if the delinquent party survives summary judgment, he or she is not barred from contesting the fact in later proceedings.[317]
- *Grant Summary Judgment:* Because a party's delinquent response cannot, alone, compel summary judg-

---

[308]*See United States v. Brace*, 1 F.4th 137, 143 (3d Cir. 2021); *F.T.C. v. E.M.A. Nationwide, Inc.*, 767 F.3d 611, 629–30 (6th Cir. 2014).

[309]*See Jackson v. Fed. Exp.*, 766 F.3d 189, 194 (2d Cir. 2014).

[310]*See Winston & Strawn, LLP v. McLean*, 843 F.3d 503, 509 (D.C. Cir. 2016). *See also Rogers v. Washington Metro. Area Transit Auth.*, 214 F. Supp. 3d 10, 14 (D.D.C. 2016) (denying opportunity); *Perkins v. Rock-Tenn Servs., Inc.*, 190 F. Supp. 3d 720, 731 (W.D. Mich. 2016), *aff'd*, 2017 WL 2829100 (6th Cir. 2017) (granting opportunity).

[311]*See* Rule 56(e)(1). *See also Grimes v. District of Columbia*, 794 F.3d 83, 92 (D.C.Cir. 2015); *Keen v. C.R. Bard, Inc.*, 480 F. Supp. 3d 624, 633 (E.D. Pa. 2020).

[312]*See* Rule 56(e)(1) advisory committee note (2010). *See also Winston & Strawn, LLP v. McLean*, 843 F.3d 503, 507 (D.C. Cir. 2016).

[313]*See* Rule 56(e)(2). *See also United States v. Mills*, 18 F.4th 573, 576 (8th Cir. 2021); *Pac. Gulf Shipping Co. v. Vigorous Shipping & Trading S.A.*, 992 F.3d 893, 900 (9th Cir. 2021).

[314]*See Warkentin v. Federated Life Ins. Co.*, 594 Fed. Appx. 900, 902–03 (9th Cir. 2014). *Compare Tanner v. McMurray*, 429 F. Supp. 3d 1047, 1069 n.63 (D.N.M. 2019), *rev'd on other grounds*, 989 F.3d 860 (10th Cir. 2021) (treating certain facts as undisputed), *with id.* at 1071 n.67 (declining to treat other facts as undisputed).

[315]*See* Rule 56(e)(2) advisory committee (2010).

[316]*See United States v. One Piece of Real Prop. Located at 5800 SW 74th Ave., Miami, Fla.*, 363 F.3d 1099, 1101-02 (11th Cir. 2004). *See also supra* Authors' Commentary to Rule 56(c) ("**Procedure #3: Content of Summary Judgment Record**").

[317]*See* Rule 56(e)(2) advisory committee note (2010).

ment,[318] summary judgment is properly granted following a delinquent response only if the standards for summary judgment are otherwise satisfied.[319] The same is true when a court treats improperly supported or improperly contested facts as undisputed.[320]

- *Other Appropriate Order:* The court may also enter some other appropriate order, designed to prompt a proper presentation of the record.[321] Nudging *pro se* litigants forward,[322] refusing to consider unsupported assertions,[323] striking (or ordering a supplementation of) a deficient submission,[324] striking off improper portions of affidavits,[325] deferring a ruling pending certain further analysis,[326] and denying summary judgment but inviting a new motion later[327] are examples.

Motions Involving *Pro Se* Litigants

In considering summary judgment motions involving *pro se* litigants, the *pro se* litigant's pleadings are construed liberally (though the court will not act as that litigant's advocate).[328] Some courts, however, direct that summary judgment may be entered against *pro se* litigants only if they are first expressly informed of the consequences of failing to come forward with contradicting evidence (*e.g.*, told he or she cannot rely merely on the allegations of the pleadings, and risks dismissal in doing so).[329] Other courts adopt this special warning duty only in

[318] *See supra* Authors' Commentary to Rule 56(e) (**"No Summary Judgment by 'Default'"**).

[319] *See* Rule 56(e)(3). *See also Banks v. Deere*, 829 F.3d 661, 668 (8th Cir. 2016); *Columbia Pictures Indus., Inc. v. Fung*, 710 F.3d 1020, 1044 (9th Cir. 2013).

[320] *See* Rule 56(e)(3) advisory committee note (2010) (even as to "deemed" undisputed facts, court "must determine the legal consequences of these facts and possible inferences from them").

[321] *See* Rule 56(e)(4). *See also Hammond v. City of Wilkes-Barre*, 600 Fed.Appx. 833, 837 n.7 (3d Cir. 2015).

[322] *See* Rule 56(e)(4) advisory committee note (2010). *See also infra* Authors' Commentary to Rule 56(e) (**"Motions Involving *Pro Se* Litigants"**).

[323] *See McGarry v. Bd. of Cty. Commissioners for Cty. of Lincoln*, 294 F. Supp. 3d 1170, 1173–74 nn. 2, 4–5 (D.N.M. 2018); *Deere & Co. v. FIMCO Inc.*, 239 F. Supp. 3d 964, 987 (W.D. Ky. 2017).

[324] *See Novak v. Mentor Worldwide LLC*, 287 F. Supp. 3d 85, 87 (D. Me. 2018).

[325] *See Phat's Bar & Grill, Inc. v. Louisville-Jefferson County Metro Gov't*, 2013 WL 142481, at *3–*4 (W.D.Ky. Jan. 11, 2013).

[326] *See Doe v. Bridges to Recovery, LLC*, 2021 WL 1321652, at *15 (C.D. Cal. Mar. 8, 2021).

[327] *See Nick's Garage, Inc. v. Progressive Cas. Ins. Co.*, 875 F.3d 107, 116 n.4 (2d Cir. 2017).

[328] *See Cardoso v. Calbone*, 490 F.3d 1194, 1197 (10th Cir. 2007). *See also supra* Authors' Commentary to Rule 8(e) (**"Motions Involving *Pro Se* Litigants"**).

[329] *See Pledger v. Lynch*, 5 F.4th 511, 525 (4th Cir. 2021); *U.S. v. Ninety Three Firearms*, 330 F.3d 414, 427 (6th Cir. 2003).

the context of incarcerated unrepresented parties;[330] as to nonprisoner unrepresented parties, those courts would require no special warning.[331]

RULE 56(f) — JUDGMENT INDEPENDENT OF THE MOTION

CORE CONCEPT

Provided the court gives the parties notice and a reasonable opportunity to respond, it may grant summary judgment in favor of a party who has not sought it, grant summary judgment on different grounds than those requested by the motion, or grant summary judgment *sua sponte*.

APPLICATIONS

2010 Amendments — Amended Rule 56(f)

Former Rule 56(f) contained the affidavit procedure for seeking to postpone a summary judgment ruling pending further discovery. That procedure has now been repositioned to amended Rule 56(d). The current content of Rule 56(f) contains three special uses of summary judgment that, though long recognized, were not formerly codified.

Summary Judgment for Non-Moving Parties

In resolving a pending motion for summary judgment, the court may grant summary judgment in favor of a party who has not requested it.[332] Before doing so, the court must give the parties notice and reasonable time to respond[333] (with a failure to do so excused only if that omission was harmless error).[334] This type of summary judgment grant might occur in at least two contexts. First, in a multi-defendant case where one co-defendant obtains summary judgment on motion, the court may enter a similar summary judgment in favor of other similarly situated but non-moving co-defendants.[335] Second, a court that denies a moving party's request for summary judgment may enter an unrequested summary judgment *against* that party and in favor of the non-moving party.[336] Such judgments are generally only entered if the court is convinced that

---

[330] *See U.S. v. Ninety Three Firearms*, 330 F.3d 414, 427–28 (6th Cir. 2003).

[331] *See U.S. v. Ninety Three Firearms*, 330 F.3d 414, 428 (6th Cir. 2003) (distinction "was only fair because parties choosing to have counsel 'must bear the risk of their attorney's mistakes,' and thus, 'a litigant who chooses himself as a legal representative should be treated no differently' ").

[332] *See* Rule 56(f)(1).

[333] *See* Rule 56(f)(1). *See also Tabura v. Kellogg USA*, 880 F.3d 544, 558 (10th Cir. 2018); *Albino v. Baca*, 747 F.3d 1162, 1176–77 (9th Cir. 2014).

[334] *See Gabb v. Wexford Health Sources, Inc.*, 945 F.3d 1027, 1034-35 (7th Cir. 2019).

[335] *See Gabb v. Wexford Health Sources, Inc.*, 945 F.3d 1027, 1034-35 (7th Cir. 2019).

[336] *See Lee v. Sixth Mount Zion Baptist Church of Pittsburgh*, 903 F.3d 113, 118 (3d Cir. 2018).

the factual record is fully developed, that the non-moving party is "clearly" entitled to judgment, and that entry of the judgment would not result in procedural prejudice.[337] Before granting such relief, the court must find that entering summary judgment is both proper on its merits and procedurally sound (that its entry does not offend fundamental fairness).[338]

Summary Judgment on Unrequested Grounds

In resolving a pending motion for summary judgment, the court may grant summary judgment on grounds not advocated by the parties.[339] Case law cautions that such authority should be exercised sparingly and with great care.[340] Before doing so, the court must give the parties notice and reasonable time to respond.[341] Some courts even foreclose such grants unless discovery is sufficiently advanced.[342] Even without proper notice, such summary judgments might be tolerated where that notice oversight proves to be harmless[343] or any objection to the absent notice was waived.[344] This is a change from prior practice which had generally foreclosed such grants[345] or limited them to only situations that would suffice for *sua sponte* summary judgments.[346]

Summary Judgment *Sua Sponte*

The court may enter summary judgment *sua sponte*.[347] In doing so, the court will apply the usual summary judgment standards, resolving all ambiguities and drawing all factual inferences in the target party's favor.[348] But the case law cautions great care in the grant of *sua sponte* summary judgments,[349] with some case law declaring them disfavored[350] or even unnecessary (because the court can always invite a party

---

[337]*See Faustin v. City & County of Denver*, 423 F.3d 1192, 1198–99 (10th Cir. 2005); *E. C. Ernst, Inc. v. General Motors Corp.*, 537 F.2d 105, 109 (5th Cir. 1976).

[338]*See Caswell v. City of Detroit Housing Com'n*, 418 F.3d 615, 617–18 (6th Cir.2005); *John G. Alden, Inc. of Mass. v. John G. Alden Ins. Agency of Fla., Inc.*, 389 F.3d 21, 25 (1st Cir. 2004).

[339]*See* Rule 56(f)(2).

[340]*See Oahn Nguyen Chung v. StudentCity.com, Inc.*, 854 F.3d 97, 103 (1st Cir. 2017).

[341]*See* Rule 56(f)(2). *See also Merechka v. Vigilant Ins. Co.*, 26 F.4th 776, 787–88 (8th Cir. 2022); *George v. Youngstown State Univ.*, 966 F.3d 446, 467 (6th Cir. 2020).

[342]*See Oahn Nguyen Chung v. StudentCity.com, Inc.*, 854 F.3d 97, 103–06 (1st Cir. 2017).

[343]*See Rains v. Jones*, 905 F.3d 545, 551–52 (8th Cir. 2018); *Oldham v. O.K. Farms, Inc.*, 871 F.3d 1147, 1150–51 (10th Cir. 2017).

[344]*See UnitedHealth Grp. Inc. v. Exec. Risk Specialty Ins. Co.*, 870 F.3d 856, 866–67 (8th Cir. 2017).

[345]*See Washburn v. Harvey*, 504 F.3d 505, 510 (5th Cir. 2007).

[346]*See Byars v. Coca-Cola Co.*, 517 F.3d 1256, 1264–65 (11th Cir. 2008).

[347]*See* Rule 56(f)(3). *See also Celotex Corp. v. Catrett*, 477 U.S. 317, 326, 106 S. Ct. 2548, 91 L. Ed. 2d 265 (1986) (noting right to enter *sua sponte* motions under Rule 56).

[348]*See NetJets Aviation, Inc. v. LHC Communications, LLC*, 537 F.3d 168, 178 (2d Cir. 2008).

[349]*See KST Data, Inc. v. DXC Tech. Co.*, 980 F.3d 709, 714 (9th Cir. 2020);

to file the motion).[351] Before granting summary judgment *sua sponte*, the court must provide advance notice of its intention and allow a reasonable time for response.[352] While such notice need not come by way of a formal document,[353] litigants must appreciate that they are targets of a summary judgment inquiry and possess that motivation when preparing the response.[354] The court's notice must identify for the parties those material facts that the court believes might not be genuinely disputed.[355] The court must also ensure that the opponent's opportunity to respond is full and fair.[356] Before entering summary judgment against a defending party, the court must allow a proper opportunity for that party to assert any affirmative defenses it may have.[357] Failure to provide these procedural safeguards is reversible error,[358] unless that error is harmless.[359]

Prior to the 2010 Amendments, certain case law practices regarding *sua sponte* summary judgments had developed over time. Some courts had held that discovery must either be completed or clearly be of no further benefit before *sua sponte* summary judgments could be granted.[360] Other courts had excused the notice and response requirement where three criteria were met: the summary judgment record was fully developed, there was no prejudice to the non-moving party, and

---

Ramsey v. Coughlin, 94 F.3d 71, 74 (2d Cir. 1996).

[350]*See Williams v. Maurer*, 9 F.4th 416, 425 n.1 (6th Cir. 2021); *A.M. v. Holmes*, 830 F.3d 1123, 1136 (10th Cir. 2016).

[351]*See ING Bank N.V. v. M/V TEMARA, IMO No. 9333929*, 892 F.3d 511, 524 n.8 (2d Cir. 2018); *Goldstein v. Fidelity and Guar. Ins. Underwriters, Inc.*, 86 F.3d 749, 751 (7th Cir. 1996).

[352]*See Lexon Ins. Co., Inc. v. Fed. Deposit Ins. Corp.*, 7 F.4th 315, 321 (5th Cir. 2021); *KST Data, Inc. v. DXC Tech. Co.*, 980 F.3d 709, 713–14 (9th Cir. 2020).

[353]*See Moore v. Equitrans, L.P.*, 27 F.4th 211, 224 (4th Cir. 2022).

[354]*See SRI Intl., Inc. v. Cisco Sys., Inc.*, 930 F.3d 1295, 1307 (Fed. Cir. 2019); *John G. Alden, Inc. of Mass. v. John G. Alden Ins. Agency of Fla., Inc.*, 389 F.3d 21, 25 (1st Cir. 2004).

[355]*See* Rule 56(f)(3). *See also ING Bank N.V. v. M/V TEMARA, IMO No. 9333929*, 892 F.3d 511, 524 (2d Cir. 2018); *Sayles v. Advanced Recovery Sys., Inc.*, 865 F.3d 246, 249 (5th Cir. 2017).

[356]*See In re 650 Fifth Ave. & Related Props.*, 830 F.3d 66, 96–97 (2d Cir. 2016); *Hotel 71 Mezz Lender LLC v. Nat'l Ret. Fund*, 778 F.3d 593, 603 (7th Cir. 2015).

[357]*See KST Data, Inc. v. DXC Tech. Co.*, 980 F.3d 709, 714 (9th Cir. 2020).

[358]*See Forrest v. Parry*, 930 F.3d 93, 110–13 (3d Cir. 2019) (reversing grant, where losing party had no reason to believe he was at risk of adverse summary judgment ruling).

[359]*See Lexon Ins. Co., Inc. v. Fed. Deposit Ins. Corp.*, 7 F.4th 315, 320–22 (5th Cir. 2021) (harmless if nonmovant has no additional evidence or, upon review, court finds no genuine dispute of material fact); *Nicholson v. Securitas Sec. Servs. USA, Inc.*, 830 F.3d 186, 188 (5th Cir. 2016) (harmless if opponent moved for reconsideration).

[360]*See Puerto Rico Elec. Power Authority v. Action Refund*, 515 F.3d 57, 64–65 (1st Cir. 2008). *See also Swatch Group Mgmt. Servs. Ltd. v. Bloomberg L.P.*, 756 F.3d 73, 80 (2d Cir. 2014) (applying same requirement under amended Rule).

the decision rested on a purely legal issue.[361]

RULE 56(g) — FAILING TO GRANT ALL OF THE REQUESTED RELIEF

CORE CONCEPT

After considering the standards for summary judgment, the court may conclude that such a judgment is not appropriate at all or not appropriate as to every claim or defense for which it was sought. Nevertheless, the inquiry might have revealed that certain material facts are not genuinely disputed. The court may (but is not required to) declare those facts as established for purposes of the case.

APPLICATIONS

2010 Amendments—Amended Rule 56(g)

Former Rule 56(g) set forth the penalties for summary judgment affidavits made in bad faith. That provision is now moved to new Rule 56(h). Rule 56(g) now contains content repositioned from former Rules 56(c) and (d), with one notable distinction. The prior language of this declaring-as-established procedure had seemed to encourage such rulings (using the verb "should"); the current Rule appears more neutral (with the verb "may").

Purpose of the "Declaring-As-Established" Procedure

The goal of this procedure is to allow trial courts to salvage some constructive result from their efforts in ruling upon otherwise denied (or partially denied) summary judgment motions.[362] Where the summary judgment inquiry demonstrates that certain material facts are not genuinely disputed, the court may declare them established for trial, even though summary judgment itself is being fully or partially denied.[363] Such declared-facts may accelerate litigations by winnowing down the number of issues that must be tried.[364]

Which Facts May Be Declared as Established

Provided the fact is a *material* one, any fact may be declared as undisputed by the court, including liability and damages

---

[361] *See DL Resources, Inc. v. FirstEnergy Solutions Corp.*, 506 F.3d 209, 223–24 (3d Cir. 2007).

[362] *See Kreg Therapeutics, Inc. v. VitalGo, Inc.*, 919 F.3d 405, 415 (7th Cir. 2019); *D'Iorio v. Winebow, Inc.*, 68 F. Supp. 3d 334, 356 (E.D.N.Y. 2014). The failure of the summary judgment motion does not defeat the availability of Rule 56(g) relief; rather, the Rule's relief becomes available precisely because the motion failed. *See Kreg Therapeutics, Inc. v. VitalGo, Inc.*, 919 F.3d 405, 415 (7th Cir. 2019).

[363] *See Singh v. George Washington Univ. Sch. of Med. & Health Sciences*, 508 F.3d 1097, 1106 (D.C. Cir. 2007); *F.D.I.C. v. Massingill*, 24 F.3d 768, 774 (5th Cir. 1994).

[364] *See Global Crossing Bandwidth, Inc. v. Locus Telecommc'n, Inc.*, 632 F. Supp. 2d 224, 238 (W.D.N.Y. 2009); *Geneva Int'l Corp. v. Petrof, Spol, S.R.O.*, 608 F. Supp. 2d 993, 1004–05 (N.D.Ill. 2009).

facts (and even particular items of damages).[365]

Standard for Declaring Facts as Established

Because this procedure is in the nature of a collateral by-product of the summary judgment inquiry itself,[366] the standard for declaring facts to be established is the same standard used in granting summary judgment.[367] The parties need not *agree* on which material facts are undisputed (or that any of them are).[368] Rather, the burden of demonstrating that a material fact is genuinely undisputed lies with the moving party, employing the same burden-of-going-forward shift used with summary judgment motions generally.[369]

District Court's Discretion

The trial judge is not required to use this procedure. Instead, the decision lies entirely within the trial judge's discretion.[370] Thus, for example, the court may decide that the task of declaring facts to be established will be more burdensome than addressing those facts through other means (like trial), or may conclude that a full trial may better illuminate those facts.[371] Nor is the court necessarily required, if it grants relief under this Rule, to set out the declared facts in a separate order,[372] or even in writing.[373]

No Interference With Opposing Party's Strategy

Parties opposing summary judgment may choose strategically to concede (or to not affirmatively dispute) a certain fact,

---

[365]*See, e.g., Barnes v. Sea Hawaii Rafting, LLC*, 889 F.3d 517, 539 (9th Cir. 2018) (seaman may establish entitlement to maintenance and expenses); *U.S. v. Univ. of Neb. at Kearney*, 940 F. Supp. 2d 974, 976–83 (D.Neb. 2013) (establishing that collegiate student housing are "dwellings" within meaning of Fair Housing Act).

[366]*See Doe v. Bibb Cty. Sch. Dist.*, 126 F. Supp. 3d 1366, 1375 (M.D. Ga. 2015) (having already filed a motion for summary judgment is a precondition of Rule 56(g) relief).

[367]*See* Rule 56(g) advisory committee note (2010). *See also California v. Campbell*, 138 F.3d 772, 780 (9th Cir. 1998); *Global Crossing Bandwidth, Inc. v. Locus Telecommc'n, Inc.*, 632 F. Supp. 2d 224, 238 (W.D.N.Y. 2009).

[368]*See Global Crossing Bandwidth, Inc. v. Locus Telecommc'n, Inc.*, 632 F. Supp. 2d 224, 238 (W.D.N.Y. 2009).

[369]*See Green v. Sun Life Assur. Co. of Canada*, 383 F. Supp. 2d 1224, 1226 (C.D. Cal. 2005).

[370]*See* Rule 56(g) advisory committee note (2010) ("Even if the court believes that a fact is not genuinely in dispute it may refrain from ordering that the fact be treated as established."). *See also Triple H Debris Removal, Inc. v. Companion Prop. & Cas. Ins. Co.*, 647 F.3d 780, 785–86 (8th Cir. 2011); *D'Iorio v. Winebow, Inc.*, 68 F. Supp. 3d 334, 356 (E.D.N.Y. 2014).

[371]*See* Rule 56(g) advisory committee note (2010). *See also Triple H Debris Removal, Inc. v. Companion Prop. & Cas. Ins. Co.*, 647 F.3d 780, 785–86 (8th Cir. 2011); *Khoday v. Symantec Corp.*, 93 F. Supp. 1067, 1090 n.7 (D.Minn. 2015) (denied, because could mislead a jury).

[372]*See U.S. Bank Nat'l Ass'n v. Verizon Commc'ns, Inc.*, 761 F.3d 409, 427 n.15 (5th Cir. 2014).

[373]*See Kreg Therapeutics, Inc. v. VitalGo, Inc.*, 919 F.3d 405, 416 (7th Cir. 2019) (issuing such orders in writing is "best practice," but not necessarily required).

and to do so for summary judgment motion purposes only. The court must take care to ensure that such strategic, procedural concessions are not used to declare a fact as established when, at trial, parties intend to contest it.[374]

Making a Separate Motion to Declare-As-Established

Under the earlier version of this procedure, courts were divided whether parties could file a freestanding, independent motion seeking to have certain facts declared as established.[375] The current language of the Rule has not resolved this uncertainty.[376] Some courts held that litigants could only seek full (or partial) summary judgments and not "declared-as-established" facts,[377] or alternatively, that any such independent motion be made only "in the wake" of such an unsuccessful full motion.[378] Other courts rejected this reasoning, and permitted the filing of distinct motions seeking "declared-as-established" rulings.[379]

Timing

The Rule sets no timing parameters for Rule 56(g) relief, beyond the obvious constraint that the court must first have determined that full or partial summary judgment will not be granted.[380]

Effect of Declared-As-Established Rulings

If the court chooses to grant them, "declared-as-established" rulings are not "judgments" and do not become "final orders" until the district court enters a final judgment.[381] Such declarations are not immutable, and they have no *res judicata* effect.[382] Nevertheless, such declarations are still rulings on a "disposi-

[374] *See also* Rule 56(g) advisory committee note (2010). *See Triple H Debris Removal, Inc. v. Companion Prop. & Cas. Ins. Co.*, 647 F.3d 780, 785–86 (8th Cir. 2011).

[375] *See Beaty v. Republic of Iraq*, 480 F. Supp. 2d 60, 100 (D.D.C. 2007) (discussing division), *rev'd on other grounds*, 556 U.S. 848, 129 S. Ct. 2183, 173 L. Ed. 2d 1193 (2009).

[376] *See Milliner v. Mut. Sec., Inc.*, 2017 WL 1064978, at *5 (N.D. Cal. Mar. 18, 2017) (noting persisting uncertainty).

[377] *See, e.g., Mullaney v. Hilton Hotels Corp.*, 634 F. Supp. 2d 1130, 1161 (D.Haw. 2009); *Patrick Schaumburg Autos., Inc. v. Hanover Ins. Co.*, 452 F. Supp. 2d 857, 867 (N.D. Ill. 2006).

[378] *See Kendall McGaw Labs., Inc. v. Community Mem. Hosp.*, 125 F.R.D. 420, 421 (D.N.J. 1989).

[379] *See, e.g., Zapata Hermanos Sucesores, S.A. v. Hearthside Baking Co., Inc.*, 313 F.3d 385, 391 (7th Cir. 2002); *McDonnell v. Cardiothoracic & Vascular Surgical Assocs., Inc.*, 2004 WL 1234138 (S.D. Ohio 2004).

[380] *See Kreg Therapeutics, Inc. v. VitalGo, Inc.*, 919 F.3d 405, 416 (7th Cir. 2019) (issuing such orders "contemporaneously" with summary judgment decision is "best practice," but not necessarily required).

[381] *See Alberty-Velez v. Corporacion de Puerto Rico Para La Difusion Publica*, 361 F.3d 1, 6 n.5 (1st Cir. 2004); *Burkhart v. Washington Metropolitan Area Transit Auth.*, 112 F.3d 1207, 1215–16 (D.C. Cir. 1997).

[382] *See Latin American Music Co. v. Media Power Group, Inc.*, 705 F.3d 34, 40–41 (1st Cir. 2013); *Burge v. Parish of St. Tammany*, 187 F.3d 452, 467 (5th Cir. 1999).

tive motion,"[383] and will be treated as "law of the case."[384] Thus, the parties are entitled to rely on the conclusiveness of the declaration[385] and, absent good reason for doing so, the district court will not generally revisit or alter facts adjudicated under Rule 56(g).[386] If the court decides that good reasons exist to alter a "declared-as-established" ruling, the court must so inform the parties and permit them an opportunity to present evidence concerning any of the revisited issues.[387]

RULE 56(h)—AFFIDAVIT OR DECLARATION SUBMITTED IN BAD FAITH

CORE CONCEPT

If the district court concludes that an affidavit or declaration submitted in a summary judgment proceeding was presented in bad faith or solely for purposes of delay, the court may order the offending party to pay reasonable expenses incurred by the party's adversary (including attorney's fees).

APPLICATIONS

2010 Amendments — Repositioned as Rule 56(h)

Rule 56(h) contains the relocated content of former Rule 56(g), with three substantive adjustments to prior practice: sanctions are now discretionary, not mandatory; an offending party is now expressly entitled to notice and an opportunity to respond; and other sanctions, beyond attorney's fees and contempt, are now explicitly authorized.

Purpose

The submission of bad faith affidavits and declarations derails, in an illegitimate way, the summary judgment process by creating the false impression of a genuine, material factual dispute that must await trial. Because the impression is not real, but dishonestly simulated, the maneuver forces the parties and the court to incur the time and costs of an unnecessary trial.[388] Rule 56(h) is intended to combat that abuse. The Rule's

---

[383] *See Burkhart v. Washington Metropolitan Area Transit Auth.*, 112 F.3d 1207, 1215–16 (D.C. Cir. 1997).

[384] *See Burge v. Parish of St. Tammany*, 187 F.3d 452, 467 (5th Cir. 1999); *Carr v. O'Leary*, 167 F.3d 1124, 1126 (7th Cir. 1999).

[385] *See Huss v. King Co., Inc.*, 338 F.3d 647, 650–51 (6th Cir. 2003); *Leddy v. Standard Drywall, Inc.*, 875 F.2d 383, 386 (2d Cir. 1989).

[386] *See Carr v. O'Leary*, 167 F.3d 1124, 1126 (7th Cir. 1999).

[387] *See Alberty-Velez v. Corporacion de Puerto Rico Para La Difusion Publica*, 361 F.3d 1, 6 n.5 (1st Cir. 2004); *Huss v. King Co., Inc.*, 338 F.3d 647, 650–51 (6th Cir. 2003). *See also Joseph P. Caulfield & Assocs., Inc. v. Litho Prods., Inc.*, 155 F.3d 883, 888 (7th Cir. 1998) (proper procedure to seek revisitation is to file motion to vacate ruling and request either that issues be added to trial or that they be resolved as matter of law in favor of moving party).

[388] *See U.S. v. Nguyen*, 655 F. Supp. 2d 1203, 1210 (S.D.Ala. 2009).

protections, however, are not frequently invoked (or granted).[389]

Express Requirements: Bad Faith or Delay

Courts may compensate a party who confronts summary judgment affidavits or declarations submitted either in bad faith or solely[390] for purposes of delay.[391] One of those two situations must be proven[392] (or both may, because the bad faith motivation may be delay).[393] Accordingly, the mere fact that a summary judgment affidavit proved to be unconvincing is not sufficient to trigger this Rule,[394] nor is the opponent's disbelief in the affidavit's veracity[395] or its conflict with other evidence.[396] Inaccurate information included negligently is also not sanctionable.[397] Instead, the circumstances must be "egregious":[398] a "deliberate or knowing act for an improper purpose,"[399] such as perjurious or blatantly false allegations or facts,[400] a contradiction without a bona fide explanation,[401] or a statement made without color, with dishonesty of belief or mo-

[389] *See Fort Hill Builders, Inc. v. National Grange Mut. Ins. Co.*, 866 F.2d 11, 16 (1st Cir. 1989); *Abdelkhaleq v. Precision Door of Akron*, 653 F. Supp. 2d 773, 787 (N.D.Ohio 2009).

[390] *DR Distribrs., LLC v. 21 Century Smoking, Inc.*, 513 F. Supp. 3d 839, 951 (N.D. Ill. 2021) (noting "solely" is "critical word," since "[t]he law rarely finds that an action occurred for a singular purpose").

[391] *See In re Gioioso*, 979 F.2d 956, 961–62 (3d Cir.1992).

[392] *See Klein v. Stahl GMBH & Co. Maschinefabrik*, 185 F.3d 98, 110 (3d Cir. 1999); *Profita v. Puckett*, 2017 WL 1491003, at *28 (D. Colo. Apr. 25, 2017).

[393] *See U.S. v. Nguyen*, 655 F. Supp. 2d 1203, 1210 (S.D.Ala. 2009).

[394] *See Am. Gen. Life Ins. v. Pasalano*, 2016 WL 3448475, at *1 (D. Utah June 20, 2016).

[395] *See Moorer v. Grumman Aerospace Corp.*, 964 F. Supp. 665, 676 (E.D. N.Y. 1997), aff'd, 162 F.3d 1148 (2d Cir. 1998).

[396] *See Thoroughman v. Savittieri*, 323 Fed.Appx. 548, 551 (9th Cir. 2009); *Turner v. Baylor Richardson Medical Center*, 476 F.3d 337, 349 (5th Cir. 2007). *See also OSA Healthcare, Inc. v. Mount Vernon Fire Ins. Co.*, 975 F. Supp. 2d 1316, 1319 (N.D. Ga. 2013) (discerning when affidavit inconsistency crosses line into fabrication "is no easy matter"). *See generally Cleveland v. Policy Mgmt. Sys. Corp.*, 526 U.S. 795, 804, 119 S. Ct. 1597, 143 L. Ed. 2d 966 (1999) (party ordinarily cannot defeat summary judgment by simply denying, in affidavit, a statement that party had earlier admitted in sworn statement absent adequate explanation for inconsistency).

[397] *See Nationwide Mut. Fire Ins. Co. v. D.R. Horton, Inc.*, 2016 WL 6828206, at *4 (S.D. Ala. Nov. 18, 2016). *See also Hunt v. Tektronix, Inc.*, 952 F. Supp. 998, 1010 (W.D.N.Y. 1997) (no sanctions where affiant's actions, though "unfortunate," were not deliberately taken in bad faith.

[398] *See Fort Hill Builders, Inc. v. National Grange Mut. Ins. Co.*, 866 F.2d 11, 16 (1st Cir. 1989); *DR Distribrs., LLC v. 21 Century Smoking, Inc.*, 513 F. Supp. 3d 839, 950 (N.D. Ill. 2021).

[399] *See Allen v. Mayo*, 2021 WL 1753948, at *10 (E.D. Va. May 4, 2021); *Rexroat v. Arizona Dep't of Educ.*, 2012 WL 5936672, at *4 (D.Ariz. Nov. 26, 2012).

[400] *See Fort Hill Builders, Inc. v. National Grange Mut. Ins. Co.*, 866 F.2d 11, 16 (1st Cir. 1989); *Jimenez v. City of New York*, 166 F. Supp. 3d 426, 430–32 (S.D.N.Y. 2016), *aff'd in part and vacated in part on other grounds*, 666 Fed. Appx. 39 (2d Cir. 2016).

[401] *See Mifflinburg Tel., Inc. v. Criswell*, 277 F. Supp. 3d 750, 807–08

tive, or asserted wantonly or to harass, delay, or for some other improper purpose.[402] And, after surveying the case law, one court added that the proof of the affidavit's impropriety must also be "clear".[403]

Express Requirement: Notice & Time to Respond

No sanctions may be imposed until the offending party is first afforded notice and a reasonable time to respond.[404]

Implied Requirements: Prejudice and Causation

Some courts require the moving party to show prejudice before sanctions are awarded,[405] and some courts will not award sanctions unless the offending document was actually considered by the judge in resolving a summary judgment motion.[406]

District Court's Discretion

Sanctions for violating this Rule are discretionary, not mandatory[407] (a change from prior practice[408]), and the breadth of that discretion is wide.[409]

Available Sanctions

The district court enjoys an array of choices to address bad faith affidavits or declarations in summary judgment practice. The courts may strike the offending affidavits,[410] compel the offenders to reimburse their adversaries for reasonable expenses

---

(M.D. Pa. 2017); *Caron v. QuicKutz, Inc.*, 2012 WL 5497869, at *20 (D.Ariz. Nov. 13, 2012), *aff'd,* 528 Fed. Appx. 993 (Fed.Cir. 2013).

[402] *See Bowers v. University of Virginia*, 2008 WL 2346033, at *4 (W.D. Va. 2008). *See also Nuzzi v. St. George Cmty. Consol. Sch. Dist. No. 258*, 688 F. Supp. 2d 815, 834 (C.D. Ill. 2010) (finding 100-page-long rambling, unsupported, "ranting" affidavits violate Rule).

[403] *See Advanced Analytics, Inc. v. Citigroup Glob. Markets, Inc.*, 2019 WL 4193941, at *4 (S.D.N.Y. Sept. 4, 2019) ("clear proof" is "one consistent principle" among courts granting Rule 56(h) relief).

[404] *See* Rule 56(h).

[405] *See Trustees of Plumbers and Steamfitters Local Union No. 43 Health and Welfare Fund v. Crawford*, 573 F. Supp. 2d 1023, 1039 (E.D. Tenn. 2008).

[406] *See, e.g., Sutton v. U.S. Small Bus. Admin.*, 92 Fed.Appx. 112, 117–18 (6th Cir.2003); *DR Distribrs., LLC v. 21 Century Smoking, Inc.*, 513 F. Supp. 3d 839, 951 (N.D. Ill. 2021).

[407] *See* Rule 56(h) advisory committee note (2010). *See also Nationwide Mut. Fire Ins. Co. v. D.R. Horton, Inc.*, 2016 WL 6828206, at *4 (S.D. Ala. Nov. 18, 2016) (noting change).

[408] *See Scott v. Metropolitan Health Corp.*, 234 Fed. Appx. 341, 345 (6th Cir. 2007). The explanation for this shift from mandatory to discretionary imposition was the drafters' observation that "courts seldom invoke the independent Rule 56 authority to impose sanctions." *See* Rule 56(h) advisory committee note (2010).

[409] *See Turner v. Baylor Richardson Medical Center*, 476 F.3d 337, 349 (5th Cir. 2007); *nVision Global Tech. Solutions, Inc. v. Cardinal Health 5, LLC*, 887 F. Supp. 2d 1240, 1260 (N.D.Ga. 2012).

[410] *See Domain Prot., LLC v. Sea Wasp, LLC*, 426 F. Supp. 3d 355, 370 (E.D. Tex. 2019); *nVision Global Tech. Solutions, Inc. v. Cardinal Health 5, LLC*, 887 F. Supp. 2d 1240, 1259 (N.D.Ga. 2012).

(including attorney's fees) incurred by the submission,[411] hold the offenders or their counsel in contempt,[412] and impose "other appropriate sanctions."[413] Moreover, false swearing could also expose the offending party to criminal prosecution.[414]

Submissions From or To *Pro Se* Litigants

Courts may apply this sanctions Rule more gently in cases involving affidavits or declarations submitted by *pro se* litigants.[415] It is uncertain whether *pro se* litigants, if victimized by sanctionable conduct, are eligible to recover expenses or "fees" under this Rule.[416]

Submissions Made in Any Summary Judgment Setting

The Rule applies to all affidavits and declarations made in a summary judgment context, including those made by both the moving and non-moving parties under Rule 56(c), as well as affidavits and declarations under Rule 56(d) seeking to postpone a summary judgment ruling.[417]

Submissions Made in Other Settings

By its terms, this Rule applies only to affidavits and declarations presented in the summary judgment context. Affidavits and declarations submitted for other purposes, or in support of relief under other Rules, are not subject to Rule 56(h).[418]

Additional Research References

Wright & Miller, *Federal Practice and Procedure* §§ 2711 to 2742
C.J.S., Federal Civil Procedure §§ 1135 to 1187 et seq., §§ 1189 to 1216 et seq.
West's Key Number Digest, Federal Civil Procedure ⚷2461 to 2559

---

[411] *See Klein v. Stahl GMBH & Co. Maschinefabrik*, 185 F.3d 98, 110 (3d Cir. 1999); *Jimenez v. City of New York*, 162 F. Supp. 3d 173, 181–83 (S.D.N.Y. 2015), *aff'd in part and vacated in part*, 666 Fed. Appx. 39 (2d Cir. 2016).

[412] *See Klein v. Stahl GMBH & Co. Maschinefabrik*, 185 F.3d 98, 110 (3d Cir. 1999).

[413] *See* Rule 56(h).

[414] *See* 18 U.S.C.A. § 1623 (person who makes knowingly false material declaration to court is subject to $10,000 fine, five years in prison, or both).

[415] *See Boggs v. Die Fliedermaus, LLP*, 286 F. Supp. 2d 291, 302 (S.D. N.Y. 2003) (sanctions inappropriate where litigant appeared *pro se*, no bad faith evidence existed, no repeated unmeritorious filings, and no prior warnings to litigant given by court).

[416] *See Coble v. Renfroe*, 2012 WL 4971997, at *2 (W.D.Wash. Oct. 17, 2012).

[417] *See Range v. Brubaker*, 2009 WL 161699, at *2 (N.D.Ind. Jan. 21, 2009) (applies to Rule 56(f) affidavits).

[418] *See Lownsberry v. Lees*, 2008 WL 4852791, at *5 (E.D.Mich. Nov. 7, 2008); *McCarley v. Household Finance Corp. III*, 2007 WL 1100330, at *2 (M.D. Ala. 2007).

RULE 57
DECLARATORY JUDGMENT

These rules govern the procedure for obtaining a declaratory judgment under 28 U.S.C. § 2201. Rules 38 and 39 govern a demand for a jury trial. The existence of another adequate remedy does not preclude a declaratory judgment that is otherwise appropriate. The court may order a speedy hearing of a declaratory-judgment action.

[Amended effective October 20, 1949; April 30, 2007, effective December 1, 2007.]

AUTHORS' COMMENTARY ON RULE 57

PURPOSE AND SCOPE

Most civil judgments award the victor some measure of coercive relief—such as money, title to land or to some other property, or an injunctive order directing that the losing party do something or refrain from doing something. Declaratory judgments are different. They simply "declare" the rights and obligations of litigants. Although they do so without any accompanying coercive relief, declaratory judgments facilitate the settling of controversies before those disagreements ripen into full-fledged violations of law or breaches of duty. And, if necessary, they can set the stage for a request for other, supplementary remedies if the declaration alone does not resolve the parties' dispute. In cases involving actual constitutional controversies, Rule 57 permits federal courts to issue declaratory judgments to determine litigants' rights and obligations. The Rule operates in conjunction with the federal Declaratory Judgment Act, 28 U.S.C.A. §§ 2201 to 02.

APPLICATIONS

Purpose

A declaratory judgment is a type of relief that pronounces the rights and obligations of litigants.[1] Its purpose is to afford litigants an early opportunity to resolve their disputes so as to avoid the threat of impending litigation,[2] and obtain both clarity in their legal relationships and the ability to make responsible decisions about their future.[3] Lacking an ultimately coercive effect capable of being enforced through contempt, it is considered a "milder" form of relief.[4] Nevertheless, it often provides very practical litigation solutions. It allows controversies to be settled before they mature into full-fledged violations of law or breaches of duty.[5] It enables probable-future-defendants to terminate a non-litigation standstill where the delay in filing a lawsuit is a plaintiff's strategy.[6] It permits defendants who are confronting multiple claims to pursue an adequate, expedient, and comparably inexpensive declaration of rights that may avoid a multiplicity of actions.[7] In each of these ways, and others, declaratory judgments provide a prudent procedural vehicle for "clearing the air."[8]

Relationship between Rule 57 and 28 U.S.C.A. § 2201

Courts have held that the federal Declaratory Judgment Act, 28 U.S.C.A. §§ 2201 to 02, is "mirrored by" and "functionally equivalent to" Rule 57.[9]

Constitutional Concerns: Subject-Matter Jurisdiction

Neither the Act nor Rule 57 creates a substantive right to litigate in federal court or expands the court's jurisdiction; instead, these provisions merely authorize a declaratory *rem-*

---

[1] *See* 28 U.S.C.A. § 2201(a).

[2] *See Severe Records, LLC v. Rich*, 658 F.3d 571, 580 (6th Cir. 2011); *Biodiversity Legal Foundation v. Badgley*, 309 F.3d 1166, 1172 (9th Cir. 2002).

[3] *See Medtronic, Inc. v. Mirowski Family Ventures, LLC*, 571 U.S. 191, 200–01, 134 S. Ct. 843, 187 L. Ed. 2d 703 (2014).

[4] *See Steffel v. Thompson*, 415 U.S. 452, 471, 94 S. Ct. 1209, 39 L. Ed. 2d 505 (1974).

[5] *See Maytag Corp. v. Int'l Union, United Auto., Aerospace & Agricultural Implement Workers of Am.*, 687 F.3d 1076, 1081–82 (8th Cir. 2012); *Vantage Trailers, Inc. v. Beall Corp.*, 567 F.3d 745, 748 (5th Cir. 2009).

[6] *See James River Ins. Co. v. Rich Bon Corp.*, 34 F.4th 1054, 1058 (11th Cir. 2022) (allowing prospective, but "stuck," defendant to seek declaration of its rights, relations, and liabilities to prospective plaintiff avoids "waiting game" that may impose serious financial/personal costs); *Shell Gulf of Mexico Inc. v. Center for Biological Diversity, Inc.*, 771 F.3d 632, 635 (9th Cir. 2014). *See generally Medtronic, Inc. v. Mirowski Family Ventures, LLC*, 571 U.S. 191, 201, 134 S. Ct. 843, 187 L. Ed. 2d 703 (2014) ("rescues" litigant from dilemma of either abandoning rights or facing lawsuit).

[7] *See Biodiversity Legal Foundation v. Badgley*, 309 F.3d 1166, 1172 (9th Cir. 2002).

[8] *See Microchip Technology Inc. v. Chamberlain Group, Inc.*, 441 F.3d 936, 943 (Fed. Cir. 2006).

[9] *See Ernst & Young v. Depositors Economic Protection Corp.*, 45 F.3d 530, 534 n.8 (1st Cir. 1995).

edy in cases otherwise properly brought in federal court.[10] Thus, a plaintiff seeking declaratory relief must establish an independent basis for the district court's subject-matter jurisdiction.[11] In diversity cases, the amount in controversy is measured by the value of the object of the litigation.[12] In federal question cases, the district courts apply the "well-pleaded complaint" rule to assess whether the plaintiff's action arises under federal law. Ergo, if the federal nature of plaintiff's lawsuit comes only from plaintiff's anticipation that the defendant will assert a federal defense, the claim likely lacks subject-matter jurisdiction.[13] When the declaratory judgment action is filed in an "inverted" posture (*i.e.*, the expected defendant files preemptively against the anticipated future claimant), it is the underlying merits claim, and not the inverted posture, that will determine whether federal question jurisdiction lies.[14]

Constitutional Concerns: Actual Controversy

The district court may only enter a declaratory judgment where the dispute between the parties is definite and concrete, affecting the parties' adverse legal interests with sufficient immediacy as to justify relief.[15] No declaratory judgment may be entered where the parties' dispute is hypothetical, abstract, or academic.[16] In other words, the dispute must be capable of being resolved by specific relief entered through a conclusive judicial decree; the ruling sought must be more than merely an

---

[10] *See Medtronic, Inc. v. Mirowski Family Ventures, LLC*, 571 U.S. 191, 197, 134 S. Ct. 843, 187 L. Ed. 2d 703 (2014); *Vaden v. Discover Bank*, 556 U.S. 49, 70 n.19, 129 S. Ct. 1262, 173 L. Ed. 2d 206 (2009); *Schilling v. Rogers*, 363 U.S. 666, 677, 80 S. Ct. 1288, 4 L. Ed. 2d 1478 (1960); *Aetna Life Ins. Co. v. Haworth*, 300 U.S. 227, 240, 57 S. Ct. 461, 81 L. Ed. 617 (1937).

[11] For further discussion on this point, see Part II of this text §§ 2.9 to 2.12 on subject-matter jurisdiction.

[12] *See Hunt v. Wash. State Apple Adver. Comm'n*, 432 U.S. 333, 347, 97 S. Ct. 2434, 53 L. Ed. 2d 383 (1977).

[13] *See Public Service Commission of Utah v. Wycoff Co., Inc.*, 344 U.S. 237, 73 S. Ct. 236, 97 L. Ed. 291 (1952). *See also Skelly Oil Co. v. Phillips Petroleum Co.*, 339 U.S. 667, 673, 70 S. Ct. 876, 94 L. Ed. 1194 (1950) ("It would turn into the federal courts a vast amount of litigation indubitably arising under State law, in the sense that the right to be vindicated was State-created, if a suit for a declaration of rights could be brought into the federal courts merely because an anticipated defense derived from federal law").

[14] *See Medtronic, Inc. v. Mirowski Family Ventures, LLC*, 571 U.S. 191, 197, 134 S. Ct. 843, 187 L. Ed. 2d 703 (2014). *See also La. Indep. Pharmacies Ass'n v. Express Scripts, Inc.*, 41 F.4th 473, 478-79 (5th Cir. 2022) (plaintiffs do not avoid well-pleaded complaint rule by seeking declaratory remedy to "recast what are in essence merely anticipated or potential federal defenses as affirmative claims") (citation omitted).

[15] *See MedImmune, Inc. v. Genentech, Inc.*, 549 U.S. 118, 127, 127 S. Ct. 764, 166 L. Ed. 2d 604 (2007); *Maryland Cas. Co. v. Pacific Coal & Oil Co.*, 312 U.S. 270, 61 S. Ct. 510, 85 L. Ed. 826 (1941); *Aetna Life Ins. Co. of Hartford, Conn. v. Haworth*, 300 U.S. 227, 57 S. Ct. 461, 81 L. Ed. 617 (1937).

[16] *See MedImmune, Inc. v. Genentech, Inc.*, 549 U.S. 118, 127, 127 S. Ct. 764, 166 L. Ed. 2d 604 (2007).

opinion advising how the law would operate on a hypothetical set of facts.[17] Whether an actual controversy exists will be measured as of the time the complaint was filed; post-filing events are not sufficient.[18]

Note: The Supreme Court has confirmed that declaratory relief is available where the plaintiff is threatened by adverse government action, and has noted (without criticism) that the lower federal courts have long agreed that declaratory relief is available where the plaintiff is threatened by adverse action from a private party.[19]

Constitutional Concerns: Standing

The actual controversy requirement also requires a plaintiff with constitutional standing—that is, a "personal stake" in the controversy, something more than a "generalized grievance" shared equally by many others.[20] Accordingly, a plaintiff must allege a personal injury-in-fact, "fairly traceable" to unlawful conduct by the defendant, and likely to be redressed by the relief that plaintiff is seeking.[21] Declaratory relief does not operate "on legal rules in the abstract," but instead only with respect to specific parties.[22] For this reason, a party lacking a qualifying standing injury cannot seek a declaratory judgment simply to have a court declare a law unconstitutional.[23] Note: apart from constitutional standing is the concept of "statutory" standing, which inquires whether a particular statute, invoked by the plaintiff, allows the cause of action and relief the lawsuit seeks.[24]

Constitutional Concerns: Ripeness/Mootness

The actual controversy requirement obligates the court to determine that the case is "ripe" for adjudication.[25] This "ripeness" must remain throughout the lawsuit. The district court

---

[17]*See California v. Texas*, 593 U.S. —, 141 S. Ct. 2104, 2115–16 (2021); *MedImmune, Inc. v. Genentech, Inc.*, 549 U.S. 118, 127, 127 S.Ct. 764, 166 L.Ed.2d 604 (2007).

[18]*See Vantage Trailers, Inc. v. Beall Corp.*, 567 F.3d 745, 748 (5th Cir. 2009).

[19]*See MedImmune, Inc. v. Genentech, Inc.*, 549 U.S. 118, 129–30, 127 S. Ct. 764, 166 L. Ed. 2d 604 (2007). *See also Southcentral Found. v. Alaska Native Tribal Health Consortium*, 983 F.3d 411, 419 (9th Cir. 2020) (mere cessation of illegal behavior in response to pending litigation does not moot case without showing that behavior could not reasonably recur).

[20]*See Warth v. Seldin*, 422 U.S. 490, 498–99, 95 S. Ct. 2197, 45 L. Ed. 2d 343 (1975).

[21]*See Steel Co. v. Citizens for a Better Env't*, 523 U.S. 83, 102–04, 118 S. Ct. 1003, 140 L. Ed. 2d 210 (1998); *Lujan v. Defs. of Wildlife*, 504 U.S. 555, 560–61, 112 S. Ct. 2130, 119 L. Ed. 2d 351 (1992). *See also California v. Texas*, 593 U.S. —, 141 S. Ct. 2104, 2113 (2021) (party at no risk of government enforcement lacks "fairly traceable" injury essential for standing).

[22]*See California v. Texas*, 593 U.S. —, 141 S. Ct. 2104, 2115 (2021).

[23]*See California v. Texas*, 593 U.S. —, 141 S. Ct. 2104, 2113–16 (2021).

[24]*See Bank of Am. Corp. v. City of Miami*, 581 U.S. —, 137 S. Ct. 1296, 1302–03, 197 L. Ed. 2d 678 (2017).

[25]*See Gagliardi v. TJCV Land Tr.*, 889 F.3d 728, 735 (11th Cir. 2018);

must decide at the time it is about to enter judgment whether an actual controversy still exists between the parties. Thus, even if an actual controversy existed at the time the lawsuit was filed, the court will not enter a declaratory judgment if later events ended the controversy and the dispute has become moot.[26]

Note: This mootness requirement may be excused when the plaintiff is able to show a substantial likelihood that the same controversy will recur in the future and would, then, still evade review under normal mootness principles.[27]

Prudential Concerns: Exercise of Discretion

Declaratory relief is never automatic or obligatory.[28] The courts have no "unflagging duty" to hear declaratory judgment cases.[29] Whether to grant or deny declaratory relief is vested in the sound discretion of the district court.[30] Likewise, the court has discretion in fashioning the relief and its extent.[31] This discretion, though wide, is not boundless; the district court may not refuse on "whim or personal disinclination" to hear a declaratory judgment action, but must instead base its refusal on good reason[32] (such as when the declaration would serve no useful purpose).[33] If the court decides not to entertain the declaratory proceeding, it may either stay or dismiss the federal action, and may enter such an order before trial or after all

---

Pic-A-State Pa., Inc. v. Reno, 76 F.3d 1294, 1298 (3d Cir. 1996).

[26]*See Preiser v. Newkirk*, 422 U.S. 395, 95 S. Ct. 2330, 45 L. Ed. 2d 272 (1975); *Golden v. Zwickler*, 394 U.S. 103, 89 S. Ct. 956, 22 L. Ed. 2d 113 (1969).

[27]*See Super Tire Engineering Co. v. McCorkle*, 416 U.S. 115, 94 S. Ct. 1694, 40 L. Ed. 2d 1 (1974).

[28]*See Wilton v. Seven Falls Co.*, 515 U.S. 277, 288, 115 S. Ct. 2137, 132 L. Ed. 2d 214 (1995).

[29]*See Rarick v. Federated Serv. Ins. Co.*, 852 F.3d 223, 225 & 227 (3d Cir. 2017). *See generally Wilton v. Seven Falls Co.*, 515 U.S. 277, 286–88, 115 S. Ct. 2137, 132 L. Ed. 2d 214 (1995).

[30]*See MedImmune, Inc. v. Genentech, Inc.*, 549 U.S. 118, 136, 127 S. Ct. 764, 166 L. Ed. 2d 604 (2007). *See also Wilton v. Seven Falls Co.*, 515 U.S. 277, 281, 115 S. Ct. 2137, 132 L. Ed. 2d 214 (1995) (even when subject-matter jurisdiction prerequisites are otherwise satisfied, district courts enjoy discretion to determine whether, in what circumstances, to entertain declaratory judgment action); *Hewitt v. Helms*, 482 U.S. 755, 762, 107 S. Ct. 2672, 96 L. Ed. 2d 654 (1987) ("The fact that a court can enter a declaratory judgment does not mean that it should"); *Public Service Commission of Utah v. Wycoff Co., Inc.*, 344 U.S. 237, 73 S. Ct. 236, 97 L. Ed. 291 (1952) (declaratory judgment statute "is an enabling act, which confers a discretion on the courts rather than an absolute right upon the litigant").

[31]*See Strawberry Water Users Ass'n v. U.S.*, 576 F.3d 1133, 1142 (10th Cir. 2009).

[32]*See Public Affairs Associates, Inc. v. Rickover*, 369 U.S. 111, 112, 82 S. Ct. 580, 7 L. Ed. 2d 604 (1962); *Commc'ns Test Design, Inc. v. Contec, LLC*, 952 F.3d 1356, 1361 (Fed. Cir. 2020).

[33]*See Cincinnati Indem. Co. v. A & K Const. Co.*, 542 F.3d 623, 625 (8th Cir. 2008).

arguments come to a close.[34]

Prudential Concerns: Factors Considered

To decide whether to entertain a declaratory judgment action, courts generally assess three concerns: efficiency, fairness, and federalism.[35] To do so, courts may weigh various factors, including: (1) the likelihood that a federal declaration will resolve the uncertainty of obligation which gave rise to the controversy; (2) the parties' convenience; (3) the public interest in settling the uncertainty; (4) the availability and relative convenience of other remedies; (5) the restraint favored when the same issues are pending in a State court; (6) avoidance of duplicative litigation; (7) preventing the declaratory action's use as a method of procedural fencing or a race for *res judicata;* and (8) (in insurance contexts) the inherent conflict of interest between an insurer's duty to defend and its attempt to characterize the action as falling within the scope of a policy exclusion.[36] (The fact that a declaratory judgment action was commenced before a later-filed coercive lawsuit is unlikely to carry dispositive weight.[37]) This list of factors in not exhaustive.[38]

- *Effect of Parallel Pending State Lawsuits:* When another lawsuit is pending in State court raising the same issues and involving the same parties, the federal court may choose to abstain from exercising jurisdiction to hear a related federal declaratory judgment action,[39] and is likely to do so[40] unless, after rigorous examination, it is assured that other factors justify proceeding.[41] (Such abstention will, however, be rare if the federal action seeks both declaratory and nondeclaratory relief.[42]) Conversely, when no such parallel lawsuits are pending

[34]*See Wilton v. Seven Falls Co.*, 515 U.S. 277, 287, 115 S. Ct. 2137, 132 L. Ed. 2d 214 (1995).

[35]*See Western World Ins. Co. v. Hoey*, 773 F.3d 755, 759 (6th Cir. 2014).

[36]*See Cardinal Health, Inc. v. Nat'l Union Fire Ins. Co.*, 29 F.4th 792, 796 (6th Cir. 2022) (listing certain factors for consideration); *Gold-Fogel v. Fogel*, 16 F.4th 790, 797–98 (11th Cir. 2021) (same).

[37]*See Morgan Drexen, Inc. v. Consumer Fin. Protection Bureau*, 785 F.3d 684, 697 (D.C.Cir. 2015) (proper question is not which was filed first, but which will best serve justice and the parties' needs).

[38]*See Morgan Drexen, Inc. v. Consumer Fin. Protection Bureau*, 785 F.3d 684, 696 (D.C.Cir. 2015); *Western World Ins. Co. v. Hoey*, 773 F.3d 755, 759–60 (6th Cir. 2014).

[39]*See Wilton v. Seven Falls Co.*, 515 U.S. 277, 282, 115 S. Ct. 2137, 132 L. Ed. 2d 214 (1995); *Brillhart v. Excess Ins. Co. of Am.*, 316 U.S. 491, 495, 62 S. Ct. 1173, 86 L. Ed. 1620 (1942).

[40]*See City of South Bend v. South Bend Common Council*, 865 F.3d 889, 893 (7th Cir. 2017) (when plaintiff is State governmental entity, it likely is abuse of discretion to issue federal declaratory judgment).

[41]*See GEICO Cas. Co. v. Isaacson*, 932 F.3d 721, 724–25 (8th Cir. 2019); *Reifer v. Westport Ins. Corp.*, 751 F.3d 129, 144–45 (3d Cir. 2014).

[42]*See Seneca Ins. Co. v. Strange Land, Inc.*, 862 F.3d 835, 841 (9th Cir.

elsewhere, the federal court still retains the discretion to decline to hear the federal case,[43] though the absence of parallel State proceedings militates heavily in favor of exercising federal jurisdiction.[44]

Statement of Circumstances Supporting Jurisdiction

If a party contests the prudence of the district court's exercise of discretion to hear a declaratory judgment claim, the court must articulate the factual circumstances supporting the award of declaratory relief,[45] unless the underlying claims are viable independently, apart from the declaratory relief request.[46]

Realignment of the Parties

In determining whether to grant a declaratory judgment, the courts may realign the parties in order to reflect the nature of the actual, underlying controversy.[47] In making this determination, the courts may consider the underlying purposes of declaratory relief, the parties' respective burdens of proof, and the best, clearest method for presenting evidence to the jury.[48] Where both sides will carry proof burdens at trial, realignment may be refused.[49]

Burden of Proof

A party seeking a declaratory judgment bears the burden of proving the existence of an actual case or controversy.[50] But assigning the ultimate merits burden of persuasion in declaratory judgment cases can prove to be nuanced. The burden of proof is considered a substantive aspect of the underlying claim.[51] Consequently, in an action seeking a declaration that the named defendant lacks some sort of right as to which that defendant would bear the burden of proof were it to file a coercive lawsuit, that defendant may well bear the burden of

---

2017); *VonRosenberg v. Lawrence*, 781 F.3d 731, 735 (4th Cir. 2015).

[43]*See Reifer v. Westport Ins. Corp.*, 751 F.3d 129, 143–44 (3d Cir. 2014) (joining majority of other Circuits in so holding).

[44]*See Reifer v. Westport Ins. Corp.*, 751 F.3d 129, 144 (3d Cir. 2014); *Vasquez v. Rackauckas*, 734 F.3d 1025, 1040–41 (9th Cir. 2013).

[45]*See Reifer v. Westport Ins. Corp.*, 751 F.3d 129, 146–47 & 146 n.22 (3d Cir. 2014); *Government Employees Ins. Co. v. Dizol*, 133 F.3d 1220, 1225 (9th Cir. 1998).

[46]*See Vasquez v. Rackauckas*, 734 F.3d 1025, 1039–40 (9th Cir. 2013).

[47]*See BASF Corp. v. Symington*, 50 F.3d 555, 557 (8th Cir. 1995).

[48]*See Fresenius Medical Care Holdings, Inc. v. Baxter Int'l, Inc.*, 2006 WL 1646110, at *1 (N.D. Cal. 2006).

[49]*See Anheuser-Busch, Inc. v. John Labatt Ltd.*, 89 F.3d 1339, 1344 (8th Cir. 1996); *L-3 Commc'ns Corp. v. OSI Systems, Inc.*, 418 F. Supp. 2d 380, 383 (S.D. N.Y. 2005).

[50]*See Cardinal Chemical Co. v. Morton Int'l Inc.*, 508 U.S. 83, 94, 113 S. Ct. 1967, 124 L. Ed. 2d 1 (1993); *Asia Vital Components Co. v. Asetek Danmark A/S*, 837 F.3d 1249, 1252 (Fed. Cir. 2016).

[51]*See Medtronic, Inc. v. Mirowski Fam. Ventures, LLC*, 571 U.S. 191, 199, 134 S. Ct. 843, 187 L. Ed. 2d 703 (2014).

proof in a declaratory judgment suit as well.[52]

Nature of Declaratory Relief

A declaratory judgment pronounces rights and relations, but by itself neither provides for nor orders any enforcement.[53] But the Declaratory Judgment Act allows the award of other, further (non-declaratory) remedies after reasonable notice and hearing.[54] Indeed, this is typical; although the parties may hope that the sought-after declaration will prompt a negotiated resolution to their dispute, declaratory relief is often a prelude to a request for further remedies.[55] Where appropriate, courts possess broad power to grant damage awards and injunctive relief in declaratory judgment actions.[56] This includes attorney's fees, if those would be available in similar non-declaratory judgment settings.[57]

Note: The Eleventh Amendment ordinarily does not preclude declaratory judgment proceedings instituted against State officials.[58]

The Existence of Other Possible Remedies

Declaratory relief is usually not foreclosed merely by showing that some adequate remedy other than a declaratory judgment exists.[59] A declaratory judgment may be entered whether or not further relief is sought or could have been awarded.[60] However, the existence of another, adequate remedy may convince the district court to exercise its discretion to deny declaratory relief in favor of some other, better remedy.[61] Moreover, where declaratory relief will not terminate the controversy, but further remedies will be sought in a different or

---

[52]*See Medtronic, Inc. v. Mirowski Fam. Ventures, LLC*, 571 U.S. 191, 193-203, 134 S. Ct. 843, 187 L. Ed. 2d 703 (2014) (in action by licensee seeking declaratory of non-infringement of a patent, defendant patent holder bears burden of proving infringement). *See also American Eagle Ins. Co. v. Thompson*, 85 F.3d 327, 331 (8th Cir. 1996) (burden remains on the party asserting the affirmative on an issue); *Utah Farm Bureau Ins. Co. v. Dairyland Ins. Co.*, 634 F.2d 1326, 1328 (10th Cir.1980) (noting divergent views on burden of proof in declaratory judgment actions).

[53]*See Drummond Coal Sales, Inc. v. Norfolk S. Ry. Co.*, 3 F.4th 605, 613 n.6 (4th Cir. 2021).

[54]*See* 28 U.S.C.A. § 2202.

[55]*See Berger v. Xerox Corp. Ret. Income Guarantee Plan*, 338 F.3d 755, 763–64 (7th Cir. 2003) ("No one wants an empty declaration.").

[56]*See Mack v. USAA Cas. Ins. Co.*, 994 F.3d 1353, 1357–58 (11th Cir. 2021); *United Teacher Assocs. Ins. Co. v. Union Labor Life Ins. Co.*, 414 F.3d 558, 570 (5th Cir. 2005).

[57]*See In re: First River Energy, L.L.C.*, 986 F.3d 914, 930 (5th Cir. 2021).

[58]*See Native Village of Noatak v. Blatchford*, 38 F.3d 1505, 1513–14 (9th Cir. 1994).

[59]*See Robinson v. Hunt Cty.*, 921 F.3d 440, 450–51 (5th Cir. 2019); *Reifer v. Westport Ins. Corp.*, 751 F.3d 129, 136 (3d Cir. 2014).

[60]*See Powell v. McCormack*, 395 U.S. 486, 89 S. Ct. 1944, 23 L. Ed. 2d 491 (1969); *Robinson v. Hunt Cty.*, 921 F.3d 440, 450–51 (5th Cir. 2019).

[61]*See National Private Truck Council, Inc. v. Oklahoma Tax Com'n*, 515 U.S. 582, 589, 115 S. Ct. 2351, 132 L. Ed. 2d 509 (1995). *Compare Ford Motor Co. v. United States*, 811 F.3d

subsequent proceeding, the declaratory judgment can be refused.[62]

Exception: Where a special statutory proceeding has been provided to adjudicate a special type of case, declaratory relief may not be available.[63]

Partial Remedy

If it exercises its discretion to hear a declaratory judgment case, the trial court is not obligated to rule on every issue presented. The court may, instead, properly choose to decide some of the issues raised and decline to decide others.[64]

Declaratory *versus* Injunctive Remedies

As between a declaratory or injunctive remedy, the district court enjoys discretion. Although a declaratory judgment cannot be enforced in contempt, it is "a real judgment, not just a bit of friendly advice"; it fixes the litigants' legal rights.[65] It is also likely to be a more simple and less elaborate order than an injunction.[66]

Rules of Procedure

All rules of procedure applicable generally to civil lawsuits apply in a declaratory judgment action.[67] Thus, for example, no declaratory relief request is properly before the court until it is pleaded in a complaint for declaratory judgment,[68] and Rule 8(a) with the *Twombly* plausibility standard governs the ade-

---

1371, 1379–80 (Fed. Cir. 2016) (justified in refusing when alternate remedy more effective), *with Capo, Inc. v. Dioptics Med. Prods., Inc.*, 387 F.3d 1352, 1358 (Fed. Cir. 2004) (abuse of discretion to deny relief when party left "helpless and immobile").

[62]*See* Rule 57 advisory committee note (1937) ("A declaratory judgment is appropriate when it will 'terminate the controversy' giving rise to the proceeding. . . . When declaratory relief will not be effective in settling the controversy, the court may decline to grant it."). *See also Duncan Place Owners Ass'n v. Danze, Inc.*, 927 F.3d 970, 977–78 (7th Cir. 2019) (relief would not settle controversy, but just "lay the groundwork" for damages claim).

[63]*See Katzenbach v. McClung*, 379 U.S. 294, 296, 85 S. Ct. 377, 13 L. Ed. 2d 290 (1964). *See generally The New York Times Co. v. Gonzales*, 459 F.3d 160, 166 (2d Cir. 2006) (such proceedings include habeas petitions and motions to vacate criminal sentences, proceedings under Civil Rights Act of 1964, and certain administrative proceedings).

[64]*See Henglein v. Colt Industries Operating Corp.*, 260 F.3d 201, 210–11 (3d Cir. 2001).

[65]*See Badger Catholic, Inc. v. Walsh*, 620 F.3d 775, 782 (7th Cir. 2010).

[66]*See Badger Catholic, Inc. v. Walsh*, 620 F.3d 775, 782 (7th Cir. 2010).

[67]*See Garanti Finansal Kiralama A.S. v. Aqua Marine & Trading Inc.*, 697 F.3d 59, 63 (2d Cir. 2012); *Cloverland-Green Spring Dairies, Inc. v. Pennsylvania Milk Marketing Bd.*, 298 F.3d 201, 210 (3d Cir. 2002) (standards for granting summary judgment in declaratory judgment case are same as for all other types of relief).

[68]*See Arizona v. City of Tucson*, 761 F.3d 1005, 1009-10 (9th Cir. 2014); *Thomas v. Blue Cross & Blue Shield Ass'n*, 594 F.3d 823, 830 (11th Cir. 2010).

quacy of such a pleading.[69]

Expedited Treatment

The district court may order a speedy hearing in declaratory judgment cases, and may move such cases to the top of the court's calendar.

Timing

Because declaratory judgments supply only a remedy, not a claim, the applicable statute of limitations will typically be the same that governs the underlying claim.[70]

Jury Trial

The right to a jury trial is preserved in declaratory judgment actions. If the issues would have been triable by a jury had something other than declaratory relief been sought, a right to a jury trial exists.[71] In such a case, entering a declaratory judgment without a jury trial can violate a party's Seventh Amendment rights.[72]

Common Uses

Classically, declaratory judgments have proved useful in insurance cases, to resolve policy coverage and interpretation disputes,[73] and in intellectual property cases, to resolve questions of validity and infringement.[74] But declaratory judgments have a far broader range. For example, they may be useful in deciding the constitutionality of government laws,[75] immunity questions,[76] status of current and future obligations,[77] land title and property rights,[78] competition and trade claims,[79] scope of

---

[69] *See Vantage Commodities Fin. Servs. I, LLC v. Assured Risk Transfer PCC, LLC*, 31 F.4th 800, 804 (D.C. Cir. 2022); *Karnatcheva v. JPMorgan Chase Bank, N.A.*, 704 F.3d 545, 547 (8th Cir. 2013).

[70] *See Petro Harvester Operating Co. v. Keith*, 954 F.3d 686, 699 (5th Cir. 2020).

[71] *See Simler v. Conner*, 372 U.S. 221, 83 S. Ct. 609, 9 L. Ed. 2d 691 (1963); *Beacon Theatres, Inc. v. Westover*, 359 U.S. 500, 79 S. Ct. 948, 3 L. Ed. 2d 988 (1959). *See also Langbord v. U.S. Dep't of Treasury*, 832 F.3d 170, 187 (3d Cir. 2016) (must look to "basic character" of suit, whether it sounds in equity or law).

[72] *See NACM-New England, Inc. v. Nat'l Ass'n of Credit Mgmt., Inc.*, 927 F.3d 1, 8 (1st Cir. 2019).

[73] *See, e.g., Aetna Life Ins. Co. of Hartford, Conn. v. Haworth*, 300 U.S. 227, 57 S. Ct. 461, 81 L. Ed. 617 (1937). *See also James River Ins. Co. v. Rich Bon Corp.*, 34 F.4th 1054, 1058 (11th Cir. 2022) ("especially helpful" in insurance contexts).

[74] *See, e.g., Kimble v. Marvel Entm't, LLC*, 135 S. Ct. 2401, 2406, 192 L. Ed. 2d 463 (2015); *Kelly Servs., Inc. v. Creative Harbor, LLC*, 846 F.3d 857, 860–76 (6th Cir. 2017).

[75] *See, e.g., Greater Baltimore Ctr. for Pregnancy Concerns, Inc. v. Mayor of Baltimore*, 683 F.3d 539, 550 (4th Cir. 2012).

[76] *See, e.g., Aetna Life Ins. Co. of Hartford, Conn. v. Haworth*, 300 U.S. 227, 57 S. Ct. 461, 81 L. Ed. 617 (1937).

[77] *See, e.g., ACI Worldwide Corp. v. Churchill Lane Assocs., LLC*, 847 F.3d 571, 575–83 (8th Cir. 2017).

[78] *See, e.g., Nixon v. AgriBank, FCB*, 686 F.3d 912, 913 (8th Cir.2012).

entitlements to beneficiaries,[80] and prisoner rights.[81]

Cautious Uses

The district courts frequently will refrain from declaratory relief in cases involving important public issues, where the concreteness of a monetary or injunctive dispute is more advisable,[82] and will often deny declaratory relief that would act to interfere with a State criminal prosecution.[83]

Improper Uses

Declaratory relief is generally not available to merely adjudicate past conduct or to proclaim that one litigant is liable to another.[84] It is also not available where a special statutory proceeding has been provided to adjudicate a certain type of case.[85] And it is often not available in federal and State tax cases, particularly where State law provides for efficient tax challenges and remedies, and where the action contests the constitutionality of a State tax provision.[86]

Effect of a Declaratory Judgment

A declaratory judgment inures directly to the benefit of the plaintiff who received it, though the relief may, as a practical matter, have far broader ramifications. Declaratory judgments enjoy an exception from claim preclusion principles, permitting a victorious plaintiff to file a second lawsuit to pursue injunctive relief or damages.[87] Issue preclusion principles apply normally; parties who have had their rights or obligations declared are ordinarily bound by that resolution in later proceedings.[88]

Appealability

Whether a declaratory judgment order is immediately appealable depends upon the nature of the court's ruling. Once

---

[79] *See, e.g., Pensacola Motor Sales Inc. v. Eastern Shore Toyota, LLC*, 684 F.3d 1211, 1222 (11th Cir. 2012).

[80] *See, e.g., Fleisher v. Standard Ins. Co.*, 679 F.3d 116, 120 (3d Cir. 2012) (ERISA dispute).

[81] *See, e.g., McFaul v. Valenzuela*, 684 F.3d 564, 569 (5th Cir. 2012).

[82] *See Public Affairs Associates, Inc. v. Rickover*, 369 U.S. 111, 82 S. Ct. 580, 7 L. Ed. 2d 604 (1962).

[83] *See Samuels v. Mackell*, 401 U.S. 66, 91 S. Ct. 764, 27 L. Ed. 2d 688 (1971).

[84] *See Spencer v. Kemna*, 523 U.S. 1, 18, 118 S. Ct. 978, 140 L. Ed. 2d 43 (1998); *Am. Civil Liberties Union v. U.S. Conference of Catholic Bishops*, 705 F.3d 44, 53 (1st Cir. 2013).

[85] *See supra* Authors' Commentary to Rule 57 ("**The Existence of Other Possible Remedies—***Exception*").

[86] *See* 28 U.S.C.A. § 2201(a). *See generally Gilbert v. United States*, 998 F.3d 410, 413–14 (9th Cir. 2021).

[87] *See Cont'l Cas. Co. v. Indian Head Indus., Inc.*, 941 F.3d 828, 835–36 (6th Cir. 2019); *ASARCO, L.L.C. v. Montana Res., Inc.*, 858 F.3d 949, 956 (5th Cir. 2017).

[88] *See* 28 U.S.C.A. § 2201(a) ("Any such declaration shall have the force and effect of a final judgment or decree. . ."). *See also Cont'l Cas. Co. v. Indian Head Indus., Inc.*, 941 F.3d 828, 835 n.1 (6th Cir. 2019); *Union de Empleados de Muelles de Puerto Rico, Inc. v. Int'l Longshoremen's Ass'n*, 884 F.3d 48, 58–59 (1st Cir. 2018).

the court disposes of all the issues presented in the declaratory judgment action (either by ruling upon them or by declining to rule upon them), the resulting judgment becomes complete, final, and appealable.[89] Conversely, if the court enters an order resolving certain of the issues presented, but expressly leaves open other issues in the case, the order is merely interlocutory and, therefore, not immediately appealable until final.[90]

Additional Research References:

Wright & Miller, *Federal Practice and Procedure* §§ 2751 to 2771, §§ 2781 to 2787

C.J.S., Declaratory Judgments §§ 1 to 24 et seq., §§ 25 to 75, §§ 76 to 126, §§ 127 to 142 et seq., §§ 143 to 165; Federal Civil Procedure §§ 1227 to 1231 et seq.

West's Key Number Digest, Declaratory Judgment ⚿1 to 395

---

[89] *See United States v. Safehouse*, 985 F.3d 225, 232-32 (3d Cir. 2021). *Cf. WM Cap. Partners 53, LLC v. Barreras, Inc.*, 975 F.3d 77, 81 (1st Cir. 2020) (granting summary judgment without also issuing accompanying declaration renders ruling non-final and unappealable).

[90] *See Henglein v. Colt Industries Operating Corp.*, 260 F.3d 201, 211 (3d Cir. 2001).

RULE 58
ENTERING JUDGMENT

(a) Separate Document. Every judgment and amended judgment must be set out in a separate document, but a separate document is not required for an order disposing of a motion:

(1) for judgment under Rule 50(b);

(2) to amend or make additional findings under Rule 52(b);

(3) for attorney's fees under Rule 54;

(4) for a new trial, or to alter or amend the judgment, under Rule 59; or

(5) for relief under Rule 60.

(b) Entering Judgment.

(1) *Without the Court's Direction.* Subject to Rule 54(b) and unless the court orders otherwise, the clerk must, without awaiting the court's direction, promptly prepare, sign, and enter the judgment when:

(A) the jury returns a general verdict;

(B) the court awards only costs or a sum certain; or

(C) the court denies all relief.

(2) *Court's Approval Required.* Subject to Rule 54(b), the court must promptly approve the form of the judgment, which the clerk must promptly enter, when:

(A) the jury returns a special verdict or a general verdict with answers to written questions; or

(B) the court grants other relief not described in this subdivision (b).

(c) Time of Entry. For purposes of these rules, judgment is entered at the following times:

(1) if a separate document is not required, when the judgment is entered in the civil docket under Rule 79(a); or

(2) if a separate document is required, when the

judgment is entered in the civil docket under Rule 79(a) and the earlier of these events occurs:

(A) it is set out in a separate document; or

(B) 150 days have run from the entry in the civil docket.

(d) Request for Entry. A party may request that judgment be set out in a separate document as required by Rule 58(a).

(e) Cost or Fee Awards. Ordinarily, the entry of judgment may not be delayed, nor the time for appeal extended, in order to tax costs or award fees. But if a timely motion for attorney's fees is made under Rule 54(d)(2), the court may act before a notice of appeal has been filed and become effective to order that the motion have the same effect under Federal Rule of Appellate Procedure 4(a)(4) as a timely motion under Rule 59.

[Amended December 27, 1946, effective March 19, 1948; January 21, 1963, effective July 1, 1963; April 22, 1993, effective December 1, 1993; April 29, 2002, effective December 1, 2002; April 30, 2007, effective December 1, 2007.]

AUTHORS' COMMENTARY ON RULE 58

PURPOSE AND SCOPE

The entry of a civil judgment usually closes the trial court's involvement with the lawsuit and opens the time for taking an appeal. Accordingly, knowing that a judgment has been entered is critical for practitioners. Rule 58 endeavors to make that date clear by ensuring that most judgments are set out separately from other documents the court may enter (so that they might be more readily noticed), by establishing the procedures for entry, and by creating a timing formula to be used if the requirements for proper entry have not been followed. The Rule also allows practitioners to nudge the court to make an entry, if one has been delayed, and to request that the trial judge allow an end-of-case motion for attorney's fees to postpone the time for taking an appeal until it has been ruled upon.

RULE 58(a)—SEPARATE DOCUMENT

CORE CONCEPT

To avoid uncertainty about when the clock for taking an appeal begins to tick, the district courts are required to set forth most judgments (and amended judgments) in a "separate document."

APPLICATIONS

Impact of 2007 "Restyling" Amendments

Rule 58(a) now contains only the "separate document" requirement. The remaining content of former Rule 58(a) has been relocated to current Rule 58(b).

The Old Separate Document Rule

Federal practice has long required that civil judgments be set forth in writing, in a "separate document," and entered on the docket. These requirements were intended to create a "bright line" for litigants and the courts in determining when finality attached and, thus, when the period for taking an appeal began.[1]

To abate any uncertainty as to when the appeal "clock" would start ticking, courts generally applied these requirements mechanically.[2] What followed was a body of interpretative case law construing and applying the "separate document" requirement that, at times, seemed confusing, even inconsistent. Some cases emphasized that rulings orally announced from the bench[3] or included within the text of a minute-order, a memorandum, or a written opinion[4] could not qualify as "judgments" under Rule 58. Other cases held that a little, but not too much, collateral discussion from the trial court might be tolerated.[5] Still other cases explained that the "separate document" requirement could be waived because it was not jurisdictional,[6] either by express agreement of the parties[7] or by failure to timely object.[8] In still other instances, some courts simply excused a "separate document" failure entirely where the circumstances made it plain that the court's decision was final.[9]

What made this situation especially troublesome was timing—until the "separate document" requirement was met, the judgment was not deemed to have been entered[10] and the time

---

[1]*See Fogade v. ENB Revocable Trust*, 263 F.3d 1274, 1285–86 (11th Cir. 2001).

[2]*See Trotter v. Regents of University of New Mexico*, 219 F.3d 1179, 1183 (10th Cir. 2000).

[3]*Atlantic Richfield Co. v. Monarch Leasing Co.*, 84 F.3d 204, 207 (6th Cir. 1996).

[4]*See U.S. v. Johnson*, 254 F.3d 279, 285 (D.C. Cir. 2001).

[5]*See Kidd v. District of Columbia*, 206 F.3d 35, 39 (D.C. Cir. 2000).

[6]*See Bankers Trust Co. v. Mallis*, 435 U.S. 381, 98 S. Ct. 1117, 55 L. Ed. 2d 357 (1978).

[7]*See Pohl v. United Airlines, Inc.*, 213 F.3d 336, 338 (7th Cir. 2000).

[8]*See American Disability Ass'n, Inc. v. Chmielarz*, 289 F.3d 1315, 1318 (11th Cir. 2002).

[9]*See Allison v. Bank One-Denver*, 289 F.3d 1223, 1232–33 (10th Cir. 2002).

[10]*See U.S. v. Indrelunas*, 411 U.S. 216, 221–22, 93 S. Ct. 1562, 36 L. Ed. 2d 202 (1973).

for filing an appeal would not begin to run.[11] A split developed among the Circuits over how to address this nagging spectre of an appeal period being postponed indefinitely by a failure to meet the exacting (but sometimes varying) requirements of a "separate document" judgment.[12]

The Current Separate Document Rule

The underlying purpose of current Rule 58 remains the same today: the "separate document" requirement is designed to ensure that litigants are alerted to the entry of judgment and to the starting of the clock for post-verdict motions or an appeal.[13] The Rule is designed to resolve the haunting question of "when is a judgment a judgment."[14] As before, the Rule achieves this goal by insisting on a "clear line of demarcation" between a judgment and an opinion or memorandum.[15] The Rule retains an austere approach to drafting judgments: the body of a proper judgment should state the relief granted and little else.[16] This austerity should make clear for the parties that an appeal-triggering event has occurred and that the appeal time has begun to run.[17] In the cause of preserving appeal periods, the current version of the "separate document" rule is applied mechanically as well.[18] But unlike under the old rule, the postponement period for the appeals clock is now capped.[19]

The "separate document" requirement applies to many categories of judgments, including summary judgments,[20] declara-

---

[11]*See Carter v. Hodge*, 726 F.3d 917, 919–20 (7th Cir. 2013) (under prior Rule, "a losing party had forever to appeal if the district court never entered a Rule 58 judgment. Forever is too long.") (citations omitted).

[12]*Compare White v. Fair*, 289 F.3d 1, 6 (1st Cir. 2002) (waiver inferred where party fails to act within 3 months to resolve separate document failure) *with Hammack v. Baroid Corp.*, 142 F.3d 266, 270 (5th Cir. 1998) (rejecting inferred waiver).

[13]*See Bankers Trust Co. v. Mallis*, 435 U.S. 381, 384, 98 S. Ct. 1117, 55 L. Ed. 2d 357 (1978) (per curiam). *See also L. Offs. of David Freydin, P.C. v. Chamara*, 24 F.4th 1122, 1128 (7th Cir. 2022) ("keeps jurisdictional lines clear").

[14]*See United Auto. Workers Local 259 Social Sec. Dept. v. Metro Auto Center*, 501 F.3d 283, 287 n.1 (3d Cir. 2007).

[15]*See Vaqueria Tres Monjitas, Inc. v. Comas-Pagan*, 772 F.3d 956, 959 (1st Cir. 2014); *In re Cendant Corp. Securities Litigation*, 454 F.3d 235, 243 (3d Cir. 2006).

[16]*See In re Cendant Corp. Securities Litigation*, 454 F.3d 235, 245 (3d Cir. 2006).

[17]*See In re Cendant Corp. Securities Litigation*, 454 F.3d 235, 245 (3d Cir. 2006).

[18]*See Vaqueria Tres Monjitas, Inc. v. Comas-Pagan*, 772 F.3d 956, 959 (1st Cir. 2014); *In re Taumoepeau*, 523 F.3d 1213, 1217 (10th Cir. 2008). *But see Wisconsin Cent. Ltd. v. TiEnergy, LLC*, 894 F.3d 851, 854 (7th Cir. 2018) (separate document failure not fatal to appellate jurisdiction if district court "otherwise indicated its intent to finally dispose of all claims").

[19]*See infra* Authors' Commentary to Rule 58(c).

[20]*See Perry v. Sheet Metal Workers' Local No. 73 Pension Fund*, 585 F.3d 358, 360–61 (7th Cir. 2009).

tory judgments,[21] preliminary injunctions,[22] forfeiture orders,[23] and orders on habeas motions.[24] It also applies to orders that, though typically merely interlocutory, are immediately appealable under the collateral order doctrine.[25]

When a "Separate Document" is *Not* Required

A separate document is not required for an order "disposing" of a Rule 50(b) renewed motion for judgment after trial, a Rule 52(b) motion to amend or make additional findings of fact, a Rule 54(d) motion for attorney's fees, a Rule 59 motion for new trial or to alter or amend a judgment, or a Rule 60 motion for relief from a judgment or order.[26] These exceptions create risks for the unwary—because a "separate document" is not required for these dispositions, the time for taking an appeal *will begin to run immediately*.[27] Dispositions by Rule 41 dismissals also might not require a separate document.[28]

Two nuances have arisen in the case law. First, because of a phrasing ambiguity, it is unclear whether every district court ruling on a post-trial motion constitutes an "amended judgment," requiring a "separate document" (the Rule's use of the phrase "disposing of" suggests possibly not).[29] Some courts navigate this uncertainty by requiring a "separate document" when a post-trial motion is granted, but not when one is denied.[30] Second, it is unclear how to treat a ruling on a mislabeled motion. One court chose to abide by the moving party's choice of labeling (even if errant); thus, a motion mis-labeled as one filed under Rule 60 will be treated for Rule 58(a) purposes as a Rule 60 motion, and the "separate document" requirement will not apply.[31]

What Qualifies as a "Separate Document"?

Except for the five exempted instances set out in the Rule's

---

[21]*See Specialized Seating, Inc. v. Greenwich Indus., LP*, 616 F.3d 722, 725–26 (7th Cir. 2010).

[22]*See C.Y. Wholesale, Inc. v. Holcomb*, 965 F.3d 541, 545 (7th Cir. 2020).

[23]*See United States v. $525,695. 24, Seized From JPMorgan Chase Bank Inv. Account #xxxxxxxx*, 869 F.3d 429, 435 (6th Cir. 2017).

[24]*See Jeffries v. U.S.*, 721 F.3d 1008, 1012–13 (8th Cir. 2013) (joining majority of Circuits in so holding). *But see Williams v. United States*, 984 F.2d 28, 29–31 (2d Cir.1993) (rejecting majority view).

[25]*See Ueckert v. Guerra*, 38 F.4th 446, 452 (5th Cir. 2022).

[26]*See* Rule 58(a)(1).

[27]*See Leavy v. Hutchison*, 952 F.3d 830, 831–32 (6th Cir. 2020); *United States v. Bradley*, 882 F.3d 390, 394 (2d Cir. 2018).

[28]*See Federated Towing & Recovery, LLC v. Praetorian Ins. Co.*, 283 F.R.D. 644, 655 (D.N.M. 2012); *Advance Capital, Inc. v. M/V ANGIE, Official No. 249544*, 273 F.R.D. 660, 661 (W.D. Wash. 2011).

[29]*See Kunz v. DeFelice*, 538 F.3d 667, 673–74 (7th Cir. 2008).

[30]*See Kunz v. DeFelice*, 538 F.3d 667, 673–74 (7th Cir. 2008). *Cf. United States v. Bradley*, 882 F.3d 390, 394 (2d Cir. 2018) (subsequent written explanation for Rule 60 motion ruling would only have reset clock if it altered earlier judgment).

[31]*See Lawuary v. United States*, 669 F.3d 864, 865–67 (7th Cir. 2012).

text,[32] every judgment (as well as partial dispositions under Rule 54(b)[33]) must be labeled "judgment" and must be set forth on a separate document.[34] Thus, a judgment that is encumbered with extraneous text, such as an "extensive" recitation of legal reasoning, analysis, facts, or procedural history, fails the separateness requirement.[35] (A very cursory explanation, however, devoid of legal analysis, may survive this examination.[36]) Ergo, neither a judicial memorandum or opinion,[37] nor marginal entry orders,[38] nor minute orders,[39] nor automated court e-mails of docketing text,[40] nor settlement decrees,[41] nor oral rulings from the bench[42] satisfy this requirement; indeed, even an otherwise qualifying judgment order that includes footnotes explaining its reasoning[43] or that is mistakenly stapled to the end of a memorandum opinion will fail this separateness requirement.[44] Thus, to qualify as a "separate document," the judgment must generally: (1) be a self-contained, separate document; (2) state the relief granted; and (3) omit the reasoning used by the district court to reach that disposition (which should, instead, appear in the court's opinion).[45]

- *Two Documents?:* The majority view holds that the separate document requirement can, in appropriate circum-

[32]*See* Rule 58(a)(1) to (a)(5). *See also supra* Authors' Commentary to Rule 58(a) (**"When a 'Separate Document' is *Not* Required"**).

[33]*See In re Cendant Corp. Securities Litigation*, 454 F.3d 235, 240 n.2 (3d Cir. 2006).

[34]*See* Rule 58(a). *See also Arzuaga v. Quiros*, 781 F.3d 29, 33 (2d Cir. 2015); *Silivanch v. Celebrity Cruises, Inc.*, 333 F.3d 355, 363 (2d Cir. 2003). *But see LeBoon v. Lancaster Jewish Community Center Ass'n*, 503 F.3d 217, 224 (3d Cir. 2007) ("No magic words are necessary").

[35]*See CX Reinsurance Co. Ltd. v. Johnson*, 977 F.3d 306, 311 (4th Cir. 2020); *Jeffries v. U.S.*, 721 F.3d 1008, 1013-14 (8th Cir. 2013).

[36]*See In re Murphy*, 679 Fed. Appx. 107, 110 (3d Cir. 2017) (referring reader to opinion for reasons); *Vaqueria Tres Monjitas, Inc. v. Comas-Pagan*, 772 F.3d 956, 959–60 (1st Cir. 2014) (single explanatory sentence, without legal analysis).

[37]*See Calumet River Fleeting, Inc. v. Int'l Union of Operating Eng'rs, Local 150, AFL–CIO*, 824 F.3d 645, 650 (7th Cir. 2016); *Witasick v. Minnesota Mut. Life Ins. Co.*, 803 F.3d 184, 187–88 (3d Cir. 2015).

[38]*See Inland Bulk Transfer Co. v. Cummins Engine Co.*, 332 F.3d 1007, 1015 n.7 (6th Cir. 2003).

[39]*See Ueckert v. Guerra*, 38 F.4th 446, 451 (5th Cir. 2022); *Vergara v. City of Chicago*, 939 F.3d 882, 885 (7th Cir. 2019); *Walters v. Wal-Mart Stores, Inc.*, 703 F.3d 1167, 1171 (10th Cir. 2013). *But see Carter v. Hodge*, 726 F.3d 917, 918-19 (7th Cir. 2013) (some minute-entries may qualify).

[40]*See Braitberg v. Charter Commc'ns, Inc.*, 836 F.3d 925, 929 (8th Cir. 2016).

[41]*See United States v. $525,695. 24, Seized From JPMorgan Chase Bank Inv. Account #xxxxxxxxx*, 869 F.3d 429, 435 (6th Cir. 2017).

[42]*See Ueckert v. Guerra*, 38 F.4th 446, 451 (5th Cir. 2022).

[43]*See Bazargani v. Radel*, 598 Fed.Appx. 829, 830 (3d Cir. 2015).

[44]*See Alinsky v. U.S.*, 415 F.3d 639, 643 (7th Cir. 2005).

[45]*See DLJ Mortg. Cap., Inc. v. Sheridan*, 975 F.3d 358, 364 (3d Cir. 2020).

stances, be met even if there is only one document (such as when the court's reasoning and analysis was conveyed orally, during oral argument or a hearing).[46]

- *Multi-Tasking Judgments:* A judgment that recites, in a single document, the disposition of multiple motions may satisfy the Rule.[47]
- *Electronic Docket Notations:* Such entries *can* qualify as a separate document, but only if they are more than merely ministerial, clerical notations and instead are self-contained, list the relief awarded, and have the signature (pen or electronic) of the judge.[48]
- *Actual or Implied Clarity:* The fact that the litigants knew, or should have known, that the contested order was intended to serve as a final judgment will not excuse a failure to meet the separateness requirement.[49] Debating over a "known-or-should-have-known" standard is precisely what Rule 58 is designed to avoid. As one court wrote: "Rule 58 is a touch-the-base requirement that lays perception aside."[50]
- *Using the "Order" Label:* The Circuits are divided as to whether a document marked "Order" can ever qualify under this Rule as a judgment, even if the "separate document" requirements are otherwise met.[51]
- *Using the "Judgment" Label:* Although Rule 58 ordinarily requires that a qualifying judgment be labeled "Judgment", the inverse is not necessarily true. If a court's ruling does not qualify as a judgment under Rule 58, labeling it that way will not make it one.[52]
- *Using "Order and Judgment" Label:* At least one court has found that the use of this label did not contravene

---

[46] *See In re Taumoepeau*, 523 F.3d 1213, 1217 (10th Cir. 2008); *In re Cendant Corp. Secs. Litig.*, 454 F.3d 235, 241–42 (3d Cir. 2006).

[47] *See Bloomgarden v. U.S. Dep't of Justice*, 319 F.R.D. 24, 25 (D.D.C. 2016).

[48] *See Witasick v. Minnesota Mut. Life Ins. Co.*, 803 F.3d 184, 187–89 (3d Cir. 2015). *But see Barber v. Shinseki*, 660 F.3d 877, 879 (5th Cir. 2011) (questioning whether electronic entries can qualify as separate documents).

[49] *See In re Cendant Corp. Secs. Litig.*, 454 F.3d 235, 241 n.4 (3d Cir. 2006).

[50] *See In re Cendant Corp. Secs. Litig.*, 454 F.3d 235, 241 n.4 (3d Cir. 2006).

[51] *See Cantu v. Moody*, 933 F.3d 414, 418 n.1 (5th Cir. 2019) ("order" rather than "judgment" label "doesn't matter"); *Local Union No. 1992 of Intern. Broth. of Elec. Workers v. Okonite Co.*, 358 F.3d 278, 285–86 (3d Cir. 2004) (same; discussing case law). *See generally* Rule 54(a) (defining "judgment" to include "a decree and any order from which an appeal lies"). *But see Kanematsu-Gosho, Ltd. v. M/T Messiniaki Aigli*, 805 F.2d 47, 48–49 (2d Cir. 1986) (per curiam) ("order" does not qualify as judgment).

[52] *See Riley v. Kennedy*, 553 U.S. 406, 419, 128 S. Ct. 1970, 1981, 170 L. Ed. 2d 837 (2008).

the "separate document" requirement.[53]

- *Curing the Defect*: An intended judgment that violates the "separate document" requirement can be remedied by the court's entry of an amended judgment.[54]
- *R&R Adoptions*: An order adopting a report and recommendation may qualify as a "separate document."[55]

Waiving the "Separate Document" Requirement

The "separate document" requirement is designed to create protection, not traps.[56] Accordingly, parties are free to wait to appeal until either (1) the judgment is placed in a "separate document" (unless, of course, that judgment is exempt from the requirement) or (2) the capped outside time period set by the Rule nears.[57] But parties can also waive their entitlement to a "separate document" and file an early appeal from a judgment that is not set out in a proper "separate document."[58] Choosing not to wait will not affect the validity of the appeal.[59]

- *Appellee Cannot Stop Early Appeals:* An appellee cannot oppose an appellant's early appeal in order to insist that the appellant first return to the district court to obtain compliance with the ministerial act of preparing a "separate document" judgment.[60] If the appellant elects to waive the right to a "separate document" and immediately appeal, the appellee cannot stop it.
- *Waiver Via Filing Post-Trial Motions*: Whether a party can waive a judgment's violation of the "separate document" requirement by the act of filing post-trial motions to the improper judgment is unclear.[61]
- *Practitioners' Safe Harbor:* Because these early appeals

---

[53]*See Vaqueria Tres Monjitas, Inc. v. Comas-Pagan*, 772 F.3d 956, 960 (1st Cir. 2014).

[54]*See Felders v. Bairett*, 885 F.3d 646, 650–51 (10th Cir. 2018); *Jackman v. Fifth Judicial Dist. Dep't of Correctional Servs.*, 728 F.3d 800, 803–04 (8th Cir. 2013).

[55]*See Jeffries v. U.S.*, 721 F.3d 1008, 1013 (8th Cir. 2013).

[56]*See Bankers Trust Co. v. Mallis*, 435 U.S. 381, 386, 98 S. Ct. 1117, 55 L. Ed. 2d 357 (1978) (per curiam) (requirement is to be "interpreted to prevent loss of the right of appeal, not to facilitate loss").

[57]*See* Rule 58(c). *See also Ueckert v. Guerra*, 38 F.4th 446, 453 (5th Cir. 2022). *See generally Shalala v. Schaefer*, 509 U.S. 292, 302-03, 113 S. Ct. 2625, 125 L. Ed. 2d 239 (1993) ("separate document" failure kept time for appeal open (applying pre-amended text)).

[58]*See Bankers Trust Co. v. Mallis*, 435 U.S. 381, 384, 98 S. Ct. 1117, 55 L. Ed. 2d 357 (1978); *Ueckert v. Guerra*, 38 F.4th 446, 453 (5th Cir. 2022).

[59]*See* Fed. R. App. P. 4(a)(7)(B). *See also In re U.S. Bureau of Prisons, Dep't of Justice*, 918 F.3d 431, 438 n.4 (5th Cir. 2019); *Felders v. Bairett*, 885 F.3d 646, 650–51 (10th Cir. 2018).

[60]*See Bankers Tr. Co. v. Mallis*, 435 U.S. 381, 382–88, 98 S. Ct. 1117, 55 L. Ed. 2d 357 (1978); *Bailey v. Potter*, 478 F.3d 409, 411 (D.C. Cir. 2007).

[61]*Compare Casey v. Albertson's Inc*, 362 F.3d 1254, 1256–59 (9th Cir. 2004) (filing Rule 60(b) motion waived objection to "separate document" failure), *with Walters v. Wal-Mart Stores, Inc.*, 703 F.3d 1167, 1171–72 (10th Cir. 2013) (filing Rule 59 or 60 motion did

are permitted, the effect grants the appellant a safe harbor. Consequently, when in doubt whether a "separate document" has been filed or not, the practitioner may always file an appeal.[62]

RULE 58(b)—ENTERING JUDGMENT

CORE CONCEPT

Judgments on a general verdict, for sums certain or costs, or that deny relief may be entered by the clerk. All other judgments must be entered by the court.

APPLICATIONS

Impact of 2007 "Restyling" Amendments

Current Rule 58(b) now contains the procedure for entering judgments (the second part of old Rule 58(a)). The displaced former Rule 58(b) has been repositioned to Rule 58(c).

Manner of Entering the Judgment

All federal judgments are entered either by the clerk or by the court:

- *By The Clerk:* Unless the court otherwise orders,[63] the clerk of court must, without awaiting any further direction from the court, promptly prepare, sign, and enter judgment when (i) the jury returns a general verdict, (ii) the court awards only costs or a sum certain, or (iii) the court denies all relief.[64]
- *By The Court:* The court must review and promptly approve the form of judgment (which the clerk then must promptly enter) when (i) the jury returns a special verdict or a general verdict accompanied by interrogatories or (ii) the court grants other relief not described above,[65] including "partial" final judgments under Rule 54(b).[66] The district court's obligation to personally "approve" the judgment may be critical. The text of judgments are often drafted by clerks and, while often satisfactory in form, they can prove troublesome when the case's disposition is complicated and a non-attorney

---

not waive objection to "separate document" failure, or shorten appeal time).

[62]*See In re Cendant Corp. Secs. Litig.*, 454 F.3d 235, 245 (3d Cir. 2006); *Borrero v. City of Chicago*, 456 F.3d 698, 701 (7th Cir. 2006).

[63]*See Passananti v. Cook County*, 689 F.3d 655, 660 (7th Cir. 2012).

[64]*See* Rule 58(b)(1). *See also Otis v. City of Chicago*, 29 F.3d 1159, 1163 (7th Cir. 1994) (Rule 58 places on clerk onus of preparing judgment). *See also Brown v. Fifth Third Bank*, 730 F.3d 698, 701 (7th Cir. 2013) (order unsigned by clerk does not satisfy Rule 58(b)).

[65]*See* Rule 58(b)(2).

[66]*See* Rule 54(b) (permitting court to direct entry of final judgment "as to one or more but fewer than all of the claims or parties only upon an express determination that there is no just reason for delay and upon an express direction for the entry of judgment").

clerk is left "at sea" without judicial guidance.[67]

Contents of Judgment

The judgment document must clearly state which parties are entitled to what relief.[68]

Transferring Judgments to Another Judicial District

A judgment for money or property entered by one federal district court may be transferred to, and executed in, another district court. Such transfers are accomplished by filing a certified copy of the judgment in the new district court *after* the judgment has become final after appeal, by the expiration of time for appeal, or when, still pending appeal, the court so orders for good cause.[69] The transferred judgment will have the same effect as any other judgment entered in the new district.[70]

RULE 58(c)—TIME OF ENTRY

CORE CONCEPT

Judgments are deemed to be entered when they are placed on the civil docket, unless a "separate document" is required. In those cases, the judgments are deemed entered when docketed if the "separate document" requirement is met, *or else* 150 days after docketing.

APPLICATIONS

Impact of 2007 "Restyling" Amendments

Current Rule 58(c) now contains the timing principles for entered judgments (formerly found in Rule 58(b)). The displaced content of Rule 58(c) has been repositioned to Rule 58(e).

Significance of Time of "Entry of Judgment"

The time for a disappointed civil litigant to take an appeal from a federal civil judgment runs from the time of "entry" of that judgment.[71] Because that time period is jurisdictional, cannot often be extended, and is appeal-dooming if not honored,[72] knowing the date of a judgment's "entry" is critical in federal practice.

---

[67]*See Rush Univ. Med. Ctr. v. Leavitt*, 535 F.3d 735, 737–38 (7th Cir. 2008). *See also Acadian Diagnostic Labs., L.L.C. v. Quality Toxicology, L.L.C.*, 965 F.3d 404, 413–14 (5th Cir. 2020) (Rule contemplates that judge "pay careful attention to the preparation of this document").

[68]*See U.S. v. Marrocco*, 578 F.3d 627, 631 n.3 (7th Cir. 2009) (document ineffectual if omits "who is entitled to what from whom") (citation omitted); *Citizens Elec. Corp. v. Bituminous Fire & Marine Ins. Co.*, 68 F.3d 1016, 1021 (7th Cir. 1995) (proper judgments say who is liable for how much, then stop).

[69]*See Stanford v. Utley*, 341 F.2d 265, 269–70 (8th Cir.1965).

[70]*See* 28 U.S.C.A. § 1963.

[71]*See* Fed. R. App. P. 4(a)(1)(A) (ordinarily, appeals must be filed within 30 days after entry). *See generally Weber v. McGrogan*, 939 F.3d 232, 241 (3d Cir. 2019).

[72]*See infra* Authors' Commentary, Part VI, Appellate Procedure § 6.3 ("**Step Two: Time for Taking An Appeal**").

Triggering "Entry of Judgment" Date

The date the clerk enters the judgment "in the civil docket" is the trigger for calculating time under Rule 58(c). The clerk is obligated by Rule 79(a) to make this entry.[73] This ministerial, administrative duty is distinct from the Rule 58(b)(2) duty of the court to approve a "separate document" judgment.

Though ministerial, this docket "entering" event is still vulnerable to a surprising amount of confusion. *First*, there may be a flurry of docketing dates associated with any given order (*e.g.*, date listed on the document, date of signing, date of filing, date of entry); only the date of entry controls for Rule 58(c) purposes.[74] *Second*, the clerk may, properly, record a "judgment" in the civil docket, even though the document so recorded fails the "separate document" requirement; in such cases, the time for appeal will usually not begin ticking until the 150-day cap expires.[75] *Third,* the syntax used by the clerk in making the entry may be ambiguous, such as a local clerk's office practice to omit the term "ENTERED" when the entry date is the same as the filed date; in those instances, the date of actual entry — albeit identified imprecisely — controls.[76] *Fourth,* the clerk may defectively enter the judgment, in which case the time for appeal again may toll until the 150-day cap expires.[77] *Fifth*, the clerk may neglect to give notice of entry, or the notice given may fail to reach the litigants; because counsel are under an affirmative duty to monitor the official dockets, failure to discover such judgment entries may have calamitous consequences on post-trial motions and appeals.[78]

Computing "Entry of Judgment" Date

A judgment must always be entered on the docket.[79] To avoid the uncertainty created by the old "separate document" requirement (which could, theoretically, have allowed months or years to pass before the appeals clock might begin to run),[80] the current Rule now imposes an outside time limit for triggering the appeal period:

---

[73]*See* Rule 79(a)(1) (clerk must maintain the civil docket); Rule 79(a)(2)(C) (judgments must be entered chronologically in the civil docket).

[74]*See United States v. Fiorelli*, 337 F.3d 282, 287 (3d Cir.2003).

[75]*See Burnley v. City of San Antonio*, 470 F.3d 189, 194–96 (5th Cir. 2006).

[76]*See Vargas Torres v. Toledo*, 672 F. Supp. 2d 261, 262–65 (D.P.R. 2009).

[77]*See, e.g., Orr v. Plumb*, 884 F.3d 923, 929–31 (9th Cir. 2018) (judgment entered by clerk without court approval); *Brown v. Fifth Third Bank*, 730 F.3d 698, 701 (7th Cir. 2013) (judgment not signed by clerk).

[78]*See United States ex rel. McAllan v. New York*, 248 F.3d 48, 53 (2d Cir. 2001) (untimely notice of appeal not rescued by clerk's office docketing problems, "because parties have an obligation to monitor the docket sheet to inform themselves of the entry of orders they wish to appeal").

[79]*See* Rule 79 (providing for entries on the official court docket).

[80]*See Weber v. McGrogan*, 939 F.3d 232, 241 (3d Cir. 2019) (150-day cap designed to ensure that appeal time "does not linger on indefinitely").

- *When "Separate Document" Required:* If a "separate document" is required, the judgment is deemed to be entered on the date when (1) it is actually entered in the civil docket, if it meets the "separate document" requirement *or* (2) 150 days elapses after entry in the civil docket, if it does not meet the "separate document" requirement.[81] Thus, the time for a civil appeal is either 30 days (the normal appeal period, assuming a Rule 58-qualifying judgment has been entered) or 180 days[82] (the normal appeal period plus 150-days, if no Rule 58-qualifying judgment was entered). Of course, at any point during the first 150 days, if the court were to discover that it had entered a deficient order, and then correct it with a proper Rule 58-qualifying judgment, a normal 30-day appeal period would begin to run from that entry.[83]
- *When "Separate Document" Not Required:* If a "separate document" is not required (*i.e.*, a Rule 50(b), 52(b), 54(d), 59, or 60 ruling), the judgment is deemed to be entered when it is entered in the civil docket.[84]

Inapplicability of the 150-Day Cap

The 150-day outside time limit is only implicated when the order in question is a final one; absent a Rule 54(b) determination, an order disposing of less than all claims or less than all parties will not become a judgment merely because 150 days has passed since its entry.[85]

Disregarding the 150-Day Cap

The 150-day outside time limit should be disregarded where it serves no purpose to apply it.[86] Thus, for example, assessing the propriety of an appeal from a collateral order should *not* be complicated by the "separate document" requirement.[87] To the contrary, appeal periods for collateral orders should start to run when the collateral order is entered, and should not await

---

[81] *See* Rule 58(c)(2). *See also Bell v. Publix Super Markets, Inc.*, 982 F.3d 468, 488 & 491–92 (7th Cir. 2020); *CX Reinsurance Co. Ltd. v. Johnson*, 977 F.3d 306, 311 (4th Cir. 2020).

[82] Subject, of course, to the impact of other Rules. *See, e.g., United States v. $525,695.24, Seized From JPMorgan Chase Bank Inv. Account #xxxxxxxx*, 869 F.3d 429, 435 (6th Cir. 2017) (210 days, not 180, when appeal taken in lawsuit involving certain federal government parties); *Morrison v. Eminence Partners II, L.P.*, 714 F. App'x 14, 16 n.1 (2d Cir. 2017) (182 days, not 180, when period expired on Saturday).

[83] *See Zaretsky v. William Goldberg Diamond Corp.*, 820 F.3d 513, 519 (2d Cir. 2016).

[84] *See* Rule 58(c)(1). *See also Kunz v. DeFelice*, 538 F.3d 667, 673–74 (7th Cir. 2008).

[85] *See Boston Prop. Exchange Transfer Co. v. Iantosca*, 720 F.3d 1, 7–9 (1st Cir. 2013); *In re Metropolitan Gov't of Nashville & Davidson County*, 606 F.3d 855, 860–61 (6th Cir. 2010).

[86] *See* Rule 58 advisory committee notes (2002).

[87] *See* Rule 58 advisory committee notes (2002).

either a "separate document" or the passing of 150 days.[88]

Special Concerns in Multidistrict Litigation (MDL)

The complexities of multi-case consolidation can create special concerns when a district court enters a dispositive ruling without also supplying a companion judgment satisfying the "separate document" requirement. Where, for example, litigants agree to a consolidated complaint for MDL use, and that complaint is later dismissed with a finality that confuses the parties, an absent "separate document" could trigger the 150-day cap and thus defeat appellate jurisdiction for all those litigants who failed to realize their time for appeal had begun to run.[89]

RULE 58(d)—REQUEST FOR ENTRY

CORE CONCEPT

Because entry of a proper judgment has serious procedural consequences (for, among other things, the time for appealing), a party may request the court to prepare one.

APPLICATIONS

Former Prohibition on Attorney-Prepared Judgments

The 2002 amendments to Rule 58(d) omitted a former express prohibition on non-requested, attorney-prepared forms of judgment. That bar had been designed to avoid delays and suitability concerns occasioned by attorney-drafting.[90] Rule 58's current language, which directs prompt entry of judgments and invites parties to move the court for a prompt entry, was thought to obviate the need for the former prohibition.[91]

Party's Request to Prompt a "Separate Document"

A party may now request the district court to enter a "separate document" judgment.[92] Allowing such requests helps protect a party's need to ensure that timing periods are promptly triggered for motions, appeals, and enforcement procedures.[93] Thus, a party may make such a request in order to cure a "separate document" deficiency with an existing judg-

---

[88] *See* Rule 58 advisory committee notes (2002).

[89] *See Bell v. Publix Super Markets, Inc.*, 982 F.3d 468, 486–92 (7th Cir. 2020).

[90] *See* Rule 58 advisory committee notes (2002). *See also Matteson v. U.S.*, 240 F.2d 517, 519 (2d Cir. 1956) (having lawyers prepare form of judgment caused delay and forced the court to sift through "excess of detail supplied by zealous advocates in their natural desire to press home all conceivable ad hoc advantages from the judgment").

[91] *See* Rule 58(d) advisory committee note (2002).

[92] *See Bell v. Publix Super Markets, Inc.*, 982 F.3d 468, 488 (7th Cir. 2020); *N. Am. Butterfly Ass'n v. Wolf*, 977 F.3d 1244, 1257 (D.C. Cir. 2020).

[93] *See* Rule 58(d) advisory committee note (2002).

ment,[94] to seek a Rule 54(b) determination that would permit an immediate partial judgment appeal,[95] or to quicken the pace for enforcement.[96] Such a request can also be made by a party who suffers a dismissal *without prejudice*, but who wishes to appeal that dismissal rather than attempt to re-plead.[97]

RULE 58(e)—COST OR FEE AWARDS

CORE CONCEPT

To facilitate a single, consolidated appeal from both a merits ruling and a ruling on an award of attorney's fees, the district court may allow a pending (but yet undecided) attorney's fees motion to suspend the time for finality.

APPLICATIONS

Impact of 2007 "Restyling" Amendments

Current Rule 58(e) now contains the costs or fees award provision, which, formerly, was found in old Rule 58(c).

Purpose

Usually, the entry of final judgment is not postponed (nor is the time for taking an appeal extended) while the district court considers requests to tax costs or award attorney's fees.[98] Concerns about resulting piecemeal litigation are considered outweighed by the need to promptly, clearly determine whether a merits appeal will be taken.[99] A Rule 58(e) motion offers an exception to this practice, which enhances judicial efficiency by allowing the appeals court to review a fees award at the same time as it reviews the merits.[100]

Effect of a Rule 58(e) Order

In order to allow a consolidated appeal of both its merits judgment and its ruling on attorney's fees, the district court may, in its discretion,[101] enter an order that treats a pending Rule 54(d)(2) motion for an award of attorney's fees as the

---

[94] *See Perry v. Sheet Metal Workers' Local No. 73 Pension Fund*, 585 F.3d 358, 362 (7th Cir. 2009).

[95] *See Jones v. Tidewater Inc.*, 2015 WL 222356, at *1 (E.D.La. Jan. 14, 2015).

[96] *See Uhl v. Komatsu Forklift Co., Ltd.*, 466 F. Supp. 2d 899, 911 (E.D. Mich. 2006), aff'd, 512 F.3d 294 (6th Cir. 2008).

[97] *See Parker v. Google, Inc.*, 242 Fed. Appx. 833, 835–36 (3d Cir. 2007).

[98] *See* Rule 58(e). *See also Ray Haluch Gravel Co. v. Central Pension Fund of Int'l Union of Operating Eng'rs & Participating Employers*, 571 U.S. 177, 186–87, 134 S. Ct. 773, 187 L. Ed. 2d 669 (2014).

[99] *See Ray Haluch Gravel Co. v. Cent. Pension Fund of Int'l Union of Operating Eng'rs & Participating Employers*, 571 U.S. 177, 186, 134 S. Ct. 773, 187 L. Ed. 2d 669 (2014).

[100] *See Hudson v. Pittsylvania Cty.*, 774 F.3d 231, 235 (4th Cir. 2014); *Kira, Inc. v. All Star Maintenance, Inc.*, 294 Fed.Appx. 139, 141 n.2 (5th Cir. 2008).

[101] *See Frommert v. Conkright*, 221 F. Supp. 3d 358, 360 (W.D.N.Y. 2016); *Electronic Privacy Info. Ctr. v. U.S. Dep't of Homeland Sec.*, 811 F. Supp. 2d 216, 225 n.2 (D.D.C. 2011).

equivalent of a Rule 59 motion.[102] If the court enters such an order, the time for appealing will not begin to run until the court decides the pending fees motion.[103] The court must, however, actually enter the Rule 58(e) order;[104] the mere fact that a litigant has requested it is not sufficient to toll.[105] Nor does tolling occur merely by the filing of some other (non-Rule 58) post-trial motion seeking an award of attorney's fees.[106] If the district court elects not to grant the order, it retains jurisdiction over the fee motion even while the merits appeal is pending,[107] which in turn deprives the appeals court of jurisdiction over that issue pending the district court's ruling.[108] A litigant who is then dissatisfied with the district court's fees decision must take a new appeal from that ruling.[109]

Prerequisites for a Rule 58(e) Order

The court may enter a Rule 58(e) order only if: (1) the motion for fees is pending and has been timely made (*i.e.*, within 14 days after entry of judgment, unless provided otherwise by statute or court order); (2) no effective notice of appeal has yet been made; and (3) a timely notice of appeal is still possible (*i.e.*, the time for appealing has not already expired).[110]

Time for Entering a Rule 58(e) Order

While it is clear that the trial court may enter a Rule 58(e) order for a *pending* fees motion, courts are divided on whether such an order may be properly entered in anticipation of a *future* fees motion.[111]

---

[102]*See* Rule 58(e). *See also Burnley v. City of San Antonio*, 470 F.3d 189, 199 (5th Cir. 2006) (noting purpose); *Gilda Marx, Inc. v. Wildwood Exercise, Inc.*, 85 F.3d 675, 680 (D.C. Cir. 1996) (desirable to have merits appeals and fees order appeals decided together).

[103]*See Ray Haluch Gravel Co. v. Central Pension Fund of Int'l Union of Operating Eng'rs & Participating Employers*, 571 U.S. 177, 187, 134 S. Ct. 773, 187 L. Ed. 2d 669 (2014). *See generally JPMorgan Chase Bank, N.A. v. Winget*, 920 F.3d 1103, 1106–08 (6th Cir. 2019) (finality does not arrive until court completes the post-judgment proceedings).

[104]*See Nutrition Distrib'n LLC v. IronMag Labs, LLC*, 978 F.3d 1068, 1071 & 1075 (9th Cir. 2020).

[105]*See Cobell v. Jewell*, 802 F.3d 12, 19 n.5 (D.C. Cir. 2015); *Hudson v. Pittsylvania Cty.*, 774 F.3d 231, 235–36 (4th Cir. 2014).

[106]*See Nutrition Distrib'n LLC v. IronMag Labs, LLC*, 978 F.3d 1068, 1071–82 (9th Cir. 2020); *House of Flavors, Inc. v. TFG-Mich., L.P.*, 700 F.3d 33, 38 (1st Cir. 2012).

[107]*See Phillips v. Tangilag*, 14 F.4th 524, 541 (6th Cir. 2021); *Kira, Inc. v. All Star Maint., Inc.*, 294 Fed.Appx. 139, 141 n.2 (5th Cir. 2008).

[108]*See McCarter v. Ret. Plan for Dist. Mngrs. of Am. Family Ins. Group*, 540 F.3d 649, 652–53 (7th Cir. 2008).

[109]*See Phillips v. Tangilag*, 14 F.4th 524, 541 (6th Cir. 2021); *T.B. ex rel. Brenneise v. San Diego Unified Sch. Dist.*, 806 F.3d 451, 466 n.2 (9th Cir. 2015).

[110]*See Ray Haluch Gravel Co. v. Central Pension Fund of Int'l Union of Operating Eng'rs & Participating Employers*, 571 U.S. 177, 187, 134 S. Ct. 773, 187 L. Ed. 2d 669 (2014); *Heck v. Triche*, 775 F.3d 265, 274–76 (5th Cir. 2014).

[111]*Compare Heck v. Triche*, 775 F.3d 265, 275–76 (5th Cir. 2014)

When the Order is *Not* Proper

The practical effect of a Rule 58(e) motion is to delay the arrival of finality and, with it, the time for taking an appeal from the court's order. The reason why district courts are authorized to grant this postponement is efficiency: to permit one, consolidated appeal from both the trial court's judgment on the merits and its ruling on attorney's fees.[112] If that goal cannot be attained, no Rule 58(e) postponement order is proper. Thus, if an appeal has already been taken from the merits ruling, if the attorney's fees motion has already been ruled upon, or if the merits judgment has already become unappealable (*e.g.*, if the appeal time has already expired), the district court has no reason or authority to issue such a postponement order.[113] Nor may a Rule 58(e) order be used with interim fee awards (fees awarded before the court decides the merits of the case).[114]

Order Applies Only to Fees, Not Costs

A postponement of finality under Rule 58(e) is, by its terms, only applicable to attorney's fee awards; finality cannot be suspended while costs are being taxed.[115]

When Fees Are an Element of the Claim Itself

Rule 58(e) applies only to extend time for resolving Rule 54(d)(2) motions. In turn, Rule 54(d)(2) sets the fee-seeking motion procedure "*unless* the substantive law requires those fees to be proved at trial as an element of damages."[116] Thus, a Rule 58(e) time extension seems unavailable for fee requests that, under applicable substantive law, cannot be pursued through Rule 54(d)(2).[117] But this distinction can prove to be nuanced and uncertain; in such cases, practitioners are wise to appeal

---

(proper), *with Robinson v. City of Harvey*, 489 F.3d 864, 868 (7th Cir. 2007) (improper, but under earlier version of Rule), *and Mendes Junior Int'l Co. v. Banco do Brasil, S.A.*, 215 F.3d 306, 312–13 (2d Cir. 2000) (improper, same).

[112] *See Burnley v. City of San Antonio*, 470 F.3d 189, 199 (5th Cir. 2006).

[113] *See Burnley v. City of San Antonio*, 470 F.3d 189, 199 (5th Cir. 2006); *Electronic Privacy Info. Ctr. v. U.S. Dep't of Homeland Sec.*, 811 F. Supp. 2d 216, 225 n.2 (D.D.C. 2011). *See also Robinson v. City of Harvey*, 489 F.3d 864, 868–69 (7th Cir. 2007) (appeal period must still be live at time of order; order may not "revive" an already-expired appeal period).

[114] *See JPMorgan Chase Bank, N.A. v. Winget*, 920 F.3d 1103, 1105–06 (6th Cir. 2019).

[115] *See Moody Nat. Bank of Galveston v. GE Life and Annuity Assur. Co.*, 383 F.3d 249, 253 (5th Cir. 2004). *See also Mahach-Watkins v. Depee*, 593 F.3d 1054, 1059 (9th Cir. 2010) (court's withholding of final decision on costs had no effect on resolution of attorney's fees motion).

[116] *See* Rule 54(d)(2) (emphasis added).

[117] *See Ray Haluch Gravel Co. v. Cent. Pension Fund of Int'l Union of Operating Eng'rs & Participating Employers*, 571 U.S. 177, 187–88, 134 S. Ct. 773, 187 L. Ed. 2d 669 (2014) (suggesting such a reading). *See generally* Rule 54(d)(2) advisory committee note (1993) (Rule 54(d)(2) procedures inapplicable "to fees recoverable as an element of damages, as when sought under the terms of a contract; such damages typically are to be claimed in a pleading and may involve issues to be resolved by a jury."). *But cf. In re*

the merits ruling at once.[118]

Additional Research References

Wright & Miller, *Federal Practice and Procedure* §§ 2781 to 2787
C.J.S., Federal Civil Procedure §§ 1227 to 1231 et seq.
West's Key Number Digest, Federal Civil Procedure ⚿2621 to 2628

Empresas Martinez Valentin Corp., 948 F.3d 448, 453–54 (1st Cir. 2020) (proper inquiry is not whether fees qualify as "part of the merits" or "compensable damages" but rather whether they were " 'incurred in the course of litigating the case' and thus could not have been determined until after the case was litigated").

[118]*See In re Empresas Martinez Valentin Corp.*, 948 F.3d 448, 455 (1st Cir. 2020) ("when in doubt, file your notice of appeal, because a premature notice, unlike a late notice, can still be effective.").

RULE 59
NEW TRIAL; ALTERING OR AMENDING A JUDGMENT

(a) In General.

(1) *Grounds for New Trial.* The court may, on motion, grant a new trial on all or some of the issues—and to any party—as follows:

(A) after a jury trial, for any reason for which a new trial has heretofore been granted in an action at law in federal court; or

(B) after a nonjury trial, for any reason for which a rehearing has heretofore been granted in a suit in equity in federal court.

(2) *Further Action After a Nonjury Trial.* After a nonjury trial, the court may, on motion for a new trial, open the judgment if one has been entered, take additional testimony, amend findings of fact and conclusions of law or make new ones, and direct the entry of a new judgment.

(b) Time to File a Motion for a New Trial. A motion for a new trial must be filed no later than 28 days after the entry of judgment.

(c) Time to Serve Affidavits. When a motion for a new trial is based on affidavits, they must be filed with the motion. The opposing party has 14 days after being served to file opposing affidavits. The court may permit reply affidavits.

(d) New Trial on the Court's Initiative or for Reasons Not in the Motion. No later than 28 days after the entry of judgment, the court, on its own, may order a new trial for any reason that would justify granting one on a party's motion. After giving the parties notice and an opportunity to be heard, the court may grant a timely motion for a new trial for a reason not stated in the motion. In either event, the court must specify the reasons in its order.

(e) Motion to Alter or Amend a Judgment. A motion to alter or amend a judgment must be filed no later than 28 days after the entry of the judgment.

[Amended effective March 19, 1948; July 1, 1966; April 27, 1995, effective December 1, 1995; April 30, 2007, effective December 1, 2007; March 26, 2009, effective December 1, 2009.]

AUTHORS' COMMENTARY ON RULE 59

PURPOSE AND SCOPE

Rule 59 is one of several post-trial motions authorized by the federal rules—joining Rule 50, which permits motions seeking judgments as a matter of law ("JMOL"s) in jury trials; Rule 52, which permits revisions to findings and judgments in bench trials; and Rule 60, which permits relief from judgments or orders. Each of these post-trial motions is addressed to the trial court that presided over the lawsuit (*i.e.,* these are not appeals).

Rule 59 permits the grant of a new trial or, in the case of a bench trial, permits the trial judge to reopen the case, receive new testimony, and amend findings and conclusions. Rule 59(e) also allows the court to alter or amend a judgment. A motion for relief under Rule 59 must be filed not later than 28 days after the entry of judgment, and that period must not be extended by the court. (Motions styled as requests for "reconsideration" are not recognized as such by the national rules, and are ordinarily treated—depending on the setting—as either Rule 54(b) motions to re-examine an interlocutory order or as post-trial motions under Rule 59(e) or Rule 60.)

In practice, parties often file two post-trial motions simultaneously: one seeking a JMOL and, alternatively, a companion motion seeking a new trial. That practice highlights an important distinction between the two motions. A JMOL motion usually seeks an outright victory; it requests that the trial court declare the moving party the winner in the dispute. A new trial motion, in contrast, usually seeks only a "do-over"; it requests that the result in the trial be cleared and a second trial be convened to hear the case anew. By combining the two motions as alternative requests for relief in the same filing, practitioners are able to press boldly for a complete victory (JMOL) but, hedging their bets if the judge is unconvinced, also offer the alternative, fall-back option of seeking the opportunity to try the case over again.

RULE 59(a)—NEW TRIALS, GENERALLY

CORE CONCEPT

In both jury and bench trials, the court may grant a new trial for any reason for which new trials (jury trials) or rehearings (bench trials) were formerly granted, such as where the verdict is against the weight of the evidence or is either excessive or inadequate, where probative evidence is newly discovered, or where conduct by the court, counsel, or the jury improperly influenced the deliberative process.

APPLICATIONS

Procedure

Motions for new trial are usually made in writing and must state with particularity the grounds for relief.[1]

Discretion of District Court

Whether the circumstances justify the granting of a new trial is a decision left to the sound discretion of the trial judge,[2] and this discretion is far greater than the court's authority to grant a motion for judgment as a matter of law.[3] So broad is this discretion that, in certain contexts, it as "virtually unassailable on appeal."[4] Although there is some dispute on the point,[5] the majority view prescribes that, in considering such motions, trial judges are not bound to view the evidence in the light most favorable to the verdict winner,[6] but may reweigh the evidence, accepting or rejecting evidence, witnesses, and other proof that the jury considered.[7] But courts must nonetheless proceed carefully, and avoid merely substituting their

---

[1] *See* Rule 7(b)(1)(A)–(C). *See also Umpleby v. Potter & Brumfield, Inc.*, 69 F.3d 209, 213 (7th Cir. 1995).

[2] *See Gasperini v. Center for Humanities, Inc.*, 518 U.S. 415, 433, 116 S. Ct. 2211, 135 L. Ed. 2d 659 (1996) ("the authority of trial judges to grant new trials . . . is large"); *Allied Chemical Corp. v. Daiflon, Inc.*, 449 U.S. 33, 101 S. Ct. 188, 66 L. Ed. 2d 193 (1980) ("confided almost entirely to the exercise of discretion on the part of the trial court").

[3] *See Rodriguez-Valentin v. Doctors' Ctr. Hosp. (Manati), Inc.*, 27 F.4th 14, 21 (1st Cir. 2022); *Echevarria v. Insight Medical, P.C.*, 72 F. Supp. 3d 442, 465–66 (S.D.N.Y. 2014).

[4] *See Crowley v. Epicept Corp.*, 883 F.3d 739, 751 (9th Cir. 2018); *Lincoln Composites, Inc. v. Firetrace USA, LLC*, 825 F.3d 453, 459 (8th Cir. 2016). *But cf. Ali v. Kipp*, 891 F.3d 59, 64 (2d Cir. 2018) (district court latitude is significant, but not limitless).

[5] *See Robinson v. McNeil Consumer Healthcare*, 671 F. Supp. 2d 975, 989 n.4 (N.D.Ill. 2009) (noting apparent division within Seventh Circuit); *Tatum v. Jackson*, 668 F. Supp. 2d 584, 598 n.10 (S.D.N.Y. 2009) (same, within Second Circuit). *But cf. Ali v. Kipp*, 891 F.3d 59, 64 (2d Cir. 2018) (must view evidence most favorably to nonmovant).

[6] *See Allied Chem. Corp. v. Daiflon, Inc.*, 449 U.S. 33, 36, 101 S. Ct. 188, 66 L. Ed. 2d 193 (1980); *Rodriguez-Valentin v. Doctors' Ctr. Hosp. (Manati), Inc.*, 27 F.4th 14, 21 (1st Cir. 2022). *See also Robinson v. McNeil Consumer Healthcare*, 671 F. Supp. 2d 975, 989 n.4 (N.D.Ill. 2009) (describing majority view as one endorsed by Professors Wright and Miller in their treatise).

[7] *See Rodriguez-Valentin v. Doctors' Ctr. Hosp. (Manati), Inc.*, 27 F.4th 14, 21 (1st Cir. 2022); *McGinnis v. Am. Home Mortgage Servicing, Inc.*, 817 F.3d 1241, 1254–55 (11th Cir. 2016).

views for a jury's without good reason.[8] (Consequently, some courts describe grants of new trials as a rare occurrence[9] and "disfavored."[10]) The task of assessing whether to grant a new trial is, obviously, a highly fact-dependent one,[11] which explains the wide discretion afforded to trial judges.[12]

Grounds for New Trials in Jury Trials

Rule 59(a) provides no list of proper reasons for which new trials may be granted in jury trials, and relies instead upon historical practice.[13] What historically justified a new trial in an action at law in the federal courts today warrants a new trial following a jury verdict.[14] Understood broadly, new trials are proper when necessary to prevent a miscarriage of justice.[15] The courts have recognized that new trials may be granted in at least[16] the following circumstances:

- *Verdict Against the Weight of Evidence:* when the district court concludes that the factfinder's verdict is against the "clear" or "great" weight of the evidence, and a new trial is therefore necessary to prevent a miscarriage of justice.[17] New trials on this ground may be granted even

---

[8]*See Leonard v. Stemtech Int'l Inc.*, 834 F.3d 376, 386 (3d Cir. 2016); *Armisted v. State Farm Mut. Auto. Ins. Co.*, 675 F.3d 989, 995 (6th Cir. 2012). *See also Rodriguez-Valentin v. Doctors' Ctr. Hosp. (Manati), Inc.*, 27 F.4th 14, 21 (1st Cir. 2022) ("trial judges do not sit as thirteenth jurors, empowered to reject any verdict with which they disagree") (cleaned up).

[9]*See Innovation Ventures, LLC v. N2G Distrib'g, Inc.*, 763 F.3d 524, 534 (6th Cir. 2014).

[10]*See Fox v. Pittsburg State Univ.*, 257 F. Supp. 3d 1112, 1145 (D. Kan. 2017); *Guidance Endodontics, LLC v. Dentsply Int'l, Inc.*, 749 F. Supp. 2d 1235, 1256 (D.N.M. 2010). *See generally Int'l Ore & Fertilizer Corp. v. SGS Control Servs., Inc.*, 38 F.3d 1279, 1287 (2d Cir.1994) (having fought once for the court's favor, the litigants should not — absent a corruption of the judicial process — be made to endure the fight anew).

[11]*See Heimlicher v. Steele*, 615 F. Supp. 2d 884, 899 (N.D.Iowa 2009).

[12]*See Max Rack, Inc. v. Core Health & Fitness, LLC*, 40 F.4th 454, 470 (6th Cir. 2022) (unlike appeals court, trial judge "had the ability to evaluate the allegedly improper conduct (and its prejudicial impact) by witnessing the conduct firsthand, not by reviewing a transcript of it secondhand").

[13]*See E.E.O.C. v. New Breed Logistics*, 783 F.3d 1057, 1065–66 (6th Cir. 2015); *Molski v. M.J. Cable, Inc.*, 481 F.3d 724, 729 (9th Cir. 2007).

[14]*See* Rule 59(a)(1)(A).

[15]*See City Select Auto Sales Inc. v. David Randall Assocs., Inc.*, 885 F.3d 154, 163 (3d Cir. 2018); *Seibert v. Jackson Cty.*, 851 F.3d 430, 438 (5th Cir. 2017).

[16]Some courts have suggested other grounds that may not neatly fit within the listed categories. *See, e.g., Doe v. Fairfax Cty. Sch. Bd.*, 1 F.4th 257, 268 (4th Cir. 2021) (new trial proper where evidence based on false evidence or otherwise result in miscarriage of justice).

[17]*See Byrd v. Blue Ridge Rural Elec. Co-op., Inc.*, 356 U.S. 525, 540, 78 S. Ct. 893, 2 L. Ed. 2d 953 (1958). *See also Oracle Corp. v. SAP AG*, 765 F.3d 1081, 1093 (9th Cir. 2014) (may be granted when "it is quite clear that the jury has reached a seriously erroneous result"). *But cf. Latino v. Kaizer*, 58 F.3d 310, 314 (7th Cir. 1995) (jury's verdict accorded greater defer-

when substantial evidence supports a jury's verdict.[18] But this authority must be exercised cautiously, so as not to overstep the rightful province of the jury.[19] Thus, because the jury's verdict should ordinarily be respected unless it constitutes a serious miscarriage of justice,[20] new trials on this ground should be a rare occurrence,[21] ordered with great restraint.[22]

- *Verdict is Excessive or Inadequate:* when the district court determines that the amount of the verdict is so unreasonable that it shocks the conscience;[23]
- *"Remittitur"*: If the court decides that the verdict is excessive, the court may offer the verdict winner a reduction—called a "remittitur"—in exchange for the court's denial of a motion for a new trial.[24] If the verdict winner accepts the court's offer, the verdict winner waives the right of appeal.[25] If remitted, the jury's verdict will be reduced to the maximum amount the jury could have awarded without being excessive.[26] A trial court's deci-

---

ence in cases involving simple issues with highly disputed facts).

[18]*See Manley v. AmBase Corp.*, 337 F.3d 237, 244 (2d Cir. 2003); *Silver Sage Partners, Ltd. v. City of Desert Hot Springs*, 251 F.3d 814, 819 (9th Cir. 2001). *But cf. Lubby Holdings LLC v. Chung*, 11 F.4th 1355, 1358 (Fed. Cir. 2021) (must be "an *absolute absence of evidence* to support the jury's verdict").

[19]*See Grant v. City of Syracuse*, 357 F. Supp. 3d 180, 192 (N.D.N.Y. 2019); *Rodriguez v. Miami-Dade Cty.*, 339 F. Supp. 3d 1279, 1290–91 (M.D. Fla. 2018); *McClure v. Country Life Ins. Co.*, 326 F. Supp. 3d 934, 940 (D. Ariz. 2018).

[20]*See City Select Auto Sales Inc. v. David Randall Assocs., Inc.*, 885 F.3d 154, 163 (3d Cir. 2018) (verdict is against "great weight" of evidence); *Raedle v. Credit Agricole Indosuez*, 670 F.3d 411, 417 (2d Cir. 2012) (verdict is "egregious").

[21]*See CFE Racing Prod., Inc. v. BMF Wheels, Inc.*, 793 F.3d 571, 591 (6th Cir. 2015); *ING Global v. United Parcel Serv. Oasis Supply Corp.*, 757 F.3d 92, 97–98 (2d Cir. 2014).

[22]*See Raedle v. Credit Agricole Indosuez*, 670 F.3d 411, 418–19 (2d Cir. 2012).

[23]*See Burke v. Regalado*, 935 F.3d 960, 1035 (10th Cir. 2019). *See also Sindi v. El-Moslimany*, 896 F.3d 1, 13 (1st Cir. 2018) (must exceed "any rational appraisal or estimate of the damage that could be based on evidence before the jury"); *Eiland v. Westinghouse Elec. Corp.*, 58 F.3d 176, 183 (5th Cir. 1995) ("contrary to right reason" or "entirely disproportionate" to injury sustained). *But see Gasperini v. Center for Humanities, Inc.*, 518 U.S. 415, 116 S. Ct. 2211, 135 L. Ed. 2d 659 (1996) (applying New York's standard which differed from federal "shocks the conscience" benchmark).

[24]*See Linn v. United Plant Guard Workers of America, Local 114*, 383 U.S. 53, 65–66, 86 S. Ct. 657, 15 L. Ed. 2d 582 (1966) (if damages award is excessive, trial judge has the "duty" to require a remittitur or grant a new trial); *Cortez v. Trans Union, LLC*, 617 F.3d 688, 715–18 (3d Cir. 2010) (describing remittitur procedure, and distinguishing constitutionally-reduced verdicts); *Atlas Food Systems and Services, Inc. v. Crane Nat. Vendors, Inc.*, 99 F.3d 587, 593 (4th Cir. 1996) (noting remittitur's history).

[25]*See Donovan v. Penn Shipping Co., Inc.*, 429 U.S. 648, 97 S. Ct. 835, 51 L. Ed. 2d 112 (1977) (per curiam).

[26]*See Sloane v. Equifax Information Services, LLC*, 510 F.3d 495, 502–03 (4th Cir. 2007); *Eiland v.*

sion on remittitur is accorded wide discretion, given that judge's ability to hear the testimony and assess the demeanor of the witnesses; a trial court's ruling that denies remittitur usually will be overturned on appeal only where the verdict is found to be so grossly excessive that the outcome is "monstrous or shocking."[27] Non-economic damages (such as pain and suffering) are usually remitted in only extraordinary circumstances.[28] Properly done, remittitur will generally not offend the Seventh Amendment's entitlement to a jury trial,[29] and may serve the laudable ends of avoiding delay and expense and limiting judicial intrusion into the jury's domain.[30]

- *"Additur":* If the court finds that the verdict is inadequate,[31] the court usually[32] may *not* offer the verdict winner an increase in verdict size—called an "additur"—in exchange for the court's denial of a motion for new trial, due to Seventh Amendment concerns.[33] Where the verdict is inadequate, the court's only option is ordering a new trial.
- *Newly Discovered Evidence:* when the district court learns of a party's newly discovered evidence. To entitle the moving party to a new trial, the newly discovered evidence generally: (1) must have existed as of the time of trial; (2) must have been excusably overlooked by the moving party, notwithstanding the moving party's diligence in attempting to discover it; (3) must be admis-

---

Westinghouse Elec. Corp., 58 F.3d 176, 183 (5th Cir. 1995). *See also Earl v. Bouchard Transp. Co., Inc.*, 917 F.2d 1320, 1328–30 (2d Cir. 1990) (adopting same rule, but discussing views on remittitur and scholarly commentary's preferences).

[27] *See Hite v. Vermeer Mfg. Co.*, 446 F.3d 858, 869–70 (8th Cir. 2006).

[28] *See Rodriguez v. Senor Frog's de la Isla, Inc.*, 642 F.3d 28, 39 (1st Cir. 2011).

[29] *See Gasperini v. Center for Humanities, Inc.*, 518 U.S. 415, 433, 116 S. Ct. 2211, 135 L. Ed. 2d 659 (1996); *Dimick v. Schiedt*, 293 U.S. 474, 486–87, 55 S. Ct. 296, 79 L. Ed. 603 (1935). Note, however, that the court ordinarily may not reduce plaintiff's damages award without first offering plaintiff a new trial. *See Hetzel v. Prince William Cnty.*, 523 U.S. 208, 211, 118 S. Ct. 1210, 140 L. Ed. 2d 336 (1998) (per curiam).

[30] *See Dwyer v. Deutsche Lufthansa, AG*, 686 F. Supp. 2d 216, 218 (E.D.N.Y. 2010).

[31] *See Bavlsik v. Gen. Motors, LLC*, 870 F.3d 800, 809 (8th Cir. 2017).

[32] *But cf., e.g., Roman v. W. Mfg., Inc.*, 691 F.3d 686, 702 (5th Cir. 2012) (permitted, if no valid dispute as to damages amount); *Pittington v. Great Smoky Mountain Lumberjack Feud, LLC*, 880 F.3d 791, 806 (6th Cir. 2018) (permitted, if parties consent or damage amount is definitive and incontrovertible); *Elm Ridge Expl. Co., LLC v. Engle*, 721 F.3d 1199, 1221 n.13 (10th Cir. 2013) (suggesting *Erie* doctrine might permit additur).

[33] *See Gasperini v. Center for Humanities, Inc.*, 518 U.S. 415, 433, 116 S. Ct. 2211, 135 L. Ed. 2d 659 (1996); *Dimick v. Schiedt*, 293 U.S. 474, 486–87, 55 S. Ct. 296, 79 L. Ed. 603 (1935).

sible; and (4) must be likely to alter the trial's outcome.[34]

- *Improper Conduct by Counsel or the Court:* when improper conduct by either an attorney[35] or the court[36] unfairly influenced the verdict. A frequent basis is error by the court in admitting or excluding evidence,[37] though to receive a new trial on that ground requires that the error affect the moving party's substantial rights.[38]
- *Improper Conduct Affecting the Jury:* when the jury verdict was not unanimous or was facially inconsistent,[39] or when the jury was improperly influenced[40] or improperly addressed by counsel,[41] or when an erroneous jury instruction likely misled or confused the jury.[42] Note, however, that after the verdict is returned, jurors usually may not impeach or alter their verdict except to testify as to improper, extrinsic influences.[43] This new trial ground is often constrained by the harmless error

---

[34]*See Colon-Millin v. Sears Roebuck De Puerto Rico, Inc.*, 455 F.3d 30, 36 n.4 (1st Cir. 2006); *Advanced Display Systems, Inc. v. Kent State University*, 212 F.3d 1272, 1284 (Fed. Cir. 2000). *See generally Jenkins v. Anton*, 922 F.3d 1257, 1263–67 (11th Cir. 2019) (parties may not "roll the dice" at trial without known-but-unavailable witness, wait to see if they win, and if not, then seek new trial).

[35]*See In re DePuy Orthopaedics, Inc., Pinnacle Hip Implant Prod. Liab. Litig.*, 888 F.3d 753, 784–86 (5th Cir. 2018) (granted, for inviting jury, in closing argument, to find product defective based on immaterial incendiary facts and other hearsay accusations); *Burke v. Regalado*, 935 F.3d 960, 1026–34 (10th Cir. 2019) (denied, where impassioned closing jury argument ruled harmless error).

[36]*See Simmons v. Bradshaw*, 879 F.3d 1157, 1161–68 (11th Cir. 2018) (granted, for improper jury instructions). *See generally Aggarwal v. Ponce School of Medicine*, 837 F.2d 17, 21–22 (1st Cir. 1988) (before conduct of judge will warrant a new trial, the moving party must be "so seriously prejudiced as to be deprived of a fair trial").

[37]*See Ruiz-Cortez v. City of Chicago*, 931 F.3d 592, 602–04 (7th Cir. 2019) (common ground for motion is claimed fundamental unfairness to movant, such as trial rulings impacting evidence). *See also Jordan v. Maxfield & Oberton Holdings, L.L.C.*, 977 F.3d 412, 417 (5th Cir. 2020); *Stampf v. Long Island R. Co.*, 761 F.3d 192, 202 (2d Cir. 2014).

[38]*See* Rule 61. *See also infra* Authors' Commentary to Rule 61 ("**Errors in Admitting or Excluding Evidence**").

[39]*See Monaco v. City of Camden*, 366 Fed.Appx. 330, 331–32 (3d Cir. 2010); *Babby v. Wilmington Dep't of Police*, 614 F. Supp. 2d 508, 512 (D.Del. 2009).

[40]*Cf. Parker v. Gladden*, 385 U.S. 363, 87 S. Ct. 468, 17 L. Ed. 2d 420 (1966) (per curiam)(statement by bailiff that defendant was "wicked fellow" who was guilty, and that higher courts would correct a guilty verdict if wrong).

[41]*See Mejias-Aguayo v. Doreste-Rodriguez*, 863 F.3d 50, 55–56 (1st Cir. 2017).

[42]*See Susan Wakeen Doll Co., Inc. v. Ashton Drake Galleries*, 272 F.3d 441, 452 (7th Cir. 2001).

[43]*See Carson v. Polley*, 689 F.2d 562, 581 (5th Cir.1982); *Smallwood v. Pearl Brewing Co.*, 489 F.2d 579, 602 (5th Cir. 1974). *But see Pena-Rodriguez v. Colorado*, 580 U.S. __, 137 S. Ct. 855, 869, 197 L. Ed. 2d 107 (2017) (holding, for criminal cases, that exception is made to no-impeachment rule where juror convicts after making clear statement showing reliance on racial stereotypes or animus).

doctrine, obligating moving parties to show that the improper conduct affected their substantive rights and was not otherwise cured (by, for example, cautionary instructions to the jury).[44]

Grounds for New Trials in Non-Jury Trials

Rule 59(a) also provides no list of proper reasons for which new trials may be granted in non-jury (bench) trials, and likewise relies upon historical practice. What historically justified a rehearing in a suit in equity in the federal courts today warrants a new trial following a bench decision.[45] New trials in equity were proper if the same circumstances would have warranted a new trial in a jury trial.[46] Given the absence of a jury as factfinder, courts seem to have narrowed the allowable grounds for a new trial in a non-jury case to three: a manifest error of law; a manifest error of fact; or newly discovered evidence.[47]

If a new trial is awarded following a bench trial, the district court may, upon retrial, open a judgment already entered, hear additional testimony, revise or add findings of fact and conclusions of law, and direct the entry of a new judgment.[48] But such motions are usually not proper platforms for new evidence which could have been offered earlier, new theories, or a rehearing on the merits.[49] Moreover, trial courts may refuse a reopening upon examining the probative value of the evidence at issue, the justification for the failure to offer it earlier, and the likelihood that the reopening will inflict undue prejudice.[50]

Burden of Proof

The burden of proving the necessity of a new trial is a heavy one, borne by the party seeking the relief.[51]

Preservation and Waiver

A party may not seek a new trial on grounds not brought contemporaneously to the trial judge's attention.[52] The courts recognize a narrow exception to this waiver rule where a trial

---

[44] *See* Rule 61 (directing that harmless errors are to be disregarded).

[45] *See* Rule 59(a)(1)(B).

[46] *See* 11 CHARLES A. WRIGHT, ARTHUR R. MILLER, MARY KAY KANE, FEDERAL PRACTICE & PROCEDURE § 2804 (2012).

[47] *See Brown v. Wright*, 588 F.2d 708, 710 (9th Cir. 1978). *See also Sedlacek v. Ocwen Loan Servicing, LLC*, 844 Fed. Appx. 110, 113 (11th Cir. 2021); *Waugh v. Williams Cos., Inc. Long Term Disability Plan*, 323 Fed. Appx. 681, 684–85 (10th Cir. 2009).

[48] *See* Rule 59(a)(2). *See also Johnson v. Hix Wrecker Service, Inc.*, 528 Fed. Appx. 636, 639 (7th Cir. 2013).

[49] *See Chavez v. City of Albuquerque*, 640 F. Supp. 2d 1340, 1343 (D.N.M. 2008).

[50] *See Precision Pine & Timber, Inc. v. United States*, 596 F.3d 817, 833–34 (Fed.Cir. 2010).

[51] *See Henderson v. Wilkie*, 966 F.3d 530, 534 (7th Cir. 2020); *Dear v. Q Club Hotel, LLC*, 933 F.3d 1286, 1302 (11th Cir. 2019).

[52] *See U.S. v. Walton*, 909 F.2d 915, 924 (6th Cir. 1990); *Guidance Endodontics, LLC v. Dentsply Int'l., Inc.*, 728 F. Supp. 2d 1170, 1185

error is so fundamental that gross injustice would result were it not corrected. Beyond this obligation of general preservation, motions for new trials (unlike Rule 50 motions for judgment as a matter of law) do not require a further pre-verdict motion, nor is a new trial motion at the district court level essential to preserving a right of appeal[53] (although when the motion attacks sufficiency of the trial evidence, this point has been cast into some doubt).[54]

Partial New Trials

The court may grant a partial new trial limited only to certain issues, provided the error justifying the new trial did not affect the determination of the remaining issues[55] and that the issue to be retried is so clearly distinct and separate from all other issues that a retrial of it alone will not be unjust.[56] When a partial new trial is granted, those portions of the original judgment that were not set aside by the court become part of the single, ultimate judgment following the new trial. Most commonly, courts have granted partial new trials on damages, following an error-free trial on liability issues, but partial new trials can be granted as to any "separable matter."[57] If, however, the trial court concludes that passion influenced the jury, a partial new trial on the issue of damages alone is ordinarily improper; the court must instead order a new trial on all issues.[58]

Comparing Rule 59 and Rule 60

Both Rule 59 and Rule 60 permit courts to grant relief from entered judgments. Beyond the timing differences between the

---

(D.N.M. 2010). *But cf. Pulla v. Amoco Oil Co.*, 72 F.3d 648, 656 (8th Cir. 1995) (party may move for new trial "based on the overwhelming evidence contrary to the verdict without ever previously raising such an objection").

[53]*See Pediatrix Screening, Inc. v. Telechem Int'l., Inc.*, 602 F.3d 541, 546–47 (3d Cir. 2010); *Fuesting v. Zimmer, Inc.*, 448 F.3d 936, 940–42 (7th Cir. 2006).

[54]*See Doe v. Fairfax Cty. Sch. Bd.*, 1 F.4th 257, 269 (4th Cir. 2021) (when party did not move for JMOL, scope of review is confined to whether *any* evidence supports jury's verdict). *But see Pediatrix Screening, Inc. v. Telechem Int'l., Inc.*, 602 F.3d 541, 546–47 (3d Cir. 2010) (rejecting suggestion that Supreme Court's decision in *Unitherm Food Systems, Inc. v. Swift-Eckrich, Inc.*, 546 U.S. 394, 126 S. Ct. 980, 163 L. Ed. 2d 974 (2006), demands further preservation); *Fuesting v. Zimmer, Inc.*, 448 F.3d 936, 940–42 (7th Cir. 2006) (same point, citing Fed. R. Evid. 103(a)).

[55]*See Anderson v. Siemens Corp.*, 335 F.3d 466, 475–76 (5th Cir. 2003); *Eximco, Inc. v. Trane Co.*, 737 F.2d 505, 513 (5th Cir.1984).

[56]*See Gasoline Products Co. v. Champlin Refining Co.*, 283 U.S. 494, 500, 51 S. Ct. 513, 75 L. Ed. 1188 (1931); *Encompass Office Sols., Inc. v. Louisiana Health Serv. & Indem. Co.*, 919 F.3d 266, 276–77 (5th Cir. 2019).

[57]*See Kirk v. Schaeffler Grp. USA, Inc.*, 887 F.3d 376, 390 (8th Cir. 2018); *Rice v. Community Health Ass'n*, 203 F.3d 283, 290 (4th Cir. 2000).

[58]*See Sanford v. Crittenden Memorial Hosp.*, 141 F.3d 882, 885 (8th Cir. 1998).

two Rules,[59] the standards for granting relief also differ. The showing for relief under Rule 60 is considered greater than that needed for Rule 59.[60]

District Court Findings and Conclusions

In granting a new trial, the district court is ordinarily under no obligation to set out supporting findings of fact and conclusions of law.[61]

Appealability

An order granting a new trial is generally interlocutory and not immediately appealable, absent a showing that the court lacked authority to enter the order.[62] An order denying a new trial is also usually not immediately appealable,[63] and perhaps not appealable at all: some courts disallow nearly all appeals from orders denying a new trial (relegating parties solely to an appeal from the underlying final judgment instead),[64] while other courts more narrowly refuse appeals when the basis for the new trial motion was that the verdict was against the weight of the evidence.[65]

RULE 59(b)—TIME TO FILE A MOTION FOR A NEW TRIAL

CORE CONCEPT

A party must file a motion for a new trial within 28 days[66] after entry of the judgment.

---

[59] *Compare* Rules 59(b), (d), (e), *with* Rule 60(c).

[60] *See Cincinnati Life Ins. Co. v. Beyrer*, 722 F.3d 939, 953 (7th Cir. 2013); *Park West Galleries, Inc. v. Hochman*, 692 F.3d 539, 545 n.3 (6th Cir. 2012).

[61] *See Jennings v. Jones*, 587 F.3d 430, 441 n.11 (1st Cir. 2009).

[62] *See Allied Chemical Corp. v. Daiflon, Inc.*, 449 U.S. 33, 101 S. Ct. 188, 66 L. Ed. 2d 193 (1980); *Schudel v. General Elec. Co.*, 120 F.3d 991, 994–95 (9th Cir. 1997).

[63] *See Clark By and Through Clark v. Heidrick*, 150 F.3d 912, 916 (8th Cir. 1998).

[64] *See Johansen v. Combustion Eng'g, Inc.*, 170 F.3d 1320, 1329 n.12 (11th Cir. 1999); *Youmans v. Simon*, 791 F.2d 341, 349 (5th Cir. 1986). *But see Grussing v. Orthopedic & Sports Med., Inc.*, 892 F.3d 953, 956 (8th Cir. 2018) (appeal permitted, but under abuse of discretion standard); *Bunn v. Oldendorff Carriers GmbH & Co. KG*, 723 F.3d 454, 468 (4th Cir. 2013) (same).

[65] *See Jocks v. Tavernier*, 316 F.3d 128, 137 (2d Cir. 2003) (Seventh Amendment forecloses review). *But cf. Gasperini v. Ctr. for Humanities, Inc.*, 518 U.S. 415, 434–39, 116 S. Ct. 2211, 135 L. Ed. 2d 659 (1996) (Seventh Amendment does not foreclose review of denial of new trial motion based on verdict excessiveness, provided review is abuse-of-discretion).

[66] This timing was set in 2009, replacing the former 10-day period which was deemed unrealistically short. *See* Rule 59 advisory committee note (2009).

APPLICATIONS

28-Day Period to *File* Motion for New Trial

This time period is for *filing*, not service.[67] Thus, a party seeking a new trial must *file* the Rule 59 motion within 28 days after the district court enters judgment on the docket.[68]

Amended Judgments

Where an amended judgment is entered which alters the legal rights or obligations of the parties, a new time period for filing Rule 59 motions might be triggered.[69]

Each Party Seeking Relief Must File

In a multi-party case, a motion by one litigant under Rule 59 will not excuse the non-filing by another litigant; each party seeking relief under this Rule must move for it.[70] Likewise, a party whose post-trial motion period has run cannot belatedly "join" a co-party's pending motion to resuscitate an otherwise expired Rule 59 filing opportunity.[71]

No Extensions

This 28-day period may not be extended by court order.[72] Over the years, two common law exceptions were recognized to this prohibition, though only one persists.[73] If an out-of-time Rule 59 motion is filed, but not objected to, the court may, in its discretion, consider and rule upon the untimely motion[74] (though such untimely motions will *not* toll the time for taking an appeal).[75] In appropriate circumstances, courts may treat an untimely Rule 59 motion as one made under Rule 60 and assess it under that Rule.[76]

---

[67] *See Schudel v. General Elec. Co.*, 120 F.3d 991, 993–94 (9th Cir. 1997) (Rule 59 requires that such motions be timely filed, not served).

[68] *See supra* Authors' Commentary to Rule 58(a)–(c) (explaining how entry date is computed).

[69] *See Walker v. Bain*, 257 F.3d 660, 670 (6th Cir. 2001).

[70] *See Hertz Corp. v. Alamo Rent-A-Car, Inc.*, 16 F.3d 1126, 1128-29 (11th Cir.1994).

[71] *See Tarlton v. Exxon*, 688 F.2d 973, 977 n.4 (5th Cir. 1982).

[72] *See* Rule 6(b)(2).

[73] *See supra* Authors' Commentary to Rule 6(b) (**"No Extensions"**).

[74] *Compare Legg v. Ulster Cty.*, 979 F.3d 101, 106, 111–13 (2d Cir. 2020) (adversary forfeits no-extensions rule by failing to contemporaneous object), *with Dill v. General American Life Ins. Co.*, 525 F.3d 612, 615–19 (8th Cir. 2008) (adversary forfeits no-extensions rule only by failing to object prior to district court's disposition of motion).

[75] *See* Fed. R. App. P. 4(a)(4)(A). *See also id.* advisory committee note (2016) (appeal time not re-started by untimely motion, even if district court had extended due date or disposed of motion without explicit reliance on untimeliness, or if opponent consents or fails to object). Previously, the majority view among the courts of appeals had migrated towards the same conclusion. *Compare, e.g., Lizardo v. United States*, 619 F.3d 273, 275-80 (3d Cir. 2010) (majority: appeal forfeited), *with Nat'l Ecological Found. v. Alexander*, 496 F.3d 466, 476 (6th Cir. 2007) (minority: appeal preserved).

[76] *See Banks v. Chicago Bd. of Educ.*, 750 F.3d 663, 665–67 (7th Cir.

3-Day Service Extension Does *Not* Apply

Because Rule 59(b) requires *filing* (not service) no later than 28 days after entry of judgment, the 3-day extension after service by mail or by certain other service methods does not apply.[77]

Timely Motion Tolls Appeal Period

A timely-filed motion for a new trial delays the finality of the underlying judgment and tolls the time for appeal until the district judge rules on the new trial motion.[78] In multi-party cases, a timely-filed new-trial motion by any party tolls the appeal time for everyone.[79] However, most courts hold that this post-trial motion tolling effect only occurs once; parties cannot toll again by filing successive post-trial motions.[80]

Motion Filed After Notice of Appeal

The filing of a notice of appeal is jurisdictional and, once filed, will ordinarily divest the district court of its jurisdiction. But, if a timely Rule 59 motion is thereafter made, the earlier-filed notice of appeal lies dormant until the district court resolves the pending motion.[81]

Appeals Filed During Pendency of Motion

A notice of appeal filed prematurely (before the trial court has ruled on a pending new trial motion) is treated as filed as of the date the trial court ultimately disposes of the pending Rule 59 motion[82] (although the notice of appeal may well need to be amended to reflect the appealed-from order).[83]

RULE 59(c)—TIME TO SERVE AFFIDAVITS

CORE CONCEPT

A party may support a motion for new trial with affidavits. In such a case, the supporting affidavits must be filed with the motion. Opposing affidavits may be filed 14 days[84] thereafter.

2014); *Feathers v. Chevron U.S.A., Inc.*, 141 F.3d 264, 268 (6th Cir. 1998).

[77]*See* Rule 6(d); *Cavaliere v. Allstate Ins. Co.*, 996 F.2d 1111, 1112–14 (11th Cir. 1993).

[78]*See* Fed. R. App. P. 4(a)(4)(A)(v).

[79]*See* Fed. R. App. P. 4(a)(4)(A). *See also New Windsor Volunteer Ambulance Corps, Inc. v. Meyers*, 442 F.3d 101, 120 (2d Cir. 2006). *See also Griggs v. Provident Consumer Disc. Co.*, 459 U.S. 56, 59–60, 103 S. Ct. 400, 74 L. Ed. 2d 225 (1982) (per curiam).

[80]*See infra* Authors' Commentary to Part VI, § 6.3 (**"Successive Post-Trial Motions"**).

[81]*See* Fed. R. App. P. 4(a)(4)(B)(i).

[82]*See* Fed. R. App. P. 4(a)(4)(B). *See also U.S. v. Holy Land Foundation for Relief & Dev't*, 722 F.3d 677, 684 (5th Cir. 2013).

[83]*See Weatherly v. Alabama State Univ.*, 728 F.3d 1263, 1270–71 (11th Cir. 2013).

[84]The Rule 59(c) time period, which had long been set at 10-days, was enlarged to 14-days by the December 2009 amendments to the Rules.

RULE 59(d)—NEW TRIAL ON THE COURT'S INITIATIVE OR FOR OTHER REASONS NOT IN THE MOTION

CORE CONCEPT

The court may grant a new trial entirely on its own initiative within 28 days[85] after entry of the judgment. Alternatively, if a timely motion for new trial has been filed by a party, the court may grant a new trial for a reason not stated in the moving papers.

APPLICATIONS

Grounds

The court may grant a new trial for any reason that a party could have permissibly requested by motion.[86] The court may initiate that relief *sua sponte* or, if a timely-filed motion is pending, may grant that relief on grounds not advanced by the movant.[87] In the latter setting, the court must first notify the parties of its intention and afford them an opportunity to be heard.[88]

Timing

A court that intends to grant a new trial on its own initiative must do so within 28 days after the entry of judgment. This period may not be extended.[89] When a court receives a motion, but decides to grant a new trial for reasons not specified in the motion, the timing is less clear. One court has held that the timing requirement does not apply to such rulings;[90] another court has held the opposite.[91]

Specifying Grounds for New Trial

When the court grants a motion for a new trial on its own initiative or on grounds different from those stated in a party's motion papers, the order must specify the grounds for the court's decision.

Other *Sua Sponte* Revisions to Judgments

Although Rule 59(d) does not expressly contemplate it, one court has approved use of the Rule to substantively amend a

---

[85] This timing was set in 2009, replacing the former 10-day period which was deemed unrealistically short. *See* Rule 59 advisory committee note (2009).

[86] *See Experience Hendrix L.L.C. v. Hendrixlicensing.com Ltd*, 762 F.3d 829, 842 (9th Cir. 2014); *Park West Galleries, Inc. v. Hochman*, 692 F.3d 539, 544 (6th Cir. 2012).

[87] *See Lesende v. Borrero*, 752 F.3d 324, 334 (3d Cir. 2014).

[88] *See Lesende v. Borrero*, 752 F.3d 324, 334–35 (3d Cir. 2014) (failure to give notice and opportunity is error); *Capitol Records, Inc. v. Thomas*, 579 F. Supp. 2d 1210, 1213 (D.Minn. 2008) (court gave notice of possible alternative grounds, accepted additional briefing, and heard oral argument).

[89] *See* Rule 6(b)(2).

[90] *See Kelly v. Moore*, 376 F.3d 481, 484 (5th Cir. 2004).

[91] *See Lesende v. Borrero*, 752 F.3d 324, 334 (3d Cir. 2014).

judgment.[92]

RULE 59(e)—MOTION TO ALTER OR AMEND A JUDGMENT

CORE CONCEPT

The court may alter or amend its judgment upon motion filed by a party within 28 days[93] after entry of the judgment.

APPLICATIONS

Purpose

The purpose of Rule 59(e) is to provide the district court with a means for correcting errors that may have "crept into the proceeding" while that court still holds jurisdiction over the case.[94] It thus gives the trial court the opportunity to cure its own mistakes (if it believes it made any)[95] and to re-examine matters encompassed in its decision on the merits.[96] Should an error be found, the rendering court's self-correction might eliminate the need for an appeal.[97]

District Court's Discretion

The decision whether to alter or amend a judgment is committed to the discretion of the trial judge,[98] absent an error of law.[99] Exercising this discretion calls upon the court to balance two competing interests—the need to bring litigation to a close and the need to render just rulings based on all the facts.[100] Relief under Rule 59(e) is an extraordinary remedy, reserved for exceptional circumstances, and granted only sparingly;[101] it is considered quite difficult to obtain.[102]

- *No Required Explanation for Denials:* Often, a court's

---

[92]*See HyperQuest, Inc. v. N'Site Solutions, Inc.*, 632 F.3d 377, 386 (7th Cir. 2011).

[93]This timing was set in 2009, replacing the former 10-day period which was deemed unrealistically short. *See* Rule 59 advisory committee note (2009).

[94]*See Sosebee v. Astrue*, 494 F.3d 583, 589 (7th Cir. 2007).

[95]*See Banister v. Davis*, 590 U.S. ___, 140 S. Ct. 1698, 1703, 207 L. Ed. 2d 58 (2020); *White v. New Hampshire Dep't of Employment Sec.*, 455 U.S. 445, 450, 102 S. Ct. 1162, 71 L. Ed. 2d 325 (1982).

[96]*See White v. New Hampshire Dept. of Employment Sec.*, 455 U.S. 445, 450–51, 102 S. Ct. 1162, 71 L. Ed. 2d 325 (1982).

[97]*See Acadian Diagnostic Labs., L.L.C. v. Quality Toxicology, L.L.C.*, 965 F.3d 404, 414 (5th Cir. 2020).

[98]*See Kaufmann v. Kijakazi*, 32 F.4th 843, 850 (9th Cir. 2022); *Uradnik v. Inter Fac. Org.*, 2 F.4th 722, 727 (8th Cir. 2021).

[99]*See Walker v. BOKF, Nat'l Ass'n*, 30 F.4th 994, 1002 (10th Cir. 2022); *Wickersham v. Ford Motor Co.*, 997 F.3d 526, 538 (4th Cir. 2021).

[100]*See Nelson v. City of Albuquerque*, 921 F.3d 925, 929 (10th Cir. 2019); *Luig v. N. Bay Enters., Inc.*, 817 F.3d 901, 907 (5th Cir. 2016).

[101]*See Kaufmann v. Kijakazi*, 32 F.4th 843, 850–51 (9th Cir. 2022); *Rollins v. Home Depot USA*, 8 F.4th 393, 396 (5th Cir. 2021).

[102]*See In re Fin. Oversight & Mgmt. Bd. for Puerto Rico*, 998 F.3d 35, 40 (1st Cir. 2021). *See also Nelson v. City of Albuquerque*, 921 F.3d 925, 929–30 (10th Cir. 2019) (trial judge

denial of a Rule 59(e) motion is not accompanied by explanation, and none is usually required.[103]

Grounds

No listing of allowable grounds for altering or amending a judgment is included in the language of Rule 59(e), and federal case law has been left to fill in that void.[104] That case law recognizes four grounds that justify such relief:

- *Intervening Change in the Law*: To qualify, the change must be to controlling law.[105]
- *Newly Discovered Evidence*: To qualify, such evidence must usually have been discovered only after trial (notwithstanding the party's diligence), be material and not merely cumulative or impeaching, and be likely to cause a new result.[106]
- *Correcting Legal Error*: To qualify, the error must be "manifest"[107] or "clear".[108]
- *Prevent Manifest Injustice*: This is a "catch-all" factor (as well as an attribute implicit in any grant of Rule 59(e) relief),[109] and generally requires a showing of prejudice that is clear, certain, and fundamentally unfair.[110]

Typically, a Rule 59(e) motion is proper, for example, where the court misunderstood the facts, a party's arguments, or the controlling law[111] or where the original judgment failed to provide that relief which the court found a party entitled to

---

lacked discretion to entertain multiple motions that propose to "reurge or elaborate" on arguments earlier made and denied). *But see Nelson v. City of Albuquerque*, 925 F.3d 1187, 1189–96 (10th Cir. 2019) (Hartz, J., dissenting from denial of en banc review) (opining that disallowing trial judge discretion to correct own mistakes, even if arguments were made before, is unwise).

[103] *See Parallel Networks, LLC v. Abercrombie & Fitch Co.*, 704 F.3d 958, 971 (Fed.Cir. 2013).

[104] *See Jenkins v. Anton*, 922 F.3d 1257, 1263 (11th Cir. 2019); *Sloas v. Ass'n of Am. R.R.s.*, 616 F.3d 380, 385 n.2 (4th Cir. 2010).

[105] *See Jennings v. Towers Watson*, 11 F.4th 335, 345 (5th Cir. 2021); *EHM Prods., Inc. v. Starline Tours of Hollywood, Inc.*, 1 F.4th 1164, 1171 (9th Cir. 2021). *See generally Banister v. Davis*, 590 U.S. __, 140 S. Ct. 1698, 1703 n.2, 207 L. Ed. 2d 58 (2020).

[106] *See Castanon v. Cathey*, 976 F.3d 1136, 1141 (10th Cir. 2020); *Cincinnati Life Ins. Co. v. Beyrer*, 722 F.3d 939, 955 (7th Cir. 2013). *See also Auto. Alignment & Body Serv., Inc. v. State Farm Mut. Auto. Ins. Co.*, 953 F.3d 707, 730 (11th Cir. 2020). *See generally Banister v. Davis*, 590 U.S. __, 140 S. Ct. 1698, 1703 n.2, 207 L. Ed. 2d 58 (2020).

[107] *See Jennings v. Towers Watson*, 11 F.4th 335, 345 (5th Cir. 2021); *Cont'l Indem. Co. v. IPFS of N.Y., LLC*, 7 F.4th 713, 717 (8th Cir. 2021).

[108] *See In re Processed Egg Prod. Antitrust Litig.*, 962 F.3d 719, 729 (3d Cir. 2020); *Pigford v. Perdue*, 950 F.3d 886, 891 (D.C. Cir. 2020).

[109] *See Morrissey v. Mayorkas*, 17 F.4th 1150, 1160 (D.C. Cir. 2021); *In re Daughtrey*, 896 F.3d 1255, 1280 (11th Cir. 2018).

[110] *See Leidos, Inc. v. Hellenic Republic*, 881 F.3d 213, 217 (D.C. Cir. 2018). *See also Burritt v. Ditlefsen*, 807 F.3d 239, 253 (7th Cir. 2015) (manifest error is "wholesale disregard, misapplication, or failure to recognize controlling precedent").

[111] *See Alpenglow Botanicals, LLC v. United States*, 894 F.3d 1187, 1203

receive.[112] But the motion is improper if it seeks no substantive change of the court's mind,[113] presents long possessed "new" information,[114] or advances positions that could have and should have been advanced prior to judgment.[115] Nor, as the case law familiarly incants, should the motion be used to merely rehash previously considered and rejected arguments,[116] though this prohibition is bounded by the court's privilege to correct an earlier mistake if convinced it made one.[117]

- *Prejudgment Interest:* Motions to add mandatory or discretionary prejudgment interest are usually proper under this Rule, provided they are timely filed[118] (though courts treat such motions as untimely if the prejudgment interest request is being raised for the first time in the Rule 59(e) motion[119]).
- *Costs or Fees:* Motions to add an award of costs[120] or attorney's fees[121] under this Rule are likely improper.

Burden of Proof

The burden of proving that Rule 59(e) warrants the

(10th Cir. 2018).

[112]*See Continental Cas. Co. v. Howard*, 775 F.2d 876, 883–84 (7th Cir. 1985).

[113]*See United States ex rel. Hoggett v. Univ. of Phoenix*, 863 F.3d 1105, 1108 (9th Cir. 2017).

[114]*See Mancini v. City of Providence by & through Lombardi*, 909 F.3d 32, 48 (1st Cir. 2018); *Alcon Research Ltd. v. Barr Labs., Inc.*, 745 F.3d 1180, 1192 (Fed. Cir. 2014).

[115]*See Banister v. Davis*, 590 U.S. —, 140 S. Ct. 1698, 1703, 207 L. Ed. 2d 58 (2020); *Exxon Shipping Co. v. Baker*, 554 U.S. 471, 485 n.5, 128 S. Ct. 2605, 171 L. Ed. 2d 570 (2008). *See generally A&C Constr. & Installation, Co. WLL v. Zurich Am. Ins. Co.*, 963 F.3d 705 (7th Cir. 2020) (trial opinions "not intended as mere first drafts, subject to revision and reconsideration at a litigant's pleasure") (citation omitted). *But cf. Cont'l Indem. Co. v. IPFS of N.Y., LLC*, 7 F.4th 713, 717 (8th Cir. 2021) (parties are not forbidden from raising issues for first time in Rule 59(e) motion, but court retains discretion to deny motion on that ground).

[116]*See Gibson v. State Farm Mut. Auto. Ins. Co.*, 994 F.3d 182, 191 (3d Cir. 2021); *PBT Real Est., LLC v. Town of Palm Beach*, 988 F.3d 1274, 1287 (11th Cir. 2021).

[117]*See 4 Pillar Dynasty LLC v. New York & Co.*, 933 F.3d 202, 217 (2d Cir. 2019) ("court still may reconsider a hastily-made earlier ruling if, upon revisiting the non-prevailing party's arguments, the court concludes that it erred"); *Hayes Family Tr. v. State Farm Fire & Cas. Co.*, 845 F.3d 997, 1005 (10th Cir. 2017) ("allows a party to reargue previously articulated positions to correct clear legal error").

[118]*See Osterneck v. Ernst & Whinney*, 489 U.S. 169, 175, 109 S. Ct. 987, 103 L. Ed. 2d 146 (1989) (mandatory prejudgment interest); *Crowe v. Bolduc*, 365 F.3d 86, 92–93 (1st Cir. 2004) (mandatory or discretionary prejudgment interest).

[119]*See First State Bank of Monticello v. Ohio Cas. Ins. Co.*, 555 F.3d 564, 572 (7th Cir. 2009). *But see Cont'l Indem. Co. v. IPFS of New York, LLC*, 7 F.4th 713, 717–19 (8th Cir. 2021) (district court not barred from granting prejudgment interest in that context, but may exercise its discretion to deny it on that basis).

[120]*See Buchanan v. Stanships, Inc.*, 485 U.S. 265, 268–69, 108 S. Ct. 1130, 99 L. Ed. 2d 289 (1988).

[121]*See White v. New Hampshire Dep't of Employment Sec.*, 455 U.S. 445, 450, 102 S. Ct. 1162, 71 L. Ed. 2d 325 (1982).

requested relief lies with the moving party.[122]

"Particularity" Requirement for Motion

All Rule 59(e) motions must satisfy the "particularity" requirement of Rule 7(b)(1).[123] Failure to do so may have dire consequences, including a loss of appeal-period suspension. Thus, a "skeleton" motion that fails to alert the court or the other litigants of the grounds for which an alteration or amendment is sought may be deemed improper and, thus, ineffective in suspending the appeal period.[124] In any event, a motion that idly asks that an earlier judgment be reconsidered (without more) is almost certainly to be denied.[125]

Time for Filing

A motion to alter or amend a judgment must be filed within 28 days after the district court enters that judgment[126] (note: this time period runs from the date of *filing*, not service or receipt).[127] An out-of-time Rule 59 motion may be treated as a Rule 60(b) motion, if the grounds asserted would support relief under that Rule.[128] If the court later amends its judgment, the timeliness of a Rule 59(e) motion is dated from that amendment only if the motion relates to content that the court altered.[129]

- *Pro Se Prisoner Plaintiffs:* The prisoner "mailbox rule" has been adopted by some courts for Rule 59(e) motions. Consequently, a *pro se* prisoner's papers may be deemed filed when deposited with the post office.[130]

---

[122] *See JTH Tax, Inc. v. Aime*, 984 F.3d 284, 292 (4th Cir. 2021); *Arabaitzis v. Unum Life Ins. Co. of Am.*, 351 F. Supp. 3d 11, 14–15 (D.D.C. 2018).

[123] *See Intera Corp. v. Henderson*, 428 F.3d 605, 611 (6th Cir. 2005).

[124] *See Talano v. Northwestern Med. Faculty Found., Inc.*, 273 F.3d 757, 760–61 (7th Cir. 2001) ("if a party could file a skeleton motion and later fill it in, the purpose of the time limitation would be defeated"). *But cf. Carlson v. CSX Transp., Inc.*, 758 F.3d 819, 826 (7th Cir. 2014) (constraining such holdings to only "extreme cases" with motions "*completely* devoid of substance").

[125] *See Wood v. Ryan*, 759 F.3d 1117, 1121 (9th Cir. 2014).

[126] *See Keith v. Bobby*, 618 F.3d 594, 597–99 (6th Cir. 2010) (period runs from date order was entered, not date it became final). *See supra* Authors' Commentary to Rule 58(a)–(c) (explaining how entry date is computed).

[127] *See Schudel v. General Elec. Co.*, 120 F.3d 991, 994 (9th Cir. 1997) (Rule 59 requires timely filing, not service). *See also Life Ins. Co. of North America v. Von Valtier*, 116 F.3d 279, 282–83 (7th Cir. 1997) (motion timely filed where delivered to district court, as required by standing chambers order, but judge delayed in transmitting it to clerk's office for formal filing).

[128] *See United States v. Garrett*, 15 F.4th 335, 339 (5th Cir. 2021).

[129] *See Progressive Indus., Inc. v. United States*, 888 F.3d 1248, 1254 (Fed. Cir. 2018); *Tru-Art Sign Co. v. Local 137 Sheet Metal Workers Int'l Ass'n*, 852 F.3d 217, 221–22 (2d Cir. 2017).

[130] *See Brown v. Taylor*, 829 F.3d 365, 368–70 (5th Cir. 2016); *Long v. Atlantic City Police Dep't*, 670 F.3d 436, 440–45 (3d Cir. 2012).

No Extensions

The court may not grant a party any extensions to this 28-day time period.[131] An untimely Rule 59(e) motion may be deemed a nullity,[132] or, in an appropriate case, treated as a Rule 60(b) motion for relief from a judgment.[133] However, a technical, electronic filing error may be excused, provided the clerk's office received the filing timely.[134] Moreover, when an untimely Rule 59(e) motion is filed, but not objected to by the non-moving party, the timeliness objection may be deemed forfeited through waiver.[135] This can prove to be a shallow comfort, though; if the trial court grants the motion, the aggrieved party may receive meaningful relief, but if the trial court denies the motion, the aggrieved party's time for taking an appeal will almost certainly be already lost.[136]

- *No 3-Day Service Extension:* Because Rule 59(e) requires *filing* (not service) no later than 28 days after entry of judgment, the 3-day extension after service by mail or by certain other service methods does not apply.[137]

Mislabeled Motions

A motion made under Rule 59(e) but which is, in substance, a Rule 50(b) motion for judgment as a matter of law,[138] a Rule 54(b) motion to reconsider an interlocutory order,[139] or a Rule 58(e) fees award motion,[140] will be treated as such.

Motions for "Reconsideration"

The Rules do not expressly authorize motions for "reconsid-

---

[131]*See* Rule 6(b).

[132]*See Quinn v. Guerrero*, 863 F.3d 353, 360 (5th Cir. 2017); *Fisher v. Kadant, Inc.*, 589 F.3d 505, 511 (1st Cir. 2009).

[133]*See Lora v. O'Heaney*, 602 F.3d 106, 111 (2d Cir. 2010); *Walker v. Astrue*, 593 F.3d 274, 279 (3d Cir. 2010).

[134]*See Shuler v. Garrett*, 715 F.3d 185, 185–87 (6th Cir. 2013) (although filed electronically under the wrong docket number, clerk received a timely filing and no prejudice was caused).

[135]*See National Ecological Foundation v. Alexander*, 496 F.3d 466, 474–75 (6th Cir. 2007) (relying on *Eberhart v. U.S.*, 546 U.S. 12, 126 S. Ct. 403, 163 L. Ed. 2d 14 (2005) (per curiam) and *Kontrick v. Ryan*, 540 U.S. 443, 124 S. Ct. 906, 157 L. Ed. 2d 867 (2004)). *See also Mobley v. C.I.A.*, 806 F.3d 568, 578 (D.C. Cir. 2015).

[136]*See* Fed. R. App. P. 4(a)(4)(A). *See also id.* advisory committee note (2016) (appeal time not re-started by untimely motion, even if district court had extended the due date or disposed of motion without explicit reliance on untimeliness, or if opponent consents or fails to object). Previously, the majority view among the courts of appeals had migrated towards the same conclusion. *See, e.g., Lizardo v. United States*, 619 F.3d 273, 276–80 (3d Cir. 2010).

[137]*See Williams v. Illinois*, 737 F.3d 473, 475–76 (7th Cir. 2013); *Albright v. Virtue*, 273 F.3d 564, 567 (3d Cir. 2001).

[138]*See Elm Ridge Exploration Co. v. Engle*, 721 F.3d 1199, 1220 (10th Cir. 2013).

[139]*See Six Dimensions, Inc. v. Perficient, Inc.*, 969 F.3d 219, 227 (5th Cir. 2020).

[140]*See Trickey v. Kaman Indus. Techs. Corp.*, 705 F.3d 788, 808 (8th Cir. 2013); *House of Flavors, Inc. v. TFG-Mich., L.P.*, 700 F.3d 33, 38 (1st Cir. 2012).

eration"[141] (although individual local Districts may).[142] Thus, a court's approach to such motions hinges on context.

When "reconsideration" is sought from an interlocutory order (*e.g.*, a denial of a motion to dismiss or for summary judgment), that motion is not properly considered under Rule 59(e) but, instead, as simply a request for the district court to revisit its earlier ruling.[143]

When "reconsideration" is sought from a judgment or other final order, such a motion will be treated *either* as one under Rule 59(e) *or* as one under Rule 60(b),[144] a classification typically dependent on the date the motion is filed. If filed within the 28-day period set for Rule 59(e) motions, the "reconsideration" will generally be treated under Rule 59(e).[145] Otherwise, the courts will likely examine the motion under Rule 60(b).[146] In either case, the applicable legal analysis will depend on the grounds asserted for the relief requested.[147]

The standards governing motions for "reconsideration" from judgments or other final orders usually track the Rule 59(e) criteria. Thus, such motions will not be granted absent "highly unusual circumstances."[148] These motions do not provide litigants with an opportunity for a "second bite at the apple"[149] or allow them, like Emperor Nero, to "fiddle as Rome burns",[150]

---

[141]*See T. B. by & through Bell v. Nw. Indep. Sch. Dist.*, 980 F.3d 1047, 1051 (5th Cir. 2020); *Peterson v. The Travelers Indem. Co.*, 867 F.3d 992, 997 (8th Cir. 2017).

[142]Local practice may set specific procedures. *See, e.g.*, *In re Greektown Holdings, LLC*, 728 F.3d 567, 573–74 (6th Cir. 2013) (Michigan procedure for "reconsideration", with accompanying "palpable defect" standard).

[143]*See supra* Authors' Commentary to Rule 54(b) (**"The Ordinary Practice (No Immediate Appeal)"**). *See also Roberts v. Winder*, 16 F.4th 1367, 1385 (10th Cir. 2021) (when asked to reconsider interlocutory orders, district courts are not constrained by "strict standards" of Rules 59(e) or 60(b)).

[144]*See T. B. by & through Bell v. Nw. Indep. Sch. Dist.*, 980 F.3d 1047, 1051 (5th Cir. 2020); *Peterson v. The Travelers Indem. Co.*, 867 F.3d 992, 997 (8th Cir. 2017).

[145]*See Carter v. City of Alton*, 922 F.3d 824, 826 n.1 (7th Cir. 2019); *Mancini v. City of Providence by & through Lombardi*, 909 F.3d 32, 47 (1st Cir. 2018).

[146]*See United States v. Garrett*, 15 F.4th 335, 339 (5th Cir. 2021); *Kohlbeck v. Wyndham Vacation Resorts, Inc.*, 7 F.4th 729, 734 n.2 (8th Cir. 2021).

[147]*See Negron-Almeda v. Santiago*, 528 F.3d 15, 20 (1st Cir. 2008); *Obriecht v. Raemisch*, 517 F.3d 489, 493–94 (7th Cir. 2008).

[148]*See McDowell v. Calderon*, 197 F.3d 1253, 1255 (9th Cir. 1999). *See also U.S. ex rel. Becker v. Westinghouse Savannah River Co.*, 305 F.3d 284, 290 (4th Cir. 2002) (simple disagreement with court's ruling will not support Rule 59(e) relief).

[149]*See Sequa Corp. v. GBJ Corp.*, 156 F.3d 136, 144 (2d Cir.1998); *Bhatnagar v. Surrendra Overseas Ltd.*, 52 F.3d 1220, 1231 (3d Cir. 1995).

[150]*Vasapolli v. Rostoff*, 39 F.3d 27, 36 (1st Cir. 1994) (Selya, J.)("Unlike the Emperor Nero, litigants cannot fiddle as Rome burns. A party who sits in silence, withholds potentially relevant information, allows his opponent to configure the summary judgment record, and acquiesces in a particular choice of law does so at his peril").

or to "ante up and play a new hand,"[151] or license a litigation "game of hopscotch" in which parties switch from one legal theory to a new one "like a bee in search of honey,"[152] or "to turn back the clock, erase the record, and try to reinvent [the] case."[153] In other words, motions for reconsideration are not vehicles for relitigating old issues.[154] But nor are they motions for "initial consideration."[155] Courts properly decline to consider new arguments or new evidence on reconsideration where those arguments or evidence were available earlier.[156]

Timely Motion Suspends Appeal Period

Like Rule 59 motions for new trial, a timely-filed Rule 59(e) motion to alter or amend the judgment suspends the time for appeal.[157] In multi-party cases, a timely-filed Rule 59 motion by any party suspends the appeal time for everyone.[158] A prematurely filed appeal during the pendency of a Rule 59(e) motion is held in abeyance until the date the district court resolves the pending motion.[159] An untimely Rule 59(e) motion generally will not suspend the time for appeal,[160] nor, generally, will a second or later post-trial motion.[161] However, the trial court's ruling on a Rule 59(e) motion may change "matters of substance" or resolve a "genuine ambiguity" in the court's original order and, in those infrequent cases, a new judgment is recognized, from which a new Rule 59(e) motion (with appeal-

---

[151]*See Markel Am. Ins. Co. v. Diaz-Santiago*, 674 F.3d 21, 33 (1st Cir. 2012) (especially when the movant is "long past being a day late and well over a dollar short").

[152]*See Cochran v. Quest Software, Inc.*, 328 F.3d 1, 11 (1st Cir. 2003) (litigants "frame the issues in a case before the trial court rules" and, once framed, should not be permitted to switch from theory to theory thereafter).

[153]*See Perez v. Lorraine Enters., Inc.*, 769 F.3d 23, 32 (1st Cir. 2014).

[154]*See Leidos, Inc. v. Hellenic Republic*, 881 F.3d 213, 217 (D.C. Cir. 2018); *Prescott v. Higgins*, 538 F.3d 32, 45 (1st Cir. 2008).

[155]*See Perrier-Bilbo v. United States*, 954 F.3d 413, 435–36 (1st Cir. 2020); *Leidos, Inc. v. Hellenic Republic*, 881 F.3d 213, 217 (D.C. Cir. 2018).

[156]*See Holder v. U.S.*, 721 F.3d 979, 986 (8th Cir. 2013); *Cincinnati Life Ins. Co. v. Beyrer*, 722 F.3d 939, 954 (7th Cir. 2013).

[157]*See* Fed. R. App. P. 4(a)(4)(A)(iv). *See also Banister v. Davis*, 590 U.S. __, 140 S. Ct. 1698, 1703, 207 L. Ed. 2d 58 (2020) (once timely Rule 59(e) motion filed, "there is no longer a final judgment to appeal from"); *Nutraceutical Corp. v. Lambert*, __ U.S. __, 139 S. Ct. 710, 717, 203 L. Ed. 2d 43 (2019) (timely motion renders otherwise final decision not final).

[158]*See* Fed. R. App. P. 4(a)(4)(A).

[159]*See* Fed. R. App. P. 4(a)(4); *Stansell v. Revolutionary Armed Forces of Colombia*, 771 F.3d 713, 745–46 (11th Cir. 2014).

[160]*See* Fed. R. App. P. 4(a)(4)(A). *See also Hanson v. Shubert*, 968 F.3d 1014, 1017–18 (9th Cir. 2020).

[161]*See Nartey v. Franciscan Health Hosp.*, 2 F.4th 1020, 1023 (7th Cir. 2021) (after Rule 59(e) motion extends appeals time, subsequent Rule 60(b) motion will not extend further); *Benson v. St. Joseph Reg'l Health Ctr.*, 575 F.3d 542, 546–47 (5th Cir. 2009) (same, two Rule 59(e) motions). *See generally infra* Authors' Commentary to Part VI, § 6.3 ("**Successive Post-Trial Motions**").

period suspension effect) may be filed.[162]

- *Appealing Correctly:* The filing of a timely, proper Rule 59(e) motion will suspend the time for filing an appeal from the original underlying *merits* ruling, and not just from the court's disposition of the Rule 59(e) motion itself[163] (but only if the appealing parties make that intent clear).[164]

Appealability

An order granting a timely-filed motion to alter or amend a judgment is immediately appealable only if it ends the litigation at the trial level.[165] An order denying such a motion likely will be immediately appealable because it usually has that litigation-ending effect at the trial level.[166]

Additional Research References

Wright & Miller, Federal Practice and Procedure §§ 2801 to 21
C.J.S., Federal Civil Procedure §§ 1061 to 1103 et seq., §§ 1233 to 1251 et seq.
West's Key Number Digest, Federal Civil Procedure ⚷2311 to 2377, ⚷2641 to 2663

---

[162] *See Andrews v. E.I. Du Pont De Nemours and Co.*, 447 F.3d 510, 516 (7th Cir. 2006) (noting exception, and that test is "whether the district court disturbed or revised legal rights settled in the original . . . order").

[163] *See Andrews v. Columbia Gas Transmission Corp.*, 544 F.3d 618, 623 n.4 (6th Cir. 2008); *Chamorro v. Puerto Rican Cars, Inc.*, 304 F.3d 1, 3 (1st Cir. 2002).

[164] *See Chamorro v. Puerto Rican Cars, Inc.*, 304 F.3d 1, 3 (1st Cir. 2002) (appeal taken only from order denying Rule 59(e) motion will generally not be considered appeal from underlying merits judgment); *Correa v. Cruisers, a Div. of KCS Intern., Inc.*, 298 F.3d 13, 21 n. 3 (1st Cir. 2002) (same).

[165] *See Hayes Family Tr. v. State Farm Fire & Cas. Co.*, 845 F.3d 997, 1003 (10th Cir. 2017) (often not appealable when they "settle nothing with finality except the fact that more litigation is on the way").

[166] *See generally* Fed. R. App. P. 4(a)(4)(A)(iv) (appeal time runs from entry of court disposing of Rule 59(e) motions).

RULE 60
RELIEF FROM A JUDGMENT OR ORDER

(a) Corrections Based on Clerical Mistakes; Oversights and Omissions. The court may correct a clerical mistake or a mistake arising from oversight or omission whenever one is found in a judgment, order, or other part of the record. The court may do so on motion or on its own, with or without notice. But after an appeal has been docketed in the appellate court and while it is pending, such a mistake may be corrected only with the appellate court's leave.

(b) Grounds for Relief from a Final Judgment, Order, or Proceeding. On motion and just terms, the court may relieve a party or its legal representative from a final judgment, order, or proceeding for the following reasons:

(1) mistake, inadvertence, surprise, or excusable neglect;

(2) newly discovered evidence that, with reasonable diligence, could not have been discovered in time to move for a new trial under Rule 59(b);

(3) fraud (whether previously called intrinsic or extrinsic), misrepresentation, or misconduct by an opposing party;

(4) the judgment is void;

(5) the judgment has been satisfied, released or discharged; it is based on an earlier judgment that has been reversed or vacated; or applying it prospectively is no longer equitable; or

(6) any other reason that justifies relief.

(c) Timing and Effect of the Motion.

(1) *Timing.* A motion under Rule 60(b) must be made within a reasonable time—and for reasons (1), (2), and (3) no more than a year after the entry of the judgment or order or the date of the proceeding.

(2) *Effect on Finality.* The motion does not affect the judgment's finality or suspend its operation.

(d) Other Powers to Grant Relief. This rule does not limit a court's power to:

(1) entertain an independent action to relieve a party from a judgment, order, or proceeding;

(2) grant relief under 28 U.S.C. § 1655 to a defendant who was not personally notified of the action; or

(3) set aside a judgment for fraud on the court.

(e) Bills and Writs Abolished. The following are abolished: bills of review, bills in the nature of bills of review, and writs of coram nobis, coram vobis, and audita querela.

[Amended effective March 19, 1948; October 20, 1949; August 1, 1987; April 30, 2007, effective December 1, 2007.]

AUTHORS' COMMENTARY ON RULE 60

PURPOSE AND SCOPE

Rule 60 is one of several post-trial motions authorized by the federal rules—joining Rule 50, which permits motions seeking judgments as a matter of law ("JMOL"s) in jury trials; Rule 52, which permits revisions to findings and judgments in bench trials; and Rule 59, which permits new trials and alterations and amendments to judgments. Each of these post-trial motions is addressed to the trial court that presided over the lawsuit (*i.e.*, these are not appeals).

Rule 60 allows courts to reopen a judgment on two grounds. Rule 60(a) permits the court to reopen a judgment that has been inaccurately memorialized, so as to ensure that the court's actual adjudicating intent is accomplished. Rule 60(b) permits judgments to be reopened for six substantive reasons; but because reopening a judgment on these bases collides with the judiciary's commitment to finality, such relief is never lightly awarded but is instead reserved for exceptional circumstances only. Rule 60(b) motions must be filed within a "reasonable time" after entry of the judgment, and, for certain reasons, that filing deadline is capped at one year. The availability of a Rule 60 motion is not intended to foreclose other avenues for post-judgment review, including the court's power to entertain independent actions for relief.

RULE 60(a)—CORRECTION BASED ON CLERICAL MISTAKES; OVERSIGHTS AND OMISSIONS

CORE CONCEPT

The district court, on its own initiative or on motion of a party, may correct clerical errors in judgments, orders, or other parts of the record, as well as errors arising from oversight or omission.

APPLICATIONS

Procedure

Motions to correct clerical errors are made to the district court that rendered the judgment sought to be corrected (some early precedent questions the authority of a transferee court to enter clerical error relief).[1]

Sua Sponte Corrections

The court *sua sponte* may raise a clerical error for correction.[2] Before doing so, however, the court must provide the parties with fair notice of its intention, allow them the opportunity to present their positions, and assure itself that no significant prejudice would follow from correcting the error.[3]

Types of Correctable Errors

Rule 60(a) is reserved for correcting "blunders in execution," not for "a change of mind."[4] Given the broad discretion the courts enjoy with Rule 60(a),[5] this distinction is pivotal. An error qualifying for correction under Rule 60(a) is quintessentially a ministerial one, never a substantively factual or legal one.[6] The distinction lies with the court's intent. Where the judgment, as entered, fails to reflect the original intention of the

---

[1]*See Tommills Brokerage Co. v. Thon*, 52 F.R.D. 200, 202 (D.P.R. 1971); *James Blackstone Mem. Ass'n v. Gulf, M. & O. R. Co.*, 28 F.R.D. 385, 385–87 (D.Conn. 1961).

[2]*See Jo Ann Howard & Assocs., P.C. v. Nat'l City Bank*, 11 F.4th 876, 885 (8th Cir. 2021); *Matter of West Texas Marketing Corp.*, 12 F.3d 497, 503 (5th Cir. 1994).

[3]*See Day v. McDonough*, 547 U.S. 198, 210, 126 S. Ct. 1675, 1684, 164 L. Ed. 2d 376 (2006).

[4]*See Tattersalls, Ltd. v. DeHaven*, 745 F.3d 1294, 1297 (9th Cir. 2014); *Sartin v. McNair Law Firm PA*, 756 F.3d 259, 265 (4th Cir. 2014).

[5]*See Diaz v. Jiten Hotel Mgmt., Inc.*, 741 F.3d 170, 174 (1st Cir. 2013); *Agro Dutch Indus. Ltd. v. U.S.*, 589 F.3d 1187, 1192 (Fed.Cir. 2009).

[6]*See Stansell v. Lopez*, 40 F.4th 1308, 1311 (11th Cir. 2022) (used to make judgments "speak the truth," not to "say something" else); *NewCSI, Inc. v. Staffing 360 Sols., Inc.*, 865 F.3d 251, 263 (5th Cir. 2017) (available where court "intended one thing but by merely clerical mistake or oversight did another"). *See generally Matter of West Texas Mktg. Corp.*, 12 F.3d 497, 504–05 (5th Cir. 1994) ("As long as the intentions of the parties are clearly defined and all the court need do is employ the judicial eraser to obliterate a mechanical or mathematical mistake, the modification will be allowed. If, on the other hand, cerebration or research into the law or planetary excursions into facts is required, Rule 60(a) will not be available . . .. It is only mindless and mechanistic mistakes, minor shifting of facts, and no new additional legal perambulations which are reachable through Rule 60(a).").

court (due to some inaccurate transcription, inadvertent omission, math error, or similar flaw in recitation), the error can be corrected with Rule 60(a).[7] Conversely, where the judgment accurately captures an intention that the court is now rethinking, Rule 60(a) does not apply.[8] The "touchstone" is "fidelity to the intent" of the original judgment.[9] But Rule 60(a) is not limited to mere typos. The Rule may be used to clarify the original order by inserting its "necessary implications" (to ensure full implementation and enforcement)[10] or by resolving an ambiguity to better reflect contemporaneous intent.[11]

Whose Errors

Relief under Rule 60(a) is available to remedy clerical mistakes committed by the court clerk, the judge, the parties, and the jury.[12]

Mislabeled Substantive Motions

An incorrectly labeled Rule 60(a) motion that actually seeks substantive alterations of a judgment may, in the court's discretion, be treated as a request for Rule 59(e) or Rule 60(b) relief.[13]

Omission of Interest Award

Correction under Rule 60(a) might be available for omitted awards of interest, but only where the court had earlier announced the award and merely neglected to fix the amount.[14] If the court was previously silent on the question of an interest award, a motion under Rule 60(a) would likely be improper.[15]

---

[7]*See Shuffle Tech Int'l, LLC v. Wolff Gaming, Inc.*, 757 F.3d 708, 709 (7th Cir. 2014); *Companion Health Serv., Inc. v. Kurtz*, 675 F.3d 75, 87 (1st Cir. 2012).

[8]*See Rivera v. PNS Stores, Inc.*, 647 F.3d 188, 193–94 (5th Cir. 2011). *See, e.g. Braun v. Ultimate Jetcharters, LLC*, 828 F.3d 501, 515–18 (6th Cir. 2016) (replacing "Ultimate Jetcharters, Inc." with "Ultimate Jetcharters, LLC"); *Pfizer Inc. v. Uprichard*, 422 F.3d 124, 129–30 (3d Cir. 2005) (inclusion of prejudgment interest proper, but order to sign settlement agreement was not); *U.S. v. Mosbrucker*, 340 F.3d 664, 665–67 (8th Cir. 2003) (permitting correction to note true status of easement tract); *Rezzonico v. H & R Block, Inc.*, 182 F.3d 144, 151 (2d Cir. 1999) (used to correct district court's omission of word "not" from judgment).

[9]*See Tattersalls, Ltd. v. DeHaven*, 745 F.3d 1294, 1298 (9th Cir. 2014). *Accord Braun v. Ultimate Jetcharters, LLC*, 828 F.3d 501, 515 (6th Cir. 2016).

[10]*See Garamendi v. Henin*, 683 F.3d 1069, 1077–80 (9th Cir. 2012).

[11]*See Meierhenry Sargent LLP v. Williams*, 992 F.3d 661, 664 (8th Cir. 2021) (to clarify reach of original ruling); *Sartin v. McNair Law Firm PA*, 756 F.3d 259, 265–66 (4th Cir. 2014) (to sharpen target of sanctions); *Tattersalls, Ltd. v. DeHaven*, 745 F.3d 1294, 1298 (9th Cir. 2014) (to implement the granting of full relief).

[12]*See Day v. McDonough*, 547 U.S. 198, 210–11, 126 S. Ct. 1675, 164 L. Ed. 2d 376 (2006); *In re Walter*, 282 F.3d 434, 440–41 (6th Cir. 2002).

[13]*See Companion Health Serv., Inc. v. Kurtz*, 675 F.3d 75, 87 (1st Cir. 2012).

[14]*See Stryker Corp. v. XL Ins. America Inc.*, 726 F. Supp. 2d 754, 789 (W.D.Mich. 2010).

[15]*See Osterneck v. Ernst & Whinney*, 489 U.S. 169, 109 S. Ct. 987, 103 L. Ed. 2d 146 (1989) (ruling that

Time for Correction

The district court may correct a Rule 60(a) error "whenever one is found."[16] Even after an appeal is taken, such mistakes can still be corrected by the district judge[17] (though, if the correction is not made pursuant to a Rule 60(a) motion filed within 28 days of judgment entry, the district court will need to seek leave from the appeals court to make the correction).[18] Corrections after the appeal is concluded may be made upon leave of the appeals court, or without leave if the corrections would not alter any appellate ruling.[19]

Implications for Appeal

A Rule 60(a) motion filed within 28 days of judgment entry suspends the time for taking an appeal.[20] An appeal from a Rule 60(a) motion filed beyond that period will likely be limited solely to the correctness of the Rule 60(a) ruling and not to the underlying merits.[21]

RULE 60(b)—OTHER GROUNDS FOR RELIEF

CORE CONCEPT

In its discretion, the district court may grant relief from a final judgment, order, or proceeding for various enumerated reasons.

APPLICATIONS

Impact of 2007 "Restyling" Amendments

In 2007, the lengthy text of former Rule 60(b) was separated into four sub-rules (now, Rules 60(b), (c), (d), and (e)). The long first sentence of the former Rule is current Rule 60(b).

Purpose

Tracing back to the original appearance of the federal civil rules, Rule 60(b) codifies the courts' inherent, discretionary power—recognized for centuries in English practice—to set

---

Rule 59(e), not Rule 60(a), is implicated in such instances). *See also Winslow v. F.E.R.C.*, 587 F.3d 1133, 1135–36 (D.C.Cir. 2009) (same, citing cases following this interpretation).

[16]*See Shuffle Tech Int'l, LLC v. Wolff Gaming, Inc.*, 757 F.3d 708, 709 (7th Cir. 2014); *Sartin v. McNair Law Firm PA*, 756 F.3d 259, 268 (4th Cir. 2014).

[17]*See Rivera v. PNS Stores, Inc.*, 647 F.3d 188, 193 (5th Cir. 2011); *Winslow v. F.E.R.C.*, 587 F.3d 1133, 1135 (D.C.Cir. 2009).

[18]*See* Rule 62.1. *See also Bancorp-South Bank v. Hazelwood Logistics Ctr., LLC*, 706 F.3d 888, 897 (8th Cir. 2013); *Home Prods. Int'l, Inc. v. United States*, 633 F.3d 1369, 1377 n.9 (Fed.Cir. 2011).

[19]*See Hartis v. Chicago Title Ins. Co.*, 694 F.3d 935, 950 (8th Cir. 2012).

[20]*See Catz v. Chalker*, 566 F.3d 839, 841–42 (9th Cir. 2009); *Dudley ex rel. Estate of Patton v. Penn-Am. Ins. Co.*, 313 F.3d 662, 665 (2d Cir. 2002). *See also* Fed. R. App. P. 4(a)(4)(A)(vi). This marked a change from former practice. *Cf. BBCA, Inc. v. United States*, 954 F.2d 1429, 1431 (8th Cir. 1992) (under pre-2009 practice, Rule 60(a) motions would not extend appeal time).

[21]*See Garamendi v. Henin*, 683 F.3d 1069, 1077–81 (9th Cir. 2012); *Rivera v. PNS Stores, Inc.*, 647 F.3d 188, 201 n.55 (5th Cir. 2011).

aside judgments where enforcement would produce an inequity.[22] This procedure endeavors to strike a balance between two often conflicting principles—that litigation be drawn to its final close and that justice be done.[23] Because upsetting a settled judgment clashes with finality,[24] such relief is considered "extraordinary,"[25] is never given lightly,[26] but awarded sparingly[27] and only when exceptional circumstances prevented acting sooner.[28] It is not available to remedy deliberate choices later shown to be unwise ones,[29] nor as a substitute for a timely appeal.[30]

Threshold Procedural Requirement — Final Judgment

Rule 60(b) relief is available only from *final* judgments, orders, and proceedings.[31] Consequently, it usually may not be used with interlocutory orders,[32] voluntary dismissals,[33] and consent decrees.[34]

Reasons for Granting Substantive Relief

Rule 60(b) provides five specified reasons for which substantive (non-clerical) relief may be granted, and adds a sixth catch-all category for reasons not otherwise specifically listed. Ordinarily, proper post-judgment relief under Rule 60(b) will not be denied simply because the moving party failed to invoke the proper reason or Rule sub-part[35]—provided, of course, that

---

[22] *See Tanner v. Yukins*, 776 F.3d 434, 438 (6th Cir. 2015).

[23] *See United Student Aid Funds, Inc. v. Espinosa*, 559 U.S. 260, 276, 130 S. Ct. 1367, 176 L. Ed. 2d 158 (2010).

[24] *See Gonzalez v. Crosby*, 545 U.S. 524, 529, 125 S. Ct. 2641, 162 L. Ed. 2d 480 (2005) (Rule's "whole purpose is to make an exception to finality").

[25] *See Unibank for Sav. v. 999 Priv. Jet, LLC*, 31 F.4th 1, 8 (1st Cir. 2022); *In re Cook Med., Inc.*, 27 F.4th 539, 542 (7th Cir. 2022).

[26] *See Tapper v. Hearn*, 833 F.3d 166, 170 (2d Cir. 2016).

[27] *See Unibank for Sav. v. 999 Priv. Jet, LLC*, 31 F.4th 1, 8 (1st Cir. 2022); *Navajo Nation v. Dep't of the Interior*, 876 F.3d 1144, 1173 (9th Cir. 2017).

[28] *See Lebahn v. Owens*, 813 F.3d 1300, 1306 (10th Cir. 2016); *Foley v. Biter*, 793 F.3d 998, 1002 (9th Cir. 2015).

[29] *See Kile v. United States*, 915 F.3d 682, 688 (10th Cir. 2019); *People for the Ethical Treatment of Animals v. United States Dep't of Health & Human Servs.*, 901 F.3d 343, 355 (D.C. Cir. 2018).

[30] *See Anderson v. City of New Orleans*, 38 F.4th 472, 478 (5th Cir. 2022); *Adams v. United States*, 911 F.3d 397, 403 (7th Cir. 2018). *See generally Banks v. Chicago Bd. of Educ.*, 750 F.3d 663, 667 (7th Cir. 2014) (generally must show relief not available in direct appeal).

[31] *See Arwa Chiropractic, P.C. v. Med-Care Diabetic & Med. Supplies, Inc.*, 961 F.3d 942, 948–49 (7th Cir. 2020).

[32] *See State Nat'l Ins. Co. v. Cty. of Camden*, 824 F.3d 399, 406 (3d Cir. 2016); *Phillips v. Sheriff of Cook Cty.*, 828 F.3d 541, 544 (7th Cir. 2016).

[33] *See Yesh Music v. Lakewood Church*, 727 F.3d 356, 361-63 (5th Cir. 2013) (surveying Circuits).

[34] *See Northeast Ohio Coalition for Homeless v. Husted*, 696 F.3d 580, 601–02 (6th Cir. 2012).

[35] *See Mendez v. Republic Bank*, 725 F.3d 651, 658 (7th Cir. 2013); *Fisher*

the substantive argument for relief is apparent.[36] But, the moving party must usually make five showings: (1) a timely motion, (2) a meritorious defense, (3) an absence of unfair prejudice to the opponent, (4) exceptional circumstances, and (5) satisfying at least one of the six subsections of this Rule.[37]

Reason 1—Mistake, Inadvertence, Surprise, or Excusable Neglect

Relief from a judgment or order may be granted for mistakes by any person, not just a party,[38] and even legal errors by the court.[39] This category may permit relief where the order or judgment results from an inability to consult with counsel,[40] a misunderstanding regarding a duty to appear,[41] a failure to receive service,[42] or, in some circumstances, an attorney's negligent failure to meet a deadline[43] or other professional misstep.[44] (Note, however, that not all courts recognize attorney negligence as capable of qualifying under this category, and those that do impose a heavy standard.[45]) This category also permits relief when the district court made a substantive error of law or fact in its judgment or order.[46]

The standard for relief under this category is a demanding one.[47] Whether relief is appropriate is assessed case by case: not every error or omission in the course of litigation will qualify as "excusable neglect",[48] nor will routine carelessness,[49] a lack of

---

v. Kadant, Inc., 589 F.3d 505, 513 (1st Cir. 2009).

[36] *See Nelson v. Napolitano*, 657 F.3d 586, 589–90 (7th Cir. 2011) (noting mistaken belief that courts are "obliged to research and construct legal arguments for parties").

[37] *See Wells Fargo Bank, N.A. v. AMH Roman Two NC, LLC*, 859 F.3d 295, 299 (4th Cir. 2017).

[38] *See Associates Discount Corp. v. Goldman*, 524 F.2d 1051, 1052 (3d Cir. 1975).

[39] *See Kemp v. United States*, ___ U.S. ___, 142 S. Ct. 1856, 1861–65 (2022) (all legal errors, not just "obvious" ones, are potential candidates for Rule 60(b)(1)).

[40] *See Falk v. Allen*, 739 F.2d 461, 464 (9th Cir.1984).

[41] *See Ellingsworth v. Chrysler*, 665 F.2d 180, 184 (7th Cir.1981).

[42] *See Blois v. Friday*, 612 F.2d 938, 940 (5th Cir.1980).

[43] *See In re Gilman*, 887 F.3d 956, 963–64 (9th Cir. 2018); *Keane v. HSBC Bank USA for Ellington Tr., Series 2007-2*, 874 F.3d 763, 764–67 (1st Cir. 2017).

[44] *See Daniels v. Agin*, 736 F.3d 70, 86–87 (1st Cir. 2013).

[45] *See Latshaw v. Trainer Wortham & Co., Inc.*, 452 F.3d 1097, 1101 (9th Cir. 2006) (surveying Circuits, and ruling that Rule 60(b)(1) does not remedy erroneous legal advice (even innocent carelessness) of counsel, explaining "[s]uch mistakes are more appropriately addressed through malpractice claims"); *Robb v. Norfolk & Western Ry. Co.*, 122 F.3d 354, 361–63 (7th Cir. 1997) (Circuit discontinues "hard-and-fast" rule barring application of Rule to attorney negligence, but sternly cautioning against expecting such relief to be granted automatically).

[46] *See Kemp v. United States*, ___ U.S. ___, 142 S. Ct. 1856, 1861–65 (2022); *Utah ex rel. Div. of Foresty, Fire & State Lands v. U.S.*, 528 F.3d 712, 722–23 (10th Cir. 2008).

[47] *See U.S. v. $23,000 in U.S. Currency*, 356 F.3d 157, 164 (1st Cir. 2004).

[48] *See Skrabec v. Town of N. Attle-*

diligence,[50] weak internal business systems,[51] preventable technology vulnerabilities,[52] a confusion concerning the Rules or the law,[53] or a party's misunderstanding of the consequences of her actions (even after advice of counsel).[54] Relief cannot be invoked merely to evade consequences of legal positions and litigation strategies undertaken, when "unsuccessful, ill-advised, or even flatly erroneous."[55] Moreover, otherwise careful clients can be penalized for omissions of their careless attorneys.[56] As a threshold showing, the moving party must demonstrate that the error made did not result from his or her own culpable conduct,[57] and instead that the party behaved with appropriate diligence.[58] To qualify as "excusable neglect", the conduct is tested against an equitable standard that weighs the totality of the circumstances;[59] among the factors the courts consider in this analysis are: (1) prejudice to the opponent; (2) length of delay and impact on the proceedings; (3) reason for the delay; and (4) the moving party's good faith.[60] The "reason-for-delay" is characterized as the "key" factor for this analysis,[61] although

---

boro, 878 F.3d 5, 9 (1st Cir. 2017); *Rodgers v. Wyoming Atty. Gen.*, 205 F.3d 1201, 1206 (10th Cir. 2000).

[49]*See Orie v. Dist. Attorney Allegheny Cty.*, 946 F.3d 187, 191 (3d Cir. 2019); *Giles v. Saint Luke's Northland-Smithville*, 908 F.3d 365, 369 (8th Cir. 2018).

[50]*See Krivak v. Home Depot U.S.A., Inc.*, 2 F.4th 601, 606 (7th Cir. 2021); *Aguiar-Carrasquillo v. Agosto-Alicea*, 445 F.3d 19, 28 (1st Cir. 2006).

[51]*See D.R.T.G. Builders, L.L.C. v. Occupational Safety & Health Rev. Comm'n*, 26 F.4th 306, 312–13 (5th Cir. 2022) (failure to establish internal processes to timely receive certified postal mail and UPS deliveries did not qualify).

[52]*See Trevino v. City of Fort Worth*, 944 F.3d 567, 571–72 (5th Cir. 2019) (defective antivirus software diverting court emails to spam folder does not qualify).

[53]*See Trevino v. City of Fort Worth*, 944 F.3d 567, 571 (5th Cir. 2019); *United States v. Davenport*, 668 F.3d 1316, 1324–25 (11th Cir. 2012).

[54]*See Cashner v. Freedom Stores, Inc.*, 98 F.3d 572, 577–78 (10th Cir. 1996).

[55]*See U.S. Commodity Futures Trading Com'n v. Kratville*, 796 F.3d 873, 896 (8th 2015). *See also Nat'l City Golf Fin. v. Scott*, 899 F.3d 412, 418 (5th Cir. 2018) (not available to unwind settlement party later regrets).

[56]*See Krivak v. Home Depot U.S.A., Inc.*, 2 F.4th 601, 607 (7th Cir. 2021); *Daniels v. Agin*, 736 F.3d 70, 86–87 (1st Cir. 2013).

[57]*See Yeschick v. Mineta*, 675 F.3d 622, 628–28 (6th Cir. 2012); *Ungar v. Palestine Liberation Org.*, 599 F.3d 79, 85 (1st Cir. 2010).

[58]*See Robinson v. Wix Filtration Corp. LLC*, 599 F.3d 403, 413 (4th Cir. 2010).

[59]*See D.R.T.G. Builders, L.L.C. v. Occupational Safety & Health Rev. Comm'n*, 26 F.4th 306, 311–12 (5th Cir. 2022); *Morrissey v. Mayorkas*, 17 F.4th 1150, 1162 (D.C. Cir. 2021). *See generally Pioneer Inv. Servs. Co. v. Brunswick Assocs. Ltd. P'ship*, 507 U.S. 380, 395, 113 S. Ct. 1489, 123 L. Ed. 2d 74 (1993). Some courts require that each of these four factors *must* be considered and weighed before ruling. *See Ahanchian v. Xenon Pictures, Inc.*, 624 F.3d 1253, 1261–62 (9th Cir. 2010).

[60]*See Orie v. Dist. Attorney Allegheny Cty.*, 946 F.3d 187, 191 (3d Cir. 2019); *Coleman Hammons Constr. Co., Inc. v. Occupational Safety & Health Review Comm'n*, 942 F.3d 279, 282–83 (5th Cir. 2019).

[61]*See Giles v. Saint Luke's*

the analysis is ordinarily not *per se* or mechanical.[62]

Note: When invoked to seek relief from a default judgment, Rule 60(b) typically obligates the moving party to show good cause, quick action in correcting the default, absence of prejudice to the non-movant, and the existence of a meritorious defense.[63] Courts may also consider whether the case implicates the public interest or would impose an especially significant financial loss.[64]

Reason 2—Newly Discovered Evidence

Relief from an order or judgment may also be granted on the basis of new evidence where: (1) the evidence has been newly discovered since trial, (2) the moving party was diligent in discovering the new evidence, (3) the new evidence is not merely cumulative or impeaching, (4) the new evidence is material, and (5) in view of the new evidence, a new trial would probably produce a different result.[65] Implicit in these elements is the recognition that the evidence must be of facts that, though in existence at the time of trial, were not discovered until after trial.[66] Relief is not necessarily foreclosed, though, merely because the party was aware of the evidence earlier (if that evidence remained inaccessible),[67] nor merely because it relates to an issue that had been earlier litigated.[68] Moreover (and implicitly), the newly discovered evidence must be both admissible and credible.[69] These requirements are strictly enforced[70] (in fact, one court requires that they be proved by clear and convincing evidence).[71] If the movant fails to meet *any* of these prerequisites, the Rule 60(b)(2) motion may be denied.[72]

Reason 3—Fraud, Misrepresentation, Other Adversary Misconduct

Relief from a judgment or order may be permitted where:

Northland-Smithville, 908 F.3d 365, 369 (8th Cir. 2018); *Skrabec v. Town of N. Attleboro*, 878 F.3d 5, 9 (1st Cir. 2017).

[62]*See Ahanchian v. Xenon Pictures, Inc.*, 624 F.3d 1253, 1261–62 (9th Cir. 2010).

[63]*See supra* Authors' Commentary to Rule 55(c). ("**Vacating a Final Judgment by Default**").

[64]*See In re OCA, Inc.*, 551 F.3d 359, 369 (5th Cir. 2008).

[65]*See Fields v. City of Chicago*, 981 F.3d 534, 554 (7th Cir. 2020); *Metzler Inv. Gmbh v. Chipotle Mexican Grill, Inc.*, 970 F.3d 133, 146–47 (2d Cir. 2020).

[66]*See LAJIM, LLC v. Gen. Elec. Co.*, 917 F.3d 933, 950 (7th Cir. 2019); *Nat'l City Golf Fin., a Div. of Nat'l City Commercial Capital Co., L.L.C. v. Scott*, 899 F.3d 412, 418 (5th Cir. 2018).

[67]*See Bain v. MJJ Prods., Inc.*, 751 F.3d 642, 646–48 (D.C. Cir. 2014).

[68]*See In re Global Energies, LLC*, 763 F.3d 1341, 1347 (11th Cir. 2014).

[69]*See Mirlis v. Greer*, 952 F.3d 36, 50 (2d Cir. 2020); *F.D.I.C. v. Arciero*, 741 F.3d 1111, 1118 (10th Cir. 2013).

[70]*See Nat'l City Golf Fin. v. Scott*, 899 F.3d 412, 418 (5th Cir. 2018); *Waddell v. Hendry County Sheriff's Office*, 329 F.3d 1300, 1309 (11th Cir. 2003).

[71]*See Luna v. Bell*, 887 F.3d 290, 294 (6th Cir. 2018).

[72]*See Jones v. Lincoln Elec. Co.*, 188 F.3d 709, 735–36 (7th Cir. 1999); *McCormack v. Citibank, N.A.*, 100 F.3d 532, 542 (8th Cir. 1996).

(1) the moving party possessed a meritorious claim at trial, (2) the adverse party engaged in fraud, misrepresentation, or other misconduct, and (3) that mischief prevented the moving party from fully and fairly presenting its case during trial.[73] (Courts are divided on whether the moving party must also show that the mischief likely altered the case's outcome;[74] in courts requiring such a showing, proving knowing or deliberate misbehavior may allow that requirement to be inferred.[75]) This category is the "lineal descendant" of the rule in equity that a court, finding fraud or undue influence, may alter or negate a written instrument.[76] Relief is reserved for judgments that were unfairly obtained, not at those that are claimed to be just factually in error.[77] Indeed, an actual factual error in the judgment may not even be required.[78] This provision is remedial, and is liberally construed.[79] It authorizes relief not only for fraud, but for misrepresentations and misconduct as well.[80] Thus, such relief may be granted to remedy belatedly uncovered misbehavior during discovery, provided it interfered substantially with the moving party's ability to fully and fairly try the case.[81]

The Rule does not define "fraud", but a typical formulation for fraud is: "the knowing misrepresentation of a material fact, or concealment of the same when there is a duty to disclose, done to induce another to act to his or her detriment."[82] Ordinarily, relief under this category is reserved for instances where a fraud was committed by the adversary (and not by the party's

---

[73] *See Fields v. City of Chicago*, 981 F.3d 534, 558 (7th Cir. 2020); *In re DePuy Orthopaedics, nc., Pinnacle Hip Implant Prod. Liab. Litig.*, 888 F.3d 753, 790 (5th Cir. 2018). *Cf. Cap Exp., LLC v. Zinus, Inc.*, 996 F.3d 1332, 1338–39 (Fed. Cir. 2021) (applying Ninth Circuit's added requirement that fraud not be discoverable through due diligence before or during proceedings, but finding that added element "questionable").

[74] *Compare Rembrandt Vision Techs., L.P. v. Johnson & Johnson Vision Care, Inc.*, 818 F.3d 1320, 1324 (Fed. Cir. 2016) (not required); *with In re Levaquin Prods. Liab. Litig.*, 739 F.3d 401, 405 (8th Cir. 2014) (absent such showing, relief may be denied).

[75] *See Aguiar-Carrasquillo v. Agosto-Alicea*, 445 F.3d 19, 28 (1st Cir. 2006).

[76] *See Ty Inc. v. Softbelly's, Inc.*, 517 F.3d 494, 498 (7th Cir. 2008).

[77] *See Trendsettah USA, Inc. v. Swisher Int'l, Inc.*, 31 F.4th 1124, 1136 (9th Cir. 2022); *Nat'l City Golf Fin. v. Scott*, 899 F.3d 412, 418–19 (5th Cir. 2018).

[78] *See Hesling v. CSX Transp., Inc.*, 396 F.3d 632, 641 (5th Cir. 2005) (proof that withheld information would have altered outcome is not required, because Rule "is aimed at judgments which were unfairly obtained, not at those which are factually incorrect").

[79] *See Hesling v. CSX Transp., Inc.*, 396 F.3d 632, 641 (5th Cir. 2005).

[80] *See Fields v. City of Chicago*, 981 F.3d 534, 558 (7th Cir. 2020) (applies to intentional and unintentional misrepresentations); *Rembrandt Vision Techs., L.P. v. Johnson & Johnson Vision Care, Inc.*, 818 F.3d 1320, 1328 (Fed. Cir. 2016) (does not require nefarious intent or purpose, and could cover accidental omissions).

[81] *See Cf. Cap Exp., LLC v. Zinus, Inc.*, 996 F.3d 1332, 1341 (Fed. Cir. 2021); *W. v. Bell Helicopter Textron, Inc.*, 803 F.3d 56, 67–72 (1st Cir. 2015).

[82] *See Info-Hold, Inc. v. Sound Merch., Inc.*, 538 F.3d 448, 455–56 (6th Cir. 2008).

own counsel or other non-adversaries).[83] Further, the fraud must generally have been perpetrated in the course of litigation, and not, for example, during an underlying commercial transaction.[84] Fraud must be proven by clear and convincing evidence.[85]

Reason 4—Void Judgment

Relief may also be granted where the judgment or order is void. This Rule's definition of a "void" judgment is narrow, however. A ruling that is alleged to be simply incorrect is not "void",[86] nor is a judgment that is merely "voidable" (based on the existence of some defense or objection).[87] The remedy for those failings is a timely appeal, for which Rule 60(b)(4) is no substitute.[88] Instead, a judgment is "void" only if it is a "legal nullity"[89] — premised on a fundamental jurisdictional or due process error.[90] As other courts have restated it, a "void" judgment is one the rendering court was powerless to enter.[91] Even then, to trigger relief, the judgment must represent a clear usurpation of judicial power (or, as many courts have written, the judgment must lack even an "arguable basis" for jurisdiction).[92] Thus, a judgment entered without subject-matter or personal jurisdiction, or which in some other manner transgressed constitutional due process or exceeded proper

[83]*See Cf. Cap Exp., LLC v. Zinus, Inc.*, 996 F.3d 1332, 1338 n.9 (Fed. Cir. 2021); *Latshaw v. Trainer Wortham & Co., Inc.*, 452 F.3d 1097, 1102 (9th Cir. 2006).

[84]*See Roger Edwards, LLC v. Fiddes & Son Ltd.*, 427 F.3d 129, 134 (1st Cir. 2005).

[85]*See Wagstaff & Cartmell, LLP v. Lewis*, 40 F.4th 830, 842 (8th Cir. 2022); *Trendsettah USA, Inc. v. Swisher Int'l, Inc.*, 31 F.4th 1124, 1136 (9th Cir. 2022).

[86]*See United Student Aid Funds, Inc. v. Espinosa*, 559 U.S. 260, 270, 130 S. Ct. 1367, 176 L. Ed. 2d 158 (2010).

[87]*See Days Inns Worldwide, Inc. v. Patel*, 445 F.3d 899, 906–08 (6th Cir. 2006) (distinguishing between void ab initio and voidable).

[88]*See United Student Aid Funds, Inc. v. Espinosa*, 559 U.S. 260, 271, 130 S. Ct. 1367, 1377, 176 L. Ed. 2d 158 (2010).

[89]*See Gillispie v. Warden, London Correctional Inst.*, 771 F.3d 323, 327 (6th Cir. 2014).

[90]*See United Student Aid Funds, Inc. v. Espinosa*, 559 U.S. 260, 271, 130 S. Ct. 1367, 1377, 176 L. Ed. 2d 158 (2010). *See also Carrasquillo-Serrano v. Municipality of Canovanas*, 991 F.3d 32, 39 (1st Cir. 2021) (two circumstances: lack of jurisdiction or court "so far exceeded a proper exercise of judicial power that a violation of the Due Process Clause results").

[91]*See Kile v. United States*, 915 F.3d 682, 686 (10th Cir. 2019); *Karsner v. Lothian*, 532 F.3d 876, 886 (D.C. Cir. 2008).

[92]*See Gater Assets Ltd. v. AO Moldovagaz*, 2 F.4th 42, 53 (2d Cir. 2021) ("plainly usurped jurisdiction" having "no arguably basis"); *Hawkins v. i-TV Digitalis Tavkozlesi zrt*, 935 F.3d 211, 221–22 (4th Cir. 2019) ("egregious", without "arguable basis"). *See also United Student Aid Funds, Inc. v. Espinosa*, 559 U.S. 260, 271, 130 S. Ct. 1367, 1377, 176 L. Ed. 2d 158 (2010) (noting no-arguable-ground prediction of lower courts, but finding no need to discuss it). *But see Bell Helicopter Textron, Inc. v. Islamic Republic of Iran*, 734 F.3d 1175, 1180–81 (D.C. Cir. 2013) (rejecting no-arguable-ground constraint).

judicial authority, is likely "void".[93] Very little discretion is accorded the district court in making this ruling; either the judgment is "void", in which case relief must be granted, or it is not.[94] Courts are divided on which party bears the burden of proof in Rule 60(b)(4) challenges: some courts impose the burden on the party who invoked the court's jurisdiction originally,[95] while others vest the burden with the movant.[96]

Reason 5—Changed Circumstances

Relief from a judgment or order may also be granted where the circumstances justifying the ruling have changed, such as (1) where the judgment is satisfied, released, or discharged, (2) where a prior judgment on which the present judgment is based has been reversed or otherwise vacated, or (3) in any other circumstance where the continued enforcement of the judgment would be inequitable (*e.g.*, a change in legislative or decisional law, or a change in critical facts).[97] These three grounds are disjunctive; any one is sufficient to justify relief.[98] This encompasses the traditional power invested in a court of equity to modify its decree when appropriate in view of changed circumstances.[99]

In evaluating such motions, the courts consider whether a substantial change in circumstances or law has occurred since the contested order was entered, whether complying with the contested order would cause extreme and unexpected hardship, and whether a good reason for modification exists.[100] The party seeking relief bears the burden of proving changed circum-

---

[93] *See United Student Aid Funds, Inc. v. Espinosa*, 559 U.S. 260, 270-71, 130 S. Ct. 1367, 176 L. Ed. 2d 158 (2010). *See also Bell v. Pulmosan Safety Equip. Corp.*, 906 F.3d 711, 714–15 (8th Cir. 2018) (failure to properly serve defendant can render resulting judgment "void").

[94] *See Sec. & Exch. Comm'n v. Novinger*, 40 F.4th 297, 301–02 (5th Cir. 2022); *Carrasquillo-Serrano v. Municipality of Canovanas*, 991 F.3d 32, 38–39 (1st Cir. 2021).

[95] *See Craig v. Ontario Corp.*, 543 F.3d 872, 876 (7th Cir. 2008). *But cf. Nagravision SA v. Gotech Int'l Tech. Ltd.*, 882 F.3d 494, 498–99 (5th Cir. 2018) (in Rule 4(k)(2) personal jurisdiction inquiry, burden begins with invoker then shifts).

[96] *See Gater Assets Ltd. v. AO Moldovagaz*, 2 F.4th 42, 53 (2d Cir. 2021) (in collateral attack on personal jurisdiction, movant must present "highly convincing" evidence).

[97] *See Agostini v. Felton*, 521 U.S. 203, 117 S. Ct. 1997, 138 L. Ed. 2d 391 (1997) (allowing relief under Rule 60(b)(5) to alter permanent injunction in light of Supreme Court's decision to overrule earlier constitutional precedent on which injunction was based); *Rufo v. Inmates of Suffolk County Jail*, 502 U.S. 367, 112 S. Ct. 748, 116 L. Ed. 2d 867 (1992) (parties seeking a modification of consent order bear burden of demonstrating "significant change" in circumstances to warrant relief from decree).

[98] *See Horne v. Flores*, 557 U.S. 433, 454, 129 S. Ct. 2579, 174 L. Ed. 2d 406 (2009).

[99] *See Frew ex rel. Frew v. Hawkins*, 540 U.S. 431, 441–42, 124 S. Ct. 899, 157 L. Ed. 2d 855 (2004).

[100] *See Horne v. Flores*, 557 U.S. 433, 447, 129 S. Ct. 2579, 174 L. Ed. 2d 406 (2009); *Rufo* v. *Inmates of Suffolk County Jail*, 502 U.S. 367, 384, 112 S. Ct. 748, 116 L. Ed. 2d 867

stances warranting relief; once that entitlement is shown, the court must modify the order.[101] The proposed modification must be "suitably tailored" to meet the new legal or factual circumstances.[102] Relief is only available where there is a prospective effect to the challenged judgment;[103] the mere fact that the law has changed since the judgment was entered[104] or that a ruling will have future collateral estoppel effect (something obviously common to many rulings)[105] or otherwise causes "some reverberations into the future"[106] does not provide the requisite "prospective" effect necessary for relief under this provision. Ordinarily, judgments that dismiss or otherwise deny injunctive relief will not possess the necessary "prospective" effect,[107] nor will money judgments because the set nature of the monetary outlay provides the finality.[108] The "satisfied, released, or discharged" clause is often invoked by parties seeking to have a judgment satisfied by the court, due to an ongoing dispute with the judgment holder over the judgment.[109] That alternative is also available in consent decree cases upon a showing of substantial compliance, although the movant's burden is considered heavy.[110] The "based-on-earlier-judgment" alternative usually requires that the prior judgment have a preclusionary (res judicata or collateral estoppel) effect, and not

---

(1992).

[101]*See Horne v. Flores*, 557 U.S. 433, 447, 129 S. Ct. 2579, 174 L. Ed. 2d 406 (2009); *Rufo v. Inmates of Suffolk Cty. Jail*, 502 U.S. 367, 383, 112 S. Ct. 748, 116 L. Ed. 2d 867 (1992).

[102]*See Rufo v. Inmates of Suffolk Cty. Jail*, 502 U.S. 367, 383, 112 S. Ct. 748, 116 L. Ed. 2d 867 (1992). *See also Nat'l Labor Relations Bd. v. Int'l Ass'n of Bridge, Structural, Ornamental & Reinforcing Ironworkers Union, Local 433*, 891 F.3d 1182, 1186 (9th Cir. 2018) (party also bears burden of proposing suitably tailored modification).

[103]*See Nat'l City Golf Fin. v. Scott*, 899 F.3d 412, 419 (5th Cir. 2018); *Prudential Ins. Co. of America v. National Park Medical Center, Inc.*, 413 F.3d 897, 903 (8th Cir. 2005). *But cf. City of Duluth v. Fond du Lac Band of Lake Superior Chippewa*, 702 F.3d 1147, 1154 (8th Cir. 2013) (prospective relief under Rule 60(b)(5) could be coupled with retrospective relief under another Rule 60(b) subpart).

[104]*See Mitchell v. United States*, 958 F.3d 775, 786–87 (9th Cir. 2020); *Kathrein v. City of Evanston*, 752 F.3d 680, 690 (7th Cir. 2014).

[105]*See Coltec Indus., Inc. v. Hobgood*, 280 F.3d 262, 271–72 (3d Cir. 2002) (if collateral estoppel effect were enough, "prospective application" would be meaningless).

[106]*See Tapper v. Hearn*, 833 F.3d 166, 170–71 (2d Cir. 2016); *Kalamazoo River Study Group v. Rockwell Intern. Corp.*, 355 F.3d 574, 587–88 (6th Cir. 2004).

[107]*See Tapper v. Hearn*, 833 F.3d 166, 171 (2d Cir. 2016) (surveying Circuits).

[108]*See Nat'l City Golf Fin., a Div. of Nat'l City Commercial Capital Co., L.L.C. v. Scott*, 899 F.3d 412, 419 (5th Cir. 2018); *Kalamazoo River Study Group v. Rockwell Intern. Corp.*, 355 F.3d 574, 587–88 (6th Cir. 2004).

[109]*See BUC Intern. Corp. v. International Yacht Council Ltd.*, 517 F.3d 1271, 1274–75 (11th Cir. 2008); *Zamani v. Carnes*, 491 F.3d 990, 995–96 (9th Cir. 2007).

[110]*See Peery v. City of Miami*, 977 F.3d 1061, 1069 & 1074–75 (11th Cir. 2020).

a mere precedential impact.[111] The courts are divided whether such relief may be granted *sua sponte*.[112]

Note: Lower courts should not apply Rule 60(b)(5) in *anticipation* of the Supreme Court's overruling of an earlier precedent. To the contrary, where one of its precedents applies directly to the circumstances at hand, even though the precedent's reasoning has been undermined by other opinions, the lower courts should follow the precedent and leave to the Supreme Court the prerogative of overruling its own decisions.[113]

Reason 6—Other Extraordinary Reasons

Finally, relief from a judgment or order may be permitted in other extraordinary circumstances[114] causing unexpected, extreme hardship.[115] The reach of Rule 60(b)(6) is broad, described as a "grand reservoir of equitable power to do justice in a particular case."[116] But while its reach is broad, its application in practice is tightly constrained.

First, this "catch-all" category and the five specific Rule 60(b) categories that precede it are mutually exclusive. If the reason for which Rule 60(b)(6) relief is sought fits topically within one of the five specific categories, an inability to satisfy that category's elements will not make the movant eligible for relief under the catch-all category.[117] (But an inability to satisfy one of the five specific categories also does not necessarily foreclose the possibility of catch-all relief on other, different grounds.[118]) "Something more" is required, and, given the breadth of the reasons captured by Rule 60(b)(1) through (b)(5), there is an

[111]*See Pirkl v. Wilkie*, 906 F.3d 1371, 1381 n.6 (Fed. Cir. 2018); *Nat'l City Golf Fin. v. Scott*, 899 F.3d 412, 419 (5th Cir. 2018).

[112]*See Baum v. Blue Moon Ventures, LLC*, 513 F.3d 181, 190 (5th Cir. 2008) (*sua sponte* grants permitted); *Dr. Jose S. Belaval, Inc. v. Perez-Perdomo*, 465 F.3d 33, 37 (1st Cir. 2006) (discussing Circuit split).

[113]*See Agostini v. Felton*, 521 U.S. 203, 117 S. Ct. 1997, 138 L. Ed. 2d 391 (1997). *See also Cano v. Baker*, 435 F.3d 1337, 1341–43 (11th Cir. 2006) (rejecting, on similar grounds, Rule 60(b)(5)'s use by former abortion plaintiff who sought to revisit her earlier abortion rights decision as wrongly decided in light of intervening medical evidence).

[114]*See, e.g., Kemp v. United States*, — U.S. —, 142 S. Ct. 1856, 1861 (2022); *Buck v. Davis*, 580 U.S. —, 137 S. Ct. 759, 197 L. Ed. 2d 1 (2017); *Gonzalez v. Crosby*, 545 U.S. 524, 535, 125 S. Ct. 2641, 162 L. Ed. 2d 480 (2005).

[115]*See Greene v. Superintendent Smithfield Sci*, 882 F.3d 443, 449 n.7 (3d Cir. 2018); *Galbert v. West Caribbean Airways*, 715 F.3d 1290, 1294 (11th Cir. 2013).

[116]*See Kile v. United States*, 915 F.3d 682, 687 (10th Cir. 2019). *Accord Henson v. Fid. Nat'l Fin., Inc.*, 943 F.3d 434, 439–40 (9th Cir. 2019).

[117]*See Kemp v. United States*, — U.S. —, 142 S. Ct. 1856, 1861 (2022); *Pioneer Inv. Servs. Co. v. Brunswick Assocs. Ltd. P'ship*, 507 U.S. 380, 393, 113 S. Ct. 1489, 123 L. Ed. 2d 74 (1993); *Liljeberg v. Health Servs. Acquisition Corp.*, 486 U.S. 847, 863 n.11, 108 S. Ct. 2194, 100 L. Ed. 2d 855 (1988).

[118]*See Johnson v. Spencer*, 950 F.3d 680, 700 (10th Cir. 2020).

understandably thin volume of cases explaining when that "something more" will be present to warrant relief under Rule 60(b)(6).[119]

Second, relief under this "catch-all" category is exceedingly rare,[120] and rests on a case-by-case,[121] highly fact-intensive balancing of finality and doing justice.[122] It does not offer an unsuccessful litigant an opportunity "to take a mulligan,"[123] and is never a substitute for direct appeal.[124] Seeking relief under Rule 60(b)(6) generally requires a showing of actual injury and the presence of circumstances beyond the movant's control that prevented timely action to protect her interests.[125] In considering such motions, courts may assess the risk of injustice to the parties and the risk that public confidence in the judicial process might be undermined.[126] There is some authority for the conclusion that this Rule is limited to setting aside a judgment or order, and may not be used to grant affirmative relief.[127] Relief on the basis of a mere change in decisional law is unlikely.[128] Some courts have ruled that Rule 60(b)(6) may be proper where a defaulted client seeks relief from judgment on the basis of an extremely gross negligence of,[129] or abandonment by,[130] counsel. But it is never available to remedy deliberate strategic choices in litigation that later prove to be unwise.[131]

Burden of Proof

Except as noted above in a sub-rule specific discussion, the

---

[119] *See East Brooks Books, Inc. v. City of Memphis*, 633 F.3d 459, 465 (6th Cir. 2011).

[120] *See In re Guidant Corp. Implantable Defibrillators Products Liability Litigation*, 496 F.3d 863, 868 (8th Cir. 2007).

[121] *See Miller v. Mays*, 879 F.3d 691, 698 (6th Cir. 2018).

[122] *See Hall v. Haws*, 861 F.3d 977, 987 (9th Cir. 2017); *West v. Carpenter*, 790 F.3d 693, 697 (6th Cir. 2015).

[123] *See Kramer v. Gates*, 481 F.3d 788, 792 (D.C. Cir. 2007).

[124] *See Banks v. Chicago Bd. of Educ.*, 750 F.3d 663, 668 (7th Cir. 2014).

[125] *See Gardner v. Martino*, 563 F.3d 981, 992 (9th Cir. 2009).

[126] *See Buck v. Davis*, 580 U.S. __, 137 S. Ct. 759 & 777–78, 772, 197 L. Ed. 2d 1 (2017); *Liljeberg v. Health Servs. Acquisition Corp.*, 486 U.S. 847, 863–64, 108 S. Ct. 2194, 100 L. Ed. 2d 855 (1988).

[127] *See Delay v. Gordon*, 475 F.3d 1039, 1044–45 (9th Cir. 2007).

[128] *See Agostini v. Felton*, 521 U.S. 203, 239, 117 S.Ct. 1997, 138 L.Ed.2d 391 (1997) ("[i]ntervening developments in the law by themselves rarely" suffice); *Crutsinger v. Davis*, 936 F.3d 265, 267 (5th Cir. 2019) (same). *But cf. Henson v. Fid. Nat'l Fin., Inc.*, 943 F.3d 434, 444–55 (9th Cir. 2019) (exceptional circumstances found to warrant relief).

[129] *See Brooks v. Yates*, 818 F.3d 532, 534 (9th Cir. 2016); *Marino v. Drug Enforcement Admin.*, 685 F.3d 1076, 1080 (D.C.Cir. 2012). *But see Giles v. Saint Luke's Northland-Smithville*, 908 F.3d 365, 370 (8th Cir. 2018) (never a vehicle for attorney incompetence / carelessness).

[130] *See Moje v. Federal Hockey League, LLC*, 792 F.3d 756, 758 (7th Cir. 2015).

[131] *See Kile v. United States*, 915 F.3d 682, 688 (10th Cir. 2019); *People for the Ethical Treatment of Animals v. United States Dep't of Health & Human Servs.*, 901 F.3d 343, 355 (D.C. Cir. 2018).

party seeking relief from a judgment or order bears the burden of demonstrating that the prerequisites for such relief are satisfied.[132] Because the relief is fundamentally equitable, equitable defenses against the moving party (*e.g.*, unclean hands) may foreclose it.[133]

Discretion of District Judge

Whether to grant relief under Rule 60(b) is left to the broad discretion of the trial court[134] (absent legal error).[135] In the case of "void" judgments attacked under Rule 60(b)(4), however, the district court's discretion is almost illusory, if it exists at all. True "void" judgments are "legal nullities", and the court's refusal to vacate such judgments is a *per se* abuse of discretion.[136]

Jurisdiction

No new independent basis for the court's jurisdiction is necessary to support a Rule 60(b) motion or ruling. Rather, such a proceeding is deemed to be a continuation of the original action, and jurisdiction to consider a later Rule 60(b) motion is not divested by subsequent events.[137]

Procedure

Motions under this Rule should be made to the court that rendered the judgment.[138] Absent a local rule dictating otherwise, the court is not required to convene a hearing on Rule 60(b) motions, but may choose to do so in its discretion.[139] The court generally does not need to enter findings of fact and conclusions of law to grant Rule 60(b) relief,[140] although a careful articulation of its analysis is advised as "helpful" and aiding

---

[132] *See D.R.T.G. Builders, L.L.C. v. Occupational Safety & Health Rev. Comm'n*, 26 F.4th 306, 312 (5th Cir. 2022); *Owens v. Republic of Sudan*, 864 F.3d 751, 819 (D.C. Cir. 2017).

[133] *See Thai-Lao Lignite (Thailand) Co. v. Gov't of Lao People's Democratic Republic*, 864 F.3d 172, 182 (2d Cir. 2017).

[134] *See Buck v. Davis*, 580 U.S. —, 137 S. Ct. 759, 777–78, 197 L. Ed. 2d 1 (2017). *See also In re Cook Med., Inc.*, 27 F.4th 539, 542 (7th Cir. 2022) ("extremely deferential").

[135] *See Cap Exp., LLC v. Zinus, Inc.*, 996 F.3d 1332, 1338 (Fed. Cir. 2021) (discretion abused when court does not apply correct law or rests ruling on clearly erroneous factfinding); *Johnson v. Spencer*, 950 F.3d 680, 701 (10th Cir. 2020) (same).

[136] *See Sec. & Exch. Comm'n v. Novinger*, 40 F.4th 297, 301–02 (5th Cir. 2022); *Kile v. United States*, 915 F.3d 682, 686 (10th Cir. 2019).

[137] *See D'Ambrosio v. Bagley*, 656 F.3d 379, 388 (6th Cir. 2011); *East Brooks Books, Inc. v. City of Memphis*, 633 F.3d 459, 465 (6th Cir. 2011).

[138] *See Board of Trustees, Sheet Metal Workers' Nat. Pension Fund v. Elite Erectors, Inc.*, 212 F.3d 1031, 1034 (7th Cir. 2000).

[139] *See Atkinson v. Prudential Property Co., Inc.*, 43 F.3d 367, 374 (8th Cir. 1994).

[140] *See Gov't of Province of Manitoba v. Zinke*, 849 F.3d 1111, 1118 (D.C. Cir. 2017); *Atkinson v. Prudential Property Co., Inc.*, 43 F.3d 367, 374 (8th Cir. 1994).

appellate review.[141]

Vacating Judgments Entered by Other Courts

Only in extraordinary circumstances may one court invoke Rule 60(b) to vacate a judgment entered by a different court; nonetheless, courts seem to possess the authority to do so in an appropriate case.[142]

Who May Seek Relief

Relief under this Rule may be requested by a party,[143] a party's legal representative,[144] or one in privity with a party.[145] Absent unusual circumstances,[146] non-parties cannot seek Rule 60(b) relief.[147]

Sua Sponte Motions

The Circuits are divided on whether a district court may, on its own initiative, grant relief from a judgment or order under Rule 60(b).[148] When such *sua sponte* relief is permitted, the courts generally demand that the parties receive notice and an opportunity to be heard before the relief is ordered.[149]

Appealability

Orders granting relief under Rule 60(b) are generally interlocutory and not immediately appealable (unless their effect ends the litigation).[150] Appeals can usually[151] be taken from orders denying Rule 60(b) relief,[152] but such appeals ordinarily implicate only the propriety of that denial, and not the underly-

[141] *See Lemoge v. U.S.*, 587 F.3d 1188, 1194 (9th Cir. 2009).

[142] *See Budget Blinds, Inc. v. White*, 536 F.3d 244, 251–55 (3d Cir. 2008). *But see Board of Trustees, Sheet Metal Workers' Nat. Pension Fund v. Elite Erectors, Inc.*, 212 F.3d 1031, 1034 (7th Cir. 2000) (ruling that courts do not have that authority).

[143] *See Pearson v. Target Corp.*, 893 F.3d 980, 984 (7th Cir. 2018) (assessing whether absent class member is "party").

[144] *See Matter of El Paso Refinery, LP*, 37 F.3d 230, 234 (5th Cir. 1994).

[145] *See Eyak Native Village v. Exxon Corp.*, 25 F.3d 773, 777 (9th Cir. 1994).

[146] *See Irvin v. Harris*, 944 F.3d 63, 69–70 (2d Cir. 2019) (allowing motion by absent class member under certain circumstances); *Pearson v. Target Corp.*, 893 F.3d 980, 984 (7th Cir. 2018) (same).

[147] *See Cook Cnty v. Texas*, 37 F.4th 1335, 1344–45 (7th Cir. 2022) (refused intervenors not entitled to relief); *Matter of Motors Liquidation Co.*, 689 Fed. Appx. 95, 96 (2d Cir. 2017) (transferor not entitled to relief).

[148] *See Van Cannon v. United States*, 890 F.3d 656, 661 (7th Cir. 2018) (describing Circuit split). *Compare U.S. v. Pauley*, 321 F.3d 578, 581 (6th Cir. 2003) (no *sua sponte* relief), *with Jo Ann Howard & Assocs., P.C. v. Nat'l City Bank*, 11 F.4th 876, 885 (8th Cir. 2021) (*sua sponte* relief permitted).

[149] *See Pierson v. Dormire*, 484 F.3d 486, 492 (8th Cir. 2007); *Fort Knox Music Inc. v. Baptiste*, 257 F.3d 108, 111 (2d Cir. 2001).

[150] *See Hayes Family Tr. v. State Farm Fire & Cas. Co.*, 845 F.3d 997, 1003–04 (10th Cir. 2017).

[151] *Cf. Gross v. Keen Grp. Sols., L.L.C.*, 18 F.4th 836, 839–40 (5th Cir. 2021) (although appealable "[m]ost of the time," Rule 60(b) denial is not final if unresolved matters remain open before district court).

[152] *See* Fed. R. App. P. 4(a)(4)(A)(vi). *See also Anderson v. City of New Orleans*, 38 F.4th 472, 478 (5th Cir. 2022); *Jackson v. Los Lunas Cmty. Program*, 880 F.3d 1176, 1190 (10th

ing judgment's merits (which ordinarily are reviewed only through a direct appeal of that judgment itself).[153]

RULE 60(c)—TIMING AND EFFECT OF MOTION

CORE CONCEPT

Relief under Rule 60(b) must be sought within a "reasonable" time after entry of the challenged judgment or order. For three of the six categories, an outside 1-year time limit is added.

APPLICATIONS

Impact of 2007 "Restyling" Amendments

In 2007, the second and third sentences of former Rule 60(b) were repositioned to current Rule 60(c).

Burden of Proof

The burden of proving that a Rule 60(b) motion was timely filed lies with the moving party.[154]

The "Void" Judgment Ground

Relief from a "void" judgment or order can be sought at any time.[155] Laches and similar finality principles generally have no effect on void judgments; the courts have held that the mere passage of time will not convert a void judgment into a proper one.[156] However, if a party attacks the court's jurisdiction and loses on that issue, the question of jurisdiction becomes *res judicata* and, accordingly, the judgment is no longer vulnerable to being voided under this Rule; instead, such a party's recourse is ordinarily limited to a direct, timely merits appeal.[157]

The Uncapped "Reasonable" Time Grounds

Relief from a judgment or order that is sought under either Reason 5 ("changed circumstances") or Reason 6 ("interests of justice") must be made "within a reasonable time" after entry of the judgment or order being challenged.[158] The courts determine whether the time of filing is "reasonable" on a case-

---

Cir. 2018).

[153] *See Browder v. Director, Dep't of Corrections of Illinois*, 434 U.S. 257, 263 n.7, 98 S. Ct. 556, 54 L. Ed. 2d 521 (1978).

[154] *See Wells Fargo Bank, N.A. v. AMH Roman Two NC, LLC*, 859 F.3d 295, 300 (4th Cir. 2017).

[155] *See Bell Helicopter Textron, Inc. v. Islamic Republic of Iran*, 734 F.3d 1175, 1179–80 (D.C. Cir. 2013); *"R" Best Produce, Inc. v. DiSapio*, 540 F.3d 115, 123–24 (2d Cir. 2008). *But see Bridgeport Music, Inc. v. Smith*, 714 F.3d 932, 942 (6th Cir. 2013) ("must be brought 'within a reasonable time' ").

[156] *See Norris v. Causey*, 869 F.3d 360, 365–66 (5th Cir. 2017); *U.S. v. One Toshiba Color Television*, 213 F.3d 147, 157–58 (3d Cir. 2000).

[157] *See Durfee v. Duke*, 375 U.S. 106, 84 S. Ct. 242, 11 L. Ed. 2d 186 (1963); *American Surety Co. v. Baldwin*, 287 U.S. 156, 53 S. Ct. 98, 77 L. Ed. 231 (1932).

[158] *See* Rule 60(c)(1). *See also Bynoe v. Baca*, 966 F.3d 972, 979–80 (9th Cir. 2020) (for Rule 60(b)(6) motions); *Lac Courte Oreilles Band of Lake Superior Chippewa Indians of Wisconsin v. Wisconsin*, 769 F.3d 543, 548 (7th Cir. 2014) (for Rule 60(b)(5) motions).

by-case basis,[159] dependent on the circumstances.[160] It is not assessed merely by the length of time that passes between discovery and filing[161] (though the greater the length, the less likely to be reasonable).[162] Importantly, the outer time boundary is not necessarily *more* than a year (but might be less than one).[163] Courts instead consider the length of delay along with its explanation, any resulting prejudice, any circumstances favoring relief, the nature of the dispute, and whether the public interest is implicated.[164] For some courts, prejudice is a pivotal inquiry.[165] In all events, Rule 60(b) cannot be invoked simply to do "an end run" around the time limits established for a taking an appeal.[166]

The 1-Year Capped "Reasonable" Time Grounds

Seeking relief from a judgment or order under any of the first three Rule 60(b) grounds must be done within a reasonable time, but in no event later than 1 year from the entry of the challenged ruling.[167] Thus, this 1-year time limit applies to Reason 1 (mistake, inadvertence, surprise),[168] Reason 2 (newly discovered evidence),[169] and Reason 3 (fraud, misrepresentation, other adversary misconduct).[170]

No Extensions to 1-Year Capped Period

Where the 1-year time limit applies, the period is "absolute" and the district court lacks the authority to extend that time.[171] However, in appropriate circumstances, an untimely Rule 60(b)

---

[159]*See Bouret-Echevarria v. Caribbean Aviation Maintenance Corp.*, 784 F.3d 37, 43 (1st Cir. 2015); *Tyler v. Anderson*, 749 F.3d 499, 510 (6th Cir. 2014).

[160]*See Thai-Lao Lignite (Thailand) Co. v. Gov't of Lao People's Democratic Republic*, 864 F.3d 172, 182 (2d Cir. 2017); *Clark v. Davis*, 850 F.3d 770, 780 (5th Cir. 2017).

[161]*See Doe v. Briley*, 562 F.3d 777, 781 (6th Cir. 2009).

[162]*See, e.g., O'Neal v. Reilly*, 961 F.3d 973, 975 (7th Cir. 2020) (year and a half not reasonable); *Quinn v. Guerrero*, 863 F.3d 353, 360 n.1 (5th Cir. 2017) (8 years not reasonable).

[163]*See Massi v. Walgreen Co.*, 337 Fed.Appx. 542, 545 (6th Cir. 2009).

[164]*See Bridgeport Music, Inc. v. Smith*, 714 F.3d 932, 942–43 (6th Cir. 2013); *Lemoge v. U.S.*, 587 F.3d 1188, 1194, 1196–97 (9th Cir. 2009).

[165]*See Salazar ex rel. Salazar v. District of Columbia*, 633 F.3d 1110, 1118–19 (D.C.Cir. 2011).

[166]*See Anderson v. City of New Orleans*, 38 F.4th 472, 478 (5th Cir. 2022).

[167]*See Pioneer Inv. Servs. Co. v. Brunswick Assocs. Ltd. P'ship*, 507 U.S. 380, 393, 113 S. Ct. 1489, 123 L. Ed. 2d 74 (1993); *In re Cook Med., Inc.*, 27 F.4th 539, 542 (7th Cir. 2022).

[168]*See Cummings v. Greater Cleveland Reg'l Transit Auth.*, 865 F.3d 844, 847 (6th Cir. 2017); *Barnett v. Neal*, 860 F.3d 570, 573 (7th Cir. 2017).

[169]*See In re G.A.D., Inc.*, 340 F.3d 331, 334 (6th Cir. 2003).

[170]*See Cap Exp., LLC v. Zinus, Inc.*, 996 F.3d 1332, 1338–39 (Fed. Cir. 2021); *United States v. McKye*, 947 F.3d 1293, 1296 (10th Cir. 2020).

[171]*See* Rule 60(c)(1). *See also In re Rumsey Land Co.*, 944 F.3d 1259, 1277 (10th Cir. 2019); *Martha Graham Sch. & Dance Found., Inc. v. Martha Graham Ctr. for Contemporary Dance, Inc.*, 466 F.3d 97, 100 (2d Cir.2006).

motion may be subject to equitable tolling[172] or, if not objected to, the timeliness objection could be forfeited.[173] Moreover, taking an appeal does not toll or extend the Rule 60(c) time period, though that period is "tethered" to the contested judgment; if the appeal substantially adjusts that judgment, a new 1-year period may open.[174]

Effect on Finality or a Judgment's Operation

The act of filing a motion for relief under Rule 60 does not affect the finality of the underlying judgment, nor does it suspend that judgment's operation.[175]

Effect on Appeals

A Rule 60 motion that is filed quickly — within the 28-day post-trial motions period — suspends the time for taking an appeal until the motion is resolved by the trial judge[176] (and, similarly, any appeal filed during such a motion's pendency lies dormant until the motion is resolved).[177] But only the first such motion has this suspension effect; second or later post-judgment motions will usually not suspend.[178] Rule 60 motions filed outside the 28-day period do not suspend the appeal time[179] (even if the opponent fails to object).[180] If such a motion is filed beyond 28 days and while an appeal is pending, the district judge is able to grant the motion only upon remand from the appeals court (although denials of the motion may be proper).[181]

---

[172]*See Weitzner v. Cynosure, Inc.*, 802 F.3d 307, 309–12 (2d Cir. 2015).

[173]*See Matter of Terrell*, 39 F.4th 888, 892 (7th Cir. 2022); *Wilburn v. Robinson*, 480 F.3d 1140, 1147–48 (D.C. Cir. 2007). *See generally Penney v. United States*, 870 F.3d 459, 462 (6th Cir. 2017) (time limit is claim-processing rule, not jurisdictional).

[174]*See Trendsettah USA, Inc. v. Swisher Int'l, Inc.*, 31 F.4th 1124, 1134–36 (9th Cir. 2022).

[175]*See* Rule 60(c)(2). *See also HSBC Bank USA, N.A. v. Townsend*, 793 F.3d 771, 792–93 (7th Cir. 2015).

[176]*See* Fed. R. App. P. 4(a)(4)(A)(vi). *See also McKenna v. Wells Fargo Bank, N.A.*, 693 F.3d 207, 213 (1st Cir. 2012); *Johnson v. Univ. of Rochester Med. Ctr.*, 642 F.3d 121, 124 (2d Cir. 2011). *See generally Banister v. Davis*, 590 U.S. __, 140 S. Ct. 1698, 1710 n.9, 207 L. Ed. 2d 58 (2020) (appeal-time suspension derives from courts' treatment of Rule 60(b) motions filed within 28 days as requests for Rule 59(e) relief).

[177]*See* Fed. R. App. P. 4(a)(4)(B)(i).

[178]*See York Group, Inc. v. Wuxi Taihu Tractor Co.*, 632 F.3d 399, 401 (7th Cir. 2011). *See also Krivak v. Home Depot U.S.A., Inc.*, 2 F.4th 601, 605–06 (7th Cir. 2021) (no suspension for Rule 60 motion, if it was preceded by appeal-suspending Rule 59(e) motion).

[179]*See Lebahn v. Owens*, 813 F.3d 1300, 1304 (10th Cir. 2016); *York Group, Inc. v. Wuxi Taihu Tractor Co.*, 632 F.3d 399, 401 (7th Cir. 2011).

[180]*See* Fed. R. App. P. 4(a)(4)(A). *See also id.* advisory committee note (2016) (appeal time not re-started by untimely motion, even if district court had extended the due date or disposed of motion without explicit reliance on untimeliness, or if opponent consents or fails to object).

[181]*See* Rule 62.1. *See also Acadian Diagnostic Labs., L.L.C. v. Quality Toxicology, L.L.C.*, 965 F.3d 404, 414–15 (5th Cir. 2020); *Home Prods. Int'l, Inc. v. United States*, 633 F.3d 1369, 1377 n.9 (Fed.Cir. 2011).

RULE 60(d)—OTHER POWERS TO GRANT RELIEF

CORE CONCEPT

Although Rule 60(a) and Rule 60(b) give the district courts specific Rule-based authority to grant relief from judgments and orders, the courts also enjoy other bases of authority to grant similar relief.

APPLICATIONS

Impact of 2007 "Restyling" Amendments

In 2007, the fourth sentence of former Rule 60(b) was repositioned to current Rule 60(d).

Relief by an Independent Action

Litigants may seek relief from a judgment or order by filing an "independent action," a proceeding that sounds in equity.[182] Independent actions are distinct from a motion under Rule 60(a) or Rule 60(b).[183] They are permitted in only exceptional cases to prevent grave miscarriages of justice.[184] An independent action may be maintained where:

(1) the judgment should not, in good conscience, be enforced;
(2) a good defense exists to the plaintiff's lawsuit;
(3) fraud, accident, or mistake prevented the defendant from obtaining the benefit of the good defense;
(4) the defendant is free of fault and negligence; *and*
(5) there is no adequate remedy at law.[185]

The Rule 60(c) time limits do not apply to independent actions in equity[186] (although courts are wary—but not necessarily prohibitive—of litigants using independent actions to avoid timeliness problems in what could otherwise be a Rule 60(b) motion).[187] If the independent action is filed in the same court that granted the judgment, ancillary jurisdiction exists—regardless of diversity or federal question jurisdiction.[188] Absent prejudice, a mislabeled independent action may be treated as a

[182]*See U.S. v. Beggerly*, 524 U.S. 38, 118 S. Ct. 1862, 141 L. Ed. 2d 32 (1998); *Mitchell v. Rees*, 651 F.3d 593, 594 (6th Cir. 2011).

[183]*See Herring v. U.S.*, 424 F.3d 384, 389 (3d Cir. 2005).

[184]*See U.S. v. Beggerly*, 524 U.S. 38, 118 S. Ct. 1862, 141 L. Ed. 2d 32 (1998); *Gillis v. Chase*, 894 F.3d 1, 3–4 (1st Cir. 2018).

[185]*See Aldana v. Del Monte Fresh Produce N.A., Inc.*, 741 F.3d 1349, 1359 (11th Cir. 2014); *Mitchell v. Rees*, 651 F.3d 593, 595 (6th Cir. 2011).

[186]*See Park West Galleries, Inc. v. Hochman*, 692 F.3d 539, 545 (6th Cir. 2012); *Robinson v. Volkswagenwerk AG*, 56 F.3d 1268, 1274 (10th Cir. 1995).

[187]*See Turner v. Pleasant*, 663 F.3d 770, 775–76 (5th Cir. 2011); *Mitchell v. Rees*, 651 F.3d 593, 597 (6th Cir. 2011).

[188]*See U.S. v. Beggerly*, 524 U.S. 38, 42–48, 118 S. Ct. 1862, 141 L. Ed. 2d 32 (1998); *Cresswell v. Sullivan & Cromwell*, 922 F.2d 60, 70 (2d Cir. 1990).

Rule 60(b) motion, and vice versa.[189]

Relief by Section 1655 of the U.S. Judiciary Code

Congress has, by statute, created a procedure for the enforcement and removal of liens, incumbrances, and clouds upon title to real or personal property. The statute provides a means for notifying the affected defendant of the pending proceeding. Defendants who do not receive prior notification may act within 1 year to have the judgment lifted and appear to defend (provided they pay any costs assessed by the court).[190]

Relief Due to Fraud on the Court

Finally, the district court also possesses the inherent power, grounded in equity, to grant relief where the judgment or order is obtained through a fraud on the court.[191] Since a ruling procured through fraud is not a true ruling at all,[192] no specific time limits apply,[193] provided relief is sought within a reasonable time.[194] The court may grant the relief on its own initiative or on motion. (Relief from this type of fraud requires a level of severity "several notches" above what is needed under Rule 60(b)(3)).[195] Movants bear the demanding burden of showing extraordinary circumstances.[196] Such fraud must be proven by clear and convincing evidence.[197] To constitute a fraud on the court, the alleged misconduct must be something more than fraud among the litigants.[198] Instead, the misconduct must be an assault on the integrity of the judicial process, which defiles the court itself or is perpetrated by officers of the court in such a manner that the impartial system of justice fails to function.[199] The misconduct must also have been unknown at the time the

---

[189] *See Mitchell v. Rees*, 651 F.3d 593, 595 (6th Cir. 2011); *United States v. Demjanjuk*, 838 F. Supp. 2d 616, 626 (N.D.Ohio 2011).

[190] *See* 28 U.S.C.A. § 1655.

[191] *Universal Oil Products Co. v. Root Refining Co.*, 328 U.S. 575, 66 S. Ct. 1176, 90 L. Ed. 1447 (1946); *Hazel-Atlas Glass Co. v. Hartford-Empire Co.*, 322 U.S. 238, 64 S. Ct. 997, 88 L. Ed. 1250 (1944).

[192] *See U.S. v. Williams*, 790 F.3d 1059, 1071 (10th Cir. 2015).

[193] *See Torres v. Bella Vista Hosp., Inc.*, 914 F.3d 15, 17–18 (1st Cir. 2019); *Kennedy v. Schneider Elec.*, 893 F.3d 414, 418 (7th Cir. 2018).

[194] *See Apotex Corp. v. Merck & Co.*, 507 F.3d 1357, 1361 (Fed.Cir.2007).

[195] *See Giasson Aerospace Sci., Inc. v. RCO Eng'g Inc.*, 872 F.3d 336, 340 (6th Cir. 2017).

[196] *See Trendsettah USA, Inc. v. Swisher Int'l, Inc.*, 31 F.4th 1124, 1132 (9th Cir. 2022) ("high standard").

[197] *See Trendsettah USA, Inc. v. Swisher Int'l, Inc.*, 31 F.4th 1124, 1132 (9th Cir. 2022); *Wickens v. Shell Oil Co.*, 620 F.3d 747, 759 (7th Cir. 2010).

[198] *See Fox ex rel. Fox v. Elk Run Coal Co.*, 739 F.3d 131, 136 (4th Cir. 2014); *Superior Seafoods, Inc. v. Tyson Foods, Inc.*, 620 F.3d 873, 878 (8th Cir. 2010).

[199] *See Hazel-Atlas Glass Co. v. Hartford-Empire Co.*, 322 U.S. 238, 245–46, 64 S. Ct. 997, 88 L. Ed. 1250 (1944); *Trendsettah USA, Inc. v. Swisher Int'l, Inc.*, 31 F.4th 1124, 1132 (9th Cir. 2022).

court acted[200] and must cause such prejudice to the moving party,[201] affecting the outcome of the case,[202] that it would be manifestly unconscionable to permit the judgment to remain.[203] Thus, the moving party must generally show (1) an officer of the court (2) committing an intentional fraud (3) directed against the court itself (4) which, in fact, succeeds in deceiving that court.[204] Fraud in the discovery process, to the extent it meets this standard, can support relief.[205]

RULE 60(e)—BILLS AND WRITS ABOLISHED

CORE CONCEPT

The old common law writs of coram nobis, coram vobis, audita querela, and bills of review are abolished in civil proceedings.[206] Filings under these ancient writs may be treated by the courts as motions for relief under Rule 60(b).[207]

Impact of 2007 "Restyling" Amendments

In 2007, the last sentence of former Rule 60(b) was repositioned to current Rule 60(e).

Many Such Writs Preserved in Criminal Cases

Although abolished by the Rules for civil cases, many such writs exist in criminal proceedings.[208]

---

[200] *See United States v. Sierra Pac. Indus., Inc.*, 862 F.3d 1157, 1168 (9th Cir. 2017). *See also Hazel-Atlas Glass Co. v. Hartford-Empire Co.*, 322 U.S. 238, 244, 64 S. Ct. 997, 88 L. Ed. 1250 (1944) ("after-discovered fraud").

[201] *See Wickens v. Shell Oil Co.*, 620 F.3d 747, 759 (7th Cir. 2010).

[202] *See United States v. Sierra Pac. Indus., Inc.*, 862 F.3d 1157, 1168 (9th Cir. 2017).

[203] *See Superior Seafoods, Inc. v. Tyson Foods, Inc.*, 620 F.3d 873, 878 (8th Cir. 2010).

[204] *See Carter v. Anderson*, 585 F.3d 1007, 1011 (6th Cir. 2009); *Herring v. United States*, 424 F.3d 384, 386 (3d Cir.2005).

[205] *See Appling v. State Farm Mut. Auto. Ins. Co.*, 340 F.3d 769, 780 (9th Cir. 2003).

[206] At the old common law, a writ of coram nobis (if sought at the King's Bench) or writ of coram vobis (if sought in the Courts of Common Pleas) were the procedural tools to correct errors of fact by petitioning to bring before the court certain facts which, if known earlier, would have prevented the entry of judgment. *See Rawlins v. Kansas*, 714 F.3d 1189, 1193–95 (10th Cir. 2013). A person against whom execution has issued or was about to issue could seek a writ of audita querela to prevent execution where the execution would be contrary to justice. *See id.* at 1192–93. Finally, a bill of review was a new action, filed in equity, that sought the correction, reversal, alteration, or explanation of a decree issued in an earlier proceeding. *See* 27A Am. Jur. 2d Equity § 256 (1996). Each of these ancient writs has been abolished—in civil actions only—by this Rule. *See* Rule 60(e).

[207] *See Green v. White*, 319 F.3d 560, 563 n.1 (3d Cir. 2003) (treating request for writ in nature of coram nobis as motion under Rule 60(b)).

[208] *See United States v. Wilkozek*, 822 F.3d 364, 368 (7th Cir. 2016) (coram nobis preserved in criminal cases); *Massey v. U.S.*, 581 F.3d 172, 174 (3d Cir. 2009) (same, audita querela).

Additional Research References

Wright & Miller, *Federal Practice and Procedure* §§ 2851 to 73
C.J.S., Federal Civil Procedure § 368, § 373, §§ 1233 to 1251 et seq.
West's Key Number Digest, Federal Civil Procedure ⚷613.1 to 613.20, ⚷2641 to 2663

RULE 61
HARMLESS ERROR

Unless justice requires otherwise, no error in admitting or excluding evidence—or any other error by the court or a party—is ground for granting a new trial, for setting aside a verdict, or for vacating, modifying, or otherwise disturbing a judgment or order. At every stage of the proceeding, the court must disregard all errors and defects that do not affect any party's substantial rights.

[Amended April 30, 2007, effective December 1, 2007.]

AUTHORS' COMMENTARY ON RULE 61

PURPOSE AND SCOPE

No matter how careful and conscientious the district judge might be, how attentive to every small detail in a case, errors can still occur. But not every trial error requires reversal, vacation, or a new trial. Instead, trial errors that do not affect a litigant's substantial rights must be disregarded by the trial judge (and, later, on appeal).

APPLICATIONS

Standard for "Harmlessness"

Rule 61 directs that errors, at all stages of the case, "must" be disregarded if they do not affect the parties' substantial rights (*i.e.*, if they are "harmless"). The Rule does not further define harmlessness, and the Supreme Court has cautioned against invoking "mandatory presumptions and rigid rules" to detect it.[1] Instead, the Court prefers "case-specific application of judgment."[2] Over the years, judges have largely been guided by a discussion of harmlessness from the criminal, statutory context, where the Court once perceived the "very plain admonition" of harmlessness as this: "Do not be technical, where technicality does not really hurt the party whose rights in the

[1]*See Shinseki v. Sanders*, 556 U.S. 396, 407, 129 S. Ct. 1696, 173 L. Ed. 2d 532 (2009).

[2]*See Shinseki v. Sanders*, 556 U.S. 396, 407, 129 S. Ct. 1696, 173 L. Ed. 2d 532 (2009).

trial and in its outcome the technicality affects."[3] Cautious about over-defining the term,[4] the Court offered two guides: if there is a sure conviction that the error did not influence, or "had but very slight effect" on, the jury, the error is harmless; but harmlessness is absent "if one cannot say, with fair assurance, after pondering all that happened without stripping the erroneous action from the whole, that the judgment was not substantially swayed by the error."[5] A more exacting definition is probably impossible, just as it is impossible to ignore the subjectivity inherent in the inquiry itself.[6] In testing for harmlessness, courts consider the entire record and assess on a case-by-case basis.[7] Every reasonable possibility of prejudice need not be disproved,[8] but harmlessness cannot be founded merely on a belief that the trial ended in a correct result.[9] Unsurprisingly, this risk of prejudice is considered greater in close cases than in more one-sided cases.[10]

Burden of Proof

The party moving for relief bears the burden of establishing that a trial error affected that party's substantial rights and, thus, was not harmless.[11] (Note, however, that the standard for harmlessness (as articulated by some courts) seems to suppose

---

[3]*See Kotteakos v. United States*, 328 U.S. 750, 759–60, 66 S. Ct. 1239, 90 L. Ed. 1557 (1946) (explaining that principle developed in era where trials had become "a game for sowing reversible error").

[4]*See Kotteakos v. United States*, 328 U.S. 750, 761, 66 S. Ct. 1239, 90 L. Ed. 1557 (1946) ("the discrimination it requires is one of judgment transcending confinement by formula or precise rule").

[5]*See Kotteakos v. United States*, 328 U.S. 750, 764–65, 66 S. Ct. 1239, 90 L. Ed. 1557 (1946). The Circuits have reformulated this inquiry in various, often seemingly inconsistent ways. *See, e.g., Bridges v. Wilson*, 996 F.3d 1094, 1099 (10th Cir. 2021) ("had a substantial influence or which leaves one in grave doubt as to whether it had such an effect on the outcome"); *Macsherry v. Sparrows Point, LLC*, 973 F.3d 212, 225 (4th Cir. 2020) (able to say, with "fair assurance," that judgment was not "substantially swayed" by error); *United States v. Johnson*, 860 F.3d 1133, 1139 (8th Cir. 2017) ("more than slight influence" on verdict); *Langbord v. U.S. Dep't of Treasury*, 832 F.3d 170, 196 (3d Cir. 2016) (en banc) (not harmless if "high probability" error did not contribute to verdict).

[6]*See U.S. v. O'Keefe*, 169 F.3d 281, 287 n. 5 (5th Cir. 1999). *Cf.* ROGER TRAYNOR, THE RIDDLE OF HARMLESS ERROR 35 (1970) ("[U]nless the appellate court believes it highly probable that the error did not affect the judgment, it should reverse").

[7]*See Bridges v. Wilson*, 996 F.3d 1094, 1099 (10th Cir. 2021); *Texas Advanced Optoelectronic Sols., Inc. v. Renesas Elecs. Am., Inc.*, 895 F.3d 1304, 1316 (Fed. Cir. 2018).

[8]*See General Motors Corp. v. New A.C. Chevrolet, Inc.*, 263 F.3d 296, 329 (3d Cir. 2001).

[9]*See Matusick v. Erie County Water Auth.*, 757 F.3d 31, 50–51 (2d Cir. 2014).

[10]*See Sims v. Great American Life Ins. Co.*, 469 F.3d 870, 886 (10th Cir. 2006).

[11]*See Palmer v. Hoffman*, 318 U.S. 109, 116, 63 S. Ct. 477, 87 L. Ed. 645 (1943). *See also Shinseki v. Sanders*, 556 U.S. 396, 409–10, 129 S. Ct. 1696, 173 L. Ed. 2d 532 (2009) (construing federal harmless error statute, 28 U.S.C.A. § 2111).

that harm may be presumed, rather than proved).[12]

Federal Law Controls

Under *Erie* principles,[13] the federal (not State) construction of the harmless error rule usually controls where the federal and State standards are inconsistent.[14]

Applies to All Errors

The harmless error rule applies to all types of errors, including most constitutional errors. The courts of appeals review rulings of the district courts under this standard as well.[15]

Errors in Rulings on Pleadings

Technical errors in pleadings will generally be discounted as harmless.[16]

Errors in Rulings on Motions

The same "substantial rights" standard applies to errors in ruling upon motions.[17] Thus, for example, an improper striking of an amended complaint was harmless if the proposed amendment would not have prevented a dismissal;[18] an improper dismissal of a claim was harmless if, in light of later discovery, it would not have survived summary judgment;[19] an improper grant of intervention was harmless if the intervenor's participa-

---

[12]*Compare Sims v. Great American Life Ins. Co.*, 469 F.3d 870, 886 (10th Cir. 2006) (must reverse unless jury's verdict was, more probably than not, unaffected by error) *with Coterel v. Dorel Juvenile Grp., Inc.*, 827 F.3d 804, 808 (8th Cir. 2016) (with only general verdict, plaintiffs could not prove that evidentiary errors were cause of their jury loss) *and Ball v. LeBlanc*, 792 F.3d 584, 591 (5th Cir. 2015) (presumes errors are harmless).

[13]*See Erie R. Co. v. Tompkins*, 304 U.S. 64, 58 S. Ct. 817, 82 L. Ed. 1188 (1938) (in diversity cases, federal courts apply federal procedure but State substantive law). *See* discussion of *Erie* Doctrine in Part II of this text.

[14]*See Hall v. Flannery*, 840 F.3d 922, 931 (7th Cir. 2016).

[15]*See* 28 U.S.C.A. § 2111 (fixing harmlessness standard for appeals). *See also McDonough Power Equipment, Inc. v. Greenwood*, 464 U.S. 548, 554, 104 S. Ct. 845, 78 L. Ed. 2d 663 (1984) (appellate courts must act in accordance with salutary policy embodied in Rule 61).

[16]*See White v. City of Chicago*, 829 F.3d 837, 844 (7th Cir. 2016) (error on pleading sufficiency deemed harmless); *Toth v. Corning Glass Works*, 411 F.2d 912, 914 (6th Cir.1969) (refusal to strike a pleading's claim deemed harmless).

[17]*See, e.g., Knight through Kerr v. Miami-Dade Cty.*, 856 F.3d 795, 807 (11th Cir. 2017) (new trial motion); *Baker Hughes Inc. v. S&S Chem., LLC*, 836 F.3d 554, 569–70 (6th Cir. 2016) (motion for summary judgment); *Citizens for Appropriate Rural Roads v. Foxx*, 815 F.3d 1068, 1079–80 (7th Cir. 2016) (motion to dismiss); *Alliance of Nonprofits for Ins., Risk Retention Group v. Kipper*, 712 F.3d 1316, 1327–28 (9th Cir. 2013) (motion for violating local rule); *Lore v. City of Syracuse*, 670 F.3d 127, 150 (2d Cir. 2012) (motions for judgment as a matter of law).

[18]*See Lopez v. Target Corp.*, 676 F.3d 1230, 1232 n.3 (11th Cir. 2012).

[19]*See Elkharwily v. Mayo Holding Co.*, 823 F.3d 462, 469 (8th Cir. 2016).

tion was inconsequential;[20] an improper dismissal of co-defendants was harmless if recovery from them was otherwise barred;[21] an improper grant of summary judgment was harmless if the verdict on claims later tried proved that the terminated claims would have failed too;[22] an improper scope of a summary judgment ruling[23] or improper consideration (or exclusion) of summary judgment affidavits and exhibits[24] was harmless where, in context, the effect could not have been prejudicial; and a reliance on clearly erroneous facts in denying a motion to decertify a class action[25] or in making a fees award[26] was harmless when other, properly found facts justified those rulings.

Errors in Admitting or Excluding Evidence

The district court enjoys broad discretion to admit or exclude evidence,[27] including expert[28] and rebuttal[29] evidence. Errors in such rulings are harmless if the party raises no objection[30] or "invited" the error through earlier questioning of a witness,[31] if the evidence wrongfully admitted or excluded was cumulative,[32] if other, uncontested evidence was sufficiently robust to support the judgment,[33] if adequate curative instructions are given,[34] or if the rulings are otherwise determined not to have caused substantial prejudice or to have substantially

---

[20]*See Prete v. Bradbury*, 438 F.3d 949, 959–60 (9th Cir. 2006).

[21]*See Bates v. City of Chicago*, 726 F.3d 951, 958 (7th Cir. 2013).

[22]*See Gareis v. 3M Co.*, 9 F.4th 812, 818–19 (8th Cir. 2021).

[23]*See Broadcast Music, Inc. v. Evie's Tavern Ellenton, Inc.*, 772 F.3d 1254, 1258 (11th Cir. 2014).

[24]*See Baker Hughes Inc. v. S&S Chem., LLC*, 836 F.3d 554, 569–70 (6th Cir. 2016); *S.E.C. v. Smart*, 678 F.3d 850, 856 (10th Cir. 2012).

[25]*See In re Samsung Top-Load Washing Mach. Mktg., Sales Pracs. & Prod. Liab. Litig.*, 997 F.3d 1077, 1093 (10th Cir. 2021).

[26]*See Dobbs v. DePuy Orthopaedics, Inc.*, 885 F.3d 455, 458 (7th Cir. 2018).

[27]*See Davis v. Velez*, 797 F.3d 192, 201 (2d Cir. 2015); *Jones v. Nat'l Am. Univ.*, 608 F.3d 1039, 1044 (8th Cir. 2010).

[28]*See Dresser-Rand Co. v. Virtual Automation Inc.*, 361 F.3d 831, 842 (5th Cir. 2004).

[29]*See Peals v. Terre Haute Police Dept.*, 535 F.3d 621, 630 (7th Cir. 2008).

[30]*See Leonard v. Stemtech Int'l Inc.*, 834 F.3d 376, 400–01 (3d Cir. 2016).

[31]*See Patterson v. Baker*, 990 F.3d 1082, 1086 (7th Cir. 2021).

[32]*See Jensen v. Solvay Chems., Inc.*, 721 F.3d 1180, 1184 (10th Cir. 2013); *Jordan v. Binns*, 712 F.3d 1123, 1137 (7th Cir. 2013).

[33]*See Langbord v. U.S. Dep't of Treasury*, 832 F.3d 170, 196–98 (3d Cir. 2016) (en banc).

[34]*See Grizzle v. Travelers Health Network, Inc.*, 14 F.3d 261, 269 (5th Cir. 1994) (court must consider curative instructions when assessing harmlessness). In ruling on the effect of the curative instructions, a court will assume that the jury obeyed the court and followed its instructions. *See also Trademark Research Corp. v. Maxwell Online, Inc.*, 995 F.2d 326, 340 (2d Cir. 1993). *Compare Davidson v. Smith*, 9 F.3d 4, 6 (2d Cir.1993) (improper testimony not cured by trial instructions) *with Trademark Research Corp. v. Maxwell Online, Inc.*, 995 F.2d 326, 331 (2d Cir.1993) (trial error deemed cured by court's instructions).

influenced the jury.[35] However, evidentiary rulings that affected the substantial rights of a party are *not* harmless, and the rulings must be reversed.[36] In making this "harmlessness" evaluation, the court views the error in light of the entire record.[37] The court considers the centrality of the evidence and the prejudicial effect of the inclusion or exclusion of the evidence.[38] The court also examines whether other evidence is "sufficiently strong" to support a conclusion that the evidentiary error had no effect on the outcome.[39] If the properly admitted evidence is not sufficient to support the verdict, the wrongful admission of evidence is not harmless.[40] Some courts begin with a "presumption of prejudice"[41] — thus, only if the court can say with fair assurance that the judgment was not substantially affected by the wrongfully admitted or excluded evidence, will the error be considered harmless.[42] Other courts seem to adopt the opposite approach.[43] The courts are particularly careful in discounting an error as harmless in close cases,[44] or where the evidence was "substantively important, inflammatory, repeated, emphasized, or unfairly self-serving."[45]

- *Effect of Multiple Errors:* Although each individual evidentiary error might not, standing alone, have affected a party's substantial rights, the court may find that the

---

[35]*See Stroup v. United Airlines, Inc.*, 26 F.4th 1147, 1168–72 (10th Cir. 2022) (contested emotional distress testimony was harmless because, in context, it was unlikely to have impacted jury); *S. Grande View Dev. Co., Inc. v. City of Alabaster*, 1 F.4th 1299, 1312 (11th Cir. 2021) (improperly admitted municipal motive evidence in just compensation case was harmless where, in context, it caused "no demonstrable effect on the ultimate verdict or other prejudice"); *Frye v. CSX Transp., Inc.*, 933 F.3d 591, 604 (6th Cir. 2019) (exclusion of photographs was harmless where relevance related to issue on which jury found in moving party's favor).

[36]*See Macsherry v. Sparrows Point, LLC*, 973 F.3d 212, 225–26 (4th Cir. 2020); *Hall v. Flannery*, 840 F.3d 922, 926–31 (7th Cir. 2016).

[37]*See Jordan v. Binns*, 712 F.3d 1123, 1137 (7th Cir. 2013).

[38]*See Standley v. Edmonds-Leach*, 783 F.3d 1276, 1284 (D.C.Cir. 2015); *Jordan v. Binns*, 712 F.3d 1123, 1137 (7th Cir. 2013).

[39]*See Jordan v. Binns*, 712 F.3d 1123, 1137 (7th Cir. 2013); *Goebel v. Denver and Rio Grande Western R.R. Co.*, 215 F.3d 1083, 1089 (10th Cir. 2000).

[40]*See S.E.C. v. Happ*, 392 F.3d 12, 28 (1st Cir. 2004); *Havrum v. U.S.*, 204 F.3d 815, 818 (8th Cir. 2000).

[41]*See Jerden v. Amstutz*, 430 F.3d 1231, 1240–41 (9th Cir. 2005).

[42]*See Barber v. City of Chicago*, 725 F.3d 702, 715 (7th Cir. 2013); *Guillemard-Ginorio v. Contreras-Gomez*, 585 F.3d 508, 534 (1st Cir. 2009).

[43]*See Stroup v. United Airlines, Inc.*, 26 F.4th 1147, 1170 (10th Cir. 2022) (movant "fails to give us persuasive grounds—based on the record before us—on which to conclude that the jury would have reached a different outcome had it *not* heard such testimony"); *Coterel v. Dorel Juvenile Grp., Inc.*, 827 F.3d 804, 808 (8th Cir. 2016) (with only general verdict, plaintiffs could not show evidentiary errors were cause of jury loss).

[44]*See Huthnance v. District of Columbia*, 722 F.3d 371, 381 (D.C.Cir. 2013); *Sims v. Great Am. Life Ins. Co.*, 469 F.3d 870, 886 (10th Cir. 2006).

[45]*See Doty v. Sewall*, 908 F.2d 1053, 1057 (1st Cir.1990).

collective effect of multiple evidentiary errors deprived the moving party of a fair trial.[46]

- *Manner of Presentation:* The harmlessness standard also applies to rulings on the manner in which evidence is presented or displayed to the jury.[47]

Error in Granting or Denying Jury Trial

The court's mistaken decision to grant a jury trial is generally harmless error,[48] but an improper denial of a jury trial is usually grounds for reversal.[49]

Errors in Seating Jurors

Errors in striking or refusing to strike prospective jurors are also measured under the harmless error standard.[50]

Errors in Jury Instructions

Jury instructions must be considered in their entirety.[51] If the charging errors would not have changed the trial result,[52] or if the parties waived the errors by failing to timely object,[53] challenges to jury instructions will be rejected as harmless.[54] Conversely, if the jury may have based their verdict on an erroneous instruction,[55] or if the instruction was otherwise

---

[46]*See Ward v. AutoZoners, LLC*, 958 F.3d 254, 273–74 & n.7 (4th Cir. 2020) (surveying Circuit division on cumulative-error doctrine in civil context).

[47]*See Miller v. Greenleaf Orthopedic Assocs., S.C.*, 827 F.3d 569, 575 (7th Cir. 2016).

[48]*See Mateyko v. Felix*, 924 F.2d 824, 828 (9th Cir. 1990). *See also Venture Properties, Inc. v. First Southern Bank*, 79 F.3d 90, 92 (8th Cir. 1996) (movant demonstrated no prejudice from court's decision to conduct a jury trial rather than a bench trial).

[49]*See Burns v. Lawther*, 53 F.3d 1237, 1241–42 (11th Cir. 1995) (harmless error rule may be applied to improper denials of trial by jury, but only if issues could have been resolved by summary judgment or judgment as matter of law); *King v. United Ben. Fire Ins. Co.*, 377 F.2d 728, 731 (10th Cir. 1967) (denial harmless where only question of law involved or where verdict for movant would have been set aside). *See also Sailor v. Hubbell, Inc.*, 4 F.3d 323, 324 (4th Cir.1993) (denial harmless if it did not affect party's rights, such as where no reasonable jury could have found in party's favor).

[50]*See Alaska Rent-A-Car, Inc. v. Avis Budget Group, Inc.*, 709 F.3d 872, 880 (9th Cir. 2013); *Avichail ex rel. T.A. v. St. John's Mercy Health Sys.*, 686 F.3d 548, 553 (8th Cir. 2012).

[51]*See American Family Mut. Ins. Co. v. Hollander*, 705 F.3d 339, 355–56 (8th Cir. 2013); *Gonzales v. Duran*, 590 F.3d 855, 862 (10th Cir. 2009).

[52]*See Czekalski v. LaHood*, 589 F.3d 449, 453 (D.C.Cir. 2009) (only if prejudicial); *Richards v. Relentless, Inc.*, 341 F.3d 35, 48 (1st Cir. 2003) (only if instruction error could have affected jury's deliberation).

[53]*See Tatum v. Moody*, 768 F.3d 806, 820 n.9 (9th Cir. 2014). *See generally Foley v. Commonwealth Elec. Co.*, 312 F.3d 517, 520 (1st Cir. 2002) (if party properly objects to jury instruction, harmless error Rule 61 applies).

[54]*See Mejias-Aguayo v. Doreste-Rodriguez*, 863 F.3d 50, 57 (1st Cir. 2017); *Helmer v. Goodyear Tire & Rubber Co.*, 828 F.3d 1195, 1199–200 (10th Cir. 2016).

[55]*See Ericsson, Inc. v. D-Link Sys., Inc.*, 773 F.3d 1201, 1235 (Fed.Cir. 2014); *Biegas v. Quickway Carriers,*

prejudicially misleading, confusing, or legally incorrect,[56] or affected a party's substantial rights,[57] a new trial is warranted.

Errors in Jury Verdict Form Interrogatories

Whether mistakes in crafting jury interrogatories on the verdict form is deemed reversible error will also be measured under the harmless error standard.[58]

Errors During / After Jury Deliberations

Mistakes in permitting juror examination of exhibits (including those admitted for demonstrative purposes only)[59] or in recalling a discharged jury for further deliberations[60] are tested under the harmless error standard.

Errors in Ruling on Counsel's Conduct During Trial

Misconduct by counsel during trial will be deemed harmless unless the court determines that the misconduct affected the verdict,[61] as will errors in permitting inappropriate counsel invitations for jury participation in a trial demonstration.[62] In testing errors occurring during argument by counsel, the court will assess (1) the argument's nature and seriousness, (2) if the opponent invited the argument, (3) if the argument could be rebutted effectively, (4) effective curative instructions, and (5) the weight of the evidence.[63]

Errors in Bench Judgments

In bench trials, errors are harmless if the record shows that the district judge would have reached the same judgment regardless of the error.[64] Thus, a judge's mistaken application of a certain method of damages valuation (one to which there

---

Inc., 573 F.3d 365, 377 (6th Cir. 2009).

[56]*See Freudeman v. Landing of Canton*, 702 F.3d 318, 324–25 (6th Cir. 2012); *Costa-Urena v. Segarra*, 590 F.3d 18, 24 (1st Cir. 2009).

[57]*See Kogut v. County of Nassau*, 789 F.3d 36, 47 (2d Cir. 2015); *Huthnance v. District of Columbia*, 722 F.3d 371, 377 (D.C.Cir. 2013).

[58]*See Helmer v. Goodyear Tire & Rubber Co.*, 828 F.3d 1195, 1199–1200 (10th Cir. 2016); *Happel v. Walmart Stores, Inc.*, 602 F.3d 820, 826–28 (7th Cir.2010).

[59]*See Baugh ex rel. Baugh v. Cuprum S.A. de C.V.*, 730 F.3d 701, 710–11 (7th Cir. 2013).

[60]*See Dietz v. Bouldin*, 579 U.S. —, 136 S. Ct. 1885, 1891–97, 195 L. Ed. 2d 161 (2016).

[61]*Cf.* Rule 39(c) (relating to advisory juries). *See Peterson v. Willie*, 81 F.3d 1033, 1036 (11th Cir. 1996) (statements made during oral arguments not reversible error unless plainly unwarranted and clearly injurious); *Westfarm Associates Ltd. Partnership v. Washington Suburban Sanitary Com'n*, 66 F.3d 669, 685 (4th Cir. 1995) (inappropriate allusion during closing argument, followed by proper instructions, not basis for reversal).

[62]*See Noel v. Artson*, 641 F.3d 580, 592 (4th Cir. 2011).

[63]*See Stollings v. Ryobi Techs., Inc.*, 725 F.3d 753, 760 (7th Cir. 2013). *See also Osterhout v. Bd. of Cnty. Commissioners of LeFlore Cnty.*, 10 F.4th 978, 989 (10th Cir. 2021) (must pervasiveness of misconduct, boundaries of evidentiary rulings, court's action to sustain objection, and curative instructions).

[64]*See United States v. AT&T, Inc.*, 916 F.3d 1029, 1046–47 (D.C. Cir. 2019); *Barber v. Ruth*, 7 F.3d 636, 641 (7th Cir. 1993).

was no testimony or other record basis) will be deemed harmless if the effect of the error caused no prejudice.[65]

Additional Research References

Wright & Miller, *Federal Practice and Procedure* §§ 2881 to 88
C.J.S., Federal Civil Procedure §§ 1062 to 1100 et seq., §§ 1241 to 1247 et seq.
West's Key Number Digest, Federal Civil Procedure ⚷2333 to 2353, ⚷2651 to 2663; Federal Courts ⚷891 to 914

---

[65] *See U.S. v. 191.07 Acres of Land*, 482 F.3d 1132, 1137 (9th Cir. 2007) (valuation error harmless because it resulted in higher award than appellants (using other method) would otherwise have received).

RULE 62
STAY OF PROCEEDINGS TO ENFORCE A JUDGMENT

(a) Automatic Stay. Except as provided in Rule 62(c) and (d), execution on a judgment and proceedings to enforce it are stayed for 30 days after its entry, unless the court orders otherwise.

(b) Stay by Bond or Other Security. At any time after judgment is entered, a party may obtain a stay by providing a bond or other security. The stay takes effect when the court approves the bond or other security and remains in effect for the time specified in the bond or other security.

(c) Stay of an Injunction, Receivership, or Patent Accounting Order. Unless the court orders otherwise, the following are not stayed after being entered, even if an appeal is taken:

(1) an interlocutory or final judgment in an action for an injunction or receivership; or

(2) a judgment or order that directs an accounting in an action for patent infringement.

(d) Injunction Pending an Appeal. While an appeal is pending from an interlocutory order or final judgment that grants, continues, modifies, refuses, dissolves, or refuses to dissolve or modify an injunction, the court may suspend, modify, restore, or grant an injunction on terms for bond or other terms that secure the opposing party's rights. If the judgment appealed from is rendered by a statutory three-judge district court, the order must be made either:

(1) by that court sitting in open session; or

(2) by the assent of all its judges, as evidenced by their signatures.

(e) Stay Without Bond on an Appeal by the United States, Its Officers, or Its Agencies. The court must not require a bond, obligation, or other security from the appellant when granting a stay on an appeal by the United States, its officers, or its agencies or on an appeal directed by a department of the federal government.

(f) Stay in Favor of a Judgment Debtor Under State Law. If a judgment is a lien on the judgment debtor's property under the law of the state where the court is located, the judgment debtor is entitled to the same stay of execution the state court would give.

(g) Appellate Court's Power Not Limited. This rule does not limit the power of the appellate court or one of its judges or justices:

(1) to stay proceedings—or suspend, modify, restore, or grant an injunction—while an appeal is pending; or

(2) to issue an order to preserve the status quo or the effectiveness of the judgment to be entered.

(h) Stay with Multiple Claims or Parties. A court may stay the enforcement of a final judgment entered under Rule 54(b) until it enters a later judgment or judgments, and may prescribe terms necessary to secure the benefit of the stayed judgment for the party in whose favor it was entered.

[Amended March 19, 1948; Oct. 20, 1949; July 19, 1961; Aug. 1, 1987; Dec. 1, 2007; As amended Dec. 1, 2009; Apr. 26, 2018, eff. Dec. 1, 2018.]

AUTHORS' COMMENTARY ON RULE 62

PURPOSE AND SCOPE

A final judgment in a federal civil case determines the litigants' rights and obligations. Whether by jury verdict, bench trial ruling, or otherwise, the judgment in the case declares the winners and losers on the issues litigated. The general rule in federal court is that such a judgment normally takes effect regardless of whether post-trial motions are pending or an appeal is intended or even filed—unless that judgment has been "stayed." Rule 62 provides the procedure for issuing "stays" of a judgment's execution and enforcement following the judgment's entry.

RULE 62(a)—AUTOMATIC STAY

CORE CONCEPT

To provide litigants a brief period to assess their next steps following the entry of a final judgment in their lawsuit, most federal civil judgments cannot be executed upon or enforced for 30 days following their entry—unless the court or another Rule provides otherwise. This 30-day stay occurs automatically, without court order or motion by any party.

APPLICATIONS

Postponement Effect

The 30-day automatic stay postpones the execution or enforcement of the judgment (in other words, a money judgment cannot be executed upon nor an injunction decree enforced),[1] unless the law or the judge provides otherwise.[2] The automatic stay does not affect whether the losing party can appeal the judgment or the running of the time for taking an appeal. Nor does the stay impact the judgment's *res judicata* effect.[3] Although there is little authority on point, it appears that for purposes of stays under Rule 62(a), time is computed using the methodology established in Rule 6(a).[4] The winning party may also request that the automatic 30-day stay be dissolved to prevent a defaulting party from potentially hiding assets during that period.[5]

Expiration of Stay Period

Once the 30-day automatic stay period expires, a party may seek the execution or enforcement of the judgment unless another subpart of Rule 62 provides otherwise.[6] If, there is no stay in place, the district court has jurisdiction to enforce its judgment.[7]

Armed Services Personnel

The Soldiers and Sailors Civil Relief Act of 1940[8] provides that a court may stay the execution of any judgment, or vacate or stay an attachment or garnishment, entered against a person in the military service.

---

[1] *See* Rule 62(a) advisory committee note (2018). *See also, e.g., In re High Sulfur Content Gasoline Prods. Liab. Litig.*, 517 F.3d 220 (5th Cir. 2008).

[2] *See Est. of Casillas v. City of Fresno*, 471 F. Supp. 3d 1035, 1036 (E.D. Cal. 2020).

[3] *See, e.g., Fish Market Nominee Corp. v. Pelofsky*, 72 F.3d 4, 7 (1st Cir. 1995).

[4] *See, e.g., KRW Sales, Inc. v. Kristel Corp.*, 154 F.R.D. 186, 188 (N.D. Ill. 1994).

[5] *Kelly Toys Holdings, LLC v. alialialiLL Store*, ___ F. Supp. 3d ___, 2022 WL 1948311, at *11 (S.D.N.Y. 2022).

[6] *See, e.g., Acevedo-Garcia v. Vera-Monroig*, 368 F.3d 49, 58 (1st Cir. 2004).

[7] *See, e.g., United States Commodity Futures Trading Commission v. Escobio*, 946 F.3d 1242 (11th Cir. 2020).

[8] *See* 50 U.S.C.A. §§ 203 to 04, App. §§ 523 to 24.

RULE 62(b)—STAY BY BOND OR OTHER SECURITY

CORE CONCEPT

The filing of post-trial motions or an appeal will not, by itself, suspend further the execution and enforcement of the contested judgment (that is, beyond the automatic stay of Rule 62(a)). Nevertheless, the movant/appellant can suspend the execution and enforcement of most judgments by posting a bond or other type of security to protect the victor during post-trial motions or an appeal, provided the bond is first approved by the district court.

APPLICATIONS

Stay Opportunity as of Right

Parties generally have the ability to obtain a further stay, beyond the stay granted automatically by Rule 62(a)[9]—provided those parties post a bond or other security with the court. Without such a stay, execution or enforcement of a federal judgment is ordinarily not delayed and can begin at the expiration of the automatic stay period.[10]

Timing

The stay authorized by this subpart takes effect when the court approves the bond or other security, and then remains in effect for the time specified in the bond or other security.

The Bond or Other Security Requirement

A bond posted to obtain a stay of execution or enforcement is usually known as a "supersedeas bond," the name of a traditional writ that was used to stay the execution of a legal judgment.[11] The bond amount will usually be set at a sum sufficient to satisfy the judgment plus the cost of interest, although the court may also require that the bond include costs and damages for delay. The court has the discretion to order a lesser bond amount or to authorize the posting of some other, different type of security.[12] Additionally, the court may order the movant to provide written notice to the opposing parties of any material disposition of the movant's assets. Failure to post a bond under this subpart will not affect a party's right to appeal, but, as noted, absent a stay, execution and enforcement can begin. An unsecured stay, which is a stay without either a

---

[9] *Crystallex Int'l Corp. v. Bolivarian Republic of Venezuela*, 24 F.4th 242, 256 (3d Cir. 2022).

[10] *See, e.g., Acevedo-Garcia v. Vera-Monroig*, 368 F.3d 49, 58 (1st Cir. 2004).

[11] *City of San Antonio, Texas v. Hotels.com, L. P.*, 141 S. Ct. 1628, 1632 (2021).

[12] *State Auto Prop. & Cas. Ins. Co. v. Sigismondi Foreign Car Specialists, Inc.*, __ F. Supp. 3d __, 2022 WL 518759, at *2 (E.D. Pa. 2022) (irrevocable letter of credit may be sufficient); *Gilead Cmty. Servs., Inc. v. Town of Cromwell*, __ F. Supp. 3d __, 2022 WL 1718036, at *5 (D. Conn. 2022) (including non-exhaustive list of factors district judge can consider in waiving bond requirement).

bond or other security, is reserved for unusual circumstances.[13]

District Court Discretion

A court has discretion to order a stay,[14] subject to the exceptions contained in Rule 62(c) and (d). The court also has discretion to establish conditions for the security of the adverse party during the pendency of the stay. Stays pending appeal constitute "extraordinary relief" on which the movant bears a heavy burden.[15]

Effect of Denial

When the court denies a stay pending disposition of a post-trial motion, the judgment is binding (and may be enforced) until vacated by the court or reversed on appeal.[16]

Procedure

Because the mere act of filing post-trial motions or an appeal does not stay execution or enforcement, litigants should file their motion for stay before the end of the automatic stay period. Once the motion for stay is made, the court has discretion to stay execution or enforcement of the judgment pending disposition of the post-trial motions.

RULE 62(c)—STAY OF AN INJUNCTION, RECEIVERSHIP, OR PATENT ACCOUNTING ORDER

CORE CONCEPT

Three categories of orders are exempted from being stayed, absent a further court order: (1) interlocutory or final judgments in actions for an injunction; (2) interlocutory or final judgment in actions for a receivership; and (3) judgments or orders directing an accounting in actions for infringement of patents.

APPLICATIONS

No Automatic Stays

Although most federal judgments benefit from the 30-day automatic stay set out in Rule 62(a), there are no routine automatic stays for these three categories of actions, even if an appeal has been taken.[17]

Discretion to Issue Stay

Notwithstanding the generally prohibitory language of Rule 62(c), district courts have discretion to grant or refuse stays in

---

[13] *Est. of Casillas v. City of Fresno*, 471 F. Supp. 3d 1035, 1036 (E.D. Cal. 2020).

[14] *Ojeda v. Metro. Transportation Auth.*, 477 F. Supp. 3d 65, 87 (S.D.N.Y. 2020).

[15] *In re Freedom Unlimited*, 489 F. Supp. 3d 1328, 1332 (S.D. Fla. 2020).

[16] *But cf.,* Fed.R.Civ.P. 62(d) (enforcement may be blocked by posting a supersedeas bond).

[17] *See, e.g., United States v. Brown*, 732 F.3d 781 (7th Cir. 2013).

these categories upon motion.[18] If the court exercises that discretion, it will usually order the movant to post security during the period of the stay or the injunction.[19] This discretion is constrained; courts may only grant such relief as may be necessary to preserve the status quo.[20]

RULE 62(d)—Injunction Pending an Appeal

CORE CONCEPT

As noted in Rule 62(c), there are no automatic stays for judgments in injunction actions, unless the court orders otherwise. Instead, a judgment that grants, continues, modifies, refuses, dissolves, or refuses to dissolve or modify an injunction ordinarily takes effect immediately. However, when an appeal is pending that challenges such a judgment, the court may suspend, modify, restore, or grant an injunction as an interim measure, awaiting the disposition of the appeal. This Rule represents an exception to the general rule that a district court lacks jurisdiction over a lawsuit while an appeal is pending.[21]

APPLICATIONS

Permissible Scope of Interim Order

This subpart applies to both final judgments and interlocutory judgments in injunction actions, and applies whether the judgment grants, continues, modifies, refuses, dissolves, or refuses to dissolve or modify an injunction. However, this subpart only allows the court to modify its injunction as an *interim* measure (in order, for example, to preserve a status quo).[22]

Time for Filing

A party may make a motion under this subpart after the notice of appeal has been filed and at any time while the appeal is pending.[23]

Place of Filing

A motion under this subpart should be made in the district court that rendered judgment, unless the movant can demonstrate that such relief is impracticable. The mere fact that the

---

[18] *See, e.g., LiButti v. U.S.*, 178 F.3d 114, 121 (2d Cir. 1999).

[19] *See, e.g., Roche Diagnostics Corp. v. Medical Automation Systems, Inc.*, 646 F.3d 424, 428 (7th Cir. 2011).

[20] *New York v. United States Dep't of Homeland Sec.*, 974 F.3d 210, 215 (2d Cir. 2020) (citing Rule 62(c), but discussing language that is now in Rule 62(d)). *See also Baum v. Blue Moon Ventures, LLC*, 513 F.3d 181, 190 n.2 (5th Cir. 2008).

[21] *Portz v. St. Cloud State Univ.*, 470 F. Supp. 3d 979, 989 (D. Minn. 2020) (court may make orders appropriate to preserve the status quo).

[22] *See, e.g., Armstrong v. Brown*, 732 F.3d 955, 959 n.6 (9th Cir. 2013); *Natural Resources Defense Council, Inc. v. Southwest Marine Inc.*, 242 F.3d 1163, 1166 (9th Cir. 2001).

[23] *See, e.g., Credit Suisse First Boston Corp. v. Grunwald*, 400 F.3d 1119, 1124 (9th Cir. 2005); *Minnesota Humane Society v. Clark*, 184 F.3d 795, 797 (8th Cir. 1999).

district court denied a preliminary judgment pending trial does not, by itself, establish that it would deny an injunction pending appeal.[24] If, however, the district court denies that relief or provides only inadequate relief, the party may press the motion in the appropriate court of appeals.[25] Where submission to a panel would prejudice the movant, the motion can be made to a single judge of the court of appeals.[26] In extraordinary circumstances, pending disposition of an application for writ of certiorari and during the pendency of an appeal to the court of appeals[27] or from a final judgment of the court of appeals,[28] a single justice of the Supreme Court, sitting as a single circuit justice, may take any action provided in Rule 62(g).[29] In addition, a judge of the court rendering the judgment may grant a stay on application for writ of certiorari to the Supreme Court.[30]

Motion Prerequisites

Courts are authorized to issue a stay to maintain the status quo or the effectiveness of the final judgment during the pendency of an appeal.[31] When a party makes a motion under this Rule, the courts will require the movant to show the following elements: (a) a strong likelihood of success on the merits of the appeal; (b) that unless the motion is granted the movant will suffer irreparable injury; (c) no substantial harm will come to other interested parties; and (d) a grant of the motion will not harm the public interest.[32] The manner in which courts weigh the four factors remains an open question, with some courts requiring parties to establish both a strong likelihood of success and irreparable injury, and other courts using a sliding scale.[33] The courts have often balanced the irreparable injury to the movant if the court did not issue the stay against the harm the stay would cause to the other parties and to the public. The governing considerations are the same whether the party ap-

---

[24] *Bos. Parent Coal. for Acad. Excellence Corp. v. Sch. Comm. of City of Bos.*, 996 F.3d 37, 43 (1st Cir. 2021).

[25] FED.R.APP. 8(a). *See Rakovich v. Wade*, 834 F.2d 673, 675 (7th Cir. 1987).

[26] FED.R.APP. 8(a).

[27] *Atiyeh v. Capps*, 449 U.S. 1312 (1981) (per Justice Rehnquist).

[28] *Graddick v. Newman*, 453 U.S. 928 (1981); *Holtzman v. Schlesinger*, 414 U.S. 1304 (1973) (per Justice Marshall).

[29] 28 U.S.C.A. § 1651(a); U.S-.Sup.Ct.R. 23.

[30] 28 U.S.C.A. § 2101(f).

[31] *Republican Nat'l Comm. v. Pelosi*, __ F. Supp. 3d __, 2022 WL 1294509, at *26 (D.D.C. 2022) (court issued an "administrative injunction" to ensure the losing party had time to seek an injunction pending appeal).

[32] *Hilton v. Braunskill*, 481 U.S. 770, 776 (1987). *See, e.g., Cuomo v. U.S. Nuclear Regulatory Com'n*, 772 F.2d 972, 974 (D.C. Cir. 1985); *Austin v. Univ. of Fla. Bd. of Trustees*, 580 F. Supp. 3d 1137, 1175 (N.D. Fla. 2022).

[33] *Austin v. Univ. of Fla. Bd. of Trustees*, 580 F. Supp. 3d 1137, 1175 (N.D. Fla. 2022) (noting that district courts rarely stay a preliminary injunction pending appeal as the test closely tracks the test for a preliminary injunction); *Alabama Ass'n of Realtors v. United States Dep't of Health & Hum. Servs.*, 539 F. Supp. 3d 211, 213-14 (D.D.C. 2021).

plies to the district court or to the appellate courts under Rule 62(g).

Requirements of the Order

An order issued under this subpart must set forth the reasons for its issuance and be specific in its terms. The court will usually order the moving party to post a bond or other security during the period of the stay or the injunction on terms that "secure the opposing party's rights."

Three-Judge District Court

When a district court of three judges, sitting by statute, renders judgment in an injunction case, a motion to stay that judgment should be addressed to all three judges. Such a court may only issue a stay pending an appeal in open court or by signature of all three judges.

RULE 62(e)—STAY WITHOUT BOND ON AN APPEAL BY THE UNITED STATES, ITS OFFICERS, OR ITS AGENCIES

CORE CONCEPT

When the party seeking the stay-pending-appeal is the United States as a party, or its officers or agencies (or when the appeal is directed by a federal department), the district court may not condition the granting of such a stay on the posting of a bond, obligation, or other security.[34] This exemption also extends to officers and agents of the United States government, and any party acting under the direction of any department or agency of the government.

RULE 62(f)—STAY IN FAVOR OF A JUDGMENT DEBTOR UNDER STATE LAW

CORE CONCEPT

If the district court's judgment creates a lien upon the debtor's property on the basis of a state law of the same state where the district court is located, a special requirement is imposed. That debtor is entitled to the same stay of execution that would have been given in state court.

APPLICATIONS

Procedure

Such stays shall operate to the same extent that state law directs a state court to enter.[35] The district court has no discretion to deny such a stay.[36] Moreover, while the normal practice anticipates that the judgment debtor will file a motion for a stay,

[34]*See, e.g., Dixon v. United States*, 900 F.3d 1257 (11th Cir. 2018).

[35]*See, e.g., Hoban v. Washington Metropolitan Area Transit Authority*, 841 F.2d 1157, 1159 (D.C. Cir. 1988).

[36]*Cf., Rodriguez-Vazquez v. Lopez-Martinez*, 345 F.3d 13, 14 (1st Cir. 2003) (citing conflicting authority).

there appears to be no requirement for such a motion and the stay can become effective even in the absence of a motion.[37]

RULE 62(g)—APPELLATE COURT'S POWER NOT LIMITED

CORE CONCEPT

The federal appeals courts are not limited by Rule 62 from issuing stays-pending-appeals; from suspending, modifying, restoring, or granting injunction pending an appeal; or from preserving the status quo or a judgment's effectiveness pending an appeal.[38]

RULE 62(h)—STAY WITH MULTIPLE CLAIMS OR PARTIES

CORE CONCEPT

A court may, under appropriate circumstances, issue a partial final judgment, thereby permitting an immediate appeal from that ruling.[39] When a court does so, it may stay enforcement of the partial final judgment until it enters some or all of the remaining judgments in the case, and may also set terms to secure the effect of the partial final judgment for the victors.

APPLICATIONS

Standards for Granting a Stay

The court has discretion to decide a motion for stay, balancing the equities of the parties and considering the administration of the case.[40]

Independent Actions

When a court consolidates several independent actions and renders judgment on one of the independent actions, this is not considered a partial judgment under Rule 54(b), and a stay will not be granted under Rule 62(h).[41]

Posting of Security

When issuing a stay of a particular judgment, the court may require security to be posted to secure that part of the judgment.[42]

---

[37]*See, e.g., Whitehead v. Food Max of Mississippi, Inc.*, 332 F.3d 796, 804–05 (5th Cir. 2003) (en banc).

[38]*In re McKenzie*, 180 U.S. 536, 551 (1901). *See also City & Cty. of San Francisco v. U.S. Citizenship & Immigr. Servs.*, 944 F.3d 773, 788 (9th Cir. 2019).

[39]*See* Rule 54(b).

[40]*See, e.g., North Penn Transfer, Inc. v. Maple Press Co.*, 176 B.R. 372, 375–77 (M.D. Pa. 1995).

[41]*In re Massachusetts Helicopter Airlines, Inc.*, 469 F.2d 439, 442 (1st Cir. 1972).

[42]*Curtiss-Wright Corp. v. General Elec. Co.*, 446 U.S. 1, 13 (1980).

Additional Research References

Wright & Miller, Federal Practice and Procedure: Civil 2d §§ 2901 to 20
C.J.S., Federal Civil Procedure § 1263; Federal Courts § 294(1 to 5) et seq.
West's Key Number Digest, Federal Courts ⟹684 to 687

RULE 62.1
INDICATIVE RULING ON A MOTION FOR RELIEF THAT IS BARRED BY A PENDING APPEAL

(a) Relief Pending Appeal. If a timely motion is made for relief that the court lacks authority to grant because of an appeal that has been docketed and is pending, the court may:

(1) defer considering the motion;

(2) deny the motion; or

(3) state either that it would grant the motion if the court of appeals remands for that purpose or that the motion raises a substantial issue.

(b) Notice to the Court of Appeals. The movant must promptly notify the circuit clerk under Federal Rule of Appellate Procedure 12.1 if the district court states that it would grant the motion or that the motion raises a substantial issue.

(c) Remand. The district court may decide the motion if the court of appeals remands for that purpose.

[Added March 26, 2009, effective December 1, 2009.]

AUTHORS' COMMENTARY ON RULE 62.1

PURPOSE AND SCOPE

Traditionally, once an appeal was taken, the district court was thereupon divested of its jurisdiction—a constraint anchored in the principle that two courts could not both possess jurisdiction over the same case at the same time. This constraint evolved with very practical exceptions. Thus, the timely filing of many post-trial motions now results in the district court retaining its jurisdiction to rule on those motions—even if an appeal has been filed.[1] But there still remains the possibility that some post-trial motions (like a motion to reopen a judgment because of newly-

[1] *See* Fed. R. App. P. 4(a)(4)(B)(i).

discovered evidence) could be timely-filed yet also outside the ordinary 28-day post-trial motion period and, thus, ineligible to preserve the district court's jurisdiction to rule.

Rule 62.1 addresses that circumstance. If a timely motion is filed in the district court which that court (due to the jurisdiction-divesting principle) lacks authority to grant, the trial judge is given three options: (1) it may defer its consideration of the motion; (2) it may deny the motion; or (3) it may inform the court of appeals either that it is inclined to grant the motion (were its jurisdiction to be restored) or that it considers the motion as raising a substantial issue that would merit further study. Given its divested jurisdiction, the third of these options is "indicative" only.[2] If the third of these options were selected, the court of appeals is authorized to respond by remanding the case back to the district court for its further consideration of the pending motion.[3]

RULE 62.1(a) RELIEF PENDING APPEAL

CORE CONCEPT

When, due to the filing of an appeal, a district court lacks the authority to rule on a timely post-trial motion, it is empowered to defer the motion, deny the motion, or notify the court of appeals of its intent to grant the motion or to consider it carefully because it raises a "substantial issue."

APPLICATIONS

Prerequisites: An Underlying Motion and a Pending Appeal

Rule 62.1(a) is applicable only to a circumstance in which a district court cannot act on a pre-existing motion[4] because a case is pending on appeal.[5]

Requirement of Timeliness

A district court has whatever authority Rule 62.1 may provide only in situations where the motion before the court was filed in a timely way.[6] If the motion is untimely, Rule 62.1 is inapplicable. A district court's orders made without jurisdiction due to a pending appeal may be construed as equivalent to

---

[2]*See Arkansas Tchr. Ret. Sys. v. State St. Bank & Tr. Co.*, 527 F. Supp. 3d 40, 47 n.1 (D. Mass. 2021).

[3]*See* Fed. R. App. P. 12.1.

[4]*See, e.g., Medgraph, Inc. v. Medtronic, Inc.*, 310 F.R.D. 208 (W.D.N.Y. 2015).

[5]*See, e.g., Singleton v. Cannizzaro*, 397 F.Supp.3d 840 (E.D. La. 2019); *Medgraph, Inc. v. Medtronic, Inc.*, 310 F.R.D. 208 (W.D.N.Y. 2015).

[6]*See, e.g., In re Checking Account Overdraft Litigation*, 754 F.3d 1290, 1294–96 (11th Cir. 2014) (Rule 62.1 motion to compel arbitration on threshold issue of arbitrability, made after district court rejected motion to compel arbitration, was unauthorized under Rule 62.1 because threshold issue had been waived); *Cf., Binta B. ex rel. S.A. v. Gordon*, 710 F.3d 608, 616 (6th Cir. 2013) (Rule 62.1 requires that issue be raised first in district court, not appellate court).

indicative rulings.[7]

Exception for Motions Which District Court May Grant

The Federal Rules of Appellate Procedure identify six post-trial motions that, if timely filed with the district court, have the effect of halting the appellate process (including the time limit for filing a notice of appeal) until the district court's disposition.[8] In other words, notwithstanding that a party may already have filed a notice of appeal, the district court is authorized to decide those post-trial motions before the appeal may proceed further. Because the application of Rule 62.1 is expressly limited to circumstances in which a district court may be prevented from granting a motion in a case pending on appeal, Rule 62.1 has no applicability to motions that fall within the scope of that list.

District Court's Authority to Deny a Motion

The applicability of Rule 62.1 is limited to circumstances in which the district court has no authority to grant a motion due to the pending appeal.[9] However, if the court is inclined to deny the motion, Rule 62.1 is no barrier.

Scope of District Court's Options

When Rule 62.1 is applicable, it provides the court with the following options. First, the court may choose to defer consideration of the motion pending outcome of the appeal. Second the court may deny the motion. Thus, notwithstanding the existence of a pending appeal, a district court is normally free to deny any motion made during the pendency of an appeal even if the court might not have had authority to grant the motion (if the court was so inclined). Third, the court may express its view that the motion would be granted if the appellate court chooses to remand the case for that purpose. Fourth, the district court may state simply that the motion raises a substantial issue.[10]

RULE 62.1(b) NOTICE TO THE COURT OF APPEALS

CORE CONCEPT

Rule 62.1(b) establishes a requirement for the party who filed the motion to notify the appellate court if the district court states that it would either grant the motion or that the motion raises a

---

[7] *See Wright v. Sumter Cty. Bd. of Elections & Registration*, 979 F.3d 1282, 1298 (11th Cir. 2020); *New York v. U.S. Dep't of Homeland Sec.*, 475 F. Supp. 3d 208, 231 (S.D.N.Y. 2020) (issuing decision on injunctive relief in the alternative as an indicative ruling, if the appellate court determined it lacked jurisdiction).

[8] Fed. R. App. P. 4(a)(4)(A)(i) – (vi).

[9] *See Justiniano v. Walker*, 986 F.3d 11, 18 (1st Cir. 2021) (Rule 60(b)(2) motion to consider new evidence after appeal was filed should have been construed as a motion under Rule 62.1).

[10] *See, e.g., Kravitz v. U.S. Dep't of Commerce*, 382 F.Supp.3d 393 (D. Md. 2019).

substantial issue.[11]

APPLICATIONS

Manner of Notice

If the notification required by Rule 62.1(b) is implicated, the manner of notification is governed by the Federal Rules of Appellate Procedure.[12] If the district court has indicated that it would either defer consideration of the motion or deny the motion, Rule 62.1(b) imposes no obligation on the movant to notify the appellate court.

RULE 62.1(c) REMAND

CORE CONCEPT

If, following the district court's "indication" of its intent, the court of appeals remands the case, the district court may then rule on the pending motion.[13]

APPLICATIONS

Grounds for Remand

A court of appeals might remand a case if the district court indicates either that it would grant the motion for relief or that the motion raises a substantial issue.[14]

Additional Research References

Wright & Miller, *Federal Practice and Procedure* § 2911
C.J.S., Federal Civil Procedure § 436

---

[11] *See, e.g., Viera v. United States*, __ F. Supp. 3d __, 2022 WL 955919, at *1 (S.D.N.Y. 2022); *Kravitz v. U.S. Dep't of Commerce*, 382 F. Supp. 3d 393 (D. Md. 2019).

[12] Fed.R.App.P. 12.1. *See also Viera v. United States*, __ F. Supp. 3d __, 2022 WL 955919, at *1 (S.D.N.Y. 2022).

[13] *See, e.g., Arlington Industries v. Bridgeport Fittings, Inc.*, 632 F.3d 1246 (Fed. Cir. 2011).

[14] *See, e.g., Henok v. Chase Home Finance, LLC*, 18 F. Supp. 3d 6 (D.D.C. 2014).

RULE 63
JUDGE'S INABILITY TO PROCEED

If a judge conducting a hearing or trial is unable to proceed, any other judge may proceed upon certifying familiarity with the record and determining that the case may be completed without prejudice to the parties. In a hearing or a nonjury trial, the successor judge must, at a party's request, recall any witness whose testimony is material and disputed and who is available to testify again without undue burden. The successor judge may also recall any other witness.

[Amended effective August 1, 1987; December 1, 1991; April 30, 2007, effective December 1, 2007.]

AUTHORS' COMMENTARY ON RULE 63

PURPOSE AND SCOPE

When, due to recusal, incapacity, retirement, death, or elevation to a higher court, a judge withdraws after a trial or hearing begins, any other judge of the court may proceed with the case. The successor judge will read the pertinent portions of the record, certify familiarity with that record, and then decide whether she or he may proceed with the case without causing prejudice to the parties. In a non-jury hearing or trial, if the successor judge proceeds with the case, he or she must recall any witnesses requested by the parties, if their testimony is material and disputed and where the witnesses are available to testify again without undue burden. In addition, the successor judge may recall any witnesses in order to become more familiar with the record.

APPLICATIONS

Caution in Relying on Pre-1992 Case Law

Rule 63 was substantially amended in late 1991 to expand the Rule's scope and to alter certain interpretations given to the Rule by the courts. Decisions that predate the 1991 amendment should be cited with care.[1]

Conditions for Inability to Proceed

A judge's withdrawal must rest on compelling reasons, such as sickness, death, disability, retirement, recusal, or disqualification.[2] A judge may not withdraw for mere personal convenience.[3]

Statement of Grounds for Withdrawal

The withdrawing judge must state on the record the reasons for his or her withdrawal.[4]

Only Applicable *After* Hearing or Trial Begins

The certification obligation of Rule 63 is only triggered if the substitution is made *after* a hearing or trial has begun; before that time, a substitution may be made without any requirement of certification by the substituting judge.[5]

Timing of Substitution

The original text of Rule 63 implied that, once a trial or hearing had begun, district judges could not be substituted unless the departing judge had already filed findings of fact and conclusions of law. The courts embraced this implication and, unless the parties stipulated otherwise, required new trials whenever the departing judge had not yet filed findings and conclusions.[6]

This "negative inference" mandate ascribed to Rule 63 was abolished in 1991. Citing the increasing length of trials in federal court and the expected concomitant increase in the number of trials interrupted by a judge's disability,[7] the drafters provided that a substitution may be made after trial commences, even in the absence of filed findings and conclusions, if the replacement judge (1) can certify his or her familiarity with the proceedings in the case to date and (2) can continue the proceedings without prejudicing the parties.

---

[1] *But see Zand v. C.I.R. Service*, 143 F.3d 1393, 1400 (11th Cir. 1998) (court may look to pre-1991 decisions for guidance given facts of particular case).

[2] *See* Rule 63 advisory committee notes (1991); 28 U.S.C.A. §§ 144 & 455 (providing for disqualification of judges). *See Atl. Specialty Ins. Co. v. Coastal Envtl. Grp. Inc.*, 945 F.3d 53, 58 (2d Cir. 2019) (death); *U.S. v. Nwoye*, 60 F. Supp. 3d 225, 227 (D.D.C. 2014) (injury); *In re Frescati Shipping Co.*, 886 F.3d 291, 298 (3d Cir. 2018) (retirement).

[3] *See* Rule 63 advisory committee notes (1991).

[4] *See* Rule 63 advisory committee notes (1991).

[5] *See Fed. Trade Comm'n v. Marshall*, 781 Fed. Appx. 599, 603–04 (9th Cir. 2019); *UWM Student Ass'n v. Lovell*, 888 F.3d 854, 857 (7th Cir. 2018).

[6] *See, e.g., In re Higginbotham*, 917 F.2d 1130, 1132 (8th Cir. 1990); *Olle v. Henry & Wright Corp.*, 910 F.2d 357, 361 (6th Cir. 1990).

[7] *See* Rule 63 advisory committee notes (1991). *See also Mergentime Corp. v. Washington Metropolitan Area Transit Authority*, 166 F.3d 1257, 1262 (D.C. Cir. 1999) (successor judges may take over at any point after trial begins, subject to certain additional responsibilities imposed).

Certifying Familiarity With the Record

Once a trial or hearing has begun, no substitute judge can replace a departing judge without first "certifying familiarity with the record."[8] It is this certification procedure that ensures that due process is not violated when the case resumes.[9] Although an express "certification" is plainly preferred,[10] the court of appeals will likely not reverse in the absence of an express certification so long as the successor judge's statements confirm compliance with the record familiarity requirement.[11] Nor will the appeals court likely reverse for unfortunate, though nonprejudicial, misstatements in the certification.[12] This certification requirement obligates the substitute judge to read and consider all relevant portions of the record.[13] What portions of the record the successor judge is required to learn depends upon the nature of the successor judge's role in the case. For example, if the successor judge inherits a jury trial before the evidence has closed, the judge must become familiar with the entire record so as to properly rule upon relevance-based evidentiary objections; but if the successor judge inherits the case after the entry of verdict or judgment, the judge need only review those portions of the record relevant to the particular issues challenged by post-trial motions.[14]

Prerequisite for Substitution

In order for a judge to be substituted, there must be an available transcript or recording to permit the replacement judge to become familiar with the proceedings that occurred prior to the substitution. The Committee Notes encourage the prompt preparation of the trial or video transcript, so as to prevent delaying the jury longer than necessary.[15]

Jury Trials

In a jury trial, the parties are not reflexively entitled to a

---

[8] *See Gaye v. Lynch*, 788 F.3d 519, 533–34 (6th Cir. 2015); *In re Reale*, 584 F.3d 27, 32 (1st Cir. 2009).

[9] *See Patelco Credit Union v. Sahni*, 262 F.3d 897, 905 (9th Cir. 2001).

[10] *See, e.g., Healey v. Murphy*, 2013 WL 1336786, at *2 (D.Mass. Mar. 29, 2013) (noting express certification); *Vescio v. Merchants Bank*, 272 B.R. 413, 420 (D. Vt. 2001), aff'd, 54 Fed. Appx. 513 (2d Cir. 2002) (same).

[11] *See Bisbal-Ramos v. City of Mayaguez*, 467 F.3d 16, 26 (1st Cir. 2006); *Mergentime Corp. v. Washington Metropolitan Area Transit Authority*, 166 F.3d 1257, 1265 (D.C. Cir. 1999). *See also United States v. Washington*, 653 F.3d 1057, 1064 (9th Cir. 2011) ("ministerial" failure to certify "does not cast doubt on the proceeding's integrity").

[12] *See In re Reale*, 584 F.3d 27, 32 n.2 (1st Cir. 2009) (finding certification's confirmation that successor judge had considered witnesses' demeanor "unfortunate" but, given record evidence, not prejudicial).

[13] *See Mergentime Corp. v. Washington Metropolitan Area Transit Authority*, 166 F.3d 1257, 1265 (D.C. Cir. 1999); *Canseco v. U.S.*, 97 F.3d 1224, 1226 (9th Cir. 1996).

[14] *See Mergentime Corp. v. Washington Metropolitan Area Transit Authority*, 166 F.3d 1257, 1265 (D.C. Cir. 1999).

[15] *See* Rule 63 advisory committee notes (1991).

new trial merely because the judge is unable to continue to preside, even when that occurs after the jury's verdict but before post-trial motions.[16] Nor, in such circumstances, do the parties have the right to insist that a witness be recalled.[17] Instead, if the successor judge can certify familiarity with the record and can determine that the proceedings are able to be completed without prejudice to the parties, nothing more is required.[18] Should the judge choose to do so, however, the successor judge has the discretion to recall a witness.[19]

Bench Trials

In a non-jury trial, the parties have the ability to insist that certain witnesses be recalled and reheard by the successor judge:

- *Testimony of Available Witness:* When a witness is available, the successor judge *must* honor a party's recall request if the witness's testimony is material, disputed, and obtainable without undue burden.[20] Even without such a request, the successor judge *may* recall any other witness discretionally[21] and *must* recall any witness whose credibility is in question but undeterminable from the record if that witness's testimony is material, disputed, and obtainable without undue burden.[22]
- *Testimony of Unavailable Witness:* If a witness has become unavailable, the successor judge can consider the testimony recorded at trial[23] or, if the testimony was not material or not disputed, may choose not to consider the testimony at all.[24]
- *Evidence Heard By Departed Judge:* In appropriate circumstances, the successor judge may base a factual finding on transcribed evidence heard by the former,

---

[16]*See Lever v. United States*, 443 F.2d 350, 351 (2d Cir. 1971) (citation omitted); *Fresquez v. BNSF Ry. Co.*, 2021 WL 857626, at *7 (D. Colo. Mar. 8, 2021) (appeal pending).

[17]*See Jackson v. State of Alabama State Tenure Com'n*, 405 F.3d 1276, 1286–87 (11th Cir. 2005).

[18]*See Jackson v. State of Alabama State Tenure Com'n*, 405 F.3d 1276, 1287 (11th Cir. 2005).

[19]*See* Rule 63.

[20]*See Centripetal Networks, Inc. v. Cisco Sys., Inc.*, 38 F.4th 1025, 1036 n.20 (Fed. Cir. 2022); *Atl. Specialty Ins. Co. v. Coastal Envtl. Grp. Inc.*, 945 F.3d 53, 65 (2d Cir. 2019). *Cf. Atl. Specialty Ins. Co.*, 945 F.3d at 68 (no obligation to recall witnesses absent party's request); *In re Reale*, 584 F.3d 27, 33 (1st Cir. 2009) (same).

[21]*See Atl. Specialty Ins. Co. v. Coastal Envtl. Grp. Inc.*, 945 F.3d 53, 65 (2d Cir. 2019).

[22]*See Canseco v. United States*, 97 F.3d 1224, 1227 (9th Cir. 1996).

[23]*See In re Petition of Frescati Shipping Co.*, 2016 WL 4035994, at *5 (E.D. Pa. July 25, 2016), *aff'd in part, vacated in part, remanded in part on other grounds*, 886 F.3d 291 (3d Cir. 2018) (may be considered as recorded deposition equivalent).

[24]*See* Rule 63 advisory committee notes (1991).

departed judge.[25]

- *Entire New Trial:* When the issues in the case are especially complex, new findings are required, unresolvable credibility issues are present, or many witnesses need to be recalled, the successor judge may grant a new trial.[26]
- *Factfinding Deference:* The involvement of a successor judge does not alter the ordinary deference that trial court factfinding enjoys on appeal, even when that factfinding is based entirely on a documentary record.[27]

Previously Litigated Issues

Unless the controlling law has changed, the successor judge will not ordinarily revisit rulings made by the withdrawing judge. However, the successor judge is required to consider and rule upon allegations of trial error properly raised in post-trial motions.[28]

Option To Enter Summary Judgment

If, after reviewing the trial transcript, the successor judge decides that no credibility determinations are required and that one party is entitled to a judgment as a matter of law, summary judgment can be entered as an alternative to the successor judge "stepping into the shoes" of the departed judge.[29]

Waiver of Right to Object to Successor Judge

Following the departure of the original judge, the litigants may be deemed to have waived any objection to the case's reassignment to a new judge if the litigants fail either to timely seek a new trial or timely object to a reassignment,[30] or fail to timely insist upon the recall of witnesses.[31] Minimally, a failure to object will likely relegate the appellate court to the very forgiving "plain error" standard of review.[32]

---

[25] *See In re Frescati Shipping Co.*, 886 F.3d 291, 298 (3d Cir. 2018).

[26] *See Centripetal Networks, Inc. v. Cisco Sys., Inc.*, 38 F.4th 1025, 1036 n.20 (Fed. Cir. 2022); *Compulife Software Inc. v. Newman*, 959 F.3d 1288, 1307 n.10 (11th Cir. 2020).

[27] *See Atl. Specialty Ins. Co. v. Coastal Envtl. Grp. Inc.*, 945 F.3d 53, 63–65 (2d Cir. 2019).

[28] *See Mergentime Corp. v. Washington Metropolitan Area Transit Authority*, 166 F.3d 1257, 1263 (D.C. Cir. 1999) (successor judge may not refuse to consider post-trial motions out of deference to original judge).

[29] *See Patelco Credit Union v. Sahni*, 262 F.3d 897, 906 (9th Cir. 2001).

[30] *See Littleton v. Pilot Travel Ctrs., LLC*, 568 F.3d 641, 648 (8th Cir. 2009) (party may not "sit back and await decision" before objecting); *Zand v. C.I.R. Service*, 143 F.3d 1393, 1400 (11th Cir. 1998) (parties had "cleverly tiptoe[d]" across a "procedural tightrope", refusing to consent to reassignment while, simultaneously, failing to seek added expense of retrial; therefore, unfavorable verdict by successor judge could not be challenged under Rule 63).

[31] *See Marantz v. Permanente Med. Group, Inc. Long Term Disability Plan*, 687 F.3d 320, 327 (7th Cir. 2012); *In re Reale*, 584 F.3d 27, 32–33 (1st Cir. 2009).

[32] *See Bisbal-Ramos v. City of Mayaguez*, 467 F.3d 16, 26 (1st Cir.

Additional Research References

Wright & Miller, *Federal Practice and Procedure: Civil 2d* §§ 2921 to 30

C.J.S., Judges §§ 35 to 68

West's Key Number Digest, Judges ⟹21, ⟹32

2006).

VIII. PROVISIONAL AND FINAL REMEDIES

RULE 64
SEIZING A PERSON OR PROPERTY

(a) Remedies Under State Law—In General. At the commencement of and throughout an action, every remedy is available that, under the law of the state where the court is located, provides for seizing a person or property to secure satisfaction of the potential judgment. But a federal statute governs to the extent it applies.

(b) Specific Kinds of Remedies. The remedies available under this rule include the following—however designated and regardless of whether state procedure requires an independent action:

- arrest;
- attachment;
- garnishment;
- replevin;
- sequestration; and
- other corresponding or equivalent remedies.

[Amended April 30, 2007, effective December 1, 2007.]

AUTHORS' COMMENTARY ON RULE 64

PURPOSE AND SCOPE

Rule 64 concerns "provisional remedies"—the seizure of a person or property, occurring *before* any final judgment is entered (but after the lawsuit initiated), designed to secure the satisfaction of any judgment that might be later entered in the lawsuit. Provisional remedies may prove important in exigent circumstances (such as when assets are at risk of slipping out of the forum or a potential debtor is threatening to decamp to locations beyond the court's reach). This sort of preliminary, anticipatory, prophylactic relief is authorized in two circumstances: where Congress approves it by federal statute or where the law of the State where the district court sits permits it. Relief under Rule 64 is infrequently sought and infrequently granted.

RULE 64(a)—REMEDIES UNDER STATE LAW—IN GENERAL

CORE CONCEPT

The pre-judgment seizure of persons and property is permitted to secure the satisfaction of a federal civil judgment if authorized by Congress or by the local state law.

APPLICATIONS

Time for Seeking a Seizure Order

A party may move the court for a seizure order under Rule 64 at any time after the federal action is commenced and, then, up to the time of judgment.[1] A party may assert a Rule 64 request as an ancillary claim in a pending action or file an independent action to do so. *Post*-judgment remedies to satisfy a judgment are available under other Rules.[2]

Sources of the Seizure Remedies

If seizure is permitted by federal statute, those provisions apply in place of any otherwise applicable state law remedy.[3] If no federal statute applies, the pre-judgment seizure remedies available (if any) are those approved under the law of the state where the district court sits.[4] But Rule 64 does not make state law remedies available beyond that state's territorial limitations.[5]

Appealability

Although coercive and injunctive in nature, pre-judgment seizures are ordinarily considered legal, not equitable, relief, and therefore are typically not immediately appealable as injunctions.[6]

---

[1] *See, e.g., Rosen v. Cascade Intern., Inc.*, 21 F.3d 1520, 1530 (11th Cir. 1994); *Credit Managers Ass'n of Southern California v. Kennesaw Life & Acc. Ins. Co.*, 25 F.3d 743, 750 (9th Cir. 1994).

[2] *See,* Rule 69 (execution (garnishment) after judgment); Rule 70 (enforcement after judgment). *See also United States for Use of Tanos v. St. Paul Mercury Ins. Co.*, 361 F.2d 838, 840 n.1 (5th Cir. 1966) (Brown, J., dissenting) (comparing Rule 64 with Rule 69); *Deegan v. Strategic Azimuth LLC*, 768 F. Supp. 2d 107, 115 n.1 (D.D.C. 2011) (comparing Rule 64 and Rule 70).

[3] *See Ditucci v. Bowser*, 985 F.3d 804, 810 (10th Cir. 2021); *United States v. Witham*, 648 F.3d 40, 44 (1st Cir. 2011).

[4] *See Pineda v. Skinner Servs., Inc.*, 22 F.4th 47, 53–54 (1st Cir. 2021); *United States v. Askins & Miller Orthopaedics, P.A.*, 924 F.3d 1348 (11th Cir. 2019).

[5] *Power Rental Op Co, LLC v. Virgin Islands Water & Power Auth.*, 515 F. Supp. 3d 1237, 1240 (M.D. Fla. 2021), *amended on denial of reconsideration*, 2021 WL 2819445 (M.D. Fla. 2021).

[6] *Crystallex Int'l Corp. v. Bolivarian Republic of Venezuela*, 24 F.4th 242, 250 (3d Cir. 2022); *Ditucci v. Bowser*, 985 F.3d 804, 808–09 (10th Cir. 2021).

RULE 64(b)—SPECIFIC KINDS OF REMEDIES

CORE CONCEPT

The types of pre-judgment seizure remedies that might be available in a federal trial court include: arrest, attachment, garnishment, replevin, sequestration, and other "corresponding or equivalent" remedies. Those types are available *if* permitted by Congress or by applicable state law, regardless of how they might be labeled and even if, under state law, a separate, independent action would usually be needed.

APPLICATIONS

Method for Obtaining Relief

Where a federal remedy exists, the procedure for obtaining relief will be provided by the relevant statute and the Rules. When relief is sought under a state remedy, state law generally supplies the procedures, except to the extent that the Rules apply. The method for obtaining relief will vary from state to state and district to district. However, in all cases a U.S. Marshal rather than a state officer would seize the goods or property.

Subject-Matter Jurisdiction

Whether asserted in a pending action or in an independent action, the types of seizures authorized by Rule 64 do not require a separate basis of subject-matter jurisdiction; the court's jurisdiction over the seizure is ancillary to the court's jurisdiction over the underlying claim.[7]

Constitutional Limitations

The seizure of a person or property without notice or a prior hearing may often be a violation of constitutional due process.[8]

Relation to Rule 65

In cases involving only money damages on an unsecured claim, a party may not use Rule 65 (governing preliminary injunctions and temporary restraining orders) to obtain a prejudgment injunction aimed at preventing dissipation of assets. Instead, such relief must be sought under other provisions, such as Rule 64's authorization to use state law prejudgment attachment provisions.[9] However, if the lawsuit also seeks equitable relief, the district court is not restricted by Rule 64 and may still grant a prejudgment injunction that freezes specific assets that are the subject of a restitution or recission

---

[7] *Peacock v. Thomas*, 516 U.S. 349, 356 (1996); *Pineda v. Skinner Servs., Inc.*, 22 F.4th 47, 53–54 (1st Cir. 2021).

[8] *See Connecticut v. Doehr*, 501 U.S. 1, 18 (1991). *See also North Georgia Finishing, Inc. v. Di-Chem, Inc.*, 419 U.S. 601 (1975).

[9] *Grupo Mexicano de Desarrollo S.A. v. Alliance Bond Fund, Inc.*, 527 U.S. 308, 330–31 (1999); *Pineda v. Skinner Servs., Inc.*, 22 F.4th 47, 53–54 (1st Cir. 2021).

claim or that preserves the power of the court to grant final injunctive relief.[10]

Armed Services Personnel

Provisional relief under Rule 64 is subject to the Soldiers' and Sailors' Civil Relief Act of 1940, which prohibits seizure of the assets of absent military personnel in many circumstances.[11]

Execution

A plaintiff who recovers judgment will likely be entitled to an execution sale of the previously seized property in satisfaction of the judgment.

Additional Research References

Wright & Miller, *Federal Practice and Procedure: Civil 2d* §§ 2931 to 40

C.J.S., Federal Civil Procedure §§ 233 to 241, § 1271

West's Key Number Digest, Attachment ⚷1 to 384; Garnishment ⚷1 to 251; Replevin ⚷1 to 135; Sequestration ⚷1 to 21

---

[10]*See, e.g., U.S. ex rel. Rahman v. Oncology Assoc.*, 198 F.3d 489, 495–97 (4th Cir. 1999). *See also De Beers Consol. Mines v. U.S.*, 325 U.S. 212, 219 (1945).

[11]50 App. U.S.C.A. §§ 501–59.

RULE 65
INJUNCTIONS AND RESTRAINING ORDERS

(a) Preliminary Injunction.

(1) *Notice.* The court may issue a preliminary injunction only on notice to the adverse party.

(2) *Consolidating the Hearing with the Trial on the Merits.* Before or after beginning the hearing on a motion for a preliminary injunction, the court may advance the trial on the merits and consolidate it with the hearing. Even when consolidation is not ordered, evidence that is received on the motion and that would be admissible at trial becomes part of the trial record and need not be repeated at trial. But the court must preserve any party's right to a jury trial.

(b) Temporary Restraining Order.

(1) *Issuing Without Notice.* The court may issue a temporary restraining order without written or oral notice to the adverse party or its attorney only if:

(A) specific facts in an affidavit or a verified complaint clearly show that immediate and irreparable injury, loss, or damage will result to the movant before the adverse party can be heard in opposition; and

(B) the movant's attorney certifies in writing any efforts made to give notice and the reasons why it should not be required.

(2) *Contents; Expiration.* Every temporary restraining order issued without notice must state the date and hour it was issued; describe the injury and state why it is irreparable; state why the order was issued without notice; and be promptly filed in the clerk's office and entered in the record. The order expires at the time after entry—not to exceed 14 days—that the court sets, unless before that time the court, for good

cause, extends it for a like period or the adverse party consents to a longer extension. The reasons for an extension must be entered in the record.

(3) *Expediting the Preliminary-Injunction Hearing.* If the order is issued without notice, the motion for a preliminary injunction must be set for hearing at the earliest possible time, taking precedence over all other matters except hearings on older matters of the same character. At the hearing, the party who obtained the order must proceed with the motion; if the party does not, the court must dissolve the order.

(4) *Motion to Dissolve.* On 2 days' notice to the party who obtained the order without notice—or on shorter notice set by the court—the adverse party may appear and move to dissolve or modify the order. The court must then hear and decide the motion as promptly as justice requires.

(c) Security. The court may issue a preliminary injunction or a temporary restraining order only if the movant gives security in an amount that the court considers proper to pay the costs and damages sustained by any party found to have been wrongfully enjoined or restrained. The United States, its officers, and its agencies are not required to give security.

(d) Contents and Scope of Every Injunction and Restraining Order.

(1) *Contents.* Every order granting an injunction and every restraining order must:

(A) state the reasons why it issued;

(B) state its terms specifically; and

(C) describe in reasonable detail—and not by referring to the complaint or other document—the act or acts restrained or required.

(2) *Persons Bound.* The order binds only the following who receive actual notice of it by personal service or otherwise:

(A) the parties;

(B) the parties' officers, agents, servants, employees, and attorneys; and

(C) other persons who are in active concert or

participation with anyone described in Rule 65(d)(2)(A) or (B).

(e) Other Laws Not Modified. These rules do not modify the following:

(1) any federal statute relating to temporary restraining orders or preliminary injunctions in actions affecting employer and employee;

(2) 28 U.S.C. § 2361, which relates to preliminary injunctions in actions of interpleader or in the nature of interpleader; or

(3) 28 U.S.C. § 2284, which relates to actions that must be heard and decided by a three-judge district court.

(f) Copyright Impoundment. This rule applies to copyright-impoundment proceedings.

[Amended effective March 19, 1948; October 20, 1949; July 1, 1966; August 1, 1987; April 23, 2001, effective December 1, 2001; April 30, 2007, effective December 1, 2007; March 26, 2009, effective December 1, 2009.]

AUTHORS' COMMENTARY ON RULE 65

PURPOSE AND SCOPE

Rule 65 permits federal courts to issue preliminary injunctions and temporary restraining orders ("TRO"s). Neither ruling is a final judgment. Instead, these are "provisional remedies," designed to "freeze" the parties' pre-dispute positions (*i.e.*, maintain the "*status quo ante*") in certain disputes where waiting for judicial intervention could result in harm so irreparable that no later ruling court could provide the injured party with meaningful relief.

Although preliminary injunctions and TROs both act to "freeze" the parties to their pre-dispute positions, the two procedures differ significantly. Preliminary injunctions may only be granted by the court after notice is given to the adverse party (and after that party has been afforded an opportunity to be heard). Temporary restraining orders are often issued more quickly and may be granted—in certain circumstances—*without* giving notice to the adverse party. But the duration of TROs is very brief: often 14 days or less. In practice, where great exigency exists, a claimant could come to court seeking a TRO first, provide the adversary notice *after* the TRO is issued, and await the court's scheduling of a preliminary injunction hearing for the coming days. There, the enjoined party would be afforded the opportunity to be heard in defense. If the court agrees with the defending party, the TRO might be "dissolved" or otherwise altered. If the court agrees with the movant, the TRO might be replaced with a preliminary injunction which could remain in place until the dispute came up for a full trial on the merits. If, at trial, the movant prevails, the preliminary injunction could be converted into a *permanent* injunction in the court's final judgment.

Rule 65 establishes the procedures for preliminary injunctions and TROs (not, as discussed below, for *permanent* injunctions). Moreover, Rule 65 does not contain the substantive standards for granting such relief—those standards are found largely in case law.

RULE 65(a)—PRELIMINARY INJUNCTION

CORE CONCEPT

The elements a party needs to prove in order to obtain a preliminary injunction are not established by this subpart, but in case law (however, those elements are discussed below, as a resource for practitioners). This subpart authorizes the court to issue preliminary injunctions, but only on notice to the opponent, and also permits the court, where appropriate, to accelerate and consolidate the trial on the merits of the dispute while it is hearing a preliminary injunction motion (so that the preliminary injunction motion and the merits trial can be considered together).

APPLICATIONS

Purpose

The purpose of a preliminary injunction is usually to maintain the status quo until the merits of a case can be decided.[1] Courts grant preliminary injunctions ordering an alteration of the status quo only in unusual circumstances where the merits clearly favor one party over another.[2] A preliminary injunction can only operate during the pendency of the case, at the end of which the court may consider whether to enter a permanent injunction.

Substantive Requirements

The substantive requirements for granting a preliminary injunction are separate from, and in addition to, the modest procedures set out in Rule 65. They are found, instead, predominantly in case law, and must be satisfied before a pre-

---

[1] *See, e.g., Resolution Trust Corp. v. Cruce*, 972 F.2d 1195, 1198 (10th Cir. 1992); *Doster v. Kendall*, ___ F. Supp. 3d ___, 2022 WL 982299, at *10 (S.D. Ohio 2022).

[2] *See, e.g., Dominion Video Satellite, Inc. v. EchoStar Satellite Corp.*, 269 F.3d 1149, 1154–55 (10th Cir. 2001); *Aoude v. Mobil Oil Corp.*, 862 F.2d 890, 893 (1st Cir. 1988).

liminary injunction may issue.[3] Although the requirements can vary by jurisdiction and type of case, federal courts generally consider the following factors in deciding whether to grant or deny a motion for a preliminary injunction:

(1) whether the potential harm to the moving party is irreparable (that is, whether the potential harm could be cured through a later award of money damages);
(2) the nature of the harm the opponent would face were the injunction granted;
(3) how others would be affected by the grant or denial of the injunction, including the impact on the public interest; and
(4) whether, in view of its position and evidence, the moving party is likely to succeed on the merits of the claim once the case comes to a full trial.[4]

Applicants for preliminary injunctive relief are generally expected to act with reasonable diligence.[5] Preliminary injunctions are considered extraordinary remedies; they are not lightly or routinely granted.[6] They are never granted as of right but are vested in the district judge's equitable discretion.[7] The pertinent inquiry is highly fact-dependent, and courts are counseled to mold any injunctive relief that they order to meet the necessities of each case.[8]

Practitioners are encouraged to consult local practice, as courts differ in the exact wording of the test and in how they choose to apply the test. Some courts tend to regard "likelihood of success" as the most important factor,[9] while others emphasize "irreparable harm." Other courts regard both as gateway factors.[10] Some courts require the movant to satisfy all four prongs,[11] while other courts use a "sliding scale," by which a strong showing on one factor may compensate for a weaker showing on another factor.[12] In addition, in particular contexts, federal statutes may expressly authorize (and set statute-

---

[3]*See Grupo Mexicano de Desarrollo S.A. v. Alliance Bond Fund, Inc.*, 527 U.S. 308, 319 (1999); *U.S. v. Cohen*, 152 F.3d 321, 324 (4th Cir. 1998).

[4]*See Winter v. Natural Resources Defense Council, Inc.*, 555 U.S. 7, 20 (2008).

[5]*See Benisek v. Lamone*, 585 U.S. —, 138 S. Ct. 1942, 1944 (2018).

[6]*See Winter v. Natural Resources Defense Council, Inc.*, 555 U.S. 7, 22 (2008); *Ass'n of Am. Publishers, Inc. v. Frosh*, — F. Supp. 3d —, 2022 WL 484926, at *5 (D. Md. 2022).

[7]*See Benisek v. Lamone*, 585 U.S. —, 138 S. Ct. 1942, 1943–44 (2018); *Ass'n of Am. Publishers, Inc. v. Frosh*, — F. Supp. 3d —, 2022 WL 484926, at *5 (D. Md. 2022).

[8]*See Rondeau v. Mosinee Paper Corp.*, 422 U.S. 49, 61–62 (1975).

[9]*Roth v. Austin*, — F. Supp. 3d —, 2022 WL 1568830, at *10 (D. Neb. 2022); *Doster v. Kendall*, — F. Supp. 3d —, 2022 WL 982299, at *11 (S.D. Ohio 2022).

[10]*Texas v. Becerra*, 577 F. Supp. 3d 527, 537 (N.D. Tex. 2021).

[11]*Bluefield Water Ass'n, Inc. v. City of Starkville*, 577 F.3d 250, 253 (5th Cir. 2009); *Savage Tavern, Inc. v. Signature Stag, LLC*, — F. Supp. 3d —, 2022 WL 686870, at *3 (N.D. Tex. 2022).

[12]*All. for the Wild Rockies v. Cottrell*, 632 F.3d 1127, 1131 (9th Cir.

specific standards for granting) injunctive relief.[13]

Applies to *Preliminary* Injunctions Only

By its terms, Rule 65 applies principally to requests for preliminary relief and, with the exception of subpart (d), does not pertain to grants or denials of *permanent* injunctions.[14]

Notice and Hearing Requirements

The court may not issue a preliminary injunction without notice to the opposing party.[15] Rule 65(a) does not, however, set out the type of required notice nor how far in advance it must be given.[16] Formal, Rule 4 service of process may not be an irreducible prerequisite.[17] The court must also hold a hearing before granting or refusing a preliminary injunction. Again, the Rule does not supply minimum requirements.[18] The Supreme Court, however, has commented that the notice/hearing requisites of the Rule "implies a hearing in which the defendant is given a fair opportunity to oppose the application and to prepare for such opposition."[19] The nature and scope of the hearing is subject to the discretion of the court.[20]

- *Supporting Evidence Need Not be Admissible at Trial:* Preliminary injunctions can be granted even where the supporting evidence lacks the requirements for admissibility at trial.[21]

Consolidation with Trial on the Merits

The court has discretion to consolidate the preliminary injunction hearing with the trial on the merits by accelerating the trial on the court's calendar, either *sua sponte*[22] or on

---

2011); *O'Hailpin v. Hawaiian Airlines, Inc.*, 583 F. Supp. 3d 1294, 1301 (D. Haw. 2022).

[13]*See, e.g., Muffley ex rel. N.L.R.B. v. Spartan Mining Co.*, 570 F.3d 534 (4th Cir. 2009).

[14]*See, e.g., Findlay Truck Line, Inc. v. Central States, Southeast & Southwest Areas Pension Fund*, 726 F.3d 738, 746 n.4 (6th Cir. 2013); *U.S. v. Criminal Sheriff, Parish of Orleans*, 19 F.3d 238 (5th Cir. 1994).

[15]*See Tumey v. Mycroft AI, Inc.*, 27 F.4th 657, 665–66 (8th Cir. 2022); *Georgia Advoc. Off. v. Jackson*, 4 F.4th 1200, __ (11th Cir. 2021).

[16]*See Tumey v. Mycroft AI, Inc.*, 27 F.4th 657, 665–66 (8th Cir. 2022); *Wyandotte Nation v. Sebelius*, 443 F.3d 1247, 1253 (10th Cir. 2006).

[17]*See Sogefi USA, Inc. v. Interplex Sunbelt, Inc.*, 538 F. Supp. 3d 620, 625 & n.7 (S.D.W. Va. 2021).

[18]*See, e.g., Alliance for Open Society International, Inc. v. United States Agency for International Development*, 911 F.3d 104 (2d Cir. 2018); *Hunter v. Hamilton County Board of Elections*, 635 F.3d 219, 246 (6th Cir. 2011).

[19]*See Granny Goose Foods, Inc. v. Bhd. of Teamsters & Auto Truck Drivers Loc. No. 70*, 415 U.S. 423, 433 (1974).

[20]*See, e.g., McDonald's Corp. v. Robertson*, 147 F.3d 1301, 1311–13 (11th Cir. 1998); *Campbell Soup Co. v. Giles*, 47 F.3d 467 (1st Cir. 1995).

[21]*University of Texas v. Camenisch*, 451 U.S. 390 (1981). *See also G.G. ex rel. Grimm v. Gloucester County School Board*, 822 F.3d 709 (4th Cir. 2016) (Rule 65 preliminary injunction does not require higher standard than Rule 56 summary judgment motions).

[22]*See, e.g., Slidewaters LLC v.*

motion.[23] Parties seeking a quick decision in the case may seek or consent to consolidation. If the case is not yet ripe for trial on the merits (as when discovery has not yet been completed), courts are hesitant to consolidate the trial with the preliminary injunction hearing.[24]

- *Timing of Order to Consolidate:* The court may order consolidation before or after commencement of the hearing on the preliminary injunction. Courts should not order consolidation unless all parties have adequate warning of the possibility of consolidation and a reasonable opportunity to prepare their positions on the merits.[25]
- *Non-Consolidation and Repetition of Evidence:* If the court does not consolidate the preliminary injunction hearing with the trial on the merits, evidence presented at the preliminary hearing is deemed preserved as part of the record. That evidence need not necessarily be repeated for trial.[26]
- *Preservation of Jury Right:* Consolidation and/or preservation of evidence for trial may not interfere with a party's right to a jury trial.[27] Thus, if the court decides a motion for a preliminary injunction by ruling on issues of fact, evidence presented on those issues of fact is preserved for trial. However, a jury will not be bound by the previous findings of fact made by the judge in the preliminary injunction hearing.[28]

Modifying or Dissolving a Preliminary Injunction

Although Rule 65(a) does not expressly address the point, a preliminary injunction will dissolve upon the entry of a final judgment in that case. Before that time, a preliminary injunction can be modified or dissolved on motion of a party who demonstrates that changed circumstances warrant a change to

---

Washington State Dep't of Lab. & Indus., 4 F.4th 747, 759 (9th Cir. 2021); *Vieira v. De Souza*, 22 F.4th 304, 307 (1st Cir. 2022).

[23]*League of United Latin Am. Citizens v. Abbott*, — F. Supp. 3d —, 2022 WL 1410729, at *34 (W.D. Tex. 2022); *Republican Nat'l Comm. v. Pelosi*, — F. Supp. 3d —, 2022 WL 1294509, at *5 (D.D.C. 2022).

[24]*Pughsley v. 3750 Lake Shore Drive Co-op. Bldg.*, 463 F.2d 1055, 1057 (7th Cir. 1972).

[25]*See University of Texas v. Camenisch*, 451 U.S. 390, 395 (1981); *Tumey v. Mycroft AI, Inc.*, 27 F.4th 657, 665–66 (8th Cir. 2022). *But cf.*, *Campaign for Family Farms v. Glickman*, 200 F.3d 1180, 1186 (8th Cir. 2000) (When dealing "with a purely legal issue on a fixed administrative standard . . .a district court may properly reach the merits in such a case without expressly ordering consolidation under Rule 65 and without giving the parties adequate notice.").

[26]*See, e.g., Attorney General of Okla. v. Tyson Foods, Inc.*, 565 F.3d 769, 776 (10th Cir. 2009); *League of United Latin Am. Citizens v. Abbott*, — F. Supp. 3d —, 2022 WL 1410729, at *34 (W.D. Tex. 2022).

[27]*See, e.g., New Windsor Volunteer Ambulance Corps v. Meyers*, 442 F.3d 101, 120 (2d Cir. 2006); *N. B. v. United States*, 552 F. Supp. 3d 387, 396 (E.D.N.Y. 2021).

[28]*See University of Texas v. Camenisch*, 451 U.S. 390, 395 (1981).

or end of the injunctive relief.[29]

Appeals

A court's decision to grant, deny, dissolve, continue, or modify a preliminary injunction is immediately appealable.[30]

Relationship to Rule 64

It now appears settled that in cases involving only money damages on an unsecured claim, a party may not use this Rule to obtain a prejudgment injunction aimed at preventing dissipation of assets. Instead, such relief must be sought under other provisions, such as Rule 64's authorization to use state law prejudgment attachment provisions.[31] However, if the lawsuit also seeks equitable relief, the district court might not be restricted by Rule 64 and could still grant a prejudgment injunction that freezes specific assets that are the subject of a restitution or recission claim or that preserves the power of the court to grant final injunctive relief.[32]

Comparison to Temporary Restraining Orders (TROs)

Temporary restraining orders (TROs) are addressed by Rule 65(b). Although both TROs and preliminary injunctions are directed at preserving the status quo until further action can be taken, the two devices are distinct in several respects. TROs may issue without notice to opponents and, if so issued, are effective for no more than 14 days (extendable once, without the opponent's consent, for a maximum of 14 additional days), whereas preliminary injunctions can remain in place for a longer period of time.[33] Courts often use TROs to maintain the status quo until there is an opportunity for a fuller hearing on a motion for a preliminary injunction.[34] Unlike preliminary injunctions, TROs are ordinarily not immediately appealable.[35]

RULE 65(b)—TEMPORARY RESTRAINING ORDER

CORE CONCEPT

Temporary restraining orders (TROs) may be issued without first providing notice to opposing parties, but only where it is

[29] *U.S. v. United Shoe Machinery Corp.*, 391 U.S. 244, 248 (1968). See also *Favia v. Indiana Univ. of Pa.*, 7 F.3d 332, 337 (3d Cir. 1993).

[30] *See* 28 U.S.C.A. § 1292(a)(1). *See also Nutrasweet Co. v. Vit-Mar Enters., Inc.*, 112 F.3d 689 (3d Cir.1997).

[31] *Grupo Mexicano de Desarrollo S.A. v. Alliance Bond Fund, Inc.*, 527 U.S. 308, 330–31 (1999).

[32] *See, e.g., U.S. ex rel. Rahman v. Oncology Associates*, 198 F.3d 489, 495–97 (4th Cir. 1999). *See also De Beers Consol. Mines v. U.S.*, 325 U.S. 212, 219 (1945); *Deckert v. Independence Shares Corp.*, 311 U.S. 282, 289 (1940) (in case where equitable remedy of recission is sought, district court has authority to issue prejudgment injunction freezing assets as means of preserving status quo pending final outcome of case).

[33] *Tumey v. Mycroft AI, Inc.*, 27 F.4th 657, 665 (8th Cir. 2022).

[34] *See, e.g., Hospital Resource Personnel, Inc. v. U.S.*, 860 F. Supp. 1554, 1556 (S.D. Ga. 1994).

[35] *See, e.g, East Bay Sanctuary Covenant v. Trump*, 909 F.3d 1219 (9th Cir. 2018).

clear that pre-issuance notice was not feasible and only when supported by the movant's affidavit or verified complaint. The duration of a TRO is limited to a maximum of 28 days (a 14-day initial period with the potential for a single 14-day renewal).

APPLICATIONS

Purpose

The purpose of a temporary restraining order is generally to preserve the status quo until the court has an opportunity to hear a request for fuller relief, such as a preliminary injunction.[36] Because a temporary restraining order implicates the due process rights of opposing parties, courts strictly enforce the limitations in this Rule.[37]

TROs on Notice to Opposing Party

This subpart is concerned principally with TROs issued *without* notice to an adversary, but a with-notice option certainly remains available in federal court. Written notice and formal service is the preferred method of giving notice. However, the court has substantial discretion to approve lesser notice.[38] If written notice is impractical, a party seeking a TRO may attempt to notify the adversary orally.

TRO Without Notice to Opposing Party

A TRO issued without first notifying the opponent is permitted but disfavored.[39] Before granting such relief, the court will require that the party seeking such relief establish the need to proceed *ex parte*, as well as all substantive case law prerequisites for a preliminary injunction.[40] Thus, to obtain a TRO without providing notice to opposing parties, the moving party must provide proof of immediate irreparable injury and a statement of the efforts made to notify the opposing party or why such notice ought not to be required.[41]

- *Irreparable Injury:* By affidavit or verified complaint,[42] the moving party must show that irreparable injury will occur if the TRO is not issued without notice and an op-

---

[36]*See, e.g., Hope v. Warden York County Prison*, 956 F.3d 156 (3d Cir. 2020).

[37]*Castillo v. Whitmer*, 479 F. Supp. 3d 565, 567-68 (W.D. Mich. 2020).

[38]*People of State of Ill. ex rel. Hartigan v. Peters*, 871 F.2d 1336, 1340 (7th Cir. 1989) ("We leave the question of what constitutes sufficient notice primarily to the district court's discretion.").

[39]*See, e.g., Aenergy, S.A. v. Republic of Angola*, 31 F.4th 119, 132 n.73 (2d Cir. 2022); *Reno Air Racing Ass'n., Inc. v. McCord*, 452 F.3d 1126, 1131 (9th Cir. 2006).

[40]*See, e.g., Phillips v. Charles Schreiner Bank*, 894 F.2d 127, 131 (5th Cir. 1990); *Norris v. Stanley*, 558 F. Supp. 3d 556, 558 (W.D. Mich. 2021).

[41]*Gibson v. Frederick Cnty., Maryland*, — F. Supp. 3d —, 2022 WL 2593710, at *1 (D. Md. 2022); *Norris v. Stanley*, 558 F. Supp. 3d 556, 558 (W.D. Mich. 2021).

[42]Fed.R.Civ.P. 65(b)(1)(A). *See also Tobey v. Chibucos*, 890 F.3d 634 n.10 (7th Cir. 2018).

portunity for the opponent to be heard.[43]

(1) *Affidavit or Verified Complaint:* The quality and detail required in an affidavit or complaint may vary, but the explanation should be sufficient for the court to assess the risk of irreparable injury and the need for prompt action.[44]

(2) *What Constitutes "Irreparable Injury":* This concept is a flexible, sometimes elusive one. It may exist when the potential loss will be difficult or impossible to calculate (possibly, lost future profits or business reputation).[45] It may also exist when the loss is of a type normally considered incompensable by money (possibly, damage to unique property or land).[46]

- *Statement Concerning Notice to Opponent:* The moving party must also explain in writing the efforts made (if any) to notify the opponent of the TRO hearing and the reasons why the court should not require further notification.[47] The court may treat failure to make reasonable efforts as a ground for denying the motion for a TRO.[48]
- *Contents of a TRO Order Issued Without Notice:* A TRO that is issued without notice must state the date and hour it was issued, must describe the injury found to be irreparable, and must explain why the court found it to be so.[49] It must also state why the order was issued without notice to the opponent.[50] It must be promptly filed in the clerk's office and entered on the official court record.[51]

Duration of a TRO

A TRO issued without notice to the opponent must expire no later than 14 days after issuance, unless an extension is

---

[43] *See, e.g., American Can Co. v. Mansukhani*, 742 F.2d 314, 321–24 (7th Cir. 1984); *Norris v. Stanley*, 558 F. Supp. 3d 556, 558 (W.D. Mich. 2021).

[44] *See, e.g., American Can Co. v. Mansukhani*, 742 F.2d 314, 321–24 (7th Cir. 1984); *Gibson v. Frederick Cnty., Maryland*, — F. Supp. 3d —, 2022 WL 2593710, at *1 (D. Md. 2022).

[45] *Rodriguez v. Molina, F. Supp. 3d* —, 2022 WL 2287805, at *2 (S.D. Iowa 2022) (stating that a parent's lawful right to connect with and visit a child constitutes irreparable harm).

[46] *Norris v. Stanley*, 558 F. Supp. 3d 556, 560 (W.D. Mich. 2021).

[47] *Norris v. Stanley*, 558 F. Supp. 3d 556, 558 (W.D. Mich. 2021); *Pagan-Gonzalez v. United States*, 544 F. Supp. 3d 217, 218-19 (D.P.R. 2021).

[48] *See, e.g., American Can Co. v. Mansukhani*, 742 F.2d 314, 321–24 (7th Cir. 1984).

[49] *See, e.g., Ben David v. Travisono*, 495 F.2d 562, 564–65 (1st Cir. 1974).

[50] *Hope v. Warden York Cty. Prison*, 972 F.3d 310, 321 (3d Cir. 2020).

[51] *See, e.g., Garcia v. Yonkers School District*, 561 F.3d 97, 106 (2d Cir. 2009).

allowed.[52] If the opponent consents to such an extension, the order may be extended for any length of time to which the parties agree[53] (typically, the TRO is converted into a preliminary injunction in such circumstances). In the absence of the opponent's consent, TROs may be extended by an additional period not greater than the length of time in the original order, and in no event for more than 14 additional days.[54] If the court issues such an extension, its reasons for doing so must be memorialized on the record.[55] The court may, of course, set the TRO to expire in a period *less* than 14 days. Even when issued *with* notice to the opponent, TROs cannot continue indefinitely unless they meet the standards required for a preliminary injunction.[56] A TRO issued by a state court prior to removal will remain in effect, but cannot exceed the time limits of this Rule, measured from the date of removal.[57]

- *Obtaining an Extension:* A party seeking a judicial extension of a TRO must move for the extension within the time limitation of the original order and must show good cause for the extension. Good cause might be a continuation of the circumstances of irreparable injury that justified the original order or such new circumstances as the TRO produced. For example, if the court is considering issuance of a preliminary injunction, extension of a TRO might be appropriate to allow the court more time to decide the preliminary injunction question.[58]

Timing of Hearing for Subsequent Preliminary Injunction

If the court grants a temporary restraining order without prior notice to opposing parties, the court must hold a hearing on an ensuing motion for a preliminary injunction "at the earli-

---

[52]*See Sampson v. Murray*, 415 U.S. 61, 86–87 (1974); *Tumey v. Mycroft AI, Inc.*, 27 F.4th 657, 665 (8th Cir. 2022).

[53]*See, e.g., Hudson v. Barr*, 3 F.3d 970, 973 (6th Cir. 1993); *In re Arthur Treacher's Franchise Litigation*, 689 F.2d 1150 (3d Cir.1982).

[54]*See, e.g., Belbacha v. Bush*, 520 F.3d 452, 455 (D.C. Cir. 2008); *Oregon Nautral Desert Ass'n v. Bushue*, ___ F. Supp. 3d ___, 2022 WL 910082, at *2 n.1 (D. Or. 2022).

[55]*But cf., Reliance Ins. Co. v. Mast Const. Co.*, 159 F.3d 1311, 1316 (10th Cir. 1998) (extension of expiration date of order does not require that operative language of order must be restated, it is sufficient that extension incorporated by reference such language as was previously laid out when order was originally granted).

[56]*See, e.g., In re Criminal Contempt Proceedings Against Gerald Crawford, Michael Warren*, 329 F.3d 131, 137 (2d Cir. 2003); *Suzie's Brewery Co. v. Anheuser-Busch Companies, LLC*, 519 F. Supp. 3d 839, 844 n.1 (D. Or. 2021). *But cf., Chicago United Industries, Ltd. v. City of Chicago*, 445 F.3d 940, 946 (7th Cir. 2006) (all TROs are subject to the time limit, not merely "without notice" TROs, citing other cases).

[57]*Uniformed Fire Officers Ass'n v. de Blasio*, 973 F.3d 41, 47 (2d Cir. 2020).

[58]*See, e.g., Joseph v. Hess Oil Virgin Islands Corp.*, 651 F.3d 348, 351 (3d Cir. 2011).

est possible time." That preliminary injunction hearing must move to the head of the court's docket, second only to preliminary injunction matters that are already pending.

Failure to Seek a Subsequent Preliminary Injunction

If a party who obtained a TRO without prior notice fails to pursue an application for a preliminary injunction at the scheduled hearing, the court will dissolve the TRO. The burden to prove clear entitlement to injunctive relief remains with the party requesting such relief.[59]

Motion to Modify or Dissolve Order

Like preliminary injunctions, TROs may be modified or dissolved on motion of a party. A party subject to a TRO issued without prior notice may move to dissolve or modify the order by providing at least 2-days' notice to all parties of a hearing on the motion to dissolve, unless the court permits less notice.[60] No specific time is prescribed for convening a hearing on a motion to modify or dissolve, though courts are directed to schedule such hearings "as expeditiously as the ends of justice require." Grounds for dissolving or modifying a TRO include a demonstration that the purpose of the order has been fulfilled or that the court lacks personal jurisdiction over the defendant.[61] An order may also be modified or dissolved if the court is persuaded that the circumstances requiring the order have changed.

Appeal

Generally, a court's decision to grant, deny, modify, continue, or dissolve a temporary restraining order is not appealable.[62]

Comparison to Preliminary Injunction

Like a TRO, a preliminary injunction is usually directed at freezing circumstances in place until there is greater opportunity to hear the merits of a case.[63] When the opposing party actually receives notice, a motion for a TRO is functionally identical to a motion for a preliminary injunction.[64] However, a preliminary injunction cannot be issued unless all parties are provided with notice of the motion for such relief,

---

[59]*Hope v. Warden York Cty. Prison*, 972 F.3d 310, 321 (3d Cir. 2020).

[60]*See Right to Life of Cent. California v. Bonta*, 562 F. Supp. 3d 947, 968 (E.D. Cal. 2021).

[61]*Alston v. www.calculator.com*, 476 F. Supp. 3d 1295, 1309 (S.D. Fla. 2020); *Nogales v. Dep't of Homeland Sec.*, 524 F. Supp. 3d 538, 542 (N.D. Tex. 2021).

[62]*See, e.g., In re Lorillard Tobacco Co.*, 370 F.3d 982, 986 (9th Cir. 2004); *Robinson v. Lehman*, 771 F.2d 772, 782 (3d Cir. 1985) (temporary restraining order not appealable unless denial of order effectively decides the case).

[63]*See, e.g., Garcia v. Yonkers School District*, 561 F.3d 97 (2d Cir. 2009); *Eastman v. United States*, __ F. Supp. 3d __, 2022 WL 2763436, at *2 (D.N.M. 2022).

[64]*Donovan v. Vance*, 576 F. Supp. 3d 816, 822 (E.D. Wash. 2021); *Texas v. Becerra*, 577 F. Supp. 3d 527, 537 (N.D. Tex. 2021).

whereas it is possible in some circumstances to obtain a TRO without first providing notice to opposing parties.[65] Preliminary injunctions may be effective for the pendency of the case, whereas TROs issued without notice are effective, with a single renewal, for a maximum of 28 days.[66] When courts grant TROs, it is often with an eye towards holding a prompt hearing on a motion for a preliminary injunction.[67] Unlike orders granting preliminary injunctions, an order granting or denying a TRO is not usually immediately appealable.[68]

RULE 65(c)—SECURITY

CORE CONCEPT

Before it may grant a preliminary injunction or temporary restraining order, the court usually must require that the moving party post a bond or other security. That bond or other security would then be available to reimburse the opponent for costs or damages the opponent might incur if it is later determined that the injunction or TRO was wrongfully issued. The amount of the required security lies with the court's discretion. No security may be required from the United States, federal officers, or federal agencies if they are the parties obtaining the injunction or TRO.

APPLICATIONS

Mandatory Nature of Posted Security

Although the language of Rule 65(c) seems to obligate a court to impose a bond, some cases treat the decision to impose a bond as a matter of discretion for the court.[69] Exceptions to the bond requirement have been recognized where there is no realistic likelihood of harm to the enjoined party, where posting a bond would impose a burden on the movant that outweighs any possible loss to the enjoined party, and when a

[65]*See, e.g., Hope v. Warden York County Prison*, 956 F.3d 156 (3d Cir. 2020); *Eastman v. United States*, __ F. Supp. 3d __, 2022 WL 2763436, at *1 (D.N.M. 2022).

[66]*Tumey v. Mycroft AI, Inc.*, 27 F.4th 657, 665 (8th Cir. 2022); *Miller v. Mitchell*, 598 F.3d 139, 145 (3d Cir. 2010) (order designated as temporary restraining order can be a preliminary injunction if it is entered for an indefinite period with notice to defendant and an appropriate hearing). *Cf., Bennett v. Medtronic, Inc.*, 285 F.3d 801, 804 (9th Cir. 2002) (if district court's order exceeds time limits of temporary restraining order, order should be reviewed under standards of preliminary injunction).

[67]*Granny Goose Foods, Inc. v. Brotherhood of Teamsters and Auto Truck Drivers Local No. 70 of Alameda County*, 415 U.S. 423 (1974).

[68]*But see., E. Bay Sanctuary Covenant v. Biden*, 993 F.3d 640, 660 (9th Cir. 2021) (TRO may be appealed if it has been effect for 30 days).

[69]*See, e.g., Pineda v. Skinner Servs., Inc.*, 22 F.4th 47, 57 (1st Cir. 2021); *BankDirect Capital Finance, LLC v. Capital Premium Financing, Inc.*, 912 F.3d 1054 (7th Cir. 2019). *But see Nichols v. Alcatel USA, Inc.*, 532 F.3d 364 (5th Cir. 2008) (failure to require bond is reversible error); *Sprint Communications Co. L.P. v. CAT Communications Intern., Inc.*, 335 F.3d 235 (3d Cir. 2003) (exceptions to bond requirement are rare).

movant seeks to enforce important federal rights or public interests.[70] In such circumstances, courts may impose a nominal bond of $1. Litigants who are unwilling or unable to post a bond can dismiss their actions.[71]

Time for Posting

If a bond is required, it must be posted when the court grants a preliminary injunction or TRO.[72] There is no requirement to post security when a party initially seeks such relief.

Amount of Security

The maximum amount of security that may be required is the court's estimate of the potential loss to a party that is proximately caused by the erroneous issuance of the injunction or order.[73] When setting the amount of security, district courts usually err on the high side because the movant still must prove its loss in order to recover the bond.[74] The court has discretion to require posting of lesser amounts than the bound party's estimated potential loss.[75] Thus, in some cases the court may limit security to a nominal amount, if such a small sum is in the interest of justice.[76] Courts have also required the moving party to post a nominal bond where the parties have failed to address the bond requirement.[77]

---

[70] *Pineda v. Skinner Servs., Inc.*, 22 F.4th 47, 57 (1st Cir. 2021); *B. P. J. v. W. Virginia State Bd. of Educ.*, 550 F. Supp. 3d 347, 357 (S.D.W. Va. 2021).

[71] *Mead Johnson & Co. v. Abbott Laboratories*, 209 F.3d 1032, 1033 (7th Cir. 2000).

[72] *Corning Inc. v. PicVue Electronics, Ltd.*, 365 F.3d 156, 158 (2d Cir. 2004); *Providence Title Co. v. Truly Title, Inc.*, 547 F. Supp. 3d 585, 613 (E.D. Tex. 2021) (allowing moving party to deposit bond within three business days of the order).

[73] *See, e.g., Hoechst Diafoil Co. v. Nan Ya Plastics Corp.*, 174 F.3d 411, 421 (4th Cir. 1999) (citing authority for bond amount of zero if no evidence supported likelihood of harm); *St. Michael's Media, Inc. v. Mayor & City Council of Baltimore*, 566 F. Supp. 3d 327, 382 (D. Md. 2021), aff'd, 2021 WL 6502220 (4th Cir. 2021).

[74] *St. Michael's Media, Inc. v. Mayor & City Council of Baltimore*, 566 F. Supp. 3d 327, 382 (D. Md. 2021), aff'd, 2021 WL 6502220 (4th Cir. 2021); *GlaxoSmithKline LLC v. Boehringer Ingelheim Pharms., Inc.*, 484 F. Supp. 3d 207, 229 (E.D. Pa. 2020), appeal dismissed sub nom. *GlaxoSmithKline LLC v. Boehringer Ingelheim Pharm*, 2020 WL 8922861 (3d Cir. 2020).

[75] *See, e.g., GoTo.com, Inc. v. Walt Disney Co.*, 202 F.3d 1199, 1211 (9th Cir. 2000); *International Ass'n of Machinists and Aerospace Workers v. Eastern Airlines, Inc.*, 925 F.2d 6 (1st Cir. 1991).

[76] *See, e.g., Davis v. Mineta*, 302 F.3d 1104 (10th Cir. 2002) ("Ordinarily, where a party is seeking to vindicate the public interest served by [federal environmental law], a minimal bond amount should be considered."); *Doe 1 v. Perkiomen Valley Sch. Dist.*, ___ F. Supp. 3d ___, 2022 WL 356868, at *28 (E.D. Pa. 2022). *But see MacDonald v. Chicago Park Dist.*, 132 F.3d 355, 358 (7th Cir. 1997) (finding error in the imposition of $100 bond upon a plaintiff of modest means as the loss to the defendant could be potentially much larger).

[77] *Schrader v. Sunday*, ___ F. Supp. 3d ___, 2022 WL 1542154, at *11 (M.D. Pa. 2022).

Inapplicability of State Law to Bond Requirement

Federal Rule of Civil Procedure 65(c), not state law, governs the amount and type of security that will be imposed.[78]

Requests for Increase in Bond

If a party believes the amount designated for the bond is insufficient to cover damages, the party may seek an increase in the bond during the time when the preliminary relief is in effect—or when the preliminary remedy has been lifted but might still be reimposed. However, once an injunction or restraining order has been reversed and will not be replaced, the amount of the bond cannot be increased.[79]

Standard for "Wrongfully Enjoined"

The majority view is that a prerequisite for an award of damages to a defendant is a finding that the defendant was wrongfully enjoined.[80] Put another way, a party has been wrongfully enjoined if it is ultimately found that the enjoined party had at all times the right to do the enjoined act.[81] If a party obtains permanent injunctive relief, even a preliminary injunction that was wrongly issued would be harmless error because the permanent injunction establishes that the defendant was not wrongfully enjoined.[82]

Judgment on Merits

A party may be wrongfully enjoined even in situations where the underlying case was not resolved on the merits. Thus, a case voluntarily dismissed without prejudice does not necessarily prevent an injured party from successfully seeking relief where the party was wrongfully restrained.[83] Moreover, it is possible that the party that prevails on the merits may nevertheless have benefitted from the issuance of a wrongful preliminary injunction.[84] Finally, a losing plaintiff may be protected from loss by the bond.[85]

---

[78] *See, e.g., Transcontinental Gas Pipe Line Co., 6.04 Acres of Land*, 910 F.3d 1130 (11th Cir. 2018).

[79] *See, e.g., Mead Johnson & Co. v. Abbott Laboratories*, 209 F.3d 1032, 1033 (7th Cir. 2000).

[80] *See, e.g., Front Range Equine Rescue v. Vilsack*, 844 F.3d 1230 (10th Cir. 2017) (party wrongfully enjoined gets presumption of recovery and the district court's discretion to deny damages is limited); *National Kidney Patients Association v. Sullivan*, 958 F.2d 1127 (D.C. Cir. 1992).

[81] *Global Naps, Inc. v. Verizon New England, Inc.*, 489 F.3d 13, 22 (1st Cir. 2007) (rejecting the minority view that injunction is wrongful only if the grant was an abuse of discretion); *Milan Exp., Inc. v. Averitt Exp., Inc.*, 254 F.3d 966 (11th Cir. 2001).

[82] *Fleet Feet, Inc. v. NIKE, Inc.*, 986 F.3d 458, 464 (4th Cir. 2021).

[83] *See, e.g., Mallet & Co. Inc. v. Lacayo*, 16 F.4th 364, 391 (3d Cir. 2021); *U.S. D.I.D. Corp. v. Windstream Communications, Inc.*, 775 F.3d 128, 139 (2d Cir. 2014).

[84] *Grupo Mexicano de Des Arrollo, S.A. v. Alliance Bond Fund, Inc.*, 527 U.S. 308, 314–17 (U.S. 1999).

[85] *See, e.g., Mallet & Co. Inc. v. Lacayo*, 16 F.4th 364, 391 (3d Cir. 2021).

Damages Recoverable

There is a presumption in favor of recovery for a wrongly enjoined party.[86] An injured party's maximum recovery is generally limited to the amount of the bond.[87] However, a party may pursue an independent action for malicious prosecution in the rare case where the elements of that tort are satisfied.[88] A party may recover attorney's fees for advice rendered in connection with proper compliance with the TRO but may not recover attorney's fees for general litigation activities.[89]

Actions Involving the United States

Rule 65(c) exempts the United States, its officers, and agencies from the obligation to post security.[90]

Relation to Rule 65.1

Rule 65.1 governs the procedures by which a party may seek recovery against security posted pursuant to Rule 65(c).

"Non-Injunction" Bonds

One prerequisite for a preliminary injunction or TRO is that the harm facing the moving party must be "irreparable." That showing of "irreparability" might be accomplished by demonstrating that the opponent would be unable to pay money damages to the moving party and, thus, that the only real, practical available remedy is an injunctive one.[91] Some courts permit the opponent to defeat this argument (and, thus, avoid being enjoined) by posting a "non-injunction" bond that could demonstrate—to both the moving party and the court—that the opponent does indeed have adequate resources to pay any resulting judgment (and, thus, that no "irreparability" exists).[92]

RULE 65(d)—CONTENTS AND SCOPE OF EVERY INJUNCTION AND RESTRAINING ORDER

CORE CONCEPT

Injunctions and restraining orders compel a party to behave in a certain manner, either to do something or to refrain from doing something. Because such orders are intended to modify a party's

[86]*Gov't Emps. Ins. Co. v. Relief Med., P.C.*, 554 F. Supp. 3d 482, 505 (E.D.N.Y. 2021); *Smart Study Co. v. Bichha123*, 505 F. Supp. 3d 322, 326 (S.D.N.Y. 2020).

[87]*W.R. Grace and Co. v. Local Union 759, Intern. Union of United Rubber, Cork, Linoleum and Plastic Workers of America*, 461 U.S. 757, 770 (1983). *See also Mallet & Co. Inc. v. Lacayo*, 16 F.4th 364, 391 (3d Cir. 2021); *Coyne-Delany Co., Inc. v. Capital Development Bd. of State of Ill.*, 717 F.2d 385, 393–94 (7th Cir. 1983).

[88]*Meyers v. Block*, 120 U.S. 206, 211 (1887).

[89]*Smart Study Co. v. B+Baby Store*, 540 F. Supp. 3d 428, 430-31 (S.D.N.Y. 2021).

[90]*Courthouse News Serv. v. New Mexico Admin. Off. of the Cts.*, 566 F. Supp. 3d 1121, 1159 (D.N.M. 2021).

[91]*See generally Lakeview Technology, Inc. v. Robinson*, 446 F.3d 655 (7th Cir. 2006).

[92]*See, e.g., Lakeview Technology, Inc. v. Robinson*, 446 F.3d 655 (7th Cir. 2006).

behavior over that party's objections, the crafting and precision of the language of the injunction or restraining order becomes especially important. This subpart prescribes the required content of every injunction or restraining order and identifies those to whom it will bind.

APPLICATIONS

Required Content—Reasons for Issuance

The injunction or order must be in a stand-alone document and contain an explanation of the reasons for its issuance.[93] However, failure of a district court to provide such an explanation does not, of itself, mandate reversal of the grant of the injunction.[94] A sufficient explanation will state specifically the facts found by the court as well as the conclusions of law upon which the court's decision is based.[95] An explanation of the reason for the court's action is usually direct, without excessive detail. A party may be held in contempt only for violating a clear and unambiguous order.[96]

- *Findings and Conclusions:* Alongside the Rule 65(d) requirement of reasons for issuance of an injunction or restraining order, Rule 52(a) provides that district courts must make findings of fact and conclusions of law when granting or denying a request for an interlocutory injunction.[97]

Required Content—Written Description of Acts Proscribed or Required

The court's order must be reduced to writing.[98] The prohibited or required acts must be described with sufficient detail and clarity so that a layperson who was bound by the order could distinguish between behavior implicated by the order and that which is not.[99] Thus, a court will ordinarily not use highly technical language unless there is no other way to de-

---

[93]*See, e.g., BankDirect Capital Finance, LLC v. Capital Premium Financing, Inc.*, 912 F.3d 1054, 1057 (7th Cir. 2019); *Advent Electronics, Inc. v. Buckman*, 112 F.3d 267 (7th Cir. 1997).

[94]*See, e.g., Test Masters Educational Services, Inc. v. Singh*, 428 F.3d 559, 577 (5th Cir. 2005).

[95]*Schmidt v. Lessard*, 414 U.S. 473, 476 (1974). *See also SEC v. Life Partners Holdings, Inc.*, 854 F.3d 765 (5th Cir. 2017).

[96]*Chevron Corp. v. Donziger*, 990 F.3d 191, 211 (2d Cir. 2021); *Hope v. Warden York Cty. Prison*, 972 F.3d 310, 322 (3d Cir. 2020).

[97]*See, e.g., Fed. Trade Comm'n v. On Point Cap. Partners LLC*, 17 F.4th 1066, 1081 (11th Cir. 2021); *Prairie Band of Potawatomi Indians v. Pierce*, 253 F.3d 1234 (10th Cir.2001).

[98]*See, e.g., In re Rockford Products Corp.*, 741 F.3d 730, 734 (7th Cir. 2013); *Lau v. Meddaugh*, 229 F.3d 121, 123 (2d Cir. 2000).

[99]*See, e.g., Union Home Mortg. Corp. v. Cromer*, 31 F.4th 356, 362 (6th Cir. 2022); *Littell v. Houston Independent School District*, 894 F.3d 616 (5th Cir. 2018). *But cf., Abbott v. Perez*, 138 S.Ct. 2305 (2018) (failure to meet specificity requirement of Rule 65(d) does not deprive appellate court of jurisdiction). *See also United States v. Askins & Miller Orthopaedics, P.A.*, 924 F.3d 1348 (11th Cir. 2019) (normally defendant need look only to four corners of injunctions, but if the stat-

scribe the acts and the parties affected are uniquely capable of understanding such language.[100] The scope of the order depends on the circumstances of the case and can be extended to legitimate activity where such a reach is necessary to protect against unlawful conduct.[101] The court should also include in the contents of its order the duration of the preliminary injunction or TRO.[102]

- *Incorporation by Reference:* Prohibited acts *may not* be described only by reference to the complaint or other documents in the action.[103] However, some courts hold that Rule 65(d) is satisfied if a document specifically describing the prohibited acts is "physically appended" to the injunction order.

Uncertainty: Clarification of Order

The Rules do not require a plaintiff to specify at the pleading stage exactly how the court would craft an appropriate injunction.[104] If a party is uncertain as to the scope of an order, it may petition the court for clarification.[105] The court has discretion to provide such clarification.[106]

Persons Bound

Rule 65(d) describes the categories of persons subject to an injunction or order: (1) the parties;[107] (2) their officers, agents, servants, employees, and attorneys;[108] and (3) other persons "in

---

ute is sufficiently specific and defendant sees what is required, an order to comply with statute can be appropriate); *Fortyune v. American Multi-Cinema, Inc.*, 364 F.3d 1075, 1087 (9th Cir. 2004) (district court has no duty to explain *how* to enforce injunction, only to explain what must or must not be done).

[100] *See, e.g., Reno Air Racing Association, Inc. v. McCord*, 452 F.3d 1126, 1134 (9th Cir. 2006).

[101] *McComb v. Jacksonville Paper Co.*, 336 U.S. 187, 192 (1949). *See, e.g., Russian Media Group, LLC v. Cable America, Inc.*, 598 F.3d 302, 307 (7th Cir. 2010).

[102] *Union Home Mortg. Corp. v. Cromer*, 31 F.4th 356, 364 (6th Cir. 2022).

[103] *Auto Driveaway Franchise Systems, LLC v. Auto Driveaway Richmond, LLC*, 928 F.3d 670 (7th Cir. 2019).

[104] *Equal Rts. Ctr. v. Uber Techs., Inc.*, 2021 WL 981011, at *13 (D.D.C. 2021).

[105] *Daniels Health Sciences, L.L.C. v. Vascular Health Sciences, L.L.C.*, 710 F.3d 579, 586 (5th Cir. 2013).

[106] *Regal Knitwear Co. v. NLRB*, 324 U.S. 9, 15 (1945).

[107] *See, e.g., U.S. v. Vitek Supply Corp.*, 151 F.3d 580 (7th Cir. 1998); *Hernandez v. O'Malley*, 98 F.3d 293, 294 (7th Cir. 1996).

[108] *See, e.g., Whiting v. Marathon County Sheriff's Dept.*, 382 F.3d 700, 704 (7th Cir. 2004) (attorney); *Planned Parenthood of Columbia/Willamette, Inc. v. American Coalition of Life Activists*, 290 F.3d 1058, 1088 n. 19 (9th Cir. 2002) (en banc) (individual employee/agent); *American Civil Liberties Union v. Johnson*, 194 F.3d 1149 (10th Cir.1999) (state's district attorneys); *Bell v. Univ. of Hartford*, 577 F. Supp. 3d 6, 14 n.2 (D. Conn. 2021) (university president). *But cf., Medical Mutual Insurance Co. of Maine v. Indian Harbor Insurance Co.*, 583 F.3d 57, 63–64 (1st Cir. 2009) (agents of company can be enjoined, but they are not personally liable if they are not parties to lawsuit).

active concert or participation" with the parties.[109] Nonparties can be bound only if they receive actual notice of the order.[110] A court may enjoin a nonparty only if the plaintiff validly invokes federal jurisdiction by satisfying the traceability and redressability requirements of standing against a defendant.[111] Courts must conduct a fact-intensive examination of the actuality of concert or participation by the nonparty, without regard to the motives that prompt the concert or participation.[112]

Successor in Interest

Persons or entities who are successors in interest to the enjoined parties will be bound by the injunction, subject to the ordinary requirements of notice.[113]

Successors in Office: Relation to Rule 25

An injunction against a public official also binds successors in office.[114] Rule 25(d), governing replacement in office while a lawsuit is pending, provides that in such circumstances, the successor in office automatically replaces the predecessor, and the lawsuits proceeds to its conclusion.[115]

Notice to Persons Bound

No one is bound by an injunction or order until that person receives fair notice of the judicial act.[116] However, formal notice, in the form of service of documents, is not necessarily required to bind a party or those in privity with a party. A party or a person in a close relationship with a party may be bound if they simply have actual knowledge of the injunction or order.[117]

Personal Jurisdiction

Persons outside the jurisdiction of the court are not subject to its orders.[118]

---

[109] *Regal Knitwear Co. v. N.L.R.B.*, 324 U.S. 9 (1945); *California Chamber of Com. v. Council for Educ. & Rsch. on Toxics*, 29 F.4th 468, 483 (9th Cir. 2022).

[110] *Uniformed Fire Officers Ass'n v. de Blasio*, 973 F.3d 41, 48 (2d Cir. 2020).

[111] *Jacobson v. Fla. Sec'y of State*, 974 F.3d 1236, 1255 (11th Cir. 2020).

[112] *Al Otro Lado v. Wolf*, 497 F. Supp. 3d 914, 929 (S.D. Cal. 2020).

[113] *See, e.g., Asetek Danmark A/S v. CMI USA, Inc.*, 852 F.3d 1352 (Fed.Cir. 2017).

[114] *See, e.g., Salt River Agricultural Improvement & Power District v. Lee*, 672 F.3d 1176, 1180 (9th Cir. 2012).

[115] Fed.R.Civ.P. 25(d).

[116] *See, e.g., ADT Security Services, Inc. v. Lisle-Woodridge Fire Protection District*, 724 F.3d 854, 873 (7th Cir. 2013).

[117] *Spallone v. U.S.*, 493 U.S. 265 (1990).

[118] *See, e.g., Next Invs., LLC v. Bank of China*, 12 F.4th 119, 132–33 (2d Cir. 2021); *R.M.S. Titanic, Inc. v. Haver*, 171 F.3d 943, 957–58 (4th Cir. 1999). *But see, Waffenschmidt v. MacKay*, 763 F.2d 711, 714 (5th Cir. 1985) (nonparties residing outside territorial jurisdiction are nevertheless subject to court's jurisdiction if they intentionally and knowingly aid and abet the violation of court's order).

Persons in Active Concert

This broad category of persons who may be subject to an injunction or order is necessarily fact-specific in application.[119] Generally, however, assignees who take an interest from a party with actual or constructive notice of an injunction or order prohibiting that party from performing a certain act relating to the interest may also be barred from performing the act.[120] Similarly, an injunction can run in favor of any unnamed member of a group, provided that the group is sufficiently identified.[121]

Another way of describing the binding effect of an injunction on non-parties is to identify two important categories of such non-parties. The first category comprises non-parties who are "legally identified" with an enjoined party. Such persons are bound if they were identified in the injunction.[122] The second category is made up of persons who act in concert with named parties in violation of an injunction.[123] However, non-parties in this group are not bound if they acted for their own purposes wholly independent of the named party.[124]

Non-parties who are uncertain as to whether they are bound by an order may seek clarification directly from the court.[125]

Permanent Injunctions

Rule 65(d)'s provisions for a satisfactory explanation of the court's decision, an adequate description of the prohibited acts, and the categories of persons bound by an injunction or order apply equally to permanent injunctions.[126]

Standing to Enforce Permanent Injunction

As is described above, there are many circumstances in which persons who are not parties may nonetheless be bound by an injunction. However, only those who are parties to a lawsuit have standing to seek enforcement of a final

---

[119]*See, e.g., Reliance Ins. Co. v. Mast Const. Co.*, 84 F.3d 372 (10th Cir. 1996) (nonparties bound include alter egos, and also those "with actual notice" who assist defendant or privy in violation of order); *U.S. v. International Broth. of Teamsters, Chauffeurs, Warehousemen and Helpers of America, AFL-CIO*, 964 F.2d 180, 184 (2d Cir. 1992).

[120]*See, e.g., Golden State Bottling Co. v. NLRB*, 414 U.S. 168, 169 (1973); *Regal Knitwear Co. v. N.L.R.B.*, 324 U.S. 9 (1945).

[121]*See, e.g., Zamecnik v. Indian Prairie School District No. 204*, 636 F.3d 874, 879 (7th Cir. 2011) (no requirement to name parties who may enforce injunction and students at the school may enforce an injunction against the school).

[122]*See, e.g., Merial, Ltd. v. Cipia Ltd.*, 681 F.3d 1283, 1304-05 (Fed. Cir. 2012).

[123]*Union Home Mortg. Corp. v. Cromer*, 31 F.4th 356, 364 n.3 (6th Cir. 2022); *Next Invs., LLC v. Bank of China*, 12 F.4th 119, 134 (2d Cir. 2021).

[124]*See, e.g., Merial, Ltd. v. Cipia Ltd.*, 681 F.3d 1283, 1304–05 (Fed. Cir. 2012).

[125]*See, e.g., Gucci America, Inc. v. Weixing Li*, 768 F.3d 122 n.9 (2d Cir. 2014).

[126]*See, e.g., Reich v. ABC/York-Estes Corp.*, 64 F.3d 316, 320 (7th Cir. 1995).

injunction.[127]

Failure to Comply with Injunction or Order

Persons within the categories of Rule 65(d) who have notice of an injunction or order and who do not comply are subject to the court's power of contempt.[128]

RULE 65(e)—OTHER LAWS NOT MODIFIED

CORE CONCEPT

Nothing in Rule 65 is to be construed to modify statutes relating to labor relations, interpleader actions, or actions subject to the jurisdiction of a three-judge court.

APPLICATION

Alterations to Courts' Injunctive Power

In each of the three areas of law addressed by Rule 65(e)—labor law, statutory interpleader, and three-judge courts—federal statutes alter the typical power of courts to issue injunctions and restraining orders. Rule 65(e) makes clear that when those statutes are applicable to a case and conflict with a provision of Rule 65, the statute governs.

RULE 65(f)—COPYRIGHT IMPOUNDMENT

CORE CONCEPT

The provisions of Rule 65 apply to copyright impoundment proceedings.

Additional Research References

Wright & Miller, *Federal Practice and Procedure* §§ 2941 to 62

C.J.S., Injunctions §§ 4 to 54, §§ 60 to 110, §§ 111 to 158, §§ 160 to 206, §§ 213 to 263, §§ 264 to 314, §§ 320 to 341

West's Key Number Digest, Injunction ⚷1001 to 1835

---

[127] *See, e.g., Planned Parenthood of Idaho, Inc. v. Wasden*, 376 F.3d 908 (9th Cir. 2004).

[128] *Gunn v. University Committee to End War in Viet Nam*, 399 U.S. 383 (1970). *See also, Reliance Ins. Co. v. Mast Const. Co.*, 84 F.3d 372, 376 (10th Cir. 1996).

RULE 65.1
PROCEEDINGS AGAINST A SECURITY PROVIDER

Whenever these rules (including the Supplemental Rules for Admiralty or Maritime Claims and Asset Forfeiture Actions) require or allow a party to give security, and security is given with one or more security providers, each provider submits to the court's jurisdiction and irrevocably appoints the court clerk as its agent for receiving service of any papers that affect its liability on the security. The security provider's liability may be enforced on motion without an independent action. The motion and any notice that the court orders may be served on the court clerk, who must promptly send a copy of each to every security provider whose address is known.

[Added July 1, 1966; amended Aug. 1, 1987; Dec. 1, 2006; Dec. 1, 2007; Apr. 26, 2018, eff. Dec. 1, 2018.]

AUTHORS' COMMENTARY ON RULE 65.1

PURPOSE AND SCOPE

Rule 65.1 provides a summary procedure by which parties can enforce their rights against a surety who has posted security.

APPLICATIONS

Scope

Rule 65.1 applies to proceedings to enforce a surety's liability on an appeal bond, a supersedeas bond, or an injunction bond posted pursuant to Rule 65(c). The Rule also applies when the Supplemental Rules for Certain Admiralty and Maritime Claims require the posting of bond.

Injunction Bonds: Rebuttable Presumption

The majority of courts hold that a party wrongfully enjoined under Rule 65 enjoys a rebuttable presumption in favor of recovering provable damages up to the limit of any bond required under Rule 65(c). Only in "rare cases" will the wrongfully enjoined party not be entitled to recovery on the bond.[1]

Alternative Procedures

Rule 65.1 is not the only means by which a party can seek to collect on a bond. Instead of employing the Rule, a party may bring an independent action against the security provider in a state or federal court.[2]

Procedure for Collecting on Bond

The appropriate method for seeking to collect from a security provider under Rule 65.1 is a motion for judgment on the bond.[3]

Timing

Generally, a party may seek recovery under Rule 65.1 once the court has terminated or altered the relief that the bond secured. Thus, if a court determines that a preliminary injunction was improvidently granted, or was of excessive scope, the party previously enjoined may then move against the bond for damages.[4]

Consent to Personal Jurisdiction

Rule 65.1 provides that when a security provider posts a bond or other security, the security provider submits to the personal jurisdiction of the court for purposes of any litigation relating to liability on the bond.[5] Personal jurisdiction is discussed in more detail earlier in this text.

Service of Process

Upon posting bond, a security provider also irrevocably appoints the clerk of court as the security provider's agent to receive service of process in matters relating to liability on the bond.

Notice

A party seeking to collect on a bond should serve the motion on the clerk of court, along with such other notice as the court may require. Rule 65.1 requires that the clerk shall "forthwith" send copies of the documents to all affected security providers whose addresses are known.

Injunction Staying Enforcement

Although Rule 65.1 is intended to provide an expeditious means of recovering damages from a bond, there are situations

---

[1] *Nintendo of America, Inc. v. Lewis Galoob Toys, Inc.*, 16 F.3d 1032, 1039 (9th Cir. 1994).

[2] *See, e.g., State of Ala. ex rel. Siegelman v. U.S. E.P.A.*, 925 F.2d 385, 388 (11th Cir. 1991).

[3] *See, e.g., Global Naps, Inc. v. Verizon New England, Inc.*, 489 F.3d 13, 20 (1st Cir. 2007); *Lyrick Studios, Inc. v. Big Idea Productions, Inc.*, 420 F.3d 388 (5th Cir. 2005).

[4] *See, e.g., American Bible Soc. v. Blount*, 446 F.2d 588, 595 n. 12 (3d Cir. 1971).

[5] *See, e.g., Instant Air Freight Co. v. C.F. Air Freight, Inc.*, 882 F.2d 797, 804 (3d Cir. 1989).

in which Rule 65.1 proceedings will be stayed. If a court enjoins proceedings against the bond, the injunction must be obeyed until it is modified or dissolved.[6]

Collecting From Principals

Although Rule 65.1 addresses the means by which a party may seek damages on a security provider's bond or other undertaking, courts also permit the use of Rule 65.1 for similar relief against a surety's principal.[7]

Subject-Matter Jurisdiction

If a party seeks in the original action to collect against a bond under Rule 65.1, the court will have supplemental jurisdiction over the claim.[8] If a party seeks to enforce a bond in an independent action, the court has subject-matter jurisdiction under 28 U.S.C.A. § 1352, governing independent actions on bonds posted pursuant to federal law.[9]

Additional Research References

Wright & Miller, *Federal Practice and Procedure* §§ 2971 to 74
C.J.S., Federal Civil Procedure §§ 1273 to 1295
West's Key Number Digest, Federal Civil Procedure ⚷2732 to 2733

---

[6] *Celotex Corp. v. Edwards*, 514 U.S. 300 (1995).

[7] *See, e.g., Willis v. Celotex Corp.*, 970 F.2d 1292 (4th Cir.1992).

[8] *See, e.g., Buddy Systems, Inc. v. Exer-Genie, Inc.*, 545 F.2d 1164, 1166 (9th Cir. 1976).

[9] *See, e.g., Milan Exp., Inc. v. Averitt Exp., Inc.*, 208 F.3d 975, 980 (11th Cir. 2000).

RULE 66
RECEIVERS

These rules govern an action in which the appointment of a receiver is sought or a receiver sues or is sued. But the practice in administering an estate by a receiver or a similar court-appointed officer must accord with the historical practice in federal courts or with a local rule. An action in which a receiver has been appointed may be dismissed only by court order.

[Amended effective March 19, 1948; October 20, 1949; April 30, 2007, effective December 1, 2007.]

AUTHORS' COMMENTARY ON RULE 66

PURPOSE AND SCOPE

A receiver is someone appointed by the court to take temporary custody of, and then work to preserve, property or other assets pending the outcome of a judicial proceeding. Typically, a receiver is appointed by the court when property or some other asset is being contested in litigation and the court is persuaded that the property or asset is in imminent danger of being lost, concealed, removed, diminished, or otherwise damaged. The purpose of a receivership—like preliminary injunctions and temporary restraining orders—is to preserve the parties' pre-dispute positions (the "*status quo ante*") while the court ponders the merits of an underlying fight.

Rule 66 provides that, when appointed by district courts, federal equity receivers must administer estates in accordance with prior federal practice and local court rules. Once an equity receiver is appointed in a particular lawsuit, the action may not thereafter be dismissed without the court's prior approval.

APPLICATIONS

Role of Federal Equity Receivers

Receivership is an extraordinary equitable remedy, justified only in extreme circumstances.[1] It is not a substantive entitlement, but an ancillary tool used to facilitate the primary relief sought in a lawsuit.[2] Acting as equity tribunals, federal courts have broad discretion and powers to determine relief in an equity receivership.[3] They appoint equity receivers to assume custody, control, and management of property that either is presently involved or is likely to become involved in litigation.[4] The receiver is charged to preserve the property, and any rents or profits the property earns, until a final disposition by the court.[5] Although typically appointed only to care for property, a federal equity receiver may be appointed where other, extraordinary circumstances compel intimate judicial supervision[6] (including, in appropriate circumstances, to aid in execution of a judgment).[7]

- *Officer of the Court:* An equity receiver is deemed to be an officer of the court, not an agent of any litigant.[8]

---

[1]*See Morgan Stanley Smith Barney LLC v. Johnson*, 952 F.3d 978, 980 (8th Cir. 2020); *Netsphere, Inc. v. Baron*, 703 F.3d 296, 305 (5th Cir. 2012).

[2]*See Gordon v. Washington*, 295 U.S. 30, 37 n. 4, 55 S. Ct. 584, 79 L. Ed. 1282 (1935) ("A receivership is only a means to reach some legitimate end sought through the exercise of the power of a court of equity. It is not an end in itself"). *Accord Kelleam v. Maryland Cas. Co. of Baltimore*, 312 U.S. 377, 381, 61 S. Ct. 595, 85 L. Ed. 899 (1941) (same). *See also ACA Fin. Guar. Corp. v. City of Buena Vista*, 298 F. Supp. 3d 834, 847 (W.D. Va. 2018), *aff'd*, 917 F.3d 206 (4th Cir. 2019) (dismissing "appointment of receiver" count as not an independent legal claim); *Roberts v. American Bank & Trust Co., Inc.*, 835 F. Supp. 2d 183, 205 (E.D.La. 2011) (receivership request denied until plaintiff first establishes valid claim for relief).

[3]*See Sec. & Exch. Comm'n v. Stanford Int'l Bank, Ltd.*, 927 F.3d 830, 840 (5th Cir. 2019); *Sec. & Exch. Comm'n v. Wells Fargo Bank, N.A.*, 848 F.3d 1339, 1343–44 (11th Cir. 2017).

[4]*See Netsphere, Inc. v. Baron*, 703 F.3d 296, 305 (5th Cir. 2012); *Gilchrist v. General Elec. Capital Corp.*, 262 F.3d 295, 302 (4th Cir. 2001).

[5]*See Morgan Stanley Smith Barney LLC v. Johnson*, 952 F.3d 978, 981 (8th Cir. 2020); *United States v. Solco I, LLC*, 962 F.3d 1244, 1246 (10th Cir. 2020). *See also Zacarias v. Stanford Int'l Bank, Ltd.*, 945 F.3d 883, 896–97 (5th Cir. 2019) (receivership undermined if claimants could "jump the queue").

[6]*See Gordon v. Washington*, 295 U.S. 30, 37, 55 S. Ct. 584, 79 L.Ed. 1282 (1935). *See also Morgan v. McDonough*, 540 F.2d 527, 534 (1st Cir. 1976) (affirming appointment of federal receiver for public high school, to implement desegregation orders). *See generally De Boer Structures (U.S.A.), Inc. v. Shaffer Tent and Awning Co.*, 187 F. Supp. 2d 910, 925 (S.D. Ohio 2001) (justified only in extreme situations).

[7]*See Gordon v. Washington*, 295 U.S. 30, 37 (1935); *Santibanez v. Wier McMahon & Co.*, 105 F.3d 234, 241 (5th Cir. 1997).

[8]*See United States v. Solco I, LLC*, 962 F.3d 1244, 1246 (10th Cir. 2020); *Zacarias v. Stanford Int'l Bank, Ltd.*, 945 F.3d 883, 896 (5th Cir. 2019).

Federal Rules Control

The Rules govern all actions in which a party seeks the appointment of a federal equity receiver, as well as all actions brought by or against the receiver once appointed.[9]

Appointment of Receivers

Rule 66 does not create a substantive right to the appointment of a receiver; a statute or general principle of equity must first justify the appointment. Federal law controls whether an equity receiver should be appointed, even in a diversity case.[10] But the Rule provides little guidance other than requiring that a receiver's appointment and work "accord with the historical practice in federal courts or with a local rule."[11] Absent explicit consent from the defendant, the plaintiff ordinarily bears the burden of showing that a receiver should be appointed.[12]

- *Who May Seek An Appointment:* The appointment of a receiver may be requested by any person having a legally recognized right to the property—a mere interest or claim to the property will not be sufficient.[13] Receivers are appointed frequently at the request of secured creditors, mortgagees, judgment creditors, and plaintiffs in shareholder derivative actions.[14]
- *Prerequisites for Appointment:* The appointment of a receiver is an extraordinary remedy, available only upon a clear showing that no remedy at law is available or adequate,[15] and that a receivership is essential to protect the property from some threatened loss or injury pending a final disposition by the court.[16] Although no precise formula exists for assessing whether a receiver ought to be appointed,[17] the courts consider various factors, including:
    - the existence of a valid claim by the party seeking

[9] *See Canada Life Assur. Co. v. LaPeter*, 563 F.3d 837, 842–43 (9th Cir. 2009); *Phelan v. Middle States Oil Corp.*, 210 F.2d 360, 363 (2d Cir. 1954).

[10] *See Morgan Stanley Smith Barney LLC v. Johnson*, 952 F.3d 978, 980 & 983 (8th Cir. 2020); *Canada Life Assur. Co. v. LaPeter*, 563 F.3d 837, 842–43 (9th Cir. 2009). *But see Hendricks & Lewis PLLC v. Clinton*, 766 F.3d 991, 999 (9th Cir. 2014) (Rule prevails over State law, but does not set different standard than State one).

[11] *See* Rule 66. *See also U.S. Bank Nat'l Ass'n v. Nesbitt Bellevue Prop. LLC*, 866 F. Supp. 2d 247, 250 (S.D.N.Y. 2012); *New York Cmty. Bank v. Sherman Ave. Assocs., LLC*, 786 F. Supp. 2d 171, 175 (D.D.C. 2011).

[12] *See U.S. Bank Nat'l Ass'n v. Nesbitt Bellevue Prop. LLC*, 866 F. Supp. 2d 247, 255 (S.D.N.Y. 2012).

[13] *See Netsphere, Inc. v. Baron*, 703 F.3d 296, 305–06 (5th Cir. 2012); *Piambino v. Bailey*, 757 F.2d 1112, 1131–32 (11th Cir. 1985).

[14] *See Santibanez v. Wier McMahon & Co.*, 105 F.3d 234, 241 (5th Cir. 1997) (by judgment creditors).

[15] *See United States v. Bradley*, 644 F.3d 1213, 1310 (11th Cir. 2011).

[16] *See Gordon v. Washington*, 295 U.S. 30, 55 S. Ct. 584, 79 L. Ed. 1282 (1935); *Aviation Supply Corp. v. R.S.B.I. Aerospace, Inc.*, 999 F.2d 314, 317 (8th Cir. 1993).

[17] *See Canada Life Assur. Co. v. LaPeter*, 563 F.3d 837, 844 (9th Cir. 2009).

the appointment;
- the imminent nature of any danger to the property, to its concealment or removal, or to its value;
- the adequacy of other legal remedies;
- the lack of a less drastic equitable remedy;
- the plaintiff's probable success in the lawsuit and the risk of irreparable injury to the property;
- whether the defendant has engaged, or may engage, in any fraudulent actions with respect to the property;
- the likelihood that appointing the receiver will do more good than harm; *and*
- whether the potential harm to the plaintiff outweighs the injury to others.[18]

Each factor need not be satisfied, so long as the court determines that its review favors the receiver's appointment.[19]

Consent to Appointment

The court may appoint a receiver where the defendant both admits liability for the claim asserted in the litigation and consents to the appointment of a receiver—provided that there has been no improper attempt by the parties to collusively manufacture federal jurisdiction.[20] Whether parties can, by contract, compel the appointment of a receiver is less clear.[21]

Discretion of the District Court

Whether to appoint a receiver lies within the district judge's sound discretion.[22]

Who May Be Appointed

The court may appoint as the receiver any person deemed capable of serving in that capacity. Ordinarily, this requires the appointment of someone who is indifferent between the

---

[18]*See Morgan Stanley Smith Barney LLC v. Johnson*, 952 F.3d 978, 980–81 (8th Cir. 2020); *Canada Life Assur. Co. v. LaPeter*, 563 F.3d 837, 844 (9th Cir. 2009).

[19]*See Morgan Stanley Smith Barney LLC v. Johnson*, 952 F.3d 978, 981 (8th Cir. 2020) (fraud is considered, but not always required); *Fleet Business Credit, L.L.C. v. Wings Restaurants, Inc.*, 291 B.R. 550, 556 (N.D. Okla. 2003) (appointing receiver where several factors weigh in favor).

[20]*See In re Reisenberg*, 208 U.S. 90, 28 S. Ct. 219, 52 L. Ed. 403 (1908).

[21]*Compare LNV Corp. v. Harrison Family Bus., LLC*, 132 F. Supp. 3d 683, 691 (D. Md. 2015) (rejecting such an argument), *with Pioneer Capital Corp. v. Environamics Corp.*, 2003 WL 345349, at *9 (D. Me. Feb. 14, 2003), *aff'd*, 2003 WL 1923765 (D. Me. Apr. 23, 2003) (existence of express contractual right to receiver, coupled with "adequate prima facie evidence of a default," may be sufficient to warrant appointment). *See also PNC Bank, Nat'l Ass'n v. Goyette Mechanical Co.*, 15 F. Supp. 3d 754, 758 (E.D. Mich. 2014) (advance consent to appointment of receiver is "strong factor" in favor of appointment).

[22]*See Morgan Stanley Smith Barney LLC v. Johnson*, 952 F.3d 978, 981 (8th Cir. 2020); *Netsphere, Inc. v. Baron*, 703 F.3d 296, 305 (5th Cir. 2012).

parties.[23] Federal law prevents the judge from appointing as a receiver any person related to the judge by consanguinity within the fourth degree,[24] a clerk or deputy of the court (absent special circumstances),[25] or a federal employee or person employed by the appointing judge.[26]

Place of Appointment

Because the appointment of a receiver is a type of *in rem* proceeding, the appointing court must enjoy a strong relationship to the contemplated receivership: a substantial portion of the defendant's business must be conducted in the host district, or a substantial portion of the anticipated receivership property must be located within the host district.

- *Conflicting Claims to Jurisdiction:* If two courts of concurrent and coordinate jurisdiction (*e.g.*, two federal courts) attempt to assert a claim to the same property, the court where the legal papers are first filed assumes exclusive jurisdiction, irrespective of whether its receiver is the first to obtain physical possession of the property. If the two courts are not of the same or concurrent jurisdiction (*e.g.*, one State and one federal court), and where the subject matter in the one litigation is not the same as in the other litigation, or where no constructive possession of the property is obtained through the filing, the court whose receiver first obtains actual possession of the property assumes exclusive jurisdiction.[27]

Notice of Appointment

Generally, the court gives notice to all parties before appointing an equity receiver. But where notice is impractical or self-defeating, or where the appointment must be made immediately, the court may appoint a receiver *ex parte*.[28]

Effect of Appointment

Once a receiver is appointed and gives the bond required by the court, the court and the receiver obtain exclusive jurisdiction of all pertinent property, no matter where it is kept.[29] To obtain jurisdiction over property outside the appointing district, the receiver must first file a copy of the complaint and appointment order in that foreign district.[30] The fees and expenses of receivership are normally a charge against the administered

---

[23] *See Liberte Capital Group, LLC v. Capwill*, 462 F.3d 543, 551 n.2 (6th Cir. 2006).

[24] 28 U.S.C.A. § 458; 18 U.S.C.A. § 1910.

[25] 28 U.S.C.A. § 957.

[26] 28 U.S.C.A. § 958.

[27] *See Harkin v. Brundage*, 276 U.S. 36, 48 S. Ct. 268, 72 L. Ed. 457 (1928).

[28] *See Arkansas La. Gas Co. v. Kroeger*, 303 F.2d 129, 132 (5th Cir. 1962).

[29] *See* 28 U.S.C.A. § 754. *See also United States v. Solco I, LLC*, 962 F.3d 1244, 1246 (10th Cir. 2020); *Liberte Capital Group, LLC v. Capwill*, 462 F.3d 543, 551 (6th Cir. 2006).

[30] 28 U.S.C.A. § 754.

property.[31]

Administration of Estates By Receivers

Traditional federal practice and, where promulgated, local court rules guide a federal equity receiver in administering the receivership property.[32] Although broad, the receiver's power is not unbridled; it does not necessarily extend to every conceivable claim relating to the receivership property.[33]

- *State Law:* The substantive law of the State in which the receivership property is located dictates the manner in which the receiver must manage and operate the receivership property.[34]
- *Federal Bankruptcy Principles:* Because bankruptcy and equity receivers share a common purpose and legal heritage, courts often consult bankruptcy principles in receivership contexts.[35]

Actions by Receivers

A federal equity receiver is authorized to commence and prosecute any action necessary to accomplish the objectives of the receivership.[36] The receiver may be directed to bring suit on specific instructions from the court, or the receiver may independently institute lawsuits pursuant to the receiver's general duties of receiving, controlling, and managing the receivership property. But a receiver's standing to sue is limited to redressing injuries to the entity in receivership.[37]

- *May Sue In Any Jurisdiction:* The receiver may bring suit in any federal district, including those districts outside the court in which the receiver was formally appointed.[38]
- *Equitable Defenses*: Receivers are deemed to have stepped into the shoes of the persons or entities for whom they act.[39] Thus, absent statutory provisions dictating otherwise, defenses that could be asserted

---

[31] *See Netsphere, Inc. v. Baron*, 703 F.3d 296, 311–13 (5th Cir. 2012) (how to assess such costs when receivership appointment was improper).

[32] *See S.E.C. v. Vescor Capital Corp.*, 599 F.3d 1189, 1193–94 (10th Cir. 2010); *Liberte Capital Group, LLC v. Capwill*, 462 F.3d 543, 551 (6th Cir. 2006).

[33] *See Sec. & Exch. Comm'n v. Stanford Int'l Bank, Ltd.*, 927 F.3d 830, 840–41 (5th Cir. 2019).

[34] *See* 28 U.S.C.A. § 959(b). *See also S.E.C. v. Vescor Capital Corp.*, 599 F.3d 1189, 1193–94 (10th Cir. 2010); *Gilchrist v. General Elec. Capital Corp.*, 262 F.3d 295, 302 (4th Cir. 2001).

[35] *See Sec. & Exch. Comm'n v. Quiros*, 966 F.3d 1195, 1199 (11th Cir. 2020); *Sec. & Exch. Comm'n v. Stanford Int'l Bank, Ltd.*, 927 F.3d 830, 840–41 (5th Cir. 2019).

[36] *See Gilchrist v. General Elec. Capital Corp.*, 262 F.3d 295, 302 (4th Cir. 2001) (when appointed, federal equity receivers may sue and be sued as provided by federal law).

[37] *See Rotstain v. Mendez*, 986 F.3d 931, 939–40 (5th Cir. 2021).

[38] 28 U.S.C.A. § 754.

[39] *See Zacarias v. Stanford Int'l Bank, Ltd.*, 945 F.3d 883, 896 (5th Cir. 2019) (under control of receiver, freed from wrongdoers' spell). *See also Isaiah*

against the original party are equally available against the party's equity receiver. However, certain equitable defenses (such as unclean hands) might not be effective against the receiver.[40]

Actions Against Receivers

A person may often sue an equity receiver, without leave of court, for any of the receiver's actions taken after the receiver was appointed and during the receiver's management and operation of the receivership property.[41] The receiver also has discretion to settle contested claims against receivership assets, provided those settlements are fair, equitable, and in the estate's best interest.[42] Ordinarily, receivers cannot be held personally liable for their obligations, liabilities, and missteps.[43]

- *Leave of Court Needed:* Leave of court is required before the receiver may be sued for claims that arise from the property owner's actions or for claims that do not challenge the receiver's actions since appointment.[44] To protect the assets (and to avoid their diminution by the costs of defending lawsuits), the receivership court may issue a blanket injunction staying all litigation against the receiver and entities under the receiver's control.[45] The court enjoys broad control over the time and manner of those proceedings.[46] Intentionally interfering with a receivership in violation of such an injunction is punishable as contempt.[47]
- *Subject to Court's General Equity Power:* Suits against receivers remain subject to the court's general equity

---

v. JPMorgan Chase Bank, 960 F.3d 1296, 1306 (11th Cir. 2020) (axiomatic that receivers obtain only rights/remedies possessed by entity in receivership).

[40]*See Isaiah v. JPMorgan Chase Bank*, 960 F.3d 1296, 1306–07 (11th Cir. 2020) (explaining when defenses will attach and when not). *See also F.D.I.C. v. O'Melveny & Myers*, 61 F.3d 17, 19 (9th Cir. 1995).

[41]28 U.S.C.A. § 959(a). *See Gilchrist v. General Elec. Capital Corp.*, 262 F.3d 295, 301 (4th Cir. 2001) (when appointed, federal equity receivers may sue and be sued as provided by federal law).

[42]*See Sec. & Exch. Comm'n v. Stanford Int'l Bank, Ltd.*, 927 F.3d 830, 840 (5th Cir. 2019).

[43]*See McNulta v. Lochridge*, 141 U.S. 327, 332, 12 S. Ct. 11, 35 L. Ed. 796 (1891). *See also Chua v. Ekonomou*, 1 F.4th 948, 954–55 (11th Cir. 2021) (receivers enjoy immunity for acts taken within scope of their authority, even if erroneous, malicious, or extrajurisdictional); *Alonso v. Weiss*, 932 F.3d 995, 1002–04 (7th Cir. 2019) (predicting that action to hold receiver personally liable would have to prove willful, deliberate misconduct).

[44]*See Barton v. Barbour*, 104 U.S. 126, 128, 26 L. Ed. 672 (1881); *Villegas v. Schmidt*, 788 F.3d 156, 158 (5th Cir. 2015).

[45]*See Sec. & Exch. Comm'n v. Stanford Int'l Bank, Ltd.*, 927 F.3d 830, 840 (5th Cir. 2019); *Liberte Capital Group, LLC v. Capwill*, 462 F.3d 543, 551–52 (6th Cir. 2006).

[46]*See Liberte Capital Group, LLC v. Capwill*, 462 F.3d 543, 552 (6th Cir. 2006).

[47]*See Liberte Capital Group, LLC v. Capwill*, 462 F.3d 543, 552 (6th Cir. 2006).

powers, which the court may exercise to achieve the ends of justice.

Jurisdiction in Actions Involving Receivers

Receivers may only sue or be sued when the district court would enjoy subject-matter jurisdiction over the dispute.

- *Diversity Cases:* In diversity jurisdiction cases, it is the citizenship of the appointed receiver, not the citizenship of the party in receivership, that is examined to determine whether complete diversity exists.[48] Expanding a receivership to include non-diverse non-parties will not necessarily defeat diversity.[49]
- *Federal Question Cases:* The district court's act of appointing a federal receiver probably will suffice to vest that district court with subject-matter jurisdiction over actions brought by or against the receiver in that district.[50] Thus, when instituted in the appointing district, suits by the receiver intended to accomplish the objectives of the receivership are deemed ancillary to the appointing court's subject-matter jurisdiction.[51] Likewise, suits may be maintained against the receiver in the receiver's appointing district even though no independent basis for subject-matter jurisdiction is present.[52]
- *Outside Appointing District:* Suits by or against receivers instituted outside the appointing district will generally require an independent basis for federal subject-matter jurisdiction.[53]

Dismissal of Actions Involving Receivers

After the court appoints a receiver in a litigation, the parties may not thereafter dismiss the litigation without first obtaining the court's approval.[54] This requirement protects against a waste of the court's time in unnecessarily establishing a receivership.

Vacating or Terminating the Receivership

The district court may vacate the order appointing the

---

[48]*See Hoagland ex rel. Midwest Transit, Inc. v. Sandberg, Phoenix & von Gontard, P.C.*, 385 F.3d 737, 738 (7th Cir. 2004); *Clarkson Co. v. Shaheen*, 544 F.2d 624, 628 (2d Cir. 1976). *See generally Mitchell v. Maurer*, 293 U.S. 237, 242, 55 S. Ct. 162, 164, 79 L. Ed. 338 (1934) (in testing diversity, "[w]e necessarily treat the primary receivers as the plaintiffs").

[49]*See Big Shoulders Cap. LLC v. San Luis & Rio Grande R.R., Inc.*, 13 F.4th 560, 565 (7th Cir. 2021).

[50]*See Gay v. Ruff*, 292 U.S. 25, 54 S. Ct. 608, 78 L. Ed. 1099 (1934).

[51]*See Pope v. Louisville, N.A. & C. Ry. Co.*, 173 U.S. 573, 19 S. Ct. 500, 43 L. Ed. 814 (1899); *Haile v. Henderson Nat. Bank*, 657 F.2d 816, 825 (6th Cir. 1981).

[52]*See Rouse v. Hornsby*, 161 U.S. 588, 16 S. Ct. 610, 40 L. Ed. 817 (1896); *Robinson v. Michigan Consol. Gas Co. Inc.*, 918 F.2d 579, 584 (6th Cir. 1990).

[53]*See U.S. v. Franklin National Bank*, 512 F.2d 245, 251 (2d Cir. 1975).

[54]*See* Rule 66.

receiver or terminate the receivership when the objectives of the receivership have been obtained or the need for the receiver has abated,[55] or when the receivership is found to have been improper in the first place.[56]

Appeals

The district court's decision to appoint a receiver may be immediately appealed.[57] The court of appeals will review the appointment under the lenient abuse of discretion standard. If the appointment is found to have been improvident, the court of appeals may reverse and tax the costs and expenses incurred in the receivership on the persons who procured the receivership.[58]

Orders refusing to wind up the receivership or refusing to take steps to accomplish the purposes thereof may also be immediately appealed.[59]

All other orders involving receivers may only be appealed after entry of a final order.[60]

Additional Research References

Wright & Miller, *Federal Practice and Procedure* §§ 2981 to 86

C.J.S., Mechanics Liens § 214; Receivers §§ 1 to 30 et seq., §§ 52 to 103 et seq., §§ 105 to 150 et seq., §§ 163 to 208 et seq., §§ 227 to 256 et seq., §§ 283 to 325 et seq., §§ 365 to 411 et seq., §§ 418 to 431 et seq.

West's Key Number Digest, Receivers ⚷1 to 220

---

[55] *See SEC v. An-Car Oil Co.*, 604 F.2d 114, 119–20 (1st Cir. 1979).

[56] *See Netsphere, Inc. v. Baron*, 703 F.3d 296, 305–11 (5th Cir. 2012).

[57] 28 U.S.C.A. § 1292(a)(2).

[58] *See Tucker v. Baker*, 214 F.2d 627, 631 (5th Cir.1954).

[59] 28 U.S.C.A. § 1292(a)(2).

[60] *See United States v. Solco I, LLC*, 962 F.3d 1244, 1250 (10th Cir. 2020) (courts narrowly construe § 1292(a)(2)); *Hewlett-Packard Co. v. Quanta Storage, Inc.*, 961 F.3d 731, 741 (5th Cir. 2020) (order declining to appoint receiver not immediately appealable).

RULE 67
DEPOSIT INTO COURT

(a) Depositing Property. If any part of the relief sought is a money judgment or the disposition of a sum of money or some other deliverable thing, a party—on notice to every other party and by leave of court—may deposit with the court all or part of the money or thing, whether or not that party claims any of it. The depositing party must deliver to the clerk a copy of the order permitting deposit.

(b) Investing and Withdrawing Funds. Money paid into court under this rule must be deposited and withdrawn in accordance with 28 U.S.C. §§ 2041 and 2042 and any like statute. The money must be deposited in an interest-bearing account or invested in a court-approved, interest-bearing instrument.

[Amended effective October 20, 1949; August 1, 1983; April 30, 2007, effective December 1, 2007.]

AUTHORS' COMMENTARY ON RULE 67

PURPOSE AND SCOPE

On occasion, parties may desire or be required to deposit money or property with the court. For example, parties may do so when a lawsuit contests title to money or other property, and the deposit is made to keep the asset safe during the litigation. Parties might do so to limit their exposure to interest on claims while the lawsuit is proceeding. Or parties may be required to do so by law, such as where stakeholders are obligated to deposit their "stake" with the court as a precondition for seeking statutory interpleader. In any event, Rule 67 establishes the procedure for making such a deposit with the court and sets the requirements for investing and withdrawing the deposit.

RULE 67(a)—DEPOSITING PROPERTY

CORE CONCEPT

A litigant may deposit with the court money or "some other deliverable thing" if a civil lawsuit seeks, as part of the requested relief, either a money judgment or the disposition of a sum of money or other deliverable thing.

APPLICATIONS

Purpose

The goal of Rule 67 is to relieve parties in possession of a contested asset of further responsibility for disbursing that asset to those who claim it.[1] Use of the Rule may, in appropriate circumstances, allow the asset's holder to make the deposit and then withdraw from the litigation as the contest for ownership ensues,[2] and may eliminate a party's liability for the accrual of interest on the asset until the case is decided.[3] The Rule has been used in federal interpleader cases[4] and for security as a condition of a stay pending appeal.[5] Rule 67 has no applicability to payments permitted or ordered in criminal cases.[6]

Court Order and Notice Required

Rule 67 deposits may only be made upon leave of court, on motion, and with notice to all other parties.[7] Whether to permit the deposit is a decision left to the sound discretion of the

[1] *See Zelaya / Cap. Int'l Judgment, LLC v. Zelaya*, 769 F.3d 1296, 1302 (11th Cir. 2014); *Alstom Caribe, Inc. v. Geo. P. Reintjes Co.*, 484 F.3d 106, 113 (1st Cir. 2007). *See generally In re Craig's Stores of Texas, Inc.*, 402 F.3d 522, 524 (5th Cir. 2005) ("Once funds are deposited, the court should determine ownership and make disbursements.").

[2] *See Alstom Caribe, Inc. v. George P. Reintjes Co.*, 484 F.3d 106, 114 (1st Cir. 2007). *See also In re 1563 28th Ave., San Francisco, CA 94112*, 333 F.R.D. 630, 635 (N.D. Cal. 2019) (interpleader plaintiff with no interest in disputed property, or in how claimants want to divide it, may be discharged from further liability by court). *See generally Cajun Elec. Power Co-op., Inc. v. Riley Stoker Corp.*, 901 F.2d 441, 444–45 (5th Cir. 1990) ("relieve the depositor of responsibility for the fund in dispute while the parties hash out their differences with respect to it").

[3] *See Cordero v. De Jesus-Mendez*, 922 F.2d 11, 18 (1st Cir. 1990) (refusing to charge interest against party who deposited money under Rule 67, because once deposit was made, duty fell on clerk of court to place money in interest bearing account). *See also Cajun Elec. Power Co-op., Inc. v. Riley Stoker Corp.*, 901 F.2d 441, 445 (5th Cir. 1990) ("may stop the accrual of interest pending a final resolution of the rights of the parties with the respect to the fund").

[4] *See Gulf State Utilities Co. v. Alabama Power Co.*, 824 F.2d 1465, 1474 (5th Cir. 1987) (suitable for use in interpleader case); *Nat'l W. Life Ins. Co. v. Borrero-Sotomayor*, 466 F. Supp. 3d 305, 309 (D.P.R. 2020). *See also In re Craig's Stores of Texas, Inc.*, 402 F.3d 522, 530–31 (5th Cir. 2005) ("continues in effect similar special provisions" in interpleader statutes and rules).

[5] *See McCollough v. Johnson, Rodenberg & Lauinger*, 2009 WL 10701734, at *1 (D. Mont. July 7, 2009). *See also Kotsopoulos v. Asturia Shipping Co.*, 467 F.2d 91, 94 (2d Cir. 1972) (by paying amount of judgment into court, party can stop running of interest against that party during pendency of appeal).

[6] *See United States v. Sun Growers of Cal.*, 212 F.3d 603, 606 (D.C. Cir. 2000).

[7] *See Garrick v. Weaver*, 888 F.2d 687, 694 (10th Cir. 1989); *Gulf States Utilities Co. v. Alabama Power Co.*, 824 F.2d 1465, 1474 (5th Cir.), *amended*, 831 F.2d 557 (5th Cir. 1987).

district court.[8]

Prerequisites for Relief

Relief under Rule 67 is available only when entitlement to the proposed-for-deposit asset is genuinely and presently at issue.[9] Thus, a motion seeking permission to make a deposit must establish that (a) the asset's ownership is contested and (b) the amount of the disputed asset is a sum-certain.[10] Accordingly, if only one entity claims entitlement, this Rule is not applicable.[11] The motion should also state the reasons for making the deposit (such as, for example, to avoid further responsibility for the deposited asset).

- *Motion by Holder:* This Rule authorizes holders of an asset to request leave to make a court deposit. It does not, however, authorize others to seek an order compelling such a deposit from someone else.[12]
- *Time for Making the Motion:* The motion may be made at any time during the life of the lawsuit.
- *Serving Clerk with Order:* If the court grants the motion, the moving party must serve the order on the clerk of court at the time of making the deposit.

Effect of Deposit on Merits of Case

This Rule offers a potential safe haven for an asset, essentially allowing a party to make the court its escrow agent.[13] But the Rule does not adjudicate rights to the asset; those

---

[8] *See Zelaya/Cap. Int'l Judgment, LLC v. Zelaya*, 769 F.3d 1296, 1300 (11th Cir. 2014); *LTV Corp. v. Gulf States Steel, Inc. of Ala.*, 969 F.2d 1050, 1063 (D.C. Cir. 1992); *Tegtmeier v. PJ Iowa, L.C.*, 189 F. Supp. 3d 811, 825 (S.D. Iowa 2016).

[9] *See Alstom Caribe, Inc. v. George P. Reintjes Co.*, 484 F.3d 106, 113 (1st Cir. 2007) (entitlement must be "genuinely in dispute" and dispute "must be extant" at time motion is filed); *Nat'l W. Life Ins. Co. v. Borrero-Sotomayor*, 466 F. Supp. 3d 305, 309 (D.P.R. 2020). *See also Tegtmeier v. PJ Iowa, L.C.*, 189 F. Supp. 3d 811, 825 (S.D. Iowa 2016) (only applies to fund in dispute).

[10] *See, e.g., Brady v. Basic Research, L.L.C.*, 312 F.R.D. 304 (E.D.N.Y. 2016).

[11] *See, e.g., Nat'l W. Life Ins. Co. v. Borrero-Sotomayor*, 466 F. Supp. 3d 305, 309 (D.P.R. 2020).

[12] *See, e.g., Cajun Elec. Power Co-op., Inc. v. Riley Stoker Corp.*, 901 F.2d 441, 444–45 (5th Cir. 1990) ("The. . . purpose [of Rule 67] is to relieve the depositor of responsibility for the fund in dispute while the parties hash out their differences with respect to it."). *Cf., Radha Geismann, M.D., P.C. v. ZocDoc, Inc.*, 909 F.3d 534 (2d Cir. 2018) (Rule 67 makes court an escrow agent, but does not by itself establish plaintiff's right to asset).

[13] *See Radha Geismann, M.D., P.C. v. ZocDoc, Inc.*, 909 F.3d 534, 541 (2d Cir. 2018) ("a procedural mechanism" permitting parties to use court "as an escrow agent"); *LTV Corp. v. Gulf States Steel, Inc. of Ala.*, 969 F.2d 1050, 1063 (D.C. Cir. 1992) ("provides a place of safekeeping for disputed funds pending the resolution of a legal dispute"). *See also Alstom Caribe, Inc. v. George P. Reintjes Co.*, 484 F.3d 106, 114 (1st Cir. 2007) (deposits "held in trust for their rightful owner").

merits questions are reserved for the underlying litigation.[14] Nor does the deposit impact the merits of the case[15] or moot the pending dispute.[16] It will not, for example, vest in another party an entitlement to collect that asset.[17]

Relation to Rules 23 and 68

Rule 23 governs much of the procedure applicable to class actions.[18] Rule 68 governs circumstances in which a defendant may offer to consent to the entry of judgment.[19] These two rules may interact when a defendant in a potential class action offers judgment to satisfy a named individual plaintiff's claim. An *unaccepted* Rule 68 offer of judgment has no force and cannot be used to render moot the possibility of class certification.[20] In the wake of this precedent in the Rule 68 context, courts have held that a defendant in a potential class action is similarly precluded from applying Rule 67 in to thwart class certification.[21]

Relation to Statutory Interpleader (28 U.S.C.A. § 1335)

Section 1335 is part of federal law governing statutory interpleader actions. One provision of § 1335 requires payment of a disputed fund into court.[22] When an interpleader action is initiated under § 1335, Rule 67 governs the circumstances in which the deposit will be made.[23]

---

[14] *See Radha Geismann, M.D., P.C. v. ZocDoc, Inc.*, 909 F.3d 534, 541 (2d Cir. 2018) ("does not itself determine who is entitled to the money"); *Fulton Dental, LLC v. Bisco, Inc.*, 860 F.3d 541, 545 (7th Cir. 2017) ("What Rule 67 is *not* is a vehicle for determining ownership; that is what the underlying litigation is for."); *LTV Corp. v. Gulf States Steel, Inc. of Ala.*, 969 F.2d 1050, 1063 (D.C. Cir. 1992) ("cannot be used as a means of altering the contractual relationships and legal duties of the parties."); *Tegtmeier v. PJ Iowa, L.C.*, 189 F. Supp. 3d 811, 825 (S.D. Iowa 2016).

[15] *See Radha Geismann, M.D., P.C. v. ZocDoc, Inc.*, 909 F.3d 534, 542 (2d Cir. 2018) ("does not affect the vitality of a plaintiff's claims"); *LTV Corp. v. Gulf States Steel, Inc.*, 969 F.2d 1050 (D.C. Cir. 1992) (does not affect rights or duties of parties).

[16] *See Conrad v. Boiron, Inc.*, 869 F.3d 536, 541 (7th Cir. 2017); *Fulton Dental, LLC v. Bisco, Inc.*, 860 F.3d 541, 545–46 (7th Cir. 2017). *See also Tegtmeier v. PJ Iowa, L.C.*, 189 F. Supp. 3d 811, 825 (S.D. Iowa 2016) (noting courts' rejection of mootness effect).

[17] *See Radha Geismann, M.D., P.C. v. ZocDoc, Inc.*, 909 F.3d 534, 542 (2d Cir. 2018).

[18] *See* Rule 23.

[19] *See* Rule 68.

[20] *See, e.g., Campbell-Ewald Co. v. Gomez*, 577 U.S. 153, 162, 136 S. Ct. 663, 193 L. Ed. 2d 571 (2016); *Radha Geismann, M.D., P.C. v. ZocDoc, Inc.*, 909 F.3d 534, 541 (2d Cir. 2018).

[21] *See, e.g., Fulton Dental, LLC v. Bisco, Inc.*, 860 F.3d 541, 544–45 (7th Cir. 2017) (rejecting any attempt to make a distinction between application of Rule 67 and Rule 68 in this context). *See also Radha Geismann, M.D., P.C. v. ZocDoc, Inc.*, 909 F.3d 534 (2d Cir. 2018) (defendant may use Rule 67 to make deposit with court, but such payment cannot nullify plaintiff's attempt to seek class relief).

[22] 28 U.S.C.A. § 1335.

[23] *See, e.g., Alstom Caribe, Inc. v. Reintjes Co.*, 484 F.3d 106 (1st Cir. 2001).

RULE 67(b)—INVESTING AND WITHDRAWING FUNDS

CORE CONCEPT

Court deposits are made with the Treasurer of the United States and are placed in an interest-bearing account or a court-approved, interest-bearing instrument. Withdrawals may be made only upon court order.

APPLICATIONS

Clerk Must Invest in Interest-Bearing Account

The clerk of court must invest any money deposited into the court in an interest-bearing account or in an interest-bearing instrument approved by the court in the name and to the credit of the court.[24]

Withdrawal of Deposit

A withdrawal request may be made upon motion to the court and notice to the U.S. Attorney, along with "full proof of the right thereto."[25] No money deposited with the court may be withdrawn without a court order permitting the withdrawal.[26]

Unclaimed Deposits

Once the right to withdraw the deposit has been adjudicated or is no longer in dispute, the withdrawal must occur within five years. If no withdrawal is made during that period, the deposited asset will be deemed forfeited and credited to the United States.[27]

Additional Research References

Wright & Miller, *Federal Practice and Procedure* §§ 2991 to 3000
C.J.S., Deposits in Court §§ 1 to 9
West's Key Number Digest, Deposits in Court ⚷1 to 12

---

[24]*See* 28 U.S.C.A. § 2041. *See also Cordero v. De Jesus-Mendez*, 922 F.2d 11, 18 (1st Cir. 1990) (responsibility "rests with the clerk of court").

[25]*See* 28 U.S.C.A. § 2042.

[26]*But cf.*, *In re Craig's Stores of Texas, Inc.*, 402 F.3d 522, 524 (5th Cir. 2005) (where money was deposited in court in a proceeding in which court was subsequently found to be lacking in jurisdiction, court could not distribute funds as it deemed just; instead, court had to return funds to party who made deposit).

[27]28 U.S.C.A. § 2042.

RULE 68
OFFER OF JUDGMENT

(a) Making an Offer; Judgment on an Accepted Offer. At least 14 days before the date set for trial, a party defending against a claim may serve on an opposing party an offer to allow judgment on specified terms, with the costs then accrued. If, within 14 days after being served, the opposing party serves written notice accepting the offer, either party may then file the offer and notice of acceptance, plus proof of service. The clerk must then enter judgment.

(b) Unaccepted Offer. An unaccepted offer is considered withdrawn, but it does not preclude a later offer. Evidence of an unaccepted offer is not admissible except in a proceeding to determine costs.

(c) Offer After Liability Is Determined. When one party's liability to another has been determined but the extent of liability remains to be determined by further proceedings, the party held liable may make an offer of judgment. It must be served within a reasonable time—but at least 14 days—before the date set for a hearing to determine the extent of liability.

(d) Paying Costs After an Unaccepted Offer. If the judgment that the offeree finally obtains is not more favorable than the unaccepted offer, the offeree must pay the costs incurred after the offer was made.

[Amended effective March 19, 1948; July 1, 1966; August 1, 1987; April 30, 2007, effective December 1, 2007; March 26, 2009, effective December 1, 2009.]

AUTHORS' COMMENTARY ON RULE 68

PURPOSE AND SCOPE

Designed to encourage the settlement of federal civil lawsuits, Rule 68 permits a defending party to make a proposal to the claimant to resolve a lawsuit on certain specified terms. The claimant then is given 14 days to accept the offer. If the claimant fails to accept the offer and later obtains a judgment equal to or less than the offer that was declined, the claimant must pay the costs the defending party incurred from the day the offer was made onward.

For purposes of this Rule, "costs" generally do not include attorney's fees or damages (but, instead, usually only a narrower range of recoverable expenses set by statute, unless Congress provides otherwise). Practitioners often find that the laudable goal of encouraging settlements is not frequently achieved by Rule 68's operation. The threat of a Rule 68 cost-shift is often not especially settlement-enticing because the size of the shiftable costs is frequently not that imposing.

Ordinary offers to settle a lawsuit do not fall within the scope of Rule 68. Settlements of lawsuits can occur in many ways and often result in the lawsuit being voluntarily dismissed without any finding of liability or any resulting, enforceable judgment. Rule 68 is different. Under Rule 68, in accordance with the defending party's proposed terms, the defending party *agrees* to the *entry of judgment*. If accepted, the claimant will have obtained a federal judgment against the defending party. If it is not accepted, the claimant may suffer the financial consequences described above.

RULE 68(a)—MAKING AN OFFER; JUDGMENT ON AN ACCEPTED OFFER

CORE CONCEPT

Only *defending* parties may make a Rule 68 offer. Such offers must be made no later than 14 days before trial. The offer must propose specific terms on which defending parties will consent to allow a judgment to be entered against them. If the claimant accepts, then the offer, the acceptance, and proof-of-service are all filed with the court. The clerk will then enter judgment.

APPLICATIONS

Purpose

The goal of Rule 68 is to encourage settlement of federal civil litigation by prompting litigants to evaluate their respective costs and risks of litigation against the likelihood of success at trial.[1] When that balance favors a prompt resolution, Rule 68 allows a defending party to present the claimant with an offer of judgment, which the claimant must then weigh against the risk of Rule 68 cost-shifting.

---

[1]See *Marek v. Chesny*, 473 U.S. 1, 5, 105 S. Ct. 3012, 87 L. Ed. 2d 1 (1985); *Long Beach Sec. Corp. v. Nat'l Credit Union Admin. Bd.*, 315 F. Supp. 3d 129, 140 (D.D.C. 2018).

Offering a Judgment

To offer a Rule 68 judgment, the defending party serves upon the claimant a written offer.[2] Once made, the offer must remain open for 14 days and is non-negotiable.[3] Although the Rule does not require it, standard practice is to serve copies of the offer upon all other parties to the case. However, until an offer is accepted by the claiming party, it is inappropriate to file a copy of the offer with the clerk's office.[4]

- *Offer to Multiple Claimants*: If an offer is made to multiple claimants, it must specify the proposed payment to each. If it fails to do so, it might not qualify for a cost-shift under this Rule.[5] However, there does not appear to be a *per se* requirement that offers of judgment apportion damages in multiple-claimant cases.[6]
- *Offer from Multiple Defendants*: If multiple defending parties collaborate in making an offer, the respective apportionment of the offered sum should be clear. Otherwise, if one or more of the offering parties is excused from the case, it may be difficult for the remaining offerors to prove that *their* offer was sufficient to trigger a cost-shift under this Rule.[7]
- *Offers by Plaintiff*: Only parties defending against a

---

[2]*See, e.g., Driver Music Co. v. Com. Union Ins. Companies*, 94 F.3d 1428, 1432 (10th Cir. 1996) (Rule 68 contemplates that offer will be in writing); *Magnuson v. Video Yesteryear*, 85 F.3d 1424, 1429 (9th Cir. 1996) (absent demonstrated special need or consent of opposing party, service by fax or Federal Express is ineffective service).

[3]*See, e.g., Kubiak v. Cnty. Of Ravalli*, 32 F.4th 1182, 1186, 1188 (9th Cir. 2022) ("widely accepted" that Rule 68 offer, "once made, is non-negotiable. . . ."; offer must remain open for 14 days and may either be accepted or rejected; "No other outcome (such as negotiation or revocation) is contemplated.") (cleaned up).

[4]*See, e.g., Kubiak v. Cnty. Of Ravalli*, 32 F.4th 1182, 1186 (9th Cir. 2022) ("The offer is filed only upon acceptance."). *See also Kason v. Amphenol Corp.*, 132 F.R.D. 197 (N.D. Ill. 1990) ("[N]o filing is permitted at the time of tender.").

[5]*See, e.g., Gavoni v. Dobbs House, Inc.*, 164 F.3d 1071, 1075–77 (7th Cir. 1999) (defendant has burden of showing that offer was more favorable than final judgment; defendant also has burden of making offer clear, and plaintiffs are entitled to "a clear baseline from which [they] may evaluate the merits of their case relative to the value of the offer"). *See also Harbor Motor Co. v. Arnell Chevrolet-Geo, Inc.*, 265 F.3d 638, 648 (7th Cir. 2001).

[6]*See, e.g., Stanczyk v. City of New York*, 752 F.3d 273, 284 (2d Cir. 2014) (Rule 68 does not require apportionment, if offer is still capable of comparison with what plaintiff was able to win). *But see Thomas v. Nat'l Football League Players' Ass'n*, 273 F.3d 1124, 1130 (D.C. Cir. 2010) (Rule 68 offer did not shift costs where only one of three plaintiffs was awarded damages).

[7]*See, e.g., Harbor Motor Co., Inc. v. Arnell Chevrolet-Geo, Inc.*, 265 F.3d 638, 647–49 (7th Cir. 2001) (one defendant won at trial, but other lost; court held plaintiff could not have estimated with any confidence what portion of offer was attributable to losing defendant, so offer was ineffective; acknowledging possibility that on different facts court might be able to calculate the share of an unapportioned offer to ascribe to each of several defendants; "We need not go so far as to conclude . . .that Rule 68 always requires an exact delineation of the manner in

claim are eligible to make an offer of judgment.[8] Unless a plaintiff is a defending party on a counterclaim, a crossclaim, or otherwise (*see* Rules 13 & 14), a plaintiff cannot make a Rule 68 offer of judgment.[9]

- *Non-Rule 68 Offers*: As noted earlier, Rule 68 authorizes a special *type* of settlement offer (*i.e.*, consent to entry of a judgment). Parties are always permitted to propose to one another a resolution of their dispute outside the scope and context of Rule 68, to which the terms of Rule 68 will not apply.[10]

Contents of Offer

A proper Rule 68 offer must propose to accept entry of judgment for a certain amount (or specific property)[11] along with "the costs then accrued."[12] The offer must provide a clear baseline from which a claimant may compare the merits of the claim to the value of the offer.[13] In construing the terms of an offer, ordinary rules of contract law apply,[14] including the tenet that ambiguities are construed against the drafter.[15]

- *Non-Money Claims*: Although it is used principally for

---

which damages are to be apportioned among multiple parties."); *Johnston v. Penrod Drilling Co.*, 803 F.2d 867, 870 (5th Cir. 1986) (plaintiff settled with one defendant, won judgment against another; court determined offer of judgment and judgment actually obtained could not be compared because "settlement may have . . . had an effect on the damage award;" noting different result if plaintiff's judgment had been won against both defendants).

[8]*See, e.g.*, *Goldberg v. Pac. Indem. Co.*, 627 F.3d 752, 756 (9th Cir. 2010) (quoting *Garcia v. Wal-Mart Stores, Inc.*, 209 F.3d 1170, 1176 (10th Cir. 2000)) ("Rule 68 only governs defendants' costs."). *Cf.*, *Amati v. City of Woodstock*, 176 F.3d 952, 958 (7th Cir. 1999) ("A plaintiff has no right to demand a Rule 68 offer."). *But cf.*, *S.A. Healy Co. v. Milwaukee Metropolitan Sewerage Dist.*, 60 F.3d 305, 310-12 (7th Cir. 1995) (Rule 68 permits offers only by parties defending claims, but in diversity case, state law permitting plaintiff's offer of settlement may be applied).

[9]*See Delta Air Lines, Inc. v. August*, 450 U.S. 346, 101 S. Ct. 1146, 67 L. Ed. 2d 287 (1981); *Felders v. Bairett*, 885 F.3d 646, 652 (10th Cir. 2018).

[10]*See, e.g.*, *Menchise v. Senterfitt*, 532 F.3d 1146, 1152 (11th Cir. 2008) (offers of settlement do not require entry of a judgment and are therefore outside the scope of Rule 68).

[11]*See, e.g.*, *Basha v. Mitsubishi Motor Credit of Am., Inc.*, 336 F.3d 451, 454–55 (5th Cir. 2003) (offer that proposed to settle all claims but did not quantify damages could not meet Rule 68 requirements); *Marryshow v. Flynn*, 986 F.2d 689, 691 (4th Cir. 1993) (offer must be for "specified amount").

[12]*See, e.g.*, *McCain v. Detroit II Auto Fin. Ctr.*, 378 F.3d 561 (6th Cir. 2004) (defendant's silence on costs means they are recoverable by plaintiff). *See also LaPierre v. City of Lawrence*, 819 F.3d 558, 564 (1st Cir. 2016) (collecting cases).

[13]*Electra v. 59 Murray Enters., Inc.*, 987 F.3d 233, 246 (2d Cir. 2021).

[14]*See, e.g.*, *Lilly v. City of New York*, 934 F.3d 222 (2d Cir. 2019) (ordinary contract principles apply); *Agema v. City of Allegan*, 826 F.3d 326 (6th Cir. 2016) (in accordance with general contract law, a counteroffer is a rejection of the original offer).

[15]*See Electra v. 59 Murray Enterprises, Inc.*, 987 F.3d 233, 244 (2d Cir. 2021) ("offer must be construed against the offeror, without looking to

claims seeking money or specific property, Rule 68 might be available in equity cases.[16]

- *What Are "Costs"?*: Although not defined in Rule 68,[17] the term "costs" is generally understood to mean only those certain categories of expenses that Congress has enumerated as "taxable" under 28 U.S.C. § 1920,[18] unless the substantive law applicable to the claims in the lawsuit prescribe further items.[19]
- *Including Costs*: An offer can meet the requirement of including costs by itemizing them specifically or with a general recital that costs are included.[20]
- *Attorney's Fees / Other Expenses as "Costs"*: If the substantive law underlying the cause of action includes attorney's fees (or other items of expenses) as "costs," then those categories may be considered "costs" for Rule 68 purposes.[21]
- *Superseding Other "Costs" Practices*: Ordinarily, a prevailing party will be awarded litigation costs.[22] The consensus view among the courts is that Rule 68 has the effect of reversing (potentially) this ordinary approach.[23] Similarly, courts have found that Rule 68 trumps the mandatory award of costs under the Fair Labor Standards Act.[24]

Timing of Offer

To be effective, a Rule 68 offer of judgment must be served on the party prosecuting a claim at least 14 days before the

extrinsic evidence."). *But see Vasconcelo v. Miami Auto Max, Inc.*, 981 F.3d 934, 943 (11th Cir. 2020) (ambiguous offer of judgment may be construed against its drafter, not ignored entirely).

[16]*See, e.g., Interfaith Cmty. Org. v. Honeywell Int'l, Inc.*, 726 F.3d 403, 408 (3d Cir. 2013) ("Rule 68 does not exempt from its purview any type of civil action."); *Chathas v. Local 134 Intern. Broth. of Elec. Workers*, 233 F.3d 508, 511 (7th Cir. 2000) ("Rule 68 offers are much more common in money cases than in equity cases, but nothing in the rule forbids its use in the latter type of case.").

[17]*But see Portillo v. Cunningham*, 872 F.3d 728, 739 (5th Cir. 2017) ("awardable costs" refers to costs governed by relevant statute or other authority).

[18]*See* Rule 54(d)(1).

[19]*See Scottsdale Ins. Co. v. Tolliver*, 636 F.3d 1273, 1278 n.7 (10th Cir. 2011).

[20]*See, e.g., Champion Produce, Inc. v. Ruby Robinson Co.*, 342 F.3d 1016, 1020 (9th Cir. 2003) (where Rule 68 offer explicitly included "pre-offer costs and attorneys' fees," judgment to which offer is compared must include those items).

[21]*See Marek v. Chesny*, 473 U.S. 1, 8-9, 105 S. Ct. 3012, 87 L. Ed. 2d 1 (1985). *See also Morjal v. City of Chicago*, 774 F.3d 419, 421-22 (7th Cir. 2014).

[22]*See* Rule 54(d)(1).

[23]*See Stanczyk v. City of New York*, 752 F.3d 273, 280-82 (2d Cir. 2014) (discussing and then embracing consensus approach); *Payne v. Milwaukee Cty.*, 288 F.3d 1021, 1027 (7th Cir. 2002).

[24]*See Vasconcelo v. Miami Auto Max, Inc.*, 981 F.3d 934, 943 (11th Cir. 2020) (discussing Rules Enabling Act).

date set for the beginning of a trial.[25] If the trial is bifurcated, the time for offering may be governed by subpart (c) of this Rule.[26]

Revoking an Offer Once Made

Except in exceptional circumstances, a Rule 68 offer cannot be revoked during the 14-day acceptance period[27] (even if summary judgment is granted in the interim on all claims in the offeror's favor)[28]—notwithstanding the otherwise applicable tenet that principles of contract law govern a Rule 68 offer and acceptance.[29]

Time for Accepting an Offer

The claimant has 14 days to accept the offer. Failure to do so will result in the offer being deemed withdrawn.[30]

Method of Accepting an Offer

The appropriate method for accepting an offer of judgment is by written notice of acceptance delivered to the party who made the offer. The offer must be accepted in its entirety, or it is deemed rejected.[31] An offer to multiple claimants may include a proviso that acceptance must be unanimous before it is effective.[32]

Entering Final Judgment on an Accepted Offer

If the claimant accepts the offer of judgment, either party may file the offer, notice of acceptance, and proof of service

---

[25]*See also Horowitch v. Diamond Aircraft Indus., Inc.*, 645 F.3d 1254, 1259 n.2 (11th Cir. 2011) ("Rule 68 instructs the parties not to file an offer of judgment with the court at the time of service.").

[26]*Delta Air Lines, Inc. v. Aug.*, 450 U.S. 346, 101 S. Ct. 1146, 67 L. Ed. 2d 287 (1981). *See also Interfaith Cmty. Org. v. Honeywell Int'l, Inc.*, 726 F.3d 403, 413 (3d Cir. 2013) (Rule 68 also applies "to disputes over attorney fees after liability has been determined").

[27]*See, e.g., Garayalde-Rios v. Municipality of Carolina*, 799 F.3d 45 (1st Cir. 2015) (Rule 68 treats offeree as essentially holding a fourteen-day option). *But cf., Perkins v. U.S. West Communications*, 138 F.3d 336 (8th Cir. 1998) (revocation permitted only for "good cause").

[28]*See, e.g., Kubiak v. Cnty. of Ravalli*, 32 F.4th 1182, 1187 (9th Cir. 2022) (relying on similar decisions from sister circuits, court held the district court properly entered judgment for plaintiff after timely acceptance of Rule 68 offer even when court granted summary judgment on all claims in favor of defendants during Rule 68's 14-day acceptance period).

[29]*See, e.g., Herrington v. Cnty. of Sonoma*, 12 F.3d 901, 907 (9th Cir. 1993) (Rule 68 is subject to standard rules of contract construction); *Dowd v. City of Los Angeles*, 28 F. Supp. 3d 1019, 1038 (C.D. Cal. 2014).

[30]*See* Rule 68(b).

[31]*See, e.g., Whitcher v. Town of Matthews*, 136 F.R.D. 582, 585 (W.D.N.C. 1991) (plaintiffs cannot both accept offer as to money damages and continue action as to equitable relief). *But cf., Gordon v. Gouline*, 81 F.3d 235 (D.C. Cir. 1996) (acceptance is effective even when conditioned upon approval of bankruptcy court).

[32]*See, e.g., Amati v. City of Woodstock*, 176 F.3d 952, 958 (7th Cir. 1999) (nothing in Rule 68 renders such a condition inoperable); *Lang v. Gates*, 36 F.3d 73, 75 (9th Cir. 1994) (requirement of unanimous consent is not invalid).

with the clerk of court. (Offers are not filed until they are accepted.) The clerk then will enter judgment consistent with the offer and acceptance.[33] Once the offer, notice of acceptance, and proof of service are filed with the court, judgment must normally be entered.[34] Except in circumstances where the literal language of Rule 68 conflicts with some other requirement of federal law, the court has no discretion to refuse to enter judgment.[35]

Trap for the Unwary—Fees and Costs

Although Rule 68 is intended to serve as an efficient, amicable means of resolving a dispute, it may sometimes become an unanticipated problem for a defendant. The problem can arise if a plaintiff accepts a Rule 68 offer, leading the defendant to believe the case is ended, only to later learn that, pursuant to a statutory allowance of, *e.g.*, attorney's fees and costs,[36] a large, additional sum is still owing to the plaintiff.[37] A prudent solution is for the defending party to include in its Rule 68 offer a clear statement that the offer encompasses all fees and costs. An offer that is silent on that point may result in additional expenses for the defendant.[38]

Settled Cases

The literal language of Rule 68 bars its use to award costs in cases that settle without going to judgment. Less certain is the result when the parties settle, and the court enters judg-

[33] *See, e.g., Kubiak v. Cnty. of Ravalli*, 32 F.4th 1182, 1187 (9th Cir. 2022) (recognizing courts' "broad agreement" over Rule 68's "mandatory and absolute" command for clerk to "automatically enter" accepted Rule 68 offer); *Mei Xing Yu v. Hasaki Rest., Inc.*, 944 F.3d 395, 400 (2d Cir. 2019); *Parental Guide of Texas, Inc. v. Thomson, Inc.*, 446 F.3d 1265, 1270 (Fed. Cir. 2006) ("[T]he entry of judgment 'is generally a ministerial act and can be performed by the clerk without any input from the court or a jury.' ").

[34] *See, e.g., Kubiak v. Cnty. of Ravalli*, 32 F.4th 1182, 1187 (9th Cir. 2022) (entering judgment is a ministerial rather than discretionary act); *Webb v. James*, 147 F.3d 617, 621 (7th Cir. 1998).

[35] *See, e.g., Me Xing Yu v. Hasaki Restaurant, Inc.*, 944 F.3d 395, 400 (2d Cir. 2019) (Rule 68(a) provides district court with no discretion; court must enter judgment); *White v. Nat'l Football League*, 756 F.3d 585, 596 (8th Cir. 2014) (district court has virtually no discretion and must enter judgment). *But cf., Gordon v. Gouline*, 81 F.3d 235, 238–39 (D.C. Cir. 1996) (in bankruptcy cases court may reject accepted offer of judgment; citing Fed. R. Bank. P. 9014; noting also that bankruptcy court is not restricted by 14-day limit for accepting offer). *See also Ramming v. Nat. Gas Pipeline Co. of Am.*, 390 F.3d 366, 371 (5th Cir. 2004) (in class action, court has duty under Rule 23 to review settlement that occurs through application of accepted offer of judgment under Rule 68).

[36] *See, e.g.*, 42 U.S.C.A. § 1988.

[37] *See, e.g., Lima v. Newark Police Dep't*, 658 F.3d 324, 329 (3d Cir. 2011).

[38] *See, e.g., Lima v. Newark Police Dep't*, 658 F.3d 324, 330–31 (3d Cir. 2011) (offer silent as to fees and costs creates additional vulnerability for defendant); *Bosley v. Min. Cnty. Comm'n*, 650 F.3d 408, 413 (4th Cir. 2011) (same analysis and result).

ment on the settlement.[39]

RULE 68(b)—UNACCEPTED OFFER

CORE CONCEPT

A Rule 68 offer of judgment that is not accepted is deemed withdrawn (though the defending party may make a subsequent offer). Unaccepted offers are inadmissible in court, except to determine costs or to challenge subject-matter jurisdiction.

APPLICATIONS

Timely Acceptance, or Deemed Withdrawal

A claimant has 14 days after receipt of service of the written offer to accept the offer of judgment.[40] If the offer is not accepted within that period, the offer is treated as withdrawn and incapable of being accepted.[41] It is possible for this 14-day period to be extended by the court under some circumstances.[42]

- *Effect of Intervening Judgment:* If, during the 14-day acceptance period, final judgment is entered against the claimant (*e.g.*, a defense motion for summary judgment is granted), the claimant's subsequent attempt at acceptance may be ruled ineffective.[43]

New Offers Following a Deemed Withdrawal (or Rejection)

Following a deemed-withdrawal of the offer (with the passing of 14 days) or an outright rejection of the offer, the offering party may renew the offer, or make a different offer, in which event a fresh 14-day period for acceptance begins to run.

---

[39] *Compare, e.g., E.E.O.C. v. Hamilton Standard Div., United Techs. Corp.*, 637 F. Supp. 1155, 1158 (D. Conn. 1986) (refusing to apply Rule 68 to case ending in settlement and stipulated dismissal), *with Lang v. Gates*, 36 F.3d 73, 77 (9th Cir. 1994) (approving application of Rule 68 to order enforcing settlement).

[40] *See, e.g., Perkins v. U.S. W. Commc'ns*, 138 F.3d 336 (8th Cir. 1998) (defendant filed motion for summary judgment; while motion was pending, defendant made offer of judgment under Rule 68; two days after offer of judgment was made, court granted defendant's summary judgment motion; plaintiff, upon notice of grant of summary judgment, accepted Rule 68 offer; held, acceptance bound defendant, notwithstanding grant of summary judgment; possible different result if defendant had conditioned offer of judgment on court's denial of summary judgment motion).

[41] *See, e.g., Kubiak v. Cnty. of Ravalli*, 32 F.4th 1182, 1186 (9th Cir. 2022); *Tejero v. Portfolio Recovery Assocs., L.L.C.*, 955 F.3d 453, 459 (5th Cir. 2020) (after 14 days without acceptance, offer is "considered withdrawn").

[42] *Minner v. Off. Depot, Inc.*, 336 F.R.D. 213, 216 (D. Colo. 2020) (defendant made Rule 68 offer on eve of plaintiff's major surgery).

[43] *See, e.g., Collar v. Abalux, Inc.*, 895 F.3d 1278 (11th Cir. 2018) (rejecting *Perkins v. U.S. West Communications*, 138 F.3d 336 (8th Cir. 1998), which held that offer remained open for full period provided by Rule 68, notwithstanding that court had entered summary judgment against plaintiff before plaintiff accepted offer).

When the Claimant Refuses to Accept an Offer for the *Full Amount* of a Claim

It may seem unusual, but a claimant might refuse (or fail to accept) an offer of judgment proposing to resolve the dispute for precisely what the pleader seeks—the full value of the claim. The effect of such a non-acceptance had, for many years, been unclear, until the U.S. Supreme Court resolved the uncertainty in 2016: an unaccepted Rule 68 offer "has no force," no matter how good the offer is.[44]

Admissibility of Evidence of an Offer of Judgment

If an offer of judgment is not accepted, the offer may not be used as evidence at trial. The only use to which a nonaccepted offer of judgment may be put is to determine costs, in the event that costs are shifted under subpart (d) of this Rule or to challenge subject-matter jurisdiction.[45]

Rule 68 in Class Action Contexts

Rule 68 can apply in class actions, but its operation in that complex litigation setting has created several uncertainties, only some of which courts have resolved.

- *Court Approval of Class Settlements:* When an offer of judgment is made in a case that has been certified as a class action, it may appear that the authority of a district judge to review and approve proposed settlements conflicts with the provision of Rule 68 that the court has no authority to approve or reject an offer of judgment that meets the requirements of Rule 68. However, the case law seems to establish that, when applicable, Rule 23 may present an exception to the limitations Rule 68 imposes on a court.[46]
- *Rule 68 Offer Made to Putative Class Representatives:*

[44]*See Campbell-Ewald Co. v. Gomez*, 577 U.S. 153, 156, 136 S. Ct. 663, 193 L.Ed.2d 571 (2016) ("Like other unaccepted contract offers, it creates no lasting right or obligation. With the offer off the table, and the defendant's continuing denial of liability, adversity between the parties persists."). *But cf. id.* at 166 ("We need not . . .now decide whether the result would be different if a defendant deposits the full amount of the plaintiff's individual claim in an account payable to the plaintiff, and the court then enters judgment for the plaintiff in that amount.").

[45]*See, e.g., O'Brien v. Ed Donnelly Enterprises, Inc.*, 575 F.3d 567, 574 (6th Cir. 2009), *abrogated on other grounds by Campbell-Ewald Co. v. Gomez*, 577 U.S. 153, 136 S. Ct. 663, 193 L. Ed. 2d 571 (2016) (offer of judgment cannot be used to support or challenge merits of claim; it can be used to determine costs or challenge subject matter jurisdiction); *Feustel v. CareerStaff Unlimited, Inc.*, 99 F. Supp. 3d 767, 775 (S.D. Ohio 2015).

[46]*See, e.g., Ramming v. Nat. Gas Pipeline Co. of Am.*, 390 F.3d 366, 371 (5th Cir. 2004) (duty of court to review settlement of class actions under Rule 23 provides potential exception to Rule 68; same result when case involves plea for injunctive relief); *Gordon v. Gouline*, 81 F.3d 235, 239–40 (D.C. Cir. 1996) (collecting cases where court held fairness hearings prior to entering judgment on Rule 68 offers); *Minner v. Off. Depot, Inc.*, 336 F.R.D. 213, 215–16 (D. Colo. 2020) (collecting cases demonstrating that application of Rule 68 offers in putative class ac-

Courts have considered whether, when such an offer is made, it renders a class uncertifiable for lack of a qualified class representative.[47] The answer to this question is resolved in part. It is settled that an *unaccepted* offer of judgment for the full statutory amount of an individual plaintiff's claim does not render a class action moot.[48] Other complexities arise if the putative class representatives accept the offer. Obviously, if such embryonic class representatives are removed from the case, the defendant is able to hinder the prospect of class certification by eliminating individual claims (potentially for a relatively small amount) and leaving unresolved the aggregate claims of a potentially much larger body of members of the entire class. Currently, courts seem to be leaning toward permitting a class representative to continue to seek certification notwithstanding that the defendant has somehow already satisfied the class representative's grievance very early in the case.[49] However, practitioners are cautioned to carefully observe local precedent on this matter and to be alert to changes.

RULE 68(c)—OFFER AFTER LIABILITY IS DETERMINED

CORE CONCEPT

Ordinarily, Rule 68 offers of judgment must be made at least 14 days before trial. When the trial is bifurcated, such that liability issues are determined first and, if needed, damages (or other extent of liability) resolved in a separate, subsequent proceeding, a "later" Rule 68 offer can be made. In such a circumstance, an offer is timely if made no less than 14 days before the damages (or extent of liability) phase of the trial is set to start.

RULE 68(d)—PAYING COSTS AFTER AN UNACCEPTED OFFER

CORE CONCEPT

A claimant need not accept an offer of judgment made by the

---

tion context is unsettled).

[47] *See* Rule 23(a)(4).

[48] *Campbell-Ewald v. Gomez*, — U.S. —, 136 S. Ct. 663, 665, 193 L. Ed. 2d 571 (2016) ("[U]naccepted settlement offer or offer of judgment does not moot a plaintiff's case . . . .").

[49] *See, e.g., Richardson v. Bledsoe*, 829 F.3d 273, 278–90 (3d Cir. 2016) (individual plaintiff's claim, though prematurely "mooted" by defendant, retains standing to pursue resolution of class certification motion); *Pitts v. Terrible Herbst, Inc.*, 653 F.3d 1081, 1091–92 (9th Cir. 2011) ("unaccepted Rule 68 offer of judgment — for the full amount of the named plaintiff's individual claim and made before the named plaintiff files a motion for class certification — does not moot a class action."). *But cf.*, *Wright v. Calumet City*, 848 F.3d 814 (7th Cir. 2017) (individual acceptance of offer of judgment precludes that plaintiff's attempt to appeal denial of class certification).

defending party. However, if the claimant obtains a later judgment that is "not more favorable" than the declined offer—that is, if it is equal to or less than what was offered—the claimant must pay the recoverable costs the defending party incurred during the period after the offer was made.

APPLICATIONS

Consequences of Nonacceptance

The consequences of not accepting a Rule 68 offer will depend on the outcome of the litigation:

- *Claimant Wins More Than Amount Offered*: If the nonaccepting claimant wins a judgment greater than the amount in the offer of judgment, the unaccepted offer has no consequence.[50] Costs are awarded normally.
- *Claimant Wins an Amount Equal to or Lesser Than Amount Offered*: If the nonaccepting claimant wins a favorable final judgment, but one only equal to or less than the amount in the offer of judgment, the nonaccepting claimant party must pay the costs the offering party incurred after it made the offer.[51] (Thus, a party that made an offer of judgment, and still lost the case, could still recover costs from the prevailing party if the loss was more modest than the offer.) The category of recoverable costs is discussed above.[52]
- *Claimant Loses*: If the nonaccepting claimant loses the

[50]*See, e.g., Brown v. Cox*, 286 F.3d 1040, 1047 (8th Cir. 2002) (plaintiff refused offer of judgment and then won judgment greater than offer; court held plaintiff's right to attorney's fees established by applicable federal civil rights law was therefore unaffected by refusal).

[51]*See, e.g., Stanczyk v. City of New York*, 752 F.3d 273, 280 (2d Cir. 2014) (three mandatory elements for fee shift: (1) defendant makes timely offer; (2) offer is rejected; (3) plaintiff wins less than offer of judgment); *Kubiak v. Cnty. of Ravalli*, 32 F.4th 1182, 1186 (9th Cir. 2022) (quoting *Radecki v. Amoco Oil Co.*, 858 F.2d 397, 402 (8th Cir. 1988)) (recognizing that "a plaintiff who receives a Rule 68 offer is in a difficult position, because a Rule 68 offer has a binding effect when refused as well as when accepted; this results from the Rule's cost-shifting mechanism, which becomes operative upon failure to accept."); *UMG Recordings, Inc. v. Shelter Capital Partners, Inc.*, 667 F.3d 1022, 1047–48 (9th Cir. 2011) (purpose of Rule 68 is to force plaintiff to "think very hard" about continuing litigation and to "compensate defendants for costs they ought not have had to incur"); *Payne v. Milwaukee Cnty.*, 288 F.3d 1021, 1025 (7th Cir. 2002) (civil rights case; prevailing plaintiff who won less than offer of judgment is not entitled to recovery attorney's fees that would otherwise have been available under federal civil rights law). *But see Capps v. Drake*, 894 F.3d 802 (7th Cir. 2018) (if plaintiff has made clear that judgment itself is the goal and has also not made a monetary claim to jury for damages, failure to win more than amount sought in pretrial settlement discussions does not trigger application of cost shifting provisions of Rule 68).

[52]*See supra* Rule 68(a) ("*What Are 'Costs'?*").

case, Rule 68—oddly—has no effect.[53] By its terms, the cost-shift granted by this subpart is triggered only when the claimant wins a judgment that is equal or less favorable than Rule 68 offer.[54]

Attorney's Fees

Rule 68 does not itself create a right to recover attorney fees.[55] However, some federal laws (such as federal civil rights laws) provide for prevailing parties (*i.e.,* two-way cost shifting) or just prevailing plaintiffs (*i.e.,* one-way cost shifting) to recover their attorney's fees as part of recoverable costs.[56] Such fee-shifting statutes often vest the court with discretion to award attorneys' fees,[57] although that discretion can be quite circumscribed.[58] With two-way cost-shifting statutes, the cost provisions for offers of judgment will apply in full to attorney's fees[59] and could entitle a defendant to recover costs that included attorney's fees.[60] With one-way cost-shifting statutes, the cost-shifting provisions for offers of judgment do not entitle

---

[53] *Hopper v. Euclid Manor Nursing Home, Inc.*, 867 F.2d 291, 295 (6th Cir. 1989) (relying on the "strict reading of the language of the rule" by the Supreme Court in *Delta Air Lines, Inc. v. Aug.*, 450 U.S. 346, 352–62, 101 S. Ct. 1146, 1150, 67 L. Ed. 2d 287 (1981)).

[54] *See Delta Air Lines, Inc. v. Aug.*, 450 U.S. 346, 352, 101 S. Ct. 1146, 67 L. Ed. 2d 287 (1981); *see also Payne v. Milwaukee Cnty.*, 288 F.3d 1021, 1025 (7th Cir. 2002) ("Had [plaintiff] not prevailed in some significant sense, [defendant] would be confined to Rule 54(d), and Rule 68 would simply have no application.").

[55] *See, e.g., McCain v. Detroit II Auto Fin. Ctr.*, 378 F.3d 561 (6th Cir. 2004) ("[T]he only way in which Rule 68 directly implicates awards of attorney's fees is in situations where such fees are made an element of 'costs'—whether by statute . . .or as a matter of contract."); *Poteete v. Capital Engineering, Inc.*, 185 F.3d 804, 807 (7th Cir. 1999) (collecting cases and holding "Rule 68 does not entitle a defendant to recover his attorneys' fees" based on the reasoning that statutes and common law principles that entitle a party to recover fees limit that entitlement to prevailing parties, and "any defendant who is entitled to invoke Rule 68 is by definition not a prevailing party").

[56] *See, e.g.*, 42 U.S.C.A. § 1988.

[57] *See, e.g.*, 42 U.S.C.A. § 1988(b).

[58] *Indep. Fed'n of Flight Attendants v. Zipes*, 491 U.S. 754, 761, 109 S. Ct. 2732, 105 L. Ed. 2d 639 (1989) (explaining narrowness of circumstances in which district court may exercise discretion to withhold fees from prevailing plaintiffs). *See also Déjà Vu v. Metro. Gov't of Nashville & Davidson Cnty., Tennessee*, 421 F.3d 417, 420 (6th Cir. 2005) ("Supreme Court has read [§ 1988] as mandatory where the plaintiff prevails and special circumstances are absent.").

[59] *See Marek v. Chesny*, 473 U.S. 1, 8-9, 105 S. Ct. 3012, 87 L. Ed. 2d 1 (1985).

[60] *See, e.g., Marek v. Chesny*, 473 U.S. 1, 105 S. Ct. 3012, 87 L. Ed. 2d 1 (1985); *Harbor Motor Co., Inc. v. Arnell Chevrolet-Geo, Inc.*, 265 F.3d 638, 646 (7th Cir. 2001) (agreeing with *Crossman*, infra, that in cases controlled by fee provision of copyright law "only prevailing parties can receive attorney's fees pursuant to rule 68;" defendant who lost case for less than offer of judgment therefore cannot recover attorney's fees; acknowledging different result in *Jordan v. Time, Inc.*, infra); *Crossman v. Marcoccio*, 806 F.2d 329, 333–34 (1st Cir. 1986) (where underlying copyright statute awards attorney's fees only to prevailing party, defendant who lost case—but for amount less than offer of judgment—

a defendant to recover attorney's fees after an unaccepted offer, but they do end the plaintiff's right to recover attorney's fees[61] or permit the court to reduce the amount of awarded fees.[62]

In calculating the amount awarded to a prevailing plaintiff in a civil rights case for the purpose of determining whether the value of the judgment exceeds the rejected offer of judgment, the district court will include costs and fees awarded, as well as the amount of the underlying judgment.[63] A defendant who loses a case cannot recover its own post-offer attorneys' fees.[64]

In civil rights cases, courts have recognized the stakes are particularly high for plaintiffs who receive a Rule 68 offer because attorney's fees in a suit under 42 U.S.C.A. § 1983 "are subject to the cost-shifting provision of Rule 68."[65]

Determining Whether Judgment Is "More Favorable"

In cases involving only money damages, it is usually not difficult to calculate whether the judgment a party won is more favorable than an earlier offer of judgment. In making this assessment, public policy interests (such as vindicating rights created by remedial statutes) should not be factored in by the court.[66] However, where a party obtains an injunction as part of a favorable judgment, the assessment can prove more

---

cannot recover attorney's fee because defendant did not prevail in case). *But see Jordan v. Time, Inc.*, 111 F.3d 102, 105 (11th Cir. 1997) (requiring plaintiff in copyright case who obtained judgment for less than offer of judgment to pay defendant's costs and fees incurred after offer was made).

[61] *See, e.g., Hescott v. City of Saginaw*, 757 F.3d 518, 530 (6th Cir. 2014). *But see Paz v. Portfolio Recovery Assocs., LLC*, 924 F.3d 949 (7th Cir. 2019) (if Congress awarded attorneys' fees on a different standard than would be applicable under Rule 68, the federal statute controls).

[62] *See, e.g., Dalal v. Alliant Techsystems, Inc.*, 182 F.3d 757 (10th Cir.1999) (affirming reduced award of attorney fees for legal work done between date of offer of judgment and date of judgment; acknowledging lack of precise formula for making calculation); *Haworth v. State of Nev.*, 56 F.3d 1048 (9th Cir. 1995) (reducing plaintiff's recovery of attorney fees because judgment was for less than the offer of judgment).

[63] *See, e.g., Hescott v. City of Saginaw*, 757 F.3d 518, 530 (6th Cir. 2014) (directing district court to combine plaintiff's award and pre-offer costs and fees to determine whether plaintiff was awarded more than offer of settlement).

[64] *See, e.g., Hescott v. City of Saginaw*, 757 F.3d 518, 528 (6th Cir. 2014) (notwithstanding Rule 68, such a defendant would not normally satisfy requirements of 42 U.S.C.A. § 1988; collecting cases). *But see Abundis v. Allstate Texas Lloyd's*, 494 F. Supp. 3d 442, 449 (S.D. Tex. 2020) (where statute defines attorneys' fees as "costs," a plaintiff who declines a Rule 68 offer and fails to obtain a more favorable judgment may not recover attorneys' fees for post-offer legal work).

[65] *See, e.g., Kubiak v. Cnty. of Ravalli*, 32 F.4th 1182, 1187 (9th Cir. 2022) (quoting *Marek v. Chesny*, 473 U.S. 1, 9, 105 S. Ct. 3012, 87 L. Ed. 2d 1 (1985) and explaining, "if a § 1983 plaintiff turns down a Rule 68 offer, goes to trial, and wins a judgment less favorable than the rejected offer, he loses his entitlement to attorney's fees as of the date of the offer.").

[66] *See, e.g., Vasconcelo v. Miami Auto Max, Inc.*, 981 F.3d 934, 944 (11th Cir. 2020).

challenging.[67] But the injunction's value should be included in the calculation in determining whether a judgment is more favorable than an earlier offer of judgment.[68]

Additional Research References

Wright & Miller, *Federal Practice and Procedure* §§ 3001 to 10. Lisnek, *Effective Negotiation and Mediation, A Lawyer's Guide.*
C.J.S., Federal Civil Procedure § 1276
West's Key Number Digest, Federal Civil Procedure ⚷2396.5, 2725

---

[67] *See, e.g., Andretti v. Borla Performance Indus., Inc.*, 426 F.3d 824, 837 (6th Cir. 2005) ("comparing the value of damages to an injunction is like comparing apples and oranges," but courts must sometimes do so in situations governed by Rule 68).

[68] *See, e.g., Reiter v. MTA New York City Transit Auth.*, 457 F.3d 224, 231 (2d Cir. 2006) ("Nothing in the language of Rule 68 suggests that a final judgment that contains equitable relief is inherently less favorable than a Rule 68 offer that contains monetary relief."); *Andretti v. Borla Performance Indus., Inc.*, 426 F.3d 824, 837 (6th Cir. 2005) ("[M]oney damages [need not be] the only measure of whether a plaintiff has obtained a 'more favorable' judgment under Rule 68.").

RULE 69
EXECUTION

(a) In General.

(1) *Money Judgment; Applicable Procedure.* A money judgment is enforced by a writ of execution, unless the court directs otherwise. The procedure on execution—and in proceedings supplementary to and in aid of judgment or execution—must accord with the procedure of the state where the court is located, but a federal statute governs to the extent it applies.

(2) *Obtaining Discovery.* In aid of the judgment or execution, the judgment creditor or a successor in interest whose interest appears of record may obtain discovery from any person—including the judgment debtor—as provided in these rules or by the procedure of the state where the court is located.

(b) Against Certain Public Officers. When a judgment has been entered against a revenue officer in the circumstances stated in 28 U.S.C. § 2006, or against an officer of Congress in the circumstances stated in 2 U.S.C. § 118, the judgment must be satisfied as those statutes provide.

[Amended effective October 20, 1949; July 1, 1970; August 1, 1987; April 30, 2007, effective December 1, 2007.]

AUTHORS' COMMENTARY ON RULE 69

PURPOSE AND SCOPE

Civil "execution" is the process of enforcing a judgment that awards money to a party. Often, invoking these procedures is unnecessary; the defeated party will simply just pay the money judgment voluntarily. Execution procedures are used when a voluntary payment is not forthcoming and the judgment winner has to collect his or her victory against a non-cooperating defeated party's assets. The chores of finding those assets, seizing them, and transforming them into the money necessary to satisfy the judgment are the roles of Rule 69. The process can prove frustrating and time-consuming. The court's assistance in this process is accomplished through its issuance of a "writ of execution." (The procedure for enforcing a non-money judgment—such as an injunction—is addressed by Rule 70.)

RULE 69(a)—IN GENERAL

CORE CONCEPT

Federal execution of a money judgment must be by "writ of execution," unless the court directs otherwise. Execution procedures must follow the federal instructions set statutorily by Congress, if any; if none, the procedures must follow the instructions established by state law in the state where the district court is sitting. Discovery in aid of execution is permitted.

APPLICATIONS

Writ of Execution

A writ of execution is a legal instrument that enforces the terms of a money judgment by formally authorizing the seizure and sale of assets belonging to the defeated party in order to satisfy the judgment.[1]

Subject-Matter Jurisdiction

Legal proceedings to collect judgments under Rule 69 are not considered actions independent of the original lawsuit, but merely a process used to enforce the court's judgment.[2] Nevertheless, a federal court must assure itself of subject matter jurisdiction in every case, even those that function to enforce a preexisting judgment.[3]

Execution Procedures

Upon obtaining a writ of execution, the judgment winner may serve the writ on the U.S. Marshal or a state officer, who will then execute upon—by attachment or otherwise—the property of the judgment debtor. Execution can occur against property of the judgment debtor that lies in the possession of third parties (such as, for example, a bank or investment company). The judgment debtor's property can be sold at an execution or sheriff's sale, thereby raising the cash used to satisfy the judgment.

- *Applicability:* This Rule and its procedures only apply to money judgments[4] entered by a federal court; they have no application to state court judgments or other types of

---

[1]*See Writ of Execution; Execution*, BLACK'S LAW DICTIONARY (11th ed. 2019).

[2]*See Bank Markazi v. Peterson*, 578 U.S. 212, 232-33 (2016). *See also Kokkonen v. Guardian Life Ins. Co. of America*, 511 U.S. 375, 379–80 (1994).

[3]*Boim v. Am. Muslims for Palestine*, 9 F.4th 545, 551–52 (7th Cir. 2021).

[4]*See, e.g., United States Commodity Futures Trading Commission v.*

judgments.[5]

- *Federal Procedures:* If a federal statute sets the type or manner of execution at issue, it governs[6] and supplants state law.[7]
- *State Procedures:* In the absence of a governing federal statutory procedure, the execution process adopted by the state where the federal court is located will govern.[8] The available state law remedies vary from jurisdiction to jurisdiction, but often include garnishment, arrest, mandamus, contempt, or the appointment of a receiver. When a state remedy is used, a party need only comply substantially with the provisions of the state remedy.[9]
- *Supplementing (or Even Supplanting) State Procedures:* Although district courts are directed to use state procedures[10] to enforce money judgments[11] (in the absence of a governing federal statute), they are also permitted to "direct otherwise." Federal courts have authority to supplement such procedures with federal practice when necessary.[12] Indeed, if state law poses an obstacle to execution, federal courts might even be able to disregard state practice entirely.[13]
- *Property Subject to the Writ of Execution:* Generally, state law will designate property of the judgment debtor that may be taken to satisfy a civil judgment. State law usually shields other categories of property (for instance, retirement accounts, trade tools, medicines, etc.) as

---

Escobio, 946 F.3d 1242 (11th Cir. 2020); *Board of Com'rs of Stark County, OH v. Cape Stone Works, Inc.*, 206 F. Supp. 2d 100, 102 (D. Mass. 2002).

[5] *See, e.g., U.S. v. Timilty*, 148 F.3d 1, 4 (1st Cir. 1998); *Threlkelt v. Tucker*, 496 F.2d 1101, 1104 (9th Cir. 1974).

[6] Federal remedies for executions in aid of judgments appear in 28 U.S.C.A. § 2001 et seq.

[7] *See, e.g., Next Invs., LLC v. Bank of China*, 12 F.4th 119, 133 (2d Cir. 2021); *Office Depot, Inc. v. Zuccarini*, 596 F.3d 696, 701 (9th Cir. 2010).

[8] *See Peacock v. Thomas*, 516 U.S. 349, 359 (1996); *Next Invs., LLC v. Bank of China*, 12 F.4th 119, 133 (2d Cir. 2021).

[9] *Duchek v. Jacobi*, 646 F.2d 415, 417 (9th Cir. 1981) (state law requiring that enforcement proceedings be held in state court may properly be disregarded).

[10] *Peacock v. Thomas*, 516 U.S. 349, 359 (1996). *See also Mendez v. Republic Bank*, 725 F.3d 651 (7th Cir. 2013).

[11] *See, e.g., Bergmann v. Michigan State Transportation Commission*, 665 F.3d 681, 684 (6th Cir. 2011).

[12] *See, e.g., U.S. v. Harkins Builders, Inc.*, 45 F.3d 830, 833 (4th Cir. 1995). *But see Credit Suisse v. U.S. Dist. Court for Cent. Dist. of California*, 130 F.3d 1342, 1344 (9th Cir. 1997) (Rule 69(a) authorizes only a writ of execution, it provides no authority for court to order payment into court); *Aetna Cas. & Sur. Co. v. Markarian*, 114 F.3d 346, 349 (1st Cir. 1997) (vacating a writ that required judgment debtor to surrender passport).

[13] *See, e.g., Hankins v. Finnel*, 964 F.2d 853, 860 (8th Cir. 1992). *But see, Cassady v. Hall*, 892 F.3d 1150 (11th Cir. 2018) (in absence of federal or state authority to garnish funds, Rule 69 cannot be used as standalone basis for writ of garnishment).

exempt from execution in that state.

- *Fees and Costs:* Fees for writs, subpoenas, keeping attached property, and for seizing, levying on, and selling property may be taxed as costs.[14]

Time for Execution

The time for execution, and the duration of the writ of execution and other execution instruments, is generally established by state law.

- *Stay of Execution:* An automatic suspension of execution on federal judgments runs for 30 days after entry.[15] Thereafter, parties may seek further suspensions of execution (for example, while post-trial motions are under consideration or an appeal is pending) as provided by Rule 62.

Immunities from Execution

The Foreign Sovereign Immunities Act provides substantial immunity for foreign sovereigns from the jurisdiction of American courts.[16] The Act also immunizes the property of foreign states from attachment and execution.[17] It appears settled, therefore, that Rule 69 can be applied only to circumstances where the Act does not provide immunity against a judgment creditor's attempt to execute against property.[18] The Eleventh Amendment to the U.S. Constitution generally bars execution against state property.[19]

Registering a Judgment in District Outside Forum State

A judgment for money or property entered by any district court may be registered in any other district court by filing a certified copy of such judgment in the other district after the judgment has become final.[20] A judgment that has been registered has the same effect as the original judgment and may be enforced as would any other judgment. A consequence, however, of registering a judgment in federal court that was previously awarded in a different federal court in a different state is that the law of the enforcing state—not the judgment state—will normally control.[21]

---

[14] *See* 28 U.S.C.A. § 1921.

[15] *See* Rule 62(a).

[16] 28 U.S.C.A. § 1604. *See, e.g., Walters v. Industrial & Commercial Bank of China, Ltd.*, 651 F.3d 280, 292 (2d Cir. 2011).

[17] 28 U.S.C.A. § 1609.

[18] *See, e.g., Walters v. Industrial and Commercial Bank of China, Ltd.*, 651 F.3d 280, 289 (2d Cir. 2011); *Rubin v. Islamic Republic of Iran*, 637 F.3d 783, 799 (7th Cir. 2011).

[19] U.S. Const. Amend. XI. *See also Carpenters Pension Fund of Baltimore v. Maryland Department of Health and Mental Hygiene*, 721 F.3d 217, 224 (4th Cir. 2013).

[20] 28 U.S.C.A. § 1963.

[21] *See, e.g., Condaire, Inc. v. Allied Piping, Inc.*, 286 F.3d 353, 357–58 (6th Cir. 2002) (collecting cases). *Cf., Gagan v. Monroe*, 269 F.3d 871, 873 (7th Cir. 2001) (because property to be executed

Discovery in Aid of Execution

An often frustrating challenge during formal execution procedures is locating assets of the defeated party to seize and sell. This subpart assists in that challenging process by permitting a re-opening of discovery for that limited purpose.[22] A party trying to enforce a judgment may use either the federal or state discovery rules to uncover information concerning assets of the debtor and to aid in executing the judgment.[23] This subpart expressly provides that such discovery may be directed toward "any person," including persons who are not parties to the lawsuit (such as a bank).[24] Although construed "liberally" and given a "very broad" scope so as to provide an efficient, effective path to execute on judgments, post-judgment execution discovery remains bounded by relevance and proportionality constraints.[25]

RULE 69(b)—AGAINST CERTAIN PUBLIC OFFICERS

CORE CONCEPT

A judgment that has been entered against a collector of the Internal Revenue Service or an officer of Congress can be converted from a *personal* obligation of that defeated party into an obligation borne solely by the United States Government.

APPLICATIONS

Obtaining a "Certificate of Probable Cause"

An internal revenue officer[26] or an officer of Congress[27] who has suffered the entry of an adverse judgment may apply to the court for a certificate of probable cause. Through that application, the court will determine whether the federal judgment debtor acted with probable and reasonable cause in performing his or her governmental duties. If the court so finds, the court will issue a certificate of probable cause.

Effect of the Certificate

The certificate of probable cause converts the action to one against the United States, thereby extinguishing the personal liability of the individual federal official. Subsequently, the judgment creditor may serve the certificate of probable cause,

---

upon was in Arizona, the forum state's law required the use of Arizona law to determine whether property was subject to execution).

[22]*See Republic of Argentina v. NML Cap., Ltd.*, 573 U.S. 134, 138 (2014).

[23]*See, e.g., Invesco High Yield Fund v. Jecklin*, 10 F.4th 900, 901 (9th Cir. 2021); *EM Ltd. v. Republic of Argentina*, 695 F.3d 201, 207 (2d Cir. 2012) (Rule 69(a)(2) discovery "is constrained principally in that it must be calculated to assist in collecting on a judgment").

[24]*See, e.g., Republic of Argentina v. NML Capital, Ltd.*, 573 U.S. 134, 138-39 (2014).

[25]*See JP Morgan Chase Bank, N.A. v. DataTreasury Corp.*, 936 F.3d 251, 256–60 (5th Cir. 2019); *Gersh v. Anglin*, 341 F.R.D. 55, 59 (D. Mont. 2022).

[26]*See* 28 U.S.C.A. § 2006.

[27]*See* 28 U.S.C.A. § 118.

along with the judgment, on the United States Treasury. The Treasury will then be obligated to pay the amount of the judgment.

Additional Research References

Wright & Miller, *Federal Practice and Procedure* §§ 3011 to 3020
C.J.S., Federal Civil Procedure §§ 1254 to 1272 et seq.
West's Key Number Digest, Execution ⚷1 to 474

RULE 70
ENFORCING A JUDGMENT FOR A SPECIFIC ACT

(a) Party's Failure to Act; Ordering Another to Act. If a judgment requires a party to convey land, to deliver a deed or other document, or to perform any other specific act and the party fails to comply within the time specified, the court may order the act to be done—at the disobedient party's expense—by another person appointed by the court. When done, the act has the same effect as if done by the party.

(b) Vesting Title. If the real or personal property is within the district, the court—instead of ordering a conveyance—may enter a judgment divesting any party's title and vesting it in others. That judgment has the effect of a legally executed conveyance.

(c) Obtaining a Writ of Attachment or Sequestration. On application by a party entitled to performance of an act, the clerk must issue a writ of attachment or sequestration against the disobedient party's property to compel obedience.

(d) Obtaining a Writ of Execution or Assistance. On application by a party who obtains a judgment or order for possession, the clerk must issue a writ of execution or assistance.

(e) Holding in Contempt. The court may also hold the disobedient party in contempt.

[April 30, 2007, effective December 1, 2007.]

AUTHORS' COMMENTARY ON RULE 70

PURPOSE AND SCOPE

Civil "enforcement" is the process of obtaining performance of a judgment that awards non-monetary relief—such as the conveyance of land, the delivery of a deed or other document, or the performance of some other act. Often, formal enforcement proceedings are unnecessary; the defeated party could simply voluntarily comply with the judgment's mandate. Enforcement procedures are needed when voluntary performance is not forthcoming and the judgment winner requires court help to coerce the judgment debtor to comply with the court's judgment. The task of obtaining compliance with a non-money judgment is the role of Rule 70. (The process of executing upon a judgment for money is addressed by Rule 69.)

RULE 70(a)—PARTY'S FAILURE TO ACT; ORDERING ANOTHER TO ACT

CORE CONCEPT

When a judgment is entered that requires a party to transfer property, to deliver a document or deed, or to perform some other act, but that party refuses to do so, the court may appoint someone else to perform that act in the disobeying person's stead. Such appointment will be at the expense of the non-performing party and will carry the same legal effect as if the act had been performed by the party himself or herself.

APPLICATIONS

Scope

This Rule applies only to parties who have failed to comply with a judgment directing them to perform specific acts within a certain time.[1] In the absence of a judgment, the Rule has no applicability.[2] The Rule authorizes the district court to issue orders to ensure that equitable relief is accomplished,[3] but unlike Rule 69, it does not require deference to state law.[4]

Application to Rule 23 Class Members

If other requirements of Rule 70 are satisfied, the Rule may also be enforced against members of Rule 23 classes who have not opted out.[5]

---

[1] *See, e.g., Analytical Engineering, Inc. v. Baldwin Filters, Inc.*, 425 F.3d 443, 449 (7th Cir. 2005). *But cf., Westlake North Property Owners Ass'n v. City of Thousand Oaks*, 915 F.2d 1301, 1304 (9th Cir. 1990) (party's attorneys cannot be sanctioned under Rule 70).

[2] *See, e.g., Deegan v. Strategic Azimuth LLC*, 768 F. Supp. 2d 107, 115 n.1 (D.D.C. 2011) (noting applicability of Rule 64 rather than Rule 70 to prejudgment relief).

[3] *See, e.g., Board of Com'rs of Stark County, OH v. Cape Stone Works, Inc.*, 206 F. Supp. 2d 100, 102 (D. Mass. 2002).

[4] *See, e.g., Bergmann v. Michigan State Transportation Commission*, 665 F.3d 681, 681 (6th Cir. 2011).

[5] *See, e.g., Dick v. Sprint Communications Co., L.P.*, 297 F.R.D. 283, 292 (W.D. Ky. 2014).

RULE 70(b)—VESTING TITLE

CORE CONCEPT

When a judgment directs a party to give to another person title to certain real or personal property and the property is located within the judicial district where the court is sitting, the court may enter a judgment that divests the party of title and then vests title in someone else. Such a judgment has the effect of a legally-executed conveyance.

APPLICATIONS

Property Within the District

If a party has failed to obey a court order pertaining to real or personal property physically located within the district in which the court sits, the court may order title transferred directly from the disobedient party to the prevailing party.

Property Outside the District

If the real or personal property is not physically located within the district in which the court sits, the court must appoint a person to convey the property. The act performed by the appointed party has the full effect as it if it were executed by the disobedient party.

Timing

Rule 70 applies to the enforcement of court orders after the entry of judgment and after the time for performing the ordered action has elapsed.[6] The Rule allows the court to hold a party in contempt for failing to perform the required action within the specified time.[7]

Content of Motion

In a written motion, the movant should allege with specificity the disobedient party's noncompliance, as well as the relief sought to remedy noncompliance.

RULE 70(c)—OBTAINING A WRIT OF ATTACHMENT OR SEQUESTRATION

CORE CONCEPT

When a judgment directs a party to perform some act but that party refuses to do so, the judgment winner can attempt to coax the disobeying party into performing by having the clerk of court issue a writ of attachment, which permits the seizure of the disobedient party's property, or a writ of sequestration, which permits placing the disobedient party's property in the possession of the court or its designee. The goal of such writs is to induce the disobeying party—on pain of such attachment or sequestra-

[6] *See, e.g., Barmat, Inc. v. U.S.*, 159 F.R.D. 578, 582 (N.D. Ga. 1994).

[7] *Alter Domus, LLC v. Winget*, 542 F. Supp. 3d 612, 619 (E.D. Mich. 2021) (refusing to sanction party where order did not contain a deadline).

tion—to do what the judgment has already ordered that party to do.

APPLICATIONS

Alternative Enforcement Remedies

The court may enforce a judgment by requiring a party to convey property or perform a specific act through the listed remedies. Upon proper motion to the clerk of court, a prevailing party may obtain a writ of attachment or sequestration authorizing seizure of the disobedient party's property or money until that party complies with a judgment.

Costs Against Disobedient Party

A court may tax against the disobedient party the costs of transferring the property or performing the specific act.

RULE 70(d)—OBTAINING A WRIT OF EXECUTION OR ASSISTANCE

CORE CONCEPT

When a judgment or order directs a party to transfer possession of property to someone else, the judgment winner can, on motion, have the clerk of court issue a writ of execution, which permits execution upon the property, or a writ of assistance, which allows others to cooperate in acquiring possession.

RULE 70(e)—HOLDING IN CONTEMPT

CORE CONCEPT

In addition to all other remedies permitted by Rule 70, the court is also authorized to hold disobeying parties in contempt.[8] Although the Rule is silent on the point, courts have considered both civil and criminal contempt sanctions.[9]

Additional Research References

Wright & Miller, *Federal Practice and Procedure* §§ 3021 to 3030

C.J.S., Assistance, Writ of § 3, § 4; Contempt § 12; Federal Civil Procedure §§ 1254 to 1260 et seq.

West's Key Number Digest, Assistance, Writ of ⚷2; Contempt ⚷20; Federal Civil Procedure ⚷2691, ⚷2695

---

[8] *See, e.g., Chesemore v. Fenkell*, 829 F.3d 803 (7th Cir. 2016).

[9] *Serenity Alpha, LLC v. Northway Mining, LLC*, 531 F. Supp. 3d 512, 518 (N.D.N.Y. 2021).

RULE 71
ENFORCING RELIEF FOR OR AGAINST A NONPARTY

When an order grants relief for a nonparty or may be enforced against a nonparty, the procedure for enforcing the order is the same as for a party.

[Amended effective August 1, 1987; April 30, 2007, effective December 1, 2007.]

AUTHORS' COMMENTARY ON RULE 71

PURPOSE AND SCOPE

Execution and enforcement of civil judgments are addressed in Rules 69 and 70. This Rule permits those same procedures to be used for or against *non-parties* when a judgment or order grants relief for a non-party or permits enforcement against a non-party. This Rule does not identify when such non-party grants or enforcements are proper. Instead, it merely supplies the procedures to be used when they are.

APPLICATIONS

Enforcement *In Favor* of a Non-party

When a non-party shares an identity of interest with a prevailing party or is an intended beneficiary of (or otherwise entitled to enforce) a court order, the court's order may be enforced in favor of that non-party in the same manner as it might be for parties.[1] The non-party must, of course, possess standing to enforce the order.[2] Thus, for example, a non-party might purchase property at a sheriff's sale that formerly belonged to a judgment debtor and that was being sold at the court's behest to satisfy that judgment. That non-party

[1]*See McKeon Prod., Inc. v. Howard S. Leight & Assocs., Inc.*, 15 F.4th 736, 742 (6th Cir. 2021); *U.S. Commodity Futures Trading Comm'n v. Escobio*, 946 F.3d 1242, 1246 (11th Cir. 2020) (noting how trial court made each investor who suffered loss an intended third-party beneficiary for Rule 71 purposes).

[2]*See, e.g., Brennan v. Nassau County*, 352 F.3d 60, 65 (2d Cir. 2003); *Beckett v. Air Line Pilots Ass'n*, 995 F.2d 280, 287-88 (D.C. Cir. 1993); *1199SEIU United Healthcare Workers E. v. PSC Cmty. Servs.*, — F. Supp. 3d —, 2022 WL 2292736, at *8–9 (S.D.N.Y. 2022).

purchaser may enforce against the judgment debtor the obligation to transfer title in the same way that a party would.[3]

Enforcement *Against* a Non-party

Orders can be enforced against non-parties in the same manner as they might be enforced against parties (provided, of course, it is lawful and constitutional to allow enforcement against that non-party).[4] Thus, for example, a non-party agent of a judgment debtor (who possesses property on the judgment debtor's behalf) may be compelled to deliver a deed to that property to the judgment winner in the same way as the judgment debtor would.[5]

Additional Research References

Wright & Miller, *Federal Practice and Procedure* §§ 3031 to 3040
C.J.S., Federal Civil Procedure § 1107
West's Key Number Digest, Federal Civil Procedure ⚷2391

---

[3] *See Peterson v. Highland Music, Inc.*, 140 F.3d 1313 (9th Cir. 1998).

[4] *See ClearOne Communications, Inc. v. Bowers*, 651 F.3d 1200, 1215–16 (10th Cir. 2011); *Irwin v. Mascott*, 370 F.3d 924, 931–32 (9th Cir. 2004).

[5] *See LiButti v. U.S.*, 178 F.3d 114 (2d Cir. 1999).

IX. SPECIAL PROCEEDINGS

RULE 71.1 CONDEMNING REAL OR PERSONAL PROPERTY

(a) Applicability of Other Rules. These rules govern proceedings to condemn real and personal property by eminent domain, except as this rule provides otherwise.

(b) Joinder of Properties. The plaintiff may join separate pieces of property in a single action, no matter whether they are owned by the same persons or sought for the same use.

(c) Complaint.

(1) *Caption.* The complaint must contain a caption as provided in Rule 10(a). The plaintiff must, however, name as defendants both the property—designated generally by kind, quantity, and location—and at least one owner of some part of or interest in the property.

(2) *Contents.* The complaint must contain a short and plain statement of the following:

(A) the authority for the taking;

(B) the uses for which the property is to be taken;

(C) a description sufficient to identify the property;

(D) the interests to be acquired; and

(E) for each piece of property, a designation of each defendant who has been joined as an owner or owner of an interest in it.

(3) *Parties.* When the action commences, the plaintiff need join as defendants only those persons who have or claim an interest in the property and whose names are then known. But before any hearing on compensation, the plaintiff must add as defendants all those persons who have or claim an interest and whose names have become known or can be found by a reasonably diligent

search of the records, considering both the property's character and value and the interests to be acquired. All others may be made defendants under the designation "Unknown Owners."

(4) *Procedure.* Notice must be served on all defendants as provided in Rule 71.1(d), whether they were named as defendants when the action commenced or were added later. A defendant may answer as provided in Rule 71.1(e). The court, meanwhile, may order any distribution of a deposit that the facts warrant.

(5) *Filing; Additional Copies.* In addition to filing the complaint, the plaintiff must give the clerk at least one copy for the defendants' use and additional copies at the request of the clerk or a defendant.

(d) Process.

(1) *Delivering Notice to the Clerk.* On filing a complaint, the plaintiff must promptly deliver to the clerk joint or several notices directed to the named defendants. When adding defendants, the plaintiff must deliver to the clerk additional notices directed to the new defendants.

(2) *Contents of the Notice.*

(A) *Main Contents.* Each notice must name the court, the title of the action, and the defendant to whom it is directed. It must describe the property sufficiently to identify it, but need not describe any property other than that to be taken from the named defendant. The notice must also state:

(i) that the action is to condemn property;

(ii) the interest to be taken;

(iii) the authority for the taking;

(iv) the uses for which the property is to be taken;

(v) that the defendant may serve an answer on the plaintiff's attorney within 21 days after being served with the notice;

(vi) that the failure to so serve an answer constitutes consent to the taking and to the court's authority to proceed with the action and fix the compensation; and

(vii) that a defendant who does not serve an answer may file a notice of appearance.

(B) *Conclusion.* The notice must conclude with the name, telephone number, and e-mail address of the plaintiff's attorney and an address within the district in which the action is brought where the attorney may be served.

(3) *Serving the Notice.*

(A) *Personal Service.* When a defendant whose address is known resides within the United States or a territory subject to the administrative or judicial jurisdiction of the United States, personal service of the notice (without a copy of the complaint) must be made in accordance with Rule 4.

(B) *Service by Publication.*

(i) A defendant may be served by publication only when the plaintiff's attorney files a certificate stating that the attorney believes the defendant cannot be personally served, because after diligent inquiry within the state where the complaint is filed, the defendant's place of residence is still unknown or, if known, that it is beyond the territorial limits of personal service. Service is then made by publishing the notice—once a week for at least three successive weeks—in a newspaper published in the county where the property is located or, if there is no such newspaper, in a newspaper with general circulation where the property is located. Before the last publication, a copy of the notice must also be mailed to every defendant who cannot be personally served but whose place of residence is then known. Unknown owners may be served by publication in the same manner by a notice addressed to "Unknown Owners."

(ii) Service by publication is complete on the

date of the last publication. The plaintiff's attorney must prove publication and mailing by a certificate, attach a printed copy of the published notice, and mark on the copy the newspaper's name and the dates of publication.

(4) *Effect of Delivery and Service.* Delivering the notice to the clerk and serving it have the same effect as serving a summons under Rule 4.

(5) *Proof of Service; Amending the Proof or Notice.* Rule 4(l) governs proof of service. The court may permit the proof or the notice to be amended.

(e) Appearance or Answer.

(1) *Notice of Appearance.* A defendant that has no objection or defense to the taking of its property may serve a notice of appearance designating the property in which it claims an interest. The defendant must then be given notice of all later proceedings affecting the defendant.

(2) *Answer.* A defendant that has an objection or defense to the taking must serve an answer within 21 days after being served with the notice. The answer must:

(A) identify the property in which the defendant claims an interest;

(B) state the nature and extent of the interest; and

(C) state all the defendant's objections and defenses to the taking.

(3) *Waiver of Other Objections and Defenses; Evidence on Compensation.* A defendant waives all objections and defenses not stated in its answer. No other pleading or motion asserting an additional objection or defense is allowed. But at the trial on compensation, a defendant—whether or not it has previously appeared or answered—may present evidence on the amount of compensation to be paid and may share in the award.

(f) Amending Pleadings. Without leave of court, the plaintiff may—as often as it wants—amend the complaint at any time before the trial on compensation. But no amendment may be made if it would result in a dismissal inconsistent with Rule 71.1(i)(1) or (2). The plaintiff need not serve a copy of an amendment, but must serve notice of the filing, as provided in Rule 5(b), on every affected party who has appeared and, as provided in Rule 71.1(d), on every affected party who has not appeared. In addition, the plaintiff must give the clerk at least one copy of each amendment for the defendants' use, and additional copies at the request of the clerk or a defendant. A defendant may appear or answer in the time and manner and with the same effect as provided in Rule 71.1(e).

(g) Substituting Parties. If a defendant dies, becomes incompetent, or transfers an interest after being joined, the court may, on motion and notice of hearing, order that the proper party be substituted. Service of the motion and notice on a nonparty must be made as provided in Rule 71.1(d)(3).

(h) Trial of the Issues.

(1) *Issues Other Than Compensation; Compensation.* In an action involving eminent domain under federal law, the court tries all issues, including compensation, except when compensation must be determined:

(A) by any tribunal specially constituted by a federal statute to determine compensation; or

(B) if there is no such tribunal, by a jury when a party demands one within the time to answer or within any additional time the court sets, unless the court appoints a commission.

(2) *Appointing a Commission; Commission's Powers and Report.*

(A) *Reasons for Appointing.* If a party has demanded a jury, the court may instead appoint a three-person commission to determine compensation because of the character, location, or quantity of the property to be condemned or for other just reasons.

(B) *Alternate Commissioners.* The court may appoint up to two additional persons to serve as alternate commissioners to hear the case and replace commissioners who, before a decision is filed, the court finds unable or disqualified to perform their duties. Once the commission renders its final decision, the court must discharge any alternate who has not replaced a commissioner.

(C) *Examining the Prospective Commissioners.* Before making its appointments, the court must advise the parties of the identity and qualifications of each prospective commissioner and alternate, and may permit the parties to examine them. The parties may not suggest appointees, but for good cause may object to a prospective commissioner or alternate.

(D) *Commission's Powers and Report.* A commission has the powers of a master under Rule 53(c). Its action and report are determined by a majority. Rule 53(d), (e), and (f) apply to its action and report.

(i) Dismissal of the Action or a Defendant.

(1) *Dismissing the Action.*

(A) *By the Plaintiff.* If no compensation hearing on a piece of property has begun, and if the plaintiff has not acquired title or a lesser interest or taken possession, the plaintiff may, without a court order, dismiss the action as to that property by filing a notice of dismissal briefly describing the property.

(B) *By Stipulation.* Before a judgment is entered vesting the plaintiff with title or a lesser interest in or possession of property, the plaintiff and affected defendants may, without a court order, dismiss the action in whole or in part by filing a stipulation of dismissal. And if the parties so stipulate, the court may vacate a judgment already entered.

(C) *By Court Order.* At any time before compensation has been determined and paid, the court may, after a motion and hearing, dismiss the action as to a piece of property. But if the plaintiff has already taken title, a lesser interest, or possession as to any part of it, the court must award compensation for the title, lesser interest, or possession taken.

(2) *Dismissing a Defendant.* The court may at any time dismiss a defendant who was unnecessarily or improperly joined.

(3) *Effect.* A dismissal is without prejudice unless otherwise stated in the notice, stipulation, or court order.

(j) Deposit and Its Distribution.

(1) *Deposit.* The plaintiff must deposit with the court any money required by law as a condition to the exercise of eminent domain and may make a deposit when allowed by statute.

(2) *Distribution; Adjusting Distribution.* After a deposit, the court and attorneys must expedite the proceedings so as to distribute the deposit and to determine and pay compensation. If the compensation finally awarded to a defendant exceeds the amount distributed to that defendant, the court must enter judgment against the plaintiff for the deficiency. If the compensation awarded to a defendant is less than the amount distributed to that defendant, the court must enter judgment against that defendant for the overpayment.

(k) Condemnation Under a State's Power of Eminent Domain. This rule governs an action involving eminent domain under state law. But if state law provides for trying an issue by jury—or for trying the issue of compensation by jury or commission or both—that law governs.

(l) Costs. Costs are not subject to Rule 54(d).

[Adopted April 30, 1951, effective August 1, 1951; amended January 21, 1963, effective July 1, 1963; April 29, 1985, effective August 1, 1985; March 2, 1987, effective August 1, 1987; April 25, 1988, effective August 1, 1988; amended by Pub.L. 100-690, Title VII, § 7050, November 18, 1988, 102 Stat. 4401 (although amendment by Pub.L. 100-690 could not be executed due to prior amendment by Court order which made the same change effective August 1, 1988); amended April 22, 1993, effective December 1, 1993; March 27, 2003, effective December 1, 2003; April 30, 2007, effective December 1, 2007; March 26, 2009, effective December 1, 2009.]

AUTHORS' COMMENTARY ON RULE 71.1

PURPOSE AND SCOPE

Federal and state governments have "eminent domain" power—the authority to take private property for public use. The "taking" (also called "condemning") of property for public use can occur, for example, when private land is needed to build a highway, a railroad spur, or an airport. The exercise of this authority by the sovereign is conditioned constitutionally on fairly compensating the landowner for the taking.[1]

RULE 71.1(a)—APPLICABILITY OF OTHER RULES

CORE CONCEPT

Rule 71.1(a) directs that, unless specifically otherwise provided in Rule 71.1, the Federal Rules of Civil Procedure govern the procedure for the condemnation of real and personal property under the power of eminent domain.[2]

APPLICATIONS

Scope

In essence, Rule 71.1 establishes two steps for condemnation in federal court. First, the rule creates an "expedited determination" of the lawfulness of the condemnation action.[3] If the first step is satisfied, the court then determines just compensation.[4]

Requirement for Substantive Cause of Action

Rule 71.1 is purely procedural and does not create a cause of action. To have a cause of action to which this rule of procedure might be applicable, a party must have a right to sue deriving from some substantive law.[5]

Condemnation of Personal Property

Rule 71.1 applies to the condemnation of personal property as an appurtenance to real property or as the sole object of the proceeding (although cases involving personal property are not

---

[1] *See* U.S. Const. amend. V ("nor shall private property be taken for public use, without just compensation").

[2] *See, e.g., Transcontinental Gas Pipe Line Co., LLC v. 6.04 Acres of Land*, 910 F.3d 1130 (11th Cir. 2018) (state law inapplicable).

[3] *See, e.g., EQT Gathering, LLC v. A Tract of Property Situated in Knott County, Kentucky*, 970 F. Supp. 2d 655, 657 (E.D. Ky. 2013).

[4] *See, e.g., EQT Gathering, LLC v. A Tract of Property Situated in Knott County, Kentucky*, 970 F. Supp. 2d 655, 657 (E.D. Ky. 2013).

[5] *See, e.g., Warren v. City of Greensboro*, 280 F.Supp.3d 780 (M.D.N.C. 2017).

common).[6]

Inverse Condemnation Proceedings

Rule 71.1 does not apply to inverse condemnation proceedings. An inverse condemnation "is a cause of action by which a landowner recovers just compensation from the government for a taking of his or her property when condemnation proceedings have not been instituted."[7] An important difference between an inverse condemnation and a direct condemnation governed by Rule 71.1 is that there is no right to a jury trial on any issue—not even compensation—in an inverse condemnation proceeding.[8]

Choice of Law

Rule 71.1 provides a uniform procedure for condemnation in federal courts.[9] State law defines the nature of the real or personal property interest, such as the meaning of property, defining what is taken, or determining the ownership of land.

Condemnation Under State Law

A district court may entertain condemnation proceedings under state law, as provided by Rule 71.1(k).

Jurisdiction and Venue

The district courts have original jurisdiction over proceedings to condemn real property for the use of the United States, its agencies, or departments.[10] Venue will be in the district court of the district in which the real property is located or, if located in different districts in the same state, in any such districts.[11]

Rule 71.1 and the Other Rules

In cases where Rule 71.1 does not provide a procedure concerning litigation, the court will apply other applicable Rules.[12]

RULE 71.1(b)—JOINDER OF PROPERTIES

CORE CONCEPT

Rule 71.1(b) permits condemnation of separate properties, including properties belonging to different owners, or properties for different public uses in the same court action.[13] Only in exceptional circumstances is the court required to conduct sepa-

---

[6]*See United States v. 8.929 Acres of Land in Arlington Cnty., Virginia*, 36 F.4th 240, 251 (4th Cir. 2022).

[7]*KLK, Inc. v. U.S. Dept. of Interior*, 35 F.3d 454, 455 n. 1 (9th Cir. 1994).

[8]*See, e.g., U.S. v. 191.07 Acres of Land*, 482 F.3d 1132, 1136 (9th Cir. 2007).

[9]*See, e.g., Alliance Pipeline L.P. v. 4.360 Acres of Land, More or Less*, 746 F.3d 362, 366 (8th Cir. 2014).

[10]28 U.S.C.A. § 1358.

[11]28 U.S.C.A. § 1403.

[12]*United States v. 8.929 Acres of Land in Arlington Cnty., Virginia*, 36 F.4th 240, 252 (4th Cir. 2022).

[13]*See, e.g., McLaughlin v. Mississippi Power Co.*, 376 F.3d 344, 354 (5th Cir. 2004) (joinder of properties under

rate trials. To eliminate jury confusion over the relative value of properties, the court may separate the evidence concerning the damages sustained by each owner.

RULE 71.1(c)—COMPLAINT

CORE CONCEPT

The requirements for a complaint under Rule 71.1(c) are different from those in an ordinary civil action. In the complaint's caption, Rule 71.1(c) requires the plaintiff to name as defendants both the property and at least one of the owners. Rule 71.1(c) does not require the plaintiff to serve a summons and a complaint on the defendants; rather the clerk of court arranges for notice to all defendants as provided in Rule 71.1(d). However, prior to a hearing on compensation, the plaintiff must join all defendants who can be ascertained from a reasonably diligent search of the records.

APPLICATIONS

Caption

The complaint's caption must include the name of the court, the title of the action, the docket number, and the name of the type of pleading being presented. The caption must name as defendants both the property and at least one of the owners. The plaintiff will name the property as the defendant by stating the kind, quantity, and location of the property.

Contents of Complaint

Rule 71.1(c) lists five requirements for inclusion in "a short and plain statement:"

(1) the authority for the taking;
(2) the use for which the property is to be taken;[14]
(3) a description of the property sufficient for identification;[15]
(4) the interests to be acquired; and
(5) for each piece of property, a designation of each defendant who has been joined as an owner or owner of an interest.

Filing of Complaint and Notice

The plaintiff must file the complaint with the clerk and provide the clerk with at least one copy for the defendants. Upon the request of the clerk or the defendants, the plaintiff must furnish additional copies. This practice differs from the normal practice under Rule 4, which requires the plaintiff to

---

Rule 71.1 is "much broader" than joinder of parties under Rules 19 and 20 and joinder of claims under Rule 18).

[14]*See, e.g., City of Arlington v. Golddust Twins Realty Corp.*, 41 F.3d 960, 964 (5th Cir. 1994).

[15]*See, e.g., Southern Natural Gas Co. v. Land, Cullman County*, 197 F.3d 1368, 1375 (11th Cir. 1999) (legal description and plat map is sufficient).

serve a summons and a copy of the complaint on the defendants.

Joining Parties at Commencement

At the commencement of an action, the plaintiff must join as defendants all persons or entities of title record having or claiming an interest in the property whose names are then known. Prior to a hearing on compensation, all other persons unascertained or unknown shall be made parties as defendants by description if their names are unknown.

Joining of Interested Parties Prior to Hearing

Prior to a hearing involving compensation, the plaintiff must add as defendants all persons who have an interest whose identities can be ascertained by a reasonably diligent search of the records,[16] and also those whose names have been learned. "Reasonably diligent" search means the type of search a title searcher would undertake, but the extent of the search required will depend upon the character and value of the property involved and the interests to be acquired. Property owners joined after the commencement of the action must be served with notice by the clerk and allowed to answer.

Failure to Join a Party

There are no indispensable parties in a condemnation action. Therefore, the failure to join a party will not defeat the plaintiff's title to the land because a condemnation action is an action *in rem.*[17] If the plaintiff's fails to join a party, the omitted party may have the right to sue for compensation in the Claims Court after the condemnation is completed.[18]

RULE 71.1(d)—PROCESS

CORE CONCEPT

Rule 71.1(d) directs that the clerk will deliver a notice of the complaint to a marshal or specially appointed person who will make personal service on the defendants.

APPLICATIONS

Content of Notice

Each notice must state:

(1) the court;
(2) the title of the action;
(3) the name of the defendant to whom it is directed;
(4) the nature of the action (condemning property);
(5) a description of the property sufficient for its identification;

---

[16] *See, e.g., Cadorette v. U.S.*, 988 F.2d 215, 224 (1st Cir. 1993).

[17] *Fulcher v. U.S.*, 632 F.2d 278, 282 (4th Cir. 1980) ("Persons not identified . . . can be impleaded as unknown.").

[18] *See, e.g., U.S. v. 194.08 Acres of Land*, 135 F.3d 1025, 1035 n. 8 (5th Cir. 1998); *Cadorette v. U.S.*, 988 F.2d 215, 225 (1st Cir. 1993).

(6) the interest to be taken;
(7) the authority for the taking;
(8) the uses for which the property is being taken;
(9) the time for answering the complaint (the defendant may serve an answer upon the plaintiff's attorney within twenty-one days after the service of the notice);
(10) the penalty for failing to answer (a consent to the taking, which permits the court to proceed to hear the action and fix compensation); and
(11) that any defendant who chooses not to file an answer may nevertheless file a notice of appearance.

The notice must, finally, include the name, telephone number, and e-mail address of the plaintiff's attorney as well as an address within the district in which the suit is brought where that attorney may be served.

Preparation of Notice

The plaintiff may prepare joint or separate notices. However, one notice must be delivered to each named defendant and need contain a description of only that property taken from the particular defendant to whom it is directed.

Filing of Notice

The plaintiff's attorney will prepare a notice and deliver it to the clerk with the complaint. Subsequently, the clerk will file and enter the complaint in the record and deliver a notice of the complaint (but not a copy of the complaint itself) to the marshal or a specially-appointed person for service.

Persons Requiring Notice

At the commencement of the case, the clerk need only provide notice to persons whose names are in the complaint. Property owners joined after the filing of the complaint must be served with notice and allowed to answer.

Service

Personal service of the notice (but without copies of the complaint) shall be made in accordance with Rule 4 upon each defendant who resides within the United States or its territories or insular possessions and whose residence is known.

Service By Publication

(1) *Persons Served by Publication:* A plaintiff may make service by publication on three types of defendants:[19]

(a) owners who do not reside in the United States, its territories, or insular possessions, and who, therefore, are beyond the territorial limits of personal service;

---

[19]*See, e.g., U.S. v. 499.472 Acres of Land More or Less in Brazoria County, Tex.*, 701 F.2d 545, 551 (5th Cir. 1983) (publication service permissible only in the explicit circumstances described in Rule 71.1(d)).

(b) owners within the state in which the complaint is filed whose place of residence is unknown after a diligent search of the records; and

(c) unknown owners.

(2) *Publication:* The plaintiff must publish the notice in a newspaper in the county where the land is located. When no newspaper exists in the county where the land is located, the plaintiff must publish the notice in a newspaper having a circulation in the area where the land is located. The plaintiff must publish the notice once a week for at least three successive weeks.

(3) *Proof of Publication:* When a plaintiff wishes to make proof of service by publication, the plaintiff's attorney must file with the court a certificate stating that the defendant cannot be served personally because the defendant's residence is beyond the personal service limits or after diligent inquiry defendant's residence is unknown. The plaintiff's attorney must attach to the certificate a printed copy of the published notice marked with the name of the newspaper and the dates of publication.

(4) *Defendants Who Cannot Be Served But Residence Known:* A defendant who cannot be personally served but whose place of residence is known must be mailed a copy of the notice prior to the date of the last publication. Service is complete on the date of the last publication.

RULE 71.1(e)—APPEARANCE OR ANSWER

CORE CONCEPT

A defendant may respond to a condemnation complaint in two ways. If the defendant intends to either contest the taking or make objections to the complaint, the defendant must file an answer. The defendant may file a motion to dismiss simultaneously with the answer that raises objections and defenses that have also been raised in the answer.[20] Alternatively, if the defendant has no defenses or objections to the taking, the defendant simply serves a notice of appearance designating the property in which the defendant has an interest. Filing a notice of appearance requires that the defendant be given notice of all subsequent proceedings that affect that defendant's interest.[21] However, regardless of whether the defendant files an answer or an appearance, a defendant may present evidence at the hearing on compensation and share in the award.[22]

---

[20] *United States v. 0.720 Acres of Land, More or Less*, __ F. Supp. 3d __, 2022 WL 1793427, at *2 (S.D. Tex. 2022); *U.S. v. 6.584 Acres of Land, more or less, Hidalgo Cty.*, 533 F. Supp. 3d 482, 494 (S.D. Tex. 2021).

[21] *Cf., U.S. v. 14.02 Acres of Land*, 547 F.3d 943, 954 (9th Cir. 2008).

[22] *See, e.g., Bank One Texas v. U.S.*, 157 F.3d 397 (5th Cir. 1998).

APPLICATIONS

Answer and Motion to Dismiss

The answer is the only responsive pleading in which defenses or objections may be asserted.[23] In the answer the defendant must identify the property, the defendant's interest in the property, and the defenses to the taking. Any defenses not properly asserted in the answer are waived.[24]

- *Motion to Dismiss:* The defendant may file a motion to dismiss simultaneously with the answer that raises objections and defenses that have also been raised in the answer.[25]

Counterclaims and Crossclaims

An answer may not contain a counterclaim or crossclaim.[26] A counterclaim must be brought in a separate action in the district court or the Court of Claims.

Timing of Answer

Within 21 days of service of the notice, the defendant must answer the complaint. This response period may be enlarged by motion, as provided by Rule 6(b).

Appearance

When the defendant has no defenses or objections to the taking or to the complaint, the defendant may serve a notice of appearance. The notice of appearance should designate the property in which the defendant claims an interest. When a defendant has filed an appearance, the defendant is entitled to receive notice of all of the proceedings affecting the defendant.[27]

RULE 71.1(f)—AMENDING PLEADINGS

CORE CONCEPT

Before the trial on the issue of just compensation, a plaintiff may amend the complaint multiple times without leave of court.[28] However, except as provided by Rule 71.1(i), the plaintiff may not amend the complaint to remove the names of defendants or claims. Within 21 days of the notice of each amended complaint, the defendant is entitled to file one amended answer as of right.

---

[23] *See, e.g., Mountain Valley Pipeline, LLC v. Western Pocahontas Properties Limited Partnership*, 918 F.3d 353 (4th Cir. 2019)

[24] *Washington Metropolitan Area Transit Authority v. Precision Small Engines*, 227 F.3d 224, 228 n. 2 (4th Cir. 2000).

[25] *United States v. 0.720 Acres of Land, More or Less*, — F. Supp. 3d —, 2022 WL 1793427, at *2 (S.D. Tex. 2022); *U.S. v. 6.584 Acres of Land, more or less, Hidalgo Cty.*, 533 F. Supp. 3d 482, 494 (S.D. Tex. 2021).

[26] *See, e.g., U.S. v. Certain Land Situated in City of Detroit*, 361 F.3d 305, 308 (6th Cir. 2004).

[27] *See, e.g., Columbia Gas Transmission, LLC v. Crawford*, 746 F. Supp. 2d 905, 909–10 (N.D. Ohio 2010).

[28] *See, e.g., Atlantic Coast Pipeline, LLC v. 0.07 Acre, More or Less, in Nelson County, Virginia*, 396 F.Supp.3d 628 (W.D. Va. 2019).

APPLICATIONS

Procedure for Amending Complaint

The plaintiff may amend the complaint by filing with the clerk the amended pleading and by serving notice of the amended pleading on each defendant. The plaintiff need not serve a copy of the amended pleading itself on defendants, a practice that differs from normal civil actions. Instead, if a defendant or the clerk requests additional copies of the amended complaint, the plaintiff must provide the clerk with additional copies.

Service to Persons Who Have Not Entered an Appearance

The plaintiff should serve notice of an amended complaint on persons who have not entered an appearance.[29]

RULE 71.1(g)—SUBSTITUTING PARTIES

CORE CONCEPT

Upon proper motion and notice of hearing, the court may order the substitution of parties when a defendant dies, becomes incompetent, or transfers an interest after the defendant's joinder. If a new party is substituted, the plaintiff must serve a copy of the motion and notice of hearing on the new party, as provided by Rule 71.1(d). Rule 25, governing substitution of parties in most civil actions, does not apply to condemnation actions.

RULE 71.1(h)—TRIAL OF THE ISSUES

CORE CONCEPT

All issues other than the issue of compensation will be decided by the court.[30] The issue of compensation will be decided by either a special tribunal, a commission, a jury, or the court, in condemnation actions instituted by the federal or state government under powers of eminent domain. Federal law may require the issue of compensation to be decided by a tribunal specially constituted by Congress. When any party demands a trial by jury, the court will decide whether to conduct a jury trial or to appoint a commission to decide the issue of compensation.

NOTE: If a commission is appointed to decide the issue of compensation, the commission must issue a report. Within 21 days after service of the commission report, parties must make and serve on the other parties and the court their objections to the report.

APPLICATIONS

Trial by Jury

When any party demands a trial by jury, the court may

[29] *See* Rule 71.1(d).

[30] *See, e.g., United States v. 8.929 Acres of Land in Arlington Cnty., Virginia*, 36 F.4th 240, 251–52 (4th Cir. 2022); *U.S. v. 480.00 Acres of Land*, 557 F.3d 1297, 1312 (11th Cir. 2009).

conduct a jury trial or may appoint a commission to decide the issue of compensation. However, there is no constitutional right to a trial by jury in condemnation cases,[31] and the jury in such cases may decide only the issue of compensation.[32]

(1) *Time for Demand:* Within the time allowed for the answer to the condemnation complaint (21 days of service of the notice of the complaint, unless an enlargement of time has extended the period) or a further time fixed by the court, any party may demand a trial by jury.

(2) *Procedure for Trial by Jury:* The trial of a condemnation action is similar to any other civil proceeding involving a trial by jury. However, the judge will determine all issues other than the amount of compensation.[33]

Trial by Commission

(1) *Appointment of Commission:* When a party demands a trial by jury, the court has discretion to appoint a commission to decide the issue of compensation rather than conducting a trial by jury.[34] Although the court is not required to make findings of fact to support its determination to appoint a commission, for purposes of appellate review the court will often state in writing its reasons for appointing a commission.

(a) *Conditions for Reference to Commission:* Courts have appointed commissions for such reasons as: local preference or habit, the preference of the Justice Department, the distance of the property from the courthouse, the complexity of the issues, the character of the land, the nature of the interest or the number of tracts taken, the need for numerous jury trials, the desirability of uniform awards, or to prevent discrimination.

(2) *Number of Commissioners:* A commission is generally composed of three persons. The court may appoint two alternate commissioners to sit at the hearing with the other commissioners.

(3) *Appointment of Commissioners:* Usually, the court will appoint commissioners and alternate commissioners. Often, the court will appoint a lawyer or ex-judge as chair of the commission and one real estate person as a member. After appointing the commissioners, the court will advise the parties of the identity and qualifications of each prospective commissioner and alternate commissioner. The parties may examine the commissioners and may, for valid cause, object to the appointment

[31] *U.S. v. Reynolds*, 397 U.S. 14, 18 (1970).

[32] *See, e.g., U.S. v. Certain Land Situated in the City of Detroit, Wayne County*, 450 F.3d 205, 208 (6th Cir. 2006).

[33] *See, e.g., U.S. v. 4.0 Acres of Land*, 175 F.3d 1133 (9th Cir. 1999).

[34] *See, U.S. v. 320.0 Acres of Land, More or Less in Monroe County, State of Fla.*, 605 F.2d 762, 828 (5th Cir. 1979) (acknowledging some contrary authority but holding that use of a commission is only for exceptional cases).

of any commissioner.[35]

(4) *Reformation and Revocation of Commission:* When the court believes the judgment of the commission has been affected by bias, the court may reform the commission by replacing some or all of the commissioners.[36] When justice so requires, such as instances of undue delay, the court may vacate the reference to the commission.

(5) *Procedure for Trial by Commission:*

(a) *Powers:* The commission will only try the issue of compensation; all other issues will be decided by the court. The commission has the same powers as a master in a non-jury trial. Proceedings before the commission are governed by Rule 53(c). The commission may regulate its proceedings, require the production of all documents, rule on the admissibility of evidence, call and examine witnesses, and permit the witnesses to be examined by the parties. These powers will be regulated indirectly by the court through its instructions to the commission in the order of reference.

(b) *Instructions:* In its order of reference, the trial judge will instruct the commissioners as to such issues as: the qualifications of expert witnesses, the weight to be given to other opinions of evidence, competent evidence of value, the best evidence of value, the manner of the hearing and the method of conducting it, the right to view the property, the limited purpose of viewing, and the kind of evidence which is inadmissible and the manner of ruling on the admissibility of evidence.

(c) *Admission of Evidence:* Although the court will control the kind of evidence which is admissible, the commission will apply the Federal Rules of Evidence when ruling on the admissibility of the evidence.

(1) *View of Property:* When necessary or conducive to a proper determination of compensation, and when not inconvenient or the cause of undue delay or expense, the commission may view the property.

(6) *Findings and Report of Commission:* A majority of the commissioners will decide the amount of compensation to award, and the commission will submit a report. The findings and the report of the commission will follow the provisions of Rule 53(e)(2). In its report, the commission must clearly show a factual basis for its findings, but need not make detailed findings. A suitable commission report will state what evidence and what measure of damages the commission accepted and

---

[35] *See, Guardian Pipeline, L.L.C. v. 950.80 Acres of Land*, 525 F.3d 554, 557–58 (7th Cir. 2008) (litigant who does not examine proposed commissioner at outset waives challenges).

[36] *See, City of Stilwell, Okl. v. Ozarks Rural Elec. Co-op. Corp.*, 166 F.3d 1064, 1069 (10th Cir. 1999) (commissioners need not have "complete and absolute impartiality").

why the commission reached its award.[37]

(7) *Objection to Commission Report:* Within 21 days after service of the commission's report, a party must make and file with the court and serve on all other parties objections to the report.[38] The party objecting to the report retains the burden of demonstrating that the report is erroneous.

(8) *Trial Court Review of Commission Report:* The trial court must adopt the report of the commission unless it finds the report to be clearly erroneous.[39] A trial court may find the report clearly erroneous when there was a substantial error in the proceedings or when the court finds that the report is unsupported by substantial evidence, is against the clear weight of the evidence,[40] or involves a misapplication of law. Courts have also found commission reports clearly erroneous when the award was grossly inadequate. When the trial court finds the report clearly erroneous, the court may examine the testimony and make its own judgment or it may recommit the matter to the commission with instructions.[41]

(9) *Commissioners' Compensation:* Commissioners will be compensated in reasonable relation to the services rendered (i.e., the bar association's minimum fee schedule). The commissioners' compensation will be charged to the plaintiff and may be included in the damage award, not taxed as costs against the award.

RULE 71.1(i)—DISMISSAL OF THE ACTION OR A DEFENDANT

CORE CONCEPT

The procedures for dismissal depend on the posture of the proceedings. Prior to a hearing or declaration of taking, the action may be dismissed as of right. Where the plaintiff has the statutory authority to file a declaration of taking, acquire an interest in the property, acquire title to the property, or take possession of the property before the entry of judgment, the case may be dismissed by stipulation of the parties or with approval of the court.[42] The defendant may file a motion to dismiss challenging the plaintiff's statutory authority to file a declaration of taking.[43] After the entry of judgment the court has discretion to vacate the judgment upon the stipulation of the parties.

---

[37] *See U.S. v. Merz*, 376 U.S. 192, 198 (1964).

[38] *See* Rule 53(f)(2).

[39] *U.S. v. Merz*, 376 U.S. 192, 198 (1964).

[40] *Georgia Power Co. v. 138.30 Acres of Land*, 596 F.2d 644 (5th Cir. 1979).

[41] *See, e.g., Southern Natural Gas Co. v. Land, Cullman County*, 197 F.3d 1368, 1375 (11th Cir. 1999); *Rockies Express Pipeline LLC v. 4.895 Acres of Land, More or Less*, 734 F.3d 424, 428–29 (6th Cir. 2013) (review is de novo).

[42] *Kirby Forest Industries, Inc. v. U.S.*, 467 U.S. 1, 12, n. 18 (1984).

[43] *United States v. 0.720 Acres of Land, More or Less*, __ F. Supp. 3d __,

APPLICATIONS

Dismissal

(1) *As of Right:* Before a hearing on compensation has begun and before the plaintiff has filed a declaration of taking as provided by statute, acquired title, acquired an interest, or taken possession of the property, the plaintiff may dismiss the action by filing a notice of dismissal stating a brief description of the property.

(2) *By Stipulation:* Before the entry of a judgment vesting plaintiff with title, an interest, or possession of the property, the parties may stipulate to a dismissal in whole or in part without an order of the court. After judgment, the parties may stipulate to a dismissal and the court may vacate the judgment and revest title in the defendant.

(3) *By Court Order:* When the hearing on compensation has begun, but the plaintiff has not filed a declaration of taking, acquired title, acquired an interest, or taken possession, the court will decide whether to grant a voluntary dismissal.[44] However, when the hearing has begun and the plaintiff has filed a declaration of taking, acquired title, acquired an interest, or taken possession, the court must award just compensation for the possession, title, or the interest taken, unless stipulated otherwise by the parties.[45]

Dismissal of Improperly and Unnecessarily Joined Parties

At any time, upon a motion or *sua sponte,* the court may dismiss a defendant who has no interest in the action but has been unnecessarily or improperly joined.

Dismissal Without Prejudice

Unless stated in the order or the stipulation, a dismissal of a condemnation proceeding is without prejudice.

RULE 71.1(j)—DEPOSIT AND ITS DISTRIBUTION

CORE CONCEPT

Rule 71.1(j) describes the procedure for the deposit of money with the court when required or permitted by statute. State substantive law will determine the amount to be deposited in state eminent domain actions, while federal substantive law will determine the amount to be deposited in federal eminent domain actions.

2022 WL 1793427, at *3 (S.D. Tex. 2022).

[44] *See, e.g., U.S. v. 4,970 Acres of Land*, 130 F.3d 712, 714–15 (5th Cir. 1997).

[45] *See, e.g., U.S. v. 4,970 Acres of Land*, 130 F.3d 712, 715 (5th Cir. 1997).

APPLICATIONS

Deposits Before Judgment

Rule 71.1(j) applies only to deposits made by the plaintiff before judgment.[46]

Government's Burden

Once the plaintiff has made a deposit with the court, Rule 71.1(j) places the burden and expenses of calculating and distributing the compensation owed to the defendants upon the plaintiff.[47]

The Declaration of Taking Act

The Declaration of Taking Act is another source of procedures when the United States seeks to condemn property and it supplements the procedures under Rule 71.1(j), relating to the deposit and distribution in eminent domain cases. Under the Act, upon the filing of a declaration of taking and a deposit of the estimated compensation with the court, title immediately vests in the federal government.[48] Like Rule 71.1, the Act does not, in and of itself, authorize a taking; the United States' ability to take title under the Act is contingent upon the United States' authority to act pursuant to statutory law.[49]

(1) *Time for Filing:* A declaration of taking may be brought at the commencement of the condemnation action and at any time before a judgment.

(2) *Certification:* The chief of the government department or bureau acquiring the land will certify that the land is within the value prescribed by Congress.

(3) *Surrender of Possession; Encumbrances:* Upon the filing of a declaration of taking, the court will fix the time and the terms upon which the parties in possession will surrender possession of the property to the plaintiff. The court may also make orders concerning encumbrances, liens, rents, taxes, assessments, insurance, etc.

(4) *Amount of Award:* The judgment will include interest from the date of the taking to the date of the award. However, no interest will be ordered on money paid into the court. When the court or the jury awards an amount greater than the deposit, the court will enter judgment against the plaintiff and in favor of the defendant for the difference plus interest.[50] When the court or the jury awards an amount less than the deposit,

---

[46] *See, e.g., U.S. v. Hirsch*, 206 F.2d 289 (2d Cir. 1953).

[47] *See, e.g., U.S. v. 818.76 Acres of Land, More or Less, in Cedar and Dade Counties*, 315 F. Supp. 758 (W.D. Mo. 1970).

[48] 40 U.S.C.A. § 3114.

[49] *United States v. Dow*, 357 U.S. 17, 23 (1958); *United States v. 162.20 Acres of Land, More or Less, Situated in Clay Cnty., State of Miss.*, 639 F.2d 299, 303 (5th Cir. 1981).

[50] *U.S. v. 9.20 Acres of Land, More or Less, Situated in Polk County, State of Iowa*, 638 F.2d 1123 (8th Cir. 1981) (deposit insufficient). *See also* 40 U.S.C.A. § 3114 *et seq.*

the court will enter judgment against the defendant and in favor of the plaintiff for the amount of overpayment. When the deposit exceeds the award, the plaintiff will obtain the excess deposit from the clerk.[51]

(5) *Deposit and Distribution:* At the time of the taking and the deposit into the court, the court may order distribution of the deposit to the known defendants.[52]

(6) *Appellate Review:* A transfer of title is not a final appealable judgment until a final judgment on compensation has been entered.[53]

RULE 71.1(k)—CONDEMNATION UNDER A STATE'S POWER OF EMINENT DOMAIN

CORE CONCEPT

Although most federal court eminent domain cases will involve the federal power of eminent domain, a state may institute an eminent domain action in a federal district court when diversity of citizenship exists between the plaintiff and the defendant and the amount in controversy exceeds $75,000, exclusive of interest and costs. Similarly, a defendant may remove a state eminent domain action to federal district court when the plaintiff initiates the suit and the defendant is not a citizen of the state in which the action is brought, and the amount in controversy exceeds $75,000, exclusive of interest and costs.[54] These state eminent domain actions must be brought in the federal district court for the district in which the land is situated.

APPLICATIONS

Choice of Law

The federal court will apply the procedure described in Rule 71.1. The court will apply state substantive condemnation law.[55]

Trial by Jury

In state eminent domain cases, the court will follow state law provisions for trial by jury or a commission.[56]

Collateral Attack of State Court Judgment

A party may not bring a federal court action challenging a state court judgment in a state eminent domain action.

RULE 71.1(*l*)—COSTS

CORE CONCEPT

Rule 71.1(l) governs the assessment of costs in condemnation

[51] *See, e.g., U.S. ex rel. Tenn. Valley Auth. v. 1.72 Acres of Land in Tennessee*, 821 F.3d 742 (6th Cir. 2016).

[52] 40 U.S.C.A. § 3114 *et seq.*

[53] *Catlin v. U.S.*, 324 U.S. 229, 243–44 (1945).

[54] 28 U.S.C.A. § 1441(a), (b).

[55] *See, e.g., City of Joliet v. New West, L.P.*, 825 F.3d 827 (7th Cir. 2016).

[56] *See, e.g., City of Joliet, Illinois v. New West, L.P.*, 825 F.3d 827 (7th Cir. 2016).

proceedings decided pursuant to Rule 71.1. The normal expenses of the proceeding will be charged to the condemnor. Expenses incurred in the distribution of the award are charged to the defendant.

APPLICATIONS

Costs Paid by Condemnor

The condemnor shall pay the normal expenses such as the bills for publication of notice, commissioners' fees, the cost of transporting commissioners and jurors to view the property, fees for attorneys representing defendants who have failed to answer, and witness' fees. These expenses shall be charged to the government and, when required, be included as damages in the award but will not be taxed against the award, except to the extent permitted by law.[57] In addition, the condemnor must pay for the expenses of a commissioner who records the deed and executes the conveyance. This provision protects private property owners from a reduction of their compensation awards, because the condemnors will typically be "prevailing parties" who would otherwise be entitled to recover costs under Rule 54.[58]

Expenses of Distribution

Expenses incurred in the distribution of the award, such as ascertaining the identity of the distributees and deciding between conflicting claimants, are chargeable against the award.[59]

Additional Research References

Wright & Miller, *Federal Practice and Procedure* §§ 3041 to 3056

C.J.S., Eminent Domain §§ 209 to 251 et seq., §§ 267 to 315 et seq., §§ 319 to 366 et seq., §§ 373 to 386 et seq.

West's Key Number Digest, Eminent Domain ⚷166 to 265(5)

---

[57] *See* Rule 71.1(*l*) advisory committee note.

[58] *See Sabal Trail Transmission, LLC v. 18.27 Acres of Land in Levy Cty.*, 2021 WL 1881404, at *20 (N.D. Fla. 2021).

[59] *See* Rule 71.1(*l*) advisory committee note.

RULE 72
MAGISTRATE JUDGES: PRETRIAL ORDER

(a) Nondispositive Matters. When a pretrial matter not dispositive of a party's claim or defense is referred to a magistrate judge to hear and decide, the magistrate judge must promptly conduct the required proceedings and, when appropriate, issue a written order stating the decision. A party may serve and file objections to the order within 14 days after being served with a copy. A party may not assign as error a defect in the order not timely objected to. The district judge in the case must consider timely objections and modify or set aside any part of the order that is clearly erroneous or is contrary to law.

(b) Dispositive Motions and Prisoner Petitions.

(1) *Findings and Recommendations.* A magistrate judge must promptly conduct the required proceedings when assigned, without the parties' consent, to hear a pretrial matter dispositive of a claim or defense or a prisoner petition challenging the conditions of confinement. A record must be made of all evidentiary proceedings and may, at the magistrate judge's discretion, be made of any other proceedings. The magistrate judge must enter a recommended disposition, including, if appropriate, proposed findings of fact. The clerk must promptly mail a copy to each party.

(2) *Objections.* Within 14 days after being served with a copy of the recommended disposition, a party may serve and file specific written objections to the proposed findings and recommendations. A party may respond to another party's objections within 14 days after being served with a copy. Unless the district judge orders otherwise, the objecting party must promptly arrange for transcribing the record, or whatever portions of it the parties agree to or

the magistrate judge considers sufficient.

(3) *Resolving Objections.* The district judge must determine de novo any part of the magistrate judge's disposition that has been properly objected to. The district judge may accept, reject, or modify the recommended disposition; receive further evidence; or return the matter to the magistrate judge with instructions.

[Former Rule 72 abrogated December 4, 1967, effective July 1, 1968; new Rule 72 adopted April 28, 1983, effective August 1, 1983; amended April 30, 1991, effective December 1, 1991; April 22, 1993, effective December 1, 1993; April 30, 2007, effective December 1, 2007; March 26, 2009, effective December 1, 2009.]

AUTHORS' COMMENTARY ON RULE 72

PURPOSE AND SCOPE

Justices of the U.S. Supreme Court, Judges of the U.S. Courts of Appeals, and Judges of the U.S. District Courts are all nominated by the President and confirmed by the Senate. They are "Article III judges," because their authority derives from Article III of the U.S. Constitution. Once they assume their posts, they serve for life. U.S. Magistrate Judges do not serve for life, but rather serve for a set term of years. Magistrate judges are not nominated by the President or confirmed by the Senate. Instead, they are selected and appointed by the U.S. District Court Judges with whom they work. The position of U.S. Magistrate Judge was created by Congress in 1968.[1] Thus, the position is a statutory rather than a constitutional one. The principal role of magistrate judges in civil litigation is to assist the district judges, while their roles in criminal prosecutions are more expansive.

Rules 72 and 73 address the civil litigation work that magistrate judges may perform. Rule 72 establishes the authority for magistrate judges to assume certain pretrial tasks in civil cases, when they are assigned those tasks by a district judge. Rule 73 sets the authority for magistrate judges to preside over both federal jury trials and federal bench trials, but only when the litigants consent.

RULE 72(a)—NONDISPOSITIVE MATTERS

CORE CONCEPT

A district court judge may refer *nondispositive* pretrial matters

[1] *See* 28 U.S.C.A. §§ 631 to 39.

to a magistrate judge for decision. Such referral is at the discretion of the district judge, who does not need the consent of the parties to refer nondispositive pretrial matters to a magistrate judge. If the district judge makes such a referral to a magistrate judge, the magistrate judge must promptly hear and rule on the matter. Objections to such rulings may be taken to the district court within 14 days. The district judge who assigned the case retains ultimate authority over the case and shall modify or set aside any portion of the magistrate judge's order found to be clearly erroneous or contrary to law.[2]

APPLICATIONS

"Nondispositive" Pretrial Matters

Nondispositive pretrial matters are those motions and matters that can arise during the preliminary processing of a federal civil case that do not entirely "dispose" of a party's claim or defense. To determine whether a motion is dispositive, courts consider whether the effect of the motion is to deny the ultimate relief sought or foreclose a defense of a party.[3] (Congress enacted a list of matters considered "dispositive," which is discussed in subpart (b) below.) A district judge may refer such matters to a magistrate judge without first obtaining the consent of the parties.[4] Examples of nondispositive motions are motions: to amend; to voluntarily dismiss a claim or lawsuit; to join claims or parties; to resolve discovery disputes;[5] to seal or unseal documents; to extend time; to compel arbitration;[6] to transfer a case to a different jurisdiction;[7] and to disqualify an attorney.[8]

Authority to Rule in Nondispositive Pretrial Matters

If a district judge refers a nondispositive pretrial matter to a magistrate judge, the magistrate judge is authorized to make a binding ruling on that nondispositive matter. The magistrate judge's ruling becomes effective when made and requires no further action by the district judge—subject, of course, to a disappointed litigant's right to object and the district judge's right of review.

Sanctions Imposed by Magistrate Judges

Magistrate judges may impose sanctions for noncompliance

---

[2] *Khoury v. Miami-Dade Cnty. Sch. Bd.*, 4 F.4th 1118, 1133 (11th Cir. 2021); *Bisig v. Time Warner Cable, Inc.*, 940 F.3d 205, 219 (6th Cir. 2019).

[3] *In re U.S. Dep't of Educ.*, 25 F.4th 692, 699 (9th Cir. 2022).

[4] *Holder v. Holder*, 392 F.3d 1009, 1022 (9th Cir. 2004).

[5] *See In re U.S. Dep't of Educ.*, 25 F.4th 692, 696–99 (9th Cir. 2022).

[6] *Bristol v. Securitas Sec. Servs. USA, Inc.*, ___ F. Supp. 3d ___, 2022 WL 1078203, at *1 n. 2 (S.D.N.Y. 2022).

[7] *In re U.S. Dep't of Educ.*, 25 F.4th 692, 699 (9th Cir. 2022).

[8] *Galloway v. Cnty. of Nassau*, ___ F. Supp. 3d ___, 2022 WL 681065, at *3 (E.D.N.Y. 2022).

with a discovery order.[9] It is less clear, however, whether magistrate judges may impose sanctions for violations of Rule 11, which governs sanctions for inappropriately filed pleadings, motions, and other papers, or are limited to just recommending such sanctions to the district court judge pursuant to Rule 72(b).[10] If a motion seeks a sanction that would be dispositive, but the magistrate judge denies the motion, the matter is not considered dispositive. Instead, the standard of review is provided by Rule 72(a) (clearly erroneous or contrary to law), rather than Rule 72(b) (de novo review upon the record).[11]

Objections to and Review of Nondispositive Pretrial Rulings

A party may object to a magistrate judge's nondispositive pretrial ruling by filing written objections within 14 days after being served with a copy of the order. Failure to make a timely objection may constitute a waiver of appellate review of the magistrate judge's order[12] or otherwise greatly curtail that party's ability to have the ruling reviewed.[13] However, the 14-day period is not jurisdictional, and the district court judge retains the discretion to review the magistrate judge's rulings in the absence of a timely objection.[14] Even if no objections are presented, the district judge may rehear or reconsider the matter *sua sponte*. If objections are filed, the district judge in the case must rule on them,[15] although, in appropriate circumstances, the lack of an express ruling by the district judge can be treated as a denial of those objections.[16] The district judge who referred the case to the magistrate judge retains ultimate authority over the case and should modify or set aside any portion of the magistrate judge's order that are be clearly erroneous or contrary to law.[17]

Review by Court of Appeals

A party may not appeal directly to the court of appeals from

---

[9] *Hutchinson v. Pfeil*, 105 F.3d 562, 566 (10th Cir. 1997); *In re Keurig Green Mountain Single-Serve Coffee Antitrust Litig.*, 341 F.R.D. 474, 492 (S.D.N.Y. 2022).

[10] *See, e.g.*, *Alpern v. Lieb*, 38 F.3d 933, 935 (7th Cir. 1994) (citing conflicting cases).

[11] *Gomez v. Martin Marietta Corp.*, 50 F.3d 1511 (10th Cir.1995).

[12] *See, e.g.*, *U.S. v. Blackledge*, 751 F.3d 188, 194 (4th Cir. 2014); *Simpson v. Lear Astronics Corp.*, 77 F.3d 1170, 1174 (9th Cir. 1996).

[13] *Sinclair Wyoming Ref. Co. v. A & B Builders, Ltd.*, 989 F.3d 747, 782 (10th Cir. 2021) (noting circuit split); *Bastidas v. Chappell*, 791 F.3d 1155 (9th Cir. 2015).

[14] *Spence v. Superintendent, Great Meadow Correctional Facility*, 219 F.3d 162, 174 (2d Cir. 2000); *Kruger v. Apfel*, 214 F.3d 784, 786–87 (7th Cir. 2000).

[15] *Devine v. Walker*, 984 F.3d 605, 607 (8th Cir. 2020).

[16] *See, e.g.*, *Fielding v. Tollaksen*, 510 F.3d 175, 179 (2d Cir. 2007); *Miller v. Automobile Club Of New Mexico, Inc.*, 420 F.3d 1098, 1117 (10th Cir. 2005).

[17] *Khoury v. Miami-Dade Cnty. Sch. Bd.*, 4 F.4th 1118, 1133 (11th Cir. 2021); *Bisig v. Time Warner Cable, Inc.*, 940 F.3d 205 (6th Cir. 2019).

a magistrate judge's nondispositive pretrial order.[18]

RULE 72(b)—DISPOSITIVE MOTIONS AND PRISONER PETITIONS

CORE CONCEPT

A district judge may also refer *dispositive* pretrial matters to a magistrate judge, but only for a recommendation (not a ruling). In reaching such a recommendation, the magistrate judge may conduct evidentiary hearings and submit proposed findings of fact as appropriate. If a party makes a timely written objection to the recommendation of the magistrate judge, the district judge must make a *de novo* review of the record.[19]

APPLICATIONS

"Dispositive" Pretrial Matters

A magistrate judge cannot make a binding ruling upon any *dispositive* pretrial matters. Instead, magistrate judges are directed to prepare a "report and recommendation" for the district judge's consideration.[20] Congress has listed by statute those pretrial matters that it considers dispositive: (1) a motion for injunctive relief; (2) a motion for judgment on the pleadings; (3) a motion for summary judgment; (4) a motion to dismiss or permit maintenance of a class action; (5) a motion to dismiss for failure to state a claim upon which relief may be granted; and (6) a motion for involuntary dismissal.[21] This statutory list, however, is deemed to be illustrative of dispositive matters, rather than exhaustive.[22]

Courts have ruled that the following situations are also considered dispositive pretrial matters for the purposes of Rule 72(b): (1) an application to proceed *in forma pauperis;*[23] (2) certain motions to amend a pleading;[24] (3) a motion for attorney's fees;[25] and (4) an order remanding a removed case back

---

[18] *United States v. O'Laughlin*, 31 F.4th 1042, 1044 (8th Cir. 2022).

[19] 28 U.S.C.A. § 636(b)(1)(C). *See also CPC Pat. Techs. Pty Ltd. v. Apple, Inc.*, 34 F.4th 801, 804 (9th Cir. 2022); *Lima v. City of E. Providence*, 17 F.4th 202, 205 (1st Cir. 2021).

[20] *See, e.g., Milwaukee Police Association v. Flynn*, 863 F.3d 636, 643 (7th Cir. 2017).

[21] 28 U.S.C.A. § 636(b)(1)(A). *See* also *CPC Pat. Techs. Pty Ltd. v. Apple, Inc.*, 34 F.4th 801, 807 (9th Cir. 2022); *Bennett v. General Caster Service of N. Gordon Co., Inc.*, 976 F.2d 995, 997 (6th Cir. 1992).

[22] *CPC Pat. Techs. Pty Ltd. v. Apple, Inc.*, 34 F.4th 801, 807 (9th Cir. 2022); *Baylor v. Mitchell Rubenstein & Associates, P.C.*, 857 F.3d 939, 946 (D.C. Cir. 2017).

[23] *Woods v. Dahlberg*, 894 F.2d 187, 187 (6th Cir. 1990).

[24] *Lundy v. Adamar of New Jersey, Inc.*, 34 F.3d 1173, 1183 (3d Cir. 1994).

[25] *Massey v. City of Ferndale*, 7 F.3d 506 (6th Cir.1993); *but see Merritt v. International Broth. of Boilermakers*, 649 F.2d 1013, 1016-18 (5th Cir. 1981) (post-judgment award of attorney's fees as sanction for misconduct in pre-trial discovery is non-dispositive as pre-trial discovery issues are inherently non-dispositive).

to state court.[26] Additionally, it is unclear whether sanctions for violations of Rule 11, which governs sanctions for inappropriately filed pleadings, motions, and other papers, are within a magistrate judge's authority under Rule 72(a), or whether the magistrate judge may only make a recommendation to the district court judge under Rule 72(b).[27]

Procedure for Dispositive Pretrial Matters

Unlike nondispositive pretrial motions (discussed in subpart (a) above), a magistrate judge who has been referred a *dispositive* pretrial matter may not rule on the dispute. Instead, magistrate judges are directed to prepare a "report and recommendation" for the district judge's consideration.[28] In coming to that recommendation, magistrate judges enjoy substantial discretion. They may conduct hearings, and they must make a record of all evidentiary proceedings. They may make a record of non-evidentiary proceedings at their discretion. Following the magistrate judge's assessment, magistrate judges must submit a recommendation to the referring district judge on how the matter ought to be resolved. When appropriate, the magistrate judge shall include proposed findings of fact with that recommendation. The clerk of the court is required to mail copies of the magistrate judge's report and recommendation to all parties.

Objecting to Magistrate Judge's Recommendation

A disappointed party may object to the magistrate judge's recommendation by filing specific, written objections within 14 days after being served with a copy of the report and recommendation. The objections should identify the portions of the recommendation to which the party objects and should state the basis for the objections.[29] The opposing party may respond to those objections within 14 days after service.

- *Waiver of Right to a Review:* A party's failure to timely object may constitute a waiver by that party of its right to have the district court review the magistrate judge's report and recommendation for specific errors,[31] although many courts impose independent obligations to review a magistrate judge's recommendations, as discussed in the

---

[26] *Vogel v. U.S. Office Products Co.*, 258 F.3d 509, 515 (6th Cir. 2001) (collecting other examples of dispositive motions); *First Union Mortg. Corp. v. Smith*, 229 F.3d 992, 996 (10th Cir. 2000).

[27] *See, e.g., Alpern v. Lieb*, 38 F.3d 933, 935 (7th Cir. 1994) (citing conflicting cases and holding that Rule 72(a) does not confer such authority on magistrate judges).

[28] *See, e.g., Milwaukee Police Association v. Flynn*, 863 F.3d 636 (7th Cir. 2017) (magistrate judge's findings and recommendation have no effect until signed by district court judge).

[29] *Deters v. Hammer*, 568 F. Supp. 3d 883, 886-87 (S.D. Ohio 2021); *P.J.E.S. by & through Escobar Francisco v. Wolf*, 502 F. Supp. 3d 492, 507 (D.D.C. 2020).

[31] *F.D.I.C. v. Hillcrest Associates*, 66 F.3d 566, 569 (2d Cir. 1995).

Review by District Court application below. Additionally, the failure to file objections may constitute a waiver of the right to appeal the district court's adoption of the recommendations.[32]

- *Obligation to Order Transcript:* A party who properly objects to a magistrate judge's recommendation will promptly arrange for a transcription of the record or portions of the record agreed upon by the parties or as directed by the magistrate judge, unless directed otherwise by the district judge.[33]

Review by District Judge

The district judge who referred a dispositive matter to a magistrate judge must conduct a *de novo* review of any portion of the report and recommendation to which a proper, timely objection has been made.[34] In doing so, the district judge may accept, reject, or modify the recommended disposition or may re-commit the matter to the magistrate judge with instructions for further consideration.[35] A district judge, under this *de novo* review standard, is not required to convene a new hearing, but is required to examine the issues upon which specific, written objections were based, either on the record or by receiving additional testimony.[36] The courts are divided on whether a district judge may consider new arguments made within the parties' written objections.[37]

The courts are also divided on whether and to what extent a district judge is obligated to review a magistrate judge's recommendation absent a timely objection; some courts impose a duty to review for clear error,[38] others consider the failure to object as a waiver of any further judicial review of the magistrate judge's decision,[39] and others require de novo review of legal conclusions.[40] If a party makes only conclusory or general objections, or simply reiterates that party's original arguments, the

---

[32] *See, e.g., Phillips ex rel. Estates of Byrd v. General Motors Corp.*, 307 F.3d 1206, 1210 (9th Cir. 2002).

[33] Rule 72(b)(2).

[34] 28 U.S.C.A. § 636(b)(1)(C). *See also CPC Pat. Techs. Pty Ltd. v. Apple, Inc.*, 34 F.4th 801, 804 (9th Cir. 2022); *Lima v. City of E. Providence*, 17 F.4th 202, 205 (1st Cir. 2021).

[35] *Mendez v. Republic Bank*, 725 F.3d 651, 661 (7th Cir. 2013); *Duke Energy Benefits Comm. v. Heafner*, __ F. Supp. 3d __, 2022 WL 1056420, at *2 (W.D.N.C. 2022).

[36] *See, e.g., USA Gymnastics v. Liberty Ins. Underwriters, Inc.*, 27 F.4th 499, 515 (7th Cir. 2022); *Arista Records LLC v. Doe*, 604 F.3d 110, 116 (2d Cir. 2010).

[37] *USA Gymnastics v. Liberty Ins. Underwriters, Inc.*, 27 F.4th 499, 515 (7th Cir. 2022) (listing cases).

[38] *Diamond v. Colonial Life & Acc. Ins. Co.*, 416 F.3d 310 (4th Cir. 2005); *United States v. Feye*, 568 F. Supp. 3d 962, 967-68 (N.D. Iowa 2021).

[39] *F.D.I.C. v. Hillcrest Associates*, 66 F.3d 566, 569 (2d Cir. 1995) (also recognizing that a narrow exception to this general rule may exist in some pro se cases); *Merchia v. United States*, 565 F. Supp. 3d 26, 51 n. 37 (D. Mass. 2021).

[40] *Stalley v. Cumbie*, __ F. Supp. 3d __, 2022 WL 504018, at *6 (M.D. Fla. 2022).

district court will review the report only for clear error.[41] Regardless of the standard of review that the district court applies when no objection is made, the district court must make some final determination on the magistrate judge's recommendation before it can become final.[42]

Dispositive Sanction Not Imposed

If a motion seeks a sanction that would be dispositive, but the magistrate judge denies the motion, the matter is not considered dispositive. Instead, the standard of review is provided by Rule 72(a) (clearly erroneous or contrary to law), rather than Rule 72(b) (de novo review upon the record).[43]

Additional Research References

Wright & Miller, *Federal Practice and Procedure* §§ 3076.1 to 3076.9
C.J.S., United States Commissioners § 3
West's Key Number Digest, United States Magistrates ⟹15 to 31

---

[41] *P.J.E.S. by & through Escobar Francisco v. Wolf*, 502 F. Supp. 3d 492, 507 (D.D.C. 2020).

[42] *Conetta v. National Hair Care Centers, Inc.*, 236 F.3d 67, 73 (1st Cir. 2001).

[43] *See, e.g., Gomez v. Martin Marietta Corp.*, 50 F.3d 1511 (10th Cir. 1995).

RULE 73
MAGISTRATE JUDGES: TRIAL BY CONSENT; APPEAL

(a) Trial by Consent. When authorized under 28 U.S.C. § 636(c), a magistrate judge may, if all parties consent, conduct a civil action or proceeding, including a jury or nonjury trial. A record must be made in accordance with 28 U.S.C. § 636(c)(5).

(b) Consent Procedure.

(1) *In General.* When a magistrate judge has been designated to conduct civil actions or proceedings, the clerk must give the parties written notice of their opportunity to consent under 28 U.S.C. § 636(c). To signify their consent, the parties must jointly or separately file a statement consenting to the referral. A district judge or magistrate judge may be informed of a party's response to the clerk's notice only if all parties have consented to the referral.

(2) *Reminding the Parties About Consenting.* A district judge, magistrate judge, or other court official may remind the parties of the magistrate judge's availability, but must also advise them that they are free to withhold consent without adverse substantive consequences.

(3) *Vacating a Referral.* On its own for good cause—or when a party shows extraordinary circumstances—the district judge may vacate a referral to a magistrate judge under this rule.

(c) Appealing a Judgment. In accordance with 28 U.S.C. § 636(c)(3), an appeal from a judgment entered at a magistrate judge's direction may be taken to the court of appeals as would any other appeal from a district-court judgment.

[Former Rule 73 abrogated December 4, 1967, effective July 1, 1968; new Rule 73 adopted April 28, 1983, effective August 1, 1983; amended March 2, 1987, effective August 1, 1987; April 22, 1993, effective December 1, 1993, April 11, 1997, effective December 1, 1997; April 30, 2007, effective December 1, 2007.]

AUTHORS' COMMENTARY ON RULE 73

PURPOSE AND SCOPE

This is the second of the two Rules concerning the use of U.S. Magistrate Judges in federal civil cases. (For a general description of U.S. Magistrate Judges and their roles, see Rule 72.) This Rule authorizes U.S. Magistrate Judges to hear full federal civil trials, either as factfinder in a bench trial or as presiding jurist in a jury trial. In effect, this Rule allows U.S. Magistrate Judges to assume the same trial role as Article III district court judges. But U.S. Magistrate Judges can only do so with the consent of the litigants. In the absence of such consent, such delegated authority would likely pose insurmountable constitutional problems.[1]

RULE 73(a)—TRIAL BY CONSENT

CORE CONCEPT

Magistrate judges may exercise case-dispositive, final adjudicative authority in federal civil cases, but only upon the consent of the parties. Upon that consent, the district judge—by court order or standing local rule—may specially designate the magistrate judge to assume that authority and conduct the trial. In such circumstances, the magistrate judge has the powers of a district judge (except the power of contempt).[2]

APPLICATIONS

Unanimous Consent

Notwithstanding the constitutional concerns that federal judicial power may only be exercised by Article III judges,[3] a magistrate judge may preside over a civil jury or non-jury trial, or otherwise exercise case-dispositive or final judgment entry authority, but only upon the free, voluntary, and unanimous consent of the parties to the litigation.[4]

Preserving the Record

Following such special designation, the magistrate judge

[1] *See generally Northern Pipeline Const. Co. v. Marathon Pipe Line Co.*, 458 U.S. 50, 58–59 (1982) (Constitution's "inexorable command" is that "[t]he judicial power of the United States must be exercised by courts having the attributes prescribed" in Article III).

[2] *See Roell v. Withrow*, 538 U.S. 580, 585 (2003) ("referral gives the magistrate judge full authority over dispositive motions").

[3] *See, e.g., Irwin v. Mascott*, 370 F.3d 924 (9th Cir. 2004).

[4] *See, e.g., Holt-Orsted v. City of Dickson*, 641 F.3d 230, 233 (6th Cir. 2011).

must decide by what means the record should be preserved, such as verbatim by a court reporter or by electronic sound recording.[5] When deciding the means of preservation of the record, the magistrate judge may consider the complexity of the case, the likelihood of appeal, the costs of recording, and time constraints.

Contempt

Magistrate judges may not hold contempt hearings. Instead, a magistrate judge may certify the facts of the potential contempt to the district judge and serve an order to show cause why the disobedient party should not be held in contempt. The district judge will then make the contempt determination and impose any sanction.[6]

RULE 73(b)—CONSENT PROCEDURE

CORE CONCEPT

Because the authority for magistrate judges to conduct civil trials depends on the consent of the litigants, the litigants will be advised of their ability to consent to a magistrate judge trial, but must also be advised that they are free to withhold that consent. The consent-confirming process is conducted by the clerk of court, without involving the district judge. Only if all parties consent will the clerk advise the district judge of the outcome of the consent-confirming process. For good cause or when a party shows exceptional circumstances, the district judge can reclaim the case.

APPLICATIONS

Clerk-Conducted Consent Procedure

At the time the action is filed, the clerk of court will notify the parties in writing of their option to proceed before a magistrate judge or to withhold their consent and proceed before the district judge.[7] To prevent the district judge from influencing the parties in their consent decision and to shield the district judge from knowing who may have refused consent, the clerk of court alone administers the consent procedure.

Time and Manner of Consent

The time for indicating a party's consent or lack of consent is set generally by local rule or court order.[8] Parties generally indicate their consent by submitting completed consent forms supplied by the clerk for this purpose.[9] Courts usually have local rules to ensure the voluntariness and willingness of consent,

---

[5] *See* 28 U.S.C. § 636(c)(5).

[6] 28 U.S.C.A. § 636(e).

[7] *See* 28 U.S.C.A. § 636(c)(2).

[8] *See, e.g., Rembert v. Apfel*, 213 F.3d 1331, 1335 n. 1 (11th Cir. 2000); *Drake v. Minnesota Min. & Mfg. Co.*, 134 F.3d 878, 883 (7th Cir. 1998).

[9] *Cf., Roell v. Withrow*, 538 U.S. 580, 586 (2003) (where non-consenting parties appear before magistrate without making further objection, magis-

such as preventing the clerk of court from notifying litigants that their case will be heard sooner by a magistrate judge or that they will receive an experienced magistrate judge. Neither the district judge, the magistrate judge, nor the clerk of court may attempt to persuade the parties to consent to a trial before a magistrate judge.[10]

- *Consent by New Parties:* In general, local rules will control the time within which new parties must exercise their right to consent to trial before a magistrate judge. The clerk of court will notify new parties of their right to consent in the same manner as the original parties. When an additional party is joined who does not consent to the participation of the magistrate judge, the district judge must hear the case.[11] Parties in default, who are on notice regarding the proceedings, impliedly consent to a magistrate judge's jurisdiction.[12]
- *Proceeding Without Party Consent:* If a magistrate judge hears a case without the consent of the parties, the resulting judgment is a "nullity."[13] However, if a party participates in a trial before a magistrate judge without objection, the court may infer that party's consent.[14]

Voluntariness of Consent

Once consent has been given and the magistrate judge has been specially designated to preside over the trial, the parties generally cannot change their minds and withdraw their consent.[15] However, a party can petition the district court to vacate its referral to the magistrate judge by showing extraordinary circumstances, or the district court may order the referral vacated on its own motion for good cause.[16] Only a district court possesses the authority to rule on a motion to withdraw consent.[17] Such authority is rarely used, never exercised routinely, and reserved for truly exceptional circumstances. For example, it has been held that a district judge may vacate a proceeding from a magistrate judge when the magistrate judge is faced with

---

trate has jurisdiction). *But see Yeldon v. Fisher*, 710 F.3d 452, 453 (2d Cir. 2013) (pro se litigant who checked "I do not consent" box, but then participated in trial before magistrate judge did not consent).

[10] *Roell v. Withrow*, 538 U.S. 580, 589 n.6 (2003).

[11] *See, e.g.*, New York Chinese TV Programs, Inc. v. U.E. Enterprises, Inc., 996 F.2d 21, 24 (2d Cir. 1993) (intervenors must also consent, even when joined after magistrate judge begins to hear case).

[12] Koch Mins. Sarl v. Bolivarian Republic of Venezuela, 2020 WL 7646764, at *10 (D.D.C. 2020).

[13] Binder v. Gillespie, 184 F.3d 1059, 1063 (9th Cir. 1999).

[14] *See Roell v. Withrow*, 538 U.S. 580, 585–91, 123 S. Ct. 1696, 155 L. Ed. 2d 775 (2003).

[15] *See Dixon v. Ylst*, 990 F.2d 478, 480 (9th Cir. 1993).

[16] 28 U.S.C.A. § 636(c)(6). *See also Branch v. Umphenour*, 936 F.3d 994 (9th Cir. 2019) (district court may make this decision on motion of a party or *sua sponte*).

[17] *See, e.g., Branch v. Umphenour*, 936 F.3d 994 (9th Cir. 2019).

extraordinary questions of law with possibly wide precedential effect.[18] This power may not be used routinely to vacate certain categories of cases from a magistrate judge.[19]

RULE 73(c)—APPEALING A JUDGMENT

CORE CONCEPT

A party dissatisfied with the judgment entered by a magistrate judge (following a trial by consent under this Rule) may appeal that judgment directly to the court of appeals in the same manner as any judgment entered by a district judge would be appealed.[20]

Additional Research References

Wright & Miller, *Federal Practice and Procedure* §§ 3077.1 to 3077.5
C.J.S., United States Commissioners § 3
West's Key Number Digest, United States Magistrates ⚷12 to 13, ⚷24 to 31

---

[18] *Gomez v. Harris*, 504 F. Supp. 1342, 1345 (D. Alaska 1981).

[19] *See, e.g., Branch v. Umphenour*, 936 F.3d 994 (9th Cir. 2019) (decision to permit withdrawal of consent to hearing before magistrate judge has a "high bar" and is not made lightly; collecting conflicting authority). *But see, e.g., Sockwell v. Phelps*, 906 F.2d 1096 n.1 (5th Cir. 1990) (summarily concluding that magistrate judge had authority to permit withdrawal of consent).

[20] *See, e.g., Holt-Orsted v. City of Dickson*, 641 F.3d 230, 233 (6th Cir. 2011) (appeal is directly to circuit court); *Dluhos v. Floating and Abandoned Vessel, Known as New York*, 162 F.3d 63, 67 (2d Cir. 1998) (consent to trial before magistrate judge waives any appeal to district judge; appeal is to circuit court).

RULE 74[1]
METHOD OF APPEAL FROM MAGISTRATE TO DISTRICT JUDGE UNDER TITLE 28, U.S.C. § 636(c)(4) AND RULE 73(d) [ABROGATED]

[1]Rules 73(d) and Rules 74, 75, and 76 provided that when a magistrate judge hears a case, the parties could choose to appeal to either the district court or the court of appeals. In 1997, the so-called "optional appeal route" to the district court was abolished by Congress. Accordingly, the Supreme Court abrogated Rules 73(d), 74, 75, and 76 effective in December 1997. Henceforth, appeals from trials conducted by magistrate judges are made only to the appropriate court of appeals.

X. DISTRICT COURTS AND CLERKS: CONDUCTING BUSINESS; ISSUING ORDERS

RULE 77
CONDUCTING BUSINESS; CLERK'S AUTHORITY; NOTICE OF AN ORDER OR JUDGMENT

(a) When Court Is Open. Every district court is considered always open for filing any paper, issuing and returning process, making a motion, or entering an order.

(b) Place for Trial and Other Proceedings. Every trial on the merits must be conducted in open court and, so far as convenient, in a regular courtroom. Any other act or proceeding may be done or conducted by a judge in chambers, without the attendance of the clerk or other court official, and anywhere inside or outside the district. But no hearing—other than one ex parte—may be conducted outside the district unless all the affected parties consent.

(c) Clerk's Office Hours; Clerk's Orders.

(1) *Hours.* The clerk's office—with a clerk or deputy on duty—must be open during business hours every day except Saturdays, Sundays, and legal holidays. But a court may, by local rule or order, require that the office be open for specified hours on Saturday or a particular legal holiday other than one listed in Rule 6(a)(6)(A).

(2) *Orders.* Subject to the court's power to suspend, alter, or rescind the clerk's action for good cause, the clerk may:

(A) issue process;

(B) enter a default;

(C) enter a default judgment under Rule 55(b)(1); and

(D) act on any other matter that does not require the court's action.

(d) Serving Notice of an Order or Judgment.

(1) *Service.* Immediately after entering an order or judgment, the clerk must serve notice of the entry, as provided in Rule 5(b), on each party who is not in default for failing to appear. The clerk must record the service on the docket. A party also may serve notice of the entry as provided in Rule 5(b).

(2) *Time to Appeal Not Affected by Lack of Notice.* Lack of notice of the entry does not affect the time for appeal or relieve—or authorize the court to relieve—a party for failing to appeal within the time allowed, except as allowed by Federal Rule of Appellate Procedure (4)(a).

[Amended effective March 19, 1948; July 1, 1963; July 1, 1968; July 1, 1971; August 1, 1987; December 1, 1991; April 23, 2001, effective December 1, 2001; April 30, 2007, effective December 1, 2007; April 25, 2014, effective December 1, 2014.]

AUTHORS' COMMENTARY ON RULE 77

PURPOSE AND SCOPE

Rule 77 contains a variety of provisions pertaining to the operations of the district court and the clerk's office. It provides that the court is always "open," and requires that the clerk's physical office be open during "business hours." It also states that trials and hearings shall be conducted in a courtroom. Finally, Rule 77 controls notice of judgments and orders.

RULE 77(a)—WHEN COURT IS OPEN

CORE CONCEPT

The district courts are deemed open at all times for purposes like filing papers, and issuing process.[1] This does not mean that the courthouse will be manned and physically open at all times.[2] Rather, papers may be filed after hours by filing them on the court's electronic filing system, delivering them to the clerk or a deputy clerk, depositing them in a designated receptacle provided

[1] *In re Bradshaw*, 283 B.R. 814, 817 (1st Cir. 2002); *In re Papst Licensing GMBH & Co. KG Litig.*, 631 F. Supp. 2d 42, 46 (D.D.C. 2009).

[2] *In re Bradshaw*, 283 B.R. 814, 818 (1st Cir. 2002).

by the clerk and authorized by local rule,[3] or even—under exceptional circumstances—leaving them with a judge.[4] Filing is not accomplished merely by delivery to the clerk's office without using an established method of filing.[5]

RULE 77(b)—PLACE FOR TRIAL AND OTHER PROCEEDINGS

CORE CONCEPT

All trials must be conducted in open court and in a regular courtroom to the extent "convenient."[6] Other proceedings, such as pretrial conferences, may be conducted in chambers or some other location.[7] However, no hearing, other than one *ex parte,* may be held outside the district without consent of all parties.

RULE 77(c)—CLERK'S OFFICE HOURS; CLERK'S ORDERS

CORE CONCEPT

At a minimum, the clerk's office must be open during business hours on all days except weekends and holidays. The hours may be expanded by local rule. The clerk's office has the power to take certain acts, such as entering default judgments and issuing process to execute judgments.[8] Such actions by the clerk's office are reviewable by the court and may be suspended, altered, or rescinded upon cause shown.[9]

RULE 77(d)—SERVING NOTICE OF AN ORDER OR JUDGMENT

CORE CONCEPT

The clerk's office must serve notice of the entry of judgment on all parties who have entered appearances[10] (but not on parties against whom default has been taken for failure to appear).[11] Typically, the notice is automatically served on all parties of rec-

---

[3]*Ticketmaster Corp. v. Tickets. Com, Inc.*, 2000 WL 525390 (C.D. Cal. 2000).

[4]*Turner v. City of Newport*, 887 F. Supp. 149 (E.D. Ky. 1995).

[5]*McIntosh v. Antonino*, 71 F.3d 29, 35 (1st Cir. 1995); *In re Fisherman's Wharf Fillet, Inc.*, 83 F. Supp. 2d 651, 657 (E.D. Va. 1999).

[6]*Steele v. Nat'l R.R. Passenger Corp.*, ___ F. Supp. 3d ___, 2022 WL 1154351, at *1 (W.D. Wash. 2022) (allowing remote testimony in light of COVID-19); *Gould Elecs. Inc. v. Livingston Cty. Rd. Comm'n*, ___ F. Supp. 3d ___, 2020 WL 3717792, at *1 (E.D. Mich. 2020) (same).

[7]*B.H. v. McDonald*, 49 F.3d 294 (7th Cir. 1995); *Crumrine v. NEG Micon USA, Inc.*, 104 F. Supp. 2d 1123, 1126 (N.D. Iowa 2000).

[8]*U.S. v. Laws*, 352 F. Supp. 2d 707, 709 (E.D. Va. 2004) (writ of garnishment).

[9]*Brady v. U.S.*, 211 F.3d 499 (9th Cir. 2000).

[10]*Braitberg v. Charter Commc'n, Inc.*, 836 F.3d 925, 929 (8th Cir. 2016); *In re WorldCom, Inc.*, 708 F.3d 327, 329 (2d Cir. 2013).

[11]*Hunter v. Shanghai Huangzhou Elec. Appliance Mfg. Co.*, 505 F. Supp. 3d 137, 144 n.2 (N.D.N.Y. 2020)

ord by the court's electronic filing system, which is sufficient.[12] However, the failure of the clerk to do so does not necessarily increase the time for appeal[13] (but the appellate courts may extend the time for appeal and may consider the failure of the clerk to send notice,[14] and the district court may reopen and extend the time for appeal if authorized by Rule 4(a)(6) of the Federal Rules of Appellate Procedure[15]). A party who wants to ensure that all other parties have notice of the judgment (and thus that the time for appeal has commenced running) may serve the notice.[16]

Additional Research References

Wright & Miller, *Federal Practice and Procedure* §§ 3081 to 3084

C.J.S., Courts § 236; Federal Civil Procedure §§ 915 et seq., § 1213; Federal Courts §§ 302 et seq.

West's Key Number Digest, Clerk of Courts ⚷1; Federal Courts ⚷971

---

[12] *See Braitberg v. Charter Commc'n, Inc.*, 836 F.3d 925, 929 (8th Cir. 2016); *Kruskal v. Martinez*, ___ F. Supp. 3d ___, 2020 WL 6888151, at *2 (D.N.M. 2020).

[13] *Maples v. Thomas*, 565 U.S. 266, 300 (2012); *Athens Cellular, Inc. v. Oconee Cty., Georgia*, 886 F.3d 1094, 1119 n.12 (11th Cir. 2018).

[14] *Maples v. Thomas*, 565 U.S. 266, 300 (2012).

[15] *Bowles v. Russell*, 551 U.S. 205, 209–10 (2007); *Athens Cellular, Inc. v. Oconee Cty., Georgia*, 886 F.3d 1094, 1119 n.12 (11th Cir. 2018).

[16] *Resendiz v. Dretke*, 452 F.3d 356, 358, (5th Cir. 2006) (only formal service pursuant to Rule 5(b) constitutes notice); *Ryan v. First Unum Life Ins. Co.*, 174 F.3d 302, 304–05 (2d Cir. 1999) (service must be by mail, not by hand delivery).

RULE 78
HEARING MOTIONS; SUBMISSION ON BRIEFS

(a) Providing a Regular Schedule for Oral Hearings. A court may establish regular times and places for oral hearings on motions.

(b) Providing for Submission on Briefs. By rule or order, the court may provide for submitting and determining motions on briefs, without oral hearings.

[Amended effective August 1, 1987; April 30, 2007, effective December 1, 2007.]

AUTHORS' COMMENTARY ON RULE 78

PURPOSE AND SCOPE

Rule 78 allows each district to enact local rules establishing regular motion days for the presentation of motions requiring a hearing. However, judges may conduct oral arguments on motions at other times. Furthermore, the districts or individual judges may also provide that motions are to be determined on briefs only, without oral argument.

RULE 78(a)—PROVIDING A REGULAR SCHEDULE FOR ORAL HEARINGS

CORE CONCEPT

The court may establish regular times for hearing arguments, but also may hear arguments at any time or place on notice that the court considers reasonable.

RULE 78(b)—PROVIDING FOR SUBMISSION ON BRIEFS

CORE CONCEPT

The court may decide motions on the papers, without oral argument.[1]

---

[1] *Kitlinski v. United States Dep't of Just.*, 994 F.3d 224, 233 (4th Cir.

Additional Research References

Wright & Miller, *Federal Practice and Procedure* §§ 3091
C.J.S., Federal Civil Procedure § 933
West's Key Number Digest, Federal Civil Procedure 1991

2021) (court's discretion); *Killer Joe Nevada, LLC v. Does 1-20*, 807 F.3d 908, 913 (8th Cir. 2015).

RULE 79
RECORDS KEPT BY THE CLERK

(a) Civil Docket.

(1) *In General.* The clerk must keep a record known as the "civil docket" in the form and manner prescribed by the Director of the Administrative Office of the United States Courts with the approval of the Judicial Conference of the United States. The clerk must enter each civil action in the docket. Actions must be assigned consecutive file numbers, which must be noted in the docket where the first entry of the action is made.

(2) *Items to be Entered.* The following items must be marked with the file number and entered chronologically in the docket:

(A) papers filed with the clerk;

(B) process issued, and proofs of service or other returns showing execution; and

(C) appearances, orders, verdicts, and judgments.

(3) *Contents of Entries; Jury Trial Demanded.* Each entry must briefly show the nature of the paper filed or writ issued, the substance of each proof of service or other return, and the substance and date of entry of each order and judgment. When a jury trial has been properly demanded or ordered, the clerk must enter the word "jury" in the docket.

(b) Civil Judgments and Orders. The clerk must keep a copy of every final judgment and appealable order; of every order affecting title to or a lien on real or personal property; and of any other order that the court directs to be kept. The clerk must keep these in the form and manner prescribed by the Director of the Administrative Office of the United States Courts with the approval of the Judicial Conference of the United States.

(c) Indexes; Calendars. Under the court's direction, the clerk must:

(1) keep indexes of the docket and of the judgments and orders described in Rule 79(b); and

(2) prepare calendars of all actions ready for trial, distinguishing jury trials from nonjury trials.

(d) Other Records. The clerk must keep any other records required by the Director of the Administrative Office of the United States Courts with the approval of the Judicial Conference of the United States.

[Amended effective March 19, 1948; October 20, 1949; July 1, 1963; April 30, 2007, effective December 1, 2007.]

AUTHORS' COMMENTARY ON RULE 79

PURPOSE AND SCOPE

Rule 79 governs the record keeping duties of the district court clerk's office. It requires the clerk's office to maintain a "docket," a list that includes each case—identified by a unique number. The docket must contain a jury-trial designation if one of the parties has demanded a jury trial (as described in Rule 38), and must list by date and description each document the parties file or the judge issues.

The clerk must also keep a copy of every final judgment and appealable order that the court issues, as well as every order affecting title to or a lien on real or personal property, any other order that the court directs the clerk to keep, and any other records the clerk's offices are ordered to maintain by the Administrative Office of the United States Courts. In addition to maintaining the docket and the final judgments, orders, and other documents, the clerk's office must maintain an index of the docket and the other documents the clerk's office is required to maintain.

RULE 79(a)—CIVIL DOCKET

CORE CONCEPT

The clerk must keep a civil docket, which is a chronological listing of each pleading, motion, brief, order, etc., filed in the case.[1] The docket may be maintained electronically.[2]

[1] *Weber v. McGrogan*, 939 F.3d 232, 241 (3d Cir. 2019); *Harmston v. City and County of San Francisco*, 627 F.3d 1273, 1279 (9th Cir. 2010).

[2] *Moncier v. Jones*, 939 F. Supp. 2d 854, 861 (M.D. Tenn. 2013).

APPLICATIONS

Description

The docket should contain a brief description of each entry.[3] Entries should be listed chronologically[4] and should show the date on which each document is entered.[5]

Jury Trial Designation

The docket should indicate if the case is to be tried before a jury.[6]

Judgments

Judgments are not effective until entered on the docket.[7]

Briefs

Although for some purposes briefs are not considered part of the official record,[8] briefs are generally filed and entered on the docket.[9]

Time for Making Docket Entry

Rule 79 does not specify the time for making entries in the docket. However, the parties' rights will not be prejudiced by a delay in entry on the docket.

RULE 79(b)—CIVIL JUDGMENTS AND ORDERS

CORE CONCEPT

The clerk's office must retain a copy of every final judgment, appealable order, order creating a lien on property, and any other order as directed by the court.[10] In practice, most courts now maintain electronic copies of all documents filed in the court, which can be accessed through the PACER system.

- *Oral Rulings:* Judges sometimes make oral rulings from the bench, and these oral rulings are sometimes, but not always, summarized in minute orders that are entered onto the docket. If these oral rulings are appealable (either as final orders or on an interlocutory basis), the practice can create some tension with Rule 79(b).[11]

---

[3] *Wilcox v. Georgetown Univ.*, 987 F.3d 143, 149 (D.C. Cir. 2021); *U.S. v. Alcantara*, 396 F.3d 189, 200 (2d Cir. 2005) (motion filed under seal should be in the docket).

[4] *Casey v. Long Island R. Co.*, 406 F.3d 142, 148 (2d Cir. 2005).

[5] *Connecticut ex rel. Blumenthal v. Crotty*, 346 F.3d 84, 92 (2d Cir. 2003).

[6] *Hentif v. Obama*, 733 F.3d 1243, 1246 (D.C. Cir. 2013).

[7] *See Ueckert v. Guerra*, 38 F.4th 446, 454 (5th Cir. 2022); *Constien v. U.S.*, 628 F.3d 1207, 1211 (10th Cir. 2010).

[8] *See United States v. Gazda*, 499 F.2d 161, 164 (3d Cir. 1974).

[9] *See* Rule 5(d).

[10] *Ueckert v. Guerra*, 38 F.4th 446, 455 (5th Cir. 2022).

[11] *Ueckert v. Guerra*, 38 F.4th 446, 455 (5th Cir. 2022).

RULE 79(c)—INDEXES; CALENDARS

CORE CONCEPT

The clerk's office must maintain an index of the civil docket and of every civil judgment, appealable order, order creating a lien on property, and other order as directed by the court. The clerk's office must also maintain a calendar of all actions ready for trial, distinguishing jury and non-jury trials.

RULE 79(d)—OTHER RECORDS

CORE CONCEPT

The Administrative Office of the United States may direct that the clerk's offices maintain other books and records.

Additional Research References

Wright & Miller, *Federal Practice and Procedure* §§ 3101 to 3107
C.J.S., Federal Civil Procedure § 933, §§ 1227 et seq.
West's Key Number Digest, Federal Civil Procedure ⚷1991, ⚷2621

RULE 80
STENOGRAPHIC TRANSCRIPT AS EVIDENCE

If stenographically reported testimony at a hearing or trial is admissible in evidence at a later trial, the testimony may be proved by a transcript certified by the person who reported it.

[Amended effective March 19, 1948; April 30, 2007, effective December 1, 2007.]

AUTHORS' COMMENTARY ON RULE 80

PURPOSE AND SCOPE

Rule 80 pertains to the use of testimony at one hearing or trial as evidence at a subsequent hearing or trial. The rule provides that a transcript certified by an official court reporter is proof of the prior testimony.[1]

Additional Research References

Wright & Miller, *Federal Practice and Procedure* §§ 3121 to 3122
C.J.S., Evidence §§ 629 to 633 et seq., §§ 652 et seq.
West's Key Number Digest, Evidence ⚷332(1), (4), ⚷340

[1] *Orr v. Bank of America, NT & SA*, 285 F.3d 764, 776 (9th Cir. 2002) (transcripts not properly certified not admitted).

XI. GENERAL PROVISIONS

RULE 81
APPLICABILITY OF THE RULES IN GENERAL; REMOVED ACTIONS

(a) Applicability to Particular Proceedings.

(1) *Prize Proceedings.* These rules do not apply to prize proceedings in admiralty governed by 10 U.S.C. §§ 7651 to 7681.

(2) *Bankruptcy.* These rules apply to bankruptcy proceedings to the extent provided by the Federal Rules of Bankruptcy Procedure.

(3) *Citizenship.* These rules apply to proceedings for admission to citizenship to the extent that the practice in those proceedings is not specified in federal statutes and has previously conformed to the practice in civil actions. The provisions of 8 U.S.C. § 1451 for service by publication and for answer apply in proceedings to cancel citizenship certificates.

(4) *Special Writs.* These rules apply to proceedings for habeas corpus and for quo warranto to the extent that the practice in those proceedings:

(A) is not specified in a federal statute, the Rules Governing Section 2254 Cases, or the Rules Governing Section 2255 Cases; and

(B) has previously conformed to the practice in civil actions.

(5) *Proceedings Involving a Subpoena.* These rules apply to proceedings to compel testimony or the production of documents through a subpoena issued by a United States officer or agency under a federal statute, except as otherwise provided by statute, by local rule, or by court order in the proceedings.

(6) *Other Proceedings.* These rules, to the extent applicable, govern proceedings under the following laws, except as these laws provide other

procedures:

(A) 7 U.S.C. §§ 292, 499g(c), for reviewing an order of the Secretary of Agriculture;

(B) 9 U.S.C., relating to arbitration;

(C) 15 U.S.C. § 522, for reviewing an order of the Secretary of the Interior;

(D) 15 U.S.C. § 715d(c), for reviewing an order denying a certificate of clearance;

(E) 29 U.S.C. §§ 159, 160, for enforcing an order of the National Labor Relations Board;

(F) 33 U.S.C. §§ 918, 921, for enforcing or reviewing a compensation order under the Longshore and Harbor Workers' Compensation Act; and

(G) 45 U.S.C. § 159, for reviewing an arbitration award in a railway-labor dispute.

(b) Scire Facias and Mandamus. The writs of scire facias and mandamus are abolished. Relief previously available through them may be obtained by appropriate action or motion under these rules.

(c) Removed Actions.

(1) *Applicability.* These rules apply to a civil action after it is removed from a state court.

(2) *Further Pleading.* After removal, repleading is unnecessary unless the court orders it. A defendant who did not answer before removal must answer or present other defenses or objections under these rules within the longest of these periods:

(A) 21 days after receiving—through service or otherwise—a copy of the initial pleading stating the claim for relief;

(B) 21 days after being served with the summons for an initial pleading on file at the time of service; or

(C) 7 days after the notice of removal is filed.

(3) *Demand for a Jury Trial.*

(A) *As Affected by State Law.* A party who, before removal, expressly demanded a jury trial in accordance with state law need not renew the demand after removal. If the state law did not require an express demand for a jury trial, a party need not make one after removal unless the court orders the parties to do so within a specified time. The court must so order at a party's request and may so order on its own. A party who fails to make a demand when so ordered waives a jury trial.

(B) *Under* Rule 38. If all necessary pleadings have been served at the time of removal, a party entitled to a jury trial under Rule 38 must be given one if the party serves a demand within 14 days after:

(i) it files a notice of removal; or

(ii) it is served with a notice of removal filed by another party.

(d) Law Applicable.

(1) *"State Law" Defined.* When these rules refer to state law, the term "law" includes the state's statutes and the state's judicial decisions.

(2) *"State" Defined.* The term "state" includes, where appropriate, the District of Columbia and any United States commonwealth or territory.

(3) *"Federal Statute" Defined in the District of Columbia.* In the United States District Court for the District of Columbia, the term "federal statute" includes any Act of Congress that applies locally to the District.

[Amended effective December 28, 1939; March 19, 1948; October 20, 1949; August 1, 1951; July 1, 1963; July 1, 1966; July 1, 1968; July 1, 1971; August 1, 1987; April 23, 2001, effective December 1, 2001; April 29, 2002, effective December 1, 2002; April 30, 2007, effective December 1, 2007; March 26, 2009, effective December 1, 2009.]

AUTHORS' COMMENTARY ON RULE 81

PURPOSE AND SCOPE

Rule 81 controls the extent to which the Federal Rules of Civil Procedure apply in an assortment of contexts. It provides that the Rules do not apply to prize proceedings in admiralty, and lists categories of proceedings where the Rules act as default provisions supplementing those provided by statute, such as admission to citizenship proceedings.

Relatedly, Rule 81 controls the manner in which the Rules apply to proceedings that are commenced in state court under one set of procedural rules, then removed to federal court and governed by a different set of rules. Rule 81(c) specifies when the federal court will require compliance with the federal procedures and when parties may rely on their satisfaction of the state procedures.

Rule 81 also abolishes two old-fashioned writs, the writ of scire facias (a writ with a variety of functions such as reviving a judgment or effecting execution) and the writ of mandamus (a writ compelling an official to take an action). Rule 81 only abolishes these writs at the trial court level, however, and courts of appeal periodically issue writs of mandamus to the district courts ordering them to take a certain action or conduct proceedings in a specified manner. Lastly, Rule 81 defines three terms: "state law;" "state;" and "federal statute."

RULE 81(a)—APPLICABILITY TO PARTICULAR PROCEEDINGS APPLICABLE

CORE CONCEPT

Rule 81(a) provides that the Rules do not apply to Prize proceedings in admiralty and lists categories of proceedings where the Rules provide default or supplemental procedures to be used as dictated by the specific statutes controlling those proceedings.

APPLICATIONS

Not Applicable to Prize Proceedings in Admiralty

The Rules do not apply to Prize proceedings in admiralty (essentially, proceedings relating to vessels, equipment, and cargo seized during armed conflict).[1]

Applicable to Supplement Statutory Procedures

The Rules supplement the statutory procedures for the following:

- Bankruptcy proceedings, to the extent provided by the Bankruptcy Rules;[2]
- Admission to citizenship proceedings;[3]
- Habeas corpus proceedings;[4]

---

[1]*Mobil Cerro Negro, Ltd. v. Bolivarian Republic of Venezuela*, 863 F.3d 96, 120 n.19 (2d Cir. 2017).

[2]*In re Lac-Megantic Train Derailment Litig.*, 999 F.3d 72, 82 (1st Cir. 2021); *Rosenberg v. DVI Receivables XIV, LLC*, 818 F.3d 1283, 1287 (11th Cir. 2016).

[3]*Kariuki v. Tarango*, 709 F.3d 495, 501 (5th Cir. 2013); *Chan v. Gantner*, 464 F.3d 289, 295 (2d Cir. 2006).

[4]*Mayle v. Felix*, 545 U.S. 644, 654–55 (2005); *Gonzalez v. Crosby*, 545 U.S. 524, 529 (2005).

- Quo warranto proceedings;[5]
- Proceedings to enforce subpoenas to testify or to produce documents issued by agencies of the United States;[6]
- Proceedings to review orders of the Secretary of Agriculture;[7]
- Proceedings arbitrated under the Federal Arbitration Act;[8]
- Proceedings to review orders of the Secretary of the Interior;[9]
- Proceedings to review orders of the Petroleum Control Boards;[10]
- Proceedings to enforce orders of the National Labor Relations Board;[11]
- Proceedings for enforcement or review of compensation orders under the Longshoremen's and Harbor Workers' Compensation Act;[12] and
- Proceedings to review arbitration awards in railway-labor disputes.[13]

RULE 81(b)—SCIRE FACIAS AND MANDAMUS

CORE CONCEPT

Rule 81(b) abolishes the Writ of Scire Facias (a writ with a variety of functions such as reviving a judgment[14] or effecting execution) and the Writ of Mandamus (a writ compelling an official to take an action).[15]

APPLICATIONS

District Court Only

Rule 81(b) abolishes the writs in the district court only.[16] Thus, a court of appeals, under appropriate circumstances,

---

[5]Rule 81(a)(4).

[6]*Acosta v. La Piedad Corp.*, 894 F.3d 947 (8th Cir. 2018); *F.T.C. v. Boehringer Ingelheim Pharm., Inc.*, 778 F.3d 142, 149 (D.C. Cir. 2015).

[7]Rule 81(a)(6)(A); *Riccelli's Produce, Inc. v. Horton Tomato Co., Inc.*, 155 F.R.D. 411 (N.D. N.Y. 1994).

[8]*Boykin v. Fam. Dollar Stores of Michigan, LLC*, 3 F.4th 832 (6th Cir. 2021) (the F.R.C.P. apply only to the extent procedures are not provided under the FAA); *O'Neal Constructors, LLC v. DRT Am., LLC*, 991 F.3d 1376, 1379 (11th Cir. 2021) (same).

[9]Rule 81(a)(6)(C).

[10]Rule 81(a)(6)(D).

[11]Rule 81(a)(6)(E).

[12]Rule 81(a)(6)(F); *Galle v. Director, Office of Workers' Compensation Programs*, 246 F.3d 440, 447 (5th Cir. 2001); *Pleasant-El v. Oil Recovery Co., Inc.*, 148 F.3d 1300, 1302 (11th Cir. 1998).

[13]Rule 81(a)(6)(G).

[14]*TDK Electronics Corp. v. Draiman*, 321 F.3d 677, 680 (7th Cir. 2003).

[15]*Plaskett v. Wormuth*, 18 F.4th 1072, 1081 (9th Cir. 2021); *Lovitky v. Trump*, 949 F.3d 753, 759 (D.C. Cir. 2020).

[16]*U.S. v. Choi*, 818 F. Supp. 2d 79, 84–85 (D.D.C. 2011).

may issue a Writ of Mandamus to a district judge.[17]

Relief Not Abolished

Only the writs themselves are abolished; the relief sought may be available through some other motion or proceeding.[18]

RULE 81(c)—REMOVED ACTIONS

CORE CONCEPT

The Rules apply to actions commenced in state court and removed to federal court. Rule 81(c) contains procedures governing the transition from state procedure to federal procedure.

APPLICATIONS

Rules Apply After Removal

When an action is commenced in state court, then removed to federal court, the Rules apply to pleadings or motions filed after the removal.[19] Thus, Rules governing the form or service of pleadings or joinder of parties would not apply to pleadings filed and served in state court prior to removal.[20]

Time for Service of Complaint

For a defendant served with the complaint before removal, state law controls the timeliness of service.[21] Rule 4(m) applies for defendants not served with the complaint prior to removal, and the 90-day deadline for service is calculated from the date of removal.[22]

Time to Remove

Even though removal occurs when a case is still pending in state court, the 30-day time period for removal is governed by the provisions in Rule 6 regarding computation of time, not by state rules regarding time computation.[23]

---

[17] *In re Nagy*, 89 F.3d 115, 116–17 (2d Cir. 1996); *U.S. v. Choi*, 818 F. Supp. 2d 79, 84–85 (D.D.C. 2011). *But see Am. Hosp. Ass'n v. Price*, 867 F.3d 160, 164 n.2 (D.C. Cir. 2017) (suggesting that even appellate courts issue mandamus relief in character, not in name).

[18] *Plaskett v. Wormuth*, 18 F.4th 1072, 1081 (9th Cir. 2021) (relief available through Mandamus Act); *Lovitky v. Trump*, 949 F.3d 753, 759 (D.C. Cir. 2020).

[19] *Williams v. Homeland Ins. Co. of New York*, 18 F.4th 806, 817 (5th Cir. 2021); *Forty Six Hundred LLC v. Cadence Educ., LLC*, 15 F.4th 70, 77 (1st Cir. 2021).

[20] *Williams v. Homeland Ins. Co. of New York*, 18 F.4th 806, 817 (5th Cir. 2021) (joinder of parties); *Cobb v. Aramark Corr. Servs., LLC*, 937 F.3d 1037, 1040 (7th Cir. 2019) (service); *In re Amerijet Intern., Inc.*, 785 F.3d 967, 974 (5th Cir. 2015) (form). *But see Pena v. City of Rio Grande City*, 879 F.3d 613, 617 (5th Cir. 2018) (allowing the plaintiff to amend the complaint, then applying the federal pleading standard).

[21] *Cooperwood v. Farmer*, 315 F.R.D. 493, 496 (N.D. Ill. 2016).

[22] *See* 28 U.S.C.A. § 1448. *See also Whidbee v. Pierce Cty.*, 857 F.3d 1019, 1023 (9th Cir. 2017); *Wallace v. Microsoft Corp.*, 596 F.3d 703, 707 (10th Cir. 2010).

[23] *Milburn v. Zurich Am. Ins. Co.*,

Time to Answer

If a defendant has not yet answered at the time of removal, the defendant may file an answer or responsive motion by the later of 7 days from the date of removal[24] or 21 days from receipt of the original pleading containing the claim (through proper service or otherwise) or service of the summons for a complaint that has been filed.[25] These timing requirements apply to any pleading asserting a claim—complaints, counterclaims, crossclaims, and impleader claims.[26] The obligation to file an answer in federal court exists even if no answer would have been required in the state court proceedings.[27] The act of removal alone does not trigger an obligation to answer a complaint that has not yet been properly served.[28]

Repleading Unnecessary

Unless the court orders otherwise,[29] pleadings filed while the action was in state court do not need to be refiled or repleaded after removal to federal court.[30]

- *Standards for Pre-Removal Pleadings*: The case law is unsettled as to the standard for pleadings filed prior to removal. While Rule 81(c)(2) states that there is no need to refile pre-removal pleadings, some courts evaluate those pleadings under federal standards and order an amended pleading when the original pleading does not satisfy the federal rules.[31] Other courts apply state pleading requirements to pre-removal pleadings.[32]

Jury Demand

Rule 81(c) contains a number of provisions explaining how jury trial demands work in cases filed in state court then removed to federal court. If a jury trial demand has been properly made in state court, no new demand is necessary.[33] If no jury trial demand was made in state court and if all pleadings were filed in state court, the parties may make a jury trial

---

334 F.R.D. 190, 191 (E.D. Mo. 2020).

[24] *D.H. Blair & Co., Inc. v. Gottdiener*, 462 F.3d 95, 102 (2d Cir. 2006); *Norsyn, Inc. v. Desai*, 351 F.3d 825, 828 (8th Cir. 2003).

[25] *Murphy Bros., Inc. v. Michetti Pipe Stringing, Inc.*, 526 U.S. 344, 346 (1999); *L.A. Pub. Ins. Adjusters, Inc. v. Nelson*, 17 F.4th 521, 524 (5th Cir. 2021).

[26] *See L.A. Pub. Ins. Adjusters, Inc. v. Nelson*, 17 F.4th 521, 524 (5th Cir. 2021) (counterclaim).

[27] *L.A. Pub. Ins. Adjusters, Inc. v. Nelson*, 17 F.4th 521, 524 (5th Cir. 2021).

[28] *Norsyn, Inc. v. Desai*, 351 F.3d 825, 829 (8th Cir. 2003).

[29] *Labertew v. Langemeier*, 846 F.3d 1028, 1034 (9th Cir. 2017) (court has authority to order repleading).

[30] *Rinsky v. Cushman & Wakefield, Inc.*, 918 F.3d 8, 17 (1st Cir. 2019); *Wasserman v. Rodacker*, 557 F.3d 635, 639 (D.C. Cir. 2009).

[31] *Pena v. City of Rio Grande City*, 879 F.3d 613, 617 (5th Cir. 2018).

[32] *In re Amerijet Int'l, Inc.*, 785 F.3d 967, 974 (5th Cir. 2015); *Roundtree v. City of New York*, 340 F.R.D. 92, 93 (S.D.N.Y. 2022).

[33] *Lutz v. Glendale Union High School*, 403 F.3d 1061, 1063–64 (9th Cir. 2005).

demand within 14 days of removal to federal court.[34] The 14 days are measured from filing the removal notice in the case of the plaintiff and from service of the notice for all other parties. If no express jury trial demand is required under state law, none will be required in the removed action unless the court so directs.[35] If a jury demand was made in the state court proceedings and the demand does not meet the state requirements but does satisfy federal requirements, it can be accepted by the federal court.[36] There remain some scenarios that are not covered by Rule 81(c). For example, in New York, jury demands may be made shortly before trial. In such cases, the court will have discretion to allow a late jury demand.[37]

RULE 81(d)—LAW APPLICABLE

CORE CONCEPT

In general, when the Rules refer to "states," they include the District of Columbia.[38] Thus, when the Rules refer to the law of the state in which the court sits, the United States District Court for the District of Columbia uses the law applied in the District of Columbia. The phrase "law of a state" includes statutes and judicial decisions.

Additional Research References

Wright & Miller, *Federal Practice and Procedure* §§ 3131 to 3134
C.J.S., Federal Civil Procedure §§ 7 to 23 et seq.
West's Key Number Digest, Federal Civil Procedure ⊜31 to 44

---

[34] *Macsherry v. Sparrows Point, LLC*, 973 F.3d 212, 227 (4th Cir. 2020); *Lutz v. Glendale Union High School*, 403 F.3d 1061, 1063–64 (9th Cir. 2005).

[35] *Bruns v. Amana*, 131 F.3d 761, 762 (8th Cir. 1997); *Syeed v. Bloomberg L.P.*, 568 F. Supp. 3d 314 (S.D.N.Y. 2021).

[36] *Wyatt v. Hunt Plywood Co., Inc.*, 297 F.3d 405, 415 (5th Cir. 2002).

[37] *See* Rule 38(b); *Syeed v. Bloomberg L.P.*, 568 F. Supp. 3d 314 (S.D.N.Y. 2021); *Felix-Hernandez v. Am. Airlines, Inc.*, 539 F. Supp. 2d 511, 512 (D.P.R. 2007).

[38] *Molock v. Whole Foods Mkt. Grp., Inc.*, 952 F.3d 293, 309 n.12 (D.C. Cir. 2020) (dissent); *Wasserman v. Rodacker*, 557 F.3d 635, 639 (D.C. Cir. 2009).

RULE 82
JURISDICTION AND VENUE UNAFFECTED

These rules do not extend or limit the jurisdiction of the district courts or the venue of actions in those courts. An admiralty or maritime claim under Rule 9(h) is governed by 28 U.S.C. § 1390.

[Amended effective October 20, 1949; July 1, 1966; April 23, 2001, effective December 1, 2001; April 30, 2007, effective December 1, 2007; April 28, 2016, effective December 1, 2016.]

AUTHORS' COMMENTARY ON RULE 82

PURPOSE AND SCOPE

Rule 82 serves a limited, but important, function. Federal courts are courts of limited subject-matter jurisdiction, meaning that they are only empowered to hear the categories of cases set forth in the Constitution and the implementing statutes enacted by Congress, as discussed in more detail in the General Concepts in Federal Practice section above. Rule 82 clarifies that the contours of the federal courts' subject-matter jurisdiction is not altered by anything in the Federal Rules of Civil Procedure.[1]

Rule 82 also provides that the Federal Rules of Civil Procedure do not affect venue in federal courts, which is controlled by federal statute. Relatedly, Rule 82 acknowledges that venue for admiralty and maritime actions is governed by 28 U.S.C.A. § 1390.

APPLICATIONS

Subject-Matter Jurisdiction Only

As a general matter, the Rules do not extend or restrict the court's subject-matter jurisdiction.[2] This principle is limited to *subject-matter* jurisdiction (*i.e.,* the type of case a district court can hear), not *personal* jurisdiction (*i.e.,* which parties must ap-

[1] *Henderson v. U.S.*, 517 U.S. 654, 664 (1996); *Laborers' Pension Fund v. Pavement Maint., Inc.*, 542 F.3d 189, 193 (7th Cir. 2008).

[2] *Waters v. Day & Zimmermann NPS, Inc.*, 23 F.4th 84, 94 (1st Cir. 2022); *Williams v. Homeland Ins. Co. of New York*, 18 F.4th 806, 817 (5th Cir. 2021).

pear and defend themselves).[3] Likewise, the Rules contain timing requirements that are often described as "jurisdictional" but do not affect the court's subject-matter jurisdiction.[4]

Venue

The Rules do not affect venue in federal court, which is generally controlled by 28 U.S.C.A. §§ 1391–1393.[5]

- *Venue for Admiralty and Maritime Cases:* The general venue statutes—28 U.S.C.A. §§ 1391–1393—do not apply to admiralty and maritime cases.[6] Admiralty and maritime cases generally have a separate venue provision to facilitate suing seamen wherever they may be found.[7]

Additional Research References

Wright & Miller, *Federal Practice and Procedure* §§ 3141 to 3142
C.J.S., Federal Civil Procedure § 19
West's Key Number Digest, Federal Civil Procedure ⚷40

---

[3]*See Mississippi Pub. Corp. v. Murphree*, 326 U.S. 438, 445 (1946); *In re Nat'l Century Fin. Ent., Inc., Inv. Litig.*, 323 F. Supp. 2d 861, 879–80 (S.D. Ohio 2004).

[4]*Kontrick v. Ryan*, 540 U.S. 443, 452–53 (2004); *Penney v. United States*, 870 F.3d 459, 462 (6th Cir. 2017).

[5]*See United States v. Foy*, 803 F.3d 128, 134 (3d Cir. 2015); *Harrison Prosthetic Cradle Inc. v. Roe Dental Lab'y, Inc.*, __ F. Supp. 3d __, 2022 WL 2203770, at *4 (N.D. Ohio 2022).

[6]*See Sunbelt Corp. v. Noble, Denton & Assoc., Inc.*, 5 F.3d 28 (3d Cir.1993); *Matter of Star & Crescent Boat Co., Inc.*, 549 F. Supp. 3d 1145, 1155 (S.D. Cal. 2021).

[7]*See* 28 U.S.C.A. § 1390; *Matter of Star & Crescent Boat Co., Inc.*, 549 F. Supp. 3d 1145, 1155 (S.D. Cal. 2021); *Travelers Prop. Cas. Co. of Am. v. Ocean Reef Charters LLC*, 324 F. Supp. 3d 366, 374 (W.D.N.Y. 2018).

RULE 83
RULES BY DISTRICT COURTS; JUDGE'S DIRECTIVES

(a) Local Rules.

(1) *In General.* After giving public notice and an opportunity for comment, a district court, acting by a majority of its district judges, may adopt and amend rules governing its practice. A local rule must be consistent with—but not duplicate—federal statutes and rules adopted under 28 U.S.C. §§ 2072 and 2075, and must conform to any uniform numbering system prescribed by the Judicial Conference of the United States. A local rule takes effect on the date specified by the district court and remains in effect unless amended by the court or abrogated by the judicial council of the circuit. Copies of rules and amendments must, on their adoption, be furnished to the judicial council and the Administrative Office of the United States Courts and be made available to the public.

(2) *Requirement of Form.* A local rule imposing a requirement of form must not be enforced in a way that causes a party to lose any right because of a nonwillful failure to comply.

(b) Procedure When There Is No Controlling Law. A judge may regulate practice in any manner consistent with federal law, rules adopted under 28 U.S.C. §§ 2072 and 2075, and the district's local rules. No sanction or other disadvantage may be imposed for noncompliance with any requirement not in federal law, federal rules, or the local rules unless the alleged violator has been furnished in the particular case with actual notice of the requirement.

[Amended effective August 1, 1985; April 27, 1995, effective December 1, 1995; April 30, 2007, effective December 1, 2007.]

AUTHORS' COMMENTARY ON RULE 83

PURPOSE AND SCOPE

Rule 83 authorizes the districts to develop local rules that only apply to actions proceeding in that district. These local rules must be published for public comment, then approved by a majority of the district judges in the district. They must be consistent with, but not duplicative of, the Federal Rules of Civil Procedure. For issues that are not controlled by either federal statute, the Federal Rules of Civil Procedure, or the district court's local rules, a district court judge may regulate proceedings in any manner consistent with those sources of procedure.

Rule 83 also imposes two limitations on the permissible consequences for failure to comply with a local rule or an individual judge's procedures. First, a local rule addressing an issue of form must not be enforced in a way that causes a party to lose a substantive right because of a nonwillful failure to comply with the local rule. Second, no sanction or other disadvantage may be imposed for noncompliance with an individual judge's procedure unless the alleged violator has been furnished in the particular case with actual notice of the procedure.

RULE 83(a)—LOCAL RULES

CORE CONCEPT

Each district court may develop local rules.[1] These local rules must be consistent with the federal rules, both in substance and in numbering. Local rules pertaining to matters of form cannot be enforced in a manner that prejudices the substantive rights of a party.

APPLICATIONS

Consistent with Federal Rules

Local rules must be consistent with,[2] and not duplicative of,[3] Acts of Congress[4] and the federal rules.[5] Additionally, numbering must be consistent with the federal rules.

[1]*Hollingsworth v. Perry*, 558 U.S. 183, 191 (2010); *Winston & Strawn, LLP v. McClean*, 843 F.3d 503, 506 (D.C. Cir. 2016).

[2]*Marcure v. Lynn*, 992 F.3d 625, 632 (7th Cir. 2021) (local rule re unopposed motions inconsistent with burden of proof under Rule 12(b)(6)); *CX Reinsurance Co. Ltd. v. Johnson*, 977 F.3d 306, 314 (4th Cir. 2020) (local rule re timing for filing a motion for attorney's fees inconsistent with Rule 54).

[3]*U.S. v. Galiczynski*, 44 F. Supp. 2d 707 (E.D. Pa. 1999), aff'd, 203 F.3d 818 (3d Cir. 1999); *Guidance Endodontics, LLC v. Dentsply Intern., Inc.*, 791 F. Supp. 2d 1014, 1017 (D.N.M. 2011).

Typical Local Rules

Local rules can cover a wide variety of topics, and vary greatly in number and scope from district to district. Some typical local rules address:

- Admission to practice before the district courts;[6]
- Admission *Pro Hac Vice;*
- Procedures for disbarment;
- Procedures for the recovery of court costs;
- Creation of divisions within the district;
- Form and number of copies of pleadings and briefs;
- Period of time for process;
- Manner for presentation of motions;
- Notice for constitutional challenges to acts of Congress;
- Continuances;
- Discovery procedures;
- Pretrial and status conferences, including pretrial statements;
- Impartial medical examinations;
- Courtroom rules and regulations, including the use of cameras and recording equipment;
- Size, selection, and instruction of the jury;
- Handling and marking of exhibits;
- Entry of judgment; and
- Motions for new trials.

Effect of Local Rule

A valid local rule has the effect of law,[7] and must be obeyed.[8] The court has authority to impose sanctions when a party violates the court's local rules.[9] However, a local rule imposing a requirement of form (as opposed to substance) may not be enforced in a manner that causes a party to lose rights for a "nonwillful" violation.[10] For example, a party should not be deprived of a right to a jury trial because it is unaware of or forgets a local rule requiring jury demands to be noted in the

---

[4] *Assoc. Against Outlier Fraud v. Huron Consulting Group, Inc.*, 817 F.3d 433, 438 n.5 (2d Cir. 2016); *In re Ricoh Co., Ltd. Patent Litig.*, 661 F.3d 1361, 1370 n.5 (Fed. Cir. 2011).

[5] *Vogel v. Harbor Plaza Ctr., LLC*, 893 F.3d 1152, 1162 (9th Cir. 2018); *Frakes v. Peoria Sch. Dist. No. 150*, 872 F.3d 545, 549 (7th Cir. 2017).

[6] *Pappas v. Philip Morris, Inc.*, 915 F.3d 889, 894 (2d Cir. 2019).

[7] *Hollingsworth v. Perry*, 558 U.S. 183, 191 (2010); *Winston & Strawn, LLP v. McClean*, 843 F.3d 503, 506 (D.C. Cir. 2016).

[8] *See Weil v. Neary*, 278 U.S. 160, 169 (1929); *Frakes v. Peoria Sch. Dist. No. 150*, 872 F.3d 545, 549 (7th Cir. 2017).

[9] *Carmona v. Wright*, 233 F.R.D. 270, 275 (N.D. N.Y. 2006); *Nick v. Morgan's Foods, Inc.*, 99 F. Supp. 2d 1056, 1061 (E.D. Mo. 2000).

[10] *Al -Qarqani v. Saudi Arabian Oil Co.*, 19 F.4th 794, 799 (5th Cir. 2021); *Pierce v. Ocwen Loan Servicing, LLC*, 987 F.3d 577, 580 (6th Cir. 2021).

caption of pleadings.[11] Likewise, a party should not lose the right to appeal if the court rejects the party's notice of appeal as not complying with the court's rules on filing.[12]

Promulgation of Local Rules

Local rules are adopted pursuant to the procedures in the Rules Enabling Act.[13]

Public Comment

Before a local rule may be enacted, it must be published for comment by the public.[14]

Obtaining Copies

Local rules are often available on the court's website. A copy of the local rules can also be obtained from the clerk's office for a nominal fee.

RULE 83(b)—PROCEDURE WHEN THERE IS NO CONTROLLING LAW

CORE CONCEPT

In the absence of a federal or local rule of procedure, judges may regulate proceedings before them as they see fit, so long as the judge's procedures are consistent with federal law, the federal rules, and local rules.[15]

APPLICATIONS

Standing Orders Consistent with Other Rules

Individual judges' standing orders or requirements must be consistent with Acts of Congress, the federal rules, and local rules.[16]

Parties Must Have Actual Notice of Court Requirements

The court may not sanction or disadvantage a party for noncompliance with a requirement not found in federal law, federal rules, or local rules unless that party has been furnished in the particular case with actual notice of the requirement.[17] Actual notice can be achieved by providing parties with a copy of the judge's requirements, by an order

---

[11]The Advisory Committee Note to the 1995 amendment to Rule 83.

[12]*Al-Qarqani v. Saudi Arabian Oil Co.*, 19 F.4th 794, 799 (5th Cir. 2021); *Pierce v. Ocwen Loan Servicing, LLC*, 987 F.3d 577, 580 (6th Cir. 2021).

[13]28 U.S.C.A. § 2071(b); *In re Dorner*, 343 F.3d 910, 913 (7th Cir. 2003); *see also Hollingsworth v. Perry*, 558 U.S. 183, 191 (2010).

[14]*In re Dorner*, 343 F.3d 910, 913 (7th Cir. 2003). *Antoine v. Atlas Turner, Inc.*, 66 F.3d 105, 108 (6th Cir. 1995).

[15]*Dietz v. Bouldin*, ___ U.S. ___, 136 S. Ct. 1885, 1892 (2016).

[16]*Chicago Studio Rental, Inc. v. Illinois Dep't of Commerce*, 940 F.3d 971, 982 (7th Cir. 2019); *Carnes v. Zamani*, 488 F.3d 1057, 1059 (9th Cir. 2007).

[17]*Massachusetts Inst. of Tech. and Elec. For Imaging, Inc. v. Abacus Software*, 462 F.3d 1344, 1359 (Fed. Cir. 2006); *Amnesty America v. Town of West Hartford*, 288 F.3d 467, 471 (2d Cir. 2002).

referencing the judge's standing orders and indicating how copies can be obtained, or by oral notice at a Rule 16 conference.[18]

Additional Research References

Wright & Miller, *Federal Practice and Procedure* §§ 3151 to 3155
C.J.S., Federal Civil Procedure § 21
West's Key Number Digest, Federal Civil Procedure ⚷25

---

[18] *See O'Connell v. Associated Wholesalers, Inc.*, 558 Fed. Appx. 286, 291 (3d Cir. 2014) (notice provided at status conference).

RULE 84
FORMS [ABROGATED]

[Abrogated (Apr. 29, 2015, eff. Dec. 1, 2015).]

2015 AMENDMENTS: The 2015 Amendments abrogated Rule 84, previously authorizing the official forms. The advisory committee note to Rule 84 states that the abrogation of Rule 84 does not alter existing pleading standards or otherwise change the requirements of Rule 8.[1] There is no longer an appendix of forms, but two nationally-uniform waiver-of-service forms are now appended to Rule 4.

---

[1]*See Summers Mfg. Co., Inc. v. Tri-Cty. AG, LLC*, 300 F. Supp. 3d 1025, 1031 n.3 (S.D. Iowa 2017) (citing cases on the standard for pleading a patent infringement claim following the abrogation of Rule 84 and Form 18). *But see Gold Crest, LLC v. Project Light, LLC*, — F. Supp. 3d. —, 2021 WL 918281, at *4 n.7 (N.D. Ohio 2021) (since form 18 was abrogated, the pleading standard is governed by *Twombly* and *Iqbal*).

RULE 85
TITLE

These rules may be cited as the Federal Rules of Civil Procedure.

[Amended April 30, 2007, effective December 1, 2007.]

AUTHORS' COMMENTARY ON RULE 85

PURPOSE AND SCOPE

The full title of the Rules is the "Federal Rules of Civil Procedure." The Rules should be cited as "Fed. R. Civ. P. —."

Additional Research References

Wright & Miller, *Federal Practice and Procedure* § 3171
C.J.S., Federal Civil Procedure §§ 7 et seq.
West's Key Number Digest, Federal Civil Procedure ⚷31

RULE 86
EFFECTIVE DATES

(a) In General. These rules and any amendments take effect at the time specified by the Supreme Court, subject to 28 U.S.C. § 2074. They govern:

(1) proceedings in an action commenced after their effective date; and

(2) proceedings after that date in an action then pending unless:

(A) the Supreme Court specifies otherwise; or

(B) the court determines that applying them in a particular action would be infeasible or work an injustice.

(b) December 1, 2007 Amendments. If any provision in Rules 1–5.1, 6–73, or 77–86 conflicts with another law, priority in time for the purpose of 28 U.S.C. § 2072(b) is not affected by the amendments taking effect on December 1, 2007.

[Amended effective March 19, 1948; October 20, 1949; July 19, 1961; July 1, 1963; April 30, 2007, effective December 1, 2007.]

AUTHORS' COMMENTARY ON RULE 86

PURPOSE AND SCOPE

On a regular basis, the Supreme Court proposes amendments to the Federal Rules of Civil Procedure to Congress, under a process described in the Judicial Rulemaking section of this book. Those amendments go into effect on December 1 of the year in which they are proposed, unless Congress acts to prevent their effectiveness. Not surprisingly, such amendments apply to all cases commenced after the effective date of the amendments. It is less intuitive how amended provisions should apply to already pending cases. Rule 86 confirms that amended provisions in the Federal Rules of Civil Procedure apply to actions commenced before the effective date of the amendments unless: a) the Supreme Court specifies otherwise; or b) the district court determines that applying them in a particular action would be infeasible or work an injustice.

RULE 86(a)—IN GENERAL

CORE CONCEPT

In general, amendments to the Rules will apply to all actions filed after the effective date of the amendments, and to proceedings in actions filed before the effective date unless the Supreme Court has specified otherwise or the court determines that application of an amended provision would not be feasible or would work an injustice.[1]

RULE 86(b)—DECEMBER 1, 2007 AMENDMENTS

CORE CONCEPT

Rule 86(b) addresses the interplay between the 2007 amendments to the Rules and the supersession clause in 28 U.S.C.A. § 2072(b). The supersession clause says that laws in conflict with one or more of the Rules shall have no further force and effect after such Rules have taken effect. In essence, the Rules are deemed to have superseded existing inconsistent laws. Because the supersession clause focuses on the sequence in time between the Rules and other laws, Rule 86(b) provides that the non-substantive changes to every Rule in the 2007 amendments do not affect the priority-in-time analysis.

---

[1] *In re Harwell*, 628 F.3d 1312, 1317 n.4 (11th Cir. 2010); *Norsoph v. Riverside Resort & Casino, Inc.*, ___ F. Supp. 3d ___, 2020 WL 641223, at *6 n.6 (D. Nev. 2020).

SUPPLEMENTAL RULES SET #1

Supplemental Rules for Admiralty or Maritime Claims and Asset Forfeiture Actions

Adopted February 28, 1966, effective July 1, 1966

The former Rules of Practice in Admiralty and Maritime Cases, promulgated by the Supreme Court on December 6, 1920, effective March 7, 1921, as revised, amended and supplemented, were rescinded, effective July 1, 1966.

Including Amendments effective December 1, 2009

RULE A
SCOPE OF RULES

(1) These Supplemental Rules apply to:

(A) the procedure in admiralty and maritime claims within the meaning of Rule 9(h) with respect to the following remedies:

(i) maritime attachment and garnishment,

(ii) actions in rem,

(iii) possessory, petitory, and partition actions, and

(iv) actions for exoneration from or limitation of liability;

(B) forfeiture actions in rem arising from a federal statute; and

(C) the procedure in statutory condemnation proceedings analogous to maritime actions in rem, whether within the admiralty and maritime jurisdiction or not. Except as otherwise provided, references in these Supplemental Rules to actions in rem include such analogous statutory condemnation proceedings.

(2) The Federal Rules of Civil Procedure also apply to the foregoing proceedings except to the extent that they are inconsistent with these Supplemental Rules.

[Added Feb. 28, 1966, eff. July 1, 1966; April 12, 2006, effective December 1, 2006.]

RULE B
IN PERSONAM ACTIONS: ATTACHMENT AND GARNISHMENT

(1) When Available; Complaint, Affidavit, Judicial Authorization, and Process. In an in personam action:

(a) If a defendant is not found within the district when a verified complaint praying for attachment and the affidavit required by Rule B(1)(b) are filed, a verified complaint may contain a prayer for process to attach the defendant's tangible or intangible personal property—up to the amount sued for—in the hands of garnishees named in the process.

(b) The plaintiff or the plaintiff's attorney must sign and file with the complaint an affidavit stating that, to the affiant's knowledge, or on information and belief, the defendant cannot be found within the district. The court must review the complaint and affidavit and, if the conditions of this Rule B appear to exist, enter an order so stating and authorizing process of attachment and garnishment. The clerk may issue supplemental process enforcing the court's order upon application without further court order.

(c) If the plaintiff or the plaintiff's attorney certifies that exigent circumstances make court review impracticable, the clerk must issue the summons and process of attachment and garnishment. The plaintiff has the burden in any post-attachment hearing under Rule E(4)(f) to show that exigent circumstances existed.

(d) (i) If the property is a vessel or tangible property on board a vessel, the summons, process, and any supplemental process must be delivered to the marshal for service.

(ii) If the property is other tangible or intangible property, the summons, process, and any supplemental process must be delivered to a person or organization authorized to serve it, who may be (A) a marshal; (B) someone under contract with the United States; (C) someone specially appointed by the court for that purpose; or, (D) in an action brought by the United States, any officer or employee of the United States.

(e) The plaintiff may invoke state-law remedies under Rule 64 for seizure of person or property for the purpose of securing satisfaction of the judgment.

(2) Notice to Defendant. No default judgment may be entered except upon proof—which may be by affidavit—that:

(a) the complaint, summons, and process of attachment or garnishment have been served on the defendant in a manner authorized by Rule 4;

(b) the plaintiff or the garnishee has mailed to the defendant the complaint, summons, and process of attachment or garnishment, using any form of mail requiring a return receipt; or

(c) the plaintiff or the garnishee has tried diligently to give notice of the action to the defendant but could not do so.

(3) Answer.

(a) By Garnishee. The garnishee shall serve an answer, together with answers to any interrogatories served with the complaint, within 21 days after service of process upon the garnishee. Interrogatories to the garnishee may be served with the complaint without leave of court. If the garnishee refuses or neglects to answer on oath as to the debts, credits, or effects of the defendant in the garnishee's hands, or any interrogatories concerning such debts, credits, and effects that may be propounded by the plaintiff, the court may award compulsory process against the garnishee. If the garnishee admits any debts, credits, or effects, they shall be held in the garnishee's hands or paid into the registry of the court, and shall be held in either case subject to the further order of the court.

(b) By Defendant. The defendant shall serve an answer within 30 days after process has been executed, whether by attachment of property or service on the garnishee.

[Added Feb. 28, 1966, eff. July 1, 1966, and amended Apr. 29, 1985, effective Aug. 1, 1985; Mar. 2, 1987, effective Aug. 1, 1987; April 17, 2000, effective December 1, 2000; April 25, 2005, effective December 1, 2005; amended March 26, 2009, effective December 1, 2009.]

RULE C
IN REM ACTIONS: SPECIAL PROVISIONS

(1) When Available. An action in rem may be brought:

(a) To enforce any maritime lien;

(b) Whenever a statute of the United States provides for a maritime action in rem or a proceeding analogous thereto.

Except as otherwise provided by law a party who may proceed in rem may also, or in the alternative, proceed in personam against any person who may be liable.

Statutory provisions exempting vessels or other property owned or possessed by or operated by or for the United States from arrest or seizure are not affected by this rule. When a statute so provides, an action against the United States or an instrumentality thereof may proceed on in rem principles.

(2) Complaint. In an action in rem the complaint must:

(a) be verified;

(b) describe with reasonable particularity the property that is the subject of the action; and

(c) state that the property is within the district or will be within the district while the action is pending.

(3) Judicial Authorization and Process.

(a) Arrest Warrant.

(i) The court must review the complaint and any supporting papers. If the conditions for an in rem action appear to exist, the court must issue an order directing the clerk to issue a warrant for the arrest of the vessel or other property that is the subject of the action.

(ii) If the plaintiff or the plaintiff's attorney certifies that exigent circumstances make court review impracticable, the clerk must promptly issue a summons and a warrant for the arrest of the vessel or other property that is the subject of the action. The plaintiff has the burden in any post-arrest hearing under Rule E(4)(f) to show that exigent circumstances existed.

(b) Service.

(i) If the property that is the subject of the action is a vessel or tangible property on board a vessel, the warrant and any supplemental process must be delivered to the marshal for service.

(ii) If the property that is the subject of the action is other property, tangible or intangible, the warrant and any supplemental process must be delivered to a person or organization authorized to enforce it, who may be: (A) a marshal; (B) someone under contract with the United States; (C) someone specially appointed by the court for that purpose; or, (D) in an action brought by the United States, any officer or employee of the United States.

(c) Deposit in Court. If the property that is the subject of the action consists in whole or in part of freight, the proceeds of property sold, or other intangible property, the clerk must issue—in addition to the warrant—a summons directing any person controlling the property to show cause why it should not be deposited in court to abide the judgment.

(d) Supplemental Process. The clerk may upon application issue supplemental process to enforce the court's order without further court order.

(4) Notice. No notice other than execution of process is required when the property that is the subject of the action has been released under Rule E(5). If the property is not released within 14 days after execution, the plaintiff must promptly—or within the time that the court allows—give public notice of the action and arrest in a newspaper designated by court order and having general circulation in the district, but publication may be terminated if the property is released before publication is completed. The notice must specify the time under Rule C(6) to file a statement of interest in or right against the seized property and to answer. This rule does not affect the notice requirements in an action to foreclose a preferred ship mortgage under 46 U.S.C. §§ 31301 et seq., as amended.

(5) **Ancillary Process.** In any action in rem in which process has been served as provided by this rule, if any part of the property that is the subject of the action has not been brought within the control of the court because it has been removed or sold, or because it is intangible property in the hands of a person who has not been served with process, the court may, on motion, order any person having possession or control of such property or its proceeds to show cause why it should not be delivered into the custody of the marshal or other person or organization having a warrant for the arrest of the property, or paid into court to abide the judgment; and, after hearing, the court may enter such judgment as law and justice may require.

(6) **Responsive Pleading; Interrogatories.**

(a) **Statement of Interest; answer.** In an action in rem:

(i) a person who asserts a right of possession or any ownership interest in the property that is the subject of the action must file a verified statement of right or interest:

(A) within 14 days after the execution of process, or

(B) within the time that the court allows;

(ii) the statement of right or interest must describe the interest in the property that supports the person's demand for its restitution or right to defend the action;

(iii) an agent, bailee, or attorney must state the authority to file a statement of right or interest on behalf of another; and

(iv) a person who asserts a right of possession or any ownership interest must serve an answer within 21 days after filing the statement of interest or right.

(b) **Interrogatories.** Interrogatories may be served with the complaint in an in rem action without leave of court. Answers to the interrogatories must be served with the answer to the complaint.

[Added Feb. 28, 1966, eff. Jul. 1, 1966, and amended Apr. 29, 1985, effective Aug. 1, 1985; Mar. 2, 1987, effective Aug. 1, 1987; Apr. 30, 1991, effective Dec. 1, 1991; April 17, 2000, effective December 1, 2000; April 29, 2002, effective December 1, 2002; April 25, 2005, effective December 1, 2005; April 12, 2006, effective December 1, 2006; amended March 26, 2009, effective December 1, 2009.]

RULE D
POSSESSORY, PETITORY, AND PARTITION ACTIONS

In all actions for possession, partition, and to try title maintainable according to the course of the admiralty practice with respect to a vessel, in all actions so maintainable with respect to the possession of cargo or other maritime property, and in all actions by one or more part owners against the others to obtain security for the return of the vessel from any voyage undertaken without their consent, or by one or more part owners against the others to obtain possession of the vessel for any voyage on giving security for its safe return, the process shall be by a warrant of arrest of the vessel, cargo, or other property, and by notice in the manner provided by Rule B(2) to the adverse party or parties.

[Added Feb. 28, 1966, eff. Jul. 1, 1966.]

RULE E
ACTIONS IN REM AND QUASI IN REM: GENERAL PROVISIONS

(1) Applicability. Except as otherwise provided, this rule applies to actions in personam with process of maritime attachment and garnishment, actions in rem, and petitory, possessory, and partition actions, supplementing Rules B, C, and D.

(2) Complaint; Security.

(a) *Complaint.* In actions to which this rule is applicable the complaint shall state the circumstances from which the claim arises with such particularity that the defendant or claimant will be able, without moving for a more definite statement, to commence an investigation of the facts and to frame a responsive pleading.

(b) *Security for Costs.* Subject to the provisions of Rule 54(d) and of relevant statutes, the court may, on the filing of the complaint or on the appearance of any defendant, claimant, or any other party, or at any later time, require the plaintiff, defendant, claimant, or other party to give security, or additional security, in such sum as the court shall direct to pay all costs and expenses that shall be awarded against the party by any interlocutory order or by the final judgment, or on appeal by any appellate court.

(3) Process.

(a) In admiralty and maritime proceedings process in rem or of maritime attachment and garnishment may be served only within the district.

(b) Issuance and Delivery. Issuance and delivery of process in rem, or of maritime attachment and garnishment, shall be held in abeyance if the plaintiff so requests.

(4) Execution of Process; Marshal's Return; Custody of Property; Procedures for Release.

(a) *In General.* Upon issuance and delivery of the

process, or, in the case of summons with process of attachment and garnishment, when it appears that the defendant cannot be found within the district, the marshal or other person or organization having a warrant shall forthwith execute the process in accordance with this subdivision (4), making due and prompt return.

(b) *Tangible Property.* If tangible property is to be attached or arrested, the marshal or other person or organization having the warrant shall take it into the marshal's possession for safe custody. If the character or situation of the property is such that the taking of actual possession is impracticable, the marshal or other person executing the process shall affix a copy thereof to the property in a conspicuous place and leave a copy of the complaint and process with the person having possession or the person's agent. In furtherance of the marshal's custody of any vessel the marshal is authorized to make a written request to the collector of customs not to grant clearance to such vessel until notified by the marshal or deputy marshal or by the clerk that the vessel has been released in accordance with these rules.

(c) *Intangible Property.* If intangible property is to be attached or arrested the marshal or other person or organization having the warrant shall execute the process by leaving with the garnishee or other obligor a copy of the complaint and process requiring the garnishee or other obligor to answer as provided in Rules B(3)(a) and C(6); or the marshal may accept for payment into the registry of the court the amount owed to the extent of the amount claimed by the plaintiff with interest and costs, in which event the garnishee or other obligor shall not be required to answer unless alias process shall be served.

(d) *Directions With Respect to Property in Custody.* The marshal or other person or organization having the warrant may at any time apply to the court for directions with respect to property that has been attached or arrested, and shall give notice of such application to any or all of the parties as the court may direct.

(e) *Expenses of Seizing and Keeping Property; Deposit.* These rules do not alter the provisions of Title 28, U.S.C., § 1921, as amended, relative to the expenses of seizing and keeping property attached or arrested and to the requirement of deposits to cover such expenses.

(f) *Procedure for Release From Arrest or Attachment.* Whenever property is arrested or attached, any person claiming an interest in it shall be entitled to a prompt hearing at which the plaintiff shall be required to show why the arrest or attachment should not be vacated or other relief granted consistent with these rules. This subdivision shall have no application to suits for seamen's wages when process is issued upon a certification of sufficient cause filed pursuant to Title 46, U.S.C. §§ 603 and 604 or to actions by the United States for forfeitures for violation of any statute of the United States.

(5) Release of Property.

(a) *Special Bond.* Whenever process of maritime attachment and garnishment or process in rem is issued the execution of such process shall be stayed, or the property released, on the giving of security, to be approved by the court or clerk, or by stipulation of the parties, conditioned to answer the judgment of the court or of any appellate court. The parties may stipulate the amount and nature of such security. In the event of the inability or refusal of the parties so to stipulate the court shall fix the principal sum of the bond or stipulation at an amount sufficient to cover the amount of the plaintiff's claim fairly stated with accrued interest and costs; but the principal sum shall in no event exceed (i) twice the amount of the plaintiff's claim or (ii) the value of the property on due appraisement, whichever is smaller. The bond or stipulation shall be conditioned for the payment of the principal sum and interest thereon at 6 per cent per annum.

(b) *General Bond.* The owner of any vessel may file

a general bond or stipulation, with sufficient surety, to be approved by the court, conditioned to answer the judgment of such court in all or any actions that may be brought thereafter in such court in which the vessel is attached or arrested. Thereupon the execution of all such process against such vessel shall be stayed so long as the amount secured by such bond or stipulation is at least double the aggregate amount claimed by plaintiffs in all actions begun and pending in which such vessel has been attached or arrested. Judgments and remedies may be had on such bond or stipulation as if a special bond or stipulation had been filed in each of such actions. The district court may make necessary orders to carry this rule into effect, particularly as to the giving of proper notice of any action against or attachment of a vessel for which a general bond has been filed. Such bond or stipulation shall be indorsed by the clerk with a minute of the actions wherein process is so stayed. Further security may be required by the court at any time.

If a special bond or stipulation is given in a particular case, the liability on the general bond or stipulation shall cease as to that case.

(c) *Release by Consent or Stipulation; Order of Court or Clerk; Costs.* Any vessel, cargo, or other property in the custody of the marshal or other person or organization having the warrant may be released forthwith upon the marshal's acceptance and approval of a stipulation, bond, or other security, signed by the party on whose behalf the property is detained or the party's attorney and expressly authorizing such release, if all costs and charges of the court and its officers shall have first been paid. Otherwise no property in the custody of the marshal, other person or organization having the warrant, or other officer of the court shall be released without an order of the court; but such order may be entered as of course by the clerk, upon the giving of approved security as provided by law and these rules, or upon the dismissal or discontinuance of the action; but the marshal or other person or organization having the warrant shall not deliver any property so released until the costs and charges of the officers of the court shall first have been paid.

(d) *Possessory, Petitory, and Partition Actions.* The foregoing provisions of this subdivision (5) do not apply to petitory, possessory, and partition actions. In such cases the property arrested shall be released only by order of the court, on such terms and conditions and on the giving of such security as the court may require.

(6) Reduction or Impairment of Security. Whenever security is taken the court may, on motion and hearing, for good cause shown, reduce the amount of security given; and if the surety shall be or become insufficient, new or additional sureties may be required on motion and hearing.

(7) Security on Counterclaim.

(a) When a person who has given security for damages in the original action asserts a counterclaim that arises from the transaction or occurrence that is the subject of the original action, a plaintiff for whose benefit the security has been given must give security for damages demanded in the counterclaim unless the court for cause shown, directs otherwise. Proceedings on the original claim must be stayed until this security is given unless the court directs otherwise.

(b) The plaintiff is required to give security under Rule E(7)(a) when the United States or its corporate instrumentality counterclaims and would have been required to give security to respond in damages if a private party but is relieved by law from giving security.

(8) Restricted Appearance. An appearance to defend against an admiralty and maritime claim with respect to which there has issued process in rem, or process of attachment and garnishment, may be expressly restricted to the defense of such claim, and in that event is not an appearance for the purposes of any other claim with respect to which such process is not available or has not been served.

(9) Disposition of Property; Sales.

(a) Interlocutory Sales; Delivery.

(i) On application of a party, the marshal, or other person having custody of the property, the court may order all or part of the property sold—with the sales proceeds, or as much of them as will satisfy the judgment, paid into court to await further orders of the court—if:

(A) the attached or arrested property is perishable, or liable to deterioration, decay, or injury by being detained in custody pending the action;

(B) the expense of keeping the property is excessive or disproportionate; or

(C) there is an unreasonable delay in securing release of the property.

(ii) In the circumstances described in Rule E(9)(a)(i), the court, on motion by a defendant or a person filing a statement of interest or right under Rule C(6), may order that the property, rather than being sold, be delivered to the movant upon giving security under these rules.

(b) *Sales; Proceeds.* All sales of property shall be made by the marshal or a deputy marshal, or by other person or organization having the warrant, or by any other person assigned by the court where the marshal or other person or organization having the warrant is a party in interest; and the proceeds of sale shall be forthwith paid into the registry of the court to be disposed of according to law.

(10) Preservation of Property. When the owner or another person remains in possession of property attached or arrested under the provisions of Rule E(4)(b) that permit execution of process without taking actual possession, the court, on a party's motion or on its own, may enter any order necessary to preserve the property and to prevent its removal.

[Added Feb. 28, 1966, eff. Jul. 1, 1966, and amended Apr. 29, 1985, effective Aug. 1, 1985; Mar. 2, 1987, effective Aug. 1, 1987; Apr. 30, 1991, effective Dec. 1, 1991; April 17, 2000, effective December 1, 2000; April 12, 2006, effective December 1, 2006.]

RULE F
LIMITATION OF LIABILITY

(1) Time for Filing Complaint; Security. Not later than six months after receipt of a claim in writing, any vessel owner may file a complaint in the appropriate district court, as provided in subdivision (9) of this rule, for limitation of liability pursuant to statute. The owner (a) shall deposit with the court, for the benefit of claimants, a sum equal to the amount or value of the owner's interest in the vessel and pending freight, or approved security therefor, and in addition such sums, or approved security therefor, as the court may from time to time fix as necessary to carry out the provisions of the statutes as amended; or (b) at the owner's option shall transfer to a trustee to be appointed by the court, for the benefit of claimants, the owner's interest in the vessel and pending freight, together with such sums, or approved security therefor, as the court may from time to time fix as necessary to carry out the provisions of the statutes as amended. The plaintiff shall also give security for costs and, if the plaintiff elects to give security, for interest at the rate of 6 percent per annum from the date of the security.

(2) Complaint. The complaint shall set forth the facts on the basis of which the right to limit liability is asserted and all facts necessary to enable the court to determine the amount to which the owner's liability shall be limited. The complaint may demand exoneration from as well as limitation of liability. It shall state the voyage if any, on which the demands sought to be limited arose, with the date and place of its termination; the amount of all demands including all unsatisfied liens or claims of lien, in contract or in tort or otherwise, arising on that voyage, so far as known to the plaintiff, and what actions and proceedings, if any, are pending thereon; whether the vessel was damaged, lost, or abandoned, and, if so, when and where; the value of the vessel at the close of the voyage or, in case of wreck, the value of her wreckage, strippings, or proceeds, if any, and where and in whose possession they are; and the amount of any pending freight recovered or recoverable. If the plaintiff elects to transfer the plaintiff's interest in the vessel to a trustee, the complaint must further show any prior paramount liens thereon, and what voyages or trips, if any, she has made since the voyage or trip on which the claims sought to be limited arose, and any existing liens arising upon any such subsequent voyage or trip, with the amounts and causes thereof, and the names and addresses of the lienors, so far as known; and whether the vessel sustained any injury upon or by reason of such subsequent voyage or trip.

(3) **Claims Against Owner; Injunction.** Upon compliance by the owner with the requirements of subdivision (1) of this rule all claims and proceedings against the owner or the owner's property with respect to the matter in question shall cease. On application of the plaintiff the court shall enjoin the further prosecution of any action or proceeding against the plaintiff or the plaintiff's property with respect to any claim subject to limitation in the action.

(4) **Notice to Claimants.** Upon the owner's compliance with subdivision (1) of this rule the court shall issue a notice to all persons asserting claims with respect to which the complaint seeks limitation, admonishing them to file their respective claims with the clerk of the court and to serve on the attorneys for the plaintiff a copy thereof on or before a date to be named in the notice. The date so fixed shall not be less than 30 days after issuance of the notice. For cause shown, the court may enlarge the time within which claims may be filed. The notice shall be published in such newspaper or newspapers as the court may direct once a week for four successive weeks prior to the date fixed for the filing of claims. The plaintiff not later than the day of second publication shall also mail a copy of the

notice to every person known to have made any claim against the vessel or the plaintiff arising out of the voyage or trip on which the claims sought to be limited arose. In cases involving death a copy of such notice shall be mailed to the decedent at the decedent's last known address, and also to any person who shall be known to have made any claim on account of such death.

(5) Claims and Answer. Claims shall be filed and served on or before the date specified in the notice provided for in subdivision (4) of this rule. Each claim shall specify the facts upon which the claimant relies in support of the claim, the items thereof, and the dates on which the same accrued. If a claimant desires to contest either the right to exoneration from or the right to limitation of liability the claimant shall file and serve an answer to the complaint unless the claim has included an answer.

(6) Information to Be Given Claimants. Within 30 days after the date specified in the notice for filing claims, or within such time as the court thereafter may allow, the plaintiff shall mail to the attorney for each claimant (or if the claimant has no attorney to the claimant) a list setting forth (a) the name of each claimant, (b) the name and address of the claimant's attorney (if the claimant is known to have one), (c) the nature of the claim, i.e., whether property loss, property damage, death, personal injury etc., and (d) the amount thereof.

(7) Insufficiency of Fund or Security. Any claimant may by motion demand that the funds deposited in court or the security given by the plaintiff be increased on the ground that they are less than the value of the plaintiff's interest in the vessel and pending freight. Thereupon the court shall cause due appraisement to be made of the value of the plaintiff's interest in the vessel and pending freight; and if the court finds that the deposit or security is either insufficient or excessive it shall order its increase or reduction. In like manner any claimant may demand that the deposit or security be increased on the ground that it is insufficient to carry out the provisions of the statutes relating to claims in respect of loss of life or bodily injury; and, after notice and hearing, the court may similarly order that the deposit or security be increased or reduced.

(8) **Objections to Claims: Distribution of Fund.** Any interested party may question or controvert any claim without filing an objection thereto. Upon determination of liability the fund deposited or secured, or the proceeds of the vessel and pending freight, shall be divided pro rata, subject to all relevant provisions of law, among the several claimants in proportion to the amounts of their respective claims, duly proved, saving, however, to all parties any priority to which they may be legally entitled.

(9) **Venue; Transfer.** The complaint shall be filed in any district in which the vessel has been attached or arrested to answer for any claim with respect to which the plaintiff seeks to limit liability; or, if the vessel has not been attached or arrested, then in any district in which the owner has been sued with respect to any such claim. When the vessel has not been attached or arrested to answer the matters aforesaid, and suit has not been commenced against the owner, the proceedings may be had in the district in which the vessel may be, but if the vessel is not within any district and no suit has been commenced in any district, then the complaint may be filed in any district. For the convenience of parties and witnesses, in the interest of justice, the court may transfer the action to any district; if venue is wrongly laid the court shall dismiss or, if it be in the interest of justice, transfer the action to any district in which it could have been brought. If the vessel shall have been sold, the proceeds shall represent the vessel for the purposes of these rules.

[Added Feb. 28, 1966, eff. Jul. 1, 1966, and amended Mar. 2, 1987, effective Aug. 1, 1987.]

RULE G
FORFEITURE ACTIONS IN REM

(1) Scope. This rule governs a forfeiture action in rem arising from a federal statute. To the extent that this rule does not address an issue, Supplemental Rules C and E and the Federal Rules of Civil Procedure also apply.

(2) Complaint. The complaint must:

(a) be verified;

(b) state the grounds for subject-matter jurisdiction, in rem jurisdiction over the defendant property, and venue;

(c) describe the property with reasonable particularity;

(d) if the property is tangible, state its location when any seizure occurred and—if different—its location when the action is filed;

(e) identify the statute under which the forfeiture action is brought; and

(f) state sufficiently detailed facts to support a reasonable belief that the government will be able to meet its burden of proof at trial.

(3) Judicial Authorization and Process.

(a) Real Property. If the defendant is real property, the government must proceed under 18 U.S.C. § 985.

(b) Other Property; Arrest Warrant. If the defendant is not real property:

(i) the clerk must issue a warrant to arrest the property if it is in the government's possession, custody, or control;

(ii) the court—on finding probable cause—must issue a warrant to arrest the property if it is not in the government's possession, custody, or control and is not subject to a judicial restraining order; and

(iii) a warrant is not necessary if the property is subject to a judicial restraining order.

(c) Execution of Process.

(i) The warrant and any supplemental process must be delivered to a person or organization authorized to execute it, who may be: (A) a marshal or any other United States officer or employee; (B) someone under contract with the United States; or (C) someone specially appointed by the court for that purpose.

(ii) The authorized person or organization must execute the warrant and any supplemental process on property in the United States as soon as practicable unless:

(A) the property is in the government's possession, custody, or control; or

(B) the court orders a different time when the complaint is under seal, the action is stayed before the warrant and supplemental process are executed, or the court finds other good cause.

(iii) The warrant and any supplemental process may be executed within the district or, when authorized by statute, outside the district.

(iv) If executing a warrant on property outside the United States is required, the warrant may be transmitted to an appropriate authority for serving process where the property is located.

(4) Notice.

(a) Notice by Publication.

(i) When Publication Is Required. A judgment of forfeiture may be entered only if the government has published notice of the action within a reasonable time after filing the complaint or at a time the court orders. But notice need not be published if:

(A) the defendant property is worth less than $1,000 and direct notice is sent under Rule G(4)(b) to every person the government can reasonably identify as a potential claimant; or

(B) the court finds that the cost of publication exceeds the property's value and that other means of notice would satisfy due process.

(ii) Content of the Notice. Unless the court orders otherwise, the notice must:

(A) describe the property with reasonable particularity;

(B) state the times under Rule G(5) to file a claim and to answer; and

(C) name the government attorney to be served with the claim and answer.

(iii) Frequency of Publication. Published notice must appear:

(A) once a week for three consecutive weeks; or

(B) only once if, before the action was filed, notice of nonjudicial forfeiture of the same property was published on an official internet government forfeiture site for at least 30 consecutive days, or in a newspaper of general circulation for three consecutive weeks in a district where publication is authorized under Rule G(4)(a)(iv).

(iv) Means of Publication. The government should select from the following options a means of publication reasonably calculated to notify potential claimants of the action:

(A) if the property is in the United States, publication in a newspaper generally circulated in the district where the action is filed, where the property was seized, or where property that was not seized is located;

(B) if the property is outside the United States, publication in a newspaper generally circulated in a district where the action is filed, in a newspaper generally circulated in the country where the property is located, or in legal notices published and generally circulated in the country where the property is located; or

(C) instead of (A) or (B), posting a notice on an official internet government forfeiture site for at least 30 consecutive days.

(b) Notice to Known Potential Claimants.

(i) Direct Notice Required. The government must

send notice of the action and a copy of the complaint to any person who reasonably appears to be a potential claimant on the facts known to the government before the end of the time for filing a claim under Rule G(5)(a)(ii)(B).

(ii) Content of the Notice. The notice must state:

(A) the date when the notice is sent;

(B) a deadline for filing a claim, at least 35 days after the notice is sent;

(C) that an answer or a motion under Rule 12 must be filed no later than 21 days after filing the claim; and

(D) the name of the government attorney to be served with the claim and answer.

(iii) Sending Notice.

(A) The notice must be sent by means reasonably calculated to reach the potential claimant.

(B) Notice may be sent to the potential claimant or to the attorney representing the potential claimant with respect to the seizure of the property or in a related investigation, administrative forfeiture proceeding, or criminal case.

(C) Notice sent to a potential claimant who is incarcerated must be sent to the place of incarceration.

(D) Notice to a person arrested in connection with an offense giving rise to the forfeiture who is not incarcerated when notice is sent may be sent to the address that person last gave to the agency that arrested or released the person.

(E) Notice to a person from whom the property was seized who is not incarcerated when notice is sent may be sent to the last address that person gave to the agency that seized the property.

(iv) When Notice Is Sent. Notice by the following means is sent on the date when it is placed in the mail, delivered to a commercial carrier, or sent by electronic mail.

(v) Actual Notice. A potential claimant who had

actual notice of a forfeiture action may not oppose or seek relief from forfeiture because of the government's failure to send the required notice.

(5) Responsive Pleadings.

(a) Filing a Claim.

(i) A person who asserts an interest in the defendant property may contest the forfeiture by filing a claim in the court where the action is pending. The claim must:

(A) identify the specific property claimed;

(B) identify the claimant and state the claimant's interest in the property;

(C) be signed by the claimant under penalty of perjury; and

(D) be served on the government attorney designated under Rule G(4)(a)(ii)(C) or (b)(ii)(D).

(ii) Unless the court for good cause sets a different time, the claim must be filed:

(A) by the time stated in a direct notice sent under Rule G(4)(b);

(B) if notice was published but direct notice was not sent to the claimant or the claimant's attorney, no later than 30 days after final publication of newspaper notice or legal notice under Rule G(4)(a) or no later than 60 days after the first day of publication on an official internet government forfeiture site; or

(C) if notice was not published and direct notice was not sent to the claimant or the claimant's attorney:

(1) if the property was in the government's possession, custody, or control when the complaint was filed, no later than 60 days after the filing, not counting any time when the complaint was under seal or when the action was stayed before execution of a warrant issued under Rule G(3)(b); or

(2) if the property was not in the govern-

ment's possession, custody, or control when the complaint was filed, no later than 60 days after the government complied with 18 U.S.C. § 985(c) as to real property, or 60 days after process was executed on the property under Rule G(3).

(iii) A claim filed by a person asserting an interest as a bailee must identify the bailor, and if filed on the bailor's behalf must state the authority to do so.

(b) Answer. A claimant must serve and file an answer to the complaint or a motion under Rule 12 within 21 days after filing the claim. A claimant waives an objection to in rem jurisdiction or to venue if the objection is not made by motion or stated in the answer.

(6) Special Interrogatories.

(a) Time and Scope. The government may serve special interrogatories limited to the claimant's identity and relationship to the defendant property without the court's leave at any time after the claim is filed and before discovery is closed. But if the claimant serves a motion to dismiss the action, the government must serve the interrogatories within 21 days after the motion is served.

(b) Answers or Objections. Answers or objections to these interrogatories must be served within 21 days after the interrogatories are served.

(c) Government's Response Deferred. The government need not respond to a claimant's motion to dismiss the action under Rule G(8)(b) until 21 days after the claimant has answered these interrogatories.

(7) Preserving, Preventing Criminal Use, and Disposing of Property; Sales.

(a) Preserving and Preventing Criminal Use of Property. When the government does not have actual possession of the defendant property the court, on motion or on its own, may enter any order necessary to preserve the property, to prevent its removal or encumbrance, or to prevent its use in a criminal offense.

(b) Interlocutory Sale or Delivery.

(i) Order to Sell. On motion by a party or a person having custody of the property, the court may order all or part of the property sold if:

(A) the property is perishable or at risk of deterioration, decay, or injury by being detained in custody pending the action;

(B) the expense of keeping the property is excessive or is disproportionate to its fair market value;

(C) the property is subject to a mortgage or to taxes on which the owner is in default; or

(D) the court finds other good cause.

(ii) Who Makes the Sale. A sale must be made by a United States agency that has authority to sell the property, by the agency's contractor, or by any person the court designates.

(iii) Sale Procedures. The sale is governed by 28 U.S.C. §§ 2001, 2002, and 2004, unless all parties, with the court's approval, agree to the sale, aspects of the sale, or different procedures.

(iv) Sale Proceeds. Sale proceeds are a substitute res subject to forfeiture in place of the property that was sold. The proceeds must be held in an interest-bearing account maintained by the United States pending the conclusion of the forfeiture action.

(v) Delivery on a Claimant's Motion. The court may order that the property be delivered to the claimant pending the conclusion of the action if the claimant shows circumstances that would permit sale under Rule G(7)(b)(i) and gives security under these rules.

(c) Disposing of Forfeited Property. Upon entry of a forfeiture judgment, the property or proceeds from selling the property must be disposed of as provided by law.

(8) Motions.

(a) **Motion To Suppress Use of the Property as Evidence.** If the defendant property was seized, a party with standing to contest the lawfulness of the seizure may move to suppress use of the property as evidence. Suppression does not affect forfeiture of the property based on independently derived evidence.

(b) **Motion To Dismiss the Action.**

(i) A claimant who establishes standing to contest forfeiture may move to dismiss the action under Rule 12(b).

(ii) In an action governed by 18 U.S.C. § 983(a)(3)(D) the complaint may not be dismissed on the ground that the government did not have adequate evidence at the time the complaint was filed to establish the forfeitability of the property. The sufficiency of the complaint is governed by Rule G(2).

(c) **Motion To Strike a Claim or Answer.**

(i) At any time before trial, the government may move to strike a claim or answer:

(A) for failing to comply with Rule G(5) or (6), or

(B) because the claimant lacks standing.

(ii) The motion:

(A) must be decided before any motion by the claimant to dismiss the action; and

(B) may be presented as a motion for judgment on the pleadings or as a motion to determine after a hearing or by summary judgment whether the claimant can carry the burden of establishing standing by a preponderance of the evidence.

(d) **Petition To Release Property.**

(i) If a United States agency or an agency's contractor holds property for judicial or nonjudicial forfeiture under a statute governed by 18 U.S.C. § 983(f), a person who has filed a claim to the property may petition for its release under § 983(f).

(ii) If a petition for release is filed before a judicial

forfeiture action is filed against the property, the petition may be filed either in the district where the property was seized or in the district where a warrant to seize the property issued. If a judicial forfeiture action against the property is later filed in another district—or if the government shows that the action will be filed in another district—the petition may be transferred to that district under 28 U.S.C. § 1404.

(e) Excessive Fines. A claimant may seek to mitigate a forfeiture under the Excessive Fines Clause of the Eighth Amendment by motion for summary judgment or by motion made after entry of a forfeiture judgment if:

(i) the claimant has pleaded the defense under Rule 8; and

(ii) the parties have had the opportunity to conduct civil discovery on the defense.

(9) Trial. Trial is to the court unless any party demands trial by jury under Rule 38.

(Added Apr. 12, 2006, eff. Dec. 1, 2006; amended March 26, 2009, effective December 1, 2009.)

SUPPLEMENTAL RULES SET #2

SUPPLEMENTAL RULES FOR SOCIAL SECURITY ACTIONS UNDER 42 U.S.C. § 405(g)

Adopted April 11, 2022, effective December 1, 2022

Following years of extensive study, these Supplemental Rules were promulgated in 2022 to bring national procedural uniformity to actions filed to obtain review of a final decision by the Commissioner of Social Security.

RULE 1
REVIEW OF SOCIAL SECURITY DECISIONS UNDER 42 U.S.C. § 405(G)

(a) Applicability of These Rules. These rules govern an action under 42 U.S.C. § 405(g) for review on the record of a final decision of the Commissioner of Social Security that presents only an individual claim.

(b) Federal Rules of Civil Procedure. The Federal Rules of Civil Procedure also apply to a proceeding under these rules, except to the extent that they are inconsistent with these rules.

RULE 2
COMPLAINT

(a) Commencing Action. An action for review under these rules is commenced by filing a complaint with the court.

(b) Contents.

(1) The complaint must:

(A) state that the action is brought under § 405(g);

(B) identify the final decision to be reviewed, including any identifying designation provided by the Commissioner with the final decision;

(C) state the name and the county of residence of the person for whom benefits are claimed;

(D) name the person on whose wage record benefits are claimed; and

(E) state the type of benefits claimed.

(2) The complaint may include a short and plain statement of the grounds for relief.

RULE 3
SERVICE

The court must notify the Commissioner of the commencement of the action by transmitting a Notice of Electronic Filing to the appropriate office within the Social Security Administration's Office of General Counsel and to the United States Attorney for the district where the action is filed. If the complaint was not filed electronically, the court must notify the plaintiff of the transmission. The plaintiff need not serve a summons and complaint under Civil Rule 4.

RULE 4
ANSWER; MOTIONS; TIME

(a) Serving the Answer. An answer must be served on the plaintiff within 60 days after notice of the action is given under Rule 3.

(b) The Answer. An answer may be limited to a certified copy of the administrative record, and to any affirmative defenses under Civil Rule 8(c). Civil Rule 8(b) does not apply.

(c) Motions Under Civil Rule 12. A motion under Civil Rule 12 must be made within 60 days after notice of the action is given under Rule 3.

(d) Time to Answer After a Motion Under Rule 4(c). Unless the court sets a different time, serving a motion under Rule 4(c) alters the time to answer as provided by Civil Rule 12(a)(4).

RULE 5
PRESENTING THE ACTION FOR DECISION

The action is presented for decision by the parties' briefs. A brief must support assertions of fact by citations to particular parts of the record.

RULE 6
PLAINTIFF'S BRIEF

The plaintiff must file and serve on the Commissioner a brief for the requested relief within 30 days after the answer is filed or 30 days after entry of an order disposing of the last remaining motion filed under Rule 4(c), whichever is later.

RULE 7
COMMISSIONER'S BRIEF

The Commissioner must file a brief and serve it on the plaintiff within 30 days after service of the plaintiff's brief.

RULE 8
REPLY BRIEF

The plaintiff may file a reply brief and serve it on the Commissioner within 14 days after service of the Commissioner's brief.

PART IV
APPENDIX OF FORMS

(See Rule 84)

INTRODUCTORY STATEMENT

Since the day they first took effect in 1938, the Federal Rules of Civil Procedure have been accompanied by an "Appendix of Forms". They were unveiled with great pride by the lead crafter of the Rules, Dean Charles E. Clark, who pronounced them a "most important part of the rules" because, he explained, "when you can't define you can at least draw pictures to show your meaning."[1] Originally, there were 34 official federal forms, a number that grew by two in 1993, and nearly all of which were substantially reworked during the 2007 "restyling" project. The forms were abrogated in 2015. The Advisory Committee Notes accompanying this abrogation opined that the Forms' purpose in 1938, while useful then, has since "been fulfilled."[2] The Committee noted the availability of various alternative sources of federal civil forms (prepared by, among others, the Administrate Office of the United States Courts, the websites of various federal district courts, and private commercial suppliers), which it concluded rendered the official set "no longer necessary."[3]

CURRENT SOURCES OF FEDERAL CIVIL FORMS

Not all federal forms were abrogated. Two remain, both for use in seeking and granting a waiver of formal service of process. They now are reprinted at the close of the text of Rule 4.

In addition to various commercially-prepared form sources, the Administration Office of the United States Courts maintains a small but important set of downloadable forms available at: http://www.uscourts.gov/forms/civil-forms. This same source also facilitates the process of locating forms preferred for use in the various federal districts.

---

[1] *See* Charles E. Clark, *Pleading Under the Federal Rules*, 12 Wyo. L.J. 177, 181 (1958).

[2] *See* Rule 84 advisory committee note (2015).

[3] *See id.* The abrogation may have been hastened by discomfort with the official pleading forms and their perceived misalignment with the U.S. Supreme Court's pleading decisions in *Bell Atlantic Corp. v. Twombly* and *Ashcroft v. Iqbal*. *See supra* Authors' Commentary to Rule 8(a) ("'*Plausible' Pleadings*"). The Advisory Committee Note endeavored to sidestep any intimation that its abrogation of the Forms was intended to adjust those pleading standards. *See* Rule 84 advisory committee note (2015) ("The abrogation of Rule 84 does not alter existing pleading standards or otherwise change the requirements of Civil Rule 8.").

PART V
MULTIDISTRICT LITIGATION

Table of Sections

Sec.

5.1 Introduction.
5.2 The Federal Multidistrict Litigation Statute, 28 U.S.C.A. § 1407.

§ 5.1 Introduction

Congress created the Judicial Panel on Multidistrict Litigation in the late 1960's in response to the challenge of efficiently and effectively managing related, protracted, and complex civil cases that were being filed in various federal courts throughout the Nation.[1] At that time, nearly 2,000 separate but related electrical equipment antitrust cases were pending in 36 different federal judicial districts.[2] To manage these numerous distinct but related antitrust cases, Chief Justice Earl Warren appointed an advisory "Coordinating Committee for Multiple Litigation," which invited counsel and district court judges to attend hearings on how to economically supervise these electrical equipment litigations.[3]

The Committee prepared and recommended more than 40 "national pretrial orders" for the cases, which were then entered voluntarily by the judges in most of the districts where these antitrust cases were pending.[4] The orders established a coordinated system of national pretrial discovery, including a central document depository available to all parties and the conduct of depositions on a coordinated, nationwide schedule.[5]

This voluntary, advisory procedure was so successful that Congress established a statutory, national multidistrict litigation court in 1968 with authority to direct the transfer of multidistrict civil cases that involve common questions of fact to a single federal district for the purpose of consolidated or coordinated nationwide pretrial proceedings.[6] This specialized court, the "Judicial Panel on Multidistrict Litigation," comprises 7 circuit and district court judges, designated from time to time by the Chief Justice, no 2 of whom may come from the same Circuit.[7]

The Judicial Panel is authorized to transfer cases for pretrial

---

[1] *See* 28 U.S.C.A. § 1407.

[2] *See* Robert A. Cahn, *A Look at the Judicial Panel on Multidistrict Litigation*, 72 F.R.D. 211, 211 (1976).

[3] *See* id. at 211–12.

[4] *See* id. at 212.

[5] *See* id.

[6] *See* 28 U.S.C.A. § 1407(a). *See generally Gelboim v. Bank of America Corp.*, 574 U.S. 405, 410, 135 S. Ct. 897, 903, 190 L. Ed. 2d 789 (2015).

[7] *See* 28 U.S.C.A. § 1407(d).

multidistrict litigation (or "MDL") treatment upon three findings: (a) that civil cases, then pending in different federal judicial districts, involve one or more common questions of fact, and that coordinated or consolidated pretrial proceedings, centralized before a single district court (b) will serve the convenience of parties and witnesses and (c) will promote the just and efficient conduct of the lawsuits.[8] If these prerequisites are met, MDL transfer to a central judicial district is appropriate, even if federal diversity jurisdiction, personal jurisdiction, or venue would otherwise be improper there over the transferred cases.[9] The resulting post-transfer authority extends only to the parties and disputes subject to the transfer; jurisdiction does not extend to those parties or disputes not brought before the transferee court.[10]

MDL treatment may be initiated by the Judicial Panel on its own initiative or upon motion by a party in any action believed to qualify for this type of coordination or consolidation.[11] A consolidation order by the Judicial Panel will ordinarily not be overturned unless it is "outlandish".[12]

If MDL treatment is granted by the Judicial Panel, the ordinary procedure follows: a single judicial district and federal judge is selected by the Judicial Panel as the MDL court for all the cases; all qualifying federal lawsuits are then transferred to that federal judge for pretrial purposes.[13] If new, later-filed federal lawsuits share a common question of fact with those already in the MDL, the Judicial Panel, upon being notified of their filing, may "tag" those new cases and transfer them to the MDL court as well.[14] Sometimes, the MDL court will invite "direct filing" of new MDL-eligible lawsuits, permitting them to be commenced in the MDL court, upon the litigants' consent to personal jurisdiction and

[8] *See* 28 U.S.C.A. § 1407(a). *See also Pinney v. Nokia, Inc.*, 402 F.3d 430, 451 (4th Cir.2005).

[9] *See Howard v. Sulzer Orthopedics, Inc.*, 382 Fed. Appx. 436, 441–42 (6th Cir. 2010); *Pinney v. Nokia, Inc.*, 402 F.3d 430, 451–52 (4th Cir.2005).

[10] *See In re Genetically Modified Rice Litig.*, 764 F.3d 864, 873 (8th Cir. 2014). Note, however, that attorneys who participate in the consolidated MDL litigations in the transferee district may, themselves, become subject to that court's personal jurisdiction for claims relating to their in-forum conduct. *See Downing v. Goldman Phipps, PLLC*, 764 F.3d 906, 913–14 (8th Cir. 2014) (finding jurisdiction over dispute alleging failing to pay into a common fund established to finance MDL litigation work).

[11] *See* 28 U.S.C.A. § 1407(c). *See also D & S Marine Servs., L.L.C. v. Lyle Props., L.L.C.*, 586 Fed. Appx. 636, 639–40 (5th Cir. 2013) (only Judicial Panel, not individual district courts, have power to transfer into MDL).

[12] *See Bennett v. Bayer Healthcare Pharms., Inc.*, 577 Fed.Appx. 616, 617-18 (7th Cir. 2014).

[13] *See Boomer v. AT & T Corp.*, 309 F.3d 404, 413 (7th Cir.2002) (MDL transfer order effective only when filed with clerk in transferee district).

[14] *See Looper v. Cook Inc.*, 20 F.4th 387, 390 (7th Cir. 2021) (describing "tag-along" process); *In re Volkswagen "Clean Diesel" Mktg., Sales Pracs., & Prod. Liab. Litig.*, 959 F.3d 1201, 1209 n.11 (9th Cir. 2020) (same).

venue.[15] Once the MDL judge obtains authority over the MDL cases, she or he will then preside over and manage a nationwide, coordinated discovery and pretrial procedures program; and, in the event the cases are not disposed of or settled by the MDL judge by the close of the pretrial stage, the lawsuits are each transferred back to their districts of origin for trial.[16] Though consolidated in the MDL, individual cases ordinarily do not lose their discrete, separate legal character or morph into a new, single, monolithic "action"[17] (at least not without deliberate action by the court and the parties to do so).[18]

During consolidation, the MDL judge may rule on case-dispositive motions (though always mindful of each claimant's right to develop his or her unique facts separately),[19] and may grant motions to dismiss both on substantive grounds[20] and for failure to abide by court scheduling orders and procedures.[21] The MDL judge may also, when circumstances warrant, resolve the consolidated cases by summary judgment.[22] Such orders—fully disposing of one or more cases, though leaving others still pending in the MDL—are usually final orders, subject to immediate appeal.[23] The MDL judge may also rule on other, non-dispositive pretrial motions (such as motions to file omnibus pleadings, to amend or otherwise adjust the pleadings, to enforce venue requirements, and to resolve discovery disputes) and may order attendance at settlement conferences.[24] The MDL judge may supervise the use of "master" complaints either for substantive, consolidated treatment or as legally inert administrative summaries of pleadings.[25]

The MDL judge may also impose litigation costs, but will usu-

---

[15]*See Looper v. Cook Inc.*, 20 F.4th 387, 390-91 (7th Cir. 2021); *Axline v. 3M Co.*, 8 F.4th 667, 670-71 (8th Cir. 2021).

[16]*See* 28 U.S.C.A. § 1407(a). *See also Gelboim v. Bank of America Corp.*, 574 U.S. 405, 413, 135 S. Ct. 897, 190 L. Ed. 2d 789 (2015); *Lexecon Inc. v. Milberg Weiss Bershad Hynes & Lerach*, 523 U.S. 26, 32, 118 S. Ct. 956, 140 L. Ed. 2d 62 (1998).

[17]*See Gelboim v. Bank of America Corp.*, 574 U.S. 405, 413, 135 S. Ct. 897, 190 L. Ed. 2d 789 (2015); *In re Nat'l Prescription Opiate Litig.*, 956 F.3d 838, 845 (6th Cir. 2020).

[18]*See Bell v. Publix Super Markets, Inc.*, 982 F.3d 468, 489 (7th Cir. 2020) (discussing practice of "consolidated amended complaints" filed in MDL); *In re Refrigerant Compressors Antitrust Litig.*, 731 F.3d 586, 590-91 (6th Cir. 2013) (same).

[19]*See In re Fosamax (Alendronate Sodium) Prod. Liab. Litig.*, 852 F.3d 268, 302 (3d Cir. 2017).

[20]*See In re African-American Slave Descendants Litig.*, 471 F.3d 754, 754–57 & 763 (7th Cir. 2006).

[21]*See In re Taxotere (Docetaxel) Prod. Liab. Litig.*, 966 F.3d 351, 356–61 (5th Cir. 2020); *Dzik v. Bayer Corp.*, 846 F.3d 211, 216 (7th Cir. 2017).

[22]*See In re Lipitor (Atorvastatin Calcium) Mktg., Sales Practices & Prod. Liab. Litig. (No II) MDL 2502*, 892 F.3d 624, 648–49 (4th Cir. 2018).

[23]*See Gelboim v. Bank of America Corp.*, 574 U.S. 405, 413-16, 135 S. Ct. 897, 190 L. Ed. 2d 789 (2015).

[24]*See In re Korean Air Lines Co.*, 642 F.3d 685, 699 (9th Cir. 2011) (collecting cases).

[25]*See In re Refrigerant Compressors Antitrust Litig.*, 731 F.3d 586,

ally allocate those costs ratably among the impacted cases.[26]

The law the MDL judge will apply during diversity-based proceedings will, ordinarily, follow the conflicts rules of the various originating transferor jurisdictions.[27] In direct-filed "tag-along" cases, the approach is usually the same—the conflicts rules of the would-be originating jurisdiction will likely apply.[28]

Remands are made by the Judicial Panel (not by the transferee judge), although the transferee judge retains a vital role of notifying the Judicial Panel (typically through a "*Suggestion to Remand*") that the coordinated or consolidated proceedings have been concluded.[29] Such a *Suggestion* by the transferee judge will be afforded "great weight."[30] The parties do not need to assert their intention to seek remand in order to preserve it; rather, a remand at the close of all pretrial proceedings is presumed.[31] But parties may request remand during the proceedings, though without the transferee judge's assent such requests carry a "strong burden of persuasion."[32] The Judicial Panel *must* remand when the coordinated or consolidated proceedings have concluded,[33] but *may*, in its "unusually broad discretion," remand when all that remains to be accomplished is case-specific.[34] The transferee judge may not self-assign the case in lieu of remand,[35] at least absent a relinquishment by the parties to their entitlement to a remand.[36] Thus, this MDL treatment is usually reserved as a vehicle for pretrial—and only pretrial—coordina-

---

590-91 (6th Cir. 2013).

[26]*See In re Avandia Mktg. Sales Practices*, 658 Fed. Appx. 29, 34-37 (3d Cir. 2016); *Winter v. Novartis Pharms. Corp.*, 739 F.3d 405, 411-12 (8th Cir. 2014).

[27]*See In re Hyundai & Kia Fuel Econ. Litig.*, 926 F.3d 539, 577 n.3 (9th Cir. 2019); *Larsen v. Citibank FSB*, 871 F.3d 1295, 1303 (11th Cir. 2017).

[28]*See Looper v. Cook Inc.*, 20 F.4th 387, 391-94 (7th Cir. 2021); *Axline v. 3M Co.*, 8 F.4th 667, 674 (8th Cir. 2021).

[29]*See In re Wilson*, 451 F.3d 161, 165 & 165 n.5 (3d Cir.2006).

[30]*See Hamer v. LivaNova Deutschland GmbH*, 994 F.3d 173, 181 (3d Cir. 2021); *In re Holiday Magic Sec. & Antitrust Litig.*, 433 F. Supp. 1125, 1126 (J.P.M.L. 1977).

[31]*See Armstrong v. LaSalle Bank Nat'l Ass'n*, 552 F.3d 613, 616 (7th Cir. 2009).

[32]*See Hamer v. LivaNova Deutschland GmbH*, 994 F.3d 173, 180 (3d Cir. 2021); *In re Holiday Magic Sec. & Antitrust Litig.*, 433 F. Supp. 1125, 1126 (J.P.M.L. 1977).

[33]*See Lexecon Inc. v. Milberg Weiss Bershad Hynes & Lerach*, 523 U.S. 26, 41, 118 S. Ct. 956, 140 L. Ed. 2d 62 (1998). *See generally Hamer v. LivaNova Deutschland GmbH*, 994 F.3d 173, 181 (3d Cir. 2021) (decision to remand ordinary turns on whether litigation benefits from further coordinated MDL proceedings).

[34]*See In re Wilson*, 451 F.3d 161, 172–73 (3d Cir.2006).

[35]*See Lexecon Inc. v. Milberg Weiss Bershad Hynes & Lerach*, 523 U.S. 26, 32-41, 118 S. Ct. 956, 140 L. Ed. 2d 62 (1998).

[36]*See In re Depuy Orthopaedics, Inc.*, 870 F.3d 345, 348 (5th Cir. 2017); *Armstrong v. LaSalle Bank Nat'l Ass'n*, 552 F.3d 613, 616-17 (7th Cir. 2009).

tion and consolidation.[37]

The extent to which a transferor court, following remand, may overrule the MDL transferee judge's orders remains unsettled; but because routine revisitations of the MDL judge's rulings would deal MDL litigants a "Return To Go" card[38] and thereby frustrate the intended goals of the MDL process,[39] the courts tend to affix law-of-the-case deference to the MDL judge's orders.[40]

The MDL procedure endeavors to achieve the economical use of the federal judiciary and the resolution of similar complex civil cases with the least cost and disruption to the parties and witnesses.[41] Consolidation or coordination may realize those aspirations by judicial disposition (on motions to dismiss or summary judgment), by settlement, or through other agreement.[42] During pretrial MDL proceedings, the MDL judge will typically look to the Federal Judicial Center's *Manual for Complex Litigation* as a primary resource for guiding the nationwide proceedings.[43] Documents are generally produced only once for hundreds or thousands of cases, with responsive documents made available to all parties at a centralized document depository. Interrogatories and requests for admissions are served on behalf of a series of related cases. Witnesses and parties, whose testimony is relevant to many cases, are deposed only once (or at least far less often than otherwise) by a select group of lead or liaison counsel. Throughout the MDL process, the transferee judge generally possesses the power to act not only on behalf of the transferee district, but also with the powers of a district judge in every district from which the consolidated cases have been transferred.[44]

The MDL judge's discretion is broad and commensurate with

---

[37]*See In re Patenaude*, 210 F.3d 135, 142 (3d Cir.2000) (MDL statute limits transferee court to only proceedings that are (1) coordinated or consolidated and (2) pretrial). *See also id.* at 144 ("pretrial" is interpreted broadly to mean all judicial proceedings that occur before trial).

[38]*See In re Pharmacy Benefit Managers Antitrust Litig.*, 582 F.3d 432, 440 (3d Cir. 2009).

[39]*See McKay v. Novartis Pharm. Corp.*, 751 F.3d 694, 703 (5th Cir. 2014).

[40]*See McKay v. Novartis Pharm. Corp.*, 751 F.3d 694, 703-05 (5th Cir. 2014) (applying law of the case principles, advising that transferor courts should rarely reverse transferee court decisions); *In re Pharmacy Benefit Managers Antitrust Litig.*, 582 F.3d 432, 443 (3d Cir. 2009) (applying law-of-the-case, and upholding transferee judge's arbitrability ruling).

[41]*See Gelboim v. Bank of America Corp.*, 574 U.S. 405, 410, 135 S. Ct. 897, 190 L. Ed. 2d 789 (2015); *In re Refrigerant Compressors Antitrust Litig.*, 731 F.3d 586, 588 (6th Cir. 2013).

[42]*See Bell v. Publix Super Markets, Inc.*, 982 F.3d 468, 489 (7th Cir. 2020).

[43]For an excellent annotated and commentary-laden version of this essential MDL resource, see David Herr's *Annotated Manual for Complex Litigation* (Thomson Reuters, revised annually) and 15 CHARLES A. WRIGHT, ARTHUR R. MILLER, EDWARD H. COOPER, RICHARD D. FREER, FEDERAL PRACTICE AND PROCEDURE §§ 3861-68 (2013).

[44]*See In re Korean Air Lines Co.*, 642 F.3d 685, 699 (9th Cir. 2011); *In re Flat Glass Antitrust Litig.*, 288 F.3d

the enormous task of managing a large litigation involving numerous litigants from across the country and posing substantial legal questions implicating pleading, discovery, expert, timeliness, choice of law, cognizable claim, and causation issues.[45] This authority encompasses the power to rule on motions relating to subpoenas issued from other judicial districts, including motions to quash.[46] But, although broad, the MDL judge's discretion is not unbounded; the judge may not, in the cause of efficiency and docketing progress, engage in "assembly-line justice,"[47] or disregard federal law or the civil rules,[48] or retain post-pretrial authority over the case through self-reassignment[49] or otherwise (absent authority to do so).[50]

Appeals from the MDL judge's pretrial orders are often (but not always) heard by the Court of Appeals for the Circuit that encompasses the MDL judge's district.[51] Sometimes, for instance, the Judicial Panel on Multidistrict Litigation may, in its discretion, elect not to permit Rule 54(b) immediate appeals (to the MDL judge's Court of Appeals) but, instead, to remand back to the originating transferor courts (with appeals, if any, to be taken to those various Courts of Appeals).[52] Likewise, when the MDL judge's order implicates a ruling compelling or sanctioning a nonparty located outside the MDL judge's district, the appeal is generally taken to the Court of Appeals for the Circuit embracing the district of the foreign discovery event.[53]

Appealability of orders disposing of some, but not all, MDL parties or claims are typically governed by usual federal appealability principles; MDL coordination or consolidation will not

---

83, 90 n. 12 (3d Cir.2002).

[45] *See In re Deepwater Horizon*, 907 F.3d 232, 235 (5th Cir. 2018); *In re Lipitor (Atorvastatin Calcium) Mktg., Sales Practices & Prod. Liab. Litig. (No II) MDL 2502*, 892 F.3d 624, 648 (4th Cir. 2018).

[46] *See In re Clients & Former Clients of Baron & Budd, P.C.*, 478 F.3d 670 (5th Cir. 2007) (per curiam).

[47] *See In re Asbestos Prods. Liab. Litig. (No. VI)*, 718 F.3d 236, 247 (3d Cir. 2013) ("efficiency must not be achieved at the expense of preventing meritorious claims from going forward"); *In re Korean Air Lines Co.*, 642 F.3d 685, 700-01 (9th Cir. 2011) (although broad, discretion does not permit court to disregard normal standards for assessing critical motions).

[48] *See In re Nat'l Prescription Opiate Litig.*, 956 F.3d 838, 844–46 (6th Cir. 2020).

[49] *See Lexecon Inc. v. Milberg Weiss Bershad Hynes & Lerach*, 523 U.S. 26, 32-41, 118 S. Ct. 956, 140 L. Ed. 2d 62 (1998).

[50] *See, e.g., Kalama v. Matson Navigation Co., Inc.*, 875 F.3d 297, 306 (6th Cir. 2017) (defendant's personal jurisdiction waiver as to one lawsuit not imputed to others); *In re Depuy Orthopaedics, Inc.*, 870 F.3d 345, 348-51 (5th Cir. 2017) (defendant's venue waiver as to certain trials not imputed to others).

[51] *See United States ex rel. Pogue v. Diabetes Treatment Ctrs. of America, Inc.*, 444 F.3d 462, 467 (6th Cir.2006).

[52] *See FedEx Ground Package Sys., Inc. v. U.S. Judicial Panel on Multidistrict Litig.*, 662 F.3d 887, 890-91 (7th Cir. 2011).

[53] *See United States ex rel. Pogue v. Diabetes Treatment Ctrs. of America, Inc.*, 444 F.3d 462, 467–68 (6th Cir. 2006).

ordinarily alter that.[54] Appealability in instances where the MDL judge issues a disposition on a consolidated complaint without also issuing a companion "separate document" judgment can be tricky.[55] The preclusive effects of MDL litigation can be complicated. For example, the decision to appeal an MDL ruling as to some consolidated defendants (and not all) will likely be preclusive once a final judgment is entered on the appeal, but perhaps not before.[56]

Over the years, MDL pretrial treatment has been granted in many different types of lawsuits,[57] including national products liability cases,[58] personal injury cases,[59] airplane disaster[60] and other large calamity cases,[61] antitrust cases,[62] securities fraud cases,[63] trade practices and consumer fraud cases,[64] intellectual property cases,[65] and a variety of other cases.[66] In its first 27 years of use, the statutory multidistrict litigation procedure had been applied to more than 39,000 federal civil cases, of which more than 90% were resolved in the MDL and prior to trial.[67] All told, over two thousand MDL's have occurred, involving some of

[54]*See In re Domestic Airline Travel Antitrust Litig.*, 3 F.4th 457, 459-61 (D.C. Cir. 2021) (no immediate appeal after district court approved settlement with two of four defendants but refused Rule 54(b) partial judgment order).

[55]*See Bell v. Publix Super Markets, Inc.*, 982 F.3d 468, 486-92 (7th Cir. 2020). *See also supra* Authors' Commentary to Rule 58(c) ("**Special Concerns in Multidistrict Litigation (MDL)**").

[56]*See In re Cygnus Telecommc'ns Tech., LLC, Patent Litig.*, 536 F.3d 1343, 1349–51 & 1350 n.1 (Fed.Cir. 2008).

[57]*See* Robert A. Cahn, *A Look at the Judicial Panel on Multidistrict Litigation*, 72 F.R.D. 211, 214 (1976).

[58]*See, e.g., In re: Am. Med. Sys., Inc., Pelvic Repair Sys. Prods. Liab. Litig.*, 844 F.Supp.2d 1359 (J.P.M.L. 2012) (MDL Nos. 2325-27); *In re Diet Drugs (Phentermine, Fenfluramine, Dexfenfluramine) Prods. Liab. Litig.*, 990 F.Supp. 834 (J.P.M.L.1998) (MDL No. 1203).

[59]*See In re: Nat'l Football League Players' Concussion Injury Litig.*, 842 F.Supp.2d 1378 (J.P.M.L. 2012) (MDL No. 2323).

[60]*See, e.g., In re Air Crash Disaster at Sioux City, Iowa, on July 19, 1989*, 128 F.R.D. 131 (J.P.M.L.1989) (MDL No. 817).

[61]*See, e.g., In re: Oil Spill by Oil Rig Deepwater Horizon in Gulf of Mexico, on Apr. 20, 2010*, 731 F.Supp.2d 1352 (J.P.M.L. 2010) (MDL No. 2179).

[62]*See, e.g., In re Delta Dental Antitrust Litig.*, 433 F. Supp. 3d 1358 (J.P.M.L. 2020) (MDL No. 2931).

[63]*See, e.g., In re: Facebook, Inc., IPO Secs. & Derivative Litig.*, 899 F.Supp.2d 1374 (J.P.M.L. 2012) (MDL No. 2389).

[64]*See, e.g., In re Juul Labs, Inc., Mktg., Sales Practices, & Prod. Liab. Litig.*, 396 F. Supp. 3d 1366, 1367 (J.P.M.L. 2019) (MDL No. 2913).

[65]*See, e.g., In re Entresto (Sacubitril/Valsartan) Patent Litig.*, 437 F. Supp. 3d 1372 (J.P.M.L. 2020) (MDL No. 2930).

[66]*See, e.g., In re Capital One Customer Data Sec. Breach Litig.*, 396 F. Supp. 3d 1364 (J.P.M.L. 2019) (MDL No. 2915); *In re South African Apartheid Litig.*, 238 F.Supp.2d 1379 (J.P.M.L. 2002) (MDL No. 1499).

[67]*See Lexecon Inc. v. Milberg Weiss Bershad Hynes & Lerach*, 523 U.S. 26, 32, 118 S. Ct. 956, 961, 140 L. Ed. 2d 62 (1998). *See also Campbell v. Boston Sci. Corp.*, 882 F.3d 70, 76 (4th Cir. 2018) (discussing MDL efficiencies in specific context).

the most challenging litigations in the history of the federal judiciary.[68] Today, a large percentage of the federal civil docket is conducted with MDL consolidations.[69] Indeed, some recent scholarship suggests MDL treatment has "supplemented and perhaps displaced the class action device as a procedural mechanism for large settlements."[70]

For a more extensive treatment of MDL practice, see David F. Herr, *Multidistrict Litigation Manual: Practice Before The Judicial Panel On Multidistrict Litigation* (Thompson-West, revised annually).

§ 5.2 The Federal Multidistrict Litigation Statute, 28 U.S.C.A. § 1407

1407. Multidistrict Litigation

(a) When civil actions involving one or more common questions of fact are pending in different districts, such actions may be transferred to any district for coordinated or consolidated pretrial proceedings. Such transfers shall be made by the judicial panel on multidistrict litigation authorized by this section upon its determination that transfers for such proceedings will be for the convenience of parties and witnesses and will promote the just and efficient conduct of such actions. Each action so transferred shall be remanded by the panel at or before the conclusion of such pretrial proceedings to the district from which it was transferred unless it shall have been previously terminated: *Provided, however*, That the panel may separate any claim, cross-claim, counter-claim, or third-party claim and remand any of such claims before the remainder of the action is remanded.

(b) Such coordinated or consolidated pretrial proceedings shall be conducted by a judge or judges to whom such actions are assigned by the judicial panel on multidistrict litigation. For this purpose, upon request of the panel, a circuit judge or a district judge may be designated and assigned temporarily for service in the transferee district by the Chief Justice of the United States or the chief judge of the circuit, as may be required, in accordance with the provisions of chapter 13 of this title. With the consent of the transferee district court, such actions may be assigned by the panel to a judge or judges of such district. The judge or judges to whom such actions are assigned, the members of the judicial panel on multidistrict litigation, and other circuit and district judges designated when needed by the panel may

[68] *See FedEx Ground Package Sys., Inc. v. U.S. Judicial Panel on Multidistrict Litig.*, 662 F.3d 887, 891 (7th Cir. 2011).

[69] *See Looper v. Cook Inc.*, 20 F.4th 387, 390 (7th Cir. 2021) (citing scholarship noting that 39% of all open federal civil cases were MDLs).

[70] *See Sullivan v. DB Invs., Inc.*, 667 F.3d 273, 334 (3d Cir. 2011) (Scirica, J., concurring) (citing Thomas E. Willging & Emery G. Lee III, *From Class Actions to Multidistrict Consolidations: Aggregate Mass–Tort Litigation after Ortiz*, 58 U. KAN. L. REV. 775, 801 (2010)).

exercise the powers of a district judge in any district for the purpose of conducting pretrial depositions in such coordinated or consolidated pretrial proceedings.

(c) Proceedings for the transfer of an action under this section may be initiated by—

(i) the judicial panel on multidistrict litigation upon its own initiative, or

(ii) motion filed with the panel by a party in any action in which transfer for coordinated or consolidated pretrial proceedings under this section may be appropriate. A copy of such motion shall be filed in the district court in which the moving party's action is pending.

The panel shall give notice to the parties in all actions in which transfers for coordinated or consolidated pretrial proceedings are contemplated, and such notice shall specify the time and place of any hearing to determine whether such transfer shall be made. Orders of the panel to set a hearing and other orders of the panel issued prior to the order either directing or denying transfer shall be filed in the office of the clerk of the district court in which a transfer hearing is to be or has been held. The panel's order of transfer shall be based upon a record of such hearing at which material evidence may be offered by any party to an action pending in any district that would be affected by the proceedings under this section, and shall be supported by findings of fact and conclusions of law based upon such record. Orders of transfer and such other orders as the panel may make thereafter shall be filed in the office of the clerk of the district court of the transferee district and shall be effective when thus filed. The clerk of the transferee district court shall forthwith transmit a certified copy of the panel's order to transfer to the clerk of the district court from which the action is being transferred. An order denying transfer shall be filed in each district wherein there is a case pending in which the motion for transfer has been made.

(d) The judicial panel on multidistrict litigation shall consist of seven circuit and district judges designated from time to time by the Chief Justice of the United States, no two of whom shall be from the same circuit. The concurrence of four members shall be necessary to any action by the panel.

(e) No proceedings for review of any order of the panel may be permitted except by extraordinary writ pursuant to the provisions of title 28, section 1651, United States Code. Petitions for an extraordinary writ to review an order of the panel to set a transfer hearing and other orders of the panel issued prior to the order either directing or denying transfer shall be filed only in the court of appeals having jurisdiction over the district in which a hearing is to be or has been held. Petitions for an extraordinary writ to review an order to transfer or orders subsequent to transfer shall be filed only in the court of appeals having jurisdiction over the transferee district. There shall be no appeal or review of an order of the panel denying a motion to transfer for consolidated or coordinated proceedings.

(f) The panel may prescribe rules for the conduct of its business not inconsistent with Acts of Congress and the Federal Rules of Civil Procedure.

(g) Nothing in this section shall apply to any action in which the United States is a complainant arising under the antitrust laws. "Antitrust laws" as used herein include those acts referred to in the Act of October 15, 1914, as amended (38 Stat. 730; 15 U.S.C. 12), and also include the Act of June 19, 1936 (49 Stat. 1526; 15 U.S.C. 13, 13a, and 13b) and the Act of September 26, 1914, as added March 21, 1938 (52 Stat. 116, 117; 15 U.S.C. 56); but shall not include section 4A of the Act of October 15, 1914, as added July 7, 1955 (69 Stat. 282; 15 U.S.C. 15a).

(h) Notwithstanding the provisions of section 1404 or subsection (f) of this section, the judicial panel on multidistrict litigation may consolidate and transfer with or without the consent of the parties, for both pretrial purposes and for trial, any action brought under section 4C of the Clayton Act.

(Added Pub.L. 90-296, § 1, Apr. 29, 1968, 82 Stat. 109, and amended Pub.L. 94-435, Title III, § 303, Sept. 30, 1976, 90 Stat. 1396.)

PART VI
APPELLATE PROCEDURE

Table of Sections

Sec.

6.1 Introduction.
6.2 Step One: Appealability.
6.3 Step Two: Time for Taking an Appeal.
6.4 Step Three: Procedure for Taking an Appeal.
6.5 Step Four: Stays Pending Appeal.
6.6 Step Five: The Appeal Process.
6.7 Step Six: Appeals to the United States Supreme Court
6.8 *Federal Rules of Appellate Procedure*.
6.9 Appendix of Forms to the *Federal Rules of Appellate Procedure*.

§ 6.1 Introduction

For many years, the rules and procedures governing federal appeals were contained within the Federal Rules of Civil Procedure. They were removed in 1968 when the new, freestanding *Federal Rules of Appellate Procedure* were promulgated. Although in-depth, rule-by-rule commentary of the federal appellate rules is beyond the scope of this text, the following summary offers a general orientation to certain prominent features of those rules (and to appellate practice generally).

§ 6.2 Step One: Appealability

CORE CONCEPT

Ordinarily, litigants may not immediately appeal each time a district court enters an unfavorable ruling against them. Instead, disgruntled litigants are typically allowed only a single appeal at the end of the case, during which all claims of trial error are bundled together for an omnibus review. But there are exceptions. Litigants must be vigilant in remembering that once a ruling becomes appealable, the time for taking that appeal has come. Delaying can be irremediable.[1]

---

[1] *See Martin v. Sullivan*, 876 F.3d 235, 236 (6th Cir. 2017) ("The losing party in a civil case has a right to appeal, but the right does not last forever," noting "strict timetable").

APPLICATIONS

Who May Appeal

Only the parties (or those who become parties) to a federal lawsuit may appeal a judgment entered in that lawsuit.[2]

Federal Appealability, Overview

The right to a federal appeal is a "creature of statute", and exists only to that extent granted by Congress.[3] Federal appellate jurisdiction is not assumed, nor can it be conferred by waiver or consent,[4] and every appellant bears the burden of showing that it exists.[5] Moreover, federal appellate courts have an independent obligation to confirm the presence of their jurisdiction, even where the parties to the appeal are prepared to concede it.[6] If federal appellate jurisdiction is absent, the appeal must be dismissed.[7] Similarly, if an appellate court determines that the trial court lacked jurisdiction over the dispute, appellate jurisdiction will exist only for the limited purpose of rectifying that error.[8]

The usual federal approach to appealability allows litigants a single appeal following the trial court's entry of its final judgment, at which time all claims of error may be raised together.[9] A contrary approach (one that would permit routine, immediate appeals after any disappointing trial court ruling) would undermine the trial court's special role in managing civil litigation[10] and result in unacceptable obstruction, burdens, delays,

---

[2]*See Marino v. Ortiz*, 484 U.S. 301, 304, 108 S.Ct. 586, 98 L.Ed.2d 629 (1988) (per curiam); *Karcher v. May*, 484 U.S. 72, 77, 108 S.Ct. 388, 98 L.Ed.2d 327 (1987).

[3]*See Abney v. U.S.*, 431 U.S. 651, 656, 97 S.Ct. 2034, 52 L.Ed.2d 651 (1977).

[4]*See New York ex rel. Bryant v. Zimmerman*, 278 U.S. 63, 66, 49 S.Ct. 61, 73 L.Ed. 184 (1928); *Barnett v. Kunkel*, 264 U.S. 16, 19, 44 S.Ct. 254, 68 L.Ed. 539 (1924).

[5]*See C.W. by & through B.W. v. Denver Cty. Sch. Dist. No. 1*, 994 F.3d 1215, 1220 (10th Cir. 2021); *Thibodeaux v. Vamos Oil & Gas Co.*, 487 F.3d 288, 293 (5th Cir. 2007).

[6]*See Bender v. Williamsport Area Sch. Dist.*, 475 U.S. 534, 541, 106 S.Ct. 1326, 89 L.Ed.2d 501 (1986).

[7]*See OFS Fitel, LLC v. Epstein, Becker & Green, P.C.*, 549 F.3d 1344, 1369 (11th Cir. 2008).

[8]*See Bender v. Williamsport Area Sch. Dist.*, 475 U.S. 534, 541, 106 S.Ct. 1326, 89 L.Ed.2d 501 (1986).

[9]*See Microsoft Corp. v. Baker*, 582 U.S. __, 137 S. Ct. 1702, 1712, 198 L. Ed. 2d 132 (2017) (general rule dating from "very foundation of our judicial system"); *Digital Equip. Corp. v. Desktop Direct, Inc.*, 511 U.S. 863, 868, 114 S.Ct. 1992, 128 L.Ed.2d 842 (1994) (single appeal may include claims of trial error from every stage of litigation). *See also Rowland v. S. Health Partners, Inc.*, 4 F.4th 422, 425 (6th Cir. 2021) (finality doctrine typically "establishes a one-case, one-appeal rule").

[10]*See Microsoft Corp. v. Baker*, 582 U.S. __, 137 S. Ct. 1702, 1712, 198 L. Ed. 2d 132 (2017); *Firestone Tire & Rubber Co. v. Risjord*, 449 U.S. 368, 374, 101 S.Ct. 669, 66 L.Ed.2d 571 (1981). *See generally Cobbledick v. U.S.*, 309 U.S. 323, 325, 60 S.Ct. 540, 84 L.Ed. 783 (1940) (judicial administration's "momentum would be arrested by permitting separate reviews of the component elements in a unified cause").

expense, and other inefficiencies.[11] Nonetheless, this usual appeal-at-the-end approach has exceptions as discussed below.

Final Decisions ("Final Orders")

Congress has vested the courts of appeals with jurisdiction to hear appeals from "final decisions" (often called "final orders") of the district courts.[12] A final order is a ruling that "ends the litigation on the merits and leaves nothing for the court to do but execute the judgment."[13] It is, usually, the ruling by which the trial court "disassociates" itself from the case,[14] typically arriving at the completion of the entire case[15] with an entry of a final judgment.[16] This approach supplies litigants with clear guidance. It ensures that litigants know that their time for appealing has come.[17] It also ordinarily limits litigants to a single appeal in most cases.[18]

Nonetheless, the final order rule has been described as "pragmatic" not rigid,[19] and "practical" not "technical."[20] Appealability will not hinge merely on whether the trial court labeled its order as "final."[21] A district court's dismissal of a lawsuit with prejudice is always likely to be final.[22] But a district court's dismissal that is technically denominated as "without prejudice" may still qualify as a final order if, in the particular circumstances, the trial judge is "finished" with the case,[23] imposes certain conditions that legally prejudices the lit-

---

[11]*See Microsoft Corp. v. Baker*, 582 U.S. —, 137 S. Ct. 1702, 1712, 198 L. Ed. 2d 132 (2017); *Bullard v. Blue Hills Bank*, 575 U.S. 496, 501, 135 S.Ct. 1686, 191 L.Ed.2d 621 (2015).

[12]*See* 28 U.S.C.A. § 1291.

[13]*See Van Cauwenberghe v. Biard*, 486 U.S. 517, 521–22, 108 S.Ct. 1945, 100 L.Ed.2d 517 (1988) (quoting *Catlin v. U.S.*, 324 U.S. 229, 233, 65 S.Ct. 631, 89 L.Ed. 911 (1945)). *See generally Behrens v. Pelletier*, 516 U.S. 299, 304, 116 S.Ct. 834, 133 L.Ed.2d 773 (1996) (finality prevents consideration of rulings that remain subject to revision).

[14]*See Bullard v. Blue Hills Bank*, 575 U.S. 496, 501, 135 S.Ct. 1686, 191 L.Ed.2d 621 (2015); *Mohawk Indus., Inc. v. Carpenter*, 558 U.S. 100, 106, 130 S.Ct. 599, 175 L.Ed.2d 458 (2009)

[15]*See Ritzen Grp., Inc. v. Jackson Masonry, LLC*, 589 U.S. —, 140 S. Ct. 582, 586, 205 L. Ed. 2d 419 (2020).

[16]*See Hall v. Hall*, 584 U.S. —, 138 S. Ct. 1118, 1124, 200 L. Ed. 2d 399 (2018); *Mohawk Industries, Inc. v. Carpenter*, 558 U.S. 100, 103, 130 S.Ct. 599, 175 L.Ed.2d 458 (2009).

[17]*See Hall v. Hall*, 584 U.S. —, 138 S. Ct. 1118, 1131, 200 L. Ed. 2d 399 (2018).

[18]*See supra* § 6.2 (**"Federal Appealability, Overview"**).

[19]*See Mohawk Indus., Inc. v. Carpenter*, 558, U.S. 100, 130, S.Ct. 599, 175 L.Ed.2d 458 (2009).

[20]*See Microsoft Corp. v. Baker*, 582 U.S. —, 137 S. Ct. 1702, 1712, 198 L. Ed. 2d 132 (2017); *Gelboim v. Bank of America Corp.*, 574 U.S. 405, 409, 135 S.Ct. 897, 190 L.Ed.2d 789 (2015).

[21]*See Riley v. Kennedy*, 553 U.S. 406, 419-20, 128 S.Ct. 1970, 170 L.Ed.2d 837 (2008); *Sullivan v. Finkelstein*, 496 U.S. 617, 628 n.7, 110 S.Ct. 2658, 110 L.Ed.2d 563 (1990).

[22]*See Carver v. Atwood*, 18 F.4th 494, 496 (5th Cir. 2021); *Card v. Principal Life Ins. Co.*, 17 F.4th 620, 623 (6th Cir. 2021).

[23]*See Corley v. Long-Lewis, Inc.*, 965 F.3d 1222, 1227–31 (11th Cir. 2020); *Hernandez v. Dart*, 814 F.3d 836, 841 (7th Cir. 2016).

igant's ability to proceed in the trial court,[24] or the dismissed party decides not to amend.[25] This "without-prejudice" setting is ripe with nuance and unpredictability.[26] Even less clear is whether a party's own, voluntary, without-prejudice dismissal of portions of a lawsuit can produce the finality needed to appeal an adverse court ruling on other portions[27]—an inquiry that may depend, in part, on whether that voluntary dismissal was acquired before an adverse, partially-dispositive order was entered or after (*i.e.*, done with the goal of manufacturing a finality that would not otherwise exist).[28] Almost all interim ("interlocutory") orders by the trial court (*e.g.*, denials of dispositive motions, discovery motions) are not considered final orders.[29] Once finality arrives, only "judgments, not statements in opinions," are appealable.[30]

Partial Final Orders (Rule 54(b))

Ordinarily, when the district court enters a judgment that disposes of less than all claims or all parties in a lawsuit, that case is not yet final (and appealable) and will not become so until all other claims affecting all other parties are finally resolved.[31] However, the district court may, in the exercise of its discretion, convert such "partial" judgments into immediately

---

[24] *See S.B. v. KinderCare Learning Ctrs., LLC*, 815 F.3d 150, 152–53 (3d Cir. 2016). *See also Sommers v. Bank of Am., N.A.*, 835 F.3d 509, 512 (5th Cir. 2016) (denial of intervention of right is appealable final order).

[25] *See Palakovic v. Wetzel*, 854 F.3d 209, 219 (3d Cir. 2017). *See also Wesco Ins. Co. v. Roderick Linton Belfance, LLP*, 39 F.4th 326, 334 (6th Cir. 2022) (attorney acknowledges intent to dismiss with prejudice).

[26] *See Corley v. Long-Lewis, Inc.*, 965 F.3d 1222, 1228 (11th Cir. 2020) ("Our precedent splinters in multiple directions on whether voluntary dismissals without prejudice are final."). *See also N. Am. Butterfly Ass'n v. Wolf*, 977 F.3d 1244, 1254-56 (D.C. Cir. 2020) (discussing division among Circuits on when dismissal becomes final if trial court grants leave to amend period, and no amendment is filed during that time window); *Zablocki v. Merchants Credit Guide Co.*, 968 F.3d 620, 622-23 (7th Cir. 2020) (same inquiry, finality arrives when repleading window lapses).

[27] *See See also Rowland v. S. Health Partners, Inc.*, 4 F.4th 422, 424-30 (6th Cir. 2021) (noting Third, Fifth, Sixth, Seventh, Eighth, Ninth, Tenth, and Eleventh Circuits agree that subsequent without-prejudice voluntary dismissals usually do not transform partial dismissal/summary judgment orders into appealable final decisions; only Second Circuit disagrees). *See generally Microsoft Corp. v. Baker*, 582 U.S. ___, 137 S. Ct. 1702, 1712–15, 198 L. Ed. 2d 132 (2017) (rejecting "voluntary-dismissal tactic" in class action context).

[28] *See United States v. Eli Lilly & Co., Inc.*, 4 F.4th 255, 261 (5th Cir. 2021) (prior without-prejudice dismissals do not deprive later decision of its finality); *Schoenfeld v. Babbitt*, 168 F.3d 1257, 1265–66 (11th Cir. 1999) (same).

[29] *See Mohawk Indus., Inc. v. Carpenter*, 558 U.S. 100, 108, 130 S. Ct. 599, 175 L. Ed. 2d 458 (2009); *Bing v. Brivo Sys., LLC*, 959 F.3d 605, 610-15 (4th Cir. 2020).

[30] *See Black v. Cutter Labs.*, 351 U.S. 292, 297, 76 S.Ct. 824, 100 L.Ed. 1188 (1956). *See generally Sexual Minorities Uganda v. Lively*, 899 F.3d 24, 29–32 (1st Cir. 2018) (prevailing party who objects to language in court's opinion generally cannot appeal).

[31] *See Rowland v. S. Health Partners, Inc.*, 4 F.4th 422, 426-27 (6th

appealable final orders by (a) finally resolving at least one claim or the rights and liabilities of at least one party, (b) expressly declaring that no just cause exists to delay the appeal from such a ruling, and (c) directing the entry of judgment on the ruling.[32]

Interlocutory Orders

Interlocutory orders are all other interim rulings by the district courts; such rulings do not purport to end the litigation, and further action in the case by the trial court is contemplated.[33] Because they are not "final orders," interlocutory rulings are generally not immediately appealable to the courts of appeals.[34] Instead, review of interlocutory orders must ordinarily wait until the district court enters its final order on the merits of the litigation. Under well-settled appellate tenets, litigants may, in the course of appealing a final order, challenge many of the preceding interlocutory rulings previously entered by the trial court.[35]

Permitted Interlocutory Appeals—Injunctions

Though they may not qualify as "final orders," interlocutory rulings that grant, continue, modify, refuse, or dissolve injunctions, or that refuse to dissolve or modify injunctions, are appealable immediately[36] (provided, of course, the injunction has not already expired by its terms).[37] This creates an exception to the general policy disfavoring piecemeal appeals,[38] and thus is construed strictly[39] and applied narrowly[40] to allow effective challenges to "orders of serious, perhaps irreparable,

---

Cir. 2021); *United States v. Eli Lilly & Co., Inc.*, 4 F.4th 255, 261 (5th Cir. 2021).

[32]*See* Rule 54(b). *See generally supra* Authors' Commentary to Rule 54(b).

[33]*See Liberty Mut. Ins. Co. v. Wetzel*, 424 U.S. 737, 744, 96 S.Ct. 1202, 47 L.Ed.2d 435 (1976) (judgments that only resolve liability issues or leave damages to be assessed are interlocutory).

[34]*See Ashcroft v. Iqbal*, 556 U.S. 662, 671, 129 S. Ct. 1937, 173 L. Ed. 2d 868 (2009) (interlocutory appeals "are the exception, not the rule").

[35]*See Ritzen Grp., Inc. v. Jackson Masonry, LLC*, 589 U.S. __, 140 S. Ct. 582, 586, 205 L. Ed. 2d 419 (2020); *Quackenbush v. Allstate Ins. Co., 517 U.S. 706, 712, 116 S. Ct. 1712, 135 L. Ed. 2d 1 (1996). See generally McLish v. Roff*, 141 U.S. 661, 665-66, 12 S. Ct. 118, 35 L. Ed. 893 (1891) ("From the very foundation of our judicial system the object and policy of the acts of congress . . . have been to save the expense and delays of repeated appeals in the same suit, and to have the whole case and every matter in controversy in it decided in a single appeal").

[36]*See* 28 U.S.C.A. § 1292(a)(1).

[37]*See Ahlman v. Barnes*, 20 F.4th 489, 493 (9th Cir. 2021); *United States v. Sec'y, Fla. Dep't of Corr.*, 778 F.3d 1223, 1228-29 (11th Cir. 2015). *See generally Calderon v. Moore*, 518 U.S. 149, 150, 116 S.Ct. 2066, 135 L.Ed.2d 453 (1996) (intervening event moots appeal if appellate court cannot grant any effectual relief).

[38]*See Gardner v. Westinghouse Broad. Co.*, 437 U.S. 478, 480, 98 S.Ct. 2451, 57 L.Ed.2d 364 (1978).

[39]*See Nwaubani v. Grossman*, 806 F.3d 677, 680 (1st Cir. 2015); *American River Transp Co. v. Ryan*, 579 F.3d 820, 824 (7th Cir. 2009).

[40]*See DM Trans, LLC v. Scott*, 38 F.4th 608, 615 (7th Cir. 2022); *Washington Metropolitan Area Transit Com'n v. Reliable Limousine Serv.*,

consequence."[41] Accordingly, an order that *specifically* grants, denies, or modifies an injunction will fall within this exception and be immediately appealable.[42] An order that has the practical effect of granting, denying, or modifying an injunctive remedy may also be immediately appealable[43] (regardless of how it was labeled or whether the parties even sought "injunctive" relief),[44] but only when it has a serious, possibly irreparable consequence and can be effectively challenged only by immediate appellate review.[45] Ordinary, routine orders by federal judges addressing the conduct or progress of a lawsuit pending before them will not usually be considered "practical" injunctions immediately appealable under this exception.[46] Additionally, an order that "modifies" an injunction is different than "interpreting" one; only the former is immediately appealable.[47] And injunctions issued by a State tribunal prior to the lawsuit's removal to federal court are usually not immediately appealable.[48]

Temporary restraining orders (TROs) are ordinarily not immediately appealable given their brief duration,[49] but if the

---

LLC, 776 F.3d 1, 8-9 (D.C.Cir. 2015).

[41] *See Gardner v. Westinghouse Broad. Co.*, 437 U.S. 478, 480, 98 S. Ct. 2451, 57 L. Ed. 2d 364 (1978) (quoting *Baltimore Contractors v. Bodinger*, 348 U.S. 176, 181, 75 S. Ct. 249, 99 L. Ed. 233 (1955)).

[42] *See Ditucci v. Bowser*, 985 F.3d 804, 808 (10th Cir. 2021); *Nat. Res. Def. Council v. Cty. of Los Angeles*, 840 F.3d 1098, 1101 (9th Cir. 2016).

[43] *See Abbott v. Perez*, 585 U.S. __, 138 S. Ct. 2305, 2319, 201 L. Ed. 2d 714 (2018); *Carson v. American Brands, Inc.*, 450 U.S. 79, 83, 101 S.Ct. 993, 67 L.Ed.2d 59 (1981). *Compare Campaign Legal Ctr. v. United States Dep't of Just.*, 34 F.4th 14, 22 (D.C. Cir. 2022) (FOIA disclosure orders are immediately appealable under § 1292(a)(1)), *with Nat'l Wildlife Fed'n v. Nat'l Marine Fisheries Serv.*, 886 F.3d 803, 824-25 (9th Cir. 2018) (order akin to routine discovery ruling not immediately appealable under § 1292(a)(2)). *But cf. Hawaii v. Trump*, 863 F.3d 1102, 1104 (9th Cir. 2017) (practical effect was merely declaratory, not injunctive).

[44] *See Abbott v. Perez*, 585 U.S. __, 138 S. Ct. 2305, 2319–20, 201 L. Ed. 2d 714 (2018); *Ditucci v. Bowser*, 985 F.3d 804, 808-09 (10th Cir. 2021).

[45] *See Carson v. Am. Brands, Inc.*, 450 U.S. 79, 84, 101 S. Ct. 993, 67 L. Ed. 2d 59 (1981). *See also Ditucci v. Bowser*, 985 F.3d 804, 808-09 (10th Cir. 2021) (qualifies if decree is equitable and compels obedience under threat of contempt)..

[46] *See Gulfstream Aerospace Corp. v. Mayacamas Corp.*, 485 U.S. 271, 279, 108 S. Ct. 1133, 99 L. Ed. 2d 296 (1988). *See also In re Braxton*, 258 F.3d 250, 259 (4th Cir. 2001) (discovery orders not immediately appealable); *Tenkku v. Normandy Bank*, 218 F.3d 926, 927 (8th Cir. 2000) (same).

[47] *See Moore v. Tangipahoa Par. Sch. Bd.*, 864 F.3d 401, 405 (5th Cir. 2017); *In re Tronox Inc.*, 855 F.3d 84, 97-98 (2d Cir. 2017). *See generally Dunlap v. Presidential Advisory Comm'n on Election Integrity*, 944 F.3d 945, 948 (D.C. Cir. 2019) (construing "modifying" narrowly ("lest we 'turn the barrier against piecemeal appeals into Swiss cheese' ") to mean actually changing parties' legal relationship to decree).

[48] *See Schuler v. Adams*, 27 F.4th 1203, 1205-10 (6th Cir. 2022); *Concordia Partners, LLC v. Pick*, 790 F.3d 277, 278–80 (1st Cir. 2015).

[49] *See Calvary Chapel of Bangor v. Mills*, 984 F.3d 21, 27 (1st Cir. 2020); *E. Bay Sanctuary Covenant v. Trump*, 932 F.3d 742, 762 (9th Cir. 2018).

contested order extends beyond the duration authorized for TROs[50] or otherwise has the practical effect of an injunction, an immediate appeal might be proper.[51]

If appellate jurisdiction exists over an injunctive ruling, that jurisdiction may extend to all matters inextricably bound up with that ruling.[52] During such an interlocutory appeal, the district court may be empowered to proceed further with the case.[53]

Permitted Interlocutory Appeals—Receivers

Though they may not qualify as "final orders," interlocutory rulings that appoint receivers[54] or refuse orders to wind up receiverships or take steps to accomplish those purposes (*i.e.*, directing disposals of property) are appealable immediately,[55] although this exception, too, is construed narrowly.[56]

Permitted Interlocutory Appeals—Admiralty

Though they may not qualify as "final orders," interlocutory decrees that determine the rights and liabilities of parties to admiralty cases in which appeals from final decrees are allowed are appealable immediately.[57] This exception encompasses orders that decide the *merits* of admiralty cases—a determination made by assessing financial realities and other practical matters[58]—and is construed narrowly[59] but still in a manner faithful to the statute's plain meaning.[60]

---

[50]*See Sampson v. Murray*, 415 U.S. 61, 86-87, 94 S. Ct. 937, 39 L. Ed. 2d 166 (1974).

[51]*See Hope v. Warden York Cnty. Prison*, 956 F.3d 156, 160-61 (3d Cir. 2020) (when "goes beyond preservation of the status quo," has "substantially and potentially irreversible" effects); *Maryville Baptist Church, Inc. v. Beshear*, 957 F.3d 610, 612 (6th Cir. 2020) ("usually is not always," and explaining inquiry). *See also Calvary Chapel of Bangor v. Mills*, 984 F.3d 21, 27 (1st Cir. 2020) (qualifying for immediate appeal "is a heavy lift").

[52]*Daves v. Dallas Cnty.*, 22 F.4th 522, 528-29 (5th Cir. 2022). *Compare Murata Mach. USA v. Daifuku Co.*, 830 F.3d 1357, 1361 (Fed. Cir. 2016) (permitting appeal), *with Tradesman Int'l, Inc. v. Black*, 724 F.3d 1004, 1010-11 (7th Cir. 2013) (refusing appeal).

[53]*See Free Speech v. Federal Election Com'n*, 720 F.3d 788, 791–92 (10th Cir. 2013); *U.S. v. Price*, 688 F.2d 204, 215 (3d Cir.1982).

[54]*See Hill on Behalf of Republic First Bancorp Inc. v. Cohen*, 40 F.4th 101, 110-11 (3d Cir. 2022) (trial court's labeling of appointee as "custodian" did not affect right of immediate receivership appeal).

[55]*See* 28 U.S.C.A. § 1292(a)(2).

[56]*See United States v. Solco I, LLC*, 962 F.3d 1244, 1250-52 (10th Cir. 2020); *Netsphere, Inc. v. Baron*, 799 F.3d 327, 331–34 (5th Cir. 2015). *Cf. Hewlett-Packard Co. v. Quanta Storage, Inc.*, 961 F.3d 731, 741 (5th Cir. 2020) (no jurisdiction over orders declining to appoint receiver).

[57]*See* 28 U.S.C.A. § 1292(a)(3).

[58]*See Minott v. M/Y BRUNELLO*, 891 F.3d 1277, 1281–82 (11th Cir. 2018); *Barnes v. Sea Hawaii Rafting, LLC*, 889 F.3d 517, 528–59 (9th Cir. 2018).

[59]*See Nat'l Shipping Co. of Saudi Arabia v. Valero Mktg. & Supply Co.*, 963 F.3d 479, 482 (5th Cir. 2020).

[60]*See In re Aramark Sports & Entm't Servs., LLC*, 831 F.3d 1264, 1274–78 (10th Cir. 2016). *See also Williamson v. Recovery Ltd. P'ship*, 731 F.3d 608, 619 (6th Cir. 2013) (dis-

Discretionary Interlocutory Appeals

The district court may, in the exercise of its discretion,[61] choose to certify certain non-final, interlocutory orders as eligible for immediate appellate review.[62] Such certification by the district court does not require the court of appeals to hear the immediate appeal; rather, the courts of appeals may refuse to do so[63] (and for almost any reason, including docket congestion).[64]

Certification by the district judge is not routinely granted ("hen's teeth rare"[65]), and is not intended for ordinary error correction,[66] but instead is reserved for "exceptional" cases.[67] Liberally granting such certifications is considered "bad policy," as it undermines the appropriate division of responsibility between federal trial and appellate courts.[68] Thus, the procedure exists to allow prompt resolution of "knotty" legal issues and to facilitate appellate review on "ephemeral" questions of law that might otherwise disappear as the record completes and finalizes.[69]

Thus, litigants seeking certification bear a heavy burden.[70]

---

cussing circuit split on "cases"/"claims" distinction).

[61] *See Swint v. Chambers County Comm'n*, 514 U.S. 35, 47, 115 S.Ct. 1203, 131 L.Ed.2d 60 (1995) (Congress conferred upon district courts "first line discretion to allow interlocutory appeals"). *See also In re Trump*, 928 F.3d 360, 369 (4th Cir. 2019) (statute directs that district courts "shall" certify for immediate appeal when criteria are met, but discretion lies "in the open-ended terms used to define the statutory criteria"). *But see In re Trump*, 928 F.3d 360, 369 (4th Cir. 2019) (discretion may be abused if premised on "whim" rather than "sound legal principles").

[62] *See* 28 U.S.C.A. § 1292(b).

[63] *See* 28 U.S.C.A. § 1292(b). *See also Van Cauwenberghe v. Biard*, 486 U.S. 517, 530, 108 S.Ct. 1945, 100 L.Ed.2d 517 (1988); *Coopers & Lybrand v. Livesay*, 437 U.S. 463, 475, 98 S.Ct. 2454, 57 L.Ed.2d 351 (1978).

[64] *See Coopers & Lybrand v. Livesay*, 437 U.S. 463, 475, 98 S.Ct. 2454, 57 L.Ed.2d 351 (1978). *See generally ICTSI Oregon, Inc. v. Int'l Longshore & Warehouse Union*, 22 F.4th 1125, 1131 (9th Cir. 2022) (akin to certiorari-granting decisions); *Drummond Co., Inc. v. Conrad & Scherer, LLP*, 885 F.3d 1324, 1336 (11th Cir. 2018) (listing discretion criteria).

[65] *See Camacho v. Puerto Rico Ports Auth.*, 369 F.3d 570, 573 (1st Cir. 2004). *See also United States ex rel. Michaels v. Agape Senior Cmty., Inc.*, 848 F.3d 330, 340 (4th Cir. 2017) (should be used "sparingly").

[66] *See Weber v. U.S.*, 484 F.3d 154, 159 n.3 (2d Cir. 2007).

[67] *See Caterpillar Inc. v. Lewis*, 519 U.S. 61, 74, 117 S.Ct. 467, 136 L.Ed.2d 437 (1996) (Congress's "design" retains "a firm final judgment rule," reserving interlocutory review for only "exceptional" cases); *Coopers & Lybrand v. Livesay*, 437 U.S. 463, 475, 98 S. Ct. 2454, 57 L. Ed. 2d 351 (1978) (only "exceptional circumstances justify a departure from the basic policy of postponing appellate review until after the entry of a final judgment").

[68] *See Moorman v. UnumProvident Corp.*, 464 F.3d 1260, 1272 (11th Cir. 2006).

[69] *See Weber v. United States*, 484 F.3d 154, 159 (2d Cir. 2007).

[70] *See OFS Fitel, LLC v. Epstein, Becker & Green, P.C.*, 549 F.3d 1344, 1358-59 (11th Cir. 2008); *Union County v. Piper Jaffray & Co.*, 525 F.3d 643, 646 (8th Cir. 2008).

They must persuade the district judge to state in writing:[71]

(1) That the order in question involves a **"controlling question of law"** (which generally means a question of "pure law", which can be resolved "quickly and cleanly" without laboring over the record[72]—such as the meaning of a regulatory, statutory, or constitutional provision or common law doctrine,[73] the resolution of which is *likely* (although not necessarily certain) to affect the future course of the litigation[74]); and

(2) There is **"substantial ground for difference of opinion"** on the legal issue the order resolves (which generally means either that there is conflicting legal authority on the disputed issue or that the issue is a particularly difficult or uncertain one of first impression);[75] and

(3) An immediate appeal from the interlocutory order may **"materially advance the ultimate termination of the litigation"** (which generally means that immediate appeal may avoid expensive and protracted litigation,[76] not that it must have a final, dispositive effect[77]).

All three criteria are required; failing to satisfy any one denies the district court the ability to grant a Rule 1292(b) certification.[78] If certification is granted, the court should specify what question of law it finds to be "controlling"—al-

---

[71] *See Metrou v. M.A. Mortenson Co.*, 781 F.3d 357, 359 (7th Cir. 2015); *Coastal Agricultural Supply, Inc. v. JP Morgan Chase Bank, N.A.*, 759 F.3d 498, 508 (5th Cir. 2014).

[72] *See ICTSI Oregon, Inc. v. Int'l Longshore & Warehouse Union*, 22 F.4th 1125, 1130 (9th Cir. 2022); *Mamani v. Berzain*, 825 F.3d 1304, 1312–13 (11th Cir. 2016).

[73] *See Ahrenholz v. Board of Trustees of Univ. of Ill.*, 219 F.3d 674, 676 (7th Cir.2000).

[74] *See Sokaogon Gaming Enter. Corp. v. Tushie-Montgomery Assocs., Inc.*, 86 F.3d 656, 659 (7th Cir.1996) ("controlling" if issue's resolution is "quite likely" to affect further course of litigation); *In re Baker & Getty Fin. Servs., Inc.*, 954 F.2d 1169, 1172 n. 8 (6th Cir.1992) ("controlling" if issue's resolution on appeal could materially affect outcome in trial court).

[75] *See In re Trump*, 874 F.3d 948, 952 (6th Cir. 2017) (shown if reasonable jurists might disagree); *McFarlin v. Conseco Servs., LLC*, 381 F.3d 1251, 1258 (11th Cir. 2004) (not shown when appeals court is in "complete and unequivocal" agreement with district court); *In re Baker & Getty Fin. Servs., Inc.*, 954 F.2d 1169, 1172 (6th Cir.1992) (shown by split among Circuits on issue); *Klinghoffer v. S.N.C. Achille Lauro Ed Altri-Gestione Motonave Achille Lauro in Amministrazione Straordinaria*, 921 F.2d 21, 25 (2d Cir.1990) (shown by difficult issues of first impression).

[76] *See ICTSI Oregon, Inc. v. Int'l Longshore & Warehouse Union*, 22 F.4th 1125, 1131 (9th Cir. 2022); *McFarlin v. Conseco Servs., LLC*, 381 F.3d 1251, 1259 (11th Cir. 2004). *See also White v. Nix*, 43 F.3d 374, 378–79 (8th Cir.1994) (when case will proceed in substantially similar manner regardless of decision on appeal, review will not "materially advance" termination of litigation).

[77] *See Sterk v. Redbox Automated Retail, LLC*, 672 F.3d 535, 536–37 (7th Cir. 2012); *Reese v. BP Exploration (Alaska) Inc.*, 643 F.3d 681, 688 (9th Cir. 2011).

[78] *See Couch v. Telescope Inc.*, 611 F.3d 629, 633 (9th Cir. 2010); *Estate of Storm v. Northwest Iowa Hosp. Corp.*, 548 F.3d 686, 687-88 (8th Cir. 2008).

though a failure to do so is not necessarily dispositive.[79] Certification is jurisdictional; if certification is not granted, the court of appeals lacks authority to hear the appeal under Section 1292(b)[80] (and the district court's refusal to certify is not, itself, usually reviewable on appeal).[81] If certification is granted, but then revoked by the trial judge before the court of appeals acquires jurisdiction, there likewise is no authority to hear the appeal.[82]

There is no express time limit for asking the trial judge to grant a Section 1292(b) certification, although unreasonably dilatory requests may be denied by the trial judge or refused by the courts of appeals.[83] If granted by the district judge, the party may petition the court of appeals within 10 days thereafter for permission to immediately appeal the certified question.[84] (An untimely petition defeats jurisdiction,[85] though courts are divided on whether a district judge can rescue a belated petition by issuing a second Section 1292(b) certification.[86]) The court of appeals may then grant immediate review, but only after assuring itself that the three certification criteria are satisfied.[87]

If granted, the scope of appellate review is then limited to the certified order, and may not reach beyond that order to consider other, uncertified rulings by the trial judge.[88] But the court of appeals may, in its discretion,[89] address any issue that

[79] *See McFarlin v. Conseco Servs., LLC*, 381 F.3d 1251, 1264 (11th Cir. 2004) ("If the district court is unsure about which of the questions, if any, that are answered by its order qualify for certification under § 1292(b), it should not certify the order for review. If convinced that a particular question does qualify, the district court should tell us which question it is.").

[80] *See In re Ford Motor Co., Bridgestone/Firestone North American Tire, LLC*, 344 F.3d 648, 654–55 (7th Cir. 2003).

[81] *See Agudas Chasidei Chabad of United States v. Russian Fed'n*, 19 F.4th 472, 476-77 (D.C. Cir. 2021) (no appellate review contemplated); *In re Ford Motor Co., Bridgestone/Firestone North American Tire, LLC*, 344 F.3d 648, 654-55 (7th Cir. 2003) (mandamus usually not proper).

[82] *See Kenosha Unified Sch. Dist. No. 1 Bd. of Educ. v. Whitaker*, 841 F.3d 730, 732 (7th Cir. 2016).

[83] *See Richardson Elecs., Ltd. v. Panache Broad. of Pa., Inc.*, 202 F.3d 957, 958 (7th Cir.2000). *See also Ahrenholz v. Board of Trustees of Univ. of Ill.*, 219 F.3d 674, 675–76 (7th Cir.2000) (petitions for certification must be filed in district court within a "reasonable time" after entry of contested order).

[84] *See* 28 U.S.C.A. § 1292(b); Fed. R. App. P. 5.

[85] *See Kennedy v. Bowser*, 843 F.3d 529, 531-36 (D.C. Cir. 2016). *See also Mei Xing Yu v. Hasaki Rest., Inc.*, 874 F.3d 94, 96–97 (2d Cir. 2017) (given circumstances, treating timely notice of appeal as petition).

[86] *See Strange On Behalf of Strange v. Islamic Republic of Iran, Interest Section*, 964 F.3d 1190, 1196–1203 (D.C. Cir. 2020) (surveying Circuit split; ruling against clock re-start).

[87] *See ICTSI Oregon, Inc. v. Int'l Longshore & Warehouse Union*, 22 F.4th 1125, 1131 (9th Cir. 2022).

[88] *See Yamaha Motor Corp., U.S.A. v. Calhoun*, 516 U.S. 199, 205, 116 S.Ct. 619, 133 L.Ed.2d 578 (1996).

[89] *See United States ex rel. Simoneaux v. E.I. duPont de Nemours*

is "fairly included" within the certified order itself;[90] review is limited by the order that is certified,[91] not by the precise question found to be controlling.[92] Other issues that are "inextricably intertwined" with the certified issue may be reached as well.[93]

Collateral Order Doctrine

In addition to Rule-based and statutory exceptions to the "final order" limitation, the Supreme Court has developed a common law "collateral order" doctrine, which recognizes that certain legal rulings—collateral to the litigation's underlying merits—may nevertheless be deemed "final" and eligible for immediate appellate review. To qualify under the collateral order doctrine, the district court's order must:

(1) Conclusively resolve

(2) An "important question" that is separate from the underlying merits

(3) Which would be effectively unreviewable if the appeal had to await entry of the final judgment.[94]

A failure to satisfy even one of these three requirements defeats the use of the collateral order doctrine.[95]

The collateral order exception represents a narrow, common law construction of the final order doctrine.[96] It is applied stringently and is never permitted to "swallow" the general prohibition against piecemeal appeals.[97] Although collateral orders typically involve a claimed right to "avoid" trial (a right which would be lost and effectively unappealable later), the Supreme Court has rejected the notion that this characteristic

---

& Co., 843 F.3d 1033, 1041 (5th Cir. 2016).

[90]*See In re Rail Freight Fuel Surcharge Antitrust Litig.—MDL No. 1869*, 34 F.4th 1, 8 (D.C. Cir. 2022). *See also ICTSI Oregon, Inc. v. Int'l Longshore & Warehouse Union*, 22 F.4th 1125, 1132-33 (9th Cir. 2022) (encompasses issues "material to" and "inextricably tied to" certified order); *Kahl v. Bureau of Nat'l Affs., Inc.*, 856 F.3d 106, 114 n.1 (D.C. Cir. 2017) (issues "logically interwoven" with certified order).

[91]*See Yamaha Motor Corp., U.S.A. v. Calhoun*, 516 U.S. 199, 205, 116 S.Ct. 619, 133 L.Ed.2d 578 (1996). *But cf. Little v. Louisville Gas & Elec. Co.*, 805 F.3d 695, 698–701 (6th Cir. 2015) ("order" means court's specific command, not entirely of the document explaining that command).

[92]*See Yamaha Motor Corp. v. Calhoun*, 516 U.S. 199, 205, 116 S.Ct. 619, 133 L.Ed.2d 578 (1996) ("it is the order that is appealable, and not the controlling question identified by the district court").

[93]*See Murray v. Metropolitan Life Ins. Co.*, 583 F.3d 173, 176 (2d Cir. 2009).

[94]*See Will v. Hallock*, 546 U.S. 345, 349, 126 S.Ct. 952, 163 L.Ed.2d 836 (2006); *Coopers & Lybrand v. Livesay*, 437 U.S. 463, 468–69, 98 S.Ct. 2454, 57 L.Ed.2d 351 (1978); *Cohen v. Beneficial Indus. Loan Corp.*, 337 U.S. 541, 546, 69 S.Ct. 1221, 93 L.Ed. 1528 (1949).

[95]*See Gulfstream Aerospace Corp. v. Mayacamas Corp.*, 485 U.S. 271, 276, 108 S.Ct. 1133, 99 L.Ed.2d 296 (1988).

[96]*See Houston Cmty. Hosp. v. Blue Cross & Blue Shield of Tex., Inc.*, 481 F.3d 265, 268 (5th Cir. 2007).

[97]*See Mohawk Indus., Inc. v. Carpenter*, 558 U.S. 100, 106, 130 S.Ct. 599, 175 L.Ed.2d 458 (2009); *Digital Equip. Corp. v. Desktop Direct, Inc.*, 511 U.S. 863, 868, 114 S.Ct. 1992, 128 L.Ed.2d 842 (1994).

alone justifies collateral order treatment.[98] Instead, the Court has ruled that true collateral orders are those that would, if not immediately reviewed, imperil "a substantial public interest" or some high order value.[99] Examples of rulings that may qualify include denials of litigation immunity,[100] of leave to litigate anonymously,[101] and to judicially seal[102] or unseal[103] documents.

Other Exceptions

Various other exceptions to the general final order principle exist,[104] though an exhaustive discussion of those nuances are beyond the scope of this text.

Additional Research References

C.J.S. Federal Courts §§ 290(1) to 291(5) et seq.
West's Key Number Digest, Federal Courts ⚷551 to 600

§ 6.3 Step Two: Time for Taking an Appeal

CORE CONCEPT

In civil cases, an appeal generally must be taken within 30 days after the entry of the disputed judgment or order, although if the United States is a party this period is extended to 60 days. Except for a few narrow exceptions, this time period may not be waived or extended. A failure to file a timely appeal will forfeit that party's right of appeal.

---

[98] *See Will v. Hallock*, 546 U.S. 345, 350–51, 126 S.Ct. 952, 958, 163 L.Ed.2d 836 (2006).

[99] *See Mohawk Indus., Inc. v. Carpenter*, 558 U.S. 100, 106-10, 130 S.Ct. 599, 175 L.Ed.2d 458 (2009) (appealing denial of attorney-client privilege assertion does not qualify); *Will v. Hallock*, 546 U.S. 345, 352, 126 S.Ct. 952, 163 L.Ed.2d 836 (2006) (offering, as examples, need to respect separation of powers, to preserve efficiency of government and initiative of officials, to respect State's dignitary interests, and to mitigate government's advantage over individual).

[100] *See P.R. Aqueduct & Sewer Auth. v. Metcalf & Eddy, Inc.*, 506 U.S. 139, 147, 113 S.Ct. 684, 121 L.Ed.2d 605 (1993) (sovereign immunity); *Mitchell v. Forsyth*, 472 U.S. 511, 526-27, 105 S.Ct. 2806, 86 L.Ed.2d 411 (1985) (absolute and qualified immunity).

[101] *See Doe v. Coll. of New Jersey*, 997 F.3d 489, 493-94 (3d Cir. 2021); *Doe v. Vill. of Deerfield*, 819 F.3d 372, 376 (7th Cir. 2016).

[102] *See Ctr. for Auto Safety v. Chrysler Grp., LLC*, 809 F.3d 1092, 1096 (9th Cir. 2016).

[103] *See DePuy Synthes Prod., Inc. v. Veterinary Orthopedic Implants, Inc.*, 990 F.3d 1364, 1368-69 (Fed. Cir. 2021).

[104] *See, e.g.*, Rule 23(f) (orders granting or denying class certification); *Cheney v. U.S. Dist. Court for D.C.*, 542 U.S. 367, 380-83, 124 S. Ct. 2576, 159 L. Ed. 2d 459 (2004) (mandamus, as permitted by 28 U.S.C.A § 1651(a)); *Forgay v. Conrad*, 47 U.S. (6 How.) 201, 201, 12 L.Ed. 404 (1848) (order directing delivery of property).

APPLICATIONS

Appeal Time is Mandatory and Jurisdictional

The applicable time periods for taking an appeal are mandatory and jurisdictional.[1] They apply to both existing parties and prospective intervenors.[2] They cannot be waived.[3] They also may not be extended, absent the few narrow exceptions discussed below.

Appeal Time When United States Is a Party

When the United States or a federal officer, employee, or agency is a party to the litigation, the parties have 60 days after the entry of the disputed judgment or order in which to take an appeal.[4] This 60-day period applies to current and former federal officers and employees, and in both official-capacity lawsuits and those individual-capacity lawsuits that concern behavior that occurred in connection with that person's duties performed on behalf of the United States.[5] The extended 60-day period applies to all parties in the case—the federal parties as well as all others.[6] However, the federal entity must be an actual party for this 60-day period to apply.[7]

Appeal Time When United States Is *Not* a Party

In all other cases, the parties have 30 days after the entry of the disputed judgment or order in which to take an appeal.[8]

When Opponent Appeals

Once one party takes an appeal, all other parties to the litigation have at least 14 days thereafter in which to take their own appeals.[9] The parties receive the benefit of this 14-day "extension" period even if the original notice of appeal is defective or otherwise is dismissed.[10] But that benefit only follows from an appeal by *another* party (and cannot be used to

---

[1] *See Bowles v. Russell*, 551 U.S. 205, 214, 127 S.Ct. 2360, 168 L.Ed.2d 96 (2007); *Browder v. Director, Dep't of Corrections*, 434 U.S. 257, 98 S.Ct. 556, 54 L.Ed.2d 521 (1978).

[2] *See Evans v. Synopsys, Inc.*, 34 F.4th 762, 769-70 (9th Cir. 2022).

[3] *See Bowles v. Russell*, 551 U.S. 205, 214, 127 S.Ct. 2360, 168 L.Ed.2d 96 (2007).

[4] *See* 28 U.S.C.A. § 2107(b); Fed. R. App. P. 4(a)(1)(A).

[5] *See* 28 U.S.C.A. § 2107(b)(4); Fed. R. App. P. 4(a)(1)(B)(iv).

[6] *See Himmelreich v. Fed. Bureau of Prisons*, 5 F.4th 653, 665 (6th Cir. 2021); *United States v. Conner*, 907 F.3d 316, 320-22 (5th Cir. 2018).

[7] *See U.S. ex rel. Eisenstein v. City of New York*, 556 U.S. 928, 931, 129 S.Ct. 2230, 173 L.Ed.2d 1255 (2009) (although aware of lawsuits, United States is not a party (and 60-day period does not apply) unless it actually intervenes).

[8] *See* 28 U.S.C.A. § 2107(a); Fed. R. App. P. 4(a)(1)(B).

[9] Fed. R. App. P. 4(a)(3) (party may file notice of appeal within 14 days after first notice of appeal was filed or within 30/60 day period prescribed in Rule 4(a), whichever is longer).

[10] *See In re Julien Co.*, 146 F.3d 420, 423 (6th Cir.1998) (applying 14-day extension rule where first appeal was dismissed for lack of standing).

bootstrap a second, corrective appeal by the same party).[11] Many courts, guided by recent U.S. Supreme Court precedent, have now ruled that this 14-day time limit, though mandatory, is not jurisdictional and may be forfeited if no objection to untimeliness is made.[12]

Appeal Time Begins To Run From Date Of "Entry"

For purposes of timeliness on appeal, the appeal period begins to run when the order is "entered" on the docket (and not when the court issues,[13] or the parties or their attorneys receive,[14] a copy). When the "separate document" requirement of Rule 58 applies, the time to appeal does not begin to run until the "separate document" prerequisite is met or the 150-day period expires[15] (although parties need not wait that long to file),[16] whichever comes first.

- *Interlocutory Order Caution:* The appeal times apply not just to appeals from final judgments, but also to appeals from appealable interlocutory orders.[17] Thus, when an appealable interlocutory order is entered—such as an injunction,[18] a Rule 54(b) partial final judgment,[19] a denial of intervention as of right,[20] or a ruling qualifying under the collateral order doctrine[21]—the relevant appeal time begins to run from the entry of that order.

Computing Time For Taking Appeal

The period within which an appeal must be taken is calculated according to the counting method set in the federal appel-

[11] *See Cruz v. Int'l Collection Corp.*, 673 F.3d 991, 1002 (9th Cir. 2012).

[12] *See, e.g., Georgia-Pac. Consumer Prod. LP v. NCR Corp.*, 40 F.4th 481, 485 (6th Cir. 2022); *Rubinstein v. Yehuda*, 38 F.4th 982, 999-1000 (11th Cir. 2022); *In re IPR Licensing, Inc.*, 942 F.3d 1363, 1370-72 (Fed. Cir. 2019). *See also Mathias v. Superintendent Frackville SCI*, 876 F.3d 462, 470-73 (3d Cir. 2017) (in deciding whether to excuse untimely-filed cross-appeal, court considers: "prejudice, merits, willfulness, and extraordinary circumstance").

[13] *See* Fed. R. App. P. 4(a)(7). *See also Lemos v. Holder*, 636 F.3d 365, 367 (7th Cir. 2011).

[14] *See Wheat v. Pfizer, Inc.*, 31 F.3d 340, 342 (5th Cir.1994).

[15] *See* Fed. R. App. P. 4(a)(7)(A). *See also* Rule 58. *See generally supra* Authors' Commentary to Rule 58.

[16] *See Shalala v. Schaefer*, 509 U.S. 292, 303, 113 S.Ct. 2625, 125 L.Ed.2d 239 (1993); *Resh v. China Agritech, Inc.*, 857 F.3d 994, 1000 (9th Cir. 2017).

[17] *See Mondis Tech. Ltd. v. LG Elecs. Inc.*, 6 F.4th 1379, 1384 (Fed. Cir. 2021).

[18] *See Sherron v. Jackson*, 323 Fed. Appx. 220, 221-22 (4th Cir. 2009) (appeal from entry of preliminary injunction dismissed because appeal was not filed within 30 days of its entry).

[19] *See Kolawole v. Sellers*, 863 F.3d 1361, 1367 (11th Cir. 2017) (appeal period begins to run when Rule 54(b) judgment is entered).

[20] *See N. Carolina State Conf. of NAACP v. Berger*, 999 F.3d 915, 923-24 (4th Cir. 2021) (if no appeal is taken within 30 days, would-be intervenor-as-of-right left without appellate review).

[21] *See Weimer v. Cty. of Fayette*, 972 F.3d 177, 184 (3d Cir. 2020) (interlocutory order appealable under collateral order doctrine must be appealed within 30 days of entry).

late rules.[22] Those rules apply unless a different method for computing time is specified.[23] In counting periods stated in units of time measured in days or longer (e.g., days, months, or years), the day that triggers the period is excluded and then every other day is included. If the period ends on a weekend or a legal holiday, the period is extended to the end of the next day that is not a weekend or legal holiday.[24] Unless otherwise specified, a day "ends" for electronic filing at midnight in the time zone of the court's principal office, and for most other filings when the clerk's office is scheduled to close.[25] Also now expressly addressed are time periods set in hours,[26] as well as the proper adjustments for federal and State holidays[27] and courthouse inaccessibility.[28]

- *Electronic Filing Caution:* Electronic filings might not be effective instantly; some courts hold that electronic filings are not complete (nor an appeal deemed "filed") until certain confirming events first occur.[29]

Extensions – By Filing Post-Trial Motions

The timely filing of the following types of post-trial motions will suspend the time for taking an appeal because their very filing causes an otherwise final order of the district court to lose its finality:[30]

- Motions for judgment as a matter of law, under Federal Rule of Civil Procedure 50(b);
- Motions to alter or supplement findings of fact, under Federal Rule of Civil Procedure 52(b);
- Motions for attorney's fees, under Federal Rule of Civil Procedure 54(d), but only if the district court extends the time for appeal in accordance with Federal Rule of Civil Procedure 58;
- Motions to alter or amend the judgment, under Federal Rule of Civil Procedure 59;
- Motions for a new trial, under Federal Rule of Civil Procedure 59; and
- Motions for relief from a judgment or order, under Federal Rule of Civil Procedure 60, but only if such mo-

---

[22]*See* Fed. R. App. P. 26(a).

[23]*See* Fed. R. App. P. 26(a).

[24]*See* Fed. R. App. P. 26(a)(1).

[25]*See* Fed. R. App. P. 26(a)(4).

[26]*See* Fed. R. App. P. 26(a)(2).

[27]*See* Fed. R. App. P. 26(a)(6).

[28]*See* Fed. R. App. P. 26(a)(3). *See generally Chao Lin v. U.S. Atty. Gen.*, 677 F.3d 1043, 1044–46 (11th Cir. 2012) (clerk's office not inaccessible when inclement weather delayed opening until 10:30 a.m., and FedEx delivered appellate petition next day).

[29]*See Sudduth v. Texas Health & Human Servs. Comm'n*, 830 F.3d 175, 177–79 (5th Cir. 2016) (not "filed" until notice is issued to user); *Franklin v. McHugh*, 804 F.3d 627, 630-32 (2d Cir. 2015) (not "filed" until last screen in filing program appears).

[30]*See* Fed. R. App. P. 4(a)(4)(A). *See generally Banister v. Davis*, 590 U.S. __, 140 S. Ct. 1698, 1703, 207 L. Ed. 2d 58 (2020); *Nutraceutical Corp. v. Lambert*, __ U.S. __, 139 S. Ct. 710, 717, 203 L. Ed. 2d 43 (2019).

tion is served within 28 days after entry of judgment.

These motions need not be successful[31] (or, perhaps, even rule-compliant[32]) to extend the appeal period. But the motions must be filed timely; an untimely filed post-trial motion will *not* suspend the appeal time[33] (nor may a court manufacture timeliness for parties by vacating a final judgment already entered so as to provide them with a new 28-day filing window).[34] Nonetheless, because post-trial timeliness is not jurisdictional, the district court may still hear an untimely post-trial motion if the non-moving party waives its timeliness objection, though doing so carries an important consequence: untimely-filed post-trial motions remain untimely for purposes of federal appeals and, thus, have no suspending effect on the time for taking an appeal (that time period *is* jurisdictional).[35] Thus, if the district court grants an untimely post-trial motion, the aggrieved party could receive meaningful relief, but if the court denies that motion, the aggrieved party's time for taking an appeal will almost certainly be already lost.[36]

Once the district court grants or denies the last still-pending, timely post-trial motion,[37] the original judgment's finality is restored and the appeals clock begins to tick[38] (assuming, of course, that the district judge's ruling results in a final order).[39]

Triggering the Appeals Clock After Post-Trial Motions

The courts of appeals are divided on whether the district court must *expressly* rule on all pending post-trial motions before the appeal clock begins ticking. The majority rule holds that the appeal time remains suspended until the trial court explicitly grants or denies the pending post-trial motions.[40] The minority view holds that the appeal period can begin to run as

---

[31] *See Stevens v. Jiffy Lube Int'l, Inc.*, 911 F.3d 1249, 1251 (9th Cir. 2018); *Urso v. U.S.*, 72 F.3d 59, 61 (7th Cir.1995).

[32] *See Al Qarqani v. Saudi Arabian Oil Co.*, 19 F.4th 794, 799-800 (5th Cir. 2021); *Ruiz v. Wing*, 991 F.3d 1130, 1138-39 (11th Cir. 2021); *Lipman v. Budish*, 974 F.3d 726, 738-40 (6th Cir. 2020).

[33] *See Ruiz v. Wing*, 991 F.3d 1130, 1137 (11th Cir. 2021); *Hanson v. Shubert*, 968 F.3d 1014, 1017-18 (9th Cir. 2020).

[34] *See Klayman v. Jud. Watch, Inc.*, 6 F.4th 1301, 1310 n.2 (D.C. Cir. 2021).

[35] *See* Fed. R. App. P. 4(a)(4)(A). *See also id.* advisory committee note (2016) (appeal time not re-started by untimely motion, even if district court had extended the due date or disposed of motion without explicit reliance on untimeliness, or if opponent consents or fails to object). Previously, the majority view among the courts of appeals had migrated towards the same conclusion. *Compare, e.g., Lizardo v. United States*, 619 F.3d 273, 275-80 (3d Cir. 2010) (majority: appeal forfeited), *with Nat'l Ecological Found. v. Alexander*, 496 F.3d 466, 476 (6th Cir. 2007) (minority: appeal preserved).

[36] *See, e.g., supra* Authors' Commentary to Rule 59(e) (**"No Extensions"**).

[37] *See* Fed. R. App. P. 4(a)(4)(A). *See also Klayman v. Jud. Watch, Inc.*, 6 F.4th 1301, 1310 (D.C. Cir. 2021).

[38] *See* Fed. R. App. P. 4(a)(4)(A). *See generally Banister v. Davis*, 590 U.S. __, 140 S. Ct. 1698, 1703, 207 L. Ed. 2d 58 (2020).

[39] *See Escribano v. Travis Cty.*, 947 F.3d 265, 269–70 (5th Cir. 2020).

[40] *See Havird Oil Co. v. Marathon Oil Co.*, 149 F.3d 283, 288 (4th Cir.1998)

soon as the district court enters the judgment (interpreting such entry as an implicit denial of the post-trial motions).[41]

Successive Post-Trial Motions

Most courts of appeals have ruled that after the time for appeal has been *once* extended by the filing of a tolling post-trial motion, the appeal period can not be suspended *again* by the filing of a *subsequent* post-trial motion.[42]

Abandoned Post-Trial Motions

If a party files timely post-trial motions, but then abandons them, the filing of those motions can be ignored; if the appeal period lapsed while those now-withdrawn motions were pending, appellate jurisdiction will likely be deemed lost.[43]

Extensions — By District Court (Neglect or Good Cause)

Upon a showing of either excusable neglect or good cause, the district court may briefly extend the time for appeal.[44] To obtain such an extension, the movant *must* seek the extension within the original appeal period itself or within 30 days after the original appeal period expires.[45] Non-party prospective intervenors may also move for an extension.[46] The district court may only extend the time for appeal for 30 days after the original appeal period expires, or for 14 days after the order granting the motion for extension is granted, whichever is later.[47] (These 30-day/14-day extension limits are mandatory but non-jurisdictional, and may be forfeited or waived.[48]) To request such an extension, an actual motion is required (merely filing a notice of appeal is not enough).[49] Motions filed before the appeal time expires may be made *ex parte* (unless the court directs otherwise); motions filed after the appeal time expires must be

---

(district court must explicitly dispose of all outstanding post-trial motions before appeal period resumes).

[41]*See Dunn v. Truck World, Inc.*, 929 F.2d 311, 313 (7th Cir.1991) (entry of judgment is implicitly order denying post-trial motion).

[42]*See Krivak v. Home Depot U.S.A., Inc.*, 2 F.4th 601, 605 (7th Cir. 2021); *Benson v. St. Joseph Reg'l Health Ctr.*, 575 F.3d 542, 546–57 (5th Cir. 2009).

[43]*See Vanderwerf v. SmithKline Beecham Corp.*, 603 F.3d 842, 845–46 (10th Cir.2010).

[44]*See* Fed. R. App. P. 4(a)(5). *See also* 28 U.S.C.A. § 2107(c).

[45]*See* Fed.R.App.P. 4(a)(5). *See also Cohen v. Empire Blue Cross & Blue Shield*, 142 F.3d 116, 118 (2d Cir.1998) (district court lacks jurisdiction to grant extension request not filed within 30-day period).

[46]*See Evans v. Synopsys, Inc.*, 34 F.4th 762, 772 (9th Cir. 2022); *CE Design, Ltd. v. Cy's Crab House N., Inc.*, 731 F.3d 725, 728–29 (7th Cir. 2013).

[47]Fed.R.App.P. 4(a)(5)(C). This 14-day period became effective in 2009; previously, the period was 10-days.

[48]*See Hamer v. Neighborhood Hous. Servs. of Chicago*, 583 U.S. __, 138 S. Ct. 13, 19-22, 199 L. Ed. 2d 249 (2017) (Congress's statute, 28 U.S.C.A. § 2107(c), permits excusable neglect/ good cause extensions, but imposes no outside cap; only non-Congressional Fed. R. App. P. 4(a)(5) sets those).

[49]*See Evans v. Synopsys, Inc.*, 34 F.4th 762, 771 & 773-75 (9th Cir. 2022); *Martin v. Sullivan*, 876 F.3d 235, 236–37 (6th Cir. 2017). *But cf. Young v. Kenney*, 949 F.3d 995, 997 (6th Cir. 2020) (courts must liberally construe filing to assess if it could reasonably be interpreted as extension motion).

made on proper notice to other parties.[50] The moving party must prove *either* excusable neglect or good cause.[51] Note, however, that the interpretation of these terms in this appellate context differs from the more forgiving interpretation given nearly identical terms in the context of Rule 6(b) of the Federal Rules of Civil Procedure.[52]

- *Excusable Neglect Defined:* Excusable neglect applies in circumstances involving fault, and seeks an extension typically made necessary by something that should have been within the movant's control.[53] It is neither a "toothless" standard nor a merciless one—equitable considerations drive the inquiry.[54] In assessing whether the neglect is "excusable," a determination vested to the district court's discretion,[55] the court will assess the risk of prejudice to the non-moving party, the length of the delay, the delay's potential impact on the proceedings, the reason for the delay (and especially whether that reason was within the reasonable control of the moving party), and the moving party's good faith.[56] These factors (and others) are not mechanically given equal weight, and the actual balance may depend on the circumstances.[57] "Excusable neglect" generally requires something more than an attorney's busy caseload or an oversight in consulting or reading the procedural rules,[58] or a clerk's failure to notify parties of a ruling they could

---

[50]*See* Fed. R. App. P. 4(a)(5)(B).

[51]*See* Fed. R. App. P. 4(a)(5)(A). *See also id.* advisory committee note (2002). *See also Ragguette v. Premier Wines & Spirits*, 691 F.3d 315, 321 n.2 (3d Cir. 2012); *Sherman v. Quinn*, 668 F.3d 421, 424–25 (7th Cir. 2012).

[52]*See Alexander v. Saul*, 5 F.4th 139, 153-54 (2d Cir. 2021).

[53]*See* Fed. R. App. P. 4(a)(5)(A) advisory committee note (2002). *See also Alexander v. Saul*, 5 F.4th 139, 142 (2d Cir. 2021); *Sherman v. Quinn*, 668 F.3d 421, 425 (7th Cir. 2012). *See generally Mayle v. Illinois*, 956 F.3d 966, 968–69 (7th Cir. 2020) (neglect is assumed; standard assesses whether that neglect is excusable).

[54]*See Abuelyaman v. Illinois State Univ.*, 667 F.3d 800, 808 (7th Cir. 2011). *Cf. Alexander v. Saul*, 5 F.4th 139, 142 (2d Cir. 2021) (taking "hard line" in conducting inquiry, observing that where rule at issue is "entirely clear," movant "will, in the ordinary course, lose").

[55]*See Alexander v. Saul*, 5 F.4th 139, 142 (2d Cir. 2021); *Sherman v. Quinn*, 668 F.3d 421, 425 (7th Cir. 2012).

[56]*See Pioneer Inv. Servs. Co. v. Brunswick Assocs. Ltd. P'ship*, 507 U.S. 380, 395, 113 S.Ct. 1489, 123 L.Ed.2d 74 (1993) (assessing "excusable neglect" in bankruptcy rules context). *See also Alexander v. Saul*, 5 F.4th 139, 142 (2d Cir. 2021); *Gould on behalf of St. Louis - Kansas City Carpenters Reg'l Council v. Bond*, 1 F.4th 583, 588 (8th Cir. 2021). *Cf. Ragguette v. Premier Wines & Spirits*, 691 F.3d 315, 325–26 (3d Cir. 2012) (listing five different non-exclusive factors).

[57]*See Treasurer, Trustees of Drury Indus., Inc. Health Care Plan & Trust v. Goding*, 692 F.3d 888, 893 (8th Cir. 2012); (excuse for delay given greatest weight); *Abuelyaman v. Illinois State Univ.*, 667 F.3d 800, 808 (7th Cir. 2011) (degree of prejudice to opponent and good faith of movant given greatest weight).

[58]*See Alexander v. Saul*, 5 F.4th 139, 143-54 (2d Cir. 2021) (denied,

have discovered by periodically checking the docket.[59]

- *Good Cause Defined:* Good cause applies in circumstances where there is no fault (excusable or otherwise), and seeks an extension typically made necessary by something that was not within the movant's control.[60] Like excusable neglect, the good-cause determination is committed to the district court's discretion.[61]

Extensions — By District Court (Non-Receipt)

If the district court determines that a party entitled to notice of the entry of a judgment or order did not timely receive that notice, the court may extend the time for appeal, but only under the following conditions:

- *Party's non-receipt within 21 days:* The court must first find that the party did not receive formal Rule 77(d) notice from the court clerk within 21 days after entry of the judgment or order[62] (the "receive" date is obviously different from a "served" date);[63] *and*
- *Party promptly moved to reopen the appeal period*: The non-noticed party must promptly move[64] the district court to reopen the appeal period within 14 days after receiving or observing written notice of the entry from any source;[65] *and*
- *Party moved no later than 180 days after entry:* The

where client failed to provide counsel with new mailing address); *Satkar Hospitality, Inc. v. Fox Television Holdings*, 767 F.3d 701, 706-09 (7th Cir. 2014) (denied, if inability or refusal to read/comprehend the Rules); *Ragguette v. Premier Wines & Spirits*, 691 F.3d 315, 321–33 (3d Cir. 2012) (denied, failure to properly task computer calendar); *Sherman v. Quinn*, 668 F.3d 421, 426–27 (7th Cir. 2012) (denied, overloaded with work). *Cf. Zipperer v. School Bd. of Seminole County*, 111 F.3d 847, 849–50 (11th Cir.1997) (granted where notice filed one-day late, mailed in-State six days before filing).

[59] *See Two-Way Media LLC v. AT & T, Inc.*, 782 F.3d 1311, 1315-17 (Fed.Cir. 2015).

[60] *See* Fed. R. App. P. 4(a)(5)(A) advisory committee note (2002); *Alexander v. Saul*, 5 F.4th 139, 147-48 (2d Cir. 2021); *Bishop v. Corsentino*, 371 F.3d 1203, 1207 (10th Cir.2004). *See also Jaburek v. Foxx*, 813 F.3d 626, 630 (7th Cir. 2016) (granted, counsel's diagnosis with gout).

[61] *See Alexander v. Saul*, 5 F.4th 139, 146-47 (2d Cir. 2021); *Nartey v. Franciscan Health Hosp.*, 2 F.4th 1020, 1024 (7th Cir. 2021).

[62] *See* 28 U.S.C.A. § 2107(c)(1); Fed. R. App. P. 4(a)(6)(A). This 21-day trigger requires actual, formal notice under Rule 77(d). Thus, if no formal Rule 77(d) notice was served within 21 days, but the party nevertheless receives informal notice of the entry, an extension of the appeal time may still be sought. *See* Fed. R. App. P. 4(a)(6)(A) advisory committee note (2005).

[63] *See* 28 U.S.C.A. § 2107(c)(2); Fed. R. App. P. 4(a)(6)(A). *See also In re WorldCom, Inc.*, 708 F.3d 327, 332–35 (2d Cir. 2013) (transmission to outdated email was not "receipt"); *Khor Chin Lim v. Courtcall Inc.*, 683 F.3d 378, 381 (7th Cir. 2012) ("receipt" occurred when letter arrived at litigant's home, even though envelope had not yet been opened).

[64] *See Martin v. Sullivan*, 876 F.3d 235, 237–38 (6th Cir. 2017) (actual motion is required; merely filing notice of appeal not sufficient).

[65] *See* Fed. R. App. P. 4(a)(6)(B). This 14-day period became effective in

maximum window for seeking an appeal extension can never last longer than 180 days (thus obligating practitioners to routinely check the court dockets, even when no formal notice has been received);[66] *and*

- *No party is prejudiced by the extension:* The court must find that no party would be prejudiced by granting an appeal period extension;[67] *and*
- *Actual extension may last only 14 days:* If an extension is granted, the non-noticed party can be given no more than an additional 14 days to file the appeal.[68] Unlike the excusable neglect/good faith extension time limits, this 14-day period is considered jurisdictional and may not be forfeited or waived.[69]

The burden of demonstrating non-receipt rests with the moving party.[70] Evidence that the order was properly mailed or transmitted over a court's official electronic filing system creates a presumption of receipt; if contested, the district court will, as factfinder, assess the evidence and determine the question of receipt or non-receipt.[71] This Rule is triggered only by non-receipt; receiving but not opening or reading the notice does not qualify for relief.[72]

Nevertheless motions for extensions due to non-receipt are still committed to the district court's discretion.[73] Thus, the district court may deny a non-receipt extension even where the moving party satisfies the technical elements of the extension

---

2009; previously, the period was 7-days. The extension window starts to run on the day the party receives or observes "written" notice from "any source" (*e.g.*, by fax, e-mail, viewing a website entry, etc.), and will last for only 14 days. *See* Fed. R. App. P. 4(a)(6)(B) advisory committee note (2005) (as revised in 2009). Oral notice, "no matter how specific, reliable, or unequivocal", will not start the period running. *Id.*

[66]*See* 28 U.S.C.A. § 2107(c)(2); Fed. R. App. P. 4(a)(6)(B).

[67]*See* 28 U.S.C.A. § 2107(c)(2); Fed. R. App. P. 4(a)(6)(C).

[68]*See* 28 U.S.C.A. § 2107(c)(2); Fed. R. App. P. 4(a)(6).

[69]*See Bowles v. Russell*, 551 U.S. 205, 208-15, 127 S. Ct. 2360, 168 L. Ed. 2d 96 (2007) (trial court's order extending for 17 days unlawfully exceed jurisdictional cap, citing 28 U.S.C.A. § 2107(c)(2)).

[70]*See Nunley v. City of Los Angeles*, 52 F.3d 792, 795 (9th Cir.1995).

[71]*See American Boat Co., Inc. v. Unknown Sunken Barge*, 567 F.3d 348, 352-53 (8th Cir. 2009) (official email notices of court's CM/ECF system are *presumed* received; absent evidence to disprove it, court may rely on presumption). *See also In re WorldCom, Inc.*, 708 F.3d 327, 334 (2d Cir. 2013) (citing advisory committee note's encouragement to prevailing parties "to send their own notice" to improve likelihood that court will reject claim of non-receipt). *But see Nunley v. City of Los Angeles*, 52 F.3d 792, 796 (9th Cir.1995) (once specific factual denial of receipt is made, court can give no further weight to presumption of receipt).

[72]*See Two-Way Media LLC v. AT & T, Inc.*, 782 F.3d 1311, 1317-18 (Fed.Cir. 2015).

[73]*See Two-Way Media LLC v. AT & T, Inc.*, 782 F.3d 1311, 1314 (Fed. Cir. 2015); *In re WorldCom, Inc.*, 708 F.3d 327, 335-41 (2d Cir. 2013). *See also United States v. Salahuddin*, 803 Fed. Appx. 663, 664 n.1 (3d Cir. 2020).

rule.[74] A denial should be supported by factfinding, especially where the justification for denial is not plain from the record.[75] Although such a denial may not be based on the court's own assessment of the underlying merits of the appeal[76] or that the moving party failed to learn of the entry of judgment independently through other means,[77] the district court may (and, sometimes, must) deny an extension when the failure of receipt was indefensibly the moving party's fault.[78] This does not, however, obligate the moving party to always to demonstrate "excusable neglect" in order to justify such relief.[79]

- *Note:* Seeking relief from orders under other rules, such as Rule 60(b), usually cannot be used to circumvent this 180-day limitation.[80] Although this inflexible 180-day time boundary sometimes "may work misfortune," it is designed to balance the interests of finality in judgments against inequity to parties.[81]

Extensions — By District Court (Fee Motions)

When a party makes a timely attorneys' fees motion under Rule 54(d), the district court may suspend the time for taking an appeal until the fees motion is resolved.[82]

Extensions – By Court of Appeals

The courts of appeals may not grant litigants an extension of the time for appeal under any circumstances.[83]

---

[74] *See In re WorldCom, Inc.*, 708 F.3d 327, 335–42 (2d Cir. 2013) (extension denied when non-receipt was caused by attorney's failure to update clerk's office's electronic filing system with his new email address). *See also Watkins v. Plantation Police Dep't*, 733 Fed. Appx. 991, 994 (11th Cir. 2018).

[75] *See Shepard v. Rangel*, 658 Fed. Appx. 365, 367 (10th Cir. 2016) (discretion "is not whim" and is reversible where basis supporting denial is not supplied).

[76] *See Kuhn v. Sulzer Orthopedics, Inc.*, 498 F.3d 365, 369–70 (6th Cir. 2007); *Arai v. American Bryce Ranches Inc.*, 316 F.3d 1066, 1069–71 (9th Cir. 2003).

[77] *See U.S. v. Withers*, 618 F.3d 1008, 1014–15 (9th Cir. 2010).

[78] *See In re WorldCom, Inc.*, 708 F.3d 327, 338-41 (2d Cir. 2013). *See also In re Chavannes*, 658 Fed. Appx. 65, 67 (3d Cir. 2016) (court may properly consider moving party's "history of untimeliness and delay" in making prejudice assessment).

[79] *See In re WorldCom, Inc.*, 708 F.3d 327, 337 (2d Cir. 2013). *See also Benavides v. Bureau of Prisons*, 79 F.3d 1211, 1214 (D.C.Cir.1996) (showings not required because court supposes that party's tardiness is not his or her fault).

[80] *See U.S. v. Winkles*, 795 F.3d 1134, 1143–44 (9th Cir. 2015); *Vencor Hosps., Inc. v. Standard Life & Acc. Ins. Co.*, 279 F.3d 1306, 1310 (11th Cir. 2002). *But see Tanner v. Yukins*, 776 F.3d 434, 441-44 (6th Cir. 2015) (permitting Rule 60(b)(6) relief in exceptional circumstances to persons who missed deadline).

[81] *See Tanner v. Yukins*, 776 F.3d 434, 440-41 (6th Cir. 2015).

[82] *See* Rule 58(e). *See also supra* Authors' Commentary to Rule 58(e).

[83] *See* Fed. R. App. P. 26(b)(1). *See also In re Fischer*, 554 F.3d 656, 657 (7th Cir. 2009); *Burnley v. City of San Antonio*, 470 F.3d 189, 192–93 (5th Cir. 2006).

Premature Appeals

A notice of appeal filed after the district court announces its decision, but before the judgment or order is formally entered, will be deemed "filed" on the day the district court formally enters the judgment or order.[84] This rule will not apply to notices of appeal filed before a ruling is even announced[85] or to appeals from orders that are plainly interlocutory and would not be immediately appealable upon entry[86] (absent a Rule 54(b) determination).[87]

A notice of appeal filed after the district court formally enters the judgment or order, but before the district court rules upon those types of post-trial motions that suspend the time for appeal, is deemed to lie dormant. The notice will become effective when the trial court rules on the outstanding post-trial motions.[88] If the appellant intends to challenge not just the original judgment but the post-trial motion ruling as well, a new or amended notice of appeal will be necessary.[89]

---

[84]*See* Fed. R. App. P. 4(a)(2). *See also FirsTier Mortg. Co. v. Investors Mortg. Ins. Co.*, 498 U.S. 269, 276, 111 S.Ct. 648, 112 L.Ed.2d 743 (1991). *See also Weston Fam. P'ship LLLP v. Twitter, Inc.*, 29 F.4th 611, 618 (9th Cir. 2022) (premature appeal filed after dismissal-with-leave-to-amend was cured when district court *sua sponte* later closed the case). *See generally Floyd v. Am. Honda Motor Co.*, 966 F.3d 1027, 1032 (9th Cir. 2020) ("There's no penalty for filing a premature notice of appeal.").

[85]*See Marshall v. Comm'r Pa. Dep't of Corr.*, 840 F.3d 92, 95 (3d Cir. 2016).

[86]*See FirsTier Mortg. Co. v. Investors Mortg. Ins. Co.*, 498 U.S. 269, 276, 111 S.Ct. 648, 112 L.Ed.2d 743 (1991). *But cf. Bonner v. Perry*, 564 F.3d 424, 427-29 (6th Cir. 2009) (notice of appeal filed after a partial disposition (that might have qualified for Rule 54(b) determination) may properly be treated as filed upon final disposition of all remaining claims).

[87]*See Brown v. Columbia Sussex Corp.*, 664 F.3d 182, 189–90 (7th Cir. 2011); *Nat'l Ass'n of Bds. of Pharmacy v. Bd. of Regents of Univ. Sys. of Ga.*, 633 F.3d 1297, 1306–07 (11th Cir. 2011). *But cf. Bielskis v. Louisville Ladder, Inc.*, 663 F.3d 887, 893 (7th Cir. 2011) (entry of Rule 58 judgment "obviates" unfiled Rule 54(b) determination).

[88]*See* Fed. R. App. P. 4(a)(4)(B). *See also Slep-Tone Entm't Corp. v. Karaoke Kandy Store, Inc.*, 782 F.3d 712, 715 (6th Cir. 2015); *U.S. v. Holy Land Foundation for Relief & Dev't*, 722 F.3d 677, 683–84 (5th Cir. 2013). This Rule represents a change in earlier practice, which held that a notice of appeal was a "nullity" if prematurely filed while post-trial motions remained pending. *See Leader Nat'l Ins. Co. v. Industrial Indem. Ins. Co.*, 19 F.3d 444, 445 (9th Cir.1994) (noting change).

[89]*See* Fed. R. App. P. 4(a)(4)(B)(ii). *See also Fed. Trade Comm'n v. Zurixx*, 26 F.4th 1172, 1176 (10th Cir. 2022) (appeal filed before court ruled on reconsideration motion did not allow appeal of that later ruling, since no new notice or amended notice was filed); *White v. United States Dep't of Just.*, 16 F.4th 539, 543 (7th Cir. 2021) (same, Rule 60(b) motion). *See generally Patten v. D.C.*, 9 F.4th 921, 929-30 (D.C. Cir. 2021) (denial of Rule 60 post-judgment motion does not merge into earlier final-judgment appeal). *But cf. Lincoln Composites, Inc. v. Firetrace USA, LLC*, 825 F.3d 453, 457 (8th Cir. 2016) (excusing failure to comply where appealing intent otherwise clear).

Additional Research References

C.J.S., Federal Courts §§ 293(5 to 17) et seq.
West's Key Number Digest, Federal Courts ⚷652 to 660.40

§ 6.4 Step Three: Procedure for Taking an Appeal

CORE CONCEPT

The procedure for taking a federal civil appeal is straightforward. The appealing parties must give proper "notice" of their intent to appeal, and must do so timely and to the proper court.

APPLICATIONS

Contents of Notice of Appeal, Generally

A "notice of appeal" is an easily-prepared, one-page form,[1] the filing of which is generally considered "a simple, nonsubstantive act."[2] In addition to typical formalities (like case caption and filer's signature block), a proper notice of appeal contains three further items: (1) the identity of the appealing parties; (2) the judgment or appealable interlocutory order being appealed; and (3) the name of the court to which the appeal is being taken.[3] These requirements are considered mandatory and jurisdictional.[4] The notice of appeal need not (and should not) set out the appealing parties' legal arguments.

Requirement #1: Naming the Appellants

An appeal is considered taken only by those parties named as appellants in the caption or body of the notice of appeal,[5] unless a party's intent to appeal is otherwise "objectively clear" from the notice.[6] Although shorthand descriptions[7] (including

---

[1]The federal appellate rules' appendix contains "suggested" notice of appeal forms, both available in edit-enabled Word format on the federal courts' website. *See* Fed. R. App. P. 3(c)(8) (referencing Forms 1A and 1B). *See also* https://www.uscourts.gov/rules-policies/current-rules-practice-procedure/appellate-rules-forms.

[2]*See Garza v. Idaho*, 586 U.S. __, 139 S. Ct. 738, 746, 203 L. Ed. 2d 77 (2019).

[3]*See* Fed. R. App. P. 3(c)(1).

[4]*See Gonzalez v. Thaler*, 565 U.S. 134, 147-48, 132 S. Ct. 641, 181 L. Ed. 2d 619 (2012); *Smith v. Barry*, 502 U.S. 244, 248, 112 S.Ct. 678, 116 L.Ed.2d 678 (1992); *Torres v. Oakland Scavenger Co.*, 487 U.S. 312, 317, 108 S.Ct. 2405, 101 L.Ed.2d 285 (1988).

[5]*See* Fed. R. App. P. 3(c)(1)(A). *See also Lokhova v. Halper*, 30 F.4th 349, 353 (4th Cir. 2022) (although omitted from notice of appeal's caption, party was identified as appellant in body of notice, which sufficed).

[6]*See* Fed. R. App. P. 3(c)(7). *See, e.g., Cooper v. Retrieval-Masters Creditors Bureau, Inc.*, 42 F.4th 688, 693-94 (7th Cir. 2022) (sanctions appeal encompassed counsel because sanctions order applied only to counsel); *S.E.C. v. Wealth Mgmt. LLC*, 628 F.3d 323,

"et al.")[8] can, on occasion, supply that requisite clarity, an express designation is by far the safer course.[9] Where clarity of a party's intent to appeal is missing, that party's right to appeal may be lost.[10] The goal is notice—to opponents and to the court—and the avoidance of gamesmanship.[11] As for appellees, they need not be separately listed in the notice of appeal.[12]

- *Pro Se Appellants:* A *pro se* appellant's notice of appeal is deemed filed on behalf of that signer's spouse and minor children (if they are parties), unless the notice of appeal "clearly indicates otherwise."[13]
- *Class Action Appellants:* A notice of appeal filed in a class action (whether or not certified as a class) is sufficient to preserve the appellate rights of unnamed class members if the notice names at least one person qualified to file the appeal as a class representative; named class members, however, must individually appeal.[14]

Requirement #2: Naming the Ruling Being Appealed

The notice of appeal must also designate the judgment (or

---

331 (7th Cir. 2010) (holders of trust entitled to appeal where no confusion existed as to their identity); *Vivendi SA v. T-Mobile USA Inc.*, 586 F.3d 689, 690 n.2 (9th Cir. 2009) (explanatory statement in Civil Appeals Docketing Statement sufficed to allow co-appellant's appeal).

[7] *See* Fed. R. App. P. 3(c)(1)(A) (giving as examples: "all plaintiffs" and "all defendants except X"). *But compare In re Motors Liquidation Co.*, 943 F.3d 125, 129 (2d Cir. 2019) ("certain Post-Closing Accident Plaintiffs" was clear), *and Air Line Pilots Ass'n v. Continental Airlines*, 125 F.3d 120 (3d Cir.1997) ("the LPP Claimants Claimants" was clear), *with Al-Qarqani v. Chevron Corp.*, 8 F.4th 1018, 1023 (9th Cir. 2021) ("Heirs of Khalid Abu al-Waleed al-Hood al-Qarqani" not clear, and failed to preserve appeal for unnamed persons), *and Batiste v. Lewis*, 976 F.3d 493, 508-09 (5th Cir. 2020) (not clear attorney, in addition to client, intended to appeal sanctions order).

[8] *See* Fed. R. App. P. 3(c)(1)(A). *See also Massie v. U.S. Dep't of Hous. & Urban Dev.*, 620 F.3d 340, 348 (3d Cir. 2010) (though disfavored, use of "et al." preserved appeal by class members). *Cf. Torres v. Oakland Scavenger Co.*, 487 U.S. 312, 318, 108 S. Ct. 2405, 101 L. Ed. 2d 285 (1988) (use of "et al." was categorically insufficient; decision altered by amendments to appellate rules in 1993).

[9] *See Olenhouse v. Commodity Credit Corp.*, 42 F.3d 1560, 1572 n. 19 (10th Cir.1994).

[10] *See Al-Qarqani v. Chevron Corp.*, 8 F.4th 1018 (9th Cir. 2021); *Cho v. Blackberry Ltd.*, 991 F.3d 155, 163-68 (2d Cir. 2021). *See generally Torres v. Oakland Scavenger Co.*, 487 U.S. 312, 314, 108 S. Ct. 2405, 101 L. Ed. 2d 285 (1988) (failure to name party in notice of appeal "constitutes a failure of that party to appeal").

[11] *See Gonzalez v. Thaler*, 565 U.S. 134, 148, 132 S. Ct. 641, 181 L. Ed. 2d 619 (2012) (otherwise, parties "could sit on the fence, await the outcome, and opt to participate only if it was favorable").

[12] *See Shifflett v. Korszniak*, 934 F.3d 356, 368 n.3 (3d Cir. 2019); *West v. United States*, 853 F.3d 520, 523 (9th Cir. 2017).

[13] *See* Fed. R. App. P. 3(c)(2). *See also Becker v. Montgomery*, 532 U.S. 757, 766–67, 121 S. Ct. 1801, 1807, 149 L. Ed. 2d 983 (2001) (rule is "ameliorative," designed to prevent an "inadvertent" loss of appeal).

[14] *See* Fed. R. App. P. 3(c)(3). *See also Cho v. Blackberry Ltd.*, 991 F.3d 155, 162-68 (2d Cir. 2021).

appealable order) that is being appealed.[15] Seasoned practitioners had usually designated only the final judgment in the lawsuit, mindful that doing so permitted appellate review not just of that judgment but also of all those preceding, interlocutory orders that were deemed to have merged into it.[16] (This appellate "merger" principle follows from the federal courts' single-appeal-at-the-end "final order" doctrine.[17]) But this had produced a trap for the unwary practitioner who, due to a misunderstanding of this merger principle or an imprudent excess of caution,[18] might have instead specifically named a particular interlocutory order in the notice of appeal, thereby inadvertently limiting the scope of the appeal and the review authority of the appellate courts.[19]

Effective December 2021, the appellate rules were amended to reduce this risk. Designating only the judgment (or, in the case of immediately appealable interlocutory orders, only that order) now is expressly deemed to encompass all other orders that merge into that designated ruling, with practitioners reminded that separately listing those merged rulings is "not necessary."[20] Moreover, the lawsuit's final judgment is considered encompassed in the notice of appeal, even when not listed, if the notice designates either (1) a ruling that adjudicates all remaining claims and the rights and liabilities of all remaining parties or (2) most types of post-trial orders.[21] Appellants are still permitted to limit their appeals to only a part of a judgment or appealable order, but only if they do so expressly.[22] Absent such an expressed limitation, a notice of appeal that contains specific designations will "not limit the scope of the notice of appeal."[23]

---

[15] *See* Fed. R. App. P. 3(c)(1)(B).

[16] *See Mid-Am. Salt, LLC v. Morris Cnty. Coop. Pricing Council*, 964 F.3d 218, 225 (3d Cir. 2020) (appeal from final judgment "will draw into question all non-final orders and rulings which produced the judgment").

[17] *See Behrens v. Pelletier*, 516 U.S. 299, 305, 116 S. Ct. 834, 838, 133 L. Ed. 2d 773 (1996); *Cohen v. Beneficial Indus. Loan Corp.*, 337 U.S. 541, 546, 69 S. Ct. 1221, 93 L. Ed. 1528 (1949). For a discussion of the final order doctrine, see *supra* Part VI § 6.2 (**"Final Decisions ('Final Orders')"**).

[18] *See Gonpo v. Sonam's Stonewalls & Art, LLC*, 41 F.4th 1, 10-11 (1st Cir. 2022) (citing advisory committee observations).

[19] *See Denault v. Ahern*, 857 F.3d 76, 81 (1st Cir. 2017) ("perilous" strategy, because counsel may later wish to rethink which issues to press on appeal but be foreclosed from doing so by narrow notice which deprives appeals court of jurisdiction over unitemized rulings).

[20] *See* Fed. R. App. P. 3(c)(4). *See also Rivera v. Kress Stores of Puerto Rico, Inc.*, 30 F.4th 98, 107 (1st Cir. 2022).

[21] *See* Fed. R. App. P. 3(c)(5). *See also* Fed. R. App. P. 3(c)(7) (judgment is considered designated if notice is filed after entry of that judgment and designates order that merged into that judgment).

[22] *See* Fed. R. App. P. 3(c)(6). *See also Rivera v. Kress Stores of Puerto Rico, Inc.*, 30 F.4th 98, 107 (1st Cir. 2022).

[23] *See* Fed. R. App. P. 3(c)(6). *See also Gonpo v. Sonam's Stonewalls & Art, LLC*, 41 F.4th 1, 11 (1st Cir. 2022)

Requirement #3: Naming the Appeals Court

The notice of appeal must identify the specific court to which the appeal is being taken[24] (unless only one proper destination is possible).[25]

Errors in Notice of Appeal

Although jurisdictional in nature,[26] the rules prescribing the proper contents of a notice of appeal are construed liberally,[27] and not hyper-technically.[28] A technical variance from the rules may be excused, if the rule requirements are functionally satisfied.[29] That function is notice, both to the court and the adversaries, of the appealing parties and the rulings to be reviewed.[30] Thus, "imperfections" in a notice of appeal will not doom that appeal "where no genuine doubt exists about who is appealing, from what judgment, to which appellate court."[31] This liberality extends to form and title, the identity of appellants, and the designation of the final judgment,[32] and may even permit a party's brief[33] or time-extension request[34] to substitute for an unfiled notice of appeal, where it provides the requisite notice. *Pro se* appeals will be assessed with special liberality.[35] Nevertheless, an appellant's subjective intentions are not enough,[36] and if the notice demanded by the rules is not satisfied either literally or functionally, the appeal will fail.[37]

(express-statement requirement "removes this trap for the unwary, while also leaving the door open for those parties who still wish to deliberately limit their notices") (cleaned up).

[24] *See* Fed. R. App. P. 3(c)(1)(C).

[25] *See United States v. Gooch*, 842 F.3d 1274, 1277 (D.C. Cir. 2016); *Jackson v. Lightsey*, 775 F.3d 170, 175-76 (4th Cir. 2014). *Cf. U.S. v. Treto-Haro*, 287 F.3d 1000, 1002 n.1 (10th Cir.2002) (failure to name correct court will not warrant dismissal where intention may be reasonably inferred).

[26] *See supra* Part VI, § 6.4 ("**Contents of Notice of Appeal, Generally**").

[27] *See Newcomb v. Wyndham Vacation Ownership, Inc.*, 999 F.3d 1134, 1137 (8th Cir. 2021); *Weimer v. Cty. of Fayette*, 972 F.3d 177, 186 (3d Cir. 2020).

[28] *See Sines v. Wilner*, 609 F.3d 1070, 1074–75 (10th Cir. 2010); *Hudson v. District of Columbia*, 558 F.3d 526, 529 (D.C.Cir. 2009).

[29] *See* Fed. R. App. P. 3(c)(7). *See also Smith v. Barry*, 502 U.S. 244, 248, 112 S.Ct. 678, 116 L.Ed.2d 678 (1992).

[30] *See Smith v. Barry*, 502 U.S. 244, 248, 112 S.Ct. 678, 116 L.Ed.2d 678 (1992).

[31] *See Becker v. Montgomery*, 532 U.S. 757, 767, 121 S. Ct. 1801, 149 L. Ed. 2d 983 (2001).

[32] *See* Fed. R. App. P. 3(c)(7).

[33] *See Taylor v. Johnson*, 257 F.3d 470, 474 (5th Cir.2001).

[34] *See Owens v. Godinez*, 860 F.3d 434, 437 (7th Cir. 2017); *United States v. Gooch*, 842 F.3d 1274, 1278 (D.C. Cir. 2016).

[35] *See United States v. Padgett*, 917 F.3d 1312, 1316 (11th Cir. 2019); *Elliott v. City of Hartford*, 823 F.3d 170, 172–73 (2d Cir. 2016).

[36] *See Smith v. Barry*, 502 U.S. 244, 248, 112 S.Ct. 678, 116 L.Ed.2d 678 (1992); *Biltcliffe v. CitiMortgage, Inc.*, 772 F.3d 925, 929-30 (1st Cir. 2014).

[37] *See Smith v. Barry*, 502 U.S. 244, 248, 112 S.Ct. 678, 116 L.Ed.2d 678 (1992). *Cf. Newcomb v. Wyndham Vacation Ownership, Inc.*, 999 F.3d 1134, 1137-38 (8th Cir. 2021) (notices "entirely deficient": they appealed "an order entered on a day when no order

Privacy Protection for Personal Data Identifiers

The vulnerability of electronically-accessible court files to privacy and security mischief prompted the adoption of special redaction and sealing privileges for certain civil cases.[38] In cases where these privileges applied at the district court level, the privileges will extend to the appeal as well.[39]

Notice Must Be *Filed* Timely

The notice of appeal must be actually *filed* with the clerk of court within the time allotted for taking an appeal.[40] Mailing or serving the notice on or before the deadline is not sufficient. For prisoners, a notice of appeal is considered timely if the prisoner complies with the appeals rules' inmate filing procedures.[41]

Place of Filing

A notice of appeal is filed with the clerk of the district court from which the appeal is taken.[42] However, mistakenly filing the notice with the court of appeals will *not* defeat the appeal. If the notice is filed timely, albeit with the court of appeals, the appeals court clerk will note the date of filing and send the notice to the clerk of the district court.[43] Filing in other, mistaken locations may doom the appeal.[44]

Electronic Filing

Represented parties *must* now file their notices of appeal[45] and subsequent appeal papers[46] electronically, unless permitted by the court (for good cause) or local rule to file nonelectronically. Unrepresented parties may file electronically only if permitted to do so by court order or local rule.[47] Filings must comply with the applicable electronic filing procedures;[48] a failure to do so can be appeal-defeating.[49] The continued vitality of precedent approving filing by physical delivery to the

---

issued, from a district court that does not exist, to a court of appeals that does not exist"). *See generally Torres v. Oakland Scavenger Co.*, 487 U.S. 312, 315-16, 108 S. Ct. 2405, 101 L. Ed. 2d 285 (1988) ("Permitting imperfect but substantial compliance with a technical [notice of appeal] requirement is not the same as waiving the requirement altogether as a jurisdictional threshold.").

[38] *See* Rule 5.2. *See also supra* Authors' Commentary to Rule 5.2.

[39] *See* Fed. R. App. P. 25(a)(5).

[40] *See* Fed. R. App. P. 3(a)(1) & 4(a)(1).

[41] *See* Fed. R. App. P. 4(c).

[42] Fed. R. App. P. 3(a).

[43] Fed. R. App. P. 4(d).

[44] *See Brooks v. SAC Wireless, LLC*, 835 Fed. Appx. 137, 138-40 (7th Cir. 2021) (*pro se* litigant's emailing of notice of appeal to district judge did not preserve appeal).

[45] *See* Rule 5(d)(3)(A). *See also* 16A Charles A. Wright, Arthur R. Miller, Edward H. Cooper, & Catherine T. Struve, Federal Practice and Procedure § 3949.1, at 51-52 (2019) (ordinarily-mandatory electronic filing rule applies to notice of appeal).

[46] *See* Fed. R. App. P. 25(a)(2)(B)(i).

[47] *See* Rule 5(d)(3)(B); Fed. R. App. P. 25(a)(2)(B)(i).

[48] *See Qureshi v. Attorney Gen. United States of Am.*, 677 Fed. Appx. 757, 761 (3d Cir. 2017) (email to court's electronic filing help desk insufficient).

[49] *See Sudduth v. Texas Health & Human Servs. Comm'n*, 830 F.3d 175,

district court's official "drop box" is unclear.[50]

Service Not Required

The appealing party need not serve the notice of appeal on all other parties; this service is made by the clerk of the district court.[51] The clerk's failure to serve the notice, however, does not defeat the appeal.[52]

- *Service Copies:* Although the appellant does not actually serve the notice of appeal on the other parties, the appellant is required to provide the clerk's office with sufficient copies of the notice for service.[53]

Joint Appeals

Joint appeals may be taken by two or more parties whose similar interests make such joinder practicable.[54] Each appealing party, however, must file a timely notice of appeal. The fact that some similarly situated parties timely appealed is immaterial; the appeal of each appealing party must be appropriately made.[55]

Consolidated Appeals

Upon its own motion or by motion of a party, the court of appeals may consolidate the appeals of different parties.[56]

Fees

Unless exempt,[57] the appealing party must pay to the district court both the district court fee for appeal and the court of appeals' docket fee.[58] Failure to pay fees should not affect the docketing of an appeal,[59] but continued nonpayment following docketing will invite dismissal for want of prosecution.[60]

177–79 (5th Cir. 2016); *Franklin v. McHugh*, 804 F.3d 627, 629-32 (2d Cir. 2015).

[50] *Cf. Pierce v. Ocwen Loan Servicing, LLC*, 987 F.3d 577, 579 (6th Cir. 2021) (permitting drop box filing, notwithstanding *local rule* mandating electronic filing); *Han Tak Lee v. Houtzdale SCI*, 798 F.3d 159, 163 (3d Cir. 2015) (same).

[51] Fed. R. App. P. 3(d)(1).

[52] Fed. R. App. P. 3(d)(3).

[53] Fed. R. App. P. 3(a)(1).

[54] Fed. R. App. P. 3(b)(1).

[55] *See Wooden v. Board of Regents of Univ. Sys. of Ga.*, 247 F.3d 1262, 1273 (11th Cir.2001).

[56] Fed. R. App. P. 3(b)(2).

[57] *See Himmelreich v. Fed. Bureau of Prisons*, 5 F.4th 653, 664 (6th Cir. 2021) (Congress has exempted federal government and those granted *in forma pauperis* status from filing fees).

[58] Fed. R. App. P. 3(e).

[59] *See* Fed. R. App. P. 3(a)(2). *See also Parissi v. Telechron, Inc.*, 349 U.S. 46, 47, 75 S. Ct. 577, 99 L. Ed. 867 (1955).

[60] *See Camacho-Valdez v. Garland*, 30 F.4th 675, 678 (7th Cir. 2022) (clerk authorized to dismiss appeal if docketing fee not paid when appeal is filed or within 14 days thereafter); *Himmelreich v. Fed. Bureau of Prisons*, 5 F.4th 653, 664 (6th Cir. 2021) (unpaid fees, without *in forma pauperis* leave, typically results in dismissal for want of prosecution). *See also, e.g.*, 1st Cir. R. 3.0(b); 5th Cir. R. 3; 6th Cir. R. 3.

Additional Research References

C.J.S. Federal Courts §§ 282 to 301(48) et seq.
West's Key Number Digest, Federal Courts ⚷521 to 956

§ 6.5 Step Four: Stays Pending Appeal

CORE CONCEPT

A party may seek a stay of judgment by filing such an application with the district court. In applications *not* involving stays of injunctions, receiverships, or accountings in patent infringement actions, a party may request a stay pending appeal by filing a bond or other security. Stay applications must be filed timely and, generally, initially in the district court.

APPLICATIONS

30-Day "Automatic" Stay

For a period of 30 days after a judgment is entered, parties are barred from executing upon the judgment or pursuing further proceedings for its enforcement.[1] This automatic stay does *not* apply to judgments involving injunctions, judgments in receivership actions, or judgments or orders directing accountings in patent infringement actions.

Time to Apply for Stay

Applications for stay generally should be filed at the earliest possible opportunity. Because the automatic stay does not apply in certain injunction, receivership, and patent infringement circumstances, appellants in those cases do not enjoy the automatic 30-day stay period and the time for execution and enforcement will immediately arrive. An appeal bond or other security must first be approved by the court before any stay is effective.[3] Consequently, a delay in seeking a stay will expose the defeated party to execution and enforcement of the judgment.

Where to Apply for Stay

Ordinarily, stays pending appeal must be filed first with the district court.[4] Only in circumstances where applying in the district court is not practicable, or where the district court has denied the request or failed to grant all the relief requested, may a party request a stay in the court of appeals.[5]

Procedure for Stay Applications in the District Court

In cases that do not involve injunctions, receivers, or accountings in patent infringement cases, the posting of an appeal bond or other security—after it has been approved by the court—will stay execution and enforcement of the judgment.[6]

In cases involving injunctions, the district court may, in its

---

[1] *See* Rule 62(a).

[3] *See* Rule 62(b).

[4] *See* Fed. R. App. P. 8(a)(1).

[5] *See* Fed. R. App. P. 8(a)(2).

[6] *See* Rule 62(b).

discretion, grant a stay of the injunction pending appeal.[7] To obtain such a stay, the moving party must generally make the traditional showing required for any injunction: strong likelihood of success on the merits, irreparable injury, no substantial harm to others, and no damage to the public interest.[8] The court may condition such a stay upon the posting of a bond or other appropriate security.[9]

Procedure for Stay Applications in the Court of Appeals

In applying for a stay in the court of appeals, the moving party must make several showings in the motion papers:[10]

a. *Proceedings Before Trial Court:* The motion must show why a stay application cannot be practicably directed to the district judge, or that the district judge has denied a stay or failed to grant all the relief requested (the district court's reasons must be set forth);

b. *Reasons for Relief:* The motion must show the reasons for the relief requested, and set forth the facts relied upon in support of that showing. Relevant parts of the record must be included and, where the facts relied upon are subject to dispute, supporting affidavits or other sworn statements must also be included;

c. *Reasonable Notice:* Reasonable notice of the motion must be given to the non-moving party;

d. *Disposition:* The motion will ordinarily be resolved by a panel or division of the court, unless exceptional circumstances justify submitting the motion to a single judge;

e. *Bond or Security:* If the motion is granted, the court of appeals can condition the stay upon the filing in the district court of a bond or other appropriate security.[11]

§ 6.6 Step Five: The Appeal Process

CORE CONCEPT

Once the appeal is timely filed, the court of appeals will send to each party a briefing notice that will schedule the filing of an Appellant's Brief, an Appellee's Brief, and an Appellant's Reply Brief. Thereafter, the court of appeals may schedule oral argument, the case will be submitted, and a written disposition on appeal will be filed.

APPLICATIONS

Effect of Appeal

Once the appeal is taken, jurisdiction over the case generally

---

[7] *See* Rule 62(c).

[8] *See supra* Author's Commentary to Rule 62(d).

[9] *See* Rule 62(c).

[10] *See* Fed. R. App. P. 8(a)(2)(A) to (2)(D).

[11] *See* Fed. R. App. P. 8(a)(2)(E).

passes from the district court to the court of appeals.[1] The district court thereafter usually enjoys only the narrow power to preform ministerial functions, issue stays and injunctions pending appeal, and, in certain instances, award counsel fees. However, under the "indicative ruling" procedure, if the district court (after being divested of jurisdiction by an appeal) states that it would grant a trial-level motion or considers such a motion to raise a "substantial issue," the court of appeals may[2] remand back to the district judge for further proceedings.[3]

Compliance With Schedule and Procedures

Failure to comply with the court of appeals' schedule and procedures is ground for such action as the court of appeals deems appropriate, including denial of the right to participate in oral argument or even dismissal of the appeal itself.[4]

Designation of the Record and Statement of Issues

The "record" on appeal consists of (1) the original papers and exhibits filed in the trial court, (2) the transcript, and (3) a certified copy of docket entries.[5] The "record" encompasses not just those exhibits admitted into evidence, but may include items presented for admission and denied by the district court.[6] Within 14 days after filing the notice of appeal, the appealing party must order those portions of the transcript that are necessary for the appeal (or file a certificate stating that no transcript will be ordered).[8] Unless the appellant orders the entire transcript, the appellant must, during this same 14-day period, file a statement of the issues for appeal and a list of the intended contents of the Appendix.[8] The appellee may thereafter serve a counter-designation of additional portions of the transcript to be included.[9]

---

[1]*See Griggs v. Provident Consumer Discount Co.*, 459 U.S. 56, 58, 103 S.Ct. 400, 74 L.Ed.2d 225 (1982) (notice of appeal is event of jurisdictional significance, conferring jurisdiction on Court of Appeals and divesting district court of control over those aspects of litigation involved in appeal).

[2]*See In re Checking Account Overdraft Litig.*, 754 F.3d 1290, 1297 (11th Cir. 2014) (appeals court retains discretion, even if indicative ruling is issued).

[3]*See* Fed. R. App. P. 12.1; *see also* Rule 62.1 (parallel district court provision).

[4]*See* Fed. R. App. P. 3(a)(2). *See also Lehman Bros. Holdings, Inc. v. Gateway Funding Diversified Mortg. Servs., L.P.*, 785 F.3d 96, 101 (3d Cir. 2015) (failure to compile record warranted forfeiture of first argument on appeal).

[5]*See* Fed. R. App. P. 10(a).

[6]*See Morton Int'l, Inc. v. A.E. Staley Mfg. Co.*, 343 F.3d 669, 682 (3d Cir.2003).

[8]*See* Fed. R. App. P. 10(b)(1). This 14-day period became effective in 2009; until then, the period was 10-days.

[8]*See* Fed. R. App. P. 10(b)(3)(A). This 14-day period became effective in 2009; until then, the period was 10-days.

[9]*See* Fed. R. App. P. 10(b)(3)(B). This 14-day period became effective in 2009; until then, the period was 10-days.

Briefing Procedures

Briefing procedures (including content, format, and length of briefs, appendices, and other submissions) are prescribed by the Appellate Rules,[10] but practitioners are also cautioned that local rules—which vary by Circuit—supplement these national procedures.

Briefing Privacy

Special redaction and sealing privileges are applied to certain civil cases in the district court (*e.g.*, social security numbers, taxpayer identification numbers, financial account numbers, birth years, and full names of minors may be presented in an abbreviated form).[11] In cases where these privileges applied at the district court level, the privileges will extend to the appeal as well.[12]

Briefing Reminders

• ***Disclosure Statement:*** The Appellate Rules require each non-governmental corporate party in every civil case to file a statement identifying each of its parent corporations and all publicly-held companies that own 10% or more of the party's stock, and to supplement that statement whenever the necessary information changes.[13]

• ***Footnote Restrictions:*** Some courts have adopted local rules that limit the use of footnotes in appellate briefs.[14]

• ***Citing "Unpublished" Decisions:*** For years, many courts of appeals forbade the citation of "unpublished", "non-precedential", "not-for-publication", or similarly labeled decisions. In 2007, the Appellate Rules invalidated this local practice. Courts of appeals may no longer prohibit or discourage the citation of such decisions[15] (although litigants citing opinions that are not publicly accessible through a commercial, legal research service, or court database must file and serve copies).[16] Courts of appeals may, however, continue to issue opinions bearing those designations, and the rules do not prescribe what effect the court must give to such decisions.[17]

Oral Argument

Oral argument is permitted generally unless the appeal is frivolous, the dispositive issues were authoritatively decided, or the decisional process would not be significantly aided by argument because the facts and legal arguments are adequately set

---

[10]*See* Fed. R. App. P. 25, 28, 28,1, 30, 31, 32.

[11]*See* Rule 5.2. *See also supra* Authors' Commentary to Rule 5.2.

[12]*See* Fed. R. App. P. 25(a)(5).

[13]Fed. R. App. P. 26.1(a)-(b).

[14]*See* 3d Cir. Loc. App. R. 32.2(a) ("Excessive footnotes in briefs are discouraged. Footnotes must be printed in the same size type utilized in the text.").

[15]Fed. R. App. P. 32.1(a). *See also id.* advisory committee note (2006).

[16]Fed. R. App. P. 32.1(b). *See also id.* advisory committee note (2006).

[17]Fed. R. App. P. 32.1. *See also id.* advisory committee note (2006).

forth in the briefs.[18] The length, scheduling, and location of argument is set by the particular court of appeals.

§ 6.7 Step Six: Appeals to the United States Supreme Court

CORE CONCEPT

A party enjoys an appeal as of right to the United States Supreme Court in only very few circumstances. In all other cases, the Supreme Court has the discretion whether to permit or refuse appeals to that Court. In practice, only a small handful of the many thousands of requests for Supreme Court review are granted each year.

APPLICATIONS

Appeals As Of Right; Time to File

Whenever a specially convened three-judge district court panel declares any Act of Congress to be unconstitutional, a direct appeal may be taken to the Supreme Court.[1] Such appeals must be filed within 30 days of the date the district court's order is entered.[2] Congress may permit other direct appeals from the district courts, and such appeals must also be filed within 30 days of the district court's action.[3]

Discretionary Appeals; Time to File

The Supreme Court may, in its discretion, grant a party appellate review from other federal and State court rulings. Supreme Court review of federal appellate court decisions may be sought by petitioning for a Writ of Certiorari[4] or by seeking a certification from the court of appeals.[5] The Supreme Court may, in its discretion, also grant a Writ of Certiorari to review decisions from the highest court of any State, but only where (a) a federal treaty or statute is drawn into question, (b) a State statute is drawn into question on federal grounds, or (c) any title, right, privilege, or immunity is specially set up or claimed under federal law.[6]

Petitions for Writs of Certiorari usually must be filed with the Supreme Court within 90 days after the entry of the disputed judgment or decree.[7]

Considerations in Granting Writs of Certiorari

The Supreme Court Rules provide a non-controlling, non-exhaustive list of the types of "compelling reasons" that may

---

[18]Fed. R. App. P. 34(a)(2).

[1]*See* 28 U.S.C.A. § 1253.

[2]*See* 28 U.S.C.A. § 2102(a).

[3]*See* 28 U.S.C.A. § 2102(b).

[4]*See* 28 U.S.C.A. § 1254(1). In Latin, "certiorari" means "to be more fully informed"; such writs of certiorari are of common law origin, and were (and are) issued by a higher court to a lower court requiring that the certified record in a case be delivered for review. *See* BLACK'S LAW DICTIONARY 275–76 (10th ed. 2014).

[5]*See* 28 U.S.C.A. § 1254(2).

[6]*See* 28 U.S.C.A. § 1257.

[7]*See* 28 U.S.C.A. § 2101; U.S. S. Ct. R. 13(1), (3).

prompt the Court to grant a Writ of Certiorari:

(1) A conflict among the federal Circuits on an "important matter";

(2) A conflict between a federal court of appeals and the highest court of a State on an "important federal question";

(3) A ruling by a court of appeals that "so far departed from the accepted and usual course of judicial proceedings" (or that sanctions such a departure by a lower court) that the Supreme Court's "supervisory power" is called for;

(4) A ruling by the highest court of a State that conflicts with the decision of another State's highest court or a federal court of appeals on an "important federal question"; or

(5) A ruling by a State court or a federal court of appeals that decides "an important question of federal law that has not been, but should be," settled by the Supreme Court, or that decides "an important federal question in a way that conflicts with relevant decisions" of the Supreme Court.[9]

§ 6.8 *Federal Rules of Appellate Procedure* (Effective July 1, 1968; amendments effective December 1, 2022)

Rule

1. Scope of Rules; Title.
2. Suspension of Rules.
3. Appeal as of Right—How Taken.
3.1 Appeal from a Judgment of a Magistrate Judge in a Civil Case [Abrogated].
4. Appeal as of Right—When Taken.
5. Appeal by Permission.
5.1 Appeal By Leave Under 28 U.S.C. § 636(c)(5) [Abrogated].
6. Appeal in a Bankruptcy Case.
7. Bond for Costs on Appeal in a Civil Case.
8. Stay or Injunction Pending Appeal.
9. Release in a Criminal Case.
10. The Record on Appeal.
11. Forwarding the Record.
12. Docketing the Appeal; Filing a Representation Statement; Filing the Record.
12.1 Remand After an Indicative Ruling by the District Court on a Motion for Relief That Is Barred by a Pending Appeal
13. Appeals from the Tax Court.
14. Applicability of Other Rules to the Review of a Tax Court Decision.
15. Review or Enforcement of an Agency Order—How Obtained; Intervention.
15.1 Briefs and Oral Argument in a National Labor Relations Board Proceeding.
16. The Record on Review or Enforcement.
17. Filing the Record.

---

[9] *See* U.S. S. Ct. R. 10(a) to (c).

18. Stay Pending Review.
19. Settlement of a Judgment Enforcing an Agency Order in Part.
20. Applicability of Rules to the Review or Enforcement of an Agency Order.
21. Writs of Mandamus and Prohibition, and Other Extraordinary Writs.
22. Habeas Corpus and Section 2255 Proceedings.
23. Custody or Release of a Prisoner in a Habeas Corpus Proceeding.
24. Proceeding In Forma Pauperis.
25. Filing and Service.
26. Computing and Extending Time.
26.1 Disclosure Statement.
27. Motions.
28. Briefs.
28.1 Cross-Appeals.
29. Brief of an Amicus Curiae.
30. Appendix to the Briefs.
31. Serving and Filing Briefs.
32. Form of Briefs, Appendices, and Other Papers.
32.1 Citing Judicial Dispositions.
33. Appeal Conferences.
34. Oral Argument.
35. En Banc Determination.
36. Entry of Judgment; Notice.
37. Interest on Judgment.
38. Frivolous Appeal—Damages and Costs.
39. Costs.
40. Petition for Panel Rehearing.
41. Mandate: Contents; Issuance and Effective Date; Stay.
42. Voluntary Dismissal.
43. Substitution of Parties.
44. Case Involving a Constitutional Question When the United States or the Relevant State Is Not a Party.
45. Clerk's Duties.
46. Attorneys.
47. Local Rules by Courts of Appeals.
48. Masters.

TITLE I. APPLICABILITY OF RULES

RULE 1. SCOPE OF RULES; DEFINITION; TITLE

(a) Scope of Rules.

(1) These rules govern procedure in the United States courts of appeals.

(2) When these rules provide for filing a motion or other document in the district court, the procedure must comply with the practice of the district court.

(b) Definition. In these rules, "state" includes the District of

Columbia and any United States commonwealth or territory.

(c) **Title.** These rules are to be known as the Federal Rules of Appellate Procedure.

RULE 2. SUSPENSION OF RULES

On its own or a party's motion, a court of appeals may—to expedite its decision or for other good cause—suspend any provision of these rules in a particular case and order proceedings as it directs, except as otherwise provided in Rule 26(b).

TITLE II. APPEAL FROM A JUDGMENT OR ORDER OF A DISTRICT COURT

RULE 3. APPEAL AS OF RIGHT—HOW TAKEN

(a) Filing the Notice of Appeal.

(1) An appeal permitted by law as of right from a district court to a court of appeals may be taken only by filing a notice of appeal with the district clerk within the time allowed by Rule 4. At the time of filing, the appellant must furnish the clerk with enough copies of the notice to enable the clerk to comply with Rule 3(d).

(2) An appellant's failure to take any step other than the timely filing of a notice of appeal does not affect the validity of the appeal, but is ground only for the court of appeals to act as it considers appropriate, including dismissing the appeal.

(3) An appeal from a judgment by a magistrate judge in a civil case is taken in the same way as an appeal from any other district court judgment.

(4) An appeal by permission under 28 U.S.C. § 1292(b) or an appeal in a bankruptcy case may be taken only in the manner prescribed by Rules 5 and 6, respectively.

(b) Joint or Consolidated Appeals.

(1) When two or more parties are entitled to appeal from a district-court judgment or order, and their interests make joinder practicable, they may file a joint notice of appeal. They may then proceed on appeal as a single appellant.

(2) When the parties have filed separate timely notices of appeal, the appeals may be joined or consolidated by the court of appeals.

(c) Contents of the Notice of Appeal.

(1) The notice of appeal must:

(A) specify the party or parties taking the appeal by naming each one in the caption or body of the notice, but an attorney representing more than one party may describe those parties with such terms as "all plaintiffs," "the defendants," "the plaintiffs A, B, et al.," or "all defendants except X";

(B) designate the judgment,—or the appealable order—from which the appeal is taken; and

(C) name the court to which the appeal is taken.

(2) A pro se notice of appeal is considered filed on behalf of the signer and the signer's spouse and minor children (if they are parties), unless the notice clearly indicates otherwise.

(3) In a class action, whether or not the class has been certified, the notice of appeal is sufficient if it names one person qualified to bring the appeal as representative of the class.

(4) The notice of appeal encompasses all orders that merge for purposes of appeal into the designated judgment or appealable order. It is not necessary to designate those orders in the notice of appeal.

(5) In a civil case, a notice of appeal encompasses the final judgment, whether or not that judgment is set out in a separate document under Federal Rule of Civil Procedure 58, if the notice designates:

(A) an order that adjudicates all remaining claims and the rights and liabilities of all remaining parties; or

(B) an order described in Rule 4(a)(4)(A).

(6) An appellant may designate only part of a judgment or appealable order by expressly stating that the notice of appeal is so limited. Without such an express statement, specific designations do not limit the scope of the notice of appeal.

(7) An appeal must not be dismissed for informality of form or title of the notice of appeal, for failure to name a party whose intent to appeal is otherwise clear from the notice, or for failure to properly designate the judgment if the notice of appeal was filed after entry of the judgment and designates an order that merged into that judgment.

(8) Forms 1A and 1B in the Appendix of Forms are suggested forms of notices of appeal.

(d) Serving the Notice of Appeal.

(1) The district clerk must serve notice of the filing of a notice of appeal by sending a copy to each party's counsel of record—excluding the appellant's—or, if a party is proceeding pro se, to the party's last known address. When a defendant in a criminal case appeals, the clerk must also serve a copy of the notice of appeal on the defendant. The clerk must promptly send a copy of the notice of appeal and of the docket entries—and any later docket entries—to the clerk of the court of appeals named in the notice. The district clerk must note, on each copy, the date when the notice of appeal was filed.

(2) If an inmate confined in an institution files a notice of ap-

peal in the manner provided by Rule 4(c), the district clerk must also note the date when the clerk docketed the notice.

(3) The district clerk's failure to serve notice does not affect the validity of the appeal. The clerk must note on the docket the names of the parties to whom the clerk sends copies, with the date of sending. Service is sufficient despite the death of a party or the party's counsel.

(e) Payment of Fees. Upon filing a notice of appeal, the appellant must pay the district clerk all required fees. The district clerk receives the appellate docket fee on behalf of the court of appeals.

RULE 3.1. APPEAL FROM A JUDGMENT OF A MAGISTRATE JUDGE IN A CIVIL CASE [ABROGATED]

RULE 4. APPEAL AS OF RIGHT—WHEN TAKEN

(a) Appeal in a Civil Case.

(1) Time for Filing a Notice of Appeal.

(A) In a civil case, except as provided in Rules 4(a)(1)(B), 4(a)(4), and 4(c), the notice of appeal required by Rule 3 must be filed with the district clerk within 30 days after entry of the judgment or order appealed from.

(B) The notice of appeal may be filed by any party within 60 days after entry of the judgment or order appealed from if one of the parties is:

(i) the United States;

(ii) a United States agency;

(iii) a United States officer or employee sued in an official capacity; or

(iv) a current or former United States officer or employee sued in an individual capacity for an act or omission occurring in connection with duties performed on the United States' behalf — including all instances in which the United States represents that person when the judgment or order is entered or files the appeal for that person.

(C) An appeal from an order granting or denying an application for a writ of error *coram nobis* is an appeal in a civil case for purposes of Rule 4(a).

(2) Filing Before Entry of Judgment. A notice of appeal filed after the court announces a decision or order—but before the entry of the judgment or order—is treated as filed on the date of and after the entry.

(3) Multiple Appeals. If one party timely files a notice of appeal, any other party may file a notice of appeal within 14 days after the date when the first notice was filed, or within the time otherwise prescribed by this Rule 4(a), whichever period ends later.

(4) Effect of a Motion on a Notice of Appeal.

(A) If a party files in the district court any of the following motions under the Federal Rules of Civil Procedure—and does so within the time allowed by those rules—the time to file an appeal runs for all parties from the entry of the order disposing of the last such remaining motion:

(i) for judgment under Rule 50(b);

(ii) to amend or make additional factual findings under Rule 52(b), whether or not granting the motion would alter the judgment;

(iii) for attorney's fees under Rule 54 if the district court extends the time to appeal under Rule 58;

(iv) to alter or amend the judgment under Rule 59;

(v) for a new trial under Rule 59; or

(vi) for relief under Rule 60 if the motion is filed no later than 28 days after the judgment is entered.

(B) (i) If a party files a notice of appeal after the court announces or enters a judgment—but before it disposes of any motion listed in Rule 4(a)(4)(A)—the notice becomes effective to appeal a judgment or order, in whole or in part, when the order disposing of the last such remaining motion is entered.

(ii) A party intending to challenge an order disposing of any motion listed in Rule 4(a)(4)(A), or a judgment's alteration or amendment upon such a motion, must file a notice of appeal, or an amended notice of appeal—in compliance with Rule 3(c)—within the time prescribed by this Rule measured from the entry of the order disposing of the last such remaining motion.

(iii) No additional fee is required to file an amended notice.

(5) Motion for Extension of Time.

(A) The district court may extend the time to file a notice of appeal if:

(i) a party so moves no later than 30 days after the time prescribed by this Rule 4(a) expires; and

(ii) regardless of whether its motion is filed before or during the 30 days after the time prescribed by this Rule 4(a) expires, that party shows excusable neglect or good cause.

(B) A motion filed before the expiration of the time prescribed in Rule 4(a)(1) or (3) may be ex parte unless the court requires otherwise. If the motion is filed after the expiration of the prescribed time, notice must be given to the other parties in accordance with local rules.

(C) No extension under this Rule 4(a)(5) may exceed 30 days after the prescribed time or 14 days after the date when the order granting the motion is entered, whichever is later.

(6) Reopening the Time to File an Appeal. The district court may reopen the time to file an appeal for a period of 14 days after the date when its order to reopen is entered, but only if all the following conditions are satisfied:

(A) the court finds that the moving party did not receive notice under Federal Rule of Civil Procedure 77(d) of the entry of the judgment or order sought to be appealed within 21 days after entry;

(B) the motion is filed within 180 days after the judgment or order is entered or within 14 days after the moving party receives notice under Federal Rule of Civil Procedure 77(d) of the entry, whichever is earlier; and

(C) the court finds that no party would be prejudiced.

(7) Entry Defined.

(A) A judgment or order is entered for purposes of this Rule 4(a):

(i) if Federal Rule of Civil Procedure 58(a) does not require a separate document, when the judgment or order is entered in the civil docket under Federal Rules of Civil Procedure 79(a); or

(ii) if Federal Rule of Civil Procedure 58(a) requires a separate document, when the judgment or order is entered in the civil docket under Federal Rule of Civil Procedure 79(a) and when the earlier of these events occurs:

- the judgment or order is set forth on a separate document, or
- 150 days have run from entry of the judgment or order in the civil docket under Federal Rule of Civil Procedure 79(a).

(B) A failure to set forth a judgment or order on a separate document when required by Federal Rule of Civil Procedure 58(a) does not affect the validity of an appeal from that judgment or order.

(b) Appeal in a Criminal Case.

(1) Time for Filing a Notice of Appeal.

(A) In a criminal case, a defendant's notice of appeal must be filed in the district court within 14 days after the later of:

(i) the entry of either the judgment or the order being appealed; or

(ii) the filing of the government's notice of appeal.

(B) When the government is entitled to appeal, its notice

of appeal must be filed in the district court within 30 days after the later of:

(i) the entry of the judgment or order being appealed; or

(ii) the filing of a notice of appeal by any defendant.

(2) Filing Before Entry of Judgment. A notice of appeal filed after the court announces a decision, sentence, or order—but before the entry of the judgment or order—is treated as filed on the date of and after the entry.

(3) Effect of a Motion on a Notice of Appeal.

(A) If a defendant timely makes any of the following motions under the Federal Rules of Criminal Procedure, the notice of appeal from a judgment of conviction must be filed within 14 days after the entry of the order disposing of the last such remaining motion, or within 14 days after the entry of the judgment of conviction, whichever period ends later. This provision applies to a timely motion:

(i) for judgment of acquittal under Rule 29;

(ii) for a new trial under Rule 33, but if based on newly discovered evidence, only if the motion is made no later than 14 days after the entry of the judgment; or

(iii) for arrest of judgment under Rule 34.

(B) A notice of appeal filed after the court announces a decision, sentence, or order—but before it disposes of any of the motions referred to in Rule 4(b)(3)(A)—becomes effective upon the later of the following:

(i) the entry of the order disposing of the last such remaining motion; or

(ii) the entry of the judgment of conviction.

(C) A valid notice of appeal is effective—without amendment—to appeal from an order disposing of any of the motions referred to in Rule 4(b)(3)(A).

(4) Motion for Extension of Time. Upon a finding of excusable neglect or good cause, the district court may—before or after the time has expired, with or without motion and notice—extend the time to file a notice of appeal for a period not to exceed 30 days from the expiration of the time otherwise prescribed by this Rule 4(b).

(5) Jurisdiction. The filing of a notice of appeal under this Rule 4(b) does not divest a district court of jurisdiction to correct a sentence under Federal Rule of Criminal Procedure 35(c), nor does the filing of a motion under 35(c) affect the validity of a notice of appeal filed before entry of the order disposing of the motion. The filing of a motion under Federal Rule of Criminal Procedure 35(a) does not suspend the time for filing a notice of appeal from a judgment of conviction.

(6) Entry Defined. A judgment or order is entered for purposes of this Rule 4(b) when it is entered on the criminal docket.

(c) Appeal by an Inmate Confined in an Institution.

(1) If an institution has a system designed for legal mail, an inmate confined there must use that system to receive the benefit of this Rule 4(c)(1). If an inmate files a notice of appeal in either a civil or a criminal case, the notice is timely if it is deposited in the institution's internal mail system on or before the last day for filing and:

(A) it is accompanied by:

(i) a declaration in compliance with 28 U.S.C. § 1746—or a notarized statement—setting out the date of deposit and stating that first-class postage is being prepaid; or

(ii) evidence (such as a postmark or date stamp) showing that the notice was so deposited and that postage was prepaid; or

(B) the court of appeals exercises its discretion to permit the later filing of a declaration or notarized statement that satisfies Rule 4(c)(1)(A)(i).

(2) If an inmate files the first notice of appeal in a civil case under this Rule 4(c), the 14-day period provided in Rule 4(a)(3) for another party to file a notice of appeal runs from the date when the district court dockets the first notice.

(3) When a defendant in a criminal case files a notice of appeal under this Rule 4(c), the 30-day period for the government to file its notice of appeal runs from the entry of the judgment or order appealed from or from the district court's docketing of the defendant's notice of appeal, whichever is later.

(d) Mistaken Filing in the Court of Appeals. If a notice of appeal in either a civil or a criminal case is mistakenly filed in the court of appeals, the clerk of that court must note on the notice the date when it was received and send it to the district clerk. The notice is then considered filed in the district court on the date so noted.

RULE 5. APPEAL BY PERMISSION

(a) Petition for Permission to Appeal.

(1) To request permission to appeal when an appeal is within the court of appeals' discretion, a party must file a petition with the circuit clerk and serve it on all other parties to the district-court action.

(2) The petition must be filed within the time specified by the statute or rule authorizing the appeal or, if no such time

is specified, within the time provided by Rule 4(a) for filing a notice of appeal.

(3) If a party cannot petition for appeal unless the district court first enters an order granting permission to do so or stating that the necessary conditions are met, the district court may amend its order, either on its own or in response to a party's motion, to include the required permission or statement. In that event, the time to petition runs from entry of the amended order.

(b) Contents of the Petition; Answer or Cross-Petition; Oral Argument.

(1) The petition must include the following:

(A) the facts necessary to understand the question presented;

(B) the question itself;

(C) the relief sought;

(D) the reasons why the appeal should be allowed and is authorized by a statute or rule; and

(E) an attached copy of:

(i) the order, decree, or judgment complained of and any related opinion or memorandum, and

(ii) any order stating the district court's permission to appeal or finding that the necessary conditions are met.

(2) A party may file an answer in opposition or a cross-petition within 10 days after the petition is served.

(3) The petition and answer will be submitted without oral argument unless the court of appeals orders otherwise.

(c) Form of Papers; Number of Copies; Length Limits. All papers must conform to Rule 32(c)(2). An original and 3 copies must be filed unless the court requires a different number by local rule or by order in a particular case. Except by the court's permission, and excluding the accompanying documents required by Rule 5(b)(1)(E):

(1) a paper produced using a computer must not exceed 5,200 words; and

(2) a handwritten or typewritten paper must not exceed 20 pages.

(d) Grant of Permission; Fees; Cost Bond; Filing the Record.

(1) Within 14 days after the entry of the order granting permission to appeal, the appellant must:

(A) pay the district clerk all required fees; and

(B) file a cost bond if required under Rule 7.

(2) A notice of appeal need not be filed. The date when the order granting permission to appeal is entered serves as the date of the notice of appeal for calculating time under

these rules.

(3) The district clerk must notify the circuit clerk once the petitioner has paid the fees. Upon receiving this notice, the circuit clerk must enter the appeal on the docket. The record must be forwarded and filed in accordance with Rules 11 and 12(c).

RULE 5.1. APPEAL BY LEAVE UNDER 28 U.S.C. § 636(C)(5) [ABROGATED]

RULE 6. APPEAL IN A BANKRUPTCY CASE

(a) Appeal From a Judgment, Order, or Decree of a District Court Exercising Original Jurisdiction in a Bankruptcy Case. An appeal to a court of appeals from a final judgment, order, or decree of a district court exercising jurisdiction under 28 U.S.C. § 1334 is taken as any other civil appeal under these rules.

(b) Appeal From a Judgment, Order, or Decree of a District Court or Bankruptcy Appellate Panel Exercising Appellate Jurisdiction in a Bankruptcy Case.

(1) **Applicability of Other Rules.** These rules apply to an appeal to a court of appeals under 28 U.S.C. § 158(d)(1) from a final judgment, order, or decree of a district court or bankruptcy appellate panel exercising appellate jurisdiction under 28 U.S.C. § 158(a) or (b), but with these qualifications:

(A) Rules 4(a)(4), 4(b), 9, 10, 11, 12(c), 13-20, 22-23, and 24(b) do not apply;

(B) the reference in Rule 3(c) to "Forms 1A and 1B in the Appendix of Forms" must be read as a reference to Form 5;

(C) when the appeal is from a bankruptcy appellate panel, "district court," as used in any applicable rule, means "appellate panel." and

(D) in Rule 12.1, "district court" includes a bankruptcy court or bankruptcy appellate panel.

(2) **Additional Rules.** In addition to the rules made applicable by Rule 6(b)(1), the following rules apply:

(A) Motion for Rehearing.

(i) If a timely motion for rehearing under Bankruptcy Rule 8022 is filed, the time to appeal for all parties runs from the entry of the order disposing of the motion. A notice of appeal filed after the district court or bankruptcy appellate panel announces or enters a judgment, order, or decree—but before disposition of the motion for rehearing—becomes effective when the order disposing of the motion for rehearing is entered.

(ii) If a party intends to challenge the order disposing

of the motion--or the alteration or amendment of a judgment, order, or decree upon the motion--then the party, in compliance with Rules 3(c) and 6(b)(1)(B), must file a notice of appeal or amended notice of appeal. The notice or amended notice must be filed within the time prescribed by Rule 4—excluding Rules 4(a)(4) and 4(b)—measured from the entry of the order disposing of the motion.

(iii) No additional fee is required to file an amended notice.

(B) The Record on Appeal.

(i) Within 14 days after filing the notice of appeal, the appellant must file with the clerk possessing the record assembled in accordance with Bankruptcy Rule 8009—and serve on the appellee—a statement of the issues to be presented on appeal and a designation of the record to be certified and made available to the circuit clerk.

(ii) An appellee who believes that other parts of the record are necessary must, within 14 days after being served with the appellant's designation, file with the clerk and serve on the appellant a designation of additional parts to be included.

(iii) The record on appeal consists of:

- the redesignated record as provided above;
- the proceedings in the district court or bankruptcy appellate panel; and
- a certified copy of the docket entries prepared by the clerk under Rule 3(d).

(C) Making the Record Available.

(i) When the record is complete, the district clerk or bankruptcy-appellate-panel clerk must number the documents constituting the record and promptly make it available to the circuit clerk. If the clerk makes the record available in paper form, the clerk will not send documents of unusual bulk or weight, physical exhibits other than documents, or other parts of the record designated for omission by local rule of the court of appeals, unless directed to do so by a party or the circuit clerk. If unusually bulky or heavy exhibits are to be made available in paper form, a party must arrange with the clerks in advance for their transportation and receipt.

(ii) All parties must do whatever else is necessary to enable the clerk to assemble the record and make it available. When the record is made available in paper form, the court of appeals may provide by rule or order that a certified copy of the docket entries be made available in place of the redesignated record. But any party may request at any time during the pendency of the appeal that the redesignated record be made available.

(D) Filing the Record. When the district clerk or bankruptcy-appellate-panel clerk has made the record available, the circuit clerk must note that fact on the docket. The date noted on the docket serves as the filing date of the record. The circuit clerk must immediately notify all parties of the filing date. [See § § 6:6, 6:7, 6:9, 7:1, 8:4]

(c) Direct Review by Permission Under 28 U.S.C. § 158(d)(2).

(1) Applicability of Other Rules. These rules apply to a direct appeal by permission under 28 U.S.C. § 158(d)(2), but with these qualifications:

(A) Rules 3-4, 5(a)(3), 6(a), 6(b), 8(a), 8(c), 9-12, 13-20, 22-23, and 24(b) do not apply;

(B) as used in any applicable rule, "district court" or "district clerk" includes--to the extent appropriate--a bankruptcy court or bankruptcy appellate panel or its clerk; and

(C) the reference to "Rules 11 and 12(c)" in Rule 5(d)(3) must be read as a reference to Rules 6(c)(2)(B) and (C).

(2) Additional Rules.

(A) The Record on Appeal. Bankruptcy Rule 8009 governs the record on appeal.

(B) Making the Record Available. Bankruptcy Rule 8010 governs completing the record and making it available.

(C) Stays Pending Appeal. Bankruptcy Rule 8007 applies to stays pending appeal.

(D) Duties of the Circuit Clerk. When the bankruptcy clerk has made the record available, the circuit clerk must note that fact on the docket. The date noted on the docket serves as the filing date of the record. The circuit clerk must immediately notify all parties of the filing date.

(E) Filing a Representation Statement. Unless the court of appeals designates another time, within 14 days after entry of the order granting permission to appeal, the attorney who sought permission must file a statement with the circuit clerk naming the parties that the attorney represents on appeal.

RULE 7. BOND FOR COSTS ON APPEAL IN A CIVIL CASE

In a civil case, the district court may require an appellant to file a bond or provide other security in any form and amount necessary to ensure payment of costs on appeal. Rule 8(b) applies to a surety on a bond given under this rule.

RULE 8. STAY OR INJUNCTION PENDING APPEAL

(a) Motion for Stay.

(1) Initial Motion in the District Court. A party must ordinarily move first in the district court for the following relief:

(A) a stay of the judgment or order of a district court pending appeal;

(B) approval of a bond or other security provided to obtain a stay of judgment; or

(C) an order suspending, modifying, restoring, or granting an injunction while an appeal is pending.

(2) Motion in the Court of Appeals; Conditions on Relief. A motion for the relief mentioned in Rule 8(a)(1) may be made to the court of appeals or to one of its judges.

(A) The motion must:

(i) show that moving first in the district court would be impracticable; or

(ii) state that, a motion having been made, the district court denied the motion or failed to afford the relief requested and state any reasons given by the district court for its action.

(B) The motion must also include:

(i) the reasons for granting the relief requested and the facts relied on;

(ii) originals or copies of affidavits or other sworn statements supporting facts subject to dispute; and

(iii) relevant parts of the record.

(C) The moving party must give reasonable notice of the motion to all parties.

(D) A motion under this Rule 8(a)(2) must be filed with the circuit clerk and normally will be considered by a panel of the court. But in an exceptional case in which time requirements make that procedure impracticable, the motion may be made to and considered by a single judge.

(E) The court may condition relief on a party's filing a bond or other security in the district court.

(b) Proceeding Against a Security Provider. If a party gives security with one or more security providers, each provider submits to the jurisdiction of the district court and irrevocably appoints the district clerk as its agent on whom any papers affecting its liability on the security may be served. On motion, a security provider's liability may be enforced in the district court without the necessity of an independent action. The motion and any notice that the district court prescribes may be served on the district clerk, who must promptly send a copy to each security provider whose address is known.

(c) Stay in a Criminal Case. Rule 38 of the Federal Rules of Criminal Procedure governs a stay in a criminal case.

RULE 9. RELEASE IN A CRIMINAL CASE

(a) Release Before Judgment of Conviction.

(1) The district court must state in writing, or orally on the record, the reasons for an order regarding the release or detention of a defendant in a criminal case. A party appealing from the order must file with the court of appeals a copy of the district court's order and the court's statement of reasons as soon as practicable after filing the notice of appeal. An appellant who questions the factual basis for the district court's order must file a transcript of the release proceedings or an explanation of why a transcript was not obtained.

(2) After reasonable notice to the appellee, the court of appeals must promptly determine the appeal on the basis of the papers, affidavits, and parts of the record that the parties present or the court requires. Unless the court so orders, briefs need not be filed.

(3) The court of appeals or one of its judges may order the defendant's release pending the disposition of the appeal.

(b) Release After Judgment of Conviction. A party entitled to do so may obtain review of a district-court order regarding release after a judgment of conviction by filing a notice of appeal from that order in the district court, or by filing a motion in the court of appeals if the party has already filed a notice of appeal from the judgment of conviction. Both the order and the review are subject to Rule 9(a). The papers filed by the party seeking review must include a copy of the judgment of conviction.

(c) Criteria for Release. The court must make its decision regarding release in accordance with the applicable provisions of 18 U.S.C. §§ 3142, 3143, and 3145(c).

RULE 10. THE RECORD ON APPEAL

(a) Composition of the Record on Appeal. The following items constitute the record on appeal:

(1) the original papers and exhibits filed in the district court;

(2) the transcript of proceedings, if any; and

(3) a certified copy of the docket entries prepared by the district clerk.

(b) The Transcript of Proceedings.

(1) Appellant's Duty to Order. Within 14 days after filing the notice of appeal or entry of an order disposing of the last timely remaining motion of a type specified in Rule 4(a)(4)(A), whichever is later, the appellant must do either of the following:

(A) order from the reporter a transcript of such parts of the proceedings not already on file as the appellant considers necessary, subject to a local rule of the court of appeals and with the following qualifications:

(i) the order must be in writing;

(ii) if the cost of the transcript is to be paid by the United States under the Criminal Justice Act, the order must so state; and

(iii) the appellant must, within the same period, file a copy of the order with the district clerk; or

(B) file a certificate stating that no transcript will be ordered.

(2) Unsupported Finding or Conclusion. If the appellant intends to urge on appeal that a finding or conclusion is unsupported by the evidence or is contrary to the evidence, the appellant must include in the record a transcript of all evidence relevant to that finding or conclusion.

(3) Partial Transcript. Unless the entire transcript is ordered:

(A) the appellant must—within the 14 days provided in Rule 10(b)(1)—file a statement of the issues that the appellant intends to present on the appeal and must serve on the appellee a copy of both the order or certificate and the statement;

(B) if the appellee considers it necessary to have a transcript of other parts of the proceedings, the appellee must, within 14 days after the service of the order or certificate and the statement of the issues, file and serve on the appellant a designation of additional parts to be ordered; and

(C) unless within 14 days after service of that designation the appellant has ordered all such parts, and has so notified the appellee, the appellee may within the following 14 days either order the parts or move in the district court for an order requiring the appellant to do so.

(4) Payment. At the time of ordering, a party must make satisfactory arrangements with the reporter for paying the cost of the transcript.

(c) Statement of the Evidence When the Proceedings Were Not Recorded or When a Transcript Is Unavailable. If the transcript of a hearing or trial is unavailable, the appellant may prepare a statement of the evidence or proceedings from the best available means, including the appellant's recollection. The statement must be served on the appellee, who may serve objections or proposed amendments within 14 days after being served. The statement and any objections or proposed amendments must then be submitted to the district court for settlement and approval. As settled and approved, the statement must be included by the district clerk in the record on appeal.

(d) Agreed Statement as the Record on Appeal. In place of the record on appeal as defined in Rule 10(a), the parties may prepare, sign, and submit to the district court a statement of the case showing how the issues presented by the appeal arose and were decided in the district court. The statement must set forth only those facts averred and proved or sought to be proved that are essential to the court's resolution of the issues. If the statement is truthful, it—together with any additions that the district court may consider necessary to a full presentation of the issues on appeal—must be approved by the district court and must then be certified to the court of appeals as the record on appeal. The district clerk must then send it to the circuit clerk within the time provided by Rule 11. A copy of the agreed statement may be filed in place of the appendix required by Rule 30.

(e) Correction or Modification of the Record.

(1) If any difference arises about whether the record truly discloses what occurred in the district court, the difference must be submitted to and settled by that court and the record conformed accordingly.

(2) If anything material to either party is omitted from or misstated in the record by error or accident, the omission or misstatement may be corrected and a supplemental record may be certified and forwarded:

(A) on stipulation of the parties;

(B) by the district court before or after the record has been forwarded; or

(C) by the court of appeals.

(3) All other questions as to the form and content of the record must be presented to the court of appeals.

RULE 11. FORWARDING THE RECORD

(a) Appellant's Duty. An appellant filing a notice of appeal must comply with Rule 10(b) and must do whatever else is necessary to enable the clerk to assemble and forward the record. If there are multiple appeals from a judgment or order, the clerk must forward a single record.

(b) Duties of Reporter and District Clerk.

(1) Reporter's Duty to Prepare and File a Transcript. The reporter must prepare and file a transcript as follows:

(A) Upon receiving an order for a transcript, the reporter must enter at the foot of the order the date of its receipt and the expected completion date and send a copy, so endorsed, to the circuit clerk.

(B) If the transcript cannot be completed within 30 days of the reporter's receipt of the order, the reporter may request the circuit clerk to grant additional time to complete it. The clerk must note on the docket the action taken and notify the parties.

(C) When a transcript is complete, the reporter must file it with the district clerk and notify the circuit clerk of the filing.

(D) If the reporter fails to file the transcript on time, the circuit clerk must notify the district judge and do whatever else the court of appeals directs.

(2) District Clerk's Duty to Forward. When the record is complete, the district clerk must number the documents constituting the record and send them promptly to the circuit clerk together with a list of the documents correspondingly numbered and reasonably identified. Unless directed to do so by a party or the circuit clerk, the district clerk will not send to the court of appeals documents of unusual bulk or weight, physical exhibits other than documents, or other parts of the record designated for omission by local rule of the court of appeals. If the exhibits are unusually bulky or heavy, a party must arrange with the clerks in advance for their transportation and receipt.

(c) Retaining the Record Temporarily in the District Court for Use in Preparing the Appeal. The parties may stipulate, or the district court on motion may order, that the district clerk retain the record temporarily for the parties to use in preparing the papers on appeal. In that event the district clerk must certify to the circuit clerk that the record on appeal is complete. Upon receipt of the appellee's brief, or earlier if the court orders or the parties agree, the appellant must request the district clerk to forward the record.

(d) [Abrogated.]

(e) Retaining the Record by Court Order.

(1) The court of appeals may, by order or local rule, provide that a certified copy of the docket entries be forwarded instead of the entire record. But a party may at any time during the appeal request that designated parts of the record be forwarded.

(2) The district court may order the record or some part of it retained if the court needs it while the appeal is pending, subject, however, to call by the court of appeals.

(3) If part or all of the record is ordered retained, the district clerk must send to the court of appeals a copy of the order and the docket entries together with the parts of the original record allowed by the district court and copies of any parts of the record designated by the parties.

(f) **Retaining Parts of the Record in the District Court by Stipulation of the Parties.** The parties may agree by written stipulation filed in the district court that designated parts of the record be retained in the district court subject to call by the court of appeals or request by a party. The parts of the record so designated remain a part of the record on appeal.

(g) **Record for a Preliminary Motion in the Court of Appeals.** If, before the record is forwarded, a party makes any of the following motions in the court of appeals:

- for dismissal;
- for release;
- for a stay pending appeal;
- for additional security on the bond on appeal or on a bond or other security provided to obtain a stay of judgment; or
- for any other intermediate order—

the district clerk must send the court of appeals any parts of the record designated by any party.

RULE 12. DOCKETING THE APPEAL; FILING A REPRESENTATION STATEMENT; FILING THE RECORD

(a) **Docketing the Appeal.** Upon receiving the copy of the notice of appeal and the docket entries from the district clerk under Rule 3(d), the circuit clerk must docket the appeal under the title of the district-court action and must identify the appellant, adding the appellant's name if necessary.

(b) **Filing a Representation Statement**. Unless the court of appeals designates another time, the attorney who filed the notice of appeal must, within 14 days after filing the notice, file a statement with the circuit clerk naming the parties that the attorney represents on appeal.

(c) **Filing the Record, Partial Record, or Certificate.** Upon receiving the record, partial record, or district clerk's certificate as provided in Rule 11, the circuit clerk must file it and immediately notify all parties of the filing date.

RULE 12.1. REMAND AFTER AN INDICATIVE RULING BY THE DISTRICT COURT ON A MOTION FOR RELIEF THAT IS BARRED BY A PENDING APPEAL

(a) **Notice to the Court of Appeals**. If a timely motion is made in the district court for relief that it lacks authority to grant because of an appeal that has been docketed and is pending, the movant must promptly notify the circuit clerk if the district court states either that it would grant the motion or that the motion raises a substantial issue.

(b) **Remand After an Indicative Ruling**. If the district court states that it would grant the motion or that the motion raises a substantial issue, the court of appeals may remand for further proceedings but retains jurisdiction unless it expressly dismisses the appeal. If the court of appeals remands but retains jurisdiction, the parties must promptly notify the circuit clerk when the district court has decided the motion on remand.

TITLE III. APPEALS FROM THE UNITED STATES TAX COURT

RULE 13. APPEALS FROM THE TAX COURT

(a) Appeal as of Right.

(1) How Obtained; Time for Filing a Notice of Appeal.

(A) An appeal as of right from the United States Tax Court is commenced by filing a notice of appeal with the Tax Court clerk within 90 days after the entry of the Tax Court's decision. At the time of filing, the appellant must furnish the clerk with enough copies of the notice to enable the clerk to comply with Rule 3(d). If one party files a timely notice of appeal, any other party may file a notice of appeal within 120 days after the Tax Court's decision is entered.

(B) If, under Tax Court rules, a party makes a timely motion to vacate or revise the Tax Court's decision, the time to file a notice of appeal runs from the entry of the order disposing of the motion or from the entry of a new decision, whichever is later.

(2) Notice of Appeal; How Filed. The notice of appeal may be filed either at the Tax Court clerk's office in the District of Columbia or by sending it to the clerk. If sent by mail the notice is considered filed on the postmark date, subject to § 7502 of the Internal Revenue Code, as amended, and the applicable regulations.

(3) Contents of the Notice of Appeal; Service; Effect of Filing and Service. Rule 3 prescribes the contents of a notice of appeal, the manner of service, and the effect of its filing and service. Form 2 in the Appendix of Forms is a suggested form of a notice of appeal.

(4) The Record on Appeal; Forwarding; Filing.

(A) Except as otherwise provided under Tax Court rules for the transcript of proceedings, the appeal is governed by the parts of Rules 10, 11, and 12 regarding the record on appeal from a district court, the time and manner of forwarding and filing, and the docketing in the court of appeals.

(B) If an appeal is taken to more than one court of appeals, the original record must be sent to the court named in the first notice of appeal filed. In an appeal to any other court of appeals, the appellant must apply to that other court to make provision for the record.

(b) Appeal by Permission. An appeal by permission is

governed by Rule 5.

RULE 14. APPLICABILITY OF OTHER RULES TO APPEALS FROM THE TAX COURT

All provisions of these rules, except Rules 4, 6-9, 15-20, and 22-23, apply to appeals from the Tax Court. References in any applicable rule (other than Rule 24(a)) to the district court and district clerk are to be read as referring to the Tax Court and its clerk.

TITLE IV. REVIEW OR ENFORCEMENT OF AN ORDER OF AN ADMINISTRATIVE AGENCY, BOARD, COMMISSION, OR OFFICER

RULE 15. REVIEW OR ENFORCEMENT OF AN AGENCY ORDER—HOW OBTAINED; INTERVENTION

(a) Petition for Review; Joint Petition.

(1) Review of an agency order is commenced by filing, within the time prescribed by law, a petition for review with the clerk of a court of appeals authorized to review the agency order. If their interests make joinder practicable, two or more persons may join in a petition to the same court to review the same order.

(2) The petition must:

(A) name each party seeking review either in the caption or the body of the petition—using such terms as "et al.," "petitioners," or "respondents" does not effectively name the parties;

(B) name the agency as a respondent (even though not named in the petition, the United States is a respondent if required by statute); and

(C) specify the order or part thereof to be reviewed.

(3) Form 3 in the Appendix of Forms is a suggested form of a petition for review.

(4) In this rule "agency" includes an agency, board, commission, or officer; "petition for review" includes a petition to enjoin, suspend, modify, or otherwise review, or a notice of appeal, whichever form is indicated by the applicable statute.

(b) Application or Cross-Application to Enforce an Order; Answer; Default.

(1) An application to enforce an agency order must be filed with the clerk of a court of appeals authorized to enforce the order. If a petition is filed to review an agency order that the court may enforce, a party opposing the petition may file a cross-application for enforcement.

(2) Within 21 days after the application for enforcement is filed, the respondent must serve on the applicant an answer to the application and file it with the clerk. If the

respondent fails to answer in time, the court will enter judgment for the relief requested.

(3) The application must contain a concise statement of the proceedings in which the order was entered, the facts upon which venue is based, and the relief requested.

(c) Service of the Petition or Application. The circuit clerk must serve a copy of the petition for review, or an application or cross-application to enforce an agency order, on each respondent as prescribed by Rule 3(d), unless a different manner of service is prescribed by statute. At the time of filing, the petitioner must:

(1) serve, or have served, a copy on each party admitted to participate in the agency proceedings, except for the respondents;

(2) file with the clerk a list of those so served; and

(3) give the clerk enough copies of the petition or application to serve each respondent.

(d) Intervention. Unless a statute provides another method, a person who wants to intervene in a proceeding under this rule must file a motion for leave to intervene with the circuit clerk and serve a copy on all parties. The motion—or other notice of intervention authorized by statute—must be filed within 30 days after the petition for review is filed and must contain a concise statement of the interest of the moving party and the grounds for intervention.

(e) Payment of Fees. When filing any separate or joint petition for review in a court of appeals, the petitioner must pay the circuit clerk all required fees.

RULE 15.1. BRIEFS AND ORAL ARGUMENT IN A NATIONAL LABOR RELATIONS BOARD PROCEEDING

In either an enforcement or a review proceeding, a party adverse to the National Labor Relations Board proceeds first on briefing and at oral argument, unless the court orders otherwise.

RULE 16. THE RECORD ON REVIEW OR ENFORCEMENT

(a) Composition of the Record. The record on review or enforcement of an agency order consists of:

(1) the order involved;

(2) any findings or report on which it is based; and

(3) the pleadings, evidence, and other parts of the proceedings before the agency.

(b) Omissions From or Misstatements in the Record. The parties may at any time, by stipulation, supply any omission from the record or correct a misstatement, or the court may so direct. If necessary, the court may direct that a supplemental record be prepared and filed.

RULE 17. FILING THE RECORD

(a) Agency to File; Time for Filing; Notice of Filing. The agency must file the record with the circuit clerk within 40 days after being served with a petition for review, unless the statute authorizing review provides otherwise, or within 40 days after it files an application for enforcement unless the respondent fails to answer or the court orders otherwise. The court may shorten or extend the time to file the record. The clerk must notify all parties of the date when the record is filed.

(b) Filing—What Constitutes.

(1) The agency must file:

(A) the original or a certified copy of the entire record or parts designated by the parties; or

(B) a certified list adequately describing all documents, transcripts of testimony, exhibits, and other material constituting the record, or describing those parts designated by the parties.

(2) The parties may stipulate in writing that no record or certified list be filed. The date when the stipulation is filed with the circuit clerk is treated as the date when the record is filed.

(3) The agency must retain any portion of the record not filed with the clerk. All parts of the record retained by the agency are a part of the record on review for all purposes and, if the court or a party so requests, must be sent to the court regardless of any prior stipulation.

RULE 18. STAY PENDING REVIEW

(a) Motion for a Stay.

(1) Initial Motion Before the Agency. A petitioner must ordinarily move first before the agency for a stay pending review of its decision or order.

(2) Motion in the Court of Appeals. A motion for a stay may be made to the court of appeals or one of its judges.

(A) The motion must:

(i) show that moving first before the agency would be impracticable; or

(ii) state that, a motion having been made, the agency denied the motion or failed to afford the relief requested and state any reasons given by the agency for its action.

(B) The motion must also include:

(i) the reasons for granting the relief requested and the facts relied on;

(ii) originals or copies of affidavits or other sworn statements supporting facts subject to dispute; and

(iii) relevant parts of the record.

(C) The moving party must give reasonable notice of the motion to all parties.

(D) The motion must be filed with the circuit clerk and normally will be considered by a panel of the court. But in an exceptional case in which time requirements make that procedure impracticable, the motion may be made to and considered by a single judge.

(b) Bond. The court may condition relief on the filing of a bond or other appropriate security.

RULE 19. SETTLEMENT OF A JUDGMENT ENFORCING AN AGENCY ORDER IN PART

When the court files an opinion directing entry of judgment enforcing the agency's order in part, the agency must within 14 days file with the clerk and serve on each other party a proposed judgment conforming to the opinion. A party who disagrees with the agency's proposed judgment must within 10 days file with the clerk and serve the agency with a proposed judgment that the party believes conforms to the opinion. The court will settle the judgment and direct entry without further hearing or argument.

RULE 20. APPLICABILITY OF RULES TO THE REVIEW OR ENFORCEMENT OF AN AGENCY ORDER

All provisions of these rules, except Rules 3–14 and 22–23, apply to the review or enforcement of an agency order. In these rules, "appellant" includes a petitioner or applicant, and "appellee" includes a respondent.

TITLE V. EXTRAORDINARY WRITS

RULE 21. WRITS OF MANDAMUS AND PROHIBITION, AND OTHER EXTRAORDINARY WRITS

(a) Mandamus or Prohibition to a Court: Petition, Filing, Service, and Docketing.

(1) A party petitioning for a writ of mandamus or prohibition directed to a court must file the petition with the circuit clerk and serve it on all parties to the proceeding in the trial court. The party must also provide a copy to the trial-court judge. All parties to the proceeding in the trial court other than the petitioner are respondents for all purposes.

(2) (A) The petition must be titled "In re [name of petitioner]."

(B) The petition must state:

(i) the relief sought;

(ii) the issues presented;

(iii) the facts necessary to understand the issue presented by the petition; and

(iv) the reasons why the writ should issue.

(C) The petition must include a copy of any order or

opinion or parts of the record that may be essential to understand the matters set forth in the petition.

(3) Upon receiving the prescribed docket fee, the clerk must docket the petition and submit it to the court.

(b) Denial; Order Directing Answer; Briefs; Precedence.

(1) The court may deny the petition without an answer. Otherwise, it must order the respondent, if any, to answer within a fixed time.

(2) The clerk must serve the order to respond on all persons directed to respond.

(3) Two or more respondents may answer jointly.

(4) The court of appeals may invite or order the trial-court judge to address the petition or may invite an amicus curiae to do so. The trial-court judge may request permission to address the petition but may not do so unless invited or ordered to do so by the court of appeals.

(5) If briefing or oral argument is required, the clerk must advise the parties, and when appropriate, the trial-court judge or amicus curiae.

(6) The proceeding must be given preference over ordinary civil cases.

(7) The circuit clerk must send a copy of the final disposition to the trial-court judge.

(c) Other Extraordinary Writs. An application for an extraordinary writ other than one provided for in Rule 21(a) must be made by filing a petition with the circuit clerk and serving it on the respondents. Proceedings on the application must conform, so far as is practicable, to the procedures prescribed in Rule 21(a) and (b).

(d) Form of Papers; Number of Copies; Length Limits. All papers must conform to Rule 32(c)(2). An original and 3 copies must be filed unless the court requires the filing of a different number by local rule or by order in a particular case. Except by the court's permission, and excluding the accompanying documents required by Rule 21(a)(2)(C):

(1) a paper produced using a computer must not exceed 7,800 words; and

(2) a handwritten or typewritten paper must not exceed 30 pages.

TITLE VI. HABEAS CORPUS; PROCEEDINGS IN FORMA PAUPERIS

RULE 22. HABEAS CORPUS AND SECTION 2255 PROCEEDINGS

(a) Application for the Original Writ. An application for a writ of habeas corpus must be made to the appropriate district court. If made to a circuit judge, the application must be transferred to the appropriate district court. If a district court denies an application made or transferred to it, renewal of the application before a circuit judge is not permitted. The applicant may, under 28 U.S.C. § 2253, appeal to the court of appeals from the district court's order denying the application.

(b) Certificate of Appealability.

(1) In a habeas corpus proceeding in which the detention complained of arises from process issued by a state court, or in a 28 U.S.C. § 2255 proceeding, the applicant cannot take an appeal unless a circuit justice or a circuit or district judge issues a certificate of appealability under 28 U.S.C. § 2253(c). If an applicant files a notice of appeal, the district clerk must send to the court of appeals the certificate (if any) and the statement described in Rule 11(a) of the Rules Governing Proceedings Under 28 U.S.C. § 2254 or § 2255 (if any), along with the notice of appeal and the file of the district-court proceedings. If the district judge has denied the certificate, the applicant may request a circuit judge to issue it.

(2) A request addressed to the court of appeals may be considered by a circuit judge or judges, as the court prescribes. If no express request for a certificate is filed, the notice of appeal constitutes a request addressed to the judges of the court of appeals.

(3) A certificate of appealability is not required when a state or its representative or the United States or its representative appeals.

RULE 23. CUSTODY OR RELEASE OF A PRISONER IN A HABEAS CORPUS PROCEEDING

(a) Transfer of Custody Pending Review. Pending review of a decision in a habeas corpus proceeding commenced before a court, justice, or judge of the United States for the release of a prisoner, the person having custody of the prisoner must not transfer custody to another unless a transfer is directed in accordance with this rule. When, upon application, a custodian shows the need for a transfer, the court, justice, or judge rendering the decision under review may authorize the transfer and substitute the successor custodian as a party.

(b) Detention or Release Pending Review of Decision Not to Release. While a decision not to release a prisoner is under review, the court or judge rendering the decision, or the court of appeals, or the Supreme Court, or a judge or justice of either court, may order that the prisoner be:

(1) detained in the custody from which release is sought;

(2) detained in other appropriate custody; or

(3) released on personal recognizance, with or without surety.

(c) Release Pending Review of Decision Ordering Release. While a decision ordering the release of a prisoner is under review, the prisoner must—unless the court or judge rendering the decision, or the court of appeals, or the Supreme Court, or a judge or justice of either court orders otherwise—be released on personal recognizance, with or without surety.

(d) Modification of the Initial Order on Custody. An initial order governing the prisoner's custody or release, including any recognizance or surety, continues in effect pending review unless for special reasons shown to the court of appeals or the Supreme Court, or to a judge or justice of either court, the order is modified or an independent order regarding custody, release, or surety is issued.

RULE 24. PROCEEDING IN FORMA PAUPERIS

(a) Leave to Proceed in Forma Pauperis.

(1) Motion in the District Court. Except as stated in Rule 24(a)(3), a party to a district-court action who desires to appeal in forma pauperis must file a motion in the district court. The party must attach an affidavit that:

(A) shows in the detail prescribed by Form 4 of the Appendix of Forms, the party's inability to pay or to give security for fees and costs;

(B) claims an entitlement to redress; and

(C) states the issues that the party intends to present on appeal.

(2) Action on the Motion. If the district court grants the motion, the party may proceed on appeal without prepaying or giving security for fees and costs, unless a statute provides otherwise. If the district court denies the motion, it must state its reasons in writing.

(3) Prior Approval. A party who was permitted to proceed in forma pauperis in the district-court action, or who was determined to be financially unable to obtain an adequate defense in a criminal case, may proceed on appeal in forma pauperis without further authorization, unless:

(A) the district court—before or after the notice of appeal is filed—certifies that the appeal is not taken in good faith or finds that the party is not otherwise entitled to proceed in forma pauperis and states in writing its reasons for the certification or finding; or

(B) a statute provides otherwise.

(4) Notice of District Court's Denial. The district clerk must immediately notify the parties and the court of appeals when the district court does any of the following:

(A) denies a motion to proceed on appeal in forma pauperis;

(B) certifies that the appeal is not taken in good faith; or

(C) finds that the party is not otherwise entitled to proceed in forma pauperis.

(5) Motion in the Court of Appeals. A party may file a motion to proceed on appeal in forma pauperis in the court of appeals within 30 days after service of the notice prescribed in Rule 24(a)(4). The motion must include a copy of the affidavit filed in the district court and the district court's statement of reasons for its action. If no affidavit was filed in the district court, the party must include the affidavit prescribed by Rule 24(a)(1).

(b) Leave to Proceed In Forma Pauperis on Appeal from the United States Tax Court or on Appeal or Review of an Administrative-Agency Proceeding. A party may file in the court of appeals a motion for leave to proceed on appeal in forma pauperis with an affidavit prescribed by Rule 24(a)(1):

(1) in an appeal from the United States Tax Court; and

(2) when an appeal or review of a proceeding before an administrative agency, board, commission, or officer proceeds directly in the court of appeals.

(c) Leave to Use Original Record. A party allowed to proceed on appeal in forma pauperis may request that the appeal be heard on the original record without reproducing any part.

TITLE VII. GENERAL PROVISIONS

RULE 25. FILING AND SERVICE

(a) Filing.

(1) Filing with the Clerk. A paper required or permitted to be filed in a court of appeals must be filed with the clerk.

(2) Filing: Method and Timeliness.

(A) Nonelectronic Filing.

(i) **In General.** For a paper not filed electronically, filing may be accomplished by mail addressed to the clerk, but filing is not timely unless the clerk receives the papers within the time fixed for filing.

(ii) **A Brief or Appendix.** A brief or appendix not filed electronically is timely filed, however, if on or before the last day for filing, it is:

• mailed to the clerk by first-class mail, or other class of mail that is at least as expeditious, postage prepaid; or

• dispatched to a third-party commercial carrier for delivery to the clerk within 3 days.

(iii) **Inmate filing.** If an institution has a system designed for legal mail, an inmate confined there must use that system to receive the benefit of this

Rule 25(a)(2)(A)(iii). A paper not filed electronically filed by an inmate is timely if it is deposited in the institution's internal mail system on or before the last day for filing and:

- it is accompanied by a declaration in compliance with 28 U.S.C. § 1746—or a notarized statement—setting out the date of deposit and stating that first-class postage is being prepaid; or evidence (such as a postmark or date stamp) showing that the paper was so deposited and that postage was prepaid; or
- the court of appeals exercises its discretion to permit the later filing of a declaration or notarized statement that satisfies Rule 25(a)(2)(C)(i).

(B) Electronic Filing and Signing.

(i) **By a Represented Person—Generally Required; Exceptions.** A person represented by an attorney must file electronically, unless nonelectronic filing is allowed by the court for good cause or is allowed or required by local rule.

(ii) **By an Unrepresented Person—When Allowed or Required.** A person not represented by an attorney:

- may file electronically only if allowed by court order or by local rule; and
- may be required to file electronically only by court order, or by a local rule that includes reasonable exceptions.

(iii) **Same as a Written Paper.** A paper filed electronically is a written paper for purposes of these rules.

(3) Filing a Motion with a Judge. If a motion requests relief that may be granted by a single judge, the judge may permit the motion to be filed with the judge; the judge must note the filing date on the motion and give it to the clerk.

(4) Clerk's Refusal of Documents. The clerk must not refuse to accept for filing any paper presented for that purpose solely because it is not presented in proper form as required by these rules or by any local rule or practice.

(5) Privacy Protection. An appeal in a case whose privacy protection was governed by Federal Rule of Bankruptcy Procedure 9037, Federal Rule of Civil Procedure 5.2, or Federal Rule of Criminal Procedure 49.1 is governed by the same rule on appeal. In all other proceedings, privacy protection is governed by Federal Rule of Civil Procedure 5.2, except that Federal Rule of Criminal Procedure 49.1 governs when an extraordinary writ is sought in a criminal case. The provisions on remote electronic access in Federal Rule of Civil Procedure 5.2(c)(1) and (2) apply in a petition for review of a benefits decision of the Railroad Retirement Board under the Railroad Retirement Act.

(b) Service of All Papers Required. Unless a rule requires service by the clerk, a party must, at or before the time of filing a paper, serve a copy on the other parties to the appeal or review. Service on a party represented by counsel must be made on the party's counsel.

(c) Manner of Service.

(1) Nonelectronic service may be any of the following:

(A) personal, including delivery to a responsible person at the office of counsel;

(B) by mail; or

(C) by third-party commercial carrier for delivery within 3 days.

(2) Electronic service of a paper may be made (A) by sending it to a registered user by filing it with the court's electronic-filing system or (B) by sending it by other electronic means that the person to be served consented to in writing.

(3) When reasonable considering such factors as the immediacy of the relief sought, distance, and cost, service on a party must be by a manner at least as expeditious as the manner used to file the paper with the court.

(4) Service by mail or by commercial carrier is complete on mailing or delivery to the carrier. Service by electronic means is complete on filing or sending, unless the party making service is notified that the paper was not received by the party served.

(d) Proof of Service.

(1) A paper presented for filing must contain either of the following if it was served other than through the court's electronic-filing system:

(A) an acknowledgment of service by the person served; or

(B) proof of service consisting of a statement by the person who made service certifying:

(i) the date and manner of service;

(ii) the names of the persons served; and

(iii) their mail or electronic addresses, facsimile numbers, or the addresses of the places of delivery, as appropriate for the manner of service.

(2) When a brief or appendix is filed by mailing or dispatch in accordance with Rule 25(a)(2)(A)(ii), the proof of service must also state the date and manner by which the document was mailed or dispatched to the clerk.

(3) Proof of service may appear on or be affixed to the papers filed.

(e) Number of Copies. When these rules require the filing or furnishing of a number of copies, a court may require a different number by local rule or by order in a particular case.

RULE 26. COMPUTING AND EXTENDING TIME

(a) Computing Time. The following rules apply in computing any time period specified in these rules, in any local rule or court order, or in any statute that does not specify a method of computing time.

(1) **Period Stated in Days or a Longer Unit.** When the period is stated in days or a longer unit of time:

(A) exclude the day of the event that triggers the period;

(B) count every day, including intermediate Saturdays, Sundays, and legal holidays; and

(C) include the last day of the period, but if the last day is a Saturday, Sunday, or legal holiday, the period continues to run until the end of the next day that is not a Saturday, Sunday, or legal holiday.

(2) **Period Stated in Hours.** When the period is stated in hours:

(A) begin counting immediately on the occurrence of the event that triggers the period;

(B) count every hour, including hours during intermediate Saturdays, Sundays, and legal holidays; and

(C) if the period would end on a Saturday, Sunday, or legal holiday, the period continues to run until the same time on the next day that is not a Saturday, Sunday, or legal holiday.

(3) **Inaccessibility of the Clerk's Office.** Unless the court orders otherwise, if the clerk's office is inaccessible:

(A) on the last day for filing under Rule 26(a)(1), then the time for filing is extended to the first accessible day that is not a Saturday, Sunday, or legal holiday; or

(B) during the last hour for filing under Rule 26(a)(2), then the time for filing is extended to the same time on the first accessible day that is not a Saturday, Sunday, or legal holiday.

(4) **"Last Day" Defined.** Unless a different time is set by a statute, local rule, or court order, the last day ends:

(A) for electronic filing in the district court, at midnight in the court's time zone;

(B) for electronic filing in the court of appeals, at midnight in the time zone of the circuit clerk's principal office;

(C) for filing under Rules 4(c)(1), 25(a)(2)(A)(ii), and 25(a)(2)(A)(iii)—and filing by mail under Rule 13(a)(2)—at the latest time for the method chosen for delivery to the post office, third-party commercial carrier, or prison mailing system; and

(D) for filing by other means, when the clerk's office is

scheduled to close.

(5) **"Next Day" Defined.** The "next day" is determined by continuing to count forward when the period is measured after an event and backward when measured before an event.

(6) **"Legal Holiday" Defined.** "Legal holiday" means:

(A) the day set aside by statute for observing New Year's Day, Martin Luther King Jr.'s Birthday, Washington's Birthday, Memorial Day, Independence Day, Labor Day, Columbus Day, Veterans' Day, Thanksgiving Day, or Christmas Day;

(B) any day declared a holiday by the President or Congress; and

(C) for periods that are measured after an event, any other day declared a holiday by the state where either of the following is located: the district court that rendered the challenged judgment or order, or the circuit clerk's principal office.

(b) Extending Time. For good cause, the court may extend the time prescribed by these rules or by its order to perform any act, or may permit an act to be done after that time expires. But the court may not extend the time to file:

(1) a notice of appeal (except as authorized in Rule 4) or a petition for permission to appeal; or

(2) a notice of appeal from or a petition to enjoin, set aside, suspend, modify, enforce, or otherwise review an order of an administrative agency, board, commission, or officer of the United States, unless specifically authorized by law.

(c) Additional Time after Certain Kinds of Service. When a party may or must act within a specified time after being served, and the paper is not served electronically on the party or delivered to the party on the date stated in the proof of service, 3 days are added after the period would otherwise expire under Rule 26(a).

RULE 26.1. DISCLOSURE STATEMENT

(a) Nongovernmental Corporations. Any nongovernmental corporation that is a party to a proceeding in a court of appeals must file a statement that identifies any parent corporation and any publicly held corporation that owns 10% or more of its stock or states that there is no such corporation. The same requirement applies to a nongovernmental corporation that seeks to intervene.

(b) Organizational Victims in Criminal Cases. In a criminal case, unless the government shows good cause, it must file a statement that identifies any organizational victim of the alleged criminal activity. If the organizational victim is a corporation, the statement must also disclose the information required by Rule 26.1(a) to the extent it can be obtained through due diligence.

(c) Bankruptcy Cases. In a bankruptcy case, the debtor, the trustee, or, if neither is a party, the appellant must file a statement that:

(1) identifies each debtor not named in the caption; and

(2) for each debtor that is a corporation, discloses the information required by Rule 26.1(a).

(d) Time for Filing; Supplemental Filing. The Rule 26.1 statement must:

(1) be filed with the principal brief or upon filing a motion, response, petition, or answer in the court of appeals, whichever occurs first, unless a local rule requires earlier filing;

(2) be included before the table of contents in the principal brief; and

(3) be supplemented whenever the information required under Rule 26.1 changes.

(e) Number of Copies. If the Rule 26.1 statement is filed before the principal brief, or if a supplemental statement is filed, an original and 3 copies must be filed unless the court requires a different number by local rule or by order in a particular case.

RULE 27. MOTIONS

(a) In General.

(1) Application for Relief. An application for an order or other relief is made by motion unless these rules prescribe another form. A motion must be in writing unless the court permits otherwise.

(2) Contents of a Motion.

(A) Grounds and relief sought. A motion must state with particularity the grounds for the motion, the relief sought, and the legal argument necessary to support it.

(B) Accompanying documents.

(i) Any affidavit or other paper necessary to support a motion must be served and filed with the motion.

(ii) An affidavit must contain only factual information, not legal argument.

(iii) A motion seeking substantive relief must include a copy of the trial court's opinion or agency's decision as a separate exhibit.

(C) Documents barred or not required.

(i) A separate brief supporting or responding to a motion must not be filed.

(ii) A notice of motion is not required.

(iii) A proposed order is not required.

(3) Response.

(A) Time to file. Any party may file a response to a motion; Rule 27(a)(2) governs its contents. The response must be filed within 10 days after service of the motion unless the court shortens or extends the time. A motion authorized by Rules 8, 9, 18, or 41 may be granted before the 10-day period runs only if the court gives reasonable notice to the parties that it intends to act sooner.

(B) Request for affirmative relief. A response may include a motion for affirmative relief. The time to respond to the new motion, and to reply to that response, are governed by Rule 27(a)(3)(A) and (a)(4). The title of the response must alert the court to the request for relief.

(4) Reply to Response. Any reply to a response must be filed within 7 days after service of the response. A reply must not present matters that do not relate to the response.

(b) Disposition of a Motion for a Procedural Order. The court may act on a motion for a procedural order—including a motion under Rule 26(b)—at any time without awaiting a response, and may, by rule or by order in a particular case, authorize its clerk to act on specified types of procedural motions. A party adversely affected by the court's, or the clerk's, action may file a motion to reconsider, vacate, or modify that action. Timely opposition filed after the motion is granted in whole or in part does not constitute a request to reconsider, vacate, or modify the disposition; a motion requesting that relief must be filed.

(c) Power of a Single Judge to Entertain a Motion. A circuit judge may act alone on any motion, but may not dismiss or otherwise determine an appeal or other proceeding. A court of appeals may provide by rule or by order in a particular case that only the court may act on any motion or class of motions. The court may review the action of a single judge.

(d) Form of Papers; Length Limits; Number of Copies.

(1) Format.

(A) Reproduction. A motion, response, or reply may be reproduced by any process that yields a clear black image on light paper. The paper must be opaque and unglazed. Only one side of the paper may be used.

(B) Cover. A cover is not required but there must be a caption that includes the case number, the name of the court, the title of the case, and a brief descriptive title indicating the purpose of the motion and identifying the party or parties for whom it is filed. If a cover is used, it must be white.

(C) **Binding.** The document must be bound in any manner that is secure, does not obscure the text, and permits the document to lie reasonably flat when open.

(D) **Paper size, line spacing, and margins.** The document must be on 8½ by 11 inch paper. The text must be double-spaced, but quotations more than two lines long may be indented and single-spaced. Headings and footnotes may be single-spaced. Margins must be at least one inch on all four sides. Page numbers may be placed in the margins, but no text may appear there.

(E) **Typeface and type styles.** The document must comply with the typeface requirements of Rule 32(a)(5) and the type-style requirements of Rule 32(a)(6).

(2) Length Limits. Except by the court's permission, and excluding the accompanying documents authorized by Rule 27(a)(2)(B):

(A) a motion or response to a motion produced using a computer must not exceed 5,200 words;

(B) a handwritten or typewritten motion or response to a motion must not exceed 20 pages;

(C) a reply produced using a computer must not exceed 2,600 words; and

(D) a handwritten or typewritten reply to a response must not exceed 10 pages.

(3) Number of Copies. An original and 3 copies must be filed unless the court requires a different number by local rule or by order in a particular case.

(e) Oral Argument. A motion will be decided without oral argument unless the court orders otherwise.

RULE 28. BRIEFS

(a) Appellant's Brief. The appellant's brief must contain, under appropriate headings and in the order indicated:

(1) a disclosure statement if required by Rule 26.1;

(2) a table of contents, with page references;

(3) a table of authorities—cases (alphabetically arranged), statutes, and other authorities—with references to the pages of the brief where they are cited;

(4) a jurisdictional statement, including:

(A) the basis for the district court's or agency's subject-matter jurisdiction, with citations to applicable statutory provisions and stating relevant facts establishing jurisdiction;

(B) the basis for the court of appeals' jurisdiction, with citations to applicable statutory provisions and stating relevant facts establishing jurisdiction;

(C) the filing dates establishing the timeliness of the appeal or petition for review; and

(D) an assertion that the appeal is from a final order or judgment that disposes of all parties' claims, or information establishing the court of appeals' jurisdiction on some other basis;

(5) a statement of the issues presented for review;

(6) a concise statement of the case setting out the facts relevant to the issues submitted for review, describing the relevant procedural history, and identifying the rulings presented for review, with appropriate references to the record (see Rule 28(e));

(7) a summary of the argument, which must contain a succinct, clear, and accurate statement of the arguments made in the body of the brief, and which must not merely repeat the argument headings;

(8) the argument, which must contain:

(A) appellant's contentions and the reasons for them, with citations to the authorities and parts of the record on which the appellant relies; and

(B) for each issue, a concise statement of the applicable standard of review (which may appear in the discussion of the issue or under a separate heading placed before the discussion of the issues);

(9) a short conclusion stating the precise relief sought; and

(10) the certificate of compliance, if required by Rule 32(g)(1)

(b) Appellee's Brief. The appellee's brief must conform to the requirements of Rule 28(a)(1)-(8) and (10), except that none of the following need appear unless the appellee is dissatisfied with the appellant's statement:

(1) the jurisdictional statement;

(2) the statement of the issues;

(3) the statement of the case; and

(4) the statement of the standard of review.

(c) Reply Brief. The appellant may file a brief in reply to the appellee's brief. Unless the court permits, no further briefs may be filed. A reply brief must contain a table of contents, with page references, and a table of authorities—cases (alphabetically arranged), statutes, and other authorities—with references to the pages of the reply brief where they are cited.

(d) References to Parties. In briefs and at oral argument, counsel should minimize use of the terms "appellant" and "appellee." To make briefs clear, counsel should use the parties' actual names or the designations used in the lower court or agency proceeding, or such descriptive terms as "the employee," "the injured person," "the taxpayer," "the ship," "the stevedore."

(e) References to the Record. References to the parts of the record contained in the appendix filed with the appellant's brief must be to the pages of the appendix. If the appendix is prepared after the briefs are filed, a party referring to the record must follow one of the methods detailed in Rule 30(c). If the original record is used under Rule 30(f) and is not consecutively paginated, or if the brief refers to an unreproduced part of the record, any reference must be to the page of the original document. For example:

- Answer p. 7;
- Motion for Judgment p. 2;
- Transcript p. 231.

Only clear abbreviations may be used. A party referring to evidence whose admissibility is in controversy must cite the pages of the appendix or of the transcript at which the evidence was identified, offered, and received or rejected.

(f) **Reproduction of Statutes, Rules, Regulations, etc.** If the court's determination of the issues presented requires the study of statutes, rules, regulations, etc., the relevant parts must be set out in the brief or in an addendum at the end, or may be supplied to the court in pamphlet form.

(g) **[Reserved]**

(h) **[Reserved]**

(i) **Briefs in a Case Involving Multiple Appellants or Appellees.** In a case involving more than one appellant or appellee, including consolidated cases, any number of appellants or appellees may join in a brief, and any party may adopt by reference a part of another's brief. Parties may also join in reply briefs.

(j) **Citation of Supplemental Authorities.** If pertinent and significant authorities come to a party's attention after the party's brief has been filed—or after oral argument but before decision—a party may promptly advise the circuit clerk by letter, with a copy to all other parties, setting forth the citations. The letter must state the reasons for the supplemental citations, referring either to the page of the brief or to a point argued orally. The body of the letter must not exceed 350 words. Any response must be made promptly and must be similarly limited.

RULE 28.1. CROSS-APPEALS

(a) **Applicability.** This rule applies to a case in which a cross-appeal is filed. Rules 28(a)–(c), 31(a)(1), 32(a)(2), and 32(a)(7)(A)–(B) do not apply to such a case, except as otherwise provided in this rule.

(b) **Designation of Appellant**. The party who files a notice of appeal first is the appellant for the purposes of this rule and Rules 30 and 34. If notices are filed on the same day, the plaintiff in the proceeding below is the appellant. These designations may be modified by the parties' agreement or by court order.

(c) Briefs. In a case involving a cross-appeal:

(1) Appellant's Principal Brief. The appellant must file a principal brief in the appeal. That brief must comply with Rule 28(a).

(2) Appellee's Principal and Response Brief. The appellee must file a principal brief in the cross-appeal and must, in the same brief, respond to the principal brief in the appeal. That appellee's brief must comply with Rule 28(a), except that the brief need not include a statement of the case unless the appellee is dissatisfied with the appellant's statement.

(3) Appellant's Response and Reply Brief. The appellant must file a brief that responds to the principal brief in the cross-appeal and may, in the same brief, reply to the response in the appeal. That brief must comply with Rule 28(a)(2)-(8) and (10), except that none of the following need appear unless the appellant is dissatisfied with the appellee's statement in the cross-appeal:

(A) the jurisdictional statement;

(B) the statement of the issues;

(C) the statement of the case; and

(D) the statement of the standard of review.

(4) Appellee's Reply Brief. The appellee may file a brief in reply to the response in the cross-appeal. That brief must comply with Rule 28(a)(2)-(3) and (10) and must be limited to the issues presented by the cross-appeal.

(5) No Further Briefs. Unless the court permits, no further briefs may be filed in a case involving a cross-appeal.

(d) Cover. Except for filings by unrepresented parties, the cover of the appellant's principal brief must be blue; the appellee's principal and response brief, red; the appellant's response and reply brief, yellow; the appellee's reply brief, gray; an intervenor's or amicus curiae's brief, green; and any supplemental brief, tan. The front cover of a brief must contain the information required by Rule 32(a)(2).

(e) Length.

(1) Page Limitation. Unless it complies with Rule 28.1(e)(2), the appellant's principal brief must not exceed 30 pages; the appellee's principal and response brief, 35 pages; the appellant's response and reply brief, 30 pages; and the appellee's reply brief, 15 pages.

(2) Type-Volume Limitation.

(A) The appellant's principal brief or the appellant's response and reply brief is acceptable if it:

(i) contains no more than 13,000 words; or

(ii) uses a monospaced face and contains no more than 1,300 lines of text.

(B) The appellee's principal and response brief is acceptable if it:

(i) contains no more than 15,300 words; or

(ii) uses a monospaced face and contains no more than 1,500 lines of text.

(C) The appellee's reply brief is acceptable if it contains no more than half of the type volume specified in Rule 28.1(e)(2)(A).

(f) Time to Serve and File a Brief. Briefs must be served and filed as follows:

(1) the appellant's principal brief, within 40 days after the record is filed;

(2) the appellee's principal and response brief, within 30 days after the appellant's principal brief is served;

(3) the appellant's response and reply brief, within 30 days after the appellee's principal and response brief is served; and

(4) the appellee's reply brief, within 21 days after the appellant's response and reply brief is served, but at least 7 days before argument unless the court, for good cause, allows a later filing.

RULE 29. BRIEF OF AN AMICUS CURIAE

(a) During Initial Consideration of a Case on the Merits.

(1) Applicability. This Rule 29(a) governs amicus filings during a court's initial consideration of a case on the merits.

(2) When Permitted. The United States or its officer or agency or a state may file an amicus-curiae brief without the consent of the parties or leave of court. Any other amicus curiae may file a brief only by leave of court or if the brief states that all parties have consented to its filing, but a court of appeals may prohibit the filing of or may strike an amicus brief that would result in a judge's disqualification.

(3) Motion for Leave to File. The motion must be accompanied by the proposed brief and state:

(A) the movant's interest; and

(B) the reason why an amicus brief is desirable and why the matters asserted are relevant to the disposition of the case.

(4) Contents and Form. An amicus brief must comply with Rule 32. In addition to the requirements of Rule 32, the cover must identify the party or parties supported and indicate whether the brief supports affirmance or reversal. An amicus brief need not comply with Rule 28, but must include the following:

(A) if the amicus curiae is a corporation, a disclosure statement like that required of parties by Rule 26.1;

(B) a table of contents, with page references;

(C) a table of authorities—cases (alphabetically arranged), statutes, and other authorities—with references to the pages of the brief where they are cited;

(D) a concise statement of the identity of the amicus curiae, its interest in the case, and the source of its authority to file;

(E) unless the amicus curiae is one listed in the first sentence of Rule 29(a)(2), a statement that indicates whether:

(i) a party's counsel authored the brief in whole or in part;

(ii) a party or a party's counsel contributed money that was intended to fund preparing or submitting the brief; and

(iii) a person—other than the amicus curiae, its members, or its counsel—contributed money that was intended to fund preparing or submitting the brief and, if so, identifies each such person;

(F) an argument, which may be preceded by a summary and which need not include a statement of the applicable standard of review; and

(G) a certificate of compliance under Rule 32(g)(1), if length is computed using a word or line limit.

(5) Length. Except by the court's permission, an amicus brief may be no more than one-half the maximum length authorized by these rules for a party's principal brief. If the court grants a party permission to file a longer brief, that extension does not affect the length of an amicus brief.

(6) Time for Filing. An amicus curiae must file its brief, accompanied by a motion for filing when necessary, no later than 7 days after the principal brief of the party being supported is filed. An amicus curiae that does not support either party must file its brief no later than 7 days after the appellant's or petitioner's principal brief is filed. A court may grant leave for later filing, specifying the time within which an opposing party may answer.

(7) Reply Brief. Except by the court's permission, an amicus curiae may not file a reply brief.

(8) Oral Argument. An amicus curiae may participate in oral argument only with the court's permission.

(b) During Consideration of Whether to Grant Rehearing.

(1) Applicability. This Rule 29(b) governs amicus filings during a court's consideration of whether to grant panel rehearing or rehearing en banc, unless a local rule or order in a case provides otherwise.

(2) When Permitted. The United States or its officer or

agency or a state may file an amicus brief without the consent of the parties or leave of court. Any other amicus curiae may file a brief only by leave of court.

(3) Motion for Leave to File. Rule 29(a)(3) applies to a motion for leave.

(4) Contents, Form, and Length. Rule 29(a)(4) applies to the amicus brief. The brief must not exceed 2,600 words.

(5) Time for Filing. An amicus curiae supporting the petition for rehearing or supporting neither party must file its brief, accompanied by a motion for filing when necessary, no later than 7 days after the petition is filed. An amicus curiae opposing the petition must file its brief, accompanied by a motion for filing when necessary, no later than the date set by the court for the response.

RULE 30. APPENDIX TO THE BRIEFS

(a) Appellant's Responsibility.

(1) Contents of the Appendix. The appellant must prepare and file an appendix to the briefs containing:

(A) the relevant docket entries in the proceeding below;

(B) the relevant portions of the pleadings, charge, findings, or opinion;

(C) the judgment, order, or decision in question; and

(D) other parts of the record to which the parties wish to direct the court's attention.

(2) Excluded Material. Memoranda of law in the district court should not be included in the appendix unless they have independent relevance. Parts of the record may be relied on by the court or the parties even though not included in the appendix.

(3) Time to File; Number of Copies. Unless filing is deferred under Rule 30(c), the appellant must file 10 copies of the appendix with the brief and must serve one copy on counsel for each party separately represented. An unrepresented party proceeding in forma pauperis must file 4 legible copies with the clerk, and one copy must be served on counsel for each separately represented party. The court may by local rule or by order in a particular case require the filing or service of a different number.

(b) All Parties' Responsibilities.

(1) Determining the Contents of the Appendix. The parties are encouraged to agree on the contents of the appendix. In the absence of an agreement, the appellant must, within 14 days after the record is filed, serve on the appellee a designation of the parts of the record the appellant intends to include in the appendix and a statement of the issues the appellant intends to present for review. The appellee may, within 14 days after receiving the designation, serve on the appellant a designation of additional parts to which it wishes to direct the court's attention. The appellant must include the designated parts in the appendix. The parties must not engage in unnecessary designation of parts of the record, because the entire record is available to the court. This paragraph applies also to a cross-appellant and a cross-appellee.

(2) Costs of Appendix. Unless the parties agree otherwise, the appellant must pay the cost of the appendix. If the appellant considers parts of the record designated by the appellee to be unnecessary, the appellant may advise the appellee, who must then advance the cost of including those parts. The cost of the appendix is a taxable cost. But if any party causes unnecessary parts of the record to be included in the appendix, the court may impose the cost of those parts on that party. Each circuit must, by local rule, provide for sanctions against attorneys who unreasonably and vexatiously increase litigation costs by including unnecessary material in the appendix.

(c) Deferred Appendix.

(1) Deferral Until After Briefs Are Filed. The court may provide by rule for classes of cases or by order in a particular case that preparation of the appendix may be deferred until after the briefs have been filed and that the appendix may be filed 21 days after the appellee's brief is served. Even though the filing of the appendix may be deferred, Rule 30(b) applies; except that a party must designate the parts of the record it wants included in the appendix when it serves its brief, and need not include a statement of the issues presented.

(2) References to the Record.

(A) If the deferred appendix is used, the parties may cite in their briefs the pertinent pages of the record. When the appendix is prepared, the record pages cited in the briefs must be indicated by inserting record page numbers, in brackets, at places in the appendix where those pages of the record appear.

(B) A party who wants to refer directly to pages of the appendix may serve and file copies of the brief within the time required by Rule 31(a), containing appropriate references to pertinent pages of the record. In that event, within 14 days after the appendix is filed, the party must serve and file copies of the brief, containing references to the pages of the appendix in place of or in addition to the references to the pertinent pages of the record. Except for the correction of typographical errors, no other changes may be made to the brief.

(d) Format of the Appendix. The appendix must begin with a table of contents identifying the page at which each part begins. The relevant docket entries must follow the table of contents. Other parts of the record must follow chronologically. When pages from the transcript of proceedings are placed in the appendix, the transcript page numbers must be shown in brackets immediately before the included pages. Omissions in the text of papers or of the transcript must be indicated by asterisks. Immaterial formal matters (captions, subscriptions, acknowledgments, etc.) should be omitted.

(e) Reproduction of Exhibits. Exhibits designated for inclusion in the appendix may be reproduced in a separate volume, or volumes, suitably indexed. Four copies must be filed with the appendix, and one copy must be served on counsel for each separately represented party. If a transcript of a proceeding before an administrative agency, board, commission, or officer was used in a district-court action and has been designated for inclusion in the appendix, the transcript must be placed in the appendix as an exhibit.

(f) Appeal on the Original Record Without an Appendix. The court may, either by rule for all cases or classes of cases or by order in a particular case, dispense with the appendix and permit an appeal to proceed on the original record with any copies of the record, or relevant parts, that the court may order the parties to file.

RULE 31. SERVING AND FILING BRIEFS

(a) Time to Serve and File a Brief.

(1) The appellant must serve and file a brief within 40 days after the record is filed. The appellee must serve and file a brief within 30 days after the appellant's brief is served. The appellant may serve and file a reply brief within 21 days after service of the appellee's brief but a reply brief must be filed at least 7 days before argument, unless the court, for good cause, allows a later filing.

(2) A court of appeals that routinely considers cases on the merits promptly after the briefs are filed may shorten the time to serve and file briefs, either by local rule or by order in a particular case.

(b) Number of Copies. Twenty-five copies of each brief must be filed with the clerk and 2 copies must be served on each unrepresented party and on counsel for each separately represented party. An unrepresented party proceeding in forma pauperis must file 4 legible copies with the clerk, and one copy must be served on each unrepresented party and on counsel for each separately represented party. The court may by local rule or by order in a particular case require the filing or service of a different number.

(c) Consequence of Failure to File. If an appellant fails to file a brief within the time provided by this rule, or within an extended time, an appellee may move to dismiss the appeal. An appellee who fails to file a brief will not be heard at oral argument unless the court grants permission.

RULE 32. FORM OF BRIEFS, APPENDICES, AND OTHER PAPERS

(a) Form of a Brief.

(1) Reproduction.

(A) A brief may be reproduced by any process that yields a clear black image on light paper. The paper must be opaque and unglazed. Only one side of the paper may be used.

(B) Text must be reproduced with a clarity that equals or exceeds the output of a laser printer.

(C) Photographs, illustrations, and tables may be reproduced by any method that results in a good copy of the original; a glossy finish is acceptable if the original is glossy.

(2) Cover. Except for filings by unrepresented parties, the cover of the appellant's brief must be blue; the appellee's, red; an intervenor's or amicus curiae's, green; any reply brief, gray; and any supplemental brief, tan. The front cover of a brief must contain:

(A) the number of the case centered at the top;

(B) the name of the court;

(C) the title of the case (see Rule 12(a));

(D) the nature of the proceeding (e.g., Appeal, Petition for Review) and the name of the court, agency, or board below;

(E) the title of the brief, identifying the party or parties for whom the brief is filed; and

(F) the name, office address, and telephone number of counsel representing the party for whom the brief is filed.

(3) Binding. The brief must be bound in any manner that is secure, does not obscure the text, and permits the brief to lie reasonably flat when open.

(4) Paper Size, Line Spacing, and Margins. The brief must be on 8½ by 11 inch paper. The text must be double-spaced, but quotations more than two lines long may be indented and single-spaced. Headings and footnotes may be single-spaced. Margins must be at least one inch on all four sides. Page numbers may be placed in the margins, but no text may appear there.

(5) Typeface. Either a proportionally spaced or a monospaced face may be used.

(A) A proportionally spaced face must include serifs, but sans-serif type may be used in headings and captions.

A proportionally spaced face must be 14-point or larger.

(B) A monospaced face may not contain more than 10½ characters per inch.

(6) Type Styles. A brief must be set in a plain, roman style, although italics or boldface may be used for emphasis. Case names must be italicized or underlined.

(7) Length.

(A) Page limitation. A principal brief may not exceed 30 pages, or a reply brief 15 pages, unless it complies with Rule 32(a)(7)(B).

(B) Type-volume limitation.

(i) A principal brief is acceptable if it:

- contains no more than 13,000 words; or
- uses a monospaced face and contains no more than 1,300 lines of text.

(ii) A reply brief is acceptable if it contains no more than half of the type volume specified in Rule 32(a)(7)(B)(i).

(b) Form of an Appendix. An appendix must comply with Rule 32(a)(1), (2), (3), and (4), with the following exceptions:

(1) The cover of a separately bound appendix must be white.

(2) An appendix may include a legible photocopy of any document found in the record or of a printed judicial or agency decision.

(3) When necessary to facilitate inclusion of odd-sized documents such as technical drawings, an appendix may be a size other than 8½ by 11 inches, and need not lie reasonably flat when opened.

(c) Form of Other Papers.

(1) Motion. The form of a motion is governed by Rule 27(d).

(2) Other Papers. Any other paper, including a petition for panel rehearing and a petition for hearing or rehearing en banc, and any response to such a petition, must be reproduced in the manner prescribed by Rule 32(a), with the following exceptions:

(A) A cover is not necessary if the caption and signature page of the paper together contain the information required by Rule 32(a)(2). If a cover is used, it must be white.

(B) Rule 32(a)(7) does not apply.

(d) Signature. Every brief, motion, or other paper filed with the court must be signed by the party filing the paper or, if the party is represented, by one of the party's attorneys.

(e) Local Variation. Every court of appeals must accept documents that comply with the form requirements of this rule and the length limits set by these rules. By local rule or order in a particular case, a court of appeals may accept documents that do not meet all the form requirements of this rule or the length limits set by these rules.

(f) **Items Excluded from Length.** In computing any length limit, headings, footnotes, and quotations count toward the limit but the following items do not:

- cover page;
- disclosure statement;
- table of contents;
- table of citations;
- statement regarding oral argument;
- addendum containing statutes, rules, or regulations;
- certificates of counsel;
- signature block;
- proof of service; and
- any item specifically excluded by these rules or by local rule.

(g) Certificate of Compliance.

(1) **Briefs and Papers That Require a Certificate.** A brief submitted under Rules 28.1(e)(2), 29(b)(4), or 32(a)(7)(B)—and a paper submitted under Rules 5(c)(1), 21(d)(1), 27(d)(2)(A), 27(d)(2)(C), 35(b)(2)(A), or 40(b)(1)—must include a certificate by the attorney, or an unrepresented party, that the document complies with the type-volume limitation. The person preparing the certificate may rely on the word or line count of the word-processing system used to prepare the document. The certificate must state the number of words—or the number of lines of monospaced type—in the document.

(2) **Acceptable Form.** Form 6 in the Appendix of Forms meets the requirements for a certificate of compliance.

RULE 32.1. CITING JUDICIAL DISPOSITIONS

(a) **Citation Permitted.** A court may not prohibit or restrict the citation of federal judicial opinions, orders, judgments, or other written dispositions that have been:

(i) designed as "unpublished," "not for publication," "non-precedential," "not precedent," or the like; and

(ii) issued on or after January 1, 2007.

(b) **Copies Required.** If a party cites a federal judicial opinion, order, judgment, or other written disposition that is not available in a publicly accessible electronic database, the party must file and serve a copy of that opinion, order, judgment, or disposition with the brief or other paper in which it is cited.

RULE 33. APPEAL CONFERENCES

The court may direct the attorneys—and, when appropriate, the parties—to participate in one or more conferences to address any matter that may aid in disposing of the proceedings, including simplifying the issues and discussing settlement. A judge or other person designated by the court may preside over the conference, which may be conducted in person or by telephone. Before a settlement conference, the attorneys must consult with their clients and obtain as much authority as feasible to settle the case. The court may, as a result of the conference, enter an order controlling the course of the proceedings or implementing any settlement agreement.

RULE 34. ORAL ARGUMENT

(a) In General.

(1) Party's Statement. Any party may file, or a court may require by local rule, a statement explaining why oral argument should, or need not, be permitted.

(2) Standards. Oral argument must be allowed in every case unless a panel of three judges who have examined the briefs and record unanimously agrees that oral argument is unnecessary for any of the following reasons:

(A) the appeal is frivolous;

(B) the dispositive issue or issues have been authoritatively decided; or

(C) the facts and legal arguments are adequately presented in the briefs and record, and the decisional process would not be significantly aided by oral argument.

(b) Notice of Argument; Postponement. The clerk must advise all parties whether oral argument will be scheduled, and, if so, the date, time, and place for it, and the time allowed for each side. A motion to postpone the argument or to allow longer argument must be filed reasonably in advance of the hearing date.

(c) Order and Contents of Argument. The appellant opens and concludes the argument. Counsel must not read at length from briefs, records, or authorities.

(d) Cross-Appeals and Separate Appeals. If there is a cross-appeal, Rule 28.1(b) determines which party is the appellant and which is the appellee for purposes of oral argument. Unless the court directs otherwise, a cross-appeal or separate appeal must be argued when the initial appeal is argued. Separate parties should avoid duplicative argument.

(e) Nonappearance of a Party. If the appellee fails to appear for argument, the court must hear appellant's argument. If the appellant fails to appear for argument, the court may hear the appellee's argument. If neither party appears, the case will be decided on the briefs, unless the court orders otherwise.

(f) Submission on Briefs. The parties may agree to submit a case for decision on the briefs, but the court may direct that the case be argued.

(g) Use of Physical Exhibits at Argument; Removal. Counsel intending to use physical exhibits other than documents at the argument must arrange to place them in the courtroom on the day of the argument before the court convenes. After the argument, counsel must remove the exhibits from the courtroom, unless the court directs otherwise. The clerk may destroy or dispose of the exhibits if counsel does not reclaim them within a reasonable time after the clerk gives notice to remove them.

RULE 35. EN BANC DETERMINATION

(a) When Hearing or Rehearing En Banc May Be Ordered. A majority of the circuit judges who are in regular active service and who are not disqualified may order that an appeal or other proceeding be heard or reheard by the court of appeals en banc. An en banc hearing or rehearing is not favored and ordinarily will not be ordered unless:

(1) en banc consideration is necessary to secure or maintain uniformity of the court's decisions; or

(2) the proceeding involves a question of exceptional importance.

(b) Petition for Hearing or Rehearing En Banc. A party may petition for a hearing or rehearing en banc.

(1) The petition must begin with a statement that either:

(A) the panel decision conflicts with a decision of the United States Supreme Court or of the court to which the petition is addressed (with citation to the conflicting case or cases) and consideration by the full court is therefore necessary to secure and maintain uniformity of the court's decisions; or

(B) the proceeding involves one or more questions of exceptional importance, each of which must be concisely stated; for example, a petition may assert that a proceeding presents a question of exceptional importance if it involves an issue on which the panel decision conflicts with the authoritative decisions of every other United States Court of Appeals that has addressed the issue.

(2) Except by the court's permission:

(A) a petition for an en banc hearing or rehearing produced using a computer must not exceed 3,900 words; and

(B) a handwritten or typewritten petition for an en banc hearing or rehearing must not exceed 15 pages.

(3) For purposes of the limits in Rule 35(b)(2), if a party files both a petition for panel rehearing and a petition for rehearing en banc, they are considered a single document even if they are filed separately, unless separate filing is

required by local rule.

(c) Time for Petition for Hearing or Rehearing En Banc. A petition that an appeal be heard initially en banc must be filed by the date when the appellee's brief is due. A petition for a rehearing en banc must be filed within the time prescribed by Rule 40 for filing a petition for rehearing.

(d) Number of Copies. The number of copies to be filed must be prescribed by local rule and may be altered by order in a particular case.

(e) Response. No response may be filed to a petition for an en banc consideration unless the court orders a response. The length limits in Rule 35(b)(2) apply to a response.

(f) Call for a Vote. A vote need not be taken to determine whether the case will be heard or reheard en banc unless a judge calls for a vote.

RULE 36. ENTRY OF JUDGMENT; NOTICE

(a) Entry. A judgment is entered when it is noted on the docket. The clerk must prepare, sign, and enter the judgment:

(1) after receiving the court's opinion—but if settlement of the judgment's form is required, after final settlement; or

(2) if a judgment is rendered without an opinion, as the court instructs.

(b) Notice. On the date when judgment is entered, the clerk must serve on all parties a copy of the opinion—or the judgment, if no opinion was written—and a notice of the date when the judgment was entered.

RULE 37. INTEREST ON JUDGMENT

(a) When the Court Affirms. Unless the law provides otherwise, if a money judgment in a civil case is affirmed, whatever interest is allowed by law is payable from the date when the district court's judgment was entered.

(b) When the Court Reverses. If the court modifies or reverses a judgment with a direction that a money judgment be entered in the district court, the mandate must contain instructions about the allowance of interest.

RULE 38. FRIVOLOUS APPEAL—DAMAGES AND COSTS

If a court of appeals determines that an appeal is frivolous, it may, after a separately filed motion or notice from the court and reasonable opportunity to respond, award just damages and single or double costs to the appellee.

RULE 39. COSTS

(a) Against Whom Assessed. The following rules apply unless the law provides or the court orders otherwise:

(1) if an appeal is dismissed, costs are taxed against the appellant, unless the parties agree otherwise;

(2) if a judgment is affirmed, costs are taxed against the appellant;

(3) if a judgment is reversed, costs are taxed against the appellee;

(4) if a judgment is affirmed in part, reversed in part, modified, or vacated, costs are taxed only as the court orders.

(b) Costs For and Against the United States. Costs for or against the United States, its agency, or officer will be assessed under Rule 39(a) only if authorized by law.

(c) Costs of Copies. Each court of appeals must, by local rule, fix the maximum rate for taxing the cost of producing necessary copies of a brief or appendix, or copies of records authorized by Rule 30(f). The rate must not exceed that generally charged for such work in the area where the clerk's office is located and should encourage economical methods of copying.

(d) Bill of Costs: Objections; Insertion in Mandate.

(1) A party who wants costs taxed must—within 14 days after entry of judgment—file with the circuit clerk and serve an itemized and verified bill of costs.

(2) Objections must be filed within 14 days after service of the bill of costs, unless the court extends the time.

(3) The clerk must prepare and certify an itemized statement of costs for insertion in the mandate, but issuance of the mandate must not be delayed for taxing costs. If the mandate issues before costs are finally determined, the district clerk must—upon the circuit clerk's request—add the statement of costs, or any amendment of it, to the mandate.

(e) Costs on Appeal Taxable in the District Court. The following costs on appeal are taxable in the district court for the benefit of the party entitled to costs under this rule:

(1) the preparation and transmission of the record;

(2) the reporter's transcript, if needed to determine the appeal;

(3) premiums paid for a bond or other security to preserve rights pending appeal; and

(4) the fee for filing the notice of appeal.

RULE 40. PETITION FOR PANEL REHEARING

(a) Time to File; Contents; Response; Action by the Court if Granted.

(1) Time. Unless the time is shortened or extended by order or local rule, a petition for panel rehearing may be filed within 14 days after entry of judgment. But in a civil case, unless an order shortens or extends the time, the petition may be filed by any party within 45 days after entry of judgment if one of the parties is:

(A) the United States;

(B) a United States agency;

(C) a United States officer or employee sued in an official capacity; or

(D) a current or former United States officer or employee sued in an individual capacity for an act or omission occurring in connection with duties performed on the United States' behalf — including all instances in which the United States represents that person when the court of appeals' judgment is entered or files the petition for that person.

(2) Contents. The petition must state with particularity each point of law or fact that the petitioner believes the court has overlooked or misapprehended and must argue in support of the petition. Oral argument is not permitted.

(3) Response. Unless the court requests, no response to a petition for panel rehearing is permitted. Ordinarily, rehearing will not be granted in the absence of such a request. If a response is requested, the requirements of Rule 40(b) apply to the response.

(4) Action by the Court. If a petition for panel rehearing is granted, the court may do any of the following:

(A) make a final disposition of the case without reargument;

(B) restore the case to the calendar for reargument or resubmission; or

(C) issue any other appropriate order.

(b) Form of Petition; Length. The petition must comply in form with Rule 32. Copies must be served and filed as Rule 31 prescribes. Except by the court's permission:

(1) a petition for panel rehearing produced using a computer must not exceed 3,900 words; and

(2) a handwritten or typewritten petition for panel rehearing must not exceed 15 pages.

RULE 41. MANDATE: CONTENTS; ISSUANCE AND EFFECTIVE DATE; STAY

(a) Contents. Unless the court directs that a formal mandate issue, the mandate consists of a certified copy of the judgment, a copy of the court's opinion, if any, and any direction about costs.

(b) When Issued. The court's mandate must issue 7 days after the time to file a petition for rehearing expires, or 7 days after entry of an order denying a timely petition for panel rehearing, petition for rehearing en banc, or motion for stay of mandate, whichever is later. The court may shorten or extend the time by order.

(c) Effective Date. The mandate is effective when issued.

(d) Staying the Mandate Pending a Petition for Certiorari.

(1) Motion to Stay. A party may move to stay the mandate pending the filing of a petition for a writ of certiorari in the Supreme Court. The motion must be served on all parties and must show that the petition would present a substantial question and that there is good cause for a stay.

(2) Duration of Stay; Extensions. The stay must not exceed 90 days, unless:

(A) the period is extended for good cause; or

(B) the party who obtained the stay notifies the circuit clerk in writing within the period of the stay:

(i) that the time for filing a petition has been extended, in which case the stay continues for the extended period; or

(ii) that the petition has been filed, in which case the stay continues until the Supreme Court's final disposition.

(3) Security. The court may require a bond or other security as a condition to granting or continuing a stay of the mandate.

(4) Issuance of Mandate. The court of appeals must issue the mandate immediately on receiving a copy of a Supreme Court order denying the petition, unless extraordinary circumstances exist.

RULE 42. VOLUNTARY DISMISSAL

(a) Dismissal in the District Court. Before an appeal has been docketed by the circuit clerk, the district court may dismiss the appeal on the filing of a stipulation signed by all parties or on the appellant's motion with notice to all parties.

(b) Dismissal in the Court of Appeals.

(1) **Stipulated Dismissal.** The circuit clerk may must dismiss a docketed appeal if the parties file a signed dismissal agreement specifying how costs are to be paid and pay any court fees that are due.

(2) **Appellant's Motion to Dismiss.** An appeal may be dismissed on the appellant's motion on terms agreed to by the parties or fixed by the court.

(3) **Other Relief.** A court order is required for any relief under Rule 42(b)(1) or (2) beyond the dismissal of an appeal—including approving a settlement, vacating an action of the district court or an administrative agency, or remanding the case to either of them.

(c) Court Approval. This Rule 42 does not alter the legal requirements governing court approval of a settlement, payment, or other consideration.

(d) Criminal Cases. A court may, by local rule, impose requirements to confirm that a defendant has consented to the dismissal of an appeal in a criminal case.

RULE 43. SUBSTITUTION OF PARTIES

(a) Death of a Party.

(1) After Notice of Appeal Is Filed. If a party dies after a notice of appeal has been filed or while a proceeding is pending in the court of appeals, the decedent's personal representative may be substituted as a party on motion filed with the circuit clerk by the representative or by any party. A party's motion must be served on the representative in accordance with Rule 25. If the decedent has no representative, any party may suggest the death on the record, and the court of appeals may then direct appropriate proceedings.

(2) Before Notice of Appeal Is Filed—Potential Appellant. If a party entitled to appeal dies before filing a notice of appeal, the decedent's personal representative—or, if there is no personal representative, the decedent's attorney of record—may file a notice of appeal within the time prescribed by these rules. After the notice of appeal is filed, substitution must be in accordance with Rule 43(a)(1).

(3) Before Notice of Appeal Is Filed—Potential Appellee. If a party against whom an appeal may be taken dies after entry of a judgment or order in the district court, but before a notice of appeal is filed, an appellant may proceed as if the death had not occurred. After the notice of appeal is filed, substitution must be in accordance with Rule 43(a)(1).

(b) Substitution for a Reason Other Than Death. If a party needs to be substituted for any reason other than death, the procedure prescribed in Rule 43(a) applies.

(c) Public Officer: Identification; Substitution.

(1) Identification of Party. A public officer who is a party to an appeal or other proceeding in an official capacity may be described as a party by the public officer's official title rather than by name. But the court may require the public officer's name to be added.

(2) Automatic Substitution of Officeholder. When a public officer who is a party to an appeal or other proceeding in an official capacity dies, resigns, or otherwise ceases to hold office, the action does not abate. The public officer's successor is automatically substituted as a party. Proceedings following the substitution are to be in the name of the substituted party, but any misnomer that does not affect the substantial rights of the parties may be disregarded. An order of substitution may be entered at any time, but failure to enter an order does not affect the substitution.

RULE 44. CASE INVOLVING A CONSTITUTIONAL QUESTION WHEN THE UNITED STATES OR THE RELEVANT STATE IS NOT A PARTY

(a) Constitutional Challenge to Federal Statute. If a party questions the constitutionality of an Act of Congress in a proceeding in which the United States or its agency, officer, or employee is not a party in an official capacity, the questioning party must give written notice to the circuit clerk immediately upon the filing of the record or as soon as the question is raised in the court of appeals. The clerk must then certify that fact to the Attorney General.

(b) Constitutional Challenge to State Statute. If a party questions the constitutionality of a statute of a State in a proceeding in which that State or its agency, officer, or employee is not a party in an official capacity, the questioning party must give written notice to the circuit clerk immediately upon the filing of the record or as soon as the question is raised in the court of appeals. The clerk must then certify that fact to the attorney general of the State.

RULE 45. CLERK'S DUTIES

(a) General Provisions.

(1) Qualifications. The circuit clerk must take the oath and post any bond required by law. Neither the clerk nor any deputy clerk may practice as an attorney or counselor in any court while in office.

(2) When Court Is Open. The court of appeals is always open for filing any paper, issuing and returning process, making a motion, and entering an order. The clerk's office with the clerk or a deputy in attendance must be open during business hours on all days except Saturdays, Sundays, and legal holidays. A court may provide by local rule or by order that the clerk's office be open for specified hours on Saturdays or on legal holidays other than New Year's Day, Martin Luther King, Jr.'s Birthday, Washington's Birthday, Memorial Day, Independence Day, Labor Day, Columbus Day, Veterans' Day, Thanksgiving Day, and Christmas Day.

(b) Records.

(1) The Docket. The circuit clerk must maintain a docket and an index of all docketed cases in the manner prescribed by the Director of the Administrative Office of the United States Courts. The clerk must record all papers filed with the clerk and all process, orders, and judgments.

(2) Calendar. Under the court's direction, the clerk must prepare a calendar of cases awaiting argument. In placing cases on the calendar for argument, the clerk must give preference to appeals in criminal cases and to other proceedings and appeals entitled to preference by law.

(3) **Other Records.** The clerk must keep other books and records required by the Director of the Administrative Office of the United States Courts, with the approval of the Judicial Conference of the United States, or by the court.

(c) **Notice of an Order or Judgment.** Upon the entry of an order or judgment, the circuit clerk must immediately serve a notice of entry on each party, with a copy of any opinion, and must note the date of service on the docket. Service on a party represented by counsel must be made on counsel.

(d) **Custody of Records and Papers.** The circuit clerk has custody of the court's records and papers. Unless the court orders or instructs otherwise, the clerk must not permit an original record or paper to be taken from the clerk's office. Upon disposition of the case, original papers constituting the record on appeal or review must be returned to the court or agency from which they were received. The clerk must preserve a copy of any brief, appendix, or other paper that has been filed.

RULE 46. ATTORNEYS

(a) **Admission to the Bar.**

(1) **Eligibility.** An attorney is eligible for admission to the bar of a court of appeals if that attorney is of good moral and professional character and is admitted to practice before the Supreme Court of the United States, the highest court of a state, another United States court of appeals, or a United States district court (including the district courts for Guam, the Northern Mariana Islands, and the Virgin Islands).

(2) **Application.** An applicant must file an application for admission, on a form approved by the court that contains the applicant's personal statement showing eligibility for membership. The applicant must subscribe to the following oath or affirmation: "I, ________, do solemnly swear [or affirm] that I will conduct myself as an attorney and counselor of this court, uprightly and according to law; and that I will support the Constitution of the United States."

(3) **Admission Procedures.** On written or oral motion of a member of the court's bar, the court will act on the application. An applicant may be admitted by oral motion in open court. But, unless the court orders otherwise, an applicant need not appear before the court to be admitted. Upon admission, an applicant must pay the clerk the fee prescribed by local rule or court order.

(b) **Suspension or Disbarment.**

(1) **Standard.** A member of the court's bar is subject to suspension or disbarment by the court if the member:

(A) has been suspended or disbarred from practice in any other court; or

(B) is guilty of conduct unbecoming a member of the court's bar.

(2) **Procedure.** The member must be given an opportunity to show good cause, within the time prescribed by the court, why the member should not be suspended or disbarred.

(3) **Order.** The court must enter an appropriate order after the member responds and a hearing is held, if requested, or after the time prescribed for a response expires, if no response is made.

(c) **Discipline.** A court of appeals may discipline an attorney who practices before it for conduct unbecoming a member of the bar or for failure to comply with any court rule. First, however, the court must afford the attorney reasonable notice, an opportunity to show cause to the contrary, and, if requested, a hearing.

RULE 47. LOCAL RULES BY COURTS OF APPEALS

(a) **Local Rules.**

(1) Each court of appeals acting by a majority of its judges in regular active service may, after giving appropriate public notice and opportunity for comment, make and amend rules governing its practice. A generally applicable direction to parties or lawyers regarding practice before a court must be in a local rule rather than an internal operating procedure or standing order. A local rule must be consistent with—but not duplicative of—Acts of Congress and rules adopted under 28 U.S.C. § 2072 and must conform to any uniform numbering system prescribed by the Judicial Conference of the United States. Each circuit clerk must send the Administrative Office of the United States Courts a copy of each local rule and internal operating procedure when it is promulgated or amended.

(2) A local rule imposing a requirement of form must not be enforced in a manner that causes a party to lose rights because of a nonwillful failure to comply with the requirement.

(b) **Procedure When There Is No Controlling Law.** A court of appeals may regulate practice in a particular case in any manner consistent with federal law, these rules, and local rules of the circuit. No sanction or other disadvantage may be imposed for noncompliance with any requirement not in federal law, federal rules, or the local circuit rules unless the alleged violator has been furnished in the particular case with actual notice of the requirement.

RULE 48. MASTERS

(a) Appointment; Powers. A court of appeals may appoint a special master to hold hearings, if necessary, and to recommend factual findings and disposition in matters ancillary to proceedings in the court. Unless the order referring a matter to a master specifies or limits the master's powers, those powers include, but are not limited to, the following:

(1) regulating all aspects of a hearing;

(2) taking all appropriate action for the efficient performance of the master's duties under the order;

(3) requiring the production of evidence on all matters embraced in the reference; and

(4) administering oaths and examining witnesses and parties.

(b) Compensation. If the master is not a judge or court employee, the court must determine the master's compensation and whether the cost is to be charged to any party.

§ 6.9 Appendix of Forms to the *Federal Rules of Appellate Procedure*

1A. Notice of Appeal to a Court of Appeals From a Judgment of a District Court.

1B. Notice of Appeal to a Court of Appeals From an Appealable Order of a District Court.

2. Notice of Appeal to a Court of Appeals From a Decision of the United States Tax Court.

3. Petition for Review of Order of an Agency, Board, Commission or Officer.

4. Affidavit Accompanying Motion for Permission to Appeal In Forma Pauperis.

5. Notice of Appeal to a Court of Appeals from a Judgment or Order of a District Court or a Bankruptcy Appellate Panel.

6. Certificate of Compliance With Rule 32(a).

Form 1A. Notice of Appeal to a Court of Appeals From a Judgment of a District Court

United States District Court for the ________

District of ________

Docket Number ________

____

A.B., Plaintiff

v. Notice of Appeal

C.D., Defendant

____

__________ (name all parties taking the appeal)* appeal to the United States Court of Appeals for the _____ Circuit from the final judgment entered on ________ (state the date the judgment was entered).

(s) __________

Attorney for _____

Address: _____

Note to inmate filers: *If you are an inmate confined in an institution and you seek the timing benefit of Fed. R. App. P. 4(c)(1), complete Form 7 (Declaration of Inmate Filing) and file that declaration along with this Notice of Appeal.*

* See Rule 3(c) for permissible ways of identifying appellants.

Form 1B. Notice of Appeal to a Court of Appeals From an Appealable Order of a District Court.

United States District Court for the _____

District of _____

Docket Number _____

____

A.B., Plaintiff

v. Notice of Appeal

C.D., Defendant

__________ (name all parties taking the appeal)* appeal to the United States Court of Appeals for the _____ Circuit from the order ________ (describe the order) entered on _____ (state the date the order was entered).

(s) __________

Attorney for _____

Address: _____

[Note to inmate filers: If you are an inmate confined in an institution and you seek the timing benefit of Fed. R. App. P. 4(c)(1), complete Form 7 (Declaration of Inmate Filing) and file that declaration along with this Notice of Appeal.]

* See Rule 3(c) for permissible ways of identifying appellants.

Form 2. Notice of Appeal to a Court of Appeals From a Decision of the United States Tax Court

United States Tax Court

Washington, D.C.

Docket Number ________

A.B., Plaintiff

v. Notice of Appeal

Commissioner of Internal Revenue, Respondent

________________ (name all parties taking the appeal)* appeal to the United States Court of Appeals for the _______ Circuit from the decision entered on ______________ (state the date the judgment was entered).

(s) ________________

Attorney for _______

Address: _______

* See Rule 3(c) for permissible ways of identifying appellants.

Form 3. Petition for Review of Order of an Agency, Board, Commission or Officer

United States Court of Appeals for the _______ Circuit

A.B., Petitioner)
)
v.) Petition for Review
)
XYZ Commission,)
Respondent

[(here name all parties bringing the petition [1])] hereby petitions the court for review of the Order of the XYZ Commission (describe the order) entered on ______, 20____.

[(s)] ____________________

Attorney for Petitioners

Address: ____________________

---

[1] See Rule 15.

Form 4. Affidavit Accompanying Motion for Permission to Appeal in Forma Pauperis

United States District Court for the ________ District of ________

<Name(s) of Plaintiff(s)>,

Plaintiff(s)
v. **Case No.** <Number>
<Name(s) of Defendant(s)>,

Defendant(s)

Affidavit in Support of Motion	**Instructions**
I swear or affirm under penalty of perjury that, because of my poverty, I cannot prepay the docket fees of my appeal or post a bond for them. I believe I am entitled to redress. I swear or affirm under penalty of perjury under United States laws that my answers on this form are true and correct. (28 U.S.C. § 1746; 18 U.S.C. § 1621.)	Complete all questions in this application and then sign it. Do not leave any blanks: if the answer to a question is "0," "none," or "not applicable (N/A)," write in that response. If you need more space to answer a question or to explain your answer, attach a separate sheet of paper identified with your name, your case's docket number, and the question number.
Signed: ____________________	Dated: ____________________

My issues on appeal are:

1. *For both you and your spouse estimate the average amount of money received from each of the following sources during the past 12 months. Adjust any amount that was received weekly, biweekly, quarterly, semiannually, or annually to show the monthly rate. Use gross amounts, that is, amounts before any deductions for taxes or otherwise.*

Income source	**Average monthly amount during the past 12 months**		**Amount expected next month**	
	You	**Spouse**	**You**	**Spouse**
Employment	$______	$______	$______	$______
Self-employment	$______	$______	$______	$______
Income from real property (such as rental income)	$______	$______	$______	$______
Interest and dividends	$______	$______	$______	$______
Gifts	$______	$______	$______	$______
Alimony	$______	$______	$______	$______
Child support	$______	$______	$______	$______
Retirement (such as social security, pensions, annuities, insurance)	$______	$______	$______	$______
Disability (such as social security, insurance payments)	$______	$______	$______	$______
Unemployment payments	$______	$______	$______	$______
Public-assistance (such as welfare)	$______	$______	$______	$______
Other (specify):				
______	$______	$______	$______	$______
Total monthly income:	$______	$______	$______	$______

2. *List your employment history for the past two years, most recent employer first. (Gross monthly pay is before taxes or other deductions.)*

Employer	**Address**	**Dates of employment**	**Gross monthly pay**
______	______	______	______
______	______	______	______
______	______	______	______

3. *List your spouse's employment history for the past two years, most recent employer first. (Gross monthly pay is before taxes or other deductions.)*

Employer	Address	Dates of employment	Gross monthly pay
______	______	______	______
______	______	______	______
______	______	______	______

4. *How much cash do you and your spouse have?* $________

Below, state any money you or your spouse have in bank accounts or in any other financial institution.

Financial institution	Type of account	Amount you have	Amount your spouse has
______	______	$______	$______
______	______	$______	$______
______	______	$______	$______

If you are a prisoner seeking to appeal a judgment in a civil action or proceeding, you must attach a statement certified by the appropriate institutional officer showing all receipts, expenditures, and balances during the last six months in your institutional accounts. If you have multiple accounts, perhaps because you have been in multiple institutions, attach one certified statement of each account.

5. *List the assets, and their values, which you own or your spouse owns. Do not list clothing and ordinary household furnishings.*

Home (Value)	**Other real estate** (Value)	**Motor vehicle #1** (Value)
______	______	Make & year: ______
______	______	Model: ______
______	______	Registration #: ______

Motor vehicle #2 (Value)	**Other assets** (Value)	**Other assets** (Value)
Make & year: ______	______	
Model: ______	______	______
Registration #: ______	______	______

6. *State every person, business, or organization owing you or your spouse money, and the amount owed.*

Person owing you or your spouse money	Amount owed to you	Amount owed to your spouse
______	______	______
______	______	______
______	______	______

7. *State the persons who rely on you or your spouse for support.*

Name [or, if under 18, initials only]	Relationship	Age
______	______	______
______	______	______
______	______	______

8. *Estimate the average monthly expenses of you and your family. Show separately the amounts paid by your spouse. Adjust any payments that are made weekly, biweekly, quarterly, semiannually, or annually to show the monthly rate.*

	You	Your Spouse
Rent or home-mortgage payment (include lot rented for mobile home)	$______	$______
Are real-estate taxes included? __ Yes __ No		
Is property insurance included? __ Yes __ No		
Utilities (electricity, heating fuel, water, sewer, and Telephone)	$______	$______
Home maintenance (repairs and upkeep)	$______	$______
Food	$______	$______
Clothing	$______	$______
Laundry and dry-cleaning	$______	$______
Medical and dental expenses	$______	$______
Transportation (not including motor vehicle payments)	$______	$______
Recreation, entertainment, newspapers, magazines, etc.	$______	$______
Insurance (not deducted from wages or included in Mortgage payments)	$______	$______
Homeowner's or renter's	$______	$______
Life	$______	$______
Health	$______	$______
Motor Vehicle	$______	$______
Other: ______________	$______	$______
Taxes (not deducted from wages or included in Mortgage payments) (specify): ______________	$______	$______
Installment payments	$______	$______

	You	Your Spouse
Motor Vehicle	$______	$______
Credit card (name): ______________	$______	$______
Department store (name): ______________	$______	$______
Other: ____________	$______	$______
Alimony, maintenance, and support paid to others	$______	$______
Regular expenses for operation of business, profession, or farm (attach detailed statement)	$______	$______
Other (specify): ____________	$______	$______
Total monthly expenses:	$______	$______

9. *Do you expect any major changes to your monthly income or expenses or in your assets or liabilities during the next 12 months?*

____ Yes ____ No If yes, describe on an attached sheet.

10. *Have you spent--or will you be spending--any money for expenses or attorney fees in connection with this lawsuit?* ____ Yes ____ No

If yes, how much? $________

11. *Provide any other information that will help explain why you cannot pay the docket fees for your appeal.*

____

____

____

12. *Provide any other information that will help explain why you cannot pay the docket fees for your appeal.*

13. *State the city and state of your legal residence.*

____

____

Your daytime phone number: (____) ________

Your age: ______ Your years of schooling: ______

Form 5. Notice of Appeal to a Court of Appeals from a Judgment or Order of a District Court or a Bankruptcy Appellate Panel

United States District Court for the ________

District of ________

File No. ________

Notice of Appeal to United States Court of Appeals for the ________________ Circuit

__________________, the plaintiff [or defendant or other party] appeals to the United States Court of Appeals for the

____________ Circuit from the final judgment [or order or decree] of the district court for the district of ____________ [or bankruptcy appellate panel of the ____________ circuit], entered in this case on ____________, 20 ___ [here describe the judgment, order, or decree] ______

The parties to the judgment [or order or decree] appealed from and the names and addresses of their respective attorneys are as follows:

Dated ____________

Signed ____________

Attorney for Appellant
Address: ____________
____

Note to inmate filers: *If you are an inmate confined in an institution and you seek the timing benefit of Fed. R. App. P. 4(c)(1), complete Form 7 (Declaration of Inmate Filing) and file that declaration along with this Notice of Appeal.*

Form 6. Certificate of Compliance with Type-Volume Limit

Certificate of Compliance With Type-Volume Limitation, Typeface Requirements, and Type Style Requirements

1.
- ☐ this document contains [*state the number of*] words, or
- ☐ this brief uses a monospaced typeface and contains [*state the number of*] lines of text.

2. This document complies with the typeface requirements of Fed. R. App. P. 32(a)(5) and the type-style requirements of Fed. R. App. P. 32(a)(6) because:
- ☐ this document has been prepared in a proportionally spaced typeface using [*state name and version of word-processing program*] in [*state font size and name of type style*], or
- ☐ this document has been prepared in a monospaced typeface using [*state name and version of word-processing program*] with [**state number of characters per inch and name of type style**].

(s)____________

Attorney for ____________
Dated: ____________

Form 7. Declaration of Inmate Filing

[insert name of court; for example,
United States District Court for the District of Minnesota]

]
Case No. ______________

I am an inmate confined in an institution. Today, ______________ *[insert date]*, I am depositing the ______________ *[insert title of document; for example, "notice of appeal"]* in this case in the institution's internal mail system. First-class postage is being prepaid either by me or by the institution on my behalf.

I declare under penalty of perjury that the foregoing is true and correct (see 28 U.S.C. § 1746; 18 U.S.C. § 1621).

Sign your name here________

Signed on ______________ *[insert date]*

Note to inmate filers: *If your institution has a system designed for legal mail, you must use that system in order to receive the timing benefit of Fed. R. App. P. 4(c)(1) or Fed. R. App. P. 25(a)(2)(A)(iii).*

Appendix 1. Length Limits Stated in the Federal Rules of Appellate Procedure

This chart summarizes the length limits stated in the Federal Rules of Appellate Procedure. Please refer to the rules for precise requirements, and bear in mind the following:

- In computing these limits, you can exclude the items listed in Rule 32(f).
- If you use a word limit or a line limit (other than the word limit in Rule 28(j)), you must file the certificate required by Rule 32(g).
- For the limits in Rules 5, 21, 27, 35, and 40:
  — You must use the word limit if you produce your document on a computer; and
  — For the limits in Rules 28.1, 29(a)(5), and 32:
- For the limits in Rules 28.1, 29(a)(5), and 32:
  — You may use the word limit or page limit, regardless of how you produce the document; or
  — You may use the line limit if you type or print your document with a monospaced typeface. A typeface is monospaced when each character occupies the same amount of horizontal space.

	Rule	Document type	Word limit	Page limit	Line limit
Permission to appeal	5(c)	• Petition for permission to appeal • Answer in opposition • Cross-petition	5,200	20	Not applicable
Extraordinary writs	21(d)	• Petition for writ of mandamus or prohibition or other extraordinary writ • Answer	7,800	30	Not applicable
Motions	27(d)(2)	• Motion • Response to a motion	5,200	20	Not applicable
	27(d)(2)	• Reply to a response to a motion	2,600	10	Not applicable
Parties' briefs (where no cross-appeal)	32(a)(7)	• Principal brief	13,000	30	1,300
	32(a)(7)	• Reply brief	6,500	15	650
Parties' briefs (where cross-appeal)	28.1(e)	• Appellant's principal brief • Appellant's response and reply brief	13,000	30	1,300
	28.1(e)	• Appellee's principal and response brief	15,300	35	1,500
	28.1(e)	• Appellee's reply brief	6,500	15	650
Party's supplemental letter	28(j)	• Letter citing supplemental authorities	350	Not applicable	Not applicable
Amicus briefs	29(a)(5)	• Amicus brief during initial consideration of case on merits	One-half the length set by the Appellate Rules for a party's principal brief	One-half the length set by the Appellate Rules for a party's principal brief	One-half the length set by the Appellate Rules for a party's principal brief

	Rule	Document type	Word limit	Page limit	Line limit
	29(b)(4)	• Amicus brief during consideration of whether to grant rehearing	2,600	Not applicable	Not applicable
Rehearing and en banc filings	35(b)(2)	• Petition for hearing en banc	3,900	15	Not applicable
	& 40(b)	• Petition for panel rehearing; petition for rehearing en banc			

Additional Research References

David G. Knibb, *Federal Court of Appeals Manual: A Manual on Practice in the United States Court of Appeals*

Charles A. Wright, Arthur R. Miller, & Edward H. Cooper, *Federal Practice and Procedure* §§ 3945 to 4000

C.J.S. Federal Courts §§ 291(1) to 301(48) et seq.

West's Key Number Digest, Federal Courts ⚷741 to 956

PART VII
TITLE 28, JUDICIARY AND JUDICIAL PROCEDURE—SELECTED PROVISIONS

Including Amendments Received through September 1, 2020

Table of Sections

Sec.

144. Bias or Prejudice of Judge.
451. Definitions.
452. Courts Always Open; Powers Unrestricted by Expiration of Sessions.
455. Disqualification of Justice, Judge, or Magistrate.
636. Jurisdiction, Powers, and Temporary Assignment.
1251. Original Jurisdiction.
1253. Direct Appeals From Decisions of Three-Judge Courts.
1254. Courts of Appeals; Certiorari; Certified Questions.
1257. State Courts; Certiorari.
1291. Final Decisions of District Courts.
1292. Interlocutory Decisions.
1331. Federal Question.
1332. Diversity of Citizenship; Amount in Controversy; Costs.
1333. Admiralty, Maritime and Prize Cases.
1334. Bankruptcy Cases and Proceedings.
1335. Interpleader.
1337. Commerce and Antitrust Regulations; Amount in Controversy, Costs.
1338. Patents, Plant Variety Protection, Copyrights, Mask Works, Trademarks, and Unfair Competition
1339. Postal Matters.
1340. Internal Revenue; Customs Duties.
1343. Civil Rights and Elective Franchise.
1345. United States as Plaintiff.
1346. United States as Defendant.
1349. Corporation Organized Under Federal Law as Party.
1357. Injuries Under Federal Laws.
1359. Parties Collusively Joined or Made.
1361. Action to Compel an Officer of the United States to Perform His Duty.
1367. Supplemental Jurisdiction.
1369. Multiparty, Multiforum Jurisdiction.
1390. Scope.
1391. Venue Generally.
1397. Interpleader.
1400. Patents and Copyrights, Mask Works, and Designs
1401. Stockholder's Derivative Action.
1402. United States as Defendant.

1404. Change of Venue.
1406. Cure of Waiver of Defects.
1407. Multidistrict Litigation.
1412. Change of Venue.
1441. Removal of Civil Actions.
1442. Federal Officers or Agencies Sued or Prosecuted.
1442a. Members of Armed Forces Sued or Prosecuted.
1443. Civil Rights Cases.
1445. Nonremovable Actions.
1446. Procedural for Removal of Civil Actions.
1447. Procedure After Removal Generally.
1448. Process After Removal.
1449. State Court Record Supplied.
1451. Definitions.
1453. Removal of Class Actions.
1631. Transfer to Cure Want of Jurisdiction.
1651. Writs.
1652. State Laws as Rules of Decision.
1653. Amendment of Pleadings to Show Jurisdiction.
1654. Appearance Personally or by Counsel.
1657. Priority of Civil Actions.
1658. Time Limitations on the Commencement of Civil Actions Arising Under Acts of Congress.
1691. Seal and Teste of Process.
1692. Process and Orders Affecting Property in Different Districts.
1695. Stockholder's Derivative Action.
1696. Service in Foreign and International Litigation.
1697. Service in Multiparty, Multiforum Actions.
1731. Handwriting.
1732. Record Made in Regular Course of Business; Photographic Copies.
1733. Government Records and Papers; Copies.
1734. Court Record Lost or Destroyed, Generally.
1735. Court Record Lost or Destroyed Where United States Interested.
1738. State and Territorial Statutes and Judicial Proceedings; Full Faith and Credit.
1739. State and Territorial Nonjudicial Records; Full Faith and Credit.
1746. Unsworn Declarations Under Penalty of Perjury.
1781. Transmittal of Letter Rogatory or Request.
1782. Assistance to Foreign and International Tribunals and to Litigants Before Such Tribunals.
1783. Subpoena of Person in Foreign Country.
1784. Contempt.
1785. Subpoenas in Multiparty, Multiforum Actions.
1821. Per Diem and Mileage Generally; Subsistence.
1826. Recalcitrant Witnesses.
1914. District Court; Filing and Miscellaneous Fees; Rules of Court.
1915. Proceedings in Forma Pauperis.
1917. District Courts; Fee on Filing Notice of or Petition for Appeal.
1920. Taxation of Costs.

1924. Verification of Bill of Costs.
1927. Counsel's Liability for Excessive Costs.
1961. Interest.
1963. Registration of Judgments for Enforcement in Other Districts.
1964. Constructive Notice of Pending Actions.
2071. Rule-Making Power Generally.
2072. Rules of Procedure and Evidence; Power to Prescribe.
2101. Supreme Court; Time for Appeal of Certiorari; Docketing; Stay.
2104. Reviews of State Court Decisions.
2106. Determination.
2107. Time for Appeal to Court of Appeals.
2111. Harmless Error.
2201. Creation of Remedy.
2202. Further Relief.
2283. Stay of State Court Proceedings.
2284. Three-Judge Court; When Required; Composition; Procedure.
2361. Process and Procedure.
2401. Time for Commencing Action Against United States.
2402. Jury Trial in Actions Against United States.
2403. Intervention by United States or a State; Constitutional Question.
2404. Death of Defendant in Damage Action.
2408. Security not Required of United States.
2411. Interest.
2412. Costs and Fees.
2413. Executions in Favor of United States.
2414. Payment of Judgments and Compromise Settlements.
2415. Time for Commencing Actions Brought by the United States.
2416. ________ Exclusions.

§ 144. Bias or Prejudice of Judge

Whenever a party to any proceeding in a district court makes and files a timely and sufficient affidavit that the judge before whom the matter is pending has a personal bias or prejudice either against him or in favor of any adverse party, such judge shall proceed no further therein, but another judge shall be assigned to hear such proceeding.

The affidavit shall state the facts and the reasons for the belief that bias or prejudice exists, and shall be filed not less than ten days before the beginning of the term at which the proceeding is to be heard, or good cause shall be shown for failure to file it within such time. A party may file only one such affidavit in any case. It shall be accompanied by a certificate of counsel of record stating that it is made in good faith.

§ 451. Definitions

As used in this title:

The term "court of the United States" includes the Supreme Court of the United States, courts of appeals, district courts constituted by chapter 5 of this title, including the Court of International Trade and any court created by Act of Congress the judges of which are entitled to hold office during good behavior.

The terms "district court" and "district court of the United States" mean the courts constituted by chapter 5 of this title.

The term "judge of the United States" includes judges of the courts of appeals, district courts, Court of International Trade and any court created by Act of Congress, the judges of which are entitled to hold office during good behavior.

The term "justice of the United States" includes the Chief Justice of the United States and the associate justices of the Supreme Court.

The term "district" and "judicial district" mean the districts enumerated in Chapter 5 of this title.

The term "department" means one of the executive departments enumerated in section 1 of Title 5, unless the context shows that such term was intended to describe the executive, legislative, or judicial branches of the government.

The term "agency" includes any department, independent establishment, commission, administration, authority, board or bureau of the United States or any corporation in which the United States has a proprietary interest, unless the context shows that such term was intended to be used in a more limited sense.

§ 452. Courts Always Open; Powers Unrestricted by Expiration of Sessions

All courts of the United States shall be deemed always open for the purpose of filing proper papers, issuing and returning process, and making motions and orders.

The continued existence or expiration of a session of court in no way affects the power of the court to do any act or take any proceeding.

§ 455. Disqualification of Justice, Judge, or Magistrate

(a) Any justice, judge, or magistrate of the United States shall disqualify himself in any proceeding in which his impartiality might reasonably be questioned.

(b) He shall also disqualify himself in the following circumstances:

(1) Where he has a personal bias or prejudice concerning a party, or personal knowledge of disputed evidentiary facts concerning the proceeding;

(2) Where in private practice he served as lawyer in the matter in controversy, or a lawyer with whom he previously practiced law served during such association as a lawyer concerning the matter, or the judge or such lawyer has been a material witness concerning it;

(3) Where he has served in governmental employment and in such capacity participated as counsel, adviser or material witness concerning the proceeding or expressed an opinion concerning the merits of the particular case in controversy;

(4) He knows that he, individually or as a fiduciary, or his spouse or minor child residing in his household, has a financial interest in the subject matter in controversy or in a party to the proceeding, or any other interest that could be substantially affected by the outcome of the proceeding;

(5) He or his spouse, or a person within the third degree of relationship to either of them, or the spouse of such a person:

(i) Is a party to the proceeding, or an officer, director, or trustee of a party;

(ii) Is acting as a lawyer in the proceeding;

(iii) Is known by the judge to have an interest that could be substantially affected by the outcome of the proceeding;

(iv) Is to the judge's knowledge likely to be a material witness in the proceeding.

(c) A judge should inform himself about his personal and fiduciary financial interests, and make a reasonable effort to inform himself about the personal financial interests of his spouse and minor children residing in his household.

(d) For the purposes of this section the following words or phrases shall have the meaning indicated:

(1) "proceeding" includes pretrial, trial, appellate review, or other stages of litigation;

(2) the degree of relationship is calculated according to the civil law system;

(3) "fiduciary" includes such relationships as executor, administrator, trustee, and guardian;

(4) "financial interest" means ownership of a legal or equitable interest, however small, or a relationship as director, adviser, or other active participant in the affairs of a party, except that:

(i) Ownership in a mutual or common investment fund that holds securities is not a "financial interest" in such securities unless the judge participates in the management of the fund;

(ii) An office in an educational, religious, charitable, fraternal, or civic organization is not a "financial interest" in securities held by the organization;

(iii) The proprietary interest of a policyholder in a mutual insurance company, of a depositor in a mutual savings association, or a similar proprietary interest, is a "financial interest" in the organization only if the outcome of the proceeding could substantially affect the value of the interest;

(iv) Ownership of government securities is a "financial interest" in the issuer only if the outcome of the proceeding could substantially affect the value of the securities.

(e) No justice, judge, or magistrate shall accept from the parties to the proceeding a waiver of any ground for disqualification enumerated in subsection (b). Where the ground for disqualification arises only under subsection (a), waiver may be accepted provided it is preceded by a full disclosure on the record of the basis for disqualification.

(f) Notwithstanding the preceding provisions of this section, if any justice, judge, magistrate, or bankruptcy judge to whom a matter has been assigned would be disqualified, after substantial judicial time has been devoted to the matter, because of the appearance or discovery, after the matter was assigned to him or her, that he or she individually or as a fiduciary, or his or her spouse or minor child residing in his or her household, has a financial interest in a party (other than an interest that could be substantially affected by the outcome), disqualification is not required if the justice, judge, magistrate judge, bankruptcy judge, spouse or minor child, as the case may be, divests himself or herself of the interest that provides the grounds for the disqualification.

§ 636. Jurisdiction, Powers, and Temporary Assignment

(a) Each United States magistrate judge serving under this chapter shall have within the district in which sessions are held by the court that appointed the magistrate judge, at other places where that court may function, and elsewhere as authorized by law—

(1) all powers and duties conferred or imposed upon United States commissioners by law or by the Rules of Criminal Procedure for the United States District Courts;

(2) the power to administer oaths and affirmations, issue orders pursuant to section 3142 of title 18 concerning release or detention of persons pending trial, and take acknowledgements, affidavits, and depositions;

(3) the power to conduct trials under section 3401, title 18, United States Code, in conformity with and subject to the limitations of that section;

(4) the power to enter a sentence for a petty offense; and

(5) the power to enter a sentence for a class A misdemeanor in a case in which the parties have consented.

(b) **(1)** Notwithstanding any provision of law to the contrary—

(A) a judge may designate a magistrate judge to hear and determine any pretrial matter pending before the court, except a motion for injunctive relief, for judgment on the pleadings, for summary judgment, to dismiss or quash an indictment or information made by the defendant, to suppress evidence in a criminal case, to dismiss or to permit maintenance of a class action, to dismiss for failure to state a claim upon which relief can be granted, and to involuntarily dismiss an action. A judge of the court may reconsider any pretrial matter under this subparagraph (A) where it has been shown that the magistrate judge's order is clearly erroneous or contrary to law.

(B) a judge may also designate a magistrate judge to conduct hearings, including evidentiary hearings, and to submit to a judge of the court proposed findings of fact and recommendations for the disposition, by a judge of the court, of any motion excepted in subparagraph (A), of applications for posttrial[1] relief made by individuals convicted of criminal offenses and of prisoner petitions challenging conditions of confinement.

(C) the magistrate judge shall file his proposed findings and recommendations under subparagraph (B) with the court and a copy shall forthwith be mailed to all parties.

Within fourteen days after being served with a copy, any party may serve and file written objections to such proposed findings and recommendations as provided by rules of court. A judge of the court shall make a de novo determination of those portions of the report or specified proposed findings or recommendations to which objection is made. A judge of the court may accept, reject, or modify, in whole or in part, the findings or recommendations made by the magistrate judge. The judge may also receive further evidence or recommit the matter to the magistrate judge with instructions.

(2) A judge may designate a magistrate judge to serve as a special master pursuant to the applicable provisions of this title and the Federal Rules of Civil Procedure for the United States district courts. A judge may designate a magistrate judge to serve as a special master in any civil case, upon consent of the parties, without regard to the provisions of rule 53(b) of the Federal Rules of Civil Procedure for the United States district courts.

(3) A magistrate judge may be assigned such additional duties as are not inconsistent with the Constitution and laws of the United States.

(4) Each district court shall establish rules pursuant to which the magistrate judges shall discharge their duties.

(c) Notwithstanding any provision of law to the contrary—

(1) Upon the consent of the parties, a full-time United States magistrate judge or a part-time United States magistrate judge who serves as a full-time judicial officer may conduct any or all proceedings in a jury or nonjury civil matter and order the entry of judgment in the case, when specially designated to exercise such jurisdiction by the district court or courts he serves. Upon the consent of the parties, pursuant to their specific written request, any other part-time magistrate judge

[1]So in original. Probably should be "post-trial".

may exercise such jurisdiction, if such magistrate judge meets the bar membership requirements set forth in section 631(b)(1) and the chief judge of the district court certifies that a full-time magistrate judge is not reasonably available in accordance with guidelines established by the judicial council of the circuit. When there is more than one judge of a district court, designation under this paragraph shall be by the concurrence of a majority of all the judges of such district court, and when there is no such concurrence, then by the chief judge.

(2) If a magistrate judge is designated to exercise civil jurisdiction under paragraph (1) of this subsection, the clerk of court shall, at the time the action is filed, notify the parties of the availability of a magistrate judge to exercise such jurisdiction. The decision of the parties shall be communicated to the clerk of court. Thereafter, either the district court judge or the magistrate judge may again advise the parties of the availability of the magistrate judge, but in so doing, shall also advise the parties that they are free to withhold consent without adverse substantive consequences. Rules of court for the reference of civil matters to magistrate judges shall include procedures to protect the voluntariness of the parties' consent.

(3) Upon entry of judgment in any case referred under paragraph (1) of this subsection, an aggrieved party may appeal directly to the appropriate United States court of appeals from the judgment of the magistrate judge in the same manner as an appeal from any other judgment of a district court. The consent of the parties allows a magistrate judge designated to exercise civil jurisdiction under paragraph (1) of this subsection to direct the entry of a judgment of the district court in accordance with the Federal Rules of Civil Procedure. Nothing in this paragraph shall be construed as a limitation of any party's right to seek review by the Supreme Court of the United States.

(4) The court may, for good cause shown on its own motion, or under extraordinary circumstances shown by any party, vacate a reference of a civil matter to a magistrate judge under this subsection.

(5) The magistrate judge shall, subject to guidelines of the Judicial Conference, determine whether the record taken pursuant to this section shall be taken by electronic sound recording, by a court reporter, or by other means.

(d) The practice and procedure for the trial of cases before officers serving under this chapter shall conform to rules promulgated by the Supreme Court pursuant to section 2072 of this title.

(e) Contempt authority.—

(1) In general.—A United States magistrate judge serving under this chapter shall have within the territorial jurisdiction prescribed by the appointment of such magistrate judge the power to exercise contempt authority as set forth in this subsection.

(2) Summary criminal contempt authority.—A magistrate judge shall have the power to punish summarily by fine or imprisonment, or both, such contempt of the authority of such magistrate judge constituting misbehavior of any person in the magistrate judge's presence so as to obstruct the administration of justice. The order of contempt shall be issued under the Federal Rules of Criminal Procedure.

(3) Additional criminal contempt authority in civil consent and misdemeanor cases.—In any case in which a United States magistrate judge presides with the consent of the parties under subsection (c) of this section, and in any misdemeanor case proceeding before a magistrate judge under section 3401 of title 18, the magistrate judge shall have the power to punish, by fine or imprisonment, or both, criminal contempt constituting disobedience or resistance to the magistrate judge's lawful writ, process, order, rule, decree, or command. Disposition of such contempt shall be conducted upon notice and hearing under the Federal Rules of Criminal Procedure.

(4) Civil contempt authority in civil consent and misdemeanor cases.—In any case in which a United States magistrate judge presides with the consent of the parties under subsection (c) of this section, and in any misdemeanor case proceeding before a magistrate judge under section 3401 of title 18, the magistrate judge may exercise the civil contempt authority of the district court. This paragraph shall not be construed to limit the authority of a magistrate judge to order sanctions under any other statute, the Federal Rules of Civil Procedure, or the Federal Rules of Criminal Procedure.

(5) Criminal contempt penalties.—The sentence imposed by a magistrate judge for any criminal contempt provided for in paragraphs (2) and (3) shall not exceed the penalties for a Class C misdemeanor as set forth in sections 3581(b)(8) and 3571(b)(6) of title 18.

(6) Certification of other contempts to the district court.—Upon the commission of any such act—

(A) in any case in which a United States magistrate judge presides with the consent of the parties under subsection (c) of this section, or in any misdemeanor case proceeding before a magistrate judge under section 3401 of title 18, that may, in the opinion of the magistrate judge, constitute a serious criminal contempt punishable by penalties exceeding those set forth in paragraph (5) of this subsection, or

(B) in any other case or proceeding under subsection (a) or (b) of this section, or any other statute, where—

(i) the act committed in the magistrate judge's presence may, in the opinion of the magistrate judge, constitute a serious criminal contempt punishable by penalties exceeding those set forth in paragraph (5) of this subsection,

(ii) the act that constitutes a criminal contempt occurs outside the presence of the magistrate judge, or

(iii) the act constitutes a civil contempt,

the magistrate judge shall forthwith certify the facts to a district judge and may serve or cause to be served, upon any person whose behavior is brought into question under this paragraph, an order requiring such person to appear before a district judge upon a day certain to show cause why that person should not be adjudged in contempt by reason of the facts so certified. The district judge shall thereupon hear the evidence as to the act or conduct complained of and, if it is such as to warrant punishment, punish such person in the same manner and to the same extent as for a contempt committed before a district judge.

(7) Appeals of magistrate judge contempt orders.—The appeal of an order of contempt under this subsection shall be made to the court of appeals in cases proceeding under subsection (c) of this section. The appeal of any other order of contempt issued under this section shall be made to the district court.

(f) In an emergency and upon the concurrence of the chief judges of the districts involved, a United States magistrate judge may be temporarily assigned to perform any of the duties specified in subsection (a), (b), or (c) of this section in a judicial district other than the judicial district for which he has been appointed. No magistrate judge shall perform any of such duties in a district to which he has been temporarily assigned until an order has been issued by the chief judge of such district specifying (1) the emergency by reason of which he has been transferred, (2) the duration of his assignment, and (3) the duties which he is authorized to perform. A magistrate judge so assigned shall not be entitled to additional compensation but shall be reimbursed for actual and necessary expenses incurred in the performance of his duties in accordance with section 635.

(g) A United States magistrate judge may perform the verification function required by section 4107 of title 18, United States Code. A magistrate judge may be assigned by a judge of any United States district court to perform the verification required by section 4108 and the appointment of counsel authorized by section 4109 of title 18, United States Code, and may perform such functions beyond the territorial limits of the United States. A magistrate judge assigned such functions shall have no authority to perform any other function within the territory of a foreign country.

(h) A United States magistrate judge who has retired may, upon the consent of the chief judge of the district involved, be recalled to serve as a magistrate judge in any judicial district by the judicial council of the circuit within which such district is located. Upon recall, a magistrate judge may receive a salary for such service in accordance with regulations promulgated by the Judicial Conference, subject to the restrictions on the payment of an annuity set forth in section 377 of this title or in subchapter III of chapter 83, and chapter 84, of title 5 which are applicable to such magistrate judge. The requirements set forth in subsections (a), (b)(3), and (d) of section 631, and paragraph (1) of subsection (b) of such section to the extent such paragraph requires membership of the bar of the location in which an individual is to serve as a magistrate judge, shall not apply to the recall of a retired magistrate judge under this subsection or section 375 of this title. Any other requirement set forth in section 631(b) shall apply to the recall of a retired magistrate judge under this subsection or section 375 of this title unless such retired magistrate judge met such requirement upon appointment or reappointment as a magistrate judge under section 361.

§ 1251. Original Jurisdiction

(a) The Supreme Court shall have original and exclusive jurisdiction of all controversies between two or more States.

(b) The Supreme Court shall have original but not exclusive jurisdiction of:

(1) All actions or proceedings to which ambassadors, other public ministers, consuls, or vice consuls of foreign states are parties;

(2) All controversies between the United States and a State;

(3) All actions or proceedings by a State against the citizens of another State or against aliens.

§ 1253. Direct Appeals from Decisions of Three-Judge Courts

Except as otherwise provided by law, any party may appeal to the Supreme Court from an order granting or denying, after notice and hearing, an interlocutory or permanent injunction in any civil action, suit or proceeding required by any Act of Congress to be heard and determined by a district court of three judges.

§ 1254. Courts of Appeals; Certiorari; Certified Questions

Cases in the courts of appeals may be reviewed by the Supreme Court by the following methods:

(1) By writ of certiorari granted upon the petition of any party to any civil or criminal case, before or after rendition of judgment or decree;

(2) By certification at any time by a court of appeals of any question of law in any civil or criminal case as to which instructions are desired, and upon such certification the Supreme Court may give binding instructions or require the entire record to be sent up for decision of the entire matter in controversy.

§ 1257. State Courts; Certiorari

(a) Final judgments or decrees rendered by the highest court of a State in which a decision could be had, may be reviewed by the Supreme Court by writ of certiorari where the validity of a treaty or statute of the United States is drawn in question or where the validity of a statute of any State is drawn in question on the ground of its being repugnant to the Constitution, treaties, or laws of the United States, or where any title, right, privilege, or immunity is specially set up or claimed under the Constitution or the treaties or statutes of, or any commission held or authority exercised under, the United States.

(b) For the purposes of this section, the term "highest court of a State" includes the District of Columbia Court of Appeals.

§ 1291. Final Decisions of District Courts

The courts of appeals (other than the United States Court of Appeals for the Federal Circuit) shall have jurisdiction of appeals from all final decisions of the district courts of the United States, the United States District Court for the District of the Canal Zone, the District Court of Guam, and the District Court of the Virgin Islands, except where a direct review may be had in the Supreme Court. The jurisdiction of the United States Court of Appeals for the Federal Circuit shall be limited to the jurisdiction described in sections 1292(c) and (d) and 1295 of this title.

§ 1292. Interlocutory Decisions

(a) Except as provided in subsections (c) and (d) of this section, the courts of appeals shall have jurisdiction of appeals from:

(1) Interlocutory orders of the district courts of the United States, the United States District Court for the District of the Canal Zone, the District Court of Guam, and the District Court of the Virgin Islands, or of the judges thereof, granting, continuing, modifying, refusing or dissolving injunctions, or refusing to dissolve or modify injunctions, except where a direct review may be had in the Supreme Court;

(2) Interlocutory orders appointing receivers, or refusing orders to wind up receiverships or to take steps to accomplish the purposes thereof, such as directing sales or other disposals of property;

(3) Interlocutory decrees of such district courts or the judges thereof determining the rights and liabilities of the parties to admiralty cases in which appeals from final decrees are allowed.

(b) When a district judge, in making in a civil action an order not otherwise appealable under this section, shall be of the opinion that such order involves a controlling question of law as to which there is substantial ground for difference of opinion and that an immediate appeal from the order may materially advance the ultimate termination of the litigation, he shall so state in writing in such order. The Court of Appeals which would have jurisdiction of an appeal of such action may thereupon, in its discretion, permit an appeal to be taken from such order, if application is made to it within ten days after the entry of the order: *Provided, however*, that application for an appeal hereunder shall not stay proceedings in the district court unless the district judge or the Court of Appeals or a judge thereof shall so order.

(c) The United States Court of Appeals for the Federal Circuit shall have exclusive jurisdiction—

(1) of an appeal from an interlocutory order or decree described in subsection (a) or (b) of this section in any case over which the court would have jurisdiction of an appeal under section 1295 of this title; and

(2) of an appeal from a judgment in a civil action for patent infringement which would otherwise be appealable to the United States Court of Appeals for the Federal Circuit and is final except for an accounting.

(d) (1) When the chief judge of the Court of International Trade issues an order under the provisions of section 256(b) of this title, or when any judge of the Court of International Trade, in issuing any other interlocutory order, includes in the order a statement that a controlling question of law is involved with respect to which there is a substantial ground for difference of opinion and that an immediate appeal from that order may materially advance the ultimate termination of the litigation, the United States Court of Appeals for the Federal Circuit may, in its discretion, permit an appeal to be taken from such order, if application is made to that Court within ten days after the entry of such order.

(2) When the chief judge of the United States Court of Federal Claims issues an order under section 798(b) of this title, or when any judge of the United States Court of Federal Claims, in issuing an interlocutory order, includes in the order a statement that a controlling question of law is involved with respect to which there is a substantial ground for difference of opinion and that an immediate appeal from that order may materially advance the ultimate termination of the litigation, the United States Court of Appeals for the Federal Circuit may, in its discretion, permit an appeal to be taken from such order, if application is made to that Court within ten days after the entry of such order.

(3) Neither the application for nor the granting of an appeal under this subsection shall stay proceedings in the Court of International Trade or in the Court of Federal Claims, as the case may be, unless a stay is ordered by a judge of the Court of International Trade or of the Court of Federal Claims or by the United States Court of Appeals for the Federal Circuit or a judge of that court.

(4) (A) The United States Court of Appeals for the Federal

Circuit shall have exclusive jurisdiction of an appeal from an interlocutory order of a district court of the United States, the District Court of Guam, the District Court of the Virgin Islands, or the District Court for the Northern Mariana Islands, granting or denying, in whole or in part, a motion to transfer an action to the United States Court of Federal Claims under section 1631 of this title.

(B) When a motion to transfer an action to the Court of Federal Claims is filed in a district court, no further proceedings shall be taken in the district court until 60 days after the court has ruled upon the motion. If an appeal is taken from the district court's grant or denial of the motion, proceedings shall be further stayed until the appeal has been decided by the Court of Appeals for the Federal Circuit. The stay of proceedings in the district court shall not bar the granting of preliminary or injunctive relief, where appropriate and where expedition is reasonably necessary. However, during the period in which proceedings are stayed as provided in this subparagraph, no transfer to the Court of Federal Claims pursuant to the motion shall be carried out.

(e) The Supreme Court may prescribe rules, in accordance with section 2072 of this title, to provide for an appeal of an interlocutory decision to the courts of appeals that is not otherwise provided for under subsection (a), (b), (c), or (d).

§ 1331. Federal Question

The district courts shall have original jurisdiction of all civil actions arising under the Constitution, laws, or treaties of the United States.

§ 1332. Diversity of Citizenship; Amount in Controversy; Costs

(a) The district courts shall have original jurisdiction of all civil actions where the matter in controversy exceeds the sum or value of $75,000, exclusive of interest and costs, and is between—

(1) citizens of different States;

(2) citizens of a State and citizens or subjects of a foreign state, except that the district courts shall not have original jurisdiction under this subsection of an action between citizens of a State and citizens or subjects of a foreign state who are lawfully admitted for permanent residence in the United States and are domiciled in the same State;

(3) citizens of different States and in which citizens or subjects of a foreign state are additional parties; and

(4) a foreign state, defined in section 1603(a) of this title, as plaintiff and citizens of a State or of different States.

(b) Except when express provision therefor is otherwise made in a statute of the United States, where the plaintiff who files the case originally in the Federal courts is finally adjudged to be entitled to recover less than the sum or value of $75,000, computed without regard to any setoff or counterclaim to which the defendant may be adjudged to be entitled, and exclusive of interest and costs, the district court may deny costs to the plaintiff and, in addition, may impose costs on the plaintiff.

(c) For the purposes of this section and section 1441 of this title—

(1) a corporation shall be deemed to be a citizen of every State and foreign state by which it has been incorporated and of the State or foreign state where it has its principal place of business, except that in any direct action against the insurer of a policy or contract of liability insurance, whether incorporated or unincorporated, to which action the insured is not joined as a party-defendant, such insurer shall be deemed a citizen of—

(A) every State and foreign state of which the insured is a citizen;

(B) every State and foreign state by which the insurer has been incorporated; and

(C) the State or foreign state where the insurer has its principal place of business; and

(2) the legal representative of the estate of a decedent shall be deemed to be a citizen only of the same State as the decedent, and the legal representative of an infant or incompetent shall be deemed to be a citizen only of the same State as the infant or incompetent.

(d) **(1)** In this subsection—

(A) the term "class" means all of the class members in a class action;

(B) the term "class action" means any civil action filed under rule 23 of the Federal Rules of Civil Procedure or similar State statute or rule of judicial procedure authorizing an action to be brought by 1 or more representative persons as a class action;

(C) the term "class certification order" means an order issued by a court approving the treatment of some or all aspects of a civil action as a class action; and

(D) the term "class members" means the persons (named or unnamed) who fall within the definition of the proposed or certified class in a class action.

(2) The district courts shall have original jurisdiction of any civil action in which the matter in controversy exceeds the sum or value of $5,000,000, exclusive of interest and costs, and is a class action in which—

(A) any member of a class of plaintiffs is a citizen of a State different from any defendant;

(B) any member of a class of plaintiffs is a foreign state or a citizen or subject of a foreign state and any defendant is a citizen of a State; or

(C) any member of a class of plaintiffs is a citizen of a

State and any defendant is a foreign state or a citizen or subject of a foreign state.

(3) A district court may, in the interests of justice and looking at the totality of the circumstances, decline to exercise jurisdiction under paragraph (2) over a class action in which greater than one-third but less than two-thirds of the members of all proposed plaintiff classes in the aggregate and the primary defendants are citizens of the State in which the action was originally filed based on consideration of—

(A) whether the claims asserted involve matters of national or interstate interest;

(B) whether the claims asserted will be governed by laws of the State in which the action was originally filed or by the laws of other States;

(C) whether the class action has been pleaded in a manner that seeks to avoid Federal jurisdiction;

(D) whether the action was brought in a forum with a distinct nexus with the class members, the alleged harm, or the defendants;

(E) whether the number of citizens of the State in which the action was originally filed in all proposed plaintiff classes in the aggregate is substantially larger than the number of citizens from any other State, and the citizenship of the other members of the proposed class is dispersed among a substantial number of States; and

(F) whether, during the 3-year period preceding the filing of that class action, 1 or more other class actions asserting the same or similar claims on behalf of the same or other persons have been filed.

(4) A district court shall decline to exercise jurisdiction under paragraph (2)—

(A) **(i)** over a class action in which—

(I) greater than two-thirds of the members of all proposed plaintiff classes in the aggregate are citizens of the State in which the action was originally filed;

(II) at least 1 defendant is a defendant—

(aa) from whom significant relief is sought by members of the plaintiff class;

(bb) whose alleged conduct forms a significant basis for the claims asserted by the proposed plaintiff class; and

(cc) who is a citizen of the State in which the action was originally filed; and

(III) principal injuries resulting from the alleged conduct or any related conduct of each defendant were incurred in the State in which the action was originally filed; and

(ii) during the 3-year period preceding the filing of that class action, no other class action has been filed asserting the same or similar factual allegations against any of the defendants on behalf of the same or other persons; or

(B) two-thirds or more of the members of all proposed plaintiff classes in the aggregate, and the primary defendants, are citizens of the State in which the action was originally filed.

(5) Paragraphs (2) through (4) shall not apply to any class action in which—

(A) the primary defendants are States, State officials, or other governmental entities against whom the district court may be foreclosed from ordering relief; or

(B) the number of members of all proposed plaintiff classes in the aggregate is less than 100.

(6) In any class action, the claims of the individual class members shall be aggregated to determine whether the matter in controversy exceeds the sum or value of $5,000,000, exclusive of interest and costs.

(7) Citizenship of the members of the proposed plaintiff classes shall be determined for purposes of paragraphs (2) through (6) as of the date of filing of the complaint or amended complaint, or, if the case stated by the initial pleading is not subject to Federal jurisdiction, as of the date of service by plaintiffs of an amended pleading, motion, or other paper, indicating the existence of Federal jurisdiction.

(8) This subsection shall apply to any class action before or after the entry of a class certification order by the court with respect to that action.

(9) Paragraph (2) shall not apply to any class action that solely involves a claim—

(A) concerning a covered security as defined under 16(f)(3)[1] of the Securities Act of 1933 (15 U.S.C. 78p(f)(3)) and section 28(f)(5)(E) of the Securities Exchange Act of 1934 (15 U.S.C. 78bb(f)(5)(E));

(B) that relates to the internal affairs or governance of a corporation or other form of business enterprise and that arises under or by virtue of the laws of the State in which such corporation or business enterprise is incorporated or organized; or

(C) that relates to the rights, duties (including fiduciary duties), and obligations relating to or created by or pursuant to any security (as defined under section 2(a)(1) of the Securities Act of 1933 (15 U.S.C. 77b(a)(1)) and the regulations issued thereunder).

(10) For purposes of this subsection and section 1453, an unincorporated association shall be deemed to be a citizen of the State where it has its principal place of business and the State under whose laws it is organized.

(11) (A) For purposes of this subsection and section 1453, a mass action shall be deemed to be a class action removable under paragraphs (2) through (10) if it otherwise meets the provisions of those paragraphs.

(B) (i) As used in subparagraph (A), the term "mass action" means any civil action (except a civil action within the scope of section 1711(2)) in which monetary relief claims of 100 or more persons are proposed to be tried jointly on the ground that the plaintiffs' claims involve common questions of law or fact, except that jurisdiction shall exist only over those plaintiffs whose claims in a mass action satisfy the jurisdictional amount requirements under subsection (a).

(ii) As used in subparagraph (A), the term "mass action" shall not include any civil action in which—

(I) all of the claims in the action arise from an event or occurrence in the State in which the action was filed, and that allegedly resulted in injuries in that State or in States contiguous to that State;

(II) the claims are joined upon motion of a defendant;

(III) all of the claims in the action are asserted on behalf of the general public (and not on behalf of individual claimants or members of a purported class) pursuant to a State statute specifically authorizing such action; or

(IV) the claims have been consolidated or coordinated solely for pretrial proceedings.

(C) (i) Any action(s) removed to Federal court pursuant to this subsection shall not thereafter be transferred to any other court pursuant to section 1407, or the rules promulgated thereunder, unless a majority of the plaintiffs in the action request transfer pursuant to section 1407.

(ii) This subparagraph will not apply—

(I) to cases certified pursuant to rule 23 of the Federal Rules of Civil Procedure; or

(II) if plaintiffs propose that the action proceed as a class action pursuant to rule 23 of the Federal Rules of Civil Procedure.

(D) The limitations periods on any claims asserted in a mass action that is removed to Federal court pursuant to this subsection shall be deemed tolled during the period that the action is pending in Federal court.

(e) The word "States", as used in this section, includes the Territories, the District of Columbia, and the Commonwealth of Puerto Rico.

[1] So in original. Reference to "16(f)(3)" probably should be preceded by "section".

§ 1333. Admiralty, Maritime and Prize Cases

The district courts shall have original jurisdiction, exclusive of the courts of the States, of:

(1) Any civil case of admiralty or maritime jurisdiction, saving to suitors in all cases all other remedies to which they are otherwise entitled.

(2) Any prize brought into the United States and all proceedings for the condemnation of property taken as prize.

§ 1334. Bankruptcy Cases and Proceedings

(a) Except as provided in subsection (b) of this section, the district courts shall have original and exclusive jurisdiction of all cases under title 11.

(b) Except as provided in subsection (e)(2), and notwithstanding any Act of Congress that confers exclusive jurisdiction on a court or courts other than the district courts, the district courts shall have original but not exclusive jurisdiction of all civil proceedings arising under title 11, or arising in or related to cases under title 11.

(c) (1) Except with respect to a case under chapter 15 of title 11, nothing in this section prevents a district court in the interest of justice, or in the interest of comity with State courts or respect for State law, from abstaining from hearing a particular proceeding arising under title 11 or arising in or related to a case under title 11.

(2) Upon timely motion of a party in a proceeding based upon a State law claim or State law cause of action, related to a case under title 11 but not arising under title 11 or arising in a case under title 11, with respect to which an action could not have been commenced in a court of the United States absent jurisdiction under this section, the district court shall abstain from hearing such proceeding if an action is commenced, and can be timely adjudicated, in a State forum of appropriate jurisdiction.

(d) Any decision to abstain or not to abstain made under subsection (c) (other than a decision not to abstain in a proceeding described in subsection (c)(2)) is not reviewable by appeal or otherwise by the court of appeals under section 158(d), 1291, or 1292 of this title or by the Supreme Court of the United States under section 1254 of this title. Subsection (c) and this subsection shall not be construed to limit the applicability of the stay provided for by section 362 of title 11, United States Code, as such section applies to an action affecting the property of the estate in bankruptcy.

(e) The district court in which a case under title 11 is commenced or is pending shall have exclusive jurisdiction—

(1) of all the property, wherever located, of the debtor as of the commencement of such case, and of property of the estate; and

(2) over all claims or causes of action that involve construction of section 327 of title 11, United States Code, or rules relating to disclosure requirements under section 327.

§ 1335. Interpleader

(a) The district courts shall have original jurisdiction of any civil action of interpleader or in the nature of interpleader filed by any person, firm, or corporation, association, or society having in his or its custody or possession money or property of the value of $500 or more, or having issued a note, bond, certificate, policy of insurance, or other instrument of value or amount of $500 or more, or providing for the delivery or payment or the loan of money or property of such amount or value, or being under any obligation written or unwritten to the amount of $500 or more, if

(1) Two or more adverse claimants, of diverse citizenship as defined in subsection (a) or (d) of section 1332 of this title, are claiming or may claim to be entitled to such money or property, or to any one or more of the benefits arising by virtue of any note, bond, certificate, policy or other instrument, or arising by virtue of any such obligation; and if (2) the plaintiff has deposited such money or property or has paid the amount of or the loan or other value of such instrument or the amount due under such obligation into the registry of the court, there to abide the judgment of the court, or has given bond payable to the clerk of the court in such amount and with such surety as the court or judge may deem proper, conditioned upon the compliance by the plaintiff with the future order or judgment of the court with respect to the subject matter of the controversy.

(b) Such an action may be entertained although the titles or claims of the conflicting claimants do not have a common origin, or are not identical, but are adverse to and independent of one another.

§ 1337. Commerce and Antitrust Regulations; Amount in Controversy, Costs

(a) The district courts shall have original jurisdiction of any civil action or proceeding arising under any Act of Congress regulating commerce or protecting trade and commerce against restraints and monopolies: Provided, however, That the district courts shall have original jurisdiction of an action brought under section 11706 or 14706 of title 49, only if the matter in controversy for each receipt or bill of lading exceeds $10,000, exclusive of interest and costs.

(b) Except when express provision therefor is otherwise made in a statute of the United States, where a plaintiff who files the case under section 11706 or 14706 of title 49, originally in the Federal courts is finally adjudged to be entitled to recover less than the sum or value of $10,000, computed without regard to any setoff or counterclaim to which the defendant may be adjudged to be entitled, and exclusive of any interest and costs, the district court may deny costs to the plaintiff and, in addition, may impose costs on the plaintiff.

(c) The district courts shall not have jurisdiction under this section of any matter within the exclusive jurisdiction of the Court of International Trade under chapter 95 of this title.

§ 1338. Patents, Plant Variety Protection, Copyrights, Mask Works, Designs, Trademarks, and Unfair Competition

(a) The district courts shall have original jurisdiction of any civil action arising under any Act of Congress relating to patents, plant variety protection, copyrights and trademarks. No State court shall have jurisdiction over any claim for relief arising under any Act of Congress relating to patents, plant variety protection, or copyrights. For purposes of this subsection, the term "State" includes any State of the United States, the District of Columbia, the Commonwealth of Puerto Rico, the United States Virgin Islands, American Samoa, Guam, and the Northern Mariana Islands.

(b) The district courts shall have original jurisdiction of any civil action asserting a claim of unfair competition when joined with a substantial and related claim under the copyright, patent, plant variety protection or trademark laws.

(c) Subsections (a) and (b) apply to exclusive rights in mask works under chapter 9 of title 17, and to exclusive rights in designs under chapter 13 of title 17, to the same extent as such subsections apply to copyrights.

§ 1339. Postal matters

The district courts shall have original jurisdiction of any civil action arising under any Act of Congress relating to the postal service.

§ 1340. Internal Revenue; Customs Duties

The district courts shall have original jurisdiction of any civil action arising under any Act of Congress providing for internal revenue, or revenue from imports or tonnage except matters within the jurisdiction of the Court of International Trade.

§ 1343. Civil Rights and Elective Franchise

(a) The district courts shall have original jurisdiction of any civil action authorized by law to be commenced by any person:

(1) To recover damages for injury to his person or property, or because of the deprivation of any right or privilege of a citizen of the United States, by any act done in furtherance of any conspiracy mentioned in section 1985 of Title 42;

(2) To recover damages from any person who fails to prevent or to aid in preventing any wrongs mentioned in section 1985 of Title 42 which he had knowledge were about to occur and power to prevent;

(3) To redress the deprivation, under color of any State law, statute, ordinance, regulation, custom or usage, of any right, privilege or immunity secured by the Constitution of the United States or by any Act of Congress providing for equal rights of citizens or of all persons within the jurisdiction of the United States;

(4) To recover damages or to secure equitable or other relief under any Act of Congress providing for the protection of civil rights, including the right to vote.

(b) For purposes of this section—

(1) the District of Columbia shall be considered to be a State; and

(2) any Act of Congress applicable exclusively to the District of Columbia shall be considered to be a statute of the District of Columbia.

§ 1345. United States As Plaintiff

Except as otherwise provided by Act of Congress, the district courts shall have original jurisdiction of all civil actions, suits or proceedings commenced by the United States, or by any agency or officer thereof expressly authorized to sue by Act of Congress.

§ 1346. United States As Defendant

(a) The district courts shall have original jurisdiction, concurrent with the United States Court of Federal Claims, of:

(1) Any civil action against the United States for the recovery of any internal-revenue tax alleged to have been erroneously or illegally assessed or collected, or any penalty claimed to have been collected without authority or any sum alleged to have been excessive or in any manner wrongfully collected under the internal-revenue laws;

(2) Any other civil action or claim against the United States, not exceeding $10,000 in amount, founded either upon the Constitution, or any Act of Congress, or any regulation of an executive department, or upon any express or implied contract with the United States, or for liquidated or unliquidated damages in cases not sounding in tort, except that the district courts shall not have jurisdiction of any civil action or claim against the United States founded upon any express or implied contract with the United States or for liquidated or unliquidated damages in cases not sounding in tort which are subject to sections 7104(b)(1) and 7107(a)(1) of title 41. For the purpose of this paragraph, an express or implied contract with the Army and Air Force Exchange Service, Navy Exchanges, Marine Corps Exchanges, Coast Guard Exchanges, or Exchange Councils of the National Aeronautics and Space Administration shall be considered an express or implied contract with the United States.

(b) (1) Subject to the provisions of chapter 171 of this title, the district courts, together with the United States District Court for the District of the Canal Zone and the District Court of the Virgin Islands, shall have exclusive jurisdiction of civil actions on claims against the United States, for money damages, accruing on and after January 1, 1945, for injury or loss of property, or personal injury or death caused by the negligent or wrongful act or omission of any employee of the Government while acting within the scope of his office or employment, under circumstances where the United States, if a private person, would be liable to the claimant in accordance with the law of the place where the act or omission occurred.

(2) No person convicted of a felony who is incarcerated while awaiting sentencing or while serving a sentence may bring a civil action against the United States or an agency, officer, or employee of the Government, for mental or emotional injury suffered while in custody without a prior showing of physical injury or the commission of a sexual act (as defined in section 2246 of Title 18).

(c) The jurisdiction conferred by this section includes jurisdiction of any set-off, counterclaim, or other claim or demand whatever on the part of the United States against any plaintiff commencing an action under this section.

(d) The district courts shall not have jurisdiction under this section of any civil action or claim for a pension.

(e) The district courts shall have original jurisdiction of any civil action against the United States provided in section 6226, 6228(a), 7426, or 7428 (in the case of the United States district court for the District of Columbia) or section 7429 of the Internal Revenue Code of 1986.

(f) The district courts shall have exclusive original jurisdiction of civil actions under section 2409a to quiet title to an estate or interest in real property in which an interest is claimed by the United States.

(g) Subject to the provisions of chapter 179, the district courts of the United States shall have exclusive jurisdiction over any civil action commenced under section 453(2) of title 3, by a covered employee under chapter 5 of such title.

§ 1349. Corporation Organized under Federal Law As Party

The district courts shall not have jurisdiction of any civil action by or against any corporation upon the ground that it was incorporated by or under an Act of Congress, unless the United States is the owner of more than one-half of its capital stock.

§ 1357. Injuries under Federal Laws

The district courts shall have original jurisdiction of any civil action commenced by any person to recover damages for any injury to his person or property on account of any act done by him, under any Act of Congress, for the protection or collection of any of the revenues, or to enforce the right of citizens of the United States to vote in any State.

§ 1359. Parties Collusively Joined or Made

A district court shall not have jurisdiction of a civil action in which any party, by assignment or otherwise, has been improperly or collusively made or joined to invoke the jurisdiction of such court.

§ 1361. Action to Compel an Officer of the United States to Perform His Duty

The district courts shall have original jurisdiction of any action in the nature of mandamus to compel an officer or employee of the United States or any agency thereof to perform a duty owed to the plaintiff.

§ 1367. Supplemental Jurisdiction

(a) Except as provided in subsections (b) and (c) or as expressly provided otherwise by Federal statute, in any civil action of which the district courts have original jurisdiction, the district courts shall have supplemental jurisdiction over all other claims that are so related to claims in the action within such original jurisdiction that they form part of the same case or controversy under Article III of the United States Constitution. Such supplemental jurisdiction shall include claims that involve the joinder or intervention of additional parties.

(b) In any civil action of which the district courts have original jurisdiction founded solely on section 1332 of this title, the district courts shall not have supplemental jurisdiction under subsection (a) over claims by plaintiffs against persons made parties under Rule 14, 19, 20, or 24 of the Federal Rules of Civil Procedure, or over claims by persons proposed to be joined as plaintiffs under Rule 19 of such rules, or seeking to intervene as plaintiffs under Rule 24 of such rules, when exercising supplemental jurisdiction over such claims would be inconsistent with the jurisdictional requirements of section 1332.

(c) The district courts may decline to exercise supplemental jurisdiction over a claim under subsection (a) if—

(1) the claim raises a novel or complex issue of State law,

(2) the claim substantially predominates over the claim or claims over which the district court has original jurisdiction,

(3) the district court has dismissed all claims over which it has original jurisdiction, or

(4) in exceptional circumstances, there are other compelling reasons for declining jurisdiction.

(d) The period of limitations for any claim asserted under subsection (a), and for any other claim in the same action that is voluntarily dismissed at the same time as or after the dismissal of the claim under subsection (a), shall be tolled while the claim is pending and for a period of 30 days after it is dismissed unless State law provides for a longer tolling period.

(e) As used in this section, the term "State" includes the District of Columbia, the Commonwealth of Puerto Rico, and any territory or possession of the United States.

§ 1369. Multiparty, Multiforum Jurisdiction

(a) In general. —The district courts shall have original jurisdiction of any civil action involving minimal diversity between adverse parties that arises from a single accident, where at least 75 natural persons have died in the accident at a discrete location, if—

(1) a defendant resides in a State and a substantial part of the accident took place in another State or other location, regardless of whether that defendant is also a resident of the State where a substantial part of the accident took place;

(2) any two defendants reside in different States, regardless of whether such defendants are also residents of the same State or States; or

(3) substantial parts of the accident took place in different States.

(b) Limitation of jurisdiction of district courts. —The district court shall abstain from hearing any civil action described in subsection (a) in which—

(1) the substantial majority of all plaintiffs are citizens of a single State of which the primary defendants are also citizens; and

(2) the claims asserted will be governed primarily by the laws of that State.

(c) Special rules and definitions. —For purposes of this section—

(1) minimal diversity exists between adverse parties if any party is a citizen of a State and any adverse party is a citizen of another State, a citizen or subject of a foreign state, or a foreign state as defined in section 1603(a) of this title;

(2) a corporation is deemed to be a citizen of any State, and a citizen or subject of any foreign state, in which it is incorporated or has its principal place of business, and is deemed to be a resident of any State in which it is incorporated or licensed to do business or is doing business;

(3) the term "injury" means—

(A) physical harm to a natural person; and

(B) physical damage to or destruction of tangible property, but only if physical harm described in subparagraph (A) exists;

(4) the term "accident" means a sudden accident, or a natural event culminating in an accident, that results in death incurred at a discrete location by at least 75 natural persons;

and

(5) the term "State" includes the District of Columbia, the Commonwealth of Puerto Rico, and any territory or possession of the United States.

(d) Intervening parties. —In any action in a district court which is or could have been brought, in whole or in part, under this section, any person with a claim arising from the accident described in subsection (a) shall be permitted to intervene as a party plaintiff in the action, even if that person could not have brought an action in a district court as an original matter.

(e) Notification of judicial panel on multidistrict litigation. —A district court in which an action under this section is pending shall promptly notify the judicial panel on multidistrict litigation of the pendency of the action.

§ 1390. Scope

(a) **Venue defined**.—As used in this chapter, the term "venue" refers to the geographic specification of the proper court or courts for the litigation of a civil action that is within the subject-matter jurisdiction of the district courts in general, and does not refer to any grant or restriction of subject-matter jurisdiction providing for a civil action to be adjudicated only by the district court for a particular district or districts.

(b) **Exclusion of certain cases**.—Except as otherwise provided by law, this chapter shall not govern the venue of a civil action in which the district court exercises the jurisdiction conferred by section 1333, except that such civil actions may be transferred between district courts as provided in this chapter.

(c) **Clarification regarding cases removed from state courts**.—This chapter shall not determine the district court to which a civil action pending in a State court may be removed, but shall govern the transfer of an action so removed as between districts and divisions of the United States district courts.

§ 1391. Venue Generally

(a) **Applicability of section**.—Except as otherwise provided by law—

(1) this section shall govern the venue of all civil actions brought in district courts of the United States; and

(2) the proper venue for a civil action shall be determined without regard to whether the action is local or transitory in nature.

(b) **Venue in general**.—A civil action may be brought in—

(1) a judicial district in which any defendant resides, if all defendants are residents of the State in which the district is located;

(2) a judicial district in which a substantial part of the events or omissions giving rise to the claim occurred, or a substantial

part of property that is the subject of the action is situated; or

(3) if there is no district in which an action may otherwise be brought as provided in this section, any judicial district in which any defendant is subject to the court's personal jurisdiction with respect to such action.

(c) **Residency.**—For all venue purposes—

(1) a natural person, including an alien lawfully admitted for permanent residence in the United States, shall be deemed to reside in the judicial district in which that person is domiciled;

(2) an entity with the capacity to sue and be sued in its common name under applicable law, whether or not incorporated, shall be deemed to reside, if a defendant, in any judicial district in which such defendant is subject to the court's personal jurisdiction with respect to the civil action in question and, if a plaintiff, only in the judicial district in which it maintains its principal place of business; and

(3) a defendant not resident in the United States may be sued in any judicial district, and the joinder of such a defendant shall be disregarded in determining where the action may be brought with respect to other defendants.

(d) **Residency of corporations in states with multiple districts.**—For purposes of venue under this chapter, in a State which has more than one judicial district and in which a defendant that is a corporation is subject to personal jurisdiction at the time an action is commenced, such corporation shall be deemed to reside in any district in that State within which its contacts would be sufficient to subject it to personal jurisdiction if that district were a separate State, and, if there is no such district, the corporation shall be deemed to reside in the district within which it has the most significant contacts.

(e) **Actions where defendant is officer or employee of the united states.**—(1) **In general.**—A civil action in which a defendant is an officer or employee of the United States or any agency thereof acting in his official capacity or under color of legal authority, or an agency of the United States, or the United States, may, except as otherwise provided by law, be brought in any judicial district in which (A) a defendant in the action resides, (B) a substantial part of the events or omissions giving rise to the claim occurred, or a substantial part of property that is the subject of the action is situated, or (C) the plaintiff resides if no real property is involved in the action. Additional persons may be joined as parties to any such action in accordance with the Federal Rules of Civil Procedure and with such other venue requirements as would be applicable if the United States or one of its officers, employees, or agencies were not a party.

(2) **Service.**—The summons and complaint in such an action shall be served as provided by the Federal Rules of Civil Procedure except that the delivery of the summons and complaint to the officer or agency as required by the rules may be made by

certified mail beyond the territorial limits of the district in which the action is brought.

(f) **Civil actions against a foreign state**.—A civil action against a foreign state as defined in section 1603(a) of this title may be brought—

(1) in any judicial district in which a substantial part of the events or omissions giving rise to the claim occurred, or a substantial part of property that is the subject of the action is situated;

(2) in any judicial district in which the vessel or cargo of a foreign state is situated, if the claim is asserted under section 1605(b) of this title;

(3) in any judicial district in which the agency or instrumentality is licensed to do business or is doing business, if the action is brought against an agency or instrumentality of a foreign state as defined in section 1603(b) of this title; or

(4) in the United States District Court for the District of Columbia if the action is brought against a foreign state or political subdivision thereof.

(g) **Multiparty, multiforum litigation**.—A civil action in which jurisdiction of the district court is based upon section 1369 of this title may be brought in any district in which any defendant resides or in which a substantial part of the accident giving rise to the action took place.

§ 1397. Interpleader

Any civil action of interpleader or in the nature of interpleader under section 1335 of this title may be brought in the judicial district in which one or more of the claimants reside.

§ 1400. Patents and Copyrights, Mask Works, and Designs

(a) Civil actions, suits, or proceedings arising under any Act of Congress relating to copyrights or exclusive rights in mask works or designs may be instituted in the district in which the defendant or his agent resides or may be found.

(b) Any civil action for patent infringement may be brought in the judicial district where the defendant resides, or where the defendant has committed acts of infringement and has a regular and established place of business.

§ 1401. Stockholder's Derivative Action

Any civil action by a stockholder on behalf of his corporation may be prosecuted in any judicial district where the corporation might have sued the same defendants.

§ 1402. United States As Defendant

(a) Any civil action in a district court against the United States under subsection (a) of section 1346 of this title may be prosecuted only:

(1) Except as provided in paragraph (2), in the judicial district where the plaintiff resides;

(2) In the case of a civil action in a district court by a corporation under paragraph (1) of subsection (a) of section 1346, in the judicial district in which is located the principal place of business or principal office or agency of the corporation; or if it has no principal place of business or principal office or agency in any judicial district (A) in the judicial district in which is located the office to which was made the return of the tax in respect of which the claim is made, or (B) if no return was made, in the judicial district in which lies the District of Columbia. Notwithstanding the foregoing provisions of this paragraph a district court, for the convenience of the parties and witnesses, in the interest of justice, may transfer any such action to any other district or division.

(b) Any civil action on a tort claim against the United States under subsection (b) of section 1346 of this title may be prosecuted only in the judicial district where the plaintiff resides or wherein the act or omission complained of occurred.

(c) Any civil action against the United States under subsection (e) of section 1346 of this title may be prosecuted only in the judicial district where the property is situated at the time of levy, or if no levy is made, in the judicial district in which the event occurred which gave rise to the cause of action.

(d) Any civil action under section 2409a to quiet title to an estate or interest in real property in which an interest is claimed by the United States shall be brought in the district court of the district where the property is located or, if located in different districts, in any of such districts.

§ 1404. Change of Venue

(a) For the convenience of parties and witnesses, in the interest of justice, a district court may transfer any civil action to any other district or division where it might have been brought or to any district or division to which all parties have consented.

(b) Upon motion, consent or stipulation of all parties, any action, suit or proceeding of a civil nature or any motion or hearing thereof, may be transferred, in the discretion of the court, from the division in which pending to any other division in the same district. Transfer of proceedings in rem brought by or on behalf of the United States may be transferred under this section without the consent of the United States where all other parties request transfer.

(c) A district court may order any civil action to be tried at any place within the division in which it is pending.

(d) Transfers from a district court of the United States to the District Court of Guam, the District Court for the Northern Mariana Islands, or the District Court of the Virgin Islands shall not be permitted under this section. As otherwise used in this section, "district court" includes the District Court of Guam, the District Court for the Northern Mariana Islands, and the District Court of the Virgin Islands, and the term "district" includes the territorial jurisdiction of that court.

§ 1406. Cure or Waiver of Defects

(a) The district court of a district in which is filed a case laying venue in the wrong division or district shall dismiss, or if it be in the interest of justice, transfer such case to any district or division in which it could have been brought.

(b) Nothing in this chapter shall impair the jurisdiction of a district court of any matter involving a party who does not interpose timely and sufficient objection to the venue.

(c) As used in this section, "district court" includes the District Court of Guam, the District Court for the Northern Mariana Islands, and the District Court of the Virgin Islands, and the term "district" includes the territorial jurisdiction of that court.

§ 1407. Multidistrict Litigation

[Note to Reader: See Part V of this text.]

§ 1412. Change of Venue

A district court may transfer a case or proceeding under title 11 to a district court for another district, in the interest of justice or for the convenience of the parties.

§ 1441. Removal of civil actions

(a) Generally.— Except as otherwise expressly provided by Act of Congress, any civil action brought in a State court of which the district courts of the United States have original jurisdiction, may be removed by the defendant or the defendants, to the district court of the United States for the district and division embracing the place where such action is pending.

(b) Removal based on diversity of citizenship.—(1) In determining whether a civil action is removable on the basis of the jurisdiction under section 1332(a) of this title, the citizenship of defendants sued under fictitious names shall be disregarded.

(2) A civil action otherwise removable solely on the basis of the jurisdiction under section 1332(a) of this title may not be removed if any of the parties in interest properly joined and served as defendants is a citizen of the State in which such action is brought.

(c) Joinder of federal law claims and state law claims.—(1) If a civil action includes—

(A) a claim arising under the Constitution, laws, or treaties of the United States (within the meaning of section 1331 of this title), and

(B) a claim not within the original or supplemental jurisdiction of the district court or a claim that has been made nonremovable by statute,

the entire action may be removed if the action would be removable without the inclusion of the claim described in subparagraph (B).

(2) Upon removal of an action described in paragraph (1), the district court shall sever from the action all claims described in paragraph (1)(B) and shall remand the severed claims to the State court from which the action was removed. Only defendants against whom a claim described in paragraph (1)(A) has been asserted are required to join in or consent to the removal under paragraph (1).

(d) Actions against foreign states.—Any civil action brought in a State court against a foreign state as defined in section 1603(a) of this title may be removed by the foreign state to the district court of the United States for the district and division embracing the place where such action is pending. Upon removal the action shall be tried by the court without jury. Where removal is based upon this subsection, the time limitations of section 1446(b) of this chapter may be enlarged at any time for cause shown.

(e) Multiparty, multiforum jurisdiction.—**(1)** Notwithstanding the provisions of subsection (b) of this section, a defendant in a civil action in a State court may remove the action to the district court of the United States for the district and division embracing the place where the action is pending if—

(A) the action could have been brought in a United States district court under section 1369 of this title; or

(B) the defendant is a party to an action which is or could have been brought, in whole or in part, under section 1369 in a United States district court and arises from the same accident as the action in State court, even if the action to be removed could not have been brought in a district court as an original matter.

The removal of an action under this subsection shall be made in accordance with section 1446 of this title, except that a notice of removal may also be filed before trial of the action in State court within 30 days after the date on which the defendant first becomes a party to an action under section 1369 in a United States district court that arises from the same accident as the action in State court, or at a later time with leave of the district court.

(2) Whenever an action is removed under this subsection and the district court to which it is removed or transferred under section 1407(j) has made a liability determination requiring further proceedings as to damages, the district court shall remand the action to the State court from which it had been removed for the determination of damages, unless the court finds that, for the convenience of parties and witnesses and in the interest of justice, the action should be retained for the determination of damages.

(3) Any remand under paragraph (2) shall not be effective until 60 days after the district court has issued an order determining liability and has certified its intention to remand the removed action for the determination of damages. An appeal with respect to the liability determination of the district court may be taken during that 60-day period to the court of appeals with appellate jurisdiction over the district court. In the event a party files such an appeal, the remand shall not be effective until the appeal has been finally disposed of. Once the remand has become effective, the liability determination shall not be subject to further review by appeal or otherwise.

(4) Any decision under this subsection concerning remand for the determination of damages shall not be reviewable by appeal or otherwise.

(5) An action removed under this subsection shall be deemed to be an action under section 1369 and an action in which jurisdiction is based on section 1369 of this title for purposes of this section and sections 1407, 1697, and 1785 of this title.

(6) Nothing in this subsection shall restrict the authority of the district court to transfer or dismiss an action on the ground of inconvenient forum.

(f) DERIVATIVE REMOVAL JURISDICTION.—The court to which a civil action is removed under this section is not precluded from hearing and determining any claim in such civil action because the State court from which such civil action is removed did not have jurisdiction over that claim.

§ 1442. Federal Officers or Agencies Sued or Prosecuted

(a) A civil action or criminal prosecution that is commenced in a State court and that is against or directed to any of the following may be removed by them to the district court of the United States for the district and division embracing the place wherein it is pending:

(1) The United States or any agency thereof or any officer (or any person acting under that officer) of the United States or of any agency thereof, in an official or individual capacity, for or relating to any act under color of such office or on account of any right, title or authority claimed under any Act of Congress for the apprehension or punishment of criminals or the collection of the revenue.

(2) A property holder whose title is derived from any such officer, where such action or prosecution affects the validity of any law of the United States.

(3) Any officer of the courts of the United States, for or relating to any act under color of office or in the performance of his duties;

(4) Any officer of either House of Congress, for or relating to any act in the discharge of his official duty under an order of such House.

(b) A personal action commenced in any State court by an alien against any citizen of a State who is, or at the time the alleged action accrued was, a civil officer of the United States and is a nonresident of such State, wherein jurisdiction is obtained by the State court by personal service of process, may be removed by the defendant to the district court of the United States for the district and division in which the defendant was served with process.

(c) Solely for purposes of determining the propriety of removal under subsection (a), a law enforcement officer, who is the defendant in a criminal prosecution, shall be deemed to have been acting under the color of his office if the officer—

(1) protected an individual in the presence of the officer from a crime of violence;

(2) provided immediate assistance to an individual who suffered, or who was threatened with, bodily harm; or

(3) prevented the escape of any individual who the officer reasonably believed to have committed, or was about to commit, in the presence of the officer, a crime of violence that resulted in, or was likely to result in, death or serious bodily injury.

(d) In this section, the following definitions apply:

(1) The terms "civil action" and "criminal prosecution" include any proceeding (whether or not ancillary to another proceeding) to the extent that in such proceeding a judicial order, including a subpoena for testimony or documents, is sought or issued. If removal is sought for a proceeding described in the previous sentence, and there is no other basis for removal, only that proceeding may be removed to the district court.

(2) The term "crime of violence" has the meaning given that term in section 16 of title 18.

(3) The term "law enforcement officer" means any employee described in subparagraph (A), (B), or (C) of section 8401(17) of title 5 and any special agent in the Diplomatic Security Service of the Department of State.

(4) The term "serious bodily injury" has the meaning given that term in section 1365 of title 18.

(5) The term "State" includes the District of Columbia, United States territories and insular possessions, and Indian country (as defined in section 1151 of title 18).

(6) The term "State court" includes the Superior Court of the District of Columbia, a court of a United States territory or insular possession, and a tribal court.

§ 1442a. Members of Armed Forces Sued or Prosecuted

A civil or criminal prosecution in a court of a State of the United States against a member of the armed forces of the United States on account of an act done under color of his office or status, or in respect to which he claims any right, title, or authority under a law of the United States respecting the armed forces thereof, or under the law of war, may at any time before the trial or final hearing thereof be removed for trial into the district court of the United States for the district where it is pending in the manner prescribed by law, and it shall thereupon be entered on the docket of the district court, which shall proceed as if the cause had been originally commenced therein and shall have full power to hear and determine the cause.

§ 1443. Civil Rights Cases

Any of the following civil actions or criminal prosecutions, commenced in a State court may be removed by the defendant to the district court of the United States for the district and division embracing the place wherein it is pending:

(1) Against any person who is denied or cannot enforce in the courts of such State a right under any law providing for the equal civil rights of citizens of the United States, or of all persons within the jurisdiction thereof;

(2) For any act under color of authority derived from any law providing for equal rights, or for refusing to do any act on the ground that it would be inconsistent with such law.

§ 1445. Nonremovable Actions

(a) A civil action in any State court against a railroad or its receivers or trustees, arising under sections 1-4 and 5-10 of the Act of April 22, 1908 (45 U.S.C. 51 to 54, 55 to 60), may not be removed to any district court of the United States.

(b) A civil action in any State court against a carrier or its receivers or trustees to recover damages for delay, loss, or injury of shipments, arising under section 11706 or 14706 of title 49, may not be removed to any district court of the United States unless the matter in controversy exceeds $10,000, exclusive of interest and costs.

(c) A civil action in any State court arising under the workmen's compensation laws of such State may not be removed to any district court of the United States.

(d) A civil action in any State court arising under section 40302 of the Violence Against Women Act of 1994 may not be removed to any district court of the United States.

§ 1446. Procedure for removal of civil actions

(a) Generally.—A defendant or defendants desiring to remove any civil action from a State court shall file in the district court of the United States for the district and division within which such action is pending a notice of removal signed pursuant to Rule 11 of the Federal Rules of Civil Procedure and containing a short and plain statement of the grounds for removal, together with a copy of all process, pleadings, and orders served upon such defendant or defendants in such action.

(b) Requirements; generally.—(1) The notice of removal of a civil action or proceeding shall be filed within 30 days after the receipt by the defendant, through service or otherwise, of a copy of the initial pleading setting forth the claim for relief upon which such action or proceeding is based, or within 30 days after the service of summons upon the defendant if such initial pleading has then been filed in court and is not required to be served on the defendant, whichever period is shorter.

(2) **(A)** When a civil action is removed solely under section 1441(a), all defendants who have been properly joined and served must join in or consent to the removal of the action.

(B) Each defendant shall have 30 days after receipt by or service on that defendant of the initial pleading or summons described in paragraph (1) to file the notice of removal.

(C) If defendants are served at different times, and a later served defendant files a notice of removal, any earlier-served defendant may consent to the removal even though that earlier-served defendant did not previously initiate or consent to removal.

(3) Except as provided in subsection (c), if the case stated by the initial pleading is not removable, a notice of removal may be filed within thirty days after receipt by the defendant, through service or otherwise, of a copy of an amended pleading, motion, order or other paper from which it may first be ascertained that the case is one which is or has become removable.

(c) Requirements; removal based on diversity of citizenship.—(1) A case may not be removed under subsection (b)(3) on the basis of jurisdiction conferred by section 1332 more than 1 year after commencement of the action, unless the district court finds that the plaintiff has acted in bad faith in order to prevent a defendant from removing the action.**(2)** If removal of a civil action is sought on the basis of the jurisdiction conferred by section 1332(a), the sum demanded in good faith in the initial pleading shall be deemed to be the amount in controversy, except that—

(A) the notice of removal may assert the amount in controversy if the initial pleading seeks—

(i) nonmonetary relief; or

(ii) a money judgment, but the State practice either does not permit demand for a specific sum or permits recovery of damages in excess of the amount demanded; and

(B) removal of the action is proper on the basis of an amount in controversy asserted under subparagraph (A) if the district court finds, by the preponderance of the evidence, that the amount in controversy exceeds the amount specified in section 1332(a).

(3) (A) If the case stated by the initial pleading is not removable solely because the amount in controversy does not exceed the amount specified in section 1332(a), information relating to the amount in controversy in the record of the State proceeding, or in responses to discovery, shall be treated as an "other paper" under subsection (b)(3).

(B) If the notice of removal is filed more than 1 year after commencement of the action and the district court finds that the plaintiff deliberately failed to disclose the actual amount in controversy to prevent removal, that finding shall be deemed bad faith under paragraph (1).

(d) Notice to adverse parties and state court.—Promptly Promptly after the filing of such notice of removal of a civil action the defendant or defendants shall give written notice thereof to all adverse parties and shall file a copy of the notice with the clerk of such State court, which shall effect the removal and the State court shall proceed no further unless and until the case is remanded.

(e) Counterclaim in 337 proceeding.—With respect to any counterclaim removed to a district court pursuant to section 337(c) of the Tariff Act of 1930, the district court shall resolve such counterclaim in the same manner as an original complaint under the Federal Rules of Civil Procedure, except that the payment of a filing fee shall not be required in such cases and the counterclaim shall relate back to the date of the original complaint in the proceeding before the International Trade Commission under section 337 of that Act.

***(g) (1)** Where the civil action or criminal prosecution that is removable under section 1442(a) is a proceeding in which a judicial order for testimony or documents is sought or issued or sought to be enforced, the 30-day requirement of subsection (b) of this section and paragraph (1) of section 1455(b) is satisfied if the person or entity desiring to remove the proceeding files the notice of removal not later than 30 days after receiving, through service, notice of any such proceeding.

ED. NOTE:

Effective January 2012, revisions to Section 1446 repositioned subpart (f), leaving that subpart empty in the current statute.

§ 1447. Procedure after Removal Generally

(a) In any case removed from a State court, the district court may issue all necessary orders and process to bring before it all proper parties whether served by process issued by the State court or otherwise.

(b) It may require the removing party to file with its clerk copies of all records and proceedings in such State court or may cause the same to be brought before it by writ of certiorari issued to such State court.

(c) A motion to remand the case on the basis of any defect other than lack of subject matter jurisdiction must be made within 30 days after the filing of the notice of removal under section 1446(a). If at any time before final judgment it appears that the district court lacks subject matter jurisdiction, the case shall be remanded. An order remanding the case may require payment of just costs and any actual expenses, including attorney fees, incurred as a result of the removal. A certified copy of the order of remand shall be mailed by the clerk to the clerk of the State court. The State court may thereupon proceed with such case.

(d) An order remanding a case to the State court from which it was removed is not reviewable on appeal or otherwise, except that an order remanding a case to the State court from which it was removed pursuant to section 1442 or 1443 of this title shall be reviewable by appeal or otherwise.

(e) If after removal the plaintiff seeks to join additional defendants whose joinder would destroy subject matter jurisdiction, the court may deny joinder, or permit joinder and remand the action to the State court.

§ 1448. Process after Removal

In all cases removed from any State court to any district court of the United States in which any one or more of the defendants has not been served with process or in which the service has not been perfected prior to removal, or in which process served proves to be defective, such process or service may be completed or new process issued in the same manner as in cases originally filed in such district court.

This section shall not deprive any defendant upon whom process is served after removal of his right to move to remand the case.

§ 1449. State Court Record Supplied

Where a party is entitled to copies of the records and proceedings in any suit or prosecution in a State court, to be used in any district court of the United States, and the clerk of such State court, upon demand, and the payment or tender of the legal fees, fails to deliver certified copies, the district court may, on affidavit reciting such facts, direct such record to be supplied by affidavit or otherwise. Thereupon such proceedings, trial, and judgment may be had in such district court, and all such process awarded, as if certified copies had been filed in the district court.

§ 1451. Definitions

For purposes of this chapter—

(1) The term "State court" includes the Superior Court of the District of Columbia.

(2) The term "State" includes the District of Columbia.

§ 1453. Removal of Class Actions

(a) Definitions. —In this section, the terms "class", "class action", "class certification order", and "class member" shall have the meanings given such terms under section 1332(d)(1).

(b) In general. —A class action may be removed to a district court of the United States in accordance with section 1446 (except that the 1-year limitation under section 1446(c)(1) shall not apply), without regard to whether any defendant is a citizen of the State in which the action is brought, except that such action may be removed by any defendant without the consent of all defendants.

(c) Review of remand orders. —

(1) In general. —Section 1447 shall apply to any removal of a case under this section, except that notwithstanding section 1447(d), a court of appeals may accept an appeal from an order of a district court granting or denying a motion to remand a class action to the State court from which it was removed if application is made to the court of appeals not more than 10 days after entry of the order.

(2) Time period for judgment. —If the court of appeals accepts an appeal under paragraph (1), the court shall complete all action on such appeal, including rendering judgment, not later than 60 days after the date on which such appeal was filed, unless an extension is granted under paragraph (3).

(3) Extension of time period. —The court of appeals may grant an extension of the 60-day period described in paragraph (2) if—

(A) all parties to the proceeding agree to such extension, for any period of time; or

(B) such extension is for good cause shown and in the interests of justice, for a period not to exceed 10 days.

(4) Denial of appeal. —If a final judgment on the appeal under paragraph (1) is not issued before the end of the period described in paragraph (2), including any extension under paragraph (3), the appeal shall be denied.

(d) Exception. —This section shall not apply to any class action that solely involves—

(1) a claim concerning a covered security as defined under section 16(f) (3) of the Securities Act of 1933 (15 U.S.C. 78p(f)(3)) and section 28(f)(5)(E) of the Securities Exchange Act of 1934 (15 U.S.C. 78bb(f)(5)(E));

(2) a claim that relates to the internal affairs or governance of a corporation or other form of business enterprise and arises under or by virtue of the laws of the State in which such corporation or business enterprise is incorporated or organized; or

(3) a claim that relates to the rights, duties (including fiduciary duties), and obligations relating to or created by or pursuant to any security (as defined under section 2(a)(1) of the Securities Act of 1933 (15 U.S.C. 77b(a)(1)) and the regulations issued thereunder).

§ 1631. Transfer to Cure Want of Jurisdiction

Whenever a civil action is filed in a court as defined in section 610 of this title or an appeal, including a petition for review of administrative action, is noticed for or filed with such a court and that court finds that there is a want of jurisdiction, the court shall, if it is in the interest of justice, transfer such action or appeal to any other such court (or, for cases within the jurisdiction of the United States Tax Court, to that court) in which the action or appeal could have been brought at the time it was filed or noticed, and the action or appeal shall proceed as if it had been filed in or noticed for the court to which it is transferred on the date upon which it was actually filed in or noticed for the court from which it is transferred.

§ 1651. Writs

(a) The Supreme Court and all courts established by Act of Congress may issue all writs necessary or appropriate in aid of their respective jurisdictions and agreeable to the usages and principles of law.

(b) An alternative writ or rule nisi may be issued by a justice or judge of a court which has jurisdiction.

§ 1652. State Laws As Rules of Decision

The laws of the several states, except where the Constitution or treaties of the United States or Acts of Congress otherwise require or provide, shall be regarded as rules of decision in civil actions in the courts of the United States, in cases where they apply.

§ 1653. Amendment of Pleadings to Show Jurisdiction

Defective allegations of jurisdiction may be amended, upon terms, in the trial or appellate courts.

§ 1654. Appearance Personally or by Counsel

In all courts of the United States the parties may plead and conduct their own cases personally or by counsel as, by the rules of such courts, respectively, are permitted to manage and conduct causes therein.

§ 1655. Lien enforcement; absent defendants

In an action in a district court to enforce any lien upon or claim to, or to remove any incumbrance or lien or cloud upon the title to, real or personal property within the district, where any defendant cannot be served within the State, or does not voluntarily appear, the court may order the absent defendant to appear or plead by a day certain.

Such order shall be served on the absent defendant personally if practicable, wherever found, and also upon the person or persons in possession or charge of such property, if any. Where personal service is not practicable, the order shall be published as the court may direct, not less than once a week for six consecutive weeks.

If an absent defendant does not appear or plead within the time allowed, the court may proceed as if the absent defendant had been served with process within the State, but any adjudication shall, as regards the absent defendant without appearance, affect only the property which is the subject of the action. When a part of the property is within another district, but within the same state, such action may be brought in either district.

Any defendant not so personally notified may, at any time within one year after final judgment, enter his appearance, and thereupon the court shall set aside the judgment and permit such defendant to plead on payment of such costs as the court deems just.

§ 1657. Priority of Civil Actions

(a) Notwithstanding any other provision of law, each court of the United States shall determine the order in which civil actions are heard and determined, except that the court shall expedite the consideration of any action brought under chapter 153 or section 1826 of this title, any action for temporary or preliminary injunctive relief, or any other action if good cause therefor is shown. For purposes of this subsection, "good cause" is shown if a right under the Constitution of the United States or a Federal Statute (including rights under section 552 of title 5) would be maintained in a factual context that indicates that a request for expedited consideration has merit.

(b) The Judicial Conference of the United States may modify the rules adopted by the courts to determine the order in which civil actions are heard and determined, in order to establish consistency among the judicial circuits.

§ 1658. Time Limitations on the Commencement of Civil Actions Arising under Acts of Congress

(a) Except as otherwise provided by law, a civil action arising under an Act of Congress enacted after the date of the enactment of this section may not be commenced later than 4 years after the cause of action accrues.

(b) Notwithstanding subsection (a), a private right of action that involves a claim of fraud, deceit, manipulation, or contrivance in contravention of a regulatory requirement concerning the securities laws, as defined in section 3(a)(47) of the Securities Exchange Act of 1934 (15 U.S.C. 78c(a)(47)), may be brought not later than the earlier of—

(1) 2 years after the discovery of the facts constituting the violation; or

(2) 5 years after such violation.

§ 1691. Seal and Teste of Process

All writs and process issuing from a court of the United States shall be under the seal of the court and signed by the clerk thereof.

§ 1692. Process and Orders Affecting Property in Different Districts

In proceedings in a district court where a receiver is appointed for property, real, personal, or mixed, situated in different districts, process may issue and be executed in any such district as if the property lay wholly within one district, but orders affecting the property shall be entered of record in each of such districts.

§ 1695. Stockholder's Derivative Action

Process in a stockholder's action in behalf of his corporation may be served upon such corporation in any district where it is organized or licensed to do business or is doing business.

§ 1696. Service in Foreign and International Litigation

(a) The district court of the district in which a person resides or is found may order service upon him of any document issued in connection with a proceeding in a foreign or international tribunal. The order may be made pursuant to a letter rogatory issued, or request made, by a foreign or international tribunal or upon application of any interested person and shall direct the manner of service. Service pursuant to this subsection does not, of itself, require the recognition or enforcement in the United States of a judgment, decree, or order rendered by a foreign or international tribunal.

(b) This section does not preclude service of such a document without an order of court.

§ 1697. Service in Multiparty, Multiforum Actions

When the jurisdiction of the district court is based in whole or in part upon section 1369 of this title, process, other than subpoenas, may be served at any place within the United States, or anywhere outside the United States if otherwise permitted by law.

§ 1731. Handwriting

The admitted or proved handwriting of any person shall be admissible, for purposes of comparison, to determine genuineness of other handwriting attributed to such person.

§ 1732. Record Made in Regular Course of Business; Photographic Copies

If any business, institution, member of a profession or calling, or any department or agency of government, in the regular course of business or activity has kept or recorded any memorandum, writing, entry, print, representation or combination thereof, of any act, transaction, occurrence, or event, and in the regular course of business has caused any or all of the same to be recorded, copied, or reproduced by any photographic, photostatic, microfilm, micro-card, miniature photographic, or other process which accurately reproduces or forms a durable medium for so reproducing the original, the original may be destroyed in the regular course of business unless its preservation is required by law. Such reproduction, when satisfactorily identified, is as admissible in evidence as the original itself in any judicial or administrative proceeding whether the original is in existence or not and an enlargement or facsimile of such reproduction is likewise admissible in evidence if the original reproduction is in existence and available for inspection under direction of court. The introduction of a reproduced record, enlargement, or facsimile does not preclude admission of the original. This subsection shall not be construed to exclude from evidence any document or copy thereof which is otherwise admissible under the rules of evidence.

§ 1733. Government Records and Papers; Copies

(a) Books or records of account or minutes of proceedings of any department or agency of the United States shall be admissible to prove the act, transaction or occurrence as a memorandum of which the same were made or kept.

(b) Properly authenticated copies or transcripts of any books, records, papers or documents of any department or agency of the United States shall be admitted in evidence equally with the originals thereof.

(c) This section does not apply to cases, actions, and proceedings to which the Federal Rules of Evidence apply.

§ 1734. Court Record Lost or Destroyed, Generally

(a) A lost or destroyed record of any proceeding in any court of the United States may be supplied on application of any interested party not at fault, by substituting a copy certified by the clerk of any court in which an authentic copy is lodged.

(b) Where a certified copy is not available, any interested person not at fault may file in such court a verified application for an order establishing the lost or destroyed record.

Every other interested person shall be served personally with a copy of the application and with notice of hearing on a day stated, not less than sixty days after service. Service may be made on any nonresident of the district anywhere within the jurisdiction of the United States or in any foreign country.

Proof of service in a foreign country shall be certified by a minister or consul of the United States in such country, under his official seal.

If, after the hearing, the court is satisfied that the statements contained in the application are true, it shall enter an order reciting the substance and effect of the lost or destroyed record. Such order, subject to intervening rights of third persons, shall have the same effect as the original record.

§ 1735. Court Record Lost or Destroyed Where United States Interested

(a) When the record of any case or matter in any court of the United States to which the United States is a party, is lost or destroyed, a certified copy of any official paper of a United States attorney, United States marshal or clerk or other certifying or recording officer of any such court, made pursuant to law, on file in any department or agency of the United States and relating to such case or matter, shall, on being filed in the court to which it relates, have the same effect as an original paper filed in such court. If the copy so filed discloses the date and amount of a judgment or decree and the names of the parties thereto, the court may enforce the judgment or decree as though the original record had not been lost or destroyed.

(b) Whenever the United States is interested in any lost or destroyed records or files of a court of the United States, the clerk of such court and the United States attorney for the district shall take the steps necessary to restore such records or files, under the direction of the judges of such court.

§ 1738. State and Territorial Statutes and Judicial Proceedings; Full Faith and Credit

The Acts of the legislature of any State, Territory, or Possession of the United States, or copies thereof, shall be authenticated by affixing the seal of such State, Territory or Possession thereto.

The records and judicial proceedings of any court of any such State, Territory or Possession, or copies thereof, shall be proved or admitted in other courts within the United States and its Territories and Possessions by the attestation of the clerk and seal of the court annexed, if a seal exists, together with a certificate of a judge of the court that the said attestation is in proper form.

Such Acts, records and judicial proceedings or copies thereof, so authenticated, shall have the same full faith and credit in every court within the United States and its Territories and Possessions as they have by law or usage in the courts of such State, Territory or Possession from which they are taken.

§ 1739. State and Territorial Nonjudicial Records; Full Faith and Credit

All nonjudicial records or books kept in any public office of any State, Territory, or Possession of the United States, or copies thereof, shall be proved or admitted in any court or office in any other State, Territory, or Possession by the attestation of the custodian of such records or books, and the seal of his office annexed, if there be a seal, together with a certificate of a judge of a court of record of the county, parish, or district in which such office may be kept, or of the Governor, or secretary of state, the chancellor or keeper of the great seal, of the State, Territory, or Possession that the said attestation is in due form and by the proper officers.

If the certificate is given by a judge, it shall be further authenticated by the clerk or prothonotary of the court, who shall certify, under his hand and the seal of his office, that such judge is duly commissioned and qualified; or, if given by such Governor, secretary, chancellor, or keeper of the great seal, it shall be under the great seal of the State, Territory, or Possession in which it is made.

Such records or books, or copies thereof, so authenticated, shall have the same full faith and credit in every court and office within the United States and its Territories and Possessions as they have by law or usage in the courts or offices of the State, Territory, or Possession from which they are taken.

§ 1746. Unsworn Declarations under Penalty of Perjury

Wherever, under any law of the United States or under any rule, regulation, order, or requirement made pursuant to law, any matter is required or permitted to be supported, evidenced, established, or proved by the sworn declaration, verification, certificate, statement, oath, or affidavit, in writing of the person making the same (other than a deposition, or an oath of office, or an oath required to be taken before a specified official other than a notary public), such matter may, with like force and effect, be supported, evidenced, established, or proved by the unsworn declaration, certificate, verification, or statement, in writing of such person which is subscribed by him, as true under penalty of perjury, and dated, in substantially the following form:

(1) If executed without the United States: "I declare *(or certify, verify, or state)* under penalty of perjury under the laws of the United States of America that the foregoing is true and correct. Executed on *(date)*.

(Signature)".

(2) If executed within the United States, its territories, possessions, or commonwealths: "I declare *(or certify, verify, or state)* under penalty of perjury that the foregoing is true and correct. Executed on *(date)*.

(Signature)".

§ 1781. Transmittal of Letter Rogatory or Request

(a) The Department of State has power, directly, or through suitable channels—

(1) to receive a letter rogatory issued, or request made, by a foreign or international tribunal, to transmit it to the tribunal, officer, or agency in the United States to whom it is addressed, and to receive and return it after execution; and

(2) to receive a letter rogatory issued, or request made, by a tribunal in the United States, to transmit it to the foreign or international tribunal, officer, or agency to whom it is addressed, and to receive and return it after execution.

(b) This section does not preclude—

(1) the transmittal of a letter rogatory or request directly from a foreign or international tribunal to the tribunal, officer, or agency in the United States to whom it is addressed and its return in the same manner; or

(2) the transmittal of a letter rogatory or request directly from a tribunal in the United States to the foreign or international tribunal, officer, or agency to whom it is addressed and its return in the same manner.

§ 1782. Assistance to Foreign and International Tribunals and to Litigants before Such Tribunals

(a) The district court of the district in which a person resides or is found may order him to give his testimony or statement or to produce a document or other thing for use in a proceeding in a foreign or international tribunal, including criminal investigations conducted before formal accusation. The order may be made pursuant to a letter rogatory issued, or request made, by a foreign or international tribunal or upon the application of any interested person and may direct that the testimony or statement be given, or the document or other thing be produced, before a person appointed by the court. By virtue of his appointment, the person appointed has power to administer any necessary oath and take the testimony or statement. The order may prescribe the practice and procedure, which may be in whole or part the practice and procedure of the foreign country or the international tribunal, for taking the testimony or statement or producing the document or other thing. To the extent that the order does not prescribe otherwise, the testimony or statement shall be taken, and the document or other thing produced, in accordance with the Federal Rules of Civil Procedure.

A person may not be compelled to give his testimony or statement or to produce a document or other thing in violation of any legally applicable privilege.

(b) This chapter does not preclude a person within the United States from voluntarily giving his testimony or statement, or producing a document or other thing, for use in a proceeding in a foreign or international tribunal before any person and in any manner acceptable to him.

§ 1783. Subpoena of Person in Foreign Country

(a) A court of the United States may order the issuance of a subpoena requiring the appearance as a witness before it, or before a person or body designated by it, of a national or resident of the United States who is in a foreign country, or requiring the production of a specified document or other thing by him, if the court finds that particular testimony or the production of the document or other thing by him is necessary in the interest of justice, and, in other than a criminal action or proceeding, if the court finds, in addition, that it is not possible to obtain his testimony in admissible form without his personal appearance or to obtain the production of the document or other thing in any other manner.

(b) The subpoena shall designate the time and place for the appearance or for the production of the document or other thing. Service of the subpoena and any order to show cause, rule, judgment, or decree authorized by this section or by section 1784 of this title shall be effected in accordance with the provisions of the Federal Rules of Civil Procedure relating to service of process on a person in a foreign country. The person serving the subpoena shall tender to the person to whom the subpoena is addressed his estimated necessary travel and attendance expenses, the amount of which shall be determined by the court and stated in the order directing the issuance of the subpoena.

§ 1784. Contempt

(a) The court of the United States which has issued a subpoena served in a foreign country may order the person who has failed to appear or who has failed to produce a document or other thing as directed therein to show cause before it at a designated time why he should not be punished for contempt.

(b) The court, in the order to show cause, may direct that any of the person's property within the United States be levied upon or seized, in the manner provided by law or court rules governing levy or seizure under execution, and held to satisfy any judgment that may be rendered against him pursuant to subsection (d) of this section if adequate security, in such amount as the court may direct in the order, be given for any damage that he might suffer should he not be found in contempt. Security under this subsection may not be required of the United States.

(c) A copy of the order to show cause shall be served on the person in accordance with section 1783(b) of this title.

(d) On the return day of the order to show cause or any later day to which the hearing may be continued, proof shall be taken. If the person is found in contempt, the court, notwithstanding any limitation upon its power generally to punish for contempt, may fine him not more than $100,000 and direct that the fine and costs of the proceedings be satisfied by a sale of the property levied upon or seized, conducted upon the notice required and in the manner provided for sales upon execution.

§ 1785. Subpoenas in Multiparty, Multiforum Actions

When the jurisdiction of the district court is based in whole or in part upon section 1369 of this title, a subpoena for attendance at a hearing or trial may, if authorized by the court upon motion for good cause shown, and upon such terms and conditions as the court may impose, be served at any place within the United States, or anywhere outside the United States if otherwise permitted by law.

§ 1821. Per Diem and Mileage Generally; Subsistence

(a) (1) Except as otherwise provided by law, a witness in attendance at any court of the United States, or before a United States Magistrate, or before any person authorized to take his deposition pursuant to any rule or order of a court of the United States, shall be paid the fees and allowances provided by this section.

(2) As used in this section, the term "court of the United States" includes, in addition to the courts listed in section 451 of this title, any court created by Act of Congress in a territory which is invested with any jurisdiction of a district court of the United States.

(b) A witness shall be paid an attendance fee of $40 per day for each day's attendance. A witness shall also be paid the attendance fee for the time necessarily occupied in going to and returning from the place of attendance at the beginning and end of such attendance or at any time during such attendance.

(c) (1) A witness who travels by common carrier shall be paid for the actual expenses of travel on the basis of the means of transportation reasonably utilized and the distance necessarily traveled to and from such witness's residence by the shortest practical route in going to and returning from the place of attendance. Such a witness shall utilize a common carrier at the most economical rate reasonably available. A receipt or other evidence of actual cost shall be furnished.

(2) A travel allowance equal to the mileage allowance which the Administrator of General Services has prescribed, pursuant to section 5704 of title 5, for official travel of employees of the Federal Government shall be paid to each witness who travels by privately owned vehicle. Computation of mileage under this paragraph shall be made on the basis of a uniformed table of distances adopted by the Administrator of General Services.

(3) Toll charges for toll roads, bridges, tunnels, and ferries, taxicab fares between places of lodging and carrier terminals, and parking fees (upon presentation of a valid parking receipt), shall be paid in full to a witness incurring such expenses.

(4) All normal travel expenses within and outside the judicial district shall be taxable as costs pursuant to section 1920 of this title.

(d) (1) A subsistence allowance shall be paid to a witness when an overnight stay is required at the place of attendance because such place is so far removed from the residence of such witness as to prohibit return thereto from day to day.

(2) A subsistence allowance for a witness shall be paid in an amount not to exceed the maximum per diem allowance prescribed by the Administrator of General Services, pursuant to section 5702(a) of title 5, for official travel in the area of attendance by employees of the Federal Government.

(3) A subsistence allowance for a witness attending in an area designated by the Administrator of General Services as a high-cost area shall be paid in an amount not to exceed the maximum actual subsistence allowance prescribed by the Administrator, pursuant to section 5702(c)(B) of title 5, for official travel in such area by employees of the Federal Government.

(4) When a witness is detained pursuant to section 3144 of title 18 for want of security for his appearance, he shall be entitled for each day of detention when not in attendance at court, in addition to his subsistence, to the daily attendance fee provided by subsection (b) of this section.

(e) An alien who has been paroled into the United States for prosecution, pursuant to section 212(d)(5) of the Immigration and Nationality Act (8 U.S.C. 1182(d)(5)), or an alien who either has admitted belonging to a class of aliens who are deportable or has been determined pursuant to section 240 of such Act (8 U.S.C. 1252(b)) to be deportable, shall be ineligible to receive the fees or allowances provided by this section.

(f) Any witness who is incarcerated at the time that his or her testimony is given (except for a witness to whom the provisions of section 3144 of title 18 apply) may not receive fees or allowances under this section, regardless of whether such a witness is incarcerated at the time he or she makes a claim for fees or allowances under this section.

§ 1826. Recalcitrant Witnesses

(a) Whenever a witness in any proceeding before or ancillary to any court or grand jury of the United States refuses without just cause shown to comply with an order of the court to testify or provide other information, including any book, paper, document, record, recording or other material, the court, upon such refusal, or when such refusal is duly brought to its attention, may summarily order his confinement at a suitable place until such time as the witness is willing to give such testimony or provide such information. No period of such confinement shall exceed the life of—

(1) the court proceeding, or

(2) the term of the grand jury, including extensions,

before which such refusal to comply with the court order occurred, but in no event shall such confinement exceed eighteen months.

(b) No person confined pursuant to subsection (a) of this section shall be admitted to bail pending the determination of an appeal taken by him from the order for his confinement if it appears that the appeal is frivolous or taken for delay. Any appeal from an order of confinement under this section shall be disposed of as soon as practicable, but not later than thirty days from the filing of such appeal.

(c) Whoever escapes or attempts to escape from the custody of any facility or from any place in which or to which he is confined pursuant to this section or section 4243 of title 18, or whoever rescues or attempts to rescue or instigates, aids, or assists the escape or attempt to escape of such a person, shall be subject to imprisonment for not more than three years, or a fine of not more than $10,000, or both.

§ 1914. District Court; Filing and Miscellaneous Fees; Rules of Court

(a) The clerk of each district court shall require the parties instituting any civil action, suit or proceeding in such court, whether by original process, removal or otherwise, to pay a filing fee of $350, except that on application for a writ of habeas corpus the filing fee shall be $5.

(b) The clerk shall collect from the parties such additional fees only as are prescribed by the Judicial Conference of the United States.

(c) Each district court by rule or standing order may require advance payment of fees.

§ 1915. Proceedings in Forma Pauperis

(a) **(1)** Subject to subsection (b), any court of the United States may authorize the commencement, prosecution or defense of any suit, action or proceeding, civil or criminal, or appeal therein, without prepayment of fees or security therefor, by a person who submits an affidavit that includes a statement of all assets such prisoner possesses that the person is unable to pay such fees or give security therefor. Such affidavit shall state the nature of the action, defense or appeal and affiant's belief that the person is entitled to redress.

(2) A prisoner seeking to bring a civil action or appeal a judgment in a civil action or proceeding without prepayment of fees or security therefor, in addition to filing the affidavit filed under paragraph (1), shall submit a certified copy of the trust fund account statement (or institutional equivalent) for the prisoner for the 6-month period immediately preceding the filing of the complaint or notice of appeal, obtained from the appropriate official of each prison at which the prisoner is or was confined.

(3) An appeal may not be taken in forma pauperis if the trial court certifies in writing that it is not taken in good faith.

(b) **(1)** Notwithstanding subsection (a), if a prisoner brings a civil action or files an appeal in forma pauperis, the prisoner shall be required to pay the full amount of a filing fee. The court shall assess and, when funds exist, collect, as a partial payment of any court fees required by law, an initial partial filing fee of 20 percent of the greater of—

(A) the average monthly deposits to the prisoner's account; or

(B) the average monthly balance in the prisoner's account for the 6-month period immediately preceding the filing of the complaint or notice of appeal.

(2) After payment of the initial partial filing fee, the prisoner shall be required to make monthly payments of 20 percent of the preceding month's income credited to the prisoner's account. The agency having custody of the prisoner shall forward payments from the prisoner's account to the clerk of the court each time the amount in the account exceeds $10 until the filing fees are paid.

(3) In no event shall the filing fee collected exceed the amount of fees permitted by statute for the commencement of a civil action or an appeal of a civil action or criminal judgment.

(4) In no event shall a prisoner be prohibited from bringing a civil action or appealing a civil or criminal judgment for the reason that the prisoner has no assets and no means by which to pay the initial partial filing fee.

(c) Upon the filing of an affidavit in accordance with subsections (a) and (b) and the prepayment of any partial filing fee as may be required under subsection (b), the court may direct payment by the United States of the expenses of (1) printing the record on appeal in any civil or criminal case, if such printing is required by the appellate court; (2) preparing a transcript of proceedings before a United States magistrate in any civil or criminal case, if such transcript is required by the district court, in the case of proceedings conducted under section 636(b) of this title or under section 3401(b) of title 18, United States Code; and (3) printing the record on appeal if such printing is required by the appellate court, in the case of proceedings conducted pursuant to section 636(c) of this title. Such expenses shall be paid when authorized by the Director of the Administrative Office of the United States Courts.

(d) The officers of the court shall issue and serve all process, and perform all duties in such cases. Witnesses shall attend as in other cases, and the same remedies shall be available as are provided for by law in other cases.

(e) **(1)** The court may request an attorney to represent any person unable to afford counsel.

(2) Notwithstanding any filing fee, or any portion thereof, that may have been paid, the court shall dismiss the case at any time if the court determines that—

(A) the allegation of poverty is untrue; or

(B) the action or appeal—

(i) is frivolous or malicious;

(ii) fails to state a claim on which relief may be granted; or

(iii) seeks monetary relief against a defendant who is immune from such relief.

(f) **(1)** Judgment may be rendered for costs at the conclusion of the suit or action as in other proceedings, but the United States shall not be liable for any of the costs thus incurred. If the United States has paid the cost of a stenographic transcript or printed record for the prevailing party, the same shall be taxed in favor of the United States.

(2) **(A)** If the judgment against a prisoner includes the payment of costs under this subsection, the prisoner shall be required to pay the full amount of the costs ordered.

(B) The prisoner shall be required to make payments for costs under this subsection in the same manner as is provided for filing fees under subsection (a)(2).

(C) In no event shall the costs collected exceed the amount of the costs ordered by the court.

(g) In no event shall a prisoner bring a civil action or appeal a judgment in a civil action or proceeding under this section if the prisoner has, on 3 or more prior occasions, while incarcerated or detained in any facility, brought an action or appeal in a court of the United States that was dismissed on the grounds that it is frivolous, malicious, or fails to state a claim upon which relief may be granted, unless the prisoner is under imminent danger of serious physical injury.

(h) As used in this section, the term 'prisoner' means any person incarcerated or detained in any facility who is accused of, convicted of, sentenced for, or adjudicated delinquent for, violations of criminal law or the terms and conditions of parole, probation, pretrial release, or diversionary program.

§ 1917. District Courts; Fee on Filing Notice of or Petition for Appeal

Upon the filing of any separate or joint notice of appeal or application for appeal or upon the receipt of any order allowing, or notice of the allowance of, an appeal or of a writ of certiorari $5 shall be paid to the clerk of the district court, by the appellant or petitioner.

§ 1920. Taxation of Costs

A judge or clerk of any court of the United States may tax as costs the following:

(1) Fees of the clerk and marshal;

(2) Fees for printed or electronically recorded manuscripts necessarily obtained for use in the case;

(3) Fees and disbursements for printing and witnesses;

(4) Fees for exemplification and the costs of making copies of any materials where copies are necessarily obtained for use in the case;

(5) Docket fees under section 1923 of this title;

(6) Compensation of court appointed experts, compensation of interpreters, and salaries, fees, expenses, and costs of special interpretation services under section 1828 of this title.

A bill of costs shall be filed in the case and, upon allowance, included in the judgment or decree.

§ 1924. Verification of Bill of Costs

Before any bill of costs is taxed, the party claiming any item of cost or disbursement shall attach thereto an affidavit, made by himself or by his duly authorized attorney or agent having knowledge of the facts, that such item is correct and has been necessarily incurred in the case and that the services for which fees have been charged were actually and necessarily performed.

§ 1927. Counsel's Liability for Excessive Costs

Any attorney or other person admitted to conduct cases in any court of the United States or any Territory thereof who so multiplies the proceedings in any case unreasonably and vexatiously may be required by the court to satisfy personally the excess costs, expenses, and attorneys' fees reasonably incurred because of such conduct.

§ 1961. Interest

(a) Interest shall be allowed on any money judgment in a civil case recovered in a district court. Execution therefor may be levied by the marshal, in any case where, by the law of the State in which such court is held, execution may be levied for interest on judgments recovered in the courts of the State. Such interest shall be calculated from the date of the entry of the judgment, at a rate equal to the weekly average 1-year constant maturity Treasury yield, as published by the Board of Governors of the Federal Reserve System, for the calendar week preceding the date of the judgment. The Director of the Administrative Office of the United States Courts shall distribute notice of that rate and any changes in it to all Federal judges.

(b) Interest shall be computed daily to the date of payment except as provided in section 2516(b) of this title and section 1304(b) of title 31, and shall be compounded annually.

(c) (1) This section shall not apply in any judgment of any court with respect to any internal revenue tax case. Interest shall be allowed in such cases at the underpayment rate or overpayment rate (whichever is appropriate) established under section 6621 of the Internal Revenue Code of 1986.

(2) Except as otherwise provided in paragraph (1) of this

subsection, interest shall be allowed on all final judgments against the United States in the United States Court of Appeals for the Federal circuit,[1] at the rate provided in subsection (a) and as provided in subsection (b).

(3) Interest shall be allowed, computed, and paid on judgments of the United States Court of Federal Claims only as provided in paragraph (1) of this subsection or in any other provision of law.

(4) This section shall not be construed to affect the interest on any judgment of any court not specified in this section.

§ 1963. Registration of Judgments for Enforcement in Other Districts

A judgment in an action for the recovery of money or property entered in any court of appeals, district court, bankruptcy court, or in the Court of International Trade may be registered by filing a certified copy of the judgment in any other district or, with respect to the Court of International Trade, in any judicial district, when the judgment has become final by appeal or expiration of the time for appeal or when ordered by the court that entered the judgment for good cause shown. Such a judgment entered in favor of the United States may be so registered any time after judgment is entered. A judgment so registered shall have the same effect as a judgment of the district court of the district where registered and may be enforced in like manner.

A certified copy of the satisfaction of any judgment in whole or in part may be registered in like manner in any district in which the judgment is a lien.

The procedure prescribed under this section is in addition to other procedures provided by law for the enforcement of judgments.

§ 1964. Constructive Notice of Pending Actions

Where the law of a State requires a notice of an action concerning real property pending in a court of the State to be registered, recorded, docketed, or indexed in a particular manner, or in a certain office or county or parish in order to give constructive notice of the action as it relates to the real property, and such law authorizes a notice of an action concerning real property pending in a United States district court to be registered, recorded, docketed, or indexed in the same manner, or in the same place, those requirements of the State law must be complied with in order to give constructive notice of such an action pending in a United States district court as it relates to real property in such State.

§ 2071. Rule-Making Power Generally

(a) The Supreme Court and all courts established by Act of

[1] So in original. Probably should be "Circuit,".

Congress may from time to time prescribe rules for the conduct of their business. Such rules shall be consistent with Acts of Congress and rules of practice and procedure prescribed under section 2072 of this title.

(b) Any rule prescribed by a court, other than the Supreme Court, under subsection (a) shall be prescribed only after giving appropriate public notice and an opportunity for comment. Such rule shall take effect upon the date specified by the prescribing court and shall have such effect on pending proceedings as the prescribing court may order.

(c) **(1)** A rule of a district court prescribed under subsection (a) shall remain in effect unless modified or abrogated by the judicial council of the relevant circuit.

(2) Any other rule prescribed by a court other than the Supreme Court under subsection (a) shall remain in effect unless modified or abrogated by the Judicial Conference.

(d) Copies of rules prescribed under subsection (a) by a district court shall be furnished to the judicial council, and copies of all rules prescribed by a court other than the Supreme Court under subsection (a) shall be furnished to the Director of the Administrative Office of the United States Courts and made available to the public.

(e) If the prescribing court determines that there is an immediate need for a rule, such court may proceed under this section without public notice and opportunity for comment, but such court shall promptly thereafter afford such notice and opportunity for comment.

(f) No rule may be prescribed by a district court other than under this section.

§ 2072. Rules of Procedure and Evidence; Power to Prescribe

(a) The Supreme Court shall have the power to prescribe general rules of practice and procedure and rules of evidence for cases in the United States district courts (including proceedings before magistrates thereof) and courts of appeals.

(b) Such rules shall not abridge, enlarge or modify any substantive right. All laws in conflict with such rules shall be of no further force or effect after such rules have taken effect.

(c) Such rules may define when a ruling of a district court is final for the purposes of appeal under section 1291 of this title.

§ 2101. Supreme Court; Time for Appeal or Certiorari; Docketing; Stay

(a) A direct appeal to the Supreme Court from any decision under section 1253 of this title, holding unconstitutional in whole or in part, any Act of Congress, shall be taken within thirty days after the entry of the interlocutory or final order, judgment or decree. The record shall be made up and the case docketed within sixty days from the time such appeal is taken under rules prescribed by the Supreme Court.

(b) Any other direct appeal to the Supreme Court which is authorized by law, from a decision of a district court in any civil action, suit or proceeding, shall be taken within thirty days from the judgment, order or decree, appealed from, if interlocutory, and within sixty days if final.

(c) Any other appeal or any writ of certiorari intended to bring any judgment or decree in a civil action, suit or proceeding before the Supreme Court for review shall be taken or applied for within ninety days after the entry of such judgment or decree. A justice of the Supreme Court, for good cause shown, may extend the time for applying for a writ of certiorari for a period not exceeding sixty days.

(d) The time for appeal or application for a writ of certiorari to review the judgment of a State court in a criminal case shall be as prescribed by rules of the Supreme Court.

(e) An application to the Supreme Court for a writ of certiorari to review a case before judgment has been rendered in the court of appeals may be made at any time before judgment.

(f) In any case in which the final judgment or decree of any court is subject to review by the Supreme Court on writ of certiorari, the execution and enforcement of such judgment or decree may be stayed for a reasonable time to enable the party aggrieved to obtain a writ of certiorari from the Supreme Court. The stay may be granted by a judge of the court rendering the judgment or decree or by a justice of the Supreme Court, and may be conditioned on the giving of security, approved by such judge or justice, that if the aggrieved party fails to make application for such writ within the period allotted therefor, or fails to obtain an order granting his application, or fails to make his plea good in the Supreme Court, he shall answer for all damages and costs which the other party may sustain by reason of the stay.

(g) The time for application for a writ of certiorari to review a decision of the United States Court of Appeals for the Armed Forces shall be as prescribed by rules of the Supreme Court.

§ 2104. Reviews of State Court Decisions

A review by the Supreme Court of a judgment or decree of a State court shall be conducted in the same manner and under the same regulations, and shall have the same effect, as if the judgment or decree reviewed had been rendered in a court of the United States.

§ 2106. Determination

The Supreme Court or any other court of appellate jurisdiction may affirm, modify, vacate, set aside or reverse any judgment, decree, or order of a court lawfully brought before it for review, and may remand the cause and direct the entry of such appropriate judgment, decree, or order, or require such further proceedings to be had as may be just under the circumstances.

§ 2107. Time for Appeal to Court of Appeals

(a) Except as otherwise provided in this section, no appeal shall bring any judgment, order or decree in an action, suit or proceeding of a civil nature before a court of appeals for review unless notice of appeal is filed, within thirty days after the entry of such judgment, order or decree.

(b) In any such action, suit, or proceeding, the time as to all parties shall be 60 days from such entry if one of the parties is—

(1) the United States;

(2) a United States agency;

(3) a United States officer or employee sued in an official capacity; or

(4) a current or former United States officer or employee sued in an individual capacity for an act or omission occurring in connection with duties performed on behalf of the United States, including all instances in which the United States represents that officer or employee when the judgment, order, or decree is entered or files the appeal for that officer or employee.

(c) The district court may, upon motion filed not later than 30 days after the expiration of the time otherwise set for bringing appeal, extend the time for appeal upon a showing of excusable neglect or good cause. In addition, if the district court finds—

(1) that a party entitled to notice of the entry of a judgment or order did not receive such notice from the clerk or any party within 21 days of its entry, and

(2) that no party would be prejudiced,

the district court may, upon motion filed within 180 days after entry of the judgment or order or within 14 days after receipt of such notice, whichever is earlier, reopen the time for appeal for a period of 14 days from the date of entry of the order reopening the time for appeal.

(d) This section shall not apply to bankruptcy matters or other proceedings under Title 11.

§ 2111. Harmless Error

On the hearing of any appeal or writ of certiorari in any case, the court shall give judgment after an examination of the record without regard to errors or defects which do not affect the substantial rights of the parties.

§ 2201. Creation of Remedy

(a) In a case of actual controversy within its jurisdiction, except with respect to Federal taxes other than actions brought under section 7428 of the Internal Revenue Code of 1986, a proceeding under section 505 or 1146 of title 11, or in any civil action involving an antidumping or countervailing duty proceeding regarding a class or kind of merchandise of a free trade area country (as defined in section 516A(f)(9) of the Tariff Act of 1930), as determined by the administering authority, any court of the United States, upon the filing of an appropriate pleading, may declare the rights and other legal relations of any interested party seeking such declaration, whether or not further relief is or could be sought. Any such declaration shall have the force and effect of a final judgment or decree and shall be reviewable as such.

(b) For limitations on actions brought with respect to drug patents see section 505 or 512 of the Federal Food, Drug, and Cosmetic Act, or section 351 of the Public Health Service Act.

§ 2202. Further Relief

Further necessary or proper relief based on a declaratory judgment or decree may be granted, after reasonable notice and hearing, against any adverse party whose rights have been determined by such judgment.

§ 2283. Stay of State Court Proceedings

A court of the United States may not grant an injunction to stay proceedings in a State court except as expressly authorized by Act of Congress, or where necessary in aid of its jurisdiction, or to protect or effectuate its judgments.

§ 2284. Three-Judge Court; When Required; Composition; Procedure

(a) A district court of three judges shall be convened when otherwise required by Act of Congress, or when an action is filed challenging the constitutionality of the apportionment of congressional districts or the apportionment of any statewide legislative body.

(b) In any action required to be heard and determined by a district court of three judges under subsection (a) of this section, the composition and procedure of the court shall be as follows:

(1) Upon the filing of a request for three judges, the judge to whom the request is presented shall, unless he determines that three judges are not required, immediately notify the chief judge of the circuit, who shall designate two other judges, at least one of whom shall be a circuit judge. The judges so designated, and the judge to whom the request was presented, shall serve as members of the court to hear and determine the action or proceeding.

(2) If the action is against a State, or officer or agency thereof, at least five days' notice of hearing of the action shall be given by registered or certified mail to the Governor and attorney general of the State.

(3) A single judge may conduct all proceedings except the trial, and enter all orders permitted by the rules of civil procedure except as provided in this subsection. He may grant a temporary restraining order on a specific finding, based on evidence submitted, that specified irreparable damage will result if the order is not granted, which order, unless previously revoked by the district judge, shall remain in force only until the hearing and determination by the district court of three judges of an application for a preliminary injunction. A single judge shall not appoint a master, or order a reference, or hear and determine any application for a preliminary or permanent injunction or motion to vacate such an injunction, or enter judgment on the merits. Any action of a single judge may be reviewed by the full court at any time before final judgment.

§ 2361. Process and Procedure

In any civil action of interpleader or in the nature of interpleader under section 1335 of this title, a district court may issue its process for all claimants and enter its order restraining them from instituting or prosecuting any proceeding in any State or United States court affecting the property, instrument or obligation involved in the interpleader action until further order of the court. Such process and order shall be returnable at such time as the court or judge thereof directs, and shall be addressed to and served by the United States marshals for the respective districts where the claimants reside or may be found.

Such district court shall hear and determine the case, and may discharge the plaintiff from further liability, make the injunction permanent, and make all appropriate orders to enforce its judgment.

§ 2401. Time for Commencing Action Against United States

(a) Except as provided by chapter 71 of title 41, every civil action commenced against the United States shall be barred unless the complaint is filed within six years after the right of action first accrues. The action of any person under legal disability or beyond the seas at the time the claim accrues may be commenced within three years after the disability ceases.

(b) A tort claim against the United States shall be forever barred unless it is presented in writing to the appropriate Federal agency within two years after such claim accrues or unless action is begun within six months after the date of mailing, by certified or registered mail, of notice of final denial of the claim by the agency to which it was presented.

§ 2402. Jury Trial in Actions Against United States

Subject to chapter 179 of this title, any action against the United States under section 1346 shall be tried by the court without a jury, except that any action against the United States under section 1346(a)(1) shall, at the request of either party to such action, be tried by the court with a jury.

§ 2403. Intervention by United States or a State; Constitutional Question

(a) In any action, suit or proceeding in a court of the United States to which the United States or any agency, officer or employee thereof is not a party, wherein the constitutionality of any Act of Congress affecting the public interest is drawn in question, the court shall certify such fact to the Attorney General, and shall permit the United States to intervene for presentation of evidence, if evidence is otherwise admissible in the case, and for argument on the question of constitutionality. The United States shall, subject to the applicable provisions of law, have all the rights of a party and be subject to all liabilities of a party as to court costs to the extent necessary for a proper presentation of the facts and law relating to the question of constitutionality.

(b) In any action, suit, or proceeding in a court of the United States to which a State or any agency, officer, or employee thereof is not a party, wherein the constitutionality of any statute of that State affecting the public interest is drawn in question, the court shall certify such fact to the attorney general of the State, and shall permit the State to intervene for presentation of evidence, if evidence is otherwise admissible in the case, and for argument on the question of constitutionality. The State shall, subject to the applicable provisions of law, have all the rights of a party and be subject to all liabilities of a party as to court costs to the extent necessary for a proper presentation of the facts and law relating to the question of constitutionality.

§ 2404. Death of Defendant in Damage Action

A civil action for damages commenced by or on behalf of the United States or in which it is interested shall not abate on the death of a defendant but shall survive and be enforceable against his estate as well as against surviving defendants.

§ 2408. Security Not Required of United States

Security for damages or costs shall not be required of the United States, any department or agency thereof or any party acting under the direction of any such department or agency on the issuance of process or the institution or prosecution of any proceeding.

Costs taxable, under other Acts of Congress, against the United States or any such department, agency or party shall be paid out of the contingent fund of the department or agency which directed the proceedings to be instituted.

§ 2411. Interest

In any judgment of any court rendered (whether against the United States, a collector or deputy collector of internal revenue, a former collector or deputy collector, or the personal representative in case of death) for any overpayment in respect of any internal-revenue tax, interest shall be allowed at the overpayment rate established under section 6621 of the Internal Revenue Code of 1986 upon the amount of the overpayment, from the date of the payment or collection thereof to a date preceding the date of the refund check by not more than thirty days, such date to be determined by the Commissioner of Internal Revenue. The Commissioner is authorized to tender by check payment of any such judgment, with interest as herein provided, at any time after such judgment becomes final, whether or not a claim for such payment has been duly filed, and such tender shall stop the running of interest, whether or not such refund check is accepted by the judgment creditor.

§ 2412. Costs and Fees

(a)(1) Except as otherwise specifically provided by statute, a judgment for costs, as enumerated in section 1920 of this title, but not including the fees and expenses of attorneys, may be awarded to the prevailing party in any civil action brought by or against the United States or any agency or any official of the United States acting in his or her official capacity in any court having jurisdiction of such action. A judgment for costs when taxed against the United States shall, in an amount established by statute, court rule, or order, be limited to reimbursing in whole or in part the prevailing party for the costs incurred by such party in the litigation.

(2) A judgment for costs, when awarded in favor of the United States in an action brought by the United States, may include an amount equal to the filing fee prescribed under section 1914(a) of this title. The preceding sentence shall not be construed as requiring the United States to pay any filing fee.

(b) Unless expressly prohibited by statute, a court may award reasonable fees and expenses of attorneys, in addition to the costs which may be awarded pursuant to subsection (a), to the prevailing party in any civil action brought by or against the United States or any agency or any official of the United States acting in his or her official capacity in any court having jurisdiction of such action. The United States shall be liable for such fees and expenses to the same extent that any other party would be liable under the common law or under the terms of any statute which specifically provides for such an award.

(c)(1) Any judgment against the United States or any agency and any official of the United States acting in his or her official capacity for costs pursuant to subsection (a) shall be paid as provided in sections 2414 and 2517 of this title and shall be in addition to any relief provided in the judgment.

(2) Any judgment against the United States or any agency and any official of the United States acting in his or her official capacity for fees and expenses of attorneys pursuant to subsection (b) shall be paid as provided in sections 2414 and 2517 of this title, except that if the basis for the award is a finding that the United States acted in bad faith, then the award shall be paid by any agency found to have acted in bad faith and shall be in addition to any relief provided in the judgment.

(d)(1)(A) Except as otherwise specifically provided by statute, a court shall award to a prevailing party other than the United States fees and other expenses, in addition to any costs awarded pursuant to subsection (a), incurred by that party in any civil action (other than cases sounding in tort), including proceedings for judicial review of agency action, brought by or against the United States in any court having jurisdiction of that action, unless the court finds that the position of the United States was substantially justified or that special circumstances make an award unjust.

(B)A party seeking an award of fees and other expenses shall, within thirty days of final judgment in the action, submit to the court an application for fees and other expenses which shows that the party is a prevailing party and is eligible to receive an award under this subsection, and the amount sought, including an itemized statement from any attorney or expert witness representing or appearing in behalf of the party stating the actual time expended and the rate at which fees and other expenses were computed. The party shall also allege that the position of the United States was not substantially justified. Whether or not the position of the United States was substantially justified shall be determined on the basis of the record (including the record with respect to the action or failure to act by the agency upon which the civil action is based) which is made in the civil action for which fees and other expenses are sought.

(C) The court, in its discretion, may reduce the amount to be awarded pursuant to this subsection, or deny an award, to the extent that the prevailing party during the course of the proceedings engaged in conduct which unduly and unreasonably protracted the final resolution of the matter in controversy.

(D) If, in a civil action brought by the United States or a proceeding for judicial review of an adversary adjudication described in section 504(a)(4) of title 5, the demand by the United States is substantially in excess of the judgment finally obtained by the United States and is unreasonable when compared with such judgment, under the facts and circumstances of the case, the court shall award to the party the fees and other expenses related to defending against the excessive demand, unless the party has committed a willful violation of law or otherwise acted in bad faith, or special circumstances make an award unjust. Fees and expenses awarded under this subparagraph shall be paid only as a consequence of appropriations provided in advance.

(2) For the purposes of this subsection—

(A) "fees and other expenses" includes the reasonable expenses of expert witnesses, the reasonable cost of any study, analysis, engineering report, test, or project which is found by the court to be necessary for the preparation of the party's case, and reasonable attorney fees (The amount of fees awarded under this subsection shall be based upon prevailing market rates for the kind and quality of the services furnished, except that (i) no expert witness shall be compensated at a rate in excess of the highest rate of compensation for expert witnesses paid by the United States; and (ii) attorney fees shall not be awarded in excess of $125 per hour unless the court determines that an increase in the cost of living or a special factor, such as the limited availability of qualified attorneys for the proceedings involved, justifies a higher fee.);

(B) "party" means (i) an individual whose net worth did not exceed $2,000,000 at the time the civil action was filed, or (ii) any owner of an unincorporated business, or any partnership, corporation, association, unit of local government, or organization, the net worth of which did not exceed $7,000,000 at the time the civil action was filed, and which had not more than 500 employees at the time the civil action was filed; except that an organization described in section 501(c)(3) of the Internal Revenue Code of 1986 (26 U.S.C. 501(c)(3)) exempt from taxation under section 501(a) of such Code, or a cooperative association as defined in section 15(a) of the Agricultural Marketing Act (12 U.S.C. 1141j(a)), may be a party regardless of the net worth of such organization or cooperative association or for purposes of subsection (d)(1)(D), a small entity as defined in section 601 of title 5;

(C) "United States" includes any agency and any official of the United States acting in his or her official capacity;

(D) "position of the United States" means, in addition to the position taken by the United States in the civil action, the action or failure to act by the agency upon which the civil action is based; except that fees and expenses may not be awarded to a party for any portion of the litigation in which the party has unreasonably protracted the proceedings;

(E) "civil action brought by or against the United States" includes an appeal by a party, other than the United States, from a decision of a contracting officer rendered pursuant to a disputes clause in a contract with the Government or pursuant to chapter 71 of title 41;

(F) "court" includes the United States Court of Federal Claims and the United States Court of Appeals for Veterans Claims;

(G) "final judgment" means a judgment that is final and not appealable, and includes an order of settlement;

(H) "prevailing party", in the case of eminent domain proceedings, means a party who obtains a final judgment (other than by settlement), exclusive of interest, the amount of which is at least as close to the highest valuation of the property involved that is attested to at trial on behalf of the property owner as it is to the highest valuation of the property involved that is attested to at trial on behalf of the Government; and

(I) "demand" means the express demand of the United States which led to the adversary adjudication, but shall not include a recitation of the maximum statutory penalty (i) in the complaint, or (ii) elsewhere when accompanied by an express demand for a lesser amount.

(3) In awarding fees and other expenses under this subsection to a prevailing party in any action for judicial review of an adversary adjudication, as defined in subsection (b)(1)(C) of section 504 of title 5, or an adversary adjudication subject to chapter 71 of title 41, the court shall include in that award fees and other expenses to the same extent authorized in subsection (a) of such section, unless the court finds that during such adversary adjudication the position of the United States was substantially justified, or that special circumstances make an award unjust.

(4) Fees and other expenses awarded under this subsection to a party shall be paid by any agency over which the party prevails from any funds made available to the agency by appropriation or otherwise.

(5)(A) Not later than March 31 of the first fiscal year beginning after the date of enactment of the John D. Dingell, Jr. Conservation, Management, and Recreation Act, and every fiscal year thereafter, the Chairman of the Administrative Conference of the United States shall submit to Congress and make publicly available online a report on the amount of fees and other expenses awarded during the preceding fiscal year pursuant to this subsection.

(B) Each report under subparagraph (A) shall describe the number, nature, and amount of the awards, the claims involved in the controversy, and any other relevant information that may aid Congress in evaluating the scope and impact of such awards.

(C)(i) Each report under subparagraph (A) shall account for all payments of fees and other expenses awarded under this subsection that are made pursuant to a settlement agreement, regardless of whether the settlement agreement is sealed or otherwise subject to a nondisclosure provision.

(ii) The disclosure of fees and other expenses required under clause (i) shall not affect any other information that is subject to a nondisclosure provision in a settlement agreement.

(D) The Chairman of the Administrative Conference of the United States shall include and clearly identify in each annual report under subparagraph (A), for each case in which an award of fees and other expenses is included in the report—

(i) any amounts paid under section 1304 of title 31 for a judgment in the case;

(ii) the amount of the award of fees and other expenses; and

(iii) the statute under which the plaintiff filed suit.

(6) As soon as practicable, and in any event not later than the date on which the first report under paragraph (5)(A) is required to be submitted, the Chairman of the Administrative Conference of the United States shall create and maintain online a searchable database containing, with respect to each award of fees and other expenses under this subsection made on or after the date of enactment of the John D. Dingell, Jr. Conservation, Management, and Recreation Act, the following information:

(A) The case name and number, hyperlinked to the case, if available.

(B) The name of the agency involved in the case.

(C) The name of each party to whom the award was made as such party is identified in the order or other court document making the award.

(D) A description of the claims in the case.

(E) The amount of the award.

(F) The basis for the finding that the position of the agency concerned was not substantially justified.

(7) The online searchable database described in paragraph (6) may not reveal any information the disclosure of which is prohibited by law or a court order.

(8) The head of each agency (including the Attorney General of the United States) shall provide to the Chairman of the Administrative Conference of the United States in a timely manner all information requested by the Chairman to comply with the requirements of paragraphs (5), (6), and (7).

(e) The provisions of this section shall not apply to any costs, fees, and other expenses in connection with any proceeding to which section 7430 of the Internal Revenue Code of 1986 applies (determined without regard to subsections (b) and (f) of such section). Nothing in the preceding sentence shall prevent the awarding under subsection (a) of this section of costs enumerated in section 1920 of this title (as in effect on October 1, 1981).

(f) If the United States appeals an award of costs or fees and other expenses made against the United States under this section and the award is affirmed in whole or in part, interest shall be paid on the amount of the award as affirmed. Such interest shall be computed at the rate determined under section 1961(a) of this title, and shall run from the date of the award through the day before the date of the mandate of affirmance.

§ 2413. Executions in Favor of United States

A writ of execution on a judgment obtained for the use of the United States in any court thereof shall be issued from and made returnable to the court which rendered the judgment, but may be executed in any other State, in any Territory, or in the District of Columbia.

§ 2414. Payment of Judgments and Compromise Settlements

Except as provided by chapter 71 of title 41, payment of final judgments rendered by a district court or the Court of International Trade against the United States shall be made on settlements by the Secretary of the Treasury. Payment of final judgments rendered by a State or foreign court or tribunal against the United States, or against its agencies or officials upon obligations or liabilities of the United States, shall be made on settlements by the Secretary of the Treasury after certification by the Attorney General that it is in the interest of the United States to pay the same.

Whenever the Attorney General determines that no appeal shall be taken from a judgment or that no further review will be sought from a decision affirming the same, he shall so certify and the judgment shall be deemed final.

Except as otherwise provided by law, compromise settlements of claims referred to the Attorney General for defense of imminent litigation or suits against the United States, or against its agencies or officials upon obligations or liabilities of the United States, made by the Attorney General or any person authorized by him, shall be settled and paid in a manner similar to judgments in like causes and appropriations or funds available for the payment of such judgments are hereby made available for the payment of such compromise settlements.

§ 2415. Time for Commencing Actions Brought by the United States

(a) Subject to the provisions of section 2416 of this title, and except as otherwise provided by Congress, every action for money damages brought by the United States or an officer or agency thereof which is founded upon any contract express or implied in law or fact, shall be barred unless the complaint is filed within six years after the right of action accrues or within one year after final decisions have been rendered in applicable administrative proceedings required by contract or by law, whichever is later: *Provided*, That in the event of later partial payment or written acknowledgment of debt, the right of action shall be deemed to accrue again at the time of each such payment or acknowledgment: *Provided further,* That an action for money damages brought by the United States for or on behalf of a recognized tribe, band or group of American Indians shall not be barred unless the complaint is filed more than six years and ninety days after the right of action accrued: *Provided further,* That an action for money damages which accrued on the date of enactment of this Act in accordance with subsection (g) brought by the United States for or on behalf of a recognized tribe, band, or group of American Indians, or on behalf of an individual Indian whose land is held in trust or restricted status, shall not be barred unless the complaint is filed sixty days after the date of publication of the list required by section 4(c) of the Indian Claims Limitation Act of 1982: *Provided*, That, for those claims that are on either of the two lists published pursuant to the Indian Claims Limitation Act of 1982, any right of action shall be barred unless the complaint is filed within (1) one year after the Secretary of the Interior has published in the Federal Register a notice rejecting such claim or (2) three years after the date the Secretary of the Interior has submitted legislation or legislative report to Congress to resolve such claim or more than two years after a final decision has been rendered in applicable administrative proceedings required by contract or by law, whichever is later.

(b) Subject to the provisions of section 2416 of this title, and except as otherwise provided by Congress, every action for money damages brought by the United States or an officer or agency thereof which is founded upon a tort shall be barred unless the complaint is filed within three years after the right of action first accrues: *Provided*, That an action to recover damages resulting from a trespass on lands of the United States; an action to recover damages resulting from fire to such lands; an action to recover for diversion of money paid under a grant program; and an action for conversion of property of the United States may be brought within six years after the right of action accrues, except that such actions for or on behalf of a recognized tribe, band or group of American Indians, including actions relating to allotted trust or restricted Indian lands, may be brought within six years and ninety days after the right of action accrues, except that such actions for or on behalf of a recognized tribe, band or group of American Indians, including actions relating to allotted trust or restricted Indian lands, or on behalf of an individual Indian whose land is held in trust or restricted status which accrued on the date of enactment of this Act in accordance with subsection (g) may be brought on or before sixty days after the date of the publication of the list required by section 4(c) of the Indian Claims Limitation Act of 1982: *Provided*, That, for those claims that are on either of the two lists published pursuant to the Indian Claims Limitation Act of 1982, any right of action shall be barred unless the complaint is filed within (1) one year after the Secretary of the Interior has published in the Federal Register a notice rejecting such claim or (2) three years after the Secretary of the Interior has submitted legislation or legislative report to Congress to resolve such claim.

(c) Nothing herein shall be deemed to limit the time for bringing an action to establish the title to, or right of possession of, real or personal property.

(d) Subject to the provisions of section 2416 of this title and except as otherwise provided by Congress, every action for the recovery of money erroneously paid to or on behalf of any civilian employee of any agency of the United States or to or on behalf of any member or dependent of any member of the uniformed services of the United States, incident to the employment or services of such employee or member, shall be barred unless the complaint is filed within six years after the right of action accrues: *Provided*, That in the event of later partial payment or written acknowledgment of debt, the right of action shall be deemed to accrue again at the time of each such payment or acknowledgment.

(e) In the event that any action to which this section applies is timely brought and is thereafter dismissed without prejudice, the action may be recommenced within one year after such dismissal, regardless of whether the action would otherwise then be barred by this section. In any action so recommenced the defendant shall not be barred from interposing any claim which would not have been barred in the original action.

(f) The provisions of this section shall not prevent the assertion, in an action against the United States or an officer or agency thereof, of any claim of the United States or an officer or agency thereof against an opposing party, a co-party, or a third party that arises out of the transaction or occurrence that is the subject matter of the opposing party's claim. A claim of the United States or an officer or agency thereof that does not arise out of the transaction or occurrence that is the subject matter of the opposing party's claim may, if time-barred, be asserted only by way of offset and may be allowed in an amount not to exceed the amount of the opposing party's recovery.

(g) Any right of action subject to the provisions of this section which accrued prior to the date of enactment of this Act shall, for purposes of this section, be deemed to have accrued on the date of enactment of this Act.

(h) Nothing in this Act shall apply to actions brought under the Internal Revenue Code or incidental to the collection of taxes imposed by the United States.

(i) The provisions of this section shall not prevent the United States or an officer or agency thereof from collecting any claim of the United States by means of administrative offset, in accordance with section 3716 of title 31.

§ 2416. Time for Commencing Actions Brought by the United States—Exclusions

For the purpose of computing the limitations periods established in section 2415, there shall be excluded all periods during which—

(a) the defendant or the res is outside the United States, its territories and possessions, the District of Columbia, or the Commonwealth of Puerto Rico; or

(b) the defendant is exempt from legal process because of infancy, mental incompetence, diplomatic immunity, or for any other reason; or

(c) facts material to the right of action are not known and reasonably could not be known by an official of the United States charged with the responsibility to act in the circumstances; or

(d) the United States is in a state of war declared pursuant to article I, section 8, of the Constitution of the United States.

PART VIII
ADVISORY COMMITTEE NOTES

§ 8.1 Introduction to the Committee Notes—The Civil Rules' "Legislative History"

The United States Supreme Court promulgated the original Federal Rules of Civil Procedure on December 20, 1937, and the Rules first became effective nine months later in September 1938. In the years since the original Rules took effect, the Supreme Court has amended the Rules many times, most recently in April 2020 with changes that took effect December 1, 2020.

The Supreme Court delegated the task of drafting the original Rules and their subsequent amendments to an Advisory Committee on Civil Rules, comprised of federal and State judges, practicing attorneys, law professors, and Department of Justice representatives. At the time the original Rules were drafted, and with every subsequent proposed amendment, the Advisory Committee has prepared "Advisory Committee Notes" that accompany each draft.[1]

Today, these Advisory Committee Notes constitute the principal source of "legislative history" for construing and interpreting the Federal Rules of Civil Procedure.[2] As one court observed, the Notes "constitute[ ] a comment on the part of the best informed body, on the subject of the scope of the Federal Rules—namely, the Committee which formulated them—and, as such, cannot be treated otherwise than with great respect."[3] The Supreme Court credits the Committee Notes as a "respected source of scholarly

[1]*See Republic of Ecuador v. Mackay*, 742 F.3d 860, 865 (9th Cir. 2014).

[2]*See Use of Notes And Statements of Advisory Committee In Construction of Rules*, 2 Fed. R. Serv. 632 (1940) (and as supplemented in 3 Fed. R. Serv. 663). *See also Gonzalez v. Thaler*, 565 U.S. 134, 164, 132 S. Ct. 641, 181 L. Ed. 2d 619 (2012) (Scalia, J., dissenting) ("a species of legislative history"); *United States v. Hayes*, 983 F.2d 78, 82 (7th Cir.1992) (analogous to legislative history, and are used to clarify "legislative intent"); *United States v. Brackeen*, 969 F.2d 827, 830 (9th Cir.1992) in construing Federal Rules of Evidence, the courts look to the Advisory Committee Notes as "legitimate sources of legislative history"); *Reed v. Binder*, 165 F.R.D. 424, 427 (D.N.J.1996) ("provide something akin to a legislative history of the Rules"). *See generally* Catherine T. Struve, *The Paradox of Delegation: Interpreting the Federal Rules of Civil Procedure*, 160 U. PA. L. Rev. 1100 (2002).

[3]*United States v. 720 Bottles Labeled 2 Fl. Oz. * * * Plantation Pure Vanilla Extract, Etc.*, 3 F.R.D. 466, 467 (E.D.N.Y.1944) (Byers, J.). *See also Heinemann v. Satterberg*, 731 F.3d 914, 917 (9th Cir. 2013) ("We pay attention to the Advisory Committee Notes.").

commentary",[4] and has instructed that the Notes are properly "relied" on[5] and afforded "weight"[6] and thus provide "a useful guide"[7] in discerning the meaning of the Rules. The Supreme Court considers the Notes to be "relevant evidence of the drafters' intent as to the meaning" of the Rules,[8] especially when the Rule language is promulgated precisely as the Advisory Committee had proposed.[9] Likewise, the later Advisory Committees' commentary on Rule amendments is entitled to similar weight.[10]

---

[4] *Tome v. United States*, 513 U.S. 150, 159, 115 S. Ct. 696, 130 L. Ed. 2d 574 (1995) (noting that author of specific Committee Note was "a distinguished commentator on the law of evidence, and he and members of the Committee consulted and considered the views, criticisms, and suggestions of the academic community in preparing the Notes"). *See also Williamson v. United States*, 512 U.S. 594, 614, 114 S. Ct. 2431, 129 L. Ed. 2d 476 (1994) (Kennedy, J., concurring) ("When as here the text of a Rule of Evidence does not answer a question that must be answered in order to apply the Rule, and when the Advisory Committee's Note does answer the question, our practice indicates that we should pay attention to the Advisory Committee's Note.").

[5] *See Corley v. U.S.*, 556 U.S. 303, 321, 129 S. Ct. 1558, 173 L. Ed. 2d 443 (2009). *See also Ross v. Williams*, 896 F.3d 958, 965 (9th Cir. 2018) ("reliable source of insight into the meaning of a rule"); *Rodriguez v. Florida Dep't of Corrections*, 748 F.3d 1073, 1076 (11th Cir. 2014) (same); *Republic of Ecuador v. Mackay*, 742 F.3d 860, 865 (9th Cir. 2014) ("particularly reliable indicator of legislative intent").

[6] *See Mississippi Publ'g Corp. v. Murphree*, 326 U.S. 438, 444, 66 S. Ct. 242, 90 L.Ed. 185 (1946). *See also Torres v. Oakland Scavenger Co.*, 487 U.S. 312, 315, 108 S. Ct. 2405, 101 L. Ed. 2d 285 (1988); *Schiavone v. Fortune*, 477 U.S. 21, 31, 106 S. Ct. 2379, 91 L. Ed. 2d 18 (1986) (superseded by Rule amendment on other grounds). *Accord O'Neal Constructors, LLC v. DRT Am., LLC*, 991 F.3d 1376, 1379-80 (11th Cir. 2021) ("nearly universally accorded great weight"); *Radtke v. Caschetta*, 822 F.3d 571, 573 (D.C. Cir. 2016) ("entitled to 'weight' "); *C.B. v. City of Sonora*, 769 F.3d 1005, 1018 (9th Cir. 2014) ("of weight"); *In re Cooper Tire & Rubber Co.*, 568 F.3d 1180, 1188 (10th Cir.2009) (must "give weight"); *United States v. Means*, 133 F.3d 444, 449 (6th Cir.1998) ("due some deference").

[7] *Tome v. United States*, 513 U.S. 150, 159, 115 S. Ct. 696, 130 L. Ed. 2d 574 (1995). *Accord In re Nat'l Football League Players Concussion Injury Litig.*, 775 F.3d 570, 576 n.6 (3d Cir. 2014) ("illuminating"); *Summers v. Delta Air Lines, Inc.*, 508 F.3d 923, 926-27 (9th Cir. 2007) ("guides our interpretation"); *Esposito v. United States*, 368 F.3d 1271, 1275 (10th Cir. 2004) (Notes "to provide parameters" for Rule's application); *United States v. Orlandez-Gamboa*, 320 F.3d 328, 331 n.2 (2d Cir.2003) ("useful guide"); *United States v. Navarro*, 169 F.3d 228, 237 (5th Cir. 1999) ("instructive").

[8] *Libretti v. United States*, 516 U.S. 29, 41, 116 S. Ct. 356, 133 L. Ed. 2d 271 (1995). *Accord Hall v. Hall*, 584 U.S. —, 138 S. Ct. 1118, 1130, 200 L. Ed. 2d 399 (2018); *Class v. United States*, 583 U.S. —, 138 S. Ct. 798, 806, 200 L. Ed. 2d 37 (2018).

[9] *See United States v. Vonn*, 535 U.S. 55, 64 n.6, 122 S. Ct. 1043, 152 L. Ed. 2d 90 (2002). *See also F.T.C. v. Boehringer Ingelheim Pharms., Inc.*, 778 F.3d 142, 154-55 (D.C.Cir. 2015); *United States v. Hodge*, 412 F.3d 479, 489 (3d Cir. 2005). *See generally Corley v. U.S.*, 556 U.S. 303, 322, 129 S. Ct. 1558, 173 L. Ed. 2d 443 (2009) ("bizarre to hold" that Congress envisioned purpose for Rule of Evidence "exactly opposite to what the Advisory Committee Notes said the rule would do").

[10] *See United States v. Anderson*, 942 F.2d 606, 611–12 (9th Cir.1991) (Notes "explain the purpose and intent

Although a formidable authority for construing the Rules, the Advisory Committee itself has acknowledged that its Notes are *not* binding on the courts:

> [S]tatements in the notes as to the purpose or effect of the rules, can have no greater force than the reasons which may be adduced to support them. The notes are not part of the rules, and the Supreme Court has not approved or otherwise assumed responsibility for them. They have no official sanction, and can have no controlling weight with the courts, when applying the rules in litigated cases.[11]

Thus, while the Advisory Committee Notes constitute "highly persuasive"[12] authority for construing and interpreting the Rules, the Notes are not controlling.[13] Like statutory legislative history, while the Committee Notes may be considered while resolving an ambiguity in a Rule's text,[14] they may not be used to contradict or supplant a Rule's plain meaning[15] or to read into a Rule additional requirements.[16] In this way, the Notes can help "supplement any deficiency" in the "explicit" language of the Rules, and, as such,

---

of the proposed rule changes").

[11]*See* Introductory Statement for Original Notes to Federal Rules of Civil Procedure.

[12]*See Campbell v. Shinseki*, 546 Fed. Appx. 874, 879 n.3 (11th Cir. 2013).

[13]*See U.S. v. Bainbridge*, 746 F.3d 943, 947 (9th Cir. 2014) (not "force of law"); *U.S. v. Petri*, 731 F.3d 833, 839 (9th Cir. 2013) (they "do not foreclose judicial consideration" of a rule's validity and meaning); *Burnley v. City of San Antonio*, 470 F.3d 189, 193 (5th Cir. 2006) (though not determinative, they are "of weight"); *Ross v. Marshall*, 426 F.3d 745, 752 n.13 (5th Cir.2005) ("do not have the force of law", but are "instructive"); *Horenkamp v. Van Winkle & Co.*, 402 F.3d 1129, 1132 (11th Cir. 2005) ("not binding" but "nearly universally accorded great weight"); *Desio v. State Farm Mut. Auto. Ins. Co.*, 339 F.R.D. 632, 641 (D. Nev. 2021) ("not determinative"); *JumpSport, Inc. v. Jumpking, Inc.*, 213 F.R.D. 329, 344 n.12 (N.D.Cal. 2003) ("not binding legal authority—at least until incorporated into law by authoritative judicial opinions"); *Reed v. Binder*, 165 F.R.D. 424, 427 (D.N.J. 1996) ("a very important source of information" which are given "considerable weight", but which are not conclusive); *United States v. Downin*, 884 F.Supp. 1474, 1479 (E.D.Cal.1995) (same effect).

[14]*See United States v. Petri*, 731 F.3d 833, 839 (9th Cir. 2013); *United States v. Lewis*, 432 F. Supp. 3d 1237, 1283 (D.N.M. 2020).

[15]*See Spirit Lake Tribe v. Jaeger*, 5 F.4th 849, 853 (8th Cir. 2021) (cannot change meaning of rule's plain language); *Whitehouse v. United States Dist. Ct. for Dist. of R.I.*, 53 F.3d 1349, 1365 (1st Cir.1995) (cannot alter unambiguous language of Rule); *United States v. Nahodil*, 36 F.3d 323, 328 (3d Cir.1994) (may not be permitted to contradict a Rule's express language). *But cf. Ostin v. State Farm Fire & Cas. Co.*, 2021 WL 1087715, at *3 (D. Colo. Mar. 22, 2021) (rejecting what would "appear" to be meaning from "literal reading" of rule, since it "may lead to conduct violating the spirit of the Federal Rules of Civil Procedure").

[16]*See Wal-Mart Stores, Inc. v. Dukes*, 564 U.S. 338, 363, 131 S. Ct. 2541, 180 L. Ed. 2d 374 (2011) ("Of course it is the Rule itself, not the Advisory Committee's description of it, that governs."). *See also Hamilton v. Wal-Mart Stores, Inc.*, 39 F.4th 575, 590 n.7 (9th Cir. 2022) (although "of weight," Notes "cannot add to" a Rule).

may be appropriately considered.[17] Moreover, if contrary rulings would render incorrect or unjust results, courts may disregard the Notes.[18]

The text of the original Advisory Committee Notes, as well as the Notes that accompanied each of the judicially promulgated amendments, are reprinted below.

§ 8.2 Full Text of the Advisory Committee Notes

I. SCOPE OF RULES—ONE FORM OF ACTION

Rule 1. Scope and Purpose of Rules

1937 ADOPTION

1. Rule 81 states certain limitations in the application of these rules to enumerated special proceedings.

2. The expression "district courts of the United States" appearing in the statute authorizing the Supreme Court of the United States to promulgate rules of civil procedure does not include the district courts held in the territories and insular possessions. See *Mookini et al. v. United States, 1938*, 303 U.S. 201, 58 S. Ct. 543, 82 L.Ed. 748.

3. These rules are drawn under the authority of the Act of June 19, 1934, U.S.C., Title 28, § 2072, formerly § 723b (Rules in actions at law; Supreme Court authorized to make), and § 2072, formerly § 723c (Union of equity and action at law rules; power of Supreme Court) and also other grants of rule making power to the Court. See Clark and Moore, A New Federal Civil Procedure—I, The Background, 44 Yale L.J. 387, 391 (1935). Under § 2072, formerly § 723b after the rules have taken effect all laws in conflict therewith are of no further force or effect. In accordance with § 2072, formerly § 723c, the Court has united the general rules prescribed for cases in equity with those in actions at law so as to secure one form of civil action and procedure for both. See Rule 2 (One Form of Action). For the former practice in equity and at law see U.S.C., Title 28, §§ 2071 and 2073, formerly §§ 723 and 730 (conferring power on the Supreme Court to make rules of practice in equity) and the Equity Rules promulgated thereunder; U.S.C., Title 28, formerly § 724 (Conformity Act); former Equity Rule 22 (Action at Law Erroneously Begun as Suit in Equity—Transfer); former Equity Rule 23 (Matters Ordinarily Determinable at Law When Arising in Suit in Equity to be Disposed of Therein); U.S.C., Title 28, former §§ 397 (Amendments to pleadings when case brought to wrong side of court), and 398 (Equitable defenses and equitable relief in actions at law).

4. With the second sentence compare U.S.C., Title 28, former § 777 (Defects of form; amendments), former § 767 (Amendment of process); former Equity Rule 19 (Amendments Generally).

1948 AMENDMENT

The amendment effective October 20, 1949, substituted the words "United States district courts" for the words "district courts of the United States."

1966 AMENDMENT

This is the fundamental change necessary to effect unification of the civil and admiralty procedure. Just as the 1938 rules abolished the distinction between actions at law and suits in equity, this change would abolish the distinction be-

---

[17] *See Thompson v. Greene*, 427 F.3d 263, 269 (4th Cir.2005).

[18] *See United States v. Hayes*, 983 F.2d 78, 82 (7th Cir.1992) ("We have not hesitated to rule in contradiction with committee notes when contrary rulings rendered incorrect or unjust results".)

tween civil actions and suits in admiralty. See also Rule 81.

1993 AMENDMENT

The purpose of this revision, adding the words "and administered" to the second sentence, is to recognize the affirmative duty of the court to exercise the authority conferred by these rules to ensure that civil litigation is resolved not only fairly, but also without undue cost or delay. As officers of the court, attorneys share this responsibility with the judge to whom the case is assigned.

2007 AMENDMENT

The language of Rule 1 has been amended as part of the general restyling of the Civil Rules to make them more easily understood and to make style and terminology consistent throughout the rules. These changes are intended to be stylistic only.

The merger of law, equity, and admiralty practice is complete. There is no need to carry forward the phrases that initially accomplished the merger.

The former reference to "suits of a civil nature" is changed to the more modern "civil actions and proceedings." This change does not affect such questions as whether the Civil Rules apply to summary proceedings created by statute. *See SEC v. McCarthy*, 322 F.3d 650 (9th Cir. 2003); *see also New Hampshire Fire Ins. Co. v. Scanlon*, 362 U.S. 404 (1960).

The Style Project

The Civil Rules are the third set of the rules to be restyled. The restyled Rules of Appellate Procedure took effect in 1998. The restyled Rules of Criminal Procedure took effect in 2002. The restyled Rules of Civil Procedure apply the same general drafting guidelines and principles used in restyling the Appellate and Criminal Rules.

1. General Guidelines

Guidance in drafting, usage, and style was provided by Bryan Garner, Guidelines for Drafting and Editing Court Rules, Administrative Office of the United States Courts (1996) and Bryan Garner, Dictionary of Modern Legal Usage (2d ed. 1995). *See also* Joseph Kimble, Guiding Principles for Restyling the Civil Rules, in Preliminary Draft of Proposed Style Revision of the Federal Rules of Civil Procedure, at x (Feb. 2005) (available at http://www.uscourts.gov/rules/Prelim_draft_proposed_pt1.pdf).

2. Formatting Changes

Many of the changes in the restyled Civil Rules result from using format to achieve clearer presentation. The rules are broken down into constituent parts, using progressively indented subparagraphs with headings and substituting vertical for horizontal lists. "Hanging indents" are used throughout. These formatting changes make the structure of the rules graphic and make the restyled rules easier to read and understand even when the words are not changed. Rule 14(a) illustrates the benefits of formatting changes.

3. Changes to Reduce Inconsistent, Ambiguous, Redundant, Repetitive, or Archaic Words

The restyled rules reduce the use of inconsistent terms that say the same thing in different ways. Because different words are presumed to have different meanings, such inconsistencies can result in confusion. The restyled rules reduce inconsistencies by using the same words to express the same meaning. For example, consistent expression is achieved without affecting meaning by the changes from "infant" in many rules to "minor" in all rules; from "upon motion or on its own initiative" in Rule 4(m) and variations in many other rules to "on motion or on its own"; and from "deemed" to "considered" in Rules 5(c), 12(e), and elsewhere. Some variations of expression have been carried forward when the context made that appropriate. As an example, "stipulate," "agree," and "consent" appear throughout the rules, and "written" qualifies these words in some places but not others. The number of variations has been reduced, but at times the former words were carried forward. None of the changes, when made, alters the rule's meaning.

The restyled rules minimize the use of inherently ambiguous words. For example, the word "shall" can mean "must," "may," or something else, depending on context. The potential for confusion is exacerbated by the fact that "shall" is no longer generally used in spoken or clearly written English. The restyled rules replace "shall" with "must," "may," or "should," depending on which one the context and established interpretation make correct in each rule.

The restyled rules minimize the use of redundant "intensifiers." These are expressions that attempt to add emphasis, but instead state the obvious and create negative implications for other rules. "The court in its discretion may" becomes "the court may"; "unless the order expressly directs otherwise" becomes "unless the court orders otherwise." The absence of intensifiers in the restyled rules does not change their substantive meaning. For example, the absence of the word "reasonable" to describe the written notice of foreign law required in Rule 44.1 does not mean that "unreasonable" notice is permitted.

The restyled rules also remove words and concepts that are outdated or redundant. The reference to "at law or in equity" in Rule 1 has become redundant with the merger of law and equity. Outdated words and concepts include the reference to "demurrers, pleas, and exceptions" in Rule 7(c); the reference to "mesne" process in Rule 77(c); and the reference in Rule 81(f) to a now-abolished official position.

The restyled rules remove a number of redundant cross-references. For example, Rule 8(b) states that a general denial is subject to the obligations of Rule 11, but all pleadings are subject to Rule 11. Removing such cross-references does not defeat application of the formerly cross-referenced rule.

4. Rule Numbers

The restyled rules keep the same rule numbers to minimize the effect on research. Subdivisions have been rearranged within some rules to achieve greater clarity and simplicity. The only change that moves one part of a rule to another is the transfer of former Rule 25(d)(2) to Rule 17(d). The restyled rules include a comparison chart to make it easy to identify transfers of provisions between subdivisions and redesignations of some subdivisions.

5. Other Changes

The style changes to the rules are intended to make no changes in substantive meaning. A very small number of minor technical amendments that arguably do change meaning were approved separately from the restyled rules, but become effective at the same time. An example is adding "e-mail address" to the information that must be included in pleadings. These minor changes occur in Rules 4(k), 9(h), 11(a), 14(b), 16(c)(1), 26(g)(1), 30(b), 31, 40, 71.1, and 78.

2015 AMENDMENT

Rule 1 is amended to emphasize that just as the court should construe and administer these rules to secure the just, speedy, and inexpensive determination of every action, so the parties share the responsibility to employ the rules in the same way. Most lawyers and parties cooperate to achieve these ends. But discussions of ways to improve the administration of civil justice regularly include pleas to discourage over-use, misuse, and abuse of procedural tools that increase cost and result in delay. Effective advocacy is consistent with—and indeed depends upon—cooperative and proportional use of procedure.

This amendment does not create a new or independent source of sanctions. Neither does it abridge the scope of any other of these rules.

Rule 2. One Form of Action

1937 ADOPTION

1. This rule modifies U.S.C., Title 28, former § 384 (Suits in equity, when not sustainable). U.S.C., Title 28, §§ 2071 to 2073, formerly §§ 723 and 730 (conferring power on the Supreme Court to make rules of practice in equity), are unaffected in so far as they relate to the rule making power in admiralty. These sections, together with § 2072, formerly § 723b (Rules in actions at law; Supreme Court authorized to make) are continued in so far as they are not inconsistent with § 2072, formerly § 723c (Union of equity and action at law rules; power of

Supreme Court). See Note 3 to Rule 1. U.S.C., Title 28, former §§ 724 (Conformity Act), 397 (Amendments to pleadings when case brought to wrong side of court) and 398 (Equitable defenses and equitable relief in actions at law) are superseded.

2. Reference to actions at law or suits in equity in all statutes should now be treated as referring to the civil action prescribed in these rules.

3. This rule follows in substance the usual introductory statements to code practices which provide for a single action and mode of procedure, with abolition of forms of action and procedural distinctions. Representative statutes are N.Y.Code 1848, Laws 1848, ch. 379, § 62; N.Y.C.P.A.1937, § 8; Calif.Code Civ.Proc. 1937, § 307; 2 Minn.Stat.Ann.1945, § 540.01; 2 Wash.Rev.Stat.Ann. Remington, 1932, §§ 153, 255.

2007 AMENDMENT

The language of Rule 2 has been amended as part of the general restyling of the Civil Rules to make them more easily understood and to make style and terminology consistent throughout the rules. These changes are intended to be stylistic only.

II. COMMENCEMENT OF ACTION; SERVICE OF PROCESS, PLEADINGS, MOTIONS AND ORDERS

Rule 3. Commencement of Action

1937 ADOPTION

1. Rule 5(e) defines what constitutes filing with the court.

2. This rule governs the commencement of all actions, including those brought by or against the United States or an officer or agency thereof, regardless of whether service is to be made personally pursuant to Rule 4(d), or otherwise pursuant to Rule 4(e).

3. With this rule compare former Equity Rule 12 (Issue of Subpoena—Time for Answer) and the following statutes (and other similar statutes) which provide a similar method for commencing an action:

U.S.C., Title 28 former:

§ 45 (District courts; practice and procedure in certain cases under interstate commerce laws)

§ 762 (Petition in suit against United States)

§ 766 (Partition suits where United States is tenant in common or joint tenant)

4. This rule provides that the first step in an action is the filing of the complaint. Under Rule 4(a) this is to be followed forthwith by issuance of a summons and its delivery to an officer for service. Other rules providing for dismissal for failure to prosecute suggest a method available to attack unreasonable delay in prosecuting an action after it has been commenced. When a federal or state statute of limitations is pleaded as a defense, a question may arise under this rule whether the mere filing of the complaint stops the running of the statute, or whether any further step is required, such as, service of the summons and complaint or their delivery to the marshal for service. The answer to this question may depend on whether it is competent for the Supreme Court, exercising the power to make rules of procedure without affecting substantive rights, to vary the operation of statutes of limitations. The requirement of Rule 4(a) that the clerk shall forthwith issue the summons and deliver it to the marshal for service will reduce the chances of such a question arising.

2007 AMENDMENTS

The caption of Rule 3 has been amended as part of the general restyling of the Civil Rules to make them more easily understood and to make style and terminology consistent throughout the rules. These changes are intended to be stylistic only.

Rule 4. Summons

1937 ADOPTION

Note to Subdivision (a). With the provision permitting additional summons upon request of the plaintiff, compare former Equity Rule 14 (Alias Subpoena) and the last sentence of former Equity Rule 12 (Issue of Subpoena—Time for Answer).

Note to Subdivision (b). This rule prescribes a form of summons which follows substantially the requirements stated in former Equity Rules 12 (Issue of Subpoena—Time for Answer) and 7 (Process, Mesne and Final).

U.S.C., Title 28, § 1691, formerly § 721 (Sealing and testing of writs) is substantially continued in so far as it applies to a summons, but its requirements as to teste of process are superseded. U.S.C., Title 28, former § 722 (Teste of Process, day of) is superseded.

See Rule 12(a) for a statement of the time within which the defendant is required to appear and defend.

Note to subdivision (c). This rule does not affect U.S.C., Title 28, § 547, formerly § 503, as amended June 15, 1935 (Marshals; duties) and such statutes as the following in so far as they provide for service of process by a marshal, but modifies them in so far as they may imply service by a marshal only:

U.S.C., Title 15:

§ 5 (Bringing in additional parties)(Sherman Act)

§ 10 (Bringing in additional parties)

§ 25 (Restraining violations; procedure)

U.S.C., Title 28, former:

§ 45 (Practice and procedure in certain cases under the interstate commerce laws)

Compare former Equity Rule 15 (Process, by Whom Served).

Note to Subdivision (d). Under this rule the complaint must always be served with the summons.

Paragraph (1). For an example of a statute providing for service upon an agent of an individual see U.S.C., Title 28, §§ 1400, 1694, formerly § 109, (Patent cases).

Paragraph (3). This enumerates the officers and agents of a corporation or of a partnership or other unincorporated association upon whom service of process may be made, and permits service of process only upon the officers, managing or general agents, or agents authorized by appointment or by law, of the corporation, partnership or unincorporated association against which the action is brought. See *Christian v. International Ass'n of Machinists, D.C.Ky.1925*, 7 F.2d 481 and *Singleton v. Order of Railway Conductors of America, D.C.Ill. 1935*, 9 F.Supp. 417. Compare *Operative Plasterers' and Cement Finishers' International Ass'n of the United States and Canada v. Case, App.D.C.1937*, 93 F.2d 56.

For a statute authorizing service upon a specified agent and requiring mailing to the defendant, see U.S.C., Title 6, § 7 (Surety companies as sureties; appointment of agents; service of process).

Paragraphs (4) and (5) provide a uniform and comprehensive method of service for all actions against the United States or an officer or agency thereof. For statutes providing for such service, see U.S.C., Title 7, §§ 217 (Proceedings for suspension of orders) 499k (Injunctions; application of injunction laws governing orders of Interstate Commerce Commission), 608c(15)(B) (Court review of ruling of Secretary of Agriculture), and 855 (making § 608c(15)(B) applicable to orders of the Secretary of Agriculture as to handlers of anti-hog-cholera serum and hog-cholera virus); U.S.C., Title 26, § 3679 (Bill in chancery to clear title to realty on which the United States has a lien for taxes); U.S.C., Title 28, former § 45 (District Courts; practice and procedure in certain cases under the interstate commerce laws) former § 763 (Petition in suit against the United States; service; appearance by district attorney), § 2409, formerly § 766 (Partition suits where United States is tenant in common or joint tenant),

§ 2410, formerly § 902 (Foreclosure of mortgages or other liens on property in which the United States has an interest). These and similar statutes are modified in so far as they prescribe a different method of service or dispense with the service of a summons.

For the Equity Rule on service, see [former] Equity Rule 13, Manner of Serving Subpoena.

Note to Subdivision (e). The provisions for the service of a summons or of notice or of an order in lieu of summons contained in U.S.C., Title 8, § 1451, formerly § 465 (Cancellation of certificates of citizenship fraudulently or illegally procured)(service by publication in accordance with state law); U.S.C., Title 28, § 1655, formerly § 118 (Absent defendants in suits to enforce liens); U.S.C., Title 35, § 72a (Jurisdiction of District Court of United States for the District of Columbia in certain equity suits where adverse parties reside elsewhere) (service by publication against parties residing in foreign countries); U.S.C., Title 38, § 445 (Action against the United States on a veteran's contract of insurance)(parties not inhabitants of or not found within the district may be served with an order of the court, personally or by publication) and similar statutes are continued by this rule. Title 24, § 378 of the Code of the District of Columbia (Publication against non-resident; those absent for six months; unknown heirs or devisees; for divorce or in rem; actual service beyond District) is continued, by this rule.

Note to Subdivision (f). This rule enlarges to some extent the present rule as to where service may be made. It does not, however, enlarge the jurisdiction of the district courts.

U.S.C., Title 28, § 1392, formerly § 113 (Suits in States containing more than one district)(where there are two or more defendants residing in different districts), former § 115 (Suits of a local nature), § 1392, formerly § 116 (Property in different districts in same state), former § 838 (Executions run in all districts of state); U.S.C., Title 47, § 13 (Action for damages against a railroad or telegraph company whose officer or agent in control of a telegraph line refuses or fails to operate such line in a certain manner—"upon any agent of the company found in such state"); U.S.C., Title 49, § 321(c) (Requiring designation of a process agent by interstate motor carriers and in case of failure so to do, service may be made upon any agent in the state) and similar statutes, allowing the running of process throughout a state, are substantially continued.

U.S.C., Title 15, §§ 5 (Bringing in additional parties)(Sherman Act), 25 (Restraining violations; procedure); U.S.C., Title 28, § 2321, formerly § 44 (Procedure in certain cases under interstate commerce laws; service of processes of court), §§ 754, 1692, formerly § 117 (Property in different states in same circuit; jurisdiction of receiver), § 2413, formerly § 839 (Executions; run in every State and Territory) and similar statutes, providing for the running of process beyond the territorial limits of a state, are expressly continued.

Note to Subdivision (g). With the second sentence compare former Equity Rule 15 (Process, by Whom Served).

Note to Subdivision (h). This rule substantially continues U.S.C., Title 28, former § 767 (Amendment of process).

1963 AMENDMENT

Subdivision (b). Under amended subdivision (e) of this rule, an action may be commenced against a nonresident of the State in which the district court is held by complying with State procedures. Frequently the form of the summons or notice required in these cases by State law differs from the Federal form of summons described in present subdivision (b) and exemplified in Form 1. To avoid confusion, the amendment of subdivision (b) states that a form of summons or notice, corresponding "as nearly as may be" to the State form, shall be employed. See also a corresponding amendment of Rule 12(a) with regard to the time to answer.

Subdivision (d)(4). This paragraph, governing service upon the United States, is amended to allow the use of certified mail as an alternative to registered mail for sending copies of the papers to the Attorney General or to a

United States officer or agency. Cf. N.J. Rule 4:5-2. See also the amendment of Rule 30(f)(1).

Subdivision (d)(7). Formerly a question was raised whether this paragraph, in the context of the rule as a whole, authorized service in original Federal actions pursuant to State statutes permitting service on a State official as a means of bringing a nonresident motorist defendant into court. It was argued in *McCoy v. Siler*, 205 F.2d 498, 501–2 (3d Cir.) (concurring opinion), cert. denied, 346 U.S. 872, 74 S. Ct. 120, 98 L.Ed. 380 (1953), that the effective service in those cases occurred not when the State official was served but when notice was given to the defendant outside the State, and that subdivision (f)(Territorial limits of effective service), as then worded, did not authorize out-of-State service. This contention found little support. A considerable number of cases held the service to be good, either by fixing upon the service on the official within the State as the effective service, thus satisfying the wording of subdivision (f) as it then stood, see *Holbrook v. Cafiero*, 18 F.R.D. 218 (D.Md.1955); *Pasternack v. Dalo*, 17 F.R.D. 420 (W.D.Pa.1955); cf. *Super Prods. Corp. v. Parkin*, 20 F.R.D. 377 (S.D.N.Y.1957), or by reading paragraph (7) as not limited by subdivision (f). See *Giffin v. Ensign*, 234 F.2d 307 (3d Cir.1956); 2 Moore's Federal Practice, ¶ 4.19 (2d ed. 1948); 1 Barron & Holtzoff, Federal Practice & Procedure § 182.1 (Wright ed. 1960); Comment, 27 U. of Chi.L.Rev. 751 (1960). See also *Olberding v. Illinois Central R. R.*, 201 F.2d 582 (6th Cir.), rev'd on other grounds, 346 U.S. 338, 74 S. Ct. 83, 98 L.Ed. 39 (1953); *Feinsinger v. Bard*, 195 F.2d 45 (7th Cir.1952).

An important and growing class of State statutes base personal jurisdiction over nonresidents on the doing of acts or on other contacts within the State, and permit notice to be given the defendant outside the State without any requirement of service on a local State official. See, e.g., Ill.Ann.Stat., c. 110, §§ 16, 17 (Smith-Hurd 1956); Wis. Stat. § 262.06 (1959). This service, employed in original Federal actions pursuant to paragraph (7), has also been held proper. See *Farr & Co. v. Cia. Intercontinental De Nav. De Cuba*, 243 F.2d 342 (2d Cir. 1957); *Kappus v. Western Hills Oil, Inc.*, 24 F.R.D. 123 (E.D.Wis.1959); *Star v. Rogalny*, 162 F.Supp. 181 (E.D.Ill.1957). It has also been held that the clause of paragraph (7) which permits service "in the manner prescribed by the law of the state," etc., is not limited by subdivision (c) requiring that service of all process be made by certain designated persons. See *Farr & Co. v. Cia. Intercontinental De Nav. De Cuba*, supra. But cf. *Sappia v. Lauro Lines*, 130 F.Supp. 810 (S.D.N.Y.1955).

The salutary results of these cases are intended to be preserved. See paragraph (7), with a clarified reference to State law, and amended subdivisions (e) and (f).

Subdivision (e). For the general relation between subdivisions (d) and (e), see 2 Moore, supra, ¶ 4.32.

The amendment of the first sentence inserting the word "thereunder" supports the original intention that the "order of court" must be authorized by a specific United States statute. See 1 Barron & Holtzoff, supra, at 731. The clause added at the end of the first sentence expressly adopts the view taken by commentators that, if no manner of service is prescribed in the statute or order, the service may be made in a manner stated in Rule 4. See 2 Moore, supra, ¶ 4.32, at 1004; Smit, International Aspects of Federal Civil Procedure, 61 Colum.L.Rev. 1031, 1036–39 (1961). But see Commentary, 5 Fed. Rules Serv. 791 (1942).

Examples of the statutes to which the first sentence relates are 28 U.S.C. § 2361 (Interpleader; process and procedure); 28 U.S.C. § 1655 (Lien enforcement; absent defendants).

The second sentence, added by amendment, expressly allows resort in original Federal actions to the procedures provided by State law for effecting service on nonresident parties (as well as on domiciliaries not found within the State). See, as illustrative, the discussion under amended subdivision (d)(7) of service pursuant to State nonresident motorist statutes and other comparable State statutes. Of particular interest is the change brought about by the reference in this sentence to State procedures for commencing actions against nonresidents by attachment and the like, accompanied by notice. Although an action commenced in a State court by attachment may be removed to the Federal court if ordinary conditions for removal are satisfied, see 28 U.S.C. § 1450; *Rorick v. Devon Syndicate, Ltd.*, 307 U.S. 299, 59 S. Ct. 877, 83 L.Ed. 1303 (1939); *Clark v. Wells*, 203 U.S. 164, 27 S. Ct. 43, 51 L.Ed. 138 (1906), there has heretofore been no provision recognized by the courts for commencing an original Federal civil action by attachment. See Currie, Attachment and Garnishment in the Federal Courts, 59 Mich.L.Rev. 337 (1961), arguing that this result came about through historical anomaly, Rule 64, which refers to attachment, garnishment, and similar procedures under State law, furnishes only provisional remedies in actions otherwise validly commenced. See *Big Vein Coal Co. v. Read*, 229 U.S. 31, 33 S. Ct. 694, 57 L.Ed. 1053 (1913); *Davis v. Ensign-Bickford Co.*, 139 F.2d 624 (8th Cir.1944); 7 Moore's Federal Practice ¶ 64.05 (2d ed. 1954); 3 Barron & Holtzoff, Federal Practice & Procedure § 1423 (Wright ed. 1958); but cf. Note, 13 So.Calif.L.Rev. 361 (1940). The amendment will now permit the institution of original Federal actions against nonresidents through the use of familiar State procedures by which property of these defendants is brought within the custody of the court and some appropriate service is made upon them.

The necessity of satisfying subject-matter jurisdictional requirements and requirements of venue will limit the practical utilization of these methods of effecting service. Within those limits, however, there appears to be no reason for denying plaintiffs means of commencing actions in Federal courts which are generally available in the State courts. See 1 Barron & Holtzoff, supra, at 374 to 80; Nordbye, Comments on Proposed Amendments to Rules of Civil Procedure for the United States District Courts, 18 F.R.D. 105, 106 (1956); Note, 34 Corn.L.Q. 103 (1948); Note, 13 So.Calif.L.Rev. 361 (1940).

If the circumstances of a particular case satisfy the applicable Federal law (first sentence of Rule 4(e), as amended) and the applicable State law (second sentence), the party seeking to make the service may proceed under the Federal or the State law, at his option.

See also amended Rule 13(a), and the Advisory Committee's Note thereto.

Subdivision (f). The first sentence is amended to assure the effectiveness of service outside the territorial limits of the State in all the cases in which any of the rules authorize service beyond those boundaries. Besides the preceding provisions of Rule 4, see Rule 71A(d)(3). In addition, the new second sentence of the subdivision permits effective service within a limited area outside the State in certain special situations, namely, to bring in additional parties to a counterclaim or cross-claim (Rule 13(h)), impleaded parties (Rule 14), and indispensable or conditionally necessary parties to a pending action (Rule 19); and to secure compliance with an order of commitment for civil contempt. In those situations effective service can be made at points not more than 100 miles distant from the courthouse in which the action is commenced, or to which it is assigned or transferred for trial.

The bringing in of parties under the 100-mile provision in the limited situations enumerated is designed to promote the objective of enabling the court to determine entire controversies. In the light of present-day facilities for communication and travel, the territorial range of the service allowed, analogous to that which applies to the service of a subpoena under Rule 45(e)(1), can hardly work hardship on the parties summoned. The provision will be especially useful in metropolitan areas spanning more than one State. Any requirements of subject-matter jurisdiction and venue will still have to be satisfied as to the parties brought in, although these requirements will be eased in some instances when the parties can be regarded as "ancillary." See *Pennsylvania R.R. v. Erie Avenue Warehouse Co.*, 302 F.2d 843 (3d Cir.1962); *Dery v. Wyer*, 265 F.2d 804 (2d Cir.1959); *United Artists Corp. v. Masterpiece Productions, Inc.*, 221 F.2d 213 (2d Cir.1955); *Lesnik v. Public Industrials Corp.*, 144 F.2d 968 (2d Cir. 1944); *Vaughn v. Terminal Transp. Co.*, 162 F.Supp. 647 (E.D.Tenn.1957); and compare the fifth paragraph of the Advisory Committee's Note to Rule 4(e), as amended. The amendment is but a moderate extension of the territorial reach of Federal process and has ample practical justification. See 2 Moore, supra, § 4.01[13] (Supp.1960); 1 Barron & Holtzoff, supra, § 184; Note, 51 Nw.U.L.Rev. 354 (1956). But cf. Nordbye, Comments on Proposed Amendments to Rules of Civil Procedure for the United States District Courts, 18 F.R.D. 105, 106 (1956).

As to the need for enlarging the territorial area in which orders of commitment for civil contempt may be served, see *Graber v. Graber*, 93 F.Supp. 281 (D. D.C.1950); *Teele Soap Mfg. Co. v. Pine Tree Products Co., Inc.*, 8 F.Supp. 546 (D. N.H.1934); *Mitchell v. Dexter*, 244 Fed. 926 (1st Cir.1917); *In re Graves*, 29 Fed. 60 (N.D.Iowa 1886).

As to the Court's power to amend subdivisions (e) and (f) as here set forth, see *Mississippi Pub. Corp. v. Murphree*, 326 U.S. 438, 66 S. Ct. 242, 90 L.Ed. 185 (1946).

Subdivision (i). The continual increase of civil litigation having international elements makes it advisable to consolidate, amplify, and clarify the provisions governing service upon parties in foreign countries. See generally Jones, International Judicial Assistance: Procedural Chaos and a Program for Reform, 62 Yale L.J. 515 (1953); Longley, Serving Process, Subpoenas and Other Documents in Foreign Territory, Proc. A.B.A., Sec.Int'l & Comp.L. 34 (1959); Smit, International Aspects of Federal Civil Procedure, 61 Colum.L.Rev. 1031 (1961).

As indicated in the opening lines of new subdivision (i), referring to the provisions of subdivision (e), the authority for effecting foreign service must be found in a statute of the United States or a statute or rule of court of the State in which the district court is held providing in terms or upon proper interpretation for service abroad upon persons not inhabitants of or found within the State. See the Advisory Committee's Note to amended Rule 4(d)(7) and Rule 4(e). For examples of Federal and State statutes expressly authorizing such service, see 8 U.S.C. § 1451(b); 35 U.S.C. §§ 146, 293; Me.Rev.Stat., ch. 22, § 70 (Supp.1961); Minn.Stat.Ann. § 303.13 (1947); N.Y.Veh. & Tfc.Law § 253. Several decisions have construed statutes to permit service in foreign countries, although the matter is not expressly mentioned in the statutes. See, e.g., *Chapman v. Superior Court*, 162 Cal.App.2d 421, 328 P.2d 23 (Dist.Ct.App.1958); *Sperry v. Fliegers*, 194 Misc. 438, 86 N.Y.S.2d 830 (Sup.Ct.1949); *Ewing v. Thompson*, 233 N.C. 564, 65 S.E.2d 17 (1951); *Rushing v. Bush*, 260 S.W.2d 900 (Tex.Ct. Civ.App.1953). Federal and State statutes authorizing service on nonresidents in such terms as to warrant the interpretation that service abroad is permissible include 15 U.S.C. §§ 77v(a), 78aa, 79y; 28 U.S.C. § 1655; 38 U.S.C. § 784(a); Ill.Ann.Stat., c. 110, §§ 16, 17 (Smith-Hurd 1956); Wis.Stat. § 262.06 (1959).

Under **subdivisions (e) and (i),** when authority to make foreign service is found in a Federal statute or statute or rule of court of a State, it is always sufficient to carry out the service in the manner indicated therein. Subdivision (i) introduces considerable further flexibility by permitting the foreign service and return thereof to be carried out in any of a number of other alternative ways that are also declared to be sufficient. Other aspects of foreign service continue to be governed by the other provisions of Rule 4. Thus, for example, subdivision (i) effects no change in the form of the summons, or the issuance of separate or additional summons, or the amendment of service.

Service of process beyond the territorial limits of the United States may involve difficulties not encountered in the case of domestic service. Service abroad may be considered by a foreign country to require the performance of judicial, and therefore "sovereign," acts within its territory, which that country may conceive to be offensive to its policy or contrary to its law. See Jones, supra, at 537. For example, a person not qualified to serve process according to the law of the foreign country may find himself subject to sanctions if he attempts service therein. See Inter-American Juridical Committee, Report on Uniformity of Legislation on International Cooperation in Judicial Procedures 20 (1952). The enforcement of a judgment in the foreign country in which the service was made may be embarrassed or prevented if the service did not comport with the law of that country. See ibid.

One of the purposes of **subdivision (i)** is to allow accommodation to the policies and procedures of the foreign country. It is emphasized, however, that the attitudes of foreign countries vary considerably and that the question of recognition of United States judgments abroad is complex. Accordingly, if enforcement is to be sought in the country of service, the foreign law should be examined before a choice is made among the methods of service allowed by subdivision (i).

Subdivision (i)(1). Subparagraph (a) of paragraph (1), permitting service by the method prescribed by the law of the foreign country for service on a person in that country in a civil action in any of its courts of general jurisdiction, provides an alternative that is likely to create least objection in the place of service and also is likely to enhance the possibilities of securing ultimate enforcement of the judgment abroad. See Report on Uniformity of Legislation on International Cooperation in Judicial Procedures, supra.

In certain foreign countries service in aid of litigation pending in other countries can lawfully be accomplished only upon request to the foreign court, which in turn directs the service to be made. In many countries this has long been a customary way of accomplishing the service. See *In re Letters Rogatory Out of First Civil Court of City of Mexico*, 261 Fed. 652 (S.D.N.Y.1919); Jones, supra, at 543; Comment, 44 Colum.L.Rev. 72 (1944); Note, 58 Yale L.J. 1193 (1949). Subparagraph (B) of paragraph (1), referring to a letter rogatory, validates this method. A proviso, applicable to this subparagraph and the preceding one, requires, as a safeguard, that the service made shall be reasonably calculated to give actual notice of the proceedings to the party. See *Milliken v. Meyer*, 311 U.S. 457, 61 S. Ct. 339, 85 L.Ed. 278 (1940).

Subparagraph (C) of paragraph (1), permitting foreign service by personal delivery on individuals and corporations, partnerships, and associations, provides for a manner of service that is not only traditionally preferred, but also is most likely to lead to actual notice. Explicit provision for this manner of service was thought desirable because a number of Federal and State statutes permitting foreign service do not specifically provide for service by personal delivery abroad, see e.g., 35 U.S.C. §§ 146, 293; 46 U.S.C. § 1292; Calif.Ins.Code § 1612; N.Y.Veh. & Tfc.Law § 253, and it also may be unavailable under the law of the country in which the service is made.

Subparagraph (D) of paragraph (1), permitting service by certain types of mail, affords a manner of service that is inexpensive and expeditious, and requires a minimum of activity within the foreign country. Several statutes specifically provide for service in a foreign country by mail, e.g., Hawaii Rev.Laws §§ 230 to 31, 230 to 32 (1955); Minn.Stat.Ann. § 303.13 (1947); N.Y.Civ. Prac.Act, § 229-b; N.Y.Veh. & Tfc.Law § 253, and it has been sanctioned by the courts even in the absence of statutory provision specifying that form of service. *Zurini v. United States*, 189 F.2d 722 (8th Cir.1951); *United States v. Cardillo*, 135 F.Supp. 798 (W.D.Pa.1955); *Autogiro Co. v. Kay Gyroplanes, Ltd.*, 55 F.Supp. 919 (D.D.C.1944). Since the reliability of postal service may vary from country to country, service by mail is proper only when it is addressed to the party to be served and a form of mail requiring a signed receipt is used. An additional safeguard is provided by the requirement that the mailing be attended to by the clerk of the court. See also the provisions of paragraph (2) of this subdivision (i) regarding proof of service by mail.

Under the applicable law it may be necessary, when the defendant is an infant or incompetent person, to deliver the summons and complaint to a guardian, committee, or similar fiduciary. In such a case it would be advisable to make service under subparagraph (A), (B), or (E).

Subparagraph (E) of paragraph (1) adds flexibility by permitting the court by order to tailor the manner of service to fit the necessities of a particular case or the peculiar requirements of the law of the country in which the service is to be made. A similar provision appears in a number of statutes, e.g., 35 U.S.C. §§ 146, 293; 38 U.S.C. § 784(a); 46 U.S.C. § 1292.

The next-to-last sentence of paragraph (1) permits service under (C) and (E) to be made by any person who is not a party and is not less than 18 years of age or who is designated by court order or by the foreign court. Cf. Rule 45(c); N.Y.Civ.Prac.Act §§ 233, 235. This alternative increases the possibility that the plaintiff will be able to find a process server who can proceed unimpeded in the foreign country; it also may improve the chances of enforcing the judgment in the country of service. Especially is the alternative valuable when authority for the foreign service is found in a statute or rule of court that limits the group of eligible process servers to designated officials or special appointees who, because directly connected with another "sovereign," may be particularly offensive to the foreign country. See generally Smit, supra, at 1040 to 41. When recourse is had to subparagraph (A) or (B) the identity of the process server always will be determined by the law of the foreign country in which the service is made.

The last sentence of paragraph (1) sets forth an alternative manner for the issuance and transmission of the summons for service. After obtaining the summons from the clerk, the plaintiff must ascertain the best manner of delivering the summons and complaint to the person, court, or officer who will make the service. Thus the clerk is not burdened with the task of determining who is permitted to serve process under the law of a particular country or the appropriate governmental or nongovernmental channel for forwarding a letter rogatory. Under (D), however, the papers must always be posted by the clerk.

Subdivision (i)(2). When service is made in a foreign country, paragraph (2) permits methods for proof of service in addition to those prescribed by subdivision (g). Proof of service in accordance with the law of the foreign country is permitted because foreign process servers, unaccustomed to the form or the requirement of return of service prevalent in the United States, have on occasion been unwilling to execute the affidavit required by Rule 4(g). See *Jones, supra*, at 537; *Longley, supra*, at 35. As a corollary of the alternate manner of service in subdivision (i)(1)(E), proof of service as directed by order of the court is permitted. The special provision for proof of service by mail is intended as an additional safeguard when that method is used. On the type of evidence of delivery that may be satisfactory to a court in lieu of a signed receipt, see *Aero Associates, Inc. v. La Metropolitana*, 183 F.Supp. 357 (S.D.N.Y.1960).

1966 AMENDMENT

The wording of Rule 4(f) is changed to accord with the amendment of Rule 13(h) referring to Rule 19 as amended.

1980 AMENDMENT

Subdivision (a). This is a technical amendment to conform this subdivision with the amendment of subdivision (c).

Subdivision (c). The purpose of this amendment is to authorize service of process to be made by any person who is authorized to make service in actions in the courts of general jurisdiction of the state in which the district court is held or in which service is made.

There is a troublesome ambiguity in Rule 4. Rule 4(c) directs that all process is to be served by the marshal, by his deputy, or by a person specially appointed by the court. But Rule 4(d)(7) authorizes service in certain cases "in the manner prescribed by the law of the state in which the district court is held. . . ."; And Rule 4(e), which authorizes service beyond the state and service in quasi in rem cases when state law permits such service, directs that "service may be made . . . under the circumstances and in the manner prescribed in the [state] statute or rule." State statutes and rules of the kind referred to in Rule 4(d)(7) and Rule 4(e) commonly designate the persons who are to make the service provided for, e.g., a sheriff or a plaintiff. When that is so, may the persons so designated by state law make service, or is service in all cases to be made by a marshal or by one specially appointed under present Rule 4(c)? The commentators have noted the ambiguity and have suggested the desirability of an amendment. See 2 Moore's Federal Practice ¶ 4.08 (1974); Wright & Miller, Federal Practice and Procedure: Civil § 1092 (1969). And the ambiguity has given rise to unfortunate results. See *United States for Use of Tanos v. St. Paul Mercury Ins. Co.*, 361

F.2d 838 (5th Cir.1966); *Veeck v. Commodity Enterprises, Inc.*, 487 F.2d 423 (9th Cir.1973).

The ambiguity can be resolved by specific amendments to Rules 4(d)(7) and 4(e), but the Committee is of the view that there is no reason why Rule 4(c) should not generally authorize service of process in all cases by anyone authorized to make service in the courts of general jurisdiction of the state in which the district court is held or in which service is made. The marshal continues to be the obvious, always effective officer for service of process.

1987 AMENDMENT

The amendments are technical. No substantive change is intended.

1993 AMENDMENT

SPECIAL NOTE: Mindful of the constraints of the Rules Enabling Act, the Committee calls the attention of the Supreme Court and Congress to new subdivision (k)(2). Should this limited extension of service be disapproved, the Committee nevertheless recommends adoption of the balance of the rule, with subdivision (k)(1) becoming simply subdivision (k). The Committee Notes would be revised to eliminate references to subdivision (k)(2). [Edit. note: Subd. (k)(2) was not disapproved.]

Purposes of Revision. The general purpose of this revision is to facilitate the service of the summons and complaint. The revised rule explicitly authorizes a means for service of the summons and complaint on any defendant. While the methods of service so authorized always provide appropriate notice to persons against whom claims are made, effective service under this rule does not assure that personal jurisdiction has been established over the defendant served.

First, the revised rule authorizes the use of any means of service provided by the law not only of the forum state, but also of the state in which a defendant is served, unless the defendant is a minor or incompetent.

Second, the revised rule clarifies and enhances the cost-saving practice of securing the assent of the defendant to dispense with actual service of the summons and complaint. This practice was introduced to the rule in 1983 by an act of Congress authorizing "service-by-mail," a procedure that effects economic service with cooperation of the defendant. Defendants that magnify costs of service by requiring expensive service not necessary to achieve full notice of an action brought against them are required to bear the wasteful costs. This provision is made available in actions against defendants who cannot be served in the districts in which the actions are brought.

Third, the revision reduces the hazard of commencing an action against the United States or its officers, agencies, and corporations. A party failing to effect service on all the offices of the United States as required by the rule is assured adequate time to cure defects in service.

Fourth, the revision calls attention to the important effect of the Hague Convention and other treaties bearing on service of documents in foreign countries and favors the use of internationally agreed means of service. In some respects, these treaties have facilitated service in foreign countries but are not fully known to the bar.

Finally, the revised rule extends the reach of federal courts to impose jurisdiction over the person of all defendants against whom federal law claims are made and who can be constitutionally subjected to the jurisdiction of the courts of the United States. The present territorial limits on the effectiveness of service to subject a defendant to the jurisdiction of the court over the defendant's person are retained for all actions in which there is a state in which personal jurisdiction can be asserted consistently with state law and the Fourteenth Amendment. A new provision enables district courts to exercise jurisdiction, if permissible under the Constitution and not precluded by statute, when a federal claim is made against a defendant not subject to the jurisdiction of any single state.

The revised rule is reorganized to make its provisions more accessible to those not familiar with all of them. Additional subdivisions in this rule allow for more captions; several overlaps among subdivisions are eliminated; and several disconnected provisions are removed, to be relocated in a new Rule 4.1.

The Caption of the Rule. Prior to this revision, Rule 4 was entitled "Process" and applied to the service of not only the summons but also other process as well, although these are not covered by the revised rule. Service of process in eminent domain proceedings is governed by Rule 71A. Service of a subpoena is governed by Rule 45, and service of papers such as orders, motions, notices, pleadings, and other documents is governed by Rule 5.

The revised rule is entitled "Summons" and applies only to that form of legal process. Unless service of the summons is waived, a summons must be served whenever a person is joined as a party against whom a claim is made. Those few provisions of the former rule which relate specifically to service of process other than a summons are relocated in Rule 4.1 in order to simplify the text of this rule.

Subdivision (a). Revised subdivision (a) contains most of the language of the former subdivision (b). The second sentence of the former subdivision (b) has been stricken, so that the federal court summons will be the same in all cases. Few states now employ distinctive requirements of form for a summons and the applicability of such a requirement in federal court can only serve as a trap for an unwary party or attorney. A sentence is added to this subdivision authorizing an amendment of a summons. This sentence replaces the rarely used former subdivision 4(h). *See* 4A Wright & Miller, *Federal Practice and Procedure* § 1131 (2d ed. 1987).

Subdivision (b). Revised subdivision (b) replaces the former subdivision (a). The revised text makes clear that the responsibility for filling in the summons falls on the plaintiff, not the clerk of the court. If there are multiple defendants, the plaintiff may secure issuance of a summons for each defendant, or may serve copies of a single original bearing the names of multiple defendants if the addressee of the summons is effectively identified.

Subdivision (c). Paragraph (1) of revised subdivision (c) retains language from the former subdivision (d)(1). Paragraph (2) retains language from the former subdivision (a), and adds an appropriate caution regarding the time limit for service set forth in subdivision (m).

The 1983 revision of Rule 4 relieved the marshals' offices of much of the burden of serving the summons. Subdivision (c) eliminates the requirement for service by the marshal's office in actions in which the party seeking service is the United States. The United States, like other civil litigants, is now permitted to designate any person who is 18 years of age and not a party to serve its summons.

The court remains obligated to appoint a marshal, a deputy, or some other person to effect service of a summons in two classes of cases specified by statute: actions brought *in forma pauperis* or by a seaman. 28 U.S.C. §§ 1915, 1916. The court also retains discretion to appoint a process server on motion of a party. If a law enforcement presence appears to be necessary or advisable to keep the peace, the court should appoint a marshal or deputy or other official person to make the service. The Department of Justice may also call upon the Marshals Service to perform services in actions brought by the United States. 28 U.S.C. § 651.

Subdivision (d). This text is new, but is substantially derived from the former subdivisions (c)(2)(C) and (D), added to the rule by Congress in 1983. The aims of the provision are to eliminate the costs of service of a summons on many parties and to foster cooperation among adversaries and counsel. The rule operates to impose upon the defendant those costs that could have been avoided if the defendant had cooperated reasonably in the manner prescribed. This device is useful in dealing with defendants who are furtive, who reside in places not easily reached by process servers, or who are outside the United States and can be served only at substantial and unnecessary expense. Illustratively, there is no useful purpose achieved by requiring a plaintiff to comply with all the formalities of service in a foreign country, including costs of translation, when suing a defendant manufacturer, fluent in English, whose products are widely distributed in the United States. *See Bankston v. Toyota Motor Corp.*, 889 F.2d 172 (8th Cir.1989).

The former text described this process as service-by-mail. This language misled some plaintiffs into thinking that service could be effected by mail without the affirmative cooperation of the defendant. *E.g., Gulley v. Mayo Foundation*, 886 F.2d 161 (8th Cir.1989). It is more accurate to describe the communication sent to the defendant as a request for a waiver of formal service.

The request for waiver of service may be sent only to defendants subject to service under subdivision (e), (f), or (h). The United States is not expected to waive service for the reason that its mail receiving facilities are inadequate to assure that the notice is actually received by the correct person in the Department of Justice. The same principle is applied to agencies, corporations, and officers of the United States and to other governments and entities subject to service under subdivision (j). Moreover, there are policy reasons why governmental entities should not be confronted with the potential for bearing costs of service in cases in which they ultimately prevail. Infants or incompetent persons likewise are not called upon to waive service because, due to their presumed inability to understand the request and its consequences, they must generally be served through fiduciaries.

It was unclear whether the former rule authorized, mailing of a request for "acknowledgement of service" to defendants outside the forum state. *See* 1 R. Casad, Jurisdiction in Civil Actions (2d Ed.) 5-29, 30 (1991) and cases cited. But, as Professor Casad observed, there was no reason not to employ this device in an effort to obtain service outside the state, and there are many instances in which it was in fact so used, with respect both to defendants within the United States and to defendants in other countries.

The opportunity for waiver has distinct advantages to a foreign defendant. By waiving service, the defendant can reduce the costs that may ultimately be taxed against it if unsuccessful in the lawsuit, including the sometimes substantial expense of translation that may be wholly unnecessary for defendants fluent in English. Moreover, a foreign defendant that waives service is afforded substantially more time to defend against the action than if it had been formally served: under Rule 12, a defendant ordinarily has only 20 days after service in which to file its answer or raise objections by motion, but by signing a waiver it is allowed 90 days after the date the request for waiver was mailed in which to submit its defenses. Because of the additional time needed for mailing and the unreliability of some foreign mail services, a period of 60 days (rather than the 30 days required for domestic transmissions) is provided for a return of a waiver sent to a foreign country.

It is hoped that, since transmission of the notice and waiver forms is a private nonjudicial act, does not purport to effect service, and is not accompanied by any summons or directive from a court, use of the procedure will not offend foreign sovereignties, even those that have withheld their assent to formal service by mail or have objected to the "service-by-mail" provisions of the former rule. Unless the addressee consents, receipt of the request under the revised rule does not give rise to any obligation to answer the lawsuit, does not provide a basis for default judgment, and does not suspend the statute of limitations in those states where the period continues to run until service. Nor are there any adverse consequences to a foreign defendant, since the provisions for shifting the expense of service to a defendant that declines to waive service apply only if the plaintiff and defendant are both located in the United States.

With respect to a defendant located in a foreign country like the United Kingdom, which accepts documents in English, whose Central Authority acts promptly in effecting service, and whose policies discourage its residents from waiving formal service, there will be little reason for a plaintiff to send the notice and request under subdivision (d) rather than use convention methods. On the other hand, the procedure offers significant potential benefits to a plaintiff when suing a defendant that, though fluent in English, is located in a country where, as a condition to formal service under a convention, documents must be translated into another language or where formal service will be otherwise costly or time-consuming.

Paragraph (1) is explicit that a timely waiver of service of a summons does not prejudice the right of a defendant to object by means of a motion authorized by Rule 12(b)(2) to the absence of jurisdiction over the defendant's person, or to assert other defenses that may be available. The only issues eliminated are those involving the sufficiency of the summons or the sufficiency of the method by which it is served.

Paragraph (2) states what the present rule implies: the defendant has a duty to avoid costs associated with the service of a summons not needed to inform the defendant regarding the commencement of an action. The text of the rule also sets forth the requirements for a Notice and Request for Waiver sufficient to put the cost-shifting provision in place. These requirements are illustrated in Forms 1A and 1B, which replace the former Form 18-A.

Paragraph (2)(A) is explicit that a request for waiver of service by a corporate defendant must be addressed to a person qualified to receive service. The general mail rooms of large organizations cannot be required to identify the appropriate individual recipient for an institutional summons.

Paragraph (2)(B) permits the use of alternatives to the United States mails in sending the Notice and Request. While private messenger services or electronic communications may be more expensive than the mail, they may be equally reliable and on occasion more convenient to the parties. Especially with respect to transmissions to foreign countries, alternative means may be desirable, for in some countries facsimile transmission is the most efficient and economical means of communication. If electronic means such as facsimile transmission are employed, the sender should maintain a record of the transmission to assure proof of transmission if receipt is denied, but a party receiving such a transmission has a duty to cooperate and cannot avoid liability for the resulting cost of formal service if the transmission is prevented at the point of receipt.

A defendant failing to comply with a request for waiver shall be given an opportunity to show good cause for the failure, but sufficient cause should be rare. It is not a good cause for failure to waive service that the claim is unjust or that the court lacks jurisdiction. Sufficient cause not to shift the cost of service would exist, however, if the defendant did not receive the request or was insufficiently literate in English to understand it. It should be noted that the provisions for shifting the cost of service apply only if the plaintiff and the defendant are both located in the United States, and accordingly a foreign defendant need not show "good cause" for its failure to waive service.

Paragraph (3) extends the time for answer if, before being served with process, the defendant waives formal service. The extension is intended to serve as an inducement to waive service and to assure that a defendant will not gain any delay by declining to waive service and thereby causing the additional time needed to effect service. By waiving service, a defendant is not called upon to respond to the complaint until 60 days from the date the notice was sent to it—90 days if the notice was sent to a foreign country—rather than within the 20 day period from date of service specified in Rule 12.

Paragraph (4) clarifies the effective date of service when service is waived; the provision is needed to resolve an issue arising when applicable law requires service of process to toll the statute of limitations. *E.g., Morse v. Elmira Country Club*, 752 F.2d 35 (2d Cir.1984). *Cf. Walker v. Armco Steel Corp.*, 446 U.S. 740, 100 S. Ct. 1978, 64 L. Ed. 2d 659 (1980).

The provisions in former subdivision (c)(2)(C)(ii) of this rule may have been misleading to some parties. Some plaintiffs, not reading the rule carefully, supposed that receipt by the defendant of the mailed complaint had the effect both of establishing the jurisdiction of the court over the defendant's person and of tolling the statute of limitations in actions in which service of the summons is required to toll the limitations period. The revised rule is clear that, if the waiver is not returned and filed, the limitations period under such a law is not tolled and the action will not otherwise proceed until formal service of process is effected.

Some state limitations laws may toll an otherwise applicable statute at the time when the defendant receives notice of the action. Nevertheless, the device of requested waiver of service is not suitable if a limitations period which is about to expire is not tolled by filing the action. Unless there is ample time, the plaintiff should proceed directly to the formal methods for service identified in subdivisions (e), (f), or (h).

The procedure of requesting waiver of service should also not be used if the time for service under subdivision (m) will expire before the date on which the waiver must be returned. While a plaintiff has been allowed additional time for service in that situation, *e.g., Prather v. Raymond Constr. Co.*, 570 F.Supp. 278 (N.D.Ga.1983), the court could refuse a request for additional time unless the defendant appears to have evaded service pursuant to subdivision (e) or (h). It may be noted that the presumptive time limit for service under subdivision (m) does not apply to service in a foreign country.

Paragraph (5) is a cost-shifting provision retained from the former rule. The costs that may be imposed on the defendant could include, for example, the cost of the time of a process server required to make contact with a defendant residing in a guarded apartment house or residential development. The paragraph is explicit that the costs of enforcing the cost-shifting provision are themselves recoverable from a defendant who fails to return the waiver. In the absence of such a provision, the purpose of the rule would be frustrated by the cost of its enforcement, which is likely to be high in relation to the small benefit secured by the plaintiff.

Some plaintiffs may send a notice and request for waiver and, without waiting for return of the waiver, also proceed with efforts to effect formal service on the defendant. To discourage this practice, the cost-shifting provisions in paragraphs (2) and (5) are limited to costs of effecting service incurred after the time expires for the defendant to return the waiver. Moreover, by returning the waiver within the time allowed and before being served with process, a defendant receives the benefit of the longer period for responding to the complaint afforded for waivers under paragraph (3).

Subdivision (e). This subdivision replaces former subdivisions (c)(2)(C)(i) and (d)(1). It provides a means for service of summons on individuals within a judicial district of the United States. Together with subdivision (f), it provides for service on persons anywhere, subject to constitutional and statutory constraints.

Service of the summons under this subdivision does not conclusively establish the jurisdiction of the court over the person of the defendant. A defendant may assert the territorial limits of the court's reach set forth in subdivision (k), including the constitutional limitations that may be imposed by the Due Process Clause of the Fifth Amendment.

Paragraph (1) authorizes service in any judicial district in conformity with state law. This paragraph sets forth the language of former subdivision (c)(2)(C)(i), which authorized the use of the law of the state in which the district court sits, but adds as an alternative the use of the law of the state in which the service is effected.

Paragraph (2) retains the text of the former subdivision (d)(1) and authorizes the use of the familiar methods of personal or abode service or service on an authorized agent in any judicial district.

To conform to these provisions, the former subdivision (e) bearing on proceedings against parties not found within the state is stricken. Likewise stricken is the first sentence of the former subdivision (f), which had restricted the authority of the federal process server to the state in which the district court sits.

Subdivision (f). This subdivision provides for service on individuals who are in a foreign country, replacing the former subdivision (i) that was added to Rule 4 in 1963. Reflecting the pattern of Rule 4 in incorporating state law limitations on the exercise of jurisdiction over persons, the former subdivision (i) limited service outside the United States to cases in which extraterritorial service was authorized by state or federal law. The new rule eliminates the requirement of explicit authorization. On occasion, service in a foreign country was held to be improper for lack of statutory authority. *E.g., Martens v. Winder*, 341 F.2d 197 (9th Cir.), *cert. denied,* 382 U.S. 937, 86 S. Ct. 391, 15 L. Ed. 2d 349 (1965). This authority, however, was found to exist by implication. *E.g., SEC v. VTR, Inc.*, 39 F.R.D. 19 (S.D.N.Y.1966). Given the substantial increase in the number of international transactions and events that are the subject of litigation in federal courts, it is appropriate to infer a general legislative authority to effect service on defendants in a foreign country.

A secondary effect of this provision for foreign service of a federal summons is to facilitate the use of federal long-arm law in actions brought to enforce the federal law against defendants who cannot be served under any state law but who can be constitutionally subjected to the jurisdiction of the federal court. Such a provision is set forth in paragraph (2) of subdivision (k) of this rule, applicable only to persons not subject to the territorial jurisdiction of any particular state.

Paragraph (1) gives effect to the Hague Convention on the Service Abroad of Judicial and Extrajudicial Documents, which entered into force for the United States on February 10, 1969. See 28 U.S.C.A., Fed.R.Civ.P. 4 (Supp.1986). This Convention is an important means of dealing with problems of service in a foreign country. *See generally* 1 B. Ristau, International Judicial Assistance §§ 4-1-1 to 4-5-2 (1990). Use of the Convention procedures, when available, is mandatory if documents must be transmitted abroad to effect service. *See Volkswagenwerk Aktiengesellschaft v. Schlunk*, 486 U.S. 694, 108 S. Ct. 2104, 100 L. Ed. 2d 722 (1988) (noting that voluntary use of these procedures may be desirable even when service could constitutionally be effected in another manner); J. Weis, *The Federal Rules and the Hague Conventions: Concerns of Conformity and Comity*, 50 U.Pitt.L.Rev. 903 (1989). Therefore, this paragraph provides that, when service is to be effected outside a judicial district of the United States, the methods of service appropriate under an applicable treaty shall be employed if available and if the treaty so requires.

The Hague Convention furnishes safeguards against the abridgment of rights of parties through inadequate notice. Article 15 provides for verification of actual notice or a demonstration that process was served by a method prescribed by the internal laws of the foreign state before a default judgment may be entered. Article 16 of the Convention also enables the judge to extend the time for appeal after judgment if the defendant shows a lack of adequate notice either to defend or to appeal the judgment, or has disclosed a prima facie case on the merits.

The Hague Convention does not specify a time within which a foreign country's Central Authority must effect service, but Article 15 does provide that alternate methods may be used if a Central Authority does not respond within six months. Generally, a Central Authority can be expected to respond much more quickly than that limit might permit, but there have been occasions when the signatory state was dilatory or refused to cooperate for substantive reasons. In such cases, resort may be had to the provision set forth in subdivision (f)(3).

Two minor changes in the text reflect the Hague Convention. First, the term "letter of request" has been added. Although these words are synonymous with "letter rogatory," "letter of request" is preferred in modern usage. The provision should not be interpreted to authorize use of a letter of request when there is in fact no treaty obligation on the receiving country to honor such a request from this country or when the United States does not extend diplomatic recognition to the foreign nation. Second, the passage formerly found in subdivision (i)(1)(B), "when service in either case is reasonably calculated to give actual notice," has been relocated.

Paragraph (2) provides alternative methods for use when internationally agreed methods are not intended to be exclusive, or where there is no international agreement applicable. It contains most of the language formerly set forth in subdivision (i) of the rule. Service by methods that would violate foreign law is not generally authorized. Subparagraphs (A) and (B) prescribe the more appropriate methods for conforming to local practice or using a local authority. Subparagraph (C) prescribes other methods authorized by the former rule.

Paragraph (3) authorizes the court to approve other methods of service not prohibited by international agreements. The Hague Convention, for example, authorizes special forms of service in cases of urgency if convention methods will not permit service within the time required by the circumstances. Other circumstances that might justify the use of additional methods include the failure of the foreign country's Central Authority to effect service within the six-month period provided by the Convention, or the refusal of the Central Authority to serve a complaint seeking punitive damages or to enforce the antitrust laws of the United States. In such cases, the court may direct a special method of service not explicitly authorized by international agreement if not prohibited by the agreement. Inasmuch as our Constitution requires that reasonable notice be given, an earnest effort should be made to devise a method of communication that is consistent with due process and minimizes offense to foreign law. A court may in some instances specially authorize use of ordinary mail. *Cf. Levin v. Ruby Trading Corp.*, 248 F.Supp. 537 (S.D.N.Y.1965).

Subdivision (g). This subdivision retains the text of former subdivision (d)(2). Provision is made for service upon an infant or incompetent person in a foreign country.

Subdivision (h). This subdivision retains the text of former subdivision (d)(3), with changes reflecting those made in subdivision (e). It also contains the provisions for service on a corporation or association in a foreign country, as formerly found in subdivision (i).

Frequent use should be made of the Notice and Request procedure set forth in subdivision (d) in actions against corporations. Care must be taken, however, to address the request to an individual officer or authorized agent of the corporation. It is not effective use of the Notice and Request procedure if the mail is sent undirected to the mail room of the organization.

Subdivision (i). This subdivision retains much of the text of former subdivisions (d)(4) and (d)(5). Paragraph (1) provides for service of a summons on the United States; it amends former subdivision (d)(4) to permit the United States attorney to be served by registered or certified mail. The rule does not authorize the use of the Notice and Request procedure of revised subdivision (d) when the United States is the defendant. To assure proper handling of mail in the United States attorney's office, the authorized mail service must be specifically addressed to the civil process clerk of the office of the United States attorney.

Paragraph (2) replaces former subdivision (d)(5). Paragraph (3) saves the plaintiff from the hazard of losing a substantive right because of failure to comply with the complex requirements of multiple service under this subdivision. That risk has proved to be more than nominal. *E.g., Whale v. United States*, 792 F.2d 951 (9th Cir.1986). This provision should be read in connection with the provisions of subdivision (c) of Rule 15 to preclude the loss of substantive rights against the United States or its agencies, corporations, or officers resulting from a plaintiff's failure to correctly identify and serve all the persons who should be named or served.

Subdivision (j). This subdivision retains the text of former subdivision (d)(6) without material change. The waiver-of-service provision is also inapplicable to actions against governments subject to service pursuant to this subdivision.

The revision adds a new paragraph (1) referring to the statute governing service of a summons on a foreign state and its political subdivisions, agencies, and instrumentalities, the Foreign Sovereign Immunities Act of 1976, 28 U.S.C. § 1608. The caption of the subdivision reflects that change.

Subdivision (k). This subdivision replaces the former subdivision (f), with no change in the title. Paragraph (1) retains the substance of the former rule in explicitly authorizing the exercise of personal jurisdiction over persons who can be reached under state long-arm law, the "100-mile bulge" provision added in 1963, or the federal interpleader act. Paragraph (1)(D) is new, but merely calls attention to federal legislation that may provide for nationwide or even worldwide service of process in cases arising under particular federal laws. Congress has provided for nationwide service of process and full exercise of territorial jurisdiction by all district courts with respect to specified federal actions. *See* 1 R. Casad, Jurisdiction in Civil Actions (2d Ed.) chap. 5 (1991).

Paragraph (2) is new. It authorizes the exercise of territorial jurisdiction over the person of any defendant against whom is made a claim arising under any federal law if that person is subject to personal jurisdiction in no state. This addition is a companion to the amendments made in revised subdivisions (e) and (f).

This paragraph corrects a gap in the enforcement of federal law. Under the former rule, a problem was presented when the defendant was a non-resident of the United States having contacts with the United States sufficient to justify the application of United States law and to satisfy federal standards of forum selection, but having insufficient contact with any single state to support jurisdiction under state long-arm legislation or meet the requirements of the Fourteenth Amendment limitation on state court territorial jurisdiction. In such cases, the defendant was shielded from the enforcement of federal law by the fortuity of a favorable limitation on the power of state courts, which was incorporated into the federal practice by the former rule. In this respect, the revision responds to the suggestion of the Supreme Court made in *Omni Capital Int'l v. Rudolf Wolff & Co., Ltd.*, 484 U.S. 97, 111 (1987).

There remain constitutional limitations on the exercise of territorial jurisdiction by federal courts over persons outside the United States. These restrictions arise from the Fifth Amendment rather than from the Fourteenth Amendment, which limits state-court reach and which was incorporated into federal practice by the reference to state law in the text of the former subdivision (e) that is deleted by this revision. The Fifth Amendment requires that any defendant have affiliating contacts with the United States sufficient to justify the exercise of personal jurisdiction over that party. *Cf. Wells Fargo & Co. v. Wells Fargo Express Co.*, 556 F.2d 406, 418 (9th Cir.1977). There also may be a further Fifth Amendment constraint in that a plaintiff's forum selection might be so inconvenient to a defendant that it would be a denial of "fair play and substantial justice" required by the due process clause, even though the defendant had significant affiliating contacts with the United States. *See DeJames v. Magnificence Carriers*, 654 F.2d 280, 286 n. 3 (3d Cir.), *cert. denied,* 454 U.S. 1085, 102 S. Ct. 642, 70 L. Ed. 2d 620 (1981). Compare *World-Wide Volkswagen Corp. v. Woodson*, 444 U.S. 286, 293–294 (1980); *Insurance Corp. of Ireland v. Compagnie des Bauxites de Guinee*, 456 U.S. 694, 702–03 (1982); *Burger King Corp. v. Rudzewicz*, 471 U.S. 462, 476–78 (1985); *Asahi Metal Indus. v. Superior Court of Cal., Solano County*, 480 U.S. 102, 108–13 (1987). *See generally* R. Lusardi, *Nationwide Service of Process: Due Process Limitations on the Power of the Sovereign*, 33 *Vill.L.Rev.* 1 (1988).

This provision does not affect the operation of federal venue legislation. *See generally* 28 U.S.C. § 1391. Nor does it affect the operation of federal law providing for the change of venue. 28 U.S.C. §§ 1404, 1406. The availability of transfer for fairness and convenience under § 1404 should preclude most conflicts between the full exercise of territorial jurisdiction permitted by this rule and the Fifth Amendment requirement of "fair play and substantial justice."

The district court should be especially scrupulous to protect aliens who reside in a foreign country from forum selections so onerous that injustice could result. "[G]reat care and reserve should be exercised when extending our notions of personal jurisdiction into the international field." *Asahi Metal Indus. v. Superior Court of Cal., Solano County*, 480 U.S. 102, 115 (1987), quoting *United States v. First Nat'l City Bank*, 379 U.S. 378, 404 (1965) (Harlan, J., dissenting).

This narrow extension of the federal reach applies only if a claim is made against the defendant under federal law. It does not establish personal jurisdiction if the only claims are those arising under state law or the law of another country, even though there might be diversity or alienage subject matter jurisdiction as to such claims. If, however, personal jurisdiction is established under this paragraph with respect to a federal claim, then 28 U.S.C. § 1367(a) provides supplemental jurisdiction over related claims against that defendant, subject to the court's discretion to decline exercise of that jurisdiction under 28 U.S.C. § 1367(c).

Subdivision (*l*). This subdivision assembles in one place all the provisions of the present rule bearing on proof of service. No material change in the rule is effected. The provision that proof of service can be amended by leave of court is retained from the former subdivision (h). *See generally* 4A Wright & Miller, *Federal Practice and Procedure* § 1132 (2d ed. 1987).

Subdivision (m). This subdivision retains much of the language of the present subdivision (j).

The new subdivision explicitly provides that the court shall allow additional time if there is good cause for the plaintiff's failure to effect service in the prescribed 120 days, and authorizes the court to relieve a plaintiff of the consequences of an application of this subdivision even if there is no good cause shown. Such relief formerly was afforded in some cases, partly in reliance on Rule 6(b). Relief may be justified, for example, if the applicable statute of limitations would bar the refiled action, or if the defendant is evading service or conceals a defect in attempted service. *E.g., Ditkof v. Owens-Illinois, Inc.*, 114 F.R.D. 104 (E.D.Mich.1987). A specific instance of good cause is set forth in paragraph (3) of this rule, which provides for extensions if necessary to correct oversights in compliance with the requirements of multiple service in actions against the United States or its officers, agencies, and corporations. The district court should also take care to protect *pro se* plaintiffs from consequences of confusion or delay attending the resolution of an *in forma pauperis* petition. *Robinson v. America's Best Contacts & Eyeglasses*, 876 F.2d 596 (7th Cir.1989).

The 1983 revision of this subdivision referred to the "party on whose behalf such service was required," rather than to the "plaintiff," a term used generically elsewhere in this rule to refer to any party initiating a claim against a person who is not a party to the action. To simplify the text, the revision returns to the usual practice in the rule of referring simply to the plaintiff even though its principles apply with equal force to defendants who may assert claims against non-parties under Rules 13(h), 14, 19, 20, or 21.

Subdivision (n). This subdivision provides for in rem and quasi-in-rem jurisdiction. Paragraph (1) incorporates any requirements of 28 U.S.C. § 1655 or similar provisions bearing on seizures or liens.

Paragraph (2) provides for other uses of quasi-in-rem jurisdiction but limits its use to exigent circumstances. Provisional remedies may be employed as a means to secure jurisdiction over the property of a defendant whose person is not within reach of the court, but occasions for the use of this provision should be rare, as where the defendant is a fugitive or assets are in imminent danger of disappearing. Until 1963, it was not possible under Rule 4 to assert jurisdiction in a federal court over the property of a defendant not personally served. The 1963 amendment to subdivision (e) authorized the use of state law procedures authorizing seizures of assets as a basis for jurisdiction. Given the liberal availability of long-arm jurisdiction, the exercise of power quasi-in-rem has become almost an anachronism. Circumstances too spare to affiliate the defendant to the forum state sufficiently to support long-arm jurisdiction over the defendant's person are also inadequate to support seizure of the defendant's assets fortuitously found within the state. *Shaffer v. Heitner*, 433 U.S. 186, 97 S. Ct. 2569, 53 L. Ed. 2d 683 (1977).

2000 AMENDMENT

Paragraph (2)(B) is added to Rule 4(i) to require service on the United States when a United States officer or employee is sued in an individual capacity for acts or omissions occurring in connection with duties performed on behalf of the United States. Decided cases provide uncertain guidance on the question whether the United States must be served in such actions. *See Vaccaro v. Dobre*, 81 F.3d 854, 856–857 (9th Cir.1996); *Armstrong v. Sears*, 33 F.3d 182, 185–187 (2d Cir.1994); *Ecclesiastical Order of the Ism of Am v. Chasin*, 845 F.2d 113, 116

(6th Cir.1988); *Light v. Wolf*, 816 F.2d 746 (D.C.Cir.1987); *see also Simpkins v. District of Columbia*, 108 F.3d 366, 368–369 (D.C.Cir.1997). Service on the United States will help to protect the interest of the individual defendant in securing representation by the United States, and will expedite the process of determining whether the United States will provide representation. It has been understood that the individual defendant must be served as an individual defendant, a requirement that is made explicit. Invocation of the individual service provisions of subdivisions (e), (f), and (g) invokes also the waiver-of-service provisions of subdivision (d).

Paragraph 2(B) reaches service when an officer or employee of the United States is sued in an individual capacity "for acts or omissions occurring in connection with the performance of duties on behalf of the United States." This phrase has been chosen as a functional phrase that can be applied without the occasionally distracting associations of such phrases as "scope of employment," "color of office," or "arising out of the employment." Many actions are brought against individual federal officers or employees of the United States for acts or omissions that have no connection whatever to their governmental roles. There is no reason to require service on the United States in these actions. The connection to federal employment that requires service on the United States must be determined as a practical matter, considering whether the individual defendant has reasonable grounds to look to the United States for assistance and whether the United States has reasonable grounds for demanding formal notice of the action.

An action against a former officer or employee of the United States is covered by paragraph (2)(B) in the same way as an action against a present officer or employee. Termination of the relationship between the individual defendant and the United States does not reduce the need to serve the United States.

Paragraph (3) is amended to ensure that failure to serve the United States in an action governed by paragraph 2(B) does not defeat an action. This protection is adopted because there will be cases in which the plaintiff reasonably fails to appreciate the need to serve the United States. There is no requirement, however, that the plaintiff show that the failure to serve the United States was reasonable. A reasonable time to effect service on the United States must be allowed after the failure is pointed out. An additional change ensures that if the United States or United States attorney is served in an action governed by paragraph 2(A), additional time is to be allowed even though no officer, employee, agency, or corporation of the United States was served.

GAP Report

The most important changes were made to ensure that no one would read the seemingly independent provisions of paragraphs 2(A) and 2(B) to mean that service must be made twice both on the United States and on the United States employee when the employee is sued in both official and individual capacities. The word "only" was added in subparagraph (A) and the new phrase "whether or not the officer or employee is sued also in an individual capacity" was inserted in subparagraph (B).

Minor changes were made to include "Employees" in the catch-line for subdivision (i), and to add "or employee" in paragraph 2(A). Although it may seem awkward to think of suit against an employee in an official capacity, there is no clear definition that separates "officers" from "employees" for this purpose. The published proposal to amend Rule 12(a)(3) referred to actions against an employee sued in an official capacity, and it seemed better to make the rules parallel by adding "employee" to Rule 4(i)(2)(A) than by deleting it from Rule 12(a)(3)(A).

2007 AMENDMENT

The language of Rule 4 has been amended as part of the general restyling of the Civil Rules to make them more easily understood and to make style and terminology consistent throughout the rules. These changes are intended to be stylistic only.

Rule 4(d)(1)(C) corrects an inadvertent error in former Rule 4(d)(2)(G). The defendant needs two copies of the waiver form, not an extra copy of the notice and request.

Rule 4(g) changes "infant" to "minor." "Infant" in the present rule means "minor." Modern word usage suggests that "minor" will better maintain the intended meaning. The same change from "infant" to "minor" is made throughout the rules. In addition, subdivision (f)(3) is added to the description of methods of service that the court may order; the addition ensures the evident intent that the court not order service by means prohibited by international agreement.

Rule 4(i)(4) corrects a misleading reference to "the plaintiff" in former Rule 4(i)(3). A party other than a plaintiff may need a reasonable time to effect service. Rule 4(i)(4) properly covers any party.

Former Rule 4(j)(2) refers to service upon an "other governmental organization subject to suit." This is changed to "any other state-created governmental organization that is subject to suit." The change entrenches the meaning indicated by the caption ("Serving a Foreign, State, or Local Government"), and the invocation of state law. It excludes any risk that this rule might be read to govern service on a federal agency, or other entities not created by state law.

The former provision describing service on interpleader claimants [former (k)(1)(C)] is deleted as redundant in light of the general provision in (k)(1)(C) recognizing personal jurisdiction authorized by a federal statute.

2015 AMENDMENT

Subdivision (d). Abrogation of Rule 84 and the other official forms requires that former Forms 5 and 6 be directly incorporated into Rule 4.

Subdivision (m). The presumptive time for serving a defendant is reduced from 120 days to 90 days. This change, together with the shortened times for issuing a scheduling order set by amended Rule 16(b)(2), will reduce delay at the beginning of litigation.

Shortening the presumptive time for service will increase the frequency of occasions to extend the time for good cause. More time may be needed, for example, when a request to waive service fails, a defendant is difficult to serve, or a marshal is to make service in an in forma pauperis action.

The final sentence is amended to make it clear that the reference to Rule 4 in Rule 71.1(d)(3)(A) does not include Rule 4(m). Dismissal under Rule 4(m) for failure to make timely service would be inconsistent with the limits on dismissal established by Rule 71.1(i)(1)(C).

Shortening the time to serve under Rule 4(m) means that the time of the notice required by Rule 15(c)(1)(C) for relation back is also shortened.

2016 AMENDMENT

Rule 4(m) is amended to correct a possible ambiguity that appears to have generated some confusion in practice. Service in a foreign country often is accomplished by means that require more than the time set by Rule 4(m). This problem is recognized by the two clear exceptions for service on an individual in a foreign country under Rule 4(f) and for service on a foreign state under Rule 4(j)(1). The potential ambiguity arises from the lack of any explicit reference to service on a corporation, partnership, or other unincorporated association. Rule 4(h)(2) provides for service on such defendants at a place outside any judicial district of the United States "in any manner prescribed by Rule 4(f) for serving an individual, except personal delivery under (f)(2)(C)(i)." Invoking service "in the manner prescribed by Rule 4(f)" could easily be read to mean that service under Rule 4(h)(2) is also service "under" Rule 4(f). That interpretation is in keeping with the purpose to recognize the delays that often occur in effecting service in a foreign country. But it also is possible to read the words for what they seem to say—service is under Rule 4(h)(2), albeit in a manner borrowed from almost all, but not quite all, of Rule 4(f).

The amendment resolves this possible ambiguity.

2017 AMENDMENT

This is a technical amendment that integrates the intended effect of the amendments adopted in 2015 and 2016.

HISTORICAL NOTE

Publisher's Note: The Order of the Supreme Court dated April 29, 2015, amended Rule 4(m) to read:

(m) Time Limit for Service. If a defendant is not served within 90 days after the complaint is filed, the court—on motion or on its own after notice to the plaintiff—must dismiss the action without prejudice against that defendant or order that service be made within a specified time. But if the plaintiff shows good cause for the failure, the court must extend the time for service for an appropriate period. This subdivision (m) does not apply to service in a foreign country under Rule 4(f) or 4(j)(1) or to service of a notice under Rule 71.1(d)(3)(A).

According to the note of the Advisory Committee, the 2015 Order intended, in part, to "make it clear that the reference to Rule 4 in Rule 71.1(d)(3)(A) does not include Rule 4(m)."

The Order of the Supreme Court dated April 28, 2016, amended Rule 4(m) to read:

(m) Time Limit for Service. If a defendant is not served within 90 days after the complaint is filed, the court—on motion or on its own after notice to the plaintiff—must dismiss the action without prejudice against that defendant or order that service be made within a specified time. But if the plaintiff shows good cause for the failure, the court must extend the time for service for an appropriate period. This subdivision (m) does not apply to service in a foreign country under Rule 4(f), 4(h)(2), or 4(j)(1).

According to the note of the Advisory Committee, the 2016 Order intended, in part, to resolve a "possible ambiguity" related to Rule 4(h)(2).

Neither the 2016 Order nor the 2016 note of the Advisory Committee referenced the 2015 Order.

For further information, see the letter to Congress from the Committee on Rules of Practice and Procedure of the Judicial Conference of the United States dated August 31, 2016.

Rule 4.1. Service of other Process

1993 ADOPTION

This is a new rule. Its purpose is to separate those few provisions of the former Rule 4 bearing on matters other than service of a summons to allow greater textual clarity in Rule 4. Subdivision (a) contains no new language.

Subdivision (b) replaces the final clause of the penultimate sentence of the former subdivision 4(f), a clause added to the rule in 1963. The new rule provides for nationwide service of orders of civil commitment enforcing decrees of injunctions issued to compel compliance with federal law. The rule makes no change in the practice with respect to the enforcement of injunctions or decrees not involving the enforcement of federally-created rights.

Service of process is not required to notify a party of a decree or injunction, or of an order that the party show cause why that party should not be held in contempt of such an order. With respect to a party who has once been served with a summons, the service of the decree or injunction itself or of an order to show cause can be made pursuant to Rule 5. Thus, for example, an injunction may be served on a party through that person's attorney. *Chagas v. United States*, 369 F.2d 643 (5th Cir.1966). The same is true for service of an order to show cause. *Waffenschmidt v. MacKay*, 763 F.2d 711 (5th Cir.1985).

The new rule does not affect the reach of the court to impose criminal contempt sanctions. Nationwide enforcement of federal decrees and injunctions is already available with respect to criminal contempt: a federal court may effect the arrest of a criminal contemnor anywhere in the United States, 28 U.S.C. § 3041, and a contemnor when arrested may be subject to removal to the district in which punishment may be imposed. Fed.R.Crim.P. 40. Thus, the present law permits criminal contempt enforcement against a contemnor wherever that person may be found.

The effect of the revision is to provide a choice of civil or criminal contempt sanctions in those situations to which it applies. Contempt proceedings, whether civil or criminal, must be brought in the court that was allegedly defied by a contumacious act. *Ex parte Bradley*, 74 U.S. (7 Wall) 364, 19 L.Ed. 214 (1869). This is so even if the offensive conduct or inaction occurred outside the district of the court in which the enforcement proceeding must be conducted. *E.g., McCourtney v. United States*, 291 Fed. 497 (8th Cir.), *cert. denied,* 263 U.S. 714, 44 S. Ct. 134, 68 L.Ed. 520 (1923). For this purpose, the rule as before does not distinguish between parties and other persons subject to contempt sanctions by reason of their relation or connection to parties.

2007 AMENDMENT

The language of Rule 4.1 has been amended as part of the general restyling of the Civil Rules to make them more easily understood and to make style and terminology consistent throughout the rules. These changes are intended to be stylistic only.

Rule 5. Service and Filing of Pleadings and other Papers

1937 ADOPTION

Note to Subdivisions (a) and (b). Compare 2 Minn.Stat. (1927) §§ 9240, 9241, 9242; N.Y.C.P.A. (1937) §§ 163, 164 and N.Y.R.C.P. (1937) Rules 20, 21; 2 Wash.Rev.Stat.Ann. (Remington, 1932) §§ 244 to 249.

Note to Subdivision (d). Compare the present practice under former Equity Rule 12 (Issue of Subpoena—Time for Answer).

1963 AMENDMENT

The words "affected thereby," stricken out by the amendment, introduced a problem of interpretation. See 1 Barron & Holtzoff, Federal Practice & Procedure 760 to 61 (Wright ed. 1960). The amendment eliminates this difficulty and promotes full exchange of information among the parties by requiring service of papers on all the parties to the action, except as otherwise provided in the rules. See also subdivision (c) of Rule 5. So, for example, a third-party defendant is required to serve his answer to the third-party complaint not only upon the defendant but also upon the plaintiff. See amended Form 22-A and the Advisory Committee's Note thereto.

As to the method of serving papers upon a party whose address is unknown, see Rule 5(b).

1970 AMENDMENT

The amendment makes clear that all papers relating to discovery which are required to be served on any party must be served on all parties, unless the court orders otherwise. The present language expressly includes notices and demands, but it is not explicit as to answers or responses as provided in Rules 33, 34, and 36. Discovery papers may be voluminous or the parties numerous, and the court is empowered to vary the requirement if in a given case it proves needlessly onerous.

In actions begun by seizure of property, service will at times have to be made before the absent owner of the property has filed an appearance. For example, a prompt deposition may be needed in a maritime action in rem. See Rules 30(a) and 30(b)(2) and the related notes. A provision is added authorizing service on the person having custody or possession of the property at the time of its seizure.

1980 AMENDMENT

Subdivision (d). By the terms of this rule and Rule 30(f)(1) discovery materials must be promptly filed, although it often happens that no use is made of the materials after they are filed. Because the copies required for filing are an added expense and the large volume of discovery filings presents serious problems of storage in some districts, the Committee in 1978 first proposed that discovery materials not be filed unless on order of the court or for use in the proceedings. But such materials are sometimes of interest to those who may have no access to them except by a requirement of filing, such as members of a class, litigants similarly situated, or the public generally. Accordingly, this amendment and a change in Rule 30(f)(1) continue the requirement of filing but make it subject to an order of the court that discovery materials not be filed unless filing is requested by the court or is effected by parties who wish to use the materials in the proceeding.

1987 AMENDMENT

The amendments are technical. No substantive change is intended.

1991 AMENDMENT

Subdivision (d). This subdivision is amended to require that the person making service under the rule certify that service has been effected. Such a requirement has generally been imposed by local rule.

Having such information on file may be useful for many purposes, including proof of service if an issue arises concerning the effectiveness of the service. The certificate will generally specify the date as well as the manner of service, but parties employing private delivery services may sometimes be unable to specify the date of delivery. In the latter circumstance, a specification of the date of transmission of the paper to the delivery service may be sufficient for the purposes of this rule.

Subdivision (e). The words *"pleading and other"* are stricken as unnecessary. Pleadings are papers within the meaning of the rule. The revision also accommodates the development of the use of facsimile transmission for filing.

Several local district rules have directed the office of the clerk to refuse to accept for filing papers not conforming to certain requirements of form imposed by local rules or practice. This is not a suitable role for the office of the clerk, and the practice exposes litigants to the hazards of time bars; for these reasons, such rules are proscribed by this revision. The enforcement of these rules and of the local rules is a role for a judicial officer. A clerk may of course advise a party or counsel that a particular instrument is not in proper form, and may be directed to so inform the court.

1993 AMENDMENT

This is a technical amendment, using the broader language of Rule 25 of the Federal Rules of Appellate Procedure. The district court—and the bankruptcy court by virtue of a cross-reference in Bankruptcy Rule 7005—can, by local rule, permit filing not only by facsimile transmissions but also by other electronic means, subject to standards approved by the Judicial Conference.

The present Rule 5(e) has authorized filing by facsimile or other electronic means on two conditions. The filing must be authorized by local rule. Use of this means of filing must be authorized by the Judicial Conference of the United States and must be consistent with standards established by the Judicial Conference. Attempts to develop Judicial Conference standards have demonstrated the value of several adjustments in the rule.

The most significant change discards the requirement that the Judicial Conference authorize local electronic filing rules. As before, each district may decide for itself whether it has the equipment and personnel required to establish electronic filing, but a district that wishes to establish electronic filing need no longer await Judicial Conference action.

The role of Judicial Conference standards is clarified by specifying that the standards are to govern technical matters. Technical standards can provide nationwide uniformity, enabling ready use of electronic filing without pausing to adjust for the otherwise inevitable variations among local rules. Judicial Conference adoption of technical standards should prove superior to specification in these rules. Electronic technology has advanced with great speed. The process of adopting Judicial Conference standards should prove speedier and more flexible in determining the time for the first uniform standards, in adjusting standards at appropriate intervals, and in sparing the Supreme Court and

Congress the need to consider technological details. Until Judicial Conference standards are adopted, however, uniformity will occur only to the extent that local rules deliberately seek to copy other local rules.

It is anticipated that Judicial Conference standards will govern such technical specifications as data formatting, speed of transmission, means to transmit copies of supporting documents, and security of communication. Perhaps more important, standards must be established to assure proper maintenance and integrity of the record and to provide appropriate access and retrieval mechanisms. Local rules must address these issues until Judicial Conference standards are adopted.

The amended rule also makes clear the equality of filing by electronic means with written filings. An electronic filing that complies with the local rule satisfies all requirements for filing on paper, signature, or verification. An electronic filing that otherwise satisfies the requirements of 28 U.S.C. s 1746 need not be separately made in writing. Public access to electronic filings is governed by the same rules as govern written filings.

The separate reference to filing by facsimile transmission is deleted. Facsimile transmission continues to be included as an electronic means.

1996 AMENDMENT

The present Rule 5(e) has authorized filing by facsimile or other electronic means on two conditions. The filing must be authorized by local rule. Use of this means of filing must be authorized by the Judicial Conference of the United States and must be consistent with standards established by the Judicial Conference. Attempts to develop Judicial Conference standards have demonstrated the value of several adjustments in the rule.

The most significant change discards the requirement that the Judicial Conference authorize local electronic filing rules. As before, each district may decide for itself whether it has the equipment and personnel required to establish electronic filing, but a district that wishes to establish electronic filing need no longer await Judicial Conference action.

The role of Judicial Conference standards is clarified by specifying that the standards are to govern technical matters. Technical standards can provide nationwide uniformity, enabling ready use of electronic filing without pausing to adjust for the otherwise inevitable variations among local rules. Judicial Conference adoption of technical standards should prove superior to specification in these rules. Electronic technology has advanced with great speed. The process of adopting Judicial Conference standards should prove speedier and more flexible in determining the time for the first uniform standards, in adjusting standards at appropriate intervals, and in sparing the Supreme Court and Congress the need to consider technological details. Until Judicial Conference standards are adopted, however, uniformity will occur only to the extent that local rules deliberately seek to copy other local rules.

It is anticipated that Judicial Conference standards will govern such technical specifications as data formatting, speed of transmission, means to transmit copies of supporting documents, and security of communication. Perhaps more important, standards must be established to assure proper maintenance and integrity of the record and to provide appropriate access and retrieval mechanisms. Local rules must address these issues until Judicial Conference standards are adopted.

The amended rule also makes clear the equality of filing by electronic means with written filings. An electronic filing that complies with the local rule satisfies all requirements for filing on paper, signature, or verification. An electronic filing that otherwise satisfies the requirements of 28 U.S.C. § 1746 need not be separately made in writing. Public access to electronic filings is governed by the same rules as govern written filings.

The separate reference to filing by facsimile transmission is deleted. Facsimile transmission continues to be included as an electronic means.

2000 AMENDMENT

Subdivision (d). Rule 5(d) is amended to provide that disclosures under Rule 26(a)(1) and (2), and discovery requests and responses under Rules 30, 31,

33, 34, and 36 must not be filed until they are used in the action. "Discovery requests" includes deposition notices and "discovery responses" includes objections. The rule supersedes and invalidates local rules that forbid, permit, or require filing of these materials before they are used in the action. The former Rule 26(a)(4) requirement that disclosures under Rule 26(a)(1) and (2) be filed has been removed. Disclosures under Rule 26(a)(3), however, must be promptly filed as provided in Rule 26(a)(3). Filings in connection with Rule 35 examinations, which involve a motion proceeding when the parties do not agree, are unaffected by these amendments.

Recognizing the costs imposed on parties and courts by required filing of discovery materials that are never used in an action, Rule 5(d) was amended in 1980 to authorize court orders that excuse filing. Since then, many districts have adopted local rules that excuse or forbid filing. In 1989 the Judicial Conference Local Rules Project concluded that these local rules were inconsistent with Rule 5(d), but urged the Advisory Committee to consider amending the rule. *Local Rules Project* at 92 (1989). The Judicial Conference of the Ninth Circuit gave the Committee similar advice in 1997. The reality of nonfiling reflected in these local rules has even been assumed in drafting the national rules. In 1993, Rule 30(f)(1) was amended to direct that the officer presiding at a deposition file it with the court or send it to the attorney who arranged for the transcript or recording. The Committee Note explained that this alternative to filing was designed for "courts which direct that depositions not be automatically filed." Rule 30(f)(1) has been amended to conform to this change in Rule 5(d).

Although this amendment is based on widespread experience with local rules, and confirms the results directed by these local rules, it is designed to supersede and invalidate local rules. There is no apparent reason to have different filing rules in different districts. Even if districts vary in present capacities to store filed materials that are not used in an action, there is little reason to continue expending court resources for this purpose. These costs and burdens would likely change as parties make increased use of audio- and videotaped depositions. Equipment to facilitate review and reproduction of such discovery materials may prove costly to acquire, maintain, and operate.

The amended rule provides that discovery materials and disclosures under Rule 26(a)(1) and (a)(2) must not be filed until they are "used in the proceeding." This phrase is meant to refer to proceedings in court. This filing requirement is not triggered by "use" of discovery materials in other discovery activities, such as depositions. In connection with proceedings in court, however, the rule is to be interpreted broadly; any use of discovery materials in court in connection with a motion, a pretrial conference under Rule 16, or otherwise, should be interpreted as use in the proceeding.

Once discovery or disclosure materials are used in the proceeding, the filing requirements of Rule 5(d) should apply to them. But because the filing requirement applies only with regard to materials that are used, only those parts of voluminous materials that are actually used need be filed. Any party would be free to file other pertinent portions of materials that are so used. *See* Fed. R. Evid. 106; *cf.* Rule 32(a)(4). If the parties are unduly sparing in their submissions, the court may order further filings. By local rule, a court could provide appropriate direction regarding the filing of discovery materials, such as depositions, that are used in proceedings.

"Shall" is replaced by "must" under the program to conform amended rules to current style conventions when there is no ambiguity.

GAP Report

The Advisory Committee recommends no changes to either the amendments to Rule 5(d) or the Committee Note as published.

2001 AMENDMENT

Rule 5(b) is restyled.

Rule 5(b)(1) makes it clear that the provision for service on a party's attorney applies only to service made under Rules 5(a) and 77(d). Service under Rules 4,

4.1, 45(b), and 71A(d)(3)—as well as rules that invoke those rules—must be made as provided in those rules.

Subparagraphs (A), (B), and (C) of Rule 5(b)(2) carry forward the method-of-service provisions of former Rule 5(b).

Subparagraph (D) of Rule 5(b)(2) is new. It authorizes service by electronic means or any other means, but only if consent is obtained from the person served. The consent must be express, and cannot be implied from conduct. Early experience with electronic filing as authorized by Rule 5(d) is positive, supporting service by electronic means as well. Consent is required, however, because it is not yet possible to assume universal entry into the world of electronic communication. Subparagraph (D) also authorizes service by nonelectronic means. The Rule 5(b)(2)(B) provision making mail service complete on mailing is extended in subparagraph (D) to make service by electronic means complete on transmission; transmission is effected when the sender does the last act that must be performed by the sender. Service by other agencies is complete on delivery to the designated agency.

Finally, subparagraph (D) authorizes adoption of local rules providing for service through the court. Electronic case filing systems will come to include the capacity to make service by using the court's facilities to transmit all documents filed in the case. It may prove most efficient to establish an environment in which a party can file with the court, making use of the court's transmission facilities to serve the filed paper on all other parties. Transmission might be by such means as direct transmission of the paper, or by transmission of a notice of filing that includes an electronic link for direct access to the paper. Because service is under subparagraph (D), consent must be obtained from the persons served.

Consent to service under Rule 5(b)(2)(D) must be in writing, which can be provided by electronic means. Parties are encouraged to specify the scope and duration of the consent. The specification should include at least the persons to whom service should be made, the appropriate address or location for such service—such as the e-mail address or facsimile machine number, and the format to be used for attachments. A district court may establish a registry or other facility that allows advance consent to service by specified means for future actions.

Rule 6(e) is amended to allow additional time to respond when service is made under Rule 5(b)(2)(D). The additional time does not relieve a party who consents to service under Rule 5(b)(2)(D) of the responsibilities to monitor the facility designated for receiving service and to provide prompt notice of any address change.

Paragraph (3) addresses a question that may arise from a literal reading of the provision that service by electronic means is complete on transmission. Electronic communication is rapidly improving, but lawyers report continuing failures of transmission, particularly with respect to attachments. Ordinarily the risk of non-receipt falls on the person being served, who has consented to this form of service. But the risk should not extend to situations in which the person attempting service learns that the attempted service in fact did not reach the person to be served. Given actual knowledge that the attempt failed, service is not effected. The person attempting service must either try again or show circumstances that justify dispensing with service.

Paragraph (3) does not address the similar questions that may arise when a person attempting service learns that service by means other than electronic means in fact did not reach the person to be served. Case law provides few illustrations of circumstances in which a person attempting service actually knows that the attempt failed but seeks to act as if service had been made. This negative history suggests there is no need to address these problems in Rule 5(b)(3). This silence does not imply any view on these issues, nor on the circumstances that justify various forms of judicial action even though service has not been made.

Changes Made After Publication and Comments

Rule 5(b)(2)(D) was changed to require that consent be "in writing."

Rule 5(b)(3) is new. The published proposal did not address the question of failed service in the text of the rule. Instead, the Committee Note included this statement: "As with other modes of service, however, actual notice that the transmission was not received defeats the presumption of receipt that arises from the provision that service is complete on transmission. The sender must take additional steps to effect service. Service by other agencies is complete on delivery to the designated agency." The addition of paragraph (3) was prompted by consideration of the draft Appellate Rule 25(c) that was prepared for the meeting of the Appellate Rules Advisory Committee. This draft provided: "Service by electronic means is complete on transmission, unless the party making service is notified that the paper was not received." Although Appellate Rule 25(c) is being prepared for publication and comment, while Civil Rule 5(b) has been published and otherwise is ready to recommend for adoption, it seemed desirable to achieve some parallel between the two rules.

The draft Rule 5(b)(3) submitted for consideration by the Advisory Committee covered all means of service except for leaving a copy with the clerk of the court when the person to be served has no known address. It was not limited to electronic service for fear that a provision limited to electronic service might generate unintended negative implications as to service by other means, particularly mail. This concern was strengthened by a small number of opinions that say that service by mail is effective, because complete on mailing, even when the person making service has prompt actual notice that the mail was not delivered. The Advisory Committee voted to limit Rule 5(b)(3) to service by electronic means because this means of service is relatively new, and seems likely to miscarry more frequently than service by post. It was suggested during the Advisory Committee meeting that the question of negative implication could be addressed in the Committee Note. There was little discussion of this possibility. The Committee Note submitted above includes a "no negative implications" paragraph prepared by the Reporter for consideration by the Standing Committee.

The Advisory Committee did not consider at all a question that was framed during the later meeting of the Appellate Rules Advisory Committee. As approved by the Advisory Committee, Rule 5(b)(3) defeats service by electronic means "if the party making service learns that the attempted service did not reach the person to be served." It says nothing about the time relevant to learning of the failure. The omission may seem glaring. Curing the omission, however, requires selection of a time. As revised, proposed Appellate Rule 25(c) requires that the party making service learn of the failure within three calendar days. The Appellate Rules Advisory Committee will have the luxury of public comment and another year to consider the desirability of this short period. If Civil Rule 5(b) is to be recommended for adoption now, no such luxury is available. This issue deserves careful consideration by the Standing Committee.

Several changes are made in the Committee Note. (1) It requires that consent "be express, and cannot be implied from conduct." This addition reflects a more general concern stimulated by a reported ruling that an e-mail address on a firm's letterhead implied consent to email service. (2) The paragraph discussing service through the court's facilities is expanded by describing alternative methods, including an "electronic link." (3) There is a new paragraph that states that the requirement of written consent can be satisfied by electronic means, and that suggests matters that should be addressed by the consent. (4) A paragraph is added to note the additional response time provided by amended Rule 6(e). (5) The final two paragraphs address newly added Rule 5(b)(3). The first explains the rule that electronic service is not effective if the person making service learns that it did not reach the person to be served. The second paragraph seeks to defeat any negative implications that might arise from limiting Rule 5(b)(3) to electronic service, not mail, not other means consented to such as commercial express service, and not service on another person on behalf of the person to be served.

Rule 6(e)

The Advisory Committee recommended that no change be made in Civil Rule 6(e) to reflect the provisions of Civil Rule 5(b)(2)(D) that, with the consent of the person to be served, would allow service by electronic or other means. Absent change, service by these means would not affect the time for acting in response to the paper served. Comment was requested, however, on the alternative that would allow an additional 3 days to respond. The alternative Rule 6(e) amendments are cast in a form that permits ready incorporation in the Bankruptcy Rules. Several of the comments suggest that the added three days should be provided. Electronic transmission is not always instantaneous, and may fail for any of a number of reasons. It may take three days to arrange for transmission in readable form. Providing added time to respond will not discourage people from asking for consent to electronic transmission, and may encourage people to give consent. The more who consent, the quicker will come the improvements that will make electronic service ever more attractive. Consistency with the Bankruptcy Rules will be a good thing, and the Bankruptcy Rules Advisory Committee believes the additional three days should be allowed.

2006 AMENDMENT

Amended Rule 5(e) acknowledges that many courts have required electronic filing by means of a standing order, procedures manual, or local rule. These local practices reflect the advantages that courts and most litigants realize from electronic filing. Courts that mandate electronic filing recognize the need to make exceptions when requiring electronic filing imposes a hardship on a party. Under amended Rule 5(e), a local rule that requires electronic filing must include reasonable exceptions, but Rule 5(e) does not define the scope of those exceptions. Experience with the local rules that have been adopted and that will emerge will aid in drafting new local rules and will facilitate gradual convergence on uniform exceptions, whether in local rules or in an amended Rule 5(e).

2007 AMENDMENT

The language of Rule 5 has been amended as part of the general restyling of the Civil Rules to make them more easily understood and to make style and terminology consistent throughout the rules. These changes are intended to be stylistic only.

Rule 5(a)(1)(E) omits the former reference to a designation of record on appeal. Appellate Rule 10 is a self-contained provision for the record on appeal, and provides for service.

Former Rule 5(b)(2)(D) literally provided that a local rule may authorize use of the court's transmission facilities to make service by non-electronic means agreed to by the parties. That was not intended. Rule 5(b)(3) restores the intended meaning—court transmission facilities can be used only for service by electronic means.

Rule 5(d)(2)(B) provides that "a" judge may accept a paper for filing, replacing the reference in former Rule 5(e) to "the" judge. Some courts do not assign a designated judge to each case, and it may be important to have another judge accept a paper for filing even when a case is on the individual docket of a particular judge. The ministerial acts of accepting the paper, noting the time, and transmitting the paper to the court clerk do not interfere with the assigned judge's authority over the action.

2018 AMENDMENT

Subdivision (b). Rule 5(b) is amended to revise the provisions for electronic service. Provision for electronic service was first made when electronic communication was not as widespread or as fully reliable as it is now. Consent of the person served to receive service by electronic means was required as a safeguard. Those concerns have substantially diminished, but have not disappeared entirely, particularly as to persons proceeding without an attorney.

The amended rule recognizes electronic service through the court's transmission facilities as to any registered user. A court may choose to allow registration only with the court's permission. But a party who registers will be subject to service through the court's facilities unless the court provides otherwise. With the consent of the person served, electronic service also may be made by means that do not utilize the court's facilities. Consent can be limited to service at a prescribed address or in a specified form, and may be limited by other conditions.

Service is complete when a person files the paper with the court's electronic-filing system for transmission to a registered user, or when one person sends it to another person by other electronic means that the other person has consented to in writing. But service is not effective if the person who filed with the court or the person who sent by other agreed-upon electronic means learns that the paper did not reach the person to be served. The rule does not make the court responsible for notifying a person who filed the paper with the court's electronic-filing system that an attempted transmission by the court's system failed. But a filer who learns that the transmission failed is responsible for making effective service.

Because Rule 5(b)(2)(E) now authorizes service through the court's facilities as a uniform national practice, Rule 5(b)(3) is abrogated. It is no longer necessary to rely on local rules to authorize such service.

Subdivision (d). Rule 5(d)(1) has provided that any paper after the complaint that is required to be served "must be filed within a reasonable time after service." Because "within" might be read as barring filing before the paper is served, "no later than" is substituted to ensure that it is proper to file a paper before it is served.

Under amended Rule 5(d)(1)(B), a certificate of service is not required when a paper is served by filing it with the court's electronic-filing system. When service is not made by filing with the court's electronic-filing system, a certificate of service must be filed with the paper or within a reasonable time after service, and should specify the date as well as the manner of service. For papers that are required to be served but must not be filed until they are used in the proceeding or the court orders filing, the certificate need not be filed until the paper is filed, unless filing is required by local rule or court order.

Amended Rule 5(d)(3) recognizes increased reliance on electronic filing. Most districts have adopted local rules that require electronic filing, and allow reasonable exceptions as required by the former rule. The time has come to seize the advantages of electronic filing by making it generally mandatory in all districts for a person represented by an attorney. But exceptions continue to be available. Nonelectronic filing must be allowed for good cause. And a local rule may allow or require nonelectronic filing for other reasons.

Filings by a person proceeding without an attorney are treated separately. It is not yet possible to rely on an assumption that pro se litigants are generally able to seize the advantages of electronic filing. Encounters with the court's system may prove overwhelming to some. Attempts to work within the system may generate substantial burdens on a pro se party, on other parties, and on the court. Rather than mandate electronic filing, filing by pro se litigants is left for governing by local rules or court order. Efficiently handled electronic filing works to the advantage of all parties and the court. Many courts now allow electronic filing by pro se litigants with the court's permission. Such approaches may expand with growing experience in the courts, along with the greater availability of the systems required for electronic filing and the increasing familiarity of most people with electronic communication. Room is also left for a court to require electronic filing by a pro se litigant by court order or by local rule. Care should be taken to ensure that an order to file electronically does not impede access to the court, and reasonable exceptions must be included in a local rule that requires electronic filing by a pro se litigant. In the beginning, this authority is likely to be exercised only to support special programs, such as one requiring e-filing in collateral proceedings by state prisoners.

A filing made through a person's electronic-filing account and authorized by that person, together with that person's name on a signature block, constitutes the person's signature.

Rule 5.1. Constitutional Challenge to a Statute—Notice, Certification, and Intervention

2006 ADOPTION

Rule 5.1 implements 28 U.S.C. § 2403, replacing the final three sentences of Rule 24(c). New Rule 5.1 requires a party that files a pleading, written motion, or other paper drawing in question the constitutionality of a federal or state statute to file a notice of constitutional question and serve it on the United States Attorney General or state attorney general. The party must promptly file and serve the notice of constitutional question. This notice requirement supplements the court's duty to certify a constitutional challenge to the United States Attorney General or state attorney general. The notice of constitutional question will ensure that the attorney general is notified of constitutional challenges and has an opportunity to exercise the statutory right to intervene at the earliest possible point in the litigation. The court's certification obligation remains, and is the only notice when the constitutionality of a federal or state statute is drawn in question by means other than a party's pleading, written motion, or other paper.

Moving the notice and certification provisions from Rule 24(c) to a new rule is designed to attract the parties' attention to these provisions by locating them in the vicinity of the rules that require notice by service and pleading.

Rule 5.1 goes beyond the requirements of § 2403 and the former Rule 24(c) provisions by requiring notice and certification of a constitutional challenge to any federal or state statute, not only those "affecting the public interest." It is better to assure, through notice, that the attorney general is able to determine whether to seek intervention on the ground that the act or statute affects a public interest. Rule 5.1 refers to a "federal statute," rather than the § 2403 reference to an "Act of Congress," to maintain consistency in the Civil Rules vocabulary. In Rule 5.1 "statute" means any congressional enactment that would qualify as an "Act of Congress."

Unless the court sets a later time, the 60-day period for intervention runs from the time a party files a notice of constitutional question or from the time the court certifies a constitutional challenge, whichever is earlier. Rule 5.1(a) directs that a party promptly serve the notice of constitutional question. The court may extend the 60-period on its own or on motion. One occasion for extension may arise if the court certifies a challenge under § 2403 after a party files a notice of constitutional question. Pretrial activities may continue without interruption during the intervention period, and the court retains authority to grant interlocutory relief. The court may reject a constitutional challenge to a statute at any time. But the court may not enter a final judgment holding a statute unconstitutional before the attorney general has responded or the intervention period has expired without response. This rule does not displace any of the statutory or rule procedures that permit dismissal of all or part of an action—including a constitutional challenge—at any time, even before service of process.

2007 AMENDMENT

The language of Rule 5.1 has been amended as part of the general restyling of the Civil Rules to make them more easily understood and to make style and terminology consistent throughout the rules. These changes are intended to be stylistic only.

Rule 5.2. Privacy Protection for Filings Made with the Court

2007 Adoption

The rule is adopted in compliance with section 205(c)(3) of the E-Government Act of 2002, Public Law 107-347. Section 205(c)(3) requires the Supreme Court to prescribe rules "to protect privacy and security concerns relating to electronic filing of documents and the public availability . . . of documents filed electronically." The rule goes further than the E-Government Act in regulating paper filings even when they are not converted to electronic form. But the number of filings that remain in paper form is certain to diminish over time. Most districts scan paper filings into the electronic case file, where they become available to the public in the same way as documents initially filed in electronic form. It is electronic availability, not the form of the initial filing, that raises the privacy and security concerns addressed in the E-Government Act.

The rule is derived from and implements the policy adopted by the Judicial Conference in September 2001 to address the privacy concerns resulting from public access to electronic case files. See http://www.privacy.uscourts.gov/Policy.htm. The Judicial Conference policy is that documents in case files generally should be made available electronically to the same extent they are available at the courthouse, provided that certain "personal data identifiers" are not included in the public file.

While providing for the public filing of some information, such as the last four digits of an account number, the rule does not intend to establish a presumption that this information never could or should be protected. For example, it may well be necessary in individual cases to prevent remote access by nonparties to any part of an account number or social security number. It may also be necessary to protect information not covered by the redaction requirement—such as driver's license numbers and alien registration numbers—in a particular case. In such cases, protection may be sought under subdivision (d) or (e). Moreover, the Rule does not affect the protection available under other rules, such as Civil Rules 16 and 26(c), or under other sources of protective authority.

Parties must remember that any personal information not otherwise protected by sealing or redaction will be made available over the internet. Counsel should notify clients of this fact so that an informed decision may be made on what information is to be included in a document filed with the court.

The clerk is not required to review documents filed with the court for compliance with this rule. The responsibility to redact filings rests with counsel and the party or non-party making the filing.

Subdivision (c) provides for limited public access in Social Security cases and immigration cases. Those actions are entitled to special treatment due to the prevalence of sensitive information and the volume of filings. Remote electronic access by nonparties is limited to the docket and the written dispositions of the court unless the court orders otherwise. The rule contemplates, however, that nonparties can obtain full access to the case file at the courthouse, including access through the court's public computer terminal.

Subdivision (d) reflects the interplay between redaction and filing under seal. It does not limit or expand the judicially developed rules that govern sealing. But it does reflect the possibility that redaction may provide an alternative to sealing.

Subdivision (e) provides that the court can by order in a particular case for good cause require more extensive redaction than otherwise required by the Rule. Nothing in this subdivision is intended to affect the limitations on sealing that are otherwise applicable to the court.

Subdivision (f) allows a person who makes a redacted filing to file an unredacted document under seal. This provision is derived from section 205(c)(3)(iv) of the E-Government Act.

Subdivision (g) allows the option to file a register of redacted information. This provision is derived from section 205(c)(3)(v) of the E-Government Act, as amended in 2004. In accordance with the E-Government Act, subdivision (g) refers to "redacted" information. The term "redacted" is intended to govern a filing that is prepared with abbreviated identifiers in the first instance, as well as a filing in which a personal identifier is edited after its preparation.

Subdivision (h) allows a person to waive the protections of the rule as to that person's own personal information by filing it unsealed and in unredacted form. One may wish to waive the protection if it is determined that the costs of redaction outweigh the benefits to privacy. If a person files an unredacted identifier by mistake, that person may seek relief from the court.

Trial exhibits are subject to the redaction requirements of Rule 5.2 to the extent they are filed with the court. Trial exhibits that are not initially filed with the court must be redacted in accordance with the rule if and when they are filed as part of an appeal or for other reasons.

Rule 6. Time

1937 ADOPTION

Note to Subdivisions (a) and (b). These are amplifications along lines common in state practices, of former Equity Rule 80 (Computation of Time—Sundays and Holidays) and of the provisions for enlargement of time found in former Equity Rules 8 (Enforcement of Final Decrees) and 16 (Defendant to Answer—Default—Decree Pro Confesso). See also Rule XIII, Rules and Forms in Criminal Cases, 1934, 292 U.S. 661, 666. Compare Ala.Code Ann. (Michie, 1928) § 13 and former Law Rule 8 of the Rules of the Supreme Court of the District of Columbia (1924), superseded in 1929 by Law Rule 8, Rules of the District Court of the United States for the District of Columbia (1937).

Note to Subdivision (c). This eliminates the difficulties caused by the expiration of terms of court. Such statutes as U.S.C., Title 28, former § 12 (Trials not discontinued by new term) are not affected. Compare Rules of the United States District Court of Minnesota, Rule 25 (Minn.Stat. (Mason, Supp. 1936), p. 1089).

Note to Subdivision (d). Compare 2 Minn.Stat. (Mason, 1927) § 9246; N.Y.R.C.P. (1937) Rules 60 and 64.

1946 AMENDMENT

Note to Subdivision (b). The purpose of the amendment is to clarify the finality of judgments. Prior to the advent of the Federal Rules of Civil Procedure, the general rule that a court loses jurisdiction to disturb its judgments, upon the expiration of the term at which they were entered, had long been the classic device which (together with the statutory limits on the time for appeal) gave finality to judgments. See note to Rule 73(a). Rule 6(c) abrogates that limit on judicial power. That limit was open to many objections, one of them being inequality of operation because, under it, the time for vacating a judgment rendered early in a term was much longer than for a judgment rendered near the end of the term.

The question to be met under Rule 6(b) is: how far should the desire to allow correction of judgments be allowed to postpone their finality? The rules contain a number of provisions permitting the vacation or modification of judgments on various grounds. Each of these rules contains express time limits on the motions for granting of relief. Rule 6(b) is a rule of general application giving wide discretion to the court to enlarge these time limits or revive them after they have expired, the only exceptions stated in the original rule being a prohibition against enlarging the time specified in Rule 59(b) and (d) for making motions for or granting new trials, and a prohibition against enlarging the time fixed by law for taking an appeal. It should also be noted that Rule 6(b) itself contains no limitation of time within which the court may exercise its discretion, and since the expiration of the term does not end its power, there is now no time limit on the exercise of its discretion under Rule 6(b).

Decisions of lower federal courts suggest that some of the rules containing time limits which may be set aside under Rule 6(b) are Rules 25, 50(b), 52(b), 60(b), and 73(g).

In a number of cases the effect of Rule 6(b) on the time limitations of these rules has been considered. Certainly the rule is susceptible of the interpretation that the court is given the power in its discretion to relieve a party from failure to act within the times specified in any of these other rules, with only the exceptions stated in Rule 6(b), and in some cases the rule has been so construed.

With regard to Rule 25(a) for substitution, it was held in *Anderson v. Brady, E.D.Ky.1941*, 1 F.R.D. 589, 4 Fed.Rules Service 25a.1, Case 1, and in *Anderson v. Yungkau, C.C.A.6, 1946*, 153 F.2d 685, certiorari granted 328 U.S. 829, 66 S.

Ct. 1025, 90 L.Ed. 1606, that under Rule 6(b) the court had no authority to allow substitution of parties after the expiration of the limit fixed in Rule 25(a).

As to Rules 50(b) for judgments notwithstanding the verdict and 52(b) for amendment of findings and vacation of judgment, it was recognized in *Leishman v. Associated Wholesale Electric Co., 1943*, 318 U.S. 203, 63 S. Ct. 543, 87 L.Ed. 714, that Rule 6(b) allowed the district court to enlarge the time to make a motion for amended findings and judgment beyond the limit expressly fixed in Rule 52(b). See Coca-Cola v. Busch, E.D.Pa.1943, 7 Fed.Rules Service, 59b.2, Case 4. Obviously, if the time limit in Rule 52(b) could be set aside under rule 6(b), the time limit in Rule 50(b) for granting judgment notwithstanding the verdict (and thus vacating the judgment entered "forthwith" on the verdict) likewise could be set aside.

As to Rule 59 on motions for a new trial, it has been settled that the time limits in Rule 59(b) and (d) for making motions for or granting new trial could not be set aside under Rule 6(b), because Rule 6(b) expressly refers to Rule 59, and forbids it. See *Safeway Stores, Inc. v. Coe, 1943*, 136 F.2d 771, 78 U.S.App. D.C. 19; *Jusino v. Morales & Tio, C.C.A.1, 1944*, 139 F.2d 946; Coca-Cola Co. v. Busch, E.D.Pa.1942, 7 Fed.Rules Service 59b.2, Case 4; *Petersen v. Chicago, Great Western Ry. Co., D.Neb.1943*, 3 F.R.D. 346, 7 Fed.Rules Service 59b.2, Case 1; *Leishman v. Associated Wholesale Electric Co., 1943*, 318 U.S. 203, 63 S. Ct. 543, 87 L.Ed. 714.

As to Rule 60(b) for relief from a judgment, it was held in *Schram v. O'Connor, E.D.Mich.1941, 5 Fed.Rules Serv. 6b.31, Case 1*, 2 F.R.D. 192, s.c., 5 Fed.Rules Serv. 6b.31, Case 2, 2 F.R.D. 192, that the six-months time limit in original Rule 60(b) for making a motion for relief from a judgment for surprise, mistake, or excusable neglect could be set aside under Rule 6(b). The contrary result was reached in *Wallace v. United States, C.C.A.2, 1944*, 142 F.2d 240, certiorari denied 323 U.S. 712, 65 S. Ct. 37, 89 L.Ed. 573; *Reed v. South Atlantic Steamship Co. of Del., D.Del.1942*, 2 F.R.D. 475, 6 Fed.Rules Serv. 60b.31, Case 1.

As to Rule 73(g), fixing the time for docketing an appeal, it was held in *Ainsworth v. Gill Glass & Fixture Co., C.C.A.3, 1939*, 104 F.2d 83, that under Rule 6(b) the district court, upon motion made after the expiration of the forty-day period, stated in Rule 73(g), but before the expiration of the ninety-day period therein specified, could permit the docketing of the appeal on a showing of excusable neglect. The contrary was held in *Mutual Benefit Health & Accident Ass'n v. Snyder, C.C.A.6, 1940*, 109 F.2d 469 and in *Burke v. Canfield, 1940*, 111 F.2d 526, 72 App.D.C. 127.

The amendment of Rule 6(b) now proposed is based on the view that there should be a definite point where it can be said a judgment is final; that the right method of dealing with the problem is to list in Rule 6(b) the various other rules whose time limits may not be set aside, and then, if the time limit in any of those other rules is too short, to amend that other rule to give a longer time. The further argument is that rule 6(c) abolished the long standing device to produce finality in judgments through expiration of the term, and since that limitation on the jurisdiction of courts to set aside their own judgments has been removed by rule 6(c), some other limitation must be substituted or judgments never can be said to be final.

In this connection reference is made to the established rule that if a motion for new trial is seasonably made, the mere making or pendency of the motion destroys the finality of the judgment, and even though the motion is ultimately denied, the full time for appeal starts anew from the date of denial. Also, a motion to amend the findings under Rule 52(b) has the same effect on the time for appeal. *Leishman v. Associated Wholesale Electric Co., 1943*, 318 U.S. 203, 63 S. Ct. 543, 87 L.Ed. 714. By the same reasoning a motion for judgment under Rule 50(b), involving as it does the vacation of a judgment entered "forthwith" on the verdict (Rule 58), operates to postpone, until an order is made, the running of the time for appeal. The Committee believes that the abolition by Rule 6(c) of the old rule that a court's power over its judgments ends with the term, requires a substitute limitation, and that unless Rule 6(b) is amended to prevent enlargement of the times specified in Rules 50(b), 52(b) and 60(b), and the limitation as to Rule 59(b) and (d) is retained, no one can say when a judgment is final. This is also true with regard to proposed Rule 59(e), which authorizes a motion to alter or amend a judgment, hence that rule is also included in the enumeration in amended Rule 6(b). In consideration of the amendment, however, it should be noted that Rule 60(b) is also to be amended so as to lengthen the six-months period originally prescribed in that rule to one year.

As to Rule 25 on substitution, while finality is not involved, the limit there fixed should be controlling. That rule, as amended, gives the court power, upon showing of a reasonable excuse, to permit substitution after the expiration of the two-year period.

As to Rule 73(g), it is believed that the conflict in decisions should be resolved and not left to further litigation, and that the rule should be listed as one whose limitation may not be set aside under Rule 6(b).

As to Rule 59(c), fixing the time for serving affidavits on motion for new trial, it is believed that the court should have authority under Rule 6(b) to enlarge the time, because, once the motion for new trial is made the judgment no longer has finality, and the extension of time for affidavits thus does not of itself disturb finality.

Other changes proposed in Rule 6(b) are merely clarifying and conforming. Thus "request" is substituted for "application" in clause (1) because an application is defined as a motion under Rule 7(b). The phrase "extend the time" is substituted for "enlarge the period" because the former is a more suitable expression and relates more clearly to both clauses (1) and (2). The final phrase in Rule 6(b), "or the period for taking an appeal as provided by law", is deleted and a reference to Rule 73(a) inserted, since it is proposed to state in that rule the time for appeal to a circuit court of appeals, which is the only appeal governed by the Federal Rules, and allows an extension of time. See Rule 72.

Subdivision (c). The purpose of this amendment is to prevent reliance upon the continued existence of a term as a source of power to disturb the finality of a judgment upon grounds other than those stated in these rules. See *Hill v. Hawes, 1944*, 320 U.S. 520, 64 S. Ct. 334, 88 L.Ed. 283; *Boaz v. Mutual Life Ins. Co. of New York, C.C.A.8, 1944*, 146 F.2d 321; *Bucy v. Nevada Construction Co., C.C.A.9, 1942*, 125 F.2d 213.

1963 AMENDMENT

Subdivision (a). This amendment is related to the amendment of Rule 77(c) changing the regulation of the days on which the clerk's office shall be open.

The wording of the first sentence of Rule 6(a) is clarified and the subdivision is made expressly applicable to computing periods of time set forth in local rules.

Saturday is to be treated in the same way as Sunday or a "legal holiday" in that it is not to be included when it falls on the last day of a computed period, nor counted as an intermediate day when the period is less than 7 days. "Legal holiday" is defined for purposes of this subdivision and amended Rule 77(c). Compare the definition of "holiday" in 11 U.S.C. § 1(18); also 5 U.S.C. § 86a; Executive Order No. 10358, "Observance of Holidays," June 9, 1952, 17 Fed.Reg. 5269. In the light of these changes the last sentence of the present subdivision, dealing with half holidays, is eliminated.

With Saturdays and State holidays made "dies non" in certain cases by the amended subdivision, computation of the usual 5-day notice of motion or the 2-day notice to dissolve or modify a temporary restraining order may work out so as to cause embarrassing delay in urgent cases. The delay can be obviated by applying to the court to shorten the time, see Rules 6(d) and 65(b).

Subdivision (b). The prohibition against extending the time for taking action under Rule 25 (Substitution of parties) is eliminated. The only limitation of time provided for in amended Rule 25 is the 90-day period following a suggestion upon the record of the death of a party within which to make a motion to substitute the proper parties for the deceased party. See Rule 25(a)(1), as amended, and the Advisory Committee's Note thereto. It is intended that the court shall have discretion to enlarge that period.

1966 AMENDMENT

P.L. 88-139, § 1, 77 Stat. 248, approved on October 16, 1963, amended 28 U.S.C. § 138 to read as follows: "The district court shall not hold formal terms." Thus Rule 6(c) is rendered unnecessary, and it is rescinded.

1967 AMENDMENT

The amendment eliminates the references to Rule 73, which is to be abrogated.

1971 AMENDMENT

The amendment adds Columbus Day to the list of legal holidays to conform the subdivision to the Act of June 28, 1968, 82 Stat. 250, which constituted Columbus Day a legal holiday effective after January 1, 1971.

The Act, which amended Title 5, U.S.C. § 6103(a), changes the day on which certain holidays are to be observed. Washington's Birthday, Memorial Day and Veterans Day are to be observed on the third Monday in February, the last Monday in May and the fourth Monday in October, respectively, rather than, as heretofore, on February 22, May 30, and November 11, respectively, Columbus Day is to be observed on the second Monday in October. New Year's Day, Independence Day, Thanksgiving Day and Christmas continue to be observed on the traditional days.

1983 AMENDMENT

Subdivision (b). The amendment confers finality upon the judgments of magistrates by foreclosing enlargement of the time for appeal except as provided in new Rule 74(a)(20 day period for demonstration of excusable neglect).

1985 AMENDMENT

Rule 6(a) is amended to acknowledge that weather conditions or other events may render the clerk's office inaccessible one or more days. Parties who are obliged to file something with the court during that period should not be penalized if they cannot do so. The amendment conforms to changes made in Federal Rule of Criminal Procedure 45(a), effective August 1, 1982.

The Rule also is amended to extend the exclusion of intermediate Saturdays, Sundays, and legal holidays to the computation of time periods less than 11 days. Under the current version of the Rule, parties bringing motions under rules with 10-day periods could have as few as 5 working days to prepare their motions. This hardship would be especially acute in the case of Rules 50(b) and (c)(2), 52(b), and 59(b), (d), and (e), which may not be enlarged at the discretion of the court. See Rule 6(b). If the exclusion of Saturdays, Sundays, and legal holidays will operate to cause excessive delay in urgent cases, the delay can be obviated by applying to the court to shorten the time. See Rule 6(b).

The Birthday of Martin Luther King, Jr., which becomes a legal holiday effective in 1986, has been added to the list of legal holidays enumerated in the Rule.

1987 AMENDMENT

The amendments are technical. No substantive change is intended.

1999 AMENDMENT

The reference to Rule 74(a) is stricken from the catalogue of time periods that cannot be extended by the district court. The change reflects the 1997 abrogation of Rule 74(a).

2001 AMENDMENT

The additional three days provided by Rule 6(e) is extended to the means of service authorized by the new paragraph (D) added to Rule 5(b), including—with the consent of the person served—service by electronic or other means. The three-day addition is provided as well for service on a person with no known address by leaving a copy with the clerk of the court.

2005 AMENDMENT

Rule 6(e) is amended to remove any doubt as to the method for extending the time to respond after service by mail, leaving with the clerk of court, electronic means, or other means consented to by the party served. Three days are added after the prescribed period otherwise expires under Rule 6(a). Intermediate Saturdays, Sundays, and legal holidays are included in counting these added three days.

If the third day is a Saturday, Sunday, or legal holiday, the last day to act is the next day that is not a Saturday, Sunday, or legal holiday. The effect of invoking the day when the prescribed period would otherwise expire under Rule 6(a) can be illustrated by assuming that the thirtieth day of a thirty-day period is a Saturday. Under Rule 6(a) the period expires on the next day that is not a Sunday or legal holiday. If the following Monday is a legal holiday, under Rule 6(a) the period expires on Tuesday. Three days are then added—Wednesday, Thursday, and Friday as the third and final day to act. If the period prescribed expires on a Friday, the three added days are Saturday, Sunday, and Monday, which is the third and final day to act unless it is a legal holiday. If Monday is a legal holiday, the next day that is not a legal holiday is the third and final day to act.

Application of Rule 6(e) to a period that is less than eleven days can be illustrated by a paper that is served by mailing on a Friday. If ten days are allowed to respond, intermediate Saturdays, Sundays, and legal holidays are excluded in determining when the period expires under Rule 6(a). If there is no legal holiday, the period expires on the Friday two weeks after the paper was mailed. The three added Rule 6(e) days are Saturday, Sunday, and Monday, which is the third and final day to act unless it is a legal holiday. If Monday is a legal holiday, the next day that is not a legal holiday is the final day to act.

2007 AMENDMENT

The language of Rule 6 has been amended as part of the general restyling of the Civil Rules to make them more easily understood and to make style and terminology consistent throughout the rules. These changes are intended to be stylistic only.

2009 AMENDMENT

Subdivision (a). Subdivision (a) has been amended to simplify and clarify the provisions that describe how deadlines are computed. Subdivision (a) governs the computation of any time period found in these rules, in any local rule or court order, or in any statute that does not specify a method of computing time. In accordance with Rule 83(a)(1), a local rule may not direct that a deadline be computed in a manner inconsistent with subdivision (a).

The time-computation provisions of subdivision (a) apply only when a time period must be computed. They do not apply when a fixed time to act is set. The amendments thus carry forward the approach taken in *Violette v. P.A. Days, Inc.*, 427 F.3d 1015, 1016 (6th Cir. 2005) (holding that Civil Rule 6(a) "does not apply to situations where the court has established a specific calendar day as a deadline"), and reject the contrary holding of *In re American Healthcare Management, Inc.*, 900 F.2d 827, 832 (5th Cir. 1990) (holding that Bankruptcy Rule 9006(a) governs treatment of date certain deadline set by court order). If, for example, the date for filing is "no later than November 1, 2007," subdivision (a) does not govern. But if a filing is required to be made "within 10 days" or "within 72 hours," subdivision (a) describes how that deadline is computed.

Subdivision (a) does not apply when computing a time period set by a statute if the statute specifies a method of computing time. *See, e.g.*, 2 U.S.C. § 394 (specifying method for computing time periods prescribed by certain statutory provisions relating to contested elections to the House of Representatives).

Subdivision (a)(1). New subdivision (a)(1) addresses the computation of time periods that are stated in days. It also applies to time periods that are stated in weeks, months, or years. *See, e.g.*, Rule 60(c)(1). Subdivision (a)(1)(B)'s directive to "count every day" is relevant only if the period is stated in days (not weeks, months or years).

Under former Rule 6(a), a period of 11 days or more was computed differently than a period of less than 11 days. Intermediate Saturdays, Sundays, and legal holidays were included in computing the longer periods, but excluded in computing the shorter periods. Former Rule 6(a) thus made computing deadlines unnecessarily complicated and led to counterintuitive results. For example, a 10-day period and a 14-day period that started on the same day usually ended on the same day — and the 10-day period not infrequently ended later than the 14-day period. See *Miltimore Sales, Inc. v. Int'l Rectifier, Inc.*, 412 F.3d 685, 686 (6th Cir. 2005).

Under new subdivision (a)(1), all deadlines stated in days (no matter the length) are computed in the same way. The day of the event that triggers the deadline is not counted. All other days — including intermediate Saturdays, Sundays, and legal holidays — are counted, with only one exception: If the period ends on a Saturday, Sunday, or legal holiday, then the deadline falls on the next day that is not a Saturday, Sunday, or legal holiday. An illustration is provided below in the discussion of subdivision (a)(5). Subdivision (a)(3) addresses filing deadlines that expire on a day when the clerk's office is inaccessible.

Where subdivision (a) formerly referred to the "act, event, or default" that triggers the deadline, new subdivision (a) refers simply to the "event" that triggers the deadline; this change in terminology is adopted for brevity and simplicity, and is not intended to change meaning.

Periods previously expressed as less than 11 days will be shortened as a practical matter by the decision to count intermediate Saturdays, Sundays, and legal holidays in computing all periods. Many of those periods have been lengthened to compensate for the change. *See, e.g.*, Rule 14(a)(1).

Most of the 10 day periods were adjusted to meet the change in computation method by setting 14 days as the new period. A 14 day period corresponds to the most frequent result of a 10 day period under the former computation method — two Saturdays and two Sundays were excluded, giving 14 days in all. A 14 day period has an additional advantage. The final day falls on the same day of the week as the event that triggered the period — the 14th day after a Monday, for example, is a Monday. This advantage of using week long periods led to adopting 7 day periods to replace some of the periods set at less than 10 days, and 21 day periods to replace 20 day periods. Thirty day and longer periods, however, were generally retained without change.

Subdivision (a)(2). New subdivision (a)(2) addresses the computation of time periods that are stated in hours. No such deadline currently appears in the Federal Rules of Civil Procedure. But some statutes contain deadlines stated in hours, as do some court orders issued in expedited proceedings.

Under subdivision (a)(2), a deadline stated in hours starts to run immediately on the occurrence of the event that triggers the deadline. The deadline generally ends when the time expires. If, however, the time period expires at a specific time (say, 2:17 p.m.) on a Saturday, Sunday, or legal holiday, then the deadline is extended to the same time (2:17 p.m.) on the next day that is not a Saturday, Sunday, or legal holiday. Periods stated in hours are not to be "rounded up" to the next whole hour. Subdivision (a)(3) addresses situations when the clerk's office is inaccessible during the last hour before a filing deadline expires.

Subdivision (a)(2)(B) directs that every hour be counted. Thus, for example, a 72-hour period that commences at 10:23 a.m. on Friday, November 2, 2007, will run until 9:23 a.m. on Monday, November 5; the discrepancy in start and end times in this example results from the intervening shift from daylight saving time to standard time.

Subdivision (a)(3). When determining the last day of a filing period stated in days or a longer unit of time, a day on which the clerk's office is not accessible because of the weather or another reason is treated like a Saturday, Sunday, or legal holiday. When determining the end of a filing period stated in hours, if the clerk's office is inaccessible during the last hour of the filing period computed under subdivision (a)(2) then the period is extended to the same time on the next day that is not a weekend, holiday, or day when the clerk's office is inaccessible.

Subdivision (a)(3)'s extensions apply "[u]nless the court orders otherwise." In some circumstances, the court might not wish a period of inaccessibility to trigger a full 24-hour extension; in those instances, the court can specify a briefer extension.

The text of the rule no longer refers to "weather or other conditions" as the reason for the inaccessibility of the clerk's office. The reference to "weather" was deleted from the text to underscore that inaccessibility can occur for reasons unrelated to weather, such as an outage of the electronic filing system. Weather can still be a reason for inaccessibility of the clerk's office. The rule does not attempt to define inaccessibility. Rather, the concept will continue to develop through caselaw, see, e.g., William G. Phelps, *When Is Office of Clerk of Court Inaccessible Due to Weather or Other Conditions for Purpose of Computing Time Period for Filing Papers under Rule 6(a) of Federal Rules of Civil Procedure*, 135 A.L.R. Fed. 259 (1996) (collecting cases). In addition, many local provisions address inaccessibility for purposes of electronic filing, *see, e.g.,* D. Kan. Rule 5.4.11 ("A Filing User whose filing is made untimely as the result of a technical failure may seek appropriate relief from the court.").

Subdivision (a)(4). New subdivision (a)(4) defines the end of the last day of a period for purposes of subdivision (a)(1). Subdivision (a)(4) does not apply in computing periods stated in hours under subdivision (a)(2), and does not apply if a different time is set by a statute, local rule, or order in the case. A local rule may, for example, address the problems that might arise if a single district has clerk's offices in different time zones, or provide that papers filed in a drop box after the normal hours of the clerk's office are filed as of the day that is date-stamped on the papers by a device in the drop box.

28 U.S.C. § 452 provides that "[a]ll courts of the United States shall be deemed always open for the purpose of filing proper papers, issuing and returning process, and making motions and orders." A corresponding provision exists in Rule 77(a). Some courts have held that these provisions permit an after-hours filing by handing the papers to an appropriate official. *See, e.g.*, Casalduc v. Diaz, 117 F.2d 915, 917 (1st Cir. 1941). Subdivision (a)(4) does not address the effect of the statute on the question of after-hours filing; instead, the rule is designed to deal with filings in the ordinary course without regard to Section 452.

Subdivision (a)(5). New subdivision (a)(5) defines the "next" day for purposes of subdivisions (a)(1)(C) and (a)(2)(C). The Federal Rules of Civil Procedure contain both forward-looking time periods and backward-looking time periods. A forward-looking time period requires something to be done within a period of time *after* an event. *See, e.g.*, Rule 59(b) (motion for new trial "must be filed no later than 28 days after entry of the judgment"). A backward-looking time period requires something to be done within a period of time before an event. *See, e.g.*, Rule 26(f) (parties must hold Rule 26(f) conference "as soon as practicable and in any event at least 21 days before a scheduling conference is held or a scheduling order is due under Rule 16(b)"). In determining what is the "next" day for purposes of subdivisions (a)(1)(C) and (a)(2)(C), one should continue counting in the same direction — that is, forward when computing a forward-looking period and backward when computing a backward-looking period. If, for example, a filing is due within 30 days *after* an event, and the thirtieth day falls on Saturday, September 1, 2007, then the filing is due on Tuesday, September 4, 2007 (Monday, September 3, is Labor Day). But if a filing is due 21 days *before* an event, and the twenty-first day falls on Saturday, September 1, then the filing is due on Friday, August 31. If the clerk's office is inaccessible on August 31, then subdivision (a)(3) extends the filing deadline forward to the next accessible day that is not a Saturday, Sunday, or legal holiday — no later than Tuesday, September 4.

Subdivision (a)(6). New subdivision (a)(6) defines "legal holiday" for purposes of the Federal Rules of Civil Procedure, including the time-computation provisions of subdivision (a). Subdivision (a)(6) continues to include within the definition of "legal holiday" days that are declared a holiday by the President or Congress.

For forward counted periods — *i.e.*, periods that are measured after an event — subdivision (a)(6)(C) includes certain state holidays within the definition of legal holidays. However, state legal holidays are not recognized in computing backward counted periods. For both forward- and backward-counted periods, the rule thus protects those who may be unsure of the effect of state holidays. For forward counted deadlines, treating state holidays the same as federal holidays extends the deadline. Thus, someone who thought that the federal courts might be closed on a state holiday would be safeguarded against an inadvertent late filing. In contrast, for backward counted deadlines, not giving state holidays the treatment of federal holidays allows filing on the state holiday itself rather than the day before. Take, for example, Monday, April 21, 2008 (Patriot's Day, a legal holiday in the relevant state). If a filing is due 14 days after an event, and the fourteenth day is April 21, then the filing is due on Tuesday, April 22 because Monday, April 21 counts as a legal holiday. But if a filing is due 14 days before an event, and the fourteenth day is April 21, the filing is due on Monday, April 21; the fact that April 21 is a state holiday does not make April 21 a legal holiday for purposes of computing this backward counted deadline. But note that if the clerk's office is inaccessible on Monday, April 21, then subdivision (a)(3) extends the April 21 filing deadline forward to the next accessible day that is not a Saturday, Sunday or legal holiday — no earlier than Tuesday, April 22.

The times set in the former rule at 1 or 5 days have been revised to 7 or 14 days. See the Note to Rule 6.

2016 AMENDMENT

Rule 6(d) is amended to remove service by electronic means under Rule 5(b)(2)(E) from the modes of service that allow 3 added days to act after being served.

Rule 5(b)(2) was amended in 2001 to provide for service by electronic means. Although electronic transmission seemed virtually instantaneous even then, electronic service was included in the modes of service that allow 3 added days to act after being served. There were concerns that the transmission might be delayed for some time, and particular concerns that incompatible systems might make it difficult or impossible to open attachments. Those concerns have been substantially alleviated by advances in technology and in widespread skill in using electronic transmission.

A parallel reason for allowing the 3 added days was that electronic service was authorized only with the consent of the person to be served. Concerns about the reliability of electronic transmission might have led to refusals of consent; the 3 added days were calculated to alleviate these concerns.

Diminution of the concerns that prompted the decision to allow the 3 added days for electronic transmission is not the only reason for discarding this indulgence. Many rules have been changed to ease the task of computing time by adopting 7-, 14-, 21-, and 28-day periods that allow "day-of-the-week" counting. Adding 3 days at the end complicated the counting, and increased the occasions for further complication by invoking the provisions that apply when the last day is a Saturday, Sunday, or legal holiday.

Electronic service after business hours, or just before or during a weekend or holiday, may result in a practical reduction in the time available to respond. Extensions of time may be warranted to prevent prejudice.

Eliminating Rule 5(b) subparagraph (2)(E) from the modes of service that allow 3 added days means that the 3 added days cannot be retained by consenting to service by electronic means. Consent to electronic service in registering for electronic case filing, for example, does not count as consent to service "by any other means" of delivery under subparagraph (F).

What is now Rule 6(d) was amended in 2005 "to remove any doubt as to the method for calculating the time to respond after service by mail, leaving with the clerk of court, electronic means, or by other means consented to by the party served." A potential ambiguity was created by substituting "after service" for the earlier references to acting after service "upon the party" if a paper or notice "is served upon the party" by the specified means. "[A]fter service" could be read to refer not only to a party that has been served but also to a party that has made service. That reading would mean that a party who is allowed a specified time to act after making service can extend the time by choosing one of the means of service specified in the rule, something that was never intended by the original rule or the amendment. Rules setting a time to act after making service include Rules 14(a)(1), 15(a)(1)(A), and 38(b)(1). "[A]fter being served" is substituted for "after service" to dispel any possible misreading.

Rules setting a time to act after making service include Rules 14(a)(1), 15(a)(1)(A), and 38(b)(1). "[A]fter being served" is substituted for "after service" to dispel any possible misreading.

III. PLEADINGS AND MOTIONS

Rule 7. Pleadings Allowed; Form of Motions

1937 ADOPTION

1. A provision designating pleadings and defining a motion is common in the State Practice Acts. See Smith-Hurd Ill.Stats. ch. 110, § 156 (Designation and order of pleadings); 2 Minn.Stat. (Mason, 1927) § 9246 (Definition of motion); and N.Y.C.P.A. (1937) § 113 (Definition of motion). Former Equity Rules 18 (Pleadings—Technical Forms Abrogated), 29 (Defenses—How Presented), and 33 (Testing Sufficiency of Defense) abolished technical forms of pleading, demurrers and pleas, and exceptions for insufficiency of an answer.

2. **Note to Subdivision (a).** This preserves the substance of former Equity Rule 31 (Reply—When Required—When Cause at Issue). Compare the English practice, English Rules under the Judicature Act (The Annual Practice, 1937) O. 23, r. r. 1, 2 (Reply to counterclaim; amended, 1933, to be subject to the rules applicable to defenses, O. 21). See O. 21, r. r. 1 to 14; O. 27, r. 13 (When pleadings deemed denied and put in issue). Under the codes the pleadings are generally limited. A reply is sometimes required to an affirmative defense in the answer. 1 Colo.Stat.Ann. (1935) § 66; Ore.Code Ann. (1930) §§ 1-614, 1-616. In other jurisdictions no reply is necessary to an affirmative defense in the answer, but a reply may be ordered by the court. N.C.Code Ann. (1935) § 525; 1 S.D.Comp.Laws (1929) § 2357. A reply to a counterclaim is usually required. Ark.Civ.Code (Crawford, 1934) §§ 123 to 125; Wis.Stat. (1935) §§ 263.20, 263.21. U.S.C.A., Title 28, former § 45 (District courts; practice and procedure in certain cases) is modified in so far as it may dispense with a reply to a counterclaim.

For amendment of pleadings, see Rule 15 dealing with amended and supplemental pleadings.

3. All statutes which use the words "petition", "bill of complaint", "plea", "demurrer", and other such terminology are modified in form by this rule.

1946 AMENDMENT

Note. This amendment [to subdivision (a)] eliminates any question as to whether the compulsory reply, where a counterclaim is pleaded, is a reply only to the counterclaim or is a general reply to the answer containing the counterclaim. The Commentary, Scope of Reply where Defendant Has Pleaded Counterclaim, 1939, 1 Fed.Rules Serv. 672; Fort Chartres and Ivy Landing Drainage and Levee District No. 5 v. Thompson, E.D.Ill.1945, 8 Fed.Rules Serv. 13.32, Case 1.

1963 AMENDMENT

Certain redundant words are eliminated and the subdivision is modified to reflect the amendment of Rule 14(a) which in certain cases eliminates the requirement of obtaining leave to bring in a third-party defendant.

1983 AMENDMENT

One of the reasons sanctions against improper motion practice have been employed infrequently is the lack of clarity of Rule 7. That rule has stated only generally that the pleading requirements relating to captions, signing, and other matters of form also apply to motions and other papers. The addition of Rule 7(b)(3) makes explicit the applicability of the signing requirement and the sanctions of Rule 11, which have been amplified.

2007 AMENDMENT

The language of Rule 7 has been amended as part of the general restyling of the Civil Rules to make them more easily understood and to make style and terminology consistent throughout the rules. These changes are intended to be stylistic only.

Former Rule 7(a) stated that "there shall be * * * an answer to a cross-claim, if the answer contains a cross-claim * * *." Former Rule 12(a)(2) provided more generally that "[a] party served with a pleading stating a cross-claim against that party shall serve an answer thereto * * *." New Rule 7(a) corrects this inconsistency by providing for an answer to a crossclaim.

For the first time, Rule 7(a)(7) expressly authorizes the court to order a reply to a counterclaim answer. A reply may be as useful in this setting as a reply to an answer, a third-party answer, or a crossclaim answer.

Former Rule 7(b)(1) stated that the writing requirement is fulfilled if the motion is stated in a written notice of hearing. This statement was deleted as redundant because a single written document can satisfy the writing requirements both for a motion and for a Rule 6(c)(1) notice.

The cross-reference to Rule 11 in former Rule 7(b)(3) is deleted as redundant. Rule 11 applies by its own terms. The force and application of Rule 11 are not diminished by the deletion.

Former Rule 7(c) is deleted because it has done its work. If a motion or pleading is described as a demurrer, plea, or exception for insufficiency, the court will treat the paper as if properly captioned.

Rule 7.1. Disclosure Statement

2002 ADOPTION

Rule 7.1 is drawn from Rule 26.1 of the Federal Rules of Appellate Procedure, with changes to adapt to the circumstances of district courts that dictate different provisions for the time of filing, number of copies, and the like. The information required by Rule 7.1(a) reflects the "financial interest" standard of Canon 3C(1)(c) of the Code of Conduct for United States Judges. This information will support properly informed disqualification decisions in situations that call for automatic disqualification under Canon 3C(1)(c). It does not cover all of the circumstances that may call for disqualification under the financial interest standard, and does not deal at all with other circumstances that may call for disqualification.

Although the disclosures required by Rule 7.1(a) may seem limited, they are calculated to reach a majority of the circumstances that are likely to call for disqualification on the basis of financial information that a judge may not know or recollect. Framing a rule that calls for more detailed disclosure will be difficult. Unnecessary disclosure requirements place a burden on the parties and on courts. Unnecessary disclosure of volumes of information may create a risk that a judge will overlook the one bit of information that might require disqualification, and also may create a risk that unnecessary disqualifications will be made rather than attempt to unravel a potentially difficult question. It has not been feasible to dictate more detailed disclosure requirements in Rule 7.1(a).

Rule 7.1 does not prohibit local rules that require disclosures in addition to those required by Rule 7.1. Developing experience with local disclosure practices and advances in electronic technology may provide a foundation for adopting more detailed disclosure requirements by future amendments of Rule 7.1.

2007 AMENDMENT

The language of Rule 7.1 has been amended as part of the general restyling of the Civil Rules to make them more easily understood and to make style and

terminology consistent throughout the rules. These changes are intended to be stylistic only.

2022 AMENDMENT

Rule 7.1(a)(1). Rule 7.1 is amended to require a disclosure statement by a nongovernmental corporation that seeks to intervene. This amendment conforms Rule 7.1 to similar recent amendments to Appellate Rule 26.1 and Bankruptcy Rule 8012(a).

Rule 7.1(a)(2). Rule 7.1 is further amended to require a party or intervenor in an action in which jurisdiction is based on diversity under 28 U.S.C. § 1332(a) to name and disclose the citizenship of every individual or entity whose citizenship is attributed to that party or intervenor. The disclosure does not relieve a party that asserts diversity jurisdiction from the Rule 8(a)(1) obligation to plead the grounds for jurisdiction, but is designed to facilitate an early and accurate determination of jurisdiction.

Two examples of attributed citizenship are provided by § 1332(c)(1) and (2), addressing direct actions against liability insurers and actions that include as parties a legal representative of the estate of a decedent, an infant, or an incompetent. Identifying citizenship in such actions is not likely to be difficult, and ordinarily should be pleaded in the complaint. But many examples of attributed citizenship arise from noncorporate entities that sue or are sued as an entity. A familiar example is a limited liability company, which takes on the citizenship of each of its owners. A party suing an LLC may not have all the information it needs to plead the LLC's citizenship. The same difficulty may arise with respect to other forms of noncorporate entities, some of them familiar—such as partnerships and limited partnerships—and some of them more exotic, such as "joint ventures." Pleading on information and belief is acceptable at the pleading stage, but disclosure is necessary both to ensure that diversity jurisdiction exists and to protect against the waste that may occur upon belated discovery of a diversity destroying citizenship. Disclosure is required by a plaintiff as well as all other parties and intervenors.

What counts as an "entity" for purposes of Rule 7.1 is shaped by the need to determine whether the court has diversity jurisdiction under § 1332(a). It does not matter whether a collection of individuals is recognized as an entity for any other purpose, such as the capacity to sue or be sued in a common name, or is treated as no more than a collection of individuals for all other purposes. Every citizenship that is attributable to a party or intervenor must be disclosed.

Discovery should not often be necessary after disclosures are made. But discovery may be appropriate to test jurisdictional facts by inquiring into such matters as the completeness of a disclosure's list of persons or the accuracy of their described citizenships. This rule does not address the questions that may arise when a disclosure statement or discovery responses indicate that the party or intervenor cannot ascertain the citizenship of every individual or entity whose citizenship may be attributed to it.

The rule recognizes that the court may limit the disclosure in appropriate circumstances. Disclosure might be cut short when a party reveals a citizenship that defeats diversity jurisdiction. Or the names of identified persons might be protected against disclosure to other parties when there are substantial interests in privacy and when there is no apparent need to support discovery by other parties to go behind the disclosure.

Disclosure is limited to individuals and entities whose citizenship is attributed to a party or intervenor. The rules that govern attribution, and the time that controls the determination of complete diversity, are matters of subject matter jurisdiction that this rule does not address. A supplemental statement is required if an event occurs after initial filing in federal court or removal to it that requires a determination of citizenships as they exist at a time after the initial filing or removal.

Rule 7.1(b). Rule 7.1(b) is amended to reflect the provisions in Rule 7.1(a) that extend the disclosure obligation to proposed intervenors and intervenors.

Rule 8. General Rules of Pleading

1937 ADOPTION

Note to Subdivision (a). See former Equity Rules 25 (Bill of Complaint—Contents), and 30 (Answer—Contents—Counterclaim). Compare 2 Ind.Stat. Ann. (Burns, 1933) §§ 2-1004, 2-1015; 2 Ohio Gen.Code Ann. (Page, 1926) §§ 11305, 11314; Utah Rev.Stat.Ann. (1933) §§ 104-7-2, 104-9-1.

See Rule 19(c) for the requirement of a statement in a claim for relief of the names of persons who ought to be parties and the reason for their omission.

See Rule 23(b) for particular requirements as to the complaint in a secondary action by shareholders.

Note to Subdivision (b). 1. This rule supersedes the methods of pleading prescribed in U.S.C., Title 19, § 508 (Persons making seizures pleading general issue and proving special matter); U.S.C. Title 35, former § 40d (Proving under general issue, upon notice, that a statement in application for an extended patent is not true), § 282, formerly § 69 (Pleading and proof in actions for infringement) and similar statutes.

2. This rule is, in part, former Equity Rule 30 (Answer—Contents—Counterclaim), with the matter on denials largely from the Connecticut practice. See Conn. Practice Book (1934) §§ 107, 108, and 122; Conn.Gen.Stat. (1930) §§ 5508 to 5514. Compare the English practice, English Rules Under the Judicature Act (The Annual Practice, 1937) O. 19, r. r. 17 to 20.

Note to Subdivision (c). This follows substantially English Rules Under the Judicature Act (The Annual Practice, 1937) O. 19, r. 15 and N.Y.C.P.A. (1937) § 242, with "surprise" omitted in this rule.

Note to Subdivision (d). The first sentence is similar to former Equity Rule 30 (Answer—Contents—Counterclaim). For the second sentence see former Equity Rule 31 (Reply—When Required—When Cause at Issue). This is similar to English Rules Under the Judicature Act (The Annual Practice, 1937) O. 19, r. r. 13, 18; and to the practice of the States.

Note to Subdivision (e). This rule is an elaboration upon former Equity Rule 30 (Answer—Contents—Counterclaim), plus a statement of the actual practice under some codes. Compare also former Equity Rule 18 (Pleadings—Technical Forms Abrogated). See Clark, Code Pleading (1928), pp. 171-4, 432-5; Hankin, Alternative and Hypothetical Pleading (1924), 33 Yale L.J. 365.

Note to Subdivision (f). A provision of like import is of frequent occurrence in the codes. Smith-Hurd Ill.Stats. ch. 110, § 157(3); 2 Minn.Stat. (Mason, 1927) § 9266; N.Y.C.P.A. (1937) § 275; 2 N.D.Comp.Laws Ann. (1913) § 7458.

1966 AMENDMENT

The change here is consistent with the broad purposes of unification.

1987 AMENDMENT

The amendments are technical. No substantive change is intended.

2007 AMENDMENT

The language of Rule 8 has been amended as part of the general restyling of the Civil Rules to make them more easily understood and to make style and terminology consistent throughout the rules. These changes are intended to be stylistic only.

The former Rule 8(b) and 8(e) cross-references to Rule 11 are deleted as redundant. Rule 11 applies by its own terms. The force and application of Rule 11 are not diminished by the deletion.

Former Rule 8(b) required a pleader denying part of an averment to "specify so much of it as is true and material and * * * deny only the remainder." "[A]nd material" is deleted to avoid the implication that it is proper to deny something that the pleader believes to be true but not material.

Deletion of former Rule 8(e)(2)'s "whether based on legal, equitable, or maritime grounds" reflects the parallel deletions in Rule 1 and elsewhere. Merger is now successfully accomplished.

2010 AMENDMENT

Subdivision (c)(1). "[D]ischarge in bankruptcy" is deleted from the list of affirmative defenses. Under 11 U.S.C. § 524(a)(1) and (2) a discharge voids a judgment to the extent that it determines a personal liability of the debtor with respect to a discharged debt. The discharge also operates as an injunction against commencement or continuation of an action to collect, recover, or offset a discharged debt. For these reasons it is confusing to describe discharge as an affirmative defense. But § 524(a) applies only to a claim that was actually discharged. Several categories of debt set out in 11 U.S.C. § 523(a) are excepted from discharge. The issue whether a claim was excepted from discharge may be determined either in the court that entered the discharge or--in most instances--in another court with jurisdiction over the creditor's claim.

Rule 9. Pleading Special Matters

1937 ADOPTION

Note to Subdivision (a). Compare former Equity Rule 25 (Bill of Complaint—Contents) requiring disability to be stated; Utah Rev.Stat.Ann. (1933) § 104-13-15, enumerating a number of situations where a general averment of capacity is sufficient. For provisions governing averment of incorporation, see 2 Minn.Stat. (Mason, 1927) § 9271; N.Y.R.C.P. (1937) Rule 93; 2 N.D.Comp.Laws Ann. (1913) §§ 7981 et seq.

Note to Subdivision (b). See English Rules Under the Judicature Act (The Annual Practice, 1937) O. 19, r. 22.

Note to Subdivision (c). The codes generally have this or a similar provision. See English Rules Under the Judicature Act (The Annual Practice, 1937) O. 19, r. 14; 2 Minn.Stat. (Mason, 1927) § 9273; N.Y.R.C.P. (1937) Rule 92; 2 N.D.Comp.Laws Ann. (1913) § 7461; 2 Wash.Rev.Stat.Ann. (Remington, 1932) § 288.

Note to Subdivision (e). The rule expands the usual code provisions on pleading a judgment by including judgments or decisions of administrative tribunals and foreign courts. Compare Ark.Civ.Code (Crawford, 1934) § 141; 2 Minn.Stat. (Mason, 1927) § 9269; N.Y.R.C.P. (1937) Rule 95; 2 Wash.Rev.Stat. Ann. (Remington, 1932) § 287.

1966 AMENDMENT

Certain distinctive features of the admiralty practice must be preserved for what are now suits in admiralty. This raises the question: After unification, when a single form of action is established, how will the counterpart of the present suit in admiralty be identifiable? In part the question is easily answered. Some claims for relief can only be suits in admiralty, either because the admiralty jurisdiction is exclusive or because no nonmaritime ground of federal jurisdiction exists. Many claims, however, are cognizable by the district courts whether asserted in admiralty or in a civil action, assuming the existence of a nonmaritime ground of jurisdiction. Thus at present the pleader has power to determine procedural consequences by the way in which he exercises the classic privilege given by the saving-to-suitors clause (28 U.S.C. § 1333) or by equivalent statutory provisions. For example, a longshoreman's claim for personal injuries suffered by reason of the unseaworthiness of a vessel may be asserted in a suit in admiralty or, if diversity of citizenship exists, in a civil action. One of the important procedural consequences is that in the civil action either party may demand a jury trial, while in the suit in admiralty there is no right to jury trial except as provided by statute.

It is no part of the purpose of unification to inject a right to jury trial into those admiralty cases in which that right is not provided by statute. Similarly as will be more specifically noted below, there is no disposition to change the present law as to interlocutory appeals in admiralty, or as to the venue of suits in admiralty; and, of course, there is no disposition to inject into the civil practice as it now is the distinctively maritime remedies (maritime attachment and garnishment, actions in rem, possessory, petitory and partition actions and limitation of liability). The unified rules must therefore provide some device for preserving the present power of the pleader to determine whether these historically maritime procedures shall be applicable to his claim or not; the pleader must be afforded some means of designating his claim as the counterpart of the present suit in admiralty, where its character as such is not clear.

The problem is different from the similar one concerning the identification of claims that were formerly suits in equity. While that problem is not free from complexities, it is broadly true that the modern counterpart of the suit in equity is distinguishable from the former action at law by the character of the relief sought. This mode of identification is possible in only a limited category of admiralty cases. In large numbers of cases the relief sought in admiralty is simple money damages, indistinguishable from the remedy afforded by the common law. This is true, for example, in the case of the longshoreman's action for personal injuries stated above. After unification has abolished the distinction between civil actions and suits in admiralty, the complaint in such an action would be almost completely ambiguous as to the pleader's intentions regarding the procedure invoked. The allegation of diversity of citizenship might be regarded as a clue indicating an intention to proceed as at present under the saving-to-suitors clause; but this, too, would be ambiguous if there were also reference to the admiralty jurisdiction, and the pleader ought not be required to forego mention of all available jurisdictional grounds.

Other methods of solving the problem were carefully explored, but the Advisory Committee concluded that the preferable solution is to allow the pleader who now has power to determine procedural consequences by filing a suit in admiralty to exercise that power under unification, for the limited instances in which procedural differences will remain, by a simple statement in his pleading to the effect that the claim is an admiralty or maritime claim.

The choice made by the pleader in identifying or in failing to identify his claim as an admiralty or maritime claim is not an irrevocable election. The rule provides that the amendment of a pleading to add or withdraw an identifying statement is subject to the principles of Rule 15.

1968 AMENDMENT

The amendment eliminates the reference to Rule 73 which is to be abrogated and transfers to Rule 9(h) the substance of Subsection (h) of Rule 73 which preserved the right to an interlocutory appeal in admiralty cases which is provided by 28 U.S.C. § 1292(a)(3).

1970 AMENDMENT

The reference to Rule 26(a) is deleted, in light of the transfer of that subdivision to Rule 30(a) and the elimination of the de bene esse procedure therefrom. See the Advisory Committee's note to Rule 30(a).

1987 AMENDMENT

The amendment is technical. No substantive change is intended.

1997 AMENDMENT

Section 1292(a)(3) of the Judicial Code provides for appeal from "[i]nterlocutory decrees of * * * district courts * * * determining the rights and liabilities of the parties to admiralty cases in which appeals from final decrees are allowed."

Rule 9(h) was added in 1966 with the unification of civil and admiralty procedure. Civil Rule 73(h) was amended at the same time to provide that the § 1292(a)(3) reference "to admiralty cases shall be construed to mean admiralty and maritime claims within the meaning of Rule 9(h)." This provision was transferred to Rule 9(h) when the Appellate Rules were adopted.

A single case can include both admiralty or maritime claims and nonadmiralty claims or parties. This combination reveals an ambiguity in the statement in present Rule 9(h) that an admiralty "claim" is an admiralty "case." An order "determining the rights and liabilities of the parties" within the meaning of § 1292(a)(3) may resolve only a nonadmiralty claim, or may simultaneously resolve interdependent admiralty and nonadmirality claims. Can appeal be taken as to the nonadmiralty matter, because it is part of a case that includes an admiralty claim, or is appeal limited to the admiralty claim?

The courts of appeals have not achieved full uniformity in applying the § 1292(a)(3) requirement that an order "determin[e] the rights and liabilities of the parties." It is common to assert that the statute should be construed narrowly, under the general policy that exceptions to the final judgment rule should be construed narrowly. This policy would suggest that the ambiguity should be resolved by limiting the interlocutory appeal right to orders that determine the rights and liabilities of the parties to an admiralty claim.

A broader view is chosen by this amendment for two reasons. The statute applies to admiralty "cases," and may itself provide for appeal from an order that disposes of a nonadmiralty claim that is joined in a single case with an admiralty claim. Although a rule of court may help to clarify and implement a statutory grant of jurisdiction, the line is not always clear between permissible implementation and impermissible withdrawal of jurisdiction. In addition, so long as an order truly disposes of the rights and liabilities of the parties within the meaning of § 1292(a)(3), it may prove important to permit appeal as to the nonadmiralty claim. Disposition of the nonadmiralty claim, for example, may make it unnecessary to consider the admiralty claim and have the same effect on the case and parties as disposition of the admiralty claim. Or the admiralty and nonadmiralty claims may be interdependent. An illustration is provided by *Roco Carriers, Ltd. v. M/V Nurnberg Express*, 899 F.2d 1292 (2d Cir.1990). Claims for losses of ocean shipments were made against two defendants, one subject to admiralty jurisdiction and the other not. Summary judgment was granted in favor of the admiralty defendant and against the nonadmiralty defendant. The nonadmiralty defendant's appeal was accepted, with the explanation that the determination of its liability was "integrally linked with the determination of non-liability" of the admiralty defendant, and that "section 1292(a)(3) is not limited to admiralty *claims;* instead, it refers to admiralty *cases.*" 899 F.2d at 1297. The advantages of permitting appeal by the nonadmiralty defendant would be particularly clear if the plaintiff had appealed the summary judgment in favor of the admiralty defendant.

It must be emphasized that this amendment does not rest on any particular assumptions as to the meaning of the § 1292(a)(3) provision that limits interlocutory appeal to orders that determine the rights and liabilities of the parties. It simply reflects the conclusion that so long as the case involves an admiralty claim and an order otherwise meets statutory requirements, the opportunity to appeal should not turn on the circumstance that the order does—or does not—dispose of an admiralty claim. No attempt is made to invoke the authority conferred by 28 U.S.C. § 1292(e) to provide by rule for appeal of an interlocutory decision that is not otherwise provided for by other subsections of § 1292.

2006 AMENDMENT

Rule 9(h) is amended to conform to the changed title of the Supplemental Rules.

2007 AMENDMENT

The language of Rule 9 has been amended as part of the general restyling of the Civil Rules to make them more easily understood and to make style and terminology consistent throughout the rules. These changes are intended to be stylistic only.

Rule 15 governs pleading amendments of its own force. The former redundant statement that Rule 15 governs an amendment that adds or withdraws a Rule 9(h) designation as an admiralty or maritime claim is deleted. The elimination of paragraph (2) means that "(3)" will be redesignated as "(2)" in Style Rule 9(h).

Rule 10. Form of Pleadings

1937 ADOPTION

The first sentence is derived in part from the opening statement of former Equity Rule 25 (Bill of Complaint—Contents). The remainder of the rule is an expansion in conformity with usual state provisions. For numbered paragraphs and separate statements, see Conn.Gen.Stat., 1930, § 5513 Smith-Hurd Ill.Stats. ch. 110, § 157(2); N.Y.R.C.P., (1937) Rule 90. For incorporation by reference, see N.Y.R.C.P., (1937) Rule 90. For written instruments as exhibits, see Smith-Hurd Ill.Stats. ch. 110, § 160.

2007 AMENDMENT

The language of Rule 10 has been amended as part of the general restyling of the Civil Rules to make them more easily understood and to make style and terminology consistent throughout the rules. These changes are intended to be stylistic only.

Rule 11. Signing of Pleadings, Motions, and other Papers; Representations to Court; Sanctions

1937 ADOPTION

This is substantially the content of former Equity Rules 24 (Signature of Counsel) and 21 (Scandal and Impertinence) consolidated and unified. Compare former Equity Rule 36 (Officers Before Whom Pleadings Verified). Compare to similar purposes, English Rules Under the Judicature Act (The Annual Practice, 1937) O. 19, r. 4, and *Great Australian Gold Mining Co. v. Martin, L. R.*, 5 Ch.Div. 1, 10 (1877). Subscription of pleadings is required in many codes. 2 Minn.Stat. (Mason, 1927) § 9265; N.Y.R.C.P. (1937) Rule 91; 2 N.D.Comp.Laws Ann. (1913) § 7455.

This rule expressly continues any statute which requires a pleading to be verified or accompanied by an affidavit, such as:

U.S.C., Title 28 former:

§ 381 (Preliminary injunctions and temporary restraining orders).

§ 762 (Suit against the United States).

U.S.C., Title 28, former § 829 (now § 1927)(Costs; attorney liable for, when) is unaffected by this rule.

For complaints which must be verified under these rules, see Rules 23(b) (Secondary Action by Shareholders) and 65 (Injunctions).

For abolition of the rule in equity that the averments of an answer under oath must be overcome by the testimony of two witnesses or of one witness sustained by corroborating circumstances. See Pa.Stat.Ann. (Purdon, 1931) see 12 P.S.Pa., § 1222; for the rule in equity itself, see *Greenfield v. Blumenthal*, 69 F.2d 294 (C.C.A. 3d.1934).

1983 AMENDMENT

Since its original promulgation, Rule 11 has provided for the striking of pleadings and the imposition of disciplinary sanctions to check abuses in the signing of pleadings. Its provisions have always applied to motions and other papers by virtue of incorporation by reference in Rule 7(b)(2). The amendment and the addition of Rule 7(b)(3) expressly confirms this applicability.

Experience shows that in practice Rule 11 has not been effective in deterring abuses. See 6 Wright & Miller, Federal Practice and Procedure: Civil § 1334 (1971). There has been considerable confusion as to (1) the circumstances that should trigger striking a pleading or motion or taking disciplinary action, (2) the standard of conduct expected of attorneys who sign pleadings and motions, and (3) the range of available and appropriate sanctions. See Rodes, Ripple & Mooney, Sanctions Imposable for Violations of the Federal Rules of Civil Procedure 64–65, Federal Judicial Center (1981). The new language is intended to reduce the reluctance of courts to impose sanctions, see Moore, Federal Practice ¶ 7.05, at 1547, by emphasizing the responsibilities of the attorney and reenforcing those obligations by the imposition of sanctions.

The amended rule attempts to deal with the problem by building upon and expanding the equitable doctrine permitting the court to award expenses, including attorney's fees, to a litigant whose opponent acts in bad faith in instituting or conducting litigation. See, e.g., *Roadway Express, Inc. v. Piper*, 447 U.S. 752 (1980); *Hall v. Cole*, 412 U.S. 1, 5 (1973). Greater attention by the district courts to pleading and motion abuses and the imposition of sanctions when appropriate, should discourage dilatory or abusive tactics and help to streamline the litigation process by lessening frivolous claims or defenses.

The expanded nature of the lawyer's certification in the fifth sentence of amended Rule 11 recognizes that the litigation process may be abused for purposes other than delay. See, e.g., *Browning Debenture Holders' Committee v. DASA Corp.*, 560 F.2d 1078 (2d Cir.1977).

The words "good ground to support" the pleading in the original rule were interpreted to have both factual and legal elements. See, e.g., *Heart Disease Research Foundation v. General Motors Corp.*, 15 Fed.R.Serv.2d 1517, 1519 (S. D.N.Y.1972). They have been replaced by a standard of conduct that is more focused.

The new language stresses the need for some prefiling inquiry into both the facts and the law to satisfy the affirmative duty imposed by the rule. The standard is one of reasonableness under the circumstances. See *Kinee v. Abraham Lincoln Fed. Sav. & Loan Ass'n*, 365 F.Supp. 975 (E.D.Pa.1973). This standard is more stringent than the original good-faith formula and thus it is expected that a greater range of circumstances will trigger its violation. See *Nemeroff v. Abelson*, 620 F.2d 339 (2d Cir.1980).

The rule is not intended to chill an attorney's enthusiasm or creativity in pursuing factual or legal theories. The court is expected to avoid using the wisdom of hindsight and should test the signer's conduct by inquiring what was reasonable to believe at the time the pleading, motion, or other paper was submitted. Thus, what constitutes a reasonable inquiry may depend on such factors as how much time for investigation was available to the signer; whether he had to rely on a client for information as to the facts underlying the pleading, motion, or other paper; whether the pleading, motion, or other paper was based on a plausible view of the law; or whether he depended on forwarding counsel or another member of the bar.

The rule does not require a party or an attorney to disclose privileged communications or work product in order to show that the signing of the pleading, motion, or other paper is substantially justified. The provisions of Rule 26(c), including appropriate orders after in camera inspection by the court, remain available to protect a party claiming privilege or work product protection.

Amended Rule 11 continues to apply to anyone who signs a pleading, motion, or other paper. Although the standard is the same for unrepresented parties, who are obliged themselves to sign the pleadings, the court has sufficient discretion to take account of the special circumstances that often arise in pro se situations. See *Haines v. Kerner*, 404 U.S. 519 (1972).

The provision in the original rule for striking pleadings and motions as sham and false has been deleted. The passage has rarely been utilized, and decisions thereunder have tended to confuse the issue of attorney honesty with the merits of the action. See generally Risinger, Honesty in Pleading and its Enforcement: Some "Striking" Problems with Fed.R.Civ.P. 11, 61 Minn.L.Rev. 1 (1976). Motions under this provision generally present issues better dealt with under Rules 8, 12, or 56. See *Murchison v. Kirby*, 27 F.R.D. 14 (S.D.N.Y.1961); 5 Wright & Miller, Federal Practice and Procedure: Civil § 1334 (1969).

The former reference to the inclusion of scandalous or indecent matter, which is itself strong indication that an improper purpose underlies the pleading, motion, or other paper, also has been deleted as unnecessary. Such matter may be stricken under Rule 12(f) as well as dealt with under the more general language of amended Rule 11.

The text of the amended rule seeks to dispel apprehensions that efforts to obtain enforcement will be fruitless by insuring that the rule will be applied when properly invoked. The word "sanctions" in the caption, for example, stresses a deterrent orientation in dealing with improper pleadings, motions or other papers. This corresponds to the approach in imposing sanctions for discovery abuses. See *National Hockey League v. Metropolitan Hockey Club*, 427 U.S. 639 (1976) (per curiam). And the words "shall impose" in the last sentence focus the court's attention on the need to impose sanctions for pleading and motion abuses. The court, however, retains the necessary flexibility to deal appropriately with violations of the rule. It has discretion to tailor sanctions to the particular facts of the case, with which it should be well acquainted.

The reference in the former text to wilfulness as a prerequisite to disciplinary action has been deleted. However, in considering the nature and severity of the sanctions to be imposed, the court should take account of the state of the attorney's or party's actual or presumed knowledge when the pleading or other paper was signed. Thus, for example, when a party is not represented by counsel, the absence of legal advice is an appropriate factor to be considered.

Courts currently appear to believe they may impose sanctions on their own motion. See *North American Foreign Trading Corp. v. Zale Corp.*, 83 F.R.D. 293 (S.D.N.Y.1979). Authority to do so has been made explicit in order to overcome the traditional reluctance of courts to intervene unless requested by one of the parties. The detection and punishment of a violation of the signing requirement, encouraged by the amended rule, is part of the court's responsibility for securing the system's effective operation.

If the duty imposed by the rule is violated, the court should have the discretion to impose sanctions on either the attorney, the party the signing attorney represents, or both, or on an unrepresented party who signed the pleading, and the new rule so provides. Although Rule 11 has been silent on the point, courts have claimed the power to impose sanctions on an attorney personally, either by imposing costs or employing the contempt technique. See 5 Wright & Miller, Federal Practice and Procedure: Civil § 1334 (1969); 2A Moore, Federal Practice ¶ 11.02, at 2104 n.8. This power has been used infrequently. The amended rule should eliminate any doubt as to the propriety of assessing sanctions against the attorney.

Even though it is the attorney whose signature violates the rule, it may be appropriate under the circumstances of the case to impose a sanction on the client. See *Browning Debenture Holders' Committee v. DASA Corp.*, supra. This modification brings Rule 11 in line with practice under Rule 37, which allows sanctions for abuses during discovery to be imposed upon the party, the attorney, or both.

A party seeking sanctions should give notice to the court and the offending party promptly upon discovering a basis for doing so. The time when sanctions are to be imposed rests in the discretion of the trial judge. However, it is anticipated that in the case of pleadings the sanctions issue under Rule 11 normally will be determined at the end of the litigation, and in the case of motions at the time when the motion is decided or shortly thereafter. The procedure obviously must comport with due process requirements. The particular format to be followed should depend on the circumstances of the situation and the severity of the sanction under consideration. In many situations the judge's participation in the proceedings provides him with full knowledge of the relevant facts and little further inquiry will be necessary.

To assure that the efficiencies achieved through more effective operation of the pleading regimen will not be offset by the cost of satellite litigation over the imposition of sanctions, the court must to the extent possible limit the scope of sanction proceedings to the record. Thus, discovery should be conducted only by leave of the court, and then only in extraordinary circumstances.

Although the encompassing reference to "other papers" in new Rule 11 literally includes discovery papers, the certification requirement in that context is governed by proposed new Rule 26(g). Discovery motions, however, fall within the ambit of Rule 11.

1987 AMENDMENT

The amendments are technical. No substantive change is intended.

1993 AMENDMENT

Purpose of revision. This revision is intended to remedy problems that have arisen in the interpretation and application of the 1983 revision of the rule. For empirical examination of experience under the 1983 rule, see, *e.g.*, New York State Bar Committee on Federal Courts, Sanctions and Attorneys' Fees (1987); T. Willging, The Rule 11 Sanctioning Process (1989); American Judicature Society, Report of the Third Circuit Task Force on Federal Rule of Civil Procedure 11 (S. Burbank ed., 1989); E. Wiggins, T. Willging, and D. Stienstra, *Report on* Rule 11 (Federal Judicial Center 1991). For book-length analyses of the case law, see G. Joseph, Sanctions: The Federal Law of Litigation Abuse (1989); J. Solovy, The Federal Law of Sanctions (1991); G. Vairo, Rule 11 Sanctions: Case Law Perspectives and Preventive Measures (1991).

The rule retains the principle that attorneys and pro se litigants have an obligation to the court to refrain from conduct that frustrates the aims of Rule 1. The revision broadens the scope of this obligation, but places greater constraints on the imposition of sanctions and should reduce the number of motions for sanctions presented to the court. New subdivision (d) removes from the ambit of this rule all discovery requests, responses, objections, and motions subject to the provisions of Rule 26 through 37.

Subdivision (a). Retained in this subdivision are the provisions requiring signatures on pleadings, written motions, and other papers. Unsigned papers are to be received by the Clerk, but then are to be stricken if the omission of the signature is not corrected promptly after being called to the attention of the attorney or pro se litigant. Correction can be made by signing the paper on file or by submitting a duplicate that contains the signature. A court may require by local rule that papers contain additional identifying information regarding the parties or attorneys, such as telephone numbers to facilitate facsimile transmissions, though, as for omission of a signature, the paper should not be rejected for failure to provide such information.

The sentence in the former rule relating to the effect of answers under oath is no longer needed and has been eliminated. The provision in the former rule that signing a paper constitutes a certificate that it has been read by the signer also has been eliminated as unnecessary. The obligations imposed under subdivision (b) obviously require that a pleading, written motion, or other paper be read before it is filed or submitted to the court.

Subdivisions (b) and (c). These subdivisions restate the provisions requiring attorneys and pro se litigants to conduct a reasonable inquiry into the law and facts before signing pleadings, written motions, and other documents, and prescribing sanctions for violation of these obligations. The revision in part expands the responsibilities of litigants to the court, while providing greater constraints and flexibility in dealing with infractions of the rule. The rule continues to require litigants to "stop-and-think" before initially making legal or factual contentions. It also, however, emphasizes the duty of candor by subjecting litigants to potential sanctions for insisting upon a position after it is no longer tenable and by generally providing protection against sanctions if they withdraw or correct contentions after a potential violation is called to their attention.

The rule applies only to assertions contained in papers filed with or submitted to the court. It does not cover matters arising for the first time during oral presentations to the court, when counsel may make statements that would not have been made if there had been more time for study and reflection. However, a litigant's obligations with respect to the contents of these papers are not measured solely as of the time they are filed with or submitted to the court, but include reaffirming to the court and advocating positions contained in those pleadings and motions after learning that they cease to have any merit. For example, an attorney who during a pretrial conference insists on a claim or defense should be viewed as "presenting to the court" that contention and would be subject to the obligations of subdivision (b) measured as of that time. Similarly, if after a notice of removal is filed, a party urges in federal court the allegations of a pleading filed in state court (whether as claims, defenses, or in disputes regarding removal or remand), it would be viewed as "presenting"—and hence certifying to the district court under Rule 11—those allegations.

The certification with respect to allegations and other factual contentions is revised in recognition that sometimes a litigant may have good reason to believe that a fact is true or false but may need discovery, formal or informal, from opposing parties or third persons to gather and confirm the evidentiary basis for the allegation. Tolerance of factual contentions in initial pleadings by plaintiffs or defendants when specifically identified as made on information and belief does not relieve litigants from the obligation to conduct an appropriate investigation into the facts that is reasonable under the circumstances; it is not a license to join parties, make claims, or present defenses without any factual basis or justification. Moreover, if evidentiary support is not obtained after a reasonable opportunity for further investigation or discovery, the party has a duty under the rule not to persist with that contention. Subdivision (b) does not require a formal amendment to pleadings for which evidentiary support is not obtained, but rather calls upon a litigant not thereafter to advocate such claims or defenses.

The certification is that there is (or likely will be) "evidentiary support" for the allegation, not that the party will prevail with respect to its contention regarding the fact. That summary judgment is rendered against a party does not necessarily mean, for purposes of this certification, that it had no evidentiary support for its position. On the other hand, if a party has evidence with respect to a contention that would suffice to defeat a motion for summary judgment based thereon, it would have sufficient "evidentiary support" for purposes of Rule 11.

Denials of factual contentions involve somewhat different considerations. Often, of course, a denial is premised upon the existence of evidence contradicting the alleged fact. At other times a denial is permissible because, after an appropriate investigation, a party has no information concerning the matter or, indeed, has a reasonable basis for doubting the credibility of the only evidence relevant to the matter. A party should not deny an allegation it knows to be true; but it is not required, simply because it lacks contradictory evidence, to admit an allegation that it believes is not true.

The changes in subdivisions (b)(3) and (b)(4) will serve to equalize the burden of the rule upon plaintiffs and defendants, who under Rule 8(b) are in effect allowed to deny allegations by stating that from their initial investigation they lack sufficient information to form a belief as to the truth of the allegation. If, after further investigation or discovery, a denial is no longer warranted, the defendant should not continue to insist on that denial. While sometimes helpful, formal amendment of the pleadings to withdraw an allegation or denial is not required by subdivision (b).

Arguments for extensions, modifications, or reversals of existing law or for creation of new law do not violate subdivision (b)(2) provided they are "nonfrivolous." This establishes an objective standard, intended to eliminate any "empty-head pure-heart" justification for patently frivolous arguments. However, the extent to which a litigant has researched the issues and found some support for its theories even in minority opinions, in law review articles, or through consultation with other attorneys should certainly be taken into account in determining whether paragraph (2) has been violated. Although arguments for a change of law are not required to be specifically so identified, a contention that is so identified should be viewed with greater tolerance under the rule.

The court has available a variety of possible sanctions to impose for violations, such as striking the offending paper; issuing an admonition, reprimand, or censure; requiring participation in seminars or other educational programs; ordering a fine payable to the court; referring the matter to disciplinary authorities (or, in the case of government attorneys, to the Attorney General, Inspector

General, or agency head), etc. *See Manual for Complex Litigation, Second,* § 42.3. The rule does not attempt to enumerate the factors a court should consider in deciding whether to impose a sanction or what sanctions would be appropriate in the circumstances; but, for emphasis, it does specifically note that a sanction may be nonmonetary as well as monetary. Whether the improper conduct was willful, or negligent; whether it was part of a pattern of activity, or an isolated event; whether it infected the entire pleading, or only one particular count or defense; whether the person has engaged in similar conduct in other litigation; whether it was intended to injure; what effect it had on the litigation process in time or expense; whether the responsible person is trained in the law; what amount, given the financial resources of the responsible person, is needed to deter that person from repetition in the same case; what amount is needed to deter similar activity by other litigants: all of these may in a particular case be proper considerations. The court has significant discretion in determining what sanctions, if any, should be imposed for a violation, subject to the principle that the sanctions should not be more severe than reasonably necessary to deter repetition of the conduct by the offending person or comparable conduct by similarly situated persons.

Since the purpose of Rule 11 sanctions is to deter rather than to compensate, the rule provides that, if a monetary sanction is imposed, it should ordinarily be paid into court as a penalty. However, under unusual circumstances, particularly for (b)(1) violations, deterrence may be ineffective unless the sanction not only requires the person violating the rule to make a monetary payment, but also directs that some or all of this payment be made to those injured by the violation. Accordingly, the rule authorizes the court, if requested in a motion and if so warranted, to award attorney's fees to another party. Any such award to another party, however, should not exceed the expenses and attorneys' fees for the services directly and unavoidably caused by the violation of the certification requirement. If, for example, a wholly unsupportable count were included in a multi-count complaint or counterclaim for the purpose of needlessly increasing the cost of litigation to an impecunious adversary, any award of expenses should be limited to those directly caused by inclusion of the improper count, and not those resulting from the filing of the complaint or answer itself. The award should not provide compensation for services that could have been avoided by an earlier disclosure of evidence or an earlier challenge to the groundless claims or defenses. Moreover, partial reimbursement of fees may constitute a sufficient deterrent with respect to violations by persons having modest financial resources. In cases brought under statutes providing for fees to be awarded to prevailing parties, the court should not employ cost-shifting under this rule in a manner that would be inconsistent with the standards that govern the statutory award of fees, such as stated in *Christiansburg Garment Co. v. EEOC*, 434 U.S. 412 (1978).

The sanction should be imposed on the persons—whether attorneys, law firms, or parties—who have violated the rule or who may be determined to be responsible for the violation. The person signing, filing, submitting, or advocating a document has a nondelegable responsibility to the court, and in most situations is the person to be sanctioned for a violation. Absent exceptional circumstances, a law firm is to be held also responsible when, as a result of a motion under subdivision (c)(1)(A), one of its partners, associates, or employees is determined to have violated the rule. Since such a motion may be filed only if the offending paper is not withdrawn or corrected within 21 days after service of the motion, it is appropriate that the law firm ordinarily be viewed as jointly responsible under established principles of agency. This provision is designed to remove the restrictions of the former rule. *Cf. Pavelic & LeFlore v. Marvel Entertainment Group*, 493 U.S. 120, 110 S. Ct. 456, 107 L. Ed. 2d 438 (1989) (1983 version of Rule 11 does not permit sanctions against law firm of attorney signing groundless complaint).

The revision permits the court to consider whether other attorneys in the firm, co-counsel, other law firms, or the party itself should be held accountable for their part in causing a violation. When appropriate, the court can make an additional inquiry in order to determine whether the sanction should be imposed on such persons, firms, or parties either in addition to or, in unusual circumstances, instead of the person actually making the presentation to the court. For example, such an inquiry may be appropriate in cases involving governmental agencies or other institutional parties that frequently impose substantial restrictions on the discretion of individual attorneys employed by it.

Sanctions that involve monetary awards (such as a fine or an award of attorney's fees) may not be imposed on a represented party for causing a violation of subdivision (b)(2), involving frivolous contentions of law. Monetary responsibility for such violations is more properly placed solely on the party's attorneys. With this limitation, the rule should not be subject to attack under the Rules Enabling Act. *See Willy v. Coastal Corp.*, 503 U.S. 131, 112 S. Ct. 1076, 117 L. Ed. 2d 280 (1992); *Business Guides, Inc. v. Chromatic Communications Enter. Inc.*, 498 U.S. 533, 111 S. Ct. 922, 112 L. Ed. 2d 1140 (1991). This restriction does not limit the court's power to impose sanctions or remedial orders that may have collateral financial consequences upon a party, such as dismissal of a claim, preclusion of a defense, or preparation of amended pleadings.

Explicit provision is made for litigants to be provided notice of the alleged violation and an opportunity to respond before sanctions are imposed. Whether the matter should be decided solely on the basis of written submissions or should be scheduled for oral argument (or, indeed, for evidentiary presentation) will depend on the circumstances. If the court imposes a sanction, it must, unless waived, indicate its reasons in a written order or on the record; the court should not ordinarily have to explain its denial of a motion for sanctions. Whether a violation has occurred and what sanctions, if any, to impose for a violation are matters committed to the discretion of the trial court; accordingly, as under current law, the standard for appellate review of these decisions will be for abuse of discretion. *See Cooter & Gell v. Hartmarx Corp.*, 496 U.S. 384, 110 S. Ct. 2447, 110 L. Ed. 2d 359 (1990) (noting, however, that an abuse would be established if the court based its ruling on an erroneous view of the law or on a clearly erroneous assessment of the evidence).

The revision leaves for resolution on a case-by-case basis, considering the particular circumstances involved, the question as to when a motion for violation of Rule 11 should be served and when, if filed, it should be decided. Ordinarily the motion should be served promptly after the inappropriate paper is filed, and, if delayed too long, may be viewed as untimely. In other circumstances, it should not be served until the other party has had a reasonable opportunity for discovery. Given the "safe harbor" provisions discussed below, a party cannot delay serving its Rule 11 motion until conclusion of the case (or judicial rejection of the offending contention).

Rule 11 motions should not be made or threatened for minor, inconsequential violations of the standards prescribed by subdivision (b). They should not be employed as a discovery device or to test the legal sufficiency or efficacy of allegations in the pleadings; other motions are available for those purposes. Nor should Rule 11 motions be prepared to emphasize the merits of a party's position, to exact an unjust settlement, to intimidate an adversary into withdrawing contentions that are fairly debatable, to increase the costs of litigation, to create a conflict of interest between attorney and client, or to seek disclosure of matters otherwise protected by the attorney-client privilege or the work-product doctrine. As under the prior rule, the court may defer its ruling (or its decision as to the identity of the persons to be sanctioned) until final resolution of the case in order to avoid immediate conflicts of interest and to reduce the disruption created if a disclosure of attorney-client communications is needed to determine whether a violation occurred or to identify the person responsible for the violation.

The rule provides that requests for sanctions must be made as a separate motion, *i.e.,* not simply included as an additional prayer for relief contained in another motion. The motion for sanctions is not, however, to be filed until at least 21 days (or such other period as the court may set) after being served. If, during this period, the alleged violation is corrected, as by withdrawing (whether formally or informally) some allegation or contention, the motion should not be filed with the court. These provisions are intended to provide a type of "safe harbor" against motions under Rule 11 in that a party will not be subject to sanctions on the basis of another party's motion unless, after receiving the motion, it refuses to withdraw that position or to acknowledge candidly that it does not currently have evidence to support a specified allegation. Under the former rule, parties were sometimes reluctant to abandon a questionable contention lest that be viewed as evidence of a violation of Rule 11; under the revision, the timely withdrawal of a contention will protect a party against a motion for sanctions.

To stress the seriousness of a motion for sanctions and to define precisely the conduct claimed to violate the rule, the revision provides that the "safe harbor" period begins to run only upon service of the motion. In most cases, however, counsel should be expected to give informal notice to the other party, whether in person or by a telephone call or letter, of a potential violation before proceeding to prepare and serve a Rule 11 motion.

As under former Rule 11, the filing of a motion for sanctions is itself subject to the requirements of the rule and can lead to sanctions. However, service of a cross motion under Rule 11 should rarely be needed since under the revision the court may award to the person who prevails on a motion under Rule 11—whether the movant or the target of the motion—reasonable expenses, including attorney's fees, incurred in presenting or opposing the motion.

The power of the court to act on its own initiative is retained, but with the condition that this be done through a show cause order. This procedure provides the person with notice and an opportunity to respond. The revision provides that a monetary sanction imposed after a court-initiated show cause order be limited to a penalty payable to the court and that it be imposed only if the show cause order is issued before any voluntary dismissal or an agreement of the parties to settle the claims made by or against the litigant. Parties settling a case should not be subsequently faced with an unexpected order from the court leading to monetary sanctions that might have affected their willingness to settle or voluntarily dismiss a case. Since show cause orders will ordinarily be issued only in situations that are akin to a contempt of court, the rule does not provide a "safe harbor" to a litigant for withdrawing a claim, defense, etc., after a show cause order has been issued on the court's own initiative. Such corrective action, however, should be taken into account in deciding what—if any—sanction to impose if, after consideration of the litigant's response, the court concludes that a violation has occurred.

Subdivision (d). Rules 26(g) and 37 establish certification standards and sanctions that apply to discovery disclosures, requests, responses, objections, and motions. It is appropriate that Rules 26 through 37, which are specially designed for the discovery process, govern such documents and conduct rather than the more general provisions of Rule 11. Subdivision (d) has been added to accomplish this result.

Rule 11 is not the exclusive source for control of improper presentations of claims, defenses, or contentions. It does not supplant statutes permitting awards of attorney's fees to prevailing parties or alter the principles governing such awards. It does not inhibit the court in punishing for contempt, in exercising its inherent powers, or in imposing sanctions, awarding expenses, or directing remedial action authorized under other rules or under 28 U.S.C. § 1927. *See Chambers v. NASCO*, 501 U.S. 32 (1991). *Chambers* cautions, however, against reliance upon inherent powers if appropriate sanctions can be imposed under provisions such as Rule 11, and the procedures specified in Rule 11—notice, opportunity to respond, and findings—should ordinarily be employed when imposing a sanction under the court's inherent powers. Finally, it should be noted that Rule 11 does not preclude a party from initiating an independent action for malicious prosecution or abuse of process.

2007 AMENDMENT

The language of Rule 11 has been amended as part of the general restyling of the Civil Rules to make them more easily understood and to make style and

terminology consistent throughout the rules. These changes are intended to be stylistic only.

Providing an e-mail address is useful, but does not of itself signify consent to filing or service by e-mail.

Rule 12. Defenses and Objections—When and How Presented—By Pleading or Motion—Motion for Judgment on the Pleadings

1937 ADOPTION

Note to Subdivision (a). 1. Compare former Equity Rules 12 (Issue of Subpoena—Time for Answer) and 31 (Reply—When Required—When Cause at Issue); 4 Mont.Rev.Codes Ann. (1935) §§ 9107, 9158; N.Y.C.P.A. (1937) § 263; N.Y.R.C.P. (1937) Rules 109 to 111.

2. U.S.C., Title 28, § 507, formerly § 763 (Petition in action against United States; service; appearance by district attorney) provides that the United States as a defendant shall have 60 days within which to answer or otherwise defend. This and other statutes which provide 60 days for the United States or an officer or agency thereof to answer or otherwise defend are continued by this rule. In so far as any statutes not excepted in Rule 81 provide a different time for a defendant to defend, such statutes are modified. See U.S.C., Title 28, former § 45 (District courts; practice and procedure in certain cases under the interstate commerce laws)(30 days).

3. Compare the last sentence of former Equity Rule 29 (Defenses—How Presented) and N.Y.C.P.A., 1937, § 283. See rule 15(a) for time within which to plead to an amended pleading.

Note to Subdivisions (b) and (d). 1. See generally former Equity Rules 29 (Defenses—How Presented), 33 (Testing Sufficiency of Defense), 43 (Defect of Parties—Resisting Objection), and 44 (Defect of Parties—Tardy Objection); N.Y.C.P.A., 1937, §§ 277 to 280; N.Y.R.C.P., 1937, Rules 106 to 112; English Rules Under the Judicature Act (The Annual Practice, 1937) O. 25, r.r. 1 to 4; Clark, Code Pleading, 1928, pp. 371–381.

2. For provisions authorizing defenses to be made in the answer or reply see English Rules Under the Judicature Act (The Annual Practice, 1937) O. 25, r.r. 1 to 4; 1 Miss.Code Ann., 1930, §§ 378, 379. Compare former Equity Rule 29 (Defenses—How Presented); U.S.C., Title 28, former § 45 (District Courts; practice and procedure in certain cases under the interstate commerce laws). U.S.C., Title 28, former § 45, substantially continued by this rule, provides: "No replication need be filed to the answer, and objections to the sufficiency of the petition or answer as not setting forth a cause of action or defense must be taken at the final hearing or by motion to dismiss the petition based on said grounds, which motion may be made at any time before answer is filed." Compare Calif.Code Civ.Proc. (Deering, 1937) § 433; 4 Nev.Comp.Laws (Hillyer, 1929) § 8600. For provisions that the defendant may demur and answer at the same time, see Calif.Code Civ.Proc. (Deering, 1937) § 431; 4 Nev.Comp.Laws (Hillyer, 1929) § 8598.

3. Former Equity Rule 29 (Defenses—How Presented) abolished demurrers and provided that defenses in point of law arising on the face of the bill should be made by motion to dismiss or in the answer, with further provision that every such point of law going to the whole or material part of the cause or causes stated might be called up and disposed of before final hearing "at the discretion of the court." Likewise many state practices have abolished the demurrer, or retain it only to attack substantial and not formal defects. See 6 Tenn.Code Ann. (Williams, 1934) § 8784; Ala.Code Ann. (Michie, 1928) § 9479; 2 Mass.Gen.Laws (Ter.Ed., 1932) ch. 231, §§ 15 to 18; Kansas Gen.Stat.Ann. (1935) §§ 60-705, 60-706.

Note to Subdivision (c). Compare former Equity Rule 33 (Testing Sufficiency of Defense); N.Y.R.C.P. (1937) Rules 111 and 112.

Note to Subdivisions (e) and (f). Compare former Equity Rules 20 (Further and Particular Statement in Pleading May Be Required) and 21 (Scandal and Impertinence); English Rules Under the Judicature Act (The Annual Practice, 1937) O. 19, r. r. 7, 7a, 7b, 8; 4 Mont.Rev.Codes Ann. (1935) §§ 9166, 9167; N.Y.C.P.A. (1937) § 247; N.Y.R.C.P. (1937) Rules 103, 115, 116, 117; Wyo.Rev.Stat.Ann. (Courtright, 1931) §§ 89-1033, 89-1034.

Note to Subdivision (g). Compare Rules of the District Court of the United States for the District of Columbia (1937) former Equity Rule 11; N.M.Rules of Pleading, Practice and Procedure, 38 N.M.Rep. vii [105-408] (1934); Wash.Gen. Rules of the Superior Courts, 1 Wash.Rev.Stat.Ann. (Remington, 1932) p. 160, Rule VI(e) and (f).

Note to Subdivision (h). Compare Calif.Code Civ.Proc. (Deering, 1937) § 434; 2 Minn.Stat. (Mason, 1927) § 9252; N.Y.C.P.A. (1937) §§ 278 and 279; Wash.Gen.Rules of the Superior Courts, 1 Wash.Rev.Stat.Ann. (Remington, 1932) p. 160, Rule VI(e). This rule continues U.S.C., Title 28, former § 80 (Dismissal or remand)(of action over which district court lacks jurisdiction), while U.S.C., Title 28, former § 399 (Amendments to show diverse citizenship) is continued by Rule 15.

1946 AMENDMENT

Note to Subdivision (a). Various minor alterations in language have been made to improve the statement of the rule. All references to bills of particulars have been stricken in accordance with changes made in subdivision (e).

Subdivision (b). The addition of defense (7), "failure to join an indispensable party", cures an omission in the rules, which are silent as to the mode of raising such failure. See Commentary, Manner of Raising Objection of Non-Joinder of Indispensable Party, 1940, 2 Fed.Rules Serv. 658, and, 1942, 5 Fed.Rules Serv. 820. In one case, *United States v. Metropolitan Life Ins. Co., E.D.Pa.1941*, 36 F.Supp. 399, the failure to join an indispensable party was raised under Rule 12(c).

Rule 12(b)(6), permitting a motion to dismiss for failure of the complaint to state a claim on which relief can be granted, is substantially the same as the old demurrer for failure of a pleading to state a cause of action. Some courts have held that as the rule by its terms refers to statements in the complaint, extraneous matter on affidavits, depositions or otherwise, may not be introduced in support of the motion, or to resist it. On the other hand, in many cases the district courts have permitted the introduction of such material. When these cases have reached circuit courts of appeals in situations where the extraneous material so received shows that there is no genuine issue as to any material question of fact and that on the undisputed facts as disclosed by the affidavits or depositions, one party or the other is entitled to judgment as a matter of law, the circuit courts, properly enough, have been reluctant to dispose of the case merely on the face of the pleading, and in the interest of prompt disposition of the action have made a final disposition of it. In dealing with such situations the Second Circuit has made the sound suggestion that whatever its label or original basis, the motion may be treated as a motion for summary judgment and disposed of as such. *Samara v. United States, C.C.A.2, 1942*, 129 F.2d 594, certiorari denied 317 U.S. 686, 63 S. Ct. 258, 87 L.Ed. 549; *Boro Hall Corp. v. General Motors Corp., C.C.A.2, 1942*, 124 F.2d 822, certiorari denied 317 U.S. 695, 63 S. Ct. 436, 87 L.Ed. 556. See, also, *Kithcart v. Metropolitan Life Ins. Co., C.C.A.8, 1945*, 150 F.2d 997.

It has also been suggested that this practice could be justified on the ground that the federal rules permit "speaking" motions. The Committee entertains the view that on motion under Rule 12(b)(6) to dismiss for failure of the complaint to state a good claim, the trial court should have authority to permit the introduction of extraneous matter, such as may be offered on a motion for summary judgment, and if it does not exclude such matter the motion should then be treated as a motion for summary judgment and disposed of in the manner and on the conditions stated in Rule 56 relating to summary judgments, and, of course, in such a situation, when the case reaches the circuit court of appeals, that court should treat the motion in the same way. The Committee believes that such practice, however, should be tied to the summary judgment rule. The term "speaking motion" is not mentioned in the rules, and if there is such a thing its limitations are undefined. Where extraneous matter is received, by tying further proceedings to the summary judgment rule the courts have a definite basis in the rules for disposing of the motion.

The Committee emphasizes particularly the fact that the summary judgment rule does not permit a case to be disposed of by judgment on the merits on affidavits, which disclose a conflict on a material issue of fact, and unless this practice is tied to the summary judgment rule, the extent to which a court, on the introduction of such extraneous matter, may resolve questions of fact on conflicting proof would be left uncertain.

The decisions dealing with this general situation may be generally grouped as follows: (1) cases dealing with the use of affidavits and other extraneous material on motions; (2) cases reversing judgments to prevent final determination on mere pleading allegations alone.

Under group (1) are: *Boro Hall Corp. v. General Motors Corp., C.C.A.2, 1942*, 124 F.2d 822, certiorari denied 317 U.S. 695, 63 S. Ct. 436, 87 L.Ed. 556; *Gallup v. Caldwell, C.C.A.3, 1941*, 120 F.2d 90; *Central Mexico Light & Power Co. v. Munch, C.C.A.2, 1940*, 116 F.2d 85; *National War Labor Board v. Montgomery Ward & Co., 1944*, 144 F.2d 528, 79 U.S.App.D.C. 200, certiorari denied 323 U.S. 774, 65 S. Ct. 134, 89 L.Ed. 619; *Urquhart v. American-La France Foamite Corp., 1944*, 144 F.2d 542, 79 U.S.App.D.C. 219; *Samara v. United States, C.C.A.2, 1942*, 129 F.2d 594; *Cohen v. American Window Glass Co., C.C.A.2, 1942*, 126 F.2d 111; *Sperry Products Inc. v. Association of American Railroads, C.C.A.2, 1942*, 132 F.2d 408; *Joint Council Dining Car Employees Local 370 v. Delaware, Lackawanna and Western R. Co., C.C.A.2, 1946*, 157 F.2d 417; *Weeks v. Bareco Oil Co., C.C.A.7, 1941*, 125 F.2d 84; *Carroll v. Morrison Hotel Corp., C.C.A.7, 1945*, 149 F.2d 404; *Victory v. Manning, C.C.A.3, 1942*, 128 F.2d 415; *Locals No. 1470, No. 1469, and No. 1512 of International Longshoremen's Association v. Southern Pacific Co., C.C.A.5, 1942*, 131 F.2d 605; *Lucking v. Delano, C.C.A.6, 1942*, 129 F.2d 283; *San Francisco Lodge No. 68 of International Association of Machinists v. Forrestal, Cal.1944*, 58 F.Supp. 466; *Benson v. Export Equipment Corp., 1945*, 164 P.2d 380, 49 N.M. 356, construing New Mexico rule identical with Rule 12(b)(6); F. E. Myers & Bros. Co. v. Goulds Pumps, Inc., N.Y.1946, 9 Fed.Rules Serv. 12b, 5 F.R.D. 132–33 Case 2. Cf. *Kohler v. Jacobs, C.C.A.5, 1943*, 138 F.2d 440; *Cohen v. United States, C.C.A.8, 1942*, 129 F.2d 733.

Under group (2) are: *Sparks v. England, C.C.A.8, 1940*, 113 F.2d 579; *Continental Collieries, Inc. v. Shober, C.C.A.3, 1942*, 130 F.2d 631; *Downey v. Palmer, C.C.A.2, 1940*, 114 F.2d 116; *DeLoach v. Crowley's Inc., C.C.A.5, 1942*, 128 F.2d 378; *Leimer v. State Mutual Life Assurance Co. of Worcester, Mass., C.C.A.8, 1940*, 108 F.2d 302; *Rossiter v. Vogel, C.C.A.2, 1943*, 134 F.2d 908, compare s.c., C.C.A.2, 1945, 148 F.2d 292; *Karl Kiefer Machine Co. v. United States Bottlers Machinery Co., C.C.A.7, 1940*, 113 F.2d 356; *Chicago Metallic Mfg. Co. v. Edward Katzinger Co., C.C.A.7, 1941*, 123 F.2d 518; *Louisiana Farmers' Protective Union, Inc. v. Great Atlantic & Pacific Tea Co. of America, Inc., C.C.A.8, 1942*, 131 F.2d 419; *Publicity Bldg. Realty Corp. v. Hannegan, C.C.A.8, 1943*, 139 F.2d 583; *Dioguardi v. Durning, C.C.A.2, 1944*, 139 F.2d 774; *Package Closure Corp. v. Sealright Co., Inc., C.C.A.2, 1944*, 141 F.2d 972; *Tahir Erk v. Glenn L. Martin Co., C.C.A.4, 1941*, 116 F.2d 865; *Bell v. Preferred Life Assurance Society of Montgomery, Ala., 1943*, 320 U.S. 238, 64 S. Ct. 5, 88 L.Ed. 15.

The addition at the end of subdivision (b) makes it clear that on a motion under Rule 12(b)(6) extraneous material may not be considered if the court excludes it, but that if the court does not exclude such material the motion shall be treated as a motion for summary judgment and disposed of as provided in Rule 56. It will also be observed that if a motion under Rule 12(b)(6) is thus converted into a summary judgment motion, the amendment insures that both parties shall be given a reasonable opportunity to submit affidavits and extraneous proofs to avoid taking a party by surprise through the conversion of the motion into a motion for summary judgment. In this manner and to this extent the amendment regularizes the practice above described. As the courts are already dealing with cases in this way, the effect of this amendment is really only to define the practice carefully and apply the requirements of the summary judgment rule in the disposition of the motion.

Subdivision (c). The sentence appended to subdivision (c) performs the same function and is grounded on the same reasons as the corresponding sentence added in subdivision (b).

Subdivision (d). The change here was made necessary because of the addition of defense (7) in subdivision (b).

Subdivision (e). References in this subdivision to a bill of particulars have been deleted, and the motion provided for is confined to one for more definite statement to be obtained only in cases where the movant cannot reasonably be required to frame an answer or other responsive pleading to the pleading in question. With respect to preparations for trial, the party is properly relegated to the various methods of examination and discovery provided in the rules for that purpose. *Slusher v. Jones, Ky.1943, 7 Fed.Rules Serv. 12e.231, Case 5*, 3 F.R.D. 168; *Best Foods, Inc. v. General Mills, Inc., D.Del.1943, 7 Fed.Rules Serv. 12e.231, Case 7*, 3 F.R.D. 275; Braden v. Callaway, Tenn.1943, 8 Fed.Rules Serv. 12e.231, Case 1 (". . . most courts . . . conclude that the definiteness required is only such as will be sufficient for the party to prepare responsive pleadings"). Accordingly, the reference to the 20 day time limit has also been eliminated, since the purpose of this present provision is to state a time period where the motion for a bill is made for the purpose of preparing for trial.

Rule 12(e) as originally drawn has been the subject of more judicial rulings than any other part of the rules, and has been much criticized by commentators, judges and members of the bar. See general discussion and cases cited in 1 Moore's Federal Practice, 1938, Cum.Supplement, § 12.07, under "Page 657"; also, Holtzoff, New Federal Procedure and the Courts, 1940, 35–41. And compare vote of Second Circuit Conference of Circuit and District Judges, June 1940, recommending the abolition of the bill of particulars; Sun Valley Mfg. Co. v. Mylish, Pa.1944, 8 Fed.Rules Serv. 12e.231, Case 6 ("Our experience . . . has demonstrated not only that 'the office of the bill of particulars is fast becoming obsolete' . . . 27 but that in view of the adequate discovery procedure available under the Rules, motions for bills of particulars should be abolished altogether."); *Walling v. American Steamship Co., N.Y.1945*, 4 F.R.D. 355, 8 Fed.Rules Serv. 12e.244, Case 8 (". . . the adoption of the rule was ill advised. It has led to confusion, duplication and delay.") The tendency of some courts freely to grant extended bills of particulars has served to neutralize any helpful benefits derived from Rule 8, and has overlooked the intended use of the rules on depositions and discovery. The words "or to prepare for trial"—eliminated by the proposed amendment—have sometimes been seized upon as grounds for compulsory statement in the opposing pleading of all the details which the movant would have to meet at the trial. On the other hand, many courts have in effect read these words out of the rule. See *Walling v. Alabama Pipe Co., Mo.1942*, 3 F.R.D. 159, 6 Fed.Rules Serv. 12e.244, Case 7; *Fleming v. Mason & Dixon Lines, Inc., Tenn.1941*, 42 F.Supp. 230; *Kellogg Co. v. National Biscuit Co., N.J.1941*, 38 F.Supp. 643; Brown v. H. L. Green Co., N.Y.1943, 7 Fed.Rules Serv. 12e.231, Case 6; Pedersen v. Standard Accident Ins. Co., Mo.1945, 8 Fed.Rules Serv. 12e.231, Case 8; *Bowles v. Ohse, Neb.1945*, 4 F.R.D. 403, 9 Fed.Rules Serv. 12e.231, Case 1; Klages v. Cohen, N.Y.1945, 9 Fed.Rules Serv. 8a.25, Case 4; Bowles v. Lawrence, Mass.1945, 8 Fed.Rules Serv. 12e.231, Case 19; McKinney Tool Mfg. Co. v. Hoyt, Ohio 1945, 9 Fed.Rules Serv. 12e.235, Case 1; *Bowles v. Jack, Minn.1945*, 5 F.R.D. 1, 9 Fed.Rules Serv. 12e.244, Case 9. And it has been urged from the bench that the phrase be stricken, *Poole v. White, W.Va.1941, 5 Fed.Rules Serv. 12e.231, Case 4*, 2 F.R.D. 40. See also Bowles v. Gabel, Mo.1946, 9 Fed.Rules Serv. 12e.244, Case 10. ("The courts have never favored that portion of the rules which undertook to justify a motion of this kind for the purpose of aiding counsel in preparing his case for trial.").

Subdivision (f). This amendment affords a specific method of raising the insufficiency of a defense, a matter which has troubled some courts, although attack has been permitted in one way or another. See *Dysart v. Remington-Rand, Inc., Conn.1939*, 31 F.Supp. 296; *Eastman Kodak Co. v. McAuley, N.Y.1941, 4 Fed.Rules Serv. 12f.21, Case 8*, 2 F.R.D. 21; *Schenley Distillers Corp. v. Renken, S.C.1940*, 34 F.Supp. 678; *Yale Transport Corp. v. Yellow Truck & Coach Mfg. Co., N.Y.1944*, 3 F.R.D. 440; *United States v. Turner Milk Co., Ill.1941, 4 Fed.Rules Serv. 12b.51, Case 3*, 1 F.R.D. 643; *Teiger v. Stephan Oderwald, Inc., N.Y.1940*, 31 F.Supp. 626; *Teplitzky v. Pennsylvania R. Co., Ill.1941*, 38 F.Supp. 535; *Gallagher v. Carroll, N.Y.1939*, 27 F.Supp. 568; *United States v. Palmer, N.Y.1939*, 28 F.Supp. 936. And see *Indemnity Ins. Co. of North America v. Pan American Airways, Inc., N.Y.1944*, 58 F.Supp. 338; Commentary, Modes of Attacking Insufficient Defenses in the Answer, 1939, 1 Fed.Rules Serv. 669, 1940, 2 Fed.Rules Serv. 640.

Subdivision (g). The change in title conforms with the companion provision in subdivision (h).

The alteration of the "except" clause requires that other than provided in subdivision (h) a party who resorts to a motion to raise defenses specified in the rule, must include in one motion all that are then available to him. Under the original rule defenses which could be raised by motion were divided into two groups which could be the subjects of two successive motions.

Subdivision (h). The addition of the phrase relating to indispensable parties is one of necessity.

1963 AMENDMENT

This amendment conforms to the amendment of Rule 4(e). See also the Advisory Committee's Note to amended Rule 4(b).

1966 AMENDMENT

Subdivision (b)(7). The terminology of this subdivision is changed to accord with the amendment of Rule 19. See the Advisory Committee's Note to Rule 19, as amended, especially the third paragraph therein before the caption "Subdivision (c)."

Subdivision (g). Subdivision (g) has forbidden a defendant who makes a preanswer motion under this rule from making a further motion presenting any defense or objection which was available to him at the time he made the first motion and which he could have included, but did not in fact include therein. Thus if the defendant moves before answer to dismiss the complaint for failure to state a claim, he is barred from making a further motion presenting the defense of improper venue, if that defense was available to him when he made his original motion. Amended subdivision (g) is to the same effect. This required consolidation of defenses and objections in a Rule 12 motion is salutary in that it works against piecemeal consideration of a case. For exceptions to the requirement of consolidation, see the last clause of subdivision (g), referring to new subdivision (h)(2).

Subdivision (h). The question has arisen whether an omitted defense which cannot be made the basis of a second motion may nevertheless be pleaded in the answer. Subdivision (h) called for waiver of "* * * defenses and objections which he [defendant] does not present * * * by motion * * * or, if he has made no motion, in his answer * * *." If the clause "if he has made no motion," was read literally, it seemed that the omitted defense was waived and could not be pleaded in the answer. On the other hand, the clause might be read as adding nothing of substance to the preceding words; in that event it appeared that a defense was not waived by reason of being omitted from the motion and might be set up in the answer. The decisions were divided. Favoring waiver, see *Keefe v. Derounian*, 6 F.R.D. 11 (N.D.Ill.1946); *Elbinger v. Precision Metal Workers Corp.*, 18 F.R.D. 467 (E.D.Wis.1956); see also *Rensing v. Turner Aviation Corp.*, 166 F.Supp. 790 (N.D.Ill.1958); *P Beiersdorf & Co. v. Duke Laboratories, Inc.*, 10 F.R.D. 282 (S.D.N.Y.1950); *Neset v. Christensen*, 92 F.Supp. 78 (E.D.N.Y.1950). Opposing waiver, see *Phillips v. Baker*, 121 F.2d 752 (9th Cir.1941); *Crum v. Graham*, 32 F.R.D. 173 (D.Mont.1963) (regretfully following the Phillips case);

see also *Birnbaum v. Birrell*, 9 F.R.D. 72 (S.D.N.Y.1948); *Johnson v. Joseph Schlitz Brewing Co.*, 33 F.Supp. 176 (E.D.Tenn.1940); *cf. Carter v. American Bus Lines, Inc.*, 22 F.R.D. 323 (D.Neb.1958).

Amend subdivision (h)(1)(A) eliminates the ambiguity and states that certain specified defenses which were available to a party when he made a preanswer motion, but which he omitted from the motion, are waived. The specified defenses are lack of jurisdiction over the person, improper venue, insufficiency of process, and insufficiency of service of process (see Rule 12(b)(2) to (5)). A party who by motion invites the court to pass upon a threshold defense should bring forward all the specified defenses he then has and thus allow the court to do a reasonably complete job. The waiver reinforces the policy of subdivision (g) forbidding successive motions.

By amended subdivision (h)(1)(B), the specified defenses, even if not waived by the operation of (A), are waived by the failure to raise them by a motion under Rule 12 or in the responsive pleading or any amendment thereof to which the party is entitled as a matter of course. The specified defenses are of such a character that they should not be delayed and brought up for the first time by means of an application to the court to amend the responsive pleading.

Since the language of the subdivisions is made clear, the party is put on fair notice of the effect of his actions and omissions and can guard himself against unintended waiver. It is to be noted that while the defenses specified in subdivision (h)(1) are subject to waiver as there provided, the more substantial defenses of failure to state a claim upon which relief can be granted, failure to join a party indispensable under Rule 19, and failure to state a legal defense to a claim (see Rule 12(b)(6), (7), (f)), as well as the defense of lack of jurisdiction over the subject matter (see Rule 12(b)(1)), are expressly preserved against waiver by amended subdivision (h)(2) and (3).

1987 AMENDMENT

The amendments are technical. No substantive change is intended.

1993 AMENDMENT

Subdivision (a) is divided into paragraphs for greater clarity, and paragraph (1)(B) is added to reflect amendments to Rule 4. Consistent with Rule 4(d)(3), a defendant that timely waives service is allowed 60 days from the date the request was mailed in which to respond to the complaint, with an additional 30 days afforded if the request was sent out of the country. Service is timely waived if the waiver is returned within the time specified in the request (30 days after the request was mailed, or 60 days if mailed out of the country) and before being formally served with process. Sometimes a plaintiff may attempt to serve a defendant with process while also sending the defendant a request for waiver of service; if the defendant executes the waiver of service within the time specified and before being served with process, it should have the longer time to respond afforded by waiving service.

The date of sending the request is to be inserted by the plaintiff on the face of the request for waiver and on the waiver itself. This date is used to measure the return day for the waiver form, so that the plaintiff can know on a day certain whether formal service of process will be necessary; it is also a useful date to measure the time for answer when service is waived. The defendant who returns the waiver is given additional time for answer in order to assure that it loses nothing by waiving service of process.

2000 AMENDMENT

Rule 12(a)(3)(B) is added to complement the addition of Rule 4(i)(2)(B). The purposes that underlie the requirement that service be made on the United States in an action that asserts individual liability of a United States officer or employee for acts occurring in connection with the performance of duties on behalf of the United States also require that the time to answer be extended to 60 days. Time is needed for the United States to determine whether to provide representation to the defendant officer or employee. If the United States provides representation, the need for an extended answer period is the same as in actions against the United States, a United States agency, or a United States officer sued in an official capacity.

An action against a former officer or employee of the United States is covered by subparagraph (3)(B) in the same way as an action against a present officer or employee. Termination of the relationship between the individual defendant and the United States does not reduce the need for additional time to answer.

GAP Report

No changes are recommended for Rule 12 as published.

2007 AMENDMENT

The language of Rule 12 has been amended as part of the general restyling of the Civil Rules to make them more easily understood and to make style and terminology consistent throughout the rules. These changes are intended to be stylistic only.

Former Rule 12(a)(4)(A) referred to an order that postpones disposition of a motion "until the trial on the merits." Rule 12(a)(4) now refers to postponing disposition "until trial." The new expression avoids the ambiguity that inheres in "trial on the merits," which may become confusing when there is a separate trial of a single issue or another event different from a single all-encompassing trial.

2009 AMENDMENT

The times set in the former rule at 10 or 20 days have been revised to 14 or 21 days. See the Note to Rule 6.

Rule 13. Counterclaim and Cross-Claim

1937 ADOPTION

1. This is substantially former Equity Rule 30 (Answer—Contents—Counterclaim), broadened to include legal as well as equitable counterclaims.

2. Compare the English practice, English Rules Under the Judicature Act (The Annual Practice, 1937) O. 19, r. r. 2 and 3, and O. 21, r. r. 10 to 17; *Beddall v. Maitland*, L.R. 17 Ch.Div. 174, 181, 182 (1881).

3. Certain states have also adopted almost unrestricted provisions concerning both the subject matter of and the parties to a counterclaim. This seems to be the modern tendency. Ark.Civ.Code (Crawford, 1934) §§ 117 (as amended) and 118; N.J.S.A. 2:27-137, 2:27-139, 2:27-141; N.Y.C.P.A. (1937) §§ 262, 266, 267 (all as amended, Laws of 1936, ch. 324), 268, 269, and 271; Wis.Stat. (1935) § 263.14(1)(c).

4. Most codes do not expressly provide for a counterclaim in the reply. Clark, Code Pleading (1928), p. 486, Ky.Codes (Carroll, 1932) Civ.Pract. § 98 does provide, however, for such counterclaim.

5. The provisions of this rule respecting counterclaims are subject to Rule 82 (Jurisdiction and Venue Unaffected). For a discussion of federal jurisdiction and venue in regard to counterclaims and cross-claims, see Shulman and Jaegerman, Some Jurisdictional Limitations in Federal Procedure (1936), 45 Yale L.J. 393, 410 et seq.

6. This rule does not affect such statutes of the United States as U.S.C., Title 28, §§ 1332, 1345, 1357, formerly § 41(1) (United States as plaintiff; civil suits at common law and in equity), relating to assigned claims in actions based on diversity of citizenship.

7. If the action proceeds to judgment without the interposition of a counterclaim as required by subdivision (a) of this rule, the counterclaim is barred. See *American Mills Co. v. American Surety Co., 1922*, 260 U.S. 360, 43 S. Ct. 149, 67 L.Ed. 306; *Marconi Wireless Telegraph Co. v. National Electric Signalling Co., N.Y.1913*, 206 F. 295; Hopkins, Federal Equity Rules (8th ed., 1933), p. 213; Simkins, Federal Practice (1934), p. 663.

8. For allowance of credits against the United States see U.S.C., Title 26, Int.Rev.Code, § 3772 (a)(1)(2)(b) (Suits for refunds of internal revenue taxes—

limitations); U.S.C., Title 28, § 2406, formerly §§ 774 (Suits by United States against individuals; credits), 775 (Suits under postal laws; credits); U.S.C., Title 31, § 227 (Offsets against judgments and claims against United States).

1946 AMENDMENT

Note to Subdivision (a). The use of the word "filing" was inadvertent. The word "serving" conforms with subdivision (e) and with usage generally throughout the rules.

The removal of the phrase "not the subject of a pending action" and the addition of the new clause at the end of the subdivision is designed to eliminate the ambiguity noted in *Prudential Insurance Co. of America v. Saxe, 1943*, 134 F.2d 16, 77 U.S.App.D.C. 144, 33–34, certiorari denied 319 U.S. 745, 63 S. Ct. 1033, 87 L.Ed. 1701. The rewording of the subdivision in this respect insures against an undesirable possibility presented under the original rule whereby a party having a claim which would be the subject of a compulsory counterclaim could avoid stating it as such by bringing an independent action in another court after the commencement of the federal action but before serving his pleading in the federal action.

Subdivision (g). The amendment is to care for a situation such as where a second mortgagee is made defendant in a foreclosure proceeding and wishes to file a cross-complaint against the mortgagor in order to secure a personal judgment for the indebtedness and foreclose his lien. A claim of this sort by the second mortgagee may not necessarily arise out of the transaction or occurrence that is the subject matter of the original action under the terms of Rule 13(g).

Subdivision (h). The change clarifies the interdependence of Rules 13(i) and 54(b).

1963 AMENDMENT

When a defendant, if he desires to defend his interest in property, is obliged to come in and litigate in a court to whose jurisdiction he could not ordinarily be subjected, fairness suggests that he should not be required to assert counterclaims, but should rather be permitted to do so at his election. If, however, he does elect to assert a counterclaim, it seems fair to require him to assert any other which is compulsory within the meaning of Rule 13(a). Clause (2), added by amendment to Rule 13(a), carries out this idea. It will apply to various cases described in Rule 4(e), as amended, where service is effected through attachment or other process by which the court does not acquire jurisdiction to render a personal judgment against the defendant. Clause (2) will also apply to actions commenced in State courts jurisdictionally grounded on attachment or the like, and removed to the Federal courts.

1966 AMENDMENT

Rule 13(h), dealing with the joinder of additional parties to a counterclaim or cross-claim, has partaken of some of the textual difficulties of Rule 19 on necessary joinder of parties. See Advisory Committee's Note to Rule 19, as amended; cf. 3 Moore's Federal Practice, par. 13.39 (2d ed. 1963), and Supp. thereto; 1A Barron & Holtzoff, Federal Practice and Procedure § 399 (Wright ed. 1960). Rule 13(h) has also been inadequate in failing to call attention to the fact that a party pleading a counterclaim or cross-claim may join additional persons when the conditions for permissive joinder of parties under Rule 20 are satisfied.

The amendment of Rule 13(h) supplies the latter omission by expressly referring to Rule 20, as amended, and also incorporates by direct reference the revised criteria and procedures of Rule 19, as amended. Hereafter, for the purpose of determining who must or may be joined as additional parties to a counterclaim or cross-claim, the party pleading the claim is to be regarded as a plaintiff and the additional parties as plaintiffs or defendants as the case may be, and amended Rules 19 and 20 are to be applied in the usual fashion. See also Rules 13(a) (compulsory counterclaims) and 22 (interpleader).

The amendment of Rule 13(h), like the amendment of Rule 19, does not attempt to regulate Federal jurisdiction or venue. See Rule 82. It should be noted, however, that in some situations the decisional law has recognized "ancillary"

Federal jurisdiction over counterclaims and cross-claims and "ancillary" venue as to parties to these claims.

1987 AMENDMENT

The amendments are technical. No substantive change is intended.

2007 AMENDMENT

The language of Rule 13 has been amended as part of the general restyling of the Civil Rules to make them more easily understood and to make style and terminology consistent throughout the rules. These changes are intended to be stylistic only.

The meaning of former Rule 13(b) is better expressed by deleting "not arising out of the transaction or occurrence that is the subject matter of the opposing party's claim." Both as a matter of intended meaning and current practice, a party may state as a permissive counterclaim a claim that does grow out of the same transaction or occurrence as an opposing party's claim even though one of the exceptions in Rule 13(a) means the claim is not a compulsory counterclaim.

2009 AMENDMENT

Rule 13(f) is deleted as largely redundant and potentially misleading. An amendment to add a counterclaim will be governed by Rule 15. Rule 15(a)(1) permits some amendments to be made as a matter of course or with the opposing party's written consent. When the court's leave is required, the reasons described in Rule 13(f) for permitting amendment of a pleading to add an omitted counterclaim sound different from the general amendment standard in Rule 15(a)(2), but seem to be administered—as they should be—according to the same standard directing that leave should be freely given when justice so requires. The independent existence of Rule 13(f) has, however, created some uncertainty as to the availability of relation back of the amendment under Rule 15(c). See 6 C. Wright, A. Miller & M. Kane, Federal Practice & Procedure: Civil 2d, § 1430 (1990). Deletion of Rule 13(f) ensures that relation back is governed by the tests that apply to all other pleading amendments.

Rule 14. Third Party Practice

1937 ADOPTION

Third-party impleader is in some aspects a modern innovation in law and equity although well known in admiralty. Because of its many advantages a liberal procedure with respect to it has developed in England, in the federal admiralty courts, and in some American state jurisdictions. See English Rules Under the Judicature Act (The Annual Practice, 1937) O. 16A, r. r. 1 to 13; United States Supreme Court Admiralty Rules (1920), Rule 56 (Right to Bring in Party Jointly Liable); 12 P.S.Pa.Ann. (1936) § 141; Wis.Stat. (1935) §§ 260.19, 260.20; N.Y.C.P.A. (1937) §§ 193(2), 211(a). Compare La.Code Pract. (Dart, 1932) §§ 378 to 388. For the practice in Texas as developed by judicial decision, see *Lottman v. Cuilla, Tex.1926*, 288 S.W. 123, 126. For a treatment of this subject see Gregory, Legislative Loss Distribution in Negligence Actions (1936); Shulman and Jaegerman, Some Jurisdictional Limitations on Federal Procedure (1936), 45 Yale L.J. 393, 417 et seq.

Third-party impleader under the former conformity act has been applied in actions at law in the federal courts. *Lowry and Co., Inc. v. National City Bank of New York, N.Y.1928*, 28 F.2d 895; *Yellow Cab Co. of Philadelphia v. Rodgers, C.C.A.3, 1932*, 61 F.2d 729.

1946 AMENDMENT

Note. The provisions in rule 14(a) which relate to the impleading of a third party who is or may be liable to the plaintiff have been deleted by the proposed amendment. It has been held that under rule 14(a) the plaintiff need not amend his complaint to state a claim against such third party if he does not wish to do so. *Satink v. Holland Township, N.J.1940*, 31 F.Supp. 229, noted, 1940, 88 U.Pa.L.Rev. 751; *Connelly v. Bender, Mich.1941*, 36 F.Supp. 368; *Whitmire v.*

Partin, Tenn.1941, 2 F.R.D. 83, 5 Fed.Rules Serv. 14a.513, Case 2; *Crim v. Lumbermen's Mutual Casualty Co., D.C.1939*, 26 F.Supp. 715; *Carbola Chemical Co., Inc. v. Trundle, N.Y.1943*, 3 F.R.D. 502, 7 Fed.Rules Serv. 14a.224, Case 1; Roadway Express, Inc. v. Automobile Ins. Co. of Hartford, Conn., Ohio 1945, 8 Fed.Rules Serv. 14a.513, Case 3. In *Delano v. Ives, Pa.1941*, 40 F.Supp. 672, the court said: ". . . the weight of authority is to the effect that a defendant cannot compel the plaintiff, who has sued him, to sue also a third party whom he does not wish to sue, by tendering in a third party complaint the third party as an additional defendant directly liable to the plaintiff." Thus impleader here amounts to no more than a mere offer of a party to the plaintiff, and if he rejects it, the attempt is a time-consuming futility. See *Satink v. Holland Township*, supra; *Malkin v. Arundel Corp., Md.1941*, 36 F.Supp. 948; also Koenigsberger, Suggestions for Changes in the Federal Rules of Civil Procedure, 1941, 4 Fed.Rules Serv. 1010. But cf. *Atlantic Coast Line R. Co. v. United States Fidelity & Guaranty Co., Ga.1943*, 52 F.Supp. 177.

Moreover, in any case where the plaintiff could not have joined the third party originally because of jurisdictional limitations such as lack of diversity of citizenship, the majority view is that any attempt by the plaintiff to amend his complaint and assert a claim against the impleaded third party would be unavailing. *Hoskie v. Prudential Ins. Co. of America, N.Y.1941*, 39 F.Supp. 305; *Johnson v. G. J. Sherrard Co., Mass.1941, 5 Fed.Rules Serv. 14a.511, Case 1*, 2 F.R.D. 164; *Thompson v. Cranston, N.Y.1942, 6 Fed.Rules Serv. 14a.511, Case 1*, 2 F.R.D. 270, affirmed, C.C.A.2d, 132 F.2d 631, certiorari denied 1943, 319 U.S. 741, 63 S. Ct. 1028, 87 L.Ed. 1698; *Friend v. Middle Atlantic Transportation Co., C.C.A.2, 1946*, 153 F.2d 778, certiorari denied 328 U.S. 865, 66 S. Ct. 1370, 90 L.Ed. 1635; *Herrington v. Jones, La.1941, 5 Fed.Rules Serv. 14a.511, Case 2*, 2 F.R.D. 108; Banks v. Employers' Liability Assurance Corp., Mo.1943, 7 Fed.Rules Serv. 14a.11, Case 2; Saunders v. Baltimore & Ohio R. Co., W.Va.1945, 9 Fed.Rules Serv. 14a.62, Case 2; Hull v. United States Rubber Co., Mich.1945, 9 Fed.Rules Serv. 14a.62, Case 3. See also concurring opinion of Circuit Judge Minton in *People of State of Illinois for Use of Trust Co. of Chicago v. Maryland Casualty Co., C.C.A.7, 1942*, 132 F.2d 850, 853. Contra: *Sklar v. Hayes, Pa.1941, 4 Fed.Rules Serv. 14a.511, Case 2*, 1 F.R.D. 594. Discussion of the problem will be found in Commentary, Amendment of Plaintiff's Pleading to Assert Claim Against Third-Party Defendant, 1942, 5 Fed.Rules Serv. 811; Commentary, Federal Jurisdiction in Third-Party Practice, 1943, 6 Fed.Rules Serv. 766; Holtzoff, Some Problems Under Federal Third-Party Practice, 1941, 3 La.L.Rev. 408, 419–420; 1 Moore's Federal Practice, 1938, Cum.Supplement § 14.08. For these reasons therefore, the words "or to the plaintiff" in the first sentence of subdivision (a) have been removed by the amendment; and in conformance therewith the words "the plaintiff" in the second sentence of the subdivision, and the words "or to the third-party plaintiff" in the concluding sentence thereof have likewise been eliminated.

The third sentence of Rule 14(a) has been expanded to clarify the right of the third-party defendant to assert any defenses which the third-party plaintiff may have to the plaintiff's claim. This protects the impleaded third-party defendant where the third-party plaintiff fails or neglects to assert a proper defense to the plaintiff's action. A new sentence has also been inserted giving the third-party defendant the right to assert directly against the original plaintiff any claim arising out of the transaction or occurrence that is the subject matter of the plaintiff's claim against the third-party plaintiff. This permits all claims arising out of the same transaction or occurrence to be heard and determined in the same action. See *Atlantic Coast Line R. Co. v. United States Fidelity & Guaranty Co., Ga.1943*, 52 F.Supp. 177. Accordingly, the next to the last sentence of subdivision (a) has also been revised to make clear that the plaintiff may, if he desires, assert directly against the third-party defendant either by amendment or by a new pleading any claim he may have against him arising out of the transaction or occurrence that is the subject matter of the plaintiff's claim against the third-party plaintiff. In such a case, the third-party defendant then is entitled to assert the defenses, counter-claims and cross-claims provided in

Rules 12 and 13.

The sentence reading "The third-party defendant is bound by the adjudication of the third-party plaintiff's liability to the plaintiff, as well as of his own to the plaintiff, or to the third-party plaintiff" has been stricken from Rule 14(a), not to change the law, but because the sentence states a rule of substantive law which is not within the scope of a procedural rule. It is not the purpose of the rules to state the effect of a judgment.

The elimination of the words "the third-party plaintiff, or any other party" from the second sentence of Rule 14(a), together with the insertion of the new phrases therein, are not changes of substance but are merely for the purpose of clarification.

1963 AMENDMENT

Under the amendment of the initial sentences of the subdivision, a defendant as a third-party plaintiff may freely and without leave of court bring in a third-party defendant if he files the third-party complaint not later than 10 days after he serves his original answer. When the impleader comes so early in the case, there is little value in requiring a preliminary ruling by the court on the propriety of the impleader.

After the third-party defendant is brought in, the court has discretion to strike the third-party claim if it is obviously unmeritorious and can only delay or prejudice the disposition of the plaintiff's claim, or to sever the third-party claim or accord it separate trial if confusion or prejudice would otherwise result. This discretion, applicable not merely to the cases covered by the amendment where the third-party defendant is brought in without leave, but to all impleaders under the rule, is emphasized in the next-to-last sentence of the subdivision, added by amendment.

In dispensing with leave of court for an impleader filed not later than 10 days after serving the answer, but retaining the leave requirement for impleaders sought to be effected thereafter, the amended subdivision takes a moderate position on the lines urged by some commentators, see Note, 43 Minn.L.Rev. 115 (1958); cf. Pa.R.Civ.P. 2252 to 53 (60 days after service on the defendant); Minn.R.Civ.P. 14.01 (45 days). Other commentators would dispense with the requirement of leave regardless of the time when impleader is effected, and would rely on subsequent action by the court to dismiss the impleader if it would unduly delay or complicate the litigation or would be otherwise objectionable. See 1A Barron & Holtzoff, Federal Practice & Procedure 649 to 50 (Wright ed. 1960); Comment, 58 Colum.L.Rev. 532, 546 (1958); cf. N.Y.Civ. Prac.Act § 193-a; Me.R.Civ.P. 14. The amended subdivision preserves the value of a preliminary screening, through the leave procedure, of impleaders attempted after the 10-day period.

The amendment applies also when an impleader is initiated by a third-party defendant against a person who may be liable to him, as provided in the last sentence of the subdivision.

1966 AMENDMENT

Rule 14 was modeled on Admiralty Rule 56. An important feature of Admiralty Rule 56 was that it allowed impleader not only of a person who might be liable to the defendant by way of remedy over, but also of any person who might be liable to the plaintiff. The importance of this provision was that the defendant was entitled to insist that the plaintiff proceed to judgment against the third-party defendant. In certain cases this was a valuable implementation of a substantive right. For example, in a case of ship collision where a finding of mutual fault is possible, one shipowner, if sued alone, faces the prospect of an absolute judgment for the full amount of the damage suffered by an innocent third-party; but if he can implead the owner of the other vessel, and if mutual fault is found, the judgment against the original defendant will be in the first instance only for a moiety of the damages; liability for the remainder will be conditioned on the plaintiff's inability to collect from the third-party defendant.

This feature was originally incorporated in Rule 14, but was eliminated by the amendment of 1946, so that under the amended rule a third party could not be impleaded on the basis that he might be liable to the plaintiff. One of the reasons for the amendment was that the Civil Rule, unlike the Admiralty Rule, did not require the plaintiff to go to judgment against the third-party defendant. Another reason was that where jurisdiction depended on diversity of citizenship the impleader of an adversary having the same citizenship as the plaintiff was not considered possible.

Retention of the admiralty practice in those cases that will be counterparts of a suit in admiralty is clearly desirable.

1987 AMENDMENT

The amendments are technical. No substantive change is intended.

2000 AMENDMENT

Subdivisions (a) and (c) are amended to reflect revisions in Supplemental Rule C(6).

GAP Report

Rule B(1)(a) was modified by moving "in an in personam action" out of paragraph (a) and into the first line of subdivision (1). This change makes it clear that all paragraphs of subdivision (1) apply when attachment is sought in an in personam action. Rule B(1)(d) was modified by changing the requirement that the clerk deliver the summons and process to the person or organization authorized to serve it. The new form requires only that the summons and process be delivered, not that the clerk effect the delivery. This change conforms to present practice in some districts and will facilitate rapid service. It matches the spirit of Civil Rule 4(b), which directs the clerk to issue the summons "to the plaintiff for service on the defendant." A parallel change is made in Rule C(3)(b).

2006 AMENDMENT

Rule 14 is amended to conform to changes in designating the paragraphs of Supplemental Rule C(6).

2007 AMENDMENT

The language of Rule 14 has been amended as part of the general restyling of the Civil Rules to make them more easily understood and to make style and terminology consistent throughout the rules. These changes are intended to be stylistic only.

Former Rule 14 twice refers to counterclaims under Rule 13. In each case, the operation of Rule 13(a) depends on the state of the action at the time the pleading is filed. If plaintiff and third-party defendant have become opposing parties because one has made a claim for relief against the other, Rule 13(a) requires assertion of any counterclaim that grows out of the transaction or occurrence that is the subject matter of that claim. Rules 14(a)(2)(B) and (a)(3) reflect the distinction between compulsory and permissive counterclaims.

A plaintiff should be on equal footing with the defendant in making third-party claims, whether the claim against the plaintiff is asserted as a counterclaim or as another form of claim. The limit imposed by the former reference to "counterclaim" is deleted.

2009 AMENDMENT

The time set in the former rule at 10 days has been revised to 14 days. See the Note to Rule 6.

Rule 15. Amended and Supplemental Pleadings

1937 ADOPTION

See generally for the present federal practice, former Equity Rules 19 (Amendments Generally), 28 (Amendment of Bill as of Course), 32 (Answer to Amended

Bill), 34 (Supplemental Pleading), and 35 (Bills of Revivor and Supplemental Bills—Form); U.S.C., Title 28, § 1653, formerly § 399 (Amendments to show diverse citizenship) and former § 777 (Defects of form; amendments). See English Rules Under the Judicature Act (The Annual Practice, 1937) O. 28, r. r. 1 to 13; O. 20, r. 4; O. 24, r. r. 1 to 3.

Note to Subdivision (a). The right to serve an amended pleading once as of course is common. 4 Mont.Rev.Codes Ann. (1935) § 9186; 1 Ore.Code Ann. (1930) § 1-904; 1 S.C.Code (Michie, 1932) § 493; English Rules Under the Judicature Act (The Annual Practice, 1937) O. 28, r. 2. Provision for amendment of pleading before trial, by leave of court, is in almost every code. If there is no statute the power of the court to grant leave is said to be inherent. Clark, Code Pleading, 1928, pp. 498, 509.

Note to Subdivision (b). Compare former Equity Rule 19 (Amendments Generally) and code provisions which allow an amendment "at any time in furtherance of justice," (e.g., Ark. Civ.Code (Crawford, 1934) § 155) and which allow an amendment of pleadings to conform to the evidence, where the adverse party has not been misled and prejudiced (e.g., N.M.Stat.Ann. (Courtright, 1929) §§ 105-601, 105-602).

Note to Subdivision (c). "Relation back" is a well recognized doctrine of recent and now more frequent application. Compare Ala.Code Ann. (Michie, 1928) § 9513; Smith-Hurd Ill.Stats. ch. 110, § 170(2); 2 Wash.Rev.Stat.Ann. (Remington, 1932) § 308-3(4). See U.S.C., Title 28, § 1653, formerly § 399 (Amendments to show diverse citizenship) for a provision for "relation back".

Note to Subdivision (d). This is an adaptation of former Equity Rule 34 (Supplemental Pleading).

1963 AMENDMENT

Rule 15(d) is intended to give the court broad discretion in allowing a supplemental pleading. However, some cases, opposed by other cases and criticized by the commentators, have taken the rigid and formalistic view that where the original complaint fails to state a claim upon which relief can be granted, leave to serve a supplemental complaint must be denied. See *Bonner v. Elizabeth Arden, Inc.*, 177 F.2d 703 (2d Cir.1949); *Bowles v. Senderowitz*, 65 F.Supp. 548 (E.D.Pa.), rev'd on other grounds, 158 F.2d 435 (3d Cir.1946), cert. denied, Senderowitz v. Fleming, 330 U.S. 848, 67 S. Ct. 1091, 91 L.Ed. 1292 (1947); cf. *La Salle Nat. Bank v. 222 East Chestnut St. Corp.*, 267 F.2d 247 (7th Cir.), cert. denied, 361 U.S. 836, 80 S. Ct. 88, 4 L. Ed. 2d 77 (1959). But see *Camilla Cotton Oil Co. v. Spencer Kellogg & Sons*, 257 F.2d 162 (5th Cir.1958); *Genuth v. National Biscuit Co.*, 81 F.Supp. 213 (S.D.N.Y.1948), app. dism., 177 F.2d 962 (2d Cir.1949); 3 Moore's Federal Practice ¶ 15.01 [5] (Supp.1960); 1A Barron & Holtzoff, Federal Practice & Procedure 820 to 21 (Wright ed. 1960). Thus plaintiffs have sometimes been needlessly remitted to the difficulties of commencing a new action even though events occurring after the commencement of the original action have made clear the right to relief.

Under the amendment the court has discretion to permit a supplemental pleading despite the fact that the original pleading is defective. As in other situations where a supplemental pleading is offered, the court is to determine in the light of the particular circumstances whether filing should be permitted, and if so, upon what terms. The amendment does not attempt to deal with such questions as the relation of the statute of limitations to supplemental pleadings, the operation of the doctrine of laches, or the availability of other defenses. All these questions are for decision in accordance with the principles applicable to supplemental pleadings generally. Cf. *Blau v. Lamb*, 191 F.Supp. 906 (S.D.N.Y. 1961); Lendonsol Amusement Corp. v. B. & Q. Assoc., Inc., 23 F.R.Serv. 15d.3, Case 1 (D.Mass.1957).

1966 AMENDMENT

Rule 15(c) is amplified to state more clearly when an amendment of a pleading changing the party against whom a claim is asserted (including an amendment to correct a misnomer or misdescription of a defendant) shall "relate back" to the date of the original pleading.

The problem has arisen most acutely in certain actions by private parties against officers or agencies of the United States. Thus an individual denied social security benefits by the Secretary of Health, Education, and Welfare may secure review of the decision by bringing a civil action against that officer within sixty days. 42 U.S.C. § 405(g) (Supp. III, 1962). In several recent cases the claimants instituted timely action but mistakenly named as defendant the United States, the Department of HEW, the "Federal Security Administration" (a nonexistent agency), and a Secretary who had retired from the office nineteen days before. Discovering their mistakes, the claimants moved to amend their complaints to name the proper defendant; by this time the statutory sixty-day period had expired. The motions were denied on the ground that the amendment "would amount to the commencement of a new proceeding and would not relate back in time so as to avoid the statutory provision * * * that suit be brought within sixty days * * *" *Cohn v. Federal Security Adm.*, 199 F.Supp. 884, 885 (W.D.N.Y.1961); see also *Cunningham v. United States*, 199 F.Supp. 541 (W.D.Mo.1958); *Hall v. Department of HEW*, 199 F.Supp. 833 (S.D.Tex. 1960); *Sandridge v. Folsom, Secretary of HEW*, 200 F.Supp. 25 (M.D.Tenn. 1959). [The Secretary of Health, Education, and Welfare has approved certain ameliorative regulations under 42 U.S.C. § 405(g). See 29 Fed.Reg. 8209 (June 30, 1964); Jacoby, The Effect of Recent Changes in the Law of "Nonstatutory" Judicial Review, 53 Geo.L.J. 19, 42–43 (1964); see also *Simmons v. United States Dept. HEW*, 328 F.2d 86 (3d Cir.1964).]

Analysis in terms of "new proceeding" is traceable to *Davis v. L. L. Cohen & Co.*, 268 U.S. 638, 45 S. Ct. 633, 69 L.Ed. 1129 (1925), and *Mellon v. Arkansas Land & Lumber Co.*, 275 U.S. 460, 48 S. Ct. 150, 72 L.Ed. 372 (1928), but those cases antedate the adoption of the Rules which import different criteria for determining when an amendment is to "relate back". As lower courts have continued to rely on the Davis and Mellon cases despite the contrary intent of the Rules, clarification of Rule 15(c) is considered advisable.

Relation back is intimately connected with the policy of the statute of limitations. The policy of the statute limiting the time for suit against the Secretary of HEW would not have been offended by allowing relation back in the situations described above. For the government was put on notice of the claim within the stated period—in the particular instances, by means of the initial delivery of process to a responsible government official (see Rule 4(d)(4) and (5)). In these circumstances, characterization of the amendment as a new proceeding is not responsive to the reality, but is merely question-begging; and to deny relation back is to defeat unjustly the claimant's opportunity to prove his case. See the full discussion by Byse, Suing the "Wrong" Defendant in Judicial Review of Federal Administrative Action: Proposals for Reform, 77 Harv.L.Rev. 40 (1963); see also Ill.Civ.P.Act § 46(4).

Much the same question arises in other types of actions against the government (see *Byse*, supra, at 45 n. 15). In actions between private parties, the problem of relation back of amendments changing defendants has generally been better handled by the courts, but incorrect criteria have sometimes been applied, leading sporadically to doubtful results. See 1A Barron & Holtzoff, Federal Practice & Procedure § 451 (Wright ed. 1960); 1 id. § 186 (1960); 2 id. § 543 (1961); 3 Moore's Federal Practice, par. 15.15 (Cum.Supp.1962); Annot., Change in Party After Statute of Limitations Has Run, 8 A.L.R.2d 6 (1949). Rule 15(c) has been amplified to provide a general solution. An amendment changing the party against whom a claim is asserted relates back if the amendment satisfies the usual condition of Rule 15(c) of "arising out of the conduct * * * set forth * * * in the original pleading," and if, within the applicable limitations period, the party brought in by amendment, first, received such notice of the institution of the action—the notice need not be formal—that he would not be prejudiced in defending the action, and, second, knew or should have known that the action would have been brought against him initially had there not been a mistake concerning the identity of the proper party. Revised Rule 15(c) goes on to provide specifically in the government cases that the first and second requirements are satisfied when the government has been notified in the manner there described (see Rules 4(d)(4) and (5)). As applied to the government cases, revised Rule 15(c) further advances the objectives of the 1961 amendment of Rule 25(d) (substitution of public officers).

The relation back of amendments changing plaintiffs is not expressly treated in revised Rule 15(c) since the problem is generally easier. Again the chief consideration of policy is that of the statute of limitations, and the attitude taken in revised Rule 15(c) toward change of defendants extends by analogy to amendments changing plaintiffs. Also relevant is the amendment of Rule 17(a) (real party in interest). To avoid forfeitures of just claims, revised Rule 17(a) would provide that no action shall be dismissed on the ground that it is not prosecuted in the name of the real party in interest until a reasonable time has been allowed for correction of the defect in the manner there stated.

1987 AMENDMENT

The amendments are technical. No substantive change is intended.

1991 AMENDMENT

The rule has been revised to prevent parties against whom claims are made from taking unjust advantage of otherwise inconsequential pleading errors to sustain a limitations defense.

Paragraph (c)(1). This provision is new. It is intended to make it clear that the rule does not apply to preclude any relation back that may be permitted under the applicable limitations law. Generally, the applicable limitations law will be state law. If federal jurisdiction is based on the citizenship of the parties, the primary reference is the law of the state in which the district court sits. *Walker v. Armco Steel Corp.*, 446 U.S. 740, 100 S. Ct. 1978, 64 L. Ed. 2d 659 (1980). If federal jurisdiction is based on a federal question, the reference may be to the law of the state governing relations between the parties. *E.g., Board of Regents v. Tomanio*, 446 U.S. 478, 100 S. Ct. 1790, 64 L. Ed. 2d 440 (1980). In some circumstances, the controlling limitations law may be federal law. *E.g., West v. Conrail, Inc.*, 481 U.S. 35, 107 S. Ct. 1538, 95 L. Ed. 2d 32 (1987). Cf. *Burlington Northern R. Co. v. Woods*, 480 U.S. 1, 107 S. Ct. 967, 94 L. Ed. 2d 1 (1987); *Stewart Organization v. Ricoh*, 487 U.S. 22, 108 S. Ct. 2239, 101 L. Ed. 2d 22 (1988). Whatever may be the controlling body of limitations law, if that law affords a more forgiving principle of relation back than the one provided in this rule, it should be available to save the claim. Accord, *Marshall v. Mulrenin*, 508 F.2d 39 (1st Cir.1974). If *Schiavone v. Fortune*, 477 U.S. 21, 106 S. Ct. 2379, 91 L. Ed. 2d 18 (1986) implies the contrary, this paragraph is intended to make a material change in the rule.

Paragraph (c)(3). This paragraph has been revised to change the result in *Schiavone v. Fortune, supra,* with respect to the problem of a misnamed defendant. An intended defendant who is notified of an action within the period allowed by Rule 4(m) for service of a summons and complaint may not under the revised rule defeat the action on account of a defect in the pleading with respect to the defendant's name, provided that the requirements of clauses (A) and (B) have been met. If the notice requirement is met within the Rule 4(m) period, a complaint may be amended at any time to correct a formal defect such as a misnomer or misidentification. On the basis of the text of the former rule, the Court reached a result in *Schiavone v. Fortune* that was inconsistent with the liberal pleading practices secured by Rule 8. See Bauer, Schiavone: *An Un-Fortune-ate Illustration of the Supreme Court's Role as Interpreter of the Federal Rules of Civil Procedure,* 63 NOTRE DAME L.REV. 720 (1988); Brussack, *Outrageous Fortune: The Case for Amending Rule 15(c) Again,* 61 S.CAL.L.REV. 671 (1988); Lewis, *The Excessive History of Federal Rule 15(c) and Its Lessons for Civil Rules Revision,* 86 MICH.L.REV. 1507 (1987).

In allowing a name-correcting amendment within the time allowed by Rule 4(m) [subdivision (m) in Rule 4 was a proposed subdivision which was withdrawn by the Supreme Court], this rule allows not only the 120 days specified in that rule, but also any additional time resulting from any extension ordered by the court pursuant to that rule, as may be granted, for example, if the defendant is a fugitive from service of the summons.

This revision, together with the revision of Rule 4(i) [revision to subdivision (i) in Rule 4 was a proposed revision which was withdrawn by the Supreme Court] with respect to the failure of a plaintiff in an action against the United States to effect timely service on all the appropriate officials, is intended to produce results contrary to those reached in *Gardner v. Gartman*, 880 F.2d 797 (4th Cir.1989), *Rys v. U.S. Postal Service*, 886 F.2d 443 (1st Cir.1989), Martin's Food & Liquor, Inc. v. U.S. Dept. of Agriculture, 14 F.R.S.3d 86 (N.D.Ill.1988). *But cf. Montgomery v. United States Postal Service*, 867 F.2d 900 (5th Cir.1989), *Warren v. Department of the Army*, 867 F.2d 1156 (8th Cir.1989); *Miles v. Department of the Army*, 881 F.2d 777 (9th Cir.1989), *Barsten v. Department of the Interior*, 896 F.2d 422 (9th Cir.1990); *Brown v. Georgia Dept. of Revenue*, 881 F.2d 1018 (11th Cir.1989).

1993 AMENDMENT

The amendment conforms the cross reference to Rule 4 to the revision of that rule.

2007 AMENDMENT

The language of Rule 15 has been amended as part of the general restyling of the Civil Rules to make them more easily understood and to make style and terminology consistent throughout the rules. These changes are intended to be stylistic only.

Former Rule 15(c)(3)(A) called for notice of the "institution" of the action. Rule 15(c)(1)(C)(i) omits the reference to "institution" as potentially confusing. What counts is that the party to be brought in have notice of the existence of the action, whether or not the notice includes details as to its "institution."

2009 AMENDMENT

Rule 15(a)(1) is amended to make three changes in the time allowed to make one amendment as a matter of course.

Former Rule 15(a) addressed amendment of a pleading to which a responsive pleading is required by distinguishing between the means used to challenge the pleading. Serving a responsive pleading terminated the right to amend. Serving a motion attacking the pleading did not terminate the right to amend, because a motion is not a "pleading" as defined in Rule 7. The right to amend survived beyond decision of the motion unless the decision expressly cut off the right to amend.

The distinction drawn in former Rule 15(a) is changed in two ways. First, the right to amend once as a matter of course terminates 21 days after service of a motion under Rule 12(b), (e), or (f). This provision will force the pleader to consider carefully and promptly the wisdom of amending to meet the arguments in the motion. A responsive amendment may avoid the need to decide the motion or reduce the number of issues to be decided, and will expedite determination of issues that otherwise might be raised seriatim. It also should advance other pretrial proceedings.

Second, the right to amend once as a matter of course is no longer terminated by service of a responsive pleading. The responsive pleading may point out issues that the original pleader had not considered and persuade the pleader that amendment is wise. Just as amendment was permitted by former Rule 15(a) in response to a motion, so the amended rule permits one amendment as a matter of course in response to a responsive pleading. The right is subject to the same 21-day limit as the right to amend in response to a motion.

The 21-day periods to amend once as a matter of course after service of a responsive pleading or after service of a designated motion are not cumulative. If a responsive pleading is served after one of the designated motions is served, for example, there is no new 21-day period.

Finally, amended Rule 15(a)(1) extends from 20 to 21 days the period to amend a pleading to which no responsive pleading is allowed and omits the provision that cuts off the right if the action is on the trial calendar. Rule 40 no longer refers to a trial calendar, and many courts have abandoned formal trial calendars. It is more effective to rely on scheduling orders or other pretrial directions to establish time limits for amendment in the few situations that otherwise might allow one amendment as a matter of course at a time that would disrupt trial preparations. Leave to amend still can be sought under Rule 15(a)(2), or at and after trial under Rule 15(b).[1]

Abrogation of Rule 13(f) establishes Rule 15 as the sole rule governing amendment of a pleading to add a counterclaim.

The times set in the former rule at 10 or 20 days have been revised to 14 or 21 days. See the Note to Rule 6.

Rule 16. Pretrial Conferences; Scheduling; Management

1937 ADOPTION

1. Similar rules of pre-trial procedure are now in force in Boston, Cleveland, Detroit, and Los Angeles, and a rule substantially like this one has been proposed for the urban centers of New York state. For a discussion of the successful operation of pre-trial procedure in relieving the congested condition of trial calendars of the courts in such cities and for the proposed New York plan, see A Proposal for Minimizing Calendar Delay in Jury Cases (Dec. 1936—published by the New York Law Society); Pre-Trial Procedure and Administration, Third Annual Report of the Judicial Council of the State of New York (1937), pages 207–243; Report of the Commission on the Administration of Justice in New York State (1934), pp. (288)–(290). See also Pre-trial Procedure in the Wayne Circuit Court, Detroit, Michigan, Sixth Annual Report of the Judicial Council of Michigan (1936), pp. 63–75; and Sunderland, The Theory and Practice of Pre-trial Procedure (Dec. 1937) 36 Mich.L.Rev. 215–226, 21 J.Am.Jud.Soc. 125. Compare the English procedure known as the "summons for directions," English Rules Under the Judicature Act (The Annual Practice, 1937) O. 38a; and a similar procedure in New Jersey, N.J.S.A. 2:27-135, 2:27-136, 2:27-160; N.J. Supreme Court Rules, 2 N.J.Misc.Rep. (1924) 1230, Rules 94, 92, 93, 95 (the last three as amended 1933, 11 N.J.Misc.Rep. (1933) 955, N.J.S.A. Tit. 2).

2. Compare the similar procedure under Rule 56(d) (Summary Judgment—Case Not Fully Adjudicated on Motion). Rule 12(g) (Consolidation of Motions), by requiring to some extent the consolidation of motions dealing with matters preliminary to trial, is a step in the same direction. In connection with clause (5) of this rule, see Rules 53(b) (Masters; Reference) and 53(e)(3) (Master's Report: In Jury Actions).

1983 AMENDMENT

Introduction

Rule 16 has not been amended since the Federal Rules were promulgated in 1938. In many respects, the rule has been a success. For example, there is evidence that pretrial conferences may improve the quality of justice rendered in the federal courts by sharpening the preparation and presentation of cases, tending to eliminate trial surprise, and improving, as well as facilitating, the settlement process. See 6 Wright & Miller, *Federal Practice and Procedure: Civil* § 1522 (1971). However, in other respects particularly with regard to case management, the rule has not always been as helpful as it might have been. Thus there has been a widespread feeling that amendment is necessary to encourage pretrial management that meets the needs of modern litigation. See *Report of the National Commission for the Review of Antitrust Laws and*

[1] If the proposed amendment to Rule 15(a)(3) ... changing the time period is approved by the Judicial Conference, the following additional sentence will be added to the Committee Note: "Amended Rule 15(a)(3) extends from 10 to 14 days the period to respond to an amended pleading."

Procedures (1979).

Major criticism of Rule 16 has centered on the fact that its application can result in over-regulation of some cases and under-regulation of others. In simple, run-of-the-mill cases, attorneys have found pretrial requirements burdensome. It is claimed that over-administration leads to a series of mini-trials that result in a waste of an attorney's time and needless expense to a client. Pollack, *Pretrial Procedures More Effectively Handled,* 65 F.R.D. 475 (1974). This is especially likely to be true when pretrial proceedings occur long before trial. At the other end of the spectrum, the discretionary character of Rule 16 and its orientation toward a single conference late in the pretrial process has led to under-administration of complex or protracted cases. Without judicial guidance beginning shortly after institution, these cases often become mired in discovery.

Four sources of criticism of pretrial have been identified. First, conferences often are seen as a mere exchange of legalistic contentions without any real analysis of the particular case. Second, the result frequently is nothing but a formal agreement on minutiae. Third, the conferences are seen as unnecessary and time-consuming in cases that will be settled before trial. Fourth, the meetings can be ceremonial and ritualistic, having little effect on the trial and being of minimal value, particularly when the attorneys attending the sessions are not the ones who will try the case or lack authority to enter into binding stipulations. See generally *McCargo v. Hedrick,* 545 F.2d 393 (4th Cir.1976); Pollack, *Pretrial Procedures More Effectively Handled,* 65 F.R.D. 475 (1974); Rosenberg, The Pretrial Conference and Effective Justice 45 (1964).

There also have been difficulties with the pretrial orders that issue following Rule 16 conferences. When an order is entered far in advance of trial, some issues may not be properly formulated. Counsel naturally are cautious and often try to preserve as many options as possible. If the judge who tries the case did not conduct the conference, he could find it difficult to determine exactly what was agreed to at the conference. But any insistence on a detailed order may be too burdensome, depending on the nature or posture of the case.

Given the significant changes in federal civil litigation since 1938 that are not reflected in Rule 16, it has been extensively rewritten and expanded to meet the challenges of modern litigation. Empirical studies reveal that when a trial judge intervenes personally at an early stage to assume judicial control over a case and to schedule dates for completion by the parties of the principal pretrial steps, the case is disposed of by settlement or trial more efficiently and with less cost and delay than when the parties are left to their own devices. Flanders, *Case Management and Court Management in United States District Courts* 17, Federal Judicial Center (1977). Thus, the rule mandates a pretrial scheduling order. However, although scheduling and pretrial conferences are encouraged in appropriate cases, they are not mandated.

Discussion

Subdivision (a); Pretrial Conferences; Objectives. The amended rule makes scheduling and case management an express goal of pretrial procedure. This is done in Rule 16(a) by shifting the emphasis away from a conference focused solely on the trial and toward a process of judicial management that embraces the entire pretrial phase, especially motions and discovery. In addition, the amendment explicitly recognizes some of the objectives of pretrial conferences and the powers that many courts already have assumed. Rule 16 thus will be a more accurate reflection of actual practice.

Subdivision (b); Scheduling and Planning. The most significant change in Rule 16 is the mandatory scheduling order described in Rule 16(b), which is based in part on Wisconsin Civil Procedure Rule 802.10. The idea of scheduling orders is not new. It has been used by many federal courts. See, *e.g.,* Southern District of Indiana, Local Rule 19.

Although a mandatory scheduling order encourages the court to become involved in case management early in the litigation, it represents a degree of judicial involvement that is not warranted in many cases. Thus, subdivision (b) permits each district court to promulgate a local rule under Rule 83 exempting certain categories of cases in which the burdens of scheduling orders exceed the administrative efficiencies that would be gained. See Eastern District of Virginia, Local Rule 12(1). Logical candidates for this treatment include social security disability matters, habeas corpus petitions, forfeitures, and reviews of certain administrative actions.

A scheduling conference may be requested either by the judge, a magistrate when authorized by district court rule, or a party within 120 days after the summons and complaint are filed. If a scheduling conference is not arranged within that time and the case is not exempted by local rule, a scheduling order must be issued under Rule 16(b), after some communication with the parties, which may be by telephone or mail rather than in person. The use of the term "judge" in subdivision (b) reflects the Advisory Committee's judgment that it is preferable that this task should be handled by a district judge rather than a magistrate, except when the magistrate is acting under 28 U.S.C. § 636(c). While personal supervision by the trial judge is preferred, the rule, in recognition of the impracticality or difficulty of complying with such a requirement in some districts, authorizes a district by local rule to delegate the duties to a magistrate. In order to formulate a practicable scheduling order, the judge, or a magistrate when authorized by district court rule, and attorneys are required to develop a timetable for the matters listed in Rule 16(b)(1) to (3). As indicated in Rule 16(b)(4) to (5), the order may also deal with a wide range of other matters. The rule is phrased permissively as to clauses (4) and (5), however, because scheduling these items at an early point may not be feasible or appropriate. Even though subdivision (b) relates only to scheduling, there is no reason why some of the procedural matters listed in Rule 16(c) cannot be addressed at the same time, at least when a scheduling conference is held.

Item (1) assures that at some point both the parties and the pleadings will be fixed, by setting a time within which joinder of parties shall be completed and the pleadings amended.

Item (2) requires setting time limits for interposing various motions that otherwise might be used as stalling techniques.

Item (3) deals with the problem of procrastination and delay by attorneys in a context in which scheduling is especially important—discovery. Scheduling the completion of discovery can serve some of the same functions as the conference described in Rule 26(f).

Item (4) refers to setting dates for conferences and for trial. Scheduling multiple pretrial conferences may well be desirable if the case is complex and the court believes that a more elaborate pretrial structure, such as that described in the *Manual for Complex Litigation,* should be employed. On the other hand, only one pretrial conference may be necessary in an uncomplicated case.

As long as the case is not exempted by local rule, the court must issue a written scheduling order even if no scheduling conference is called. The order, like pretrial orders under the former rule and those under new Rule 16(c), normally will "control the subsequent course of the action." See Rule 16(e). After consultation with the attorneys for the parties and any unrepresented parties—a formal motion is not necessary—the court may modify the schedule on a showing of good cause if it cannot reasonably be met despite the diligence of the party seeking the extension. Since the scheduling order is entered early in the litigation, this standard seems more appropriate than a "manifest injustice" or "substantial hardship" test. Otherwise, a fear that extensions will not be granted may encourage counsel to request the longest possible periods for completing pleading, joinder, and discovery. Moreover, changes in the court's calendar sometimes will oblige the judge or magistrate when authorized by district court rule to modify the scheduling order.

The district courts undoubtedly will develop several prototype scheduling orders for different types of cases. In addition, when no formal conference is held, the court may obtain scheduling information by telephone, mail, or otherwise. In many instances this will result in a scheduling order better suited to the individual case than a standard order, without taking the time that would be required by a formal conference.

Rule 16(b) assures that the judge will take some early control over the litigation, even when its character does not warrant holding a scheduling conference. Despite the fact that the process of preparing a scheduling order does not always bring the attorneys and judge together, the fixing of time limits serves

> to stimulate litigants to narrow the areas of inquiry and advocacy to those they believe are truly relevant and material. Time limits not only compress the amount of time for litigation, they should also reduce the amount of resources invested in litigation. Litigants are forced to establish discovery priorities and thus to do the most important work first.

Report of the National Commission for the Review of Antitrust Laws and Procedures 28 (1979).

Thus, except in exempted cases, the judge or a magistrate when authorized by district court rule will have taken some action in every case within 120 days after the complaint is filed that notifies the attorneys that the case will be moving toward trial. Subdivision (b) is reenforced by subdivision (f), which makes it clear that the sanctions for violating a scheduling order are the same as those for violating a pretrial order.

Subdivision (c); Subjects to be Discussed at Pretrial Conferences. This subdivision expands upon the list of things that may be discussed at a pretrial conference that appeared in original Rule 16. The intention is to encourage better planning and management of litigation. Increased judicial control during the pretrial process accelerates the processing and termination of cases. Flanders, *Case Management and Court Management in United States District Courts,* Federal Judicial Center (1977). See also *Report of the National Commission for the Review of Antitrust Laws and Procedures* (1979).

The reference in Rule 16(c)(1) to "formulation" is intended to clarify and confirm the court's power to identify the litigable issues. It has been added in the hope of promoting efficiency and conserving judicial resources by identifying the real issues prior to trial, thereby saving time and expense for everyone. See generally *Meadow Gold Prods. Co. v. Wright*, 278 F.2d 867 (D.C.Cir.1960). The notion is emphasized by expressly authorizing the elimination of frivolous claims or defenses at a pretrial conference. There is no reason to require that this await a formal motion for summary judgment. Nor is there any reason for the court to wait for the parties to initiate the process called for in Rule 16(c)(1).

The timing of any attempt at issue formulation is a matter of judicial discretion. In relatively simple cases it may not be necessary or may take the form of a stipulation between counsel or a request by the court that counsel work together to draft a proposed order.

Counsel bear a substantial responsibility for assisting the court in identifying the factual issues worthy of trial. If counsel fail to identify an issue for the court, the right to have the issue tried is waived. Although an order specifying the issues is intended to be binding, it may be amended at trial to avoid manifest injustice. See Rule 16(e). However, the rule's effectiveness depends on the court employing its discretion sparingly.

Clause (6) acknowledges the widespread availability and use of magistrates. The corresponding provision in the original rule referred only to masters and limited the function of the reference to the making of "findings to be used as evidence" in a case to be tried to a jury. The new text is not limited and broadens the potential use of a magistrate to that permitted by the Magistrate's Act.

Clause (7) explicitly recognizes that it has become commonplace to discuss settlement at pretrial conferences. Since it obviously eases crowded court dockets and results in savings to the litigants and the judicial system, settlement should be facilitated at as early a stage of the litigation as possible. Although it is not the purpose of Rule 16(b)(7) to impose settlement negotiations on unwilling litigants, it is believed that providing a neutral forum for discussing the subject might foster it. See Moore's Federal Practice ¶ 16.17; 6 Wright & Miller, *Federal Practice and Procedure: Civil* § 1522 (1971). For instance, a judge to whom a case has been assigned may arrange, on his own motion or at a party's request, to have settlement conferences handled by another member of the court or by a magistrate. The rule does not make settlement conferences mandatory because they would be a waste of time in many cases. See Flanders, *Case Management and Court Management in the United States District Courts,* 39, Federal Judicial Center (1977). Requests for a conference from a party indicating a willingness to talk settlement normally should be honored, unless thought to be frivolous or dilatory.

A settlement conference is appropriate at any time. It may be held in conjunction with a pretrial or discovery conference, although various objectives of pretrial management, such as moving the case toward trial, may not always be compatible with settlement negotiations, and thus a separate settlement conference may be desirable. See 6 Wright & Miller, *Federal Practice and Procedure: Civil* § 1522, at p. 571 (1971).

In addition to settlement, Rule 16(c)(7) refers to exploring the use of procedures other than litigation to resolve the dispute. This includes urging the litigants to employ adjudicatory techniques outside the courthouse. See, for example, the experiment described in Green, Marks & Olson, *Settling Large Case Litigation: An Alternative Approach,* 11 Loyola of L.A. L.Rev. 493 (1978).

Rule 16(c)(10) authorizes the use of special pretrial procedures to expedite the adjudication of potentially difficult or protracted cases. Some district courts obviously have done so for many years. See Rubin, *The Managed Calendar: Some Pragmatic Suggestions About Achieving the Just, Speedy and Inexpensive Determination of Civil Cases in Federal Courts,* 4 Just. Sys. J. 135 (1976). Clause 10 provides an explicit authorization for such procedures and encourages their use. No particular techniques have been described; the Committee felt that flexibility and experience are the keys to efficient management of complex cases. Extensive guidance is offered in such documents as the *Manual for Complex Litigation.*

The rule simply identifies characteristics that make a case a strong candidate for special treatment. The four mentioned are illustrative, not exhaustive, and overlap to some degree. But experience has shown that one or more of them will be present in every protracted or difficult case and it seems desirable to set them out. See Kendig, *Procedures for Management of Non-Routine Cases,* 3 Hofstra L.Rev. 701 (1975).

The last sentence of subdivision (c) is new. See Wisconsin Civil Procedure Rule 802.11(2). It has been added to meet one of the criticisms of the present practice described earlier and insure proper preconference preparation so that the meeting is more than a ceremonial or ritualistic event. The reference to "authority" is not intended to insist upon the ability to settle the litigation. Nor should the rule be read to encourage the judge conducting the conference to compel attorneys to enter into stipulations or to make admissions that they consider to be unreasonable, that touch on matters that could not normally have been anticipated to arise at the conference, or on subjects of a dimension that normally require prior consultation with and approval from the client.

Subdivision (d); Final Pretrial Conference. This provision has been added to make it clear that the time between any final pretrial conference (which in a simple case may be the only pretrial conference) and trial should be as short as possible to be certain that the litigants make substantial progress with the case and avoid the inefficiency of having that preparation repeated when there is a delay between the last pretrial conference and trial. An optimum time of 10 days to two weeks has been suggested by one federal judge. Rubin, *The Managed Calendar: Some Pragmatic Suggestions About Achieving the Just, Speedy and Inexpensive Determination of Civil Cases in Federal Courts,* 4 Just. Sys. J. 135, 141 (1976). The Committee, however, concluded that it would be inappropriate to fix a precise time in the rule, given the numerous variables that could bear on the matter. Thus the timing has been left to the court's discretion.

At least one of the attorneys who will conduct the trial for each party must be present at the final pretrial conference. At this late date there should be no doubt as to which attorney or attorneys this will be. Since the agreements and stipulations made at this final conference will control the trial, the presence of lawyers who will be involved in it is especially useful to assist the judge in structuring the case, and to lead to a more effective trial.

Subdivision (e); Pretrial Orders. Rule 16(e) does not substantially change the portion of the original rule dealing with pretrial orders. The purpose of an order is to guide the course of the litigation and the language of the original rule making that clear has been retained. No compelling reason has been found for major revision, especially since this portion of the rule has been interpreted and clarified by over forty years of judicial decisions with comparatively little difficulty. See 6 Wright & Miller, *Federal Practice and Procedure: Civil* §§ 1521 to 30 (1971). Changes in language therefore have been kept to a minimum to avoid confusion.

Since the amended rule encourages more extensive pretrial management than did the original, two or more conferences may be held in many cases. The language of Rule 16(e) recognizes this possibility and the corresponding need to issue more than one pretrial order in a single case.

Once formulated, pretrial orders should not be changed lightly; but total inflexibility is undesirable. See, *e.g., Clark v. Pennsylvania R.R. Co.*, 328 F.2d 591 (2d Cir.1964). The exact words used to describe the standard for amending the pretrial order probably are less important than the meaning given them in practice. By not imposing any limitation on the ability to modify a pretrial order, the rule reflects the reality that in any process of continuous management what is done at one conference may have to be altered at the next. In the case of the final pretrial order, however, a more stringent standard is called for and the words "to prevent manifest injustice," which appeared in the original rule, have been retained. They have the virtue of familiarity and adequately describe the restraint the trial judge should exercise.

Many local rules make the plaintiff's attorney responsible for drafting a proposed pretrial order, either before or after the conference. Others allow the court to appoint any of the attorneys to perform the task, and others leave it to the court. See Note, *Pretrial Conference: A Critical Examination of Local Rules Adopted by Federal District Courts,* 64 Va.L.Rev. 467 (1978). Rule 16 has never addressed this matter. Since there is no consensus about which method of drafting the order works best and there is no reason to believe that nationwide uniformity is needed, the rule has been left silent on the point. See *Handbook for Effective Pretrial Procedure,* 37 F.R.D. 225 (1964).

Subdivision (f); Sanctions. Original Rule 16 did not mention the sanctions that might be imposed for failing to comply with the rule. However, courts have not hesitated to enforce it by appropriate measures. See, *e.g., Link v. Wabash R. Co.*, 370 U.S. 626 (1962) (district court's dismissal under Rule 41(b) after plaintiff's attorney failed to appear at a pretrial conference upheld); *Admiral Theatre Corp. v. Douglas Theatre*, 585 F.2d 877 (8th Cir.1978) (district court has discretion to exclude exhibits or refuse to permit the testimony of a witness not listed prior to trial in contravention of its pretrial order).

To reflect that existing practice, and to obviate dependence upon Rule 41(b) or the court's inherent power to regulate litigation, *cf. Societe Internationale Pour Participations Industrielles et Commerciales, S.A. v. Rogers*, 357 U.S. 197, 78 S. Ct. 1087, 2 L. Ed. 2d 1255 (1958), Rule 16(f) expressly provides for imposing sanctions on disobedient or recalcitrant parties, their attorneys, or both in four types of situations. Rodes, Ripple & Mooney, *Sanctions Imposable for Violations of the Federal Rules of Civil Procedure* 65–67, 80–84, Federal Judicial Center (1981). Furthermore, explicit reference to sanctions reenforces the rule's intention to encourage forceful judicial management.

Rule 16(f) incorporates portions of Rule 37(b)(2), which prescribes sanctions for failing to make discovery. This should facilitate application of Rule 16(f), since courts and lawyers already are familiar with the Rule 37 standards. Among the sanctions authorized by the new subdivision are: preclusion order, striking a pleading, staying the proceeding, default judgment, contempt, and charging a party, his attorney, or both with the expenses, including attorney's fees, caused by noncompliance. The contempt sanction, however, is only available for a violation of a court order. The references in Rule 16(f) are not exhaustive.

As is true under Rule 37(b)(2), the imposition of sanctions may be sought by either the court or a party. In addition, the court has discretion to impose whichever sanction it feels is appropriate under the circumstances. Its action is reviewable under the abuse-of-discretion standard. See *National Hockey League v. Metropolitan Hockey Club, Inc.*, 427 U.S. 639, 96 S. Ct. 2778, 49 L. Ed. 2d 747 (1976).

1987 AMENDMENT

The amendments are technical. No substantive change is intended.

1993 AMENDMENT

Subdivision (b). One purpose of this amendment is to provide a more appropriate deadline for the initial scheduling order required by the rule. The former rule directed that the order be entered within 120 days from the filing of the complaint. This requirement has created problems because Rule 4(m) allows 120 days for service and ordinarily at least one defendant should be available to participate in the process of formulating the scheduling order. The revision provides that the order is to be entered within 90 days after the date a defendant first appears (whether by answer or by a motion under Rule 12) or, if earlier (as may occur in some actions against the United States or if service is waived under Rule 4), within 120 days after service of the complaint on a defendant. The longer time provided by the revision is not intended to encourage unnecessary delays in entering the scheduling order. Indeed, in most cases the order can and should be entered at a much earlier date. Rather, the additional time is intended to alleviate problems in multi-defendant cases and should ordinarily be adequate to enable participation by all defendants initially named in the action.

In many cases the scheduling order can and should be entered before this deadline. However, when setting a scheduling conference, the court should take into account the effect this setting will have in establishing deadlines for the parties to meet under revised Rule 26(f) and to exchange information under revised Rule 26(a)(1). While the parties are expected to stipulate to additional time for making their disclosures when warranted by the circumstances, a scheduling conference held before defendants have had time to learn much about the case may result in diminishing the value of the Rule 26(f) meeting, the parties' proposed discovery plan, and indeed the conference itself.

New paragraph (4) has been added to highlight that it will frequently be desirable for the scheduling order to include provisions relating to the timing of disclosures under Rule 26(a). While the initial disclosures required by Rule 26(a)(1) will ordinarily have been made before entry of the scheduling order, the timing and sequence for disclosure of expert testimony and of the witnesses and exhibits to be used at trial should be tailored to the circumstances of the case and is a matter that should be considered at the initial scheduling conference. Similarly, the scheduling order might contain provisions modifying the extent of discovery (*e.g.*, number and length of depositions) otherwise permitted under these rules or by a local rule.

The report from the attorneys concerning their meeting and proposed discovery plan, as required by revised Rule 26(f), should be submitted to the court before the scheduling order is entered. Their proposals, particularly regarding matters on which they agree, should be of substantial value to the court in setting the timing and limitations on discovery and should reduce the time of the court needed to conduct a meaningful conference under Rule 16(b). As under the prior rule, while a scheduling order is mandated, a scheduling conference is not. However, in view of the benefits to be derived from the litigants and a judicial officer meeting in person, a Rule 16(b) conference should, to the extent practicable, be held in all cases that will involve discovery.

This subdivision, as well as subdivision (c)(8), also is revised to reflect the new title of United States Magistrate Judges pursuant to the Judicial Improvements Act of 1990.

Subdivision (c). The primary purposes of the changes in subdivision (c) are to call attention to the opportunities for structuring of trial under Rules 42, 50, and 52 and to eliminate questions that have occasionally been raised regarding the authority of the court to make appropriate orders designed either to facilitate settlement or to provide for an efficient and economical trial. The prefatory language of this subdivision is revised to clarify the court's power to enter appropriate orders at a conference notwithstanding the objection of a party. Of course settlement is dependent upon agreement by the parties and, indeed, a conference is most effective and productive when the parties participate in a spirit of cooperation and mindful of their responsibilities under Rule 1.

Paragraph (4) is revised to clarify that in advance of trial the court may address the need for, and possible limitations on, the use of expert testimony under Rule 702 of the Federal Rules of Evidence. Even when proposed expert testimony might be admissible under the standards of Rules 403 and 702 of the evidence rules, the court may preclude or limit such testimony if the cost to the litigants—which may include the cost to adversaries of securing testimony on the same subjects by other experts—would be unduly expensive given the needs of the case and the other evidence available at trial.

Paragraph (5) is added (and the remaining paragraphs renumbered) in recognition that use of Rule 56 to avoid or reduce the scope of trial is a topic that can, and often should, be considered at a pretrial conference. Renumbered paragraph (11) enables the court to rule on pending motions for summary adjudication that are ripe for decision at the time of the conference. Often, however, the potential use of Rule 56 is a matter that arises from discussions during a conference. The court may then call for motions to be filed.

Paragraph (6) is added to emphasize that a major objective of pretrial conferences should be to consider appropriate controls on the extent and timing of discovery. In many cases the court should also specify the times and sequence for disclosure of written reports from experts under revised Rule 26(a)(2)(B) and perhaps direct changes in the types of experts from whom written reports are required. Consideration should also be given to possible changes in the timing or form of the disclosure of trial witnesses and documents under Rule 26(a)(3).

Paragraph (9) is revised to describe more accurately the various procedures that, in addition to traditional settlement conferences, may be helpful in settling litigation. Even if a case cannot immediately be settled, the judge and attorneys can explore possible use of alternative procedures such as mini-trials, summary jury trials, mediation, neutral evaluation, and nonbinding arbitration that can lead to consensual resolution of the dispute without a full trial on the merits. The rule acknowledges the presence of statutes and local rules or plans that may authorize use of some of these procedures even when not agreed to by the parties. See 28 U.S.C. §§ 473(a)(6), 473(b)(4), 651 to 58; Section 104(b)(2), Pub.L. 101-650. The rule does not attempt to resolve questions as to the extent a court would be authorized to require such proceedings as an exercise of its inherent powers.

The amendment of paragraph (9) should be read in conjunction with the sentence added to the end of subdivision (c), authorizing the court to direct that, in appropriate cases, a responsible representative of the parties be present or available by telephone during a conference in order to discuss possible settlement of the case. The sentence refers to participation by a party or its representative. Whether this would be the individual party, an officer of a corporate party, a representative from an insurance carrier, or someone else would depend on the circumstances. Particularly in litigation in which governmental agencies or large amounts of money are involved, there may be no one with on-the-spot settlement authority, and the most that should be expected is access to a person who would have a major role in submitting a recommendation to the body or board with ultimate decision-making responsibility. The selection of the appropriate representative should ordinarily be left to the party and its counsel. Finally, it should be noted that the unwillingness of a party to be available, even by telephone, for a settlement conference may be a clear signal that the time and expense involved in pursuing settlement is likely to be unproductive and that personal participation by the parties should not be required.

The explicit authorization in the rule to require personal participation in the manner stated is not intended to limit the reasonable exercise of the court's inherent powers, *e.g., G. Heileman Brewing Co. v. Joseph Oat Corp.*, 871 F.2d 648 (7th Cir.1989), or its power to require party participation under the Civil Justice Reform Act of 1990. See 28 U.S.C. § 473(b)(5) (civil justice expense and delay reduction plans adopted by district courts may include requirement that representatives "with authority to bind [parties] in settlement discussions" be available during settlement conferences).

New paragraphs (13) and (14) are added to call attention to the opportunities for structuring of trial under Rule 42 and under revised Rules 50 and 52.

Paragraph (15) is also new. It supplements the power of the court to limit the extent of evidence under Rules 403 and 611(a) of the Federal Rules of Evidence, which typically would be invoked as a result of developments during trial. Limits on the length of trial established at a conference in advance of trial can provide the parties with a better opportunity to determine priorities and exercise selectivity in presenting evidence than when limits are imposed during trial. Any such limits must be reasonable under the circumstances, and ordinarily the court should impose them only after receiving appropriate submissions from the parties outlining the nature of the testimony expected to be presented through various witnesses, and the expected duration of direct and cross-examination.

2006 AMENDMENT

The amendment to Rule 16(b) is designed to alert the court to the possible need to address the handling of discovery of electronically stored information early in the litigation if such discovery is expected to occur. Rule 26(f) is amended to direct the parties to discuss discovery of electronically stored information if such discovery is contemplated in the action. Form 35 is amended to call for a report to the court about the results of this discussion. In many instances, the court's involvement early in the litigation will help avoid difficulties that might otherwise arise.

Rule 16(b) is also amended to include among the topics that may be addressed in the scheduling order any agreements that the parties reach to facilitate discovery by minimizing the risk of waiver of privilege or work-product protection. Rule 26(f) is amended to add to the discovery plan the parties' proposal for the court to enter a case-management or other order adopting such an agreement. The parties may agree to various arrangements. For example, they may agree to initial provision of requested materials without waiver of privilege or protection to enable the party seeking production to designate the materials desired or protection for actual production, with the privilege review of only those materials to follow. Alternatively, they may agree that if privileged or protected information is inadvertently produced, the producing party may by timely notice assert the privilege or protection and obtain return of the materials without waiver. Other arrangements are possible. In most circumstances, a party who receives information under such an arrangement cannot assert that production of the information waived a claim of privilege or of protection as trial-preparation material.

An order that includes the parties' agreement may be helpful in avoiding delay and excessive cost in discovery. *See Manual for Complex Litigation* (4th) § 11.446. Rule 16(b)(6) recognizes the propriety of including such agreements in the court's order. The rule does not provide the court with authority to enter such a case-management or other order without party agreement, or limit the court's authority to act on motion.

2007 AMENDMENT

The language of Rule 16 has been amended as part of the general restyling of the Civil Rules to make them more easily understood and to make style and

terminology consistent throughout the rules. These changes are intended to be stylistic only.

When a party or its representative is not present, it is enough to be reasonably available by any suitable means, whether telephone or other communication device.

2015 AMENDMENT

The provision for consulting at a scheduling conference by "telephone, mail, or other means" is deleted. A scheduling conference is more effective if the court and parties engage in direct simultaneous communication. The conference may be held in person, by telephone, or by more sophisticated electronic means.

The time to issue the scheduling order is reduced to the earlier of 90 days (not 120 days) after any defendant has been served, or 60 days (not 90 days) after any defendant has appeared. This change, together with the shortened time for making service under Rule 4(m), will reduce delay at the beginning of litigation. At the same time, a new provision recognizes that the court may find good cause to extend the time to issue the scheduling order. In some cases it may be that the parties cannot prepare adequately for a meaningful Rule 26(f) conference and then a scheduling conference in the time allowed. Litigation involving complex issues, multiple parties, and large organizations, public or private, may be more likely to need extra time to establish meaningful collaboration between counsel and the people who can supply the information needed to participate in a useful way. Because the time for the Rule 26(f) conference is geared to the time for the scheduling conference or order, an order extending the time for the scheduling conference will also extend the time for the Rule 26(f) conference. But in most cases it will be desirable to hold at least a first scheduling conference in the time set by the rule.

Three items are added to the list of permitted contents in Rule 16(b)(3)(B).

The order may provide for preservation of electronically stored information, a topic also added to the provisions of a discovery plan under Rule 26(f)(3)(C). Parallel amendments of Rule 37(e) recognize that a duty to preserve discoverable information may arise before an action is filed.

The order also may include agreements incorporated in a court order under Evidence Rule 502 controlling the effects of disclosure of information covered by attorney-client privilege or work-product protection, a topic also added to the provisions of a discovery plan under Rule 26(f)(3)(D).

Finally, the order may direct that before filing a motion for an order relating to discovery the movant must request a conference with the court. Many judges who hold such conferences find them an efficient way to resolve most discovery disputes without the delay and burdens attending a formal motion, but the decision whether to require such conferences is left to the discretion of the judge in each case.

HISTORICAL NOTES

Change of Name

Reference to United States magistrate or to magistrate deemed to refer to United States magistrate judge pursuant to section 321 of Pub.L. 101-650, set out as a note under section 631 of this title.

IV. PARTIES

Rule 17. Parties Plaintiff and Defendant; Capacity

1937 ADOPTION

Note to Subdivision (a). The real party in interest provision, except for the last clause which is new, is taken verbatim from former Equity Rule 37 (Parties Generally—Intervention), except that the word "expressly" has been omitted. For similar provisions see N.Y.C.P.A., 1937, § 210; Wyo.Rev.Stat.Ann., 1931, §§ 89-501, 89-502, 89-503; English Rules Under the Judicature Act (The Annual

Practice, 1937) O. 16, r. 8. See, also former Equity Rule 41 (Suit to Execute Trusts of Will—Heir as Party). For examples of statutes of the United States providing particularly for an action for the use or benefit of another in the name of the United States, see U.S.C., Title 40, § 270b (Suit by persons furnishing labor and material for work on public building contracts * * * may sue on a payment bond, "in the name of the United States for the use of the person suing"); and U.S.C., Title 25, § 201 (Penalties under laws relating to Indians—how recovered). Compare U.S.C., Title 26, Int.Rev.Code [1939], § 3745(c) (Suits for penalties, fines, and forfeitures, under this title, where not otherwise provided for, to be in name of United States).

Note to Subdivision (b). For capacity see generally Clark and Moore, A New Federal Civil Procedure—II. Pleadings and Parties, 44 Yale L.J. 1291, 1312–1317, 1935, and specifically *Coppedge v. Clinton, C.C.A.10, 1934*, 72 F.2d 531 (natural person); *David Lupton's Sons Co. v. Automobile Club of America, 1912*, 32 S. Ct. 711, 225 U.S. 489, 56 L.Ed. 1177, Ann.Cas.1914A, 699 (corporation); *Puerto Rico v. Russell & Co., 1933*, 288 U.S. 476, 53 S. Ct. 447, 77 L.Ed. 903, (unincorporated assn.); *United Mine Workers of America v. Coronado Coal Co., 1922, 42 assn. S. Ct. 570*, 259 U.S. 344, 42 S. Ct. 570, 66 L.Ed. 975, 27 A.L.R. 762 (federal substantive right enforced against unincorporated association by suit against the association in its common name without naming all its members as parties). This rule follows the existing law as to such associations, as declared in the case last cited above. Compare *Moffat Tunnel League v. United States*, 289 U.S. 113, 53 S. Ct. 543, 77 L.Ed. 1069 (1933). See note to Rule 23, clause (1).

Note to Subdivision (c). The provision for infants and incompetent persons is substantially former Equity Rule 70 (Suits by or Against Incompetents) with slight additions. Compare the more detailed English provisions, English Rules Under the Judicature Act (The Annual Practice, 1937) O. 16, r. r. 16 to 21.

1946 AMENDMENT

Note. The new matter [in subdivision (b)] makes clear the controlling character of Rule 66 regarding suits by or against a federal receiver in a federal court.

1948 AMENDMENT

The amendment effective October 20, 1949, deleted the words "Rule 66" at the end of subdivision (b) and substituted the words "Title 28, U.S.C., §§ 754 and 959(a)."

1966 AMENDMENT

The minor change in the text of the rule is designed to make it clear that the specific instances enumerated are not exceptions to, but illustrations of, the rule. These illustrations, of course, carry no negative implication to the effect that there are not other instances of recognition as the real party in interest of one whose standing as such may be in doubt. The enumeration is simply of cases in which there might be substantial doubt as to the issue but for the specific enumeration. There are other potentially arguable cases that are not excluded by the enumeration. For example, the enumeration states that the promisee in a contract for the benefit of a third party may sue as real party in interest; it does not say, because it is obvious, that the third-party beneficiary may sue (when the applicable law gives him that right.)

The rule adds to the illustrative list of real parties in interest a bailee—meaning, of course, a bailee suing on behalf of the bailor with respect to the property bailed. (When the possessor of property other than the owner sues for an invasion of the possessory interest he is the real party in interest.) The word "bailee" is added primarily to preserve the admiralty practice whereby the owner of a vessel as bailee of the cargo, or the master of the vessel as bailee of both vessel and cargo, sues for damage to either property interest or both. But there is no reason to limit such a provision to maritime situations. The owner of a warehouse in which household furniture is stored is equally entitled to sue on behalf of the numerous owners of the furniture stored. Cf. *Gulf Oil Corp. v.*

Gilbert, 330 U.S. 501, 67 S. Ct. 839, 91 L.Ed. 1055 (1947).

The provision that no action shall be dismissed on the ground that it is not prosecuted in the name of the real party in interest until a reasonable time has been allowed, after the objection has been raised, for ratification, substitution, etc., is added simply in the interests of justice. In its origin the rule concerning the real party in interest was permissive in purpose: it was designed to allow an assignee to sue in his own name. That having been accomplished, the modern function of the rule in its negative aspect is simply to protect the defendant against a subsequent action by the party actually entitled to recover, and to insure generally that the judgment will have its proper effect as res judicata.

This provision keeps pace with the law as it is actually developing. Modern decisions are inclined to be lenient when an honest mistake has been made in choosing the party in whose name the action is to be filed—in both maritime and nonmaritime cases. See *Levinson v. Deupree*, 345 U.S. 648, 73 S. Ct. 914, 97 L. Ed. 2d 1319 (1953); *Link Aviation, Inc. v. Downs*, 325 F.2d 613 (D.C.Cir. 1963). The provision should not be misunderstood or distorted. It is intended to prevent forfeiture when determination of the proper party to sue is difficult or when an understandable mistake has been made. It does not mean, for example, that, following an airplane crash in which all aboard were killed, an action may be filed in the name of John Doe (a fictitious person), as personal representative of Richard Roe (another fictitious person), in the hope that at a later time the attorney filing the action may substitute the real name of the real personal representative of a real victim, and have the benefit of suspension of the limitation period. It does not even mean, when an action is filed by the personal representative of John Smith, of Buffalo, in the good faith belief that he was aboard the flight, that upon discovery that Smith is alive and well, having missed the fatal flight, the representative of James Brown, of San Francisco, an actual victim, can be substituted to take advantage of the suspension of the limitation period. It is, in cases of this sort, intended to insure against forfeiture and injustice—in short, to codify in broad terms the salutary principle of *Levinson v. Deupree*, 345 U.S. 648, 73 S. Ct. 914, 97 L. Ed. 2d 1319 (1953), and *Link Aviation, Inc. v. Downs*, 325 F.2d 613 (D.C.Cir.1963).

1987 AMENDMENT

The amendments are technical. No substantive change is intended.

1988 AMENDMENT

The amendment is technical. No substantive change is intended.

2007 AMENDMENT

The language of Rule 17 has been amended as part of the general restyling of the Civil Rules to make them more easily understood and to make style and terminology consistent throughout the rules. These changes are intended to be stylistic only.

Rule 17(d) incorporates the provisions of former Rule 25(d)(2), which fit better with Rule 17.

Rule 18. Joinder of Claims and Remedies

1937 ADOPTION

Note to Subdivision (a). 1. Recent development, both in code and common law states, has been toward unlimited joinder of actions. See Smith-Hurd Ill.Stats. ch. 110, § 168; N.J.S.A. 2:27-37, as modified by N.J.Sup.Ct.Rules, Rule 21, 2 N.J.Misc. 1208 (1924); N.Y.C.P.A. (1937) § 258 as amended by Laws of 1935, ch. 339.

2. This provision for joinder of actions has been patterned upon former Equity Rule 26 (Joinder of Causes of Action) and broadened to include multiple parties. Compare the English practice, English Rules Under the Judicature Act (The Annual Practice, 1937) O. 18, r. r. 1 to 9 (noting rules 1 and 6). The earlier American codes set forth classes of joinder, following the now abandoned New York rule. See N.Y.C.P.A. § 258 before amended in 1935; Compare Kan.Gen.

Stat.Ann. (1935) § 60-601; Wis.Stat. (1935) § 263.04 for the more liberal practice.

3. The provisions of this rule for the joinder of claims are subject to Rule 82 (Jurisdiction and Venue Unaffected). For the jurisdictional aspects of joinder of claims, see Shulman and Jaegerman. Some Jurisdictional Limitations on Federal Procedure (1936), 45 Yale L.J. 393, 397–410. For separate trials of joined claims, see rule 42(b).

Note to Subdivision (b). This rule is inserted to make it clear that in a single action a party should be accorded all the relief to which he is entitled regardless of whether it is legal or equitable or both. This necessarily includes a deficiency judgment in foreclosure actions formerly provided for in former Equity Rule 10 (Decree for Deficiency in Foreclosures, Etc.). In respect to fraudulent conveyances the rule changes the former rule requiring a prior judgment against the owner (*Braun v. American Laundry Mach. Co., N.Y.1932*, 56 F.2d 197) to conform to the provisions of the Uniform Fraudulent Conveyance Act, §§ 9 and 10. See McLaughlin, Application of the Uniform Fraudulent Conveyance Act, 46 Harv.L.Rev. 404, 444 (1933).

1966 AMENDMENT

The Rules "proceed upon the theory that no inconvenience can result from the joinder of any two or more matters in the pleadings, but only from trying two or more matters together which have little or nothing in common." Sunderland, The New Federal Rules, 45 W.Va.L.Q. 5, 13 (1938); see Clark, Code Pleading 58 (2d ed. 1947). Accordingly, Rule 18(a) has permitted a party to plead multiple claims of all types against an opposing party, subject to the court's power to direct an appropriate procedure for trying the claims. See Rules 42(b), 20(b), 21.

The liberal policy regarding joinder of claims in the pleadings extends to cases with multiple parties. However, the language used in the second sentence of Rule 18(a)—"if the requirements of Rules 19 [necessary joinder of parties], 20 [permissive joinder of parties], and 22 [interpleader] are satisfied"—has led some courts to infer that the rules regulating joinder of parties are intended to carry back to Rule 18(a) and to impose some special limits on joinder of claims in multiparty cases. In particular, Rule 20(a) has been read as restricting the operation of Rule 18(a) in certain situations in which a number of parties have been permissively joined in an action. In *Federal Housing Admr. v. Christianson*, 26 F.Supp. 419 (D.Conn.1939), the indorsee of two notes sued the three comakers of one note, and sought to join in the action a count on a second note which had been made by two of the three defendants. There was no doubt about the propriety of the joinder of the three parties defendant, for a right to relief was being asserted against all three defendants which arose out of a single "transaction" (the first note) and a question of fact or law "common" to all three defendants would arise in the action. See the text of Rule 20(a). The court, however, refused to allow the joinder of the count on the second note, on the ground that this right to relief, assumed to arise from a distinct transaction, did not involve a question common to all the defendants but only two of them. For analysis of the Christianson case and other authorities, see 2 Barron & Holtzoff, Federal Practice & Procedure, § 533.1 (Wright ed. 1961); 3 Moore's Federal Practice, par. 18.04[3] (2d ed. 1963).

If the court's view is followed, it becomes necessary to enter at the pleading stage into speculations about the exact relation between the claim sought to be joined against fewer than all the defendants properly joined in the action, and the claims asserted against all the defendants. Cf. Wright, Joinder of Claims and Parties Under Modern Pleading Rules, 36 Minn.L.Rev. 580, 605–06 (1952). Thus if it could be found in the Christianson situation that the claim on the second note arose out of the same transaction as the claim on the first or out of a transaction forming part of a "series," and that any question of fact or law with respect to the second note also arose with regard to the first, it would be held that the claim on the second note could be joined in the complaint. See 2 Barron & Holtzoff, supra, at 199; see also id. at 198 n. 60.4; cf. 3 Moore's Federal Practice, supra, at 1811. Such pleading niceties provide a basis for delaying and wasteful maneuver. It is more compatible with the design of the Rules to allow the claim to be joined in the pleading, leaving the question of possible separate trial of that claim to be later decided. See 2 Barron & Holtzoff, supra, § 533.1; Wright, supra, 36 Minn.L.Rev. at 604–11; Developments in the Law—Multiparty Litigation in the Federal Courts, 71 Harv. 874, 970–71 (1958); Commentary, Relation Between Joinder of Parties and Joinder of Claims, 5 F.R.Serv. 822 (1942). It is instructive to note that the court in the Christianson case, while holding that the claim on the second note could not be joined as a matter of pleading, held open the possibility that both claims would later be consolidated for trial under Rule 42(a). See 26 F.Supp. 419.

Rule 18(a) is now amended not only to overcome the Christianson decision and similar authority, but also to state clearly, as a comprehensive proposition, that a party asserting a claim (an original claim, counterclaim, cross-claim, or third-party claim) may join as many claims as he has against an opposing party. See *Noland Co., Inc. v. Graver Tank & Mfg. Co.*, 301 F.2d 43, 49–51 (4th Cir.1962); but cf. *C. W. Humphrey Co. v. Security Alum. Co.*, 31 F.R.D. 41 (E.D. Mich.1962). This permitted joinder of claims is not affected by the fact that there are multiple parties in the action. The joinder of parties is governed by other rules operating independently.

It is emphasized that amended Rule 18(a) deals only with pleading. As already indicated, a claim properly joined as a matter of pleading need not be proceeded with together with the other claims if fairness or convenience justifies separate treatment.

Amended Rule 18(a), like the rule prior to amendment, does not purport to deal with questions of jurisdiction or venue which may arise with respect to claims properly joined as a matter of pleading. See Rule 82.

See also the amendment of Rule 20(a) and the Advisory Committee's Note thereto.

Free joinder of claims and remedies is one of the basic purposes of unification of the admiralty and civil procedure. The amendment accordingly provides for the inclusion in the rule of maritime claims as well as those which are legal and equitable in character.

1987 AMENDMENT

The amendments are technical. No substantive change is intended.

2007 AMENDMENT

The language of Rule 18 has been amended as part of the general restyling of the Civil Rules to make them more easily understood and to make style and terminology consistent throughout the rules. These changes are intended to be stylistic only.

Modification of the obscure former reference to a claim "heretofore cognizable only after another claim has been prosecuted to a conclusion" avoids any uncertainty whether Rule 18(b)'s meaning is fixed by retrospective inquiry from some particular date.

Rule 19. Joinder of Persons Needed for Just Adjudication

1937 ADOPTION

Note to Subdivision (a). The first sentence with verbal differences (e. g., "united" interest for "joint" interest) is to be found in former Equity Rule 37 (Parties Generally—Intervention). Such compulsory joinder provisions are common. Compare Alaska Comp.Laws (1933) § 3392 (containing in same sentence a "class suit" provision); Wyo.Rev.Stat.Ann. (Courtright, 1931) § 89-515 (immediately followed by "class suit" provisions, § 89-516). See also former Equity Rule 42 (Joint and Several Demands). For example of a proper case for involuntary plaintiff, see *Independent Wireless Telegraph Co. v. Radio Corp. of America, 1926*, 269 U.S. 459, 46 S. Ct. 166, 70 L.Ed. 357.

The joinder provisions of this rule are subject to Rule 82 (Jurisdiction and Venue Unaffected).

Note to Subdivision (b). For the substance of this rule see former Equity Rule 39 (Absence of Persons Who Would be Proper Parties) and U.S.C., Title 28, § 1391, formerly § 111 (When part of several defendants cannot be served); *Camp v. Gress, 1919*, 250 U.S. 308, 39 S. Ct. 478, 63 L.Ed. 997. See also the second and third sentences of former Equity Rule 37 (Parties Generally—Intervention).

Note to Subdivision (c). For the substance of this rule see the fourth subdivision of former Equity Rule 25 (Bill of Complaint—Contents).

1966 AMENDMENT

GENERAL CONSIDERATIONS

Whenever feasible, the persons materially interested in the subject of an action—see the more detailed description of these persons in the discussion of new subdivision (a) below—should be joined as parties so that they may be heard and a complete disposition made. When this comprehensive joinder cannot be accomplished—a situation which may be encountered in Federal courts because of limitations on service of process, subject matter jurisdiction, and venue—the case should be examined pragmatically and a choice made between the alternatives of proceeding with the action in the absence of particular interested persons, and dismissing the action.

Even if the court is mistaken in its decision to proceed in the absence of an interested person, it does not by that token deprive itself of the power to adjudicate as between the parties already before it through proper service of process. But the court can make a legally binding adjudication only between the parties actually joined in the action. It is true that an adjudication between the parties before the court may on occasion adversely affect the absent person as a practical matter, or leave a party exposed to a later inconsistent recovery by the absent person. These are factors which should be considered in deciding whether the action should proceed, or should rather be dismissed; but they do not themselves negate the court's power to adjudicate as between the parties who have been joined.

DEFECTS IN THE ORIGINAL RULE

The foregoing propositions were well understood in the older equity practice, see Hazard, Indispensable Party: The Historical Origin of a Procedural Phantom, 61 Colum.L.Rev. 1254 (1961), and Rule 19 could be and often was applied in consonance with them. But experience showed that the rule was defective in its phrasing and did not point clearly to the proper basis of decision.

Textual defects.—(1) The expression "persons * * * who ought to be parties if complete relief is to be accorded between those already parties," appearing in original subdivision (b), was apparently intended as a description of the persons whom it would be desirable to join in the action, all questions of feasibility of joinder being put to one side; but it was not adequately descriptive of those persons.

(2) The word "indispensable," appearing in original subdivision (b), was apparently intended as an inclusive reference to the interested persons in whose absence it would be advisable, all factors having been considered, to dismiss the action. Yet the sentence implied that there might be interested persons, not "indispensable," in whose absence the action ought also to be dismissed. Further, it seemed at least superficially plausible to equate the word "indispensable" with the expression "having a joint interest," appearing in subdivision (a). See *United States v. Washington Inst. of Tech., Inc.*, 138 F.2d 25, 26 (3d Cir.1943); cf. *Chidester v. City of Newark*, 162 F.2d 598 (3d Cir.1947). But persons holding an interest technically "joint" are not always so related to an action that it would be unwise to proceed without joining all of them, whereas persons holding an interest not technically "joint" may have this relation to an action. See Reed, Compulsory Joinder of Parties in Civil Actions, 55 Mich.L.Rev. 327, 356 ff., 483 (1957).

(3) The use of "indispensable" and "joint interest" in the context of original Rule 19 directed attention to the technical or abstract character of the rights or

obligations of the persons whose joinder was in question, and correspondingly distracted attention from the pragmatic considerations which should be controlling.

(4) The original rule, in dealing with the feasibility of joining a person as a party to the action, besides referring to whether the person was "subject to the jurisdiction of the court as to both service of process and venue," spoke of whether the person could be made a party "without depriving the court of jurisdiction of the parties before it." The second quoted expression used "jurisdiction" in the sense of the competence of the court over the subject matter of the action, and in this sense the expression was apt. However, by a familiar confusion, the expression seems to have suggested to some that the absence from the lawsuit of a person who was "indispensable" or "who ought to be [a] part[y]" itself deprived the court of the power to adjudicate as between the parties already joined. See *Samuel Goldwyn, Inc. v. United Artists Corp.*, 113 F.2d 703, 707 (3d Cir.1940); *McArthur v. Rosenbaum Co. of Pittsburgh*, 180 F.2d 617, 621 (3d Cir. 1950); cf. *Calcote v. Texas Pac. Coal & Oil Co.*, 157 F.2d 216 (5th Cir.1946), cert. denied, 329 U.S. 782, 67 S. Ct. 205, 91 L.Ed. 671 (1946), noted in 56 Yale L.J. 1088 (1947); Reed, supra, 55 Mich.L.Rev. at 332–34.

Failure to point to correct basis of decision. The original rule did not state affirmatively what factors were relevant in deciding whether the action should proceed or be dismissed when joinder of interested persons was infeasible. In some instances courts did not undertake the relevant inquiry or were misled by the "jurisdiction" fallacy. In other instances there was undue preoccupation with abstract classifications of rights or obligations, as against consideration of the particular consequences of proceeding with the action and the ways by which these consequences might be ameliorated by the shaping of final relief or other precautions.

Although these difficulties cannot be said to have been general analysis of the cases showed that there was good reason for attempting to strengthen the rule. The literature also indicated how the rule should be reformed. See Reed, supra (discussion of the important case of Shields v. Barrow, 17 How. (58 U.S.) 130 (1854), appears at 55 Mich.L.Rev. p. 340 ff.); Hazard, supra; N.Y. Temporary Comm. on Courts, First Preliminary Report, Legis.Doc.1957, No. 6(b), pp. 28, 233; N. Y. Judicial Council, Twelfth Ann.Rep., Legis.Doc.1946, No. 17, p. 163; Joint Comm. on Michigan Procedural Revision, Final Report, Pt. III, p. 69 (1960); Note, Indispensable Parties in the Federal Courts, 65 Harv.L.Rev. 1050 (1952); Developments in the Law—Multiparty Litigation in the Federal Courts, 71 Harv.L.Rev. 874, 879 (1958); Mich.Gen. Court Rules, R. 205 (effective Jan. 1, 1963); N.Y.Civ.Prac.Law & Rules, § 1001 (effective Sept. 1, 1963).

THE AMENDED RULE

New subdivision (a) defines the persons whose joinder in the action is desirable. Clause (1) stresses the desirability of joining those persons in whose absence the court would be obliged to grant partial or "hollow" rather than complete relief to the parties before the court. The interests that are being furthered here are not only those of the parties, but also that of the public in avoiding repeated lawsuits on the same essential subject matter. Clause (2)(i) recognizes the importance of protecting the person whose joinder is in question against the practical prejudice to him which may arise through a disposition of the action in his absence. Clause (2)(ii) recognizes the need for considering whether a party may be left, after the adjudication, in a position where a person not joined can subject him to a double or otherwise inconsistent liability. See Reed, supra, 55 Mich.L.Rev. at 330, 338; Note, supra, 65 Harv.L.Rev. at 1052–57; Developments in the Law, supra, 71 Harv.L.Rev. at 881–85.

The subdivision (a) definition of persons to be joined is not couched in terms of the abstract nature of their interests—"joint," "united," "separable," or the like. See N.Y. Temporary Comm. on Courts, First Preliminary Report, supra; Developments in the Law, supra, at 880. It should be noted particularly, however, that the description is not at variance with the settled authorities holding that a tortfeasor with the usual "joint-and-several" liability is merely a permissive party to an action against another with like liability. See 3 Moore's Federal Practice 2153 (2d ed. 1963); 2 Barron & Holtzoff, Federal Practice & Procedure § 513.8 (Wright ed. 1961). Joinder of these tortfeasors continues to be regulated by Rule 20; compare Rule 14 on third-party practice.

If a person as described in subdivision (a)(1)–(2) is amenable to service of process and his joinder would not deprive the court of jurisdiction in the sense of competence over the action, he should be joined as a party; and if he has not been joined, the court should order him to be brought into the action. If a party joined has a valid objection to the venue and chooses to assert it, he will be dismissed from the action.

Subdivision (b).—When a person as described in subdivision (a)(1)–(2) cannot be made a party, the court is to determine whether in equity and good conscience the action should proceed among the parties already before it, or should be dismissed. That this decision is to be made in the light of pragmatic considerations has often been acknowledged by the courts. See *Roos v. Texas Co.*, 23 F.2d 171 (2d Cir.1927), cert. denied, 277 U.S. 587, 48 S. Ct. 434, 72 L.Ed. 1001 (1928); *Niles-Bement-Pond Co. v. Iron Moulders' Union*, 254 U.S. 77, 80, 41 S. Ct. 39, 65 L.Ed. 145 (1920). The subdivision sets out four relevant considerations drawn from the experience revealed in the decided cases. The factors are to a certain extent overlapping, and they are not intended to exclude other considerations which may be applicable in particular situations.

The first factor brings in a consideration of what a judgment in the action would mean to the absentee. Would the absentee be adversely affected in a practical sense, and if so, would the prejudice be immediate and serious, or remote and minor? The possible collateral consequences of the judgment upon the parties already joined are also to be appraised. Would any party be exposed to a fresh action by the absentee, and if so, how serious is the threat? See the elaborate discussion in Reed, supra; cf. *A. L. Smith Iron Co. v. Dickson*, 141 F.2d 3 (2d Cir.1944); *Caldwell Mfg. Co. v. Unique Balance Co.*, 18 F.R.D. 258 (S. D.N.Y.1955).

The second factor calls attention to the measures by which prejudice may be averted or lessened. The "shaping of relief" is a familiar expedient to this end. See, e. g., the award of money damages in lieu of specific relief where the latter might affect an absentee adversely. *Ward v. Deavers*, 203 F.2d 72 (D.C.Cir. 1953); *Miller & Lux, Inc. v. Nickel*, 141 F.Supp. 41 (N.D.Cal.1956). On the use of "protective provisions," see *Roos v. Texas Co.*, supra; *Atwood v. Rhode Island Hosp. Trust Co.*, 275 Fed. 513, 519 (1st Cir.1921), cert. denied, 257 U.S. 661, 42 S. Ct. 270, 66 L.Ed. 422 (1922); cf. *Stumpf v. Fidelity Gas Co.*, 294 F.2d 886 (9th Cir.1961); and the general statement in *National Licorice Co. v. National Labor Relations Board*, 309 U.S. 350, 363, 60 S. Ct. 569, 84 L.Ed. 799 (1940).

Sometimes the party is himself able to take measures to avoid prejudice. Thus a defendant faced with a prospect of a second suit by an absentee may be in a position to bring the latter into the action by defensive interpleader. See *Hudson v. Newell*, 172 F.2d 848, 852 mod., 174 F.2d 546 (5th Cir.1949); *Gauss v. Kirk*, 198 F.2d 83, 86 (D.C.Cir.1952); *Abel v. Brayton Flying Service, Inc.*, 248 F.2d 713, 716 (5th Cir.1957) (suggestion of possibility of counterclaim under Rule 13(h)); cf. *Parker Rust-Proof Co. v. Western Union Tel. Co.*, 105 F.2d 976 (2d Cir.1939), cert. denied, 308 U.S. 597 (1939). So also the absentee may sometimes be able to avert prejudice to himself by voluntarily appearing in the action or intervening on an ancillary basis. See Developments in the Law, supra, 71 Harv.L.Rev. at 882; Annot., Intervention or Subsequent Joinder of Parties as Affecting Jurisdiction of Federal Court Based on Diversity of Citizenship, 134 A.L.R. 335 (1941); *Johnson v. Middleton*, 175 F.2d 535 (7th Cir.1949); *Kentucky Nat. Gas Corp. v. Duggins*, 165 F.2d 1011 (6th Cir.1948); *McComb v. McCormack*, 159 F.2d 219 (5th Cir.1947). The court should consider whether this, in turn, would impose undue hardship on the absentee (For the possibility of the court's informing an absentee of the pendency of the action, see comment under subdivision (c) below.)

The third factor—whether an "adequate" judgment can be rendered in the absence of a given person—calls attention to the extent of the relief that can be accorded among the parties joined. It meshes with the other factors, especially the "shaping of relief" mentioned under the second factor. Cf. *Kroese v. General Steel Castings Corp.*, 179 F.2d 760 (3d Cir.1950), cert. denied, 339 U.S. 983, 70 S. Ct. 1026, 94 L.Ed. 1386 (1950).

The fourth factor, looking to the practical effects of a dismissal, indicates that the court should consider whether there is any assurance that the plaintiff, if dismissed, could sue effectively in another forum where better joinder would be possible. See *Fitzgerald v. Haynes*, 241 F.2d 417, 420 (3d Cir.1957); *Fouke v. Schenewerk*, 197 F.2d 234, 236 (5th Cir.1952); cf. *Warfield v. Marks*, 190 F.2d 178 (5th Cir.1951).

The subdivision uses the word "indispensable" only in a conclusory sense, that is, a person is "regarded as indispensable" when he cannot be made a party and, upon consideration of the factors above mentioned, it is determined that in his absence it would be preferable to dismiss the action, rather than to retain it.

A person may be added as a party at any stage of the action on motion or on the court's initiative (see Rule 21); and a motion to dismiss, on the ground that a person has not been joined and justice requires that the action should not proceed in his absence, may be made as late as the trial on the merits (see Rule 12(h)(2), as amended; cf. Rule 12(b)(7), as amended). However, when the moving party is seeking dismissal in order to protect himself against a later suit by the absent person (subdivision (a)(2)(ii)), and is not seeking vicariously to protect the absent person against a prejudicial judgment (subdivision (a)(2)(i)), his undue delay in making the motion can properly be counted against him as a reason for denying the motion. A joinder question should be decided with reasonable promptness, but decision may properly be deferred if adequate information is not available at the time. Thus the relationship of an absent person to the action, and the practical effects of an adjudication upon him and others, may not be sufficiently revealed at the pleading stage; in such a case it would be appropriate to defer decision until the action was further advanced. Cf. Rule 12(d).

The amended rule makes no special provision for the problem arising in suits against subordinate Federal officials where it has often been set up as a defense that some superior officer must be joined. Frequently this defense has been accompanied by or intermingled with defenses of sovereign community or lack of consent of the United States to suit. So far as the issue of joinder can be isolated from the rest, the new subdivision seems better adapted to handle it than the predecessor provision. See the discussion in *Johnson v. Kirkland*, 290 F.2d 440, 446–47 (5th Cir.1961) (stressing the practical orientation of the decisions); *Shaughnessy v. Pedreiro*, 349 U.S. 48, 54, 75 S. Ct. 591, 99 L.Ed. 868 (1955). Recent legislation, P.L. 87-748, 76 Stat. 744, approved October 5, 1962, adding §§ 1361, 1391(e) to Title 28, U.S.C., vests original jurisdiction in the District Courts over actions in the nature of mandamus to compel officials of the United States to perform their legal duties, and extends the range of service of process and liberalizes venue in these actions. If, then, it is found that a particular official should be joined in the action, the legislation will make it easy to bring him in.

Subdivision (c) parallels the predecessor subdivision (c) of Rule 19. In some situations it may be desirable to advise a person who has not been joined of the fact that the action is pending, and in particular cases the court in its discretion may itself convey this information by directing a letter or other informal notice to the absentee.

Subdivision (d) repeats the exception contained in the first clause of the predecessor subdivision (a).

1987 AMENDMENT

The amendments are technical. No substantive change is intended.

2007 AMENDMENT

The language of Rule 19 has been amended as part of the general restyling of the Civil Rules to make them more easily understood and to make style and

terminology consistent throughout the rules. These changes are intended to be stylistic only.

Former Rule 19(b) described the conclusion that an action should be dismissed for inability to join a Rule 19(a) party by carrying forward traditional terminology: "the absent person being thus regarded as indispensable." "Indispensable" was used only to express a conclusion reached by applying the tests of Rule 19(b). It has been discarded as redundant.

Rule 20. Permissive Joinder of Parties

1937 ADOPTION

The provisions for joinder here stated are in substance the provisions found in England, California, Illinois, New Jersey, and New York. They represent only a moderate expansion of the present federal equity practice to cover both law and equity actions.

With this rule compare also former Equity Rules 26 (Joinder of Causes of Action), 37 (Parties Generally—Intervention), 40 (Nominal Parties), and 42 (Joint and Several Demands).

The provisions of this rule for the joinder of parties are subject to rule 82 (Jurisdiction and Venue Unaffected).

Note to Subdivision (a). The first sentence is derived from English Rules Under the Judicature Act (The Annual Practice, 1937) O. 16, r. 1. Compare Calif.Code Civ.Proc. (1937) §§ 378, 379a; Smith-Hurd Ill.Stats. ch. 110, §§ 147 to 148; N.J.S.A. 2:27-24, 2:27-25, 2:27-38; N.Y.C.P.A. (1937) §§ 209, 211. The second sentence is derived from English Rules Under the Judicature Act (The Annual Practice, 1937) O. 16, r. 4. The third sentence is derived from O. 16, r. 5, and the fourth from O. 16, r. r. 1 and 4.

Note to Subdivision (b). This is derived from English Rules Under the Judicature Act (The Annual Practice, 1937) O. 16, r. r. 1 and 5.

1966 AMENDMENT

See the amendment of Rule 18(a) and the Advisory Committee's Note thereto. It has been thought that a lack of clarity in the antecedent of the word "them," as it appeared in two places in Rule 20(a), contributed to the view, taken by some courts, that this rule limited the joinder of claims in certain situations of permissive party-joinder. Although the amendment of Rule 18(a) should make clear that this view is untenable, it has been considered advisable to amend Rule 20(a) to eliminate any ambiguity. See 2 Barron & Holtzoff, Federal Practice & Procedure 202 (Wright Ed. 1961).

A basic purpose of unification of admiralty and civil procedure is to reduce barriers to joinder; hence the reference to "any vessel," etc.

1987 AMENDMENT

The amendments are technical. No substantive change is intended.

2007 AMENDMENT

The language of Rule 20 has been amended as part of the general restyling of the Civil Rules to make them more easily understood and to make style and terminology consistent throughout the rules. These changes are intended to be stylistic only.

Rule 21. Misjoinder and Non-Joinder of Parties

1937 ADOPTION

See English Rules Under the Judicature Act (The Annual Practice, 1937) O. 16, r. 11. See also former Equity Rules 43 (Defect of Parties—Resisting Objection) and 44 (Defect of Parties—Tardy Objection).

For separate trials see Rules 13(i) (Counterclaims and Cross-Claims: Separate Trials; Separate Judgments), 20(b) (Permissive Joinder of Parties: Separate Trials), and 42(b) (Separate Trials, generally) and the note to the latter rule.

2007 AMENDMENT

The language of Rule 21 has been amended as part of the general restyling of the Civil Rules to make them more easily understood and to make style and terminology consistent throughout the rules. These changes are intended to be stylistic only.

Rule 22. Interpleader

1937 ADOPTION

The first paragraph provides for interpleader relief along the newer and more liberal lines of joinder in the alternative. It avoids the confusion and restrictions that developed around actions of strict interpleader and actions in the nature of interpleader. Compare *John Hancock Mutual Life Insurance Co. v. Kegan et al., D.C.Md.1938*, 22 F.Supp. 326. It does not change the rules on service of process, jurisdiction, and venue, as established by judicial decision.

The second paragraph allows an action to be brought under the recent interpleader statute when applicable. By this paragraph all remedies under the statute are continued, but the manner of obtaining them is in accordance with these rules. For temporary restraining orders and preliminary injunctions under this statute, see Rule 65(e).

This rule substantially continues such statutory provisions as U.S.C., Title 38, § 445 (Actions on claims; jurisdiction; parties; procedure; limitation; witnesses; definitions)(actions upon veterans' contracts of insurance with the United States), providing for interpleader by the United States where it acknowledges indebtedness under a contract of insurance with the United States; U.S.C., Title 49, § 97 (Interpleader of conflicting claimants)(by carrier which has issued bill of lading). See Chafee, The Federal Interpleader Act of 1936: I and II (1936), 45 Yale L.J. 963, 1161.

1948 AMENDMENT

The amendment effective October 20, 1949, substituted the reference to "Title 28, U.S.C., §§ 1335, 1397, and 2361," at the end of the first sentence of paragraph (2), in lieu of the reference to "Section 24(26) of the Judicial Code, as amended, U.S.C., Title 28, § 41(26)." The amendment also substituted the words "those provisions" in the second sentence of paragraph (2) for the words "that section."

1987 AMENDMENT

The amendment is technical. No substantive change is intended.

2007 AMENDMENT

The language of Rule 22 has been amended as part of the general restyling of the Civil Rules to make them more easily understood and to make style and terminology consistent throughout the rules. These changes are intended to be stylistic only.

Rule 23. Class Actions

1937 ADOPTION

Note to Subdivision (a). This is a substantial restatement of former Equity Rule 38 (Representatives of Class) as that rule has been construed. It applies to all actions, whether formerly denominated legal or equitable. For a general analysis of class actions, effect of judgment, and requisites of jurisdiction see Moore, Federal Rules of Civil Procedure: Some Problems Raised by the Preliminary Draft, 25 Georgetown L.J. 551, 570 et seq., 1937; Moore and Cohn, Federal Class Actions, 32 Ill.L.Rev. 307, 1937; Moore and Cohn, Federal Class Actions—Jurisdiction and Effect of Judgment, 32 Ill.L.Rev. 555–567, 1938; Lesar, Class Suits and the Federal Rules, 22 Minn.L.Rev. 34, 1937; cf. Arnold and James, Cases on Trials, Judgments and Appeals, 1936, 175; and see Blume,

Jurisdictional Amount in Representative Suits, 15 Minn.L.Rev. 501, 1931.

The general test of former Equity Rule 38 (Representatives of Class) that the question should be "one of common or general interest to many persons constituting a class so numerous as to make it impracticable to bring them all before the court," is a common test. For states which require the two elements of a common or general interest and numerous persons, as provided for in former Equity Rule 38, see Del.Ch. Rule 113; Fla.Comp.Gen.Laws Ann. (Supp., 1936) § 4918(7); Georgia Code, 1933, § 37-1002, and see English Rules Under the Judicature Act (The Annual Practice, 1937) O. 16, r. 9. For statutory provisions providing for class actions when the question is one of common or general interest or when the parties are numerous, see Ala.Code Ann. (Michie, 1928) § 5701; 2 Ind.Stat.Ann. (Burns, 1933) § 2-220; N.Y.C.P.A.1937, § 195; Wis.Stat. 1935, § 260.12. These statutes have, however, been uniformly construed as though phrased in the conjunctive. See *Garfein v. Stiglitz*, 260 Ky. 430, 86 S.W.2d 155, 1935. The rule adopts the test of former Equity Rule 38, but defines what constitutes a "common or general interest". Compare with code provisions which make the action dependent upon the propriety of joinder of the parties. See Blume, The "Common Questions" Principle in the Code Provision for Representative Suits, 30 Mich.L.Rev. 878, 1932. For discussion of what constitutes "numerous persons" see Wheaton, Representative Suits Involving Numerous Litigants, 19 Corn.L.Q. 399 (1934); Note, 36 Harv.L.Rev. 89 (1922).

Clause (1). Joint, Common, or Secondary Right. This clause is illustrated in actions brought by or against representatives of an unincorporated association. See *Oster v. Brotherhood of Locomotive Firemen and Enginemen, 1921*, 114 A. 377, 271 Pa. 419; *Pickett v. Walsh, 1906*, 78 N.E. 753, 192 Mass. 572, 6 L.R.A.,N.S. 1067; *Colt v. Hicks, 1932*, 179 N.E. 335, 97 Ind.App. 177. Compare rule 17(b) as to when an unincorporated association has capacity to sue or be sued in its common name; *United Mine Workers of America v. Coronado Coal Co., 1922*, 259 U.S. 344, 42 S. Ct. 570, 66 L.Ed. 975, 27 A.L.R. 762 (an unincorporated association was sued as an entity for the purpose of enforcing against it a federal substantive right); Moore, Federal Rules of Civil Procedure: Some Problems Raised by the Preliminary Draft, 25 Georgetown L.J. 551, 566 (for discussion of jurisdictional requisites when an unincorporated association sues or is sued in its common name and jurisdiction is founded upon diversity of citizenship). For an action brought by representatives of one group against representatives of another group for distribution of a fund held by an unincorporated association, see *Smith v. Swormstedt, 1853*, 14 L.Ed. 942, 16 How. 288. Compare *Christopher et al. v. Brusselback, 1938*, 302 U.S. 500, 58 S. Ct. 350, 82 L.Ed. 388.

For an action to enforce rights held in common by policyholders against the corporate issuer of the policies, see *Supreme Tribe of Ben Hur v. Cauble, 1921*, 255 U.S. 356, 41 S. Ct. 338, 65 L.Ed. 673. See also *Terry v. Little, 1880*, 101 U.S. 216, 25 L.Ed. 864; *John A. Roebling's Sons Co. v. Kinnicutt, D.C.N.Y.1917*, 248 F. 596, dealing with the right held in common by creditors to enforce the statutory liability of stockholders.

Typical of a secondary action is a suit by stockholders to enforce a corporate right. For discussion of the general nature of these actions see *Ashwander v. Tennessee Valley Authority, 1936*, 297 U.S. 288, 56 S. Ct. 466, 80 L.Ed. 688; Glenn, The Stockholder's Suit—Corporate and Individual Grievances, 33 Yale L.J. 580 (1924); McLaughlin, Capacity of Plaintiff-Stockholder to Terminate a Stockholder's Suit, 46 Yale L.J. 421 (1937). See also Subdivision (b) of this rule which deals with Shareholder's Action; Note, 15 Minn.L.Rev. 453 (1931).

Clause (2). A creditor's action for liquidation or reorganization of a corporation is illustrative of this clause. An action by a stockholder against certain named defendants as representatives of numerous claimants presents a situation converse to the creditor's action.

Clause (3). See *Everglades Drainage League v. Napoleon Broward Drainage Dist., D.C.Fla.1918*, 253 F. 246; *Gramling v. Maxwell, D.C.N.C.1931*, 52 F.2d 256, approved in 1932, 30 Mich.L.Rev. 624; *Skinner v. Mitchell, 1921*, 197 P. 569, 108 Kan. 861; *Duke of Bedford v. Ellis, 1901*, A.C. 1, for class actions when there were numerous persons and there was only a question of law or fact common to them; and see Blume, The "Common Questions" Principle in the Code Provision for Representative Suits, 30 Mich.L.Rev. 878 (1932).

Note to Subdivision (b). This is former Equity Rule 27 (Stockholder's Bill) with verbal changes. See also *Hawes v. Oakland, 1882*, 104 U.S. 450, 26 L.Ed. 827 and former Equity Rule 94, promulgated January 23, 1882, 104 U.S. IX.

Note to Subdivision (c). See McLaughlin, Capacity of Plaintiff-Stockholder to Terminate a Stockholder's Suit, 46 Yale L.J. 421 (1937).

SUPPLEMENTARY NOTE OF ADVISORY COMMITTEE REGARDING THIS RULE

Note. Subdivision (b), relating to secondary actions by shareholders, provides among other things, that in such an action the complainant "shall aver (1) that the plaintiff was a shareholder at the time of the transaction of which he complains or that his share thereafter devolved on him by operation of law * * *".

As a result of the decision in *Erie R. Co. v. Tompkins, 1938*, 304 U.S. 64, 58 S. Ct. 817, 82 L.Ed. 1188 (decided April 25, 1938, after this rule was promulgated by the Supreme Court, though before it took effect) a question has arisen as to whether the provision above quoted deals with a matter of substantive right or is a matter of procedure. If it is a matter of substantive law or right, then under *Erie R. Co. v. Tompkins*, clause (1) may not be validly applied in cases pending in states whose local law permits a shareholder to maintain such actions, although not a shareholder at the time of the transactions complained of. The Advisory Committee, believing the question should be settled in the courts, proposes no change in Rule 23 but thinks rather that the situation should be explained in an appropriate note.

The rule has a long history. In *Hawes v. Oakland, 1882*, 104 U.S. 450, 26 L.Ed. 827, the Court held that a shareholder could not maintain such an action unless he owned shares at the time of the transactions complained of, or unless they devolved on him by operation of law. At that time the decision in *Swift v. Tyson, 1842*, 41 U.S. 1, 10 L.Ed. 865, 16 Peters 1, was the law, and the federal courts considered themselves free to establish their own principles of equity jurisprudence, so the Court was not in 1882 and has not been, until *Erie R. Co. v. Tompkins* in 1938, concerned with the question whether *Hawes* v. *Oakland* dealt with substantive right or procedure.

Following the decision in *Hawes* v. *Oakland*, and at the same term, the Court, to implement its decision, adopted former Equity Rule 94, which contained the same provision above quoted from Rule 23 F.R.C.P. The provision in former Equity Rule 94 was later embodied in former Equity Rule 27, of which the present Rule 23 is substantially a copy.

In *City of Quincy v. Steel, 1887*, 120 U.S. 241, 245, 7 S. Ct. 520, 30 L.Ed. 624, the Court referring to *Hawes v. Oakland* said: "In order to give effect to the principles there laid down, this Court at that term adopted [former] Rule 94 of the rules of practice for courts of equity of the United States."

Some other cases dealing with former Equity Rules 94 or 27 prior to the decision in *Erie R. Co. v. Tompkins* are *Dimpfel v. Ohio & Miss. R. R., 1884*, 110 U.S. 209, 3 S. Ct. 573, 28 L.Ed. 121; *Illinois Central R. Co. v. Adams, 1901*, 180 U.S. 28, 34, 21 S. Ct. 251, 45 L.Ed. 410; *Venner v. Great Northern Ry., 1908*, 209 U.S. 24, 30, 28 S. Ct. 328, 52 L.Ed. 666; *Jacobson v. General Motors Corp., N.Y.1938*, 22 F.Supp. 255, 257. These cases generally treat *Hawes v. Oakland* as establishing a "principle" of equity, or as dealing not with jurisdiction but with the "right" to maintain an action, or have said that the defense under the equity rule is analogous to the defense that the plaintiff has no "title" and results in a dismissal "for want of equity."

Those state decisions which held that a shareholder acquiring stock after the event may maintain a derivative action are founded on the view that it is a right belonging to the shareholder at the time of the transaction and which passes as a right to the subsequent purchaser. See *Pollitz v. Gould, 1911*, 94 N.E. 1088, 202 N.Y. 11.

The first case arising after the decision in *Erie R. Co. v. Tompkins* in which this problem was involved, was *Summers v. Hearst, N.Y.1938*, 23 F.Supp. 986. It concerned former Equity Rule 27, as Federal Rule 23 was not then in effect. In a well considered opinion Judge Leibell reviewed the decisions and said: "The federal cases that discuss this section of [former] Rule 27 support the view that it states a principle of substantive law." He quoted *Pollitz v. Gould, 1911*, 94 N.E. 1088, 202 N.Y. 11, as saying that the United States Supreme Court "seems to have been more concerned with establishing this rule as one of practice than of substantive law" but that "whether it be regarded as establishing a principle of law or a rule of practice, this authority has been subsequently followed in the United States courts."

He then concluded that, although the federal decisions treat the equity rule as "stating a principle of substantive law", if "[former] Equity Rule 27 is to be modified or revoked in view of *Erie R. Co. v. Tompkins*, it is not the province of this Court to suggest it, much less impliedly to follow that course by disregarding the mandatory provisions of the Rule."

Some other federal decisions since 1938 touch the question.

In *Piccard v. Sperry Corporation, N.Y.1941*, 36 F.Supp. 1006, 1009–10, affirmed without opinion, C.C.A.2d 1941, 120 F.2d 328, a shareholder, not such at the time of the transactions complained of, sought to intervene. The court held an intervenor was as much subject to Rule 23 as an original plaintiff; and that the requirement of Rule 23(b) was "a matter of practice," not substance, and applied in New York where the state law was otherwise, despite *Erie R. Co. v. Tompkins.* In *York v. Guaranty Trust Co. of New York, C.C.A.2, 1944*, 143 F.2d 503, reversed on other grounds 326 U.S. 99, 65 S. Ct. 1464, 89 L.Ed. 2079, the court said: "Restrictions on the bringing of stockholders' actions, such as those imposed by F.R.C.P. 23(b) or other state statutes are procedural," citing the Picard and other cases.

In *Gallup v. Caldwell, C.C.A.3, 1941*, 120 F.2d 90, 95, arising in New Jersey, the point was raised but not decided, the court saying that it was not satisfied that the then New Jersey rule differed from Rule 23(b), and that "under the circumstances the proper course was to follow Rule 23(b)."

In *Mullins v. DeSoto Securities Co., La.1942*, 45 F.Supp. 871, 878, the point was not decided, because the court found the Louisiana rule to be the same as that stated in Rule 23(b).

In *Toebelman v. Missouri-Kansas Pipe Line Co., Del.1941*, 41 F.Supp. 334, 340, the court dealt only with another part of rule 23(b), relating to prior demands on the stockholders and did not discuss *Erie R. Co. v. Tompkins* or its effect on the rule.

In *Perrott v. United States Banking Corp., Del.1944*, 53 F.Supp. 953, it appeared that the Delaware law does not require the plaintiff to have owned shares at the time of the transaction complained of. The court sustained Rule 23(b), after discussion of the authorities, saying:

"It seems to me the rule does not go beyond procedure. * * * Simply because a particular plaintiff cannot qualify as a proper party to maintain such an action does not destroy or even whittle at the cause of action. The cause of action exists until a qualified plaintiff can get it started in a federal court."

In Bankers Nat. Corp. v. Barr, N.Y.1945, 9 Fed.Rules Serv. 23b.11, Case 1, the court held Rule 23(b) to be one of procedure, but that whether the plaintiff was a stockholder was a substantive question to be settled by state law.

The New York rule, as stated in *Pollitz v. Gould*, supra, has been altered by an act of the New York Legislature, Chapter 667, Laws of 1944, effective April 9, 1944, General Corporation Law, § 61, which provides that "in any action brought by a shareholder in the right of a * * * corporation, it must appear that the plaintiff was a stockholder at the time of the transaction of which he complains, or that his stock thereafter devolved upon him by operation of law." At the same time a further and separate provision was enacted, requiring under certain circumstances the giving of security for reasonable expenses and attorney's fees, to which security the corporation in whose right the action is brought and the defendants therein may have recourse. (Chapter 668, Laws of 1944, effective April 9, 1944, General Corporation Law, § 61-b.) These provisions are aimed at so-called "strike" stockholders' suits and their attendant abuses. *Shielcrawt v. Moffett, 1945*, 61 N.E.2d 435, 294 N.Y. 180; *Noel Associates, Inc. v. Merrill, 1944*, 53 N.Y.S.2d 143, 184 Misc. 646.

Insofar as § 61 is concerned, it has been held that the section is procedural in nature. *Klum v. Clinton Trust Co., 1944*, 48 N.Y.S.2d 267, 183 Misc. 340; *Noel Associates, Inc. v. Merrill*, supra. In the latter case the court pointed out that "The 1944 amendment to Section 61 rejected the rule laid down in the Pollitz case and substituted, in place thereof, in its precise language, the rule which has long prevailed in the Federal Courts and which is now Rule 23(b) * * *". There is, nevertheless, a difference of opinion regarding the application of the statute to pending actions. See *Klum v. Clinton Trust Co.*, supra (applicable); *Noel Associates, Inc. v. Merrill*, supra (inapplicable).

With respect to § 61-B, which may be regarded as a separate problem, *Noel Associates, Inc. v. Merrill*, supra, it has been held that even though the statute is procedural in nature—a matter not definitely decided—the Legislature evinced no intent that the provisions should apply to actions pending when it became effective. *Shielcrawt v. Moffett*, supra. As to actions instituted after the effective date of the legislation, the constitutionality of § 61-b is in dispute. See *Wolf v. Atkinson, 1944*, 49 N.Y.S.2d 703, 182 Misc. 675 (constitutional); *Citron v. Mangel Stores Corp., Sup.Ct.1944*, 50 N.Y.S.2d 416 (unconstitutional); Zlinkoff, The American Investor and the Constitutionality of Section 61-B of the New York General Corporation Law, 1945, 54 Yale L.J. 352.

New Jersey also enacted a statute, similar to Chapters 667 and 668 of the New York Law. See P.L.1945, Ch. 131, R.S.Cum.Supp. 14:3-15. The New Jersey provision similar to Chapter 668, § 61-B, differs, however, in that it specifically applies retroactively. It has been held that this provision is procedural and hence will not govern a pending action brought against a New Jersey corporation in the New York courts. *Shielcrawt v. Moffett, 1945*, 56 N.Y.S.2d 134, 184 Misc. 1074.

See, also generally, 2 Moore's Federal Practice, 1938, 2250–2253, and Cum.Supplement § 23.05.

The decisions here discussed show that the question is a debatable one, and that there is respectable authority for either view, with a recent trend towards the view that Rule 23(b)(1) is procedural. There is reason to say that the question is one which should not be decided by the Supreme Court ex parte, but left to await a judicial decision in a litigated case, and that in the light of the material in this note, the only inference to be drawn from a failure to amend rule 23(b) would be that the question is postponed to await a litigated case.

The Advisory Committee is unanimously of the opinion that this course should be followed.

If, however, the final conclusion is that the rule deals with a matter of substantive right, then the rule should be amended by adding a provision that Rule 23(b)(1) does not apply in jurisdictions where state law permits a shareholder to maintain a secondary action, although he was not a shareholder at the time of the transactions of which he complains.

1966 AMENDMENT

Difficulties with the original rule. The categories of class actions in the original rule were defined in terms of the abstract nature of the rights involved: the so-called "true" category was defined as involving "joint, common, or secondary rights"; the "hybrid" category, as involving "several" rights related to "specific property"; the "spurious" category, as involving "several" rights affected by a common question and related to common relief. It was thought that the definitions accurately described the situations amenable to the class-suit device, and also would indicate the proper extent of the judgment in each category, which would in turn help to determine the res judicata effect of the judgment if questioned in a later action. Thus the judgments in "true" and "hybrid" class actions would extend to the class (although in somewhat different ways); the judgment in a "spurious" class action would extend only to the parties including intervenors. See Moore, Federal Rules of Civil Procedure: Some Problems Raised by the Preliminary Draft, 25 Geo.L.J. 551, 570–76 (1937).

In practice the terms "joint," "common," etc., which were used as the basis of the Rule 23 classification proved obscure and uncertain. See Chafee, Some Problems of Equity 245–46, 256–57 (1950); Kalven & Rosenfield, The Contemporary Function of the Class Suit, 8 U. of Chi.L.Rev. 684, 707 & n. 73 (1941); Keeffe, Levy & Donovan, Lee Defeats Ben Hur, 33 Corn.L.Q. 327, 329–36 (1948); Developments in the Law: Multiparty Litigation in the Federal Courts, 71 Harv.L.Rev. 874, 931 (1958); Advisory Committee's Note to Rule 19, as amended. The courts had considerable difficulty with these terms. See, e.g., *Gullo v. Veterans' Co-op Housing Assn.*, 13 F.R.D. 11 (D.D.C.1952); *Shipley v. Pittsburgh & L. E. R. Co.*, 70 F.Supp. 870 (W.D.Pa.1947); *Deckert v. Independence Shares Corp.*, 27 F.Supp. 763 (E.D.Pa.1939), rev'd, 108 F.2d 51 (3d Cir.1939), rev'd, 311 U.S. 282, 61 S. Ct. 229, 85 L.Ed. 189 (1940), on remand, 39 F.Supp. 592 (E.D.Pa.1941), rev'd sub nom. Pennsylvania Co. for Ins. on Lives v. Deckert, 123 F.2d 979 (3d Cir.1941) (see Chafee, supra, at 264 to 65).

Nor did the rule provide an adequate guide to the proper extent of the judgments in class actions. First, we find instances of the courts classifying actions as "true" or intimating that the judgments would be decisive for the class where these results seemed appropriate but were reached by dint of depriving the word "several" of coherent meaning. See, e.g., *System Federation No. 91 v. Reed*, 180 F.2d 991 (6th Cir.1950); *Wilson v. City of Paducah*, 100 F.Supp. 116 (W.D. Ky.1951); *Citizens Banking Co. v. Monticello State Bank*, 143 F.2d 261 (8th Cir. 1944); *Redmond v. Commerce Trust Co.*, 144 F.2d 140 (8th Cir.1944), cert. denied, 323 U.S. 776, 65 S. Ct. 187, 89 L.Ed. 620 (1944); *United States v. American Optical Co.*, 97 F.Supp. 66 (N.D.Ill.1951); *National Hairdressers' & C. Assn. v. Philad Co.*, 34 F.Supp. 264 (D.Del.1940); 41 F.Supp. 701 (D.Del.1941), aff'd mem., 129 F.2d 1020 (3d Cir.1942). Second, we find cases classified by the courts as "spurious" in which, on a realistic view, it would seem fitting for the judgments to extend to the class. See, e.g., *Knapp v. Bankers Sec. Corp.*, 17 F.R.D. 245 (E.D.Pa.1954), aff'd 230 F.2d 717 (3d Cir.1956); *Giesecke v. Denver Tramway Corp.*, 81 F.Supp. 957 (D.Del.1949); *York v. Guaranty Trust Co.*, 143 F.2d 503 (2d Cir.1944), rev'd on grounds not here relevant, 326 U.S. 99, 65 S. Ct. 1464, 89 L.Ed. 2079 (1945) (see Chafee, supra, at 208); cf. *Webster Eisenlohr, Inc. v. Kalodner*, 145 F.2d 316, 320 (3d Cir.1944), cert. denied, 325 U.S. 867, 65 S. Ct. 1404, 89 L.Ed. 1986 (1945). But cf. the early decisions, *Duke of Bedford v. Ellis*, [1901] A.C. 1; *Sheffield Waterworks v. Yeomans*, L.R. 2 Ch.App. 8 (1866); *Brown v. Vermuden*, 1 Ch.Cas. 272, 22 Eng.Rep. 796 (1676).

The "spurious" action envisaged by original Rule 23 was in any event an anomaly because, although denominated a "class" action and pleaded as such, it was supposed not to adjudicate the rights or liabilities of any person not a party. It was believed to be an advantage of the "spurious" category that it would invite decisions that a member of the "class" could, like a member of the class in a "true" or "hybrid" action, intervene on an ancillary basis without being required to show an independent basis of Federal jurisdiction, and have the benefit of the date of the commencement of the action for purposes of the statute of limitations. See 3 Moore's Federal Practice, pars. 23.10[1], 23.12 (2d ed. 1963). These results were attained in some instances but not in others. On the statute of limitations, see *Union Carbide & Carbon Corp. v. Nisley*, 300 F.2d 561 (10th Cir.1961), pet. cert. dism., 371 U.S. 801, 83 S. Ct. 13, 9 L. Ed. 2d 46 (1962); but cf. *P. W. Husserl, Inc. v. Simplicity Pattern Co.*, 25 F.R.D. 264 (S.D. N.Y.1960); *Athas v. Day*, 161 F.Supp. 916 (D.Colo.1958). On ancillary intervention, see *Amen v. Black*, 234 F.2d 12 (10th Cir.1956), cert. granted, 352 U.S. 888, 77 S. Ct. 127, 1 L. Ed. 2d 84 (1956), dism. on stip., 355 U.S. 600, 78 S. Ct. 530, 2 L. Ed. 2d 523 (1958); but cf. *Wagner v. Kemper*, 13 F.R.D. 128 (W.D.Mo. 1952). The results, however, can hardly depend upon the mere appearance of a "spurious" category in the rule; they should turn on more basic considerations. See discussion of subdivision (c)(1) below.

Finally, the original rule did not squarely address itself to the question of the measures that might be taken during the course of the action to assure procedural fairness, particularly giving notice to members of the class, which may in turn be related in some instances to the extension of the judgment to the class. See Chafee, supra, at 230 to 31; Keeffe, Levy & Donovan, supra; Developments in the Law, supra, 71 Harv.L.Rev. at 937–38; Note Binding Effect of Class Actions, 67 Harv.L.Rev. 1059, 1062–65 (1954); Note, Federal Class Actions: A Suggested Revision of Rule 23, 46 Colum.L.Rev. 818, 833–36 (1946); Mich.Gen.Court R. 208.4 (effective Jan. 1, 1963); Idaho R.Civ.P. 23(d); Minn.R.Civ.P. 23.04; N.Dak.R.Civ.P. 23(d).

The amended rule describes in more practical terms the occasions for maintaining class actions; provides that all class actions maintained to the end as such will result in judgments including those whom the court finds to be members of the class, whether or not the judgment is favorable to the class; and refers to the measures which can be taken to assure the fair conduct of these actions.

Subdivision (a) states the prerequisites for maintaining any class action in terms of the numerousness of the class making joinder of the members impracticable, the existence of questions common to the class, and the desired qualifications of the representative parties. See Weinstein, Revision of Procedure: Some Problems in Class Actions, 9 Buffalo L.Rev. 433, 458–59 (1960); 2 Barron & Holtzoff, Federal Practice & Procedure § 562, at 265, § 572, at 351 to 52 (Wright ed. 1961). These are necessary but not sufficient conditions for a class action. See, e.g., *Giordano v. Radio Corp. of Am.*, 183 F.2d 558, 560 (3d Cir.1950); *Zachman v. Erwin*, 186 F.Supp. 681 (S.D.Tex.1959); *Baim & Blank, Inc. v. Warren-Connelly Co., Inc.*, 19 F.R.D. 108 (S.D.N.Y.1956). Subdivision (b) describes the additional elements which in varying situations justify the use of a class action.

Subdivision (b)(1). The difficulties which would be likely to arise if resort were had to separate actions by or against the individual members of the class here furnish the reasons for, and the principal key to, the propriety and value of utilizing the class-action device. The considerations stated under clauses (A) and (B) are comparable to certain of the elements which define the persons whose joinder in an action is desirable as stated in Rule 19(a), as amended. See amended Rule 19(a)(2)(i) and (ii), and the Advisory Committee's Note thereto; Hazard, Indispensable Party: The Historical Origin of a Procedural Phantom, 61 Colum.L.Rev. 1254, 1259–60 (1961); cf. 3 Moore, supra, par. 23.08 at 3435.

Clause (A): One person may have rights against, or be under duties toward, numerous persons constituting a class, and be so positioned that conflicting or varying adjudications in lawsuits with individual members of the class might establish incompatible standards to govern his conduct. The class action device can be used effectively to obviate the actual or virtual dilemma which would thus confront the party opposing the class. The matter has been stated thus: "The felt necessity for a class action is greatest when the courts are called upon to order or sanction the alteration of the status quo in circumstances such that a large number of persons are in a position to call on a single person to alter the status quo, or to complain if it is altered, and the possibility exists that [the] actor might be called upon to act in inconsistent ways." Louisell & Hazard, Pleading and Procedure: State and Federal 719 (1962); see *Supreme Tribe of Ben Hur v. Cauble*, 255 U.S. 356, 366–67, 41 S. Ct. 338, 65 L.Ed. 673 (1921). To illustrate: Separate actions by individuals against a municipality to declare a bond issue invalid or condition or limit it, to prevent or limit the making of a particular appropriation or to compel or invalidate an assessment, might create a risk of inconsistent or varying determinations. In the same way, individual litigations of the rights and duties of riparian owners, or of landowners' rights and duties respecting a claimed nuisance, could create a possibility of incompatible adjudications. Actions by or against a class provide a ready and fair means of achieving unitary adjudication. See *Maricopa County Mun.Water Con. Dist. v. Looney*, 219 F.2d 529 (9th Cir.1955); *Rank v. Krug*, 142 F.Supp. 1, 154–59 (S.D. Cal.1956), on app., *State of California v. Rank*, 293 F.2d 340, 348 (9th Cir.1961); *Gart v. Cole*, 263 F.2d 244 (2d Cir.1959), cert. denied 359 U.S. 978, 79 S. Ct.

898, 3 L. Ed. 2d 929 (1959); cf. *Martinez v. Maverick Cty. Water Con. & Imp. Dist.*, 219 F.2d 666 (5th Cir.1955); 3 Moore, supra, par. 23.11[2], at 3458 to 59.

Clause (B): This clause takes in situations where the judgment in a nonclass action by or against an individual member of the class, while not technically concluding the other members, might do so as a practical matter. The vice of an individual action would lie in the fact that the other members of the class, thus practically concluded, would have had no representation in the lawsuit. In an action by policy holders against a fraternal benefit association attacking a financial reorganization of the society, it would hardly have been practical, if indeed it would have been possible, to confine the effects of a validation of the reorganization to the individual plaintiffs. Consequently a class action was called for with adequate representation of all members of the class. See *Supreme Tribe of Ben Hur v. Cauble*, 255 U.S. 356, 41 S. Ct. 338, 65 L.Ed. 673 (1921); *Waybright v. Columbian Mut. Life Ins. Co.*, 30 F.Supp. 885 (W.D.Tenn.1939); cf. Smith v. Swormstedt, 16 How. (57 U.S.) 288 (1853). For much the same reason actions by shareholders to compel the declaration of a dividend, the proper recognition and handling of redemption or pre-emption rights, or the like (or actions by the corporation for corresponding declarations of rights), should ordinarily be conducted as class actions, although the matter has been much obscured by the insistence that each shareholder has an individual claim. See *Knapp v. Bankers Securities Corp.*, 17 F.R.D. 245 (E.D.Pa.1954), aff'd, 230 F.2d 717 (3d Cir.1956); *Giesecke v. Denver Tramway Corp.*, 81 F.Supp. 957 (D.Del.1949); *Zahn v. Transamerica Corp.*, 162 F.2d 36 (3d Cir.1947); *Speed v. Transamerica Corp.*, 100 F.Supp. 461 (D.Del.1951); *Sobel v. Whittier Corp.*, 95 F.Supp. 643 (E.D.Mich.1951), app. dism., 195 F.2d 361 (6th Cir.1952); *Goldberg v. Whittier Corp.*, 111 F.Supp. 382 (E.D.Mich.1953); *Dann v. Studebaker-Packard Corp.*, 288 F.2d 201 (6th Cir.1961); *Edgerton v. Armour & Co.*, 94 F.Supp. 549 (S.D. Cal.1950); *Ames v. Mengel Co.*, 190 F.2d 344 (2d Cir.1951). These shareholders' actions are to be distinguished from derivative actions by shareholders dealt with in new Rule 23.1. The same reasoning applies to an action which charges a breach of trust by an indenture trustee or other fiduciary similarly affecting the members of a larger class of security holders or other beneficiaries, and which requires an accounting or like measures to restore the subject of the trust. See *Boesenberg v. Chicago T. & T. Co.*, 128 F.2d 245 (7th Cir.1942); *Citizens Banking Co. v. Monticello State Bank*, 143 F.2d 261 (8th Cir.1944); *Redmond v. Commerce Trust Co.*, 144 F.2d 140 (8th Cir.1944), cert. denied, 323 U.S. 776, 65 S. Ct. 187, 89 L.Ed. 620 (1944); cf. *York v. Guaranty Trust Co.*, 143 F.2d 503 (2d Cir.1944), rev'd on grounds not here relevant, 326 U.S. 99, 65 S. Ct. 1464, 89 L.Ed. 2079 (1945).

In various situations an adjudication as to one or more members of the class will necessarily or probably have an adverse practical effect on the interests of other members who should therefore be represented in the lawsuit. This is plainly the case when claims are made by numerous persons against a fund insufficient to satisfy all claims. A class action by or against representative members to settle the validity of the claims as a whole, or in groups, followed by separate proof of the amount of each valid claim and proportionate distribution of the fund, meets the problem. Cf. *Dickinson v. Burnham*, 197 F.2d 973 (2d Cir.1952), cert. denied, 344 U.S. 875, 73 S. Ct. 169, 97 L.Ed. 678 (1952); 3 Moore, supra, at par. 23.09. The same reasoning applies to an action by a creditor to set aside a fraudulent conveyance by the debtor and to appropriate the property to his claim, when the debtor's assets are insufficient to pay all creditors' claims. See *Heffernan v. Bennett & Armour*, 110 Cal.App.2d 564, 243 P.2d 846 (1952); cf. *City & County of San Francisco v. Market Street Ry.*, 95 Cal.App.2d 648, 213 P.2d 780 (1950). Similar problems, however, can arise in the absence of a fund either present or potential. A negative or mandatory injunction secured by one of a numerous class may disable the opposing party from performing claimed duties toward the other members of the class or materially affect his ability to do so. An adjudication as to movie "clearances and runs" nominally affecting only one exhibitor would often have practical effects on all the exhibitors in the same territorial area. Cf. *United States v. Paramount*

Pictures, Inc., 66 F.Supp. 323, 341–46 (S.D.N.Y.1946); 334 U.S. 131, 144–48, 68 S. Ct. 915, 92 L.Ed. 1260 (1948). Assuming a sufficiently numerous class of exhibitors, a class action would be advisable. (Here representation of subclasses of exhibitors could become necessary; see subdivision (c)(3)(B).)

Subdivision (b)(2). This subdivision is intended to reach situations where a party has taken action or refused to take action with respect to a class, and final relief of an injunctive nature or of a corresponding declaratory nature, settling the legality of the behavior with respect to the class as a whole, is appropriate. Declaratory relief "corresponds" to injunctive relief when as a practical matter it affords injunctive relief or serves as a basis for later injunctive relief. The subdivision does not extend to cases in which the appropriate final relief relates exclusively or predominantly to money damages. Action or inaction is directed to a class within the meaning of this subdivision even if it has taken effect or is threatened only as to one or a few members of the class, provided it is based on grounds which have general application to the class.

Illustrative are various actions in the civil-rights field where a party is charged with discriminating unlawfully against a class, usually one whose members are incapable of specific enumeration. See *Potts v. Flax*, 313 F.2d 284 (5th Cir.1963); *Bailey v. Patterson*, 323 F.2d 201 (5th Cir.1963), cert. denied, 376 U.S. 910, 84 S. Ct. 666, 11 L. Ed. 2d 609 (1964); *Brunson v. Board of Trustees of School District No. 1, Clarendon Cty., S.C.*, 311 F.2d 107 (4th Cir.1962), cert. denied, 373 U.S. 933, 83 S. Ct. 1538, 10 L. Ed. 2d 690 (1963); *Green v. School Bd. of Roanoke, Va.*, 304 F.2d 118 (4th Cir.1962); *Orleans Parish School Bd. v. Bush*, 242 F.2d 156 (5th Cir.1957), cert. denied, 354 U.S. 921, 77 S. Ct. 1380, 1 L. Ed. 2d 1436 (1957); *Mannings v. Board of Public Inst. of Hillsborough County, Fla.*, 277 F.2d 370 (5th Cir.1960); *Northcross v. Board of Ed. of City of Memphis*, 302 F.2d 818 (6th Cir.1962), cert. denied, 370 U.S. 944, 82 S. Ct. 1586, 8 L. Ed. 2d 810 (1962); *Frasier v. Board of Trustees of Univ. of N. C.*, 134 F.Supp. 589 (M.D.N.C.1955, 3-judge court), aff'd, 350 U.S. 979, 76 S. Ct. 467, 100 L.Ed. 848 (1956). Subdivision (b)(2) is not limited to civil-rights cases. Thus an action looking to specific or declaratory relief could be brought by a numerous class of purchasers, say retailers of a given description, against a seller alleged to have undertaken to sell to that class at prices higher than those set for other purchasers, say retailers of another description, when the applicable law forbids such a pricing differential. So also a patentee of a machine, charged with selling or licensing the machine on condition that purchasers or licensees also purchase or obtain licenses to use an ancillary unpatented machine, could be sued on a class basis by a numerous group of purchasers or licensees, or by a numerous group of competing sellers or licensors of the unpatented machine, to test the legality of the "tying" condition.

Subdivision (b)(3). In the situations to which this subdivision relates, class-action treatment is not as clearly called for as in those described above, but it may nevertheless be convenient and desirable depending upon the particular facts. Subdivision (b)(3) encompasses those cases in which a class action would achieve economies of time, effort, and expense, and promote uniformity of decision as to persons similarly situated, without sacrificing procedural fairness or bringing about other undesirable results. Cf. Chafee, supra, at 201.

The court is required to find, as a condition of holding that a class action may be maintained under this subdivision, that the questions common to the class predominate over the questions affecting individual members. It is only where this predominance exists that economies can be achieved by means of the class-action device. In this view, a fraud perpetrated on numerous persons by the use of similar misrepresentations may be an appealing situation for a class action, and it may remain so despite the need, if liability is found, for separate determination of the damages suffered by individuals within the class. On the other hand, although having some common core, a fraud case may be unsuited for treatment as a class action if there was material variation in the representations made or in the kinds or degrees of reliance by the persons to whom they were addressed. See *Oppenheimer v. F. J. Young & Co., Inc.*, 144 F.2d 387 (2d Cir.1944); *Miller v. National City Bank of N. Y.*, 166 F.2d 723 (2d Cir.1948); and for like problems in other contexts, see *Hughes v. Encyclopaedia Britannica*, 199 F.2d 295 (7th Cir.1952); *Sturgeon v. Great Lakes Steel Corp.*, 143 F.2d 819 (6th Cir.1944). A "mass accident" resulting in injuries to numerous persons is ordinarily not appropriate for a class action because of the likelihood that significant questions, not only of damages but of liability and defenses of liability, would be present, affecting the individuals in different ways. In these circumstances an action conducted nominally as a class action would degenerate in practice into multiple lawsuits separately tried. See *Pennsylvania R.R. v. United States*, 111 F.Supp. 80 (D.N.J.1953); cf. Weinstein, supra, 9 Buffalo L.Rev. at 469. Private damage claims by numerous individuals arising out of concerted antitrust violations may or may not involve predominating common questions. See *Union Carbide & Carbon Corp. v. Nisley*, 300 F.2d 561 (10th Cir.1961), pet. cert. dism., 371 U.S. 801, 83 S. Ct. 13, 9 L. Ed. 2d 46 (1962); cf. *Weeks v. Bareco Oil Co.*, 125 F.2d 84 (7th Cir.1941); *Kainz v. Anheuser-Busch, Inc.*, 194 F.2d 737 (7th Cir.1952); *Hess v. Anderson, Clayton & Co.*, 20 F.R.D. 466 (S.D.Cal.1957).

That common questions predominate is not itself sufficient to justify a class action under subdivision (b)(3), for another method of handling the litigious situation may be available which has greater practical advantages. Thus one or more actions agreed to by the parties as test or model actions may be preferable to a class action; or it may prove feasible and preferable to consolidate actions. Cf. Weinstein, supra, 9 Buffalo L.Rev. at 438–54. Even when a number of separate actions are proceeding simultaneously, experience shows that the burdens on the parties and the courts can sometimes be reduced by arrangements for avoiding repetitious discovery or the like. Currently the Coordinating Committee on Multiple Litigation in the United States District Courts (a subcommittee of the Committee on Trial Practice and Technique of the Judicial Conference of the United States) is charged with developing methods for expediting such massive litigation. To reinforce the point that the court with the aid of the parties ought to assess the relative advantages of alternative procedures for handling the total controversy, subdivision (b)(3) requires, as a further condition of maintaining the class action, that the court shall find that that procedure is "superior" to the others in the particular circumstances.

Factors (A)–(D) are listed, non-exhaustively, as pertinent to the findings. The court is to consider the interests of individual members of the class in controlling their own litigations and carrying them on as they see fit. See *Weeks v. Bareco Oil Co.*, 125 F.2d 84, 88–90, 93–94 (7th Cir.1941) (anti-trust action); see also *Pentland v. Dravo Corp.*, 152 F.2d 851 (3d Cir.1945), and Chafee, supra, at 273 to 75, regarding policy of Fair Labor Standards Act of 1938, § 16(b), 29 U.S.C. § 216(b), prior to amendment by Portal-to-Portal Act of 1947, § 5(a). [The present provisions of 29 U.S.C. § 216(b) are not intended to be affected by Rule 23, as amended.]

In this connection the court should inform itself of any litigation actually pending by or against the individuals. The interests of individuals in conducting separate lawsuits may be so strong as to call for denial of a class action. On the other hand, these interests may be theoretic rather than practical; the class may have a high degree of cohesion and prosecution of the action through representatives would be quite unobjectionable, or the amounts at stake for individuals may be so small that separate suits would be impracticable. The burden that separate suits would impose on the party opposing the class, or upon the court calendars, may also fairly be considered. (See the discussion, under subdivision (c)(2) below, of the right of members to be excluded from the class upon their request.)

Also pertinent is the question of the desirability of concentrating the trial of the claims in the particular forum by means of a class action, in contrast to allowing the claims to be litigated separately in forums to which they would ordinarily be brought. Finally, the court should consider the problems of management which are likely to arise in the conduct of a class action.

Subdivision (c)(1). In order to give clear definition to the action, this provision requires the court to determine, as early in the proceedings as may be practicable, whether an action brought as a class action is to be so maintained.

The determination depends in each case on satisfaction of the terms of subdivision (a) and the relevant provisions of subdivision (b).

An order embodying a determination can be conditional; the court may rule, for example, that a class action may be maintained only if the representation is improved through intervention of additional parties of a stated type. A determination once made can be altered or amended before the decision on the merits if, upon fuller development of the facts, the original determination appears unsound. A negative determination means that the action should be stripped of its character as a class action. See subdivision (d)(4). Although an action thus becomes a nonclass action, the court may still be receptive to interventions before the decision on the merits so that the litigation may cover as many interests as can be conveniently handled; the questions whether the intervenors in the nonclass action shall be permitted to claim "ancillary" jurisdiction or the benefit of the date of the commencement of the action for purposes of the statute of limitations are to be decided by reference to the laws governing jurisdiction and limitations as they apply in particular contexts.

Whether the court should require notice to be given to members of the class of its intention to make a determination, or of the order embodying it, is left to the court's discretion under subdivision (d)(2).

Subdivision (c)(2) makes special provision for class actions maintained under subdivision (b)(3). As noted in the discussion of the latter subdivision, the interests of the individuals in pursuing their own litigations may be so strong here as to warrant denial of a class action altogether. Even when a class action is maintained under subdivision (b)(3), this individual interest is respected. Thus the court is required to direct notice to the members of the class of the right of each member to be excluded from the class upon his request. A member who does not request exclusion may, if he wishes, enter an appearance in the action through his counsel; whether or not he does so, the judgment in the action will embrace him.

The notice, setting forth the alternatives open to the members of the class, is to be the best practicable under the circumstances, and shall include individual notice to the members who can be identified through reasonable effort. (For further discussion of this notice, see the statement under subdivision (d)(2) below.)

Subdivision (c)(3). The judgment in a class action maintained as such to the end will embrace the class, that is, in a class action under subdivision (b)(1) or (b)(2), those found by the court to be class members; in a class action under subdivision (b)(3), those to whom the notice prescribed by subdivision (c)(2) was directed, excepting those who requested exclusion or who are ultimately found by the court not to be members of the class. The judgment has this scope whether it is favorable or unfavorable to the class. In a (b)(1) or (b)(2) action the judgment "describes" the members of the class, but need not specify the individual members; in a (b)(3) action the judgment "specifies" the individual members who have been identified and described the others.

Compare subdivision (c)(4) as to actions conducted as class actions only with respect to particular issues. Where the class-action character of the lawsuit is based solely on the existence of a "limited fund," the judgment, while extending to all claims of class members against the fund, has ordinarily left unaffected the personal claims of nonappearing members against the debtor. See 3 Moore, supra, par. 23.11[4].

Hitherto, in a few actions conducted as "spurious" class actions and thus nominally designed to extend only to parties and others intervening before the determination of liability, courts have held or intimated that class members might be permitted to intervene after a decision on the merits favorable to their interests, in order to secure the benefits of the decision for themselves, although they would presumably be unaffected by an unfavorable decision. See, as to the propriety of this so-called "one-way" intervention in "spurious" actions, the conflicting views expressed in *Union Carbide & Carbon Corp. v. Nisley*, 300 F.2d 561 (10th Cir.1961), pet. cert. dism., 371 U.S. 801, 83 S. Ct. 13, 9 L. Ed. 2d 46 (1962); *York v. Guaranty Trust Co.*, 143 F.2d 503, 529 (2d Cir.1944), rev'd on grounds not here relevant, 326 U.S. 99, 65 S. Ct. 1464, 89 L.Ed. 2079 (1945); *Pentland v. Dravo Corp.*, 152 F.2d 851, 856 (3d Cir.1945); *Speed v. Transamerica Corp.*, 100 F.Supp. 461, 463 (D.Del.1951); *State Wholesale Grocers v. Great Atl. & Pac. Tea Co.*, 24 F.R.D. 510 (N.D.Ill.1959); *Alabama Ind. Serv. Stat. Assn. v. Shell Pet. Corp.*, 28 F.Supp. 386, 390 (N.D.Ala.1939); *Tolliver v. Cudahy Packing Co.*, 39 F.Supp. 337, 339 (E.D.Tenn.1941); *Kalven & Rosenfield*, supra, 8 U. of Chi.L.Rev. 684 (1941); Comment, 53 Nw.U.L.Rev. 627, 632–33 (1958); Developments in the Law, supra, 71 Harv.L.Rev. at 935; 2 Barron & Holtzoff, supra, § 568; but cf. *Lockwood v. Hercules Powder Co.*, 7 F.R.D. 24, 28–29 (W.D. Mo.1947); *Abram v. San Joaquin Cotton Oil Co.*, 46 F.Supp. 969, 976–77 (S.D. Cal.1942); Chafee, supra, at 280, 285; 3 Moore, supra, par. 23.12, at 3476. Under proposed subdivision (c)(3), one-way intervention is excluded; the action will have been early determined to be a class or nonclass action, and in the former case the judgment, whether or not favorable, will include the class, as above stated.

Although thus declaring that the judgment in a class action includes the class, as defined, subdivision (c)(3) does not disturb the recognized principle that the court conducting the action cannot predetermine the res judicata effect of the judgment; this can be tested only in a subsequent action. See Restatement, Judgments § 86, comment (h), § 116 (1942). The court, however, in framing the judgment in any suit brought as a class action, must decide what its extent or coverage shall be, and if the matter is carefully considered, questions of res judicata are less likely to be raised at a later time and if raised will be more satisfactorily answered. See Chafee, supra, at 294; Weinstein, supra, 9 Buffalo L.Rev. at 460.

Subdivision (c)(4). This provision recognizes that an action may be maintained as a class action as to particular issues only. For example, in a fraud or similar case the action may retain its "class" character only through the adjudication of liability to the class; the members of the class may thereafter be required to come in individually and prove the amounts of their respective claims.

Two or more classes may be represented in a single action. Where a class is found to include subclasses divergent in interest, the class may be divided correspondingly, and each subclass treated as a class.

Subdivision (d) is concerned with the fair and efficient conduct of the action and lists some types of orders which may be appropriate.

The court should consider how the proceedings are to be arranged in sequence, and what measures should be taken to simplify the proof and argument. See subdivision (d)(1). The orders resulting from this consideration, like the others referred to in subdivision (d), may be combined with a pretrial order under Rule 16, and are subject to modification as the case proceeds.

Subdivision (d)(2) sets out a non-exhaustive list of possible occasions for orders requiring notice to the class. Such notice is not a novel conception. For example, in "limited fund" cases, members of the class have been notified to present individual claims after the basic class decision. Notice has gone to members of a class so that they might express any opposition to the representation, see *United States v. American Optical Co.*, 97 F.Supp. 66 (N.D.Ill.1951), and 1950–51 CCH Trade Cases 64573–74 (par. 62869); cf. *Weeks v. Bareco Oil Co.*, 125 F.2d 84, 94 (7th Cir.1941), and notice may encourage interventions to improve the representation of the class. Cf. *Oppenheimer v. F. J. Young & Co.*, 144 F.2d 387 (2d Cir.1944). Notice has been used to poll members on a proposed modification of a consent decree. See record in *Sam Fox Publishing Co. v. United States*, 366 U.S. 683, 81 S. Ct. 1309, 6 L. Ed. 2d 604 (1961).

Subdivision (d)(2) does not require notice at any stage, but rather calls attention to its availability and invokes the court's discretion. In the degree that there is cohesiveness or unity in the class and the representation is effective, the need for notice to the class will tend toward a minimum. These indicators suggest that notice under subdivision (d)(2) may be particularly useful and advisable in certain class actions maintained under subdivision (b)(3), for example, to permit members of the class to object to the representation. Indeed, under subdivision (c)(2), notice must be ordered, and is not merely discretionary, to give the members in a subdivision (b)(3) class action an opportunity to secure exclusion from the class. This mandatory notice pursuant to subdivision (c)(2), together with any discretionary notice which the court may find it advisable to give under subdivision (d)(2), is designed to fulfill requirements of due process to which the class action procedure is of course subject. See *Hansberry v. Lee*, 311 U.S. 32, 61 S. Ct. 115, 85 L.Ed. 22 (1940); *Mullane v. Central Hanover Bank & Trust Co.*, 339 U.S. 306, 70 S. Ct. 652, 94 L.Ed. 865 (1950); cf. *Dickinson v. Burnham*, 197 F.2d 973, 979 (2d Cir.1952), and studies cited at 979 n. 4; see also *All American Airways, Inc. v. Elderd*, 209 F.2d 247, 249 (2d Cir.1954); *Gart v. Cole*, 263 F.2d 244, 248–49 (2d Cir.1959), cert. denied, 359 U.S. 978, 79 S. Ct. 898, 3 L. Ed. 2d 929 (1959).

Notice to members of the class, whenever employed under amended Rule 23, should be accommodated to the particular purpose but need not comply with the formalities for service of process. See Chafee, supra, at 230 to 31; *Brendle v. Smith*, 7 F.R.D. 119 (S.D.N.Y.1946). The fact that notice is given at one stage of the action does not mean that it must be given at subsequent stages. Notice is available fundamentally "for the protection of the members of the class or otherwise for the fair conduct of the action" and should not be used merely as a device for the undesirable solicitation of claims. See the discussion in *Cherner v. Transitron Electronic Corp.*, 201 F.Supp. 934 (D.Mass.1962); *Hormel v. United States*, 17 F.R.D. 303 (S.D.N.Y.1955).

In appropriate cases the court should notify interested government agencies of the pendency of the action or of particular steps therein.

Subdivision (d)(3) reflects the possibility of conditioning the maintenance of a class action, e.g., on the strengthening of the representation, see subdivision (c)(1) above; and recognizes that the imposition of conditions on intervenors may be required for the proper and efficient conduct of the action.

As to orders under **subdivision (d)(4)**, see subdivision (c)(1) above.

Subdivision (e) requires approval of the court, after notice, for the dismissal or compromise of any class action.

1987 AMENDMENT

The amendments are technical. No substantive change is intended.

1998 AMENDMENT

Subdivision (f). This permissive interlocutory appeal provision is adopted under the power conferred by 28 U.S.C. § 1292(e). Appeal from an order granting or denying class certification is permitted in the sole discretion of the court of appeals. No other type of Rule 23 order is covered by this provision. The court of appeals is given unfettered discretion whether to permit the appeal, akin to the discretion exercised by the Supreme Court in acting on a petition for certiorari. This discretion suggests an analogy to the provision in 28 U.S.C. § 1292(b) for permissive appeal on certification by a district court. Subdivision (f), however, departs from the § 1292(b) model in two significant ways. It does not require that the district court certify the certification ruling for appeal, although the district court often can assist the parties and court of appeals by offering advice on the desirability of appeal. And it does not include the potentially limiting requirements of § 1292(b) that the district court order "involve[] a controlling question of law as to which there is substantial ground for difference of opinion and that an immediate appeal from the order may materially advance the ultimate termination of the litigation."

The courts of appeals will develop standards for granting review that reflect the changing areas of uncertainty in class litigation. The Federal Judicial Center study supports the view that many suits with class-action allegations present familiar and almost routine issues that are no more worthy of immediate appeal than many other interlocutory rulings. Yet several concerns justify expansion of present opportunities to appeal. An order denying certification may confront the plaintiff with a situation in which the only sure path to appellate review is by proceeding to final judgment on the merits of an individual claim that, standing alone, is far smaller than the costs of litigation. An order granting certification, on the other hand, may force a defendant to settle rather than incur the costs of defending a class action and run the risk of potentially ruinous liability. These concerns can be met at low cost by establishing in the court of appeals a discretionary power to grant interlocutory review in cases that show appeal-worthy certification issues.

Permission to appeal may be granted or denied on the basis of any consideration that the court of appeals finds persuasive. Permission is most likely to be granted when the certification decision turns on a novel or unsettled question of law, or when, as a practical matter, the decision on certification is likely dispositive of the litigation.

The district court, having worked through the certification decision, often will be able to provide cogent advice on the factors that bear on the decision whether to permit appeal. This advice can be particularly valuable if the certification decision is tentative. Even as to a firm certification decision, a statement of reasons bearing on the probable benefits and costs of immediate appeal can help focus the court of appeals decision, and may persuade the disappointed party that an attempt to appeal would be fruitless.

The 10-day period for seeking permission to appeal is designed to reduce the risk that attempted appeals will disrupt continuing proceedings. It is expected that the courts of appeals will act quickly in making the preliminary determination whether to permit appeal. Permission to appeal does not stay trial court proceedings. A stay should be sought first from the trial court. If the trial court refuses a stay, its action and any explanation of its views should weigh heavily with the court of appeals.

Appellate Rule 5 has been modified to establish the procedure for petitioning for leave to appeal under subdivision (f).

Changes Made after Publication (GAP Report)

No changes were made in the text of Rule 23(f) as published.

Several changes were made in the published Committee Note. (1) References to 28 U.S.C. § 1292(b) interlocutory appeals were revised to dispel any implication that the restrictive elements of § 1292(b) should be read into Rule 23(f). New emphasis was placed on court of appeals discretion by making explicit the analogy to certiorari discretion. (2) Suggestions that the new procedure is a "modest" expansion of appeal opportunities, to be applied with "restraint," and that permission "almost always will be denied when the certification decision turns on case-specific matters of fact and district court discretion," were deleted. It was thought better simply to observe that courts of appeals will develop standards "that reflect the changing areas of uncertainty in class litigation."

2003 AMENDMENT

Subdivision (c). Subdivision (c) is amended in several respects. The requirement that the court determine whether to certify a class "as soon as practicable after commencement of an action" is replaced by requiring determination "at an early practicable time." The notice provisions are substantially revised.

Paragraph (1). Subdivision (c)(1)(A) is changed to require that the determination whether to certify a class be made "at an early practicable time." The "as soon as practicable" exaction neither reflect s prevailing practice nor captures the many valid reasons that may justify deferring the initial certification decision. See Willging, Hooper & Niemic, Empirical Study of Class Actions in Four Federal District Courts: Final Report to the Advisory Committee on Civil Rules 26–36 (Federal Judicial Center 1996).

Time may be needed to gather information necessary to make the certification decision. Although an evaluation of the probable outcome on the merits is not properly part of the certification decision, discovery in aid of the certification decision often includes information required to identify the nature of the issues that actually will be presented at trial. In this sense it is appropriate to conduct controlled discovery into the "merits," limited to those aspects relevant to making the certification decision on an informed basis. Active judicial supervision may be required to achieve the most effective balance that expedites an informed certification determination without forcing an artificial and ultimately wasteful division between "certification discovery" and "merits discovery." A critical need is to determine how the case will be tried. An increasing number of courts require a party requesting class certification to present a "trial plan" that describes the issues likely to be presented at trial and tests whether they are susceptible of class-wide proof. See Manual For Complex Litigation Third, § 21.213, p. 44; § 30.11, p. 214; § 30.12, p. 215.

Other considerations may affect the timing of the certification decision. The party opposing the class may prefer to win dismissal or summary judgment as to the individual plaintiffs without certification and without binding the class that might have been certified. Time may be needed to explore designation of class counsel under Rule 23(g), recognizing that in many cases the need to progress toward the certification determination may require designation of interim counsel under Rule 23(g)(2)(A).

Although many circumstances may justify deferring the certification decision, active management may be necessary to ensure that the certification decision is not unjustifiably delayed.

Subdivision (c)(1)(C) reflects two amendments. The provision that a class certification "may be conditional" is deleted. A court that is not satisfied that the requirements of Rule 23 have been met should refuse certification until they have been met. The provision that permits alteration or amendment of an order granting or denying class certification is amended to set the cut-off point at final judgment rather than "the decision on the merits." This change avoids the possible ambiguity in referring to "the decision on the merits." Following a determination of liability, for example, proceedings to define the remedy may demonstrate the need to amend the class definition or subdivide the class. In this setting the final judgment concept is pragmatic. It is not the same as the concept used for appeal purposes, but it should be flexible, particularly in protract ed litigation.

The authority to amend an order under Rule 23(c)(1) before final judgment does not restore the practice of "one-way intervention" that was rejected by the 1966 revision of Rule 23. A determination of liability after certification, however, may show a need to amend the class definition. Decertification may be warranted after further proceedings.

If the definition of a class certified under Rule 23(b)(3) is altered to include members who have not been afforded notice and an opportunity to request exclusion, notice—including an opportunity to request exclusion—must be directed to the new class members under Rule 23(c)(2)(B).

Paragraph (2). The first change made in Rule 23(c)(2) is to call attention to the court's authority—already established in part by Rule 23(d)(2)—to direct notice of certification to a Rule 23(b)(1) or (b)(2) class. The present rule expressly requires notice only in actions certified under Rule 23(b)(3). Members of classes certified under Rules 23(b)(1) or (b)(2) have interests that may deserve protection by notice.

The authority to direct notice to class members in a (b)(1) or (b)(2) class action should be exercised with care. For several reasons, there may be less need for notice than in a (b)(3) class action. There is no right to request exclusion from a (b)(1) or (b)(2) class. The characteristics of the class may reduce the need for formal notice. The cost of providing notice, moreover, could easily cripple actions that do not seek damages. The court may decide not to direct notice after balancing the risk that notice costs may deter the pursuit of class relief against the benefits of notice.

When the court does direct certification notice in a (b)(1) or (b)(2) class action, the discretion and flexibility established by subdivision (c)(2)(A) extend to the method of giving notice. Notice facilitates the opportunity to participate. Notice calculated to reach a significant number of class members often will protect the interests of all. Informal methods may prove effective. A simple posting in a place visited by many class members, directing attention to a source of more detailed information, may suffice. The court should consider the costs of notice in relation to the probable reach of inexpensive methods.

If a Rule 23(b)(3) class is certified in conjunction with a (b)(2) class, the (c)(2)(B) notice requirements must be satisfied as to the (b)(3) class.

The direction that class-certification notice be couched in plain, easily understood language is a reminder of the need to work unremittingly at the difficult task of communicating with class members. It is difficult to provide information about most class actions that is both accurate and easily understood by class members who are not themselves lawyers. Factual uncertainty, legal complexity, and the complication of class-action procedure raise the barriers high. The Federal Judicial Center has created illustrative clear-notice forms that provide a helpful starting point for actions similar to those described in the forms.

Subdivision (e). Subdivision (e) is amended to strengthen the process of reviewing proposed class-action settlements. Settlement may be a desirable means of resolving a class action. But court review and approval are essential to assure adequate representation of class members who have not participated in shaping the settlement.

Paragraph (1). Subdivision (e)(1)(A) expressly recognizes the power of a class representative to settle class claims, issues, or defenses.

Rule 23(e)(1)(A) resolves the ambiguity in former Rule 23(e)'s reference to dismissal or compromise of "a class action." That language could be—and at times was—read to require court approval of settlements with putative class representatives that resolved only individual claims. See Manual for Complex Litigation Third, § 30.41. The new rule requires approval only if the claims, issues, or defenses of a certified class are resolved by a settlement, voluntary dismissal, or compromise.

Subdivision (e)(1)(B) carries forward the notice requirement of present Rule 23(e) when the settlement binds the class through claim or issue preclusion; notice is not required when the settlement binds only the individual class representatives. Notice of a settlement binding on the class is required either when the settlement follows class certification or when the decisions on certification and settlement proceed simultaneously.

Reasonable settlement notice may require individual notice in the manner required by Rule 23(c)(2)(B) for certification notice to a Rule 23(b)(3) class. Individual notice is appropriate, for example, if class members are required to take action—such as filing claims—to participate in the judgment, or if the court orders a settlement opt-out opportunity under Rule 23(e)(3).

Subdivision (e)(1)(C) confirms and mandates the already common practice of holding hearings as part of the process of approving settlement, voluntary dismissal, or compromise that would bind members of a class.

Subdivision (e)(1)(C) states the standard for approving a proposed settlement that would bind class members. The settlement must be fair, reasonable, and adequate. A helpful review of many factors that may deserve consideration is provided by *In re: Prudential Ins. Co. America Sales Practice Litigation Agent Actions*, 148 F.3d 283, 316–324 (3d Cir. 1998). Further guidance can be found in the Manual for Complex Litigation.

The court must make findings that support the conclusion that the settlement is fair, reasonable, and adequate. The findings must be set out in sufficient detail to explain to class members and the appellate court the factors that bear on applying the standard.

Settlement review also may provide an occasion to review the cogency of the initial class definition. The terms of the settlement themselves, or objections, may reveal divergent interests of class members and demonstrate the need to redefine the class or to designate subclasses. Redefinition of a class certified under Rule 23(b)(3) may require notice to new class members under Rule 23(c)(2)(B). See Rule 23(c)(1)(C).

Paragraph (2). Subdivision (e)(2) requires parties seeking approval of a settlement, voluntary dismissal, or compromise under Rule 23(e)(1) to file a statement identifying any agreement made in connection with the settlement. This provision does not change the basic requirement that the parties disclose all terms of the settlement or compromise that the court must approve under Rule 23(e)(1). It aims instead at related undertakings that, although seemingly separate, may have influenced the terms of the settlement by trading away possible advantages for the class in return for advantages for others. Doubts should be resolved in favor of identification.

Further inquiry into the agreements identified by the parties should not become the occasion for discovery by the parties or objectors. The court may direct the parties to provide to the court or other parties a summary or copy of the full terms of any agreement identified by the parties. The court also may direct the parties to provide a summary or copy of any agreement not identified by the parties that the court considers relevant to its review of a proposed settlement. In exercising discretion under this rule, the court may act in steps, calling first for a summary of any agreement that may have affected the settlement and then for a complete version if the summary does not provide an adequate basis for review. A direction to disclose a summary or copy of an agreement may raise concerns of confidentiality. Some agreements may include information that merits protection against general disclosure. And the court must provide an opportunity to claim work-product or other protections.

Paragraph (3). Subdivision (e)(3) authorizes the court to refuse to approve a settlement unless the settlement affords class members a new opportunity to request exclusion from a class certified under Rule 23(b)(3) after settlement terms are known. An agreement by the parties themselves to permit class members to elect exclusion at this point by the settlement agreement may be one factor supporting approval of the settlement. Often there is an opportunity to opt out at this point because the class is certified and settlement is reached in circumstances that lead to simultaneous notice of certification and notice of settlement. In these cases, the basic opportunity to elect exclusion applies without further complication. In some cases, particularly if settlement appears imminent at the time of certification, it may be possible to achieve equivalent protection by deferring notice and the opportunity to elect exclusion until actual settlement terms are known. This approach avoids the cost and potential confusion of providing two notices and makes the single notice more meaningful. But notice should not be delayed unduly after certification in the hope of settlement.

Rule 23(e)(3) authorizes the court to refuse to approve a settlement unless the settlement affords a new opportunity to elect exclusion in a case that settles after a certification decision if the earlier opportunity to elect exclusion provided with the certification notice has expired by the time of the settlement notice. A decision to remain in the class is likely to be more carefully considered and is better informed when settlement terms are known.

The opportunity to request exclusion from a proposed settlement is limited to members of a (b)(3) class. Exclusion may be requested only by individual class members; no class member may purport to opt out other class members by way of another class action.

The decision whether to approve a settlement that does not allow a new opportunity to elect exclusion is confided to the court's discretion. The court may make this decision before directing notice to the class under Rule 23(e)(1)(B) or after the Rule 23(e)(1)(C) hearing. Many factors may influence the court's decision. Among these are changes in the information available to class members since expiration of the first opportunity to request exclusion, and the nature of the individual class members' claims.

The terms set for permitting a new opportunity to elect exclusion from the proposed settlement of a Rule 23(b)(3) class action may address concerns of potential misuse. The court might direct, for example, that class members who elect exclusion are bound by rulings on the merits made before the settlement was proposed for approval. Still other terms or conditions may be appropriate.

Paragraph (4). Subdivision (e)(4) confirms t he right of class members to object to a proposed settlement, voluntary dismissal, or compromise. The right is defined in relation to a disposition that, because it would bind the class, requires court approval under subdivision (e)(1)(C).

Subdivision (e)(4)(B) requires court approval for withdrawal of objections made under subdivision (e)(4)(A). Review follows automatically if the objections are withdrawn on terms that lead to modification of the settlement with the class. Review also is required if the objector formally withdraws the objections. If the objector simply abandons pursuit of the objection, the court may inquire into the circumstances.

Approval under paragraph (4)(B) may be given or denied with little need for further inquiry if the objection and the disposition go only to a protest that the individual treatment afforded the objector under the proposed settlement is unfair because of factors that distinguish the objector from other class members. Different considerations may apply if the objector has protested that the proposed settlement is not fair, reasonable, or adequate on grounds that apply generally to a class or subclass. Such objections, which purport to represent class-wide interests, may augment the opportunity for obstruction or delay. If such objections are surrendered on terms that do not affect the class settlement or the objector's participation in the class settlement, the court often can approve withdrawal of the objections without elaborate inquiry.

Once an objector appeals, control of the proceeding lies in the court of appeals. The court of appeals may undertake review and approval of a settlement with the objector, perhaps as part of appeal settlement procedures, or may remand to the district court to take advantage of the district court's familiarity with the action and settlement.

Subdivision (g). Subdivision (g) is new. It responds to the reality that the selection and activity of class counsel are often critically important to the successful handling of a class action. Until now, courts have scrutinized proposed class counsel as well as the class representative under Rule 23(a)(4). This experience has recognized the importance of judicial evaluation of the proposed lawyer for the class, and this new subdivision builds on that experience rather than introducing an entirely new element into the class certification process. Rule 23(a)(4) will continue to call for scrutiny of the proposed class representative, while this subdivision will guide the court in assessing proposed class counsel as part of the certification decision. This subdivision recognizes the importance of class counsel, states the obligation to represent the interests of the class, and provides a framework for selection of class counsel. The procedure and standards for appointment vary depending on whether there are multiple applicants to be class counsel. The new subdivision also provides a method by which the court may make directions from the outset about the potential fee award to class counsel in the event the action is successful.

Paragraph (1) sets out the basic requirement that class counsel be appointed if a class is certified and articulates the obligation of class counsel to represent the interests of the class, as opposed to the potentially conflicting interests of individual class members. It also sets out the factors the court should consider in assessing proposed class counsel.

Paragraph (1)(A) requires that the court appoint class counsel to represent the class. Class counsel must be appointed for all classes, including each subclass that the court certifies to represent divergent interests.

Paragraph (1)(A) does not apply if "a statute provides otherwise." This recognizes that provisions of the Private Securities Litigation Reform Act of 1995, Pub. L. No. 104-67, 109 Stat. 737 (1995) (codified in various sections of 15 U.S.C.), contain directives that bear on selection of a lead plaintiff and the retention of counsel. This subdivision does not purport to supersede or to affect the interpretation of those provisions, or any similar provisions of other legislation.

Paragraph 1(B) recognizes t hat t he primary responsibility of class counsel, resulting from appointment as class counsel, is to represent the best interests of the class. The rule thus establishes the obligation of class counsel, an obligation that may be different from the customary obligations of counsel to individual clients. Appointment as class counsel means that the primary obligation of counsel is to the class rather than to any individual members of it. The class representatives do not have an unfettered right to "fire" class counsel. In the same vein, the class representatives cannot command class counsel to accept or reject a settlement proposal. To the contrary, class counsel must determine whether seeking the court's approval of a settlement would be in the best interests of the class as a whole.

Paragraph (1)(C) articulates the basic responsibility of the court to appoint class counsel who will provide the adequate representation called for by paragraph (1)(B). It identifies criteria that must be considered and invites the court to consider any other pertinent matters. Although couched in terms of the court's duty, the listing also informs counsel seeking appointment about the topics that should be addressed in an application for appointment or in the motion for class certification.

The court may direct potential class counsel to provide additional information about the topics mentioned in paragraph (1)(C) or about any other relevant topic. For example, the court may direct applicants to inform the court concerning any agreements about a prospective award of attorney fees or nontaxable costs, as such agreements may sometimes be significant in the selection of class counsel. The court might also direct that potential class counsel indicate how parallel litigation might be coordinated or consolidated with t he action before the court.

The court may also direct counsel to propose terms for a potential award of attorney fees and nontaxable costs. Attorney fee awards are an important feature of class action practice, and attention to this subject from the outset may often be a productive technique. Paragraph (2)(C) therefore authorizes the court to provide directions about attorney fees and costs when appointing class counsel. Because there will be numerous class actions in which this information is not likely to be useful, the court need not consider it in all class actions.

Some information relevant to class counsel appointment may involve matters that include adversary preparation in a way that should be shielded from disclosure to other parties. An appropriate protective order may be necessary to preserve confidentiality.

In evaluating prospective class counsel, the court should weigh all pertinent factors. No single factor should necessarily be determinative in a given case. For example, the resources counsel will commit to the case must be appropriate to its needs, but the court should be careful not to limit consideration t o lawyers with the greatest resources.

If, after review of all applicants, the court concludes that none would be satisfactory class counsel, it may deny class certification, reject all applications, recommend that an application be modified, invite new applications, or make any other appropriate order regarding selection and appointment of class counsel.

Paragraph (2). This paragraph sets out the procedure that should be followed in appointing class counsel. Although it affords substantial flexibility, it provides the framework for appointment of class counsel in all class actions. For counsel who filed the action, the materials submitted in support of the motion for class certification may suffice to justify appointment so long as the information described in paragraph (g)(1)(C) is included. If there are other applicants, they ordinarily would file a formal application detailing their suitability for the position.

In a plaintiff class action the court usually would appoint as class counsel only an attorney or attorneys who have sought appointment. Different considerations may apply in defendant class actions.

The rule states that the court should appoint "class counsel." In many instances, the applicant will be an individual attorney. In other cases, however, an entire firm, or perhaps numerous attorneys who are not otherwise affiliated but are collaborating on the action will apply. No rule of thumb exists to determine when such arrangements are appropriate; the court should be alert to the need for adequate staffing of the case, but also to the risk of overstaffing or an ungainly counsel structure.

Paragraph (2)(A) authorizes the court to designate interim counsel during the pre-certification period if necessary to protect the interests of the putative class. Rule 23(c)(1)(B) directs that the order certifying the class include appointment of class counsel. Before class certification, however, it will usually be important for an attorney to take action to prepare for the certification decision. The amendment to Rule 23(c)(1) recognizes that some discovery is often necessary for that determination. It also may be important to make or respond to motions before certification. Settlement may be discussed before certification. Ordinarily, such work is handled by the lawyer who filed the action. In some cases, however, there may be rivalry or uncertainty that makes formal designation of interim counsel appropriate. Rule 23(g)(2)(A) authorizes the court to designate interim counsel to act on behalf of the putative class before the certification decision is made. Failure to make the formal designation does not prevent the attorney who filed the action from proceeding in it. Whether or not formally designated interim counsel, an attorney who acts on behalf of the class before certification must act in the best interests of the class as a whole. For example, an attorney who negotiates a pre-certification settlement must seek a settlement that is fair, reasonable, and adequate for the class.

Rule 23(c)(1) provides that the court should decide whether to certify the class "at an early practicable time," and directs that class counsel should be appointed in the order certifying the class. In some cases, it may be appropriate for the court to allow a reasonable period after commencement of the action for filing applications to serve as class counsel. The primary ground for deferring appointment would be that there is reason to anticipate competing applications to serve as class counsel. Examples might include instances in which more than one class action has been filed, or in which other attorneys have filed individual actions on behalf of putative class members. The purpose of facilitating competing applications in such a case is to afford the best possible representation for the class. Another possible reason for deferring appointment would be that the initial applicant was found inadequate, but it seems appropriate to permit additional applications rather than deny class certification.

Paragraph (2)(B) states the basic standard the court should use in deciding whether to certify the class and appoint class counsel in the single applicant situation—that the applicant be able to provide the representation called for by paragraph (1)(B) in light of the factors identified in paragraph (1)(C).

If there are multiple adequate applicants, paragraph (2)(B) directs the court to select the class counsel best able to represent the interests of the class. This decision should also be made using the factors outlined in paragraph (1)(C), but in the multiple applicant situation the court is to go beyond scrutinizing the adequacy of counsel and make a comparison of the strengths of the various applicants. As with the decision whether to appoint the sole applicant for the posit ion, no single factor should be dispositive in selecting class counsel in cases in which there are multiple applicants. The fact that a given attorney filed the instant action, for example, might not weigh heavily in the decision if that lawyer had not done significant work identifying or investigating claims. Depending on the nature of the case, one important consideration might be the applicant's existing attorney-client relationship with the proposed class representative.

Paragraph (2)(C) builds on the appointment process by authorizing the court to include provisions regarding attorney fees in the order appointing class counsel. Courts may find it desirable to adopt guidelines for fees or nontaxable costs, or to direct class counsel to report to the court at regular intervals on the efforts undertaken in the action, to facilitate the court's later determination of a reasonable attorney fee.

Subdivision (h). Subdivision (h) is new. Fee awards are a powerful influence on the way attorneys initiate, develop, and conclude class actions. Class action attorney fee awards have heretofore been handled, along with all other attorney fee awards, under Rule 54(d)(2), but that rule is not addressed to the particular concerns of class actions. This subdivision is designed to work in tandem with new subdivision (g) on appointment of class counsel, which may afford an opportunity for the court to provide an early framework for an eventual fee award, or for monitoring the work of class counsel during the pendency of the action.

Subdivision (h) applies to "an action certified as a class action." This includes cases in which there is a simultaneous proposal for class certification and settlement even though technically the class may not be certified unless the court approves the settlement pursuant to review under Rule 23(e). When a settlement is proposed for Rule 23(e) approval, either after certification or with a request for certification, notice to class members about class counsel's fee motion would ordinarily accompany the notice to the class about the settlement proposal itself.

This subdivision does not undertake to create new grounds for an award of attorney fees or nontaxable costs. Instead, it applies when such awards are authorized by law or by agreement of the parties. Against that background, it provides a format for all awards of attorney fees and nontaxable costs in connection with a class action, not only the award to class counsel. In some situations, there may be a basis for making an award to other counsel whose work produced a beneficial result for the class, such as attorneys who acted for the class before certification but were not appointed class counsel, or attorneys who represented objectors to a proposed settlement under Rule 23(e) or to the fee motion of class counsel. Other situations in which fee awards are authorized by law or by agreement of the parties may exist.

This subdivision authorizes an award of "reasonable" attorney fees and nontaxable costs. This is the customary term for measurement of fee awards in cases in which counsel may obtain an award of fees under the "common fund" theory that applies in many class actions, and is used in many fee-shifting statutes. Depending on the circumstances, courts have approached the determination of what is reasonable in different ways. In particular, there is some variation among courts about whether in "common fund" cases the court should use the lodestar or a percentage method of determining what fee is reasonable. The rule does not attempt to resolve the question whether the lodestar or percentage approach should be viewed as preferable.

Active judicial involvement in measuring fee awards is singularly important to the proper operation of the class-action process. Continued reliance on caselaw development of fee-award measures does not diminish the court's responsibility. In a class action, the district court must ensure that the amount and mode of payment of attorney fees are fair and proper whether the fees come from a common fund or are otherwise paid. Even in the absence of objections, the court bears this responsibility.

Courts discharging this responsibility have looked to a variety of factors. One fundamental focus is the result actually achieved for class members, a basic consideration in any case in which fees are sought on the basis of a benefit achieved for class members. The Private Securities Litigation Reform Act of 1995 explicitly makes this factor a cap for a fee award in actions to which it applies. See 15 U.S.C. §§ 77z-1(a)(6); 78u-4(a)(6) (fee award should not exceed a "reasonable percentage of the amount of any damages and prejudgment interest actually paid to the class"). For a percentage approach to fee measurement, results achieved is the basic starting point.

In many instances, the court may need to proceed with care in assessing the value conferred on class members. Settlement regimes that provide for future payments, for example, may not result in significant actual payments to class members. In this connection, the court may need to scrutinize the manner and operation of any applicable claims procedure. In some cases, it may be appropriate to defer some portion of the fee award until actual payouts to class members are known. Settlements involving nonmonetary provisions for class members also deserve careful scrutiny to ensure that these provisions have actual value to the class. On occasion the court's Rule 23(e) review will provide a solid basis for t his sort of evaluation, but in any event it is also important to assessing the fee award for the class.

At the same time, it is important to recognize that in some class actions the monetary relief obtained is not the sole determinant of an appropriate attorney fees award. Cf. *Blanchard v. Bergeron*, 489 U.S. 87, 95 (1989) (cautioning in an individual case against an "undesirable emphasis" on "the importance of the recovery of damages in civil rights litigation" that might "shortchange efforts to seek effective injunctive or declaratory relief").

Any directions or orders made by the court in connection with appointing class counsel under Rule 23(g) should weigh heavily in making a fee award under this subdivision.

Courts have also given weight to agreements among the parties regarding the fee motion, and to agreements between class counsel and others about the fees claimed by the motion. Rule 54(d)(2)(B) provides: "If directed by the court, the motion shall also disclose the terms of any agreement with respect to fees to be paid for the services for which claim is made." The agreement by a settling party not to oppose a fee application up to a certain amount, for example, is worthy of consideration, but the court remains responsible to determine a reasonable fee. "Side agreements" regarding fees provide at least perspective pertinent to an appropriate fee award.

In addition, courts may take account of the fees charged by class counsel or other attorneys for representing individual claimants or objectors in the case. In determining a fee for class counsel, the court's objective is to ensure an overall fee that is fair for counsel and equitable within the class. In some circumstances individual fee agreements between class counsel and class members might have provisions inconsistent with those goals, and the court might determine that adjustments in the class fee award were necessary as a result.

Finally, it is important to scrutinize separately the application for an award covering nontaxable costs. If costs were addressed in the order appointing class counsel, those directives should be a presumptive starting point in determining what is an appropriate award.

Paragraph (1). Any claim for an award of attorney fees must be sought by motion under Rule 54(d)(2), which invokes the provisions for timing of appeal in Rule 58 and Appellate Rule 4. Owing to the distinctive features of class action fee motions, however, the provisions of t his subdivision control disposition of fee motions in class actions, while Rule 54(d)(2) applies to matters not addressed in this subdivision.

The court should direct when the fee motion must be filed. For motions by class counsel in cases subject to court review of a proposed settlement under Rule 23(e), it would be important to require the filing of at least the initial motion in time for inclusion of information about the motion in the notice to the class about the proposed settlement that is required by Rule 23(e). In cases litigated to judgment, the court might also order class counsel's motion to be filed promptly so that notice to the class under t his subdivision (h) can be given.

Besides service of the motion on all parties, notice of class counsel's motion for attorney fees must be "directed to the class in a reasonable manner." Because members of the class have an interest in the arrangements for payment of class counsel whether that payment comes from the class fund or is made directly by another party, notice is required in all instances. In cases in which settlement approval is contemplated under Rule 23(e), notice of class counsel's fee motion should be combined with notice of the proposed settlement, and the provision regarding notice to the class is parallel to the requirements for notice under Rule 23(e). In adjudicated class actions, the court may calibrate the notice to avoid undue expense.

Paragraph (2). A class member and any party from whom payment is sought may object to the fee motion. Other parties—for example, nonsettling defendants—may not object because they lack a sufficient interest in the amount the court awards. The rule does not specify a time limit for making an objection. In setting the date objections are due, the court should provide sufficient time after the full fee motion is on file to enable potential objectors to examine the motion.

The court may allow an objector discovery relevant to the objections. In determining whether to allow discovery, the court should weigh the need for the information against the cost and delay that would attend discovery. See Rule 26(b)(2). One factor in determining whether to authorize discovery is the completeness of the material submitted in support of the fee motion, which depends in part on the fee measurement standard applicable to the case. If the motion provides thorough information, the burden should be on the objector to justify discovery to obtain further information.

Paragraph (3). Whether or not there are formal objections, the court must determine whether a fee award is justified and, if so, set a reasonable fee. The rule does not require a formal hearing in all cases. The form and extent of a hearing depend on the circumstances of the case. The rule does require findings and conclusions under Rule 52(a).

Paragraph (4). By incorporating Rule 54(d)(2), this provision gives the court broad authority to obtain assistance in determining the appropriate amount to award. In deciding whether to direct submission of such questions to a special master or magistrate judge, the court should give appropriate consideration to the cost and delay that such a process might entail.

2007 AMENDMENT

The language of Rule 23 has been amended as part of the general restyling of the Civil Rules to make them more easily understood and to make style and terminology consistent throughout the rules. These changes are intended to be stylistic only.

Amended Rule 23(d)(2) carries forward the provisions of former Rule 23(d) that recognize two separate propositions. First, a Rule 23(d) order may be combined with a pretrial order under Rule 16. Second, the standard for amending the Rule 23(d) order continues to be the more open-ended standard for amending Rule 23(d) orders, not the more exacting standard for amending Rule 16 orders.

As part of the general restyling, intensifiers that provide emphasis but add no meaning are consistently deleted. Amended Rule 23(f) omits as redundant the explicit reference to court of appeals discretion in deciding whether to permit an interlocutory appeal. The omission does not in any way limit the unfettered discretion established by the original rule.

2009 AMENDMENT

The time set in the former rule at 10 days has been revised to 14 days. See the Note to Rule 6.

2018 AMENDMENT

Rule 23 is amended mainly to address issues related to settlement, and also to take account of issues that have emerged since the rule was last amended in 2003.

Subdivision (c)(2). As amended, Rule 23(e)(1) provides that the court must direct notice to the class regarding a proposed class-action settlement only after determining that the prospect of class certification and approval of the proposed settlement justifies giving notice. This decision has been called "preliminary approval" of the proposed class certification in Rule 23(b)(3) actions. It is common to send notice to the class simultaneously under both Rule 23(e)(1) and Rule 23(c)(2)(B), including a provision for class members to decide by a certain date whether to opt out. This amendment recognizes the propriety of this combined notice practice.

Subdivision (c)(2) is also amended to recognize contemporary methods of giving notice to class members. Since *Eisen v. Carlisle & Jacquelin*, 417 U.S. 156 (1974), interpreted the individual notice requirement for class members in Rule 23(b)(3) class actions, many courts have read the rule to require notice by first class mail in every case. But technological change since 1974 has introduced other means of communication that may sometimes provide a reliable additional or alternative method for giving notice. Although first class mail may often be the preferred primary method of giving notice, courts and counsel have begun to employ new technology to make notice more effective. Because there is no reason to expect that technological change will cease, when selecting a method or methods of giving notice courts should consider the capacity and limits of current technology, including class members' likely access to such technology.

Rule 23(c)(2)(B) is amended to take account of these changes. The rule continues to call for giving class members "the best notice that is practicable." It does not specify any particular means as preferred. Although it may sometimes be true that electronic methods of notice, for example email, are the most promising, it is important to keep in mind that a significant portion of class members in certain cases may have limited or no access to email or the Internet.

Instead of preferring any one means of notice, therefore, the amended rule relies on courts and counsel to focus on the means or combination of means most likely to be effective in the case before the court. The court should exercise its discretion to select appropriate means of giving notice. In providing the court with sufficient information to enable it to decide whether to give notice to the class of a proposed class-action settlement under Rule 23(e)(1), it would ordinarily be important to include details about the proposed method of giving notice and to provide the court with a copy of each notice the parties propose to use.

In determining whether the proposed means of giving notice is appropriate, the court should also give careful attention to the content and format of the notice and, if notice is given under both Rule 23(e)(1) and Rule 23(c)(2)(B), any claim form class members must submit to obtain relief.

Counsel should consider which method or methods of giving notice will be most effective; simply assuming that the "traditional" methods are best may disregard contemporary communication realities. The ultimate goal of giving notice is to enable class members to make informed decisions about whether to opt out or, in instances where a proposed settlement is involved, to object or to make claims. Rule 23(c)(2)(B) directs that the notice be "in plain, easily understood language." Means, format, and content that would be appropriate for class members likely to be sophisticated, for example in a securities fraud class action, might not be appropriate for a class having many members likely to be less sophisticated. The court and counsel may wish to consider the use of class notice experts or professional claims administrators.

Attention should focus also on the method of opting out provided in the notice. The proposed method should be as convenient as possible, while protecting against unauthorized opt-out notices.

Subdivision (e). The introductory paragraph of Rule 23(e) is amended to make explicit that its procedural requirements apply in instances in which the court has not certified a class at the time that a proposed settlement is presented to the court. The notice required under Rule 23(e)(1) then should also satisfy the notice requirements of amended Rule 23(c)(2)(B) for a class to be certified under Rule 23(b)(3), and trigger the class members' time to request exclusion. Information about the opt-out rate could then be available to the court when it considers final approval of the proposed settlement.

Subdivision (e)(1). The decision to give notice of a proposed settlement to the class is an important event. It should be based on a solid record supporting the conclusion that the proposed settlement will likely earn final approval after notice and an opportunity to object. The parties must provide the court with information sufficient to determine whether notice should be sent. At the time they seek notice to the class, the proponents of the settlement should ordinarily provide the court with all available materials they intend to submit to support approval under Rule 23(e)(2) and that they intend to make available to class members. The amended rule also specifies the standard the court should use in deciding whether to send notice—that it likely will be able both to approve the settlement proposal under Rule 23(e)(2) and, if it has not previously certified a class, to certify the class for purposes of judgment on the proposal.

The subjects to be addressed depend on the specifics of the particular class action and proposed settlement. But some general observations can be made.

One key element is class certification. If the court has already certified a class, the only information ordinarily necessary is whether the proposed settlement calls for any change in the class certified, or of the claims, defenses, or issues regarding which certification was granted. But if a class has not been certified, the parties must ensure that the court has a basis for concluding that it likely will be able, after the final hearing, to certify the class. Although the standards for certification differ for settlement and litigation purposes, the court cannot make the decision regarding the prospects for certification without a suitable basis in the record. The ultimate decision to certify the class for purposes of settlement cannot be made until the hearing on final approval of the proposed settlement. If the settlement is not approved, the parties' positions regarding certification for settlement should not be considered if certification is later sought for purposes of litigation.

Regarding the proposed settlement, many types of information might appropriately be provided to the court. A basic focus is the extent and type of benefits that the settlement will confer on the members of the class. Depending on the nature of the proposed relief, that showing may include details of the contemplated claims process and the anticipated rate of claims by class members. Because some funds are frequently left unclaimed, the settlement agreement ordinarily should address the distribution of those funds.

The parties should also supply the court with information about the likely range of litigated outcomes, and about the risks that might attend full litigation. Information about the extent of discovery completed in the litigation or in parallel actions may often be important. In addition, as suggested by Rule 23(b)(3)(B), the parties should provide information about the existence of other pending or anticipated litigation on behalf of class members involving claims that would be released under the proposal.

The proposed handling of an award of attorney's fees under Rule 23(h) ordinarily should be addressed in the parties' submission to the court. In some cases, it will be important to relate the amount of an award of attorney's fees to the expected benefits to the class. One way to address this issue is to defer some or all of the award of attorney's fees until the court is advised of the actual claims rate and results.

Another topic that normally should be considered is any agreement that must be identified under Rule 23(e)(3).

The parties may supply information to the court on any other topic that they regard as pertinent to the determination whether the proposal is fair, reasonable, and adequate. The court may direct the parties to supply further information about the topics they do address, or to supply information on topics they do not address. The court should not direct notice to the class until the parties' submissions show it is likely that the court will be able to approve the proposal after notice to the class and a final approval hearing.

Subdivision (e)(2). The central concern in reviewing a proposed class-action settlement is that it be fair, reasonable, and adequate. Courts have generated lists of factors to shed light on this concern. Overall, these factors focus on comparable considerations, but each circuit has developed its own vocabulary for expressing these concerns. In some circuits, these lists have remained essentially unchanged for thirty or forty years. The goal of this amendment is not to displace any factor, but rather to focus the court and the lawyers on the core concerns of procedure and substance that should guide the decision whether to approve the proposal.

A lengthy list of factors can take on an independent life, potentially distracting attention from the central concerns that inform the settlement-review process. A circuit's list might include a dozen or more separately articulated factors. Some of those factors—perhaps many—may not be relevant to a particular case or settlement proposal. Those that are relevant may be more or less important to the particular case. Yet counsel and courts may feel it necessary to address every factor on a given circuit's list in every case. The sheer number of factors can distract both the court and the parties from the central concerns that bear on review under Rule 23(e)(2).

This amendment therefore directs the parties to present the settlement to the court in terms of a shorter list of core concerns, by focusing on the primary procedural considerations and substantive qualities that should always matter to the decision whether to approve the proposal.

Approval under Rule 23(e)(2) is required only when class members would be bound under Rule 23(c)(3). Accordingly, in addition to evaluating the proposal itself, the court must determine whether it can certify the class under the standards of Rule 23(a) and (b) for purposes of judgment based on the proposal.

Paragraphs (A) and (B). These paragraphs identify matters that might be described as "procedural" concerns, looking to the conduct of the litigation and of the negotiations leading up to the proposed settlement. Attention to these matters is an important foundation for scrutinizing the substance of the proposed settlement. If the court has appointed class counsel or interim class counsel, it will have made an initial evaluation of counsel's capacities and experience. But the focus at this point is on the actual performance of counsel acting on behalf of the class.

The information submitted under Rule 23(e)(1) may provide a useful starting point in assessing these topics. For example, the nature and amount of discovery in this or other cases, or the actual outcomes of other cases, may indicate whether counsel negotiating on behalf of the class had an adequate information base. The pendency of other litigation about the same general subject on behalf of class members may also be pertinent. The conduct of the negotiations may be important as well. For example, the involvement of a neutral or court-affiliated mediator or facilitator in those negotiations may bear on whether they were conducted in a manner that would protect and further the class interests. Particular attention might focus on the treatment of any award of attorney's fees, with respect to both the manner of negotiating the fee award and its terms.

Paragraphs (C) and (D). These paragraphs focus on what might be called a "substantive" review of the terms of the proposed settlement. The relief that the settlement is expected to provide to class members is a central concern. Measuring the proposed relief may require evaluation of any proposed claims process; directing that the parties report back to the court about actual claims experience may be important. The contents of any agreement identified under Rule 23(e)(3) may also bear on the adequacy of the proposed relief, particularly regarding the equitable treatment of all members of the class.

Another central concern will relate to the cost and risk involved in pursuing a litigated outcome. Often, courts may need to forecast the likely range of possible classwide recoveries and the likelihood of success in obtaining such results. That forecast cannot be done with arithmetic accuracy, but it can provide a benchmark for comparison with the settlement figure.

If the class has not yet been certified for trial, the court may consider whether certification for litigation would be granted were the settlement not approved.

Examination of the attorney-fee provisions may also be valuable in assessing the fairness of the proposed settlement. Ultimately, any award of attorney's fees must be evaluated under Rule 23(h), and no rigid limits exist for such awards. Nonetheless, the relief actually delivered to the class can be a significant factor in determining the appropriate fee award.

Often it will be important for the court to scrutinize the method of claims processing to ensure that it facilitates filing legitimate claims. A claims processing method should deter or defeat unjustified claims, but the court should be alert to whether the claims process is unduly demanding.

Paragraph (D) calls attention to a concern that may apply to some class action settlements—inequitable treatment of some class members vis-a-vis others. Matters of concern could include whether the apportionment of relief among class members takes appropriate account of differences among their claims, and whether the scope of the release may affect class members in different ways that bear on the apportionment of relief.

Subdivisions (e)(3) and (e)(4). Headings are added to subdivisions (e)(3) and (e)(4) in accord with style conventions. These additions are intended to be stylistic only.

Subdivision (e)(5). The submissions required by Rule 23(e)(1) may provide information critical to decisions whether to object or opt out. Objections by class members can provide the court with important information bearing on its determination under Rule 23(e)(2) whether to approve the proposal.

Subdivision (e)(5)(A). The rule is amended to remove the requirement of court approval for every withdrawal of an objection. An objector should be free to withdraw on concluding that an objection is not justified. But Rule 23(e)(5)(B)(i) requires court approval of any payment or other consideration in connection with withdrawing the objection.

The rule is also amended to clarify that objections must provide sufficient specifics to enable the parties to respond to them and the court to evaluate them. One feature required of objections is specification whether the objection asserts interests of only the objector, or of some subset of the class, or of all class members. Beyond that, the rule directs that the objection state its grounds "with specificity." Failure to provide needed specificity may be a basis for rejecting an objection. Courts should take care, however, to avoid unduly burdening class members who wish to object, and to recognize that a class member who is not represented by counsel may present objections that do not adhere to technical legal standards.

Subdivision (e)(5)(B). Good-faith objections can assist the court in evaluating a proposal under Rule 23(e)(2). It is legitimate for an objector to seek payment for providing such assistance under Rule 23(h).

But some objectors may be seeking only personal gain, and using objections to obtain benefits for themselves rather than assisting in the settlement-review process. At least in some instances, it seems that objectors—or their counsel—have sought to obtain consideration for withdrawing their objections or dismissing appeals from judgments approving class settlements. And class counsel sometimes may feel that avoiding the delay produced by an appeal justifies providing payment or other consideration to these objectors. Although the payment may advance class interests in a particular case, allowing payment perpetuates a system that can encourage objections advanced for improper purposes.

The court-approval requirement currently in Rule 23(e)(5) partly addresses this concern. Because the concern only applies when consideration is given in connection with withdrawal of an objection, however, the amendment requires approval under Rule 23(e)(5)(B)(i) only when consideration is involved. Although such payment is usually made to objectors or their counsel, the rule also requires court approval if a payment in connection with forgoing or withdrawing an objection or appeal is instead to another recipient. The term "consideration" should be broadly interpreted, particularly when the withdrawal includes some arrangements beneficial to objector counsel. If the consideration involves a payment to counsel for an objector, the proper procedure is by motion under Rule 23(h) for an award of fees.

Rule 23(e)(5)(B)(ii) applies to consideration in connection with forgoing, dismissing, or abandoning an appeal from a judgment approving the proposal. Because an appeal by a class-action objector may produce much longer delay than an objection before the district court, it is important to extend the court-approval requirement to apply in the appellate context. The district court is best positioned to determine whether to approve such arrangements; hence, the rule requires that the motion seeking approval be made to the district court.

Until the appeal is docketed by the circuit clerk, the district court may dismiss the appeal on stipulation of the parties or on the appellant's motion. See Fed. R. App. P. 42(a). Thereafter, the court of appeals has authority to decide whether to dismiss the appeal. This rule's requirement of district court approval of any consideration in connection with such dismissal by the court of appeals has no effect on the authority of the court of appeals to decide whether to dismiss the appeal. It is, instead, a requirement that applies only to providing consideration in connection with forgoing, dismissing, or abandoning an appeal.

Subdivision (e)(5)(C). Because the court of appeals has jurisdiction over an objector's appeal from the time that it is docketed in the court of appeals, the procedure of Rule 62.1 applies. That procedure does not apply after the court of appeals' mandate returns the case to the district court.

Subdivision (f). As amended, Rule 23(e)(1) provides that the court must direct notice to the class regarding a proposed class-action settlement only after determining that the prospect of eventual class certification justifies giving notice. But this decision does not grant or deny class certification, and review under Rule 23(f) would be premature. This amendment makes it clear that an appeal under this rule is not permitted until the district court decides whether to certify the class.

The rule is also amended to extend the time to file a petition for review of a class-action certification order to 45 days whenever a party is the United States, one of its agencies, or a United States officer or employee sued for an act or omission occurring in connection with duties performed on the United States' behalf. In such a case, the extension applies to a petition for permission to appeal by any party. The extension recognizes—as under Rules 4(i) and 12(a) and Appellate Rules 4(a)(1)(B) and 40(a)(1)—that the United States has a special need for additional time in regard to these matters. It applies whether the officer or employee is sued in an official capacity or an individual capacity. An action against a former officer or employee of the United States is covered by this provision in the same way as an action against a present officer or employee. Termination of the relationship between the individual defendant and the United States does not reduce the need for additional time.

Rule 23.1. Derivative Actions by Shareholders

1966 ADDITION

A derivative action by a shareholder of a corporation or by a member of an unincorporated association has distinctive aspects which require the special provisions set forth in the new rule. The next-to-the-last sentence recognizes that the question of adequacy of representation may arise when the plaintiff is one of a group of shareholders or members. Cf. 3 Moore's Federal Practice, par. 23.08 (2d ed. 1963).

The court has inherent power to provide for the conduct of the proceedings in a derivative action, including the power to determine the course of the proceedings and require that any appropriate notice be given to shareholders or members.

1987 AMENDMENT

The amendments are technical. No substantive change is intended.

2007 AMENDMENT

The language of Rule 23.1 has been amended as part of the general restyling of the Civil Rules to make them more easily understood and to make style and terminology consistent throughout the rules. These changes are intended to be stylistic only.

Rule 23.2. Actions Relating to Unincorporated Associations

1966 ADDITION

Although an action by or against representatives of the membership of an unincorporated association has often been viewed as a class action, the real or main purpose of this characterization has been to give "entity treatment" to the association when for formal reasons it cannot sue or be sued as a jural person under Rule 17(b). See Louisell & Hazard, Pleading and Procedure: State and Federal 718 (1962); 3 Moore's Federal Practice, par. 23.08 (2d ed. 1963); Story, J. in *West v. Randall*, 29 Fed.Cas. 718, 722–23, No. 17,424 (C.C.D.R.I.1820);

and, for examples, *Gibbs v. Buck*, 307 U.S. 66, 59 S. Ct. 725, 83 L.Ed. 1111 (1939); *Tunstall v. Brotherhood of Locomotive F. & E.*, 148 F.2d 403 (4th Cir. 1945); *Oskoian v. Canuel*, 269 F.2d 311 (1st Cir.1959). Rule 23.2 deals separately with these actions, referring where appropriate to Rule 23.

2007 AMENDMENT

The language of Rule 23.2 has been amended as part of the general restyling of the Civil Rules to make them more easily understood and to make style and terminology consistent throughout the rules. These changes are intended to be stylistic only.

Rule 24. Intervention

1937 ADOPTION

The right to intervene given by the following and similar statutes is preserved, but the procedure for its assertion is governed by this rule:

U.S.C., Title 28, former:

§ 45a (Special attorneys; participation by Interstate Commerce Commission; intervention)(in certain cases under interstate commerce laws)

§ 48 (Suits to be against United States; intervention by United States)

§ 401 (Intervention by United States; constitutionality of Federal statute)

U.S.C., Title 40:

§ 276a-2(b) (Bonds of contractors for public buildings or works; rights of persons furnishing labor and materials).

Compare with the last sentence of former Equity Rule 37 (Parties Generally—Intervention). This rule amplifies and restates the present federal practice at law and in equity. For the practice in admiralty see Admiralty Rules 34 (How Third Party May Intervene) and 42 (Claims Against Proceeds in Registry). See generally Moore and Levi, Federal Intervention: I The Right to Intervene and Reorganization (1936), 45 Yale L.J. 565. Under the codes two types of intervention are provided, one for the recovery of specific real or personal property (2 Ohio Gen.Code Ann. (Page, 1926) § 11263; Wyo.Rev.Stat.Ann. (Courtright, 1931) § 89-522), and the other allowing intervention generally when the applicant has an interest in the matter in litigation (1 Colo.Stat.Ann. (1935) Code Civ.Proc. § 22; La.Code Pract. (Dart, 1932) Arts. 389 to 394; Utah Rev.Stat.Ann. (1933) § 104-3-24). The English intervention practice is based upon various rules and decisions and falls into the two categories of absolute right and discretionary right. For the absolute right see English Rules Under the Judicature Act (The Annual Practice, 1937) O. 12, r. 24 (admiralty), r. 25 (land), r. 23 (probate); O. 57, r. 12 (execution); J.A. (1925) §§ 181, 182, 183(2) (divorce); *In re Metropolitan Amalgamated Estates, Ltd.*, (1912) 2 Ch. 497 (receivership); *Wilson v. Church*, 9 Ch.D. 552 (1878) (representative action). For the discretionary right see O. 16, r. 11 (nonjoinder) and Re Fowler, 142 L.T.Jo. 94 (Ch.1916), *Vavasseur v. Krupp*, 9 Ch.D. 351 (1878) (persons out of the jurisdiction).

1946 AMENDMENT

Note to Subdivision (a). The addition to subdivision (a)(3) covers the situation where property may be in the actual custody of some other officer or agency—such as the Secretary of the Treasury—but the control and disposition of the property is lodged in the court wherein the action is pending.

Subdivision (b). The addition in subdivision (b) permits the intervention of governmental officers or agencies in proper cases and thus avoids exclusionary constructions of the rule. For an example of the latter, see *Matter of Bender Body Co., Ref. Ohio 1942*, 47 F.Supp. 224, app'd as moot, N.E. Ohio 1942, 47 F.Supp. 224, 234, holding that the Administrator of the Office of Price Administration, then acting under the authority of an Executive Order of the President, could not intervene in a bankruptcy proceeding to protest the sale of assets above ceiling prices. Compare, however, *Securities and Exchange Commission v. United States Realty & Improvement Co., 1940*, 310 U.S. 434, 60 S. Ct. 1044, 84 L.Ed. 1293, where permissive intervention of the Commission to protect the public interest in an arrangement proceeding under Chapter XI of the Bankruptcy Act was upheld. See also dissenting opinion in *Securities and Exchange Commission v. Long Island Lighting Co., C.C.A.2d 1945*, 148 F.2d 252, judgment vacated as moot and case remanded with direction to dismiss complaint, 1945, 325 U.S. 833, 65 S. Ct. 1085, 89 L.Ed. 1961. For discussion see Commentary, Nature of Permissive Intervention Under Rule 24b, 1940, 3 Fed.Rules Serv. 704; Berger, Intervention by Public Agencies in Private Litigation in the Federal Courts, 1940, 50 Yale L.J. 65.

Regarding the construction of subdivision (b)(2), see *Allen Calculators, Inc., v. National Cash Register Co., 1944*, 322 U.S. 137, 64 S. Ct. 905, 88 L.Ed. 1188.

1948 AMENDMENT

The amendment effective Oct. 20, 1949, substituted the reference to "Title 28, U.S.C., § 2403" at the end of subdivision (c) for the reference to "the Act of August 24, 1937, c. 754, § 1."

1963 AMENDMENT

This amendment conforms to the amendment of Rule 5(a). See the Advisory Committee's Note to that amendment.

1966 AMENDMENT

In attempting to overcome certain difficulties which have arisen in the application of present Rule 24(a)(2) and (3), this amendment draws upon the revision of the related Rules 19 (joinder of persons needed for just adjudication) and 23 (class actions), and the reasoning underlying that revision.

Rule 24(a)(3) as amended in 1948 provided for intervention of right where the applicant established that he would be adversely affected by the distribution or disposition of property involved in an action to which he had not been made a party. Significantly, some decided cases virtually disregarded the language of this provision. Thus Professor Moore states: "The concept of a fund has been applied so loosely that it is possible for a court to find a fund in almost any in personam action." 4 Moore's Federal Practice, par. 24.09[3], at 55 (2d ed. 1962), and see, e.g., *Formulabs, Inc. v. Hartley Pen Co.*, 275 F.2d 52 (9th Cir.1960). This development was quite natural, for Rule 24(a)(3) was unduly restricted. If an absentee would be substantially affected in a practical sense by the determination made in an action, he should, as a general rule, be entitled to intervene, and his right to do so should not depend on whether there is a fund to be distributed or otherwise disposed of. Intervention of right is here seen to be a kind of counterpart to Rule 19(a)(2)(i) on joinder of persons needed for a just adjudication: where, upon motion of a party in an action, an absentee should be joined so that he may protect his interest which as a practical matter may be substantially impaired by the disposition of the action, he ought to have a right to intervene in the action on his own motion. See Louisell & Hazard, Pleading and Procedure: State and Federal 749–50 (1962).

The general purpose of original Rule 24(a)(2) was to entitle an absentee, purportedly represented by a party, to intervene in the action if he could establish with fair probability that the representation was inadequate. Thus, where an action is being prosecuted or defended by a trustee, a beneficiary of the trust should have a right to intervene if he can show that the trustee's representation of his interest probably is inadequate; similarly a member of a class should have the right to intervene in a class action if he can show the inadequacy of the representation of his interest by the representative parties before the court.

Original Rule 24(a)(2), however, made it a condition of intervention that "the applicant is or may be bound by a judgment in the action," and this created difficulties with intervention in class actions. If the "bound" language was read literally in the sense of res judicata, it could defeat intervention in some meritorious cases. A member of a class to whom a judgment in a class action extended by its terms (see Rule 23(c)(3), as amended) might be entitled to show in a later action, when the judgment in the class action was claimed to operate as res judicata against him, that the "representative" in the class action had not in fact adequately represented him. If he could make this showing, the class-

substitution is not required, but may be entered at any time if a party desires or the court thinks fit.

The general term "public officer" is used in preference to the enumeration which appears in the present rule. It comprises Federal, State, and local officers.

The expression "in his official capacity" is to be interpreted in its context as part of a simple procedural rule for substitution; care should be taken not to distort its meaning by mistaken analogies to the doctrine of sovereign immunity from suit or the Eleventh Amendment. The amended rule will apply to all actions brought by public officers for the government, and to any action brought in form against a named officer, but intrinsically against the government or the office or the incumbent thereof whoever he may be from time to time during the action. Thus the amended rule will apply to actions against officers to compel performance of official duties or to obtain judicial review of their orders. It will also apply to actions to prevent officers from acting in excess of their authority or under authority not validly conferred, cf. *Philadelphia Co. v. Stimson*, 223 U.S. 605, 32 S. Ct. 340, 56 L.Ed. 570 (1912), or from enforcing unconstitutional enactments, cf. *Ex parte Young*, 209 U.S. 123, 28 S. Ct. 441, 52 L.Ed. 714 (1908); *Ex parte La Prade*, 289 U.S. 444, 53 S. Ct. 682, 77 L.Ed. 1311 (1933). In general it will apply whenever effective relief would call for corrective behavior by the one then having official status and power, rather than one who has lost that status and power through ceasing to hold office. Cf. *Land v. Dollar*, 330 U.S. 731, 67 S. Ct. 1009, 91 L.Ed. 1209 (1947); *Larson v. Domestic & Foreign Commerce Corp.*, 337 U.S. 682, 69 S. Ct. 1457, 93 L.Ed. 1628 (1949). Excluded from the operation of the amended rule will be the relatively infrequent actions which are directed to securing money judgments against the named officers enforceable against their personal assets; in these cases Rule 25(a)(1), not Rule 25(d), applies to the question of substitution. Examples are actions against officers seeking to make them pay damages out of their own pockets for defamatory utterances or other misconduct in some way related to the office, see *Barr v. Matteo*, 360 U.S. 564, 79 S. Ct. 1335, 3 L. Ed. 2d 1434 (1959); *Howard v. Lyons*, 360 U.S. 593, 79 S. Ct. 1331, 3 L. Ed. 2d 1454 (1959); *Gregoire v. Biddle*, 177 F.2d 579 (2d Cir.1949), cert. denied, 339 U.S. 949, 70 S. Ct. 803, 94 L.Ed. 1363 (1950). Another example is the anomalous action for a tax refund against a collector of internal revenue, see *Ignelzi v. Granger*, 16 F.R.D. 517 (W.D.Pa. 1955), 28 U.S.C. § 2006, 4 Moore, supra, ¶ 25.05, p. 531; but see 28 U.S.C. § 1346(a)(1), authorizing the bringing of such suits against the United States rather than the officer.

Automatic substitution under the amended rule, being merely a procedural device for substituting a successor for a past officeholder as a party, is distinct from and does not affect any substantive issues which may be involved in the action. Thus a defense of immunity from suit will remain in the case despite a substitution.

Where the successor does not intend to pursue the policy of his predecessor which gave rise to the lawsuit, it will be open to him, after substitution, as plaintiff to seek voluntary dismissal of the action, or as defendant to seek to have the action dismissed as moot or to take other appropriate steps to avert a judgment or decree. Contrast *Ex parte La Prade*, supra; *Allen v. Regents of the University System*, 304 U.S. 439, 58 S. Ct. 980, 82 L.Ed. 1448 (1938); *McGrath v. National Assn. of Mfgrs.*, 344 U.S. 804, 73 S. Ct. 31, 97 L.Ed. 627 (1952); *Danenberg v. Cohen*, 213 F.2d 944 (7th Cir.1954).

As the present amendment of Rule 25(d)(1) eliminates a specified time period to secure substitution of public officers, the reference in Rule 6(b) (regarding enlargement of time) to Rule 25 will no longer apply to these public-officer substitutions.

As to substitution on appeal, the rules of the appellate courts should be consulted.

Subdivision (d)(2). This provision, applicable in "official capacity" cases as described above, will encourage the use of the official title without any mention of the officer individually, thereby recognizing the intrinsic character of the action and helping to eliminate concern with the problem of substitution. If for any reason it seems desirable to add the individual's name, this may be done upon motion or on the court's initiative; thereafter the procedure of amended Rule 25(d)(1) will apply if the individual named ceases to hold office.

For examples of naming the officer or title rather than the officeholder, see *Annot.*, 102 A.L.R. 943; *Comment,* 50 Mich.L.Rev. 443, 450 (1952); cf. 26 U.S.C. § 7484. Where an action is brought by or against a board or agency with continuity of existence, it has been often decided that there is no need to name the individual members and substitution is unnecessary when the personnel changes. 4 Moore, supra, ¶ 25.09, p. 536. The practice encouraged by amended Rule 25(d)(2) is similar.

1963 AMENDMENT

Present Rule 25(a)(1), together with present Rule 6(b), results in an inflexible requirement that an action be dismissed as to a deceased party if substitution is not carried out within a fixed period measured from the time of the death. The hardships and inequities of this unyielding requirement plainly appear from the cases. See, e. g., *Anderson v. Yungkau*, 329 U.S. 482, 67 S. Ct. 428, 91 L.Ed. 436 (1947); *Iovino v. Waterson*, 274 F.2d 41 (1959), cert. denied, Carlin v. Iovino, 362 U.S. 949, 80 S. Ct. 860, 4 L. Ed. 2d 867 (1960); *Perry v. Allen*, 239 F.2d 107 (5th Cir.1956); *Starnes v. Pennsylvania R. R.*, 26 F.R.D. 625 (E.D.N.Y.), aff'd per curiam, 295 F.2d 704 (2d Cir.1961), cert. denied, 369 U.S. 813, 82 S. Ct. 688, 7 L. Ed. 2d 612 (1962); *Zdanok v. Glidden Co.*, 28 F.R.D. 346 (S.D.N.Y.1961). See also 4 Moore's Federal Practice ¶ 25.01[9] (Supp.1960); 2 Barron & Holtzoff, Federal Practice & Procedure § 621, at 420 to 21 (Wright ed. 1961).

The amended rule establishes a time limit for the motion to substitute based not upon the time of the death, but rather upon the time information of the death is provided by means of a suggestion of death upon the record, i. e., service of a statement of the fact of the death. Cf. Ill.Ann.Stat., c. 110, § 54(2) (Smith-Hurd 1956). The motion may not be made later than 90 days after the service of the statement unless the period is extended pursuant to Rule 6(b), as amended. See the Advisory Committee's Note to amended Rule 6(b). See also the new Official Form 30.

A motion to substitute may be made by any party or by the representative of the deceased party without awaiting the suggestion of death. Indeed, the motion will usually be so made. If a party or the representative of the deceased party desires to limit the time within which another may make the motion, he may do so by suggesting the death upon the record.

A motion to substitute made within the prescribed time will ordinarily be granted, but under the permissive language of the first sentence of the amended rule ("the court may order") it may be denied by the court in the exercise of a sound discretion if made long after the death—as can occur if the suggestion of death is not made or is delayed—and circumstances have arisen rendering it unfair to allow substitution. Cf. *Anderson v. Yungkau, supra, 329 U.S. at 485, 486, 67 S. Ct. at 430, 431*, 91 L.Ed. 436, where it was noted under the present rule that settlement and distribution of the estate of a deceased defendant might be so far advanced as to warrant denial of a motion for substitution even though made within the time limit prescribed by that rule. Accordingly, a party interested in securing substitution under the amended rule should not assume that he can rest indefinitely awaiting the suggestion of death before he makes his motion to substitute.

1987 AMENDMENT

The amendments are technical. No substantive change is intended.

2007 AMENDMENT

The language of Rule 25 has been amended as part of the general restyling of the Civil Rules to make them more easily understood and to make style and terminology consistent throughout the rules. These changes are intended to be stylistic only.

V. DEPOSITIONS AND DISCOVERY

ADVISORY COMMITTEE'S EXPLANATORY STATEMENT CONCERNING 1970 AMENDMENTS OF THE DISCOVERY RULES

This statement is intended to serve as a general introduction to the amendments of Rules 26–37, concerning discovery, as well as related amendments of other rules. A separate note of customary scope is appended to amendments proposed for each rule. This statement provides a framework for the consideration of individual rule changes.

CHANGES IN THE DISCOVERY RULES

The discovery rules, as adopted in 1938, were a striking and imaginative departure from tradition. It was expected from the outset that they would be important, but experience has shown them to play an even larger role than was initially foreseen. Although the discovery rules have been amended since 1938, the changes were relatively few and narrowly focused, made in order to remedy specific defects. The amendments now proposed reflect the first comprehensive review of the discovery rules undertaken since 1938. These amendments make substantial changes in the discovery rules. Those summarized here are among the more important changes.

Scope of Discovery. New provisions are made and existing provisions changed affecting the scope of discovery: (1) The contents of insurance policies are made discoverable (Rule 26(b)(2)). (2) A showing of good cause is no longer required for discovery of documents and things and entry upon land (Rule 34). However, a showing of need is required for discovery of "trial preparation" materials other than a party's discovery of his own statement and a witness' discovery of his own statement; and protection is afforded against disclosure in such documents of mental impressions, conclusions, opinions, or legal theories concerning the litigation. (Rule 26(b)(3)). (3) Provision is made for discovery with respect to experts retained for trial preparation, and particularly those experts who will be called to testify at trial (Rule 26(b)(4)). (4) It is provided that interrogatories and requests for admission are not objectionable simply because they relate to matters of opinion or contention, subject of course to the supervisory power of the court (Rules 33(b), 36(a)). (5) Medical examination is made available as to certain nonparties. (Rule 35(a)).

Mechanics of Discovery. A variety of changes are made in the mechanics of the discovery process, affecting the sequence and timing of discovery, the respective obligations of the parties with respect to requests, responses, and motions for court orders, and the related powers of the court to enforce discovery requests and to protect against their abusive use. A new provision eliminates the automatic grant of priority in discovery to one side (Rule 26(d)). Another provides that a party is not under a duty to supplement his responses to requests for discovery, except as specified (Rule 26(e)).

Other changes in the mechanics of discovery are designed to encourage extrajudicial discovery with a minimum of court intervention. Among these are the following: (1) The requirement that a plaintiff seek leave of court for early discovery requests is eliminated or reduced, and motions for a court order under Rule 34 are made unnecessary. Motions under Rule 35 are continued. (2) Answers and objections are to be served together and an enlargement of the time for response is provided. (3) The party seeking discovery, rather than the objecting party, is made responsible for invoking judicial determination of discovery disputes not resolved by the parties. (4) Judicial sanctions are tightened with respect to unjustified insistence upon or objection to discovery. These changes bring Rules 33, 34, and 36 substantially into line with the procedure now provided for depositions.

Failure to amend Rule 35 in the same way is based upon two considerations. First, the Columbia Survey (described below) finds that only about 5 percent of medical examinations require court motions, of which about half result in court orders. Second and of greater importance, the interest of the person to be examined in the privacy of his person was recently stressed by the Supreme Court in *Schlagenhauf v. Holder*, 379 U.S. 104, 85 S. Ct. 234, 13 L. Ed. 2d 152 (1964). The court emphasized the trial judge's responsibility to assure that the medical examination was justified, particularly as to its scope.

Rearrangement of Rules. A limited rearrangement of the discovery rules has been made, whereby certain provisions are transferred from one rule to another. The reasons for this rearrangement are discussed below in a separate section of this statement and the details are set out in a table at the end of this statement.

Optional Procedures. In two instances, new optional procedures have been made available. A new procedure is provided to a party seeking to take the deposition of a corporation or other organization (Rule 30(b)(6)). A party on whom interrogatories have been served requesting information derivable from his business records may under specified circumstances produce the records rather than give answers (Rule 33(c)).

Other Changes. This summary of changes is by no means exhaustive. Various changes have been made in order to improve, tighten, or clarify particular provisions, to resolve conflicts in the case law, and to improve language. All changes, whether mentioned here or not, are discussed in the appropriate note for each rule.

A FIELD SURVEY OF DISCOVERY PRACTICE

Despite widespread acceptance of discovery as an essential part of litigation, disputes have inevitably arisen concerning the values claimed for discovery and abuses alleged to exist. Many disputes about discovery relate to particular rule provisions or court decisions and can be studied in traditional fashion with a view to specific amendment. Since discovery is in large measure extrajudicial, however, even these disputes may be enlightened by a study of discovery "in the field." And some of the larger questions concerning discovery can be pursued only by a study of its operation at the law office level and in unreported cases.

The Committee, therefore, invited the Project for Effective Justice of Columbia Law School to conduct a field survey of discovery. Funds were obtained from the Ford Foundation and the Walter E. Meyer Research Institute of Law, Inc. The survey was carried on under the direction of Prof. Maurice Rosenberg of Columbia Law School. The Project for Effective Justice has submitted a report to the Committee entitled "Field Survey of Federal Pretrial Discovery" (hereafter referred to as the Columbia Survey). The Committee is deeply grateful for the benefit of this extensive undertaking and is most appreciative of the cooperation of the Project and the funding organizations. The Committee is particularly grateful to Professor Rosenberg who not only directed the survey but has given much time in order to assist the Committee in assessing the results.

The Columbia Survey concludes, in general, that there is no empirical evidence to warrant a fundamental change in the philosophy of the discovery rules. No widespread or profound failings are disclosed in the scope or availability of discovery. The costs of discovery do not appear to be oppressive, as a general matter, either in relation to ability to pay or to the stakes of the litigation. Discovery frequently provides evidence that would not otherwise be available to the parties and thereby makes for a fairer trial or settlement. On the other hand, no positive evidence is found that discovery promotes settlement.

More specific findings of the Columbia Survey are described in other Committee notes, in relation to particular rule provisions and amendments. Those interested in more detailed information may obtain it from the Project for Effective Justice.

REARRANGEMENT OF THE DISCOVERY RULES

The present discovery rules are structured entirely in terms of individual discovery devices, except for Rule 27 which deals with perpetuation of testimony, and Rule 37 which provides sanctions to enforce discovery. Thus, Rules 26 and 28 to 32 are in terms addressed only to the taking of a deposition of a party or third person. Rules 33 to 36 then deal in succession with four additional discovery devices: Written interrogatories to parties, production for inspection of documents and things, physical or mental examination and requests for admission.

Under the rules as promulgated in 1938, therefore, each of the discovery devices was separate and self-contained. A defect of this arrangement is that there is no natural location in the discovery rules for provisions generally applicable to all discovery or to several discovery devices. From 1938 until the present, a few amendments have applied a discovery provision to several rules. For example, in 1948, the scope of deposition discovery in Rule 26(b) and the provision for protective orders in Rule 30(b) were incorporated by reference in Rules 33 and 34. The arrangement was adequate so long as there were few provisions governing discovery generally and these provisions were relatively simple.

As will be seen, however, a series of amendments are now proposed which govern most or all of the discovery devices. Proposals of a similar nature will probably be made in the future. Under these circumstances, it is very desirable, even necessary, that the discovery rules contain one rule addressing itself to discovery generally.

Rule 26 is obviously the most appropriate rule for this purpose. One of its subdivisions, Rule 26(b), in terms governs only scope of deposition discovery, but it has been expressly incorporated by reference in Rules 33 and 34 and is treated by courts as setting a general standard. By means of a transfer to Rule 26 of the provisions for protective orders now contained in Rule 30(b), and a transfer from Rule 26 of provisions addressed exclusively to depositions, Rule 26 is converted into a rule concerned with discovery generally. It becomes a convenient vehicle for the inclusion of new provisions dealing with the scope, timing, and regulation of discovery. Few additional transfers are needed. See table showing rearrangement of rules, set out below.

There are, to be sure, disadvantages in transferring any provision from one rule to another. Familiarity with the present pattern, reinforced by the references made by prior court decisions and the various secondary writings about the rules, is not lightly to be sacrificed. Revision of treatises and other reference works is burdensome and costly. Moreover, many States have adopted the existing pattern as a model for their rules.

On the other hand, the amendments now proposed will in any event require revision of texts and reference works as well as reconsideration by States following the Federal model. If these amendments are to be incorporated in an understandable way, a rule with general discovery provisions is needed. As will be seen, the proposed rearrangement produces a more coherent and intelligible pattern for the discovery rules taken as a whole. The difficulties described are those encountered whenever statutes are reexamined and revised. Failure to rearrange the discovery rules now would freeze the present scheme, making future change even more difficult.

TABLE SHOWING REARRANGEMENT OF RULES

Existing Rule No.	New Rule No.
26(a)	30(a), 31(a)
26(c)	30(c)
26(d)	32(a)
26(e)	32(b)
26(f)	32(c)
30(a)	30(b)

Existing Rule No.	New Rule No.
30(b)	26(c)
32	32(d)

Rule 26. General Provisions Governing Discovery; Duty of Disclosure

1937 ADOPTION

Note to Subdivision (a). This rule freely authorizes the taking of depositions under the same circumstances and by the same methods whether for the purpose of discovery or for the purpose of obtaining evidence. Many states have adopted this practice on account of its simplicity and effectiveness, safeguarding it by imposing such restrictions upon the subsequent use of the deposition at the trial or hearing as are deemed advisable. See Ark.Civ.Code (Crawford, 1934) §§ 606 to 607; Calif.Code Civ.Proc. (Deering, 1937) § 2021; 1 Colo.Stat. Ann. (1935) Code Civ.Proc. § 376; Idaho Code Ann. (1932) § 16-906; Ill.Rules of Pract., Rule 19 (Smith-Hurd Ill.Stats. c. 110, § 259.19); Smith-Hurd Ill.Stats. c. 51, § 24; 2 Ind.Stat.Ann. (Burns, 1933) §§ 2-1501, 2-1506; Ky.Codes (Carroll, 1932) Civ.Pract. § 557; 1 Mo.Rev.Stat. (1929) § 1753; 4 Mont.Rev.Codes Ann. (1935) § 10645; Neb.Comp.Stat. (1929) ch. 20, §§ 1246 to 7; 4 Nev.Comp.Laws (Hillyer, 1929) § 9001; 2 N.H.Pub.Laws (1926) ch. 337, § 1; N.C.Code Ann. (1935) § 1809; 2 N.D.Comp.Laws Ann. (1913) §§ 7889 to 7897; 2 Ohio Gen.Code Ann. (Page, 1926) §§ 11525-6; 1 Ore.Code Ann. (1930) tit. 9, § 1503; 1 S.D.Comp. Laws (1929) §§ 2713-16; Vernon's Ann.Civ.Stats.Tex. arts. 3738, 3752, 3769; Utah Rev.Stat.Ann. (1933) § 104-51-7; Wash.Rules of Practice adopted by the Supreme Ct., Rule 8, 2 Wash.Rev.Stat.Ann. (Remington, 1932) § 308-8; W.Va.Code (1931) ch. 57, art. 4, § 1. Compare former Equity Rules 47 (Depositions—To be Taken in Exceptional Instances); 54 (Depositions Under Revised Statutes, Sections 863, 865, 866, 867—Cross-Examination); 58 (Discovery—Interrogatories—Inspection and Production of Documents—Admission of Execution or Genuineness).

This and subsequent rules incorporate, modify, and broaden the provisions for depositions under U.S.C., Title 28, former §§ 639 (Depositions *de bene esse*; when and where taken; notice), 640 (Same; mode of taking). 641 (Same; transmission to court), 644 (Depositions under *dedimus potestatem* and *in perpetuam*), 646 (Deposition under *dedimus potestatem*; how taken). These statutes are superseded in so far as they differ from this and subsequent rules. U.S.C., Title 28, § 643 (Depositions; taken in mode prescribed by State laws) is superseded by the third sentence of Subdivision (a).

While a number of states permit discovery only from parties or their agents, others either make no distinction between parties or agents of parties and ordinary witnesses, or authorize the taking of ordinary depositions, without restriction, from any persons who have knowledge of relevant facts. See Ark.Civ. Code (Crawford, 1934) §§ 606 to 607; 1 Idaho Code Ann. (1932) § 16-906; Ill.Rules of Pract., Rule 19 (Smith-Hurd Ill.Stats. c. 110, § 259.19); Smith-Hurd Ill.Stats. c. 51, § 24; 2 Ind.Stat.Ann. (Burns, 1933) § 2-1501; Ky.Codes (Carroll, 1932) Civ.Pract. §§ 554 to 558; 2 Md.Ann.Code (Bagby, 1924) Art. 35, § 21; 2 Minn.Stat. (Mason, 1927) § 9820; Mo.St.Ann. §§ 1753, 1759, pp. 4023, 4026; Neb.Comp.Stat. (1929) ch. 20, §§ 1246 to 7; 2 N.H.Pub.Laws (1926) ch. 337, § 1; 2 N.D.Comp.Laws Ann. (1913) § 7897; 2 Ohio Gen.Code Ann. (Page, 1926) §§ 11525 to 6; 1 S.D.Comp.Laws (1929) §§ 2713 to 16; Vernon's Ann.Civil Stats.Tex. arts. 3738, 3752, 3769; Utah Rev.Stat.Ann. (1933) § 104-51-7; Wash.Rules of Practice adopted by Supreme Ct., Rule 8, 2 Wash.Rev.Stat.Ann. (Remington, 1932) § 308-8; W.Va.Code (1931) ch. 57, art. 4, § 1.

The more common practice in the United States is to take depositions on notice by the party desiring them, without any order from the court, and this has been followed in these rules. See Calif.Code Civ.Proc. (Deering, 1937) § 2031; 2

Fla.Comp.Gen.Laws Ann. (1927) §§ 4405 to 7; 1 Idaho Code Ann. (1932) § 16-902; Ill.Rules of Pract., Rule 19 (Smith-Hurd Ill.Stats. c. 110, § 259.19); Smith-Hurd Ill.Stats. c. 51, § 24; 2 Ind.Stat.Ann. (Burns, 1933) § 2-1502; Kan.Gen. Stat.Ann. (1935) § 60-2827; Ky.Codes (Carroll, 1932) Civ.Pract. § 565; 2 Minn.Stat. (Mason, 1927) § 9820; Mo.St.Ann. § 1761, p. 4029; 4 Mont.Rev.Codes Ann. (1935) § 10651; Nev.Comp.Laws (Hillyer, 1929) § 9002; N.C.Code Ann. (1935) § 1809; 2 N.D.Comp.Laws Ann. (1913) § 7895; Utah Rev.Stat.Ann. (1933) § 104-51-8.

Note to Subdivision (b). While the old chancery practice limited discovery to facts supporting the case of the party seeking it, this limitation has been largely abandoned by modern legislation. See Ala.Code Ann. (Michie, 1928) §§ 7764 to 7773; 2 Ind.Stat.Ann. (Burns, 1933) §§ 2-1028, 2-1506, 2-1728—2-1732; Iowa Code (1935) § 11185; Ky.Codes (Carroll, 1932) Civ.Pract. §§ 557, 606(8); La.Code Pract. (Dart, 1932) arts. 347 to 356; 2 Mass.Gen.Laws (Ter.Ed., 1932) ch. 231, §§ 61 to 67; Mo.St.Ann. §§ 1753, 1759, pp. 4023, 4026; Neb.Comp. Stat. (1929) §§ 20-1246, 20-1247; 2 N.H.Pub.Laws (1926) ch. 337, § 1; 2 Ohio Gen.Code Ann. (Page, 1926) §§ 11497, 11526; Vernon's Ann.Civ.Stats.Tex. arts. 3738, 3753, 3769; Wis.Stat. (1935) § 326.12; Ontario Consol.Rules of Pract. (1928) Rules 237 to 347; Quebec Code of Civ.Proc. (Curran, 1922) §§ 286 to 290.

Note to Subdivisions (d), (e), and (f). The restrictions here placed upon the use of depositions at the trial or hearing are substantially the same as those provided in U.S.C., Title 28, former § 641, for depositions taken, *de bene esse*, with the additional provision that any deposition may be used when the court finds the existence of exceptional circumstances. Compare English Rules Under the Judicature Act (The Annual Practice, 1937) O. 37, r. 18 (with additional provision permitting use of deposition by consent of the parties). See also former Equity Rule 64 (Former Depositions, Etc. May be Used Before Master); and 2 Minn.Stat. (Mason, 1927) § 9835 (Use in a subsequent action of a deposition filed in a previously dismissed action between the same parties and involving the same subject matter).

1946 AMENDMENT

Note to Subdivision (a). The amendment eliminates the requirement of leave of court for the taking of a deposition except where a plaintiff seeks to take a deposition within 20 days after the commencement of the action. The retention of the requirement where a deposition is sought by a plaintiff within 20 days of the commencement of the action protects a defendant who has not had an opportunity to retain counsel and inform himself as to the nature of the suit; the plaintiff, of course, needs no such protection. The present rule forbids the plaintiff to take a deposition, without leave of court, before the answer is served. Sometimes the defendant delays the serving of an answer for more than 20 days, but as 20 days are sufficient time for him to obtain a lawyer, there is no reason to forbid the plaintiff to take a deposition without leave merely because the answer has not been served. In all cases, Rule 30(a) empowers the court, for cause shown, to alter the time of the taking of a deposition, and Rule 30(b) contains provisions giving ample protection to persons who are unreasonably pressed. The modified practice here adopted is along the line of that followed in various states. See e. g., 8 Mo.Rev.Stat.Ann.1939, § 1917; 2 Burns' Ind.Stat.Ann.1933, § 2-1506.

Subdivision (b). The amendments to subdivision (b) make clear the broad scope of examination and that it may cover not only evidence for use at the trial but also inquiry into matters in themselves inadmissible as evidence but which will lead to the discovery of such evidence. The purpose of discovery is to allow a broad search for facts, the names of witnesses, or any other matters which may aid a party in the preparation or presentation of his case. *Engl v. Aetna Life Ins. Co., C.C.A.2, 1943*, 139 F.2d 469; Mahler v. Pennsylvania R. Co., N.Y.1945, 8 Fed.Rules Serv. 33.351, Case 1. In such a preliminary inquiry admissibility at trial should not be the test as to whether the information sought is within the scope of proper examination. Such a standard unnecessarily curtails the utility of discovery practice. Of course, matters entirely without bearing either as direct evidence or as leads to evidence are not within the scope of inquiry, but to the extent that the examination develops useful information, it functions successfully as an instrument of discovery, even if it produces no testimony directly admissible. *Lewis v. United Air Lines Transport Corp., Conn.1939*, 27 F.Supp. 946; *Engl v. Aetna Life Ins. Co.*, supra; *Mahler v. Pennsylvania R. Co.*, supra; Bloomer v. Sirian Lamp Co., Del.1944, 8 Fed.Rules Serv. 26b.31, Case 3; Rosseau v. Langley, N.Y.1945, 9 Fed.Rules Serv. 34.41, Case 1 (Rule 26 contemplates "examinations not merely for the narrow purpose of adducing testimony which may be offered in evidence but also for the broad discovery of information which may be useful in preparation for trial."); Olson Transportation Co. v. Socony-Vacuum Co., Wis.1944, 8 Fed.Rules Serv. 34.41, Case 2 (". . . the Rules . . . permit 'fishing' for evidence as they should."); Note, 1945, 45 Col.L.Rev. 482. Thus hearsay, while inadmissible itself, may suggest testimony which properly may be proved. Under Rule 26(b) several cases, however, have erroneously limited discovery on the basis of admissibility, holding that the word "relevant" in effect meant "material and competent under the rules of evidence". *Poppino v. Jones Store Co., Mo.1940*, 1 F.R.D. 215, 3 Fed.Rules Serv. 26b.5, Case 1; *Benevento v. A & P Food Stores, Inc., N.Y.1939*, 26 F.Supp. 424. Thus it has been said that inquiry might not be made into statements or other matters which, when disclosed, amounted only to hearsay. See *Maryland, for Use of Montvila v. Pan-American Bus Lines, Inc., Md.1940*, 1 F.R.D. 213, 3 Fed.Rules Serv. 26b.211, Case 3; *Gitto v. "Italia", Societa Anonima Di Navigazione, N.Y.1940*, 31 F.Supp. 567; *Rose Silk Mills Inc. v. Insurance Co. of North America, N.Y.1939*, 29 F.Supp. 504; *Colpak v. Hetterick, N.Y.1941*, 40 F.Supp. 350; *Matthies v. Peter F. Connolly Co., N.Y.1941, 6 Fed.Rules Serv. 30a.22, Case 1*, 2 F.R.D. 277; *Matter of Examination of Citizens Casualty Co. of New York, N.Y.1942*, 3 F.R.D. 171, 7 Fed.Rules Serv. 26b.211, Case 1; United States v. Silliman, N.J.1944, 8 Fed.Rules Serv. 26b.52, Case 1. The contrary and better view, however, has often been stated. See, e. g., *Engl v. Aetna Life Ins. Co.*, supra; *Stevenson v. Melady, N.Y.1940, 3 Fed.Rules Serv. 26b.31, Case 1*, 1 F.R.D. 329; *Lewis v. United Air Lines Transport Corp.*, supra; *Application of Zenith Radio Corp., Pa.1941, 4 Fed.Rules Serv. 30b.21, Case 1*, 1 F.R.D. 627; *Steingut v. Guaranty Trust Co. of New York, N.Y.1941*, 1 F.R.D. 723, 4 Fed.Rules Serv. 26b.5, Case 2; *De Seversky v. Republic Aviation Corp., N.Y.1941*, 2 F.R.D. 183, 5 Fed.Rules Serv. 26b.31, Case 5; *Moore v. George A. Hormel & Co., N.Y.1942, 6 Fed.Rules Serv. 30b.41, Case 1*, 2 F.R.D. 340; *Hercules Powder Co. v. Rohm & Haas Co., Del.1943, 7 Fed.Rules Serv. 45b.311, Case 2*, 3 F.R.D. 302; *Bloomer v. Sirian Lamp Co.*, supra; Crosby Steam Gage & Valve Co. v. Manning, Maxwell & Moore, Inc., Mass.1944, 8 Fed.Rules Serv. 26b.31, Case 1; Patterson Oil Terminals, Inc. v. Charles Kurz & Co., Inc., Pa.1945, 9 Fed.Rules Serv. 33.321, Case 2; *Pueblo Trading Co. v. Reclamation Dist. No. 1500, Cal.1945, 9 Fed.Rules Serv. 33.321, Case 4*, 4 F.R.D. 471. See also discussion as to the broad scope of discovery in *Hoffman v. Palmer, C.C.A.2, 1942*, 129 F.2d 976, 995–997, affirmed 318 U.S. 109, 63 S. Ct. 477, 87 L.Ed. 645; Note, 1945, 45 Col.L.Rev. 482.

1963 AMENDMENT

This amendment conforms to the amendment of Rule 28(b). See the next-to-last paragraph of the Advisory Committee's Note to that amendment.

1966 AMENDMENT

The requirement that the plaintiff obtain leave of court in order to serve notice of taking of a deposition within 20 days after commencement of the action gives rise to difficulties when the prospective deponent is about to become unavailable for examination. The problem is not confined to admiralty, but has been of special concern in that context because of the mobility of vessels and their personnel. When Rule 26 was adopted as Admiralty Rule 30A in 1961, the problem was alleviated by permitting depositions *de bene esse*, for which leave of court is not required. See Advisory Committee's Note to Admiralty Rule 30A (1961).

A continuing study is being made in the effort to devise a modification of the

20-day rule appropriate to both the civil and admiralty practice to the end that Rule 26(a) shall state a uniform rule applicable alike to what are now civil actions and suits in admiralty. Meanwhile, the exigencies of maritime litigation require preservation, for the time being at least, of the traditional *de bene esse* procedure for the post-unification counterpart of the present suit in admiralty. Accordingly, the amendment provides for continued availability of that procedure in admiralty and maritime claims within the meaning of Rule 9(h).

1970 AMENDMENT

A limited rearrangement of the discovery rules is made, whereby certain rule provisions are transferred, as follows: Existing Rule 26(a) is transferred to Rules 30(a) and 31(a). Existing Rule 26(c) is transferred to Rule 30(c). Existing Rules 26(d), (e), and (f) are transferred to Rule 32. Revisions of the transferred provisions, if any, are discussed in the notes appended to Rules 30, 31, and 32. In addition, Rule 30(b) is transferred to Rule 26(c). The purpose of this rearrangement is to establish Rule 26 as a rule governing discovery in general. (The reasons are set out in the Advisory Committee's explanatory statement.)

Subdivision (a)—Discovery Devices. This is a new subdivision listing all of the discovery devices provided in the discovery rules and establishing the relationship between the general provisions of Rule 26 and the specific rules for particular discovery devices. The provision that the frequency of use of these methods is not limited confirms existing law. It incorporates in general form a provision now found in Rule 33.

Subdivision (b)—Scope of Discovery. This subdivision is recast to cover the scope of discovery generally. It regulates the discovery obtainable through any of the discovery devices listed in Rule 26(a).

All provisions as to scope of discovery are subject to the initial qualification that the court may limit discovery in accordance with these rules. Rule 26(c) (transferred from 30(b)) confers broad powers on the courts to regulate or prevent discovery even though the materials sought are within the scope of 26(b), and these powers have always been freely exercised. For example, a party's income tax return is generally held not privileged, 2A Barron & Holtzoff, Federal Practice and Procedure, § 65.2 (Wright ed. 1961), and yet courts have recognized that interests in privacy may call for a measure of extra protection. *E.g., Wiesenberger v. W. E. Hutton & Co.*, 35 F.R.D. 556 (S.D.N.Y.1964). Similarly, the courts have in appropriate circumstances protected materials that are primarily of an impeaching character. These two types of materials merely illustrate the many situations, not capable of governance by precise rule, in which courts must exercise judgment. The new subsections in Rule 26(d) do not change existing law with respect to such situations.

Subdivision (b)(1)—In General. The language is changed to provide for the scope of discovery in general terms. The existing subdivision, although in terms applicable only to depositions, is incorporated by reference in existing Rules 33 and 34. Since decisions as to relevance to the subject matter of the action are made for discovery purposes well in advance of trial, a flexible treatment of relevance is required and the making of discovery, whether voluntary or under court order, is not a concession or determination of relevance for purposes of trial. *Cf.* 4 Moore's Federal Practice ¶ 26-16[1] (2d ed. 1966).

Subdivision (b)(2)—Insurance Policies. Both the cases and commentators are sharply in conflict on the question whether defendant's liability insurance coverage is subject to discovery in the usual situation when the insurance coverage is not itself admissible and does not bear on another issue in the case. Examples of Federal cases requiring disclosure and supporting comments: *Cook v. Welty*, 253 F.Supp. 875 (D.D.C.1966) (cases cited); *Johanek v. Aberle*, 27 F.R.D. 272 (D.Mont.1961); Williams, Discovery of Dollar Limits in Liability Policies in Automobile Tort Cases, 10 Ala.L.Rev. 355 (1958); Thode, Some Reflections on the 1957 Amendments to the Texas Rules, 37 Tex.L.Rev. 33, 40–42 (1958). Examples of Federal cases refusing disclosure and supporting comments: *Bisserier v. Manning*, 207 F.Supp. 476 (D.N.J.1962); *Cooper v. Stender*, 30 F.R.D. 389 (E.D.Tenn.1962); Frank, Discovery and Insurance, Coverage, 1959

Ins.L.J. 281; Fournier, Pre-trial Discovery of Insurance Coverage and Limits, 28 Ford.L.Rev. 215 (1959).

The division in reported cases is close. State decisions based on provisions similar to the federal rules are similarly divided. See cases collected in 2A Barron & Holtzoff, Federal Practice and Procedure § 647.1, nn. 45.5, 45.6 (Wright ed. 1961). It appears to be difficult if not impossible to obtain appellate review of the issue. Resolution by rule amendment is indicated. The question is essentially procedural in that it bears upon preparation for trial and settlement before trial, and courts confronting the question, however they have decided it, have generally treated it as procedural and governed by the rules.

The amendment resolves this issue in favor of disclosure. Most of the decisions denying discovery, some explicitly, reason from the text of Rule 26(b) that it permits discovery only of matters which will be admissible in evidence or appear reasonably calculated to lead to such evidence; they avoid considerations of policy, regarding them as foreclosed. See *Bisserier* v. *Manning*, supra. Some note also that facts about a defendant's financial status are not discoverable as such, prior to judgment with execution unsatisfied, and fear that, if courts hold insurance coverage discoverable, they must extend the principle to other aspects of the defendant's financial status. The cases favoring disclosure rely heavily on the practical significance of insurance in the decisions lawyers make about settlement and trial preparation. In *Clauss v. Danker*, 264 F.Supp. 246 (S.D.N.Y.1967), the court held that the rules forbid disclosure but called for an amendment to permit it.

Disclosure of insurance coverage will enable counsel for both sides to make the same realistic appraisal of the case, so that settlement and litigation strategy are based on knowledge and not speculation. It will conduce to settlement and avoid protracted litigation in some cases, though in others it may have an opposite effect. The amendment is limited to insurance coverage, which should be distinguished from any other facts concerning defendant's financial status (1) because insurance is an asset created specifically to satisfy the claim; (2) because the insurance company ordinarily controls the litigation; (3) because information about coverage is available only from defendant or his insurer; and (4) because disclosure does not involve a significant invasion of privacy.

Disclosure is required when the insurer "may be liable" on part or all of the judgment. Thus, an insurance company must disclose even when it contests liability under the policy, and such disclosure does not constitute a waiver of its claim. It is immaterial whether the liability is to satisfy the judgment directly or merely to indemnify or reimburse another after he pays the judgment.

The provision applies only to persons "carrying on an insurance business" and thus covers insurance companies and not the ordinary business concern that enters into a contract of indemnification. *Cf.* N.Y.Ins.Law § 41. Thus, the provision makes no change in existing law on discovery of indemnity agreements other than insurance agreements by persons carrying on an insurance business. Similarly, the provision does not cover the business concern that creates a reserve fund for purposes of self-insurance.

For some purposes other than discovery, an application for insurance is treated as a part of the insurance agreement. The provision makes clear that, for discovery purposes, the application is not to be so treated. The insurance application may contain personal and financial information concerning the insured, discovery of which is beyond the purpose of this provision.

In no instance does disclosure make the facts concerning insurance coverage admissible in evidence.

Subdivision (b)(3)—Trial Preparation: Materials. Some of the most controversial and vexing problems to emerge from the discovery rules have arisen out of requests for the production of documents or things prepared in anticipation of litigation or for trial. The existing rules make no explicit provision for such materials. Yet, two verbally distinct doctrines have developed, each conferring a qualified immunity on these materials—the "good cause" requirement in Rule 34 (now generally held applicable to discovery of documents via deposition under Rule 45 and interrogatories under Rule 33) and the work-product doctrine of *Hickman v. Taylor*, 329 U.S. 495, 67 S. Ct. 385, 91 L.Ed. 451 (1947). Both demand a showing of justification before production can be had, the one of "good cause" and the other variously described in the *Hickman* case: "necessity or justification," "denial * * * would unduly prejudice the preparation of petitioner's case," or "cause hardship or injustice" 329 U.S. at 509–510.

In deciding the *Hickman* case, the Supreme Court appears to have expressed a preference in 1947 for an approach to the problem of trial preparation materials by judicial decision rather than by rule. Sufficient experience has accumulated, however, with lower court applications of the *Hickman* decision to warrant a reappraisal.

The major difficulties visible in the existing case law are (1) confusion and disagreement as to whether "good cause" is made out by a showing of relevance and lack of privilege, or requires an additional showing of necessity, (2) confusion and disagreement as to the scope of the *Hickman* work-product doctrine, particularly whether it extends beyond work actually performed by lawyers, and (3) the resulting difficulty of relating the "good cause" required by Rule 34 and the "necessity or justification" of the work-product doctrine, so that their respective roles and the distinctions between them are understood.

Basic Standard.—Since Rule 34 in terms requires a showing of "good cause" for the production of all documents and things, whether or not trial preparation is involved, courts have felt that a single formula is called for and have differed over whether a showing of relevance and lack of privilege is enough or whether more must be shown. When the facts of the cases are studied, however, a distinction emerges based upon the type of materials. With respect to documents not obtained or prepared with an eye to litigation, the decisions, while not uniform, reflect a strong and increasing tendency to relate "good cause" to a showing that the documents are relevant to the subject matter of the action. *E.g., Connecticut Mutual Life Ins. Co. v. Shields*, 17 F.R.D. 273 (S.D.N.Y.1955), with cases cited; *Houdry Process Corp. v. Commonwealth Oil Refining Co.*, 24 F.R.D. 58 (S.D.N.Y.1959); see *Bell v. Commercial Ins. Co.*, 280 F.2d 514, 517 (3d Cir.1960). When the party whose documents are sought shows that the request for production is unduly burdensome or oppressive, courts have denied discovery for lack of "good cause" although they might just as easily have based their decision on the protective provisions of existing Rule 30(b) (new Rule 26(c)). *E.g., Lauer v. Tankrederi*, 39 F.R.D. 334 (E.D.Pa.1966).

As to trial-preparation materials, however, the courts are increasingly interpreting "good cause" as requiring more than relevance. When lawyers have prepared or obtained the materials for trial, all courts require more than relevance; so much is clearly commanded by *Hickman*. But even as to the preparatory work of nonlawyers, while some courts ignore work-product and equate "good cause" with relevance, *e.g., Brown v. New York, N. H. & H. R. R.*, 17 F.R.D. 324 (S.D.N.Y.1955), the more recent trend is to read "good cause" as requiring inquiry into the importance of and need for the materials as well as into alternative sources for securing the same information. In *Guilford Nat'l Bank v. Southern Ry.*, 297 F.2d 921 (4th Cir.1962), statements of witnesses obtained by claim agents were held not discoverable because both parties had had equal access to the witnesses at about the same time, shortly after the collision in question. The decision was based solely on Rule 34 and "good cause"; the court declined to rule on whether the statements were work-products. The court's treatment of "good cause" is quoted at length and with approval in *Schlagenhauf v. Holder*, 379 U.S. 104, 117–118, 85 S. Ct. 234, 13 L. Ed. 2d 152 (1964). See also *Mitchell v. Bass*, 252 F.2d 513 (8th Cir.1958); *Hauger v. Chicago, R. I. & Pac. R. R.*, 216 F.2d 501 (7th Cir.1954); *Burke v. United States*, 32 F.R.D. 213 (E.D.N.Y.1963). While the opinions dealing with "good cause" do not often draw an explicit distinction between trial preparation materials and other materials, in fact an overwhelming proportion of the cases in which a special showing is required are cases involving trial preparation materials.

The rules are amended by eliminating the general requirement of "good cause" from Rule 34 but retaining a requirement of a special showing for trial preparation materials in this subdivision. The required showing is expressed, not in terms of "good cause" whose generality has tended to encourage confusion and controversy, but in terms of the elements of the special showing to be made: substantial need of the materials in the preparation of the case and inability without undue hardship to obtain the substantial equivalent of the materials by other means.

These changes conform to the holdings of the cases, when viewed in light of their facts. Apart from trial preparation, the fact that the materials sought are documentary does not in and of itself require a special showing beyond relevance and absence of privilege. The protective provisions are of course available, and if the party from whom production is sought raises a special issue of privacy (as with respect to income tax returns or grand jury minutes) or points to evidence primarily impeaching, or can show serious burden or expense, the court will exercise its traditional power to decide whether to issue a protective order. On the other hand, the requirement of a special showing for discovery of trial preparation materials reflects the view that each side's informal evaluation of its case should be protected, that each side should be encouraged to prepare independently, and that one side should not automatically have the benefit of the detailed preparatory work of the other side. See Field and McKusick, Maine Civil Practice 264 (1959).

Elimination of a "good cause" requirement from Rule 34 and the establishment of a requirement of a special showing in this subdivision will eliminate the confusion caused by having two verbally distinct requirements of justification that the courts have been unable to distinguish clearly. Moreover, the language of the subdivision suggests the factors which the courts should consider in determining whether the requisite showing has been made. The importance of the materials sought to the party seeking them in preparation of his case and the difficulty he will have obtaining them by other means are factors noted in the *Hickman* case. The courts should also consider the likelihood that the party, even if he obtains the information by independent means, will not have the substantial equivalent of the documents the production of which he seeks.

Consideration of these factors may well lead the court to distinguish between witness statements taken by an investigator, on the one hand, and other parts of the investigative file, on the other. The court in *Southern Ry. v. Lanham*, 403 F.2d 119 (5th Cir.1968), while it naturally addressed itself to the "good cause" requirements of Rule 34, set forth as controlling considerations the factors contained in the language of this subdivision. The analysis of the court suggests circumstances under which witness statements will be discoverable. The witness may have given a fresh and contemporaneous account in a written statement while he is available to the party seeking discovery only a substantial time thereafter. *Lanham, supra* at 127–128; *Guilford, supra* at 926. Or he may be reluctant or hostile. *Lanham, supra* at 128–129; *Brookshire v. Pennsylvania RR*, 14 F.R.D. 154 (N.D.Ohio 1953); *Diamond v. Mohawk Rubber Co.*, 33 F.R.D. 264 (D.Colo.1963). Or he may have a lapse of memory. *Tannenbaum v. Walker*, 16 F.R.D. 570 (E.D.Pa.1954). Or he may probably be deviating from his prior statement. *Cf. Hauger v. Chicago, R. I. & Pac. RR*, 216 F.2d 501 (7th Cir.1954). On the other hand, a much stronger showing is needed to obtain evaluative materials in an investigator's reports. *Lanham, supra* at 131–133; *Pickett v. L. R. Ryan, Inc.*, 237 F.Supp. 198 (E.D.S.C.1965).

Materials assembled in the ordinary course of business, or pursuant to public requirements unrelated to litigation, or for other nonlitigation purposes are not under the qualified immunity provided by this subdivision. *Goosman v. A. Duie Pyle, Inc.*, 320 F.2d 45 (4th Cir.1963); *cf. United States v. New York Foreign Trade Zone Operators, Inc.*, 304 F.2d 792 (2d Cir.1962). No change is made in the existing doctrine, noted in the *Hickman* case, that one party may discover relevant facts known or available to the other party, even though such facts are contained in a document which is not itself discoverable.

Treatment of Lawyers; Special Protection of Mental Impressions, Conclusions, Opinions, and Legal Theories Concerning the Litigation.—

The courts are divided as to whether the work-product doctrine extends to the preparatory work only of lawyers. The *Hickman* case left this issue open since the statements in that case were taken by a lawyer. As to courts of appeals compare *Alltmont v. United States*, 177 F.2d 971, 976 (3d Cir.1949), *cert. denied*, 339 U.S. 967, 70 S. Ct. 999, 94 L.Ed. 1375 (1950) (*Hickman* applied to statements obtained by FBI agents on theory it should apply to "all statements of prospective witnesses which a party has obtained for his trial counsel's use"), with *Southern Ry. v. Campbell*, 309 F.2d 569 (5th Cir.1962) (statements taken by claim agents not work-product), and *Guilford Nat'l Bank v. Southern Ry.*, 297 F.2d 921 (4th Cir.1962) (avoiding issue of work-product as to claim agents, deciding case instead under Rule 34 "good cause"). Similarly, the district courts are divided on statements obtained by claim agents, compare, *e.g.*, *Brown v. New York, N. H. & H. R. R.*, 17 F.R.D. 324 (S.D.N.Y.1955) with *Hanke v. Milwaukee Electric Ry. & Transp. Co.*, 7 F.R.D. 540 (E.D.Wis.1947); Investigators, compare *Burke v. United States*, 32 F.R.D. 213 (E.D.N.Y.1963) with *Snyder v. United States*, 20 F.R.D. 7 (E.D.N.Y.1956); and Insurers, compare *Gottlieb v. Bresler*, 24 F.R.D. 371 (D.D.C.1959) with *Burns v. Mulder*, 20 F.R.D. 605 (E.D. Pa.1957). See 4 Moore's Federal Practice ¶ 26.23[8.1] (2d ed. 1966); 2A Barron & Holtzoff, Federal Practice and Procedure § 652.2 (Wright ed. 1961).

A complication is introduced by the use made by courts of the "good cause" requirement of Rule 34, as described above. A court may conclude that trial preparation materials are not work-product because not the result of lawyer's work and yet hold that they are not producible because "good cause" has not been shown. *Cf. Guilford Nat'l Bank v. Southern Ry.*, 297 F.2d 921 (4th Cir. 1962), cited and described above. When the decisions on "good cause" are taken into account, the weight of authority affords protection of the preparatory work of both lawyers and nonlawyers (though not necessarily to the same extent) by requiring more than a showing of relevance to secure production.

Subdivision (b)(3) reflects the trend of the cases by requiring a special showing, not merely as to materials prepared by an attorney, but also as to materials prepared in anticipation of litigation or preparation for trial by or for a party or any representative acting on his behalf. The subdivision then goes on to protect against disclosure the mental impressions, conclusions, opinions, or legal theories concerning the litigation of an attorney or other representative of a party. The *Hickman* opinion drew special attention to the need for protecting an attorney against discovery of memoranda prepared from recollection of oral interviews. The courts have steadfastly safeguarded against disclosure of lawyers' mental impressions and legal theories, as well as mental impressions and subjective evaluations of investigators and claim-agents. In enforcing this provision of the subdivision, the courts will sometimes find it necessary to order disclosure of a document but with portions deleted.

Rules 33 and 36 have been revised in order to permit discovery calling for opinions, contentions, and admissions relating not only to fact but also to the application of law to fact. Under those rules, a party and his attorney or other representative may be required to disclose, to some extent, mental impressions, opinions, or conclusions. But documents or parts of documents containing these matters are protected against discovery by this subdivision. Even though a party may ultimately have to disclose in response to interrogatories or requests to admit, he is entitled to keep confidential documents containing such matters prepared for internal use.

Party's Right to Own Statement.—An exception to the requirement of this subdivision enables a party to secure production of his own statement without any special showing. The cases are divided. Compare, *e.g.*, *Safeway Stores, Inc. v. Reynolds*, 176 F.2d 476 (D.C.Cir.1949); *Shupe v. Pennsylvania R. R.*, 19 F.R.D. 144 (W.D.Pa.1956); with *e.g.*, *New York Central R. R. v. Carr*, 251 F.2d 433 (4th Cir.1957); *Belback v. Wilson Freight Forwarding Co.*, 40 F.R.D. 16 (W. D.Pa.1966).

Courts which treat a party's statement as though it were that of any witness overlook the fact that the party's statement is, without more, admissible in evidence. Ordinarily, a party gives a statement without insisting on a copy because he does not yet have a lawyer and does not understand the legal consequences of his actions. Thus, the statement is given at a time when he functions at a disadvantage. Discrepancies between his trial testimony and earlier statement may result from lapse of memory or ordinary inaccuracy; a written statement produced for the first time at trial may give such discrepancies a prominence which they do not deserve. In appropriate cases the court may order a party to be deposed before his statement is produced. *E.g., Smith v. Central Linen Service Co.*, 39 F.R.D. 15 (D.Md.1966); *McCoy v. General Motors Corp.*, 33 F.R.D. 354 (W.D.Pa.1963).

Commentators strongly support the view that a party be able to secure his statement without a showing. 4 Moore's Federal Practice ¶ 26.23[8.4] (2d ed. 1966); 2A Barron & Holtzoff, Federal Practice and Procedure § 652.3 (Wright ed. 1961); see also Note, Developments in the Law—Discovery, 74 Harv.L.Rev. 940, 1039 (1961). The following states have by statute or rule taken the same position: *Statutes*: Fla.Stat.Ann. § 92.33; Ga.Code Ann. § 38-2109(b); La.Stat. Ann.R.S. 13:3732; Mass.Gen.Laws Ann. c. 271, § 44; Minn.Stat.Ann. § 602.01; N.Y.C.P.L.R. § 3101(e); *Rules*: Mo.R.C.P. 56.01(a); N.Dak.R.C.P. 34(b); Wyo.R. C.P. 34(b); *cf.* Mich.G.C.R. 306.2.

In order to clarify and tighten the provision on statements by a party, the term "statement" is defined. The definition is adapted from 18 U.S.C. § 3500(e) (Jencks Act). The statement of a party may of course be that of plaintiff or defendant, and it may be that of an individual or of a corporation or other organization.

Witness' Right to Own Statement.—A second exception to the requirement of this subdivision permits a non-party witness to obtain a copy of his own statement without any special showing. Many, though not all, of the considerations supporting a party's right to obtain his statement apply also to the non-party witness. Insurance companies are increasingly recognizing that a witness is entitled to a copy of his statement and are modifying their regular practice accordingly.

Subdivision (b)(4)—Trial Preparation: Experts. This is a new provision dealing with discovery of information (including facts and opinions) obtained by a party from an expert retained by that party in relation to litigation or obtained by the expert and not yet transmitted to the party. The subdivision deals separately with those experts whom the party expects to call as trial witnesses and with those experts who have been retained or specially employed by the party but who are not expected to be witnesses. It should be noted that the subdivision does not address itself to the expert whose information was not acquired in preparation for trial but rather because he was an actor or viewer with respect to transactions or occurrences that are part of the subject matter of the lawsuit. Such an expert should be treated as an ordinary witness.

Subsection (b)(4)(A) deals with discovery of information obtained by or through experts who will be called as witnesses at trial. The provision is responsive to problems suggested by a relatively recent line of authorities. Many of these cases present intricate and difficult issues as to which expert testimony is likely to be determinative. Prominent among them are food and drug, patent, and condemnation cases. See, *e.g., United States v. Nysco Laboratories, Inc.*, 26 F.R.D. 159, 162 (E.D.N.Y.1960) (food and drug); *E. I. du Pont De Nemours & Co. v. Phillips Petroleum Co.*, 24 F.R.D. 416, 421 (D.Del.1959) (patent); *Cold Metal Process Co. v. Aluminum Co. of America*, 7 F.R.D. 425 (N.D.Ohio 1947), *aff'd, Sachs v. Aluminum Co. of America*, 167 F.2d 570 (6th Cir.1948) (same); *United States v. 50.34 Acres of Land*, 13 F.R.D. 19 (E.D.N.Y. 1952) (condemnation).

In cases of this character, a prohibition against discovery of information held by expert witnesses produces in acute form the very evils that discovery has been created to prevent. Effective cross-examination of an expert witness requires advance preparation. The lawyer even with the help of his own experts frequently cannot anticipate the particular approach his adversary's expert will take or the data on which he will base his judgment on the stand. McGlothlin, Some Practical Problems in Proof of Economic, Scientific, and Technical Facts,

23 F.R.D 467, 478 (1958). A California study of discovery and pretrial in condemnation cases notes that the only substitute for discovery of experts' valuation materials is "lengthy—and often fruitless—cross-examination during trial," and recommends pretrial exchange of such material. Calif.Law Rev.Comm'n, Discovery in Eminent Domain Proceedings 707 to 710 (Jan. 1963). Similarly, effective rebuttal requires advance knowledge of the line of testimony of the other side. If the latter is foreclosed by a rule against discovery, then the narrowing of issues and elimination of surprise which discovery normally produces are frustrated.

These considerations appear to account for the broadening of discovery against experts in the cases cited where expert testimony was central to the case. In some instances, the opinions are explicit in relating expanded discovery to improved cross-examination and rebuttal at trial. *Franks v. National Dairy Products Corp.*, 41 F.R.D. 234 (W.D.Tex.1966); *United States v. 23.76 Acres*, 32 F.R.D. 593 (D.Md.1963); see also an unpublished opinion of Judge Hincks, quoted in *United States v. 48 Jars, etc.*, 23 F.R.D. 192, 198 (D.D.C.1958). On the other hand, the need for a new provision is shown by the many cases in which discovery of expert trial witnesses is needed for effective cross-examination and rebuttal, and yet courts apply the traditional doctrine and refuse disclosure. *E.g., United States v. Certain Parcels of Land*, 25 F.R.D. 192 (N.D.Cal.1959); *United States v. Certain Acres*, 18 F.R.D. 98 (M.D.Ga.1955).

Although the trial problems flowing from lack of discovery of expert witnesses are most acute and noteworthy when the case turns largely on experts, the same problems are encountered when a single expert testifies. Thus, subdivision (b)(4)(A) draws no line between complex and simple cases, or between cases with many experts and those with but one. It establishes by rule substantially the procedure adopted by decision of the court in *Knighton v. Villian & Fassio*, 39 F.R.D. 11 (D.Md.1965). For a full analysis of the problem and strong recommendations to the same effect, see Friedenthal, Discovery and Use of an Adverse Party's Expert Information, 14 Stan.L.Rev. 455, 485–488 (1962); Long, Discovery and Experts under the Federal Rules of Civil Procedure, 38 F.R.D. 111 (1965).

Past judicial restrictions on discovery of an adversary's expert, particularly as to his opinions, reflect the fear that one side will benefit unduly from the other's better preparation. The procedure established in subsection (b)(4)(A) holds the risk to a minimum. Discovery is limited to trial witnesses, and may be obtained only at a time when the parties know who their expert witnesses will be. A party must as a practical matter prepare his own case in advance of that time, for he can hardly hope to build his case out of his opponent's experts.

Subdivision (b)(4)(A) provides for discovery of an expert who is to testify at the trial. A party can require one who intends to use the expert to state the substance of the testimony that the expert is expected to give. The court may order further discovery, and it has ample power to regulate its timing and scope and to prevent abuse. Ordinarily, the order for further discovery shall compensate the expert for his time, and may compensate the party who intends to use the expert for past expenses reasonably incurred in obtaining facts or opinions from the expert. Those provisions are likely to discourage abusive practices.

Subdivision (b)(4)(B) deals with an expert who has been retained or specially employed by the party in anticipation of litigation or preparation for trial (thus excluding an expert who is simply a general employee of the party not specially employed on the case), but who is not expected to be called as a witness. Under its provisions, a party may discover facts known or opinions held by such an expert only on a showing of exceptional circumstances under which it is impracticable for the party seeking discovery to obtain facts or opinions on the same subject by other means.

Subdivision (b)(4)(B) is concerned only with experts retained or specially consulted in relation to trial preparation. Thus the subdivision precludes discovery against experts who were informally consulted in preparation for trial, but not retained or specially employed. As an ancillary procedure, a party may on a proper showing require the other party to name experts retained or specially employed, but not those informally consulted.

These new provisions of subdivision (b)(4) repudiate the few decisions that have held an expert's information privileged simply because of his status as an expert, *e.g., American Oil Co. v. Pennsylvania Petroleum Products Co.*, 23 F.R.D. 680, 685–686 (D.R.I.1959). See Louisell, Modern California Discovery 315–316 (1963). They also reject as ill-considered the decisions which have sought to bring expert information within the work-product doctrine. See *United States v. McKay*, 372 F.2d 174, 176–177 (5th Cir.1967). The provisions adopt a form of the more recently developed doctrine of "unfairness". See *e.g., United States v. 23.76 Acres of Land*, 32 F.R.D. 593, 597 (D.Md.1963); Louisell, *supra*, at 317–318; 4 Moore's Federal Practice ¶ 26.24 (2d ed. 1966).

Under subdivision (b)(4)(C), the court is directed or authorized to issue protective orders, including an order that the expert be paid a reasonable fee for time spent in responding to discovery, and that the party whose expert is made subject to discovery be paid a fair portion of the fees and expenses that the party incurred in obtaining information from the expert. The court may issue the latter order as a condition of discovery, or it may delay the order until after discovery is completed. These provisions for fees and expenses meet the objection that it is unfair to permit one side to obtain without cost the benefit of an expert's work for which the other side has paid, often a substantial sum. *E.g., Lewis v. United Air Lines Transp. Corp.*, 32 F.Supp. 21 (W.D.Pa.1940); *Walsh v. Reynolds Metals Co.*, 15 F.R.D. 376 (D.N.J.1954). On the other hand, a party may not obtain discovery simply by offering to pay fees and expenses. *Cf. Boynton v. R. J. Reynolds Tobacco Co.*, 36 F.Supp. 593 (D.Mass.1941).

In instances of discovery under subdivision (b)(4)(B), the court is directed to award fees and expenses to the other party, since the information is of direct value to the discovering party's preparation of his case. In ordering discovery under (b)(4)(A)(ii), the court has discretion whether to award fees and expenses to the other party; its decision should depend upon whether the discovering party is simply learning about the other party's case or is going beyond this to develop his own case. Even in cases where the court is directed to issue a protective order, it may decline to do so if it finds that manifest injustice would result. Thus, the court can protect, when necessary and appropriate, the interests of an indigent party.

Subdivision (c)—Protective Orders. The provisions of existing Rule 30(b) are transferred to this subdivision (c), as part of the rearrangement of Rule 26. The language has been changed to give it application to discovery generally. The subdivision recognizes the power of the court in the district where a deposition is being taken to make protective orders. Such power is needed when the deposition is being taken far from the court where the action is pending. The court in the district where the deposition is being taken may, and frequently will, remit the deponent or party to the court where the action is pending.

In addition, drafting changes are made to carry out and clarify the sense of the rule. Insertions are made to avoid any possible implication that a protective order does not extend to "time" as well as to "place" or may not safeguard against "undue burden or expense."

The new reference to trade secrets and other confidential commercial information reflects existing law. The courts have not given trade secrets automatic and complete immunity against disclosure, but have in each case weighed their claim to privacy against the need for disclosure. Frequently, they have been afforded a limited protection. See *e.g., Covey Oil Co. v. Continental Oil Co.*, 340 F.2d 993 (10th Cir.1965); *Julius M. Ames Co. v. Bostitch, Inc.*, 235 F.Supp. 856 (S.D.N.Y.1964).

The subdivision contains new matter relating to sanctions. When a motion for a protective order is made and the court is disposed to deny it, the court may go a step further and issue an order to provide or permit discovery. This will bring the sanctions of Rule 37(b) directly into play. Since the court has heard the contentions of all interested persons, an affirmative order is justified. See Rosenberg, Sanctions to Effectuate Pretrial Discovery, 58 Col.L.Rev. 480, 492–493

(1958). In addition, the court may require the payment of expenses incurred in relation to the motion.

Subdivision (d)—Sequence and Priority. This new provision is concerned with the sequence in which parties may proceed with discovery and with related problems of timing. The principal effects of the new provision are first, to eliminate any fixed priority in the sequence of discovery, and second, to make clear and explicit the court's power to establish priority by an order issued in a particular case.

A priority rule developed by some courts, which confers priority on the party who first serves notice of taking a deposition, is unsatisfactory in several important respects:

First, this priority rule permits a party to establish a priority running to all depositions as to which he has given earlier notice. Since he can on a given day serve notice of taking many depositions he is in a position to delay his adversary's taking of depositions for an inordinate time. Some courts have ruled that deposition priority also permits a party to delay his answers to interrogatories and production of documents. *E.g., E. I. duPont de Nemours & Co. v. Phillips Petroleum Co.*, 23 F.R.D. 237 (D.Del.1959); *but cf. Sturdevant v. Sears, Roebuck & Co.*, 32 F.R.D. 426 (W.D.Mo.1963).

Second, since notice is the key to priority, if both parties wish to take depositions first a race results. See *Caldwell-Clements, Inc. v. McGraw-Hill Pub. Co.*, 11 F.R.D. 156 (S.D.N.Y.1951) (description of tactics used by parties). But the existing rules on notice of deposition create a race with runners starting from different positions. The plaintiff may not give notice without leave of court until 20 days after commencement of the action, whereas the defendant may serve notice at any time after commencement. Thus, a careful and prompt defendant can almost always secure priority. This advantage of defendants is fortuitous, because the purpose of requiring plaintiff to wait 20 days is to afford defendant an opportunity to obtain counsel, not to confer priority.

Third, although courts have ordered a change in the normal sequence of discovery on a number of occasions, *e.g., Kaeppler v. James H. Matthews & Co.*, 200 F.Supp. 229 (E.D.Pa.1961); *Park & Tilford Distillers Corp. v. Distillers Co.*, 19 F.R.D. 169 (S.D.N.Y.1956) and have at all times avowed discretion to vary the usual priority, most commentators are agreed that courts in fact grant relief only for "the most obviously compelling reasons." 2A Barron & Holtzoff, Federal Practice and Procedure 44 to 47 (Wright ed. 1961); see also Younger, Priority of Pretrial Examination in the Federal Courts—A Comment, 34 N.Y.U.L.Rev. 1271 (1959); Freund, The Pleading and Pretrial of an Antitrust Claim, 46 Corn.L.Q. 555, 564 (1964). Discontent with the fairness of actual practice has been evinced by other observers. Comment, 59 Yale L.J. 117, 134–136 (1949); Yudkin, Some Refinements in Federal Discovery Procedure, 11 Fed.B.J. 289, 296–297 (1951); Developments in the Law-Discovery, 74 Harv.L.Rev. 940, 954–958 (1961).

Despite these difficulties, some courts have adhered to the priority rule, presumably because it provides a test which is easily understood and applied by the parties without much court intervention. It thus permits deposition discovery to function extrajudicially, which the rules provide for and the courts desire. For these same reasons, courts are reluctant to make numerous exceptions to the rule.

The Columbia Survey makes clear that the problem of priority does not affect litigants generally. It found that most litigants do not move quickly to obtain discovery. In over half of the cases, both parties waited at least 50 days. During the first 20 days after commencement of the action—the period when defendant might assure his priority by noticing depositions—16 percent of the defendants acted to obtain discovery. A race could not have occurred in more than 16 percent of the cases and it undoubtedly occurred in fewer. On the other hand, five times as many defendants as plaintiffs served notice of deposition during the first 19 days. To the same effect, see Comment, Tactical Use and Abuse of Depositions Under the Federal Rules, 59 Yale L.J. 117, 134 (1949).

These findings do not mean, however, that the priority rule is satisfactory or that a problem of priority does not exist. The court decisions show that parties do battle on this issue and carry their disputes to court. The statistics show that these court cases are not typical. By the same token, they reveal that more extensive exercise of judicial discretion to vary the priority will not bring a flood of litigation, and that a change in the priority rule will in fact affect only a small fraction of the cases.

It is contended by some that there is no need to alter the existing priority practice. In support, it is urged that there is no evidence that injustices in fact result from present practice and that, in any event, the courts can and do promulgate local rules, as in New York, to deal with local situations and issue orders to avoid possible injustice in particular cases.

Subdivision (d) is based on the contrary view that the rule of priority based on notice is unsatisfactory and unfair in its operation. Subdivision (d) follows an approach adapted from Civil Rule 4 of the District Court for the Southern District of New York. That rule provides that starting 40 days after commencement of the action, unless otherwise ordered by the court, the fact that one party is taking a deposition shall not prevent another party from doing so "concurrently." In practice, the depositions are not usually taken simultaneously; rather, the parties work out arrangements for alternation in the taking of depositions. One party may take a complete deposition and then the other, or, if the depositions are extensive, one party deposes for a set time, and then the other. See *Caldwell-Clements, Inc. v. McGraw-Hill Pub. Co.*, 11 F.R.D. 156 (S.D. N.Y.1951).

In principle, one party's initiation of discovery should not wait upon the other's completion, unless delay is dictated by special considerations. Clearly the principle is feasible with respect to all methods of discovery other than depositions. And the experience of the Southern District of New York shows that the principle can be applied to depositions as well. The courts have not had an increase in motion business on this matter. Once it is clear to lawyers that they bargain on an equal footing, they are usually able to arrange for an orderly succession of depositions without judicial intervention. Professor Moore has called attention to Civil Rule 4 and suggested that it may usefully be extended to other areas. 4 Moore's Federal Practice 1154 (2d ed. 1966).

The court may upon motion and by order grant priority in a particular case. But a local court rule purporting to confer priority in certain classes of cases would be inconsistent with this subdivision and thus void.

Subdivision (e)—Supplementation of Responses. The rules do not now state whether interrogatories (and questions at deposition as well as requests for inspection and admissions) impose a "continuing burden" on the responding party to supplement his answers if he obtains new information. The issue is acute when new information renders substantially incomplete or inaccurate an answer which was complete and accurate when made. It is essential that the rules provide an answer to this question. The parties can adjust to a rule either way, once they know what it is. See 4 Moore's Federal Practice ¶ 33.25[4] (2d ed. 1966).

Arguments can be made both ways. Imposition of a continuing burden reduces the proliferation of additional sets of interrogatories. Some courts have adopted local rules establishing such a burden. E.g., E.D.Pa.R. 20(f), quoted in *Taggart v. Vermont Transp. Co.*, 32 F.R.D. 587 (E.D.Pa.1963); D.Me.R. 15(c). Others have imposed the burden by decision. *E.g., Chenault v. Nebraska Farm Products, Inc.*, 9 F.R.D. 529, 533 (D.Neb.1949). On the other hand, there are serious objections to the burden, especially in protracted cases. Although the party signs the answers, it is his lawyer who understands their significance and bears the responsibility to bring answers up to date. In a complex case all sorts of information reaches the party, who little understands its bearing on answers previously given to interrogatories. In practice, therefore, the lawyer under a continuing burden must periodically recheck all interrogatories and canvass all new information. But a full set of new answers may no longer be needed by the interrogating party. Some issues will have been dropped from the case, some questions are now seen as unimportant, and other questions must in any event be reformulated. See *Novick v. Pennsylvania R. R.*, 18 F.R.D. 296, 298 (W.D.Pa. 1955).

Subdivision (e) provides that a party is not under a continuing burden except as expressly provided. Cf. Note, 68 Harv.L.Rev. 673, 677 (1955). An exception is made as to the identity of persons having knowledge of discoverable matters, because of the obvious importance to each side of knowing all witnesses and because information about witnesses routinely comes to each lawyer's attention. Many of the decisions on the issue of a continuing burden have in fact concerned the identity of witnesses. An exception is also made as to expert trial witnesses in order to carry out the provisions of Rule 26(b)(4). See *Diversified Products Corp. v. Sports Center Co.*, 42 F.R.D. 3 (D.Md.1967).

Another exception is made for the situation in which a party, or more frequently his lawyer, obtains actual knowledge that a prior response is incorrect. This exception does not impose a duty to check the accuracy of prior responses, but it prevents knowing concealment by a party or attorney. Finally, a duty to supplement may be imposed by order of the court in a particular case (including an order resulting from a pretrial conference) or by agreement of the parties. A party may of course make a new discovery request which requires supplementation of prior responses.

The duty will normally be enforced, in those limited instances where it is imposed, through sanctions imposed by the trial court, including exclusion of evidence, continuance, or other action, as the court may deem appropriate.

1980 AMENDMENT

Subdivision (f). This subdivision is new. There has been widespread criticism of abuse of discovery. The Committee has considered a number of proposals to eliminate abuse, including a change in Rule 26(b)(1) with respect to the scope of discovery and a change in Rule 33(a) to limit the number of questions that can be asked by interrogatories to parties.

The Committee believes that abuse of discovery, while very serious in certain cases, is not so general as to require such basic changes in the rules that govern discovery in all cases. A very recent study of discovery in selected metropolitan districts tends to support its belief. P. Connolly, E. Holleman, & M. Kuhlman, Judicial Controls and the Civil Litigative Process: Discovery (Federal Judicial Center, 1978). In the judgment of the Committee abuse can best be prevented by intervention by the court as soon as abuse is threatened.

To this end this subdivision provides that counsel who has attempted without success to effect with opposing counsel a reasonable program or plan for discovery is entitled to the assistance of the court.

It is not contemplated that requests for discovery conferences will be made routinely. A relatively narrow discovery dispute should be resolved by resort to Rules 26(c) or 37(a), and if it appears that a request for a conference is in fact grounded in such a dispute, the court may refer counsel to those rules. If the court is persuaded that a request is frivolous or vexatious, it can strike it. See Rules 11 and 7(b)(2).

A number of courts routinely consider discovery matters in preliminary pretrial conferences held shortly after the pleadings are closed. This subdivision does not interfere with such a practice. It authorizes the court to combine a discovery conference with a pretrial conference under Rule 16 if a pretrial conference is held sufficiently early to prevent or curb abuse.

1983 AMENDMENT

Excessive discovery and evasion or resistance to reasonable discovery requests pose significant problems. Recent studies have made some attempt to determine the sources and extent of the difficulties. See Brazil, *Civil Discovery: Lawyers' Views of its Effectiveness, Principal Problems and Abuses,* American Bar Foundation (1980); Connolly, Holleman & Kuhlman, *Judicial Controls and the Civil Litigative Process: Discovery,* Federal Judicial Center (1978); Ellington, *A Study of Sanctions for Discovery Abuse,* Department of Justice (1979); Schroeder

& Frank, *The Proposed Changes in the Discovery Rules,* 1978 Ariz. St. L.J. 475.

The purpose of discovery is to provide a mechanism for making relevant information available to the litigants. "Mutual knowledge of all the relevant facts gathered by both parties is essential to proper litigation." *Hickman v. Taylor*, 329 U.S. 495, 507, 67 S. Ct. 385, 91 L.Ed. 451 (1947). Thus the spirit of the rules is violated when advocates attempt to use discovery tools as tactical weapons rather than to expose the facts and illuminate the issues by overuse of discovery or unnecessary use of defensive weapons or evasive responses. All of this results in excessively costly and time-consuming activities that are disproportionate to the nature of the case, the amount involved, or the issues or values at stake.

Given our adversary tradition and the current discovery rules, it is not surprising that there are many opportunities if not incentives, for attorneys to engage in discovery that, although authorized by the broad, permissive terms of the rules, nevertheless results in delay. See Brazil, *The Adversary Character of Civil Discovery: A Critique and Proposals for Change*, 31 Vand.L.Rev. 1259 (1978). As a result, it has been said that the rules have "not infrequently [been] exploited to the disadvantage of justice." *Herbert v. Lando*, 441 U.S. 153, 179, 99 S. Ct. 1635, 60 L. Ed. 2d 115 (1979) (Powell, J., concurring). These practices impose costs on an already overburdened system and impede the fundamental goal of the "just, speedy, and inexpensive determination of every action." Fed.R. Civ.P. 1.

Subdivision (a); Discovery Methods. The deletion of the last sentence of Rule 26(a)(1), which provided that unless the court ordered otherwise under Rule 26(c) "the frequency of use" of the various discovery methods was not to be limited, is an attempt to address the problem of duplicative, redundant, and excessive discovery and to reduce it. The amendment, in conjunction with the changes in Rule 26(b)(1), is designed to encourage district judges to identify instances of needless discovery and to limit the use of the various discovery devices accordingly. The question may be raised by one of the parties, typically on a motion for a protective order, or by the court on its own initiative. It is entirely appropriate to consider a limitation on the frequency of use of discovery at a discovery conference under Rule 26(f) or at any other pretrial conference authorized by these rules. In considering the discovery needs of a particular case, the court should consider the factors described in Rule 26(b)(1).

Subdivision (b); Discovery Scope and Limits. Rule 26(b)(1) has been amended to add a sentence to deal with the problem of over-discovery. The objective is to guard against redundant or disproportionate discovery by giving the court authority to reduce the amount of discovery that may be directed to matters that are otherwise proper subjects of inquiry. The new sentence is intended to encourage judges to be more aggressive in identifying and discouraging discovery overuse. The grounds mentioned in the amended rule for limiting discovery reflect the existing practice of many courts in issuing protective orders under Rule 26(c). See, *e.g., Carlson Cos. v. Sperry & Hutchinson Co.*, 374 F.Supp. 1080 (D.Minn.1973); *Dolgow v. Anderson*, 53 F.R.D. 661 (E.D.N.Y.1971); *Mitchell v. American Tobacco Co.*, 33 F.R.D. 262 (M.D.Pa.1963); *Welty v. Clute*, 1 F.R.D. 446 (W.D.N.Y.1940). On the whole, however, district judges have been reluctant to limit the use of the discovery devices. See, *e.g., Apco Oil Corp. v. Certified Transp., Inc.*, 46 F.R.D. 428 (W.D.Mo.1969). See generally 8 Wright & Miller, *Federal Practice and Procedure: Civil* §§ 2036, 2037, 2039, 2040 (1970).

The first element of the standard, Rule 26(b)(1)(i), is designed to minimize redundancy in discovery and encourage attorneys to be sensitive to the comparative costs of different methods of securing information. Subdivision (b)(1)(ii) also seeks to reduce repetitiveness and to oblige lawyers to think through their discovery activities in advance so that full utilization is made of each deposition, document request, or set of interrogatories. The elements of Rule 26(b)(1)(iii) address the problem of discovery that is disproportionate to the individual lawsuit as measured by such matters as its nature and complexity, the importance of the issues at stake in a case seeking damages, the limitations on a financially weak litigant to withstand extensive opposition to a discovery program or to respond to discovery requests, and the significance of the substantive issues, as measured in philosophic, social, or institutional terms. Thus the rule recognizes that many cases in public policy spheres, such as employment practices, free speech, and other matters, may have importance far beyond the monetary amount involved. The court must apply the standards in an even-handed manner that will prevent use of discovery to wage a war of attrition or as a device to coerce a party, whether financially weak or affluent.

The rule contemplates greater judicial involvement in the discovery process and thus acknowledges the reality that it cannot always operate on a self-regulating basis. See Connolly, Holleman & Kuhlman, *Judicial Controls and the Civil Litigative Process: Discovery* 77, Federal Judicial Center (1978). In an appropriate case the court could restrict the number of depositions, interrogatories, or the scope of a production request. But the court must be careful not to deprive a party of discovery that is reasonably necessary to afford a fair opportunity to develop and prepare the case.

The court may act on motion, or its own initiative. It is entirely appropriate to resort to the amended rule in conjunction with a discovery conference under Rule 26(f) or one of the other pretrial conferences authorized by the rules.

Subdivision (g); Signing of Discovery Requests, Responses, and Objections. Rule 26(g) imposes an affirmative duty to engage in pretrial discovery in a responsible manner that is consistent with the spirit and purposes of Rules 26 through 37. In addition, Rule 26(g) is designed to curb discovery abuse by explicitly encouraging the imposition of sanctions. The subdivision provides a deterrent to both excessive discovery and evasion by imposing a certification requirement that obliges each attorney to stop and think about the legitimacy of a discovery request, a response thereto, or an objection. The term "response" includes answers to interrogatories and to requests to admit as well as responses to production requests.

If primary responsibility for conducting discovery is to continue to rest with the litigants, they must be obliged to act responsibly and avoid abuse. With this in mind, Rule 26(g), which parallels the amendments to Rule 11, requires an attorney or unrepresented party to sign each discovery request, response, or objection. Motions relating to discovery are governed by Rule 11. However, since a discovery request, response, or objection usually deals with more specific subject matter than motions or papers, the elements that must be certified in connection with the former are spelled out more completely. The signature is a certification of the elements set forth in Rule 26(g).

Although the certification duty requires the lawyer to pause and consider the reasonableness of his request, response, or objection, it is not meant to discourage or restrict necessary and legitimate discovery. The rule simply requires that the attorney make a reasonable inquiry into the factual basis of his response, request, or objection.

The duty to make a "reasonable inquiry" is satisfied if the investigation undertaken by the attorney and the conclusions drawn therefrom are reasonable under the circumstances. It is an objective standard similar to the one imposed by Rule 11. See the Advisory Committee Note to Rule 11. See also *Kinee v. Abraham Lincoln Fed. Sav. & Loan Ass'n*, 365 F.Supp. 975 (E.D.Pa.1973). In making the inquiry, the attorney may rely on assertions by the client and on communications with other counsel in the case as long as that reliance is appropriate under the circumstances. Ultimately what is reasonable is a matter for the court to decide on the totality of the circumstances.

Rule 26(g) does not require the signing attorney to certify the truthfulness of the client's factual responses to a discovery request. Rather, the signature certifies that the lawyer has made a reasonable effort to assure that the client has provided all the information and documents available to him that are responsive to the discovery demand. Thus, the lawyer's certification under Rule 26(g) should be distinguished from other signature requirements in the rules, such as those in Rules 30(e) and 33.

Nor does the rule require a party or an attorney to disclose privileged communications or work product in order to show that a discovery request, response, or objection is substantially justified. The provisions of Rule 26(c), including appropriate orders after *in camera* inspection by the court, remain available to protect a party claiming privilege or work product protection.

The signing requirement means that every discovery request, response, or objection should be grounded on a theory that is reasonable under the precedents or a good faith belief as to what should be the law. This standard is heavily dependent on the circumstances of each case. The certification speaks as of the time it is made. The duty to supplement discovery responses continues to be governed by Rule 26(e).

Concern about discovery abuse has led to widespread recognition that there is a need for more aggressive judicial control and supervision. *ACF Industries, Inc. v. EEOC*, 439 U.S. 1081, 99 S. Ct. 865, 59 L. Ed. 2d 52 (1979) (certiorari denied) (Powell, J., dissenting). Sanctions to deter discovery abuse would be more effective if they were diligently applied "not merely to penalize those whose conduct may be deemed to warrant such a sanction, but to deter those who might be tempted to such conduct in the absence of such a deterrent." *National Hockey League v. Metropolitan Hockey Club*, 427 U.S. 639, 643, 96 S. Ct. 2778, 49 L. Ed. 2d 747 (1976). See also Note, *The Emerging Deterrence Orientation in the Imposition of Discovery Sanctions,* 91 Harv.L.Rev. 1033 (1978). Thus the premise of Rule 26(g) is that imposing sanctions on attorneys who fail to meet the rule's standards will significantly reduce abuse by imposing disadvantages therefor.

Because of the asserted reluctance to impose sanctions on attorneys who abuse the discovery rules, see Brazil, *Civil Discovery: Lawyers' Views of its Effectiveness, Principal Problems and Abuses,* American Bar Foundation (1980); Ellington, *A Study of Sanctions for Discovery Abuse,* Department of Justice (1979), Rule 26(g) makes explicit the authority judges now have to impose appropriate sanctions and requires them to use it. This authority derives from Rule 37, 28 U.S.C. § 1927, and the court's inherent power. See *Roadway Express, Inc. v. Piper*, 447 U.S. 752, 100 S. Ct. 2455, 65 L. Ed. 2d 488 (1980); *Martin v. Bell Helicopter Co.*, 85 F.R.D. 654, 661–62 (D.Col.1980); Note, *Sanctions Imposed by Courts on Attorneys Who Abuse the Judicial Process*, 44 U.Chi.L.Rev. 619 (1977). The new rule mandates that sanctions be imposed on attorneys who fail to meet the standards established in the first portion of Rule 26(g). The nature of the sanction is a matter of judicial discretion to be exercised in light of the particular circumstances. The court may take into account any failure by the party seeking sanctions to invoke protection under Rule 26(c) at an early stage in the litigation.

The sanctioning process must comport with due process requirements. The kind of notice and hearing required will depend on the facts of the case and the severity of the sanction being considered. To prevent the proliferation of the sanction procedure and to avoid multiple hearings, discovery in any sanction proceeding normally should be permitted only when it is clearly required by the interests of justice. In most cases the court will be aware of the circumstances and only a brief hearing should be necessary.

1987 AMENDMENT

The amendments are technical. No substantive change is intended.

1993 AMENDMENT

Subdivision (a). Through the addition of paragraphs (1)–(4), this subdivision imposes on parties a duty to disclose, without awaiting formal discovery requests, certain basic information that is needed in most cases to prepare for trial or make an informed decision about settlement. The rule requires all parties (1) early in the case to exchange information regarding potential witnesses, documentary evidence, damages, and insurance, (2) at an appropriate time during the discovery period to identify expert witnesses and provide a detailed written statement of the testimony that may be offered at trial through specially retained experts, and (3) as the trial date approaches to identify the particular evidence that may be offered at trial. The enumeration in Rule 26(a) of items to be disclosed does not prevent a court from requiring by order or local rule that the parties disclose additional information without a discovery request. Nor are parties precluded from using traditional discovery methods to obtain further information regarding these matters, as for example asking an expert during a deposition about testimony given in other litigation beyond the four-year period specified in Rule 26(a)(2)(B).

A major purpose of the revision is to accelerate the exchange of basic information about the case and to eliminate the paper work involved in requesting such information, and the rule should be applied in a manner to achieve those objectives. The concepts of imposing a duty of disclosure were set forth in Brazil, *The Adversary Character of Civil Discovery: A Critique and Proposals for Change*, 31 *Vand.L.Rev.* 1348 (1978), and Schwarzer, *The Federal Rules, the Adversary Process, and Discovery Reform*, 50 *U.Pitt.L.Rev.* 703, 721–23 (1989).

The rule is based upon the experience of district courts that have required disclosure of some of this information through local rules, court-approved standard interrogatories, and standing orders. Most have required pretrial disclosure of the kind of information described in Rule 26(a)(3). Many have required written reports from experts containing information like that specified in Rule 26(a)(2)(B). While far more limited, the experience of the few state and federal courts that have required pre-discovery exchange of core information such as is contemplated in Rule 26(a)(1) indicates that savings in time and expense can be achieved, particularly if the litigants meet and discuss the issues in the case as a predicate for this exchange and if a judge supports the process, as by using the results to guide further proceedings in the case. Courts in Canada and the United Kingdom have for many years required disclosure of certain information without awaiting a request from an adversary.

Paragraph (1). As the functional equivalent of court-ordered interrogatories, this paragraph requires early disclosure, without need for any request, of four types of information that have been customarily secured early in litigation through formal discovery. The introductory clause permits the court, by local rule, to exempt all or particular types of cases from these disclosure requirement *[sic]* or to modify the nature of the information to be disclosed. It is expected that courts would, for example, exempt cases like Social Security reviews and government collection cases in which discovery would not be appropriate or would be unlikely. By order the court may eliminate or modify the disclosure requirements in a particular case, and similarly the parties, unless precluded by order or local rule, can stipulate to elimination or modification of the requirements for that case. The disclosure obligations specified in paragraph (1) will not be appropriate for all cases, and it is expected that changes in these obligations will be made by the court or parties when the circumstances warrant.

Authorization of these local variations is, in large measure, included in order to accommodate the Civil Justice Reform Act of 1990, which implicitly directs districts to experiment during the study period with differing procedures to reduce the time and expense of civil litigation. The civil justice delay and expense reduction plans adopted by the courts under the Act differ as to the type, form, and timing of disclosures required. Section 105(c)(1) of the Act calls for a report by the Judicial Conference to Congress by December 31, 1995, comparing experience in twenty of these courts; and section 105(c)(2)(B) contemplates that some changes in the Rules may then be needed. While these studies may indicate the desirability of further changes in Rule 26(a)(1), these changes probably could not become effective before December 1998 at the earliest. In the meantime, the present revision puts in place a series of disclosure obligations that, unless a court acts affirmatively to impose other requirements or indeed to reject all such requirements for the present, are designed to eliminate certain discovery, help focus the discovery that is needed, and facilitate preparation for trial or settlement.

Subparagraph (A) requires identification of all persons who, based on the investigation conducted thus far, are likely to have discoverable information relevant to the factual disputes between the parties. All persons with such information should be disclosed, whether or not their testimony will be supportive of the position of the disclosing party. As officers of the court, counsel are expected to disclose the identity of those persons who may be used by them as witnesses or who, if their potential testimony were known, might reasonably be expected to be deposed or called as a witness by any of the other parties. Indicating briefly the general topics on which such persons have information should not be burdensome, and will assist other parties in deciding which depositions will actually be needed.

Subparagraph (B) is included as a substitute for the inquiries routinely made about the existence and location of documents and other tangible things in the possession, custody, or control of the disclosing party. Although, unlike subdivision (a)(3)(C), an itemized listing of each exhibit is not required, the disclosure should describe and categorize, to the extent identified during the initial investigation, the nature and location of potentially relevant documents and records, including computerized data and other electronically-recorded information, sufficiently to enable opposing parties (1) to make an informed decision concerning which documents might need to be examined, at least initially, and (2) to frame their document requests in a manner likely to avoid squabbles resulting from the wording of the requests. As with potential witnesses, the requirement for disclosure of documents applies to all potentially relevant items then known to the party, whether or not supportive of its contentions in the case.

Unlike subparagraphs (C) and (D), subparagraph (B) does not require production of any documents. Of course, in cases involving few documents a disclosing party may prefer to provide copies of the documents rather than describe them, and the rule is written to afford this option to the disclosing party. If, as will be more typical, only the description is provided, the other parties are expected to obtain the documents desired by proceeding under Rule 34 or through informal requests. The disclosing party does not, by describing documents under subparagraph (B), waive its right to object to production on the basis of privilege or work product protection, or to assert that the documents are not sufficiently relevant to justify the burden or expense of production.

The initial disclosure requirements of subparagraphs (A) and (B) are limited to identification of potential evidence "relevant to disputed facts alleged with particularity in the pleadings." There is no need for a party to identify potential evidence with respect to allegations that are admitted. Broad, vague, and conclusory allegations sometimes tolerated in notice pleading—for example, the assertion that a product with many component parts is defective in some unspecified manner—should not impose upon responding parties the obligation at that point to search for and identify all persons possibly involved in, or all documents affecting, the design, manufacture, and assembly of the product. The greater the specificity and clarity of the allegations in the pleadings, the more complete should be the listing of potential witnesses and types of documentary evidence. Although paragraphs (1)(A) and (1)(B) by their terms refer to the factual disputes defined in the pleadings, the rule contemplates that these issues would be informally refined and clarified during the meeting of the parties under subdivision (f) and that the disclosure obligations would be adjusted in the light of these discussions. The disclosure requirements should, in short, be applied with common sense in light of the principles of Rule 1, keeping in mind the salutary purposes that the rule is intended to accomplish. The litigants should not indulge in gamesmanship with respect to the disclosure obligations.

Subparagraph (C) imposes a burden of disclosure that includes the functional equivalent of a standing Request for Production under Rule 34. A party claiming damages or other monetary relief must, in addition to disclosing the calculation of such damages, make available the supporting documents for inspection and copying as if a request for such materials had been made under Rule 34. This obligation applies only with respect to documents then reasonably available to it and not privileged or protected as work product. Likewise, a party would not be expected to provide a calculation of damages which, as in many patent infringement actions, depends on information in the possession of another party or person.

Subparagraph (D) replaces subdivision (b)(2) of Rule 26, and provides that liability insurance policies be made available for inspection and copying. The last two sentences of that subdivision have been omitted as unnecessary, not to signify any change of law. The disclosure of insurance information does not thereby render such information admissible in evidence. See Rule 411, Federal Rules of Evidence. Nor does subparagraph (D) require disclosure of applications for insurance, though in particular cases such information may be discoverable in accordance with revised subdivision (a)(5).

Unless the court directs a different time, the disclosures required by subdivision (a)(1) are to be made at or within 10 days after the meeting of the parties under subdivision (f). One of the purposes of this meeting is to refine the factual disputes with respect to which disclosures should be made under paragraphs (1)(A) and (1)(B), particularly if an answer has not been filed by a defendant, or, indeed, to afford the parties an opportunity to modify by stipulation the timing or scope of these obligations. The time of this meeting is generally left to the parties provided it is held at least 14 days before a scheduling conference is held or before a scheduling order is due under Rule 16(b). In cases in which no scheduling conference is held, this will mean that the meeting must ordinarily be held within 75 days after a defendant has first appeared in the case and hence that the initial disclosures would be due no later than 85 days after the first appearance of a defendant.

Before making its disclosures, a party has the obligation under subdivision (g)(1) to make a reasonable inquiry into the facts of the case. The rule does not demand an exhaustive investigation at this stage of the case, but one that is reasonable under the circumstances, focusing on the facts that are alleged with particularity in the pleadings. The type of investigation that can be expected at this point will vary based upon such factors as the number and complexity of the issues; the location, nature, number, and availability of potentially relevant witnesses and documents; the extent of past working relationships between the attorney and the client, particularly in handling related or similar litigation; and of course how long the party has to conduct an investigation, either before or after filing of the case. As provided in the last sentence of subdivision (a)(1), a party is not excused from the duty of disclosure merely because its investigation is incomplete. The party should make its initial disclosures based on the pleadings and the information then reasonably available to it. As its investigation continues and as the issues in the pleadings are clarified, it should supplement its disclosures as required by subdivision (e)(1). A party is not relieved from its obligation of disclosure merely because another party has not made its disclosures or has made an inadequate disclosure.

It will often be desirable, particularly if the claims made in the complaint are broadly stated, for the parties to have their Rule 26(f) meeting early in the case, perhaps before a defendant has answered the complaint or had time to conduct other than a cursory investigation. In such circumstances, in order to facilitate more meaningful and useful initial disclosures, they can and should stipulate to a period of more than 10 days after the meeting in which to make these disclosures, at least for defendants who had no advance notice of the potential litigation. A stipulation at an early meeting affording such a defendant at least 60 days after receiving the complaint in which to make its disclosures under subdivision (a)(1)—a period that is two weeks longer than the time formerly specified for responding to interrogatories served with a complaint—should be adequate and appropriate in most cases.

Paragraph (2). This paragraph imposes an additional duty to disclose information regarding expert testimony sufficiently in advance of trial that opposing parties have a reasonable opportunity to prepare for effective cross examination and perhaps arrange for expert testimony from other witnesses. Normally the court should prescribe a time for these disclosures in a scheduling order under Rule 16(b), and in most cases the party with the burden of proof on an issue should disclose its expert testimony on that issue before other parties are required to make their disclosures with respect to that issue. In the absence of such a direction, the disclosures are to be made by all parties at least 90 days before the trial date or the date by which the case is to be ready for trial, except that an additional 30 days is allowed (unless the court specifies another time) for disclosure of expert testimony to be used solely to contradict or rebut the testimony that may be presented by another party's expert. For a discussion of procedures that have been used to enhance the reliability of expert testimony, see M. Graham, *Expert Witness Testimony and the Federal Rules of Evidence: Insuring Adequate Assurance of Trustworthiness,* 1986 *U.Ill.L.Rev.* 90.

Paragraph (2)(B) requires that persons retained or specially employed to provide expert testimony, or whose duties as an employee of the party regularly involve the giving of expert testimony, must prepare a detailed and complete written report, stating the testimony the witness is expected to present during direct examination, together with the reasons therefor. The information disclosed under the former rule in answering interrogatories about the "substance" of expert testimony was frequently so sketchy and vague that it rarely dispensed with the need to depose the expert and often was even of little help in preparing for a deposition of the witness. Revised Rule 37(c)(1) provides an incentive for full disclosure; namely, that a party will not ordinarily be permitted to use on direct examination any expert testimony not so disclosed. Rule 26(a)(2)(B) does not preclude counsel from providing assistance to experts in preparing the reports, and indeed, with experts such as automobile mechanics, this assistance may be needed. Nevertheless, the report, which is intended to set forth the substance of the direct examination, should be written in a manner that reflects the testimony to be given by the witness and it must be signed by the witness.

The report is to disclose the data and other information considered by the expert and any exhibits or charts that summarize or support the expert's opinions. Given this obligation of disclosure, litigants should no longer be able to argue that materials furnished to their experts to be used in forming their opinions—whether or not ultimately relied upon by the expert—are privileged or otherwise protected from disclosure when such persons are testifying or being deposed.

Revised subdivision (b)(4)(A) authorizes the deposition of expert witnesses. Since depositions of experts required to prepare a written report may be taken only after the report has been served, the length of the deposition of such experts should be reduced, and in many cases the report may eliminate the need for a deposition. Revised subdivision (e)(1) requires disclosure of any material changes made in the opinions of an expert from whom a report is required, whether the changes are in the written report or in testimony given at a deposition.

For convenience, this rule and revised Rule 30 continue to use the term "expert" to refer to those persons who will testify under Rule 702 of the Federal Rules of Evidence with respect to scientific, technical, and other specialized matters. The requirement of a written report in paragraph (2)(B), however, applies only to those experts who are retained or specially employed to provide such testimony in the case or whose duties as an employee of a party regularly involve the giving of such testimony. A treating physician, for example, can be deposed or called to testify at trial without any requirement for a written report. By local rule, order, or written stipulation, the requirement of a written report may be waived for particular experts or imposed upon additional persons who will provide opinions under Rule 702.

Paragraph (3). This paragraph imposes an additional duty to disclose, without any request, information customarily needed in final preparation for trial. These disclosures are to be made in accordance with schedules adopted by the court under Rule 16(b) or by special order. If no such schedule is directed by the court, the disclosures are to be made at least 30 days before commencement of the trial. By its terms, rule 26(a)(3) does not require disclosure of evidence to be used solely for impeachment purposes; however, disclosure of such evidence—as well as other items relating to conduct of trial—may be required by local rule or a pretrial order.

Subparagraph (A) requires the parties to designate the persons whose testimony they may present as substantive evidence at trial, whether in person or by deposition. Those who will probably be called as witnesses should be listed separately from those who are not likely to be called but who are being listed in order to preserve the right to do so if needed because of developments during trial. Revised Rule 37(c)(1) provides that only persons so listed may be used at trial to present substantive evidence. This restriction does not apply unless the omission was "without substantial justification" and hence would not bar an unlisted witness if the need for such testimony is based upon developments during trial that could not reasonably have been anticipated—*e.g.,* a change of testimony.

Listing a witness does not obligate the party to secure the attendance of the person at trial, but should preclude the party from objecting if the person is called to testify by another party who did not list the person as a witness.

Subparagraph (B) requires the party to indicate which of these potential witnesses will be presented by deposition at trial. A party expecting to use at trial a deposition not recorded by stenographic means is required by revised Rule 32 to provide the court with a transcript of the pertinent portions of such depositions. This rule requires that copies of the transcript of a nonstenographic deposition be provided to other parties in advance of trial for verification, an obvious concern since counsel often utilize their own personnel to prepare transcripts from audio or video tapes. By order or local rule, the court may require that parties designate the particular portions of stenographic depositions to be used at trial.

Subparagraph (C) requires disclosure of exhibits, including summaries (whether to be offered in lieu of other documentary evidence or to be used as an aid in understanding such evidence), that may be offered as substantive evidence. The rule requires a separate listing of each such exhibit, though it should permit voluminous items of a similar or standardized character to be described by meaningful categories. For example, unless the court has otherwise directed, a series of vouchers might be shown collectively as a single exhibit with their starting and ending dates. As with witnesses, the exhibits that will probably be offered are to be listed separately from those which are unlikely to be offered but which are listed in order to preserve the right to do so if needed because of developments during trial. Under revised Rule 37(c)(1) the court can permit use of unlisted documents the need for which could not reasonably have been anticipated in advance of trial.

Upon receipt of these final pretrial disclosures, other parties have 14 days (unless a different time is specified by the court) to disclose any objections they wish to preserve to the usability of the deposition testimony or to the admissibility of the documentary evidence (other than under Rules 402 and 403 of the Federal Rules of Evidence). Similar provisions have become commonplace either in pretrial orders or by local rules, and significantly expedite the presentation of evidence at trial, as well as eliminate the need to have available witnesses to provide "foundation" testimony for most items of documentary evidence. The listing of a potential objection does not constitute the making of that objection or require the court to rule on the objection; rather, it preserves the right of the party to make the objection when and as appropriate during trial. The court may, however, elect to treat the listing as a motion "in limine" and rule upon the objections in advance of trial to the extent appropriate.

The time specified in the rule for the final pretrial disclosures is relatively close to the trial date. The objective is to eliminate the time and expense in making these disclosures of evidence and objections in those cases that settle shortly before trial, while affording a reasonable time for final preparation for trial in those cases that do not settle. In many cases, it will be desirable for the court in a scheduling or pretrial order to set an earlier time for disclosures of evidence and provide more time for disclosing potential objections.

Paragraph (4). This paragraph prescribes the form of disclosures. A signed written statement is required, reminding the parties and counsel of the solemnity of the obligations imposed; and the signature on the initial or pretrial disclosure is a certification under subdivision (g)(1) that it is complete and correct as of the time when made. Consistent with Rule 5(d), these disclosures are to be filed with the court unless otherwise directed. It is anticipated that many courts will direct that expert reports required under paragraph (2)(B) not be filed until needed in connection with a motion or for trial.

Paragraph (5). This paragraph is revised to take note of the availability of revised Rule 45 for inspection from non-parties of documents and premises without the need for a deposition.

Subdivision (b). This subdivision is revised in several respects. First, former paragraph (1) is subdivided into two paragraphs for ease of reference and to avoid renumbering of paragraphs (3) and (4). Textual changes are then made in new paragraph (2) to enable the court to keep tighter rein on the extent of discovery. The information explosion of recent decades has greatly increased both the potential cost of wide-ranging discovery and the potential for discovery to be used as an instrument for delay or oppression. Amendments to Rules 30, 31, and 33 place presumptive limits on the number of depositions and interrogatories, subject to leave of court to pursue additional discovery. The revisions in Rule 26(b)(2) are intended to provide the court with broader discretion to impose additional restrictions on the scope and extent of discovery and to authorize courts that develop case tracking systems based on the complexity of cases to increase or decrease by local rule the presumptive number of depositions and interrogatories allowed in particular types or classifications of cases. The revision also dispels any doubt as to the power of the court to impose limitations on the length of depositions under Rule 30 or on the number of requests for admission under Rule 36.

Second, former paragraph (2), relating to insurance, has been relocated as part of the required initial disclosures under subdivision (a)(1)(D), and revised to provide for disclosure of the policy itself.

Third, paragraph (4)(A) is revised to provide that experts who are expected to be witnesses will be subject to deposition prior to trial, conforming the norm stated in the rule to the actual practice followed in most courts, in which depositions of experts have become standard. Concerns regarding the expense of such depositions should be mitigated by the fact that the expert's fees for the deposition will ordinarily be borne by the party taking the deposition. The requirement under subdivision (a)(2)(B) of a complete and detailed report of the expected testimony of certain forensic experts may, moreover, eliminate the need for some such depositions or at least reduce the length of the depositions. Accordingly, the deposition of an expert required by subdivision (a)(2)(B) to provide a written report may be taken only after the report has been served.

Paragraph (4)(C), bearing on compensation of experts, is revised to take account of the changes in paragraph (4)(A).

Paragraph (5) is a new provision. A party must notify other parties if it is withholding materials otherwise subject to disclosure under the rule or pursuant to a discovery request because it is asserting a claim of privilege or work product protection. To withhold materials without such notice is contrary to the rule, subjects the party to sanctions under Rule 37(b)(2), and may be viewed as a waiver of the privilege or protection.

The party must also provide sufficient information to enable other parties to evaluate the applicability of the claimed privilege or protection. Although the person from whom the discovery is sought decides whether to claim a privilege or protection, the court ultimately decides whether, if this claim is challenged, the privilege or protection applies. Providing information pertinent to the applicability of the privilege or protection should reduce the need for in camera examination of the documents.

The rule does not attempt to define for each case what information must be provided when a party asserts a claim of privilege or work product protection. Details concerning time, persons, general subject matter, etc., may be appropriate if only a few items are withheld, but may be unduly burdensome when voluminous documents are claimed to be privileged or protected, particularly if the items can be described by categories. A party can seek relief through a protective order under subdivision (c) if compliance with the requirement for providing this information would be an unreasonable burden. In rare circumstances some of the pertinent information affecting applicability of the claim, such as the identity of the client, may itself be privileged; the rule provides that such information need not be disclosed.

The obligation to provide pertinent information concerning withheld privileged materials applies only to items "otherwise discoverable." If a broad discovery request is made—for example, for all documents of a particular type during a twenty year period—and the responding party believes in good faith that production of documents for more than the past three years would be unduly burdensome, it should make its objection to the breadth of the request and, with respect to the documents generated in that three year period, produce the unprivileged documents and describe those withheld under the claim of privilege. If the court later rules that documents for a seven year period are properly discoverable, the documents for the additional four years should then be either produced (if not privileged) or described (if claimed to be privileged).

Subdivision (c). The revision requires that before filing a motion for a protective order the movant must confer—either in person or by telephone—with the other affected parties in a good faith effort to resolve the discovery dispute without the need for court intervention. If the movant is unable to get opposing parties even to discuss the matter, the efforts in attempting to arrange such a conference should be indicated in the certificate.

Subdivision (d). This subdivision is revised to provide that formal discovery—as distinguished from interviews of potential witnesses and other informal discovery—not commence until the parties have met and conferred as required by subdivision (f). Discovery can begin earlier if authorized under Rule 30(a)(2)(C) (deposition of person about to leave the country) or by local rule, order, or stipulation. This will be appropriate in some cases, such as those involving requests for a preliminary injunction or motions challenging personal jurisdiction. If a local rule exempts any types of cases in which discovery may be needed from the requirement of a meeting under Rule 26(f), it should specify when discovery may commence in those cases.

The meeting of counsel is to take place as soon as practicable and in any event at least 14 days before the date of the scheduling conference under Rule 16(b) or the date a scheduling order is due under Rule 16(b). The court can assure that discovery is not unduly delayed either by entering a special order or by setting the case for a scheduling conference.

Subdivision (e). This subdivision is revised to provide that the requirement for supplementation applies to all disclosures required by subdivisions (a)(1)–(3). Like the former rule, the duty, while imposed on a "party," applies whether the corrective information is learned by the client or by the attorney. Supplementations need not be made as each new item of information is learned but should be made at appropriate intervals during the discovery period, and with special promptness as the trial date approaches. It may be useful for the scheduling order to specify the time or times when supplementations should be made.

The revision also clarifies that the obligation to supplement responses to formal discovery requests applies to interrogatories, requests for production, and requests for admissions, but not ordinarily to deposition testimony. However, with respect to experts from whom a written report is required under subdivision (a)(2)(B), changes in the opinions expressed by the expert whether in the report or at a subsequent deposition are subject to a duty of supplemental disclosure under subdivision (e)(1).

The obligation to supplement disclosures and discovery responses applies whenever a party learns that its prior disclosures or responses are in some material respect incomplete or incorrect. There is, however, no obligation to provide supplemental or corrective information that has been otherwise made known to the parties in writing or during the discovery process, as when a witness not previously disclosed is identified during the taking of a deposition or when an expert during a deposition corrects information contained in an earlier report.

Subdivision (f). This subdivision was added in 1980 to provide a party threatened with abusive discovery with a special means for obtaining judicial intervention other than through discrete motions under Rules 26(c) and 37(a). The amendment envisioned a two-step process: first, the parties would attempt to frame a mutually agreeable plan; second, the court would hold a "discovery conference" and then enter an order establishing a schedule and limitations for the conduct of discovery. It was contemplated that the procedure, an elective one triggered on request of a party, would be used in special cases rather than as a routine matter. As expected, the device has been used only sparingly in most courts, and judicial controls over the discovery process have ordinarily been imposed through scheduling orders under Rule 16(b) or through rulings on discovery motions.

The provisions relating to a conference with the court are removed from subdivision (f). This change does not signal any lessening of the importance of judicial supervision. Indeed, there is a greater need for early judicial involvement to consider the scope and timing of the disclosure requirements of Rule 26(a) and the presumptive limits on discovery imposed under these rules or by local rules. Rather, the change is made because the provisions addressing the use of conferences with the court to control discovery are more properly included in Rule 16, which is being revised to highlight the court's powers regarding the discovery process.

The desirability of some judicial control of discovery can hardly be doubted. Rule 16, as revised, requires that the court set a time for completion of discovery and authorizes various other orders affecting the scope, timing, and extent of discovery and disclosures. Before entering such orders, the court should consider the views of the parties, preferably by means of a conference, but at the least through written submissions. Moreover, it is desirable that the parties' proposals regarding discovery be developed through a process where they meet in person, informally explore the nature and basis of the issues, and discuss how discovery can be conducted most efficiently and economically.

As noted above, former subdivision (f) envisioned the development of proposed discovery plans as an optional procedure to be used in relatively few cases. The revised rule directs that in all cases not exempted by local rule or special order the litigants must meet in person and plan for discovery. Following this meeting, the parties submit to the court their proposals for a discovery plan and can begin formal discovery. Their report will assist the court in seeing that the timing and scope of disclosures under revised Rule 26(a) and the limitations on the extent of discovery under these rules and local rules are tailored to the circumstances of the particular case.

To assure that the court has the litigants' proposals before deciding on a scheduling order and that the commencement of discovery is not delayed unduly, the rule provides that the meeting of the parties take place as soon as practicable and in any event at least 14 days before a scheduling conference is held or before a scheduling order is due under Rule 16(b). (Rule 16(b) requires that a scheduling order be entered within 90 days after the first appearance of a defendant or, if earlier, within 120 days after the complaint has been served on any defendant.) The obligation to participate in the planning process is imposed on all parties that have appeared in the case, including defendants who, because of a pending Rule 12 motion, may not have yet filed an answer in the case. Each such party should attend the meeting, either through one of its attorneys or in person if unrepresented. If more parties are joined or appear after the initial meeting, an additional meeting may be desirable.

Subdivision (f) describes certain matters that should be accomplished at the meeting and included in the proposed discovery plan. This listing does not exclude consideration of other subjects, such as the time when any dispositive motions should be filed and when the case should be ready for trial.

The parties are directed under subdivision (a)(1) to make the disclosures required by that subdivision at or within 10 days after this meeting. In many cases the parties should use the meeting to exchange, discuss, and clarify their respective disclosures. In other cases, it may be more useful if the disclosures are delayed until after the parties have discussed at the meeting the claims and defenses in order to define the issues with respect to which the initial disclosures should be made. As discussed in the Notes to subdivision (a)(1), the parties may also need to consider whether a stipulation extending this 10-day period would be appropriate, as when a defendant would otherwise have less than 60 days after being served in which to make its initial disclosure. The parties should also discuss at the meeting what additional information, although not subject to the disclosure requirements, can be made available informally without the necessity for formal discovery requests.

The report is to be submitted to the court within 10 days after the meeting and should not be difficult to prepare. In most cases counsel should be able to agree that one of them will be responsible for its preparation and submission to the court. Form 35 has been added in the Appendix to the Rules, both to illustrate the type of report that is contemplated and to serve as a checklist for the meeting.

The litigants are expected to attempt in good faith to agree on the contents of the proposed discovery plan. If they cannot agree on all aspects of the plan, their report to the court should indicate the competing proposals of the parties on those items, as well as the matters on which they agree. Unfortunately, there may be cases in which, because of disagreements about time or place or for other reasons, the meeting is not attended by all parties or, indeed, no meeting takes place. In such situations, the report—or reports—should describe the circumstances and the court may need to consider sanctions under Rule 37(g).

By local rule or special order, the court can exempt particular cases or types of cases from the meet-and-confer requirement of subdivision (f). In general this should include any types of cases which are exempted by local rule from the requirement for a scheduling order under Rule 16(b), such as cases in which there will be no discovery (*e.g.,* bankruptcy appeals and reviews of social security determinations). In addition, the court may want to exempt cases in which discovery is rarely needed (*e.g.,* government collection cases and proceedings to enforce administrative summonses) or in which a meeting of the parties might be impracticable (*e.g.,* actions by unrepresented prisoners). Note that if a court exempts from the requirements for a meeting any types of cases in which discovery may be needed, it should indicate when discovery may commence in those cases.

Subdivision (g). Paragraph (1) is added to require signatures on disclosures, a requirement that parallels the provisions of paragraph (2) with respect to discovery requests, responses, and objections. The provisions of paragraph (3) have been modified to be consistent with Rules 37(a)(4) and 37(c)(1); in combination, these rules establish sanctions for violation of the rules regarding disclosures and discovery matters. Amended Rule 11 no longer applies to such violations.

2000 AMENDMENT

Purposes of amendments. The Rule 26(a)(1) initial disclosure provisions are amended to establish a nationally uniform practice. The scope of the disclosure obligation is narrowed to cover only information that the disclosing party may use to support its position. In addition, the rule exempts specified categories of proceedings from initial disclosure, and permits a party who contends that disclosure is not appropriate in the circumstances of the case to present its objections to the court, which must then determine whether disclosure should be made. Related changes are made in Rules 26(d) and (f).

The initial disclosure requirements added by the 1993 amendments permitted local rules directing that disclosure would not be required or altering its operation. The inclusion of the "opt out" provision reflected the strong opposition to initial disclosure felt in some districts, and permitted experimentation with differing disclosure rules in those districts that were favorable to disclosure. The local option also recognized that—partly in response to the first publication in 1991 of a proposed disclosure rule—many districts had adopted a variety of disclosure programs under the aegis of the Civil Justice Reform Act. It was hoped that developing experience under a variety of disclosure systems would support eventual refinement of a uniform national disclosure practice. In addition, there was hope that local experience could identify categories of actions in which disclosure is not useful.

A striking array of local regimes in fact emerged for disclosure and related features introduced in 1993. *See* D. Stienstra, *Implementation of Disclosure in United States District Courts, With Specific Attention to Courts' Responses to Selected Amendments to Federal Rule of Civil Procedure 26* (Federal Judicial Center, March 30, 1998) (describing and categorizing local regimes). In its final report to Congress on the CJRA experience, the Judicial Conference recommended reexamination of the need for national uniformity, particularly in regard to initial disclosure. Judicial Conference, *Alternative Proposals for Reduction of Cost and Delay: Assessment of Principles, Guidelines and Techniques,* 175 F.R.D. 62, 98 (1997).

At the Committee's request, the Federal Judicial Center undertook a survey in 1997 to develop information on current disclosure and discovery practices. *See* T. Willging, J. Shapard, D. Stienstra & D. Miletich, *Discovery and Disclosure Practice, Problems, and Proposals for Change* (Federal Judicial Center, 1997). In addition, the Committee convened two conferences on discovery involving lawyers from around the country and received reports and recommendations on possible discovery amendments from a number of bar groups. Papers and other proceedings from the second conference are published in 39 Boston Col. L. Rev. 517–840 (1998).

The Committee has discerned widespread support for national uniformity. Many lawyers have experienced difficulty in coping with divergent disclosure and other practices as they move from one district to another. Lawyers surveyed by the Federal Judicial Center ranked adoption of a uniform national disclosure rule second among proposed rule changes (behind increased availability of judges to resolve discovery disputes) as a means to reduce litigation expenses without interfering with fair outcomes. *Discovery and Disclosure Practice, supra*, at 44 to 45. National uniformity is also a central purpose of the Rules Enabling Act of 1934, as amended, 28 U.S.C. §§ 2072 to 2077.

These amendments restore national uniformity to disclosure practice. Uniformity is also restored to other aspects of discovery by deleting most of the provisions authorizing local rules that vary the number of permitted discovery events or the length of depositions. Local rule options are also deleted from Rules 26(d) and (f).

Subdivision(a)(1). The amendments remove the authority to alter or opt out of the national disclosure requirements by local rule, invalidating not only formal local rules but also informal "standing" orders of an individual judge or court that purport to create exemptions from—or limit or expand—the disclosure provided under the national rule. *See* Rule 83. Case-specific orders remain proper, however, and are expressly required if a party objects that initial disclosure is not appropriate in the circumstances of the action. Specified categories of proceedings are excluded from initial disclosure under subdivision (a)(1)(E). In addition, the parties can stipulate to forgo disclosure, as was true before. But even in a case excluded by subdivision (a)(1)(E) or in which the parties stipulate to bypass disclosure, the court can order exchange of similar information in managing the action under Rule 16.

The initial disclosure obligation of subdivisions (a)(1)(A) and (B) has been narrowed to identification of witnesses and documents that the disclosing party may use to support its claims or defenses. "Use" includes any use at a pretrial conference, to support a motion, or at trial. The disclosure obligation is also triggered by intended use in discovery, apart from use to respond to a discovery request; use of a document to question a witness during a deposition is a common example. The disclosure obligation attaches both to witnesses and documents a party intends to use and also to witnesses and to documents the party intends to use if—in the language of Rule 26(a)(3)—"the need arises."

A party is no longer obligated to disclose witnesses or documents, whether favorable or unfavorable, that it does not intend to use. The obligation to disclose information the party may use connects directly to the exclusion sanction of Rule 37(c)(1). Because the disclosure obligation is limited to material that the party may use, it is no longer tied to particularized allegations in the pleadings. Subdivision (e)(1), which is unchanged, requires supplementation if information later acquired would have been subject to the disclosure requirement. As case preparation continues, a party must supplement its disclosures when it determines that it may use a witness or document that it did not previously intend to use.

The disclosure obligation applies to "claims and defenses," and therefore requires a party to disclose information it may use to support its denial or rebuttal of the allegations, claim, or defense of another party. It thereby bolsters the requirements of Rule 11(b)(4), which authorizes denials "warranted on the evidence," and disclosure should include the identity of any witness or document that the disclosing party may use to support such denials.

Subdivision (a)(3) presently excuses pretrial disclosure of information solely for impeachment. Impeachment information is similarly excluded from the initial disclosure requirement.

Subdivisions (a)(1)(C) and (D) are not changed. Should a case be exempted from initial disclosure by Rule 26(a)(1)(E) or by agreement or order, the insurance information described by subparagraph (D) should be subject to discovery, as it would have been under the principles of former Rule 26(b)(2), which was added in 1970 and deleted in 1993 as redundant in light of the new initial disclosure obligation.

New subdivision (a)(1)(E) excludes eight specified categories of proceedings from initial disclosure. The objective of this listing is to identify cases in which there is likely to be little or no discovery, or in which initial disclosure appears unlikely to contribute to the effective development of the case. The list was developed after a review of the categories excluded by local rules in various districts from the operation of Rule 16(b) and the conference requirements of subdivision (f). Subdivision (a)(1)(E) refers to categories of "proceedings" rather than categories of "actions" because some might not properly be labeled "actions." Case designations made by the parties or the clerk's office at the time of filing do not control application of the exemptions. The descriptions in the rule are generic and are intended to be administered by the parties—and, when needed, the courts—with the flexibility needed to adapt to gradual evolution in the types of proceedings that fall within these general categories. The exclusion of an action for review on an administrative record, for example, is intended to reach a proceeding that is framed as an "appeal" based solely on an administrative record. The exclusion should not apply to a proceeding in a form that commonly permits admission of new evidence to supplement the record. Item (vii), excluding a proceeding ancillary to proceedings in other courts, does not refer to bankruptcy proceedings; application of the Civil Rules to bankruptcy proceedings is determined by the Bankruptcy Rules.

Subdivision (a)(1)(E) is likely to exempt a substantial proportion of the cases in most districts from the initial disclosure requirement. Based on 1996 and 1997 case filing statistics, Federal Judicial Center staff estimate that, nationwide, these categories total approximately one-third of all civil filings.

The categories of proceedings listed in subdivision (a)(1)(E) are also exempted from the subdivision (f) conference requirement and from the subdivision (d) moratorium on discovery. Although there is no restriction on commencement of discovery in these cases, it is not expected that this opportunity will often lead to abuse since there is likely to be little or no discovery in most such cases. Should a defendant need more time to respond to discovery requests filed at the beginning of an exempted action, it can seek relief by motion under Rule 26(c) if the plaintiff is unwilling to defer the due date by agreement.

Subdivision (a)(1)(E)'s enumeration of exempt categories is exclusive. Although a case-specific order can alter or excuse initial disclosure, local rules or "standing" orders that purport to create general exemptions are invalid. *See* Rule 83.

The time for initial disclosure is extended to 14 days after the subdivision (f) conference unless the court orders otherwise. This change is integrated with corresponding changes requiring that the subdivision (f) conference be held 21 days before the Rule 16(b) scheduling conference or scheduling order, and that the report on the subdivision (f) conference be submitted to the court 14 days after the meeting. These changes provide a more orderly opportunity for the parties to review the disclosures, and for the court to consider the report. In many instances, the subdivision (f) conference and the effective preparation of the case would benefit from disclosure before the conference, and earlier disclosure is encouraged.

The presumptive disclosure date does not apply if a party objects to initial disclosure during the subdivision (f) conference and states its objection in the subdivision (f) discovery plan. The right to object to initial disclosure is not intended to afford parties an opportunity to "opt out" of disclosure unilaterally. It does provide an opportunity for an objecting party to present to the court its position that disclosure would be "inappropriate in the circumstances of the action." Making the objection permits the objecting party to present the question to the judge before any party is required to make disclosure. The court must then rule on the objection and determine what disclosures—if any—should be made. Ordinarily, this determination would be included in the Rule 16(b) scheduling order, but the court could handle the matter in a different fashion. Even when circumstances warrant suspending some disclosure obligations, others—such as the damages and insurance information called for by subdivisions (a)(1)(C) and (D)—may continue to be appropriate.

The presumptive disclosure date is also inapplicable to a party who is "first served or otherwise joined" after the subdivision (f) conference. This phrase refers to the date of service of a claim on a party in a defensive posture (such as a defendant or third-party defendant), and the date of joinder of a party added as a claimant or an intervenor. Absent court order or stipulation, a new party has 30 days in which to make its initial disclosures. But it is expected that later-added parties will ordinarily be treated the same as the original parties when the original parties have stipulated to forgo initial disclosure, or the court has ordered disclosure in a modified form.

Subdivision (a)(3). The amendment to Rule 5(d) forbids filing disclosures under subdivisions (a)(1) and (a)(2) until they are used in the proceeding, and this change is reflected in an amendment to subdivision (a)(4). Disclosures under subdivision (a)(3), however, may be important to the court in connection with the final pretrial conference or otherwise in preparing for trial. The requirement that objections to certain matters be filed points up the court's need to be provided with these materials. Accordingly, the requirement that subdivision (a)(3) materials be filed has been moved from subdivision (a)(4) to subdivision (a)(3), and it has also been made clear that they—and any objections—should be filed "promptly."

Subdivision (a)(4). The filing requirement has been removed from this subdivision. Rule 5(d) has been amended to provide that disclosures under subdivisions (a)(1) and (a)(2) must not be filed until used in the proceeding. Subdivision (a)(3) has been amended to require that the disclosures it directs, and objections to them, be filed promptly. Subdivision (a)(4) continues to require that all disclosures under subdivisions (a)(1), (a)(2), and (a)(3) be in writing, signed, and served.

"Shall" is replaced by "must" under the program to conform amended rules to current style conventions when there is no ambiguity.

GAP Report

The Advisory Committee recommends that the amendments to Rules 26(a)(1)(A) and (B) be changed so that initial disclosure applies to information the disclosing party "may use to support" its claims or defenses. It also recommends changes in the Committee Note to explain that disclosure requirement. In addition, it recommends inclusion in the Note of further explanatory matter regarding the exclusion from initial disclosure provided in new Rule 26(a)(1)(E) for actions for review on an administrative record and the impact of these exclusions on bankruptcy proceedings. Minor wording improvements in the Note are also proposed.

Subdivision (b)(1). In 1978, the Committee published for comment a proposed amendment, suggested by the Section of Litigation of the American Bar Association, to refine the scope of discovery by deleting the "subject matter" language. This proposal was withdrawn, and the Committee has since then made other changes in the discovery rules to address concerns about overbroad discovery. Concerns about costs and delay of discovery have persisted nonetheless, and other bar groups have repeatedly renewed similar proposals for amendment to this subdivision to delete the "subject matter" language. Nearly one-third of the lawyers surveyed in 1997 by the Federal Judicial Center endorsed narrowing the scope of discovery as a means of reducing litigation expense without interfering with fair case resolutions. *Discovery and Disclosure Practice, supra*, at 44 to 45 (1997). The Committee has heard that in some instances, particularly cases involving large quantities of discovery, parties seek to justify discovery requests that sweep far beyond the claims and defenses of the parties on the ground that they nevertheless have a bearing on the "subject matter" involved in the action.

The amendments proposed for subdivision (b)(1) include one element of these earlier proposals but also differ from these proposals in significant ways. The similarity is that the amendments describe the scope of party- controlled discovery in terms of matter relevant to the claim or defense of any party. The court, however, retains authority to order discovery of any matter relevant to the subject matter involved in the action for good cause. The amendment is designed to involve the court more actively in regulating the breadth of sweeping or contentious discovery. The Committee has been informed repeatedly by lawyers that involvement of the court in managing discovery is an important method of controlling problems of inappropriately broad discovery. Increasing the availability of judicial officers to resolve discovery disputes and increasing court management of discovery were both strongly endorsed by the attorneys surveyed by the Federal Judicial Center. *See Discovery and Disclosure Practice, supra*, at 44. Under the amended provisions, if there is an objection that discovery goes beyond material relevant to the parties' claims or defenses, the court would become involved to determine whether the discovery is relevant to the claims or defenses and, if not, whether good cause exists for authorizing it so long as it is relevant to the subject matter of the action. The good-cause standard warranting broader discovery is meant to be flexible.

The Committee intends that the parties and the court focus on the actual claims and defenses involved in the action. The dividing line between information relevant to the claims and defenses and that relevant only to the subject matter of the action cannot be defined with precision. A variety of types of information not directly pertinent to the incident in suit could be relevant to the claims or defenses raised in a given action. For example, other incidents of the same type, or involving the same product, could be properly discoverable under the revised standard. Information about organizational arrangements or filing systems of a party could be discoverable if likely to yield or lead to the discovery of admissible information. Similarly, information that could be used to impeach a likely witness, although not otherwise relevant to the claims or defenses, might be properly discoverable. In each instance, the determination whether such information is discoverable because it is relevant to the claims or defenses depends on the circumstances of the pending action.

The rule change signals to the court that it has the authority to confine discovery to the claims and defenses asserted in the pleadings, and signals to the parties that they have no entitlement to discovery to develop new claims or defenses that are not already identified in the pleadings. In general, it is hoped that reasonable lawyers can cooperate to manage discovery without the need for judicial intervention. When judicial intervention is invoked, the actual scope of discovery should be determined according to the reasonable needs of the action. The court may permit broader discovery in a particular case depending on the circumstances of the case, the nature of the claims and defenses, and the scope of the discovery requested.

The amendments also modify the provision regarding discovery of information not admissible in evidence. As added in 1946, this sentence was designed to make clear that otherwise relevant material could not be withheld because it was hearsay or otherwise inadmissible. The Committee was concerned that the "reasonably calculated to lead to the discovery of admissible evidence" standard set forth in this sentence might swallow any other limitation on the scope of discovery. Accordingly, this sentence has been amended to clarify that information must be relevant to be discoverable, even though inadmissible, and that discovery of such material is permitted if reasonably calculated to lead to the discovery of admissible evidence. As used here, "relevant" means within the scope of discovery as defined in this subdivision, and it would include information relevant to the subject matter involved in the action if the court has ordered discovery to that limit based on a showing of good cause.

Finally, a sentence has been added calling attention to the limitations of subdivision (b)(2)(i), (ii), and (iii). These limitations apply to discovery that is otherwise within the scope of subdivision (b)(1). The Committee has been told repeatedly that courts have not implemented these limitations with the vigor that was contemplated. *See 8 Federal Practice & Procedure* § 2008.1 at 121. This otherwise redundant cross-reference has been added to emphasize the need for active judicial use of subdivision (b)(2) to control excessive discovery. *Cf. Crawford-El v. Britton*, 118 S. Ct. 1584, 1597 (1998) (quoting Rule 26(b)(2) (iii) and stating that "Rule 26 vests the trial judge with broad discretion to tailor discovery narrowly").

GAP Report

The Advisory Committee recommends changing the rule to authorize the court to expand discovery to any "matter"—not "information"—relevant to the subject matter involved in the action. In addition, it recommends additional clarifying material in the Committee Note about the impact of the change on some commonly disputed discovery topics, the relationship between cost-bearing under Rule 26(b)(2) and expansion of the scope of discovery on a showing of good cause, and the meaning of "relevant" in the revision to the last sentence of current subdivision (b)(1). In addition, some minor clarifications of language changes have been proposed for the Committee Note.

Subdivision (b)(2). Rules 30, 31, and 33 establish presumptive national limits on the numbers of depositions and interrogatories. New Rule 30(d)(2) establishes a presumptive limit on the length of depositions. Subdivision (b)(2) is amended to remove the previous permission for local rules that establish different presumptive limits on these discovery activities. There is no reason to believe that unique circumstances justify varying these nationally-applicable presumptive limits in certain districts. The limits can be modified by court order or agreement in an individual action, but "standing" orders imposing different presumptive limits are not authorized. Because there is no national rule limiting the number of Rule 36 requests for admissions, the rule continues to authorize local rules that impose numerical limits on them. This change is not intended to interfere with differentiated case management in districts that use this technique by case-specific order as part of their Rule 16 process.

Subdivision (d). The amendments remove the prior authority to exempt cases by local rule from the moratorium on discovery before the subdivision (f) conference, but the categories of proceedings exempted from initial disclosure under subdivision (a)(1)(E) are excluded from subdivision (d). The parties may agree to disregard the moratorium where it applies, and the court may so order in a case, but "standing" orders altering the moratorium are not authorized.

Subdivision (f). As in subdivision (d), the amendments remove the prior authority to exempt cases by local rule from the conference requirement. The Committee has been informed that the addition of the conference was one of the most successful changes made in the 1993 amendments, and it therefore has determined to apply the conference requirement nationwide. The categories of proceedings exempted from initial disclosure under subdivision (a)(1)(E) are exempted from the conference requirement for the reasons that warrant exclusion from initial disclosure. The court may order that the conference need not occur in a case where otherwise required, or that it occur in a case otherwise exempted by subdivision (a)(1)(E). "Standing" orders altering the conference requirement for categories of cases are not authorized.

The rule is amended to require only a "conference" of the parties, rather than a "meeting." There are important benefits to face-to-face discussion of the topics to be covered in the conference, and those benefits may be lost if other means of conferring were routinely used when face-to- face meetings would not impose burdens. Nevertheless, geographic conditions in some districts may exact costs far out of proportion to these benefits. The amendment allows the court by case-specific order to require a face-to- face meeting, but "standing" orders so requiring are not authorized.

As noted concerning the amendments to subdivision (a)(1), the time for the conference has been changed to at least 21 days before the Rule 16 scheduling conference, and the time for the report is changed to no more than 14 days after the Rule 26(f) conference. This should ensure that the court will have the report well in advance of the scheduling conference or the entry of the scheduling order.

Since Rule 16 was amended in 1983 to mandate some case management activities in all courts, it has included deadlines for Completing these tasks to ensure that all courts do so within a reasonable time. Rule 26(f) was fit into this scheme when it was adopted in 1993. It was never intended, however, that the national requirements that certain activities be completed by a certain time should delay case management in districts that move much faster than the national rules direct, and the rule is therefore amended to permit such a court to adopt a local rule that shortens the period specified for the completion of these tasks.

"Shall" is replaced by "must," "does," or an active verb under the program to conform amended rules to current style conventions when there is no ambiguity.

GAP Report

The Advisory Committee recommends adding a sentence to the published amendments to Rule 26(f) authorizing local rules shortening the time between the attorney conference and the court's action under Rule 16(b), and addition to the Committee Note of explanatory material about this change to the rule. This addition can be made without republication in response to public comments.

2006 AMENDMENT

Subdivision (a). Rule 26(a)(1)(B) is amended to parallel Rule 34(a) by recognizing that a party must disclose electronically stored information as well as documents that it may use to support its claims or defenses. The term "electronically stored information" has the same broad meaning in Rule 26(a)(1) as in Rule 34(a). This amendment is consistent with the 1993 addition of Rule 26(a)(1)(B). The term "data compilations" is deleted as unnecessary because it is a subset of both documents and electronically stored information.

Subdivision (a)(1)(E). Civil forfeiture actions are added to the list of exemptions from Rule 26(a)(1) disclosure requirements. These actions are governed by new Supplemental Rule G. Disclosure is not likely to be useful.

Subdivision (b)(2). The amendment to Rule 26(b)(2) is designed to address issues raised by difficulties in locating, retrieving, and providing discovery of some electronically stored information. Electronic storage systems often make it easier to locate and retrieve information. These advantages are properly taken into account in determining the reasonable scope of discovery in a particular case. But some sources of electronically stored information can be accessed only with substantial burden and cost. In a particular case, these burdens and costs may make the information on such sources not reasonably accessible.

It is not possible to define in a rule the different types of technological features that may affect the burdens and costs of accessing electronically stored information. Information systems are designed to provide ready access to information used in regular ongoing activities. They also may be designed so as to provide ready access to information that is not regularly used. But a system may retain information on sources that are accessible only by incurring substantial burdens or costs. Subparagraph (B) is added to regulate discovery from such sources.

Under this rule, a responding party should produce electronically stored information that is relevant, not privileged, and reasonably accessible, subject to the (b)(2)(C) limitations that apply to all discovery. The responding party must also identify, by category or type, the sources containing potentially responsive information that it is neither searching nor producing. The identification should, to the extent possible, provide enough detail to enable the requesting party to evaluate the burdens and costs of providing the discovery and the likelihood of finding responsive information on the identified sources.

A party's identification of sources of electronically stored information as not reasonably accessible does not relieve the party of its common-law or statutory duties to preserve evidence. Whether a responding party is required to preserve unsearched sources of potentially responsive information that it believes are not reasonably accessible depends on the circumstances of each case. It is often useful for the parties to discuss this issue early in discovery.

The volume of—and the ability to search—much electronically stored information means that in many cases the responding party will be able to produce information from reasonably accessible sources that will fully satisfy the parties' discovery needs. In many circumstances the requesting party should obtain and evaluate the information from such sources before insisting that the responding party search and produce information contained on sources that are not reasonably accessible. If the requesting party continues to seek discovery of information from sources identified as not reasonably accessible, the parties should discuss the burdens and costs of accessing and retrieving the information, the needs that may establish good cause for requiring all or part of the requested discovery even if the information sought is not reasonably accessible, and conditions on obtaining and producing the information that may be appropriate.

If the parties cannot agree whether, or on what terms, sources identified as not reasonably accessible should be searched and discoverable information produced, the issue may be raised either by a motion to compel discovery or by a motion for a protective order. The parties must confer before bringing either motion. If the parties do not resolve the issue and the court must decide, the responding party must show that the identified sources of information are not reasonably accessible because of undue burden or cost. The requesting party may need discovery to test this assertion. Such discovery might take the form of requiring the responding party to conduct a sampling of information contained on the sources identified as not reasonably accessible; allowing some form of inspection of such sources; or taking depositions of witnesses knowledgeable about the responding party's information systems.

Once it is shown that a source of electronically stored information is not reasonably accessible, the requesting party may still obtain discovery by showing good cause, considering the limitations of Rule 26(b)(2)(C) that balance the costs and potential benefits of discovery. The decision whether to require a responding party to search for and produce information that is not reasonably accessible depends not only on the burdens and costs of doing so, but also on whether those burdens and costs can be justified in the circumstances of the case. Appropriate considerations may include: (1) the specificity of the discovery request; (2) the quantity of information available from other and more easily accessed sources; (3) the failure to produce relevant information that seems likely to have existed but is no longer available on more easily accessed sources; (4) the likelihood of finding relevant, responsive information that cannot be obtained from other, more easily accessed sources; (5) predictions as to the importance and usefulness of the further information; (6) the importance of the issues at stake in the litigation; and (7) the parties' resources.

The responding party has the burden as to one aspect of the inquiry—whether the identified sources are not reasonably accessible in light of the burdens and costs required to search for, retrieve, and produce whatever responsive information may be found. The requesting party has the burden of showing that its need for the discovery outweighs the burdens and costs of locating, retrieving, and producing the information. In some cases, the court will be able to determine whether the identified sources are not reasonably accessible and whether the requesting party has shown good cause for some or all of the discovery, consistent with the limitations of Rule 26(b)(2)(C), through a single proceeding or presentation. The good-cause determination, however, may be complicated because the court and parties may know little about what information the sources identified as not reasonably accessible might contain, whether it is relevant, or how valuable it may be to the litigation. In such cases, the parties may need some focused discovery, which may include sampling of the sources, to learn more about what burdens and costs are involved in accessing the information, what the information consists of, and how valuable it is for the litigation in light of information that can be obtained by exhausting other opportunities for discovery.

The good-cause inquiry and consideration of the Rule 26(b)(2)(C) limitations are coupled with the authority to set conditions for discovery. The conditions may take the form of limits on the amount, type, or sources of information required to be accessed and produced. The conditions may also include payment by the requesting party of part or all of the reasonable costs of obtaining information from sources that are not reasonably accessible. A requesting party's willingness to share or bear the access costs may be weighed by the court in determining whether there is good cause. But the producing party's burdens in reviewing the information for relevance and privilege may weigh against permitting the requested discovery.

The limitations of Rule 26(b)(2)(C) continue to apply to all discovery of electronically stored information, including that stored on reasonably accessible electronic sources.

Subdivision (b)(5). The Committee has repeatedly been advised that the risk of privilege waiver, and the work necessary to avoid it, add to the costs and delay of discovery. When the review is of electronically stored information, the risk of waiver, and the time and effort required to avoid it, can increase substantially because of the volume of electronically stored information and the difficulty in ensuring that all information to be produced has in fact been reviewed. Rule 26(b)(5)(A) provides a procedure for a party that has withheld information on the basis of privilege or protection as trial-preparation material to make the claim so that the requesting party can decide whether to contest the claim and the court can resolve the dispute. Rule 26(b)(5)(B) is added to provide a procedure for a party to assert a claim of privilege or trial-preparation material protection after information is produced in discovery in the action and, if the claim is contested, permit any party that received the information to present the matter to the court for resolution.

Rule 26(b)(5)(B) does not address whether the privilege or protection that is asserted after production was waived by the production. The courts have developed principles to determine whether, and under what circumstances, waiver results from inadvertent production of privileged or protected information. Rule 26(b)(5)(B) provides a procedure for presenting and addressing these issues. Rule 26(b)(5)(B) works in tandem with Rule 26(f), which is amended to direct the parties to discuss privilege issues in preparing their discovery plan, and which, with amended Rule 16(b), allows the parties to ask the court to include in an order any agreements the parties reach regarding issues of privilege or trial-preparation material protection. Agreements reached under Rule 26(f)(4) and orders including such agreements entered under Rule 16(b)(6) may be considered when a court determines whether a waiver has occurred. Such agreements and orders ordinarily control if they adopt procedures different from those in Rule 26(b)(5)(B).

A party asserting a claim of privilege or protection after production must give notice to the receiving party. That notice should be in writing unless the circumstances preclude it. Such circumstances could include the assertion of the claim during a deposition. The notice should be as specific as possible in identifying the information and stating the basis for the claim. Because the receiving party must decide whether to challenge the claim and may sequester the information and submit it to the court for a ruling on whether the claimed privilege or protection applies and whether it has been waived, the notice should be sufficiently detailed so as to enable the receiving party and the court to understand the basis for the claim and to determine whether waiver has occurred. Courts will continue to examine whether a claim of privilege or protection was made at a reasonable time when delay is part of the waiver determination under the governing law.

After receiving notice, each party that received the information must promptly return, sequester, or destroy the information and any copies it has. The option of sequestering or destroying the information is included in part because the receiving party may have incorporated the information in protected trial-preparation materials. No receiving party may use or disclose the information pending resolution of the privilege claim. The receiving party may present to the court the questions whether the information is privileged or protected as trial-preparation material, and whether the privilege or protection has been waived. If it does so, it must provide the court with the grounds for the privilege or protection specified in the producing party's notice, and serve all parties. In presenting the question, the party may use the content of the information only to the extent permitted by the applicable law of privilege, protection for trial-preparation material, and professional responsibility.

If a party disclosed the information to nonparties before receiving notice of a claim of privilege or protection as trial-preparation material, it must take reasonable steps to retrieve the information and to return it, sequester it until the claim is resolved, or destroy it.

Whether the information is returned or not, the producing party must preserve the information pending the court's ruling on whether the claim of privilege or of protection is properly asserted and whether it was waived. As with claims made under Rule 26(b)(5)(A), there may be no ruling if the other parties do not contest the claim.

Subdivision (f). Rule 26(f) is amended to direct the parties to discuss discovery of electronically stored information during their discovery-planning conference. The rule focuses on "issues relating to disclosure or discovery of electronically stored information"; the discussion is not required in cases not involving electronic discovery, and the amendment imposes no additional requirements in those cases. When the parties do anticipate disclosure or discovery of electronically stored information, discussion at the outset may avoid later difficulties or ease their resolution.

When a case involves discovery of electronically stored information, the issues to be addressed during the Rule 26(f) conference depend on the nature and extent of the contemplated discovery and of the parties' information systems. It may be important for the parties to discuss those systems, and accordingly important for counsel to become familiar with those systems before the conference. With that information, the parties can develop a discovery plan that takes into account the capabilities of their computer systems. In appropriate cases identification of, and early discovery from, individuals with special knowledge of a party's computer systems may be helpful.

The particular issues regarding electronically stored information that deserve attention during the discovery planning stage depend on the specifics of the given case. *See Manual for Complex Litigation* (4th) § 40.25(2) (listing topics for discussion in a proposed order regarding meet-and-confer sessions). For example, the parties may specify the topics for such discovery and the time period for which discovery will be sought. They may identify the various sources of such information within a party's control that should be searched for electronically stored information. They may discuss whether the information is reasonably accessible to the party that has it, including the burden or cost of retrieving and reviewing the information. *See* Rule 26(b)(2)(B). Rule 26(f)(3) explicitly directs the parties to discuss the form or forms in which electronically stored information might be produced. The parties may be able to reach agreement on the forms of production, making discovery more efficient. Rule 34(b) is amended to permit a requesting party to specify the form or forms in which it wants electronically stored information produced. If the requesting party does not specify a form, Rule 34(b) directs the responding party to state the forms it intends to use in the production. Early discussion of the forms of production may facilitate the application of Rule 34(b) by allowing the parties to determine what forms of production will meet both parties' needs. Early identification of disputes over the forms of production may help avoid the expense and delay of searches or productions using inappropriate forms.

Rule 26(f) is also amended to direct the parties to discuss any issues regarding preservation of discoverable information during their conference as they develop a discovery plan. This provision applies to all sorts of discoverable information, but can be particularly important with regard to electronically stored information. The volume and dynamic nature of electronically stored information may complicate preservation obligations. The ordinary operation of computers involves both the automatic creation and the automatic deletion or overwriting of certain information. Failure to address preservation issues early in the litigation increases uncertainty and raises a risk of disputes.

The parties' discussion should pay particular attention to the balance between the competing needs to preserve relevant evidence and to continue routine operations critical to ongoing activities. Complete or broad cessation of a party's routine computer operations could paralyze the party's activities. *Cf. Manual for Complex Litigation* (4th) § 11.422 ("A blanket preservation order may be prohibitively expensive and unduly burdensome for parties dependent on computer systems for their day-to-day operations.") The parties should take account of these considerations in their discussions, with the goal of agreeing on reasonable preservation steps.

The requirement that the parties discuss preservation does not imply that courts should routinely enter preservation orders. A preservation order entered over objections should be narrowly tailored. Ex parte preservation orders should issue only in exceptional circumstances.

Rule 26(f) is also amended to provide that the parties should discuss any issues relating to assertions of privilege or of protection as trial-preparation materials, including whether the parties can facilitate discovery by agreeing on procedures for asserting claims of privilege or protection after production and whether to ask the court to enter an order that includes any agreement the parties reach. The Committee has repeatedly been advised about the discovery difficulties that can result from efforts to guard against waiver of privilege and work-product protection. Frequently parties find it necessary to spend large amounts of time reviewing materials requested through discovery to avoid waiving privilege. These efforts are necessary because materials subject to a claim of privilege or protection are often difficult to identify. A failure to withhold even one such item may result in an argument that there has been a waiver of privilege as to all other privileged materials on that subject matter. Efforts to avoid the risk of waiver can impose substantial costs on the party producing the material and the time required for the privilege review can substantially delay access for the party seeking discovery.

These problems often become more acute when discovery of electronically stored information is sought. The volume of such data, and the informality that attends use of e-mail and some other types of electronically stored information, may make privilege determinations more difficult, and privilege review correspondingly more expensive and time consuming. Other aspects of electronically stored information pose particular difficulties for privilege review. For example, production may be sought of information automatically included in electronic files but not apparent to the creator or to readers. Computer programs may retain draft language, editorial comments, and other deleted matter (sometimes referred to as "embedded data" or "embedded edits") in an electronic file but not make them apparent to the reader. Information describing the history, tracking, or management of an electronic file (sometimes called "metadata") is usually not apparent to the reader viewing a hard copy or a screen image. Whether this information should be produced may be among the topics discussed in the Rule 26(f) conference. If it is, it may need to be reviewed to ensure that no privileged information is included, further complicating the task of privilege review.

Parties may attempt to minimize these costs and delays by agreeing to protocols that minimize the risk of waiver. They may agree that the responding party will provide certain requested materials for initial examination without waiving any privilege or protection—sometimes known as a "quick peek." The requesting party then designates the documents it wishes to have actually produced. This designation is the Rule 34 request. The responding party then responds in the usual course, screening only those documents actually requested for formal production and asserting privilege claims as provided in Rule 26(b)(5)(A). On other occasions, parties enter agreements—sometimes called "clawback agreements"—that production without intent to waive privilege or protection should not be a waiver so long as the responding party identifies the documents mistakenly produced, and that the documents should be returned under those circumstances. Other voluntary arrangements may be appropriate depending on the circumstances of each litigation. In most circumstances, a party who receives information under such an arrangement cannot assert that production of the information waived a claim of privilege or of protection as trial-preparation material.

Although these agreements may not be appropriate for all cases, in certain cases they can facilitate prompt and economical discovery by reducing delay before the discovering party obtains access to documents, and by reducing the cost and burden of review by the producing party. A case-management or other order including such agreements may further facilitate the discovery process. Form 35 is amended to include a report to the court about any agreement regarding protections against inadvertent forfeiture or waiver of privilege or protection that the parties have reached, and Rule 16(b) is amended to recognize that the court may include such an agreement in a case-management or other order. If the parties agree to entry of such an order, their proposal should be included in the report to the court.

Rule 26(b)(5)(B) is added to establish a parallel procedure to assert privilege or protection as trial-preparation material after production, leaving the question of waiver to later determination by the court.

2007 AMENDMENT

The language of Rule 26 has been amended as part of the general restyling of the Civil Rules to make them more easily understood and to make style and terminology consistent throughout the rules. These changes are intended to be stylistic only.

Former Rule 26(a)(5) served as an index of the discovery methods provided by later rules. It was deleted as redundant. Deletion does not affect the right to pursue discovery in addition to disclosure.

Former Rule 26(b)(1) began with a general statement of the scope of discovery that appeared to function as a preface to each of the five numbered paragraphs that followed. This preface has been shifted to the text of paragraph (1) because it does not accurately reflect the limits embodied in paragraphs (2), (3), or (4), and because paragraph (5) does not address the scope of discovery.

The reference to discovery of "books" in former Rule 26(b)(1) was deleted to achieve consistent expression throughout the discovery rules. Books remain a proper subject of discovery.

Amended Rule 26(b)(3) states that a party may obtain a copy of the party's own previous statement "on request." Former Rule 26(b)(3) expressly made the request procedure available to a nonparty witness, but did not describe the procedure to be used by a party. This apparent gap is closed by adopting the request procedure, which ensures that a party need not invoke Rule 34 to obtain a copy of the party's own statement.

Rule 26(e) stated the duty to supplement or correct a disclosure or discovery response "to include information thereafter acquired." This apparent limit is not reflected in practice; parties recognize the duty to supplement or correct by providing information that was not originally provided although it was available at the time of the initial disclosure or response. These words are deleted to reflect the actual meaning of the present rule.

Former Rule 26(e) used different phrases to describe the time to supplement or correct a disclosure or discovery response. Disclosures were to be supplemented "at appropriate intervals." A prior discovery response must be "seasonably * * * amend[ed]." The fine distinction between these phrases has not been observed in practice. Amended Rule 26(e)(1)(A) uses the same phrase for disclosures and discovery responses. The party must supplement or correct "in a timely manner."

Former Rule 26(g)(1) did not call for striking an unsigned disclosure. The omission was an obvious drafting oversight. Amended Rule 26(g)(2) includes disclosures in the list of matters that the court must strike unless a signature is provided "promptly * * * after being called to the attorney's or party's attention."

Former Rule 26(b)(2)(A) referred to a "good faith" argument to extend existing law. Amended Rule 26(b)(1)(B)(i) changes this reference to a "nonfrivolous" argument to achieve consistency with Rule 11(b)(2).

As with the Rule 11 signature on a pleading, written motion, or other paper, disclosure and discovery signatures should include not only a postal address but also a telephone number and electronic-mail address. A signer who lacks one or more of those addresses need not supply a nonexistent item.

Rule 11(b)(2) recognizes that it is legitimate to argue for establishing new law. An argument to establish new law is equally legitimate in conducting discovery.

2010 AMENDMENT

Rule 26. Rules 26(a)(2) and (b)(4) are amended to address concerns about expert discovery. The amendments to Rule 26(a)(2) require disclosure regarding expected expert testimony of those expert witnesses not required to provide expert reports and limit the expert report to facts or data (rather than "data or other information," as in the current rule) considered by the witness. Rule 26(b)(4) is amended to provide work-product protection against discovery regarding draft expert disclosures or reports and--with three specific exceptions--communications between expert witnesses and counsel.

In 1993, Rule 26(b)(4)(A) was revised to authorize expert depositions and Rule 26(a)(2) was added to provide disclosure, including--for many experts--an extensive report. Many courts read the disclosure provision to authorize discovery of all communications between counsel and expert witnesses and all draft reports. The Committee has been told repeatedly that routine discovery into attorney-expert communications and draft reports has had undesirable effects. Costs have risen. Attorneys may employ two sets of experts--one for purposes of consultation and another to testify at trial--because disclosure of their collaborative interactions with expert consultants would reveal their most sensitive and confidential case analyses. At the same time, attorneys often feel compelled to adopt a guarded attitude toward their interaction with testifying experts that impedes effective communication, and experts adopt strategies that protect against discovery but also interfere with their work.

Subdivision (a)(2)(B). Rule 26(a)(2)(B)(ii) is amended to provide that disclosure include all "facts or data considered by the witness in forming" the opinions to be offered, rather than the "data or other information" disclosure prescribed in 1993. This amendment is intended to alter the outcome in cases that have relied on the 1993 formulation in requiring disclosure of all attorney-expert communications and draft reports. The amendments to Rule 26(b)(4) make this change explicit by providing work-product protection against discovery regarding draft reports and disclosures or attorney-expert communications.

The refocus of disclosure on "facts or data" is meant to limit disclosure to material of a factual nature by excluding theories or mental impressions of counsel. At the same time, the intention is that "facts or data" be interpreted broadly to require disclosure of any material considered by the expert, from whatever source, that contains factual ingredients. The disclosure obligation extends to any facts or data "considered" by the expert in forming the opinions to be expressed, not only those relied upon by the expert.

Subdivision (a)(2)(C). Rule 26(a)(2)(C) is added to mandate summary disclosures of the opinions to be offered by expert witnesses who are not required to provide reports under Rule 26(a)(2)(B) and of the facts supporting those opinions. This disclosure is considerably less extensive than the report required by Rule 26(a)(2)(B). Courts must take care against requiring undue detail, keeping in mind that these witnesses have not been specially retained and may not be as responsive to counsel as those who have.

This amendment resolves a tension that has sometimes prompted courts to require reports under Rule 26(a)(2)(B) even from witnesses exempted from the report requirement. An (a)(2)(B) report is required only from an expert described in (a)(2)(B).

A witness who is not required to provide a report under Rule 26(a)(2)(B) may both testify as a fact witness and also provide expert testimony under Evidence Rule 702, 703, or 705. Frequent examples include physicians or other health care professionals and employees of a party who do not regularly provide expert testimony. Parties must identify such witnesses under Rule 26(a)(2)(A) and provide the disclosure required under Rule 26(a)(2)(C). The (a)(2)(C) disclosure obligation does not include facts unrelated to the expert opinions the witness will present.

Subdivision (a)(2)(D). This provision (formerly Rule 26(a)(2)(C)) is amended slightly to specify that the time limits for disclosure of contradictory or rebuttal evidence apply with regard to disclosures under new Rule 26(a)(2)(C), just as they do with regard to reports under Rule 26(a)(2)(B).

Subdivision (b)(4). Rule 26(b)(4)(B) is added to provide work-product protection under Rule 26(b)(3)(A) and (B) for drafts of expert reports or disclosures. This protection applies to all witnesses identified under Rule 26(a)(2)(A), whether they are required to provide reports under Rule 26(a)(2)(B) or are the subject of disclosure under Rule 26(a)(2)(C). It applies regardless of the form in which the draft is recorded, whether written, electronic, or otherwise. It also applies to drafts of any supplementation under Rule 26(e); see Rule 26(a)(2)(E).

Rule 26(b)(4)(C) is added to provide work-product protection for attorney-expert communications regardless of the form of the communications, whether oral, written, electronic, or otherwise. The addition of Rule 26(b)(4)(C) is designed to protect counsel's work product and ensure that lawyers may interact with retained experts without fear of exposing those communications to searching discovery. The protection is limited to communications between an expert witness required to provide a report under Rule 26(a)(2)(B) and the attorney for the party on whose behalf the witness will be testifying, including any "preliminary" expert opinions. Protected "communications" include those between the party's attorney and assistants of the expert witness. The rule does not itself protect communications between counsel and other expert witnesses, such as those for whom disclosure is required under Rule 26(a)(2)(C). The rule does not exclude protection under other doctrines, such as privilege or independent development of the work-product doctrine.

The most frequent method for discovering the work of expert witnesses is by deposition, but Rules 26(b)(4)(B) and (C) apply to all forms of discovery.

Rules 26(b)(4)(B) and (C) do not impede discovery about the opinions to be offered by the expert or the development, foundation, or basis of those opinions.

For example, the expert's testing of material involved in litigation, and notes of any such testing, would not be exempted from discovery by this rule. Similarly, inquiry about communications the expert had with anyone other than the party's counsel about the opinions expressed is unaffected by the rule. Counsel are also free to question expert witnesses about alternative analyses, testing methods, or approaches to the issues on which they are testifying, whether or not the expert considered them in forming the opinions expressed. These discovery changes therefore do not affect the gatekeeping functions called for by *Daubert v. Merrell Dow Pharmaceuticals, Inc.*, 509 U.S. 579 (1993), and related cases.

The protection for communications between the retained expert and "the party's attorney" should be applied in a realistic manner, and often would not be limited to communications with a single lawyer or a single law firm. For example, a party may be involved in a number of suits about a given product or service, and may retain a particular expert witness to testify on that party's behalf in several of the cases. In such a situation, the protection applies to communications between the expert witness and the attorneys representing the party in any of those cases. Similarly, communications with in-house counsel for the party would often be regarded as protected even if the in-house attorney is not counsel of record in the action. Other situations may also justify a pragmatic application of the "party's attorney" concept.

Although attorney-expert communications are generally protected by Rule 26(b)(4)(C), the protection does not apply to the extent the lawyer and the expert communicate about matters that fall within three exceptions. But the discovery authorized by the exceptions does not extend beyond those specific topics. Lawyer-expert communications may cover many topics and, even when the excepted topics are included among those involved in a given communication, the protection applies to all other aspects of the communication beyond the excepted topics.

First, under Rule 26(b)(4)(C)(i) attorney-expert communications regarding compensation for the expert's study or testimony may be the subject of discovery. In some cases, this discovery may go beyond the disclosure requirement in Rule 26(a)(2)(B)(vi). It is not limited to compensation for work forming the opinions to be expressed, but extends to all compensation for the study and testimony provided in relation to the action. Any communications about additional benefits to the expert, such as further work in the event of a successful result in the present case, would be included. This exception includes compensation for work done by a person or organization associated with the expert. The objective is to permit full inquiry into such potential sources of bias.

Second, under Rule 26(b)(4)(C)(ii) discovery is permitted to identify facts or data the party's attorney provided to the expert and that the expert considered in forming the opinions to be expressed. The exception applies only to communications "identifying" the facts or data provided by counsel; further communications about the potential relevance of the facts or data are protected.

Third, under Rule 26(b)(4)(C)(iii) discovery regarding attorney-expert communications is permitted to identify any assumptions that counsel provided to the expert and that the expert relied upon in forming the opinions to be expressed. For example, the party's attorney may tell the expert to assume the truth of certain testimony or evidence, or the correctness of another expert's conclusions. This exception is limited to those assumptions that the expert actually did rely on in forming the opinions to be expressed. More general attorney-expert discussions about hypotheticals, or exploring possibilities based on hypothetical facts, are outside this exception.

Under the amended rule, discovery regarding attorney-expert communications on subjects outside the three exceptions in Rule 26(b)(4)(C), or regarding draft expert reports or disclosures, is permitted only in limited circumstances and by court order. A party seeking such discovery must make the showing specified in Rule 26(b)(3)(A)(ii)--that the party has a substantial need for the discovery and cannot obtain the substantial equivalent without undue hardship. It will be rare for a party to be able to make such a showing given the broad disclosure and discovery otherwise allowed regarding the expert's testimony. A party's failure to provide required disclosure or discovery does not show the need and hardship required by Rule 26(b)(3)(A); remedies are provided by Rule 37.

In the rare case in which a party does make this showing, the court must protect against disclosure of the attorney's mental impressions, conclusions, opinions, or legal theories under Rule 26(b)(3)(B). But this protection does not extend to the expert's own development of the opinions to be presented; those are subject to probing in deposition or at trial.

Former Rules 26(b)(4)(B) and (C) have been renumbered (D) and (E), and a slight revision has been made in (E) to take account of the renumbering of former (B).

2015 AMENDMENT

Rule 26(b)(1) is changed in several ways.

Information is discoverable under revised Rule 26(b)(1) if it is relevant to any party's claim or defense and is proportional to the needs of the case. The considerations that bear on proprtionality are moved from present Rule 26(b)(2)(C)(iii), slightly rearranged and with one additio.

Most of what now appears in Rule 26(b)(2)(C)(iii) was first adopted in 1983. The 1983 provision was explicitly adopted as part of the scope of discovery defined by Rule 26(b)(1). Rule 26(b)(1) directed the court to limit the frequency or extent of use of discovery if it determined that "the discovery is unduly burdensome or expensive, taking into account the needs of the case, the amount in controversy, limitations on the parties' resources, and the importance of the issues at stake in the litigation." At the same time, Rule 26(g) was added. Rule 26(g) provided that signing a discovery request, response, or objection certified that the request, response, or objection was "not unreasonable or unduly burdensome or expensive, given the needs of the case, the discovery already had in the case, the amount in controversy, and the importance of the issues at stake in the litigation." The parties thus shared the responsibility to honor these limits on the scope of discovery.

The 1983 Committee Note stated that the new provisions were added "to deal with the problem of over-discovery. The objective is to guard against redundant or disproportionate discovery by giving the court authority to reduce the amount of discovery that may be directed to matters that are otherwise proper subjects of inquiry. The new sentence is intended to encourage judges to be more aggressive in identifying and discouraging discovery overuse. The grounds mentioned in the amended rule for limiting discovery reflect the existing practice of many courts in issuing protective orders under Rule 26(c) ... On the whole, however, district judges have been reluctant to limit the use of the discovery devices."

The clear focus of the 1983 provisions may have been softened, although inadvertently, by the amendments made in 1993. The 1993 Committee Note explained: "[F]ormer paragraph (b)(1) [was] subdivided into two paragraphs for ease of reference and to avoid renumbering of paragraphs (3) and (4). Subdividing the paragraphs, however, was done in a way that could be read to separate the proportionality provisions as limitations, no longer an integral part of the (b)(1) scope provisions. That appearance was immediately offset by the next statement in the Note: Textual changes are then made in new paragraph (2) to enable the court to keep tighter rein on the extent of discovery.

The 1993 amendments added two factors to the considerations that bear on limiting discovery: whether "the burden or expense of the proposed discovery outweighs its likely benefit," and "the importance of the proposed discovery in resolving the issues." Addressing these and other limitations added by the 1993 discovery amendments, the Committee Note stated that [t]he revisions in Rule 26(b)(2) are intended to provide the court with broader discretion to impose additional restrictions on the scope and extent of discovery...'

The relationship between Rule 26(b)(1) and (2) was further addressed by an amendment made in 2000 that added a new sentence at the end of (b)(1): "All discovery is subject to the limitations imposed by Rule 26(b)(2)(i), (ii), and (iii)[now Rule 26(b)(2)(C)]." The Committee Note recognized that "[t]hese limitations apply to discovery that is otherwise within the scope of subdivision (b)(1)." It explained that the Committee had been told repeatedly that courts were not using these limitations as originally intended. "This otherwise redundant cross-reference has been added to emphasize the need for active judicial use of subdivision (b)(2) to control excessive discovery."

The present amendment restores the proportionality factors to their original place in defining the scope of discovery. This change reinforces the Rule 26(g) obligation of the parties to consider these factors in making discovery requests, responses, or objections.

Restoring the proportionality calculation to Rule 26(b)(1) does not change the existing responsibilities of the court and the parties to consider proportionality, and the change does not place on the party seeking discovery the burden of addressing all proportionality considerations.

Nor is the change intended to permit the opposing party to refuse discovery simply by making a boilerplate objection that it is not proportional. The parties and the court have a collective responsibility to consider the proportionality of all discovery and consider it in resolving discovery disputes.

The parties may begin discovery without a full appreciation of the factors that bear on proportionality. A party requesting discovery, for example, may have little information about the burden or expense of responding. A party requested to provide discovery may have little information about the importance of the discovery in resolving the issues as understood by the requesting party. Many of these uncertainties should be addressed and reduced in the parties' Rule 26(f) conference and in scheduling and pretrial conferences with the court. But if the parties continue to disagree, the discovery dispute could be brought before the court and the parties' responsibilities would remain as they have been since 1983. A party claiming undue burden or expense ordinarily has far better information — perhaps the only information — with respect to that part of the determination. A party claiming that a request is important to resolve the issues should be able to explain the ways in which the underlying information bears on the issues as that party understands them. The court's responsibility, using all the information provided by the parties, is to consider these and all the other factors in reaching a case-specific determination of the appropriate scope of discovery.

The direction to consider the parties' relative access to relevant information adds new text to provide explicit focus on considerations already implicit in present Rule 26(b)(2)(C)(iii). Some cases involve what often is called "information asymmetry." One party — often an individual plaintiff — may have very little discoverable information. The other party may have vast amounts of information, including information that can be readily retrieved and information that is more difficult to retrieve. In practice these circumstances often mean that the burden of responding to discovery lies heavier on the party who has more information, and properly so.

Restoring proportionality as an express component of the scope of discovery warrants repetition of parts of the 1983 and 1993 Committee Notes that must not be lost from sight. The 1983 Committee Note explained that "[t]he rule contemplates greater judicial involvement in the discovery process and thus acknowledges the reality that it cannot always operate on a self-regulating basis." The 1993 Committee Note further observed that "[t]he information explosion of recent decades has greatly increased both the potential cost of wide-ranging discovery and the potential for discovery to be used as an instrument for delay or oppression." What seemed an explosion in 1993 has been exacerbated by the advent of e-discovery. The present amendment again reflects the need for continuing and close judicial involvement in the cases that do not yield readily to the ideal of effective party management. It is expected that discovery will be effectively managed by the parties in many cases. But there will be important occasions for judicial management, both when the parties are legitimately unable to resolve important differences and when the parties fall short of effective, cooperative management on their own.

It also is important to repeat the caution that the monetary stakes are only one factor, to be balanced against other factors. The 1983 Committee Note recognized "the significance of the substantive issues, as measured in philosophic, social, or institutional terms. Thus the rule recognizes that many cases in public policy spheres, such as employment practices, free speech, and other matters, may have importance far beyond the monetary amount involved." Many other substantive areas also may involve litigation that seeks relatively small amounts of money, or no money at all, but that seeks to vindicate vitally important personal or public values.

So too, consideration of the parties' resources does not foreclose discovery requests addressed to an impecunious party, nor justify unlimited discovery requests addressed to a wealthy party. The 1983 Committee Note cautioned that "[t]he court must apply the standards in an even-handed manner that will prevent use of discovery to wage a war of attrition or as a device to coerce a party, whether financially weak or affluent."

The burden or expense of proposed discovery should be determined in a realistic way. This includes the burden or expense of producing electronically stored information. Computer-based methods of searching such information continue to develop, particularly for cases involving large volumes of electronically stored information. Courts and parties should be willing to consider the opportunities for reducing the burden or expense of discovery as reliable means of searching electronically stored information become available.

A portion of present Rule 26(b)(1) is omitted from the proposed revision. After allowing discovery of any matter relevant to any party's claim or defense, the present rule adds: "including the existence, description, nature, custody, condition, and location of any documents or other tangible things and the identity and location of persons who know of any discoverable matter." Discovery of such matters is so deeply entrenched in practice that it is no longer necessary to clutter the long text of Rule 26 with these examples. The discovery identified in these examples should still be permitted under the revised rule when relevant and proportional to the needs of the case. Framing intelligent requests for electronically stored information, for example, may require detailed information about another party's information systems and other information resources.

The amendment deletes the former provision authorizing the court, for good cause, to order discovery of any matter relevant to the subject matter involved in the action. The Committee has been informed that this language is rarely invoked. Proportional discovery relevant to any party's claim or defense suffices, given a proper understanding of what is relevant to a claim or defense. The distinction between matter relevant to a claim or defense and matter relevant to the subject matter was introduced in 2000. The 2000 Note offered three examples of information that, suitably focused, would be relevant to the parties' claims or defenses. The examples were "other incidents of the same type, or involving the same product"; "information about organizational arrangements or filing systems"; and "information that could be used to impeach a likely witness." Such discovery is not foreclosed by the amendments. Discovery that is relevant to the parties' claims or defenses may also support amendment of the pleadings to add a new claim or defense that affects the scope of discovery.

The former provision for discovery of relevant but inadmissible information that appears "reasonably calculated to lead to the discovery of admissible evidence" is also deleted. The phrase has been used by some, incorrectly, to define the scope of discovery. As the Committee Note to the 2000 amendments observed, use of the "reasonably calculated" phrase to define the scope of discovery "might swallow any other limitation on the scope of discovery." The 2000 amendments sought to prevent such misuse by adding the word "Relevant" at the beginning of the sentence, making clear that " 'relevant' means within the scope of discovery as defined in this subdivision..." The "reasonably calculated" phrase has continued to create problems, however, and is removed by these amendments. It is replaced by the direct statement that "Information within this scope of discovery need not be admissible in evidence to be discoverable." Discovery of nonprivileged information not admissible in evidence remains available so long as it is otherwise within the scope of discovery.

Rule 26(b)(2)(C)(iii) is amended to reflect the transfer of the considerations that bear on proportionality to Rule 26(b)(1). The court still must limit the frequency or extent of proposed discovery, on motion or on its own, if it is outside the scope permitted by Rule 26(b)(1).

Rule 26(c)(1)(B) is amended to include an express recognition of protective orders that allocate expenses for disclosure or discovery. Authority to enter such orders is included in the present rule, and courts already exercise this authority. Explicit recognition will forestall the temptation some parties may feel to contest this authority. Recognizing the authority does not imply that cost-shifting should become a common practice. Courts and parties should continue to assume that a responding party ordinarily bears the costs of responding.

Rule 26(d)(2) is added to allow a party to deliver Rule 34 requests to another party more than 21 days after that party has been served even though the parties have not yet had a required Rule 26(f) conference. Delivery may be made by any party to the party that has been served, and by that party to any plaintiff and any other party that has been served. Delivery does not count as service; the requests are considered to be served at the first Rule 26(f) conference. Under Rule 34(b)(2)(A) the time to respond runs from service. This relaxation of the discovery moratorium is designed to facilitate focused discussion during the Rule 26(f) conference. Discussion at the conference may produce changes in the requests. The opportunity for advance scrutiny of requests delivered before the Rule 26(f) conference should not affect a decision whether to allow additional time to respond.

Rule 26(d)(3) is renumbered and amended to recognize that the parties may stipulate to case-specific sequences of discovery.

Rule 26(f)(3) is amended in parallel with Rule 16(b)(3) to add two items to the discovery plan — issues about preserving electronically stored information and court orders under Evidence Rule 502.

Rule 27. Depositions Before Action or Pending Appeal

1937 ADOPTION

Note to Subdivision (a). This rule offers a simple method of perpetuating testimony in cases where it is usually allowed under equity practice or under modern statutes. See *Arizona v. California, 1934*, 292 U.S. 341, 54 S. Ct. 735, 78 L.Ed. 1298; *Todd Engineering Dry Dock and Repair Co. v. United States, C.C.A.5, 1929*, 32 F.2d 734; *Hall v. Stout*, 4 Del.Ch. 269 (1871). For comparable state statutes see Ark.Civ.Code (Crawford, 1934) §§ 666 to 670; Calif.Code Civ.Proc. (Deering, 1937) 2083 to 2089; Smith-Hurd Ill.Stats. c. 51, §§ 39 to 46; Iowa Code (1935) §§ 11400 to 11407; 2 Mass.Gen.Laws (Ter.Ed., 1932) ch. 233, §§ 46 to 63; N.Y.C.P.A. (1937) § 295; Ohio Gen.Code Ann. (Throckmorton, 1936) §§ 12216 to 12222; Va.Code Ann. (Michie, 1936) § 6235; Wis.Stat. (1935) §§ 326.27 to 326.29. The appointment of an attorney to represent absent parties or parties not personally notified, or a guardian ad litem to represent minors and incompetents, is provided for in several of the above statutes.

Note to Subdivision (b). This follows the practice approved in *Richter v. Union Trust Co., 1885*, 115 U.S. 55, 5 S. Ct. 1162, 29 L.Ed. 345, by extending the right to perpetuate testimony to cases pending an appeal.

Note to Subdivision (c). This preserves the right to employ a separate action to perpetuate testimony under U.S.C., Title 28, former § 644 (Depositions under *dedimus potestatem* and *in perpetuum*) as an alternate method.

1946 AMENDMENT

Note. Since the second sentence in subdivision (a)(3) refers only to depositions, it is arguable that Rules 34 and 35 are inapplicable in proceedings to perpetuate testimony. The new matter [in subdivision (a)(3) and (b)] clarifies. A conforming change is also made in subdivision (b).

1948 AMENDMENT

The amendment effective October 1949, substituted the words "United States district court" in subdivision (a)(1) and (4) in place of the words "district court of the United States."

1971 AMENDMENT

The reference intended in this subdivision is to the rule governing the use of depositions in court proceedings. Formerly Rule 26(d), that rule is now Rule 32(a). The subdivision is amended accordingly.

1987 AMENDMENT

The amendments are technical. No substantive change is intended.

2005 AMENDMENT

The outdated cross-reference to former Rule 4(d) is corrected to incorporate all Rule 4 methods of service. Former Rule 4(d) has been allocated to many different subdivisions of Rule 4. Former Rule 4(d) did not cover all categories of defendants or modes of service, and present Rule 4 reaches further than all of former Rule 4. But there is no reason to distinguish between the different categories of defendants and modes of service encompassed by Rule 4. Rule 4 service provides effective notice. Notice by such means should be provided to any expected adverse party that comes within Rule 4.

Other changes are made to conform Rule 27(a)(2) to current style conventions.

2007 AMENDMENT

The language of Rule 27 has been amended as part of the general restyling of the Civil Rules to make them more easily understood and to make style and terminology consistent throughout the rules. These changes are intended to be stylistic only.

2009 AMENDMENT

The time set in the former rule at 20 days has been revised to 21 days. See the Note to Rule 6.

Rule 28. Persons Before Whom Depositions May Be Taken

1937 ADOPTION

In effect this rule is substantially the same as U.S.C., Title 28, former § 639 (Depositions *de bene esse*; when and where taken: notice). U.S.C., Title 28, former § 642 (Depositions, acknowledgments, and affidavits taken by notaries public) does not conflict with Subdivision (a).

1946 AMENDMENT

Note. The added language [in subdivision (a)] provides for the situation, occasionally arising, when depositions must be taken in an isolated place where there is no one readily available who has the power to administer oaths and take testimony according to the terms of the rule as originally stated. In addition, the amendment affords a more convenient method of securing depositions in the case where state lines intervene between the location of various witnesses otherwise rather closely grouped. The amendment insures that the person appointed shall have adequate power to perform his duties. It has been held that a person authorized to act in the premises, as, for example, a master, may take testimony outside the district of his appointment. *Consolidated Fastener Co. v. Columbian Button & Fastener Co., C.C.N.Y.1898*, 85 Fed. 54; *Mathieson Alkali Works v. Arnold Hoffman & Co., C.C.A.1, 1929*, 31 F.2d 1.

1963 AMENDMENT

The amendment of clause (1) is designed to facilitate depositions in foreign countries by enlarging the class of persons before whom the depositions may be taken on notice. The class is no longer confined, as at present, to a secretary of embassy or legation, consul general, consul, vice consul, or consular agent of the United States. In a country that regards the taking of testimony by a foreign official in aid of litigation pending in a court of another country as an infringement upon its sovereignty, it will be expedient to notice depositions before officers of the country in which the examination is taken. See generally Symposium Letters Rogatory (Grossman ed. 1956); Doyle, Taking Evidence by Deposition and Letters Rogatory and Obtaining Documents in Foreign Territory. Proc.A.B.A., Sec.Int'l & Comp.L. 37 (1959); Heilpern, Procuring Evidence Abroad, 14 Tul.L.Rev. 29 (1939); Jones, International Judicial Assistance: Procedural Chaos and a Program for Reform, 62 Yale L.J. 515, 526–29 (1953); Smit. International Aspects of Federal Civil Procedure. 61 Colum.L.Rev. 1031, 1056–58 (1961).

Clause (2) of amended subdivision (b), like the corresponding provision of subdivision (a) dealing with depositions taken in the United States, makes it clear that the appointment of a person by commission in itself confers power upon him to administer any necessary oath.

It has been held that a letter rogatory will not be issued unless the use of a notice or commission is shown to be impossible or impractical. See, *e.g., United States v. Matles*, 154 F.Supp. 574 (E.D.N.Y.1957); *The Edmund Fanning*, 89 F.Supp. 282 (E.D.N.Y.1950); *Branyan v. Koninklijke Luchtvaart Maatschappij*, 13 F.R.D. 425 (S.D.N.Y.1953). See also *Ali Akber Kiachif v. Philco International Corp.*, 10 F.R.D. 277 (S.D.N.Y.1950). The intent of the fourth sentence of the amended subdivision is to overcome this judicial antipathy and to permit a sound choice between depositions under a letter rogatory and on notice or by commission in the light of all the circumstances. In a case in which the foreign country will compel a witness to attend or testify in aid of a letter rogatory but not in aid of a commission, a letter rogatory may be preferred on the ground that it is less expensive to execute, even if there is plainly no need for compulsive process. A letter rogatory may also be preferred when it cannot be demonstrated that a witness will be recalcitrant or when the witness states that he is willing to testify voluntarily, but the contingency exists that he will change his mind at the last moment. In the latter case, it may be advisable to issue both a commission and a letter rogatory, the latter to be executed if the former fails. The choice between a letter rogatory and a commission may be conditioned by other factors, including the nature and extent of the assistance that the foreign country will give to the execution of either.

In executing a letter rogatory the courts of other countries may be expected to follow their customary procedure for taking testimony. See *United States v. Paraffin Wax, 2255 Bags*, 23 F.R.D. 289 (E.D.N.Y.1959). In many non-common-law countries the judge questions the witness, sometimes without first administering an oath, the attorneys put any supplemental questions either to the witness or through the judge, and the judge dictates a summary of the testimony, which the witness acknowledges as correct. See *Jones, supra*, at 530 to 32; *Doyle, supra*, at 39 to 41. The last sentence of the amended subdivision provides, contrary to the implications of some authority, that evidence recorded in such a fashion need not be excluded on that account. See *The Mandu*, 11 F.Supp. 845 (E.D.N.Y.1935). But cf. *Nelson v. United States*, 17 Fed.Cas. 1340 (No. 10,116)(C.C.D.Pa.1816); *Winthrop v. Union Ins. Co.*, 30 Fed.Cas. 376 (No. 17901)(C.C.D.Pa.1807). The specific reference to the lack of an oath or a verbatim transcript is intended to be illustrative. Whether or to what degree the value or weight of the evidence may be affected by the method of taking or recording the testimony is left for determination according to the circumstances of the particular case, cf. *Uebersee Finanz-Korporation, A. G. v. Brownell*, 121 F.Supp. 420 (D.D.C.1954); *Danisch v. Guardian Life Ins. Co.*, 19 F.R.D. 235 (S.D.N.Y.1956); the testimony may indeed be so devoid of substance or probative value as to warrant its exclusion altogether.

Some foreign countries are hostile to allowing a deposition to be taken in their country, especially by notice or commission, or to lending assistance in the taking of a deposition. Thus compliance with the terms of amended subdivision (b) may not in all cases ensure completion of a deposition abroad. Examination of the law and policy of the particular foreign country in advance of attempting a deposition is therefore advisable. See 4 Moore's Federal Practice ¶¶ 28.05–28.08 (2d ed. 1950).

1980 AMENDMENT

The amendments are clarifying.

1987 AMENDMENT

The amendment is technical. No substantive change is intended.

1993 AMENDMENT

This revision is intended to make effective use of the Hague Convention on the Taking of Evidence Abroad in Civil or Commercial Matters, and of any similar treaties that the United States may enter into in the future which provide procedures for taking depositions abroad. The party taking the deposition is ordinarily obliged to conform to an applicable treaty or convention if an effective deposition can be taken by such internationally approved means, even though a verbatim transcript is not available or testimony cannot be taken under oath. For a discussion of the impact of such treaties upon the discovery process, and of the application of principles of comity upon discovery in countries not signatories to a convention, see *Société Nationale Industrielle Aérospatiale v. United States District Court*, 482 U.S. 522, 107 S. Ct. 2542, 96 L. Ed. 2d 461 (1987).

The term "letter of request" has been substituted in the rule for the term "letter rogatory" because it is the primary method provided by the Hague Convention. A letter rogatory is essentially a form of letter of request. There are several other minor changes that are designed merely to carry out the intent of the other alterations.

2007 AMENDMENT

The language of Rule 28 has been amended as part of the general restyling of the Civil Rules to make them more easily understood and to make style and terminology consistent throughout the rules. These changes are intended to be stylistic only.

Rule 29. Stipulations Regarding Discovery Procedure

1970 AMENDMENT

There is no provision for stipulations varying the procedures by which methods of discovery other than depositions are governed. It is common practice for parties to agree on such variations, and the amendment recognizes such agreements and provides a formal mechanism in the rules for giving them effect. Any stipulation varying the procedures may be superseded by court order, and stipulations extending the time for response to discovery under Rules 33, 34, and 36 require court approval.

1993 AMENDMENT

This rule is revised to give greater opportunity for litigants to agree upon modifications to the procedures governing discovery or to limitations upon discovery. Counsel are encouraged to agree on less expensive and time-consuming methods to obtain information, as through voluntary exchange of documents, use of interviews in lieu of depositions, etc. Likewise, when more depositions or interrogatories are needed than allowed under these rules or when more time is needed to complete a deposition than allowed under a local rule, they can, by agreeing to the additional discovery, eliminate the need for a special motion addressed to the court.

Under the revised rule, the litigants ordinarily are not required to obtain the court's approval of these stipulations. By order or local rule, the court can, however, direct that its approval be obtained for particular types of stipulations; and, in any event, approval must be obtained if a stipulation to extend the 30-day period for responding to interrogatories, requests for production, or requests for admissions would interfere with dates set by the court for completing discovery, for hearing of a motion, or for trial.

2007 AMENDMENT

The language of Rule 29 has been amended as part of the general restyling of the Civil Rules to make them more easily understood and to make style and terminology consistent throughout the rules. These changes are intended to be stylistic only.

Rule 30. Depositions upon Oral Examination

1937 ADOPTION

Note to Subdivision (a). This is in accordance with common practice. See U.S.C., Title 28, former § 639 (Depositions *de bene esse*; when and where taken; notice), the relevant provisions of which are incorporated in this rule; West's Ann.Code Civ.Proc. § 2031; and statutes cited in respect to notice in the Note to Rule 26(a). The provision for enlarging or shortening the time of notice has been added to give flexibility to the rule.

Note to Subdivisions (b) and (d). These are introduced as a safeguard for the protection of parties and deponents on account of the unlimited right of discovery given by Rule 26.

Note to Subdivisions (c) and (e). These follow the general plan of former Equity Rule 51 (Evidence Taken Before Examiners, Etc.) and U.S.C., Title 28, former § 640 (Depositions *de bene esse*; mode of taking), and former § 641 (Same; transmission to court), but are more specific. They also permit the deponent to require the officer to make changes in the deposition if the deponent is not satisfied with it. See also former Equity Rule 50 (Stenographer—Appointment—Fees.)

Note to Subdivision (f). Compare former Equity Rule 55 (Depositions Deemed Published When Filed.)

Note to Subdivision (g). This is similar to 2 Minn.Stat. (Mason, 1927) § 9833, but is more extensive.

1963 AMENDMENT

This amendment corresponds to the change in Rule 4(d)(4). See Advisory Committee's Note to that amendment.

1970 AMENDMENT

Subdivision (a). This subdivision contains the provisions of existing Rule 26(a), transferred here as part of the rearrangement relating to Rule 26. Existing Rule 30(a) is transferred to 30(b). Changes in language have been made to conform to the new arrangement.

This subdivision is further revised in regard to the requirement of leave of court for taking a deposition. The present procedure, requiring a plaintiff to obtain leave of court if he serves notice of taking a deposition within 20 days after commencement of the action, is changed in several respects. First, leave is required by reference to the time the deposition is to be taken rather than the date of serving notice of taking. Second, the 20-day period is extended to 30 days and runs from the service of summons and complaint on any defendant, rather than the commencement of the action. Cf. Ill.S. Ct.R. 19-1, S-H Ill.Ann. Stat. § 101.19-1. Third, leave is not required beyond the time that defendant initiates discovery, thus showing that he has retained counsel. As under the present practice, a party not afforded a reasonable opportunity to appear at a deposition, because he has not yet been served with process, is protected against use of the deposition at trial against him. See Rule 32(a), transferred from 26(d). Moreover, he can later redepose the witness if he so desires.

The purpose of requiring the plaintiff to obtain leave of court is, as stated by the Advisory Committee that proposed the present language of Rule 26(a), to protect "a defendant who has not had an opportunity to retain counsel and inform himself as to the nature of the suit." Note to 1948 amendment of Rule 26(a), quoted in 3A Barron & Holtzoff, Federal Practice and Procedure 455 to 456 (Wright ed. 1958). In order to assure defendant of this opportunity, the period is lengthened to 30 days. This protection, however, is relevant to the time of taking the deposition, not to the time that notice is served. Similarly, the protective period should run from the service of process rather than the filing of the complaint with the court. As stated in the note to Rule 26(d), the courts have used the service of notice as a convenient reference point for assigning priority in taking depositions, but with the elimination of priority in new Rule 26(d) the reference point is no longer needed. The new procedure is consistent in principle with the provisions of Rules 33, 34, and 36 as revised.

Plaintiff is excused from obtaining leave even during the initial 30-day period if he gives the special notice provided in subdivision (b)(2). The required notice must state that the person to be examined is about to go out of the district where the action is pending and more than 100 miles from the place of trial, or out of the United States, or on a voyage to sea, and will be unavailable for examination unless deposed within the 30-day period. These events occur most often in maritime litigation, when seamen are transferred from one port to another or are about to go to sea. Yet, there are analogous situations in nonmaritime litigation, and although the maritime problems are more common, a rule limited to claims in the admiralty and maritime jurisdiction is not justified.

In the recent unification of the civil and admiralty rules, this problem was temporarily met through addition in Rule 26(a) of a provision that depositions *de bene esse* may continue to be taken as to admiralty and maritime claims within the meaning of Rule 9(h). It was recognized at the time that "a uniform rule applicable alike to what are now civil actions and suits in admiralty" was clearly preferable, but the *de bene esse* procedure was adopted "for the time being at least." See Advisory Committee's Note in Report of the Judicial Conference: Proposed Amendments to Rules of Civil Procedure 43 to 44 (1966).

The changes in Rule 30(a) and the new Rule 30(b)(2) provide a formula applicable to ordinary civil as well as maritime claims. They replace the provision for depositions *de bene esse*. They authorize an early deposition without leave of court where the witness is about to depart and, unless his deposition is promptly taken, (1) it will be impossible or very difficult to depose him before trial or (2) his deposition can later be taken but only with substantially increased effort and expense. *Cf. S. S. Hai Chang*, 1966 A.M.C. 2239 (S.D.N.Y.1966), in which the deposing party is required to prepay expenses and counsel fees of the other party's lawyer when the action is pending in New York and depositions are to be taken on the West Coast. Defendant is protected by a provision that the deposition cannot be used against him if he was unable through exercise of diligence to obtain counsel to represent him.

The distance of 100 miles from place of trial is derived from the *de bene esse* provision and also conforms to the reach of a subpoena of the trial court, as provided in Rule 45(e). See also S.D.N.Y.Civ.R. 5(a). Some parts of the *de bene esse* provision are omitted from Rule 30(b)(2). Modern deposition practice adequately covers the witness who lives more than 100 miles away from place of trial. If a witness is aged or infirm, leave of court can be obtained.

Subdivision (b). Existing Rule 30(b) on protective orders has been transferred to Rule 26(c), and existing Rule 30(a) relating to the notice of taking deposition has been transferred to this subdivision. Because new material has been added, subsection numbers have been inserted.

Subdivision (b)(1). If a subpoena duces tecum is to be served, a copy thereof or a designation of the materials to be produced must accompany the notice. Each party is thereby enabled to prepare for the deposition more effectively.

Subdivision (b)(2). This subdivision is discussed in the note to subdivision (a), to which it relates.

Subdivision (b)(3). This provision is derived from existing Rule 30(a), with a minor change of language.

Subdivision (b)(4). In order to facilitate less expensive procedures, provision is made for the recording of testimony by other than stenographic means—*e.g.*, by mechanical, electronic, or photographic means. Because these methods give rise to problems of accuracy and trustworthiness, the party taking the deposition is required to apply for a court order. The order is to specify how the testimony is to be recorded, preserved, and filed, and it may contain whatever additional safeguards the court deems necessary.

Subdivision (b)(5). A provision is added to enable a party, through service of notice, to require another party to produce documents or things at the taking of his deposition. This may now be done as to a nonparty deponent through use of a subpoena duces tecum as authorized by Rule 45, but some courts have held that documents may be secured from a party only under Rule 34. See 2A Barron & Holtzoff, Federal Practice and Procedure § 644.1 n. 83.2, § 792 n. 16 (Wright ed. 1961). With the elimination of "good cause" from Rule 34, the reason for this restrictive doctrine has disappeared. *Cf.* N.Y.C.P.L.R. § 3111.

Whether production of documents or things should be obtained directly under Rule 34 or at the deposition under this rule will depend on the nature and volume of the documents or things. Both methods are made available. When the documents are few and simple, and closely related to the oral examination, ability to proceed via this rule will facilitate discovery. If the discovering party insists on examining many and complex documents at the taking of the deposition, thereby causing undue burdens on others, the latter may, under Rules 26(c) or 30(d), apply for a court order that the examining party proceed via Rule 34 alone.

Subdivision (b)(6). A new provision is added, whereby a party may name a corporation, partnership, association, or governmental agency as the deponent and designate the matters on which he requests examination, and the organization shall then name one or more of its officers, directors, or managing agents, or other persons consenting to appear and testify on its behalf with respect to matters known or reasonably available to the organization. *Cf.* Alberta, Sup.Ct.R. 255. The organization may designate persons other than officers, directors, and managing agents, but only with their consent. Thus, an employee or agent who has an independent or conflicting interest in the litigation—for example, in a personal injury case—can refuse to testify on behalf of the organization.

This procedure supplements the existing practice whereby the examining party designates the corporate official to be deposed. Thus, if the examining party believes that certain officials who have not testified pursuant to this subdivision have added information, he may depose them. On the other hand, a court's decision whether to issue a protective order may take account of the availability and use made of the procedures provided in this subdivision.

The new procedure should be viewed as an added facility for discovery, one which may be advantageous to both sides as well as an improvement in the deposition process. It will reduce the difficulties not encountered in determining, prior to the taking of a deposition, whether a particular employee or agent is a "managing agent." See Note, Discovery Against Corporations Under the Federal Rules, 47 Iowa L.Rev. 1006–1016 (1962). It will curb the "bandying" by which officers or managing agents of a corporation are deposed in turn but each disclaims knowledge of facts that are clearly known to persons in the organization and thereby to it. *Cf. Haney v. Woodward & Lothrop, Inc.*, 330 F.2d 940, 944 (4th Cir.1964). The provision should also assist organizations which find that an unnecessarily large number of their officers and agents are being deposed by a party uncertain of who in the organization has knowledge. Some courts have held that under the existing rules a corporation should not be burdened with choosing which person is to appear for it. *E.g., United States v. Gahagan Dredging Corp.*, 24 F.R.D. 328, 329 (S.D.N.Y.1958). This burden is not essentially different from that of answering interrogatories under Rule 33, and is in any case lighter than that of an examining party ignorant of who in the corporation has knowledge.

Subdivision (c). A new sentence is inserted at the beginning, representing the transfer of existing Rule 26(c) to this subdivision. Another addition conforms to the new provision in subdivision (b)(4).

The present rule provides that transcription shall be carried out unless all parties waive it. In view of the many depositions taken from which nothing useful is discovered, the revised language provides that transcription is to be performed if any party requests it. The fact of the request is relevant to the exercise of the court's discretion in determining who shall pay for transcription.

Parties choosing to serve written questions rather than participate personally in an oral deposition are directed to serve their questions on the party taking the deposition, since the officer is often not identified in advance. Confidentiality is preserved, since the questions may be served in a sealed envelope.

Subdivision (d). The assessment of expenses incurred in relation to motions made under this subdivision (d) is made subject to the provisions of Rule 37(a). The standards for assessment of expenses are more fully set out in Rule 37(a), and these standards should apply to the essentially similar motions of this subdivision.

Subdivision (e). The provision relating to the refusal of a witness to sign his deposition is tightened through insertion of a 30-day time period.

Subdivision (f)(1). A provision is added which codifies in a flexible way the procedure for handling exhibits related to the deposition and at the same time assures each party that he may inspect and copy documents and things produced by a nonparty witness in response to a subpoena duces tecum. As a general rule and in the absence of agreement to the contrary or order of the court, exhibits produced without objection are to be annexed to and returned with the deposition, but a witness may substitute copies for purposes of marking and he may obtain return of the exhibits. The right of the parties to inspect exhibits for identification and to make copies is assured. *Cf.* N.Y.C.P.L.R. § 3116(c).

1971 AMENDMENT

The subdivision permits a party to name a corporation or other form of organization as a deponent in the notice of examination and to describe in the notice the matters about which discovery is desired. The organization is then obliged to designate natural persons to testify on its behalf. The amendment clarifies the procedure to be followed if a party desires to examine a non-party organization through persons designated by the organization. Under the rules, a subpoena rather than a notice of examination is served on a non-party to compel attendance at the taking of a deposition. The amendment provides that a subpoena may name a non-party organization as the deponent and may indicate the matters about which discovery is desired. In that event, the non-party organization must respond by designating natural persons, who are then obliged to testify as to matters known or reasonably available to the organization. To insure that a non-party organization that is not represented by counsel has knowledge of its duty to designate, the amendment directs the party seeking discovery to advise of the duty in the body of the subpoena.

1972 AMENDMENT

Subdivision (c). Existing Rule 43(b), which is to be abrogated, deals with the use of leading questions, the calling, interrogation, impeachment, and scope of cross-examination of adverse parties, officers, etc. These topics are dealt with in many places in the Rules of Evidence. Moreover, many pertinent topics included in the Rules of Evidence are not mentioned in Rule 43(b), e.g. privilege. A reference to the Rules of Evidence generally is therefore made in subdivision (c) of Rule 30.

1980 AMENDMENT

Subdivision (b)(4). It has been proposed that electronic recording of depositions be authorized as a matter of course, subject to the right of a party to seek an order that a deposition be recorded by stenographic means. The Committee is not satisfied that a case has been made for a reversal of present practice. The amendment is made to encourage parties to agree to the use of electronic recording of depositions so that conflicting claims with respect to the potential of electronic recording for reducing costs of depositions can be appraised in the light of greater experience. The provision that the parties may stipulate that depositions may be recorded by other than stenographic means seems implicit in Rule 29. The amendment makes it explicit. The provision that the stipulation or order shall designate the person before whom the deposition is to be taken is added to encourage the naming of the recording technician as that person, eliminating the necessity of the presence of one whose only function is to administer the oath. See Rules 28(a) and 29.

Subdivision (b)(7). Depositions by telephone are now authorized by Rule 29 upon stipulation of the parties. The amendment authorizes that method by order of the court. The final sentence is added to make it clear that when a deposition is taken by telephone it is taken in the district and at the place where the witness is to answer the questions rather than that where the questions are propounded.

Subdivision (f)(1). For the reasons set out in the Note following the amendment of Rule 5(d), the court may wish to permit the parties to retain depositions unless they are to be used in the action. The amendment of the first paragraph permits the court to so order.

The amendment of the second paragraph is clarifying. The purpose of the paragraph is to permit a person who produces materials at a deposition to offer copies for marking and annexation to the deposition. Such copies are a "substitute" for the originals, which are not to be marked and which can thereafter be used or even disposed of by the person who produces them. In the light of that purpose, the former language of the paragraph had been justly termed "opaque." Wright & Miller, Federal Practice and Procedure: Civil § 2114.

1987 AMENDMENT

The amendments are technical. No substantive change is intended.

1993 AMENDMENT

Subdivision (a). Paragraph (1) retains the first and third sentences from the former subdivision (a) without significant modification. The second and fourth sentences are relocated.

Paragraph (2) collects all provisions bearing on requirements of leave of court to take a deposition.

Paragraph (2)(A) is new. It provides a limit on the number of depositions the parties may take, absent leave of court or stipulation with the other parties. One aim of this revision is to assure judicial review under the standards stated in Rule 26(b)(2) before any side will be allowed to take more than ten depositions in a case without agreement of the other parties. A second objective is to emphasize that counsel have a professional obligation to develop a mutual cost-effective plan for discovery in the case. Leave to take additional depositions should be granted when consistent with the principles of Rule 26(b)(2), and in some cases the ten-per-side limit should be reduced in accordance with those same principles. Consideration should ordinarily be given at the planning meeting of the parties under Rule 26(f) and at the time of a scheduling conference under Rule 16(b) as to enlargements or reductions in the number of depositions, eliminating the need for special motions.

A deposition under Rule 30(b)(6) should, for purposes of this limit, be treated as a single deposition even though more than one person may be designated to testify.

In multi-party cases, the parties on any side are expected to confer and agree as to which depositions are most needed, given the presumptive limit on the number of depositions they can take without leave of court. If these disputes cannot be amicably resolved, the court can be requested to resolve the dispute or permit additional depositions.

Paragraph (2)(B) is new. It requires leave of court if any witness is to be deposed in the action more than once. This requirement does not apply when a deposition is temporarily recessed for convenience of counsel or the deponent or to enable additional materials to be gathered before resuming the deposition. If significant travel costs would be incurred to resume the deposition, the parties should consider the feasibility of conducting the balance of the examination by telephonic means.

Paragraph (2)(C) revises the second sentence of the former subdivision (a) as to when depositions may be taken. Consistent with the changes made in Rule 26(d), providing that formal discovery ordinarily not commence until after the litigants have met and conferred as directed in revised Rule 26(f), the rule requires leave of court or agreement of the parties if a deposition is to be taken before that time (except when a witness is about to leave the country).

Subdivision (b). The primary change in subdivision (b) is that parties will be authorized to record deposition testimony by nonstenographic means without first having to obtain permission of the court or agreement from other counsel.

Former subdivision (b)(2) is partly relocated in subdivision (a)(2)(C) of this rule. The latter two sentences of the first paragraph are deleted, in part because they are redundant to Rule 26(g) and in part because Rule 11 no longer applies to discovery requests. The second paragraph of the former subdivision (b)(2), relating to use of depositions at trial where a party was unable to obtain counsel in time for an accelerated deposition, is relocated in Rule 32.

New paragraph (2) confers on the party taking the deposition the choice of the method of recording, without the need to obtain prior court approval for one taken other than stenographically. A party choosing to record a deposition only by videotape or audiotape should understand that a transcript will be required by Rule 26(a)(3)(B) and Rule 32(c) if the deposition is later to be offered as evidence at trial or on a dispositive motion under Rule 56. Objections to the nonstenographic recording of a deposition, when warranted by the circumstances, can be presented to the court under Rule 26(c).

Paragraph (3) provides that other parties may arrange, at their own expense, for the recording of a deposition by a means (stenographic, visual, or sound) in addition to the method designated by the person noticing the deposition. The former provisions of this paragraph, relating to the court's power to change the date of a deposition, have been eliminated as redundant in view of Rule 26(c)(2).

Revised paragraph (4) requires that all depositions be recorded by an officer designated or appointed under Rule 28 and contains special provisions designed to provide basic safeguards to assure the utility and integrity of recordings taken other than stenographically.

Paragraph (7) is revised to authorize the taking of a deposition not only by telephone but also by other remote electronic means, such as satellite television, when agreed to by the parties or authorized by the court.

Subdivision (c). Minor changes are made in this subdivision to reflect those made in subdivision (b) and to complement the new provisions of subdivision (d)(1), aimed at reducing the number of interruptions during depositions.

In addition, the revision addresses a recurring problem as to whether other potential deponents can attend a deposition. Courts have disagreed, some holding that witnesses should be excluded through invocation of Rule 615 of the evidence rules, and others holding that witnesses may attend unless excluded by an order under Rule 26(c)(5). The revision provides that other witnesses are not automatically excluded from a deposition simply by the request of a party. Exclusion, however, can be ordered under Rule 26(c)(5) when appropriate; and, if exclusion is ordered, consideration should be given as to whether the excluded witnesses likewise should be precluded from reading, or being otherwise informed about, the testimony given in the earlier depositions. The revision addresses only the matter of attendance by potential deponents, and does not attempt to resolve issues concerning attendance by others, such as members of the public or press.

Subdivision (d). The first sentence of new paragraph (1) provides that any objections during a deposition must be made concisely and in a non-argumentative and non-suggestive manner. Depositions frequently have been unduly prolonged, if not unfairly frustrated, by lengthy objections and colloquy, often suggesting how the deponent should respond. While objections may, under the revised rule, be made during a deposition, they ordinarily should be limited to those that under Rule 32(d)(3) might be waived if not made at that time, *i.e.*, objections on grounds that might be immediately obviated, removed, or cured, such as to the form of a question or the responsiveness of an answer. Under Rule 32(b), other objections can, even without the so-called "usual stipulation" preserving objections, be raised for the first time at trial and therefore should be kept to a minimum during a deposition.

Directions to a deponent not to answer a question can be even more disruptive than objections. The second sentence of new paragraph (1) prohibits such directions except in the three circumstances indicated: to claim a privilege or protection against disclosure (*e.g.,* as work product), to enforce a court directive limiting the scope or length of permissible discovery, or to suspend a deposition to enable presentation of a motion under paragraph (3).

Paragraph (2) is added to this subdivision to dispel any doubts regarding the power of the court by order or local rule to establish limits on the length of depositions. The rule also explicitly authorizes the court to impose the cost resulting from obstructive tactics that unreasonably prolong a deposition on the person engaged in such obstruction. This sanction may be imposed on a non-party witness as well as a party or attorney, but is otherwise congruent with Rule 26(g).

It is anticipated that limits on the length of depositions prescribed by local rules would be presumptive only, subject to modification by the court or by agreement of the parties. Such modifications typically should be discussed by the parties in their meeting under Rule 26(f) and included in the scheduling order required by Rule 16(b). Additional time, moreover, should be allowed under the revised rule when justified under the principles stated in Rule 26(b)(2). To reduce the number of special motions, local rules should ordinarily permit—and indeed encourage—the parties to agree to additional time, as when, during the taking of a deposition, it becomes clear that some additional examination is needed.

Paragraph (3) authorizes appropriate sanctions not only when a deposition is unreasonably prolonged, but also when an attorney engages in other practices that improperly frustrate the fair examination of the deponent, such as making improper objections or giving directions not to answer prohibited by paragraph (1). In general, counsel should not engage in any conduct during a deposition that would not be allowed in the presence of a judicial officer. The making of an excessive number of unnecessary objections may itself constitute sanctionable conduct, as may the refusal of an attorney to agree with other counsel on a fair apportionment of the time allowed for examination of a deponent or a refusal to agree to a reasonable request for some additional time to complete a deposition, when that is permitted by the local rule or order.

Subdivision (e). Various changes are made in this subdivision to reduce problems sometimes encountered when depositions are taken stenographically. Reporters frequently have difficulties obtaining signatures—and the return of depositions—from deponents. Under the revision pre-filing review by the deponent is required only if requested before the deposition is completed. If review is requested, the deponent will be allowed 30 days to review the transcript or recording and to indicate any changes in form or substance. Signature of the deponent will be required only if review is requested and changes are made.

Subdivision (f). Minor changes are made in this subdivision to reflect those made in subdivision (b). In courts which direct that depositions not be automatically filed, the reporter can transmit the transcript or recording to the attorney taking the deposition (or ordering the transcript or record), who then becomes custodian for the court of the original record of the deposition. Pursuant to subdivision (f)(2), as under the prior rule, any other party is entitled to secure a copy of the deposition from the officer designated to take the deposition; accordingly, unless ordered or agreed, the officer must retain a copy of the recording or the stenographic notes.

2000 AMENDMENT

Subdivision (d). Paragraph (1) has been amended to clarify the terms regarding behavior during depositions. The references to objections "to evidence" and limitations "on evidence" have been removed to avoid disputes about what is "evidence" and whether an objection is to, or a limitation is on, discovery instead. It is intended that the rule apply to any objection to a question or other issue arising during a deposition, and to any limitation imposed by the court in connection with a deposition, which might relate to duration or other matters.

The current rule places limitations on instructions that a witness not answer only when the instruction is made by a "party." Similar limitations should apply with regard to anyone who might purport to instruct a witness not to answer a question. Accordingly, the rule is amended to apply the limitation to instructions by any person. The amendment is not intended to confer new authority on nonparties to instruct witnesses to refuse to answer deposition questions. The amendment makes it clear that, whatever the legitimacy of giving such instructions, the nonparty is subject to the same limitations as parties.

Paragraph (2) imposes a presumptive durational limitation of one day of seven hours for any deposition. The Committee has been informed that overlong depositions can result in undue costs and delays in some circumstances. This limitation contemplates that there will be reasonable breaks during the day for lunch and other reasons, and that the only time to be counted is the time occupied by the actual deposition. For purposes of this durational limit, the deposition of each person designated under Rule 30(b)(6) should be considered a separate deposition. The presumptive duration may be extended, or otherwise altered, by agreement. Absent agreement, a court order is needed. The party seeking a court order to extend the examination, or otherwise alter the limitations, is expected to show good cause to justify such an order.

Parties considering extending the time for a deposition—and courts asked to order an extension—might consider a variety of factors. For example, if the witness needs an interpreter, that may prolong the examination. If the examination will cover events occurring over a long period of time, that may justify allowing additional time. In cases in which the witness will be questioned about numerous or lengthy documents, it is often desirable for the interrogating party to send copies of the documents to the witness sufficiently in advance of the deposition so that the witness can become familiar with them. Should the witness nevertheless not read the documents in advance, thereby prolonging the deposition, a court could consider that a reason for extending the time limit. If the examination reveals that documents have been requested but not produced, that may justify further examination once production has occurred. In multi-party cases, the need for each party to examine the witness may warrant additional time, although duplicative questioning should be avoided and parties with similar interests should strive to designate one lawyer to question about areas of common interest. Similarly, should the lawyer for the witness want to examine the witness, that may require additional time. Finally, with regard to expert witnesses, there may more often be a need for additional time—even after the submission of the report required by Rule 26(a)(2)—for full exploration of the theories upon which the witness relies.

It is expected that in most instances the parties and the witness will make reasonable accommodations to avoid the need for resort to the court. The limitation is phrased in terms of a single day on the assumption that ordinarily a single day would be preferable to a deposition extending over multiple days; if alternative arrangements would better suit the parties, they may agree to them. It is also assumed that there will be reasonable breaks during the day. Preoccupation with timing is to be avoided.

The rule directs the court to allow additional time where consistent with Rule 26(b)(2) if needed for a fair examination of the deponent. In addition, if the deponent or another person impedes or delays the examination, the court must authorize extra time. The amendment makes clear that additional time should also be allowed where the examination is impeded by an "other circumstance," which might include a power outage, a health emergency, or other event.

In keeping with the amendment to Rule 26(b)(2), the provision added in 1993 granting authority to adopt a local rule limiting the time permitted for depositions has been removed. The court may enter a case-specific order directing shorter depositions for all depositions in a case or with regard to a specific witness. The court may also order that a deposition be taken for limited periods on several days.

Paragraph (3) includes sanctions provisions formerly included in paragraph (2). It authorizes the court to impose an appropriate sanction on any person responsible for an impediment that frustrated the fair examination of the deponent. This could include the deponent, any party, or any other person involved in the deposition. If the impediment or delay results from an "other circumstance" under paragraph (2), ordinarily no sanction would be appropriate.

Former paragraph (3) has been renumbered (4) but is otherwise unchanged.

Subdivision (f)(1): This subdivision is amended because Rule 5(d) has been amended to direct that discovery materials, including depositions, ordinarily should not be filed. The rule already has provisions directing that the lawyer who arranged for the transcript or recording preserve the deposition. Rule 5(d) provides that, once the deposition is used in the proceeding, the attorney must file it with the court.

"Shall" is replaced by "must" or "may" under the program to conform amended rules to current style conventions when there is no ambiguity.

GAP Report

The Advisory Committee recommends deleting the requirement in the published proposed amendments that the deponent consent to extending a deposition beyond one day, and adding an amendment to Rule 30(f)(1) to conform to the published amendment to Rule 5(d) regarding filing of depositions. It also recommends conforming the Committee Note with regard to the deponent veto, and adding material to the Note to provide direction on computation of the durational limitation on depositions, to provide examples of situations in which the parties might agree—or the court order—that a deposition be extended, and to make clear that no new authority to instruct a witness is conferred by the amendment. One minor wording improvement in the Note is also suggested.

2007 AMENDMENT

The language of Rule 30 has been amended as part of the general restyling of the Civil Rules to make them more easily understood and to make style and terminology consistent throughout the rules. These changes are intended to be stylistic only.

The right to arrange a deposition transcription should be open to any party, regardless of the means of recording and regardless of who noticed the deposition.

"[O]ther entity" is added to the list of organizations that may be named as deponent. The purpose is to ensure that the deposition process can be used to reach information known or reasonably available to an organization no matter what abstract fictive concept is used to describe the organization. Nothing is gained by wrangling over the place to fit into current rule language such entities as limited liability companies, limited partnerships, business trusts, more exotic common-law creations, or forms developed in other countries.

2015 AMENDMENT

Rule 30 is amended in parallel with Rules 31 and 33 to reflect the recognition of proportionality in Rule 26(b)(1).

2020 AMENDMENT

Rule 30(b)(6) is amended to respond to problems that have emerged in some cases. Particular concerns raised have included overlong or ambiguously worded lists of matters for examination and inadequately prepared witnesses. This amendment directs the serving party and the named organization to confer before or promptly after the notice or subpoena is served about the matters for examination. The amendment also requires that a subpoena notify a nonparty organization of its duty to confer and to designate each person who will testify. It facilitates collaborative efforts to achieve the proportionality goals of the 2015 amendments to Rules 1 and 26(b)(1).

Candid exchanges about the purposes of the deposition and the organization's information structure may clarify and focus the matters for examination, and enable the organization to designate and to prepare an appropriate witness or witnesses, thereby avoiding later disagreements. It may be productive also to discuss "process" issues, such as the timing and location of the deposition, the number of witnesses and the matters on which each witness will testify, and any other issue that might facilitate the efficiency and productivity of the deposition.

The amended rule directs that the parties confer either before or promptly after the notice or subpoena is served. If they begin to confer before service, the discussion may be more productive if the serving party provides a draft of the proposed list of matters for examination, which may then be refined as the parties confer. The process of conferring may be iterative. Consistent with Rule 1, the obligation is to confer in good faith about the matters for examination, but the amendment does not require the parties to reach agreement. In some circumstances, it may be desirable to seek guidance from the court.

When the need for a Rule 30(b)(6) deposition is known early in the case, the Rule 26(f) conference may provide an occasion for beginning discussion of these topics. In appropriate cases, it may also be helpful to include reference to Rule 30(b)(6) depositions in the discovery plan submitted to the court under Rule 26(f)(3) and in the matters considered at a pretrial conference under Rule 16.

Because a Rule 31 deposition relies on written questions rather than a description with reasonable particularity of the matters for examination, the duty to confer about the matters for examination does not apply when an organization is deposed under Rule 31(a)(4).

Rule 31. Depositions upon Written Questions

1937 ADOPTION

This rule is in accordance with common practice. In most of the states listed in the Note to Rule 26(a), provisions similar to this rule will be found in the statutes which in their respective statutory compilations follow those cited in the Note to Rule 26(a).

1970 AMENDMENT

Confusion is created by the use of the same terminology to describe both the taking of a deposition upon "written interrogatories" pursuant to this rule and the serving of "written interrogatories" upon parties pursuant to Rule 33. The distinction between these two modes of discovery will be more readily and clearly grasped through substitution of the word "questions" for "interrogatories" throughout this rule.

Subdivision (a). A new paragraph is inserted at the beginning of this subdivision to conform to the rearrangement of provisions in Rules 26(a), 30(a), and 30(b).

The revised subdivision permits designation of the deponent by general description or by class or group. This conforms to the practice for depositions on oral examination.

The new procedure provided in Rule 30(b)(6) for taking the deposition of a corporation or other organization through persons designated by the organization is incorporated by reference.

The service of all questions, including cross, redirect, and recross, is to be made on all parties. This will inform the parties and enable them to participate fully in the procedure.

The time allowed for service of cross, redirect, and recross questions has been extended. Experience with the existing time limits shows them to be unrealistically short. No special restriction is placed on the time for serving the notice of taking the deposition and the first set of questions. Since no party is required to serve cross questions less than 30 days after the notice and questions are served, the defendant has sufficient time to obtain counsel. The court may for cause shown enlarge or shorten the time.

Subdivision (d). Since new Rule 26(c) provides for protective orders with respect to all discovery, and expressly provides that the court may order that one discovery device be used in place of another, subdivision (d) is eliminated as unnecessary.

1987 AMENDMENT

The amendments are technical. No substantive change is intended.

1993 AMENDMENT

Subdivision (a). The first paragraph of subdivision (a) is divided into two subparagraphs, with provisions comparable to those made in the revision of Rule 30. Changes are made in the former third paragraph, numbered in the revision as paragraph (4), to reduce the total time for developing cross-examination, redirect, and recross questions from 50 days to 28 days.

2007 AMENDMENT

The language of Rule 31 has been amended as part of the general restyling of the Civil Rules to make them more easily understood and to make style and terminology consistent throughout the rules. These changes are intended to be stylistic only.

The party who noticed a deposition on written questions must notify all other parties when the deposition is completed, so that they may make use of the deposition. A deposition is completed when it is recorded and the deponent has either waived or exercised the right of review under Rule 30(e)(1).

2015 AMENDMENT

Rule 31 is amended in parallel with Rules 30 and 33 to reflect the recognition of proportionality in Rule 26(b)(1).

Rule 32. Use of Depositions in Court Proceedings

1937 ADOPTION

This rule is in accordance with common practice. In most of the states listed in the note to Rule 26, provisions similar to this rule will be found in the statutes which in their respective statutory compilations follow those cited in the note to Rule 26.

1970 AMENDMENT

As part of the rearrangement of the discovery rules, existing subdivisions (d), (e), and (f) of Rule 26 are transferred to Rule 32 as new subdivisions (a), (b), and (c). The provisions of Rule 32 are retained as subdivision (d) of Rule 32 with appropriate changes in the lettering and numbering of subheadings. The new rule is given a suitable new title. A beneficial byproduct of the rearrangement is that provisions which are naturally related to one another are placed in one rule.

A change is made in new Rule 32(a), whereby it is made clear that the rules of evidence are to be applied to depositions offered at trial as though the deponent were then present and testifying at trial. This eliminates the possibility of certain technical hearsay objections which are based, not on the contents of deponent's testimony, but on his absence from court. The language of present Rule 26(d) does not appear to authorize these technical objections, but it is not entirely clear. Note present Rule 26(e), transferred to Rule 32(b); see 2A Barron & Holtzoff, Federal Practice and Procedure 164 to 166 (Wright ed. 1961).

An addition in Rule 32(a)(2) provides for use of a deposition of a person designated by a corporation or other organization, which is a party, to testify on its behalf. This complements the new procedure for taking the deposition of a corporation or other organization provided in Rules 30(b)(6) and 31(a). The addition is appropriate, since the deposition is in substance and effect that of the corporation or other organization which is a party.

A change is made in the standard under which a party offering part of a deposition in evidence may be required to introduce additional parts of the deposition. The new standard is contained in a proposal made by the Advisory Committee on Rules of Evidence. See Rule 1-07 and accompanying Note, Preliminary Draft of Proposed Rules of Evidence for the United States District Courts and Magistrates 21–22 (March, 1969).

References to other rules are changed to conform to the rearrangement, and minor verbal changes have been made for clarification. The time for objecting to written questions served under Rule 31 is slightly extended.

1972 AMENDMENT

Subdivision (c). The concept of "making a person one's own witness" appears to have had significance principally in two respects: impeachment and waiver of incompetency. Neither retains any vitality under the Rules of Evidence. The old prohibition against impeaching one's own witness is eliminated by Evidence Rule 607. The lack of recognition in the Rules of Evidence of state rules of incompetency in the Dead Man's area renders it unnecessary to consider aspects of waiver arising from calling the incompetent party-witness. Subdivision (c) is deleted because it appears to be no longer necessary in the light of the Rules of Evidence.

1980 AMENDMENT

Subdivision (a)(1). Rule 801(d) of the Federal Rules of Evidence permits a prior inconsistent statement of a witness in a deposition to be used as substantive evidence. And Rule 801(d)(2) makes the statement of an agent or servant admissible against the principal under the circumstances described in the Rule. The language of the present subdivision is, therefore, too narrow.

Subdivision (a)(4). The requirement that a prior action must have been dismissed before depositions taken for use in it can be used in a subsequent action was doubtless an oversight, and the courts have ignored it. See Wright & Miller, Federal Practice and Procedure: Civil § 2150. The final sentence is added to reflect the fact that the Federal Rules of Evidence permit a broader use of depositions previously taken under certain circumstances. For example, Rule 804(b)(1) of the Federal Rules of Evidence provides that if a witness is unavailable, as that term is defined by the rule, his deposition in any earlier proceeding can be used against a party to the prior proceeding who had an opportunity and similar motive to develop the testimony of the witness.

1987 AMENDMENT

The amendment is technical. No substantive change is intended.

1993 AMENDMENT

Subdivision (a). The last sentence of revised subdivision (a) not only includes the substance of the provisions formerly contained in the second paragraph of Rule 30(b)(2), but adds a provision to deal with the situation when a party, receiving minimal notice of a proposed deposition, is unable to obtain a court ruling on its motion for a protective order seeking to delay or change the place of the deposition. Ordinarily a party does not obtain protection merely by the filing of a motion for a protective order under Rule 26(c); any protection is dependent upon the court's ruling. Under the revision, a party receiving less than 11 days notice of a deposition can, provided its motion for a protective order is filed promptly, be spared the risks resulting from nonattendance at the deposition held before its motion is ruled upon. Although the revision of Rule 32(a) covers only the risk that the deposition could be used against the non-appearing movant, it should also follow that, when the proposed deponent is the movant, the deponent would have "just cause" for failing to appear for purposes of Rule 37(d)(1). Inclusion of this provision is not intended to signify that 11 days' notice is the minimum advance notice for all depositions or that greater than 10 days should necessarily be deemed sufficient in all situations.

Subdivision (c). This new subdivision, inserted at the location of a subdivision previously abrogated, is included in view of the increased opportunities for video-recording and audio-recording of depositions under revised Rule 30(b). Under this rule a party may offer deposition testimony in any of the forms authorized under Rule 30(b) but, if offering it in a nonstenographic form, must provide the court with a transcript of the portions so offered. On request of any party in a jury trial, deposition testimony offered other than for impeachment purposes is to be presented in a nonstenographic form if available, unless the court directs otherwise. Note that under Rule 26(a)(3)(B) a party expecting to use nonstenographic deposition testimony as substantive evidence is required to provide other parties with a transcript in advance of trial.

2007 AMENDMENT

The language of Rule 32 has been amended as part of the general restyling of the Civil Rules to make them more easily understood and to make style and terminology consistent throughout the rules. These changes are intended to be stylistic only.

Former Rule 32(a) applied "[a]t the trial or upon the hearing of a motion or an interlocutory proceeding." The amended rule describes the same events as "a hearing or trial."

The final paragraph of former Rule 32(a) allowed use in a later action of a deposition "lawfully taken and duly filed in the former action." Because of the 2000 amendment of Rule 5(d), many depositions are not filed. Amended Rule 32(a)(8) reflects this change by excluding use of an unfiled deposition only if filing was required in the former action.

2009 AMENDMENT

The times set in the former rule at less than 11 days and within 5 days have been revised to 14 days and 7 days. See the Note to Rule 6.

Rule 33. Interrogatories to Parties

1937 ADOPTION

This rule restates the substance of former Equity Rule 58 (Discovery—Interrogatories—Inspection and Production of Documents—Admission of Execution or Genuineness), with modifications to conform to these rules.

1946 AMENDMENT

Note. The added second sentence in the first paragraph of Rule 33 conforms with a similar change in Rule 26(a) and will avoid litigation as to when the interrogatories may be served. Original rule 33 does not state the times at which parties may serve written interrogatories upon each other. It has been the accepted view, however, that the times were the same in Rule 33 as those stated in Rule 26(a). *United States v. American Solvents & Chemical Corp. of California, Del.1939*, 30 F.Supp. 107; *Sheldon v. Great Lakes Transit Corp., N.Y.1942*, 2 F.R.D. 272, 5 Fed.Rules Serv. 33.11, Case 3; *Musher Foundation, Inc., v. Alba Trading Co., N.Y.1941*, 42 F.Supp. 281, 2 Moore's Federal Practice, 1938, 2621. The time within which leave of court must be secured by a plaintiff has been fixed at 10 days, in view of the fact that a defendant has 10 days within which to make objections in any case, which should give him ample time to engage counsel and prepare.

Further in the first paragraph of Rule 33, the word "service" is substituted for "delivery" in conformance with the use of the word "serve" elsewhere in the rule and generally throughout the rules. See also Note to Rule 13(a) herein. The portion of the rule dealing with practice on objections has been revised so as to afford a clearer statement of the procedure. The addition of the words "to interrogatories to which objection is made" insures that only the answers to the objectionable interrogatories may be deferred, and that the answers to interrogatories not objectionable shall be forthcoming within the time prescribed in the rule. Under the original wording, answers to all interrogatories may be withheld until objections, sometimes to but a few interrogatories, are determined. The amendment expedites the procedure of the rule and serves to eliminate the strike value of objections to minor interrogatories. The elimination of the last sentence of the original rule is in line with the policy stated subsequently in this note.

The added second paragraph in Rule 33 contributes clarity and specificity as to the use and scope of interrogatories to the parties. The field of inquiry will be as broad as the scope of examination under Rule 26(b). There is no reason why interrogatories should be more limited than depositions, particularly when the former represent an inexpensive means of securing useful information. See Hoffman v. Wilson Line, Inc., Pa.1946, 9 Fed.Rules Serv. 33.514, Case 2; *Brews-*

ter v. Technicolor, Inc., N.Y.1941, 2 F.R.D. 186, 5 Fed.Rules Serv. 33.319, Case 3; *Kingsway Press, Inc. v. Farrell Publishing Corp., N.Y.1939*, 30 F.Supp. 775. Under present Rule 33 some courts have unnecessarily restricted the breadth of inquiry on various grounds. See *Auer v. Hershey Creamery Co., N.J.1939, 2 Fed.Rules Serv. 33.31, Case 2*, 1 F.R.D. 14; *Tudor v. Leslie, Mass.1940*, 1 F.R.D. 448, 4 Fed.Rules Serv. 33.324, Case 1. Other courts have read into the rule the requirement that interrogation should be directed only towards "important facts", and have tended to fix a more or less arbitrary limit as to the number of interrogatories which could be asked in any case. See *Knox v. Alter, Pa.1942*, 2 F.R.D. 337, 6 Fed.Rules Serv. 33.352, Case 1; *Byers Theaters, Inc. v. Murphy, Va.1940, 3 Fed.Rules Serv. 33.31, Case 3*, 1 F.R.D. 286; *Coca-Cola Co. v. Dixi-Cola Laboratories, Inc., Md.1939*, 30 F.Supp. 275. See also comment on these restrictions in Holtzoff, Instruments of Discovery under Federal Rules of Civil Procedure, 1942, 41 Mich.L.Rev. 205, 216–217. Under amended Rule 33, the party interrogated is given the right to invoke such protective orders under Rule 30(b) as are appropriate to the situation. At the same time, it is provided that the number of or number of sets of interrogatories to be served may not be limited arbitrarily or as a general policy to any particular number, but that a limit may be fixed only as justice requires to avoid annoyance, expense, embarrassment or oppression in individual cases. The party interrogated, therefore, must show the necessity for limitation on that basis. It will be noted that in accord with this change the last sentence of the present rule, restricting the sets of interrogatories to be served, has been stricken. In *J. Schoeneman, Inc. v. Brauer, Mo.1940*, 1 F.R.D. 292, 3 Fed.Rules Serv. 33.31, Case 2, the court said: "Rule 33 * * * has been interpreted * * * as being just as broad in its implications as in the case of depositions * * * It makes no difference therefore, how many interrogatories are propounded. If the inquiries are pertinent the opposing party cannot complain." To the same effect, see Canuso v. City of Niagara Falls, N.Y.1945, 8 Fed.Rules Serv. 33.352, Case 1; *Hoffman v. Wilson Line, Inc.*, supra.

By virtue of express language in the added second paragraph of Rule 33, as amended, any uncertainty as to the use of the answers to interrogatories is removed. The omission of a provision on this score in the original rule has caused some difficulty. See e.g., *Bailey v. New England Mutual Life Ins. Co., Cal.1940*, 1 F.R.D. 494, 4 Fed.Rules Serv. 33.46, Case 1.

The second sentence of the second paragraph in Rule 33, as amended, concerns the situation where a party wishes to serve interrogatories on a party after having taken his deposition, or vice versa. It has been held that an oral examination of a party, after the submission to him and answer of interrogatories, would be permitted. *Howard v. State Marine Corp., N.Y.1940, 4 Fed.Rules Serv. 33.62, Case 1*, 1 F.R.D. 499; *Stevens v. Minder Construction Co., N.Y.1943*, 3 F.R.D. 498, 7 Fed.Rules Serv. 30b.31, Case 2. But objections have been sustained to interrogatories served after the oral deposition of a party had been taken. *McNally v. Simons, N.Y.1940, 3 Fed.Rules Serv. 33.61, Case 1*, 1 F.R.D. 254; *Currier v. Currier, N.Y.1942*, 3 F.R.D. 21, 6 Fed.Rules Serv. 33.61, Case 1, Rule 33, as amended, permits either interrogatories after a deposition or a deposition after interrogatories. It may be quite desirable or necessary to elicit additional information by the inexpensive method of interrogatories where a deposition has already been taken. The party to be interrogated, however, may seek a protective order from the court under Rule 30(b) where the additional deposition or interrogation works a hardship or injustice on the party from whom it is sought.

1970 AMENDMENT

Subdivision (a). The mechanics of the operation of Rule 33 are substantially revised by the proposed amendment, with a view to reducing court intervention. There is general agreement that interrogatories spawn a greater percentage of objections and motions than any other discovery device. The Columbia Survey shows that, although half of the litigants resorted to depositions and about one-third used interrogatories, about 65 percent of the objections were made with respect to interrogatories and 26 percent related to depositions. See also Speck, The Use of Discovery in United States District Courts, 60 Yale L.J. 1132, 1144, 1151 (1951); Note, 36 Minn.L.Rev. 364, 379 (1952).

The procedures now provided in Rule 33 seem calculated to encourage objections and court motions. The time periods now allowed for responding to interrogatories—15 days for answers and 10 days for objections—are too short. The Columbia Survey shows that tardy response to interrogatories is common, virtually expected. The same was reported in Speck, *supra,* 60 Yale L.J. 1132, 1144. The time pressures tend to encourage objections as a means of gaining time to answer.

The time for objections is even shorter than for answers, and the party runs the risk that if he fails to object in time he may have waived his objections. *E.g., Cleminshaw v. Beech Aircraft Corp.*, 21 F.R.D. 300 (D.Del.1957); See 4 Moore's Federal Practice, ¶ 33.27 (2d ed. 1966); 2A Barron & Holtzoff, Federal Practice and Procedure 372 to 373 (Wright ed. 1961). It often seems easier to object than to seek an extension of time. Unlike Rules 30(d) and 37(a), Rule 33 imposes no sanction of expenses on a party whose objections are clearly unjustified.

Rule 33 assures that the objections will lead directly to court, through its requirement that they be served with a notice of hearing. Although this procedure does not preclude an out-of-court resolution of the dispute, the procedure tends to discourage informal negotiations. If answers are served and they are thought inadequate, the interrogating party may move under Rule 37(a) for an order compelling adequate answers. There is no assurance that the hearing on objections and that on inadequate answers will be heard together.

The amendment improves the procedure of Rule 33 in the following respects:

(1) The time allowed for response is increased to 30 days and this time period applies to both answers and objections, but a defendant need not respond in less than 45 days after service of the summons and complaint upon him. As is true under existing law, the responding party who believes that some parts or all of the interrogatories are objectionable may choose to seek a protective order under new Rule 26(c) or may serve objections under this rule. Unless he applies for a protective order, he is required to serve answers or objections in response to the interrogatories, subject to the sanctions provided in Rule 37(d). Answers and objections are served together, so that a response to each interrogatory is encouraged, and any failure to respond is easily noted.

(2) In view of the enlarged time permitted for response, it is no longer necessary to require leave of court for service of interrogatories. The purpose of this requirement—that defendant have time to obtain counsel before a response must be made—is adequately fulfilled by the requirement that interrogatories be served upon a party with or after service of the summons and complaint upon him.

Some would urge that the plaintiff nevertheless not be permitted to serve interrogatories with the complaint. They fear that a routine practice might be invited, whereby form interrogatories would accompany most complaints. More fundamentally, they feel that, since very general complaints are permitted in present-day pleading, it is fair that the defendant have a right to take the lead in serving interrogatories. (These views apply also to Rule 36.) The amendment of Rule 33 rejects these views, in favor of allowing both parties to go forward with discovery, each free to obtain the information he needs respecting the case.

(3) If objections are made, the burden is on the interrogating party to move under Rule 37(a) for a court order compelling answers, in the course of which the court will pass on the objections. The change in the burden of going forward does not alter the existing obligation of an objecting party to justify his objections. *E.g., Pressley v. Boehlke*, 33 F.R.D. 316 (W.D.N.C.1963). If the discovering party asserts that an answer is incomplete or evasive, again he may look to Rule 37(a) for relief, and he should add this assertion to his motion to overrule objections. There is no requirement that the parties consult informally concerning their differences, but the new procedure should encour-

age consultation, and the court may by local rule require it.

The proposed changes are similar in approach to those adopted by California in 1961. See Calif.Code Civ.Proc. § 2030(a). The experience of the Los Angeles Superior Court is informally reported as showing that the California amendment resulted in a significant reduction in court motions concerning interrogatories. Rhode Island takes a similar approach. See R. 33, R.I.R.Civ. Proc. Official Draft, p. 74 (Boston Law Book Co.).

A change is made in subdivision (a) which is not related to the sequence of procedures. The restriction to "adverse" parties is eliminated. The courts have generally construed this restriction as precluding interrogatories unless an issue between the parties is disclosed by the pleadings—even though the parties may have conflicting interests. *E.g., Mozeika v. Kaufman Construction Co.*, 25 F.R.D. 233 (E.D.Pa.1960) (plaintiff and third-party defendant); *Biddle v. Hutchinson*, 24 F.R.D. 256 (M.D.Pa.1959) (codefendants). The resulting distinctions have often been highly technical. In *Schlagenhauf v. Holder*, 379 U.S. 104, 85 S. Ct. 234, 13 L. Ed. 2d 152 (1964), the Supreme Court rejected a contention that examination under Rule 35 could be had only against an "opposing" party, as not in keeping "with the aims of a liberal, nontechnical application of the Federal Rules." 379 U.S. at 116. Eliminating the requirement of "adverse" parties from Rule 33 brings it into line with all other discovery rules.

A second change in subdivision (a) is the addition of the term "governmental agency" to the listing of organizations whose answers are to be made by any officer or agent of the organization. This does not involve any change in existing law. Compare the similar listing in Rule 30(b)(6).

The duty of a party to supplement his answers to interrogatories is governed by a new provision in Rule 26(c).

Subdivision (b). There are numerous and conflicting decisions on the question whether and to what extent interrogatories are limited to matters "of fact," or may elicit opinions, contentions, and legal conclusions. Compare, *e.g., Payer, Hewitt & Co. v. Bellanca Corp.*, 26 F.R.D. 219 (D.Del.1960) (opinions bad); *Zinsky v. New York Central R. R.*, 36 F.R.D. 680 (N.D.Ohio 1964) (factual opinion or contention good, but legal theory bad); *United States v. Carter Products, Inc.*, 28 F.R.D. 373 (S.D.N.Y.1961) (factual contentions and legal theories bad) with *Taylor v. Sound Steamship Lines, Inc.*, 100 F.Supp. 388 (D.Conn. 1951) (opinions good); *Bynum v. United States*, 36 F.R.D. 14 (E.D.La.1964) (contentions as to facts constituting negligence good). For lists of the many conflicting authorities, see 4 Moore's Federal Practice ¶ 33.17 (2d ed. 1966); 2A Barron & Holtzoff, *Federal Practice and Procedure* § 768 (Wright ed. 1961).

Rule 33 is amended to provide that an interrogatory is not objectionable merely because it calls for an opinion or contention that relates to fact or the application of law to fact. Efforts to draw sharp lines between facts and opinions have invariably been unsuccessful, and the clear trend of the cases is to permit "factual" opinions. As to requests for opinions or contentions that call for the application of law to fact, they can be most useful in narrowing and sharpening the issues, which is a major purpose of discovery. See *Diversified Products Corp. v. Sports Center Co.*, 42 F.R.D. 3 (D.Md.1967); Moore, *supra*; Field & McKusick, Maine Civil Practice § 26.18 (1959). On the other hand, under the new language interrogatories may not extend to issues of "pure law," *i.e.*, legal issues unrelated to the facts of the case. *Cf. United States v. Maryland & Va. Milk Producers Assn., Inc.*, 22 F.R.D. 300 (D.D.C.1958).

Since interrogatories involving mixed questions of law and fact may create disputes between the parties which are best resolved after much or all of the other discovery has been completed, the court is expressly authorized to defer an answer. Likewise, the court may delay determination until pretrial conference, if it believes that the dispute is best resolved in the presence of the judge.

The principal question raised with respect to the cases permitting such interrogatories is whether they reintroduce undesirable aspects of the prior pleading practice, whereby parties were chained to misconceived contentions or theories, and ultimate determination on the merits was frustrated. See James, *The*

Revival of Bills of Particulars under the Federal Rules, 71 Harv.L.Rev. 1473 (1958). But there are few if any instances in the recorded cases demonstrating that such frustration has occurred. The general rule governing the use of answers to interrogatories is that under ordinary circumstances they do not limit proof. See, *e.g., McElroy v. United Air Lines, Inc.*, 21 F.R.D. 100 (W.D.Mo. 1957); *Pressley v. Boehlke*, 33 F.R.D. 316, 317 (W.D.N.C.1963). Although in exceptional circumstances reliance on an answer may cause such prejudice that the court will hold the answering party bound to his answer, *e.g., Zielinski v. Philadelphia Piers, Inc.*, 139 F.Supp. 408 (E.D.Pa.1956), the interrogating party will ordinarily not be entitled to rely on the unchanging character of the answers he receives and cannot base prejudice on such reliance. The rule does not affect the power of a court to permit withdrawal or amendment of answers to interrogatories.

The use of answers to interrogatories at trial is made subject to the rules of evidence. The provisions governing use of depositions, to which Rule 33 presently refers, are not entirely apposite to answers to interrogatories, since deposition practice contemplates that all parties will ordinarily participate through cross-examination. See 4 Moore's Federal Practice ¶ 33.29[1] (2d ed. 1966).

Certain provisions are deleted from subdivision (b) because they are fully covered by new Rule 26(c) providing for protective orders and Rules 26(a) and 26(d). The language of the subdivision is thus simplified without any change of substance.

Subdivision (c). This is a new subdivision, adopted from Calif.Code Civ.Proc. § 2030(c), relating especially to interrogatories which require a party to engage in burdensome or expensive research into his own business records in order to give an answer. The subdivision gives the party an option to make the records available and place the burden of research of the party who seeks the information. "This provision, without undermining the liberal scope of interrogatory discovery, places the burden of discovery upon its potential benefitee," Louisell, Modern California Discovery, 124–125 (1963), and alleviates a problem which in the past has troubled Federal courts. See Speck, The Use of Discovery in United States District Courts, 60 Yale L.J. 1132, 1142–1144 (1951). The interrogating party is protected against abusive use of this provision through the requirement that the burden of ascertaining the answer be substantially the same for both sides. A respondent may not impose on an interrogating party a mass of records as to which research is feasible only for one familiar with the records. At the same time, the respondent unable to invoke this subdivision does not on that account lose the protection available to him under new Rule 26(c) against oppressive or unduly burdensome or expensive interrogatories. And even when the respondent successfully invokes the subdivision, the court is not deprived of its usual power, in appropriate cases, to require that the interrogating party reimburse the respondent for the expense of assembling his records and making them intelligible.

1980 AMENDMENT

Subdivision (c). The Committee is advised that parties upon whom interrogatories are served have occasionally responded by directing the interrogating party to a mass of business records or by offering to make all of their records available, justifying the response by the option provided by this subdivision. Such practices are an abuse of the option. A party who is permitted by the terms of this subdivision to offer records for inspection in lieu of answering an interrogatory should offer them in a manner that permits the same direct and economical access that is available to the party. If the information sought exists in the form of compilations, abstracts or summaries then available to the responding party, those should be made available to the interrogating party. The final sentence is added to make it clear that a responding party has the duty to specify, by category and location, the records from which answers to interrogatories can be derived.

1993 AMENDMENT

Purpose of Revision. The purpose of this revision is to reduce the frequency and increase the efficiency of interrogatory practice. The revision is based on experience with local rules. For ease of reference, subdivision (a) is divided into two subdivisions and the remaining subdivisions renumbered.

Subdivision (a). Revision of this subdivision limits interrogatory practice. Because Rule 26(a)(1)(3) requires disclosure of much of the information previously obtained by this form of discovery, there should be less occasion to use it. Experience in over half of the district courts has confirmed that limitations on the number of interrogatories are useful and manageable. Moreover, because the device can be costly and may be used as a means of harassment, it is desirable to subject its use to the control of the court consistent with the principles stated in Rule 26(b)(2), particularly in multi-party cases where it has not been unusual for the same interrogatory to be propounded to a party by more than one of its adversaries.

Each party is allowed to serve 25 interrogatories upon any other party, but must secure leave of court (or a stipulation from the opposing party) to serve a larger number. Parties cannot evade this presumptive limitation through the device of joining as "subparts" questions that seek information about discrete separate subjects. However, a question asking about communications of a particular type should be treated as a single interrogatory even though it requests that the time, place, persons present, and contents be stated separately for each such communication.

As with the number of depositions authorized by Rule 30, leave to serve additional interrogatories is to be allowed when consistent with Rule 26(b)(2). The aim is not to prevent needed discovery, but to provide judicial scrutiny before parties make potentially excessive use of this discovery device. In many cases it will be appropriate for the court to permit a larger number of interrogatories in the scheduling order entered under Rule 16(b).

Unless leave of court is obtained, interrogatories may not be served prior to the meeting of the parties under Rule 26(f).

When a case with outstanding interrogatories exceeding the number permitted by this rule is removed to federal court, the interrogating party must seek leave allowing the additional interrogatories, specify which twenty-five are to be answered, or resubmit interrogatories that comply with the rule. Moreover, under Rule 26(d), the time for response would be measured from the date of the parties' meeting under Rule 26(f). See Rule 81(c), providing that these rules govern procedures after removal.

Subdivision (b). A separate subdivision is made of the former second paragraph of subdivision (a). Language is added to paragraph (1) of this subdivision to emphasize the duty of the responding party to provide full answers to the extent not objectionable. If, for example, an interrogatory seeking information about numerous facilities or products is deemed objectionable, but an interrogatory seeking information about a lesser number of facilities or products would not have been objectionable, the interrogatory should be answered with respect to the latter even though an objection is raised as to the balance of the facilities or products. Similarly, the fact that additional time may be needed to respond to some questions (or to some aspects of questions) should not justify a delay in responding to those questions (or other aspects of questions) that can be answered within the prescribed time.

Paragraph (4) is added to make clear that objections must be specifically justified, and that unstated or untimely grounds for objection ordinarily are waived. Note also the provisions of revised Rule 26(b)(5), which require a responding party to indicate when it is withholding information under a claim of privilege or as trial preparation materials.

These provisions should be read in light of Rule 26(g), authorizing the court to impose sanctions on a party and attorney making an unfounded objection to an interrogatory.

Subdivisions (c) and (d). The provisions of former subdivisions (b) and (c) are renumbered.

2006 AMENDMENT

Rule 33(d) is amended to parallel Rule 34(a) by recognizing the importance of electronically stored information. The term "electronically stored information" has the same broad meaning in Rule 33(d) as in Rule 34(a). Much business information is stored only in electronic form; the Rule 33(d) option should be available with respect to such records as well.

Special difficulties may arise in using electronically stored information, either due to its form or because it is dependent on a particular computer system. Rule 33(d) allows a responding party to substitute access to documents or electronically stored information for an answer only if the burden of deriving the answer will be substantially the same for either party. Rule 33(d) states that a party electing to respond to an interrogatory by providing electronically stored information must ensure that the interrogating party can locate and identify it "as readily as can the party served," and that the responding party must give the interrogating party a "reasonable opportunity to examine, audit, or inspect" the information. Depending on the circumstances, satisfying these provisions with regard to electronically stored information may require the responding party to provide some combination of technical support, information on application software, or other assistance. The key question is whether such support enables the interrogating party to derive or ascertain the answer from the electronically stored information as readily as the responding party. A party that wishes to invoke Rule 33(d) by specifying electronically stored information may be required to provide direct access to its electronic information system, but only if that is necessary to afford the requesting party an adequate opportunity to derive or ascertain the answer to the interrogatory. In that situation, the responding party's need to protect sensitive interests of confidentiality or privacy may mean that it must derive or ascertain and provide the answer itself rather than invoke Rule 33(d).

2007 AMENDMENT

The language of Rule 33 has been amended as part of the general restyling of the Civil Rules to make them more easily understood and to make style and terminology consistent throughout the rules. These changes are intended to be stylistic only.

The final sentence of former Rule 33(a) was a redundant cross-reference to the discovery moratorium provisions of Rule 26(d). Rule 26(d) is now familiar, obviating any need to carry forward the redundant cross-reference.

Former Rule 33(b)(5) was a redundant reminder of Rule 37(a) procedure and is omitted as no longer useful.

Former Rule 33(c) stated that an interrogatory "is not necessarily objectionable merely because an answer * * * involves an opinion or contention * * *." "[I]s not necessarily" seemed to imply that the interrogatory might be objectionable merely for this reason. This implication has been ignored in practice. Opinion and contention interrogatories are used routinely. Amended Rule 33(a)(2) embodies the current meaning of Rule 33 by omitting "necessarily."

2015 AMENDMENT

Rule 33 is amended in parallel with Rules 30 and 31 to reflect the recognition of proportionality in Rule 26(b)(1).

Rule 34. Production of Documents and Things and Entry upon Land for Inspection and Other Purposes

1937 ADOPTION

In England orders are made for the inspection of documents, English Rules Under the Judicature Act (The Annual Practice, 1937) O. 31, r. r. 14, et seq., or for the inspection of tangible property or for entry upon land, O. 50, r. 3. Michigan provides for inspection of damaged property when such damage is the ground of the action. Mich.Court Rules Ann. (Searl, 1933) Rule 41, § 2.

Practically all states have statutes authorizing the court to order parties in possession or control of documents to permit other parties to inspect and copy them before trial. See Ragland, Discovery Before Trial (1932) Appendix, p. 267, setting out the statutes.

Compare former Equity Rule 58 (Discovery—Interrogatories—Inspection and Production of Documents—Admission of Execution or Genuineness)(fifth paragraph).

1946 AMENDMENT

Note. The changes in clauses (1) and (2) correlate the scope of inquiry permitted under Rule 34 with that provided in Rule 26(b), and thus remove any ambiguity created by the former differences in language. As stated in Olson Transportation Co. v. Socony-Vacuum Oil Co., E.D.Wis.1944, 8 Fed.Rules Serv. 34.41, Case 2 "* * * Rule 34 is a direct and simple method of discovery." At the same time the addition of the words following the term "parties" makes certain that the person in whose custody, possession, or control the evidence reposes may have the benefit of the applicable protective orders stated in Rule 30(b). This change should be considered in the light of the proposed expansion of Rule 30(b).

An objection has been made that the word "designated" in Rule 34 has been construed with undue strictness in some district court cases so as to require great and impracticable specificity in the description of documents, papers, books, etc., sought to be inspected. The Committee, however, believes that no amendment is needed, and that the proper meaning of "designated" as requiring specificity has already been delineated by the Supreme Court. See *Brown v. United States, 1928*, 276 U.S. 134, 143, 48 S. Ct. 288, 290, 72 L.Ed. 500 ("The subpoena * * * specifies * * * with reasonable particularity the subjects to which the documents called for related."); *Consolidated Rendering Co. v. Vermont, 1908*, 207 U.S. 541, 543–544, 28 S. Ct. 178, 179, 52 L.Ed. 327 ("We see no reason why all such books, papers and correspondence which related to the subject of inquiry, and were described with reasonable detail, should not be called for and the company directed to produce them. Otherwise, the State would be compelled to designate each particular paper which it desired, which presupposes an accurate knowledge of such papers, which the tribunal desiring the papers would probably rarely, if ever, have.").

1970 AMENDMENT

Rule 34 is revised to accomplish the following major changes in the existing rule: (1) to eliminate the requirement of good cause; (2) to have the rule operate extrajudicially; (3) to include testing and sampling as well as inspecting or photographing tangible things; and (4) to make clear that the rule does not preclude an independent action for analogous discovery against persons not parties.

Subdivision (a). Good cause is eliminated because it has furnished an uncertain and erratic protection to the parties from whom production is sought and is now rendered unnecessary by virtue of the more specific provisions added to Rule 26(b) relating to materials assembled in preparation for trial and to experts retained or consulted by parties.

The good cause requirement was originally inserted in Rule 34 as a general protective provision in the absence of experience with the specific problems that would arise thereunder. As the note to Rule 26(b)(3) on trial preparation materials makes clear, good cause has been applied differently to varying classes of documents, though not without confusion. It has often been said in court opinions that good cause requires a consideration of need for the materials and of alternative means of obtaining them, i.e., something more than relevance and lack of privilege. But the overwhelming proportion of the cases in which the formula of good cause has been applied to require a special showing are those involving trial preparation. In practice, the courts have not treated documents as having a special immunity to discovery simply because of their being documents. Protection may be afforded to claims of privacy or secrecy or of undue burden or expense under what is now Rule 26(c) (previously Rule 30(b)). To be sure, an appraisal of "undue" burden inevitably entails consideration of the needs of the party seeking discovery. With special provisions added to govern trial preparation materials and experts, there is no longer any occasion to retain the requirement of good cause.

The revision of Rule 34 to have it operate extrajudicially, rather than by court order, is to a large extent a reflection of existing law office practice. The Columbia Survey shows that of the litigants seeking inspection of documents or things, only about 25 percent filed motions for court orders. This minor fraction nevertheless accounted for a significant number of motions. About half of these motions were uncontested and in almost all instances the party seeking production ultimately prevailed. Although an extrajudicial procedure will not drastically alter existing practice under Rule 34—it will conform to it in most cases—it has the potential of saving court time in a substantial though proportionately small number of cases tried annually.

The inclusion of testing and sampling of tangible things and objects or operations on land reflects a need frequently encountered by parties in preparation for trial. If the operation of a particular machine is the basis of a claim for negligent injury, it will often be necessary to test its operating parts or to sample and test the products it is producing. *Cf.* Mich.Gen.Ct.R. 310.1(1)(1963) (testing authorized).

The inclusive description of "documents" is revised to accord with changing technology. It makes clear that Rule 34 applies to electronic data compilations from which information can be obtained only with the use of detection devices, and that when the data can as a practical matter be made usable by the discovering party only through respondent's devices, respondent may be required to use his devices to translate the data into usable form. In many instances, this means that respondent will have to supply a printout of computer data. The burden thus placed on respondent will vary from case to case, and the courts have ample power under Rule 26(c) to protect respondent against undue burden or expense, either by restricting discovery or requiring that the discovering party pay costs. Similarly, if the discovering party needs to check the electronic source itself, the court may protect respondent with respect to preservation of his records, confidentiality of nondiscoverable matters, and costs.

Subdivision (b). The procedure provided in Rule 34 is essentially the same as that in Rule 33, as amended, and the discussion in the note appended to that rule is relevant to Rule 34 as well. Problems peculiar to Rule 34 relate to the specific arrangements that must be worked out for inspection and related acts of copying, photographing, testing, or sampling. The rule provides that a request for inspection shall set forth the items to be inspected either by item or category, describing each with reasonable particularity, and shall specify a reasonable time, place, and manner of making the inspection.

Subdivision (c). Rule 34 as revised continues to apply only to parties. Comments from the bar make clear that in the preparation of cases for trial it is occasionally necessary to enter land or inspect large tangible things in the possession of a person not a party, and that some courts have dismissed independent actions in the nature of bills in equity for such discovery on the ground that Rule 34 is preemptive. While an ideal solution to this problem is to provide for discovery against persons not parties in Rule 34, both the jurisdictional and procedural problems are very complex. For the present, this subdivision makes clear that Rule 34 does not preclude independent actions for discovery against persons not parties.

1980 AMENDMENT

Subdivision (b). The Committee is advised that, "It is apparently not rare for parties deliberately to mix critical documents with others in the hope of obscuring significance." Report of the Special Committee for the Study of Discovery Abuse, Section of Litigation of the American Bar Association (1977) 22. The sentence added by this subdivision follows the recommendation of the Report.

1987 AMENDMENT

The amendment is technical. No substantive change is intended.

1991 AMENDMENT

This amendment reflects the change effected by revision of Rule 45 to provide for subpoenas to compel non-parties to produce documents and things and to submit to inspections of premises. The deletion of the text of the former paragraph is not intended to preclude an independent action for production of documents or things or for permission to enter upon land, but such actions may no longer be necessary in light of this revision.

1993 AMENDMENT

The rule is revised to reflect the change made by Rule 26(d), preventing a party from seeking formal discovery prior to the meeting of the parties required by Rule 26(f). Also, like a change made in Rule 33, the rule is modified to make clear that, if a request for production is objectionable only in part, production should be afforded with respect to the unobjectionable portions.

When a case with outstanding requests for production is removed to federal court, the time for response would be measured from the date of the parties' meeting. See Rule 81(c), providing that these rules govern procedures after removal.

2006 AMENDMENT

Subdivision (a). As originally adopted, Rule 34 focused on discovery of "documents" and "things." In 1970, Rule 34(a) was amended to include discovery of data compilations, anticipating that the use of computerized information would increase. Since then, the growth in electronically stored information and in the variety of systems for creating and storing such information has been dramatic. Lawyers and judges interpreted the term "documents" to include electronically stored information because it was obviously improper to allow a party to evade discovery obligations on the basis that the label had not kept pace with changes in information technology. But it has become increasingly difficult to say that all forms of electronically stored information, many dynamic in nature, fit within the traditional concept of a "document." Electronically stored information may exist in dynamic databases and other forms far different from fixed expression on paper. Rule 34(a) is amended to confirm that discovery of electronically stored information stands on equal footing with discovery of paper documents. The change clarifies that Rule 34 applies to information that is fixed in a tangible form and to information that is stored in a medium from which it can be retrieved and examined. At the same time, a Rule 34 request for production of "documents" should be understood to encompass, and the response should include, electronically stored information unless discovery in the action has clearly distinguished between electronically stored information and "documents."

Discoverable information often exists in both paper and electronic form, and the same or similar information might exist in both. The items listed in Rule 34(a) show different ways in which information may be recorded or stored. Images, for example, might be hard-copy documents or electronically stored information. The wide variety of computer systems currently in use, and the rapidity of technological change, counsel against a limiting or precise definition of electronically stored information. Rule 34(a)(1) is expansive and includes any type of information that is stored electronically. A common example often sought in discovery is electronic communications, such as e-mail. The rule covers—either as documents or as electronically stored information—information "stored in any medium," to encompass future developments in computer technology. Rule 34(a)(1) is intended to be broad enough to cover all current types of computer-based information, and flexible enough to encompass future changes and developments.

References elsewhere in the rules to "electronically stored information" should be understood to invoke this expansive approach. A companion change is made to Rule 33(d), making it explicit that parties choosing to respond to an interrogatory by permitting access to responsive records may do so by providing access to electronically stored information. More generally, the term used in Rule 34(a)(1) appears in a number of other amendments, such as those to Rules 26(a)(1), 26(b)(2), 26(b)(5)(B), 26(f), 34(b), 37(f), and 45. In each of these rules, electronically stored information has the same broad meaning it has under Rule

34(a)(1). References to "documents" appear in discovery rules that are not amended, including Rules 30(f), 36(a), and 37(c)(2). These references should be interpreted to include electronically stored information as circumstances warrant.

The term "electronically stored information" is broad, but whether material that falls within this term should be produced, and in what form, are separate questions that must be addressed under Rules 26(b), 26(c), and 34(b).

The Rule 34(a) requirement that, if necessary, a party producing electronically stored information translate it into reasonably usable form does not address the issue of translating from one human language to another. *See In re Puerto Rico Elect. Power Auth.*, 687 F.2d 501, 504–510 (1st Cir.1982).

Rule 34(a)(1) is also amended to make clear that parties may request an opportunity to test or sample materials sought under the rule in addition to inspecting and copying them. That opportunity may be important for both electronically stored information and hard-copy materials. The current rule is not clear that such testing or sampling is authorized; the amendment expressly permits it. As with any other form of discovery, issues of burden and intrusiveness raised by requests to test or sample can be addressed under Rules 26(b)(2) and 26(c). Inspection or testing of certain types of electronically stored information or of a responding party's electronic information system may raise issues of confidentiality or privacy. The addition of testing and sampling to Rule 34(a) with regard to documents and electronically stored information is not meant to create a routine right of direct access to a party's electronic information system, although such access might be justified in some circumstances. Courts should guard against undue intrusiveness resulting from inspecting or testing such systems.

Rule 34(a)(1) is further amended to make clear that tangible things must—like documents and land sought to be examined—be designated in the request.

Subdivision (b). Rule 34(b) provides that a party must produce documents as they are kept in the usual course of business or must organize and label them to correspond with the categories in the discovery request. The production of electronically stored information should be subject to comparable requirements to protect against deliberate or inadvertent production in ways that raise unnecessary obstacles for the requesting party. Rule 34(b) is amended to ensure similar protection for electronically stored information.

The amendment to Rule 34(b) permits the requesting party to designate the form or forms in which it wants electronically stored information produced. The form of production is more important to the exchange of electronically stored information than of hard-copy materials, although a party might specify hard copy as the requested form. Specification of the desired form or forms may facilitate the orderly, efficient, and cost-effective discovery of electronically stored information. The rule recognizes that different forms of production may be appropriate for different types of electronically stored information. Using current technology, for example, a party might be called upon to produce word processing documents, e-mail messages, electronic spreadsheets, different image or sound files, and material from databases. Requiring that such diverse types of electronically stored information all be produced in the same form could prove impossible, and even if possible could increase the cost and burdens of producing and using the information. The rule therefore provides that the requesting party may ask for different forms of production for different types of electronically stored information.

The rule does not require that the requesting party choose a form or forms of production. The requesting party may not have a preference. In some cases, the requesting party may not know what form the producing party uses to maintain its electronically stored information, although Rule 26(f)(3) is amended to call for discussion of the form of production in the parties' prediscovery conference.

The responding party also is involved in determining the form of production. In the written response to the production request that Rule 34 requires, the responding party must state the form it intends to use for producing electronically stored information if the requesting party does not specify a form or if the responding party objects to a form that the requesting party specifies. Stating the intended form before the production occurs may permit the parties to identify and seek to resolve disputes before the expense and work of the production occurs. A party that responds to a discovery request by simply producing electronically stored information in a form of its choice, without identifying that form in advance of the production in the response required by Rule 34(b), runs a risk that the requesting party can show that the produced form is not reasonably usable and that it is entitled to production of some or all of the information in an additional form. Additional time might be required to permit a responding party to assess the appropriate form or forms of production.

If the requesting party is not satisfied with the form stated by the responding party, or if the responding party has objected to the form specified by the requesting party, the parties must meet and confer under Rule 37(a)(2)(B) in an effort to resolve the matter before the requesting party can file a motion to compel. If they cannot agree and the court resolves the dispute, the court is not limited to the forms initially chosen by the requesting party, stated by the responding party, or specified in this rule for situations in which there is no court order or party agreement.

If the form of production is not specified by party agreement or court order, the responding party must produce electronically stored information either in a form or forms in which it is ordinarily maintained or in a form or forms that are reasonably usable. Rule 34(a) requires that, if necessary, a responding party "translate" information it produces into a "reasonably usable" form. Under some circumstances, the responding party may need to provide some reasonable amount of technical support, information on application software, or other reasonable assistance to enable the requesting party to use the information. The rule does not require a party to produce electronically stored information in the form it which it is ordinarily maintained, as long as it is produced in a reasonably usable form. But the option to produce in a reasonably usable form does not mean that a responding party is free to convert electronically stored information from the form in which it is ordinarily maintained to a different form that makes it more difficult or burdensome for the requesting party to use the information efficiently in the litigation. If the responding party ordinarily maintains the information it is producing in a way that makes it searchable by electronic means, the information should not be produced in a form that removes or significantly degrades this feature.

Some electronically stored information may be ordinarily maintained in a form that is not reasonably usable by any party. One example is "legacy" data that can be used only by superseded systems. The questions whether a producing party should be required to convert such information to a more usable form, or should be required to produce it at all, should be addressed under Rule 26(b)(2)(B).

Whether or not the requesting party specified the form of production, Rule 34(b) provides that the same electronically stored information ordinarily need be produced in only one form.

2007 AMENDMENT

The language of Rule 34 has been amended as part of the general restyling of the Civil Rules to make them more easily understood and to make style and terminology consistent throughout the rules. These changes are intended to be stylistic only.

The final sentence in the first paragraph of former Rule 34(b) was a redundant cross-reference to the discovery moratorium provisions of Rule 26(d). Rule 26(d) is now familiar, obviating any need to carry forward the redundant cross-reference.

The redundant reminder of Rule 37(a) procedure in the second paragraph of former Rule 34(b) is omitted as no longer useful.

2015 AMENDMENT

Several amendments are made in Rule 34, aimed at reducing the potential to impose unreasonable burdens by objections to requests to produce.

Rule 34(b)(2)(A) is amended to fit with new Rule 26(d)(2). The time to respond to a Rule 34 request delivered before the parties' Rule 26(f) conference is 30 days after the first Rule 26(f) conference.

Rule 34(b)(2)(B) is amended to require that objections to Rule 34 requests be stated with specificity. This provision adopts the language of Rule 33(b)(4), eliminating any doubt that less specific objections might be suitable under Rule 34. The specificity of the objection ties to the new provision in Rule 34(b)(2)(C) directing that an objection must state whether any responsive materials are being withheld on the basis of that objection. An objection may state that a request is overbroad, but if the objection recognizes that some part of the request is appropriate the objection should state the scope that is not overbroad. Examples would be a statement that the responding party will limit the search to documents or electronically stored information created within a given period of time prior to the events in suit, or to specified sources. When there is such an objection, the statement of what has been withheld can properly identify as matters "withheld" anything beyond the scope of the search specified in the objection.

Rule 34(b)(2)(B) is further amended to reflect the common practice of producing copies of documents or electronically stored information rather than simply permitting inspection. The response to the request must state that copies will be produced. The production must be completed either by the time for inspection specified in the request or by another reasonable time specifically identified in the response. When it is necessary to make the production in stages the response should specify the beginning and end dates of the production.

Rule 34(b)(2)(C) is amended to provide that an objection to a Rule 34 request must state whether anything is being withheld on the basis of the objection. This amendment should end the confusion that frequently arises when a producing party states several objections and still produces information, leaving the requesting party uncertain whether any relevant and responsive information has been withheld on the basis of the objections. The producing party does not need to provide a detailed description or log of all documents withheld, but does need to alert other parties to the fact that documents have been withheld and thereby facilitate an informed discussion of the objection. An objection that states the limits that have controlled the search for responsive and relevant materials qualifies as a statement that the materials have been "withheld."

Rule 35. Physical and Mental Examinations of Persons

1937 ADOPTION

Physical examination of parties before trial is authorized by statute or rule in a number of states. See Ariz.Rev.Code Ann. (Struckmeyer, 1928) § 4468; Mich. Court Rules Ann. (Searl, 1933) Rule 41, § 2; 2 N.J.Comp.Stat. (1910); N.Y.C. P.A. (1937) § 306; 1 S.D.Comp.Laws (1929) § 2716A; 3 Wash.Rev.Stat.Ann. (Remington, 1932) § 1230-1.

Mental examination of parties is authorized in Iowa. Iowa Code (1935) ch. 491-F1. See McCash, The Evolution of the Doctrine of Discovery and Its Present Status in Iowa, 20 Ia.L.Rev. 68 (1934).

The constitutionality of legislation providing for physical examination of parties was sustained in *Lyon v. Manhattan Railway Co., 1894*, 37 N.E. 113, 142 N.Y. 298, and *McGovern v. Hope, 1899*, 42 A. 830, 63 N.J.L. 76. In *Union Pacific Ry. Co. v. Botsford, 1891*, 141 U.S. 250, 11 S. Ct. 1000, 35 L.Ed. 734, it was held that the court could not order the physical examination of a party in the absence of statutory authority. But in *Camden and Suburban Ry. Co. v. Stetson, 1900*, 177 U.S. 172, 20 S. Ct. 617, 44 L.Ed. 721 where there was statutory authority for such examination, derived from a state statute made operative by the conformity act, the practice was sustained. Such authority is now found in the present rule made operative by the Act of June 19, 1934, c. 651, U.S.C., Title 28, § 2072, formerly §§ 723b (Rules in actions at law; Supreme Court authorized to make) and 723c (Union of equity and action at law rules; power of Supreme Court).

1970 AMENDMENT

Subdivision (a). Rule 35(a) has hitherto provided only for an order requiring a party to submit to an examination. It is desirable to extend the rule to provide for an order against the party for examination of a person in his custody or under his legal control. As appears from the provisions of amended Rule 37(b)(2) and the comment under that rule, an order to "produce" the third person imposes only an obligation to use good faith, efforts to produce the person.

The amendment will settle beyond doubt that a parent or guardian suing to recover for injuries to a minor may be ordered to produce the minor for examination. Further, the amendment expressly includes blood examination within the kinds of examinations that can be ordered under the rule. See *Beach v. Beach*, 114 F.2d 479 (D.C.Cir.1940), Provisions similar to the amendment have been adopted in at least 10 States; Calif.Code Civ.Proc. § 2032; Ida.R. Civ.P. 35; Ill. S-H Ann. c. 110A, § 215; Md.R.P. 420; Mich.Gen.Ct.R. 311; Minn.R. Civ.P. 35; Mo.Vern.Ann.R.Civ.P. 60.01; N.Dak.R.Civ.P. 35; N.Y.C.P.L. § 3121; Wyo.R.Civ.P. 35.

The amendment makes no change in the requirements of Rule 35 that, before a court order may issue the relevant physical or mental condition must be shown to be "in controversy" and "good cause" must be shown for the examination. Thus, the amendment has no effect on the recent decision of the Supreme Court in *Schlagenhauf v. Holder*, 379 U.S. 104, 85 S. Ct. 234, 13 L. Ed. 2d 152 (1964), stressing the importance of these requirements and applying them to the facts of the case. The amendment makes no reference to employees of a party. Provisions relating to employees in the State statutes and rules cited above appear to have been virtually unused.

Subdivision (b)(1). This subdivision is amended to correct an imbalance in Rule 35(b)(1) as heretofore written. Under that text, a party causing a Rule 35(a) examination to be made is required to furnish to the party examined, on request, a copy of the examining physician's report. If he delivers this copy, he is in turn entitled to receive from the party examined reports of all examinations of the same condition previously or later made. But the rule has not in terms entitled the examined party to receive from the party causing the Rule 35(a) examination any reports of earlier examinations of the same condition to which the latter may have access. The amendment cures this defect. See La.Stat. Ann., Civ.Proc. art 1495 (1960); Utah R.Civ.P. 35(c).

The amendment specifies that the written report of the examining physician includes results of all tests made, such as results of X-rays and cardiograms. It also embodies changes required by the broadening of Rule 35(a) to take in persons who are not parties.

Subdivision (b)(3). This new subdivision removes any possible doubt that reports of examination may be obtained although no order for examination has been made under Rule 35(a). Examinations are very frequently made by agreement, and sometimes before the party examined has an attorney. The courts have uniformly ordered that reports be supplied, see 4 Moore's Federal Practice ¶ 35.06, n. 1 (2d ed. 1966); 2A Barron & Holtzoff, Federal Practice and Procedure § 823, n. 22 (Wright ed. 1961), and it appears best to fill the technical gap in the present rule.

The subdivision also makes clear that reports of examining physicians are discoverable not only under Rule 35(b), but under other rules as well. To be sure, if the report is privileged, then discovery is not permissible under any rule other than Rule 35(b) and it is permissible under Rule 35(b) only if the party requests a copy of the report of examination made by the other party's doctor. *Sher v. De Haven*, 199 F.2d 777 (D.C.Cir.1952), *cert. denied* 345 U.S. 936, 73 S. Ct. 797, 97 L.Ed. 1363 (1953). But if the report is unprivileged and is subject to discovery under the provisions of rules other than Rule 35(b)—such as Rules 34 or 26(b)(3) or (4)—discovery should not depend upon whether the person examined demands a copy of the report. Although a few cases have suggested the contrary, *e.g., Galloway v. National Dairy Products Corp.*, 24 F.R.D. 362 (E. D.Pa.1959), the better considered district court decisions hold that Rule 35(b) is not preemptive. *E.g., Leszynski v. Russ*, 29 F.R.D. 10, 12 (D.Md.1961) and cases cited. The question was recently given full consideration in *Buffington v. Wood*, 351 F.2d 292 (3d Cir.1965), holding that Rule 35(b) is not preemptive.

1987 AMENDMENT

The amendments are technical. No substantive change is intended.

1991 AMENDMENT

The revision authorizes the court to require physical or mental examinations conducted by any person who is suitably licensed or certified.

The rule was revised in 1988 by Congressional enactment to authorize mental examinations by licensed clinical psychologists. This revision extends that amendment to include other certified or licensed professionals, such as dentists or occupational therapists, who are not physicians or clinical psychologists, but who may be well-qualified to give valuable testimony about the physical or mental condition that is the subject of dispute.

The requirement that the examiner be *suitably* licensed or certified is a new requirement. The court is thus expressly authorized to assess the credentials of the examiner to assure that no person is subjected to a court-ordered examination by an examiner whose testimony would be of such limited value that it would be unjust to require the person to undergo the invasion of privacy associated with the examination. This authority is not wholly new, for under the former rule, the court retained discretion to refuse to order an examination, or to restrict an examination. 8 WRIGHT & MILLER, FEDERAL PRACTICE & PROCEDURE § 2234 (1986 Supp.). The revision is intended to encourage the exercise of this discretion, especially with respect to examinations by persons having narrow qualifications.

The court's responsibility to determine the suitability of the examiner's qualifications applies even to a proposed examination by a physician. If the proposed examination and testimony calls for an expertise that the proposed examiner does not have, it should not be ordered, even if the proposed examiner is a physician. The rule does not, however, require that the license or certificate be conferred by the jurisdiction in which the examination is conducted.

2007 AMENDMENT

The language of Rule 35 has been amended as part of the general restyling of the Civil Rules to make them more easily understood and to make style and terminology consistent throughout the rules. These changes are intended to be stylistic only.

Rule 36. Requests for Admission

1937 ADOPTION

Compare similar rules: Former Equity Rule 58 (last paragraph, which provides for the admission of the execution and genuineness of documents); English Rules Under the Judicature Act (The Annual Practice, 1937) O. 32; Ill.Rev.Stat. (1937) ch. 110, § 182 and Rule 18 (Ill.Rev.Stat. (1937) ch. 110, § 259.18); 2 Mass.Gen.Laws (Ter.Ed., 1932) ch. 231, § 69; Mich. Court Rules Ann. (Searl, 1933) Rule 42; N.J.Comp.Stat. (2 Cum.Supp. 1911 to 1924); N.Y.C. P.A. (1937) §§ 322, 323; Wis.Stat. (1935) § 327.22.

1946 AMENDMENT

Note. The first change in the first sentence of Rule 36(a) and the addition of the new second sentence, specifying when requests for admissions may be served, bring Rule 36 in line with amended Rules 26(a) and 33. There is no reason why these rules should not be treated alike. Other provisions of Rule 36(a) give the party whose admissions are requested adequate protection.

The second change in the first sentence of the rule [subdivision (a)] removes any uncertainty as to whether a party can be called upon to admit matters of fact other than those set forth in relevant documents described in and exhibited with the request. In *Smyth v. Kaufman, C.C.A.2, 1940*, 114 F.2d 40, it was held that the word "therein", now stricken from the rule [said subdivision] referred to the request and that a matter of fact not related to any document could be presented to the other party for admission or denial. The rule of this case is now clearly stated.

The substitution of the word "served" for "delivered" in the third sentence of the amended rule [said subdivision] is in conformance with the use of the word "serve" elsewhere in the rule and generally throughout the rules. See also notes to Rules 13(a) and 33 herein. The substitution [in said subdivision] of "shorter or longer" for "further" will enable a court to designate a lesser period than 10 days for answer. This conforms with a similar provision already contained in Rule 33.

The addition of clause (2) [in said subdivision] specifies the method by which a party may challenge the propriety of a request to admit. There has been considerable difference of judicial opinion as to the correct method, if any, available to secure relief from an allegedly improper request. See Commentary, Methods of Objecting to Notice to Admit, 1942, 5 Fed.Rules Serv. 835; *International Carbonic Engineering Co. v. Natural Carbonic Products, Inc., S.D.Cal.1944*, 57 F.Supp. 248. The changes in clause (1) are merely of a clarifying and conforming nature.

The first of the added last two sentences [in said subdivision] prevents an objection to a part of a request from holding up the answer, if any, to the remainder. See similar proposed change in Rule 33. The last sentence strengthens the rule by making the denial accurately reflect the party's position. It is taken, with necessary changes, from Rule 8(b).

1970 AMENDMENT

Rule 36 serves two vital purposes, both of which are designed to reduce trial time. Admissions are sought, first to facilitate proof with respect to issues that cannot be eliminated from the case, and secondly, to narrow the issues by eliminating those that can be. The changes made in the rule are designed to serve these purposes more effectively. Certain disagreements in the courts about the proper scope of the rule are resolved. In addition, the procedural operation of the rule is brought into line with other discovery procedures, and the binding effect of an admission is clarified. See generally Finman, The Request for Admissions in Federal Civil Procedure, 71 Yale L.J. 371 (1962).

Subdivision (a). As revised, the subdivision provides that a request may be made to admit any matters within the scope of Rule 26(b) that relate to statements or opinions of fact or of the application of law to fact. It thereby eliminates the requirement that the matters be "of fact." This change resolves conflicts in the court decisions as to whether a request to admit matters of "opinion" and matters involving "mixed law and fact" is proper under the rule. As to "opinion," compare, *e.g., Jackson Buff Corp. v. Marcelle*, 20 F.R.D. 139 (E.D.N.Y.1957); *California v. The S. S. Jules Fribourg*, 19 F.R.D. 432 (N.D.Cal.1955), with *e.g., Photon, Inc. v. Harris Intertype, Inc.*, 28 F.R.D. 327 (D.Mass.1961); *Hise v. Lockwood Grader Corp.*, 153 F.Supp. 276 (D.Neb.1957). As to "mixed law and fact" the majority of courts sustain objections, *e.g., Minnesota Mining and Mfg. Co. v. Norton Co.*, 36 F.R.D. 1 (N.D.Ohio 1964), but *McSparran v. Hanigan*, 225 F.Supp. 628 (E.D.Pa.1963) is to the contrary.

Not only is it difficult as a practical matter to separate "fact" from "opinion," see 4 Moore's Federal Practice ¶ 36.04 (2d ed. 1966); cf. 2A Barron & Holtzoff, Federal Practice and Procedure 317 (Wright ed. 1961), but an admission on a matter of opinion may facilitate proof or narrow the issues or both. An admission of a matter involving the application of law to fact may, in a given case, even more clearly narrow the issues. For example, an admission that an employee acted in the scope of his employment may remove a major issue from the trial. In *McSparran* v. *Hanigan*, *supra*, plaintiff admitted that "the premises on which said accident occurred, were occupied or under the control" of one of the defendants, 225 F.Supp. at 636. This admission, involving law as well as fact, removed one of the issues from the lawsuit and thereby reduced the proof required at trial. The amended provision does not authorize requests for admissions of law unrelated to the facts of the case.

Requests for admission involving the application of law to fact may create disputes between the parties which are best resolved in the presence of the judge after much or all of the other discovery has been completed. Power is therefore expressly conferred upon the court to defer decision until a pretrial conference is held or until a designated time prior to trial. On the other hand, the court should not automatically defer decision; in many instances, the importance of the admission lies in enabling the requesting party to avoid the burdensome accumulation of proof prior to the pretrial conference.

Courts have also divided on whether an answering party may properly object to request for admission as to matters which that party regards as "in dispute". Compare, *e.g., Syracuse Broadcasting Corp. v. Newhouse*, 271 F.2d 910, 917 (2d Cir.1959); *Driver v. Gindy Mfg. Corp.*, 24 F.R.D. 473 (E.D.Pa.1959); with *e.g., McGonigle v. Baxter*, 27 F.R.D. 504 (E.D.Pa.1961); *United States v. Ehbauer*, 13 F.R.D. 462 (W.D.Mo.1952). The proper response in such cases is an answer. The very purpose of the request is to ascertain whether the answering party is prepared to admit or regards the matter as presenting a genuine issue for trial. In his answer, the party may deny, or he may give as his reason for inability to admit or deny the existence of a genuine issue. The party runs no risk of sanctions if the matter is genuinely in issue since Rule 37(c) provides a sanction of costs only when there are no good reasons for a failure to admit.

On the other hand, requests to admit may be so voluminous and so framed that the answering party finds the task of identifying what is in dispute and what is not unduly burdensome. If so, the responding party may obtain a protective order under Rule 26(c). Some of the decisions sustaining objections on "disputability" grounds could have been justified by the burdensome character of the requests. See *e.g., Syracuse Broadcasting Corp.* v. *Newhouse*, *supra*.

Another sharp split of authority exists on the question whether a party may base his answer on lack of information or knowledge without seeking out additional information. One line of cases has held that a party may answer on the basis of such knowledge as he has at the time he answers. *E.g., Jackson Buff Corp. v. Marcelle*, 20 F.R.D. 139 (E.D.N.Y.1957); *Sladek v. General Motors Corp.*, 16 F.R.D. 104 (S.D.Iowa 1954). A larger group of cases, supported by commentators, has taken the view that if the responding party lacks knowledge, he must inform himself in reasonable fashion. *E.g., Hise v. Lockwood Grader Corp.*, 153 F.Supp. 276 (D.Neb.1957); *E. H. Tate Co. v. Jiffy Enterprises, Inc.*, 16 F.R.D. 571 (E.D.Pa.1954); Finman, *supra*, 71 Yale L.J. 371, 404–409; 4 Moore's Federal Practice ¶ 36.04 (2d ed. 1966); 2A Barron & Holtzoff, Federal Practice and Procedure 509 (Wright ed. 1961).

The rule as revised adopts the majority view, as in keeping with a basic principle of the discovery rules that a reasonable burden may be imposed on the parties when its discharge will facilitate preparation for trial and ease the trial process. It has been argued against this view that one side should not have the burden of "proving" the other side's case. The revised rule requires only that the answering party make reasonable inquiry and secure such knowledge and information as are readily obtainable by him. In most instances, the investigation will be necessary either to his own case or to preparation for rebuttal. Even when it is not, the information may be close enough at hand to be "readily obtainable." Rule 36 requires only that the party state that he has taken these steps. The sanction for failure of a party to inform himself before he answers lies in the award of costs after trial, as provided in Rule 37(c).

The requirement that the answer to a request for admission be sworn is deleted, in favor of a provision that the answer be signed by the party or by his attorney. The provisions of Rule 36 make it clear that admissions function very much as pleadings do. Thus, when a party admits in part and denies in part, his admission is for purposes of the pending action only and may not be used against him in any other proceeding. The broadening of the rule to encompass mixed questions of law and fact reinforces this feature. Rule 36 does not lack a sanction for false answers; Rule 37(c) furnishes an appropriate deterrent.

The existing language describing the available grounds for objection to a request for admission is eliminated as neither necessary nor helpful. The statement that objection may be made to any request which is "improper" adds nothing to the provisions that the party serve an answer or objection addressed to each matter and that he state his reasons for any objection. None of the other discovery rules sets forth grounds for objection, except so far as all are subject to the general provisions of Rule 26.

Changes are made in the sequence of procedures in Rule 36 so that they conform to the new procedures in Rules 33 and 34. The major changes are as follows:

(1) The normal time for response to a request for admissions is lengthened from 10 to 30 days, conforming more closely to prevailing practice. A defendant need not respond, however, in less than 45 days after service of the summons and complaint upon him. The court may lengthen or shorten the time when special situations require it.

(2) The present requirement that the plaintiff wait 10 days to serve requests without leave of court is eliminated. The revised provision accords with those in Rules 33 and 34.

(3) The requirement that the objecting party move automatically for a hearing on his objection is eliminated, and the burden is on the requesting party to move for an order. The change in the burden of going forward does not modify present law on burden of persuasion. The award of expenses incurred in relation to the motion is made subject to the comprehensive provisions of Rule 37(a)(4).

(4) A problem peculiar to Rule 36 arises if the responding party serves answers that are not in conformity with the requirements of the rule—for example, a denial is not "specific," or the explanation of inability to admit or deny is not "in detail." Rule 36 now makes no provision for court scrutiny of such answers before trial, and it seems to contemplate that defective answers bring about admissions just as effectively as if no answer had been served. Some cases have so held. *E.g., Southern Ry. Co. v. Crosby*, 201 F.2d 878 (4th Cir.1953); *United States v. Laney*, 96 F.Supp. 482 (E.D.S.C.1951).

Giving a defective answer the automatic effect of an admission may cause unfair surprise. A responding party who purported to deny or to be unable to admit or deny will for the first time at trial confront the contention that he has made a binding admission. Since it is not always easy to know whether a denial is "specific" or an explanation is "in detail," neither party can know how the court will rule at trial and whether proof must be prepared. Some courts, therefore, have entertained motions to rule on defective answers. They have at times ordered that amended answers be served, when the defects were technical, and at other times have declared that the matter was admitted. *E.g., Woods v. Stewart*, 171 F.2d 544 (5th Cir.1948); *SEC v. Kaye, Real & Co.*, 122 F.Supp. 639 (S.D.N.Y.1954); *Sieb's Hatcheries, Inc. v. Lindley*, 13 F.R.D. 113 (W.D.Ark. 1952). The rule as revised conforms to the latter practice.

Subdivision (b). The rule does not now indicate the extent to which a party is bound by his admission. Some courts view admissions as the equivalent of sworn testimony. *E.g., Ark-Tenn Distributing Corp. v. Breidt*, 209 F.2d 359 (3d Cir.1954); *United States v. Lemons*, 125 F.Supp. 686 (W.D.Ark.1954); 4 Moore's Federal Practice ¶ 36.08 (2d ed. 1966 Supp.). At least in some jurisdictions a party may rebut his own testimony, *e.g., Alamo v. Del Rosario*, 98 F.2d 328 (D.C.Cir.1938), and by analogy an admission made pursuant to Rule 36 may likewise be thought rebuttable. The courts in *Ark-Tenn* and *Lemons, supra*, reasoned in this way, although the results reached may be supported on different grounds. In *McSparran v. Hanigan*, 225 F.Supp. 628, 636–637 (E.D.Pa. 1963), the court held that an admission is conclusively binding, though noting the confusion created by prior decisions.

The new provisions give an admission a conclusively binding effect, for purposes only of the pending action, unless the admission is withdrawn or amended. In form and substance a Rule 36 admission is comparable to an admission in pleadings or a stipulation drafted by counsel for use at trial, rather than to an evidentiary admission of a party. Louisell, Modern California

Discovery § 8.07 (1963); 2A Barron & Holtzoff, *Federal Practice and Procedure* § 838 (Wright ed. 1961). Unless the party securing an admission can depend on its binding effect, he cannot safely avoid the expense of preparing to prove the very matters on which he has secured the admission, and the purpose of the rule is defeated. Field & McKusick, Maine Civil Practice § 36.4 (1959); Finman, *supra*, 71 Yale L.J. 371, 418–426; Comment, 56 Nw.U.L.Rev. 679, 682–683 (1961).

Provision is made for withdrawal or amendment of an admission. This provision emphasizes the importance of having the action resolved on the merits, while at the same time assuring each party that justified reliance on an admission in preparation for trial will not operate to his prejudice. *Cf. Moosman v. Joseph P. Blitz, Inc.*, 358 F.2d 686 (2d Cir.1966).

1987 AMENDMENT

The amendments are technical. No substantive change is intended.

1993 AMENDMENT

The rule is revised to reflect the change made by Rule 26(d), preventing a party from seeking formal discovery until after the meeting of the parties required by Rule 26(f).

2007 AMENDMENT

The language of Rule 36 has been amended as part of the general restyling of the Civil Rules to make them more easily understood and to make style and terminology consistent throughout the rules. These changes are intended to be stylistic only.

The final sentence of the first paragraph of former Rule 36(a) was a redundant cross-reference to the discovery moratorium provisions of Rule 26(d). Rule 26(d) is now familiar, obviating any need to carry forward the redundant cross-reference. The redundant reminder of Rule 37(c) in the second paragraph was likewise omitted.

Rule 37. Failure to Make Disclosure or Cooperate in Discovery: Sanctions

1937 ADOPTION

The provisions of this rule authorizing orders establishing facts or excluding evidence or striking pleadings, or authorizing judgments of dismissal or default, for refusal to answer questions or permit inspection or otherwise make discovery, are in accord with *Hammond Packing Co. v. Arkansas, 1909*, 212 U.S. 322, 29 S. Ct. 370, 53 L.Ed. 530, 15 Ann.Cas. 645, which distinguishes between the justifiable use of such measures as a means of compelling the production of evidence, and their unjustifiable use, as in *Hovey v. Elliott, 1897*, 167 U.S. 409, 17 S. Ct. 841, 42 L.Ed. 215, for the mere purpose of punishing for contempt.

1948 AMENDMENT

The amendment effective October 1949, substituted the reference to "Title 28, U.S.C., § 1783" in subdivision (e) for the reference to "the Act of July 3, 1926, c. 762, § 1 (44 Stat. 835), U.S.C., Title 28, § 711."

1970 AMENDMENT

Rule 37 provides generally for sanctions against parties or persons unjustifiably resisting discovery. Experience has brought to light a number of defects in the language of the rule as well as instances in which it is not serving the purposes for which it was designed. See Rosenberg, *Sanctions to Effectuate Pretrial Discovery*, 58 Col.L.Rev. 480 (1958). In addition, changes being made in other discovery rules require conforming amendments to Rule 37.

Rule 37 sometimes refers to a "failure" to afford discovery and at other times to a "refusal" to do so. Taking note of this dual terminology, courts have imported into "refusal" a requirement of "willfulness." See *Roth v. Paramount*

Pictures Distributing Corp., 8 F.R.D. 31 (W.D.Pa.1948); *Campbell v. Johnson*, 101 F.Supp. 705, 707 (S.D.N.Y.1951). In *Societe Internationale v. Rogers*, 357 U.S. 197, 78 S. Ct. 1087, 2 L. Ed. 2d 1255 (1958), the Supreme Court concluded that the rather random use of these two terms in Rule 37 showed no design to use them with consistently distinctive meanings, that "refused" in Rule 37(b)(2) meant simply a failure to comply, and that willfulness was relevant only to the selection of sanctions, if any, to be imposed. Nevertheless, after the decision in *Societe*, the court in *Hinson v. Michigan Mutual Liability Co.*, 275 F.2d 537 (5th Cir.1960) once again ruled that "refusal" required willfulness. Substitution of "failure" for "refusal" throughout Rule 37 should eliminate this confusion and bring the rule into harmony with the *Societe Internationale* decision. See Rosenberg, *supra*, 58 Col.L.Rev. 480, 489–490 (1958).

Subdivision (a). Rule 37(a) provides relief to a party seeking discovery against one who, with or without stated objections, fails to afford the discovery sought. It has always fully served this function in relation to depositions, but the amendments being made to Rules 33 and 34 give Rule 37(a) added scope and importance. Under existing Rule 33, a party objecting to interrogatories must make a motion for court hearing on his objections. The changes now made in Rules 33 and 37(a) make it clear that the interrogating party must move to compel answers, and the motion is provided for in Rule 37(a). Existing Rule 34, since it requires a court order prior to production of documents or things or permission to enter on land, has no relation to Rule 37(a). Amendments of Rules 34 and 37(a) create a procedure similar to that provided for Rule 33.

Subdivision (a)(1). This is a new provision making clear to which court a party may apply for an order compelling discovery. Existing Rule 37(a) refers only to the court in which the deposition is being taken; nevertheless, it has been held that the court where the action is pending has "inherent power" to compel a party deponent to answer. *Lincoln Laboratories, Inc. v. Savage Laboratories, Inc.*, 27 F.R.D. 476 (D.Del.1961). In relation to Rule 33 interrogatories and Rule 34 requests for inspection, the court where the action is pending is the appropriate enforcing tribunal. The new provision eliminates the need to resort to inherent power by spelling out the respective roles of the court where the action is pending and the court where the deposition is taken. In some instances, two courts are available to a party seeking to compel answers from a party deponent. The party seeking discovery may choose the court to which he will apply, but the court has power to remit the party to the other court as a more appropriate forum.

Subdivision (a)(2). This subdivision contains the substance of existing provisions of Rule 37(a) authorizing motions to compel answers to questions put at depositions and to interrogatories. New provisions authorize motions for orders compelling designation under Rules 30(b)(6) and 31(a) and compelling inspection in accordance with a request made under Rule 34. If the court denies a motion, in whole or part, it may accompany the denial with issuance of a protective order. Compare the converse provision in Rule 26(c).

Subdivision (a)(3). This new provision makes clear that an evasive or incomplete answer is to be considered, for purposes of subdivision (a), a failure to answer. The courts have consistently held that they have the power to compel adequate answers. *E.g., Cone Mills Corp. v. Joseph Bancroft & Sons Co.*, 33 F.R.D. 318 (D.Del.1963). This power is recognized and incorporated into the rule.

Subdivision (a)(4). This subdivision amends the provisions for award of expenses, including reasonable attorney's fees, to the prevailing party or person when a motion is made for an order compelling discovery. At present, an award of expenses is made only if the losing party or person is found to have acted without substantial justification. The change requires that expenses be awarded unless the conduct of the losing party or person is found to have been substantially justified. The test of "substantial justification" remains, but the change in language is intended to encourage judges to be more alert to abuses occurring in the discovery process.

On many occasions, to be sure, the dispute over discovery between the parties is genuine, though ultimately resolved one way or the other by the court. In such cases, the losing party is substantially justified in carrying the matter to court. But the rules should deter the abuse implicit in carrying or forcing a discovery dispute to court when no genuine dispute exists. And the potential or actual imposition of expenses is virtually the sole formal sanction in the rules to deter a party from pressing to a court hearing frivolous requests for or objections to discovery.

The present provision of Rule 37(a) that the court shall require payment if it finds that the defeated party acted without "substantial justification" may appear adequate, but in fact it has been little used. Only a handful of reported cases include an award of expenses, and the Columbia Survey found that in only one instance out of about 50 motions decided under Rule 37(a) did the court award expenses. It appears that the courts do not utilize the most important available sanction to deter abusive resort to the judiciary.

The proposed change provides in effect that expenses should ordinarily be awarded unless a court finds that the losing party acted justifiably in carrying his point to court. At the same time, a necessary flexibility is maintained, since the court retains the power to find that other circumstances make an award of expenses unjust—as where the prevailing party also acted unjustifiably. The amendment does not significantly narrow the discretion of the court, but rather presses the court to address itself to abusive practices. The present provision that expenses may be imposed upon either the party or his attorney or both is unchanged. But it is not contemplated that expenses will be imposed upon the attorney merely because the party is indigent.

Subdivision (b). This subdivision deals with sanctions for failure to comply with a court order. The present captions for subsections (1) and (2) entitled, "Contempt" and "Other Consequences," respectively, are confusing. One of the consequences listed in (2) is the arrest of the party, representing the exercise of the contempt power. The contents of the subsections show that the first authorizes the sanction of contempt (and no other) by the court in which the deposition is taken, whereas the second subsection authorizes a variety of sanctions, including contempt, which may be imposed by the court in which the action is pending. The captions of the subsections are changed to reflect their contents.

The scope of Rule 37(b)(2) is broadened by extending it to include any order "to provide or permit discovery," including orders issued under Rules 37(a) and 35. Various rules authorize orders for discovery—*e.g.*, Rule 35(b)(1), Rule 26(c) as revised, Rule 37(d). See Rosenberg, *supra*, 58 Col.L.Rev. 480, 484–486. Rule 37(b)(2) should provide comprehensively for enforcement of all these orders. *Cf. Societe Internationale v. Rogers*, 357 U.S. 197, 207, 78 S. Ct. 1087, 1093, 2 L. Ed. 2d 1255 (1958). On the other hand, the reference to Rule 34 is deleted to conform to the changed procedure in that rule.

A new subsection (E) provides that sanctions which have been available against a party for failure to comply with an order under Rule 35(a) to submit to examination will now be available against him for his failure to comply with a Rule 35(a) order to produce a third person for examination, unless he shows that he is unable to produce the person. In this context, "unable" means in effect "unable in good faith." See *Societe Internationale v. Rogers*, 357 U.S. 197, 78 S. Ct. 1087, 2 L. Ed. 2d 1255 (1958).

Subdivision (b)(2) is amplified to provide for payment of reasonable expenses caused by the failure to obey the order. Although Rules 37(b)(2) and 37(d) have been silent as to award of expenses, courts have nevertheless ordered them on occasion. *E.g., United Sheeplined Clothing Co. v. Arctic Fur Cap Corp.*, 165 F.Supp. 193 (S.D.N.Y.1958); *Austin Theatre, Inc. v. Warner Bros. Pictures, Inc.*, 22 F.R.D. 302 (S.D.N.Y.1958). The provision places the burden on the disobedient party to avoid expenses by showing that his failure is justified or that special circumstances make an award of expenses unjust. Allocating the burden in this way conforms to the changed provisions as to expenses in Rule 37(a), and is particularly appropriate when a court order is disobeyed.

An added reference to directors of a party is similar to a change made in subdivision (d) and is explained in the note to that subdivision. The added reference to persons designated by a party under Rules 30(b)(6) or 31(a) to testify on behalf of the party carries out the new procedure in those rules for taking a deposition of a corporation or other organization.

Subdivision (c). Rule 37(c) provides a sanction for the enforcement of Rule 36 dealing with requests for admission. Rule 36 provides the mechanism whereby a party may obtain from another party in appropriate instances either (1) an admission, or (2) a sworn and specific denial or (3) a sworn statement "setting forth in detail the reasons why he cannot truthfully admit or deny." If the party obtains the second or third of these responses, in proper form, Rule 36 does not provide for a pretrial hearing on whether the response is warranted by the evidence thus far accumulated. Instead, Rule 37(c) is intended to provide posttrial relief in the form of a requirement that the party improperly refusing the admission pay the expenses of the other side in making the necessary proof at trial.

Rule 37(c), as now written, addresses itself in terms only to the sworn denial and is silent with respect to the statement of reasons for an inability to admit or deny. There is no apparent basis for this distinction, since the sanction provided in Rule 37(c) should deter all unjustified failures to admit. This omission in the rule has caused confused and diverse treatment in the courts. One court has held that if a party give inadequate reasons, he should be treated before trial as having denied the request, so that Rule 37(c) may apply. *Bertha Bldg. Corp. v. National Theaters Corp.*, 15 F.R.D. 339 (E.D.N.Y.1954). Another has held that the party should be treated as having admitted the request. Heng Hsin Co. v. Stern, Morgenthau & Co., 20 Fed.Rules Serv. 36a.52, Case 1 (S.D.N.Y. Dec. 10, 1954). Still another has ordered a new response, without indicating what the outcome should be if the new response were inadequate. *United States Plywood Corp. v. Hudson Lumber Co.*, 127 F.Supp. 489, 497–498 (S.D.N.Y.1954). See generally Finman, *The Request for Admissions in Federal Civil Procedure*, 71 Yale L.J. 371, 426–430 (1962). The amendment eliminates this defect in Rule 37(c) by bringing within its scope all failures to admit.

Additional provisions in Rule 37(c) protect a party from having to pay expenses if the request for admission was held objectionable under Rule 36(a) or if the party failing to admit had reasonable ground to believe that he might prevail on the matter. The latter provision emphasizes that the true test under Rule 37(c) is not whether a party prevailed at trial but whether he acted reasonably in believing that he might prevail.

Subdivision (d). The scope of subdivision (d) is broadened to include responses to requests for inspection under Rule 34, thereby conforming to the new procedures of Rule 34.

Two related changes are made in subdivision (d): the permissible sanctions are broadened to include such orders "as are just"; and the requirement that the failure to appear or respond be "wilful" is eliminated. Although Rule 37(d) in terms provides for only three sanctions, all rather severe, the courts have interpreted it as permitting softer sanctions than those which it sets forth. *E.g., Gill v. Stolow*, 240 F.2d 669 (2d Cir.1957); *Saltzman v. Birrel*, 156 F.Supp. 538 (S.D.N.Y.1957); 2A Barron & Holtzoff, *Federal Practice and Procedure* 554 to 557 (Wright ed. 1961). The rule is changed to provide the greater flexibility as to sanctions which the cases show is needed.

The resulting flexibility as to sanctions eliminates any need to retain the requirement that the failure to appear or respond be "wilful." The concept of "wilful failure" is at best subtle and difficult, and the cases do not supply a bright line. Many courts have imposed sanctions without referring to willfulness. *E.g., Milewski v. Schneider Transportation Co.*, 238 F.2d 397 (6th Cir.1956); *Dictograph Products, Inc. v. Kentworth Corp.*, 7 F.R.D. 543 (W.D.Ky.1947). In addition, in view of the possibility of light sanctions, even a negligent failure should come within Rule 37(d). If default is caused by counsel's ignorance of Federal practice, *cf. Dunn v. Pennsylvania R. R.*, 96 F.Supp. 597 (N.D.Ohio 1951), or by his preoccupation with another aspect of the case, *cf. Maurer-Neuer, Inc. v. United Packinghouse Workers*, 26 F.R.D. 139 (D.Kan.1960), dismissal of the action and default judgment are not justified, but the imposition of expenses and fees may well be. "Willfulness" continues to play a role, along with various other factors, in the choice of sanctions. Thus, the scheme conforms to Rule 37(b) as construed by the Supreme Court in *Societe Internationale v. Rogers*, 357 U.S. 197, 208, 78 S. Ct. 1087, 1094, 2 L. Ed. 2d 1255 (1958).

A provision is added to make clear that a party may not properly remain completely silent even when he regards a notice to take his deposition or a set of interrogatories or requests to inspect as improper and objectionable. If he desires not to appear or not to respond, he must apply for a protective order. The cases are divided on whether a protective order must be sought. Compare *Collins v. Wayland*, 139 F.2d 677 (9th Cir.1944), *cert. den.* 322 U.S. 744, 64 S. Ct. 1151, 88 L.Ed. 1576; *Bourgeois v. El Paso Natural Gas Co.*, 20 F.R.D. 358 (S.D.N.Y.1957); *Loosley v. Stone*, 15 F.R.D. 373 (S.D.Ill.1954), with *Scarlatos v. Kulukundis*, 21 F.R.D. 185 (S.D.N.Y.1957); *Ross v. True Temper Corp.*, 11 F.R.D. 307 (N.D.Ohio 1951). Compare also Rosenberg, *supra*, 58 Col.L.Rev. 480, 496 (1958) with 2A Barron & Holtzoff, Federal Practice and Procedure 530 to 531 (Wright ed. 1961). The party from whom discovery is sought is afforded, through Rule 26(c), a fair and effective procedure whereby he can challenge the request made. At the same time, the total noncompliance with which Rule 37(d) is concerned may impose severe inconvenience or hardship on the discovering party and substantially delay the discovery process. *Cf.* 2B Barron & Holtzoff, Federal Practice and Procedure 306 to 307 (Wright ed. 1961) (response to a subpoena).

The failure of an officer or managing agent of a party to make discovery as required by present Rule 37(d) is treated as the failure of the party. The rule as revised provides similar treatment for a director of a party. There is slight warrant for the present distinction between officers and managing agents on the one hand and directors on the other. Although the legal power over a director to compel his making discovery may not be as great as over officers or managing agents, *Campbell v. General Motors Corp.*, 13 F.R.D. 331 (S.D.N.Y.1952), the practical differences are negligible. That a director's interests are normally aligned with those of his corporation is shown by the provisions of old Rule 26(d)(2), transferred to 32(a)(2) (deposition of director of party may be used at trial by an adverse party for any purpose) and of Rule 43(b) (director of party may be treated at trial as a hostile witness on direct examination by any adverse party). Moreover, in those rare instances when a corporation is unable through good faith efforts to compel a director to make discovery, it is unlikely that the court will impose sanctions. *Cf. Societe Internationale v. Rogers*, 357 U.S. 197, 78 S. Ct. 1087, 2 L. Ed. 2d 1255 (1958).

Subdivision (e). The change in the caption conforms to the language of 28 U.S.C. § 1783, as amended in 1964.

Subdivision (f). Until recently, costs of a civil action could be awarded against the United States only when expressly provided by Act of Congress, and such provision was rarely made. See H.R.Rep.No. 1535, 89th Cong., 2d Sess., 2 to 3 (1966). To avoid any conflict with this doctrine, Rule 37(f) has provided that expenses and attorney's fees may not be imposed upon the United States under Rule 37. See 2A Barron & Holtzoff, *Federal Practice and Procedure* 857 (Wright ed.1961).

A major change in the law was made in 1966, 80 Stat. 308, 28 U.S.C. § 2412 (1966), whereby a judgment for costs may ordinarily be awarded to the prevailing party in any civil action brought by or against the United States. Costs are not to include the fees and expenses of attorneys. In light of this legislative development, Rule 37(f) is amended to permit the award of expenses and fees against the United States under Rule 37, but only to the extent permitted by statute. The amendment brings Rule 37(f) into line with present and future statutory provisions.

1980 AMENDMENT

Subdivision (b)(2). New Rule 26(f) provides that if a discovery conference is held, at its close the court shall enter an order respecting the subsequent conduct of discovery. The amendment provides that the sanctions available for violation of other court orders respecting discovery are available for violation of the discovery conference order.

Subdivision (e). Subdivision (e) is stricken. Title 28, U.S.C. § 1783 no longer refers to sanctions. The subdivision otherwise duplicates Rule 45(e)(2).

Subdivision (g). New Rule 26(f) imposes a duty on parties to participate in good faith in the framing of a discovery plan by agreement upon the request of any party. This subdivision authorizes the court to award to parties who participate in good faith in an attempt to frame a discovery plan the expenses incurred in the attempt if any party or his attorney fails to participate in good faith and thereby causes additional expense.

Failure of United States to Participate in Good Faith in Discovery. Rule 37 authorizes the court to direct that parties or attorneys who fail to participate in good faith in the discovery process pay the expenses, including attorneys' fees, incurred by other parties as a result of that failure. Since attorneys' fees cannot ordinarily be awarded against the United States (28 U.S.C. § 2412), there is often no practical remedy for the misconduct of its officers and attorneys. However, in the case of a government attorney who fails to participate in good faith in discovery, nothing prevents a court in an appropriate case from giving written notification of that fact to the Attorney General of the United States and other appropriate heads of offices or agencies thereof.

1987 AMENDMENT

The amendments are technical. No substantive change is intended.

1993 AMENDMENT

Subdivision (a). This subdivision is revised to reflect the revision of Rule 26(a), requiring disclosure of matters without a discovery request.

Pursuant to new subdivision (a)(2)(A), a party dissatisfied with the disclosure made by an opposing party may under this rule move for an order to compel disclosure. In providing for such a motion, the revised rule parallels the provisions of the former rule dealing with failures to answer particular interrogatories. Such a motion may be needed when the information to be disclosed might be helpful to the party seeking the disclosure but not to the party required to make the disclosure. If the party required to make the disclosure would need the material to support its own contentions, the more effective enforcement of the disclosure requirement will be to exclude the evidence not disclosed, as provided in subdivision (c)(1) of this revised rule.

Language is included in the new paragraph and added to the subparagraph (B) that requires litigants to seek to resolve discovery disputes by informal means before filing a motion with the court. This requirement is based on successful experience with similar local rules of court promulgated pursuant to Rule 83.

The last sentence of paragraph (2) is moved into paragraph (4).

Under revised paragraph (3), evasive or incomplete disclosures and responses to interrogatories and production requests are treated as failures to disclose or respond. Interrogatories and requests for production should not be read or interpreted in an artificially restrictive or hypertechnical manner to avoid disclosure of information fairly covered by the discovery request, and to do so is subject to appropriate sanctions under subdivision (a).

Revised paragraph (4) is divided into three subparagraphs for ease of reference, and in each the phrase "after opportunity for hearing" is changed to "after affording an opportunity to be heard" to make clear that the court can consider such questions on written submissions as well as on oral hearings.

Subparagraph (A) is revised to cover the situation where information that should have been produced without a motion to compel is produced after the motion is filed but before it is brought on for hearing. The rule also is revised to provide that a party should not be awarded its expenses for filing a motion that could have been avoided by conferring with opposing counsel.

Subparagraph (C) is revised to include the provision that formerly was contained in subdivision (a)(2) and to include the same requirement of an opportunity to be heard that is specified in subparagraphs (A) and (B).

Subdivision (c). The revision provides a self-executing sanction for failure to make a disclosure required by Rule 26(a), without need for a motion under subdivision (a)(2)(A).

Paragraph (1) prevents a party from using as evidence any witnesses or information that, without substantial justification, has not been disclosed as required by Rules 26(a) and 26(e)(1). This automatic sanction provides a strong inducement for disclosure of material that the disclosing party would expect to use as evidence, whether at a trial, at a hearing, or on a motion, such as one under Rule 56. As disclosure of evidence offered solely for impeachment purposes is not required under those rules, this preclusion sanction likewise does not apply to that evidence.

Limiting the automatic sanction to violations "without substantial justification," coupled with the exception for violations that are "harmless," is needed to avoid unduly harsh penalties in a variety of situations: *e.g.,* the inadvertent omission from a Rule 26(a)(1)(A) disclosure of the name of a potential witness known to all parties; the failure to list as a trial witness a person so listed by another party; or the lack of knowledge of a pro se litigant of the requirement to make disclosures. In the latter situation, however, exclusion would be proper if the requirement for disclosure had been called to the litigant's attention by either the court or another party.

Preclusion of evidence is not an effective incentive to compel disclosure of information that, being supportive of the position of the opposing party, might advantageously be concealed by the disclosing party. However, the rule provides the court with a wide range of other sanctions—such as declaring specified facts to be established, preventing contradictory evidence, or, like spoliation of evidence, allowing the jury to be informed of the fact of nondisclosure—that, though not self-executing, can be imposed when found to be warranted after a hearing. The failure to identify a witness or document in a disclosure statement would be admissible under the Federal Rules of Evidence under the same principles that allow a party's interrogatory answers to be offered against it.

Subdivision (d). This subdivision is revised to require that, where a party fails to file any response to interrogatories or a Rule 34 request, the discovering party should informally seek to obtain such responses before filing a motion for sanctions.

The last sentence of this subdivision is revised to clarify that it is the pendency of a motion for protective order that may be urged as an excuse for a violation of subdivision (d). If a party's motion has been denied, the party cannot argue that its subsequent failure to comply would be justified. In this connection, it should be noted that the filing of a motion under Rule 26(c) is not self-executing—the relief authorized under that rule depends on obtaining the court's order to that effect.

Subdivision (g). This subdivision is modified to conform to the revision of Rule 26(f).

2000 AMENDMENT

Subdivision (c)(1). When this subdivision was added in 1993 to direct exclusion of materials not disclosed as required, the duty to supplement discovery responses pursuant to Rule 26(e)(2) was omitted. In the face of this omission, courts may rely on inherent power to sanction for failure to supplement as required by Rule 26(e)(2), *see* 8 *Federal Practice & Procedure* § 2050 at 607 to 09, but that is an uncertain and unregulated ground for imposing sanctions. There is no obvious occasion for a Rule 37(a) motion in connection with failure to supplement, and ordinarily only Rule 37(c)(1) exists as rule-based authority for sanctions if this supplementation obligation is violated.

The amendment explicitly adds failure to comply with Rule 26(e)(2) as a ground for sanctions under Rule 37(c)(1), including exclusion of withheld materials. The rule provides that this sanction power only applies when the failure to supplement was "without substantial justification." Even if the failure was not substantially justified, a party should be allowed to use the material that was not disclosed if the lack of earlier notice was harmless.

"Shall" is replaced by "is" under the program to conform amended rules to current style conventions when there is no ambiguity.

GAP Report

The Advisory Committee recommends that the published amendment proposal be modified to state that the exclusion sanction can apply to failure "to amend a prior response to discovery as required by Rule 26(e)(2)." In addition, one minor phrasing change is recommended for the Committee Note.

2006 AMENDMENT

Subdivision (f). Subdivision (f) is new. It focuses on a distinctive feature of computer operations, the routine alteration and deletion of information that attends ordinary use. Many steps essential to computer operation may alter or destroy information, for reasons that have nothing to do with how that information might relate to litigation. As a result, the ordinary operation of computer systems creates a risk that a party may lose potentially discoverable information without culpable conduct on its part. Under Rule 37(f), absent exceptional circumstances, sanctions cannot be imposed for loss of electronically stored information resulting from the routine, good-faith operation of an electronic information system.

Rule 37(f) applies only to information lost due to the "routine operation of an electronic information system"—the ways in which such systems are generally designed, programmed, and implemented to meet the party's technical and business needs. The "routine operation" of computer systems includes the alteration and overwriting of information, often without the operator's specific direction or awareness, a feature with no direct counterpart in hard-copy documents. Such features are essential to the operation of electronic information systems.

Rule 37(f) applies to information lost due to the routine operation of an information system only if the operation was in good faith. Good faith in the routine operation of an information system may involve a party's intervention to modify or suspend certain features of that routine operation to prevent the loss of information, if that information is subject to a preservation obligation. A preservation obligation may arise from many sources, including common law, statutes, regulations, or a court order in the case. The good faith requirement of Rule 37(f) means that a party is not permitted to exploit the routine operation of an information system to thwart discovery obligations by allowing that operation to continue in order to destroy specific stored information that it is required to preserve. When a party is under a duty to preserve information because of pending or reasonably anticipated litigation, intervention in the routine operation of an information system is one aspect of what is often called a "litigation hold." Among the factors that bear on a party's good faith in the routine operation of an information system are the steps the party took to comply with a court order in the case or party agreement requiring preservation of specific electronically stored information.

Whether good faith would call for steps to prevent the loss of information on sources that the party believes are not reasonably accessible under Rule 26(b)(2) depends on the circumstances of each case. One factor is whether the party reasonably believes that the information on such sources is likely to be discoverable and not available from reasonably accessible sources.

The protection provided by Rule 37(f) applies only to sanctions "under these rules." It does not affect other sources of authority to impose sanctions or rules of professional responsibility.

This rule restricts the imposition of "sanctions." It does not prevent a court from making the kinds of adjustments frequently used in managing discovery if a party is unable to provide relevant responsive information. For example, a court could order the responding party to produce an additional witness for deposition, respond to additional interrogatories, or make similar attempts to provide substitutes or alternatives for some or all of the lost information.

2007 AMENDMENT

The language of Rule 37 has been amended as part of the general restyling of the Civil Rules to make them more easily understood and to make style and terminology consistent throughout the rules. These changes are intended to be stylistic only.

2013 AMENDMENT

Rule 37(b) is amended to conform to amendments made to Rule 45, particularly the addition of Rule 45(f) providing for transfer of a subpoena-related motion to the court where the action is pending. A second sentence is added to Rule 37(b)(1) to deal with contempt of orders entered after such a transfer. The Rule 45(f) transfer provision is explained in the Committee Note to Rule 45.

2015 AMENDMENT

Subdivision (a). Rule 37(a)(3)(B)(iv) is amended to reflect the common practice of producing copies of documents or electronically stored information rather than simply permitting inspection. This change brings item (iv) into line with paragraph (B), which provides a motion for an order compelling "production, or inspection."

Subdivision (e). Present Rule 37(e), adopted in 2006, provides: "Absent exceptional circumstances, a court may not impose sanctions under these rules on a party for failing to provide electronically stored information lost as a result of the routine, good-faith operation of an electronic information system." This limited rule has not adequately addressed the serious problems resulting from the continued exponential growth in the volume of such information. Federal circuits have established significantly different standards for imposing sanctions or curative measures on parties who fail to preserve electronically stored information. These developments have caused litigants to expend excessive effort and money on preservation in order to avoid the risk of severe sanctions if a court finds they did not do enough.

New Rule 37(e) replaces the 2006 rule. It authorizes and specifies measures a court may employ if information that should have been preserved is lost, and specifies the findings necessary to justify these measures. It therefore forecloses reliance on inherent authority or state law to determine when certain measures should be used. The rule does not affect the validity of an independent tort claim for spoliation if state law applies in a case and authorizes the claim.

The new rule applies only to electronically stored information, also the focus of the 2006 rule. It applies only when such information is lost. Because electronically stored information often exists in multiple locations, loss from one source may often be harmless when substitute information can be found elsewhere.

The new rule applies only if the lost information should have been preserved in the anticipation or conduct of litigation and the party failed to take reasonable steps to preserve it. Many court decisions hold that potential litigants have a duty to preserve relevant information when litigation is reasonably foreseeable. Rule 37(e) is based on this common-law duty; it does not attempt to create a new duty to preserve. The rule does not apply when information is lost before a duty to preserve arises.

In applying the rule, a court may need to decide whether and when a duty to preserve arose. Courts should consider the extent to which a party was on notice that litigation was likely and that the information would be relevant. A variety of events may alert a party to the prospect of litigation. Often these events provide only limited information about that prospective litigation, however, so that the scope of information that should be preserved may remain uncertain. It is important not to be blinded to this reality by hindsight arising from familiarity with an action as it is actually filed.

Although the rule focuses on the common-law obligation to preserve in the anticipation or conduct of litigation, courts may sometimes consider whether there was an independent requirement that the lost information be preserved. Such requirements arise from many sources — statutes, administrative regulations, an order in another case, or a party's own information-retention protocols. The court should be sensitive, however, to the fact that such independent preservation requirements may be addressed to a wide variety of concerns unrelated to the current litigation. The fact that a party had an independent obligation to preserve information does not necessarily mean that it had such a duty with respect to the litigation, and the fact that the party failed to observe some other preservation obligation does not itself prove that its efforts to preserve were not reasonable with respect to a particular case.

The duty to preserve may in some instances be triggered or clarified by a court order in the case. Preservation orders may become more common, in part because Rules 16(b)(3)(B)(iii) and 26(f)(3)(C) are amended to encourage discovery plans and orders that address preservation. Once litigation has commenced, if the parties cannot reach agreement about preservation issues, promptly seeking judicial guidance about the extent of reasonable preservation may be important.

The rule applies only if the information was lost because the party failed to take reasonable steps to preserve the information. Due to the ever-increasing volume of electronically stored information and the multitude of devices that generate such information, perfection in preserving all relevant electronically stored information is often impossible. As under the current rule, the routine, good-faith operation of an electronic information system would be a relevant factor for the court to consider in evaluating whether a party failed to take reasonable steps to preserve lost information, although the prospect of litigation may call for reasonable steps to preserve information by intervening in that routine operation. This rule recognizes that "reasonable steps" to preserve suffice; it does not call for perfection. The court should be sensitive to the party's sophistication with regard to litigation in evaluating preservation efforts; some litigants, particularly individual litigants, may be less familiar with preservation obligations than others who have considerable experience in litigation.v Because the rule calls only for reasonable steps to preserve, it is inapplicable when the loss of information occurs despite the party's reasonable steps to preserve. For example, the information may not be in the party's control. Or information the party has preserved may be destroyed by events outside the party's control — the computer room may be flooded, a "cloud" service may fail, a malign software attack may disrupt a storage system, and so on. Courts may, however, need to assess the extent to which a party knew of and protected against such risks.

Another factor in evaluating the reasonableness of preservation efforts is proportionality. The court should be sensitive to party resources; aggressive preservation efforts can be extremely costly, and parties (including governmental parties) may have limited staff and resources to devote to those efforts. A party may act reasonably by choosing a less costly form of information preservation, if it is substantially as effective as more costly forms. It is important that counsel become familiar with their clients' information systems and digital data — including social media — to address these issues. A party urging that preservation requests are disproportionate may need to provide specifics about these matters in order to enable meaningful discussion of the appropriate preservation regime.

When a party fails to take reasonable steps to preserve electronically stored information that should have been preserved in the anticipation or conduct of litigation, and the information is lost as a result, Rule 37(e) directs that the initial focus should be on whether the lost information can be restored or replaced through additional discovery. Nothing in the rule limits the court's powers under Rules 16 and 26 to authorize additional discovery. Orders under Rule 26(b)(2)(B) regarding discovery from sources that would ordinarily be considered inaccessible or under Rule 26(c)(1)(B) on allocation of expenses may be pertinent to solving such problems. If the information is restored or replaced, no further measures should be taken. At the same time, it is important to emphasize that efforts to restore or replace lost information through discovery should be proportional to the apparent importance of the lost information to claims or defenses in the litigation. For example, substantial measures should not be employed to restore or replace information that is marginally relevant or duplicative.

Subdivision (e)(1). This subdivision applies only if information should have been preserved in the anticipation or conduct of litigation, a party failed to take reasonable steps to preserve the information, information was lost as a result, and the information could not be restored or replaced by additional discovery. In addition, a court may resort to (e)(1) measures only "upon finding prejudice to another party from loss of the information." An evaluation of prejudice from the loss of information necessarily includes an evaluation of the information's importance in the litigation.

The rule does not place a burden of proving or disproving prejudice on one party or the other. Determining the content of lost information may be a difficult task in some cases, and placing the burden of proving prejudice on the party that did not lose the information may be unfair. In other situations, however, the content of the lost information may be fairly evident, the information may appear to be unimportant, or the abundance of preserved information may appear sufficient to meet the needs of all parties. Requiring the party seeking curative measures to prove prejudice may be reasonable in such situations. The rule leaves judges with discretion to determine how best to assess prejudice in particular cases.

Once a finding of prejudice is made, the court is authorized to employ measures "no greater than necessary to cure the prejudice." The range of such measures is quite broad if they are necessary for this purpose. There is no all-purpose hierarchy of the severity of various measures; the severity of given measures must be calibrated in terms of their effect on the particular case. But authority to order measures no greater than necessary to cure prejudice does not require the court to adopt measures to cure every possible prejudicial effect. Much is entrusted to the court's discretion.

In an appropriate case, it may be that serious measures are necessary to cure prejudice found by the court, such as forbidding the party that failed to preserve information from putting on certain evidence, permitting the parties to present evidence and argument to the jury regarding the loss of information, or giving the jury instructions to assist in its evaluation of such evidence or argument, other than instructions to which subdivision (e)(2) applies. Care must be taken, however, to ensure that curative measures under subdivision (e)(1) do not have the effect of measures that are permitted under subdivision (e)(2) only on a finding of intent to deprive another party of the lost information's use in the litigation. An example of an inappropriate (e)(1) measure might be an order striking pleadings related to, or precluding a party from offering any evidence in support of, the central or only claim or defense in the case. On the other hand, it may be appropriate to exclude a specific item of evidence to offset prejudice caused by failure to preserve other evidence that might contradict the excluded item of evidence.

Subdivision (e)(2). This subdivision authorizes courts to use specified and very severe measures to address or deter failures to preserve electronically stored information, but only on finding that the party that lost the information acted with the intent to deprive another party of the information's use in the litigation. It is designed to provide a uniform standard in federal court for use of these serious measures when addressing failure to preserve electronically stored information. It rejects cases such as *Residential Funding Corp. v. DeGeorge Financial Corp.*, 306 F.3d 99 (2d Cir. 2002), that authorize the giving of adverse-inference instructions on a finding of negligence or gross negligence.

Adverse-inference instructions were developed on the premise that a party's intentional loss or destruction of evidence to prevent its use in litigation gives rise to a reasonable inference that the evidence was unfavorable to the party responsible for loss or destruction of the evidence. Negligent or even grossly negligent behavior does not logically support that inference. Information lost through negligence may have been favorable to either party, including the party that lost it, and inferring that it was unfavorable to that party may tip the balance at trial in ways the lost information never would have. The better rule for the negligent or grossly negligent loss of electronically stored information is to preserve a broad range of measures to cure prejudice caused by its loss, but to limit the most severe measures to instances of intentional loss or destruction.

Similar reasons apply to limiting the court's authority to presume or infer that the lost information was unfavorable to the party who lost it when ruling on a pretrial motion or presiding at a bench trial. Subdivision (e)(2) limits the ability of courts to draw adverse inferences based on the loss of information in these circumstances, permitting them only when a court finds that the information was lost with the intent to prevent its use in litigation.

Subdivision (e)(2) applies to jury instructions that permit or require the jury to presume or infer that lost information was unfavorable to the party that lost it. Thus, it covers any instruction that directs or permits the jury to infer from the loss of information that it was in fact unfavorable to the party that lost it. The subdivision does not apply to jury instructions that do not involve such an inference. For example, subdivision (e)(2) would not prohibit a court from allowing the parties to present evidence to the jury concerning the loss and likely relevance of information and instructing the jury that it may consider that evidence, along with all the other evidence in the case, in making its decision. These measures, which would not involve instructing a jury it may draw an adverse inference from loss of information, would be available under subdivision (e)(1) if no greater than necessary to cure prejudice. In addition, subdivision (e)(2) does not limit the discretion of courts to give traditional missing evidence instructions based on a party's failure to present evidence it has in its possession at the time of trial.

Subdivision (e)(2) requires a finding that the party acted with the intent to deprive another party of the information's use in the litigation. This finding may be made by the court when ruling on a pretrial motion, when presiding at a bench trial, or when deciding whether to give an adverse inference instruction at trial. If a court were to conclude that the intent finding should be made by a jury, the court's instruction should make clear that the jury may infer from the loss of the information that it was unfavorable to the party that lost it only if the jury first finds that the party acted with the intent to deprive another party of the information's use in the litigation. If the jury does not make this finding, it may not infer from the loss that the information was unfavorable to the party that lost it.

Subdivision (e)(2) does not include a requirement that the court find prejudice to the party deprived of the information. This is because the finding of intent required by the subdivision can support not only an inference that the lost information was unfavorable to the party that intentionally destroyed it, but also an inference that the opposing party was prejudiced by the loss of information that would have favored its position. Subdivision (e)(2) does not require any further finding of prejudice.

Courts should exercise caution, however, in using the measures specified in (e)(2). Finding an intent to deprive another party of the lost information's use in the litigation does not require a court to adopt any of the measures listed in subdivision (e)(2). The remedy should fit the wrong, and the severe measures authorized by this subdivision should not be used when the information lost was relatively unimportant or lesser measures such as those specified in subdivision (e)(1) would be sufficient to redress the loss.

VI. TRIALS

Rule 38. Jury Trial of Right

1937 ADOPTION

This rule provides for the preservation of the constitutional right of trial by jury as directed in the enabling act (act of June 19, 1934, 48 Stat. 1064, U.S.C., Title 28, former § 2072, formerly § 723c), and it and the next rule make definite provision for claim and waiver of jury trial, following the method used in many

American states and in England and the British Dominions. Thus the claim must be made at once on initial pleading or appearance under Ill.Rev.Stat. (1937) ch. 110, § 188; 6 Tenn.Code Ann. (Williams, 1934) § 8734; compare Wyo.Rev.Stat.Ann. (1931) § 89-1320 (with answer or reply); within 10 days after the pleadings are completed or the case is at issue under 2 Conn.Gen.Stat. (1930) § 5624; Hawaii Rev.Laws (1935) § 4101; 2 Mass.Gen.Laws (Ter.Ed.1932) ch. 231, § 60; 3 Mich.Comp.Laws (1929) § 14263; Mich. Court Rules Ann. (Searl, 1933) Rule 33 (15 days); England (until 1933) O. 36, r. r. 2 and 6; and Ontario Jud. Act (1927) § 57(1)(4 days, or, where prior notice of trial, 2 days from such notice); or at a definite time varying under different codes, from 10 days before notice of trial to 10 days after notice, or, as in many, when the case is called for assignment, Ariz.Rev.Code Ann. (Struckmeyer, 1928) § 3802; Calif.Code Civ.Proc. (Deering, 1937) § 631, par. 4; Iowa Code (1935) § 10724; 4 Nev.Comp. Laws (Hillyer, 1929) § 8782; N.M.Stat.Ann. (Courtright, 1929) § 105-814; N.Y.C. P.A. (1937) § 426, subdivision 5 (applying to New York, Bronx, Richmond, Kings, and Queens Counties); R.I.Pub.Laws (1929), ch. 1327, amending R.I.Gen.Laws (1923) ch. 337, § 6; Utah Rev.Stat.Ann. (1933) § 104-23-6; 2 Wash.Rev.Stat.Ann. (Remington, 1932) § 316; England (4 days after notice of trial), Administration of Justice Act (1933) § 6 and amended rule under the Judicature Act (The Annual Practice, 1937), O. 36, r. 1; Australia High Court Procedure Act (1921) § 12, Rules, O. 33, r. 2; Alberta Rules of Ct. (1914) 172, 183, 184; British Columbia Sup.Ct.Rules (1925) O. 36, r. r. 2, 6, 11, and 16; New Brunswick Jud. Act (1927) O. 36, r. r. 2 and 5. See James Trial by Jury and the New Federal Rules of Procedure (1936), 45 Yale L.J. 1022.

Rule 81(c) provides for claim for jury trial in removed actions.

The right to trial by jury as declared in U.S.C., Title 28, § 1873, formerly § 770 (Trial of issues of fact; by jury; exceptions), and similar statutes, is unaffected by this rule. This rule modifies U.S.C., Title 28, former § 773 (Trial of issues of fact; by court).

1966 AMENDMENT

See Note to Rule 9(h), supra.

1987 AMENDMENT

The amendments are technical. No substantive change is intended.

1993 AMENDMENT

Language requiring the filing of a jury demand as provided in subdivision (d) is added to subdivision (b) to eliminate an apparent ambiguity between the two subdivisions. For proper scheduling of cases, it is important that jury demands not only be served on other parties, but also be filed with the court.

2007 AMENDMENT

The language of Rule 38 has been amended as part of the general restyling of the Civil Rules to make them more easily understood and to make style and terminology consistent throughout the rules. These changes are intended to be stylistic only.

2009 AMENDMENT

The times set in the former rule at 10 days have been revised to 14 days. See the Note to Rule 6.

Rule 39. Trial by Jury or by the Court

1937 ADOPTION

The provisions for express waiver of jury trial found in U.S.C., Title 28, former § 773 (Trial of issues of fact; by court) are incorporated in this rule. See Rule 38, however, which extends the provisions for waiver of jury. U.S.C., Title 28, former § 772 (Trial of issues of fact; in equity in patent causes) is unaffected by this rule. When certain of the issues are to be tried by jury and others by the court, the court may determine the sequence in which such issues shall be tried.

See *Liberty Oil Co. v. Condon Nat. Bank*, 260 U.S. 235, 43 S. Ct. 118, 67 L.Ed. 232 (1922).

A discretionary power in the courts to send issues of fact to the jury is common in state procedure. Compare Calif.Code Civ.Proc. (Deering, 1937) § 592; 1 Colo.Stat.Ann. (1935) Code Civ.Proc., Ch. 12, § 191; Conn.Gen.Stat. (1930) § 5625; 2 Minn.Stat. (Mason, 1927) § 9288; 4 Mont.Rev.Codes Ann. (1935) § 9327; N.Y.C.P.A. (1937) § 430; 2 Ohio Gen.Code Ann. (Page, 1926) § 11380; 1 Okla.Stat.Ann. (Harlow, 1931) § 351 [12 Okl.St.Ann. § 557]; Utah Rev.Stat.Ann. (1933) § 104-23-5; 2 Wash.Rev.Stat.Ann. (Remington, 1932) § 315; Wis.Stat. (1935) § 270.07. See former Equity Rule 23 (Matters Ordinarily Determinable at Law When Arising in Suit in Equity to be Disposed of Therein) and U.S.C., Title 28, former § 772 (Trial of issues of fact; in equity in patent causes); *Colleton Merc. Mfg. Co. v. Savannah River Lumber Co., C.C.A.4, 1922*, 280 F. 358; *Fed. Res. Bk. of San Francisco v. Idaho Grimm Alfalfa Seed Growers' Ass'n, C.C.A.9, 1925*, 8 F.2d 922, certiorari denied 270 U.S. 646, 46 S. Ct. 347, 70 L.Ed. 778; *Watt v. Starke, 1879*, 101 U.S. 247, 25 L.Ed. 826.

2007 AMENDMENT

The language of Rule 39 has been amended as part of the general restyling of the Civil Rules to make them more easily understood and to make style and terminology consistent throughout the rules. These changes are intended to be stylistic only.

Rule 40. Assignment of Cases for Trial

1937 ADOPTION

U.S.C., Title 28, former § 769 (Notice of case for trial) is modified. See former Equity Rule 56 (On Expiration of Time for Depositions, Case Goes on Trial Calendar). See also former Equity Rule 57 (Continuances).

For examples of statutes giving precedence, see U.S.C., Title 28, formerly § 47 (now §§ 1253, 2101, 2325)(Injunctions as to orders of Interstate Commerce Commission); formerly § 380 (now §§ 1253, 2101, 2284) (Injunctions alleged unconstitutionality of state statutes); formerly § 380a (now §§ 1253, 2101, 2284)(Same; Constitutionality of federal statute); former § 768 (Priority of cases where a state is party); Title 15, § 28 (Antitrust laws; suits against monopolies expedited); Title 22, § 240 (Petition for restoration of property seized as munitions of war, etc.); and Title 49, § 44 (Proceedings in equity under interstate commerce laws; expedition of suits).

2007 AMENDMENT

The language of Rule 40 has been amended as part of the general restyling of the Civil Rules to make them more easily understood and to make style and terminology consistent throughout the rules. These changes are intended to be stylistic only.

The best methods for scheduling trials depend on local conditions. It is useful to ensure that each district adopts an explicit rule for scheduling trials. It is not useful to limit or dictate the provisions of local rules.

Rule 41. Dismissal of Actions

1937 ADOPTION

Note to Subdivision (a). Compare Ill.Rev.Stat. (1937) c. 110, § 176, and English Rules Under the Judicature Act (The Annual Practice, 1937) O. 26.

Provisions regarding dismissal in such statutes as U.S.C., Title 8, § 164 (Jurisdiction of district courts in immigration cases) and U.S.C., Title 31, § 232 (Liability of persons making false claims against United States; suits) are preserved by paragraph (1).

Note to Subdivision (b). This provides for the equivalent of a nonsuit on motion by the defendant after the completion of the presentation of evidence by the plaintiff. Also, for actions tried without a jury, it provides the equivalent of the directed verdict practice for jury actions which is regulated by Rule 50.

1946 AMENDMENT

Note to Subdivision (a). The insertion of the reference to Rule 66 correlates Rule 41(a)(1) with the express provisions concerning dismissal set forth in amended Rule 66 on receivers.

The change in Rule 41(a)(1)(i) gives the service of a motion for summary judgment by the adverse party the same effect in preventing unlimited dismissal as was originally given only to the service of an answer. The omission of reference to a motion for summary judgment in the original rule was subject to criticism. 3 Moore's Federal Practice, 1938, 3037–3038, n. 12. A motion for summary judgment may be forthcoming prior to answer, and if well taken will eliminate the necessity for an answer. Since such a motion may require even more research and preparation than the answer itself, there is good reason why the service of the motion, like that of the answer, should prevent a voluntary dismissal by the adversary without court approval.

The word "generally" has been stricken from Rule 41(a)(1)(ii) in order to avoid confusion and to conform with the elimination of the necessity for special appearance by original Rule 12(b).

Subdivision (b). In some cases tried without a jury, where at the close of plaintiff's evidence the defendant moves for dismissal under Rule 41(b) on the ground that plaintiff's evidence is insufficient for recovery, the plaintiff's own evidence may be conflicting or present questions of credibility. In ruling on the defendant's motion, questions arise as to the function of the judge in evaluating the testimony and whether findings should be made if the motion is sustained. Three circuits hold that as the judge is the trier of the facts in such a situation his function is not the same as on a motion to direct a verdict, where the jury is the trier of the facts, and that the judge in deciding such a motion in a non-jury case may pass on conflicts of evidence and credibility, and if he performs that function of evaluating the testimony and grants the motion on the merits, findings are required. *Young v. United States, C.C.A.9, 1940*, 111 F.2d 823; *Gary Theatre Co. v. Columbia Pictures Corporation, C.C.A.7, 1941*, 120 F.2d 891; *Bach v. Friden Calculating Machine Co., Inc., C.C.A.6, 1945*, 148 F.2d 407. Cf. *Mateas v. Fred Harvey, a Corporation, C.C.A.9, 1945*, 146 F.2d 989. The Third Circuit has held that on such a motion the function of the court is the same as on a motion to direct in a jury case, and that the court should only decide whether there is evidence which would support a judgment for the plaintiff, and therefore, findings are not required by Rule 52. *Federal Deposit Insurance Corp. v. Mason, C.C.A.3, 1940*, 115 F.2d 548; *Schad v. Twentieth Century-Fox Film Corp., C.C.A.3, 1943*, 136 F.2d 991. The added sentence in Rule 41(b) incorporates the view of the Sixth, Seventh and Ninth Circuits. See also 3 Moore's Federal Practice, 1938, Cum.Supplement § 41.03, under "Page 3045"; Commentary, The Motion to Dismiss in Non-Jury Cases, 1946, 9 Fed.Rules Serv., Comm.Pg. 41b.14.

1963 AMENDMENT

Under the present text of the second sentence of this subdivision, the motion for dismissal at the close of the plaintiff's evidence may be made in a case tried to a jury as well as in a case tried without a jury. But, when made in a jury-tried case, this motion overlaps the motion for a directed verdict under Rule 50(a), which is also available in the same situation. It has been held that the standard to be applied in deciding the Rule 41(b) motion at the close of the plaintiff's evidence in a jury-tried case is the same as that used upon a motion for a directed verdict made at the same stage; and, just as the court need not make findings pursuant to Rule 52(a) when it directs a verdict, so in a jury-tried case it may omit these findings in granting the Rule 41(b) motion. See generally *O'Brien v. Westinghouse Electric Corp.*, 293 F.2d 1, 5–10 (3d Cir.1961).

As indicated by the discussion in the *O'Brien* case, the overlap has caused confusion. Accordingly, the second and third sentences of Rule 41(b) are amended to provide that the motion for dismissal at the close of the plaintiff's evidence shall apply only to non-jury cases (including cases tried with an advisory jury). Hereafter the correct motion in jury-tried cases will be the motion for a directed verdict. This involves no change of substance. It should be noted that the court upon a motion for a directed verdict may in appropriate circumstances deny that motion and grant instead a new trial, or a voluntary dismissal without prejudice under Rule 41(a)(2). See 6 Moore's Federal Practice ¶ 59.08[5] (2d ed. 1954); cf. *Cone v. West Virginia Pulp & Paper Co.*, 330 U.S. 212, 217, 67 S. Ct. 752, 755, 91 L.Ed. 849 (1947).

The first sentence of Rule 41(b), providing for dismissal for failure to prosecute or to comply with the Rules or any order of court, and the general provisions of the last sentence remain applicable in jury as well as non-jury cases.

The amendment of the last sentence of Rule 41(b) indicates that a dismissal for lack of an indispensable party does not operate as an adjudication on the merits. Such a dismissal does not bar a new action, for it is based merely "on a plaintiff's failure to comply with a precondition requisite to the Court's going forward to determine the merits of his substantive claim." See *Costello v. United States*, 365 U.S. 265, 284–288, 81 S. Ct. 534, 544–546, 5 L. Ed. 2d 551 & n. 5 (1961); *Mallow v. Hinde*, 6 L.Ed. 599, 12 Wheat. (25 U.S.) 193 (1827); Clark, Code Pleading 602 (2d ed. 1947); Restatement of Judgments § 49, comm. a, b (1942). This amendment corrects an omission from the rule and is consistent with an earlier amendment, effective in 1948, adding "the defense of failure to join an indispensable party" to clause (1) of Rule 12(h).

1966 AMENDMENT

The terminology is changed to accord with the amendment of Rule 19. See that amended rule and the Advisory Committee's Note thereto.

1968 AMENDMENT

The amendment corrects an inadvertent error in the reference to amended Rule 23.

1987 AMENDMENT

The amendment is technical. No substantive change is intended.

1991 AMENDMENT

Language is deleted that authorized the use of this rule as a means of terminating a non-jury action on the merits when the plaintiff has failed to carry a burden of proof in presenting the plaintiff's case. The device is replaced by the new provisions of Rule 52(c), which authorize entry of judgment against the defendant as well as the plaintiff, and earlier than the close of the case of the party against whom judgment is rendered. A motion to dismiss under Rule 41 on the ground that a plaintiff's evidence is legally insufficient should now be treated as a motion for judgment on partial findings as provided in Rule 52(c).

2007 AMENDMENT

The language of Rule 41 has been amended as part of the general restyling of the Civil Rules to make them more easily understood and to make style and terminology consistent throughout the rules. These changes are intended to be stylistic only.

When Rule 23 was amended in 1966, Rules 23.1 and 23.2 were separated from Rule 23. Rule 41(a)(1) was not then amended to reflect the Rule 23 changes. In 1968 Rule 41(a)(1) was amended to correct the cross-reference to what had become Rule 23(e), but Rules 23.1 and 23.2 were inadvertently overlooked. Rules 23.1 and 23.2 are now added to the list of exceptions in Rule 41(a)(1)(A). This change does not affect established meaning. Rule 23.2 explicitly incorporates Rule 23(e), and thus was already absorbed directly into the exceptions in Rule 41(a)(1). Rule 23.1 requires court approval of a compromise or dismissal in language parallel to Rule 23(e) and thus supersedes the apparent right to dismiss by notice of dismissal.

Rule 42. Consolidation; Separate Trials

1937 ADOPTION

Subdivision (a) is based upon U.S.C. Title 28, former § 734 (Orders to save costs; consolidation of causes of like nature) but in so far as the statute differs from this rule, it is modified.

For comparable statutes dealing with consolidation see Ark.Dig.Stat. (Crawford & Moses, 1921) § 1081; Cal.Code Civ.Proc. § 1048; N.M.Stat.Ann. (Courtright, 1929), § 105-828; N.Y.C.P.A. (1937) §§ 96, 96a, and 97; American Judicature Society, Bulletin XIV, (1919) Art. 26.

For severance or separate trials, see Calif.Code Civ.Proc. § 1048; N.Y.C.P.A. (1937) § 96; American Judicature Society, Bulletin XIV (1919) Art. 3, § 2 and Art. 10, § 10. See also the third sentence of former Equity Rule 29 (Defenses—How Presented) providing for discretionary separate hearing and disposition before trial of pleas in bar or abatement, and see also Rule 12(d) of these rules for preliminary hearings of defenses and objections.

For the entry of separate judgments, see Rule 54(b) (Judgment at Various Stages).

1966 AMENDMENT

In certain suits in admiralty separation for trial of the issues of liability and damages (or of the extent of liability other than damages, such as salvage and general average) has been conducive to expedition and economy, especially because of the statutory right to interlocutory appeal in admiralty cases (which is of course preserved by these Rules). While separation of issues for trial is not to be routinely ordered, it is important that it be encouraged where experience has demonstrated its worth. Cf. Weinstein, Routine Bifurcation of Negligence Trials, 14 Vand.L.Rev. 831 (1961).

In cases (including some cases within the admiralty and maritime jurisdiction) in which the parties have a constitutional or statutory right of trial by jury, separation of issues may give rise to problems. See *e.g., United Air Lines, Inc. v. Wiener*, 286 F.2d 302 (9th Cir.1961). Accordingly, the proposed change in Rule 42 reiterates the mandate of Rule 38 respecting preservation of the right to jury trial.

2007 AMENDMENT

The language of Rule 42 has been amended as part of the general restyling of the Civil Rules to make them more easily understood and to make style and terminology consistent throughout the rules. These changes are intended to be stylistic only.

Rule 43. Taking of Testimony

1937 ADOPTION

Note to Subdivision (a). The first sentence is a restatement of the substance of U.S.C., Title 28, former § 635 (Proof in common-law actions), formerly § 637 (now §§ 2072, 2073)(Proof in equity and admiralty), and former Equity Rule 46 (Trial—Testimony Usually Taken in Open Court—Rulings on Objections to Evidence). This rule abolishes in patent and trademark actions, the practice under former Equity Rule 48 of setting forth in affidavits the testimony in chief of expert witnesses whose testimony is directed to matters of opinion. The second and third sentences on admissibility of evidence and Subdivision (b) on contradiction and cross-examination modify U.S.C., Title 28, formerly § 725 (now § 1652) (Laws of states as rules of decision) insofar as that statute has been construed to prescribe conformity to state rules of evidence. Compare Callihan and Ferguson, *Evidence and the new Federal Rules of Civil Procedure*, 45 Yale L.J. 622 (1936), and *Same*: 2, 47 Yale L.J. 195 (1937). The last sentence modifies to the extent indicated U.S.C., Title 28, § 631 (Competency of witnesses governed by State laws).

Note to Subdivision (b). See 4 Wigmore on Evidence (2d ed., 1923) §§ 1885 et seq.

Note to Subdivision (c). See former Equity Rule 46 (Trial—Testimony Usually Taken in Open Court—Rulings on Objections to Evidence). With the last sentence compare *Dowagiac Mfg. Co. v. Lochren*, 143 Fed. 211 (C.C.A. 8 1906). See also *Blease v. Garlington*, 92 U.S. 1, 23 L.Ed. 521 (1876); *Nelson v. United States*, 201 U.S. 92, 114, 26 S. Ct. 358, 365, 50 L.Ed. 673 (1906); *Unkle v. Wills*, 281 Fed. 29 (8th.Cir.1922).

See Rule 61 for harmless error in either the admission or exclusion of evidence.

Note to Subdivision (d). See former Equity Rule 78 (Affirmation in Lieu of Oath) and U.S.C. Title 1, § 1 (Words importing singular number, masculine gender, etc.; extended application), providing for affirmation in lieu of oath.

SUPPLEMENTARY NOTE ON ADVISORY COMMITTEE REGARDING RULES 43 AND 44

Note. These rules have been criticized and suggested improvements offered by commentators. 1 Wigmore on Evidence, 3d ed. 1940, 200–204; Green, The Admissibility of Evidence Under the Federal Rules, 1941, 55 Harv.L.Rev. 197. Cases indicate, however, that the rule is working better than these commentators had expected. *Boerner v. United States, C.C.A.2d, 1941*, 117 F.2d 387, cert. den., 1941, 313 U.S. 587, 61 S. Ct. 1120, 85 L.Ed. 1542; *Mosson v. Liberty Fast Freight Co., C.C.A.2d, 1942*, 124 F.2d 448; *Hartford Accident & Indemnity Co. v. Olivier, C.C.A. 5th, 1941*, 123 F.2d 709; *Anzano v. Metropolitan Life Ins. Co. of New York, C.C.A.3d, 1941*, 118 F.2d 430; *Franzen v. E. I. DuPont De Nemours & Co., C.C.A.3d, 1944*, 146 F.2d 837; *Fakouri v. Cadais, C.C.A. 5th, 1945*, 147 F.2d 667; *In re C. & P. Co., S.D.Cal.1945*, 63 F.Supp. 400, 408. But cf. United States v. Aluminum Co. of America, S.D.N.Y.1938, 1 Fed.Rules Serv. 43a.3, Case 1; Note, 1946, 46 Col.L.Rev. 267. While consideration of a comprehensive and detailed set of rules of evidence seems very desirable, it has not been feasible for the Committee so far to undertake this important task. Such consideration should include the adaptability to federal practice of all or parts of the proposed Code of Evidence of the American Law Institute. See Armstrong, Proposed Amendments to Federal Rules of Civil Procedure, 4 F.R.D. 124, 137–138.

1966 AMENDMENT

Note to Subdivision (f). This new subdivision authorizes the court to appoint interpreters (including interpreters for the deaf), to provide for their compensation, and to tax the compensation as costs. Compare proposed subdivision (b) of Rule 28 of the Federal Rules of Criminal Procedure.

1972 AMENDMENTS

Rule 43, entitled Evidence, has heretofore served as the basic rule of evidence for civil cases in federal courts. Its very general provisions are superseded by the detailed provisions of the new Rules of Evidence. The original title and many of the provisions of the rule are, therefore, no longer appropriate.

Subdivision (a). The provision for taking testimony in open court is not duplicated in the Rules of Evidence and is retained. Those dealing with admissibility of evidence and competency of witnesses, however, are no longer needed or appropriate since those topics are covered at large in the Rules of Evidence. They are accordingly deleted. The language is broadened, however, to take account of acts of Congress dealing with the taking of testimony, as well as of the Rules of Evidence and any other rules adopted by the Supreme Court.

Subdivision (b). The subdivision is no longer needed or appropriate since the matters with which it deals are treated in the Rules of Evidence. The use of leading questions, both generally and in the interrogation of an adverse party or witness identified with him, is the subject of Evidence Rule 611(c). Who may impeach is treated in Evidence Rule 607, and scope of cross-examination is covered in Evidence Rule 611(b). The subdivision is accordingly deleted.

Subdivision (c). Offers of proof and making a record of excluded evidence are treated in Evidence Rule 103. The subdivision is no longer needed or appropriate and is deleted.

1987 AMENDMENT

The amendment is technical. No substantive change is intended.

1996 AMENDMENT

Rule 43(a) is revised to conform to the style conventions adopted for simplifying the present Civil Rules. The only intended changes of meaning are described below.

The requirement that testimony be taken "orally" is deleted. The deletion makes it clear that testimony of a witness may be given in open court by other means if the witness is not able to communicate orally. Writing or sign language are common examples. The development of advanced technology may enable testimony to be given by other means. A witness unable to sign or write by hand may be able to communicate through a computer or similar device.

Contemporaneous transmission of testimony from a different location is permitted only on showing good cause in compelling circumstances. The importance of presenting live testimony in court cannot be forgotten. The very ceremony of trial and the presence of the factfinder may exert a powerful force for truthtelling. The opportunity to judge the demeanor of a witness face-to-face is accorded great value in our tradition. Transmission cannot be justified merely by showing that it is inconvenient for the witness to attend the trial.

The most persuasive showings of good cause and compelling circumstances are likely to arise when a witness is unable to attend trial for unexpected reasons, such as accident or illness, but remains able to testify from a different place. Contemporaneous transmission may be better than an attempt to reschedule the trial, particularly if there is a risk that other—and perhaps more important—witnesses might not be available at a later time.

Other possible justifications for remote transmission must be approached cautiously. Ordinarily depositions, including video depositions, provide a superior means of securing the testimony of a witness who is beyond the reach of a trial subpoena, or of resolving difficulties in scheduling a trial that can be attended by all witnesses. Deposition procedures ensure the opportunity of all parties to be represented while the witness is testifying. An unforeseen need for the testimony of a remote witness that arises during trial, however, may establish good cause and compelling circumstances. Justification is particularly likely if the need arises from the interjection of new issues during trial or from the unexpected inability to present testimony as planned from a different witness.

Good cause and compelling circumstances may be established with relative ease if all parties agree that testimony should be presented by transmission. The court is not bound by a stipulation, however, and can insist on live testimony. Rejection of the parties' agreement will be influenced, among other factors, by the apparent importance of the testimony in the full context of the trial.

A party who could reasonably foresee the circumstances offered to justify transmission of testimony will have special difficulty in showing good cause and the compelling nature of the circumstances. Notice of a desire to transmit testimony from a different location should be given as soon as the reasons are known, to enable other parties to arrange a deposition, or to secure an advance ruling on transmission so as to know whether to prepare to be present with the witness while testifying.

No attempt is made to specify the means of transmission that may be used. Audio transmission without video images may be sufficient in some circumstances, particularly as to less important testimony. Video transmission ordinarily should be preferred when the cost is reasonable in relation to the matters in dispute, the means of the parties, and the circumstances that justify transmission. Transmission that merely produces the equivalent of a written statement ordinarily should not be used.

Safeguards must be adopted that ensure accurate identification of the witness and that protect against influence by persons present with the witness. Accurate transmission likewise must be assured.

Other safeguards should be employed to ensure that advance notice is given to all parties of foreseeable circumstances that may lead the proponent to offer testimony by transmission. Advance notice is important to protect the opportunity to argue for attendance of the witness at trial. Advance notice also ensures an opportunity to depose the witness, perhaps by video record, as a means of supplementing transmitted testimony.

2007 AMENDMENT

The language of Rule 43 has been amended as part of the general restyling of the Civil Rules to make them more easily understood and to make style and terminology consistent throughout the rules. These changes are intended to be stylistic only.

Rule 44. Proof of Official Record

1937 ADOPTION

This rule provides a simple and uniform method of proving public records, and entry or lack of entry therein, in all cases including those specifically provided for by statutes of the United States. Such statutes are not superseded, however, and proof may also be made according to their provisions whenever they differ from this rule.

Some of those statutes are:

U.S.C., Title 28, former:

§ 661 (Copies of department or corporation records and papers; admissibility; seal)

§ 662 (Same; in office of General Counsel of the Treasury)

§ 663 (Instruments and papers of Comptroller of Currency; admissibility)

§ 664 (Organization certificates of national banks; admissibility)

§ 665 (Transcripts from books of Treasury in suits against delinquents; admissibility)

§ 666 (Same; certificate by Secretary or Assistant Secretary)

§ 670 (Admissibility of copies of statements of demands by Post Office Department)

§ 671 (Admissibility of copies of post office records and statement of accounts)

§ 672 (Admissibility of copies of records in General Land Office)

§ 673 (Admissibility of copies of records, and so forth, of Patent Office)

§ 674 (Copies of foreign letters patent as prima facie evidence)

§ 675 (Copies of specifications and drawings of patents admissible)

§ 676 (Extracts from Journals of Congress admissible when injunction of secrecy removed)

§ 677 (Copies of records in offices of United States consuls admissible)

§ 678 (Books and papers in certain district courts)

§ 679 (Records in clerks' offices, western district of North Carolina)

§ 680 (Records in clerks' offices of former district of California)

§ 681 (Original records lost or destroyed; certified copy admissible)

§ 682 (Same; when certified copy not obtainable)

§ 685 (Same; certified copy of official papers)

§ 687 (Authentication of legislative acts; proof of judicial proceedings of State)

§ 688 (Proofs of records in offices not pertaining to courts)

§ 689 (Copies of foreign records relating to land titles)

§ 695 (Writings and records made in regular course of business; admissibility)

§ 695e (Foreign documents on record in public offices; certification)

U.S.C., Title 1:

§ 112 (Statutes at large; contents; admissibility in evidence)

§ 113 ("Little and Brown's" edition of laws and treaties competent evidence of Acts of Congress)

§ 204 (Codes and supplements as establishing prima facie the laws of United States and District of Columbia, etc.)

§ 208 (Copies of supplements to Code of Laws of United States and of District of Columbia Code and supplements; conclusive evidence of original)
U.S.C., Title 5:
§ 490 (Records of Department of Interior; authenticated copies as evidence)
U.S.C., Title 6:
§ 7 (Surety Companies as sureties; appointment of agents; service of process)
U.S.C., Title 8:
§ 9a (Citizenship of children of persons naturalized under certain laws; repatriation of native-born women married to aliens prior to September 22, 1922; copies of proceedings)
§ 1443 (Regulations for execution of naturalization laws; certified copies of papers as evidence)
§ 1443 (Certifications of naturalization records; authorization; admissibility as evidence)
U.S.C., Title 11:
§ 44(d), (e), (f), (g) (Bankruptcy court proceedings and orders as evidence)
U.S.C., Title 15:
§ 127 (Trade-mark records in Patent Office; copies as evidence)
U.S.C., Title 20:
§ 52 (Smithsonian Institution; evidence of title to site and buildings)
U.S.C., Title 25:
§ 6 (Bureau of Indian Affairs; seal; authenticated and certified documents; evidence)
U.S.C., Title 31:
§ 46 (Laws governing General Accounting Office; copies of books, records, etc., thereof as evidence)
U.S.C., Title 38:
§ 11g (Seal of Veterans' Administration; authentication of copies of records)
U.S.C., Title 40:
§ 238 (National Archives; seal; reproduction of archives; fee; admissibility in evidence of reproductions)
§ 270c (Bonds of contractors for public works; right of person furnishing labor or material to copy of bond)
U.S.C., Title 43:
§§ 57 to 59 (Copies of land surveys, etc., in certain states and districts admissible as evidence)
§ 83 (General Land Office registers and receivers; transcripts of records as evidence)
U.S.C., Title 46:
§ 823 (Records of Maritime Commission; copies; publication of reports; evidence)
U.S.C., Title 47:
§ 154(m) (Federal Communications Commission; copies of reports and decisions as evidence)
§ 412 (Documents filed with Federal Communications Commission as public records; prima facie evidence; confidential records)
U.S.C., Title 49:
§ 14(3) (Interstate Commerce Commission reports and decisions; printing and distribution of copies)
§ 16(13) (Copies of schedules, tariffs, etc., filed with Interstate Commerce Commission as evidence)
§ 19a(i) (Valuation of property of carriers by Interstate Commerce Commission; final published valuations as evidence)

SUPPLEMENTARY NOTE OF ADVISORY COMMITTEE REGARDING RULES 43 AND 44

For supplementary note of Advisory Committee on this rule, see note under Rule 43.

1966 AMENDMENT

Subdivision (a)(1). These provisions on proof or official records kept within the United States are similar in substance to those heretofore appearing in

Rule 44. There is a more exact description of the geographical areas covered. An official record kept in one of the areas enumerated qualifies for proof under subdivision (a)(1) even though it is not a United States official record. For example, an official record kept in one of these areas by a government in exile falls within subdivision (a)(1). It also falls within subdivision (a)(2) which may be availed of alternatively. *Cf. Banco de Espana v. Federal Reserve Bank*, 114 F.2d 438 (2d Cir.1940).

Subdivision (a)(2). Foreign official records may be proved, as heretofore, by means of official publications thereof. See *United States v. Aluminum Co. of America*, 1 F.R.D. 71 (S.D.N.Y.1939). Under this rule a document that, on its face, appears to be an official publication, is admissible, unless a party opposing its admission into evidence shows that it lacks that character.

The rest of subdivision (a)(2) aims to provide greater clarity, efficiency, and flexibility in the procedure for authenticating copies of foreign official records.

The reference to attestation by "the officer having the legal custody of the record," hitherto appearing in Rule 44, has been found inappropriate for official records kept in foreign countries where the assumed relation between custody and the authority to attest does not obtain. See 2B Barron & Holtzoff, Federal Practice & Procedure § 992 (Wright ed. 1961). Accordingly it is provided that an attested copy may be obtained from any person authorized by the law of the foreign country to make the attestation without regard to whether he is charged with responsibility for maintaining the record or keeping it in his custody.

Under Rule 44 a United States foreign service officer has been called on to certify to the authority of the foreign official attesting the copy as well as the genuineness of his signature and his official position. See Schlesinger, Comparative Law 57 (2d ed. 1959); Smit, International Aspects of Federal Civil Procedure, 61 Colum.L.Rev. 1031, 1063 (1961); 22 C.F.R. § 92.41(a), (e)(1958). This has created practical difficulties. For example, the question of the authority of the foreign officer might raise issues of foreign law which were beyond the knowledge of the United States officer. The difficulties are met under the amended rule by eliminating the element of the authority of the attesting foreign official from the scope of the certifying process, and by specifically permitting use of the chain-certificate method. Under this method, it is sufficient if the original attestation purports to have been issued by an authorized person and is accompanied by a certificate of another foreign official whose certificate may in turn be followed by that of a foreign official of higher rank. The process continues until a foreign official is reached as to whom the United States foreign service official (or a diplomatic or consular officer of the foreign country assigned or accredited to the United States) has adequate information upon which to base a "final certification." See *New York Life Ins. Co. v. Aronson*, 38 F.Supp. 687 (W.D.Pa.1941); 22 C.F.R. § 92.37 (1958).

The final certification (a term used in contradistinction to the certificates prepared by the foreign officials in a chain) relates to the incumbency and genuineness of signature of the foreign official who attested the copy of the record or, where the chain-certificate method is used, of a foreign official whose certificate appears in the chain, whether that certificate is the last in the chain or not. A final certification may be prepared on the basis of material on file in the consulate or any other satisfactory information.

Although the amended rule will generally facilitate proof of foreign official records, it is recognized that in some situations it may be difficult or even impossible to satisfy the basic requirements of the rule. There may be no United States consul in a particular foreign country; the foreign officials may not cooperate, peculiarities may exist or arise hereafter in the law or practice of a foreign country. See *United States v. Grabina*, 119 F.2d 863 (2d Cir.1941); and, generally, Jones, International Judicial Assistance: Procedural Chaos and a Program for Reform, 62 Yale L.J. 515, 548–49 (1953). Therefore the final sentence of subdivision (a)(2) provides the court with discretion to admit an attested copy of a record without a final certification, or an attested summary of a record with or without a final certification. See Rep. of Comm. on Comparative Civ. Proc. & Prac., Proc. A.B.A., Sec. Int'l & Comp. L. 123, 130 to 131 (1952);

Model Code of evidence §§ 517, 519 (1942). This relaxation should be permitted only when it is shown that the party has been unable to satisfy the basic requirements of the amended rule despite his reasonable efforts. Moreover, it is specially provided that the parties must be given a reasonable opportunity in these cases to examine into the authenticity and accuracy of the copy or summary.

Subdivision (b). This provision relating to proof of lack of record is accommodated to the changes made in subdivision (a).

Subdivision (c). The amendment insures that international agreements of the United States are unaffected by the rule. Several consular conventions contain provisions for reception of copies or summaries of foreign official records. See e.g., Consular Conv. with Italy, May 8, 1878, art. X, 20 Stat. 725, T.S. No. 178 (Dept. State 1878). See also 28 U.S.C. §§ 1740 to 42, 1745; *Fakouri v. Cadais*, 149 F.2d 321 (5th Cir.1945), cert. denied, 326 U.S. 742, 66 S. Ct. 54, 90 L.Ed. 443 (1945); 5 Moore's Federal Practice, par. 44.05 (2d ed. 1951).

1987 AMENDMENT

The amendments are technical. No substantive change is intended.

1991 AMENDMENT

The amendment to paragraph (a)(1) strikes the references to specific territories, two of which are no longer subject to the jurisdiction of the United States, and adds a generic term to describe governments having a relationship with the United States such that their official records should be treated as domestic records.

The amendment to paragraph (a)(2) adds a sentence to dispense with the final certification by diplomatic officers when the United States and the foreign country where the record is located are parties to a treaty or convention that abolishes or displaces the requirement. In that event the treaty or convention is to be followed. This changes the former procedure for authenticating foreign official records only with respect to records from countries that are parties to the Hague Convention Abolishing the Requirement of Legalization for Foreign Public Documents. Moreover, it does not affect the former practice of attesting the records, but only changes the method of certifying the attestation.

The Hague Public Documents Convention provides that the requirement of a final certification is abolished and replaced with a model *apostille*, which is to be issued by officials of the country where the records are located. See Hague Public Documents Convention, Arts. 2 to 4. The *apostille* certifies the signature, official position, and seal of the attesting officer. The authority who issues the *apostille* must maintain a register or card index showing the serial number of the *apostille* and other relevant information recorded on it. A foreign court can then check the serial number and information on the *apostille* with the issuing authority in order to guard against the use of fraudulent *apostilles*. This system provides a reliable method for maintaining the integrity of the authentication process, and the *apostille* can be accorded greater weight than the normal authentication procedure because foreign officials are more likely to know the precise capacity under their law of the attesting officer than would an American official. See generally Comment, *The United States and the Hague Convention Abolishing the Requirement of Legalization for Foreign Public Documents*, 11 HARV. INT'L L.J. 476, 482, 488 (1970).

2007 AMENDMENT

The language of Rule 44 has been amended as part of the general restyling of the Civil Rules to make them more easily understood and to make style and terminology consistent throughout the rules. These changes are intended to be stylistic only.

Rule 44.1. Determination of Foreign Law

1966 ADDITIONS

Rule 44.1 is added by amendment to furnish Federal courts with a uniform and effective procedure for raising and determining an issue concerning the law of a foreign country.

To avoid unfair surprise, the first sentence of the new rule requires that a party who intends to raise an issue of foreign law shall give notice thereof. The uncertainty under Rule 8(a) about whether foreign law must be pleaded—compare *Siegelman v. Cunard White Star, Ltd.*, 221 F.2d 189 (2d Cir.1955), and *Pedersen v. United States*, 191 F.Supp. 95 (D.Guam 1961), with *Harrison v. United Fruit Co.*, 143 F.Supp. 598 (S.D.N.Y.1956)—is eliminated by the provision that the notice shall be "written" and "reasonable." It may, but need not be, incorporated in the pleadings. In some situations the pertinence of foreign law is apparent from the outset; accordingly the necessary investigation of that law will have been accomplished by the party at the pleading stage, and the notice can be given conveniently in the pleadings. In other situations the pertinence of foreign law may remain doubtful until the case is further developed. A requirement that notice of foreign law be given only through the medium of the pleadings would tend in the latter instances to force the party to engage in a peculiarly burdensome type of investigation which might turn out to be unnecessary; and correspondingly the adversary would be forced into a possible wasteful investigation. The liberal provisions for amendment of the pleadings afford help if the pleadings are used as the medium of giving notice of the foreign law; but it seems best to permit a written notice to be given outside of and later than the pleadings, provided the notice is reasonable.

The new rule does not attempt to set any definite limit on the party's time for giving the notice of an issue of foreign law; in some cases the issue may not become apparent until the trial and notice then given may still be reasonable. The stage which the case had reached at the time of the notice, the reason proffered by the party for his failure to give earlier notice, and the importance to the case as a whole of the issue of foreign law sought to be raised, are among the factors which the court should consider in deciding a question of the reasonableness of a notice. If notice is given by one party it need not be repeated by any other and serves as a basis for presentation of material on the foreign law by all parties.

The second sentence of the new rule describes the materials to which the court may resort in determining an issue of foreign law. Heretofore the district courts, applying Rule 43(a), have looked in certain cases to State law to find the rules of evidence by which the content of foreign-country law is to be established. The State laws vary; some embody procedures which are inefficient, time consuming and expensive. See, generally, Nussbaum, Proving the Law of Foreign Countries, 3 Am.J.Comp.L. 60 (1954). In all events the ordinary rules of evidence are often inapposite to the problem of determining foreign law and have in the past prevented examination of material which could have provided a proper basis for the determination. The new rule permits consideration by the court of any relevant material, including testimony, without regard to its admissibility under Rule 43. Cf. N.Y. Civ. Prac. Law & Rules, R. 4511 (Effective Sept. 1, 1963); 2 Va. Code Ann. tit. 8, § 8-273; 2 W. Va. Code Ann. § 5711.

In further recognition of the peculiar nature of the issue of foreign law, the new rule provides that in determining this law the court is not limited by material presented by the parties; it may engage in its own research and consider any relevant material thus found. The court may have at its disposal better foreign law materials than counsel have presented, or may wish to reexamine and amplify material that has been presented by counsel in partisan fashion or in insufficient detail. On the other hand, the court is free to insist on a complete presentation by counsel.

There is no requirement that the court give formal notice to the parties of its intention to engage in its own research on an issue of foreign law which has been raised by them, or of its intention to raise and determine independently an issue not raised by them. Ordinarily the court should inform the parties of material it has found diverging substantially from the material which they have presented; and in general the court should give the parties an opportunity to analyze and counter new points upon which it proposes to rely. See Schlesinger, Comparative Law 142 (2d ed. 1959); Wyzanski, A Trial Judge's Freedom and

Responsibility, 65 Harv.L.Rev. 1281, 1296 (1952); cf. *Siegelman v. Cunard White Star, Ltd.*, supra, 221 F.2d at 197. To require, however, that the court give formal notice from time to time as it proceeds with its study of the foreign law would add an element of undesirable rigidity to the procedure for determining issues of foreign law.

The new rule refrains from imposing an obligation on the court to take "judicial notice" of foreign law because this would put an extreme burden on the court in many cases; and it avoids use of the concept of "judicial notice" in any form because of the uncertain meaning of that concept as applied to foreign law. See, e.g., Stern, Foreign Law in the Courts: Judicial Notice and Proof, 45 Calif. L.Rev. 23, 43 (1957). Rather the rule provides flexible procedures for presenting and utilizing material on issues of foreign law by which a sound result can be achieved with fairness to the parties.

Under the third sentence, the court's determination of an issue of foreign law is to be treated as a ruling on a question of "law," not "fact," so that appellate review will not be narrowly confined by the "clearly erroneous" standard of Rule 52(a). *Cf.* Uniform Judicial Notice of Foreign Law Act § 3; Note, 72 Harv.L.Rev. 318 (1958).

The new rule parallels Article IV of the Uniform Interstate and International Procedure Act, approved by the Commissioners on Uniform State Laws in 1962, except that section 4.03 of Article IV states that "[t]he court, not the jury" shall determine foreign law. The new rule does not address itself to this problem, since the Rules refrain from allocating functions as between the court and the jury. See Rule 38(a). It has long been thought, however, that the jury is not the appropriate body to determine issues of foreign law. See, e.g., Story, Conflict of Laws, § 638 (1st ed. 1834, 8th ed. 1883); 1 Greenleaf, Evidence, § 486 (1st ed. 1842, 16th ed. 1899); 4 Wigmore, Evidence § 2558 (1st ed. 1905); 9 id. § 2558 (3d ed. 1940). The majority of the States have committed such issues to determination by the court. See Article 5 of the Uniform Judicial Notice of Foreign Law Act, adopted by twenty-six states, 9A U.L.A. 318 (1957) (Suppl.1961, at 134); N.Y.Civ.Prac.Law & Rules, R. 4511 (effective Sept. 1, 1963); Wigmore, loc. cit. And Federal courts that have considered the problem in recent years have reached the same conclusion without reliance on statute. See *Jansson v. Swedish American Line*, 185 F.2d 212, 216 (1st Cir.1950); *Bank of Nova Scotia v. San Miguel*, 196 F.2d 950, 957, n. 6 (1st Cir.1952); *Liechti v. Roche*, 198 F.2d 174 (5th Cir.1952); *Daniel Lumber Co. v. Empresas Hondurenas, S.A.*, 215 F.2d 465 (5th Cir.1954).

1972 AMENDMENT

Since the purpose of the provision is to free the judge, in determining foreign law, from any restrictions imposed by evidence rules, a general reference to the Rules of Evidence is appropriate and is made.

1987 AMENDMENT

The amendment is technical. No substantive change is intended.

2007 AMENDMENT

The language of Rule 44.1 has been amended as part of the general restyling of the Civil Rules to make them more easily understood and to make style and terminology consistent throughout the rules. These changes are intended to be stylistic only.

Rule 45. Subpoena

1937 ADOPTION

This rule applies to subpoenas *ad testificandum* and *duces tecum* issued by the district courts for attendance at a hearing or a trial, or to take depositions. It does not apply to the enforcement of subpoenas issued by administrative officers and commissions pursuant to statutory authority. The enforcement of such subpoenas by the district courts is regulated by appropriate statutes. Many of these statutes do not place any territorial limits on the validity of subpoenas so issued, but provide that they may be served anywhere within the United States. Among such statutes are the following:

U.S.C., Title 7, §§ 222 and 511n (Secretary of Agriculture)

U.S.C., Title 15, § 49 (Federal Trade Commission)

U.S.C., Title 15, §§ 77v(b), 78u(c), 79r(d) (Securities and Exchange Commission)

U.S.C., Title 16, §§ 797(g) and 825f (Federal Power Commission)

U.S.C., Title 19, § 1333(b) (Tariff Commission)

U.S.C., Title 22, §§ 268, 270d and 270e (International Commissions, etc.)

U.S.C., Title 26, §§ 614, 619(b) [see 7456] (Board of Tax Appeals)

U.S.C., Title 26, § 1523(a) [see 7608] (Internal Revenue Officers)

U.S.C., Title 29, § 161 (Labor Relations Board)

U.S.C., Title 33, § 506 (Secretary of Army)

U.S.C., Title 35, §§ 54 to 56 [now 24] (Patent Office proceedings)

U.S.C., Title 38, [former] § 133 (Veterans' Administration)

U.S.C., Title 41, § 39 (Secretary of Labor)

U.S.C., Title 45, § 157 Third. (h)(Board of Arbitration under Railway Labor Act)

U.S.C., Title 45, § 222(b) (Investigation Commission under Railroad Retirement Act of 1935)

U.S.C., Title 46, § 1124(b) (Maritime Commission)

U.S.C., Title 47, § 409(c) and (d) (Federal Communications Commission)

U.S.C., Title 49, § 12(2) and (3) (Interstate Commerce Commission)

U.S.C., Title 49, § 173a [see 1484] (Secretary of Commerce)

Note to Subdivisions (a) and (b). These simplify the form of subpoena as provided in U.S.C., Title 28, former § 655 (Witnesses; subpoena; form; attendance under); and broaden U.S.C., Title 28, former § 636 (Production of books and writings) to include all actions, and to extend to any person. With the provision for relief from an oppressive or unreasonable subpoena *duces tecum*, compare N.Y.C.P.A. (1937) § 411.

Note to Subdivision (c). This provides for the simple and convenient method of service permitted under many state codes; e.g., N.Y.C.P.A. (1937) §§ 220, 404, J.Ct.Act, § 191; 3 Wash.Rev.Stat.Ann. (Remington, 1932) § 1218. Compare Equity Rule 15 (Process, by Whom Served).

For statutes governing fees and mileage of witnesses see:

U.S.C., Title 28, former sections:

§ 600a [now 1871] (Per diem; mileage)

§ 600c [now 1821, 1823] (Amount per diem and mileage for witnesses; subsistence)

§ 600d [former] (Fees and mileage in certain states)

§ 601 [former] (Witnesses; fees; enumeration)
§ 602 [now 1824] (Fees and mileage of jurors and witnesses)
§ 603 [see Title 5, §§ 5515, 5537] (No officer of court to have witness fees)

Note to Subdivision (d). The method provided in paragraph (1) for the authorization of the issuance of subpoenas has been employed in some districts. See *Henning v. Boyle, N.Y.1901*, 112 F. 397. The requirement of an order for the issuance of a subpoena *duces tecum* is in accordance with U.S.C., Title 28, former § 647 (Deposition under *dedimus potestatem*; subpoena *duces tecum*). The provisions of paragraph (2) are in accordance with common practice. See U.S.C., Title 28, former § 648 (Deposition under *dedimus potestatem*; witnesses, when required to attend); N.Y.C.P.A. (1937) § 300; 1 N.J.Rev.Stat. (1937) 2:27-174.

Note to Subdivision (e). The first paragraph continues the substance of U.S.C., Title 28, [former] § 654 (Witnesses; subpoenas; may run into another district). Compare U.S.C., Title 11, [former] § 69 (Referees in bankruptcy; contempts before)(production of books and writings) which is not affected by this rule. For examples of statutes which allow the court, upon proper application and cause shown, to authorize the clerk of the court to issue a subpoena for a witness who lives in another district and at a greater distance than 100 miles from the place of the hearing or trial, see:

U.S.C., Title 15:
§ 23 (Suits by United States; subpoenas for witnesses)(under anti-trust laws).
U.S.C., Title 38:
§ 445 [now 784] (Actions on claims; jurisdiction; parties; procedure; limitation; witnesses; definitions)(Veterans' insurance contracts).

The second paragraph continues the present procedure applicable to certain witnesses who are in foreign countries. See U.S.C., Title 28, §§ 711 [now 1783] (Letters rogatory to take testimony of witness, addressed to court of foreign country; failure of witness to appear; subpoena) and former § 713 [now 1783] (Service of Subpoena on witness in foreign country).

Note to Subdivision (f). Compare [former] Equity Rule 52 (Attendance of Witnesses Before Commissioner, Master, or Examiner).

1946 AMENDMENT

Note to Subdivision (b). The added words, "or tangible things" in subdivision (b) merely make the rule for the subpoena duces tecum at the trial conform to that of subdivision (d) for the subpoena at the taking of depositions. The insertion of the words "or modify" in clause (1) affords desirable flexibility.

Subdivision (d). The added last sentence of amended subdivision (d)(1) properly gives the subpoena for documents or tangible things the same scope as provided in Rule 26(b), thus promoting uniformity. The requirement in the last sentence of original Rule 45(d)(1)—to the effect that leave of court should be obtained for the issuance of such a subpoena—has been omitted. This requirement is unnecessary and oppressive on both counsel and court, and it had been criticized by district judges. There is no satisfactory reason for a differentiation between a subpoena for the production of documentary evidence by a witness at a trial (Rule 45(a)) and for the production of the same evidence at the taking of a deposition. Under this amendment, the person subpoenaed may obtain the protection afforded by any of the orders permitted under Rule 30(b) or Rule 45(b). See *Application of Zenith Radio Corp., Pa.1941, 4 F.Rules Serv. 30b.21, Case 1*, 1 F.R.D. 627; *Fox v. House, Okla.1939*, 29 F.Supp. 673; *United States of America for the Use of Tilo Roofing Co., Inc. v. J. Slotnik Co., Conn.1944*, 3 F.R.D. 408.

The changes in subdivision (d)(2) give the court the same power in the case of residents of the district as is conferred in the case of non-residents, and permit the court to fix a place for attendance which may be more convenient and accessible for the parties than that specified in the rule.

1948 AMENDMENT

The amendment effective October 1949, substituted the reference to "Title 28, U.S.C., § 1783" at the end of subdivision (e)(2) for the reference to "the Act of

July 3, 1926, c. 762, §§ 1, 3 (44 Stat. 835), U.S.C., Title 28, § 713."

1970 AMENDMENT

At present when a subpoena duces tecum is issued to a deponent, he is required to produce the listed materials at the deposition, but is under no clear compulsion to permit their inspection and copying. This results in confusion and uncertainty before the time the deposition is taken, with no mechanism provided whereby the court can resolve the matter. Rule 45(d)(1), as revised, makes clear that the subpoena authorizes inspection and copying of the materials produced. The deponent is afforded full protection since he can object, thereby forcing the party serving the subpoena to obtain a court order if he wishes to inspect and copy. The procedure is thus analogous to that provided in Rule 34.

The changed references to other rules conform to changes made in those rules. The deletion of words in the clause describing the proper scope of the subpoena conforms to a change made in the language of Rule 34. The reference to Rule 26(b) is unchanged but encompasses new matter in that subdivision. The changes make it clear that the scope of discovery through a subpoena is the same as that applicable to Rule 34 and the other discovery rules.

1980 AMENDMENT

Subdivision (d)(1). The amendment defines the term "proof of service" as used in the first sentence of the present subdivision. For want of a definition, the district court clerks have been obliged to fashion their own, with results that vary from district to district. All that seems required is a simple certification on a copy of the notice to take a deposition that the notice has been served on every other party to the action. That is the proof of service required by Rule 25(d) of both the Federal Rules of Appellate Procedure and the Supreme Court Rules.

Subdivision (e)(1). The amendment makes the reach of a subpoena of a district court at least as extensive as that of the state courts of general jurisdiction in the state in which the district court is held. Under the present rule the reach of a district court subpoena is often greater, since it extends throughout the district. No reason appears why it should be less, as it sometimes is because of the accident of district lines. Restrictions upon the reach of subpoenas are imposed to prevent undue inconvenience to witnesses. State statutes and rules of court are quite likely to reflect the varying degrees of difficulty and expense attendant upon local travel.

1985 AMENDMENT

Present Rule 45(d)(2) has two sentences setting forth the territorial scope of deposition subpoenas. The first sentence is directed to depositions taken in the judicial district in which the deponent resides; the second sentence addresses situations in which the deponent is not a resident of the district in which the deposition is to take place. The Rule, as currently constituted, creates anomalous situations that often cause logistical problems in conducting litigation.

The first sentence of the present Rule states that a deponent may be required to attend only in the *county* wherein that person resides or is employed or transacts business in person, that is, where the person lives or works. Under this provision a deponent can be compelled, without court order, to travel from one end of that person's home county to the other, no matter how far that may be. The second sentence of the Rule is somewhat more flexible, stating that someone who does not reside in the district in which the deposition is to be taken can be required to attend in the county where the person is served with the subpoena, *or* within 40 miles from the place of service.

Under today's conditions there is no sound reason for distinguishing between residents of the district or county in which a deposition is to be taken and nonresidents, and the Rule is amended to provide that any person may be subpoenaed to attend a deposition within a specified radius from that person's residence, place of business, or where the person was served. The 40-mile radius has been increased to 100 miles.

1987 AMENDMENT

The amendments are technical. No substantive change is intended.

1991 AMENDMENT

Purposes of Revision. The purposes of this revision are (1) to clarify and enlarge the protections afforded persons who are required to assist the court by giving information or evidence; (2) to facilitate access outside the deposition procedure provided by Rule 30 to documents and other information in the possession of persons who are not parties; (3) to facilitate service of subpoenas for depositions or productions of evidence at places distant from the district in which an action is proceeding; (4) to enable the court to compel a witness found within the state in which the court sits to attend trial; (5) to clarify the organization of the text of the rule.

Subdivision (a). This subdivision is amended in seven significant respects.

First, Paragraph (a)(3) modifies the requirement that a subpoena be issued by the clerk of court. Provision is made for the issuance of subpoenas by attorneys as officers of the court. This revision perhaps culminates an evolution. Subpoenas were long issued by specific order of the court. As this became a burden to the court, general orders were made authorizing clerks to issue subpoenas on request. Since 1948, they have been issued in blank by the clerk of any federal court to any lawyer, the clerk serving as stationer to the bar. In allowing counsel to issue the subpoena, the rule is merely a recognition of present reality.

Although the subpoena is in a sense the command of the attorney who completes the form, defiance of a subpoena is nevertheless an act in defiance of a court order and exposes the defiant witness to contempt sanctions. In *ICC v. Brimson*, 154 U.S. 447, 14 S. Ct. 1125, 38 L.Ed. 1047 (1894), the Court upheld a statute directing federal courts to issue subpoenas to compel testimony before the ICC. In *CAB v. Hermann*, 353 U.S. 322, 77 S. Ct. 804, 1 L. Ed. 2d 852 (1957), the Court approved as established practice the issuance of administrative subpoenas as a matter of absolute agency right. And in *NLRB v. Warren Co.*, 350 U.S. 107, 76 S. Ct. 185, 100 L.Ed. 96 (1955), the Court held that the lower court had no discretion to withhold sanctions against a contemnor who violated such subpoenas. The 1948 revision of Rule 45 put the attorney in a position similar to that of the administrative agency, as a public officer entitled to use the court's contempt power to investigate facts in dispute. Two courts of appeals have touched on the issue and have described lawyer-issued subpoenas as mandates of the court. *Waste Conversion, Inc. v. Rollins Environmental Services (NJ), Inc.*, 893 F.2d 605 (3d Cir.1990); *Fisher v. Marubeni Cotton Corp.*, 526 F.2d 1338, 1340 (8th Cir.1975). Cf. *Young v. United States ex rel. Vuitton et Fils S.A.*, 481 U.S. 787, 821, 107 S. Ct. 2124, 2145, 95 L. Ed. 2d 740 (1987) (Scalia, J., concurring). This revision makes the rule explicit that the attorney acts as an officer of the court in issuing and signing subpoenas.

Necessarily accompanying the evolution of this power of the lawyer as officer of the court is the development of increased responsibility and liability for the misuse of this power. The latter development is reflected in the provisions of subdivision (c) of this rule, and also in the requirement imposed by paragraph (3) of this subdivision that the attorney issuing a subpoena must sign it.

Second, Paragraph (a)(3) authorizes attorneys in distant districts to serve as officers authorized to issue commands in the name of the court. Any attorney permitted to represent a client in a federal court, even one admitted pro haec vice, has the same authority as a clerk to issue a subpoena from any federal court for the district in which the subpoena is served and enforced. In authorizing attorneys to issue subpoenas from distant courts, the amended rule effectively authorizes service of a subpoena anywhere in the United States by an attorney representing any party. This change is intended to ease the administrative burdens of inter-district law practice. The former rule resulted in delay and expense caused by the need to secure forms from clerks' offices some distance from the place at which the action proceeds. This change does not enlarge the burden on the witness.

Pursuant to Paragraph (a)(2), a subpoena for a deposition must still issue from the court in which the deposition or production would be compelled. Accordingly, a motion to quash such a subpoena if it overbears the limits of the subpoena power must, as under the previous rule, be presented to the court for the district in which the deposition would occur. Likewise, the court in whose name the subpoena is issued is responsible for its enforcement.

Third, in order to relieve attorneys of the need to secure an appropriate seal to affix to a subpoena issued as an officer of a distant court, the requirement that a subpoena be under seal is abolished by the provisions of Paragraph (a)(1).

Fourth, Paragraph (a)(1) authorizes the issuance of a subpoena to compel a non-party to produce evidence independent of any deposition. This revision spares the necessity of a deposition of the custodian of evidentiary material required to be produced. A party seeking additional production from a person subject to such a subpoena may serve an additional subpoena requiring additional production at the same time and place.

Fifth, Paragraph (a)(2) makes clear that the person subject to the subpoena is required to produce materials in that person's control whether or not the materials are located within the district or within the territory within which the subpoena can be served. The non-party witness is subject to the same scope of discovery under this rule as that person would be as a party to whom a request is addressed pursuant to Rule 34.

Sixth, Paragraph (a)(1) requires that the subpoena include a statement of the rights and duties of witnesses by setting forth in full the text of the new subdivisions (c) and (d).

Seventh, the revised rule authorizes the issuance of a subpoena to compel the inspection of premises in the possession of a non-party. Rule 34 has authorized such inspections of premises in the possession of a party as discovery compelled under Rule 37, but prior practice required an independent proceeding to secure such relief ancillary to the federal proceeding when the premises were not in the possession of a party. Practice in some states has long authorized such use of a subpoena for this purpose without apparent adverse consequence.

Subdivision (b). Paragraph (b)(1) retains the text of the former subdivision (c) with minor changes.

The reference to the United States marshal and deputy marshal is deleted because of the infrequency of the use of these officers for this purpose. Inasmuch as these officers meet the age requirement, they may still be used if available.

A provision requiring service of prior notice pursuant to Rule 5 of compulsory pretrial production or inspection has been added to paragraph (b)(1). The purpose of such notice is to afford other parties an opportunity to object to the production or inspection, or to serve a demand for additional documents or things. Such additional notice is not needed with respect to a deposition because of the requirement of notice imposed by Rule 30 or 31. But when production or inspection is sought independently of a deposition, other parties may need notice in order to monitor the discovery and in order to pursue access to any information that may or should be produced.

Paragraph (b)(2) retains language formerly set forth in subdivision (e) and extends its application to subpoenas for depositions or production.

Paragraph (b)(3) retains language formerly set forth in paragraph (d)(1) and extends its applications to subpoenas for trial or hearing or production.

Subdivision (c). This provision is new and states the rights of witnesses. It is not intended to diminish rights conferred by Rules 26 to 37 or any other authority.

Paragraph (c)(1) gives specific application to the principle stated in Rule 26(g) and specifies liability for earnings lost by a non-party witness as a result of a misuse of the subpoena. No change in existing law is thereby effected. Abuse of a subpoena is an actionable tort, *Board of Ed. v. Farmingdale Classroom Teachers Ass'n*, 38 N.Y.2d 397, 380 N.Y.S.2d 635, 343 N.E.2d 278 (1975), and the duty of the attorney to the non-party is also embodied in Model Rule of Professional Conduct 4.4. The liability of the attorney is correlative to the expanded power of the attorney to issue subpoenas. The liability may include the cost of fees to collect attorneys' fees owed as a result of a breach of this duty.

Paragraph (c)(2) retains language from the former subdivision (b) and paragraph (d)(1). The 10-day period for response to a subpoena is extended to 14 days to avoid the complex calculations associated with short time periods under Rule 6 and to allow a bit more time for such objections to be made.

A non-party required to produce documents or materials is protected against significant expense resulting from involuntary assistance to the court. This provision applies, for example, to a non-party required to provide a list of class members. The court is not required to fix the costs in advance of production, although this will often be the most satisfactory accommodation to protect the party seeking discovery from excessive costs. In some instances, it may be preferable to leave uncertain costs to be determined after the materials have been produced, provided that the risk of uncertainty is fully disclosed to the discovering party. See, *e.g., United States v. Columbia Broadcasting System, Inc.*, 666 F.2d 364 (9th Cir.1982).

Paragraph (c)(3) explicitly authorizes the quashing of a subpoena as a means of protecting a witness from misuse of the subpoena power. It replaces and enlarges on the former subdivision (b) of this rule and tracks the provisions of Rule 26(c). While largely repetitious, this rule is addressed to the witness who may read it on the subpoena, where it is required to be printed by the revised paragraph (a)(1) of this rule.

Subparagraph (c)(3)(A) identifies those circumstances in which a subpoena must be quashed or modified. It restates the former provisions with respect to the limits of mandatory travel that are set forth in the former paragraphs (d)(2) and (e)(1), with one important change. Under the revised rule, a federal court can compel a witness to come from any place in the state to attend trial, whether or not the local state law so provides. This extension is subject to the qualification provided in the next paragraph, which authorizes the court to condition enforcement of a subpoena compelling a non-party witness to bear substantial expense to attend trial. The traveling non-party witness may be entitled to reasonable compensation for the time and effort entailed.

Clause (c)(3)(A)(iv) requires the court to protect all persons from undue burden imposed by the use of the subpoena power. Illustratively, it might be unduly burdensome to compel an adversary to attend trial as a witness if the adversary is known to have no personal knowledge of matters in dispute, especially so if the adversary would be required to incur substantial travel burdens.

Subparagraph (c)(3)(B) identifies circumstances in which a subpoena should be quashed unless the party serving the subpoena shows a substantial need and the court can devise an appropriate accommodation to protect the interests of the witness. An additional circumstance in which such action is required is a request for costly production of documents; that situation is expressly governed by subparagraph (b)(2)(B).

Clause (c)(3)(B)(i) authorizes the court to quash, modify, or condition a subpoena to protect the person subject to or affected by the subpoena from unnecessary or unduly harmful disclosures of confidential information. It corresponds to Rule 26(c)(7).

Clause (c)(3)(B)(ii) provides appropriate protection for the intellectual property of the non-party witness; it does not apply to the expert retained by a party, whose information is subject to the provisions of Rule 26(b)(4). A growing problem has been the use of subpoenas to compel the giving of evidence and information by unretained experts. Experts are not exempt from the duty to give evidence, even if they cannot be compelled to prepare themselves to give effective testimony, *e.g., Carter-Wallace, Inc. v. Otte*, 474 F.2d 529 (2d Cir.1972), but compulsion to give evidence may threaten the intellectual property of experts denied the opportunity to bargain for the value of their services. See generally Maurer, *Compelling the Expert Witness: Fairness and Utility Under the Federal Rules of Civil Procedure*, 19 GA.L.REV. 71 (1984); Note, *Discovery and Testimony of Unretained Experts*, 1987 DUKE L.J. 140. Arguably the compulsion to testify can be regarded as a "taking" of intellectual property. The rule establishes the right of such persons to withhold their expertise, at least unless the party seeking it makes the kind of showing required for a conditional denial of a motion to quash as provided in the final sentence of subparagraph (c)(3)(B); that requirement is the same as that necessary to secure work product under Rule 26(b)(3) and gives assurance of reasonable compensation. The Rule thus approves the accommodation of competing interests exemplified in *United States v. Columbia Broadcasting System Inc.*, 666 F.2d 364 (9th Cir.1982). See also *Wright v. Jeep Corporation*, 547 F.Supp. 871 (E.D.Mich.1982).

As stated in *Kaufman v. Edelstein*, 539 F.2d 811, 822 (2d Cir.1976), the district court's discretion in these matters should be informed by "the degree to which the expert is being called because of his knowledge of facts relevant to the case rather than in order to give opinion testimony; the difference between testifying to a previously formed or expressed opinion and forming a new one; the possibility that, for other reasons, the witness is a unique expert; the extent to which the calling party is able to show the unlikelihood that any comparable witness will willingly testify; and the degree to which the witness is able to show that he has been oppressed by having continually to testify. . . ."

Clause (c)(3)(B)(iii) protects non-party witnesses who may be burdened to perform the duty to travel in order to provide testimony at trial. The provision requires the court to condition a subpoena requiring travel of more than 100 miles on reasonable compensation.

Subdivision (d). This provision is new. Paragraph (d)(1) extends to non-parties the duty imposed on parties by the last paragraph of Rule 34(b), which was added in 1980.

Paragraph (d)(2) is new and corresponds to the new Rule 26(b)(5) [paragraph (5) in Rule 26(b) was a proposed paragraph which was withdrawn by the Supreme Court]. Its purpose is to provide a party whose discovery is constrained by a claim of privilege or work product protection with information sufficient to evaluate such a claim and to resist if it seems unjustified. The person claiming a privilege or protection cannot decide the limits of that party's own entitlement.

A party receiving a discovery request who asserts a privilege or protection but fails to disclose that claim is at risk of waiving the privilege or protection. A person claiming a privilege or protection who fails to provide adequate information about the privilege or protection claim to the party seeking the information is subject to an order to show cause why the person should not be held in contempt under subdivision (e). Motions for such orders and responses to motions are subject to the sanctions provisions of Rules 7 and 11.

A person served a subpoena that is too broad may be faced with a burdensome task to provide full information regarding all that person's claims to privilege or work product protection. Such a person is entitled to protection that may be secured through an objection made pursuant to paragraph (c)(2).

Subdivision (e). This provision retains most of the language of the former subdivision (f).

"Adequate cause" for a failure to obey a subpoena remains undefined. In at least some circumstances, a non-party might be guilty of contempt for refusing to obey a subpoena even though the subpoena manifestly overreaches the appropriate limits of the subpoena power. *E.g., Walker v. City of Birmingham*, 388 U.S. 307, 87 S. Ct. 1824, 18 L. Ed. 2d 1210 (1967). But, because the command of the subpoena is not in fact one uttered by a judicial officer, contempt should be very sparingly applied when the non-party witness has been overborne by a party or attorney. The language added to subdivision (f) is intended to assure that result where a non-party has been commanded, on the signature of an attorney, to travel greater distances than can be compelled pursuant to this rule.

2005 AMENDMENT

This amendment closes a small gap in regard to notifying witnesses of the manner for recording a deposition. A deposition subpoena must state the method for recording the testimony.

Rule 30(b)(2) directs that the party noticing a deposition state in the notice the manner for recording the testimony, but the notice need not be served on the deponent. The deponent learns of the recording method only if the deponent is a party or is informed by a party. Rule 30(b)(3) permits another party to designate an additional method of recording with prior notice to the deponent and the other parties. The deponent thus has notice of the recording method when an additional method is designated. This amendment completes the notice provisions to ensure that a nonparty deponent has notice of the recording method when the recording method is described only in the deposition notice.

A subpoenaed witness does not have a right to refuse to proceed with a deposition due to objections to the manner of recording. But under rare circumstances, a nonparty witness might have a ground for seeking a protective order under Rule 26(c) with regard to the manner of recording or the use of the deposition if recorded in a certain manner. Should such a witness not learn of the manner of recording until the deposition begins, undesirable delay or complication might result. Advance notice of the recording method affords an opportunity to raise such protective issues.

Other changes are made to conform Rule 45(a)(2) to current style conventions.

2006 AMENDMENTS

Rule 45 is amended to conform the provisions for subpoenas to changes in other discovery rules, largely related to discovery of electronically stored information. Rule 34 is amended to provide in greater detail for the production of electronically stored information. Rule 45(a)(1)(C) is amended to recognize that electronically stored information, as defined in Rule 34(a), can also be sought by subpoena. Like Rule 34(b), Rule 45(a)(1) is amended to provide that the subpoena can designate a form or forms for production of electronic data. Rule 45(c)(2) is amended, like Rule 34(b), to authorize the person served with a subpoena to object to the requested form or forms. In addition, as under Rule 34(b), Rule 45(d)(1)(B) is amended to provide that if the subpoena does not specify the form or forms for electronically stored information, the person served with the subpoena must produce electronically stored information in a form or forms in which it is usually maintained or in a form or forms that are reasonably usable. Rule 45(d)(1)(C) is added to provide that the person producing electronically stored information should not have to produce the same information in more than one form unless so ordered by the court for good cause.

As with discovery of electronically stored information from parties, complying with a subpoena for such information may impose burdens on the responding person. Rule 45(c) provides protection against undue impositions on nonparties. For example, Rule 45(c)(1) directs that a party serving a subpoena "shall take reasonable steps to avoid imposing undue burden or expense on a person subject to the subpoena," and Rule 45(c)(2)(B) permits the person served with the subpoena to object to it and directs that an order requiring compliance "shall protect a person who is neither a party nor a party's officer from significant expense resulting from" compliance. Rule 45(d)(1)(D) is added to provide that the responding person need not provide discovery of electronically stored information from sources the party identifies as not reasonably accessible, unless the court orders such discovery for good cause, considering the limitations of Rule 26(b)(2)(C), on terms that protect a nonparty against significant expense. A parallel provision is added to Rule 26(b)(2).

Rule 45(a)(1)(B) is also amended, as is Rule 34(a), to provide that a subpoena is available to permit testing and sampling as well as inspection and copying. As in Rule 34, this change recognizes that on occasion the opportunity to perform testing or sampling may be important, both for documents and for electronically stored information. Because testing or sampling may present particular issues of burden or intrusion for the person served with the subpoena, however, the protective provisions of Rule 45(c) should be enforced with vigilance when such demands are made. Inspection or testing of certain types of electronically stored information or of a person's electronic information system may raise issues of confidentiality or privacy. The addition of sampling and testing to Rule 45(a) with regard to documents and electronically stored information is not meant to create a routine right of direct access to a person's electronic information system, although such access might be justified in some circumstances. Courts should guard against undue intrusiveness resulting from inspecting or testing such systems.

Rule 45(d)(2) is amended, as is Rule 26(b)(5), to add a procedure for assertion of privilege or of protection as trial-preparation materials after production. The receiving party may submit the information to the court for resolution of the privilege claim, as under Rule 26(b)(5)(B).

Other minor amendments are made to conform the rule to the changes described above.

2007 AMENDMENT

The language of Rule 45 has been amended as part of the general restyling of the Civil Rules to make them more easily understood and to make style and terminology consistent throughout the rules. These changes are intended to be stylistic only.

The reference to discovery of "books" in former Rule 45(a)(1)(C) was deleted to achieve consistent expression throughout the discovery rules. Books remain a proper subject of discovery.

Former Rule 45(b)(1) required "prior notice" to each party of any commanded production of documents and things or inspection of premises. Courts have agreed that notice must be given "prior" to the return date, and have tended to converge on an interpretation that requires notice to the parties before the subpoena is served on the person commanded to produce or permit inspection. That interpretation is adopted in amended Rule 45(b)(1) to give clear notice of general present practice.

The language of former Rule 45(d)(2) addressing the manner of asserting privilege is replaced by adopting the wording of Rule 26(b)(5). The same meaning is better expressed in the same words.

2013 AMENDMENT

Rule 45 was extensively amended in 1991. The goal of the present amendments is to clarify and simplify the rule. The amendments recognize the court where the action is pending as the issuing court, permit nationwide service of a subpoena, and collect in a new subdivision (c) the previously scattered provisions regarding place of compliance. These changes resolve a conflict that arose after the 1991 amendment about a court's authority to compel a party or party officer to travel long distances to testify at trial; such testimony may now be required only as specified in new Rule 45(c). In addition, the amendments introduce authority in new Rule 45(f) for the court where compliance is required to transfer a subpoena-related motion to the court where the action is pending on consent of the person subject to the subpoena or in exceptional circumstances.

Subdivision (a). This subdivision is amended to provide that a subpoena issues from the court where the action is pending. Subdivision (a)(3) specifies that an attorney authorized to practice in that court may issue a subpoena, which is consistent with current practice.

In Rule 45(a)(1)(D), "person" is substituted for "party" because the subpoena may be directed to a nonparty.

Rule 45(a)(4) is added to highlight and slightly modify a notice requirement first included in the rule in 1991. Under the 1991 amendments, Rule 45(b)(1) required prior notice of the service of a "documents only" subpoena to the other parties. Rule 45(b)(1) was clarified in 2007 to specify that this notice must be served before the subpoena is served on the witness.

The Committee has been informed that parties serving subpoenas frequently fail to give the required notice to the other parties. The amendment moves the notice requirement to a new provision in Rule 45(a) and requires that the notice include a copy of the subpoena. The amendments are intended to achieve the original purpose of enabling the other parties to object or to serve a subpoena for additional materials.

Parties desiring access to information produced in response to the subpoena will need to follow up with the party serving it or the person served to obtain such access. The rule does not limit the court's authority to order notice of receipt of produced materials or access to them. The party serving the subpoena should in any event make reasonable provision for prompt access.

Subdivision (b). The former notice requirement in Rule 45(b)(1) has been moved to new Rule 45(a)(4).

Rule 45(b)(2) is amended to provide that a subpoena may be served at any place within the United States, removing the complexities prescribed in prior versions.

Subdivision (c). Subdivision (c) is new. It collects the various provisions on where compliance can be required and simplifies them. Unlike the prior rule, place of service is not critical to place of compliance. Although Rule 45(a)(1)(A)(iii) permits the subpoena to direct a place of compliance, that place must be selected under Rule 45(c).

Rule 45(c)(1) addresses a subpoena to testify at a trial, hearing, or deposition. Rule 45(c)(1)(A) provides that compliance may be required within 100 miles of where the person subject to the subpoena resides, is employed, or regularly conducts business in person. For parties and party officers, Rule 45(c)(1)(B)(i) provides that compliance may be required anywhere in the state where the person resides, is employed, or regularly conducts business in person. When an order under Rule 43(a) authorizes testimony from a remote location, the witness can be commanded to testify from any place described in Rule 45(c)(1).

Under Rule 45(c)(1)(B)(ii), nonparty witnesses can be required to travel more than 100 miles within the state where they reside, are employed, or regularly transact business in person only if they would not, as a result, incur "substantial expense." When travel over 100 miles could impose substantial expense on the witness, the party that served the subpoena may pay that expense and the court can condition enforcement of the subpoena on such payment.

Because Rule 45(c) directs that compliance may be commanded only as it provides, these amendments resolve a split in interpreting Rule 45's provisions for subpoenaing parties and party officers. Compare *In re Vioxx Products Liability Litigation*, 438 F. Supp. 2d 664 (E.D. La. 2006) (finding authority to compel a party officer from New Jersey to testify at trial in New Orleans), with *Johnson v. Big Lots Stores, Inc.*, 251 F.R.D. 213 (E.D. La. 2008) (holding that Rule 45 did not require attendance of plaintiffs at trial in New Orleans when they would have to travel more than 100 miles from outside the state). Rule 45(c)(1)(A) does not authorize a subpoena for trial to require a party or party officer to travel more than 100 miles unless the party or party officer resides, is employed, or regularly transacts business in person in the state.

Depositions of parties, and officers, directors, and managing agents of parties need not involve use of a subpoena. Under Rule 37(d)(1)(A)(i), failure of such a witness whose deposition was properly noticed to appear for the deposition can lead to Rule 37(b) sanctions (including dismissal or default but not contempt) without regard to service of a subpoena and without regard to the geographical limitations on compliance with a subpoena. These amendments do not change that existing law; the courts retain their authority to control the place of party depositions and impose sanctions for failure to appear under Rule 37(b).

For other discovery, Rule 45(c)(2) directs that inspection of premises occur at those premises, and that production of documents, tangible things, and electronically stored information may be commanded to occur at a place within 100 miles of where the person subject to the subpoena resides, is employed, or regularly conducts business in person. Under the current rule, parties often agree that production, particularly of electronically stored information, be transmitted by electronic means. Such arrangements facilitate discovery, and nothing in these amendments limits the ability of parties to make such arrangements.

Rule 45(d)(3)(A)(ii) directs the court to quash any subpoena that purports to compel compliance beyond the geographical limits specified in Rule 45(c).

Subdivision (d). Subdivision (d) contains the provisions formerly in subdivision (c). It is revised to recognize the court where the action is pending as the issuing court, and to take account of the addition of Rule 45(c) to specify where compliance with a subpoena is required.

Subdivision (f). Subdivision (f) is new. Under Rules 45(d)(2)(B), 45(d)(3), and 45(e)(2)(B), subpoena-related motions and applications are to be made to the court where compliance is required under Rule 45(c). Rule 45(f) provides authority for that court to transfer the motion to the court where the action is pending. It applies to all motions under this rule, including an application under Rule 45(e)(2)(B) for a privilege determination.

Subpoenas are essential to obtain discovery from nonparties. To protect local nonparties, local resolution of disputes about subpoenas is assured by the limitations of Rule 45(c) and the requirements in Rules 45(d) and (e) that motions be made in the court in which compliance is required under Rule 45(c). But transfer to the court where the action is pending is sometimes warranted. If the person subject to the subpoena consents to transfer, Rule 45(f) provides that the court where compliance is required may do so.

In the absence of consent, the court may transfer in exceptional circumstances, and the proponent of transfer bears the burden of showing that such circumstances are present. The prime concern should be avoiding burdens on local nonparties subject to subpoenas, and it should not be assumed that the issuing court is in a superior position to resolve subpoena-related motions. In some circumstances, however, transfer may be warranted in order to avoid disrupting the issuing court's management of the underlying litigation, as when that court has already ruled on issues presented by the motion or the same issues are likely to arise in discovery in many districts. Transfer is appropriate only if such interests outweigh the interests of the nonparty served with the subpoena in obtaining local resolution of the motion. Judges in compliance districts may find it helpful to consult with the judge in the issuing court presiding over the underlying case while addressing subpoena-related motions.

If the motion is transferred, judges are encouraged to permit telecommunications methods to minimize the burden a transfer imposes on nonparties, if it is necessary for attorneys admitted in the court where the motion is made to appear in the court in which the action is pending. The rule provides that if these attorneys are authorized to practice in the court where the motion is made, they may file papers and appear in the court in which the action is pending in relation to the motion as officers of that court.

After transfer, the court where the action is pending will decide the motion. If the court rules that discovery is not justified, that should end the matter. If the court orders further discovery, it is possible that retransfer may be important to enforce the order. One consequence of failure to obey such an order is contempt, addressed in Rule 45(g). Rule 45(g) and Rule 37(b)(1) are both amended to provide that disobedience of an order enforcing a subpoena after transfer is contempt of the issuing court and the court where compliance is required under Rule 45(c). In some instances, however, there may be a question about whether the issuing court can impose contempt sanctions on a distant nonparty. If such circumstances arise, or if it is better to supervise compliance in the court where compliance is required, the rule provides authority for retransfer for enforcement. Although changed circumstances may prompt a modification of such an order, it is not expected that the compliance court will reexamine the resolution of the underlying motion.

Subdivision (g). Subdivision (g) carries forward the authority of former subdivision (e) to punish disobedience of subpoenas as contempt. It is amended to make clear that, in the event of transfer of a subpoena-related motion, such disobedience constitutes contempt of both the court where compliance is required under Rule 45(c) and the court where the action is pending. If necessary for effective enforcement, Rule 45(f) authorizes the issuing court to transfer its order after the motion is resolved.

The rule is also amended to clarify that contempt sanctions may be applied to a person who disobeys a subpoena-related order, as well as one who fails entirely to obey a subpoena. In civil litigation, it would be rare for a court to use contempt sanctions without first ordering compliance with a subpoena, and the order might not require all the compliance sought by the subpoena. Often contempt proceedings will be initiated by an order to show cause, and an order to comply or be held in contempt may modify the subpoena's command. Disobedience of such an order may be treated as contempt.

The second sentence of former subdivision (e) is deleted as unnecessary.

Rule 46. Exceptions Unnecessary

1937 ADOPTION

Abolition of formal exceptions is often provided by statute. See Ill.Rev.Stat. (1937), ch. 110, § 204; Neb.Comp.Stat. (1929) § 20-1139; N.M.Stat.Ann. (Courtright, 1929) § 105-830; 2 N.D.Comp.Laws Ann. (1913) § 7653; Ohio Code Ann. (Throckmorton, 1936) § 11560; 1 S.D.Comp.Laws (1929) § 2542; Utah Rev.Stat.Ann. (1933) §§ 104-39-2, 104-24-18; Va.Rules of Court, Rule 22, 163 Va. v. xii (1935); Wis.Stat. (1935) § 270.39. Compare N.Y.C.P.A. (1937) §§ 583, 445, and 446, all as amended by L.1936, ch. 915. Rule 51 deals with objections to the court's instructions to the jury.

U.S.C., Title 28, former § 776 (Bill of exceptions; authentication; signing of by judge) and former § 875 (Review of findings in cases tried without a jury) are superseded insofar as they provide for formal exceptions, and a bill of exceptions.

1987 AMENDMENT

The amendments are technical. No substantive change is intended.

2007 AMENDMENTS

The language of Rule 46 has been amended as part of the general restyling of the Civil Rules to make them more easily understood and to make style and terminology consistent throughout the rules. These changes are intended to be stylistic only.

Rule 47. Selection of Jurors

1937 ADOPTION

Note to Subdivision (a). This permits a practice found very useful by federal trial judges. For an example of a state practice in which the examination by the court is supplemented by further inquiry by counsel see Rule 27 of the Code of Rules for the District Courts of Minnesota, 186 Minn. xxxiii (1932), 3 Minn.Stat. (Mason, Supp.1936) Appendix 4, p. 1062.

Note to Subdivision (b). The provision for an alternate juror is one often found in modern state codes. See N.C.Code (1935) § 2330(a); Ohio Gen.Code Ann. (Page, Supp.1926 to 1935) § 11419-47; Pa.Stat.Ann. (Purdon, Supp.1936) Title 17, § 1153; compare U.S.C., Title 28, § 417a (Alternate jurors in criminal trials); 1 N.J.Rev.Stat. (1937) 2:91A-1, 2:91A-2, 2:91A-3.

Provisions for qualifying, drawing, and challenging of jurors are found in U.S.C., Title 28, former:

- § 411 (Qualifications and exemptions)
- § 412 (Manner of drawing)
- § 413 (Apportioned in district)
- § 415 (Not disqualified because of race or color)
- § 416 (Venire; service and return)
- § 417 (Talesmen for petit jurors)
- § 418 (Special juries)
- § 423 (Jurors not to serve more than once a year)
- § 424 (Challenges)

and D.C.Code (1930) Title 18, §§ 341 to 360 (Juries and Jury Commission) and Title 6, § 366 (Peremptory challenges).

1966 AMENDMENT

The revision of this subdivision brings it into line with the amendment of Rule 24(c) of the Federal Rules of Criminal Procedure. That rule previously allowed four alternate jurors, as contrasted with the two allowed in civil cases, and the amendments increase the number to a maximum of six in all cases. The Advisory Committee's Note to amended Criminal Rule 24(c) points to experience demonstrating that four alternates may not be enough in some lengthy criminal trials; and the same may be said of civil trials. The Note adds:

"The words 'or are found to be' are added to the second sentence to make clear that an alternate juror may be called in the situation where it is first discovered during the trial that a juror was unable or disqualified to perform his duties at the time he was sworn."

1991 AMENDMENT

Subdivision (b). The former provision for alternate jurors is stricken and the institution of the alternate juror abolished.

The former rule reflected the long-standing assumption that a jury would consist of exactly twelve members. It provided for additional jurors to be used as substitutes for jurors who are for any reason excused or disqualified from service after the commencement of the trial. Additional jurors were traditionally designated at the outset of the trial, and excused at the close of the evidence if they had not been promoted to full service on account of the elimination of one of the original jurors.

The use of alternate jurors has been a source of dissatisfaction with the jury system because of the burden it places on alternates who are required to listen to the evidence but denied the satisfaction of participating in its evaluation.

Subdivision (c). This provision makes it clear that the court may in appropriate circumstances excuse a juror during the jury deliberations without causing a mistrial. Sickness, family emergency or juror misconduct that might occasion a mistrial are examples of appropriate grounds for excusing a juror. It is not grounds for the dismissal of a juror that the juror refuses to join with fellow jurors in reaching a unanimous verdict.

2007 AMENDMENTS

The language of Rule 47 has been amended as part of the general restyling of the Civil Rules to make them more easily understood and to make style and terminology consistent throughout the rules. These changes are intended to be stylistic only.

Rule 48. Number of Jurors—Participation in Verdict

1937 ADOPTION

For provisions in state codes, compare Utah Rev.Stat.Ann. (1933) § 48-0-5 (In civil cases parties may agree in open court on lesser number of jurors); 2 Wash.Rev.Stat.Ann. (Remington, 1932) § 323 (Parties may consent to any number of jurors not less than three).

1991 AMENDMENT

The former rule was rendered obsolete by the adoption in many districts of local rules establishing six as the standard size for a civil jury.

It appears that the minimum size of a jury consistent with the Seventh Amendment is six. *Cf. Ballew v. Georgia*, 435 U.S. 223, 98 S. Ct. 1029, 55 L. Ed. 2d 234 (1978) (holding that a conviction based on a jury of less than six is a denial of due process of law). If the parties agree to trial before a smaller jury, a verdict can be taken, but the parties should not other than in exceptional circumstances be encouraged to waive the right to a jury of six, not only because of the constitutional stature of the right, but also because smaller juries are more erratic and less effective in serving to distribute responsibility for the exercise of judicial power.

Because the institution of the alternate juror has been abolished by the proposed revision of Rule 47, it will ordinarily be prudent and necessary, in order to provide for sickness or disability among jurors, to seat more than six jurors. The use of jurors in excess of six increases the representativeness of the jury and harms no interest of a party. Ray v. Parkside Surgery Center, 13 F.R.Serv. 585 (6th Cir.1989).

If the court takes the precaution of seating a jury larger than six, an illness occurring during the deliberation period will not result in a mistrial, as it did formerly, because all seated jurors will participate in the verdict and a sufficient number will remain to render a unanimous verdict of six or more.

In exceptional circumstances, as where a jury suffers depletions during trial and deliberation that are greater than can reasonably be expected, the parties may agree to be bound by a verdict rendered by fewer than six jurors. The court should not, however, rely upon the availability of such an agreement, for the use of juries smaller than six is problematic for reasons fully explained in *Ballew v. Georgia, supra.*

2007 AMENDMENTS

The language of Rule 48 has been amended as part of the general restyling of the Civil Rules to make them more easily understood and to make style and terminology consistent throughout the rules. These changes are intended to be stylistic only.

2009 AMENDMENTS

Jury polling is added as new subdivision (c), which is drawn from Criminal Rule 31(d) with minor revisions to reflect Civil Rules Style and the parties' opportunity to stipulate to a nonunanimous verdict.

Rule 49. Special Verdicts and Interrogatories

1937 ADOPTION

The Federal courts are not bound to follow state statutes authorizing or requiring the court to ask a jury to find a special verdict or to answer interrogatories. *Victor-American Fuel Co. v. Peccarich*, 209 Fed. 568 (C.C.A. 8th., 1913), cert. den. 232 U.S. 727, 34 S. Ct. 603, 58 L.Ed. 817 (1914); *Spokane and I. E. R. Co. v. Campbell*, 217 Fed. 518 (C.C.A. 9th., 1914), affd. 241 U.S. 497, 36 S. Ct. 683, 60 L.Ed. 1125 (1916); Simkins, Federal Practice (1934) § 186. The power of a territory to adopt by statute the practice under Subdivision (b) has been sustained. *Walker v. New Mexico and Southern Pacific R. R.*, 165 U.S. 593, 17 S. Ct. 421, 41 L.Ed. 837 (1897); *Southwestern Brewery and Ice Co. v. Schmidt*, 226 U.S. 162, 33 S. Ct. 68, 57 L.Ed. 170 (1912).

Compare Wis.Stat. (1935) §§ 270.27, 270.28 and 270.30; Green, A New Development in Jury Trial (1927), 13 A.B.A.J. 715; Morgan, A Brief History of Special Verdicts and Special Interrogatories, 1923, 32 Yale L.J. 575.

The provisions of U.S.C., Title 28, formerly § 400(3) (now §§ 2201, 2202) (Declaratory judgments authorized; procedure) permitting the submission of issues of fact to a jury are covered by this rule.

1963 AMENDMENT

This amendment conforms to the amendment of Rule 58. See the Advisory Committee's Note to Rule 58, as amended.

1987 AMENDMENT

The amendments are technical. No substantive change is intended.

2007 AMENDMENTS

The language of Rule 49 has been amended as part of the general restyling of the Civil Rules to make them more easily understood and to make style and terminology consistent throughout the rules. These changes are intended to be stylistic only.

Rule 50. Judgment As a Matter of Law in Jury Trials; Alternative Motion for New Trial; Conditional Rulings

1937 ADOPTION

Note to Subdivision (a). The present federal rule is changed to the extent that the formality of an express reservation of rights against waiver is no longer necessary. See *Sampliner v. Motion Picture Patents Co.*, 254 U.S. 233, 41 S. Ct. 79, 65 L.Ed. 240 (1920); *Union Indemnity Co. v. United States*, 74 F.2d 645 (C.C.A. 6th., 1935). The requirement that specific grounds for the motion for a directed verdict must be stated settles a conflict in the federal cases. See Simkins, Federal Practice (1934) § 189.

Note to Subdivision (b). For comparable state practice upheld under the conformity act, see *Baltimore and Carolina Line v. Redman*, 295 U.S. 654, 55 S. Ct. 890, 79 L.Ed. 1636 (1935); compare *Slocum v. New York Life Ins. Co.*, 228 U.S. 364, 33 S. Ct. 523, 57 L.Ed. 879, Ann.Cas. 1914D, 1029 (1913).

See *Northern Ry. Co. v. Page*, 274 U.S. 65, 47 S. Ct. 491, 71 L.Ed. 929 (1927), following the Massachusetts practice of alternative verdicts, explained in Thorndike, *Trial by Jury in United States Courts*, 26 Harv.L.Rev. 732 (1913). See also Thayer, Judicial Administration, 63 U. of Pa.L.Rev. 585, 600–601, and note 32 (1915); Scott, Trial by Jury and the Reform of Civil Procedure, 31 Harv.L.Rev. 669, 685 (1918); Comment, 34 Mich.L.Rev. 93, 98 (1935).

1963 AMENDMENT

Subdivision (a). The practice, after the court has granted a motion for a directed verdict, of requiring the jury to express assent to a verdict they did not reach by their own deliberations serves no useful purpose and may give offense to the members of the jury. See 2B Barron & Holtzoff, Federal Practice & Procedure § 1072, at 367 (Wright ed. 1961); Blume, Origin and Development of the Directed Verdict, 48 Mich.L.Rev. 555, 582–85, 589–90 (1950). The final sentence of the subdivision, added by amendment, provides that the court's order granting a motion for a directed verdict is effective in itself, and that no action need be taken by the foreman or other members of the jury. See Ariz.R.Civ.P. 50(c); cf. Fed.R.Crim.P. 29(a). No change is intended in the standard to be applied in deciding the motion. To assure this interpretation, and in the interest of simplicity, the traditional term, "directed verdict," is retained.

Subdivision (b). A motion for judgment notwithstanding the verdict will not lie unless it was preceded by a motion for a directed verdict made at the close of all the evidence.

The amendment of the second sentence of this subdivision sets the time limit for making the motion for judgment n. o. v. at 10 days after the entry of judgment, rather than 10 days after the reception of the verdict. Thus the time provision is made consistent with that contained in Rule 59(b) (time for motion for new trial) and Rule 52(b) (time for motion to amend findings by the court).

Subdivision (c) deals with the situation where a party joins a motion for a new trial with his motion for judgment n. o. v., or prays for a new trial in the alternative, and the motion for judgment n. o. v. is granted. The procedure to be followed in making rulings on the motion for the new trial, and the consequences of the rulings thereon, were partly set out in *Montgomery Ward & Co. v. Duncan*, 311 U.S. 243, 253, 61 S. Ct. 189, 195, 85 L.Ed. 147 (1940), and have been further elaborated in later cases. See *Cone v. West Virginia Pulp & Paper Co.*, 330 U.S. 212, 67 S. Ct. 752, 91 L.Ed. 849 (1947); *Globe Liquor Co., Inc. v. San Roman*, 332 U.S. 571, 68 S. Ct. 246, 92 L.Ed. 177 (1948); *Fountain v. Filson*, 336 U.S. 681, 69 S. Ct. 754, 93 L.Ed. 971 (1949); *Johnson v. New York, N. H. & H. R. R. Co.*, 344 U.S. 48, 73 S. Ct. 125, 97 L.Ed. 77 (1952). However, courts as well as counsel have often misunderstood the procedure, and it will be helpful to summarize the proper practice in the text of the rule. The amendments do not alter the effects of a jury verdict or the scope of appellate review.

In the situation mentioned, **subdivision (c)(1)** requires that the court make a "conditional" ruling on the new-trial motion, i.e., a ruling which goes on the assumption that the motion for judgment n. o. v. was erroneously granted and will be reversed or vacated; and the court is required to state its grounds for the conditional ruling. **Subdivision (c)(1)** then spells out the consequences of a reversal of the judgment in the light of the conditional ruling on the new-trial motion.

If the motion for new trial has been conditionally granted, and the judgment is reversed, "the new trial shall proceed unless the appellate court has otherwise ordered." The party against whom the judgment n. o. v. was entered below may, as appellant, besides seeking to overthrow that judgment, also attack the conditional grant of the new trial. And the appellate court, if it reverses the judgment n. o. v., may in an appropriate case also reverse the conditional grant of the new trial and direct that judgment be entered on the verdict. See *Bailey v. Slentz*, 189 F.2d 406 (10th Cir.1951); *Moist Cold Refrigerator Co. v. Lou Johnson Co.*, 249 F.2d 246 (9th Cir.1957), cert. denied, 356 U.S. 968, 78 S. Ct. 1008, 2 L. Ed. 2d 1074 (1958); *Peters v. Smith*, 221 F.2d 721 (3d Cir.1955); *Dailey v. Timmer*, 292 F.2d 824 (3d Cir. 1961), explaining *Lind v. Schenley Industries, Inc.*, 278 F.2d 79 (3d Cir.), cert. denied, 364 U.S. 835, 81 S. Ct. 58, 5 L. Ed. 2d 60 (1960); *Cox v. Pennsylvania R. R.*, 120 A.2d 214 (D.C.Mun.Ct.App. 1956); 3 Barron & Holtzoff, Federal Practice & Procedure § 1302.1 at 346 to 47 (Wright ed. 1958); 6 Moore's Federal Practice ¶ 59.16 at 3915 n. 8a (2d ed. 1954).

If the motion for a new trial has been conditionally denied, and the judgment is reversed, "subsequent proceedings shall be in accordance with the order of the appellate court." The party in whose favor judgment n. o. v. was entered below may, as appellee, besides seeking to uphold that judgment, also urge on the appellate court that the trial court committed error in conditionally denying the new trial. The appellee may assert this error in his brief, without taking a cross-appeal. *Cf. Patterson v. Pennsylvania R. R.*, 238 F.2d 645, 650 (6th Cir. 1956); *Hughes v. St. Louis Nat. L. Baseball Club, Inc.*, 359 Mo. 993, 997, 224 S.W.2d 989, 992 (1949). If the appellate court concludes that the judgment cannot stand, but accepts the appellee's contention that there was error in the conditional denial of the new trial, it may order a new trial in lieu of directing the entry of judgment upon the verdict.

Subdivision (c)(2), which also deals with the situation where the trial court has granted the motion for judgment n. o. v., states that the verdict-winner may apply to the trial court for a new trial pursuant to Rule 59 after the judgment n. o. v. has been entered against him. In arguing to the trial court in opposition to the motion for judgment n. o. v., the verdict-winner may, and often will, contend that he is entitled, at the least, to a new trial, and the court has a range of discretion to grant a new trial or (where plaintiff won the verdict) to order a dismissal of the action without prejudice instead of granting judgment n. o. v. See *Cone v. West Virginia Pulp & Paper Co., supra, 330 U.S. at 217, 218, 67 S. Ct. at 755, 756*, 91 L.Ed. 849. Subdivision (c)(2) is a reminder that the verdict-winner is entitled, even after entry of judgment n. o. v. against him, to move for a new trial in the usual course. If in these circumstances the motion is granted, the judgment is superseded.

In some unusual circumstances, however, the grant of the new-trial motion may be only conditional, and the judgment will not be superseded. See the situation in *Tribble v. Bruin*, 279 F.2d 424 (4th Cir.1960) (upon a verdict for plaintiff, defendant moves for and obtains judgment n. o. v.; plaintiff moves for a new trial on the ground of inadequate damages; trial court might properly have granted plaintiff's motion, conditional upon reversal of the judgment n. o. v.).

Even if the verdict-winner makes no motion for a new trial, he is entitled upon his appeal from the judgment n. o. v. not only to urge that that judgment should be reversed and judgment entered upon the verdict, but that errors were committed during the trial which at the least entitle him to a new trial.

Subdivision (d) deals with the situation where judgment has been entered on the jury verdict, the motion for judgment n. o. v. and any motion for a new trial having been denied by the trial court. The verdict-winner, as appellee, besides seeking to uphold the judgment may urge upon the appellate court that in case the trial court is found to have erred in entering judgment on the verdict, there are grounds for granting him a new trial instead of directing the entry of judgment for his opponent. In appropriate cases the appellate court is not precluded from itself directing that a new trial be had. See *Weade v. Dichmann, Wright & Pugh, Inc.*, 337 U.S. 801, 69 S. Ct. 1326, 93 L.Ed. 1704 (1949). Nor is it precluded in proper cases from remanding the case for a determination by the trial court as to whether a new trial should be granted. The latter course is advisable where the grounds urged are suitable for the exercise of trial court discretion.

Subdivision (d) does not attempt a regulation of all aspects of the procedure where the motion for judgment n. o. v. and any accompanying motion for a new trial are denied, since the problems have not been fully canvassed in the decisions and the procedure is in some respects still in a formative stage. It is, however, designed to give guidance on certain important features of the practice.

1987 AMENDMENT

The amendments are technical. No substantive change is intended.

1991 AMENDMENT

Subdivision (a). The revision of this subdivision aims to facilitate the exercise by the court of its responsibility to assure the fidelity of its judgment to the controlling law, a responsibility imposed by the Due Process Clause of the Fifth Amendment. *Cf. Galloway v. United States*, 319 U.S. 372, 63 S. Ct. 1077, 87 L.Ed. 1458 (1943).

The revision abandons the familiar terminology of *direction of verdict* for several reasons. The term is misleading as a description of the relationship between judge and jury. It is also freighted with anachronisms some of which are the subject of the text of former subdivision (a) of this rule that is deleted in this revision. Thus, it should not be necessary to state in the text of this rule that a motion made pursuant to it is not a waiver of the right to jury trial, and only the antiquities of directed verdict practice suggest that it might have been. The term "judgment as a matter of law" is an almost equally familiar term and appears in the text of Rule 56; its use in Rule 50 calls attention to the relationship between the two rules. Finally, the change enables the rule to refer to preverdict and post-verdict motions with a terminology that does not conceal the common identity of two motions made at different times in the proceeding.

If a motion is denominated a motion for directed verdict or for judgment notwithstanding the verdict, the party's error is merely formal. Such a motion should be treated as a motion for judgment as a matter of law in accordance with this rule.

Paragraph (a)(1) articulates the standard for the granting of a motion for judgment as a matter of law. It effects no change in the existing standard. That existing standard was not expressed in the former rule, but was articulated in long-standing case law. *See generally* Cooper, *Directions for Directed Verdicts: A Compass for Federal Courts*, 55 MINN.L.REV. 903 (1971). The expressed standard makes clear that action taken under the rule is a performance of the court's duty to assure enforcement of the controlling law and is not an intrusion on any responsibility for factual determinations conferred on the jury by the Seventh Amendment or any other provision of federal law. Because this standard is also used as a reference point for entry of summary judgment under 56(a), it serves to link the two related provisions.

The revision authorizes the court to perform its duty to enter judgment as a matter of law at any time during the trial, as soon as it is apparent that either party is unable to carry a burden of proof that is essential to that party's case. Thus, the second sentence of paragraph (a)(1) authorizes the court to consider a motion for judgment as a matter of law as soon as a party has completed a presentation on a fact essential to that party's case. Such early action is appropriate when economy and expedition will be served. In no event, however, should the court enter judgment against a party who has not been apprised of the materiality of the dispositive fact and been afforded an opportunity to present any available evidence bearing on that fact. In order further to facilitate the exercise of the authority provided by this rule, Rule 16 is also revised [not revised as of date of this commentary] to encourage the court to schedule an order of trial that proceeds first with a presentation on an issue that is likely to be dispositive, if such an issue is identified in the course of pretrial. Such scheduling can be appropriate where the court is uncertain whether favorable action should be taken under Rule 56. Thus, the revision affords the court the alternative of denying a motion for summary judgment while scheduling a separate trial of the issue under Rule 42(b) or scheduling the trial to begin with a presentation on that essential fact which the opposing party seems unlikely to be able to maintain.

Paragraph (a)(2) retains the requirement that a motion for judgment be made prior to the close of the trial, subject to renewal after a jury verdict has been rendered. The purpose of this requirement is to assure the responding party an opportunity to cure any deficiency in that party's proof that may have been overlooked until called to the party's attention by a late motion for judgment. Cf. *Farley Transp. Co. v. Santa Fe Trail Transp. Co.*, 786 F.2d 1342 (9th Cir.1985) ("If the moving party is then permitted to make a later attack on the evidence through a motion for judgment notwithstanding the verdict or an appeal, the opposing party may be prejudiced by having lost the opportunity to present additional evidence before the case was submitted to the jury"); *Benson v. Allphin*, 786 F.2d 268 (7th Cir.1986) ("the motion for directed verdict at the close of all the evidence provides the nonmovant an opportunity to do what he can to remedy the deficiencies in his case . . ."); *McLaughlin v. The Fellows Gear Shaper Co.*, 786 F.2d 592, 4 F.R.Serv.3d 607 (3d Cir.1986) (per Adams, J., dissenting: "This Rule serves important practical purposes in ensuring that neither party is precluded from presenting the most persuasive case possible and in preventing unfair surprise after a matter has been submitted to the jury"). At one time, this requirement was held to be of constitutional stature, being compelled by the Seventh Amendment. Cf. *Slocum v. New York Life Insurance Co.*, 228 U.S. 364, 33 S. Ct. 523, 57 L.Ed. 879 (1913). But cf. *Baltimore & Carolina Line v. Redman*, 295 U.S. 654, 55 S. Ct. 890, 79 L.Ed. 1636 (1935).

The second sentence of paragraph (a)(2) does impose a requirement that the moving party articulate the basis on which a judgment as a matter of law might be rendered. The articulation is necessary to achieve the purpose of the requirement that the motion be made before the case is submitted to the jury, so that the responding party may seek to correct any overlooked deficiencies in the proof. The revision thus alters the result in cases in which courts have used various techniques to avoid the requirement that a motion for a directed verdict be made as a predicate to a motion for judgment notwithstanding the verdict. E.g., *Benson v. Allphin*, 786 F.2d 268 (7th Cir.1986) ("this circuit has allowed something less than a formal motion for directed verdict to preserve a party's right to move for judgment notwithstanding the verdict"). *See generally* 9 WRIGHT & MILLER, FEDERAL PRACTICE AND PROCEDURE § 2537 (1971 and Supp.). The information required with the motion may be supplied by explicit reference to materials and argument previously supplied to the court.

This subdivision deals only with the entry of judgment and not with the resolution of particular factual issues as a matter of law. The court may, as before, properly refuse to instruct a jury to decide an issue if a reasonable jury could on the evidence presented decide that issue in only one way.

Subdivision (b). This provision retains the concept of the former rule that the post-verdict motion is a renewal of an earlier motion made at the close of the evidence. One purpose of this concept was to avoid any question arising under the Seventh Amendment. *Montgomery Ward & Co. v. Duncan*, 311 U.S. 243, 61 S. Ct. 189, 85 L.Ed. 147 (1940). It remains useful as a means of defining the appropriate issue posed by the post-verdict motion. A post-trial motion for judgment can be granted only on grounds advanced in the pre-verdict motion. *E.g., Kutner Buick, Inc. v. American Motors Corp.*, 868 F.2d 614 (3d Cir.1989).

Often it appears to the court or to the moving party that a motion for judgment as a matter of law made at the close of the evidence should be reserved for a post-verdict decision. This is so because a jury verdict for the moving party moots the issue and because a preverdict ruling gambles that a reversal may result in a new trial that might have been avoided. For these reasons, the court may often wisely decline to rule on a motion for judgment as a matter of law made at the close of the evidence, and it is not inappropriate for the moving party to suggest such a postponement of the ruling until after the verdict has been rendered.

In ruling on such a motion, the court should disregard any jury determination for which there is no legally sufficient evidentiary basis enabling a reasonable jury to make it. The court may then decide such issues as a matter of law and enter judgment if all other material issues have been decided by the jury on the basis of legally sufficient evidence, or by the court as a matter of law.

The revised rule is intended for use in this manner with Rule 49. Thus, the court may combine facts established as a matter of law either before trial under Rule 56 or at trial on the basis of the evidence presented with other facts determined by the jury under instructions provided under Rule 49 to support a proper judgment under this rule.

This provision also retains the former requirement that a post-trial motion under the rule must be made within 10 days after entry of a contrary judgment. The renewed motion must be served and filed as provided by Rule 5. A purpose of this requirement is to meet the requirements of F.R.App.P. 4(a)(4).

Subdivision (c). Revision of this subdivision conforms the language to the change in diction set forth in subdivision (a) of this revised rule.

Subdivision (d). Revision of this subdivision conforms the language to that of the previous subdivisions.

1993 AMENDMENT

This technical amendment corrects an ambiguity in the text of the 1991 revision of the rule, which, as indicated in the Notes, was not intended to change the existing standards under which "directed verdicts" could be granted. This amendment makes clear that judgments as a matter of law in jury trials may be entered against both plaintiffs and defendants and with respect to issues or defenses that may not be wholly dispositive of a claim or defense.

1995 AMENDMENT

The only change, other than stylistic, intended by this revision is to prescribe a uniform explicit time for filing of post-judgment motions under this rule—no later than 10 days after entry of the judgment. Previously, there was an inconsistency in the wording of Rules 50, 52, and 59 with respect to whether certain post-judgment motions had to be filed, or merely served, during that period. This inconsistency caused special problems when motions for a new trial were joined with other post-judgment motions. These motions affect the finality of the judgment, a matter often of importance to third persons as well as the parties and the court. The Committee believes that each of these rules should be revised to require filing before end of the 10-day period. Filing is an event that can be determined with certainty from court records. The phrase "no later than" is used—rather than "within"—to include post-judgment motions that sometimes are filed before actual entry of the judgment by the clerk. It should be noted that under Rule 6(a) Saturdays, Sundays, and legal holidays are excluded in measuring the 10-day period, and that under Rule 5 the motions when filed are to contain a certificate of service on other parties.

2006 AMENDMENT

The language of Rule 50(a) has been amended as part of the general restyling of the Civil Rules to make them more easily understood and to make style and terminology consistent throughout the rules. These changes are intended to be stylistic only.

Rule 50(b) is amended to permit renewal of any Rule 50(a) motion for judgment as a matter of law, deleting the requirement that a motion be made at the close of all the evidence. Because the Rule 50(b) motion is only a renewal of the preverdict motion, it can be granted only on grounds advanced in the preverdict motion. The earlier motion informs the opposing party of the challenge to the sufficiency of the evidence and affords a clear opportunity to provide additional evidence that may be available. The earlier motion also alerts the court to the opportunity to simplify the trial by resolving some issues, or even all issues, without submission to the jury. This fulfillment of the functional needs that underlie present Rule 50(b) also satisfies the Seventh Amendment. Automatic reservation of the legal questions raised by the motion conforms to the decision in *Baltimore & Carolina Line v. Redman*, 297 U.S. 654 (1935).

This change responds to many decisions that have begun to move away from requiring a motion for judgment as a matter of law at the literal close of all the evidence. Although the requirement has been clearly established for several decades, lawyers continue to overlook it. The courts are slowly working away from the formal requirement. The amendment establishes the functional approach that courts have been unable to reach under the present rule and makes practice more consistent and predictable.

Many judges expressly invite motions at the close of all the evidence. The amendment is not intended to discourage this useful practice.

Finally, an explicit time limit is added for making a posttrial motion when the trial ends without a verdict or with a verdict that does not dispose of all issues suitable for resolution by verdict. The motion must be made no later than 10 days after the jury was discharged.

2007 AMENDMENTS

The language of Rule 50 has been amended as part of the general restyling of the Civil Rules to make them more easily understood and to make style and terminology consistent throughout the rules. These changes are intended to be stylistic only.

Former Rule 50(b) stated that the court reserves ruling on a motion for judgment as a matter of law made at the close of all the evidence "[i]f, for any reason, the court does not grant" the motion. The words "for any reason" reflected the proposition that the reservation is automatic and inescapable. The ruling is reserved even if the court explicitly denies the motion. The same result follows under the amended rule. If the motion is not granted, the ruling is reserved.

Amended Rule 50(e) identifies the appellate court's authority to direct the entry of judgment. This authority was not described in former Rule 50(d), but was recognized in *Weisgram v. Marley Co.*, 528 U.S. 440 (2000), and in *Neely v. Martin K. Eby Construction Company*, 386 U.S. 317 (1967). When Rule 50(d) was drafted in 1963, the Committee Note stated that "[s]ubdivision (d) does not attempt a regulation of all aspects of the procedure where the motion for judgment n.o.v. and any accompanying motion for a new trial are denied * * *." Express recognition of the authority to direct entry of judgment does not otherwise supersede this caution.

2009 AMENDMENTS

Former Rules 50, 52, and 59 adopted 10 day periods for their respective post judgment motions. Rule 6(b) prohibits any expansion of those periods. Experience has proved that in many cases it is not possible to prepare a satisfactory post judgment motion in 10 days, even under the former rule that excluded intermediate Saturdays, Sundays, and legal holidays. These time periods are particularly sensitive because Appellate Rule 4 integrates the time to appeal with a timely motion under these rules. Rather than introduce the prospect of uncertainty in appeal time by amending Rule 6(b) to permit additional time, the former 10 day periods are expanded to 28 days. Rule 6(b) continues to prohibit expansion of the 28 day period.

Rule 51. Instructions to Jury: Objection

1937 ADOPTION

Supreme Court Rule 8 requires exceptions to the charge of the court to the jury which shall distinctly state the several matters of law in the charge to which exception is taken. Similar provisions appear in the rules of the various Circuit Courts of Appeals.

1987 AMENDMENT

Although Rule 51 in its present form specifies that the court shall instruct the jury only after the arguments of the parties are completed, in some districts (typically those in states where the practice is otherwise) it is common for the parties to stipulate to instruction before the arguments. The purpose of the amendment is to give the court discretion to instruct the jury either before or after argument. Thus, the rule as revised will permit resort to the long-standing federal practice or to an alternative procedure, which has been praised because it gives counsel the opportunity to explain the instructions, argue their application to the facts and thereby give the jury the maximum assistance in determining the issues and arriving at a good verdict on the law and the evidence. As an ancillary benefit, this approach aids counsel by supplying a natural outline so that arguments may be directed to the essential fact issues which the jury must decide. See generally Raymond, *Merits and Demerits of the Missouri System of Instructing Juries*, 5 St. Louis U.L.J. 317 (1959). Moreover, if the court instructs before an argument, counsel then know the precise words the court has chosen and need not speculate as to the words the court will later use in its instructions. Finally, by instructing ahead of argument the court has the attention of the jurors when they are fresh and can give their full attention to the court's instructions. It is more difficult to hold the attention of jurors after lengthy arguments.

2003 AMENDMENT

Rule 51 is revised to capture many of the interpretations that have emerged in practice. The revisions in text will make uniform the conclusions reached by a majority of decisions on each point. Additions also are made to cover some practices that cannot now be anchored in the text of Rule 51.

Scope. Rule 51 governs instructions to the trial jury on the law that governs the verdict. A variety of other instructions cannot practicably be brought within Rule 51. Among these instructions are preliminary instructions to a venire, and cautionary or limiting instructions delivered in immediate response to events at trial.

Requests. Subdivision (a) governs requests. Apart from the plain error doctrine recognized in subdivision (d)(2), a court is not obliged to instruct the jury on issues raised by the evidence unless a party requests an instruction. The revised rule recognizes the court's authority to direct that requests be submitted before trial.

The close-of-the-evidence deadline may come before trial is completed on all potential issues. Trial may be formally bifurcated or may be sequenced in some less formal manner. The close of the evidence is measured by the occurrence of two events: completion of all intended evidence on an identified phase of the trial and impending submission to the jury with instructions.

The risk in directing a pretrial request deadline is that trial evidence may raise new issues or reshape issues the parties thought they had understood. Courts need not insist on pretrial requests in all cases. Even if the request time is set before trial or early in the trial, subdivision (a)(2)(A) permits requests after the close of the evidence to address issues that could not reasonably have been anticipated at the earlier time for requests set by the court.

Subdivision (a)(2)(B) expressly recognizes the court's discretion to act on an untimely request. The most important consideration in exercising the discretion confirmed by subdivision (a)(2)(B) is the importance of the issue to the case—the closer the issue lies to the "plain error" that would be recognized under subdivision (d)(2), the better the reason to give an instruction. The cogency of the reason for failing to make a timely request also should be considered. To be considered under subdivision (a)(2)(B) a request should be made before final instructions and before final jury arguments. What is a "final" instruction and argument depends on the sequence of submitting the case to the jury. If separate portions of the case are submitted to the jury in sequence, the final arguments and final instructions are those made on submitting to the jury the portion of the case addressed by the arguments and instructions.

Instructions. Subdivision (b)(1) requires the court to inform the parties, before instructing the jury and before final jury arguments related to the instruction, of the proposed instructions as well as the proposed action on instruction requests. The time limit is addressed to final jury arguments to reflect the practice that allows interim argument s during trial in complex cases; it may not be feasible to develop final instructions before such interim arguments. It is enough that counsel know of the intended instructions before making final arguments addressed to the issue. If the trial is sequenced or bifurcated, the final arguments addressed to an issue may occur before the close of the entire trial.

Subdivision (b)(2) complements subdivision (b)(1) by carrying forward the opportunity to object established by present Rule 51. It makes explicit the opportunity to object on the record, ensuring a clear memorial of the objection.

Subdivision (b)(3) reflects common practice by authorizing instructions at any time after trial begins and before the jury is discharged.

Objections. Subdivision (c) states the right to object to an instruction or the failure to give an instruction. It carries forward the formula of present Rule 51 requiring that the objection state distinctly the matter objected to and the grounds of the objection, and makes explicit the requirement that the objection be made on the record. The provisions on the time to object make clear that it is timely to object promptly after learning of an instruction or action on a request when the court has not provided advance information as required by subdivision (b)(1). The need to repeat a request by way of objection is continued by new subdivision (d)(1)(B) except where the court made a definitive ruling on the record.

Preserving a claim of error and plain error. Many cases hold that a proper request for a jury instruction is not alone enough to preserve the right to appeal failure to give the instruction. The request must be renewed by objection. This doctrine is appropriate when the court may not have sufficiently focused on the request, or may believe that the request has been granted in substance although in different words. But this doctrine may also prove a trap for the unwary who fail to add an objection after the court has made it clear that the request has been considered and rejected on the merits.

Subdivision (d)(1)(B) establishes authority to review the failure to grant a timely request, despite a failure to add an objection, when the court has made a definitive ruling on the record rejecting the request.

Many circuits have recognized that an error not preserved under Rule 51 may be reviewed in exceptional circumstances. The language adopted to capture these decisions in subdivision (d)(2) is borrowed from Criminal Rule 52. Although the language is the same, the context of civil litigation often differs from the context of criminal prosecution; actual application of the plain-error standard takes account of the differences. The Supreme Court has summarized application of Criminal Rule 52 as involving four elements: (1) there must be an error; (2) the error must be plain; (3) the error must affect substantial rights; and (4) the error must seriously affect the fairness, integrity, or public reputation of judicial proceedings. *Johnson v. U.S.*, 520 U.S. 461, 466–467, 469–470 (1997). (The Johnson case quoted the fourth element from its decision in a civil action, *U.S. v. Atkinson*, 297 U.S. 157, 160 (1936): "In exceptional circumstances, especially in criminal cases, appellate courts, in the public interest, may, of their own motion, notice errors to which no exception has been taken, if the errors are obvious, or if they otherwise substantially affect the fairness, integrity, or public reputation of judicial proceedings.")

The court's duty to give correct jury instructions in a civil action is shaped by at least four factors.

The factor most directly implied by a "plain" error rule is the obviousness of the mistake. The importance of the error is a second major factor. The costs of correcting an error reflect a third factor that is affected by a variety of circumstances. In a case that seems close to the fundamental error line, account also may be taken of the impact a verdict may have on nonparties.

2007 AMENDMENTS

The language of Rule 51 has been amended as part of the general restyling of the Civil Rules to make them more easily understood and to make style and

terminology consistent throughout the rules. These changes are intended to be stylistic only.

Rule 52. Findings by the Court; Judgment on Partial Findings

1937 ADOPTION

See Former Equity Rule 70 1/2, as amended Nov. 25, 1935, (Findings of Fact and Conclusions of Law) and U.S.C., Title 28, former § 764 (Opinion, findings, and conclusions in action against United States) which are substantially continued in this rule. The provisions of U.S.C., Title 28, former §§ 773 (Trial of issues of fact; by court) and 875 (Review in cases tried without a jury) are superseded in so far as they provide a different method of finding facts and a different method of appellate review. The rule stated in the third sentence of **Subdivision (a)** accords with the decisions on the scope of the review in modern federal equity practice. It is applicable to all classes of findings in cases tried without a jury whether the finding is of a fact concerning which there was conflict of testimony, or of a fact deduced or inferred from uncontradicted testimony. See *Silver King Coalition Mines Co. v. Silver King Consolidated Mining Co., C.C.A.8, 1913*, 204 F. 166, certiorari denied 229 U.S. 624, 33 S. Ct. 1051, 57 L.Ed. 1356; *Warren v. Keep, 1894*, 155 U.S. 265, 15 S. Ct. 83, 39 L.Ed. 144; *Furrer v. Ferris, 1892*, 145 U.S. 132, 12 S. Ct. 821, 36 L.Ed. 649; *Tilghman v. Proctor, 1888*, 125 U.S. 136, 149, 8 S. Ct. 894, 901, 31 L.Ed. 664; *Kimberly v. Arms, 1889*, 129 U.S. 512, 524, 9 S. Ct. 355, 359, 32 L.Ed. 764. Compare *Kaeser & Blair, Inc. v. Merchants' Ass'n, C.C.A.6, 1933*, 64 F.2d 575, 576; *Dunn v. Trefry, C.C.A.1, 1919*, 260 F. 147, 148.

In the following states findings of fact are required in all cases tried without a jury (waiver by the parties being permitted as indicated at the end of the listing): Arkansas, Civ.Code (Crawford, 1934) § 364; California, Code Civ.Proc. (Deering, 1937) §§ 632, 634; Colorado, 1 Stat.Ann. (1935) Code Civ.Proc. §§ 232, 291 (in actions before referees or for possession of and damages to land); Connecticut, Gen.Stats. §§ 5660, 5664; Idaho, 1 Code Ann. (1932) §§ 7-302 through 7-305; Massachusetts (equity cases), 2 Gen.Laws (Ter.Ed., 1932) ch. 214, § 23; Minnesota, 2 Stat. (Mason, 1927) § 9311; Nevada, 4 Comp.Laws (Hillyer, 1929) §§ 8783 to 8784; New Jersey, Sup.Ct.Rule 113, 2 N.J.Misc. 1197, 1239 (1924); New Mexico, Stat.Ann. (Courtright, 1929) § 105-813; North Carolina, Code (1935) § 569; North Dakota, 2 Comp.Laws Ann. (1913) § 7641; Oregon, 2 Code Ann. (1930) § 2-502; South Carolina, Code (Michie, 1932) § 649; South Dakota, 1 Comp.Laws (1929) §§ 2525 to 2526; Utah, Rev.Stat.Ann. (1933) §§ 104-26-2, 104-26-3; Vermont (where jury trial waived), Pub.Laws (1933) § 2069; Washington, 2 Rev.Stat.Ann. (Remington, 1932) § 367; Wisconsin, Stat. (1935) § 270.33. The parties may waive this requirement for findings in California, Idaho, North Dakota, Nevada, New Mexico, Utah, and South Dakota.

In the following states the review of findings of fact in all non-jury cases, including jury waived cases, is assimilated to the equity review: Alabama, Code Ann. (Michie, 1928) §§ 9498, 8599; California, Code Civ.Proc. (Deering, 1937) § 956a; but see 20 Calif.Law Rev. 171 (1932); Colorado, *Johnson v. Kountze, 1895*, 43 P. 445, 21 Colo. 486, semble; Illinois, *Baker v. Hinrichs, 1934*, 194 N.E. 284, 359 Ill. 138; *Weininger v. Metropolitan Fire Ins. Co., 1935*, 195 N.E. 420, 359 Ill. 584, 98 A.L.R. 169; Minnesota, *State Bank of Gibbon v. Walter, 1926*, 208 N.W. 423, 167 Minn. 37, 38; *Waldron v. Page, 1934*, 253 N.W. 894, 191 Minn. 302; New Jersey, N.J.S.A. 2:27-241, 2-27-363, as interpreted in *Bussy v. Hatch, 1920*, 111 A. 546, 95 N.J.L. 56; New York, *York Mortgage Corporation v. Clotar Const. Corp., 1930*, 172 N.E. 265, 254 N.Y. 128, 133; North Dakota, Comp.Laws Ann. (1913) § 7846, as amended by N.D.Laws 1933, c. 208; *Milnor Holding Co. v. Holt, 1933*, 248 N.W. 315, 63 N.D. 362, 370; Oklahoma, *Wichita Mining and Improvement Co. v. Hale, 1908*, 94 P. 530, 20 Okl. 159, 167; South Dakota, *Randall v. Burk Township*, 4 S.D. 337, 57 N.W. 4 (1893); Texas, *Custard v. Flowers, 1929*, 14 S.W.2d 109; Utah, Rev.Stat.Ann. (1933) § 104-41-5; Vermont, *Roberge v. Troy, 1933*, 105 Vt. 134, 163 A. 770; Washington, 2

Rev.Stat.Ann. (Remington, 1932) §§ 309 to 316; *McCullough v. Puget Sound Realty Associates, 1913*, 136 Pac. 1146, 76 Wash. 700, but see *Cornwall v. Anderson, 1915*, 148 P. 1, 85 Wash. 369; West Virginia, *Kinsey v. Carr, 1906*, 55 S.E. 1004, 60 W.Va. 449, semble; Wisconsin, Stat. (1935) § 251.09; *Campbell v. Sutliff, 1927*, 214 N.W. 374, 193 Wis. 370; *Gessler v. Erwin Co., 1924*, 193 N.W. 363, 182 Wis. 315.

For examples of an assimilation of the review of findings of fact in cases tried without a jury to the review at law as made in several states, see Clark and Stone, Review of Findings of Fact, 4 U. of Chi.L.Rev. 190, 215 (1937).

1946 AMENDMENT

Note to Subdivision (a). The amended rule makes clear that the requirement for findings of fact and conclusions of law thereon applies in a case with an advisory jury. This removes an ambiguity in the rule as originally stated, but carries into effect what has been considered its intent. 3 Moore's Federal Practice, 1938, 3119. *Hurwitz v. Hurwitz, 1943*, 136 F.2d 796, 78 U.S.App.D.C. 66.

The two sentences added at the end of Rule 52(a) eliminate certain difficulties which have arisen concerning findings and conclusions. The first of the two sentences permits findings of fact and conclusions of law to appear in an opinion or memorandum of decision. See, e.g., *United States v. One 1941 Ford Sedan, Tex.1946*, 65 F.Supp. 84. Under original Rule 52(a) some courts have expressed the view that findings and conclusions could not be incorporated in an opinion. *Detective Comics, Inc. v. Bruns Publications, N.Y.1939*, 28 F.Supp. 399; *Pennsylvania Co. for Insurance on Lives & Granting Annuities v. Cincinnati & L. E. R. Co., Ohio 1941*, 43 F.Supp. 5; *United States v. Aluminum Co. of America, N.Y.1941*, 2 F.R.D. 224, 5 Fed.Rules Serv. 52a.11, Case 3; see also s. c., 44 F.Supp. 97. But, to the contrary, see *Wellman v. United States, Mass.1938*, 25 F.Supp. 868; *Cook v. United States, Mass.1939*, 26 F.Supp. 253; *Proctor v. White, Mass.1939*, 28 F.Supp. 161; *Green Valley Creamery, Inc. v. United States, C.C.A.1, 1939*, 108 F.2d 342. See also *Matton Oil Transfer Corp. v. The Dynamic, C.C.A.2, 1941*, 123 F.2d 999; *Carter Coal Co. v. Litz, C.C.A.4, 1944*, 140 F.2d 934; *Woodruff v. Heiser, C.C.A.10, 1945*, 150 F.2d 869; Coca Cola Co. v. Busch, Pa.1943, 7 Fed.Rules Serv. 59b.2, Case 4; Oglebay, Some Developments in Bankruptcy Law, 1944, 18 J. of Nat'l Ass'n of Ref. 68, 69. Findings of fact aid in the process of judgment and in defining for future cases the precise limitations of the issues and the determination thereon. Thus they not only aid the appellate court on review, *Hurwitz v. Hurwitz, 1943*, 136 F.2d 796, 78 U.S.App.D.C. 66, but they are an important factor in the proper application of the doctrines of res judicata and estoppel by judgment. Nordbye, Improvements in Statement of Findings of Fact and Conclusions of Law, 1 F.R.D. 25, 26–27; *United States v. Forness, C.C.A.2, 1942*, 125 F.2d 928, certiorari denied 316 U.S. 694, 62 S. Ct. 1293, 86 L.Ed. 1764. These findings should represent the judge's own determination and not the long, often argumentative statements of successful counsel. *United States v. Forness*, supra: *United States v. Crescent Amusement Co., 1944*, 323 U.S. 173, 65 S. Ct. 254, 89 L.Ed. 160. Consequently, they should be a part of the judge's opinion and decision, either stated therein or stated separately. *Matton Oil Transfer Corp. v. The Dynamic*, supra. But the judge need only make brief, definite, pertinent findings and conclusions upon the contested matters; there is no necessity for over-elaboration of detail or particularization of facts. *United States v. Forness*, supra; *United States v. Crescent Amusement Co.*, supra. See also *Petterson Lighterage & Towing Corp. v. New York Central R. Co., C.C.A.2d, 1942*, 126 F.2d 992; *Brown Paper Mill Co., Inc. v. Irwin, C.C.A.8, 1943*, 134 F.2d 337; *Allen Bradley Co. v. Local Union No. 3, I. B. E. W., C.C.A.2, 1944*, 145 F.2d 215, reversed on other grounds 325 U.S. 797, 65 S. Ct. 1533, 89 L.Ed. 1939; Young v. Murphy, Ohio 1946, 9 Fed.Rules Serv. 52a.11, Case 2.

The last sentence of Rule 52(a) as amended will remove any doubt that findings and conclusions are unnecessary upon decision of a motion, particularly one under Rule 12 or Rule 56, except as provided in amended Rule 41(b). As so holding, see *Thomas v. Peyser, App.D.C.1941*, 118 F.2d 369; *Schad v. Twentieth*

Century-Fox Corp., C.C.A.3, 1943, 136 F.2d 991; *Prudential Ins. Co. of America v. Goldstein, N.Y.1942*, 43 F.Supp. 767; *Somers Coal Co. v. United States, Ohio 1942*, 2 F.R.D. 532, 6 Fed.Rules Serv. 52a.1, Case 1; *Pen-Ken Oil & Gas Corp. v. Warfield Natural Gas Co., Ky.1942*, 2 F.R.D. 355, 5 Fed.Rules Serv. 52a.1, Case 3; also Commentary, Necessity of Findings of Fact, 1941, 4 Fed.Rules Serv. 936.

1963 AMENDMENT

This amendment conforms to the amendment of Rule 58. See the Advisory Committee's Note to Rule 58, as amended.

1983 AMENDMENT

Rule 52(a) has been amended to revise its penultimate sentence to provide explicitly that the district judge may make the findings of fact and conclusions of law required in nonjury cases orally. Nothing in the prior text of the rule forbids this practice, which is widely utilized by district judges. See Christensen, *A Modest Proposal for Immeasurable Improvement,* 64 A.B.A.J. 693 (1978). The objective is to lighten the burden on the trial court in preparing findings in nonjury cases. In addition, the amendment should reduce the number of published district court opinions that embrace written findings.

1985 AMENDMENT

Rule 52(a) has been amended (1) to avoid continued confusion and conflicts among the circuits as to the standard of appellate review of findings of fact by the court, (2) to eliminate the disparity between the standard of review as literally stated in Rule 52(a) and the practice of some courts of appeals, and (3) to promote nationwide uniformity. See Note, *Rule 52(a): Appellate Review of Findings of Fact Based on Documentary or Undisputed Evidence*, 49 Va.L.Rev. 506, 536 (1963).

Some courts of appeal have stated that when a trial court's findings do not rest on demeanor evidence and evaluation of a witness' credibility, there is no reason to defer to the trial court's findings and the appellate court more readily can find them to be clearly erroneous. See, e.g., *Marcum v. United States*, 621 F.2d 142, 144–45 (5th Cir.1980). Others go further, holding that appellate review may be had without application of the "clearly erroneous" test since the appellate court is in as good a position as the trial court to review a purely documentary record. See, *e.g., Atari, Inc. v. North American Philips Consumer Electronics Corp.*, 672 F.2d 607, 614 (7th Cir.), cert. denied, 459 U.S. 880, 103 S. Ct. 176, 74 L. Ed. 2d 145 (1982); *Lydle v. United States*, 635 F.2d 763, 765 n. 1 (6th Cir.1981); *Swanson v. Baker Indus., Inc.*, 615 F.2d 479, 483 (8th Cir.1980); *Taylor v. Lombard*, 606 F.2d 371, 372 (2d Cir.1979), *cert. denied,* 445 U.S. 946, 100 S. Ct. 1346, 63 L. Ed. 2d 781 (1980); *Jack Kahn Music Co. v. Baldwin Piano & Organ Co.*, 604 F.2d 755, 758 (2d Cir.1979); *John R. Thompson Co. v. United States*, 477 F.2d 164, 167 (7th Cir.1973).

A third group has adopted the view that the "clearly erroneous" rule applies in all nonjury cases even when findings are based solely on documentary evidence or on inferences from undisputed facts. See, *e.g., Maxwell v. Sumner*, 673 F.2d 1031, 1036 (9th Cir.), *cert. denied,* 459 U.S. 976, 103 S. Ct. 313, 74 L. Ed. 2d 291 (1982); *United States v. Texas Education Agency*, 647 F.2d 504, 506–07 (5th Cir.1981), *cert. denied,* 454 U.S. 1143, 102 S. Ct. 1002, 71 L. Ed. 2d 295 (1982); *Constructora Maza, Inc. v. Banco de Ponce*, 616 F.2d 573, 576 (1st Cir. 1980); *In re Sierra Trading Corp.*, 482 F.2d 333, 337 (10th Cir.1973); *Case v. Morrisette*, 475 F.2d 1300, 1306–07 (D.C.Cir.1973).

The commentators also disagree as to the proper interpretation of the Rule. *Compare* Wright, *The Doubtful Omniscience of Appellate Courts,* 41 Minn.L. Rev. 751, 769–70 (1957) (language and intent of Rule support view that "clearly erroneous" test should apply to all forms of evidence), *and* 9 C. Wright & A. Miller, *Federal Practice and Procedure: Civil § 2587*, at 740 (1971) (language of the Rule is clear), *with* 5A J. Moore, Federal Practice ¶ 52.04, 2687–88 (2d ed. 1982) (Rule as written supports broader review of findings based on non-demeanor testimony).

The Supreme Court has not clearly resolved the issue. See, *Bose Corp. v.*

Consumers Union of United States, Inc., 466 U.S. 485, 498, 104 S. Ct. 1949, 1958, 80 L. Ed. 2d 502 (1984); *Pullman-Standard v. Swint*, 456 U.S. 273, 293, 102 S. Ct. 1781, 1792, 72 L. Ed. 2d 66 (1982); *United States v. General Motors Corp.*, 384 U.S. 127, 141 n. 16, 86 S. Ct. 1321, 1328 n. 16, 16 L. Ed. 2d 415 (1966); *United States v. United States Gypsum Co.*, 333 U.S. 364, 394–96, 68 S. Ct. 525, 541–542, 92 L.Ed. 746 (1948).

The principal argument advanced in favor of a more searching appellate review of findings by the district court based solely on documentary evidence is that the rationale of Rule 52(a) does not apply when the findings do not rest on the trial court's assessment of credibility of the witnesses but on an evaluation of documentary proof and the drawing of inferences from it, thus eliminating the need for any special deference to the trial court's findings. These considerations are outweighed by the public interest in the stability and judicial economy that would be promoted by recognizing that the trial court, not the appellate tribunal, should be the finder of the facts. To permit courts of appeals to share more actively in the fact-finding function would tend to undermine the legitimacy of the district courts in the eyes of litigants, multiply appeals by encouraging appellate retrial of some factual issues, and needlessly reallocate judicial authority.

1991 AMENDMENT

Subdivision (c) is added. It parallels the revised Rule 50(a), but is applicable to non-jury trials. It authorizes the court to enter judgment at any time that it can appropriately make a dispositive finding of fact on the evidence.

The new subdivision replaces part of Rule 41(b), which formerly authorized a dismissal at the close of the plaintiff's case if the plaintiff had failed to carry an essential burden of proof. Accordingly, the reference to Rule 41 formerly made in subdivision (a) of this rule is deleted.

As under the former Rule 41(b), the court retains discretion to enter no judgment prior to the close of the evidence.

Judgment entered under this rule differs from a summary judgment under Rule 56 in the nature of the evaluation made by the court. A judgment on partial findings is made after the court has heard all the evidence bearing on the crucial issue of fact, and the finding is reversible only if the appellate court finds it to be "clearly erroneous." A summary judgment, in contrast, is made on the basis of facts established on account of the absence of contrary evidence or presumptions; such establishments of fact are rulings on questions of law as provided in Rule 56(a) and are not shielded by the "clear error" standard of review.

1993 AMENDMENT

This technical amendment corrects an ambiguity in the text of the 1991 revision of the rule, similar to the revision being made to Rule 50. This amendment makes clear that judgments as a matter of law in nonjury trials may be entered against both plaintiffs and defendants and with respect to issues or defenses that may not be wholly dispositive of a claim or defense.

1995 AMENDMENT

The only change, other than stylistic, intended by this revision is to require that any motion to amend or add findings after a nonjury trial must be filed no later than 10 days after entry of the judgment. Previously, there was an inconsistency in the wording of Rules 50, 52, and 59 with respect to whether certain post-judgment motions had to be filed, or merely served, during that period. This inconsistency caused special problems when motions for a new trial were joined with other post-judgment motions. These motions affect the finality of the judgment, a matter often of importance to third persons as well as the parties and the court. The Committee believes that each of these rules should be revised to require filing before end of the 10-day period. Filing is an event that can be determined with certainty from court records. The phrase "no later than" is used—rather than "within"—to include post-judgment motions that sometimes are filed before actual entry of the judgment by the clerk. It should be noted that under Rule 6(a) Saturdays, Sundays, and legal holidays are excluded in measuring the 10-day period, and that under Rule 5 the motions when filed are to contain a certificate of service on other parties.

2007 AMENDMENTS

The language of Rule 52 has been amended as part of the general restyling of the Civil Rules to make them more easily understood and to make style and terminology consistent throughout the rules. These changes are intended to be stylistic only.

Former Rule 52(a) said that findings are unnecessary on decisions of motions "except as provided in subdivision (c) of this rule." Amended Rule 52(a)(3) says that findings are unnecessary "unless these rules provide otherwise." This change reflects provisions in other rules that require Rule 52 findings on deciding motions. Rules 23(e), 23(h), and 54(d)(2)(C) are examples.

Amended Rule 52(a)(5) includes provisions that appeared in former Rule 52(a) and 52(b). Rule 52(a) provided that requests for findings are not necessary for purposes of review. It applied both in an action tried on the facts without a jury and also in granting or refusing an interlocutory injunction. Rule 52(b), applicable to findings "made in actions tried without a jury," provided that the sufficiency of the evidence might be "later questioned whether or not in the district court the party raising the question objected to the findings, moved to amend them, or moved for partial findings." Former Rule 52(b) did not explicitly apply to decisions granting or refusing an interlocutory injunction. Amended Rule 52(a)(5) makes explicit the application of this part of former Rule 52(b) to interlocutory injunction decisions.

Former Rule 52(c) provided for judgment on partial findings, and referred to it as "judgment as a matter of law." Amended Rule 52(c) refers only to "judgment," to avoid any confusion with a Rule 50 judgment as a matter of law in a jury case. The standards that govern judgment as a matter of law in a jury case have no bearing on a decision under Rule 52(c).

2009 AMENDMENTS

Former Rules 50, 52, and 59 adopted 10 day periods for their respective post judgment motions. Rule 6(b) prohibits any expansion of those periods. Experience has proved that in many cases it is not possible to prepare a satisfactory post judgment motion in 10 days, even under the former rule that excluded intermediate Saturdays, Sundays, and legal holidays. These time periods are particularly sensitive because Appellate Rule 4 integrates the time to appeal with a timely motion under these rules. Rather than introduce the prospect of uncertainty in appeal time by amending Rule 6(b) to permit additional time, the former 10 day periods are expanded to 28 days. Rule 6(b) continues to prohibit expansion of the 28 day period.

Rule 53. Masters

1937 ADOPTION

Note to Subdivision (a). This is a modification of former Equity Rule 68 (Appointment and Compensation of Masters).

Note to Subdivision (b). This is substantially the first sentence of former Equity Rule 59 (Reference to Master—Exceptional, Not Usual) extended to actions formerly legal. See *Ex parte Peterson, 1920*, 253 U.S. 300, 40 S. Ct. 543, 64 L.Ed. 919.

Note to Subdivision (c). This is former Equity Rules 62 (Powers of Master) and 65 (Claimants Before Master Examinable by Him) with slight modifications. Compare former Equity Rules 49 (Evidence Taken Before Examiners, Etc.) and 51. (Evidence Taken Before Examiners, Etc.).

Note to Subdivision (d). (1) This is substantially a combination of the second sentence of former Equity Rule 59 (Reference to Master—Exceptional, Not Usual) and former Equity Rule 60 (Proceedings Before Master). Compare former Equity Rule 53 (Notice of Taking Testimony Before Examiner, Etc.).

(2) This is substantially former Equity Rule 52 (Attendance of Witnesses Before Commissioner, Master, or Examiner).

(3) This is substantially former Equity Rule 63 (Form of Accounts Before Master).

Note to Subdivision (e). This contains the substance of former Equity Rules 61 (Master's Report—Documents Identified but not Set Forth), 61½ (Master's Report—Presumption as to Correctness—Review), and 66 (Return of Master's Report—Exceptions—Hearing), with modifications as to the form and effect of the report and for inclusion of reports by auditors, referees, and examiners, and references in actions formerly legal. Compare former Equity Rules 49 (Evidence Taken Before Examiners, Etc.) and 67 (Costs on Exceptions to Master's Report). See *Camden v. Stuart, 1892*, 144 U.S. 104, 12 S. Ct. 585, 36 L.Ed. 363; *Ex parte Peterson, 1920*, 253 U.S. 300, 40 S. Ct. 543, 64 L.Ed. 919.

1966 AMENDMENT

These changes are designed to preserve the admiralty practice whereby difficult computations are referred to a commissioner or assessor, especially after an interlocutory judgment determining liability. As to separation of issues for trial see Rule 42(b).

1983 AMENDMENT

Subdivision (a). The creation of full-time magistrates, who serve at government expense and have no nonjudicial duties competing for their time, eliminates the need to appoint standing masters. Thus the prior provision in Rule 53(a) authorizing the appointment of standing masters is deleted. Additionally, the definition of "master" in subdivision (a) now eliminates the superseded office of commissioner.

The term "special master" is retained in Rule 53 in order to maintain conformity with 28 U.S.C. § 636(b)(2), authorizing a judge to designate a magistrate "to serve as a special master pursuant to the applicable provisions of this title and the Federal Rules of Civil Procedure for the United States District Courts." Obviously, when a magistrate serves as a special master, the provisions for compensation of masters are inapplicable, and the amendment to subdivision (a) so provides.

Although the existence of magistrates may make the appointment of outside masters unnecessary in many instances, see, *e.g., Gautreaux v. Chicago Housing Authority*, 384 F.Supp. 37 (N.D.Ill.1974), mandamus denied *sub nom.,* Chicago Housing Authority v. Austin, 511 F.2d 82 (7th Cir.1975); *Avco Corp. v. American Tel. & Tel. Co.*, 68 F.R.D. 532 (S.D.Ohio 1975), such masters may prove useful when some special expertise is desired or when a magistrate is unavailable for lengthy and detailed supervision of a case.

Subdivision (b). The provisions of 28 U.S.C. § 636(b)(2) not only permit magistrates to serve as masters under Rule 53(b) but also eliminate the exceptional condition requirement of Rule 53(b) when the reference is made with the consent of the parties. The amendment to subdivision (b) brings Rule 53 into harmony with the statute by exempting magistrates, appointed with the consent of the parties, from the general requirement that some exceptional condition requires the reference. It should be noted that subdivision (b) does not address the question, raised in recent decisional law and commentary, as to whether the exceptional condition requirement is applicable when *private masters* who are not magistrates are appointed with the consent of the parties. See Silberman, *Masters and Magistrates Part II: The American Analogue,* 50 N.Y.U. L.Rev. 1297, 1354 (1975).

Subdivision (c). The amendment recognizes the abrogation of Federal Rule 43(c) by the Federal Rules of Evidence.

Subdivision (f). The new subdivision responds to confusion flowing from the dual authority for references of pretrial matters to magistrates. Such references can be made, with or without the consent of the parties, pursuant to Rule 53 or under 28 U.S.C. § 636(b)(1)(A) and (b)(1)(B). There are a number of distinctions between references made under the statute and under the rule. For example, under the statute nondispositive pretrial matters may be referred to a magistrate, without consent, for final determination with reconsideration by the district judge if the magistrate's order is clearly erroneous or contrary to law. Under the rule, however, the appointment of a master, without consent of the parties, to supervise discovery would require some exceptional condition (Rule 53(b)) and would subject the proceedings to the report procedures of Rule 53(e). If an order of reference does not clearly articulate the source of the court's authority the resulting proceedings could be subject to attack on grounds of the magistrate's noncompliance with the provisions of Rule 53. This subdivision therefore establishes a presumption that the limitations of Rule 53 are not applicable unless the reference is specifically made subject to Rule 53.

A magistrate serving as a special master under 28 U.S.C. § 636(b)(2) is governed by the provisions of Rule 53, with the exceptional condition requirement lifted in the case of a consensual reference.

1987 AMENDMENT

The amendments are technical. No substantive change is intended.

1991 AMENDMENT

The purpose of the revision is to expedite proceedings before a master. The former rule required only a filing of the master's report, with the clerk then notifying the parties of the filing. To receive a copy, a party would then be required to secure it from the clerk. By transmitting directly to the parties, the master can save some efforts of counsel. Some local rules have previously required such action by the master.

1993 AMENDMENT

This revision is made to conform the rule to changes made by the Judicial Improvements Act of 1990.

2003 AMENDMENT

Rule 53 is revised extensively to reflect changing practices in using masters. From the beginning in 1938, Rule 53 focused primarily on special masters who perform trial functions. Since then, however, courts have gained experience with masters appointed to perform a variety of pretrial and post-trial functions. See Willging, Hooper, Leary, Miletich, Reagan, & Shapard, Special Masters' Incidence and Activity, (Federal Judicial Center 2000). This revised Rule 53 recognizes that in appropriate circumstances masters may properly be appointed to perform these functions and regulates such appointments. Rule 53 continues to address trial masters as well, but permits appointment of a trial master in an action to be tried to a jury only if the parties consent. The new rule clarifies the provisions that govern the appointment and function of masters for all purposes. Rule 53(g) also changes the standard of review for findings of fact made or recommended by a master. The core of the original Rule 53 remains, including its prescription that appointment of a master must be the exception and not the rule.

Special masters are appointed in many circumstances outside the Civil Rules. Rule 53 applies only to proceedings that Rule 1 brings within its reach.

Subdivision (a)(1). District judges bear primary responsibility for the work of their courts. A master should be appointed only in limited circumstances. Subdivision (a)(1) describes three different standards, relating to appointments by consent of the parties, appointments for trial duties, and appointments for pretrial or post-trial duties.

Consent Masters. Subparagraph (a)(1)(A) authorizes appointment of a master with the parties' consent. Party consent does not require that the court make the appointment; the court retains unfettered discretion to refuse appointment.

Trial Masters. Use of masters for the core functions of trial has been progressively limited. These limits are reflected in the provisions of subparagraph (a)(1)(B) that restrict appointments to exercise trial functions. The Supreme Court gave clear direction to this trend in *La Buy v. Howes Leather Co.*, 352 U.S. 249 (1957); earlier roots are sketched in *Los Angeles Brush Mfg. Corp. v.*

James, 272 U.S. 701 (1927). As to nonjury trials, this trend has developed through elaboration of the "exceptional condition" requirement in present Rule 53(b). This phrase is retained, and will continue to have the same force as it has developed. Although the provision that a reference "shall be the exception and not the rule" is deleted, its meaning is embraced for this setting by the exceptional condition requirement.

Subparagraph (a)(1)(B)(ii) carries forward the approach of present Rule 53(b), which exempts from the "exceptional condition" requirement "matters of account and of difficult computation of damages." This approach is justified only as to essentially ministerial determinations that require mastery of much detailed information but that do not require extensive determinations of credibility.

Evaluations of witness credibility should only be assigned to a trial master when justified by an exceptional condition.

The use of a trial master without party consent is abolished as to matters to be decided by a jury unless a statute provides for this practice.

Abolition of the direct power to appoint a trial master as t o issues to be decided by a jury leaves the way free to appoint a trial master with the consent of all parties. A trial master should be appointed in a jury case, with consent of the parties and concurrence of the court, only if the parties waive jury trial with respect to the issues submitted to the master or if the master's findings are to be submitted to the jury as evidence in the manner provided by former Rule 53(e)(3). In no circumstance may a master be appointed to preside at a jury trial.

The central function of a trial master is to preside over an evidentiary hearing on the merits of the claims or defenses in the action. This function distinguishes the trial master from most functions of pretrial and post-trial masters. If any master is to be used for such matters as a preliminary injunction hearing or a determination of complex damages issues, for example,

the master should be a trial master. The line, however, is not distinct. A pretrial master might well conduct an evidentiary hearing on a discovery dispute, and a post-trial master might conduct evidentiary hearings on questions of compliance.

Rule 53 has long provided authority to report the evidence without recommendations in nonjury trials. This authority is omitted from Rule 53(a)(1)(B). In some circumstances a master may be appointed under Rule 53(a)(1)(A) or (C) to take evidence and report without recommendations.

For nonjury cases, a master also may be appointed to assist the court in discharging trial duties other than conducting an evidentiary hearing.

Pretrial and Post-Trial Masters. Subparagraph (a)(1)(C) authorizes appointment of a master to address pretrial or post-trial matters. Appointment is limited t o matters t hat cannot be addressed effectively and in a timely fashion by an available district judge or magistrate judge of the district. A master's pretrial or post-trial duties may include matters that could be addressed by a judge, such as reviewing discovery documents for privilege, or duties t hat might not be suitable for a judge. Some forms of settlement negotiations, investigations, or administration of an organization are familiar examples of duties that a judge might not feel free to undertake.

Magistrate Judges. Particular attention should be paid to the prospect that a magistrate judge may be available for special assignments. United States magistrate judges are authorized by statute to perform many pretrial functions in civil actions. 28 U.S.C. § 636(b)(1). Ordinarily a district judge who delegates these functions should refer them to a magistrate judge acting as magistrate judge.

There is statutory authority to appoint a magistrate judge as special master. 28 U.S.C. § 636(b)(2). In special circumstances, or when expressly authorized by a statute other than § 636(b)(2), it may be appropriate to appoint a magistrate judge as a master when needed to perform functions outside those listed in § 636(b)(1). There is no apparent reason to appoint a magistrate judge to perform as master duties that could be performed in the role of magistrate judge. Party consent is required for trial before a magistrate judge, moreover, and this requirement should not be undercut by resort to Rule 53 unless specifically authorized by statute; see 42 U.S.C. § 2000e-5(f)(5).

Pretrial Masters. The appointment of masters to participate in pretrial proceedings has developed extensively over the last two decades as some district courts have felt the need for additional help in managing complex litigation. This practice is not well regulated by present Rule 53, which focuses on masters as trial participants. Rule 53 is amended to confirm the authority to appoint—and to regulate the use of—pretrial masters.

A pretrial master should be appointed only when the need is clear. Direct judicial performance of judicial functions may be particularly important in cases that involve important public issues or many parties. At the extreme, a broad delegation of pretrial responsibility as well as a delegation of trial responsibilities can run afoul of Article III.

A master also may be appointed to address matters that blur the divide between pretrial and trial functions. The court's responsibility to interpret patent claims as a matter of law, for example, may be greatly assisted by appointing a master who has expert knowledge of the field in which the patent operates. Review of the master's findings will be de novo under Rule 53(g)(4), but the advantages of initial determination by a master may make the process more effective and timely than disposition by the judge acting alone. Determination of foreign law may present comparable difficulties. The decision whether to appoint a master to address such matters is governed by subdivision (a)(1)(C), not the trial-master provisions of subdivision (a)(1)(B).

Post-Trial Masters. Courts have come to rely on masters to assist in framing and enforcing complex decrees. Present Rule 53 does not directly address this practice. Amended Rule 53 authorizes appointment of post-trial masters for these and similar purposes. The constraint of subdivision (a)(1)(C) limits this practice to cases in which the master's duties cannot be performed effectively and in a timely fashion by an available district judge or magistrate judge of the district.

Reliance on a master is appropriate when a complex decree requires complex policing, particularly when a party has proved resistant or intransigent. This practice has been recognized by the Supreme Court, see *Local 28, Sheet Metal Workers' Internat. Assn. v. EEOC*, 478 U.S. 421, 481–482 (1986). The master's role in enforcement may extend to investigation in ways that are quite unlike the traditional role of judicial officers in an adversary system.

Expert Witness Overlap. This rule does not address the difficulties that arise when a single person is appointed to perform overlapping roles as master and as court-appointed expert witness under Evidence Rule 706. Whatever combination of functions is involved, the Rule 53(a)(1)(B) limit that confines trial masters to issues to be decided by the court does not apply to a person who also is appointed as an expert witness under Evidence Rule 706.

Subdivision (a)(2) and (3). Masters are subject to the Code of Conduct for United States Judges, with exceptions spelled out in the Code. Special care must be taken to ensure that there is no actual or apparent conflict of interest involving a master. The standard of disqualification is established by 28 U.S.C. § 455. The affidavit required by Rule 53(b)(3) provides an important source of information about possible grounds for disqualification, but careful inquiry should be made at the time of making t he initial appointment. The disqualification standards established by § 455 are strict. Because a master is not a public judicial officer, it may be appropriate to permit the parties to consent to appointment of a particular person as master in circumstances that would require disqualification of a judge. The judge must be careful to ensure that no party feels any pressure to consent, but with such assurances—and with the judge's own determination that there is no troubling conflict of interests or disquieting appearance of impropriety—consent may justify an otherwise barred appointment.

One potential disqualification issue is peculiar to the master's role. It may happen that a master who is an attorney represents a client whose litigation is assigned to the judge who appointed the attorney as master. Other parties to the litigation may fear that the attorney-master will gain special respect from the judge. A flat prohibition on appearance before the appointing judge during the time of service as master, however, might in some circumstances unduly limit t he opportunity to make a desirable appointment. These matters may be regulated to some extent by state rules of professional responsibility. The question of present conflicts, and t he possibility of future conflicts, can be considered at the time of appointment. Depending on the circumstances, the judge may consider it appropriate to impose a non-appearance condition on the lawyer-master, and perhaps on the master's firm as well.

Subdivision (b). The order appointing a pretrial master is vitally important in informing the master and the parties about the nature and extent of the master's duties and authority. Care must be taken to make the order as precise as possible. The parties must be given notice and opportunity to be heard on the question whether a master should be appointed and on the terms of the appointment. To the extent possible, the notice should describe the master's proposed duties, time to complete the duties, standards of review, and compensation. Often it will be useful to engage the parties in the process of identifying the master, inviting nominations, and reviewing potential candidates. Party involvement may be particularly useful if a pretrial master is expected to promote settlement.

The hearing requirement of Rule 53(b)(1) can be satisfied by an opportunity to make written submissions unless the circumstances require live testimony.

Rule 53(b)(2) requires precise designation of the master's duties and authority. Clear identification of any investigating or enforcement duties is particularly important. Clear delineation of topics for any reports or recommendations is also an important part of this process. And it is important to protect against delay by establishing a time schedule for performing the assigned duties. Early designation of the procedure for fixing the master's compensation also may provide useful guidance to the parties.

Ex parte communications between a master and the court present troubling questions. Ordinarily the order should prohibit such communications, assuring that the parties know where authority is lodged at each step of the proceedings. Prohibiting ex parte communications between master and court also can enhance the role of a settlement master by assuring the parties that settlement can be fostered by confidential revelations that will not be shared with the court. Yet there may be circumstances in which the master's role is enhanced by the opportunity for ex parte communications with the court. A master assigned to help coordinate multiple proceedings, for example, may benefit from off-the-record exchanges with the court about logistical matters. The rule does not directly regulate these matters. It requires only that the court exercise its discretion and address the topic in the order of appointment.

Similarly difficult questions surround ex part e communications between a master and the parties. Ex parte communications may be essential in seeking to advance settlement. Ex parte communications also may prove useful in other settings, as with in camera review of documents to resolve privilege questions.

In most settings, however, ex parte communications with the parties should be discouraged or prohibited. The rule requires that the court address the topic in the order of appointment.

Subdivision (b)(2)(C) provides that the appointment order must state the nature of the materials to be preserved and filed as the record of the master's activities, and (b)(2)(D) requires that the order state the method of filing the record. It is not feasible to prescribe the nature of the record without regard to the nature of the master's duties. The records appropriate to discovery duties may be different from those appropriate to encouraging settlement, investigating possible violations of a complex decree, or making recommendations for trial findings. A basic requirement, however, is that the master must make and file a complete record of the evidence considered in making or recommending findings of fact on the basis of evidence. The order of appointment should routinely include this requirement unless the nature of the appointment precludes any prospect that the master will make or recommend evidence-based findings of fact. In some circumstances it may be appropriate for a party to file materials directly with the court as provided by Rule 5(e), but in many circumstances filing with the court may be inappropriate. Confidentiality is important with respect to many materials that may properly be considered by a master. Materials in the record can be transmitted to the court, and filed, in connection with review of a master's order, report, or recommendations under subdivisions (f) and (g). Independently of review proceedings, the court may direct filing of any materials that it wishes to make part of the public record.

The provision in subdivision (b)(2)(D) that the order must state the standards for reviewing the master's orders, findings, or recommendations is a reminder of t he provisions of subdivision (g)(3) that recognize stipulations for review less searching than the presumptive requirement of de novo decision by the court. Subdivision (b)(2)(D) does not authorize the court to supersede the limits of subdivision (g)(3).

In setting the procedure for fixing the master's compensation, it is useful at the outset to establish specific guidelines to control total expense. The court has power under subdivision (h) to change the basis and terms for determining compensation after notice to the parties.

Subdivision (b)(3) permits entry of the order appointing a master only after the master has filed an affidavit disclosing whether there is any ground for

disqualification under 28 U.S.C. § 455. If the affidavit discloses a possible ground for disqualification, the order can enter only if the court determines that there is no ground for disqualification or if the parties, knowing of the ground for disqualification, consent with the court's approval to waive the disqualification.

The provision in Rule 53(b)(4) for amending the order of appointment is as import ant as the provisions for the initial order. Anything that could be done in the initial order can be done by amendment. The hearing requirement can be satisfied by an opportunity to make written submissions unless the circumstances require live testimony.

Subdivision (c). Subdivision (c) is a simplification of the provisions scattered throughout present Rule 53. It is intended to provide the broad and flexible authority necessary to discharge the master's responsibilities. The most important delineation of a master's authority and duties is provided by the Rule 53(b) appointing order.

Subdivision (d). The subdivision (d) provisions for evidentiary hearings are reduced from t he extensive provisions in current Rule 53. This simplification of the rule is not intended to diminish the authority that may be delegated to a master. Reliance is placed on the broad and general terms of subdivision (c).

Subdivision (e). Subdivision (e) provides that a master's order must be filed and entered on the docket. It must be promptly served on the parties, a task ordinarily accomplished by mailing or other means as permitted by Rule 5(b). In some circumstances it may be appropriate to have the clerk's office assist the master in mailing the order to the parties.

Subdivision (f). Subdivision (f) restates some of the provisions of present Rule 53(e)(1). The report is the master's primary means of communication with the court. The materials to be provided to support review of the report will depend on the nature of the report. The master should provide all portions of the record preserved under Rule 53(b)(2)(C) that the master deems relevant to the report. The parties may designate additional materials from the record, and may seek permission to supplement the record with evidence. The court may direct that additional materials from the record be provided and filed. Given the wide array of tasks that may be assigned to a pretrial master, there may be circumstances that justify sealing a report or review record against public access—a report on continuing or failed settlement efforts is the most likely example. A post-trial master may be assigned duties in formulating a decree that deserve similar protection. Such circumstances may even justify denying access to the report or review materials by the parties, although this step should be taken only for the most compelling reasons. Sealing is much less likely to be appropriate with respect to a trial master's report.

Before formally making an order, report, or recommendations, a master may find it helpful to circulate a draft to the parties for review and comment. The usefulness of this practice depends on the nature of the master's proposed action.

Subdivision (g). The provisions of subdivision (g)(1), describing the court's powers to afford a hearing, take evidence, and act on a master's order, report, or recommendations are drawn from present Rule 53(e)(2), but are not limited, as present Rule 53(e)(2) is limited, to the report of a trial master in a nonjury action. The requirement that the court must afford an opportunity to be heard can be satisfied by taking written submissions when the court acts on the report without taking live testimony.

The subdivision (g)(2) time limits for objecting to—or seeking adoption or modification of—a master's order, report, or recommendations, are important. They are not jurisdictional. Although a court may properly refuse to entertain untimely review proceedings, the court may excuse the failure to seek timely review. The basic time period is lengthened to 20 days because the present 10-day period may be too short to permit thorough study and response to a complex report dealing with complex litigation. If no party asks the court to act on a master's report, the court is free to adopt the master's action or to disregard it at any relevant point in the proceedings.

Subdivision (g)(3) establishes the standards of review for a master's findings of fact or recommended findings of fact. The court must decide de novo all objections to findings of fact made or recommended by the master unless the parties stipulate, with the court's consent, t hat t he findings will be reviewed for clear error or—with respect to a master appointed on the parties' consent or appointed to address pretrial or post-trial matters—that the findings will be final. Clear-error review is more likely to be appropriate with respect to findings that do not go to the merits of the underlying claims or defenses, such as findings of fact bearing on a privilege objection to a discovery request. Even if no objection is made, the court is free to decide the facts de novo; to review for clear error if an earlier approved stipulation provided clear-error review; or to withdraw its consent to a stipulation for clear-error review or finality, and then to decide de novo. If the court withdraws its consent to a stipulation for finality or clear-error review, it may reopen the opportunity to object.

Under Rule 53(g)(4), the court must decide de novo all objections to conclusions of law made or recommended by a master. As with findings of fact, the court also may decide conclusions of law de novo when no objection is made.

Apart from factual and legal questions, masters often make determinations that, when made by a trial court, would be treated as matters of procedural discretion. The court may set a standard for review of such matters in the order of appointment, and may amend the order to establish the standard. If no standard is set by the original or amended order appointing the master, review of procedural matters is for abuse of discretion. The subordinate role of the master means that the trial court's review for abuse of discretion may be more searching than the review that an appellate court makes of a trial court.

If a master makes a recommendation on any matter that does not fall within Rule 53(g)(3), (4), or (5), the court may act on the recommendation under Rule 53(g)(1).

Subdivision (h). The need to pay compensation is a substantial reason for care in appointing private persons as masters.

Payment of the master's fees must be allocated among the parties and any property or subject-matter within the court's control. The amount in controversy and the means of the parties may provide some guidance in making the allocation. The nature of the dispute also may be important—parties pursuing matters of public interest, for example, may deserve special protection. A party whose unreasonable behavior has occasioned the need to appoint a master, on the other hand, may properly be charged all or a major portion of the master's fees. It may be proper to revise an interim allocation after decision on the merits. The revision need not await a decision that is final for purposes of appeal, but may be made to reflect disposition of a substantial portion of the case.

The basis and terms for fixing compensation should be stated in the order of appointment. The court retains power to alter the initial basis and terms, after notice and an opportunity to be heard, but should protect the parties against unfair surprise.

The provision of former Rule 53(a) that the "provision for compensation shall not apply when a United States Magistrate Judge is designated to serve as a master" is deleted as unnecessary. Other provisions of law preclude compensation.

Subdivision (i). Rule 53(i) carries forward unchanged former Rule 53(f).

2007 AMENDMENTS

The language of Rule 53 has been amended as part of the general restyling of the Civil Rules to make them more easily understood and to make style and terminology consistent throughout the rules. These changes are intended to be stylistic only.

2009 AMENDMENTS

The time set in the former rule at 20 days has been revised to 21 days. See the Note to Rule 6.

VII. JUDGMENT

Rule 54. Judgments; Costs

1937 ADOPTION

Note to Subdivision (a). The second sentence is derived substantially from former Equity Rule 71 (Form of Decree).

Note to Subdivision (b). This provides for the separate judgment of equity and code practice. See Wis.Stat. (1935) § 270.54; Compare N.Y.C.P.A. (1937) § 476.

Note to Subdivision (c). For the limitation on default contained in the first sentence, see 2 N.D.Comp.Laws Ann. (1913) § 7680; N.Y.C.P.A. (1937) § 479. Compare English Rules Under the Judicature Act (The Annual Practice, 1937) O. 13, r.r. 3 to 12. The remainder is a usual code provision. It makes clear that a judgment should give the relief to which a party is entitled, regardless of whether it is legal or equitable or both. This necessarily includes the deficiency judgment in foreclosure cases formerly provided for by Equity Rule 10 (Decree for Deficiency in Foreclosures, Etc.).

Note to Subdivision (d). For the present rule in common law actions, see *Ex parte Peterson*, 253 U.S. 300, 40 S. Ct. 543, 64 L.Ed. 919 (1920); Payne, Costs in Common Law Actions in the Federal Courts (1935), 21 Va.L.Rev. 397.

The provisions as to costs in actions *in forma pauperis* contained in U.S.C., Title 28, former §§ 832 to 836 are unaffected by this rule. Other sections of U.S.C., Title 28, which are unaffected by this rule are: former §§ 815 (Costs; plaintiff not entitled to, when), 821 (Costs; infringement of patent; disclaimer), 825 (Costs; several actions), 829 (Costs; attorney liable for, when), and 830 (Costs; bill of; taxation).

The provisions of the following and similar statutes as to costs against the United States and its officers and agencies are specifically continued:

U.S.C., Title 15, §§ 77v(a), 78aa, 79y (Securities and Exchange Commission)

U.S.C., Title 16, § 825p (Federal Power Commission)

U.S.C., Title 26, §§ 3679(d) and 3745(d) (Internal revenue actions)

U.S.C., Title 26, § 3770(b)(2) (Reimbursement of costs of recovery against revenue officers)

U.S.C., Title 28, former § 817 (Internal revenue actions)

U.S.C., Title 28, former § 836 (United States—actions *in forma pauperis*)

U.S.C., Title 28, former § 842 (Actions against revenue officers)

U.S.C., Title 28, former § 870 (United States—in certain cases)

U.S.C., Title 28, former § 906 (United States—foreclosure actions)

U.S.C., Title 47, § 401 (Communications Commission)

The provisions of the following and similar statutes as to costs are unaffected:

U.S.C., Title 7, § 210(f) (Actions for damages based on an order of the Secretary of Agriculture under Stockyards Act)

U.S.C., Title 7, § 499g(c) (Appeals from reparations orders of Secretary of Agriculture under Perishable Commodities Act)

U.S.C., Title 8, § 45 (Action against district attorneys in certain cases)

U.S.C., Title 15, § 15 (Actions for injuries due to violation of antitrust laws)

U.S.C., Title 15, § 72 (Actions for violation of law forbidding importation or sale of articles at less than market value or wholesale prices)

U.S.C., Title 15, § 77k (Actions by persons acquiring securities registered with untrue statements under Securities Act of 1933)

U.S.C., Title 15, § 78i(e) (Certain actions under the Securities Exchange Act of 1934)

U.S.C., Title 15, § 78r (Similar to 78i(e))

U.S.C., Title 15, § 96 (Infringement of trade-mark—damages)

U.S.C., Title 15, § 99 (Infringement of trade-mark—injunctions)

U.S.C., Title 15, § 124 (Infringement of trade-mark—damages)

U.S.C., Title 19, § 274 (Certain actions under customs law)

U.S.C., Title 30, § 32 (Action to determine right to possession of mineral lands in certain cases)

U.S.C., Title 31, §§ 232 and 234 (Action for making false claims upon United States)

U.S.C., Title 33, § 926 (Actions under Harbor Workers' Compensation Act)

U.S.C., Title 35, § 67 (Infringement of patent—damages)

U.S.C., Title 35, § 69 (Infringement of patent—pleading and proof)

U.S.C., Title 35, § 71 (Infringement of patent—when specification too broad)

U.S.C., Title 45, § 153p (Actions for non-compliance with an order of National R. R. Adjustment Board for payment of money)

U.S.C., Title 46, § 38 (Action for penalty for failure to register vessel)

U.S.C., Title 46, § 829 (Action based on non-compliance with an order of Maritime Commission for payment of money)

U.S.C., Title 46, § 941 (Certain actions under Ship Mortgage Act)

U.S.C., Title 46, § 1227 (Actions for damages for violation of certain provisions of the Merchant Marine Act, 1936)

U.S.C., Title 47, § 206 (Actions for certain violations of Communications Act of 1934)

U.S.C., Title 49, § 16(2) (Action based on non-compliance with an order of I.C.C. for payment of money)

1946 AMENDMENT

Note. The historic rule in the federal courts has always prohibited piecemeal disposal of litigation and permitted appeals only from final judgments except in those special instances covered by statute. *Hohorst v. Hamburg-American Packet Co., 1893*, 148 U.S. 262, 13 S. Ct. 590, 37 L.Ed. 443; *Rexford v. Brunswick-Balke-Collender Co., 1913*, 228 U.S. 339, 33 S. Ct. 515, 57 L.Ed. 864; *Collins v. Miller, 1920*, 252 U.S. 364, 40 S. Ct. 347, 64 L.Ed. 616. Rule 54(b) was originally adopted in view of the wide scope and possible content of the newly created "civil action" in order to avoid the possible injustice of a delay in judgment of a distinctly separate claim to await adjudication of the entire case. It was not designed to overturn the settled federal rule stated above, which, indeed, has more recently been reiterated in *Catlin v. United States, 1945*, 324 U.S. 229, 65 S. Ct. 631, 89 L.Ed. 911. See also *United States v. Florian, 1941*, 312 U.S. 656, 61 S. Ct. 713, 85 L.Ed. 1105; *Reeves v. Beardall, 1942*, 316 U.S. 283, 62 S. Ct. 1085, 86 L.Ed. 1478.

Unfortunately, this was not always understood, and some confusion ensued. Hence situations arose where district courts made a piecemeal disposition of an action and entered what the parties thought amounted to a judgment, although a trial remained to be had on other claims similar or identical with those disposed of. In the interim the parties did not know their ultimate rights, and accordingly took an appeal, thus putting the finality of the partial judgment in question. While most appellate courts have reached a result generally in accord with the intent of the rule, yet there have been divergent precedents and division of views which have served to render the issues more clouded to the parties appellant. It hardly seems a case where multiplicity of precedents will tend to remove the problem from debate. The problem is presented and discussed in the following cases: *Atwater v. North American Coal Corp., C.C.A.2, 1940*, 111 F.2d 125; *Rosenblum v. Dingfelder, C.C.A.2, 1940*, 111 F.2d 406; *Audi-Vision, Inc. v. RCA Mfg. Co., Inc., C.C.A.2, 1943*, 136 F.2d 621; *Zalkind v. Scheinman, C.C.A.2, 1943*, 139 F.2d 895; *Oppenheimer v. F. J. Young & Co., Inc., C.C.A.2, 1944*, 144 F.2d 387; *Libbey-Owens-Ford Glass Co. v. Sylvania Industrial Corp., C.C.A.2, 1946*, 154 F.2d 814, certiorari denied 328 U.S. 859, 66 S. Ct. 1353, 90 L.Ed. 1630; *Zarati Steamship Co. v. Park Bridge Corp., C.C.A.2, 1946*, 154 F.2d 377; *Baltimore and Ohio R. Co. v. United Fuel Gas Co., C.C.A.4, 1946*, 154 F.2d 545; *Jefferson Electric Co. v. Sola Electric Co., C.C.A.7, 1941*, 122 F.2d 124; *Leonard v. Socony-Vacuum Oil Co., C.C.A.7, 1942*, 130 F.2d 535; *Markham v. Kasper, C.C.A.7, 1945*, 152 F.2d 270; *Hanney v. Franklin Fire Ins. Co. of Philadelphia, C.C.A.9, 1944*, 142 F.2d 864; *Toomey v. Toomey, 1945*, 149 F.2d 19, 80 U.S.App. D.C. 77.

In view of the difficulty thus disclosed, the Advisory Committee in its two preliminary drafts of proposed amendments attempted to redefine the original rule with particular stress upon the interlocutory nature of partial judgments which did not adjudicate all claims arising out of a single transaction or occurrence. This attempt appeared to meet with almost universal approval from those of the profession commenting upon it, although there were, of course, helpful suggestions for additional changes in language or clarification of detail. But cf. Circuit Judge Frank's dissenting opinion in *Libbey-Owens-Ford Glass Co. v. Sylvania Industrial Corp.*, supra, n.21 of the dissenting opinion. The Committee, however, became convinced on careful study of its own proposals that the seeds of ambiguity still remained, and that it had not completely solved the problem of piecemeal appeals. After extended consideration, it concluded that a retention of the older federal rule was desirable and that this rule needed only the exercise of a discretionary power to afford a remedy in the infrequent harsh case to provide a simple, definite, workable rule. This is afforded by amended Rule 54(b). It re-establishes an ancient policy with clarity and precision. For the possibility of staying execution where not all claims are disposed of under Rule 54(b), see amended Rule 62(h).

1961 AMENDMENT

This rule permitting appeal, upon the trial court's determination of "no just reason for delay," from a judgment upon one or more but less than all the claims in an action, has generally been given a sympathetic construction by the courts and its validity is settled. *Reeves v. Beardall*, 316 U.S. 283, 62 S. Ct. 1085, 86 L.Ed. 1478 (1942); *Sears, Roebuck & Co. v. Mackey*, 351 U.S. 427, 76 S. Ct. 895, 100 L.Ed. 1297 (1956); *Cold Metal Process Co. v. United Engineering & Foundry Co.*, 351 U.S. 445, 76 S. Ct. 904, 100 L.Ed. 1311 (1956).

A serious difficulty has, however, arisen because the rule speaks of claims but nowhere mentions parties. A line of cases has developed in the circuits consistently holding the rule to be inapplicable to the dismissal, even with the requisite trial court determination, of one or more but less than all defendants jointly charged in an action, i. e. charged with various forms of concerted or related wrongdoing or related liability. See *Mull v. Ackerman*, 279 F.2d 25 (2d Cir.1960); *Richards v. Smith*, 276 F.2d 652 (5th Cir.1960); *Hardy v. Bankers Life & Cas. Co.*, 222 F.2d 827 (7th Cir.1955); *Steiner v. 20th Century-Fox Film Corp.*, 220 F.2d 105 (9th Cir.1955). For purposes of Rule 54(b) it was arguable that there were as many "claims" as there were parties defendant and that the rule in its present text applied where less than all of the parties were dismissed, cf. *United Artist Corp. v. Masterpiece Productions, Inc.*, 221 F.2d 213, 215 (2d Cir.1955); *Bowling Machines, Inc. v. First Nat. Bank*, 283 F.2d 39 (1st Cir. 1960); but the Courts of Appeals are now committed to an opposite view.

The danger of hardship through delay of appeal until the whole action is concluded may be at least as serious in the multiple-parties situations as in multiple-claims cases, see *Pabellon v. Grace Line, Inc.*, 191 F.2d 169, 179 (2d Cir.1951), cert. denied, 342 U.S. 893, 72 S. Ct. 201, 96 L.Ed. 669 (1951), and courts and commentators have urged that Rule 54(b) be changed to take in the former. See *Reagan v. Traders & General Ins. Co.*, 255 F.2d 845 (5th Cir.1958); *Meadows v. Greyhound Corp.*, 235 F.2d 233 (5th Cir.1956); *Steiner v. 20th Century-Fox Film Corp.*, supra; 6 Moore's Federal Practice ¶ 54.34[2] (2d ed. 1953); 3 Barron & Holtzoff, *Federal Practice & Procedure* § 1193.2 (Wright ed. 1958); *Developments in the Law—Multiparty Litigation,* 71 Harv.L.Rev. 874, 981 (1958); Note, 62 Yale L.J. 263, 271 (1953); Ill.Ann.Stat. ch. 110, § 50(2) (Smith-Hurd 1956). The amendment accomplishes this purpose by referring explicitly to parties.

There has been some recent indication that interlocutory appeal under the provisions of 28 U.S.C. § 1292(b), added in 1958, may now be available for the multiple-parties cases here considered. See *Jaftex Corp. v. Randolph Mills, Inc.*, 282 F.2d 508 (2d Cir.1960). The Rule 54(b) procedure seems preferable for those cases, and § 1292(b) should be held inapplicable to them when the rule is enlarged as here proposed. See *Luckenbach Steamship Co., Inc. v. H. Muehlstein & Co., Inc.*, 280 F.2d 755, 757 (2d Cir.1960); 1 Barron & Holtzoff, supra, § 58.1, p. 321 (Wright ed. 1960).

1987 AMENDMENT

The amendment is technical. No substantive change is intended.

1993 AMENDMENT

Subdivision (d). This revision adds paragraph (2) to this subdivision to provide for a frequently recurring form of litigation not initially contemplated by the rules—disputes over the amount of attorneys' fees to be awarded in the large number of actions in which prevailing parties may be entitled to such awards or in which the court must determine the fees to be paid from a common fund. This revision seeks to harmonize and clarify procedures that have been developed through case law and local rules.

Paragraph (1). Former subdivision (d), providing for taxation of costs by the clerk, is renumbered as paragraph (1) and revised to exclude applications for attorneys' fees.

Paragraph (2). This new paragraph establishes a procedure for presenting claims for attorneys' fees, whether or not denominated as "costs." It applies also to requests for reimbursement of expenses, not taxable as costs, when recoverable under governing law incident to the award of fees. *Cf. West Virginia Univ. Hosp. v. Casey*, 499 U.S. 83 (1991), holding, prior to the Civil Rights Act of 1991, that expert witness fees were not recoverable under 42 U.S.C. § 1988. As noted in subparagraph (A), it does not, however, apply to fees recoverable as an element of damages, as when sought under the terms of a contract; such damages typically are to be claimed in a pleading and may involve issues to be resolved by a jury. Nor, as provided in subparagraph (E), does it apply to awards of fees as sanctions authorized or mandated under these rules or under 28 U.S.C. § 1927.

Subparagraph (B) provides a deadline for motions for attorneys' fees—14 days after final judgment unless the court or a statute specifies some other time. One purpose of this provision is to assure that the opposing party is informed of the claim before the time for appeal has elapsed. Prior law did not prescribe any specific time limit on claims for attorneys' fees. *White v. New Hampshire Dep't of Employment Sec.*, 455 U.S. 445, 102 S. Ct. 1162, 71 L. Ed. 2d 325 (1982). In many nonjury cases the court will want to consider attorneys' fee issues immediately after rendering its judgment on the merits of the case. Note that the time for making claims is specifically stated in some legislation, such as the Equal Access to Justice Act, 28 U.S.C. § 2412(d)(1)(B) (30-day filing period).

Prompt filing affords an opportunity for the court to resolve fee disputes shortly after trial, while the services performed are freshly in mind. It also enables the court in appropriate circumstances to make its ruling on a fee request in time for any appellate review of a dispute over fees to proceed at the same time as review on the merits of the case.

Filing a motion for fees under this subdivision does not affect the finality or the appealability of a judgment, though revised Rule 58 provides a mechanism by which prior to appeal the court can suspend the finality to resolve a motion for fees. If an appeal on the merits of the case is taken, the court may rule on the claim for fees, may defer its ruling on the motion, or may deny the motion without prejudice, directing under subdivision (d)(2)(B) a new period for filing after the appeal has been resolved. A notice of appeal does not extend the time for filing a fee claim based on the initial judgment, but the court under subdivision (d)(2)(B) may effectively extend the period by permitting claims to be filed after resolution of the appeal. A new period for filing will automatically begin if a new judgment is entered following a reversal or remand by the appellate court or the granting of a motion under Rule 59.

The rule does not require that the motion be supported at the time of filing with the evidentiary material bearing on the fees. This material must of course be submitted in due course, according to such schedule as the court may direct in light of the circumstances of the case. What is required is the filing of a motion sufficient to alert the adversary and the court that there is a claim for fees and the amount of such fees (or a fair estimate).

If directed by the court, the moving party is also required to disclose any fee agreement, including those between attorney and client, between attorneys sharing a fee to be awarded, and between adversaries made in partial settlement of a dispute where the settlement must be implemented by court action as may be required by Rules 23(e) and 23.1 or other like provisions. With respect to the fee arrangements requiring court approval, the court may also by local rule require disclosure immediately after such arrangements are agreed to. *E.g.*, Rule 5 of United States District Court for the Eastern District of New York; *cf. In re "Agent Orange" Product Liability Litigation (MDL 381)*, 611 F.Supp. 1452, 1464 (E.D.N.Y.1985).

In the settlement of class actions resulting in a common fund from which fees will be sought, courts frequently have required that claims for fees be presented in advance of hearings to consider approval of the proposed settlement. The rule does not affect this practice, as it permits the court to require submissions of fee claims in advance of entry of judgment.

Subparagraph (C) assures the parties of an opportunity to make an appropriate presentation with respect to issues involving the evaluation of legal services. In some cases, an evidentiary hearing may be needed, but this is not required in every case. The amount of time to be allowed for the preparation of submissions both in support of and in opposition to awards should be tailored to the particular case.

The court is explicitly authorized to make a determination of the liability for fees before receiving submissions by the parties bearing on the amount of an award. This option may be appropriate in actions in which the liability issue is doubtful and the evaluation issues are numerous and complex.

The court may order disclosure of additional information, such as that bearing on prevailing local rates or on the appropriateness of particular services for which compensation is sought.

On rare occasion, the court may determine that discovery under Rules 26 to 37 would be useful to the parties. *Compare* Rules Governing Section 2254 Cases in the U.S. District Courts, Rule 6. *See* Note, *Determining the Reasonableness of Attorneys' Fees—the Discoverability of Billing Records*, 64 *B.U.L.Rev.* 241 (1984). In complex fee disputes, the court may use case management techniques to limit the scope of the dispute or to facilitate the settlement of fee award disputes.

Fee awards should be made in the form of a separate judgment under Rule 58 since such awards are subject to review in the court of appeals. To facilitate review, the paragraph provides that the court set forth its findings and conclusions as under Rule 52(a), though in most cases this explanation could be quite brief.

Subparagraph (D) explicitly authorizes the court to establish procedures facilitating the efficient and fair resolution of fee claims. A local rule, for example, might call for matters to be presented through affidavits, or might provide for issuance of proposed findings by the court, which would be treated as accepted by the parties unless objected to within a specified time. A court might also consider establishing a schedule reflecting customary fees or factors affecting fees within the community, as implicitly suggested by Justice O'Connor in *Pennsylvania v. Delaware Valley Citizens' Council*, 483 U.S. 711, 733, 107 S. Ct. 3078, 3091, 97 L. Ed. 2d 585 (1987) (O'Connor, J., concurring)(how particular markets compensate for contingency). *Cf. Thompson v. Kennickell*, 710 F.Supp. 1 (D.D.C.1989) (use of findings in other cases to promote consistency). The parties, of course, should be permitted to show that in the circumstances of the case such a schedule should not be applied or that different hourly rates would be appropriate.

The rule also explicitly permits, without need for a local rule, the court to refer issues regarding the amount of a fee award in a particular case to a master under Rule 53. The district judge may designate a magistrate judge to act as a master for this purpose or may refer a motion for attorneys' fees to a magistrate judge for proposed findings and recommendations under Rule 72(b). This authorization eliminates any controversy as to whether such references are permitted under Rule 53(b) as "matters of account and of difficult computation of damages" and whether motions for attorneys' fees can be treated as the equivalent of a dispositive pretrial matter that can be referred to a magistrate judge. For consistency and efficiency, all such matters might be referred to the same magistrate judge.

Subparagraph (E) excludes from this rule the award of fees as sanctions under these rules or under 28 U.S.C. § 1927.

2002 AMENDMENT

Subdivision (d)(2)(C) is amended to delete the requirement that judgment on a motion for attorney fees be set forth in a separate document. This change complements the amendment of Rule 58(a)(1), which deletes the separate document requirement for an order disposing of a motion for attorney fees under Rule 54. These changes are made to support amendment of Rule 4 of the Federal Rules of Appellate Procedure. It continues to be important that a district court make clear its meaning when it intends an order to be the final disposition of a motion for attorney fees.

The requirement in subdivision (d)(2)(B) that a motion for attorney fees be not only filed but also served no later than 14 days after entry of judgment is changed to require filing only, to establish a parallel with Rules 50, 52, and 59. Service continues to be required under Rule 5(a).

2003 AMENDMENT

Rule 54(d)(2)(D) is revised to reflect amendments to Rule 53.

2007 AMENDMENTS

The language of Rule 54 has been amended as part of the general restyling of the Civil Rules to make them more easily understood and to make style and terminology consistent throughout the rules. These changes are intended to be stylistic only.

The words "or class member" have been removed from Rule 54(d)(2)(C) because Rule 23(h)(2) now addresses objections by class members to attorney-fee motions. Rule 54(d)(2)(C) is amended to recognize that Rule 23(h) now controls those aspects of attorney-fee motions in class actions to which it is addressed.

2009 AMENDMENTS

Former Rule 54(d)(1) provided that the clerk may tax costs on 1 day's notice. That period was unrealistically short. The new 14 day period provides a better opportunity to prepare and present a response. The former 5 day period to serve a motion to review the clerk's action is extended to 7 days to reflect the change in the Rule 6(a) method for computing periods of less than 11 days.

Rule 55. Default

1937 ADOPTION

This represents the joining of the equity decree *pro confesso* (former Equity Rules 12 (Issue of Subpoena—Time for Answer), 16 (Defendant to Answer—Default—Decree *Pro Confesso*), 17 (Decree *Pro Confesso* to be Followed by Final Decree—Setting Aside Default), 29 (Defenses—How Presented), 31 (Reply—When Required—When Cause at Issue)) and the judgment by default now governed by U.S.C., Title 28, former § 724 (Conformity Act). For dismissal of an action for failure to comply with these rules or any order of the court, see Rule 41(b).

Note to Subdivision (a). The provision for the entry of default comes from the Massachusetts practice, 2 Mass.Gen. Laws (Ter.Ed., 1932) ch. 231, § 57. For affidavit of default, see 2 Minn.Stat. (Mason, 1927) § 9256.

Note to Subdivision (b). The provision in paragraph (1) for the entry of judgment by the clerk when plaintiff claims a sum certain is found in the N.Y.C. P.A. (1937) § 485, in Calif.Code Civ.Proc. (Deering, 1937) § 585(1), and in Conn. Practice Book (1934) § 47. For provisions similar to paragraph (2), compare Calif.Code, *supra*, § 585(2); N.Y.C.P.A. (1937) § 490; 2 Minn.Stat. (Mason, 1927) § 9256(3); 2 Wash.Rev.Stat.Ann. (Remington, 1932) § 411(2); U.S.C., Title 28, § 1874, formerly § 785 (Action to recover forfeiture in bond) and similar statutes are preserved by the last clause of paragraph (2).

Note to Subdivision (e). This restates substantially the last clause of U.S.C., Title 28, former § 763 (Action against the United States under the Tucker Act). As this rule governs in all actions against the United States, U.S.C., Title 28, former § 45 (Practice and procedure in certain cases under the interstate commerce laws) and similar statutes are modified in so far as they contain anything inconsistent therewith.

SUPPLEMENTARY NOTE OF ADVISORY COMMITTEE REGARDING THIS RULE

Note. The operation of Rule 55(b) (Judgment) is directly affected by the Soldiers' and Sailors' Civil Relief Act of 1940, 50 U.S.C., Appendix, §§ 501 et seq. Section 200 of the Act [50 U.S.C.A. Appendix, § 520] imposes specific requirements which must be fulfilled before a default judgment can be entered, e.g., *Ledwith v. Storkan, D.Neb.1942, 6 Fed.Rule Serv. 60b.24, Case 2*, 2 F.R.D. 539, and also provides for the vacation of a judgment in certain circumstances. See discussion in Commentary, Effect of Conscription Legislation on the Federal Rules, 1940, 3 Fed.Rules Serv. 725; 3 Moore's Federal Practice, 1938, Cum.Supplement § 55.02.

1987 AMENDMENT

The amendments are technical. No substantive change is intended.

2007 AMENDMENTS

The language of Rule 55 has been amended as part of the general restyling of the Civil Rules to make them more easily understood and to make style and terminology consistent throughout the rules. These changes are intended to be stylistic only.

Former Rule 55(a) directed the clerk to enter a default when a party failed to plead or otherwise defend "as provided by these rules." The implication from the reference to defending "as provided by these rules" seemed to be that the clerk should enter a default even if a party did something showing an intent to defend, but that act was not specifically described by the rules. Courts in fact have rejected that implication. Acts that show an intent to defend have frequently prevented a default even though not connected to any particular rule. "[A]s provided by these rules" is deleted to reflect Rule 55(a)'s actual meaning.

Amended Rule 55 omits former Rule 55(d), which included two provisions. The first recognized that Rule 55 applies to described claimants. The list was incomplete and unnecessary. Rule 55(a) applies Rule 55 to any party against whom a judgment for affirmative relief is requested. The second provision was a redundant reminder that Rule 54(c) limits the relief available by default judgment.

2009 AMENDMENTS

The time set in the former rule at 3 days has been revised to 7 days. See the Note to Rule 6.

2015 AMENDMENT

Rule 55(c) is amended to make plain the interplay between Rules 54(b), 55(c), and 60(b). A default judgment that does not dispose of all of the claims among all parties is not a final judgment unless the court directs entry of final judgment under Rule 54(b). Until final judgment is entered, Rule 54(b) allows revision of the default judgment at any time. The demanding standards set by Rule 60(b) apply only in seeking relief from a final judgment.

Rule 56. Summary Judgment

1937 ADOPTION

This rule is applicable to all actions, including those against the United States or an officer or agency thereof.

Summary judgment procedure is a method for promptly disposing of actions in which there is no genuine issue as to any material fact. It has been extensively used in England for more than 50 years and has been adopted in a number of American states. New York, for example, has made great use of it. During the first nine years after its adoption there, the records of New York county alone show 5,600 applications for summary judgments. Report of the Commission on the Administration of Justice in New York State (1934), p. 383. See also Third Annual Report of the Judicial Council of the State of New York (1937), p. 30.

In England it was first employed only in cases of liquidated claims, but there has been a steady enlargement of the scope of the remedy until it is now used in actions to recover land or chattels and in all other actions at law, for liquidated or unliquidated claims, except for a few designated torts and breach of promise of marriage. English Rules Under the Judicature Act (The Annual Practice, 1937) O. 3, r. 6; Orders 14, 14A, and 15; see also O. 32, r. 6, authorizing an application for judgment at any time upon admissions. In Michigan (3 Comp.Laws (1929) § 14260) and Illinois (Smith-Hurd Ill.Stats. c. 110, §§ 181, 259.15, 259.16), it is not limited to liquidated demands. New York (N.Y.R.C.P. (1937) Rule 113; see also Rule 107) has brought so many classes of actions under the operation of the rule that the Commission on Administration of Justice in New York State (1934) recommend that all restrictions be removed and that the remedy be available "in any action" (p. 287). For the history and nature of the summary judgment procedure and citations of state statutes, see Clark and Samenow, The Summary Judgment (1929), 38 Yale L.J. 423.

Note to Subdivision (d). See Rule 16 (Pre-Trial Procedure; Formulating Issues) and the **Note** thereto.

Note to Subdivisions (e) and (f). These are similar to rules in Michigan. Mich. Court Rules Ann. (Searl, 1933) Rule 30.

1946 AMENDMENT

Note to Subdivision (a). The amendment allows a claimant to move for a summary judgment at any time after the expiration of 20 days from the commencement of the action or after service of a motion for summary judgment by the adverse party. This will normally operate to permit an earlier motion by the claimant than under the original rule, where the phrase "at any time after the pleading in answer thereto has been served" operates to prevent a claimant from moving for summary judgment, even in a case clearly proper for its exercise, until a formal answer has been filed. Thus in *Peoples Bank v. Federal Reserve Bank of San Francisco, Cal. 1944*, 58 F.Supp. 25, the plaintiff's countermotion for a summary judgment was stricken as premature, because the defendant had not filed an answer. Since Rule 12(a) allows at least 20 days for an answer, that time plus the 10 days required in Rule 56(c) means that under original Rule 56(a) a minimum period of 30 days necessarily has to elapse in every case before the claimant can be heard on his right to a summary judgment. An extension of time by the court or the service of preliminary motions of any kind will prolong that period even further. In many cases this merely represents unnecessary delay. See *United States v. Adler's Creamery, Inc., C.C.A.2, 1939*, 107 F.2d 987. The changes are in the interest of more expeditious litigation. The 20-day period, as provided, gives the defendant an opportunity to secure counsel and determine a course of action. But in a case where the defendant himself makes a motion for summary judgment within that time, there is no reason to restrict the plaintiff and the amended rule so provides.

Subdivision (c). The amendment of Rule 56(c), by the addition of the final sentence, resolves a doubt expressed in *Sartor v. Arkansas Natural Gas Corp., 1944*, 321 U.S. 620, 64 S. Ct. 724, 88 L.Ed. 967. See also Commentary, Summary Judgment as to Damages, 1944, 7 Fed. Rules Serv. 974; *Madeirense do Brasil S/A v. Stulman-Emrick Lumber Co., C.C.A.2d, 1945*, 147 F.2d 399, certiorari denied 325 U.S. 861, 65 S. Ct. 1201, 89 L.Ed. 1982. It makes clear that although the question of recovery depends on the amount of damages, the summary judgment rule is applicable and summary judgment may be granted in a proper case. If the case is not fully adjudicated it may be dealt with as provided in subdivision (d) of Rule 56, and the right to summary recovery determined by a preliminary order, interlocutory in character, and the precise amount of recovery left for trial.

Subdivision (d). Rule 54(a) defines "judgment" as including a decree and "any order from which an appeal lies." Subdivision (d) of Rule 56 indicates clearly, however, that a partial summary "judgment" is not a final judgment, and, therefore, that it is not appealable, unless in the particular case some statute allows an appeal from the interlocutory order involved. The partial summary judgment is merely a pretrial adjudication that certain issues shall be deemed established for the trial of the case. This adjudication is more nearly akin to the preliminary order under Rule 16, and likewise serves the purpose of speeding up litigation by eliminating before trial matters wherein there is no genuine issue of fact. See *Leonard v. Socony-Vacuum Oil Co., C.C.A.7, 1942*, 130 F.2d 535; *Biggins v. Oltmer Iron Works, C.C.A.7, 1946*, 154 F.2d 214, 3 Moore's Federal Practice, 1938, 3190–3192. Since interlocutory appeals are not allowed, except where specifically provided by statute, see 3 Moore, op. cit. supra, 3155–3156, this interpretation is in line with that policy, *Leonard v. Socony-Vacuum Oil Co.*, supra. See also *Audi-Vision, Inc. v. RCA Mfg. Co., C.C.A.2, 1943*, 136 F.2d 621; *Toomey v. Toomey, App.D.C. 1945*, 149 F.2d 19, 80 U.S.App.D.C. 77; *Biggins v. Oltmer Iron Works*, supra; *Catlin v. United States, 1945*, 324 U.S. 229, 65 S. Ct. 631, 89 L.Ed. 911.

1963 AMENDMENT

Subdivision (c). By the amendment "answers to interrogatories" are included among the materials which may be considered on motion for summary judgment. The phrase was inadvertently omitted from the rule, see 3 Barron & Holtzoff, Federal Practice & Procedure 159 to 60 (Wright ed. 1958), and the courts have generally reached by interpretation the result which will hereafter be required by the text of the amended rule. See Annot., 74 A.L.R.2d 984 (1960).

Subdivision (e). The words "answers to interrogatories" are added in the third sentence of this subdivision to conform to the amendment of subdivision (c).

The last two sentences are added to overcome a line of cases, chiefly in the Third Circuit, which has impaired the utility of the summary judgment device. A typical case is as follows: A party supports his motion for summary judgment by affidavits or other evidentiary matter sufficient to show that there is no genuine issue as to a material fact. The adverse party, in opposing the motion, does not produce any evidentiary matter, or produces some but not enough to establish that there is a genuine issue for trial. Instead, the adverse party rests on averments of his pleadings which on their face present an issue. In this situation Third Circuit cases have taken the view that summary judgment must be denied, at least if the averments are "well-pleaded," and not suppositious, conclusory, or ultimate. See *Frederick Hart & Co., Inc. v. Recordgraph Corp.*, 169 F.2d 580 (3d Cir.1948); *United States ex rel. Kolton v. Halpern*, 260 F.2d 590 (3d Cir.1958); *United States ex rel. Nobles v. Ivey Bros. Constr. Co., Inc.*, 191 F.Supp. 383 (D.Del.1961); *Jamison v. Pennsylvania Salt Mfg. Co.*, 22 F.R.D. 238 (W.D.Pa.1958); *Bunny Bear, Inc. v. Dennis Mitchell Industries*, 139 F.Supp. 542 (E.D.Pa.1956); *Levy v. Equitable Life Assur. Society*, 18 F.R.D. 164 (E.D.Pa. 1955).

The very mission of the summary judgment procedure is to pierce the pleadings and to assess the proof in order to see whether there is a genuine need for trial. The Third Circuit doctrine, which permits the pleadings themselves to stand in the way of granting an otherwise justified summary judgment, is incompatible with the basic purpose of the rule. See 6 Moore's Federal Practice 2069 (2d ed. 1953); 3 Barron & Holtzoff, supra, § 1235.1.

It is hoped that the amendment will contribute to the more effective utilization of the salutary device of summary judgment.

The amendment is not intended to derogate from the solemnity of the pleadings. Rather it recognizes that, despite the best efforts of counsel to make his pleadings accurate, they may be overwhelmingly contradicted by the proof available to his adversary.

Nor is the amendment designed to affect the ordinary standards applicable to the summary judgment motion. So, for example: Where an issue as to a material fact cannot be resolved without observation of the demeanor of witnesses in order to evaluate their credibility, summary judgment is not appropriate. Where the evidentiary matter in support of the motion does not establish the absence of a genuine issue, summary judgment must be denied even if no opposing evidentiary matter is presented. And summary judgment may be inappropriate where the party opposing it shows under subdivision (f) that he cannot at the time present facts essential to justify his opposition.

1987 AMENDMENT

The amendments are technical. No substantive change is intended.

2007 AMENDMENTS

The language of Rule 56 has been amended as part of the general restyling of the Civil Rules to make them more easily understood and to make style and terminology consistent throughout the rules. These changes are intended to be stylistic only.

Former Rule 56(a) and (b) referred to summary-judgment motions on or against a claim, counterclaim, or crossclaim, or to obtain a declaratory judgment. The list was incomplete. Rule 56 applies to third-party claimants, intervenors, claimants in interpleader, and others. Amended Rule 56(a) and (b) carry forward the present meaning by referring to a party claiming relief and a party against whom relief is sought.

Former Rule 56(c), (d), and (e) stated circumstances in which summary judgment "shall be rendered," the court "shall if practicable" ascertain facts existing without substantial controversy, and "if appropriate, shall" enter summary judgment. In each place "shall" is changed to "should." It is established that although there is no discretion to enter summary judgment when there is a genuine issue as to any material fact, there is discretion to deny summary judgment when it appears that there is no genuine issue as to any material fact. *Kennedy v. Silas Mason Co.*, 334 U.S. 249, 256–257 (1948). Many lower court decisions are gathered in 10A Wright, Miller & Kane, Federal Practice & Procedure: Civil 3d, § 2728. "Should" in amended Rule 56(c) recognizes that courts will seldom exercise the discretion to deny summary judgment when there is no genuine issue as to any material fact. Similarly sparing exercise of this discretion is appropriate under Rule 56(e)(2). Rule 56(d)(1), on the other hand, reflects the more open-ended discretion to decide whether it is practicable to determine what material facts are not genuinely at issue.

Former Rule 56(d) used a variety of different phrases to express the Rule 56(c) standard for summary judgment—that there is no genuine issue as to any material fact. Amended Rule 56(d) adopts terms directly parallel to Rule 56(c).

2009 AMENDMENTS

The timing provisions for summary judgment are outmoded. They are consolidated and substantially revised in new subdivision (c)(1). The new rule allows a party to move for summary judgment at any time, even as early as the commencement of the action. If the motion seems premature both subdivision (c)(1) and Rule 6(b) allow the court to extend the time to respond. The rule does set a presumptive deadline at 30 days after the close of all discovery.

The presumptive timing rules are default provisions that may be altered by an order in the case or by local rule. Scheduling orders are likely to supersede the rule provisions in most cases, deferring summary-judgment motions until a stated time or establishing different deadlines. Scheduling orders tailored to the needs of the specific case, perhaps adjusted as it progresses, are likely to work better than default rules. A scheduling order may be adjusted to adopt the parties' agreement on timing, or may require that discovery and motions occur in stages — including separation of expert-witness discovery from other discovery.

Local rules may prove useful when local docket conditions or practices are incompatible with the general Rule 56 timing provisions.

If a motion for summary judgment is filed before a responsive pleading is due from a party affected by the motion, the time for responding to the motion is 21 days after the responsive pleading is due.

2010 AMENDMENT

Rule 56 is revised to improve the procedures for presenting and deciding summary-judgment motions and to make the procedures more consistent with those already used in many courts. The standard for granting summary judgment remains unchanged. The language of subdivision (a) continues to require that there be no genuine dispute as to any material fact and that the movant be entitled to judgment as a matter of law. The amendments will not affect continuing development of the decisional law construing and applying these phrases.

Subdivision (a). Subdivision (a) carries forward the summary-judgment standard expressed in former subdivision (c), changing only one word--genuine "issue" becomes genuine "dispute." "Dispute" better reflects the focus of a summary-judgment determination. As explained below, "shall" also is restored to the place it held from 1938 to 2007.

The first sentence is added to make clear at the beginning that summary judgment may be requested not only as to an entire case but also as to a claim, defense, or part of a claim or defense. The subdivision caption adopts the common phrase "partial summary judgment" to describe disposition of less than the whole action, whether or not the order grants all the relief requested by the motion.

"Shall" is restored to express the direction to grant summary judgment. The word "shall" in Rule 56 acquired significance over many decades of use. Rule 56 was amended in 2007 to replace "shall" with "should" as part of the Style Project, acting under a convention that prohibited any use of "shall." Comments on proposals to amend Rule 56, as published in 2008, have shown that neither of the choices available under the Style Project conventions -- "must" or "should"--is suitable in light of the case law on whether a district court has discretion to deny summary judgment when there appears to be no genuine dispute as to any material fact. Compare Anderson v. Liberty Lobby, Inc., 477 U.S. 242, 255 (1986)("Neither do we suggest that the trial courts should act other than with caution in granting summary judgment or that the trial court may not deny summary judgment in a case in which there is reason to believe that the better course would be to proceed to a full trial. Kennedy v. Silas Mason Co., 334 U.S. 249 * * * (1948))," with Celotex Corp. v. Catrett, 477 U.S. 317, 322 (1986)("In our view, the plain language of Rule 56(c) mandates the entry of summary judgment, after adequate time for discovery and upon motion, against a party who fails to make a showing sufficient to establish the existence of an element essential to that party's case, and on which that party will bear the burden of proof at trial."). Eliminating "shall" created an unacceptable risk of changing the summary-judgment standard. Restoring "shall" avoids the unintended consequences of any other word.

Subdivision (a) also adds a new direction that the court should state on the record the reasons for granting or denying the motion. Most courts recognize this practice. Among other advantages, a statement of reasons can facilitate an appeal or subsequent trial-court proceedings. It is particularly important to state the reasons for granting summary judgment. The form and detail of the statement of reasons are left to the court's discretion.

The statement on denying summary judgment need not address every available reason. But identification of central issues may help the parties to focus further proceedings.

Subdivision (b). The timing provisions in former subdivisions (a) and (c) are superseded. Although the rule allows a motion for summary judgment to be filed at the commencement of an action, in many cases the motion will be premature until the nonmovant has had time to file a responsive pleading or other pretrial proceedings have been had. Scheduling orders or other pretrial orders can regulate timing to fit the needs of the case.

Subdivision (c). Subdivision (c) is new. It establishes a common procedure for several aspects of summary-judgment motions synthesized from similar elements developed in the cases or found in many local rules.

Subdivision (c)(1) addresses the ways to support an assertion that a fact can or cannot be genuinely disputed. It does not address the form for providing the required support. Different courts and judges have adopted different forms including, for example, directions that the support be included in the motion, made part of a separate statement of facts, interpolated in the body of a brief or memorandum, or provided in a separate statement of facts included in a brief or memorandum.

Subdivision (c)(1)(A) describes the familiar record materials commonly relied upon and requires that the movant cite the particular parts of the materials that support its fact positions. Materials that are not yet in the record--including materials referred to in an affidavit or declaration--must be placed in the record. Once materials are in the record, the court may, by order in the case, direct that the materials be gathered in an appendix, a party may voluntarily submit an appendix, or the parties may submit a joint appendix. The appendix procedure also may be established by local rule. Pointing to a specific location in an appendix satisfies the citation requirement. So too it may be convenient to direct that a party assist the court in locating materials buried in a voluminous record.

Subdivision (c)(1)(B) recognizes that a party need not always point to specific record materials. One party, without citing any other materials, may respond or reply that materials cited to dispute or support a fact do not establish the absence or presence of a genuine dispute. And a party who does not have the trial burden of production may rely on a showing that a party who does have the trial burden cannot produce admissible evidence to carry its burden as to the fact.

Subdivision (c)(2) provides that a party may object that material cited to support or dispute a fact cannot be presented in a form that would be admissible in evidence. The objection functions much as an objection at trial, adjusted for the pretrial setting. The burden is on the proponent to show that the material is admissible as presented or to explain the admissible form that is anticipated. There is no need to make a separate motion to strike. If the case goes to trial, failure to challenge admissibility at the summary-judgment stage does not forfeit the right to challenge admissibility at trial.

Subdivision (c)(3) reflects judicial opinions and local rules provisions stating that the court may decide a motion for summary judgment without undertaking an independent search of the record. Nonetheless, the rule also recognizes that a court may consider record materials not called to its attention by the parties.

Subdivision (c)(4) carries forward some of the provisions of former subdivision (e)(1). Other provisions are relocated or omitted. The requirement that a sworn or certified copy of a paper referred to in an affidavit or declaration be attached to the affidavit or declaration is omitted as unnecessary given the requirement in subdivision (c)(1)(A) that a statement or dispute of fact be supported by materials in the record.

A formal affidavit is no longer required. 28 U.S.C. § 1746 allows a written unsworn declaration, certificate, verification, or statement subscribed in proper form as true under penalty of perjury to substitute for an affidavit.

Subdivision (d). Subdivision (d) carries forward without substantial change the provisions of former subdivision (f).

A party who seeks relief under subdivision (d) may seek an order deferring the time to respond to the summary-judgment motion.

Subdivision (e). Subdivision (e) addresses questions that arise when a party fails to support an assertion of fact or fails to properly address another party's assertion of fact as required by Rule 56(c). As explained below, summary judgment cannot be granted by default even if there is a complete failure to respond to the motion, much less when an attempted response fails to comply with Rule 56(c) requirements. Nor should it be denied by default even if the movant completely fails to reply to a nonmovant's response. Before deciding on other possible action, subdivision (e)(1) recognizes that the court may afford an opportunity to properly support or address the fact. In many circumstances this opportunity will be the court's preferred first step.

Subdivision (e)(2) authorizes the court to consider a fact as undisputed for purposes of the motion when response or reply requirements are not satisfied. This approach reflects the "deemed admitted" provisions in many local rules. The fact is considered undisputed only for purposes of the motion; if summary judgment is denied, a party who failed to make a proper Rule 56 response or reply remains free to contest the fact in further proceedings. And the court may choose not to consider the fact as undisputed, particularly if the court knows of record materials that show grounds for genuine dispute.

Subdivision (e)(3) recognizes that the court may grant summary judgment only if the motion and supporting materials--including the facts considered undisputed under subdivision (e)(2)--show that the movant is entitled to it. Considering some facts undisputed does not of itself allow summary judgment. If there is a proper response or reply as to some facts, the court cannot grant summary judgment without determining whether those facts can be genuinely disputed. Once the court has determined the set of facts--both those it has chosen to consider undisputed for want of a proper response or reply and any that cannot be genuinely disputed despite a procedurally proper response or reply--it must determine the legal consequences of these facts and permissible inferences from them.

Subdivision (e)(4) recognizes that still other orders may be appropriate. The choice among possible orders should be designed to encourage proper presentation of the record. Many courts take extra care with pro se litigants, advising them of the need to respond and the risk of losing by summary judgment if an adequate response is not filed. And the court may seek to reassure itself by some examination of the record before granting summary judgment against a pro se litigant.

Subdivision (f). Subdivision (f) brings into Rule 56 text a number of related procedures that have grown up in practice. After giving notice and a reasonable time to respond the court may grant summary judgment for the nonmoving party; grant a motion on legal or factual grounds not raised by the parties; or consider summary judgment on its own. In many cases it may prove useful first to invite a motion; the invited motion will automatically trigger the regular procedure of subdivision (c).

Subdivision (g). Subdivision (g) applies when the court does not grant all the relief requested by a motion for summary judgment. It becomes relevant only after the court has applied the summary judgment standard carried forward in subdivision (a) to each claim, defense, or part of a claim or defense, identified by the motion. Once that duty is discharged, the court may decide whether to apply the summary-judgment standard to dispose of a material fact that is not genuinely in dispute. The court must take care that this determination does not interfere with a party's ability to accept a fact for purposes of the motion only. A nonmovant, for example, may feel confident that a genuine dispute as to one or a few facts will defeat the motion, and prefer to avoid the cost of detailed response to all facts stated by the movant. This position should be available without running the risk that the fact will be taken as established under subdivision (g) or otherwise found to have been accepted for other purposes.

If it is readily apparent that the court cannot grant all the relief requested by the motion, it may properly decide that the cost of determining whether some potential fact disputes may be eliminated by summary disposition is greater than the cost of resolving those disputes by other means, including trial. Even if the court believes that a fact is not genuinely in dispute it may refrain from ordering that the fact be treated as established. The court may conclude that it is better to leave open for trial facts and issues that may be better illuminated by the trial of related facts that must be tried in any event.

Subdivision (h). Subdivision (h) carries forward former subdivision (g) with three changes. Sanctions are made discretionary, not mandatory, reflecting the experience that courts seldom invoke the independent Rule 56 authority to impose sanctions. See Cecil & Cort, Federal Judicial Center Memorandum on Federal Rule of Civil Procedure 56(g) Motions for Sanctions (April 2, 2007). In addition, the rule text is expanded to recognize the need to provide notice and a reasonable time to respond. Finally, authority to impose other appropriate sanctions also is recognized.

Rule 57. Declaratory Judgments

1937 ADOPTION

The fact that a declaratory judgment may be granted "whether or not further relief is or could be prayed" indicates that declaratory relief is alternative or cumulative and not exclusive or extraordinary. A declaratory judgment is appropriate when it will "terminate the controversy" giving rise to the proceeding. Inasmuch as it often involves only an issue of law on undisputed or relatively undisputed facts, it operates frequently as a summary proceeding, justifying docketing the case for early hearing as on a motion, as provided for in California (Code Civ.Proc. (Deering, 1937) § 1062a), Michigan (3 Comp.Laws (1929) § 13904), and Kentucky (Codes (Carroll, 1932) Civ.Prac. § 639a-3).

The "controversy" must necessarily be "of a justiciable nature, thus excluding an advisory decree upon a hypothetical state of facts." *Ashwander v. Tennessee Valley Authority, 1936*, 297 U.S. 288, 325, 56 S. Ct. 466, 473, 80 L.Ed. 688, 699. The existence or non-existence of any right, duty, power, liability, privilege, disability, or immunity or of any fact upon which such legal relations depend, or of a status, may be declared. The petitioner must have a practical interest in the declaration sought and all parties having an interest therein or adversely affected must be made parties or be cited. A declaration may not be rendered if a special statutory proceeding has been provided for the adjudication of some special type of case, but general ordinary or extraordinary legal remedies, whether regulated by statute or not, are not deemed special statutory proceedings.

When declaratory relief will not be effective in settling the controversy, the court may decline to grant it. But the fact that another remedy would be equally effective affords no ground for declining declaratory relief. The demand for relief shall state with precision the declaratory judgment desired, to which may be joined a demand for coercive relief, cumulatively or in the alternative; but when coercive relief only is sought but is deemed ungrantable or inappropriate, the court may *sua sponte,* if it serves a useful purpose, grant instead a declaration of rights. *Hasselbring v. Koepke, 1933*, 248 N.W. 869, 263 Mich. 466, 93 A.L.R. 1170. Written instruments, including ordinances and statutes, may be construed before or after breach at the petition of a properly interested party, process being served on the private parties or public officials interested. In other respects the Uniform Declaratory Judgment Act affords a guide to the scope and function of the federal act. Compare *Aetna Life Insurance Co. v. Haworth, 1937*, 300 U.S. 227, 57 S. Ct. 461, 81 L.Ed. 617, 108 A.L.R. 1000; *Nashville, Chattanooga & St. Louis Ry. v. Wallace, 1933*, 288 U.S. 249, 53 S. Ct. 345, 77 L.Ed. 730, 87 A.L.R. 1191; *Gully, Tax Collector v. Interstate Natural Gas Co.*, 82 F.2d 145 (C.C.A. 5, 1936); *Ohio Casualty Ins. Co. v. Plummer, Tex.1935*, 13 F.Supp. 169; Borchard, Declaratory Judgments (1934), *passim.*

1948 AMENDMENT

The Amendment effective October 1949, substituted the reference to "Title 28, U.S.C., § 2201" in the first sentence for the reference to "Section 274(d) of the Judicial Code, as amended, U.S.C., Title 28, § 400."

2007 AMENDMENTS

The language of Rule 57 has been amended as part of the general restyling of the Civil Rules to make them more easily understood and to make style and terminology consistent throughout the rules. These changes are intended to be stylistic only.

Rule 58. Entry of Judgment

1937 ADOPTION

See Wis.Stat.1935, § 270.31 (judgment entered forthwith on verdict of jury unless otherwise ordered), § 270.65 (where trial is by the court, entered by direction of the court), § 270.63 (entered by clerk on judgment on admitted claim for money). Compare 1 Idaho Code Ann.1932, § 7-1101, and 4 Mont.Rev. Codes Ann.1935, § 9403, which provides that judgment in jury cases be entered by clerk within 24 hours after verdict unless court otherwise directs. Conn.Practice Book 1934, § 200, provides that all judgments shall be entered within one week after rendition. In some States such as Washington, 2 Rev.Stat.Ann.Remington, 1932, § 431, in jury cases the judgment is entered two days after the return of verdict to give time for making motion for new trial; § 435 (*ibid.*), provides that all judgments shall be entered by the clerk, subject to the court's direction.

1946 AMENDMENT

Note. The reference to Rule 54(b) is made necessary by the amendment of that rule.

Two changes have been made in Rule 58 in order to clarify the practice. The substitution of the more inclusive phrase "all relief be denied" for the words "there be no recovery", makes it clear that the clerk shall enter the judgment forthwith in the situations specified without awaiting the filing of a formal judgment approved by the court. The phrase "all relief be denied" covers cases such as the denial of a bankrupt's discharge and similar situations where the relief sought is refused but there is literally no denial of a "recovery".

The addition of the last sentence in the rule emphasizes that judgments are to be entered promptly by the clerk without waiting for the taxing of costs. Certain district court rules, for example, Civil Rule 22 of the Southern District of New York—until its annulment Oct. 1, 1945, for conflict with this rule—and the like rule of the Eastern District of New York, are expressly in conflict with this provision, although the federal law is of long standing and well settled. *Fowler v. Hamill, 1891*, 139 U.S. 549, 11 S. Ct. 663, 35 L.Ed. 266; Craig v. The Hartford, C.C.Cal.1856, Fed.Cas.No.3,333; *Tuttle v. Claflin, C.C.A.2, 1895*, 66 F. 7, certiorari denied 166 U.S. 721, 17 S. Ct. 992, 41 L.Ed. 1187; *Prescott & A. C. Ry. Co. v. Atchison, T. & S. F. R. Co., C.C.A.2, 1897*, 84 F. 213; *Stallo v. Wagner, C.C.A.2, 1917*, 245 F. 636, 639–40; *Brown v. Parker, C.C.A.8, 1899*, 97 F. 446; *Allis-Chalmers v. United States, C.C.A.7, 1908*, 162 F. 679. And this applies even though state law is to the contrary. *United States v. Nordbye, C.C.A.8, 1935*, 75 F.2d 744, 746, certiorari denied 296 U.S. 572, 56 S. Ct. 103, 80 L.Ed. 404. Inasmuch as it has been held that failure of the clerk thus to enter judgment is a "misprision" "not to be excused", *The Washington, C.C.A.2, 1926*, 16 F.2d 206, such a district court rule may have serious consequences for a district court clerk. Rules of this sort also provide for delay in entry of the judgment contrary to Rule 58. See *Commissioner of Internal Revenue v. Bedford's Estate, 1945*, 325 U.S. 283, 65 S. Ct. 1157, 89 L.Ed. 1611.

1963 AMENDMENT

Under the present rule a distinction has sometimes been made between judgments on general jury verdicts, on the one hand, and, on the other, judgments upon decisions of the court that a party shall recover only money or costs or that all relief shall be denied. In the first situation, it is clear that the clerk should enter the judgment without awaiting a direction by the court unless the court otherwise orders. In the second situation it was intended that the clerk should similarly enter the judgment forthwith upon the court's decision; but because of the . . . separate listing in the rule, and the use of the phrase "upon receipt of the direction," the rule has sometimes been interpreted as requiring the clerk to await a separate direction of the court. All these judgments are usually uncomplicated, and should be handled in the same way. The amended rule accordingly deals with them as a single group in clause (1)(substituting the expression "only a sum certain" for the present expression "only money"), and requires the clerk to prepare, sign, and enter them forthwith, without awaiting court direction, unless the court makes a contrary order. (The clerk's duty is ministerial and may be performed by a deputy clerk in the name of the clerk. See 28 U.S.C. § 956; cf. *Gilbertson v. United States*, 168 Fed. 672 (7th Cir. 1909).) The more complicated judgments described in clause (2) must be approved by the court before they are entered.

Rule 58 is designed to encourage all reasonable speed in formulating and entering the judgment when the case has been decided. Participation by the attorneys through the submission of forms of judgment involves needless expenditure of time and effort and promotes delay, except in special cases where counsel's assistance can be of real value. See *Matteson v. United States*, 240 F.2d 517, 518–19 (2d Cir.1956). Accordingly, the amended rule provides that attorneys shall not submit forms of judgment unless directed to do so by the court. This applies to the judgments mentioned in clause (2) as well as clause (1).

Hitherto some difficulty has arisen, chiefly where the court has written an opinion or memorandum containing some apparently directive or dispositive words, e.g., "the plaintiff's motion [for summary judgment] is granted," see *United States v. F. & M. Schaefer Brewing Co.*, 356 U.S. 227, 229, 78 S. Ct. 674, 676, 2 L. Ed. 2d 721 (1958). Clerks on occasion have viewed these opinions or memoranda as being in themselves a sufficient basis for entering judgment in the civil docket as provided by Rule 79(a). However, where the opinion or memorandum has not contained all the elements of a judgment or where the judge has later signed a formal judgment, it has become a matter of doubt whether the purported entry of judgment was effective, starting the time running for post-verdict motions and for the purpose of appeal. See id.; and compare *Blanchard v. Commonwealth Oil Co.*, 294 F.2d 834 (5th Cir.1961); *United States v. Higginson*, 238 F.2d 439 (1st Cir.1956); *Danzig v. Virgin Isle Hotel, Inc.*, 278 F.2d 580 (3d Cir.1960); *Sears v. Austin*, 282 F.2d 340 (9th Cir.1960), with *Matteson v. United States*, supra; *Erstling v. Southern Bell Tel. & Tel. Co.*, 255 F.2d 93 (5th Cir.1958); *Barta v. Oglala Sioux Tribe*, 259 F.2d 553 (8th Cir.1958), cert. denied, 358 U.S. 932, 79 S. Ct. 320, 3 L. Ed. 2d 304 (1959); *Beacon Fed. S. & L. Assn. v. Federal Home L. Bank Bd.*, 266 F.2d 246 (7th Cir.), cert. denied, 361 U.S. 823, 80 S. Ct. 70, 4 L. Ed. 2d 67 (1959); *Ram v. Paramount Film D. Corp.*, 278 F.2d 191 (4th Cir.1960).

The amended rule eliminates these uncertainties by requiring that there be a judgment set out on a separate document—distinct from any opinion or memorandum—which provides the basis for the entry of judgment. That judgments shall be on separate documents is also indicated in Rule 79(b); and see General Rule 10 of the U. S. District Courts for the Eastern and Southern Districts of New York; *Ram v. Paramount Film D. Corp.*, supra, at 194.

See the amendment of Rule 79(a) and the new specimen forms of judgment, Forms 31 and 32.

See also Rule 55(b)(1) and (2) covering the subject of judgments by default.

1993 AMENDMENT

Ordinarily the pendency or post-judgment filing of a claim for attorney's fees will not affect the time for appeal from the underlying judgment. *See Budinich v. Becton Dickinson & Co.*, 486 U.S. 196, 108 S. Ct. 1717, 100 L. Ed. 2d 178 (1988). Particularly if the claim for fees involves substantial issues or is likely to be affected by the appellate decision, the district court may prefer to defer consideration of the claim for fees until after the appeal is resolved. However, in many cases it may be more efficient to decide fee questions before an appeal is taken so that appeals relating to the fee award can be heard at the same time as appeals relating to the merits of the case. This revision permits, but does not require, the court to delay the finality of the judgment for appellate purposes under revised Fed.R.App.P. 4(a) until the fee dispute is decided. To accomplish this result requires entry of an order by the district court before the time a notice of appeal becomes effective for appellate purposes. If the order is entered, the motion for attorney's fees is treated in the same manner as a timely motion under Rule 59.

2002 AMENDMENT

Rule 58 has provided that a judgment is effective only when set forth on a separate document and entered as provided in Rule 79(a). This simple separate document requirement has been ignored in many cases. The result of failure to enter judgment on a separate document is that the time for making motions under Rules 50, 52, 54(d)(2)(B), 59, and some motions under Rule 60, never begins to run. The time to appeal under Appellate Rule 4(a) also does not begin to run. There have been few visible problems with respect to Rule 50, 52, 54(d)(2)(B), 59, or 60 motions, but there have been many and horridly confused problems under Appellate Rule 4(a). These amendments are designed to work in conjunction with Appellate Rule 4(a) to ensure that appeal time does not linger on indefinitely, and to maintain the integration of the time periods set for Rules 50, 52, 54(d)(2)(B), 59, and 60 with Appellate Rule 4(a).

Rule 58(a) preserves the core of the present separate document requirement, both for the initial judgment and for any amended judgment. No attempt is made to sort through the confusion that some courts have found in addressing the elements of a separate document. It is easy to prepare a separate document that recites the terms of the judgment without offering additional explanation or citation of authority. Forms 31 and 32 provide examples.

Rule 58 is amended, however, to address a problem that arises under Appellate Rule 4(a). Some courts treat such orders as those that deny a motion for new trial as a "judgment," so that appeal time does not start to run until the order is entered on a separate document. Without attempting to address the question whether such orders are appealable, and thus judgments as defined by Rule 54(a), the amendment provides that entry on a separate document is not required for an order disposing of the motions listed in Appellate Rule 4(a). The enumeration of motions drawn from the Appellate Rule 4(a) list is generalized by omitting details that are important for appeal time purposes but that would unnecessarily complicate the separate document requirement. As one example, it is not required that any of the enumerated motions be timely. Many of the enumerated motions are frequently made before judgment is entered. The exemption of the order disposing of the motion does not excuse the obligation to set forth the judgment itself on a separate document. And if disposition of the motion results in an amended judgment, the amended judgment must be set forth on a separate document.

Rule 58(b) discards the attempt to define the time when a judgment becomes "effective." Taken in conjunction with the Rule 54(a) definition of a judgment to include "any order from which an appeal lies," the former Rule 58 definition of effectiveness could cause strange difficulties in implementing pretrial orders that are appealable under interlocutory appeal provisions or under expansive theories of finality. Rule 58(b) replaces the definition of effectiveness with a new provision that defines the time when judgment is entered. If judgment is promptly set forth on a separate document, as should be done when required by Rule 58(a)(1), the new provision will not change the effect of Rule 58. But in the cases in which court and clerk fail to comply with this simple requirement, the motion time periods set by Rules 50, 52, 54, 59, and 60 begin to run after expiration of 150 days from entry of the judgment in the civil docket as required by Rule 79(a).

A companion amendment of Appellate Rule 4(a)(7) integrates these changes with the time to appeal.

The new all-purpose definition of the entry of judgment must be applied with common sense to other questions that may turn on the time when judgment is entered. If the 150-day provision in Rule 58(b)(2)(B)—designed to integrate the time for post-judgment motions with appeal time—serves no purpose, or would defeat the purpose of another rule, it should be disregarded. In theory, for example, the separate document requirement continues to apply to an interlocutory order that is appealable as a final decision under collateral-order doctrine. Appealability under collateral-order doctrine should not be complicated by failure to enter the order as a judgment on a separate document—there is little reason to force trial judges to speculate about the potential appealability of every order, and there is no means to ensure that the trial judge will always reach the same conclusion as the court of appeals. Appeal time should start to run when the collateral order is entered without regard to creation of a separate document and without awaiting expiration of the 150 days provided by Rule 58(b)(2). Drastic surgery on Rules 54(a) and 58 would be required to address this and related issues, however, and it is better to leave this conundrum to the pragmatic disregard that seems its present fate. The present amendments do not seem to make matters worse, apart from one false appearance. If a pretrial order is set forth on a separate document that meets the requirements of Rule 58(b), the time to move for reconsideration seems to begin to run, perhaps years before final judgment. And even if there is no separate document, the time to move for reconsideration seems to begin 150 days after entry in the civil docket. This apparent problem is resolved by Rule 54(b), which expressly permits revision of all orders not made final under Rule 54(b) "at any time before the entry of judgment adjudicating all the claims and the rights and liabilities of all the parties."

New Rule 58(d) replaces the provision that attorneys shall not submit forms of judgment except on direction of the court. This provision was added to Rule 58 to avoid the delays that were frequently encountered by the former practice of directing the attorneys for the prevailing party to prepare a form of judgment, and also to avoid the occasionally inept drafting that resulted from attorney-prepared judgments. See *11 Wright, Miller & Kane, Federal Practice & Procedure: Civil 2d, § 2786*. The express direction in Rule 58(a)(2) for prompt action by the clerk, and by the court if court action is required, addresses this concern. The new provision allowing any party to move for entry of judgment on a separate document will protect all needs for prompt commencement of the periods for motions, appeals, and execution or other enforcement.

2007 AMENDMENTS

The language of Rule 58 has been amended as part of the general restyling of the Civil Rules to make them more easily understood and to make style and terminology consistent throughout the rules. These changes are intended to be stylistic only.

Rule 59. New Trials; Amendment of Judgments

1937 ADOPTION

This rule represents an amalgamation of the petition for rehearing of former Equity Rule 69 (Petition for Rehearing) and the motion for new trial of 28 U.S.C., § 2111, formerly § 391 (New trials; harmless error), made in the light of the experience and provision of the code States. Compare Calif.Code Civ.Proc., Deering, 1937, §§ 656 to 663a, 28 U.S.C., § 2111, formerly § 391 (New trials; harmless error) is thus substantially continued in this rule. U.S.C., Title 28, former § 840 (Executions; stay on conditions) is modified in so far as it contains time provisions inconsistent with **Subdivision (b)**. For the effect of the motion for new trial upon the time for taking an appeal see *Morse v. United States, 1926*, 270 U.S. 151, 46 S. Ct. 241, 70 L.Ed. 518; *Aspen Mining and Smelting Co. v. Billings, 1893*, 150 U.S. 31, 14 S. Ct. 4, 37 L.Ed. 986.

For partial new trials which are permissible under **Subdivision (a)**, see *Gasoline Products Co., Inc. v. Champlin Refining Co., 1931*, 283 U.S. 494, 51 S. Ct. 513, 75 L.Ed. 1188; *Schuerholz v. Roach, C.C.A.4, 1932*, 58 F.2d 32; *Simmons v. Fish, 1912*, 97 N.E. 102, 210 Mass. 563, Am.Ann.Cas. 1912D, 588 (sustaining and recommending the practice and citing federal cases and cases in accord from about sixteen states and contra from three States). The procedure in several States provides specifically for partial new trials. Ariz.Rev.Code Ann., Struckmeyer, 1928, § 3852; Calif.Code Civ.Proc., Deering, 1937, §§ 657, 662; Smith-Hurd Ill.Stats., 1937, c. 110, § 216 (Par. (f)); Md.Ann.Code, Bagby, 1924, Art. 5, §§ 25, 26; Mich.Court Rules Ann., Searl, 1933, Rule 47, § 2; Miss.Sup.Ct. Rule 12, 161 Miss. 903, 905, 1931; N.J.Sup.Ct.Rules 131, 132, 147, 2 N.J.Misc. 1197, 1246 to 1251, 1255, 1924, 2 N.D.Comp.Laws Ann., 1913, § 7844, as amended by N.D.Laws 1927, ch. 214.

1946 AMENDMENT

Note to Subdivision (b). With the time for appeal to a circuit court of appeals reduced in general to 30 days by the proposed amendment of Rule 73(a), the utility of the original "except" clause, which permits a motion for a new trial on the ground of newly discovered evidence to be made before the expiration of the time for appeal, would have been seriously restricted. It was thought advisable, therefore, to take care of this matter in another way. By amendment of Rule 60(b), newly discovered evidence is made the basis for relief from a judgment, and the maximum time limit has been extended to one year. Accordingly the amendment of Rule 59(b) eliminates the "except" clause and its specific treatment of newly discovered evidence as a ground for a motion for new trial. This ground remains, however, as a basis for a motion for new trial served not later than 10 days after the entry of judgment. See also Rule 60(b).

As to the effect of a motion under subdivision (b) upon the running of appeal time, see amended Rule 73(a) and Note.

Subdivision (e). This subdivision has been added to care for a situation such as that arising in *Boaz v. Mutual Life Ins. Co. of New York, C.C.A.8, 1944*, 146 F.2d 321, and makes clear that the district court possesses the power asserted in that case to alter or amend a judgment after its entry. The subdivision deals only with alteration or amendment of the original judgment in a case and does not relate to a judgment upon motion as provided in Rule 50(b). As to the effect of a motion under subdivision (e) upon the running of appeal time, see amended Rule 73(a) and Note.

The title of Rule 59 has been expanded to indicate the inclusion of this subdivision.

1966 AMENDMENT

By narrow interpretation of Rule 59(b) and (d), it has been held that the trial court is without power to grant a motion for a new trial, timely served, by an order made more than 10 days after the entry of judgment, based upon a ground not stated in the motion but perceived and relied on by the trial court sua sponte. *Freid v. McGrath*, 133 F.2d 350 (D.C.Cir.1942); *National Farmers Union Auto. & Cas. Co. v. Wood*, 207 F.2d 659 (10th Cir.1953); *Bailey v. Slentz*, 189 F.2d 406 (10th Cir.1951); *Marshall's U. S. Auto Supply, Inc. v. Cashman*, 111 F.2d 140 (10th Cir.1940), cert. denied, 311 U.S. 667, 61 S. Ct. 26, 85 L.Ed. 428 (1940); but see *Steinberg v. Indemnity Ins. Co.*, 36 F.R.D. 253 (E.D.La.1964).

The result is undesirable. Just as the court has power under Rule 59(d) to grant a new trial of its own initiative within the 10 days, so it should have power, when an effective new trial motion has been made and is pending, to decide it on grounds thought meritorious by the court although not advanced in the motion. The second sentence added by amendment to Rule 59(d) confirms the court's power in the latter situation, with provision that the parties be afforded a hearing before the power is exercised. See 6 Moore's Federal Practice, par. 59.09[2] (2d ed. 1953).

In considering whether a given ground has or has not been advanced in the motion made by the party, it should be borne in mind that the particularity called for in stating the grounds for a new trial motion is the same as that required for all motions by Rule 7(b)(1). The latter rule does not require ritualistic detail but rather a fair indication to court and counsel of the substance of the grounds relied on. See *Lebeck v. William A. Jarvis, Inc.*, 250 F.2d 285 (3d Cir.1957); *Tsai v. Rosenthal*, 297 F.2d 614 (8th Cir.1961); *General Motors Corp. v. Perry*, 303 F.2d 544 (7th Cir.1962); *cf. Grimm v. California Spray-Chemical Corp.*, 264 F.2d 145 (9th Cir.1959); *Cooper v. Midwest Feed Products Co.*, 271 F.2d 177 (8th Cir.1959).

1995 AMENDMENT

The only change, other than stylistic, intended by this revision is to add explicit time limits for filing motions for a new trial, motions to alter or amend a judgment, and affidavits opposing a new trial motion. Previously, there was an inconsistency in the wording of Rules 50, 52, and 59 with respect to whether certain post-judgment motions had to be filed, or merely served, during the prescribed period. This inconsistency caused special problems when motions for a new trial were joined with other post-judgment motions. These motions affect the finality of the judgment, a matter often of importance to third persons as well as the parties and the court. The Committee believes that each of these rules should be revised to require filing before end of the 10-day period. Filing is an event that can be determined with certainty from court records. The phrase "no later than" is used—rather than "within"—to include post-judgment motions that sometimes are filed before actual entry of the judgment by the clerk. It should be noted that under Rule 5 the motions when filed are to contain a certificate of service on other parties. It also should be noted that under Rule 6(a) Saturdays, Sundays, and legal holidays are excluded in measuring the 10-day period, but that Bankruptcy Rule 9006(a) excludes intermediate Saturdays, Sundays, and legal holidays only in computing periods less than 8 days.

2007 AMENDMENTS

The language of Rule 59 has been amended as part of the general restyling of the Civil Rules to make them more easily understood and to make style and terminology consistent throughout the rules. These changes are intended to be stylistic only.

2009 AMENDMENTS

Former Rules 50, 52, and 59 adopted 10 day periods for their respective post judgment motions. Rule 6(b) prohibits any expansion of those periods. Experience has proved that in many cases it is not possible to prepare a satisfactory post judgment motion in 10 days, even under the former rule that excluded intermediate Saturdays, Sundays, and legal holidays. These time periods are particularly sensitive because Appellate Rule 4 integrates the time to appeal with a timely motion under these rules. Rather than introduce the prospect of uncertainty in appeal time by amending Rule 6(b) to permit additional time, the former 10 day periods are expanded to 28 days. Rule 6(b) continues to prohibit expansion of the 28 day period.

Former Rule 59(c) set a 10 day period after being served with a motion for new trial to file opposing affidavits. It also provided that the period could be extended for up to 20 days for good cause or by stipulation. The apparent 20 day limit on extending the time to file opposing affidavits seemed to conflict with the Rule 6(b) authority to extend time without any specific limit. This tension between the two rules may have been inadvertent. It is resolved by deleting the former Rule 59(c) limit. Rule 6(b) governs. The underlying 10 day period was extended to 14 days to reflect the change in the Rule 6(a) method for computing periods of less than 11 days.

Rule 60. Relief from Judgment or Order

1937 ADOPTION

Note to Subdivision (a). See former Equity Rule 72 (Correction of Clerical Mistakes in Orders and Decrees); Mich. Court Rules Ann. (Searl, 1933) Rule 48,

§ 3; 2 Wash.Rev.Stat.Ann. (Remington, 1932) § 464(3); Wyo.Rev.Stat.Ann., (Courtright, 1931) § 89-2301(3). For an example of a very liberal provision for the correction of clerical errors and for amendment after judgment, see Va.Code Ann. (Michie, 1936) §§ 6329, 6333.

Note to Subdivision (b). Application to the court under this subdivision does not extend the time for taking an appeal, as distinguished from the motion for new trial. This section is based upon Calif.Code Civ.Proc. (Deering, 1937) § 473. See also N.Y.C.P.A., 1937, § 108; 2 Minn.Stat., Mason, 1927, § 9283.

For the independent action to relieve against mistake, etc. see Dobie, Federal Procedure, pages 760–765, compare 639; and Simkins, Federal Practice, ch. CXXI, pp. 820–830, and ch. CXXII, pp. 831–834, compare § 214.

1946 AMENDMENT

Note to Subdivision (a). The amendment incorporates the view expressed in *Perlman v. 322 West Seventy-Second Street Co., Inc., C.C.A.2, 1942*, 127 F.2d 716, 3 Moore's Federal Practice, 1938, 3276, and further permits correction after docketing, with leave of the appellate court. Some courts have thought that upon the taking of an appeal the district court lost its power to act. See *Schram v. Safety Investment Co., Mich.1942*, 45 F.Supp. 636; also *Miller v. United States, C.C.A.7, 1940*, 114 F.2d 267.

Note to Subdivision (b). When promulgated, the rules contained a number of provisions, including those found in Rule 60(b), describing the practice by a motion to obtain relief from judgments, and these rules, coupled with the reservation in Rule 60(b) of the right to entertain a new action to relieve a party from a judgment, were generally supposed to cover the field. Since the rules have been in force, decisions have been rendered that the use of bills of review, coram nobis, or audita querela, to obtain relief from final judgments is still proper, and that various remedies of this kind still exist although they are not mentioned in the rules and the practice is not prescribed in the rules. It is obvious that the rules should be complete in this respect and define the practice with respect to any existing rights or remedies to obtain relief from final judgments. For extended discussion of the old common law writs and equitable remedies, the interpretation of Rule 60, and proposals for change, see Moore and Rogers, Federal Relief from Civil Judgments, 1946, 55 Yale L.J. 623. See also 3 Moore's Federal Practice, 1938, 3254 et seq.; Commentary, Effect of Rule 60b on Other Methods of Relief From Judgment, 1941, 4 Fed.Rules Serv. 942, 945; *Wallace v. United States, C.C.A.2, 1944*, 142 F.2d 240, certiorari denied 323 U.S. 712, 65 S. Ct. 37, 89 L.Ed. 573.

The reconstruction of Rule 60(b) has for one of its purposes a clarification of this situation. Two types of procedure to obtain relief from judgments are specified in the rules as it is proposed to amend them. One procedure is by motion in the court and in the action in which the judgment was rendered. The other procedure is by a new or independent action to obtain relief from a judgment, which action may or may not be begun in the court which rendered the judgment. Various rules, such as the one dealing with a motion for new trial and for amendment of judgments, Rule 59, one for amended findings, Rule 52, and one for judgment notwithstanding the verdict, Rule 50(b), and including the provisions of Rule 60(b) as amended, prescribe the various types of cases in which the practice by motion is permitted. In each case there is a limit upon the time within which resort to a motion is permitted, and this time limit may not be enlarged under Rule 6(b). If the right to make a motion is lost by the expiration of the time limits fixed in these rules, the only other procedural remedy is by a new or independent action to set aside a judgment upon those principles which have heretofore been applied in such an action. Where the independent action is resorted to, the limitations of time are those of laches or statutes of limitations. The Committee has endeavored to ascertain all the remedies and types of relief heretofore available by coram nobis, coram vobis, audita querela, bill of review, or bill in the nature of a bill of review. See Moore and Rogers, Federal Relief from Civil Judgments, 1946, 55 Yale L.J. 623, 659–682. It endeavored then to amend the rules to permit, either by motion or by independent action, the granting of various kinds of relief from judgments which were permitted in the federal courts prior to the adoption of these rules, and the amendment concludes with a provision abolishing the use of bills of review and the other common law writs referred to, and requiring the practice to be by motion or by independent action.

To illustrate the operation of the amendment, it will be noted that under Rule 59(b) as it now stands, without amendment, a motion for new trial on the ground of newly discovered evidence is permitted within ten days after the entry of the judgment, or after that time upon leave of the court. It is proposed to amend Rule 59(b) by providing that under that rule a motion for new trial shall be served not later than ten days after the entry of the judgment, whatever the ground be for the motion, whether error by the court or newly discovered evidence. On the other hand, one of the purposes of the bill of review in equity was to afford relief on the ground of newly discovered evidence long after the entry of the judgment. Therefore, to permit relief by a motion similar to that heretofore obtained on bill of review, Rule 60(b) as amended permits an application for relief to be made by motion, on the ground of newly discovered evidence, within one year after judgment. Such a motion under Rule 60(b) does not affect the finality of the judgment, but a motion under Rule 59, made within 10 days, does affect finality and the running of the time for appeal.

If these various amendments, including principally those to Rule 60(b), accomplish the purpose for which they are intended, the federal rules will deal with the practice in every sort of case in which relief from final judgments is asked, and prescribe the practice. With reference to the question whether, as the rules now exist, relief by coram nobis, bills of review, and so forth, is permissible, the generally accepted view is that the remedies are still available, although the precise relief obtained in a particular case by use of these ancillary remedies is shrouded in ancient lore and mystery. See *Wallace v. United States, C.C.A.2, 1944*, 142 F.2d 240, certiorari denied 323 U.S. 712, 65 S. Ct. 37, 89 L.Ed. 573; *Fraser v. Doing, App.D.C.1942*, 130 F.2d 617; *Jones v. Watts, C.C.A.5, 1944*, 142 F.2d 575; *Preveden v. Hahn, N.Y.1941*, 36 F.Supp. 952; *Cavallo v. Agwilines, Inc., N.Y.1942, 6 Fed.Rules Serv. 60b.31, Case 2*, 2 F.R.D. 526; *McGinn v. United States, D.Mass.1942, 6 Fed.Rules Serv. 60b.51, Case 3*, 2 F.R.D. 562; City of Shattuck, Oklahoma ex rel. Versluis v. Oliver, Okl.1945, 8 Fed.Rules Serv. 60b.31, Case 3; Moore and Rogers, Federal Relief from Civil Judgments, 1946, 55 Yale L.J. 623, 631–653; 3 Moore's Federal Practice, 1938, 3254 et seq.; Commentary Effect of Rule 60b on Other Methods of Relief from Judgments, op. cit. supra. Cf. *Norris v. Camp, C.C.A.10, 1944*, 144 F.2d 1; *Reed v. South Atlantic Steamship Co. of Delaware, Del.1942*, 2 F.R.D. 475, 6 Fed.Rules Serv. 60b.31, Case 1; *Laughlin v. Berens, D.C.1945, 8 Fed.Rules Serv. 60b.51, Case 1*, 73 W.L.R. 209.

The transposition of the words "the court" and the addition of the word "and" at the beginning of the first sentence are merely verbal changes. The addition of the qualifying word "final" emphasizes the character of the judgments, orders or proceedings from which Rule 60(b) affords relief; and hence interlocutory judgments are not brought within the restrictions of the rule, but rather they are left subject to the complete power of the court rendering them to afford such relief from them as justice requires.

The qualifying pronoun "his" has been eliminated on the basis that it is too restrictive, and that the subdivision should include the mistake or neglect of others which may be just as material and call just as much for supervisory jurisdiction as where the judgment is taken against the party through *his* mistake, inadvertence, etc.

Fraud, whether intrinsic or extrinsic, misrepresentation, or other misconduct of an adverse party are express grounds for relief by motion under amended subdivision (b). There is no sound reason for their exclusion. The incorporation of fraud and the like within the scope of the rule also removes confusion as to the proper procedure. It has been held that relief from a judgment obtained by extrinsic fraud could be secured by motion within a "reasonable time," which might be after the time stated in the rule had run. *Fiske v. Buder, C.C.A.8,*

1942, 125 F.2d 841; see also inferentially *Bucy v. Nevada Construction Co., C.C.A.9, 1942*, 125 F.2d 213. On the other hand, it has been suggested that in view of the fact that fraud was omitted from original Rule 60(b) as a ground for relief, an independent action was the only proper remedy. Commentary, Effect of Rule 60b on Other Methods of Relief From Judgment, 1941, 4 Fed.Rules Serv. 942, 945. The amendment settles this problem by making fraud an express ground for relief by motion; and under the saving clause, fraud may be urged as a basis for relief by independent action insofar as established doctrine permits. See Moore and Rogers Federal Relief from Civil Judgments, 1946, 55 Yale L.J. 623, 653–659; 3 Moore's Federal Practice, 1938, 3267 et seq. And the rule expressly does not limit the power of the court, when fraud has been perpetrated upon it, to give relief under the saving clause. As an illustration of this situation, see *Hazel-Atlas Glass Co. v. Hartford-Empire Co., 1944*, 322 U.S. 238, 64 S. Ct. 997, 88 L.Ed. 1250.

The time limit for relief by motion in the court and in the action in which the judgment was rendered has been enlarged from six months to one year.

It should be noted that Rule 60(b) does not assume to define substantive law as to the grounds for vacating judgments, but merely prescribes the practice in proceedings to obtain relief. It should also be noted that under § 200(4) of the Soldiers' and Sailors' Civil Relief Act of 1940, 50 U.S.C., Appendix, §§ 501 et seq. [§ 520(4)], a judgment rendered in any action or proceeding governed by the section may be vacated under certain specified circumstances upon proper application to the court.

1948 AMENDMENT

The amendment effective October 1949, substituted the reference to "Title 28, U.S.C., § 1655," in the next to the last sentence of subdivision (b), for the reference to "Section 57 of the Judicial Code, U.S.C., Title 28, § 118."

1987 AMENDMENT

The amendment is technical. No substantive change is intended.

2007 AMENDMENTS

The language of Rule 60 has been amended as part of the general restyling of the Civil Rules to make them more easily understood and to make style and terminology consistent throughout the rules. These changes are intended to be stylistic only.

The final sentence of former Rule 60(b) said that the procedure for obtaining any relief from a judgment was by motion as prescribed in the Civil Rules or by an independent action. That provision is deleted as unnecessary. Relief continues to be available only as provided in the Civil Rules or by independent action.

Rule 61. Harmless Error

1937 ADOPTION

A combination of U.S.C., Title 28, § 2111, former § 391 (New trials; harmless error) and former § 777 (Defects of form; amendments) with modifications. See *McCandless v. United States, 1936*, 298 U.S. 342, 56 S. Ct. 764, 80 L.Ed. 1205. Compare former Equity Rule 72 (Correction of Clerical Mistakes in Orders and Decrees); and last sentence of former Equity Rule 46 (Trial—Testimony Usually Taken in Open Court—Rulings on Objections to Evidence). For the last sentence see the last sentence of former Equity Rule 19 (Amendments Generally).

2007 AMENDMENTS

The language of Rule 61 has been amended as part of the general restyling of the Civil Rules to make them more easily understood and to make style and terminology consistent throughout the rules. These changes are intended to be stylistic only.

Rule 62. Stay of Proceedings to Enforce a Judgment

1937 ADOPTION

Note to Subdivision (a). The first sentence states the substance of the last sentence of U.S.C., Title 28, former § 874 (Supersedeas). The remainder of the subdivision states the substance of the last clause of U.S.C., Title 28, § 1292, formerly § 227 (Appeals in proceedings for injunctions; receivers; and admiralty), and of §§ 1292, 2107, formerly § 227a (Appeals in suits in equity for infringement of letters patent for inventions; stay of proceedings for accounting), but extended to include final as well as interlocutory judgments.

Note to Subdivision (b). This modifies U.S.C., Title 28, former § 840 (Executions; stay on conditions).

Note to Subdivision (c). Compare former Equity Rule 74 (Injunction Pending Appeal); and *Cumberland Telephone and Telegraph Co. v. Louisiana Public Service Commission, 1922*, 260 U.S. 212, 43 S. Ct. 75, 67 L.Ed. 217. See Simkins, Federal Practice (1934), § 916, in regard to the effect of appeal on injunctions and the giving of bonds. See U.S.C., Title 6 (Official and Penal Bonds) for bonds by surety companies. For statutes providing for a specially constituted district court of three judges, see:

U.S.C., Title 7:

§ 217 (Proceedings for suspension of orders of Secretary of Agriculture under Stockyards Act)—by reference.

§ 499k (Injunctions; application of injunction laws governing orders of Interstate Commerce Commission to orders of Secretary of Agriculture under Perishable Commodities Act)—by reference.

U.S.C., Title 15:

§ 28 (Antitrust laws; suits against monopolies expedited)

U.S.C., Title 28 former:

§ 47 (Injunctions as to orders of Interstate Commerce Commission, etc.)

§ 380 (Injunctions; alleged unconstitutionality of State statutes)

§ 380a (Same; constitutionality of federal statute)

U.S.C., Title 49:

§ 44 (Suits in equity under interstate commerce laws; expedition of suits)

Note to Subdivision (d). This modifies U.S.C., Title 28, former § 874 (Supersedeas). See Rule 36(2), Rules of the Supreme Court of the United States, which governs supersedeas bonds on direct appeals to the Supreme Court, and Rule 73(d), of these rules, which governs supersedeas bonds on appeals to a circuit court of appeals. The provisions governing supersedeas bonds in both kinds of appeals are substantially the same.

Note to Subdivision (e). This states the substance of U.S.C., Title 28, § 2408, formerly § 870 (Bond; not required of the United States).

Note to Subdivision (f). This states the substance of U.S.C., Title 28, former § 841 (Executions; stay of one term) with appropriate modification to conform to the provisions of Rule 6(c) as to terms of court.

1946 AMENDMENT

Note to Subdivision (a). [This subdivision not amended]. Sections 203 and 204 of the Soldiers' and Sailors' Civil Relief Act of 1940, 50 U.S.C., Appendix, §§ 501 et seq. [§§ 523, 524], provide under certain circumstances for the issuance and continuance of a stay of execution of any judgment or order entered against a person in military service. See *Bowsman v. Peterson, Neb.1942*, 45 F.Supp. 741. Section 201 of the Act [50 U.S.C., App. § 521] permits under certain circumstances the issuance of a stay of any action or proceeding at any stage thereof, where either the plaintiff or defendant is a person in military service. See also note to Rule 64 herein.

Subdivision (b). This change was necessary because of the proposed addition to Rule 59 of subdivision (e).

Subdivision (h). In proposing to revise Rule 54(b), the Committee thought it advisable to include a separate provision in Rule 62 for stay of enforcement of a final judgment in cases involving multiple claims.

1948 AMENDMENT

The amendment effective October 1949, deleted at the end of subdivision (g) the following language which originally appeared after the word "entered": "and these rules do not supersede the provisions of Section 210 of the Judicial Code, as amended, U.S.C., Title 28, former § 47a, or of other statutes of the United States to the effect that stays pending appeals to the Supreme Court may be granted only by that court or a justice thereof."

1961 AMENDMENT

The amendment adopted Apr. 17, 1961, effective July 19, 1961, eliminated words "on some but not all of the claims presented in the action" which followed "final judgment."

1987 AMENDMENT

The amendment is technical. No substantive change is intended.

2007 AMENDMENTS

The language of Rule 62 has been amended as part of the general restyling of the Civil Rules to make them more easily understood and to make style and terminology consistent throughout the rules. These changes are intended to be stylistic only.

The final sentence of former Rule 62(a) referred to Rule 62(c). It is deleted as an unnecessary. Rule 62(c) governs of its own force.

2009 AMENDMENTS

The time set in the former rule at 10 days has been revised to 14 days. See the Note to Rule 6.

2018 AMENDMENT

Subdivisions (a), (b), (c), and (d) of former Rule 62 are reorganized and the provisions for staying a judgment are revised.

The provisions for staying an injunction, receivership, or order for a patent accounting are reorganized by consolidating them in new subdivisions (c) and (d). There is no change in meaning. The language is revised to include all of the words used in 28 U.S.C. § 1292(a)(1) to describe the right to appeal from interlocutory actions with respect to an injunction, but subdivisions (c) and (d) apply both to interlocutory injunction orders and to final judgments that grant, refuse, or otherwise deal with an injunction.

New Rule 62(a) extends the period of the automatic stay to 30 days. Former Rule 62(a) set the period at 14 days, while former Rule 62(b) provided for a court-ordered stay "pending disposition of" motions under Rules 50, 52, 59, and 60. The time for making motions under Rules 50, 52, and 59, however, was later extended to 28 days, leaving an apparent gap between expiration of the automatic stay and any of those motions (or a Rule 60 motion) made more than 14 days after entry of judgment. The revised rule eliminates any need to rely on inherent power to issue a stay during this period. Setting the period at 30 days coincides with the time for filing most appeals in civil actions, providing a would-be appellant the full period of appeal time to arrange a stay by other means. A 30-day automatic stay also suffices in cases governed by a 60-day appeal period.

Amended Rule 62(a) expressly recognizes the court's authority to dissolve the automatic stay or supersede it by a court-ordered stay. One reason for dissolving the automatic stay may be a risk that the judgment debtor's assets will be dissipated. Similarly, it may be important to allow immediate enforcement of a judgment that does not involve a payment of money. The court may address the risks of immediate execution by ordering dissolution of the stay only on condition that security be posted by the judgment creditor. Rather than dissolve the stay, the court may choose to supersede it by ordering a stay that lasts longer or requires security.

Subdivision 62(b) carries forward in modified form the supersedeas bond provisions of former Rule 62(d). A stay may be obtained under subdivision (b) at any time after judgment is entered. Thus a stay may be obtained before the automatic stay has expired, or after the automatic stay has been lifted by the court. The new rule's text makes explicit the opportunity to post security in a form other than a bond. The stay takes effect when the court approves the bond or other security and remains in effect for the time specified in the bond or security—a party may find it convenient to arrange a single bond or other security that persists through completion of post-judgment proceedings in the trial court and on through completion of all proceedings on appeal by issuance of the appellate mandate. This provision does not supersede the opportunity for a stay under 28 U.S.C. § 2101(f) pending review by the Supreme Court on certiorari. Finally, subdivision (b) changes the provision in former subdivision (d) that "an appellant" may obtain a stay. Under new subdivision (b), "a party" may obtain a stay. For example, a party may wish to secure a stay pending disposition of post-judgment proceedings after expiration of the automatic stay, not yet knowing whether it will want to appeal.

Rule 62.1. Indicative Ruling on a Motion for Relief That is Barred by a Pending Appeal

2009 ADOPTION

This new rule adopts for any motion that the district court cannot grant because of a pending appeal the practice that most courts follow when a party makes a Rule 60(b) motion to vacate a judgment that is pending on appeal. After an appeal has been docketed and while it remains pending, the district court cannot grant a Rule 60(b) motion without a remand. But it can entertain the motion and deny it, defer consideration, or state that it would grant the motion if the court of appeals remands for that purpose or state that the motion raises a substantial issue. Experienced lawyers often refer to the suggestion for remand as an "indicative ruling." (Appellate Rule 4(a)(4) lists six motions that, if filed within the relevant time limit, suspend the effect of a notice of appeal filed before or after the motion is filed until the last such motion is disposed of. The district court has authority to grant the motion without resorting to the indicative ruling procedure.)

This clear procedure is helpful whenever relief is sought from an order that the court cannot reconsider because the order is the subject of a pending appeal. Rule 62.1 does not attempt to define the circumstances in which an appeal limits or defeats the district court's authority to act in the face of a pending appeal. The rules that govern the relationship between trial courts and appellate courts may be complex, depending in part on the nature of the order and the source of appeal jurisdiction. Rule 62.1 applies only when those rules deprive the district court of authority to grant relief without appellate permission. If the district court concludes that it has authority to grant relief without appellate permission, it can act without falling back on the indicative ruling procedure.

To ensure proper coordination of proceedings in the district court and in the appellate court, the movant must notify the circuit clerk under Federal Rule of Appellate Procedure 12.1 if the district court states that it would grant the motion or that the motion raises a substantial issue. Remand is in the court of appeals' discretion under Appellate Rule 12.1.

Often it will be wise for the district court to determine whether it in fact would grant the motion if the court of appeals remands for that purpose. But a motion may present complex issues that require extensive litigation and that may either be mooted or be presented in a different context by decision of the issues raised on appeal. In such circumstances the district court may prefer to state that the motion raises a substantial issue, and to state the reasons why it prefers to decide only if the court of appeals agrees that it would be useful to decide the motion before decision of the pending appeal. The district court is not bound to grant the motion after stating that the motion raises a substantial issue; further proceedings on remand may show that the motion ought not be granted.

Rule 63. Inability of a Judge to Proceed

1937 ADOPTION

This rule adapts and extends the provisions of U.S.C., Title 28, former § 776 (Bill of exceptions; authentication; signing of by judge) to include all duties to be performed by the judge after verdict or judgment. The statute is therefore superseded.

1987 AMENDMENT

The amendments are technical. No substantive change is intended.

1991 AMENDMENT

The revision substantially displaces the former rule. The former rule was limited to the disability of the judge, and made no provision for disqualification or possible other reasons for the withdrawal of the judge during proceedings. In making provision for other circumstances, the revision is not intended to encourage judges to discontinue participation in a trial for any but compelling reasons. Cf. *United States v. Lane*, 708 F.2d 1394, 1395–1397 (9th Cir.1983). Manifestly, a substitution should not be made for the personal convenience of the court, and the reasons for a substitution should be stated on the record.

The former rule made no provision for the withdrawal of the judge during the trial, but was limited to disqualification after trial. Several courts concluded that the text of the former rule prohibited substitution of a new judge prior to the points described in the rule, thus requiring a new trial, whether or not a fair disposition was within reach of a substitute judge. *E.g., Whalen v. Ford Motor Credit Co.*, 684 F.2d 272 (4th Cir.1982, en banc) *cert. denied*, 459 U.S. 910, 103 S. Ct. 216, 74 L. Ed. 2d 172 (1982) (jury trial); *Arrow-Hart, Inc. v. Philip Carey Co.*, 552 F.2d 711 (6th Cir.1977) (non-jury trial). *See generally* Comment, *The Case of the Dead Judge: Fed.R.Civ.P. 63: Whalen v. Ford Motor Credit Co.*, 67 MINN.L.REV. 827 (1983).

The increasing length of federal trials has made it likely that the number of trials interrupted by the disability of the judge will increase. An efficient mechanism for completing these cases without unfairness is needed to prevent unnecessary expense and delay. To avoid the injustice that may result if the substitute judge proceeds despite unfamiliarity with the action, the new Rule provides, in language similar to Federal Rule of Criminal Procedure 25(a), that the successor judge must certify familiarity with the record and determine that the case may be completed before that judge without prejudice to the parties. This will necessarily require that there be available a transcript or a videotape of the proceedings prior to substitution. If there has been a long but incomplete jury trial, the prompt availability of the transcript or videotape is crucial to the effective use of this rule, for the jury cannot long be held while an extensive transcript is prepared without prejudice to one or all parties.

The revised text authorizes the substitute judge to make a finding of fact at a bench trial based on evidence heard by a different judge. This may be appropriate in limited circumstances. First, if a witness has become unavailable, the testimony recorded at trial can be considered by the successor judge pursuant to F.R.Ev. 804, being equivalent to a recorded deposition available for use at trial pursuant to Rule 32. For this purpose, a witness who is no longer subject to a subpoena to compel testimony at trial is unavailable. Secondly, the successor judge may determine that particular testimony is not material or is not disputed, and so need not be reheard. The propriety of proceeding in this manner may be marginally affected by the availability of a videotape record; a judge who has reviewed a trial on videotape may be entitled to greater confidence in his or her ability to proceed.

The court would, however, risk error to determine the credibility of a witness not seen or heard who is available to be recalled. Cf. *Anderson v. City of Bessemer City NC*, 470 U.S. 564, 575, 105 S. Ct. 1504, 1512, 84 L. Ed. 2d 518 (1985); *Marshall v. Jerrico Inc.*, 446 U.S. 238, 242, 100 S. Ct. 1610, 1613, 64 L. Ed. 2d 182 (1980). See also *United States v. Raddatz*, 447 U.S. 667, 100 S. Ct. 2406, 65

L. Ed. 2d 424 (1980).

2007 AMENDMENTS

The language of Rule 63 has been amended as part of the general restyling of the Civil Rules to make them more easily understood and to make style and terminology consistent throughout the rules. These changes are intended to be stylistic only.

VIII. PROVISIONAL AND FINAL REMEDIES

NOTES OF ADVISORY COMMITTEE ON RULES 1991 AMENDMENT

The purpose of the revision is to divide this chapter of the Rules into two. No substantive change is effected.

Rule 64. Seizure of Person or Property

1937 ADOPTION

This rule adopts the existing federal law, except that it specifies the applicable state law to be that of the time when the remedy is sought. Under U.S.C., Title 28, former § 726 (Attachments as provided by state laws) the plaintiff was entitled to remedies by attachment or other process which were on June 1, 1872, provided by the applicable state law, and the district courts might, from time to time, by general rules, adopt such state laws as might be in force. This statute is superseded as are district court rules which are rendered unnecessary by the rule.

Lis pendens. No rule concerning *lis pendens* is stated, for this would appear to be a matter of substantive law affecting state laws of property. It has been held that in the absence of a state statute expressly providing for the recordation of notice of the pendency of federal actions, the commencement of a federal action is notice to all persons affected. *King v. Davis, Va.1903*, 137 F. 198. It has been held, however, that when a state statute does so provide expressly, its provisions are binding. *United States v. Calcasieu Timber Co., C.C.A.5, 1916*, 236 F. 196.

For statutes of the United States on attachment, see, e.g.:

U.S.C., Title 28 former:

§ 737 (Attachment in postal suits)
§ 738 (Attachment; application for warrant)
§ 739 (Attachment; issue of warrant)
§ 740 (Attachment; trial of ownership of property)
§ 741 (Attachment; investment of proceeds of attached property)
§ 742 (Attachment; publication of attachment)
§ 743 (Attachment; personal notice of attachment)
§ 744 (Attachment; discharge; bond)
§ 745 (Attachment; accrued rights not affected)
§ 746 (Attachments dissolved in conformity with State laws)

For statutes of the United States on garnishment, see, e.g.:

U.S.C., Title 28 former:

§ 748 (Garnishees in suits by United States against a corporation)
§ 749 (Same; issue tendered on denial of indebtedness)
§ 750 (Same; garnishee failing to appear)

For statutes of the United States on arrest, see, e.g.:

U.S.C., Title 28 former:

§ 376 (Writs of ne exeat)
§ 755 (Special bail in suits for duties and penalties)
§ 756 (Defendant giving bail in one district and committed in another)
§ 757 (Defendant giving bail in one district and committed in another; defendant held until judgment in first suit)

§ 758 (Bail and affidavits; taking by commissioners)
§ 759 (Calling of bail in Kentucky)
§ 760 (Clerks may take bail de bene esse)
§ 843 (Imprisonment for debt)
§ 844 (Imprisonment for debt; discharge according to State laws)
§ 845 (Imprisonment for debt; jail limits)

For statutes of the United States on replevin, see, e.g.:

U.S.C., Title 28:

§ 2463, formerly § 747 (Replevy of property taken under revenue laws).

SUPPLEMENTARY NOTE OF ADVISORY COMMITTEE REGARDING THIS RULE

Note. Sections 203 and 204 of the Soldiers' and Sailors' Civil Relief Act of 1940, 50 U.S.C., Appendix, §§ 523 and 524, provide under certain circumstances for the issuance and continuance of a stay of the execution of any judgment entered against a person in military service, or the vacation or stay of any attachment or garnishment directed against such person's property, money, or debts in the hands of another. See also note to Rule 62 herein.

2007 AMENDMENTS

The language of Rule 64 has been amended as part of the general restyling of the Civil Rules to make them more easily understood and to make style and terminology consistent throughout the rules. These changes are intended to be stylistic only.

Former Rule 64 stated that the Civil Rules govern an action in which any remedy available under Rule 64(a) is used. The Rules were said to govern from the time the action is commenced if filed in federal court, and from the time of removal if removed from state court. These provisions are deleted as redundant. Rule 1 establishes that the Civil Rules apply to all actions in a district court, and Rule 81(c)(1) adds reassurance that the Civil Rules apply to a removed action "after it is removed."

Rule 65. Injunctions

1937 ADOPTION

Note to Subdivisions (a) and (b). These are taken from U.S.C., Title 28, former § 381 (Injunctions; preliminary injunctions and temporary restraining orders).

Note to Subdivision (c). Except for the last sentence, this is substantially U.S.C., Title 28, former § 382 (Injunctions; security on issuance of). The last sentence continues the following and similar statutes which expressly except the United States or an officer or agency thereof from such security requirements: U.S.C., Title 15, §§ 77t(b), 78u(e), and 79r(f) (Securities and Exchange Commission). It also excepts the United States or an officer or agency thereof from such security requirements in any action in which a restraining order or interlocutory judgment of injunction issues in its favor whether there is an express statutory exception from such security requirements or not.

See U.S.C., Title 6 (Official and Penal Bonds) for bonds by surety companies.

Note to Subdivision (d). This is substantially U.S.C., Title 28, former § 383 (Injunctions; requisites of order; binding effect).

Note to Subdivision (e). The words "relating to temporary restraining orders and preliminary injunctions in actions affecting employer and employee" are words of description and not of limitation.

Compare former Equity Rule 73 (Preliminary Injunctions and Temporary Restraining Orders) which is substantially equivalent to the statutes.

For other statutes dealing with injunctions which are continued, see e.g.:

U.S.C., Title 28, former:

§ 46 (Suits to enjoin orders of Interstate Commerce Commission to be against United States)

§ 47 (Injunctions as to orders of Interstate Commerce Commission; appeal to

Supreme Court; time for taking)
§ 378 (Injunctions; when granted)
§ 379 (Injunctions; stay in State courts)
§ 380 (Injunctions; alleged unconstitutionality of State statutes; appeal to Supreme Court)
§ 380a (Injunctions; constitutionality of Federal statute; application for hearing; appeal to Supreme Court)
U.S.C., Title 7:
§ 216 (Court proceedings to enforce orders; injunction)
§ 217 (Proceedings for suspension of orders)
U.S.C., Title 15:
§ 4 (Jurisdiction of courts; duty of district attorney; procedure)
§ 25 (Restraining violations; procedure)
§ 26 (Injunctive relief for private parties; exceptions)
§ 77t(b) (Injunctions and prosecution of offenses)

1946 AMENDMENT

Note. It has been held that in actions on preliminary injunction bonds the district court has discretion to grant relief in the same proceeding or to require the institution of a new action on the bond. *Russell v. Farley, 1881*, 105 U.S. 433, 466, 26 L.Ed. 1060. It is believed, however, that in all cases the litigant should have a right to proceed on the bond in the same proceeding, in the manner provided in Rule 73(f) for a similar situation. The paragraph added to Rule 65(c) insures this result and is in the interest of efficiency. There is no reason why Rules 65(c) and 73(f) should operate differently. Compare § 50, sub. n of the Bankruptcy Act, 11 U.S.C. § 78, sub. n, under which actions on all bonds furnished pursuant to the Act may be proceeded upon summarily in the bankruptcy court. See 2 Collier on Bankruptcy, 14th ed. by Moore and Oglebay, 1853–1854.

1948 AMENDMENT

The amendment effective October 1949, changed subdivision (e) in the following respects: in the first clause the amendment substituted the words "any statute of the United States" for the words "the Act of October 15, 1914, ch. 323, §§ 1 and 20 (38 Stat. 730), U.S.C., Title 29, §§ 52 and 53, or the Act of March 23, 1932, ch. 90 (47 Stat. 70), U.S.C., Title 29, ch. 6"; in the second clause of subdivision (e) the amendment substituted the reference to "Title 28, U.S.C., § 2361" for the reference to "Section 24(26) of the Judicial Code as amended, U.S.C., Title 28, § 41(26)"; and the third clause was amended to read "Title 28, U.S.C., § 2284," etc., as at present, instead of "the Act of August 24, 1937, ch. 754, § 3, relating to actions to enjoin the enforcement of acts of Congress."

1966 AMENDMENT

Subdivision (a)(2). This new subdivision provides express authority for consolidating the hearing of an application for a preliminary injunction with the trial on the merits. The authority can be exercised with particular profit when it appears that a substantial part of evidence offered on the application will be relevant to the merits and will be presented in such form as to qualify for admission on the trial proper. Repetition of evidence is thereby avoided. The fact that the proceedings have been consolidated should cause no delay in the disposition of the application for the preliminary injunction, for the evidence will be directed in the first instance to that relief, and the preliminary injunction, if justified by the proof, may be issued in the course of the consolidated proceedings. Furthermore, to consolidate the proceedings will tend to expedite the final disposition of the action. It is believed that consolidation can be usefully availed of in many cases.

The subdivision further provides that even when consolidation is not ordered, evidence received in connection with an application for a preliminary injunction which would be admissible on the trial on the merits forms part of the trial record. This evidence need not be repeated on the trial. On the the other hand, repetition is not altogether prohibited. That would be impractical and unwise.

For example, a witness testifying comprehensively on the trial who has previously testified upon the application for a preliminary injunction might sometimes be hamstrung in telling his story if he could not go over some part of his prior testimony to connect it with his present testimony. So also, some repetition of testimony may be called for where the trial is conducted by a judge who did not hear the application for the preliminary injunction. In general, however, repetition can be avoided with an increase of efficiency in the conduct of the case and without any distortion of the presentation of evidence by the parties.

Since an application for a preliminary injunction may be made in an action in which, with respect to all or part of the merits, there is a right to trial by jury, it is appropriate to add the caution appearing in the last sentence of the subdivision. In such a case the jury will have to hear all the evidence bearing on its verdict, even if some part of the evidence has already been heard by the judge alone on the application for the preliminary injunction.

The subdivision is believed to reflect the substance of the best current practice and introduces no novel conception.

Subdivision (b). In view of the possibly drastic consequence of a temporary restraining order, the opposition should be heard, if feasible, before the order is granted. Many judges have properly insisted that, when time does not permit of formal notice of the application to the adverse party, some expedient, such as telephonic notice to the attorney for the adverse party, be resorted to if this can reasonably be done. On occasion, however, temporary restraining orders have been issued without any notice when it was feasible for some fair, although informal, notice to be given. See the emphatic criticisms in *Pennsylvania R. Co. v. Transport Workers Union*, 278 F.2d 693, 694 (3d Cir.1960); *Arvida Corp. v. Sugarman*, 259 F.2d 428, 429 (2d Cir.1958); *Lummus Co. v. Commonwealth Oil Ref. Co., Inc.*, 297 F.2d 80, 83 (2d Cir.1961), cert. denied, 368 U.S. 986, 82 S. Ct. 601, 7 L. Ed. 2d 524 (1962).

Heretofore the first sentence of subdivision (b), in referring to a notice "served" on the "adverse party" on which a "hearing" could be held, perhaps invited the interpretation that the order might be granted without notice if the circumstances did not permit of a formal hearing on the basis of a formal notice. The subdivision is amended to make it plain that informal notice, which may be communicated to the attorney rather than the adverse party, is to be preferred to no notice at all.

Before notice can be dispensed with, the applicant's counsel must give his certificate as to any efforts made to give notice and the reasons why notice should not be required. This certificate is in addition to the requirement of an affidavit or verified complaint setting forth the facts as to the irreparable injury which would result before the opposition could be heard.

The amended subdivision continues to recognize that a temporary restraining order may be issued without any notice when the circumstances warrant.

Subdivision (c). Original Rules 65 and 73 contained substantially identical provisions for summary proceedings against sureties on bonds required or permitted by the rules. There was fragmentary coverage of the same subject in the Admiralty Rules. Clearly, a single comprehensive rule is required, and is incorporated as Rule 65.1.

1987 AMENDMENT

The amendments are technical. No substantive change is intended.

2001 AMENDMENT

New subdivision (f) is added in conjunction with abrogation of the antiquated Copyright Rules of Practice adopted for proceedings under the 1909 Copyright Act. Courts have naturally turned to Rule 65 in response to the apparent inconsistency of the former Copyright Rules with the discretionary impoundment procedure adopted in 1976, 17 U.S.C. § 503(a). Rule 65 procedures also have assuaged well-founded doubts whether the Copyright Rules satisfy more contemporary requirements of due process. See, e.g., *Religious Technology Center v. Netcom On-Line Communication Servs., Inc.*, 923 F.Supp. 1231,

1260–1265 (N.D.Cal.1995); *Paramount Pictures Corp. v. Doe*, 821 F.Supp. 82 (E.D.N.Y.1993); *WPOW, Inc. v. MRLJ Enterprises*, 584 F.Supp. 132 (D.D.C.1984).

A common question has arisen from the experience that notice of a proposed impoundment may enable an infringer to defeat the court's capacity to grant effective relief. Impoundment may be ordered on an ex parte basis under subdivision (b) if the applicant makes a strong showing of the reasons why notice is likely to defeat effective relief. Such no-notice procedures are authorized in trademark infringement proceedings, see 15 U.S.C. § 1116(d), and courts have provided clear illustrations of the kinds of showings that support ex parte relief. See *Matter of Vuitton et Fils S.A.*, 606 F.2d 1 (2d Cir.1979); *Vuitton v. White*, 945 F.2d 569 (3d Cir.1991). In applying the tests for no-notice relief, the court should ask whether impoundment is necessary, or whether adequate protection can be had by a less intrusive form of no-notice relief shaped as a temporary restraining order.

This new subdivision (f) does not limit use of trademark procedures in cases that combine trademark and copyright claims. Some observers believe that trademark procedures should be adopted for all copyright cases, a proposal better considered by Congressional processes than by rulemaking processes.

2007 AMENDMENTS

The language of Rule 65 has been amended as part of the general restyling of the Civil Rules to make them more easily understood and to make style and terminology consistent throughout the rules. These changes are intended to be stylistic only.

The final sentence of former Rule 65(c) referred to Rule 65.1. It is deleted as unnecessary. Rule 65.1 governs of its own force.

Rule 65(d)(2) clarifies two ambiguities in former Rule 65(d). The former rule was adapted from former 28 U.S.C. § 363, but omitted a comma that made clear the common doctrine that a party must have actual notice of an injunction in order to be bound by it. Amended Rule 65(d) restores the meaning of the earlier statute, and also makes clear the proposition that an injunction can be enforced against a person who acts in concert with a party's officer, agent, servant, employee, or attorney.

2009 AMENDMENTS

The time set in the former rule at 10 days has been revised to 14 days. See the Note to Rule 6.

Rule 65.1. Security: Proceedings against Sureties

1966 ADDITION

See Note to Rule 65.

1987 AMENDMENT

The amendments are technical. No substantive change is intended.

2006 AMENDMENT

Rule 65.1 is amended to conform to the changed title of the Supplemental Rules.

2007 AMENDMENTS

The language of Rule 65.1 has been amended as part of the general restyling of the Civil Rules to make them more easily understood and to make style and terminology consistent throughout the rules. These changes are intended to be stylistic only.

2018 AMENDMENT

Rule 65.1 is amended to reflect the amendments of Rule 62. Rule 62 allows a party to obtain a stay of a judgment "by providing a bond or other security." Limiting Rule 65.1 enforcement procedures to sureties might exclude use of those procedures against a security provider that is not a surety. All security providers, including sureties, are brought into Rule 65.1 by these amendments. But the reference to "bond" is retained in Rule 62 because it has a long history.

The word "mail" is changed to "send" to avoid restricting the method of serving security providers.

Rule 66. Receivers Appointed by Federal Courts

1946 AMENDMENT

Note. The title of Rule 66 has been expanded to make clear the subject of the rule, i. e., federal equity receivers.

The first sentence added to Rule 66 prevents a dismissal by any party, after a federal equity receiver has been appointed, except upon leave of court. A party should not be permitted to oust the court and its officer without the consent of that court. See Civil Rule 31(e), Eastern District of Washington.

The second sentence added at the beginning of the rule deals with suits by or against a federal equity receiver. The first clause thereof eliminates the formal ceremony of an ancillary appointment before suit can be brought by a receiver, and is in accord with the more modern state practice, and with more expeditious and less expensive judicial administration. 2 Moore's Federal Practice, 1938, 2088–2091. For the rule necessitating ancillary appointment, see *Sterrett v. Second Nat. Bank, 1918*, 248 U.S. 73, 39 S. Ct. 27, 63 L.Ed. 135; *Kelley v. Queeney, W.D.N.Y.1941*, 41 F.Supp. 1015; see also *McCandless v. Furlaud, 1934*, 293 U.S. 67, 55 S. Ct. 42, 79 L.Ed. 202. This rule has been extensively criticized. First, Extraterritorial Powers of Receivers, 1932, 27 Ill.L.Rev. 271; Rose, Extraterritorial Actions by Receivers, 1933, 17 Minn.L.Rev. 704; Laughlin, The Extraterritorial Powers of Receivers, 1932, 45 Harv.L.Rev. 429; Clark and Moore, A New Federal Civil Procedure—II, Pleadings and Parties, 1935, 44 Yale L.J.1291, 1312–1315; Note, 1932, 30 Mich.L.Rev. 1322. See also comment in *Bicknell v. Lloyd-Smith, C.C.A.2, 1940*, 109 F.2d 527, certiorari denied 311 U.S. 650, 61 S. Ct. 15, 85 L.Ed. 416. The second clause of the sentence merely incorporates the well-known and general rule that, absent statutory authorization, a federal receiver cannot be sued without leave of the court which appointed him, applied in the federal courts since *Barton v. Barbour, 1881*, 104 U.S. 126, 26 L.Ed. 672. See also 1 Clark on Receivers, 2d ed., § 549. Under 28 U.S.C., § 959, formerly § 125, leave of court is unnecessary when a receiver is sued "in respect of any act or transaction of his in carrying on the business" connected with the receivership property, but such suit is subject to the general equity jurisdiction of the court in which the receiver was appointed, so far as justice necessitates.

Capacity of a state court receiver to sue or be sued in federal court is governed by Rule 17(b).

The last sentence added to Rule 66 assures the application of the rules in all matters except actual administration of the receivership estate itself. Since this implicitly carries with it the applicability of those rules relating to appellate procedure, the express reference thereto contained in Rule 66 has been stricken as superfluous. Under Rule 81(a)(1) the rules do not apply to bankruptcy proceedings except as they may be made applicable by order of the Supreme Court. Rule 66 is applicable to what is commonly known as a federal "chancery" or "equity" receiver, or similar type of court officer. It is not designed to regulate or affect receivers in bankruptcy, which are governed by the Bankruptcy Act and the General Orders. Since the Federal Rules are applicable in bankruptcy by virtue of General Orders in Bankruptcy 36 and 37 only to the extent that they are not inconsistent with the Bankruptcy Act or the General Orders, Rule 66 is not applicable to bankruptcy receivers. See 1 Collier on Bankruptcy, 14th ed. by Moore and Oglebay, ¶¶ 2.23–2.36.

1948 AMENDMENT

The amendment effective October 1949, deleted a sentence which formerly appeared immediately following the first sentence and which read as follows: "A receiver shall have the capacity to sue in any district court without ancillary appointment; but actions against a receiver may not be commenced without leave of the court appointing him except when authorized by a statute of the United States."

2007 AMENDMENTS

The language of Rule 66 has been amended as part of the general restyling of the Civil Rules to make them more easily understood and to make style and terminology consistent throughout the rules. These changes are intended to be stylistic only.

Rule 67. Deposit in Court

1937 ADOPTION

This rule provides for deposit in court generally, continuing similar special provisions contained in such statutes as U.S.C., Title 28, §§ 1335, 1397, 2361, formerly § 41(26) (Original jurisdiction of bills of interpleader, and of bills in the nature of interpleader). See generally *Howard v. United States, 1902*, 184 U.S. 676, 22 S. Ct. 543, 46 L.Ed. 754; United States Supreme Court Admiralty Rules (1920), Rules 37 (Bringing Funds into Court), 41 (Funds in Court Registry), and 42 (Claims Against Proceeds in Registry). With the first sentence, compare English Rules Under the Judicature Act (The Annual Practice, 1937) O. 22, r. 1(1).

1948 AMENDMENT

The amendment effective October 1949 substituted the reference to "Title 28, U.S.C., §§ 2041, and 2042" for the reference to "Sections 995 and 996, Revised Statutes, as amended, U.S.C., Title 28, §§ 851, 852." The amendment also added the words "as amended" following the citation of the Act of June 26, 1934, c. 756, § 23, and, in the parenthetical citation immediately following, added the reference to "58 Stat. 845."

1983 AMENDMENT

Rule 67 has been amended in three ways. The first change is the addition of the clause in the first sentence. Some courts have construed the present rule to permit deposit only when the party making it claims no interest in the fund or thing deposited. *E.g., Blasini-Stern v. Beech-Nut Life Savers Corp.*, 429 F.Supp. 533 (D.Puerto Rico 1975); *Dinkins v. General Aniline & Film Corp.*, 214 F.Supp. 281 (S.D.N.Y.1963). However, there are situations in which a litigant may wish to be relieved of responsibility for a sum or thing, but continue to claim an interest in all or part of it. In these cases the deposit-in-court procedure should be available; in addition to the advantages to the party making the deposit, the procedure gives other litigants assurance that any judgment will be collectable. The amendment is intended to accomplish that.

The second change is the addition of a requirement that the order of deposit be served on the clerk of the court in which the sum or thing is to be deposited. This is simply to assure that the clerk knows what is being deposited and what his responsibilities are with respect to the deposit. The latter point is particularly important since the rule as amended contemplates that deposits will be placed in interest-bearing accounts; the clerk must know what treatment has been ordered for the particular deposit.

The third change is to require that any money be deposited in an interest-bearing account or instrument approved by the court.

2007 AMENDMENTS

The language of Rule 67 has been amended as part of the general restyling of the Civil Rules to make them more easily understood and to make style and terminology consistent throughout the rules. These changes are intended to be stylistic only.

Rule 68. Offer of Judgment

1937 ADOPTION

See 2 Minn.Stat. (Mason, 1927) § 9323; 4 Mont.Rev.Codes Ann. (1935) § 9770; N.Y.C.P.A. (1937) § 177.

For the recovery of costs against the United States, see Rule 54(d).

1946 AMENDMENT

Note. The third sentence of Rule 68 has been altered to make clear that evidence of an unaccepted offer is admissible in a proceeding to determine the costs of the action but is not otherwise admissible.

The two sentences substituted for the deleted last sentence of the rule assure a party the right to make a second offer where the situation permits—as, for example, where a prior offer was not accepted but the plaintiff's judgment is nullified and a new trial ordered, whereupon the defendant desires to make a second offer. It is implicit, however, that as long as the case continues—whether there be a first, second or third trial—and the defendant makes no further offer, his first and only offer will operate to save him the costs from the time of that offer if the plaintiff ultimately obtains a judgment less than the sum offered. In the case of successive offers not accepted, the offeror is saved the costs incurred after the making of the offer which was equal to or greater than the judgment ultimately obtained. These provisions should serve to encourage settlements and avoid protracted litigation.

The phrase "before the trial begins," in the first sentence of the rule, has been construed in *Cover v. Chicago Eye Shield Co., C.C.A.7, 1943*, 136 F.2d 374, certiorari denied 320 U.S. 749, 64 S. Ct. 53, 88 L.Ed. 445.

1966 AMENDMENT

This logical extension of the concept of offer of judgment is suggested by the common admiralty practice of determining liability before the amount of liability is determined.

1987 AMENDMENT

The amendments are technical. No substantive change is intended.

2007 AMENDMENTS

The language of Rule 68 has been amended as part of the general restyling of the Civil Rules to make them more easily understood and to make style and terminology consistent throughout the rules. These changes are intended to be stylistic only.

2009 AMENDMENTS

Former Rule 68 allowed service of an offer of judgment more than 10 days before the trial begins, or — if liability has been determined — at least 10 days before a hearing to determine the extent of liability. It may be difficult to know in advance when trial will begin or when a hearing will be held. The time is now measured from the date set for trial or hearing; resetting the date establishes a new time for serving the offer.

The former 10-day periods are extended to 14 days to reflect the change in the Rule 6(a) method for computing periods less than 11 days.

Rule 69. Execution

1937 ADOPTION

Note to Subdivision (a). This follows in substance U.S.C., Title 28, former § 727 (Executions as provided by State laws) and former § 729 (Proceedings in vindication of civil rights), except that, as in the similar case of attachments (see note to Rule 64), the rule specifies the applicable State law to be that of the time when the remedy is sought, and thus renders unnecessary, as well as supersedeas, local district court rules.

Statutes of the United States on execution, when applicable, govern under this rule. Among these are:

U.S.C., Title 12:

§ 91 (Transfers by bank and other acts in contemplation of insolvency)

§ 632 (Jurisdiction of United States district courts in cases arising out of foreign banking jurisdiction where Federal reserve bank a party)

U.S.C., Title 19:

§ 199 (Judgments for customs duties, how payable)

U.S.C., Title 26:

§ 1610(a) (Surrender of property subject to distraint)

U.S.C., Title 28, former:

§ 122 (Creation of new district or transfer of territory; lien)

§ 350 (Time for making application for appeal or certiorari; stay pending application for certiorari)

§ 489 (District Attorneys; reports to Department of Justice)

§ 574 (Marshals, fees enumerated)

§ 786 (Judgments for duties; collected in coin)

§ 811 (Interest on judgments)

§ 838 (Executions; run in all districts of State)

§ 839 (Executions; run in every State and Territory)

§ 840 (Executions; stay on conditions), as modified by Rules 62(b)

§ 841 (Executions; stay of one term), as modified by Rule 62(f)

§ 842 (Executions; against officers of revenue in cases of probable cause), as incorporated in Subdivision (b) of this rule

§ 843 (Imprisonment for debt)

§ 844 (Imprisonment for debt; discharge according to State laws)

§ 845 (Imprisonment for debt; jail limits)

§ 846 (Fieri Facias; appraisal of goods; appraisers)

§ 847 (Sales; real property under order or decree)

§ 848 (Sales; personal property under order or decree)

§ 849 (Sales; necessity of notice)

§ 850 (Sales; death of marshal after levy or after sale)

§ 869 (Bond in former error and on appeal) as incorporated in Rule 73(c)

§ 874 (Supersedeas), as modified by Rules 62(d) and 73(d)

U.S.C., Title 31:

§ 195 (Purchase on execution)

U.S.C., Title 33:

§ 918 (Collection of defaulted payments)

U.S.C., Title 49:

§ 74(g) (Causes of action arising out of Federal control of railroads; execution and other process)

Special statutes of the United States on exemption from execution are also continued. Among these are:

U.S.C., Title 2:

§ 118 (Actions against officers of Congress for official acts)

U.S.C., Title 5:

§ 729 (Federal employees retirement annuities not subject to assignment, execution, levy, or other legal process)

U.S.C., Title 10:

§ 610 (Exemption of enlisted men from arrest on civil process)

U.S.C., Title 22, former:

§ 21(h) (Foreign service retirement and disability system; establishment; rules and regulations; annuities; nonassignable; exemption from legal process)

U.S.C., Title 33:

§ 916 (Assignment and exemption from claims of creditors) Longshoremen's and Harborworkers' Compensation Act

U.S.C., Title 38:

§ 54 (Attachment, levy or seizure of moneys due pensioners prohibited)

§ 393 (Army and Navy Medal of Honor Roll; pensions additional to other pensions; liability to attachment, etc.) Compare Title 34, § 365(c) (Medal of

Honor Roll; special pension to persons enrolled)

§ 618 (Benefits exempt from seizure under process and taxation; no deductions for indebtedness to United States)

U.S.C., Title 43:

§ 175 (Exemption from execution of homestead land)

U.S.C., Title 48:

§ 1371*o* (Panama Canal and railroad retirement annuities, exemption from execution and so forth)

SUPPLEMENTARY NOTE OF ADVISORY COMMITTEE REGARDING THIS RULE

Note. With respect to the provisions of the Soldiers' and Sailors' Civil Relief Act of 1940, 50 U.S.C. Appendix, §§ 501 et seq., see Notes to Rules 62 and 64 herein.

1948 AMENDMENT

The amendment effective October 1949 substituted the citation of "Title 28, U.S.C. § 2006" in subdivision (b) in place of the citation to "Section 989, Revised Statutes, U.S.C. Title 28, § 842".

1970 AMENDMENT

The amendment assures that, in aid of execution on a judgment, all discovery procedures provided in the rules are available and not just discovery via the taking of a deposition. Under the present language, one court has held that Rule 34 discovery is unavailable to the judgment creditor. *M. Lowenstein & Sons, Inc. v. American Underwear Mfg. Co.*, 11 F.R.D. 172 (E.D.Pa.1951). Notwithstanding the language, and relying heavily on legislative history referring to Rule 33, the Fifth Circuit has held that a judgment creditor may invoke Rule 33 interrogatories. *United States v. McWhirter*, 376 F.2d 102 (5th Cir. 1967). But the court's reasoning does not extend to discovery except as provided in Rules 26 to 33. One commentator suggests that the existing language might properly be stretched to all discovery, 7 Moore's Federal Practice ¶ 69.05[1] (2d ed. 1966), but another believes that a rules amendment is needed. 3 Barron & Holtzoff, Federal Practice and Procedure 1484 (Wright ed. 1958). Both commentators and the court in *McWhirter* are clear that, as a matter of policy, Rule 69 should authorize the use of all discovery devices provided in the rules.

1987 AMENDMENT

The amendments are technical. No substantive change is intended.

2007 AMENDMENTS

The language of Rule 69 has been amended as part of the general restyling of the Civil Rules to make them more easily understood and to make style and terminology consistent throughout the rules. These changes are intended to be stylistic only.

Amended Rule 69(b) incorporates directly the provisions of 2 U.S.C. § 118 and 28 U.S.C. § 2006, deleting the incomplete statement in former Rule 69(b) of the circumstances in which execution does not issue against an officer.

Rule 70. Judgment for Specific Acts; Vesting Title

1937 ADOPTION

Compare former Equity Rules 7 (Process, Mesne and Final), 8 (Enforcement of Final Decrees), and 9 (Writ of Assistance). To avoid possible confusion, both old and new denominations for attachment (sequestration) and execution (assistance) are used in this rule. Compare with the provision in this rule that the judgment may itself vest title, 6 Tenn.Ann.Code (Williams, 1934) § 10594; 2 Conn.Gen.Stat. (1930) § 5455; N.M.Stat.Ann. (Courtright, 1929) § 117-117; 2 Ohio Gen.Code Ann. (Page, 1926) § 11590; and England, Supreme Court of Judicature Act (1925) § 47.

2007 AMENDMENTS

The language of Rule 70 has been amended as part of the general restyling of the Civil Rules to make them more easily understood and to make style and

terminology consistent throughout the rules. These changes are intended to be stylistic only.

Rule 71. Process in Behalf of and Against Persons Not Parties

1937 ADOPTION

Compare former Equity Rule 11 (Process in Behalf of and Against Persons Not Parties). Compare also *Terrell v. Allison, 1875*, 22 L.Ed. 634, 21 Wall. 289; *Farmers' Loan and Trust Co. v. Chicago and A. Ry. Co., C.C.Ind.1890*, 44 F. 653; *Robert Findlay Mfg. Co. v. Hygrade Lighting Fixture Corp., N.Y.1923*, 288 F. 80; Thompson v. Smith, C.C.Minn.1870, Fed.Cas.No.13,977.

1987 AMENDMENT

The amendments are technical. No substantive change is intended.

2007 AMENDMENTS

The language of Rule 71 has been amended as part of the general restyling of the Civil Rules to make them more easily understood and to make style and terminology consistent throughout the rules. These changes are intended to be stylistic only.

IX. SPECIAL PROCEEDINGS

NOTES OF ADVISORY COMMITTEE ON RULES 1991 ADDITION

This chapter heading is to be inserted between Rule 71 and Rule 71A.

Rule 71.1. Condemnation of Property

1951 ADDITION

The Court will remember that at its conference on December 2, 1948, the discussion was confined to subdivision (h) of the rule (* * *), the particular question being whether the tribunal to award compensation should be a commission or a jury in cases where the Congress has not made specific provision on the subject. The Advisory Committee was agreed from the outset that a rule should not be promulgated which would overturn the decision of the Congress as to the kind of tribunal to fix compensation, provided that the system established by Congress was found to be working well. We found two instances where the Congress had specified the kind of tribunal to fix compensation. One case was the District of Columbia (U.S.C., Title 40, §§ 361 to 386 (now D.C.Code, 1951 Ed., Title 16-619 to 16-644)) where a rather unique system exists under which the court is required in all cases to order the selection of a "jury" of five from among not less than twenty names drawn from "the special box provided by law." They must have the usual qualifications of jurors and in addition must be freeholders of the District and not in the service of the United States or the District. That system has been in effect for many years, and our inquiry revealed that it works well under the conditions prevailing in the District, and is satisfactory to the courts of the District, the legal profession and to property owners.

The other instance is that of the Tennessee Valley Authority, where the act of Congress (U.S.C. Title 16, § 831x), provides that compensation is fixed by three disinterested commissioners appointed by the court, whose award goes before the District Court for confirmation or modification. The Advisory Committee made a thorough inquiry into the practical operation of the TVA commission system. We obtained from counsel for the TVA the results of their experience, which afforded convincing proof that the commission system is preferable under the conditions affecting TVA and that the jury system would not work satisfactorily. We then, under date of February 6, 1947, wrote every Federal judge who had ever sat in a TVA condemnation case, asking his views as to whether the commission system is satisfactory and whether a jury system should be preferred. Of 21 responses from the judges 17 approved the commission system and opposed the substitution of a jury system for the TVA. Many of the judges went further and opposed the use of juries in any condemnation cases. Three of the judges preferred the jury system, and one dealt only with the TVA provision for a three judge district court. The Advisory Committee has not considered abolition of the three judge requirement of the TVA Act, because it seemed to raise a question of jurisdiction, which cannot be altered by rule. Nevertheless the Department of Justice continued its advocacy of the jury system for its asserted expedition and economy; and others favored a uniform procedure. In consequence of these divided counsels the Advisory Committee was itself divided, but in its May 1948 Report to the Court recommended the following rule as approved by a majority (* * *):

(h) Trial. If the action involves the exercise of the power of eminent domain under the law of the United States, any tribunal specially constituted by an Act of Congress governing the case for the trial of the issue of just compensation shall be the tribunal for the determination of that issue; but if there is no such specially constituted tribunal any party may have a trial by jury of the issue of just compensation by filing a demand therefor within the time allowed for answer or within such further time as the court may fix. Trial of all issues shall otherwise be by the court.

The effect of this was to preserve the existing systems in the District of Columbia and in TVA cases, but to provide for a jury to fix compensation in all other cases.

Before the Court's conference of December 2, 1948, the Chief Justice informed the Committee that the Court was particularly interested in the views expressed by Judge John Paul, Judge of the United States District Court for the Western District of Virginia, in a letter from him to the chairman of the Advisory Committee, dated February 13, 1947. Copies of all the letters from judges who had sat in TVA cases had been made available to the Court, and this letter from Judge Paul is one of them. Judge Paul strongly opposed jury trials and recommended the commission system in large projects like the TVA, and his views seemed to have impressed the Court and to have been the occasion for the conference.

The reasons which convinced the Advisory Committee that the use of commissioners instead of juries is desirable in TVA cases were these:

1. The TVA condemns large areas of land of similar kind, involving many owners. Uniformity in awards is essential. The commission system tends to prevent discrimination and provide for uniformity in compensation. The jury system tends to lack of uniformity. Once a reasonable and uniform standard of values for the area has been settled by a commission, litigation ends and settlements result.
2. Where large areas are involved many small landowners reside at great distances from the place where a court sits. It is a great hardship on humble people to have to travel long distances to attend a jury trial. A commission may travel around and receive the evidence of the owner near his home.
3. It is impracticable to take juries long distances to view the premises.
4. If the cases are tried by juries the burden on the time of the courts is excessive.

These considerations are the very ones Judge Paul stressed in his letter. He pointed out that they applied not only to the TVA but to other large governmental projects, such as flood control, hydroelectric power, reclamation, national forests, and others. So when the representatives of the Advisory Committee appeared at the Court's conference December 2, 1948, they found it difficult to justify the proposed provision in subdivision (h) of the rule that a jury should be used to fix compensation in all cases where Congress had not specified the tribunal. If our reasons for preserving the TVA system were sound, provision for a jury in similar projects of like magnitude seemed unsound.

Aware of the apparent inconsistency between the acceptance of the TVA system and the provision for a jury in all other cases, the members of the Committee attending the conference of December 2, 1948, then suggested that in the other cases the choice of jury or commission be left to the discretion of the District Court, going back to a suggestion previously made by Committee members and reported at page 15 of the Preliminary Draft of June 1947. They called the attention of the Court to the fact that the entire Advisory Committee had not been consulted about this suggestion and proposed that the draft be returned to the Committee for further consideration, and that was done.

The proposal we now make for subdivision (h) is as follows:

(h) Trial. If the action involves the exercise of the power of eminent domain under the law of the United States, any tribunal specially constituted by an Act of Congress governing the case for the trial of the issue of just compensation shall be the tribunal for the determination of that issue; but if there is no such specially constituted tribunal any party may have a trial by jury of the issue of just compensation by filing a demand therefor within the time allowed for answer or within such further time as the court may fix, unless the court in its discretion orders that, because of the character, location, or quantity of the property to be condemned, or for other reasons in the interest of justice, the issue of compensation shall be determined by a commission of three persons appointed by it. If a commission is appointed it shall have the powers of a master provided in subdivision (c) of Rule 53 and proceedings before it shall be governed by the provisions of paragraphs (1) and (2) of subdivision (d) of Rule 53. Its action and report shall be determined by a majority and its findings and report shall have the effect, and be dealt with by the court in accordance with the practice, prescribed in paragraph (2) of subdivision (e) of Rule 53. Trial of all issues shall otherwise be by the court.

In the 1948 draft the Committee had been almost evenly divided as between jury or commission and that made it easy for us to agree on the present draft. It would be difficult to state in a rule the various conditions to control the District Court in its choice and we have merely stated generally the matters which should be considered by the District Court.

The rule as now drafted seems to meet Judge Paul's objection. In large projects like the TVA the court may decide to use a commission. In a great number of cases involving only sites for buildings or other small areas, where use of a jury is appropriate, a jury may be chosen. The District Court's discretion may also be influenced by local preference or habit, and the preference of the Department of Justice and the reasons for its preference will doubtless be given weight. The Committee are convinced that there are some types of cases in which use of a commission is preferable and others in which a jury may be appropriately used, and that it would be a mistake to provide that the same kind of tribunal should be used in all cases. We think the available evidence clearly leads to that conclusion.

When this suggestion was made at the conference of December 2, 1948, representatives of the Department of Justice opposed it, expressing opposition to the use of a commission in any case. Their principal ground for opposition to commissions was then based on the assertion that the commission system is too expensive because courts allow commissioners too large compensation. The obvious answer to that is that the compensation of commissioners ought to be fixed or limited by law, as was done in the TVA Act, and the agency dealing with appropriations—either the Administrative Office or some other interested department of the government—should correct that evil, if evil there be, by obtaining such legislation. Authority to promulgate rules of procedure does not include power to fix compensation of government employees. The Advisory Committee is not convinced that even without such legislation the commission system is more expensive than the jury system. The expense of jury trials includes not only the per diem and mileage of the jurors impaneled for a case but like items for the entire venire. In computing cost of jury trials, the salaries of court officials, judges, clerks, marshals and deputies must be considered. No figures have been given to the Committee to establish that the cost of the commission system is the greater.

We earnestly recommend the rule as now drafted for promulgation by the

Court, in the public interest.

The Advisory Committee have given more time to this rule, including time required for conferences with the Department of Justice to hear statements of its representatives, than has been required by any other rule. The rule may not be perfect but if faults develop in practice they may be promptly cured. Certainly the present conformity system is atrocious.

Under state practices, just compensation is normally determined by one of three methods: by commissioners; by commissioners with a right of appeal to and trial de novo before a jury; and by a jury, without a commission. A trial to the court or to the court including a master are, however, other methods that are occasionally used. Approximately 5 states use only commissioners; 23 states use commissioners with a trial de novo before a jury; and 18 states use only the jury. This classification is advisedly stated in approximate terms, since the same state may utilize diverse methods, depending upon different types of condemnations or upon the locality of the property, and since the methods used in a few states do not permit of a categorical classification. To reject the proposed rule and leave the situation as it is would not satisfy the views of the Department of Justice. The Department and the Advisory Committee agree that the use of a commission, with appeal to a jury, is a wasteful system.

The Department of Justice has a voluminous "Manual on Federal Eminent Domain," the 1940 edition of which has 948 pages with an appendix of 73 more pages. The title page informs us the preparation of the manual was begun during the incumbency of Attorney General Cummings, was continued under Attorney General Murphy, and completed during the incumbency of Attorney General Jackson. The preface contains the following statement:

It should also be mentioned that the research incorporated in the manual would be of invaluable assistance in the drafting of a new uniform code, or rules of court, for federal condemnation proceedings, which are now greatly confused, not only by the existence of over seventy federal statutes governing condemnations for different purposes—statutes which sometimes conflict with one another—but also by the countless problems occasioned by the requirements of conformity to state law. Progress of the work has already demonstrated that the need for such reform exists.

It is not surprising that more than once Attorneys General have asked the Advisory Committee to prepare a federal rule and rescue the government from this morass.

The Department of Justice has twice tried and failed to persuade the Congress to provide that juries shall be used in all condemnation cases. The debates in Congress show that part of the opposition to the Department of Justice's bills came from representatives opposed to jury trials in all cases, and in part from a preference for the conformity system. Our present proposal opens the door for district judges to yield to local preferences on the subject. It does much for the Department's points of view. It is a great improvement over the present so-called conformity system. It does away with the wasteful "double" system prevailing in 23 states where awards by commissions are followed by jury trials.

Aside from the question as to the choice of a tribunal to award compensation, the proposed rule would afford a simple and improved procedure.

We turn now to an itemized explanation of the other changes we have made in the 1948 draft. Some of these result from recent amendments to the Judicial Code. Others result from a reconsideration by the Advisory Committee of provisions which we thought could be improved.

1. In the amended Judicial Code, the district courts are designated as "United States District Courts" instead of "District Courts of the United States," and a corresponding change has been made in the rule.

2. After the 1948 draft was referred back to the committee, the provision in subdivision (c)(2), relating to naming defendants, * * * which provided that the plaintiff shall add as defendants all persons having or claiming an interest in that property whose names can be ascertained by a search of the records to the extent commonly made by competent searchers of title in the vicinity "in light of

the type and value of the property involved," the phrase in quotation marks was changed to read, "in the light of the character and value of the property involved and the interests to be acquired."

The Department of Justice made a counter proposal * * * that there be substituted the words "reasonably diligent search of the records, considering the type." When the American Bar Association thereafter considered the draft, it approved the Advisory Committee's draft of this subdivision, but said that it had no objection to the Department's suggestion. Thereafter, in an effort to eliminate controversy, the Advisory Committee accepted the Department's suggestion as to (c)(2), using the word "character" instead of the word "type."

The Department of Justice also suggested that in subdivision (d)(3)(ii) relating to service by publication, the search for a defendant's residence as a preliminary to publication be limited to the state in which the complaint is filed. Here again the American Bar Association's report expressed the view that the Department's suggestion was unobjectionable and the Advisory Committee thereupon adopted it.

3. Subdivision (k) of the 1948 draft is as follows:

(k) Condemnation Under a State's Power of Eminent Domain. If the action involves the exercise of the power of eminent domain under the law of a state, the practice herein prescribed may be altered to the extent necessary to observe and enforce any condition affecting the substantial rights of a litigant attached by the state law to the exercise of the state's power of eminent domain.

Occasionally condemnation cases under a state's power of eminent domain reach a United States District Court because of diversity of citizenship. Such cases are rare, but provision should be made for them.

The 1948 draft of (k) required a district court to decide whether a provision of state law specifying the tribunal to award compensation is or is not a "condition" attached to the exercise of the state's power. On reconsideration we concluded that it would be wise to redraft (k) so as to avoid that troublesome question. As to conditions in state laws which affect the substantial rights of a litigant, the district courts would be bound to give them effect without any rule on the subject. Accordingly we present two alternative revisions. One suggestion supported by a majority of the Advisory Committee is as follows:

(k) Condemnation Under a State's Power of Eminent Domain. The practice herein prescribed governs in actions involving the exercise of the power of eminent domain under the law of a state, provided that if the state law makes provision for trial of any issue by jury, or for trial of the issue of compensation by jury or commission or both, that provision shall be followed.

The other is as follows:

(k) Condemnation Under a State's Power of Eminent Domain. The practice herein prescribed governs in actions involving the exercise of the power of eminent domain under the law of a state, provided that if the state law gives a right to a trial by jury such a trial shall in any case be allowed to the party demanding it within the time permitted by these rules, and in that event no hearing before a commission shall be had.

The first proposal accepts the state law as to the tribunals to fix compensation, and in that respect leaves the parties in precisely the same situation as if the case were pending in a state court, including the use of a commission with appeal to a jury, if the state law so provides. It has the effect of avoiding any question as to whether the decisions in *Erie R. Co. v. Tompkins* and later cases have application to a situation of this kind.

The second proposal gives the parties a right to a jury trial if that is provided for by state law, but prevents the use of both commission and jury. Those members of the Committee who favor the second proposal do so because of the obvious objections to the double trial with a commission and appeal to a jury. As the decisions in *Erie R. Co. v. Tompkins* and later cases may have a bearing on this point, and the Committee is divided, we think both proposals should be placed before the Court.

4. The provision * * * of the 1948 draft * * * prescribing the effective date of

the rule was drafted before the recent amendment of the Judicial Code on that subject. On May 10, 1950, the President approved an act which amended section 2072 of Title 28, United States Code, to read as follows:

Such rules shall not take effect until they have been reported to Congress by the Chief Justice at or after the beginning of a regular session thereof but not later than the first day of May, and until the expiration of 90 days after they have been thus reported.

To conform to the statute now in force, we suggest a provision as follows:

Effective Date. This Rule 71A and the amendment to Rule 81(a) will take effect on August 1, 1951. Rule 71A governs all proceedings in actions brought after it takes effect and also all further proceedings in actions then pending, except to the extent that in the opinion of the court its application in a particular action pending when the rule takes effect would not be feasible or would work injustice, in which event the former procedure applies.

If the rule is not reported to Congress by May 1, 1951, this provision must be altered.

5. We call attention to the fact that the proposed rule does not contain a provision for the procedure to be followed in order to exercise the right of the United States to take immediate possession or title, when the condemnation proceeding is begun. There are several statutes conferring such a right which are cited in the original notes to the May 1948 draft * * *. The existence of this right is taken into account in the rule. In paragraph (c)(2), * * * it is stated: "Upon the commencement of the action, the plaintiff need join as defendants only the persons having or claiming an interest in the property whose names are then known." That is to enable the United States to exercise the right to immediate title or possession without the delay involved in ascertaining the names of all interested parties. The right is also taken into account in the provision relating to dismissal (paragraph (i), subdivisions (1), (2), and (3), * * *); also in paragraph (j) relating to deposits and their distribution.

The Advisory Committee considered whether the procedure for exercising the right should be specified in the rule and decided against it, as the procedure now being followed seems to be giving no trouble, and to draft a rule to fit all the statutes on the subject might create confusion.

The American Bar Association has taken an active interest in a rule for condemnation cases. In 1944 its House of Delegates adopted a resolution which among other things resolved:

That before adoption by the Supreme Court of the United States of any redraft of the proposed rule, time and opportunity should be afforded to the bar to consider and make recommendations concerning any such redraft.

Accordingly, in 1950 the revised draft was submitted to the American Bar Association and its section of real property, probate and trust law appointed a committee to consider it. That committee was supplied with copies of the written statement from the Department of Justice giving the reasons relied on by the Department for preferring a rule to use juries in all cases. The Advisory Committee's report was approved at a meeting of the section of real property law, and by the House of Delegates at the annual meeting of September 1950. The American Bar Association report gave particular attention to the question whether juries or commissions should be used to fix compensation, approved the Advisory Committee's solution appearing in their latest draft designed to allow use of commissions in projects comparable to the TVA, and rejected the proposal for use of juries in all cases.

In November 1950 a committee of the Federal Bar Association, the chairman of which was a Special Assistant to the Attorney General, made a report which reflected the attitude of the Department of Justice on the condemnation rule.

Aside from subdivision (h) about the tribunal to award compensation the final draft of the condemnation rule here presented has the approval of the American Bar Association and, we understand, the Department of Justice, and we do not know of any opposition to it. Subdivision (h) has the unanimous approval of the Advisory Committee and has been approved by the American Bar Association.

The use of commissions in TVA cases, and, by fair inference, in cases comparable to the TVA, is supported by 17 out of 20 judges who up to 1947 had sat in TVA cases. The legal staff of the TVA has vigorously objected to the substitution of juries for commissions in TVA cases. We regret to report that the Department of Justice still asks that subdivision (h) be altered to provide for jury trials in all cases where Congress has not specified the tribunal. We understand that the Department approves the proposal that the system prevailing in 23 states for the "double" trial, by commission with appeal to and trial de novo before a jury, should be abolished, and also asks that on demand a jury should be substituted for a commission, in those states where use of a commission alone is now required. The Advisory Committee has no evidence that commissions do not operate satisfactorily in the case of projects comparable to the TVA.

ORIGINAL REPORT

General Statement. 1. Background. When the Advisory Committee was formulating its recommendations to the Court concerning rules of procedure, which subsequently became the Federal Rules of 1938, the Committee concluded at an early stage not to fix the procedure in condemnation cases. This is a matter principally involving the exercise of the federal power of eminent domain, as very few condemnation cases involving the state's power reach the United States District Courts. The Committee's reasons at that time were that inasmuch as condemnation proceedings by the United States are governed by statutes of the United States, prescribing different procedure for various agencies and departments of the government, or, in the absence of such statutes, by local state practice under the Conformity Act (40 U.S.C., [former] sec. 258), it would be extremely difficult to draft a uniform rule satisfactory to the various agencies and departments of the government and to private parties; and that there was no general demand for a uniform rule. The Committee continued in that belief until shortly before the preparation of the April 1937 Draft of the Rules, when the officials of the Department of Justice having to do with condemnation cases urgently requested the Committee to propose rules on this subject. The Committee undertook the task and drafted a Condemnation Rule which appeared for the first time as Rule 74 of the April 1937 Draft. After the publication and distribution of this initial draft many objections were urged against it by counsel for various governmental agencies, whose procedure in condemnation cases was prescribed by federal statutes. Some of these agencies wanted to be excepted in whole or in part from the operation of the uniform rule proposed in April 1937. And the Department of Justice changed its position and stated that it preferred to have government condemnations conducted by local attorneys familiar with the state practice, which was applied under the Conformity Act where the Acts of Congress do not prescribe the practice; that it preferred to work under the Conformity Act without a uniform rule of procedure. The profession generally showed little interest in the proposed uniform rule. For these reasons the Advisory Committee in its Final Report to the Court in November 1937 proposed that all of Rule 74 be stricken and that the Federal Rules be made applicable only to appeals in condemnation cases. See note to Rule 74 of the Final Report.

Some six or seven years later when the Advisory Committee was considering the subject of amendments to the Federal Rules both government officials and the profession generally urged the adoption of some uniform procedure. This demand grew out of the volume of condemnation proceedings instituted during the war, and the general feeling of dissatisfaction with the diverse condemnation procedures that were applicable in the federal courts. A strongly held belief was that both the sovereign's power to condemn and the property owner's right to compensation could be promoted by a simplified rule. As a consequence the Committee proposed a Rule 71A on the subject of condemnation in its Preliminary Draft of May 1944. In the Second Preliminary Draft of May 1945 this earlier proposed Rule 71A was, however, omitted. The Committee did not then feel that it had sufficient time to prepare a revised draft satisfactory to it which would meet legitimate objections made to the draft of May 1944. To avoid unduly delaying the proposed amendments to existing rules the Committee concluded to proceed in the regular way with the preparation of the amendments to these rules and deal with the question of a condemnation rule as an independent matter. As a consequence it made no recommendations to the Court on condemnation in its Final Report of Proposed Amendments of June 1946; and the amendments which the Court adopted in December 1946 did not deal with condemnation. After concluding its task relative to amendments, the Committee returned to a consideration of eminent domain, its proposed Rule 71A of May 1944, the suggestions and criticisms that had been presented in the interim, and in June 1947 prepared and distributed to the profession another draft of a proposed condemnation rule. This draft contained several alternative provisions, specifically called attention to and asked for opinion relative to these matters, and in particular as to the constitution of the tribunal to award compensation. The present draft was based on the June 1947 formulation in light of the advice of the profession on both matters of substance and form.

2. Statutory Provisions. The need for a uniform condemnation rule in the federal courts arises from the fact that by various statutes Congress has prescribed diverse procedures for certain condemnation proceedings, and, in the absence of such statutes, has prescribed conformity to local state practice under 40 U.S.C. § 258. This general conformity adds to the diversity of procedure since in the United States there are multifarious methods of procedure in existence. Thus in 1931 it was said that there were 269 different methods of judicial procedure in different classes of condemnation cases and 56 methods of nonjudicial or administrative procedure. First Report of Judicial Council of Michigan, 1931, § 46, pp. 55 to 56. These numbers have not decreased. Consequently, the general requirement of conformity to state practice and procedure, particularly where the condemnor is the United States, leads to expense, delay and uncertainty. In advocacy of a uniform federal rule, see Armstrong, Proposed Amendments to Federal Rules for Civil Procedure 1944, 4 F.R.D. 124, 134; id., Report of the Advisory Committee on Federal Rules of Civil Procedure Recommending Amendments, 1946, 5 F.R.D. 339, 357.

There are a great variety of Acts of Congress authorizing the exercise of the power of eminent domain by the United States and its officers and agencies. These statutes for the most part do not specify the exact procedure to be followed, but where procedure is prescribed, it is by no means uniform.

The following are instances of Acts which merely authorize the exercise of the power without specific declaration as to the procedure:

U.S.C., Title 16:

§ 404c-11 (Mammoth Cave National Park; acquisition of lands, interests in lands or other property for park by the Secretary of the Interior).

§ 426d (Stones River National Park; acquisition of land for parks by the Secretary of the Army).

§ 450aa (George Washington Carver National Monument; acquisition of land by the Secretary of the Interior).

§ 517 (National forest reservation; title to lands to be acquired by the Secretary of Agriculture).

U.S.C., Title 42:

§§ 1805(b)(5), 1813(b) (Atomic Energy Act).

The following are instances of Acts which authorized condemnation and declare that the procedure is to conform with that of similar actions in state courts:

U.S.C., Title 16:

§ 423k (Richmond National Battlefield Park; acquisition of lands by the Secretary of the Interior).

§ 714 (Exercise by water power licensee of power of eminent domain).

U.S.C., Title 24:

§ 78 (Condemnation of land for the former National Home for Disabled Volunteer Soldiers).

U.S.C., Title 33:

§ 591 (Condemnation of lands and materials for river and harbor improvement by the Secretary of the Army).

U.S.C., Title 40:

§ 257 (Condemnation of realty for sites for public building and for other public uses by the Secretary of the Treasury authorized).

§ 258 (Same procedure).

U.S.C., Title 50:

§ 171 (Acquisition of land by the Secretary of the Army for national defense).

§ 172 (Acquisition of property by the Secretary of the Army, etc., for production of lumber).

§ 632 App. (Second War Powers Act, 1942; acquisition of real property for war purposes by the Secretary of the Army, the Secretary of the Navy and others).

The following are Acts in which a more or less complete code of procedure is set forth in connection with the taking:

U.S.C., Title 16:

§ 831x (Condemnation by Tennessee Valley Authority).

U.S.C., Title 40:

§§ 361 to 386 (now D.C. Code, 1951 Ed., Title 16-619 to 16-644) (Acquisition of lands in District of Columbia for use of United States; condemnation).

3. Adjustment of Rule to Statutory Provisions. While it was apparent that the principle of uniformity should be the basis for a rule to replace the multiple diverse procedures set out above, there remained a serious question as to whether an exception could properly be made relative to the method of determining compensation. Where Congress had provided for conformity to state law the following were the general methods in use: an initial determination by commissioners, with appeal to a judge; an initial award, likewise made by commissioners, but with the appeal to a jury; and determination by a jury without a previous award by commissioners. In two situations Congress had specified the tribunal to determine the issue of compensation: condemnation by the Tennessee Valley Authority; and condemnation in the District of Columbia. Under the TVA procedure the initial determination of value is by three disinterested commissioners, appointed by the court, from a locality other than the one in which the land lies. Either party may except to the award of the commission;

in that case the exceptions are to be heard by three district judges (unless the parties stipulate for a lesser number), with a right of appeal to the circuit court of appeals. The TVA is a regional agency. It is faced with the necessity of acquiring a very substantial acreage within a relatively small area, and charged with the task of carrying on within the Tennessee Valley and in cooperation with the local people a permanent program involving navigation and flood control, electric power, soil conservation, and general regional development. The success of this program is partially dependent upon the good will and cooperation of the people of the Tennessee Valley, and this in turn partially depends upon the land acquisition program. Disproportionate awards among landowners would create dissatisfaction and ill will. To secure uniformity in treatment Congress provided the rather unique procedure of the three-judge court to review de novo the initial award of the commissioners. This procedure has worked to the satisfaction of the property owners and the TVA. A full statement of the TVA position and experience is set forth in Preliminary Draft to Proposed Rule to Govern Condemnation Cases (June, 1947) 15–19. A large majority of the district judges with experience under this procedure approve it, subject to some objection to the requirement for a three-judge district court to review commissioners' awards. A statutory three-judge requirement is, however, jurisdictional and must be strictly followed. *Stratton v. St. Louis, Southwestern Ry. Co., 1930*, 282 U.S. 10, 51 S. Ct. 8, 75 L.Ed. 135; *Ayrshire Collieries Corp. v. United States, 1947*, 331 U.S. 132, 67 S. Ct. 1168, 91 L.Ed. 1391. Hence except insofar as the TVA statute itself authorizes the parties to stipulate for a court of less than three judges, the requirement must be followed, and would seem to be beyond alteration by court rule even if change were thought desirable. Accordingly the TVA procedure is retained for the determination of compensation in TVA condemnation cases. It was also thought desirable to retain the specific method Congress had prescribed for the District of Columbia, which is a so-called jury of five appointed by the court. This is a local matter and the specific treatment accorded by Congress has given local satisfaction.

Aside from the foregoing limited exceptions dealing with the TVA and the District of Columbia, the question was whether a uniform method for determining compensation should be a commission with appeal to a district judge, or a commission with appeal to a jury, or a jury without a commission. Experience with the commission on a nationwide basis, and in particular with the utilization of a commission followed by an appeal to a jury, has been that the commission is time consuming and expensive. Furthermore, it is largely a futile procedure where it is preparatory to jury trial. Since in the bulk of states a land owner is entitled eventually to a jury trial, since the jury is a traditional tribunal for the determination of questions of value, and since experience with juries has proved satisfactory to both government and land owner, the right to jury trial is adopted as the general rule. Condemnation involving the TVA and the District of Columbia are the two exceptions. See Note to Subdivision (h), infra.

Note to Subdivision (a). As originally promulgated the Federal rules governed appeals in condemnation proceedings but were not otherwise applicable. Rule 81(a)(7). Pre-appeal procedure, in the main, conformed to state procedure. See statutes and discussion, supra. The purpose of Rule 71A is to provide a uniform procedure for condemnation in the federal district courts, including the District of Columbia. To achieve this purpose Rule 71A prescribes such specialized procedure as is required by condemnation proceedings, otherwise it utilizes the general framework of the Federal Rules where specific detail is unnecessary. The adoption of Rule 71A, of course, renders paragraph (7) of Rule 81(a) unnecessary.

The promulgation of a rule for condemnation procedure is within the rule-making power. The Enabling Act [Act of June 19, 1934, c. 651, §§ 1, 2 (48 Stat. 1064), 28 U.S.C., former §§ 723b, 723c, now § 2072] gives the Supreme Court "the power to prescribe, by general rules * * * the forms of process, writs, pleadings, and motions, and the practice and procedure in civil actions at law." Such rules, however, must not abridge, enlarge, or modify substantive rights. In *Kohl v. United States, 1875*, 91 U.S. 367, 23 L.Ed. 449, a proceeding instituted by the United States to appropriate land for a postoffice site under a statute enacted for such purpose, the Supreme Court held that "a proceeding to take land in virtue of the government's eminent domain, and determining the compensation to be made for it, is * * * a suit at common law, when initiated in a court." See, also, *Madisonville Traction Co. v. St. Bernard Mining Co., 1905*, 196 U.S. 239, 25 S. Ct. 251, 49 L.Ed. 462, infra, under subdivision (k). And the Conformity Act, 40 U.S.C., § 258, which is superseded by Rule 71A, deals only with "practice, pleadings, forms and proceedings and not with matters of substantive laws." *United States v. 243.22 Acres of Land in Village of Farmingdale, Town of Babylon, Suffolk County, N.Y., D.C.N.Y.1942*, 43 F.Supp. 561, affirmed 129 F.2d 678, certiorari denied 317 U.S. 698, 63 S. Ct. 441, 87 L.Ed. 558.

Rule 71A affords a uniform procedure for all cases of condemnation invoking the national power of eminent domain, and, to the extent stated in subdivision (k), for cases invoking a state's power of eminent domain; and supplants all statutes prescribing a different procedure. While the almost exclusive utility of the rule is for the condemnation of real property, it also applies to the condemnation of personal property, either as an incident to real property or as the sole object of the proceeding, when permitted or required by statute. See 38 U.S.C., § 438j (World War Veterans' Relief Act); 42 U.S.C., §§ 1805, 1811, 1813 (Atomic Energy Act); 50 U.S.C., § 79 (Nitrates Act); 50 U.S.C., §§ 161 to 166 (Helium Gas Act). Requisitioning of personal property with the right in the owner to sue the United States, where the compensation cannot be agreed upon (see 42 U.S.C., § 1813, supra, for example) will continue to be the normal method of acquiring personal property and Rule 71A in no way interferes with or restricts any such right. Only where the law requires or permits the formal procedure of condemnation to be utilized will the rule have any applicability to the acquisition of personal property.

Rule 71A is not intended to and does not supersede the Act of February 26, 1931, c. 307, §§ 1 to 5 (46 Stat. 1421), 40 U.S.C., §§ 258a to 258e, which is a supplementary condemnation statute, permissive in its nature and designed to permit the prompt acquisition of title by the United States, pending the condemnation proceeding, upon a deposit in court. See *United States v. 76,800 Acres, More or Less, of Land, in Bryan and Liberty Counties, Ga., D.C.Ga.1942*, 44 F.Supp. 653; *United States v. 17,280 Acres of Land, More or Less, Situated in Saunders County, Neb., D.C.Neb.1942*, 47 F.Supp. 267. The same is true insofar as the following or any other statutes authorize the acquisition of title or the taking of immediate possession:

U.S.C., Title 33:

§ 594 (When immediate possession of land may be taken; for a work of river and harbor improvements).

U.S.C., Title 42:

§ 1813(b) (When immediate possession may be taken under Atomic Energy Act).

U.S.C., Title 50:

§ 171 (Acquisition of land by the Secretary of the Army for national defense).

§ 632 App. (Second War Powers Act, 1942; Acquisition of real property for war purposes by the Secretary of the Army, the Secretary of the Navy, and others).

Note to Subdivision (b). This subdivision provides for broad joinder in accordance with the tenor of other rules such as Rule 18. To require separate condemnation proceedings for each piece of property separately owned would be unduly burdensome and would serve no useful purpose. And a restriction that only properties may be joined which are to be acquired for the same public use would also cause difficulty. For example, a unified project to widen a street, construct a bridge across a navigable river, and for the construction of approaches to the level of the bridge on both sides of the river might involve acquiring property for different public uses. Yet it is eminently desirable that the plaintiff may in one proceeding condemn all the property interests and rights necessary to carry out this project. Rule 21 which allows the court to sever and proceed separately with any claim against a party, and Rule 42(b) giving the court broad discretion to order separate trials give adequate protection to all defendants in condemnation proceedings.

Note to Subdivision (c). Since a condemnation proceeding is in rem and since a great many property owners are often involved, paragraph (1) requires the property to be named and only one of the owners. In other respects the caption will contain the name of the court, the title of the action, file number, and a designation of the pleading as a complaint in accordance with Rule 10(a).

Since the general standards of pleading are stated in other rules, paragraph (2) prescribes only the necessary detail for condemnation proceedings. Certain statutes allow the United States to acquire title or possession immediately upon commencement of an action. See the Act of February 26, 1931, c. 307, §§ 1 to 5 (46 Stat. 1421), 40 U.S.C., §§ 258a to 258e, supra; and 33 U.S.C., § 594, 42 U.S.C., § 1813(b), 50 U.S.C., §§ 171, 632, supra. To carry out the purpose of such statutes and to aid the condemnor in instituting the action even where title is not acquired at the outset, the plaintiff is initially required to join as defendants only the persons having or claiming an interest in the property whose names are then known. This in no way prejudices the property owner, who must eventually be joined as a defendant, served with process, and allowed to answer before there can be any hearing involving the compensation to be paid for his piece of property. The rule requires the plaintiff to name all persons having or claiming an interest in the property of whom the plaintiff has learned and, more importantly, those appearing of record. By charging the plaintiff with the necessity to make "a search of the records of the extent commonly made by competent searchers of title in the vicinity in light of the type and value of the property involved" both the plaintiff and property owner are protected. Where a short term interest in property of little value is involved, as a two or three year easement over a vacant land for purposes of ingress and egress to other property, a search of the records covering a long period of time is not required. Where on the other hand fee simple title in valuable property is being condemned the search must necessarily cover a much longer period of time and be commensurate with the interests involved. But even here the search is related to the type made by competent title searchers in the vicinity. A search that extends back to the original patent may be feasible in some midwestern and western states and be proper under certain circumstances. In the Atlantic seaboard states such a search is normally not feasible nor desirable. There is a common sense business accommodation of what title searchers can and should do. For state statutes requiring persons appearing as owners or otherwise interested in the property to be named as defendants, see 3 Colo.Stat.Ann., 1935, c. 61, § 2; Ill.Ann.Stat., Smith-Hurd, c. 47, § 2; 1 Iowa Code, 1946, § 472.3; Kans.Stat.Ann., 1935, § 26-101; 2 Mass.Laws Ann., 1932, c. 80A, § 4; 7 Mich.Stat.Ann., 1936, § 8.2; 2 Minn.Stat., Mason, 1927, § 6541; 20 N.J.Stat. Ann., 1939, § 1-2; 3 Wash.Revised Stat., Remington, 1932, Title 6, § 891. For state provisions allowing persons whose names are not known to be designated under the descriptive term of "unknown owner", see Hawaii Revised Laws, 1945, c. 8, § 310 ("Such [unknown] defendant may be joined in the petition under a fictitious name."); Ill.Ann.Stat., Smith-Hurd, c. 47, § 2 ("Persons interested, whose names are unknown, may be made parties defendant by the description of the unknown owners; * * *"); Maryland Code Ann., 1939, Art. 33A, § 1 ("In case any owner or owners is or are not known, he or they may be described in such petition as the unknown owner or owners, or the unknown heir or heirs of a deceased owner."); 2 Mass.Laws Ann., 1932, c. 80A, § 4

("Persons not in being, unascertained or unknown who may have an interest in any of such land shall be made parties respondent by such description as seems appropriate, * * *"); New Mex.Stat.Ann., 1941, § 25-901 ("the owners * * * shall be parties defendant, by name, if the names are known, and by description of the unknown owners of the land therein described, if their names are unknown."); Utah Code Ann., 1943, § 104-61-7 ("The names of all owners and claimants of the property, if known, or a statement that they are unknown who must be styled defendants").

The last sentence of paragraph (2) enables the court to expedite the distribution of a deposit, in whole or in part, as soon as pertinent facts of ownership, value and the like are established. See also subdivision (j).

The signing of the complaint is governed by Rule 11.

Note to Subdivision (d). In lieu of a summons, which is the initial process in other civil actions under Rule 4(a), subdivision (d) provides for a notice which is to contain sufficient information so that the defendant in effect obtains the plaintiff's statement of his claim against the defendant to whom the notice is directed. Since the plaintiff's attorney is an officer of the court and to prevent unduly burdening the clerk of the court, paragraph (1) of subdivision (d) provides that plaintiff's attorney shall prepare and deliver a notice or notices to the clerk. Flexibility is provided by the provision for joint or several notices and for additional notices. Where there are only a few defendants it may be convenient to prepare but one notice directed to all the defendants. In other cases where there are many defendants it will be more convenient to prepare two or more notices; but in any event a notice must be directed to each named defendant. Paragraph (2) provides that the notice is to be signed by the plaintiff's attorney. Since the notice is to be delivered to the clerk, the issuance of the notice will appear of record in the court. The clerk should forthwith deliver the notice or notices for service to the marshal or to a person specially appointed to serve the notice. Rule 4(a). The form of the notice is such that, in addition to informing the defendant of the plaintiff's statement of claim, it tells the defendant precisely what his rights are. Failure on the part of the defendant to serve an answer constitutes a consent to the taking and to the authority of the court to proceed to fix compensation therefor, but it does not preclude the defendant from presenting evidence as to the amount of compensation due him or in sharing the award of distribution. See subdivision (e); Form 28.

While under Rule 4(f) the territorial limits of a summons are normally the territorial limits of the state in which the district court is held, the territorial limits for personal service of a notice under Rule 71A(d)(3) are those of the nation. This extension of process is here proper since the aim of the condemnation proceeding is not to enforce any personal liability and the property owner is helped not imposed upon, by the best type of service possible. If personal service cannot be made either because the defendant's whereabouts cannot be ascertained, or, if ascertained, the defendant cannot be personally served, as where he resides in a foreign country such as Canada or Mexico, then service by publication is proper. The provisions for this type of service are set forth in the rule and are in no way governed by 28 U.S.C., § 118.

Note to Subdivision (e). Departing from the scheme of Rule 12, subdivision (e) requires all defenses and objections to be presented in an answer and does not authorize a preliminary motion. There is little need for the latter in condemnation proceedings. The general standard of pleading is governed by other rules, particularly Rule 8, and this subdivision (e) merely prescribes what matters the answer should set forth. Merely by appearing in the action a defendant can receive notice of all proceedings affecting him. And without the necessity of answering a defendant may present evidence as to the amount of compensation due him, and he may share in the distribution of the award. See also subdivision (d)(2); Form 28.

Note to Subdivision (f). Due to the number of persons who may be interested in the property to be condemned, there is a likelihood that the plaintiff will need to amend his complaint, perhaps many times, to add new parties or state new issues. This subdivision recognizes that fact and does not burden the court with applications by the plaintiff for leave to amend. At the same time all defendants are adequately protected; and their need to amend the answer is adequately protected by Rule 15 which is applicable by virtue of subdivision (a) of this Rule 71A.

Note to Subdivision (g). A condemnation action is a proceeding in rem. Commencement of the action as against a defendant by virtue of his joinder pursuant to subdivision (c)(2) is the point of cut-off and there is no mandatory requirement or substitution because of a subsequent change of interest, although the court is given ample power to require substitution. Rule 25 is inconsistent with subdivision (g) and hence inapplicable. Accordingly, the time periods of Rule 25 do not govern to require dismissal nor to prevent substitution.

Note to Subdivision (h). This subdivision prescribes the method for determining the issue of just compensation in cases involving the federal power of eminent domain. The method of jury trial provided by subdivision (h) will normally apply in cases involving the state power by virtue of subdivision (k).

Congress has specially constituted a tribunal for the trial of the issue of just compensation in two instances: condemnation under the Tennessee Valley Authority Act; and condemnation in the District of Columbia. These tribunals are retained for reasons set forth in the General Statement: 3. Adjustment of Rule to Statutory Provisions, supra. Subdivision (h) also has prospective application so that if Congress should create another special tribunal, that tribunal will determine the issue of just compensation. Subject to these exceptions the general method of trial of that issue is to be by jury if any party demands it, otherwise that issue, as well as all other issues, are to be tried by the court.

As to the TVA procedure that is continued, U.S.C., Title 16, § 831x requires that three commissioners be appointed to fix the compensation; that exceptions to their award are to be heard by three district judges (unless the parties stipulate for a lesser number) and that the district judges try the question de novo; that an appeal to the circuit court of appeals may be taken within 30 days from the filing of the decision of the district judges; and that the circuit court of appeals shall on the record fix compensation "without regard to the awards of findings theretofore made by the commissioners or the district judges." The mode of fixing compensation in the District of Columbia, which is also continued, is prescribed in U.S.C., Title 40, §§ 361 to 386. Under § 371 the court is required in all cases to order the selection of a jury of five from among not less than 20 names, drawn "from the special box provided by law." They must have the usual qualifications of jurors and in addition must be freeholders of the District, and not in the service of the United States or the District. A special oath is administered to the chosen jurors. The trial proceeds in the ordinary way, except that the jury is allowed to separate after they have begun to consider their verdict.

There is no constitutional right to jury trial in a condemnation proceeding, *Bauman v. Ross, 1897*, 167 U.S. 548, 17 S. Ct. 966, 42 L.Ed. 270. See, also, Hines, Does the Seventh Amendment to the Constitution of the United States Require Jury Trials in all Condemnation Proceedings?, 1925, 11 Va.L.Rev. 505; Blair, Federal Condemnation Proceedings and the Seventh Amendment, 1927, 41 Harv.L.Rev. 29; 3 Moore's Federal Practice, 1938, 3007. Prior to Rule 71A, jury trial in federal condemnation proceedings was however, enjoyed under the general conformity statute, 40 U.S.C., § 258, in states which provided for jury trial. See generally, 2 Lewis, Eminent Domain, 3d ed. 1909, §§ 509, 510; 3 Moore, op. cit. supra. Since the general conformity statute is superseded by Rule 71A, see supra under subdivision (a), and since it was believed that the rule to be substituted should likewise give a right to jury trial, subdivision (h) establishes that method as the general one for determining the issue of just compensation.

Note to Subdivision (i). Both the right of the plaintiff to dismiss by filing a notice of dismissal and the right of the court to permit a dismissal are circumscribed to the extent that where the plaintiff has acquired the title or a lesser interest or possession, viz., any property interest for which just compensation should be paid, the action may not be dismissed, without the defendant's consent, and the property owner remitted to another court, such as the Court of Claims, to recover just compensation for the property right taken. Circuity of action is thus prevented without increasing the liability of the plaintiff to pay just compensation for any interest that is taken. Freedom of dismissal is accorded, where both the condemnor and condemnee agree, up to the time of the entry of judgment vesting plaintiff with title. And power is given to the court, where the parties agree, to vacate the judgment and thus revest title in the property owner. In line with Rule 21, the court may at any time drop a defendant who has been unnecessarily or improperly joined as where it develops that he has no interest.

Note to Subdivision (j). Whatever the substantive law is concerning the necessity of making a deposit will continue to govern. For statutory provisions concerning deposit in court in condemnation proceedings by the United States, see U.S.C., Title 40, § 258a; U.S.C., Title 33, § 594—acquisition of title and possession statutes referred to in note to subdivision (a), supra. If the plaintiff is invoking the state's power of eminent domain the necessity of deposit will be governed by the state law. For discussion of such law, see 1 Nichols, Eminent Domain, 2d ed. 1917, §§ 209–216. For discussion of the function of deposit and the power of the court to enter judgment in cases both of deficiency and overpayment, see *United States v. Miller, 1943*, 317 U.S. 369, 63 S. Ct. 276, 87 L.Ed. 336, 147 A.L.R. 55, rehearing denied 318 U.S. 798, 63 S. Ct. 557, 87 L.Ed. 1162 (judgment in favor of plaintiff for overpayment ordered).

The court is to make distribution of the deposit as promptly as the facts of the case warrant. See also subdivision (c)(2).

Note to Subdivision (k). While the overwhelming number of cases that will be brought in the federal courts under this rule will be actions involving the federal power of eminent domain, a small percentage of cases may be instituted in the federal court or removed thereto on the basis of diversity or alienage which will involve the power of eminent domain under the law of a state. See *Boom Co. v. Patterson, 1878*, 98 U.S. 403, 25 L.Ed. 206; *Searl v. School District No. 2, 1888*, 124 U.S. 197, 8 S. Ct. 460, 31 L.Ed. 415; *Madisonville Traction Co. v. Saint Bernard Mining Co., 1905*, 196 U.S. 239, 25 S. Ct. 251, 49 L.Ed. 462. In the Madisonville case, and in cases cited therein, it has been held that condemnation actions brought by state corporations in the exercise of a power delegated by the state might be governed by procedure prescribed by the laws of the United States, whether the cases were begun in or removed to the federal court. See, also, *Franzen v. Chicago, M. & St. P. Ry. Co., C.C.A.7th, 1921*, 278 F. 370, 372.

Any condition affecting the substantial right of a litigant attached by state law is to be observed and enforced, such as making a deposit in court where the power of eminent domain is conditioned upon so doing. (See also subdivision (j)). Subject to this qualification, subdivision (k) provides that in cases involving the state power of eminent domain, the practice prescribed by other subdivisions of Rule 71A shall govern.

Note to Subdivision (*l*). Since the condemnor will normally be the prevailing party and since he should not recover his costs against the property owner, Rule 54(d), which provides generally that costs shall go to the prevailing party, is made inapplicable. Without attempting to state what the rule on costs is, the effect of subdivision (*l*) is that costs shall be awarded in accordance with the law that has developed in condemnation cases. This has been summarized as follows: "Costs of condemnation proceedings are not assessable against the condemnee, unless by stipulation he agrees to assume some or all of them. Such normal expenses of the proceeding as bills for publication of notice, commissioners' fees, the cost of transporting commissioners and jurors to take a view, fees for attorneys to represent defendants who have failed to answer, and witness' fees, are properly charged to the government, though not taxed as costs. Similarly, if it is necessary that a conveyance be executed by a commissioner, the United States pay his fees and those for recording the deed. However, the distribution of the award is a matter in which the United States has no legal interest. Expenses incurred in ascertaining the identity of distributees and deciding between conflicting claimants are properly chargeable against the award, not against the United States, although United States attorneys are expected to aid the court in such matters as amici curiae." Lands Division Manual 861. For other discussion and citation, see *Grand River Dam Authority v. Jarvis, C.C.A. 10th, 1942*, 124 F.2d 914. Costs may not be taxed against the United States except to the extent permitted by law. *United States v. 125.71 Acres of Land in Loyalhanna Tp., Westmoreland County, Pa., D.C.Pa.1944*, 54 F.Supp. 193; Lands Division Manual 859. Even if it were thought desirable to allow the property owner's costs to be taxed against the United States, this is a matter for legislation and not court rule.

1963 AMENDMENT

This amendment conforms to the amendment of Rule 4(f).

1985 AMENDMENT

Rule 71A(h) provides that except when Congress has provided otherwise, the issue of just compensation in a condemnation case may be tried by a jury if one of the parties so demands, unless the court in its discretion orders the issue determined by a commission of three persons. In 1980, the Comptroller General of the United States in a Report to Congress recommended that use of the commission procedure should be encouraged in order to improve and expedite the trial of condemnation cases. The Report noted that long delays were being caused in many districts by such factors as crowded dockets, the precedence given criminal cases, the low priority accorded condemnation matters, and the high turnover of Assistant United States Attorneys. The Report concluded that revising Rule 71A to make the use of the commission procedure more attractive might alleviate the situation.

Accordingly, Rule 71A(h) is being amended in a number of respects designed to assure the quality and utility of a Rule 71A commission. First, the amended Rule will give the court discretion to appoint, in addition to the three members of a commission, up to two additional persons as alternate commissioners who would hear the case and be available, at any time up to the filing of the decision by the three-member commission, to replace any commissioner who becomes unable or disqualified to continue. The discretion to appoint alternate commissioners can be particularly useful in protracted cases, avoiding expensive retrials that have been required in some cases because of the death or disability of a commissioner. Prior to replacing a commissioner an alternate would not be present at, or participate in, the commission's deliberations.

Second, the amended Rule requires the court, before appointment, to advise the parties of the identity and qualifications of each prospective commissioner and alternate. The court then may authorize the examination of prospective appointees by the parties and each party has the right to challenge for cause. The objective is to insure that unbiased and competent commissioners are appointed.

The amended Rule does not prescribe a qualification standard for appointment to a commission, although it is understood that only persons possessing background and ability to appraise real estate valuation testimony and to award fair and just compensation on the basis thereof would be appointed. In most situations the chairperson should be a lawyer and all members should have some background qualifying them to weigh proof of value in the real estate field and, when possible, in the particular real estate market embracing the land in question.

The amended Rule should give litigants greater confidence in the commission procedure by affording them certain rights to participate in the appointment of commission members that are roughly comparable to the practice with regard to jury selection. This is accomplished by giving the court permission to allow the parties to examine prospective commissioners and by recognizing the right of each party to object to the appointment of any person for cause.

1987 AMENDMENT

The amendments are technical. No substantive change is intended.

1988 AMENDMENT

The amendment is technical. No substantive change is intended.

1993 AMENDMENT

The references to the subdivisions of Rule 4 are deleted in light of the revision of that rule.

2003 AMENDMENT

The references to specific subdivisions of Rule 53 are deleted or revised to reflect amendments of Rule 53.

2007 AMENDMENTS

The language of Rule 71A has been amended as part of the general restyling of the Civil Rules to make them more easily understood and to make style and terminology consistent throughout the rules. These changes are intended to be stylistic only.

Former Rule 71A has been redesignated as Rule 71.1 to conform to the designations used for all other rules added with the original numbering system.

Rule 71.1(e) allows a defendant to appear without answering. Former form 28 (now form 60) includes information about this right in the Rule 71.1(d)(2) notice. It is useful to confirm this practice in the rule.

The information that identifies the attorney is changed to include telephone number and electronic-mail address, in line with similar amendments to Rules 11(a) and 26(g)(1).

2009 AMENDMENTS

The times set in the former rule at 20 days have been revised to 21 days. See the Note to Rule 6.

Rule 72. Magistrate Judges; Pretrial Orders

1983 ADDITION

Subdivision (a). This subdivision addresses court-ordered referrals of nondispositive matters under 28 U.S.C. § 636(b)(1)(A). The rule calls for a written order of the magistrate's disposition to preserve the record and facilitate review. An oral order read into the record by the magistrate will satisfy this requirement.

No specific procedures or timetables for raising objections to the magistrate's rulings on nondispositive matters are set forth in the Magistrates Act. The rule fixes a 10-day period in order to avoid uncertainty and provide uniformity that will eliminate the confusion that might arise if different periods were prescribed by local rule in different districts. It also is contemplated that a party who is successful before the magistrate will be afforded an opportunity to respond to objections raised to the magistrate's ruling.

The last sentence of subdivision (a) specifies that reconsideration of a magistrate's order, as provided for in the Magistrates Act, shall be by the district judge to whom the case is assigned. This rule does not restrict experimentation by the district courts under 28 U.S.C. § 636(b)(3) involving references of matters other than pretrial matters, such as appointment of counsel, taking of default judgments, and acceptance of jury verdicts when the judge is unavailable.

Subdivision (b). This subdivision governs court-ordered referrals of dispositive pretrial matters and prisoner petitions challenging conditions of confinement, pursuant to statutory authorization in 28 U.S.C. § 636(b)(1)(B). This rule does not extend to habeas corpus petitions, which are covered by the specific rules relating to proceedings under Sections 2254 and 2255 of Title 28.

This rule implements the statutory procedures for making objections to the magistrate's proposed findings and recommendations. The 10-day period, as specified in the statute, is subject to Rule 6(e) which provides for an additional 3-day period when service is made by mail. Although no specific provision appears in the Magistrates Act, the rule specifies a 10-day period for a party to respond to objections to the magistrate's recommendation.

Implementing the statutory requirements, the rule requires the district judge to whom the case is assigned to make a de novo determination of those portions of the report, findings, or recommendations to which timely objection is made. The term "de novo" signifies that the magistrate's findings are not protected by the clearly erroneous doctrine, but does not indicate that a second evidentiary hearing is required. See United States v. Raddatz, 417 [447] U.S. 667 (1980). See also Silberman, *Masters and Magistrates Part II: The American Analogue,* 50 N.Y.U.L.Rev. 1297, 1367 (1975). When no timely objection is filed, the court need only satisfy itself that there is no clear error on the face of the record in order to accept the recommendation. See *Campbell v. United States Dist. Court*, 501 F.2d 196, 206 (9th Cir.1974), cert. denied, 419 U.S. 879, 95 S. Ct. 143, 42 L. Ed. 2d 119, quoted in House Report No. 94-1609, 94th Cong. 2d Sess. (1976) at 3. Compare *Park Motor Mart, Inc. v. Ford Motor Co.*, 616 F.2d 603 (1st Cir. 1980). Failure to make timely objection to the magistrate's report prior to its adoption by the district judge may constitute a waiver of appellate review of the district judge's order. See *United States v. Walters*, 638 F.2d 947 (6th Cir.1981).

1991 AMENDMENT

This amendment is intended to eliminate a discrepancy in measuring the 10 days for serving and filing objections to a magistrate's action under subdivisions (a) and (b) of this Rule. The rule as promulgated in 1983 required objections to the magistrate's handling of nondispositive matters to be served and filed within 10 days of entry of the order, but required objections to dispositive motions to be made within 10 days of being served with a copy of the recommended disposition. Subdivision (a) is here amended to conform to subdivision (b) to avoid any confusion or technical defaults, particularly in connection with magistrate orders that rule on both dispositive and nondispositive matters.

The amendment is also intended to assure that objections to magistrate's orders that are not timely made shall not be considered. *Compare* Rule 51.

1993 AMENDMENT

This revision is made to conform the rule to changes made by the Judicial Improvements Act of 1990.

2007 AMENDMENTS

The language of Rule 72 has been amended as part of the general restyling of the Civil Rules to make them more easily understood and to make style and terminology consistent throughout the rules. These changes are intended to be stylistic only.

2009 AMENDMENTS

The times set in the former rule at 10 days have been revised to 14 days. See the Note to Rule 6.

Rule 73. Magistrate Judges; Trial by Consent and Appeal

1983 ADDITION

Subdivision (a). This subdivision implements the broad authority of the 1979 amendments to the Magistrates Act, 28 U.S.C. § 636(c), which permit a magistrate to sit in lieu of a district judge and exercise civil jurisdiction over a case, when the parties consent. See McCabe, *The Federal Magistrate Act of 1979,* 16 Harv.J.Legis. 343, 364–79 (1979). In order to exercise this jurisdiction, a magistrate must be specially designated under 28 U.S.C. § 636(c)(1) by the district court or courts he serves. The only exception to a magistrate's exercise of civil jurisdiction, which includes the power to conduct jury and nonjury trials and decide dispositive motions, is the contempt power. A hearing on contempt is to be conducted by the district judge upon certification of the facts and an order to show cause by the magistrate. See 28 U.S.C. § 639(e). In view of 28 U.S.C. § 636(c)(1) and this rule, it is unnecessary to amend Rule 58 to provide that the decision of a magistrate is a "decision by the court" for the purposes of that rule and a "final decision of the district court" for purposes of 28 U.S.C. § 1291 governing appeals.

Subdivision (b). This subdivision implements the blind consent provision of 28 U.S.C. § 636(c)(2) and is designed to ensure that neither the judge nor the magistrate attempts to induce a party to consent to reference of a civil matter under this rule to a magistrate. See House Rep. No. 96-444, 96th Cong. 1st Sess. 8 (1979).

The rule opts for a uniform approach in implementing the consent provision by directing the clerk to notify the parties of their opportunity to elect to proceed before a magistrate and by requiring the execution and filing of a consent form or forms setting forth the election. However, flexibility at the local level is preserved in that local rules will determine how notice shall be communicated to the parties, and local rules will specify the time period within which an election must be made.

The last paragraph of subdivision (b) reiterates the provision in 28 U.S.C. § 636(c)(6) for vacating a reference to the magistrate.

Subdivision (c). Under 28 U.S.C. § 636(c)(3), the normal route of appeal from the judgment of a magistrate—the only route that will be available unless the parties otherwise agree in advance—is an appeal by the aggrieved party "directly to the appropriate United States court of appeals from the judgment of the magistrate in the same manner as an appeal from any other judgment of a district court." The quoted statutory language indicates Congress' intent that the same procedures and standards of appealability that govern appeals from district court judgments govern appeals from magistrates' judgments.

Subdivision (d). 28 U.S.C. § 636(c)(4) offers parties who consent to the exercise of civil jurisdiction by a magistrate an alternative appeal route to that provided in subdivision (c) of this rule. This optional appellate route was provided by Congress in recognition of the fact that not all civil cases warrant the same appellate treatment. In cases where the amount in controversy is not great and there are no difficult questions of law to be resolved, the parties may desire to avoid the expense and delay of appeal to the court of appeals by electing an appeal to the district judge. See McCabe, *The Federal Magistrate Act of 1979,* 16 Harv.J.Legis. 343, 388 (1979). This subdivision provides that the parties may elect the optional appeal route at the time of reference to a magistrate. To this end, the notice by the clerk under subdivision (b) of this rule shall explain the appeal option and the corollary restriction on review by the court of appeals. This approach will avoid later claims of lack of consent to the avenue of appeal. The choice of the alternative appeal route to the judge of the district court should be made by the parties in their forms of consent. Special appellate rules to govern appeals from a magistrate to a district judge appear in new Rules 74 through 76.

1987 AMENDMENT

The amendment is technical. No substantive change is intended.

1993 AMENDMENT

This revision is made to conform the rule to changes made by the Judicial Improvements Act of 1990. The Act requires that, when being reminded of the availability of a magistrate judge, the parties be advised that withholding of consent will have no "adverse substantive consequences." They may, however, be advised if the withholding of consent will have the adverse procedural consequence of a potential delay in trial.

1997 AMENDMENT

The Federal Courts Improvement Act of 1996 repealed the former provisions of 28 U.S.C. § 636(c)(4) and (5) that enabled parties that had agreed to trial before a magistrate judge to agree also that appeal should be taken to the district court. Rule 73 is amended to conform to this change. Rules 74, 75, and 76 are abrogated for the same reason. The portions of Form 33 and Form 34 that referred to appeals to the district court also are deleted.

2007 AMENDMENTS

The language of Rule 73 has been amended as part of the general restyling of the Civil Rules to make them more easily understood and to make style and

terminology consistent throughout the rules. These changes are intended to be stylistic only.

Rule 74. Method of Appeal From Magistrate Judge to District Judge Under Title 28, U.S.C. § 636(c)(4) and Rule 73(d)

ABROGATED

2007 AMENDMENT

Rule 74 was abrogated in 1997 to reflect repeal of the statute providing for appeal from a magistrate judge's judgment to the district court. The rule number is reserved for possible future use.

Rule 75. Proceedings on Appeal from Magistrate Judge to District Judge under Rule 73(d)

ABROGATED

2007 AMENDMENT

Rule 75 was abrogated in 1997 to reflect repeal of the statute providing for appeal from a magistrate judge's judgment to the district court. The rule number is reserved for possible future use.

Rule 76. Judgment of the District Judge on the Appeal under Rule 73(d) and Costs

ABROGATED

2007 AMENDMENT

Rule 76 was abrogated in 1997 to reflect repeal of the statute providing for appeal from a magistrate judge's judgment to the district court. The rule number is reserved for possible future use.

X. DISTRICT COURTS AND CLERKS

Rule 77. District Courts and Clerks

1937 ADOPTION

This rule states the substance of U.S.C., Title 28, § 452, formerly § 13 (Courts open as courts of admiralty and equity). Compare former Equity Rules 1 (District Court Always Open For Certain Purposes—Orders at Chambers), 2 (Clerk's Office Always Open, Except, Etc.), 4 (Notice of Orders), and 5 (Motions Grantable of Course by Clerk).

1946 AMENDMENT

Note. Rule 77(d) has been amended to avoid such situations as the one arising in *Hill v. Hawes, 1944*, 320 U.S. 520, 64 S. Ct. 334, 88 L.Ed. 283. In that case, an action instituted in the District Court for the District of Columbia, the clerk failed to give notice of the entry of a judgment for defendant as required by Rule 77(d). The time for taking an appeal then was 20 days under Rule 10 of the Court of Appeals (later enlarged by amendment to thirty days), and due to lack of notice of the entry of judgment the plaintiff failed to file his notice of appeal within the prescribed time. On this basis the trial court vacated the original judgment and then re-entered it, whereupon notice of appeal was filed. The Court of Appeals dismissed the appeal as taken too late. The Supreme Court, however, held that although Rule 77(d) did not purport to attach any consequence to the clerk's failure to give notice as specified, the terms of the rule were such that the appellant was entitled to rely on it, and the trial court in such a case, in the exercise of a sound discretion, could vacate the former judgment and enter a new one, so that the appeal would be within the allowed time.

Because of Rule 6(c), which abolished the old rule that the expiration of the term ends a court's power over its judgment, the effect of the decision in *Hill v. Hawes* is to give the district court power, in its discretion and without time limit, and long after the term may have expired, to vacate a judgment and reenter it for the purpose of reviving the right of appeal. This seriously affects the finality of judgments. See also proposed Rule 6(c) and note; proposed Rule 60(b) and note; and proposed Rule 73(a) and note.

Rule 77(d) as amended makes it clear that notification by the clerk of the entry of a judgment has nothing to do with the starting of the time for appeal; that time starts to run from the date of entry of judgment and not from the date of notice of the entry. Notification by the clerk is merely for the convenience of litigants. And lack of such notification in itself has no effect upon the time for appeal; but in considering an application for extension of time for appeal as provided in Rule 73(a), the court may take into account, as one of the factors affecting its decision, whether the clerk failed to give notice as provided in Rule 77(d), or the party failed to receive the clerk's notice. It need not, however, extend the time for appeal merely because the clerk's notice was not sent or received. It would, therefore, be entirely unsafe for a party to rely on absence of notice from the clerk of the entry of a judgment, or to rely on the adverse party's failure to serve notice of the entry of a judgment. Any party may, of course, serve timely notice of the entry of a judgment upon the adverse party and thus preclude a successful application, under Rule 73(a), for the extension of the time for appeal.

1963 AMENDMENT

Subdivision (c). The amendment authorizes closing of the clerk's office on Saturday as far as civil business is concerned. However, a district court may require its clerk's office to remain open for specified hours on Saturdays or "legal holidays" other than those enumerated ("Legal holiday" is defined in Rule 6(a), as amended.) The clerk's offices of many district courts have customarily remained open on some of the days appointed as holidays by State law. This practice could be continued by local rule or order.

Subdivision (d). This amendment conforms to the amendment of Rule 5(a). See the Advisory Committee's Note to that amendment.

1968 AMENDMENT

The provisions of Rule 73(a) are incorporated in Rule 4(a) of the Federal Rules of Appellate Procedure.

1971 AMENDMENT

The amendment adds Columbus Day to the list of legal holidays. See the Note accompanying the amendment of Rule 6(a).

1987 AMENDMENT

The amendments are technical. No substantive change is intended. The Birthday of Martin Luther King, Jr. is added to the list of national holidays in Rule 77.

1991 AMENDMENT

This revision is a companion to the concurrent amendment to Rule 4 of the Federal Rules of Appellate Procedure. The purpose of the revisions is to permit district courts to ease strict sanctions now imposed on appellants whose notices of appeal are filed late because of their failure to receive notice of entry of a judgment. See, e.g. *Tucker v. Commonwealth Land Title Ins. Co.*, 800 F.2d 1054 (11th Cir.1986); *Ashby Enterprises, Ltd. v. Weitzman, Dym & Associates*, 780 F.2d 1043 (D.C.Cir.1986); *In re OPM Leasing Services, Inc.*, 769 F.2d 911 (2d Cir.1985); *Spika v. Village of Lombard, Ill.*, 763 F.2d 282 (7th Cir.1985); *Hall v. Community Mental Health Center of Beaver County*, 772 F.2d 42 (3d Cir.1985); *Wilson v. Atwood v. Stark*, 725 F.2d 255 (5th Cir. en banc), *cert. dismissed*, 468 U.S. 1222, 105 S. Ct. 17, 82 L. Ed. 2d 912 (1984); *Case v. BASF Wyandotte*, 737 F.2d 1034 (Fed.Cir.1984), cert. denied, 469 U.S. 982, 105 S. Ct. 386, 83 L. Ed.

2d 321 (1984); *Hensley v. Chesapeake & Ohio R.R. Co.*, 651 F.2d 226 (4th Cir. 1981); *Buckeye Cellulose Corp. v. Braggs Electric Construction Co.*, 569 F.2d 1036 (8th Cir.1978).

Failure to receive notice may have increased in frequency with the growth in the caseload in the clerks' offices. The present strict rule imposes a duty on counsel to maintain contact with the court while a case is under submission. Such contact is more difficult to maintain if counsel is outside the district, as is increasingly common, and can be a burden to the court as well as counsel.

The effect of the revisions is to place a burden on prevailing parties who desire certainty that the time for appeal is running. Such parties can take the initiative to assure that their adversaries receive effective notice. An appropriate procedure for such notice is provided in Rule 5.

The revised rule lightens the responsibility but not the workload of the clerk's offices, for the duty of that office to give notice of entry of judgment must be maintained.

2001 AMENDMENT

Rule 77(d) is amended to reflect changes in Rule 5(b). A few courts have experimented with serving Rule 77(d) notices by electronic means on parties who consent to this procedure. The success of these experiments warrants express authorization. Because service is made in the manner provided in Rule 5(b), party consent is required for service by electronic or other means described in Rule 5(b)(2)(D). The same provision is made for a party who wishes to ensure actual communication of the Rule 77(d) notice by also serving notice.

Changes Made After Publication and Comments

Rule 77(d) was amended to correct an oversight in the published version. The clerk is to note "service," not "mailing," on the docket.

2007 AMENDMENTS

The language of Rule 77 has been amended as part of the general restyling of the Civil Rules to make them more easily understood and to make style and terminology consistent throughout the rules. These changes are intended to be stylistic only.

2014 AMENDMENTS

The amendment corrects an inadvertent failure to revise the cross-reference to Rule 6(a) when what was Rule 6(a)(4)(A) became 6(a)(6)(A).

Rule 78. Motion Day

1937 ADOPTION

Compare former Equity Rule 6 (Motion Day) with the first paragraph of this rule. The second paragraph authorizes a procedure found helpful for the expedition of business in some of the federal and state courts. See Rule 43(e) of these rules dealing with evidence on motions. Compare Civil Practice Rules of the Municipal Court of Chicago (1935), Rules 269, 270, 271.

1987 AMENDMENT

The amendment is technical. No substantive change is intended.

2007 AMENDMENTS

The language of Rule 78 has been amended as part of the general restyling of the Civil Rules to make them more easily understood and to make style and terminology consistent throughout the rules. These changes are intended to be stylistic only.

Rule 16 has superseded any need for the provision in former Rule 78 for orders for the advancement, conduct, and hearing of actions.

Rule 79. Books and Records Kept by the Clerk and Entries Therein

1937 ADOPTION

Compare Equity Rule 3 (Books Kept by Clerk and Entries Therein). In connection with this rule, see also the following statutes of the United States:

U.S.C., Title 5:

§ 301 (Officials for investigation of official acts, records and accounts of marshals, attorneys, clerks of courts, United States commissioners, referees and trustees)

§ 318 (Accounts of district attorneys)

U.S.C., Title 28, former:

§ 556 (Clerks of district courts; books open to inspection)

§ 567 (Same; accounts)

§ 568 (Same; reports and accounts of moneys received; dockets)

§ 813 (Indices of judgment debtors to be kept by clerks)

And see "Instructions to United States Attorneys, Marshals, Clerks and Commissioners" issued by the Attorney General of the United States.

1946 AMENDMENT

Note to Subdivision (a). The amendment substitutes the Director of the Administrative Office of the United States Courts, acting subject to the approval of the Judicial Conference of Senior Circuit Judges, in the place of the Attorney General as a consequence of and in accordance with the provisions of the act establishing the Administrative Office and transferring functions thereto. Act of August 7, 1939, ch. 501, §§ 1 to 7, 53 Stat. 1223, 28 U.S.C. formerly §§ 444 to 450 (now §§ 601 to 610).

Subdivision (b). The change in this subdivision does not alter the nature of the judgments and orders to be recorded in permanent form but it does away with the express requirement that they be recorded in a book. This merely gives latitude for the preservation of court records in other than book form, if that shall seem advisable, and permits with the approval of the Judicial Conference and adoption of such modern, space-saving methods as microphotography. See Proposed Improvements in the Administration of the Offices of Clerks of United States District Courts, prepared by the Bureau of the Budget, 1941, 38–42. See also Rule 55, Federal Rules of Criminal Procedure [following section 687 of Title 18 U.S.C.].

Subdivision (c). The words "Separate and" have been deleted as unduly rigid. There is no sufficient reason for requiring that the indices in all cases be separate; on the contrary, the requirement frequently increases the labor of persons searching the records as well as the labor of the clerk's force preparing them. The matter should be left to administrative discretion.

The other changes in the subdivision merely conform with those made in subdivision (b) of the rule.

Subdivision (d). Subdivision (d) is a new provision enabling the Administrative Office, with the approval of the Judicial Conference, to carry out any improvements in clerical procedure with respect to books and records which may be deemed advisable. See report cited in Note to subdivision (b), supra.

1948 AMENDMENT

The amendment effective October 1949 substituted the name, "Judicial Conference of the United States," for "Judicial Conference of Senior Circuit Judges," in the first sentence of subdivision (a), and in subdivisions (b) and (d).

1963 AMENDMENT

The terminology is clarified without any change of the prescribed practice. See amended Rule 58, and the Advisory Committee's Note thereto.

2007 AMENDMENTS

The language of Rule 79 has been amended as part of the general restyling of the Civil Rules to make them more easily understood and to make style and

terminology consistent throughout the rules. These changes are intended to be stylistic only.

Rule 80. Stenographer; Stenographic Report or Transcript As Evidence

1937 ADOPTION

Note to Subdivision (a). This follows substantially former Equity Rule 50 (Stenographer—Appointment—Fees). [This subdivision was abrogated. See amendment note of Advisory Committee below.]

Note to Subdivision (b). See Reports of Conferences of Senior Circuit Judges with the Chief Justice of the United States (1936), 22 A.B.A.J. 818, 819, (1937), 24 A.B.A.J. 75, 77. [This subdivision was abrogated. See amendment note of Advisory Committee below.]

Note to Subdivision (c). Compare Iowa Code (1935) § 11353.

1946 AMENDMENT

Note. Subdivisions (a) and (b) of rule 80 have been abrogated because of Public Law 222, 78th Cong., ch. 3, 2d Sess., approved Jan. 20, 1944, 28 U.S.C. formerly § 9a (now §§ 550, 604, 753, 1915, 1920), providing for the appointment of official stenographers for each district court, prescribing their duties, providing for the furnishing of transcripts, the taxation of the fees therefor as costs and other related matters. This statute has now been implemented by Congressional appropriation available for the fiscal year beginning July 1, 1945.

Subdivision (c) of Rule 80 (Stenographic Report or Transcript as Evidence) has been retained unchanged.

2007 AMENDMENTS

The language of Rule 80 has been amended as part of the general restyling of the Civil Rules to make them more easily understood and to make style and terminology consistent throughout the rules. These changes are intended to be stylistic only.

XI. GENERAL PROVISIONS

Rule 81. Applicability in General

1937 ADOPTION

Note to Subdivision (a). Paragraph (1): Compare the enabling act, act of June 19, 1934, U.S.C., Title 28, formerly § 723b (now § 2072)(Rules in actions at law; Supreme Court authorized to make) and formerly § 723c (now § 2072)(Union of equity and action at law rules; power of Supreme Court). For the application of these rules in bankruptcy and copyright proceedings, see Orders xxxvi and xxxvii in Bankruptcy and Rule 1 of Rules of Practice and Procedure under § 25 of the copyright act, act of March 4, 1909, U.S.C., Title 17, § 25 (now § 101)(Infringement and rules of procedure).

For examples of statutes which are preserved by paragraph (2) see: U.S.C., Title 8, ch. 9 (Naturalization); Title 28, former ch. 14 (Habeas corpus); Title 28, former §§ 377a to 377c (Quo warranto); and such forfeiture statutes as U.S.C., Title 7, former § 116 (Misbranded seeds, confiscation), and Title 21, formerly § 14 (now § 334(b))(Pure Food and Drug Act—condemnation of adulterated or misbranded food; procedure). See also *Four Hundred and Forty-Three Cans of Frozen Egg Product v. U.S.*, 226 U.S. 172, 33 S. Ct. 50, 57 L.Ed. 174 (1912).

For examples of statutes which under paragraph (7) will continue to govern procedure in condemnation cases, see U.S.C., Title 40, § 258 (Condemnation of realty for sites for public building, etc., procedure); U.S.C., Title 16, § 831x (Condemnation by Tennessee Valley Authority); U.S.C., Title 40, § 120 (Acquisition of lands for public use in District of Columbia); Title 40, ch. 7 (Acquisition of lands in District of Columbia for use of United States; condemnation).

Note to Subdivision (b). Some statutes which will be affected by this subdivision are:

U.S.C., Title 7:

§ 222 (Federal Trade Commission powers adopted for enforcement of Stockyards Act)(By reference to Title 15, § 49)

U.S.C., Title 15:

§ 49 (Enforcement of Federal Trade Commission orders and antitrust laws)

§ 77t(c) (Enforcement of Securities and Exchange Commission orders and Securities Act of 1933)

§ 78u(f) (Same; Securities Exchange Act of 1934)

§ 79r(g) (Same; Public Utility Holding Company Act of 1935)

U.S.C., Title 16:

§ 820 (Proceedings in equity for revocation or to prevent violations of license of Federal Power Commission licensee)

§ 825m-b (Mandamus to compel compliance with Federal Water Power Act, etc.)

U.S.C., Title 19:

§ 1333(c) (Mandamus to compel compliance with orders of Tariff Commission, etc.)

U.S.C., Title 28, former:

§ 377 (Power to issue writs)

§ 572 (Fees, attorneys, solicitors and proctors)

§ 778 (Death of parties; substitution of executor or administrator). Compare Rule 25(a) (Substitution of parties; death), and the note thereto.

U.S.C., Title 33:

§ 495 (Removal of bridges over navigable waters)

U.S.C., Title 45:

§ 88 (Mandamus against Union Pacific Railroad Company)

§ 153(p) (Mandamus to enforce orders of Adjustment Board under Railway Labor Act)

§ 185 (Same; National Air Transport Adjustment Board)(By reference to § 153)

U.S.C., Title 47:

§ 11 (Powers of Federal Communications Commission)

§ 401(a) (Enforcement of Federal Communications Act and orders of Commission)

§ 406 (Same; compelling furnishing of facilities; mandamus)

U.S.C., Title 49:

§ 19a(*l*) (Mandamus to compel compliance with Interstate Commerce Act)

§ 20(9) (Jurisdiction to compel compliance with interstate commerce laws by mandamus)

For comparable provisions in state practice see Ill. Rev. Stat. (1937), ch. 110, § 179; Calif. Code Civ. Proc. (Deering, 1937) § 802.

Note to Subdivision (c). Such statutes as the following dealing with the removal of actions are substantially continued and made subject to these rules:

U.S.C., Title 28, former:

§ 71 (Removal of suits from state courts)

§ 72 (Same; procedure)

§ 73 (Same; suits under grants of land from different states)

§ 74 (Same; causes against persons denied civil rights)

§ 75 (Same; petitioner in actual custody of state court)

§ 76 (Same; suits and prosecutions against revenue officers)

§ 77 (Same; suits by aliens)

§ 78 (Same; copies of records refused by clerk of state court)

§ 79 (Same; previous attachment bonds or orders)

§ 80 (Same; dismissal or remand)

§ 81 (Same; proceedings in suits removed)

§ 82 (Same; record; filing and return)

§ 83 (Service of process after removal)

U.S.C., Title 28, formerly § 72 (now §§ 1446, 1447), *supra*, however, is modified by shortening the time for pleading in removed actions.

Note to Subdivision (e). The last sentence of this subdivision modifies U.S.C., Title 28, formerly § 725 (now § 1652)(Laws of States as rules of decision) in so far as that statute has been construed to govern matters of procedure and to exclude state judicial decisions relative thereto.

1946 AMENDMENT

Note to Subdivision (a). Despite certain dicta to the contrary, *Lynn v. United States, C.C.A5, 1940*, 110 F.2d 586; *Mount Tivy Winery, Inc. v. Lewis, Cal.1942*, 42 F.Supp. 636, it is manifest that the rules apply to actions against the United States under the Tucker Act. See *United States to Use of Foster Wheeler Corp. v. American Surety Co. of New York, N.Y.1939*, 25 F.Supp. 700; *Boerner v. United States, N.Y.1939*, 26 F.Supp. 769; *United States v. Gallagher, C.C.A.9, 1945*, 151 F.2d 556. Rules 1 and 81 provides that the rules shall apply to all suits of a civil nature, whether cognizable as cases at law or in equity, except those specifically excepted; and the character of the various proceedings excepted by express statement in Rule 81, as well as the language of the rules generally, shows that the term "civil action" [Rule 2] includes actions against the United States. Moreover, the rules in many places expressly make provision for the situation wherein the United States is a party as either plaintiff or defendant. See Rules 4(d)(4), 12(a), 13(d), 25(d), 37(f), 39(c), 45(c), 54(d), 55(e), 62(e), and 65(c). In *United States v. Sherwood, 1941*, 312 U.S. 584, 61 S. Ct. 767, 85 L.Ed. 1058, the Solicitor General expressly conceded in his brief for the United States that the rules apply to Tucker Act cases. The Solicitor General stated: "The Government, of course, recognizes that the Federal Rules of Civil Procedure apply to cases brought under the Tucker Act." (Brief for the United States, p. 31). Regarding *Lynn v. United States, supra*, the Solicitor General stated: "The Government, of course, recognizes that the Federal Rules of Civil Procedure apply to cases brought under the Tucker Act." (Brief for the United States, p. 31). Regarding *Lynn* v. *United States*, *supra,* the Solicitor General said: "In *Lynn* v. *United States* . . . the Circuit Court of Appeals for the Fifth Circuit went beyond the Government's contention there, and held that an action under the Tucker Act is neither an action at law nor a suit in equity and, seemingly, that the Federal Rules of Civil Procedure are, therefore, inapplicable. We think the suggestion is erroneous. Rules 4(d), 12(a), 39(c), and 55(e) expressly contemplate suits against the United States, and nothing in the Enabling Act (48 Stat. 1064, 28 U.S.C. § 2072, formerly §§ 723b, 723c) suggests that the Rules are inapplicable to Tucker Act proceedings, which in terms are to accord with court rules and their subsequent modifications (Sec. 4, Act of March 3, 1887, 24 Stat. 505, 28 U.S.C. §§ 2071, 2072, formerly § 761)." (Brief for the United States, p. 31, n. 17.)

United States v. *Sherwood, supra,* emphasizes, however, that the application of the rules in Tucker Act cases affects only matters of procedure and does not operate to extend jurisdiction. See also Rule 82. In the Sherwood case, the New York Supreme Court, acting under § 795 of the New York Civil Practice Act, made an order, authorizing Sherwood, as a judgment creditor, to maintain a suit under the Tucker Act to recover damages from the United States for breach of its contract with the judgment debtor, Kaiser, for construction of a post office building. Sherwood brought suit against the United States and Kaiser in the District Court for the Eastern District of New York. The question before the United States Supreme Court was whether a United States District Court had jurisdiction to entertain a suit against the United States wherein private parties were joined as parties defendant. It was contended that either the Federal Rules of Civil Procedure or the Tucker Act, or both, embodied the consent of the United States to be sued in litigations in which issues between the plaintiff and third persons were to be adjudicated. Regarding the effect of the Federal Rules, the Court declared that nothing in the rules, so far as they may be applicable in Tucker Act cases, authorized the maintenance of any suit against the United States to which it had not otherwise consented. The matter involved was not one of procedure but of jurisdiction, the limits of which were marked by the consent of the United States to be sued. The jurisdiction thus limited is unaffected by the Federal Rules of Civil Procedure.

Subdivision (a)(2). The added sentence makes it clear that the rules have not superseded the requirements of U.S.C., Title 28, § 2253, formerly § 466. *Schenk v. Plummer, C.C.A.9, 1940,* 113 F.2d 726.

For correct application of the rules in proceedings for forfeiture of property for violation of a statute of the United States, such as under U.S.C., Title 22, § 405 (seizure of war materials intended for unlawful export) or U.S.C., Title 21, § 334(b) (Federal Food, Drug, and Cosmetic Act; formerly Title 21, U.S.C., § 14, Pure Food and Drug Act), see *Reynal v. United States, C.C.A.5, 1945,* 153 F.2d 929; *United States v. 108 Boxes of Cheddar Cheese, D.Iowa 1943,* 3 F.R.D. 40.

Subdivision (a)(3). The added sentence makes it clear that the rules apply to appeals from proceedings to enforce administrative subpoenas. See *Perkins v. Endicott Johnson Corp., C.C.A.2d, 1942,* 128 F.2d 208, affirmed 317 U.S. 501, 63 S. Ct. 339, 87 L.Ed. 424; *Walling v. News Printing, Inc., C.C.A.3, 1945,* 148 F.2d 57; *McCrone v. United States, 1939,* 307 U.S. 61, 59 S. Ct. 685, 83 L.Ed. 1108. And, although the provision allows full recognition of the fact that the rigid application of the rules in the proceedings themselves may conflict with the summary determination desired, *Goodyear Tire & Rubber Co. v. National Labor Relations Board, C.C.A.6, 1941,* 122 F.2d 450; *Cudahy Packing Co. v. National Labor Relations Board, C.C.A.10, 1941,* 117 F.2d 692, it is drawn so as to permit application of any of the rules in the proceedings whenever the district court deems them helpful. See, e.g., *Peoples Natural Gas Co. v. Federal Power Commission, App.D.C.1942,* 127 F.2d 153, certiorari denied 316 U.S. 700, 62 S. Ct. 1298, 86 L.Ed. 1769; *Martin v. Chandis Securities Co., C.C.A.9th, 1942,* 128 F.2d 731. Compare the application of the rules in summary proceedings in bankruptcy under General Order 37. See 1 Collier on Bankruptcy, 14th ed. by Moore and Oglebay, 326–327; 2 Collier, op.cit.supra, 1401–1402; 3 Collier, op.cit.supra, 228–231; 4 Collier, op.cit.supra, 1199–1202.

Subdivision (a)(6). Section 405 of U.S.C., Title 8 originally referred to in the last sentence of paragraph (6), has been repealed and § 1451, formerly § 738, U.S.C.A., Title 8, has been enacted in its stead. The last sentence of paragraph (6) has, therefore, been amended in accordance with this change. The sentence has also been amended so as to refer directly to the statute regarding the provision of time for answer, thus avoiding any confusion attendant upon a change in the statute.

That portion of subdivision (a)(6) making the rules applicable to proceedings for enforcement or review of compensation orders under the Longshoremen's and Harbor Workers' Compensation Act [33 U.S.C. §§ 901 et seq.] was added by an amendment made pursuant to order of the Court, December 28, 1939, effective three months subsequent to the adjournment of the 76th Congress, January 3, 1941.

Subdivision (c). The change in subdivision (c) effects more speedy trials in removed actions. In some states many of the courts have only two terms a year. A case, if filed 20 days before a term, is returnable to that term, but if filed less than 20 days before a term, is returnable to the following term, which convenes six months later. Hence, under the original wording of Rule 81(c), where a case is filed less than 20 days before the term and is removed within a few days but before answer, it is possible for the defendant to delay interposing his answer or presenting his defenses by motion for six months or more. The rule as amended prevents this result.

Subdivision (f). The use of the phrase "the United States or an officer or agency thereof" in the rules (as e.g., in Rule 12(a) and amended Rule 73(a)) could raise the question of whether "officer" includes a collector of internal revenue, a former collector, or the personal representative of a deceased collector, against whom suits for tax refunds are frequently instituted. Difficulty might ensue for the reason that a suit against a collector or his representative has been held to be a personal action. *Sage v. United States, 1919,* 250 U.S. 33, 39 S. Ct. 415, 63 L.Ed. 828; *Smietanka v. Indiana Steel Co., 1921,* 257 U.S. 1, 42 S.

Ct. 1, 66 L.Ed. 99; *United States v. Nunnally Investment Co., 1942*, 316 U.S. 258, 62 S. Ct. 1064, 86 L.Ed. 1455. The addition of subdivision (f) to Rule 81 dispels any doubts on the matter and avoids further litigation.

1948 AMENDMENT

The amendment effective October 1949, substituted the words "United States District Court" for the words "District Court of the United States" in the last sentence of subdivision (a)(1) and in the first and third sentences of subdivision (e). The amendment substituted the words "United States district courts" in lieu of "district courts of the United States" in subdivision (a)(4) and (5) and in the first sentence of subdivision (c).

The amendment effective October 20, 1949, also made the following changes:

In subdivision (a)(1), the reference to "Title 17, U.S.C." was substituted for the reference to "the Act of March 4, 1909, c. 320, § 25 (35 Stat. 1081), as amended, U.S.C., Title 17, § 25."

In subdivision (a)(2) the reference to "Title 28, U.S.C., § 2253" was substituted for "U.S.C., Title 28, § 466."

In subdivision (a)(3) the reference in the first sentence to "Title 9, U.S.C.," was substituted for "the Act of February 12, 1925, c. 213 (43 Stat. 883), U.S.C., Title 9".

In subdivision (a)(5), the words "as amended" were inserted after the parenthetical citation of "(49 Stat. 453)," and after the citations of "Title 29, §§ 159 and 160," former references to subdivisions "(e), (g), and (i)" were deleted.

In subdivision (a)(6) after the words "These rules" at the beginning of the first sentence, the following words were deleted: "do not apply to proceedings under the Act of September 13, 1888, c. 1015, § 13 (25 Stat. 479), as amended, U.S.C., Title 8, [former] § 282, relating to deportation of Chinese; they". Also in the first sentence, after the parenthetical citation of "(44 Stat. 1434, 1436)," the words "as amended" were added. In the last sentence, the words "October 14, 1940, c. 876, § 338 (54 Stat. 1158)" were inserted in lieu of the words "June 29, 1906, c. 3592, § 15 (34 Stat. 601), as amended."

In subdivision (c), the word "all" originally appearing in the first sentence between the words "govern" and "procedure" was deleted. In the third sentence, the portion beginning with the words "20 days after the receipt" and including all the remainder of that sentence was substituted for the following language: "the time allowed for answer by the law of the state or within 5 days after the filing of the transcript of the record in the district court of the United States, whichever period is longer, but in any event within 20 days after the filing of the transcript". In the fourth or last sentence, after the words at the beginning of the sentence, "If at the time of removal all necessary pleadings have been," the word "served" was inserted in lieu of the word "filed," and the concluding words of the sentence, "petition for removal is filed if he is the petitioner," together with the final clause immediately following, were substituted for the words "record of the action is filed in the district court of the United States."

1963 AMENDMENT

Subdivision (a)(4). This change reflects the transfer of functions from the Secretary of Commerce to the Secretary of the Interior made by 1939 Reorganization Plan No. II, § 4(e), 53 Stat. 1433.

Subdivision (a)(6). The proper current reference is to the 1952 statute superseding the 1940 statute.

Subdivision (c). Most of the cases have held that a party who has made a proper express demand for jury trial in the State court is not required to renew the demand after removal of the action. *Zakoscielny v. Waterman Steamship Corp.*, 16 F.R.D. 314 (D.Md.1954); *Talley v. American Bakeries Co.*, 15 F.R.D. 391 (E.D.Tenn.1954); *Rehrer v. Service Trucking Co.*, 15 F.R.D. 113 (D.Del. 1953); 5 Moore's Federal Practice ¶ 38.39[3] (2d ed. 1951); 1 Barron & Holtzoff, Federal Practice & Procedure § 132 (Wright ed. 1960). But there is some authority to the contrary. *Petsel v. Chicago, B. & Q. R. Co.*, 101 F.Supp. 1006 (S.D.Iowa 1951); *Nelson v. American Nat. Bank & Trust Co.*, 9 F.R.D. 680 (E.D.Tenn.

1950). The amendment adopts the preponderant view.

In order still further to avoid unintended waivers of jury trial, the amendment provides that where by State law applicable in the court from which the case is removed a party is entitled to jury trial without making an express demand, he need not make a demand after removal. However, the district court for calendar or other purposes may on its own motion direct the parties to state whether they demand a jury, and the court must make such a direction upon the request of any party. Under the amendment a district court may find it convenient to establish a routine practice of giving these directions to the parties in appropriate cases.

Subdivision (f). The amendment recognizes the change of nomenclature made by Treasury Dept. Order 150-26(2), 18 Fed.Reg. 3499 (1953).

As to a special problem arising under Rule 25 (Substitution of parties) in actions for refund of taxes, see the Advisory Committee's Note to the amendment of Rule 25(d), effective July 19, 1961; and 4 Moore's Federal Practice ¶ 25.09 at 531 (2d Ed. 1950).

1966 AMENDMENT

See Note to Rule 1, supra.

Statutory proceedings to forfeit property for violation of the laws of the United States, formerly governed by the admiralty rules, will be governed by the unified and supplemental rules. See Supplemental Rule A.

Upon the recommendation of the judges of the United States District Court for the District of Columbia, the Federal Rules of Civil Procedure are made applicable to probate proceedings in that court. The exception with regard to adoption proceedings is removed because the court no longer has jurisdiction of those matters; and the words "mental health" are substituted for "lunacy" to conform to the current characterization in the District.

The purpose of the amendment to paragraph (3) is to permit the deletion from Rule 73(a) of the clause "unless a shorter time is provided by law." The 10 day period fixed for an appeal under 45 U.S.C. § 159 is the only instance of a shorter time provided for appeals in civil cases. Apart from the unsettling effect of the clause, it is eliminated because its retention would preserve the 15 day period heretofore allowed by 28 U.S.C. § 2107 for appeals from interlocutory decrees in admiralty, it being one of the purposes of the amendment to make the time for appeals in civil and admiralty cases uniform under the unified rules. See Advisory Committee's Note to subdivision (a) of Rule 73.

1967 AMENDMENT

The amendments eliminate inappropriate references to appellate procedure.

1971 AMENDMENT

Title 28, U.S.C., § 2243 now requires that the custodian of a person detained must respond to an application for a writ of habeas corpus "within three days unless for good cause additional time, not exceeding twenty days, is allowed." The amendment increases to forty days the additional time that the district court may allow in habeas corpus proceedings involving persons in custody pursuant to a judgment of a state court. The substantial increase in the number of such proceedings in recent years has placed a considerable burden on state authorities. Twenty days has proved in practice too short a time in which to prepare and file the return in many such cases. Allowance of additional time should, of course, be granted only for good cause.

While the time allowed in such a case for the return of the writ may not exceed forty days, this does not mean that the state must necessarily be limited to that period of time to provide for the federal court the transcript of the proceedings of a state trial or plenary hearing if the transcript must be prepared after the habeas corpus proceeding has begun in the federal court.

1987 AMENDMENT

The amendments are technical. No substantive change is intended.

2001 AMENDMENT

Former Copyright Rule 1 made the Civil Rules applicable to copyright proceedings except to the extent the Civil Rules were inconsistent with Copyright Rules. Abrogation of the Copyright Rules leaves the Civil Rules fully applicable to copyright proceedings. Rule 81(a)(1) is amended to reflect this change.

The District of Columbia Court Reform and Criminal Procedure Act of 1970, Pub.L. 91-358, 84 Stat. 473, transferred mental health proceedings formerly held in the United States District Court for the District of Columbia to local District of Columbia courts. The provision that the Civil Rules do not apply to these proceedings is deleted as superfluous.

The reference to incorporation of the Civil Rules in the Federal Rules of Bankruptcy Procedure has been restyled.

Changes Made After Publication and Comments

The Committee Note was amended to correct the inadvertent omission of a negative. As revised, it correctly reflects the language that is stricken from the rule.

2002 AMENDMENT

This amendment brings Rule 81(a)(2) into accord with the Rules Governing § 2254 and § 2255 proceedings. In its present form, Rule 81(a)(2) includes return-time provisions that are inconsistent with the provisions in the Rules Governing §§ 2254 and 2255. The inconsistency should be eliminated, and it is better that the time provisions continue to be set out in the other rules without duplication in Rule 81. Rule 81 also directs that the writ be directed to the person having custody of the person detained. Similar directions exist in the § 2254 and § 2255 rules, providing additional detail for applicants subject to future custody. There is no need for partial duplication in Rule 81.

The provision that the civil rules apply to the extent that practice is not set forth in the § 2254 and § 2255 rules dovetails with the provisions in Rule 11 of the § 2254 rules and Rule 12 of the § 2255 rules.

2007 AMENDMENTS

The language of Rule 81 has been amended as part of the general restyling of the Civil Rules to make them more easily understood and to make style and terminology consistent throughout the rules. These changes are intended to be stylistic only.

Rule 81(c) has been revised to reflect the amendment of 28 U.S.C. § 1446(a) that changed the procedure for removal fiom a petition for removal to a notice of removal.

Former Rule 81(e), drafted before the decision in *Erie R.R. v. Tompkins*, 304 U.S. 64 (1938), defined state law to include "the statutes of that state and the state judicial decisions construing them." The *Erie* decision reinterpreted the Rules of Decision Act, now 28 U.S.C. § 1652, recognizing that the "laws" of the states include the common law established by judicial decisions. Long-established practice reflects this understanding, looking to state common law as well as statutes and court rules when a Civil Rule directs use of state law. Amended Rule 81(d)(1) adheres to this practice, including all state judicial decisions, not only those that construe state statutes.

Former Rule 81(f) is deleted. The office of district director of internal revenue was abolished by restructuring under the Internal Revenue Service Restructuring and Reform Act of 1998, Pub.L. 105-206, July 22, 1998, 26 U.S.C. § 1 Note.

2009 AMENDMENTS

[Subdivision (c)] The times set in the former rule at 5, 10, and 20 days have been revised to 7, 14, and 21 days, respectively. See the Note to Rule 6.

[Subdivision (d)] Several Rules incorporate local state practice. Rule 81(d) now provides that "the term 'state' includes, where appropriate, the District of Columbia." The definition is expanded to include any commonwealth or territory of the United States. As before, these entities are included only "where appropriate." They are included for the reasons that counsel incorporation of state practice. For example, state holidays are recognized in computing time under Rule 6(a). Other, quite different, examples are Rules 64(a), invoking state law for prejudgment remedies, and 69(a)(1), relying on state law for the procedure on execution. Including commonwealths and territories in these and other rules avoids the gaps that otherwise would result when the federal rule relies on local practice rather than provide a uniform federal approach. Including them also establishes uniformity between federal courts and local courts in areas that may involve strong local interests, little need for uniformity among federal courts, or difficulty in defining a uniform federal practice that integrates effectively with local practice.

Adherence to a local practice may be refused as not "appropriate" when the local practice would impair a significant federal interest.

Rule 82. Jurisdiction and Venue Unaffected

1937 ADOPTION

These rules grant extensive power of joining claims and counterclaims in one action, but, as this rule states, such grant does not extend federal jurisdiction. The rule is declaratory of existing practice under the former Federal Equity Rules with regard to such provisions as former Equity Rule 26 on Joinder of Clauses of Action and former Equity Rule 30 on Counterclaims. Compare Shulman and Jaegerman, Some Jurisdictional Limitations on Federal Procedure, 45 Yale L.J. 393 (1936).

1948 AMENDMENT

The amendment effective October 1949, substituted the words "United States district courts" for "district courts of the United States."

1966 AMENDMENT

Title 28, U.S.C., § 1391(b) provides: "A civil action wherein jurisdiction is not founded solely on diversity of citizenship may be brought only in the judicial district where all defendants reside, except as otherwise provided by law." This provision cannot appropriately be applied to what were formerly suits in admiralty. The rationale of decisions holding it inapplicable rests largely on the use of the term "civil action": i.e., a suit in admiralty is not a "civil action" within the statute. By virtue of the amendment to Rule 1, the provisions of Rule 2 convert suits in admiralty into civil actions. The added sentence is necessary to avoid an undesirable change in existing law with respect to venue.

2001 AMENDMENT

The final sentence of Rule 82 is amended to delete the reference to 28 U.S.C. § 1393, which has been repealed.

Style Comment

The recommendation that the change be made without publication carries with it a recommendation that style changes not be made. Styling would carry considerable risks. The first sentence of Rule 82, for example, states that the Civil Rules do not "extend or limit the jurisdiction of the United States district courts." That sentence is a flat lie if "jurisdiction" includes personal or quasi-in rem jurisdiction. The styling project on this rule requires publication and comment.

2007 AMENDMENT

The language of Rule 82 has been amended as part of the general restyling of the Civil Rules to make them more easily understood and to make style and terminology consistent throughout the rules. These changes are intended to be stylistic only.

2016 AMENDMENT

Rule 82 is amended to reflect the enactment of 28 U.S.C. § 1390 and the repeal of § 1392.

Rule 83. Rules by District Courts; Judge's Directives

1937 ADOPTION

This rule substantially continues U.S.C., Title 28, § 2071, formerly § 731 (Rules of practice in district courts) with the additional requirement that copies of such rules and amendments be furnished to the Supreme Court of the United States. See former Equity Rule 79 (Additional Rules by District Court). With the last sentence compare United States Supreme Court Admiralty Rules, 1920, Rule 44 (Right of Trial Courts to Make Rules of Practice)(originally promulgated in 1842).

1985 AMENDMENT

Rule 83, which has not been amended since the Federal Rules were promulgated in 1938, permits each district to adopt local rules not inconsistent with the Federal Rules by a majority of the judges. The only other requirement is that copies be furnished to the Supreme Court.

The widespread adoption of local rules and the modest procedural prerequisites for their promulgation have led many commentators to question the soundness of the process as well as the validity of some rules. See 12 C. Wright & A. Miller, *Federal Practice and Procedure: Civil* § 3152, at 217 (1973); Caballero, *Is There an Over-Exercise of Local Rule-Making Powers by the United States District Courts?,* 24 Fed. Bar News 325 (1977). Although the desirability of local rules for promoting uniform practice within a district is widely accepted, several commentators also have suggested reforms to increase the quality, simplicity, and uniformity of the local rules. See Note, *Rule 83 and the Local Federal Rules,* 67 Colum.L.Rev. 1251 (1967), and Comment, *The Local Rules of Civil Procedure in the Federal District Courts—A Survey*, 1966 Duke L.J. 1011.

The amended Rule attempts, without impairing the procedural validity of existing local rules, to enhance the local rulemaking process by requiring appropriate public notice of proposed rules and an opportunity to comment on them. Although some district courts apparently consult the local bar before promulgating rules, many do not, which has led to criticism of a process that has district judges consulting only with each other. See 12 C. Wright & A. Miller, *supra,* § 3152, at 217; Blair, *The New Local Rules for Federal Practice in Iowa,* 23 Drake L.Rev. 517 (1974). The new language subjects local rulemaking to scrutiny similar to that accompanying the Federal Rules, administrative rulemaking, and legislation. It attempts to assure that the expert advice of practitioners and scholars is made available to the district court before local rules are promulgated. See Weinstein, Reform of Court Rule-Making Procedures 84–87, 127–37, 151 (1977).

The amended Rule does not detail the procedure for giving notice and an opportunity to be heard since conditions vary from district to district. Thus, there is no explicit requirement for a public hearing, although a district may consider that procedure appropriate in all or some rulemaking situations. See generally, Weinstein, supra, at 117–37, 151. The new Rule does not foreclose any other form of consultation. For example, it can be accomplished through the mechanism of an "Advisory Committee" similar to that employed by the Supreme Court in connection with the Federal Rules themselves.

The amended Rule provides that a local rule will take effect upon the date specified by the district court and will remain in effect unless amended by the district court or abrogated by the judicial council. The effectiveness of a local rule should not be deferred until approved by the judicial council because that might unduly delay promulgation of a local rule that should become effective immediately, especially since some councils do not meet frequently. Similarly, it was thought that to delay a local rule's effectiveness for a fixed period of time would be arbitrary and that to require the judicial council to abrogate a local rule within a specified time would be inconsistent with its power under 28 U.S.C. § 332 (1976) to nullify a local rule at any time. The expectation is that the judicial council will examine all local rules, including those currently in effect, with an eye toward determining whether they are valid and consistent with the Federal Rules, promote inter-district uniformity and efficiency, and do not undermine the basic objectives of the Federal Rules.

The amended Rule requires copies of local rules to be sent upon their promulgation to the judicial council and the Administrative Office of the United States Courts rather than to the Supreme Court. The Supreme Court was the appropriate filing place in 1938, when Rule 83 originally was promulgated, but the establishment of the Administrative Office makes it a more logical place to develop a centralized file of local rules. This procedure is consistent with both the Criminal and the Appellate Rules. See Fed.R.Crim.P. 57(a); Fed.R.App.P. 47. The Administrative Office also will be able to provide improved utilization of the file because of its recent development of a Local Rules Index.

The practice pursued by some judges of issuing standing orders has been controversial, particularly among members of the practicing bar. The last sentence in Rule 83 has been amended to make certain that standing orders are not inconsistent with the Federal Rules or any local district court rules. Beyond that, it is hoped that each district will adopt procedures, perhaps by local rule, for promulgating and reviewing single-judge standing orders.

1995 AMENDMENT

Subdivision (a). This rule is amended to reflect the requirement that local rules be consistent not only with the national rules but also with Acts of Congress. The amendment also states that local rules should not repeat Acts of Congress or national rules.

The amendment also requires that the numbering of local rules conform with any uniform numbering system that may be prescribed by the Judicial Conference. Lack of uniform numbering might create unnecessary traps for counsel and litigants. A uniform numbering system would make it easier for an increasingly national bar and for litigants to locate a local rule that applies to a particular procedural issue.

Paragraph (2) is new. Its aim is to protect against loss of rights in the enforcement of local rules relating to matters of form. For example, a party should not be deprived of a right to a jury trial because its attorney, unaware of—or forgetting—a local rule directing that jury demands be noted in the caption of the case, includes a jury demand only in the body of the pleading. The proscription of paragraph (2) is narrowly drawn—covering only violations attributable to nonwillful failure to comply and only those involving local rules directed to matters of form. It does not limit the court's power to impose substantive penalties upon a party if it or its attorney contumaciously or willfully violates a local rule, even one involving merely a matter of form. Nor does it affect the court's power to enforce local rules that involve more than mere matters of form—for example, a local rule requiring parties to identify evidentiary matters relied upon to support or oppose motions for summary judgment.

Subdivision (b). This rule provides flexibility to the court in regulating practice when there is no controlling law. Specifically, it permits the court to regulate practice in any manner consistent with Acts of Congress, with rules adopted under 28 U.S.C. §§ 2072 and 2075, and with the district local rules.

This rule recognizes that courts rely on multiple directives to control practice. Some courts regulate practice through the published Federal Rules and the local rules of the court. Some courts also have used internal operating procedures, standing orders, and other internal directives. Although such directives continue to be authorized, they can lead to problems. Counsel or litigants may be unaware of various directives. In addition, the sheer volume of directives may impose an unreasonable barrier. For example, it may be difficult to obtain copies of the directives. Finally, counsel or litigants may be unfairly sanctioned for failing to comply with a directive. For these reasons, the amendment to this rule disapproves imposing any sanction or other disadvantage on a person for noncompliance with such an internal directive, unless the alleged violator has been furnished actual notice of the requirement in a particular case.

There should be no adverse consequence to a party or attorney for violating special requirements relating to practice before a particular court unless the party or attorney has actual notice of those requirements. Furnishing litigants with a copy outlining the judge's practices—or attaching instructions to a notice setting a case for conference or trial—would suffice to give actual notice, as would an order in a case specifically adopting by reference a judge's standing order and indicating how copies can be obtained.

2007 AMENDMENTS

The language of Rule 83 has been amended as part of the general restyling of the Civil Rules to make them more easily understood and to make style and terminology consistent throughout the rules. These changes are intended to be stylistic only.

Rule 84. Forms

1937 ADOPTION

In accordance with the practice found useful in many codes, provision is here made for a limited number of official forms which may serve as guides in pleading. Compare 2 Mass.Gen.Laws (Ter.Ed., 1932) ch. 231, § 147, Forms 1 to 47; English Annual Practice (1937) Appendix A to M, inclusive; Conn.Practice Book (1934) Rules, 47 to 68, pp. 123 to 427.

1946 AMENDMENT

Note. The amendment serves to emphasize that the forms contained in the Appendix of Forms are sufficient to withstand attack under the rules under which they are drawn, and that the practitioner using them may rely on them to that extent. The circuit courts of appeals generally have upheld the use of the forms as promoting desirable simplicity and brevity of statement. *Sierocinski v. E. I. DuPont DeNemours & Co., C.C.A.3, 1939*, 103 F.2d 843; *Swift & Co. v. Young, C.C.A.4, 1939*, 107 F.2d 170; *Sparks v. England, C.C.A.8, 1940*, 113 F.2d 579; *Ramsouer v. Midland Valley R. Co., C.C.A.8, 1943*, 135 F.2d 101. And the forms as a whole have met with widespread approval in the courts. See cases cited in 1 Moore's Federal Practice, 1938, Cum. Supplement § 8.07, under "Page 554"; see also Commentary, The Official Forms, 1941, 4 Fed.Rules Serv. 954. In Cook, "Facts" and "Statements of Fact", 1937, 4 U.Chi.L.Rev. 233, 245–246, it is said with reference to what is now Rule 84: ". . . pleaders in the federal courts are not to be left to guess as to the meaning of [the] language" in Rule 8(a) regarding the form of the complaint. "All of which is as it should be. In no other way can useless litigation be avoided." Ibid. The amended rule will operate to discourage isolated results such as those found in *Washburn v. Moorman Mfg. Co., Cal.1938*, 25 F.Supp. 546; *Employers' Mutual Liability Ins. Co. of Wisconsin v. Blue Line Transfer Co., Mo.1941*, 2 F.R.D. 121, 5 Fed.Rules Serv. 12e.235, Case 2.

2007 AMENDMENTS

The language of Rule 84 has been amended as part of the general restyling of the Civil Rules to make them more easily understood and to make style and terminology consistent throughout the rules. These changes are intended to be stylistic only.

2015 AMENDMENT

Rule 84 was adopted when the Civil Rules were established in 1938 "to indicate, subject to the provisions of these rules, the simplicity and brevity of statement which the rules contemplate." The purpose of providing illustrations for the rules, although useful when the rules were adopted, has been fulfilled. Accordingly, recognizing that there are many excellent alternative sources for forms, including the Administrative Office of the United States Courts, Rule 84 and the Appendix of Forms are no longer necessary and have been abrogated.

Rule 85. Title

2007 AMENDMENTS

The language of Rule 85 has been amended as part of the general restyling of the Civil Rules to make them more easily understood and to make style and

terminology consistent throughout the rules. These changes are intended to be stylistic only.

Rule 86. Effective Date

1937 ADOPTION

See former Equity Rule 81 (These Rules Effective February 1, 1913—Old Rules Abrogated).

1946 AMENDMENT

Effective Date of 1946 Amendment. The first regular session of the 80th Congress adjourned sine die on Friday, Dec. 19, 1947, therefore the amendments to Rules 6, 7, 12, 13, 14, 17, 24, 26, 27, 28, 33, 34, 36, 41, 45, 52, 54, 56, 58, 59, 60, 62, 65, 66, 68, 73, 75, 77, 79, 80, 81, 84, and 86, became effective Mar. 19, 1948 as provided for in subsection (b) of this rule.

1948 AMENDMENT

Effective Date of 1948 Amendment. The first regular session of the 81st Congress adjourned sine die on Oct. 19, 1949, therefore the amendments to Rules 1, 17, 22, 24, 25, 27, 37, 45, 57, 60, 65, 66, 67, 69, 72 to 76, 79, 81, 82, and 86 and to forms 1, 19, 22, 23, and 27 became effective on Oct. 20, 1949, following the adjournment as provided for in subsection (c) of this rule.

1966 AMENDMENT

Effective Date of 1966 Amendment; Transmission to Congress; Rescission. Sections 2 to 4 of the Order of the Supreme Court, dated Feb. 28, 1966, 383 U.S. 1031, provided:

"2. That the foregoing amendments and additions to the Rules of Civil Procedure shall take effect on July 1, 1966, and shall govern all proceedings in actions brought thereafter and also in all further proceedings in actions then pending, except to the extent that in the opinion of the court their application in a particular action then pending would not be feasible or would work injustice, in which event the former procedure applies.

"3. That the Chief Justice be, and he hereby is, authorized to transmit to the Congress the foregoing amendments and additions to the Rules of Civil Procedure in accordance with the provisions of Title 28, U.S.C., §§ 2072 and 2073.

"4. That: (a) subdivision (c) of Rule 6 of the Rules of Civil Procedure for the United States District Courts promulgated by this court on December 20, 1937, effective September 16, 1938; (b) Rule 2 of the Rules for Practice and Procedure under section 25 of An Act To amend and consolidate the Acts respecting copyright, approved March 4, 1909, promulgated by this court on June 1, 1909, effective July 1, 1909; and (c) the Rules of Practice in Admiralty and Maritime Cases, promulgated by this court on December 6, 1920, effective March 7, 1921, as revised, amended and supplemented, be, and they hereby are, rescinded, effective July 1, 1966."

1970 AMENDMENT

Effective Date of 1970 Amendments; Transmission to Congress. Sections 2 and 3 of the Order of the Supreme Court, dated Mar. 30, 1970, provided:

"2. That the foregoing amendments to the Rules of Civil Procedure shall take effect on July 1, 1970, and shall govern all proceedings in actions brought thereafter and also in all further proceedings in actions then pending, except to the extent that in the opinion of the court their application in a particular action then pending would not be feasible or would work injustice, in which event the former procedure applies.

"3. That the Chief Justice be, and he hereby is, authorized to transmit to the Congress the foregoing amendments to the Rules of Civil Procedure in accordance with the provisions of Title 28, U.S.C. § 2072."

2007 AMENDMENTS

The language of Rule 86 has been amended as part of the general restyling of the Civil Rules to make them more easily understood and to make style and terminology consistent throughout the rules. These changes are intended to be stylistic only.

The subdivisions that provided a list of the effective dates of the original Civil

Rules and amendments made up to 1963 are deleted as no longer useful.

Rule 86(b) is added to clarify the relationship of amendments taking effect on December 1, 2007, to other laws for the purpose of applying the "supersession" clause in 28 U.S.C. § 2072(b). Section 2072(b) provides that a law in conflict with an Enabling Act Rule "shall be of no further force or effect after such rule[] ha[s] taken effect." The amendments that take effect on December 1, 2007, result from the general restyling of the Civil Rules and from a small number of technical revisions adopted on a parallel track. None of these amendments is intended to affect resolution of any conflict that might arise between a rule and another law. Rule 86(b) makes this intent explicit. Any conflict that arises should be resolved by looking to the date the specific conflicting rule provision first became effective.

SUPPLEMENTAL RULES FOR CERTAIN ADMIRALTY AND MARITIME CLAIMS

Rule A. Scope of Rules

1966 ADOPTION

Certain distinctively maritime remedies must be preserved in unified rules. The commencement of an action by attachment or garnishment has heretofore been practically unknown in federal jurisprudence except in admiralty, although the amendment of Rule 4(e) effective July 1, 1963, makes available that procedure in accordance with state law. The maritime Proceeding in rem is unique, except as it has been emulated by statute, and is closely related to the substantive maritime law relating to liens. Arrest of the vessel or other maritime property is an historic remedy in controversies over title or right to possession, and in disputes among co-owners over the vessel's employment. The statutory right to limit liability is limited to owners of vessels, and has its own complexities. While the unified federal rules are generally applicable to these distinctive proceedings, certain special rules dealing with them are needed.

Arrest of the person and imprisonment for debt are not included because there remedies are not peculiarly maritime. The practice is not uniform but conforms to state law. See 2 Benedict § 286 [Note: reference is to the 6th Edition of Benedict on Admiralty and not to the current 7th Edition]; 28 U.S.C., § 2007; FRCP 64, 69. The relevant provisions of Admiralty Rules 2, 3, and 4 are unnecessary or obsolete.

No attempt is here made to compile a complete and self-contained code governing these distinctively maritime remedies. The more limited objective is to carry forward the relevant provisions of the former Rules of Practice for Admiralty and Maritime Cases, modernized and revised to some extent but still in the context of history and precedent. Accordingly, these Rules are not to be construed as limiting or impairing the traditional power of a district court, exercising the admiralty and maritime jurisdiction, to adapt its Procedures and its remedies in the individual case, consistently with these rules, to secure the just, speedy, and inexpensive determination of every action. (*See Swift & Co. Packers v. Compania Columbiana Del Caribe, S/A 339 U.S. 684*, 70 S. Ct. 861, 94 L.Ed. 1206 (1950); Rule 1). In addition, of course, the district courts retain the power to make local rules not inconsistent with these rules. *See* Rule 83; cf. Admiralty Rule 44.

2006 AMENDMENT

Rule A is amended to reflect the adoption of Rule G to govern procedure in civil forfeiture actions. Rule G(1) contemplates application of other Supplemental Rules to the extent that Rule G does not address an issue. One example is the Rule E(4)(c) provision for arresting intangible property.

Rule B. In Personam Actions: Attachment and Garnishment

1966 ADOPTION

Subdivision (1).

This preserves the traditional maritime remedy of attachment and garnishment, and carries forward the relevant substance of Admiralty Rule 2. In addition, or in the alternative, provision is made for the use of similar state remedies made available by the amendment of Rule 4(e) effective July 1, 1963. On the effect of appearance to defend against attachment see Rule E(8).

The rule follows closely the language of Admiralty Rule 2. No change is made with respect to the property subject to attachment. No change is made in the condition that makes the remedy available. The rules have never defined the clause, "if the defendant shall not be found within the district," and no definition is attempted here. The subject seems one best left for the time being to development on a case-by-case basis. The proposal does shift from the marshal (on whom it now rests in theory) to the plaintiff the burden of establishing that the defendant cannot be found in the district.

A change in the context of the practice is brought about by Rule 4(f), which will enable summons to be served throughout the state instead of, as heretofore, only within the district. The Advisory Committee considered whether the rule on attachment and garnishment should be correspondingly changed to permit those remedies only when the defendant cannot be found within the state and concluded that the remedy should not be so limited.

The effect is to enlarge the class of cases in which the plaintiff may proceed by attachment or garnishment although jurisdiction of the person of the defendant may be independently obtained. This is possible at the present time where, for example, a corporate defendant has appointed an agent within the district to accept service of process but is not carrying on activities there sufficient to subject it to jurisdiction. (*Seawind Compania, S.A v. Crescent Line, Inc.*, 320 F.2d 580 (2d Cir.1963)), or where, though the foreign corporation's activities in the district are sufficient to subject it personally to the jurisdiction, there is in the district no officer on whom process can be served (*United States v. Cia. Naviera Continental, S.A.*, 178 F.Supp. 561, (S.D.N.Y.1959)).

Process of attachment or garnishment will be limited to the district. See Rule E(3)(a).

Subdivision (2).

The former Admiralty Rules did not provide for notice to the defendant in attachment and garnishment proceedings. None is required by the principles of due process, since it is assumed that the garnishee or custodian of the property attached will either notify the defendant or be deprived of the right to plead the judgment as a defense in an action against him by the defendant. *Harris v. Balk*, 198 U.S. 215, 25 S. Ct. 625, 49 L.Ed. 1023 (1905); *Pennoyer v. Neff, 95 U.S. (5 Otto) 714*, 24 L.Ed. 565 (1878). Modern conceptions of fairness, however, dictate that actual notice be given to persons known to claim an interest in the property that is the subject of the action where that is reasonably practicable. In attachment and garnishment proceedings the persons whose interests will be affected by the judgment are identified by the complaint. No substantial burden is imposed on the plaintiff by a simple requirement that he notify the defendant of the action by mail.

In the usual case the defendant is notified of the pendency of the proceedings by the garnishee or otherwise, and appears to claim the property and to make his answer. Hence notice by mail is not routinely required in all cases, but only in those in which the defendant has not appeared prior to the time when a default judgment is demanded. The rule therefore provides only that no default judgment shall be entered except upon proof of notice, or of inability to give notice despite diligent efforts to do so. Thus the burden of giving notice is further minimized.

In some cases the plaintiff may prefer to give notice by serving process in the usual way instead of simply by mail. (Rule 4(d).) In particular, if the defendant is in a foreign country the plaintiff may wish to utilize the modes of notice recently provided to facilitate compliance with foreign laws and procedures (Rule 4(i)). The rule provides for these alternatives.

The rule does not provide for notice by publication because there is no problem concerning unknown claimants, and publication has little utility in proportion to its expense where the identity of the defendant is known.

Subdivision (3).

Subdivision (a) incorporates the substance of Admiralty Rule 36.

The Admiralty Rules were silent as to when the garnishee and the defendant were to answer. See also 2 Benedict ch. XXIV [Reference is to the 6th Edition of Benedict on Admiralty and not to the current 7th Edition].

The rule proceeds on the assumption that uniform and definite Periods of time for responsive pleadings should be substituted for return days (see the discussion under Rule C(6), below). Twenty days seems sufficient time for the garnishee to answer (cf. FRCP 12(a)), and an additional 10 days should suffice for the defendant. When allowance is made for the time required for notice to reach the defendant this gives the defendant in attachment and garnishment approximately the same time that defendants have to answer when personally served.

1985 AMENDMENT

Rule B(1) has been amended to provide for judicial scrutiny before the issuance of any attachment or garnishment process. Its purpose is to eliminate doubts as to whether the Rule is consistent with the principles of procedural due process enunciated by the Supreme Court in *Sniadach v. Family Finance Corp.*, 395 U.S. 337, 89 S. Ct. 1820, 23 L. Ed. 2d 349 (1969); and later developed in *Fuentes v. Shevin*, 407 U.S. 67, 92 S. Ct. 1983, 32 L. Ed. 2d 556 (1972); *Mitchell v. W.T. Grant Co.*, 416 U.S. 600, 94 S. Ct. 1895, 40 L. Ed. 2d 406 (1974); and *North Georgia Finishing, Inc. v. Di-Chem, Inc.*, 419 U.S. 601, 95 S. Ct. 719, 42 L. Ed. 2d 751 (1975). Such doubts were raised in *Grand Bahama Petroleum Co. v. Canadian Transportation Agencies, Ltd.*, 450 F.Supp. 447 (W. D.Wash.1978); and *Schiffahartsgesellschaft Leonhardt & Co. v. A. Bottacchi S.A. de Navegacion*, 552 F.Supp. 771 (S.D.Ga.1982), which was reversed, 732 F.2d 1543 (11th Cir.1984). *But compare Polar Shipping Ltd. v. Oriental Shipping Corp.*, 680 F.2d 627 (9th Cir.1982), in which a majority of the panel upheld the constitutionality of Rule B because of the Unique commercial context in which it is invoked. practice described in Rule B(1) has been adopted in districts by local rule. E.g., N.D. Calif. Local Rule 603.3; W.D.Wash. Local Admiralty Rule 15(d).

The rule envisions that the order will issue when the plaintiff makes a prima facie showing that he has a maritime claim against the defendant in the amount sued for and the defendant is not present in the district. A simple order with conclusory findings is contemplated. The reference to review by the "court" is broad enough to embrace review by a magistrate as well as by a district judge.

The new provision recognizes that in some situations, such as when the judge is unavailable and the ship is about to depart from the jurisdiction, it will be impracticable, if not impossible, to secure the judicial review contemplated by Rule B(1). When "exigent circumstances" exist, the rule enables the plaintiff to secure the issuance of the summons and process of attachment and garnishment, subject to a later showing that the necessary circumstances actually existed. This provision is intended to provide a safety valve without undermining the requirement of preattachment scrutiny. Thus, every effort to secure judicial review, including conducting a hearing by telephone, should be pursued before resorting to the exigent-circumstances procedure.

Rule B(1) also has been amended so that the garnishee shall be named in the "process" rather than in the "complaint." This should solve the problem presented in *Filia Compania Naviera, S.A. v. Petroship, S.A.*, 1983 A.M.C. 1 (S.D.

N.Y.1982), and eliminate any need for an additional judicial review of the complaint and affidavit when a garnishee is added.

1987 AMENDMENT

The amendments are technical No substantive change is intended.

2000 AMENDMENT

Rule B(1) is amended in two ways, and style changes have been made.

The service provisions of Rule C(3) are adopted in paragraph (d), providing alternatives to service by a marshal if the property to be seized is not a vessel or tangible property on board a vessel.

The provision that allows the plaintiff to invoke state attachment and garnishment remedies is amended to reflect the 1993 amendments of Civil Rule 4. Former Civil Rule 4(e), incorporated in Rule B(1), allowed general use of state quasi-in-rem jurisdiction if the defendant was not an inhabitant of, or found within, the state. Rule 4(e) was replaced in 1993 by Rule 4(n)(2), which permits use of state law to seize a defendant's assets only if personal jurisdiction over the defendant cannot be obtained in the district where the action is brought. Little purpose would be served by incorporating Rule 4(n)(2) in Rule B, since maritime attachment and garnishment are available whenever the defendant is not found within the district, a concept that allows attachment or garnishment even in some circumstances in which personal jurisdiction also can be asserted. In order to protect against any possibility that elimination of the reference to state quasi-in-rem jurisdiction remedies might seem to defeat continued use of state security devices, paragraph (e) expressly incorporates Civil Rule 64. Because Rule 64 looks only to security, not jurisdiction, the former reference to Rule E(8) is deleted as no longer relevant.

Rule B(2)(a) is amended to reflect the 1993 redistribution of the service provisions once found in Civil Rule 4(d) and (i). These provisions are now found in many different subdivisions of Rule 4. The new reference simply incorporates Rule 4, without designating the new subdivisions, because the function of Rule B(2) is simply to describe the methods of notice that suffice to support a default judgment. Style changes also have been made.

2005 AMENDMENT

Rule B(1) is amended to incorporate the decisions in *Heidmar, Inc. v. Anomina Ravennate Di Armamento Sp.A. of Ravenna*, 132 F.3d 264, 267–268 (5th Cir. 1998), and *Navieros InterAmericanos, S.A. v. M/V Vasilia Express*, 120 F.3d 304, 314–315 (1st Cir.1997). The time for determining whether a defendant is "found" in the district is set at the time of filing the verified complaint that prays for attachment and the affidavit required by Rule B(1)(b). As provided by Rule B(1)(b), the affidavit must be filed with the complaint. A defendant cannot defeat the security purpose of attachment by appointing an agent for service of process after the complaint and affidavit are filed. The complaint praying for attachment need not be the initial complaint. So long as the defendant is not found in the district, the prayer for attachment may be made in an amended complaint; the affidavit that the defendant cannot be found must be filed with the amended complaint.

2009 AMENDMENT

The time set in the former rule at 20 days has been revised to 21 days. See the Note to Rule 6.

Rule C. In Rem Actions: Special Provisions

1966 ADOPTION

Subdivision (1).

This rule is designed not only to preserve the proceeding in rem as it now exists in admiralty cases, but to preserve the substance of Admiralty Rules 13 to 18. The general reference to enforcement of any maritime lien is believed to state the existing law, and is an improvement over the enumeration in the former Admiralty Rules, which is repetitious and incomplete (e.g., there was no reference to general average). The reference to any maritime lien is intended to include liens created by state law which are enforceable in admiralty.

The main concern of Admiralty Rules 13 to 18 was with the question whether certain actions might be brought in rem or also, or in the alternative, in personam. Essentially, therefore, these rules deal with questions of substantive law, for in general an action in rem may be brought to enforce any maritime lien, and no action in personam may be brought when the substantive law imposes no personal liability.

These rules may be summarized as follows:

1. Cases in which the plaintiff may proceed in rem and/or in personam:

a. Suits for seamen's wages;

b. Suits by materialmen for supplies, repairs, etc.;

c. Suits for pilotage;

d. Suits for collision damages;

e. Suits founded on mere maritime hypothecation;

f. Suits for salvage.

2. Cases in which the plaintiff may proceed only in personam:

a. Suits for assault and beating.

3. Cases in which the plaintiff may proceed only in rem:

a. Suits on bottomry bonds.

The coverage is incomplete, since the rules omit mention of many cases in which the plaintiff may proceed in rem or in personam. This revision proceeds on the principle that it is preferable to make a general statement as to the availability of the remedies, leaving out conclusions on matters of substantive law. Clearly it is not necessary to enumerate the cases listed under Item 1, above, nor to try to complete the list.

The rule eliminates the provision of Admiralty Rule 15 that actions for assault and beating may be brought only in personam. A preliminary study fails to disclose any reason for the rule. It is subject to so many exceptions that it is calculated to deceive rather than to inform. A seaman may sue in rem when he has been beaten by a fellow member of the crew so vicious as to render the vessel unseaworthy, *The Rolph*, 293 Fed. 269, aff'd 299 Fed. 52 (9th Cir.1923), or where the theory of the action is that a beating by the master is a breach of the obligation under the shipping articles to treat the seaman with proper kindness, *The David Evans*, 187 Fed. 775 (C.C.A. 9, 1911); and a passenger may sue in rem on the theory that the assault is a breach of the contract of passage, *The Western States*, 159 Fed. 354 (2d Cir.1908). To say that an action for money damages may be brought only in personam seems equivalent to saying that a maritime lien shall not exist; and that, in turn, seems equivalent to announcing a rule of substantive law rather than a rule of procedure. Dropping the rule will leave it to the courts to determine whether a lien exists as a matter of substantive law.

The specific reference to bottomry bonds is omitted because, as a matter of hornbook substantive law, there is no personal liability on such bonds.

Subdivision (2).

This incorporates the substance of Admiralty Rules 21 and 22.

Subdivision (3).

Derived from Admiralty Rules 10 and 37. The provision that the warrant is to be issued by the clerk is new, but is assumed to state existing law.

There is remarkably little authority bearing on Rule 37, although the subject would seem to be an important one. The rule appears on its face to have provided for a sort of ancillary process, and this may well be the case when tangible property, such as a vessel, is arrested, and intangible property such as freight is incidentally involved. It can easily happen, however, that the only property against which the action may be brought is intangible, as where the owner of a vessel under charter has a lien on subfreights. See 2 Benedict § 299 and cases cited. (Reference is to the 6th Edition of Benedict on Admiralty and not to the current 7th Edition). In such cases it would seem that the order to the person holding the fund is equivalent to original process, taking the place of the warrant for arrest. That being so, it would also seem that (1) there should be some provision for notice, comparable to that given when tangible property is arrested, and (2) it should not be necessary, as Rule 37 provided, to petition the court for issuance of the process, but that it should issue as of course. Accordingly the substance of Rule 37 is included in the rule covering ordinary process, and notice will be required by Rule C(4). Presumably the rules omit any requirement of notice in these cases because the holder of the funds (e.g., the cargo owner) would be required on general principles *(cf. Harris v. Balk*, 198 U.S. 215, 25 S. Ct. 625, 49 L.Ed. 1023 (1905)) to notify his obligee (*e.g.*, the charterer); but in actions in rem such notice seems plainly inadequate because there may be adverse claims to the fund (*e.g.*, there may be liens against the subfreights for seamen's wages, etc.). *Compare* Admiralty Rule 9.

Subdivision (4).

This carries forward the notice provision of Admiralty Rule 10, with one modification. Notice by publication is too expensive and ineffective a formality to be routinely required. When, as usually happens, the vessel or other property is released on bond or otherwise there is no point in publishing notice; the vessel is freed from the claim of the plaintiff and no other interest in the vessel can be affected by the proceedings. If, however, the vessel is not released, general notice is required in order that all persons, including unknown claimants, may appear and be heard, and in order that the judgment in rem shall be binding on all the world.

Subdivision (5).

This incorporates the substance of Admiralty Rule 9.

There are remarkably few cases dealing directly with the rule. In *The George Prescott*, 10 Fed.Cas. 222 (No. 5,339) (E.D.N.Y.1865), the master and crew of a vessel libeled her for wages, and other lienors also filed libels. One of the lienors suggested to the court that prior to the arrest of the vessel the master had removed the sails, and asked that he be ordered to produce them. He admitted removing the sails and selling them, justifying on the ground that he held a mortgage on the vessel. He was ordered to pay the proceeds into court. *Cf. United States v. The Zarco*, 187 F.Supp. 371 (S.D.Cal.1960), where an armature belonging to a vessel subject to a preferred ship mortgage was in possession of a repairman claiming a lien.

It is evident that, though the rule has had a limited career in the reported cases, it is a potentially important one. It is also evident that the rule is framed in terms narrower than the principle that supports it. There is no apparent reason for limiting it to ships and their appurtenances (2 Benedict § 299) [Reference is to the 6th Edition of Benedict on Admiralty and not to the current 7th Edition]. Also, the reference to "third parties" in the existing rule seems unfortunate. In *The George Prescott*, the person who removed and sold the sails was a plaintiff in the action, and relief against him was just as necessary as if he had been a stranger.

Another situation in which process of this kind would seem to be useful is that in which the principal property that is the subject of the action is a vessel, but her pending freight is incidentally involved. The warrant of arrest, and notice of its service, should be all that is required by way of original process and notice; ancillary process without notice should suffice as to the incidental intangibles.

The distinction between Admiralty Rules 9 and 37 is not at once apparent but seems to be this: Where the action was against Property that could not be seized by the marshal because it was intangible, the original process was required to be similar to that issued against a garnishee, and general notice was required (though not provided for by the present rule; *cf.* Advisory Committee's Note to Rule C(3)). Under Admiralty Rule 9 property had been arrested and general notice had been given, but some of the property had been removed or for some other reason could not be arrested. Here no further notice was necessary.

The rule also makes provision for this kind of situation: The proceeding is against a vessel's pending freight only; summons has been served on the person supposedly holding the funds, and general notice has been given; it develops that another person holds all or part of the funds. Ancillary process should be available here without further notice.

Subdivision (6).

Adherence to the practice of return days seems unsatisfactory. The practice varies significantly from district to district. A uniform rule should be provided so that any claimant or defendant can readily determine when he is required to file or serve a claim or answer.

A virtue of the return-day practice is that it requires claimants to come forward and identify themselves at an early stage of the proceedings—before they could fairly be required to answer. The draft is designed to preserve this feature of the present practice by requiring early filing of the claim. The time schedule contemplated in the draft is closely comparable to the present practice in the Southern District of New York, where the claimant has a minimum of 8 days to claim and three weeks thereafter to answer.

This rule also incorporates the substance of Admiralty Rule 25. The present rule's emphasis on "the true and bona fide owner" is omitted, since anyone having the right to possession can claim (2 Benedict § 324) [Reference is to the 6th Edition of Benedict on Admiralty and not to the current 7th Edition].

1985 AMENDMENT

Rule C(3) has been amended to provide for judicial scrutiny before the issuance of any warrant of arrest. Its purpose is to eliminate any doubt as to the rule's constitutionality under the *Sniadach* line of cases. *Sniadach v. Family Finance Corp.*, 395 U.S. 337, 89 S. Ct. 1820, 23 L. Ed. 2d 349 (1969); *Fuentes v. Shevin*, 407 U.S. 67, 92 S. Ct. 1983, 32 L. Ed. 2d 556 (1972); *Mitchell v. W. T. Grant Co.*, 416 U.S. 600, 94 S. Ct. 1895, 40 L. Ed. 2d 406 (1974); and *North Georgia Finishing, Inc. v. Di-Chem, Inc.*, 419 U.S. 601, 95 S. Ct. 719, 42 L. Ed. 2d 751 (1975). This was thought desirable even though both the Fourth and the Fifth Circuits have upheld the existing rule. *Amstar Corp. v. S/S Alexandros T.*, 664 F.2d 904 (4th Cir.1981); *Merchants National Bank of Mobile v. The Dredge General G.L. Gillespie*, 663 F.2d 1338 (5th Cir.1981), *cert. dismissed,* 456 U.S. 966, 102 S. Ct. 2263, 72 L. Ed. 2d 865 (1982). A contrary view was taken by Judge Tate in the *Merchants National Bank* case and by the district court in *Alyeska Pipeline Service Co. v. The Vessel Bay Ridge*, 509 F.Supp. 1115 (D.Alaska 1981), *appeal dismissed*, 703 F.2d 381 (9th Cir.1983).

The rule envisions that the order will issue upon a prima facie showing that the plaintiff has an action in rem against the defendant in the amount sued for and that the property is within the district. A simple order with conclusory findings is contemplated. The reference to review by the "court" is broad enough to embrace a magistrate as well as a district judge.

The new provision recognizes that in some situations, such as when a judge is unavailable and the vessel is about to depart from the jurisdiction, it will be impracticable, if not impossible, to secure the judicial review contemplated by Rule C(3). When "exigent circumstances" exist, the rule enables the plaintiff to secure the issuance of the summons and warrant of arrest, subject to a later showing that the necessary circumstances actually existed. This provision is intended to provide a safety valve without undermining the requirement of pre-arrest scrutiny. Thus, every effort to secure judicial review, including conducting a hearing by telephone, should be pursued before invoking the exigent-circumstances procedure.

The foregoing requirements for prior court review or proof of exigent circumstances do not apply to actions by the United States for forfeitures for federal statutory violations. In such actions a prompt hearing is not constitutionally required, *United States v. Eight Thousand Eight Hundred and Fifty Dollars*, 461 U.S. 555, 103 S. Ct. 2005, 76 L. Ed. 2d 143 (1983); *Calero-Toledo v. Pearson Yacht Leasing Co.*, 416 U.S. 663, 94 S. Ct. 2080, 40 L. Ed. 2d 452 (1974), and could prejudice the government in its prosecution of the claimants as defendants in parallel criminal proceedings since the forfeiture hearing could be misused by the defendants to obtain by way of civil discovery information to which they would not otherwise be entitled and subject the government and the courts to the unnecessary burden and expense of two hearings rather than one.

1987 AMENDMENT

The amendments are technical. No substantive change is intended.

1991 AMENDMENT

These amendments are designed to conform the rule to Fed.R.Civ.P. 4, as amended. As with recent amendments to Rule 4, it is intended to relieve the Marshals Service of the burden of using its limited personnel and facilities for execution of process in routine circumstances. Doing so may involve a contractual arrangement with a person or organization retained by the government to perform these services, or the use of other government officers and employees, or the special appointment by the court of persons available to perform suitably.

The seizure of a vessel, with or without cargo, remains a task assigned to the Marshal. Successful arrest of a vessel frequently requires the enforcement presence of an armed government official and the cooperation of the United States Coast Guard and other governmental authorities. If the marshal is called upon to seize the vessel, it is expected that the same officer will also be responsible for the seizure of any property on board the vessel at the time of seizure that is to be the object of arrest or attachment.

2000 AMENDMENT

Style changes have been made throughout the revised portions of Rule C. Several changes of meaning have been made as well.

Subdivision 2. In rem jurisdiction originally extended only to property within the judicial district. Since 1986, Congress has enacted a number of jurisdictional and venue statutes for forfeiture and criminal matters that in some circumstances permit a court to exercise authority over property outside the district. 28 U.S.C. § 1355(b)(1) allows a forfeiture action in the district where an act or omission giving rise to forfeiture occurred, or in any other district where venue is established by § 1395 or by any other statute. Section 1355(b)(2) allows an action to be brought as provided in (b)(1) or in the United States District Court for the District of Columbia when the forfeiture property is located in a foreign country or has been seized by authority of a foreign government. Section 1355(d) allows a court with jurisdiction under § 1355(b) to cause service in any other district of process required to bring the forfeiture property before the court. Section 1395 establishes venue of a civil proceeding for forfeiture in the district where the forfeiture accrues or the defendant is found; in any district where the property is found; in any district into which the property is brought, if the property initially is outside any judicial district; or in any district where the vessel is arrested if the proceeding is an admiralty proceeding to forfeit a vessel. Section 1395(e) deals with a vessel or cargo entering a port of entry closed by the President, and transportation to or from a state or section declared to be in insurrection. 18 U.S.C. § 981(h) creates expanded jurisdiction and venue over property located elsewhere that is related to a criminal prosecution pending in the district. These amendments, and related amendments of Rule E(3), bring these Rules into step with the new statutes. No change is made as to admiralty and maritime proceedings that do not involve a forfeiture governed by one of the new statutes.

Subdivision (2) has been separated into lettered paragraphs to facilitate understanding.

Subdivision (3). Subdivision (3) has been rearranged and divided into lettered paragraphs to facilitate understanding.

Paragraph (b)(i) is amended to make it clear that any supplemental process addressed to a vessel or tangible property on board a vessel, as well as the original warrant, is to be served by the marshal.

Subdivision (4). Subdivision (4) has required that public notice state the time for filing an answer, but has not required that the notice set out the earlier time for filing a statement of interest or claim. The amendment requires that both times be stated.

A new provision is added, allowing termination of publication if the property is released more than 10 days after execution but before publication is completed. Termination will save money, and also will reduce the risk of confusion as to the status of the property.

Subdivision (6). Subdivision (6) has applied a single set of undifferentiated provisions to civil forfeiture proceedings and to in rem admiralty proceedings. Because some differences in procedure are desirable, these proceedings are separated by adopting a new paragraph (a) for civil forfeiture proceedings and recasting the present rule as paragraph (b) for in rem admiralty proceedings. The provision for interrogatories and answers is carried forward as paragraph (c). Although this established procedure for serving interrogatories with the complaint departs from the general provisions of Civil Rule 26(d), the special needs of expedition that often arise in admiralty justify continuing the practice.

Both paragraphs (a) and (b) require a statement of interest or right rather than the "claim" formerly required. The new wording permits parallel drafting, and facilitates cross-references in other rules. The substantive nature of the statement remains the same as the former claim. The requirements of (a) and (b) are, however, different in some respects.

In a forfeiture proceeding governed by paragraph (a), a statement must be filed by a person who asserts an interest in or a right against the property involved. This category includes every right against the property, such as a lien, whether or not it establishes ownership or a right to possession. In determining who has an interest in or a right against property, courts may continue to rely on precedents that have developed the meaning of "claims" or "claimants" for the purpose of civil forfeiture proceedings.

In an admiralty and maritime proceeding governed by paragraph (b), a statement is filed only by a person claiming a right of possession or ownership. Other claims against the property are advanced by intervention under Civil Rule 24, as it may be supplemented by local admiralty rules. The reference to ownership includes every interest that qualifies as ownership under domestic or foreign law. If an ownership interest is asserted, it makes no difference whether its character is legal, equitable, or something else.

Paragraph (a) provides more time than paragraph (b) for filing a statement. Admiralty and maritime in rem proceedings often present special needs for prompt action that do not commonly arise in forfeiture proceedings.

Paragraphs (a) and (b) do not limit the right to make a restricted appearance under Rule E(8).

2002 AMENDMENT

Rule C(3) is amended to reflect the provisions of 18 U.S.C. § 985, enacted by the Civil Asset Forfeiture Reform Act of 2000, 114 Stat. 202, 214 to 215. Section 985 provides, subject to enumerated exceptions, that real property that is the subject of a civil forfeiture action is not to be seized until an order of forfeiture is entered. A civil forfeiture action is initiated by filing a complaint, posting notice, and serving notice on the property owner. The summons and arrest procedure is no longer appropriate.

Rule C(6)(a)(i)(A) is amended to adopt the provision enacted by 18 U.S.C. § 983(a)(4)(A), shortly before Rule C(6)(a)(i)(A) took effect, that sets the time for filing a verified statement as 30 days rather than 20 days, and that sets the first alternative event for measuring the 30 days as the date of service of the Government's complaint.

Rule C(6)(a)(iii) is amended to give notice of the provision enacted by 18 U.S.C. § 983(a)(4)(B) that requires that the answer in a forfeiture proceeding be filed within 20 days. Without this notice, unwary litigants might rely on the provision of Rule 5(d) that allows a reasonable time for filing after service.

Rule C(6)(b)(iv) is amended to change the requirement that an answer be filed within 20 days to a requirement that it be served within 20 days. Service is the ordinary requirement, as in Rule 12(a). Rule 5(d) requires filing within a reasonable time after service.

2005 AMENDMENT

Rule C(6)(b)(i)(A) is amended to delete the reference to a time 10 days after completed publication under Rule C(4). This change corrects an oversight in the amendments made in 2000. Rule C(4) requires publication of notice only if the property that is the subject of the action is not released within 10 days after execution of process. Execution of process will always be earlier than publication.

2006 AMENDMENT

Rule C is amended to reflect the adoption of Rule G to govern procedure in civil forfeiture actions.

2008 AMENDMENT

Supplemental Rule C(6)(a)(i) is amended to correct an inadvertent omission in the 2006 amendment to Rule C. The amendment is technical and stylistic in nature. No substantive change is intended.

2009 AMENDMENT

The times set in the former rule at 10 or 20 days have been revised to 14 or 21 days. See the Note to Rule 6.

Rule D. Possessory, Petitory, and Partition Actions

1966 ADOPTION

This carries forward the substance of Admiralty Rule 19.

Rule 19 provided the remedy of arrest in controversies involving title and possession in general. See The Tilton, 23 Fed.Cas.1277 (No. 14,054) (C.C.D.Mass.1830). In addition it provided that remedy in controversies between co-owners respecting the employment of a vessel. It did not deal comprehensively with controversies between co-owners, omitting the remedy of partition. Presumably the omission is traceable to the fact that, when the rules were originally promulgated, concepts of substantive law (sometimes stated as concepts of jurisdiction) denied the remedy of partition except where the parties in disagreement were the owners of equal shares. *See The Steamboat Orleans*, 36 U.S. (11 Pet.) 175, 9 L.Ed. 677 (1837). The Supreme Court has now removed any doubt as to the jurisdiction of the district courts to partition a vessel, and has held in addition that no fixed principle of federal admiralty law limits the remedy to the case of equal shares. *Madruga v. Superior Court*, 346 U.S. 556, 74 S. Ct. 298, 98 L.Ed. 290 (1954). It is therefore appropriate to include a reference to partition in the rule.

Rule E. Actions in Rem and Quasi in Rem: General Provisions

1966 ADOPTION

Subdivisions (1), (2).

Adapted from Admiralty Rule 24. The rule is based on the assumption that there is no more need for security for costs in maritime personal actions than in civil cases generally, but that there is reason to retain the requirement for actions in which property is seized. As to proceedings for limitation of liability see Rule F(1).

Subdivision (3).

The Advisory Committee has concluded for practical reasons that process requiring seizure of property should continue to be served only within the geographical limits of the district. Compare Rule B(1), continuing the condition that process of attachment and garnishment may be served only if the defendant is not found within the district.

The provisions of Admiralty Rule 1 concerning the persons by whom process is to be served will be superseded by FRCP 4(c).

Subdivision (4).

This rule is intended to preserve the provisions of Admiralty Rules 10 and 36 relating to execution of process, custody of property seized by the marshal, and the marshal's return. It is also designed to make express provision for matters not heretofore covered.

The provision relating to clearance in subdivision (b) is suggested by Admiralty Rule 44 of the District of Maryland.

Subdivision (d) is suggested by English Rule 12, Order 75.

28 U.S.C., § 1921 as amended in 1962 contains detailed provisions relating to the expenses of seizing and preserving property attached or arrested.

Subdivision (5).

In addition to Admiralty Rule 11 (see Rule E(9)), the release of property seized on process of attachment or in rem was dealt with by Admiralty Rules 5, 6, 12, and 57, and 28 U.S.C., § 2464 (formerly Rev.Stat. § 941). The rule consolidates these provisions and makes them uniformly applicable to attachment and garnishment and actions in rem.

The rule restates the substance of Admiralty Rule 5. Admiralty Rule 12 dealt only with ships arrested on in rem process. Since the same ground appears to be covered more generally by 28 U.S.C., § 2464, the subject matter of Rule 12 is omitted. The substance of Admiralty Rule 57 is retained. 28 U.S.C., § 2464 is incorporated with changes of terminology, and with a substantial change as to the amount of the bond. See 2 Benedict 395 n. 1a [Reference is to the 6th Edition of Benedict on Admiralty and not to the current 7th Edition.] *The Lotosland*, 2 F.Supp. 42 (S.D.N.Y.1933). The provision for general bond is enlarged to include the contingency of attachment as well as arrest of the vessel.

Subdivision (6).

Adapted from Admiralty Rule 8.

Subdivision (7).

Derived from Admiralty Rule 50.

Title 46, U.S.C. § 783 extends the principle of Rule 50 to the Government when sued under the Public Vessels Act, presumably on the theory that the credit of the Government is the equivalent of the best security. The rule adopts this principle and extends it to all cases in which the Government is defendant although the Suits in Admiralty Act contains no parallel provisions.

Subdivision (8).

Under the liberal joinder provisions of unified rules the plaintiff will be enabled to join with maritime actions in rem, or maritime actions in personam with process of attachment and garnishment, claims with respect to which such process is not available, including nonmaritime claims. Unification should not, however, have the result that, in order to defend against an admiralty and maritime claim with respect to which process in rem or quasi in rem has been served, the claimant or defendant must subject himself personally to the jurisdiction of the court with reference to other claims with respect to which such process is not available or has not been served, especially when such other claims are nonmaritime. So far as attachment and garnishment are concerned this principle holds true whether process is issued according to admiralty tradition and the Supplemental Rules or according to Rule 4(e) as incorporated by Rule B(1).

A similar problem may arise with respect to civil actions other than admiralty and maritime claims within the meaning of Rule 9(h). That is to say, in an ordinary civil action, whether maritime or not, there may be joined in one action claims with respect to which process of attachment and garnishment is available under state law and Rule 4(e) and claims with respect to which such process is not available or has not been served. The general Rules of Civil Procedure do not specify whether an appearance in such cases to defend the claim with respect to which process of attachment and garnishment has issued is an appearance for the purposes of the other claims. In that context the question has been considered best left to case-by-case development. Where admiralty and maritime claims within the meaning of Rule 9(h) are concerned, however, it seems important to include a specific provision to avoid an unfortunate and unintended effect of unification. No inferences whatever as to the effect of such an appearance in an ordinary civil action should be drawn from the specific provision here and the absence of such a provision in the general Rules.

Subdivision (9).

Adapted from Admiralty Rules 11, 12, and 40. Subdivision (a) is necessary because of various provisions as to disposition of property in forfeiture proceedings. In addition to particular statutes, note the provisions of 28 U.S.C., §§ 2461 to 65.

The provision of Admiralty Rule 12 relating to unreasonable delay was limited to ships but should have broader application. See 2 Benedict 404 [Reference is to the 6th Edition of Benedict on Admiralty and not to the current 7th Edition]. Similarly, both Rules 11 and 12 were limited to actions, in rem, but should equally apply to attached property.

1985 AMENDMENT

Rule E(4)(f) makes available the type of prompt post-seizure hearing in proceedings under Supplemental Rules B and C that the Supreme Court has called for in a number of cases arising in other contexts. See *North Georgia Finishing, Inc. v. Di-Chem, Inc.*, 419 U.S. 601, 95 S. Ct. 719, 42 L. Ed. 2d 751 (1975); *Mitchell v. W.T. Grant Co.*, 416 U.S. 600, 94 S. Ct. 1895, 40 L. Ed. 2d 406 (1974). Although post-attachment and post-arrest hearings always have been available on motion, an explicit statement emphasizing promptness and elaborating the procedure has been lacking in the Supplemental Rules. Rule E(4)(f) is designed to satisfy the constitutional requirement of due process by guaranteeing to the shipowner a prompt post-seizure hearing at which he can attack the complaint, the arrest, the security demanded, or any other alleged deficiency in the proceedings. The amendment also is intended to eliminate the previously disparate treatment under local rules of defendants whose property has been seized pursuant to Supplemental Rules B and C.

The new Rule E(4)(f) is based on a proposal by the Maritime Law Association of the United States and on local admiralty rules in the Eastern, Northern, and Southern Districts of New York. E.D.N.Y. Local Rule 13; N.D.N.Y. Local Rule 13; S.D.N.Y. Local Rule 12. Similar provisions have been adopted by other maritime districts. E.g., N.D.Calif. Local Rule 603.4; W.D.La. Local Admiralty Rule 21. Rule E(4)(f) will provide uniformity in practice and reduce constitutional uncertainties.

Rule E(4)(f) is triggered by the defendant or any other person with an interest in the property seized. Upon an oral or written application similar to that used in seeking a temporary restraining order, see Rule 65(b), the court is required to hold a hearing as promptly as possible to determine whether to allow the arrest or attachment to stand. The plaintiff has the burden of showing why the seizure should not be vacated. The hearing also may determine the amount of security to be granted or the propriety of imposing counter-security to protect the defendant from an improper seizure.

The foregoing requirements for prior court review or proof of exigent circumstances do not apply to actions by the United States for forfeitures for federal statutory violations. In such actions a prompt hearing is not constitutionally required, *United States v. Eight Thousand Eight Hundred and Fifty Dollars*, 461 U.S. 555, 103 S. Ct. 2005, 76 L. Ed. 2d 143 (1983); *Calero-Toledo v. Pearson Yacht Leasing Co.*, 416 U.S. 663, 94 S. Ct. 2080, 40 L. Ed. 2d 452 (1974), and could prejudice the government in its prosecution of the claimants as defendants in parallel criminal proceedings since the forfeiture hearing could be misused by the defendants to obtain by way of civil discovery information to which they would not otherwise be entitled and subject the government and the courts to the unnecessary burden and expense of two hearings rather than one.

1987 AMENDMENT

The amendments are technical. No substantive change is intended.

1991 AMENDMENT

These amendments are designed to conform this rule to Fed.R.Civ.P. 4, as amended. They are intended to relieve the Marshals Service of the burden of using its limited personnel and facilities for execution of process in routine circumstances. Doing so may involve a contractual arrangement with a person or organization retained by the government to perform these services, or the use of other government officers and employees, or the special appointment by the court of persons available to perform suitably.

2000 AMENDMENT

Style changes have been made throughout the revised portions of Rule E. Several changes of meaning have been made as well.

Subdivision (3). Subdivision (3) is amended to reflect the distinction drawn in Rule C(2)(c) and (d). Service in an admiralty or maritime proceeding still must be made within the district, as reflected in Rule C(2)(c), while service in forfeiture proceedings may be made outside the district when authorized by statute, as reflected in Rule C(2)(d).

Subdivision (7). Subdivision (7)(a) is amended to make it clear that a plaintiff need give security to meet a counterclaim only when the counterclaim is asserted by a person who has given security to respond in damages in the original action.

Subdivision (8). Subdivision (8) is amended to reflect the change in Rule B(1)(e) that deletes the former provision incorporating state quasi-in-rem jurisdiction. A restricted appearance is not appropriate when state law is invoked only for security under Civil Rule 64, not as a basis of quasi-in-rem jurisdiction. But if state law allows a special, limited, or restricted appearance as an incident of the remedy adopted from state law, the state practice applies through Rule 64 "in the manner provided by" state law.

Subdivision (9). Subdivision 9(b)(ii) is amended to reflect the change in Rule C(6) that substitutes a statement of interest or right for a claim.

Subdivision (10). Subdivision 10 is new. It makes clear the authority of the court to preserve and to prevent removal of attached or arrested property that remains in the possession of the owner or other person under Rule E(4)(b).

2006 AMENDMENT

Rule E is amended to reflect the adoption of Rule G to govern procedure in civil forfeiture actions.

Rule F. Limitation of Liability

1966 ADOPTION

Subdivision (1).

The amendments of 1936 to the Limitation Act superseded to some extent the provisions of Admiralty Rule 51, especially with respect to the time of filing the complaint and with respect to security. The rule here incorporates in substance the 1936 amendment of the Act (46 U.S.C., § 185) with a slight modification to make it clear that the complaint may be filed at any time not later than six months after a claim has been lodged with the owner.

Subdivision (2).

Derived from Admiralty Rules 51 and 53.

Subdivision (3).

This is derived from the last sentence of 46 U.S.C. § 185 and the last paragraph of Admiralty Rule 51.

Subdivision (4).

Derived from Admiralty Rule 51.

Subdivision (5).

Derived from Admiralty Rules 52 and 53.

Subdivision (6).

Derived from Admiralty Rule 52.

Subdivision (7).

Derived from Admiralty Rule 52 and 46 U.S.C., § 185.

Subdivision (8).

Derived from Admiralty Rule 52.

Subdivision (9).

Derived from Admiralty Rule 54. The provision for transfer is revised to conform closely to the language of 28 U.S.C. §§ 1404(a) and 1406(a), though it retains the existing rule's provision for transfer to any district for convenience. The revision also makes clear what has been doubted: that the court may transfer if venue is wrongly laid.

1987 AMENDMENT

The amendments are technical. No substantive change is intended.

Rule G. Forfeiture Actions In Rem

2006 ADOPTION

Rule G is added to bring together the central procedures that govern civil forfeiture actions. Civil forfeiture actions are in rem proceedings, as are many admiralty proceedings. As the number of civil forfeiture actions has increased, however, reasons have appeared to create sharper distinctions within the framework of the Supplemental Rules. Civil forfeiture practice will benefit from distinctive provisions that express and focus developments in statutory, constitutional, and decisional law. Admiralty practice will be freed from the pressures that arise when the needs of civil forfeiture proceedings counsel interpretations of common rules that may not be suitable for admiralty proceedings.

Rule G generally applies to actions governed by the Civil Asset Forfeiture Reform Act of 2000 (CAFRA) and also to actions excluded from it. The rule refers to some specific CAFRA provisions; if these statutes are amended, the rule should be adapted to the new provisions during the period required to amend the rule. Rule G is not completely self-contained. Subdivision (1) recognizes the need to rely at times on other Supplemental Rules and the place of the Supplemental Rules within the basic framework of the Civil Rules.

Supplemental Rules A, C, and E are amended to reflect the adoption of Rule G.

Subdivision (1). Rule G is designed to include the distinctive procedures that govern a civil forfeiture action. Some details, however, are better supplied by relying on Rules C and E. Subdivision (1) incorporates those rules for issues not addressed by Rule G. This general incorporation is at times made explicit—subdivision (7)(b)(v), for example, invokes the security provisions of Rule E. But Rules C and E are not to be invoked to create conflicts with Rule G. They are to be used only when Rule G, fairly construed, does not address the issue.

The Civil Rules continue to provide the procedural framework within which Rule G and the other Supplemental Rules operate. Both Rule G(1) and Rule A state this basic proposition. Rule G, for example, does not address pleadings amendments. Civil Rule 15 applies, in light of the circumstances of a forfeiture action.

Subdivision (2). Rule E(2)(a) requires that the complaint in an admiralty action "state the circumstances from which the claim arises with such particularity that the defendant or claimant will be able, without moving for a more definite statement, to commence an investigation of the facts and to frame a responsive pleading." Application of this standard to civil forfeiture actions has evolved to the standard stated in subdivision (2)(f). The complaint must state sufficiently detailed facts to support a reasonable belief that the government will be able to meet its burden of proof at trial. *See U.S. v. Mondragon*, 313 F.3d 862 (4th Cir. 2002). Subdivision (2)(f) carries this forfeiture case law forward without change.

Subdivision (3). Subdivision (3) governs in rem process in a civil forfeiture action.

Paragraph (a). Paragraph (a) reflects the provisions of 18 U.S.C. § 985.

Paragraph (b). Paragraph (b) addresses arrest warrants when the defendant is not real property. Subparagraph (i) directs the clerk to issue a warrant if the property is in the government's possession, custody, or control. If the property is not in the government's possession, custody, or control and is not subject to a restraining order, subparagraph (ii) provides that a warrant issues only if the court finds probable cause to arrest the property. This provision departs from former Rule C(3)(a)(i), which authorized issuance of summons and warrant by the clerk without a probable-cause finding. The probable-cause finding better protects the interests of persons interested in the property. Subparagraph (iii) recognizes that a warrant is not necessary if the property is subject to a judicial restraining order. The government remains free, however, to seek a warrant if it anticipates that the restraining order may be modified or vacated.

Paragraph (c). Subparagraph (ii) requires that the warrant and any supplemental process be served as soon as practicable unless the property is already in the government's possession, custody, or control. But it authorizes the court to order a different time. The authority to order a different time recognizes that the government may have secured orders sealing the complaint in a civil forfeiture action or have won a stay after filing. The seal or stay may be ordered for reasons, such as protection of an ongoing criminal investigation, that would be defeated by prompt service of the warrant. Subparagraph (ii) does not reflect any independent ground for ordering a seal or stay, but merely reflects the consequences for execution when sealing or a stay is ordered. A court also may order a different time for service if good cause is shown for reasons unrelated to a seal or stay. Subparagraph (iv) reflects the uncertainty surrounding service of an arrest warrant on property not in the United States. It is not possible to identify in the rule the appropriate authority for serving process in all other countries. Transmission of the warrant to an appropriate authority, moreover, does not ensure that the warrant will be executed. The rule requires only that the warrant be transmitted to an appropriate authority.

Subdivision (4). Paragraph (a). Paragraph (a) reflects the traditional practice of publishing notice of an in rem action.

Subparagraph (i) recognizes two exceptions to the general publication requirement. Publication is not required if the defendant property is worth less than $1,000 and direct notice is sent to all reasonably identifiable potential claimants as required by subdivision (4)(b). Publication also is not required if the cost would exceed the property's value and the court finds that other means of notice would satisfy due process. Publication on a government-established internet forfeiture site, as contemplated by subparagraph (iv), would be at a low marginal publication cost, which would likely be the cost to compare to the property value.

Subparagraph (iv) states the basic criterion for selecting the means and method of publication. The purpose is to adopt a means reasonably calculated to reach potential claimants. The government should choose from among these means a method that is reasonably likely to reach potential claimants at a cost reasonable in the circumstances.

If the property is in the United States and newspaper notice is chosen, publication may be where the action is filed, where the property was seized, or—if the property was not seized—where the property is located. Choice among these places is influenced by the probable location of potential claimants.

If the property is not in the United States, account must be taken of the sensitivities that surround publication of legal notices in other countries. A foreign country may forbid local publication. If potential claimants are likely to be in the United States, publication in the district where the action is filed may be the best choice. If potential claimants are likely to be located abroad, the better choice may be publication by means generally circulated in the country where the property is located.

Newspaper publication is not a particularly effective means of notice for most potential claimants. Its traditional use is best defended by want of affordable alternatives. Paragraph (iv)(C) contemplates a government-created internet forfeiture site that would provide a single easily identified means of notice. Such a site could allow much more direct access to notice as to any specific property than publication provides.

Paragraph (b). Paragraph (b) is entirely new. For the first time, Rule G expressly recognizes the due process obligation to send notice to any person who reasonably appears to be a potential claimant.

Subparagraph (i) states the obligation to send notice. Many potential claimants will be known to the government because they have filed claims during the administrative forfeiture stage. Notice must be sent, however, no matter what source of information makes it reasonably appear that a person is a potential claimant. The duty to send notice terminates when the time for filing a claim expires.

Notice of the action does not require formal service of summons in the manner required by Rule 4 to initiate a personal action. The process that begins an in rem forfeiture action is addressed by subdivision (3). This process commonly gives notice to potential claimants. Publication of notice is required in addition to this process. Due process requirements have moved beyond these traditional means of notice, but are satisfied by practical means that are reasonably calculated to accomplish actual notice.

Subparagraph (ii)(B) directs that the notice state a deadline for filing a claim that is at least 35 days after the notice is sent. This provision applies both in actions that fall within 18 U.S.C. § 983(a)(4)(A) and in other actions. Section 983(a)(4)(A) states that a claim should be filed no later than 30 days after service of the complaint. The variation introduced by subparagraph (ii)(B) reflects the procedure of § 983(a)(2)(B) for nonjudicial forfeiture proceedings. The nonjudicial procedure requires that a claim be filed "not later than the deadline set forth in a personal notice letter (which may be not earlier than 35 days after the date the letter is sent) * * *." This procedure is as suitable in a civil forfeiture action as in a nonjudicial forfeiture proceeding. Thirty-five days after notice is sent ordinarily will extend the claim time by no more than a brief period; a claimant anxious to expedite proceedings can file the claim before the deadline; and the government has flexibility to set a still longer period when circumstances make that desirable.

Subparagraph (iii) begins by stating the basic requirement that notice must be sent by means reasonably calculated to reach the potential claimant. No attempt is made to list the various means that may be reasonable in different circumstances. It may be reasonable, for example, to rely on means that have already been established for communication with a particular potential claimant. The government's interest in choosing a means likely to accomplish actual notice is bolstered by its desire to avoid post-forfeiture challenges based on arguments that a different method would have been more likely to accomplish actual notice. Flexible rule language accommodates the rapid evolution of communications technology.

Notice may be directed to a potential claimant through counsel, but only to counsel already representing the claimant with respect to the seizure of the property, or in a related investigation, administrative forfeiture proceeding, or criminal case.

Subparagraph (iii)(C) reflects the basic proposition that notice to a potential claimant who is incarcerated must be sent to the place of incarceration. Notice directed to some other place, such as a pre-incarceration residence, is less likely to reach the potential claimant. This provision does not address due process questions that may arise if a particular prison has deficient procedures for delivering notice to prisoners. *See Dusenbery v. U.S.*, 534 U.S. 161 (2002).

Items (D) and (E) of subparagraph (iii) authorize the government to rely on an address given by a person who is not incarcerated. The address may have been given to the agency that arrested or released the person, or to the agency that seized the property. The government is not obliged to undertake an independent investigation to verify the address.

Subparagraph (iv) identifies the date on which notice is considered to be sent for some common means, without addressing the circumstances for choosing among the identified means or other means. The date of sending should be determined by analogy for means not listed. Facsimile transmission, for example, is sent upon transmission. Notice by personal delivery is sent on delivery.

Subparagraph (v), finally, reflects the purpose to effect actual notice by providing that a potential claimant who had actual notice of a forfeiture proceeding cannot oppose or seek relief from forfeiture because the government failed to comply with subdivision (4)(b).

Subdivision (5). Paragraph (a). Paragraph (a) establishes that the first step of contesting a civil forfeiture action is to file a claim. A claim is required by 18 U.S.C. § 983(a)(4)(A) for actions covered by § 983. Paragraph (a) applies this procedure as well to actions not covered by § 983. "Claim" is used to describe this first pleading because of the statutory references to claim and claimant. It functions in the same way as the statement of interest prescribed for an admiralty proceeding by Rule C(6), and is not related to the distinctive meaning of "claim" in admiralty practice.

If the claimant states its interest in the property to be as bailee, the bailor must be identified. A bailee who files a claim on behalf of a bailor must state the bailee's authority to do so.

The claim must be signed under penalty of perjury by the person making it. An artificial body that can act only through an agent may authorize an agent to sign for it. Excusable inability of counsel to obtain an appropriate signature may be grounds for an extension of time to file the claim.

Paragraph (a)(ii) sets the time for filing a claim. Item (C) applies in the relatively rare circumstance in which notice is not published and the government did not send direct notice to the claimant because it did not know of the claimant or did not have an address for the claimant.

Paragraph (b). Under 18 U.S.C. § 983(a)(4)(B), which governs many forfeiture proceedings, a person who asserts an interest by filing a claim "shall file an answer to the Government's complaint for forfeiture not later than 20 days after the date of the filing of the claim." Paragraph (b) recognizes that this statute works within the general procedures established by Civil Rule 12. Rule 12(a)(4) suspends the time to answer when a Rule 12 motion is served within the time allowed to answer. Continued application of this rule to proceedings governed by § 983(a)(4)(B) serves all of the purposes advanced by Rule 12(a)(4), *see U. S. v. $8,221,877.16*, 330 F.3d 141 (3d Cir.2003); permits a uniform procedure for all civil forfeiture actions; and recognizes that a motion under Rule 12 can be made only after a claim is filed that provides background for the motion.

Failure to present an objection to in rem jurisdiction or to venue by timely motion or answer waives the objection. Waiver of such objections is familiar. An answer may be amended to assert an objection initially omitted. But Civil Rule 15 should be applied to an amendment that for the first time raises an objection to in rem jurisdiction by analogy to the personal jurisdiction objection provision in Civil Rule 12(h)(1)(B). The amendment should be permitted only if it is permitted as a matter of course under Rule 15(a).

A claimant's motion to dismiss the action is further governed by subdivisions (6)(c), (8)(b), and (8)(c).

Subdivision (6). Subdivision (6) illustrates the adaptation of an admiralty procedure to the different needs of civil forfeiture. Rule C(6) permits interrogatories to be served with the complaint in an in rem action without limiting the subjects of inquiry. Civil forfeiture practice does not require such an extensive departure from ordinary civil practice. It remains useful, however, to permit the government to file limited interrogatories at any time after a claim is filed to gather information that bears on the claimant's standing. Subdivisions (8)(b) and (c) allow a claimant to move to dismiss only if the claimant has standing, and recognize the government's right to move to dismiss a claim for lack of standing. Subdivision (6) interrogatories are integrated with these provisions in that the interrogatories are limited to the claimant's identity and relationship to the defendant property. If the claimant asserts a relationship to the property as bailee, the interrogatories can inquire into the bailor's interest in the property and the bailee's relationship to the bailor. The claimant can accelerate the time to serve subdivision (6) interrogatories by serving a motion to dismiss—the interrogatories must be served within 20 days after the motion is served. Integration is further accomplished by deferring the government's obligation to respond to a motion to dismiss until 20 days after the claimant moving to dismiss has answered the interrogatories.

Special interrogatories served under Rule G(6) do not count against the presumptive 25-interrogatory limit established by Rule 33(a). Rule 33 procedure otherwise applies to these interrogatories.

Subdivision (6) supersedes the discovery "moratorium" of Rule 26(d) and the broader interrogatories permitted for admiralty proceedings by Rule C(6).

Subdivision (7). Paragraph (a). Paragraph (a) is adapted from Rule E(9)(b). It provides for preservation orders when the government does not have actual possession of the defendant property. It also goes beyond Rule E(9) by recognizing the need to prevent use of the defendant property in ongoing criminal offenses.

Paragraph (b). Paragraph (b)(i)(C) recognizes the authority, already exercised in some cases, to order sale of property subject to a defaulted mortgage or to defaulted taxes. The authority is narrowly confined to mortgages and tax liens; other lien interests may be addressed, if at all, only through the general good-cause provision. The court must carefully weigh the competing interests in each case.

Paragraph (b)(i)(D) establishes authority to order sale for good cause. Good cause may be shown when the property is subject to diminution in value. Care should be taken before ordering sale to avoid diminished value.

Paragraph (b)(iii) recognizes that if the court approves, the interests of all parties may be served by their agreement to sale, aspects of the sale, or sale procedures that depart from governing statutory procedures.

Paragraph (c) draws from Rule E(9)(a), (b), and (c). Disposition of the proceeds as provided by law may require resolution of disputed issues. A mortgagee's claim to the property or sale proceeds, for example, may be disputed on the ground that the mortgage is not genuine. An undisputed lien claim, on the other hand, may be recognized by payment after an interlocutory sale.

Subdivision (8). Subdivision (8) addresses a number of issues that are unique to civil forfeiture actions.

Paragraph (a). Standing to suppress use of seized property as evidence is governed by principles distinct from the principles that govern claim standing. A claimant with standing to contest forfeiture may not have standing to seek suppression. Rule G does not of itself create a basis of suppression standing that does not otherwise exist.

Paragraph (b). Paragraph (b)(i) is one element of the system that integrates the procedures for determining a claimant's standing to claim and for deciding a claimant's motion to dismiss the action. Under paragraph (c)(ii), a motion to dismiss the action cannot be addressed until the court has decided any government motion to strike the claim or answer. This procedure is reflected in the (b)(i) reminder that a motion to dismiss the forfeiture action may be made only by a claimant who establishes claim standing. The government, moreover, need not respond to a claimant's motion to dismiss until 20 days after the claimant has answered any subdivision (6) interrogatories.

Paragraph (b)(ii) mirrors 18 U.S.C. § 983(a)(3)(D). It applies only to an action independently governed by § 983(a)(3)(D), implying nothing as to actions outside § 983(a)(3)(D). The adequacy of the complaint is measured against the pleading requirements of subdivision (2), not against the quality of the evidence available to the government when the complaint was filed.

Paragraph (c). As noted with paragraph (b), paragraph (c) governs the procedure for determining whether a claimant has standing. It does not address the principles that govern claim standing.

Paragraph (c)(i)(A) provides that the government may move to strike a claim or answer for failure to comply with the pleading requirements of subdivision (5) or to answer subdivision (6) interrogatories. As with other pleadings, the court should strike a claim or answer only if satisfied that an opportunity should not be afforded to cure the defects under Rule 15. Not every failure to respond to subdivision (6) interrogatories warrants an order striking the claim. But the special role that subdivision (6) plays in the scheme for determining claim standing may justify a somewhat more demanding approach than the general approach to discovery sanctions under Rule 37.

Paragraph (c)(ii) directs that a motion to strike a claim or answer be decided before any motion by the claimant to dismiss the action. A claimant who lacks standing is not entitled to challenge the forfeiture on the merits.

Paragraph (c)(ii) further identifies three procedures for addressing claim standing. If a claim fails on its face to show facts that support claim standing, the claim can be dismissed by judgment on the pleadings. If the claim shows facts that would support claim standing, those facts can be tested by a motion for summary judgment. If material facts are disputed, precluding a grant of summary judgment, the court may hold an evidentiary hearing. The evidentiary hearing is held by the court without a jury. The claimant has the burden to establish claim standing at a hearing; procedure on a government summary judgment motion reflects this allocation of the burden.

Paragraph (d). The hardship release provisions of 18 U.S.C. § 983(f) do not apply to a civil forfeiture action exempted from § 983 by § 983(i).

Paragraph (d)(ii) reflects the venue provisions of 18 U.S.C. § 983(f)(3)(A) as a guide to practitioners. In addition, it makes clear the status of a civil forfeiture action as a "civil action" eligible for transfer under 28 U.S.C. § 1404. A transfer decision must be made on the circumstances of the particular proceeding. The district where the forfeiture action is filed has the advantage of bringing all related proceedings together, avoiding the waste that flows from consideration of different parts of the same forfeiture proceeding in the court where the warrant issued or the court where the property was seized. Transfer to that court would serve consolidation, the purpose that underlies nationwide enforcement of a seizure warrant. But there may be offsetting advantages in retaining the petition where it was filed. The claimant may not be able to litigate, effectively or at all, in a distant court. Issues relevant to the petition may be better litigated where the property was seized or where the warrant issued. One element, for example, is whether the claimant has sufficient ties to the community to provide assurance that the property will be available at the time of trial. Another is whether continued government possession would prevent the claimant from working. Determining whether seizure of the claimant's automobile prevents work may turn on assessing the realities of local public transit facilities.

Paragraph (e). The Excessive Fines Clause of the Eighth Amendment forbids an excessive forfeiture. *U.S. v. Bajakajian*, 524 U.S. 321 (1998). 18 U.S.C. § 983(g) provides a "petition" "to determine whether the forfeiture was constitutionally excessive" based on finding "that the forfeiture is grossly disproportional to the offense." Paragraph (e) describes the procedure for § 983(g) mitigation petitions and adopts the same procedure for forfeiture actions that fall outside § 983(g). The procedure is by motion, either for summary judgment or for mitigation after a forfeiture judgment is entered. The claimant must give notice of this defense by pleading, but failure to raise the defense in the initial answer may be cured by amendment under Rule 15. The issues that bear on mitigation often are separate from the issues that determine forfeiture. For that reason it may be convenient to resolve the issue by summary judgment before trial on the forfeiture issues. Often, however, it will be more convenient to determine first whether the property is to be forfeited. Whichever time is chosen to address mitigation, the parties must have had the opportunity to conduct civil discovery on the defense. The extent and timing of discovery are governed by the ordinary rules.

Subdivision (9). Subdivision (9) serves as a reminder of the need to demand jury trial under Rule 38. It does not expand the right to jury trial. *See U.S. v. One Parcel of Property Located at 32 Medley Lane*, 2005 WL 465241 (D.Conn. 2005), ruling that the court, not the jury, determines whether a forfeiture is constitutionally excessive.

2009 AMENDMENTS

The times set in the former rule at 20 days have been revised to 21 days. See the Note to Rule 6.

PART IX
FEDERAL RULES OF EVIDENCE FOR UNITED STATES COURTS

Effective July 1, 1975

Reflecting Latest Amendments Effective December 1, 2020

The Federal Rules of Evidence Style Project

In 2011 the Evidence Rules became the fourth set of national procedural rules to be restyled. The restyled Rules of Appellate Procedure took effect in 1998. The restyled Rules of Criminal Procedure took effect in 2002. The restyled Rules of Civil Procedure took effect in 2007. The restyled Rules of Evidence apply the same general drafting guidelines and principles used in restyling the Appellate, Criminal, and Civil Rules.

1. General Guidelines

Guidance in drafting, usage, and style was provided by Bryan Garner, *Guidelines for Drafting and Editing Court Rules,* Administrative Office of the United States Courts (1969) and Bryan Garner, *A Dictionary of Modern Legal Usage* (2d ed. 1995). *See also* Joseph Kimble, *Guiding Principles for Restyling the Civil Rules*, in *Preliminary Draft of Proposed Style Revision of the Federal Rules of Civil Procedure,* at page x (Feb. 2005) (available at http://www.uscourts.gov/rules/Prelim_draft_proposed_pt1.pdf); Joseph Kimble, *Lessons in Drafting from the New Federal Rules of Civil Procedure*, 12 Scribes J. Legal Writing __ (2008–2009).

2. Formatting Changes

Many of the changes in the restyled Evidence Rules result from using format to achieve clearer presentations. The rules are broken down into constituent parts, using progressively indented subparagraphs with headings and substituting vertical for horizontal lists. "Hanging indents" are used throughout. These formatting changes make the structure of the rules graphic and make the restyled rules easier to read and understand even when the words are not changed. Rules 103, 404(b), 606(b), and 612 illustrate the benefits of formatting changes.

3. Changes to Reduce Inconsistent, Ambiguous, Redundant, Repetitive, or Archaic Words

The restyled rules reduce the use of inconsistent terms that say the same thing in different ways. Because different words are presumed to have different meanings, such inconsistencies can result in confusion. The restyled rules reduce inconsistencies by using the same words to express the same meaning. For example, consistent expression is achieved by not switching between "accused" and "defendant" or between "party opponent" and "opposing party" or between the various formulations of civil and criminal action/case/proceeding.

The restyled rules minimize the use of inherently ambiguous words. For example, the word "shall" can mean "must," "may," or something else, depending on context. The potential for confusion is exacerbated by the fact the word "shall" is no longer generally used in spoken or clearly written English. The restyled rules replace "shall" with "must," "may," or "should," depending on which one the context and established interpretation make correct in each rule.

The restyled rules minimize the use of redundant "intensifiers." These are expressions that attempt to add emphasis, but instead state the obvious and create negative implications for other rules. The absence of intensifiers in the restyled rules does not change their substantive meaning. *See, e.g.,* Rule 104(c) (omitting "in all cases"); Rule 602 (omitting "but need not"); Rule 611(b) (omitting "in the exercise of discretion").

The restyled rules also remove words and concepts that are outdated or redundant.

4. *Rule Numbers*

The restyled rules keep the same numbers to minimize the effect on research. Subdivisions have been rearranged within some rules to achieve greater clarity and simplicity.

5. *No Substantive Change*

The Committee made special efforts to reject any purported style improvement that might result in a substantive change in the application of a rule. The Committee considered a change to be "substantive" if any of the following conditions were met:

a. Under the existing practice in any circuit, the change could lead to a different result on a question of admissibility (e.g., a change that requires a court to provide either a less or more stringent standard in evaluating the admissibility of particular evidence);

b. Under the existing practice in any circuit, it could lead to a change in the procedure by which an admissibility decision is made (e.g., a change in the time in which an objection must be made, or a change in whether a court must hold a hearing on an admissibility question);

c. It alters the structure of a rule in a way that may alter the approach that courts and litigants have used to think about, and argue about, questions of admissibility (e.g., merging Rules 104(a) and 104(b) into a single subdivision); or

d. It changes a "sacred phrase" — phrases that have become so familiar in practice that to alter them would be unduly disruptive. Examples in the Evidence Rules include "unfair prejudice" and "truth of the matter asserted."

Table of Rules

ARTICLE I. GENERAL PROVISIONS

Rule

101 Scope; Definitions

102 Purpose

103 Rulings on Evidence

104 Preliminary Questions

105 Limiting Evidence That Is Not Admissible Against Other Parties or for Other Purposes

106 Remainder of or Related Writings or Recorded Statements

ARTICLE II. JUDICIAL NOTICE

201 Judicial Notice of Adjudicative Facts

ARTICLE III. PRESUMPTIONS IN CIVIL CASES

301 Presumptions in Civil Cases Generally

302 Applying State Law to Presumptions in Civil Cases

ARTICLE IV. RELEVANCE AND ITS LIMITS
401 Test for Relevant Evidence
402 General Admissibility of Relevant Evidence
403 Excluding Relevant Evidence for Prejudice, Confusion, Waste of Time, or Other Reasons
404 Character Evidence; Other Crimes, Wrongs or Acts
405 Methods of Proving Character
406 Habit; Routine Practice
407 Subsequent Remedial Measures
408 Compromise Offers and Negotiations
409 Offers to Pay Medical and Similar Expenses
410 Pleas, Plea Discussions, and Related Statements
411 Liability Insurance
412 Sex-Offense Cases: The Victim's Sexual Behavior or Predisposition
413 Similar Crimes in Sexual-Assault Cases
414 Similar Crimes in Child-Molestation Cases
415 Similar Acts in Civil Cases Involving Sexual Assault or Child Molestation
ARTICLE V. PRIVILEGES
501 Privilege in General
502 Attorney-Client Privilege and Work Product; Limitations on Waiver
ARTICLE VI. WITNESSES
601 Competency to Testify in General
602 Need for Personal Knowledge
603 Oath or Affirmation to Testify Truthfully
604 Interpreter
605 Judge's Competency as a Witness
606 Juror's Competency as a Witness
607 Who May Impeach a Witness
608 A Witness's Character for Truthfulness or Untruthfulness
609 Impeachment by Evidence of a Criminal Conviction
610 Religious Beliefs or Opinions
611 Mode and Order of Examining Witnesses and Presenting Evidence
612 Writing Used to Refresh a Witness's Memory
613 Witness's Prior Statement
614 Court's Calling or Examining a Witness
615 Excluding Witnesses
ARTICLE VII. OPINIONS AND EXPERT TESTIMONY
701 Opinion Testimony by Lay Witnesses
702 Testimony by Expert Witnesses
703 Bases of an Expert's Opinion Testimony
704 Opinion on an Ultimate Issue
705 Disclosing the Facts or Data Underlying an Expert's Opinion
706 Court-Appointed Expert Witnesses
ARTICLE VIII. HEARSAY
801 Definitions That Apply to This Article; Exclusions from Hearsay
802 The Rule Against Hearsay
803 Exceptions to the Rule Against Hearsay — Regardless of Whether the Declarant Is Available as a Witness

804 Exceptions to the Rule Against Hearsay — When the Declarant Is Unavailable as a Witness
805 Hearsay Within Hearsay
806 Attacking and Supporting the Declarant's Credibility
807 Residual Exception
ARTICLE IX. AUTHENTICATION AND IDENTIFICATION
901 Authenticating or Identifying Evidence
902 Evidence That Is Self-Authenticating
903 Subscribing Witness's Testimony
ARTICLE X. CONTENTS OF WRITINGS, RECORDINGS, AND PHOTOGRAPHS
1001 Definitions That Apply to This Article
1002 Requirement of the Original
1003 Admissibility of Duplicates
1004 Admissibility of Other Evidence of Content
1005 Copies of Public Records to Prove Content
1006 Summaries to Prove Content
1007 Testimony or Statement of a Party to Prove Content
1008 Functions of the Court and Jury
ARTICLE XI. MISCELLANEOUS RULES
1101 Applicability of the Rules
1102 Amendments
1103 Title

ARTICLE I. GENERAL PROVISIONS

RULE 101. SCOPE; DEFINITIONS

(a) **Scope.** These rules apply to proceedings in United States courts. The specific courts and proceedings to which the rules apply, along with exceptions, are set out in Rule 1101.

(b) **Definitions.** In these rules:

(1) "civil case" means a civil action or proceeding;

(2) "criminal case" includes a criminal proceeding;

(3) "public office" includes a public agency;

(4) "record" includes a memorandum, report, or data compilation;

(5) a "rule prescribed by the Supreme Court" means a rule adopted by the Supreme Court under statutory authority; and

(6) a reference to any kind of written material or any other medium includes electronically stored information.

RULE 102. PURPOSE

These rules should be construed so as to administer every proceeding fairly, eliminate unjustifiable expense and delay, and promote the development of evidence law, to the end of ascertaining the truth and securing a just determination.

RULE 103. RULINGS ON EVIDENCE

(a) **Preserving a Claim of Error.** A party may claim error in a ruling to admit or exclude evidence only if the error affects a substantial right of the party and:

(1) if the ruling admits evidence, a party, on the record:

(A) timely objects or moves to strike; and

(B) states the specific ground, unless it was apparent from the context; or

(2) if the ruling excludes evidence, a party informs the court of its substance by an offer of proof, unless the substance was apparent from the context.

(b) **Not Needing to Renew an Objection or Offer of Proof.** Once the court rules definitively on the record — either before or at trial — a party need not renew an objection or offer of proof to preserve a claim of error for appeal.

(c) **Court's Statement About the Ruling; Directing an Offer of Proof.** The court may make any statement about the character or form of the evidence, the objection made, and the ruling. The court may direct that an offer of proof be made in question-and-answer form.

(d) **Preventing the Jury from Hearing Inadmissible Evidence.** To the extent practicable, the court must conduct a jury trial so that inadmissible evidence is not suggested to the jury by any means.

(e) **Taking Notice of Plain Error.** A court may take notice of a plain error affecting a substantial right, even if the claim of error was not properly preserved.

RULE 104. PRELIMINARY QUESTIONS

(a) **In General.** The court must decide any preliminary question about whether a witness is qualified, a privilege exists, or evidence is admissible. In so deciding, the court is not bound by evidence rules, except those on privilege.

(b) **Relevance That Depends on a Fact.** When the relevance of evidence depends on whether a fact exists, proof must be introduced sufficient to support a finding that the fact does exist. The court may admit the proposed evidence on the condition that the proof be introduced later.

(c) **Conducting a Hearing So That the Jury Cannot Hear It.** The court must conduct any hearing on a preliminary question so that the jury cannot hear it if:

(1) the hearing involves the admissibility of a confession;

(2) a defendant in a criminal case is a witness and so requests; or

(3) justice so requires.

(d) **Cross-Examining a Defendant in a Criminal Case.** By testifying on a preliminary question, a defendant in a criminal case does not become subject to cross-examination on other issues in the case.

(e) Evidence Relevant to Weight and Credibility. This rule does not limit a party's right to introduce before the jury evidence that is relevant to the weight or credibility of other evidence.

RULE 105. LIMITING EVIDENCE THAT IS NOT ADMISSIBLE AGAINST OTHER PARTIES OR FOR OTHER PURPOSES

If the court admits evidence that is admissible against a party or for a purpose — but not against another party or for another purpose — the court, on timely request, must restrict the evidence to its proper scope and instruct the jury accordingly.

RULE 106. REMAINDER OF OR RELATED WRITINGS OR RECORDED STATEMENTS

If a party introduces all or part of a writing or recorded statement, an adverse party may require the introduction, at that time, of any other part — or any other writing or recorded statement — that in fairness ought to be considered at the same time.

ARTICLE II. JUDICIAL NOTICE

RULE 201. JUDICIAL NOTICE OF ADJUDICATIVE FACTS

(a) Scope. This rule governs judicial notice of an adjudicative fact only, not a legislative fact.

(b) Kinds of Facts That May Be Judicially Noticed. The court may judicially notice a fact that is not subject to reasonable dispute because it:

- **(1)** is generally known within the trial court's territorial jurisdiction; or
- **(2)** can be accurately and readily determined from sources whose accuracy cannot reasonably be questioned.

(c) Taking Notice. The court:

- **(1)** may take judicial notice on its own; or
- **(2)** must take judicial notice if a party requests it and the court is supplied with the necessary information.

(d) Timing. The court may take judicial notice at any stage of the proceeding.

(e) Opportunity to Be Heard. On timely request, a party is entitled to be heard on the propriety of taking judicial notice and the nature of the fact to be noticed. If the court takes judicial notice before notifying a party, the party, on request, is still entitled to be heard.

(f) Instructing the Jury. In a civil case, the court must instruct the jury to accept the noticed fact as conclusive. In a criminal case, the court must instruct the jury that it may or may not accept the noticed fact as conclusive.

ARTICLE III. PRESUMPTIONS IN CIVIL CASES

RULE 301. PRESUMPTIONS IN CIVIL CASES GENERALLY

In a civil case, unless a federal statute or these rules provide otherwise, the party against whom a presumption is directed has the burden of producing evidence to rebut the presumption. But this rule does not shift the burden of persuasion, which remains on the party who had it originally.

RULE 302. APPLYING STATE LAW TO PRESUMPTIONS IN CIVIL CASES

In a civil case, state law governs the effect of a presumption regarding a claim or defense for which state law supplies the rule of decision.

ARTICLE IV. RELEVANCE AND ITS LIMITS

RULE 401. TEST FOR RELEVANT EVIDENCE

Evidence is relevant if:

(a) it has any tendency to make a fact more or less probable than it would be without the evidence; and

(b) the fact is of consequence in determining the action.

RULE 402. GENERAL ADMISSIBILITY OF RELEVANT EVIDENCE

Relevant evidence is admissible unless any of the following provides otherwise:

- the United States Constitution;
- a federal statute;
- these rules; or
- other rules prescribed by the Supreme Court.

Irrelevant evidence is not admissible.

RULE 403. EXCLUDING RELEVANT EVIDENCE FOR PREJUDICE, CONFUSION, WASTE OF TIME, OR OTHER REASONS

The court may exclude relevant evidence if its probative value is substantially outweighed by a danger of one or more of the following: unfair prejudice, confusing the issues, misleading the jury, undue delay, wasting time, or needlessly presenting cumulative evidence.

RULE 404. CHARACTER EVIDENCE; OTHER CRIMES, WRONGS OR ACTS

(a) Character Evidence.

(1) ***Prohibited Uses.*** Evidence of a person's character or character trait is not admissible to prove that on a particular occasion the person acted in accordance with the character or trait.

(2) ***Exceptions for a Defendant or Victim in a Criminal Case.*** The following exceptions apply in a criminal case:

(A) a defendant may offer evidence of the defendant's pertinent trait, and if the evidence is admitted, the prosecutor may offer evidence to rebut it;

(B) subject to the limitations in Rule 412, a defendant may offer evidence of an alleged victim's pertinent trait, and if the evidence is admitted, the prosecutor may:

(i) offer evidence to rebut it; and

(ii) offer evidence of the defendant's same trait; and

(C) in a homicide case, the prosecutor may offer evidence of the alleged victim's trait of peacefulness to rebut evidence that the victim was the first aggressor.

(3) ***Exceptions for a Witness.*** Evidence of a witness's character may be admitted under Rules 607, 608, and 609.

(b) **Other Crimes, Wrongs, or Acts.**

(1) ***Prohibited Uses.*** Evidence of any other crime, wrong, or act is not admissible to prove a person's character in order to show that on a particular occasion the person acted in accordance with the character.

(2) ***Permitted Uses.*** This evidence may be admissible for another purpose, such as proving motive, opportunity, intent, preparation, plan, knowledge, identity, absence of mistake, or lack of accident.

(3) ***Notice in a Criminal Case.*** In a criminal case, the prosecutor must:

(A) provide reasonable notice of any such evidence that the prosecutor intends to offer at trial, so that the defendant has a fair opportunity to meet it;

(B) articulate in the notice the permitted purpose for which the prosecutor intends to offer the evidence and the reasoning that supports the purpose; and

(C) do so in writing before trial—or in any form during trial if the court, for good cause, excuses lack of pretrial notice.

RULE 405. METHODS OF PROVING CHARACTER

(a) **By Reputation or Opinion.** When evidence of a person's character or character trait is admissible, it may be proved by testimony about the person's reputation or by testimony in the form of an opinion. On cross-examination of the character witness, the court may allow an inquiry into relevant specific instances of the person's conduct.

(b) **By Specific Instances of Conduct.** When a person's character or character trait is an essential element of a charge, claim, or defense, the character or trait may also be proved by relevant specific instances of the person's conduct.

RULE 406. HABIT; ROUTINE PRACTICE

Evidence of a person's habit or an organization's routine practice may be admitted to prove that on a particular occasion the person or organization acted in accordance with the habit or routine practice. The court may admit this evidence regardless of whether it is corroborated or whether there was an eyewitness.

RULE 407. SUBSEQUENT REMEDIAL MEASURES

When measures are taken that would have made an earlier injury or harm less likely to occur, evidence of the subsequent measures is not admissible to prove:

- negligence;
- culpable conduct;
- a defect in a product or its design; or
- a need for a warning or instruction.

But the court may admit this evidence for another purpose, such as impeachment or — if disputed — proving ownership, control, or the feasibility of precautionary measures.

RULE 408. COMPROMISE OFFERS AND NEGOTIATIONS

(a) Prohibited Uses. Evidence of the following is not admissible — on behalf of any party — either to prove or disprove the validity or amount of a disputed claim or to impeach by a prior inconsistent statement or a contradiction:

(1) furnishing, promising, or offering — or accepting, promising to accept, or offering to accept — a valuable consideration in compromising or attempting to compromise the claim; and

(2) conduct or a statement made during compromise negotiations about the claim — except when offered in a criminal case and when the negotiations related to a claim by a public office in the exercise of its regulatory, investigative, or enforcement authority.

(b) Exceptions. The court may admit this evidence for another purpose, such as proving a witness's bias or prejudice, negating a contention of undue delay, or proving an effort to obstruct a criminal investigation or prosecution.

RULE 409. OFFERS TO PAY MEDICAL AND SIMILAR EXPENSES

Evidence of furnishing, promising to pay, or offering to pay medical, hospital, or similar expenses resulting from an injury is not admissible to prove liability for the injury.

RULE 410. PLEAS, PLEA DISCUSSIONS, AND RELATED STATEMENTS

(a) Prohibited Uses. In a civil or criminal case, evidence of the following is not admissible against the defendant who made the plea or participated in the plea discussions:

(1) a guilty plea that was later withdrawn;

(2) a nolo contendere plea;

(3) a statement made during a proceeding on either of those pleas under Federal Rule of Criminal Procedure 11 or a comparable state procedure; or

(4) a statement made during plea discussions with an attorney for the prosecuting authority if the discussions did not result in a guilty plea or they resulted in a later-withdrawn guilty plea.

(b) Exceptions. The court may admit a statement described in Rule 410(a)(3) or (4):

(1) in any proceeding in which another statement made during the same plea or plea discussions has been introduced, if in fairness the statements ought to be considered together; or

(2) in a criminal proceeding for perjury or false statement, if the defendant made the statement under oath, on the record, and with counsel present.

RULE 411. LIABILITY INSURANCE

Evidence that a person was or was not insured against liability is not admissible to prove whether the person acted negligently or otherwise wrongfully. But the court may admit this evidence for another purpose, such as proving a witness's bias or prejudice or proving agency, ownership, or control.

RULE 412. SEX-OFFENSE CASES: THE VICTIM'S SEXUAL BEHAVIOR OR PREDISPOSITION

(a) Prohibited Uses. The following evidence is not admissible in a civil or criminal proceeding involving alleged sexual misconduct:

(1) evidence offered to prove that a victim engaged in other sexual behavior; or

(2) evidence offered to prove a victim's sexual predisposition.

(b) Exceptions.

(1) ***Criminal Cases.*** The court may admit the following evidence in a criminal case:

(A) evidence of specific instances of a victim's sexual behavior, if offered to prove that someone other than the defendant was the source of semen, injury, or other physical evidence;

(B) evidence of specific instances of a victim's sexual behavior with respect to the person accused of the sexual misconduct, if offered by the defendant to prove consent or if offered by the prosecutor; and

(C) evidence whose exclusion would violate the defendant's constitutional rights.

(2) ***Civil Cases.*** In a civil case, the court may admit evidence offered to prove a victim's sexual behavior or sexual predisposition if its probative value substantially outweighs the danger of harm to any victim and of unfair prejudice to any party. The court may admit evidence of a victim's reputation only if the victim has placed it in controversy.

(c) **Procedure to Determine Admissibility.**

(1) ***Motion.*** If a party intends to offer evidence under Rule 412(b), the party must:

(A) file a motion that specifically describes the evidence and states the purpose for which it is to be offered;

(B) do so at least 14 days before trial unless the court, for good cause, sets a different time;

(C) serve the motion on all parties; and

(D) notify the victim or, when appropriate, the victim's guardian or representative.

(2) ***Hearing.*** Before admitting evidence under this rule, the court must conduct an in camera hearing and give the victim and parties a right to attend and be heard. Unless the court orders otherwise, the motion, related materials, and the record of the hearing must be and remain sealed.

(d) **Definition of "Victim."** In this rule, "victim" includes an alleged victim.

RULE 413. SIMILAR CRIMES IN SEXUAL-ASSAULT CASES

(a) **Permitted Uses.** In a criminal case in which a defendant is accused of a sexual assault, the court may admit evidence that the defendant committed any other sexual assault. The evidence may be considered on any matter to which it is relevant.

(b) **Disclosure to the Defendant.** If the prosecutor intends to offer this evidence, the prosecutor must disclose it to the defendant, including witnesses' statements or a summary of the expected testimony. The prosecutor must do so at least 15 days before trial or at a later time that the court allows for good cause.

(c) **Effect on Other Rules.** This rule does not limit the admission or consideration of evidence under any other rule.

(d) **Definition of "Sexual Assault."** In this rule and Rule 415, "sexual assault" means a crime under federal law or under state law (as "state" is defined in 18 U.S.C. § 513) involving:

(1) any conduct prohibited by 18 U.S.C. chapter 109A;

(2) contact, without consent, between any part of the defendant's body — or an object — and another person's genitals or anus;

(3) contact, without consent, between the defendant's genitals or anus and any part of another person's body;
(4) deriving sexual pleasure or gratification from inflicting death, bodily injury, or physical pain on another person; or
(5) an attempt or conspiracy to engage in conduct described in subparagraphs (1)-(4).

RULE 414. SIMILAR CRIMES IN CHILD-MOLESTATION CASES

(a) **Permitted Uses.** In a criminal case in which a defendant is accused of child molestation, the court may admit evidence that the defendant committed any other child molestation. The evidence may be considered on any matter to which it is relevant.

(b) **Disclosure to the Defendant.** If the prosecutor intends to offer this evidence, the prosecutor must disclose it to the defendant, including witnesses' statements or a summary of the expected testimony. The prosecutor must do so at least 15 days before trial or at a later time that the court allows for good cause.

(c) **Effect on Other Rules.** This rule does not limit the admission or consideration of evidence under any other rule.

(d) **Definition of "Child" and "Child Molestation."** In this rule and Rule 415:
(1) "child" means a person below the age of 14; and
(2) "child molestation" means a crime under federal law or under state law (as "state" is defined in 18 U.S.C. § 513) involving:
(A) any conduct prohibited by 18 U.S.C. chapter 109A and committed with a child;
(B) any conduct prohibited by 18 U.S.C. chapter 110;
(C) contact between any part of the defendant's body — or an object — and a child's genitals or anus;
(D) contact between the defendant's genitals or anus and any part of a child's body;
(E) deriving sexual pleasure or gratification from inflicting death, bodily injury, or physical pain on a child; or
(F) an attempt or conspiracy to engage in conduct described in subparagraphs (A)-(E).

RULE 415. SIMILAR ACTS IN CIVIL CASES INVOLVING SEXUAL ASSAULT OR CHILD MOLESTATION

(a) **Permitted Uses.** In a civil case involving a claim for relief based on a party's alleged sexual assault or child molestation, the court may admit evidence that the party committed any other sexual assault or child molestation. The evidence may be considered as provided in Rules 413 and 414.

(b) **Disclosure to the Opponent.** If a party intends to offer this evidence, the party must disclose it to the party against whom it will be offered, including witnesses' statements or a summary of the expected testimony. The party must do so at least 15 days before trial or at a later time that the court allows for good cause.

(c) **Effect on Other Rules.** This rule does not limit the admission or consideration of evidence under any other rule.

ARTICLE V. PRIVILEGES

RULE 501. PRIVILEGE IN GENERAL

The common law — as interpreted by United States courts in the light of reason and experience — governs a claim of privilege unless any of the following provides otherwise:

- the United States Constitution;
- a federal statute; or
- rules prescribed by the Supreme Court.

But in a civil case, state law governs privilege regarding a claim or defense for which state law supplies the rule of decision.

RULE 502. ATTORNEY-CLIENT PRIVILEGE AND WORK PRODUCT; LIMITATIONS ON WAIVER

The following provisions apply, in the circumstances set out, to disclosure of a communication or information covered by the attorney-client privilege or work-product protection.

(a) **Disclosure Made in a Federal Proceeding or to a Federal Office or Agency; Scope of a Waiver.** When the disclosure is made in a federal proceeding or to a federal office or agency and waives the attorney-client privilege or work-product protection, the waiver extends to an undisclosed communication or information in a federal or state proceeding only if:

(1) the waiver is intentional;

(2) the disclosed and undisclosed communications or information concern the same subject matter; and

(3) they ought in fairness to be considered together.

(b) **Inadvertent Disclosure.** When made in a federal proceeding or to a federal office or agency, the disclosure does not operate as a waiver in a federal or state proceeding if:

(1) the disclosure is inadvertent;

(2) the holder of the privilege or protection took reasonable steps to prevent disclosure; and

(3) the holder promptly took reasonable steps to rectify the error, including (if applicable) following Federal Rule of Civil Procedure 26(b)(5)(B).

(c) **Disclosure Made in a State Proceeding.** When the

disclosure is made in a state proceeding and is not the subject of a state-court order concerning waiver, the disclosure does not operate as a waiver in a federal proceeding if the disclosure:

(1) would not be a waiver under this rule if it had been made in a federal proceeding; or

(2) is not a waiver under the law of the state where the disclosure occurred.

(d) **Controlling Effect of a Court Order.** A federal court may order that the privilege or protection is not waived by disclosure connected with the litigation pending before the court — in which event the disclosure is also not a waiver in any other federal or state proceeding.

(e) **Controlling Effect of a Party Agreement.** An agreement on the effect of disclosure in a federal proceeding is binding only on the parties to the agreement, unless it is incorporated into a court order.

(f) **Controlling Effect of this Rule.** Notwithstanding Rules 101 and 1101, this rule applies to state proceedings and to federal court-annexed and federal court-mandated arbitration proceedings, in the circumstances set out in the rule. And notwithstanding Rule 501, this rule applies even if state law provides the rule of decision.

(g) **Definitions.** In this rule:

(1) "attorney-client privilege" means the protection that applicable law provides for confidential attorney-client communications; and

(2) "work-product protection" means the protection that applicable law provides for tangible material (or its intangible equivalent) prepared in anticipation of litigation or for trial.

ARTICLE VI. WITNESSES

RULE 601. COMPETENCY TO TESTIFY IN GENERAL

Every person is competent to be a witness unless these rules provide otherwise. But in a civil case, state law governs the witness's competency regarding a claim or defense for which state law supplies the rule of decision.

RULE 602. NEED FOR PERSONAL KNOWLEDGE

A witness may testify to a matter only if evidence is introduced sufficient to support a finding that the witness has personal knowledge of the matter. Evidence to prove personal knowledge may consist of the witness's own testimony. This rule does not apply to a witness's expert testimony under Rule 703.

RULE 603. OATH OR AFFIRMATION TO TESTIFY TRUTHFULLY

Before testifying, a witness must give an oath or affirmation to testify truthfully. It must be in a form designed to impress that duty on the witness's conscience.

RULE 604. INTERPRETER

An interpreter must be qualified and must give an oath or affirmation to make a true translation.

RULE 605. JUDGE'S COMPETENCY AS A WITNESS

The presiding judge may not testify as a witness at the trial. A party need not object to preserve the issue.

RULE 606. JUROR'S COMPETENCY AS A WITNESS

(a) **At the Trial.** A juror may not testify as a witness before the other jurors at the trial. If a juror is called to testify, the court must give a party an opportunity to object outside the jury's presence.

(b) **During an Inquiry into the Validity of a Verdict or Indictment.**

(1) ***Prohibited Testimony or Other Evidence.*** During an inquiry into the validity of a verdict or indictment, a juror may not testify about any statement made or incident that occurred during the jury's deliberations; the effect of anything on that juror's or another juror's vote; or any juror's mental processes concerning the verdict or indictment. The court may not receive a juror's affidavit or evidence of a juror's statement on these matters.

(2) ***Exceptions.*** A juror may testify about whether:

(A) extraneous prejudicial information was improperly brought to the jury's attention;

(B) an outside influence was improperly brought to bear on any juror; or

(C) a mistake was made in entering the verdict on the verdict form.

RULE 607. WHO MAY IMPEACH A WITNESS

Any party, including the party that called the witness, may attack the witness's credibility.

RULE 608. A WITNESS'S CHARACTER FOR TRUTHFULNESS OR UNTRUTHFULNESS

(a) **Reputation or Opinion Evidence.** A witness's credibility may be attacked or supported by testimony about the witness's reputation for having a character for truthfulness or untruthfulness, or by testimony in the form of an opinion about that character. But evidence of truthful character is admissible only after the witness's character for truthfulness has been attacked.

(b) **Specific Instances of Conduct.** Except for a criminal conviction under Rule 609, extrinsic evidence is not admissible to prove specific instances of a witness's conduct in order to attack or support the witness's character for truthfulness. But the court may, on cross-examination, allow them to be inquired into if they are probative of the character for truthfulness or untruthfulness of:

(1) the witness; or

(2) another witness whose character the witness being cross-examined has testified about.

By testifying on another matter, a witness does not waive any privilege against self-incrimination for testimony that relates only to the witness's character for truthfulness.

RULE 609. IMPEACHMENT BY EVIDENCE OF A CRIMINAL CONVICTION

(a) **In General.** The following rules apply to attacking a witness's character for truthfulness by evidence of a criminal conviction:

(1) for a crime that, in the convicting jurisdiction, was punishable by death or by imprisonment for more than one year, the evidence:

(A) must be admitted, subject to Rule 403, in a civil case or in a criminal case in which the witness is not a defendant; and

(B) must be admitted in a criminal case in which the witness is a defendant, if the probative value of the evidence outweighs its prejudicial effect to that defendant; and

(2) for any crime regardless of the punishment, the evidence must be admitted if the court can readily determine that establishing the elements of the crime required proving — or the witness's admitting — a dishonest act or false statement.

(b) **Limit on Using the Evidence After 10 Years.** This subdivision (b) applies if more than 10 years have passed since the witness's conviction or release from confinement for it, whichever is later. Evidence of the conviction is admissible only if:

(1) its probative value, supported by specific facts and circumstances, substantially outweighs its prejudicial effect; and

(2) the proponent gives an adverse party reasonable written notice of the intent to use it so that the party has a fair opportunity to contest its use.

(c) **Effect of a Pardon, Annulment, or Certificate of Rehabilitation.** Evidence of a conviction is not admissible if:

(1) the conviction has been the subject of a pardon, annulment, certificate of rehabilitation, or other equivalent pro-

cedure based on a finding that the person has been rehabilitated, and the person has not been convicted of a later crime punishable by death or by imprisonment for more than one year; or

(2) the conviction has been the subject of a pardon, annulment, or other equivalent procedure based on a finding of innocence.

(d) **Juvenile Adjudications.** Evidence of a juvenile adjudication is admissible under this rule only if:

(1) it is offered in a criminal case;

(2) the adjudication was of a witness other than the defendant;

(3) an adult's conviction for that offense would be admissible to attack the adult's credibility; and

(4) admitting the evidence is necessary to fairly determine guilt or innocence.

(e) **Pendency of an Appeal.** A conviction that satisfies this rule is admissible even if an appeal is pending. Evidence of the pendency is also admissible.

RULE 610. RELIGIOUS BELIEFS OR OPINIONS

Evidence of a witness's religious beliefs or opinions is not admissible to attack or support the witness's credibility.

RULE 611. MODE AND ORDER OF EXAMINING WITNESSES AND PRESENTING EVIDENCE

(a) **Control by the Court; Purposes.** The court should exercise reasonable control over the mode and order of examining witnesses and presenting evidence so as to:

(1) make those procedures effective for determining the truth;

(2) avoid wasting time; and

(3) protect witnesses from harassment or undue embarrassment.

(b) **Scope of Cross-Examination.** Cross-examination should not go beyond the subject matter of the direct examination and matters affecting the witness's credibility. The court may allow inquiry into additional matters as if on direct examination.

(c) **Leading Questions.** Leading questions should not be used on direct examination except as necessary to develop the witness's testimony. Ordinarily, the court should allow leading questions:

(1) on cross-examination; and

(2) when a party calls a hostile witness, an adverse party, or a witness identified with an adverse party.

RULE 612. WRITING USED TO REFRESH A WITNESS'S MEMORY

(a) **Scope.** This rule gives an adverse party certain options when a witness uses a writing to refresh memory:

(1) while testifying; or

(2) before testifying, if the court decides that justice requires the party to have those options.

(b) **Adverse Party's Options; Deleting Unrelated Matter.** Unless 18 U.S.C. § 3500 provides otherwise in a criminal case, an adverse party is entitled to have the writing produced at the hearing, to inspect it, to cross-examine the witness about it, and to introduce in evidence any portion that relates to the witness's testimony. If the producing party claims that the writing includes unrelated matter, the court must examine the writing in camera, delete any unrelated portion, and order that the rest be delivered to the adverse party. Any portion deleted over objection must be preserved for the record.

(c) **Failure to Produce or Deliver the Writing.** If a writing is not produced or is not delivered as ordered, the court may issue any appropriate order. But if the prosecution does not comply in a criminal case, the court must strike the witness's testimony or — if justice so requires — declare a mistrial.

RULE 613. WITNESS'S PRIOR STATEMENT

(a) **Showing or Disclosing the Statement During Examination.** When examining a witness about the witness's prior statement, a party need not show it or disclose its contents to the witness. But the party must, on request, show it or disclose its contents to an adverse party's attorney.

(b) **Extrinsic Evidence of a Prior Inconsistent Statement.** Extrinsic evidence of a witness's prior inconsistent statement is admissible only if the witness is given an opportunity to explain or deny the statement and an adverse party is given an opportunity to examine the witness about it, or if justice so requires. This subdivision (b) does not apply to an opposing party's statement under Rule 801(d)(2).

RULE 614. COURT'S CALLING OR EXAMINING A WITNESS

(a) **Calling.** The court may call a witness on its own or at a party's request. Each party is entitled to cross-examine the witness.

(b) **Examining.** The court may examine a witness regardless of who calls the witness.

(c) **Objections.** A party may object to the court's calling or examining a witness either at that time or at the next opportunity when the jury is not present.

RULE 615. EXCLUDING WITNESSES

At a party's request, the court must order witnesses excluded so that they cannot hear other witnesses' testimony. Or the court may do so on its own. But this rule does not authorize excluding:

(a) a party who is a natural person;

(b) an officer or employee of a party that is not a natural person, after being designated as the party's representative by its attorney;

(c) a person whose presence a party shows to be essential to presenting the party's claim or defense; or

(d) a person authorized by statute to be present.

ARTICLE VII. OPINIONS AND EXPERT TESTIMONY

RULE 701. OPINION TESTIMONY BY LAY WITNESSES

If a witness is not testifying as an expert, testimony in the form of an opinion is limited to one that is:

(a) rationally based on the witness's perception;

(b) helpful to clearly understanding the witness's testimony or to determining a fact in issue; and

(c) not based on scientific, technical, or other specialized knowledge within the scope of Rule 702.

RULE 702. TESTIMONY BY EXPERT WITNESSES

A witness who is qualified as an expert by knowledge, skill, experience, training, or education may testify in the form of an opinion or otherwise if:

(a) the expert's scientific, technical, or other specialized knowledge will help the trier of fact to understand the evidence or to determine a fact in issue;

(b) the testimony is based on sufficient facts or data;

(c) the testimony is the product of reliable principles and methods; and

(d) the expert has reliably applied the principles and methods to the facts of the case.

RULE 703. BASES OF AN EXPERT'S OPINION TESTIMONY

An expert may base an opinion on facts or data in the case that the expert has been made aware of or personally observed. If experts in the particular field would reasonably rely on those kinds of facts or data in forming an opinion on the subject, they need not be admissible for the opinion to be admitted. But if the facts or data would otherwise be inadmissible, the proponent of the opinion may disclose them to the jury only if their probative value in helping the jury evaluate the opinion substantially outweighs their prejudicial effect.

RULE 704. OPINION ON AN ULTIMATE ISSUE

(a) In General — Not Automatically Objectionable. An

opinion is not objectionable just because it embraces an ultimate issue.

(b) Exception. In a criminal case, an expert witness must not state an opinion about whether the defendant did or did not have a mental state or condition that constitutes an element of the crime charged or of a defense. Those matters are for the trier of fact alone.

RULE 705. DISCLOSING THE FACTS OR DATA UNDERLYING AN EXPERT'S OPINION

Unless the court orders otherwise, an expert may state an opinion — and give the reasons for it — without first testifying to the underlying facts or data. But the expert may be required to disclose those facts or data on cross-examination.

RULE 706. COURT-APPOINTED EXPERT WITNESSES

(a) Appointment Process. On a party's motion or on its own, the court may order the parties to show cause why expert witnesses should not be appointed and may ask the parties to submit nominations. The court may appoint any expert that the parties agree on and any of its own choosing. But the court may only appoint someone who consents to act.

(b) Expert's Role. The court must inform the expert of the expert's duties. The court may do so in writing and have a copy filed with the clerk or may do so orally at a conference in which the parties have an opportunity to participate. The expert:

(1) must advise the parties of any findings the expert makes;

(2) may be deposed by any party;

(3) may be called to testify by the court or any party; and

(4) may be cross-examined by any party, including the party that called the expert.

(c) Compensation. The expert is entitled to a reasonable compensation, as set by the court. The compensation is payable as follows:

(1) in a criminal case or in a civil case involving just compensation under the Fifth Amendment, from any funds that are provided by law; and

(2) in any other civil case, by the parties in the proportion and at the time that the court directs — and the compensation is then charged like other costs.

(d) Disclosing the Appointment to the Jury. The court may authorize disclosure to the jury that the court appointed the expert.

(e) Parties' Choice of Their Own Experts. This rule does not limit a party in calling its own experts.

ARTICLE VIII. HEARSAY

RULE 801. DEFINITIONS THAT APPLY TO THIS ARTICLE; EXCLUSIONS FROM HEARSAY

(a) Statement. "Statement" means a person's oral assertion, written assertion, or nonverbal conduct, if the person intended it as an assertion.

(b) Declarant. "Declarant" means the person who made the statement.

(c) Hearsay. "Hearsay" means a statement that:

(1) the declarant does not make while testifying at the current trial or hearing; and

(2) a party offers in evidence to prove the truth of the matter asserted in the statement.

(d) Statements That Are Not Hearsay. A statement that meets the following conditions is not hearsay:

(1) ***A Declarant-Witness's Prior Statement.*** The declarant testifies and is subject to cross-examination about a prior statement, and the statement:

(A) is inconsistent with the declarant's testimony and was given under penalty of perjury at a trial, hearing, or other proceeding or in a deposition;

(B) is consistent with the declarant's testimony and is offered;

(i) to rebut an express or implied charge that the declarant recently fabricated it or acted from a recent improper influence or motive in so testifying; or

(ii) to rehabilitate the declarant's credibility as a witness when attacked on another ground; or

(C) identifies a person as someone the declarant perceived earlier.

(2) ***An Opposing Party's Statement.*** The statement is offered against an opposing party and:

(A) was made by the party in an individual or representative capacity;

(B) is one the party manifested that it adopted or believed to be true;

(C) was made by a person whom the party authorized to make a statement on the subject;

(D) was made by the party's agent or employee on a matter within the scope of that relationship and while it existed; or

(E) was made by the party's coconspirator during and in furtherance of the conspiracy.

The statement must be considered but does not by itself establish the declarant's authority under (C); the existence or scope of the relationship under (D); or the existence of the conspiracy or participation in it under (E).

RULE 802. THE RULE AGAINST HEARSAY

Hearsay is not admissible unless any of the following provides otherwise:

- a federal statute;
- these rules; or
- other rules prescribed by the Supreme Court.

RULE 803. EXCEPTIONS TO THE RULE AGAINST HEARSAY — REGARDLESS OF WHETHER THE DECLARANT IS AVAILABLE AS A WITNESS

The following are not excluded by the rule against hearsay, regardless of whether the declarant is available as a witness:

(1) ***Present Sense Impression.*** A statement describing or explaining an event or condition, made while or immediately after the declarant perceived it.

(2) ***Excited Utterance.*** A statement relating to a startling event or condition, made while the declarant was under the stress of excitement that it caused.

(3) ***Then-Existing Mental, Emotional, or Physical Condition.*** A statement of the declarant's then-existing state of mind (such as motive, intent, or plan) or emotional, sensory, or physical condition (such as mental feeling, pain, or bodily health), but not including a statement of memory or belief to prove the fact remembered or believed unless it relates to the validity or terms of the declarant's will.

(4) ***Statement Made for Medical Diagnosis or Treatment.*** A statement that:

(A) is made for — and is reasonably pertinent to — medical diagnosis or treatment; and

(B) describes medical history; past or present symptoms or sensations; their inception; or their general cause.

(5) ***Recorded Recollection.*** A record that:

(A) is on a matter the witness once knew about but now cannot recall well enough to testify fully and accurately;

(B) was made or adopted by the witness when the matter was fresh in the witness's memory; and

(C) accurately reflects the witness's knowledge.

If admitted, the record may be read into evidence but may be received as an exhibit only if offered by an adverse party.

(6) ***Records of a Regularly Conducted Activity.*** A record of an act, event, condition, opinion, or diagnosis if:

(A) the record was made at or near the time by — or from information transmitted by — someone with knowledge;

(B) the record was kept in the course of a regularly conducted activity of a business, organization, occupation, or calling, whether or not for profit;

(C) making the record was a regular practice of that activity;

(D) all these conditions are shown by the testimony of the custodian or another qualified witness, or by a certification that complies with Rule 902(11) or (12) or with a statute permitting certification; and

(E) the opponent does not show that the source of information or the method or circumstances of preparation indicate a lack of trustworthiness.

(7) ***Absence of a Record of a Regularly Conducted Activity.*** Evidence that a matter is not included in a record described in paragraph (6) if:

(A) the evidence is admitted to prove that the matter did not occur or exist;

(B) a record was regularly kept for a matter of that kind; and

(C) the opponent does not show that the possible source of the information or other circumstances indicate a lack of trustworthiness.

(8) ***Public Records.*** A record or statement of a public office if:

(A) it sets out:

(i) the office's activities;

(ii) a matter observed while under a legal duty to report, but not including, in a criminal case, a matter observed by law-enforcement personnel; or

(iii) in a civil case or against the government in a criminal case, factual findings from a legally authorized investigation; and

(B) the opponent does not show that the source of information or other circumstances indicate a lack of trustworthiness.

(9) ***Public Records of Vital Statistics.*** A record of a birth, death, or marriage, if reported to a public office in accordance with a legal duty.

(10) ***Absence of a Public Record.*** Testimony--or a certification under Rule 902--that a diligent search failed to disclose a public record or statement if:

(A) the testimony or certification is admitted to prove that

(i) the record or statement does not exist; or

(ii) a matter did not occur or exist, if a public office regularly kept a record or statement for a matter of that kind; and

(B) in a criminal case, a prosecutor who intends to offer a certification provides written notice of that intent at least 14 days before trial, and the defendant does not object in writing within 7 days of receiving the notice--unless the court sets a different time for the notice or the objection.

(11) ***Records of Religious Organizations Concerning Personal or Family History.*** A statement of birth, legitimacy, ancestry, marriage, divorce, death, relationship by blood or marriage, or similar facts of personal or family history, contained in a regularly kept record of a religious organization.

(12) ***Certificates of Marriage, Baptism, and Similar Ceremonies.*** A statement of fact contained in a certificate:

(A) made by a person who is authorized by a religious organization or by law to perform the act certified;

(B) attesting that the person performed a marriage or similar ceremony or administered a sacrament; and

(C) purporting to have been issued at the time of the act or within a reasonable time after it.

(13) ***Family Records.*** A statement of fact about personal or family history contained in a family record, such as a Bible, genealogy, chart, engraving on a ring, inscription on a portrait, or engraving on an urn or burial marker.

(14) ***Records of Documents That Affect an Interest in Property.*** The record of a document that purports to establish or affect an interest in property if:

(A) the record is admitted to prove the content of the original recorded document, along with its signing and its delivery by each person who purports to have signed it;

(B) the record is kept in a public office; and

(C) a statute authorizes recording documents of that kind in that office.

(15) ***Statements in Documents That Affect an Interest in Property.*** A statement contained in a document that purports to establish or affect an interest in property if the matter stated was relevant to the document's purpose — unless later dealings with the property are inconsistent with the truth of the statement or the purport of the document.

(16) ***Statements in Ancient Documents.*** A statement in a document that was prepared before January 1, 1998, and whose authenticity is established.

(17) ***Market Reports and Similar Commercial Publications.*** Market quotations, lists, directories, or other compilations that are generally relied on by the public or by persons in particular occupations.

(18) ***Statements in Learned Treatises, Periodicals, or Pamphlets.*** A statement contained in a treatise, periodical, or pamphlet if:

(A) the statement is called to the attention of an expert witness on cross-examination or relied on by the expert on direct examination; and

(B) the publication is established as a reliable authority by the expert's admission or testimony, by another expert's testimony, or by judicial notice.

If admitted, the statement may be read into evidence but not received as an exhibit.

(19) ***Reputation Concerning Personal or Family History.*** A reputation among a person's family by blood, adoption, or marriage — or among a person's associates or in the community — concerning the person's birth, adoption, legitimacy, ancestry, marriage, divorce, death, relationship by blood, adoption, or marriage, or similar facts of personal or family history.

(20) ***Reputation Concerning Boundaries or General History.*** A reputation in a community — arising before the controversy — concerning boundaries of land in the community or customs that affect the land, or concerning general historical events important to that community, state, or nation.

(21) ***Reputation Concerning Character.*** A reputation among a person's associates or in the community concerning the person's character.

(22) ***Judgment of a Previous Conviction.*** Evidence of a final judgment of conviction if:

(A) the judgment was entered after a trial or guilty plea, but not a nolo contendere plea;

(B) the conviction was for a crime punishable by death or by imprisonment for more than a year;

(C) the evidence is admitted to prove any fact essential to the judgment; and

(D) when offered by the prosecutor in a criminal case for a purpose other than impeachment, the judgment was against the defendant.

The pendency of an appeal may be shown but does not affect admissibility.

(23) ***Judgments Involving Personal, Family, or General History, or a Boundary.*** A judgment that is admitted to prove a matter of personal, family, or general history, or boundaries, if the matter:

(A) was essential to the judgment; and

(B) could be proved by evidence of reputation.

(24) **[*Other Exceptions.*]** [Transferred to Rule 807.]

RULE 804. EXCEPTIONS TO THE RULE AGAINST HEARSAY — WHEN THE DECLARANT IS UNAVAILABLE AS A WITNESS

(a) Criteria for Being Unavailable. A declarant is considered to be unavailable as a witness if the declarant:

(1) is exempted from testifying about the subject matter of the declarant's statement because the court rules that a privilege applies;

(2) refuses to testify about the subject matter despite a court order to do so;

(3) testifies to not remembering the subject matter;

(4) cannot be present or testify at the trial or hearing because of death or a then-existing infirmity, physical illness, or mental illness; or

(5) is absent from the trial or hearing and the statement's proponent has not been able, by process or other reasonable means, to procure:

(A) the declarant's attendance, in the case of a hearsay exception under Rule 804(b)(1) or (6); or

(B) the declarant's attendance or testimony, in the case of a hearsay exception under Rule 804(b)(2), (3), or (4).

But this subdivision (a) does not apply if the statement's proponent procured or wrongfully caused the declarant's unavailability as a witness in order to prevent the declarant from attending or testifying.

(b) The Exceptions. The following are not excluded by the rule against hearsay if the declarant is unavailable as a witness:

(1) ***Former Testimony.*** Testimony that:

(A) was given as a witness at a trial, hearing, or lawful deposition, whether given during the current proceeding or a different one; and

(B) is now offered against a party who had — or, in a civil case, whose predecessor in interest had — an opportunity and similar motive to develop it by direct, cross-, or redirect examination.

(2) ***Statement Under the Belief of Imminent Death.*** In a prosecution for homicide or in a civil case, a statement that the declarant, while believing the declarant's death to be imminent, made about its cause or circumstances.

(3) ***Statement Against Interest.*** A statement that:

(A) a reasonable person in the declarant's position would have made only if the person believed it to be true because, when made, it was so contrary to the declarant's proprietary or pecuniary interest or had so great a tendency to invalidate the declarant's claim against someone else or to expose the declarant to civil or criminal liability; and

(B) is supported by corroborating circumstances that clearly indicate its trustworthiness, if it is offered in a criminal case as one that tends to expose the declarant to criminal liability.

(4) ***Statement of Personal or Family History.*** A statement about:

(A) the declarant's own birth, adoption, legitimacy, ancestry, marriage, divorce, relationship by blood, adoption, or marriage, or similar facts of personal or family history, even though the declarant had no way of acquiring personal knowledge about that fact; or

(B) another person concerning any of these facts, as well as death, if the declarant was related to the person by blood, adoption, or marriage or was so intimately associated with the person's family that the declarant's information is likely to be accurate.

(5) [***Other Exceptions.***] [Transferred to Rule 807.]

(6) ***Statement Offered Against a Party That Wrongfully Caused the Declarant's Unavailability.*** A statement offered against a party that wrongfully caused — or acquiesced in wrongfully causing — the declarant's unavailability as a witness, and did so intending that result.

RULE 805. HEARSAY WITHIN HEARSAY

Hearsay within hearsay is not excluded by the rule against hearsay if each part of the combined statements conforms with an exception to the rule.

RULE 806. ATTACKING AND SUPPORTING THE DECLARANT'S CREDIBILITY

When a hearsay statement — or a statement described in Rule 801(d)(2)(C), (D), or (E) — has been admitted in evidence, the declarant's credibility may be attacked, and then supported, by any evidence that would be admissible for those purposes if the declarant had testified as a witness. The court may admit evidence of the declarant's inconsistent statement or conduct, regardless of when it occurred or whether the declarant had an opportunity to explain or deny it. If the party against whom the statement was admitted calls the declarant as a witness, the party may examine the declarant on the statement as if on cross-examination.

RULE 807. RESIDUAL EXCEPTION

(a) **In General.** Under the following conditions, a hearsay statement is not excluded by the rule against hearsay even if the statement is not admissible under a hearsay exception in Rule 803 or 804:

(1) the statement is supported by sufficient guarantees of

trustworthiness—after considering the totality of circumstances under which it was made and evidence, if any, corroborating the statement; and

(2) it is more probative on the point for which it is offered than any other evidence that the proponent can obtain through reasonable efforts.

(b) Notice. The statement is admissible only if the proponent gives an adverse party reasonable notice of the intent to offer the statement—including its substance and the declarant's name—so that the party has a fair opportunity to meet it. The notice must be provided in writing before the trial or hearing—or in any form during the trial or hearing if the court, for good cause, excuses a lack of earlier notice.

ARTICLE IX. AUTHENTICATION AND IDENTIFICATION

RULE 901. AUTHENTICATING OR IDENTIFYING EVIDENCE

(a) In General. To satisfy the requirement of authenticating or identifying an item of evidence, the proponent must produce evidence sufficient to support a finding that the item is what the proponent claims it is.

(b) Examples. The following are examples only — not a complete list — of evidence that satisfies the requirement:

(1) ***Testimony of a Witness with Knowledge.*** Testimony that an item is what it is claimed to be.

(2) ***Nonexpert Opinion About Handwriting.*** A nonexpert's opinion that handwriting is genuine, based on a familiarity with it that was not acquired for the current litigation.

(3) ***Comparison by an Expert Witness or the Trier of Fact.*** A comparison with an authenticated specimen by an expert witness or the trier of fact.

(4) ***Distinctive Characteristics and the Like.*** The appearance, contents, substance, internal patterns, or other distinctive characteristics of the item, taken together with all the circumstances.

(5) ***Opinion About a Voice.*** An opinion identifying a person's voice — whether heard firsthand or through mechanical or electronic transmission or recording — based on hearing the voice at any time under circumstances that connect it with the alleged speaker.

(6) ***Evidence About a Telephone Conversation.*** For a telephone conversation, evidence that a call was made to the number assigned at the time to:

(A) a particular person, if circumstances, including self-identification, show that the person answering was the one called; or

(B) a particular business, if the call was made to a business and the call related to business reasonably transacted over the telephone.

(7) ***Evidence About Public Records.*** Evidence that:

(A) a document was recorded or filed in a public office as authorized by law; or

(B) a purported public record or statement is from the office where items of this kind are kept.

(8) ***Evidence About Ancient Documents or Data Compilations.*** For a document or data compilation, evidence that it:

(A) is in a condition that creates no suspicion about its authenticity;

(B) was in a place where, if authentic, it would likely be; and

(C) is at least 20 years old when offered.

(9) ***Evidence About a Process or System.*** Evidence describing a process or system and showing that it produces an accurate result.

(10) ***Methods Provided by a Statute or Rule.*** Any method of authentication or identification allowed by a federal statute or a rule prescribed by the Supreme Court.

RULE 902. EVIDENCE THAT IS SELF-AUTHENTICATING

The following items of evidence are self-authenticating; they require no extrinsic evidence of authenticity in order to be admitted:

(1) ***Domestic Public Documents That Are Sealed and Signed.*** A document that bears:

(A) a seal purporting to be that of the United States; any state, district, commonwealth, territory, or insular possession of the United States; the former Panama Canal Zone; the Trust Territory of the Pacific Islands; a political subdivision of any of these entities; or a department, agency, or officer of any entity named above; and

(B) a signature purporting to be an execution or attestation.

(2) ***Domestic Public Documents That Are Not Sealed but Are Signed and Certified.*** A document that bears no seal if:

(A) it bears the signature of an officer or employee of an entity named in Rule 902(1)(A); and

(B) another public officer who has a seal and official duties within that same entity certifies under seal — or its equivalent — that the signer has the official capacity and that the signature is genuine.

(3) ***Foreign Public Documents.*** A document that purports to be signed or attested by a person who is authorized by a foreign country's law to do so. The document must be accompanied by a final certification that certifies the genuineness of the signature and official position of the signer or attester — or of any foreign official whose certificate of genuineness relates to the signature or attestation or is in a chain of certificates of genuineness relating to the signature or attestation. The certification may be made by a secretary of a United States embassy or legation; by a consul general, vice consul, or consular agent of the United States; or by a diplomatic or consular official of the foreign country assigned or accredited to the United States. If all parties have been given a reasonable opportunity to investigate the document's authenticity and accuracy, the court may, for good cause, either:

(A) order that it be treated as presumptively authentic without final certification; or

(B) allow it to be evidenced by an attested summary with or without final certification.

(4) ***Certified Copies of Public Records.*** A copy of an official record — or a copy of a document that was recorded or filed in a public office as authorized by law — if the copy is certified as correct by:

(A) the custodian or another person authorized to make the certification; or

(B) a certificate that complies with Rule 902(1), (2), or (3), a federal statute, or a rule prescribed by the Supreme Court.

(5) ***Official Publications.*** A book, pamphlet, or other publication purporting to be issued by a public authority.

(6) ***Newspapers and Periodicals.*** Printed material purporting to be a newspaper or periodical.

(7) ***Trade Inscriptions and the Like.*** An inscription, sign, tag, or label purporting to have been affixed in the course of business and indicating origin, ownership, or control.

(8) ***Acknowledged Documents.*** A document accompanied by a certificate of acknowledgment that is lawfully executed by a notary public or another officer who is authorized to take acknowledgments.

(9) ***Commercial Paper and Related Documents.*** Commercial paper, a signature on it, and related documents, to the extent allowed by general commercial law.

(10) ***Presumptions Under a Federal Statute.*** A signature, document, or anything else that a federal statute declares to be presumptively or prima facie genuine or authentic.

(11) ***Certified Domestic Records of a Regularly Conducted Activity.*** The original or a copy of a domestic record that meets the requirements of Rule 803(6)(A)-(C), as shown by a certification of the custodian or another qualified person that complies with a federal statute or a rule prescribed by the Supreme Court. Before the trial or hearing, the proponent must give an adverse party reasonable written notice of the intent to offer the record — and must make the record and certification available for inspection — so that the party has a fair opportunity to challenge them.

(12) ***Certified Foreign Records of a Regularly Conducted Activity.*** In a civil case, the original or a copy of a foreign record that meets the requirements of Rule 902(11), modified as follows: the certification, rather than complying with a federal statute or Supreme Court rule, must be signed in a manner that, if falsely made, would subject the maker to a criminal penalty in the country where the certification is signed. The proponent must also meet the notice requirements of Rule 902(11).

(13) ***Certified Records Generated by an Electronic Process or System.*** A record generated by an electronic process or system that produces an accurate result, as shown by a certification of a qualified person that complies with the certification requirements of Rule 902(11) or (12). The proponent must also meet the notice requirements of Rule 902(11).

(14) ***Certified Data Copied from an Electronic Device, Storage Medium, or File.*** Data copied from an electronic device, storage medium, or file, if authenticated by a process of digital identification, as shown by a certification of a qualified person that complies with the certification requirements of Rule 902(11) or (12). The proponent also must meet the notice requirements of Rule 902(11).

RULE 903. SUBSCRIBING WITNESS'S TESTIMONY

A subscribing witness's testimony is necessary to authenticate a writing only if required by the law of the jurisdiction that governs its validity.

ARTICLE X. CONTENTS OF WRITINGS, RECORDINGS, AND PHOTOGRAPHS

RULE 1001. DEFINITIONS THAT APPLY TO THIS ARTICLE

In this article:

(a) A "writing" consists of letters, words, numbers, or their equivalent set down in any form.

(b) A "recording" consists of letters, words, numbers, or their equivalent recorded in any manner.

(c) A "photograph" means a photographic image or its equivalent stored in any form.

(d) An "original" of a writing or recording means the writing or recording itself or any counterpart intended to have the same effect by the person who executed or issued it. For electronically stored information, "original" means any printout — or other output readable by sight — if it accurately reflects the information. An "original" of a photograph includes the negative or a print from it.

(e) A "duplicate" means a counterpart produced by a mechanical, photographic, chemical, electronic, or other equivalent process or technique that accurately reproduces the original.

RULE 1002. REQUIREMENT OF THE ORIGINAL

An original writing, recording, or photograph is required in order to prove its content unless these rules or a federal statute provides otherwise.

RULE 1003. ADMISSIBILITY OF DUPLICATES

A duplicate is admissible to the same extent as the original unless a genuine question is raised about the original's authenticity or the circumstances make it unfair to admit the duplicate.

RULE 1004. ADMISSIBILITY OF OTHER EVIDENCE OF CONTENT

An original is not required and other evidence of the content of a writing, recording, or photograph is admissible if:

(a) all the originals are lost or destroyed, and not by the proponent acting in bad faith;

(b) an original cannot be obtained by any available judicial process;

(c) the party against whom the original would be offered had control of the original; was at that time put on notice, by pleadings or otherwise, that the original would be a subject of proof at the trial or hearing; and fails to produce it at the trial or hearing; or

(d) the writing, recording, or photograph is not closely related to a controlling issue.

RULE 1005. COPIES OF PUBLIC RECORDS TO PROVE CONTENT

The proponent may use a copy to prove the content of an official record — or of a document that was recorded or filed in a public office as authorized by law — if these conditions are met: the record or document is otherwise admissible; and the copy is certified as correct in accordance with Rule 902(4) or is testified to be correct by a witness who has compared it with the original. If no such copy can be obtained by reasonable diligence, then the proponent may use other evidence to prove the content.

RULE 1006. SUMMARIES TO PROVE CONTENT

The proponent may use a summary, chart, or calculation to prove the content of voluminous writings, recordings, or photographs that cannot be conveniently examined in court. The proponent must make the originals or duplicates available for examination or copying, or both, by other parties at a reasonable time and place. And the court may order the proponent to produce them in court.

RULE 1007. TESTIMONY OR STATEMENT OF A PARTY TO PROVE CONTENT

The proponent may prove the content of a writing, recording, or photograph by the testimony, deposition, or written statement of the party against whom the evidence is offered. The proponent need not account for the original.

RULE 1008. FUNCTIONS OF THE COURT AND JURY

Ordinarily, the court determines whether the proponent has fulfilled the factual conditions for admitting other evidence of the content of a writing, recording, or photograph under Rule 1004 or 1005. But in a jury trial, the jury determines — in accordance with Rule 104(b) — any issue about whether:

(a) an asserted writing, recording, or photograph ever existed;

(b) another one produced at the trial or hearing is the original; or

(c) other evidence of content accurately reflects the content.

ARTICLE XI. MISCELLANEOUS RULES

RULE 1101. APPLICABILITY OF THE RULES

(a) To Courts and Judges. These rules apply to proceedings before:

- United States district courts;
- United States bankruptcy and magistrate judges;
- United States courts of appeals;
- the United States Court of Federal Claims; and
- the district courts of Guam, the Virgin Islands, and the Northern Mariana Islands.

(b) To Cases and Proceedings. These rules apply in:

- civil cases and proceedings, including bankruptcy, admiralty, and maritime cases;
- criminal cases and proceedings; and
- contempt proceedings, except those in which the court may act summarily.

(c) Rules on Privilege. The rules on privilege apply to all stages of a case or proceeding.

(d) Exceptions. These rules — except for those on privilege — do not apply to the following:

(1) the court's determination, under Rule 104(a), on a preliminary question of fact governing admissibility;

(2) grand-jury proceedings; and

(3) miscellaneous proceedings such as:

- extradition or rendition;
- issuing an arrest warrant, criminal summons, or search warrant;
- a preliminary examination in a criminal case;
- sentencing;
- granting or revoking probation or supervised release; and
- considering whether to release on bail or otherwise.

(e) Other Statutes and Rules. A federal statute or a rule prescribed by the Supreme Court may provide for admitting or excluding evidence independently from these rules.

RULE 1102. AMENDMENTS

These rules may be amended as provided in 28 U.S.C. § 2072.

RULE 1103. TITLE

These rules may be cited as the Federal Rules of Evidence.

PART X
USCOURTS.GOV

In past years, Part X of this Handbook presented a Directory of Federal Court locations/contact information and a Directory of Federal Judges. Even annually updated, however, these directories were inevitably out-of-date before they were printed, due to the persistent natural evolution of court personnel and infrastructure. Fortunately, all the information once printed in these directories is now offered in greater and more dynamic detail through the Federal Courts website: www.uscourts.gov

On the Federal Courts website, there is a Federal Court Finder button that enables users to find a federal court by location or court name. This feature includes appellate, district, and bankruptcy courts within its scope, and is enhanced with links to a Google map tool.

Under the Judges & Judgeships tab of the website, there is a wealth of information concerning the various types of federal judges, authorized judgeships, judicial vacancies, judicial milestones, judicial compensation, and standards of judicial conduct. Under the same tab, there is also a link to a directory of judges on the Federal Judicial Center's website (www.fjc.gov/history/judges) where one can find biographical information, from 1789 to present, on presidentially appointed federal judges

The Rules & Policies tab of the Federal Courts website also offers a treasure trove of information relating to the development and amendment of federal court rules. Under this tab, there are detailed explanations of the rulemaking process and extensive records of the rulemaking committees involved in that process. (For a quick, more abbreviated introduction to this rulemaking process, see Part I, §§ 1.3 to 1.6 of this text.) There are also links to all national federal rules and forms currently in effect, to local rules prescribed by district courts and courts of appeal, to pending rules and forms amendments, and to proposed amendments published for public comment.

Other tabs on the Federal Courts website present information on the overall role and administration of the federal judiciary, a bank of national court forms that can be used in all federal courts, a fee schedule for various types of courts, links to court records (including the PACER and CM/ECF systems for electronic access to or filing of documents in particular cases), and a variety of statistical data and analytical reports concerning the business of the federal judiciary. There is also a button where users can access a Judiciary News page. On that page, one can sign up to be notified by email of any news updates.

An excursion to www.uscourts.gov will never disappoint.

Abbreviations

Rule. . . . . Federal Rules of Civil Procedure (Part III)
Evid. Rule. . . . . Federal Rules of Evidence (Part X)
Form. . . . . Forms Appendix to Federal Rules of Civil Procedure (Part IV)
Auth. Comm. [ ]. . . Author's Commentary to [ ] (Part III)
Juris. [ ]. . . . . Federal Jurisdiction and Venue [ ] (Part II)

INDEX

Abbreviations
Rule
Federal Rules of Civil Procedure (Part III)
Evid. Rule
Federal Rules of Evidence (Part X)
Form
Forms Appendix to Federal Rules of Civil Procedure (Part IV)
Auth. Comm. [ ]
Author's Commentary to [ ] (Part III)
Juris. [ ]
Federal Jurisdiction and Venue [ ] (Part II)

ABATEMENT OF ACTIONS
Substitution of parties where public officer was party, Rule 25(d).

ABSENCE
Hearsay exception,
Declarant from hearing and proponent of statement unable to procure his attendance, "unavailability as witness" as including, Evid. Rule 804.
Entry in records of regularly conducted activity, Evid. Rule 803.
Public record or entry, Evid. Rule 803.
Joinder, persons needed for just adjudication, Rule 19(a).
Witness, waiver, signing, depositions upon oral examination, Rule 30(e).

ABSTRACTS
Business records, interrogatories, Rule 33(c).

ACCEPTANCE
Offer of Judgment, Auth. Comm. Rule 68.

ACCIDENT
Absence of, admissibility of evidence of other wrongs or acts to prove, Evid. Rule 404.

ACCORD AND SATISFACTION
Affirmative defense, Rule 8(c).

ACCOUNTS AND ACCOUNTING
Complaint in action on, form of, Form 4.
Default judgment, necessity of taking account, Rule 55(b)(2).
Masters, statement of accounts, Rule 53(d)(3); Auth. Comm. Rule 53(d)(3).
Reference to master, Rule 53(b).
Stay of judgment for accounting for infringement, Rule 62(a); Auth. Comm. Rule 62(a).

ACCUSED
Character evidence, Evid. Rule 404.
Juvenile adjudication of witness other than, evidence of, impeachment of witness, Evid. Rule 609.
Self-incrimination privilege not waived when examined respecting matters relating only to credibility, Evid. Rule 608.

ACCUSED—Cont'd
Testimony on preliminary matter, cross-examination as to other issues, Evid. Rule 104.

ACTIONS AND PROCEEDINGS
Appeal and Review, generally, this index.
Applicability of rules, Rule 81(a); Evid. Rule 1101; Auth. Comm. Rules 2 and 81(a).
Capacity to Sue or Be Sued, Rule 17(b).
Civil action, one form of action, Rule 2; Auth. Comm. Rule 2.
Class Actions, generally, this index.
Commencement, Rule 3; Auth. Comm. Rule 3.
Consolidation for trial or hearing, Rule 42(a); Auth. Comm. Rule 42(a).
Costs, generally, this index.
Counterclaims, generally, this index.
Criminal Actions and Procedure, generally, this index.
Cross-Claims, generally, this index.
Default Judgments, generally, this index.
Dismissal, generally, this index.
Evidence, generally, this index.
Factual findings resulting from investigation, hearsay exception, Evid. Rule 803.
Governed by original rules and amendments, Rule 86; Auth. Comm. Rule 86.
In rem, maritime, third-party complaint, Rule 14(a).
Independent action for relief from judgment, Rule 60(b).
Injunction, generally, this index.
Instructions to Jury, generally, this index.
Interpleader, generally, this index.
Intervention, generally, this index.
Joinder, generally, this index.
Judgments and Decrees, generally, this index.
Jury, generally, this index.
Miscellaneous proceedings, inapplicability, Evid. Rule 1101.
Motions, generally, this index.
Parties, generally, this index.
Petitory Actions, generally, this index.
Possessory Actions, generally, this index.
Presumptions, generally, this index.
Privileges and Immunities, generally, this index.
Process, generally, this index.
Real Party in Interest, Rule 17(a).
Rules as governing, Evid. Rule 101.
Shareholders, derivative actions, Rule 23.1.
Statutory proceedings, Auth. Comm. Rule 1.
Sureties, proceedings against, Rule 65.1.
Termination of action as to claim or party disposed of by judgment, Rule 54(b).
Third-Party Practice, generally, this index.
Trial, generally, this index.
Trial By Court, generally, this index.
Unincorporated associations, Rule 23.2.
Verdict, generally, this index.
Witnesses, generally, this index.

ADDRESS
Letters rogatory, Rule 28(b).
Plaintiff's address to appear in summons, Rule 4(b).

ADJOURNMENT
Master's proceeding, failure of party to appear at time and place appointed, Rule 53(d); Auth. Comm. Rule 53(d).

ADJUDICATIVE FACTS
Judicial notice, Evid. Rule 201.

ADMINISTRATION
Fairness in, purpose and construction of rules, Evid. Rule 102.

ADMINISTRATIVE OFFICE OF THE UNITED STATES COURTS
Clerk to keep records required by director, Rule 79(d).
Director to prescribe form of civil docket, Rule 79(a).

ADMINISTRATORS
Prosecution of action, Rule 17(a).

ADMIRALTY OR MARITIME CLAIMS
FRCP Supplemental Rules, Rules A-F.

ADMISSIBILITY OF EVIDENCE
See, also, Relevant Evidence, generally, this index.
Authentication, generally, this index.
Business records, 28 U.S.C.A. § 1732.
Character Evidence, generally, this index.
Compromise and offers to compromise, Evid. Rule 408.
Confessions, hearings on, conducting out of hearing of jury, Evid. Rule 104.
Control, subsequent remedial measures to prove, Evid. Rule 407.
Court records, 28 U.S.C.A. §§ 1734-35.
Depositions, use in court proceedings, Rule 32(a); Auth. Comm. Rule 32(a).
Objections to, Rule 32(b); Auth. Comm. Rule 32(b).
Foreign documents, 28 U.S.C.A. § 174.
Government records, 28 U.S.C.A. § 1733.
Guilty, offer to plead or withdrawn plea of, Evid. Rule 410.
Handwriting, 28 U.S.C.A. § 1731.
Hearsay, generally, this index.
Liability insurance, issue of negligence or wrongful action, Evid. Rule 411.
Limited admissibility, Evid. Rule 105.
Medical and similar expenses, payment, proof of liability for injury, Evid. Rule 409.
Nolo contendere, plea of or offer to plead, Evid. Rule 410.
Official foreign record, attested copy, Rule 44(a)(2); Auth. Comm. Rule 44(a)(2).
Opinions and Expert Testimony, generally, this index.
Ownership, subsequent remedial measures to prove, Evid. Rule 407.
Patent documents, 28 U.S.C.A. §§ 1744-1745.
Pendency of appeal, evidence of conviction of crime, impeachment of witness, Evid. Rule 609.
Postmaster demand, 28 U.S.C.A. § 1743.
Precautionary measures, feasibility, subsequent remedial measures to prove, Evid. Rule 407.
Preliminary questions concerning, court determination, Evid. Rule 104.

ADMISSIBILITY OF EVIDENCE—Cont'd
Prior inconsistent statement of witness, extrinsic evidence of, Evid. Rule 613.
Questions of, Evid. Rule 104.
Questions of fact preliminary to, inapplicability, Evid. Rule 1101.
Religious beliefs or opinions, Evid. Rule 610.
Remainder of or related writings or recorded statements, Evid. Rule 106.
Rulings on, objection, Evid. Rule 103.
Sex offenses, victims past behavior, Evid. Rule 412.
State and territorial records, 28 U.S.C.A. §§ 1738-1739.
Subsequent remedial measures, Evid. Rule 407.
Trial, insurance agreements, information concerning, Rule 26(b); Auth. Comm. Rule 26(b)(2).
Victims past behavior, sex offenses, Evid. Rule 412.

ADMISSIONS
Conference to obtain admissions of facts and documents, Rule 16; Auth. Comm. Rule 16.
Effect of, Rule 36(b); Auth. Comm. Rule 36(b).
Party opponent, hearsay, extrinsic evidence of prior inconsistent statement of witness, applicability, provisions respecting, Evid. Rule 613.
Pending action only, Rule 36(b); Auth. Comm. Rule 36(b).
Pleading, failure to deny, Rule 8(d); Auth. Comm. Rule 8.
Prohibition against use in other proceedings, Rule 36(b).
Requests for, Rule 36; Auth. Comm. Rule 36.
See, also, Discovery, generally, this index.
Answer, service, requisites of, etc., Rule 36(a); Auth. Comm. Rule 36(a).
Copies of documents served with, Rule 36(a); Auth. Comm. Rule 36(a).
Denials, Auth. Comm. Rule 36(a).
Effect of admission, Rule 36(b); Auth. Comm. Rule 36(b).
Expenses,
Award of, Rule 36(a); Auth. Comm. Rule 36(a).
Failure to admit genuineness of document or truth of matter requested, Rule 37(c); Auth. Comm. Rule 37(c).
Failure to respond, Auth. Comm. Rule 36(a).
Form of, Form 25.
Method of obtaining discovery, Rule 26(a); Auth. Comm. Rule 26(a).
Motion to determine sufficiency of answers or objections, Rule 36(a); Auth. Comm. Rule 36(a).
Objections, service, requisites of, etc., Rule 36(a); Auth. Comm. Rule 36(a).
Orders, sufficiency of answers or objections, Rule 36(a).
Pre-trial conference or prior to trial, final disposition, Rule 36(a).
Scope, Rule 36(a); Auth. Comm. Rule 36(a).
Scope of, Rule 26(b); Auth. Comm. Rule 26(b).
Service, time of, Rule 36(a); Auth. Comm. Rule 36(a).
Stipulations, extension of time, responses to, approval of court, Rule 29.
Summary judgment rendered where admissions show no genuine issue, etc., Rule 56(c).
Supplementing responses, Auth. Comm. Rules 26(e) and 36(a).
Withdrawal or amendment, Rule 36(b); Auth. Comm. Rule 36(b).
Writings, recordings or photographs, contents of proved by, Evid. Rule 1007.

ADOPTION
Hearsay exception,
Reputation concerning, Evid. Rule 803.
Statement of declarant concerning, Evid. Rule 804.
Written statement as prior statement concerning action or subject matter made by party or person, obtaining of discovery, Rule 26(b); Auth. Comm. Rule 26(b)(3).

ADOPTION BY REFERENCE
Auth. Comm. Rules 10(b) and (c).

ADVANCEMENT
Causes on docket, Rule 78.

ADVERSE PARTIES
Parties, this index.

ADVISORY COMMITTEE NOTES
Generally, Part VII (text of original Notes and Notes to amendments)
Effect, Auth. Comm. Rule 1.

ADVISORY JURY
Trial by court with advisory jury, Rules 39(c) and 52(a); Auth. Comm. Rule 39(c).

AFFIDAVITS
Contempt for filing affidavit for summary judgment in bad faith, Rule 56(g); Auth. Comm. Rule 56(g).
Default judgment, Rule 55; Auth. Comm. Rule 55.
Motion based on facts appearing of record, hearing on affidavits, Rule 43(e); Auth. Comm. Rule 7(b).
New trial, time for serving no motion for, Rule 59(c).
Opposing affidavits,
Made in bad faith, Rule 56(g).
Time for service, Rule 6(d).
Rule 11, effect on, Auth. Comm. Rule 11.
Service of Process, this index.
Summary judgment, Rule 56.
Temporary restraining order, notice, Rule 65(b).

AFFIRMATIONS
Oaths and Affirmations, generally, this index.

AFFIRMATIVE DEFENSES
Pleading, Rule 8(c); Auth. Comm. Rule 8(c).
Reply to, Auth. Comm. Rule 7(a)
Service of pleadings, numerous defendants, Rule 5(c).
Sua Sponte assertion, Auth. Comm. Rule 8.

AGE
Witness, inability to attend or testify, depositions, use in court proceedings, Rule 32(a); Auth. Comm. Rule 32(a).

AGENCIES OF UNITED STATES
Actions of, set aside by reviewing authority, facts subject to trial de novo, rules applicable in part, Evid. Rule 1101.

AGENCIES OF UNITED STATES—Cont'd
Amended pleadings against the United States, Rule 15(c)(3).
Answer or reply, time for service, Rule 12(a).
Appeal, stay without bond or security, Rule 62(e).
Definition of, 28 U.S.C.A. § 451.
Depositions,
Introduction in evidence as making deponent witness of introducing party, nonapplicability, Rule 32(c).
Oral examination, Rule 30(b).
Failure of officer, etc., to attend at own deposition, sanctions, Rule 37(d).
Failure to comply with order compelling designation, sanctions, Rule 37(b).
Motion for order compelling designation, Rule 37(a).
Use in court proceedings, Rule 32(a).
Written questions, Rule 31(a).
Failure of officer, etc., to attend at own deposition, sanctions, Rule 37(d).
Failure to comply with order compelling answer, sanctions, Rule 37(b).
Motion for order compelling answer, Rule 37(a).
Documents of under or not under seal, self-authentication, Evid. Rule 902.
Interrogatories, service of, Rule 33(a).
Process, amendment of pleading, change of party, Rule 15(c).
Records and reports, hearsay exception, Evid. Rule 803.
Restraining order or preliminary injunction, security, Rule 65(c).
Service of summons and complaint, Rules 4(d)(4), (5).
Subpoena,
Application of rules, Rule 81(a).
Naming as deponent and advising nonparty organization as to designation of officers, etc., Rule 30(b).
Tender of fees and mileage, Rule 45(b).
Suits in the name of the United States, Rule 17(a).

AGENTS AND AGENCY
Consular agent, authentication of official record, Rule 44(a).
Discovery, trial and litigation, need of materials, Rule 26(b).
Hearsay, statements by agents which are not, Evid. Rule 801.
Liability, insurance against, admissibility to prove agency, Evid. Rule 411.
Managing Agent, generally, this index.
Service of process,
Agent of United States, Rules 4(d)(4), (5).
Process, admiralty or maritime claims, actions in rem and quasi in rem, Supp. Rule E(4)(b).
Summons and complaint, Rule 4(d).

AGGREGATION
Satisfying requirements for amount in controversy, Jurisdiction, Juris. § 2.12.

AGREEMENTS, PARTIES
Physical and mental examinations, Rule 35(b); Auth. Comm. Rule 35(b).
Supplementing responses to request for discovery, Rule 26(e); Auth. Comm. Rule 26(e).

AGRICULTURAL PRODUCTS OR COMMODITIES
Associations of producers, monopolizing or restraining trade, cease and desist orders, review, rules applicable in part, Evid. Rule 1101.

AIRCRAFT
Prize, applicability of rules in part, Evid. Rule 1101.

ALIENS
Venue and, Venue, Juris. § 2.14.

ALTERATION
Class actions, orders, Rule 23(d).
Judgment,
Stay of proceedings pending motion for, Rule 62(b).
Time for service of motion for, Rule 59(e).
Order, class action maintainable, determination, Rule 23(c).

AMBIGUITIES IN PLEADINGS
Motion to make more definite statement, Rule 12(e); Auth. Comm. Rule 12(e).

AMENDMENT
Admission, Rule 36(b).
Class actions, orders, Rule 23(d).
Conclusions of law on motion for new trial, Rule 59(a).
Effective date of amendments to rules, Rule 86.
Findings of court, Rule 52(b); Auth. Comm. Rule 52(b).
Extension of time, Rule 6(b).
Motion for new trial, Rule 59(a).
Stay of proceedings to enforce judgment pending disposition of motion to amend, Rule 62(b); Auth. Comm. Rule 62(b).
Judgments and decrees,
Stay of proceedings pending motion for, Rule 62(b); Auth. Comm. Rule 62(b).
Time for service of motion, Rule 59(e).
Method of, Evid. Rule 1102.
Order, class action maintainable, determination, Rule 23(c).
Pleadings, Rule 15.
Admiralty and maritime claims, identifying statement, Rule 9(h).
Class actions, orders, Rule 23(d).
Commencement of amended complaints, Auth. Comm. Rule 3.
Condemnation proceedings, Rule 71A(f).
Conform to evidence, Rule 15(b).
Omission, defense, waiver, Rule 12(h).
Omitted counterclaims, Rule 13(f).
Pre-trial procedure, Rule 16.
Relation back, Rule 15(c).
Right to Amend, Rule 15(a).
Prior responses to request for discovery, Rule 26(e); Auth. Comm. Rule 26(e).
Process or proof of service, Rule 4(h).
Rules by district courts, Rule 83.
Rules of Criminal Procedure, provisions concerning offer to plead guilty, nolo contendere, etc., Evid. Rule 410.
Serving amended complaints, Auth Comm. Rule 4.
Substitution of parties, rule 25.

AMOUNT
Jurisdiction, form of allegation, Form 2.
Liability, determination, further proceedings, offer of judgment, Rule 68.

AMOUNT IN CONTROVERSY
Subject matter jurisdiction, Jurisdiction, Juris. § 2.12.

ANCIENT DOCUMENTS
Authentication and identification, conformity with requirements, Evid. Rule 901.
Statements in, hearsay exception, Evid. Rule 803.

ANCILLARY PROCESS
Admiralty or maritime claims, actions in rem, Supp. Rule C(5).

ANNEXATION
Exhibits, depositions upon oral examination, Rule 30(f); Auth. Comm. Rule 30(f).

ANNOYANCE
Depositions upon oral examination, motion to terminate or limit, Rule 30(d); Auth. Comm. Rule 30(d).
Protective orders relating to depositions, grounds for, Rule 26(c).

ANNULMENT
Conviction, subject of, impeachment of witness by evidence of conviction of crime, effect, Evid. Rule 609.

ANSWER
Pleadings, this index.

ANTI-SMUGGLING ACT
Appealability, Auth. Comm. Appeals.
Fines, penalties and forfeitures, action for, applicability of rules in part, Evid. Rule 1101.

APPEAL AND REVIEW
Generally, Part IV.
Admiralty, Auth. Comm. Appeals
Admissibility of evidence, pendency of appeal, impeachment of witness by evidence of conviction of crime, Evid. Rule 609.
Agricultural products, association of producers, monopolizing or restraining trade, cease and desist orders, rules applicable in part, Evid. Rule 1101.
Aliens, action respecting naturalization and revocation thereof, rules applicable in part, Evid. Rule 1101.
Appealability, Auth. Comm. Appeals.
Application of rules to, Rules 81(a)(2), (3).
Aquatic products, cease and desist orders, restraint of trade by association engaged in catching, etc., applicability of rules in part, Evid. Rule 1101.
Availability to appellate court, withheld portion of writing used to refresh memory, Evid. Rule 612.
Briefing during, Appeals § 6.6.
Collateral orders, Appeals § 6.2.
Correction of clerical errors in judgments, orders and record during pendency of appeal, Rule 60(a).
Costs, taxation by clerk, Rule 54(d).
Court of appeals, appeals to, notice, form, Form 27.
Depositions pending appeal, Rule 27(b); Auth. Comm. Rule 27(b).
District of Columbia courts, application of rules to appeals, Rule 81(a)(1).
Extension of time for taking appeal to court of appeals, Rule 6(b).

APPEAL AND REVIEW—Cont'd

Federal agency actions set aside by reviewing court, facts subject to trial de novo, rules applicable in part, Evid. Rule 1101.
Fees on filing notice of appeal, 28 U.S.C.A. § 1917.
Final orders, Appeals. § 6.2.
Findings by court, request for purpose of review, Rule 52(a).
Habeas corpus cases, certification of probable cause in certain cases, Rule 81(a).
Harmless errors, Rule 61; 28 U.S.C.A. § 2111.
Injunction,
  Appealability, Auth. Comm. Appeals.
  Pending appeal, Rule 62(c); Auth. Comm. Rule 62(c).
  Suspending, modifying or granting by appellate court pending appeal, Rule 62(g); Auth. Comm. Rule 62(g).
Interlocutory orders, Appeals. § 6.2.
Judgment,
  Copy, clerk to keep correct copy of final judgment, Rule 79(b).
  Triggering time for appeal, Auth. Comm. Rule 58.
Longshoremen's and Harbor Workers' Compensation Act, review, application of rules, Rule 81(a)(6).
Magistrate judges,
  Judgment entered upon direction of, Rule 73(c), (d); Auth. Comm. Rule 73(c), (d).
  Judgment of district judge on appeal by consent, Rule 76; Auth. Comm. Rule 76.
  Method of appeal to district judge, Rule 74; Auth. Comm. Rule 74.
  Proceedings on appeal to district judge, Rule 75; Auth. Comm. Rule 75.
Notice of appeal, form on appeal to, Form 27; Auth. Comm. Appeals; Appeals § 6.4.
Oral argument, Appeals, § 6.6.
Pendency of appeal,
  As not rendering evidence of conviction inadmissible, impeachment by evidence of conviction of crime, Evid. Rule 609.
  Judgment of previous conviction, admissibility, hearsay exception, Evid. Rule 803.
Perishable agricultural products, unfair conduct, reparation order respecting, rules applicable in part, Evid. Rule 1101.
Petroleum products, application for certificate of clearance for shipment in interstate commerce, order denying, applicability of rules in part, Evid. Rule 1101.
Post-trial motions, effect of, Appeals § 6.3.
Preliminary injunction, Auth. Comm. Rule 65(a).
Procedure for appeals, Auth. Comm. Appeals.
Receivers, Auth. Comm. Appeals.
Record on appeal, service, Rule 5(a).
Relief from failure to appeal within time, lack of notice of entry of judgment, Rule 77(d); Auth. Comm. Rule 77(d).
Status quo, order preserving pending appeal, Rule 62(g).
Stay pending appeal, Rule 62; Auth. Comm. Rule 62; Appeals § 6.5; 28 U.S.C.A. § 2283.
Supersedeas bond, Rule 62(d); Auth. Comm. Rule 62(d).
Supreme Court, appeals to, Appeals § 6.7.
Temporary restraining order, Auth. Comm. Rule 65(b).

APPEAL AND REVIEW—Cont'd
Time,
Appeal to court of appeals, Rule 6(b); Auth. Comm. Appeals.
Extension of time for taking, Rule 6(b); Auth. Comm. Appeals.
Lack of notice of entry of judgment, Rule 77(d); Auth. Comm. Rule 77(d).
Premature appeals, Auth. Comm. Appeals
Supersedeas bond, giving, Rule 62(d); Auth. Comm. Rule 62(d).

APPEARANCE
Generally, 28 U.S.C.A. § 1654.
Admiralty or maritime claims, actions in rem and quasi in rem, restricted, Supp. Rule E(8).
Authentication and identification, conformity with requirements, Evid. Rule 901.
Civil docket entry in, Rule 79(a).
Condemnation proceedings, Rule 71A(e); Auth. Comm. Rule 71A(e).
Required for service, Rule 5(a); Auth. Comm. Rule 5(a).
"Special" appearance, Auth. Comm. Rule 12(b)(2).

APPLICATION
Bankruptcy proceedings, Rule 81(a)(1).
Intervention, Rule 24.
Personal property, rules governing procedure for condemnation, Rule 71A(a); Auth. Comm. Rule 71A(a).
Preliminary injunction, consolidation, hearing with trial on merits, Rule 65(a)(2).

APPOINTMENT
Interpreters, Rule 43(f); Auth. Comm. Rule 43(f).
Master, Rule 53(a); Auth. Comm. Rule 53(a).
Persons for service of process, Rule 4(c).
Receivers, Auth. Comm. Rule 66.

AQUATIC PRODUCTS
Cease and desist orders, restraint of trade by association engaged in catching, etc., applicability of rules in part, Evid. Rule 1101.

ARBITRATION AND AWARD
Affirmative defenses, Rule 8(c).
Applicability of rules to, Rule 81(a)(3); Auth. Comm. Rule 81(a).

ARREST
Satisfaction of judgment ultimately to be entered, Rule 64.
Third-party complaint references, admiralty and maritime claims, Rule 14(a).
United States vessels, etc., exemptions, supplemental rules inapplicable, Supp. Rule C(1).
Warrants, issuance, proceedings for, inapplicability, Evid. Rule 1101.

ARTS
Learned treatises, statements in, hearsay exception, Evid. Rule 803.

ASSESSOR
Included in term "master", Rule 53(a).

ASSIGNMENT OF ERRORS ON APPEAL
Instructions, giving or failure to give, Rule 51.

ASSISTANCE
Writ of, possession, delivery of, Rule 70; Auth. Comm. Rule 70.

ASSISTANT UNITED STATES ATTORNEY
Service on of summons and complaint against United States, Rule 4(d)(4).

ASSOCIATIONS AND SOCIETIES
Capacity to sue or be sued, Rule 17(b).
Depositions,
Introduction in evidence as making deponent witness of introducing party, nonapplicability, Rule 32(c).
Oral examination, Rule 30(b); Auth. Comm. Rule 30(b)(6).
Failure of officer, director, etc., to attend at own deposition, sanctions, Rule 37(d); Auth. Comm. Rule 37(d).
Failure to comply with order compelling designation, sanctions, Rule 37(b).
Motion for order compelling designation, Rule 37(a).
Use in court proceedings, Rule 32(a).
Written questions, Rule 31(a); Auth. Comm. Rule 31(a).
Failure of officer, director, etc., to attend at own deposition, sanctions, Rule 37(d); Auth. Comm. Rule 37(d).
Motion for order compelling answer, Rule 37(a).
Interrogatories, service of, Rule 33(a).
Officer, director or managing agent of adverse party, examination and cross examination, Rule 43(b).
Pleading capacity to sue or be sued, Rule 9(a).
Service on, Rule 4(d); Auth. Comm. Rule 4(d).
Subpoena, naming as deponent and advising nonparty, organization as to designation of officers, etc., Rule 30(b); Auth. Comm. Rule 30(b)(6).
Unincorporate associations, Rule 23.2; Auth. Comm. Rule 23.2.
Witnesses, interrogation, Rule 43(b).

ASSUMPTION OF RISK
Affirmative defense, Rule 8(c).

ATTACHMENT
Opposing party bringing suit upon claim, court not acquiring jurisdiction to render personal judgment pleader need not state claim, Rule 13(a).
Property of person disobeying judgment directing performance of specific acts, Rule 70; Auth. Comm. Rule 70.
Seizure of person or property, availability of remedy, Rule 64.

ATTACKING CREDIBILITY OF WITNESSES
Credibility of Witnesses, this index.

ATTESTATION
Official records, authentication, Rule 44(a); Auth. Comm. Rule 44(a).

ATTORNEY GENERAL
Notice of intervention, Rule 24(c).
Process, amendment of pleading, change of party, Rule 15(c).
Service of summons and complaint against United States, Rule 4(d)(4).

ATTORNEY'S FEES
Class Actions, Auth. Comm. Rule 23.
Costs, Auth. Comm. Rule 54(d).

ATTORNEY'S FEES—Cont'd
Depositions,
Failure of party to attend at own deposition, Rule 37(d); Auth. Comm. Rule 37(d).
Oral examination, failure to attend or to serve subpoena, payment, Rule 30(g); Auth. Comm. Rule 30(g).
Discovery,
Failure to comply with order compelling, Rule 37(b); Auth. Comm. Rule 37(b).
Requests, signing of, sanctions, Rule 26(g); Auth. Comm. Rule 26(g).
Documents, failure to admit genuineness, Rule 37(c).
Entry upon land, etc., for inspection and other purposes, failure of party to respond to request for inspection, Rule 37(d).
Interrogatories, failure of party to serve answers to, Rule 37(d).
Motion for order to compel discovery, Rule 37(a); Auth. Comm. Rule 37(a).
Offer of judgment, Auth. Comm. Rule 68.
Pleadings, motions, etc., signing of, sanctions, Rule 11.
Pretrial conference, failure to appear, sanctions, Rule 16(f).
Pretrial order, failure to obey, sanctions, Rule 16(f).
Production of documents or things, failure of party to respond to request for inspection, Rule 37(d).
Scheduling conference, failure to appear, sanctions, Rule 16(f).
Scheduling order, failure to obey, sanctions, Rule 16(f).
Summary judgment, fees imposed on person filing affidavit in bad faith, Rule 56(g).
Truth of matter, failure to admit, Rule 37(c); Auth. Comm. Rule 37(c).
United States, discovery proceedings, Rule 37(f).

ATTORNEYS
Appearances, 28 U.S.C.A. § 1654.
Depositions upon oral examination, notice, signing certification, Rule 30(b).
Discovery, trial and litigation preparation, need of materials, Rule 26(b); Auth. Comm. Rule 26(b)(3).
Fees. Attorney's Fees, generally, this index.
Interpleader, Auth. Comm. Rule 22.
Interrogatories, signing answers to, Rule 33(a); Auth. Comm. Rule 33(a).
Master, submission of draft of report for suggestions, Rule 53(e).
Notice,
Court of proposed action upon requests for instructions, Rule 51.
Meeting on order of reference, Rule 53(d); Auth. Comm. Rule 53(d).
Temporary restraining order, Rule 65(b).
Officer or employee of party not natural person designated as representative by attorney, exclusion, provisions governing exclusion of witnesses as not authorizing, Evid. Rule 615.
Pleadings, signing by attorney of record, Rule 11.
Pre-trial conference, Rule 16.
Prior statements of witnesses, request to show or disclose to opposing counsel, Evid. Rule 613.
Service of process,
Admiralty or maritime claims, limitation of liability, Supp. Rule F(4).
Pleadings, etc., Rule 5(b).
Service upon attorneys, Auth. Comm. Rule 4.

ATTORNEYS—Cont'd
Signature, answers or objections to requests for admission, Rule 36(a).
Submission, forms of judgment, Rule 58.
Summons to state name and address of plaintiff's attorney, Rule 4(b).

AUDIT
Business records, interrogatories, Rule 33(c).

AUDITA QUERELA
Writ abolished, Rule 60(b).

AUDITOR
Included in term "master," Rule 53(a).

AUTHENTICATION
Acknowledged documents, self-authentication, Evid. Rule 902.
Ancient documents, conformity with requirements, Evid. Rule 901.
Commercial paper and related documents, self-authentication, Evid. Rule 902.
Comparison by trier or expert witness, conformity with requirements, Evid. Rule Rule 901.
Contents, conformity with requirements, Evid. Rule 901.
Data compilation, conformity with requirements, Evid. Rule 901.
Distinctive characteristics and the like, conformity with requirements, Evid. Rule 901.
Extrinsic evidence of authenticity, condition precedent to admissibility not required respecting certain documents, etc., Evid. Rule 902.
General provisions, Evid. Rule 901.
Illustrations, Evid. Rule 901.
Methods provided by statute or rule, Evid. Rule 901.
Newspapers and periodicals, self-authentication, Evid. Rule 902.
Nonexpert opinion on handwriting, conformity with requirements, Evid. Rule 901.
Notary public, documents accompanied by certificate of acknowledgment executed by, self-authentication, Evid. Rule 902.
Official publications, self-authentication, Evid. Rule 902.
Official record, Rule 44(a); Auth. Comm. Rule 44(a).
Presumptions under Acts of Congress, genuineness or authenticity of signature, document or other matter, Evid. Rule 902.
Process or system used to produce result, etc., conformity with requirements, Evid. Rule 901.
Proof of identification, admissibility of other crimes, wrongs or acts, Evid. Rule 404.
Public records and reports, conformity with requirements, Evid. Rule 901.
Requirement of, Evid. Rule 901.
Self-authentication, Evid. Rule 902.
Subscribing witness, testimony unnecessary, Evid. Rule 903.
Telephone conversations, conformity with requirements, Evid. Rule 901.
Testimony of witness with knowledge, conformity with requirements, Evid. Rule 901.
Trade inscriptions and the like, self-authentication, Evid. Rule 902.
Voice identification, conformity with requirements, Evid. Rule 901.

AVOIDANCE
Pleading matters constituting an avoidance, Rule 8(c).

AVOIDANCE—Cont'd
Service of pleadings, numerous defendants, Rule 5(c).

BAD FAITH
Affidavits in support of summary judgment, Rule 56(g).
Depositions upon oral examination, motion to terminate or limit, Rule 30(d); Auth. Comm. Rule 30(d).
Motions, pleadings and other documents filed in court, Rule 11.

BAIL
Release on, proceedings, inapplicability, Evid. Rule 1101.

BAILEES
Prosecution of action, Rule 17(a).

BANKRUPTCY
Applicability of rules, Evid. Rules 101, 1101.

BAPTISMAL RECORDS
Hearsay exception, Evid. Rule 803.

BIAS OR PREJUDICE
Compromise and offers to compromise claims, admissibility of evidence to prove, Evid. Rule 408.
Exclusion of relevant evidence on grounds of unfair prejudice, Evid. Rule 403.
Extraneous prejudicial information improperly brought to jury's attention, testimony of juror respecting, Evid. Rule 606.
Insurance against liability, evidence of, admissibility to prove, Evid. Rule 411.

BIBLES
Hearsay exception, statements in bible concerning personal or family history, Evid. Rule 803.

BILLS OF REVIEW
Abolished, Rule 60(b).

BIRTHS
Hearsay, this index.

BIVENS ACTIONS
Service issues in, Auth. Comm. Rule 4.

BOARDS AND COMMISSIONS
Pleading decision, Rule 9(e).

BONDS (OFFICERS AND FIDUCIARIES)
General bond, admiralty or maritime claims, actions in rem and quasi in rem, release, property, Supp. Rules E(5)(b), (c).
Injunction pending appeal, Rule 62(c).
Interpleader, Auth. Comm. Rule 22 and Statutory Interpleader.
Preliminary injunction, Rule 65(c); Auth. Comm. Rule 65(c).
Proceedings against sureties, Rule 65.1.
Removal, abolition of requirement for bond, Removal, Juris. § 2.17.
Shareholder derivative suits, Auth. Comm. Rule 23.1.
Special bond, admiralty or maritime claims, actions in rem and quasi in rem, release, property, Supp.Rules E(5)(a) to (c).
Stay pending appeal, Rule 62.
Surety, Rule 65.1.

BONDS (OFFICERS AND FIDUCIARIES)—Cont'd
Temporary restraining order, Rule 65(c); Auth. Comm. Rule 65(c).

BOOKS AND PAPERS
Clerk to keep, Rule 79(d).
Discovery, scope of, Rule 26(b).
Documents, generally, this index.
Master, compelling production, Rule 53(c).
Official, self-authentication, Evid. Rule 902.
Subpoena for production, Rule 45(a); Auth. Comm. Rule 45(a).

BOUNDARIES
Reputation concerning or judgment as to, hearsay exception, Evid. Rule 803.

BRIEFS
Appeal from magistrate to district judge, Rule 75(c), (d); Auth. Comm. Rule 75(c), (d).
Appeal to courts of appeal, Auth. Comm. Appeals.
Supporting or opposing Motions, Auth. Comm. Rule 7(b).

BURDEN OF PROOF
Class Certification, Auth. Comm. Rule 23.
Presumption as not shifting, Evid. Rule 301.

BUSINESS RECORDS
Admissibility, 28 U.S.C.A. § 1732.
Interrogatories, option to produce, Rule 33(c); Auth. Comm. Rule 33(c).

CALENDARS
Assignment of cases for trial, Rule 40; Auth. Comm. Rule 40.
Clerk to prepare, Rule 79(c).
Declaratory judgment case advanced on calendar, Rule 57.
Pre-trial calendar, establishment by rule, Rule 16.

CANAL ZONE
Documents of under or not under seal, self-authentication, Evid. Rule 902.

CAPACITY
Capacity to sue or be sued, Rule 17(b).
Pleading capacity of party, Rule 9(a); Auth. Comm. Rule 9(a).

CAPITAL PUNISHMENT
Death Penalty, generally, this index.

CAPTIONS
Alterations to, effect of, Auth. Comm. Rule 10(a).
Motions and other papers, Rule 7(b).
Names of parties, Auth. Comm. Rule 10(a).
Pleading, Rule 10(a); Auth. Comm. Rule 10(a).

CASES
Same as civil actions, Auth. Comm. Rule 2.

CERTIFICATE OF SERVICE
Filing, Rule 5(d).

CERTIFICATES AND CERTIFICATION
See, also, specific index headings.
Attorneys, temporary restraining order, notice, Rule 65(b).
Authentication of official record, Rule 44(a); Auth. Comm. Rule 44(a).
Class Actions, Rule 23(c); Auth. Comm. Rule 23(c).
Depositions,
Oral examination, officer taking, Rule 30(f).
Written questions, officer taking, Rule 31(a).
Foreign public documents, signature and official position of executing or attesting person, etc., Evid. Rule 902.
Marriage, baptismal, etc., hearsay exception, Evid. Rule 803.
Probable cause in certain appeals in habeas corpus cases, Rule 81(a).

CERTIFIED COPIES
Public records, self-authentication, Evid. Rule 902.
Summary judgment, copies attached to affidavit supporting or opposing, Rule 56(e).

CERTIFIED MAIL
Depositions upon oral examination, filing of, Rule 30(f).
Service of summons and complaint on United States or officers or agencies thereof, Rule 4(d).

CERTIFIED PUBLIC ACCOUNTANT
Statement of accounts, evidence before master, Rule 53(d)(3); Auth. Comm. Rule 53(d)(3).

CHALLENGES
Jury, Rule 47(b); Auth. Comm. Rule 47(b).

CHAMBERS
Business which may be conducted at, Rule 77(b); Auth. Comm. Rule 77(b).

CHANGES
Depositions upon oral examination, form or substance, Rule 30(e); Auth. Comm. Rule 30(e).
Party, amendment of pleading, relation back, Rule 15(c).

CHARACTER EVIDENCE
Generally, Evid. Rule 404.
Accused, Evid. Rule 404.
Hearsay exception, reputation as to character, Evid. Rule 803.
Methods of proving character, Evid. Rule 405.
Not admissible to prove conduct, exceptions, Evid. Rule 404.
Notice, prosecution intent to use, evidence of other crimes, Evid. Rule 404.
Opinion. Reputation or opinion evidence, generally, post.
Other crimes, wrongs or acts, evidence of, admissibility, Evid. Rule 404.
Reputation or opinion evidence, Evid. Rule 608.
Methods of proving character, Evid. Rule 405.
Specific instances of conduct, methods of proving character, Evid. Rule 405.
Victims, Evid. Rule 404.
Witnesses, Evid. Rules 404, 607 to 609.

CHARGES
Copies, depositions upon oral examination, Rule 30(f); Auth. Comm. Rule 30(f).

CHARTS

Hearsay exception, statement of fact concerning personal or family history contained in, Evid. Rule 803.

Production of documents or things, generally, post.

CHILDREN

Infants, generally, this index.

CHRISTMAS DAY

Clerks of court, business hours for office, exception concerning opening, Rule 77(c).

"Legal holiday" as including for purposes of computing time, Rule 6(a).

CITATION

Generally, Evid. Rule 1103.

Rules cited as Federal Rules of Civil Procedure, Rule 85.

CITIZENSHIP

Diversity, jurisdiction, form of allegation, Form 2.

Diversity of citizenship, cases involving, competency of witnesses, determination, Evid. Rule 601.

Proceedings for admission to citizenship, applicability of rules to, Rules 81(a)(2), (6).

Subject matter jurisdiction, Jurisdiction, Juris. § 2.12.

CIVIL ACTIONS

Actions and Proceedings, generally, this index.

CIVIL DOCKET

See Docket

CLAIMANT

Interpleader, Rule 22 and Statutory Interpleader; Auth. Comm. Rule 22 and Statutory Interpleader.

Third-party practice references, admiralty and maritime claims, Rule 14(a).

CLAIMS

Character or trait of character as essential element, proof of specific instances of conduct, Evid. Rule 405.

Competency of witness, state law as determining unless federal law supplies rule of decision, Evid. Rule 601.

Compromise and offers to compromise, admissibility, Evid. Rule 408.

Discovery, sanctions for failure to comply with order compelling, refusal to allow support or opposition to, Rule 37(b).

Joinder, Rule 18(a).

Privilege of witness, person, etc., state law as determining unless federal law supplies rule of decision, Evid. Rule 501.

United States Claims Court, generally, this index.

CLASS ACTIONS

Generally, Rule 23.

Joinder, persons needed for just adjudication, Rule 19(d).

Shareholders, derivative actions, Rule 23.1.

Unincorporated associations, actions relating to, Rule 23.2.

CLASS REPRESENTATIVES

Generally, Rule 23(a); Auth. Comm. Rule 23.

CLERGY

Marriage, baptismal and similar certificates, statements respecting, hearsay exception, Evid. Rule 803.

CLERICAL MISTAKES

Correction of, Rule 60(a).

CLERKS OF COURT

Agent, service, surety, proceedings against, Rule 65.1.
Books kept by clerk, Rule 79.
Business hours, Rule 77(c); Auth. Comm. Rule 77(c).
Calendars to be prepared by, Rule 79(c).
Chambers, attendance of clerk at, Rule 77(b).
Copy of,
  Final judgment or appealable order to be kept, Rule 79(b).
  Order of reference to be furnished to master, Rule 53(d).
Costs taxed by, Rule 54(d).
Default judgment entered by, Rules 55(a), (b)(1).
Entries in books kept by clerk of district court, Rule 79.
Execution to enforce judgment directing delivery of possession issued by, Rule 70.
Filing pleadings and papers with court, Rule 5(e).
Indexes for civil docket and civil judgments and orders, Rule 79(c).
Judgment,
  Entered by, Rule 58.
  Indices, Rule 79(c).
Local rule or order of district court, office to be opened for specified hours on Saturdays or particular legal holidays, Rule 77(c).
Master to file report with clerk, Rule 53(e); Auth. Comm. Rule 53(e)(1).
  Filing of report by master, Rule 53(e).
  Orders or judgments given by clerk, Rule 77(d); Auth. Comm. Rule 77(d).
Office, Rule 77(c).
Orders this index.
Records to be kept, Rule 79(d).
Release, property, admiralty or maritime claims, actions in rem and quasi in rem, Supp. Rule E(5)(c).
Review of taxation of costs by clerk, Rule 54(d).
Saturdays, Sundays and legal holidays, exception, business hours, Rule 77(c).
Service, pleading or other papers by leaving copy with clerk of court, Rule 5(b).
Summons, issuance, signature, and delivery for service on filing of complaint, Rule 4(a).
Writ of assistance issued by, Rule 70; Auth. Comm. Rule 70.

COLLECTOR OF CUSTOMS

Clearance of vessels, admiralty or maritime claims, actions in rem and quasi in rem, Supp. Rule E(4)(b).

COLLECTOR OF INTERNAL REVENUE

Judgment against, satisfaction of, Rule 69(b); Auth. Comm. Rule 69(b).

COLLUSIVE INVOCATION OF JURISDICTION

Subject matter jurisdiction, Jurisdiction, Juris. § 2.12.

COLUMBUS DAY

Clerks of court, business hours for office, exceptions concerning opening, Rule 77(c).

"Legal holiday" as including for purposes of computing time, Rule 6(a).

COMMENCEMENT OF ACTION

Diversity cases, Auth. Comm. Rule 3.

Federal question cases, Auth. Comm. Rule 3.

Filing of complaint, Rule 3.

Pauper and prisoner plaintiffs, Auth. Comm. Rule 3

COMMERCIAL PAPER

Self-authentication, Evid. Rule 902.

COMMISSION BY COURT

Foreign countries, persons authorized to take deposition, Rule 28(b); Auth. Comm. Rule 28(b).

COMMISSIONER

Included in term "master", Rule 53(a).

COMMITTEE

Incompetent person, action or defense, Rule 17(c).

COMMUNITIES

Reputation concerning boundaries or general history, hearsay exception, Evid. Rule 803.

COMPENSATION AND SALARIES

Experts appointed by court, Evid. Rule 706.

Interpreters, Rule 43(f); Auth. Comm. Rule 43(f).

Master, Rule 53(a); Auth. Comm. Rule 53(a).

COMPETENCY OF WITNESSES

Witnesses, this index.

COMPILATIONS

Business records, interrogatories, Rule 33(c).

COMPLAINT

Pleadings, this index.

COMPLICATED ISSUES

Reference to master, Rule 53(b).

COMPROMISE AND SETTLEMENT

Admissibility, Evid. Rule 408.

Class actions, Rule 23(e).

Derivative actions by shareholders, Rule 23.1.

Settlement Classes, Auth. Comm. Rule 23.

Unincorporated associations, actions relating to, Rule 23.2.

COMPULSORY

Counterclaims, pleading, Rule 13(a).

Process, admiralty or maritime claims, refusal by garnishee to answer, Supp. Rule B(3).

COMPUTERS

Printout, etc., shown to reflect data accurately, "original" as including, contents of writings, etc., Evid. Rule 1001.

CONCISENESS

Pleading, Rule 8(e)(1).

CONCLUSIONS OF LAW

Amendment on motion for new trial, Rule 59(a).
Findings by court, Rule 52(a); Auth. Comm. Rule 52(a).
Master, setting forth in report, Rule 53(e).

CONCURRENT JURISDICTION

Subject matter jurisdiction, Jurisdiction, Juris. § 2.11.

CONDEMNATION OF PROPERTY

Generally, Rule 71A; Auth. Comm. Rule 71A.
Commission, Rule 71A; Auth. Comm. Rule 71A(h).
Complaint, Form 29.
Criminal libel for under Federal Food, Drug and Cosmetic Act, applicability of rules in part, Evid. Rule 1101.
Notice, Form 28.

CONDITIONAL RULINGS

Grant of motion, judgment as a matter of law, Rule 50; Auth. Comm. Rule 50(c).

CONDITIONS PRECEDENT

Pleading, Rule 9(c); Auth. Comm. Rule 9(c).

CONFESSIONS

Hearings on, conducting out of hearing of jury, Evid. Rule 104.

CONFLICT OF LAWS

Capacity to sue or be sued, Rule 17(b).

CONGRESS

Authentication or identification, methods provided by, Evid. Rule 901.
Privilege of witnesses, etc., law governing, exception, Evid. Rule 501.
Relevant evidence admissible except as otherwise provided by Act of, Evid. Rule 402.
Signature, document or other matter, presumption of genuineness or authenticity, Act of respecting, Evid. Rule 902.

CONSENT

Parties,
Order for trial by jury, Rule 39(c); Auth. Comm. Rule 39(c).
Trial by court, Rule 39(a); Auth. Comm. Rule 39(a).
Withdrawal of demand for jury trial, Rule 38(d); Auth. Comm. Rule 38(d).
Personal jurisdiction, Jurisdiction, Juris. § 2.4.
Release, property, admiralty or maritime claims, actions in rem and quasi in rem, Supp. Rule E(5)(c).
Unanimity and removal, Removal.
Venue, generally, this index.

CONSERVATOR

Infant or incompetent, action or defense, Rule 17(c).

CONSIDERATION
Pleading failure of consideration as defense, Rule 8(c).

CONSOLIDATION
Actions for trial or hearing, Rule 42(a); Auth. Comm. Rule 42(a).
Defenses in motion, Rule 12(g); Auth. Comm. Rule 12(g).
Multidistrict Litigation Rules (Part V).
Pleadings to do justice, Rule 8(f).
Preliminary injunction hearing with trial on merits, Rule 65(a)(2).

CONSPIRACY
Statement by co-conspirator of party during course and in furtherance of, not hearsay, Evid. Rule 801.

CONSTITUTION OF UNITED STATES
Certifying constitutional questions, 28 U.S.C.A. § 2403.
Privilege of witnesses, etc., law governing, exception, Evid. Rule 501.
Relevant evidence admissible except as otherwise provided by, Evid. Rule 402.

CONSTRUCTION OF RULES
Generally, Auth. Comm. Rule 1; Evid. Rule 102.

CONSUL GENERAL
Foreign public documents, final certification, genuineness of signature, etc., Evid. Rule 902.

CONSULS AND CONSULAR AGENTS
Authentication of official record, Rule 44(a).
Depositions, taking, Rule 28(b).

CONSULTANTS
Discovery, trial and litigation, preparation, need of material, Rule 26(b); Auth. Comm. Rule 26(b)(4).

CONTEMPT
Applicability of rules to proceedings respecting, Evid. Rule 1101.
Depositions, refusal to answer, etc., Rule 37(b); Auth. Comm. Rule 37(b).
Discovery, sanction for failure to comply with order compelling, Rule 37(b); Auth. Comm. Rule 37(b).
Foreign country subpoenas, 28 U.S.C.A. § 1784.
Judgment directing performance of specific acts, disobedience, Rule 7.
Service, persons required to respond to order of commitment, places outside state but within United States, Rule 4(f).
Subpoena, disobedience, Rule 45(e); Auth. Comm. Rule 45(e).
Summary judgment, filing affidavit in bad faith, Rule 56(g).
Witnesses, failure to appear before master, Rule 53(d); Auth. Comm. Rule 53(d)(2).

CONTENTS, DEPOSITIONS UPON
Oral examination, notice of taking, Rule 30(b).
Written questions, notice, Rule 31(a).

CONTINUANCES
Summary judgment, continuance to procure opposing affidavit, Rule 56(f); Auth. Comm. Rule 56(f).

CONTRADICTING
Testimony of deponent, use of deposition in court proceedings, Rule 32(a); Auth. Comm. Rule 32(a).
Witnesses, Rule 43(b).

CONTRIBUTION
Liability, third-party practice, admiralty and maritime claims, Rule 14(c).

CONTRIBUTORY NEGLIGENCE
Affirmative defenses, Rule 8(c).

CONTROL
Inscriptions, signs, etc., purporting to be affixed in course of business and indicating, self-authentication, Evid. Rule 902.
Insurance against liability, admissibility for purpose of proving, Evid. Rule 411.
Subsequently remedial measures, admissibility to prove, Evid. Rule 407.

CONVERSION
Complaint in action for, form of, Form 11.

CONVICTION
Impeachment of witness, evidence of conviction of crime, Evid. Rule 609.
Judgment of previous conviction, hearsay exception, Evid. Rule 803.

COPIES
Business records, interrogatories, Rule 33(c); Auth. Comm. Rule 33(c).
Complaint, furnishing for service, Rule 4(d).
Depositions,
Oral examination, Rule 30(f); Auth. Comm. Rule 30(f).
Written questions, Rule 31(b).
Documents, service with requests for admission, Rule 36(a); Auth. Comm. Rule 36(a).
Foreign official records, authentication, Rule 44(a)(2); Auth. Comm. Rule 44(a)(2).
Order for, Rule 27(a), (b).
Order of reference, clerk to furnish to master, Rule 53(d).
Process, execution, admiralty or maritime claims, actions in rem and quasi in rem, Supp. Rules E(4)(b), (c).
Production of documents or things, generally, post.
Service, interrogatories, answers and objections to, time, Rule 33(a).
Summons, furnishing for service, Rule 4(d).
Written instruments, exhibit as part of pleading, Rule 10(c).

COPYRIGHTS
Complaint in action for infringement, form of, Form 17.
Inapplicability of rules to proceedings relating to, Rule 81(a).

CORAM NOBIS
Writ abolished, Rule 60(b).

CORAM VOBIS
Writ abolished, Rule 60(b).

CORPORATIONS
Agency of United States, service on, Rule 4(d).
Capacity to sue or be sued, determination, Rule 17(b).

CORPORATIONS—Cont'd
Citizenship, subject matter jurisdiction, Jurisdiction, Juris. § 2.12.
Depositions,
Introduction in evidence as making deponent witness of introducing party, nonapplicability, Rule 32(c).
Oral examination, Rule 30(b); Auth. Comm. Rule 30(b)(6).
Failure of officer, director, etc., to attend at own deposition, sanctions, Rule 37(d); Auth. Comm. Rule 37(d).
Failure to comply with order compelling designation, sanctions, Rule 37(b).
Motion for order compelling designation, Rule 37(a).
Use in court proceedings, Rule 32(a); Auth. Comm. Rule 32(a).
Written questions, Rule 31(a).
Failure of officer, etc., to attend at own deposition, sanctions, Rule 37(d); Auth. Comm. Rule 37(d).
Failure to comply with order compelling answer, sanctions, Rule 37(b).
Motion for order compelling answer, Rule 37(a).
Interrogatories, service of, Rule 33(a).
Service, Rule 4(d) and 4(f); Auth. Comm. Rule 4(d) and 4(f).
Shareholders, derivative actions, Rule 23.1.
Subpoena, naming as deponent and advising nonparty organization as to designation of officers, etc., Rule 30(b); Auth. Comm. Rule 30(b)(6).
Venue and, Venue; Juris. § 2.14; Auth. Comm. Rule 13.
Witnesses, interrogation, Rule 43(b).

CORPORATE DISCLOSURE
Statement of, Rule 7.1; Auth. Comm. Rule 7.1.

CORRECTION
Clerical errors in judgments, orders, etc., during pendency of appeal, Rule 60(a).

COSMETICS
Criminal libel for condemnation, exclusion of imports or other proceedings, applicability of rules in part, Evid. Rule 1101.

COSTS
Appeal from magistrate to district judge by consent, Rule 76(c); Auth. Comm. Rule 76(c).
Attorney's fees, Auth. Comm. Rule 54(d).
Condemnation of property, Rule 71A(l); Auth. Comm. Rule 71A(l).
Default judgment including costs, Rule 55(b).
Delay of entry of judgment for taxing of costs, Rule 58.
Deposition expenses, Auth. Comm. Rule 54(d).
Discovery requests, etc., signing of, sanctions, Rule 26(g); Auth. Comm. Rule 26(g).
Evidence of offer of judgment in proceeding to determine costs, Rule 68.
Exemplification fees, Auth. Comm, Rule 54(d).
Expert fees, Auth. Comm. Rule 54(d)
Masters Auth. Comm. Rule 54(d).
Notice, cost in class actions, Rule 23(c)(2); Auth. Comm. Rule 23.
Offer of judgment affecting, Rule 68.
Pretrial conference, failure to appear, sanctions, Rule 16(f).
Pretrial order, failure to obey, sanctions, Rule 16(f).
Prevailing party, Auth. Comm. Rule 54(d).

COSTS—Cont'd
Previously dismissed action, Rule 41(d); Auth. Comm. Rule 41(d).
Printing fees, Auth. Comm. Rule 54(d).
Restraining order or preliminary injunction, security, Rule 65(c).
Scheduling conference, failure to appear, sanctions, Rule 16(f).
Scheduling order, failure to obey, sanctions, Rule 16(f).
Signing of pleadings, motions, etc., sanctions, Rule 11.
Summary judgment, affidavits presented in bad faith, Rule 56(g).
Taxation,
Entry of judgment not delayed for, Rule 58.
Interpreter's compensation, Rule 43(f); Auth. Comm. Rule 43(f).
Prevailing party, Rule 54(d); Auth. Comm. Rule 54(d).
Types, 28 U.S.C.A. § 1920.
United States, actions in volumes, 28 U.S.C.A. § 2412.
Verification before taxing, 28 U.S.C.A. § 1924.
Vexatious conduct by counsel, 28 U.S.C.A. § 1927.
Witness fees, Auth. Comm. Rule 54(d).

COUNSELORS
Attorneys, generally, this index.

COUNTERCLAIMS
Generally, Rules 7(a), 13; Auth. Comm. Rule 7(a).
Additional parties, determinations, service territorial limits, Rule 4(f).
Default judgment against counterclaimants, Rule 55(d).
Dismissal, Rules 41(a), (c); Auth. Comm. Rule 41(a)(2), (c).
Entry of judgment disposing of, Rule 54(b).
Form, Form 20.
Counterclaim for interpleader, Form 21.
Interpleader, Rule 22 and Auth. Comm. Statutory Interpleader.
Joinder, Rule 18(a).
Judgment, Rule 13(i).
On one or more but fewer than all claims, Rule 54(b).
Jurisdiction and, Jurisdiction, Juris. § 2.4.
Mistake in designation of defense, Rule 8(c); Auth. Comm. Rule 8(c).
Relation to Rules 19 and 20, Rule 13(h).
Reply, Rule 7(a); Auth. Comm. Rule 7(a).
Time of service, Rule 12(a).
Requisites, Rule 8(a); Auth. Comm. Rule 8(a).
Separate trial, Rule 42(b).
Service of pleadings, numerous defendants, Rule 5(c).
Summary judgment, Rule 56.
Third party practice, Rule 14(a).
Time for reply by United States, Rule 12(a).
Venue and, Venue, Juris. § 2.14.
Voluntary dismissal, Rule 41(a)(2); Auth. Comm. Rule 41(a)(2), (c).

COUNTS
Pleading in separate counts, Auth. Comm. Rule 10(b).

COURT OF CLAIMS
United States Claims Court, generally, this index.

COURT PROCEEDINGS
Depositions, use in, Rule 32; Auth. Comm. Rule 32.

COURTS
Always open, 28 U.S.C.A. § 452.
Calling and interrogation of witnesses, Evid. Rule 614.
Clerks of Court, generally, this index.
Court of Claims. United States Claims Court, generally, this index.
Defined,
Generally, 28 U.S.C.A. § 451.
Applicability of evidence rules, Evid. Rule 1101.
Discovery,
Failure to comply with order compelling, sanctions by, Rule 37(b); Auth. Comm. Rule 37(b).
Motion for order to compel, Rule 37(a); Auth. Comm. Rule 37(a).
Discretion of Court, generally, this index.
District courts, generally, this index.
Dockets, generally, this index
Experts, appointment, Evid. Rule 706.
Filing of papers after complaint with court, Rule 5(d).
Judges, generally, this index.
Mode and order of interrogating witnesses and presenting evidence, control of, Evid. Rule 611.
Official record, authentication, Rule 44(a)(1); Auth. Comm. Rule 44(a)(1).
Orders, generally, this index.
Own motion, exclusion of witnesses so that other witnesses cannot be heard, Evid. Rule 615.
Rules as governing proceedings in, Auth. Comm. Rule 1; Evid. Rule 101.
Supreme Court, generally, this index.
Three judge courts and injunctions, Rule 65(e).
United States Claims Court, generally, this index.
Writings, recordings, or photographs,
Contents, functions respecting, Evid. Rule 1008.
Voluminous, production, Evid. Rule 1006.

COURTS OF APPEALS, APPEAL TO
Appellate jurisdiction,
Final decisions, 28 U.S.C.A. § 1291.
Interlocutory decisions, 28 U.S.C.A. § 1292.
Applicability of rules, Evid. Rule 1101.
Extension of time, Rule 6(b).
Notice of appeal, form of, Form 27.
Procedure, Auth. Comm. Appeals.
Time for appeal to, 28 U.S.C.A. § 2107.

CREDIBILITY OF WITNESSES
Attacking or supporting,
By evidence in form of opinion or reputation, Evid. Rule 608.
Credibility of declarant, hearsay statements, Evid. Rule 806.
Cross-examination, scope limited to matters affecting, Evid. Rule 610.
Impeachment,
By evidence of conviction of crime, Evid. Rule 609.

CREDIBILITY OF WITNESSES—Cont'd
Impeachment,—Cont'd
Persons who may impeach, Evid. Rule 607.
Preliminary questions, rule concerning as not limiting right of party to introduce evidence respecting, Evid. Rule 104.
Religious beliefs or opinions, admissibility to impair or enhance, Evid. Rule 610.
Self-incrimination privilege not waived when accused or other witness examined respecting matters relating only to, Evid. Rule 608.
Specific instances of conduct to attack or support, Evid. Rule 608.
Supporting. Attacking or supporting, generally, ante.
Who may impeach, Evid. Rule 607.

CRIMINAL ACTIONS AND PROCEDURE
Applicability of rules, Evid. Rule 1101.
Character evidence, evidence of other crimes, admissibility, Evid. Rule 404.
Character of victim, homicide case, Evid. Rule 404.
Conviction, generally, this index.
Eligibility for removal, Removal, Juris. § 2.17.
Federal Food, Drug and Cosmetic Act, criminal libel for condemnation, exclusion of imports, or other proceedings under, applicability of rules, in part, Evid. Rule 1101.
Habeas Corpus, generally, this index.
Homicide, generally, this index.
Investigations of. Criminal Investigations, generally, this index.
Judicial notice, instructions to jury, Evid. Rule 201.
Jury, generally, this index.
Obstruction of criminal prosecution, compromise and offers to compromise claims, admissibility of evidence respecting to prove, Evid. Rule 408.
Other crimes or wrongs, prosecution intent to introduce, notice, Evid. Rule 404.
Perjury, generally, this index.
Plea of Guilty, generally, this index.
Plea of Nolo Contendere, generally, this index.
Police officers and law enforcement personnel, matters observed by, hearsay, public records and reports, exception and exclusion, Evid. Rule 803.
Preliminary examination, inapplicability of rules, Evid. Rule 1101.
Summonses, issuance, inapplicability, Evid. Rule 1101.
Trial, generally, this index.
Writing used to refresh memory, failure to produce or deliver, striking of testimony or declaration of mistrial, Evid. Rule 612.

CRIMINAL INVESTIGATIONS
Factual findings resulting from, hearsay exception, Evid. Rule 803.
Obstruction, compromise and offers to compromise claims, admissibility to prove effort respecting, Evid. Rule 408.

CROSS-CLAIMS
Generally, Rules 7 and 13; Auth. Comm. Rule 7(a).
Additional parties, determination, service territorial limits, Rule 4(f).
Answer to cross-claim if answer contains a cross-claim, Rule 7(a); Auth. Comm. Rule 7(a).
Default judgment against cross-claimant, Rule 55(d).
Dismissal, Rule 41(c); Auth. Comm. Rule 41(c).
Entry of judgment disposing of, Rule 54(b).

CROSS-CLAIMS—Cont'd
Form, Form 20.
Joinder, Rule 18(a).
Judgment on one or more but fewer than all the claims, Rule 54(b).
Jurisdiction and Jurisdiction, Juris. § 2.4.
Relation to Rules 19 and 20, Rule 13(h).
Requisites, Rule 8(a); Auth. Comm. Rule 8(a).
Separate trial, Rule 42(b); Auth. Comm. Rule 42(b).
Service of pleadings, numerous defendants, Rule 5(c).
Summary judgment, Rule 56.
Third party practice, Rule 14(a).
Time for answer by United States, etc., Rule 12(a).
Venue and, Venue, Juris. § 2,14; Auth. Comm. Rule 13.

CROSS-EXAMINATION
Accused testifying on preliminary matter, examination as to other issues in case, Evid. Rule 104.
Conviction of crime, impeachment, credibility of witness by evidence of, Evid. Rule 609.
Court, witnesses called by, Evid. Rule 614.
Depositions upon oral examination, Rule 30(c); Auth. Comm. Rule 30(c).
Disclosure of facts or data underlying expert opinion, Evid. Rule 705.
Experts appointed by court, Evid. Rule 706.
Hearsay statements, examination of declarant by party against whom admitted, Evid. Rule 806.
Leading questions, Evid. Rule 611.
Relevant specific instances of conduct, methods of proving character of person, Evid. Rule 405.
Scope of, mode and order of interrogation and presentation of evidence, Evid. Rule 611.
Witnesses, Rule 43(b).
Writing used to refresh memory, witness using, Evid. Rule 612.

CRYPTS
Hearsay exception, statements concerning engravings on, Evid. Rule 803.

CULPABILITY
Conduct, subsequent remedial measures, admissibility to prove, Evid. Rule 407.

CUMULATIVE EVIDENCE
Exclusion of relevant evidence due to needless presentation of, Evid. Rule 403.

CUSTODY
Property, admiralty or maritime claims, actions in rem and quasi in rem, Supp.Rule E(4).

CUSTOMS DUTIES
Fines and penalties, actions for, application of rules in part, Evid. Rule 1101.
Searches, seizures, and forfeitures, actions for, applicability of rules in part, Evid. Rule 1101.

DAMAGES
Computation, reference to master, Rule 53(b).
Default judgment, determination of amount of damages, Rule 55(b)(2).
Pleading, special damages, Rule 9(g).

DAMAGES—Cont'd
Restraining order or preliminary injunction, security, Rule 65(c).
Summary judgment, Rule 56(c).
Unliquidated damages, pleading, Auth. Comm. Rule 8(a).

DATA COMPILATIONS
Production of Documents or Things, generally, this index.
Regularly conducted activity, hearsay exception, Evid. Rule 803.
"Writings" and "recordings" as including, contents of writings, etc., Evid. Rule 1001.

DEATH
Hearsay, this index.
Party, substitution, Rule 25(a).
Suggestion of death upon the record under rule concerning, form of, Form 30.
Public officers, substitution of party, Rule 25(d).
Witness, depositions, use in court proceedings, Rule 32(a); Auth. Comm. Rule 32(a).

DEATH PENALTY
Impeachment, credibility of witness, evidence of conviction of crime punishable by death, court determination, probative value, Evid. Rule 609.
Judgment of previous conviction of crime punishable by death, evidence of, hearsay exception, Evid. Rule 803.

DEBT
Complaint in action for, form of, Form 13.

DECEDENTS
Actions on behalf of and subject matter jurisdiction, Jurisdiction.

DECLARATORY JUDGMENTS
Generally, Rule 57; Auth. Comm. Rule 57.
Actual controversy required, Auth. Comm. Rule 57.
Appealability, Auth. Comm. Rule 57.
Creation of remedy, 28 U.S.C.A. § 2201.
Cumulative remedy, Auth. Comm. Rule 57.
Discretion of court in granting, Auth. Comm. Rule 57.
Expedited treatment, Auth. Comm. Rule 57.
Factors for, Auth. Comm. Rule 57.
Further relief, 28 U.S.C.A. § 2202.
Jury trial, Auth. Comm. Rule 57.
Mootness, Auth. Comm. Rule 57.
Realignment of parties, Auth. Comm. Rule 57.
Ripeness as requirement of, Auth. Comm. Rule 57.
Subject matter jurisdiction required, Jurisdiction; Auth. Comm. Rule 57.
Summary judgment, Rule 56.
Tax cases, Auth. Comm. Rule 57.

DECLARATORY RELIEF
Class actions, Rule 23(b).

DECREES
Judgments and Decrees, generally, this index.

DEFAULT JUDGMENTS
Generally, Rule 55; Auth. Comm. Rule 55.
Contested motions, Auth. Comm. Rule 55.
Demand for judgment, Rule 54(c); Auth. Comm. Rule 54(c).
Discovery, sanction for failure to comply with order compelling, Rule 37(b).
Entry of default, Rule 55(a); Auth. Comm. Rule 55(a).
Judgment by default, Rule 55(b); Auth. Comm. Rule 55(b).
Entry by Clerk of Court, Rule 55(b); Auth. Comm. Rule 55(b).
Entry by Court, Rule 55(b); Auth. Comm. Rule 55(b).
Military defendants, default against, Rule 55(b); Auth. Comm. Rule 55(b).
Multiple defendants, Rule 55(b); Auth. Comm. Rule 55(b).
Pleading,
Failure to plead as grounds for entering default, Rule 55(a).
Relief demanded by, Rule 54(c).
Relief awarded, Rule 54(c).
Setting aside default, Rule 55(c); Auth. Comm. Rule 55(c).
Summons as notice to defendant, judgment by default will be entered on failure to appeal and defend, Rule 4(b).
United States, default against, Rule 55(e); Auth. Comm. Rule 55(e).

DEFECTIVE PLEADING
Statement of claim, permission granted for service of supplemental pleadings, Rule 15(d).

DEFENSES
"Built-It" defenses, Auth. Comm. Rule 12(b)(6).
Character or trait of character as essential element, proof of specific instances of conduct, Evid. Rule 405.
Competency of witness, state law as determining unless federal law supplies rule of decision, Evid. Rule 601.
Consolidation of defenses, Rule 12(g); Auth. Comm. Rule 12(g).
Implied waiver of, Auth. Comm. Rule 12(h).
Motions, this index.
Pleadings, this index.
Privilege of witness, person, etc., state law as determining unless federal law supplies rule of decision respecting, Evid. Rule 501.
Waiver of defenses, Rule 12(h); Auth. Comm. Rule 12(h).

DEFINITIONS
Declarant, hearsay, Evid. Rule 801.
Duplicate, contents of, Evid. Rule 1001.
Hearsay, Evid. Rule 801.
Judge, applicability of rules, Evid. Rule 1101.
Original of writing or recording, contents, Evid. Rule 1001.
Photographs, contents of, Evid. Rule 1001.
Psychologists, mental examinations, Rule 35.
Recordings, contents of, Evid. Rule 1001.
Relevant evidence, Evid. Rule 401.
Statements, hearsay, Evid. Rule 801.
Statements which are not hearsay, Evid. Rule 801.
Unavailability as a witness, hearsay exceptions, Evid. Rule 804.
Writings, contents of, Evid. Rule 1001.

DELAY
Compromise and offers to compromise claims, admission of evidence negativing contention of undue delay, Evid. Rule 408.
Discovery, prohibition, Rule 26(d).
Elimination of unjustifiable delay, purpose and construction of rules, Evid. Rule 102.
Entry of judgment, taxing of costs, Rule 58.
Exclusion of relevant evidence on grounds of undue delay or waste of time, Evid. Rule 403.

DELIVERY
Copy of pleadings, etc., meaning of term, Rule 5(b).
Process,
United States attorney, etc., amendment of pleading, change of party, Rule 15(c).
Report of examiner, physical and mental examinations, Rule 35(b); Auth. Comm. Rule 35(b).

DEMAND
Corporate action, demand for as prerequisite to shareholder derivative suits, Rule 23.1; Auth. Comm. Rule 23.1.
Judgment, demand for, Rule 54(c).
Jury trial, Rule 38(b); Auth. Comm. Rule 38(b).
Removed action, Rule 81(c); Auth. Comm. Rule 81(c).
Service, Rule 5(a).

DEMURRERS
Abolished, Rule 7(c).

DENIALS
Form, Rule 8(b); Auth. Comm. Rule 8(b).

DEPOSITIONS
See, also, Discovery, generally, this index.
Admissibility under rules of evidence, use in court proceedings, Rule 32(a); Auth. Comm. Rule 32(a).
Affidavits for summary judgment supplemented or opposed by depositions, Rule 56(e).
Agencies of United States, this index.
Associations and Societies, this index.
Before action, Rule 27(a); Auth. Comm. Rule 27(a).
Certification, Rule 30(f); Auth. Comm. Rule 30(f).
Changes to transcript, Rule 30(e); Auth. Comm. Rule 30(e).
Competency, relevancy, or materiality of testimony, objections to, Rule 32(d); Auth. Comm. Rule 32(d).
Competency of witness, objections to, Rule 32(d); Auth. Comm. Rule 32(d).
Completion of, errors and irregularities in, effect of, Rule 32(d).
Contradicting or impeaching testimony of deponent, use of, Rule 32(a); Auth. Comm. Rule 32(a).
Corporations, this index.
Court appointed experts, Evid. Rule 706.
Cross-examination of deponent, taking depositions before action, Rule 27(a)(2).
Death of witness, use in court proceedings, Rule 32(a); Auth. Comm. Rule 32(a).

DEPOSITIONS—Cont'd
Disqualification of,
Officer, objections to, Rule 32(d); Auth. Comm. Rule 32(d).
Person taking, for interest, Rule 28(c); Auth. Comm. Rule 28(c).
Examination of deponent, Rules 27(a), 30; Auth. Comm. Rules 27(a), 30.
Exceptional circumstances requiring use in court proceedings, Rule 32(a); Auth. Comm. Rule 32(a).
Expenses and Expenditures, this index.
Failure to attend, Rule 30(g).
Foreign countries, persons before whom taken, Rule 28(b); Auth. Comm. Rule 28(b).
Hearing, motions, use at, Rule 32(a); Auth. Comm. Rule 32(a).
Inability of witness to attend or testify because of age, illness, etc., use in court proceedings, Rule 32(a); Auth. Comm. Rule 32(a).
Interlocutory proceedings, use of, Rule 32(a).
Interrogatories, Rules 31, 33.
Introduction,
Of other parts, use in court proceedings, Rule 32(a); Auth. Comm. Rule 32(a).
Letters rogatory, foreign countries, persons before whom depositions may be taken, Rule 28(b); Auth. Comm. Rule 28(b).
Notice, this index.
Number of depositions, Rule 30(a); Rule 31(a); Auth. Comm. Rule 30(a); Auth. Comm. Rule 31(a).
Oath or affirmation, power to administer oaths, Rule 28(a).
Objections, Rule 30(c); Auth. Comm. Rule 30(c).
Errors and irregularities in, Rule 32(d); Auth. Comm. Rule 32(d).
Subpoena for taking, Rule 45(c).
To admissibility in court proceedings, Rule 32(b); Auth. Comm. Rule 32(b).
Officers, persons before whom taken, Rule 28; Auth. Comm. Rule 28.
Oral examination, Rule 30.
Attorney's signature on special notice as constituting certification, Rule 30(b).
Certification and filing by officer taking, Rule 30(f); Auth. Comm. Rule 30(f).
Changes in form or substance, Rule 30(e); Auth. Comm. Rule 30(e).
Completion or adjournment of examination before applying for order to compel answer, Rule 37(a).
Contents, notice, Rule 30(b); Auth. Comm. Rule 30(b)(1).
Copies, charges for, Rule 30(f).
Enlargement or shortening of time for taking. Rule 30(b).
Errors and irregularities occurring at, effect of, Rule 32(d).
Evasive or incomplete answer, defined, motion for order to compel, Rule 37(a).
Evidence taken subject to objections, Rule 30(c); Auth. Comm. Rule 30(c).
Exhibits, Rule 30(f); Auth. Comm. Rule 30(f).
Expenses, award of, motion to terminate or limit, Rule 30(d); Auth. Comm. Rule 30(d).
Failure of party,
Giving notice of taking to attend payment, expenses and attorney's fees, Rule 30(g); Auth. Comm. Rule 30(g).
To attend at own depositions, sanctions, Rule 37(d); Auth. Comm. Rule 37(b), (d).
Failure to comply with order compelling answer, sanctions, Rule 37(b).
General requirements for notice, Rule 30(b); Auth. Comm. Rule 30(b)(1).

DEPOSITIONS—Cont'd
Oral examination, Rule 30.—Cont'd
Illness, absence, or refusal of witness to sign, Rule 30(e).
Leave of court, Rule 30(a) et seq.; Auth. Comm. Rule 30.
Method of obtaining discovery, Rule 26(a).
Motion,
For order to compel answer, Rule 37(a).
To terminate or limit, Rule 30(d); Auth. Comm. Rule 30(d).
Nonstenographic recording, Rules 30(b) and 32(c); Auth. Comm. Rules 30(b)(3) and 32(c).
Notice, Rule 30(b) et seq.; Auth. Comm. Rule 30(b) and 32(c).
Oath of witness, Rule 30(c); Auth. Comm. Rule 30(c).
Objections, Rule 30(c); Auth. Comm. Rule 30(c).
To errors and irregularities occurring at, Rule 32(d).
Orders, this index.
Organizations, Rule 30(b); Auth. Comm. Rule 30(b)(6).
Procedure for examination and cross-examination, Rule 30(c); Auth. Comm. Rule 30(c).
Production of documents or things, request for, accompanying notice, Rule 30(b); Auth. Comm. Rule 30(b)(5).
Prompt notice of filing, Rule 30(f).
Record of, Rule 30(c); Auth. Comm. Rule 30(c).
Rejection on motion to suppress for refusal to sign, Rule 30(e).
Requirements, Rule 30(b); Auth. Comm. Rule (b).
Sanctions, certification concerning special notice, Rule 30(b).
Signature of witness, Rule 30(e); Auth. Comm. Rule 30(e).
Special notice, obviation of leave of court, Rule 30(b); Auth. Comm. Rule 30(b)(2).
Stipulation, waiver of signing, Rule 30(e).
Submission to witness, Rule 30(e).
Subpoena, Rule 45(a); Auth. Comm. Rule 45.
Compelling attendance of witnesses, Rule 30(a).
Failure of party giving notice of taking to serve, expenses and attorney's fees, payment, Rule 30(g); Auth. Comm. Rule 30(g).
Naming of deponent or advising non-party organization concerning designation of officers, etc., Rule 30(b); Auth. Comm. Rule 30(b)(6).
Subpoena duces tecum, designation of materials to be produced, inclusion in notice, Rule 30(b); Auth. Comm. Rule 30(b)(5).
Suspension of taking, Rule 30(d); Auth. Comm. Rule 30(d).
Time for taking, Rule 30(a) et seq.; Auth. Comm. Rule 30(a).
When leave of court not required, Rule 30(a).
Written questions in lieu of, Rule 30(c); Auth. Comm. Rule 30(c).
Orders, this index.
Outside United States, witness, use in court proceedings, Rule 32(a).
Partnership, this index.
Pending appeal, Rule 27(b); Auth. Comm. Rule 27(b).
Persons before whom taken, Rule 28; Auth. Comm. Rule 28.
Petition for depositions before action, Rule 27(a)(1); Auth. Comm. Rule 27(a).
Physical and mental examinations, examiners agreement not precluding, Rule 35(b).

DEPOSITIONS—Cont'd
Place of,
Trial or hearing, witness more than 100 miles from, use in court proceedings, Rule 32(a); Auth. Comm. Rule 32(a).
Prior actions or proceedings in United States or State courts, effect on use, Rule 32(a); Auth. Comm. Rule 32(a).
Protective orders, Rule 26(c); Auth. Comm. Rule 26(c).
Registered or certified mail, sending to clerk of court for filing, Rule 30(f).
Return of, errors and irregularities in, effect of, Rule 32(d).
Service, notice of taking before action, Rule 27(a)(2); Auth. Comm. Rule 27(a).
Signing, Rule 30(e); Auth. Comm. Rule 30(e).
Stipulations as to taking, Rule 29; Auth. Comm. Rule 29.
Subpoenas,
Attendance at deposition, Rule 45(a).
Failure to procure attendance of witness, use in court proceedings, Rule 32(a); Auth. Comm. Rule 32(a).
Oral examination,
Compelling attendance of witnesses, Rule 30(a).
Failure of party giving notice to serve, payment, expenses and attorney's fees, Rule 30(g); Auth. Comm. Rule 30(g).
Naming of deponent and advising nonparty organization concerning designation of officers, etc., Rule 30(b); Auth. Comm. Rule 30(b)(6).
Use in court proceedings upon failure of witness to attend, Rule 32(a); Auth. Comm. Rule 32(a).
Written questions, compelling attendance of witness, Rule 31(a); Auth. Comm. Rule 31(a).
Substitution of parties, effect on use, Rule 32(a); Auth. Comm. Rule 32(a).
Summary judgment,
Continuance to procure depositions opposing, Rule 56(f).
Rendered where depositions show no genuine issue, etc., Rule 56(e).
Telephone, Rule 30(b)(7).
Time, this index.
Trial, use at, Rule 32(a); Auth. Comm. Rule 32(a).
United States, this index.
Use of in court proceedings, Rule 32; Auth. Comm. Rule 32.
Venue, this index.
Writings, recordings or photographs, proof of contents, Evid. Rule 1007.
Written questions, Rule 31; Auth. Comm. Rule 31.
Certification, Rule 31(a).
Contents, notice, Rule 31(a); Auth. Comm. Rule 31(a).
Copies, Rule 31(b).
Cross, redirect and recross questions, service of, Rule 31(a); Auth. Comm. Rule 31(a).
Enlargement or shortening of time for service, Rule 31(a).
Evasive or incomplete answer, defined, motion for order to compel, Rule 37(a).
Failure of party to attend at own deposition, sanctions, Rule 37(d).
Failure to comply with order compelling answer, sanctions, Rule 37(b).
Filing, Rule 31(a).
Notice of, Rule 31(c); Auth. Comm. Rule 31(c).
In lieu of oral examination, Rule 30(c); Auth. Comm. Rule 30(c).
Mailing, Rule 31(b).

DEPOSITIONS—Cont'd
Written questions, Rule 31; Auth. Comm. Rule 31.—Cont'd
Method of obtaining discovery, Rule 26(a).
Motion for order to compel answer, Rule 37(a).
Notice, Rule 31(a) et seq.; Auth. Comm. Rule 31(a).
Objections to form of, Rule 32(d); Auth. Comm. Rule 32(d).
Place of examination, Rule 45(d).
Preparation of record, Rule 31(d).
Prisoners, leave of court, Rule 31(a); Auth. Comm. Rule 31(a).
Service, Rule 31(a); Auth. Comm. Rule 31(a).
Subpoena, Rule 45(a).
Compelling attendance of witness, Rule 31(a); Auth. Comm. Rule 31(a).
Taking by officer, Rule 31(b); Auth. Comm. Rule 31(b).
Time for taking, Rule 31(a); Auth. Comm. Rule 31(a).

DEPOSITS
Condemnation proceedings, Rule 71A(j); Auth. Comm. Rule 71A(j).
Condition to exercise of power of eminent domain, Rule 71A(j).
In court, Rule 67.
Security, appeal to court of appeals, Rule 73(c).

DEPUTY MARSHAL
Process service, Rule 4(c).

DERIVATIVE ACTIONS BY SHAREHOLDERS
Generally, Rule 23.1.

DESCRIPTIVE TITLE
Notice or commission may designate persons before whom deposition to be taken, Rule 28(b).

DESIGN
Hearsay exceptions, statements respecting, Evid. Rule 803.

DESTRUCTION
Originals of records, writings or photographs, admissibility, other evidence of contents, Evid. Rule 1004.

DIAGNOSES
Examiners report, physical and mental examinations, Rule 35(b).

DIRECTED VERDICT
Extension of time, Rule 6(b).
Judgment as a matter of law, Rule 50; Auth. Comm. Rule 50.
Stay of proceedings to enforce judgment pending disposition of motion, Rule 62(b); Auth. Comm. Rule 62(b).

DIRECTORIES
Use and reliance on by public or persons in particular occupations, hearsay exception, Evid. Rule 803.

DIRECTORS
Witnesses, interrogation, Rule 43(b).

DISCHARGE
In bankruptcy, pleading as affirmative defense, Rule 8(c).

DISCLOSURE
Discovery disclosures generally, Rule 26(a); Auth. Comm. Rule 26(a).
Expert witnesses, Rule 26(a)(2); Auth. Comm. Rule 26(a)(2).
Facts of data underlying expert opinion, Evid. Rule 705.
Form of disclosures, Rule 26(a)(4); Auth. Comm. Rule 26(a)(4).
Initial disclosures, Rule 26(a)(1); Auth. Comm. Rule 26(a)(1).
Pretrial disclosures, Rule 26(a)(3); Auth. Comm. Rule 26(a)(3).
To jury, court appointment of expert witnesses, Evid. Rule 706.

DISCLOSURE OF MENTAL IMPRESSIONS, ETC., OF REPRESENTATIVE
Discovery, protective order against, Rule 26(b)(3); Auth. Comm. Rule 26(b)(3).

DISCLOSURE STATEMENT (Conflicts of Interest Notice)
Generally, Auth. Comm. Rule 7.1.
Collateral Effects, Auth. Comm. Rule 7.1.

DISCOVERY
Generally, Rule 26; Auth. Comm. Rule 26.
Attorney's Fees, generally, this index.
Delay prohibited, Rule 26(d).
Depositions, generally, this index.
Disclosures, generally, this index.
Discovery plan; Rule 26(f); Auth. Comm. Rule 26(f).
Entry upon Land, generally, this index.
Expenses and Expenditures, this index.
Expert witnesses, Rule 26(a)(2); Rule 26(b)(4); Auth. Comm. Rule 26(a)(2); Auth. Comm. Rule 26(b)(4).
Failure to make, sanctions, Rule 37; Auth. Comm. Rule 37.
Fees, etc., expert witnesses, trial or litigation preparation, Rule 26(b); Auth. Comm. Rule 26(b)(4).
Foreign country, subpoena of person in, Rule 37(e).
Frequency, use of methods, limitation prohibited, Rule 26(a).
Initial disclosures, Rule 26(a)(1); Auth. Comm. Rule 26(a)(1).
Insurance agreements, existence and contents, Rule 26(b); Auth. Comm. Rule 26(b)(2).
Interrogatories, generally, this index.
Judgment or execution, obtaining in aid of, Rule 69(a).
Jurisdictional discovery, Auth. Comm. Rule 72(b)(2).
Meeting, Rule 26(f); Auth. Comm. Rule 26(f).
Methods,
Of obtaining, Rule 26(a); Auth. Comm. Rule 26(a).
Use, timing and sequence for, Rule 26(d); Auth. Comm. Rule 26(d).
Modification of procedures, stipulations, Rule 29; Auth. Comm. Rule 29.
Motions, this index.
Objections, Rule 26(b); Auth. Comm. Rules 33, 34.
Signature, Rule 26(g); Auth. Comm. Rule 26(g).
Orders, this index.
Physical and Mental Examinations, generally, this index.
Pretrial disclosures, Rule 26(a)(3); Auth. Comm. Rule 26(a)(3).
Privileges, Rule 26(b); Auth. Comm. Rule 26(6).
Production of Documents or Things, generally, this index.
Protective Orders, this index.

DISCOVERY—Cont'd

Request for, responses to,

Extension of time, stipulations, approval of court, Rule 29; Auth. Comm. Rule 29.

Signature, Rule 26(g); Auth. Comm. Rule 26(g).

Supplementation of, Rule 26(e); Auth. Comm. Rule 26(e).

Requests for admissions. Admissions, this index.

Sanctions, Auth. Comm. Rule 37.

Scope, Rule 26(b); Auth. Comm. Rule 26(b).

Sequence, use of methods, Rule 26(d); Auth. Comm. Rule 26 (d).

Service, papers relating to, Rule 5(a).

Signature of discovery documents, Rule 26(g); Auth. Comm. Rule 26(g).

State practice, applicability, proceedings in aid of judgment or execution, Rule 69(a); Auth. Comm. Rule 69(a).

Statements previously made by parties or persons, of action or subject matter, obtaining of, Rule 26(b); Auth. Comm. Rule 26(b)(3).

Stipulations regarding procedure, Rule 29; Auth. Comm. Rule 29.

Summary judgment, continuance to procure discovery opposing, Rule 56(f).

Supplementation of responses, Rule 26(e); Auth. Comm. Rule 26(e).

Time, methods, use of, Rule 26(d); Auth. Comm. Rule 26(d).

Trial or litigation preparation,

Expert witnesses, Rule 26(b).

Substantial need of materials, Rule 26(b); Auth. Comm. Rule 26(b)(3).

Witnesses, Rule 26 et seq.

DISCRETION OF COURT

Bond for injunctions or temporary restraining orders, Rule 65(c); Auth. Comm. Rule 65(c).

Class actions,

Additional notice, Rule 23(d).

Certification, Rule 23(c).

Dismissal or compromise, Rule 23(e).

Counterclaims and crossclaims,

After-acquired or late maturing counterclaims, Rule 13(e).

Omitted counterclaims, Rule 13(f).

Separate trials, Rule 13(i).

Disclosure to jury, court appointment of expert witnesses, Evid. Rule 706.

Dismissal for failure to join indispensable party, Rule 19(b); Auth. Comm. Rule 19(b).

Interpreters, compensation, taxation as costs, Rule 43(f); Auth. Comm. Rule 43(f).

Joinder and separate trials, Rules 20(b) and 21; Auth. Comm. Rules 20(b), 21.

Judicial notice, adjudicative facts, Evid. Rule 201.

Jury trial, court to order, Rule 39(b).

Leave to amend pleadings, Rule 15(a), (b).

Leave to supplement pleadings, Rule 15(d).

Magnitude of sanctions, Rule 11; Auth. Comm. Rule 11.

Master, adjournment of proceedings, Rule 53(d).

Scope, cross-examination, Evid. Rule 611.

Supplemental Jurisdiction and, Jurisdiction, Juris. § 2.13.

Unincorporated associations, suits involving, Auth. Comm. Rule 23.2.

DISHONESTY

Impeachment of witness by evidence of conviction of crime involving, Evid. Rule 609.

DISMISSAL

Generally, Rule 41; Auth. Comm. Rule 41.
Action for condemnation of property, Rule 71A(i); Auth. Comm. Rule 71A(i).
Appealability of orders on motions to dismiss, Auth. Comm. Rule 12.
Claims of opposing party, judgment on counterclaim or cross-claim, Rule 13(i).
Class actions, Rule 23(e).
Determination by court when joinder not feasible, Rule 19(b).
Costs of previously dismissed action, Rule 41(d).
Counterclaims and Crossclaims, Rule 41(e).
Discovery, sanction for failure to comply with order compelling, Rule 37(b); Auth. Comm. Rule 37(b).
Discovery postponed during pending motion, Auth. Comm. Rule 12(b)(6).
Failure to prosecute, Auth. Comm. Rule 41(b).
Inappropriate forum and, Forum non Conveniens.
Involuntary dismissal, Rule 41(b); Auth. Comm. Rule 41(b).
Joined party, Rule 19(a).
Dismissal for failure to join party, Rules 12(b)(7), 19(b); Auth. Comm. Rules 12(b)(7), 19(b).
Jurisdiction, lack of, Jurisdiction, Juris. §§ 2.1-2.13.
Motions,
Failure of pleading to state claim on which relief can be granted, Rule 12(b).
Findings of fact and conclusions of law, Rule 52(a).
Form of, Form 19.
Notice of dismissal, Auth. Comm. Rule 41(a).
Personal jurisdiction, lack of, Rule 12(b)(2); Jurisdiction; Auth. Comm. Rule 12(b)(2).
Prejudice, Auth. Comm. Rule 41.
Process, dismissal for insufficient, Rule 12(b)(4); Auth. Comm. Rule 12(b)(4).
Prosecution not in name of real party in interest, Rule 17(a).
Receivers, order of court for dismissal of action wherein receiver has been appointed, Rule 66.
Sanctions, Rule 11; Auth. Comm. Rule 11.
Service, dismissal for insufficient, Rule 12(b)(5); Auth. Comm. Rule 12(b)(5).
Service not completed within 120 days from commencement, Rule 4(j); Auth. Comm. Rules 3, 4(j).
Shareholder derivative actions, Rule 23.1.
Stipulation of dismissal; Auth. Comm. Rule 41(a).
Subject matter, lack of jurisdiction, Rule 12(b)(1), (h); Jurisdiction; Auth. Comm. Rule 12(b)(1), (h).
Substitution of parties, failure to serve motion for within certain time after death, Rule 25(a).
Third party claim, Rule 41(c).
Unincorporated associations, actions relating to, Rule 23.2.
Venue, improper, Rule 12(b)(3); Auth. Comm. Rule 12(b)(3).
Voluntary dismissal, Rule 41(a); Auth. Comm. Rule 41(a).
While motion pending, Auth. Comm. Rule 12(b)(6).

DISPOSITION OF PROPERTY
Admiralty or maritime claims, actions in rem and quasi in rem, Supp. Rule E(9).

DISTRICT
Definition of, 28 U.S.C.A. § 451.
Depositions, sanctions by court where taken, failure to comply with order compelling answer, Rule 37(b); Auth. Comm. Rule 37(b).
Documents of under or not under seal, self-authentication, Evid. Rule 902.
Official record, authentication, Rule 44(a)(1); Auth. Comm. Rule 44(a)(1).
Pending action, person about to go out of, depositions upon oral examination, leave of court not required, Rule 30(b); Auth. Comm. Rule 30(b)(2).
Venue and, Venue, Juris. § 2.14.

DISTRICT COURTS
Appeal, fees upon filing notice of, 28 U.S.C.A. § 1917.
Applicability of rules, Evid. Rule 1101.
Definition of, 28 U.S.C.A. § 451.
Fees of, 28 U.S.C.A. § 1914.
Hearings conducted outside district, Rule 77(b).
Jurisdiction of,
Antitrust Commerce, 28 U.S.C.A. § 1337.
Civil rights, 28 U.S.C.A. § 1343.
Collusive joinder, 28 U.S.C.A. § 1359.
Corporations, 28 U.S.C.A. § 1349.
Diversity, 28 U.S.C.A. § 1332.
Federal question, 28 U.S.C.A. § 1331.
Federal inquiries, 28 U.S.C.A. § 1357.
Foreign states, 28 U.S.C.A. § 1330.
Interpleader, 28 U.S.C.A. § 1335.
Officers, 28 U.S.C.A. § 1361.
Supplemental jurisdiction, 28 U.S.C.A. § 1367.
United States as party, 28 U.S.C.A. §§ 1345, 1346.
Local rules, computation of time, Rule 6(a).
Motion day, Rule 78.
Open, court to remain open, Rule 77(a); Auth. Comm. Rule 77(a).
Open court, trial conducted in, Rule 77(b); Auth. Comm. Rule 77(b).
Three-Judge panels, 28 U.S.C.A. § 2284.

DISTRICT DIRECTOR OF INTERNAL REVENUE
"Officer" as including, Rule 81(f).

DISTRICT OF COLUMBIA
Subject matter jurisdiction and, Jurisdiction, Juris. §§ 2.12-2.13.

DISTRICT OF COLUMBIA COURTS
Applicability of rules, Rule 81(a), (e); Auth. Comm. Rule 81(a).

DIVERSITY OF CITIZENSHIP
Removal in cases based on diversity jurisdiction, Removal, Juris. § 2.16.
Subject matter jurisdiction, Jurisdiction, Juris. § 2.12.
Venue and diversity cases, Venue, Juris. § 2.14.

DIVISIONS
Venue and divisions within federal judicial districts, Venue, Juris. § 2.14.

DIVORCE

Hearsay exception,

Records of, Evid. Rule 803.

Statement of declarant concerning, Evid. Rule 804.

DOCKETS

Appeal to,

Correction of clerical mistakes in judgments and orders before docketing appeal, Rule 60(a).

Court of appeals, extension of time for docketing, Rule 6(b).

Civil docket, Rule 79(a); Auth. Comm. Rule 79(a).

Jury trial, designation, Rule 39(a).

Note of mailing notice of entry of order or judgment, Rule 77(d).

DOCUMENTS

Admission of genuineness. Admissions, generally, this index.

Ancient Documents, generally, this index.

Authentication, generally, this index.

Discovery,

Need requirement, litigation or trial, preparation, Rule 26(b); Auth. Comm. Rule 26(b)(2).

Scope of, Rule 26(b); Auth. Comm. Rule 26(b).

Disobedience to judgment directing delivery, Rule 70.

Foreign official documents, 28 U.S.C.A. § 1741.

Masters, compelling production, Rule 53(c).

Order for production, Rule 27(a), (b).

Patent documents, 28 U.S.C.A. §§ 1744-1745.

Pleading official document, Rule 9(d).

Postmaster demand, 28 U.S.C.A. § 1743.

Production of documents or things, generally, this index.

Subpoenas, response, Rule 45(d).

DOMESTIC OFFICIAL RECORDS

Authentication, Rule 44(a)(1); Auth. Comm. Rule 44(a)(1).

DOMICILE

Parties, capacity to sue or be sued, Rule 17(b).

Subject matter jurisdiction and citizenship, Jurisdiction, Juris. § 2.12.

DRAWINGS

Production of documents or things, generally, this index.

DRUGS

Criminal libel for condemnation, exclusion of imports or other proceedings, applicability of rules in part, Evid. Rule 1101.

DUE PROCESS

Personal jurisdiction, quasi in rem jurisdiction, in rem jurisdiction, Jurisdiction.

DURESS

Pleading as affirmative defense, Rule 8(c).

DWELLING HOUSE

Service of pleading, etc., Rule 5(b).

E-MAIL
Substituted service by, Auth. Comm. Rule 4(f).

EFFECTIVE DATE
Offer to plead guilty, nolo contendere, etc., provisions concerning, Evid. Rule 410.
Original rules and amendments, Rule 86; Auth. Comm. Rule 86.

ELECTRICAL RECORDING
Obtaining prior statement concerning action or subject matter by party or person, Rule 26(b).

EMBARRASSMENT
Depositions upon oral examination, motion to terminate or limit, Rule 30(d); Auth. Comm. Rule 30(d).
Protective orders relating to depositions, grounds for, Rule 26(c); Auth. Comm. Rule 26(c).

EMINENT DOMAIN
Condemnation of Property, generally, this index.

EMOTION
Hearsay exceptions, statement respecting, Evid. Rule 803.

EMPLOYEES
Officers and Employees, generally, this index.
Employer and Employee,
Preliminary injunctions and temporary restraining orders, Rule 65(e).

ENGRAVINGS
Rings, urns, crypts or tombstones, statements concerning, hearsay exception, Evid. Rule 803.

ENLARGEMENT OF TIME
Extension of Time, generally, this index.

ENTRY
Answers to interrogatories where harmonious with general verdict, etc., Rule 49(b); Auth. Comm. Rule 49(b).
Judgments and Decrees, this index.

ENTRY UPON LAND
See, also, Discovery, generally, this index.
Failure of party to respond to request for inspection, sanctions, Rule 37(d).
Failure to comply with order compelling inspection, sanctions, Rule 37(b).
Method of obtaining discovery, Rule 26(a).
Motion for order to compel inspection, Rule 37(a).
Objections, Rule 34(b).
Procedure, Rule 34(b); Auth. Comm. Rule 34(b).
Requests, Rule 34(a), (b); Auth. Comm. Rule 34(a), (b).
Responses to requests, Rule 34(b); Auth. Comm. Rule 34(b).
Scope of, Rule 34(a); Auth. Comm. Rule 34(a).
Service, requests, Rule 34(a), (b); Auth. Comm. Rule 34(b).
Stipulations, extension of time, responses to, approval of court, Rule 29.

EQUITABLE TOLLING
Auth. Comm. Rule 23.

EQUITY

Amount in controversy for subject matter jurisdiction, Jurisdiction.
Application of rules, Rule 1; Auth. Comm. Rule 1.
Determination by court whenever joinder not feasible, Rule 19(b).
Equity principles, Auth. Comm. Rule 2.
Injunction, generally, this index.
Joinder of claims, Rule 18(a).
Pleading, statement of separate claims or defenses, Rule 8(e)(2).

ERRORS AND IRREGULARITIES

Clerical errors in judgment, Rule 60(a).
Depositions, use in court proceedings, effect of, Rule 32(d).
Effect of erroneous rulings, Evid. Rule 103.
Plain error affecting substantial rights, notice, Evid. Rule 103.

ESTOPPEL

Pleading as affirmative defense, Rule 8(c).

EVIDENCE

Action to perpetuate testimony, Rule 27(c); Auth. Comm. Rule 27(c).
Affidavits, hearing of motion based on facts appearing of record, Rule 43(e).
Affirmation in lieu of oath, Rule 43(d).
Amendment of pleading to conform to evidence, Rule 15(b).
Character Evidence, generally, this index.
Compelling giving of testimony, application of rules, Rule 81(a).
Costs, evidence of offer of judgment in proceeding to determine costs, Rule 68.
Credibility of Witnesses, generally, this index.
Depositions, generally, this index.
Discovery, generally, this index.
Documents, generally, this index.
Findings of fact by court, objection, Rule 52(b).
Foreign law, determination, Rule 44.1; Auth. Comm. Rule 44.1.
Form and admissibility, Rule 43(a).
Harmless error in admitting or excluding, Rule 61.
Hearsay, generally, this index.
Interpreters, Rule 43(f).
Letters rogatory, exclusion, Rule 28(b).
Master, Rule 53; Auth. Comm. Rule 53(d)(3), (e)(3).
Motions, Rule 43(e).
Official record, Rule 44; Auth. Comm. Rule 44.
Perpetuation by action, Rule 27(c).
Pre-trial procedure, Rule 16.
Preliminary injunction hearing, admissibility upon trial, Rule 65(a)(2).
Presumptions, generally, this index.
Production of Documents or Things, generally, this index.
Record,
  Evidence by master, Rule 53(c).
Relevant Evidence, generally, this index.
Scope of examination and cross-examination of witness, Rule 43(b).
Stenographic report or transcript as evidence, Rule 80(c); Auth. Comm. Rule 80(c).
Subpoena for production, Rule 45.

EVIDENCE—Cont'd
Transcript of evidence, filing by master with report, Rule 53(e).
United States, establishing claim on default, Rule 55(e).
Voluntary dismissal before introduction of evidence at trial, Rule 41(c).

EX PARTE PROCEEDINGS
Master, failure of party to appear at time and place appointed, Rule 53(b); Auth. Comm. Rule 53(d)(1).
Temporary restraining orders, Rule 65(b); Auth. Comm. Rule 65(b).

EXAMINATION
Accounting parties before master, Rule 53(d); Auth. Comm. Rule 53(d)(3).
Business records, interrogatories, Rule 33(c).
Cross-Examination, generally, this index.
Deponent, Rule 26(b), (c).
Order for examination, Rule 27(a); Auth. Comm. Rule 27(a).
Jurors, Rule 47(a); Auth. Comm. Rule 47(a).
Physical and mental examinations, generally, post.
Voluminous writings, recordings or photographs, originals or duplicates, availability for, Evid. Rule 1006.
Witnesses, Rule 43(b).
Master, Rule 53(c); Auth. Comm. Rule 53(c).
Prior statements, Evid. Rule 613.

EXAMINER
Included in term "master," Rule 53(a).

EXCEPTIONAL CIRCUMSTANCES
Depositions use in court proceedings, Rule 32(a); Auth. Comm. Rule 32(a).
Discovery, nontrial expert witnesses, trial or litigation preparation, Rule 26(b); Auth. Comm. Rule 26(b)(4).

EXCEPTIONS
Formal exceptions to rulings unnecessary, Rule 46; Auth. Comm. Rule 46.
Insufficiency of pleadings, abolished, Rule 7(c).

EXCESSIVE FUNDS OR SECURITY
Admiralty or maritime claims, limitation of liability, Supp. Rule F(7).

EXCITEMENT
Hearsay exceptions, excited utterance, Evid. Rule 803.

EXCLUSION OF EVIDENCE
Admissibility of Evidence, generally, this index.

EXCLUSIVE JURISDICTION
Subject matter jurisdiction, Jurisdiction, Juris. § 2.11.

EXCUSABLE NEGLECT
Extension of time, Rule 6(b).
Judgment, relief from judgment on ground of, Rule 60(b).

EXECUTION
Generally, Rule 69; Auth. Comm. Rule 69.
Civil docket, entry in, Rule 79(a).
Compensation of master against delinquent party, Rule 53(a); Auth. Comm. Rule 53(a).

EXECUTION—Cont'd
Discovery in aid of, Rule 69(a).
Possession, execution to enforce judgment directing delivery of possession, Rule 70.
Process, admiralty or maritime claims, actions in rem and quasi in rem, Supp.Rule E(4).
Stay, Rule 62; Auth. Comm. Rule 62.
Time for issuing, Rule 62(a); Auth. Comm. Rule 62(a).
United States, actions involving, 28 U.S.C.A. § 2413.

EXECUTORS AND ADMINISTRATORS
Prosecution of action, Rule 17(a).

EXEMPTIONS
U.S. vessels, etc., arrest, etc., supplemental rules inapplicable, Supp. Rule C(1).

EXHIBITS
Depositions upon oral examination, Rule 30(f); Auth. Comm. Rule 30(f).
Hearsay exception, receipt as,
Learned treatises, Evid. Rule 803.
Recorded recollection, Evid. Rule 803.
Masters, filing with report, Rule 53(e).
Motion, bringing in third-party defendant, form of, Form 22-B.
Part of pleading, Rule 10(c).

EXPENSES AND EXPENDITURES
Depositions,
Failure of party to attend at own deposition, Rule 37(d); Auth. Comm. Rule 37(d).
Motions for protective orders, Rule 26(c); Auth. Comm. Rule 26(c).
Oral examination,
Failure to attend or to serve subpoena, payment, Rule 30(g); Auth. Comm. Rule 30(g).
Motion to terminate or limit, Rule 30(d); Auth. Comm. Rule 30(d).
Taxed as costs, Auth. Comm. Rule 54(d).
Discovery,
Expert witnesses, trial or litigation preparation, testifying and non-testifying, Rule 26(b); Auth. Comm. Rule 26(b)(4).
Failure to comply with order compelling, Rule 37(b); Auth. Comm. Rule 37(b).
Documents, failure to admit genuineness, Rule 37(c).
Elimination, unjustifiable expense, purpose and construction of rules, Evid. Rule 102.
Entry upon land, etc., for inspection and other purposes, failure of party to respond to request for inspection, Rule 37(d); Auth. Comm. Rule 37(d).
Exemplified document, Auth. Comm. Rule 54(d).
Expert witnesses, Auth. Comm. Rule 54(d).
Interrogatories, failure of party to serve answers to, Rule 37(d); Auth. Comm. Rule 37(d).
Medical and similar expenses, payment, admissibility to prove liability for injury, Evid. Rule 409.
Motion, for order,
Refusal to furnish prior statements by person of action or subject matter upon request, Rule 26(b).

EXPENSES AND EXPENDITURES—Cont'd
Motion, for order,—Cont'd
To compel discovery, Rule 37(a); Auth. Comm. Rule 37(a).
Printing, Auth. Comm. Rule 54(d).
Production of documents or things, failure of party to respond to request for inspection, Rule 37(d); Auth. Comm. Rule 37(d).
Requests for admission, Rule 36(a); Auth. Comm. Rule 36(a).
Sanctions, Rule 11.
United States, discovery proceedings, Rule 37(f).
Witnesses, Auth. Comm. Rule 54(d).

EXPERT WITNESSES
Opinions and Expert Testimony, generally, this index.

EXTENSION OF TIME
Generally, Rule 6(b); Auth. Comm. Rule 6(b).
Affidavits opposing new trial, time for serving, Rule 59(c).
Answers or objections to requests for admission, Rule 36(a); Auth. Comm. Rule 36(a).
Courthouse inaccessible, Rule 6(b); Auth. Comm. Rule 6(b).
Depositions,
Oral examination, taking, Rule 30(b).
Written questions, service, Rule 31(a).
Discovery, responses to, approval of court, stipulations, Rule 29; Auth. Comm. Rule 29.
Holidays, Rule 6(b); Auth. Comm. Rule 6(b).
Interrogatories, service, copies of answers and objections to, Rule 33(a); Auth. Comm. Rule 33(a).
Responses to request for production of documents or things and entry upon land, etc., for inspection and other purposes, Rule 34(b); Auth. Comm. Rule 34(b).
Return, habeas corpus writ of or show cause order, Rule 8(a).
Service by mail, Rule 6(e); Auth. Comm. Rule 6(e).
Temporary restraining order, Rule 65(b).
Weekends, Rule 6(b); Auth. Comm. Rule 6(b).

EXTRADITION
Proceedings, inapplicability, Evid. Rule 1101.

FACSIMILE TRANSMISSION
Filing by, Rule 5(e).
Service by, Auth. Comm. Rule 5.

FACTS
Expert witnesses, trial or litigation preparation, discovery, Rule 26(b).
Statements or opinions of. Admissions, generally, this index.
Taken to be established, discovery, sanctions for failure to comply with order compelling, Rule 37(b); Auth. Comm. Rule 37(b).

FAILURE OF CONSIDERATION
Pleading as affirmative defense, Rule 8(c).

FAIR CONDUCT
Class actions, orders, Rule 23(d).

FAMILY HISTORY OR RECORDS
Hearsay, this index.

FEDERAL AGENCIES
Agencies of United States, generally, this index.

FEDERAL EMPLOYER'S LIABILITY ACT
Complaint for negligence under, form of, Form 14.

FEDERAL EXPRESS
Service via overnight carriers, Auth. Comm. Rule 5(6)

FEDERAL FOOD, DRUG, AND COSMETIC ACT
Criminal libel for condemnation, exclusion of imports, or other proceedings, applicability of rules in part, Evid. Rule 1101.

FEDERAL OFFICERS AND EMPLOYEES
Officers and Employees, generally, this index.

FEDERAL QUESTION
Existence, jurisdiction, form of allegation, Form 2.
Removal in cases based on federal question jurisdiction, Removal, Juris. § 2.16.
Subject matter jurisdiction, Jurisdiction, Juris. 2.11.

FEES
Appeal, fees upon filing notice of, 28 U.S.C.A. § 1917.
Attorney's Fees, generally, this index.
Discovery, expert witnesses, trial or litigation preparation, testifying and nontestifying, Rule 26(b); Auth. Comm. Rules 26(b).
District Court fees, 28 U.S.C.A. § 1914.
Filing fees, Auth. Comm. Rule 3 & Rule 5(e).
Marshall fees, 28 U.S.C.A. § 1921.
Service fees, Auth. Comm. Rule 4(e).
Special appointments for service of process, Rule 4(c).

FELLOW SERVANT
Pleading injury by as affirmative defense, Rule 8(c).

FETAL DEATHS
Records of, hearsay exception, Evid. Rule 803.

FICTICIOUS NAME PARTIES
Propriety of, Auth Comm. Rule 10.

FILE NUMBERS
Actions entered in civil docket, assignment, Rule 79(a).

FILING
Briefs on appeal from magistrate to district judge, Rule 75(c); Auth. Comm. Rule 75(c).
Complaint, admiralty or maritime claims, limitation of liability, Supp. Rule F(1).
Depositions upon,
Oral examination, officer taking, Rule 30(f); Auth. Comm. Rule 30(f).
Written questions, Rule 31(b); Auth. Comm. Rule 31(c).
Discovery papers, Auth. Comm. Rule 5(d).
Electronic means, filing by, Auth. Comm. Rule 5(e).
Facsimile transmission, Rule 5(e); Auth. Comm. Rule 5(e).

FILING—Cont'd
Fees, Auth. Comm. Rule 3 & Rule 5(e).
Judge, filing with, Auth. Comm. Rule 5(e).
Master's reports, Rule 53(e); Auth. Comm. Rule 53(e)(1).
Papers after complaint, Rule 5(d).
Pleading,
Complaint,
Commencement of civil action, Rule 3.
Issuance of summons, Rule 4(a)(b).
Numerous defendants, Rule 5(c).
Prisoners, filing by, Auth. Comm. Rule 5(e).
Reasonable time for filing, Auth. Comm. Rule 5(d).
Seizure actions, Auth. Comm. Rule 5(a).
Temporary restraining order, Rule 65(b).
Time for, Rule 5(d); Auth. Comm. 5(d).
With the court, defined, Rule 5(e); Auth. Comm. Rule 5(e).

FINDINGS
Amendment of findings, Rule 52(b); Auth. Comm. Rule 52(b).
Extension of time, Rule 6(b).
Motion for new trial, Rule 59(a).
Stay of proceedings to enforce judgment pending disposition of motion to amend, Rule 62(b).
Class actions maintainable, Rule 23(b).
Court, findings by, Rule 52; Auth. Comm. Rule 52.
Master, findings of, Rule 53(e); Auth. Comm. Rule 53(e)(1).
Findings by court, Rule 52(a); Auth. Comm. Rule 52(a).
Motion for amendment of findings by court, Rule 52(b); Auth. Comm. Rule 52(b).
Partial findings, judgment on, Rule 52; Auth. Comm. Rule 52(c).
Special verdict, Rule 49(a).
Stay of proceedings to enforce judgment pending disposition of motion to amend, Rule 62(b).
Unanimity of jurors, Rule 48.

FINES AND PENALTIES
Customs duties, actions for, application of rules in part, Evid. Rule 1101.
Death Penalty, generally, this index.
Sentence and Punishment, generally, this index.
Witnesses, failure to appear before master, Rule 53(d); Auth. Comm. Rule 53(d)(2).

FOOD
Criminal libel for condemnation, exclusion of imports or other proceedings, applicability of rules in part, Evid. Rule 1101.

FOREIGN CORPORATIONS
Service, Rule 4(d).

FOREIGN COUNTRIES
Depositions, persons before whom taken, Rule 28(b); Auth. Comm. Rule 28(b).
Discovery, subpoena of person in, Rule 37(e).
Foreign and international tribunals, assistance to, 28 U.S.C.A. § 1782.
Removal in suits against, Removal.

FOREIGN COUNTRIES—Cont'd
Service in, alternative provisions for, Rule 4(i).
Subpoena directed to witness in foreign country, Rule 45(b); Auth. Comm. Rule 45(b); 28 U.S.C.A. § 1783.
Venue and, Venue, Juris. § 2.14.

FOREIGN DIPLOMATIC AND CONSULAR OFFICERS
Certification, genuineness of signature and official position of executing or attesting person, etc., foreign public documents, Evid. Rule 902.
Foreign and international tribunals, assistance to, 28 U.S.C.A. § 1782.

FOREIGN DOCUMENTS
Certification, genuineness of signature and official position of executing or attesting person, etc., Evid. Rule 902.

FOREIGN GOVERNMENTS AND AGENCIES
Service on, Auth. Comm. Rule 4(d).

FOREIGN JUDGMENTS
Pleading, Rule 9(e).

FOREIGN LAW
Determination, Rule 44.1; Auth. Comm. Rule 44.1.

FOREIGN OFFICIAL RECORDS
Authentication, Rule 44(a)(2); Auth. Comm. Rule 44(a)(2).

FOREIGN SERVICE
Certification, signatures, etc., foreign public documents, authority of consular agents, vice consul, etc., Evid. Rule 902.

FORFEITURES
Deposition, property, admiralty or maritime claims, actions in rem and quasi in rem, Supp. Rule, E(9)(a).

FORM OF ACTION
One form of action, civil action, Rule 2; Auth. Comm. Rule 2.

FORMER DISTRICT DIRECTOR OR COLLECTOR OF INTERNAL REVENUE
"Officer" as including, Rule 81(f).

FORMS
Answer, Form 21.
  Intervener, Form 23.
  Presenting defenses, Form 20.
Appendix Forms, intent to indicate simplicity and brevity of statement contemplated, Rule 84.
Complaint. Pleadings, generally, this index.
Counterclaim, Form 20.
  Interpleader, Form 21.
Cross-claim, Form 20.
Evidence, Rule 43(a).
Exhibit accompanying motion, bringing in third-party defendant, Form 22-B.
Judgment on,
  Decision by the court, Form 32.
  Jury verdict, Form 31.

FORMS—Cont'd
Jurisdiction, allegation of, Form 2.
Motions,
Bringing in third-party defendant, Form 22-B.
Dismissal of complaint, Form 19.
Intervention as defendant, Form 23.
Production of documents, form of, Form 24.
Technical forms not required, Rule 8(e)(1).
Notice,
Appeal to court of appeals, Form 27.
Bringing in third-party defendant, Form 22-B.
Condemnation of property, Form 28.
Intervention as defendant, Form 23.
Lawsuit, Form 1A.
Motion,
Dismiss complaint, Form 19.
Production of documents, Form 24.
Pleadings, this index.
Purpose of, Rule 84.
Request,
For admission, Form 25.
Production of documents or things, Form 24.
Statement of accounts before master, Rule 53(d); Auth. Comm. Rule 53(d)(3).
Subpoenas, Rule 45(a); Auth. Comm. Rule 45(a).
Suggestion of death upon the record under rule concerning substitution of parties, Form 30.
Summons, Rule 4(b), Form 1.
Third-party defendant, summons against, Forms 22-a, 22-A.
Third-party practice, Forms 22, 22-A.
Waiver of service, Form 1B.
Request for, Form 1A.

FORUM NON CONVENIENS
Deference to plaintiff and, Forum non Conveniens, Juris. § 2.15.
Remedy for inappropriate forum,
Dismissal of action, Forum non Conveniens, Juris. § 2.15 & Auth. Comm. Rule 12(b)(3).
Transfer of action, Forum non Conveniens, Juris. § 2.15.

FRAUD
Pleading, Rule 9(b); Auth. Comm. Rule 9(b).
Relief from judgment, Rule 60(b).

FRAUDULENT CONVEYANCES
Complaint in action to set aside, form of, Form 13.
Joinder of remedy, Rule 18(b).

GARNISHMENT
Availability of, Rule 64.

GENEALOGIES
Statement of personal or family history contained in, hearsay exception, Evid. Rule 803.

GOOD CAUSE
Failure to timely serve process, Auth. Comm. Rule 4(m).
Motion for protective orders relating to depositions, Rule 26(c); Auth. Comm. Rule 26(c).
Physical and mental examinations, order for, Rule 35(a); Auth. Comm. Rule 35(a).

GOODS SOLD AND DELIVERED
Complaint, Form 5.

GOVERNMENTAL AGENCIES
Agencies of United States, generally, this index.

GOVERNMENTAL ORGANIZATION
Service of summons and complaint, Rule 4(d); Auth. Comm. Rule 4(d).

GOVERNMENTS
Privilege of, general rule, Evid. Rule 501.

GRAND JURY
Proceedings before, inapplicability, Evid. Rule 1101.

GRAPHS
Production of documents or things, generally, post.

GROUNDS
Class actions maintainable, Rule 23(b).
New trial, Rule 59(d).

GROUP PLEADING
Limitations upon, Auth. Comm. Rule 9(b) & Rule 10(b).

GUAM
District court, applicability of rules, Evid. Rule 1101.
Subject matter jurisdiction, Jurisdiction, Juris. §§ 2.12-2.13.

GUARDIANS
Action or defense by representative, Rule 17(a), (c).

GUILTY
Plea of Guilty, generally, this index.

HABEAS CORPUS
Applicability of rules in part, Evid. Rule 1101.
Application of rules to, Rule 81(a); Auth. Comm. Rule 81(a).
Direction of writ or show cause order to person having custody, Rule 81(a); Auth. Comm. Rule 81(a).
Return of writ or show cause order, time, Rule 81(a); Auth. Comm. Rule 81(a).

HABIT
Relevant evidence, Evid. Rule 406.

HANDWRITING
Admissibility, 28 U.S.C.A. § 1731.
Writings, generally, this index.

HARASSMENT
Witnesses, control of mode and order of interrogation and presentation of evidence to protect from, Evid. Rule 611.

HARMLESS ERROR
Disregard of error not affecting substantial rights, Rule 61; Auth. Comm. Rule 61; 28 U.S.C.A. § 2111.

HEALTH
Hearsay exceptions, statements respecting, Evid. Rule 803.

HEARINGS
Conducted outside district, Rule 77(b).
Consolidation of actions for hearing, Rule 42(a); Auth. Comm. Rule 42(a).
Discovery, order to compel, award of expenses, Rule 37(a); Auth. Comm. Rule 37(a).
Inability of judge to proceed, Rule 63.
Judicial notice, adjudicative facts, opportunity to be heard as to propriety of taking, Evid. Rule 201.
Jury, this index.
Motions,
Depositions, use of, Rule 32(a).
Without oral hearing, determination of, Rule 78; Auth. Comm. Rule 78.
New trial, Rule 59(d).
Preliminary hearing on defenses in pleading, etc., Rule 12(d); Auth. Comm. Rule 12(d).
Preliminary injunction, consolidation with trial on merits, Rule 65(a)(2).
Service of notice, Rule 6(d).
Subpoena for attendance at, Rule 45(a).
Successor judges, Rule 63.
Temporary restraining order, Rule 65(b).
Voluntary dismissal before introduction of evidence, Rule 41(c).

HEARSAY
Generally, Evid. Rule 802.
Absence of,
Declarant from hearing and proponent of statement unable to procure attendance of, "unavailability as witness" as including, exception, Evid. Rule 804.
Entry in records of regularly conducted activity, exception, Evid. Rule 803.
Public record or entry, exception, Evid. Rule 803.
Admission by party-opponent, statements which are not hearsay, Evid. Rule 801.
Adoption,
Reputation concerning, exception, Evid. Rule 803.
Statement of declarant concerning, exception, Evid. Rule 804.
Agent or servant, statements by not hearsay, Evid. Rule 801.
Ancestry, records of religious organizations, exception, Evid. Rule 803.
Attacking and supporting credibility of declarant, Evid. Rule 806.
Availability of declarant immaterial, Evid. Rule 803.
Baptismal certificates, exception, Evid. Rule 803.
Births,
Records of, exception, Evid. Rule 803.
Statement of declarant concerning, exception, Evid. Rule 804.
Bodily health, statements respecting, exception, Evid. Rule 803.
Boundaries, reputation concerning or judgment as to, exception, Evid. Rule 803.
Certificates, marriage, baptismal, etc., exception, Evid. Rule 803.
Commercial publications, exception, Evid. Rule 803.

HEARSAY—Cont'd
Criminal liability, statement tending to expose declarant to and offered to exculpate accused, admissibility, exception, Evid. Rule 804.
Cross-examination by party against whom statement of declarant admitted, Evid. Rule 806.
Death,
Declarant unable to be present or to testify at hearing because of, "unavailability as witness" as including, exception, Evid. Rule 804.
Records of, exception, Evid. Rule 803.
Statement under belief of impending death, exception, Evid. Rule 804.
Declarant, defined, Evid. Rule 801.
Definitions, Evid. Rule 801.
Design, statements respecting, exception, Evid. Rule 803.
Divorce,
Records of, exception, Evid. Rule 803.
Statement of declarant concerning, exception, Evid. Rule 804.
Engravings, rings, urns, crypts or tombstones, statements concerning, exception, Evid. Rule 803.
Exceptions, enumeration of, Evid. Rules 803, 804.
Excited utterance, statement relating to, exception, Evid. Rule 803.
Existing mental, emotional, or physical condition, statement respecting, exception, Evid. Rule 803.
Factual findings resulting from investigation, civil actions and criminal cases, public records and reports, exception, Evid. Rule 803.
Family bibles, statements of personal or family history in, exception, Evid. Rule 803.
Family history or records,
Reputation concerning, exception, Evid. Rule 803.
Statement of, exception, Evid. Rule 804.
Fetal deaths, records of, exception, Evid. Rule 803.
Former testimony, exception, Evid. Rule 804.
Genealogies, statement of personal or family history contained in, exception, Evid. Rule 803.
General listing, reputation concerning or judgment as to, exception, Evid. Rule 803.
Impending death, statement under belief of, exception, Evid. Rule 804.
Inability of declarant to be present or testify at hearing because of death, etc., "unavailability as witness" as including, exceptions, Evid. Rule 804.
Intent, statements respecting, exception, Evid. Rule 803.
Interest, statement against, exception, Evid. Rule 804.
Judgment,
As to personal, family or general history or boundaries, exception, Evid. Rule 803.
Previous convictions, exception, Evid. Rule 803.
Lack of memory of subject matter of his statement, declarant testifying to, "unavailability as witness" as including, exceptions, Evid. Rule 804.
Learned treatises, exception, Evid. Rule 803.
Legitimacy, statement of declarant concerning, exception, Evid. Rule 804.
Market reports, exception, Evid. Rule 803.
Marriage,
Records of, exception, Evid. Rule 803.
Statement of declarant concerning, exception, Evid. Rule 804.

HEARSAY—Cont'd
Matters not excluded by hearsay rule, declarant,
Available as witness, Evid. Rule 803.
Unavailable as witness, Evid. Rule 804.
Medical diagnosis or treatment, statements for purposes of, exception, Evid. Rule 803.
Memoranda, recollections, exception, Evid. Rule 803.
Motive, statements respecting, exception, Evid. Rule 803.
Pain, statements respecting, exception, Evid. Rule 803.
Personal history. Family history or records, generally, ante.
Police officers and law enforcement personnel, matters observed by, public records and reports, exception and exclusion, Evid. Rule 803.
Present sense impression, statement describing, etc., exception, Evid. Rule 803.
Previous conviction, judgment of, exception, Evid. Rule 803.
Procurement or wrongdoing of proponent of statement, declarant not available as witness if his exemption, refusal, etc., is due to, exception, Evid. Rule 804.
Property, record of or statements in documents affecting an interest in, exception, Evid. Rule 803.
Public records and reports, exceptions, Evid. Rule 803.
Recorded recollection, exception, Evid. Rule 803.
Refusing to testify concerning subject matter of statement despite court order to do so, declarant persisting in, "unavailability as witness" as including exceptions, Evid. Rule 804.
Regularly conducted activity, records of, exception, Evid. Rule 803.
Relationship by blood or marriage, records of religious organizations, exception, Evid. Rule 803.
Religious organizations, records of, exception, Evid. Rule 803.
Reputation,
As to character, exception, Evid. Rule 803.
Concerning boundaries or general history, exception, Evid. Rule 803.
Ruling of court, declarant exempted by on ground of privilege from testifying concerning subject matter of his statement, "unavailability as witness" as including, exception, Evid. Rule 804.
Statements,
Defined, Evid. Rule 801.
Not specifically covered in enumerated exceptions, exception of, Evid. Rules 803, 804.
Which are not hearsay, Evid. Rule 801.
Unavailability as a witness, defined, Evid. Rule 804.
Urns, crypts or tombstones, statement concerning engravings on, exception, Evid. Rule 803.
Vital statistics, records of, exception, Evid. Rule 803.
Within hearsay, exclusion, Evid. Rule 805.

HISTORY
Hearsay, generally, this index.

HOLIDAYS
Excluded in computing time, Auth. Comm. Rule 6.

HOMICIDE
Statement under belief of impending death, criminal prosecution, hearsay exception, Evid. Rule 804.

HOMICIDE—Cont'd
Victim, character of, as peaceful or aggressive, Evid. Rule 404.

HOSPITALS
Expenses, payment, admissibility to prove liability for injury, Evid. Rule 409.

HOSTILE WITNESSES
Leading questions, interrogation by, Evid. Rule 611.

HYPOTHETICAL STATEMENT
Claim or defense, Rule 8(e)(2).

IDENTIFICATION
Documents and things produced for inspection, depositions upon oral examination, Rule 30(f).
Expert witnesses, trial preparation, interrogatories, Rule 26(b); Auth. Comm. Rule 26(b)(4).
Persons with knowledge of discoverable matter,
Discovery, scope of, Rule 26(b).
Supplementation of responses to request for discovery, Rule 26(e); Auth. Comm. Rule 26(e).

ILLEGALITY
Pleading as affirmative defense, Rule 8(c).

ILLEGITIMACY
Legitimacy and Illegitimacy, generally, this index.

ILLNESS OF WITNESS
Inability to attend or testify, depositions, use in court proceedings, Rule 32(a); Auth. Comm. Rule 32(a).
Waiver, signing depositions upon oral examination, Rule 30(e).

IMMUNITY
From service, Auth. Comm. Rule 4.

IMPAIRMENT OF SECURITY
Admiralty or maritime claims, actions in rem and quasi in rem, Supp. Rule E(6).

IMPEACHMENT OF WITNESSES
Generally, Rule 43 (b).
Conviction of crime, evidence of, Evid. Rule 609.
Deposition in court proceedings, use of, Rule 32(a); Auth. Comm. Rule 32(a).
Guilty, offer to plead or withdraw plea of, statements respecting, admissibility, Evid. Rule 410.
Juvenile adjudications, evidence of, admissibility, Evid. Rule 609.
Nolo contendere, plea of or offer to plead, statements respecting, admissibility, Evid. Rule 410.
Party calling witness, Evid. Rule 607.
Persons who may impeach, Evid. Rule 607.
Subsequent remedial measures, admissibility for purpose of, Evid. Rule 407.

IMPLEADER ACTIONS
Generally, Rule 14.
Subject matter jurisdiction, jurisdiction, Juris. § 2.13.

IMPORTS AND EXPORTS
Exclusion of imports under Federal Food, Drug, and Cosmetic Act, applicability of rules in part, Evid. Rule 1101.

IMPRISONMENT OF WITNESS
Inability to attend or testify, depositions, use in court proceedings, Rule 32(a); Auth. Comm. Rule 32(a).

IN FORMA PAUPERIS
Commencement of action, Auth. Comm. Rule 3.
Fees, 28 U.S.C.A., § 1915.

IN PERSONAM ACTIONS
Interpleader, Auth. Comm. Rule 22 and Statutory Interpleader.
Personal jurisdiction, Jurisdiction, Juris. §§ 2.3-2.7.

IN REM ACTIONS, ADMIRALTY OR MARITIME CLAIMS
Applicability, supplemental rules, Supp. Rule A.
General provisions, Supp. Rule E.
Jurisdiction, Jurisdiction, Juris. § 2.9.
Special proceedings, Supp. Rule C.
Statutory condemnation proceedings, inclusion, Supp. Rule A.

INADVERTENCE
Relief from judgment on ground of, Rule 60(b).

INCOMPETENT PERSONS
Subject matter jurisdiction, Jurisdiction.

INCOMPETENT PERSONS, PARTIES
Generally, Rule 17(c).
Default judgment entry against, Rules 55(b)(1, 2).
Depositions, taking before action, Rule 27(a)(2).
Service of summons and complaint, Rule 4(d); Auth. Comm. Rule 4(d).
Substitution, Rule 25(b).

INDEMNITOR
Discovery, trial and litigation, preparation of materials, Rule 26(b).

INDEPENDENCE DAY
Clerks of court, business hours for office, exceptions concerning opening, Rule 77(c).
"Legal holiday" as including for purposes of computing time, Rule 6(a).

INDICES
Civil docket and civil judgments and orders, Rule 79(c).

INDICTMENT AND INFORMATION
Inquiry into validity, testimony of juror in connection with, restriction and exception, Evid. Rule 606.

INDISPENSABLE PARTY
Determination by court, Rule 19(b).

INDORSEMENT
Admiralty or maritime claims, actions in rem and quasi in rem, bond or stipulation, Supp. Rule E(5)(b).
Temporary restraining order, Rule 65(b).

INFANTS

Default judgment entered against, Rules 55(b)(1), (2).
Depositions, taking before action, Rule 27(a).
Parties, Rule 17(c).
Service of summons and complaint, Rule 4(d); Auth. Comm. Rule 4(d).
Subject matter jurisdiction, Jurisdiction, Juris. § 2.12.

INFERENCES

Opinions and Expert Testimony, generally, this index.
Presumptions, generally, this index.

INFIRMITY OF WITNESS

Inability to attend or testify, depositions, use in court proceedings, Rule 32(a); Auth. Comm. Rule 32(a).

INFORMATION

Discovery, generally, this index.

INFRINGEMENT

Complaint in action for infringement of,
Copyright, Form 17.
Patent, Form 16.
Stay of judgment for accounting for infringement, Rule 62(a).

INJUNCTION

Generally, Rule 65.
Class actions, Rule 23(b).
Preliminary injunction or temporary restraining order, Rule 65.

INNOCENCE

Conviction of crime subject of pardon, annulment, etc., based on findings of, impeachment by evidence of conviction, effect, Evid. Rule 609.

INSANE PERSONS

Incompetent Persons, Parties, generally, this index.

INSPECTION

Business records, interrogatories, Rule 33(c); Auth. Comm. Rule 33(c).
Documents and things produced for inspection, depositions upon oral examination, Rule 30(f).
Entry Upon Land, generally, this index.
Order for, Rule 27.
Production of Documents or Things, generally, this index.
Writing used to refresh memory, right of adverse party, Evid. Rule 612.

INSTRUCTIONS TO JURY

Generally, Rule 51; Auth. Comm. Rule 51.
Answers to interrogatories and rendering general verdict, instruction to enable, Rule 49(b); Auth. Comm. Rule 49(b).
Judicial notice, Evid. Rule 201.
Limited admissibility of evidence, Evid. Rule 105.
Objections, Rule 51; Auth. Comm. Rule 51.
Special verdict, Rule 49(a); Auth. Comm. Rule 49(a).

INSUFFICIENCY OF FUND OR SECURITY

Admiralty or maritime claims, limitation of liability, Supp. Rule F(7).

INSULAR POSSESSION
Documents of under or not under seal, self-authentication, Evid. Rule 902.
Official record, authentication, Rule 44(a)(1).

INSURANCE AGREEMENTS
Admissibility in evidence at trial, Rule 26(b); Auth. Comm. Rule 26(b)(2).
Discovery, existence and contents, Rule 26(b); Auth. Comm. Rule 26(b)(2).
Liability, evidence, person insured against, admissibility on issue of negligence or wrongful action, Evid. Rule 411.

INSURANCE COMPANIES
Subject matter jurisdiction, Jurisdiction.

INSURER
Discovery, trial and litigation preparation, need of materials, Rule 26(b); Auth. Comm. Rule 26(b)(2).

INTANGIBLE PROPERTY
Admiralty or maritime claims, actions in rem, ancillary process, Supp. Rule C(5).
Custody, etc., admiralty or maritime claims, action in rem and quasi in rem, Supp. Rule E(4)(c).

INTENT
Pleading, Rule 9(b).
Proof of, admissibility of other crimes, wrongs or acts, Evid. Rule 404.

INTEREST
Civil cases, 28 U.S.C.A. § 1961.
Class actions, protection, Rule 23(a).
Depositions, disqualification for taking, Rule 28(c); Auth. Comm. Rule 28(c).
In,
Property, etc., inability to protect, right to intervene, Rule 24(a).
Subject of action, joinder, persons needed for just adjudication, Rule 19(a).
Prejudgment interest, motions for, Auth. Comm. Rule 59(e).
Statement against, hearsay exception, Evid. Rule 804.
Transfer of, substitution of new party, Rule 25(c); Auth. Comm. Rule 25(c).

INTERLOCUTORY
Injunction, findings of facts and conclusions of law, Rule 52(a); Auth. Comm. Rule 52(a).
Order, admiralty or maritime claims, actions in rem and quasi in rem, security, Supp. Rule E(9)(b).
Proceeding, depositions, use of, Rule 32(a).
Sales, admiralty or maritime claims, actions in rem and quasi in rem, Supp. Rule E(9)(b).

INTERNAL PATTERNS
Authentication and identification, conformity with requirements, Evid. Rule 901.

INTERNAL REVENUE OFFICER
Execution against, Rule 69(b); Auth. Comm. Rule 69(b).

INTERPLEADER
Generally, Rule 22 and 28 U.S.C.A. § 1335.
Competency of witnesses, determination, Evid. Rule 601.

INTERPLEADER—Cont'd
Complaint for interpleader and declaratory relief, form of, Form 18.
Counterclaim for interpleader, form of, Form 21; Auth. Comm. Rule 22 and Statutory Interpleader.
Injunction in action of, Rule 65(e).
Process and procedure, 28 U.S.C.A. § 2361.
Venue, 28 U.S.C.A. § 1397.

INTERPRETERS
Appointment and compensation, Rule 43(f).
Subject to rules relating to qualification as expert, Evid. Rule 604.

INTERROGATION
Witnesses, by court, Evid. Rule 614.

INTERROGATORIES
See, also, Discovery, generally, this index.
Generally, Rule 33(a) et seq.; Auth. Comm. Rule 33.
Adverse parties, Rule 43(b).
Answer, Rule 33(a); Auth. Comm. Rule 33(a).
Business records, option to produce, Rule 33(c); Auth. Comm. Rule 33(c).
Copies of answers and objections, service, time, Rule 33(a); Auth. Comm. Rule 33(a).
Evasive or incomplete answer, defined, motion for order to compel, Rule 37(a).
Examination of accounting parties before master, Rule 53(d)(3).
Expert witnesses, Rule 26(b); Auth. Comm. Rule § 26(b)(4) and 33(b).
Failure of party to serve answers or objections, to, sanctions, Rule 37(b).
Failure to comply with order compelling answer, sanction, Rule 37(d); Auth. Comm. Rule 37(d).
General verdict accompanied by answer to interrogatories, Rule 49(b); Auth. Comm. Rule 49(b).
Method of obtaining discovery, Rule 26(a).
Motion for order to compel answer, Rule 37(a); Auth. Comm. Rule 37(a).
Number of interrogatories, Rule 33(a); Auth. Comm. Rule 33(a).
Objections to, Rule 33(b); Auth. Comm. Rule 33(b).
Orders, this index.
Privileged information, Auth. Comm. Rule 33(b).
Scope of, Rule 33(b); Auth. Comm. Rule 33(b).
Service, Rule 33(a); Auth. Comm. Rule 33(a).
Special interrogatories to jury, Rule 49; Auth. Comm. Rule 49.
Stipulations, extension of time, responses to, approval of court, Rule 29; Auth. Comm. Rule 29.
Submission to jury with forms for a general verdict, Rule 49(b); Auth. Comm. Rule 49(b).
Summary judgment,
Affidavits for, supplemented or opposed by answers to, Rule 56(e).
Rendered where answers show no genuine issue, etc., Rule 56(c).
Supplement, duty to, Rule 26(e); Auth. Comm. Rules 26(e) and 33(a).
Time of service, Rule 33(a); Auth. Comm. Rule 33(a).
Trial, use at, Rule 33(b); Auth. Comm. Rule 33(b).

INTERVENTION
Generally, Rule 24.
Form, Form 23.
Subject matter jurisdiction, jurisdiction, Juris. § 2.13; Auth. Comm. Rule 24(a).
United States, intervention by, 28 U.S.C.A. § 2403.

INTRODUCTION OF DESIGNATED MATTERS IN EVIDENCE
Prohibition, sanction for failure to comply with order compelling discovery, Rule 37(b); Auth. Comm. Rule 37(b).

INVESTIGATION
Criminal Investigations, generally, this index.
Factual findings resulting from, hearsay exception, Evid. Rule 803.
Foreign official records, Rule 44(a)(2).
Foreign public documents, authenticity and accuracy, Evid. Rule 902.

INVOLUNTARY DISMISSAL
Procedure, Rule 41(b); Auth. Comm. Rule 41(b).

INVOLUNTARY PLAINTIFF
Refusal to join, Rule 19(a).

IRREPARABLE INJURY
Preliminary injunctions and temporary restraining orders, Auth. Comm. Rule 65.

ISSUANCE OF PROCESS
Admiralty or maritime claims, actions in rem and quasi in rem, Supp. Rule E(3)(b).

ISSUES
Capacity of party, pleading, Rule 9(a).
Confusion of, exclusion of relevant evidence on grounds of, Evid. Rule 403.
Fact in issue,
Expert testimony, Evid. Rule 702.
Opinion testimony by lay witnesses, Evid. Rule 701.
Jury trial,
Specification of issues in demand for, Rule 38(c); Auth. Comm. Rule 38(c).
Trial of issues, Rule 39(a); Auth. Comm. Rule 39(a).
Pre-trial procedure, Rule 16.
Separate trial, Rule 42(b).
Trial by court, Rule 39(b).
Ultimate issue, opinion on, Evid. Rule 704.

JOINDER
Claims, Rule 18(a); Auth. Comm. Rule 2.
Dismissal for failure to join, Rules 12(b)(7), 19(b); Auth. Comm. Rules 12(b)(7), 19(b).
Parties, this index.
Property in condemnation proceeding, Rule 71A(b); Auth. Comm. Rule 71A(b).
Remedies, Rules 18(b), 21.
Removal and, Removal.
Subject matter jurisdiction
Third-party practice, Rule 14.

JOINT HEARING
Order of court, Rule 42(a); Auth. Comm. Rule 42(a).

JUDGES

Appointment of masters, Rule 53(a).
Competency as witness, Evid. Rule 605.
Definition of,
Generally, 28 U.S.C.A. § 451.
Applicability of evidence rules, Evid.Rule 1101.
Inability to proceed, Rule 63 & Auth. Comm. Rule 63.
Management-Judges, generally, this index.
Official record, authentication, Rule 44(a)(1).
Permit for filing pleading and papers with him, Rule 5(e).
Successor judges, Rule 63.

JUDGMENT AS A MATTER OF LAW

Generally, Rule 50; Auth. Comm. Rule 50.

JUDGMENTS AND DECREES

Amendment or alteration, Rule 59(e); Auth. Comm. Rule 59(e).
Stay of proceedings pending disposition of motion for, Rule 62(b).
Time for service of motion, Rule 59(e).
Appeal from magistrate to district judge by consent, Rule 76; Auth. Comm. Rule 76.
Appeal upon certification by district judge, Rule 54(b); Auth. Comm. Rule 54(b).
Attachment of property of person disobeying judgment for specific acts, Rule 70; Auth. Comm. Rule 70.
Attorneys, submission of forms, Rule 58.
Bills of review abolished, Rule 60(b).
Certification, Rule 54(b); Auth. Comm. Rule 54(b).
Civil docket, entry in, Rule 79(a).
Class actions, Rule 23(c).
Clerical mistakes, correction of, Rule 60(a).
Clerk to enter, Rule 58.
Contempt by disobeying judgment directing performance of specific acts, Rule 70; Auth. Comm. Rule 70.
Copies, clerk to keep correct copy of every final judgment, Rule 79(b).
Counterclaim or cross-claim, Rule 13(i).
Entry of judgment disposing of, Rule 54(b).
Decision by the court, form of, Form 32.
Declaratory judgments, this index.
Decree included in judgment, Rule 54(a).
Default Judgments, generally, this index.
Defined, Rule 54(a); Auth. Comm. Rule 54(a).
Demand for judgment, Rule 54(c); Auth. Comm. Rules 8(a) and 54(c).
Determination by court whenever joinder not feasible, Rule 19(b).
Discovery in aid of, Rule 69(a).
Effective when set forth on separate document and entered, Rule 58.
Enforcement of judgment for payment of money. Execution, generally, ante.
Entry of judgment, Rule 58; Auth. Comm. Rule 58.
Actions tried upon facts without jury or with an advisory jury, findings by court, Rule 52(a).
Appeal timeliness, Rule 58; Auth. Comm. Rule 58.
Disposing of multiple claims or multiple parties, Rule 54(b).

JUDGMENTS AND DECREES—Cont'd
Entry of judgment, Rule 58; Auth. Comm. Rule 58.—Cont'd
General verdict and answers to interrogatories harmonious with each other, etc., Rule 49(b); Auth. Comm. Rule 49(b).
New judgment on motion for new trial, Rule 59(a).
Partial findings, Rule 52; Auth. Comm. Rule 52(c).
Taxation of costs, entry not delayed by, Auth. Comm. Rule 58.
Excusable neglect as ground for relief from, Rule 60(b).
Finality, unaffected by motion for relief on ground of mistake, inadvertence, surprise or excusable neglect, Rule 60(b).
Fraud, relief from judgment, Rule 60(b).
General verdict accompanied by answers to interrogatories, entry of judgment, Rule 58.
Hearsay exception,
Personal, family or general history, or boundaries, judgment as proof of, Evid. Rule 803.
Previous conviction judgment, evidence of, Evid. Rule 803.
Inadvertence as ground for relief from, Rule 60(b).
Indices to be kept by clerk of every judgment, Rule 79(c).
Inequitable prospective application, relief from judgment, Rule 60(b).
Judge to approve form upon special verdict or general verdict accompanied by answers to interrogatories, etc., Rule 58.
Jury verdict, form of, Form 31.
Misconduct, relief from judgment, Rule 60(b).
Mistake as ground for relief from, Rule 60(b).
Modification, errors not affecting substantial rights not ground for, Rule 61.
Motions,
Alter or amend,
Extension of time, Rule 6(b).
Time for service, Rule 59(e).
Correction of clerical mistakes, Rule 60(a); Auth. Comm. Rule 60(a).
Findings of fact and conclusions of law, Rule 52(a).
Judgment on the pleadings, Rule 12(c); Auth. Comm. Rule 12(c).
Multiple claims or parties, Rule 54(b); Auth. Comm. Rule 54(b).
Raising objections to evidence to sustain findings by court, Rule 52(b).
Relief on ground of mistake, inadvertence, surprise or excusable neglect, Rule 60(b); Auth. Comm. Rule 60(b).
Time for making motion, Rule 60(b); Auth. Comm. Rule 60(b).
Stay of enforcement, Rule 62(h).
Stay of proceedings to enforce judgment pending motion to alter or amend, Rule 62(b); Auth. Comm. Rule 62(b).
New trial, stay of proceedings to enforce on motion for new trial, Rule 62(b); Auth. Comm. Rule 62(b).
Newly discovered evidence, relief from judgment, Rule 60(b).
Notice of entry, Rule 58, Rule 77(d).
Notice of motion for correction of clerical mistakes, Rule 60(a).
Notwithstanding the verdict, judgment as a matter of law, Rule 50; Auth. Comm. Rule 50.
Offer of judgment, Rule 68.
Service, Rule 5(a).
Opening judgment on motion for new trial, Rule 59(a).
Order included in meaning of "judgment," Rule 54(a).

JUDGMENTS AND DECREES—Cont'd
Partial findings, Rule 52; Auth. Comm. Rule 52(c).
Personal judgment, court not acquiring jurisdiction to render, opposing party bringing suit upon claim by attachment, etc., pleader need not state claim, Rule 13(a).
Personal representatives, relief from judgment on ground of mistake, inadvertence, surprise or excusable neglect, Rule 60(b).
Pleading, Rule 9(e); Auth. Comm. Rule 9(c).
Recitals of pleading not required, Rule 54(a).
Possession, enforcement of judgment directing delivery, Rule 70; Auth. Comm. Rule 70.
Recitals, Rule 54(a).
Record of prior proceedings, recitals of record not required, Rule 54(a).
Recovery by party only of sum certain or costs or that relief shall be denied, entry of judgment, Rule 58.
Registration of foreign judgments, 28 U.S.C.A. § 1963.
Relief, limitations on, Rule 54(c); Auth. Comm. Rules 2, 54(c).
Relief from judgment, Rule 60; Auth. Comm. Rule 60.
Extension of time, Rule 6(b).
Stay of proceedings to enforce judgment pending disposition of motion, Rule 62(b); Auth. Comm. Rule 62(b).
Report of master, recitals of report not required, Rule 54(a).
Reversal, relief from, Rule 60(b).
Satisfaction, admiralty or maritime claims, actions in rem or quasi in rem, sales, Supp. Rule E(9)(b).
Satisfied, released or discharged, relief from, Rule 60(b).
Security on stay of proceedings to enforce, Rule 62(b); Auth. Comm. Rule 62(b).
Separate document, setting forth on, Rule 58.
Separate judgment as to one or more but fewer than all claims, Rule 54(b).
Sequestration of property of person disobeying judgment for specific acts, Rule 70; Auth. Comm. Rule 70.
Setting aside judgment,
Power to set aside unaffected by motion for relief on ground of mistake, inadvertence, surprise or excusable neglect, Rule 60(b).
Special verdict, entry of judgment on, Rule 58.
Specific acts, performance of judgment directing specific acts, Rule 70; Auth. Comm. Rule 70.
State law, staying enforcement in accordance to state law, Rule 62(f).
Stay,
Judgment on one or more but fewer than all of the claims or parties, Rule 62(h).
Proceedings to enforce, Rule 62; Auth. Comm. Rule 60.
Separate judgment as to one or more but fewer than all claims, Rule 62(h).
Summary Judgment, generally, this index.
Surprise as ground for relief from, Rule 60(b).
Suspension by motion for relief on ground of mistake, inadvertence, surprise or excusable neglect, Rule 60(b).
Termination of action as to claim disposed of, Rule 54(b).
Third-party claim, Rule 54(b).
Third-party practice, admiralty and maritime claims, Rule 14(c).
Time,
Extension of time for relief from judgment, Rule 6(b).

JUDGMENTS AND DECREES—Cont'd
Time,—Cont'd
Motion,
Alter or amend judgment, extension of time, Rule 6(b).
Relief on ground of mistake, inadvertence, surprise or excusable neglect, Rule 60(b).
Proceedings to enforce, Rule 62(a).
Title, judgment vesting title in another, Rule 70; Auth. Comm. Rule 70.
Transferring judgment, Rule 58; Auth. Comm. Rule 58.
United States, stay of judgment against, Rule 62(e); Auth. Comm. Rule 62(e).
Vacation, errors not affecting substantial rights not ground for, Rule 61.
Verdict submitted on written interrogatories to jury, Rule 49(b); Auth. Comm. Rule 49(b).
Void judgment, relief from, Rule 60(b).
Writs of coram nobis, coram vobis and audita querela abolished, Rule 60(b).

JUDICIAL NOTICE
Adjudicative facts, Evid. Rule 201.
Learned treatises, statements in, hearsay exception, Evid. Rule 803.

JUDICIAL PANEL ON MULTIDISTRICT LITIGATION
Generally, this index.

JUDICIAL REVIEW
Appeal and Review, generally, this index.

JURISDICTION
Generally, Part II.
Amendment of pleadings to show, 28 U.S.C.A. § 1653.
Amount in controversy, subject matter jurisdiction, Jurisdiction, Juris. § 2.12.
Citizenship,
Corporations and, subject matter jurisdiction, Jurisdiction, Juris. § 2.12.
Subject matter jurisdiction, Jurisdiction, Juris. § 2.12.
Class actions, Auth. Comm. Rule 23.
Collusive invocation of jurisdiction, subject matter jurisdiction, Jurisdiction, Juris. § 2.12.
Concurrent jurisdiction, subject matter jurisdiction, Jurisdiction, Juris. § 2.11.
Consent, personal jurisdiction, Jurisdiction, Juris. § 2.4.
Corporate citizenship, subject matter jurisdiction, Jurisdiction, Juris. § 2.12.
Counterclaims and crossclaims, Juris. § 2.4, Auth. Comm. Rule 13.
Decedents, subject matter jurisdiction, Jurisdiction, Juris. § 2.12.
Declaratory judgments, subject matter jurisdiction, Jurisdiction, Juris. § 2.12.
Dismissal for lack of, operation and effect, Rule 41(b); Jurisdiction, Juris. §§ 2.2-2.13.
Dismissal for lack of personal jurisdiction, Auth. Comm. Rule 12(b)(2); Jurisdiction, Juris. §§ 2.1-2.2.
Dismissal for lack of subject matter jurisdiction, Auth. Comm. Rule 12(b)(1); Jurisdiction, Juris. §§ 2.1, 2.10.
District of Columbia, subject matter jurisdiction, Jurisdiction, Juris. §§ 2.12-2.13.
Diversity jurisdiction, subject matter jurisdiction, Jurisdiction, Juris. § 2.12.
Generally, 28 U.S.C.A. § 1331.

JURISDICTION—Cont'd
Domicile,
Citizenship and, subject matter jurisdiction, Jurisdiction, Juris. § 2.12.
Due Process, requirements of in cases involving personal jurisdiction, quasi in rem jurisdiction, and in rem jurisdiction, Jurisdiction, Juris. §§ 2.1-2.9.
Equity cases, amount in controversy and, subject matter jurisdiction, Jurisdiction, Juris. § 2.12.
Exclusive jurisdiction, subject matter jurisdiction, Jurisdiction, Juris. § 2.11.
Federal question, Jurisdiction, Juris. § 2.11.
Generally, 28 U.S.C.A. § 1332.
Guam, subject matter jurisdiction, Jurisdiction, Juris. §§ 2.12-2.13.
Incompetent persons, subject matter jurisdiction, Jurisdiction, Juris. § 2.12.
Infants, subject matter jurisdiction, Jurisdiction, Juris. § 2.12.
In personam jurisdiction, Jurisdiction, Juris. §§ 2.1-2.7.
In rem jurisdiction, Jurisdiction, Juris. § 2.9.
Insurance Companies, subject matter jurisdiction, Jurisdiction, Juris. § 2.12.
Interpleader, Auth. Comm. Rule 22 and Statutory Interpleader.
Generally, 28 U.S.C.A. § 1335.
Intervention and subject matter jurisdiction, Auth. Comm. Rule 24(a).
Joinder of party, improper jurisdiction, Rule 19(a).
Lack of, defense, Rule 12(h).
Intervention and subject matter jurisdiction, Auth. Comm. Rule 24(a).
Legal certainty, amount in controversy and, subject matter jurisdiction, Jurisdiction, Juris. § 2.12.
Long-arm statutes, personal jurisdiction, Jurisdiction, Juris. § 2.5.
Minimum contacts, personal jurisdiction, Jurisdiction, Juris. § 2.4.
Motion to dismiss complaint for lack of jurisdiction, form of, Form 19.
Personal jurisdiction, Jurisdiction, Juris. §§ 2.3-2.7.
Pleading, Auth. Comm. Rule 8(a).
Judgment or decision, necessity of setting forth matter showing jurisdiction, Rule 9(e).
Jurisdiction, form of allegations, Form 2.
Preliminary injunctions, Auth. Comm. Rule 65(d).
Puerto Rico, subject matter jurisdiction, Jurisdiction, Juris. §§ 2.12-2.13.
Quasi in rem jurisdiction, Jurisdiction, Juris. §§ 2.8, 2.10.
Remedy for failure of jurisdiction, Jurisdiction, Juris. §§ 2.1-2.13.
Removal and subject matter jurisdiction, Removal, Juris. § 2.16.
Rules not to extend or limit, Rule 82; Auth. Comm. Rule 1.
Sanctions, applicability when court lacks jurisdiction, Auth. Comm. Rule 11.
Shareholder derivative suits, Auth. Comm. Rule 23.1.
Subject matter jurisdiction, Jurisdiction, Juris. §§ 2.10-2.13.
Supplemental jurisdiction, subject matter jurisdiction, Jurisdiction, Juris. § 2.13.
Generally, 28 U.S.C.A. § 1367.
Sureties, proceedings against, Rule 65.1.
"Tag" jurisdiction, jurisdiction, Juris., § 2.4.
Temporary restraining orders, Rule 65(d).
Timing, citizenship and, subject matter jurisdiction, Jurisdiction.
Transfer to cure lack of jurisdiction, 28 U.S.C.A. § 1631.
Transient jurisdiction, personal jurisdiction, Jurisdiction, Juris. § 2.4.
Third-party practice, Auth. Comm. Rule 14 (a), (b), and (c).

JURISDICTION—Cont'd
Unincorporated associations,
Subject matter jurisdiction, Jurisdiction; Auth. Comm. Rule 23.2.
United States Territories, subject matter jurisdiction, Jurisdiction, Juris. §§ 2.12-2.13.
Virgin Islands, subject matter jurisdiction, Jurisdiction, Juris. § § 2.12-2.13.
Waiver, personal jurisdiction, Jurisdiction, Juris. § 2.4.

JURISDICTIONAL DISCOVERY
Generally, Auth. Comm. Rule 12(b)(1), 12(b)(2), 12(b)(3).

JURY
Advisory jury, Rules 39(c), 52(a); Auth. Comm. Rule 39(c).
Calendar to designate cases as jury actions, Rule 79(c).
Calling and interrogation of witnesses by court, objection to made when jury not present, Evid. Rule 614.
Comparison by with specimens which have been authenticated, Evid. Rule 901.
Competency of juror as witness, Evid. Rule 606.
Complicated issues, reference to master, Rule 53(b); Auth. Comm. Rule 53(b).
Declaratory judgment, Rule 57; Auth. Comm. Rule 57.
Default judgment, determination of amount of damages by, Rule 55(b)(2).
Demand for, Rule 38(b); Auth. Comm. Rule 38(b).
Removed action, Rule 81(c); Auth. Comm. Rule 81(c).
Right of court to order in absence of demand, Rule 39(b); Auth. Comm. Rule 39(b).
Disclosure to, court appointment, expert witnesses, Evid. Rule 706.
Entry of demand in civil docket, Rule 79(a).
Examination of jurors, Rule 47(a); Auth. Comm. Rule 47(a).
Excusing juror, Rule 47(c); Auth. Comm. Rule 47(c).
Extraneous prejudicial information improperly brought to jury's attention, testimony of juror respecting, Evid. Rule 606.
Findings, unanimity, Rule 48; Auth. Comm. Rule 48.
Hearing,
Admissibility of confessions, conducting out of presence of, Evid. Rule 104.
Rulings on evidence, Evid. Rule 103.
Inquiry into validity of indictment, testimony of juror, restriction and exception, Evid. Rule 606.
Instructions to Jury, generally, this index.
Judgment as a matter of law, Rule 50; Auth. Comm. Rule 50.
Jurors, selection, Rule 47; Auth. Comm. Rule 47.
Misleading, exclusion of relevant evidence on grounds of, Evid. Rule 403.
Number of jurors, Rule 48; Auth. Comm. Rule 48.
Objections to questions to witnesses, Rule 43(c).
Outside influence improperly brought to bear on juror, testimony of juror respecting, Evid. Rule 606.
Peremptory challenges, Rule 47(b); Auth. Comm. Rule 47(b).
Preliminary injunction, Rule 65(a)(2).
Reference to master, Rule 53(b); Auth. Comm. Rule 53(b).
Removed action, Rule 81(c); Auth. Comm. Rule 81(c).
Reports of master, Rule 53(e).
Right preserved, Rule 38(a).
Separate trials, Rule 42(b); Auth. Comm. Rule 42(b).

JURY—Cont'd

Size of jury, Rule 48; Auth. Comm. Rule 48.
Specification of issues, Rule 38(c); Auth. Comm. Rule 38(c).
Stipulations for trial by court, Rule 39(a); Auth. Comm. Rule 39(a).
United States, jury finals in actions against, 28 U.S.C.A. § 2402.
Waiver, Rule 38(d); Auth. Comm. Rule 38(d).
Failure of party to make demand for jury trial upon removal of action from state court, Rule 81(c).
Withdrawal of demand for, Rule 38(d); Auth. Comm. Rule 38(d).
Writings, recordings or photographs, admissibility of evidence of contents, functions respecting, Evid. Rule 1008.

JUSTICES

Judges, generally, this index.

JUVENILE DELINQUENTS AND OFFENDERS

Adjudication, impeachment of witness by evidence of, admissibility, Evid. Rule 609.

KING, BIRTHDAY OF MARTIN LUTHER KING, JR.

"Legal holiday" for purpose of computation of time, Rule 6(a).

KNOWLEDGE

Lack of personal knowledge, testimony of witness, Evid. Rule 602.
Pleading, Rule 9(b).
Proof of, admissibility of evidence of other crimes, wrongs or acts, Evid. Rule 404.
Recorded recollection, hearsay exception, Evid. Rule 803.
Scientific, technical or specialized, testimony by experts, Evid. Rule 702.
Testimony of witness with, authentication and identification, conformity with requirements, Evid. Rule 901.

LABELS

Purporting to be affixed in course of business and indicating ownership, control or origin, self-authentication, Evid. Rule 902.

LABOR DAY

Clerks of court, business hours for office, exception concerning opening, Rule 77(c).
"Legal holiday" for purposes of computing time, Rule 6(a).

LABOR RELATIONS

Preliminary injunctions and temporary restraining orders, Rule 65(e).

LACHES

Pleading as defense, Rule 8(c).

LAND

Entry Upon Land, generally, this index.

LAW

Application of rules, Rule 1.
Governing, capacity to sue or be sued, Rule 17(b).

LAW ENFORCEMENT PERSONNEL

Matters observed by, public records and reports, hearsay exception, Evid. Rule 803.

LAWYERS
Attorneys, generally, this index.

LEADING QUESTIONS
Witnesses, Rule 43(b); Evid. Rule 611.

LEAVE OF COURT
Depositions upon,
Oral examination, Rule 30; Auth. Comm. Rule 30(a).
Written questions, prisoners, Rule 31(a); Auth. Comm. Rule 31(a).
Requests for admission, Rule 36(a).

LEGAL HOLIDAYS
Clerks of court, business hours, Rule 77(c).
Computation of time, Rule 6(a).
Defined, Rule 6(a).

LEGAL REPRESENTATIVES
Replacing real party in interest, Rule 17(a); Auth. Comm. Rule 17(a).
Judgment against, relief on ground of mistake, inadvertence, surprise or excusable neglect, Rule 60(b).

LEGITIMACY AND ILLEGITIMACY
Hearsay exception,
Records of, Evid. Rule 803.
Statement of declarant concerning, Evid. Rule 804.

LETTERS ROGATORY
Assistance to foreign and international tribunals, 28 U.S.C.A. § 1782.
Foreign countries, persons before whom depositions may be taken, Rule 28(b); Auth. Comm. Rule 28(b).
Transmittal, 28 U.S.C.A. § 1781.

LICENSE
Pleading as defense, Rule 8(c).

LIENS
Maritime, enforcement, action in rem, Supp. Rule C(1).

LIMITATION
Depositions upon oral examination, motion for, Rule 30(d); Auth. Comm. Rule 30(d).
Liability, admiralty or maritime claims, Supp. Rule F.
Applicability, supplemental rules, Supp. Rule A.
Pleading as defense, Rule 8(c).

LISTS
Use and reliance on by public or persons in particular occupations, hearsay exception, Evid. Rule 803.

LITIGATION
Anticipation of, discovery, preparation for, Rule 26(b); Auth. Comm. Rule 26(b)(3).
Discovery of documents and tangible things, preparation and anticipation of, need of materials, Rule 26(b); Auth. Comm. Rule 26(b)(3).

LOCAL RULES
Authorization and Nature, Rule 83; Auth. Comm. Rule 83.

LONG-ARM STATUTES
Personal jurisdiction and, personal jurisdiction, Jurisdiction.

LONGSHOREMEN'S AND HARBOR WORKERS' COMPENSATION ACT
Applicability of rules to review proceedings under, Rule 81(a)(6).

LOSS
Originals of records, writings or photographs, admissibility, other evidence of contents, Evid. Rule 1004.

MAGISTRATE JUDGES
Generally, Rules 72-76.
Appeal and Review, this index.
Appeal after trial, Rules 73, 74; Auth. Comm. Rules 73, 74.
Appeal to district judge, Rules 74-76, Form 34; Auth. Comm. Rules 74-76.
Applicability of rules, Evid. Rules 101, 1101.
Consent to jurisdiction, Forms 33, 34.
"Court" as including, applicability of rules, Evid. Rule 1101.
Election of appeal to district judge, Form 34.
"Judge" as including, applicability of rules, Evid. Rule 1101.
Judgment on appeal to district judge by consent, Rule 76; Auth. Comm. Rule 76.
Minor and petty offenses, trial of, applicability of rules in part, Evid. Rule 1101.
Pretrial matters, Rule 72; Auth. Comm. Rule 72.
Rule governing masters, when subject to, Rule 53(f).
Rules as governing proceedings before, Evid. Rules 101, 1101.
Sanctions, authority to order, Auth. Comm. Rule 11.
Trial by consent, Rule 73; Auth. Comm. Rule 73.

MAGNETIC IMPULSE
"Writings" and "recordings" as including, contents of writings, etc., Evid. Rule 1001.

MAIL
Certified Mail, generally, this index.
Depositions upon written questions, Rule 31(b).
Notice,
Entry of orders or judgments by clerk, Rule 77(d).
Filing of report by master, Rule 53(e); Auth. Comm. Rule 53(e)(1).
Process, U. S. attorney, etc., amendment of pleading change of party, Rule 15(c).
Registered Mail, generally, this index.
Service of process,
Additional time after service by mail, Rule 6(e); Auth. Comm. Rule 6(e).
Deposited with post office, service complete, Auth. Comm. Rule 5(b).
Pleading and other papers, Rule 5(b); Auth. Comm. Rule 5(b).
Summons and complaint on defendant, Rule 4(c).
Sureties, proceedings against, Rule 65.1.
United States, Rule 4(i).
Waiver of service by mail, Rule 4(d).

MALICE
Pleading, Rule 9(b).

MANAGING AGENT
Service of summons or complaint, Rule 4(d).
Witnesses, interrogation, Rule 43(b).

MANDAMUS
Abolition of writ, Rule 81(b).

MARIANA ISLANDS
District court, applicability of rules, Evid. Rule 1101.

MARITIME CASES
Admiralty or Maritime Claims, generally, this index.

MARITIME PRIZE
Applicability of rules in part, Evid. Rule 1101.

MARKET QUOTATIONS
Hearsay exception, Evid. Rule 803.

MARRIAGE
Hearsay exception,
Records of, Evid. Rule 803.
Statement of declarant concerning, Evid. Rule 804.

MARSHALS
Fees of, 28 U.S.C.A. § 1921.
Process, service, Rule 4(c).

MASTER AND SERVANT
Complaint for negligence under Federal Employer's Liability Act, form of, Form 14.
Injunctions in proceedings affecting, Rule 65(e).

MASTERS
Generally, Rule 53; Auth. Comm. Rule 53.
Costs, Recovery of, Auth. Comm. Rule 54(d)
Defined, Rule 53(a).
Findings,
Acceptance by court in action tried without jury or with advisory jury, Rules 52(a), 53(e).
Court, Rule 52(a); Auth. Comm. Rule 52(a).
Magistrate subject to rule governing masters, when, Rule 53(f); Auth. Comm. Rule 53(f).
Powers, Rule 53(c).
Report, Rule 53; Auth. Comm. Rule 53(e).
Judgment not required to recite, Rule 54(a).

MATTER OF LAW
Judgment as a matter of law, Rule 50; Auth. Comm. Rule 50(a).

MEASURING OF PROPERTY OR OBJECTS
Entry upon land, etc., for inspection and other purposes, generally, ante.

MECHANICAL OR ELECTRONIC RECORDING
Obtaining prior statement concerning action or subject matter by party or person, Rule 26(b); Auth. Comm. Rule 26(b)(3).

MECHANICAL OR ELECTRONIC RECORDING—Cont'd
"Writings" and "recordings" as including, contents of writings, etc., Evid. Rule 1001.

MEDICAL AND SURGICAL CARE AND ASSISTANCE
Expenses, payment, admissibility to prove liability for injury, Evid. Rule 409.
Hearsay exceptions, statements concerning medical diagnosis or treatment, Evid. Rule 803.

MEDICINE
Learned treatises, statements in, hearsay exception, Evid. Rule 803.

MEMORANDUM
Hearsay exceptions, Evid. Rule 803.

MEMORIAL DAY
Clerks of court, business hours for office, exceptions concerning opening, Rule 77(c).
"Legal holiday" as including for purposes of computing time, Rule 6(a).

MEMORY
Lack of, declarant testifying to, concerning subject matter of his statement, "unavailability as witness" as including, hearsay exception, Evid. Rule 804.
Writing used to refresh, Evid. Rule 612.

MENTAL CAPACITY OR CONDITION
Hearsay exceptions, statements respecting, Evid. Rule 803.

MENTAL EXAMINATIONS
Physical and mental examinations, generally, this index.

MENTAL HEALTH PROCEEDINGS
Nonapplicability of rules in U.S. District Court for District of Columbia, Rule 81(a).

MENTAL ILLNESS OR INFIRMITY
Declarant unable to be present or to testify at hearing because of, "unavailability as witness" as including, hearsay exception, Evid. Rule 804.

MERCHANT MARINE ACT
Complaint for damages under, form of, Form 15.

MILEAGE
Tender on delivery of copy of subpoena, Rule 45(b); Auth. Comm. Rule 45(b).

MINIMUM CONTACTS
Personal jurisdiction and, personal jurisdiction, Jurisdiction.

MINORS
Infants, generally, this index.

MISCELLANEOUS PROCEEDINGS
Inapplicability of rules, Evid. Rule 1101.

MISCELLANEOUS RULES
Generally, Evid. Rule 1101 et seq.

MISCONDUCT
Relief from judgment, order or proceeding, Rule 60(b).

MISJOINDER
Parties, Rule 21.

MISNOMERS
Substitution proceedings involving public officers, disregarding when not substantial, Rule 25(d).

MISTAKES
Absence of, proof, admissibility of evidence of other crimes, wrongs or acts, Evid. Rule 404.
Correction of clerical mistakes, Rule 60(a).
Judgment, relief from judgment on ground of mistake, Rule 60(b).
Party's identity, amendment of pleading, relation back, Rule 15(c).
Pleading, Rule 9(b); Auth. Comm. Rule 9(b).
Designation of defense, Rule 8(c).

MISTRIAL
Writing used to refresh memory, criminal cases, failure to produce or deliver, ground for, Evid. Rule 612.

MODIFICATION
Discovery procedures, stipulations, Rule 29; Auth. Comm. Rule 29.
Master's report by court, Rule 53(e); Auth. Comm. Rule 53(e).
Preliminary injunctions, Auth. Comm. rule 65(a).

MONEY
Had and received, complaint in action for, form of, Form 8.
Lent, complaint in action for, form for, Form 6.
Paid, complaint in action for money paid by mistake, form of, Form 7.

MORE DEFINITE STATEMENT
Motion for, Rule 12(e); Auth. Comm. Rule 12(e).

MOTION DAY
Generally, Rule 78.

MOTION PICTURES
"Photographs" as including, contents of photographs, etc., Evid. Rule 1001.

MOTIONS
Admission, withdrawal or amendment, Rule 36(b); Auth. Comm. Rule 36(b).
Adoption of statement by reference, Rule 10(c).
Advisory jury, Rule 39(c).
Amending motions, Auth. Comm. Rule 12(g).
Amend pleadings, Rule 15.
Amendment of findings of court, Rule 52(b); Auth. Comm. Rule 52(b).
Application to court for,
Action on report of master, Rule 53(e).
Order, Rule 7(b)(1); Auth. Comm. Rule 7(b).
Attachments, Auth. Comm. Rule 7(b).
Bringing in third-party defendant, form of, Form 22-B.
Consolidation, defenses in, Rule 12(g); Auth. Comm. Rule 12(g).
Correction of clerical mistakes, Rule 60(a).
Depositions,
Oral examination, termination or limitation, Rule 30(d); Auth. Comm. Rule 30(d).

MOTIONS—Cont'd
Depositions,—Cont'd
Use of, hearings on, Rule 32(a).
Discovery,
Protective orders relating to depositions, Rule 26(c); Auth. Comm. Rule 26(c).
Sequence, methods, use in, Rule 26(d).
Dismissal, this index.
Extension of time, Rule 6(b); Auth. Comm. Rule 12(a).
Filing, Auth. Comm. Rule 7(b).
Findings of fact and conclusions of law unnecessary on decision of motion, Rule 52(a).
Form of, Auth. Comm. Rule 7(b) & 12(b).
Forms, this index.
Intervention, Rule 24(c).
Defendant, form of, Form 23.
Judgments and Decrees, this index.
Judgment as a matter of law, Rule 50.
Jury trial, order by court, Rule 39(b).
Local rules governing, Auth. Comm. Rule 7(b.)
Manipulative motions. Auth. Comm. Rule 12(a).
More definite and certain pleading, Rule 12(e); Auth. Comm. Rule 12(e).
New Trials, this index.
Notice of motion,
Bringing in third-party defendant, form of, Form 22-B.
Correction of clerical mistakes, Rule 60(a).
Dismissal of complaint, form of, Form 19.
Intervention as defendant, form of, Form 23.
Order compelling discovery, Rule 37(a); Auth. Comm. Rule 37(a).
Sureties, proceedings against, Rule 65.1.
Oral hearing, Rule 78; Auth. Comm. Rule 7(b).
Oral motions, Auth. Comm. Rule 7(b).
Orders,
Attached to Motions, Auth. Comm. Rule 7(b).
Compelling discovery, Rule 37(a); Auth. Comm. Rule 37(a).
Depositions,
Failure of party to attend at own deposition, sanctions, Rule 37(d).
Oral examination, IR3§ Annexation of original material to, Rule 30(f). IR3§ Recording of, Rule 30(b). IR3§ Termination or limitation, Rule 30(d).
Discovery, expert witnesses, trial preparation, Rule 26(b).
Entry upon land, failure of party to respond to request for inspection, sanctions, Rule 37(d).
Examiners report, physical and mental examinations, delivery, Rule 35(b).
Interrogatories,
Failure of party to respond to request for inspection, sanctions, Rule 37(d).
Failure of party to serve answers to, sanctions, Rule 37(d).
Objections to or failure to answer, Rule 33(a).
Physical and mental examinations, Rule 35(a).
Production of documents or things and entry upon land, etc., for inspection and other purposes, Rule 34(b).
Partial & pending motions, Auth. Comm. Rule 12(a).

MOTIONS—Cont'd
Particularity, Rule 7(b)(1).
Pleadings, this index.
Preliminary hearing on motions, Rule 12(d); Auth. Comm. Rule 12(d).
Reconsideration, Auth. Comm. Rule 59(e).
Scheduling, Rule 78.
Service of process, Rules 5(a), 6(d); Auth. Comm. Rule 7(b).
Alter or amend judgment, Rule 59(e).
Dismiss action for or lack of, form of, Form 19.
Intervention, Rule 24(c).
New trial, Rule 59(b).
Substitution of parties, Rule 25.
Summary judgment, Rule 56(c).
Severance or separate trial, third-party claim, Rule 14(a).
Signature, Rule 11; Auth. Comm. Rule 7(b).
Application of rules to motions and other papers, Rule 7(b), (c).
Sanctions, Rule 11.
Striking,
Pleading, Rule 12(f); Auth. Comm. Rule 12(f).
Third-party claim, Rule 14(a).
Substitution of parties, Rule 25.
Sufficiency, determination of answers or objections to requests for admission, Rule 36(a); Auth. Comm. Rule 36(a).
Summary judgment, this index.
Supplemental pleadings, Rule 15(d).
Suppression, depositions,
Errors and irregularities in completion and return of, Rule 32(d).
Oral examination, refusal to sign, rejection, Rule 30(e).
Sureties, liability, enforcement, Rule 65.1.
Technical forms not required, Rule 8(e)(1).
Temporary restraining order, Rule 65(b).
Third-party complaint, service, leave to make, Rule 14(a).
Time,
Enlargement, Rule 6(b).
Joinder, Auth. Comm. Rule 19.
Judgment on the pleading, Rule 12(c).
Motion on enumerated defenses, Auth. Comm. Rule 12(b).
New trial, Rule 59(b).
Person defending for summary judgment, Rule 56(b).
Relief from judgment on ground of mistake, inadvertence, surprise or excusable neglect, Rule 60(b).
Service, Rule 6(d); Auth. Comm. Rule 6(d).
Summary judgment by claimant, Rule 56(a).
Tolling during pendency of motion, Auth. Comm. Rule 12(a).
Waiver of defenses, Rule 12(h); Auth. Comm. Rule 12(h).
Writing, Rule 7(b)(1); Auth. Comm. Rule 7(b).

MOTIVE
Hearsay exceptions, statements respecting, Evid. Rule 803.
Proof of, admissibility of evidence of other crimes, wrongs or acts, Evid. Rule 404.

MULTIDISTRICT LITIGATION
Generally, see Part V Auth. Comm.
Introduction, Part V Auth. Comm.
Rules of Judicial Panel on, Part V.
Statute, Part V & 28 U.S.C.A. § 1407.

MULTIPLE CLAIMS OR PARTIES, JUDGMENT
Generally, Rule 54(b); Auth. Comm. Rule 2.
Stay of enforcement, Rule 62(h); Auth. Comm. Rule 62(h).

MUNICIPAL CORPORATIONS
Service of summons and complaint, Rule 4(d).

MURDER
Homicide, generally, this index.

NAMES
Depositions, notice or commission may designate persons before whom to be taken, Rule 28(b).
Nonjoinder, persons, needed for just adjudication, pleading, Rule 19(c).
Pleading setting forth name of parties, etc., in caption, Rule 10(a).
Summons, form and requisites, Rule 4(b).

NATIONAL LABOR RELATIONS BOARD
Inapplicability of rules to proceedings to enforce orders, Rule 81(a)(5).

NATIONS
Reputation concerning boundaries or general history important to nation in which located, hearsay exception, Evid. Rule 803.

NATURALIZATION
Applicability of rules to proceedings, Rule 81(a).
Review, action respecting naturalization and revocation thereof, rules applicable in part, Evid. Rule 1101.

NEGLIGENCE
Pleadings, this index.
Subsequent remedial measures, admissibility to prove, Evid. Rule 407.

NEGOTIATIONS
Compromise, claims, conduct or statements made, admissibility, Evid. Rule 408.

NEW TRIALS
Generally, Rule 59; Auth. Comm. Rule 59.
Additur, Auth. Comm. Rule 59(a).
Against weight of evidence, Auth. Comm. Rule 59(a).
Alternative motion, judgment as a matter of law, Rule 50; Auth. Comm. Rule 50(b).
Answers to written interrogatories inconsistent with general verdict, Rule 49(b); Auth. Comm. Rule 49(b).
Discretion in granting, Auth. Comm. Rule 59(a).
Grounds for new trial, Rule 59(a); Auth. Comm. Rule 59(a).
Harmless error not ground for, Rule 61.
Improper conduct by Counsel, Court, or Jury, Auth. Comm. Rule 59(a).
Judgment as a matter of law, alternative motion with, Rule 50; Auth. Comm. Rule 50(b).

NEW TRIALS—Cont'd
Motions, Rule 59(d).
Affidavits, in support of motion, Rule 59(c); Auth. Comm. Rule 59(c).
Appealability, Auth. Comm. 59(a).
Extension of time, Rule 6(b).
Judgment as a matter of law motion, alternative, Rule 50; Auth. Comm. Rule 50(b).
Time for moving, Rule 59(b); Auth. Comm. Rule 59(b).
Newly discovered evidence, Auth. Comm. Rule 59(a).
Order for, Rule 59(d); Auth. Comm. Rule 59(d).
Extension of time, Rule 6(b).
Partial new trial, Auth. Comm. 59(a).
Remittitur, Auth. Comm. Rule 59(a).
Stay of execution or proceedings to enforce judgment on motion for, Rule 62(b); Auth. Comm. Rule 62(b).
Time for making, Auth. Comm. Rule 59(b).
Waiver of right to seek, Auth. Comm. 59(a).

NEW YEAR'S DAY
Clerks of court, business hours for office, exceptions concerning opening, Rule 77(c).
"Legal holiday" as including for purposes of computing time, Rule 6(a).

NEWLY DISCOVERED EVIDENCE
Relief from judgment, order or proceeding, Rule 60(b).

NEWSPAPERS
Notice, admiralty or maritime claims,
Actions in rem, Supp. Rule C(4).
Limitation of liability, Supp.Rule F(4).
Printed material purporting to be, self-authentication, Evid. Rule 902.

NEXT FRIEND
Action by infant or incompetent person, Rule 17(c).

NOLO CONTENDERE
Plea of Nolo Contendere, generally, this index.

NONJOINDER
Persons needed for just adjudication, pleading, reasons, Rule 19(c).

NONRESIDENTS
Form of summons, etc., to correspond to requirement of statute or rule of state court pursuant to which service was made, Rule 4(b).
Service on, Rule 4(e).
Subpoena requiring attendance for taking deposition, Rule 45(b).

NOTARY PUBLIC
Documents accompanied by certificate of acknowledgment executed by, self-authentication, Evid. Rule 902.

NOTICE
Acceptance of offer of judgment, Rule 68.
Adjournment of proceedings before master, Rule 53(d).
Amendment of pleading, change of party, relation back, Rule 15(c).
Appeal, form, Form 27.

NOTICE—Cont'd
Application for order of court to speed proceedings of master, Rule 53(d).
Attorneys, this index.
Class actions, Rule 23(c) and (d); Auth. Comm. Rule 23.
Condemnation of property, form, Form 28.
Default judgment, application for, Rule 55(b).
Depositions,
Effect of errors and irregularities in, Rule 32(d); Auth. Comm. Rule 32(d).
Filing, Rule 31(c); Auth. Comm. Rule 31(c).
Oral examination, Rule 30(b); Auth. Comm. Rule 30(b).
Taking,
In foreign country, Rule 28(b); Auth. Comm. Rule 28(b).
Stipulations, Rule 29; Auth. Comm. Rule 29.
Written questions, Rule 31(a); Auth. Comm. Rule 31(a).
Derivative actions by shareholders, dismissal or compromise, Rule 23.1.
Dismissal, Rule 41(a); Auth. Comm. Rule 41(a).
Extension of time, Rule 6(b).
Filing,
Depositions upon,
Oral examination, Rule 30(f); Auth. Comm. Rule 30(f).
Written questions, Rule 31(c); Auth. Comm. Rule 31(c).
Pleading, Rule 5(c).
Report by master, Rule 53(e); Auth. Comm. Rule 53(e)(1).
Foreign law, determination, pleadings, Rule 44.1; Auth. Comm. Rule 44.1.
Forms, this index.
Hearing of motion, fulfillment of requirement as to motion in writing, Rule 7(b).
Judgments, entry, Rule 58.
Judicial Notice, generally, this index.
Jurisdiction and, Juris. § § 2.6-2.9.
Lawsuit, form, Form 1A.
Magistrate jurisdiction, consent, Rule 73(b); Auth. Comm. Rule 73(b).
Mail, this index.
Meeting on order of reference, Rule 53(d).
Motions, this index.
New trial, Rule 59(d).
Orders,
Notice of entry, Rule 77(d); Auth. Comm. Rule 77(d).
Physical and mental examinations, Rule 35(a).
Placing of actions on trial calendar, Rule 40.
Preliminary injunction, Rule 65(a).
Rules, amendments, Rule 83.
Service of process, Rule 5.
Application for default judgment, Rule 55(b).
Condemnation proceedings, Rule 71A(d); Auth. Comm. Rule 71A(d).
Depositions upon oral examination, Rule 30(b).
Entry of order or judgment, Rule 77(d); Auth. Comm. Rule 77(d).
Hearing, Rule 6(d).
Party not inhabitant of or found within state, Rule 4(e).
Form to correspond to that required by statute or rule of state court, Rule 4(b).
Taking depositions before action, Rule 27(a)(2); Auth. Comm. Rule 27(a).

NOTICE—Cont'd
Service of process, Rule 5.—Cont'd
Third-party complaint, leave on a motion upon notice, Rule 14(a).
Shareholder derivative suits, Rule 23.1.
Special notice, depositions upon oral examination, Rule 30(b); Auth. Comm. Rule 30(b)(2).
Summons as notice to defendant judgment by default will be entered on failure to appear, Rule 4(b).
Surety, Auth. Comm. Rule 65.1.
Taxation of costs by clerk, Rule 54(d).
Temporary restraining order, Rule 65(b).
Time,
Enlargement, Rule 6(b).
Hearing, service, Rule 6(d).
Magistrate, appeal to district judge from, Rule 74; Auth. Comm. Rule 74(b).
Taxation of cost, Rule 54(d).

NUMBER
Claims, cross-claims, etc., separate trial, Rule 42(b).
Class actions, Rule 23(a); Auth. Comm. Rule 23.
Expert witnesses, pre-trial limitation, Rule 16.
Pleading, separate claims or defenses, Rule 8(e)(2).
Shareholder derivative actions, Auth. Comm. Rule 23.1.
Unincorporated associations, actions involving, Auth. Comm. Rule 23.2.

OATHS AND AFFIRMATIONS
Affirmation in lieu of oath, Rule 43(d).
Interpreters, Evid. Rule 604.
Witnesses, this index.

OBJECTIONS
Calling and interrogation of witnesses by court, Evid. Rule 614.
Competency of judge as witness, necessity of making, Evid. Rule 605.
Depositions, this index.
Discovery, Rule 26(b).
Findings of fact by court, Rule 52(b).
Instructions, Rule 51; Auth. Comm. Rule 51.
Interrogatories, Rules 33(a, b); Auth. Comm. Rule 33(b).
Failure of party to serve, sanctions, Rule 37(d).
Juror, testimony by, Evid. Rule 606.
Magistrate's recommended disposition, Rule 72(b); Auth. Comm. Rule 72(b).
Master's report, Rule 53(e); Auth. Comm. Rule 53(e).
Motions, omission, effect, Rule 12(g).
Pleading, Rule 12.
Production of documents or things and entry upon land, etc., for inspection and other purposes, Rule 34(b); Auth. Comm. Rule 34(a).
Requests for admission, service, requisites of, etc., Rule 36(a); Auth. Comm. Rule 36(a).
Rulings,
Absence of objection as not prejudicial, Rule 46.
Admissibility of evidence, Evid. Rule 103.
Sufficiency, motion for determination on request for admission, Rule 36(a); Auth. Comm. Rule 36(a).

OBJECTIONS—Cont'd
Writing used to refresh memory, preservation, portion withheld over objections and availability on appeal, Evid. Rule 612.

OFFENSES
Crimes and Offenses, generally, this index.

OFFER OF JUDGMENT
Generally, Rule 68.

OFFER OF PROOF
Rulings on evidence, Evid. Rule 103.
Witnesses, probable proof on objection made, Rule 43(c).

OFFERS
Compromise and offers to compromise, admissibility, Evid. Rule 408.
Plea of guilty or of nolo contendere, admissibility, Evid. Rule 410.

OFFICERS AND EMPLOYEES
Depositions, generally, this index.
Documents under or not under seal, self-authentication, Evid. Rule 902.
Governmental organizations, service on, Rule 4(d).
Marriage, baptismal and similar certificates, statements respecting, hearsay exception, Evid. Rule 803.
Parties, termination of office, substitution, Rule 25(d).
Pleading decision, Rule 9(e).
Proof of record, Rule 44.
Public officers in official capacity, description as party by, Rule 25(d).
Service, summons and complaint on defendant, Rule 4(d).
United States,
  Appeal, stay without bond or security, Rule 62(e); Auth. Comm. Rule 62(e).
  Compelling giving of testimony, etc., application of rules, Rule 81(a).
  Definition, Rule 81(f).
  Process, amendment of pleading, change of party, Rule 15(c).
  Restraining order or preliminary injunction, security, Rule 65(c).
  Tender of fees and mileage, delivery of copy of subpoena, Rule 45(b).
  Time for, service of answer or reply, Rule 12(a).
  Witnesses, interrogation, Rule 43(b).
Venue and federal officers, Venue, Juris. § 2.14.

OFFICIAL ACTS
Pleading, Rule 9(d); Auth. Comm. Rule 9(d).

OFFICIAL PUBLICATIONS
Self-authentication, Evid. Rule 902.

OFFICIAL RECORDS
Authentication, Rule 44(a); Auth. Comm. Rule 44(a).
Lack of record, Rule 44(b); Auth. Comm. Rule 44(b).

OPEN COURT
Trial conducted in, Rule 77(b); Auth. Comm. Rule 77(b).

OPINIONS AND EXPERT TESTIMONY
  Generally, Evid. Rule 702.
Admissions, generally, ante.

OPINIONS AND EXPERT TESTIMONY—Cont'd
Bases of opinion testimony by experts, Evid. Rule 703.
Evidence as to personal knowledge of witness subject to provisions respecting, Evid. Rule 602.
Character Evidence, this index.
Comparison by trier or expert witness, authentication and identification, conformity with requirements, Evid. Rule 901.
Compensation, court appointed experts, Evid. Rule 706.
Court appointed experts, Evid. Rule 706.
Disclosure of facts or data underlying expert opinion, Evid. Rule 705.
Findings, expert witness appointed by court to advise party of, Evid. Rule 706.
Identity of, supplementation of responses to request for discovery, Rule 26(e); Auth. Comm. Rule 26(e).
Interpreters, subject to rules relating to qualification as expert, Evid. Rule 604.
Lay witnesses, Evid. Rule 701.
Limitation of number, pre-trial conference, for, Rule 16.
Nonexpert opinion on handwriting, authentication and identification, conformity with requirements, Evid. Rule 901.
Trial by court, Rule 52(a).
Trial or litigation preparation, discovery, Rule 26(b); Auth. Comm. Rule 30(b)(4).
Ultimate issue, opinion on, Evid. Rule 704.

OPPOSING PARTY
Actions by, class actions maintainable, Rule 23(b).

OPPRESSION
Depositions upon oral examination, motion to terminate or limit, Rule 30(d); Auth. Comm. Rule 30(d).
Protective orders relating to depositions, grounds for, Rule 26(c); Auth. Comm. Rule 26(c).

ORAL EXAMINATION
Depositions, this index.

ORDERS
Admissions, requests for, expenses on failure to admit, Rule 37(c).
Civil docket, entry in, Rule 79(a).
Class actions,
Altering prior rulings, Rule 23(d).
Approving settlement, Rule 23(e).
Determination whether maintainable, Rule 23(c).
Clerical mistakes, correction of, Rule 60(a).
Clerks of court,
Copy of every appealable order or order affecting title, etc., kept by, Rule 79(b).
Indexes to be kept by, Rule 79(c).
Orders grantable by, Rule 77(c).
Computation, time, Rule 6(a).
Conduct, class actions, Rule 23(d).
Consolidation, preliminary injunction hearing with trial on merits, Rule 65(a)(2).
Depositions, Rule 27(a); Auth. Comm. Rule 27(a).
Failure of party to attend at own deposition, sanctions, Rule 37(d).

ORDERS—Cont'd

Depositions, Rule 27(a); Auth. Comm. Rule 27(a).—Cont'd
Oral examination, Rule 30(a) et seq.
Annexation of original material to, Rule 30(f).
Manner of recording, Rule 30(b).
Record of, Rule 30(c).
Termination or limitation, Rule 30(d).
Discovery,
Compelling, Rules 37(a, b); Auth. Comm. Rules 37(a, b).
Failure to comply with order compelling sanctions, Rule 37(b); Auth. Comm. Rule 37(b).
Limitation, use of methods, Rule 26(a); Auth. Comm. Rule 26(c).
Sanctions upon failure to comply with order compelling, Rule 37(b).
Scope of, limitation, Rule 26(b); Auth. Comm. Rule 26(c).
Statements previously made of action or subject matter by parties or persons, refusal, request to furnish, Rule 26(b); Auth. Comm. Rule 26(b)(3).
Stipulations regarding procedure, Rule 29.
Trial preparation, expert witnesses, Rule 26(b); Auth. Comm. Rule 26(b)(4).
Dismissal of action,
For condemnation of property, Rule 71A(i); Auth. Comm. Rule 71A(i).
Wherein receiver has been appointed, Rule 66.
Documents, failure to admit genuineness, award of expenses, Rule 37(c).
Entry upon land, failure of party to respond to request for inspection, sanctions, Rule 37(d).
Examiners report, physical and mental examinations, delivery, Rule 35(b).
Exceptions unnecessary, Rule 46.
Exclusion of witnesses, Evid. Rule 615.
Fraud, relief from order, Rule 60(b).
In lieu of summons, service upon party not inhabitant of or found within state, Rule 4(e).
Form to correspond to that required by statute or state court rule, Rule 4(b), (e).
Interrogatories,
Answers to, Rule 33(b).
Failure of party to serve answers to, sanctions, Rule 37(d).
Objections to or failure to answer, Rule 33(a).
Joinder, persons needed for just adjudication, Rule 19(a).
Judgment includes order, Rule 54(a).
Mental examination, Rule 27(a, b).
Misconduct of party, relief from order, Rule 60(b).
Motions, this index.
Multiple claims or involving multiple parties, termination of action, Rule 54(b).
New trial, Rule 59(d).
Newly discovered evidence, relief from order, Rule 60(b).
Notice of entry given by clerk, Rule 77(d).
Physical and mental examinations, Rule 35(a).
Pretrial order after conference, Rule 16(e).
Production of documents or things, failure of party to respond to request for inspection, sanctions, Rule 37(d).
Protective Orders, generally, this index.
Reference to master, Rules 53(c, d).

ORDERS—Cont'd

Responses to request for discovery, duty to supplement, imposition by, Rule 26(e); Auth. Comm. Rule 26(e).

Failure to obey scheduling or pretrial order, Rule 16(f).

Violation of duties relating to documents filed with court, Rule 11.

Scheduling, pretrial conference, Rule 16(b).

Separate trials, Rule 20(b).

Service, Rule 5(a).

Pleading, numerous defendants, Rule 5(c).

Signing of pleadings, motions, etc., sanctions, Rule 11.

Speed proceedings of master, Rule 53(d).

Substitution of parties, public officers ceasing to hold office, Rule 25(d).

Sufficiency of answers or objections to requests for admission, Rule 36(a).

Truth of matter, failure to admit, award of expenses, Rule 37(c).

Unincorporated associations, actions relating to, Rule 23.2.

Voluminous writings, recordings or photographs, production, Evid. Rule 1006.

Voluntary dismissal, Rule 41(a)(2); Auth. Comm. Rule 41(a)(2).

Writing used to refresh memory, excising matters not related to subject matter of testimony and remainder delivered to entitled party, Evid. Rule 612.

ORGANIZATIONS

Depositions upon oral examination, Rule 30(b); Auth. Comm. Rule 30(b)(6).

ORIGIN

Inscriptions, signs, etc., purporting to be affixed in course of business and indicating self-authentication, Evid. Rule 902.

OVERNIGHT COURIERS

Service via, Auth. Comm. Rule 5(b).

OWNERSHIP

Admiralty or maritime claims against limitation of liability, Supp. Rule F(3).

Inscriptions, signs, etc., purporting to be affixed in course of business and indicating self-authentication, Evid. Rule 902.

Insurance against liability, admissibility for purpose of proving, Evid. Rule 411.

PAIN

Hearsay exceptions, statements respecting, Evid. Rule 803.

PAMPHLETS

Learned treatises, statements in, hearsay exception, Evid. Rule 803.

Official, self-authentication, Evid. Rule 902.

PANAMA CANAL

Canal Zone, generally, this index.

PAPERS

Books and Papers, generally, this index.

PARAGRAPHS

Pleading, Rule 10(b).

PARDON

Impeachment of witness by evidence of conviction subject of, effect, Evid. Rule 609.

PARTIAL FINDINGS
Judgment on, Rule 52; Auth. Comm. Rule 52(c).

PARTICULARITY
Pleading,
Conditions precedent, Rule 9(c).
Shareholder derivative actions, Rule 23.1; Auth. Comm. Rule 23.1.

PARTIES
Additional parties,
Amending pleadings to add parties or change a party's name, Rule 15(a), (c)(3).
Determination, pending action, counterclaim or cross-claim, service, territorial limits, Rule 4(f).
Indispensable parties, Rule 19(b); Auth. Comm. rule 19(b).
Joinder, counterclaim or cross-claim, Rule 13(h).
Admissions, generally, this index.
Adverse parties,
Calling as witness, Rule 43(b).
Extrinsic evidence, prior inconsistent statement of witness, opportunity to interrogate respecting, Evid. Rule 613.
Leading questions, interrogation by, Evid. Rule 611.
Writing used to refresh memory, rights respecting, Evid. Rule 612.
Capacity to sue or be sued, determination, Rule 17(b).
Change of, amendment of pleadings, relation back, Rule 15(c).
Class actions, class representatives and other class members, Rule 23; Auth. Comm. Rule 23.
Compensation of master, payment, Rule 53(a); Auth. Comm. Rule 53(a).
Consent, this index.
Corporation, capacity to sue or be sued, Rule 17(b).
Credibility of witnesses, attacking, Evid. Rule 607.
Cross-claim against coparty, Rule 13(g).
Cross-Examination, generally, this index.
Death, substitution, Rule 25(a).
Defendant,
Bringing in third party, Rule 14(a).
Depositions, generally, this index.
Discovery, Rule 26 et seq.
Dismissal for lack of an indispensable party, Rule 41(b).
Experts of own selection, calling, Evid. Rule 706.
Failure to join, Rule 12(b).
Impeachment of own witness, Evid. Rule 607.
Incompetent Persons, Parties, generally, this index.
Indispensable party,
Defining indispensable parties, Rule 19(b); Auth. Comm. Rule 19(b).
Dismissal for lack of, Rule 41(b).
Infants, Rule 17(c).
Interpleader, generally, this index.
Interrogatories, generally, this index.
Intervention, Rule 24.
Form, Form 23.

PARTIES—Cont'd
Joinder, Rules 19 to 21.
Additional parties, counterclaim or cross-claim, Rule 13(h).
Class actions, impracticability, Rule 23(a).
Dismissal for failure to join, Rule 41(d).
Misjoinder or nonjoinder, Rules 12(b, h), 21.
Service, places outside state but within United States, Rule 4(f).
Judicial notice, opportunity to be heard as to propriety of taking, Evid. Rule 201.
Motion,
Asserting defense of failure to state claim on which relief can be granted, Rule 12(b).
Bringing in third-party defendant, form of, Form 22-B.
Multiple parties, judgment, Rule 54(b).
Stay of enforcement, Rule 62(h); Auth. Comm. Rule 62(h).
Natural person, exclusion, provisions respecting exclusion of witnesses as not authorizing, Evid. Rule 615.
Needed for just adjudication,
Defense, failure to join, Rule 12(b)(7); Rule 12(h).
Joinder, Rule 19.
Notice, generally, this index.
Officer, etc., of party not natural person designated as representative by attorney, exclusion, provisions governing exclusion of witnesses as not authorizing, Evid. Rule 615.
Opinions and Expert Testimony, generally, this index.
Partnership, capacity to sue or to be sued, Rule 17(b).
Physical and Mental Examinations, generally, this index.
Plaintiff,
Bringing in third party, Rule 14.
Default judgment against, Rule 55(d).
Real party in interest, Rule 17(a).
Voluntary dismissal, Rule 41(a); Auth. Comm. Rule 41(a).
Pleadings, this index.
Presence essential to presentation of cause, exclusion of, provision respecting exclusion of witnesses as not authorizing, Evid. Rule 615.
Process in behalf of and against persons not parties, Rule 71; Auth. Comm. Rule 71.
Public officer, substitution, Rule 25(d).
Real party in interest, prosecution of action, Rule 17(a).
Receiver, law governing capacity to sue or be sued, Rule 17(b).
Representative capacity, capacity to sue or be sued, Rule 17(b).
Representative parties, class actions, Rule 23(a).
Separate Trials, Rule 20(b).
Service of pleadings and papers, Rule 5(b, c).
Substitution, Rule 25.
Condemnation proceedings, Rule 71A(g); Auth. Comm. Rule 71A(g).
Suggestion of death upon the record under rule concerning, form of, Form 30.
Suggestion, lack of jurisdiction, Rule 12(h).
Third-Party Practice, generally, this index.
Transfer of interest, substitution, Rule 25(c).
United States, action for use or benefit of another, Rule 17(a).

PARTIES—Cont'd
Writings, recordings or photographs, proof of contents of by testimony or written admission of, Evid. Rule 1007.

PARTITION ACTIONS, ADMIRALTY OR MARITIME CLAIMS
Actions in rem and quasi in rem, applicability, Supp. Rule E(1).
Applicability, supplemental rules, Supp. Rule A.
Process and notice, Supp. Rule D.
Release, property, Supp. Rule E(5)(d).

PARTNERSHIP
Capacity to sue or be sued, Rule 17(b).
Depositions,
Introduction in evidence as making deponent witness of introducing party, nonapplicability, Rule 32(c).
Oral examination, Rule 30(b).
Failure of officer, director, etc., to attend at own deposition, sanctions, Rule 37(d).
Failure to comply with order compelling designation, sanctions, Rule 37(b).
Motion for order to compel designation, Rule 37(a).
Use in court proceedings, Rule 32(a).
Written questions, Rule 31(a).
Failure of officer, etc., to attend at own deposition, sanctions, Rule 37(d).
Failure to comply with order compelling answer, sanctions, Rule 37(b).
Motion for order compelling answer, Rule 37(a).
Interrogatories, service of, Rule 33(a).
Service on, Rule 4(d); Auth. Comm. Rule 4(d).
Subpoena, naming as deponent and advising nonparty organization as to designation of officers, etc., Rule 30(b).
Witnesses, interrogation, Rule 43(b).

PAST BEHAVIOR
Victims of sex offenses, relevance, Evid. Rule 412.

PATENTS
Complaint in action for infringement, form of, Form 16.
Stay of judgment for accounting for infringement, Rule 62(a).

PAYMENT
Complaint for money paid by mistake, form of, Form 7.
Pleading as affirmative defense, Rule 8(c).

PAYMENT INTO COURT
Generally, Rule 67.
Admiralty or maritime claims,
Actions in rem, Supp.Rule C(5).
Actions in rem and quasi in rem, Supp. Rule E(4)(c).
Sale, proceeds, Supp. Rule E(9)(c).
Interpleader, Auth. Comm. Rule 22 and Statutory Interpleader.

PENALTIES
Fines and Penalties, generally, this index.

PENDING ACTIONS
Additional parties, determination service territorial limits, Rule 4(f).

PENDING ACTIONS—Cont'd
Counterclaims, Rule 13(a).
Discovery, failure to comply with order compelling, sanctions by court, Rule 37(b); Auth. Comm. Rule 37(b).

PEREMPTORY CHALLENGES
Jury, Rule 47(b); Auth. Comm. Rule 47(b).

PERIODICALS
Hearsay exception,
Commercial publications, use and reliance on by public or persons in particular occupations, Evid. Rule 803.
Learned treatises, statements in, Evid. Rule 803.
Self-authentication,
Official publications, Evid. Rule 902.
Printed material purporting to be, Evid. Rule 902.

PERISHABLE AGRICULTURAL COMMODITIES
Reparation order, unfair conduct, review, rules applicable in part, Evid. Rule 1101.

PERJURY
Guilty, offer to plead or withdrawn plea of, statement respecting, admissibility in subsequent prosecution of declarant, Evid. Rule 410.
Impeachment of witness by evidence of conviction of crime involving false statements, Evid. Rule 609.
Nolo contendere, plea of or offer to plead, statements respecting, admissibility, subsequent prosecution of declarant, Evid. Rule 410.

PERMISSIVE
Counterclaims, pleading, Rule 13(b).
Crossclaims, pleading, Rule 13(g).
Intervention, parties, Rule 24(b).
Joinder, parties, Rule 20.

PERPETUATION OF TESTIMONY
Proceedings for, Rule 27; Auth. Comm. Rule 27.

PERSONAL HISTORY
Hearsay, generally, this index.

PERSONAL INJURIES
Medical and similar expenses, payment, admissibility to prove liability, Evid. Rule 409.

PERSONAL JURISDICTION
Lack of, defense, Rule 12(b)(2), (h); Jurisdiction; Auth. Comm. Rule 12(b)(2).
Venue and, Venue, Juris. § 2.14.

PERSONAL PROPERTY
Application of rules governing procedure for condemnation, Rule 71A(a); Auth. Comm. Rule 71A(a).

PERSONAL REPRESENTATIVE
"Officer" as including personal representative of deceased district director or collector of internal revenue, Rule 81(f).

PERSONAL SERVICE
Notice, condemnation proceedings, Rule 71A(d); Auth. Comm. Rule 71A(d).
Summons and complaint, Rule 4(d).

PETROLEUM AND PETROLEUM PRODUCTS
Certificate of clearance, shipment in interstate commerce, denial, application, review, order respecting, applicability, rules in part, Evid. Rule 1101.

PETROLEUM CONTROL BOARDS
Inapplicability of rules to review orders of, Rule 81(a).

PHONO-RECORDS
Production of Documents or Things, generally, this index.

PHOTOGRAPHS
Collateral matters, other evidence of contents, Evid. Rule 1004.
Copies of, duplicates, admissibility, Evid. Rule 1003.
Definitions, Evid. Rule 1001.
Duplicates, defined, Evid. Rule 1001.
Functions of court and jury, Evid. Rule 1008.
Loss or destruction of originals, other evidence of contents, Evid. Rule 1004.
Opponent, original in possession of, other evidence of contents, Evid. Rule 1004.
Order for, Rule 27(a), (b).
Original,
  Defined, Evid. Rule 1001.
  Not obtainable, other evidence of contents, Evid. Rule 1004.
Other evidence of, admissibility, Evid. Rule 1004.
Photographing, "writings" and "recordings" as including, Evid. Rule 1001.
Production of Documents or Things, generally, this index.
Proof of, requirement of original, exception, Evid. Rule 1002.
Property or objects. Entry Upon Land, generally, this index.
Testimony, deposition or written admission of party, proof by, Evid. Rule 1007.
Voluminous photographs, summaries of, Evid. Rule 1006.

PHOTOSTATS
"Writings" and "recordings" as including, contents of writings, etc., Evid. Rule 1001.

PHYSICAL AND MENTAL EXAMINATIONS
See, also, Discovery, generally, this index.
  Generally, Rule 35; Auth. Comm. Rule 35.
Agreement of parties, Rule 35(b); Auth. Comm. Rule 35(b).
Cost of examination, Auth. Comm. Rule 35(a).
Deposition of examiner, Rule 35(b).
Discovery, examiners report, Rule 35(b); Auth. Comm. Rule 35(b).
Effect, failure or refusal to make report, Rule 35(b); Auth. Comm. Rule 35(b).
Examiners report, Rule 35(b); Auth. Comm. Rule 35(b).
Expert witnesses, litigation or trial preparation, Rule 26(b).
Failure to comply with order compelling, sanctions, Rule 37(b), Auth. Comm. Rules 35(a) and 37(b).
Method of obtaining discovery, Rule 26(a).
Motion, Auth. Comm. Rule 35(a).
Notice, Rule 35(a).
Order, Rule 35(a); Auth. Comm. Rule 35(a).

PHYSICAL AND MENTAL EXAMINATIONS—Cont'd
Prior or future reports by examiner, request for, Rule 35(b); Auth. Comm. Rule 35(b).
Psychologists, Rule 35; Auth. Comm. Rule 35(a).
Waiver, privilege of prior examination reports, Rule 35(b); Auth. Comm. Rule 35(b).

PHYSICAL CONDITION
Hearsay exception,
Declarant unable to be present or to testify at hearing because of existing physical infirmity, "unavailability as witness" as including, Evid. Rule 804.
Statements respecting, Evid. Rule 803.

PLACE
Deposition, taking, stipulations, Rule 29.
Physical and mental examinations, Rule 35(a); Auth. Comm. Rule 35(a).
Pleading, averments, Rule 9(f).
Trial. Venue, generally, this index.

PLAINTIFF
Parties, this index.

PLANS
Hearsay exceptions, statements respecting, Evid. Rule 803.
Proof of, admissibility of evidence of other crimes, wrongs or acts, Evid. Rule 404.

PLEA OF GUILTY
Admissibility, Evid. Rule 410.
Judgment of conviction entered after, evidence of, hearsay exception, Evid. Rule 803.
Withdrawn, admissibility, civil or criminal actions, Evid. Rule 410.

PLEA OF NOLO CONTENDERE
Admissibility, Evid. Rule 410.

PLEADINGS
Accord and satisfaction, affirmative defense, Rule 8(c).
Account, form of complaint in action on, Form 4.
Additional claims for relief, service, Rule 5(a).
Admiralty jurisdiction, Auth. Comm. Rule 8(a).
Admission by failure to deny, Rule 8(d); Auth. Comm. Rule 8(d).
Adoption by reference, Rule 10(c).
Affirmative defenses, Rule 8(c); Auth. Comm. Rule 8(c).
Allowed, Rule 7; Auth. Comm. Rule 7(a).
Alternative statement of claim or defense, Rules 8(a, e); Auth. Comm. Rule 8(e).
Ambiguity, motion for more definite statement, Rule 12(e).
Amendment, this index.
Answer,
Allowed, Rule 7(a).
Condemnation proceedings, Rule 71A(e); Auth. Comm. Rule 71A(e).
Depositions,
Motion for order to compel, Rule 37(a).
Sanctions for failure to comply with order compelling answer, Rule 37(b).

PLEADINGS—Cont'd

Answer,—Cont'd
Extension of time to serve, Auth. Comm. Rule 12(a).
Evasive or incomplete answer, defined, motion for order to compel discovery, Rule 37(a).
Form of, Forms 20, 21, 23.
General verdict accompanied by answer to interrogatory, Rule 49(b).
Interrogatories, Rule 33(a) et seq.
Affidavits for summary judgments supplemented or opposed by, Rule 56(e).
Failure of party to serve, sanctions, Rule 37(d).
Motion for order to compel, Rule 37(a).
Summary judgment rendered where answers show no genuine issue, etc., Rule 56(c).
Use of, Rule 33(b).
Written, submission to jury with form in general verdict, Rule 49(b).
Intervener, form of, Form 23.
Removed action, Rule 81(c); Auth. Comm. Rule 81(c).
Requisites of, after requests for admission, service, requisites, etc., Rule 36(a).
Sufficiency of, motion for determination on request for admission, Rule 36(a).
Time for service and reply, Rule 12(a); Auth. Comm. Rule 12(a).
United States, time to serve, Rule 12(a); Auth. Comm. Rule 12(a).
Arbitration and award, affirmative defense, Rule 8(c).
Associations, capacity to sue or be sued, Rule 9(a).
Assumption of risk, affirmative defense, Rule 8(c).
Authority to sue or be sued, Rule 9(a); Auth. Comm. Rule 9(a).
Avoidance, matters constituting, Rule 8(c).
Board's decision, Rule 9(e).
Capacity of party to sue or be sued, Rule 9(a); Auth. Comm. Rule 9(a).
Caption, Rule 10(a); Auth. Comm. Rule 10(a).
Signing, etc., application of rules to motions and other papers, Rule 7(b)(2).
Claims for relief, requisites, Rule 8(a); Auth. Comm. Rule 8(a).
Complaint,
Account, form of complaint in action on, Form 4.
Commencement of action by filing, Rule 3.
Commencement of amended complaints, Auth. Comm. Rule 3.
Condemnation of property, Rule 71A(c); Form 29.
Conversion, form of complaint in action for, Form 11.
Debt, form of complaint in action for, Form 13.
Fraudulent conveyances, form of complaint in action to set aside, Form 13.
Goods sold and delivered, form of complaint for, Form 5.
Infringement of,
Copyright, form of complaint in action for, Form 17.
Patent, form of complaint in action for, Form 16.
Interpleader and declaratory relief, form of complaint in action for, Form 18.
Jurisdiction, form of allegation, Form 2.
Merchant Marine Act, form of complaint in action for damages under, Form 15.
Money,
Had and received, form of complaint in action for, Form 8.
Lent, form of complaint in action for, Form 6.
Paid by mistake, form of complaint in action for, Form 7.

PLEADINGS—Cont'd
Complaint,—Cont'd
Motion to dismiss, form of, Form 19.
Names of all parties to be included in title of action, Rule 10(a).
Negligence, form of complaint in action for, Form 9.
Federal Employer's Liability Act, Form 14.
Plaintiff unable to determine person responsible, Form 10.
Pleadings allowed, Rule 7(a); Auth. Comm. Rule 7(a).
Promissory note, form of complaint in action on, Form 3.
Separate counts, Rule 10(b).
Service, Rule 4(d).
Specific performance, contract to convey land, form of complaint in action for, Form 12.
Summons,
Notice to defendant, judgment will be entered as demanded in complaint on failure to appear, Rule 4(b).
Service together with summons, Rule 4(d).
Third-party complaint, form of, Forms 22, 22-A.
Third-party defendant, complaint against, form of, Form 22-A.
Third-party practice, Rule 14(a).
Title of action, Rule 10(a).
Unfair competition, form of complaint in action for, Form 17.
Compulsory counterclaim, Rule 13(a).
Conciseness, requirement, Rule 8(e)(1); Auth. Comm. Rule 8.
Condemnation proceedings, Rule 71A; Auth. Comm. Rule 71A.
Condition of the mind, Rule 9(b); Auth. Comm. Rule 9(b).
Conditions precedent, Rule 9(c); Auth. Comm. Rule 9(c).
Consolidation, defenses in motion, Rule 12(g).
Construction to do justice, Rule 8(f).
Contributory negligence, affirmative defense, Rule 8(c).
Conversion, form of complaint in action for, Form 11.
Counterclaims, generally, this index.
Crossclaims, generally, this index.
Damages, special damages, Rule 9(g); Auth. Comm. Rule 9(g).
Debt, form of complaint in action for, Form 13.
Default judgment,
Entered on failure to plead, Rule 55(a).
Relief demanded by pleading, Rule 54(c).
Defective service of supplemental pleading granted even though defective in statement of claim, Rule 15(d).
Defenses, Rules 8(b), (c), 12; Auth. Comm. Rule 8(b), (c).
Alternative allegation, Rule 8(e).
Answer presenting, form of, Form 20.
Consolidation in motion, Rule 12(g).
Discovery, sanctions for failure to comply with order compelling, refusal to allow support or opposition to, Rule 37(b).
Hypothetical statement, Rule 8(e).
Motion to strike for insufficient defense, Rule 12(f).
Omission from motion, Rule 12(h).
Effect, Rule 12(g).
Removed action, Rule 81(c).

PLEADINGS—Cont'd
Defenses, Rules 8(b), (c), 12; Auth. Comm. Rule 8(b), (c).—Cont'd
Separate count, Rule 10(b).
Summary judgment, Rule 56(e).
Third-party practice, Rule 14(a).
Waiver or preservation, Rule 12(h).
Demurrers abolished, Rule 7(c).
Denial,
"Conclusion of law" denials, Auth. Comm. Rule 8(c) & 8(d).
Form of, Rule 8(b).
"Lack of information" denials, Auth. Comm. Rule 8(b).
Performance or occurrence of conditions precedent, Rule 9(c); Auth. Comm. Rule 9(c).
"Speaks for itself" denials, Auth. Comm. Rule 8(b) & 8(d).
"Strict proof demanded" denials, Auth. Comm. Rule 8(b) & 8(d).
Directness, requirement, Rule 8(e)(1).
Discharge in bankruptcy, affirmative defense, Rule 8(c).
Dismissal before responsive pleading is served, Rule 41(c); Auth. Comm. Rule 41(a)(1).
Diversity jurisdiction, Auth. Comm. Rule 8(a).
Duress, affirmative defense, Rule 8(c).
Estoppel as affirmative defense, Rule 8(c).
Exceptions for insufficiency of pleading abolished, Rule 7(c).
Exhibits, part of pleading, Rule 10(c).
Existence of party, Rule 9(a).
Failure of consideration as affirmative defense, Rule 8(c).
Failure to make statement more definite and certain, Rule 12(e).
Federal question, Auth. Comm. Rule 8(a).
Fellow servant, injury by as affirmative defense, Rule 8(c).
File number, setting forth in caption, Rule 10(a).
Filing with the court, defined, Rule 5(e).
Foreign judgment, Rule 9(e); Auth. Comm. Rule 9(e).
Foreign law, determination, notice, Rule 44.1; Auth. Comm. Rule 44.1.
Forms, Rule 10.
Account, action on, Form 4.
Answer, Forms 20, 21.
Conversion, action for, Form 11.
Debt, action for, Form 13.
Fraudulent conveyances, action to set aside, Form 13.
Goods sold and delivered, action for, Form 5.
Infringement of,
Copyright, action for, Form 17.
Patent, action for, Form 16.
Interpleader and declaratory relief, action for, Form 18.
Jurisdiction, form of allegation, Form 2.
Merchant Marine Act, action for damages under, Form 15.
Money,
Had and received, action for, Form 8.
Lent, action for, Form 6.
Paid by mistake, action for, Form 7.

PLEADINGS—Cont'd
Forms, Rule 10.—Cont'd
Negligence, action for, Form 9.
Federal Employer's Liability Act, action for, Form 14.
Plaintiff is unable to determine person responsible, Form 10.
Promissory note, action on, Form 3.
Reason for omitting party, Form 26.
Specific performance, contract to convey land, action for, Form 12.
Technical forms not required, Rule 8(e).
Unfair competition, action for, Form 17.
Fraud, Rule 9(b); Auth. Comm. Rule 9(b).
Affirmative defense, Rule 8(c).
Fraudulent conveyance,
Form of complaint in action to set aside, Form 13.
Joinder of remedies, Rule 18(b).
General denial, Rule 8(b); Auth. Comm. Rule 8(b).
General rules, Rule 8; Auth. Comm. Rule 8.
Goods sold and delivered, form of complaint in action for, Form 5.
Group pleading, Auth. Comm. Rule 9(b).
Hypothetical statement of claim or defense, Rule 8(e); Auth. Comm. Rule 8(e).
Illegality as defense, Rule 8(c).
Immaterial or impertinent matter, motion to strike, Rule 12(f); Auth. Comm. Rule 12(f).
Inconsistent statement of claim or defense, Rule 8(e); Auth. Comm. Rule8(e).
Incorporation by reference, Rule 10(c).
Information and belief, Auth. Comm. Rule 9(b).
Infringement of,
Copyright, form of complaint in action for, Form 17.
Patent, form of complaint in action for, Form 16.
Intent, Rule 9(b); Auth. Comm. Rule 9(b).
Interpleader and declaratory relief, form of complaint in action for, Form 18.
Joinder for counterclaims and crossclaims, Rule 13(h).
Joinder of claims and remedies, Rule 18.
Joinder of parties, Rules 19-21.
Judgment, Rule 9(e); Auth. Comm. Rule 9(e).
Not to contain recitals of pleadings, Rule 54(a).
Jurisdiction, form of allegation, Form 2.
Amend pleadings to show, 28 U.S.C.A. § 1653.
Knowledge, Rule 9(b); Auth. Comm. Rule 9(b).
Laches as defense, Rule 8(c).
License as defense, Rule 8(c).
Mail, service, Rule 5(b).
Malice, Rule 9(b); Auth. Comm. Rule 9(b).
Merchant Marine Act, form of complaint in action for damages under, Form 15.
Mistake, Rule 9(b); Auth. Comm. Rule 9(b).
Designation of defense, Rule 8(c).
Money,
Had and received, form of complaint in action for, Form 8.
Lent, form of complaint in action for, Form 6.
Paid by mistake, form of complaint in action for, Form 7.

PLEADINGS—Cont'd
Motions,
Dismiss, form of, Form 19.
Judgment on the pleading, Rule 12(c).
Manipulative, Auth. Comm. Rule 12(a).
More definite statement, Rule 12(e).
Partial & pending motions, Auth. Comm. Rule 12(a).
Strike, Rule 12(f).
Summary judgment, Rules 12(b, c).
Supplemental pleading, service, Rule 15(d).
Names, parties in title of action, Rule 10(a).
Negative averments, raising issue as to capacity of party, etc., Rule 9(a).
Negligence,
Federal Employer's Liability Act, Form 14.
Form of complaint in action for, Form 9.
Plaintiff unable to determine person responsible, Form 10.
New claims for relief, service, Rule 5(a).
"Notice" pleading, Auth. Comm. Rule 8(b).
Number of separate claims or defenses, Rule 8(e)(2).
Numerous defendants, service of pleading of defendants, Rule 5(c).
Objections, Rule 12.
Officer's decision, Rule 9(e).
Official document or act, Rule 9(d); Auth. Comm. Rule 9(d).
Omitted,
Counterclaim, Rule 13(f).
Persons, setting forth names, Rule 19(c).
Paragraphs, numbering, contents, etc., Rule 10(b); Auth. Comm. Rule 10(b).
Partial pending motion, tolling responsive pleading time, Auth. Comm. Rule 12(a).
Particularity, conditions precedent, Rule 9(c); Auth. Comm. Rule 9(c).
Parties,
Defense, failure to join party needed, for just adjudication, Rules 12(b, h).
Form of allegation of reason for omitting party, Form 26.
Title of action, Rule 10(a).
Payment as defense, Rule 8(c).
Pending Motion, tolling responsive pleading time, Auth. Comm. Rule 12(a).
Permissive counterclaims, Rule 13(b).
Personal jurisdiction, Auth. Comm. Rule 8(a).
Place, Rule 9(f); Auth. Comm. Rule 9(f).
Pleas for insufficiency of pleading abolished, Rule 7(c).
Preliminary hearing on defenses, etc., Rule 12(d).
Presentation of matters outside the pleading, Rules 12(b, c).
Promissory note, form of complaint in action on, Form 3.
Quasi judicial tribunal's decision, Rule 9(e).
Reasons for nonjoinder of persons needed for just adjudication, Rules 12(b), (h).
Redundant matters, motion to strike, Rule 12(f); Auth. Comm. Rule 12(f).
Reference,
Adoption of statement by reference, Rule 10(c); Auth. Comm. Rule 10(c).
Paragraph by number in succeeding pleadings, Rule 10(b); Auth. Comm. Rule 10(b).
Release as defense, Rule 8(c).

PLEADINGS—Cont'd
Removed cases, repleading after removal, Rule 81(c); Auth. Comm. Rule 81(c).
Reply, generally, this index.
Representative capacity of party suing or sued, Rule 9(a); Auth. Comm. Rule 9(a).
Res judicata as defense, Rule 8(c).
Responsive pleading,
Admission by failure to deny, Rule 8(d); Auth. Comm. Rule 8(d).
Omission, defenses, waiver, Rule 12(h).
Time for serving, Rule 12(A).
Scandalous matter, motion to strike, Rule 12(f); Auth. Comm. Rule 12(f).
Service, Rule 5.
Supplemental pleading, Rule 15(d).
Time, Rule 12(a).
Shareholder derivative actions,
Particularity, Rule 23.1.
Verification, Rule 23.1.
Signature, Rule 11.
Application of rules to motions and other papers, Rule 7(b).
Sanctions, Rule 11.
Statements, Rule 8(e).
Special damages, Rule 9(g); Auth. Comm. Rule 9(g).
Special matters, Rule 9.
Specific performance, contract to convey land, form of complaint in action for, Form 12.
Statement,
Identifying, admiralty and maritime claims, Rule 9(h); Auth. Comm. Rule 9(h).
Separate claims or defenses, admiralty and maritime claims, Rule 8(e)(2).
Statute of Frauds as defense, Rule 8(c).
Statute of Limitations as defense, Rule 8(c).
Striking out, Rule 12(f).
Discovery, sanction for failure to comply with order compelling, Rule 37(b); Auth. Comm. Rule 37(b).
Failure to make more definite statement, Rule 12(e).
Summary judgment, Rules 12(b, c).
Rendered where pleadings show no genuine issue, etc., Rule 56(c).
Supplemental jurisdiction, Auth. Comm. Rule 8(a).
Supplemental pleading, Rule 15(d).
Technical forms not required, Rule 8(e)(1).
Third-Party Practice, generally, this index.
Time, Rule 9(f); Auth. Comm. Rule 9(f).
Amendments, Rule 15(a), (b), and (c).
Dismissal of action, Rule 41(a).
Service, Rule 12(a).
Summary judgment, Rule 56(a).
Title of action, setting forth in caption, Rule 10(a).
Two or more statements of claim or defense, Rule 8(e).
Unfair competition, form of complaint in action for, Form 17.
United States,
Counterclaim against, Rule 13(d).

PLEADINGS—Cont'd
United States,—Cont'd
Time for answer or reply, Rule 12(a).
Unliquidated damages, Auth. Comm. Rule 8(a).
Unserved pleadings, effect of, Auth. Comm. Rule 5.
Venue, Statement of basis, Auth. Comm. Rule 8(a).
Verification. Complaint, ante.
Waiver of defenses and objections, Rule 8(c).

PLEAS
Plea of Guilty, generally, this index.
Plea of Nolo Contendere, generally, this index.

PLEAS, INSUFFICIENCY OF PLEADINGS
Exceptions abolished, Rule 7(c).

POLICE OR PATROLMEN
Matters observed by, public records and reports, hearsay exception, Evid. Rule 803.

POLITICAL SUBDIVISIONS
Documents of under or not under seal, self-authentication, Evid. Rule 902.
Privilege of, general rule, Evid. Rule 501.

PORTRAITS
Family, statements concerning inscriptions on, hearsay exception, Evid. Rule 803.

POSSESSION
Judgment directing delivery of possession, Rule 70; Auth. Comm. Rule 70.
Vessel, admiralty or maritime claims, process and notice, Supp. Rule D.

PRAYER
Claims for relief, Rule 8(a).
Default judgment, relief prayed for, Rule 54(c).

PREFERENCE
Cases on trial calendar, Rule 40.
Declaratory judgment, Rule 57.
Interrogatories, answers to, orders concerning, Rule 33(b).
Requests for admission, final disposition, Rule 36(a).

PREFERRED SHIP MORTGAGE
Foreclosure, actions in rem, inapplicable, Supp.Rule C(4).

PREJUDGMENT INTEREST
Motions for, Auth. Comm. Rule 59(e).

PREJUDICE
Bias or Prejudice, generally, this index.

PRELIMINARY EXAMINATIONS
Criminal cases, inapplicability of rules, Evid. Rule 1101.

PRELIMINARY HEARING
Pleading, Rule 12(d).

PRELIMINARY INJUNCTIONS
Generally, Rule 65.

PRELIMINARY QUESTIONS
Generally, Evid. Rule 104.
Fact, inapplicability of rules, Evid. Rule 1101.

PRESERVATION
Writing used to refresh memory, portion withheld over objections, Evid. Rule 612.

PRESERVATION OF DEFENSES
Generally, Rule 12(h).

PRESUMPTIONS
Civil actions and proceedings, Evid. Rule 301.
Applicability of state law, Evid. Rule 302.
Foreign public documents, treatment as authentic, Evid. Rule 902.
Signatures, documents or other matters, genuineness or authenticity, Act of Congress respecting, Evid. Rule 902.

PRETRIAL CONFERENCE
Generally, Rule 16; Auth. Comm. Rule 16.

PREVAILING PARTY
Costs, Rule 54(d); Auth. Comm. Rule 54(d).

PRINTING
"Writings" and "recordings" as including, contents of writings, etc., Evid. Rule 1001.

PRISONERS, DEPOSITIONS
Oral examination, leave of court, Rule 30(a); Auth. Comm. Rule 30(a).
Use in court proceedings, Rule 32(a); Auth. Comm. Rule 32(a).
Written questions, leave of court, Rule 31(a); Auth. Comm. Rule 31(a).

PRIVATE CORPORATIONS
Corporations, generally, this index.

PRIVILEGES AND IMMUNITIES
Generally, Evid. Rule 501.
Existence of, preliminary questions concerning, court determination, Evid. Rule 104.
Ruling of court, grounds, exempting declarant from testifying concerning subject matter of his statement, "unavailability as witness" as including, hearsay exception, Evid. Rule 804.
Subpoenas, response, Rule 45(d); Auth. Comm. Rule 45(d).

PRIZE PROCEEDINGS IN ADMIRALTY
Applicability of rules in part, Evid. Rule 1101.
Nonapplicability of rules, Rule 81(a).

PROBATION
Granting or revoking, proceedings for, inapplicability, Evid. Rule 1101.

PROCEEDINGS
Actions and Proceedings, generally, this index.

PROCESS

Generally, Rule 4; 28 U.S.C.A. § § 1691-1696.
Amendment, Rule 4(h).
Behalf of and against persons not parties, Rule 71; Auth. Comm. Rule 71.
Change of party, amendment of pleading, Rule 15(c).
Civil docket, entry in, Rule 79(a).
Condemnation of property, Rule 71A(d); Auth. Comm. 71A(d).
Defense of insufficiency, Rule 12(b)(4), (h); Auth. Comm. Rule 12(b)(4).
Foreign and international litigations, 28 U.S.C.A. § 1696.
Motion to dismiss complaint for failure to serve, form of, Form 19.
Opposing party bringing suit upon claim by, court not acquiring jurisdiction to render personal judgment, pleader need not state claim, Rule 13(a).
Receivers, 28 U.S.C.A. § 1692.
Sealed, 28 U.S.C.A. § 1691.
Service of Process, generally, this index.
Stockholder's derivative actions, 28 U.S.C.A. § 1695.
Summons, generally, this index.
Third-party practice, Rule 14(a).
Used to produce result, etc., authentication and identification, conformity with requirements, Evid. Rule 901.

PROCESS SERVERS

Plaintiff selects, Auth. Comm. Rule 4(c).

PRODUCTION OF DOCUMENTS OR THINGS

See, also, Discovery, generally, this index.
Application of rules, Rule 81(a).
Compelling production, Rules 37(a) and 45(c); Auth. Comm. Rule 37(a).
Computer Data, Auth. Comm. Rule 34(b).
Depositions upon oral examination, inspection during, identification, etc., Rule 30(f).
Failure to,
Comply with order compelling inspection, sanctions, Rule 37(b); Auth. Comm. Rule 37(b).
Respond to request for inspection, sanctions, Rule 37(d); Auth. Comm. Rule 37(d).
Method of obtaining discovery, Rule 26(a).
Motion for order to compel inspection, Rule 37(a).
Motion for protective order, Rule 26(c); Auth. Comm. Rules 26(c) and 34(a).
Notice for taking deposition upon oral examination accompanied by request for, Rule 30(b); Auth. Comm. Rule 30(b)(5).
Objections, Rule 34(b); Auth. Comm. Rule 34(b).
Persons not parties, independent action against, Rule 34(c); Auth. Comm. Rule 34(c).
Procedure, Rule 34(b); Auth. Comm. Rule 34(b).
Requests, Rule 34(a), (b); Auth. Comm. Rule 34(a), (b).
Form of, Form 24.
Responses to requests, Rule 34(b); Auth. Comm. Rule 34(b).
Scope of, Rule 34(a); Auth. Comm. Rule 34(a).
Service, requests, Rule 34(a), (b); Auth. Comm. Rule 34(b).
Stipulations, extension of time, responses to approval of court, Rule 29.
Subpoenas, Rule 45; Auth. Comm. Rule 45(a).

PRODUCTION OF DOCUMENTS OR THINGS—Cont'd
Time for service and answer, Rule 34(b); Auth. Comm. Rule 34(b).
Voluminous writings, recordings or photographs, court order, Evid. Rule 1006.

PROMISSORY NOTE
Complaint in action on form of, Form 3.

PROOF
Evidence, generally, this index.

PROPERTY
Constructive notice of pending actions concerning, 28 U.S.C.A. § 1964.
Records of or statements in documents affecting an interest in, hearsay exception, Evid. Rule 803.

PROPERTY DISPOSITION
Admiralty or maritime claims, actions in rem and quasi in rem, Supp. Rule E(9).

PROPOSED AMENDMENTS, 1993
Federal Rules of Civil Procedure, Part IA.
Federal Rules of Evidence, Evid.Rules 101, 705, and 1101.

PROTECTIVE ORDERS
Generally, Rule 26(c); Auth. Comm. Rule 26(c).
Discovery,
Denial of motion for order compelling, Rule 37(a); Auth. Comm. Rule 37(a).
Failure of parties to take certain actions, excuse discovery objectionable, Rule 37(d).
Materials, trial or litigation preparation, disclosure of mental impressions, etc., of party representative, Rule 26(b); Auth. Comm. Rule 26(b).
Expenses, award of, motions for, Rule 26(c); Auth. Comm. Rule 26(c).

PSEUDONYM LITIGATION
Propriety of, Auth. Comm. Rule 10.

PSYCHOLOGISTS AND PSYCHOLOGY
Mental examination of persons, Rule 35; Auth. Comm. Rule 35(a).

PUBLIC CORPORATIONS
Corporations, generally, this index.

PUBLIC OFFICERS
Officers and Employees, generally, this index.

PUBLIC RECORDS
Records and Recordation, generally, this index.

PUBLICATION
Official records, evidence, Rule 44(a)(1); Auth. Comm. Rule 44(a)(1).

PUBLICATIONS (MAGAZINES, ETC.)
Pamphlets, generally, this index.
Periodicals, generally, this index.

PUERTO RICO
Subject matter jurisdiction and, Jurisdiction.

PUNISHMENT
Sentence and Punishment, generally, this index.

PURPOSE OF RULES
Generally, Evid. Rule 102.

QUASI IN REM ACTIONS
See generally, Jurisdiction, this index.
Service, Auth. Comm. Rule 4(e).

QUASI JUDICIAL TRIBUNAL
Pleading judgment or decision, Rule 9(e).

QUESTIONS OF LAW OR FACT
Common to class, actions, Rules 23(a, b).
Foreign law, determination, Rule 44.1; Auth. Comm. Rule 44.1.

QUO WARRANTO
Applicability of rules to, Rule 81(a)(2).

RAILROAD LABOR DISPUTES
Applicability of rules to, Rule 81(a)(3).

"RAMBO"-STYLE LITIGATION TACTICS
Contrary to Rule 1 mandate, Auth. Comm. Rule 1.

RAPE
Victims, relevance of past behavior, Evid. Rule 412.

REAL PARTY IN INTEREST
Prosecution in name of, Rule 17(a).

RECEIVERS
Generally, Rule 66; Auth. Comm. Rule 66.
Actions by and against receivers, Auth. Comm. Rule 66.
Appeals regarding, Auth. Comm. Rule 66.
Appointment, Auth. Comm. Rule 66.
Discretion, Auth. Comm. Rule 66.
Dismissal, Auth. Comm. Rule 66.
Equitable defenses by and against, Auth. Comm. Rule 66.
Jurisdiction, Auth. Comm. Rule 66.
Law governing capacity to sue or be sued, Rule 17(b).
Process, 28 U.S.C.A. § 1692.
Role, Auth. Comm. Rule 66.
Stay of judgment, Rule 62(a); Auth. Comm. Rule 62(a).
Terminating or vacating, Auth. Comm. Rule 66.

RECITALS
Judgment, Rule 54(a).

RECONSIDERATION
Motions for, Auth. Comm. Rule 59(e).

RECORDS AND RECORDATION
Appeal from magistrate to district judge, Rule 75(b); Auth. Comm. Rule 75(b).
Authentication, Rule 44(a); Auth. Comm. Rule 44.
Authentication and identification, conformity with requirements, Evid. Rule 901.
Business records, option to produce, interrogatories, Rule 33(c); Auth. Comm. Rule 33(c).
Admissibility of, 28 U.S.C.A. § 1732.

RECORDS AND RECORDATION—Cont'd
Certified copies, self-authentication, Evid. Rule 902.
Clerical mistakes, correction of, Rule 60(a).
Clerk to keep, Rule 79(d).
Congressional journals, 28 U.S.C.A. § 1736.
Consular papers, 28 U.S.C.A. § 1740.
Contents of,
Collateral matters, other evidence of contents, Evid. Rule 1004.
Copies of, duplicates, admissibility, Evid. Rule 1003.
Definitions, Evid. Rule 1001.
Duplicates, defined, Evid. Rule 1001.
Functions of court and jury, Evid. Rule 1008.
Loss or destruction of originals, other evidence of contents, Evid. Rule 1004.
Official records, proof of, Evid. Rule 1005.
Opponent, original in possession of, other evidence of contents, Evid. Rule 1004.
Original,
Defined, Evid. Rule 1001.
Not obtainable, other evidence of contents, Evid. Rule 1004.
Other evidence of, admissibility, Evid. Rule 1004.
Proof of, requirement of original, exception, Evid. Rule 1002.
Recordings, defined, Evid. Rule 1001.
Testimony or deposition or written admission of party, proof by, Evid. Rule 1007.
Voluminous recordings, summaries of, Evid. Rule 1006.
Court records, 28 U.S.C.A. § § 1734-1735.
Depositions upon,
Oral examination, order, manner, Rules 30(b, c).
Written questions, preparation by officer, Rule 31(b).
Examination, depositions upon oral examination, Rule 30(c).
Excluded evidence, Rule 43(c).
Family history or records. Hearsay, generally, this index.
Findings by the court, Rule 52(a); Auth. Comm. Rule 52(a).
Foreign documents, 28 U.S.C.A. § 1741.
Government records, 28 U.S.C.A. § 1733.
Hearsay, generally, this index.
Judgment not required to recite record of prior proceedings, Rule 54(a).
Magistrate, proceedings before, Rules 72(b), 73(a).
Master, record of evidence, Rule 53(c).
Extension of time for filing, Rule 6(b).
Service, Rule 5(a).
Offer of proof and ruling on, Evid. Rule 103.
Officer's bond, 28 U.S.C.A. § 1737.
Preliminary injunction hearing, evidence, Rule 65(a)(2).
Proof of, Rule 44; Auth. Comm. Rule 44.
State and territorial records, 28 U.S.C.A. § § 1738-1739.
Statements, remainder or part of, introduction, Evid. Rule 106.
Summaries, contents of voluminous recordings, Evid. Rule 1006.

REDUCTION OF SECURITY
Admiralty or maritime claims, actions in rem and quasi in rem, Supp. Rule E(6).

REDUNDANCY

Pleading, motion to strike, Rule 12(f); Auth. Com. Rule 12(f).

REFERENCE AND REFEREES

Bankruptcy, this index.

Default judgment, reference to determine account or amount of damages, Rule 55(b).

Magistrate, Rule 73; Auth. Comm. Rule 73(a).

Master, Rule 53(b), (d); Auth. Comm. Rule 53.

Notice of meeting, Rule 53(d).

Paragraphs by number in succeeding pleading, Rule 10(b).

Pleading, adoption of statement by reference, Rule 10(c).

Pre-trial determination as to preliminary reference, Rule 16.

Referee as included in term master, Rule 53(a).

REGISTERED MAIL

Depositions,

Sending to clerk of court for filing, Rule 30(f).

Upon oral examination, filing of, Rule 30(f).

Service of summons on United States or officers or agencies thereof, Rule 4(d).

REHABILITATION

Certificate of, conviction subject of, impeachment of witness by evidence of conviction of crime, effect, Evid. Rule 609.

RELATION BACK

Amended pleadings, Rule 15(c).

RELATIVES

Blood or marriage, relationship by, records of religious organizations, hearsay exception, Evid. Rule 803.

RELEASE

Pleading as defense, Rule 8(c).

RELEVANT EVIDENCE

See, also, Admissibility of Evidence, generally, this index.

Character Evidence, generally, this index.

Defined, Evid. Rule 401.

Exclusion on grounds of prejudice, confusion, waste of time or needless presentation of cumulative evidence, Evid. Rule 403.

Fulfillment, condition of fact, relevancy of evidence dependent upon, admission, Evid. Rule 104.

Generally, admissible, Evid. Rule 402.

Habit of person, Evid. Rule 406.

Irrelevant evidence inadmissible, Evid. Rule 402.

Sex offenses, victims past behavior, Evid. Rule 412.

Subsequent remedial measures, Evid. Rule 407.

Victims past behavior, sex offenses, Evid. Rule 412.

RELIGIOUS BELIEFS OR OPINIONS

Credibility of witness, admissibility to impair or enhance, Evid. Rule 610.

RELIGIOUS ORGANIZATIONS

Records of, hearsay exception, Evid. Rule 803.

REMAND
Inappropriate removal, remedy for, Removal.

REMEDY
Failure of jurisdiction and, Jurisdiction.
Failure of venue and, Venue.
Inappropriate forum and, Forum non Conveniens.
Misjoinder of party, Rule 21.

REMOVAL
Generally, Removal, Juris. § § 2.16-2.17, 28 U.S.C.A. § § 1441-1451.
Bond, Removal.
Civil rights cases, 28 U.S.C.A. § 1443.
Consent to removal, Removal, Juris. § 2.16.
Criminal actions, Removal, Juris. § 2.17.
Diversity of citizenship jurisdiction, Removal, Juris. § 2.16, 28 U.S.C.A. § 1441.
Federal question jurisdiction, Removal, Juris. § 2.16, 28 U.S.C.A. § 1441.
Foreign states, suits against and removal, Removal, Juris. § 2.16, 28 U.S.C.A. § 1441.
Inappropriate removal and remedy, Removal, Juris. § 2.16, 28 U.S.C.A. § 1447.
Joinder of non-removable claims, Removal, Juris. § 2.16.
Nonremovable actions, 28 U.S.C.A. § 1445.
Procedure for removal, Removal, Juris. § 2.17, 28 U.S.C.A. § § 1446-1448.
Remand when removal inappropriate, Removal, Juris. § 2.16, 28 U.S.C.A. § 1447.
Remedy for inappropriate removal, Removal, Juris. § 2.17, 28 U.S.C.A. § 1447.
Sanctions in removal cases, Removal, Juris. § 2.17.
Subject matter jurisdiction and removal, Removal, Juris. § 2.16.
Time, Removal, Juris. § 2.17.
Unanimous consent, Removal, Juris. § 2.16.
Venue and removal, Removal, Juris. § 2.16.

REMOVED CASES
See generally, Removal, this index.
Application of rules, Rule 81(c); Auth. Comm. Rule 81(c).
Jury demand, Rule 81(c); Auth. Comm. Rule 81(c).
Service of process, Auth. Comm. Rule 4.
Time to Answer, Rule 81(c); Auth. Comm. Rule 81(c).
Without regard to citizenship of parties, competency of witnesses, state law as determining, exception, Evid. Rule 601.

REPLEADING
Removed cases, Rule 81(c); Auth. Comm. Rule 81(c).

REPLEVIN
Availability of remedy, Rule 64.

REPLY
Generally, Rule 7(a); Auth. Comm. Rule 7(a).
Affidavits, motion for new trial, Rule 59(c).
Briefs, in summary, judgment context, Auth. Comm. Rule 56(c).
Time for, Rule 12(a).

REPORTS
Authentication and identification, conformity with requirements, Evid. Rule 901.

REPORTS—Cont'd
Evidence on trial by court, Rule 43(c).
Hearsay exception,
Public reports, Evid. Rule 803.
Regularly conducted activity, Evid. Rule 803.
Masters, ante.
Mental examinations, psychologists, Rule 35.
Physical and mental examinations, Rule 35(b); Auth. Comm. Rule 35(b).

REPRESENTATIVES
Action on behalf of infant or incompetent, Rule 17(c).
Capacity to sue or be sued, determination, Rule 17(b).
Class actions, Rule 23; Auth. Comm. Rule 23.
Deceased party, motion for substitution made by, Rule 25(a).
Intervention, Auth. Comm. Rule 24(a).
Party,
Discovery, trial and litigation preparation, need of materials, Rule 26(b).
Protective order against disclosures of mental impressions, etc., in discovery, Rule 26(b).
Unincorporated associations, actions involving, Auth. Comm. rule 23.2.

REPUTATION
Hearsay, this index.

REQUESTS
Findings by court, Rule 52(a); Auth. Comm. Rule 52(a).
For admissions, Admissions, this index.
Instruction, Rule 51; Auth. Comm. Rule 51.
Judicial notice, opportunity to be heard as to propriety of taking, Evid. Rule 201.
Limited admissibility of evidence, Evid. Rule 105.
Physical and mental examinations, prior to future reports of examiner, Rule 35(b).
Prior statements of witnesses, showing or disclosing to opposing counsel, Evid. Rule 613.
Production of documents or things and entry upon land, etc., for inspection and other purposes, Rules 34(a), (b); Auth. Comm. Rule 34(b).
Form of, Form 24.
Generally, Production of Documents or Things, this index.
Record of evidence by master, Rule 53(c).

RES JUDICATA
Pleading as defense, Rule 8(c).

RESIDENCE OF PARTY
Venue and, Venue, Juris. § 2.14.

RESPONSES
Depositions, upon written questions, taking by officer, Rule 31(b); Auth. Comm. Rule 31(b).
Request for,
Discovery,
Extension of time, stipulations, approval of court, Rule 29; Auth. Comm. Rule 29.
Supplementation of, Rule 26(e); Auth. Comm. Rule 26(e).

RESPONSES—Cont'd
Request for,—Cont'd
Production of documents or things and entry upon land, etc., for inspection and other purposes, Rule 34(b); Auth. Comm. Rule 34(b).
Form of, Form 24.

RESTRAINING ORDERS
Form and scope, Rule 65(d).
Security, Rule 65(c).

RETURN
Documents and things produced for inspection, depositions upon oral examination, Rule 30(f).
Habeas corpus, writ of or show cause order, time, Rule 81(a); Auth. Comm. Rule 81(a).
Marshal, admiralty or maritime claims, actions in rem and quasi in rem, execution, process, Supp.Rule E(4).

REVERSAL
Judgment as a matter of law, alternative new trial motion, Rule 50.

REVIEW
Appeal and Review, generally, this index.

RICO (Racketeer Influenced & Corrupt Organizations Act)
RICO Case Statements, Auth. Comm. Rule 12(e).

RINGS
Engravings, statements concerning, hearsay exception, Evid. Rule 803.

ROUTINE PRACTICE
Organizations, relevant evidence, Evid. Rule 406.

RULES
Amendment, notice, Rule 83.
Construction, Auth. Comm. Rule 1.
District court's power to establish, Rule 83; Auth. Comm. Rule 83.
Effective date, Rule 86; Auth. Comm. Rule 86.
"Just", "Speedy", "Inexpensive" mandate, Auth. Comm. Rule 1.
State laws, as rules of decision, 28 U.S.C.A. § 1652.
Supreme Court, this index.

RULES OF CRIMINAL PROCEDURE
Supercedure of provisions concerning offer to plead guilty, nolo contendere, etc., by amendment to, Evid. Rule 410.

RULINGS ON EVIDENCE
Generally, Evid. Rule 103.

SALES
Complaint in action for goods sold and delivered, form of, Form 5.

SAMPLES
Production of Documents or Things, generally, this index.
Property or objects. Entry Upon Land, generally, this index.

SANCTIONS
Appeal from magistrate, Rule 74(d).

SANCTIONS—Cont'd
Depositions upon oral examination, certification of special notice, Rule 30(b).
Discovery, failure to make, Rule 37; Auth. Comm. Rule 37.
Pleadings and other documents filed in court, Rule 11.
Pretrial order, Rule 16(f)
Removal, applicability of Rule 11 sanctions to, Removal.
Subpoenas, excessive burden, Rule 45(c); Auth. Comm. Rule 45(c).
Title, Rule 85.

SATURDAY
Clerks of court, business hours, Rule 77(c).
Computation of time, Rule 6(a).
Discovery requests, etc., signing, Rule 26(g).
Pretrial conference, failure to appear, Rule 16(f).
Pretrial order, failure to obey, Rule 16(f).
Scheduling conference, failure to appear, Rule 16(f).
Scheduling order, failure to obey, Rule 16(f).
Signing of pleadings, motions, etc., Rule 11.

SCANDALOUS MATTER
Motion to strike, Rule 12(f).

SCIENCES
Learned treatises, statements in, hearsay exception, Evid. Rule 803.

SCIRE FACIAS
Abolition of writ, Rule 81(b).

SCOPE OF RULES
Generally, Rule 1; Evid. Rule 101.
Judicial notice, adjudicative facts, rule respecting, Evid. Rule 201.

SEA VOYAGE
Depositions upon oral examination, leave of court not required, Rule 30(b); Auth. Comm. Rule 30(b)(2).

SEALS
Authentication of official record, Rule 44(a).
Domestic public documents under or not under, extrinsic evidence of authenticity as condition precedent to admissibility not required, Evid. Rule 902.
Summons, Rule 4(b).

SEAMEN
Destitute seamen, transportation to U. S., actions for penalties for refusal of, applicability of rules in part, Evid. Rule 1101.
Foreign diplomatic and consular officers, disputes between seamen, applicability of rules in part, Evid. Rule 1101.

SEARCHES AND SEIZURES
Person or property, Rule 64; Auth. Comm. Rule 64.
Property,
Service in action begun by, Rule 5(a).
Warrants, issuance, proceedings for, inapplicability, Evid. Rule 1101.

SECRETARY OF AGRICULTURE
Inapplicability of rules to proceedings to review orders, Rule 81(a).

SECRETARY OF EMBASSY OR LEGATION
Authentication of official record, Rule 44(a); Auth. Comm. Rule 44(a)(2).

SECRETARY OF INTERIOR
Inapplicability of rules to proceedings to review orders of, Rule 81(a).

SECURITY
Injunctions, Rule 65(c).
Pending appeal, Rule 62(c); Auth. Comm. Rule 62(c).
Master not to retain report as security for compensation, Rule 53(a).
Proceedings against sureties, Rule 65.1.
Stay of proceedings to enforce judgment, Rule 62(b).
Surety, Rule 65.1.

SEIZURE
Searches and Seizures, generally, this index.

SELF-INCRIMINATION
Not waived by accused or other witness when examined respecting matters relating only to credibility, Evid. Rule 608.

SENSATION
Hearsay exceptions, statement respecting, Evid. Rule 803.

SENTENCE AND PUNISHMENT
See, also, Fines and Penalties, generally, this index.
Death Penalty, generally, this index.
Impeaching credibility of witness, conviction of crime punishable by imprisonment exceeding one year, court determination, probative value, Evid. Rule 609.
Judgment of previous conviction, crime punishable by imprisonment exceeding one year, evidence of, hearsay exception, Evid. Rule 803.
Motions to vacate, set aside or correct, applicability of rules in part, Evid. Rule 1101.
Proceedings, inapplicability, Evid. Rule 1101.

SEPARATE
Actions, risk created, class actions maintainable, Rule 23(b).
Judgment as to one or more but fewer than all claims, staying enforcement, Rule 62(h); Auth. Comm. Rule 62(h).
Summons, issuance against defendants, Rule 4(a).
Trials, Rule 42(b); Auth. Comm. Rule 42(b).
Generally, this index.

SEPARATE DOCUMENT RULE
Requirement of, Rule 58; Auth. Comm. Rule 58.

SEQUESTRATION
Property of person disobeying judgment directing performance of specific acts, Rule 70; Auth. Comm. Rule 70.

SERVICE OF PROCESS
Generally, Rule 4, 4.1.
Adults, service on, Auth. Comm. Rule 4(e)-(f).
Affidavits, Rule 4.1.
New trial, Rule 59(c).

SERVICE OF PROCESS—Cont'd
Affidavits, Rule 4.1.—Cont'd
Supporting motion, Rule 6(d).
Agents and Agency, this index.
Amended complaints, Auth. Comm. Rule 4.
Answer, time, Rule 12(a).
Answers or objections to requests for admission, Rule 36(a).
Appearance, Rule 5(a); Auth. Comm. Rule 5(a).
Associations, service on, Rule 4(h); Auth. Comm. Rule 4(h).
Attorney, original service or, Auth. Comm. Rule 4(e).
Attorney, pleading and other papers, Rule 5(b); Auth. Comm. Rule 5(b).
Attorney General of United States, Rule 4(h).
Burden of proving proper service, Auth. Comm. Rule 4.
Business, service at, Auth. Comm. Rule 4(e).
Certificate of service, filing, Rule 5(d).
Certified mail, summons and complaint against United States or officers or agencies thereof, Rule 4(h).
Clerk of court, agent, proceeding against sureties, Rule 65.1.
Corporations, service on, Rule 4(h); Auth. Comm. Rule 4(h).
Cross, redirect and recross questions, depositions upon written questions, Rule 31(a).
Defense, insufficiency, Rules 12(b), (h).
Demand, Rule 5(a).
Jury trial, failure to serve as waiver, Rule 38(d).
Depositions upon questions in lieu of oral examination, Rule 30(c).
Discovery, papers relating to, Rule 5(a).
Dismissal,
If not made within 120 days, Rule 4(m); Auth. Comm. Rule 3; Auth. Comm. Rule 4(m).
Insufficient service, Rule 12(b)(5); Auth. Comm. Rule 12(b)(5).
Dwelling House, service at, Auth. Comm. Rule 4(e).
Electronic service, Rule 5(b); Auth. Comm. Rule 5(b).
E-Mail service, Auth. Comm. Rule 4(f).
Facsimile service, Rule 5(b); Auth. Comm. Rule 5(b)
Federal officers, agents, corporations, service on, Rule 4(i); Auth. Comm. Rule 4(i).
Foreign corporations, service on, Rule 4(f); Auth. Comm. Rule 4(f).
Foreign countries,
Alternative provisions for, Rule 4(j); Auth. Comm. Rule 4(j).
Serving associations in, Rule 4(h).
Serving corporations in, Rule 4(h).
Serving individuals in, Rule 4(f).
Serving infants/incompetents in, Rule 4(g).
Serving partnerships in, Rule 4(h).
Foreign governments and agencies, service on, Rule 4(j); Auth. Comm. Rule 4(j).
Good cause required for service outside 120 days, Auth. Comm. Rule 4(m).
Governments and municipalities, service on, Rule 4(j); Auth. Comm. Rule 4(j).
Hague service, Auth. Comm. Rule 4(f) & 4(j).
How made, Rule 5(b).
Immunity from service, Auth. Comm. Rule 4.

SERVICE OF PROCESS—Cont'd
Individuals, service on, Rule 4(e); Rule 4(f); Auth. Comm. Rule 4(e) & 4(f).
Infants and incompetent persons, service on, Rule 4(g); Auth. Comm. Rule 4(g).
Interrogatories, Rule 33(a).
Failure of party to serve answers or objections to, sanctions, Rule 37(d).
Intervention, Rule 24(c).
Jurisdiction, distinct from service procedures, Auth. Comm. Rule 4.
Local governments, service on, Rule 4(j); Auth. Comm. Rule 4(j).
Long-arm statutes, Rule 4(k); Auth. Comm. Rule 4(k).
Maids, service on, Auth. Comm. Rule 4(e).
Mail, this index.
Marshal, service by, Rule 4(c); Auth. Comm. Rule 4(c).
Motions, this index.
New Claims, new parties, Auth. Comm. Rule 5(b).
Notice, this index.
Numerous defendants, Rule 5(c); Auth. Comm. Rule 5(c).
Objections, depositions,
Errors and irregularities in notice, Rule 32(d).
Written questions, form of, Rule 32(d).
Offer of judgment, Rules 5(a), 68.
Order in lieu of summons, party not inhabitant of or not found within state, Rule 4(k).
Orders of court, Rule 5(a).
"Otherwise provided by federal law", Auth. Comm. Rule 4.
Papers other than pleading and process, Rule 5.
Parties not inhabitant of or found within state, Rule 4(k).
Foreign countries, alternative provisions for service in, Rule 4(j).
Partnerships, service on, Rule 4(h); Auth. Comm. Rule 4(h).
Personal service, notice, condemnation proceedings, Rule 71A(d); Auth. Comm. Rule 71A(d).
Personal service on defendant, Rule 4(e).
Pleadings, this index.
Prisoners, service on, Auth. Comm. Rule 5(b).
Process other than complaint or summons, Rule 4.1.
Process server, Auth. Comm. Rule 4(c).
Proof of service, Rule 4(l); Auth. Comm. Rule 4(l).
Parties not inhabitant of or found within state, alternative provisions for service in foreign countries, Rule 4(i).
Property, seizure of, Rule 4(n).
Publication,
Condemnation proceedings, Rule 71A(d); Auth. Comm. Rule 71A(d).
Depositions, taking before action, Rule 27(a)(2).
Record on appeal, Rule 5(a).
Registered mail, summons and complaint against United States or officers or agencies thereof, Rule 4(h).
Removed cases, Auth. Comm. Rule 4.
Requests for,
Admission, Rule 36(a).
Production of documents or things and entry upon land, etc., for inspection and other purposes, Rules 34(a, b).

SERVICE OF PROCESS—Cont'd
Responses to requests for production of documents or things and entry upon land, etc., for inspection and other purposes, Rule 34(b).
Return of service, Auth. Comm. Rule 4(l).
Amendment, Auth. Comm. Rule 4(l).
Seizure of property in action begun by, Rule 5(a); Auth. Comm. Rule 5(a).
State governments, service on, Rule 4(j); Auth. Comm. Rule 4(j).
Subpoena, Rule 45.
Discovery, person in foreign country, Rule 37(e).
Substitution of parties, motion, Rule 25.
Summons, this index.
Territorial limits of effective service, Rule 4(k); Auth. Comm. Rule 4(k).
Third-party practice, Rule 14(a).
Time,
Affidavits for new trial, Rule 59(c).
Answer, Rule 12(a).
Answers or objections to requests for admission, Rule 36(a).
Certification of class actions, Auth. Comm. Rule 23(c)(2).
Copies of answers and objections to interrogatories, Rule 33(a).
Extensions for service time, Rule 4(m); Auth. Comm. Rule 4(m).
Interrogatories, Rule 33(a).
Motion, Rule 6(d).
Summary judgment, Rule 56(c).
Notice,
Application for default judgment, Rule 55(b)(2).
Hearing, Rule 6(d).
Objections to subpoenas, Rule 45(c).
Offer of judgment, Rule 68.
Reply to counterclaim, Rule 12(a).
Requests for,
Admission, Rule 36(a).
Production of documents or things and entry upon land, etc., for inspection and other purposes, Rule 34(b).
Responses to requests for production of documents or things and entry upon land, etc., for inspection and other purposes, Rule 34(b).
Substitution of parties, motion for, Rule 25(a).
Summons, time limit for service, Rule 4(m).
United States, service on government, officer, agency, Rule 4(i); Auth. Comm. Rule 4(i).
Venue, distinct from service procedures, Auth. Comm. Rule 4.
Waiver of service, Rule 4(d); Auth. Comm. Rule 4(d).
When required, Rule 5(a).

SETTING ASIDE
Default judgment, Rule 55(c); Auth. Comm. Rule 55(c).
Findings of fact by court, Rule 52(a).
Judgment, ante.
Verdict,
Errors not affecting substantial rights not ground for, Rule 61.

SETTLEMENT
Compromise and Settlement, generally, this index.

SEX OFFENSES
Victims, relevance of past behavior, Evid. Rule 412.

SHAREHOLDERS DERIVATIVE ACTIONS
Generally, Rule 23.1.
Process, 28 U.S.C.A. § 1695.
Venue, 28 U.S.C.A. § 1401.

SHIPPING
Prize, applicability of rules in part, Evid. Rule 1101.
Seamen, generally, this index.

SHORT TITLE
Generally, Evid. Rule 1103.

SHORTENING OF TIME
Extension of time, generally, ante.

SHOW CAUSE ORDERS
Habeas corpus, generally, ante.

SIGNATURE
Answer or objection to requests for admission, Rule 36(a).
Depositions upon oral examination, Rule 30(e); Auth. Comm. Rule 30(e).
Notice of, attorneys, constituting certification, Rule 30(b).
Discovery requests, responses and objections, Rule 26(g); Auth. Comm. Rule 26(g).
Duty to sign pleadings and other documents, Rule 11.
Foreign official records, authentication, Rule 44(a)(2); Auth. Comm. Rule 44(a)(2).
Foreign public documents, certification, genuineness and official position of executing or attesting person, etc., Evid. Rule 902.
Interrogatories, answers to, Rule 33(a); Auth. Comm. Rule 33(a).
Motions, this index.
Objections to answers to interrogatories, Rule 33(a).
Pleadings, this index.
Self-authentication,
Commercial paper and related documents, Evid. Rule 902.
Domestic public documents under or not under seal, Evid. Rule 902.
Summons by clerk, Rule 4(b).
Written statement as prior statement concerning action or subject matter made by party or person, obtaining of discovery, Rule 26(b).

SIGNS
Purporting to be affixed in course of business and indicating ownership, control or origin, self-authentication, Evid. Rule 902.

SPECIAL
Appearances, Auth. Comm. Rule 12(b)(2).
Appointments, service of process, Rule 4(c).
Damages, pleading, Rule 9(g); Auth. Comm. Rule 9(g).
Master, appointment, Rule 53(a), (b).
Matters, pleading, Rule 9; Auth. Comm. Rule 9.
Verdict,
Entry of judgment on, Rule 58.

SPECIAL—Cont'd
Verdict,—Cont'd
Requirement of return, Rule 49(a); Auth. Comm. Rule 49(a).

SPECIFIC PERFORMANCE, CONTRACT TO CONVEY LAND
Complaint in action for, form of, Form 12.
Disobedience to judgment directing execution of conveyance, Rule 70; Auth. Comm. Rule 70.

SPECIMENS
Comparison by trier or expert witness, authentication and identification, conformity with requirements, Evid. Rule 901.

"SPIRIT" OF RULES
Influence in interpreting Rules, Auth. Comm. Rule 1.

STAKEHOLDER
Generally, Auth. Comm. Rule 22 and Statutory Interpleader.

STANDING
Shareholder derivative actions, Rule 23.1; Auth. Comm. Rule 23.1.

STATE
Documents of under or not under seal, self-authentication, Evid. Rule 902.
"Legal holiday" as including day appointed as holiday by state in which district court is held, computation of time, Rule 6(a).
Official record, authentication, Rule 44(a)(1); Auth. Comm. Rule 44(a)(1).
Practice, execution and discovery in aid of, applicability, Rule 69(a); Auth. Comm. Rule 69(a).
Service of summons and complaint, Rule 4(d).

STATE AGENCIES
Documents of under or not under seal, self-authentication, Evid. Rule 902.

STATE COURTS
Prior actions or proceedings, depositions, effect on use of, Rule 32(a).
State in which district court is held, rule, service upon party not inhabitant of or found within state, Rule 4(e).
Form to correspond to that required by, Rule 4(b).

STATE LAW
Application to,
Condemnation under state law, Rule 71A(k); Auth. Comm. Rule 71A(k).
Service,
State in which district court is held, Rule 4(d).
Upon party not inhabitant of or found within state, state in which court is held, Rule 4(e).
Foreign countries, alternative provisions for service in, Rule 4(i).
Competency of witness, cases involving diversity of citizenship or interpleader, determination in accordance with, exception, Evid. Rule 601.
Demand for jury trial made in accordance with, demand not needed after removal to district court, Rule 81(c); Auth. Comm. Rule 81(c).
Presumptions, applicability in civil actions and proceedings, Evid. Rule 302.
Privilege of witness, state, etc., determination in accordance with, exception, Evid. Rule 501.

STATE OFFICERS AND EMPLOYEES
Public Officers and Employees, generally, this index.

STATEMENT
Claim, failure, defense, Rules 12(b, h).
Depositions upon oral examination, changes of form or substance, Rule 30(e); Auth. Comm. Rule 30(e).
Extrinsic evidence of prior inconsistent statement of witness, admissibility, Evid. Rule 613.
Facts,
Admissions, generally, ante.
False statements. Perjury, generally, this index.
Guilty, offer to plead or withdrawn plea of, statements made in connection with, admissibility, Evid. Rule 410.
Hearsay, this index.
Lack of official record, admissibility, Rule 44(b); Auth. Comm. Rule 44(b).
Legal defense to claim, failure, Rule 12(h).
Made in compromise of claim negotiations, admissibility, Evid. Rule 408.
Nolo contendere, plea of, statement made in connection with, admissibility, Evid. Rule 410.
Perjury, generally, this index.
Pleading, admiralty or maritime claims, Rule 9(h).
Previously made by parties or persons of action or subject matter, obtaining of, discovery, Rule 26(b); Auth. Comm. Rule 26(b)(3).
Prior statements of witnesses, examination concerning, Evid. Rule 613.
Recorded, remainder or part of, introduction, Evid. Rule 106.

STATES
Documents of under or not under seal, self-authentication, Evid. Rule 902.
Laws of. State Laws, generally, this index.
Privilege of, general rule, Evid. Rule 501.
Reputation concerning boundaries or general history important to state in which located, hearsay exception, Evid. Rule 803.

STATUTE OF FRAUDS
Pleading as defense, Rule 8(c).

STATUTE OF LIMITATIONS
Civil actions arising under Act of Congress, 28 U.S.C.A. § 1658, Auth. Comm. Rule 23.
Pleading as defense, Rule 8(c).
Tolling, through filing complaint, Auth. Comm. Rule 3.

STATUTES
Authentication or identification, methods provided by, Evid. Rule 901.
Computation, time, Rule 6(a).
Maritime action in rem, Supp.Rule C(1).
Question arising under, jurisdiction, form of allegation, Form 2.
Right to intervene, conferring, Rule 24(a).
Service, application, Rule 4(d).
Party not inhabitant of or found within state, Rule 4(e).
Foreign countries, alternative provisions for service in, Rule 4(i).
Form to correspond to that required by, Rule 4(b).
Territorial limits of effective service, Rule 4(f).

STATUTES—Cont'd
State Laws, generally, this index.

STAY
Accounting in action for infringement of patent, Rule 62(a); Auth. Comm. Rule 62(a).
Appeal without bond, United States or officer or agency thereof, Rule 62(e); Auth. Comm. Rule 62(e).
Appellate court's powers, Rule 62(g); Auth. Comm. Rule 62(g).
Approval of supersedeas bond by court, Rule 62(d); Auth. Comm. Rule 62(d).
Bond for stay in favor of United States, Rule 62(e); Auth. Comm. Rule 62(e).
Discovery, sanction for failure to comply with order compelling, Rule 37(b).
District judge decision on consent appeal from magistrate, Rule 76(b); Auth. Comm. Rule 76(b).
Execution, Rules 62, 62(b).
Injunction judgment, Rule 62(a); Auth. Comm. Rule 62(a).
Judgments and Decrees, this index.
Payment of costs of previously dismissed action, Rule 41(d).
Receivership judgment, Rule 62(a); Auth. Comm. Rule 62(a).
State law, stay according to, Rule 62(f); Auth. Comm. Rule 62(f).
Supersedeas bond for stay on appeal, Rule 62(d); Auth. Comm. Rule 62(d).
United States or agency thereof, stay in favor of, Rule 62(e); Auth. Comm. Rule 62(e).

STENOGRAPHERS
Report or transcript as evidence, Rule 80(c); Auth. Comm. Rule 80(c).

STENOGRAPHIC
Recording, obtaining prior statement concerning action or subject matter by party or person, Rule 26(b).
Transcription, depositions upon oral examination, Rule 30(b), (c); Auth. Comm. Rule 30(c).

STIPULATIONS
Depositions,
Taking, Rule 29; Auth. Comm. Rule 29.
Upon oral examination, waiver of signing, Rule 30(e).
Discovery procedure, Rule 29; Auth. Comm. Rule 29.
Dismissal, Rule 41(a); Auth. Comm. Rule 41(a).
Action for condemnation of property, Rule 71A(i); Auth. Comm. Rule 71A(i).
Findings of master, Rule 53(e); Auth. Comm. Rule 53(e)(4).
Jury verdict, unanimity and size of jury, Rule 48; Auth. Comm. Rule 48.
New trial, stipulations extending time for filing, Rule 59(c).
Proceedings against sureties, Rule 65.1.
Trial by court, Rule 39(a); Auth. Comm. Rule 39(a).

STRIKING OF PLEADING
Generally, Rule 12(f); Auth. Comm. Rule 12(f).
Discovery, sanction for failure to comply with order compelling, Rule 37(b); Auth. Comm. Rule 37(b).
Failure to make more definite statement, Rule 12(e).
Third-party claim, Rule 14(a).

SUBCLASSES
Treatment, class actions, Rule 23(c).

SUBJECT MATTER
Expert witnesses, trial preparation interrogatories, Rule 26(b).
Lack of jurisdiction, defense, Rule 12(b)(1), (h); Jurisdiction; Auth. Comm. Rule 12(b)(1).
Requirements, subject matter jurisdiction, Jurisdiction, Juris. § § 2.10-2.13.

SUBPOENA DUCES TECUM
Designation of materials in notice to take deposition upon oral examination, Rules 30(b), 45(a); Auth. Comm. Rules 30(b)(5), 45(a).

SUBPOENAS
Generally, Rule 45; Auth. Comm. Rule 45.
Depositions, this index.
Discovery, person in foreign country, Rule 37(e).
Failure to obey, contempt, Rule 45(e); Auth. Comm. Rule 45(e).
Foreign countries, persons in, 28 U.S.C.A. § 1783.
Contempt, 28 U.S.C.A. § 1784.
Form, Rule 45(a); Auth. Comm. Rule 45(a).
Master, procuring attendance of witnesses, Rule 53(d).
Objections, Rule 45(c); Auth. Comm. Rule 45(c).
Production of documents, application of rules, Rule 81(a).
Protection of persons subject to, Rule 45; Auth. Comm. Rule 45(c).
Service, Rule 45(b); Auth. Comm. Rule 45(b).

SUBSTANCE
Authentication and identification, conformity with requirements, Evid. Rule 901.

SUBSTANTIAL RIGHTS
Disregard of error not affecting, Rule 61.

SUBSTITUTION
Copies, documents and things produced for inspection, depositions, upon oral examination, Rule 30(f).
Parties, Rule 25.
Condemnation proceedings, Rule 71A(g); Auth. Comm. Rule 71A(g).
Depositions, effect on use of, Rule 32(a); Auth. Comm. Rule 32(a).
Suggestion of death upon the record under rule concerning, form of, Form 30.

SUCCESSORS OF DECEASED PARTY
Motion for substitution made by, Rule 25(a).
Suggestion of death, Rule 25(a); Auth. Comm. Rule 25(a).

SUM CERTAIN
Defined, Auth. Comm. Rule 55.

SUMMARIES
Business records, interrogatories, Rule 33(c).
Foreign official records, evidence, Rule 44(a)(2).
Voluminous writings, recordings or photographs, contents of, Evid. Rule 1006.

SUMMARY JUDGMENT
Generally, Rule 56; Auth. Comm. Rule 56.

SUMMARY JUDGMENT—Cont'd
Affidavits, Rule 56(e); Auth. Comm. Rule 56(e).
Bad faith affidavits, Rule 56(g).
Pro se drafters, Auth. Comm. Rule 56(g).
Unavailable affidavits, Rule 56(f); Auth. Comm. Rule 56(f).
Verified complaints and statements in place of, Auth. Comm. Rule 56(e).
Appealability of rulings on motions for, Auth. Comm. Rule 56(c).
Authenticating exhibits, Auth. Comm. Rule 56(e).
Burden of proving, Auth. Comm. Rule 56(c).
Credibility questions, Auth. Comm. Rule 56(c).
Cross motions for, Auth. Comm. Rule 56(c).
Discovery while summary judgment pending, Rule 56(f).
Distinct from dismissal or judgment on pleadings or judgment as a matter of law, Auth. Comm. Rule 56.
Findings of fact and conclusions of law, Rule 52(a).
Form of, Auth. Comm. Rule 56(c).
Hearings on motions for, Auth. Comm. Rule 56(c).
Law of the case on, Auth. Comm. Rule 56(c) & 54(d).
Motions, Rules 12(b), (c), 56.
Multiple motions for, Auth. Comm. Rule 56(c).
Non-moving party, Auth. Comm. Rule 56(c).
Oral argument, Auth. Comm. Rule 56(c).
Oral testimony, Auth. Comm. Rule 56(c).
Partial summary judgment, Rule 56(c)-(d); Auth. Comm. Rule 56(c)-(d).
Premature, Auth. Comm. Rule 56(a)-(b).
Procedure for making, Rule 56(c); Auth. Comm. Rule 56(c).
Purpose of, Auth. Comm. Rule 56(c).
Reasonable inferences, Auth. Comm. Rule 56(c).
Reply briefs, Auth. Comm. Rule 56(c).
Standards for entering, Rule 56(c); Auth. Comm. Rule 56(c).
State of mind questions, Auth. Comm. Rule 56(c).
Stipulated facts on motion for, Auth. Comm. Rule 56(c).
Sua sponte, Auth. Comm. Rule 56(c).
Time, dismissal of action, Rule 41(a).
Uncontested motions, Auth. Comm. Rule 56(c).
Unrepresented party warning, Auth. Comm. Rule 56(c).
Who may make, Rule 56(a)-(b); Auth. Comm. Rule 56(a)-(b).

SUMMONS
Generally, Rule 4.
Criminal, proceedings for, inapplicability, Evid. Rule 1101.
Forms, this index.
Issued by clerk, Rule 4(a); (b).
Service of process, Rule 4.
Action against officer or employee of United States, 28 § 1391.
Application of rule to service of pleading, Rule 5(a).
Party not inhabitant of or found within state, Rule 4(k).
Foreign countries, alternative provisions for service in, Rule 4(j).
Third-party practice, Rule 14(a).
Waiver, Form 1B.
Request for, Form 1A.

SUMMONS—Cont'd
Third-party defendant, Forms 22, 22-A.
Time limit for service, Rule 4(m).

SUNDAY
Clerks of court, business hours, Rule 77(c).
Computation of time, Rule 6(a).

SUPERSEDEAS BOND
Stay on appeal, Rule 62(d); Auth. Comm. Rule 62(d).

SUPPLEMENTAL JURISDICTION
Generally, 28 U.S.C.A. § 1367.
Subject matter jurisdiction and, Jurisdiction.
Timeliness of state law claims invoking, Auth. Comm. Rule 2.

SUPPLEMENTAL PLEADING
Service, Rule 15(d).

SUPPLEMENTAL PROCESS
Actions in rem, Supp. Rule C(3).

SUPPLEMENTARY PROCEEDINGS
Execution, Rule 69(a); Auth. Comm. Rule 62(a).

SUPPLEMENTATION OF RESPONSES
Request for discovery, Rule 26(e); Auth. Comm. Rule 26(e).

SUPPORTING CREDIBILITY OF WITNESSES
Credibility of Witnesses, this index.

SUPREME COURT
Abatement, review of matters in, 28 U.S.C.A. § 2105.
Appellate jurisdiction, Generally, Appeals § 6.7.
Courts of appeals, decisions from, 28 U.S.C.A. § 1254.
District courts, decisions from, 28 U.S.C.A. § 1253.
State courts, decisions from, 28 U.S.C.A. § 1257.
Determinations by, 28 U.S.C.A. § 2106.
Original jurisdiction, 28 U.S.C.A. § 1251.
Privilege of witnesses, etc., law governing, exception, Evid. Rule 501.
Rules of court,
Authentication and identification, methods provided by, Evid. Rule 901.
Hearsay, not admissible except as provided by, Evid. Rule 802.
Relevant evidence admissible except as otherwise prescribed by, Evid. Rule 402.
State court decisions, review of, 28 U.S.C.A. § 2104.
Time for appeal and certiorari, 28 U.S.C.A. § 2101.
Writs of certiorari, Appeals § 6.7.

SURETIES
Discovery, trial and litigation preparation, need of materials, Rule 26(b).
Proceedings against, Rule 65.1.

SURPRISE
Relief from judgment on ground of, Rule 60(b).

SURVEYS OF PROPERTY OR OBJECTS
Entry Upon Land, generally, this index.

SYSTEM
Used to produce result, etc., authentication and identification, conformity with requirements, Evid. Rule 901.

TABULATIONS
Use and reliance on by public or persons in particular occupations, hearsay exception, Evid. Rule 803.

TAGS
Purporting to be affixed in course of business and indicating ownership, control or origin, self-authentication, Evid. Rule 902.

TANGIBLE PROPERTY
Discovery,
Need requirement, litigation or trial, preparation, Rule 26(b).
Scope of, Rule 26(b).

TECHNICAL FORM OF PLEADING
Not required, Rule 8(e)(1).

TELEGRAPHS AND TELEPHONES
Authentication and identification, telephone conversations, conformity with requirements, Evid. Rule 901.

TEMPORARY RESTRAINING ORDER
Generally, Rules 65(b), (c), (e).

TERRITORIAL LIMITS
Service, process, admiralty or maritime claims, actions in rem and quasi in rem, Supp. Rule E(3)(a).

TERRITORIES
Documents of under or not under seal, self-authentication, Evid. Rule 902.
Official record, authentication, Rule 44(a)(1).

TESTIMONY
See specific index headings.

TESTS
Production of Documents or Things, generally, this index.
Property or objects. Entry Upon Land, generally, this index.
Results, report of examiner, physical and mental examinations, Rule 35(b); Auth. Comm. Rule 35(b).

THANKSGIVING DAY
Clerks of court, business hours for office, exception concerning opening, Rule 77(c).
"Legal holiday" as including for purposes of computing time, Rule 6(a).

THIRD-PARTY PRACTICE
Generally, Rule 14.
Answer, service of third-party complaint, Rule 7(a).
Claim,
Dismissal, Rule 41(c); Auth. Comm. Rule 41(c).
Entry of judgment disposing of, Rule 54(b).

THIRD-PARTY PRACTICE—Cont'd
Claim,—Cont'd
Joinder, Rule 18(a).
Judgment on one or more but fewer than all claims, Rule 54(b).
Requisites, Rule 8(a).
Separate trial, Rule 42(b).
Complaint,
Form, Forms 22, 22-A.
Summoning person not an original party, Rule 7(a).
Service, places outside state but within United States, Rule 4(f).
Third-party defendant,
Motion to bring in, form of, Form 22-B.
Summons and complaint against, form of, Forms 22, 22-A.
Third-party plaintiff, default judgment against, Rule 55(d).

THREE-JUDGE COURTS
Injunction pending appeal, Rule 62(c).

TIME
Acceptance of offer of judgment, Rule 68; Auth. Comm. Rule 68.
Additional time for proceeding or act after service by mail, Rule 6(e).
Admissions, request for, answers or objections to, Rule 36(a); Auth. Comm. Rule 36(a).
Amending pleadings as of right, Rule 15(a).
Appeal and Review, this index.
Briefs on appeal from magistrate to district judge, filing, Rule 75(c); Auth. Comm. Rule 75(c).
Certification of class actions, Auth. Comm. Rule 23(c)(2).
Citizenship and timing for subject matter jurisdiction, Jurisdiction.
Defendant bringing in third-party, Rule 14(a).
Delay, generally, this index.
Depositions,
Oral examination, Rule 30(a) et seq.; Auth. Comm. Rule 30(a).
Taking, stipulations, Rule 29; Auth. Comm. Rule 29.
Written questions, Rule 31(a); Auth. Comm. Rule 31(a).
Discovery, methods, use, Rule 26(d); Auth. Comm. Rule 26(d).
Dismissal of action, prosecution not in name of real party in interest, Rule 17(a).
Effective date of amendment, Rule 86; Auth. Comm. Rule 86.
Execution, time for issuing, Rule 62(a).
Extension of Time, generally, this index.
Filing papers after complaint with court, Rule 5(d).
Holidays, excluded in computing time, Auth. Comm. Rule 6.
How computed, Auth. Comm. Rule 6.
Inaccessible, when courthouse is, Auth. Comm. Rule 6(a).
Injunctions, Auth. Comm. Rule 65.
Intervention, Rule 24; Auth. Comm. Rule 24.
Involuntary dismissal, Rule 41(b).
Judicial notice, taking, Evid. Rule 201.
Judgments and Decrees, this index.
Limit, impeachment by evidence of conviction of crime, Evid. Rule 609.
Mail, additional time for proceeding after service by, Rule 6(e); Auth. Comm. Rule 6(e).

TIME—Cont'd
Meeting of parties on order of reference, Rule 53(d).
Motions, this index.
Needless consumption of, court control of mode and order of interrogating witnesses and presenting evidence to avoid, Evid. Rule 611.
New requests for supplementation of prior responses to requests for discovery, Rule 26(e).
Notice, this index.
Objections to report of master, Rule 53(e); Auth. Comm. Rule 53(e).
Offer of judgment, Rule 68.
Opposing affidavits on motion for new trial, Rule 59(c).
Permission to amend pleadings, Rule 15(a) and (b).
Physical and mental examinations, Rule 35(a); Auth. Comm. Rule 35(a).
Pleadings, this index.
Proof of service, Rule 4(g).
Relation back of amended pleadings, Rule 15(c).
Removal, Removal, Juris. § 2.17.
Return, habeas corpus, writ of or show cause order, Rule 81(a); Auth. Comm. Rule 81(a).
Review of taxation of costs by clerk, Rule 54(d).
Rules become effective, Rule 86; Auth. Comm. Rule 86.
Saturdays, excluded in computing time, Auth. Comm. Rule 6.
Service of Process, this index.
Substitution of parties, Auth. Comm. Rule 25.
Summary judgment, Rule 56(a).
Summons, time limit for service, Rule 4(j).
Summons to show time for appearance by defendant, Rule 4(b).
Sundays, excluded in computing time, Auth. Comm. Rule 6.
Supersedeas bond, time for giving, Rule 62(d); Auth. Comm. Rule 62(d).
Surety, proceeding against, Auth. Comm. Rule 65.1.
Temporary restraining order, Rule 65(b).
Third-party practice, Rule 14(a).
Voluntary dismissal, Rule 41(a); Auth. Comm. Rule 41(a).
Waste of, exclusion of relevant evidence on grounds of, Evid. Rule 403.

TITLE
Action, setting forth in caption of pleading, Rule 10(a).
Judgment vesting title in another, Rule 70; Auth. Comm. Rule 70.
Rules, Rule 85.

TOMBSTONES
Engravings on, statements concerning, hearsay exceptions, Evid. Rule 803.

TRADE INSCRIPTIONS
Purporting to be affixed in course of business and indicating ownership, control or origin, self-authentication, Evid. Rule 902.

TRADE SECRETS
Disclosure, subpoenas requiring, relief from, Rule 45(c); Auth. Comm. Rule 45(c).

TRANSCRIPT
Evidence, master, filing with report, Rule 53(e).
Master, filing of transcript of proceedings with report, Rule 53(e).

TRANSCRIPT—Cont'd
Stenographic transcript as evidence, Rule 80(c); Auth. Comm. Rule 80(c).

TRANSCRIPTION
Obtaining prior statement concerning action or subject matter by party or person, Rule 26(b); Auth. Comm. Rule 26(b)(3).

TRANSFER
Improper venue and remedy for, Venue, Juris. § 2.14.
Inappropriate forum and remedy for, Forum non Conveniens, Juris. § 2.15.
Multidistrict Litigation Rules (Part V).

TRANSIENT JURISDICTION
Personal jurisdiction and, Jurisdiction, Juris. § 2.4.

TRAVEL FEES
Special appointments for service of process to save, Rule 4(c).

TREATISES
Learned, statements in, hearsay exception, Evid. Rule 803.

TRIAL
Assignment of cases for trial, Rule 40.
Condemnation proceedings, Rule 71A(h); Auth. Comm. Rule 71A(h).
Consolidation,
  Actions for trial, Rule 42(a); Auth. Comm. Rule 42(a).
  With preliminary injunction hearing, Rule 65(a)(2).
Court trial. Trial By Court, generally, this index.
Depositions, use of, Rule 32(a); Auth. Comm. Rule 32(a).
Directed Verdict, generally, this index.
Discovery,
  Documents and tangible things, need of materials in preparation for, Rule 26(b).
  Preparation for, expert witnesses, Rule 26(b).
Evidence, generally, this index.
Inability of judge to proceed, Rule 63; Auth. Comm. Rule 63.
Instructions to jury, Rule 51; Auth. Comm. Rule 51.
Interrogatories, use at, Rule 33(b).
Jury, generally, this index.
Magistrates, trial by consent, Rule 73; Auth. Comm. Rule 73.
  Costs and Fees in actions involving, 28 U.S.C.A. § 2412.
New Trials, generally, this index.
Objections, generally, this index.
Open court, trial conducted in, Rule 77(b); Auth. Comm. Rule 77(b).
Pretrial procedure, Rule 16.
Separate trials, Rule 42(b); Auth. Comm. Rule 42(b).
  Joinder of parties, Rule 20(b).
  Judgment on counterclaim or crossclaim, Rule 13(i).
  Misjoinder, Rule 21.
  Third party claim, Rule 14(a).
Subpoena for attendance at, Rule 45(a); Auth. Comm. Rule 45(a).
Successor judges, Rule 63; Auth. Comm. Rule 63.
Venue, generally, this index.
Verdict, generally, this index.

TRIAL—Cont'd
Voluntary dismissal before introduction of evidence, Rule 41(c).
Witnesses, generally, this index.
Writing used to refresh memory, criminal cases, failure to produce or deliver, ground for mistrial, Evid. Rule 612.

TRIAL BY COURT
Advisory jury, Rule 52(a).
Dismissal motion by defendant, Rule 41(b).
Finding, Rule 52; Auth. Comm. Rule 52.
Issues, Rule 39(b).
Motion by defendant for dismissal, Rule 41(b).
Opinion or memorandum of decision, Rule 52(a); Auth. Comm. Rule 52.
Partial findings, judgment on, Rule 52; Auth. Comm. Rule 52.
Record of excluded evidence, Rule 43(c).
Reference to magistrate, Rule 72.
Reference to master, Rule 53(b); Auth. Comm. Rule 53(b).
Reports of master, Rule 53(e); Auth. Comm. Rule 53(e).
Stipulations for, Rule 39(a); Auth. Comm. Rule 39(a).

TRIAL BY JURY
Jury, generally, this index.

TRIAL DE NOVO
Federal agency actions set aside, facts subject to, rules applicable in part, Evid. Rule 1101.

TRIER OF FACT
Jury, generally, this index.

TRUST TERRITORY OF PACIFIC ISLANDS
Documents of under or not under seal, self-authentication, Evid. Rule 902.

TRUSTS AND TRUSTEES
Prosecution of action, Rule 17(a).

TYPEWRITING
"Writings" and "recordings" as including, contents of writings, etc., Evid. Rule 1001.

UNDERTAKINGS
Bonds(Officers and Fiduciaries), generally, this index.

UNDUE
Burden or expense, protective orders relating to depositions, grounds for, Rule 26(c); Auth. Comm. Rule 26(c).
Hardship, trial and litigation preparation, discovery, need of materials, Rule 26(b).

UNFAIR COMPETITION
Complaint in action for, form of, Form 17.

UNINCORPORATED ASSOCIATION
Actions relating to, Rule 23.2.
Capacity to sue or be sued, Rule 17(b).
Shareholders, derivative actions, Rule 23.1
Subject matter jurisdiction, Jurisdiction.

UNINCORPORATED ASSOCIATION—Cont'd
Venue and, Venue.

UNITED STATES
Action for benefit of another to be brought in name of United States, Rule 17(a).
Agencies of United States, generally, this index.
Answer to complaint, etc., time, Rule 12(a).
Appeal, stay without bond or security, Rule 62(e); Auth. Comm. Rule 62(e).
Bond for stay of judgment against, Rule 62(e).
Costs imposed against, Rule 54(d).
Counterclaim against, Rule 13(d).
Death of defendant in actions involving, 28 U.S.C.A. § 2404.
Default against, Rule 55(e); Auth. Comm. Rule 55(e).
Depositions, Rule 55(e).
Persons before whom taken, Rule 28(a); Auth. Comm. Rule 28(a).
Upon oral examination, leave of court not required where person about to leave, Rule 30(b); Auth. Comm. Rule 30(b)(2).
Use in court proceedings where witness outside of, Rule 32(a); Auth. Comm. Rule 32(a).
Discovery, expenses and fees allowable, Rule 37(f).
Documents of under or not under seal, self-authentication, Evid. Rule 902.
Executions in favor of, 28 U.S.C.A. § 2413.
Interest against, 28 U.S.C.A. § 2411.
Intervention by, 28 U.S.C.A. § 2403.
Judgments against, 28 U.S.C.A. § 2414.
Jury trials in actions against, 28 U.S.C.A. § 2402.
Officers and Employees, this index.
Official record, authentication, Rule 44(a)(1); Auth. Comm. Rule 44(a)(1).
Process, amendment of pleading, change of party, Rule 15(c).
Reply to counterclaim, time, Rule 12(a).
Security not required of, 28 U.S.C.A. § 2408.
Service of summons and complaint on, Rule 4(d); Auth. Comm. Rule 4(d).
Stay in favor of, Rule 62(e); Auth. Comm. Rule 62(e).
Subpoena,
Compelling giving of testimony, etc., application of rules, Rule 81(a).
Tender of fees and mileage, Rule 45(b).
Territories and subject matter jurisdiction, Jurisdiction.
Time for commencing action against, 28 U.S.C.A. § 2401.
Time for commencing actions by, 28 U.S.C.A. § § 2415-2416.
Venue and, Venue, Juris. § 2.14.

UNITED STATES ATTORNEY
Process, amendment of pleading, change of party, Rule 15(c).
Service on, Rules 4(d), 12(a).

UNITED STATES CLAIMS COURT
Applicability of rules, Evid. Rule 1101.

UNITED STATES LAWS
Preference of actions on trial calendar, Rule 40.

UNITED STATES MARSHAL
Marshals, generally, this index.

UNITED STATES TERRITORIES

Subject matter jurisdiction and, Jurisdiction.

URNS

Hearsay exception, statement concerning inscriptions on, Evid. Rule 803.

VACATION OF JUDGMENT

Judgment as a matter of law, alternative new trial motion, Rule 50; Auth. Comm. Rule 50.

VENUE

Generally, Juris. § 2.14; 28 U.S.C.A. § § 1391-1412.
Aliens, and Venue, Juris. § 2.14.
Change of, Juris. § 2.14; 28 U.S.C.A. § § 1404, 1406, 1412.
Class actions, Auth. Comm. Rule 23.
Corporations, and Venue, Juris. § 2.14.
Counterclaims and crossclaims, and Venue, Juris. § 2.14, Auth. Comm. Rule 13 (a), (b), (e), (g) and (h).
Defense, improper venue, Rules 12(b, h).
Generally, 28 U.S.C.A. § § 1404, 1406.
Depositions,
Failure to comply with order compelling answer, sanctions in district where deposition taken, Rule 37(b).
Oral examination, leave of court not required where person more than 100 miles from place of trial, Rule 30(b).
Use in court proceedings where witness outside of, Rule 32(a).
Discovery, motion for order compelling, Rule 37(a).
Dismissal for improper venue, Rule 12(b)(3); Rule 41(b); Auth. Comm. Rule 12(b)(3).
Motion, form of, Form 19.
District courts, and Venue, Juris. § 2.14.
Diversity of citizenship, and Venue, Juris. § 2.14.
Division, within federal judicial district, and Venue, Juris. § 2.14.
Foreign countries, and venue, Juris. § 2.14.
Interpleader, Auth. Comm. Rule 22 and 28 U.S.C.A. § 1335.
Joinder of party, improper venue, Rule 19(a).
Multidistrict litigation, 28 U.S.C.A. § 1407; Multidistrict Litigation Rules (Part V)..
Multiple defendants or multiple claims, venue over, Auth. Comm. Rule12(b)(3).
Personal jurisdiction, and Venue, Juris. § § 2.1, 2.14.
Pleading, Auth. Comm. Rule 8(a).
Remedy for improper venue, Juris. § 2.14.
Removal and, Removal, Juris. § 2.17.
Residence, and Venue, Juris. § 2.14.
Rules not to extend or limit, Rule 82; Auth. Comm. Rule 82.
Shareholder derivative actions, Auth. Comm. Rule 23.1.
Third-party practice, Auth. Comm. Rule 14 (a), (b) and (c).
Transfer for improper venue, Juris. § 2.14; 28 U.S.C.A. § § 1406, 1412.
Unincorporated associations, and Venue, Juris. § 2.14.
United States, and Venue, Juris. § 2.14.
Generally, 28 U.S.C.A. § 1402.

VERDICT

Civil docket, entry in, Rule 79(a).
Directed Verdict, generally, this index.
General verdict,
Accompanied by answer to interrogatory, Rule 49(b); Auth. Comm. Rule 49(b).
Entry of judgment on, Rule 58.
Inquiry into validity, testimony of juror in connection with, restriction and exception, Evid. Rule 606.
Judgment on jury verdict, form of, Form 31.
Setting aside,
Errors not affecting substantial rights not ground for, Rule 61.
Special verdicts, 49(a); Auth. Comm. Rule 49(a).
Unanimity of jurors, Rule 48; Auth. Comm. Rule 48.

VERIFICATION

Copies, documents and things produced for inspection, depositions upon oral examination, Rule 30(f).
Pleadings, this index.
Requirement generally abolished, subject to exceptions, Rule 11.
Shareholder derivative actions, rule 23.1; Auth. Comm. Rule 23.1.
Unsworn declarations, 28 U.S.C.A. § 1746.

VESSELS

Prize, applicability of rules in part, Evid. Rule 1101.

VETERANS DAY

Clerks of court, business hours for office, exception concerning opening, Rule 77(c).
"Legal holiday" as including for purposes of computing time, Rule 6(a).

VICE CONSUL

Authentication of official record, Rule 44(a).

VICTIMS

Character evidence, Evid. Rule 404.
Sex offenses, relevance of past behavior, Evid. Rule 412.

VIDEOTAPES

"Photographs" as including, contents of photographs, etc., Evid. Rule 1001.

VIRGIN ISLANDS

District court, applicability of rules, Evid. Rule 1101.
Subject matter jurisdiction, jurisdiction, Juris. § 2.12.

VITAL STATISTICS

Records of, hearsay exception, Evid. Rule 803.

VOICES

Identification, authentication and identification, conformity with requirements, Evid. Rule 901.

VOLUNTARY DISMISSAL

Effect, etc., Rule 41(a); Auth. Comm. Rule 41(a).
Time for, Rule 41(a); Auth. Comm. Rule 41(a).

WAIVER
Compulsory counterclaims, Auth. Comm. Rule 13(a).
Defenses, Rule 12(h).
Depositions,
Objections to because of errors and irregularities in, Rule 32(d); Auth. Comm. Rule 32(d).
Oral examination, signing of, Rule 30(e); Auth. Comm. Rule 30(e).
Jury trial, Rule 38(d); Auth. Comm. Rule 38(d).
Objections to personal jurisdiction, Jurisdiction, Juris. § 2.4.
Physical and mental examination report, prior reports, privilege, effect of, Rule 35(b); Auth. Comm. Rule 35(b).
Pleading as defense, Rule 8(c).
Service, Rule 4(d); Auth. Comm. Rule 4(d).
Trial by jury,
Failure of party to make demand for jury trial upon removal of actions from state court, Rule 81(c); Auth. Comm. Rule 81(c).
Omission of instruction on issue of fact raised by evidence or pleading, Rule 49(a); Auth. Comm. Rule 49(a).
Untimely Objection, Auth. Comm. Rule 17(a).

WASHINGTON'S BIRTHDAY
Clerks of court, business hours for office, exceptions concerning opening, Rule 77(c).
"Legal holiday" as including for purposes of computing time, Rule 6(a).

WEATHER
Effects on computing time, Auth. Comm. Rule 6(a).

WEIGHT OF EVIDENCE
Preliminary questions, rule concerning as not limiting right of party to introduce evidence respecting, Evid. Rule 104.

WILLS
Statement of memory or belief relating to execution, revocation, etc., hearsay, exclusion, Evid. Rule 803.

WITHDRAWAL
Admission, Rule 36(b); Auth. Comm. Rule 36(b).
Demand for jury trial, Rule 38(d); Auth. Comm. Rule 38(d).
Deposits in court, Rule 67.
Offer of judgment, Rule 68.

WITNESSES
Attacking or supporting credibility. Credibility of Witnesses, this index.
Bias or Prejudice, generally, this index.
Calling and interrogation of by court, Evid. Rule 614.
Certified public accountant before master, statement of accounts as evidence, Rule 53(d).
Character evidence, Evid. Rules 404, 607 to 609.
Compelling giving of testimony, application of rules, Rule 81(a).
Competency,
Generally, Rule 43(a); Evid. Rule 601.
Determination, Rule 43(a).
Judge, Evid. Rule 605.

WITNESSES—Cont'd
Competency,—Cont'd
Jurors, Evid. Rule 606.
Credibility of Witnesses, generally, this index.
Cross-Examination, generally, this index.
Depositions, generally, this index.
Discovery, generally, this index.
Examination, Rule 43(b).
Master, Rule 53(c).
Prior statements of, Evid. Rule 613.
Exclusion of, Evid. Rule 615.
Expert witnesses. Opinions and Expert Testimony, generally, this index.
Extrinsic evidence of prior inconsistent statement of, Evid. Rule 613.
Harassment or undue embarrassment, control by court of mode and order of interrogating witnesses and presenting evidence to protect from, Evid. Rule 611.
Hostile witnesses, interrogation by leading questions, Evid. Rule 611.
Illness of Witness, generally, this index.
Impeachment of Witnesses, generally, this index.
Interrogation, mode and order of, control by court, Evid. Rule 611.
Lack of personal knowledge, Evid. Rule 602.
Leading questions, Rule 43 (b); Evid. Rule 611.
Master, proceedings before, Rule 53; Auth. Comm. Rule 53(d)(2).
Notice, other crimes or wrongs, intent of prosecution to introduce, Evid. Rule 404.
Oaths and affirmations, Evid. Rule 603.
Affirmation in lieu of oath, Rule 43(d); Auth. Comm. Rule 43(d).
Interpreters, Evid. Rule 604.
Powers of master, Rule 53(c).
Opinions and Expert Testimony, generally, this index.
Per diem, mileage, subsistence, 28 U.S.C.A. § 1821.
Perjury, generally, this index.
Personal knowledge, evidence to prove, Evid. Rule 602.
Pre-trial conference to limit number, Rule 16.
Prior statements of, examination concerning, Evid. Rule 613.
Privileges and Immunities, generally, this index.
Qualification, preliminary questions concerning, court determination, Evid. Rule 104.
Recalcitrant witnesses, 28 U.S.C.A. § 1826.
Recalling, successor judges, Rule 63.
Subscribing witness, testimony of unnecessary to authenticate writing, exception, Evid. Rule 903.

WORDS AND PHRASES
Definitions, generally, this index.

WRITINGS
Answer or objection to requests for admission, Rule 36(a).
Containing matter not related to subject matter of testimony, excising and ordering delivery of remainder to party entitled thereto, refreshing memory, Evid. Rule 612.

WRITINGS—Cont'd
Contents of,
Collateral matters, other evidence of contents, Evid. Rule 1004.
Copies of, duplicates, admissibility of, Evid. Rule 1003.
Definitions, Evid. Rule 1001.
Duplicates, defined, Evid. Rule 1001.
Functions of court and jury, Evid. Rule 1008.
Loss or destruction of originals, other evidence of contents, Evid. Rule 1004.
Opponent, original in possession of, other evidence of contents, Evid. Rule 1004.
Original,
Defined, Evid. Rule 1001.
Not obtainable other evidence of contents, Evid. Rule 1004.
Other evidence of admissibility, Evid. Rule 1004.
Proof of, requirement of original, exception, Evid. Rule 1002.
Testimony, deposition or written admission of party, proof by, Evid. Rule 1007.
Voluminous writings, summaries of, Evid. Rule 1006.
Writings, defined, Evid. Rule 1001.
Depositions upon oral examination, taking of, notice, Rule 30(b).
Discovery procedure, stipulations regarding, Rule 29.
Examination by court in camera, writing used to refresh memory, Evid. Rule 612.
Handwriting, 28 U.S.C.A. § 1731.
Interrogatories, answers to, Rule 33(a).
Motions, Rule 7(b)(1).
Nonexpert opinion on handwriting, authentication and identification, conformity with requirements, Evid. Rule 901.
Objections,
Subpoena for inspection, Rule 45(c).
To form of depositions upon written questions, Rule 32(d).
Physical and mental examinations, report of examiner, Rule 35(b).
Production of Documents or Things, generally, this index.
Remainder or part of, introduction, Evid. Rule 106.
Subscribing witness, testimony of unnecessary to authenticate, exception, Evid. Rule 903.
Summaries of voluminous writings, Evid. Rule 1006.
Use to refresh memory, Evid. Rule 612.

WRITS
Applicability of Rules, Rules 81(a, b).
Assistance, judgment directing delivery of possession, Rule 70; Auth. Comm. Rule 70.
Audita querela, coram nobis, etc., abolished, Rule 60(b).
Execution, generally, this index.
Habeas Corpus, generally, this index.
Issuance of, 28 U.S.C.A. § 1651.

WRITTEN INTERROGATORIES
Interrogatories, generally, this index.

WRITTEN QUESTIONS
Depositions, this index.

X-RAYS
"Photographs" as including, contents of photographs, etc., Evid. Rule 1001.